We sincerely appreciate
your assistance in our wedding.
Ben & Becky Wright

Hammond Publications Advisory Board

Library of Congress Cataloging in Publication Data
Hammond Incorporated.
Hammond citation world atlas.
Includes glossary and index.
1. Atlases.   I. Title.   II. Title: Citation world
atlas.
G1021.H267 1982   912   82-81115
ISBN 0-8437-1254-6   AACR2
ISBN 0-8437-1255-4 (pbk.)

Contents

Gazetteer-Index of the World

This alphabetical list of grand divisions, countries, states, colonial possessions, etc., gives area in both square miles and square kilometers, population, capital or chief town, and index references and page numbers on which they are shown on the largest scale. The index reference shows the square on the respective map in which the name of the entry may be located.

Country	Area Square Miles	Area Square Kilometers	Population	Capital or Chief Town	Index Ref.	Page No.
*Afghanistan	250,775	649,507	15,540,000	Kabul	A 2	68
Africa	11,707,000	30,321,130	469,000,000	......		102
Alabama, U.S.A.	51,705	133,916	3,893,888	Montgomery	......	195
Alaska, U.S.A.	591,004	1,530,700	401,851	Juneau	......	196
*Albania	11,100	28,749	2,590,600	Tiranë	E 5	45
Alberta, Canada	255,285	661,185	2,207,856	Edmonton	......	182
*Algeria	919,591	2,381,740	17,422,000	Algiers	D 3	106
American Samoa	77	199	32,395	Pago Pago	J 7	87
Andorra	188	487	31,000	Andorra la Vella	G 1	33
*Angola	481,351	1,246,700	7,078,000	Luanda	C 6	114
Anguilla	35	91	6,519	The Valley	F 3	156
Antarctica	5,500,000	14,245,000	....	......		5
*Antigua and Barbuda	171	443	72,000	St. John's	G 3	156
*Argentina	1,072,070	2,776,661	27,862,771	Buenos Aires	......	143
Arizona, U.S.A.	114,000	295,260	2,718,425	Phoenix	......	198
Arkansas, U.S.A.	53,187	137,754	2,286,435	Little Rock	......	202
Ascension Island, St. Helena	34	88	719	Georgetown	A 5	102
Asia	17,128,500	44,362,815	2,633,000,000	......		54
*Australia	2,966,136	7,682,300	13,548,448	Canberra	......	88
*Austria	32,375	83,851	7,507,000	Vienna	B 3	40
*Bahamas	5,382	13,939	223,455	Nassau	C 1	156
*Bahrain	240	622	358,857	Manama	F 4	58
*Bangladesh	55,126	142,776	87,052,024	Dacca	G 4	68
*Barbados	166	430	249,000	Bridgetown	B 8	161
*Belgium	11,781	30,513	9,855,110	Brussels	E 7	27
*Belize	8,867	22,966	144,857	Belmopan	C 2	154
*Benin	43,483	112,620	3,338,240	Porto-Novo	E 6	106
Bermuda	21	54	67,761	Hamilton	H 3	156
*Bhutan	18,147	47,000	1,298,000	Thimphu	G 3	68
*Bolivia	424,163	1,098,582	5,600,000	La Paz; Sucre	......	136
*Botswana	224,764	582,139	819,000	Gaborone	C 4	119
*Brazil	3,284,426	8,506,663	119,024,600	Brasília	......	132
British Columbia, Canada	366,253	948,596	2,716,301	Victoria	......	184
British Indian Ocean Terr.	29	75	2,000	(London, U.K.)	L10	54
Brunei	2,226	5,765	212,840	Bandar Seri Begawan	E 4	85
*Bulgaria	42,823	110,912	8,862,000	Sofia	F 4	45
*Burma	261,789	678,034	32,913,000	Rangoon	B 2	72
*Burundi	10,747	27,835	4,021,910	Bujumbura	E 4	114
California, U.S.A.	158,706	411,049	23,667,565	Sacramento	......	204
*Cambodia (Kampuchea)	69,898	181,036	5,200,000	Phnom Penh	E 4	72
*Cameroon	183,568	475,441	8,503,000	Yaoundé	B 2	114
*Canada	3,851,787	9,976,139	24,105,163	Ottawa	......	162
*Cape Verde	1,557	4,033	324,000	Praia	B 8	106
Cayman Islands	100	259	16,677	Georgetown	B 3	156
*Central African Republic	242,000	626,780	2,284,000	Bangui	C 2	114
Central America	197,480	511,475	21,000,000	......		154
Ceylon, see Sri Lanka						
*Chad	495,752	1,283,998	4,309,000	N'Djamena	C 4	111
Channel Islands	75	194	133,000	St. Helier; St. Peter Port	E 8	13
*Chile	292,257	756,946	11,198,789	Santiago	......	138
*China, People's Rep. of	3,691,000	9,559,690	958,090,000	Peking (Beijing)	......	77
China, Republic of (Taiwan)	13,971	36,185	16,609,961	Taipei	K 7	77
*Colombia	439,513	1,138,339	27,520,000	Bogotá	......	126
Colorado, U.S.A.	104,091	269,596	2,889,735	Denver	......	208
*Comoros	719	1,862	290,000	Moroni	G 2	119
*Congo	132,046	342,000	1,537,000	Brazzaville	B 4	114
Connecticut, U.S.A.	5,018	12,997	3,107,576	Hartford	......	210
Cook Islands	91	236	18,128	Avarua	K 7	87
*Costa Rica	19,575	50,700	2,245,000	San José	E 5	154
*Cuba	44,206	114,494	9,706,369	Havana	......	158
*Cyprus	3,473	8,995	629,000	Nicosia	E 5	62
*Czechoslovakia	49,373	127,876	15,276,799	Prague	C 2	41
Delaware, U.S.A.	2,044	5,294	594,317	Dover	R 3	245
*Denmark	16,629	43,069	5,124,000	Copenhagen	......	21
District of Columbia, U.S.A.	69	179	638,432	Washington	F 5	244
*Djibouti	8,880	23,000	386,000	Djibouti	H 5	111
*Dominica	290	751	74,089	Roseau	E 7	161
*Dominican Republic	18,704	48,443	5,431,000	Santo Domingo	D 6	158
*Ecuador	109,483	283,561	8,354,000	Quito	C 3	128
*Egypt	386,659	1,001,447	41,572,000	Cairo	E 2	110
*El Salvador	8,260	21,393	4,813,000	San Salvador	C 4	154
England, U.K.	50,516	130,836	46,220,955	London	......	13
*Equatorial Guinea	10,831	28,052	244,000	Malabo	A 3	114
*Ethiopia	471,776	1,221,900	31,065,000	Addis Ababa	G 5	110
Europe	4,057,000	10,507,630	676,000,000	......		7
Faerøe Islands, Denmark	540	1,399	41,969	Tórshavn	B 2	21
Falkland Islands & Dependencies	6,198	16,053	1,855	Stanley	E 8	120
*Fiji	7,055	18,272	588,068	Suva	H 8	87
*Finland	130,128	337,032	4,788,000	Helsinki	O 6	18
Florida, U.S.A.	58,664	151,940	9,746,342	Tallahassee	......	212
*France	210,038	543,998	53,788,000	Paris	......	28
French Guiana	35,135	91,000	64,000	Cayenne	E 3	131
French Polynesia	1,544	4,000	137,382	Papeete	L 8	87
*Gabon	103,346	267,666	551,000	Libreville	B 4	114
*Gambia	4,127	10,689	601,000	Banjul	A 6	106
Georgia, U.S.A.	58,910	152,577	5,463,105	Atlanta	......	217
*Germany, East (German Democratic Republic)	41,768	108,179	16,737,000	Berlin (East)	......	22
*Germany, West (Federal Republic)	95,985	248,601	61,658,000	Bonn	......	22
*Ghana	92,099	238,536	11,450,000	Accra	D 7	106
Gibraltar	2.28	5.91	29,760	Gibraltar	D 4	33
*Great Britain & Northern Ireland (United Kingdom)	94,399	244,493	55,672,000	London	......	10
*Greece	50,944	131,945	9,599,000	Athens	F 6	45
Greenland	840,000	2,175,600	49,773	Nûk (Godthåb)	B12	4
*Grenada	133	344	110,000	St. George's	G 4	156
Guadeloupe & Dependencies	687	1,779	319,000	Basse-Terre	F 4	156
Guam	209	541	105,821	Agaña	E 4	87
*Guatemala	42,042	108,889	7,262,419	Guatemala	B 3	154
*Guinea	94,925	245,856	5,143,284	Conakry	B 6	106
*Guinea-Bissau	13,948	36,125	777,214	Bissau	A 6	106
*Guyana	83,000	214,970	820,000	Georgetown	B 3	131
*Haiti	10,694	27,697	5,009,000	Port-au-Prince	C 5	158
Hawaii, U.S.A.	6,471	16,760	964,691	Honolulu	......	218
Holland, see Netherlands						
*Honduras	43,277	112,087	3,691,000	Tegucigalpa	D 3	154
Hong Kong	403	1,044	5,022,000	Victoria	H 7	77
*Hungary	35,919	93,030	10,709,536	Budapest	D 3	41
*Iceland	39,768	103,000	228,785	Reykjavík	B 1	21
Idaho, U.S.A.	83,564	216,431	944,038	Boise	......	220
Illinois, U.S.A.	56,345	145,934	11,426,596	Springfield	......	222
*India	1,269,339	3,287,588	683,810,051	New Delhi	D 4	68
Indiana, U.S.A.	36,185	93,719	5,490,260	Indianapolis	......	227
*Indonesia	788,430	2,042,034	147,383,075	Jakarta	D 7	85
Iowa, U.S.A.	56,275	145,752	2,913,808	Des Moines	......	229
*Iran	636,293	1,648,000	37,447,000	Tehran	F 4	66
*Iraq	172,476	446,713	12,767,000	Baghdad	C 4	66
*Ireland	27,136	70,282	3,440,427	Dublin	......	17
Ireland, Northern, U.K.	5,452	14,121	1,543,000	Belfast	F 2	17
Isle of Man	227	588	64,000	Douglas	C 3	13
*Israel	7,847	20,324	3,878,000	Jerusalem	B 4	65
*Italy	116,303	301,225	57,140,000	Rome	......	34
*Ivory Coast	124,504	322,465	7,920,000	Abidjan	C 7	106
*Jamaica	4,411	11,424	2,161,000	Kingston	......	158
*Japan	145,730	377,441	117,057,485	Tokyo	......	81
*Jordan	35,000	90,650	2,152,273	Amman	D 3	65
*Kampuchea (Cambodia)	69,898	181,036	5,200,000	Phnom Penh	E 4	72
Kansas, U.S.A.	82,277	213,097	2,364,236	Topeka	......	232
Kentucky, U.S.A.	40,409	104,659	3,660,257	Frankfort	......	237
*Kenya	224,960	582,646	15,327,061	Nairobi	G 3	115
Kiribati	291	754	56,213	Bairiki	J 6	87
Korea, North	46,540	120,539	17,914,000	P'yŏngyang	D 3	80
Korea, South	38,175	98,873	37,448,836	Seoul	D 5	80
*Kuwait	6,532	16,918	1,355,827	Al Kuwait	E 4	58
*Laos	91,428	236,800	3,721,000	Vientiane	D 3	72
*Lebanon	4,015	10,399	3,161,000	Beirut	F 6	62
*Lesotho	11,720	30,355	1,339,000	Maseru	D 5	119
*Liberia	43,000	111,370	1,873,000	Monrovia	C 7	106
*Libya	679,358	1,759,537	2,856,000	Tripoli	B 2	110
Liechtenstein	61	158	25,220	Vaduz	J 2	39
Louisiana, U.S.A.	47,752	123,678	4,206,312	Baton Rouge	......	202
*Luxembourg	999	2,587	364,000	Luxembourg	J 9	27
Macau	6	16	271,000	Macau	H 7	77
*Madagascar	226,657	587,041	8,742,000	Antananarivo	H 3	119
Maine, U.S.A.	33,265	86,156	1,125,027	Augusta	......	243
*Malawi	45,747	118,485	5,968,000	Lilongwe	F 6	114
Malaya, Malaysia	50,806	131,588	11,138,227	Kuala Lumpur	D 6	72
*Malaysia	128,308	332,318	13,435,588	Kuala Lumpur	D 6 / E 4	72 / 85
*Maldives	115	298	143,046	Male	L 9	54
*Mali	464,873	1,204,021	6,906,000	Bamako	C 6	106
*Malta	122	316	343,970	Valletta	E 7	34

*Member of the United Nations.

GAZETTEER-INDEX OF THE WORLD

Country	Area Square Miles	Square Kilometers	Population	Capital or Chief Town	Index Ref.	Page No.
Manitoba, Canada	250,999	650,087	1,017,323	Winnipeg		179
Martinique	425	1,101	308,000	Fort-de-France	D 5	161
Maryland, U.S.A.	10,460	27,091	4,216,975	Annapolis		245
Massachusetts, U.S.A.	8,284	21,456	5,737,037	Boston		249
*Mauritania	419,229	1,085,803	1,634,000	Nouakchott	B 5	106
*Mauritius	790	2,046	959,000	Port Louis	G 5	119
Mayotte	144	373	47,300	Dzaoudzi	G 2	119
*Mexico	761,601	1,972,546	67,395,826	Mexico City		150
Michigan, U.S.A.	58,527	151,585	9,262,078	Lansing		250
Midway Islands	1.9	4.9	468		J 3	87
Minnesota, U.S.A.	84,402	218,601	4,075,970	St. Paul		255
Mississippi, U.S.A.	47,689	123,515	2,520,638	Jackson		256
Missouri, U.S.A.	69,697	180,515	4,916,759	Jefferson City		261
Monaco	368 acres	149 hectares	25,029	Monaco	G 6	28
*Mongolia	606,163	1,569,962	1,594,800	Ulaanbaatar	E 2	77
Montana, U.S.A.	147,046	380,849	786,690	Helena		262
Montserrat	40	104	12,073	Plymouth	G 3	157
*Morocco	172,414	446,550	20,242,000	Rabat	C 2	106
*Mozambique	303,769	786,762	12,130,000	Maputo	E 4	119
Namibia (South-West Africa)	317,827	823,172	1,200,000	Windhoek	B 3	118
Nauru	7.7	20	7,254	Yaren (district)	G 6	87
Nebraska, U.S.A.	77,355	200,349	1,569,825	Lincoln		264
*Nepal	54,663	141,577	14,179,301	Kathmandu	E 3	68
*Netherlands	15,892	41,160	14,227,000	The Hague; Amsterdam	F 5	27
Netherlands Antilles	390	1,010	246,000	Willemstad	E 4	156
Nevada, U.S.A.	110,561	286,353	800,493	Carson City		266
New Brunswick, Canada	28,354	73,437	688,926	Fredericton		170
New Caledonia & Dependencies	7,335	18,998	133,233	Nouméa	G 8	87
Newfoundland, Canada	156,184	404,517	561,996	St. John's		166
New Hampshire, U.S.A.	9,279	24,033	920,610	Concord		268
New Hebrides, see Vanuatu						
New Jersey, U.S.A.	7,787	20,168	7,364,823	Trenton		273
New Mexico, U.S.A.	121,593	314,926	1,302,981	Santa Fe		274
New York, U.S.A.	49,108	127,190	17,558,072	Albany		276
*New Zealand	103,736	268,676	3,167,357	Wellington		100
*Nicaragua	45,698	118,358	2,703,000	Managua	D 4	154
*Niger	489,189	1,267,000	5,098,427	Niamey	F 5	106
*Nigeria	357,000	924,630	82,643,000	Lagos	F 6	106
Niue	100	259	3,843	Alofi	K 7	87
North America	9,363,000	24,250,170	370,000,000			146
North Carolina, U.S.A.	52,669	136,413	5,881,813	Raleigh		281
North Dakota, U.S.A.	70,702	183,118	652,717	Bismarck		282
Northern Ireland, U.K.	5,452	14,121	1,543,000	Belfast	F 2	17
Northwest Territories, Canada	1,304,896	3,379,683	44,684	Yellowknife	G 3	187
*Norway	125,053	323,887	4,092,000	Oslo	F 7	18
Nova Scotia, Canada	21,425	55,491	837,789	Halifax		168
Ohio, U.S.A.	41,330	107,045	10,797,624	Columbus		284
Oklahoma, U.S.A.	69,956	181,186	3,025,290	Oklahoma City		288
*Oman	120,000	310,800	891,000	Muscat	G 6	58
Ontario, Canada	412,580	1,068,582	8,551,733	Toronto		175, 177
Oregon, U.S.A.	97,073	251,419	2,633,149	Salem		291
Pacific Islands, Territory of the	533	1,380	133,732	Saipan	F 5	87
*Pakistan	310,403	803,944	83,782,000	Islamabad	B 3	68
*Panama	29,761	77,082	1,830,175	Panamá	G 6	154
*Papua New Guinea	183,540	475,369	3,006,799	Port Moresby	E 6	87
*Paraguay	157,047	406,752	2,973,000	Asunción		144
Pennsylvania, U.S.A.	45,308	117,348	11,863,895	Harrisburg		294
Persia, see Iran						
*Peru	496,222	1,285,215	17,031,221	Lima		128
*Philippines	115,707	299,681	47,914,017	Manila		82
Pitcairn Islands	18	47	61	Adamstown	O 8	87
*Poland	120,725	312,678	35,815,000	Warsaw		47
*Portugal	35,549	92,072	9,933,000	Lisbon	B 3	32
Prince Edward Island, Canada	2,184	5,657	121,328	Charlottetown	E 2	168
Puerto Rico	3,515	9,104	3,186,076	San Juan		161
*Qatar	4,247	11,000	220,000	Doha	F 4	58
Québec, Canada	594,857	1,540,680	6,377,518	Québec		172, 174
Réunion	969	2,510	491,000	St-Denis	F 5	119
Rhode Island, U.S.A.	1,212	3,139	947,154	Providence	H 5	249
Rhodesia, see Zimbabwe						
*Romania	91,699	237,500	22,048,305	Bucharest	F 3	45
*Rwanda	10,169	26,337	4,819,317	Kigali	E 4	114
Sabah, Malaysia	29,300	75,887	1,002,608	Kota Kinabalu	F 4	85
Saint Christopher (St. Kitts)-Nevis	104	269	44,404	Basseterre	F 3	156
Saint Helena & Dependencies	162	420	5,147	Jamestown	B 6	102
*Saint Lucia	238	616	115,783	Castries	G 6	161
Saint Pierre & Miquelon	93.5	242	5,840	Saint-Pierre	C 4	166
*Saint Vincent & the Grenadines	150	388	124,000	Kingstown	G 4	157
San Marino	23.4	60.6	19,149	San Marino	D 3	34
*São Tomé e Príncipe	372	963	85,000	São Tomé	F 8	106
Sarawak, Malaysia	48,202	124,843	1,294,753	Kuching	E 5	85
Saskatchewan, Canada	251,699	651,900	957,025	Regina		181
*Saudi Arabia	829,995	2,149,687	8,367,000	Riyadh	D 4	58
Scotland, U.K.	30,414	78,772	5,117,146	Edinburgh		15
*Senegal	75,954	196,720	5,508,000	Dakar	A 5	106
*Seychelles	145	375	63,000	Victoria	H 5	119
Siam, see Thailand						
*Sierra Leone	27,925	72,325	3,470,000	Freetown	B 7	106
*Singapore	226	585	2,413,945	Singapore	F 6	72
*Solomon Islands	11,500	29,785	221,000	Honiara	G 6	87
*Somalia	246,200	637,658	3,645,000	Mogadishu	H 3	115
*South Africa	455,318	1,179,274	23,771,970	Cape Town; Pretoria	C 5	118
South America	6,875,000	17,806,250	245,000,000			120
South Carolina, U.S.A.	31,113	80,583	3,121,833	Columbia		296
South Dakota, U.S.A.	77,116	199,730	690,768	Pierre		298
South-West Africa (Namibia)	317,827	823,172	1,200,000	Windhoek	B 3	118
*Spain	194,881	504,742	37,430,000	Madrid	E 7	33
*Sri Lanka	25,332	65,610	14,850,001	Colombo	E 7	68
*Sudan	967,494	2,505,809	18,691,000	Khartoum	E 4	110
*Suriname	55,144	142,823	352,041	Paramaribo	C 3	131
*Swaziland	6,705	17,366	547,000	Mbabane	E 5	119
*Sweden	173,665	449,792	8,320,000	Stockholm	J 8	18
Switzerland	15,943	41,292	6,365,960	Bern	G 4	39
*Syria	71,498	185,180	8,979,000	Damascus	G 5	62
Taiwan	13,971	36,185	16,609,961	Taipei	K 7	77
*Tanzania	363,708	942,003	17,527,560	Dar es Salaam	F 5	114
Tennessee, U.S.A.	42,144	109,153	4,591,120	Nashville		237
Texas, U.S.A.	266,807	691,030	14,229,288	Austin		303
*Thailand	198,455	513,998	46,455,000	Bangkok	D 3	72
*Togo	21,622	56,000	2,472,000	Lomé	E 7	106
Tokelau	3.9	10	1,575	Fakaofo	J 6	87
Tonga	270	699	90,128	Nuku'alofa	J 8	87
*Trinidad and Tobago	1,980	5,128	1,067,108	Port-of-Spain	G 5	157
Tristan da Cunha, St. Helena	38	98	251	Edinburgh	J 7	2
*Tunisia	63,378	164,149	6,367,000	Tunis	F 1	106
*Turkey	300,946	779,450	45,217,556	Ankara	D 3	62
Turks and Caicos Islands	166	430	7,436	Cockburn Town, Grand Turk	D 2	156
Tuvalu	9.78	25.33	7,349	Fongafale, Funafuti	H 6	87
*Uganda	91,076	235,887	12,630,076	Kampala	F 3	114
*Ukrainian S.S.R., U.S.S.R.	233,089	603,700	49,755,000	Kiev	D 5	52
*Union of Soviet Socialist Republics	8,649,490	22,402,179	262,436,227	Moscow		48
*United Arab Emirates	32,278	83,600	1,040,275	Abu Dhabi	F 5	58
*United Kingdom	94,399	244,493	55,672,000	London		10
*United States of America	3,623,420	9,384,658	226,504,825	Washington		188
*Upper Volta	105,869	274,200	6,908,000	Ouagadougou	D 6	106
*Uruguay	72,172	186,925	2,899,000	Montevideo		145
Utah, U.S.A.	84,899	219,888	1,461,037	Salt Lake City		304
*Vanuatu	5,700	14,763	112,596	Vila	G 7	87
Vatican City	108.7 acres	44 hectares	728		B 6	34
*Venezuela	352,143	912,050	13,913,000	Caracas		124
Vermont, U.S.A.	9,614	24,900	511,456	Montpelier		268
*Vietnam	128,405	332,569	52,741,766	Hanoi	E 3	72
Virginia, U.S.A.	40,767	105,587	5,346,818	Richmond		307
Virgin Islands, British	59	153	12,000	Road Town	H 1	157
Virgin Islands, U.S.A.	132	342	95,591	Charlotte Amalie	A 4	161
Wake Island	2.5	6.5	302	Wake Islet	G 4	87
Wales, U.K.	8,017	20,764	2,790,462	Cardiff	D 5	13
Wallis and Futuna	106	275	9,192	Mata Utu	J 7	87
Washington, U.S.A.	68,139	176,480	4,132,180	Olympia		310
Western Sahara	102,703	266,000	76,425		B 3	106
*Western Samoa	1,133	2,934	151,983	Apia	J 7	87
West Virginia, U.S.A.	24,231	62,758	1,950,279	Charleston		312
*White Russian S.S.R. (Byelorussian S.S.R.), U.S.S.R.	80,154	207,600	9,560,000	Minsk	C 4	52
Wisconsin, U.S.A.	56,153	145,436	4,705,521	Madison		317
World (land)	57,970,000	150,142,300	4,415,000,000			1, 2
Wyoming, U.S.A.	97,809	253,325	469,557	Cheyenne		319
*Yemen, People's Democratic Rep. of	111,101	287,752	1,969,000	Aden	E 7	58
*Yemen Arab Republic	77,220	200,000	6,456,189	San'a	D 6	58
*Yugoslavia	98,766	255,804	22,471,000	Belgrade	C 3	45
Yukon Territory, Canada	207,075	536,324	22,684	Whitehorse	E 3	186
*Zaire	905,063	2,344,113	28,291,000	Kinshasa	D 4	114
*Zambia	290,586	752,618	5,679,808	Lusaka	E 7	114
*Zimbabwe	150,803	390,580	7,360,000	Harare (Salisbury)	D 3	119

Introduction to the Maps and Indexes

The following notes have been added to aid the reader in making the best use of this atlas. Though he may be familiar with maps and map indexes, the publisher believes that a quick review of the material below will add to his enjoyment of this reference work.

Arrangement — The Plan of the Atlas. The atlas has been designed with maximum convenience for the user as its objective. All geographically related information pertaining to a country or region appears on adjacent pages, eliminating the task of searching throughout the entire volume for data on a given area. Thus, the reader will find, conveniently assembled, political, topographic, economic and special maps of a political area or region, accompanied by detailed map indexes, statistical data, and illustrations of the national flags of the area.

The sequence of country units in this American-designed atlas is international in arrangement. Units on the world as a whole are followed by a section on the polar regions which, in turn, is followed by pages devoted to Europe and its countries. Every continent map is accompanied by special population distribution, climatic and vegetation maps of that continent. Following the maps of the European continent and its countries, the geographic sequence plan proceeds as follows: Asia, the Pacific and Australia, Africa, South America, North America, and ends with detailed coverage on the United States.

Political Maps — The Primary Reference Tool. The most detailed maps in each country unit are the *political maps.* It is our feeling that the reader is likely to refer to these maps more often than to any other in the book when confronted by such questions as — Where? How big? What is it near? Answering these common queries is the function of the political maps. Each political map stresses *political* phenomena — countries, internal political divisions, boundaries, cities and towns. The major political unit or units, shown on the map, are banded in distinctive colors for easy identification and delineation. First-order political subdivisions (states, provinces, counties on the state maps) are shown, scale permitting.

The reader is advised to make use of the *legend* appearing under the title on each political map. Map *symbols,* the special "language" of maps, are explained in the legend. Each variety of dot, circle, star or interrupted line has a special meaning which should be clearly understood by the user so that he may interpret the map data correctly.

Each country has been portrayed at a *scale* commensurate with its political, areal, economic or tourist importance. In certain cases, a whole map unit may be devoted to a single nation if that nation is considered to be of prime interest to most atlas users. In other cases, several nations will be shown on a single map if, as separate entities, they are of lesser relative importance. Areas of dense settlement and important significance within a country have been enlarged and portrayed in inset maps inserted on the margins of the main map. The scale of each map is indicated as a fractional representation (1:1,000,000). The reader is advised to refer to the linear or "bar" scale appearing on each map or map inset in order to determine the distance between points.

The *projection* system used for each map is noted near the title of the map. Map projections are the special graphic systems used by cartographers to render the curved three-dimensional surface of the globe on a flat surface. Optimum map projections determined by the attributes of the area have been used by the publishers for each map in the atlas.

A word here as to the choice of place names on the maps. Throughout the atlas names appear, with a few exceptions, in their local official spellings. However, conventional Anglicized spellings are used for major geographical divisions and for towns and topographic features for which English forms exist; i.e., "Spain" instead of "España" or "Munich" instead of "München." Names of this type are normally followed by the local official spelling in parentheses. As an aid to the user the indexes are cross-referenced for all current and most former spellings of such names.

Names of cities and towns in the United States follow the forms listed in the *Post Office Directory* of the United States Postal Service. Domestic physical names follow the decisions of the Board on Geographic Names, U.S. Department of the Interior, and of various state geographic name boards.

It is the belief of the publishers that the boundaries shown in a general reference atlas should reflect current geographic and political realities. This policy has been followed consistently in the atlas. The presentation of *de facto* boundaries in cases of territorial dispute between various nations does not imply the political endorsement of such boundaries by the publisher, but simply the honest representation of boundaries as they exist at the time of the printing of the atlas maps.

Indexes — Pinpointing a Location. Each political map is accompanied by a comprehensive index of the place names appearing on the map. If you are unfamiliar with the location of a particular geographical place and wish to find its position within the confines of the subject area of the map, consult the map index as your first step. The name of the feature sought will be found in its proper alphabetical sequence with a key reference letter-number combination corresponding to its location on the map. After noting the key reference letter-number combination for the place name, turn to the map. The place name will be found within the square formed by the two lines of latitude and the two lines of longitude which enclose the co-ordinates — i.e., the marginal letters and numbers. The diagram below illustrates the system of indexing.

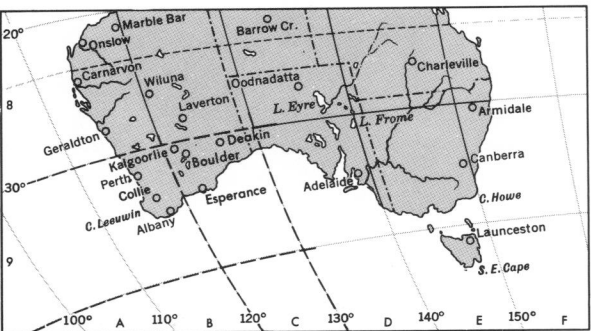

In the case of maps consisting entirely of insets, the place name is found near the intersection point of the imaginary lines connecting the co-ordinates at right angles. See below.

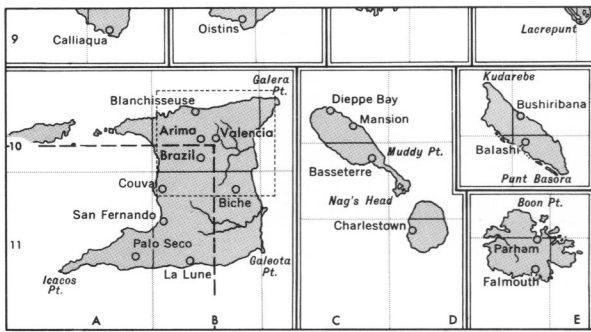

Where space on the map has not permitted giving the complete form of the place name, the complete form is shown in the index. Where a place is known by more than one name or by various spellings of the same name, the different forms have been included in the index. Physical features are listed under their proper names and not according to their generic terms; that is to say, Rio Negro will be found under Negro and not under Rio Negro. On the other hand, Rio Grande will be found under Rio Grande. Accompanying most index entries for cities and towns, and for other political units, are *population figures* for the particular entries. The large number of population figures in the atlas makes this work one of the most comprehensive statistical sources available to the public today. The population figures have been taken from the latest official censuses and estimates of the various nations.

Population and area figures for countries and major political units are listed in bold type *fact lists* on the margins of the indexes. In addition, the capital, largest city, highest point, monetary unit, principal languages and the prevailing religions of the country concerned are also listed. The Gazetteer-Index of the World on the preceding pages provides a quick reference index for countries and other important areas. Though population and area figures for each major unit area also found in the map section, the Gazetteer-Index provides a conveniently arranged statistical comparison contained in two pages.

All index entries for cities and towns in the United States are preceded by a five-digit postal ZIP code number applying to the community. This useful feature permits the reader to address his mail so that it will be routed and delivered more efficiently and quickly by the U.S. Postal Service. A dagger (†) designates those places that do not possess a post office. The ZIP code number listed in such cases refers to that of the nearest post office. An asterisk (*) marks those larger cities which are divided into multiple ZIP code areas. Using the single ZIP code number listed in such cases will direct your letter to the proper city with dispatch. However, if the precise ZIP code number of the address within the city is needed, it is suggested that the reader refer to the latest National ZIP Code Directory at his local post office. This detailed guide lists every street in a multiple ZIP code city with the proper ZIP code for the street.

Relief Maps. Accompanying each political map is a relief map of the area. The purpose of the relief map is to illustrate the surface configuration (TOPOGRAPHY) of the region. A shading technique in color simulates the relative ruggedness of the terrain — plains, plateaus, valleys, hills and mountains. Graded colors, ranging from greens for lowlands, yellows for intermediate elevations to browns in the highlands, indicate the height above sea level of each part of the land. A vertical scale at the margin of the map shows the approximate height in meters and feet represented by each color.

Economic Maps — Agriculture, Industry and Resources. One of the most interesting features that will be found in each country unit is the economic map. From this map one can determine the basic activities of a nation as expressed through its economy. A perusal of the map yields a full understanding of the area's economic geography and natural resources.

The agricultural economy is manifested in two ways: color bands and commodity names. The color bands express broad categories of *dominant land use*, such as, cereal belts, forest lands, livestock range lands, nonagricultural wastes. The red commodity names, on the other hand, pinpoint the areas of production of *specific* crops; i.e., wheat, cotton, sugar beets, etc.

Major mineral occurrences are denoted by standard letter symbols appearing in blue. The relative size of the letter symbols signifies the relative importance of the deposit.

The manufacturing sector of the economy is presented by means of diagonal line patterns expressing the various *industrial areas* of consequence within a country.

The fishing industry is represented by names of commercial fish species appearing offshore in blue letters. Major waterpower sites are designated by blue symbols.

The publishers have tried to make this work the most comprehensive and useful atlas available, and it is hoped that it will prove a valuable reference work. Any constructive suggestions from the reader will be welcomed.

Sources and Acknowledgments

A multitude of sources goes into the making of a large-scale reference work such as this. To list them all would take many pages and would consume space better devoted to the maps and reference materials themselves. However, certain general sources were very useful in preparing this work and are listed below.

STATISTICAL OFFICE OF THE UNITED NATIONS.
Demographic Yearbook. New York. Issued annually.

STATISTICAL OFFICE OF THE UNITED NATIONS.
Statistical Yearbook. New York. Issued annually.

THE GEOGRAPHER, U.S. DEPARTMENT OF STATE.
International Boundary Study papers. Washington. Various dates.

THE GEOGRAPHER, U.S. DEPARTMENT OF STATE.
Geographic Notes. Washington. Various dates.

UNITED STATES BOARD ON GEOGRAPHIC NAMES.
Decisions on Geographic Names in the United States. Washington. Various dates.

UNITED STATES BOARD ON GEOGRAPHIC NAMES.
Official Standard Names Gazetteers. Washington. Various dates.

CANADIAN PERMANENT COMMITTEE ON GEOGRAPHICAL NAMES.
Gazetteer of Canada series. Ottawa. Various dates.

UNITED STATES POSTAL SERVICE.
National Five Digit ZIP Code and Post Office Directory. Washington. 1982.

UNITED STATES POSTAL SERVICE.
Postal Bulletin. Washington. Issued weekly.

UNITED STATES DEPARTMENT OF THE INTERIOR. BUREAU OF MINES.
Minerals Yearbook. 4 vols. Washington. Various dates.

UNITED STATES GEOLOGICAL SURVEY.
Elevations and distances in the United States. Reston, Va. 1980.

CARTACTUAL.
Cartactual — Topical Map Service. Budapest. Issued bimonthly.

AMERICAN GEOGRAPHICAL SOCIETY.
Focus. New York. Issued ten times a year.

THE AMERICAN UNIVERSITY.
Foreign Area Studies. Washington. Various dates.

CENTRAL INTELLIGENCE AGENCY.
General reference maps. Washington. Various dates.

A sample list of sources used for specific countries follows:

Afghanistan
CENTRAL STATISTICS OFFICE.
Preliminary Results of the First Afghan Population Census 1979. Kabul.

Albania
DREJTORIA E STATISTIKËS.
1979 Census. Tiranë.

Burundi
SERVICE NATIONAL DES ÉTUDES ET STATISTIQUES.
1979 Census. Bujumbura.

French Polynesia
INSTITUT NATIONAL DE LA STATISTIQUE ET DES ÉTUDES ÉCONOMIQUES.
Recensement Général de la Population 1977. Papeete.

Guinea-Bissau
DEPARTAMENTO CENTRAL DE RECENSEAMENTO.
Recenseamento Geral da População 1979. Bissau.

Hungary
HUNGARIAN CENTRAL STATISTICAL OFFICE.
1980 Census. Budapest.

Kuwait
CENTRAL OFFICE OF STATISTICS.
1980 Census. Al Kuwait.

Malawi
NATIONAL STATISTICAL OFFICE.
Population Census 1977. Zomba.

Panama
DIRECCIÓN DE ESTADISTICA Y CENSO.
Censos Nacionales de 1980. Panamá.

Papua New Guinea
BUREAU OF STATISTICS.
National Population Census 1980. Port Moresby.

Philippines
NATIONAL CENSUS AND STATISTICS OFFICE.
1980 Census of Population. Manila.

Romania
DIRECŢIA CENTRALĂ DE STATISTICĂ.
1979 Estimates. Bucharest.

Rwanda
BUREAU NATIONAL DE RECENSEMENT.
Recensement Général de la Population 1978. Kigali.

Saint Lucia
CENSUS OFFICE.
1980 Population Census. Castries.

Singapore
DEPARTMENT OF STATISTICS.
Census of Population 1980. Singapore.

Tanzania
BUREAU OF STATISTICS.
1978 Population Census. Dar es Salaam.

U.S.S.R.
CENTRAL STATISTICAL ADMINISTRATION.
1979 Census. Moscow.

United States
BUREAU OF THE CENSUS.
1980 Census of Population. Washington.

Vanuatu
CENSUS OFFICE.
1979 Population Census. Port Vila.

Zambia
CENTRAL STATISTICAL OFFICE.
1980 Census of Population and Housing. Lusaka.

Glossary of Abbreviations

A

A. A. F. — Army Air Field
Acad. — Academy
A. C. T. — Australian Capital Territory
adm. — administration; administrative
A. F. B. — Air Force Base
Afgh., Afghan. — Afghanistan
Afr. — Africa
Ala. — Alabama
Alb. — Albania
Alg. — Algeria
Alta. — Alberta
Amer. — American
Amer. Samoa — American Samoa
And. — Andorra
Ant., Antarc. — Antarctica
Ant. & Bar. — Antigua and Barbuda
Ar. — Arabia
arch. — archipelago
Arg. — Argentina
Ariz. — Arizona
Ark. — Arkansas
A. S. S. R. — Autonomous Soviet
        Socialist Republic
Aust. — Austria
Aust. Cap. Terr. — Australian Capital
        Territory
Austr., Austral. — Australian, Australia
aut. — autonomous
Aut. Obl. — Autonomous Oblast

B

B. — bay
Bah. — Bahamas
Barb. — Barbados
Battlef. — Battlefield
Bch. — Beach
Belg. — Belgium
Berm. — Bermuda
Bol. — Bolivia
Bots. — Botswana
Br. — Branch
Br. — British
Braz. — Brazil
Br. Col. — British Columbia
Br. Ind. Oc. Terr. — British Indian
        Ocean Territory
Bulg. — Bulgaria

C

C. — cape
Calif. — California
Can. — Canada
can. — canal
cap. — capital
Cent. Afr. Rep. — Central African
        Republic
Cent. Amer. — Central America
C. G. Sta. — Coast Guard Station
C. H. — Court House
chan. — channel
Chan. Is. — Channel Islands
Chem. Ctr. — Chemical Center
co. — county
C. of G. H. — Cape of Good Hope
Col. — Colombia
Colo. — Colorado
comm. — commissary
Conn. — Connecticut
cont. — continent
cord. — cordillera (mountain range)
C. Rica — Costa Rica
C. S. — County Seat
C. Verde — Cape Verde
Czech. — Czechoslovakia

D

D. C. — District of Columbia
Del. — Delaware
Dem. — Democratic
Den. — Denmark
depr. — depression
dept. — department
des. — desert
dist., dist's — district, districts
div. — division
Dom. Rep. — Dominican Republic

E

E. — East
Ec., Ecua. — Ecuador
E. Ger. — East Germany
elec. div. — électoral division
El Salv. — El Salvador
Eng. — England
Equat. Guinea, Eq. Guin — Equatorial
        Guinea

escarp. — escarpment
est. — estuary
Eth. — Ethiopia

F

Falk. Is. — Falkland Islands
Fin. — Finland
Fk., Fks. — Fork, Forks
Fla. — Florida
for. — forest
Fr. — France, French
Fr. Gui. — French Guiana
Fr. Poly. — French Polynesia
Ft. — Fort

G

G. — gulf
Ga. — Georgia
Game Res. — Game Reserve
Ger. — Germany
geys. — geyser
Gibr. — Gibraltar
glac. — glacier
gov. — governorate
Gr. — Group
Greenl. — Greenland
Gren. — Grenada
Gt. Brit. — Great Britain
Guad. — Guadeloupe
Guat. — Guatemala
Guinea-Biss. — Guinea-Bissau
Guy. — Guyana

H

har., harb., hbr. — harbor
hd. — head
highl. — highland, highlands
Hist. — Historic, Historical
Hond. — Honduras
Hts. — Heights
Hung. — Hungary

I

i., isl. — island, isle
I. C. — independent city
Ice., Icel. — Iceland
Ida. — Idaho
Ill. — Illinois
Ind. — Indiana
ind. city — independent city
Indon. — Indonesia
Ind. Res. — Indian Reservation
int. div. — internal division
inten. — intendency
Int'l — International
Ire. — Ireland
is., isls. — islands
Isr. — Israel
isth. — isthmus
Iv. Coast — Ivory Coast

J

Jam. — Jamaica
Jct. — Junction

K

Kans. — Kansas
Ky. — Kentucky

L

L. — Lake, Loch, Lough
La. — Louisiana
Lab. — Laboratory
lag. — lagoon
Ld. — Land
Leb. — Lebanon
Les. — Lesotho
Liecht. — Liechtenstein
Lux. — Luxembourg

M

Mad., Madag. — Madagascar
Man. — Manitoba
Mart. — Martinique
Mass. — Massachusetts
Maur. — Mauritania
Md. — Maryland
met. area — metropolitan area
Mex. — Mexico
Mich. — Michigan
Minn. — Minnesota
Miss. — Mississippi
Mo. — Missouri
Mon. — Monument
Mong. — Mongolia
Mont. — Montana
Mor. — Morocco

Moz., Mozamb. — Mozambique
mt. — mount
mtn. — mountain

N

N., No., North. — North, Northern
N. Amer. — North America
Nam., Namib. — Namibia
N. A. S. — Naval Air Station
Nat'l — National
Nat'l Cem. — National Cemetery
Nat'l Mem. Park — National Memorial
        Park
Nat'l Mil. Park — National Military
        Park
Nat'l Pkwy. — National Parkway
Nav. Base — Naval Base
Nav. Sta. — Naval Station
N. B., N. Br. — New Brunswick
N. C. — North Carolina
N. Dak. — North Dakota
Nebr. — Nebraska
Neth. — Netherlands
Neth. Ant. — Netherlands Antilles
Nev. — Nevada
New Bruns. — New Brunswick
New Cal., New Caled. — New Caledonia
Newf. — Newfoundland
New Hebr. — New Hebrides
N. H. — New Hampshire
Nic. — Nicaragua
N. Ire. — Northern Ireland
N. J. — New Jersey
N. Mex. — New Mexico
Nor. — Norway, Norwegian
North. — Northern
North. Terr., No. Terr. — Northern
        Territory
        (Australia)
N. S. — Nova Scotia
N. S. W., N.S. Wales — New South Wales
N. W. T., N. W. Terrs. — Northwest
        Territories
        (Canada)
N. Y. — New York
N. Z., N. Zealand — New Zealand

O

Obl. — Oblast
O. F. S. — Orange Free State
Okla. — Oklahoma
Okr. — Okrug
Ont. — Ontario
Ord. Depot — Ordnance Depot
Oreg. — Oregon

P

Pa. — Pennsylvania
Pac. Is. — Pacific Islands,
        Territory of the
Pak. — Pakistan
Pan. — Panama
Papua N. G. — Papua New Guinea
Par. — Paraguay
par. — parish
passg. — passage
P.D.R. Yemen — People's Democratic
        Republic of Yemen
P. E. I. — Prince Edward Island
pen. — peninsula
Phil., Phil. Is. — Philippines
Pk. — Park
pk. — peak
plat. — plateau
P. N. G. — Papua New Guinea
Pol. — Poland
Port. — Portugal, Portuguese
Pr. Edward I. — Prince Edward Island
pref. — prefecture
P. Rico — Puerto Rico
prom. — promontory
prov. — province, provincial
pt. — point

Q

Que. — Québec
Queens. — Queensland

R

R. — River
ra. — range
Rec., Recr. — Recreation, Recreational
reg. — region
Rep. — Republic
res. — reservoir
Res. — Reservation, Reserve
R. I. — Rhode Island

riv. — river
Rom. — Romania

S

S. — South
Sa. — Sierra, Serra
S. Afr., S. Africa — South Africa
salt dep. — salt deposit
salt des. — salt desert
S. Amer. — South America
São T. & Pr. — São Tomé
        and Príncipe
Sask. — Saskatchewan
Saudi Ar. — Saudi Arabia
S. Aust., S. Austral. — South Australia
S. C. — South Carolina
Scot. — Scotland
Sd. — Sound
S. Dak. — South Dakota
Sen. — Senegal
sen. dist. — senatorial district
Seych. — Seychelles
S. F. S. R. — Soviet Federated Socialist
        Republic
Sing. — Singapore
S. Leone — Sierra Leone
S. Marino — San Marino
Sol. Is. — Solomon Islands
Sp. — Spanish
Spr., Sprs. — Spring, Springs
S. S. R. — Soviet Socialist Republic
St., Ste. — Saint, Sainte
Sta. — Station
St. Chris.-Nevis — Saint Christopher-
        Nevis
St. P. & M. — Saint Pierre and
        Miquelon
St. Vin. & Grens. — St. Vincent & The
        Grenadines
str., strs. — strait, straits
Sur. — Suriname
S. W. Afr. — South-West Africa
Swaz. — Swaziland
Switz. — Switzerland

T

Tanz. — Tanzania
Tas. — Tasmania
Tenn. — Tennessee
terr., terrs. — territory, territories
Tex. — Texas
Thai. — Thailand
trad. — traditional
Trin. & Tob. — Trinidad and Tobago
Tun. — Tunisia
twp. — township

U

U.A.E. — United
        Arab Emirates
U. K. — United Kingdom
Upp. Volta — Upper Volta
urb. area — urban area
Urug. — Uruguay
U. S. — United States
U. S. S. R. — Union of Soviet Socialist
        Republics

V

Va. — Virginia
Ven., Venez. — Venezuela
V. I. (Br.) — Virgin Islands (British)
V. I. (U. S.) — Virgin Islands (U. S.)
Vic. — Victoria
Viet. — Vietnam
Vill. — Village
vol. — volcano
Vt. — Vermont

W

W. — West, Western
Wash. — Washington
W. Aust., W. Austral. — Western
        Australia
W. Ger. — West Germany
W. Indies — West Indies
Wis. — Wisconsin
W. Samoa — Western Samoa
W. Va. — West Virginia
Wyo. — Wyoming

Y

Yugo. — Yugoslavia
Yukon — Yukon Territory

Z

Zim. — Zimbabwe

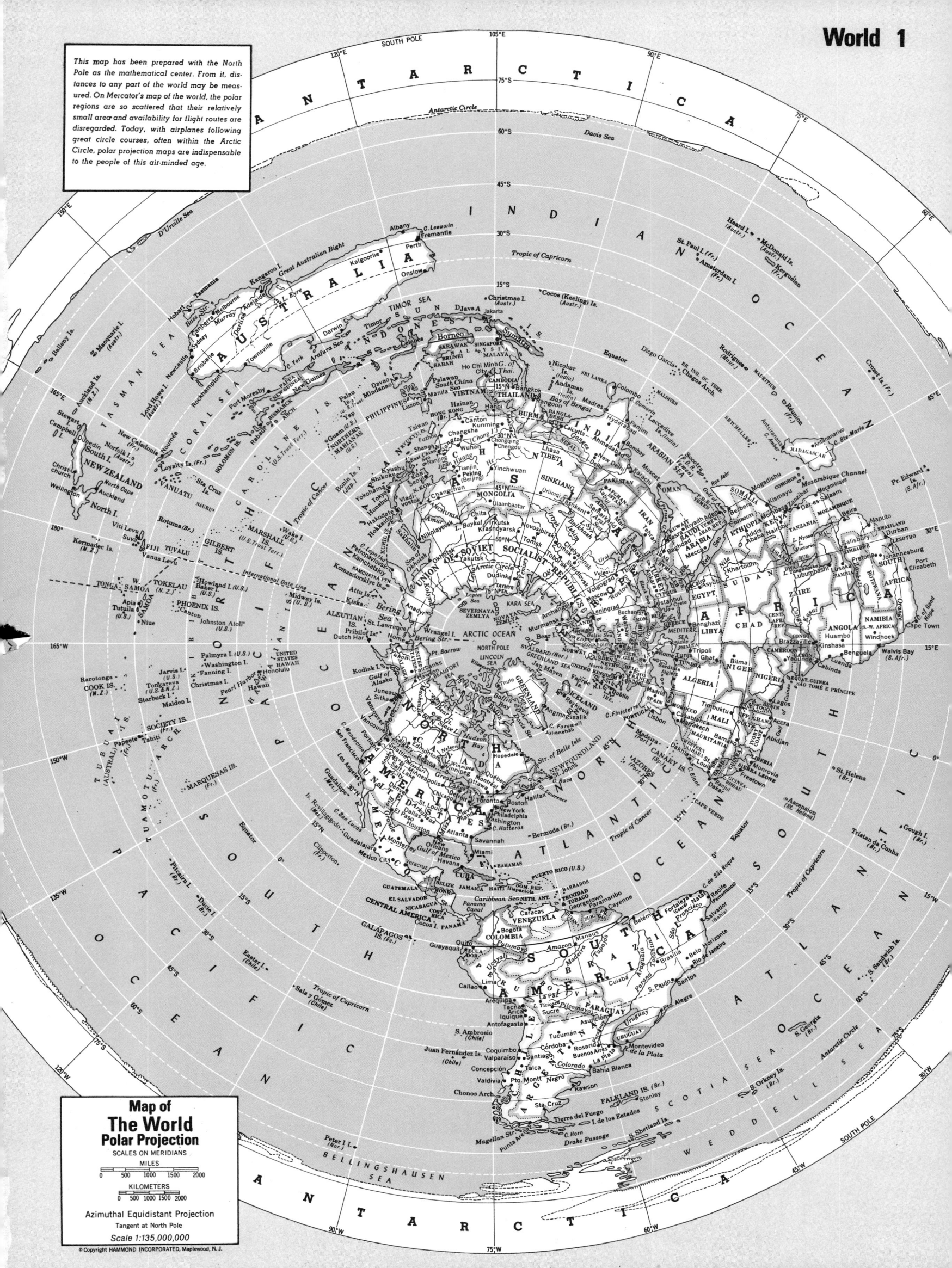

This map has been prepared with the North Pole as the mathematical center. From it, distances to any part of the world may be measured. On Mercator's map of the world, the polar regions are so scattered that their relatively small area and availability for flight routes are disregarded. Today, with airplanes following great circle courses, often within the Arctic Circle, polar projection maps are indispensable to the people of this air-minded age.

Map of The World Polar Projection

SCALES ON MERIDIANS

MILES

0   500   1000   1500   2000

KILOMETERS

0   500   1000   1500   2000

Azimuthal Equidistant Projection

Tangent at North Pole

Scale 1:135,000,000

© Copyright HAMMOND INCORPORATED, Maplewood, N. J.

The World

BRIESEMEISTER ELLIPTICAL
EQUAL-AREA PROJECTION

Capitals of Countries ....⊛
Other Capitals.............................⊛
International Boundaries..... – – –

Scale 1:80,000,000

Time Zones

STANDARD	Areas using half hour deviations.
TIME	
ZONES	Areas not using zone system.

NOTE: Standard time zones in the U.S.S.R. are always advanced one hour.

LAND AREA 57,970,000 sq. mi.
(150,142,300 sq. km.)
WATER AREA 139,781,000 sq. mi.
(362,032,790 sq. km.)
TOTAL SURFACE AREA 197,751,000 sq.mi.
(512,175,090 sq. km.)
POPULATION 4,415,000,000

Antarctica

AZIMUTHAL EQUIDISTANT PROJECTION

Scale 1:62,000,000

© Copyright HAMMOND INCORPORATED, Maplewood, N.J.

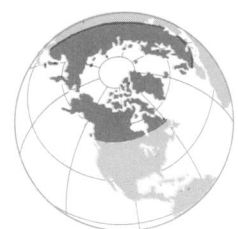

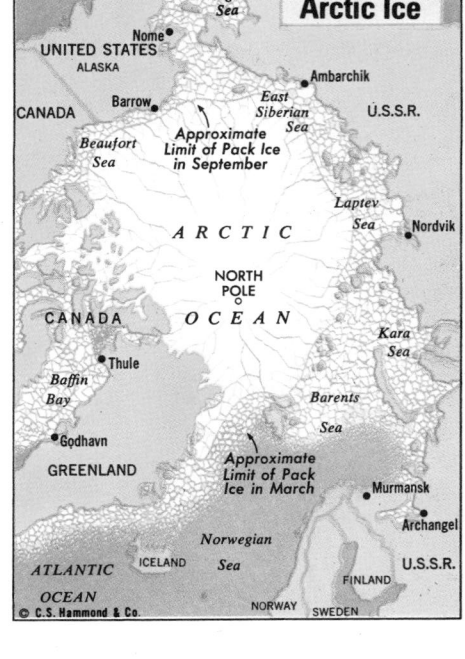

Arctic Ocean

AZIMUTHAL EQUIDISTANT PROJECTION

SCALE OF MILES
0 100 200   400   600

SCALE OF KILOMETERS
0   200 400 600 800 1000

Scale 1:41,000,000

EXPLORERS' ROUTES

Peary 1909
Byrd 1926
Amundsen, Ellsworth & Nobile 1926
Anderson in U.S.S. Nautilus 1958

By ship   By sledge
By airplane   By dirigible
By nuclear submarine

© Copyright HAMMOND INCORPORATED, Maplewood, N.J.

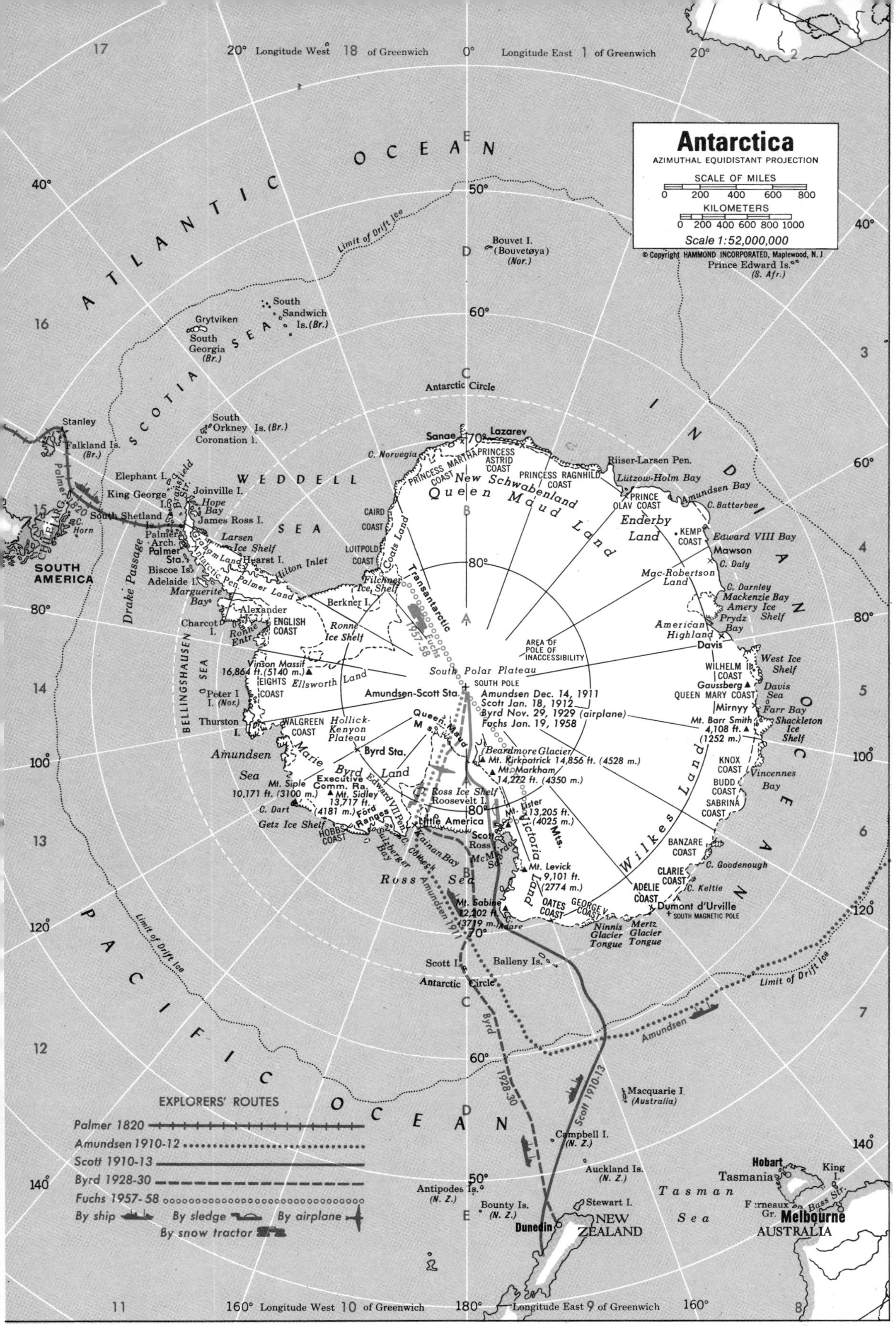

Antarctica
AZIMUTHAL EQUIDISTANT PROJECTION

SCALE OF MILES
0 200 400 600 800

KILOMETERS
0 200 400 600 800 1000

Scale 1:52,000,000

© Copyright HAMMOND INCORPORATED, Maplewood, N.J.

EXPLORERS' ROUTES

Palmer 1820
Amundsen 1910-12
Scott 1910-13
Byrd 1928-30
Fuchs 1957-58

By ship   By sledge   By airplane
By snow tractor

Amundsen Dec. 14, 1911
Scott Jan. 18, 1912
Byrd Nov. 29, 1929 (airplane)
Fuchs Jan. 19, 1958

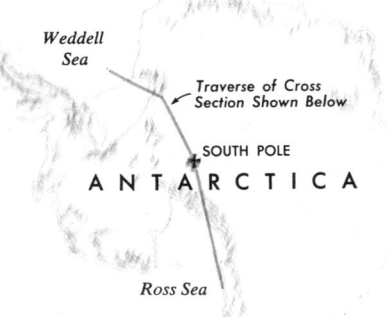

Weddell Sea

Traverse of Cross Section Shown Below

SOUTH POLE

ANTARCTICA

Ross Sea

Antarctic Cross Section: Weddell Sea to Ross Sea

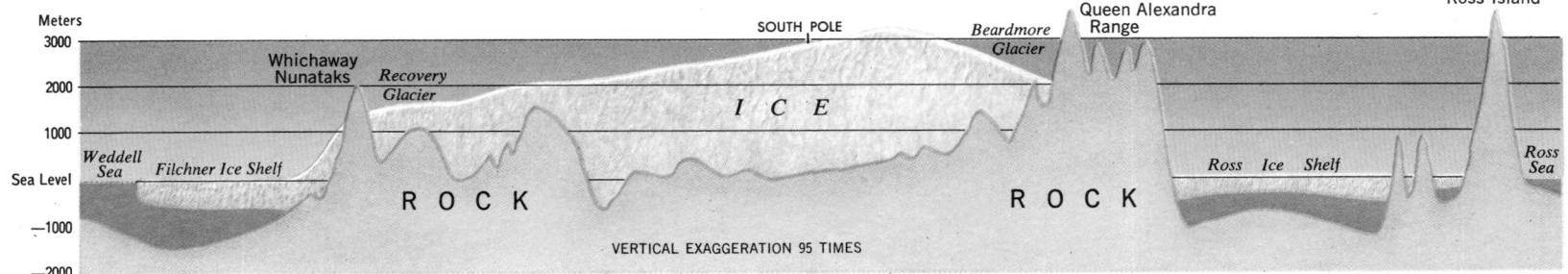

VERTICAL EXAGGERATION 95 TIMES

Information Based on American Geographical Society's "Antarctic Map Folio Series"

Europe — Polyconic Projection — Scale 1:20,800,000

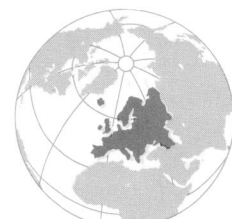

AREA 4,057,000 sq. mi.
(10,507,630 sq. km.)
POPULATION 676,000,000
LARGEST CITY Paris
HIGHEST POINT El'brus 18,510 ft.
(5,642 m.)
LOWEST POINT Caspian Sea -92 ft.
(-28 m.)

Population Distribution

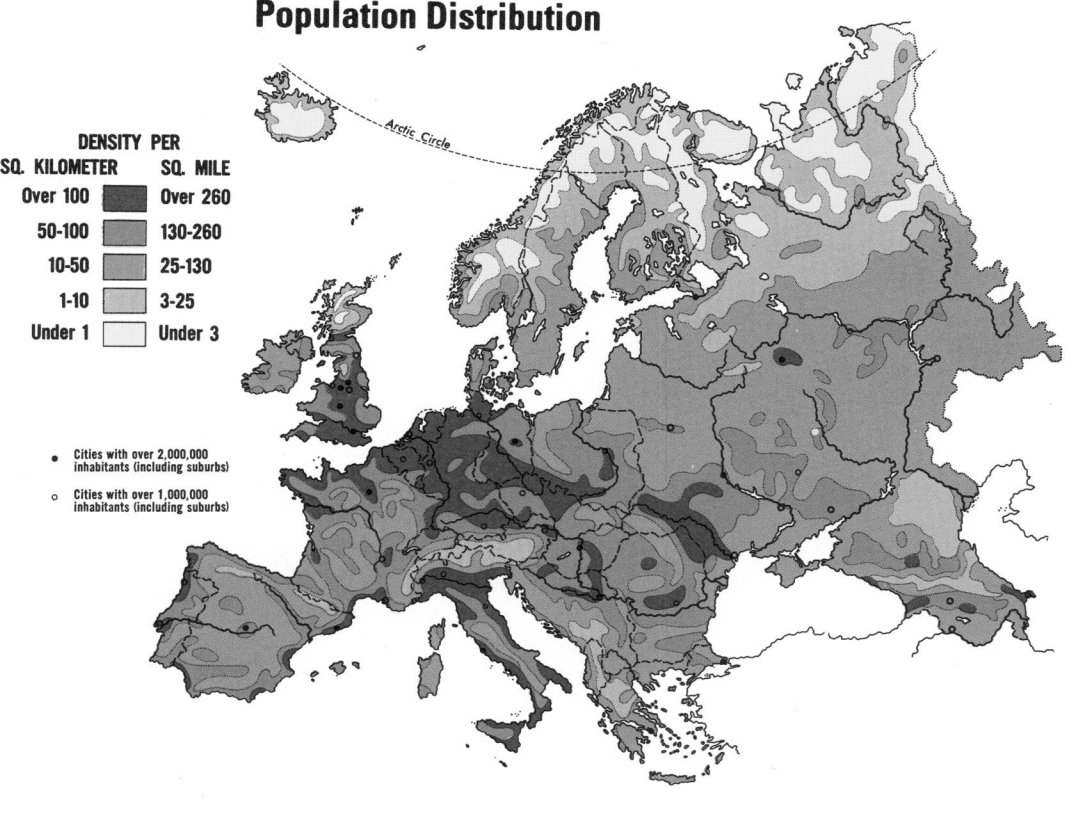

DENSITY PER

SQ. KILOMETER	SQ. MILE
Over 100	Over 260
50-100	130-260
10-50	25-130
1-10	3-25
Under 1	Under 3

• Cities with over 2,000,000
inhabitants (including suburbs)

○ Cities with over 1,000,000
inhabitants (including suburbs)

Vegetation

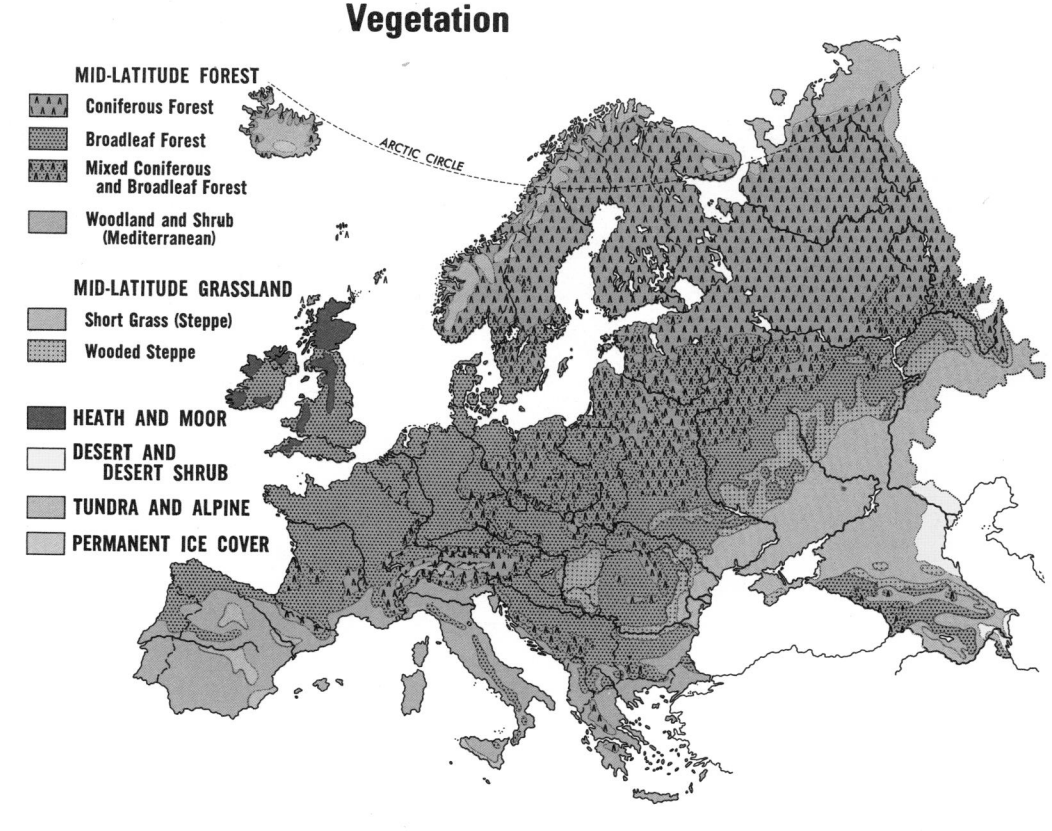

MID-LATITUDE FOREST

- Coniferous Forest
- Broadleaf Forest
- Mixed Coniferous and Broadleaf Forest
- Woodland and Shrub (Mediterranean)

MID-LATITUDE GRASSLAND

- Short Grass (Steppe)
- Wooded Steppe

HEATH AND MOOR

DESERT AND DESERT SHRUB

TUNDRA AND ALPINE

PERMANENT ICE COVER

© Copyright HAMMOND INCORPORATED, Maplewood, N.J.

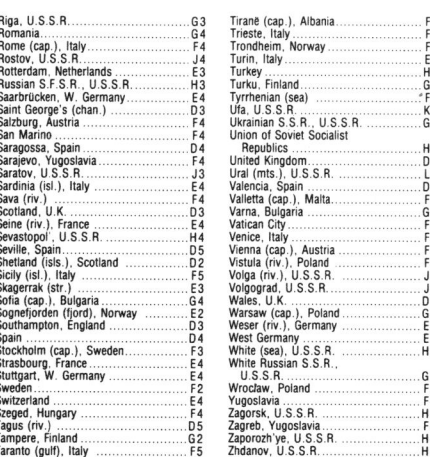

30°   20°   10°   0°   10°   20°   30°   40°   50°   60°

60°

Hom
ICELAND
Reykjavik
Fontur

NORWEGIAN
SEA

Arctic Circle

BARENTS
SEA

Kolguyev I.
Kanin
Pen.
Chechnaya Bay
Pechora

Nordkapp
Sørøy
Hammerfest

Vesterålen
Lofoten

Kiruna
Kemi

Murmansk

Kola
Pen.

WHITE
SEA

Archangel

Northern Dvina

Faerøe Is.
(Den.)

Shetland
Is.

Glittertind
8,110 ft.
(2,470 m.)
Bergen

Trondheim

Oulu

FINLAND

Lake
Onega

UNION OF

Hebrides
Orkney
Is.

Hardangerfjord
Moray Firth

Aberdeen
Ben Nevis
4,406 ft.
(1,343 m.)
Glasgow

Sundsvall

Tampere

Lake
Ladoga

Leningrad

Volga

Gor'kiy

Belfast
UK
IRELAND
Dublin

IRISH SEA
Liverpool

UNITED

KINGDOM

NORTH

SEA

Lindesnes

Skagerrak

Oslo

Västerås
Stockholm
Åland
Is.
Gotland
Hiiumaa

Helsinki

Saaremaa

Riga

Minsk

Moscow

SOCIAL

C. Clear

St. Georges Chan.

Birmingham

Land's End

DENMARK

Kattegat

Göteborg

Copenhagen

Bornholm

Rügen
Gdansk

Western Dvina

50°

ATLANTIC

OCEAN

English Channel

Channel Is.
(U.K.)

London

Le Havre

Seine

Paris

NETHERLANDS
Amsterdam

BELGIUM
Brussels
LUX
Cologne
Bonn

Frisian Is.

Hamburg
Elbe

WEST

GERMANY

Leipzig

EAST

Berlin

GERMANY

POLAND

Warsaw
Vistula

Łódź

Oder

Prague

Bug

Kiev

Dnieper

Khar'kov

Don

Nantes

Loire

FRANCE

Stuttgart

Munich

Vienna

CZECHOSLOVAKIA

Brno

Cracow

L'vov

Donetsk

Bay of
Biscay

Finisterre

Bordeaux

Dordogne

Garonne

Lyon

Rhône

SWITZ.
Bern

AUSTRIA
Graz
Budapest

HUNGARY

Cluj-Napoca

Carpathian Mts.

Odessa

SEA OF
AZOV

Crimea

Krasnodar

Porto

PORTUGAL

Douro

Pyrenees

Ebro

Turin

Milan

Genoa

Venice
San Marino

Zagreb
Sava

Belgrade

ROMANIA

Bucharest

Danube

BLACK SEA

40°

Lisbon

Tagus

SPAIN
Madrid

Guadiana

Zaragoza

Barcelona

Valencia

Gulf
of
Lions

Marseille
MONACO

Corsica

VATICAN CITY
Rome

Naples

SAN MARINO

ADRIATIC SEA

YUGOSLAVIA

Skopje

Sofia

BULGARIA

Balkan Mts.

Istanbul

Bosporus

Ankara

TURKEY

C. de São
Vicente

Cádiz

Minorca
Balearic Is.
Majorca
Ibiza

Sardinia

TYRRHENIAN
SEA

Tirane

Thessaloniki

Dardanelles

Lésvos

C. Finistre

Str. of Gibraltar

Tangier

GIBRALTAR
(U.K.)

Oran

Algiers

Palermo

Sicily

Etna
11,053 ft.
(3,369 m.)

C. Teulada

IONIAN
SEA

Athens

Crete

C. Tainaron

Rhodes

CYPRUS
Nicosia

LEBANON
Beirut

Rabat

Casablanca

MOROCCO

ALGERIA

AFRICA

Constantine

TUNISIA

C. Bon
Tunis

C. Passero

MALTA
Valletta

MEDITERRANEAN   SEA

Longitude West of   Greenwich   0°   Longitude East of   Greenwich

Vegetation/Relief

SCALE OF MILES
0   100   200   300   400   500   600   700   800   900   1000
SCALE OF KILOMETERS
0   100   200   300   400   500   600   700   800   900   1000

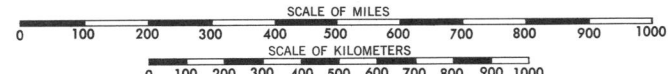

Capitals of Countries .... ⊛
International Boundaries ....
Canals ....

Depths in Fathoms

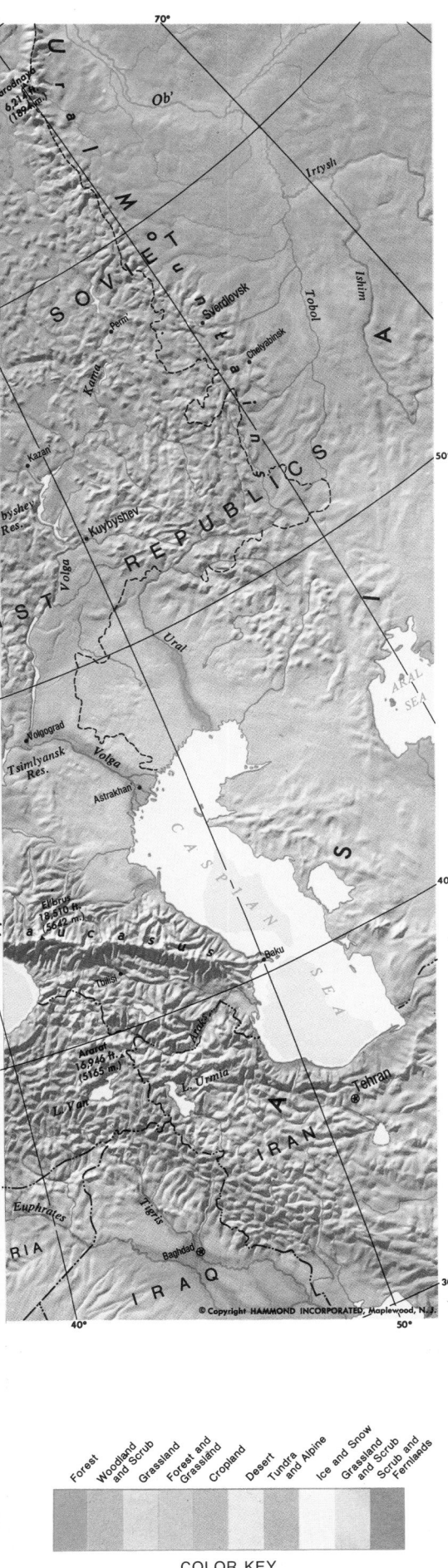

COLOR KEY

Forest | Woodland and Scrub | Grassland | Forest and Grassland | Cropland | Desert | Tundra and Alpine | Ice and Snow | Grassland and Scrub | Scrub and Farmlands

Rainfall

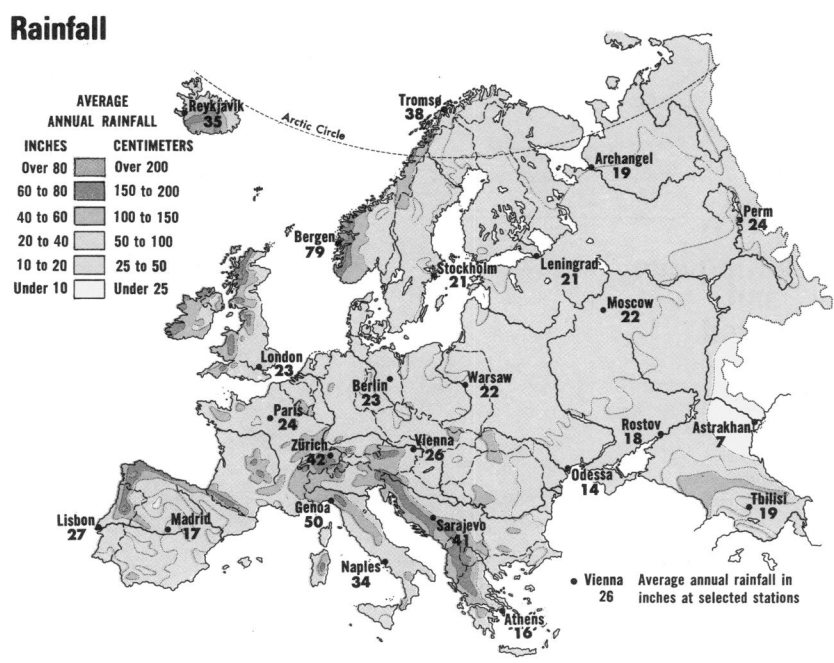

AVERAGE ANNUAL RAINFALL

INCHES	CENTIMETERS
Over 80	Over 200
60 to 80	150 to 200
40 to 60	100 to 150
20 to 40	50 to 100
10 to 20	25 to 50
Under 10	Under 25

Reykjavik 35 — Tromsø 38 — Archangel 19 — Perm 24 — Bergen 79 — Stockholm 21 — Leningrad 21 — Moscow 22 — London 23 — Berlin 23 — Warsaw 22 — Rostov 18 — Astrakhan 7 — Paris 24 — Vienna 26 — Zürich 42 — Odessa 14 — Tbilisi 19 — Lisbon 27 — Madrid 17 — Genoa 50 — Sarajevo 41 — Naples 34 — Athens 16

• Vienna 26   Average annual rainfall in inches at selected stations

Average January Temperature

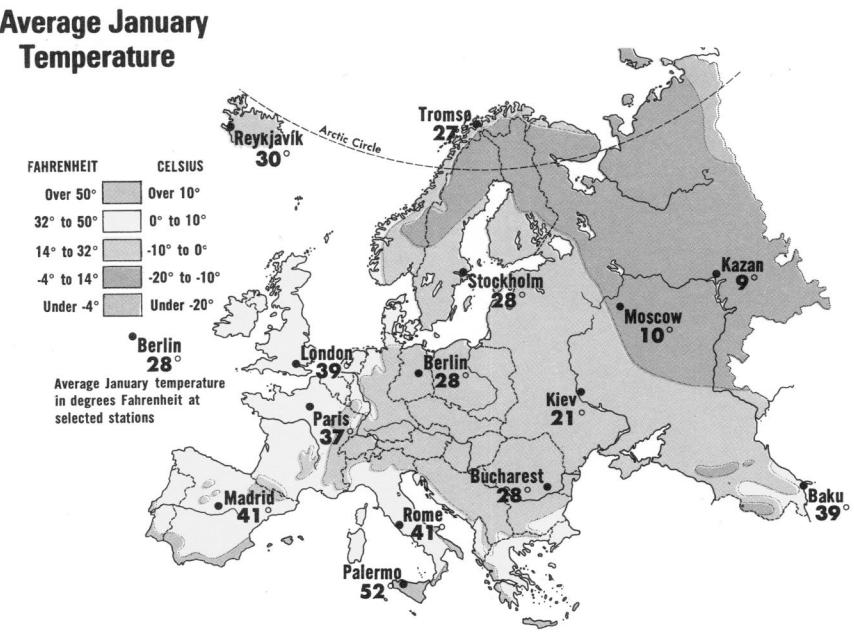

FAHRENHEIT	CELSIUS
Over 50°	Over 10°
32° to 50°	0° to 10°
14° to 32°	-10° to 0°
-4° to 14°	-20° to -10°
Under -4°	Under -20°

• Berlin 28°   Average January temperature in degrees Fahrenheit at selected stations

Reykjavík 30° — Tromsø 27° — Stockholm 28° — Kazan 9° — Moscow 10° — London 39° — Berlin 28° — Kiev 21° — Paris 37° — Bucharest 28° — Baku 39° — Madrid 41° — Rome 41° — Palermo 52°

Average July Temperature

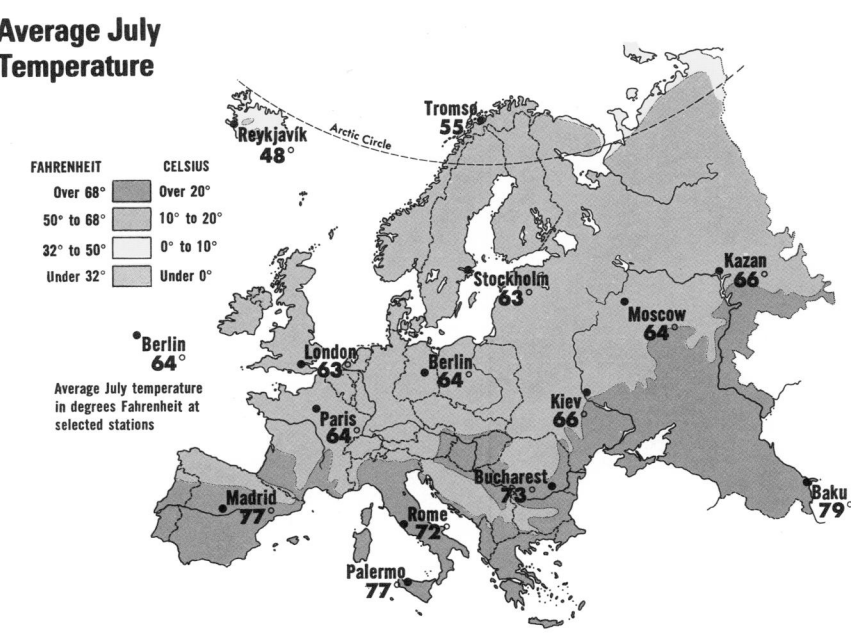

FAHRENHEIT	CELSIUS
Over 68°	Over 20°
50° to 68°	10° to 20°
32° to 50°	0° to 10°
Under 32°	Under 0°

• Berlin 64°   Average July temperature in degrees Fahrenheit at selected stations

Reykjavík 48° — Tromsø 55° — Stockholm 63° — Kazan 66° — Moscow 64° — London 63° — Berlin 64° — Kiev 66° — Paris 64° — Bucharest 73° — Baku 79° — Madrid 77° — Rome 72° — Palermo 77°

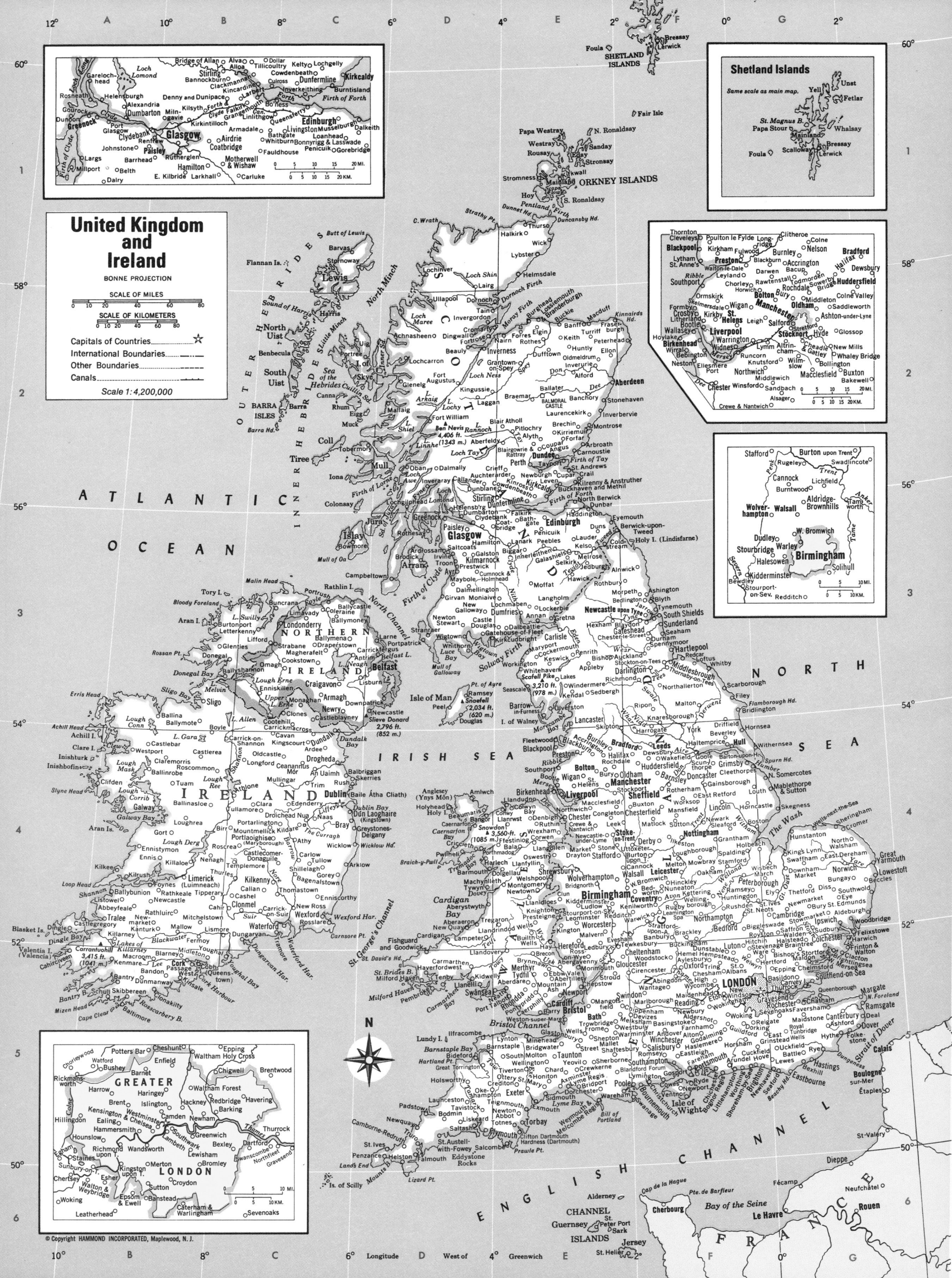

United Kingdom and Ireland

BONNE PROJECTION

SCALE OF MILES

SCALE OF KILOMETERS

Capitals of Countries............★
International Boundaries............
Other Boundaries............
Canals............

Scale 1:4,200,000

Shetland Islands

Same scale as main map.

GREATER LONDON

© Copyright HAMMOND INCORPORATED, Maplewood, N.J.

UNITED KINGDOM

AREA 94,399 sq. mi. (244,493 sq. km.)
POPULATION 55,672,000
CAPITAL London
LARGEST CITY London
HIGHEST POINT Ben Nevis 4,406 ft. (1,343 m.)
MONETARY UNIT pound sterling
MAJOR LANGUAGES English, Gaelic, Welsh
MAJOR RELIGIONS Protestantism, Roman Catholicism

IRELAND

AREA 27,136 sq. mi. (70,282 sq. km.)
POPULATION 3,440,427
CAPITAL Dublin
LARGEST CITY Dublin
HIGHEST POINT Carrantuohill 3,415 ft. (1,041 m.)
MONETARY UNIT Irish pound
MAJOR LANGUAGES English, Gaelic (Irish)
MAJOR RELIGION Roman Catholicism

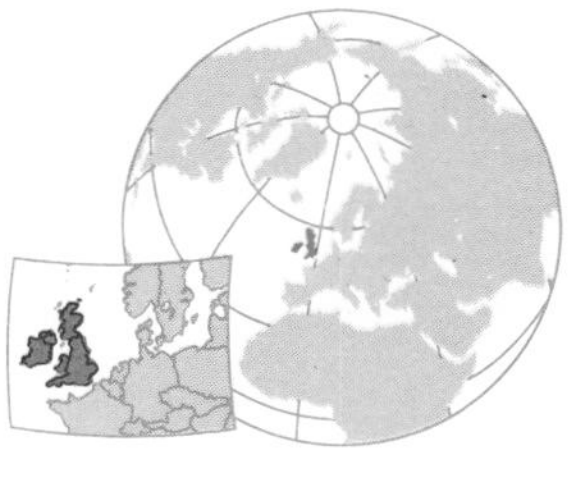

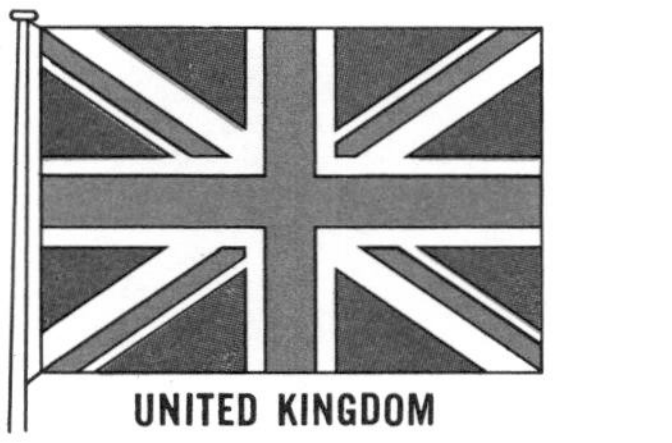

UNITED KINGDOM

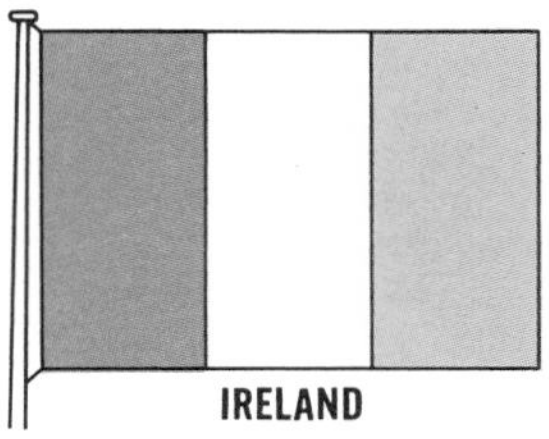

IRELAND

ENGLAND

COUNTIES

Avon, 920,200 E 6
Bedfordshire, 491,700 G 5
Berkshire, 659,000 F 6
Buckinghamshire, 512,000 G 6
Cambridgeshire, 563,000 G 5
Cheshire, 916,400 E 4
Cleveland, 567,900 F 3
Cornwall, 405,200 C 7
Cumbria, 473,600 D 3
Derbyshire, 887,600 F 5
Devon, 942,100 D 7
Dorset, 575,800 E 7
Durham, 610,400 F 3
East Sussex, 655,600 H 7
Essex, 1,426,200 H 6
Gloucestershire, 491,500 E 6
Greater London, 7,028,200 H 8
Greater Manchester, 2,684,100 H 2
Hampshire, 1,456,100 F 6
Hereford and Worcester, 594,200 E 5
Hertfordshire, 937,300 G 6
Humberside, 848,600 G 4
Isle of Wight, 111,300 F 7
Isles of Scilly, 1,900 A 7
Kent, 1,448,100 H 6
Lancashire, 1,375,500 E 4
Leicestershire, 837,900 F 5
Lincolnshire, 524,500 G 4
London, Greater, 7,028,200 H 8
Manchester, Greater, 2,684,100 H 2
Merseyside, 1,578,000 G 2
Norfolk, 662,500 H 5
Northamptonshire, 505,900 G 5
Northumberland, 287,300 E 2
North Yorkshire, 653,000 F 3
Nottinghamshire, 977,500 F 4
Oxfordshire, 541,800 F 6
Salop, 359,000 E 5
Somerset, 404,400 E 6
South Yorkshire, 1,318,300 F 4
Staffordshire, 997,600 E 5
Suffolk, 577,600 H 5
Surrey, 1,002,900 G 6
Sussex, East, 655,600 H 7
Sussex, West, 623,400 G 7
Tyne and Wear, 1,182,900 H 3
Warwickshire, 471,000 F 5
West Midlands, 2,743,300 F 5
West Sussex, 623,400 G 7
West Yorkshire, 2,072,500 J 1
Wiltshire, 512,800 E 6
Yorkshire, North, 653,000 F 3
Yorkshire, South, 1,318,300 F 4
Yorkshire, West, 2,072,500 J 1

CITIES and TOWNS

Abingdon, 20,130 F 6
Accrington, 36,470 H 1
Adwick le Street, 17,650 K 2
Aldeburgh, 2,750 J 5
Aldershot, 33,750 G 8
Aldridge Brownhills, 89,370 E 5
Alfreton, 21,560 F 4
Alnwick, 7,300 F 2
Altrincham, 40,800 H 2
Amersham, ⊙17,254 G 7
Andover, 27,620 F 6
Appleby, 2,240 E 3
Arnold, 35,090 F 4
Arundel, 2,390 G 7
Ashford, 36,380 H 6
Ashington, 24,720 F 2
Ashton-under-Lyne, 48,500 H 2
Axminster, ⊙4,515 D 7
Aycliffe, ⊙20,203 F 3
Aylesbury, 41,420 G 7
Bacup, 14,990 H 1
Bakewell, 4,100 J 2
Banbury, 31,060 F 5
Banstead, 44,100 H 8
Barking, 153,800 H 8
Barnet, 305,200 H 7
Barnsley, 74,730 J 2
Barnstaple, 17,820 D 6
Barrow-in-Furness, 73,400 D 3
Barton-upon-Humber, 7,750 G 4
Basildon, 135,720 J 8
Basingstoke, 60,910 F 6
Bath, 83,100 E 6
Batley, 41,630 J 1
Battle, ⊙4,987 H 7
Bebington, 62,500 G 2
Bedford, 74,390 G 5
Bedlington, 27,200 F 2
Bedworth, 41,600 F 5
Beeston and Stapleford, 65,360 F 5
Benfleet, 49,180 J 8
Bentley with Arksey, 22,320 F 4
Berkhamsted, 15,920 G 7
Beverley, 16,920 G 4
Bexhill, 34,680 H 7
Bexley, 213,500 H 8
Biddulph, 18,720 H 2
Birkenhead, 135,750 G 2
Birmingham, 1,058,800 F 5
Bishop Auckland, 32,940 E 3
Bishop's Stortford, 21,720 H 6
Blackburn, 101,670 H 1
Blackpool, 149,000 G 1
Blaydon, 31,940 H 3
Blyth, 35,390 F 2
Bodmin, 10,430 C 7
Bognor Regis, 34,620 G 7
Boldon, 24,430 J 3
Bolton, 154,480 H 2
Bootle, 71,160 G 2
Boston, 26,700 G 5
Bournemouth, 144,100 F 7
Bracknell, ⊙34,067 G 8
Bradford, 458,900 J 1
Braintree and Bocking, 26,300 H 6
Brent, 256,500 H 8
Brentwood, 58,690 J 8
Bridgwater, 26,700 E 6
Bridlington, 26,920 G 3
Bridport, 6,660 E 7
Brigg, 4,870 G 4
Brighowe, 35,320 J 1
Brightlingsea, 7,170 J 6
Brighton, 156,500 G 7
Bristol, 416,300 E 6
Broadstairs and Saint Peter's, 21,670 J 6
Bromley, 299,100 H 8
Bromsgrove, 41,430 E 5
Buckfastleigh, 2,870 C 7
Buckingham, 5,290 G 6
Bude-Stratton, 5,750 C 7
Bungay, 4,120 J 5
Burgess Hill, 20,030 G 7
Burnham-on-Crouch, 4,920 H 6
Burnley, 74,300 H 1
Burntwood, ⊙23,088 F 5
Burton upon Trent, 49,480 F 5
Bury, 69,550 H 2
Bury Saint Edmunds, 26,800 H 5
Bushey, 24,500 H 7
Buxton, 20,050 J 2
Caister-on-Sea, ⊙6,287 J 5
Camborne-Redruth, 43,970 B 7
Cambridge, 106,400 G 5
Camden, 185,800 H 8
Cannock, 56,440 E 5
Canterbury, 115,600 H 6
Canvey Island, 29,550 J 8
Carlisle, 99,600 D 3
Carlton, 46,690 F 5
Caterham and Warlingham, 35,840 H 8
Chatham, 59,550 J 8
Cheadle and Gatley, 62,460 H 2
Chelmsford, 58,320 J 7
Cheltenham, 75,910 E 6
Chertsey, 45,070 G 8
Chesham, 20,830 G 7
Cheshunt, 45,750 H 7
Chester, 117,200 G 2
Chesterfield, 69,480 J 2
Chester-le-Street, 20,720 J 3
Chichester, 20,940 G 7
Chigwell, 54,220 H 8
Chippenham, 18,550 E 6
Chorley, 31,800 G 2
Christchurch, 31,610 F 7
Cirencester, 14,500 E 6
Clacton, 39,380 J 6
Clay Cross, 9,630 J 2
Cleator Moor, ⊙7,686 D 3
Cleethorpes, 37,200 H 4
Clevedon, 15,140 D 6
Clun, ⊙1,261 D 6
Coalville, 28,740 F 5
Cockermouth, 6,480 D 3
Colchester, 79,600 H 6
Colne, 19,030 H 1
Colne Valley, 21,190 J 2
Congleton, 21,500 H 2
Consett, 35,080 H 3
Corby, 48,850 G 5
Coventry, 336,800 F 5
Cowes, 19,190 F 7
Crawley, 72,600 G 6
Crewe and Nantwich, 98,100 E 4
Cromer, 5,720 J 5
Crook and Willington, 21,120 E 3
Crosby, 56,750 G 2
Croydon, 330,600 H 8
Cuckfield, 26,500 G 6
Darlington, 85,120 F 3
Dartford, 44,130 J 8
Darton, 15,710 J 2
Darwen, 29,290 H 1
Deal, 26,840 J 6
Dearne, 24,780 K 2
Denton, 38,110 H 2
Derby, 213,700 F 5
Dewsbury, 50,560 J 1
Didcot, ⊙14,277 F 6
Doncaster, 81,530 F 4
Dorking, 22,410 G 8
Dover, 34,160 J 6
Downham Market, 4,120 H 5
Droitwich, 13,950 E 5
Dronfield, 20,000 J 2
Dudley, 187,110 E 5
Dunstable, 32,090 G 6
Durham, 88,800 J 3
Ealing, 293,800 H 8
Eastbourne, 73,200 H 7
East Grinstead, 19,420 G 6
Eastleigh, 46,340 F 7
East Retford, 18,260 G 4
Egham, 30,320 G 8
Egremont, ⊙7,253 D 3
Eling, ⊙20,006 F 7
Ellesmere, ⊙2,630 E 5
Ellesmere Port, 63,870 G 2
Enfield, 260,900 H 7
Epsom and Ewell, 70,700 G 8
Esher, 63,970 H 8
Eston, ⊙46,219 F 3
Eton, 4,950 G 8
Evesham, 14,090 F 5
Exeter, 93,300 D 7
Exminster, ⊙3,181 D 7
Exmouth, 26,840 D 7
Falmouth, 17,530 B 7
Fareham, 86,300 F 7
Farnborough, 43,520 G 8
Farnham, 33,140 G 8
Farnworth, 26,110 H 2
Faversham, 15,010 H 6
Felixstowe, 19,460 J 6
Felling, 38,990 J 3
Filey, 5,660 G 3
Fleet, 22,930 G 8
Fleetwood, 30,070 D 4
Folkestone, 45,610 J 6
Formby, 24,850 G 2
Framlingham, ⊙2,258 J 5
Frimley and Camberley, 47,390 G 8
Fulwood, 22,910 G 1
Gainsborough, 17,440 G 4
Gateshead, 91,230 J 3
Gillingham, Dorset, ⊙4,050 E 6
Gillingham, Kent, 93,900 J 8
Glastonbury, 6,580 E 6
Glossop, 24,820 J 2
Gloucester, 91,600 E 6
Godalming, 18,840 G 8
Golborne, 28,720 G 2
Goole, 17,920 G 4
Gosport, 82,300 F 7
Grange, 3,520 E 3
Grantham, 27,830 G 5
Gravesend, 53,500 J 8
Great Baddow, ⊙18,755 J 7
Great Torrington, 3,430 C 7
Great Yarmouth, 49,410 J 5
Greenwich, 207,200 H 8
Grimsby, 93,800 G 4
Guildford, 58,470 G 8
Guisborough, 14,860 F 3
Hackney, 192,500 H 8
Hale, 17,080 H 2
Halesowen, 54,120 E 5
Halifax, 88,580 J 1
Haltemprice, 54,850 G 4
Haltwhistle, ⊙3,511 E 2
Hammersmith, 170,000 H 8
Haringey, 228,200 H 8
Harlow, 79,160 H 7
Harrogate, 64,620 J 1
Harrow, 200,200 G 8
Hartlepool, 97,100 F 3
Harwich, 15,280 J 6
Haslingden, 15,140 H 1
Hastings, 74,600 H 7
Hatfield, ⊙25,359 H 7
Havant and Waterloo, 112,430 G 7
Haverhill, 14,550 H 5
Havering, 239,200 J 8
Hayle, ⊙5,378 B 7
Hazel Grove and Bramhall, 40,400 H 2
Heanor, 24,590 F 4
Hebburn, 23,150 J 3
Hedon, 3,010 G 4
Hemel Hempstead, 71,150 G 7
Hereford, 47,800 E 5
Hertford, 20,760 H 7
Hetton, 16,810 J 3
Hexham, 9,820 E 3
Heywood, 31,720 H 2
High Wycombe, 61,190 G 8
Hillingdon, 230,800 G 8
Hinckley, 49,310 F 5
Hinderwell, ⊙2,551 G 3
Hitchin, 29,190 G 6
Hoddesdon, 27,510 H 7
Holmfirth, 19,790 J 2
Horley, ⊙18,593 H 8
Hornsea, 7,280 G 4
Horsham, 26,770 G 6
Horwich, 16,670 G 2
Houghton-le-Spring, 33,150 J 3
Hounslow, 199,100 G 8
Hove, 72,000 G 7
Hoylake, 32,000 G 2
Hoyland Nether, 15,500 J 2
Hucknall, 27,110 F 4
Huddersfield, 130,060 J 2
Hugh Town, ⊙1,958 A 8
Hull, 276,600 G 4
Hunstanton, 4,140 H 5
Huntingdon and Godmanchester, 17,200 G 5
Huyton-with-Roby, 65,950 G 2
Hyde, 37,040 H 2
Ilfracombe, 9,350 C 6
Ilkeston, 33,690 F 5
Immingham, ⊙10,259 G 4
Ipswich, 121,500 J 5
Islington, 171,600 H 8
Jarrow, 28,510 J 3
Kendal, 22,440 E 3
Kenilworth, 19,730 F 5
Kensington and Chelsea, 161,400 G 8
Keswick, 4,790 D 3
Kettering, 44,480 G 5
Keynsham, 18,970 E 6
Kidderminster, 49,960 E 5
Kidsgrove, 22,690 E 4
King's Lynn, 29,990 H 5
Kingston upon Thames, 135,600 H 8
Kingswood, 30,450 E 6
Kirkburton, 20,320 J 2
Kirkby, 59,100 G 2
Kirkby Lonsdale, ⊙1,506 E 3
Kirkby Stephen, ⊙1,539 E 3
Knutsford, 14,840 H 2
Lambeth, 290,300 H 8
Lancaster, 126,300 E 3
Leatherhead, 40,830 G 8
Leeds, 744,500 J 1
Leek, 19,460 H 2
Leicester, 289,400 F 5
Leigh, 46,390 H 2
Leighton-Linslade, 22,590 F 7
Letchworth, 31,520 G 6
Lewes, 14,170 H 7
Lewisham, 237,300 H 8
Leyland, 23,690 G 1
Lichfield, 23,690 F 5
Lincoln, 73,700 G 4
Liskeard, 5,360 C 7
Litherland, 23,530 G 2
Littlehampton, 20,320 G 7

(continued on following page)

ENGLAND

AREA 50,516 sq. mi. (130,836 sq. km.)
POPULATION 46,220,955
CAPITAL London
LARGEST CITY London
HIGHEST POINT Scafell Pike 3,210 ft. (978 m.)

WALES

AREA 8,017 sq. mi. (20,764 sq. km.)
POPULATION 2,790,462
LARGEST CITY Cardiff
HIGHEST POINT Snowdon 3,560 ft. (1,085 m.)

SCOTLAND

AREA 30,414 sq. mi. (78,772 sq. km.)
POPULATION 5,117,146
CAPITAL Edinburgh
LARGEST CITY Glasgow
HIGHEST POINT Ben Nevis 4,406 ft. (1,343 m.)

NORTHERN IRELAND

AREA 5,452 sq. mi. (14,121 sq. km.)
POPULATION 1,543,000
CAPITAL Belfast
LARGEST CITY Belfast
HIGHEST POINT Slieve Donard 2,796 ft. (852 m.)

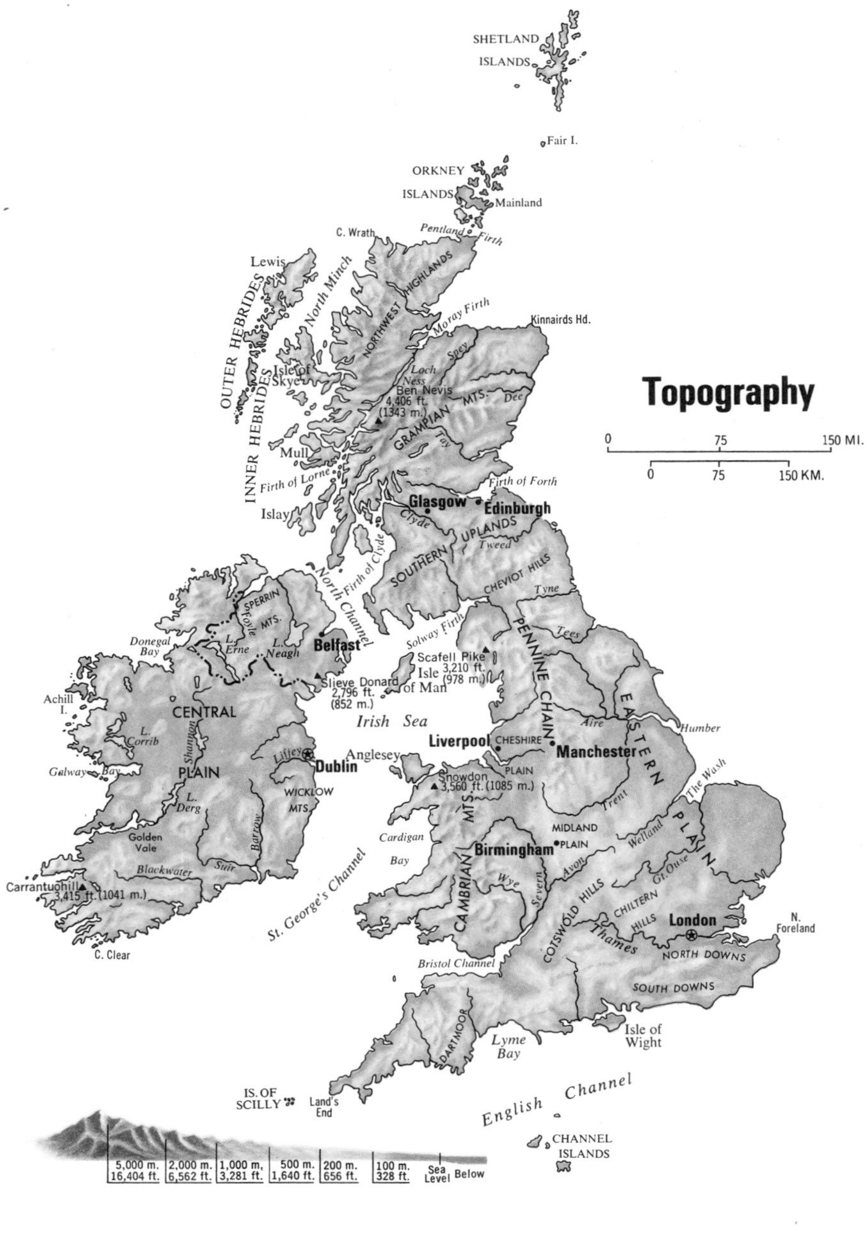

Topography
0
75
150 MI.
0
75
150 KM.
SHETLAND ISLANDS
Fair I.
ORKNEY ISLANDS
Mainland
C. Wrath
Pentland Firth
Lewis
OUTER HEBRIDES
North Minch
NORTHWEST HIGHLANDS
Moray Firth
Kinnairds Hd.
Isle of Skye
Spey
Loch Ness
Ben Nevis 4,406 ft. (1343 m.)
GRAMPIAN MTS.
Dee
INNER HEBRIDES
Mull
Firth of Lorne
Tay
Firth of Forth
Islay
Glasgow
Edinburgh
Clyde
SOUTHERN UPLANDS
Tweed
Firth of Clyde
CHEVIOT HILLS
Tyne
North Channel
SPERRIN MTS.
Lough Neagh
Belfast
Donegal Bay
L. Erne
Solway Firth
Tees
Scafell Pike 3,210 ft. (978 m.)
Isle of Man
Slieve Donard 2,796 ft. (852 m.)
PENNINE CHAIN
Achill I.
CENTRAL PLAIN
Irish Sea
Aire
EASTERN PLAIN
Humber
L. Corrib
Shannon
Liffey
Dublin
Anglesey
Liverpool
CHESHIRE PLAIN
Manchester
Trent
The Wash
Galway Bay
WICKLOW MTS.
Snowdon 3,560 ft. (1085 m.)
L. Derg
Cardigan Bay
CAMBRIAN MTS.
MIDLAND PLAIN
Welland
Barrow
Birmingham
Golden Vale
Suir
Blackwater
Severn
Avon
Gt. Ouse
Carrantuohill 3,415 ft. (1041 m.)
St. George's Channel
Wye
COTSWOLD HILLS
CHILTERN HILLS
London
N. Foreland
Thames
NORTH DOWNS
C. Clear
Bristol Channel
SOUTH DOWNS
DARTMOOR
Lyme Bay
Isle of Wight
IS. OF SCILLY
Land's End
English Channel
CHANNEL ISLANDS
5,000 m. 16,404 ft.
2,000 m. 6,562 ft.
1,000 m. 3,281 ft.
500 m. 1,640 ft.
200 m. 656 ft.
100 m. 328 ft.
Sea Level
Below

Liverpool, 539,700 G 2
Loftus, 7,850 G 3
London (cap.), 7,028,200 H 8
London, ★12,332,900 H 8
Long Eaton, 33,560 F 5
Longbenton, 50,120 J 3
Looe, 4,060 C 7
Loughborough, 49,010 F 5
Lowestoft, 53,260 J 5
Ludlow, ⊙7,466 E 5
Luton, 164,500 G 6
Lydd, 4,670 H 7
Lyme Regis, 3,460 E 7
Lymington, 36,780 F 7
Lynton, 1,770 D 6
Lytham Saint Anne's, 42,120 G 1
Mablethorpe and Sutton, 6,750 H 4
Macclesfield, 45,420 H 2
Maidenhead, 48,210 G 8
Maidstone, 72,110 J 8
Maldon, 14,350 H 6
Malmesbury, 2,550 E 6
Malton, 4,010 G 3
Malvern, 30,420 E 5
Manchester, 490,000 H 2
Mangotsfield, 23,000 E 6
Mansfield, 58,450 K 2
Mansfield Woodhouse, 25,400 F 4
March, 14,560 H 5
Margate, 50,290 J 6
Market Harborough, 15,230 G 5
Marlborough, 6,370 F 6
Matlock, 20,300 J 2
Melton Mowbray, 20,680 G 5
Merton, 169,400 H 8
Middlesbrough, 153,900 F 3
Middleton, 53,340 H 2
Middlewich, 7,600 H 2
Mildenhall, ⊙9,269 H 5
Millom, ⊙7,101 D 3
Milton Keynes, 89,900 G 5
Minehead, 8,230 D 6
Moretonhampstead, ⊙1,440 C 7
Morpeth, 14,450 F 2
Mundesley, ⊙1,536 J 5
Nelson, 31,220 H 1
Neston, 18,210 G 2
Newark, 24,760 G 4
Newbury, 24,850 F 6
Newcastle upon Tyne, 295,800 H 3
Newcastle-under-Lyme, 75,940 E 4
Newham, 228,900 H 8
Newhaven, 9,970 H 7
Newport, 22,430 F 7
New Romney, 3,830 J 7
Newton Abbot, 19,940 D 7
Newton-le-Willows, 21,780 H 2
New Windsor, 29,660 G 8
Northallerton F 3
Northam, 8,310 C 6
Northampton, 128,290 F 5
Northfleet, 27,150 J 8
North Sunderland, ⊙1,725 F 2
Northwich, 17,710 H 2
Norton, 5,580 G 3
Norton-Radstock, 15,900 E 6
Norwich, 119,200 J 5
Nottingham, 280,300 F 5
Nuneaton, 69,210 F 5
Oadby, 20,700 F 5
Oakham, 7,280 G 5
Okehampton, 4,000 D 7
Oldham, 103,690 H 2
Ormskirk, 28,860 G 2
Oswaldtwistle, 14,270 H 1
Oxford, 117,400 F 6
Padstow, ⊙2,802 B 7
Penryn, 5,660 B 7
Penzance, 19,360 B 7
Peterborough, 118,900 G 5
Peterlee, ⊙21,846 J 3
Plymouth, 259,100 C 7
Polperro, ⊙1,491 C 7
Poole, 110,600 E 7
Porlock, ⊙1,290 D 6
Portishead, 9,680 E 6
Portland, 14,860 E 7
Portslade-by-Sea, 18,040 G 7
Portsmouth, 198,500 F 7
Potters Bar, 24,670 H 7
Poulton-le-Fylde, 16,340 G 1
Preston, 94,760 G 1
Prestwich, 32,850 H 2
Queenborough, 31,550 H 6
Radcliffe, 29,630 H 2
Ramsbottom, 16,710 H 2
Ramsgate, 40,090 J 6
Rawtenstall, 20,950 H 1
Rayleigh, 26,740 J 8
Reading, 131,200 G 8
Redbridge, 231,600 H 8
Redcar, ⊙46,325 F 3
Redditch, 44,750 E 5
Reigate, 55,600 H 8
Richmond upon Thames, 166,800 H 8
Rickmansworth, 29,030 G 8
Ripley, 18,060 F 4
Rochdale, 93,780 H 2
Rochester, 56,030 J 8
Rothbury, ⊙1,818 E 2
Rotherham, 84,770 K 2
Royal Leamington Spa, 44,950 F 5
Royal Tunbridge Wells, 44,800 H 6
Rugby, 60,380 F 5
Rugeley, 24,440 E 5
Runcorn, 42,730 G 2
Rushden, 21,840 G 5
Ryde, 23,170 F 7
Rye, 4,530 H 7
Ryton, 15,170 H 3
Saddleworth, 21,340 J 2
Saint Agnes, ⊙4,747 B 7
Saint Albans, 123,800 H 7
Saint Austell-with-Fowey, 32,710 C 7
Saint Columb Major, ⊙3,953 B 7
Saint Helens, 104,890 G 2
Saint Ives, Cornwall, 9,760 B 7
Saint Neots, 17,940 G 5
Salcombe, 2,370 D 7
Sale, 59,060 H 2
Salford, 261,100 H 2
Salisbury, 35,460 F 6
Saltburn and Marske-by-the-Sea, 21,170 G 3
Sandbach, 14,280 H 2
Sandown-Shanklin, 14,800 F 7
Sandwich, 4,420 J 6
Saxmundham, 1,820 J 5
Scarborough, 43,300 G 3
Scunthorpe, 68,100 G 4
Seaford, 18,020 H 7
Seaham, 22,470 J 3
Seascale, ⊙2,106 D 3
Seaton, 4,500 D 7
Seaton Valley, 35,880 J 3
Sedbergh, ⊙2,741 E 3
Selsey, ⊙6,491 G 7
Sevenoaks, 18,160 J 8
Shaftesbury, 4,180 E 7
Sheffield, 558,000 J 2
Sherborne, 9,230 E 7
Sheringham, 4,940 J 5
Shildon, 15,360 F 3
Shoreham-by-Sea, 19,620 G 7
Shrewsbury, 56,120 E 5
Silloth, ⊙2,662 D 3
Sittingbourne and Milton, 32,830 H 6
Skelmersdale, 35,850 G 2
Skelton and Brotton, 15,930 G 3
Sleaford, 8,050 G 5
Slough, 89,060 G 8
Solihull, 108,230 F 5
Southampton, 213,700 F 7
Southend-on-Sea, 159,300 H 6
Southport, 86,030 G 1
South Shields, 96,900 J 3
Southwark, 224,900 H 8
Southwold, 1,960 J 5
Sowerby Bridge, 15,700 H 1
Spalding, 17,040 G 5
Spenborough, 41,460 J 1
Spennymoor, 19,050 F 3
Stafford, 54,860 E 5
Staines, 56,380 G 8
Stamford, 14,980 G 5
Stanley, 42,280 H 3
Staveley, 17,620 K 2
Stevenage, 72,600 G 6
Stockport, 138,350 H 2
Stockton-on-Tees, 165,400 F 3
Stoke-on-Trent, 256,200 E 4
Stourbridge, 56,530 E 5
Stourport-on-Severn, 19,430 E 5
Stowmarket, 9,020 J 5
Stratford-upon-Avon, 20,080 F 5
Stretford, 52,450 H 2
Stroud, 19,600 E 6
Sudbury, 8,860 H 5
Sunbury-on-Thames, 40,070 G 8
Sunderland, 214,820 J 3
Sutton, 166,700 H 8
Sutton Bridge, ⊙3,113 H 5
Sutton in Ashfield, 40,330 K 2
Swadlincote, 21,060 F 5
Swanage, 8,000 E 7
Swindon, 90,680 F 6
Tamworth, 46,960 F 5
Taunton, 37,570 D 6
Tavistock, ⊙7,620 C 7
Telford, ⊙79,451 E 5
Tenbury, ⊙2,151 E 5
Tewkesbury, 9,210 E 6
Thetford, 15,690 H 5
Thirsk, ⊙2,884 F 3
Thornaby-on-Tees, ⊙42,385 F 3
Thorne, ⊙16,694 F 4
Thornton Cleveleys, 27,090 G 1
Thurrock, 127,700 J 8
Tiverton, 16,190 D 7
Todmorden, 14,540 H 1
Tonbridge, 31,410 H 6
Torbay, 109,900 D 7
Torpoint, 6,840 C 7
Tower Hamlets, 146,100 H 8
Tow Law, 2,460 H 4
Trowbridge, 20,120 E 6
Truro, 15,690 B 7
Turton, 22,800 H 2
Tynemouth, 67,090 J 3
Upton upon Severn, ⊙2,048 E 5
Urmston, 44,130 H 2
Uttoxeter, 9,100 E 5
Ventnor, 6,980 F 7
Wainfleet All Saints, ⊙1,116 H 4
Wakefield, 306,500 J 2
Wallasey, 94,520 G 2
Wallsend, 45,490 J 3
Walsall, 182,430 E 5
Waltham Forest, 223,700 H 8
Waltham Holy Cross, 14,810 H 7
Walton and Weybridge, 51,270 G 8
Walton-le-Dale, 27,660 G 1
Wandsworth, 284,600 H 8
Wantage, 8,490 F 6
Ware, 14,900 H 7
Wareham, 4,630 E 7
Warley, 161,260 E 5
Warminster, 14,440 E 6
Warrington, 65,320 G 2
Warwick, 17,870 F 5
Washington, 27,720 J 3
Watchet, 2,980 D 6
Watford, 77,000 H 7
Wellingborough, 39,570 G 5
Wells, 8,960 E 6
Wells-next-the-Sea, 2,450 H 5
Welwyn, 39,900 H 7
Wem, ⊙3,411 E 5
West Bridgford, 28,340 F 5
West Bromwich, 162,740 F 5
West Mersea, 4,730 H 6
Westminster, 216,100 H 8
Weston-super-Mare, 51,960 D 6
Weymouth and Melcombe Regis, 41,080 E 7
Whickham, 29,710 J 3
Whitchurch, ⊙7,142 E 5
Whitehaven, 26,260 D 3
Whitley Bay, 37,010 J 3
Widnes, 58,330 G 2
Wigan, 80,920 G 2
Wigston, 31,650 F 5
Wilmslow, 31,250 H 2
Wilton, 4,090 F 6
Winchester, 88,900 F 6
Windermere, 7,860 E 3
Winsford, 26,920 E 4
Wirral, 27,510 G 2
Wisbech, 16,990 H 5
Witham, 19,730 H 6
Withernsea, 6,300 H 4
Wivenhoe, 5,630 J 6
Woking, 79,300 G 8
Wokingham, 22,390 G 8
Wolverhampton, 266,400 E 5
Wombwell, 17,850 K 2
Woodhall Spa, 2,420 G 4
Woodley and Sandford, ⊙24,581 G 8
Woodstock, 2,070 F 6
Wooler, ⊙1,833 E 2
Worcester, 73,900 E 5
Workington, 28,260 D 3
Worksop, 36,590 F 4
Worsbrough, 15,180 J 2
Worsley, 49,530 H 2
Worthing, 89,100 G 7
Wymondham, 9,390 J 5
Yateley, ⊙16,505 G 8
Yeovil, 26,180 E 7
York, 101,900 F 4

OTHER FEATURES

Aire (riv.) F 4
Atlantic Ocean A 7
Avon (riv.) F 5
Avon (riv.) F 7
Axe Edge (mt.) H 2
Barnstaple (bay) C 6
Beachy (head) H 7
Bigbury (bay) C 7
Blackwater (riv.) H 6
Bristol (chan.) C 6
Brown Willy (mt.) C 7
Cheviot (hills) E 2
Cheviot, The (mt.) E 2
Chiltern (hills) G 6
Cleveland (hills) F 3
Colne (riv.) G 8
Cornwall (cape) B 7
Cotswold (hills) E 6
Cross Fell (mt.) E 3
Cumbrian (mts.) D 3
Dart (riv.) D 7
Dartmoor National Park C 7
Dee (riv.) D 4
Derwent (riv.) G 3
Derwent (riv.) H 3
Don (riv.) F 4
Dorset Heights (hills) E 7
Dove (riv.) J 2
Dover (str.) J 7
Dungeness (prom.) J 7
Dunkery (hill) D 6
Eddystone (rocks) C 7
Eden (riv.) E 3
English (chan.) D 8
Esk (riv.) D 2
Exe (riv.) D 7
Exmoor National Park D 6
Fens, The (reg.) G 5
Flamborough (head) G 3
Formby (head) G 2
Foulness Island (pen.) J 6
Gibraltar (pt.) H 4
Great Ouse (riv.) H 5
Hartland (pt.) C 6
High Willhays (mt.) C 7
Hodder (riv.) H 1
Holderness (pen.), 43,900 G 4
Holy (isl.), 189 F 2
Humber (riv.) G 4
Irish (sea) B 4
Kennet (riv.) F 6
Lake District National Park D 3
Land's End (prom.) B 7
Lea (riv.) G 6
Lincoln Wolds (hills) G 4
Lindisfarne (Holy) (isl.), 189 F 2
Liverpool (bay) D 4
Lizard, The (pen.), 7,371 B 8
Lundy (isl.), 49 C 6
Lune (riv.) E 3
Lyme (bay) D 7
Manacle (pt.) C 7
Medway (riv.) H 6
Mendip (hills) E 6
Mersea (isl.), 4,423 J 6
Mersey (riv.) G 2
Morecambe (bay) D 3
Mounts (bay) B 7
Naze, The (prom.) J 6
Nene (riv.) H 5
New (for.) F 6
North (sea) J 4
North Downs (hills) G 6
North Foreland (prom.) J 6
Northumberland National Park E 2
North York Moors National Park G 3
Orford Ness (prom.) J 5
Ouse (riv.) G 4
Ouse (riv.) G 6
Parrett (riv.) E 6
Peak District National Park F 4
Peak, The (mt.) J 2
Peel Fell (mt.) E 2
Pennine Chain (range) E 3
Plymouth (sound) C 7
Portland, Bill of (pt.) E 7
Prawle (pt.) D 7
Purbeck, Isle of (pen.), 39,500 F 7
Ribble (riv.) E 4
Saint Alban's (head) F 7
Saint Bees (head) D 3
Saint Martin's (isl.), 106 A 8
Saint Mary's (isl.), 1,958 A 8
Scafell Pike (mt.) D 3
Scilly (isls.), 1,900 A 7
Selsey Bill (prom.) G 7
Severn (riv.) E 6
Sheppey (isl.), 31,550 J 6
Sherwood (for.) F 4
Skiddaw (mt.) D 3
Solent (chan.) F 7
Solway (firth) D 3
South Downs (hills) G 7
Spithead (chan.) F 7
Spurn (head) H 4
Stonehenge (ruins) F 6
Stour (riv.) E 7
Stour (riv.) H 8
Stour (riv.) J 6
Swale (riv.) F 3
Tamar (riv.) C 7
Taw (riv.) D 7
Tees (riv.) F 3
Test (riv.) F 6
Thames (riv.) H 6
Tintagel (head) C 7
Torridge (riv.) C 7
Trent (riv.) F 4
Tresco (isl.), 246 A 8
Tweed (riv.) E 2
Tyne (riv.) F 3
Ure (riv.) F 3
Ver (riv.) H 7
Walney, Isle of (isl.), 11,241 D 3
Wash, The (bay) H 5
Weald, The (reg.) H 6
Wear (riv.) F 3
Weaver (riv.) G 2
Welland (riv.) G 5
Wey (riv.) G 6
Wharfe (riv.) E 3
Wirral (pen.), 432,900 G 2
Witham (riv.) G 4
Wolds, The (hills) G 4
Wye (riv.) D 5
Wyre (riv.) F 2
Yare (riv.) J 5
Yorkshire Dales National Park E 3

CHANNEL ISLANDS

CITIES and TOWNS

Saint Anne E 8
Saint Helier (cap.), Jersey, ⊙28,135 E 8
Saint Peter Port (cap.), Guernsey, ⊙16,303 E 8
Saint Sampson's, ⊙6,534 E 8

OTHER FEATURES

Alderney (isl.), 1,686 E 8
Guernsey (isl.), 51,351 E 8
Herm (isl.), 96 E 8
Jersey (isl.), 72,629 E 8
Sark (isl.), 590 E 8

ISLE of MAN

CITIES and TOWNS

Castletown, 2,620 C 3
Douglas (cap.), 20,389 C 3
Laxey, 1,170 C 3
Michael, 408 C 3
Onchan, 4,807 C 3
Peel, 3,081 C 3
Port Erin, 1,714 C 3
Port Saint Mary, 1,508 C 3
Ramsey, 5,048 C 3

OTHER FEATURES

Ayre (pt.) C 3
Calf of Man (isl.) C 3
Langness (prom.) C 3
Snaefell (mt.) C 3
Spanish (head) C 3

WALES

COUNTIES

Clwyd, 376,000 D 4
Dyfed, 323,100 C 6
Gwent, 439,600 D 6
Gwynedd, 225,100 C 4
Mid Glamorgan, 540,400 D 6
Powys, 101,500 D 5
South Glamorgan, 389,200 A 7
West Glamorgan, 371,900 D 6

CITIES and TOWNS

Aberaeron, 1,340 C 5
Abercarn, 18,370 B 6
Aberdare, 38,030 A 6
Abertillery, 20,550 B 6
Amlwch, 3,630 C 4
Bala, 1,650 D 5
Bangor, 16,030 C 4
Barmouth, 2,070 C 5
Barry, 42,780 B 7
Beaumaris, 2,090 C 4
Bedwellty, 25,460 B 6
Bethesda, 4,180 D 4
Betws-y-Coed, 720 D 4
Brecknock (Brecon), 6,460 D 6
Brecon, 6,460 D 6
Bridgend, 14,690 A 7
Brynmawr, 5,970 B 6
Builth Wells, 1,480 D 5
Burry Port, 5,990 C 6
Caernarfon, 8,840 C 4
Caerphilly, 42,190 B 6
Cardiff, 281,500 B 7
Cardigan, 3,830 C 5
Chepstow, 8,260 E 6
Chirk, ⊙3,564 D 5
Colwyn Bay, 25,370 D 4
Criccieth, 1,590 C 5
Cwmamman, 3,950 D 6
Cwmbran, 32,980 B 6
Denbigh, 8,420 D 4
Dolgellau, 2,430 D 5
Ebbw Vale, 25,670 B 6
Ffestiniog, 5,510 D 5
Fishguard and Goodwick, 5,020 B 5
Flint, 15,070 G 2
Gelligaer, 33,820 A 6
Harlech, ⊙332 C 5
Haverfordwest, 8,930 B 6
Hawarden, ⊙20,389 G 2
Hay, 1,200 D 5
Holywell, 8,570 G 2
Kidwelly, 3,090 C 6
Knighton, 2,190 D 5
Llandeilo, 1,780 C 6
Llandovery, 2,040 D 5
Llandrindod Wells, 3,460 D 5
Llandudno, 17,700 D 4
Llanelli, 25,870 C 6
Llanfairfechan, 3,800 D 4
Llangefni, 4,070 C 4
Llangollen, 3,050 D 5
Llanguicke, ⊙15,029 D 6
Llanidloes, 2,390 D 5
Llantrisant, ⊙27,490 A 7
Llanwrtyd Wells, 460 D 5
Llwchwr, 27,530 D 6
Machynlleth, 1,830 D 5
Maesteg, 21,100 D 6
Menai Bridge, 2,730 C 4
Merthyr Tydfil, 61,500 A 6
Milford Haven, 13,960 B 6
Mold, 8,700 G 2
Montgomery, 1,000 D 5
Mountain Ash, 27,710 A 6
Mynyddislwyn, 15,590 B 6
Narberth, 970 C 6
Neath, 27,280 D 6
Nefyn, ⊙2,086 C 5
Newcastle Emlyn, 690 C 5
Newport, Dyfed, ⊙1,062 C 5
Newport, Gwent, 110,090 B 6
New Quay, 760 C 5
Newtown, 6,400 D 5
Neyland, 2,690 B 6
Ogmore and Garw, 19,680 A 6
Pembroke, 14,570 C 6
Penarth, 24,180 B 7
Penmaenmawr, 4,050 C 4
Pontypool, 36,710 B 6
Pontypridd, 34,180 A 6
Porthcawl, 14,980 D 6
Porthmadog, 3,900 C 5
Port Talbot, 58,200 D 6
Prestatyn, 15,480 D 4
Presteigne, 1,330 D 5
Pwllheli, 4,020 C 5
Rhondda, 85,400 A 6
Rhyl, 22,150 D 4
Risca, 15,780 B 6
Ruthin, 4,780 D 4
Saint David's, ⊙1,638 B 6
Swansea, 190,800 C 6
Tenby, 4,930 C 6
Tredegar, 17,450 B 6
Tywyn, 3,850 C 5
Welshpool, 7,370 D 5
Wrexham, 39,530 E 4

OTHER FEATURES

Anglesey (isl.), 64,500 C 4
Aran Fawddwy (mt.) C 5
Bardsey (isl.), 9 C 5
Berwyn (mts.) D 5
Black (mts.) D 6
Braich-y-Pwll (prom.) C 5
Brecon Beacons (mt.) D 6
Brecon Beacons National Park D 6
Caldy (isl.), 70 C 6
Cambrian (mts.) D 5
Cardigan (bay) C 5
Carmarthen (bay) C 6
Cemmaes (head) C 5
Dee (riv.) D 4
Dovey (riv.) D 5
Ely (riv.) B 7
Gower (pen.), 17,220 C 6
Great Ormes (head) C 4
Holy (isl.), 13,715 C 4
Lleyn (pen.), 25,800 C 5
Menai (str.) C 4
Milford Haven (inlet) B 6
Pembrokeshire Coast National Park C 6
Plynlimon (mt.) D 5
Preseli (mts.) C 6
Radnor (for.) D 5
Rhymney (riv.) B 6
Saint Brides (bay) B 6
Saint David's (head) B 6
Saint George's (chan.) B 5
Saint Gowans (head) C 6
Severn (riv.) E 5
Snowdon (mt.) D 4
Snowdonia National Park D 4
Taff (riv.) B 7
Teifi (riv.) C 5
Towy (riv.) D 6
Tremadoc (bay) C 5
Usk (riv.) B 6
Wye (riv.) D 5
Ynys Môn (Anglesey) (isl.), 64,500 C 4

★Population of met. area.
⊙Population of parish.

SCOTLAND
(map on page 15)

REGIONS

Borders, 99,409 E 5
Central, 269,281 D 4
Dumfries and Galloway, 143,667 E 5
Fife, 336,339 E 4
Grampian, 448,772 F 3
Highland, 182,044 D 3
Lothian, 754,008 E 5
Orkney (islands area), 17,675 E 1
Shetland (islands area), 18,494 F 2
Strathclyde, 2,504,909 C 4
Tayside, 401,987 E 4
Western Isles (islands area), 29,615 A 3

CITIES and TOWNS

Aberchirder, 877 F 3
Aberdeen, 210,362 F 3
Aberdour, 1,576 D 1
Aberfeldy, 1,552 E 4
Aberfoyle, 793 D 4
Aberlady, 737 F 4
Aberlour, 842 E 3
Abernethy, 776 E 4
Aboyne, 1,040 F 3
Acharacle, ⊙764 C 4
Achiltibuie, ⊙1,564 C 3
Achnasheen, ⊙1,078 C 3
Ae, 239 E 5
Airdrie, 38,491 C 2
Alexandria, 9,758 A 1
Alford, 764 F 3
Alloa, 13,558 C 1
Alness, 2,560 D 3
Altnaharra, ⊙1,227 D 2
Alva, 4,593 C 1
Alyth, 1,738 E 4
Ancrum, 266 F 5
Annan, 6,250 E 6
Annat, ⊙550 C 3
Annbank Station, 2,530 D 5
Applecross, ⊙550 C 3
Arbroath, 22,706 F 4
Ardavasar, ⊙449 B 3
Ardersier, 942 E 3
Ardgay, 193 D 3
Ardrishaig, 946 C 4
Ardrossan, 11,072 D 5
Armadale, 7,200 C 2
Arrochar, 543 D 4
Ascog, 230 A 2
Auchenblae, 339 F 4
Auchencairn, 215 E 6
Auchinleck, 4,883 D 5
Auchterarder, 1,738 E 4
Auchtermuchty, 1,426 E 4
Auldearn, 405 E 3
Aviemore, 1,224 E 3
Avoch, 776 D 3
Ayr, 47,990 D 5
Ayton, 410 F 5
Bailivanish, 347 A 3
Baillieston, 7,671 B 2
Balallan, 283 B 2
Balerno, 3,576 D 2
Balfron, 1,149 B 1
Ballantrae, 262 C 5
Ballater, 981 F 3
Ballingry, 4,332 D 1
Ballinluig, 188 E 4
Balloch, Highland, 572 D 3
Balloch, Strathclyde, 1,484 B 1
Baltasound, 246 G 2
Banchory, 2,435 F 3
Banff, 3,832 F 3
Bankfoot, 868 E 4
Bankhead, 1,492 F 3
Bannockburn, 5,889 C 1
Barrhead, 18,736 B 2
Barrhill, 236 D 5
Barvas, 279 B 2
Bathgate, 14,038 C 2
Bayble, 543 B 2
Bearsden, 25,128 B 2
Beattock, 309 E 5
Beauly, 1,141 D 3
Beith, 5,859 D 5
Bellsbank, 3,066 D 5
Bellshill, 18,166 C 2
Berriedale, ⊙1,927 E 2
Bieldside, 1,137 F 3
Biggar, 1,718 E 5
Birnam, 659 E 4
Bishopbriggs, 21,570 B 2
Bishopton, 2,931 B 2
Blackburn, 7,636 C 2
Blackford, 529 E 4
Blair Atholl, 437 E 4
Blairgowrie and Rattray, 5,681 E 4
Blanefield, 835 B 1
Blantyre, 13,992 B 2
Blyth Bridge, ⊙441 E 5
Bo'ness, 12,959 C 1
Boat of Garten, 406 E 3
Boddam, 1,429 G 3
Bonar Bridge, 519 D 3
Bonhill, 4,385 B 1
Bonnybridge, 5,701 C 1
Bonnyrigg and Lasswade, 7,429 D 2
Bowmore, 947 B 5
Braemar, 394 E 3
Breasclete, 234 B 2
Brechin, 6,759 F 4
Bridge of Allan, 4,638 C 1
Bridge of Don, 4,086 F 3
Bridge of Weir, 4,724 A 2
Brightons, 3,106 C 1
Broadford, 310 B 3
Brodick, 630 C 5
Brora, 1,436 E 2
Broxburn, 7,776 D 1
Buchlyvie, 412 B 1
Buckhaven and Methil, 17,930 F 4
Buckie, 8,145 E 3
Bucksburn, 6,567 F 3
Bunessan, ⊙585 B 4
Burghead, 1,321 E 3
Burnmouth, 300 F 5
Burntisland, 5,626 D 1
Cairndow, ⊙874 D 4
Cairnryan, 199 D 6
Callander, 1,805 D 4
Cambuslang, 14,607 B 2
Campbeltown, 6,428 C 5
Cannich, 203 D 3
Canonbie, 234 F 5
Caol, 3,719 C 4
Carbost, ⊙772 B 3
Cardenden, 6,802 D 1
Carloway, 178 B 2
Carluke, 8,864 E 5
Carnoustie, 6,838 F 4
Carnwath, 1,246 E 5
Carradale, 262 C 5
Carrbridge, 416 E 3
Carron, 2,626 C 1
Carsphairn, 186 D 5
Castlebay, 284 A 4
Castle Douglas, 3,384 E 6
Castle Kennedy, 307 D 6
Castletown, 902 E 2
Catrine, 2,681 D 5
Cawdor, 111 E 3
Chirnside, 888 F 5
Chryston, 8,322 C 2
Clackmannan, 3,248 C 1
Clarkston, 8,404 B 2
Closeburn, 225 E 5
Clovulin, ⊙315 C 4
Clydebank, 47,538 B 2
Coalburn, 1,460 E 5
Coatbridge, 50,806 C 2
Cockburnspath, 233 F 5
Cockenzie and Port Seton, 3,539 D 1
Coldingham, 423 F 5
Coldstream, 1,393 F 5
Coll, 305 B 2
Colmonell, 218 D 5
Comrie, 1,119 E 4
Connel, 300 C 4
Cononbridge, 914 D 3
Corpach, 1,296 C 4
Coupar Angus, 2,010 E 4
Cove and Kilcreggan, 1,402 A 1
Cove Bay, 765 F 3
Cowdenbeath, 10,215 D 1
Cowie, 2,751 C 1
Craigellachie, 382 E 3
Craignure, ⊙544 C 4
Crail, 1,033 F 4
Crawford, 384 E 5
Creetown, 769 D 6
Crieff, 5,718 E 4
Crimond, 313 G 3
Crinan, ⊙462 C 4
Cromarty, 492 E 3
Crosshill, 535 D 5
Crossmichael, 317 D 6
Cruden Bay, 528 G 3
Cullen, 1,199 F 3
Culross, 504 C 1
Cults, 3,336 F 3
Cumbernauld, 41,200 C 1
Cumnock and Holmhead, 6,298 D 5
Cupar, 6,607 E 4
Currie, 6,764 D 2
Dailly, 1,258 D 5
Dalbeattie, 3,659 E 6
Daliburgh, 261 A 3
Dalkeith, 9,713 D 2
Dalmally, 283 D 4
Dalmellington, 1,949 D 5
Dalry, 5,833 D 5
Dalrymple, 1,336 D 5
Darvel, 3,177 D 5
Daviot, ⊙513 D 3
Denholm, 581 F 5
Denny and Dunipace, 10,424 C 1
Dervaig, ⊙1,081 B 4
Dingwall, 4,275 D 3
Dollar, 2,573 E 4
Dornoch, 880 D 3
Douglas, 1,843 E 5
Doune, 859 D 4
Drongan, 3,609 D 5
Drumbeg, ⊙833 C 2
Drummore, 336 D 6
Drumnadrochit, 359 D 3
Drymen, 659 B 1
Dufftown, 1,481 E 3
Dumbarton, 25,469 B 1
Dumfries, 29,259 E 5
Dunbar, 4,609 F 4
Dunbeath, 161 E 2
Dunbeg, 939 C 4
Dunblane, 5,222 E 4
Dundee, 194,732 F 4
Dundonald, 2,256 D 5
Dunfermline, 52,098 D 1
Dunkeld, 273 E 4
Dunning, 564 E 4
Dunoon, 8,759 A 2
Dunragit, 323 D 6
Duns, 1,812 F 5
Duntochter, 3,532 B 2
Dunure, 452 D 5
Dunvegan, 301 B 3
Dyce, 2,733 F 3
Eaglesfield, 581 E 5
Eaglesham, 2,788 D 5
Earlston, 1,415 F 5
East Calder, 2,690 D 2
East Kilbride, 71,200 B 2
East Linton, 882 F 5
Eastriggs, 1,455 E 5
Ecclefechan, 844 E 5
Edinburgh (cap.), 470,085 D 1
Edzell, 658 F 4
Elderslie, 5,204 B 2
Elgin, 17,042 E 3
Elie and Earlsferry, 807 F 4
Ellon, 2,855 F 3
Embo, 260 E 3
Errol, 762 E 4
Evanton, 562 D 3
Eyemouth, 2,704 F 5
Fairlie, 1,029 D 5
Falkirk, 36,901 C 1
Falkland, 998 E 4
Fallin, 3,159 C 1
Fauldhouse, 5,247 C 2
Ferness, ⊙287 E 3
Ferryden, 740 F 4
Findhorn, 664 E 3
Findochty, 1,229 E 3
Fintry, 296 B 1
Fochabers, 1,238 E 3
Forfar, 11,179 F 4
Forres, 5,317 E 3
Fort Augustus, 670 D 3
Forth, 2,929 C 2
Fortrose, 1,150 D 3
Fort William, 4,370 C 4
Foyers, 276 D 3
Fraserburgh, 10,930 G 3
Friockheim, 807 F 4
Furnace, 220 C 4
Fyvie, 405 F 3
Gairloch, 125 C 3
Galashiels, 12,808 F 5
Galston, 4,256 D 5
Gardenstown, 892 F 3
Garelochhead, 1,552 A 1
Gargunnock, 457 B 1
Garlieston, 385 D 6
Garmouth, 352 E 3
Garrabost, 307 B 2
Gartmore, 253 B 1
Gatehouse-of-Fleet, 835 D 6
Giffnock, 10,987 B 2
Gifford, 575 F 5
Girvan, 7,597 D 5
Glamis, 190 F 4
Glasgow, 880,617 B 2
Glasgow, ★1,674,789 B 2
Glenbarr, ⊙691 C 5
Glencaple, 275 E 5
Glencoe, 195 C 4
Glenelg, ⊙1,468 C 3
Glenluce, 725 D 6
Glenrothes, 31,400 E 4
Golspie, 1,374 E 3
Gordon, 320 F 5
Gorebridge, 3,426 D 2
Gourock, 11,192 A 1
Grangemouth, 24,430 C 1
Grantown-on-Spey, 1,578 E 3
Greenlaw, 574 F 5
Greenock, 67,275 A 2
Gretna, 1,907 E 5
Gullane, 1,701 F 4
Haddington, 6,767 F 5
Halkirk, 679 E 2
Hamilton, 45,495 C 2
Hamnavoe, 307 G 2
Harthill, 4,712 C 2
Hatton, 315 G 3
Hawick, 16,484 F 5
Heathhall, 1,365 E 5
Helensburgh, 13,327 A 1
Helmsdale, 727 E 2
Hill of Fearn, 233 D 3
Hillside, 692 F 4
Hillswick, ⊙696 G 2
Hopeman, 1,248 E 3
Huntly, 4,078 F 3
Hurlford, 4,294 D 5
Inchnadamph, ⊙833 D 2
Innellan, 922 A 2
Innerleithen, 2,293 E 5
Insch, 881 F 3
Inveraray, 473 C 4
Inverbervie, 853 F 4
Invercassley, ⊙1,067 D 3
Invergordon, 2,385 D 3
Invergowrie, 1,389 E 4
Inverie, ⊙1,468 C 3
Inverkeithing, 6,102 D 1
Inverness, 35,801 D 3
Inverurie, 5,534 F 3
Irvine, 48,500 D 5
Isle of Whithorn, 222 D 6
Jedburgh, 3,953 F 5
John O'Groats, 195 E 2
Johnshaven, 544 F 4
Johnstone, 23,251 B 2
Kames, 230 C 5
Keiss, 344 E 2
Keith, 4,192 F 3
Kelso, 4,934 F 5
Kelty, 6,573 D 1
Kemnay, 1,042 F 3
Kenmore, 211 E 4
Kilbarchan, 2,669 A 2
Kilbirnie, 8,259 A 2
Kilchoan, ⊙764 B 4
Kildonan, ⊙1,105 E 2
Killearn, 1,086 B 1
Killin, 600 D 4
Kilmacolm, 3,348 A 2
Kilmarnock, 50,175 D 5
Kilmaurs, 2,518 D 5
Kilninver, ⊙247 C 4
Kilrenny and Anstruther, 2,951 F 4
Kilsyth, 10,210 B 1
Kilwinning, 8,460 D 5
Kinbrace, ⊙1,105 E 2
Kincardine, 3,278 C 1
Kinghorn, 2,163 D 1
Kingussie, 1,036 D 3
Kinlochewe, ⊙1,794 C 3
Kinlochleven, 1,243 D 4
Kinloch Rannoch, 241 D 4
Kinloss, 2,378 E 3
Kinross, 2,829 E 4
Kintore, 970 F 3
Kippen, 529 B 1
Kirkcaldy, 50,207 D 1
Kirkcolm, 346 C 6
Kirkconnel, 3,318 E 5
Kirkcowan, 354 D 6
Kirkcudbright, 2,690 E 6
Kirkhill, 210 D 3
Kirkintilloch, 26,664 B 2
Kirkmuirhill, 2,575 E 5
Kirkton of Glenisla, ⊙331 E 4
Kirkwall, 4,777 E 2
Kirriemuir, 4,295 E 4
Kyleakin, 268 C 3
Kyle of Lochalsh, 687 C 3
Kylestrome, ⊙745 D 2
Ladybank, 1,216 E 4
Laggan, 393 D 3
Lairg, 572 D 2
Lamlash, 613 C 5
Lanark, 8,842 E 5
Langholm, 2,509 E 5
Larbert, 4,922 C 1
Largs, 9,461 A 2
Larkhall, 15,926 E 5
Lauder, 639 F 5
Laurencekirk, 1,416 F 4

(continued)

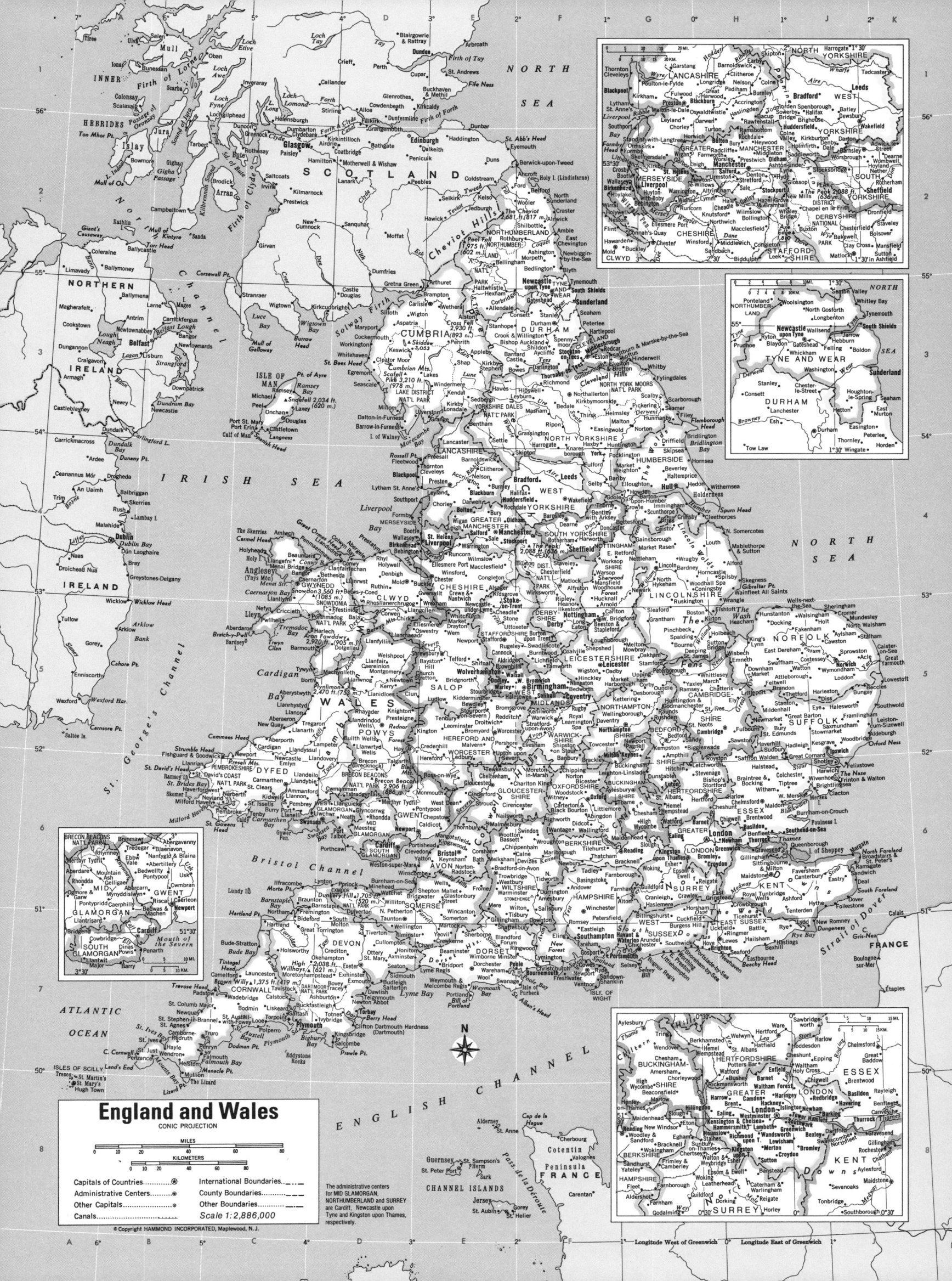

England and Wales

CONIC PROJECTION

MILES

KILOMETERS

Capitals of Countries..........⊛
Administrative Centers..........◉
Other Capitals..........◉
Canals..........

International Boundaries..........
County Boundaries..........
Other Boundaries..........

The administrative centers for MID GLAMORGAN, NORTHUMBERLAND and SURREY are Cardiff, Newcastle upon Tyne and Kingston upon Thames, respectively.

Scale 1:2,886,000

© Copyright HAMMOND INCORPORATED, Maplewood, N.J.

Longitude West of Greenwich   Longitude East of Greenwich

Lennoxtown, 3,070 . . . B 1
Lerwick, 6,195 . . . G 2
Leslie, 3,303 . . . E 4
Lesmahagow, 3,906 . . . E 5
Leswalt, 237 . . . C 6
Letham, 804 . . . F 4
Leuchars, 2,482 . . . F 4
Leurbost, 461 . . . B 2
Leven, 9,507 . . . F 4
Leverburgh, 223 . . . B 3
Lhanbryde, 1,184 . . . E 3
Lilliesleaf, 212 . . . F 5
Limekilns, 812 . . . D 1
Linlithgow, 6,098 . . . C 1
Linwood, 10,510 . . . B 2
Lionel, 187 . . . B 2
Livingston, 21,900 . . . C 2
Loanhead, 5,971 . . . D 2
Lochailort, ⊙673 . . . C 4
Lochaline, 213 . . . C 4
Lochans, 355 . . . D 6
Locharbriggs, 2,561 . . . E 5
Lochawe, 200 . . . C 4
Lochboisdale, 382 . . . A 3
Lochcarron, 204 . . . C 3
Lochgelly, 7,754 . . . D 1
Lochgilphead, 1,217 . . . C 4
Lochgoilhead, 216 . . . D 4
Lochinver, 283 . . . C 2
Lochmaben, 1,304 . . . E 5
Lochmaddy, 307 . . . A 3
Lochore, 2,994 . . . D 1
Lochwinnoch, 2,064 . . . A 2
Lockerbie, 3,135 . . . E 5
Lossiemouth and Branderburgh, 5,817 . . . E 3
Lumsden, 248 . . . F 3
Luncarty, 584 . . . E 4
Lybster, 554 . . . E 2
Lyness, ⊙454 . . . E 2
Macduff, 3,682 . . . F 3
Machrihanish, 212 . . . C 5
Maidens, 536 . . . D 5
Mallaig, 903 . . . C 4
Markinch, 2,366 . . . E 4
Mauchline, 3,612 . . . D 5
Maud, 634 . . . F 3
Maybole, 4,703 . . . D 5
Mayfield, 8,232 . . . D 2
Meigle, 357 . . . E 4
Melrose, 2,197 . . . F 5
Melvaig, ⊙1,794 . . . C 3
Methlick, 315 . . . F 3
Methven, 806 . . . E 4
Mid Yell, 220 . . . G 2
Millport, 1,161 . . . A 2
Milnathort, 1,099 . . . E 4
Milngavie, 10,846 . . . B 1
Minnigaff, 658 . . . D 6
Mintlaw, 657 . . . F 3
Moffat, 2,041 . . . E 5
Moniaive, 342 . . . E 5
Monifieth, 7,100 . . . F 4
Montrose, 4,704 . . . F 4
Morar, 184 . . . C 4
Motherwell and Wishaw, 72,991 . . . C 2
Muirkirk, 2,607 . . . E 5
Muir of Ord, 1,339 . . . D 3
Musselburgh, 17,045 . . . D 2
Muthill, 672 . . . E 4
Nairn, 5,821 . . . E 3
Neilston, 4,358 . . . B 2
Nethy Bridge, 431 . . . E 3
New Abbey, 339 . . . E 6
Newarthill, 7,003 . . . C 2
Newburgh, Fife, 2,124 . . . E 4
Newburgh, Grampian, 447 . . . G 3
Newcastleton, 903 . . . F 5
New Cumnock, 5,077 . . . D 5
New Deer, 601 . . . F 3
New Galloway, 337 . . . D 5
Newmains, 6,847 . . . C 2
Newmarket, 613 . . . B 2
Newmill, 449 . . . E 3
Newmilns and Greenholm, 3,509 . . . D 5
New Pitsligo, 1,125 . . . F 3
Newport-on-Tay, 3,762 . . . F 4
New Scone, 3,830 . . . E 4
Newtongrange, 4,555 . . . D 2
Newton Mearns, 6,901 . . . B 2
Newtonmore, 894 . . . D 3
Newton Stewart, 1,983 . . . D 6
Newtown Saint Boswells, 1,101 . . . F 5
Newtyle, 664 . . . E 4
North Berwick, 4,317 . . . F 4
North Tolsta, 527 . . . B 2
Oakley, 3,499 . . . C 1
Oban, 6,515 . . . C 4
Old Kilpatrick, 3,256 . . . B 2
Oldmeldrum, 1,103 . . . F 3
Oykel Bridge, ⊙742 . . . D 3
Paisley, 94,833 . . . B 2
Palnackie, 225 . . . E 6
Patna, 2,867 . . . D 5
Peebles, 6,049 . . . E 5
Penicuik, 10,476 . . . D 2
Penpont, 364 . . . E 5
Perth, 43,098 . . . E 4
Peterculter, 3,226 . . . F 3
Peterhead, 14,846 . . . G 3
Pierowall, ⊙735 . . . E 1
Pitlochry, 2,468 . . . E 4
Pitmedden, 313 . . . F 3
Pittenweem, 1,548 . . . F 4
Plockton, 288 . . . C 3
Poolewe, ⊙1,794 . . . C 3
Port Appin, ⊙2,172 . . . C 4
Port Askaig, ⊙1,795 . . . B 5
Port Bannatyne, 730 . . . A 2
Port Charlotte, 240 . . . B 5
Port Ellen, 932 . . . B 5
Port Glasgow, 22,189 . . . A 2
Portgordon, 814 . . . F 3
Portknockie, 1,217 . . . F 3
Portmahomack, 226 . . . E 3
Portpatrick, 643 . . . C 6
Portree, 1,374 . . . B 3
Portsoy, 1,717 . . . F 3
Port William, 517 . . . D 6
Prestonpans, 3,272 . . . D 1
Prestwick, 13,218 . . . D 5
Queensferry, 5,339 . . . D 1
Reay, 283 . . . E 2
Renfrew, 18,880 . . . B 2
Renton, 3,443 . . . A 1
Rhu, 1,540 . . . A 1
Rhynie, 333 . . . F 3
Rigside, 1,195 . . . E 5
Rosehearty, 1,220 . . . F 3
Rosneath, 946 . . . A 1
Rothes, 1,240 . . . E 3
Rothesay, 6,285 . . . A 2
Rutherglen, 24,091 . . . B 2
Saint Abbs, 203 . . . F 5
Saint Andrews, 12,837 . . . F 4
Saint Combs, 738 . . . G 3
Saint Cyrus, 340 . . . F 4
Saint Margaret's Hope, 210 . . . F 2
Saint Monance, 1,205 . . . F 4
Saline, 831 . . . C 1
Saltcoats, 14,861 . . . D 5
Sandbank, 850 . . . A 1
Sandhead, 248 . . . D 6
Sandwick, 603 . . . B 2
Sanquhar, 2,030 . . . D 5
Sauchie, 6,082 . . . C 1
Scalasaig, ⊙137 . . . B 4
Scalloway, 896 . . . G 2
Scarinish, ⊙875 . . . B 4
Scourie, ⊙745 . . . C 2
Scrabster, 273 . . . E 2
Selkirk, 5,635 . . . F 5
Shader, 258 . . . B 2
Shawbost, 458 . . . B 2
Shieldaig, ⊙550 . . . C 3
Shotts, 9,512 . . . C 2
Skateraw, 674 . . . F 3
Skelmorlie, 1,535 . . . A 2
Skipness, ⊙765 . . . C 5
Slamannan, 1,584 . . . C 2
Spean Bridge, 235 . . . D 4
Springholm, 340 . . . E 5
Stanley, 1,385 . . . E 4
Stenhousemuir, 8,203 . . . C 1
Stevenston, 11,786 . . . D 5
Stewarton, 5,165 . . . D 5
Stirling, 29,799 . . . C 1
Stonehaven, 4,837 . . . F 4
Stonehouse, 7,900 . . . D 5
Stornoway, 5,371 . . . B 2
Stow, 485 . . . F 5
Strachan, ⊙390 . . . F 4
Strachur Bay, ⊙678 . . . C 4
Stranraer, 10,174 . . . C 6
Strathaven, 5,464 . . . D 5
Strathpeffer, 874 . . . D 3
Strichen, 962 . . . F 3
Stromeferry, ⊙1,724 . . . C 3
Stromness, 1,680 . . . E 2
Strontian, ⊙764 . . . C 4
Struan, ⊙772 . . . B 3
Swinton, 235 . . . F 5
Tain, 2,057 . . . D 3
Tarbert, Strathclyde, 1,391 . . . C 5
Tarbert, W. Isles, 479 . . . B 3
Tarbolton, 2,224 . . . D 5
Tarland, 452 . . . F 3
Tayport, 2,848 . . . F 4
Thornhill, Central, 443 . . . D 4
Thornhill, Dumf. & Gall., 1,510 . . . E 5
Thurso, 9,113 . . . E 2
Tillicoultry, 4,320 . . . C 1
Tobermory, 652 . . . B 4
Tolob, ⊙2,033 . . . G 2
Tomatin, 214 . . . D 3
Tomintoul, 306 . . . E 3
Torphins, 499 . . . F 3
Tradespark, 425 . . . E 3
Tranent, 7,212 . . . F 5
Troon, 11,656 . . . D 5
Tullibody, 6,082 . . . C 1
Turriff, 3,051 . . . F 3
Tweedsmuir, ⊙105 . . . E 5
Twynholm, 274 . . . D 6
Tyndrum, ⊙1,153 . . . D 4
Uddingston, 5,278 . . . B 2
Uig, Highland, 103 . . . B 3
Uig, W. Isles, ⊙1,948 . . . A 2
Ullapool, 807 . . . C 3
Uphall, 3,035 . . . C 1
Viewpark, 9,812 . . . C 2
Walkerburn, 842 . . . F 5
Watten, 347 . . . E 2
Wemyss Bay, 323 . . . A 2
West Barns, 659 . . . F 5
West Calder, 2,005 . . . C 2
West Kilbride, 3,883 . . . D 5
West Linton, 705 . . . D 2
Whitburn, 11,647 . . . C 2
Whitehills, 875 . . . F 3
Whithorn, 990 . . . D 6
Whiting Bay, 352 . . . C 5
Wick, 7,804 . . . E 2
Wigtown, 1,118 . . . D 6
Winchburgh, 2,409 . . . D 1
Yetholm, 435 . . . F 5

OTHER FEATURES

A'Chralaig (mt.) . . . C 3
Ailsa Craig (isl.), 3 . . . C 5
Almond (riv.) . . . E 4
Annan (riv.) . . . E 5
Appin (dist.), 2,006 . . . C 4
Ardgour (dist.), 315 . . . C 4
Ardle (riv.) . . . E 4
Ardnamurchan (pen.), 764 . . . B 4
Argyll (dist.), 4,940 . . . C 4
Arkaig, Loch (lake) . . . C 4
Arran (isl.), 3,564 . . . C 5
Askival (mt.) . . . B 4
Assynt (dist.), 833 . . . C 2
Athol (dist.), 1,082 . . . D 4
Atlantic Ocean . . . B 2
Avon (riv.) . . . C 1
Avon (riv.) . . . E 3
Awe, Loch (lake) . . . C 4
Ayr (riv.) . . . D 5
Ayr, Heads of (cape) . . . D 5
Badenoch (dist.), 2,717 . . . D 4
Baleshare (isl.), 64 . . . A 3
Balmoral Castle . . . E 3
Barra (sound) . . . A 3
Barra (isl.), 1,005 . . . A 4
Barra (head) . . . A 4
Barra Isles (isls.), 1,092 . . . A 4
Battock (mt.) . . . F 4
Beauly (riv.) . . . D 3
Beinn Dearg (mt.) . . . D 3
Beinn a Ghlo (mt.) . . . E 4
Bell Rock (isl.), 3 . . . F 4
Ben Alder (mt.) . . . D 4
Ben Avon (mt.) . . . E 3
Benbecula (isl.), 1,355 . . . A 3
Ben Cruachan (mt.) . . . C 4
Ben Lawers (mt.) . . . D 4
Ben Lui (mt.) . . . D 4
Ben Macdhui (mt.) . . . E 3
Ben Mhor (mt.) . . . A 3
Ben More (mt.) . . . B 4
Ben More (mt.) . . . D 4
Ben More Assynt (mt.) . . . D 2
Ben Nevis (mt.) . . . D 4
Bernera (isl.), 276 . . . B 2
Berneray (isl.), 131 . . . A 3
Berneray (isl.), 6 . . . A 4
Bidean nam Bian (mt.) . . . D 4
Black Isle (pen.), 7,209 . . . D 3
Blackwater (res.) . . . D 4
Boisdale, Loch (inlet) . . . A 3
Bracadale, Loch (inlet) . . . B 3
Braemar (dist.), 7,624 . . . E 3
Breadalbane (dist.), 3,649 . . . D 4
Bressay (isl.), 248 . . . G 2
Broad (bay) . . . B 2
Broad Law (mt.) . . . E 5
Broom, Loch (inlet) . . . C 3
Brough Ness (prom.) . . . F 2
Buchan (dist.), 40,089 . . . F 3
Buddon Ness (prom.) . . . F 4
Burray (isl.), 209 . . . F 2
Burrow (head) . . . D 6
Bute (isl.), 8,423 . . . C 5
Bute (sound) . . . C 5
Butt of Lewis (prom.) . . . B 2
Cairn Gorm (mt.) . . . E 3
Cairngorm (mts.) . . . E 3
Cairn Toul (mt.) . . . E 3
Caledonian (canal) . . . D 3
Canna (isl.), 22 . . . B 3
Carn Ban (mt.) . . . D 3
Carn Eige (mt.) . . . C 3
Carrick (dist.), 21,425 . . . D 5
Carron (riv.) . . . C 1
Carron (riv.) . . . C 3
Cheviot (hills) . . . F 5
Cheviot, The (mt.) . . . F 5
Clisham (mt.) . . . B 3
Clyde (riv.) . . . D 5
Clyde (firth) . . . D 5
Coll (isl.), 144 . . . B 4
Colonsay (isl.), 137 . . . B 4
Copinsay (isl.), 3 . . . F 2
Cowal (dist.), 15,548 . . . C 4
Creag Meagaidh (mt.) . . . D 4
Cromarty (firth) . . . D 3
Cuillin (hills) . . . B 3
Cuillin (sound) . . . B 3
Dee (riv.) . . . D 5
Dee (riv.) . . . F 3
Dennis (head) . . . F 1
Deveron (riv.) . . . F 3
Don (riv.) . . . F 3
Doon (riv.) . . . D 5
Dornoch (firth) . . . E 3
Duirinish (dist.), 1,085 . . . B 3
Duncansby (head) . . . F 2
Dunnet (head) . . . E 2
Earn (riv.) . . . E 4
Earn, Loch (lake) . . . D 4
Eday (isl.), 179 . . . F 1
Eddrachillis (bay) . . . C 2
Eden (riv.) . . . F 4
Egilsay (isl.), 39 . . . F 1
Eigg (isl.), 69 . . . B 4
Eil, Loch (lake) . . . C 4
Eishort, Loch (inlet) . . . B 3
Enard (bay) . . . C 2
Eriboll, Loch (inlet) . . . D 2
Ericht, Loch (lake) . . . D 4
Eriskay (isl.), 219 . . . A 3
Erisort, Loch (inlet) . . . B 2
Esk (riv.) . . . F 5
Etive, Loch (inlet) . . . C 4
Ewe, Loch (inlet) . . . C 3
Eye (pen.), 850 . . . B 2
Fair Isle (isl.), 65 . . . F 3
Fetlar (isl.), 88 . . . G 2
Fife Ness (prom.) . . . F 4
Findhorn (riv.) . . . E 3
Flannan (isls.), 3 . . . A 2
Formartine (dist.), 10,768 . . . F 3
Forth (riv.) . . . B 1
Forth (firth) . . . F 4
Forth and Clyde (canal) . . . B 2
Foula (isl.), 33 . . . F 2
Fyne, Loch (inlet) . . . C 5
Galloway (dist.), 54,972 . . . D 5
Galloway, Mull of (prom.) . . . D 6
Gare Loch (inlet) . . . A 1
Garioch (dist.), 6,863 . . . F 3
Garry, Loch (lake) . . . D 3
Gigha (isl.), 174 . . . C 5
Girdle Ness (prom.) . . . F 3
Glass (riv.) . . . D 3
Glen More (dist.), 55,035 . . . D 3
Goat Fell (mt.) . . . C 5
Gometra (isl.), 10 . . . B 4
Grampian (mts.) . . . D 4
Great Cumbrae (isl.), 1,296 . . . A 2
Gruinard (bay) . . . C 3
Hallandale (riv.) . . . E 2
Harris (sound) . . . A 3
Harris (dist.), 2,175 . . . B 3
Hebrides (sea) . . . B 3
Hebrides, Inner (isls.), 14,881 . . . B 4
Hebrides, Outer (isls.), 29,615 . . . A 3
Helmsdale (riv.) . . . E 2
Herma Ness (prom.) . . . G 2
Holy (isl.), 10 . . . C 5
Holy Loch (inlet) . . . A 1
Hoy (isl.), 419 . . . E 2
Inchcape (Bell Rock) (isl.), 3 . . . F 4
Inchkeith (isl.), 3 . . . D 1
Indaal, Loch (inlet) . . . B 5
Inner (sound) . . . C 3
Inner Hebrides (isls.), 14,881 . . . B 4
Iona (isl.), 145 . . . B 4
Isla (riv.) . . . E 4
Islay (isl.), 3,816 . . . B 5
Jura (isl.), 210 . . . C 5
Jura (sound) . . . C 5
Katrine, Loch (lake) . . . D 4
Kerrera (isl.), 27 . . . C 4
Kilbrannan (sound) . . . C 5
Kinnairds (head) . . . G 3
Kintyre (pen.), 10,077 . . . C 5
Kintyre, Mull of (prom.) . . . C 5
Knapdale (dist.), 4,082 . . . C 5
Kyle of Tongue (inlet) . . . D 2
Laggan (bay) . . . B 5
Lammermuir (hills) . . . F 5
Lennox (hills) . . . B 1
Leven (lake) . . . E 4
Leven, Loch (inlet) . . . D 4
Lewis (dist.), 20,047 . . . B 2
Liddel Water (riv.) . . . F 5
Linnhe, Loch (inlet) . . . C 4
Lismore (isl.), 166 . . . C 4
Little Minch (sound) . . . B 3
Lochaber (dist.), 13,813 . . . D 4
Lochnagar (mt.) . . . E 4
Lochy, Loch (lake) . . . D 3
Lomond, Loch (lake) . . . D 4
Long, Loch (inlet) . . . D 4
Lorne (dist.), 12,162 . . . C 4
Lorne (firth) . . . C 4
Loyal, Loch (lake) . . . D 2
Luce (bay) . . . D 6
Luing (isl.), 151 . . . C 4
Lyon (riv.) . . . D 4
Machers, The (pen.), 6,192 . . . D 6
Mainland (isl.), 12,747 . . . E 1
Mainland (isl.), 12,944 . . . G 2
Mar (dist.), 23,931 . . . F 3
Maree, Loch (lake) . . . C 3
May, Isle of (isl.), 10 . . . F 4
Merrick (mt.) . . . D 5
Minginish (dist.), 772 . . . B 3
Moidart (dist.), 155 . . . C 4
Monach (sound) . . . A 3
Monadhliath (mts.) . . . D 3
Moorfoot (hills) . . . E 5
Moray (firth) . . . E 3
Moriston (riv.) . . . D 3
Morven (dist.), 398 . . . C 4
Morven (mt.) . . . E 2
Muck (isl.), 24 . . . B 4
Muckle Flugga (isl.), 3 . . . G 2
Mull (isl.), 2,024 . . . C 4
Mull (head) . . . F 1
Mull (sound) . . . C 4
Nairn (riv.) . . . D 3
na Keal, Loch (inlet) . . . B 4
Naver (riv.) . . . D 2
Ness, Loch (lake) . . . D 3
Nevis, Loch (inlet) . . . C 3
Nith (riv.) . . . E 5
North (chan.) . . . C 5
North (sound) . . . F 1
North (sound) . . . G 4
North Esk (riv.) . . . F 4
North Minch (sound) . . . B 3
North Ronaldsay (isl.), 134 . . . F 1
North Uist (isl.), 1,469 . . . A 3
Oa, Mull of (prom.) . . . B 5
Ochil (hills) . . . E 4
Oich (riv.) . . . D 3
Orchy (riv.) . . . D 4
Orkney (isls.), 17,675 . . . F 1
Oronsay (isl.), 2 . . . B 4
Outer Hebrides (isls.), 29,615 . . . A 3
Oykel (riv.) . . . D 3
Pabbay (isl.), 4 . . . A 3
Papa Stour (isl.), 24 . . . F 2
Papa Westray (isl.), 106 . . . F 1
Paps of Jura (mt.) . . . C 5
Park (dist.), 210 . . . B 2
Peel Fell (mt.) . . . F 5
Pentland (hills) . . . D 2
Pentland (firth) . . . E 2
Pladda (isl.), 2 . . . C 5
Quoich, Loch (lake) . . . C 3
Raasay (isl.), 163 . . . C 3
Rannoch (dist.), 1,177 . . . D 4
Rannoch, Loch (lake) . . . D 4
Rhinns, The (pen.), 8,295 . . . C 6
Roag, Loch (inlet) . . . B 2
Rona (isl.), 3 . . . B 3
Ross of Mull (pen.), 585 . . . B 4
Rousay (isl.), 181 . . . E 1
Rudha Hunish (cape) . . . B 3
Rudh Re (cape) . . . C 3
Rum (isl.), 40 . . . B 3
Ryan, Loch (inlet) . . . C 5
Saint Kilda (isl.), 65 . . . A 2
Saint Magnus (bay) . . . F 2
Sanda (isl.), 9 . . . C 5
Sanday (isl.), 11 . . . B 3
Sanday (isl.), 592 . . . F 1
Scalpay (isl.), 483 . . . B 3
Scalpay (isl.), 5 . . . C 3
Scapa Flow (chan.) . . . E 2
Scarp (isl.), 12 . . . A 2
Scridain, Loch (inlet) . . . B 4
Scurdie Ness (prom.) . . . F 4
Seaforth, Loch (inlet) . . . B 3
Seil (isl.), 326 . . . C 4
Sgurr a Choire Ghlais (mt.) . . . D 3
Sgurr Alasdair (mt.) . . . B 3
Sgurr Mor (mt.) . . . D 3
Sgurr na Lapaich (mt.) . . . C 3
Shapinsay (isl.), 346 . . . F 1
Shetland (isls.), 18,494 . . . G 2
Shiant (sound) . . . B 3
Shiel, Loch (lake) . . . C 4
Shin (falls) . . . D 3
Shin, Loch (lake) . . . D 2
Shona (isl.), 17 . . . C 4
Sidlaw (hills) . . . E 4
Sinclair's (bay) . . . E 2
Skye, Isle of (isl.), 7,183 . . . B 3
Sleat (pt.) . . . B 4
Sleat (dist.), 449 . . . C 3
Small Isles (isls.), 171 . . . B 4
Snizort, Loch (inlet) . . . B 3
Soay (isl.), 5 . . . B 3
Solway (firth) . . . E 6
South Esk (riv.) . . . F 4
South Ronaldsay (isl.), 776 . . . F 2
South Uist (isl.), 2,281 . . . A 3
Spean (riv.) . . . D 4
Spey (riv.) . . . E 3
Start (pt.) . . . F 1
Stinchar (riv.) . . . D 5
Strathbogie (dist.), 7,959 . . . F 3
Strathmore (valley) . . . E 4
Strathspey (dist.), 6,668 . . . E 3
Strathy (pt.) . . . E 2
Stroma (isl.), 8 . . . E 2
Stronsay (isl.), 436 . . . F 1
Sumburgh (head) . . . G 2
Sunart, Loch (inlet) . . . C 4
Swona (isl.), 3 . . . E 2
Taransay (isl.), 5 . . . A 3
Tarbat Ness (prom.) . . . E 3
Tarbert, East Loch (inlet) . . . B 3
Tarbert, Loch (inlet) . . . B 5
Tarbert, West Loch (inlet) . . . A 3
Tay (riv.) . . . E 4
Tay (firth) . . . F 4
Tay, Loch (lake) . . . D 4
Teith (riv.) . . . D 4
Teviot (riv.) . . . F 5
Thurso (riv.) . . . E 2
Tiree (isl.), 875 . . . B 4
Tolsta (head) . . . B 2
Tor Ness (prom.) . . . E 2
Torridon, Loch (inlet) . . . C 3
Trossachs, The (valley) . . . D 4
Trotternish (dist.), 1,948 . . . B 3
Tweed (riv.) . . . F 5
Tyne (riv.) . . . F 5
Ulva (isl.), 23 . . . B 4
Unst (isl.), 1,124 . . . G 2
Vaternish (dist.), 162 . . . B 3
Vatersay (isl.), 77 . . . A 4
West Burra (isl.), 501 . . . G 2
Westray (firth) . . . E 1
Westray (isl.), 735 . . . E 1
Whalsay (isl.), 870 . . . G 2
White Coomb (mt.) . . . E 5
Wigtown (bay) . . . D 6
Wrath (cape) . . . C 2
Wyre (isl.), 36 . . . F 1
Yarrow (riv.) . . . E 5
Yell (isl.), 1,143 . . . G 2
Ythan (riv.) . . . F 3

★Population of met. area
⊙Population of parish.

Agriculture, Industry and Resources

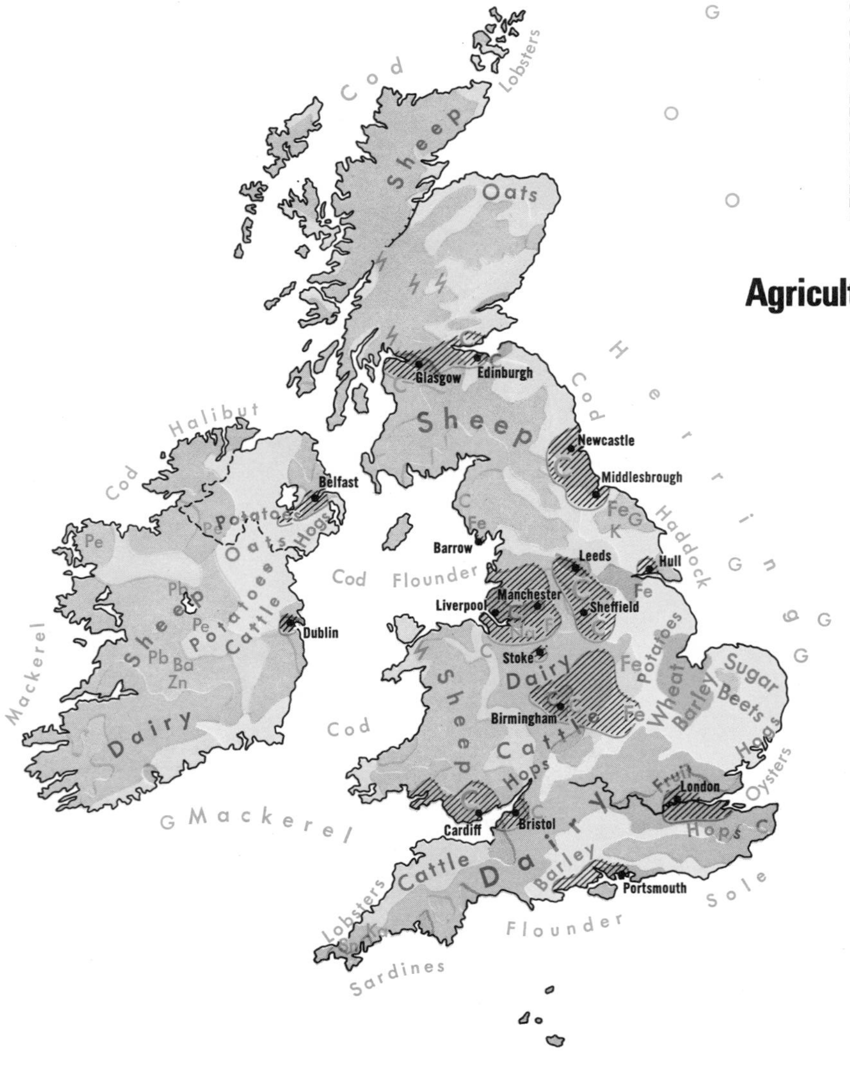

DOMINANT LAND USE

- Cereals (chiefly oats, barley)
- Truck Farming, Horticulture
- Dairy, Mixed Farming
- Livestock, Mixed Farming
- Pasture Livestock

MAJOR MINERAL OCCURRENCES

Ba	Barite	Na	Salt
C	Coal	O	Petroleum
F	Fluorspar	Pb	Lead
Fe	Iron Ore	Pe	Peat
G	Natural Gas	Sn	Tin
K	Potash	Zn	Zinc
Ka	Kaolin (china clay)		

Water Power
Major Industrial Areas

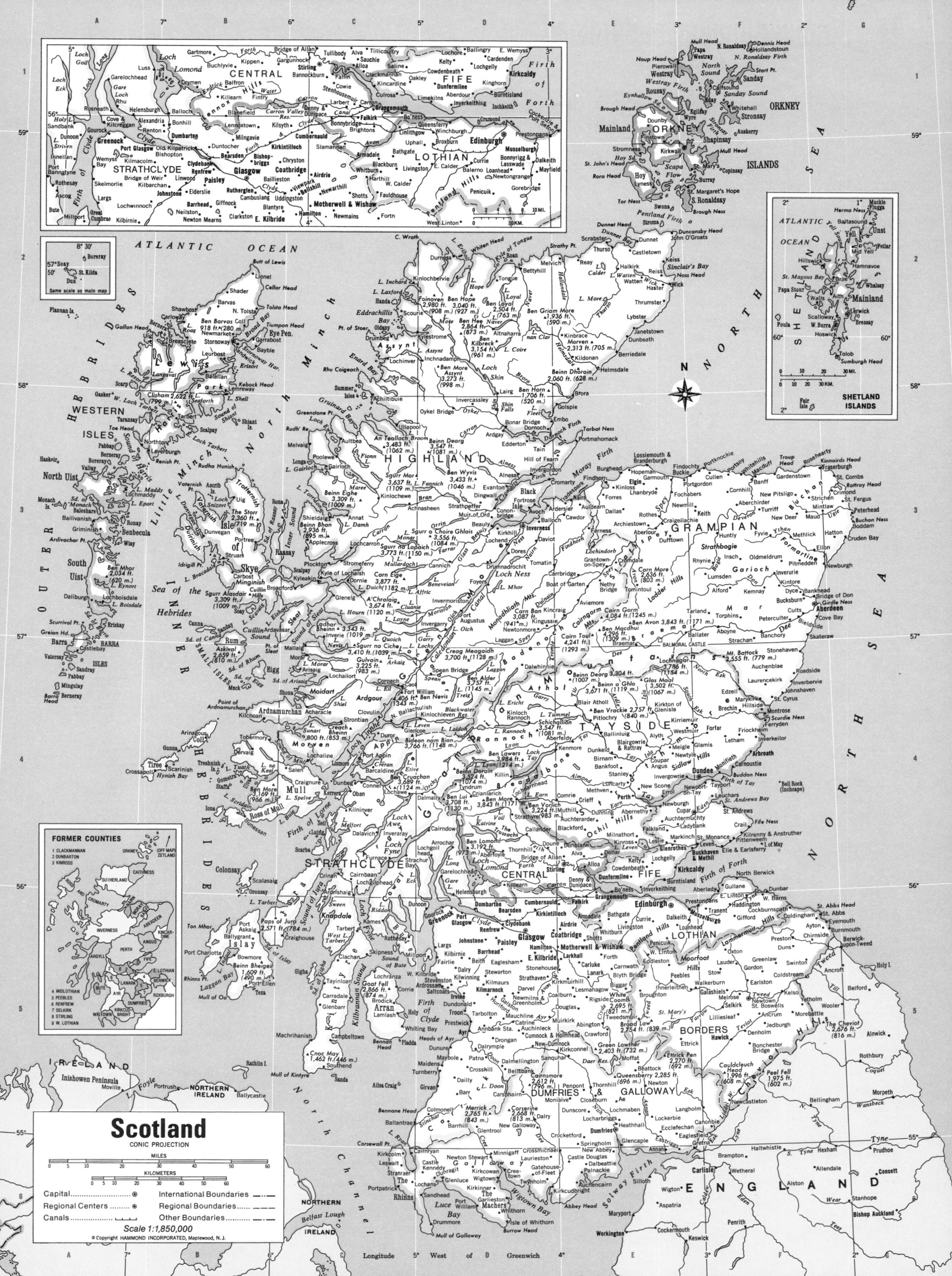

Scotland

CONIC PROJECTION

MILES

KILOMETERS

Capital..............................⊛   International Boundaries _____
Regional Centers...............⊙   Regional Boundaries _____
Canals..............................   Other Boundaries _____

Scale 1:1,850,000

© Copyright HAMMOND INCORPORATED, Maplewood, N.J.

FORMER COUNTIES

1 CLACKMANNAN
2 DUNBARTON
3 KINROSS
4 MIDLOTHIAN
5 PEEBLES
6 RENFREW
7 SELKIRK
8 STIRLING
9 W. LOTHIAN

SHETLAND ISLANDS

ORKNEY ISLANDS

16 United Kingdom and Ireland
(continued)

IRELAND

COUNTIES

Carlow, 34,237 ... H 6
Cavan, 52,618 ... G 4
Clare, 75,008 ... D 6
Cork, 352,883 ... D 7
Donegal, 108,344 ... K 2
Dublin, 852,219 ... J 5
Galway, 149,223 ... D 5
Kerry, 112,772 ... B 7
Kildare, 71,977 ... H 5
Kilkenny, 61,473 ... G 6
Laoighis, 45,259 ... G 6
Leitrim, 28,360 ... E 3
Leix (Laoighis), 45,259 ... G 6
Limerick, 140,459 ... D 7
Longford, 28,250 ... F 4
Louth, 74,951 ... J 4
Mayo, 109,525 ... C 4
Meath, 71,729 ... H 4
Monaghan, 46,242 ... H 3
Offaly, 51,829 ... F 5
Roscommon, 53,519 ... E 4
Sligo, 50,275 ... D 3
Tipperary, 123,565 ... F 6
Waterford, 77,315 ... F 7
Westmeath, 53,570 ... G 5
Wexford, 86,351 ... H 7
Wicklow, 66,295 ... J 5

CITIES and TOWNS

Abbeydorney, 188 ... B 7
Abbeyfeale, 1,337 ... C 7
Abbeylara, ‡290 ... F 4
Abbeyleix, 1,033 ... G 6
Achill Sound, ‡1,163 ... B 4
Aclare, ‡336 ... D 3
Adare, 545 ... D 6
Aghada-Farsid-Rostellan, 461 ... E 8
Aghadoe, ‡497 ... B 7
Aghagower, ‡693 ... C 4
Ahascragh, 221 ... E 5
Annagry, 201 ... E 1
Annascaul, 236 ... B 7
An Uaimh, 4,605 ... H 4
An Uaimh, *6,665 ... H 4
Ardagh, Limerick, 213 ... C 7
Ardagh, Longford, ‡974 ... F 4
Ardara, 683 ... E 2
Ardee, *3,183 ... H 4
Ardee, 3,096 ... H 4
Ardfert, 286 ... B 7
Ardfinnan, 510 ... F 7
Ardmore, 233 ... F 8
Ardrahan, ‡239 ... D 5
Arklow, 6,948 ... J 6
Arthurstown, 1,188 ... H 7
Arva, 370 ... F 4
Ashford, 341 ... J 5
Askeaton, 844 ... D 6
Athboy, 705 ... H 4
Athea, 328 ... C 7
Athenry, 1,240 ... D 5
Athleague, ‡955 ... E 4
Athlone, 9,825 ... F 5
Athlone, *11,611 ... F 5
Athy, 4,270 ... H 6
Athy, *4,654 ... H 6
Aughrim, 451 ... J 6
Avoca, ‡620 ... J 6
Bagenalstown (Muinebeag), 2,321 ... H 6
Baile Átha Cliath (Dublin) (cap.), 567,866 ... K 5
Bailieborough, 1,293 ... G 4
Balbriggan, 3,741 ... J 4
Balla, 293 ... C 4
Ballaghaderreen, 1,121 ... E 4
Ballina, Mayo, 6,063 ... C 3
Ballina, *6,369 ... C 3
Ballina, Tipperary, 336 ... E 6
Ballinagh, 459 ... G 4
Ballinakill, 300 ... G 6
Ballineen ... D 8
Ballinamore, 808 ... F 3
Ballinasloe, 5,969 ... E 5
Ballincollig-Carrigrohane, 2,110 ... D 8
Ballindine, 232 ... C 4
Ballingarry, Limerick, 422 ... D 7
Ballingarry, Tipperary, ‡574 ... F 6
Ballinlough, 242 ... D 4
Ballinrobe, 1,272 ... C 4
Ballintober, ‡867 ... E 4
Ballintra, 197 ... E 2
Ballisodare, 486 ... E 3
Ballivor, 287 ... H 4
Ballybay, 754 ... G 3
Ballybay, *1,159 ... G 3
Ballybofey-Stranorlar, 2,214 ... F 2
Ballybunion, 1,287 ... B 7
Ballycanew, ‡460 ... J 6
Ballycarney, ‡294 ... J 6
Ballycastle, ‡724 ... C 3
Ballyconnell, 421 ... F 3
Ballycotton, 389 ... F 8
Ballydehob, 253 ... C 8
Ballyduff, 406 ... B 7
Ballygar, 359 ... E 4
Ballygeary, 725 ... J 7
Ballyhaise, 274 ... G 3
Ballyhaunis, 1,093 ... D 4
Ballyheigue, 450 ... B 7
Ballyjamesduff, 673 ... G 4
Ballylanders, 266 ... E 7
Ballylongford, 504 ... B 6
Ballymahon, 707 ... F 4
Ballymakeery, 272 ... C 8
Ballymore, ‡447 ... F 5
Ballymore Eustace, 433 ... J 5
Ballymote, 952 ... D 3
Ballyporeen, ‡810 ... E 7
Ballyragget, 519 ... G 6
Ballyroan, ‡478 ... G 6
Ballyshannon, 2,325 ... E 3
Ballytore, ‡580 ... H 5
Baltimore, 200 ... C 9
Baltinglass, 909 ... H 6
Baltray, 236 ... J 4
Banagher, 1,052 ... F 5
Bandon, 2,257 ... D 8
Bandon, *4,071 ... D 8
Bannow, ‡798 ... H 7
Bansha, 184 ... E 7
Bantry, 2,579 ... C 8
Barna, ‡1,734 ... C 5
Belmullet, 744 ... B 3
Belturbet, 1,092 ... G 3
Bennettsbridge, 367 ... G 6
Birr, 3,319 ... F 5
Birr, *3,881 ... F 5
Blanchardstown, 3,279 ... H 5
Blarney, 1,128 ... D 8
Blessington, 637 ... J 5
Boherbue, 372 ... C 7
Borris, 430 ... H 6
Borris-in-Ossory, 276 ... F 6
Borrisokane, 769 ... E 6
Borrisoleigh, 471 ... E 6
Boyle, 1,727 ... E 4
Boyle, *1,939 ... E 4
Bray, 14,467 ... K 5
Bray, *15,841 ... K 5
Bri Chualann (Bray), 14,467 ... K 5
Broadford, 226 ... C 7
Brosna, 250 ... C 7
Bruff, 547 ... D 7
Bruree, 243 ... D 7
Bunbeg-Derrybeg, 878 ... E 1
Bunclody-Carrickduff, 929 ... H 6
Buncrana, 2,955 ... G 1
Buncrana, *3,334 ... G 1
Bundoran, 1,337 ... E 3
Burtonport, ‡1,288 ... E 2
Buttevant, 1,045 ... D 7
Cahir, 1,747 ... F 7
Cahirciveen, 1,547 ... A 8
Callan, 1,283 ... G 7
Camolin, 306 ... J 6
Campile, 231 ... H 7
Cappamore, 567 ... E 6
Cappawhite, 305 ... E 6
Cappoquin, 872 ... F 7
Carbury, ‡894 ... H 5
Carlingford, 559 ... J 3
Carlow, 9,588 ... H 6
Carlow, *10,399 ... H 6
Carndonagh, 1,146 ... G 1
Carnew, 570 ... H 6
Carrickmacross, 2,100 ... H 4
Carrickmacross, *2,475 ... H 4
Carrick-on-Shannon, 1,854 ... F 4
Carrick-on-Suir, 5,006 ... F 7
Carrigaholt, ‡493 ... B 6
Carrigaline, 951 ... E 8
Carrigallen, 230 ... F 4
Carrigart, ‡753 ... F 1
Carrigtwohill, 622 ... E 8
Carrowkeel, ‡326 ... G 1
Cashel, 2,692 ... F 7
Castlebar, 5,979 ... C 4
Castlebar, *6,476 ... C 4
Castlebellingham, 407 ... J 4
Castleblayney, 2,118 ... H 3
Castleblayney, *2,395 ... H 3
Castlecomer-Donaguile, 1,244 ... G 6
Castledermot, 583 ... H 6
Castlefin, 610 ... F 2
Castlegregory, 216 ... A 7
Castleisland, 1,929 ... B 7
Castlemartyr, 491 ... E 8
Castlepollard, 693 ... G 4
Castlerea, 1,752 ... D 4
Castletown, ‡504 ... F 6
Castletownbere, 812 ... B 8
Castletownroche, 399 ... D 7
Castletownshend, 170 ... C 9
Causeway, 215 ... B 7
Cavan, 3,273 ... G 3
Cavan, *4,312 ... G 3
Ceanannus Mór, 2,391 ... G 4
Ceanannus Mór, *2,653 ... G 4
Celbridge, 1,568 ... H 5
Charlestown-Bellahy, 677 ... D 4
Charleville (Rathluirc), 2,232 ... D 7
Clara, 2,156 ... F 5
Claregalway, ‡594 ... D 5
Claremorris, 1,718 ... C 4
Clashmore, ‡379 ... F 8
Clifden, 790 ... B 5
Cloghan, 404 ... F 5
Clogh-Chatsworth, 324 ... G 6
Clogheen, 530 ... F 7
Clogherhead, 649 ... J 4
Clonakilty, 2,430 ... D 8
Clonaslee, 285 ... F 5
Clondalkin, 7,009 ... J 5
Clonegal, 202 ... H 6
Clones, 2,164 ... G 3
Clonfert, ‡430 ... E 5
Clonmany, ‡936 ... G 1
Clonmel, 11,622 ... F 7
Clonmel, *12,291 ... F 7
Clonmellon, 328 ... H 4
Clonroche, 222 ... H 7
Clontuskert, 351 ... E 4
Cloone, ‡460 ... F 4
Cloughjordan, 480 ... E 6
Cloyne, 654 ... E 8
Coachford, 290 ... D 8
Cóbh, 6,076 ... E 8
Cóbh, *7,141 ... E 8
Coill Dubh, 920 ... H 5
Collon, 262 ... J 4
Collooney, 546 ... E 3
Cong, 233 ... C 4
Convoy, 654 ... F 2
Coolaney, ‡352 ... D 3
Coolgreany, ‡603 ... J 6
Cootehill, 1,415 ... G 3
Cootehill, *1,542 ... G 3
Cork, 128,645 ... E 8
Cork, *134,430 ... E 8
Corofin, 342 ... C 6
Courtmacsherry, 210 ... D 8
Courtown Harbour, 291 ... J 6
Creeslough, 269 ... F 1
Crookhaven, ‡400 ... B 9
Croom, 756 ... D 6
Crosshaven, 1,222 ... E 8
Crossmolina, 1,077 ... C 3
Crusheen, ‡405 ... D 6
Culdaff, ‡621 ... G 1
Daingean, 492 ... G 5
Delvin, 223 ... G 4
Dingle, 1,401 ... A 7
Doaghbeg, ‡701 ... F 1
Donabate, 426 ... J 5
Donegal, 1,725 ... F 2
Doneraile, 799 ... D 7
Dooagh-Keel, 649 ... A 4
Doon, 387 ... E 6
Douglas, ‡4,448 ... D 8
Drimoleague, 415 ... C 8
Drishane, ‡1,548 ... C 7
Drogheda, 19,762 ... J 4
Drogheda, *20,095 ... J 4
Droichead Nua, 5,053 ... H 5
Droichead Nua, *6,444 ... H 5
Dromahair, 177 ... E 3
Drumcar, ‡1,215 ... J 4
Drumconrath, ‡1,044 ... H 4
Drumkeerin, ‡467 ... E 3
Drumlish, 205 ... F 4
Drumshanbo, 576 ... E 3
Dublin (cap.), 567,866 ... K 5
Dublin, *679,748 ... K 5
Duleek, 658 ... J 4
Duncannon, 228 ... H 7
Dundalk, 21,672 ... H 3
Dundalk, *23,816 ... H 3
Dunfanaghy, 303 ... F 1
Dungarvan, 5,583 ... F 7
Dungloe, 940 ... E 2
Dunkineely, 288 ... E 2
Dún Laoghaire, 53,171 ... K 5
Dún Laoghaire, *98,379 ... K 5
Dunlavin, 423 ... H 5
Dunleer, 855 ... J 4
Dunmanway, 1,392 ... C 8
Dunmore, 522 ... D 4
Dunmore East, 656 ... G 7
Dunshaughlin, ‡283 ... H 5
Durrow, Laoighis, 596 ... G 6
Durrow, Offaly, ‡441 ... F 5
Easky, 184 ... D 3
Edenderry, 2,953 ... G 5
Edenderry, *3,116 ... G 5
Elphin, 489 ... E 4
Emyvale, 281 ... G 3
Ennis, 5,972 ... D 6
Ennis, *10,840 ... D 6
Enniscorthy, 5,704 ... J 7
Enniscorthy, *6,642 ... J 7
Enniskerry, 772 ... J 5
Ennistymon, 1,013 ... C 6
Eyrecourt, 314 ... E 5
Fahan, ‡1,023 ... G 1
Falcarragh, 506 ... E 1
Feakle, ‡398 ... D 6
Fenit, 360 ... B 7
Ferbane, 1,064 ... F 5
Fermoy, 3,237 ... E 7
Fermoy, *4,033 ... E 7
Ferns, 712 ... J 6
Fethard, Tipperary, 1,064 ... F 7
Fethard, Wexford, ‡637 ... H 7
Foxford, 868 ... C 4
Foynes, 624 ... C 6
Frankford (Kilcormac), 1,089 ... F 5
Frenchpark, ‡693 ... E 4
Freshford, 585 ... G 6
Galbally, 258 ... E 7
Galway, 27,726 ... C 5
Galway, *29,375 ... C 5
Geashill, ‡751 ... G 5
Glandore, ‡695 ... C 8
Glanmire-Riverstown, 1,113 ... E 8
Glanworth, 335 ... E 7
Glenamaddy, 315 ... D 4
Glenbeigh, 266 ... B 7
Glencolumbkille, ‡787 ... D 2
Glengarriff, 244 ... C 8
Glenties, 734 ... E 2
Glenville, ‡264 ... D 7
Glin, 623 ... C 6
Golden, ‡640 ... F 7
Gorey, 2,946 ... J 6
Gorey, *3,024 ... J 6
Gormanston, ‡1,384 ... J 4
Gort, 975 ... D 5
Gowran, 402 ... G 6
Graiguenamanagh-Tinnahinch, 1,303 ... H 6
Granard, 1,054 ... F 4
Greencastle, 322 ... H 1
Greenore, 882 ... J 4
Greystones-Delgany, 4,517 ... K 5
Gurteen, 165 ... D 3
Hacketstown, 574 ... H 6
Headford, 673 ... C 5
Holycross, ‡902 ... F 6
Hospital, 525 ... E 7
Inchigeelagh, ‡516 ... C 8
Inishannon, 190 ... D 8
Inistioge, 179 ... G 7
Inniscrone, 582 ... C 3
Johnstown, 303 ... G 6
Kanturk, 2,063 ... D 7
Keel-Dooagh, 649 ... A 4
Kells, ‡423 ... G 6
Kells (Ceanannus Mór), 2,391 ... G 4
Kenmare, 903 ... B 8
Kilbaha, ‡471 ... B 6
Kilbeggan, 635 ... G 5
Kilcar, 273 ... D 2
Kilcock, 827 ... H 5
Kilconnell, ‡629 ... E 5
Kilcoole, 679 ... K 5
Kilcormac, 1,089 ... F 5
Kilcullen, 880 ... H 5
Kildare, 3,137 ... H 5
Kildysart, 239 ... C 6
Kilfenora, ‡441 ... C 6
Kilfinane, 561 ... D 7
Kilgarvan, 228 ... B 8
Kilkee, 1,287 ... B 6
Kilkelly, 225 ... D 4
Kilkenny, 9,838 ... G 6
Kilkenny, *13,306 ... G 6
Killala, 368 ... C 3
Killaloe, 871 ... D 6
Killarney, 7,184 ... C 7
Killarney, *7,541 ... C 7
Killavullen, 221 ... D 7
Killenaule, 592 ... F 6
Killeshandra, 432 ... F 3
Killimor, 221 ... E 5
Killinaboy, ‡297 ... C 6
Killorglin, 1,150 ... B 7
Killucan-Rathwire, 290 ... G 4
Killybegs, 1,094 ... E 2
Kilmacrennan, 274 ... F 1
Kilmacthomas, 396 ... G 7
Kilmallock, 1,170 ... D 7
Kilmeadan, ‡262 ... G 7
Kilmihill, 284 ... C 6
Kilmoganny, 181 ... G 7
Kilmore Quay, 273 ... H 7
Kilmurry, ‡387 ... C 6
Kilnaleck, 273 ... G 4
Kilronan, 243 ... B 5
Kilrush, 2,671 ... C 6
Kilsheelan, ‡665 ... F 7
Kiltimagh, 978 ... C 4
Kilworth, 360 ... E 7
Kingscourt, 1,016 ... H 4
Kingstown (Dún Laoghaire), 53,171 ... K 5
Kinlough, 160 ... E 3
Kinnegad, 362 ... G 5
Kinnitty, ‡420 ... F 5
Kinsale, 1,622 ... D 8
Kinsale, *1,989 ... D 8
Kinvara, 293 ... D 5
Knightstown, 236 ... A 8
Knock, ‡1,202 ... D 4
Knocklong, 248 ... D 7
Knocknagashel, 168 ... C 7
Labasheeda, ‡468 ... C 6
Laghey, ‡625 ... E 2
Lahinch, 455 ... C 6
Lanesborough-Ballyleague, 906 ... E 4
Laracor, ‡404 ... H 4
Laytown-Bettystown-Mornington, 1,882 ... J 4
Leenane, ‡271 ... B 4
Leighlindridge, 379 ... H 6
Leitrim, ‡544 ... F 3
Leixlip, 2,402 ... H 5
Letterkenny, 4,930 ... F 2
Letterkenny, *5,207 ... F 2
Lifford, 1,121 ... F 2
Limerick, 57,161 ... D 6
Limerick, *63,002 ... D 6
Liscarroll, 231 ... D 7
Lisdoonvarna, 459 ... C 5
Lismore, 884 ... F 7
Lismore, *1,041 ... F 7
Listowel, 3,021 ... C 7
Littleton, 322 ... F 6
Longford, 3,876 ... F 4
Longford, *4,791 ... F 4
Lorrha, ‡685 ... E 5
Loughrea, 3,075 ... E 5
Louisburgh, 310 ... B 4
Louth, 208 ... J 4
Lucan-Doddsborough, 4,245 ... J 5
Luimneach (Limerick), 57,161 ... D 6
Lusk, 553 ... J 4
Macroom, 2,256 ... C 8
Malahide, 3,834 ... J 5
Malin, ‡552 ... G 1
Mallow, 5,901 ... D 7
Mallow, *6,506 ... D 7
Manorhamilton, 858 ... E 3
Manulla, ‡660 ... C 4
Maryborough (Portlaoighise), 3,902 ... G 5
Maynooth, 1,296 ... H 5
Meathas Truim, 546 ... G 4
Midleton, 3,075 ... E 8
Midleton, *4,666 ... E 8
Milford, 763 ... F 1
Millstreet, 1,319 ... D 7
Milltown, 260 ... A 7
Miltown-Malbay, 677 ... C 6
Minard, ‡397 ... A 7
Mitchelstown, 2,783 ... E 7
Moate, 1,378 ... F 5
Mohill, 868 ... F 4
Monaghan, 5,256 ... G 3
Monasterevan, 1,619 ... H 5
Moneygall, 282 ... F 6
Monivea, ‡405 ... D 5
Mooncoin, 413 ... G 7
Mount Bellew, 275 ... D 5
Mountcharles, 445 ... E 2
Mountmellick, 2,595 ... G 5
Mountmellick, *2,864 ... G 5
Mountrath, 1,098 ... F 5
Moville, 1,089 ... G 1
Moycullen, ‡498 ... C 5
Moynalty, ‡583 ... H 4
Muff, 240 ... G 1
Muinebeag, 2,321 ... H 6
Mullagh, 293 ... H 4
Mullaghmore, ‡629 ... D 3
Mullinahone, 262 ... F 7
Mullinavat, 343 ... G 7
Mullingar, 6,790 ... G 4
Mullinger, *9,245 ... G 4
Naas, 5,078 ... H 5
Navan (An Uaimh), 4,605 ... H 4
Nenagh, 5,085 ... E 6
Nenagh, *5,174 ... E 6
Newbliss, ‡547 ... G 3
Newbridge (Droichead Nua), 5,053 ... H 5
Newcastle, 2,549 ... D 7
Newcastle, *2,680 ... D 7
Newmarket, 886 ... C 7
Newmarket-on-Fergus, 1,052 ... D 6
New Pallas, ‡1,271 ... E 6
Newport, Mayo, 420 ... C 4
Newport, Tipperary, 582 ... E 6
New Ross, 4,775 ... H 7
New Ross, *5,153 ... H 7
Newtownforbes, ‡495 ... F 4
Newtownmountkennedy, 882 ... J 5
Newtownsandes, 268 ... C 6
O'Briensbridge-Montpelier, 237 ... D 6
Oldcastle, 759 ... G 4
Old Leighlin, ‡309 ... G 6
Oola, 348 ... E 6
Oranmore, 440 ... D 5
Oughterard, 628 ... C 5
Passage East, 408 ... G 7
Passage West, 2,709 ... E 8
Patrickswell, 415 ... D 6
Pettigo, 332 ... F 2
Piltown, 456 ... G 7
Portarlington, 3,117 ... G 5
Portlaoighise, 3,902 ... G 5
Portlaoighise, *6,470 ... G 5
Portlaw, 1,166 ... G 7
Portmarnock, 1,726 ... J 5
Portumna, 913 ... E 5
Queenstown (Cóbh), 6,076 ... E 8
Rahan, ‡531 ... F 5
Ramelton, 807 ... F 1
Raphoe, 945 ... F 2
Rathangan, 868 ... G 5
Rathcoole, 1,740 ... J 5
Rathcormac, 191 ... E 7
Rathdowney, 892 ... F 6
Rathdrum, 1,141 ... J 6
Rathgormuck, ‡231 ... F 7
Rathkeale, 1,543 ... D 7
Rathluirc, 2,232 ... D 7
Rathmore, 437 ... J 5
Rathmullen, 486 ... F 1
Rathnew-Merrymeeting, 954 ... J 6
Rathowen, ‡294 ... F 4
Rathvilly, 230 ... H 6
Ratoath, 300 ... J 5
Riverstown, 236 ... E 3
Rockcorry, 233 ... H 3
Rosapenna, ‡822 ... F 1
Roscommon, 1,556 ... E 4
Roscommon, *2,821 ... E 4
Roscrea, 3,855 ... F 6
Rosscarbery, 309 ... C 8
Rosses Point, 464 ... D 3
Rosslare, 588 ... J 7
Rosslare Harbour (Ballygeary), 725 ... J 7
Roundstone, 204 ... A 5
Roundwood, 260 ... J 5
Rush, 2,633 ... J 4
Saint Johnston, 463 ... F 2
Scarriff, 619 ... E 6
Schull, 457 ... B 8
Scotstown, 264 ... H 3
Shanagolden, 231 ... C 6
Shannon Airport, 3,657 ... D 6
Shannon Bridge, 188 ... F 5
Shercock, 313 ... G 4
Shillelagh, 246 ... J 6
Shinrone, 365 ... F 5
Shrule, 288 ... C 4
Sixmilebridge, 567 ... D 6
Skerries, 3,044 ... J 4
Skibbereen, 2,104 ... C 8
Slane, 483 ... H 4
Sligo, 14,080 ... E 3
Sligo, *14,456 ... E 3
Sneem, 285 ... B 8
Spiddal, ‡819 ... C 5
Stepaside, 748 ... J 5
Stradbally, Laoighis, 891 ... G 5
Stradbally, Waterford, 158 ... F 7
Strokestown, 563 ... E 4
Swanlinbar, 257 ... F 3
Swinford, 1,105 ... C 4
Swords, 4,133 ... J 5
Taghmon, 369 ... H 7
Tallaght, 6,174 ... J 5
Tallow, 883 ... F 7
Tarbert, 485 ... C 6
Teltown, ‡739 ... H 4
Templemore, 2,174 ... F 6
Templetuohy, 197 ... F 6
Termonfeckin, 328 ... J 4
Thomastown, 1,270 ... G 7
Thurles, 6,840 ... F 6
Thurles, *7,087 ... F 6
Timoleague, 257 ... D 8
Tinahely, 450 ... H 6
Tipperary, 4,631 ... E 7
Tipperary, *4,717 ... E 7
Toomevara, 272 ... E 6
Tralee, 12,287 ... B 7
Tralee, *13,263 ... B 7
Tramore, 3,792 ... G 7
Trim, 1,700 ... H 4
Trim, *2,255 ... H 4
Tuam, 3,808 ... D 4
Tuam, *4,952 ... D 4
Tubbercurry, 959 ... D 3
Tulla, 415 ... D 6
Tullamore, 6,809 ... G 5
Tullamore, *7,474 ... G 5
Tullaroan, ‡301 ... G 6
Tullow, 1,838 ... H 6
Tullow, *1,945 ... H 6
Tynagh, ‡452 ... E 5
Tyrrellspass, 289 ... G 5
Urlingford, 652 ... F 6
Virginia, 583 ... G 4
Waterford, 31,968 ... G 7
Waterford, *33,676 ... G 7
Waterville, 547 ... A 8
Westport, 3,023 ... C 4
Wexford, 11,849 ... H 7
Wexford, *13,293 ... H 7
Whitegate, 370 ... E 8
Wicklow, 3,786 ... K 6
Wicklow, *3,915 ... K 6
Woodenbridge, ‡620 ... J 6
Woodford, 198 ... E 5
Youghal, 5,445 ... F 8
Youghal, *5,626 ... F 8

OTHER FEATURES

Achill (isl.), 3,129 ... A 4
Allen (lake) ... E 3
Allen, Bog of (marsh) ... H 5
Aran (isl.), 773 ... D 2
Aran (isls.), 1,499 ... B 5
Arklow (bank) ... K 6
Arrow (lake) ... E 3
Awbeg (riv.) ... D 7
Ballinskelligs (bay) ... A 8
Ballycotton (bay) ... F 8
Ballyheige (bay) ... B 7
Ballyhoura (hills) ... E 7
Ballyteige (bay) ... H 7
Bandon (riv.) ... D 8
Bann (riv.) ... J 6
Bantry (bay) ... B 8
Barrow (riv.) ... H 7
Baurtregaum (mt.) ... A 7
Bear (isl.), 288 ... B 8
Blacksod (bay) ... A 3
Blackstairs (mt.) ... H 6
Blackwater (riv.) ... D 7
Blackwater (riv.) ... H 4
Blasket (isls.) ... A 7
Bloody Foreland (prom.) ... E 1
Blue Stack (mts.) ... E 2
Boderg (lake) ... E 4
Boggeragh (mts.) ... D 7
Boyne (riv.) ... J 4
Brandon (head) ... A 7
Bride (riv.) ... E 7
Broad Haven (harb.) ... B 3
Brosna (riv.) ... F 5
Bull, The (isl.), 5 ... A 8
Caha (mts.) ... B 8
Carlingford (inlet) ... J 3
Carnsore (pt.) ... J 7
Carrantuohill (mt.) ... B 7
Clare (riv.) ... D 5
Clare (isls.), 168 ... A 4
Clear (cape) ... B 9
Clear (isl.), 192 ... C 9
Clew (bay) ... B 4
Comeragh (mts.) ... F 7
Conn (lake) ... C 3
Connacht (prov.), 390,902 ... C 4
Connemara (dist.), 7,599 ... B 5
Cork (harb.) ... E 8
Corrib (lake) ... C 5
Courtmacsherry (bay) ... D 8
Curragh, The ... H 5
Dee (riv.) ... H 4
Deel (riv.) ... D 7
Deele (riv.) ... F 2
Derg (lake) ... E 6
Derravaragh (lake) ... G 4
Derryveagh (mts.) ... E 2
Dingle (bay) ... A 7
Donegal (bay) ... D 3
Drum (hills) ... F 7
Dublin (bay) ... J 5
Dundalk (bay) ... J 4
Dunmanus (bay) ... B 8
Dursey (isl.), 38 ... A 8
Ennell (lake) ... G 5
Erne (riv.) ... E 3
Errigal (mt.) ... E 1
Erris (head) ... A 3
Fanad (head) ... F 1
Fastnet Rock (isl.), 3 ... B 9
Feale (riv.) ... C 7
Fergus (riv.) ... D 6
Finn (riv.) ... F 2
Finn (riv.) ... G 3
Flesk (riv.) ... C 7
Foyle (inlet) ... G 1
Foyle (riv.) ... G 2
Galley (head) ... D 9
Galtee (mts.) ... E 7
Galtymore (mt.) ... E 7
Galway (bay) ... C 5
Gara (lake) ... D 4
Garadice (lake) ... F 3
Gill (lake) ... E 3
Glyde (riv.) ... H 4
Golden Vale (plain) ... E 7
Gorumna (isl.), 1,108 ... B 5
Gowna (lake) ... G 4
Grand (canal) ... G 5
Greenore (pt.) ... J 7
Gweebarra (bay) ... D 2
Hags (head) ... B 6
Helvick (head) ... G 7
Hook (head) ... H 7
Horn (head) ... E 1
Iar Connacht (dist.), 10,774 ... C 5
Inishbofin (isl.), 236 ... A 4
Inishbofin (isl.), 103 ... E 1
Inisheer (isl.), 313 ... B 5
Inishmaan (isl.), 319 ... C 5
Inishmore (isl.), 864 ... B 5
Inishowen (head) ... H 1
Inishowen (pen.), 24,109 ... G 1
Inishtrahull (isl.), 3 ... G 1
Inishturk (isls.), 83 ... A 4
Inny (riv.) ... A 8
Inny (riv.) ... F 4
Inver (bay) ... E 2
Ireland's Eye (isl.) ... K 5
Irish (sea) ... K 4
Joyce's Country (dist.), 2,021 ... B 4
Kenmare (riv.) ... A 8
Kerry (head) ... A 7
Key (lake) ... E 3
Kilkieran (bay) ... B 5
Killala (bay) ... C 3
Killary (harb.) ... A 4
Kinsale (harb.) ... E 8
Kippure (mt.) ... J 5
Knockboy (mt.) ... B 8
Knockmealdown (mts.) ... F 7
Lady's Island Lake (inlet) ... J 7
Lambay (isl.), 24 ... K 4
Laune (riv.) ... B 7
Leane (lake) ... B 7
Leane (lake) ... G 4
Lee (riv.) ... D 8
Leinster (mt.) ... H 6
Leinster (prov.), 1,498,140 ... G 5
Lettermullan (isl.), 221 ... B 5
Liffey (riv.) ... H 5
Liscannor (bay) ... B 6
Long Island (bay) ... B 9
Loop (head) ... A 6
Lugnaquillia (mt.) ... J 5
Macgillicuddy's Reeks (mts.) ... B 7
Macnean (lake) ... F 3
Maigue (riv.) ... D 6
Maine (riv.) ... C 7
Malin (head) ... F 1
Mask (lake) ... C 4
Maumturk (mts.) ... B 5
Melvin (lake) ... E 3
Mizen (head) ... B 9
Moher (cliffs) ... B 6
Monavullagh (mts.) ... F 7
Moy (riv.) ... C 3
Mulkear (riv.) ... E 6
Mullaghareirk (mts.) ... C 7
Mulroy (bay) ... F 1
Munster (prov.), 882,002 ... D 7
Mweelrea (mt.) ... B 4
Mweenish (isl.), 198 ... B 5
Nagles (mts.) ... E 7
Nenagh (riv.) ... E 6
Nephin (mt.) ... C 3
Nore (riv.) ... G 7
North (sound) ... B 5
Omey (isl.), 34 ... A 5
Oughter (lake) ... G 3
Ovoca (riv.) ... J 6
Owenmore (riv.) ... D 3
Owey (isl.), 51 ... D 1
Paps, The (mt.) ... C 7
Partry (mts.) ... C 4
Pollaphuca (res.) ... J 5
Punchestown ... H 5
Rathlin O'Birne (isl.), 3 ... C 2
Ree (lake) ... F 5
Roaringwater (bay) ... B 9
Rosses (bay) ... D 1
Rosskeeragh (pt.) ... D 3
Royal (canal) ... G 4
Saint Finan's (bay) ... A 8
Saint George's (chan.) ... K 7
Saint John's (pt.) ... D 2
Saltee (isls.) ... H 7
Seven (heads) ... D 8
Seven Hogs, The (isls.) ... A 7
Shannon (riv.) ... E 6
Sheeffry (hills) ... B 4
Sheelin (lake) ... G 4
Sheep Haven (harb.) ... F 1
Sheeps (head) ... B 8
Sherkin (isl.), 82 ... C 9
Silvermine (mts.) ... E 6
Slaney (riv.) ... H 7
Slieve Aughty (mts.) ... D 5
Slieve Bloom (mts.) ... F 5
Slieve Gamph (mts.) ... D 3
Slievenaman (mt.) ... F 7
Sligo (bay) ... D 3
Slyne (head) ... A 5
South (sound) ... C 5
Stacks (mts.) ... B 7
Suck (riv.) ... E 5
Suir (riv.) ... G 7
Swilly (inlet) ... F 1
Tara (hill) ... H 4
Tory (isl.), 273 ... E 1
Tory (sound) ... E 1
Tralee (bay) ... B 7
Trawbreaga (bay) ... F 1
Ulster (part) (prov.), 207,204 ... G 2
Valencia (Valentia) (isl.), 770 ... A 8
Valentia (isl.), 770 ... A 8
Waterford (harb.) ... G 7
Wexford (bay) ... J 7
Wicklow (head) ... K 6
Wicklow (mts.) ... J 6
Youghal (bay) ... F 8

NORTHERN IRELAND

DISTRICTS

Antrim, 37,600 ... J 2
Ards, 52,100 ... K 2
Armagh, 47,500 ... H 3
Ballymena, 52,200 ... J 2
Ballymoney, 22,700 ... J 1
Bainbridge, 28,800 ... J 3
Belfast, 368,200 ... J 2
Carrickfergus, 27,500 ... K 2
Castlereagh, 63,600 ... K 2
Coleraine, 44,900 ... H 1
Cookstown, 27,500 ... H 2
Craigavon, 71,200 ... J 3
Down, 48,800 ... K 3
Dungannon, 43,000 ... H 3
Fermanagh, 50,900 ... F 3
Larne, 29,000 ... K 2
Limavady, 25,000 ... H 1
Lisburn, 80,800 ... J 2
Londonderry, 86,600 ... G 2
Magherafelt, 32,200 ... H 2
Mourne (Newry and Mourne), 75,300 ... J 3
Moyle, 13,400 ... J 1
Newtownabbey, 71,500 ... J 2
North Down, 59,600 ... K 2
Omagh, 41,800 ... G 2
Strabane, 35,500 ... G 2

CITIES and TOWNS

Ahoghill, ‡1,929 ... J 2
Annalong, 1,001 ... K 3
Antrim, 8,351 ... J 2
Ardglass, 1,052 ... K 3
Armagh, 13,606 ... H 3
Armoy, ‡1,051 ... J 1
Augher, ‡1,986 ... G 3
Aughnacloy, ‡1,885 ... H 3
Ballycastle, 2,899 ... J 1
Ballyclare, 5,155 ... J 2
Ballygawley, ‡2,165 ... G 3
Ballykelly, 1,116 ... G 1
Ballymena, 23,386 ... J 2
Ballymoney, 5,697 ... J 1
Ballynahinch, 3,485 ... J 3
Banbridge, 7,968 ... J 3
Bangor, 35,260 ... K 2
Belfast (cap.), 353,700 ... J 2
Belfast, *551,940 ... J 2
Bellaghy, ‡2,265 ... H 2
Belleek, ‡2,487 ... E 3
Beragh, ‡2,137 ... G 2
Bessbrook, 2,619 ... J 3
Brookeborough, ‡2,534 ... G 3
Broughshane, 1,288 ... J 2
Bushmills, 1,288 ... J 1
Caledon, ‡1,828 ... H 3
Carnlough, 1,416 ... J 2
Carrickfergus, 16,603 ... K 2
Carrowdore, 2,548 ... K 2
Castledawson, 1,162 ... H 2
Castlederg, 1,766 ... F 2
Castlewellan, 1,488 ... K 3
Claudy, ‡2,507 ... G 2
Clogher, ‡1,888 ... G 3
Coalisland, 3,614 ... H 2
Coleraine, 16,354 ... H 1
Comber, 5,575 ... K 2
Cookstown, 6,965 ... H 2
Craigavon, 12,740 ... J 3
Crossgar, 1,098 ... K 3
Crossmaglen, 1,085 ... H 3
Crumlin, 1,450 ... J 2
Cullybackey, 1,649 ... J 2
Derrygonnelly, ‡2,539 ... F 3
Dervock, ‡1,191 ... J 1
Donaghadee, 4,008 ... K 2
Downpatrick, 7,918 ... K 3
Draperstown, ‡2,247 ... H 2
Dromore, Bainbridge, 2,848 ... J 3
Dromore, Omagh, ‡2,224 ... G 3
Drumquin, ‡1,982 ... F 2
Dundrum, ‡2,245 ... K 3
Dungannon, 8,190 ... H 3
Dungiven, 1,536 ... H 2
Dunnamanagh, ‡2,242 ... G 2
Ederny and Kesh, ‡2,497 ... F 2
Enniskillen, 9,679 ... F 3
Feeny, ‡1,459 ... H 2
Fintona, 1,190 ... G 3
Fivemiletown, ‡1,649 ... G 3
Garvagh, ‡2,363 ... H 2
Gilford, 1,592 ... J 3
Glenarm, ‡1,728 ... J 2
Glenavy, ‡2,360 ... J 2
Glynn, ‡1,872 ... K 2
Gortin, ‡2,033 ... G 2
Greyabbey, ‡2,646 ... K 2
Hillsborough, 1,021 ... J 3
Holywood, 9,892 ... K 2
Irvinestown, 1,457 ... F 3
Keady, 2,145 ... H 3
Kells, ‡2,560 ... J 2
Kesh, ‡2,497 ... F 3
Kilkeel, 4,090 ... K 3
Killough, ‡3,295 ... K 3
Killyleagh, 2,359 ... K 3
Kilrea, 1,196 ... H 2
Kircubbin, 1,075 ... K 3
Larne, 18,482 ... K 2
Limavady, 6,004 ... H 1
Lisburn, 31,836 ... J 2
Lisnaskea, 1,443 ... G 3
Londonderry, 51,200 ... G 2
Loughbrickland, ‡2,056 ... J 3
Maghera, 2,085 ... H 2
Magherafelt, 4,704 ... H 2
Markethill, ‡2,352 ... H 3
Millisle, 1,172 ... K 2
Moneymore, 1,178 ... H 2
Moy, ‡2,349 ... H 3
Moygashel, 1,086 ... H 3
Newcastle, 4,647 ... J 3
Newry, 20,279 ... J 3
Newtownabbey, 58,114 ... K 2
Newtownards, 15,484 ... K 2
Newtownbutler, ‡2,663 ... G 3
Newtownhamilton, ‡1,936 ... H 3
Newtownstewart, 1,433 ... G 2
Omagh, 14,594 ... G 2
Pomeroy, ‡1,786 ... H 2
Portaferry, 1,730 ... K 3
Portavogie, 1,310 ... K 3
Portglenone, ‡2,061 ... H 2
Portrush, 5,376 ... H 1
Portstewart, 5,085 ... H 1
Randalstown, 2,799 ... J 2
Rathfriland, 1,886 ... J 3
Rostrevor, 1,617 ... J 3
Saintfield, ‡2,198 ... K 3
Sion Mills, 1,588 ... G 2
Sixmilecross, ‡1,980 ... G 2
Stewartstown, ‡1,759 ... H 2
Strabane, 9,413 ... G 2
Strangford, ‡1,987 ... K 3
Tandragee, 1,725 ... J 3
Tempo, ‡2,282 ... G 3
Trillick, ‡2,167 ... G 3
Warrenpoint, 4,291 ... J 3
Whitehead, 2,642 ... K 2

OTHER FEATURES

Bann (riv.) ... H 2
Belfast (inlet) ... K 2
Blackwater (riv.) ... H 3
Bush (riv.) ... H 1
Derg (riv.) ... F 2
Divis (mt.) ... J 2
Dundrum (bay) ... K 3
Erne (lake) ... F 3
Foyle (inlet) ... G 1
Foyle (riv.) ... G 2
Giant's Causeway ... H 1
Lagan (riv.) ... K 2
Larne (inlet) ... K 2
Magee, Island (pen.), 1,581 ... K 2
Magilligan (pt.) ... H 1
Main (riv.) ... J 2
Mourne (mts.) ... J 3
Mourne (riv.) ... G 2
Neagh (lake) ... J 2
North (chan.) ... K 1
Rathlin (isl.), 109 ... J 1
Red (bay) ... K 1
Roe (riv.) ... H 1
Saint John's (pt.) ... K 3
Slieve Donard (mt.) ... K 3
Sperrin (mts.) ... G 2
Strangford (inlet) ... K 3
Torr (head) ... K 1
Ulster (part) (prov.), 1,537,200 ... G 2
Upper Lough Erne (lake) ... F 3

*City and suburbs.
‡Population of district.

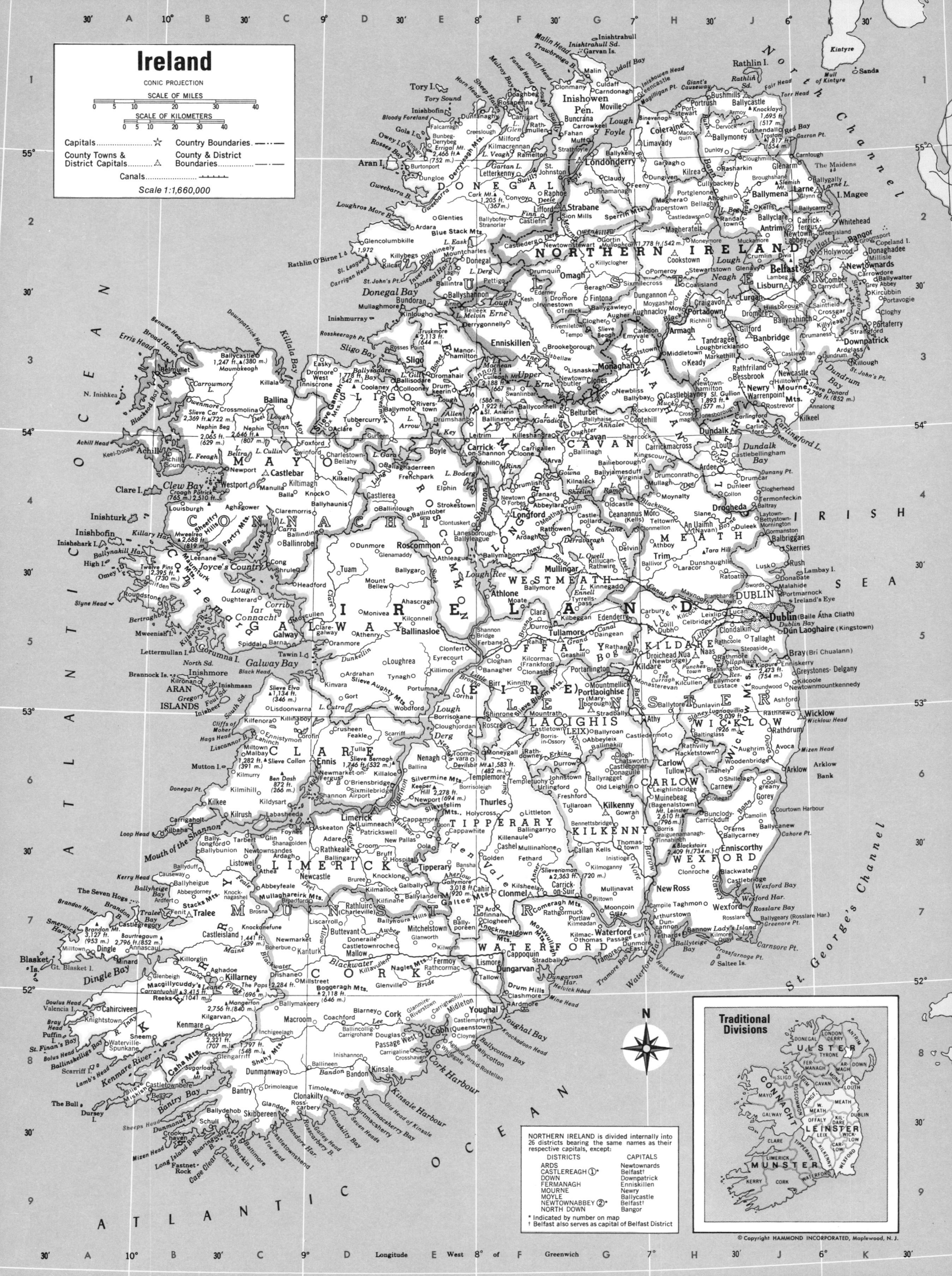

Ireland

CONIC PROJECTION

SCALE OF MILES

0 5 10 20 30 40

SCALE OF KILOMETERS

0 5 10 20 30 40

Capitals............................ ☆
County Towns &
District Capitals............... △
Canals..............................

Country Boundaries. — ∙ — ∙ —
County & District
Boundaries.....................

Scale 1:1,660,000

Traditional Divisions

NORTHERN IRELAND is divided internally into 26 districts bearing the same names as their respective capitals, except:

DISTRICTS	CAPITALS
ARDS	Newtownards
CASTLEREAGH ① *	Belfast †
DOWN	Downpatrick
FERMANAGH	Enniskillen
MOURNE	Newry
MOYLE	Ballycastle
NEWTOWNABBEY ②	Belfast †
NORTH DOWN	Bangor

* Indicated by number on map
† Belfast also serves as capital of Belfast District

© Copyright HAMMOND INCORPORATED, Maplewood, N.J.

Longitude West 8° of Greenwich

Svalbard

NORWEGIAN SEA

STOCKHOLM

NORWEGIAN SEA

ATLANTIC OCEAN

NORTH SEA

DENMARK

WEST GERMANY

EAST GERMANY

POLAND

ARCTIC OCEAN

BARENTS SEA

GULF OF BOTHNIA

BALTIC SEA

U. S. S. R.

Norway, Sweden, Finland and Denmark

CONIC PROJECTION

SCALE OF MILES

0   50   100   150

SCALE OF KILOMETERS

0   50   100   150   200

Capitals of Countries .... ☆
Administrative Centers .... △
International Boundaries .... —·—·—
Internal Boundaries .... —··—··—
Canals .... ━━━

Scale 1:7,440,000

SUBDIVISIONS
Indicated by Numbers
Counties in NORWAY

1 Akershus   G 6
2 Vestfold   G 7
3 Østfold   G 7
4 Oslo   G 7

Oslo is the administrative
center for Akershus and
Oslo County.

Counties in SWEDEN

5 Göteborg och
   Bohus   G 7
6 Västmanland   K 7
7 Södermanland K 7
8 Östergötland J 7
9 Malmöhus   H 9
10 Kristianstad J 8

AREA 125,053 sq. mi. (323,887 sq. km.)
POPULATION 4,092,000
CAPITAL Oslo
LARGEST CITY Oslo
HIGHEST POINT Glittertinden 8,110 ft. (2,472 m.)
MONETARY UNIT krone
MAJOR LANGUAGE Norwegian
MAJOR RELIGION Protestantism

AREA 173,665 sq. mi. (449,792 sq. km.)
POPULATION 8,320,000
CAPITAL Stockholm
LARGEST CITY Stockholm
HIGHEST POINT Kebnekaise 6,946 ft. (2,117 m.)
MONETARY UNIT krona
MAJOR LANGUAGE Swedish
MAJOR RELIGION Protestantism

AREA 130,128 sq. mi. (337,032 sq. km.)
POPULATION 4,788,000
CAPITAL Helsinki
LARGEST CITY Helsinki
HIGHEST POINT Haltiatunturi 4,343 ft. (1,324 m.)
MONETARY UNIT markka
MAJOR LANGUAGES Finnish, Swedish
MAJOR RELIGION Protestantism

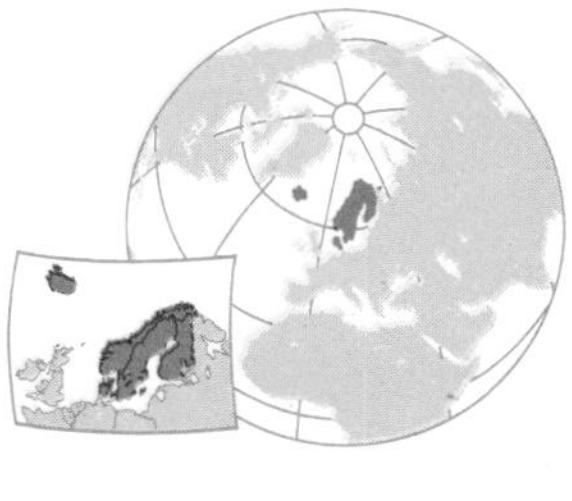

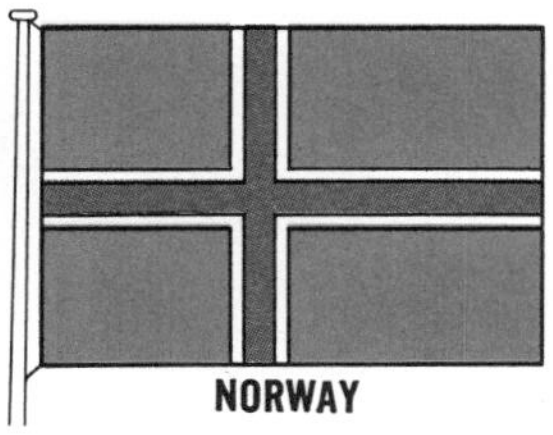
NORWAY

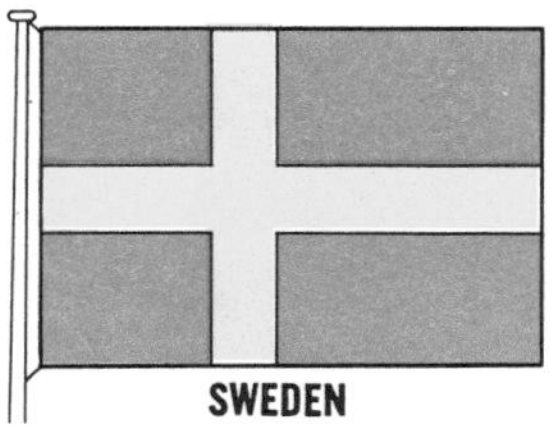
SWEDEN

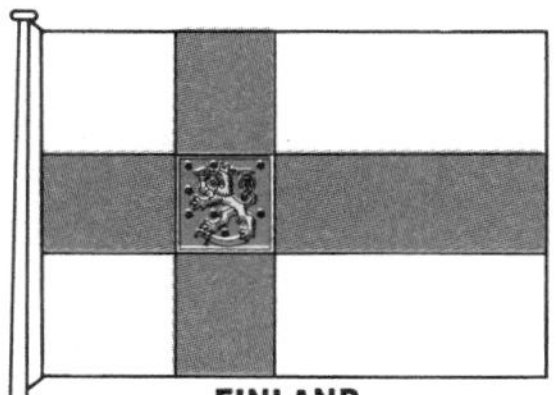
FINLAND

FINLAND

PROVINCES

- Ahvenanmaa 22,380 ... L6
- Åland (Ahvenanmaa) 22,380 ... L6
- Häme 662,500 ... O6
- Keski-Suomi 241,770 ... O5
- Kuopio 252,023 ... P5
- Kymi 346,478 ... Q6
- Lappi 196,792 ... P3
- Mikkeli 211,453 ... P6
- Oulu 406,309 ... P4
- Pohjois-Karjala 179,065 ... Q5
- Turku ja Pori 697,988 ... N6
- Uusimaa 1,085,625 ... O6
- Vaasa 425,283 ... N5

CITIES and TOWNS

- Äänekoski 10,725 ... O5
- Åbo (Turku) 164,857 ... N6
- Alavus 10,285 ... N5
- Borgaå 18,740 ... O6
- Ekenäs 7,391 ... N6
- Espoo 117,090 ... O6
- Forssa 18,442 ... N6
- Haapajärvi 7,791 ... O5
- Hämeenlinna 40,761 ... O6
- Hamina 11,055 ... P6
- Hangö 10,374 ... N7
- Hanko (Hangö) 10,374 ... N7
- Harjavalta 8,445 ... M6
- Heinola 15,350 ... P6
- Helsinki (cap.) 502,961 ... O6
- Helsinki* 794,746 ... O6
- Huutokoski† 6,458 ... P5
- Hyvinkää 35,865 ... O6
- Iisalmi 21,159 ... P5
- Ikaalinen 8,364 ... N6
- Imatra 35,590 ... Q6
- Ivalo 2,661 ... P2
- Jakobstad 20,397 ... N5
- Jämsä 12,526 ... O6
- Järvenpää 16,259 ... O6
- Joensuu 41,429 ... R5
- Jyväskylä 61,209 ... O5
- Jyväskylä* 84,185 ... O5
- Kajaani 20,583 ... P4
- Kalajoki 3,624 ... N4
- Kankaanpää 12,564 ... M6
- Karhula 21,834 ... P6
- Karis 8,152 ... N6
- Karjaa (Karis) 8,152 ... N6
- Karkkila 8,678 ... N6
- Kauniainien 6,219 ... O6
- Kauttua 3,297 ... M6
- Kelloselkä† 8,200 ... Q3
- Kemi 27,893 ... O4
- Kemijärvi 12,951 ... P3
- Kerava 19,966 ... O6
- Kokemäki 10,188 ... N6
- Kokkola 22,096 ... N5
- Kotka 34,026 ... P6
- Kotka* 60,235 ... P6
- Kouvola 29,383 ... P6
- Kouvola* 59,507 ... P6
- Kristiinankaupunki (Kristinestad) 9,331 ... N5
- Kristinestad 9,331 ... N5
- Kuhmo 4,150 ... Q4
- Kuopio 71,684 ... Q5
- Kurikka 11,177 ... M5
- Kuusamo 4,449 ... Q4
- Kuusankoski 22,342 ... P6
- Lahti 94,864 ... O6
- Lahti* 112,129 ... O6
- Lappeenranta 52,682 ... P6
- Lapua 15,189 ... N5
- Lieksa 20,274 ... R5
- Loimaa 6,575 ... N6
- Lovisa 8,674 ... P6
- Maarianhamina (Mariehamn) 9,574 ... M7
- Mänttä 7,910 ... O6
- Mariehamn 9,574 ... M7
- Mikkeli 27,112 ... P6
- Naantali 7,814 ... M6
- Nokia 22,308 ... N6
- Nurmes 11,721 ... Q5
- Nykarleby 7,408 ... N5
- Oulainen 7,322 ... O4
- Oulu 93,707 ... O4
- Oulu* 103,044 ... O4
- Outokumpu 10,736 ... Q5
- Parainen 10,170 ... M6
- Parkano 8,518 ... N6
- Pieksämäki 12,923 ... P5
- Pietarsaari (Jakobstad) 20,397 ... N5
- Pori 80,343 ... M6
- Pori* 86,635 ... M6
- Posio† 6,205 ... Q3
- Pudasjärvi† 12,594 ... P4
- Raahe 15,379 ... O4
- Raisio 14,271 ... M6
- Rauma 29,081 ... M6
- Riihimäki 24,106 ... O6
- Rovaniemi 28,411 ... O3
- Saarijärvi 2,714 ... O5
- Salo 19,176 ... N6
- Savonlinna 28,336 ... Q6
- Seinäjoki 22,123 ... N5
- Sodankylä 3,304 ... P3
- Sotkamo 2,316 ... Q4
- Suolahti 5,936 ... O5
- Suonenjoki 9,286 ... P5
- Tammisaari (Ekenäs) 7,391 ... N6
- Tampere 168,118 ... N6
- Tampere* 220,920 ... N6
- Toijala 8,080 ... N6
- Tornio 19,971 ... O4
- Turku 164,857 ... N6
- Turku* 217,423 ... N6
- Turtola† 5,852 ... O3
- Ulvila† 8,040 ... N6
- Uusikaarlepyy (Nykarleby) 7,408 ... N5
- Uusikaupunki 11,915 ... M6
- Vaasa 54,402 ... M5
- Vaasa* 58,224 ... M5
- Valkeakoski 22,588 ... N6
- Vammala 16,363 ... N6
- Varkaus 24,450 ... Q5
- Vasa (Vaasa) 54,402 ... M5
- Vuotso† 10,186 ... P2
- Ylivieska 10,827 ... O4

OTHER FEATURES

- Åland (isls.) ... L6
- Baltic (sea) ... K9
- Bothnia (gulf) ... M5
- Finland (gulf) ... P7
- Hailuoto (isl.) ... O4
- Haltiatunturi (mt.) ... M2
- Hangöudd (prom.) ... N7
- Haukivesi (lake) ... Q5
- Iijoki (riv.) ... O4
- Inari (lake) ... P2
- Ivalojoki (riv.) ... P2
- Juojärvi (lake) ... Q5
- Kalajoki (riv.) ... O4
- Kallavesi (lake) ... P5
- Karlö (Hailuoto) (isl.) ... O4
- Keitele (lake) ... O5
- Kemijärvi (lake) ... Q3
- Kemijoki (riv.) ... O3
- Kiantajärvi (lake) ... Q4
- Kilpisjärvi (lake) ... M2
- Kitinen (riv.) ... P3
- Kivijärvi (lake) ... O5
- Koitere (lake) ... R5
- Kuusamojärvi (lake) ... Q4
- Längelmävesi (lake) ... O6
- Lapland (reg.) ... O2
- Lappajärvi (lake) ... O5
- Lapuanjoki (riv.) ... N5
- Lestijärvi (lake) ... O5
- Lokka (res.) ... Q3
- Muojärvi (lake) ... R4
- Muonio (riv.) ... M2
- Näsijärvi (lake) ... O6
- Onkivesi (lake) ... P5
- Orihvesi (lake) ... Q5
- Oulujärvi (lake) ... P4
- Oulujoki (riv.) ... O4
- Ounasjoki (riv.) ... O3
- Päijänne (lake) ... O6
- Pielinen (lake) ... Q5
- Puruvesi (lake) ... Q6
- Puulavesi (lake) ... P5
- Pyhäjärvi (lake) ... O5
- Pyhäjärvi (lake) ... M6
- Saimaa (lake) ... Q6
- Siikajoki (riv.) ... O4
- Simojärvi (lake) ... P3
- Simojoki (riv.) ... O4
- Tana (riv.) ... P2
- Tornio (riv.) ... O3
- Vallgrund (isl.) ... M5
- Ylikitka (lake) ... Q3

NORWAY

COUNTIES

- Akershus 355,196 ... G6
- Aust-Agder 86,216 ... E7
- Buskerud 209,684 ... F6
- Finnmark 79,373 ... O2
- Hedmark 183,465 ... G6
- Hordaland 386,492 ... E6
- Møre og Romsdal 231,944 ... E5
- Nordland 243,233 ... J3
- Nord-Trøndelag 122,886 ... H4
- Oppland 178,259 ... F6
- Oslo (city) 462,732 ... D3
- Østfold 228,546 ... G7
- Rogaland 287,653 ... E7
- Sogn og Fjordane 103,135 ... E6
- Sør-Trøndelag 241,361 ... G5
- Telemark 158,853 ... F7
- Troms 144,111 ... L2
- Vest-Agder 131,659 ... E7
- Vestfold 182,433 ... G7

CITIES and TOWNS

- Ålesund 40,868 ... D5
- Ålgård 2,322 ... D7
- Alta 5,582 ... N2
- Åndalsnes 2,574 ... F5
- Årdalstangen 2,360 ... F6
- Arendal 11,701 ... F7
- Arendal* 21,228 ... F7
- Årnes 2,267 ... G6
- Askim 8,413 ... E4
- Bamble† 7,031 ... F7
- Barentsburg ... C2
- Bergen 213,434 ... D6
- Bodø 31,077 ... J3
- Borge† 3,294 ... H2
- Brønnøysund 3,130 ... G4
- Dombås 1,114 ... F5
- Drammen 50,777 ... C4
- Drammen* 56,521 ... C4
- Drøbak 4,538 ... D4
- Eidsvoll 2,906 ... G6
- Eigersund 11,379 ... D7
- Elverum 7,391 ... G6
- Farsund 8,908 ... E7
- Flekkefjord 8,750 ... E7
- Flora 8,822 ... D6
- Fredrikstad 29,024 ... D4
- Fredrikstad* 51,141 ... D4
- Gjøvik 25,963 ... G6
- Grimstad 13,091 ... F7
- Halden 27,087 ... G7
- Hamar 16,418 ... G6
- Hamar* 25,138 ... G6
- Hammerfest 7,610 ... N1
- Hammerfest* 8,005 ... N1
- Harstad 21,125 ... K2
- Haugesund 27,386 ... D7
- Haugesund* 29,277 ... D7
- Hermansverk 706 ... E6
- Holmestrand 8,246 ... C4
- Holmsbu 273 ... D4
- Honningsvag 3,780 ... O1
- Horten 13,746 ... D4
- Horten* 17,246 ... D4
- Kirkenes 4,466 ... Q2
- Kongsberg 19,854 ... F7
- Kongsvinger 16,146 ... H6
- Kopervik 4,221 ... D7
- Kornsjø† 6,079 ... G7
- Kragerø 5,249 ... F7
- Kristiansand 59,488 ... F8
- Kristiansund 18,847 ... E5
- Kvinnherad† 2,898 ... E6
- Larvik 9,097 ... C4
- Larvik* 19,202 ... C4
- Lenvik† 11,098 ... L2
- Levanger 5,066 ... G5
- Lillehammer 21,248 ... F6
- Lillesand 3,028 ... F7
- Lillestrøm† 11,550 ... E3
- Longyearbyen ... D2
- Lysaker† 81,612 ... D3
- Mandal 11,579 ... E7
- Meråker† 2,907 ... G5
- Mo 21,033 ... J3
- Molde 20,334 ... E5
- Mosjøen 9,341 ... H4
- Moss 25,786 ... D4
- Moss* 27,430 ... D4
- Mysen 3,760 ... G7
- Namsos 11,452 ... G4
- Narvik 19,582 ... K2
- Nesttun† 11,519 ... D6
- Nittedal† 8,889 ... D3
- Notodden 12,970 ... F7
- Nøtterøy 11,944 ... D4
- Ny-Ålesund ... C2
- Odda 7,401 ... E6
- Oppdal 2,173 ... F5
- Orkanger 3,685 ... F5
- Oslo (cap.) 462,732 ... D3
- Oslo* 645,413 ... D3
- Porsgrunn 31,709 ... G7
- Rakkestad 2,392 ... G7
- Ringerike 30,156 ... C3
- Risør 6,560 ... F7
- Rjukan 5,334 ... F7
- Røros 3,041 ... G5
- Sandefjord 33,350 ... C4
- Sandnes 33,934 ... D7
- Sandvika† 34,337 ... C3
- Sarpsborg 12,889 ... D4
- Sarpsborg* 36,449 ... D4
- Selje† 3,386 ... D5
- Ski 9,081 ... D4
- Skien 47,105 ... F7
- Stavanger 86,639 ... D7
- Stavern 2,604 ... D4
- Steinkjer 20,553 ... G4
- Stor-Elvdal† 2,993 ... G6
- Sunndalsøra 5,114 ... F5
- Sveagruva ... D2
- Svolvaer 3,942 ... J2
- Tønsberg 9,964 ... D4
- Tønsberg* 36,374 ... D4
- Tromsø 43,830 ... L2
- Trondheim 134,910 ... F5
- Ullensvang† 2,326 ... E6
- Vadsø 6,019 ... Q1
- Vardø 3,875 ... R1
- Vik 1,019 ... E6
- Volda 3,511 ... E5
- Voss 5,944 ... E6

OTHER FEATURES

- Alsten (isl.) ... H4
- Andøya (isl.) ... J2
- Barduelv (riv.) ... L2
- Bellsund ... C2
- Bjørnafjorden (fjord) ... D6
- Bjornøya (isl.) ... D3
- Boknafjord (fjord) ... D7
- Bremanger (isl.) ... D6
- Dønna (isl.) ... H3
- Dovrefjell (hills) ... F5
- Edgeøya (isl.) ... E2
- Femundsjø (lake) ... G5
- Folda (fjord) ... G4
- Folda (fjord) ... J3
- Frohavet (bay) ... F5
- Frøya (isl.) ... F5
- Glittertinden (mt.) ... F6
- Hardangervidda (plat.) ... E6
- Hardangerfjord (fjord) ... D7
- Hinlopenstreten (str.) ... C1
- Hinnøya (isl.) ... K2
- Hitra (isl.) ... F5
- Hopen (isl.) ... E2
- Isfjorden (fjord) ... C2
- Jostedalsbreen (glac.) ... E6
- Kjölen (mts.) ... K3
- Kongsfjorden (fjord) ... B2
- Kvaløya (isl.) ... O1
- Lågen (riv.) ... G6
- Laksefjorden (fjord) ... P1
- Langøy (isl.) ... J2
- Lapland (reg.) ... K2
- Leka (isl.) ... G4
- Lindesnes (cape) ... E8
- Lista (pen.) ... E7
- Lofoten (isls.) ... H2
- Lopphavet (bay) ... M1
- Magerøya (isl.) ... P1
- Moskenesøya (isl.) ... H3
- Namsen (riv.) ... H4
- Nordaustlandet (isl.) ... D1
- Nordfjord (fjord) ... E6
- Nordkapp (pt.) ... C1
- Nordkinn (headland) ... Q1
- Nordkinn (pen.) ... P1
- North Cape (Nordkapp) (pt.) ... P1
- Norwegian (sea) ... F3
- Ofotfjorden (fjord) ... K2
- Oslofjord (fjord) ... D4
- Otra (riv.) ... E7
- Otterøya (isl.) ... E5
- Pasvikelv (riv.) ... Q2
- Platen, Kapp (pt.) ... D1
- Porsangen (fjord) ... O1
- Rana (fjord) ... H3
- Rauma (riv.) ... F5
- Ringvassøy (isl.) ... L2
- Romsdalsfjorden (fjord) ... E5
- Saltfjorden (fjord) ... J3
- Seiland (isl.) ... N1
- Senja (isl.) ... K2
- Skagerrak (str.) ... F8
- Smøla (isl.) ... E5
- Sognafjorden (fjord) ... D6
- Sørkapp (pt.) ... C2
- Sorøya (isl.) ... N1
- Spitsbergen (isl.) ... C2
- Storfjorden (fjord) ... D2
- Sulitjelma (mt.) ... J3
- Svalbard (isls.) ... C3
- Tana (riv.) ... P1
- Tanafjord (fjord) ... Q1
- Tokke (riv.) ... F7
- Trondheimsfjorden (fjord) ... G5
- Tyrifjord (lake) ... C3
- Vaerøy (isl.) ... H3
- Vagåvatn (lake) ... F6
- Vannøy (isl.) ... L1
- Varangerhalvøya (pen.) ... Q1
- Varangerfjord (fjord) ... Q2
- Vega (isl.) ... G4
- Vesterålen (isls.) ... J2
- Vestfjord (fjord) ... H3
- Vestvågøya (isl.) ... H3
- Vikna (isls.) ... G4

SWEDEN

COUNTIES

- Älvsborg 418,150 ... H7
- Blekinge 155,391 ... J8
- Gävleborg 294,595 ... K6
- Göteborg och Bohus 714,660 ... G7
- Gotland 54,447 ... L8
- Halland 219,767 ... H8
- Jämtland 133,559 ... J5
- Jönköping 301,905 ... H8
- Kalmar 240,768 ... K8
- Kopparberg 281,082 ... J6
- Kristianstad 272,090 ... J8

(continued on following page)

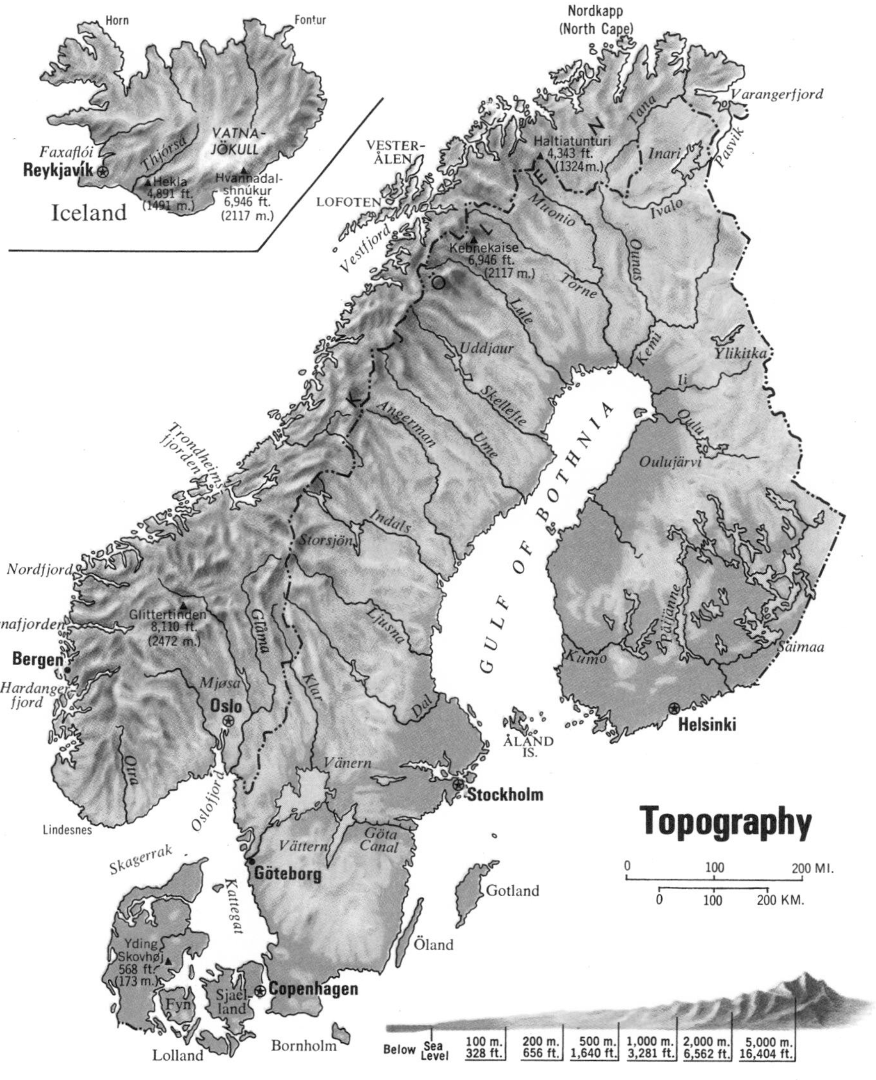
Horn
Fontur
Faxaflói
Reykjavík
VATNA-JÖKULL
Hekla 4,891 ft. (1491 m.)
Hvannadal-shnúkur 6,946 ft. (2117 m.)
Iceland
Nordkapp (North Cape)
Varangerfjord
VESTER-ÅLEN
LOFOTEN
Vestfjord
Haltiatunturi 4,343 ft. (1324 m.)
Kebnekaise 6,946 ft. (2117 m.)
Tana
Inari
Pasvik
Ivalo
Muonio
Ounas
Torne
Lule
Kemi
Ylikitka
Uddjaur
Ii
Skellefte
Ume
Ångerman
Oulu
Oulujärvi
Trondheimsfjorden
GULF OF BOTHNIA
Indals
Storsjön
Nordfjord
Sognafjorden
Glittertinden 8,110 ft. (2472 m.)
Bergen
Hardangerfjord
Glåma
Ljusna
Päijänne
Saimaa
Kumo
Mjøsa
Oslo
Klar
Dal
Helsinki
ÅLAND IS.
Vänern
Otra
Oslofjord
Stockholm
Lindesnes
Skagerrak
Vättern
Göta Canal
Göteborg
Kattegat
Gotland
Öland
Yding Skovhøj 568 ft. (173 m.)
Fyn
Sjælland
Copenhagen
Lolland
Bornholm
Topography
0 100 200 MI.
0 100 200 KM.
Below Sea Level
100 m. 328 ft.
200 m. 656 ft.
500 m. 1,640 ft.
1,000 m. 3,281 ft.
2,000 m. 6,562 ft.
5,000 m. 16,404 ft.

20 Norway, Sweden, Finland, Denmark and Iceland

(continued)

Kronoberg 169,454 J8
Malmöhus 740,137 H9
Norrbotten 264,215 L3
Örebro 273,994 J7
Östergötland 387,104 J7
Skaraborg 263,382 H7
Södermanland 252,030 K7
Stockholm 1,493,052 L7
Uppsala 229,879 K7
Värmland 284,442 H7
Västerbotten 236,367 K4
Västernorrland 268,202 K5
Västmanland 259,872 K7

CITIES and TOWNS

Åhus 6,125 J9
Alingsås 18,892 H7
Älmhult 7,390 H8
Alvesta 7,261 J8
Älvsbyn 4,707 M4
Åmål 9,556 H7
Ånge 3,760 J5
Ängelholm 16,016 H8
Arboga 11,819 J7
Arbrå 2,734 K6
Årjäng† 2,596 H7
Arvidsjaur 4,194 L4
Arvika 13,934 H7
Åseda 2,465 J8
Askim 17,609 G8
Åtvidaberg 8,436 K7
Avesta 19,095 J6
Bålsta 8,243 G1
Båstad 2,452 H8
Bengtsfors 3,535 H7
Boden 19,590 M4
Bollnäs 13,305 K6
Bollstabruk 3,548 L5
Borås 67,537 H8
Borås* 187,710 H8
Borgholm 2,789 K8
Borlänge 40,158 J6
Brunflo 3,460 J5
Dalby† 4,013 H6
Danderyd† 36,596 H1
Dannemora 291 K6
Edsbyn 4,388 J6
Eksjö 9,686 J8
Emmaboda 5,652 J8
Enköping 18,541 G1
Eskilstuna 66,409 K7
Eslöv 13,629 H9
Fagersta† 14,778 J6
Falkenberg 14,148 H8
Falköping 15,126 H7
Falun 30,073 J6
Färjestaden 2,995 K8
Filipstad 7,835 H7
Finspång 16,346 J7
Flen 6,770 K7
Forshaga 6,000 H7
Frösö 10,274 J5
Frövi 2,583 J7
Gällivare 8,669 M3
Gamleby 3,666 J8
Gävle 67,454 K6
Gimo 3,154 K6
Gislaved 8,564 H8
Gnesta 3,835 G2
Göteborg 444,540 G8
Göteborg* 690,767 G8
Hagfors 8,060 H6
Hällefors 7,862 J7
Hallsberg 6,799 J7
Hallstahammar 13,583 K7
Hallstavik 5,162 L6
Halmstad 49,558 H8
Haparanda 5,031 N4
Härnösand 18,971 L5
Hässleholm 16,813 H8
Hedemora 7,039 K6
Helsingborg 80,986 H8
Helsingborg* 215,894 H8
Hjo 4,615 J7
Hofors 11,459 K6
Höganäs 10,866 H8
Holmsund 5,467 M5
Hörnefors 2,441 L5
Huddinge 48,339 H1
Hudiksvall 15,004 K6
Hultsfred 5,763 K8
Husum 2,517 L5
Hyltebruk 3,469 H8
Iggesund 4,448 K6
Järna 6,237 G2
Jokkmokk 3,186 L3
Jönköping 78,650 H8
Jönköping* 131,499 H8
Kalix 7,668 N4
Kalmar 32,049 K8
Karlshamn 17,447 J8
Karlskoga† 35,425 J7
Karlskrona 33,414 J8
Karlstad 51,243 H7
Katrineholm 22,884 K7
Kinna 13,676 H8
Kiruna 25,410 L3
Kisa 4,323 J7
Köping 20,059 J7
Kopparberg 3,942 J7
Kramfors 7,719 L5
Kristianstad 30,780 J9
Kristinehamn 21,146 H7
Kumla 11,451 J7
Kungälv† 12,764 G8
Kungsbacka† 11,986 G8
Kvissleby 3,413 K5
Laholm 3,898 H8
Landskrona 29,486 H9
Långshyttan 2,744 K6
Laxå 5,166 J7
Leksand 4,410 J6
Lessebo 2,991 J8
Lidingö 30,098 H1
Lidköping 21,001 H7
Lindesberg 8,247 J7
Linköping 80,274 K7
Linköping* 132,839 K7
Ljungby 12,969 J8
Ljusdal 7,075 J6
Ljusne 3,578 K6
Ludvika 18,217 J6
Luleå 42,139 N4
Lund 55,047 H9
Lycksele 8,586 L4
Lysekil 7,815 G7
Malmberget 10,239 M3
Malmö 241,191 H9
Malmö* 453,339 H9
Malung 6,211 H6
Mariefred 2,553 F1
Mariestad 16,454 H7
Markaryd 4,266 H8
Märsta 17,066 K7
Marstrand 1,168 G8
Mellerud 3,579 H7
Mjölby 12,488 J7
Mölndal† 47,248 H8
Mönsterås 5,005 K8
Mora 8,772 J6
Motala 29,454 J7
Nacka 19,708 H1
Nässjö 18,634 J8
Nora 5,515 J7
Norberg 5,438 K6
Norrköping 85,244 K7
Norrköping* 163,206 K7
Norrtälje 12,784 L7
Nybro 13,010 J8
Nyköping 30,352 K7
Nynäshamn 11,070 L7
Ockelbo 2,810 K6
Olofström 10,096 J8
Örebro 117,877 J7
Örebro* 171,440 J7
Örnsköldsvik 29,514 L5
Orrefors 919 J8
Orsa 5,099 J6
Oskarshamn 19,021 K8
Östersund 40,056 J5
Östhammar 1,783 L6
Oxelösund 13,862 K7
Piteå 16,169 M4
Rättvik 4,087 J6
Rimbo 3,404 L7
Ronneby 12,086 J8
Säffle 11,428 H7
Sala 11,216 K7
Saltsjöbaden 8,113 J1
Sandviken 27,994 K6
Säter 4,297 J6
Sävsjö 4,913 J8
Sigtuna 4,780 H1
Simrishamn 5,834 J9
Skanör med Falsterbo 4,909 H9
Skara 10,138 H7
Skellefteå 29,353 M4
Skövde 29,945 H7
Skutskär 7,174 K6
Smedjebacken 8,418 J6
Söderhamn 14,673 K6
Söderköping 5,310 K7
Södertälje 58,408 G1
Sollefteå 8,923 K5
Sollentuna† 40,905 H1
Solna† 53,992 H1
Sölvesborg 7,292 J9
Stenungsund 8,361 G7
Stockholm (cap.) 665,550 G1
Stockholm* 1,357,183 G1
Storuman 2,587 K4
Storvik 2,748 K6
Strängnäs 10,255 F1
Strömstad 4,735 G7
Strömsund 4,119 K5
Sundbyberg† 27,058 G1
Sundsvall 52,268 K5
Sunne 4,273 H7
Surahammar 6,509 J7
Sveg 2,608 J5
Svenljunga 3,189 H8
Täby† 41,285 H1
Tibro 8,476 J7
Tidaholm 8,039 J7
Tierp 5,005 K6
Timrå 11,416 K5
Tomelilla 5,371 J9
Torsby 3,632 H6
Torshälla 8,231 K7
Tranås 14,854 J7
Trelleborg 22,559 H9
Trollhättan 42,499 H7
Trosa 3,128 K7
Uddevalla 32,700 G7
Ulricehamn 7,827 H8
Umeå 49,715 M5
Uppsala 101,850 K7
Uppsala* 157,202 L7
Vadstena 5,294 J7
Vaggeryd 3,974 J8
Valdemarsvik 3,558 K7
Vallentuna 10,477 H1
Vänersborg 20,510 G7
Vännäs 3,876 L5
Vansbro 2,708 H6
Vara 3,049 H7
Varberg 19,467 G8
Värnamo 15,726 J8
Västerås 98,858 K7
Västerås* 147,508 K7
Västerhaninge 14,125 H1
Västervik 21,239 K8
Vaxholm† 3,744 J1
Växjö 40,328 J8
Vetlanda 12,358 J8
Vilhelmina 4,060 K4
Vimmerby 7,405 J8
Virserum 2,495 J8
Visby 19,886 L8
Ystad 14,286 H9

OTHER FEATURES

Ångermanälven (riv.) K5
Åsnen (lake) J8
Baltic (sea) K9
Bolmen (lake) H8
Bothnia (gulf) N4
Dalälven (riv.) K6
Fårö (isl.) L8
Göta (canal) J7
Göta (riv.) H7
Gotland (isl.) L8
Gräsö (isl.) L6
Hanöbukten (bay) J9
Hjälmaren (lake) J7
Hoburgen (cliff) L8
Hornslandet (pen.) K6
Indalsälven (riv.) H5
Kalixälv (riv.) N3
Kalmarsund (sound) K8
Kattegat (str.) G8
Kebnekaise (mt.) L3
Kölen (mts.) K3
Klarälv (riv.) H6
Lapland (reg.) M2
Ljusnan (riv.) H5
Luleälv (riv.) M4
Mälaren (lake) G1
Muonioälv (riv.) M2
Öland (isl.) K8
Öresund (sound) H9
Ornö (isl.) J2
Österdalälven (riv.) H6
Piteälv (riv.) M4
Siljan (lake) J6
Skagerrak (str.) F8
Sommen (lake) J8
Stora Lulevatten (lake) L3
Storsjön (lake) J5
Sulitelma (mt.) K3
Torneälv (riv.) M3
Uddjaur (lake) L4
Umeälv (riv.) L4
Vänern (lake) H7
Västerdalälven (riv.) H6
Vättern (lake) J7

*City and suburbs.
†Population of commune.
†Population of parish.

DENMARK

COUNTIES

Århus 534,333 D5
Bornholm 47,241 F9
Copenhagen (commune) 622,612 F6
Faerøe Islands 41,969 B2
Frederiksberg (commune) 101,874 F6
Frederiksborg 260,825 E5
Fyn 433,765 D7
København (Copenhagen) (commune) 622,612 F6
Københaven 616,571 F6
Nordjylland 457,165 D4
Ribe 198,153 B7
Ringkøbing 242,006 B5
Roskilde 154,314 E6
Sønderjylland 238,502 C7
Storstrøm 252,780 E7
Vejle 306,809 C6
Vestsjaelland 259,484 E6
Viborg 221,002 C4

CITIES and TOWNS

Åbenrå 15,196 C7
Åbybro 2,897 C3
Åkirkeby 2,001 F9
Ålborg 154,582 D4
Ålestrup 1,926 C4
Århus 245,941 D5
Års 4,266 C4
Århup 1,675 D7
AErøskøbing 1,223 D8
Agerbaek 935 B6
Allingaåbro 1,385 D5
Allinge-Sandvig 1,991 F8
Ansager 1,157 B6
Arden 1,303 C4
Asaå 1,344 D3
Askov 904 C7
Asnaes 1,413 E6
Assens, Århus 1,341 D4
Assens, Fyn 5,139 D7
Augustenborg 2,628 D8
Auning 1,516 D5
Avlum 1,729 B5
Baelum 1,169 D4
Bagenkop 776 D8
Ballerup 50,673 F6
Bandholm 693 E8
Bedsted 965 B4
Birkerød 13,663 F6
Bjerringbro 4,761 C5
Bogense 2,861 D6
Bolderslev 774 C8
Børkop 1,410 C6
Borup 1,591 E7
Braedstrup 2,163 C6
Bramming 3,678 B7
Brande 4,784 B6
Bredebro 1,173 B7
Broager 2,143 C8
Brønderslev 10,247 C3
Brørup 2,584 C7
Brovst 4,200 C3
Bryrup 579 C5
Christiansfeld 1,994 C7
Copenhagen (cap.) 603,368 F6
Copenhagen* 1,327,940 F6
Dronninglund 4,661 D3
Dybvad 805 D3
Ebeltoft 3,017 D5
Egernsund 1,323 C8
Egtved 1,311 C6
Ejby 1,372 C7
Esbjerg 68,097 B7
Faåborg 6,495 D7
Fakse 2,720 F7
Fakse Ladeplads 1,799 F7
Farsø 2,821 C4
Farum 9,936 F6
Fjerritslev 2,134 C3
Fredensborg 4,709 F6
Fredericia 36,157 C6
Frederiksberg 101,874 F6
Frederikshavn 24,846 D3
Frederikssund 11,272 E6
Frederiksvaerk 8,903 E6
Fuglebjerg 1,094 E7
Gedser 1,200 F8
Gedsted 1,006 C4
Gelsted 1,307 C7
Gentofte 77,744 F6
Gilleleje 2,943 F5
Give 2,366 C6
Glamsbjerg 2,226 D7
Glostrup 28,326 F6
Glumsø 1,027 E7
Glyngøre 1,071 C4
Gørding 1,261 B7
Gørlev 1,542 E7
Graested 1,654 F5
Gram 2,061 C7
Graåsten 2,947 C8
Grenaå 12,569 D5
Grindsted 7,558 B6
Haårby 1,506 D7
Haderslev 20,042 C7
Hadsten 3,914 C5
Hadsund 3,652 D4
Hals 1,654 D3
Hammel 3,247 C5
Hammerum 3,227 C5
Hanstholm 1,716 B3
Harboør 1,359 B4
Haårlev 1,228 F7
Hasle 18
Haslev 6,925 E7
Havdrup 1,833 F6
Hedensted 2,659 C6
Hellebaek 2,911 F5
Helsinge 3,613 F6
Helsingør 42,425 F6
Herning 32,973 B5
Hillerød 23,963 F6
Hinnerup 2,061 D5
Hirtshals 6,861 C2
Hjallerup 1,573 C3
Hjerm 647 B5
Hjørring 19,692 C3
Hobro 8,737 C4
Højer 1,416 B8
Højslev 1,641 C4
Holbaek 19,485 E6
Holeby 1,434 E8
Holstebro 25,006 B5
Holsted 1,390 B6
Høng 2,488 E7
Hornslet 2,561 D5
Horsens 44,120 C6
Hørsholm 19,346 F6
Hørve 1,139 E6
Hov 635 D6
Humlum 546 B4
Hundested 5,443 E6
Hurup 2,287 B4
Hvidbjerg 994 B4
Hvide Sande 2,129 A6
Ikast 9,222 C5
Jelling 1,540 C6
Jerslev 798 D3
Juelsminde 1,991 D6
Jyderup 2,901 E6
Kalundborg 12,248 D6
Karise 1,184 F7
Karup 1,694 C5
Kastrup† 17,391 F6
Kerteminde 5,007 D7
Kibaek 1,279 B5
Kjellerup 3,245 C5
Klitmøller 542 B3
København (Copenhagen) (cap.) 603,368 F6
Køge 18,608 F7
Kolding 41,602 C7
Kolind 1,036 D5
Korsør 15,502 E7
Kvaerndrup 891 D7
Langaå 2,320 C5
Lem 1,026 B5
Lemvig 6,448 B4
Løgstør 3,633 C4
Løgumkloster 2,091 B7
Lohals 580 D7
Løjt Kirkeby 1,203 C7
Løkken 1,345 C3
Løsning 1,967 C6
Lundby 747 E7
Lunderskov 1,494 C7
Lyngby 61,516 F6
Malling 1,584 D5
Mariager 1,692 D4
Maribo 5,287 E8
Marstal 4,124 D8
Middelfart 13,315 C7

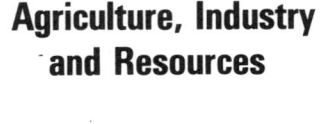

Agriculture, Industry and Resources

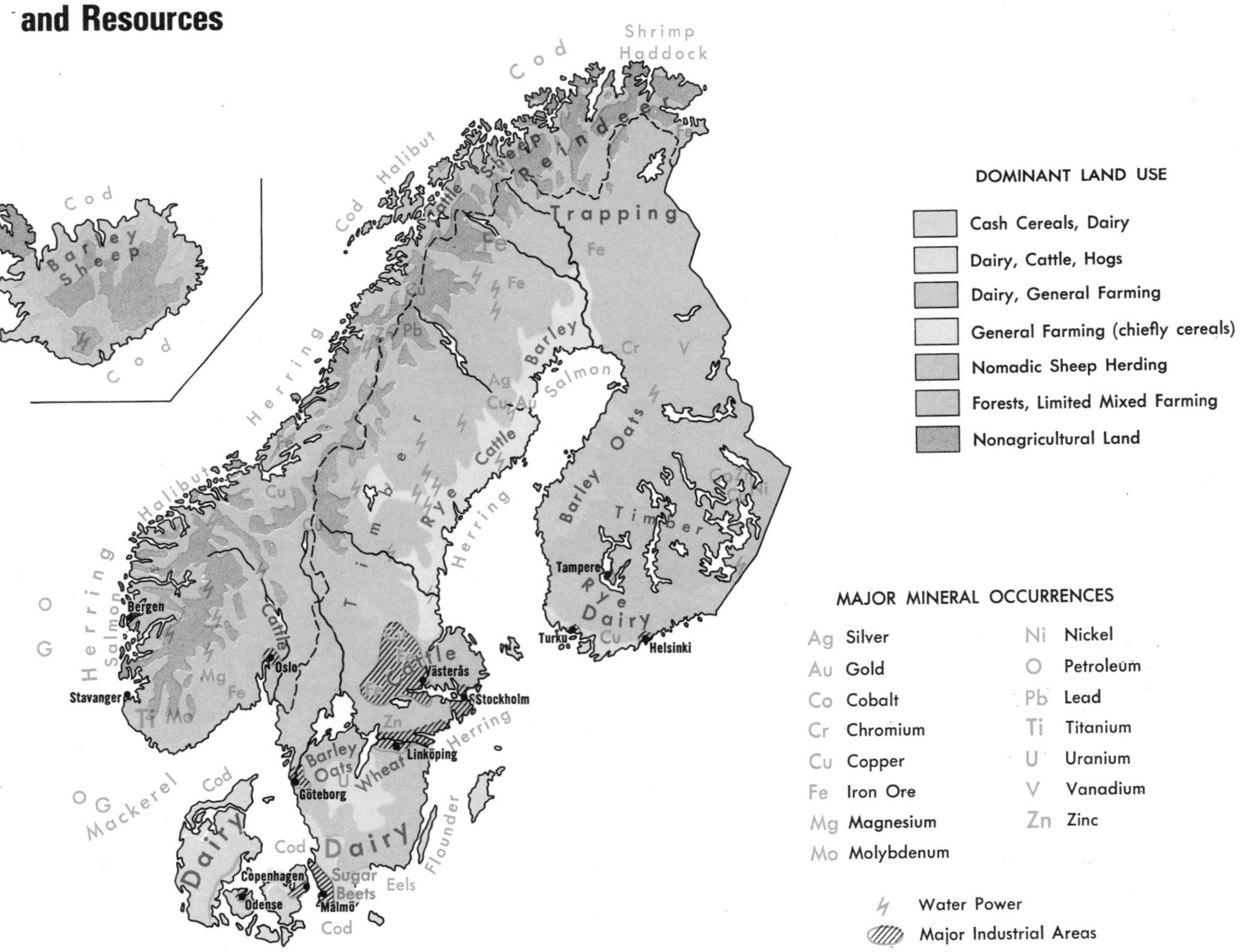

Shrimp
Haddock
Cod
Halibut
Cattle
Sheep
Reindeer
Trapping
Fe
Cu
Pb
Barley
Cr
V
Ag
Au
Salmon
Herring
Timber
Rye
Oats
Tampere
Dairy
Turku
Helsinki
Bergen
Oslo
Stavanger
Mg
Ti
Mo
Västerås
Stockholm
Zn
Linköping
Wheat
Göteborg
Mackerel
Copenhagen
Odense
Malmö
Sugar Beets
Eels
Flounder
DOMINANT LAND USE
Cash Cereals, Dairy
Dairy, Cattle, Hogs
Dairy, General Farming
General Farming (chiefly cereals)
Nomadic Sheep Herding
Forests, Limited Mixed Farming
Nonagricultural Land
MAJOR MINERAL OCCURRENCES
Ag Silver
Au Gold
Co Cobalt
Cr Chromium
Cu Copper
Fe Iron Ore
Mg Magnesium
Mo Molybdenum
Ni Nickel
O Petroleum
Pb Lead
Ti Titanium
U Uranium
V Vanadium
Zn Zinc
Water Power
Major Industrial Areas

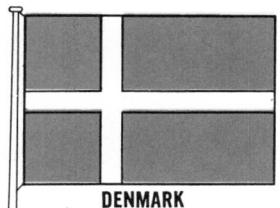

DENMARK

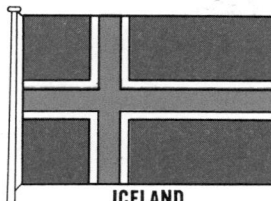

ICELAND

DENMARK

AREA 16,629 sq. mi. (43,069 sq. km.)
POPULATION 5,124,000
CAPITAL Copenhagen
LARGEST CITY Copenhagen
HIGHEST POINT Yding Skovhøj 568 ft. (173 m.)
MONETARY UNIT krone
MAJOR LANGUAGE Danish
MAJOR RELIGION Protestantism

ICELAND

AREA 39,768 sq. mi. (103,000 sq. km.)
POPULATION 228,785
CAPITAL Reykjavík
LARGEST CITY Reykjavík
HIGHEST POINT Hvannadalshnúkur 6,952 ft. (2,119 m.)
MONETARY UNIT króna
MAJOR LANGUAGE Icelandic
MAJOR RELIGION Protestantism

OTHER FEATURES

FÆRØE ISLANDS

CITIES and TOWNS

OTHER FEATURES

ICELAND

CITIES and TOWNS

OTHER FEATURES

*City and suburbs

Denmark and Iceland
CONIC PROJECTION
SCALE OF MILES
SCALE OF KILOMETERS
Capitals of Countries
Capitals of Counties (amter)
International Boundaries
Internal Boundaries
Scale 1:2,300,000
Denmark is divided into fourteen Counties plus Copenhagen and Frederiksberg communes.
© Copyright HAMMOND INCORPORATED, Maplewood, N. J.
Faerøe Islands
ICELAND
JUTLAND (JYLLAND)
SKAGERRAK
KATTEGAT
NORTH SEA
BALTIC SEA
SWEDEN
GERMANY
COPENHAGEN
BORNHOLM
Longitude 10° East of Greenwich

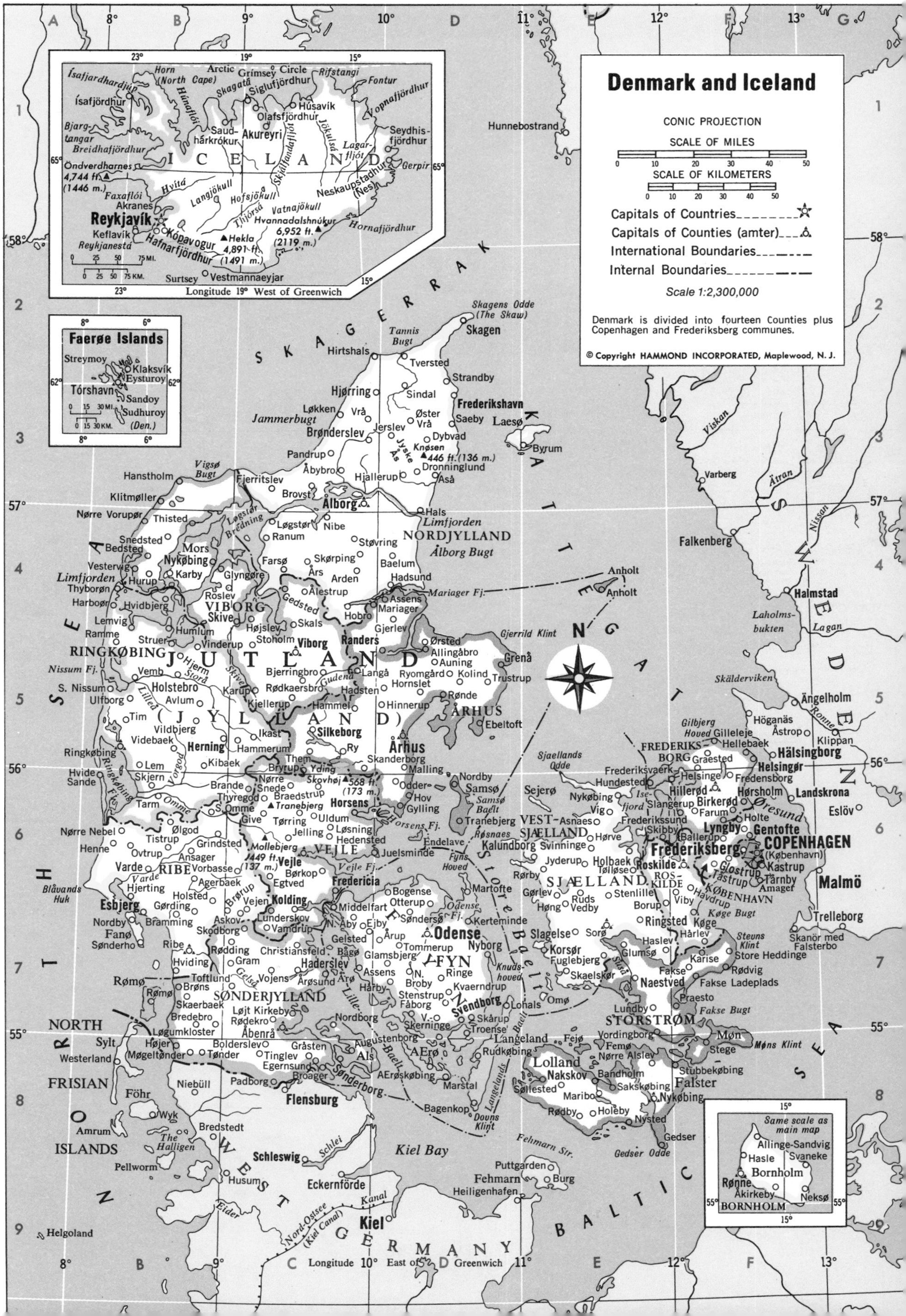

Germany

CONIC PROJECTION

SCALE OF MILES

SCALE OF KILOMETERS

Capitals of Countries .... ★
State and District Capitals .... ◉
International Boundaries ....
State and District Boundaries ....
Canals ....

Scale 1:3,040,000

East Germany is divided into districts bearing the same name as their respective capitals.

Berlin

© Copyright HAMMOND INCORPORATED, Maplewood, N.J.

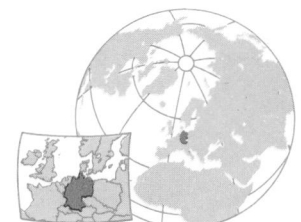

AREA 95,985 sq. mi. (248,601 sq. km.)
POPULATION 61,658,000
CAPITAL Bonn
LARGEST CITY Berlin (West)
HIGHEST POINT Zugspitze 9,718 ft. (2,962 m.)
MONETARY UNIT Deutsche mark
MAJOR LANGUAGE German
MAJOR RELIGIONS Protestantism, Roman
Catholicism

AREA 41,768 sq. mi. (108,179 sq. km.)
POPULATION 16,737,000
CAPITAL Berlin (East)
LARGEST CITY Berlin (East)
HIGHEST POINT Fichtelberg 3,983 ft. (1,214 m.)
MONETARY UNIT East German mark
MAJOR LANGUAGE German
MAJOR RELIGIONS Protestantism, Roman
Catholicism

WEST GERMANY

EAST GERMANY

Topography

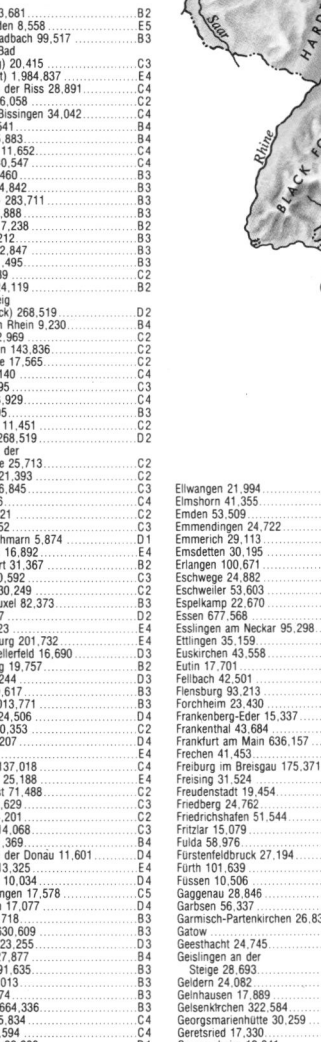

0   50   100 MI.
0   50   100 KM.

	100 m.	200 m.	500 m.	1,000 m.	2,000 m.	5,000 m.
Below Sea Level	328 ft.	656 ft.	1,640 ft.	3,281 ft.	6,562 ft.	16,404 ft.

(continued on following page)

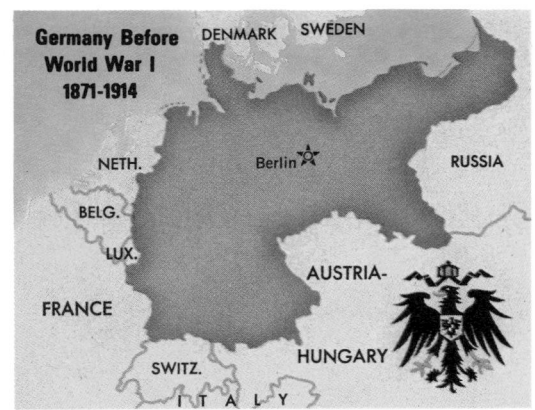

Germany Before World War I 1871-1914

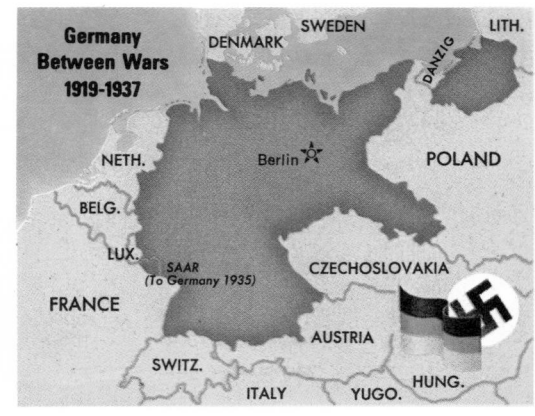

Germany Between Wars 1919-1937

Occupied Germany 1945-1949

Agriculture, Industry and Resources

DOMINANT LAND USE

- Wheat, Sugar Beets
- Cereals (chiefly rye, oats, barley)
- Potatoes, Rye
- Dairy, Livestock
- Mixed Cereals, Dairy
- Truck Farming
- Grapes, Fruit
- Forests

MAJOR MINERAL OCCURRENCES

Ag	Silver	K	Potash
Ba	Barite	Lg	Lignite
C	Coal	Na	Salt
Cu	Copper	O	Petroleum
Fe	Iron Ore	Pb	Lead
G	Natural Gas	U	Uranium
Gr	Graphite	Zn	Zinc

⚡ Water Power

▨ Major Industrial Areas

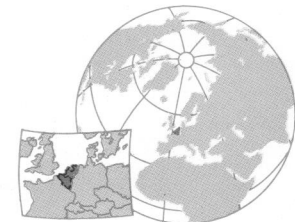

AREA 15,892 sq. mi. (41,160 sq. km.)
POPULATION 14,227,000
CAPITALS The Hague, Amsterdam
LARGEST CITY Amsterdam
HIGHEST POINT Vaalserberg 1,056 ft. (322 m.)
MONETARY UNIT guilder (florin)
MAJOR LANGUAGE Dutch
MAJOR RELIGIONS Protestantism, Roman Catholicism

AREA 11,781 sq. mi. (30,513 sq. km.)
POPULATION 9,855,110
CAPITAL Brussels
LARGEST CITY Brussels (greater)
HIGHEST POINT Botrange 2,277 ft. (694 m.)
MONETARY UNIT Belgian franc
MAJOR LANGUAGES French (Walloon), Flemish
MAJOR RELIGION Roman Catholicism

AREA 999 sq. mi. (2,587 sq. km.)
POPULATION 364,000
CAPITAL Luxembourg
LARGEST CITY Luxembourg
HIGHEST POINT Ardennes Plateau 1,825 ft. (556 m.)
MONETARY UNIT Luxembourg franc
MAJOR LANGUAGES Luxembourgeois (Letzeburgisch), French, German
MAJOR RELIGION Roman Catholicism

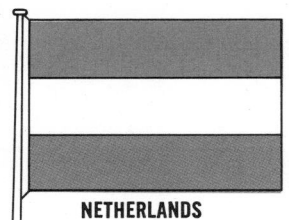

NETHERLANDS

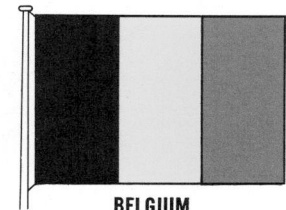

BELGIUM

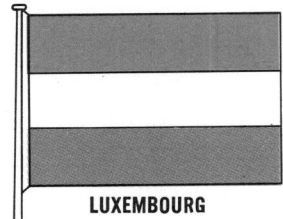

LUXEMBOURG

BELGIUM

PROVINCES

Antwerp 1,533,249	F6
Brabant 2,176,373	F7
East Flanders 1,310,117	D7
Hainaut 1,317,453	D7
Liège 1,008,905	H7
Limburg 652,547	G7
Luxembourg 217,310	G9
Namur 380,561	F8
West Flanders 1,054,429	B7

CITIES and TOWNS†

Aalst 46,659	D7
Aalter 9,173	C6
Aarlen (Arlon) 13,745	H9
Aarschot 12,474	F7
Aat (Ath) 11,842	D7
Alken 8,677	G7
Alost (Aalst) 46,659	D7
Amay 7,617	G7
Andenne 8,091	G8
Anderlecht 103,796	B9

Anderlues 12,176	E8
Ans 3,426	H7
Antoing 3,426	C7
Antwerp 224,543	E6
Antwerp* 928,000	E6
Antwerpen (Antwerp) 224,543	E6
Ardooie 7,081	C7
Arendonk 9,919	G6
Arlon 13,745	H9
As 5,496	H6
Asse 6,583	E7
Ath 11,842	D7
Attert	H9
Aubange 3,761	H9
Audenarde (Oudenaarde) 26,615	D7
Auderghem 34,546	C9
Auvelais 8,287	F8
Aywaille 3,850	H8
Baerle-Hertog	F6
Balen 15,110	G6
Basse-Sambre	F8
Bastenaken (Bastogne) 6,816	H9
Bastogne 6,816	H9
Beernem	C6
Beloeil	D7
Berchem 50,241	F6

Berchem-Sainte-Agathe 19,087	B9
Bergen (Mons) 59,362	E8
Beringen	G6
Bertogne	H8
Bertrix 4,562	G9
Beveren 15,913	E6
Bilzen 7,178	G7
Binche 10,098	E8
Blankenberge 13,969	C6
Bocholt 6,497	H6
Boom 16,584	E6
Borgerhout 49,002	E6
Borgloon 3,412	G7
Borgworm (Waremme) 10,956	G7
Bourg-Léopold (Leopoldsburg) 9,593	G6
Boussu 11,474	D8
Braine-l'Alleud 18,531	E7
Braine-le-Comte 11,957	D7
Brecht	F6
Bredene 9,244	B6
Bree 10,389	H6
Bruges 117,220	C6
Brugge (Bruges) 117,220	C6
Brussels (cap.)* 1,054,970	C9
Bruxelles (Brussels)	

(cap.)* 1,054,970	C9
Cerfontaine	E8
Charleroi 23,689	E8
Charleroi* 458,000	E8
Chastre	E8
Châtelet 14,752	D7
Chièvres 3,283	D7
Chimay 3,288	E8
Chiny	G9
Ciney 7,536	G8
Comblain-au-Pont 3,582	G8
Comines 8,192	B7
Courcelles 17,015	E8
Courtrai (Kortrijk) 44,961	C7
Couvin 4,234	F8
Damme	C6
De Haan	C6
Deinze 16,711	C7
Denderleeuw 9,925	D7
Dendermonde 22,119	E6
De Panne 6,985	B6
Dessel 7,505	G6
Destelbergen	D6
Deurne 80,766	F6
Diest 10,799	F7
Diksmuide 6,669	B6

Dilbeek 15,108	B9
Dilsen	H6
Dinant 9,747	G8
Dison 8,466	H7
Dixmude (Diksmuide) 6,669	B6
Doische	F8
Doornik (Tournai) 32,794	C7
Dour 10,059	D8
Drogenbos 4,840	B10
Duffel 13,802	F6
Durbuy	H8
Ecaussinnes 6,630	E7
Edingen (Enghien) 4,115	D7
Eeklo 19,144	D6
Eghezée	F7
Eigenbrakel (Braine-l'Alleud) 18,531	E7
Ekeren 27,648	E6
Ellezelles 3,906	D7
Enghien 4,115	D7
Erezée	G8
Erquelinnes 4,471	E8
Esneux 6,183	H7
Essen 10,795	F6
Estampuis	C7
Etterbeek 51,030	B9

Eupen 14,879	J7
Evere 26,957	C9
Evergem 12,886	D6
Farciennes	E8
Fernelmont	F7
Ferrières	H8
Filemalle 8,135	G7
Fleurus 8,523	E8
Florennes 4,107	F8
Forest 55,135	B9
Fosses-La-Ville 3,972	F8
Frameries 11,224	D8
Froidchapelle	E8
Furnes (Veurne) 9,496	B6
Ganshoren 21,147	B9
Geel 29,346	F6
Geldenaken (Jodoigne) 4,132	F7
Gembloux-sur-Orneau 11,249	F7
Genk 57,913	H7
Gent (Ghent) 148,860	D6
Geraardsbergen 17,533	D7
Gerpinnes	F8
Ghent 148,860	D6
Ghent* 477,000	D6
Gistel	B6
Gooik	C9
Gouvy	H8
Grammont (Geraardsbergen) 17,533	D7
Grez-Doiceau	F7
Grimbergen	E7
Haacht 4,436	F7
Habay	H9
Hal (Halle) 20,017	E7
Halen 5,322	G7
Halle 20,017	E7
Hamme 17,559	E6
Hamois	G8
Hamont-Achel 6,893	H6
Hannuit (Hannut) 7,232	G7
Hannut 7,232	G7
Harelbeke 18,498	C7
Hasselt 39,663	G7
Hastière	F8
Heist-Knokke 27,582	C6
Heist-op-den-Berg 13,472	F6
Hensies	D8
Herentals 18,639	F6
Herne	E7
Herselt 7,412	F6
Herstal 29,600	H7
Herve 4,118	H7
Heuvelland	B7
Hoboken 33,693	E6
Hoei (Huy) 12,736	G8
Hoeselt 6,884	G7
Honnelles	D8
Hoogstraten 4,381	F6
Hotton	G8
Huy 12,736	G8
Ichtegem	B6
Ieper 20,825	B7
Ingelmunster 10,245	C7
Ittre	E7
Ixelles 86,450	C9
Izegem 22,928	C7
Jabbeke	B6
Jemappes 18,632	D8
Jette 40,013	B9
Jodoigne 4,132	F7
Kalmthout 12,724	F6
Kapellen 13,352	F6
Kasterlee	F6
Kinrooi	H6
Knokke-Heist 27,582	C6
Koekelare 7,807	B6
Koekelberg 17,570	B9
Koksijde	B6
Kontich 14,432	E6
Kortemark 5,904	C6
Kortrijk 44,961	C7
Kraainem 11,390	C9
La Louvière 23,310	E8
La Louvière* 113,259	E8
Lanaken 8,659	H7
Landen 5,740	G7
Langemark-Poelkapelle 5,457	B7
Lasne	E7
Lede 10,316	D7
Léglise	H9
Leopoldsburg 9,593	G6
Le Roeulx	E8
Lessen (Lessines) 8,906	D7
Lessines 8,906	D7
Leuven 30,623	F7
Leuze-en-Hainaut 7,185	D7
Libin	G9
Libramont-Chevigny 2,975	G9
Lichtervelde 7,459	C6
Liedekerke 10,482	D7
Liège 145,573	H7
Liège* 622,000	H7
Lier 28,416	F6
Lierre (Lier) 28,416	F6
Limbourg 3,762	J7
Limburg (Limbourg) 3,762	J7
Linkebeek 4,265	C10

Linter	G7
Lochristi	D6
Lokeren 26,740	D6
Lommel 21,984	G6
Lontzen	H9
Looz (Borgloon) 3,412	G7
Lo-Reninge	B7
Louvain (Leuven) 30,623	F7
Luik (Liège) 145,573	H7
Lummen	G7
Maaseik 8,622	H6
Maasmechelen	H7
Machelen 7,057	C9
Maldegem 14,474	C6
Malines (Mechelen) 65,466	F6
Malmédy 6,464	J8
Manage	E7
Manhay	H8
Marche-en-Famenne 4,567	G8
Marchin 4,206	G8
Mechelen 65,466	F6
Meerhout 8,567	G6
Meise	E7
Menen (Menen) 22,037	C7
Menin (Menen) 22,037	C7
Merchtem 8,986	E7
Merelbeke 13,837	D6
Merksem 39,768	E6
Merksplas 5,065	F6
Messancy 3,150	H9
Mettet 3,372	F8
Meulebeke 10,458	C7
Middelkerke	B6
Moeskroen (Mouscron) 37,311	C7
Mol 28,823	G6
Molenbeek-Saint-Jean 68,411	B9
Momignies	E8
Mons 59,362	E8
Montigny-le-Tilleul	E8
Moorslede	B7
Mortsel 28,012	E6
Mouscron 37,311	C7
Namen (Namur) 32,269	F8
Namur 32,269	F8
Nassogne	G8
Nazareth	D7
Neerpelt 8,771	G6
Neufchâteau 2,670	G9
Nevele	D6
Nieuport (Nieuwpoort) 8,273	B6
Nieuwpoort 8,273	B6
Nijvel (Nivelles) 16,126	E7
Ninove 12,428	D7
Nivelles 16,126	E7
Ohey	G8
Onhaye	F8
Oostende (Ostend) 71,227	B6
Oostkamp 8,999	C6
Opwijk 9,699	E7
Ostend 71,227	B6
Oudenaarde 26,615	D7
Oudenburg	B6
Oud-Turnhout 9,245	G6
Oupeye	H7
Overijse 16,181	F7
Overpelt 10,470	G6
Paliseul	G9
Peer 7,201	G6
Péruwelz 7,878	D8
Philippeville 2,076	E8
Plombières	F7
Poperinge 12,671	B7
Profondeville	F8
Putte 6,953	F6
Quaregnon 17,688	D8
Quévy	D8
Quiévrain 5,510	D8
Raeren 3,655	J7
Ravels	G6
Rebecq 3,744	E7
Renaix (Ronse) 25,056	D7
Rendeux	H8
Retie 6,619	G6
Rochefort 4,357	G8
Roeselare 40,428	C7
Ronse 25,056	D7
Roulers (Roeselare) 40,428	C7
Rouvroy	G9
Ruiselede	C6
Sainte-Ode	H8
Saint-Georges-sur-Meuse 6,003	G7
Saint-Gilles 55,055	B9
Saint-Hubert 3,091	G8
Saint-Josse-ten-Noode 23,633	C9
Saint-Nicolas (Sint-Niklaas) 49,214	E6
Saint-Trond (Sint-Truiden) 21,473	G7
Saint-Vith (Sankt Vith) 3,001	J8
Sankt Vith 3,001	J8
Schaerbeek 118,950	C9
Schoten 29,914	F6
Seraing 40,545	G7
's-Gravenbrakel (Braine-le-Comte) 11,957	D7
Sint-Laurens	D6
Sint-Niklaas 49,214	E6

(continued on following page)

Agriculture, Industry and Resources

DOMINANT LAND USE

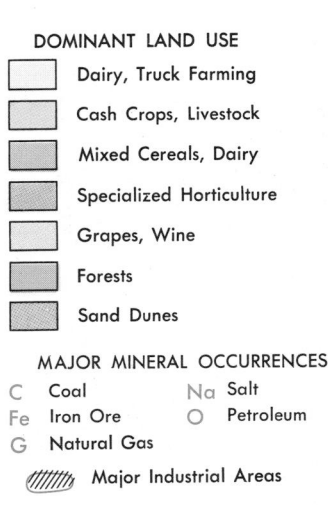

- Dairy, Truck Farming
- Cash Crops, Livestock
- Mixed Cereals, Dairy
- Specialized Horticulture
- Grapes, Wine
- Forests
- Sand Dunes

MAJOR MINERAL OCCURRENCES

C	Coal	Na	Salt
Fe	Iron Ore	O	Petroleum
G	Natural Gas		

Major Industrial Areas

26 Netherlands, Belgium and Luxembourg
(continued)

Sint-Pieters-Leeuw 16,856 ..... B9
Sint-Truiden 21,473 ..... G7
Soignies 12,006 ..... D7
Somme-Leuze G8
Spa 9,504 ..... H8
Sprimont H8
Staden 5,499 ..... B7
Stavelot 4,723 ..... H8
Steenokkerzeel 4,037 ..... C9
Stekene E6
Stoumont H8
Tamise (Temse) 14,950 ..... E6
Tellin G8
Temse 14,950 ..... E6
Tenneville H8
Termonde (Dendermonde) 22,119 ..... E6
Tessenderlo 11,778 ..... G6
Theux 5,316 ..... H8
Thuin 5,777 ..... E8
Tielt 14,077 ..... C7
Tielt-Winge 3,743 ..... F7
Tienen 24,134 ..... F7
Tintigny G9
Tirlemont (Tienen) 24,134 ..... F7
Tongeren 20,136 ..... G7
Tongres (Tongeren) 20,136 ..... G7
Torhout 15,156 ..... C6
Tournai 32,794 ..... C7
Trois-Ponts H8
Tubeke (Tubize) 11,507 ..... E7
Tubize 11,507 ..... E7
Turnhout 38,007 ..... F6
Uccle 78,909 ..... B9
Ukkel (Uccle) 78,909 ..... B9
Vaux-sur-Sûre H9
Verviers 33,587 ..... H7
Veurne 9,496 ..... B6
Vielsalm 3,587 ..... H8
Vilvoorde 34,633 ..... F7
Vilvorde (Vilvoorde) 34,633 ..... F7
Viroinval F8
Virton 3,558 ..... H9
Visé 6,880 ..... H7
Vleteren B7
Vorst (Forest) 55,135 ..... B9
Vresse-sur-Semois F9
Waarschoot 7,905 ..... D6
Wachtebeke D6
Waregem 17,725 ..... C7
Waremme 10,956 ..... G7
Waterloo 17,764 ..... E7
Watermaal-Bosvoorde
(Watermael-Boitsfort C9
Watermael-Boitsfort 25,123 ..... C9
Waver (Wavre) 11,767 ..... F7
Wavre 11,767 ..... F7
Wellin G8
Wemmel 12,631 ..... B9
Wervik 12,672 ..... B7
Westerlo 14,173 ..... F6
Westmalle F6
Wetteren 20,816 ..... D7
Wezembeek-Oppem 10,899 ..... D9
Wezet (Visé) 6,880 ..... H7
Willebroek 15,726 ..... E6
Wilrijk 43,485 ..... E6
Wingene 7,140 ..... C6
Woluwe-Saint-Lambert 47,360 ..... C9
Woluwe-Saint-Pierre 40,884 ..... C9
Ypres (Ieper) 20,825 ..... B7
Zaventem 10,625 ..... C9
Zedelgem C6
Zeebrugge C6
Zele 18,585 ..... E6
Zelzate 12,785 ..... D6
Zemst E7
Zinnik (Soignies) 12,006 ..... D7
Zonhoven 13,484 ..... G6
Zottegem 21,461 ..... D7
Zuienkerke C6

OTHER FEATURES

Albert, (canal) F6
Ardennes, (for.) F9
Botrange, (mt.) J8
Dender, (riv.) D7
Deûle, (riv.) B7
Dyle, (riv.) F7
Hohe Venn, (plat.) H8
Lesse, (riv.) F8
Lys, (riv.) B7
Mark, (riv.) F6
Meuse, (riv.) F8
Nethe, (riv.) F6
North, (sea) D4
Ourthe, (riv.) G8
Rupel, (riv.) F7
Sambre, (riv.) D8
Schelde (Scheldt), (riv.) C7
Scheldt, (riv.) C7
Schnee Eifel, (plat.) J8
Semois, (riv.) G9
Senne, (riv.) E7
Vaalserberg, (mt.) J7
Vesdre, (riv.) H7
Weisserstein, (mt.) J8
Yser, (riv.) B7
Zitterwald, (plat.) J8

LUXEMBOURG

CITIES and TOWNS

Clervaux 916 ..... J8
Diekirch† 5,059 ..... J9
Differdange 9,287 ..... H9
Dudelange† 14,615 ..... J10
Echternach† 3,792 ..... J9
Esch-sur-Alzette† 27,574 ..... J9
Ettelbruck† 5,990 ..... J9
Grevenmacher† 2,918 ..... J9
Luxembourg (cap.) 78,272 ..... J9
Mamer 3,123 ..... H9
Mersch 1,869 ..... J9
Pétange 6,234 ..... H9
Remich† 12,138 ..... J9
Vianden† 1,520 ..... J9
Wiltz 1,601 ..... H9

OTHER FEATURES

Alzette, (riv.) J9
Clerf, (riv.) J8
Eisling, (mts.) H9
Mosel, (riv.) J9
Our, (riv.) J9
Sauer, (riv.) J9

NETHERLANDS

PROVINCES

Drenthe 405,924 ..... K3
Dronten 15,343 ..... H4
Friesland 560,614 ..... H2
Gelderland 1,639,997 ..... H4
Groningen 540,062 ..... K2
Limburg 1,051,620 ..... H6
North Brabant 1,967,261 ..... F5
North Holland 2,295,875 ..... F3
Overijssel 985,569 ..... J4
South Holland 3,048,648 ..... E5
Utrecht 867,909 ..... G4
Zeeland 332,286 ..... D6
Zuidelijke
IJsselmeerpolders 14,231 ..... H4

CITIES and TOWNS†

Aalsmeer 20,779 ..... F4
Aalten 17,486 ..... K5
Aardenburg 3,869 ..... C6
Akkrum 5,044 ..... H2
Alkmaar 65,199 ..... F3
Almelo 62,634 ..... K4
Alphen aan de Rijn 46,065 ..... F4
Amersfoort 87,784 ..... G4
Amstelveen 71,803 ..... B5
Amsterdam (cap.) 751,156 ..... B4
Amsterdam* 987,205 ..... B4
Andijk 5,301 ..... G3
Apeldoorn 134,055 ..... H4
Apeldoorn* 237,231 ..... H4
Appingedam 13,295 ..... K2
Arnhem 126,051 ..... H4
Arnhem* 281,126 ..... H4
Assen 43,783 ..... K3
Asten 12,295 ..... H6
Axel 12,072 ..... D6
Baarle-Nassau 5,583 ..... F6
Baarn 25,045 ..... G4
Barneveld 34,189 ..... H4
Bath E6
Beilen 12,948 ..... K3
Bemmel 14,218 ..... H5
Bergeijk 9,009 ..... G6
Bergen 14,306 ..... F3
Bergen op Zoom 40,770 ..... E5
Bergum 28,047 ..... H2
Berkel 9,367 ..... F5
Berkhout 5,167 ..... F3
Beverwijk 37,551 ..... F4
Blerick J6
Bloemendaal 17,940 ..... E4
Blokzijl H3
Bodegraven 15,848 ..... F4
Bolsward 9,934 ..... H2
Borculo 9,859 ..... J4
Borger 12,017 ..... K3
Borne 18,216 ..... K4
Boskoop 12,985 ..... F4
Boxmeer 12,662 ..... H5
Boxtel 22,465 ..... G5
Breda 118,086 ..... F5
Breda* 151,182 ..... F5
Breezand F3
Breskens C6
Brielle 10,620 ..... E5
Brouwershaven 3,263 ..... D5
Brummen 20,460 ..... J4
Brunssum 26,116 ..... J7
Buiksloot C4
Bussum 37,848 ..... G4
Capelle 35,696 ..... F5
Coevorden 13,089 ..... K3
Colijnsplaat D5
Culemborg 17,682 ..... G5
Cuyk 15,366 ..... H5
Dalen 5,084 ..... K3
De Bilt 32,588 ..... G4
Dedemsvaart 12,975 ..... J3
De Koog F2
Delft 86,103 ..... E4
Delfzijl 23,316 ..... K2
Den Burg 12,132 ..... F2
Denekamp 11,533 ..... L4
Den Helder 60,421 ..... F3
Deurne 26,539 ..... H6
Deventer 65,557 ..... J4
Didam 14,263 ..... J5
De Wijk 4,631 ..... J3
Diemen 13,704 ..... C5
Dieren J4
Diever 3,162 ..... J3
Dinxperlo 7,296 ..... K5
Dirksland 6,495 ..... E5
Doesburg 9,759 ..... J4
Doetinchem 34,915 ..... J5
Dokkum 11,203 ..... H2
Domburg 3,874 ..... C5
Dongen 19,219 ..... F5
Doorn 11,966 ..... G4
Dordrecht 101,840 ..... F5
Dordrecht* 186,793 ..... F5
Drachten 45,390 ..... J2
Driebergen 17,022 ..... G4
Dronten 16,544 ..... H3
Druten 11,113 ..... H5
Echt 17,035 ..... H6
Edam-Volendam 21,507 ..... G4
Ede 79,897 ..... H4
Egmond aan Zee 5,734 ..... E3
Eindhoven 192,562 ..... G6
Eindhoven* 358,234 ..... G6
Elburg 18,082 ..... H4
Elst 16,686 ..... H5
Emmeloord 34,467 ..... H3
Emmen 86,700 ..... K3
Enkhuizen 13,430 ..... G3
Enschede 141,597 ..... K4
Enschede* 239,015 ..... K4
Epe 32,267 ..... H4
Erica K3
Ermelo 23,835 ..... H4
Etten-Leur 26,167 ..... F5
Europoort E5
Flushing 43,806 ..... C6
Franeker 11,415 ..... H2
Geertruidenberg 6,185 ..... F5
Geldermalsen 8,952 ..... G5
Geldrop 25,879 ..... H6
Geleen 35,910 ..... H7
Gemert 15,267 ..... H5
Gendringen 19,086 ..... J5
Genemuiden 6,058 ..... H3
Gennep 14,773 ..... H5
Giessendam-Hardinxveld 15,523 ..... F5
Giethoorn J3
Gilze 19,603 ..... F5
Goes 28,505 ..... D6
Goirle 13,447 ..... G5
Goor 11,435 ..... K4
Gorinchem 28,337 ..... G5
Gorredijk J2
Gouda 56,403 ..... F4
Graauw E6
Gramsbergen 5,866 ..... K3
Grave 9,492 ..... H5
Groenlo 8,693 ..... K4
Groesbeek 18,094 ..... H5
Groningen 163,357 ..... K2
Groningen* 201,662 ..... K2
Grouw 8,567 ..... H2
Haamstede 4,575 ..... D5
Haarlem 164,672 ..... F4
Haarlem* 232,048 ..... F4
Haarlemmermeer
(Hoofddorp) 72,046 ..... F4
Hague, The (cap.) 479,369 ..... E4
Hague, The* 682,452 ..... E4
Halfweg 4,456 ..... B4
Hallum H2
Hardenberg 28,489 ..... J3
Harderwijk 28,508 ..... H4
Hardinxveld-Giessendam 15,523 ..... G5
Harlingen 14,533 ..... G2
Hasselt 5,817 ..... J3
Hattem 11,074 ..... H4
Heemskert 31,728 ..... F3
Heemstede 27,376 ..... F4
Heer H7
Heerde 16,833 ..... H4
Heerenveen 34,948 ..... H3
Heerhugowaard 26,019 ..... F3
Heerlen 71,500 ..... J7
Heesch 8,659 ..... G5
Heiloo 20,524 ..... F3
Hellendoorn 32,068 ..... J4
Hellevoetsluis 14,186 ..... E5
Helmond 59,249 ..... H6
Hengelo, Gelderland 8,015 ..... J4
Hengelo, Overijssel 72,281 ..... K4
Heusden 5,542 ..... G5
Hillegom 17,489 ..... E4
Hilvarenbeek 8,408 ..... G6
Hilversum 94,041 ..... G4
Hilversum* 110,498 ..... G4
Hippolytushoef 7,847 ..... G3
Hoek D6
Hoek van Holland (Hook of
Holland) D4
Hoensbroek 22,441 ..... H7
Holijsloot C4
Hollum H2
Holwerd H2
Hoofddorp
(Haarlemmermeer) 72,046 ..... F4
Hoogeveen 42,673 ..... J3
Hoogezand-Sappemeer 33,860 ..... K2
Hoogkarspel 5,112 ..... G3
Hook of Holland D4
Hoorn 24,609 ..... G3
Horst 16,242 ..... H6
Huissen 11,049 ..... H5
Huizen 25,603 ..... G4
Hulst 17,283 ..... E6
IJmuiden 6,633 ..... E4
IJsselstein 15,450 ..... F4
Ilpendam 3,310 ..... C4
Joure 14,329 ..... H3
Kampen 29,488 ..... H3
Katwijk aan Zee 37,437 ..... E4
Kerkdriel 7,584 ..... G5
Kerkrade 46,609 ..... J7
Kesteren 8,257 ..... G5
Klazienaveen 9,520 ..... L3
Kollum 11,887 ..... J2
Krimpen aan den IJssel 26,396 ..... F5
Landsmeer 8,082 ..... C4
Laren 13,615 ..... G4
Leek 15,713 ..... J2
Leerdam 15,030 ..... F5
Leeuwarden 85,074 ..... H2
Leiden 99,891 ..... E4
Leiden* 167,554 ..... E4
Lelystad H3
Lemmer 10,013 ..... H3
Lisse 19,182 ..... F4
Lith 5,088 ..... G5
Lochem 17,274 ..... J4
Lonneker K4
Loon op Zand 18,000 ..... G5
Losser 20,688 ..... L4
Maarssen 18,346 ..... F4
Maasbree 9,462 ..... H6
Maassluis 28,170 ..... E5
Maastricht 111,044 ..... H7
Maastricht* 145,862 ..... H7
Margraten 3,318 ..... H7
Medemblik 6,432 ..... G3
Meerssen 8,414 ..... H7
Meppel 21,057 ..... J3
Middelburg 36,372 ..... C6
Middelharnis 14,245 ..... E5
Middenmeer F3
Millingen aan den Rijn 5,035 ..... J5
Moerdijk F5
Monnickendam 8,127 ..... C4
Montfoort 3,442 ..... G4
Muiden 6,567 ..... G4
Muntendam 4,147 ..... K2
Naaldwijk 24,117 ..... E4
Naarden 17,319 ..... G4
Nagele H3
Neede 10,842 ..... K4
Nes 3,012 ..... H2
Nieuwegein 22,648 ..... G4
Nieuwe-Pekela 5,086 ..... L2
Nieuwkoop 8,923 ..... F4
Nieuw-Schoonebeek 7,556 ..... L3
Nijkerk 21,615 ..... H4
Nijmegen 148,493 ..... H5
Nijmegen* 213,981 ..... H5
Noordwijk 22,386 ..... E4
Norg 6,041 ..... J2
Numansdorp 7,072 ..... E5
Nunspeet 21,340 ..... H4
Odoorn 11,973 ..... K3
Oisterwijk 16,263 ..... G5
Oldenzaal 26,624 ..... K4
Olst 8,480 ..... J4
Ommen 16,136 ..... J3
Onstwedde K2
Oostburg 18,461 ..... C6
Oosterhout 40,077 ..... F5
Ooosterwolde 5,845 ..... J2
Oostmahorn J2
Oostzaan 6,336 ..... C4
Ootmarsum 3,901 ..... K4
Oss 45,643 ..... H5
Otterlo H4
Oud-Beijerland 14,251 ..... E5
Ouddorp 9,091 ..... D5
Oudenbosch 11,061 ..... E5
Oude-Pekela 8,067 ..... K2
Oudewater 6,870 ..... F4
Purmerend 32,614 ..... F4
Putten 18,243 ..... H4
Raalte 23,598 ..... J4
Renkum 34,547 ..... H5
Reusel 6,901 ..... G6
Rheden 49,755 ..... J4
Rhenen 16,893 ..... H5
Ridderkerk 45,069 ..... F5
Rijnsburg 10,698 ..... F4
Rijssen 20,008 ..... J4
Rijswijk 54,123 ..... E4
Roden 16,437 ..... J2
Roermond 36,695 ..... J6
Roosendaal 51,685 ..... F5
Rotterdam 614,767 ..... E5
Rotterdam* 1,016,505 ..... E5
Rutten H3
Ruurlo 7,557 ..... J4
Sappemeer-Hoogezand 33,860 ..... K2
Schagen 13,929 ..... F3
Scheveningen E4
Schiedam 78,068 ..... E5
Schijndel 18,658 ..... G5
Schiphol B5
Schoonhoven 10,753 ..... F5
's Gravendeel 7,242 ..... E5
's Gravenhage (The Hague)
(cap.) 479,369 ..... E4
's Gravenhage* 682,452 ..... E4
's Gravenzande 15,833 ..... E4
's Heerenberg 18,326 ..... J5
's Hertogenbosch 86,184 ..... G5
Simpelveld 6,783 ..... H7
Sint Annaland E5
Sint Jacobiparochie H2
Sittard 34,278 ..... H6
Sliedrecht 21,839 ..... F5
Slochteren 13,447 ..... K2
Sloten, North Holland B5
Sloterdijk B4
Sluis 3,140 ..... C6
Smilde 8,247 ..... K3
Sneek 28,123 ..... H2
Soest 40,165 ..... G4
Soesterberg G4
Stadskanaal 13,946 ..... L3
Staphorst 11,608 ..... J3
Steenbergen 12,930 ..... E5
Steenwijk 20,721 ..... J3
Stiens 7,711 ..... H2
Swifterbant H3
Tegelen 18,386 ..... J6
Ter Apel L3
Termunten 4,803 ..... K2
Terneuzen 33,731 ..... D6
Tholen 17,213 ..... E5
Tiel 24,974 ..... G5
Tilburg 151,513 ..... G5
Tilburg* 212,510 ..... G5
Twello 22,542 ..... J4
Uden 28,946 ..... H5
Uithoorn 22,812 ..... F4
Uithuizen 5,194 ..... K2
Ulrum 3,665 ..... J2
Urk 9,397 ..... H3
Utrecht 250,887 ..... G4
Utrecht* 464,357 ..... G4
Vaals 11,057 ..... H7
Vaassen 7,225 ..... H4
Valkenswaard 27,121 ..... H6
Veendam 26,168 ..... K2
Veenendaal 35,845 ..... G4
Veenhuizen J2
Veere 4,252 ..... D5
Veghel 22,308 ..... H5
Veldhoven 30,030 ..... G6
Velp J5
Velsen 64,035 ..... F4
Venlo 61,659 ..... J6
Venraij 31,526 ..... H6
Vianen 12,821 ..... G5
Vlaardingen 78,311 ..... E5
Vlagtwedde 16,719 ..... L3
Vlijmen 13,515 ..... G5
Vlissingen (Flushing) 43,806 ..... C6
Volendam-Edam 21,507 ..... G4
Voorburg 45,209 ..... E4
Voorst 22,542 ..... J4
Vorden 7,276 ..... J4
Vriezenveen 16,025 ..... K4
Vught 23,261 ..... G5
Waalre 13,219 ..... G6
Waalwijk 25,977 ..... F5
Wageningen 28,659 ..... H5
Wamel 8,979 ..... H5
Warmenhuizen 3,818 ..... F3
Weert 36,850 ..... H6
Weesp 17,037 ..... C5
West-Terschelling 4,542 ..... G2
Wierden 20,618 ..... K4
Wijhe 6,888 ..... J4
Wijk bij Duurstede 7,927 ..... G5
Wijk en Aalburg 9,266 ..... F5
Winschoten 19,760 ..... L2
Winsum 5,007 ..... K2
Winterswijk 27,413 ..... K5
Woensdrecht 9,101 ..... E6
Woerden 22,064 ..... F4
Wolvega 22,812 ..... J3
Workum 4,135 ..... G3
Zaandam (Zaanstad) 124,795 ..... B4
Zaandam (Zaanstad)* 137,371 ..... B4
Zaltbommel 8,010 ..... G5
Zandvoort 16,289 ..... E4
Zeist 58,630 ..... G4
Zevenaar 26,560 ..... J5
Zevenbergen 13,307 ..... E5
Zierikzee 8,816 ..... D5
Zundert 12,444 ..... F6
Zutphen 29,188 ..... J4
Zwartsluis 4,391 ..... H3
Zwijndrecht 38,271 ..... E5
Zwolle 77,826 ..... J3

OTHER FEATURES

Alkmaardermeer (lake) F3
Ameland (isl.) H2
Bergumermeer (lake) J2
Beulaker Wijde (lake) H3
Borndiep (chan.) H2
De Fluessen (lake) G3
De Honte (bay) D6
De Peel (reg.) H6
De Twente (reg.) K4
De Zaan (riv.) B4
Dollard (bay) L2
Dommel (riv.) H6
Duiveland (isl.) D5
Eastern Scheldt (est.) D5
Eems (riv.) K2
Eijerlandsche Gat (str.) F2
Flevoland Polders 35,618 ..... G4
Friesche Gat (chan.) J2
Frisian, West (isls.) G2
Galgenberg (hill) H4
Goeree (isl.) D5
Grevelingen (str.) E5
Griend (isl.) G2
Groninger Wad (sound) J2
Groote IJ Polder B4
Haarlemmermeer Polder 72,046 ..... B5
Haringvliet (str.) E5
Het IJ (est.) C4
Hoek van Holland (cape) D5
Hondsrug (hills) K3
Houtrak Polder A4
Hunse (riv.) K3
IJmeer (bay) C4
IJssel (riv.) J4
IJsselmeer (lake) G3
Lauwers (chan.) J1
Lauwers Zee (bay) J2
Lek (riv.) F5
Lemelerberg (hill) J4
Lower Rhine (riv.) H5
Maas (riv.) G5
Mark (riv.) F6
Marken (isl.) G4
Markerwaard Polder G3
Marsdiep (chan.) F3
North (sea) E3
North Beveland (isl.) D5
North East Polder 34,467 ..... H3
North Holland (canal) C4
North Sea (canal) F4
Old Rhine (riv.) E4
Oostzaan Polder 6,336 ..... B4
Orange (canal) K3
Overflakkee (isl.) E5
Pinke Gat (chan.) H2
Regge (riv.) K4
Rhine (riv.) J5
Roer (riv.) J6
Rottumeplaat (isl.) J1
Rottumeroog (isl.) J1
Schiermonnikoog (isl.) J1
Schouwen (isl.) D5
Slotermeer (lake) H3
Sneekermeer (lake) H2
South Beveland (isl.) D6
Terschelling (isl.) G2
Texel (isl.) F2
Tjeukemeer (lake) H3
Tjonger (riv.) J3
Vaalserberg (mt.) J7
Vecht (riv.) F4
Vechte (riv.) J3
Veersche Meer (lake) D5
Veluwe (reg.) H4
Vlieland (isl.) F2
Vliestroom (str.) G2
Voorne (isl.) D5
Waal (riv.) G5
Waddenzee (sound) G2
Walcheren (isl.) C5
Wester Eems (chan.) K1
Western Scheldt (De Honte)
(bay) D6
West Frisian (isls.) F2
Westgat (chan.) F3
Wieringermeer Polder 11,870 ..... G3
Wilhelmina (canal) G6
Willems (canal) G5

*City and suburbs.
†Population of cities in Belgium & Netherlands are communes

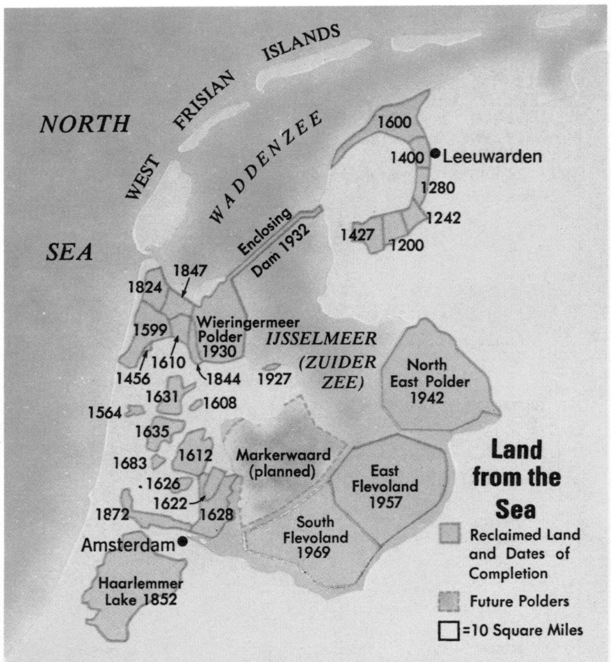

For centuries the Dutch have been renowned for the drainage of marshes and the construction of polders, i.e., arable land reclaimed from the sea. Future projects will convert much of the present IJsselmeer to agricultural land.

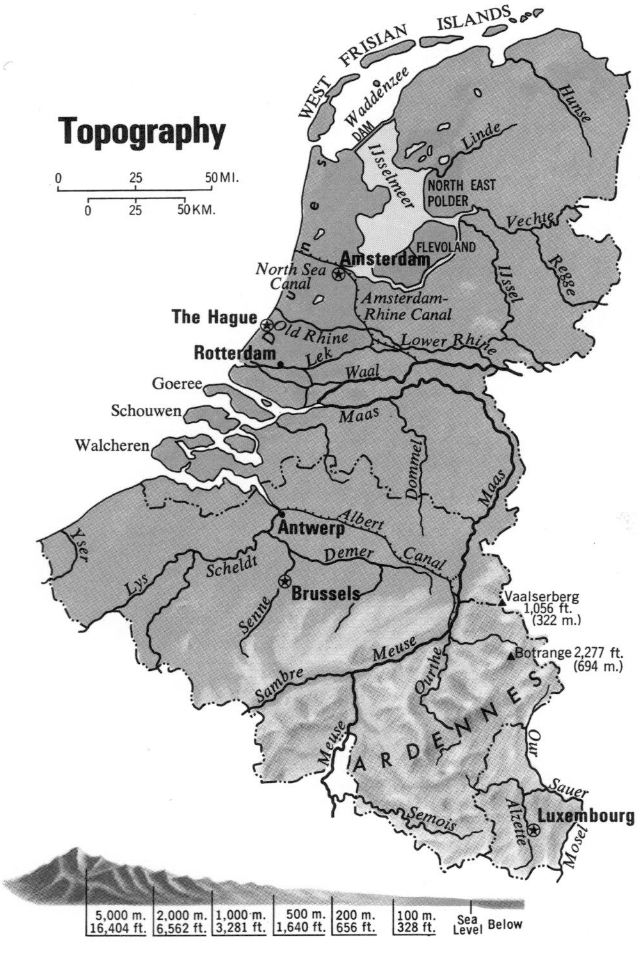

Netherlands, Belgium and Luxembourg

CONIC PROJECTION

SCALE OF MILES

0 5 10 20 30 40

SCALE OF KILOMETERS

0 5 10 20 30 40 50

Capitals of Countries .... ☆
Provincial Capitals .... △
International Boundaries .... ▬ ▪ ▬ ▪
Provincial Boundaries .... ▬ ▬
Canals .... ▬ ▪ ▪ ▬

Scale 1:1,670,000

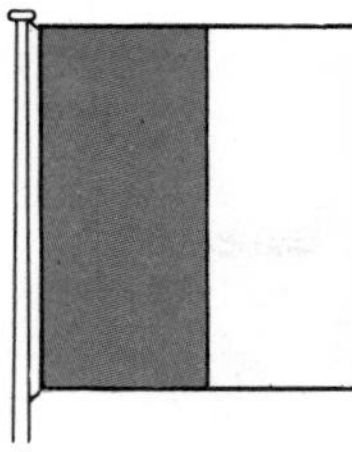

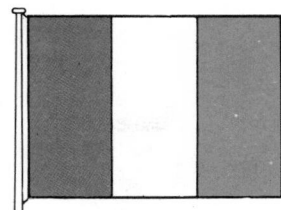

AREA 210,038 sq. mi. (543,998 sq. km.)
POPULATION 53,788,000
CAPITAL Paris
LARGEST CITY Paris
HIGHEST POINT Mont Blanc 15,771 ft. (4,807 m.)
MONETARY UNIT franc
MAJOR LANGUAGE French
MAJOR RELIGION Roman Catholicism

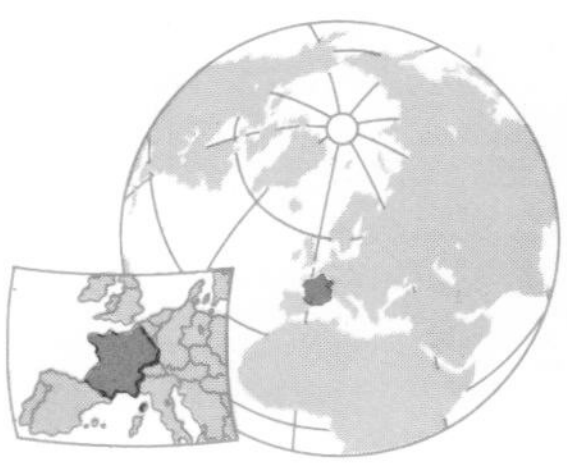

DEPARTMENTS

Ain 376,477	F4
Aisne 533,862	E3
Allier 378,406	E4
Alpes-de-Haute-Provence 112,178	G5
Alpes-Maritimes 816,681	G6
Ardèche 257,065	F5
Ardennes 309,306	F3
Ariège 137,857	D6
Aube 284,823	E3
Aude 272,366	E6
Aveyron 278,306	E5
Bas-Rhin 882,121	G3
Belfort (terr.) 128,125	G4
Bouches-du-Rhône 1,632,974	F6
Calvados 560,967	C3
Cantal 166,549	E5
Charente 337,064	D5
Charente-Maritime 497,859	C5
Cher 316,350	E4
Corrèze 240,363	D5
Corse du Sud 128,634	B6
Côte-d'Or 456,070	F4
Côtes-du-Nord 525,556	B3
Creuse 146,214	D4
Deux-Sèvres 335,829	C4
Dordogne 373,179	D5
Doubs 471,082	G4
Drôme 361,847	F5
Essonne 923,063	E3
Eure 422,952	D3
Eure-et-Loir 335,151	D3
Finistère 804,088	A3
Gard 494,575	F6
Gers 175,366	D6
Gironde 1,061,480	C5
Haute-Corse 161,208	B6
Haute-Garonne 777,431	D6
Haute-Loire 205,491	E5
Haute-Marne 212,304	F3
Hautes-Alpes 97,358	G5
Haute-Saône 222,254	G4
Haute-Savoie 447,795	G5
Hautes-Pyrénées 227,222	D6
Haute-Vienne 352,149	D5
Haut-Rhin 635,209	G4
Hauts-de-Seine 1,438,930	A2
Hérault 648,202	E6
Ille-et-Vilaine 702,199	C3
Indre 248,523	D4
Indre-et-Loire 478,601	D4
Isère 860,339	F5
Jura 238,856	F4
Landes 288,323	C5
Loire 742,396	F5
Loire-Atlantique 934,499	C4
Loiret 490,189	E4
Loir-et-Cher 283,686	D4
Lot 150,778	D5
Lot-et-Garonne 292,616	D5
Lozère 74,825	E5
Maine-et-Loire 629,849	C4
Manche 451,662	C3
Marne 530,399	F3
Mayenne 261,789	C3
Meurthe-et-Moselle 722,588	G3
Meuse 203,904	F3
Morbihan 563,588	B4
Moselle 1,006,373	G3
Nièvre 245,212	E4
Nord 2,510,738	E2
Oise 606,320	E3
Orne 293,523	C3
Paris (city) 2,299,830	B2
Pas-de-Calais 1,403,035	E2
Puy-de-Dôme 580,033	E5
Pyrénées-Atlantiques 534,748	C6
Pyrénées-Orientales 299,506	E6
Rhône 1,429,647	F5
Saône-et-Loire 569,810	F4
Sarthe 490,385	D3
Savoie 305,118	G5
Seine-et-Marne 755,762	E3
Seine-Saint-Denis 1,322,127	C1
Somme 538,462	E3
Tarn 338,024	E6
Tarn-et-Garonne 183,314	D5
Val-de-Marne 1,215,713	C1
Val-d'Oise 840,885	E3
Var 626,093	G6
Vaucluse 390,446	F6
Vendée 450,641	C4
Vienne 357,366	D4
Vosges 397,957	G3
Yonne 299,851	E4
Yvelines 1,082,255	D3

CITIES and TOWNS

Abbeville 25,252	D2
Agde 9,856	E6
Agen 33,763	D5
Aix-en-Provence 91,665	F6
Aix-les-Bains 21,884	G5
Ajaccio 47,065	B7
Albert 11,746	E2
Albertville 16,630	G5
Albi 43,942	E6
Alençon 32,917	D3
Alès 33,315	E5
Ambérieu-en-Bugey 9,294	F5
Amboise 10,498	D4
Amiens 129,453	D3
Ancenis 6,689	C4
Angers 136,603	C4
Angoulême 46,293	D5
Annecy 53,058	G5
Annonay 19,234	F5
Antibes 44,226	G6
Antony 57,450	B2
Apt 9,735	F6
Arcachon 13,856	C5
Argentan 16,063	D3
Argenteuil 101,542	A1
Arles 37,337	F6
Armentières 23,850	E2
Arras 45,804	E2
Asnières-sur-Seine 75,328	A1
Aubagne 26,145	F6
Aubenas 11,967	F5
Aubervilliers 72,859	B1
Auch 18,767	D6
Audincourt 18,570	G4
Aulnay-sous-Bois 77,982	B1
Auray 10,006	B4
Aurignac 744	D6
Aurillac 29,458	E5
Autun 19,441	F4
Auxerre 36,039	E4
Auxonne 6,414	F4
Avallon 8,518	E4
Avignon 73,482	F6
Avion 22,860	E2
Avranches 10,128	C3
Ax-les-Thermes 1,456	D6
Bagnères-de-Bigorre 9,080	D6
Bagnolet 35,858	B2
Bagnols-sur-Cèze 13,111	F5
Barbizon 1,189	E3
Barcelonnette 2,523	G5
Barfleur 701	C3
Bar-le-Duc 19,188	F3
Bar-sur-Aube 7,227	F3
Bastia 45,387	B6
Bayeux 13,381	C3
Bayonne 41,281	C6
Beaucaire 10,189	F6
Beaune 16,386	F4
Beauvais 53,493	E3
Belfort 54,469	G4
Belley 6,612	F5
Berck 14,104	D2
Bergerac 25,488	D5
Bernay 9,928	D3
Besançon 119,803	G4
Béthune 26,208	E2
Béziers 79,213	E6
Biarritz 27,453	C6
Blois 49,134	D4
Bobigny 43,041	B1
Bogny-sur-Meuse 6,845	F3
Bolbec 12,347	D3
Bondy 48,285	B1
Bonneville 6,717	G4
Bordeaux 220,830	C5
Boulogne-Billancourt 103,527	A2
Boulogne-sur-Mer 48,309	D2
Bourg-en-Bresse 40,052	F4
Bourges 75,200	E4
Bourgoin-Jallieu 18,504	F5
Bressuire 9,778	C4
Brest 163,940	A3
Briançon 8,523	G5
Brignoles 8,784	G6
Brioude 7,756	E5
Brive-la-Gaillarde 49,276	D5
Bruay-en-Artois 25,544	E2
Caen 116,987	C3
Cahors 19,288	D5
Calais 73,009	D2
Caluire-et-Cuire 43,024	F5
Cambrai 38,706	E2
Cannes 70,226	G6
Carcassonne 38,887	D6
Carmaux 11,970	E5
Carpentras 20,169	F5
Castelnaudary 8,947	E6
Castelsarrasin 6,562	D6
Castres 41,037	E6
Cavaillon 17,383	F6
Châlons-sur-Marne 50,870	F3
Chalon-sur-Saône 55,495	F4
Chambéry 52,286	F5
Chambord 166	D4
Chamonix-Mont-Blanc 6,246	G5
Champigny-sur-Marne 80,189	C2
Chantilly 10,517	E3
Charenton-le-Pont 20,383	B2
Charleville-Mézières 59,513	F3
Chartres 38,574	D3
Châteaubriant 12,417	C4
Château-du-Loir 5,598	D4
Châteaudun 14,634	D3
Château-Gontier 8,301	C4
Châteauroux 53,166	D4
Château-Thierry 13,379	E3
Châtellerault 33,811	D4
Châtillon 26,562	B2
Châtillon-sur-Seine 7,367	F4
Chatou 26,415	A1
Chaumont 26,568	F3
Chauny 14,324	E3
Chelles 24,192	C1
Cherbourg 31,333	C3
Chinon 5,378	D4
Choisy-le-Roi 38,629	B2
Cholet 49,887	C4
Clamart 52,881	A2
Clermont 7,834	E3
Clermont-Ferrand 153,379	E5
Clichy 47,731	B1
Cluny 4,335	F4
Cluses 12,713	G4
Cognac 21,567	C5
Colmar 58,585	G3
Colombes 83,241	A1
Commentry 8,074	E4
Commercy 6,918	F3
Compiègne 37,009	E3
Concarneau 15,096	A4
Cosne-Cours-sur-Loire 9,768	E4
Coudekerque-Branche 24,702	E2
Coulommiers 11,363	E3
Courbevoie 54,391	A1
Coutances 8,286	C3
Creil 31,893	E3
Crépy-en-Valois 10,661	E3
Créteil 58,665	B2
Cusset 13,672	E4
Dax 18,019	C6
Deauville 5,655	C3
Decazeville 9,318	E5
Decize 6,853	E4
Denain 26,096	E2
Dieppe 25,607	D3
Digne 13,140	G5
Digoin 10,449	F4
Dijon 149,899	F4
Dinan 13,303	B3
Dinard 9,211	B3
Dôle 28,109	F4
Domrémy-la-Pucelle 190	F3
Douai 43,954	E2
Douarnenez 17,851	A3
Doullens 6,806	E2
Draguignan 19,653	G6
Drancy 64,258	B1
Dreux 31,503	D3
Dunkirk (Dunkerque) 78,171	E2
Elbeuf 18,642	D3
Épernay 29,286	E3
Épinal 39,000	G3
Épinay-sur-Seine 46,458	B1
Erstein 6,494	G3
Étampes 18,810	E3
Étaples 10,423	D2
Eu 8,349	D3
Évreux 46,181	D3
Évry 15,300	E3
Falaise 8,133	C3
Fécamp 20,835	D3
Figeac 8,675	D5
Firminy 23,776	F5
Flers 18,590	C3
Foix 9,569	D6
Fontainebleau 16,436	E3
Fontenay-le-Comte 12,301	C4
Fontenay-sous-Bois 46,200	C2
Forbach 24,812	G3
Fougères 26,260	C3
Fourmies 15,318	F2
Fréjus 27,805	G6
Gagny 36,714	C1
Gaillac 7,653	D6
Gap 24,962	G5
Gardanne 8,175	F6
Gennevillers 50,154	B1
Gentilly 16,843	B2
Gex 3,959	G4
Gien 13,817	E4
Gif 10,866	E3
Gisors 7,591	D3
Givet 7,787	F2
Givors 19,356	F5
Granville 12,869	C3
Grasse 24,260	G6
Graulhet 11,099	E6
Gray 8,718	F4
Grenoble 165,431	F5
Guebwiller 10,477	G4
Guéret 14,418	D4
Guingamp 9,269	B3
Guise 6,642	E3
Haguenau 23,023	G3
Harfleur 9,857	D3
Hautmont 19,130	F2
Hayange 8,479	F3
Hazebrouck 18,867	E2
Hendaye 9,404	C6
Hénin-Beaumont 26,296	E2
Hennebont 8,978	B4
Héricourt 8,481	G4
Hirson 11,909	F3
Honfleur 8,995	D3
Hyères 29,366	G6
Issoire 13,560	E5
Issoudun 15,065	D4
Issy-les-Moulineaux 47,355	A2
Istres 10,127	F6
Ivry-sur-Seine 62,804	B2
Joigny 10,825	E3
La Baule-Escoublac 13,854	B4
La Ciotat 29,290	F6
La Courneuve 37,917	B1
La Flèche 12,743	C4
La Grand-Combe 9,406	E5
L'Aigle 9,198	D3
Landerneau 13,983	B3
Langres 10,745	F4
Lannion 13,692	B3
Laon 27,420	E3
La Pallice	C4
La Rochelle 72,936	C4
La Roche-sur-Yon 40,789	C4
La Seyne-sur-Mer 50,059	F6
Laval 50,734	C3
Lavelanet 9,278	E6
Le Blanc 7,431	D4
Le Blanc-Mesnil 49,062	B1
Le Bourget 10,520	B1
Le Cateau 8,680	E2
Le Chesnay 24,590	A2
Le Creusot 31,643	F4
Le Havre 216,917	C3
Le Mans 150,289	C3
Lens 39,973	E2
Le Puy 24,793	F5
Les Andelys 7,524	D3
Les Sables-d'Olonne 17,157	B4
Le Teil 7,993	F5
Le Tréport 6,463	D2
Levallois-Perret 52,460	A1
Lézignan-Corbières 6,929	E6
Libourne 21,265	C5
Liévin 33,040	E2
Lille 171,010	E2
Limoges 136,059	D5
Limoux 9,595	E6
Lisieux 24,972	D3
Livry-Gargan 32,879	C1
Lodève 7,131	E6
Longwy 20,107	F3
Lons-le-Saunier 20,897	F4
Lorient 68,655	B4
Loudéac 7,173	B3
Loudun 7,060	D4
Lourdes 17,685	C6
Louviers 17,919	D3
Luçon 8,834	C4
Lunel 12,392	E6
Lunéville 22,438	G3
Lure 8,538	G4
Luxeuil-les-Bains 10,061	G4
Lyon 454,265	F5
Mâcon 39,130	F4
Maisons-Alfort 53,963	B2
Maisons-Laffitte 23,465	A1
Malakoff 34,100	A2
Manosque 17,256	G6
Mantes-la-Jolie 42,408	D3
Marmande 13,223	C5
Marseille 901,421	F6
Martigues 26,850	F6
Maubeuge 34,152	F2
Mayenne 11,278	C3
Mazamet 13,148	E6
Meaux 41,831	E3
Mehun-sur-Yèvre 6,533	E4
Melun 36,913	E3
Mende 10,040	E5
Menton 24,736	G6
Metz 110,939	G3
Meudon 31,294	A2
Millau 20,401	E5
Mimizan 6,826	C5
Mirecourt 7,160	G3
Moissac 7,403	D5
Montargis 18,021	E3
Montauban 35,344	D5
Montbard 7,477	F4
Montbéliard 29,968	G4
Montbrison 9,945	E5
Montceau-les-Mines 28,093	F4
Mont-de-Marsan 24,812	C6
Mont-Dore 2,074	E5
Montélimar 25,422	F5
Montfort 2,701	C3
Montigny-les-Metz 24,208	G3
Montluçon 56,337	E4
Montmédy 1,859	F3
Montpellier 178,136	E6
Montreuil, Seine-Saint-Denis 96,441	B2
Montrouge 40,189	B2
Mont-Saint-Michel 88	C3
Morlaix 15,919	B3
Morteau 6,515	G4
Moulins 25,856	E4
Moyeuvre-Grande 12,448	G3
Mulhouse 116,494	G4
Muret 13,041	D6
Nancy 106,906	G3
Nanterre 94,441	A1
Nantes 252,537	C4
Narbonne 36,525	E6
Nemours 11,159	E3
Neufchâteau 8,582	F3
Neuilly-sur-Seine 65,941	A1
Nevers 45,122	E4
Nice 331,002	G6
Nîmes 123,914	F6
Niort 59,297	C4
Nogent-le-Rotrou 12,284	D3
Noisy-le-Sec 37,674	B1
Noyon 13,784	E3
Oloron-Sainte-Marie 11,616	C6
Orange 19,847	F5
Orléans 88,503	D3
Orly 26,090	B2
Orthez 9,639	C6
Oullins 27,731	F5
Oyonnax 22,548	F4
Pamiers 12,906	D6
Pantin 42,651	B1
Paray-le-Monial 11,523	F4
Paris (cap.) 2,291,554	B2
Parthenay 12,549	C4
Pau 81,560	C6
Périgueux 34,779	D5
Péronne 8,358	E3
Perpignan 101,198	E6
Pessac 50,333	C5
Pézenas 6,768	E6
Pithiviers 9,976	E3
Poitiers 78,739	D4
Pont-à-Mousson 14,461	G3
Pontarlier 17,778	G4
Pontivy 9,478	B3
Pont-l'Abbe 6,618	A4
Pontoise 26,702	E3
Port-de-Bouc 20,448	F6
Port-Saint-Louis-du-Rhône 9,649	F6
Port-Vendres 5,448	E6
Privas 9,385	F5
Provins 12,281	E3
Puteau 35,366	A2
Quimper 50,856	A4
Quimperlé 9,783	B4
Rambouillet 18,446	D3
Redon 9,528	C4
Reims 177,320	E3
Remiremont 10,250	G3
Rennes 194,094	C3

(continued on following page)

Topography

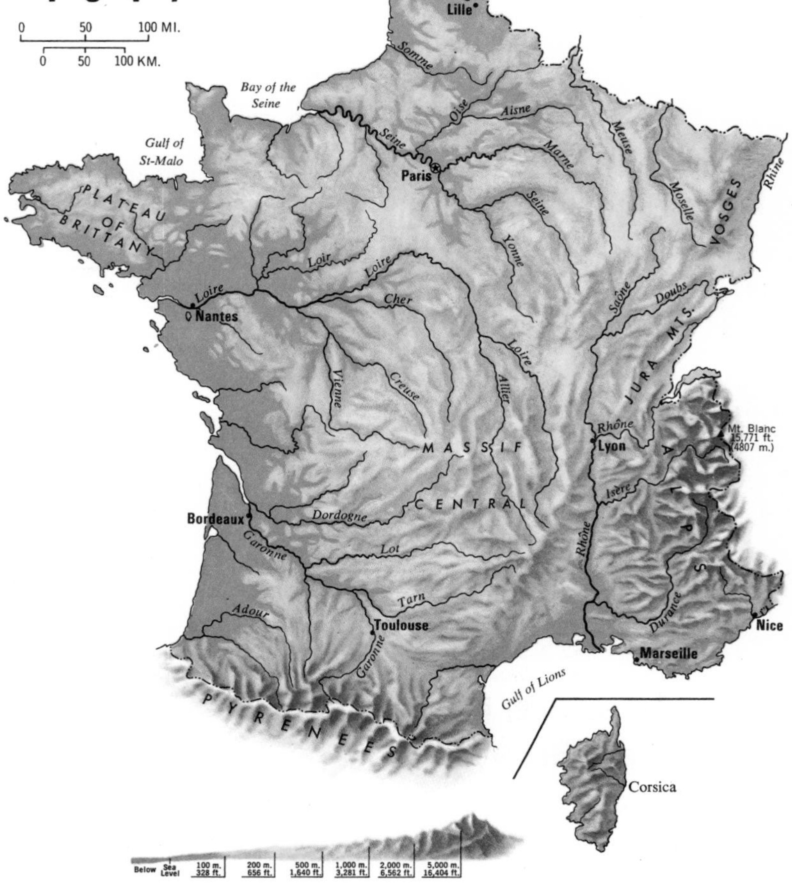
0 50 100 MI.
0 50 100 KM.
Lille
Somme
Bay of the Seine
Oise
Aisne
Meuse
Rhine
Gulf of St-Malo
Seine
Paris
Marne
Moselle
VOSGES
PLATEAU OF BRITTANY
Loir
Loire
Yonne
Saône
Doubs
Nantes
Cher
JURA MTS.
Vienne
Creuse
Allier
Rhône
Mt. Blanc 15,771 ft. (4807 m.)
Lyon
MASSIF CENTRAL
Isère
ALPS
Bordeaux
Dordogne
Garonne
Lot
Tarn
Durance
Nice
Adour
Toulouse
Marseille
Gulf of Lions
PYRENEES
Corsica
Below Sea Level
100 m. 328 ft.
200 m. 656 ft.
500 m. 1,640 ft.
1,000 m. 3,281 ft.
2,000 m. 6,562 ft.
5,000 m. 16,404 ft.

Historic Provinces

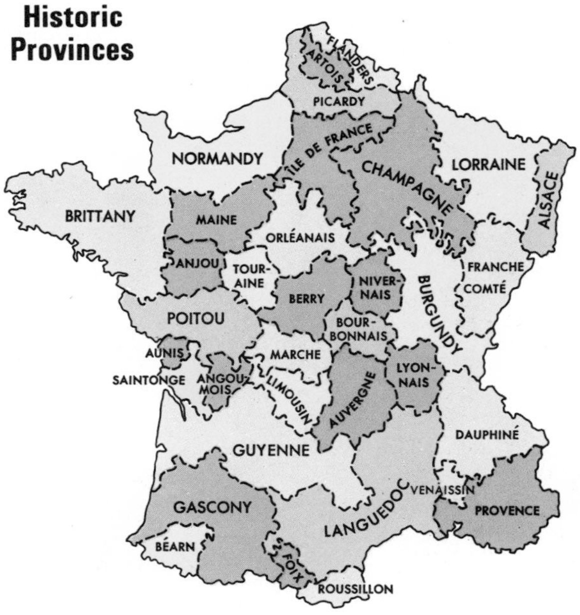
FLANDERS
ARTOIS
PICARDY
NORMANDY
ÎLE DE FRANCE
CHAMPAGNE
LORRAINE
ALSACE
BRITTANY
MAINE
ORLÉANAIS
ANJOU
TOUR-AINE
FRANCHE COMTÉ
BERRY
NIVER-NAIS
BURGUNDY
POITOU
BOUR-BONNAIS
AUNIS
MARCHE
SAINTONGE
ANGOU-MOIS
LIMOUSIN
AUVERGNE
LYON-NAIS
GUYENNE
DAUPHINÉ
VENAISSIN
GASCONY
LANGUEDOC
PROVENCE
BÉARN
FOIX
ROUSSILLON

A resident of the city of Caen thinks of himself as a Norman rather than as a citizen of the modern department of Calvados. In spite of the passing of nearly two centuries, the historic provinces which existed before 1790 command the local patriotism of most Frenchmen.

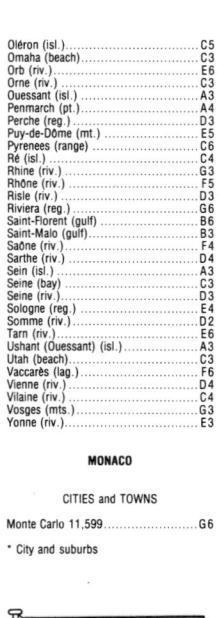
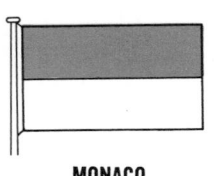

Wine Regions

Climate, soil and variety of grape planted determine the quality of wine. Long, hot and fairly dry summers with cool, humid nights constitute an ideal climate. The nature of the soil is such a determining influence that identical grapes planted in Bordeaux, Burgundy and Champagne, will yield wines of widely different types.

Agriculture, Industry and Resources

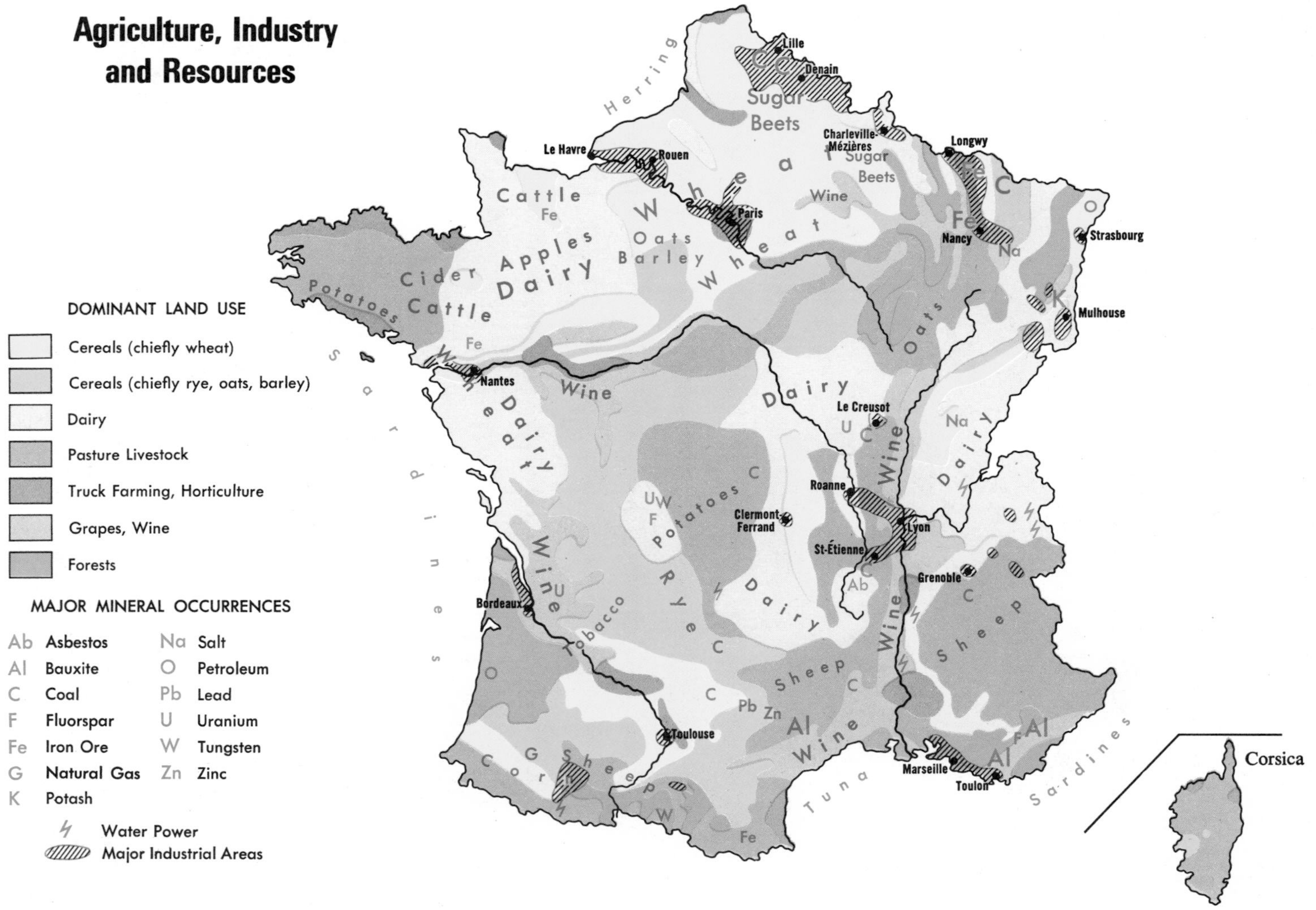

DOMINANT LAND USE

- Cereals (chiefly wheat)
- Cereals (chiefly rye, oats, barley)
- Dairy
- Pasture Livestock
- Truck Farming, Horticulture
- Grapes, Wine
- Forests

MAJOR MINERAL OCCURRENCES

Ab Asbestos
Al Bauxite
C   Coal
F   Fluorspar
Fe Iron Ore
G   Natural Gas
K   Potash
Na Salt
O   Petroleum
Pb Lead
U   Uranium
W   Tungsten
Zn Zinc

⚡ Water Power
▨ Major Industrial Areas

SPAIN

PROVINCES

Álava 204,323 E1
Albacete 335,026 E3
Alicante 920,105 F3
Almería 375,004 E4
Ávila 203,798 D2
Badajoz 687,599 C3
Baleares 558,287 H3
Barcelona 3,929,194 G2
Burgos 358,075 E1
Cáceres 457,777 C3
Cádiz 885,433 D4
Castellón 385,823 G2
Ciudad Real 507,650 D3
Córdoba 724,116 D3
Cuenca 247,158 E2
Gerona 414,397 H1
Granada 733,375 E4
Guadalajara 147,732 E2
Guipúzcoa 631,003 E1
Huelva 397,683 C4
Huesca 222,238 F1
Jaén 661,146 E4
La Coruña 1,004,188 B1
Las Palmas 579,710 C4
León 548,721 C1
Lérida 347,015 G2
Logroño 235,713 E1
Lugo 415,052 C1
Madrid 3,792,561 E2
Málaga 867,330 D4
Murcia 832,313 F4
Navarra 464,867 F1
Orense 413,733 C1
Oviedo 1,045,635 C1
Palencia 198,763 D1
Pontevedra 750,701 B1
Salamanca 371,607 C2
Santa Cruz de Tenerife 590,514 B5
Santander 467,138 D1
Segovia 162,770 D2
Sevilla 1,327,190 D4
Soria 114,956 E2
Tarragona 431,961 G2
Teruel 170,284 F2
Toledo 468,925 D3
Valencia 1,767,327 F3
Valladolid 412,572 D2
Vizcaya 1,043,310 E1
Zamora 251,934 D2
Zaragoza 760,186 F2

CITIES and TOWNS

Adra 10,851 E4
Aguilar 12,893 D4
Aguilas 15,525 F4
Alagón 5,114 F2
Alayor 5,124 J3
Albacete 82,607 F3
Albox 5,072 E4
Alburquerque 7,530 C3
Alcalá de Guadaira 28,781 D4
Alcalá de Henares 59,783 G4
Alcalá de los Gazules 5,262 D4
Alcalá la Real 9,849 E4
Alcanar 5,961 G2
Alcañiz 10,229 F2
Alcantarilla 19,895 F4
Alcaudete 8,557 E4
Alcázar de San Juan 24,620 E3
Alcira 30,493 F3
Alcora 6,711 F2
Alcoy 61,371 F3
Alfaro 8,766 F1
Algeciras 74,754 D4
Algemesí 21,158 F3
Alhama de Granada 6,148 E4
Alhama de Murcia 9,274 F4
Alicante 177,918 F3
Almadén 10,713 D3
Almagro 9,066 E3
Almansa 16,965 F3
Almendralejo 21,929 C3
Almería 104,008 E4
Almodóvar del Campo 7,310 D3
Almonte 9,960 C4
Almuñécar 7,812 E4
Álora 8,209 D4
Altea 7,262 G3
Amposta 11,767 G2
Andorra 6,485 F2
Andújar 25,962 D3
Antequera 28,039 D4
Aracena 5,390 C4
Aranda de Duero 18,183 E2
Aranjuez 28,559 E2
Archena 7,118 F3
Archidona 6,084 D4
Arcos de la Frontera 16,217 D4
Arenas de San Pedro 5,225 D2
Arenys de Mar 8,325 H2
Arévalo 5,807 D2
Argamasilla de Alba 6,192 E3
Arganda 11,876 G4
Arnedo 9,809 E1
Arrecife 21,310 C4
Arroyo de la Luz 8,130 C3
Artá 5,284 H3
Arucas 9,095 B5
Aspe 13,229 F3
Astorga 11,794 C1
Ávila de los
Caballeros 30,958 D2
Avilés 67,186 C1
Ayamonte 9,897 C4
Ayora 5,249 F3
Azpeitia 7,835 E1
Azuaga 10,719 D3
Badajoz 80,793 C3
Badalona 162,888 H2
Baena 16,496 D4
Baeza 12,607 E4
Bailén 13,207 E3
Balaguer 11,676 G2
Bañolas 9,807 H1
Baracaldo 108,757 E1
Barbastro 13,243 F1
Barcarrota 5,012 C3
Barcelona 1,741,144 H2
Barcelona‡ 2,000,000 H2
Baza 14,290 E4
Beas de Segura 6,592 E3
Béjar 16,804 D2
Bélmez 5,161 D3
Benavente 11,779 D1
Benicarló 12,831 G2
Berga 11,163 G1
Berja 7,081 E4
Bermeo 16,714 E1
Betanzos 7,283 B1
Bilbao 393,179 E1
Bilbao‡ 450,000 E1
Binéfar 6,821 G2
Blanes 15,810 H2
Borjas Blancas 4,991 G2
Bujalance 8,236 D4
Bullas 8,131 F4
Burgos 118,366 E1
Burriana 21,298 G3
Cabeza del Buey 8,704 D3
Cabra 16,177 D4

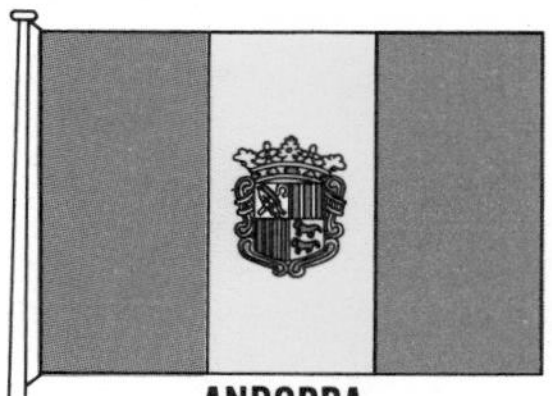

ANDORRA

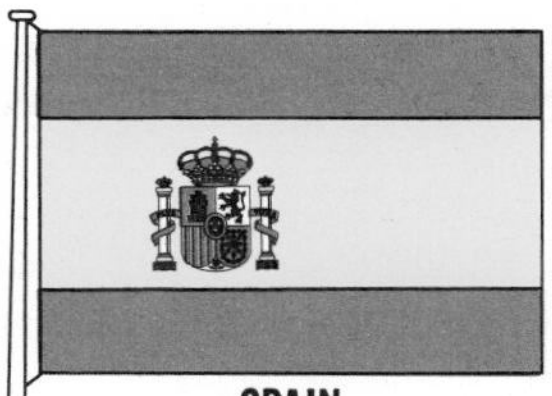

SPAIN

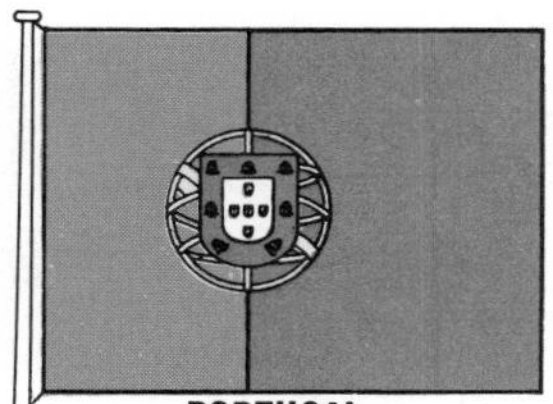

PORTUGAL

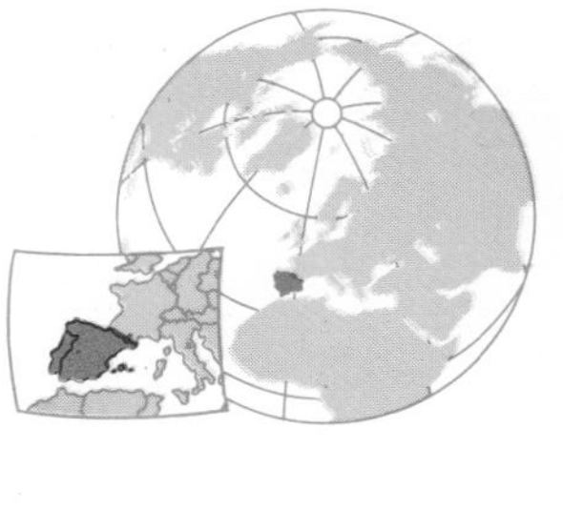

SPAIN

AREA 194,881 sq. mi. (504,742 sq. km.)
POPULATION 37,430,000
CAPITAL Madrid
LARGEST CITY Madrid
HIGHEST POINT Pico de Teide 12,172 ft. (3,710 m.) (Canary Is.); Mulhacén 11,411 ft. (3,478 m.) (mainland)
MONETARY UNIT peseta
MAJOR LANGUAGES Spanish, Catalan, Basque, Galician, Valencian
MAJOR RELIGION Roman Catholicism

PORTUGAL

AREA 35,549 sq. mi. (92,072 sq. km.)
POPULATION 9,933,000
CAPITAL Lisbon
LARGEST CITY Lisbon
HIGHEST POINT Malhão da Estrela 6,532 ft. (1,991 m.)
MONETARY UNIT escudo
MAJOR LANGUAGE Portuguese
MAJOR RELIGION Roman Catholicism

ANDORRA

AREA 188 sq. mi. (487 sq. km.)
POPULATION 31,000
CAPITAL Andorra la Vella
MONETARY UNITS French franc, Spanish peseta
MAJOR LANGUAGE Catalan
MAJOR RELIGION Roman Catholicism

GIBRALTAR

AREA 2.28 sq. mi. (5.91 sq. km.)
POPULATION 29,760
CAPITAL Gibraltar
MONETARY UNIT pound sterling
MAJOR LANGUAGES English, Spanish
MAJOR RELIGION Roman Catholicism

Cáceres 53,108 C3
Cádiz 135,743 C4
Calahorra 16,315 E1
Calasparra 7,238 F3
Calatayud 16,524 F2
Calella 9,696 H2
Callosa de Ensarriá 5,701 G3
Calzada de Calatrava 5,751 E3
Campanario 7,722 D3
Campillos 7,014 D4
Campo de Criptana 12,604 E3
Candás 5,517 D1
Candeleda 5,153 D2
Cangas de Narcea 4,826 C1
Caniles 5,099 E4
Caravaca de le Cruz 10,411 E3
Carballo 5,542 B1
Carcagente 18,223 F3
Carmona 22,832 D4
Cartagena 52,312 F4
Caspe 8,766 G2
Cassá de la Selva 5,248 H2
Castellón de la Plana 79,773 G2
Castro del Río 10,087 D4
Castro-Urdiales 8,369 E1
Castuera 8,060 D3
Caudete 7,332 F3
Cazalla de la Sierra 5,382 D4
Cazorla 6,938 E4
Cehegín 9,661 F3
Cervera 5,693 G2
Ceuta 60,639 D5
Chiclana de la Frontera 22,986 C4
Chiva 5,394 F3
Ciempozuelos 9,185 F5
Cieza 22,929 F3
Ciudadela 13,701 H2
Ciudad Real 39,931 D3
Ciudad-Rodrigo 11,694 C2
Cocentaina 8,375 F3
Coín 14,190 D4
Colmenar de Oreja 4,930 G5
Colmenar Viejo 12,886 F4
Constantina 10,227 D4
Consuegra 10,026 E3
Córdoba 216,049 D4
Corella 5,850 F1
Coria 8,083 C3
Coria del Río 18,085 C4
Corral de Almaguer 8,006 E3
Crevillente 15,749 F3
Cuéllar 6,118 D2
Cuenca 33,980 E2
Cullera 15,128 F3
Daimiel 17,710 E3
Denia 14,514 G3
Dolores 5,420 F3
Don Benito 21,351 C3
Dos Hermanas 36,921 D4
Durango 20,403 E1
Écija 27,295 D4
Eibar 36,729 E1
Ejea de los Caballeros 9,766 F1
El Arahal 14,703 D4
Elche 101,271 F3
Elda 41,404 F3
Elizondo 2,516 F1
El Puerto de Santa
María 36,451 C4
Espejo 5,925 D4
Estella 10,371 E1
Estepa 9,376 D4
Estepona 18,560 D4
Felanitx 9,100 H3
Ferrol del Caudillo 75,464 B1
Figueras 22,087 H1
Fraga 9,665 G2
Fregenal de la Sierra 6,826 C3
Fuengirola 20,597 D4
Fuente de Cantos 5,967 C3
Fuenterrabiá 2,350 E1
Fuentes de Andalucía 8,257 D4
Gandía 30,702 F3
Gerona 37,095 H2
Getafe 68,680 F4
Gijón 159,806 D1
Granada 185,799 E4
Granollers 30,066 H2
Guadalajara 30,924 E2
Guadix 15,311 E4
Guareña 7,706 C3
Guernica y Luno 12,046 E1
Haro 8,393 E1
Hellín 15,934 F3
Herencia 8,212 E3
Hinojosa del Duque 9,873 D3
Hortaleza G4
Hospitalet 241,978 H2
Huelma 5,260 E4
Huelva 96,689 C4
Huercal-Overa 5,158 F4
Huesca 33,076 F1
Huéscar 6,384 E4
Ibiza 16,943 G3
Igualada 27,941 G2
Inca 16,930 H3
Irún 38,014 F1
Iscar 5,192 D2
Isla Cristina 11,402 C4
Iznalloz 4,814 E4
Jaca 9,936 F1
Jaén 71,145 E4
Jaraíz de la Vera 6,379 D2
Játiva 20,934 F3
Jávea 6,228 G3
Jerez de la Frontera 112,411 C4
Jerez de los Caballeros 8,607 C3
Jijona 8,117 F3
Jódar 11,973 E4
Jumilla 16,407 F3
La Almunia de Doña
Godina 4,835 F2
La Bañeza 8,480 C1
La Bisbal 6,374 H1
La Carolina 13,138 E3
La Coruña 184,372 B1
La Granja (San
Ildefonso) 3,198 E2
La Guardia 4,967 B2
La Línea de la
Concepción 51,021 D4
La Orotava 8,246 B4
La Palma del Condado 9,256 C4
La Puebla 9,923 H3
La Puebla de Montalbán 6,629 D3
La Rambla 6,525 D4
Laredo 9,114 E1
La Roda 11,460 E3
La Solana 13,894 E3
Las Palmas de Gran
Canaria 260,368 B4
Las Pedroñeras 5,846 E3
La Unión 9,998 F4
Lebrija 15,081 D4
Leganés 57,537 F4
León 99,702 D1
Lérida 73,148 G2
Linares 45,330 E3
Liria 11,323 F3
Llerena 5,728 C3
Llivia 801 G1
Llodio 15,587 E1
Lluctmayor 9,630 H3
Logroño 83,117 E1
Loja 11,549 D4
Lora del Río 15,741 D4
Lorca 25,208 F4
Los Santos de Maimona 7,899 C3
Los Yébenes 5,477 E3
Lucena 21,527 D4
Lugo 53,504 C1
Madrid (cap.) 3,146,071 F4
Madrid‡ 3,500,000 F4
Madridejos 9,948 E3
Madroñera 5,397 D3
Mahón 17,802 J3
Málaga 334,988 D4
Málaga‡ 400,000 D4
Malagón 7,732 E3
Malpartida de Cáceres 5,054 C3
Manacor 20,266 H3
Mancha Real 7,547 E4
Manlleu 13,169 H1
Manresa 52,526 G2
Manzanares 15,024 E3
Marbella 19,648 D4
Marchena 16,227 D4
Marín 10,948 B1
Martos 16,395 E4
Mataró 73,129 H2
Medina del Campo 16,345 D2
Medina de Rioseco 4,874 D2
Medina-Sidonia 7,523 D4
Mérida 36,916 C3
Miajadas 8,042 D3
Mieres 22,790 D1
Minas de Ríotinto 3,939 C4
Miranda de Ebro 29,355 E1
Moguér 7,629 C4
Mollerusa 6,685 G2
Monesterio 5,923 C3
Monforte 14,002 C1
Monóvar 9,071 F3
Montehermoso 5,952 C2
Montellano 6,658 D4
Montijo 11,931 C3
Montilla 18,670 D4
Montoro 9,295 D3
Monzón 14,089 G2
Mora 10,523 E3
Moratalla 5,101 E3
Morón de la Frontera 25,662 D4
Mota del Cuervo 5,130 E3
Motril 25,121 E4
Mula 9,168 F3
Munera 5,003 E3
Murcia 102,242 F4
Navalcarnero 6,212 F4
Navalmoral de la Mata 9,650 D3
Nerja 7,413 E4
Nerva 10,830 C4
Novelda 16,867 F3
Nules 9,027 F3
Ocaña 5,603 E3
Oliva 16,717 F3
Oliva de la Frontera 8,560 C3
Olivenza 7,616 C3
Olot 18,062 H1
Olvera 9,825 D4
Onda 13,012 F3
Onteniente 23,685 F3
Orense 63,542 C1
Orihuela 17,610 F3
Osuna 17,384 D4
Oviedo 130,021 C1
Padul 6,377 E4
Palafrugell 10,421 H2
Palamós 7,679 H2
Palencia 58,327 D2
Palma 191,416 H3
Palma del Río 15,075 D4
Pamplona 142,686 F1
Pego 8,861 F3
Peñafiel 4,794 E2
Peñaranda de
Bracamonte 6,094 D2
Peñarroya-Pueblonuevo 15,649 D3
Pinos-Puente 7,634 E4
Plasencia 26,897 C2
Pola de Lena 5,760 D1
Pollensa 7,625 H3
Ponferrada 22,838 C1
Pontevedra 27,118 B1
Porcuna 8,169 D4
Port-Bou 2,230 H1
Portugalete 45,589 E1
Posadas 7,245 D4
Pozoblanco 13,280 D3
Pozuelo de Alarcón 14,041 D2
Priego de Córdoba 12,676 D4
Puente-Genil 22,888 D4
Puertollano 50,609 D3
Puerto Real 13,993 D4
Puigcerdá 4,418 G1
Quesada 6,965 E4
Quintana de la Serena 5,171 D3
Quintanar de la Orden 7,764 E3
Reinosa 10,863 D1
Requena 9,836 F3
Reus 47,240 G2
Ripoll 9,283 H1
Ronda 22,094 D4
Roquetas 5,617 G2
Rosas 5,448 H1
Rota 20,021 C4
Rute 8,294 D4
Sabadell 148,223 H2
Sagunto 17,052 F3
Salamanca 125,132 D2
Sallent 7,118 H2
Salobreña 5,961 E4
Salt 5,572 H1
Sama 9,863 D1
San Carlos de la
Rápita 8,946 G2
San Clemente 6,016 E3
San Feliu de
Guíxols 12,006 H2
San Fernando 59,309 C4
San Ildefonso 3,198 E2

Agriculture, Industry and Resources

DOMINANT LAND USE

- Cereals (chiefly wheat)
- Livestock (chiefly sheep, goats)
- Mixed Cereals, Livestock
- Olives, Fruit
- Grapes, Fruit, Nuts, Mixed Cereals
- Forests
- Nonagricultural Land

MAJOR MINERAL OCCURRENCES

Ag	Silver	Na	Salt
C	Coal	O	Petroleum
Cu	Copper	Pb	Lead
Fe	Iron Ore	Py	Pyrites
G	Natural Gas	Sb	Antimony
Hg	Mercury	Sn	Tin
K	Potash	U	Uranium
Lg	Lignite	W	Tungsten
Mg	Magnesium	Zn	Zinc

Water Power
Major Industrial Areas

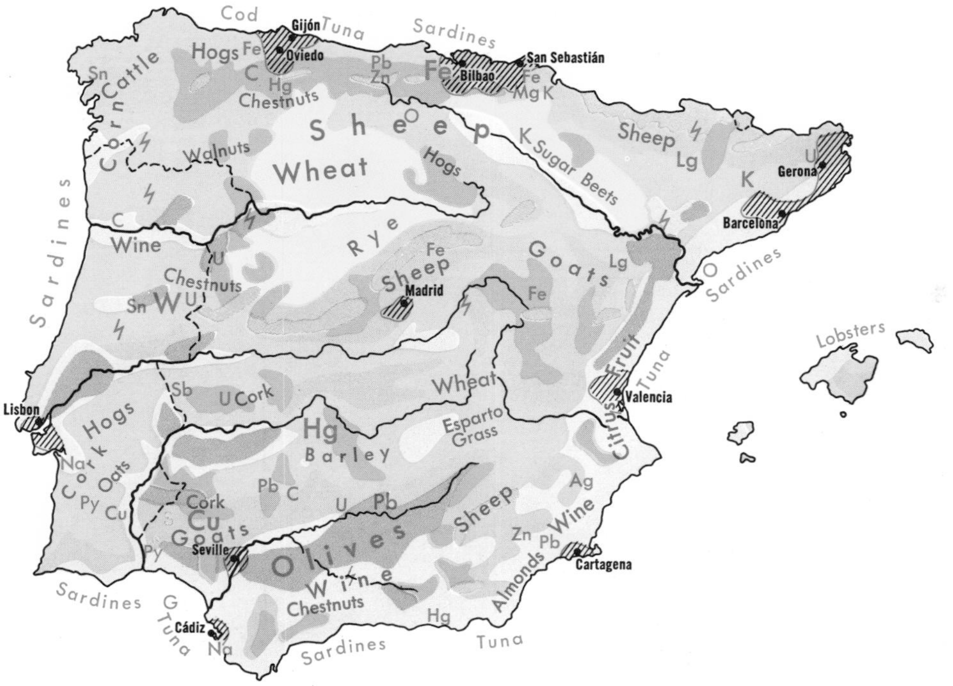

(continued on following page)

San Lorenzo de El
  Escorial 8,098 ....E2
Sanlúcar de Barrameda 29,483 ...C4
Sanlúcar la Mayor 6,121 ....C4
San Roque 8,224 ....D4
San Sebastián 159,557 ....E1
Santa Cruz de la Palma 10,393 ...B4
Santa Cruz de Mudela 6,354 ......E3
Santa Cruz de Tenerife 74,910 ...B4
Santa Eugenia 5,946 ....B1
Santa Fé 8,990 ....D4
Sant Feliu 560,000 ....D4
Santander 130,019 ....D1
Santiago 51,620 ....B1
Santo Domingo de la
  Calzada 5,638 ....E1
Santoña 9,546 ....E1
San Vicente de
  Alcántara 7,006 ....C3
Saragossa 449,319 ....F2
Saragossa‡ 500,000 ....F2
Segorbe 6,962 ....F3
Segovia 41,880 ....D2
Seo de Urgel 6,604 ....G1
Seville 511,447 ....C4
Seville‡ 560,000 ....D4
Sitges 8,906 ....G2
Socuéllamos 12,610 ....E3
Sóller 6,470 ....H2
Solsona 5,346 ....G2
Sonseca 6,594 ....D3
Soria 24,744 ....E2
Sotrondio 5,914 ....D1
Sueca 20,019 ....F3
Tabernes de Valldigna 13,962 .....G3
Tafalla 8,858 ....F1
Talavera de la Reina 39,889 ......D2
Tarancón 8,238 ....E3
Tarazona 11,067 ....E2
Tarazona de la Mancha 5,952 ......E3
Tarifa 9,201 ....D4
Tarragona 53,548 ....G2
Tarrasa 134,481 ....G2
Tárrega 9,036 ....G2
Tauste 6,832 ....F2
Telde 13,257 ....B5
Teruel 20,614 ....F2

Tobarra 5,887 ....F3
Toledo 43,905 ....D3
Tolosa 15,164 ....F1
Tomelloso 26,041 ....E3
Tordesillas 5,815 ....D2
Toro 8,455 ....D2
Torredonjimeno 12,507 ....D4
Torrejón de Ardoz 21,081 ....G4
Torrelavega 19,933 ....D1
Torremolinos 20,484 ....D4
Torrente 38,397 ....F3
Torreviaja 9,431 ....F4
Torrijos 6,362 ....D3
Torrox 5,583 ....D4
Tortosa 20,030 ....G2
Totana 12,714 ....F4
Trigueros 6,280 ....C4
Trujillo 9,024 ....D3
Tudela 20,942 ....F1
Úbeda 28,306 ....E3
Ubrique 13,166 ....C4
Utiel 9,168 ....F3
Utrera 28,287 ....D4
Valdemoro 6,263 ....F4
Valdepeñas 24,018 ....E3
Valencia 626,675 ....F3
Valencia‡ 700,000 ....F3
Valencia de Alcántara 5,963 ......C3
Valladolid 227,511 ....D2
Vall de Uxó 23,976 ....F3
Vallecas G4
Valls 14,189 ....G2
Valverde del Camino 10,566 ....C4
Vejer de la Frontera 6,184 ....C4
Vélez-Málaga 20,794 ....D4
Vendrell 7,951 ....G2
Vera 4,903 ....F4
Vergara 11,541 ....E1
Vicálvaro G4
Vich 23,449 ....H2
Vilafranca del
  Penedés 16,875 ....G2
Villacañas 9,883 ....E3
Villacarrillo 9,452 ....E3
Villafranca de los

Barros 12,610 ....C3
Villagarcla 6,601 ....B1
Villajoyosa 12,573 ....F3
Villanueva de Córdoba 11,270 .....D3
Villanueva del Arzobispo 8,076 ...E3
Villanueva de la Serena 16,687 ...D3
Villanueva de los
  Infantes 8,154 ....E3
Villanueva y Geltrú 35,714 ....G2
Villarreal de los
  Infantes 29,482 ....F3
Villarrobledo 19,698 ....E3
Villarrubia de los Ojos 9,144 ....E3
Villaverde G4
Villena 23,483 ....F3
Vinaroz 13,727 ....G2
Vitoria 124,791 ....E1
Yecla 19,352 ....F3
Zafra 11,583 ....C3
Zalamea de la Serena 6,017 ....D3
Zamora 48,791 ....D2
Zaragoza (Saragossa) 449,319 .....F2

OTHER FEATURES

Alborán (isl.) E5
Alcaraz, Sierra de (range) E3
Alcudia (bay) H3
Almanzor (mt.) D2
Almanzora (riv.) F4
Andalusia (reg.) D4
Aneto (peak) G1
Aragón (reg.) F2
Arosa, Ria de (est.) B1
Asturias (reg.) C1
Balaitous (mt.) F1
Balearic Islands
  (isls.) H3
Barbate (riv.) D4
Biscay (bay) D1
Cabrera (isl.) H3
Cádiz (Gulf) C4
Cala Burras (pt.) D4
Canary (isls.) B4
Cantabrian (range) C1
Catalonia (reg.) G2

Cinca (riv.) G2
Columbretes (isls.) G3
Costa Brava (reg.) H2
Costa de Sola (Costa del Sol)
  (reg.) D4
Creus (cape) H1
Cuenca, Sierra de (range) F3
Demanda, Sierra de la (range) E1
Douro (riv.) C2
Duero (Douro) (riv.) C2
Ebro (riv.) G2
Eresma (riv.) D2
Esla (riv.) D2
Estats (peak) G1
Estremadura (reg.) C3
Finisterre (cape) B1
Formentera (isl.) H3
Formentor (cape) H2
Fuerteventura (isl.) C4
Galicia (reg.) B1
Gata (cape) F4
Gata (mts.) C2
Genil (riv.) D4
Gibraltar (str.) D5
Gomera (isl.) B5
Gran Canaria (isl.) B5
Gredos, Sierra de (range) D2
Guadalimar (riv.) E3
Guadalquivir (riv.) C4
Guadarrama, Sierra de (range) D2
Guadarrama (riv.) F4
Guadiana (riv.) D3
Gúdar, Sierra de (range) F2
Henares (riv.) G4
Hierro (isl.) A5
Ibiza (isl.) G3
Jalón (riv.) E2
Jarama (riv.) F4
Júcar (riv.) F3
Lanzarote (isl.) C4
La Palma (isl.) A4
León (reg.) C1
Llobregat (riv.) H2
Majorca (isl.) H3
Mallorca (Majorca)
  (isl.) H3

Mancha, La (reg.) E3
Manzanares (riv.) F4
Marismas, Las (marsh) C4
Mar Menor (lag.) F4
Mayor (cape) E1
Menorca (Minorca) (isl.) J2
Miño (riv.) B1
Minorca (isl.) J2
Moncayo, Sierra de (range) F2
Montserrat (mt.) G2
Morena, Sierra (range) E3
Mulhacén (mt.) E4
Murcia (reg.) F3
Nao (cape) G3
Navia (riv.) C1
Nevada, Sierra (mts.) E4
New Castile (reg.) E3
Odiel (riv.) C4
Old Castile (reg.) D2
Órbigo (riv.) D1
Palos (cape) F4
Peñalara (mt.) E2
Peñas (cape) D1
Peña Vieja (mt.) D1
Peníbética, Sistema (range) E4
Perdido (mt.) G1
Pyrenees (range) F1

Rosas (gulf) H1
San Jorge (gulf) G2
Segura (riv.) F3
Sil (riv.) C1
Tagus (riv.) D3
Tajo (Tagus) (riv.) D3
Teide, Pico de (peak) B5
Tenerife (isl.) B5
Ter (riv.) H1
Tinto (riv.) C4
Toledo (mts.) E3
Tortosa (cape) G3
Trafalgar (cape) C4
Turia (riv.) F3
Urgel, Llanos de (plain) G2
Valencia (gulf) G3
Valencia (reg.) F3
Valencia, Albufera de (lag.) G3
Vascongadas (reg.) E1

CITIES and TOWNS

PORTUGAL

DISTRICTS

Aveiro 545,230 ....B2

Beja 204,440 ....C3
Braga 609,415 ....B2
Bragança 180,395 ....C2
Castelo Branco 254,355 ....C3
Coimbra 399,380 ....B2
Évora 178,475 ....C3
Faro 268,040 ....B4
Funchal 251,135 ....A2
Guarda 210,720 ....C2
Leiria 376,940 ....B3
Lisbon 1,568,020 ....A1
Oporto (Porto) 1,309,560 ....B2
Portalegre 145,545 ....C3
Porto 1,309,560 ....B2
Santarém 427,995 ....B3
Setúbal 469,555 ....B3
Viana do Castelo 250,510 ....B2
Vila Real 265,605 ....C2
Viseu 410,795 ....C2

CITIES and TOWNS

PORTUGAL

Abrantes 11,775 ....B3
Águeda 9,343 ....B2
Albufeira 7,479 ....B4
Alcácer do Sal 13,187 ....B3
Alcântara 23,699 ....A1

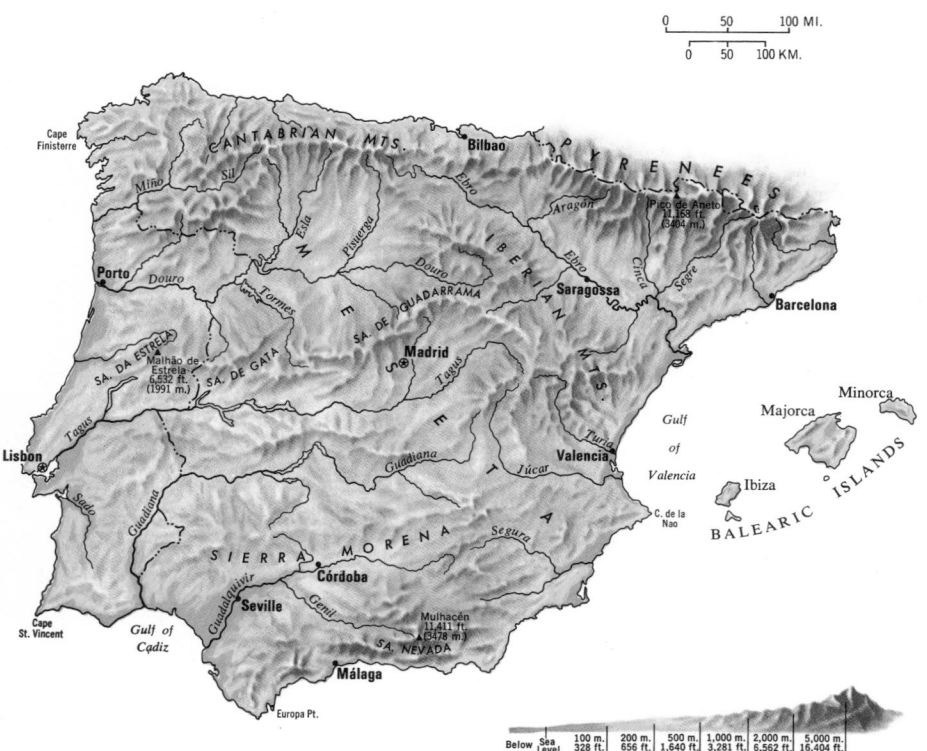

Topography

0   50   100 MI.

0   50   100 KM.

| Below Sea Level | 100 m. 328 ft. | 200 m. 656 ft. | 500 m. 1,640 ft. | 1,000 m. 3,281 ft. | 2,000 m. 6,562 ft. | 5,000 m. 16,404 ft. |

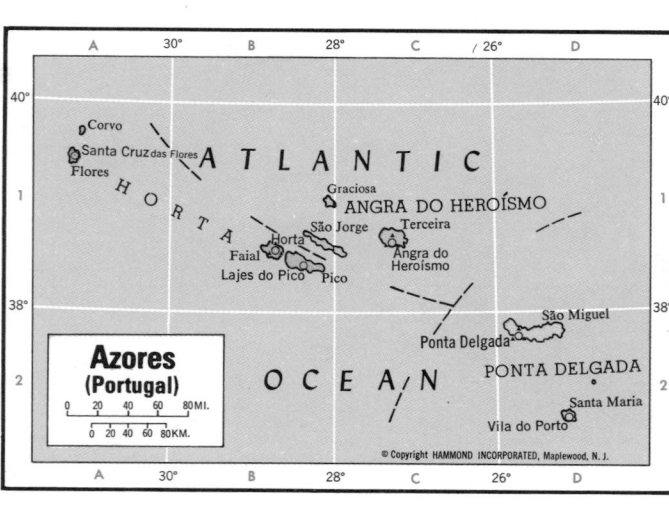

Azores
(Portugal)

0 20 40 60 80 MI.

0 20 40 60 80 KM.

© Copyright HAMMOND INCORPORATED, Maplewood, N.J.

AZORES

INTERNAL DIVISIONS

Angra do Heroísmo
  (dist.) 83,500 ....C1
Horta (dist.) 38,700 ....A1
Ponta Delgada (dist.) 153,700 ....D2

CITIES and TOWNS

Angra do Heroísmo 13,795 ....C1
Horta 6,145 ....B1
Lajes do Pico 2,147 ....B1
Ponta Delgada 20,195 ....C2
Santa Cruz das Flores 1,880 ......A1
Vila do Porto 4,149 ....D2

OTHER FEATURES

Azores (isls.) A2
Corvo (isl.) B1
Faial (isl.) B1
Flores (isl.) A1
Graciosa (isl.) C1
Pico (isl.) C1
Santa Maria (isl.) D2
São Jorge (isl.) B1
São Miguel (isl.) C2
Terceira (isl.) C1

PORTUGAL is divided for administrative purposes into 22 districts bearing the same names as their respective capitals.

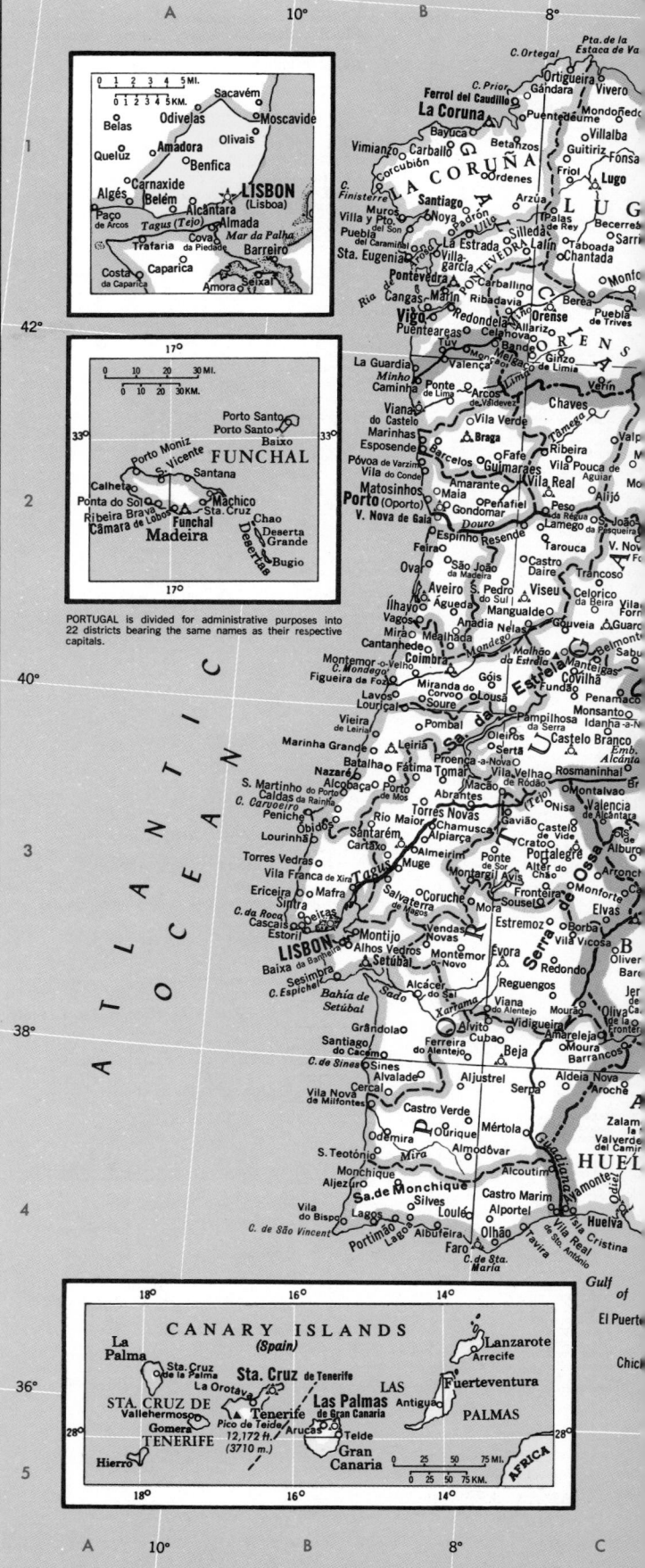

Alcobaça 4,799 ....B3
Aldeia Nova de São
 Bento 5,228 ....C4
Algés 18,010 ....A1
Alhos Vedros 7,915 ....B3
Aljustrel 7,473 ....B4
Almada 38,990 ....A1
Almeirim 8,780 ....B3
Alpiarça 7,623 ....B3
Alportel 7,632 ....C2
Amadora 65,870 ....A1
Amarante 6,067 ....B2
Amora 10,330 ....A1
Aveiro 19,905 ....B2
Avis 1,686 ....C3
Baixa da Banheira 18,550 ....B3
Barreiro 53,690 ....B1
Batalha 6,673 ....B3
Beja 14,760 ....B4
Belas 12,001 ....A1
Belém 19,043 ....A1
Benfica 39,459 ....A1
Borba 4,879 ....C3
Braga 48,735 ....B2
Bragança 9,310 ....C2
Caldas da Rainha 13,070 ....B3
Câmara de Lobos 14,068 ....A2

Campo Maior 7,405 ....C3
Cantanhede 6,734 ....B2
Caparica 13,315 ....A1
Carnaxide 38,309 ....A1
Cartaxo 6,628 ....B3
Cascais 14,925 ....B3
Castelo Branco 18,740 ....C3
Cercal 5,021 ....B4
Chaves 11,465 ....C2
Coimbra 55,985 ....B2
Coruche 17,461 ....B3
Cova da Piedade 21,000 ....A1
Covilhã 26,530 ....C2
Elvas 10,305 ....C3
Espinho 11,745 ....B2
Estoril 15,740 ....A1
Estremoz 9,565 ....C3
Évora 23,665 ....C3
Fafe 8,142 ....B2
Faro 20,470 ....B4
Fátima 6,433 ....B3
Feira 5,222 ....B2
Ferreira do Alentejo 6,153 ....B4
Figueira da Foz 10,485 ....B2
Funchal 38,340 ....A2
Fundão 5,081 ....C2
Gondomar 14,105 ....B2

Grândola 9,698 ....B3
Guarda 9,735 ....C2
Guimarães 24,280 ....B2
Ílhavo 11,083 ....B2
Lagoa 5,694 ....B4
Lagos 10,359 ....B4
Lamego 10,350 ....C2
Lavos 5,051 ....B2
Leiria 7,540 ....B3
Lisboa (Lisbon) (cap.) 769,410 ....A1
Lisbon‡ 1,100,000 ....A1
Loulé 12,777 ....B4
Lourical 6,087 ....B3
Lourinhã 7,340 ....B3
Lousã 7,341 ....B2
Machico 10,905 ....A2
Mafra 7,149 ....B3
Manguade 4,839 ....C2
Marinha Grande 18,548 ....B3
Matosinhos 22,505 ....B2
Mêda 4,760 ....C2
Mirandela 5,203 ....C2
Monchique 8,566 ....B4
Montemor-o-Novo 9,284 ....B3
Montijo 26,730 ....B3
Moscavide 21,765 ....A1

Moura 9,351 ....C3
Nazaré 8,553 ....B3
Odemira 6,793 ....B4
Odivelas 26,020 ....A1
Oeiras 14,880 ....A1
Olhão 11,155 ....C4
Olivais 55,138 ....A1
Oporto (Porto) 300,925 ....B2
Ovar 16,004 ....B2
Paço de Arcos 11,791 ....A1
Penafiel 6,463 ....B2
Peniche 12,555 ....B3
Peso da Régua 5,376 ....C2
Pombal 12,508 ....B3
Ponta do Sol 5,599 ....A2
Ponte de Sor 9,951 ....C3
Portalegre 10,970 ....C3
Portimão 10,300 ....B4
Porto 300,925 ....B2
Póvoa de Varzim 17,415 ....B2
Proença-a-Nova 4,792 ....B3
Queluz 25,845 ....A1
Redondo 6,858 ....C3
Reguengos de Monsaraz 5,806 ....C3
Ribeira Brava 7,416 ....A2
Rio Maior 10,206 ....B3
Sacavém 12,625 ....A1

Salvaterra de Magos 6,265 ....B3
Santa Cruz 6,348 ....A2
Santarém 16,850 ....B3
Santiago do Cacem 5,887 ....B3
São Brás de Alportel
 (Alportel) 7,632 ....C4
São João da Madeira 14,225 ....B2
São Teotónio 6,146 ....B4
São Vicente 5,147 ....A2
Serta 7,991 ....B3
Sesimbra 16,614 ....B3
Setúbal 49,670 ....B3
Silves 9,493 ....B4
Sines 6,996 ....B3
Sintra 15,994 ....B3
Sovre 7,620 ....C2
Tavira 10,263 ....C4
Tomar 10,905 ....B3
Torres Novas 13,806 ....B3
Torres Vedras 14,833 ....B3
Trafaria 6,145 ....A1
Vagos 5,802 ....B2
Vendas Novas 8,979 ....B3
Viana do Castelo 12,510 ....B2
Vila de Conde 16,485 ....B2
Vila Franca de Xira 13,070 ....B3

Vila Nova de Gaia
 Gaia 50,805 ....B2
Vila Real Real 10,050 ....C2
Vila Real de Santo
 Antonio 10,320 ....C4
Viseu 16,140 ....B2

OTHER FEATURES

Atlantic Ocean A3
Carvoeiroeiro (cape) A3
Desertartas (isls.) A2
Douro (riv.) B2
Espichel (cape) A3
Estrela, Serra da (mts.) C2
Guadiana (riv.) B4
Lima (riv.) B2
Madeira (isls.) A2
Madeira (isls.) B2
Minho (riv.) B1
Mira (riv.) B4
Monchique, Serra de (mts.) B4
Mondego (riv.) B2
Ossa, Serra da (mts.) C3
Porto Santo (isl.) B2
Roca (cape) B3

Sadu (riv.) B3
São Vincent (cape) B4
Santa Marla (cape) C4
Setúbal (bay) B3
Tagus (riv.) B3
Tâmega (riv.) C2
Tejo (Tagus) (riv.) B3
Xarrama (riv.) B3

ANDORRA

CITIES and TOWNS

Andorra la Vella (cap.) 12,000 ....G1

GIBRALTAR

Gibraltar 29,760 ....D4

PHYSICAL FEATURES

Europa (pt.) D4

‡Population of metropolitan area.

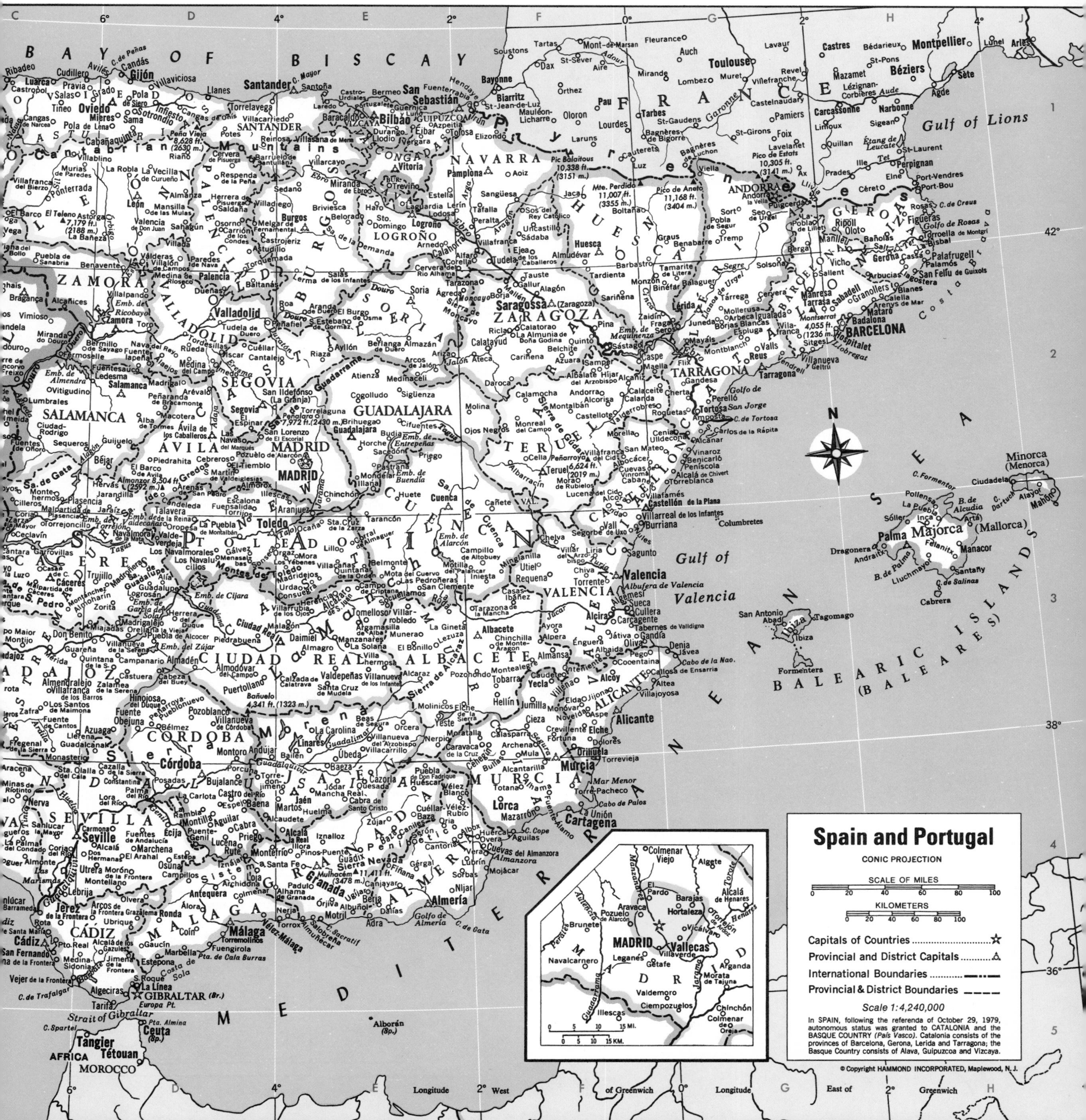

© Copyright HAMMOND INCORPORATED, Maplewood, N.J.

Spain and Portugal

CONIC PROJECTION

SCALE OF MILES
0 20 40 60 80 100

KILOMETERS
0 20 40 60 80 100

Capitals of Countries ....☆
Provincial and District Capitals ....△
International Boundaries ....
Provincial & District Boundaries ___ ___

Scale 1:4,240,000

In SPAIN, following the referenda of October 29, 1979, autonomous status was granted to CATALONIA and the BASQUE COUNTRY (País Vasco). Catalonia consists of the provinces of Barcelona, Gerona, Lerida and Tarragona; the Basque Country consists of Alava, Guipuzcoa and Vizcaya.

Italy

CONIC PROJECTION

SCALE OF MILES

0 20 40 60 80 100

SCALE OF KILOMETERS

0 20 40 60 80 100

Capitals of Countries	☆
Regional Capitals	⬡
Provincial Capitals	△
International Boundaries	— · · — · · —
Regional Boundaries	— · — · —

Scale 1: 4,710,000

The regions are subdivided into provinces bearing the same names as their respective capitals, except:

PROVINCE	CAPITAL
MASSA-CARRARA	Massa
PESARO-URBINO	Pesaro

Vatican City

SCALE

0 300 600

Rome and Environs

0 5 10 15M.

0 5 10 15KM.

© Copyright HAMMOND INCORPORATED, Maplewood, N.J.

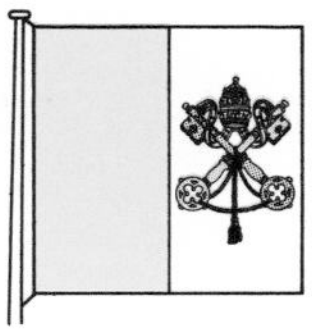

VATICAN CITY

AREA 108.7 acres (44 hectares)
POPULATION 728

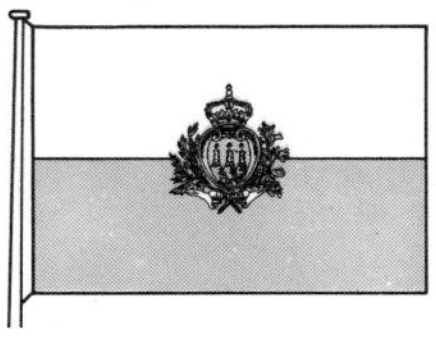

SAN MARINO

AREA 23.4 sq. mi. (60.6 sq. km.)
POPULATION 19,149

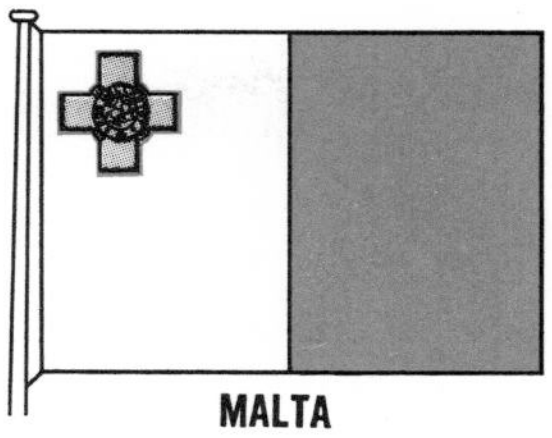

MALTA

AREA 122 sq. mi. (316 sq. km.)
POPULATION 343,970
CAPITAL Valletta
LARGEST CITY Sliema
HIGHEST POINT 787 ft. (240 m.)
MONETARY UNIT Maltese pound
MAJOR LANGUAGES Maltese, English
MAJOR RELIGION Roman Catholicism

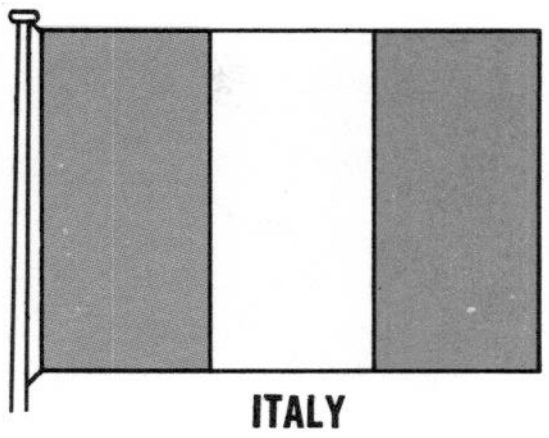

ITALY

AREA 116,303 sq. mi. (301,225 sq. km.)
POPULATION 57,140,000
CAPITAL Rome
LARGEST CITY Rome
HIGHEST POINT Dufourspitze (Mte. Rosa) 15,203 ft. (4,634 m.)
MONETARY UNIT lira
MAJOR LANGUAGE Italian
MAJOR RELIGION Roman Catholicism

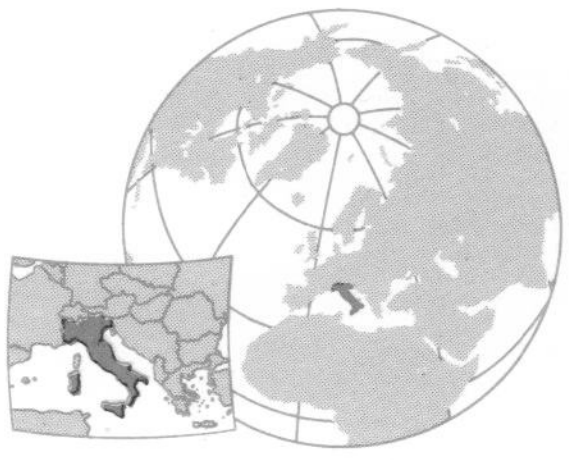

ITALY

REGIONS

Abruzzi 1,166,664 ..... D3
Aosta 109,150 ..... A2
Apulia (Puglia) 3,582,787 ..... F4
Basilicata 603,064 ..... F4
Calabria 1,988,051 ..... F5
Campania 5,059,348 ..... E4
Emilia-Romagna 3,846,755 ..... C2
Friuli-Venezia Giulia 1,213,532 ..... D1
Latium (Lazio) 4,689,482 ..... D3
Liguria 1,853,578 ..... B2
Lombardy 8,543,657 ..... B2
Marche 1,359,907 ..... D3
Molise 319,807 ..... E4
Piedmont 4,432,313 ..... A2
Sardinia 1,473,800 ..... B4
Sicily 4,680,715 ..... D6
Trentino-Alto Adige 841,886 ..... C1
Tuscany 3,473,097 ..... C3
Umbria 775,783 ..... D3
Veneto 2,109,502 ..... D3

PROVINCES

Agrigento 454,045 ..... D6
Alessandria 483,183 ..... B2
Ancona 416,611 ..... D3
Aosta 109,150 ..... A2
Arezzo 306,340 ..... C3
Ascoli Piceno 340,758 ..... D3
Asti 218,547 ..... B2
Avellino 427,509 ..... E4
Bari 1,351,288 ..... F4
Belluno 221,155 ..... D1
Benevento 286,499 ..... E4
Bergamo 829,019 ..... B2
Bologna 918,844 ..... C2
Bolzano-Bozen 414,041 ..... C1
Brescia 957,686 ..... C2
Brindisi 366,027 ..... G4
Cagliari 802,888 ..... B5
Caltanissetta 282,069 ..... D6
Campobasso 227,641 ..... E4
Caserta 677,959 ..... E4
Catania 938,273 ..... E6
Catanzaro 718,069 ..... F5
Chieti 351,567 ..... E3
Como 720,463 ..... B2
Cosenza 691,659 ..... F5
Cremona 334,281 ..... B2
Cuneo 540,504 ..... A2
Enna 202,131 ..... E6
Ferrara 383,639 ..... C2
Florence 1,146,367 ..... C3
Foggia 657,292 ..... E4
Forlì 565,470 ..... D2
Frosinone 422,630 ..... D4
Genoa 1,087,973 ..... B2
Gorizia 142,412 ..... D2
Grosseto 216,315 ..... C3
Imperia 225,127 ..... B3
Isernia 92,166 ..... E4
L'Aquila 293,066 ..... D3
La Spezia 244,435 ..... B2
Latina 376,238 ..... D4
Lecce 696,503 ..... G4
Leghorn 335,265 ..... C3
Lucca 380,356 ..... C3
Macerata 286,155 ..... D3
Mantua 376,892 ..... C2
Massa-Carrara 200,955 ..... C2
Matera 194,629 ..... F4
Messina 654,703 ..... E5
Milan 3,903,685 ..... B2
Modena 553,852 ..... C2
Naples 2,709,929 ..... E4
Novara 496,811 ..... B2
Nuoro 273,021 ..... B4
Padua 762,998 ..... C2
Palermo 1,124,015 ..... D5
Parma 395,497 ..... C2
Pavia 526,389 ..... B2
Perugia 552,936 ..... D3
Pesaro e Urbino 316,383 ..... D3
Pescara 264,981 ..... E3
Piacenza 284,881 ..... B2
Pisa 375,933 ..... C3
Pistoia 254,335 ..... C2
Pordenone 253,906 ..... D2
Potenza 408,435 ..... E4
Ragusa 255,047 ..... E6
Ravenna 351,876 ..... D2
Reggio di Calabria 578,323 ..... E5
Reggio nell'Emilia 392,696 ..... C2
Rieti 143,162 ..... D3
Rome 3,490,377 ..... F6
Rovigo 251,908 ..... C2
Salerno 957,452 ..... E4
Sassari 397,891 ..... B4
Savona 296,043 ..... B2
Siena 257,221 ..... C3
Sondrio 169,149 ..... B1
Syracuse 365,039 ..... E6
Taranto 511,677 ..... F4
Teramo 257,080 ..... D3
Terni 222,847 ..... D3
Trapani 405,393 ..... D5
Trento 427,845 ..... C1
Treviso 668,620 ..... D2
Trieste 300,304 ..... E2
Turin 2,287,016 ..... A2
Udine 516,910 ..... D1
Varese 725,823 ..... B2
Venice 807,251 ..... D2
Vercelli 406,252 ..... B2
Verona 733,595 ..... C2
Vicenza 677,884 ..... C2
Viterbo 257,075 ..... C3

CITIES and TOWNS

Acireale 34,081 ..... E6
Acqui Terme 20,099 ..... B2
Acri 8,150 ..... F5
Adrano 31,988 ..... E6
Adria 11,951 ..... D2
Agira 11,262 ..... E6
Agnone 3,965 ..... E4
Agrigento 40,513 ..... D6
Agropoli 9,413 ..... E4
Alassio 13,512 ..... A2
Alatri 5,710 ..... D4
Alba 23,522 ..... B2
Albano Laziale 15,561 ..... F7
Albenga 13,397 ..... B3
Albino 8,837 ..... B2
Alcamo 41,448 ..... D6
Alessandria 78,644 ..... B2
Alghero 28,454 ..... B4
Altamura 44,879 ..... F4
Amalfi 4,205 ..... E4
Amantea 6,132 ..... E5
Amelia 4,331 ..... D3
Ancona 88,427 ..... D3
Andria 76,405 ..... F4
Anguillara Sabazia 3,241 ..... F6
Anzio 14,966 ..... D4
Aosta 35,053 ..... A2
Aprilia 18,412 ..... D4
Aragona 11,213 ..... D6
Arezzo 56,693 ..... C3
Argenta 6,682 ..... D2
Ariano Irpino 9,796 ..... E4
Ariccia 7,287 ..... F7
Artena 5,034 ..... F7
Ascoli Piceno 43,041 ..... D3
Assisi 4,630 ..... D3
Asti 62,277 ..... B2
Atessa 3,079 ..... E3
Atri 4,686 ..... D3
Augusta 32,501 ..... E6
Avellino 44,750 ..... E4
Aversa 46,536 ..... E4
Avezzano 26,456 ..... D3
Avigliano 5,400 ..... E4
Avola 29,089 ..... E6
Bagheria 32,465 ..... D5
Barcellona Pozzo di Gotto 25,280 ..... E5
Bari 339,110 ..... F4
Barletta 75,116 ..... F4
Bassano del Grappa 33,002 ..... C2
Bellagio 3,258 ..... B2
Belluno 22,180 ..... D1
Benevento 48,523 ..... E4
Bergamo 127,553 ..... B2
Biancavilla 18,743 ..... E6
Biella 46,453 ..... B2
Bisceglie 45,014 ..... F4
Bitonto 39,714 ..... F4
Bitti 4,606 ..... B4
Bologna 493,282 ..... C2
Bolzano (Bolzen) 102,806 ..... C1
Bondeno 7,451 ..... C2
Bonorva 5,232 ..... B4
Bordighera 8,994 ..... A3
Borgo 4,013 ..... C1
Borgomanero 16,655 ..... B2
Bórgo San Lorenzo 7,699 ..... C2
Bosa 8,045 ..... B4
Boves 3,896 ..... A2
Bra 18,399 ..... A2
Bracciano 7,681 ..... C3
Brescia 189,092 ..... C2
Bressanone 12,261 ..... C1
Brindisi 76,612 ..... G4
Bronte 17,823 ..... E6
Brunico 5,175 ..... D1
Budrio 5,635 ..... C2
Busto Arsizio 72,400 ..... B2
Cagli 4,356 ..... D3
Cagliari 211,015 ..... B5
Caltagirone 34,444 ..... E6
Caltanissetta 52,838 ..... D6
Camaiore 8,578 ..... C3
Camerino 4,644 ..... D3
Campobasso 35,551 ..... E4
Campo Tures 1,325 ..... C1
Canicatti 28,761 ..... E6
Canosa di Puglia 30,263 ..... E4
Cantù 28,617 ..... B2
Capua 13,938 ..... E4
Caravaggio 11,298 ..... B2
Carbonia 23,031 ..... B5
Carini 14,255 ..... D5
Carloforte 6,671 ..... B5
Carmagnola 16,469 ..... A2
Carpi 41,789 ..... C2
Carrara 56,236 ..... C2
Casale Monferrato 35,156 ..... B2
Casalmaggiore 6,374 ..... C2
Cascina-Navacchio 28,263 ..... C3
Caserta 51,621 ..... E4
Cassano allo Ionio 9,661 ..... F5
Cassino 14,747 ..... D4
Castelfranco Veneto 16,042 ..... D2
Castel Gandolfo 2,965 ..... F7
Castellammare del Golfo 13,144 ..... D5
Castellammare di Stabia 64,341 ..... E4
Castel San Pietro Terme 6,985 ..... C2
Castelvetrano 29,167 ..... D6
Castiglion Fiorentino 3,797 ..... C3
Castrovillari 15,207 ..... F5
Catania 403,390 ..... E6
Catanzaro 52,054 ..... F5
Caulonia 3,402 ..... F5
Cava de'Tirreni 33,868 ..... E4
Cavarzere 7,917 ..... D2
Cecina 19,415 ..... C3
Cefalù 11,043 ..... E5
Ceglie Messapico 17,512 ..... F4
Celano 9,531 ..... D3
Cerignola 44,648 ..... E4
Cernobbio 8,026 ..... B2
Cerveteri 5,239 ..... E6
Cesano 2,883 ..... F6
Cesena 49,915 ..... D2
Cesenatico 12,805 ..... D2
Chiari 12,017 ..... C2
Chiavari 29,950 ..... B2
Chieri 27,548 ..... A2
Chieti 31,895 ..... E3
Chioggia 24,044 ..... D2
Chivasso 21,369 ..... A2
Ciampino 36,728 ..... F7
Cittadella 9,321 ..... C2
Città di Castello 18,880 ..... C3
Cittanova 11,045 ..... F5
Cividale del Friuli 8,345 ..... D1
Civitavecchia 41,305 ..... C3
Clusone-Fiorine 6,428 ..... C2
Codroipo 6,117 ..... D2
Colle di Val d'Elsa 8,657 ..... C3
Comacchio 10,437 ..... D2
Comiso 24,508 ..... E6
Como 73,257 ..... B2
Conegliano 28,635 ..... D2
Conversano 16,805 ..... F4
Corato 38,163 ..... F4
Cori 6,829 ..... F7
Corigliano Calabro 14,518 ..... F5
Corleone 11,057 ..... D6
Correggio 11,415 ..... C2
Cortina d'Ampezzo 7,285 ..... D1
Cortona 3,482 ..... C3
Cosenza 94,565 ..... F5
Courmayeur 1,401 ..... A2
Crema 26,061 ..... B2
Cremona 75,988 ..... B2
Crotone 44,081 ..... F5
Cuneo 41,633 ..... A2
Cuorgnè 6,752 ..... A2
Desenzano del Garda 14,624 ..... C2
Diano Marina 6,001 ..... B3
Domodossola 18,562 ..... A1
Dorgali 6,714 ..... B4
Eboli 19,787 ..... E4
Edolo 3,707 ..... C1
Empoli 30,526 ..... C3
Enna 27,351 ..... E6
Este 12,992 ..... C2
Fabriano 18,355 ..... D3
Faenza 36,241 ..... D2
Fano 31,238 ..... D3
Fasano 21,247 ..... F4
Favara 27,940 ..... D6
Feltre 11,806 ..... C1
Fermo 17,521 ..... D3
Ferrandina 8,372 ..... F4
Ferrara 97,507 ..... C2
Fidenza 18,064 ..... B2
Fiesole 3,772 ..... C3
Finale Emilia 7,474 ..... C2
Finale Ligure 11,461 ..... B2
Firenze (Florence) 441,654 ..... C3
Fiumicino 13,180 ..... F7
Florence 441,654 ..... C3
Floridia 16,562 ..... E6
Foggia 136,436 ..... E4
Foligno 26,887 ..... D3
Fondi 16,472 ..... D4
Forlì 83,303 ..... D2
Formia 18,978 ..... D4
Fossano 15,857 ..... A2
Fossombrone 5,882 ..... D3
Francavilla Fontana 30,347 ..... F4
Frascati 14,217 ..... F7
Frosinone 34,066 ..... D4
Gaeta 21,973 ..... D4
Galatina 22,137 ..... G4
Galatone 13,880 ..... F4
Gallarate 43,773 ..... B2
Gallipoli 16,878 ..... F4
Garessio 3,359 ..... A2
Gela 66,845 ..... E6
Gemona 6,863 ..... D1
Genoa 787,011 ..... B2
Genova (Genoa) 787,011 ..... B2
Genzano di Roma 14,147 ..... F7
Giarre 18,233 ..... E6
Gioia del Colle 23,299 ..... F4
Gioiosa Ionica 3,811 ..... F5
Giovinazzo 17,768 ..... F4
Giulianova 17,926 ..... E3
Gorizia 35,912 ..... D2
Gravina in Puglia 32,006 ..... F4
Grosseto 48,309 ..... C3
Grottaferrata 10,639 ..... F7
Grottaglie 23,556 ..... F4
Guardiagrele 4,122 ..... E3
Guastalla 7,639 ..... C2
Gubbio 12,371 ..... D3
Guidonia 8,413 ..... F6
Iglesias 24,472 ..... B5
Imola 42,111 ..... C2
Imperia 37,585 ..... B3
Isernia 12,290 ..... E4
Ivrea 26,530 ..... B2
Jesi 33,011 ..... D3
Ladispoli 6,625 ..... E6
Lagonegro 5,613 ..... E4
La Maddalena 10,405 ..... B4
Lanciano 19,652 ..... E3
Lanusei 5,508 ..... B5
Lanuvio 2,970 ..... F7
L'Aquila 36,233 ..... D3
Larino 5,166 ..... E4
La Spezia 121,254 ..... B2
Latina 53,003 ..... D4
Lauria 4,927 ..... E4
Lavello 11,486 ..... E4
Lecce 80,114 ..... G4
Lecco 53,165 ..... B2
Leghorn 170,369 ..... C3
Legnago 15,534 ..... C2
Lendinara 7,079 ..... C2
Lentini 31,429 ..... E6
Leonforte 16,317 ..... E6
Lerici 5,407 ..... B2
Licata 40,997 ..... D6
Lido di Ostia 61,492 ..... F7
Lido di Venezia 18,794 ..... D2
Lipari 3,886 ..... E5
Livigno 2,135 ..... C1
Livorno (Leghorn) 170,369 ..... C3
Lodi 42,489 ..... B2
Lonigo 6,368 ..... C2
Lucca 54,280 ..... C3
Lucera 29,355 ..... E4
Lugo 19,497 ..... D2
Macerata 33,470 ..... D3
Macomer 9,433 ..... B4
Maglie 13,326 ..... G4
Manduria 25,194 ..... F4
Manfredonia 44,463 ..... F4
Mantua 59,529 ..... C2
Marino 12,135 ..... F7
Marsala 34,150 ..... D6
Marsciano 5,372 ..... D3
Martina Franca 31,811 ..... F4
Massa 56,591 ..... C2
Massafra 22,610 ..... F4
Massa Marittima 6,438 ..... C3
Matera 43,026 ..... F4
Mazara del Vallo 37,441 ..... D6
Mazzarino 14,981 ..... E6
Melfi 13,355 ..... E4
Menfi 12,386 ..... D6
Merano 30,951 ..... C1
Mesagne 26,955 ..... G4
Messina 203,937 ..... E5
Mestre 184,818 ..... D2
Milan 1,724,557 ..... B2
Milazzo 18,576 ..... E5
Minturno 2,428 ..... D4
Mirandola 11,551 ..... C2
Mira Taglio 10,194 ..... D2
Mistretta 6,631 ..... E6
Modena 149,029 ..... C2
Modica 31,074 ..... E6
Mola di Bari 23,778 ..... F4
Molfetta 63,250 ..... F4
Moncalieri 49,953 ..... A2
Mondovì Breo 12,524 ..... A2
Monfalcone 29,589 ..... D2
Monopoli 29,776 ..... F4
Monreale 19,348 ..... D5
Monselice 9,047 ..... C2
Montalto Uffugo 3,173 ..... E5
Montebelluna 9,573 ..... D2
Montefiascone 6,885 ..... D3
Montepulciano 4,069 ..... C3
Monterotondo 15,869 ..... F6
Monte Sant'Angelo 17,756 ..... F4
Montevarchi 16,849 ..... C3
Monza 110,735 ..... B2
Mortara 13,929 ..... B2
Naples 1,214,775 ..... E4
Nardò 24,142 ..... F4
Narni 6,213 ..... D3
Naro 13,171 ..... D6
Nettuno 20,927 ..... D4
Nicastro 27,206 ..... F5
Nicosia 13,982 ..... E6
Niscemi 23,925 ..... E6
Nizza Monferrato 7,532 ..... B2
Nocera Inferiore 44,415 ..... E4
Noto 21,606 ..... E6
Novara 92,634 ..... B2
Novi Ligure 29,944 ..... B2
Nuoro 30,551 ..... B4
Olbia 20,998 ..... B4
Oliena 7,030 ..... B4
Orbetello 6,884 ..... C3
Oristano 20,966 ..... B5
Ortona 11,966 ..... E3
Orvieto 8,813 ..... D3
Osimo 12,034 ..... D3
Ostia Antica 2,583 ..... F7
Ostuni 27,241 ..... F4
Otranto 3,707 ..... G4
Ozieri 9,149 ..... B4
Pachino 20,427 ..... E6
Padua 210,950 ..... C2
Palazzolo Acreide 8,981 ..... E6
Palermo 556,374 ..... D5
Palestrina 9,239 ..... F7
Palma di Montechiaro 22,381 ..... D6
Palmi 14,405 ..... E5
Palombara Sabina 5,292 ..... F6
Pantelleria 3,116 ..... C6
Paola 11,330 ..... E5
Parma 151,967 ..... C2
Partanna 10,303 ..... D6
Partinico 25,447 ..... D6
Paterno 41,504 ..... E6
Patti 7,500 ..... E5
Pavia 80,639 ..... B2
Pavullo nel Frignano 5,026 ..... C2
Penne 5,889 ..... D3
Pergine Valsugana 6,248 ..... C1
Pergola 3,866 ..... D3
Perugia 65,975 ..... D3
Pesaro 72,104 ..... D3
Pescara 125,391 ..... E3
Pescia 9,918 ..... C3
Piacenza 100,001 ..... B2
Piazza Armerina 21,754 ..... E6
Pietrasanta 6,620 ..... B3
Pinerolo 33,935 ..... A2
Piombino 35,641 ..... C3
Piove di Sacco 7,035 ..... C2
Pisa 91,156 ..... C3
Pisticci 11,239 ..... F4
Pistoia 55,403 ..... C2
Poggibonsi 21,271 ..... C3
Pomezia 11,915 ..... F7
Pont Canavese 4,075 ..... A2
Pontecorvo 5,986 ..... D4
Pontinia 3,166 ..... D4
Pontremoli 5,222 ..... B2
Popoli 5,372 ..... E3
Pordenone 43,230 ..... D2
Portocivitanova 25,773 ..... D3
Porto Empedocle 15,986 ..... D6
Portoferraio 7,579 ..... C3
Portofino 720 ..... B2
Portogruaro 12,258 ..... D2
Portomaggiore 6,343 ..... C2
Porto Recanati 5,389 ..... D3
Porto Torres 15,422 ..... B4
Potenza 46,869 ..... E4
Pozzallo 12,199 ..... E6
Pozzuoli 53,546 ..... D4
Prato 108,385 ..... C3
Prima Porta 11,393 ..... F6
Priverno 9,950 ..... D4
Putignano 19,290 ..... F4
Quartu Sant'Elena 29,715 ..... B5
Ragusa 55,751 ..... E6
Rapallo 22,272 ..... B2
Ravenna 75,153 ..... D2
Recanati 10,176 ..... D3
Reggio di Calabria 110,291 ..... E5
Reggio nell'Emilia 102,337 ..... C2
Rho 39,206 ..... B2
Riesi 15,855 ..... E6
Rieti 26,775 ..... D3
Rimini 101,579 ..... D2
Rionero in Vulture 11,230 ..... E4
Riva del Garda 8,513 ..... C2
Roccastrada 2,629 ..... C3
Rome (cap.) 2,535,018 ..... F6
Ronciglione 5,900 ..... C3
Rossano 12,119 ..... F5
Rovereto 26,827 ..... C2
Rovigo 31,124 ..... C2
Ruvo di Puglia 23,133 ..... F4

(continued on following page)

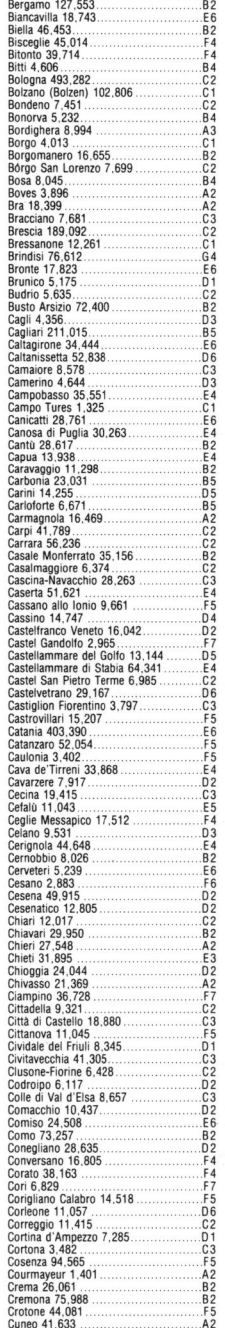

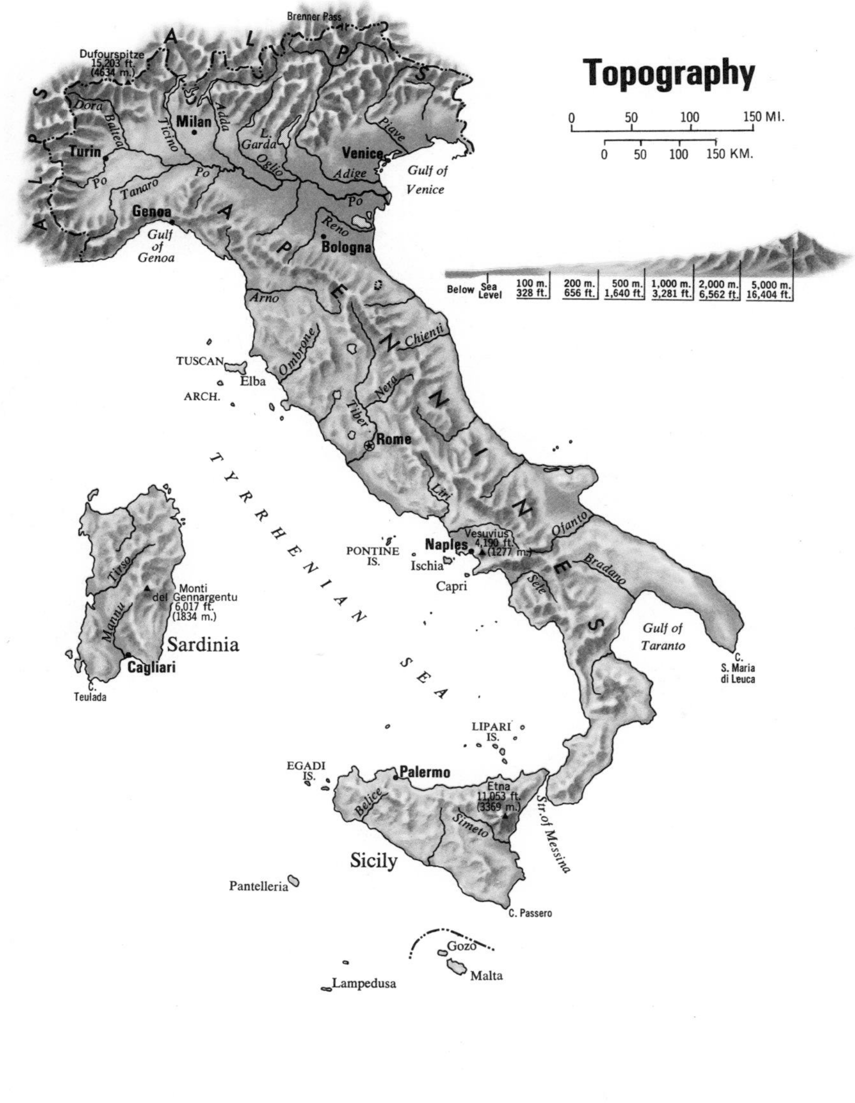
Topography
0 50 100 150 MI.
0 50 100 150 KM.
Below Sea Level
100 m. 328 ft.
200 m. 656 ft.
500 m. 1,640 ft.
1,000 m. 3,281 ft.
2,000 m. 6,562 ft.
5,000 m. 16,404 ft.
Brenner Pass
Dufourspitze 15,203 ft. (4634 m.)
A L P S
Dora Baltea
Milan
Adda
Ticino
Garda
Oglio
Piave
Venice
Adige
Gulf of Venice
Turin
Po
Tanaro
Genoa
Gulf of Genoa
Reno
Bologna
A P E N N I N E S
Arno
Chienti
Ombrone
Tiber
Nera
Rome
TUSCAN ARCH.
Elba
T Y R R H E N I A N S E A
Liri
PONTINE IS.
Naples
Vesuvius 4,190 ft. (1277 m.)
Ischia
Capri
Ofanto
Bradano
Sele
Gulf of Taranto
C. S. Maria di Leuca
Tirso
Monti del Gennargentu 6,017 ft. (1834 m.)
Mannu
Sardinia
Cagliari
C. Teulada
LIPARI IS.
EGADI IS.
Palermo
Etna 11,053 ft. (3369 m.)
Belice
Simeto
Str. of Messina
Sicily
Pantelleria
C. Passero
Gozo
Malta
Lampedusa

(continued)

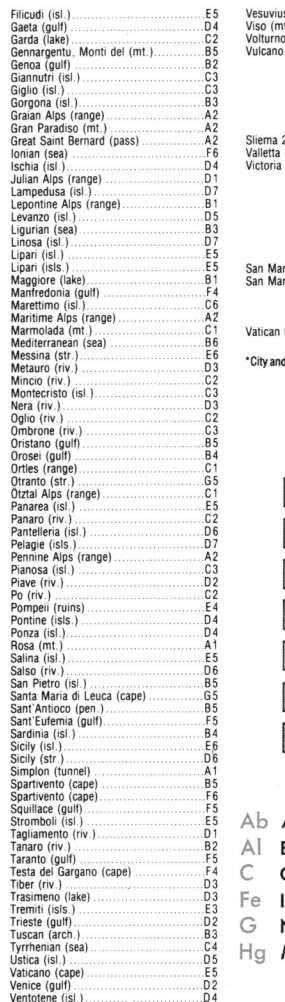

Sabaudia 4,501 .... D4
Saint Vincent 3,737 .... A2
Sala Consilina 8,177 .... E4
Salemi 10,180 .... D6
Salerno 146,534 .... E4
Salsomaggiore Terme 13,677 .... B2
Saluzzo 13,929 .... A2
Sambiase 10,567 .... F5
San Bartolomeo in Galdo 6,943 .... E4
San Benedetto del Tronto 40,108 .... E3
San Cataldo 19,609 .... D6
San Giovanni in Fiore 16,116 .... F5
San Giovanni in Persiceto 12,151 .... C2
San Marco in Lamis 15,817 .... E4
San Miniato 3,245 .... C3
Sannicandro Garganico 17,939 .... E4
San Remo 47,684 .... A3
Sansepolcro 11,443 .... C3
San Severino Marche 6,447 .... D3
San Severo 49,622 .... E4
Santa Maria Capua Vetere 31,077 .... E4
Sant'Elpidio a Mare 4,446 .... E3
Santeramo in Colle 19,758 .... F4
San Vito 3,901 .... B5
San Vito al Tagliamento 6,328 .... D2
San Vito dei Normanni 18,447 .... F4
San Vito Romano 3,256 .... F6
Saronno 32,477 .... B2
Sarroch 3,560 .... B5
Sassari 94,312 .... B4
Sassuolo 33,451 .... C2
Savigliano 14,036 .... A2
Savona 76,274 .... B2
Schio 27,890 .... C2
Sciacca 29,803 .... D6
Scicli 18,405 .... E6
Segni 7,193 .... F7
Senigallia 25,413 .... D3
Sesto Fiorentino 41,636 .... C3
Sestri Levante 18,331 .... B2
Settebagni 5,022 .... F6
Sezze 7,043 .... D4
Siderno 8,023 .... F5
Siena 56,539 .... C3
Siniscola 6,149 .... B4
Sinnai 8,499 .... B5
Siracusa (Syracuse) 93,006 .... E6
Sondrio 19,724 .... B1
Sora 14,031 .... D4
Soresina 9,300 .... C2
Sorrento 13,078 .... E4
Sorso 10,741 .... B4
Spoleto 18,013 .... D3
Squinzano 14,053 .... G4
Stresa 3,758 .... B2
Sulmona 18,221 .... D3
Susa 5,773 .... A2
Suzzara 12,013 .... C2
Syracuse 93,006 .... E6
Taormina 6,696 .... E6
Taranto 205,158 .... F4
Tarquinia 10,300 .... C3
Taurianova 12,198 .... E5
Tempio Pausania 10,382 .... B4
Teramo 31,163 .... D3
Termini Imerese 24,085 .... D6
Termoli 13,986 .... E3
Terni 75,873 .... D3
Terracina 24,092 .... D4
Terralba 8,551 .... B5
Tirano 7,413 .... C1
Tivoli 28,393 .... F6
Todi 5,705 .... D3
Tolentino 11,642 .... D3
Torino (Turin) 1,181,698 .... A2
Torre Annunziata 71,068 .... E4
Torre del Greco 74,752 .... E4
Torremaggiore 16;171 .... E4
Tortona 24,165 .... B2
Trani 40,508 .... F4
Trapani 90,305 .... D5
Trento 64,272 .... C1
Treviglio 21,920 .... B2
Treviso 87,447 .... D2
Tricase 10,481 .... G5
Trieste 257,259 .... E2
Trino 8,722 .... B2
Turin 1,181,698 .... A2
Udine 97,544 .... D2
Umbertide 6,640 .... D3
Urbino 7,735 .... D3
Valdagno 20,342 .... C2
Valenza 20,533 .... B2
Valmontone 6,543 .... F7
Varallo Pombia 3,118 .... B2
Varazze 11,676 .... B2
Varese 65,978 .... B2
Vasto 17,295 .... E3
Velletri 22,020 .... F7
Venafro 5,156 .... E4
Venezia (Venice) 108,082 .... D2
Venice 108,082 .... D2
Venosa 10,993 .... E4
Ventimiglia 20,343 .... A3
Verbania 29,894 .... B2
Vercelli 54,934 .... B2
Veroli 2,793 .... D4
Verona 227,032 .... C2
Viadana 6,667 .... C2
Viareggio 49,965 .... C3
Vibo Valentia 18,005 .... F5
Vicenza 99,451 .... C2
Vicovaro 3,005 .... F6
Vigevano 62,855 .... B2
Villacidro 12,651 .... B5
Villafranca di Verona 11,762 .... C2
Viterbo 39,291 .... C3
Vittoria 43,673 .... E6
Vittorio Veneto 25,476 .... D1
Vizzini 8,583 .... E6
Voghera 37,316 .... B2
Volterra 10,732 .... C3
Zagarolo 4,232 .... F7

OTHER FEATURES

Adda (riv.) B2
Adige (riv.) C2
Adriatic (sea) E3
Alicudi (isl.) E5
Apennines, Central (range) D3
Apennines, Northern (range) B2
Apennines, Southern (range) E4
Arno (riv.) C3
Asinara (isl.) B4
Bernina, Piz (peak) B1
Blanc (mt.) A2
Bolsena (lake) C3
Bonifacio (str.) B4
Bracciano (lake) D3
Brenner (pass) C1
Capraia (isl.) B3
Capri (isl.) E4
Carbonara (cape) B5
Carnic Alps (range) D1
Castellammare (gulf) D5
Circeo (cape) D4
Como (lake) B1
Cottian Alps (range) A2
Dolomite Alps (range) C1
Dora Baltea (riv.) A2
Dora Riparia (riv.) A2
Egadi (isls.) C6
Elba (isl.) C3
Etna (vol.) E6
Favignana (isl.) D6
Filicudi (isl.) E5
Gaeta (gulf) D4
Garda (lake) C2
Gennargentu, Monti del (mt.) B5
Genoa (gulf) B2
Giannutri (isl.) C3
Giglio (isl.) C3
Gorgona (isl.) B3
Graian Alps (range) A2
Gran Paradiso (mt.) A2
Great Saint Bernard (pass) A2
Ionian (sea) F6
Ischia (isl.) D4
Julian Alps (range) D1
Lampedusa (isl.) D7
Lepontine Alps (range) B1
Levanzo (isl.) D5
Ligurian (sea) B3
Linosa (isl.) D7
Lipari (isl.) E5
Lipari (isls.) E5
Maggiore (lake) B1
Manfredonia (gulf) F4
Marettimo (isl.) C6
Maritime Alps (range) A2
Marmolada (mt.) C1
Mediterranean (sea) B6
Messina (str.) E6
Metauro (riv.) D3
Mincio (riv.) C2
Montecristo (isl.) C3
Nera (riv.) D3
Oglio (riv.) C2
Ombrone (riv.) C3
Oristano (gulf) B5
Orosei (gulf) B4
Ortles (range) C1
Otranto (str.) G5
Ötztal Alps (range) C1
Panarea (isl.) E5
Panaro (riv.) C2
Pantelleria (isl.) D6
Pelagie (isls.) D7
Pennine Alps (range) A2
Pianosa (isl.) C3
Piave (riv.) D2
Po (riv.) C2
Pompeii (ruins) E4
Pontine (isls.) D4
Ponza (isl.) D4
Rosa (mt.) A1
Salina (isl.) E5
Salso (riv.) D6
San Pietro (isl.) B5
Santa Maria di Leuca (cape) G5
Sant'Antioco (pen.) B5
Sant'Eufemia (gulf) F5
Sardinia (isl.) B4
Sicily (isl.) E6
Sicily (str.) D6
Simplon (tunnel) A1
Spartivento (cape) B5
Spartivento (cape) F6
Squillace (gulf) F5
Stromboli (isl.) E5
Tagliamento (riv.) D1
Tanaro (riv.) B2
Taranto (gulf) F5
Testa del Gargano (cape) F4
Tiber (riv.) D3
Trasimeno (lake) D3
Tremiti (isls.) E3
Trieste (gulf) D2
Tuscan (arch.) B3
Tyrrhenian (sea) C4
Ustica (isl.) D5
Vaticano (cape) E5
Venice (gulf) D2
Ventotene (isl.) D4
Vesuvius (vol.) E4
Viso (mt.) A2
Volturno (riv.) E4
Vulcano (isl.) E5

MALTA

CITIES and TOWNS

Sliema 20,095 .... E7
Valletta (cap.) 14,042 .... E7
Victoria 5,249 .... E6

SAN MARINO

CITIES and TOWNS

San Marino (cap.) 4,628 .... D3
San Marino* 5,410 .... D3

VATICAN CITY

Vatican City 728 .... B6

*City and suburbs.

Agriculture, Industry and Resources

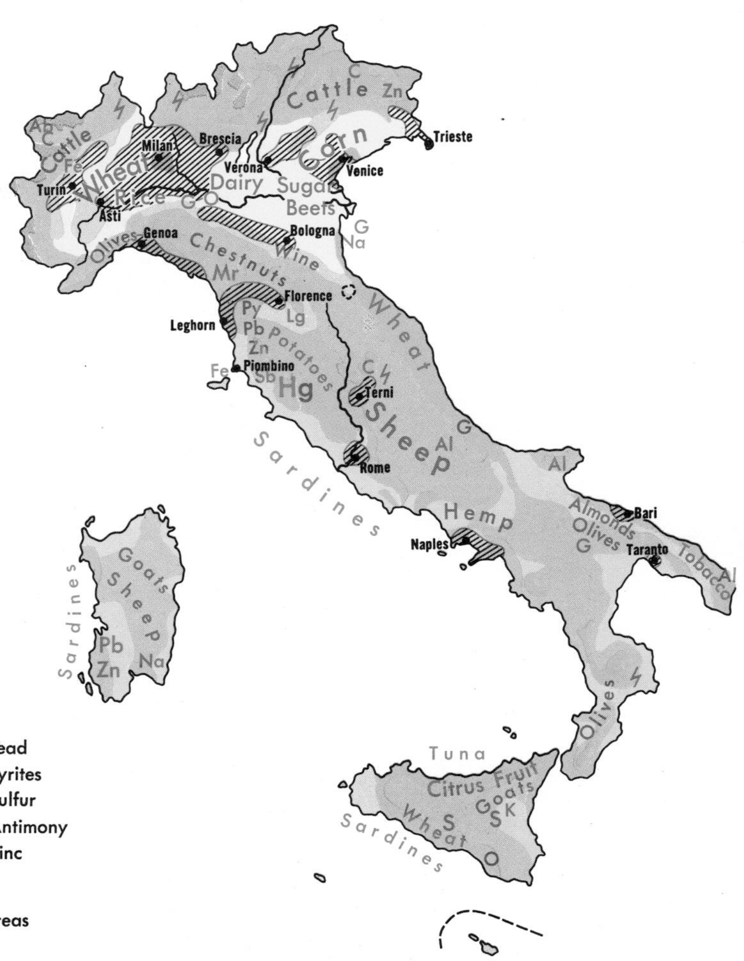

Cattle
Wheat
Rice
Milan
Brescia
Verona
Venice
Trieste
Turin
Asti
Genoa
Dairy
Corn
Sugar Beets
Bologna
Olives
Chestnuts
Wine
Florence
Leghorn
Piombino
Potatoes
Wheat
Terni
Sheep
Rome
Sardines
Hemp
Naples
Bari
Taranto
Almonds
Olives
Tobacco
Goats
Sheep
Tuna
Citrus Fruit
Goats

DOMINANT LAND USE

- Wheat, Rice, Dairy
- Pasture Livestock
- Cereals, Livestock
- Fruit, Truck and Mixed Farming
- Grapes, Wine
- Forests
- Nonagricultural Land

MAJOR MINERAL OCCURRENCES

Ab	Asbestos	K	Potash	Pb	Lead
Al	Bauxite	Lg	Lignite	Py	Pyrites
C	Coal	Mr	Marble	S	Sulfur
Fe	Iron Ore	Na	Salt	Sb	Antimony
G	Natural Gas	O	Petroleum	Zn	Zinc
Hg	Mercury				

Water Power

Major Industrial Areas

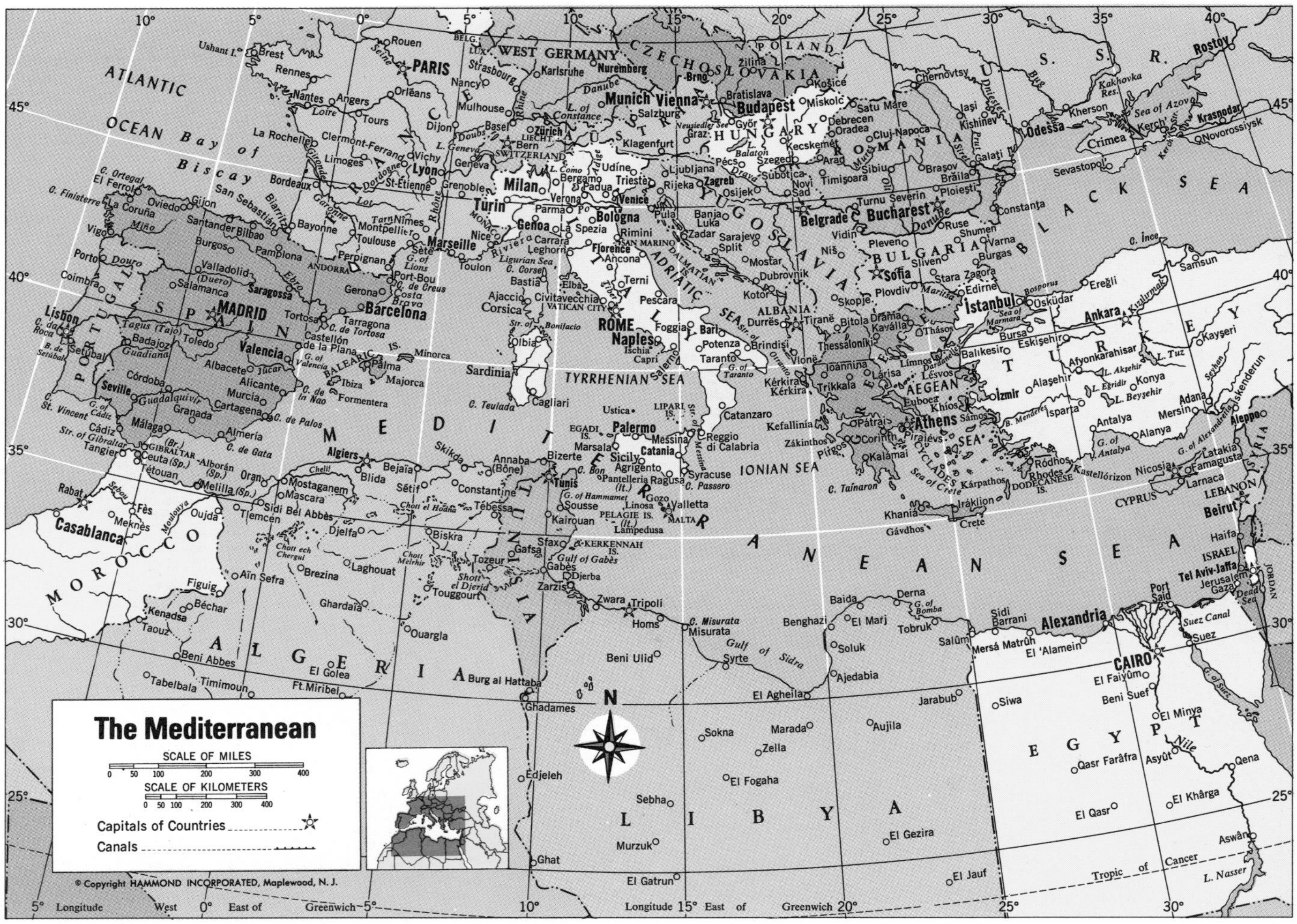

ATLANTIC
OCEAN
Bay of Biscay
WEST GERMANY
CZECHOSLOVAKIA
POLAND
HUNGARY
RUMANIA
YUGOSLAVIA
BULGARIA
ALBANIA
SWITZERLAND
BLACK SEA
TYRRHENIAN SEA
IONIAN SEA
AEGEAN SEA
MEDITERRANEAN SEA
MOROCCO
ALGERIA
LIBYA
EGYPT
TURKEY
PARIS
MADRID
ROME
Munich
Vienna
Budapest
Belgrade
Bucharest
Sofia
Athens
Istanbul
Ankara
Algiers
Tunis
Tripoli
Alexandria
CAIRO
Barcelona
Marseille
Milan
Turin
Genoa
Naples
Palermo
Casablanca
The Mediterranean
SCALE OF MILES
SCALE OF KILOMETERS
Capitals of Countries
Canals
© Copyright HAMMOND INCORPORATED, Maplewood, N. J.
Longitude West 0° East of Greenwich

SWITZERLAND

AREA 15,943 sq. mi. (41,292 sq. km.)
POPULATION 6,365,960
CAPITAL Bern
LARGEST CITY Zürich
HIGHEST POINT Dufourspitze
(Mte. Rosa) 15,203 ft. (4,634 m.)
MONETARY UNIT Swiss franc
MAJOR LANGUAGES German, French,
Italian, Romansch
MAJOR RELIGIONS Protestantism,
Roman Catholicism

LIECHTENSTEIN

AREA 61 sq. mi. (158 sq. km.)
POPULATION 25,220
CAPITAL Vaduz
LARGEST CITY Vaduz
HIGHEST POINT Grauspitze 8,527 ft.
(2,599 m.)
MONETARY UNIT Swiss franc
MAJOR LANGUAGE German
MAJOR RELIGION Roman Catholicism

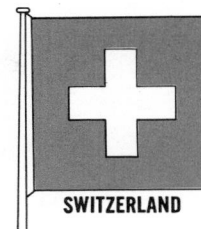

SWITZERLAND

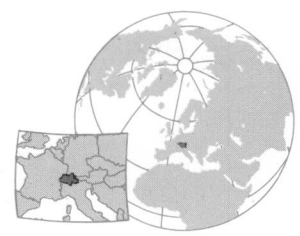

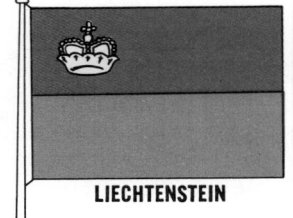

LIECHTENSTEIN

Languages

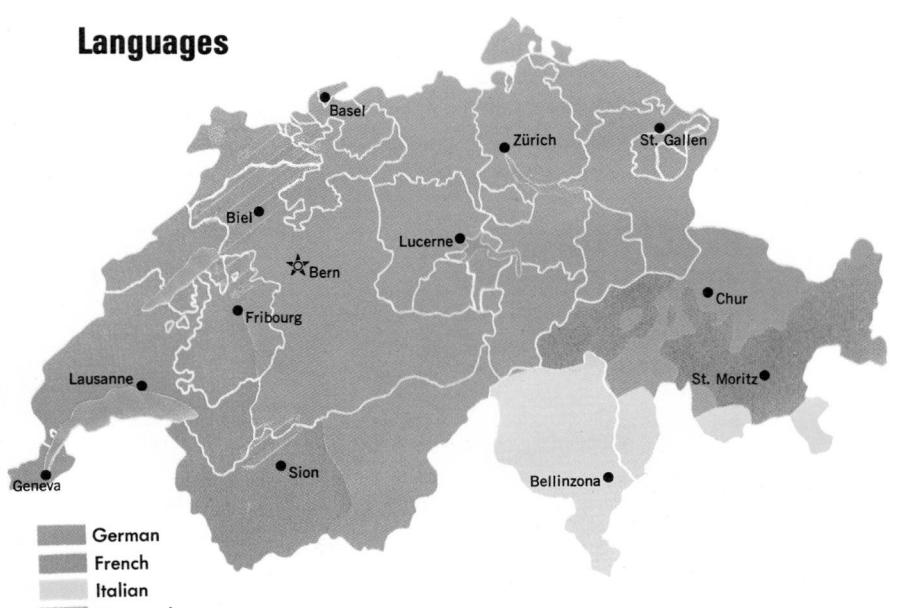

German
French
Italian
Romansch

Switzerland is a multilingual nation with four official languages. 70% of the people speak German, 19% French, 10% Italian and 1% Romansch.

Agriculture, Industry and Resources

DOMINANT LAND USE

Cereals, Dairy
Pasture Livestock
General Farming, Livestock
Fruit, Truck, Mixed Farming
Forests
Nonagricultural Land

⚡ Water Power
▨ Major Industrial Areas

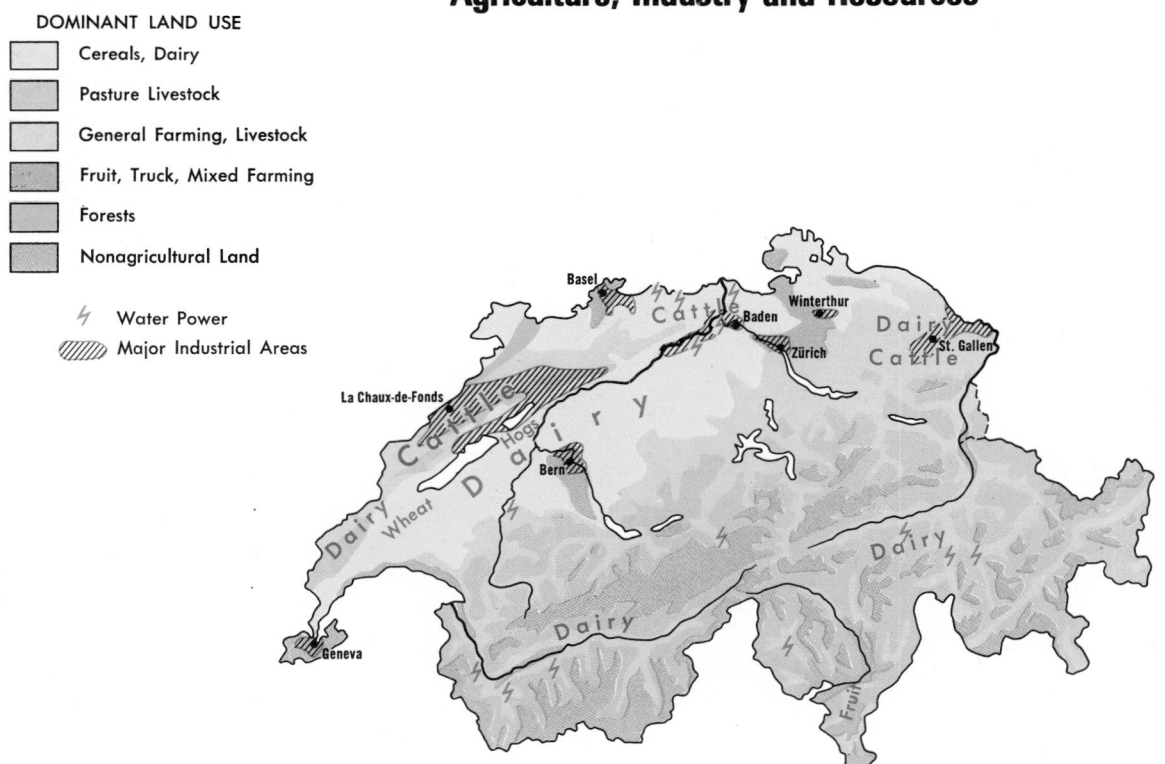

SWITZERLAND

CANTONS

Aargau 442,400 .... F2
Appenzell, Ausser
  Rhoden 46,700 .... H2
Appenzell, Inner Rhoden 13,500 .... H2
Baselland 219,500 .... E2
Baselstadt 209,700 .... E1
Bern 920,900 .... D2
Fribourg 181,600 .... D3
Geneva (Genève) 338,600 .... B4
Glarus 35,700 .... H3
Graubünden (Grisons) 164,300 .... H3
Grisons (Graubünden) 164,300 .... H3
Jura 67,200 .... D2
Lucerne (Luzern) 292,900 .... F2
Luzern 292,900 .... C3
Neuchâtel 162,200 .... C3
Nidwalden 26,900 .... F3
Obwalden 25,400 .... F3
Sankt Gallen 385,000 .... H2
Schaffhausen 69,300 .... G1
Schwyz 93,100 .... G2
Soleure (Solothurn) 221,800 ...... E2
Solothurn 221,800 .... E2
Thurgau 183,500 .... H1
Ticino 264,400 .... G4
Uri 34,000 .... G3
Valais 214,000 .... D4
Vaud 523,500 .... B3
Zug 73,600 .... G2
Zürich 1,117,300 .... G2

CITIES and TOWNS

Aadorf 3,022 .... G2
Aarau 16,881 .... F2
Aarau* 51,800 .... F2

Aarberg 3,122 .... D2
Aarburg 5,943 .... E2
Adelboden 3,326 .... E3
Adliswil 15,920 .... F2
Aeschi bei Spiez 1,402 .... E3
Affoltern am Albis 7,363 .... F2
Affoltern im Emmental 1,223 ...... C4
Aigle 6,532 .... C4
Airolo 2,140 .... G3
Alle 1,615 .... D2
Allschwil 17,638 .... D1
Alpnach 3,277 .... F3
Altdorf 8,647 .... G3
Altstätten 9,084 .... J2
Amriswil 7,601 .... H1
Andelfingen 1,453 .... G1
Andermatt 1,589 .... G3
Appenzell 5,217 .... H2
Arbedo-Castione 2,456 .... G4
Arbon 12,227 .... H1
Arbon* 15,400 .... H1
Ardon 1,498 .... D4
Arosa 2,717 .... J3
Arth 7,580 .... F2
Ascona 4,086 .... G4
Attalens 1,116 .... C3
Au 4,944 .... J2
Aubonne 1,983 .... B4
Avenches 2,235 .... D3
Baar 14,074 .... F2
Baden 14,115 .... F2
Baden* 66,800 .... F2
Bad Ragaz 3,713 .... H2
Balerna 3,885 .... G5
Balsthal 5,607 .... E2
Bäretswil 2,733 .... G2
Basel 199,600 .... E1
Basel* 379,700 .... E1
Bassecourt 2,985 .... D2
Bätterkinden 1,757 .... E2

Bauma 3,159 .... G2
Beatenberg 1,263 .... E3
Beinwil am See 2,520 .... F2
Belfaux 1,075 .... D3
Bellingen 4,769 .... H4
Bellinzona 16,979 .... H4
Bellinzona* 31,000 .... H4
Belp 6,981 .... D3
Berg 1,039 .... H1
Bern (cap.) 154,700 .... D3
Bern* 285,300 .... D3
Beromünster 1,552 .... F2
Bettlach 4,046 .... D2
Bex 5,069 .... D4
Biasca 4,696 .... H4
Biberist 7,769 .... D2
Biel 63,400 .... D2
Biel**89,900 .... D2
Bière 1,252 .... B3
Binningen 15,344 .... D1
Bischofszell 4,233 .... H1
Blumenstein 1,049 .... E3
Bodio 1,425 .... G4
Bolligen 26,121 .... E3
Boltigen 1,519 .... D3
Bonaduz 1,289 .... H3
Boncourt 1,528 .... C2
Bönigen 1,738 .... E3
Boswil 1,904 .... F2
Boudry 4,372 .... C3
Bourg Saint-Pierre 236 .... D5
Breil-Brigels 1,215 .... H3
Breitenbach 2,455 .... E2
Bremgarten 4,873 .... F2
Brienz 2,796 .... E3
Brig 5,191 .... F4
Brissago 2,120 .... G4
Brittnau 2,888 .... E2
Broc 1,842 .... D3
Brugg 8,635 .... F2
Brusio 1,344 .... K4
Bubendorf 2,070 .... E2
Bubikon 3,244 .... G2
Buchs 8,454 .... H2
Bülach 11,043 .... G1
Bulle 7,556 .... D3
Buochs 3,232 .... F3
Büren an der Aare 3,085 .... D2
Burgdorf 15,888 .... E2
Burgdorf* 18,400 .... E2
Bürglen, Thurgau 1,920 .... H1
Bürglen, Uri 3,401 .... G3
Bussigny-près-Lausanne 4,509 .... B3
Bütschwil 3,270 .... H2
Carouge 14,055 .... B4
Castagnola 4,430 .... G4
Cazis 1,687 .... H3
Cernier 1,717 .... C2
Chalais 1,651 .... E4
Cham 8,209 .... F2
Chamoson 2,049 .... D4
Charmey 1,155 .... D3
Château-d'Oex 3,203 .... D4
Châtel-Saint-Denis 2,842 .... C3
Chêne-Bougeries 8,670 .... B4
Chavornay 1,521 .... C3
Chexbres 1,607 .... C3
Chiasso 8,868 .... G5
Chippis 1,561 .... E4
Chur 32,400 .... J3
Churwalden 1,052 .... J3
Claro 1,143 .... G4
Collombey-Muraz 2,279 .... C4
Collonge-Bellerive 3,541 .... B4
Conthey 4,259 .... D4
Coppet 1,097 .... B4
Corcelles-près-Payerne 1,256 .... C3
Corgémont 1,645 .... D2
Cossonay 1,529 .... B3
Courgenay 1,954 .... D2
Courrendlin 2,656 .... D2
Courroux 1,788 .... D2
Courtelary 1,462 .... C2
Courtételle 1,864 .... D2
Couvet 3,481 .... C3
Cully 1,535 .... C4
Davos 10,238 .... J3
Degersheim 3,400 .... H2
Delémont 11,797 .... D2
Derendingen 4,917 .... E2
Dielsdorf 2,691 .... F1
Diemtigen 1,913 .... D3
Diepoldsau 3,311 .... J2
Diessenhofen 2,532 .... G1
Dietikon 22,705 .... F2
Disentis-Muster 2,319 .... G3
Domat-Ems 5,701 .... H3
Dombresson 1,109 .... C2
Dornach 5,258 .... E2
Döttingen 3,380 .... F1
Dübendorf 19,639 .... G2
Düdingen 4,932 .... D3
Dürnten 4,820 .... G2
Dürrenroth 1,084 .... E2
Ebnat-Kappel 5,131 .... H2
Echallens 1,643 .... C3
Ecublens 6,379 .... B3
Egg 5,250 .... G2
Eggiwil 2,391 .... E3
Eglisau 2,160 .... G1
Egnach 3,466 .... H1

(continued on following page)

Switzerland and Liechtenstein

(continued)

Topography

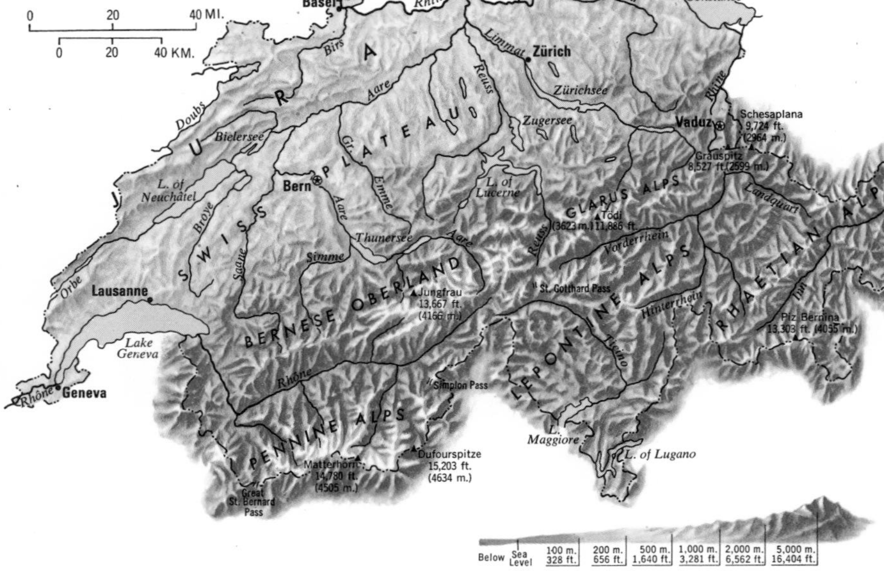

0 20 40 MI.
0 20 40 KM.
Basel
Rhine
Thur
L. of Constance
Birs
Limmat
Zürich
Zürichsee
Reuss
Rhine
Doubs
Bielersee
Aare
Zugersee
Vaduz
Schesaplana 9,724 ft. (2964 m.)
Grauspitz 8,527 ft. (2599 m.)
L. of Neuchâtel
Bern
Emme
L. of Lucerne
GLARUS ALPS
Tödi 11,886 ft. (3623 m.)
Landquart
Broye
SWISS PLATEAU
JURA
Thunersee
Aare
Vorderrhein
RHAETIAN ALPS
Saane
Simme
BERNESE OBERLAND
Jungfrau 13,667 ft. (4166 m.)
St. Gotthard Pass
Hinterrhein
Inn
Orbe
Lausanne
Lake Geneva
Rhône
Geneva
LEPONTINE ALPS
Ticino
Piz Bernina 13,303 ft. (4055 m.)
Simplon Pass
PENNINE ALPS
Maggiore
L. of Lugano
Matterhorn 14,780 ft. (4505 m.)
Dufourspitze 15,203 ft. (4634 m.)
Great St. Bernard Pass
Below Sea Level
100 m. 328 ft.
200 m. 656 ft.
500 m. 1,640 ft.
1,000 m. 3,281 ft.
2,000 m. 6,562 ft.
5,000 m. 16,404 ft.

Einsiedeln 10,020 ... G2
Elgg 2,970 ... G2
Emmen 22,040 ... F2
Engelberg 2,841 ... F3
Ennenda 2,762 ... H2
Entlebuch 3,310 ... F3
Erlach 1,052 ... D2
Erlenbach im Simmental 1,436 ... E3
Ermatingen 1,787 ... H1
Erstfeld 4,516 ... G3
Eschenbach 3,387 ... G2
Escholzmatt 3,161 ... E3
Estavayer-le-Lac 3,439 ... C3
Evolène 1,403 ... D4
Faido 1,866 ... G4
Felsberg 1,321 ... H3
Feuerthalen 3,118 ... G1
Flawil 8,474 ... H2
Fleurier 4,124 ... C3
Flims 1,936 ... H3
Flüelen 1,731 ... G3
Flums 4,474 ... H2
Frauenfeld 17,576 ... G1
Freienbach 8,429 ... G2
Fribourg 41,600 ... D3
Fribourg* 53,500 ... D3
Frick 3,112 ... E1
Frutigen 5,796 ... E3
Fully 3,643 ... D4
Gais 2,344 ... H2
Gelterkinden 5,157 ... E2
Geneva (Genève) 163,100 ... B4
Geneva (Genève)* 320,200 ... B4
Gersau 1,753 ... G2
Gimel 1,205 ... B3
Giornico 1,389 ... G4
Giswil 2,760 ... F3
Giubiasco 5,796 ... H4
Gland 2,404 ... B4
Glarus 6,189 ... H2
Glattfelden 2,857 ... F1
Glis 3,389 ... E4
Gordola 2,586 ... G4
Gossau 12,793 ... H2
Grabs 4,245 ... H2
Grächen 1,063 ... E4
Grandson 2,135 ... C3
Grenchen 20,051 ... D2
Grenchen* 28,300 ... D2
Grindelwald 3,511 ... E3
Grosswangen 2,213 ... F2
Gruyères 1,234 ... D3
Gstaad ... D4
Gsteig 865 ... D4
Guggisberg 1,739 ... D3
Gurtnellen 1,048 ... G3
Guttingen 1,060 ... H1
Hallau 1,836 ... F1
Heiden 3,716 ... H2
Heimberg 3,046 ... E3
Hérémence 1,484 ... D4
Hergiswil 4,364 ... F3
Herisau 14,597 ... H2
Herzogenbuchsee 5,140 ... E2
Hilterfingen 3,647 ... E3
Hinwil 6,547 ... G2
Hitzkirch 1,468 ... F2
Hochdorf 5,222 ... F2
Horgen 15,691 ... G2
Huttwil 4,800 ... E2
Igis 5,283 ... J3
Ilanz 1,783 ... H3
Illnau 13,693 ... G2
Ingenbohl 5,111 ... G2
Innertkirchen 1,064 ... F3
Ins 2,435 ... D2
Interlaken 4,735 ... E3
Jegenstorf 2,858 ... D2
Jenaz 1,124 ... J3
Jona 9,286 ... G2
Jungfraujoch ... E3
Kaltbrunn 2,751 ... H2
Kandersteg 957 ... E4
Kerns 3,807 ... F3
Kerzers 2,688 ... D3
Kirchberg, Bern 3,595 ... E2
Kirchberg, St. Gallen 6,309 ... G2
Kleinlützel 1,271 ... D2
Klingnau 2,545 ... F1
Klosters Dorf 3,534 ... J3
Kloten 16,388 ... G2
Koblenz 1,439 ... F1
Kölliken 3,219 ... F2
Köniz 33,800 ... D3
Konolfingen 4,137 ... E3
Kreuzlingen 15,760 ... H1
Kriens 20,409 ... F2
Krummenau 1,904 ... H2
Küsnacht 12,193 ... G2
Küssnacht am Rigi 7,956 ... F2
Küttigen 4,181 ... F2
L'Abbaye 1,319 ... B3
La Chaux-de-Fonds 42,500 ... C2
Lachen 4,914 ... G2
Lancy 20,523 ... B4
La Neuveville 3,917 ... D2
Langenthal 13,077 ... E2
Langenthal* 22,100 ... E2
Langnau am Albis 4,879 ... G2
Langnau in Emmental 8,950 ... E3
La Roche 1,069 ... D3
La Sarraz 1,190 ... C3
La Tour-de-Peilz 8,864 ... C4
Läufelfingen 1,243 ... E2
Laufen 4,723 ... D2
Laufenburg 2,128 ... F1
Laupen 2,139 ... D3
Lauperswil 2,542 ... E3
Lausanne 136,100 ... C3
Lausanne* 228,700 ... C3
Lauterbrunnen 3,431 ... E3
Le Brassus 5,465 ... B3
Le Châble 4,541 ... D4
Le Chenit (Le Brassus) 5,465 ... B3
Le Landeron 2,768 ... C2
Le Locle 14,452 ... C2
Le Mont-sur-Lausanne 2,692 ... C3
Lengau 4,736 ... D2
Lenk 1,876 ... D4
Le Noirmont 1,516 ... C2
Lens 2,052 ... D4
Lenzburg 7,594 ... F2
Les Bois 1,110 ... C2
Les Ponts-de-Martel 1,327 ... C2
Leuk 2,796 ... E4
Leukerbad 1,056 ... E4
Leysin 2,752 ... C4
Liechtensteig 2,131 ... H2
Liestal 12,500 ... E2
Liestal-Sissach* 40,800 ... E2
Linthal 1,458 ... H3
Littau 13,495 ... F2
Locarno 14,143 ... G4
Locarno* 39,200 ... G4
Lodrino 1,075 ... G4
Lotzwil 2,323 ... E2
Lucens 2,144 ... C3
Lucerne 70,200 ... F2
Lucerne* 158,600 ... F2
Lugano 22,280 ... G4
Lugano* 64,200 ... G4
Lungern 1,813 ... F3
Luthern 1,706 ... E2
Lutry 4,994 ... C3
Lützelflüh 3,842 ... E3
Luzern (Lucerne) 70,200 ... F2
Lyss 8,131 ... D2
Maienfeld 1,542 ... J2
Malans 1,294 ... J3
Malleray 1,969 ... D2
Malters 5,100 ... F2
Malvaglia 1,099 ... H4
Männedorf 7,419 ... G2
Marbach 1,265 ... E3
Martigny 10,478 ... C4
Meilen 9,881 ... G2
Meiringen 3,759 ... F3
Melide 1,315 ... G5
Mellingen 3,211 ... F2
Mels 5,969 ... H2
Mendrisio 6,223 ... G5
Menzingen 3,483 ... G2
Menznau 2,185 ... E2
Mesocco 1,376 ... H4
Meyrin 14,255 ... B4
Minusio 5,027 ... G4
Möhlin 6,003 ... E1
Mollis 2,628 ... H2
Montana 1,725 ... D4
Monthey 10,114 ... C4
Montreux 20,421 ... C4
Morges 11,931 ... B3
Morges* 17,200 ... B3
Moudon 3,773 ... C3
Moutier 8,794 ... D2
Müllheim 1,620 ... G1
Mümliswil-Ramiswil 2,702 ... E2
Münchenbuchsee 6,459 ... E2
Münsingen 8,350 ... E3
Muotathal 2,763 ... G3
Muri 4,853 ... F2
Muri bei Bern 3,057 ... E3
Mürren ... E3
Murten 4,256 ... D3
Muttenz 15,518 ... E1
Näfels 3,739 ... H2
Naters 5,517 ... E4
Nebikon 1,378 ... F2
Nendaz 4,051 ... D4
Nesslau 1,934 ... H2
Netstal 2,771 ... H2
Neuchâtel 38,400 ... C3
Neuchâtel* 61,700 ... C3
Neuenegg 3,452 ... D3
Neuhausen am Rheinfall 12,103 ... G1
Neunkirch 1,239 ... F1
Nidau 7,962 ... D2
Niederbipp 3,293 ... E2
Niederurnen 3,354 ... G2
Nunningen 1,450 ... E2
Nyon 11,424 ... B4
Oberägeri 2,992 ... G2
Oberburg 3,015 ... E2
Oberdiessbach 2,145 ... E3
Oberdorf 1,953 ... E2
Oberriet 6,123 ... J2
Obersiggenthal 6,623 ... F1
Oberzwil 4,659 ... H2
Oensingen 3,387 ... E2
Oftringen 9,189 ... E2
Ollon 4,470 ... D4
Olten 21,209 ... E2
Olten* 49,000 ... E2
Opfikon 11,115 ... G2
Orbe 4,522 ... C3
Orsières 2,470 ... D4
Ouchy ... C4
Paradiso 3,101 ... G5
Payerne 6,899 ... C3
Penthalaz 1,701 ... C3
Péry 1,486 ... D2
Peseux 5,578 ... C3
Pfaffnau 2,584 ... E2
Pieterlen 3,485 ... D2
Plaffeien 1,448 ... D3
Pontresina 1,646 ... J3
Porrentruy 7,827 ... C2
Port-Valais 1,363 ... C4
Poschiavo 3,563 ... J4
Prangins 1,466 ... B4
Pratteln 15,127 ... E1
Pully 15,917 ... C4
Quinto 1,490 ... G3
Rafz 2,215 ... G1
Ramsen 1,217 ... G1
Rapperswil 8,713 ... G2
Raron 1,257 ... E4
Regensdorf 8,566 ... F2
Reichenbach im Kandertal 2,900 ... E3
Reiden 3,275 ... F2
Reinach in Aargau 5,862 ... F2
Reinach in Baselland 13,419 ... E2
Renan 1,094 ... C2
Renens 17,391 ... C3
Rheinau 2,075 ... G1
Rheineck 3,275 ... J2
Rheinfelden 6,866 ... E1
Richterswil 7,380 ... G2
Riehen 21,026 ... E1
Riggisberg 2,193 ... E3
Riva San Vitale 1,607 ... G5
Rivera 1,146 ... G4
Roggwil 3,403 ... E2
Rolle 3,658 ... B4
Romanshorn 8,329 ... H1
Romont 3,276 ... C3
Rorschach 11,963 ... H2
Rorschach* 24,200 ... H2
Rosenlaui ... F3
Rothrist 5,883 ... E2
Roveredo 2,037 ... H4
Rüeggisberg 1,857 ... E3
Rumlang 5,677 ... G2
Rüschegg 1,346 ... D3
Ruswil 4,756 ... F2
Rüthi 1,493 ... J2
Rüti, Zürich 9,546 ... G2
Saanen 5,840 ... D4
Sachseln 3,059 ... F3
Saignelégier 1,745 ... D2
Saint-Aubin-Sauges 2,058 ... C3
Saint-Blaise 2,586 ... D2
Sainte-Croix 6,240 ... B3
Saint-Imier 6,740 ... D2
Saint-Légier-La Chiésaz 2,230 ... C4
Saint-Martin 1,120 ... E4
Saint-Maurice 3,808 ... C4
Saint Moritz 5,699 ... J3
Saint Niklaus 2,043 ... E4
Saint-Prex 2,306 ... B4
Saint Stephan 1,213 ... D3
Saint-Ursanne 1,073 ... D2
Samedan 2,574 ... J3
Sankt Gallen 81,900 ... H2
Sankt Gallen* 90,400 ... H2
Sankt Margrethen 5,101 ... J2
Sargans 4,058 ... H2
Sarnen 6,952 ... F3
Satigny 1,877 ... A4
Savièse 3,585 ... D4
Saxon 2,409 ... D4
Schaffhausen 36,800 ... G1
Schaffhausen* 55,800 ... G1
Schänis 2,355 ... H2
Schattdorf 3,292 ... G3
Scherzingen 1,420 ... H1
Schiers 2,342 ... J3
Schinznach-Dorf 1,154 ... F2
Schleitheim 1,544 ... G1
Schlieren 11,869 ... F2
Schönenwerd 4,793 ... E2
Schübelbach 4,395 ... G2
Schüpfheim 3,773 ... F3
Schwanden 2,823 ... H2
Schwyz 12,194 ... G2
Scuol 1,686 ... K3
Sempach 1,619 ... F2
Seon 3,628 ... F2
Seuzach 3,258 ... G1
Sevelen 2,742 ... H2
Sierre 11,017 ... D4
Signau 2,642 ... E3
Sigriswil 3,540 ... E3
Silenen 2,338 ... G3
Sils im Domleschg 762 ... H3
Silvaplana 714 ... J4
Sins 2,435 ... F2
Sion 21,925 ... D4
Sirnach 3,706 ... G2
Sissach 4,938 ... E2
Solothurn (Soleure) 17,708 ... E2
Solothurn* 35,600 ... E2
Somvix 1,555 ... G3
Sonvico 1,129 ... G4
Spiez 9,911 ... E3
Stäfa 9,937 ... G2
Stalden 1,121 ... E4
Stans 5,180 ... F3
Steckborn 3,752 ... G1
Steffisburg 12,621 ... E3
Stein 1,763 ... E1
Stein am Rhein 2,751 ... G1
Suhr 7,223 ... F2
Sulgen 1,834 ... H1
Sumiswald 5,334 ... E2
Sursee 7,052 ... F2
Tafers 2,021 ... D3
Täuffelen 1,761 ... D2
Tavannes 3,869 ... D2
Tavetsch 1,273 ... G3
Teufen 5,300 ... H2
Thal 4,919 ... J2
Thalwil 13,591 ... G2
Thayngen 3,640 ... G1
Therwil 5,412 ... E1
Thun 37,000 ... E3
Thun* 63,600 ... E3
Thunstetten 2,483 ... E2
Thusis 2,381 ... H3
Trachselwald 1,199 ... E2
Tramelan 5,549 ... D2
Trimmis 1,109 ... J3
Troistorrents 2,208 ... C4
Trub 1,833 ... E3
Trun 1,607 ... G3
Turbenthal 2,939 ... G2
Uetendorf 3,132 ... E3
Unterägeri 4,671 ... G2
Unteriberg 1,344 ... G2
Unterkulm 2,596 ... F2
Unterseen 4,192 ... E3
Untervaz 1,230 ... H3
Urnäsch 2,313 ... H2
Uster 21,819 ... G2
Utzenstorf 3,193 ... E2
Uznach 3,984 ... H2
Uzwil 9,133 ... H2
Vallorbe 4,028 ... B3
Vaz-Obervaz 2,003 ... J3
Vechigen 3,595 ... E3
Vernayaz 1,356 ... D4
Versoix 5,627 ... B4
Vevey 17,957 ... C4
Vevey-Montreux* 62,300 ... C4
Villeneuve 3,705 ... C4
Visp 5,252 ... E4
Vouvry 1,851 ... C4
Vuadens 1,278 ... C3
Wädenswil 15,695 ... G2
Wahlern 4,832 ... D3
Wald 8,185 ... G2
Waldenburg 1,449 ... E2
Waldkirch 2,669 ... H2
Walenstadt 3,446 ... H2
Wallisellen 10,415 ... G2
Walzenhausen 2,082 ... J2
Wangen an der Aare 2,013 ... E2
Wängi 2,730 ... H1
Wartau 3,604 ... H2

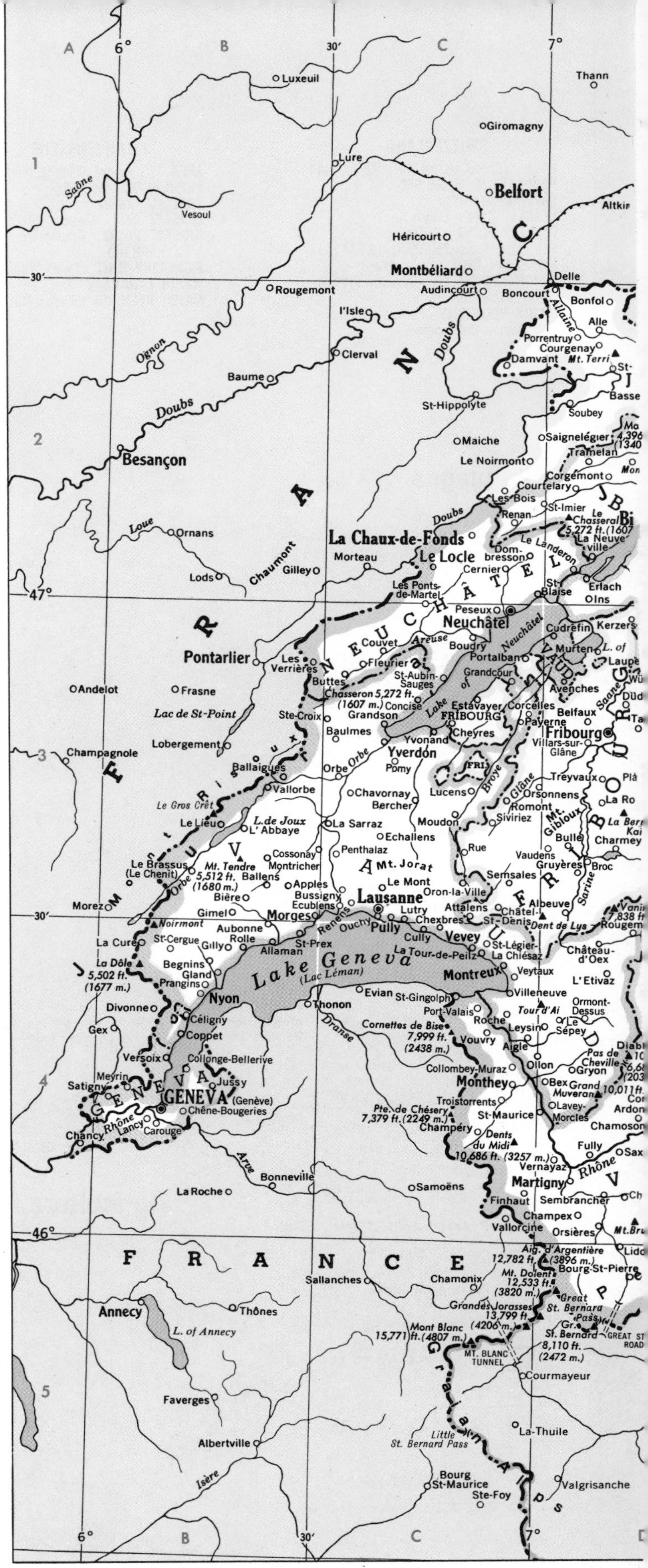

A
B
C
6°
30′
7°
Luxeuil
Thann
Giromagny
Lure
Saône
Vesoul
Belfort
Altkirch
Héricourt
Montbéliard
Delle
Rougemont
Audincourt
Boncourt
Bonfol
Alle
L'Isle
Ognon
Doubs
Porrentruy
Courgenay
Damvant
Mt. Terri
Clerval
Baume
St-Hippolyte
Soubey
Doubs
Besançon
Maiche
Le Noirmont
Saignelégier
Tramelan
Corgémont
Courtelary
Les Bois
Renan
St-Imier
Chasseral 5,272 ft. (1607 m.)
La Neuveville
Loue
Ornans
La Chaux-de-Fonds
Le Locle
Le Landeron
Morteau
Chaumont
Gilley
Lods
Les Ponts-de-Martel
Cernier
St-Blaise
Erlach
Ins
47°
Peseux
Neuchâtel
Kerzers
Couvet
Areuse
Boudry
Portalban
Murten
L. of Murten
Pontarlier
Les Verrières
Fleurier
Buttes
St-Aubin-Sauges
Grandcour
Avenches
Andelot
Frasne
Chasseron 5,272 ft. (1607 m.)
Concise
Estavayer
Corcelles
Lac de St-Point
Ste-Croix
Grandson
FRIBOURG
Payerne
Belfaux
Fribourg
Lobergement
Baulmes
Yvonand
Cheyres
Villars-sur-Glâne
Champagnole
Orbe
Yverdon
Pomy
Ballaigues
Vallorbe
Lucens
Treyvaux
Le Gros Crêt
Chavornay
Bercher
Orsonnens
Romont
Moudon
Siviriez
Le Lieu
L. de Joux
L'Abbaye
La Sarraz
Echallens
Penthalaz
Rue
Vaudens
Gruyères
Broc
Le Brassus (Le Chenit)
Mt. Tendre 5,512 ft. (1680 m.)
Montricher
Ballens
Cossonay
Mt. Jorat
Semsales
Bière
Apples
Bussigny
Ecublens
Lausanne
Le Mont
Oron-la-Ville
Morez
Gimel
Morges
Lutry
Attalens
Châtel-St-Denis
Albeuve
30′
Noirmont
St-Cergue
Renens
Ouchy
Pully
Chexbres
Cully
Dent de Lys
Rougemont
La Cure
Aubonne
Rolle
St-Prex
Vevey
La Tour-de-Peilz
St-Légier
La Chiésaz
Château-d'Oex
Gilly
La Dôle 5,502 ft. (1677 m.)
Begnins
Gland
Prangins
Lake Geneva
(Lac Léman)
Montreux
Veytaux
L'Etivaz
Nyon
Evian
St-Gingolph
Villeneuve
Divonne
Thonon
Port-Valais
Tour d'Ai
Ormont-Dessus
Céligny
Coppet
Dranse
Cornettes de Bise 7,999 ft. (2438 m.)
Leysin
Le Sépey
Gex
Roche
Vouvry
Aigle
Versoix
Collonge-Bellerive
Collombey-Muraz
Ollon
Gryon
Meyrin
Jussy
Monthey
Bex
Satigny
GENEVA
Chêne-Bougeries
Troistorrents
Grand Muveran 10,011 ft.
Lavey-Morcles
Chamoson
Chancy
Lancy
Carouge
Pte. de Chésery 7,379 ft. (2249 m.)
St-Maurice
Champéry
Dents du Midi 10,686 ft. (3257 m.)
Fully
Vernayaz
Saxon
Arve
Bonneville
Martigny
Rhône
La Roche
Samoëns
Finhaut
Sembrancher
Champex
Vallorcine
Orsières
46°
F
R
A
N
C
E
Aig. d'Argentière 12,782 ft. (3896 m.)
Mt. Dolent 12,533 ft. (3820 m.)
Bourg-St-Pierre
Sallanches
Chamonix
Great St. Bernard Pass
Annecy
Thônes
Grandes Jorasses 13,799 ft. (4206 m.)
Gr. St. Bernard 8,110 ft. (2472 m.)
GREAT ST. BERNARD ROAD TUNNEL
L. of Annecy
Mont Blanc 15,771 ft. (4807 m.)
MT. BLANC TUNNEL
Courmayeur
Faverges
Little St. Bernard Pass
La Thuile
Albertville
Isère
Bourg St-Maurice
Ste-Foy
Valgrisanche
1
2
3
4
5

Wattwil 8,566 ... H2
Weesen 1,308 ... H2
Weggis 2,517 ... F2
Weinfelden 8,621 ... H1
Wettingen 19,900 ... F2
Wetzikon 13,469 ... G2
Wil 14,646 ... H2
Wil* 20,500 ... H2
Wilchingen 1,066 ... F1
Wilderswil 1,666 ... E3
Wildhaus 1,104 ... H2
Willisau 2,728 ... F2
Wimmis 1,833 ... E3
Windisch 7,444 ... F1
Winterthur 93,500 ... G1
Winterthur* 110,100 ... G1
Wohlen 12,024 ... F2
Wohlen* 16,000 ... F2
Wohlen bei Bern 4,190 ... D3
Wolfenschiessen 1,470 ... F3
Wolhusen 3,556 ... F2
Worb 9,526 ... E3
Wünnewil 3,652 ... D3
Wynigen 1,986 ... E2
Yverdon 20,538 ... C3
Yvonand 1,321 ... C3
Zell, Luzern 1,590 ... E2
Zell, Zürich 4,008 ... G2
Zermatt 3,101 ... E4
Zizers 1,913 ... J3
Zofingen 9,292 ... F2
Zollikofen 9,069 ... E3
Zollikon 12,117 ... G2
Zug 22,972 ... G2
Zug* 51,300 ... G2
Zuoz 1,165 ... J3
Zürich 401,600 ... F2
Zürich* 718,100 ... F2
Zurzach 3,098 ... F1
Zweisimmen 2,738 ... D3

OTHER FEATURES

Aa (riv.) ... F3
Aare (riv.) ... E3
Ägerisee (lake) ... G2
Aiguille d'Argentière (mt.) ... C5
Aletschhorn (mt.) ... F4
Aroser Rothorn (mt.) ... J3
Ault (peak) ... H3
Balmhorn (mt.) ... E4
Bernese Oberland (reg.) ... E3
Bernina (peak) ... J4
Bernina (pass) ... K4
Bielersee (lake) ... D2
Bietschhorn (mt.) ... E4
Birs (riv.) ... D2
Blinnenhorn (mt.) ... F4
Blümlisalp (mt.) ... E3
Bodensee (Constance) (lake) ... H1
Borgne (riv.) ... D4
Breithorn (mt.) ... E5
Breithorn (mt.) ... E4
Brienzer Rothorn (mt.) ... F3
Brienzersee (lake) ... F3
Broye (riv.) ... C3
Buchegg (mts.) ... D2
Buin (peak) ... K3
Campo Tencia (peak) ... G4
Chasseron (mt.) ... C3
Churfirsten (mt.) ... H2
Clariden (mt.) ... G3
Constance (lake) ... H1
Cornettes de Bise (mts.) ... C4
Dammastock (mt.) ... F3
Davos (valley) ... J3
Dent Blanche (mt.) ... E4
Dent de Lys (mt.) ... D4

Switzerland and Liechtenstein

CONIC PROJECTION

SCALE OF MILES

0 5 10 20 30

SCALE OF KILOMETERS

0 5 10 20 30 40 50

Capitals of Countries.............................☆
Capitals of Cantons..............................◉
International Boundaries.....................▬ ▪ ▬ ▪ ▬
Canals..▬▬▬

Scale 1:1,140,000

© Copyright HAMMOND INCORPORATED, Maplewood, N.J.

Longitude 8° East of Greenwich

Austria, Czechoslovakia and Hungary

AUSTRIA

PROVINCES

Burgenland 272,119 .... D3
Carinthia 525,728 .... B3
Lower Austria 1,414,161 .... C2
Salzburg 401,766 .... B3
Styria 1,192,442 .... C3
Tirol 540,771 .... A3
Upper Austria 1,223,444 .... B2
Vienna (city) 1,614,841 .... D2
Vorarlberg 271,473 .... A3

CITIES and TOWNS†

Admont 3,126 .... C3
Allentsteig 2,783 .... C2
Altheim 4,766 .... B2
Althofen 3,886 .... C3
Amstetten 13,330 .... C2
Andau 3,058 .... D3
Arnoldstein 6,740 .... B3
Aspang Markt 2,316 .... D3
Attnang-Puchheim 7,837 .... B2
Bad Aussee 5,039 .... B3
Baden 22,631 .... D2
Badgastein 5,228 .... B3
Bad Goisern 6,360 .... B3
Bad Hofgastein 5,525 .... B3
Bad Ischl 12,740 .... B3
Bad Leonfelden 2,712 .... C2
Bad Sankt-Leonhard im
Lavanttal 4,882 .... C3
Berndorf 8,371 .... C3
Bischofshofen 9,417 .... B3
Bludenz 12,050 .... A3
Bramberg am Wildkogel 3,129 .... B3
Braunau am Inn 16,432 .... B2
Bregenz 22,839 .... A3
Bruck an der Leitha 7,506 .... D2
Bruck an der Mur 16,359 .... C3
Deutsch Feistritz 3,820 .... C3
Deutschkreutz 3,673 .... D3
Deutsch Landsberg 6,614 .... C3
Deutsch Wagram 4,481 .... D2
Dornbirn 33,810 .... A3
Ebenfurth 2,272 .... D3
Ebensee 9,413 .... B3
Eferding 3,014 .... B2
Eggenburg 3,730 .... C2
Ehrwald 2,198 .... A3
Eisenerz 11,563 .... C3
Eisenkappel-Vellach 3,761 .... C3
Eisenstadt 10,059 .... D3
Enns 9,622 .... C2
Feldbach 3,887 .... C3
Feldkirch 21,214 .... A3
Feldkirchen in
Kärnten 11,188 .... B3
Ferlach 7,621 .... C3
Fieberbrunn 3,651 .... B3
Fohnsdorf 11,169 .... C3
Frankenmarkt 2,960 .... B3
Frauenkirchen 2,749 .... D3
Freistadt 5,956 .... C2
Freidberg 2,504 .... D3
Friesach 7,257 .... C3
Frohnleiten 5,081 .... C3
Fulpmes 2,553 .... A3
Fürstenfeld 6,054 .... C3
Gaming 4,181 .... C3
Gänserndorf 4,211 .... D2
Gleisdorf 4,921 .... C3
Gloggnitz 7,078 .... D3
Gmünd, Carinthia 2,267 .... B3
Gmünd, Lower Austria 6,323 .... C2
Gmunden 12,270 .... B3
Golling an der Salzach 3,089 .... B3
Götzis 7,931 .... A3
Gratwein 2,747 .... C3
Graz 251,900 .... C3
Graz* 314,200 .... C3
Grein 2,767 .... C2
f21Grieskirchen 4,519 .... B2
Grosssiegharts 3,288 .... C2
Grünburg 3,775 .... C3
Güssing 3,675 .... D3
Haag 5,060 .... C2
Hainburg an der Donau 6,009 .... D2
Hainfeld 3,897 .... C2
Hallein 14,371 .... B3
Hallstatt 1,303 .... B3
Hartberg 5,702 .... C3
Haslach an der Mühl 2,636 .... C2
Heidenreichstein 4,340 .... C2
Heiligenblut 1,324 .... B3
Hermagor-Preseggersee 7,531 .... B3
Herzogenburg 7,299 .... C2
Hohenau an der March 3,591 .... D2
Hohenberg 2,016 .... C3
Hohenems 11,487 .... A3
Hollabrunn 6,563 .... D2
Hopfgarten in Nordtirol 4,784 .... B3
Horn 6,264 .... C2
Hüttenberg 3,251 .... C3
Imst 5,855 .... A3
Innsbruck 115,800 .... A3
Innsbruck* 167,200 .... A3
Jenbach 5,868 .... A3
Jennersdorf 4,210 .... C3
Judenburg 11,346 .... C3
Kapfenberg 26,001 .... C3
Kappl 2,156 .... A3
Kaprun 2,604 .... B3
Kindberg 6,128 .... C3
Kirchdorf an der Krems 3,471 .... C3
Kitzbühel 7,995 .... B3
Klagenfurt 74,326 .... C3
Klagenfurt* 112,600 .... C3
Klosterneuburg 21,912 .... D2
Knittelfeld 14,517 .... C3
Köflach 12,612 .... C3
Königswiesen 2,921 .... C2
Korneuburg 8,892 .... D2
Kössen 2,764 .... B3
Kötschach-Mauthen 3,740 .... B3
Krems an der Donau 21,733 .... C2
Kufstein 12,766 .... A3
Kundl 3,020 .... A3
Laa an der Thaya 5,455 .... D2
Laakirchen 7,664 .... B3
Lambach 3,301 .... C2
Landeck 7,388 .... A3
Längenfeld 2,838 .... A3
Langenlois 4,957 .... C2
Langenwang 4,071 .... C3
Lavamünd 4,120 .... C3
Leibnitz 6,646 .... C3
Lenzing 5,385 .... B3
Leoben 35,153 .... C3
Lienz 11,696 .... B3
Liezen 6,244 .... C3
Lilienfeld 3,126 .... C3
Linz 205,700 .... C2
Linz* 356,500 .... C2
Lustenau 15,239 .... A3
Mannersdorf am
Leithagebirge 4,012 .... D3
Marchegg 2,678 .... D2
Mariazell 2,298 .... C3
Matrei in Osttirol 4,003 .... B3
Mattersburg 5,417 .... D3
Mattighofen 4,344 .... B2
Mauerkirchen 2,237 .... B2
Mautern in Steiermark 2,536 .... C3
Mauthausen 4,419 .... C2
Mauthen-Kötschach 3,750 .... B3
Mayrhofen 3,174 .... A3
Melk 5,108 .... C2
Mistelbach an der Zaya 6,306 .... D2
Mittersill 4,361 .... B3
Mödling 18,712 .... D2
Mondsee 2,141 .... B3
Murau 2,710 .... C3
Mürzzuschlag 11,564 .... C3
Neuberg an der Mürz 2,183 .... C3
Neumarkt am Wallersee 3,267 .... B3
Neunkirchen 10,922 .... C3
Neusiedl am See 3,999 .... D3
Neustift im Stubaital 2,789 .... A3
Ober Grafendorf 4,109 .... C2
Oberndorf bei Salzburg 3,293 .... B3
Obervellach 2,420 .... B3
Oberwart 5,661 .... D3
Paternion 5,805 .... B3
Perg 4,872 .... C2
Peuerbach 2,161 .... B2
Pfunds 2,043 .... A3
Pinkafeld 4,610 .... C3
Pöchlarn 3,199 .... C2
Pörtschach am
Wörthersee 2,511 .... C3
Poysdorf 5,774 .... D2
Pregarten 3,249 .... C2
Raabs an der Thaya 4,194 .... C2
Radenthein 6,847 .... B3
Radkersburg 2,000 .... C3
Radstadt 3,585 .... B3
Rankweil 8,440 .... A3
Rechnitz 3,412 .... D3
Reichenau an der Rax 4,053 .... C3
Retz 4,780 .... D2
Ried im Innkreis 10,534 .... B2
Rottenmann 4,781 .... C3
Saalfelden am Steinernen
Meer 10,172 .... B3
Salzburg 122,100 .... B3
Salzburg* 213,430 .... B3
Sankt Aegyd am Neuwalde 3,165 .... C3
Sankt Anton am Arlberg 2,086 .... A3
Sankt Johann in Tirol 5,942 .... B3
Sankt Michael im Lungau 2,839 .... B3
Sankt Michael in
Obersteiermark 3,717 .... C3
Sankt Michael im Lungau 2,839 .... B3
Sankt Paul im Lavanttal 6,721 .... C3
Sankt Pölten 43,300 .... C2
Sankt Valentin 8,715 .... C2
Sankt Veit an der Glan 11,047 .... C3
Sankt Wolfgang im
Salzkammergut 2,746 .... B3
Schärding 5,874 .... B2
Scheibbs 4,419 .... C2
Schladming 3,460 .... B3
Schrems 3,393 .... C2
Schruns 3,607 .... A3
Schwarzach im Pongau 3,616 .... B3
Schwaz 10,253 .... A3
Schwechat 14,997 .... D2
Schwertberg 3,881 .... C2
Sierning 8,162 .... C2
Sillian 1,988 .... B3
Solbad Hall in Tirol 12,335 .... A3
Spital am Pyhrn 2,315 .... C3
Spittal an der Drau 13,690 .... B3
Steinach 2,698 .... A3
Steyr 40,578 .... C2
Stockerau 12,634 .... D2
Strassburg 2,850 .... C3
Tamsweg 5,060 .... B3
Telfs 6,589 .... A3
Ternitz 10,287 .... D3
Traiskirchen 8,878 .... D2
Traun 20,843 .... C2
Trieben 4,639 .... C3
Trofaiach 8,731 .... C3
Tulln 7,705 .... D2
Velden am Wörthersee 7,306 .... C3
Vienna (cap.) 1,700,000 .... D2
Vienna* 1,858,700 .... D2
Villach 50,979 .... B3
Vöcklabruck 10,627 .... B2
Voitsberg 11,094 .... C3
Völkermarkt 10,772 .... C3
Vordernberg 2,508 .... C3
Waidhofen an der Thaya 4,200 .... C2
Waidhofen an der Ybbs 5,218 .... C3
Weitensfeld-Flattnitz 5,206 .... B3
Weitra 3,250 .... C2
Weiz 8,241 .... C3
Wels 47,279 .... C2
Weyer Markt 2,518 .... C3
Wien (Vienna) (cap.) 1,700,000 .... D2
Wiener Neustadt 34,774 .... D3
Wildon 2,002 .... C3
Wilhelmsburg 6,307 .... C2
Wolfsberg 31,176 .... C3
Wörgl 7,811 .... A3
Ybbs an der Donau 6,422 .... C2
Zams 3,120 .... A3
Zell am See 7,456 .... B3
Zell am Ziller 1,882 .... A3
Zeltweg 8,431 .... C3
Zirl 4,157 .... A3
Zistersdorf 3,412 .... D2
Zwettl-Niederösterreich 11,624 .... C2

OTHER FEATURES

AllgÄu Alps (mts.) A3
Bavarian Alps (mts.) A3
Bodensee (Constance) (lake) A3
Brenner (pass) A3
Carnic Alps (mts.) B3
Constance (lake) A3
Danube (riv.) C2
Donau (Danube) (riv.) D2
Drau (riv.) C3
Enns (riv.) C3
Grossglockner (mt.) B3
Hohe Tauern (range) B3
Inn (riv.) B2
Karawanken (range) C3
March (riv.) D2
Mühlviertel (reg.) C2
Mur (riv.) C3
Neusiedler See (lake) D3
Niedere Tauern (range) B3
Ötztal Alps (mts.) A3
Raab (riv.) C3
Rhine (riv.) A3
Salzach (riv.) B2
Salzkammergut (reg.) B3
Semmering (pass) C3
Thaya (riv.) C2
Traun (riv.) C2
Wildspitze (mt.) A3
Zugspitze (mt.) A3

CZECHOSLOVAKIA

REPUBLICS

Czech Socialist Rep. 9,964,338 .... B1
Slovak Socialist Rep. 4,670,409 .... E2

REGIONS

Bratislava (city) 333,000 .... D2
Jihočeský 662,002 .... C2
Jihomoravský 1,966,850 .... D2
Praha (city) 1,161,200 .... C1
Severočeský 1,122,035 .... C1
Severomoravský 1,849,286 .... D2
Středočeský 1,193,041 .... C2
Středoslovenský 1,436,351 .... E2
Východočeský 1,214,581 .... C1
Východoslovenský 1,298,481 .... F2
Západočeský 865,094 .... B2
Západoslovenský 1,610,542 .... D2

CITIES and TOWNS

Aš 120,000 .... B1
Austerlitz (Slavkov) D2
Bánovce nad Bebravou 11,400 .... E2
Banská Bystrica 53,000 .... E2
Banská štiavnica 7,486 .... E2
Bardejov 17,400 .... F2
Benešov 11,100 .... C2
Beroun 17,600 .... B2
Bílina 17,800 .... B1
Blansko 13,800 .... D2
Boskovice 8,531 .... D2
Brandýs nad Labem-Stará
Boleslavv 333,000 .... C1
Bratislava 333,000 .... D2
Břeclav 21,100 .... D2
Brezno 14,800 .... E2
Brno 335,700 .... D2
Broumov 7,782 .... D1
Bruntál 12,300 .... D2
Bystřice nad
Pernštejnem 6,471 .... D2
Bystřice pod
Hostýnem 6,681 .... D2
Bytča 6,922 .... E2
Čadca 16,800 .... E2
Čalovo 6,591 .... D3
Čáslav 10,200 .... C2
Česká Lípa 18,600 .... C1
Česká Třebová 14,700 .... D2
České Budějovice 80,800 .... C2
Český Brod 6,640 .... C1
Český Krumlov 12,000 .... C2
Český Těšín 17,200 .... E2
Cheb 27,000 .... B1
Choceň 8,198 .... D1
Chodov 14,400 .... B1
Chomutov 44,200 .... B1
Chotěboř 6,692 .... C2
Chrudim 18,800 .... C2
Čierny Balog 6,435 .... E2
Děčín 46,500 .... C1
Detva 13,100 .... E2
Dobříš 6,378 .... C2
Dobruška 5,779 .... D1
Dolný Kubín 9,900 .... E2
Domažlice 9,100 .... B2
Dubnica nad Váhom 11,300 .... E2
Duchcov 9,712 .... B1
Dunajská Streda 13,000 .... D3
Dvory nad Žitavou 5,847 .... E3
Dvů Králové nad
Labem 16,800 .... C1
Falknov (Sokolov) 23,900 .... B1
Fil'akovo 7,822 .... E2
Frenštát pod
Radhoštěm 8,516 .... E2
Frýdek-Místek 43,800 .... E2
Frýdlant v.
Čechách 5,948 .... C1
Frýdlant nad
Ostravicí 6,250 .... E2
Galanta 12,300 .... D2
Gottwaldov 84,300 .... D2
Handlová 16,200 .... E2
Havířov 85,000 .... E2
Havlíčkův Brod 19,200 .... C2
Hlinsko 8,890 .... D2
Hlohovec 15,200 .... D2
Hlučín 15,300 .... E2
Hnúšt'a-Likier E2
Hodonín 22,600 .... D2
Holešov 9,091 .... D2
Holíč 7,602 .... D2
Holice 6,151 .... C1
Horažd'ovice B2
Hořice v
Podkrkonoší 7,715 .... C1
Horná Štubňa E2
Horní Benešov D2
Horní Libina D2
Hořovice 5,665 .... C2
Horšovský Týn B2
Hostinné C1
Hradec Králové 85,600 .... C1
Hranice 13,300 .... D2
Hrinova 7,800 .... E2
Hronov 9,767 .... D1
Hrušovany D2
Humenné 22,200 .... G2
Humpolec 7,810 .... C2
Hurbanovo E3
Hustopeče D2
Ilava E2
Ivančice 7,314 .... D2

Topography

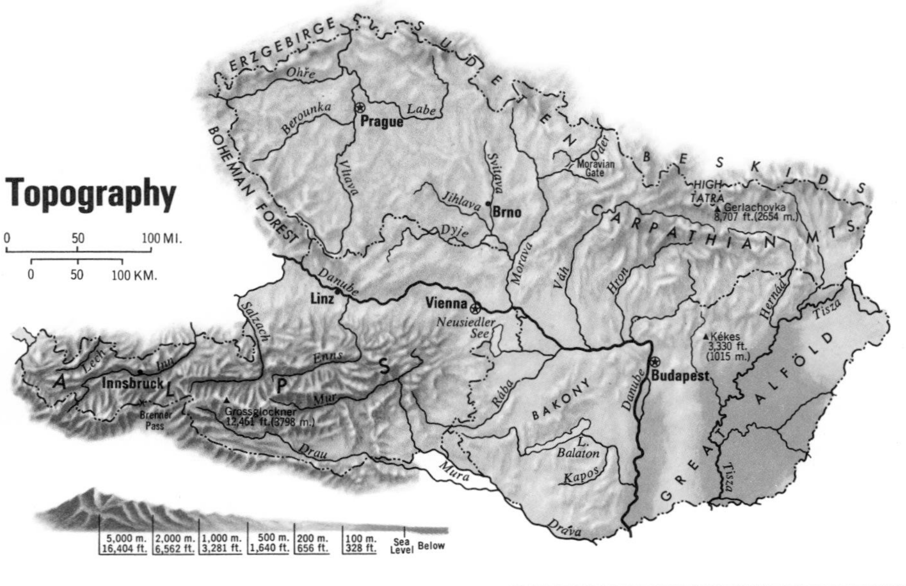

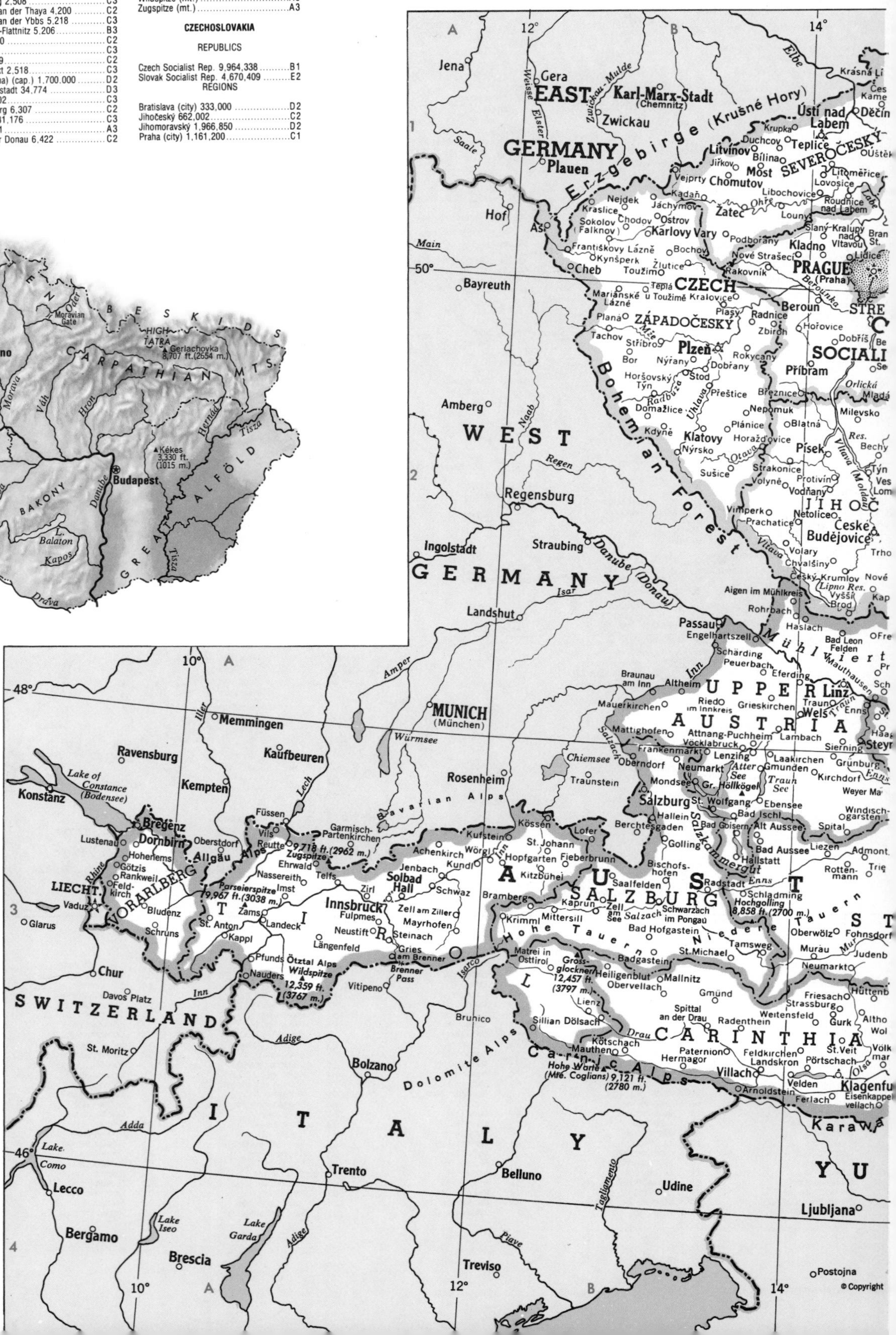

AREA 32,375 sq. mi. (83,851 sq. km.)
POPULATION 7,507,000
CAPITAL Vienna
LARGEST CITY Vienna
HIGHEST POINT Grossglockner 12,457 ft. (3,797 m.)
MONETARY UNIT schilling
MAJOR LANGUAGE German
MAJOR RELIGION Roman Catholicism

AREA 49,373 sq. mi. (127,876 sq. km.)
POPULATION 15,276,799
CAPITAL Prague
LARGEST CITY Prague
HIGHEST POINT Gerlachovka 8,707 ft. (2,654 m.)
MONETARY UNIT koruna
MAJOR LANGUAGES Czech, Slovak
MAJOR RELIGIONS Roman Catholicism, Protestantism

AREA 35,919 sq. mi. (93,030 sq. km.)
POPULATION 10,709,536
CAPITAL Budapest
LARGEST CITY Budapest
HIGHEST POINT Kékes 3,330 ft. (1,015 m.)
MONETARY UNIT forint
MAJOR LANGUAGE Hungarian
MAJOR RELIGIONS Roman Catholicism, Protestantism

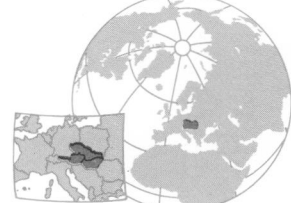

AUSTRIA

CZECHOSLOVAKIA

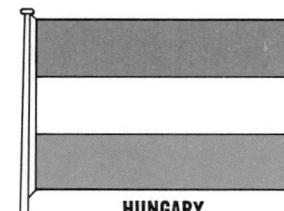

HUNGARY

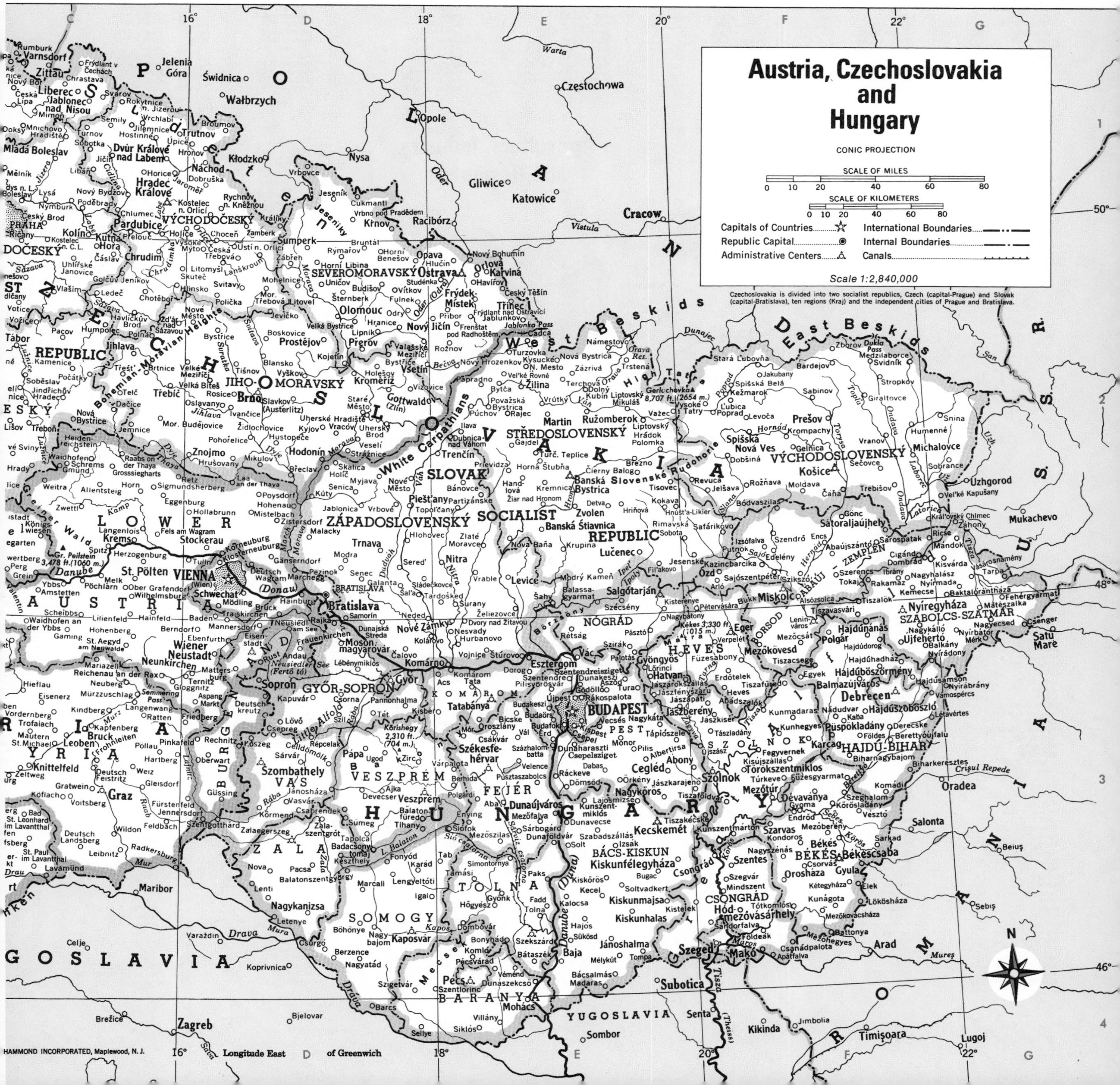

Austria, Czechoslovakia and Hungary

CONIC PROJECTION

SCALE OF MILES
0 10 20 40 60 80

SCALE OF KILOMETERS
0 10 20 40 60 80

Capitals of Countries...........★ International Boundaries_____
Republic Capital...................◉ Internal Boundaries_____
Administrative Centers..........△ Canals...................

Scale 1:2,840,000

Czechoslovakia is divided into two socialist republics, Czech (capital-Prague) and Slovak (capital-Bratislava), ten regions (Kraj) and the independent cities of Prague and Bratislava.

HAMMOND INCORPORATED, Maplewood, N.J.

(continued)

Jablonec nad Nisou 36,300 C1
Jablonica D2
Jablunkov 9,405 E2
Jáchymov B1
Jakubany F2
Jaroměř 11,600 C1
Jelšava F2
Jemnice C2
Jeseník 10,900 D1
Jesenské F2
Jevíčko D2
Jičín 13,200 C1
Jihlava 44,500 C2
Jilemnice C1
Jindřichův Hradec 15,700 C2
Jiřkov 11,400 B1
Kadaň 18,100 B1
Kamenice C2
Kaplice C2
Karlovy Vary 43,300 B1
Karviná 79,100 E2
Kdyně B2
Kežmarok 11,000 F2
Kladno 61,200 B1
Klatovy 18,500 B2
Kojetín 5,852 D2
Kokava nad Rimavicou 5,391 E2
Kolárovo 10,500 D3
Kolín 29,100 C1
Komárno 28,200 D3
Košice 169,100 F2
Kostelec nad Orlicí 5,575 D1
Král'ovský Chlmec 5,329 G2
Kralupy nad Vltavou 16,900 C1
Kraslice 6,733 B1
Kremnica 5,941 E2
Krnov 25,000 D1
Kroměříž 23,200 D2
Krompachy 6,332 F2
Krupina 6,627 E2
Krupka 8,301 B1
Kutná Hora 19,200 C2
Kyjov 10,700 D2
Kynšperk 5,524 B1
Kysucké Nové Mesto 11,700 E2
Lanškroun 8,683 D2
Levice 19,000 E2
Levoča 10,100 F2
Libáň C1
Liberec 75,600 C1
Moravě 6,581 D2
Nové Město nad Váhom 15,900 D2
Nové Strašecí B1
Nové Zámky 27,300 D3
Nový Bohumín 16,700 E2
Nový Bor 7,621 C1
Nový Bydžov 6,824 C1
Nový Hrozenkov E2
Nový Jičín 21,400 E2
Nymburk 13,600 C1
Nýřany 6,204 B2
Nýrsko B2
Odry D2
Olomouc 82,800 D2
Opava 53,800 E2
Orlová 25,500 E2
Ostrava 293,500 E2
Ostrov 18,200 B1
Pardubice 78,500 C1
Partizánske 15,100 E2
Pelhřimov 11,900 C2
Pezinok 13,100 D2
Piešt'any 25,400 D2
Písek 25,100 C2
Plzeň 155,000 B2
Počátky C2
Podbořany B1
Poděbrady 13,400 C1
Pohořelice D2
Polička 6,529 D2
Polná C2
Polomka E2
Poprad 25,800 F2
Považská Bystrica 19,300 E2
Prachatice 7,900 B2
Prague (Praha) (cap.) 1,161,200 C1
Přelouč 6,251 C1
Přerov 43,500 D2
Prešov 61,000 F2
Přeštice B2
Příbor 7,726 E2
Příbram 31,300 B2
Prievidza 30,900 E2
Prostějov 44,200 D2
Protivín C2
Púchov 9,306 E2
Radnice B2
Rajec E2
Rakovník 14,200 B1
Štúrovo 8,287 E3
Šumperk 25,900 D1
Šurany 6,693 E2
Sušice 10,300 B2
Svárov C1
Svidník 4,600 F2
Svitavy 15,000 D2
Tábor 28,100 C2
Tachov 11,400 B2
Telč 5,285 C2
Teplice 52,300 B1
Tišnov 8,263 D2
Topol'čany 17,500 D2
Třebíč 23,900 C2
Trebišov 13,700 F2
Třeboň 6,068 C2
Trenčín 38,800 E2
Třešt' 5,053 C2
Třinec 32,000 E2
Trnava 48,600 D2
Trutnov 24,500 D1
Turnov 13,600 C1
Turzovka 6,107 E2
Uherské Hradiště 32,100 D2
Uherský Brod 12,800 D2
Uničov 10,800 D2
Úpice 6,323 C1
Ústí nad Labem 74,900 C1
Ústí nad Orlicí 13,700 D2
Valašské Meziříčí 19,400 D2
Varnsdorf 14,700 C1
Važec E2
Vejprty B1
Velká Bíteš D2
Velká Bystřice D2
Vel'ké Kapušany G2
Velké Meziříčí 7,590 D2
Vel'ké Rovné E2
Veselí nad Lužnicí C2
Veselí nad Moravou 11,500 D2
Vimperk 5,749 B2
Vítkov 5,138 D2
Vizovice D2
Vlašim 8,873 C2
Vodňany 5,620 C2
Vojnice E3
Volary B2
Volyně B2
Votice C2
Jablunka (pass) E2
Jeseníky (mts.) D1
Jihlava (riv.) D2
Krušné Hory (Erzgebirge) (mts.) B1
Labe (riv.) C1
Lipno (res.) C2
Lužnice (riv.) C2
Moldau (Vltava) (riv.) C2
Morava (riv.) D2
Nitra (riv.) E2
Oder (Odra) (riv.) D2
Ohře (riv.) B1
Ondava (riv.) F2
Orava (riv.) E2
Orlická (res.) C2
Sázava (riv.) C2
Slovenské Rudohorie (mts.) E2
Sudeten (mts.) C1
Svitava (riv.) D2
Svratka (riv.) D2
Tatra, High (mts.) E2
Torysa (riv.) F2
Úhlava (riv.) B2
Váh (riv.) D2
Vltava (riv.) C2
White Carpathians (mts.) E2

HUNGARY

COUNTIES

Bács-Kiskun 568,532 E3
Baranya 434,030 E4
Békés 436,987 F3
Borsod-Abaúj-Zemplén 808,924 F2
Budapest (city) 2,060,170 E3
Csongrád 456,862 F3
Fejér 421,568 E3
Győr-Sopron 428,476 D3
Hajdú-Bihar 552,417 F3
Heves 350,874 F3
Komárom 321,579 E3
Nógrád 239,907 E3
Pest 973,486 E3
Somogy 360,308 D3
Szabolcs-Szatmár 593,746 G3
Szolnok 446,379 F3
Tolna 266,414 E3
Vas 285,527 D3
Csenger 4,792 G3
Csepel 71,693 E3
Csepreg 4,079 D3
Csongrád 22,202 E3
Csorna 12,131 D3
Csorvás 6,826 F3
Csurgó 5,463 D3
Dabas 13,075 E3
Debrecen 192,484 F3
Derecske 9,579 F3
Dévaványa 11,208 F3
Devecser 5,482 D3
Dombóvár 19,917 E3
Dombrád 6,328 F2
Dömsöd 6,545 E3
Dorog 10,754 E3
Dunaföldvár 10,318 E3
Dunaharaszti 15,788 E3
Dunakeszi 25,187 E3
Dunaszekcső 2,999 E3
Dunaújváros 60,694 E3
Dunavecse 4,521 E3
Edelény 9,559 F2
Eger 61,283 F3
Egyek 7,956 F3
Elek 6,032 F3
Enes 2,565 F2
Endrőd 8,136 F3
Enying 7,518 E3
Érd 41,210 E3
Erdőtelek 4,250 F3
Esztergom 30,476 E3
Fadd 4,805 E3
Fegyvernek 8,421 F3
Fehérgyarmat 6,729 G3
Földeák 3,855 F3
Földes 5,293 F2
Fonyód 3,957 D3
Füzesabony 6,965 F3
Füzesgyarmat 7,097 F3
Gödöllő 28,057 E3
Gönc 2,875 F2
Gyoma 10,392 F3
Gyöngyös 36,927 E3
Gyönk 2,507 E3
Győr 123,618 D3
Gyula 34,514 F3
Hajdúböszörmény 32,145 F3
Hajdúdorog 10,118 F3
Hajdúhadház 13,626 F3
Körmend 11,787 D3
Körösladány 6,565 F3
Kőszeg 12,705 D3
Kunágota 4,622 F3
Kunhegyes 10,116 F3
Kunmadaras 7,343 F3
Kunszentmárton 11,103 F3
Kunszentmiklós 7,952 E3
Lajosmizse 12,872 E3
Lébénymiklós 6,190 D3
Lengyeltóti 3,389 D3
Leninváros 18,667 F3
Lenti 8,106 D3
Létavértes 9,106 G3
Letenye 4,395 D3
Lőkösháza 2,514 F3
Lőrinci 10,679 E3
Madaras 4,519 E3
Makó 29,943 F3
Mándok 5,093 G2
Marcali 12,485 D3
Mátészalka 17,709 G3
Mélykút 7,640 E3
Mérk 3,211 G3
Mezőberény 12,702 F3
Mezőcsát 6,729 F3
Mezőfalva 5,008 E3
Mezőhegyes 8,631 F3
Mezőkovácsháza 7,473 F3
Mezőkövesd 18,435 F3
Mezőszilas 2,792 E3
Mezőtúr 22,018 F3
Mindszent 8,730 F3
Miskolc 206,727 F2
Mohács 21,385 E4
Monor 16,838 E3
Mór 12,066 E3
Mosonmagyaróvár 29,732 D3
Nádudvar 9,447 F3
Nagyatád 12,946 D3
Nagybajom 4,402 D3
Nagyecsed 8,225 G3
Nagyhalász 6,437 F2
Nagykálló 11,282 F3
Nagykanizsa 48,494 D3
Nagykáta 11,922 E3
Nagykőrös 27,900 E3
Nagyszénás 7,124 F3
Nyírábrány 4,509 G3
Nyíradony 7,146 G3
Szarvas 20,598 F3
Szécsény 5,690 E2
Százhalombatta 13,963 E3
Szeged 171,342 E3
Szeghalom 9,736 F3
Szegvár 6,395 F3
Székesfehérvár 103,197 E3
Szekszárd 34,592 E3
Szendrő 4,098 F2
Szentendre 16,844 E3
Szentes 35,326 F3
Szentgotthárd 5,837 D3
Szentlőrinc 3,926 E3
Szerencs 8,612 F2
Szigetvár 12,114 D3
Szikszó 6,419 F2
Szil 2,073 D3
Szolnok 75,203 F3
Szombathely 82,830 D3
Tab 3,922 E3
Tamási 7,602 E3
Tápiószele 5,575 E3
Tapolca 17,161 D3
Tarpa 3,436 G2
Tata 24,114 E3
Tatabánya 75,942 E3
Tét 4,441 D3
Tiszacsege 6,263 F3
Tiszaföldvár 12,560 F3
Tiszafüred 12,259 F3
Tiszakécske 12,378 E3
Tiszalök 6,230 F2
Tiszavasvári 13,292 F3
Tokaj 4,845 F2
Tolna 8,997 E3
Tompa 5,365 E3
Törökszentmiklós 25,551 F3
Tótkomlós 8,803 F3
Tura 8,235 E3
Túrkeve 11,393 F3
Újfehértó 14,412 F3
Újpest 80,384 E3
Újszász 7,098 F2
Vác 34,837 E3
Vál 2,488 E3
Vámospércs 5,213 F3
Várpalota 28,293 E3
Vásárosnamény 8,637 G2
Vasvár 4,275 D3
Vecsés 19,193 E3

Agriculture, Industry and Resources

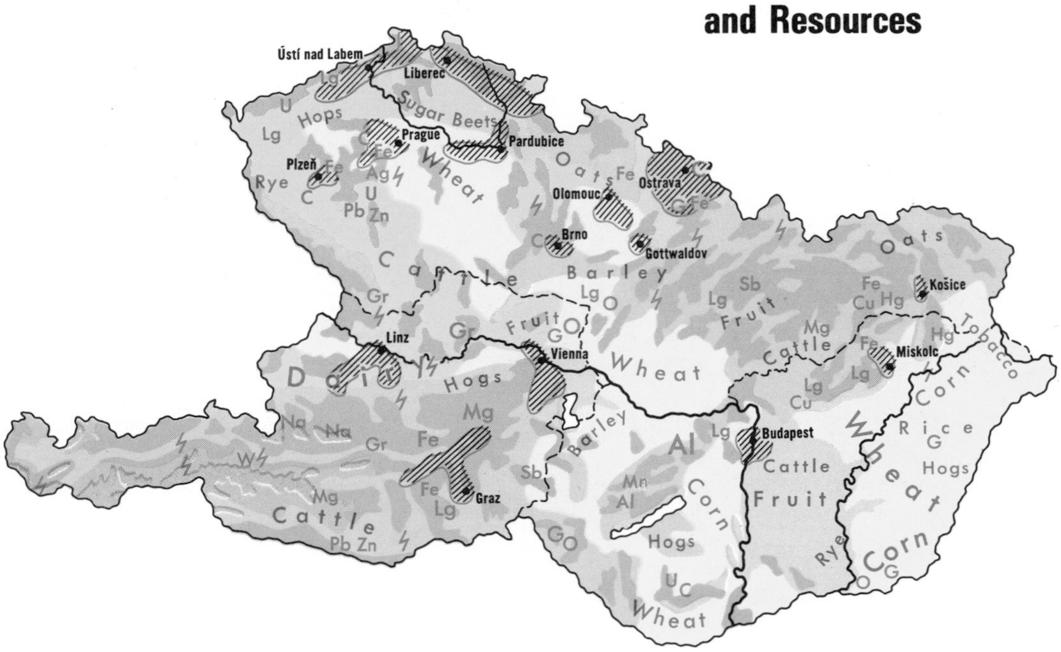

Ústí nad Labem
Liberec
Sugar Beets
Hops
Prague
Pardubice
Plzeň
Rye
Wheat
Oats
Olomouc
Ostrava
Brno
Gottwaldov
Cattle
Barley
Oats
Košice
Linz
Vienna
Fruit
Wheat
Cattle
Miskolc
Tobacco
Dairy
Hogs
Corn
Budapest
Rice
Cattle
Fruit
Hogs
Wheat
Graz
Cattle
Corn
Hogs
Wheat

DOMINANT LAND USE

- Cereals (chiefly wheat, corn)
- Other Cereals, Livestock, Dairy
- General Farming, Livestock
- General Farming, Truck Farming
- Pasture Livestock
- Grapes, Wine
- Forests
- Nonagricultural Land

MAJOR MINERAL OCCURRENCES

Ag	Silver	Mg	Magnesium
Al	Bauxite	Mn	Manganese
C	Coal	Na	Salt
Cu	Copper	O	Petroleum
Fe	Iron Ore	Pb	Lead
G	Natural Gas	Sb	Antimony
Gr	Graphite	U	Uranium
Hg	Mercury	W	Tungsten
Lg	Lignite	Zn	Zinc

Water Power

Major Industrial Areas

Lidice C1
Lipník nad Bečvou 7,358 D2
Liptovský Mikuláš 19,400 E2
Litoměřice 19,700 C1
Litomyšl 8,112 D2
Litovel 5,805 D2
Litvínov 23,300 B1
Lomnice C2
Louny 15,200 B1
Lovosice 9,323 C1
L'ubica F2
Lučenec 23,300 E2
Lysá nad Labem 9,920 C1
Malacky 13,200 D2
Mariánské Lázně 14,600 B2
Martin 47,800 E2
Medzilaborce F2
Mělník 17,800 C1
Michalovce 23,600 G2
Mikulov 6,267 D2
Milevsko 7,091 C2
Mimoň 6,773 C1
Mladá Boleslav 36,900 C1
Mladá Vožice C2
Mnichovo Hradiště 5,239 C1
Modra 7,219 D2
Modrý Kameň 6,200 E2
Mohelnice 6,050 D2
Moldava nad Bodvou 5,397 F2
Moravská Třebová 9,052 D2
Moravské Budějovice 5,576 D2
Most 59,400 B1
Myjava 6,657 D2
Náchod 19,300 D1
Námestovo E2
Neded D2
Nejdek 8,187 B1
Nepomuk B2
Nesvady 5,453 E3
Netolice C2
Nitra 50,000 E2
Nová Baňa 6,218 E2
Nová Bystrica E2
Nová Bystřice C2
Nové Hrady C2
Nové Město na Moravě 6,581 D2
Revúca 5,901 F2
Říčany u Prahy 8,407 C2
Rimavská Sobota 5,800 E2
Rokycany 12,800 B2
Rokytnice nad Jizerou C1
Rosice D2
Roudnice nad Labem 11,800 C1
Rožňava 12,400 F2
Rožnov pod Radhoštěm 11,600 E2
Rumburk C1
Ružomberok 22,600 E2
Rychnov nad Kněžnou 7,500 D1
Rýmařov 7,522 D2
Sabinov 5,473 F2
Šafárikovo F2
Šahy 5,049 E2
Šal'a 15,200 D2
Samorín 8,287 D2
Sečovce 5,744 F2
Sedlčany C2
Semily 8,200 C1
Senec 8,544 D2
Senica 12,300 D2
Sereď 12,500 D2
Skalica 11,100 D2
Skuteč D2
Sládečkovce 5,598 D2
Slaný 13,200 C1
Slavkov D2
Snina 10,900 G2
Soběslav 6,140 C2
Sobotka C1
Sobrance G2
Sokolov 23,900 B1
Spišská Belá F2
Spišská Nová Ves 26,100 F2
Stará L'ubovňa 5,800 F2
Staré Město 6,293 D2
Šternberk 13,700 D2
Stod B2
Strakonice 19,000 B2
Strážnice 5,482 D2
Stříbro B2
Stropkov 5,645 F2
Studénka 9,744 D2
Vráble E2
Vracov D2
Vranov nad Teplou 14,700 F2
Vrbno pod Pradědem 5,594 D1
Vrbovce D1
Vrbové D2
Vrchlabí 11,700 C1
Vrútky 5,756 E2
Vsetín 24,100 D2
Vyškov 15,100 D2
Vysoké Mýto 8,830 D2
Vysoké Tatry F2
Vyšší Brod C2
Zábřeh 11,300 D2
Žamberk 5,040 D1
Žatec 17,400 B1
Zázrivá E2
Zbiroh B2
Zborov F2
Žd'ár nad Sázavou 17,800 C2
Želiezovce 5,478 E2
Žiar nad Hronom 14,800 E2
Židlochovice D2
Žilina 56,000 E2
Zlaté Moravce 10,300 E2
Zlín (Gottwaldov) 84,300 D2
Žlutice B1
Znojmo 28,500 D2
Zvolen 29,000 E2

OTHER FEATURES

Berounka (riv.) C2
Beskids, East (mts.) F1
Beskids, West (mts.) E2
Bohemian (for.) B2
Bohemian-Moravian Heights (hills) C2
Danube (riv.) C2
Dunajec (riv.) F2
Dyje (riv.) D2
Erzgebirge (mts.) B1
Gerlachovka (mt.) E2
Hornád (riv.) F2
Hron (riv.) E2
Ipel' (riv.) E2
Veszprém 386,740 D3
Zala 316,610 D3

CITIES and TOWNS

Aba 4,271 E3
Abádszalók 6,386 F3
Abaújszántó 4,209 F2
Abony 15,624 E3
Ács 8,423 E3
Ajka 29,601 D3
Albertirsa 11,252 E3
Alsózsolca 5,045 F2
Arló 4,203 F2
Aszód 6,218 E3
Bácsalmás 9,025 E3
Badacsonytomaj 2,933 D3
Baja 38,456 E3
Baktalórántháza 3,736 G2
Balassagyarmat 18,534 E2
Balatonfüred 12,599 D3
Balkány 7,667 G3
Balmazújváros 17,371 F3
Barcs 11,448 D4
Bátaszék 7,274 E3
Battonya 9,324 F3
Békés 22,287 F3
Békéscsaba 67,266 F3
Berettyóújfalu 16,406 F3
Berzence 3,406 D3
Bicske 10,720 E3
Biharkeresztes 4,788 F3
Biharnagybajom 4,093 F3
Böhönye 3,215 D3
Bonyhád 14,841 E3
Budafok 40,623 E3
Budaörs 13,958 E3
Budakeszi 10,429 E3
Budapest (cap.) 2,060,170 E3
Bugak 4,989 E3
Cegléd 40,567 E3
Celldömölk 12,533 D3
Cigánd 4,767 F2
Csabrendek 3,045 D3
Csákvár 5,238 E3
Csanádpalota 4,642 F3
Hajdúnánás 18,146 F3
Hajdúsámson 7,492 F3
Hajdúszoboszló 23,374 F3
Hajós 5,113 E3
Hatvan 24,790 E3
Heves 10,943 F3
Hódmezővásárhely 54,481 F3
Hőgyész 3,534 E3
Ibrány 7,037 F2
Izsák 7,686 E3
Izsófalva 6,816 F2
Jánoshalma 12,534 E3
Jánosháza 3,274 D3
Jászapáti 10,424 E3
Jászárokszállás 10,139 E3
Jászberény 31,347 E3
Jászfényszaru 6,869 E3
Jászkarajenő 4,101 E3
Jászkisér 6,816 F3
Jászladány 7,823 F3
Kaba 6,654 F2
Kalocsa 18,613 E3
Kaposvár 72,330 D3
Kapuvár 11,243 D3
Karád 2,754 D3
Karcag 25,264 F3
Kazincbarcika 37,481 F2
Kecel 10,493 E3
Kecskemét 91,929 E3
Kemecse 4,583 F2
Keszthely 21,671 D3
Kétegyháza 4,728 F3
Kisbér 4,562 D3
Kiskőrös 15,499 E3
Kiskunfélegyháza 35,339 E3
Kiskunhalas 30,552 E3
Kiskunmajsa 14,439 E3
Kispest 65,106 E3
Kistelek 8,544 E3
Kisterenye 6,844 E2
Kisújszállás 13,699 F3
Kisvárda 17,828 G2
Komádi 8,765 F3
Komárom 19,955 E3
Komló 30,301 E3
Kondoros 7,319 F3
Nyírbátor 13,388 G3
Nyíregyháza 108,156 F3
Nyírmada 4,744 F2
Örkény 5,013 E3
Orosháza 36,243 F3
Oroszlány 20,604 E3
Ózd 48,521 F2
Pacsa 1,984 D3
Paks 19,514 E3
Pannonhalma 3,731 D3
Pápa 32,202 D3
Pásztó 7,962 E3
Pécs 168,788 E3
Pécsvárad 3,672 E3
Pétervására 2,753 F3
Pilis 9,055 E3
Pilisvörösvár 10,217 E3
Polgár 9,429 F3
Polgárdi 5,767 E3
Püspökladány 15,730 F3
Pusztaszabolcs 5,794 E3
Putnok 7,103 F2
Ráckeve 7,534 E3
Rajka 2,448 D3
Rakamaz 5,407 F2
Rákospalota 60,983 E3
Répcelak 1,997 D3
Ricse 2,992 G2
Sajószentpéter 13,992 F2
Salgótarján 49,320 E2
Sándorfalva 5,949 F3
Sárbogárd 11,178 E3
Sarkad 11,937 F3
Sárospatak 15,316 F2
Sárvár 15,126 D3
Sátoraljaújhely 19,252 F2
Sellye 2,804 D4
Siklós 10,567 E4
Simontornya 4,892 E3
Siófok 20,084 E3
Solt 6,911 E3
Soltvadkert 7,934 E3
Sopron 53,930 D3
Sükösd 4,430 E3
Sümeg 6,229 D3
Szabadszállás 8,223 E3
Velence 3,463 E3
Vémend 2,293 E3
Verpelét 4,622 F2
Veszprém 54,898 D3
Vésztő 9,815 F3
Villány 2,764 E4
Záhony 3,049 G2
Zalaegerszeg 39,671 D3
Zalaszentgrót 5,346 D3
Zirc 5,980 D3

OTHER FEATURES

Bakony (mts.) D3
Balaton (lake) D3
Berettyó (riv.) F3
Bükk (mts.) F2
Csepelsziget (isl.) E3
Danube (riv.) E3
Dráva (riv.) D3
Duna (Danube) (riv.) E3
Fertő tó (Neusiedler See) (lake) D3
Great Alföld (plain) F3
Hernád (riv.) F2
Kapos (riv.) D3
Kékes (mt.) E3
Körös (riv.) F3
Maros (riv.) F3
Mátra (mts.) E3
Mecsek (mts.) D3
Mura (riv.) D3
Rába (riv.) D3
Sajó (riv.) F2
Sárviz csatorna (canal) E3
Sió csatorna (canal) E3
Szentendreisziget (isl.) E3
Tisza (riv.) F3
Zala (riv.) D3

*City and suburbs.
†Population of Austrian cities are communes.

YUGOSLAVIA

AREA 98,766 sq. mi. (255,804 sq. km.)
POPULATION 22,471,000
CAPITAL Belgrade
LARGEST CITY Belgrade
HIGHEST POINT Triglav 9,393 ft. (2,863 m.)
MONETARY UNIT Yugoslav dinar
MAJOR LANGUAGES Serbo-Croation, Slovenian, Macedonian, Montenegrin, Albanian
MAJOR RELIGIONS Eastern Orthodoxy, Roman Catholicism, Islam

ALBANIA

AREA 11,100 sq. mi. (28,749 sq. km.)
POPULATION 2,590,600
CAPITAL Tiranë
LARGEST CITY Tiranë
HIGHEST POINT Korab 9,026 ft. (2,751 m.)
MONETARY UNIT lek
MAJOR LANGUAGE Albanian
MAJOR RELIGIONS Islam, Eastern Orthodoxy, Roman Catholicism

ROMANIA

AREA 91,699 sq. mi. (237,500 sq. km.)
POPULATION 22,048,305
CAPITAL Bucharest
LARGEST CITY Bucharest
HIGHEST POINT Moldoveanul 8,343 ft. (2,543 m.)
MONETARY UNIT leu
MAJOR LANGUAGES Romanian, Hungarian
MAJOR RELIGION Eastern Orthodoxy

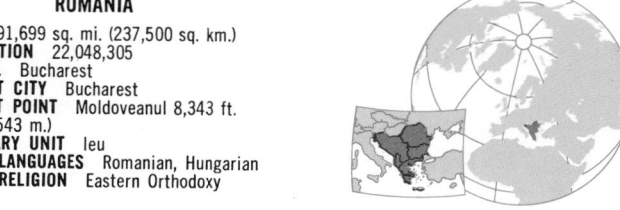

BULGARIA

AREA 42,823 sq. mi. (110,912 sq. km.)
POPULATION 8,862,000
CAPITAL Sofia
LARGEST CITY Sofia
HIGHEST POINT Musala 9,597 ft. (2,925 m.)
MONETARY UNIT lev
MAJOR LANGUAGE Bulgarian
MAJOR RELIGION Eastern Orthodoxy

GREECE

AREA 50,944 sq. mi. (131,945 sq. km.)
POPULATION 9,599,000
CAPITAL Athens
LARGEST CITY Athens
HIGHEST POINT Olympus 9,570 ft. (2,917 m.)
MONETARY UNIT drachma
MAJOR LANGUAGE Greek
MAJOR RELIGION Eastern (Greek) Orthodoxy

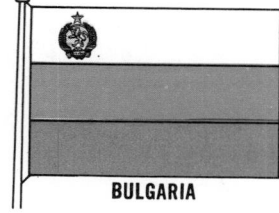

BULGARIA

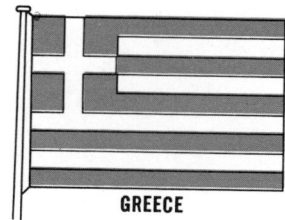

GREECE

YUGOSLAVIA

ALBANIA

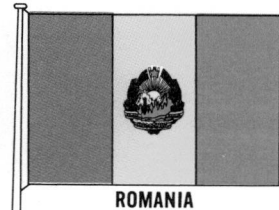

ROMANIA

Agriculture, Industry and Resources

DOMINANT LAND USE

- Cereals (chiefly wheat, corn)
- Mixed Farming, Horticulture
- Pasture Livestock
- Tobacco, Cotton
- Grapes, Wine
- Forests
- Nonagricultural Land

MAJOR MINERAL OCCURRENCES

Ab	Asbestos	Mg	Magnesium
Ag	Silver	Mn	Manganese
Al	Bauxite	Mr	Marble
C	Coal	Na	Salt
Cr	Chromium	Ni	Nickel
Cu	Copper	O	Petroleum
Fe	Iron Ore	Pb	Lead
G	Natural Gas	Sb	Antimony
Hg	Mercury	U	Uranium
Lg	Lignite	Zn	Zinc

⚡ Water Power
▨ Major Industrial Areas

ALBANIA

CITIES and TOWNS

Berat 25,700	D5
Çorovode	E5
Burrel	D5
Delvine 6,000	D6
Durrës (Durazzo) 53,800	D5
Elbasan 41,700	E5
Ersekë	E5
Fier 23,000	D5
Gjirokastër 17,100	D5
Kavajë 18,700	D5
Korçë 47,300	E5
Krujë 7,900	D5
Kuçovë (Stalin) 14,000	D5
Kukës 6,100	E4
Leskovik	E5
Lezhë	D5
Lushnje 18,900	D5
Memaliaj	D5
Peqin	D5
Përmet	D5
Peshkopi 6,600	E5
Pogradec 10,100	E5
Pukë	E4
Sarandë 8,700	E6
Shëngjin	D5
Shijak 6,200	D5
Shkodër 55,300	D5
Stalin 14,000	D5
Tepelenë	D5
Tiranë (Tirana) (cap.) 171,300	E5
Vlorë 50,000	D5

OTHER FEATURES

Adriatic (sea)	B4
Drin (riv.)	E4
Korab (mt.)	E5
Ohrid (lake)	E5
Otranto (str.)	D5
Prespa (lake)	E5
Sazan (isl.)	D5
Scutari (lake)	D4
Vijosë (riv.)	D5

BULGARIA

CITIES and TOWNS

Akhtopol 938	H4
Aitatar 3,249	H4
Ardino 5,080	G5
Asenovgrad 43,049	G5
Aytos 20,967	H4
Balchik 11,070	J4
Bansko 10,011	F5
Belogradchik 6,892	F4
Berkovitsa 16,253	F4
Blagoevgrad 50,043	F5
Botevgrad 17,789	F4
Bregovo 5,567	F3
Breznik 4,699	F4
Burgas 144,449	H4
Byala 10,564	H4
Byala Slatina 15,788	G4
Chirpan 20,595	G4
Devin 7,120	F5
Dimitrovgrad 45,596	G4
Dobrich (Tolbukhin) 86,184	H4
Dryanovo 9,804	G4
Elena 7,008	G4
Elin Pelin 5,499	F4
Elkhovo 12,397	H4
Gabrovo 75,034	G4
General-Toshevo 8,928	H4
Godech 5,225	F4
Gorna Oryakhovitsa 34,157	H4
Gotse Delchev 17,015	F5
Grudovo 9,871	H4
Ikhtiman 11,482	F4
Isperikh 10,500	H4
Ivaylovgrad 3,900	H5
Karapelit	H4
Karlovo 25,472	G4
Karnobat 21,480	H4
Kavarna 10,872	J4
Kazanlŭk 53,607	G4
Kharmanli 19,240	H5
Khaskovo 75,031	G4
Kotel 8,229	H4
Krumovgrad 5,211	H5
Kubrat 9,826	H4
Kula 5,667	F4
Kŭrdzhali 41,757	G5
Kyustendil 48,239	F4
Lom 30,538	F4
Lovech 43,858	G4

Lukovit 10,400	G4
Malko Tŭrnovo 4,233	H4
Maritsa 8,664	H4
Michurin 4,434	H4
Mikhaylovgrad 40,064	F4
Momchilgrad 8,185	G5
Nesebŭr 6,768	H4
Nikopol 5,563	G4
Nova Zagora 21,872	H4
Novi Pazar 15,751	H4
Omurtag 9,067	H4
Oryakhovo 14,012	F4
Panagyurishte 20,649	F4
Pazardzhik 65,577	F4
Pernik 84,432	F4
Peshtera 16,882	F4
Petrich 24,381	F5
Pirdop 8,248	G4
Pleven 107,567	G4
Plovdiv 300,242	G4
Pomorie 11,960	H4
Popina	H3
Popovo 19,428	H4
Provadiya 15,143	H4
Radomir 10,436	F4
Razgrad 42,486	H4
Razlog 13,690	F5
Rositsa	H4
Ruse 160,351	H4
Samokov 25,763	F4
Sandanski 19,003	F5
Sevlievo 24,421	G4
Shabla 4,471	J4
Shumen 83,525	H4
Silistra 58,270	H3
Simeonovgrad (Maritsa) 8,664	H4
Sliven 90,137	H4
Smolyan 29,032	G5
Smyadovo 5,020	H4
Sofia (cap.) 965,728	F4
Sozopol 3,877	H4
Stanke Dimitrov 42,034	F4
Stara Zagora 122,200	G4
Svilengrad 15,150	G5
Svishtov 29,412	G4
Teteven 12,555	G4
Tolbukhin 86,184	H4
Topolovgrad 7,230	H4
Troyan 23,692	G4
Trŭn 3,435	F4
Tŭrgovishte 38,796	H4
Tutrakan 11,447	H4
Varna 251,654	J4
Veliko Tŭrnovo 56,497	G4
Vidin 53,030	F4
Vratsa 61,265	F4
Yambol 75,861	H4
Zimnitsa	H4
Zlatograd 7,732	G5

OTHER FEATURES

Balkan (mts.)	G4
Black (sea)	J4
Danube (riv.)	H4
Dunav (Danube) (riv.)	H4
Emine (cape)	J4
Iskŭr (riv.)	G4
Kaliakra (cape)	J4
Maritsa (riv.)	G4
Mesta (riv.)	F5
Midzhur (mt.)	F4
Musala (mt.)	F4
Osŭm (riv.)	G4
Rhodope (mts.)	G5
Rujen (mt.)	G5
Struma (riv.)	F5
Timok (riv.)	F3
Tundzha (riv.)	H4
Vit (riv.)	G4

GREECE

REGIONS

Aegean Islands 417,813	G6
Athens, Greater 2,566,775	F7
Áyion Óros (aut. dist.) 1,732	G5
Central Greece and Euboea 966,543	F6
Crete 456,642	G9
Epirus 310,334	E6
Ionian Islands 184,443	D6
Macedonia 1,888,952	F5
Pelopónnisos 986,912	F7
Thessaly 659,913	F6
Thrace 329,582	G5

CITIES and TOWNS

Agrinion 30,973	E6
Aiyina 5,704	F7

Alyión 18,829	F6
Alexandroúpolis 22,995	H5
Alivérion 4,414	G6
Almirós 5,680	F6
Amaliás 14,177	E7
Amfilokhía 4,668	E6
Ámfissa 6,605	F6
Andíssa 1,762	H6
Andravídha 3,046	E6
Ándros 1,827	G7
Áno Viánnos 1,431	G8
Anóyia 2,750	G8
Ardhéa 3,555	F5
Areópolis 674	F7
Argalastí 1,621	F6
Árgos 18,890	F7
Argostólion 7,060	E6
Arkhángelos 3,016	J7
Árnaia 2,424	F5
Árta 19,498	E6
Astipálaia 787	H7
Atalándi 4,581	F6
Athens (cap.) 867,023	F7
Athens* 2,566,775	F7
Ayía 3,241	F6
Áyioi Kírikos 1,083	H7
Áyios Matthaíos 1,596	D6
Áyios Nikólaos 5,002	G8
Candia (Iráklion) 77,506	G8
Canea (Khaniá) 40,564	G8
Corinth 20,773	F7
Delfí 1,185	F6
Delvinákion 1,067	E6
Dhidhimótikhon 8,388	H5
Dhíkaia 1,222	H5
Dhmítsana 996	F7
Dhomokós 1,991	F6
Dráma 29,692	G5
Édhessa 13,967	F5
Elassón 7,200	F6
Elevtheroúpolis 4,888	G5
Ermoúpolis 13,502	G7
Fársala 6,967	F6
Filiátes 2,579	E6
Filiatrá 5,919	E7
Filippiás 3,248	E6
Flórina 11,164	E5
Gargaliánoi 5,888	E7
Grevená 8,106	E5
Ídhra 2,381	F7
Ierápetra 7,055	G8
Igoumenítsa 4,109	E6
Ioánnina 40,130	E6
Íos 1,270	G7
Iráklion 77,506	G8
Istíaia 4,059	F6
Itháki 2,293	E6
Kalámai 39,133	F7
Kalampáka 5,453	E6
Kalávrita 1,948	F6
Kálimnos 6,492	H7
Kándanos 403	F8
Kardhítsa 25,685	F6
Kariá 1,350	E6
Karíaí 301	G5
Káristos 3,550	G6
Kárpathos 1,363	H8
Karpenísion 4,414	E6
Kastéllion (Kíssamos) 2,996	F8
Kastéllion 1,152	G8
Kastoría 15,407	E5
Katákolon 690	E7
Kateríni 28,808	F5
Kavála 46,234	G5
Kéa 693	G7
Kérkira 28,630	D6
Khalkís 36,300	F6
Khaniá 40,564	G8
Khíos 24,084	H6
Khóra Sfakíon 246	G8
Kiáton 7,392	F6
Kilkís 10,538	F5
Kími 2,772	F6
Kipárissía 3,882	E7
Kíssamos 2,996	F8
Klthíra 349	G8
Komotiní 28,896	G5
Kónitsa 3,150	E5
Koropí 9,367	F7
Kos 7,828	H7
Kozáni 23,240	E5
Kranidhion 3,657	F7
Lagkadá 1,350	F7
Lamía 37,872	F6
Langadhás 6,707	F5
Langadhía	F7
Lárisa 72,336	F6
Lávrion 8,283	G7
Leonídhion 3,181	F7
Levádhia 15,445	F6
Levkás 8,769	E6
Limenária 1,507	G5

(continued on following page)

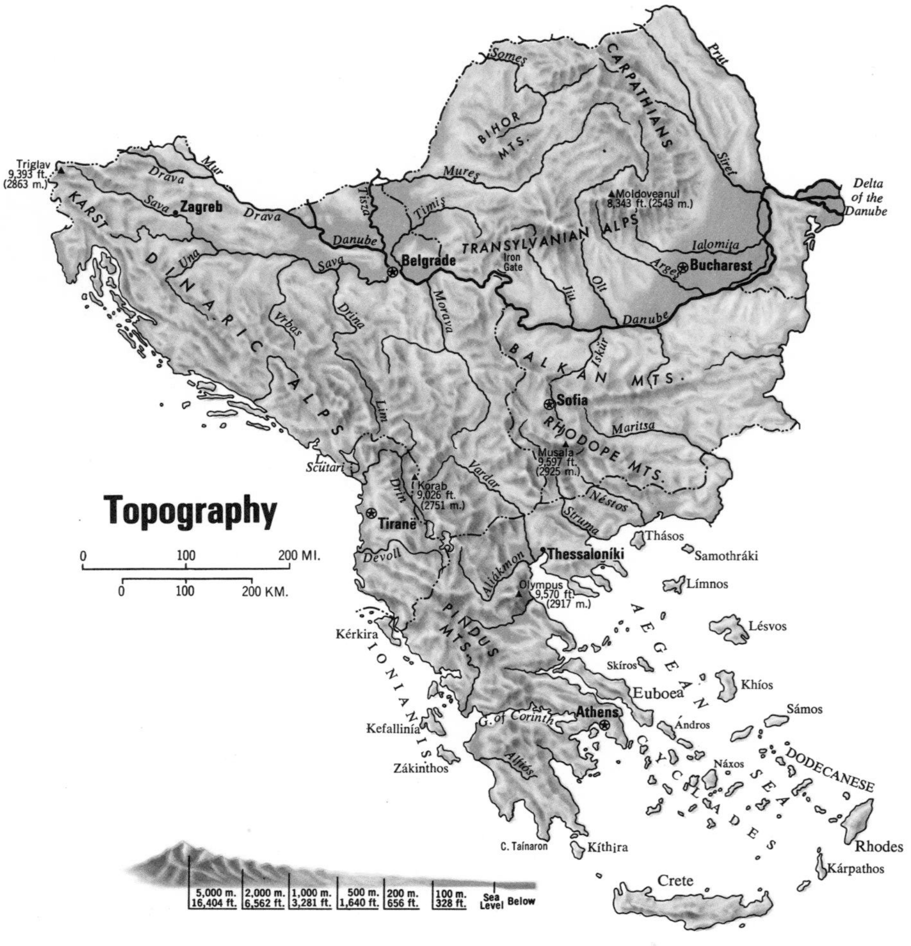
Topography
0 100 200 MI.
0 100 200 KM.
Triglav 9,393 ft. (2863 m.)
Zagreb
Belgrade
Bucharest
Sofia
Tirane
Thessaloníki
Athens
Scutari
Moldoveanul 8,343 ft. (2543 m.)
Musala 9,597 ft. (2925 m.)
Korab 9,026 ft. (2751 m.)
Olympus 9,570 ft. (2917 m.)
Iron Gate
Delta of the Danube
CARPATHIANS
BIHOR MTS.
TRANSYLVANIAN ALPS
BALKAN MTS.
RHODOPE MTS.
PINDUS MTS.
DINARIC ALPS
KARST
Somes
Prut
Siret
Mureş
Timiş
Tisza
Drava
Mur
Sava
Una
Vrbas
Drina
Lim
Morava
Danube
Ialomiţa
Argeş
Olt
Jiu
Iskur
Maritsa
Vardar
Drin
Devoll
Nestos
Struma
Aliákmon
Alfiós
Thásos
Samothráki
Límnos
Lésvos
Khíos
Sámos
Skíros
Euboea
Ándros
Náxos
Kérkira
Kefallinía
Zákinthos
G. of Corinth
C. Taínaron
Kíthira
Crete
Rhodes
Kárpathos
AEGEAN SEA
IONIAN SEA
CYCLADES
DODECANESE
5,000 m. 16,404 ft.
2,000 m. 6,562 ft.
1,000 m. 3,281 ft.
500 m. 1,640 ft.
200 m. 656 ft.
100 m. 328 ft.
Sea Level
Below

Límni 2,394 .... F6
Líndos 700 .... J7
Litókhoron 5,561 .... F5
Lixoúrion 3,364 .... E6
Loutrá Aidhipsoú 2,195 .... F6
Marathón 1,976 .... G6
Megalópolis 3,357 .... E7
Mégara 17,294 .... F6
Meligalá 1,724 .... F7
Mesolóngion 11,614 .... E6
Messíni 6,625 .... E7
Métsovon 2,823 .... E6
Mikínai 390 .... F7
Mílos 850 .... G7
Mírina 3,982 .... G6
Míthimna 1,414 .... G6
Mitilíni 23,426 .... H6
Moîrai 2,948 .... G8
Moláoi 2,484 .... F7
Monólithos 247 .... H7
Moúdhros 1,024 .... G6
Náousa 17,375 .... F5
Návpaktos 8,170 .... F6
Návplion 9,281 .... F7
Náxos 2,892 .... G7
Neápolis 3,070 .... F7
Neméa 4,356 .... F7
Néon Karlóvasi 4,401 .... H7
Nestórion 1,143 .... E5
Nigríta 7,301 .... F5
Oinóî 188 .... F6
Orestías 10,727 .... H5
Paramithía 2,747 .... E6
Pátrai 111,607 .... E6
Pérdika 1,198 .... E6
Péta 2,116 .... E6
Pílos 2,258 .... E7
Piraiévs (Piraeus) 187,362 .... F7
Pírgos 20,599 .... E7
Piryí 1,455 .... G6
Píthion 1,047 .... H5
Plomárion 4,353 .... H6
Políkastron 5,279 .... F5
Políkhnitos 4,152 .... G6
Políyiros 3,707 .... F5
Póros 4,051 .... F7
Préveza 11,439 .... E6
Psakhná 4,650 .... F6
Psári 622 .... E7
Ptolemaís 16,588 .... E5
Réthimnon 14,969 .... G8
Rhodes (Ródhos) 32,092 .... J7
Salamís 18,256 .... F6
Salonika
(Thessaloníki) 345,799 .... F5
Sámi 957 .... E6
Sámos 5,146 .... H7
Samothráki 508 .... G5
Sápai 2,456 .... G5
Sérrai 39,897 .... F5
Sérvia 3,834 .... F5
Siátista 4,852 .... E5
Sidhirókastron 6,363 .... F5
Sími 2,344 .... H7
Sitía 6,167 .... H8
Skíathos 3,707 .... F6
Skíros 1,925 .... G6
Skópelos 2,545 .... F6
Souflíon 5,637 .... H5
Sparta 10,549 .... F7
Spétsai 3,427 .... F7
Spíli 789 .... G8
Stavrós 1,700 .... F5
Stílis 4,427 .... F6
Thásos 2,052 .... G5
Thessaloníki 345,799 .... F5
Thessaloníki* 482,361 .... F5
Thíra 1,322 .... G7
Thívai 15,971 .... F6
Timbákion 3,229 .... G8
Tínos 3,423 .... G7
Tírnavos 10,451 .... F6
Tríkkala 34,794 .... E6
Trípolis 20,209 .... F7
Vámos 652 .... F8
Vartholomión 3,015 .... E7
Vathí 2,491 .... H7
Velvendós 4,063 .... F5
Vérroia 29,528 .... F5
Vólos 51,290 .... F6
Vónitsa 3,324 .... E6
Vrondádhes 4,253 .... G6
Xánthi 24,867 .... G5
Yerolimín 73 .... F7
Yiannitsá 18,151 .... F5
Yíthion 4,915 .... F7
Zákinthos 9,339 .... E7
Zante (Zákinthos) 9,339 .... E7

OTHER FEATURES

Aegean (sea) G6
Akrítas (cape) E7
Aktí (pen.) G5
Amorgós (isl.) G7
Anáfi (isl.) G7
Andikíthira (isl.) F8
Ándros (isl.) G7
Arda (riv.) G5
Argolís (gulf) F7
Astipálaia (isl.) H7
Áthos (mt.) G5
Áyios Evstrátios
(isl.) G6
Áyios Yeóryios (cape) G5
Cephalonia (Kefallinía)
(isl.) E6
Corfu (Kérkira) (isl.) D6
Corinth (gulf) F6
Crete (isl.) G8
Crete (sea) G7
Cyclades (isls.) G7
Día (isl.) G8
Dodecanese (isls.) H8
Euboea (Évvoia)
(isl.) G6
Évros (riv.) H5
Évvoia (isl.) G6
Gávdhos (isl.) F8
Ídhi (mt.) G8
Ikaría (isl.) G7
Ionian (sea) D7
Íos (isl.) G7
Itháki (Ithaca) (isl.) E6
Kafirévs (cape) G6
Kálimnos (isl.) H7
Kárpathos (isl.) H8
Kásos (isl.) H8
Kassándra (pen.) F6
Kéa (isl.) G7
Kefallinía (isl.) E6
Kérkira (isl.) D6
Khálki (isl.) H7
Khaniá (gulf) G8
Khíos (isl.) G6
Kímolos (isl.) G7
Kiparissía (gulf) E7
Kíthira (isl.) F7
Kíthnos (isl.) G7
Kos (isl.) H7
Kriós (cape) F8
Kríti (Crete) (isl.) G8
Lakonía (gulf) F7
Léros (isl.) H7
Lésvos (isl.) G6
Levítha (isl.) H7
Levkás (isl.) E6
Límnos (isl.) G6
Maléa (cape) F7
Matapan (Taínaron) (cape) F7
Merabéllou (gulf) H8
Mesará (gulf) G8
Messíni (gulf) E7
Míkonos (isl.) G7
Mílos (isl.) G7
Mirtóön (sea) F7
Náxos (isl.) G7
Néstos (riv.) G5
Nísiros (isl.) H7
Northern Sporades (isls.) F6
Olympia (isls.) E7
Olympus (mt.) F5
Parnassus (mt.) F6
Páros (isl.) G7
Pátmos (isl.) H7
Paxoí (isl.) D6
Pindus (mts.) E6
Piniós (riv.) E6
Prespa (lake) E5
Psará (isl.) G6
Psevdhókavos (cape) G6
Rhodes (isl.) H7
Rhodope (mts.) G5
Salonika (Thermaic) (gulf) F6
Sámos (isl.) H7
Samothráki (isl.) G5
Saría (isl.) H8
Saronic (gulf) F7
Sérifos (isl.) G7
Sídheros (cape) H8
Sífnos (isl.) G7
Sími (isl.) H7
Síros (isl.) G7
Sithoniá (pen.) F5
Skíros (isl.) G6
Spátha (cape) F8
Strimón (gulf) G5
Strofádhes (isls.) E7
Taínaron (cape) F7
Thásos (isl.) G5
Thermaic (gulf) F6
Thíra (isl.) G7
Tílos (isl.) H7
Tínos (isl.) G7
Toronaic (gulf) F5
Vardar (riv.) E5
Voîvíïs (lake) F6
Vólvi (lake) F5
Voúxa (cape) F8
Zákinthos (Zante)
(isl.) E7

ROMANIA

CITIES and TOWNS

Aiud 25,173 .... F2
Alba Iulia 44,552 .... F2
Alexandria 38,296 .... G3
Anina 11,594 .... E3
Arad 161,568 .... E2
Babadag 8,423 .... J3
Bacău 131,413 .... H2
Baia de Aramă 5,065 .... F3
Baia Mare 112,893 .... F2
Băile Herculane 4,606 .... F3
Băileşti 21,246 .... F3
Balş 16,091 .... G3
Beiuş 9,992 .... F2
Bereşti Tîrg H2
Bicaz 9,490 .... G2
Bîrlad 59,059 .... H2
Bistriţa 47,562 .... G2
Bivolari H2
Blaj 21,678 .... F2
Borşa 25,287 .... G2
Botoşani 69,881 .... H2
Brad 18,391 .... F2
Brăila 203,983 .... H3
Braşov 259,108 .... G3
Bucharest (Bucureşti)
(cap.) 1,832,015 .... G3
Bucharest* 1,960,097 .... G3
Buhuşi 20,204 .... H2
Buzău 106,738 .... H3
Buziaş 8,310 .... E3
Calafat 16,421 .... F3
Călăraşi 58,960 .... H3
Caracal 31,159 .... G3
Caransebeş 27,429 .... F3
Carei 24,496 .... F2
Cernavodă 14,686 .... J3
Chişineu Criş 9,344 .... E2
Cîmpeni 7,722 .... F2
Cîmpia Turzii 23,745 .... F2
Cîmpina 33,259 .... H3
Cîmpulung 33,448 .... G3
Cîmpulung Moldovenesc 19,270 .... G2
Cisnădie 21,114 .... G3
Cluj-Napoca 274,095 .... F2
Cogealac J3
Comaneşti 18,177 .... H2
Constanţa 279,308 .... J3
Corabia 20,454 .... G4
Costeşti 10,446 .... G3
Craiova 220,893 .... F3
Cujmir F3
Curtea de Argeş 23,555 .... G3
Dăbuleni F4
Dăeni J3
Darabani 12,207 .... H1
Dej 35,396 .... F2
Deta 6,956 .... E3
Deva 68,290 .... F3
Dorohoi 23,121 .... H2
Drăgăneşti Olt 11,606 .... G3
Drăgăşani 16,290 .... F3
Drobeta-Turnu Severin 80,114 .... F3
Făgăraş 34,762 .... G3
Fălçiu J2
Fălticeni 22,463 .... H2
Făurei 3,620 .... H3
Feteşti 28,730 .... H3
Focşani 62,275 .... H3
Folteşti H3
Găeşti 13,384 .... G3
Galaţi 252,884 .... H3
Gheorghe Gheorghiu-Dej 41,297 .... H2
Gheorghieni 20,592 .... G2
Gherla 19,303 .... G2
Giurgiu 53,241 .... G3
Haţeg 9,706 .... F3
Hîrlău 8,135 .... H2
Hîrşova 8,434 .... J3
Huedin 8,557 .... F2
Hunedoara 83,159 .... F3
Huşi 24,329 .... J2
Iaşi 262,493 .... H2
Ineu 10,414 .... E2
Isaccea 5,283 .... J3
Jibou F2
Jimbolia 15,325 .... E3
Lipova 12,427 .... E2
Luduş 15,771 .... G2
Lugoj 48,558 .... F3
Lupeni 28,251 .... F3
Mangalia 27,263 .... J4
Medgidia 43,691 .... J3
Mediaş 68,442 .... G2
Miercurea Ciuc 38,097 .... G2
Mizil 14,294 .... H3
Mociu G2
Moineşti 21,015 .... H2
Moldova Nouă 18,498 .... E3
Moreni 17,743 .... G3
Nădlac 8,407 .... E2
Năsăud 8,646 .... G2
Negreşti 7,435 .... H2
Ocna Mureş 16,381 .... G2
Odobeşti 8,440 .... H3
Odorheiu Secuiesc 33,392 .... G2
Olteniţa 25,536 .... H3
Oradea 175,400 .... E2
Orăştie 18,769 .... F3
Oraviţa 13,628 .... E3
Orşova 14,873 .... F3
Panciu 7,772 .... H3
Paşcani 26,937 .... H2
Pătulele F3
Pechea H3
Pecica E2
Periam E2
Petrila 25,087 .... F3
Petroşeni 42,316 .... F3
Piatra Neamţ 84,192 .... G2
Pincota 7,494 .... E2
Piteşti 125,029 .... G3
Pleniţa F3
Ploieşti 207,009 .... H3
Poenari Burchi G3
Poiana Mare F4
Pucioasa 14,056 .... G3
Rădăuţi 24,222 .... G2
Reghin 31,948 .... G2
Reşiţa 90,698 .... E3
Rîmnicu Sărat 29,815 .... H3
Rîmnicu Vîlcea 75,070 .... G3
Roman 56,466 .... H2
Roşiori de Vede 28,832 .... G3
Săcele 29,391 .... G3
Salonta 19,698 .... E2
Satu Mare 108,152 .... F2
Săveni 7,913 .... H1
Sebeş 27,448 .... F3
Sebiş 6,401 .... F2
Segarcea 8,783 .... F3
Sfîntu Gheorghe 51,210 .... G3
Sfîntu Gheorghe J3
Sibiu 156,854 .... G3
Sighetu Marmaţiei 38,879 .... F2
Sighişoara 32,296 .... G2
Şimleul Silvaniei 14,780 .... F2
Sinaia 14,215 .... G3
Sînnicolaul Mare 13,565 .... E2
Siret 6,677 .... G1
Slănic 8,017 .... G3
Slatina 54,954 .... G3
Slobozia 35,207 .... H3
Solca 4,835 .... G2
Sovata 10,745 .... G2
Ştefăneşti H2
Strehaia 11,431 .... F3
Suceava 66,857 .... G2
Sulina 5,240 .... J3
Tăşnad 10,441 .... F2
Techirghiol 11,228 .... J3
Tecuci 37,928 .... H3
Timişoara 281,320 .... E3
Tinca F2
Tîrgovişte 71,533 .... G3
Tîrgu Cărbuneşti 7,536 .... F3
Tîrgu Frumos 6,428 .... H2
Tîrgu Jiu 70,629 .... F3
Tîrgu Mureş 129,284 .... G2
Tîrgu Neamţ 15,756 .... G2
Tîrgu Ocna 12,960 .... H2
Tîrgu Secuiesc 18,265 .... H2
Tîrnăveni 27,799 .... F2
Topliţa 14,347 .... G2
Tulcea 67,091 .... J3
Turda 57,972 .... F2
Turnu Măgurele 30,003 .... G4
Urlaţa 10,900 .... H3
Urziceni 13,500 .... H3
Vasile Roaită J3
Vaslui 44,134 .... H2
Vatra Dornei 16,748 .... G2
Videle 11,323 .... G3
Vişeul de Sus 20,697 .... F2
Viziru H3
Zalău 36,158 .... F2
Zărneşti 23,378 .... G3
Zimnicea 15,111 .... G4

OTHER FEATURES

Argeş (riv.) G3
Bîrlad (riv.) H2
Black (sea) J4
Brăila (marshes) H3
Buzău (riv.) H3
Carpathian (mts.) G2
Crişul Alb (riv.) F2
Crişul Repede (riv.) F2
Danube (delta) J3
Danube (riv.) H4
Ialomiţa (marshes) J3
Ialomiţa (riv.) H3
Jijia (riv.) H2
Jiu (riv.) F3
Moldoveanul (mt.) G3
Mureş (riv.) E2
Olt (riv.) G3
Peleaga (mt.) F3
Pietrosul (mt.) G2
Prut (riv.) J2
Siret (riv.) H2
Someş (riv.) F2
Timiş (riv.) E3
Tîrnava Mare (riv.) G2
Transylvanian Alps (mts.) G3

YUGOSLAVIA

INTERNAL DIVISIONS

Bosnia and Hercegovina
(rep.) 3,710,965 .... C3
Croatia (rep.) 4,396,397 .... C3
Kosovo (aut. reg.) 1,240,919 .... E4
Macedonia (rep.) 1,623,598 .... E5
Montenegro (rep.) 527,207 .... D4
Serbia (rep.) 8,401,673 .... E3
Slovenia (rep.) 1,697,068 .... B2
Vojvodina (aut.
prov.) 1,953,980 .... D3

CITIES and TOWNS

Aleksinac 11,943 .... E4
Apatin 17,501 .... D3
Arendjelovac 15,659 .... E3
Bačka Topola 16,028 .... D3
Bakar B3
Banja Luka 85,786 .... C3
Bar 3,594 .... D4
Bečej 26,616 .... E3
Bela Crkva 11,137 .... E3
Belgrade (cap.) 727,945 .... E3
Beli Manastir 7,325 .... D3
Beograd (Belgrade)
(cap.) 727,945 .... E3
Berovo 5,053 .... F5
Bihać 24,155 .... B3
Bijeljina 24,888 .... D3
Bijelo Polje 9,298 .... D4
Bileća 4,083 .... D4
Biograd 3,595 .... B4
Bitola 64,467 .... E5
Bjelovar 21,019 .... C3
Blato 5,591 .... C4
Bled 4,710 .... A2
Bor 27,520 .... E3
Bosanska Dubica 9,191 .... C3
Bosanska Gradiška 9,742 .... C3
Bosanska Kostajnica 2,535 .... B3
Bosanska Krupa 8,947 .... C3
Bosanski Brod 10,113 .... D3
Bosanski Novi 9,861 .... C3
Bosanski Petrovac 4,113 .... C3
Bosanski Šamac 4,949 .... D3
Brčko 25,575 .... D3
Brežice 3,271 .... B3
Budva 2,483 .... D4
Bugojno 9,079 .... C3
Čačak 38,890 .... E4
Čakovec 11,766 .... C2
Čapljina 4,677 .... C4
Caribrod (Dimitrovgrad) 5,449 .... F4
Cazin 1,213 .... B3
Celje 30,827 .... B2
Cetinje 12,089 .... D4
Ćuprija 17,691 .... E4
Daruvar 8,478 .... C3
Debar 8,597 .... E5
Derventa 11,887 .... C3
Dimitrovgrad 5,449 .... F4
Djakovica 29,499 .... E4
Djakovo 15,833 .... D3
Doboj 18,073 .... C3
Donji Vakuf 4,928 .... C3
Drvar 6,237 .... C3
Dubrovnik 31,213 .... C4
Fiume (Rijeka) 128,883 .... B3
Foča 9,370 .... D4
Gacko 1,641 .... D4
Gevgelija 9,319 .... F5
Glamoč 2,627 .... C3
Gnjilane 21,359 .... E4
Gornji Milanovac 11,114 .... D3
Gornji Vakuf 2,429 .... C4
Gospić 8,238 .... B3
Gostivar 18,805 .... E5
Gračac 3,228 .... B3
Gračanica 9,302 .... D3
Gradačac 7,571 .... D3
Grubišno Polje 2,771 .... C3
Gusinje 2,616 .... D4
Herceg Novi 6,645 .... D4
Ivangrad 11,373 .... E4
Ivanjica 5,719 .... E4
Jajce 9,221 .... C3
Jesenice 16,163 .... A2
Kanjiža 11,348 .... D2
Karlovac 47,046 .... B3
Kavadarci 17,974 .... E5
Kičevo 14,189 .... E5
Kikinda 37,392 .... E3
Kladanj 3,255 .... D3
Ključ 3,466 .... C3
Knin 7,279 .... C3
Knjaževac 11,734 .... F4
Kočani 16,611 .... F5
Kočevje 7,277 .... B3
Kolašin 2,111 .... D4
Konjic 9,161 .... D4
Koper 16,683 .... A3
Koprivnica 16,398 .... C2
Kosovska Mitrovica 42,526 .... E4
Kostajnica 9,161 .... C3
Kotor 5,728 .... D4
Kragujevac 72,080 .... E3
Kraljevo 28,065 .... E4
Kranj 26,341 .... B2
Križevci 8,501 .... C2
Krk 1,500 .... B3
Krško 4,451 .... B3
Kruševac 29,902 .... E4
Kulen Vakuf 1,078 .... B3
Kumanovo 44,791 .... E4
Kutina 10,892 .... C3
Leskovac 46,050 .... E4
Livno 7,223 .... C4
Ljubinje 785 .... D4
Ljubljana 169,064 .... B3
Ljubuški 2,891 .... C4
Loznica 13,513 .... D3
Maglaj 5,869 .... D3
Makarska 6,589 .... C4
Maribor 94,976 .... B2
Modriča 7,406 .... D3
Mostar 47,821 .... D4
Murska Sobota 9,665 .... C2
Našice 5,836 .... C3
Negotin 11,325 .... F3
Nevesinje 3,077 .... D4
Nikšić 28,940 .... D4
Nin 1,782 .... B3
Niš 128,231 .... F4
Nova Gorizia A2
Nova Gradiška 11,765 .... C3
Novi 2,682 .... B3
Novi Pazar 28,696 .... E4
Novi Sad 143,591 .... D3
Novo Mesto 9,553 .... B3
Novska 5,168 .... C3
Ogulin 9,975 .... B3
Ohrid 26,352 .... E5
Omiš 3,515 .... C4
Opatija 9,238 .... A3
Osijek 94,989 .... D3
Pag 2,318 .... B3
Pančevo 53,979 .... E3
Paraćin 21,555 .... E4
Peć 41,783 .... E4
Petrinja 12,296 .... B3
Piran 5,485 .... A3
Pirot 29,658 .... F4
Plav 3,072 .... D4
Pljevlja 14,459 .... D4
Plŏce 4,257 .... C4
Pola (Pula) 47,117 .... A3
Poreč 4,512 .... A3
Postojna 6,085 .... B3
Požarevac 33,336 .... E3
Preševo 7,634 .... E4
Priboj 12,556 .... D4
Prijedor 22,379 .... C3
Prijepolje 7,960 .... D4
Prilep 48,045 .... E5
Priština 71,264 .... E4
Prizren 41,875 .... E4
Prokuplje 20,617 .... E4
Prozor 1,420 .... C4
Ptuj 9,245 .... C2
Pula 47,117 .... A3
Rab 1,675 .... B3
Radoviš 9,373 .... F5
Ragusa (Dubrovnik) 31,213 .... C4
Raška 3,935 .... E4
Ravne na Koroškem 6,529 .... B2
Rijeka 128,883 .... B3
Rogatica 4,801 .... D4
Rovinj 8,998 .... A3
Rožaj E4
Ruma 24,180 .... D3
Šabac 43,539 .... D3
Samobor 7,821 .... B3
Sanski Most 8,718 .... C3
Sarajevo 245,058 .... D4
Senj 4,927 .... B3
Senta 24,694 .... D3
Šibenik 29,619 .... C4
Šid 11,867 .... D3
Sinj 4,705 .... C4
Sisak 37,215 .... C3
Sjenica 9,118 .... E4
Škofja Loka 4,971 .... A2
Skopje 308,117 .... E5
Skradin 893 .... B4
Slavonska Požega 18,160 .... C3
Slavonski Brod 38,829 .... D3
Smederevo 39,200 .... E3
Smederevska Palanka 18,837 .... E3
Sombor 44,210 .... D3
Split 150,739 .... C4
Srebrenica 3,101 .... D3
Sremska Mitrovica 32,569 .... D3
Štip 27,218 .... F5
Stolac 3,862 .... D4
Ston 407 .... C4
Struga 11,369 .... E5
Strumica 22,770 .... F5
Subotica 89,476 .... D2
Surdulica 7,048 .... F4
Svetozarevo 27,812 .... E4
Svilajnac 7,848 .... E3
Teslić 4,940 .... C3
Tetovo 35,293 .... E5
Titograd 54,639 .... D4
Titovo Užice 35,465 .... D4
Titov Veles 35,583 .... E5
Travnik 12,745 .... C3
Trbovlje 16,393 .... B2
Trebinje 3,553 .... D4
Trogir 6,162 .... C4
Trstenik 7,167 .... E4
Tržič 4,435 .... B2
Tuzla 53,836 .... D3
Ub 3,785 .... E3
Ulcinj 7,472 .... D5
Umag 3,228 .... A3
Uroševac E4
Valjevo 26,655 .... D3
Varaždin 34,662 .... B2
Vareš 7,632 .... D3
Velenje 11,225 .... B2
Velika Plana E3
Veliki Bečkerek
(Zrenjanin) 60,201 .... E3
Vinkovci 29,257 .... D3
Virovitica 16,389 .... C3
Višegrad 4,753 .... D4
Visoko 9,365 .... D4
Vlasenica 4,033 .... D3
Vranje 25,909 .... F4
Vrbas 22,502 .... D3
Vršac 33,573 .... E3
Vučitrn 11,701 .... E4
Vukovar 29,500 .... D3
Žabljak 1,023 .... D4
Zadar 43,588 .... B3
Zagreb 561,773 .... C3
Zaječar 27,724 .... E4
Zara (Zadar) 43,588 .... B3
Zenica 49,522 .... C3
Žepče 3,177 .... D3
Zrenjanin 60,201 .... E3
Zvornik 8,498 .... D3

OTHER FEATURES

Adriatic (sea) B4
Bobotov Kuk (mt.) D4
Bosna (riv.) D3
Brač (isl.) C4
Cazma (riv.) C3
Cres (isl.) B3
Čvrsnica (mt.) C4
Dalmatia (reg.) C4
Danube (riv.) E3
Dinaric Alps (mts.) B3
Drava (riv.) C3
Drina (riv.) D3
Dugi Otok (isl.) B3
Hvar (isl.) C4
Ibar (riv.) E4
Istria (pen.) A3
Kamenjak (cape) A3
Kladovo F3
Korab (mt.) E5
Korčula (isl.) C4
Kornat (isl.) B4
Krk (isl.) B3
Kupa (riv.) B3
Kvarner (gulf) B3
Lastovo (Lagosta) (isl.) C4
Lim (riv.) D4
Lošinj (isl.) B3
Midzhur (mt.) F4
Mljet (isl.) C4
Morava (riv.) E3
Mur (riv.) B2
Neretva (riv.) D4
Ohrid (lake) E5
Pag (isl.) B3
Palagruža (Pelagosa) (isl.) C4
Prespa (lake) E5
Rab (isl.) B3
Rujen (mt.) F4
Sava (riv.) D3
Scutari (lake) D4
Slavonia (reg.) C3
Šolta (isl.) C4
Tara (riv.) D4
Timok (riv.) F3
Tisa (riv.) E3
Triglav (mt.) A2
Una (riv.) C3
Vardar (riv.) E5
Vis (isl.) C4
Vrbas (riv.) C3
Žirje (isl.) B4

*City and suburbs.

The Balkan States

CONIC PROJECTION

SCALE OF MILES

0 25 50 75 100 125 150 175

SCALE OF KILOMETERS

0 25 50 75 100 125 150 175

Capitals of Countries _____ ☆
Administrative Centers _____ ▲
International Boundaries _____
Major Internal Boundaries ____ _ _
Minor Internal Boundaries ___ .....
Canals _____

Scale 1:6,150,000

BULGARIA and GREECE are divided into counties and departments, respectively. Because of the scale no attempt has been made to delimit and name these sub-divisions; their administrative centers have, however, been designated.

The larger divisions named in Greece are well-known geographical regions, without administrative function.

ROMANIA consists of thirty-nine counties and three cities of regional status, Bucharest, Constanţa and Petroşeni. Scale does not permit delimiting these counties.

ALBANIA is divided into twenty-seven districts. Scale does not permit the delimitation of these divisions.

YUGOSLAVIA is a federation of six republics. The Serbian republic includes an autonomous province (Vojvodina), and an autonomous region (Kosovo).

© Copyright HAMMOND INCORPORATED, Maplewood, N.J.

Topography

0   50   100 MI.

0   50   100 KM.

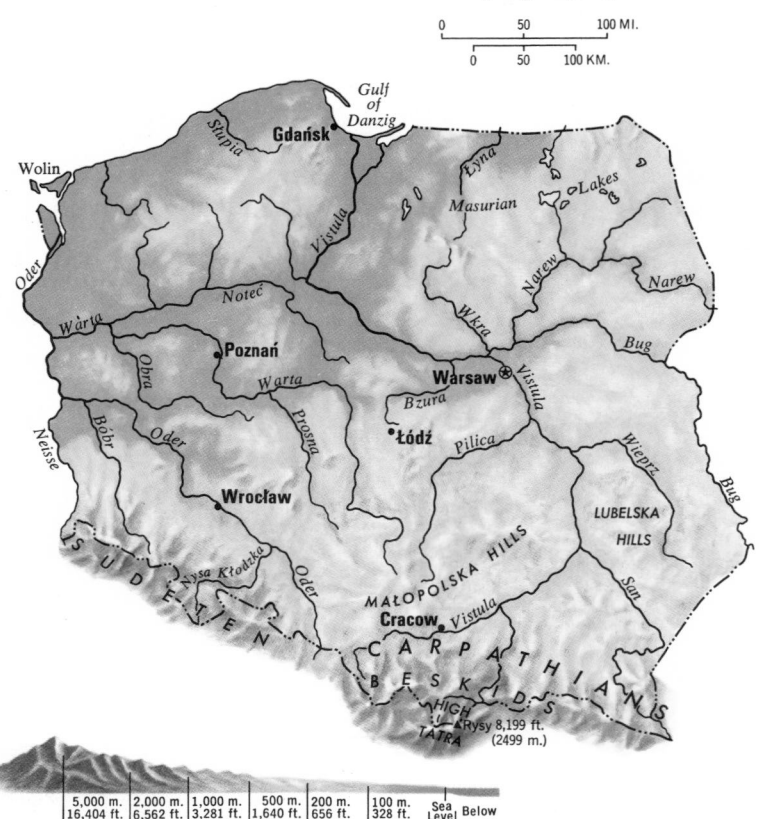

Gulf of Danzig

Wolin

Gdańsk

Słupia   Łyna   Masurian   Lakes

Oder   Vistula   Narew

Notec   Wkra   Narew

Wàrta   Bzura   Warsaw   Vistula   Bug

Neisse   Bóbr   Obra   Oder   Prosna   Warta   Pilica   Łódź   Wieprz   Bug

Poznań

Wrocław   LUBELSKA HILLS

SUDETEN   Nysa Kłodzka   Oder   MAŁOPOLSKA HILLS   San   Vistula   Cracow

CARPATHIANS   BESKIDS

HIGH TATRA   Rysy 8,199 ft. (2499 m.)

| 5,000 m. 16,404 ft. | 2,000 m. 6,562 ft. | 1,000 m. 3,281 ft. | 500 m. 1,640 ft. | 200 m. 656 ft. | 100 m. 328 ft. | Sea Level | Below |

Agriculture, Industry and Resources

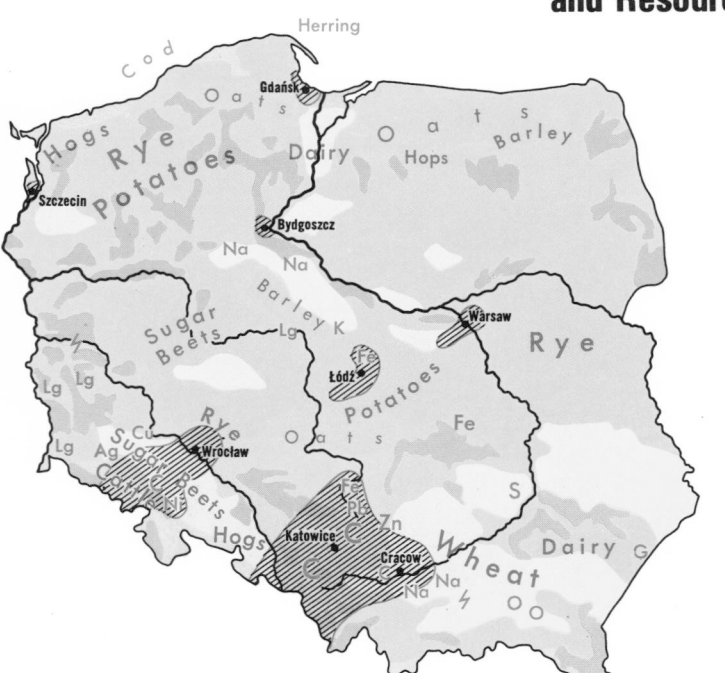

Cod   Herring

Gdańsk   Oats

Hogs   Rye   Oats   Dairy   Hops   Barley

Potatoes   Szczecin   Bydgoszcz   Na   Na   Barley   K   Lg   Warsaw   Rye

Sugar Beets   Łódź   Potatoes   Fe

Lg   Lg   Rye   Oats   S

Lg   Sugar Beets   Ag   Wrocław   Dairy   G

Cu   Katowice   Zn   Wheat   O   O

Hogs   Cracow   Na   Na

MAJOR MINERAL OCCURRENCES

Ag	Silver	Na	Salt
C	Coal	Ni	Nickel
Cu	Copper	O	Petroleum
Fe	Iron Ore	Pb	Lead
G	Natural Gas	S	Sulfur
K	Potash	Zn	Zinc
Lg	Lignite		

⚡ Water Power

▨ Major Industrial Areas

DOMINANT LAND USE

☐ Cereals (chiefly wheat)

☐ Rye, Oats, Barley, Potatoes

☐ General Farming, Livestock

☐ Forests

BALTIC SEA   LITHUANIA

DANZIG   Niemen

GERMANY

Oder   Stettin   Vilna

Berlin   Poznań   Vistula   Bug   Brest   Pinsk   U. S. S. R.

Warsaw

GERMANY   Neisse   Warta   Oder

Breslau   Cracow   Lwów

Poland 1938

0   50   100 MILES

CZECHOSLOVAKIA   Dniester

HUNGARY   ROMANIA

BALTIC SEA   Niemen

U. S. S. R.

Gdańsk (Danzig)   Vilna

Oder   Szczecin (Stettin)

Berlin   Poznań   Vistula   Bug   Brest   Pinsk

GERMANY   Warsaw

Neisse   Warta

Wrocław (Breslau)   Oder

Cracow   L'vov (Lwów)

Poland 1945

0   50   100 MILES

CZECHOSLOVAKIA   Dniester

HUNGARY   ROMANIA

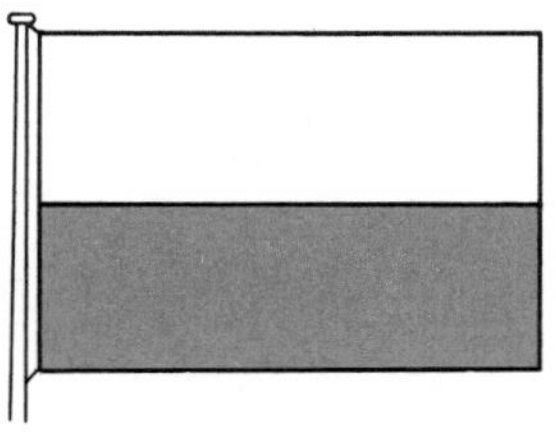

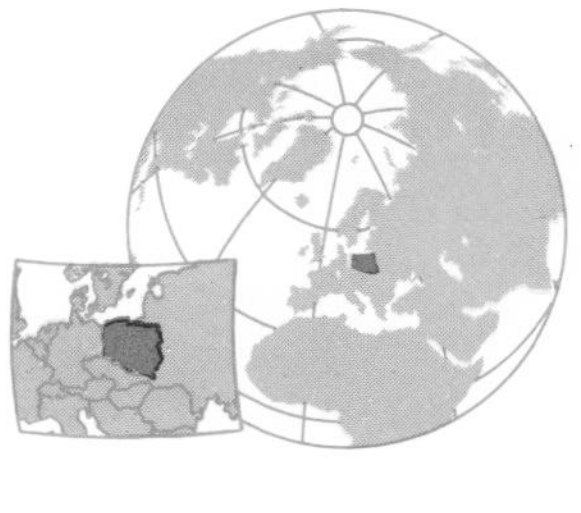

AREA 120,725 sq. mi. (312,678 sq. km.)
POPULATION 35,815,000
CAPITAL Warsaw
LARGEST CITY Warsaw
HIGHEST POINT Rysy 8,199 ft. (2,499 m.)
MONETARY UNIT zloty
MAJOR LANGUAGE Polish
MAJOR RELIGION Roman Catholicism

Braniewo 12,100 .... D1
Breslau (Wrocław) 461,900 .... C3
Brieg (Brzeg) 30,780 .... C3
Brodnica 17,300 .... D2
Brzeg 30,780 .... C3
Brzeg Dolny 10,800 .... C3
Brzesko 9,701 .... E3
Busko Zdrój 11,100 .... E3
Bydgoszcz 280,460 .... C2
Bytom 186,993 .... A3
Bytów 10,642 .... C1
Chełm 38,789 .... F3
Chełmno 17,906 .... D2
Chełmza 14,200 .... D2
Chodziez 14,100 .... C2
Chojnice 23,500 .... C2
Chojnów 11,000 .... B3
Chorzów 151,338 .... B4
Choszczno 9,800 .... B2
Chrzanów 29,300 .... B4
Ciechanów 28,500 .... E2
Cieplice
  Śląskie-Zdrój 15,400 .... B3
Cieszyn 25,234 .... D4
Cracow 651,300 .... E4
Czechowice-Dziedzice 25,400 .... D4
Czeladź 31,843 .... B4
Częstochowa 187,613 .... D3
Dąbrowa Górnicza 61,660 .... B3
Danzig (Gdańsk) 364,285 .... D1
Darłowo 11,200 .... C1
Dębica 22,900 .... E3
Dęblin 14,600 .... E3
Dębno 10,700 .... B2
Działdowo 10,100 .... E2
Dzierzoniów 32,800 .... C3
Elbing (Elblag) 89,835 .... D1
Ełk 27,188 .... F2
Gdańsk 364,285 .... D1
Gdynia 190,125 .... D1
Gizycko 18,200 .... E1
Gleiwitz (Gliwice) 170,912 .... A4
Głogów (Glogau) 20,226 .... C3
Głowno 12,800 .... D2
Głubczyce 11,300 .... C3
Głuchołazy 13,200 .... C3
Gniezno 50,643 .... C2
Goleniów 14,600 .... B2
Gorlice 15,200 .... E4
Gorzów Wielkopolski 74,267 .... B2
Gostyń 13,000 .... C3
Gostynin 12,000 .... D2
Grajewo 11,200 .... F2
Grodzisk Mazowiecki 20,400 .... E2
Grójec 10,300 .... E3
Grudziądz 75,511 .... D2
Grünberg (Zielona
  Góra) 59,700 .... B3
Gryfice 13,200 .... B2
Guben (Gubin) 14,600 .... B3
Hajnowka m4,345 .... F2
Hindenburg (Zabrze) 199,400 .... A4
Hirschberg (Jelenia
  Góra) 55,720 .... B3
Hrubieszów 14,999 .... F3
Iława 16,400 .... D2
Inowrocław 54,817 .... D2
Jarocin 18,100 .... C3
Jarosław 29,000 .... F4
Jasło 17,025 .... E4
Jastrzębie Zdroj 34,400 .... D3
Jaworzno 63,271 .... B4
Jędrzejów 13,264 .... E3
Jelenia Góra 55,720 .... B3
Kalisz 81,227 .... D3
Kamienna Góra 21,000 .... B3
Kartuzy 10,558 .... C1
Katowice 303,264 .... B4
Kedzierzyn-Koźle 45,600 .... C3
Kępno 10,151 .... C3
Kętrzyn 19,300 .... E1
Kielce 125,952 .... E3
Kłobuck 12,600 .... D3
Kłodzko 26,000 .... C3
Kluczbork 18,000 .... D3
Knurów 28,400 .... A4
Kolberg (Kołobrzeg) 25,419 .... B1
Koło 13,100 .... D2
Kołobrzeg 25,419 .... B1
Konin 40,600 .... D2
Końskie 13,100 .... E3
Konstantynów
  Łódzki 12,800 .... D3
Kościan 18,700 .... C2
Kościerzyna 18,914 .... C1
Köslin (Koszalin) 64,414 .... C1
Kostrzyń 11,200 .... B2
Koszalin 64,414 .... C1
Kraków (Cracow) 651,300 .... E4
Krapkowice 13,800 .... D3
Kraśnik Fabryczny 14,600 .... F3
Krasnystaw 12,495 .... F3
Krosno 26,500 .... E4
Krotoszyn 21,900 .... C3
Krynica 10,200 .... E4
Küstrin 11,200 .... B2
Kutno 30,000 .... D2
Kwidzin 23,104 .... D2
Łancut 12,049 .... F3
Landsberg (Gorzów
  Wielkepolski) 74,267 .... B2
Łaziska Górne 10,800 .... A4
Lębork 25,000 .... C1
Łęczyca 13,900 .... D2
Legionowo 20,800 .... E2
Legnica 75,843 .... C3
Leszcyny 12,200 .... A4
Leszno 33,890 .... C3
Libiaz 10,600 .... D3
Lidzbark Warmiński 12,900 .... E1
Liegnitz (Legnica) 75,843 .... C3
Lipno 10,900 .... D2
Łódź 777,800 .... D3
Łomza 25,500 .... F2
Łowicz 20,400 .... D2
Lubań 17,200 .... B3
Lubartów 10,000 .... F3
Lubin 28,400 .... C3
Lublin 235,937 .... F3
Lubliniec 19,800 .... D3
Luboń 16,400 .... C2
Lubsko 12,600 .... B3
Łuków 15,500 .... F3
Malbork (Marienburg) 30,900 .... D1
Międzyrzec Podlaski 13,500 .... F3
Międzyrzecz 14,900 .... B2
Mielec 26,800 .... E3
Mikłów 21,300 .... B4
Mińsk Mazowiecki 24,200 .... E2
Mława 20,007 .... E2
Mońki 9,560 .... F2
Morąg 9,681 .... E2
Mrągowo 13,400 .... E2
Myślenice 12,100 .... E4
Mysłowice 44,737 .... C4
Myszków 18,000 .... D3
Nakło nad Notecia 16,800 .... C2
Namysłów 11,076 .... C3
Neisse (Nysa) 31,837 .... C3
Nidzica 9,642 .... E2
Nisko 10,000 .... E3
Nowa Ruda 18,100 .... C3
Nowa Sól 33,300 .... B3
Nowy Dwor Mazowiecki 16,900 .... E2
Nowy Sącz 41,103 .... E4
Nowy Targ 21,900 .... E4
Nysa 31,837 .... C3
Oborniki 10,200 .... C2
Oława 17,746 .... C3
Oleśnica 27,500 .... C3
Olkusz 15,800 .... D3
Olsztyn 94,119 .... E2
Opoczno 12,168 .... E3
Opole 86,510 .... C3
Oppeln 86,510 .... C3
Orzesze 9,600 .... A4
Ostróda 21,300 .... D2
Ostrołęka 21,981 .... E2
Ostrów Mazowiecka 15,000 .... E2
Ostrów Wielkopolski 49,530 .... C3
Ostrowiec
  Świętokrzyski 49,958 .... E3
Oświęcim 39,600 .... D3
Otwock 39,863 .... E2
Ozorków 18,200 .... D3
Pabianice 62,275 .... D3
Piekary Śląskie 36,300 .... B4
Piła 43,778 .... C2
Pionki 13,600 .... E3
Piotrków Trybunalski 59,683 .... D3
Pisz 11,100 .... E2
Pleszew 13,348 .... C3
Płock 71,727 .... D2
Płońsk 11,619 .... E2
Police 12,700 .... B2
Poznań 469,085 .... C2
Prudnik 20,300 .... C3
Pruszcz Gdanski 13,000 .... D1
Pruszków 42,961 .... E2
Przasnysz 11,100 .... E2
Przemyśl 53,228 .... F4
Puck 9,500 .... D1
Puławy 34,800 .... F3
Pułtusk 12,600 .... E2
Rabka 10,700 .... D4
Racibórz 40,418 .... C3
Radom 158,640 .... E3
Radomsko 31,179 .... D3
Ratibor (Racibórz) 40,418 .... C3
Rawa Mazowiecka 9,800 .... E3
Rawicz 14,100 .... C3
Ruda Śląska 142,407 .... B4
Rumia 23,300 .... D1
Rybnik 43,415 .... D3
Rypin 10,029 .... D2
Rzeszów 82,192 .... F4
Sandomierz 16,800 .... E3
Sanok 21,600 .... F4
Schneidemühl (Piła) 36,600 .... C2
Schweidnitz
  (Świdnica) 47,542 .... C3
Siedlce 38,983 .... F2
Siemianowice
  Śląskie 67,278 .... B4
Sieradz 18,500 .... D3
Sierpc 12,700 .... D2
Skarzysko-Kamienna 39,194 .... E3
Skawina 15,900 .... D4
Skierniewice 25,590 .... E2
Sławno 10,700 .... C1
Słubice 12,000 .... B2
Słupsk 68,311 .... C1
Sochaczew 20,500 .... E2
Sokółka 10,023 .... F2
Sokołów Podlaski 9,569 .... F2
Sopot 47,573 .... D1
Sosnowiec 144,652 .... B4
Śrem 15,600 .... C2
Środa Śląska 10,259 .... C3
Środa Wielkopolska 14,800 .... C2
Stalowa Wola 29,768 .... F3
Starachowice 42,807 .... E3
Stargard Szceciński 44,400 .... B2
Starogard Gdański 33,400 .... D2
Stary Sacz 57,400 .... E4
Stettin (Szczecin) 337,294 .... B2
Stolp (Słupsk) 68,311 .... C1
Strzegom 14,000 .... C3
Strzelce Opolskie 14,700 .... D3
Strzelin 9,800 .... C3
Sulechów 10,200 .... B2
Suwałki 25,360 .... F1
Swarzędz 12,100 .... C2
Świdnica 47,542 .... C3
Świdnik 21,900 .... F3
Świdwin 12,500 .... B2
Świebodzice 18,500 .... C3
Świebodzin 14,900 .... B2
Świecie 17,900 .... D2
Świętochłowice 57,633 .... A4
Świnoujście
  (Swinemünde) 27,900 .... B1
Szamotuły 14,600 .... C2
Szczecin 337,204 .... B2
Szczecinek 28,600 .... C2
Szczytno 17,371 .... E2
Szprotawa 11,200 .... B3
Tarnobrzeg 18,800 .... E3
Tarnów 85,514 .... E4
Tarnowskie Góry 34,200 .... A3
Tczew 40,794 .... D1
Tomaszów Lubelski 12,329 .... F3
Tomaszów Mazowiecki 54,911 .... E3
Toruń 129,152 .... D2
Trzcianka 10,900 .... C2
Trzebinia-Siersza C4
Turek 18,500 .... D2
Tychy 71,384 .... B4
Ustka 9,900 .... C1
Wąbrzeźno 11,800 .... D2
Wadowice 11,700 .... D4
Wągrowiec 15,600 .... C2
Wałbrzych 125,048 .... C3
Wałcz 18,900 .... C2
Waldenburg
  (Wałbrzych) 125,048 .... C3
Warsaw (Warszawa)
  (cap.) 1,377,100 .... E2
Wejherowo 33,600 .... D1
Wieliczka 13,600 .... E3
Wieluń 14,300 .... D3
Wisła 9,800 .... D4
Włocławek 77,169 .... D2
Wodzisław Śląski 25,600 .... D4
Wolin 35,458 .... B2
Wołomin 24,000 .... E2
Wołów 10,500 .... C3
Wrocław 523,318 .... C3
Września 17,800 .... C2
Wschowa 10,000 .... C3
Wyszków E2
Ząbki 16,000 .... E2
Ząbkowice Śląskie 13,800 .... C3
Zabrze 197,214 .... A4
Zagań 21,400 .... B3
Zakopane 27,039 .... D4
Zambrów 14,082 .... E2
Zamość 34,734 .... F3
Zary 28,300 .... B3
Zawiercie 39,410 .... D3
Zduńska Wola 29,066 .... D3
Zgierz 42,838 .... D3
Zgorzelec 28,400 .... B3
Ziębice 9,700 .... C3
Zielona Góra 73,156 .... B3
Złocieniec 10,100 .... C2
Złotoryja 12,200 .... C3
Złotów 11,600 .... C2
Znin 9,600 .... C2
Zyrardów 33,196 .... E2
Zywiec 22,400 .... D4

OTHER FEATURES

Baltic (sea) B1
Beskids (range) D4
Brda (riv.) C2
Brynica (riv.) B4
Bug (riv.) F2
Danzig (Gdańsk) (gulf) D1
Dukla (pass) E4
Dunajec (riv.) E4
Gwda (riv.) C2
Hel (pen.) D1
High Tatra (range) D4
Kłodnica (riv.) A4
Łyna (riv.) E1
Mamry, Jezioro (lake) E1
Masurian (lkes) E2
Narew (riv.) E2
Neisse (riv.) B3
Noteć (riv.) B2
Nysa Kłodzka (riv.) C3
Nysa Łuzycka (Neisse)
  (riv.) B3
Oder (riv.) B2
Orava (res.) D4
Pilica (riv.) D3
Pomeranian (bay) B1
Prosna (riv.) C3
Przemsza (riv.) B4
Rysy (mt.) D4
San (riv.) F3
Słupia (riv.) C1
Śniardwy, Jezioro (lake) E2
Sudeten (range) B3
Uznam (Usedom) (isl.) B1
Vistula (riv.) D2
Warmia (reg.) D1
Warta (riv.) B2
Wieprz (riv.) F3
Wisła (Vistula) (riv.) D2
Wkra (riv.) E2
Wolin (Wollin) (isl.) B2

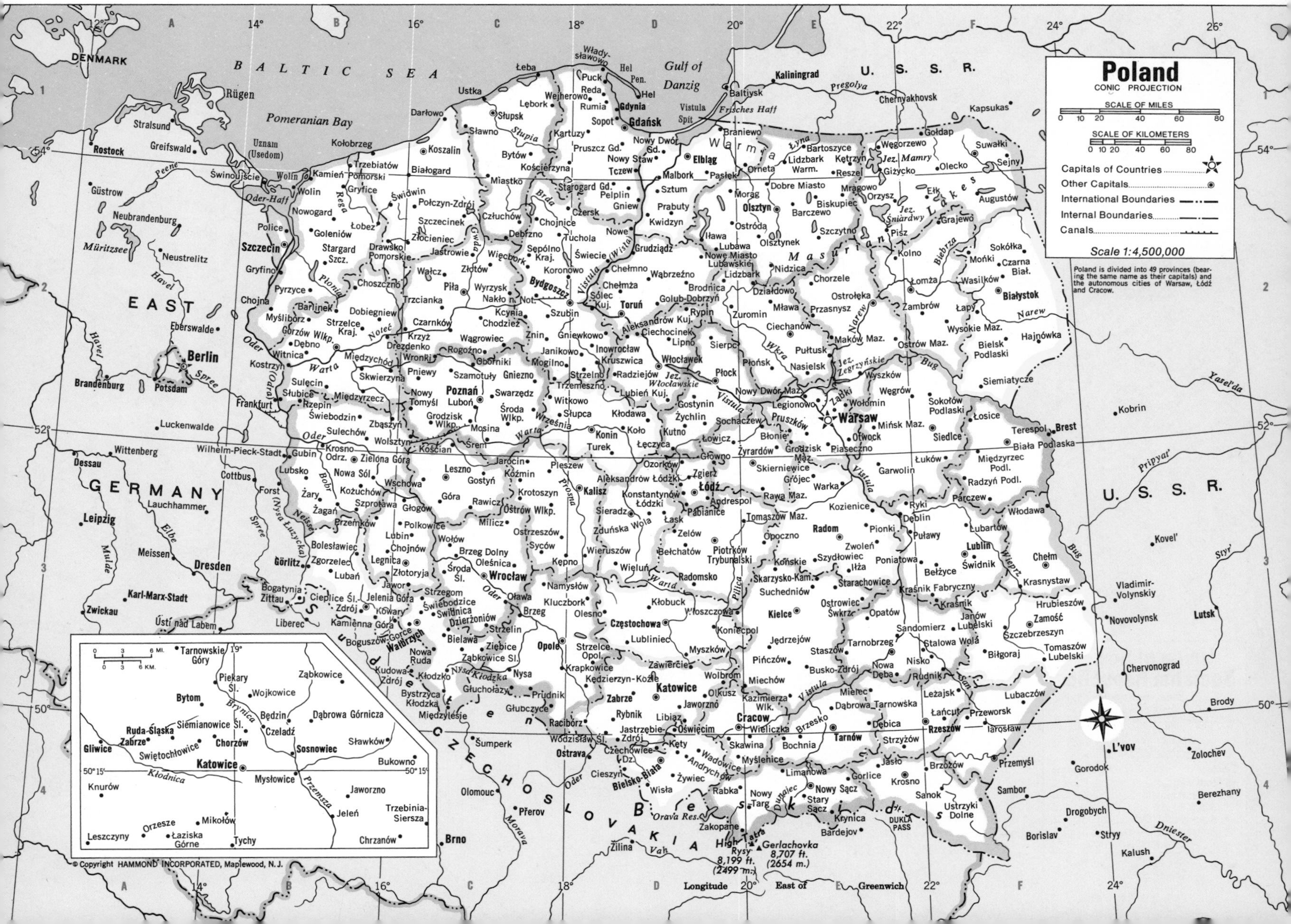

UNION REPUBLICS

Armenian S.S.R.	3,031,000	E6
Azerbaidzhan S.S.R.	6,028,000	E5
Estonian S.S.R.	1,466,000	C4
Georgian S.S.R.	5,015,000	D5
Kazakh S.S.R.	14,684,000	G5
Kirgiz S.S.R.	3,529,000	H5
Latvian S.S.R.	2,521,000	C4
Lithuanian S.S.R.	3,398,000	C4
Moldavian S.S.R.	3,947,000	C5
Russian S.F.S.R.	137,551,000	D4
Tadzhik S.S.R.	3,801,000	H6
Turkmen S.S.R.	2,759,000	F6
Ukrainian S.S.R.	49,755,000	C5
Uzbek S.S.R.	15,391,000	G5
White Russian S.S.R.	9,560,000	C4

INTERNAL DIVISIONS

Abkhaz A.S.S.R.	505,000	E5
Adygey Aut. Obl.	405,000	D5
Adzhar A.S.S.R.	354,000	E5
Aginsk Buryat Aut. Okr.	69,000	M4
Bashkir A.S.S.R.	3,849,000	F4
Buryat A.S.S.R.	900,000	M4
Chechen-Ingush		
A.S.S.R.	1,154,000	E5
Chukchi Aut. Okr.	133,000	R3
Chuvash A.S.S.R.	1,292,000	E4
Dagestan A.S.S.R.	1,628,000	E5
Evenki Aut. Okr.	16,000	K3
Gorno-Altay Aut. Obl.	172,000	J4
Gorno-Badakhshan Aut.		
Obl.	127,000	H6
Jewish Aut. Obl.	190,000	O5
Kabardin-Balkar		

A.S.S.R.	674,000	E5
Kalmuck A.S.S.R.	294,000	E5
Karachay-Cherkess Aut.		
Obl.	368,000	E5
Karakalpak A.S.S.R.	904,000	G5
Karelian A.S.S.R.	736,000	D3
Khakass Aut. Obl.	500,000	J4
Khanty-Mansi Aut. Okr.	569,000	G3
Komi A.S.S.R.	1,119,000	F3
Komi-Permyak Aut. Okr.	173,000	F4
Koryak Aut. Okr.	34,000	R3
Mari A.S.S.R.	703,000	E4
Mordvinian A.S.S.R.	991,000	E4
Nagorno-Karabakh Aut.		
Obl.	161,000	E6
Nakhichevan' A.S.S.R.	239,000	E6
Nenets Aut. Okr.	47,000	F3
North Ossetian		
A.S.S.R.	597,000	E5
South Ossetian Aut.		
Obl.	98,000	E5
Tatar A.S.S.R.	3,436,000	F4
Taymyr Aut. Okr.	44,000	J2
Tuvinian A.S.S.R.	267,000	K4
Udmurt A.S.S.R.	1,494,000	F4
Ust'-Ordynskiy Buryat Aut.		
Okr.	133,000	L4
Yakut A.S.S.R.	839,000	N3
Yamal-Nenets Aut. Okr.	158,000	H3

CITIES and TOWNS

Abakan 128,000		K4
Abay 34,245		J4
Abaza 15,202		J4
Achinsk 117,000		K4

Agata		K3
Aginskoye 7,922		M4
Akmolinsk		
(Tselinograd) 234,000		H4
Aksay 10,010		G5
Aktas		G5
Aktash		O4
Aktyubinsk 191,000		F4
Aldan 17,689		N4
Aleksandrovsk-Sakhalinskiy		
20,342		P5
Alekseyevka 18,041		J4
Aleysk 32,487		J4
Alga 12,000		F5
Aliskerovo		R3
Allakh-Yun'		N4
Alma-Ata 910,000		H5
Almaznyy		M3
Ambarchik		R3
Amderma		F3
Amursk 24,010		O3
Anadyr' 7,703		S3
Andizhan 230,000		H5
Angarsk 239,000		L4
Angren		H5
Anzhero-Sudzhensk 105,000		J4
Aral'sk 37,722		G5
Archangel		
(Arkhangel'sk) 385,000		E3
Arkalyk 15,108		G4
Armavir 162,000		E5
Arsen'yev 60,000		O5
Artem 69,000		O5
Artemovskiy		M4
Arys' 26,414		G5
Arzamas 93,000		E4
Asbest 79,000		G4

Ashkhabad 312,000		F6
Asino 29,395		J4
Astrakhan' 461,000		E5
Atbasar 37,228		G4
Atka		Q3
Ayaguz 35,827		J5
Ayan		O4
Aykhal		M3
Bagdarin		M4
Baku* 1,022,000		E6
Baku* 1,550,000		F5
Balakovo 152,000		E4
Balashov 93,000		E4
Baley 27,215		M4
Balkhash 78,000		H5
Balykchi 22,397		H5
Bam		N4
Barabinsk 37,274		H4
Baranovichi 131,000		C4
Barnaul 533,000		J4
Batagay 10,000		O3
Batumi 123,000		E5
Baykit		K3
Baykonyr		G5
Bayram-Ali 31,987		G6
Belgorod 240,000		D4
Belogorsk 67,000		N4
Belomorsk 16,595		D3
Beloretsk 71,000		F4
Belovo 112,000		J4
Berdichev 80,000		C5
Berdsk 67,000		J4
Berezniki 185,000		F4
Berezovo 6,000		G3
Beringovskiy		T3
Bikin 17,473		O5
Bira		O5

Birobidzhan 69,000		O5
Biruni		G5
Biysk 212,000		J4
Blagoveshchensk 172,000		N4
Bobruysk 192,000		C4
Bodaybo 19,000		M4
Borisoglebsk 68,000		E4
Borzya 27,815		M4
Bratsk 214,000		L4
Brest 177,000		C4
Brindakit		N4
Bryansk 394,000		D4
Bugul'ma 80,000		F4
Bukachacha 10,000		M4
Bukhara 185,000		G5
Bulun		N2
Buzuluk 76,000		F4
Chadan		K4
Chapayevsk 85,000		F4
Chara		M4
Chardzhou 140,000		G6
Charsk 10,100		J5
Cheboksary 308,000		E4
Chegdomyn 16,499		O4
Chelkar 19,377		F5
Chelyabinsk 1,030,000		G4
Cheremkhovo 77,000		L4
Cherepovets 266,000		D4
Cherkessk 91,000		E5
Chernigov 238,000		D4
Chernogorsk 71,000		K4
Chernovtsy 219,000		C5
Chernyshevsk 10,000		M4
Cherskiy		Q3
Chimbay 18,899		F5
Chimkent 322,000		H5
Chirchik 132,000		H5

Chita 303,000		M4
Chokurdakh		P2
Chumikan		O4
Dal'negorsk 33,506		O5
Dal'nerechensk 28,224		O5
Daugavpils 116,000		C4
Denau		G6
Dikson		J2
Dimitrovgrad 106,000		F4
Dnepropetrovsk 1,066,000		D5
Donetsk 1,021,000		D5
Drogobych 66,000		C5
Druzhba		J5
Druzhina		P3
Dudinka 19,701		K3
Dushanbe 494,000		G6
Dzerzhinsk 257,000		E4
Dzhalal-Abad 55,000		H5
Dzhalinda		N4
Dzhambul 264,000		H5
Dzhetygara 32,169		G4
Dzhezkazgan 89,000		G5
Dzhusaly 20,658		G5
Egvekinot		S3
Ekibastuz 66,000		H4
Ekimchan		O4
El'dikan		O3
Elista 70,000		E5
Emba 17,820		F5
Engel's 161,000		E4
Erivan 1,019,000		E6
Evensk		Q3
Fergana 176,000		H5
Fort-Shevchenko 12,000		F5
Frolovo 33,398		E5
Frunze 533,000		H5

Gasan-Kuli		F6
Gol'chikha		J2
Gomel' 383,000		D4
Gor'kiy 1,344,000		E4
Gorno-Altaysk 34,413		J4
Gornyak 16,643		J4
Grodno 195,000		C4
Groznyy 375,000		E5
Gubakha 33,243		F4
Gulistan 30,879		H5
Gur'yev 131,000		F5
Gusinoozersk 10,000		L4
Gyda		H2
Igarka 15,624		J3
Igrim		G3
Ilanskiy 22,852		K4
Indiga		E3
Inta 51,000		F3
Ishim 63,000		G4
Isil'kul' 25,958		H4
Ivano-Frankovsk 150,000		C5
Ivanovo 465,000		E4
Ivdel 15,308		G3
Izhevsk 549,000		F4
Izmail 83,000		C5
Kachkanar 34,117		F4
Kagan 34,117		G5
Kalachinsk 20,809		H4
Kalakan		M4
Kalinin 412,000		D4
Kaliningrad 355,000		B4
Kalmykovo		F5
Kaluga 265,000		D4
Kamen'-na-Obi 35,604		H4

Union of Soviet Socialist Republics

CONIC PROJECTION

SCALE OF MILES
0 100 200 300 400 500 600

SCALE OF KILOMETERS
0 100 200 300 400 500 600

Capitals
- ★ National
- ☆ Union Republic
- ◎ A.S.S.R.
- ◎ Autonomous Oblast
- ◎ Autonomous Okrug

Boundaries

Scale 1:30,400,000

ADMINISTRATIVE DIVISIONS NOT NAMED ON MAP

	Division	Ref.		Division	Ref.
1.	Abkhaz A.S.S.R.	E5	13.	Khakass Aut. Oblast	J4
2.	Adygey Aut. Oblast	D5	14.	Komi-Permyak Aut. Okrug	F4
3.	Adzhar A.S.S.R.	E5	15.	Mari A.S.S.R.	E4
4.	Aginsk Buryat		16.	Mordvinian A.S.S.R.	E4
	Autonomous Okrug	M4	17.	Nagorno-Karabakh Aut. Oblast	E5
5.	Chechen-Ingush A.S.S.R.	E5	18.	Nakhichevan' A.S.S.R.	E6
6.	Chuvash A.S.S.R.	E4	19.	North Ossetian A.S.S.R.	E5
7.	Gorno-Altay Aut. Oblast	J4	20.	South Ossetian Aut. Oblast	E5
8.	Gorno-Badakhshan Aut. Obl.	H6	21.	Tatar A.S.S.R.	F4
9.	Jewish Aut. Oblast	O5	22.	Tuvinian A.S.S.R.	K4
10.	Kabardin-Balkar A.S.S.R.	E5	23.	Udmurt A.S.S.R.	F4
11.	Karachay-Cherkess Aut. Oblast	E5	24.	Ust'-Ordynsk Buryat	
12.	Karakalpak A.S.S.R.	G5		Autonomous Okrug	L4

AREA 8,649,490 sq. mi. (22,402,179 sq. km.)
POPULATION 262,436,227
CAPITAL Moscow
LARGEST CITY Moscow
HIGHEST POINT Communism Peak 24,599 ft. (7,498 m.)
MONETARY UNIT ruble
MAJOR LANGUAGES Russian, Ukrainian, White Russian, Uzbek, Azerbaidzhani, Tatar, Georgian, Lithuanian, Armenian, Yiddish, Latvian, Mordvinian, Kirgiz, Tadzhik, Estonian, Kazakh, Moldavian (Romanian), German, Chuvash, Turkmenian, Bashkir
MAJOR RELIGIONS Eastern (Russian) Orthodoxy, Islam, Judaism, Protestantism (Baltic States)

Kamenskoye	R3	Kavalerovo 16,415	O5
Kamensk-Ural'skiy 187,000	G4	Kazan' 993,000	F4
Kamyshin 112,000	E4	Kem' 21,025	D3
Kandalaksha 42,656	C3	Kemerovo 471,000	J4
Kansk 101,000	K4	Kentau 52,000	G5
Kapchagay	H5	Kerki 10,000	G6
Kara	G3	Khabarovsk 528,000	O5
Karaganda 572,000	H5	Khandyga	O3
Karasuk 22,637	H4	Khanty-Mansiysk 24,754	H3
Karatau 26,962	H5	Khar'kov 1,444,000	D4
Karazhal 17,702	H5	Khatanga	L2
Kargasok	J4	Kherson 319,000	D5
Karpinsk	F4	Khilok 17,000	M4
Karshi 108,000	G6	Khiva 24,139	F5
Kartaly 42,801	G4	Khodzheyli 36,435	F5
Katangli	P4	Kholmsk 37,412	P5
Kattakurgan 53,000	G5	Khorog 12,295	H6
Kaunas 370,000	C4	Kiev 2,144,000	D4

UNION REPUBLICS

	AREA (sq. mi.)	AREA (sq. km.)	POPULATION	CAPITAL and LARGEST CITY
RUSSIAN S.F.S.R.	6,592,812	17,075,400	137,551,000	Moscow 7,831,000
KAZAKH S.S.R.	1,048,300	2,715,100	14,684,000	Alma-Ata 910,000
UKRAINIAN S.S.R.	233,089	603,700	49,755,000	Kiev 2,144,000
TURKMEN S.S.R.	188,455	488,100	2,759,000	Ashkhabad 312,000
UZBEK S.S.R.	173,591	449,600	15,391,000	Tashkent 1,780,000
WHITE RUSSIAN S.S.R.	80,154	207,600	9,560,000	Minsk 1,262,000
KIRGIZ S.S.R.	76,641	198,500	3,529,000	Frunze 533,000
TADZHIK S.S.R.	55,251	143,100	3,801,000	Dushanbe 494,000
AZERBAIDZHAN S.S.R.	33,436	86,600	6,028,000	Baku 1,022,000
GEORGIAN S.S.R.	26,911	69,700	5,015,000	Tbilisi 1,066,000
LITHUANIAN S.S.R.	25,174	65,200	3,398,000	Vilna 481,000
LATVIAN S.S.R.	24,595	63,700	2,521,000	Riga 835,000
ESTONIAN S.S.R.	17,413	45,100	1,466,000	Tallinn 430,000
MOLDAVIAN S.S.R.	13,012	33,700	3,947,000	Kishinev 503,000
ARMENIAN S.S.R.	11,506	29,800	3,031,000	Erivan 1,019,000

Kirensk 10,000	L4	Krasnokamsk 56,000	F4	Leninakan 207,000	E5	Miass 150,000	G4	Nazarovo 54,000	K4
Kirov 390,000	E4	Krasnotur'insk 61,000	G3	Leningrad 4,073,000	D4	Michurinsk 101,000	E4	Nazyvayevsk 15,792	H4
Kirovabad 232,000	E5	Krasnoural'sk 39,743	G4	Leningrad* 4,588,000	D4	Millerovo 34,627	E5	Nebit-Dag 71,000	F6
Kirovograd 237,000	D5	Krasnovodsk 53,000	F5	Leninogorsk 54,000	J5	Minsk 1,262,000	C4	Nefteyugansk 52,000	H3
Kirovskiy	H5	Krasnoyarsk 796,000	K4	Leninsk	O5	Minsk* 1,276,000	C4	Nel'kan	O4
Kiselevsk 122,000	J4	Kremenchug 210,000	D5	Leninsk-Kuznetskiy 132,000	J4	Minusinsk 56,000	K4	Nepa	L4
Kishinev 503,000	C5	Krivoy Rog 650,000	D5	Leninskoye	O5	Mirnyy 23,826	M3	Neryungri	N4
Kizel 46,264	F4	Kudymkar 26,350	F4	Lenkoran' 35,505	E6	Mogilev 290,000	D4	Nevel'sk 20,726	P5
Kizyl-Arvat 21,671	F6	Kul'sary 16,427	F5	Lensk 16,758	M3	Mogocha 17,884	N4	Nikolayev 440,000	D5
Klaipeda 176,000	B4	Kulunda 15,264	H4	Lesosibirsk	K4	Molodechno 73,000	C4	Nikolayevsk-na-Amure 30,082	P4
Kokand 153,000	H5	Kulyab 55,000	H6	Lesozavodsk 34,957	O5	Monchegorsk 51,000	C3	Nikol'skoye	R4
Kokchetav 103,000	H4	Kum-Dag 10,000	F6	Liepāja 108,000	B4	Moscow* 8,011,000	D4	Nizhneudinsk 39,743	K4
Kolomna 147,000	D4	Kungur 80,000	F4	Lipetsk 396,000	E4	Moscow (cap.) 7,831,000	D4	Nizhnevartovsk 109,000	H3
Kolpashevo 24,911	J4	Kupino 20,799	H4	Luga 31,905	D4	Motygino 10,000	K4	Nizhneyansk	O3
Komsomol'sk 15,385	G4	Kurgan 310,000	G4	Lutsk 137,000	C4	Mozyr' 73,000	C4	Nizhniy Tagil 398,000	G4
Komsomol'sk-na-Amure 264,000	O4	Kurgan-Tyube 34,620	G6	L'vov 667,000	C4	Murgab	H6	Nordvik-Ugol'naya	M2
Kondopoga 27,908	D3	Kursk 375,000	D4	Lys'va 75,000	F4	Murmansk 381,000	D3	Noril'sk 180,000	J3
Kopeysk 146,000	G4	Kushka	G6	Magadan 121,000	P4	Muynak 12,000	F5	Novaya Kazanka	F5
Korf	T3	Kustanay 165,000	G4	Magdagachi 15,059	N4	Mys Shmidta	T3	Novgorod 186,000	D4
Korsakov 38,210	P5	Kutaisi 194,000	E5	Magnitogorsk 406,000	G4	Nadym	H3	Novoalexandrovsk 34,815	G5
Koslan	E3	Kuybyshev 1,216,000	F4	Makhachkala 251,000	E5	Nagornyy	N4	Novokazalinsk 34,815	G5
Kostroma 255,000	E4	Kuybyshev 40,166	H4	Makinsk 22,850	H4	Nakhichevan' 33,279	E6	Novokuznetsk 541,000	J4
Kotlas 61,000	E3	Kyakhta 15,316	L4	Mama	S3	Nakhodka 133,000	O5	Novomoskovsk 147,000	E4
Kovel' 33,351	C4	Kyusyur	O3	Markovo	S3	Nal'chik 207,000	E5	Novorossiysk 159,000	D5
Kovrov 143,000	E4	Kyzyl 66,000	K4	Mary (Merv) 74,000	G6	Namangan 227,000	H5	Novosibirsk 1,312,000	J4
Kozhevnikovo	J4	Kyzyl-Orda 156,000	G5	Maykop 128,000	D5	Naryan-Mar 16,864	F3	Novozybkov 34,433	D4
Krasino	F2	Labytnangi	G3	Mednogorsk 38,024	F4	Naryn 21,098	H5	Novyy Port	H3
Krasnodar 560,000	E5	Lebedinyy	N4	Medvezh'yegorsk 17,465	D3	Navoi 84,000	G6	Novyy Uren' 18,073	F5
Krasnokamensk 51,000	M4	Leninabad 130,000	G5	Mezen'	E3			Novyy Urengoy	H3
								Nukus 109,000	G5

Topography

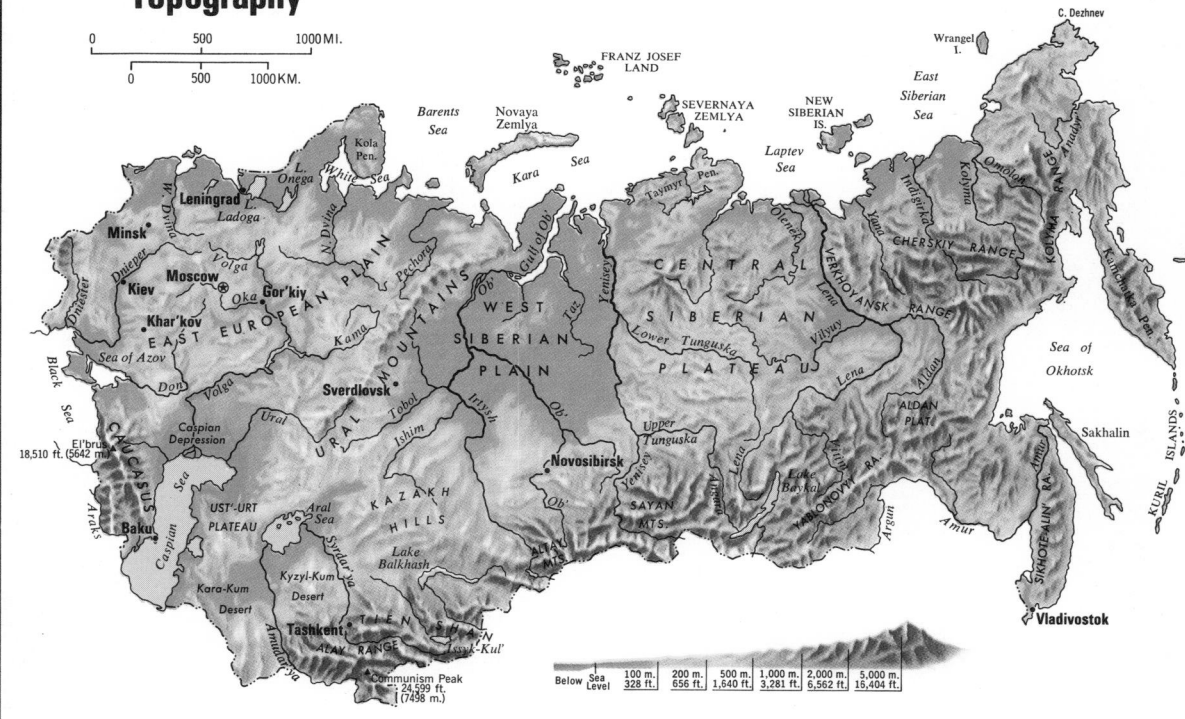

(continued)

Nyandoma 23,366 .... E3
Nyurba M3
Obluch'ye 17,000 .... N5
Odessa 1,046,000 .... D5
Okha 30,890 .... P4
Okhotsk P4
Olëkminsk N3
Olënek M3
Omsk 1,014,000 .... H4
Omsukchan Q3
Omutninsk 28,777 .... F4
Onega 25,047 .... D3
Ordzhonikidze 279,000 .... E5
Orel 305,000 .... D4
Orenburg 459,000 .... F4
Orotukan Q3
Orsk 247,000 .... F4
Osh 169,000 .... H5
Ostrogozhsk 29,921 .... D4
Oymyakon O3
Ozernovskiy Q4
Palana 2,735 .... R4
Panfilov 19,173 .... H5
Pärnu 51,000 .... C4
Partizansk 48,345 .... O5
Pavlodar 273,000 .... H4
Pechenga D2
Pechora 56,000 .... F3
Peleduy M4
Penza 483,000 .... E4
Perkatkin T2
Perm' 999,000 .... F4
Pervoural'sk 129,000 .... F4
Petropavlovsk 207,000 .... G4
Petropavlovsk-Kamchatskiy 215,000 .... R4
Petrovsk-Zabaykal'skiy 28,313 .... L4
Petrozavodsk 234,000 .... D3
Pevek S3
Pikol'skiy 32,862 .... G5
Pinsk 90,000 .... C4
Plastun O5
Podol'sk 202,000 .... D4
Pokrovsk N3
Poligus K3
Poltava 279,000 .... D5
Polyarnyy 15,321 .... D3
Ponoy E3
Poronaysk 23,610 .... P5
Prikumsk 35,768 .... E5
Progress 10,000 .... O5
Prokop'yevsk 266,000 .... J4
Provideniya T3
Przheval'sk 51,000 .... H5
Pskov 176,000 .... C4
Pushkin 90,000 .... C4
Raychikhinsk 25,157 .... N5
Riga 835,000 .... C4
Rostov-na-Donu 934,000 .... E5
Rovno 179,000 .... C4
Rubtsovsk 157,000 .... J4
Ruch'i E3
Rudnyy 110,000 .... G4
Ryazan' 453,000 .... E4
Rybach'ye H5
Rybinsk 239,000 .... D4
Rzhev 69,000 .... D4
Saksaul'skiy F5
Salekhard 21,929 .... G3
Sal'sk 57,000 .... E5
Samagaltay K4
Samarkand 477,000 .... G6
Sangar N3
Saran' 55,000 .... H5
Saransk 263,000 .... E4
Sarapul 107,000 .... F4
Saratov 856,000 .... E4
Sarkand 18,296 .... J5
Segezha 28,810 .... D3
Semipalatinsk 283,000 .... H4
Serakhs G6
Serov 101,000 .... G4
Serpukhov 140,000 .... D4
Sevastopol' 301,000 .... D5
Severobaykal'sk M4
Severodvinsk 197,000 .... E3
Severo-Kuril'sk 8,000 .... Q4
Severoural'sk 29,880 .... G3
Severo-Yeniseysk K3
Shadrinsk 82,000 .... G4
Shakhtinsk 50,000 .... H5
Shakhty 209,000 .... E5
Shar'ya 25,788 .... E4
Shchuchinsk 40,432 .... H4
Shenkursk E3
Shevchenko 111,000 .... F5
Shilka 16,065 .... M4
Shimanovsk 16,880 .... N4
Shushenskoye 10,000 .... K4
Šiauliai 118,000 .... C4
Siktyakh N3
Simferopol' 302,000 .... D5
Skovorodino 10,000 .... N4
Slavgorod 32,908 .... H4
Slobodskoy 34,374 .... E4
Slyudyanka 20,639 .... L4
Smolensk 276,000 .... D4
Snezhnogorsk J3
Sochi 287,000 .... D5
Sokol 48,253 .... E4
Solikamsk 101,000 .... F3
Sortavala 22,188 .... C3
Sosnogorsk 24,688 .... F3
Sosnovo-Ozerskoye M4
Sovetskaya Gavan' 28,455 .... P5
Spassk-Dal'niy 53,000 .... O5
Srednekolymsk Q3
Sretensk 16,000 .... M4
Stalingrad (Volgograd) 929,000 .... E5
Stavropol' 258,000 .... E5
Stepanakert 30,293 .... E6
Sterlitamak 220,000 .... F4
Strezhevoy H3
Sukhana M3
Sukhumi 114,000 .... D5
Sumy 228,000 .... D4
Suntar M3
Surgut 107,000 .... H3
Susuman 12,000 .... P3
Sverdlovsk 1,211,000 .... F4
Svobodnyy 75,000 .... N4
Syktyvkar 171,000 .... F3
Syzran' 178,000 .... E4
Taganrog 276,000 .... D5
Takhiatash F5
Takhta-Bazar G6
Taksimo M4
Taldy-Kurgan 88,000 .... H5
Talgar 31,273 .... H5
Tallinn 430,000 .... C4
Tambey G2
Tambov 270,000 .... E4
Tara 22,358 .... H4
Tarko-Sale H3
Tartu 105,000 .... C4
Tashauz 84,000 .... F5
Tashkent 1,780,000 .... G5
Tatarsk 29,589 .... H4
Tavda G4
Tayshet 34,232 .... K4
Tazovskiy J3
Tbilisi 1,066,000 .... E5
Tedzhen 25,708 .... F6
Tekeli 29,846 .... H5
Temirtau 213,000 .... H4
Termez 57,000 .... G6
Ternopol' 144,000 .... C5
Tiksi N2
Tobol'sk 62,000 .... G4
Togliatti (Tol'yatti) 502,000 .... F4
Tokmak 59,000 .... H5
Tommot 8,000 .... N4
Tomsk 421,000 .... J4
Tot'ma E4
Troitsk 88,000 .... G4
Tselinograd 234,000 .... H4
Tskhinvali 30,311 .... E5
Tula 514,000 .... D4
Tulun 52,000 .... L4
Tura 3,528 .... L3
Turan K4
Turgay G5
Turkestan 67,000 .... G5
Tynda N4
Tyumen' 359,000 .... G4
Uelen T3
Ufa 969,000 .... F4
Uglegorsk 17,921 .... P5
Ukhta 87,000 .... F3
Ulan-Ude 300,000 .... L4
Ul'yanovsk 464,000 .... E4
Ural'sk 167,000 .... F4
Uray 17,385 .... G3
Urgench 100,000 .... G5
Ushtobe 24,484 .... H5
Usol'ye-Sibirskoye 103,000 .... L4
Ussuriysk 147,000 .... O5
Ust'-Ilimsk 69,000 .... L4
Ust'-Kamchatsk 10,000 .... R4
Ust'-Kamenogorsk 274,000 .... J5
Ust'-Kut 50,000 .... L4
Ust'-Kuyga O3
Ust'-Maya O3
Ust'-Nera P3
Ust'-Omchug P3
Ust'-Olenëk M2
Ust'-Ordynskiy 10,693 .... L4
Ust'-Port J2
Vanavara L3
Vanino 15,401 .... P5
Velikiye Luki 102,000 .... D4
Velikiy Ustyug 36,737 .... E3
Vel'sk 21,899 .... E3
Ventspils 40,467 .... B4
Verkhnevilyuysk N3
Verkniy At-Uryakh Q3
Verkhoyansk 2,000 .... N3
Vilna (Vilnius) 481,000 .... C4
Vilyuysk N3
Vinnitsa 314,000 .... C5
Vitebsk 297,000 .... D4
Vitimskiy M4
Vladimir 296,000 .... D4
Vladivostok 550,000 .... O5
Volgograd 929,000 .... E5
Volochanka K2
Vologda 237,000 .... E4
Vorkuta 100,000 .... G3
Voronezh 783,000 .... E4
Voroshilovgrad 463,000 .... E5
Vostochnyy O5
Votkinsk 90,000 .... F4
Voy-Vozh 10,000 .... F3
Vyazemskiy 18,365 .... O5
Vyborg 76,000 .... C3
Vyshniy Volochek 72,000 .... D4
Yakutsk 152,000 .... N3
Yalutorsk 25,426 .... G4
Yamsk Q4
Yaroslavl' 597,000 .... D4
Yartsevo J4
Yelets 112,000 .... D4
Yelizovo 10,000 .... Q4
Yeniseysk 19,880 .... K4
Yermak 28,133 .... H4
Yermentau 15,276 .... H4
Yesil' 15,000 .... G4
Yessey L3
Yoshkar-Ola 201,000 .... E4
Yurga 78,000 .... J4
Yuzhno-Sakhalinsk 140,000 .... P5
Zabaykal'sk M5
Zakamensk 10,000 .... L4
Zaozernyy 27,216 .... K4
Zaporozh'ye 781,000 .... D5
Zarafshan G5
Zavitinsk 19,009 .... O4
Zaysan 10,000 .... J5
Zeya 16,684 .... N4
Zhatay O3
Zhdanov 503,000 .... D5
Zheleznogorsk-Ilimskiy 22,179 .... L4
Zhigalovo L4
Zhigansk N3
Zhitomir 244,000 .... C4
Zima 41,567 .... L4
Zlatoust 198,000 .... F4
Zyryanka Q3

OTHER FEATURES

Alakol' (lake) J5
Alazeya (riv.) Q3
Aldan (plat.) N4
Aldan (riv.) O3
Alexandra Land (isl.) E1
Altay (mts.) J5
Amga (riv.) O3
Amgun' (riv.) O4
Amudar'ya (riv.) G5
Amur (riv.) O4
Anabar (riv.) M2
Anadyr' (gulf) T3
Anadyr' (range) S3
Anadyr' (riv.) S3
Angara (riv.) K4
Aniva (cape) P5
Aral (sea) F5
Arctic Ocean K1
Argun' (riv.) M4
Arkticheskiy Institut (isls.) H2
Atrek (riv.) F6
Ayon (isl.) R2
Azov (sea) D5
Balkhash (lake) H5
Baltic (sea) B4
Barents (sea) D2
Baykal (lake) L4
Baykal (mts.) L4
Beloye (lake) D3
Belyy (isl.) G2
Bering (isl.) R4
Bering (sea) S4
Bering (str.) U3
Bet-Pak-Dala (des.) H5
Black (sea) D5
Bol'shevik (isl.) K2
Bol'shoy Lyakhovskiy (isl.) P2
Bolvanskiy Nos (cape) G2
Bratsk (res.) L4
Caspian (sea) F6
Caucasus (mts.) E5
Chelyuskin (cape) M2
Cherskiy (range) P3
Chu (riv.) H5
Chukchi (pen.) T3
Chukchi (sea) T2
Chulym (riv.) J4
Chuna (riv.) K4
Chunya (riv.) K3
Communism (peak) H6
Crimea (pen.) D5
Dezhnev (cape) T3
Dmitriya Lapteva (str.) O2
Dnieper (riv.) D5
Dniester (riv.) C5
Don (riv.) E5
Donets (riv.) D5
Dulgalakh (riv.) O3
Dvina, Northern (riv.) E3
Dvina, Western (riv.) C4
Dzhugdzhur (range) O4
East Siberian (sea) S2
Emba (riv.) F5
Faddeyevskiy (isl.) P2
Finland (gulf) C4
Franz Josef Land (isls.) F1
George Land (isl.) E1
Gizhiga (bay) Q3
Govena (cape) R4
Graham Bell (isl.) G1
Gyda (pen.) H2
Gydan (Kolyma) (range) Q3
Hiiumaa (isl.) C4
Ili (riv.) H5
Imandra (lake) D3
Indigirka (riv.) P3
Irtysh (riv.) H4
Ishim (riv.) G4
Issyk-Kul' (lake) H5
Iturup (isl.) P5
Japan (sea) O6
Kakhovka (res.) D5
Kamchatka (pen.) Q4
Kanin (pen.) E3
Kanin Nos (cape) E3
Kara (sea) G2
Kara-Bogaz-Gol (gulf) F5
Karaginskiy (isl.) R4
Kara-Kum (canal) F6
Kara-Kum (des.) F5
Karskiye Vorota (str.) F2
Khanka (lake) O5
Kharasavey (cape) G2
Kheta (riv.) K2
Klyuchevskaya Sopka (vol.) Q4
Kola (pen.) D3
Kolguyev (isl.) E3
Kolyma (range) Q3
Kolyma (riv.) Q3
Komandorskiye (isls.) R4
Komsomolets (isl.) L1
Koni (pen.) Q4
Koryak (range) S3
Kotel'nyy (isl.) O2
Kotuy (riv.) L3
Kuma (riv.) E5
Kura (riv.) E6
Kuril (isls.) P5
Kuybyshev (res.) F4
Kyzyl-Kum (des.) G5
Ladoga (lake) D3
La Pérouse (str.) P5
Laptev (sea) N2
Lena (riv.) N3
Little Yenisey (riv.) K4
Long (str.) S2
Lopatka (cape) Q4
Lower Tunguska (riv.) K3
Lyatkhovskiye (isls.) O2
Mangyshlak (pen.) F5
Markha (riv.) M3
Matochkin Shar (str.) F2
Maya (riv.) O4
Mezen' (riv.) E3
Murgab (riv.) G6
Nadym (riv.) H3
Narodnaya (mt.) G3
Navarin (cape) T3
New Siberian (isls.) P2
Northern Dvina (riv.) E3
Novaya Sibir' (isl.) Q2
Novaya Zemlya (isls.) F2
Ob' (gulf) H3
Ob' (riv.) G3
October Revolution (isl.) L2
Oka (riv.) L4
Okhotsk (sea) P4
Olëkma (riv.) N4
Olënek (bay) N2
Olënek (riv.) M3
Oloy (range) R3
Olyutorskiy (cape) S4
Omolon (riv.) Q3
Omoloy (riv.) O3
Onega (lake) D3
Onega (riv.) D3
Ozernoy (cape) R4
Paramushir (isl.) Q4
Pechora (riv.) F3
Peipus (lake) C4
Penzhina (bay) R3
Pioner (isl.) J2
Pobeda (peak) J5
Pur (riv.) H3
Pyasina (riv.) J2
Riga (gulf) C4
Rybachiy (pen.) D2
Rybinsk (res.) D4
Saaremaa (isl.) B4
Sakhalin (gulf) P4
Sakhalin (isl.) P4
Sannikova (str.) O2
Sary Su (riv.) H5
Sayan (mts.) K4
Selemdzha (riv.) O4
Sergeya Kirova (isls.) J2
Severnaya Zemlya (isls.) L1
Shantar (isls.) O4
Shelagskiy (cape) R2
Shelekhov (gulf) Q4
Siberia (reg.) 38,524,000 .... M3
Sikhote-Alin' (range) O5
Stanovoy (range) N4
Stony Tunguska (riv.) K3
Syrdar'ya (riv.) G5
Tannu-Ola (range) K5
Tatar (str.) P4
Taymyr (lake) K2
Taymyr (pen.) L2
Taymyr (riv.) K2
Taz (riv.) J3
Tengiz (lake) G4
Terpeniye (cape) P5
Tobol (riv.) G4
Tsimlyansk (res.) E5
Tym (riv.) J3
Tyung (riv.) M3
Uda (riv.) O4
Ulutau (mts.) G5
Ural (mts.) F4
Ural (riv.) F5
Urup (isl.) Q5
Ussuri (riv.) O5
Ust'-Urt (plat.) F5
Vakh (riv.) J3
Velikaya (riv.) S3
Verkhoyansk (range) N3
Vil'kitskogo (str.) L2
Vilyuy (range) M3
Vilyuy (res.) M3
Vilyuy (riv.) L3
Vitim (riv.) M4
Volga (riv.) E5
Western Dvina (riv.) C4
White (sea) D3
Wiese (isl.) H2
Wilczek Land (isl.) G1
Wrangel (isl.) T2
Yablonovyy (range) M4
Yamal (pen.) G2
Yana (riv.) O3
Yelizavety (cape) P4
Yenisey (riv.) J3
Zaysan (lake) J5
Zeya (riv.) N4
Zhelaniye (cape) H2

*City and suburbs.

Agriculture, Industry and Resources

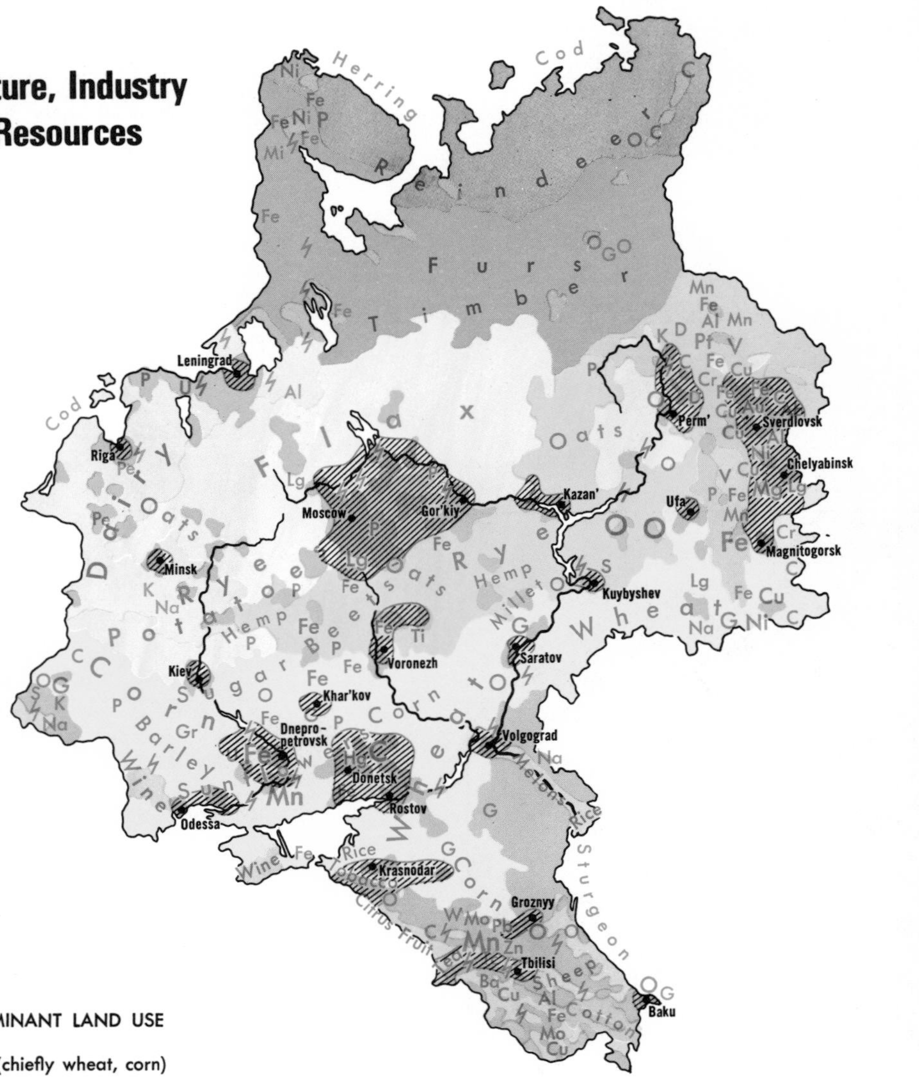

Herring
Cod
Reindeer
Furs
Timber
Flax
Oats
Rye
Potatoes
Hemp
Millet
Wheat
Sugar Beets
Corn
Barley
Wine
Rice
Sturgeon
Sheep
Cotton
Leningrad
Riga
Moscow
Gor'kiy
Kazan'
Perm'
Sverdlovsk
Chelyabinsk
Ufa
Magnitogorsk
Minsk
Kuybyshev
Voronezh
Saratov
Kiev
Khar'kov
Dnepro-petrovsk
Volgograd
Donetsk
Rostov
Odessa
Krasnodar
Groznyy
Tbilisi
Baku

DOMINANT LAND USE

- Cereals (chiefly wheat, corn)
- Cereals (chiefly wheat, rye, oats)
- Dairy, Hogs, Livestock
- Livestock, Dairy
- Pasture Livestock
- Truck Farming, Potatoes, Vegetables, Dairy
- Flax, Dairy, Potatoes
- Cotton
- Vineyards, Orchards, Horticulture
- Sheep Herding, Limited Agriculture
- Forests
- Nonagricultural Land

MAJOR MINERAL OCCURRENCES

Ab	Asbestos	Hg	Mercury	Pb	Lead
Al	Bauxite	K	Potash	Pe	Peat
Au	Gold	Lg	Lignite	Pt	Platinum
Ba	Barite	Mg	Magnesium	S	Sulfur, Pyrites
C	Coal	Mi	Mica	Tc	Talc
Cr	Chromium	Mn	Manganese	Ti	Titanium
Cu	Copper	Mo	Molybdenum	U	Uranium
D	Diamonds	Na	Salt	V	Vanadium
Fe	Iron Ore	Ni	Nickel	W	Tungsten
G	Natural Gas	O	Petroleum	Zn	Zinc
Gr	Graphite	P	Phosphates		

Water Power
Major Industrial Areas

Agriculture, Industry and Resources

DOMINANT LAND USE

- Cereals (chiefly wheat, corn)
- Livestock, Dairy
- Truck Farming, Potatoes, Vegetables, Dairy
- Cotton
- Sheep Herding, Limited Agriculture
- Forests
- Nonagricultural Land

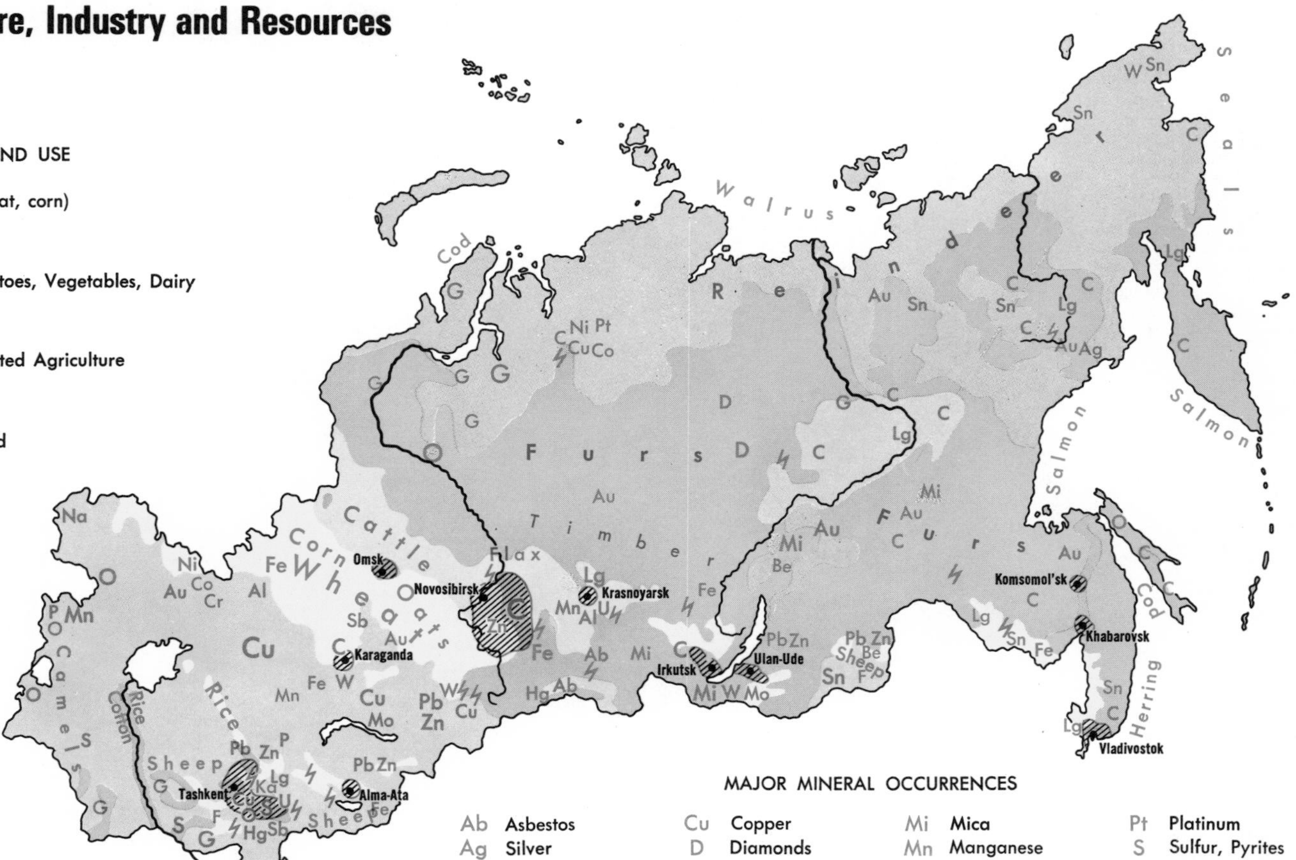

MAJOR MINERAL OCCURRENCES

Ab	Asbestos	Cu	Copper	Mi	Mica	Pt	Platinum
Ag	Silver	D	Diamonds	Mn	Manganese	S	Sulfur, Pyrites
Al	Bauxite	F	Fluorspar	Mo	Molybdenum	Sb	Antimony
Au	Gold	Fe	Iron Ore	Na	Salt	Sn	Tin
Be	Beryl	G	Natural Gas	Ni	Nickel	U	Uranium
C	Coal	Hg	Mercury	O	Petroleum	W	Tungsten
Co	Cobalt	Ka	Kaolin	P	Phosphates	Zn	Zinc
Cr	Chromium	Lg	Lignite	Pb	Lead		

⚡ Water Power   ▨ Major Industrial Areas

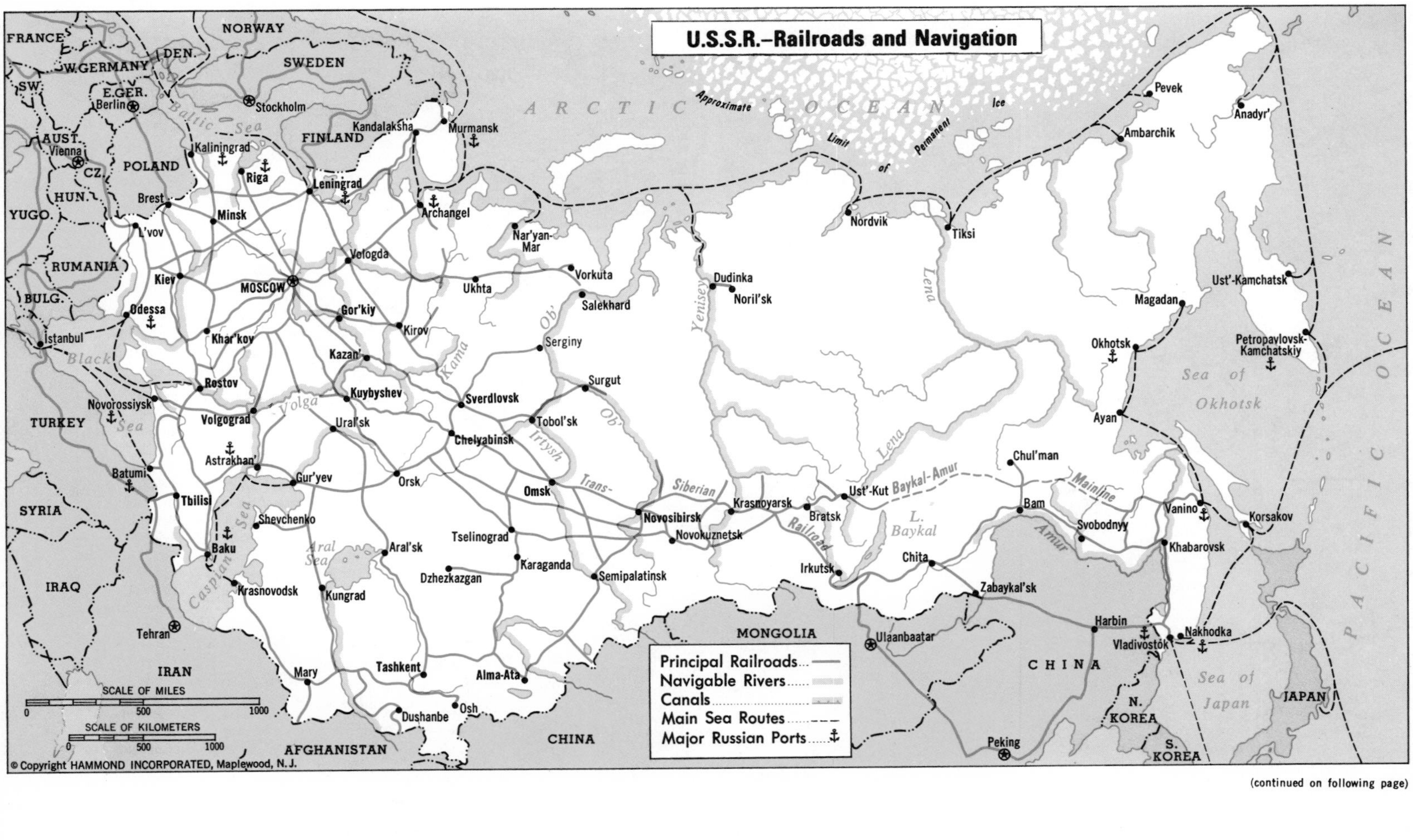

U.S.S.R.—Railroads and Navigation

Principal Railroads
Navigable Rivers
Canals
Main Sea Routes
Major Russian Ports ⚓

SCALE OF MILES
0   1000

SCALE OF KILOMETERS
0   500   1000

© Copyright HAMMOND INCORPORATED, Maplewood, N.J.

(continued on following page)

Union of Soviet Socialist Republics
European Part

CONIC PROJECTION

SCALE OF MILES

SCALE OF KILOMETERS

National Capitals .... ☆
Capitals of Union Republics .... ⬠
Administrative Centers .... △
International boundaries ....
Union Republic boundaries ....
A.S.S.R., Oblast, Kray boundaries ....
Autonomous Oblast boundaries ....
Autonomous Okrug boundaries ....

Scale 1:13,250,000

The government of the United States has not recognized the incorporation of Estonia, Latvia and Lithuania into the Soviet Union.

Administrative Divisions bear same names as their respective Capitals or Centers, except:

Abkhaz A.S.S.R.	Sukhumi	F6
Adygey Aut. Oblast	Maykop	F6
Adzhar A.S.S.R.	Batumi	F6
Bashkir A.S.S.R.	Ufa	J4
Chechen-Ingush A.S.S.R.	Groznyy	G6
Chuvash A.S.S.R.	Cheboksary	G3
Crimean Oblast	Simferopol'	D6
Dagestan A.S.S.R.	Makhachkala	G6
Kabardin-Balkar A.S.S.R.	Nal'chik	F6
Kalmuck A.S.S.R.	Elista	F5
Karachay-Cherkess Aut. Obl.	Cherkessk	F6
Karelian A.S.S.R.	Petrozavodsk	D2
Komi A.S.S.R.	Syktyvkar	H2
Komi-Permyak Aut. Okrug	Kudymkar	H3
Mari A.S.S.R.	Yoshkar-Ola	G3
Mordvinian A.S.S.R.	Saransk	G4
Nagorno-Karabakh Aut. Obl.	Stepanakert	G7
Nenets Aut. Okrug	Nar'yan-Mar	H1
North Ossetian A.S.S.R.	Ordzhonikidze	F6
South Ossetian Aut. Obl.	Tskhinvali	F6
Tatar A.S.S.R.	Kazan'	G3
Trans-Carpathian Oblast	Uzhgorod	B5
Udmurt A.S.S.R.	Izhevsk	H3
Volyn Oblast	Lutsk	C4

© Copyright HAMMOND INCORPORATED, Maplewood, N.J.

U.S.S.R. — EUROPEAN

UNION REPUBLICS

Armenian S.S.R. 3,031,000	F6
Azerbaidzhan S.S.R. 6,028,000	G6
Estonian S.S.R. 1,466,000	C3
Georgian S.S.R. 5,015,000	F6
Latvian S.S.R. 2,521,000	B3
Lithuanian S.S.R. 3,398,000	B3
Moldavian S.S.R. 3,947,000	C5
Russian S.F.S.R. 137,551,000	F3
Ukrainian S.S.R. 49,755,000	D5
White Russian S.S.R. 9,560,000	C4

INTERNAL DIVISIONS

Abkhaz A.S.S.R. 505,000	F6
Adygey Aut. Obl. 405,000	F6
Adzhar A.S.S.R. 354,000	F6
Bashkir A.S.S.R. 3,849,000	J4
Chechen-Ingush A.S.S.R. 1,154,000	G6
Chuvash A.S.S.R. 1,292,000	G3
Crimean Oblast 2,183,000	D6
Dagestan A.S.S.R. 1,628,000	G6
Kabardin-Balkar A.S.S.R. 674,000	F6
Kalmuck A.S.S.R. 294,000	G5
Karachav-Cherkess Aut. Obl. 368,000	F6
Karelian A.S.S.R. 736,000	D2
Komi A.S.S.R. 1,119,000	H2
Komi-Permyak Aut. Okr. 173,000	J4
Mari A.S.S.R. 703,000	G3
Mordvinian A.S.S.R. 991,000	G4
Nagorno-Karabakh Aut. Obl. 161,000	G7
Nakhichevan' A.S.S.R. 239,000	G7
Nenets Aut. Okr. 47,000	H1
North Ossetian A.S.S.R. 597,000	F6
South Ossetian Aut. Obl. 98,000	F6
Tatar A.S.S.R. 3,436,000	G3
Trans-Carpathian Oblast 1,155,000	B5
Udmurt A.S.S.R. 1,494,000	H3
Volyn Oblast 1,015,000	C4

CITIES and TOWNS

Abdulino 26,010	H4
Agdam 21,277	G6
Agryz 19,267	H4
Akhaltsikhe 18,972	F6
Akhtubinsk 43,466	H3
Akhty	G6
Akhtyrka 41,354	E4
Akkerman (Belgorod-Dnestrovskiy) 32,928	D5
Alagir 18,161	F6
Alatyr' 43,499	G4
Alaverdi 21,311	F6
Aleksandriya 82,000	D5
Aleksandrovsk 18,286	J3
Alekseyevka 25,562	F4
Aleksin 67,000	E4
Ali-Bayramly 33,828	G7
Al'met'yevsk 110,000	H3
Alushta 22,016	D6
Amderma	K1
Anapa 29,900	E6
Apatity 62,000	D1
Apsheronsk 32,867	F6
Archangel (Arkhangel'sk) 385,000	F2
Armavir 162,000	F6
Arzamas 93,000	F3
Astara	G7
Astrakhan' 461,000	G5
Atkarsk 28,881	F4
Azov 75,000	F5
Bakhchisaray 15,912	D6
Baku 1,022,000	H6
Baku * 1,550,000	H6
Balakhna 36,542	F3
Balaklava	D6
Balakovo 152,000	G4
Balashov 93,000	F4
Baltiysk 20,300	A4
Baranovichi 131,000	C4
Barysh 20,792	G4
Bataysk 90,000	E5
Batumi 123,000	F6
Belaya Tserkov' 151,000	D4
Belebey 32,460	H4
Belev 17,733	E4
Belgorod 240,000	E4
Belgorod-Dnestrovskiy 32,928	D5
Belomorsk 16,595	D2
Belorechensk 35,970	F6
Beloretsk 71,000	J4
Belozersk	F3
Bel'tsy 125,000	C5
Belush'ya Guba	H1
Bendery 101,000	C5
Berdichev 80,000	C5
Berdyansk 122,000	E5
Berezniki 185,000	J3
Beslan 26,893	F6
Bezhetsk 30,030	E3
Birsk 29,607	J3
Bobrov 17,977	F4
Bobruysk 192,000	C4
Bologoye 33,949	D3
Bor 63,000	G3
Borislav 33,800	B5
Borisoglebsk 68,000	F4
Borisov 112,000	C4
Borovichi 60,000	D3
Brest 177,000	B4
Bryansk 394,000	D4
Bugul'ma 80,000	H4
Buguruslan 54,000	H4
Buturlinovka 21,643	F4
Buy 29,946	F3
Buynaksk 37,946	G6
Buzuluk 76,000	H4
Bykhov 17,371	C4
Cāsis 17,696	C3
Chadyr-Lunga 20,474	C5
Chapayevsk 85,000	G4
Chaykovskiy 48,034	H3
Cheboksary 308,000	G3
Cherdyn'	J2
Cherepovets 266,000	E3
Cherkassy 228,000	D5
Cherkessk 91,000	F6
Chernigov 238,000	D4
Chernovtsy 219,000	C5
Chernushka 21,106	J3
Chervonograd 55,000	B4
Chiatura 25,474	F6
Chistopol' 64,000	G3
Chortkov 19,183	B5
Chudovo	D3
Chusovoy 56,000	J3
Danilov 17,593	F3
Dankov 20,030	E4
Daugavpils 116,000	C3
Dedovsk 20,123	H4
Derbent 70,000	G6
Dimitrovgrad 106,000	G4
Dneprodzerzhinsk 250,000	D5
Dnepropetrovsk 1,066,000	D5
Dobrush 16,809	D4
Dobryanka 18,349	J3
Donetsk 1,021,000	E5
Dorogobuzh 66,000	B5
Dubna 55,000	E3
Dubna	E4

Dubno 25,442	C4
Dvinsk (Daugavpils) 116,000	C3
Dyat'kovo 26,825	D4
Dzerzhinsk 257,000	F3
Dzhankoy 43,459	D5
Dzhul'fa	G7
Echmiadzin 31,819	F6
Elektrostal' 139,000	E3
Elista 70,000	F5
El'ton	G5
Engel's 161,000	G4
Erivan 1,019,000	F6
Fastov 51,000	D4
Feodosiya 76,000	D5
Frolovo 33,398	F5
Furmanov 40,155	F3
Gagra 23,025	F6
Galich 19,374	F3
Gandzha (Kirovabad) 232,000	G6
Gatchina 75,000	C3
Gay 28,250	J4
Gaysin 23,741	C5
Gdov	C3
Gelendzhik 29,086	E6
Genichesk 20,031	E5
Georgiu-Dezh 52,000	F4
Glazov 81,000	H3
Globokoye	C3
Glukhov 27,096	D4
Gomel' 383,000	D4
Gori 56,000	F6
Gorki 22,117	D4
Gor'kiy 1,344,000	F3
Gorlovka 336,000	E5
Gorodets 34,229	F3
Gremikha	E1
Gremyachinsk 29,975	J3
Grodno 195,000	B4
Groznyy 375,000	G6
Gryazi 41,292	F4
Gubakha 33,243	J3
Gubkin 65,000	E4
Gudauta	F6
Gudermes 32,445	G6
Gukovo 68,000	F5
Gus'-Khrustal'nyy 72,000	F3
Imishli 17,839	G7
Inta 51,000	J1
Inza 19,060	G4
Ishimbay 57,000	J4
Ivano-Frankovsk 150,000	B5
Ivanovo 465,000	F3
Izberbash 17,299	G6
Izhevsk 549,000	H3
Izmail 83,000	C5
Izyum 61,000	E5
Jékabpils 22,440	C2
Jelgava 68,000	B3
Jurmala 61,000	B2
Kadiyevka (Stakhanov) 108,000	E5
Kafan 29,916	G7
Kagul 26,249	C5
Kakhovka 28,472	D5
Kalach 18,475	F4
Kalach-na-Donu 20,795	F5
Kalinin 412,000	E3
Kaliningrad, Kaliningrad 355,000	B4
Kaliningrad, Moscow Oblast 133,000	E3
Kalinkovichi 23,918	C4
Kaluga 265,000	E4
Kalush 60,000	B5
Kamenets-Podol'skiy 81,000	C5
Kamenka, Penza 30,067	F4
Kamensk-Shakhtinskiy 72,000	F5
Kamyshin 112,000	G4
Kanash 40,682	G3
Kandalaksha 42,656	D1
Karachayevsk	F6
Karachev 15,972	E4
Karimī 17,678	J3
Kasimov 33,066	F4
Kaspiysk 38,990	G6
Kaunas 370,000	B4
Kazan' 993,000	G3
Kazatin 26,649	C5
Kem' 21,025	D2
Kerch' 157,000	E5
Keret'	D1
Khachmas 22,313	H6
Khadyzhensk 17,856	E6
Khar'kov 1,444,000	E5
Khasavyurt 65,000	G6
Khashuri 24,469	F6
Kherson 319,000	D5
Khmel'nitskiy 172,000	C5
Khotin	C5
Khust 23,810	B5
Khvalynsk 16,249	G4
Kiev 2,144,000	D4
Kiliya 24,276	C5
Kimovsk 44,490	E4
Kimry 58,000	E3
Kinel' 39,373	H4
Kineshma 101,000	F3
Kirishi 27,252	D3
Kirov, Kaluga 29,355	D4
Kirov, Kirov 390,000	G3
Kirovabad 232,000	G6
Kirovakan 146,000	F6
Kirovo-Chepetsk 71,000	H3
Kirovograd 237,000	D5
Kirovsk 38,484	D1
Kirsanov 21,795	F4
Kishinev 503,000	C5
Kislovodsk 101,000	F6
Kizel 46,264	J3
Kizlyar 29,745	G6
Klaipeda 176,000	B3
Klintsy 67,000	D4
Kobrin 24,935	B4
Kobuleti 18,051	F6
Kohtla-Järve 73,000	C3
Kolomiya 52,000	B5
Kolomna 147,000	E4
Kolpino 114,000	D3
Kommunarsk 120,000	E5
Komrat 21,369	C5
Komsomol'skiy 17,078	K1
Kondopoga 27,908	D2
Königsberg (Kaliningrad) 355,000	B4
Konotop 82,000	D4
Konstantinovka 112,000	E5
Korenovsk 26,323	F6
Korosten' 65,000	C4
Korostyshev 21,153	C4
Kovel' 33,351	C4
Kovrov 143,000	F3
Kovylkino 17,300	F4
Kramatorsk 178,000	E5
Krasnoarmeysk 60,000	G4
Krasnodar 560,000	F6
Krasnograd 18,386	E5
Krasnokamsk 56,000	H3
Krasnoslobodsk 17,749	J3
Krasnovishersk	J2
Krasnyy Kut 17,087	G4
Krasnyy Luch 106,000	E5

Krasnyy Sulin 41,684	F5
Kremenchug 210,000	D5
Krichev 25,682	D4
Krivoy Rog 650,000	D5
Krolevets 18,307	D4
Kronshtadt 39,477	C3
Kropotkin 70,000	F5
Krymsk 41,430	E6
Kubla 18,871	D4
Kudymkar 26,350	H3
Kulebaki 46,252	F3
Kumertau 52,000	J4
Kunda	J3
Kungur 80,000	J3
Kupyansk 30,055	E4
Kursk 375,000	E4
Kutaisi 194,000	F6
Kuvandyk 22,914	J4
Kuybyshev 1,216,000	H4
Kuznetsk 94,000	G4
Kuzomen'	E1
Lalinsk 54,000	H3
Lakhdenpokh'ya	C2
Lebedin 29,240	D4
Leninakan 207,000	F6
Leningrad 4,073,000	C3
Leningrad * 4,588,000	C3
Leningorsk 54,000	H4
Lenkoran' 35,505	G7
L'gov 25,110	E4
Lida 66,000	C4
Liepāja 108,000	B3
Likholslavl'	E3
Lipetsk 396,000	E4
Lischansk 119,000	E5
Livny 37,290	E4
Lodeynoye Pole 19,632	D2
Lozovaya 53,000	E5
Lubny 54,000	D4
Luga 31,905	C3
Lutsk 137,000	C4
L'vov (Lwów) 667,000	B5
Lys'va 75,000	J3
Lyubertsy 160,000	E3
Lyubotin 33,324	E5
Lyudinovo 33,871	D4
Makeyevka 436,000	E5
Makhachkala 251,000	G6
Makharadze 21,679	F6
Malaya Vishera 15,381	D3
Malgobek 20,548	F6
Manturovo 21,510	F3
Marganets 50,000	D5
Mariupol' (Zhdanov) 503,000	E5
Marks 17,132	G4
Maykop 128,000	F6
Mednogorsk 38,024	J4
Medvezh'yegorsk 17,465	D2
Melenki 18,545	F3
Meleuz 24,851	J4
Melitopol' 161,000	E5
Memel (Klaipeda) 176,000	B3
Merefa 29,985	E5
Mezen'	F1
Michurinsk 101,000	F4
Mikhaylovka 58,000	F4
Millerovo 34,627	F5
Mineral'nye Vody 67,000	F6
Mingechaur 60,000	G6
Minsk 1,262,000	C4
Minsk * 1,276,000	C4
Mirgorod 28,407	D5
Mogilev 290,000	C4
Mogilev-Podol'skiy 26,051	C5
Molodechno 73,000	C4
Molotov (Perm') 999,000	J3
Monchegorsk 51,000	D1
Morshansk 44,245	F4
Moscow (Moskva)	E3
Moscow (cap.) 7,831,000	E3
Kostroma 255,000	F3
Moskrin 29,196	F3
Mozhaysk 20,321	E3
Mozdok 38,930	F6
Mozyr' 73,000	C4
Mtsensk 27,833	E4
Mukachevo 72,000	B5
Murmansk 381,000	D1
Mytishchi 141,000	E3
Naberezhnye Chelny 301,000	H3
Nakhichevan' 33,279	G7
Nal'chik 207,000	F6
Narva 73,000	D3
Nar'yan-Mar 16,864	H1
Nasosnaya 40,038	H6
Nazran 26,833	F6
Nechitsa 60,000	C4
Nerekhta 25,722	F3
Nevel' 17,804	D3
Nevinnomyssk 104,000	F6

Nezhin 70,000	D4
Nikel' 21,299	C1
Nikolayev 440,000	D5
Nikol'sk 20,740	G3
Nikopol' 146,000	D5
Nizhnekamsk 134,000	H3
Nizhniy Lomov 17,460	F4
Nizhniy Novgorod (Gor'kiy) 1,344,000	F3
Nosovka 19,430	D4
Novaya Kakhovka 52,000	D5
Novgorod 186,000	D3
Novgorod-Severskiy	D4
Novoanninskiy 20,461	F4
Novocherkassk 183,000	F5
Novograd-Volynskiy 41,194	C4
Novogrudok 19,374	C4
Novokuybyshevsk 109,000	G4
Novomoskovsk 147,000	E4
Novopolotsk 67,000	C3
Novorossiysk 159,000	E6
Novoshakhtinsk 104,000	F5
Novotroitsk 95,000	J4
Novoukrainka 19,554	D5
Novouzensk	G4
Novovolynsk 41,187	B4
Novovyatsk 26,408	G3
Novozybkov 34,433	D4
Nurlat 17,533	H4
Nyandoma 23,366	F2
Nytva 17,491	H3
Nyuvchim	H2
Obninsk 73,000	E3
Ochamchira 18,718	F6
Odessa 1,046,000	D5
Oktyabr'sk 33,981	G4
Oktyabr'skiy 88,000	H4
Okulovka 19,194	D3
Olenegorsk 21,485	D1
Olonets	D2
Omutninsk 28,777	H3
Onega 25,047	E2
Ordzhonikidze 279,000	F6
Orel 305,000	E4
Orenburg 459,000	J4
Orgeyev 25,798	C5
Orsha 112,000	D4
Orsk 247,000	J4
Osa 15,038	J3
Osipenko (Berdyansk) 122,000	E5
Osipovichi 19,705	C4
Ostashkov 23,419	D3
Ostrogozhsk 29,921	E4
Ostrov 22,369	C3
Otradnyy 44,426	H4
Panevežys 102,000	B3
Pärnu 51,000	C3
Pavlograd 107,000	E5
Pavlovo 68,000	F3
Pechenga	D1
Pechora 56,000	J2
Penza 483,000	G4
Perm' 999,000	J3
Pervomaysk 72,000	D5
Petrokrepost'	D3
Petrovsk 30,953	G4
Petrozavodsk 234,000	D2
Petsamo (Pechenga)	D1
Pikalevo 20,000	D3
Podol'sk 202,000	E3
Podporoz'ye 21,545	D2
Pokhvistnevo 26,125	H4
Polonnoye 22,484	C4
Polotsk 71,000	C3
Poltava 279,000	D5
Polyarnyy 15,321	D1
Ponoy	F1
Poti 45,979	F6
Povenets	D2
Povorino 20,591	F4
Prikumsk 35,768	F5
Priluki 65,000	D4
Priozersk 18,000	C3
Primorsk	C3
Primorsko-Akhtarsk 25,981	E5
Priozersk 16,052	C2
Privolzhskiy 23,041	G4
Priyutovo 21,351	H4
Prokhladnyy 40,074	F6
Pskov 176,000	C3
Pugachev 33,963	G4
Pushkin 90,000	C3
Pyatigorsk 107,000	F6
Rabocheostrovsk	D1
Rakvere 17,891	C3
Rechitsa 60,000	C4
Reni 19,625	C5
Revel (Tallinn) 430,000	C3

Rēzekne 30,803	C3
Riga 835,000	B3
Romny 53,000	D4
Roslavl' 56,000	D4
Rossosh' 36,438	F4
Rostov 30,815	E3
Rostov-na-Donu 934,000	F5
Rovno 179,000	C4
Rtishchevo 37,146	F4
Rubezhnoye 66,000	E5
Rustavi 129,000	G6
Ruzayevka 41,084	G4
Ryazan' 453,000	E4
Ryazhsk 25,425	F4
Rybinsk 239,000	E3
Rybnitsa 32,266	C5
Rzhev 69,000	D3
Safonovo 53,000	D3
Saki 24,208	D5
Salavat 137,000	H4
Sal'sk 57,000	F5
Sal'yany 24,429	G7
Samara (Kuybyshev) 1,216,000	H4
Sambor 29,253	B5
Saransk 263,000	G4
Sarapul 107,000	H3
Saratov 856,000	G4
Sasovo 27,228	F4
Segezha 28,810	D2
Semenov 23,633	F3
Semilukі 18,221	F4
Sengiley	G4
Serdobol (Sortavala) 22,188	D2
Serdobsk 33,783	F4
Sergach 20,000	G3
Serpukhov 140,000	E4
Sevastopol' 301,000	D6
Severodonetsk 113,000	E5
Severodvinsk 197,000	E2
Severomorsk 50,000	D1
Shakhty 209,000	F5
Shakhun'ya 20,009	G3
Shar'ya 25,788	G3
Shchekino 70,000	E4
Shchigry 17,133	E4
Sheki 43,158	G6
Shemakha 17,986	G6
Shepetovka 38,707	C4
Shostka 82,000	D4
Shpola 19,806	D5
Shumerlya 33,816	G3
Shuya 72,000	F3
Siauliai 118,000	B3
Sibay 37,656	J4
Simferopol' 302,000	D6
Skadovsk	D5
Skopin 24,429	F4
Slantsy 41,146	C3
Slavuta 25,573	C4
Slavyansk 140,000	E5
Slavyansk-na-Kubani 54,000	E5
Slobodskoy 34,374	H3
Slonim 30,279	B4
Slutsk 35,609	C4
Smela 62,000	D5
Smolensk 276,000	D4
Sochi 287,000	E6
Sokol 46,843	F3
Soligorsk 65,000	C4
Solikamsk 101,000	J3
Sol'-Iletsk 22,257	J4
Sorochinsk 23,235	H4
Soroki 21,924	C5
Sortavala 22,188	D2
Sosnogorsk 24,688	H2
Sovetsk (Tilsit) 38,456	B4
Sovetsk 17,022	G3
Stakhanov 108,000	E5
Stalingrad (Volgograd) 929,000	F5
Staraya Russa 34,577	D3
Staryy Oskol 115,000	E4
Stavropol' 258,000	F6
Sterlitamak 220,000	J4
Stupino 70,000	E4
Sudak	E6
Sukhumi 114,000	F6
Sumgait 190,000	H6
Sumy 228,000	E4
Svetlogorsk 69,000	C4
Svetlograd 40,265	F5
Syktyvkar 171,000	H2
Syzran' 178,000	G4
Taganrog 276,000	E5
Talinn 430,000	C3
Tallinn 430,000	C3
Tambov 270,000	F4
Tartu 105,000	C3
Taurage 19,461	B3
Tbilisi 1,066,000	F6
Telavi 21,179	F6

Telšiai 20,220	B3
Temryuk 23,172	E5
Ternopol' 144,000	C5
Teykovo 41,607	E3
Tiflis (Tbilisi) 1,066,000	F6
Tikhoretsk 64,000	F5
Tikhvin 59,000	D3
Tilsit (Sovetsk) 38,456	B4
Timashevsk 29,055	F5
Tiraspol' 139,000	C5
Togliatti (Tol'yatti) 502,000	G4
Tokmak 59,000	E5
Toropets 16,863	D3
Torzhok 45,443	E3
Troitsko-Pechorsk	J2
Tskhinvali 30,311	F6
Tuapse 60,000	E6
Tukums 14,800	B3
Tula 514,000	E4
Tutayev 16,839	E3
Tuymazy 37,027	H4
Tver' (Kalinin) 412,000	E3
Tyrnyauz 18,253	F6
Uchaly 21,808	J4
Ufa 969,000	J4
Uglich 35,463	E3
Ukmerge 21,663	C3
Ul'yanovsk 464,000	G4
Uman' 79,000	D5
Unecha 21,749	D4
Ungeny 17,228	C5
Uryupinsk 38,192	F4
Usinsk	J1
Usman' 20,150	F4
Uvarovo 24,946	F4
Uzhgorod 91,000	B5
Uzlovaya 65,000	E4
Valga 16,795	C3
Valmiera 20,331	C2
Valuyki 29,093	E4
Vasil'kov 26,741	D4
Velikiye Luki 102,000	D3
Velikiy Ustyug 36,737	F2
Vel'sk 21,899	F2
Ventspils 40,467	B3
Vereshchagino 23,585	H3
Vichuga 52,000	F3
Vijpuri (Vyborg) 76,000	C2
Vileyka	C4
Vilna (Vilnius) 481,000	C4
Vinnitsa 314,000	C5
Virandur 20,580	B5
Vitebsk 297,000	C3
Vladimir 296,000	F3
Vladimir-Volynskiy 28,412	B4
Volgodonsk 91,000	F5
Volgograd 929,000	F5
Volkhov 47,025	D3
Volkovysk 28,266	B4
Vologda 237,000	F3
Vol'sk 66,000	G4
Volzhsk 52,000	G3
Volzhskiy 209,000	F5
Vorkuta 100,000	K1
Voronezh 783,000	F4
Voroshilovgrad 463,000	E5
Voskresensk 76,000	E3
Votkinsk 90,000	H3
Voznesensk 36,457	D5
Vyatskiye Polyany 32,729	H3
Vyaz'ma 52,000	D3
Vyborg 76,000	C2
Vyksa 54,000	F3
Vyshniy Volochek 72,000	D3
Yalta 80,000	D6
Yanaul 20,115	J3
Yaroslavl' 597,000	E3
Yartsevo 36,662	D3
Yefremov 53,000	E4
Yelabuga 31,728	H3
Yelets 112,000	E4
Yenakiyevo 114,000	E5
Yershov 21,731	G4
Yessentuki 78,000	F6
Yevlakh 29,462	G6
Yevpatoria 93,000	D6
Yeysk 71,000	E5
Yoshkar-Ola 201,000	G3
Yur'yevets 20,144	F3
Zagorsk 107,000	E3
Zapolyarnyy 22,084	C1
Zaporozh'ye 781,000	E5
Zelenodol'sk 85,000	G3
Zelenokumsk 29,691	F6
Zernograd 20,324	F5
Zhdanov 503,000	E5
Zheleznodorozhnyy 76,000	H2
Zheleznogorsk 65,000	E4
Zhigulevsk 52,130	G4

Zhitomir 244,000	C4
Zhlobin 25,359	D4
Zhmerinka 36,195	C5
Zhodino 22,083	C4
Zhovtnevoye 31,102	D5
Znamenka 27,393	D5
Zolotonosha 27,639	D5
Zugdidi 39,896	F6
Zuyevka 17,001	H3

OTHER FEATURES

Apsheron (pen.)	H6
Araks (riv.)	G7
Azov (sea)	E5
Baltic (sea)	B3
Barents (sea)	E1
Belaya (riv.)	H3
Beloye (lake)	E2
Black (sea)	D6
Bug (riv.)	B4
Bug (riv.)	D5
Caspian (sea)	G6
Caucasus (mts.)	F6
Crimea (pen.)	D5
Desna (riv.)	D4
Dnieper (riv.)	D5
Dniester (riv.)	C5
Don (riv.)	F5
Donets (riv.)	E5
Dvina (bay)	E2
Dvina, Northern (riv.)	F2
Dvina, Western (riv.)	C3
Dykh-Tau (mt.)	F6
El'brus (mt.)	F6
Finland (gulf)	B3
Hiiumaa (isl.)	B3
Il'men' (lake)	D3
Imandra (lake)	D1
Kakhovka (res.)	D5
Kama (riv.)	H2
Kandalaksha (gulf)	D1
Kanin (pen.)	G1
Kara (sea)	K1
Karskiye Vorota (str.)	J1
Kazbek (mt.)	F6
Khopor (riv.)	F4
Kola (pen.)	E1
Kolguyev (isl.)	G1
Kuban' (riv.)	F6
Kura (riv.)	G6
Kuybyshev (res.)	G4
Ladoga (lake)	D2
Lapland (reg.)	D1
Mezen' (riv.)	F2
Moksha (riv.)	F4
Narodnaya (mt.)	J1
Niemen (riv.)	B4
Novaya Zemlya (isls.)	H1
Oka (riv.)	F4
Onega (bay)	E2
Onega (lake)	D2
Onega (riv.)	E2
Pechora (riv.)	H1
Peipus (lake)	C3
Pripet (marshes)	C4
Pripyat' (riv.)	C4
Psël (riv.)	D5
Riga (gulf)	B3
Rybachiy (pen.)	D1
Rybinsk (res.)	E3
Saaremaa (isl.)	B3
Samara (riv.)	H4
Sevan (lake)	F6
Sura (riv.)	G4
Svir' (riv.)	D2
Terek (riv.)	G6
Timan (ridge)	H2
Tsil'ma (riv.)	H1
Tsimlyansk (res.)	F5
Tuloma (riv.)	D1
Ural (riv.)	J4
Ural (mts.)	J3
Usa (riv.)	K1
Valday (hills)	D3
Vaygach (isl.)	K1
Velikaya (riv.)	C3
Volga (riv.)	G5
Volga-Don (canal)	F5
Volgograd (res.)	G4
Volkhov (riv.)	D3
Vorskla (riv.)	E4
Vyatka (riv.)	H3
Vychegda (riv.)	H2
White (sea)	E2
Yamantau (mt.)	J4
Yugorskiy (pen.)	K1

BALTIC STATES

Alytus 55,000	C3
Biržai 11,400	C2
Cēsis 17,696	C2
Daugava (Western Dvina) (riv.)	D2
Daugavpils 116,000	D3
Dobele 10,100	B2
Druskininkai 11,200	C3
Dvina, Western (riv.)	C2
Finland (gulf)	D1
Gauja (riv.)	C2
Haapsalu 11,483	B1
Hiiumaa (isl.)	B1
Jēkabpils 22,400	C2
Jelgava 68,000	B2
Jonava 14,400	C3
Jurmala 61,000	B2
Kapsukas 28,763	B3
Kaunas 370,000	B3
Kedainiai 19,677	C3
Kihnu (isl.)	B1
Kingisepp (Kuressaare) 12,140	B1
Kivioli 11,153	D1
Klaipeda 176,000	A3
Kohtla-Järve 73,000	D1
Kretinga 13,000	A3
Kuldīga 12,300	A2
Kuressaare 12,140	B1
Liepāja 108,000	A2
Lubāna (lake)	D2

Niemen (riv.)	A3
Ogre 15,708	C2
Paneveżys 102,000	C2
Pärnu 51,000	C1
Plunge 13,600	D1
Radviliskis 16,841	B3
Rakvere 17,891	D1
Rēzekne 30,803	D2
Riga (cap.) Latvia 835,000	C2
Riga (gulf)	B2
Saaremaa (isl.)	B1
Saldus 10,000	B2
Šiauliai 118,000	B3
Šiliamae 13,505	D1
Šilute 12,400	A3
Tallinn (cap.)	A3
Estonia 430,000	C1
Tapa 10,037	D1
Tartu 105,000	D1
Taurage 19,461	B3
Telšiai 20,220	B2
Tukums 14,800	B2
Ukmerge 21,663	C3
Utena 13,300	C3
Valga 16,795	D2
Valmiera 20,331	C2
Venta (riv.)	B2
Ventspils 40,467	A2
Vilkaviskis 11,400	B3
Viljandi 21,808	C1
Vilna 481,000	C3
Vormsi (isl.)	B1
Võrtsjärv (lake)	D1
Võru 15,398	D2
Western Dvina (riv.)	C2

*City and suburbs.

MAP SECTION

20° Longitude A East 22° of B Greenwich 24° Gulf 26° Finland 28° E

Tallinn Paldiski Keila Kehra Loksa Kunda Narva
Haapsalu Türi Paide Jögeva Jörva-Jaani Mustvee L. Peipus Kallaste
ESTONIA
Saaremaa Muhu Pärnu Sindi Viljandi Vörtsjärv Tartu Rapina Pskov
Kuressaare Kihnu Killingi-Nõmme Mõisaküla Tõrva Antsla Vöru Petseri
Ruhnu Ainaži Salacgriva Valka Valga
Ventspils Dundaga Mazsalaca Valmiera Smiltene Ape Alūksne Vilaka
Piltene Roja Mērsrags Limbaži Cēsis Ligatne Gulbene Balvi
Riga Sigulda
Liepāja Durbe Kuldiga Saldus Dobele Jelgava Jurmala Ogre Madona Kārsava
Grobiņa Priekule Auce Bauska Jaunjelgava Plaviņas Rēzekne Ludza
R.S.F.S.R.
Mažeikiai Naujoji Akmene Zagare Joniškis Birżai Nereta Preiļi Dagda
Palanga Kretinga Plunge Radviliškis Pasvalys Rokiškis Subata Daugavpils Krāslava
Klaipeda (Memel) Rietavas Kelmė Šiauliai Panevėžys Zarasai Griva
Priekule Silute Skaudvilė Raseiniai Anykščiai Utena Sniečkus
LITHUANIA
Taurage Kedainiai Ukmerge
WHITE RUSSIAN S.S.R.
Jurbarkas Vilkija Jonava Širvintos
Kaliningrad (Königsberg) Neman (Ragnit) Kaunas Kazlu-Rūda Vievis
(Insterburg) Sakiai Trakai **Vilna** (Vilnius)
Pregolya Chernyakhovsk Kybartai Prienai
R.S.F.S.R. Ozersk Kapsukas Varėna
Ketrzyn Gižycko Suwalki Lazdijai Ališkas
POLAND Augustów Druskininkai

© Copyright HAMMOND INCORPORATED, Maplewood, N.J.

The government of the United States has not recognized the incorporation of Estonia Latvia and Lithuania into the Soviet Union nor does it recognize other post-war territorial changes shown on this map. The flags shown here were the official flags of the independent Baltic States prior to 1939.

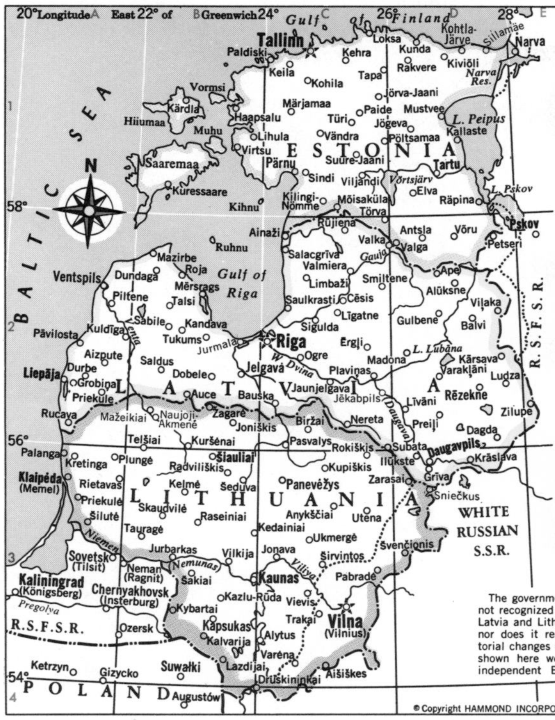

The Baltic States

SCALE OF MILES
0 25 50 75 100
SCALE OF KILOMETERS
0 30 60 90 120 150 180

Capitals	☆
International Boundaries	▬ ▪ ▬
Union Republic Boundaries	▬ ▬
Prewar boundaries of the Baltic States where divergent from present boundaries	▪▪▪▪▪

ESTONIA

LATVIA

LITHUANIA

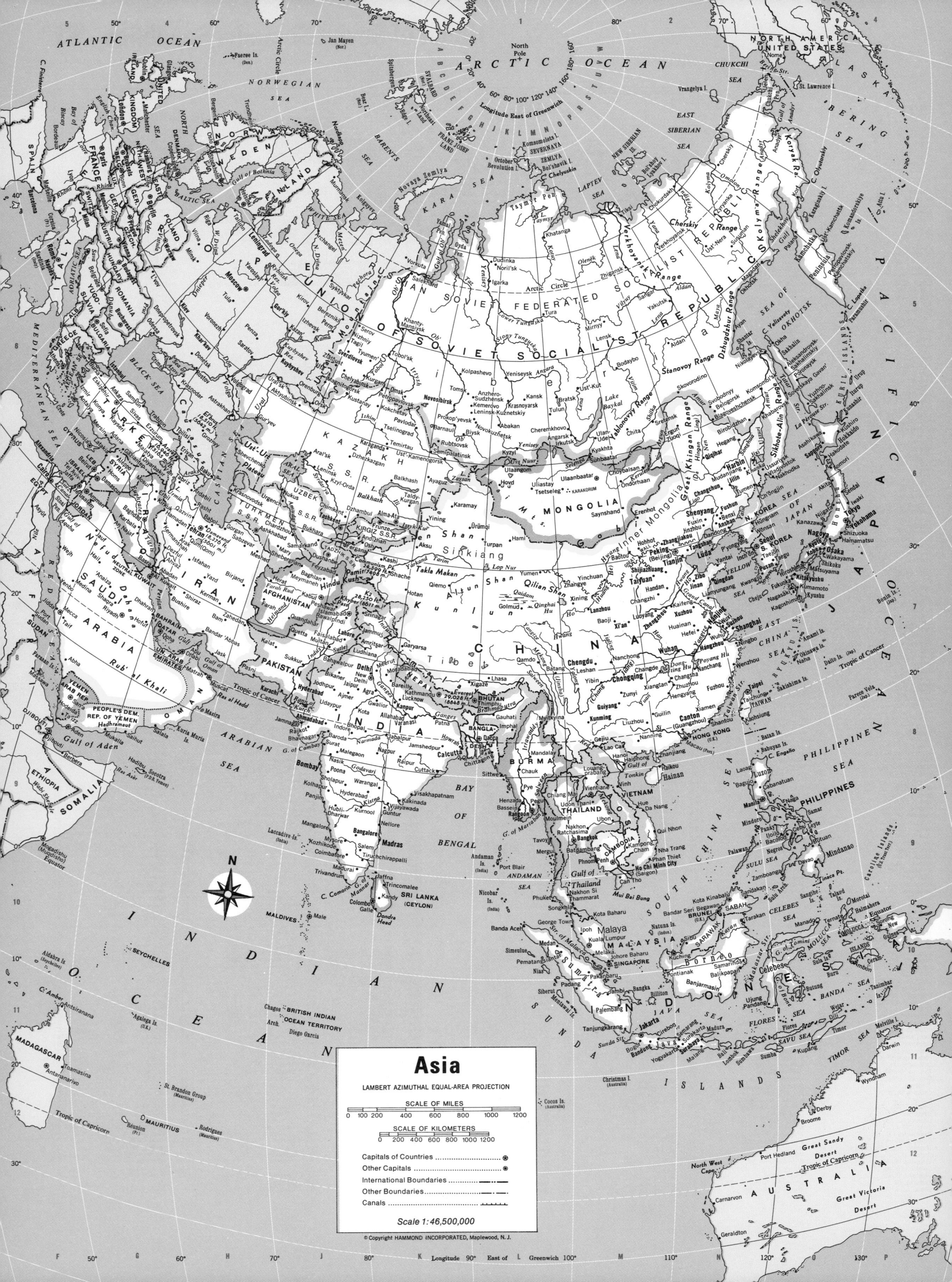

Asia

LAMBERT AZIMUTHAL EQUAL-AREA PROJECTION

SCALE OF MILES

0 100 200   400   600   800   1000   1200

SCALE OF KILOMETERS

0 200 400 600 800 1000 1200

Capitals of Countries .... ⊛
Other Capitals .... ⊙
International Boundaries .... ▬▬▬▬
Other Boundaries .... ▬·▬·▬
Canals .... ┼┼┼┼┼┼

Scale 1: 46,500,000

© Copyright HAMMOND INCORPORATED, Maplewood, N.J.

Population Distribution

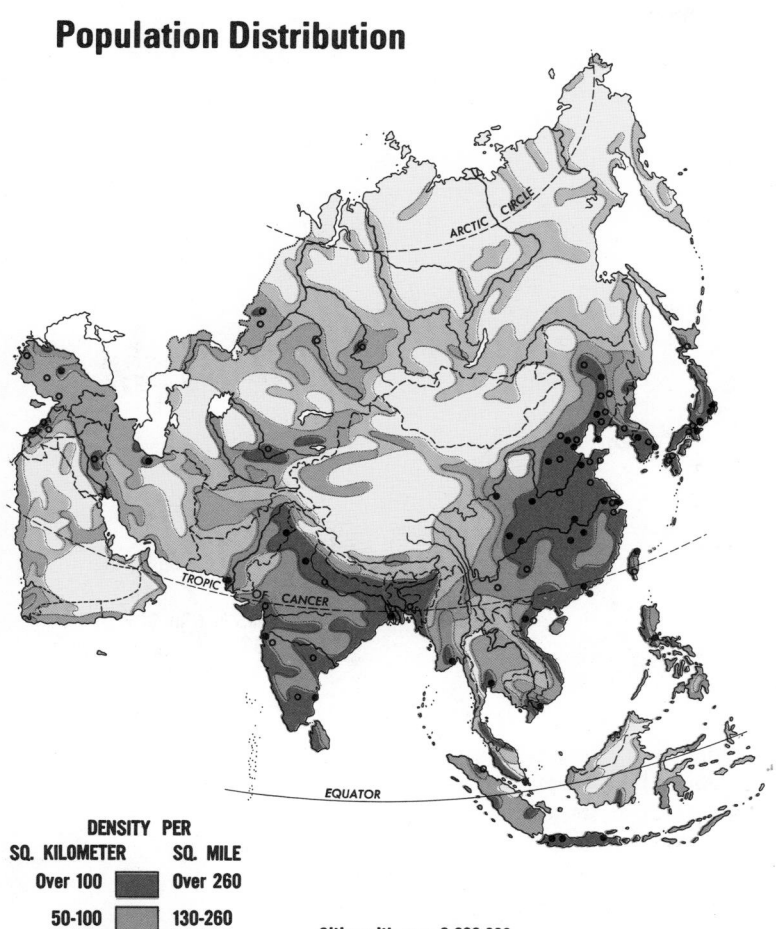

AREA 17,128,500 sq. mi.
(44,362,815 sq. km.)
POPULATION 2,633,000,000
LARGEST CITY Tokyo
HIGHEST POINT Mt. Everest 29,028 ft.
(8,848 m.)
LOWEST POINT Dead Sea -1,296 ft.
(-395 m.)

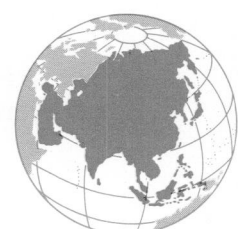

Vegetation

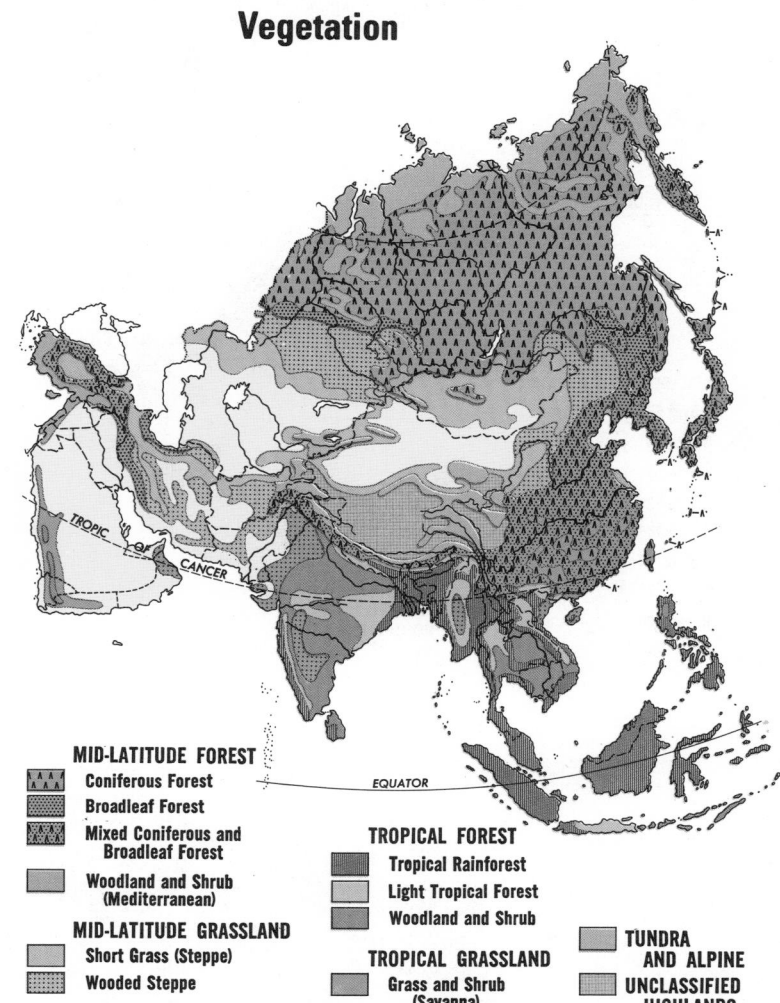

DENSITY PER

SQ. KILOMETER	SQ. MILE
Over 100	Over 260
50-100	130-260
10-50	25-130
1-10	3-25
Under 1	Under 3

• Cities with over 2,000,000 inhabitants (including suburbs)

○ Cities with over 1,000,000 inhabitants (including suburbs)

MID-LATITUDE FOREST
Coniferous Forest
Broadleaf Forest
Mixed Coniferous and Broadleaf Forest
Woodland and Shrub (Mediterranean)

MID-LATITUDE GRASSLAND
Short Grass (Steppe)
Wooded Steppe

DESERT AND DESERT SHRUB

TROPICAL FOREST
Tropical Rainforest
Light Tropical Forest
Woodland and Shrub

TROPICAL GRASSLAND
Grass and Shrub (Savanna)
Wooded Savanna

TUNDRA AND ALPINE

UNCLASSIFIED HIGHLANDS

Average January Temperature

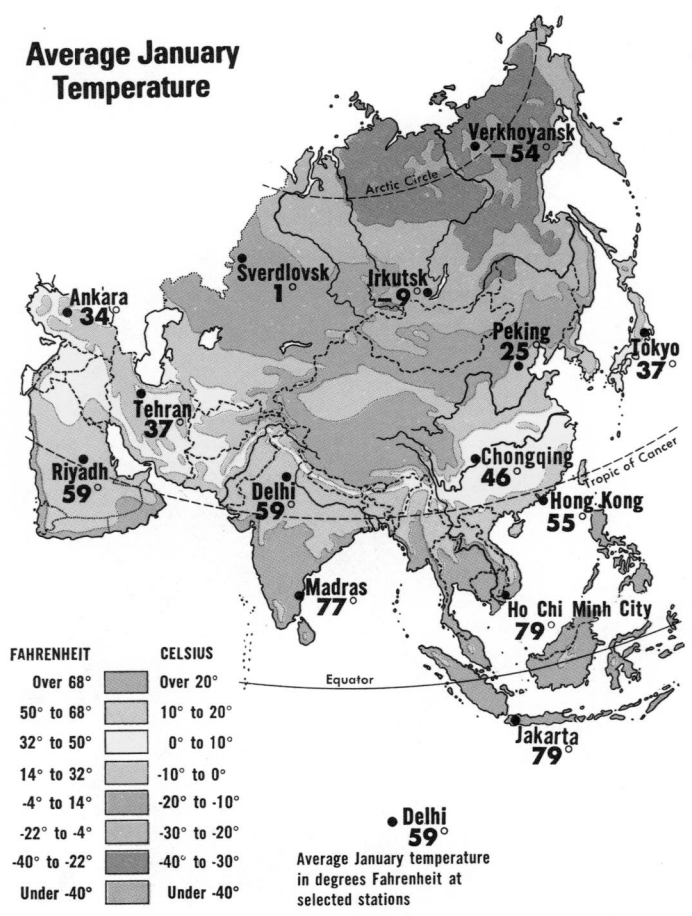

Verkhoyansk −54°
Sverdlovsk 1°
Irkutsk −9°
Peking 25°
Tokyo 37°
Ankara 34°
Tehran 37°
Chongqing 46°
Hong Kong 55°
Riyadh 59°
Delhi 59°
Madras 77°
Ho Chi Minh City 79°
Jakarta 79°

FAHRENHEIT	CELSIUS
Over 68°	Over 20°
50° to 68°	10° to 20°
32° to 50°	0° to 10°
14° to 32°	−10° to 0°
−4° to 14°	−20° to −10°
−22° to −4°	−30° to −20°
−40° to −22°	−40° to −30°
Under −40°	Under −40°

• Delhi
59°
Average January temperature
in degrees Fahrenheit at
selected stations

Average July Temperature

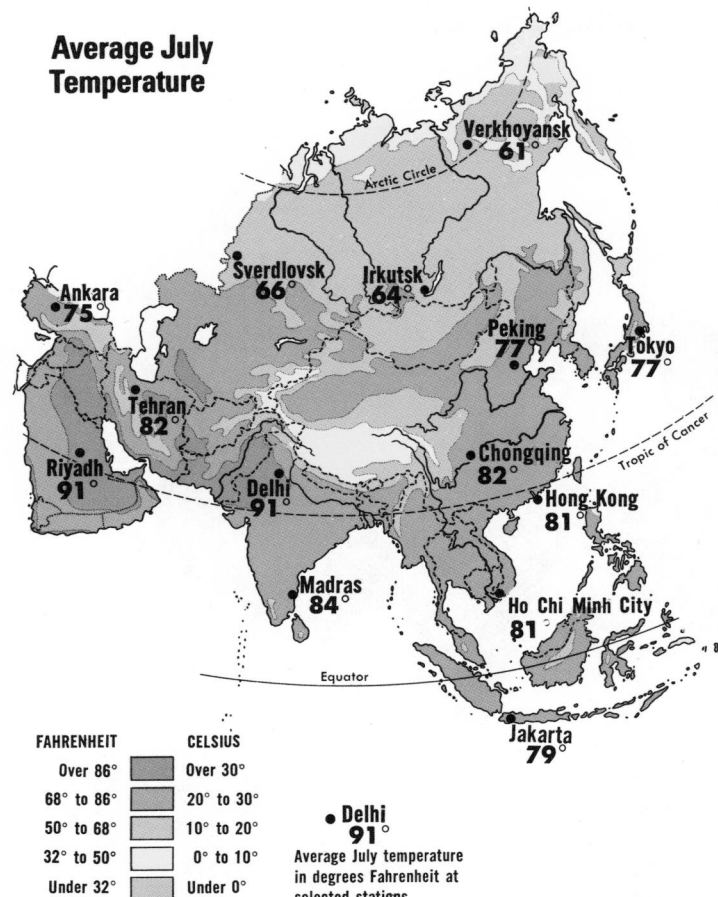

Verkhoyansk 61°
Sverdlovsk 66°
Irkutsk 64°
Peking 77°
Tokyo 77°
Ankara 75°
Tehran 82°
Chongqing 82°
Hong Kong 81°
Riyadh 91°
Delhi 91°
Madras 84°
Ho Chi Minh City 81°
Jakarta 79°

FAHRENHEIT	CELSIUS
Over 86°	Over 30°
68° to 86°	20° to 30°
50° to 68°	10° to 20°
32° to 50°	0° to 10°
Under 32°	Under 0°

• Delhi
91°
Average July temperature
in degrees Fahrenheit at
selected stations

Rainfall

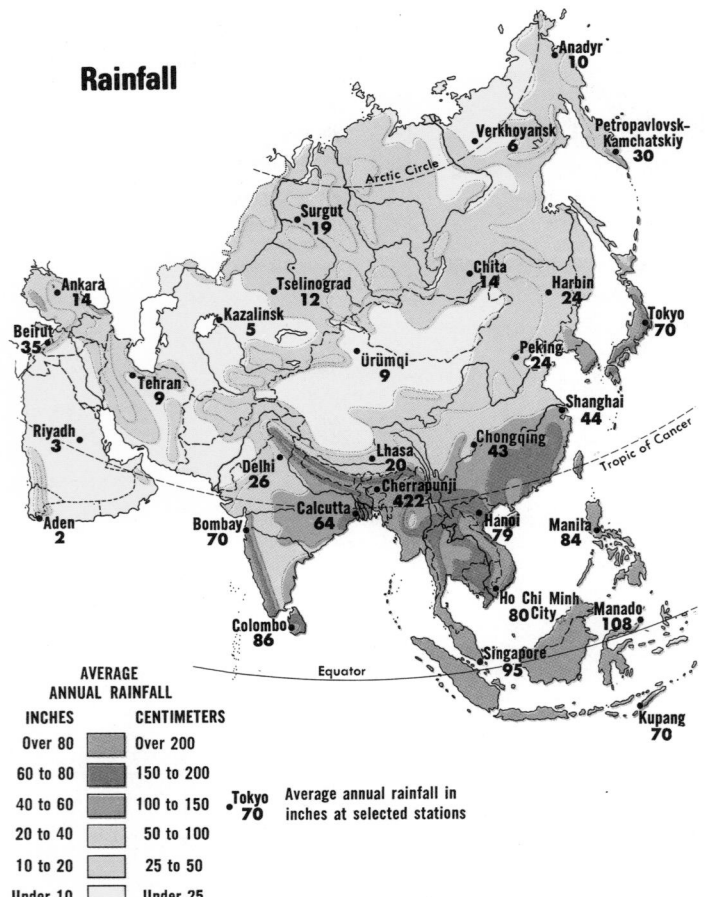

Anadyr 10
Petropavlovsk-Kamchatskiy 30
Verkhoyansk 6
Surgut 19
Chita 14
Harbin 24
Tokyo 70
Ankara 14
Tselinograd 12
Kazalinsk 5
Ürümqi 9
Peking 24
Beirut 35
Shanghai 44
Tehran 9
Lhasa 20
Chongqing 43
Riyadh 3
Delhi 26
Cherrapunji 422
Hanoi 79
Manila 84
Calcutta 64
Aden 2
Bombay 70
Ho Chi Minh City 80
Manado 108
Colombo 86
Singapore 95
Kupang 70

AVERAGE ANNUAL RAINFALL

INCHES	CENTIMETERS
Over 80	Over 200
60 to 80	150 to 200
40 to 60	100 to 150
20 to 40	50 to 100
10 to 20	25 to 50
Under 10	Under 25

• Tokyo
70
Average annual rainfall in
inches at selected stations

Vegetation/Relief

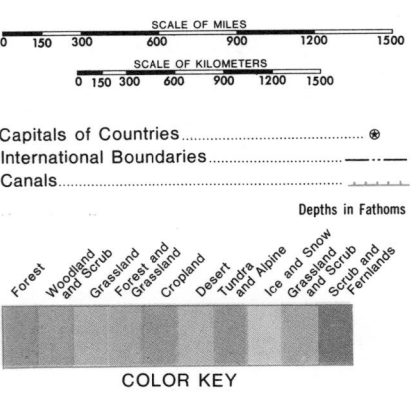

SCALE OF MILES
0 150 300 600 900 1200 1500

SCALE OF KILOMETERS
0 150 300 600 900 1200 1500

Capitals of Countries.............................⊛
International Boundaries.........................
Canals...

Depths in Fathoms

Forest
Woodland and Scrub
Grassland
Forest and Grassland
Cropland
Desert
Tundra and Alpine
Ice and Snow
Grassland and Scrub
Scrub and Fernlands

COLOR KEY

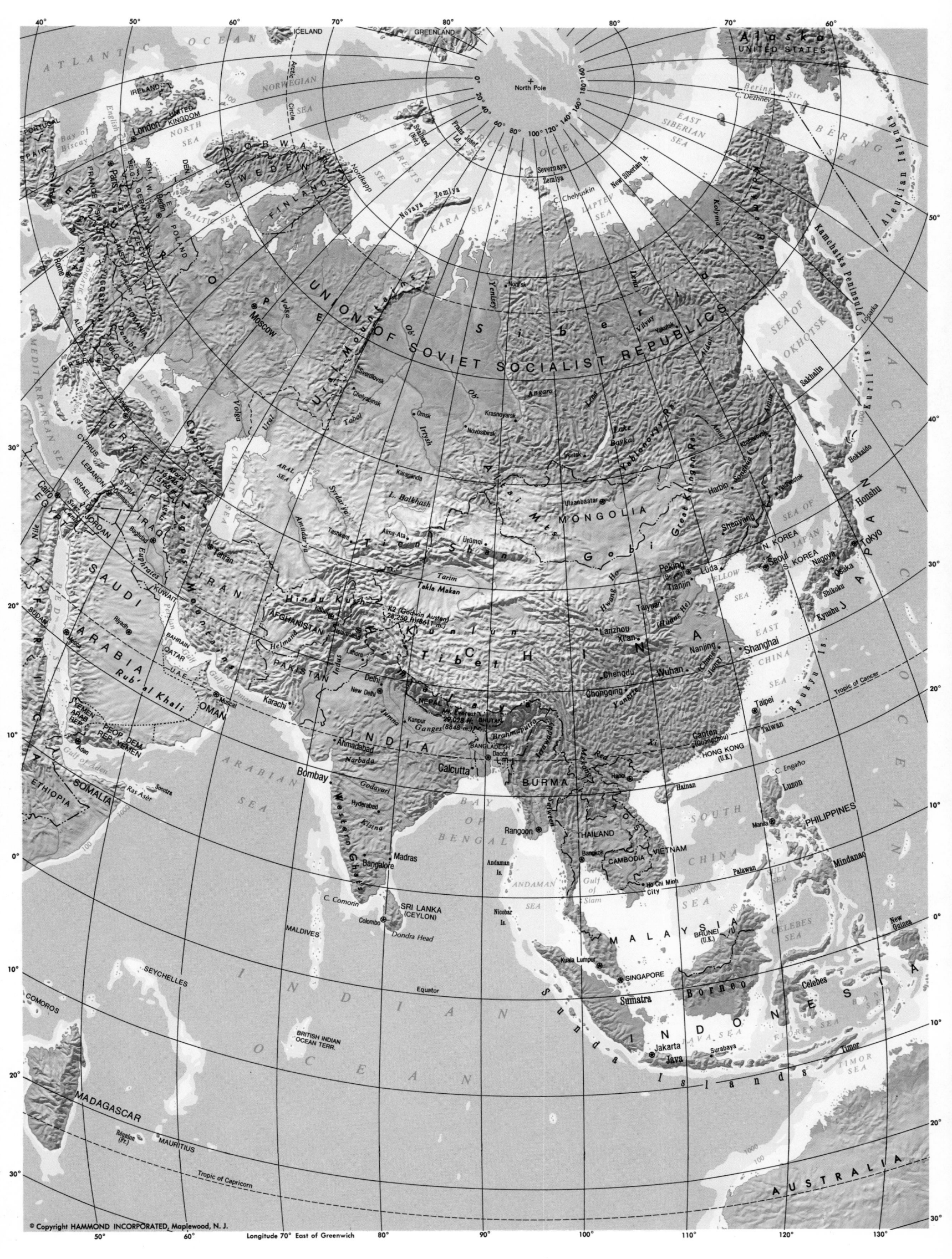

Longitude 70° East of Greenwich

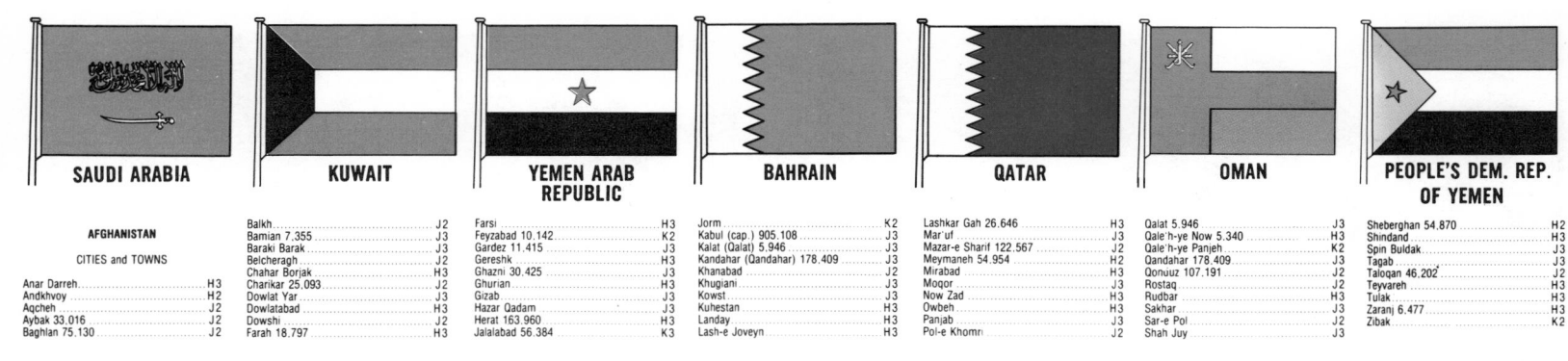

| SAUDI ARABIA | KUWAIT | YEMEN ARAB REPUBLIC | BAHRAIN | QATAR | OMAN | PEOPLE'S DEM. REP. OF YEMEN |

AFGHANISTAN

CITIES and TOWNS

Anar Darreh H3	Balkh J2	Farsi H3	Jorm K2	Lashkar Gah 26.646 .... H3	Qalat 5.946 .... J3	Sheberghan 54.870 .... H2
Andkhvoy H2	Bamian 7.355 .... J3	Feyzabad 10.142 .... K2	Kabul (cap.) 905.108 .... J3	Mar'uf J3	Qale'h-ye Now 5.340 .... H3	Shindand H3
Aqcheh J2	Baraki Barak J3	Gardez 11.415 .... J3	Kalat (Qalat) 5.946 .... J3	Mazar-e Sharif 122.567 .... H2	Qale'h-ye Panjeh K2	Spin Buldak J3
Aybak 33.016 .... J2	Belcheragh H2	Gereshk H3	Kandahar (Qandahar) 178.409 .... J2	Meymaneh 54.954 .... H2	Qandahar 178.409 .... J3	Tagab J3
Baghlan 75.130 .... J2	Chahar Borjak H3	Ghazni 30.425 .... J3	Khanabad J2	Mirabad H3	Qandahar 178.409 .... J2	Taloqan 46.202 .... J2
	Charikar 25.093 .... J3	Ghurian H3	Khugiani J3	Mogor J3	Qonuuz 107.191 .... J2	Teyvareh H3
	Dowlat Yar H3	Gizab J3	Kowst J3	Now Zad H3	Rostaq J2	Tulak H3
	Dowlatabad J2	Hazar Qadam J3	Kuhestan H3	Owbeh H3	Rudbar H3	Zarani 6.477 .... H3
	Dowshi J3	Herat 163.960 .... H3	Landay H3	Panjab J3	Sakhar J3	Zibak K2
	Farah 18.797 .... H3	Jalalabad 56.384 .... K3	Lash-e Joveyn H3	Pol-e Khomri J2	Sar-e Pol J2	
					Shah Juy J3	

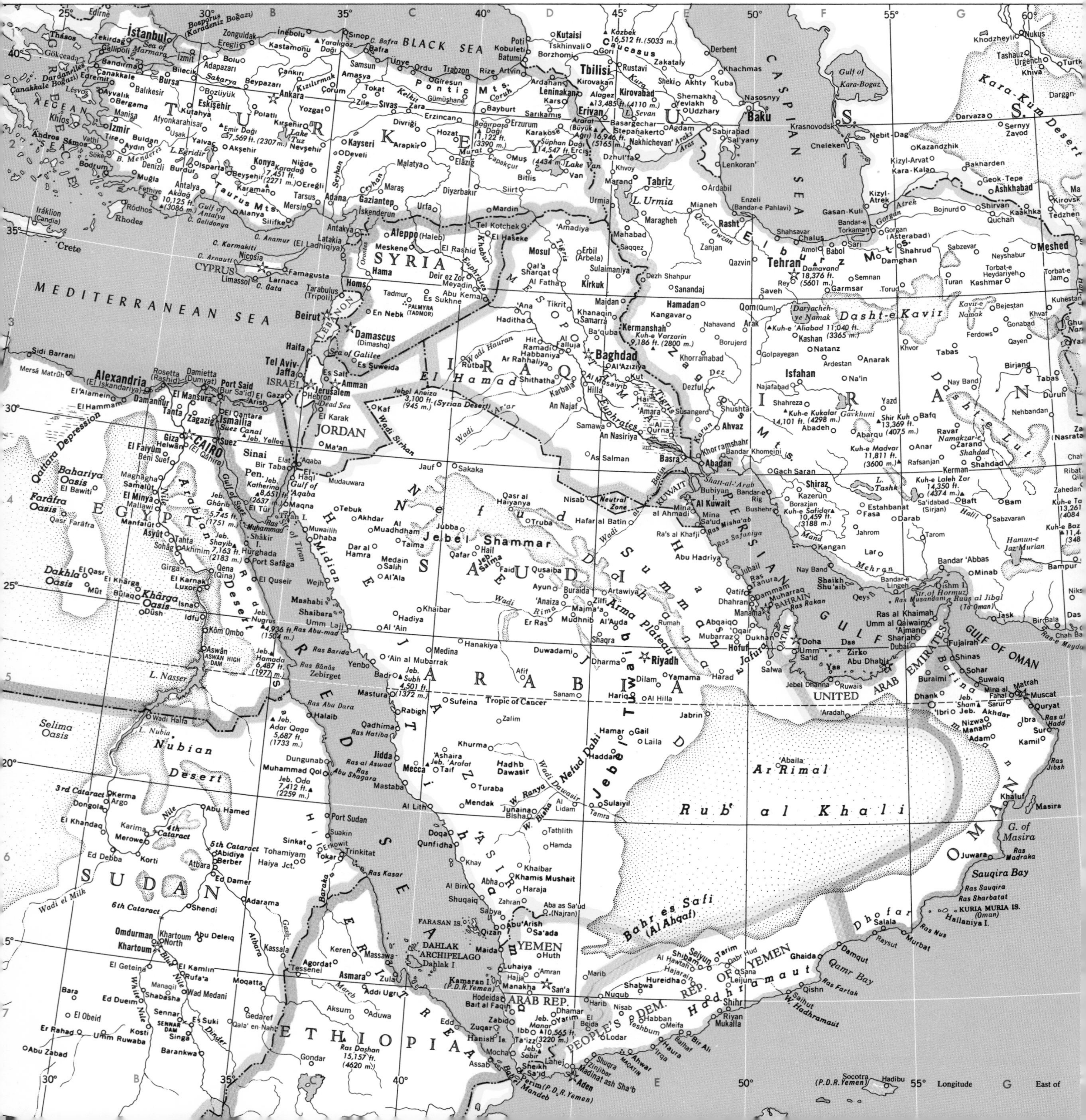

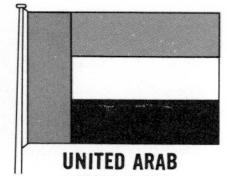

UNITED ARAB EMIRATES

OTHER FEATURES

Farah Rud (riv.) H3
Gowd-e Zerreh (depr.) H4
Harirud (riv.) H3
Helmand (riv.) J3
Hindu Kush (mts.) J2
Kabul (riv.) K3
Konar (riv.) K2
Lurah (riv.) J3

Margow, Dasht-e (des.) H3
Murghab (riv.) H2
Namaksar (salt lake) H3
Paropamisus (mts.) H3
Rigestan (reg.) H3

BAHRAIN
CITIES and TOWNS

Manama (cap.) 88,785 ....F4
Muharraq 37,732 ....F4

GAZA STRIP
CITIES and TOWNS

Gaza* 118,272 ....B3

IRAN
CITIES and TOWNS

Abadan 296,081 ....E3
Abadeh 16,000 ....F3
Abarqu 8,000 ....F3
Ahvaz 329,006 ....E3

Amol 68,782 ....F2
Anar 463 ....G3
Anarak 2,038 ....F3
Arak 114,507 ....E3
Ardabil 147,404 ....E2
Ardestan 5,868 ....F3
Asterabad (Gorgan) 88,348 ....F2
Babol 67,790 ....F2
Bafq 5,000 ....G3
Baft 6,000 ....G4

(continued on following page)

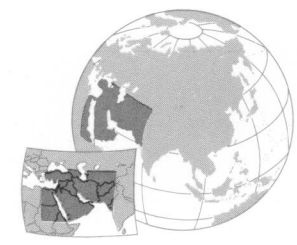

SAUDI ARABIA
AREA 829,995 sq. mi. (2,149,687 sq. km.)
POPULATION 8,367,000
CAPITAL Riyadh
MONETARY UNIT Saudi riyal
MAJOR LANGUAGE Arabic
MAJOR RELIGION Islam

KUWAIT
AREA 6,532 sq. mi. (16,918 sq. km.)
POPULATION 1,355,827
CAPITAL Al Kuwait
MONETARY UNIT Kuwaiti dinar
MAJOR LANGUAGE Arabic
MAJOR RELIGION Islam

YEMEN ARAB REPUBLIC
AREA 77,220 sq. mi. (200,000 sq. km.)
POPULATION 6,456,189
CAPITAL San'a
MONETARY UNIT Yemeni rial
MAJOR LANGUAGE Arabic
MAJOR RELIGION Islam

BAHRAIN
AREA 240 sq. mi. (622 sq. km.)
POPULATION 358,857
CAPITAL Manama
MONETARY UNIT Bahraini dinar
MAJOR LANGUAGE Arabic
MAJOR RELIGION Islam

QATAR
AREA 4,247 sq. mi. (11,000 sq. km.)
POPULATION 220,000
CAPITAL Doha
MONETARY UNIT Qatari riyal
MAJOR LANGUAGE Arabic
MAJOR RELIGION Islam

OMAN
AREA 120,000 sq. mi. (310,800 sq. km.)
POPULATION 891,000
CAPITAL Muscat
MONETARY UNIT Omani rial
MAJOR LANGUAGE Arabic
MAJOR RELIGION Islam

PEOPLE'S DEM. REP. OF YEMEN
AREA 111,101 sq. mi. (287,752 sq. km.)
POPULATION 1,969,000
CAPITAL Aden
MONETARY UNIT Yemeni dinar
MAJOR LANGUAGE Arabic
MAJOR RELIGION Islam

UNITED ARAB EMIRATES
AREA 32,278 sq. mi. (83,600 sq. km.)
POPULATION 1,040,275
CAPITAL Abu Dhabi
MONETARY UNIT dirham
MAJOR LANGUAGE Arabic
MAJOR RELIGION Islam

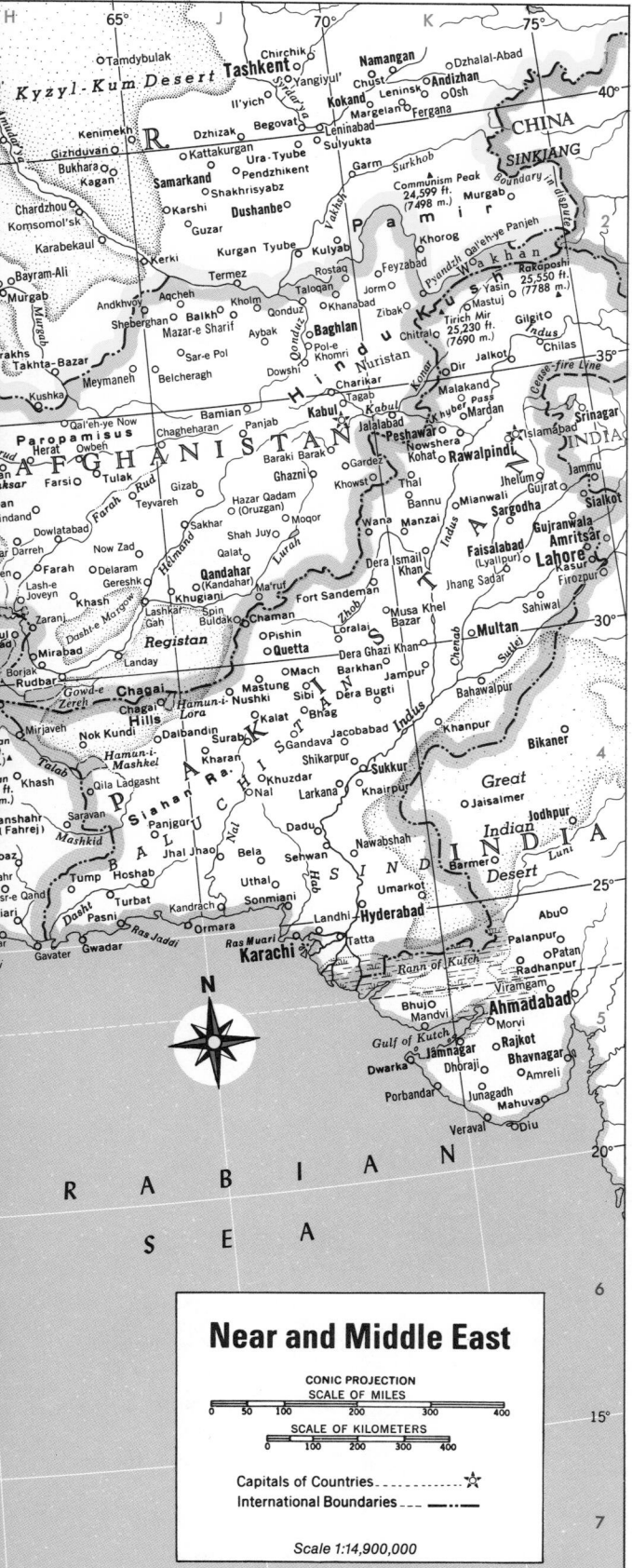

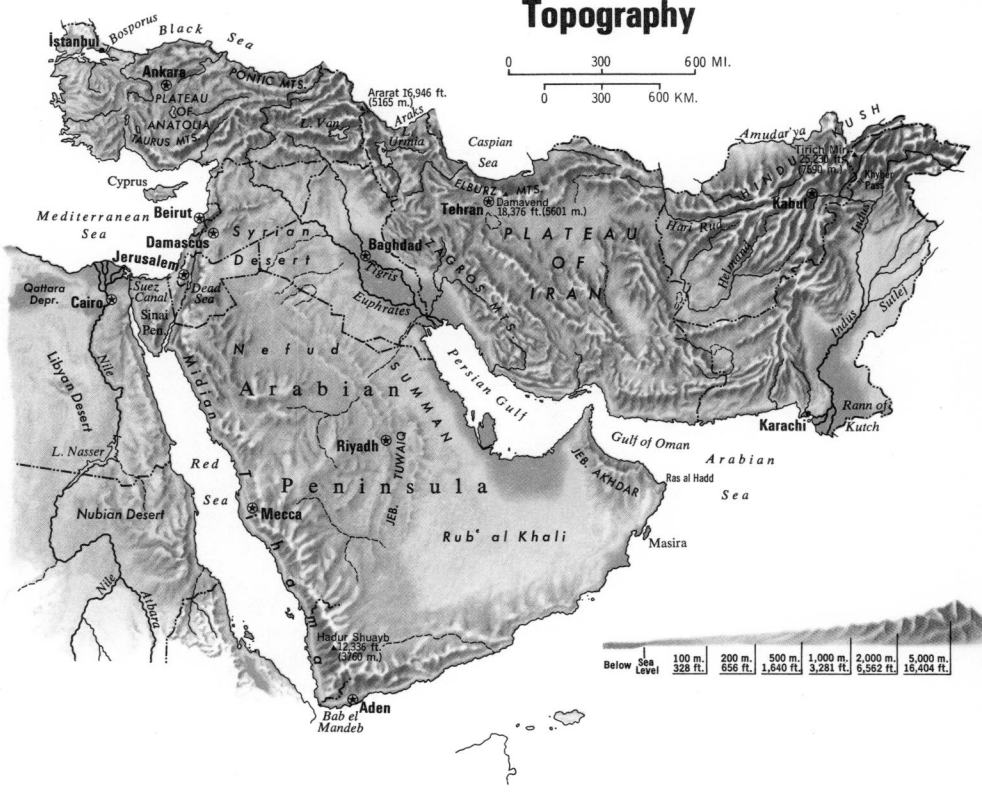

Topography

Near and Middle East
CONIC PROJECTION
SCALE OF MILES
SCALE OF KILOMETERS
Capitals of Countries .... ☆
International Boundaries ___ __ _
Scale 1:14,900,000

© Copyright HAMMOND INCORPORATED, Maplewood, N.J.

Near and Middle East

(continued)

Bam 22,000 ... G4
Bampur 1,585 ... H4
Bandar 'Abbas 89,103 ... G4
Bandar-e Lengeh 4,920 ... F4
Bandar-e Pahlavi (Enzeli) 55,978 ... E2
Bandar-e Rig 1,889 ... F4
Bandar-e Torkaman 13,000 ... F2
Bandar Khomeini 6,000 ... E3
Bejestan 3,823 ... G3
Bir Bala 103 ... G4
Birjand 25,854 ... G3
Bojnurd 31,248 ... G2
Borazjan 20,000 ... F4
Borujerd 100,103 ... E3
Bushehr 57,681 ... F4
Chah Bahar 1,800 ... H4
Chalus 15,000 ... F2
Damghan 13,000 ... F2
Darab 13,000 ... G4
Dashtiari ... H4
Dezful 110,287 ... E3
Dezh Shahpur 1,384 ... E2
Enzeli 55,978 ... E2
Estahbanat 18,187 ... F4
Fahrej (Iranshahr) 5,000 ... H4
Fasa 19,000 ... F4
Ferdows 11,000 ... G3
Gach Saran ... F3
Garmsar 4,723 ... F2
Golpayegan 20,515 ... F3
Gonabad 8,000 ... G3
Gorgan 88,348 ... F2
Hamadan 155,846 ... E3
Iranshahr 5,000 ... H4
Isfahan 617,825 ... F3
Jahrom 38,236 ... F4
Jask 1,078 ... G4
Kangan 2,682 ... F4
Kangavar 9,414 ... E3
Kashan 84,545 ... F3
Kashmar 17,000 ... G2
Kazerun 51,309 ... F4
Kerman 140,309 ... G3
Kermanshah 290,861 ... E3
Khash 7,439 ... H4
Khorramabad 104,928 ... E3
Khorramshahr 146,709 ... E3
Khvor 2,912 ... G3
Khvoy 70,040 ... E2
Lar 22,000 ... F4
Mahabad 28,610 ... E2
Maragheh 60,820 ... E2
Marand 24,000 ... E2
Meshed 670,180 ... H2
Mianeh 28,447 ... E2
Minab 4,228 ... G2
Mirjaveh 11,000 ... H4
Nahavand 24,000 ... E3
Na'in 5,925 ... F3
Najafabad 76,236 ... F3
Nasratabad (Zabol) 20,000 ... H3
Natanz 4,370 ... F3
Nehbandan 2,130 ... G3
Neyshabur 59,101 ... G2
Nikshahr ... H4
Pahlevi (Enzeli) 55,978 ... E2
Qasr-e Qand 1,879 ... H4
Qayen 6,000 ... G3
Qazvin 138,527 ... E2
Qom 246,831 ... F3
Quchan 29,133 ... G2
Qum (Qom) 246,831 ... F3
Rafsanjan 21,000 ... G3
Rasht 187,203 ... E2
Ravar 5,074 ... G3
Rey 102,825 ... F2
Reza'iyeh (Urmia) 163,991 ... D2
Sabzevar 69,174 ... G2
Sabzvaran 7,000 ... G4
Sai'dabad 20,000 ... G4
Sanandaj 95,834 ... E2
Saqqez 17,000 ... E2
Saravan ... H4
Sari 70,936 ... F2
Saveh 17,565 ... F2
Semnan 31,058 ... F2
Shahdad 2,777 ... G3
Shahreza 34,220 ... F3
Shahrud 30,767 ... G2
Shahsavar 12,000 ... F2
Shiraz 416,408 ... F4
Shirvan 11,000 ... G2
Shustar 24,000 ... E3
Sirjan (Sai'dabad) 20,000 ... G4
Susangerd 21,000 ... E3
Tabas 10,000 ... G3
Tabas-Masina (Tabas) 466 ... H3
Tabriz 598,576 ... E2
Tarom 394 ... G4
Tehran (cap.) 4,496,159 ... F2
Torbat-e Heydariyeh 30,106 ... G2
Torbat-e Jam 13,000 ... H2
Torud 721 ... F2
Turan ... G2
Turbat-i-Shaikh Jam 13,000 ... H2
Urmia 163,991 ... D2
Yazd 135,978 ... F3
Yazdan ... H3
Zabol 20,000 ... H3
Zahedan 92,628 ... H4
Zanjan 99,967 ... E2
Zarand 5,000 ... G3

OTHER FEATURES

Araks (riv.) ... E2
Atrek (riv.) ... G2
Bazman, Kuh-e (mt.) ... H4
Damavand (mt.) ... F2
Dez (riv.) ... E3
Elburz (mts.) ... F2
Gavkhuni (lake) ... F3
Gorgan (riv.) ... F2
Halil (riv.) ... G4
Jaz Murian, Hamun-e (marsh) ... G4
Karun (riv.) ... E3
Kavir, Dasht-e (salt des.) ... G3
Kavir-e Namak (salt des.) ... G3
Lut, Dasht-e (des.) ... G3
Maidani, Ras (cape) ... G4
Mand Rud (riv.) ... F4
Mashkid (riv.) ... H4
Mehran (riv.) ... F4
Namak, Daryacheh-ye (salt lake) ... F3
Namaksar (salt lake) ... H3
Namakzar-e Shahdad (salt lake) ... G3
Oman (gulf) ... G5
Persian (gulf) ... F4
Qeys (isl.) ... F4
Qezel Owzan (riv.) ... E2
Qeshm (isl.) ... G4
Safidar, Kuh-e (mt.) ... F4
Shaikh Shua'ib (isl.) ... F4
Shir Kuh (mt.) ... F3
Taftan, Kuh-e (mt.) ... H4
Talab (riv.) ... H4
Tashk (lake) ... F4
Urmia (lake) ... E2
Zagros (mts.) ... E3

IRAQ

CITIES and TOWNS

Al'Aziziya 7,450 ... E3
Al Falluja 38,072 ... D3
Al Fatha† 15,329 ... D2
Al Musaiyib 15,955 ... D3
Al Qurna 5,638 ... E3
'Amadiya 2,578 ... D2
'Amara 64,847 ... E3
'Ana 15,729 ... D3
An Najaf 128,096 ... D3
An Nasiriya 60,405 ... E3
Arbela (Erbil) 90,320 ... D2
Ar Rahhaliya 1,579 ... D3
As Salman 3,584 ... E3
Baghdad (cap.) 502,503 ... E3
Baghdad* 1,745,328 ... E3
Baq'uba 34,575 ... D3
Basra 313,327 ... E3
Erbil 90,320 ... D2
Habbaniya 14,405 ... D3
Haditha 6,870 ... D3
Hai 16,988 ... E3
Hilla 84,717 ... D3
Hit 9,131 ... D3
Karbal'a 83,301 ... D3
Khanaqin 23,522 ... D3
Kirkuk 167,413 ... D2
Kirkuk* 176,794 ... D2
Kut 42,116 ... E3
Maidan 354 ... E3
Mosul 315,157 ... D2
Qala' Sharqat 2,434 ... D2
Ramadi 28,723 ... D3
Rutba 5,091 ... D3
Samarra 24,746 ... D3
Samawa 33,473 ... D3
Shithatha 2,326 ... D3
Sulaimaniya 86,822 ... E2
Tikrit 9,921 ... D3

OTHER FEATURES

'Aneiza, Jebel (mt.) ... C3
'Ara'r, Wadi (dry riv.) ... D3
Batin, Wadi al (dry riv.) ... E4
Euphrates (riv.) ... E3
Hauran, Wadi (dry riv.) ... D3
Mesopotamia (reg.) ... D3
Syrian (El Hamad) (des.) ... D3
Tigris (riv.) ... E3

KUWAIT

CITIES and TOWNS

Al Kuwait (cap.) 181,774 ... E4
Mina al Ahmadi ... E4
Mina Saud ... E4

OTHER FEATURES

Bubiyan (isl.) ... E4
Persian (gulf) ... F4

OMAN

CITIES and TOWNS

Adam ... G5
Buraimi ... G5
Dhank ... G5
Ibra ... G5
I'bri ... G5
Juwara ... G6
Kamil ... G5
Khaluf ... G5
Khasab ... G4
Manah ... G5
Masqat (Muscat) (cap.) 7,500 ... G5
Matrah 15,000 ... G5
Mina al Fahal ... G5
Murbat ... G6
Muscat (cap.) 7,500 ... G5
Nizwa ... G5
Quryat ... G5
Raysut (Risut) ... F6
Salala 4,000 ... F6
Sarur ... G5
Shinas ... G5
Sohar ... G5
Sur ... G5
Suwaiq ... G5

OTHER FEATURES

Akhdar, Jebel (range) ... G5
Batina (reg.) ... G5
Dhofar (reg.) ... F6
Hadd, Ras al (cape) ... G5
Jibsh, Ras (cape) ... G5
Kuria Muria (isls.) ... G6
Madraka, Ras (cape) ... G6
Masira (gulf) ... G6
Masira (isl.) ... G5
Musandam, Ras (cape) ... G4
Nus, Ras (cape) ... G6
Oman (gulf) ... G5
Oman (reg.) ... G5
Ruus al Jibal (dist.) ... G4
Sauqira (bay) ... G6
Sauqira, Ras (cape) ... G6
Sham, Jebel (mt.) ... G5
Sharbatat, Ras (cape) ... G6

QATAR

CITIES and TOWNS

Doha (cap.) 150,000 ... F4
Dukhan ... F4
Umm Sai'd ... F5

OTHER FEATURES

Persian (gulf) ... F4
Rakan, Ras (cape) ... F4

SAUDI ARABIA

CITIES and TOWNS

Aba as Sau'd 47,501 ... D6
'Abaila ... F5
Abha 30,150 ... D6
Abqaiq ... E4
Abu 'Arish ... D6
Abu Hadriya ... E4
'Ain al Mubarrak ... C5
Al 'Ain ... C4
Al 'Ala ... C4
Al 'Auda ... E4
Al Birk ... D6
Al Hilla ... E5
Al Lidam ... D5
Al Lith ... C5
Al Muadhdam ... C4
'Anaiza ... D4
Artawiya ... E4
'Ashaira ... D5
Ayun ... D4
Badr ... C5
Buraida 69,940 ... D4
Dam ... D5
Dammam 127,844 ... F4
Dar al Hamra ... C4
Dhaba ... C4
Dhahran ... E4
Dharma ... E5
Dilam ... E5
Doqa ... D6
Duwadami ... D5
Er Ras ... D4
Faid ... D4
Gail ... E5
Haddar ... E5
Hadiya ... C4
Hafar al Batin ... E4
Hail 40,502 ... D4
Hamar ... E5
Hamda ... D6
Hanakiya ... D5
Haql ... C4
Harad ... E5
Haraja ... D6
Hariq ... E5
Hofuf 101,271 ... E4
Jabrin ... E5
Jauf ... C4
Jidda 561,104 ... C5
Jizan (Qizan) 32,812 ... D6
Jubail ... F4
Jubba ... D4
Junaina ... D5
Kaf ... C3
Khaibar, 'Asir ... D5
Khaibar, Hejaz ... C4
Khamis Mushait 49,581 ... D6
Khay ... D6
Khurma ... D5
Laila ... E5
Majmaa' ... D4
Maqna ... C4
Marib ... E6
Mastaba ... C5
Mastura ... C5
Mecca 366,801 ... C5
Medain Salih ... C4
Medina 198,186 ... D5
Mendak ... D5
Mina Sau'd ... E4
Mubarraz 54,325 ... E4
Mudhnib ... D4
Muwailih ... C4
Najran (Aba as Sau'd) 47,501 ... D6
Nisab ... D4
O'qair ... E4
Qadhima ... C5
Qafar ... D4
Qasr al Haiyanya ... D4
Qatif ... E4
Qizan 32,812 ... D6
Qunfidha ... D6
Qusaiba ... D4
Rabigh ... C5
Ra's al Khafji ... E4
Ras Tanura ... F4
Riyadh (cap.) 666,840 ... E5
Rumah ... E4
Sabya ... D6
Sakaka ... D4
Salwa ... F5
Shaqra ... D4
Shuqaiq ... D6
Sufeina ... D5
Sulaiyil ... E5
Taif 204,857 ... D5
Taima ... C4
Tamra ... E5
Tathlith ... D6
Tebuk (Tabuk) 74,825 ... C4
Truba ... D4
Turaba ... D5
Umm Lajj ... C4
Wejh ... C4
Yamama ... E5
Yenbo ... C5
Zahran ... D6
Zalim ... D5
Zilfi ... E4

OTHER FEATURES

Abu-Mad, Ras (cape) ... C5
'Aneiza, Jebel (mt.) ... C3
'Aqaba (gulf) ... C4
Arafat, Jebel (mt.) ... D5
'Ara'r, Wadi (dry riv.) ... D3
Arma (plat.) ... E4
Aswad, Ras al (cape) ... C5
Bahr es Safi (des.) ... E6
Barida, Ras (cape) ... C5
Bisha, Wadi (dry riv.) ... D5
Dahana (des.) ... E4
Dawasir, Wadi (dry riv.) ... E5
Dawasir, Hadhb (range) ... D5
Farasan (isls.) ... D6
Hatiba, Ras (cape) ... C5
Jafura (des.) ... F5
Mashabi (isl.) ... C4
Midian (dist.) ... C4
Mishaa'b, Ras (cape) ... E4
Nefud (des.) ... D4
Nefud Dahi (des.) ... D5
Persian (gulf) ... F4
Ranya, Wadi (dry riv.) ... D5
Red (sea) ... C5
Rima, Wadi (dry riv.) ... D4
Rimal, Ar (des.) ... F5
Rub al Khali (des.) ... F5
Safaniya, Ras (cape) ... E4
Salma, Jebel (mts.) ... D4
Shaibara (isl.) ... C4
Shammar, Jebel (plat.) ... D4
Sirhan, Wadi (dry riv.) ... C3
Subh, Jebel (mt.) ... C5
Summan (plat.) ... E4
Tihama (reg.) ... C5
Tiran (isl.) ... C4
Tiran (str.) ... C4
Tuwaiq, Jebel (range) ... E5

UNITED ARAB EMIRATES

CITIES and TOWNS

Abu Dhabi (cap.) 347,000 ... F5
'AJman ... G4
'Aradah ... F5
Buraimi ... G5
Dubai ... F4
Fujairah ... G4
Jebel Dhanna ... F5
Ras al Khaimah ... G4
Ruwais ... F5
Sharjah ... F4
Umm al Qaiwain ... G4

OTHER FEATURES

Das (isl.) ... F4
Oman (gulf) ... G5
Yas (isl.) ... F5
Zirko (isl.) ... F5

WEST BANK

CITIES and TOWNS

Hebron 38,309 ... C3

OTHER FEATURES

Dead (sea) ... C3

YEMEN ARAB REP.

CITIES and TOWNS

'Amran ... D6
Bait al Faqih ... D7
Dhamar 19,467 ... D7
El Beida 5,975 ... E7
Hajja 5,814 ... D6
Harib ... E7
Hodeida 80,314 ... D7
Huth ... D6
Ibb 19,066 ... D7
Luhaiya ... D6
Marib 292 ... D6
Mocha ... D7
Saa'da 4,252 ... D6
Sana' (cap.) 134,588 ... D6
Sheikh Sai'd ... D7
Tai'zz 78,642 ... D7
Yarim ... D7
Zabid ... D7

OTHER FEATURES

Hanish (isls.) ... D7
Manar, Jebel (mt.) ... D7
Mandeb, Bab el (str.) ... D7
Red (sea) ... C5
Sabir, Jebel (mt.) ... D7
Tihama (reg.) ... C5
Zuqar (isl.) ... D7

YEMEN, PEOPLE'S DEM. REPUBLIC OF

CITIES and TOWNS

Aden (cap.) 240,370 ... E7
Ahwar ... E7
Balhaf ... E7
Bir 'Ali ... E7
Damqut ... F6
Ghaida ... F6
Habban ... E7
Hadibu ... F7
Hajarain ... E6
Haura ... E7
Hureidha ... E6
I'rqa ... E7
Lahej ... E7
Leijun ... E6
Lodar ... E7
Madinat ash Shab' ... E7
Meifa ... E7
Mukalla 45,000 ... E7
Nisab ... E7
Nuqub ... E6
Qishn ... F6
Riyan ... E7
Saihut ... F6
Seiyun 20,000 ... E6
Shabwa ... E6
Shibam ... E6
Shihr ... E7
Shuqra ... E7
Tarim ... E6
Yeshbum ... E7
Zinjibar ... E7

OTHER FEATURES

Fartak, Ras (cape) ... F6
Hadhramaut (dist.) ... E7
Hadhramaut, Wadi (dry riv.) ... F7
Kamaran (isl.) ... D6
Perim (isl.) ... D7
Socotra (isl.) ... F7

*City and suburbs.

Agriculture, Industry and Resources

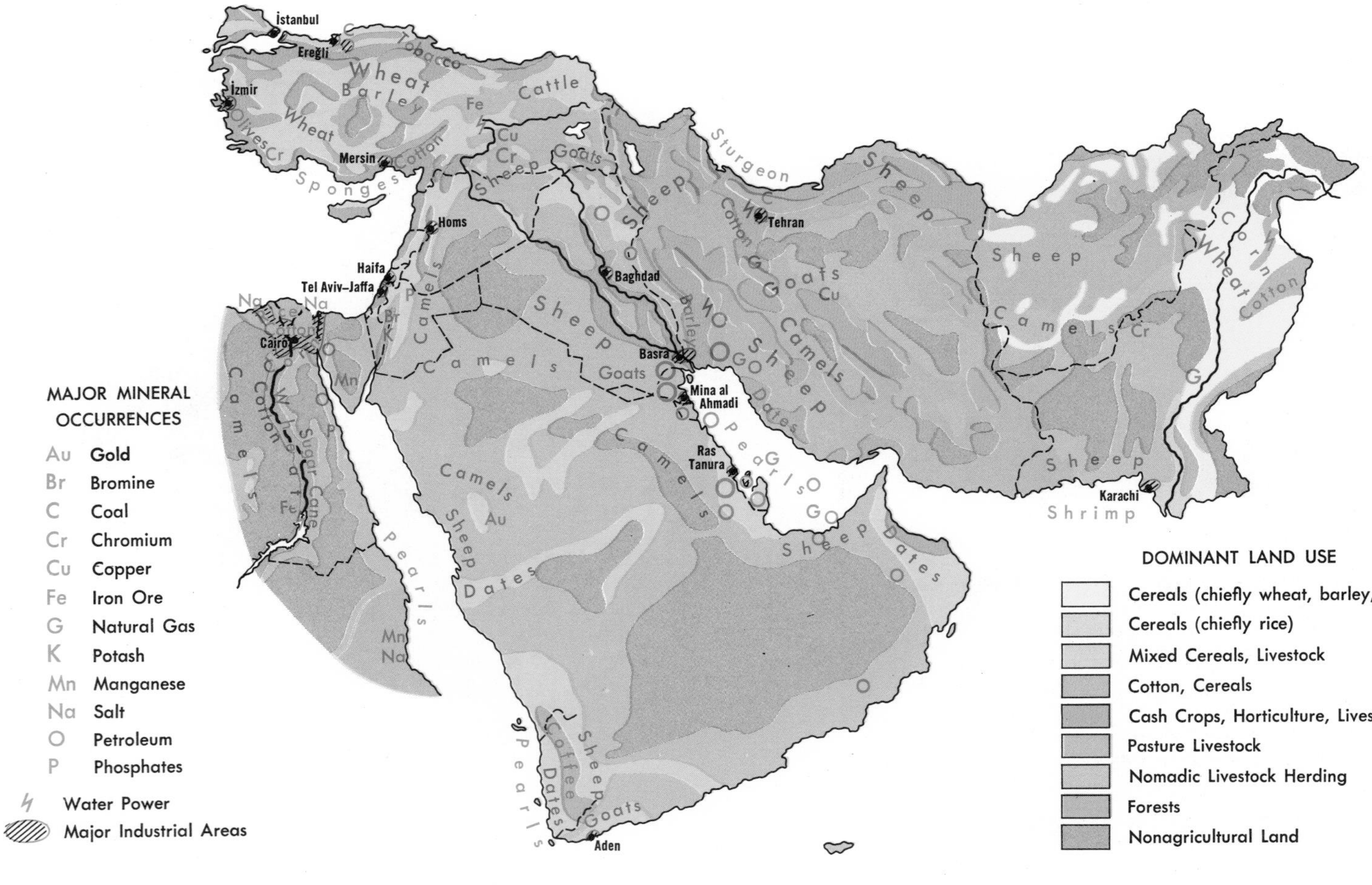

İstanbul
Ereğli
İzmir
Mersin
Homs
Haifa
Tel Aviv–Jaffa
Cairo
Baghdad
Tehran
Basra
Mina al Ahmadi
Ras Tanura
Karachi
Aden
Wheat
Barley
Tobacco
Cattle
Olives
Cotton
Sponges
Sheep
Goats
Camels
Sturgeon
Dates
Pearls
Corn
Shrimp
Sugar Cane
Coffee
MAJOR MINERAL OCCURRENCES
Au Gold
Br Bromine
C Coal
Cr Chromium
Cu Copper
Fe Iron Ore
G Natural Gas
K Potash
Mn Manganese
Na Salt
O Petroleum
P Phosphates
Water Power
Major Industrial Areas
DOMINANT LAND USE
Cereals (chiefly wheat, barley, corn)
Cereals (chiefly rice)
Mixed Cereals, Livestock
Cotton, Cereals
Cash Crops, Horticulture, Livestock
Pasture Livestock
Nomadic Livestock Herding
Forests
Nonagricultural Land

TURKEY

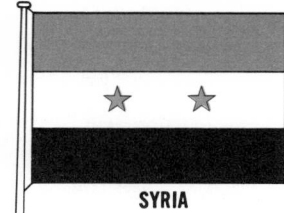
SYRIA

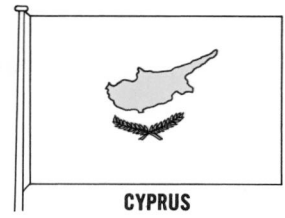
LEBANON

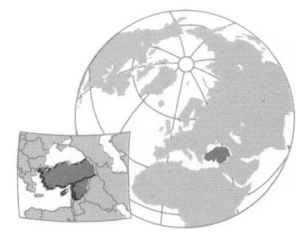
CYPRUS

AREA 300,946 sq. mi. (779,450 sq. km.)
POPULATION 45,217,556
CAPITAL Ankara
LARGEST CITY Istanbul
HIGHEST POINT Ararat 16,946 ft. (5,165 m.)
MONETARY UNIT Turkish lira
MAJOR LANGUAGE Turkish
MAJOR RELIGION Islam

AREA 71,498 sq. mi. (185,180 sq. km.)
POPULATION 8,979,000
CAPITAL Damascus
LARGEST CITY Damascus
HIGHEST POINT Hermon 9,232 ft. (2,814 m.)
MONETARY UNIT Syrian pound
MAJOR LANGUAGES Arabic, French, Kurdish, Armenian
MAJOR RELIGIONS Islam, Christianity

AREA 4,015 sq. mi. (10,399 sq. km.)
POPULATION 3,161,000
CAPITAL Beirut
LARGEST CITY Beirut
HIGHEST POINT Qurnet es Sauda 10,131 ft. (3,088 m.)
MONETARY UNIT Lebanese pound
MAJOR LANGUAGES Arabic, French
MAJOR RELIGIONS Christianity, Islam

AREA 3,473 sq. mi. (8,995 sq. km.)
POPULATION 629,000
CAPITAL Nicosia
LARGEST CITY Nicosia
HIGHEST POINT Troödos 6,406 ft. (1,953 m.)
MONETARY UNIT Cypriot pound
MAJOR LANGUAGES Greek, Turkish, English
MAJOR RELIGIONS Eastern (Greek) Orthodoxy, Islam

CYPRUS

CITIES and TOWNS

Dhali 2,970 .... E5
Episkopi 2,150 .... E5
Famagusta 38,960 ...... F5
Ktima E5
Kyrenia 3,892 .... E5
Kythrea 3,400 .... E5
Lapithos 3,600 .... E5
Larnaca 19,608 .... E5
Lefka 3,650 .... E5
Limassol 79,641 .... E5
Morphou 9,040 .... E5
Nicosia (cap.) 115,718 .. E5
Paphos 8,984 .... E5
Polis 2,200 .... E5
Rizokarpasso 3,600 ..... E5
Yialousa 2,750 .... E5

OTHER FEATURES

Andreas (cape) F5
Arnauti (cape) E5
Gata (cape) E5
Greco (cape) F5
Kormakiti (cape) E5
Troodos (mt.) E5

LEBANON

CITIES and TOWNS

A'leih 18,630 .... F6
Amyun 7,926 .... F5
Baa'lbek 15,560 .... G5
Batrun 5,976 .... F5
Beirut (cap.) 474,870 .. F6
Beirut* 938,940 .... F6
Hermil 2,652 .... G5
Merj U'yun 9,318 .... F6
Rasheiya 6,731 .... F6
Rayak 1,480 .... F6
Saida 32,200 .... F6
Sidon (Saida) 32,200 ... F6
Sur 16,483 .... F6
Tripoli (Tarabulus) 127,611 ... F5

Tyre (Sur) 16,483 ...... F6
Zahle 53,121 .... F6
Zegharta 18,210 .... G5

OTHER FEATURES

Lebanon (mts.) F6
Leontes (Litani) (riv.) ... F6
Litani (riv.) F6
Sauda, Qurnet es (mt.) .. G5

SYRIA

PROVINCES

Aleppo 1,316,872 ...... G4
Damascus 1,457,934 ... G6
Deir ez Zor 292,780 .... H5
Dera' 230,481 .... G6
El Quneitra 16,490 ..... F6
Es Suweida 139,650 .... G6
Hama 514,748 .... G5
Haseke 468,506 .... J4
Homs 546,176 .... G5
Idlib 383,695 .... G5
Latakia 389,552 .... F5
Rashid 243,736 .... H5
Tartus 302,065 .... G5

CITIES and TOWNS

Abu Kemal 6,907 ...... J5
A'in el A'rab 4,529 ..... H4
Aleppo 639,428 .... G4
Azaz 13,923 .... G4
Baniyas 8,537 .... F5
Busra G6
Damascus (cap.) 836,668 ... G6
Deir ez Zor 66,164 ..... H5
Dera' 27,651 .... G6
Dimashq (Damascus) (cap.) 836,668 ... G6
Duma 30,050 .... G6
El Bab 27,366 .... G4
El Haseke 32,746 ...... J4
El Ladhiqiya (Latakia) 125,716 ... F5
El Quryatein G5
El Quneitra 17,752 ..... F6
El Rashid 37,151 .... H5

En Nebk 16,334 .... G5
Es Suweide 29,524 ..... G6
Et Tell el Abyad H4
Haffe 4,656 .... G5
Haleb (Aleppo) 639,428 ... G4
Hama 137,421 .... G5
Harim 6,837 .... G4
Homs 215,423 .... G5
Idlib 34,515 .... G5
Izra 3,226 .... G6
Jeble 15,715 .... F5
Jerablus 8,610 .... J3
Jisr esh Shughur 13,131 ... G5
Khan Sheikhun G5
Latakia 125,716 .... F5
Masyaf 7,058 .... G5
Membij 13,796 .... G4
Meskene H5
Meyadin 12,515 .... J5
Qala'i es Salihiye J5
Qamishliye 31,448 ..... J4
Quteife 4,993 .... G6
Raqqa (El Rashid) 37,151 ... H5
Sabkha 3,375 .... H5
Safita 9,650 .... G5
Selemiya 21,677 .... G5
Tadmur 10,670 .... H5
Tartus 29,842 .... F5
Telkalakh 6,242 .... F5
Zebdani 10,010 .... G6

OTHER FEATURES

A'mrit (ruins) F5
Arwad (Ruad) (isl.) F5
A'si (Orontes) (riv.) G5
Druz, Jebel ed (mts.) ... G6
El Furat (riv.) H4
Euphrates (El Furat) (riv.) ... H4
Hermon (mt.) F6
Khabur (riv.) J5
Orontes (riv.) G5
Palmyra (Tadmor) (ruins) ... H5
Ruwaq, Jebel er (mts.) ... G6

TURKEY

PROVINCES

Adana 1,240,475 ...... F4

Adiyaman 346,892 ..... H4
Afyonkarahisar 579,171 ... D3
Agri 330,201 .... K3
Amasya 322,806 .... F2
Ankara 2,585,293 ...... D3
Antalya 669,357 .... D4
Artvin 228,026 .... J2
Aydin 609,869 .... B4
Balikesir 789,255 ...... B3
Bilecik 137,120 .... D2
Bingöl 210,804 .... J3
Bitlis 218,305 .... J3
Bolu 428,704 .... D2
Burdur 222,896 .... C4
Bursa 961,639 .... C2
Çanakkale 369,385 .... B2
Çankiri 265,468 .... E2
Çorum 547,580 .... F2
Denizli 560,916 .... C4
Diyarbakir 651,233 .... H4
Edirne 340,732 .... B2
Elâziğ 417,924 .... H3
Erzincan 283,683 ...... H3
Erzurum 746,666 ...... J3
Eskişehir 495,097 ..... D3
Gaziantep 715,939 .... G4
Giresun 463,587 .... H2
Gümüşhane 293,673 .. H2
Hakkâri 126,036 .... K4
Hatay 744,113 .... G4
İçel 714,817 .... F4
Isparta 322,685 .... D4
İstanbul 3,904,588 .... C2
İzmir 1,673,966 .... B3
Kahramanmaraş 641,480 ... G3
Kars 707,398 .... K2
Kastamonu 438,243 ... E2
Kayseri 676,809 .... F3
Kirklareli 268,399 ..... B2
Kirşehir 232,853 ...... F3
Kocaeli 477,736 .... C2
Konya 1,422,461 ...... E4
Kütahya 470,423 ...... C3
Malatya 574,558 ...... H3
Manisa 872,375 .... B3
Mardin 519,687 .... J4
Muğla 400,796 .... B4
Muş 267,203 .... J3
Nevşehir 249,308 ..... F3
Niğde 463,121 .... F4

Ordu 664,290 .... G2
Rize 336,278 .... J2
Sakarya 495,649 ...... D2
Samsun 906,381 ...... F2
Siirt 381,503 .... J4
Sinop 267,605 .... E2
Sivas 741,713 .... G3
Tekirdağ 319,987 ..... B2
Tokat 599,166 .... G2
Trabzon 719,008 ..... H2
Tunceli 164,591 ...... H3
Urfa 597,277 .... H4
Uşak 229,679 .... C3
Van 386,314 .... K3
Yozgat 500,371 ...... F3
Zonguldak 836,156 ... D2

CITIES and TOWNS

Acigol 3,934 .... F3
Acipayam 5,046 ...... C4
Adalia (Antalya) 130,774 ... D4
Adana 475,384 .... F4
Adapazari 114,130 .... D2
Adilcevaz 9,022 ...... K3
Adiyaman 43,782 .... H4
Afşin 18,231 .... G3
Afyonkarahisar 60,150 ... D3
Ağlasun 4,288 .... D4
Ağli 3,399 .... E2
Ağri (Karaköse) 35,284 ... K3
Ahlat 7,995 .... K3
Akçaabat 10,756 ..... H2
Akçakale 7,366 ...... G4
Akçakoca 9,066 ...... D2
Akdağmadeni 7,909 .. F3
Akhisar 53,357 .... B3
Aksaray 45,564 ...... F3
Akşehir 35,544 ...... D3
Akseki 5,141 .... D4
Akviran 3,799 .... E4
Akyazi 12,438 .... D2
Alaca 12,552 .... F2
Alaçam 2,321 .... F2
Alaçam 10,013 ...... F2
Alanya 18,520 .... D4
Alaşehir 23,243 ..... C3
Alexandretta (İskenderun) 107,437 ... G4
Aliağa 5,727 .... B3

Alibeyköyü 33,387 ... D6
Almus 4,225 .... G2
Alpu 3,718 .... D3
Altindağ 512,392 ... E2
Altinova 6,980 ...... B3
Altintaş 3,386 ...... C3
Altinözü 5,158 ..... G4
Alucra 7,070 .... H2
Amasra 4,369 ...... E2
Amasya 41,496 .... G2
Anamur 21,475 .... E4
Andirin 5,018 ...... G4
Ankara (cap.) 1,701,004 ... E3
Antakya 77,518 .... G4
Antalya 130,774 ... D4
Antioch (Antakya) 77,518 ... G4
Araç 3,594 .... E2
Aralik 4,155 .... L3
Arapkir 8,436 ...... H3
Ardahan 16,285 ... K2
Ardanuç 2,942 .... K2
Arguvan 2,461 .... H3
Arhavi 6,311 ...... J2
Arpaçay 2,651 .... K2
Arsin 6,557 .... H2
Artova 2,813 ...... G2
Artvin 13,390 ..... J2
Aşkale 10,817 .... J3
Avanos 8,635 ..... F3
Ayancik 7,202 .... F2
Ayaş 4,575 .... E2
Aybasti 13,180 ... G2
Aydin 59,579 ..... B4
Aydincik 6,739 ... E4
Ayrancı 2,664 .... E4
Ayvacik 3,120 ... B3
Ayvalik 18,041 .. B3
Babadağ 5,890 .. C4
Babaeski 17,090 .. B2
Bafra 34,288 .... F2
Bahçe 10,212 .... G4
Bakirköy 200,942 .. D6
Baklan 3,327 ..... C4
Balâ 4,107 .... E3
Balikesir 99,443 .. B3
Balya 2,362 ...... B3
Banaz 6,264 ..... C3
Bandirma 45,752 .. B2
Bartin 18,409 .... E2

Başkale 8,558 .... K3
Başmakçı 5,925 ... C4
Batman 64,384 ... J4
Bayat 4,671 ...... F2
Bayburt 20,156 ... J2
Bayindir 14,078 .. B3
Baykan 2,690 .... J3
Bayramiç 6,385 .. B3
Bergama 29,749 .. B3
Beşiktaş 174,931 .. D6
Beşiri 4,165 ...... J4
Besni 16,313 ..... G4
Beykoz 76,804 ... D6
Beyoglu 230,532 .. D6
Beypazari 14,963 .. D2
Beyşehir 15,060 .. D4
Beytüşşebap 2,766 .. K4
Biga 15,188 ...... B2
Bigadiç 7,535 .... C3
Bilecik 11,269 ... C2
Bingöl (Çapakçur) 22,047 .. J3
Birecik 20,104 ... H4
Bismil 12,775 .... J4
Bitlis 25,054 .... J3
Bodrum 7,858 ... B4
Boğazliyan 10,329 .. F3
Bolu 32,812 ..... D2
Bolvadin 29,218 .. D3
Bor 16,560 ...... F4
Borçka 4,636 .... J2
Bornova 45,096 .. B3
Boyabat 13,139 .. F2
Bozdoğan 7,218 .. C4
Bozkir 5,294 .... E4
Bozkurt 2,948 ... F2
Bozova 5,462 ... H4
Bozüyük 15,197 .. C3
Bucak 15,090 ... D4
Bulancak 14,153 .. H2
Bulanik 8,296 ... K3
Buldan 11,115 .. C3
Bünyan 12,277 .. G3
Burdur 36,633 .. D4
Burhaniye 12,800 .. B3
Bursa 346,103 .. C2
Büyükada D6
Büyükdere D5
Çal 3,274 .... C3
Çala 2,450 ...... K2
Çaldiran 3,366 .. K3

(continued on following page)

Agriculture, Industry and Resources

DOMINANT LAND USE

Cereals (chiefly wheat, barley), Livestock

Cash Crops, Horticulture, Livestock

Pasture Livestock

Nomadic Livestock Herding

Forests

Nonagricultural Land

MAJOR MINERAL OCCURRENCES

Ab   Asbestos
Al   Bauxite
C   Coal
Cr   Chromium
Cu   Copper
Fe   Iron Ore
Hg   Mercury
Mg   Magnesium

Na   Salt
O   Petroleum
P   Phosphates
Pb   Lead
Py   Pyrites
Sb   Antimony
Zn   Zinc

⚡   Water Power
▨   Major Industrial Areas

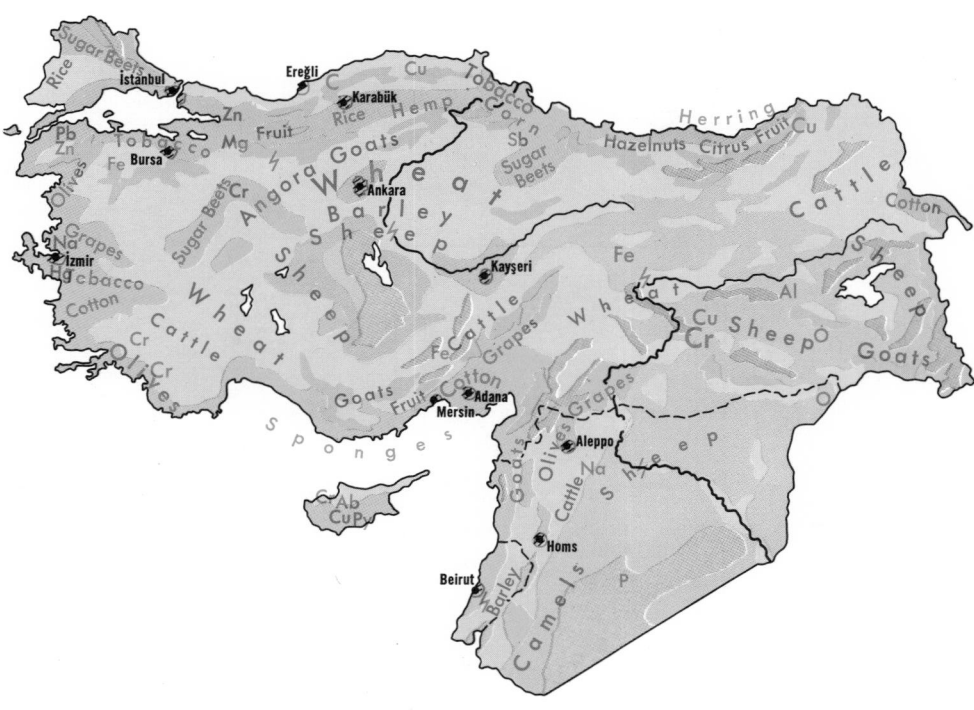

Place	Pop.	Ref.
Çalköy	3,002	C3
Çamardı	2,419	F4
Çameli	2,502	C4
Çamlıdere	4,386	E2
Çan	11,797	B2
Çanakkale	30,788	B6
Çandır	6,986	F3
Çankaya	895,005	E3
Çankırı	28,512	E2
Çardak	4,232	C6
Çarşamba	23,973	G2
Çatak	2,366	K4
Çatalca	7,693	C2
Çatalzeytin	2,271	F1
Çay	12,200	D3
Çaycuma	8,118	D2
Çayeli	13,480	J2
Çayıralan	8,071	F3
Çayırlı	4,580	J3
Çekerek	3,796	F2
Çelikhan	5,066	H3
Çemişkezek	3,048	H3
Çerkeş	3,780	D2
Çerkezköy	8,428	C2
Çermik	9,749	H3
Çeşme	5,284	B3
Çetinkaya	3,616	G3
Ceyhan	62,909	F4
Ceylanpınar	20,171	H4
Çiçekdağı	3,203	F3
Çide	3,520	E1
Çifteler	8,163	D3
Cihanbeyli	10,079	E3
Çıldır	2,260	K2
Çine	11,308	B4
Çivril	7,721	C3
Cizre	15,557	K4
Çölemerik	11,735	K4
Çorlu	40,134	C2
Çorum	64,852	F2
Çubuk	5,479	E2
Çukurca	3,019	K4
Çumra	19,225	E4
Çüngüş	2,616	H3
Daday	2,528	E1
Darende	8,055	G3
Dazkırı	3,912	C4
Delice	3,462	E3
Demirci	15,016	C3
Demirkent	4,204	E4
Demirköy	4,257	B2
Denizli	106,902	C4
Dereli	4,188	H2
Derik	13,292	J4
Derinkuyu	5,618	F3
Develi	17,323	F3
Devrek	9,164	D2
Devrekani	4,014	E1
Dicle	5,247	J3
Dikili	6,916	B3
Dirmil	3,476	C4
Divriği	12,302	H3
Diyadin	5,094	K3
Diyarbakır	169,535	H4
Doğanbey	3,077	J3
Doğanhisar	9,487	D3
Doğanşehir	10,280	G3
Döger	3,478	D3
Doğubeyazıt	17,612	K3
Domaniç	2,729	C3
Dörtyol	19,390	F4
Dumlu	4,206	J2
Durağan	3,259	F1
Dursunbey	8,615	C3
Düzce	32,129	D2
Eceabat	3,642	B6
Edirne	63,001	B2
Edremit	26,110	B3
Eflani	3,793	E2
Eğirdir	9,799	D4
Elazığ	131,415	H3
Elbistan	26,048	G3
Eldivan	3,302	E2
Eleşkirt	8,202	K3
Elmalı	10,184	C4
Emet	6,239	C3
Emirdağ	13,184	D3
Emirgazi	5,244	E4
Enez	2,486	B2
Erciş	20,315	K3
Erciş	22,351	K3
Erdek	8,685	B2
Erdemli	19,936	F4
Ereğli	45,992	D2
Ereğli	50,354	E4
Ergani	27,598	H3
Erh	3,924	
Eruh	5,340	K4
Erzin	15,314	G4
Erzincan	60,351	H3
Erzurum	162,973	H3
Eskimalatya	10,182	H3
Eskipazar	2,865	E2
Eskişehir	259,952	D3
Esme	7,828	C3
Espiye	8,168	H2
Eynesil	6,081	H2
Ezine	9,359	B3
Fakılı	4,173	F3
Fatih	504,127	C2
Fatsa	19,758	G2
Feke	5,576	F4
Fethiye	12,700	C4
Fevzipaşa	5,495	F4
Fındıklı	5,008	J2
Finike	4,200	C4
Foça	4,829	B3
Gallipoli	13,466	C5
Gaziantep	300,882	G4
Gazipaşa	6,696	D4
Gebze	33,110	C2
Gediz	10,649	C3
Gelibolu (Gallipoli)	13,466	C5
Gemerek	5,769	G3
Gemlik	20,704	C2
Genç	7,671	J3
Genezin	4,925	F3
Gerçüş	4,393	J4
Gerede	8,259	E2
Gerger	2,773	H3
Germencik	10,558	B4
Gerze	7,313	F1
Gevaş	6,333	K3
Geyve	7,806	D2
Giresun	38,236	H2
Gökçe	4,470	B2
Göksun	10,481	G3
Gölbaşı	15,103	H4
Gölcük	33,279	C2
Göle	7,680	K2
Gölhisar	7,095	C4
Gölköy	10,022	G2
Gölmarmara	11,982	B3
Gördes	7,909	C3
Görele	8,079	H2
Göynücek	2,600	F2
Göynük	2,519	D2
Güdül	4,746	E2
Gülnar	6,344	E4
Gülşehir	6,188	F3
Gümüş	3,066	F2
Gümüşhacıköy	12,789	F2
Gümüşhane	11,166	H2
Güney	7,154	C3
Gürün	9,138	G3
Hacıbektaş	5,032	F3
Hacılar	15,622	F4
Hadim	10,467	E4
Hafik	5,398	G3
Hakkâri (Çölemerik)	11,735	K4
Halfeti	3,689	G4
Hamur	2,267	K3
Hanak	2,581	K2
Hani	7,559	H3
Harput	3,231	H3
Haruniye	12,837	F4
Hassa	10,926	G4
Hatay (Antakya)	77,518	G4
Havran	7,552	B3
Havsa	4,298	B2
Havza	15,341	F2
Haymana	6,123	E3

Turkey is divided into provinces bearing the same names as their capital towns, except:

Province	Capital	Ref.
AĞRI	Karaköse	K3
BİNGÖL	Çapakçur	J3
HAKKÂRİ	Çölemerik	K4
HATAY	Antakya	G4
İÇEL	Mersin	F4
KOCAELİ	İzmit	C2
SAKARYA	Adapazarı	D2
TUNCELİ	Kalan	H3

Turkey, Syria, Lebanon and Cyprus 63

Hayrabolu 12,331 ..... B2
Hazro 4,896 ..... J3
Hekimhan 11,818 ..... G3
Hendek 15,291 ..... D2
Hilvan 6,473 ..... H4
Hinis 10,226 ..... J3
Hisarönü 4,485 ..... E2
Hizan 2,545 ..... K3
Hopa 9,089 ..... J2
Horasan 7,724 ..... K2
Hozat 5,796 ..... H3
Içel (Mersin) 152,236 ..... F4
Idil 4,862 ..... J4
Iğdir 29,542 ..... K3
Ilgaz 6,624 ..... E2
Ilgin 11,830 ..... D3
Ilica 8,947 ..... J3
Imranli 5,667 ..... H2
Incesu 7,089 ..... F3
Inebolu 6,824 ..... E2
Inegöl 37,805 ..... C2
Inönü 4,152 ..... D3
Ipsala 6,829 ..... B2
Ipsile 2,328 ..... G2
Iskenderun 107,437 ..... G4
Iskilip 16,588 ..... F2
Islâhiye 20,683 ..... G4
Isparta 62,870 ..... D4
Ispir 3,929 ..... J2
Istanbul 2,547,364 ..... D6
Ivrindi 3,730 ..... B3
Izmir 636,834 ..... B3
Izmit 165,483 ..... D2
Iznik 11,614 ..... C2
Kadiköy 354,957 ..... D6
Kadinhani 11,802 ..... E3
Kadirli 34,779 ..... F4
Kağithane 164,448 ..... D6
Kağizman 11,517 ..... K2
Kâhta 15,602 ..... H4
Kalan 11,637 ..... H3
Kale 3,399 ..... C4
Kalecik 4,707 ..... E2
Kaman 16,516 ..... E3
Kandira 10,187 ..... D2
Kangal 5,937 ..... G3
Karabük 69,182 ..... E2
Karacabey 21,648 ..... C2
Karahalli 5,539 ..... C3
Karaisali 2,316 ..... F4
Karakoçan 5,604 ..... H3
Karaköse (Ağri) 35,284 ..... K3

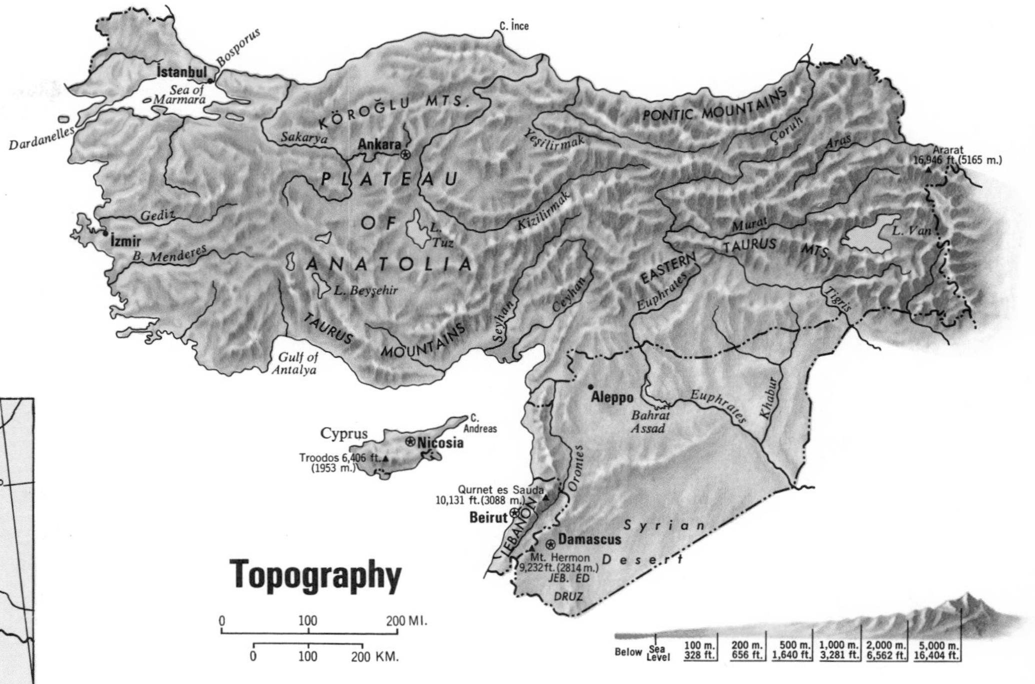

Topography
Istanbul
Bosporus
Sea of Marmara
Dardanelles
C. Ince
KÖROĞLU MTS.
PONTIC MOUNTAINS
Sakarya
Ankara
Yeşilirmak
Çoruh
Aras
Ararat 16,946 ft. (5165 m.)
PLATEAU OF ANATOLIA
L. Tuz
Kizilirmak
Gediz
Izmir
B. Menderes
L. Beyşehir
Murat
TAURUS MTS.
EASTERN
Euphrates
L. Van
Tigris
Seyhan
Ceyhan
TAURUS MOUNTAINS
Gulf of Antalya
Aleppo
Bahrat Assad
Euphrates
Khabur
Cyprus
Nicosia
C. Andreas
Troodos 6,406 ft. (1953 m.)
Orontes
Qurnet es Sauda 10,131 ft. (3088 m.)
Beirut
LEBANON
Damascus
Mt. Hermon 9,232 ft. (2814 m.)
JEB. ED DRUZ
Syrian Desert
0 100 200 MI.
0 100 200 KM.
Below Sea Level
100 m. 328 ft.
200 m. 656 ft.
500 m. 1,640 ft.
1,000 m. 3,281 ft.
2,000 m. 6,562 ft.
5,000 m. 16,404 ft.

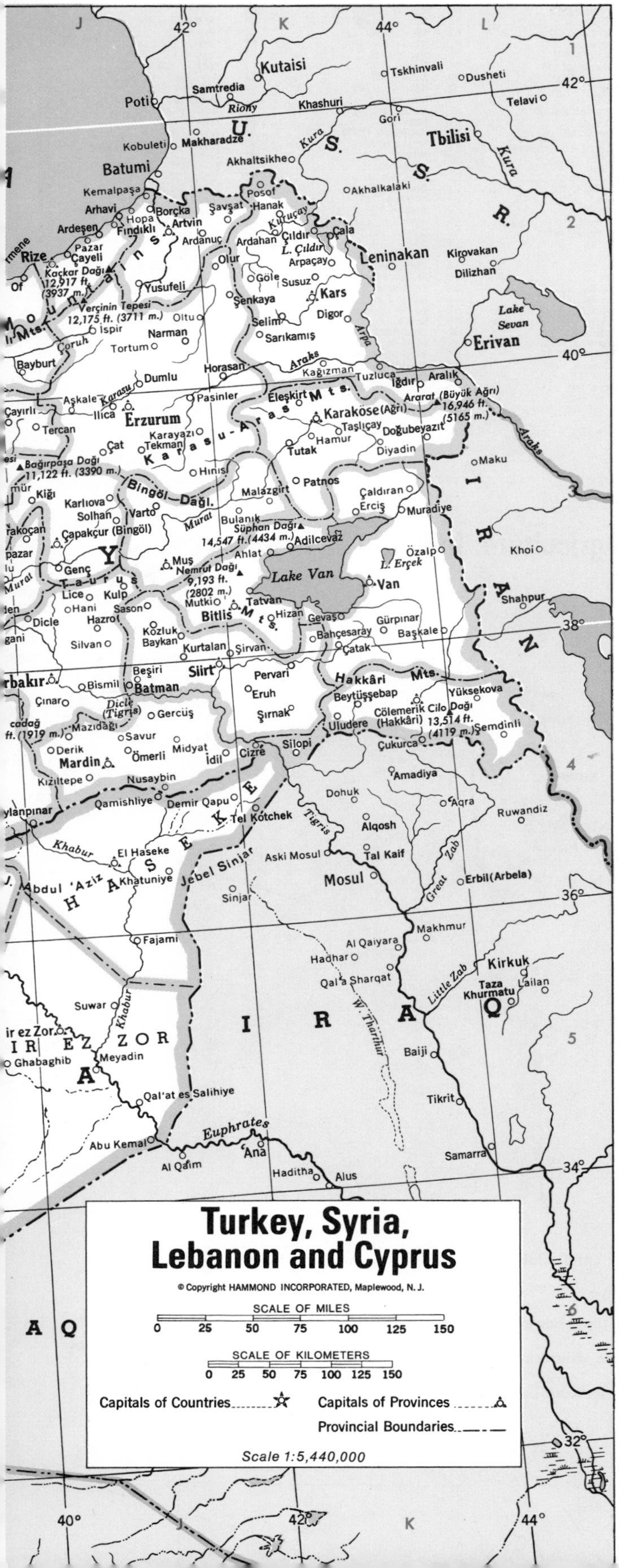

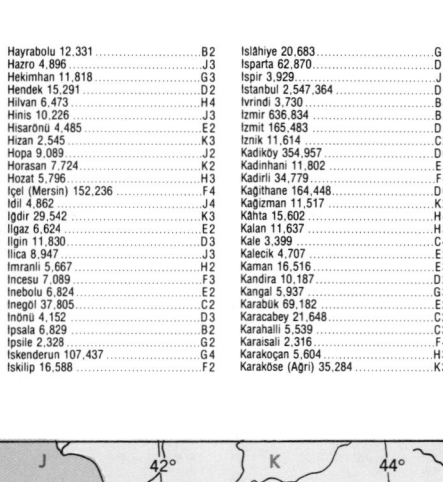

Turkey, Syria, Lebanon and Cyprus
© Copyright HAMMOND INCORPORATED, Maplewood, N. J.
SCALE OF MILES
0 25 50 75 100 125 150
SCALE OF KILOMETERS
0 25 50 75 100 125 150
Capitals of Countries
Capitals of Provinces
Provincial Boundaries
Scale 1:5,440,000
Kutaisi
Tskhinvali
Dusheti
Samtredia
Poti
Rioni
Khashuri
Telavi
Gori
Tbilisi
Kobuleti
Makharadze
Batumi
Akhaltsikhe
Akhalkalaki
Kemalpaşa
Arhavi
Hopa
Borçka
Şavşat
Artvin
Ardeşen
Findikli
Ardanuç
Ardahan
Çildir
Pazar
Rize
Çayeli
Olur
Arpaçay
Leninakan
Kirovakan
Dilizhan
Kaçkar Daği 12,917 ft. (3937 m.)
Yusufeli
Göle
Susuz
Kars
Verçinin Tepesi 12,175 ft. (3711 m.)
Şenkaya
Digor
Oltu
Lake Sevan
Ispir
Selim
Narman
Sarikamiş
Erivan
Tortum
Bayburt
Dumlu
Horasan
Kağizman
Tuzluca
Iğdir
Aralik
Pasinler
Araks
Ararat (Büyük Ağri) 16,946 ft. (5165 m.)
Aşkale
Ilica
Erzurum
Karaköse (Ağri)
Taşliçay
Doğubeyazit
Tercan
Karayazi
Tekman
Çat
Hamur
Tutak
Diyadin
Maku
Bağirpaşa Daği 11,122 ft. (3390 m.)
Hinis
Patnos
Kiği
Malazgirt
Karliova
Varto
Bingöl Daği
Çaldiran
Erciş
Muradiye
Solhan
Çapakçur (Bingöl)
Bulanik
Süphan Daği 14,547 ft. (4434 m.)
Adilcevaz
Ahlat
Özalp
Khoi
Muş
Nemrut Daği 9,193 ft. (2802 m.)
Lake Van
Erçek
Genç
Mutki
Van
Lice
Kulp
Tatvan
Shahpur
Hani
Sason
Hizan
Gevaş
Gürpinar
Dicle
Hazro
Kozluk
Bitlis
Bahçesaray
Başkale
Baykan
Kurtalan
Şirvan
Çatak
Silvan
Beşiri
Siirt
Pervari
Hakkâri
Bismil
Batman
Eruh
Beytüşşebap
Yüksekova
Çinar
Gerciş
Şirnak
Çölemerik (Hakkâri)
Cilo Daği 13,514 ft. (4119 m.)
Şemdinli
Mazidaği
Savur
Uludere
Derik
Midyat
Silopi
Çukurca
Mardin
Ömerli
Idil
Cizre
Kiziltepe
Nusaybin
Amadiya
Dohuk
Qamishliye
Demir Qapu
Aqra
Ruwandiz
Tel Kotchek
Tigris
Alqosh
Khabur
El Haseke
Aski Mosul
Tal Kaif
Khatuniye
Jebel Sinjar
Mosul
Erbil (Arbela)
Sinjar
Great Zab
Fajami
Makhmur
Al Qaiyara
Hadhar
Kirkuk
Qal'a Sharqat
Little Zab
Taza Khurmatu
Lailan
Suwar
ZOR
IRAQ
Baiji
Ghabaghib
Meyadin
Qal'at es Salihiye
Tikrit
Euphrates
Abu Kemal
Ana
Al Qaim
Haditha
Alus
Samarra

Karaman 43,759 ..... E4
Karamanli 5,904 ..... C4
Karapinar 19,589 ..... E4
Karasu 11,600 ..... D2
Karataş 5,598 ..... F4
Karayaka 4,242 ..... G2
Karayazi 3,595 ..... J3
Kargi 5,021 ..... F2
Karliova 3,631 ..... J3
Kars 54,892 ..... K2
Karşiyaka 171,600 ..... B3
Kartal 53,073 ..... D6
Kaş 2,493 ..... C4
Kastamonu 29,993 ..... F2
Kavak, Çanakkale 3,932 ..... C5
Kavak, Samsun 3,964 ..... F2
Kayseri 207,037 ..... F3
Kazanli 4,461 ..... F4
Kazimkarabekir 4,086 ..... E4
Keban 5,800 ..... H3
Keçiborlu 7,096 ..... D4
Keles 2,423 ..... C3
Kelkit 6,928 ..... H2
Kemah 3,038 ..... H3
Kemaliye 3,014 ..... H3
Kemalpaşa 7,572 ..... J2
Kemerburgaz 7,234 ..... D5
Kemirhisar 6,205 ..... F4
Kepsut 4,704 ..... C3
Keşan 27,088 ..... B2
Keşap 5,264 ..... H2
Keskin 10,540 ..... E3
Kiği 5,598 ..... J3
Kilimli 26,649 ..... D2
Kilis 54,055 ..... G4
Kinik 11,785 ..... B3
Kiraz 5,284 ..... C3
Kirikhan 38,118 ..... G4
Kirikkale 137,874 ..... E3
Kirkağaç 15,078 ..... B3
Kirklareli 33,265 ..... B2
Kirşehir 41,415 ..... F3
Kizilcahamam 7,050 ..... E2
Kizilhisar 11,119 ..... C4
Kiziltepe 21,531 ..... J4
Kizilviran 3,260 ..... E4
Kocaeli (Izmit) 165,483 ..... D2
Koçarli 5,182 ..... B4
Konya 246,727 ..... E4
Korkuteli 10,334 ..... D4
Köyceğiz 4,612 ..... C4
Koyulhisar 3,861 ..... G2
Kozakli 6,200 ..... F3
Kozan 32,045 ..... F4
Kozlu 27,322 ..... D2
Kozluk 6,197 ..... J3
Küçükköy 56,411 ..... C6
Kula 10,807 ..... C3
Kulp 4,474 ..... J3
Kulu 11,707 ..... E3
Kumkale 1,752 ..... B6
Kumluca 7,704 ..... D4
Küre 2,378 ..... E2
Kurşunlu 6,562 ..... E2
Kurtalan 7,001 ..... J3
Kuşadasi 10,269 ..... B4
Kütahya 82,442 ..... C3
Kuyucak 6,039 ..... C4
Lâdik 6,785 ..... G2
Lâpseki 3,727 ..... C6
Lice 8,625 ..... J3
Lüleburgaz 32,401 ..... B2
Maden 15,151 ..... H3
Mağara 4,314 ..... G3
Mahmudiye 5,240 ..... D3
Malatya 154,505 ..... H3
Malazgirt 13,094 ..... K3
Malkara 14,399 ..... B2
Maltepe 66,343 ..... D6
Manavgat 10,804 ..... D4
Manisa 78,114 ..... B3
Manyas 4,410 ..... B3
Maraş
(Kahramanmaraş) 135,782 ..... G4
Mardin 36,629 ..... J4
Marmaris 5,596 ..... C4
Mazgirt 3,141 ..... H3
Mazidaği 4,842 ..... J4
Mecitözü 6,066 ..... F2
Menemen 18,464 ..... B3
Mengen 2,459 ..... D2
Meriç 3,922 ..... B2
Mersin 152,236 ..... F4
Merzifon 30,801 ..... F2
Mesudiye 4,294 ..... F4
Midyat 16,905 ..... J4
Midye 2,003 ..... C2
Mihaliççik 4,004 ..... D3
Milâs 17,929 ..... B4
Mucur 9,398 ..... F3
Mudanya 8,399 ..... C2
Mudurnu 3,905 ..... D2
Muğla 24,178 ..... C4
Muradiye 6,334 ..... K3
Muş 27,761 ..... J3
Mustafakemalpaşa 27,706 ..... C3
Mut 11,466 ..... E4
Mutki 2,815 ..... J3
Muttalip 3,917 ..... D3
Nallihan 7,883 ..... D2
Narman 4,607 ..... J2
Nazilli 52,176 ..... C4
Nevşehir 30,203 ..... F3
Niğde 31,844 ..... F4
Niksar 19,156 ..... G2
Nizip 36,190 ..... G4
Nurhak 5,330 ..... G4
Nusaybin 23,684 ..... J4
Ödemiş 37,364 ..... C3
Of 10,376 ..... J2
Oğuzeli 7,194 ..... G4
Oltu 10,093 ..... J2
Ömerli 4,738 ..... J4
Ordu 47,481 ..... G2
Orhaneli 3,335 ..... C3
Orhangazi 12,181 ..... C2
Orta 3,596 ..... E2
Ortaca 8,604 ..... C4
Ortakaraviran 3,856 ..... E4
Ortaköy, Çorum 2,657 ..... F2
Ortaköy, Niğde 6,371 ..... F3
Osmancik 11,921 ..... F2
Osmaneli 4,789 ..... D2
Osmaniye 61,581 ..... G4
Ovacik, Tunceli 2,248 ..... H3
Özalp 4,188 ..... K3
Palu 5,489 ..... H3
Pasinler 14,267 ..... J3
Patnos 15,918 ..... K3
Pazar, Rize 8,856 ..... J2
Pazar, Tokat 4,337 ..... G2
Pazarcik 15,943 ..... G4
Pazaryeri 5,633 ..... C3
Pera (Beyoğlu) 230,532 ..... D6
Perşembe 6,701 ..... G2
Pertek 4,176 ..... H3
Pervari 4,126 ..... K4
Pinarbaşi 9,503 ..... G3
Pinarhisar 10,523 ..... B2
Polatli 35,267 ..... E3
Posof 2,209 ..... K2
Pozanti 5,408 ..... F4
Pülümür 3,442 ..... H3
Pütürge 4,878 ..... H3
Refahiye 6,570 ..... H3
Reşadiye 9,022 ..... G2
Reyhanli 25,749 ..... G4
Rize 36,044 ..... J2
Şabanözü 3,442 ..... E2
Safranbolu 14,793 ..... E2
Saimbeyli 3,622 ..... G4
Sakarya (Adapazari) 114,130 ..... D2
Salihli 45,514 ..... C3
Samandaği 22,540 ..... F4
Samsat 2,083 ..... H4
Samsun 168,478 ..... F2
Sandikli 13,181 ..... D3
Sapanca 9,040 ..... D2
Şaphane 3,919 ..... C3
Sarayköy 10,513 ..... C4
Sarayönü 8,946 ..... E3
Sarigöl 6,979 ..... C3
Sarikamiş 21,262 ..... K2
Sarikaya 5,160 ..... F3
Sariköy 4,695 ..... B2
Sarioğlan 3,245 ..... G3
Sariyer 79,329 ..... D5
Sariz 3,591 ..... G3
Şarkikaraağaç 4,772 ..... D3
Şarkişla 12,763 ..... G3
Şarköy 5,396 ..... B2
Sason 3,211 ..... J3
Savaştepe 7,179 ..... B3
Şavşat 3,078 ..... K2
Savur 4,983 ..... J4
Seben 2,471 ..... D2
Şebinkalahisar 10,214 ..... H2
Şefaatli 6,769 ..... F3
Seferihisar 6,484 ..... B3
Selçuk 12,251 ..... B3
Selendi 4,457 ..... C3
Selim 3,569 ..... K2
Selimiye 2,989 ..... B4
Senirkent 8,247 ..... D3
Şenkaya 3,190 ..... K2
Şereflikoçhisar 20,523 ..... E3
Serik 14,161 ..... D4
Seydişehir 25,651 ..... D4
Seyitgazi 2,819 ..... D3
Siirt 35,654 ..... J4
Şile 4,062 ..... C2
Silifke 19,257 ..... E4
Silivri 8,525 ..... C2
Silopi 4,460 ..... K4
Silvan 29,599 ..... J3
Simav 11,601 ..... C3
Sincanli 3,847 ..... D3
Sindirgi 7,818 ..... C3
Sinop 16,098 ..... F2
Şiran 5,048 ..... H2
Şirnak 10,587 ..... K4
Şirvan 5,166 ..... K3
Sivas 149,201 ..... G3
Sivasli 4,394 ..... C3
Siverek 40,990 ..... H4
Sivrihisar 8,713 ..... D3
Smyrna (Izmir) 636,834 ..... B3
Söğüt 5,329 ..... D3
Söke 35,407 ..... B4
Solhan 7,014 ..... J3
Soma 23,713 ..... B3
Sorgun 14,081 ..... F3
Şuhut 8,154 ..... D3
Sulakyurt 4,311 ..... E2
Sultandaği 4,017 ..... D3
Sultanhani 5,112 ..... E3
Suluova 21,278 ..... F2
Sungurlu 21,641 ..... F2
Sürmene 8,096 ..... J2
Sürüç 20,395 ..... H4
Suşehri 10,863 ..... H2
Susurluk 14,000 ..... C3
Susuz 5,006 ..... K2
Sütçüler 2,721 ..... D4
Tarsus 102,186 ..... F4
Taşkent 7,098 ..... E4
Taşköprü 8,146 ..... F2
Taşliçay 3,684 ..... K3
Taşova 6,516 ..... F4
Tatvan 29,271 ..... K3
Tavas 9,728 ..... C4
Tavşanli 19,575 ..... C3
Tefenni 4,280 ..... C4
Tekirdağ 41,257 ..... B2
Tercan 6,068 ..... J3
Terme 15,660 ..... G2
Tire 30,694 ..... B3
Tirebolu 7,385 ..... H2
Tokat 48,588 ..... G2
Tomarza 6,548 ..... F3
Tömük 7,660 ..... F4
Tonya 10,544 ..... H2
Torbali 17,237 ..... B3
Tortum 4,110 ..... J2
Torul 3,221 ..... H2
Tosya 17,515 ..... F2
Trabzon 97,210 ..... H2
Trebizond (Trabzon) 97,210 ..... H2
Tunceli (Kalan) 11,637 ..... H3
Turgutlu 47,009 ..... B3
Turhal 39,170 ..... F2
Türkeli 2,194 ..... F2
Türkoğlu 9,207 ..... G4
Tutak 4,325 ..... K3
Tuzluca 5,209 ..... K3
Tuzlukçu 4,613 ..... D3
Ula 5,117 ..... C4
Ulaş 2,469 ..... G3
Ulubey 4,214 ..... C3
Uluborlu 10,016 ..... D3
Uludere 4,050 ..... K4
Ulukişla 6,336 ..... F4
Umurbey 2,754 ..... C6
Ünye 23,366 ..... G2
Urfa 132,934 ..... H4
Ürgüp 6,758 ..... F3
Urla 13,903 ..... B3
Uşak 58,578 ..... C3
Üsküdar 202,957 ..... D6
Üzümlü 4,365 ..... D4
Uzunköprü 27,005 ..... B2
Vakfikebir 12,556 ..... H2
Van 63,663 ..... K3
Varto 5,572 ..... J3
Vezirköprü 11,705 ..... F2
Viranşehir 26,244 ..... H4
Vize 8,203 ..... B2
Yahyali 13,738 ..... F3
Yalova, Istanbul 27,289 ..... C2
Yalvaç 18,305 ..... D3
Yaprakli 3,020 ..... E2
Yatağan 4,903 ..... C4
Yayladaği 4,471 ..... F5
Yenice, Çanakkale 4,004 ..... B3
Yenice, Içel 4,106 ..... F4
Yenice, Zonguldak 5,791 ..... E2
Yeniceoba 5,740 ..... E3
Yeniköy, Istanbul D6
Yenimahalle 198,643 ..... E3
Yenişehir 15,188 ..... C2
Yerkesik 2,381 ..... C4
Yerköy 19,927 ..... F3
Yeşilhisar 10,409 ..... F3
Yeşilköy D6
Yeşilova, Burdur 3,685 ..... C4
Yeşilova, Niğde 5,237 ..... E3
Yeşilyurt 7,451 ..... H3
Yildizeli 7,043 ..... G3
Yozgat 32,501 ..... F3
Yüksekova 7,329 ..... L4
Yumurtalik 2,442 ..... F4
Yunak 6,187 ..... D3
Yusufeli 3,050 ..... J2
Zara 10,376 ..... G3
Zeytinburnu 123,548 ..... D6
Zeytindağ 3,517 ..... B3
Zile 32,157 ..... G2
Zivarik 2,703 ..... E3
Zonguldak 90,221 ..... D2

OTHER FEATURES

Abydos (ruins) B6
Aci (lake) C4
Adalar (isl.) D6
Aegean (sea) A3
Ağri, Büyuk (Ararat)
(mt.) L3
Akdağ (mt.) C4
Aladağ (mt.) F4
Alexandretta (gulf) F4
Amanos (mts.) G4
Anamur (cape) E5
Anatolia (reg.) D3
Ankara (riv.) D3
Antalya (gulf) D4
Anti-Taurus (mts.) G3
Araks (riv.) K2
Ararat (mt.) L3
Arpa (riv.) K2
Baba (cape) A3
Bati Firat (riv.) H3
Beyşehir (lake) D4
Black (sea) E1
Bosporus (str.) C2
Bozcaada (isl.) A3
Burgaz (isl.) D6
Büyük Ağri (Ararat)
(mt.) L3
Çanakkale Boğazi (Dardanelles) (str.) B6
Çandarli (gulf) B3
Canik (mts.) G2
Ceyhan (riv.) F4
Cilo Daği (mt.) K4
Çoruh (riv.) J2
Dardanelles (str.) B6
Dicle (riv.) J4
Eastern Taurus (mts.) J3
Ephesus (ruins) B3
Erciyas Daği (mt.) F3
Ergene (riv.) B2
Euphrates (Firat) (riv.) G4
Firat (riv.) G4
Gediz (riv.) C3
Gelidonya (cape) D4
Gökçeada (isl.) A2
Göksu (riv.) E4
Helles (cape) B6
Heybeli (isl.) D6
Ilium (ruins) B6
Imroz (Gökçeada)
(isl.) A2
Ince (cape) F1
Istranca (mts.) B2
Kaçkar Daği (mt.) J2
Karadeniz Boğazi (Bosporus)
(str.) C2
Karasu-Aras (mts.) J3
Kelkit (riv.) G2
Kerme (gulf) B4
Keşiş Tepesi (mt.) H3
Kizilirmak (riv.) F2
Koca (riv.) C3
Köroğlu (mts.) E2
Küre (mts.) E2
Mandalya (gulf) B4
Marmara (isl.) B2
Marmara (sea) C2
Menderes, Büyük (riv.) C4
Meriç (riv.) B2
Murat (riv.) H3
Pontic (mts.) H2
Porsuk (riv.) D3
Prinkipo (Adalar) (isl.) D6
Sakarya (riv.) D2
Saros (gulf) B2
Seyhan (riv.) F4
Simav (riv.) C3
Sinop (cape) F1
Sultan (mts.) D3
Süphan Daği (mt.) K3
Taurus (mts.) D4
Tigris (Dicle) J4
Troy (Ilium) (ruins) B6
Tuz (lake) E3
Van (lake) K3
Yeşilirmak (riv.) G2

* City and suburbs

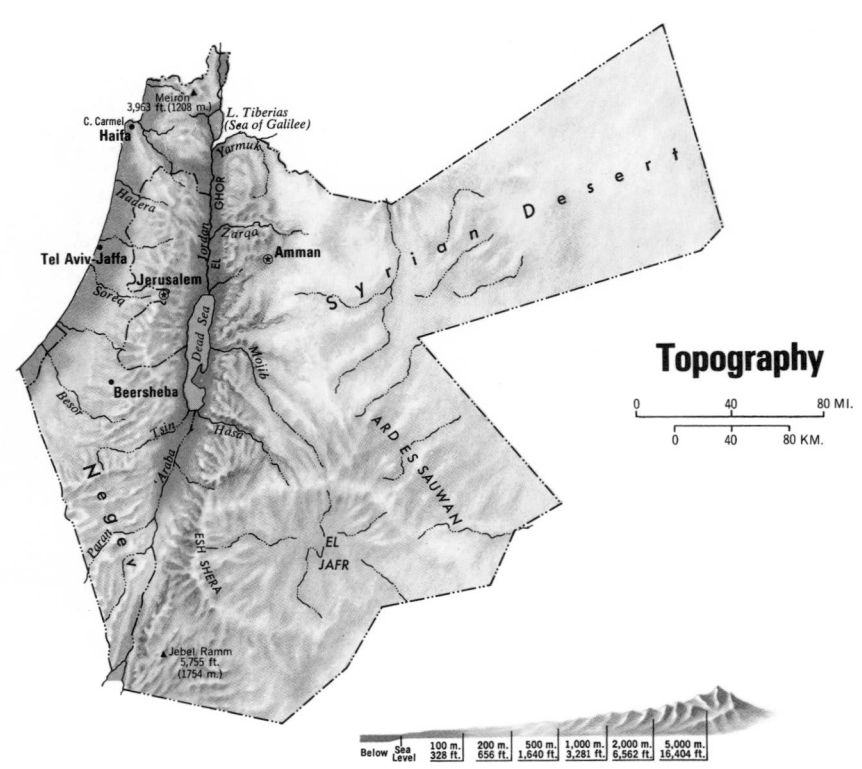

Topography

```
0        40        80 MI.
0        40        80 KM.
```

```
Below  Sea    100 m.  200 m.  500 m.  1,000 m.  2,000 m.  5,000 m.
Level  Level  328 ft. 656 ft. 1,640 ft. 3,281 ft. 6,562 ft. 16,404 ft.
```

ISRAEL

DISTRICTS

Central 572,300	B3
Haifa 480,800	C2
Jerusalem 338,600	B4
Northern 473,700	C2
Southern 351,300	B5
Tel Aviv 905,100	B3

CITIES and TOWNS

Acre 34,400	C2
Afiqim 1,243	D2
'Afula 17,400	C2
Ahuzzam 407	B4
Akko (Acre) 34,400	C2
Arad 5,400	C5
'Arrabe 6,000	C2
Ashdod 40,500	B4
Ashdot Yaa'qov 1,197	D2
Ashqelon 43,100	A4
Atlit 1,516	B2
Avihayil 579	B3
Bat Shelomo 218	B2
Bat Yam 124,100	A3
Be'eri 390	A5
Be'er Menuha	D5
Beersheba (Be'er Sheva) 101,000	B5
Be'er Tuveya 602	B4
Beit Guvrin	B4
Bene Beraq 74,100	B3
Bet Qama 228	B4
Bet She'an 11,300	D3
Bet Shemesh 10,100	B4
Binyamina 2,701	B2
Carmel	C2
Dafna 577	D1
Dalyat al-Karmel 6,200	B2
Dan 498	D1
Dimona 23,700	D4
Dor 195	B2
E'in Gedi	C5
E'in Harod 1,372	C2
Elat	D6
Elath (Elat) 12,800	D6
El 'Auja	D5
Elyakim 568	C2
Elyashiv 435	B3
Even Yehuda 3,464	B3
Gal'on 356	B4
Gat 430	B4
Gedera 5,400	B4
Gerofit	B6
Gesher 360	C2
Gesher Haziv 238	C1
Gevara'm 283	B4
Gilat 561	B5
Ginnosar 473	C2
Giv'atayim 48,500	B3
Giv'at Brenner 1,505	B4
Giv'at Hayyim 1,360	B3
Habonim 189	B2
Hadera 31,900	B2
Haifa 227,800	B2
Haifa* 367,400	B2
Hatseva	D5
Hazerim 127	B5

Hazor Hagelilit	D2
Helez 466	B4
Herzeliyya 41,200	B3
Hod Hasharon 13,500	B3
Hodiyya 400	B4
Holon 121,200	B3
Iksal 2,156	C2
Jerusalem (cap.) 376,000	C4
Jish 1,498	C1
Kafar Kanna 5,200	C2
Kafr Yasif 2,975	C1
Karkur-Pardes Hanna 13,600	C3
Kefar Blum 565	D1
Kefar Gila'di 701	C1
Kefar Ruppin 306	D3
Kefar Sava 26,500	B3
Kefar Vitkin 808	B3
Kefar Zekhariya 420	B4
Kinneret 909	D2
Lod (Lydda) 30,500	B4
Lydda 30,500	B4
Magen 149	A5
Maa'lot-Tarshiha	C1
Malkiya	D1
Mash 'Abbe Sade 238	B6
Mavqi'm 177	B4
Megiddo	C2
Metula 261	D1
Migdal 688	C2
Migdal Ha E'meq	C2
Mikhmoret 608	B3
Mishmar Hanegev 336	B5
Mishmar Hayarden	D1
Mivtahim 398	A5
Mizpe Ramon 331	B5
Moza Illit 219	C4
Mughar 4,010	B2
Muqeible 459	C2
Nahariyya 24,000	C1
Nazareth 33,300	C2
Nazerat I'llit	C2
Negba 453	B4
Nes Ziyyona 11,700	B4
Netanya 70,700	B3
Netivot	B5
Nevatim 436	B5
Newe Yam 211	B2
Newe Zohar	C5
Nir Yitzhaq 209	A5
Nizzanim 479	B4
Ofaqim	B5
O'mer	B5
Oron	C6
Or Yehuda	B4
Pardes Hanna-Karkur 13,600	B2
Peduyim 361	A5
Petah Tiqwa 112,000	B3
Qadima 2,937	B3
Qalansuwa	B3
Qedma 157	B4
Qiryat Atta	C2
Qiryat Bialik 18,000	C2
Qiryat Gat 19,200	B4
Qiryat Mal'akhi	B4
Qiryat Motzkin 17,600	C2
Qiryat Shemona 15,200	C1
Qiryat Tivo'n 9,800	C2
Qiryat Yam 19,800	C2
Raa'nana 14,900	B3
Ramat Gan 120,900	B3

Ramat Hasharon 20,100	B3
Rame 2,986	C2
Ramla 34,100	B4
Rehovot 39,200	B4
Re'im 155	A5
Revadim 175	B4
Revivim 258	D5
Rishon Le Ziyyon 51,900	B4
Rosh Ha 'Ayin	B3
Rosh Pinna 700	B4
Ruhama 497	B4
Saa'd 418	B5
Safad (Zefat) 13,600	C1
Sakhnin 8,400	C2
Sede Boqer	D5
Sederot	B5
Sedom	C5
Sedot Yam 511	B2
Shave Ziyyon 269	C1
Shefara'm 11,800	C2
Shefayim 614	B3
Shoval 393	B5
Tabiye 11,700	C3
Tel Aviv-Jaffa 343,300	B3
Tel Aviv-Jaffa* 1,219,900	B3
Tiberias 23,800	C2
Tirat Hakarmel 14,400	B2
Tirat Zevi 353	D3
Tur'an 2,304	C2
Umm e! Fahm 13,300	C2
Urim 203	B5
Uzza 487	B4
Yad Mordekhai 416	A4
Yagur 1,266	C2
Yahav	D5
Yavne 10,100	B4
Yavne'el 1,580	D2
Yehud 8,900	B3
Yeroham 5,800	B6
Yesodot 293	B4
Yesud Hamaa'la 428	D1
Yiftah	D1
Yirka 2,715	C2
Yotvata	D5
Zavdi'el 396	B4
Ze'elim 148	A5
Zefat 13,600	C1
Zikhron Yaa'qov 6,500	B2
Zippori 241	C2

OTHER FEATURES

Aqaba (gulf)	D6
'Araba, Wadi (valley)	D5
Beer Sheva (dry riv.)	B5
Besor (riv.)	B5
Carmel (cape)	B2
Carmel (mt.)	C2
Dead (sea)	C4
Galilee, Sea of (Tiberias) (lake)	D2
Galilee (reg.)	C2
Gerar (dry riv.)	B5
Hadera (dry riv.)	B3
Haniqra, Rosh (cape)	C1
Jordan (riv.)	D3
Judaea (reg.)	C4
Lakhish (dry riv.)	B4
Meiron (mt.)	C1
Negev (reg.)	D5

Archaeological Sites in Palestine

■ Major Excavations

```
Miles
0   10   20   30
```

© Copyright HAMMOND INCORPORATED

Agriculture, Industry and Resources

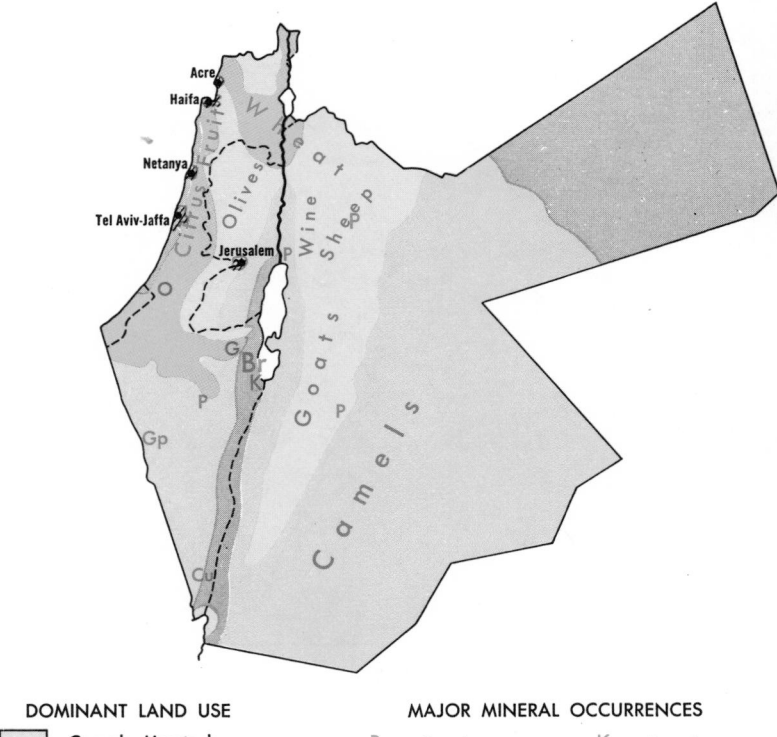

DOMINANT LAND USE

- Cereals, Livestock
- Cash Crops, Horticulture
- Nomadic Livestock Herding
- Nonagricultural Land

MAJOR MINERAL OCCURRENCES

Br	Bromine	K	Potash
Cu	Copper	O	Petroleum
G	Natural Gas	P	Phosphates
Gp	Gypsum		

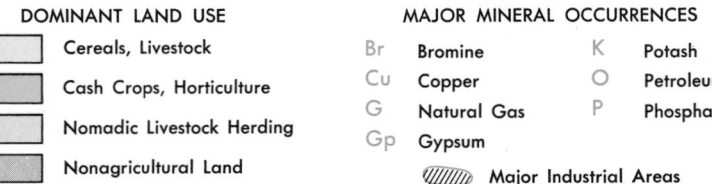 Major Industrial Areas

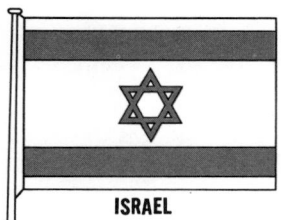

ISRAEL

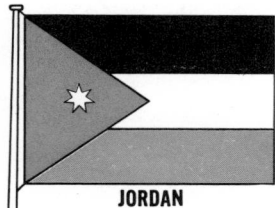

JORDAN

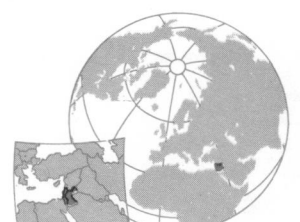

ISRAEL

AREA 7,847 sq. mi. (20,324 sq. km.)
POPULATION 3,878,000
CAPITAL Jerusalem
LARGEST CITY Tel Aviv-Jaffa
HIGHEST POINT Meiran 3,963 ft.
(1,208 m.)
MONETARY UNIT shekel
MAJOR LANGUAGES Hebrew, Arabic
MAJOR RELIGIONS Judaism, Islam,
Christianity

JORDAN

AREA (East Bank) 35,000 sq. mi.
(90,650 sq. km.)
POPULATION 2,152,273
CAPITAL Amman
LARGEST CITY Amman
HIGHEST POINT Jeb. Ramm 5,755 ft.
(1,754 m.)
MONETARY UNIT Jordanian dinar
MAJOR LANGUAGE Arabic
MAJOR RELIGION Islam

Qishon (riv.)	C2
Ramon (mt.)	D5
Rubin (dry riv.)	B4
Tabor (mt.)	C2
Tiberias (lake)	D2
Yarmuk (riv.)	D2
Yarqon (riv.)	B3

OTHER FEATURES

Golan Heights	D1
West Bank	C3

JORDAN

GOVERNORATES

'Ajlun 506,000	D3
Amman 1,000,000	D4
El Balqa 113,000	D4
El Karak 93,000	E5
Maa'n 62,000	D5

GAZA STRIP

CITIES and TOWNS

'Abasan 1,481	A5
Bani Suheila 7,561	A5
Beit Hanun 4,756	A4
Deir el Balah 10,854	A5
Deir el Balah* 18,118	A5
Gaza 87,793	A5
Gaza* 118,272	A5
Jabaliya 10,508	A4
Jabaliya* 43,604	A4
Khan Yunis 29,522	A5
Khan Yunis* 52,997	A5
Rafah 10,812	A5
Rafah* 49,812	A5

CITIES and TOWNS

'Ajlun⊙ 42,000	D3
Amman (cap.) 711,850	D4
'Anjara 3,163	D3
'Aqaba 15,000	D6
Bala'ma 769	E3
Baqura 3,042	D2
Damiya 483	D3
Dana 844	D5
Deir Abu Sai'd 1,927	D3
Dhira'	D5
El 'Al 492	D4
El Husn 3,728	D3
El Karak 10,000	E4
El Kitta 987	D3
El Madwar 164	E3
El Mafraq 15,500	E3
El Majdal 259	E5
El Quweira 268	E5
El Yaduda 251	D4
Er Rafid 787	D2
Er Ramtha 19,000	E2
Er Rumman 293	D3
Er Ruseifa 6,200	D4
Esh Shaubak 01	D5
Es Sahab 2,580	E4
Es Salt 24,000	D3
Es Sukhna 649	E3
Et Tafila 17,000	D5
Et Taiyiba 2,606	D2
Ez Zarqa 263,400	E3
Harima 635	D2
Hawara 2,342	D4
Hisban 718	D4
I'bbin 1,364	D3
Irbid 136,770	D2
Jarash⊙ 29,000	D3
Kitim 1,026	D3
Kufrinja 3,922	D3
Kuraiyima	D3
Ma'daba 125	D2
Maa'n⊙ 9,500	D5
Ma'daba 22,600	D4
Mai'n 1,271	D4
Manja 353	D4
Nau'r 2,382	D4
Nitil 348	D4
Qumeim 955	D2
Ra's en Naqb 225	E5
Safut 4,210	D3
Samar 716	D4
Sarih 3,390	D3
Suweilih 3,457	D3
Suweima 315	D4
Um Jauza 582	D4
Wadi es Sir 4,455	D4
Wadi Musa 654	E5
Waqqas 2,321	D2
Zuweiza 126	D4

WEST BANK

CITIES AND TOWNS

'Ajja 1,322	C3
'Anabta 3,426	C2
Anin 914	C2
'Anza 807	C3
'Aqaba 1,127	C3
'Aqrabe 2,501	C3
Ariha (Jericho) 5,312	C4
'Arraba 4,231	C3
'Arura 849	C3
'Attil 3,808	C3
Beit Fajjar 2,474	C4
Beit Hanina 1,177	C4
Beit Jala 6,041	C4
Beit Lahm (Bethlehem) 14,439	C4
Beit Nuba 1,350	C4
Beit Sahur 5,380	C4
Bethlehem 14,439	C4
Biddu 1,259	C4
Birqin 2,036	C3
Bir Zeit 2,311	C4
Burqa 2,477	C3
Deir Ballut 1,058	C3
Deir Sharaf 973	C3
Dhahiriya 4,875	B5
Duma 524	C3
Dura 4,954	C4
El Bira 9,674	C4
El Bira* 13,037	C4
El Khalil (Hebron) 38,309	C4
Er Rihiya 679	C5
Ez Zababida 1,474	C3
Falama 162	C3
Halhul 6,041	C4
Haris 641	C3
Hebron 38,309	C4
Idna 3,713	B4
I'mwas 1,955	B4
Jaba 2,817	C3
Jalama 784	C2
Jalbun 914	C3
Jalud 221	C3
Jenin 8,346	C3
Jenin* 13,365	C3
Jericho 5,312	C4
Jericho* 6,931	C4
Jifna 655	C4
Kharas 1,364	C4
Nablus (Nablus) 41,799	C3
Nahhalin 1,109	C4
Nil'in 1,227	C4
Qabalan 1,380	C3
Qabatiya 6,005	C3
Qaffin 2,480	C3
Qalqiliya 8,926	C3
Qibya 926	C3
Rafidiya 1,123	C3
Ramallah 12,134	C4
Rammun 1,198	C4
Rantis 897	C3
Salfit 3,201	C3
Samu 3,784	C5
Shuf'at 14,000	C4
Shuweika 2,332	C3
Silat Dhahr 2,104	C3
Sinjil 1,823	C3
Siris 1,285	C3
Tammun 2,952	C3
Tarqumiya 2,412	C4
Tubas 5,262	C3
Tulkarm 10,255	C3
Tulkarm* 15,275	C3
Tur 12,200	C4
Yab'ad 4,857	C3
Yabrud 277	C4
Yamun 4,384	C3
Yatta 7,281	C5
Zububa 633	C2

OTHER FEATURES

'Ajlun (range)	D3
Aqaba (gulf)	D6
'Araba, Wadi (valley)	D5
Dead (sea)	D4
Ebal (mt.)	C3
El Ghor (reg.)	C6
El Lisan (pen.)	D5
Hasa, Wadi el (dry riv.)	E5
Jordan (riv.)	D3
Judaea (reg.)	C4
Khirbet Qumran (site)	D4
Mashash, Wadi (dry riv.)	D5
Nebo (mt.)	D4
Petra (ruins)	D5
Ramm, Jebel (mt.)	D5
Samaria (reg.)	C3
Shallala, Wadi esh (dry riv.)	D4
Shu'eib, Wadi (dry riv.)	D4
Tell 'Asur (mt.)	C4
Yabis, Wadi el (dry riv.)	D3
Zarqa (riv.)	D3

*City and suburbs.
⊙ Population of subdivision.

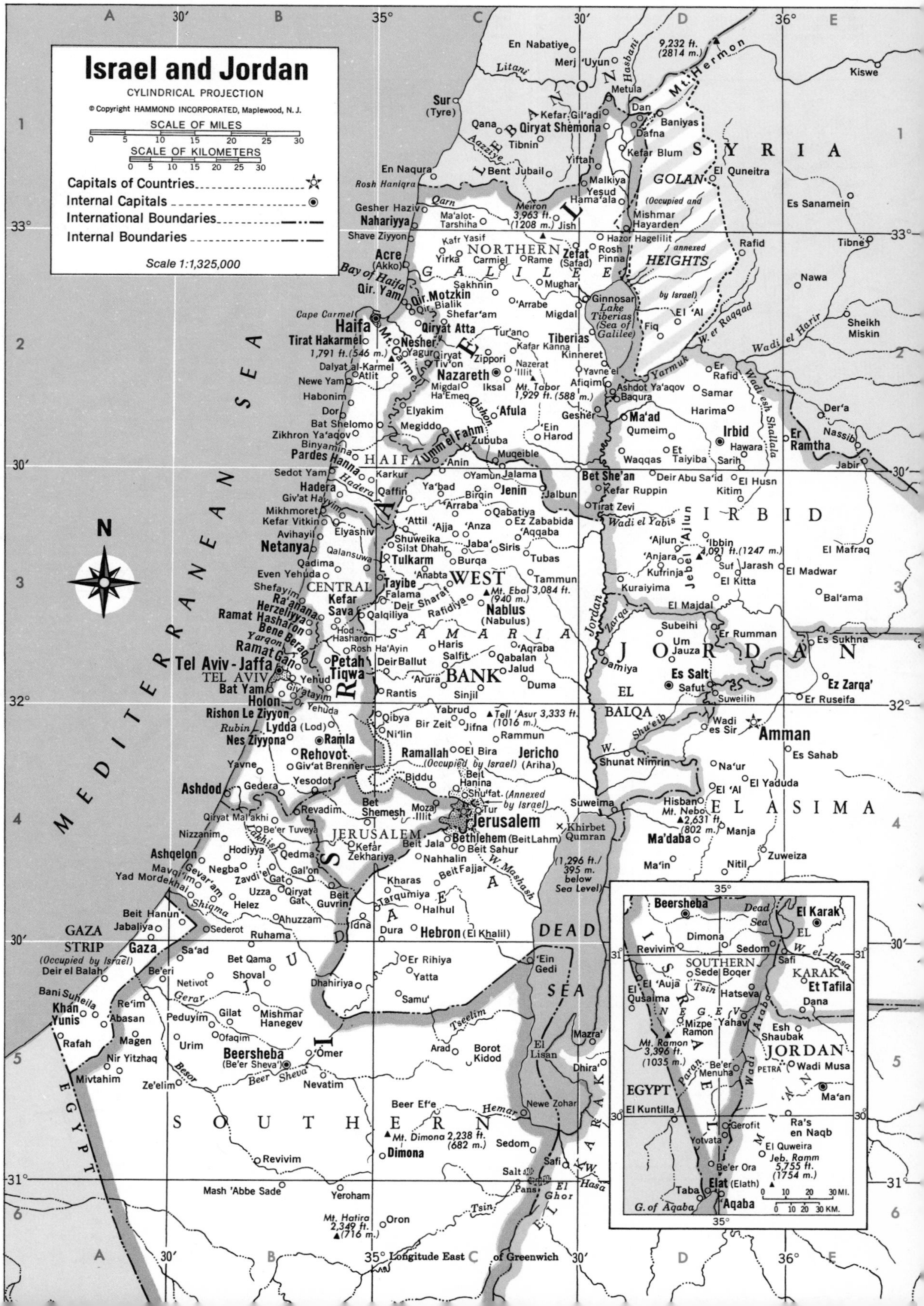

Israel and Jordan

CYLINDRICAL PROJECTION

© Copyright HAMMOND INCORPORATED, Maplewood, N.J.

SCALE OF MILES
0 5 10 15 20 25 30

SCALE OF KILOMETERS
0 5 10 15 20 25 30

Capitals of Countries ☆
Internal Capitals ⊙
International Boundaries
Internal Boundaries

Scale 1:1,325,000

IRAN

INTERNAL DIVISIONS

Azerbaijan, East
(prov.) 3,194,543 ....E1
Azerbaijan, West
(prov.) 1,404,875 ....D1
Bakhtiari
(prov.) 394,300 ....F4
Boyer Ahmediyeh and Kohkiluyeh
(governor 244,750 ....G5
Bushehr (prov.) 345,427 ....G6
Central (Markazi)
(prov.) 6,921,283 ....G3
Esfahan (Istahan)
(prov.) 1,974,938 ....H4
Fars (prov.) 2,020,947 ....H6
Gilan (prov.) 1,577,800 ....F2
Hamadan (governorate) 1,086,512 ....F3
Hormozgan (prov.) 463,419 ....J7
Ilam (prov.) 244,222 ....F4
Istahan (prov.) 1,974,938 ....H4
Kerman (prov.) 1,088,045 ....K6
Kermanshahan (prov.) 1,016,199 ....E3
Khorasan (prov.) 3,266,650 ....K3
Khuzestan (prov.) 2,176,612 ....F5
Kordestan (Kurdistan)
(prov.) 781,889 ....E3
Lorestan (Luristan)
(governorate) 924,848 ....F4
Mazandaran (prov.) 2,384,226 ....H2
Semnan (governorate) 485,875 ....J3
Sistan and Baluchestan
(prov.) 659,297 ....M6
Yazd (governorate) 356,218 ....J5
Zanjan (governorate) 579,000 ....F2

CITIES and TOWNS

Abadan 296,061 ....F5
Abadeh 16,000 ....H5
Abarqu 8,000 ....H5
Abhar 24,000 ....F2
Agha Jari 24,195 ....F5
Ahvaz (Ahwaz) 329,006 ....F5
Amol 68,782 ....H2
Anarak 2,038 ....H4
Andimeshk 16,000 ....F4
Arak 114,507 ....F3
Ardabil 147,404 ....F1
Asadabad 7,000 ....F3
Asterabad (Gorgan) 88,348 ....J2
Babol 67,790 ....H2
Babol Sar 7,237 ....H2
Bafq 5,000 ....J5
Baft 6,000 ....K6
Bahramabad (Rafsanjan) 21,000 ....K5
Bajgiran 1,151 ....L2
Bam 22,000 ....L6
Bampur 1,585 ....M7
Bandar A'bbas 89,103 ....J7
Bandar-e Deylam 3,691 ....G5
Bandar-e Lengeh 4,920 ....J7
Bandar-e Mas'hur 17,000 ....F5
Bandar-e Pahlavi
(Enzeli) 55,978 ....F2
Bandar-e Rig 1,889 ....G6
Bandar-e Torkaman 13,000 ....H2
Bandar Khomeini 6,000 ....F5
Bandar Shahpur 6,000 ....F5
Bastak 2,473 ....J7
Bastam 3,296 ....J2

Behbehan 39,874 ....G5
Behshahr 26,032 ....H2
Bejestan 3,623 ....K3
Bijar 12,000 ....E3
Birjand 25,854 ....L4
Bojnurd 31,248 ....K2
Borazjan 20,000 ....G6
Borujerd 100,103 ....F3
Bowkan 9,000 ....E2
Bushehr (Bushire) 57,681 ....G6
Chah Bahar 1,800 ....M8
Chalus 15,000 ....G2
Damavand 5,319 ....H3
Damghan 13,000 ....J3
Daran 4,609 ....G4
Darreh Gaz 11,000 ....L2
Deheq 4,115 ....G4
Dehkhvaregan 6,000 ....D2
Delijan 6,000 ....G3
Dezful 110,287 ....F4
Duzdab (Dezful) 110,287 ....F4
Duzdab (Zahedan) 92,628 ....M6
Enzeli 55,978 ....F2
Esfahan (Istahan) 671,820 ....G4
Estahabanate 18,187 ....J6
Evaz 4,609 ....J7
Ezna 5,000 ....F3
Fahrej (Iranshahr) 5,000 ....M7
Farman 8,000 ....J6
Farrashband 3,532 ....G6
Fasa 19,000 ....H6
Ferdows 11,000 ....K3
Firuzabad 8,718 ....H6
Firuzkuh 4,684 ....H3
Fowman 9,000 ....F2
Gach Saran G5
Ganaveh 9,000 ....G6

Garmsar 4,723 ....H3
Gavater M8
Golpayegan 20,515 ....G4
Golshan (Tabas) 10,000 ....K4
Gomishan 6,000 ....J2
Gonabad 8,000 ....L3
Gonbad-e Kavus 59,868 ....J2
Gorgan (Gurgan) 88,348 ....J2
Haft Gel 10,000 ....F5
Hamadan 155,846 ....F3
Hashtpar 5,000 ....F2
Herowabad 5,422 ....F2
Homayunshahr 46,836 ....G4
Hormoz 2,569 ....J7
Hoveyzeh 4,722 ....F5
Ilam 15,000 ....F4
Iranshahr 5,000 ....M7
Isfahan 671,825 ....G4
Izeh 1,983 ....F5
Jahrom 38,236 ....H6
Jajarm 3,641 ....K2
Jolfa 1,078 ....E1
Kakhk 4,043 ....L3
Kangan 2,682 ....G7
Kangavar 9,414 ....F3
Karaj 138,774 ....G3
Kashan 84,545 ....G3
Kashmar 24,000 ....L3
Kazerun 51,309 ....G6
Kazvin (Qazvin) 138,527 ....G3
Kerman 140,309 ....K5
Kermanshah 290,861 ....E3
Khaf 5,000 ....L3
Khash 7,439 ....M6
Khiyav 9,000 ....E1
Khomein 3,054 ....G3
Khorramabad 104,928 ....F4
Khorramshahr 146,709 ....F5
Khvaf 5,000 ....L3

Khvonsar 10,947 ....F4
Khvor 2,912 ....J4
Khvoy (Khoi) 70,040 ....D1
Kord Kuy 9,855 ....J2
Lahijan 25,725 ....F2
Lahijan 138,527 ....F2
Lar 22,000 ....J7
Mahabad 28,610 ....D2
Mahallat 12,000 ....G4
Mahan 8,000 ....K5
Maku 17,000 ....D1
Malamir (Izeh) 1,983 ....F5
Malayer 28,434 ....F3
Maragheh 60,820 ....D2
Marand 24,000 ....D1
Marv Dasht 25,498 ....H6
Mashhad (Meshed) 670,180 ....L2
Masjed Soleyman 77,161 ....F5
Mehran 664 ....E4
Meybod 15,000 ....J4
Meshed-i-Sar 6,000 ....H2
Miandowab 19,000 ....D2
Mianeh 28,447 ....E2
Minab 4,228 ....K7
Mirjaveh 5,000 ....M6
Nahavand 24,000 ....F3
Nain 5,925 ....H4
Najafabad 76,236 ....G4
Nasrabad (Zabol) 20,000 ....M6
Natanz 4,370 ....H4
Neyriz 16,114 ....H6
Neyshabur 59,101 ....L2
Nishapur (Neyshabur) 59,101 ....L2
Nosratabad 20,000 ....L6
Now Shahr 8,000 ....G2
Oshnoviyeh 5,000 ....D2

Pahlevi (Enzeli) 55,978 ....F2
Pazanan 81 ....F5
Qasr-e-Shirin 15,094 ....E3
Qayen 6,000 ....L4
Qazvin 138,527 ....F2
Qom 246,831 ....G3
Qorveh 2,929 ....E3
Quchan 29,193 ....L2
Qum (Qom) 246,831 ....G3
Rafsanjan 21,000 ....K5
Ramhormoz 9,000 ....F5
Ramsar 12,000 ....G2
Rasht 187,203 ....F2
Ravar 5,074 ....K5
Resht (Rasht) 187,203 ....F2
Rey 102,825 ....G3
Rezaiyeh (Urmia) 163,991 ....D2
Rigan 8,255 ....L6
Rud Sar 7,460 ....G2
Sabzevar 69,791 ....K2
Sabzevaran 7,000 ....K6
Sa'i'dabad 20,000 ....J6
Sanandaj 95,834 ....E3
Saqqez 17,000 ....E2
Sarab 16,000 ....E2
Sarakhs 3,461 ....M2
Saravan 4,012 ....N7
Sar Dasht 6,000 ....D2
Sar Eskand Khan 3,153 ....E2
Sari 70,936 ....H2
Savanat (Estahbanat) 18,187 ....J6
Saveh 17,565 ....G3
Semnan 31,058 ....H3
Shadegan 6,000 ....F5
Shahabad 12,000 ....E3
Shahdad 2,777 ....K5
Shahi 63,289 ....H2
Shahin Dezh 4,195 ....D2

Shahistan (Saravan) 4,012 ....N7
Shahpur 13,161 ....D1
Shahreza 34,220 ....G4
Shahr Kord 24,000 ....G4
Shahrud 30,767 ....J3
Shahsavar 12,000 ....G2
Sharafkaneh 1,000 ....H6
Shiraz 416,408 ....H6
Shirvan 11,000 ....L2
Shush 1,433 ....F4
Shushtar 24,000 ....F4
Sinneh (Sananda) 95,834 ....E3
Sirjan (Sai'dabad) 20,000 ....J6
Sivand 1,811 ....H5
Songor 10,433 ....E3
Sufian 2,914 ....E1
Sultanabad (Kashmar) 17,000 ....L3
Susangerd 21,000 ....F5
Tabas 10,000 ....K4
Tabriz 598,576 ....E1
Taft 7,000 ....J5
Tajrish 157,486 ....G3
Takestan 13,485 ....F2
Tehran (cap.) 4,496,159 ....G3
Torbat-e-Heydariyeh 30,106 ....L3
Torbat-e Jam 13,000 ....M3
Tun (Ferdows) 11,000 ....K3
Turbat-i-Shaikh Jam 13,000 ....M3
Urmia 163,991 ....D2
Varamin 11,183 ....G3
Yazd (Yezd) 135,978 ....J5
Yazd-e Khvast 3,544 ....H5
Zabol 20,000 ....M6
Zahedan 92,628 ....M6
Zanjan 99,967 ....F2
Zarand 7,000 ....K5
Zarqam 7,000 ....H6
Zenjan (Zanjan) 99,967 ....F2

Iran and Iraq

CONIC PROJECTION

SCALE OF MILES

0 25 50 100 150 200

SCALE OF KILOMETERS

0 25 50 100 150 200

Capitals of Countries .... ★
Capitals of Provinces .... △
Capitals of Governorates ...... ◉
International Boundaries ...... ____ ___
Provincial Boundaries .... ____ ____
Governorate Boundaries ...... ____ ____

Scale 1:8,160,000

Iran consists of fifteen provinces called ostans. Attached to seven of these provinces are eight governorates.

OTHER FEATURES

Aji Chai (riv.)	E1
A'rabi (isl.)	G7
Araks (Aras) (riv.)	E1
Atrak (Atrek) (riv.)	J2
Bakhtegan (lake)	J6
Baluchistan (reg.)	M7
Bampur (riv.)	M7
Behistun (ruins)	E3
Caspian (sea)	G1
Damavend (Demavend) (mt.)	G3
Dez (riv.)	F4
Elburz (mts.)	G2
Farsi (isl.)	G7
Gorgan (riv.)	G2
Hari Rud (riv.)	M3
Karkheh (riv.)	E4
Karun (riv.)	F5
Kashaf Rud (riv.)	M2
Khark (Kharg) (isl.)	G6
Kuh (cape)	K8
Kurang (riv.)	G4
Laristan (reg.)	J7
Makran (reg.)	M8
Mand Rud (riv.)	G6
Mehran (riv.)	J7
Namaksar (lake)	M4
Nezwar (mt.)	H3
Oman (gulf)	M8
Pasargadae (ruins)	H5
Persepolis (ruins)	H5
Persian (gulf)	F6
Qareh Su (riv.)	E1
Qareh Su (riv.)	G3
Qeshm (isl.)	J7
Qezel Owzam (riv.)	F2
Safid Rud (riv.)	F2

Shaikh Shua'ib (isl.)	H7
Shelagh (riv.)	M5
Shirvan (riv.)	E3
Shur (riv.)	J7
Siah Kuh (mt.)	L3
Silup (riv.)	M8
Susa (ruins)	F4
Talab (riv.)	N6
Tashk (lake)	J6
Urmia (lake)	D2
Zagros (mts.)	E4
Zarineh (riv.)	E2
Zilbir (riv.)	D1
Zohreh (riv.)	F5

IRAQ

GOVERNORATES

Anbar	B4
An Najaf	D4
Babil	D4
Basra	E5
Dhi Qar	E5
Dohuk	C2
Diyala	D4
Erbil	D2
Karbala	B4
Maysan	E5
Muthanna	D5
Ninawa	B3
Qadisiya	D4
Salahuddin	C3
Sulaimaniya	D3
Tamin	D3
Wasit	D4

CITIES and TOWNS

Ad Diwaniya 60,553	D5
A'faq 5,390	D4
Al A'ziziya 7,450	D4
Al Falluja 38,072	C4
Al Fathat 15,329	C3
A'li Gharbi 15,456	E4
A'li Sharqi 8,398	E4
Al Kufa 30,862	D4
Al Musaiyib 15,955	D4
Al Q'aim 3,372	B3
Al Qaiyara 3,060	C3
Al Qosh 3,863	C2
Al Qurna 5,638	E5
A'madiya 2,578	D2
A'mara 64,847	E5
A'na 15,729	B3
An Najaf 128,096	D5
An Nasiriya 60,405	D5
A'qra 8,659	D2
Arbela (Erbil) 90,320	C2
Aski Mosul 643	C2
As Salman 1,789	D5
Az Zubair 41,408	E5
Badra 3,564	D4
Baghdad (cap.) 502,503	D4
Baghdad* 1,745,328	D4
Baiji 6,785	C3
Baq'uba 34,575	D4
Basra 313,327	E5
Dohuk 16,998	C2
Erbil 90,320	D2
Fao 15,399	F6
Habbaniya 14,405	C4
Haditha 6,870	C3
Hai 16,988	E4
Halabja 11,206	D3
Hilla 84,717	D4
Hindiya 16,436	C4
Hit 9,131	C4
Karbal'a 83,301	C4
Khanaqin 23,522	D3
Kifri 8,500	D3
Kirkuk 167,413	D3
Kirkuk* 176,794	D3
Kubaisa 4,023	C4
Kut 42,116	D4
Makhmur 2,556	C3
Mandali 11,262	D4
Mosul 315,157	C2
Muqdadiyah 12,181	D4
Naft Kaneh	D3
Na'maniya 11,943	D4
Qal'at Diza 6,250	D2
Ramadi 28,723	C4
Rania 4,090	D2
Refai 7,681	E5
Rumaitha 10,222	D5
Rutba 5,091	B4
Ruwandiz 5,801	D2
Sad'iya 5,285	D3
Samarra 24,746	C3
Samawa 33,473	D5
Shaikh Saa'd 2,958	E4
Shaqlawa 6,814	D2
Shatra 18,822	E5
Sinjar 7,942	B2
Sulaimaniya 86,822	D3
Tal Kaif 7,482	C2
Taza Khurmatu 2,681	C3
Tikrit 9,921	C3
Tuz Khurmatu 13,860	D3
Zakho 14,790	C2

OTHER FEATURES

Adhaim (riv.)	D3
Aneiza, Jebel (mt.)	A4
A'rab, Shatt-al- (riv.)	F5
A'ra'r, Wadi (dry riv.)	B5
Babylon (ruins)	D4
Batin, Wadi al (dry riv.)	E6
Ctesiphon (ruins)	D4
Darbandikhan (dam)	D3
Euphrates (riv.)	D4
Great Zab (riv.)	C2
Hauran, Wadi (dry riv.)	B4
Little Zab (riv.)	C3
Mesopotamia (reg.)	B3
Nineveh (ruins)	C2
Sad'iya, Hor (lake)	E5
Saniya, Hor (lake)	E5
Shai'b Hisb, Wadi (dry riv.)	C5
Sinjar, Jebel (mts.)	B2
Siyah Kuh (mt.)	B4
Syrian (des.)	B4
Tigris (riv.)	E4
Ubaiyidh, Wadi (dry riv.)	B5
Ur (ruins)	E5

*City and suburbs.
†Population of commune.

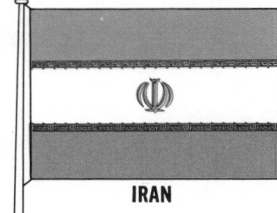

IRAN

IRAQ

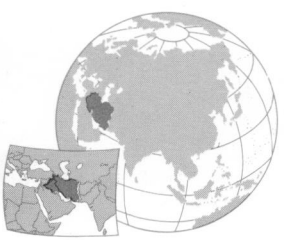

AREA 636,293 sq. mi. (1,648,000 sq. km.)
POPULATION 37,447,000
CAPITAL Tehran
LARGEST CITY Tehran
HIGHEST POINT Damavand 18,376 ft. (5,601 m.)
MONETARY UNIT Iranian rial
MAJOR LANGUAGES Persian, Azerbaijani, Kurdish
MAJOR RELIGION Islam

AREA 172,476 sq. mi. (446,713 sq. km.)
POPULATION 12,767,000
CAPITAL Baghdad
LARGEST CITY Baghdad
HIGHEST POINT Haji Ibrahim 11,811 ft. (3,600 m.)
MONETARY UNIT Iraqi dinar
MAJOR LANGUAGES Arabic, Kurdish
MAJOR RELIGION Islam

Topography

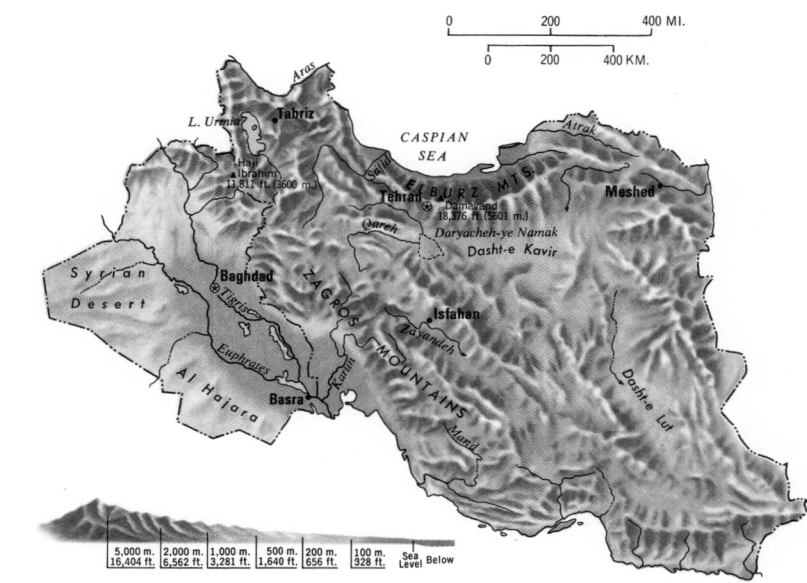

0   200   400 MI.
0   200   400 KM.

5,000 m. / 16,404 ft. — 2,000 m. / 6,562 ft. — 1,000 m. / 3,281 ft. — 500 m. / 1,640 ft. — 200 m. / 656 ft. — 100 m. / 328 ft. — Sea Level / Below

Agriculture, Industry and Resources

DOMINANT LAND USE

- Cereals, Livestock
- Cash Crops, Horticulture, Livestock
- Pasture Livestock
- Nomadic Livestock Herding
- Forests
- Nonagricultural Land

MAJOR MINERAL OCCURRENCES

C	Coal
Cr	Chromium
Cu	Copper
Fe	Iron Ore
G	Natural Gas
Mn	Manganese
Na	Salt
O	Petroleum
Pb	Lead
S	Sulfur, Pyrites
Zn	Zinc

⚡ Water Power
▨ Major Industrial Areas

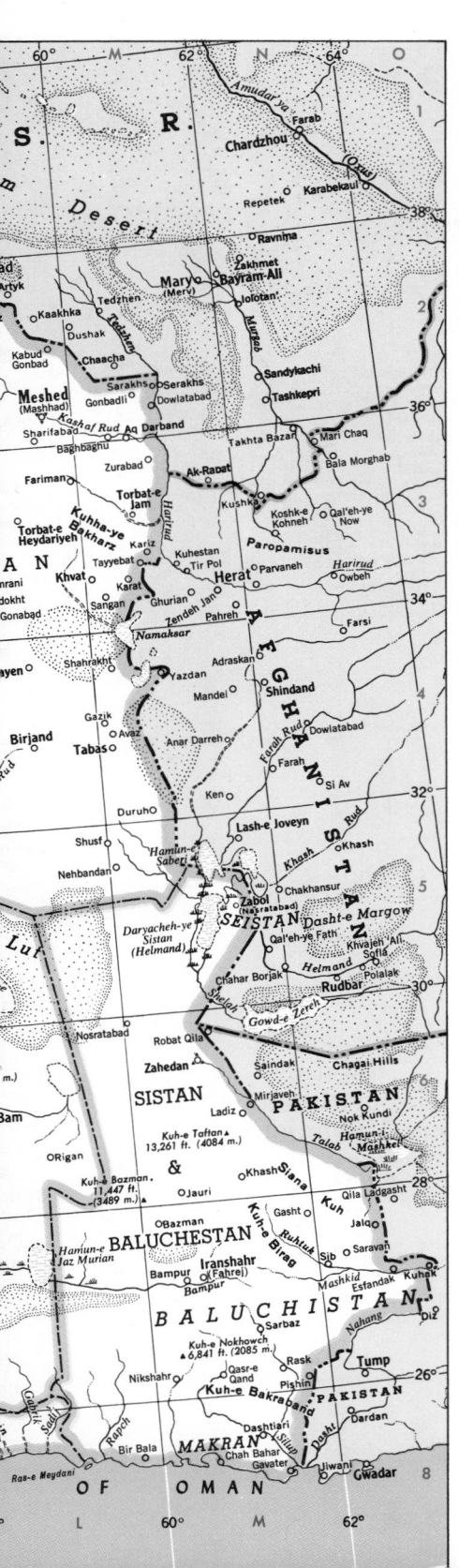

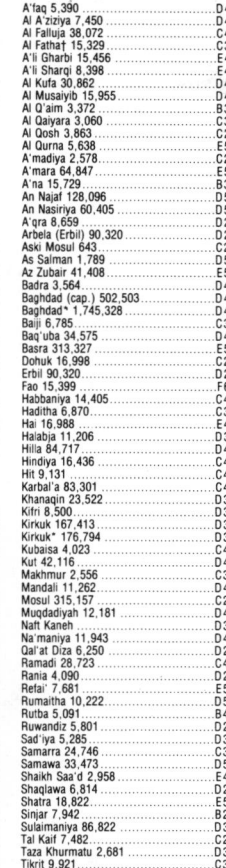

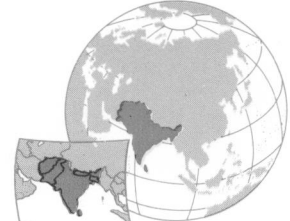

INDIA

AREA 1,269,339 sq. mi. (3,287,588 sq. km.)
POPULATION 683,810,051
CAPITAL New Delhi
LARGEST CITY Calcutta (greater)
HIGHEST POINT Nanda Devi 25,645 ft. (7,817 m.)
MONETARY UNIT Indian rupee
MAJOR LANGUAGES Hindi, English, Bihari, Telugu, Marathi, Bengali, Tamil, Gujarati, Rajasthani, Kanarese, Malayalam, Oriya, Punjabi, Assamese, Kashmiri, Urdu
MAJOR RELIGIONS Hinduism, Islam, Christianity, Sikhism, Buddhism, Jainism, Zoroastrianism, Animism

PAKISTAN

AREA 310,403 sq. mi. (803,944 sq. km.)
POPULATION 83,782,000
CAPITAL Islamabad
LARGEST CITY Karachi
HIGHEST POINT K2 (Godwin Austen) 28,250 ft. (8,611 m.)
MONETARY UNIT Pakistani rupee
MAJOR LANGUAGES Urdu, English, Punjabi, Pushtu, Sindhi, Baluchi, Brahui
MAJOR RELIGIONS Islam, Hinduism, Sikhism, Christianity, Buddhism

SRI LANKA (CEYLON)

AREA 25,332 sq. mi. (65,610 sq. km.)
POPULATION 14,850,001
CAPITAL Colombo
LARGEST CITY Colombo
HIGHEST POINT Pidurutalagala 8,281 ft. (2,524 m.)
MONETARY UNIT Sri Lanka rupee
MAJOR LANGUAGES Sinhala, Tamil, English
MAJOR RELIGIONS Buddhism, Hinduism, Christianity, Islam

AFGHANISTAN

AREA 250,775 sq. mi. (649,507 sq. km.)
POPULATION 15,540,000
CAPITAL Kabul
LARGEST CITY Kabul
HIGHEST POINT Nowshak 24,557 ft. (7,485 m.)
MONETARY UNIT afghani
MAJOR LANGUAGES Pushtu, Dari, Uzbek
MAJOR RELIGION Islam

NEPAL

AREA 54,663 sq. mi. (141,577 sq. km.)
POPULATION 14,179,301
CAPITAL Kathmandu
LARGEST CITY Kathmandu
HIGHEST POINT Mt. Everest 29,028 ft. (8,848 m.)
MONETARY UNIT Nepalese rupee
MAJOR LANGUAGES Nepali, Maithili, Tamang, Newari, Tharu
MAJOR RELIGIONS Hinduism, Buddhism

MALDIVES

AREA 115 sq. mi. (298 sq. km.)
POPULATION 143,046
CAPITAL Male
LARGEST CITY Male
HIGHEST POINT 20 ft. (6 m.)
MONETARY UNIT Maldivian rupee
MAJOR LANGUAGE Divehi
MAJOR RELIGION Islam

BHUTAN

AREA 18,147 sq. mi. (47,000 sq. km.)
POPULATION 1,298,000
CAPITAL Thimphu
LARGEST CITY Thimphu
HIGHEST POINT Kula Kangri 24,784 ft. (7,554 m.)
MONETARY UNIT ngultrum
MAJOR LANGUAGES Dzongka, Nepali
MAJOR RELIGIONS Buddhism, Hinduism

BANGLADESH

AREA 55,126 sq. mi. (142,776 sq. km.)
POPULATION 87,052,024
CAPITAL Dacca
LARGEST CITY Dacca
HIGHEST POINT Keokradong 4,034 ft. (1,230 m.)
MONETARY UNIT taka
MAJOR LANGUAGES Bengali, English
MAJOR RELIGIONS Islam, Hinduism, Christianity

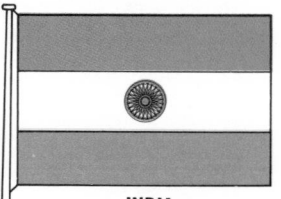

INDIA

PAKISTAN

SRI LANKA (CEYLON)

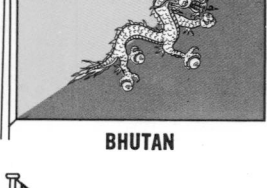

BHUTAN

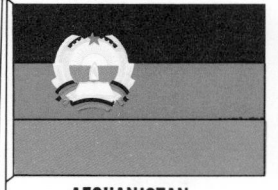

AFGHANISTAN

MALDIVES

BANGLADESH

NEPAL

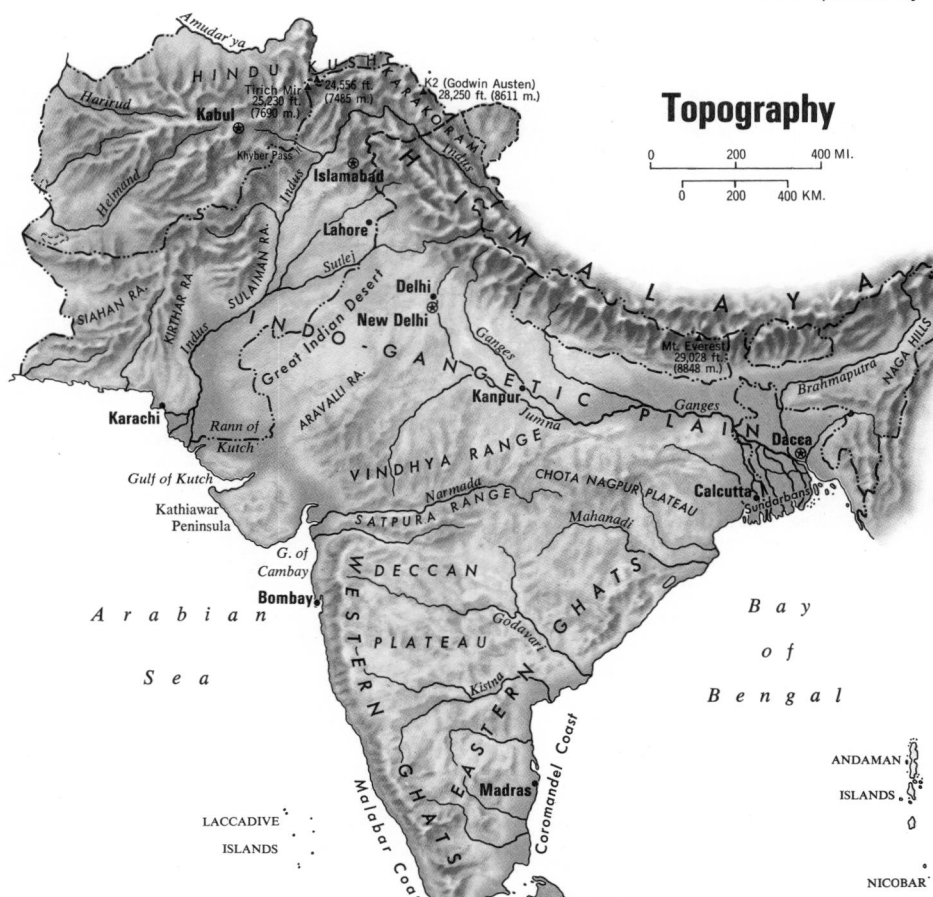

Topography

(continued)

Assam (state) 19,902,826 ... G3
Bihar (state) 69,823,154 ... F4
Chandigarh (terr.) 450,061 ... D2
Dadra and Nagar Haveli (terr.) 103,677 ... C4
Delhi (terr.) 6,196,414 ... D3
Goa, Daman and Diu (terr.) 1,082,117 ... C4
Gujarat (state) 33,960,905 ... C4
Haryana (state) 12,850,902 ... D3
Himachal Pradesh (state) 4,237,569 ... D2
Jammu and Kashmir (state) 5,981,600 ... D2
Karnataka (state) 37,043,451 ... D6
Kerala (state) 25,403,217 ... D6
Lakshadweep (terr.) 40,237 ... C6
Madhya Pradesh (state) 52,131,717 ... D4
Maharashtra (state) 62,693,898 ... C5
Manipur (state) 1,433,691 ... G4
Meghalaya (state) 1,327,874 ... G3
Mizoram (terr.) 487,774 ... G4
Nagaland (state) 773,281 ... G3
Orissa (state) 26,272,054 ... E5
Pondicherry (terr.) 604,136 ... E6
Punjab (state) 16,669,755 ... D2
Rajasthan (state) 34,102,912 ... C3
Sikkim (state) 315,682 ... F3
Tamil Nadu (state) 48,297,456 ... D6
Tripura (state) 2,060,189 ... G4
Uttar Pradesh (state) 110,858,019 ... D3
West Bengal (state) 54,485,560 ... F4

CITIES and TOWNS

Abu 9,840 ... C4
Abu Road 25,331 ... C4
Achalpur 42,326 ... D4
Addanki 10,223 ... D5
Adilabad 30,368 ... D5
Adoni 85,311 ... D5
Agartala 59,625 ... G4
Agartala□ 100,264 ... G4
Agra 591,917 ... D3
Agra□ 634,622 ... D3
Ahmadabad 1,591,832 ... C4
Ahmadabad□ 1,741,522 ... C4
Ahmadnagar 118,236 ... C5
Ahmadnagar□ 148,405 ... C5
Aizwal 31,740 ... G4
Ajanta ... D4
Ajmer 262,851 ... C3
Akola 168,438 ... D4
Alibag 11,913 ... C5
Aligarh 252,314 ... D3
Alipore ... F2
Allahabad 490,622 ... E3
Allahabad□ 513,036 ... E3
Alleppey-Cochin 160,166 ... D7
Almora 19,671 ... D3
Along 3,524 ... G3
Alwar 100,378 ... D3
Amalner 55,544 ... C4
Ambala 83,633 ... D2
Ambala□ 186,168 ... D2
Ambikapur 23,087 ... E4
Amravati 193,800 ... D4
Amreli 39,520 ... C4
Amritsar 407,628 ... C2
Amritsar□ 458,029 ... C2
Anakapalle 57,273 ... E5
Anantapur 80,069 ... D6
Anantnag 27,643 ... D2
Andheri ... B7
Andul 3,602 ... F2
Arcot 30,230 ... D6
Arrah 92,919 ... E3
Aruppukkottai 62,223 ... D7
Arvi 26,494 ... D4
Asansol 155,968 ... F4
Asansol□ 241,792 ... F4
Aurangabad, Bihar 18,714 ... E4
Aurangabad, Maharashtra 150,483 ... D5
Aurangabad□ 165,253 ... D5
Azamgarh 40,963 ... E3
Badagara 53,938 ... D6
Bagalkot 51,746 ... D5
Bahraich 73,931 ... E3
Baidyabati 54,130 ... F1
Balaghat 27,872 ... E4
Balasore 46,239 ... F4
Ballia 47,101 ... E3
Bally 38,892 ... F1
Balotra 17,595 ... C3
Balrampur 36,191 ... E3
Balurghat 67,088 ... F3
Banda 50,575 ... D3
Bandar (Machilipatnam) 112,612 ... E5
Bandra ... B7
Bangalore 1,540,741 ... D6
Bangalore□ 1,653,779 ... D6
Bankura 79,129 ... F4
Bansberia 61,748 ... F1
Banswara 27,363 ... C4
Baramati 27,912 ... C5
Baramula 26,334 ... C2
Baranagar 136,842 ... F1
Barasat 42,642 ... F1
Barbil 24,342 ... F4
Bareilly 296,248 ... D3
Bareilly□ 326,106 ... D3
Baripada 28,725 ... F4
Barmer 38,630 ... C3
Baroda (Vadodara) 466,696 ... C4
Barpeta 26,479 ... G3
Barrackpore 96,889 ... F1
Barrackpore□ 198,255 ... F1
Barsi 62,374 ... D5
Baruipur 20,501 ... F2
Barwani 22,099 ... D4
Basim 32,496 ... D4
Basirhat 63,816 ... F4
Bassein 30,594 ... C5
Bastar ... E5
Batala 58,200 ... D2
Baudh 8,891 ... E4
Bauria 10,610 ... E2
Beawar 66,114 ... C3
Belgaum 192,427 ... C5
Belgaum□ 213,872 ... C5
Bellary 125,183 ... D5
Benares (Varanasi) 583,856 ... E3
Berhampore 72,605 ... F4
Berhampur 117,662 ... F5
Bettiah 51,018 ... E3
Betul 30,862 ... D4
Bhadrak 40,487 ... F4
Bhadravati 40,203 ... D6
Bhadravati□ 101,358 ... D6
Bhadreswar 45,586 ... F1
Bhagalpur 172,202 ... F4
Bhandara 39,423 ... E4
Bhandup ... B7
Bhanjanagar 12,353 ... E4
Bharatpur 68,036 ... D3
Bharuch 91,589 ... C4
Bhatapara 20,980 ... E4
Bhatinda 53,684 ... C2
Bhatkal 18,732 ... C6
Bhatpara 204,750 ... F1
Bhavnagar 225,358 ... C4
Bhavnagar□ 225,974 ... C4
Bhawanipatna 22,808 ... E5
Bhilai 157,173 ... E4
Bhilwara 82,155 ... C3
Bhimavaram 63,762 ... E5
Bhimunipatnam 14,291 ... E5
Bhind 42,371 ... D3
Bhinmal 14,050 ... C3
Bhir (Bir) 49,965 ... D5
Bhiwandi 79,576 ... C5
Bhiwani 73,086 ... D3
Bhopal 298,022 ... D4
Bhor 10,708 ... C5
Bhubaneswar 105,491 ... F4
Bhuj 52,177 ... B4
Bhusawal 96,800 ... D4
Bhusawal□ 104,708 ... D4
Bidar 50,670 ... D5
Bihar 100,046 ... F3
Bijapur, Karnataka 103,931 ... D5
Bijapur, Madhya Pradesh 5,289 ... E5
Bijnor 43,290 ... D3
Bikaner 188,518 ... C3
Bikaner□ 208,894 ... C3
Bilaspur 98,410 ... E4
Bina-Itawa 33,106 ... D4
Bir 49,965 ... D5
Birmitrapur 28,063 ... E4
Bobbili 30,649 ... E5
Bodhan 37,589 ... D5
Bodinayakkanur 54,176 ... D6
Bolangir 35,748 ... E4
Bombay (Greater)* 5,970,575 ... B7
Bomdila 2,264 ... G3
Broach (Bharuch) 91,589 ... C4
Budaun 72,204 ... D3
Budge-Budge 51,039 ... F2
Bundi 34,279 ... D3
Burdwan 143,318 ... F4
Burhanpur 105,246 ... D4
Calcutta 3,148,746 ... F2
Calcutta□ 7,031,382 ... F2
Calicut (Kozhikode) 333,979 ... D6
Cambay 62,097 ... C4
Cannanore 55,162 ... C6
Cawnpore (Kanpur) 1,154,388 ... E3
Chaibasa 35,386 ... F4
Chamba 11,814 ... D2
Champdani 58,596 ... F1
Chanderi 10,294 ... D4
Chandernagore 75,238 ... F1
Chandigarh 218,743 ... D2
Chandigarh□ 232,940 ... D2
Chandrapur 75,134 ... D5
Chapra 83,101 ... F3
Chatrapur 10,835 ... F5
Chembur ... B7
Cherrapunji⊙ 83,987 ... G3
Chhatarpur 32,271 ... D4
Chhindwara 53,492 ... D4
Chidambaram 48,811 ... E6
Chik Ballapur 29,227 ... D6
Chikmagalur 41,639 ... D6
Chingleput 38,419 ... E6
Chiplun 20,942 ... C5
Chirala 54,487 ... E5
Chitorgarh 25,917 ... C4
Chitradurga 50,254 ... D6
Chittoor 63,035 ... D6
Churachandpur 8,706 ... G4
Churu 52,502 ... D3
Chushul ... D2
Cocanada (Kakinada) 164,200 ... E5
Cochin-Alleppey 439,066 ... D6
Coimbatore 356,368 ... D6
Coimbatore□ 736,203 ... D6
Colachel 18,819 ... D7
Cooch Behar 53,684 ... F3
Coondapoor 23,831 ... C6
Cuddalore 101,335 ... E6
Cuddapah 66,195 ... D6
Cumbum 9,745 ... D5
Cuttack 194,068 ... F4
Cuttack□ 205,759 ... F4
Dabhoi 37,892 ... C4
Daltonganj 32,367 ... E4
Damoh 59,489 ... D4
Dapoli 6,296 ... C5
Darbhanga 132,059 ... F3
Darjeeling 42,873 ... F3
Datia 36,439 ... D3
Davangere 121,110 ... D6
Deesa 28,324 ... C4
Dehra Dun 166,073 ... D2
Dehra Dun□ 203,464 ... D2
Delhi 3,287,883 ... D3
Delhi□ 3,647,023 ... D3
Demchok ... D2
Deogarh, Orissa 8,906 ... E4
Deoghar, Bihar 40,356 ... F4
Deolali 55,436 ... C5
Deoria 38,161 ... E3
Dewas 51,545 ... D4
Dhamtari 34,546 ... E4
Dhanbad 79,838 ... F4
Dhanbad□ 434,031 ... F4
Dhar 36,172 ... C4
Dharmsala 10,939 ... D2
Dharwar-Hubli 379,166 ... C5
Dhenkanal 19,615 ... E4
Dholpur 31,865 ... D3
Dhond 16,583 ... C5
Dhoraji 59,773 ... C4
Dhubri 36,503 ... G3
Dhulia 137,129 ... C4
Dibrugarh 80,348 ... G3
Digboi 16,538 ... H3
Dindigul 128,429 ... D6
Diphu 10,200 ... G3
Dispur 1,725 ... G3
Diu 6,214 ... C4
Dohad 44,506 ... C4
Domjor 10,896 ... F1
Dudhi 5,084 ... E4
Dum Dum 31,363 ... F1
Dum Dum□ 273,812 ... F1
Dungarpur 19,773 ... C4
Durg 67,892 ... E4
Durgapur 206,638 ... F4
Dwarka 17,801 ... B4
Eluru 127,023 ... E5
English Bazar 61,335 ... F3
Erode 105,111 ... D6
Etawah 85,894 ... D3
Faizabad-cum-Ayodhya 102,835 ... E3
Faridabad 85,762 ... D3
Farrukhabad-cum-Fatehgarh 102,768 ... D3
Farrukhabad-cum-Fatehgarh□ 110,835 ... D3
Fatehpur, Rajasthan 34,929 ... C3
Fatehpur, Uttar Pradesh 54,665 ... E3
Firozabad 133,863 ... D3
Firozpur 49,545 ... C2
Gadag-Betgeri 95,426 ... D5
Gadwal 21,828 ... D5
Gandhinagar 24,055 ... C4
Ganganagar 90,042 ... C3
Gangapur 27,453 ... D3
Gangtok 12,000 ... F3
Garden Reach 154,913 ... F2
Garulia 44,271 ... F1
Gauhati 123,783 ... G3
Gauhati□ 200,377 ... G3
Gaya 179,884 ... F4
Ghat Kopar 34,256 ... B7
Ghaziabad 118,836 ... D3
Ghaziabad□ 127,700 ... D3
Ghazipur 45,635 ... E3
Goalpara 16,703 ... G3
Godhra 66,403 ... C4
Gonda 52,662 ... E3
Gondal 54,928 ... C4
Gondia 77,992 ... E4
Gorakhpur 230,911 ... E3
Goregaon ... B7
Gudur 33,778 ... D6
Gulbarga 145,588 ... D5
Guna 40,006 ... D4
Guntakal 66,320 ... D5
Guntur 269,991 ... D5
Gurais ... D2
Gwalior 384,772 ... D3
Gwalior□ 406,140 ... D3
Haflong 5,197 ... G3
Hanle ... D2
Hanumangarh 30,017 ... C3
Harda 28,504 ... D4
Hardoi 46,639 ... E3
Hardwar 77,864 ... D2
Hassan 51,325 ... D6
Hathras 74,349 ... D3
Hazaribagh 54,818 ... F4
Hindupur 42,959 ... D6
Hinganghat 44,349 ... D4
Hingoli 31,948 ... D5
Hissar 89,437 ... D3
Honavar 12,444 ... C6
Hooghly-Chinsura 105,241 ... F1
Hoshangabad 27,011 ... D4
Hospet 65,196 ... D5
Howrah 737,877 ... F2
Hubli-Dharwar 379,166 ... C5
Hyderabad 1,607,396 ... D5
Hyderabad□ 1,796,339 ... D5
Ichchapuram 15,850 ... F5
Ichhapur 11,975 ... F1
Imphal 100,366 ... G4
Indore 543,381 ... D4
Indore□ 560,936 ... D4
Itanagar⊙ 18,787 ... G3
Itarsi 44,191 ... D4
Jabalpur 426,224 ... D4
Jabalpur□ 534,845 ... D4
Jagdalpur 31,344 ... E5
Jagtial 30,900 ... D5
Jaipur 615,258 ... D3
Jaipur□ 636,768 ... D3
Jaisalmer 16,578 ... C3
Jajpur 16,707 ... F4
Jalgaon 106,711 ... D4
Jalna 91,099 ... D4
Jalor 15,478 ... C3
Jalpaiguri 55,159 ... F3
Jamalpur 61,731 ... F3
Jammu 155,338 ... D2
Jammu□ 164,207 ... D2
Jamnagar 214,816 ... B4
Jamnagar□ 227,640 ... B4
Jamshedpur 341,576 ... F4
Jamshedpur□ 456,146 ... F4
Jaora 37,235 ... D4
Jaunpur 80,737 ... E3
Jeypore 34,319 ... E5
Jhalawar 20,035 ... D4
Jhansi 173,292 ... D3
Jhansi□ 198,135 ... D3
Jharsuguda 24,727 ... E4
Jhunjhunu 32,024 ... D3
Jind 38,161 ... D3
Jodhpur 317,612 ... C3
Jorhat 30,247 ... G3
Jubbulpore (Jabalpur) 426,224 ... D4
Juhu ... B7
Jullundur 296,106 ... D2
Jullundur□ 329,830 ... D2
Junagadh 95,485 ... B4
Kadayanallur 50,295 ... D7
Kadiri 33,810 ... D6
Kakinada 164,200 ... E5
Kalyan 99,547 ... C5
Kamarhati 169,404 ... F1
Kamptee 53,412 ... D4
Kanchipuram 110,657 ... E6
Kanchrapara 78,768 ... F1
Kandla 17,995 ... C4
Kandukur 16,654 ... E5
Kanker 9,278 ... E4
Kannauj 28,187 ... D3
Kanpur 1,154,388 ... E3
Kanpur□ 1,275,242 ... E3
Karad 42,329 ... C5
Karaikudi 55,449 ... D7
Karanja 31,150 ... D4
Kargil 2,390 ... D2
Karikal 26,080 ... E6
Karkal 18,593 ... C6
Karnal 92,784 ... D3
Karwar 27,770 ... C6
Kasaragod 34,984 ... C6
Kasganj 46,467 ... D3
Katarnian Ghat ... E3
Katihar 67,014 ... F3
Katni (Murwara) 54,864 ... E4
Kavali 29,616 ... E6
Kavaratti 4,420 ... C6
Kawardha 11,226 ... E4
Kendrapara 20,079 ... F4
Keonjhar 19,340 ... F4
Khamgaon 53,692 ... D4
Khamman 56,919 ... D5
Khandwa 84,517 ... D4
Kharagpur 61,783 ... F4
Khardah 32,302 ... F1
Khurda 15,879 ... F4
Kirkee 65,497 ... C5
Kishangarh 37,405 ... D3
Kishtwar 5,276 ... D2
Kohima 21,545 ... G3
Kolar 43,418 ... D6
Kolar Gold Fields 76,112 ... D6
Kolhapur 259,050 ... C5
Konnagar 34,424 ... F1
Koppal 27,277 ... D5
Koraput 21,505 ... E5
Korba 30,963 ... E4
Kota 212,991 ... D3
Kottaguden 75,542 ... E5
Kottayam 59,714 ... D7
Kotturu 12,873 ... D6
Kovur 16,846 ... E6
Kozhikode 333,979 ... D6
Krishnanagar 85,923 ... F4
Kulu 8,958 ... D2
Kumbakonam 113,130 ... D6
Kumta 19,112 ... C6
Kurla ... B7
Kurnool 136,710 ... D5
Laful⊙ 8,161 ... G7
Lansdowne 6,670 ... D3
Latur 70,156 ... D5
Leh 5,519 ... D2
Lohardaga 17,087 ... E4
Lucknow 749,239 ... E3
Lucknow□ 813,982 ... E3
Ludhiana 397,850 ... D2
Ludhiana□ 401,176 ... D2
Lumding 29,253 ... G3
Lungleh 6,019 ... G4
Machilipatnam 112,612 ... E5
Madh ... B7
Madhubani 32,919 ... F3
Madras 2,469,449 ... E6
Madras□ 3,169,930 ... E6
Madugula 8,376 ... E5
Madurai 549,114 ... D7
Madurai□ 711,501 ... D7
Mahabaleshwar 7,318 ... C5
Mahbubnagar 51,756 ... D5
Mahe 8,972 ... D6
Mahim 11,344 ... C5
Mahoba 29,707 ... D3
Mahuva 39,497 ... C4
Malad ... B6
Malakanagiri 7,494 ... E5
Malegaon 191,847 ... C4
Maler Kotla 48,536 ... D2
Malkapur 35,476 ... D4
Malvan 17,579 ... C5
Mandi 16,849 ... D2
Mandla 24,406 ... E4
Mandsaur 52,347 ... C4
Mandvi 27,849 ... B4
Manendragarh 11,936 ... E4
Mangalore 165,174 ... C6
Mangrol 27,183 ... B4
Manmad 29,571 ... C4
Mannargudi 42,783 ... E6
Manori ... B6
Margao 41,655 ... C5
Marmagao 44,065 ... C5
Mathura 132,028 ... D3
Mau 64,058 ... E3
Mayuram 60,195 ... D6
Meerut 270,993 ... D3
Mehsana 51,598 ... C4
Mercara 19,357 ... D6
Mhow 59,037 ... D4
Midnapore 71,326 ... F4
Miraj 77,606 ... D5
Mirzapur-cum-Vindhyachal 105,939 ... E4
Modasa 22,483 ... C4
Mokokchung 17,423 ... G3
Monghyr 102,474 ... F3
Mora ... B7
Moradabad 258,590 ... D3
Morena 44,901 ... D3
Morvi 60,976 ... C4
Mulund ... B6
Murud 11,210 ... C5
Murwara 54,864 ... E4
Muzaffarnagar 114,783 ... D3
Muzaffarpur 126,379 ... E3
Mysore 355,685 ... D6
Nadiad 108,269 ... C4
Nagapattinam 68,026 ... E6
Nagaur 36,448 ... C3
Nagercoil 141,288 ... D7
Nagina 37,066 ... D3
Nagpur 866,076 ... D4
Nagpur□ 930,459 ... D4
Nahan 16,017 ... D2
Naihati 82,080 ... F1
Naini Tal 23,986 ... D3
Nainpur 14,683 ... E4
Nalgonda 33,126 ... D5
Nander 126,538 ... D5
Nandurbar 54,070 ... C4
Nandyal 63,193 ... D5
Narayanpet 21,744 ... D5
Narnaul 31,875 ... D3
Narsimhapur 25,552 ... D4
Narsinghgarh 13,814 ... D4
Nasik 176,091 ... C5
Nasirabad 25,732 ... C3
Navsari 72,979 ... C4
Nellore 133,590 ... E6
New Delhi (cap.) 301,801 ... D3
Nhava-Sheva ... B7
Nimach 47,113 ... D4
Nipani 35,116 ... C5
Nirmal 28,529 ... D5
Nizamabad 115,640 ... D5
North Lakhimpur 20,094 ... G3
Nova Goa (Panaji) 34,953 ... C5
Nowgong, Assam 56,537 ... G3
Nowgong, Madhya Pradesh 10,248 ... D3
Okha Port 10,687 ... B4
Ongole 53,330 ... E5
Ootacamund 63,310 ... D6
Orai 42,513 ... D3
Osmanabad 27,279 ... D5
Pachmarhi 1,212 ... D4
Palanpur 42,114 ... C4
Palayankottai 70,070 ... D7
Palghat 95,788 ... D6
Pali 49,834 ... C3
Palni 49,575 ... D6
Panaji 34,953 ... C5
Panchur 59,021 ... F2
Pandharpur 53,638 ... D5
Panihati 148,046 ... F1
Panipat 87,981 ... D3
Panna 22,316 ... E4
Panruti 34,065 ... D6
Paradip ... F4
Parbhani 61,570 ... D5
Parlakhemundi 26,917 ... E5
Partapgarh 17,402 ... C4
Parvatipuram 30,025 ... E5
Pasighat 5,116 ... G3
Patan 64,519 ... C4
Pathankot 76,355 ... D2
Patiala 148,686 ... D2
Patiala□ ... D2
Patna 473,001 ... F3
Patna□ ... F3
Pauni 17,781 ... E4
Phalodi 17,379 ... C3
Phulbani 10,677 ... E4
Pilibhit 68,273 ... D3
Pokaran 7,769 ... C3
Pondicherry 90,537 ... E6
Ponnani 35,723 ... D6
Poona (Pune)□ ... C5
Porbandar 96,881 ... B4
Porbandar□ ... B4
Port Blair 26,218 ... G6
Porto Novo 17,412 ... E6
Proddatur 70,822 ... D6
Puduchcheri (Pondicherry) 90,537 ... E6
Pudukkottai 66,384 ... D6
Pune 856,105 ... C5
Puri 72,674 ... F5
Purli 31,078 ... D5
Purnea 56,484 ... F3
Purulia 57,708 ... F4
Puttur 17,483 ... D6
Quilon 124,208 ... D7
Radhanpur 18,360 ... C4
Raichur 79,831 ... D5
Raigarh 46,745 ... E4
Raipur 174,518 ... E4
Raipur□ ... E4
Rajahmundry 165,912 ... E5
Rajahmundry□ ... E5
Rajapalaiyam 86,952 ... D7
Rajapur 9,017 ... C5
Rajgarh 11,475 ... D4
Rajkot 300,612 ... C4
Rajnandgaon 41,183 ... E4
Rajpipla 25,769 ... C4
Rajpur 34,393 ... F2
Rajpura 14,840 ... D2
Rameswarem 16,755 ... D7
Rampur, Him. Pradesh 2,623 ... D2
Rampur, Uttar Pradesh 161,417 ... D3
Ranchi 175,934 ... F4
Ratangarh 31,506 ... C3
Ratlam 106,666 ... C4
Ratnagiri 37,551 ... C5
Raurkela 47,076 ... F4
Raxaul 12,064 ... E3
Rayagada 25,064 ... E5
Renigunta 8,567 ... E6
Rewa 69,182 ... E4
Rishra 63,486 ... F1
Robertsganj 7,093 ... E4
Roha 8,631 ... C5
Rohtak 124,783 ... C5
Sadiya⊙ 64,252 ... H3

British India

U.S.S.R.
GILGIT AGENCY
AFGHANISTAN
KASHMIR & JAMMU
N.W. FRONTIER PROV.
PUNJAB
PUNJAB STATES
TIBET
CHINA
IRAN
BALUCHISTAN
Indus
BAHAWALPUR (PUNJ. ST.)
DELHI
RAMPUR
NEPAL
SIKKIM
BHUTAN
Brahmaputra
ASSAM
PUNJ. ST.
RAJPUTANA
UNITED PROVINCES
AJMER-MERWARA
SIND
Gwadar (Oman)
GWALIOR
E. ST.
KHASI HILLS
Ganges
BENARES
BIHAR
MANIPUR
WESTERN INDIA
CENTRAL INDIA
EASTERN STATES
BENGAL
TRIPURA (E. ST.)
Arabian Sea
GUJARAT ST.
Chandernagore (Fr.)
BURMA
CENTRAL PROVINCES
E. ST.
ORISSA
BERAR
Diu (Port.)
Damão (Port.)
BOMBAY
EASTERN STATES
Bay of Bengal
HYDERABAD
DECCAN STATES
Yanaon (Fr.)
Gôa (Port.)
MADRAS
MYSORE
COORG
Bangalore (Br.)
Andaman Islands (Br.)
Mahé (Fr.)
Pondichéry (Fr.)
Karikal (Fr.)
M. ST.
Laccadive Islands (Madras)
Cochin (Br.)
MADRAS STATES
CEYLON
Nicobar Islands (Br.)

British India. *The provinces of British India were directly administered by Britain. A few areas were leased from the Indian princes.*

Indian States. *The Indian States, sometimes referred to as the "Native" or "Princely States," were under the nominal control of maharajas or other hereditary princes.*

Possessions of Other Countries in India

State or Provincial Boundaries

Other Internal Boundaries

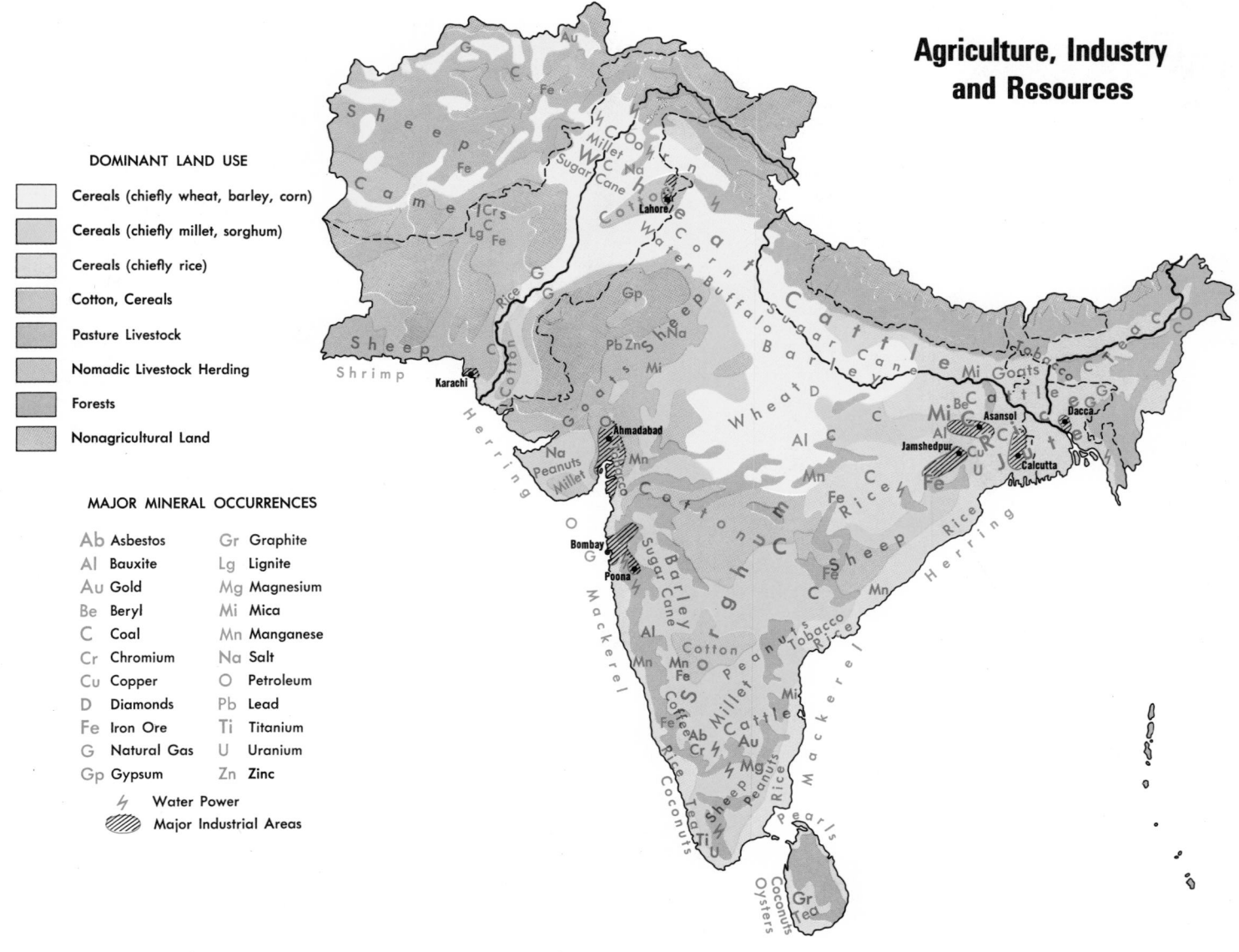

Agriculture, Industry and Resources

DOMINANT LAND USE

- Cereals (chiefly wheat, barley, corn)
- Cereals (chiefly millet, sorghum)
- Cereals (chiefly rice)
- Cotton, Cereals
- Pasture Livestock
- Nomadic Livestock Herding
- Forests
- Nonagricultural Land

MAJOR MINERAL OCCURRENCES

Ab Asbestos
Al Bauxite
Au Gold
Be Beryl
C Coal
Cr Chromium
Cu Copper
D Diamonds
Fe Iron Ore
G Natural Gas
Gp Gypsum

Gr Graphite
Lg Lignite
Mg Magnesium
Mi Mica
Mn Manganese
Na Salt
O Petroleum
Pb Lead
Ti Titanium
U Uranium
Zn Zinc

⚡ Water Power
▨ Major Industrial Areas

Burma, Thailand, Indochina and Malaya

CONIC PROJECTION

SCALE OF MILES

SCALE OF KILOMETERS

International Boundaries ------------
Division and State Boundaries ---·-·--
Capitals of Countries ------------ ☆
Division and State Capitals ------------ ◉

Scale 1:10,000,000

© Copyright HAMMOND INCORPORATED, Maplewood, N. J.

Longitude East 96° of Greenwich

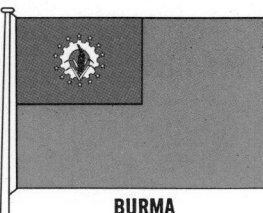

BURMA

THAILAND

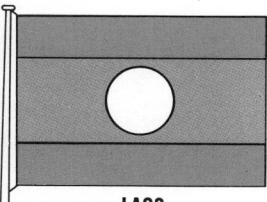

LAOS

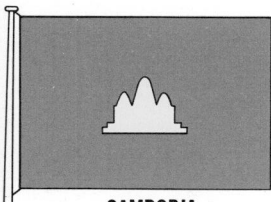

CAMBODIA

VIETNAM

MALAYSIA

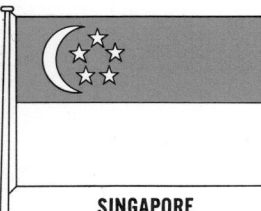

SINGAPORE

BURMA

AREA 261,789 sq. mi. (678,034 sq. km.)
POPULATION 32,913,000
CAPITAL Rangoon
LARGEST CITY Rangoon
HIGHEST POINT Hkakabo Razi 19,296 ft. (5,881 m.)
MONETARY UNIT kyat
MAJOR LANGUAGES Burmese, Karen, Shan, Kachin, Chin, Kayah, English
MAJOR RELIGIONS Buddhism, tribal religions

THAILAND

AREA 198,455 sq. mi. (513,998 sq. km.)
POPULATION 46,455,000
CAPITAL Bangkok
LARGEST CITY Bangkok
HIGHEST POINT Doi Inthanon 8,452 ft. (2,576 m.)
MONETARY UNIT baht
MAJOR LANGUAGES Thai, Lao, Chinese, Khmer, Malay
MAJOR RELIGIONS Buddhism, tribal religions

LAOS

AREA 91,428 sq. mi. (236,800 sq. km.)
POPULATION 3,721,000
CAPITAL Vientiane
LARGEST CITY Vientiane
HIGHEST POINT Phou Bia 9,252 ft. (2,820 m.)
MONETARY UNIT kip
MAJOR LANGUAGE Lao
MAJOR RELIGIONS Buddhism, tribal religions

CAMBODIA

AREA 69,898 sq. mi. (181,036 sq. km.)
POPULATION 5,200,000
CAPITAL Phnom Penh
LARGEST CITY Phnom Penh
HIGHEST POINT 5,948 ft. (1,813 m.)
MONETARY UNIT riel
MAJOR LANGUAGE Khmer (Cambodian)
MAJOR RELIGION Buddhism

VIETNAM

AREA 128,405 sq. mi. (332,569 sq. km.)
POPULATION 52,741,766
CAPITAL Hanoi
LARGEST CITY Ho Chi Minh City (Saigon)
HIGHEST POINT Fan Si Pan 10,308 ft. (3,142 m.)
MONETARY UNIT dong
MAJOR LANGUAGES Vietnamese, Thai, Muong, Meo, Yao, Khmer, French, Chinese, Cham
MAJOR RELIGIONS Buddhism, Taoism, Confucianism, Roman Catholicism, Cao-Dai

MALAYSIA

AREA 128,308 sq. mi. (332,318 sq. km.)
POPULATION 13,435,588
CAPITAL Kuala Lumpur
LARGEST CITY Kuala Lumpur
HIGHEST POINT Mt. Kinabalu 13,455 ft. (4,101 m.)
MONETARY UNIT ringgit
MAJOR LANGUAGES Malay, Chinese, English, Tamil, Dayak, Kadazan
MAJOR RELIGIONS Islam, Confucianism, Buddhism, tribal religions, Hinduism, Taoism, Christianity, Sikhism

SINGAPORE

AREA 226 sq. mi. (585 sq. km.)
POPULATION 2,413,945
CAPITAL Singapore
LARGEST CITY Singapore
HIGHEST POINT Bukit Timah 581 ft. (177 m.)
MONETARY UNIT Singapore dollar
MAJOR LANGUAGES Chinese, Malay, Tamil, English, Hindi
MAJOR RELIGIONS Confucianism, Buddhism, Taoism, Hinduism, Islam, Christianity

Topography

0   200   400 MI.
0   200   400 KM.

5,000 m. 2,000 m. 1,000 m. 500 m. 200 m. 100 m. Sea Level
16,404 ft. 6,562 ft. 3,281 ft. 1,640 ft. 656 ft. 328 ft. Below

(continued on following page)

(continued)

Agriculture, Industry and Resources

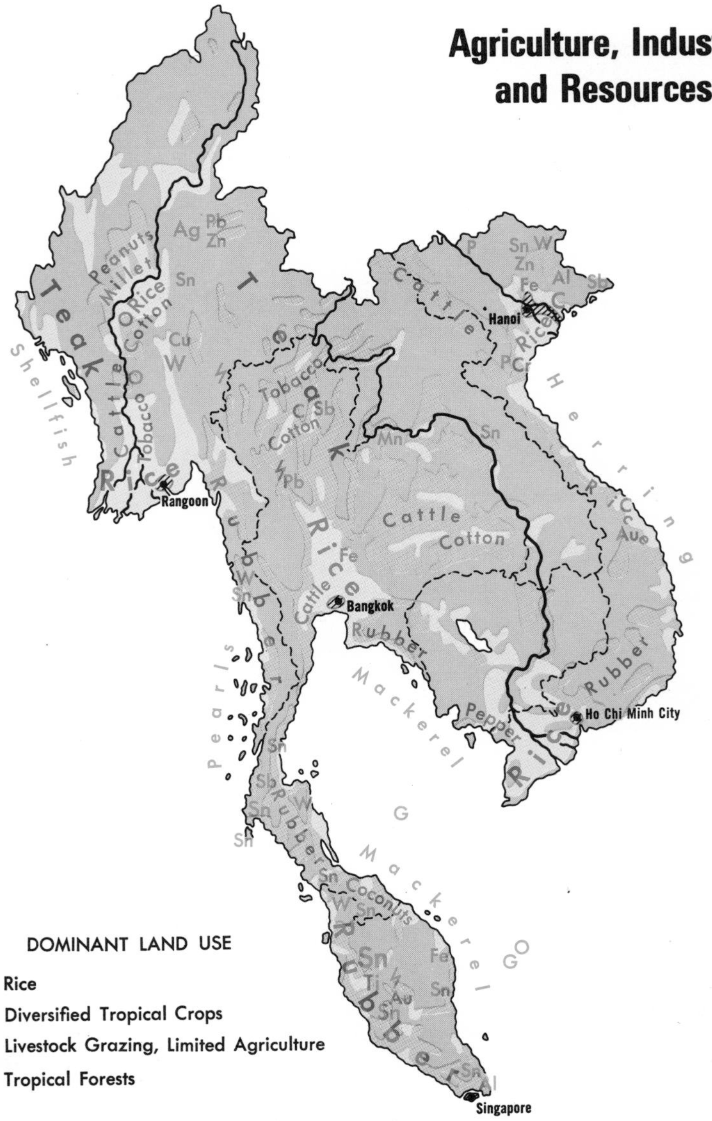

DOMINANT LAND USE

- Rice
- Diversified Tropical Crops
- Livestock Grazing, Limited Agriculture
- Tropical Forests

MAJOR MINERAL OCCURRENCES

Ag	Silver	Cu	Copper	O	Petroleum	Sn	Tin
Al	Bauxite	Fe	Iron Ore	P	Phosphates	Ti	Titanium
Au	Gold	G	Natural Gas	Pb	Lead	W	Tungsten
C	Coal	Mn	Manganese	Sb	Antimony	Zn	Zinc
Cr	Chromium						

Water Power

Major Industrial Areas

Bilauktaung (range) C4
Chaukan (pass) C1
Cheduba (isl.) B3
Chin (hills) B2
Chindwin (riv.) B2
Coco (chan.) B4
Combermere (bay) B3
Daung Kyun (isl.) C4
Dawna (range) C3
Great Coco (isl.) B4
Great Tenasserim (riv.) C4
Heinze Chaung (bay) C4
Heywood (chan.) B3
Hka, Nam (riv.) C2
Hkakabo Razi (mt.) C1
Indawgyi (lake) C1
Inle (lake) C2
Irrawaddy (riv.) B3
Irrawaddy, Mouths of the (delta) B4
Kadan Kyun (isl.) C4
Kaladan (riv.) B2
Kalegauk (isl.) C4
Khao Luang (mt.) C5
Lanbi Kyun (isl.) C5
Launglon Bok (isls.) C4
Loi Leng (mt.) C2
Manipur (riv.) B2
Martaban (gulf) C4
Mekong (riv.) D2
Mergui (arch.) C5
Mon (riv.) B2
Mu (riv.) B2
Negrais (cape) B3
Pakchan (riv.) C5
Pangsau (pass) C1
Pawn, Nam (riv.) C2
Pegu Yoma (mts.) B3
Preparis (isl.) B4
Ramree (isl.) B3
Salween (riv.) C3
Shan (plat.) C2
Sittang (riv.) C3
Taungthonton (mt.) B1
Tavoy (pt.) C4
Tenasserim (isl.) C4
Teng, Nam (riv.) C2
Three Pagodas (pass) C4
Victoria (mt.) B2

CAMBODIA (KAMPUCHEA)

CITIES and TOWNS

Batdambang (Battambang) D4
Choam Khsant E4
Kampong Cham E4
Kampong Chhnang D4
Kampong Khleang E4
Kampong Saom D5
Kampong Spoe E5
Kampong Thum E4
Kampong Trabek E5
Kampot E5
Kaoh Nhek E4
Kracheh E4
Krong Kaoh Kong D4
Krong Keb E5
Kulen E4
Lumphat E4
Moung Roessei D4
Pailin D4
Paoy Pet D4
Phnom Penh (cap.) c. 300,000 .... E5
Phnum Tbeng Meanchey E4
Phsar Ream D5
Phumi Banam E5
Phumi Phsar E4
Phumi Prek Kak E4
Phumi Samraong D4
Pouthisat D4
Prek Pouthi E5
Prey Veng E5
Pursat (Pouthisat) D4
Rovieng Tbong E4
Sambor E4
Senmonoron E4
Siempang E4
Siemreab D4
Sisophon D4
Sre Ambel D5
Sre Khtum E4
Stoeng Treng E4
Suong E5
Svay Rieng E5
Takev E5
Virochey E4

OTHER FEATURES

Angkor Wat (ruins) E4
Dangrek (mts.) D4
Drang, la (riv.) E4
Joncs (plain) E5
Khong, Se (riv.) E4
Kong, Kaoh (isl.) D5
Mekong (riv.) E4
Rung, Kaoh (isl.) D5
San, Se (riv.) E4
Sen, Stoeng (riv.) E4
Srepok (riv.) E4
Tang, Kaoh (isl.) D5
Thailand (gulf) D5
Tonle Sap (lake) D4
Wai, Poulo (isls.) D5

LAOS

CITIES and TOWNS

Attapu 2,750 .... E4
Ban Khon E4
Ban Lahanam E3
Borikan D3
Champasak 3,500 .... E4
Dônghén E3
Khamkeut⊙ 31,206 .... E3
Louang Namtha 1,459 .... D2
Louangphrabang 7,596 .... D3
Muang Hinboun 1,750 .... E3
Muang Kènthao D3
Muang Khammoun 5,500 .... E3
Muang Không 1,750 .... E4
Muang Khôngxédôn 2,000 .... E4
Muang Khoua D2
Muang May E4
Muang Ou Tai D2
Muang Paktha D2
Muang Phin E3
Muang Tahoi E3
Muang Vapi E4
Muang Xaignabouri (Sayaboury) 2,500 .... D3
Mounlapamôk E4
Napè E3
Nong Het E3
Pakxé 8,000 .... E4
Phiafai⊙ 17,216 .... E4
Phôngsali 2,500 .... D2
San Nua (Sam Neua) 3,000 .... E2
Saravan 2,350 .... E4
Savannakhét 8,500 .... E3
Sayaboury (Muang Xaignabouri) 2,500 .... D3
Thakhek (Muang Khammouan) 5,500 .... E3
Tourakom D3
Viangchan (Vientiane) 132,253 .... D3
Vientiane (cap.) 132,253 .... D3
Xiangkhoang 3,500 .... D3

OTHER FEATURES

Bolovens (plat.) E4
Hou, Nam (riv.) D2
Jars (plain) D3
Mekong (riv.) D3
Ou, Nam (riv.) D2
Phou Bia (mt.) D3
Phou Cô Pi (mt.) E3
Phou Loi (mt.) D2
Rao Co (mt.) E3
Se Khong (riv.) E4
Tha, Nam (riv.) D2
Xianghoang (plat.) D3

MALAYA, MALAYSIA*

STATES

Federal Territory 937,875 .... D7
Johor (Johore) 1,601,504 .... D7
Kedah 1,102,200 .... D6
Kelantan 877,575 .... D6
Melaka 453,153 .... D7
Negeri Sembilan 563,955 .... D7
Pahang 770,644 .... D7
Perak 1,762,288 .... D6
Perlis 147,726 .... D6
Pinang (Penang) 911,586 .... D6
Selangor 1,467,441 .... D7
Terengganu 542,280 .... D6

CITIES and TOWNS

Alor Gajah 2,222 .... D7
Alor Setar 66,260 .... D6
Bandar Maharani (Muar) 61,218 .... D7
Bandar Penggaram (Batu Pahat) 53,291 .... D7
Batu Gajah 10,692 .... D6
Batu Pahat 53,291 .... D7
Bentong 22,683 .... D7
Butterworth 61,187 .... D6
Chukai 12,514 .... D6
Gemas 5,214 .... D7
George Town (Pinang) 269,603 .... C6
Ipoh 247,953 .... D6
Johor Baharu (Johore Bharu) 136,234 .... F5
Kampar 26,591 .... D6
Kangar 8,758 .... D6
Kelang 113,611 .... D7
Keluang 43,272 .... D7
Kota Baharu 55,124 .... D6
Kota Tinggi 8,725 .... F5
Kuala Dungun 17,560 .... D6
Kuala Lipis 9,270 .... D6
Kuala Lumpur (cap.) 451,977 .... D7
Kuala Lumpur* 937,875 .... D7
Kuala Pilah 12,508 .... D7
Kuala Rompin 1,384 .... D7
Kuala Selangor 3,132 .... D7
Kuala Terengganu 53,320 .... D6
Kuantan 43,358 .... D7
Kulai 11,841 .... F5
Lumut 3,255 .... D6
Malacca (Melaka) 87,160 .... D7
Mawai F5
Melaka 87,160 .... D7
Mersing 18,246 .... E7
Muar 61,218 .... D7
Pekan 4,682 .... D7
Pekan Nanas 9,003 .... E5
Pinang (George Town) 269,603 .... C6
Pontian Kechil 8,349 .... E5
Port Dickson 10,300 .... D7
Port Kelang D7
Port Weld 3,233 .... D6
Raub 18,433 .... D7
Segamat 17,796 .... D7
Seremban 80,921 .... D7
Sungai Petani 35,959 .... C6
Taiping 54,645 .... D6
Tanah Merah 7,012 .... D6
Telok Anson 44,524 .... D6
Tumpat 10,673 .... D6

OTHER FEATURES

Aur, Pulau (isl.) E7
Belumut, Gunong (mt.) D7
Gelang, Tanjong (pt.) D6
Johor, Sungai (riv.) F5
Johore (str.) E6
Kelantan, Sungai (riv.) D6
Langkawi, Pulau (isl.) C6
Ledang, Gunong (mt.) D7
Lima, Pulau (isl.) F6
Malacca (str.) D7
Malay (pen.) D6
Pahang, Sungai (riv.) D7
Pangkor, Pulau (isl.) D6
Perak, Gunong (mt.) D6
Perhentian, Kepulauan (isls.) D6
Pulai, Sungai (riv.) E5
Ramunia, Tanjong (pt.) F6
Redang, Pulau (isl.) D6
Sedili Kechil, Tanjong (pt.) F5
Tahan, Gunong (mt.) D6
Temiang, Bukit (mt.) D6
Tenggol, Pulau (isl.) D6
Tinggi, Pulau (isl.) E7

SINGAPORE

CITIES and TOWNS

Jurong 50,974 .... E6
Nee Soon 37,641 .... F6
Serangoon 89,558 .... F6
Singapore (cap.) 2,413,945 .... F6

OTHER FEATURES

Keppel (harb.) F6
Main (str.) F6
Singapore (str.) F6
Tekong Besar, Pulau (isl.) F6

THAILAND (SIAM)

CITIES and TOWNS

Ang Thong 7,267 .... C4
Ayutthaya (Phra Nakhon Si Ayutthaya) 37,213 .... D4
Ban Aranyaprathet 12,276 .... D4
Bangkok (cap.) 1,867,297 .... D4
Bangkok* 2,495,312 .... D4
Bang Lamung D4
Bang Saphan C5
Ban Kantang 9,247 .... C6
Ban Kapong C5
Ban Khlong Yai D5
Ban Kui Nua D4
Ban Ngon D3
Ban Pak Phanang 13,590 .... D5
Banphot Phisai C3
Ban Pua D3
Ban Sattahip D4
Ban Tha Uthen D3
Bua Chum D4
Buriram 16,431 .... D4
Chachoengsao 22,106 .... D4
Chai Badan D4
Chai Buri D3
Chainat 9,944 .... D4
Chaiya C5
Chaiyaphum 12,540 .... D4
Chang Khoeng C3
Chanthaburi 15,479 .... D4
Chiang Dao C3
Chiang Khan D3
Chiang Mai 83,729 .... C3
Chiang Rai 13,927 .... C3
Chiang Saen C2
Chon Buri 39,367 .... D4
Chumphon 11,643 .... C5
Den Chai C3
Hat Yai 47,953 .... C6
Hot C3
Hua Hin 21,426 .... D4
Kalasin 14,960 .... D3
Kamphaeng Phet 12,378 .... C3
Kanchanaburi 16,397 .... C4
Khanu C3
Khemmarat E4
Khon Kaen 29,431 .... D3
Khorat (Nakhon Ratchasima) 66,071 .... D4
Krabi 8,764 .... C5
Krung Thep (Bangkok) (cap.) 1,867,297 .... D4
Kumphawapi D3
Lae D3
Lampang 40,100 .... C3
Lamphun 11,309 .... C3
Lang Suan 4,020 .... C5
Loei 10,137 .... D3
Lom Sak 10,597 .... D3
Lop Buri 23,112 .... D4
Mae Hong Son 3,981 .... C3
Maha Sarakham 19,707 .... D3
Mukdahan E3
Nakhon Nayok 8,185 .... D4
Nakhon Pathom 34,300 .... C4
Nakhon Phanom 20,385 .... D3
Nakhon Ratchasima 66,071 .... D4
Nakhon Sawan 46,853 .... D4
Nakhon Si Thammarat 40,671 .... D5
Nan 17,738 .... D3
Nang Rong D4
Narathiwat 21,256 .... D6
Ngao D3
Nong Khai 21,150 .... D3
Pattani 21,938 .... D6
Phanat Nikhom 10,514 .... D4
Phangnga 5,738 .... C5
Phatthalung 13,336 .... D6
Phayao 20,346 .... C3
Phet Buri 27,755 .... C4
Phetchabun 6,240 .... D3
Phichai D3
Phichit 10,814 .... D3
Phitsanulok 33,883 .... D3
Phon Phisai D3
Phrae 17,555 .... D3
Phra Nakhon Si Ayutthaya 37,213 .... D4
Phuket 34,362 .... C6
Phutthaisong D4
Prachin Buri 14,167 .... D4
Prachuap Khiri Khan 9,075 .... D5
Pran Buri D4
Rahaeng (Tak) 16,317 .... C3
Ranong 10,301 .... C5
Rat Buri 32,271 .... C4
Rayong 14,846 .... D4
Roi Et 20,242 .... D4
Rong Kwang D3
Sakon Nakhon 18,943 .... E3
Samut Prakan 46,632 .... D4
Samut Sakhon 33,619 .... D4
Samut Songkhram 23,574 .... C4
Sara Buri 25,025 .... D4
Satun 7,315 .... C6
Sawankhalok 8,387 .... C3
Selaphum E3
Sing Buri 9,050 .... D4
Singora (Songkhla) 41,193 .... D6
Sisaket 13,662 .... E4
Songkhla 41,193 .... D6
Sukhothai 15,488 .... D3
Suphan Buri 18,768 .... C4
Surat Thani 24,923 .... C5
Surin 16,342 .... D4
Suwannaphum D4
Tak 16,317 .... C3
Takua Pa 7,825 .... C5
Thoen C3
Thon Buri 628,015 .... D4
To Mo D6
Trang 32,985 .... C6
Trat 7,917 .... D4
Ubon 40,650 .... E4
Udon Thani 56,218 .... D3
Uthai Thani 10,525 .... C4
Uttaradit 12,022 .... D3
Warin Chamrap 21,520 .... E4
Yala 30,051 .... D6
Yasothon 12,079 .... D4

OTHER FEATURES

Amya (pass) C4
Bilauktaung (range) C4
Chang, Ko (isl.) D4
Chao Phraya, Mae Nam (riv.) D4
Chi, Mae Nam (riv.) D3
Dangrek (Dong Rak) (mts.) D4
Doi Inthanon (mt.) C3
Doi Pha Hom Pok (mt.) C2
Doi Pia Fai (mt.) D4
Kao Prawa (mt.) C3
Khao Luang (mt.) C5
Khwae Noi, Mae Nam (riv.) C4
Kra (isth.) C5
Kut, Ko (isl.) D5
Laem Pho (cape) D6
Laem Talumphuk (cape) D5
Lanta, Ko (isl.) C6
Luang (mt.) C5
Mae Klong, Mae Nam (riv.) C4
Mekong (riv.) E3
Mun, Mae Nam (riv.) D4
Nan, Mae Nam (riv.) D3
Nong Lahan (lake) D3
Pakchan (riv.) C5
Pa Sak, Mae Nam (riv.) D4
Phangan, Ko (isl.) D5
Phuket, Ko (isl.) C5
Ping, Mae Nam (riv.) C3
Samui (str.) D5
Samui, Ko (isl.) D5
Siam (Thailand) (gulf) D5
Tao, Ko (isl.) C5
Tapi, Mae Nam (riv.) C5
Terutao, Ko (isl.) C6
Tha Chin, Mae Nam (riv.) C4
Thale Luang (lag.) D6
Thalu, Ko (isls.) C5
Three Pagodas (pass) C4
Wang, Mae Nam (riv.) C3

VIETNAM

CITIES and TOWNS

An Loc (Binh Long) 15,276 .... E5
An Nhon F4
An Tuc (An Khe) F4
Ap Long Ha F5
Ap Vinh Hao F5
Bac Can E2
Bac Giang E2
Bac Lieu 53,841 .... E5
Bac Ninh 22,560 .... E2
Ba Don E3
Bai Thuong E3
Ban Me Thuot 68,771 .... F4
Bao Ha D2
Bao Lac E2
Bien Hoa 87,135 .... E5
Binh Long (An Loc) 15,276 .... E5
Binh Son F4
Bo Duc E4
Bong Son (Hoai Nhon) F4
Cam Ranh 118,111 .... F5
Can Tho 182,424 .... E5
Cao Bang E2
Cao Lanh 16,482 .... E5
Chau Phu 37,175 .... E5
Chu Lai F4
Con Cuong E3
Cua Rao E3
Da Lat 105,072 .... F5
Dam Doi E5
Da Nang 492,194 .... E3
Dien Bien Phu D2
Dong Hoi E3
Duong Dong D5
Gia Dinh E5
Go Cong 33,191 .... E5
Ha Giang E2
Haiphong* 1,279,067 .... E2
Hanoi (cap.)* 2,570,905 .... E2
Ha Tien E5
Ha Tinh E3
Hau Bon E4
Hoa Binh E2
Hoa Da F5
Hoai Nhon F4
Ho Chi Minh City (Saigon)* 3,419,678 .... E5
Hoi An 45,059 .... F4
Hoi Xuan E2
Hon Chong E5
Hon Gai 100,000 .... E2
Hue 209,043 .... E3
Huong Khe E3
Ke Bao E2
Khanh Hoa F4
Khanh Hung 59,015 .... E5
Khe Sanh E3
Kien Hung E5
Kontum 33,554 .... E4
Lac Giao (Ban Me Thuot) 68,771 .... E4
Lai Chau D2
Lang Son 15,071 .... E2
Lao Cai E2
Loc Ninh E5
Long Xuyen 72,658 .... E5
Mo Duc F4
Mong Cai E2
Muong Khuong E2
My Tho 119,892 .... E5
Nam Dinh E2
Nghia Lo D2
Nha Trang 216,227 .... F4
Ninh Binh E3
Phan Rang 33,377 .... F5
Phan Thiet 80,122 .... F5
Phu Cuong 28,267 .... E5
Phu Lang Thuong (Bac Giang) E2
Phuc Loi E3
Phu Dien E3
Phu Ly E2
Phu My F4
Phu Qui E3
Phu Rieng E5
Phu Tho 10,888 .... E2
Phu Vinh 48,485 .... E5
Pleiku 23,720 .... E4
Quang Nam E4
Quang Ngai 14,119 .... F4
Quang Tri 15,874 .... E3
Quang Yen E2
Quan Long 59,331 .... E5
Qui Nhon 213,757 .... F4
Rach Gia 104,161 .... E5
Ron E3
Sa Dec 51,867 .... E5
Saigon (Ho Chi Minh City)* 3,419,678 .... E5
Song Cau F4
Son Ha F4
Son La D2
Son Tay 19,213 .... E2
Tam Ky 38,532 .... F4
Tam Quan F4
Tan An 38,082 .... E5
Tay Ninh 22,957 .... E5
Thai Binh 14,739 .... E2
Thai Nguyen E2
Thanh Hoa 31,211 .... E3
Thanh Tri E5
That Khe E2
Tien Yen E2
Tra Vinh (Phu Vinh) 48,485 .... E5
Truc Giang 68,629 .... E5
Trung Khanh Phu E2
Tuyen Quang E2
Tuy Hoa 63,552 .... F4
Van Hoa E2
Van Ninh F4
Van Yen E2
Vinh 43,954 .... E3
Vinh Long 30,667 .... E5
Vinh Yen E2
Vu Liet E3
Vung Tau 108,436 .... E5
Xuan Loc E5
Yen Bai E2

OTHER FEATURES

Bach Long Vi, Dao (isl.) F2
Ba Den, Nui (mt.) E5
Bai Bung, Mui (Ca Mau) (pt.) E5
Black (riv.) D2
Ca Mau (Mui Bai Bung) (pt.) E5
Cam Ranh, Vinh (bay) F5
Cat Ba, Dao (isl.) E2
Chon May, Vung (bay) F3
Cu Lao, Hon (isls.) F5
Deux Frères, Les (isls.) E5
Dinh, Mui (cape) F5
Fan Si Pan (mt.) D2
Ia Drang (riv.) E4
Joncs (plain) E5
Kontum (plat.) E4
Khoai, Hon (isl.) E5
Lang Bian, Nui (mts.) E4
Lay, Mui (cape) E3
Mekong, Mouths of the (delta) E5
Nam Tram, Mui (cape) F4
Nightingale (Bach Long Vi) (isl.) F2
Panjang, Hon (Hon Tho Chau) (isl.) D5
Phu Quoc, Dao (isl.) D5
Rao Co (mt.) E3
Red (riv.) E2
Se San (riv.) E4
Sip Song Chau Thai (mts.) D2
Song Ba (riv.) F4
Song Ca (riv.) E3
Song Cai (riv.) E4
South China (sea) F4
Tonkin (gulf) E3
Varella, Mui (cape) F4
Wai, Poulo (isls.) E4
Yang Sin, Chu (mt.) F4

*See Southeast Asia, p. 85 for other part of Malaysia.

*City and suburbs.
⊙Population of district.

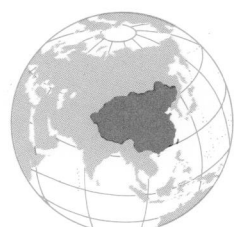

CHINA (MAINLAND)
AREA 3,691,000 sq. mi. (9,559,690 sq. km.)
POPULATION 958,090,000
CAPITAL Peking (Beijing)
LARGEST CITY Shanghai
HIGHEST POINT Mt. Everest 29,028 ft. (8,848 m.)
MONETARY UNIT yuan
MAJOR LANGUAGES Chinese, Chuang, Uigur, Yi, Tibetan, Miao, Mongol, Kazakh
MAJOR RELIGIONS Confucianism, Buddhism, Taoism, Islam

CHINA (TAIWAN)
AREA 13,971 sq. mi. (36,185 sq. km.)
POPULATION 16,609,961
CAPITAL Taipei
LARGEST CITY Taipei
HIGHEST POINT Yü Shan 13,113 ft. (3,997 m.)
MONETARY UNIT new Taiwan yüan (dollar)
MAJOR LANGUAGES Chinese, Formosan
MAJOR RELIGIONS Confucianism, Buddhism, Taoism, Christianity, tribal religions

MONGOLIA
AREA 606,163 sq. mi. (1,569,962 sq. km.)
POPULATION 1,594,800
CAPITAL Ulaanbaatar
LARGEST CITY Ulaanbaatar
HIGHEST POINT Tabun Bogdo 14,288 ft. (4,355 m.)
MONETARY UNIT tughrik
MAJOR LANGUAGES Khalkha Mongolian, Kazakh (Turkic)
MAJOR RELIGION Buddhism

HONG KONG
AREA 403 sq. mi. (1,044 sq. km.)
POPULATION 5,022,000
CAPITAL Victoria
MONETARY UNIT Hong Kong dollar
MAJOR LANGUAGES Chinese, English
MAJOR RELIGIONS Confucianism, Buddhism, Christianity

MACAU
AREA 6 sq. mi. (16 sq. km.)
POPULATION 271,000
CAPITAL Macau
MONETARY UNIT pataca
MAJOR LANGUAGES Chinese, Portuguese
MAJOR RELIGIONS Confucianism, Buddhism, Taoism, Christianity

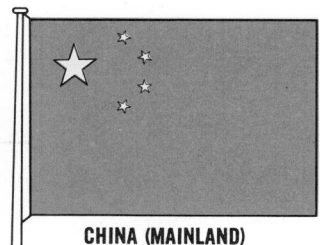

CHINA (MAINLAND)

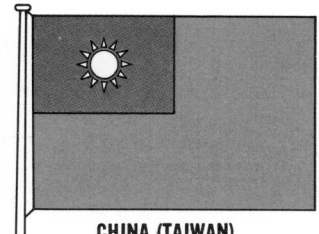

CHINA (TAIWAN)

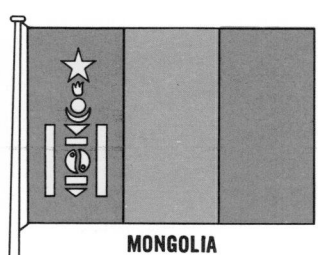

MONGOLIA

CHINA

PROVINCES

Anhui (Anhwei) 47,130,000	J5
Chekiang (Zhejiang) 37,510,000	K6
Fujian (Fukien) 24,500,000	J6
Gansu (Kansu) 18,730,000	E3
Guangdong (Kwangtung) 55,930,000	H7
Guangxi Zhuangzu (Kwangsi Chuang Aut. Reg.) 34,020,000	G7
Guizhou (Kweichow) 26,860,000	G6
Heilongkiang (Heilungkiang) 33,760,000	K2
Hebei (Hopei) 50,570,000	J4
Henan (Honan) 70,660,000	H5
Hubei (Hupei) 45,750,000	H5
Hunan 51,660,000	H6
Inner Mongolian Aut. Reg. (Nei Monggol) 8,900,000	H3
Jiangxi (Kiangsi) 31,830,000	J6
Jiangsu (Kiangsu) 58,340,000	K5
Jilin (Kirin) 24,740,000	L3
Kansu (Gansu) 18,730,000	E3
Kiangsi (Jiangxi) 31,830,000	J6
Kiangsu (Jiangsu) 58,340,000	K5
Kirin (Jilin) 24,740,000	L3
Kwangsi Chuang Aut. Reg. (Guangxi Zhuang 34,020,000	G7
Kwangtung (Guangdong) 55,930,000	H7
Kweichow (Guizhou) 26,860,000	G6
Liaoning 37,430,000	K3
Nei Monggol (Inner Mongolian Aut. Reg.) 8,900,000	H3
Ningxia Huizu (Ningsia Hui Aut. Reg.) 3,660,000	F3
Qinghai (Tsinghai) 3,650,000	E4
Shaanxi (Shensi) 27,790,000	G5
Shanxi (Shansi) 24,340,000	H4
Shandong (Shantung) 71,600,000	J4
Sichuan (Szechwan) 97,070,000	F5
Sinkiang-Uigur Aut. Reg. (Xinjiang) Uygur 12,330,000	B3
Taiwan 16,609,961	K7
Tibet Aut. Reg. (Xizang) 1,790,000	B5
Tsinghai (Qinghai) 3,650,000	E4
Xinjiang Uygur (Sinkiang-Uigur Aut. Reg.) 12,330,000	B3
Xizang (Tibet Aut. Reg.) 1,790,000	B5
Yunnan 30,920,000	F7
Zhejiang (Chekiang) 37,510,000	K6

CITIES AND TOWNS†

Aba	F5
Abagnar (Silinhot)	J3
Aihui (Aigun) (Heihe)	L1
Aksu (Aqsu)	B3
Altay	C2
Alxa Youqi	F4
Alxa Zuoqi	F4
Amoy (Xiamen) 400,000	J7
Anda (Anta)	L2
Ankang	G5
Anqing (Anking) 160,000	J5
Anshan 1,500,000	K3
Anshun	G6
Antu	L3
Anxi	E3
Anxi	E3
Anyang 225,000	H4
Aqsu (Aksu)	B3
Aratürük (Yiwu)	D3
Ar Horqin	K3
Arixang (Wenquan)	B3
Artux (Atushi)	A4
Bachu (Maralwexi)	A4
Baicheng, Jilin	K2
Baicheng (Bay), Xinjiang Uygur	B3
Bairin Zuoqi	J3
Baoding (Paoting) 350,000	J4
Baoji (Paoki) 275,000	G5
Baoshan	E7
Baoting	G8
Baotou (Paotow) 800,000	G3
Bargrax (Bohu)	C3
Batang	E5
Bay (Baicheng)	B3
Bayan Obo	G3
Ba Xian	J4
Bei'an (Pehan) 130,000	L2
Beihai (Pakhoi) 175,000	G7
Beijing (Peking) (cap.)● 8,500,000	J3
Bengbu (Pengpu) 400,000	J5
Benxi (Penki) 750,000	K3
Bohu (Bagrax)	C3
Bole	B3
Bortala (Bole)	B3
Boshan	J4
Bo Xian (Pohsien)	J5
Butha	K2
Cangzhou (Tsangchow)	J4
Canton (Guangzhou) 2,300,000	H7
Chamdo (Qamdo)	E5
Changchih (Changzhi)	H4
Changchow (Changzhou) 400,000	J5
Changchow (Zhangzhou)	J7
Changchun 1,500,000	K3
Changde (Changteh) 225,000	H6
Changhua 137,236	K7
Changji	C3
Changjiang	G8
Changsha 850,000	H6
Changteh (Changde) 225,000	H6
Changyeh (Zhangye)	F4
Changzhi (Changchih)	H4
Changzhou (Changchow) 400,000	K5
Chankiang (Zhanjiang) 220,000	H7
Chao'an (Chaochow)	J7
Chaochow (Chao'an)	J7
Chaotung (Zhaotong)	F6
Chaoyang, Liaoning	K3
Chaoyang, Guangdong	J7
Charkhlia (Ruoqiang)	C4
Chefoo (Yantai) 180,000	K4
Chengchow (Zhengzhou) 1,500,000	H5
Chengde (Chengteh) 200,000	J3
Chengdu (Chengtu) 2,000,000	F5
Chen Xian	H6
Cherchen (Qiemo)	C4
Chiai 238,713	K7
Chifeng	J3
Chinchow (Jinzhou) 750,000	K3
Chindu	E5
Chinkiang (Zhenjiang) 250,000	J5
Chinsi (Jinxi)	K3
Chinwangtao (Qinhuangdao) 400,000	K4
Chishui	G6
Chongqing (Chungking) 3,500,000	G6
Chüanchow (Quanzhou) 130,000	J7
Chuchow (Zhuzhou) 350,000	H6
Chuguchak (Tacheng)	B2
Chumatien (Zhumadian)	H5
Chungking (Chongqing) 3,500,000	G6
Chungshan (Zhongshan) 135,000	H7
Da'an (Talai)	K2
Dali	F6
Dandong (Tantung) 450,000	K3
Dan Xian	G8
Da Qaidam	E4
Datong (Tatung), Shanxi 300,000	H3
Datong, Qinghai	F4
Da Xian	G5
Dazhai	H4
Dengkou	G3
Deyang	F5
Dezhou (Tehchow)	J4
Dingxing	H4
Dongchuan	F6
Dongfang	G8
Dongsheng	H4
Dongtai	K5
Dorbiljin (Emin)	B2
Dukou	F6
Dulan	E4
Dunhua (Tunhwa)	L3
Dunhuang	E3
Duolun	J3
Duyun	G6
Duyun (Tüyün)	G6
Ejin	F3
Emin (Dorbiljin)	B2
Ergun Youqi	K1
Ergun Zuoqi	K1
Ertai	C2
Fatshan (Foshan)	H7

China and Mongolia Transportation

Railroads	————
Under Construction	‑ ‑ ‑ ‑
Connecting Roads	————
Navigable Rivers	
Canals	
Major Seaports	‡

© Copyright HAMMOND INCORPORATED, Maplewood, N.J.

(continued on following page)

Foochow (Fuzhou) 900,000	J6	Huadian	L3	Kiamusze (Jiamusi) 275,000	M2	Mudanjiang		Shangrao (Shangjao) 100,000	J6	Sinsiang (Xinxiang) 300,000	H4	Tart	D4
Foshan (Fatshan)	H7	Huaibei	J5	Kian (Ji'an) 100,000	J6	(Mutankiang) 400,000	M3	Shangshui 100,000	J5	Siping (Szeping) 180,000	L3	Tatung (Datong) 300,000	H3
Fowyang (Fuyang)	J5	Huaide (Hwaiteh)	K3	Kienyang (Qianyang)	H6	Mukden (Shenyang) 3,750,000	K3	Shanshan (Piqan)	D3	Socho (Shache)	A4	Taxkorgan	A4
Fushun 1,700,000	K3	Huainan 350,000	J5	Kingtehchen		Muli	F6	Shantou (Swatow) 400,000	J7	Soochow (Suzhou) 1,300,000	K5	Techow (Dezhou)	J4
Fusingchen (Simao)	F7	Hualien	K7	(Jingdezhen) 300,000	J6	Naqqu	D5	Shaoguan (Shiukwan) 125,000	H7	Suao	K7	Tengchow	E6
Fu Xian, Liaoning	K4	Huangling	G4	Kinhwa (Jinhua)	J6	Nanchang 900,000	J6	Shaoxing (Shaohing) 225,000	K5	Süchow (Xuzhou) 1,500,000	J5	Tianjin	E4
Fu Xian, Shaanxi	G4	Huangshi 200,000	J5	Kirin (Jilin) 1,200,000	L3	Nanchong (Nanchung) 275,000	G5	Shaoyang 275,000	H6	Suifenhe	M3	Tianshui 100,000	G5
Fuxin (Fusin) 350,000	K3	Huangzhong	F4	Kisi (Jixi) 350,000	M2	Nanjing (Nanking) 2,000,000	J5	Shashi 125,000	H5	Suihua	L2	Tianshui 100,000	G5
Fuyang (Fowyang)	J5	Huizhou	H7	Kiukiang (Jiujiang) 120,000	J6	Nanning 375,000	G7	Shenyang (Mukden) 3,750,000	K3	Suining	G5	Tieling	L3
Fuyu, Heilongjiang	K2	Hulin	M2	Kokiu (Geju) 250,000	F7	Nanping	J6	Shigatse (Xigazê)	C6	Suzhou (Soochow) 1,300,000	K5	Tienshsui (Tianshui) 100,000	F5
Fuyu, Jilin	L2	Hunchun	M3	Kongmoon (Jiangmen) 150,000	H7	Nantong 300,000	K5	Shihezi (Shihhotzu)	C3	Swatow (Shantou) 400,000	J7	Tientsin (Tianjin) 7,210,000	J4
Fuyuan, Heilongjiang	M2	Hunjiang	L3	Korla	C3	Nanyang	H5	Shijiazhuang		Szeping (Siping) 180,000	K3	Tingri	C6
Fuyuan, Yunnan	F7	Hwainan (Huainan) 350,000	J5	Kuldja (Yining) 160,000	B3	Napo	G7	(Shihkiachwang) 1,500,000	J4	Tai'an	J4	Togtoh	H3
Fuyun	C2	Hwaiteh (Huaide)	K3	Kumul (Hami)	D3	Neijiang (Neikiang) 240,000	G6	Shiquanhe	A5	Taibus	H3	Toksu (Xinhe)	B3
Fuzhou (Foochow),		Hwangshih (Huangshi) 200,000	J5	Künes (Xinyuan)	B3	Nenjiang	L2	Shiukwan (Shaoyuan) 125,000	H7	Taichow (Taizhou) 275,000	K5	Toksun	D3
Fujian 900,000	J6	Ichang (Yichang) 150,000	H5	Kunming 1,700,000	F6	Ningbo (Ningpo) 350,000	K6	Shiyan	H5	Taichung 565,255	K7	Tonghua (Tungchwan)	L3
Fuzhou, Jiangxi	J6	Ichun (Yichun) 200,000	L2	Kuqa	C3	Ningpo (Ningbo) 350,000	K6	Shizuishan (Shihsuishan)	G4	Taigu	H4	Tongjiang (Tungkiang)	M2
Ganzhou (Kanchow) 135,000	H6	Ilan	K7	Kuytun	C3	Ningxia (Yinchuan,		Shuangcheng	L2	Tainan 541,390	J7	Tongling	J5
Ganyrsa (Gartok)	B5	Ipin (Yibin) 275,000	F6	Kwangchow (Canton) 2,300,000	H7	Yinchuan) 175,000	G4	Shuangyashan 150,000	M2	Taipei 2,108,193	K7	Tongliao	K3
Gejiu (Kokiu) 250,000	F7	Jamusi (Kiamusze) 275,000	M2	Kweilin (Guilin) 225,000	G6	Niya (Minfeng)	B4	Shuo Xian	H4	Taitung	K7	Tongren	G6
Golmud (Golmo)	D4	Ji'an (Kian) 100,000	J6	Kweisui (Hohhot) 700,000	H3	Ongniud	J3	Sian (Xi'an) 1,900,000	G5	Taiyuan 2,725,000	H4	Tongyu	K3
Gonghe	F4	Jiangmen (Kongmoon) 150,000	H7	Kweiyang (Guiyang) 1,500,000	G6	Oroqen	K1	Siangfan (Xiangfan) 150,000	H5	Taizhou (Taichow) 275,000	K5	Tsangchow (Cangzhou)	J4
Guangyuan	G5	Jiangmen 120,000	J6	Lanzhou (Lanchow) 1,500,000	G4	Paicheng (Baicheng)	K2	Siangtan (Xiangtan) 300,000	H6	Talai (Da'an, Dalai)	K2	Tsiaotso (Jiaozuo) 300,000	H4
Guan Xian	F5	Jian'ou	J6	Lenghu	D4	Pakhoi (Beihai) 175,000	G7	Sianyang (Xianyang) 125,000	G5	Tali (Dali)	E6	Tsinan (Jinan) 1,500,000	J4
Guangzhou (Canton) 2,300,000	H7	Jiaozuo (Tsiaotso) 300,000	H4	Lengshuijiang	H6	Paoding (Baoding) 350,000	J4	Silinhot (Abnagar)	J3	Tangjiang	J6	Tsingkiang (Qingjiang) 110,000	J5
Guilin (Kweilin) 225,000	G6	Jiaxing (Kashing)	K5	Leshan (Loshan) 250,000	F6	Paotow (Baotou) 800,000	G3	Simao (Fusingchen)	F7	Tangshan 1,200,000	J4	Tsingshih (Jinshi) 100,000	H5
Guiyang (Kweiyang)		Jiayuguan	E4	Lhasa 175,000	D6	Pehan (Bei'an) 130,000	L2	Sinchu 208,038	K7	Tantung (Dandong) 450,000	K3	Tsingtao (Qingdao) 1,900,000	K4
Guizhou 1,500,000	G6	Jieyang	J7	Lhazê (Lhatse)	C6	Peking (Beijing)		Singtai (Xingtai)	H4	Tao'an	K3	Tsining (Jining), Nei
Guiyang, Hunan	H6	Jilin (Kirin) 1,200,000	L3	Lianyungang		(cap.) ● 8,500,000	J4	Sining (Xining) 250,000	F4	Taoyuan 105,841	K6	Monggol 160,000	H3
Gulja (Yining) 160,000	B3	Jinan (Tsinan) 1,500,000	J4	(Lienyünkang) 300,000	J5	Pengpu (Bengbu) 400,000	J5						
Guma (Pishan)	A4	Jingdezhen		Liaoyang 250,000	K3	Penki (Benxi) 750,000	K3						
Guyang	G4	(Kingtehchen) 300,000	J6	Liaoyuan 300,000	L3	Pingdingshan	H5						
Guyuan	J3	Jinghong	F7	Lijiang	F6	Pingliang	G4						
Gyaca	D6	Jingxi	G7	Linfen	H4	Pingtung 165,360	K7						
Gyangzê	C6	Jing Xian, Anhui	J5	Lingling	H6	Pingxiang, Guangxi Zhuangzu	G7						
Habahe	C2	Jing Xian, Hunan	H6	Linhe	G3	Pingxiang, Jiangxi	H6						
Haikou (Hoihow) 500,000	H7	Jinguyan	F4	Linqing (Lintsing)	J4	Piqan (Shanshan)	D3						
Hailar	D3	Jinhua (Kinhwa)	J6	Linxi	J3	Pishan (Guma)	A4						
Hami (Kumul)	D3	Jining (Tsining), Nei		Linxia (Linsia)	F4	Pohsien (Bo Xian)	J5						
Hancheng	H4	Monggol 160,000	H3	Liuzhou (Liuchow) 250,000	G7	Qamdo	E5						
Hanchung (Hanzhong) 120,000	G5	Jining (Tsining), Shandong	J4	Loho (Luohe)	H5	Qarkilik (Ruoqiang)	C4						
Handan (Hantan) 500,000	J4	Jinshi (Tsingshih) 100,000	H6	Longjiang	K2	Qianyang (Kienyang)	H6						
Hangzhou (Hangchow) 1,100,000	J5	Jinxi (Chinsi)	K3	Lopnur (Yuli)	C3	Qiemo (Qarqan)	C4						
Hantan (Handan) 500,000	H4	Jinzhou (Chinchow) 750,000	K3	Loshan (Leshan) 250,000	F6	Qingdao (Tsingtao) 1,900,000	K4						
Hanzhong (Hanchung) 120,000	G5	Jiujiang (Kiukiang) 120,000	J6	Loyang (Luoyang) 750,000	H5	Qingjiang, Jiangxi	J6						
Harbin 2,750,000	L2	Jiuquan (Kiuchüan)	E4	Lu'an	J5	Qingjiang, Anhui 110,000	J5						
Hebi	H4	Jixi (Kisi) 350,000	M2	Luchow (Luzhou) 225,000	G6	Qinhuangdao							
Hechuan (Hochwan)	G5	Juichin (Ruijin)	J6	Luda (Lüta) 4,000,000	K4	(Chinwangtao) 400,000	K4						
Hefei (Hofei) 400,000	J5	Jun Xian	H5	Luohe	H5	Qionghai	H8						
Hegang (Hokang) 350,000	L2	Kaba (Habahe)	C2	Luoyang (Loyang) 750,000	H5	Qiqihar (Tsitsihar) 1,500,000	K2						
Heihe (Aihui) (Aigun)	L1	Kaifeng 330,000	H5	Lüshun	K4	Qitai	C3						
Hekou	F7	Kaili	G6	Lüta (Lüda) 4,000,000	K4	Qog	G3						
Hengchun	K7	Kaiyuan, Liaoning	K3	Luxi	F7	Qoqek (Tacheng)	B2						
Hengshan	G4	Kaiyuan, Yunnan	F7	Luzhou (Luchow) 225,000	G6	Quanzhou (Chüanchow) 130,000	J7						
Hengyang 310,000	H6	Kalgan (Zhangjiakou) 1,000,000	J3	Ma'anshan	J5	Qu Xian, Sichuan	G5						
Hepu (Hoppo)	G7	Kanchow (Ganzhou) 135,000	H6	Manas	C3	Qu Xian, Zhejiang	J6						
Hexigten	J3	Kangding	F5	Manchouli (Manchouli)	J2	Qüxü	D6						
Hezuo	F5	Kaohsiung 1,028,334	J7	Manchouli (Manchouli)	J2	Ruijin (Juichin)	J6						
Hochwan (Hechuan)	G5	Karakax (Kara Kashi) (Moyu)	A4	Maoming (Mowming)	H7	Ruoqiang (Qarkilik)	C4						
Hofei (Hefei) 400,000	J5	Karamay	B2	Maralwexi (Bachu)	A4	Rutog	A5						
Hohhot (Huhehot) 700,000	H3	Karghalik (Yecheng)	A4	Mengcheng	J5	Sanmenxia	H5						
Hoihow (Haikou) 500,000	H7	Kashi (Kashgar) 175,000	A4	Mengzi	F7	Sanming	J6						
Hokang (Hegang) 350,000	L2	Kashing (Jiaxing)	K5	Mianyang, Hubei	H5	Sêrxü	E5						
Hoppo (Hepu)	G7	Kaxgar (Kashi) 175,000	A4	Mianyang, Sichuan	G5	Shache (Yarkand)	A4						
Horgin Youyi Qianqi		Keelung 342,604	K7	Minfeng (Niya)	B4	Shandan	F4						
(Ulanhot) 100,000	K2	Kenli	J4	Minle	F4	Shangdu	H3						
Hotan	B4	Keriya (Yutian)	B4	Mowming (Maoming)	H7	Shanghai ● 10,980,000	K5						
Houma	H4	Khotan (Hotan)	B4	Moyu (Karakax)	A4	Shangqui (Shangkiu) 250,000	J5						
Hsüchang (Xuchang)	H5												

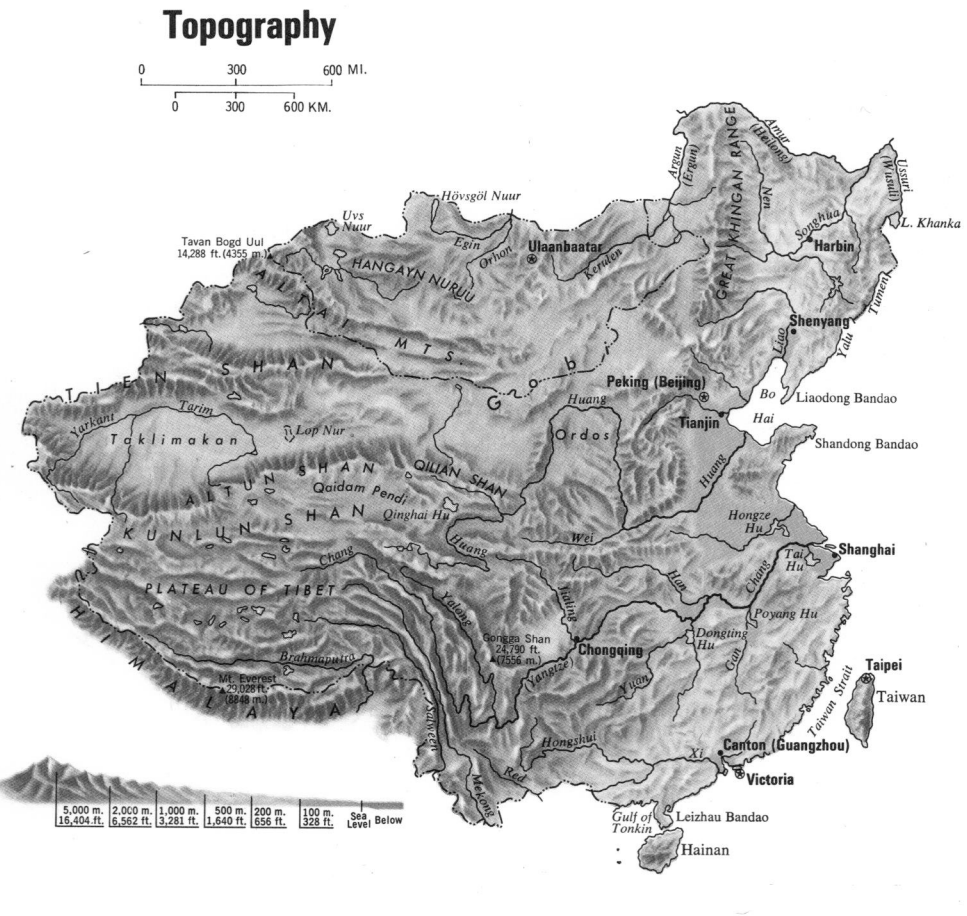

Topography

0   300   600 MI.

0   300   600 KM.

5,000 m. 2,000 m. 1,000 m. 500 m. 200 m. 100 m. Sea
16,404 ft. 6,562 ft. 3,281 ft. 1,640 ft. 656 ft. 328 ft. Level Below

On this map Chinese place-names have been rendered according to the Pinyin spelling system within the area controlled by the People's Republic of China. Alphabetically listed below are selected Chinese place-names spelled in the traditional manner, followed by the equivalent Pinyin form.

Amoy (Hsiamen)	Xiamen	Kirin	Jilin	Sian	Xi'an
Anhwei	Anhui	Kiukiang	Jiujiang	Siangtan	Xiangtan
Canton		Kwangsi	Guangxi	Sining	Xining
(Kwangchow)	Guangzhou	Kwangtung	Guangdong	Sinkiang-	
Chefoo (Yentai)	Yantai	Kweichow	Guizhou	Uighur	Xinjiang Uygur
Chekiang	Zhejiang	Kweilin	Guilin	Soochow	Suzhou
Chengchow	Zhengzhou	Kweiyang	Guiyang	Süchow	Xuzhou
Chengtu	Chengdu	Lanchow	Lanzhou	Swatow	Shantou
Chungking	Chongqing	Liuchow	Liuzhou	Szechwan	Sichuan
Foochow	Fuzhou	Loyang	Luoyang	Tachai	Dazhai
Fukien	Fujian	Lüta	Lüda	Tatung	Datong
Hangchow	Hangzhou	Mutankiang	Mudanjiang	Tibet	Xizang
Heilungkiang	Heilongjiang	Nanking	Nanjing	Tientsin	Tianjin
Hofei	Hefei	Ningpo	Ningbo	Tsinan	Jinan
Honan	Henan	Ningsia Hui	Ningxia Huizu	Tsingtao	Qingdao
Hopei	Hebei	Paoting	Baoding	Tsining	Jining
Huhehot	Hohhot	Paotow	Baotou	Tsitsihar	Qiqihar
Hupeh	Hubei	Peking	Beijing	Tsunyi	Zunyi
Hwainan	Huainan	Penki	Benxi	Tungchwan	Tongchuan
Inner Mongolia	Nei Monggol	Pishan	Guma	Tzepo	Zibo
Kansu	Gansu	Shanghai	Shanghai	Urumchi	Ürümqi
Kiangsi	Jiangxi	Shansi	Shanxi	Wusih	Wuxi
Kiangsu	Jiangsu	Shantung	Shandong	Yenan	Yan'an
Kingtehchen	Jingdezhen	Shensi	Shaanxi	Yinchwan	Yinchuan
		Shihkiachwang	Shijiazhuang		

(continued on following page)

China and Mongolia

SCALE OF MILES
0 100 200 300 400 500

SCALE OF KILOMETERS
0 100 200 300 400 500

Capitals of Countries ...... ⊛   International Boundaries ......
Provincial Capitals .... ⊙   Provincial Boundaries ....
Canals ....   Walls ....

Scale 1:19,100,000

© Copyright HAMMOND INCORPORATED, Maplewood, N.J.

† Populations of mainland cities, excluding Peking (Beijing), Shanghai and Tianjin (Tientsin), courtesy of Kingsley Davis, Office of Int'l Pop. and Research, Inst. of Int'l Studies Univ. of California.

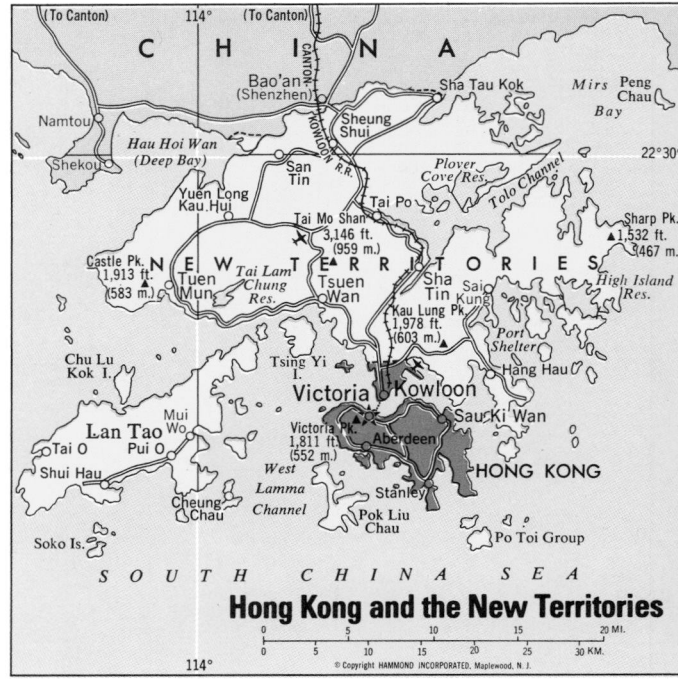

Hong Kong and the New Territories

© Copyright HAMMOND INCORPORATED, Maplewood, N.J.

Agriculture, Industry and Resources

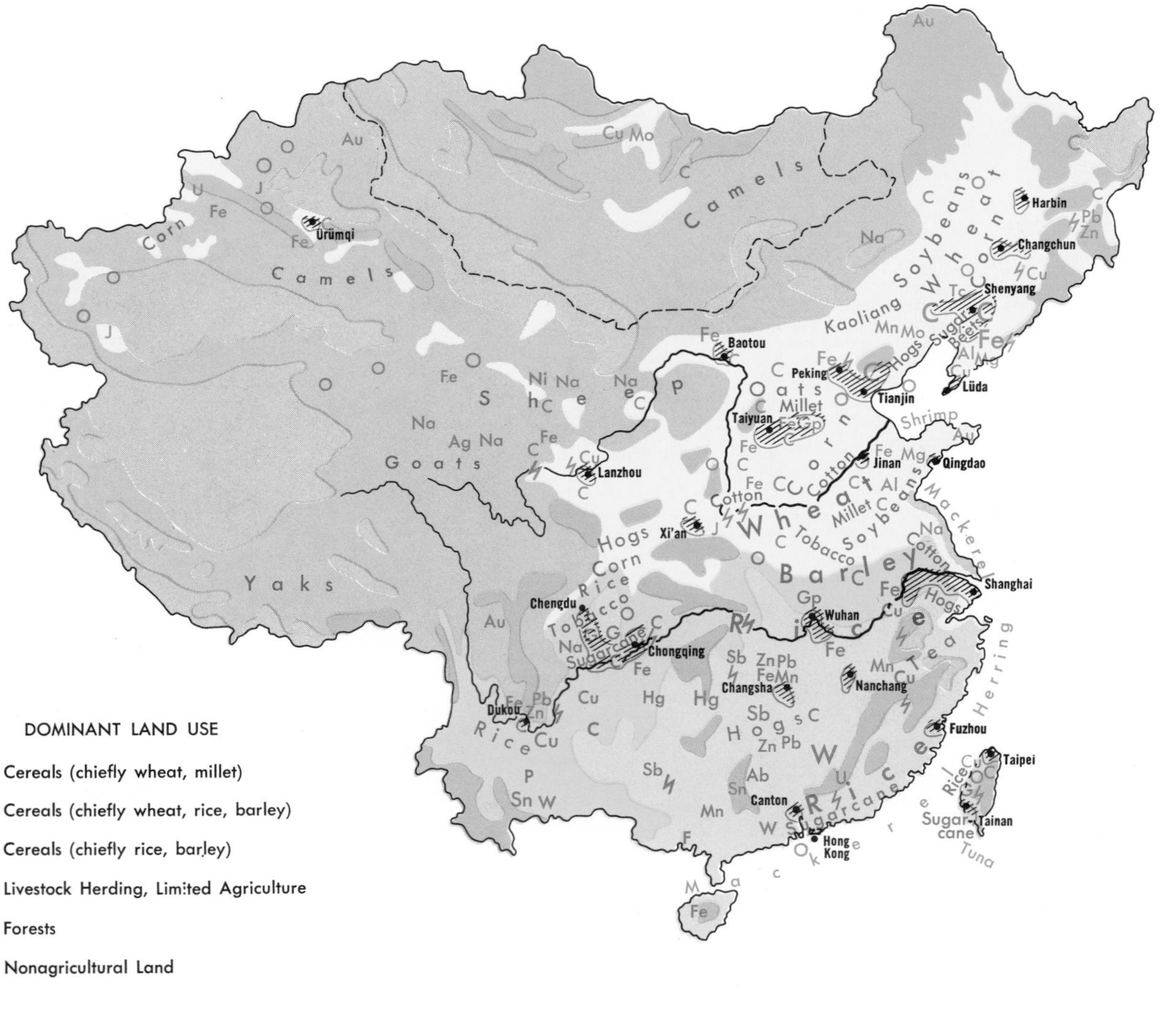

MAJOR MINERAL OCCURRENCES

Ab	Asbestos
Ag	Silver
Al	Bauxite
Au	Gold
C	Coal
Cu	Copper
F	Fluorspar
Fe	Iron Ore
G	Natural Gas
Gp	Gypsum
Hg	Mercury
J	Jade
Mg	Magnesium
Mn	Manganese
Mo	Molybdenum
Na	Salt
Ni	Nickel
O	Petroleum
P	Phosphates
Pb	Lead
Sb	Antimony
Sn	Tin
Tc	Talc
U	Uranium
W	Tungsten
Zn	Zinc

⚡ Water Power

▨ Major Industrial Areas

DOMINANT LAND USE

- Cereals (chiefly wheat, millet)
- Cereals (chiefly wheat, rice, barley)
- Cereals (chiefly rice, barley)
- Livestock Herding, Limited Agriculture
- Forests
- Nonagricultural Land

AREA 145,730 sq. mi. (377,441 sq. km.)
POPULATION 117,057,485
CAPITAL Tokyo
LARGEST CITY Tokyo
HIGHEST POINT Fuji 12,389 ft. (3,776 m.)
MONETARY UNIT yen
MAJOR LANGUAGE Japanese
MAJOR RELIGIONS Buddhism, Shintoism

AREA 46,540 sq. mi. (120,539 sq. km.)
POPULATION 17,914,000
CAPITAL P'yŏngyang
LARGEST CITY P'yŏngyang
HIGHEST POINT Paektu 9,003 ft. (2,744 m.)
MONETARY UNIT won
MAJOR LANGUAGE Korean
MAJOR RELIGIONS Confucianism, Buddhism, Ch'ondogyo

AREA 38,175 sq. mi. (98,873 sq. km.)
POPULATION 37,448,836
CAPITAL Seoul
LARGEST CITY Seoul
HIGHEST POINT Halla 6,398 ft. (1,950 m.)
MONETARY UNIT won
MAJOR LANGUAGE Korean
MAJOR RELIGIONS Confucianism, Buddhism, Ch'ondogyo, Christianity

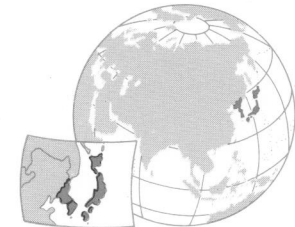

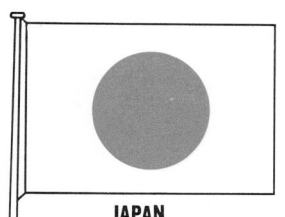

JAPAN

NORTH KOREA

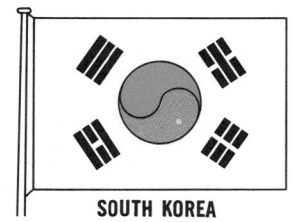

SOUTH KOREA

JAPAN

PREFECTURES

Aichi 5,923,569 .....H6
Akita 1,232,481 .....J4
Aomori 1,468,646 .....K3
Chiba 4,149,147 .....P2
Ehime 1,465,215 .....F7
Fukui 773,599 .....G5
Fukuoka 4,292,963 .....D7
Fukushima 1,970,616 .....K5
Gifu 1,867,978 .....H6
Gumma 1,756,480 .....J5
Hiroshima 2,646,324 .....E6
Hokkaido 5,338,206 .....K2
Hyogo 4,992,140 .....H7
Ibaraki 2,342,198 .....K5
Ishikawa 1,069,872 .....H5
Iwate 1,385,563 .....K4
Kagawa 961,292 .....G6
Kagoshima 1,723,902 .....E8
Kanagawa 6,397,748 .....O2
Kochi 808,397 .....F7
Kumamoto 1,715,273 .....E7
Kyoto 2,424,856 .....J7
Mie 1,626,002 .....H6
Miyagi 1,955,267 .....K4
Miyazaki 1,085,055 .....E8
Nagano 2,017,564 .....J5
Nagasaki 1,571,912 .....D7
Nara 1,077,491 .....J8
Niigata 2,391,938 .....J5
Oita 1,190,314 .....E7
Okayama 1,814,305 .....F6
Okinawa 1,042,572 .....N6
Osaka 8,278,925 .....J8
Saga 837,674 .....E7

Saitama 4,821,340 .....O2
Shiga 985,621 .....J7
Shimane 768,886 .....F6
Shizuoka 3,308,799 .....H6
Tochigi 1,698,003 .....K5
Tokushima 805,166 .....G7
Tokyo 11,673,554 .....O2
Tottori 581,311 .....F6
Toyama 1,070,791 .....H5
Wakayama 1,072,118 .....H6
Yamagata 1,220,302 .....K4
Yamaguchi 1,555,218 .....E6
Yamanashi 783,050 .....J6

CITIES and TOWNS

Abashiri 43,825 .....M1
Ageo 146,358 .....O2
Aikawa 13,546 .....H4
Aizuwakamatsu 108,650 .....J5
Ajigasawa 18,086 .....J3
Akashi 234,905 .....H8
Aki 24,480 .....F7
Akita 261,246 .....J4
Akkeshi 16,778 .....M2
Akune 30,295 .....E7
Amagasaki 545,783 .....H8
Amagi 42,725 .....E7
Anan 60,439 .....G7
Aomori 264,222 .....K3
Asahi 34,028 .....K6
Asahikawa 320,526 .....L2
Ashibetsu 36,520 .....L2
Ashikaga 162,359 .....J5
Ashiya 76,211 .....H8
Atami 51,437 .....J6
Atsugi 108,955 .....O2
Awaji 9,623 .....H8

Ayabe 43,490 .....G6
Beppu 133,894 .....E7
Bibai 38,416 .....L2
Biratori 9,331 .....L2
Chiba 659,356 .....P2
Chichibu 61,798 .....J5
Chigasaki 152,023 .....O3
Chitose 61,031 .....L2
Chofu 175,924 .....O2
Choshi 90,374 .....K6
Daito 110,829 .....J8
Ebetsu 77,624 .....K2
Eniwa 39,884 .....K2
Esashi, Hokkaido 10,172 .....L1
Esashi, Hokkaido 14,409 .....J3
Esashi, Iwate 36,336 .....K4
Fuchu, Hiroshima 50,217 .....F6
Fuchu, Tokyo 182,474 .....O2
Fuji 199,195 .....J6
Fujieda 90,358 .....J6
Fujisawa 265,975 .....O3
Fukagawa 36,000 .....L2
Fukuchiyama 60,003 .....G6
Fukue 32,018 .....D7
Fukui 231,364 .....G5
Fukuoka 1,002,201 .....D7
Fukushima 246,531 .....K5
Fukuyama 329,714 .....F6
Funabashi 423,101 .....P2
Furukawa 54,356 .....K4
Gifu 408,707 .....H6
Gobo 30,272 .....G7
Gose 37,554 .....J8
Gosen 39,376 .....J5
Goshogawara 49,040 .....K3
Gotsu 27,992 .....F6
Habikino 94,160 .....J8
Haboro 13,624 .....K1

Hachinohe 224,366 .....K3
Hachioji 322,580 .....O2
Hadano 103,663 .....O3
Hagi 52,724 .....E6
Hakodate 307,453 .....K3
Hakui 28,726 .....H5
Hamada 50,316 .....E6
Hamamatsu 468,884 .....H6
Hanamaki 65,826 .....K4
Hanno 55,926 .....O2
Haramachi 43,483 .....K5
Hayama 24,026 .....O3
Higashiosaka 524,750 .....J8
Hikone 85,066 .....H6
Himeji 436,086 .....G6
Hirari 61,789 .....H5
Hino 126,847 .....O2
Hirakata 297,618 .....J7
Hirara 29,301 .....L7
Hirata 30,942 .....F6
Hiratsuka 195,635 .....O3
Hiroo 11,399 .....L2
Hirosaki 164,911 .....K3
Hiroshima 852,611 .....E6
Hitachi 202,383 .....K5
Hitachiota 35,322 .....K5
Hitoyoshi 41,118 .....E7
Hofu 105,540 .....E6
Hondo 40,432 .....E7
Honjo 40,488 .....J4
Hyuga 53,448 .....E7
Ibaraki 210,286 .....J7
Ibusuki 32,339 .....E8
Ichihara 194,068 .....P3
Ichikawa 319,291 .....P2
Ichinohe 21,433 .....K3
Ichinomiya 238,463 .....H6
Ichinoseki 59,122 .....K4

Ide 9,112 .....J7
Iida 77,112 .....H6
Iizuka 75,417 .....E6
Ikeda, Hokkaido 12,306 .....L2
Ikeda, Osaka 100,268 .....H7
Ikoma 48,848 .....J8
Ikuno 6,658 .....G6
Imabari 119,726 .....F6
Imari 60,913 .....D7
Imazu 11,519 .....H6
Ina 54,468 .....H6
Isahaya 73,341 .....D7
Ise 104,957 .....H6
Ishigaki 34,657 .....L7
Ishige 19,220 .....P2
Ishinomaki 115,085 .....K4
Ishioka 43,679 .....K5
Itami 171,978 .....H7
Ito 68,072 .....J6
Itoigawa 36,646 .....H5
Itoman 39,363 .....N6
Iwaizumi 20,219 .....L4
Iwakuni 111,069 .....E6
Iwami 16,063 .....G6
Iwamizawa 72,305 .....L2
Iwanai 25,823 .....K2
Iwasaki 4,437 .....J3
Iwata 67,665 .....H6
Iwatsuki 83,825 .....O2
Iyo 27,805 .....F7
Izuhara 18,460 .....D6
Izumiotsu 66,250 .....J8
Izumisano 86,139 .....G6
Izumo 71,568 .....F6
Joetsu 123,418 .....H5
Joyo 58,923 .....J7

Kadoma 143,238 .....J7
Kaga 71,599 .....H5
Kagoshima 456,827 .....E8
Kaizuka 79,506 .....H8
Kakogawa 169,293 .....G6
Kamaishi 68,981 .....L4
Kamakura 165,552 .....O3
Kameoka 58,184 .....J7
Kamiisco 27,229 .....K3
Kaminoyama 37,858 .....J4
Kamiyaku 8,668 .....E8
Kamo 8,953 .....J7
Kanazawa 395,263 .....H5
Kanonji 44,131 .....F6
Kanoya 67,951 .....E8
Kanuma 81,799 .....J5
Karatsu 75,224 .....D7
Kaseda 24,969 .....D8
Kashihara 95,701 .....J8
Kashiwa 203,065 .....P2
Kashiwara 63,586 .....J8
Kashiwazaki 80,351 .....J5
Kasugai 213,867 .....H6
Kasukabe 121,639 .....O2
Katsuta 79,996 .....K5
Katsuura 26,755 .....K6
Kawachinagano 66,936 .....J8
Kawagoe 225,465 .....O2
Kawaguchi 345,538 .....J8
Kawanishi 115,773 .....H7
Kawasaki 1,014,951 .....O2
Kesennuma 66,616 .....K4
Kikonai 10,034 .....K3
Kimitsu 76,016 .....O3
Kiryu 134,239 .....J5
Kisarazu 96,840 .....P3
Kishiwada 174,952 .....J8
Kitaibaraki 44,332 .....K5

Kitakami 48,759 .....K4
Kitakata 37,471 .....J5
Kitakyushu 1,058,058 .....E6
Kitami 91,519 .....L2
Kizu 11,890 .....J7
Kobayashi 38,325 .....E8
Kobe 1,360,605 .....H7
Kochi 280,962 .....F7
Kodaira 156,181 .....O2
Kofu 193,879 .....J6
Koga 55,973 .....J5
Koganei 102,714 .....O2
Kokubu 31,660 .....E8
Komagane 30,318 .....H6
Komatsu 100,273 .....H5
Koriyama 264,628 .....K5
Koshigaya 195,917 .....O2
Koyama 16,394 .....E8
Kubohama 17,817 .....F7
Kuji 38,122 .....K3
Kuki 45,797 .....O2
Kumagaya 131,485 .....J5
Kumamoto 488,166 .....E7
Kumano 27,026 .....J7
Kumiyama 11,540 .....J7
Kunitachi 65,207 .....F6
Kurashiki 392,755 .....F6
Kurayoshi 50,785 .....F6
Kuroiso 42,349 .....K5
Kurume 204,474 .....E7
Kushikino 30,456 .....E8
Kushima 30,038 .....E8
Kushimoto 18,997 .....G7
Kushiro 206,840 .....M2
Kyonan 13,067 .....O3
Kyoto 1,461,059 .....J7
Machida 255,305 .....O2
Maebashi 250,241 .....J5
Maihara 12,845 .....G6
Maizuru 97,780 .....G6
Makubetsu 18,444 .....L2
Makurazaki 29,685 .....O3
Mashike 9,312 .....K2
Masuda 50,734 .....E6
Matsubara 132,462 .....H8
Matsue 127,440 .....F6
Matsumae 18,307 .....J3
Matsuo 47,888 .....O3
Matsumoto 185,595 .....H5
Matsusaka 108,893 .....H6
Matsuto 36,170 .....H5
Matsuyama 367,323 .....F7
Mihara 83,679 .....F6
Miki 53,731 .....H7
Mikuni 21,602 .....G5
Minamata 36,782 .....E7
Minobu 10,345 .....H6
Minoo 79,621 .....J7
Misawa 37,437 .....K3
Mitaka 164,950 .....O2
Mito 197,953 .....K5
Mitsukaido 38,820 .....P2
Miyako 61,912 .....L4
Miyakonojo 118,289 .....E8
Miyazaki 234,347 .....E8
Miyazu 30,194 .....G6
Miyoshi 37,193 .....F6
Mizusawa 52,266 .....K4
Mobara 64,942 .....K6
Mombetsu 32,825 .....L1
Monbetsu 15,029 .....L2
Mooka 47,345 .....K5
Mori 17,030 .....K2
Moriguchi 178,383 .....J7
Morioka 216,223 .....K4
Motobu 17,823 .....H6
Muko 45,886 .....J7
Murakami 32,939 .....J4
Muroran 158,715 .....K2
Muroto 26,660 .....G7
Musashino 139,508 .....O2
Mutsu 44,646 .....K3
Nachikatsuura 23,596 .....H7
Nagahama, Ehime 13,144 .....F7
Nagahama, Shiga 54,064 .....H6
Nagano 306,637 .....J5
Nagaoka, Kyoto 65,557 .....J7
Nagaoka, Niigata 171,742 .....J5
Nagaokakyo 65,557 .....J7
Nagasaki 450,194 .....D7
Nagato 27,327 .....E6
Nago 65,797 .....N6
Nagoya 2,079,740 .....H6
Naha 295,006 .....N6
Nakaminato 33,147 .....K5
Nakamura 34,437 .....F7
Nakasato 14,248 .....K3
Nakatsu 59,111 .....E7
Nanao 49,493 .....H5
Nankoku 42,832 .....F7
Nara 257,538 .....J8
Narashino 117,852 .....P2
Nayoro 35,145 .....L1
Naze 46,359 .....N6
Nemuro 45,817 .....M2
Neyagawa 254,311 .....J7
Nichinan 52,171 .....E8
Niigata 423,188 .....J5
Niihama 131,712 .....F6
Niimi 30,014 .....F6
Niitsu 58,970 .....J5
Nishinomiya 400,622 .....H8

Agriculture, Industry and Resources

DOMINANT LAND USE

- Cereals, Cash Crops
- Truck Farming, Horticulture
- Mixed Farming, Dairy
- Rice
- Forests, Scrub

MAJOR MINERAL OCCURRENCES

Ag Silver
Au Gold
C Coal
Cu Copper
Fe Iron Ore
G Natural Gas
Gr Graphite
Mg Magnesium

Mn Manganese
Mo Molybdenum
O Petroleum
Pb Lead
Py Pyrites
U Uranium
W Tungsten
Zn Zinc

⚡ Water Power
▨ Major Industrial Areas

(continued on following page)

80 Japan and Korea
(continued)

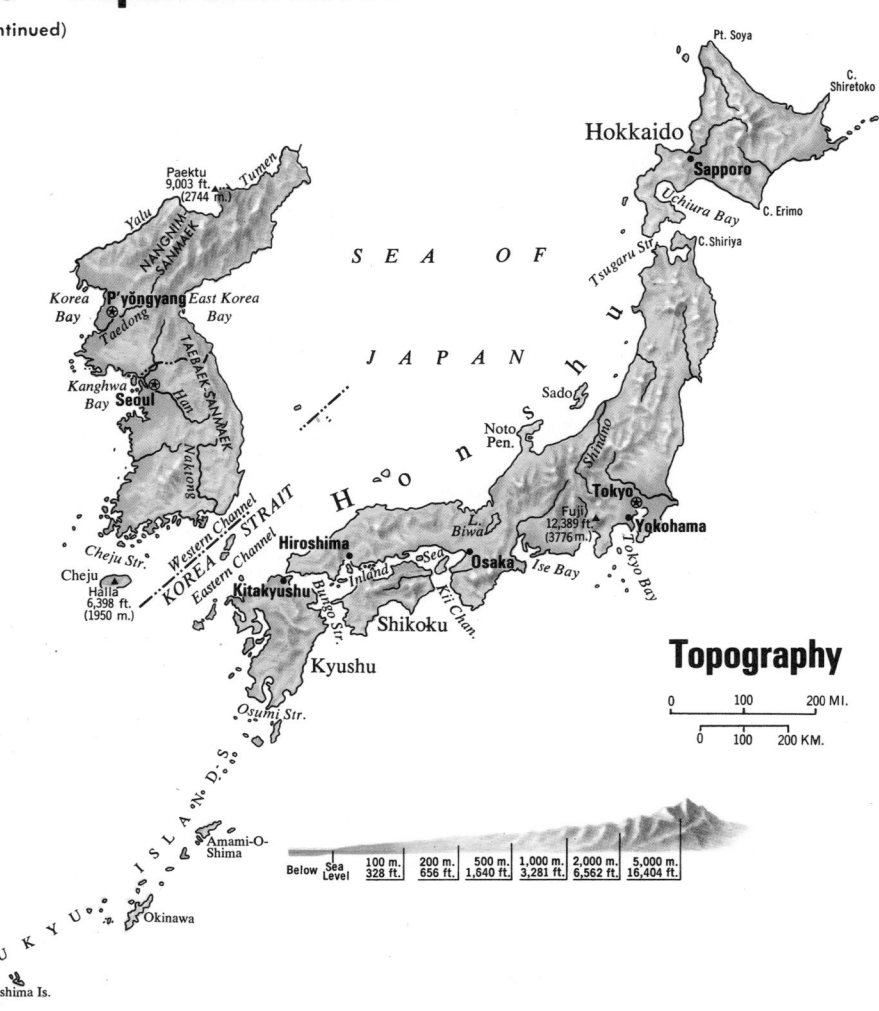

Topography

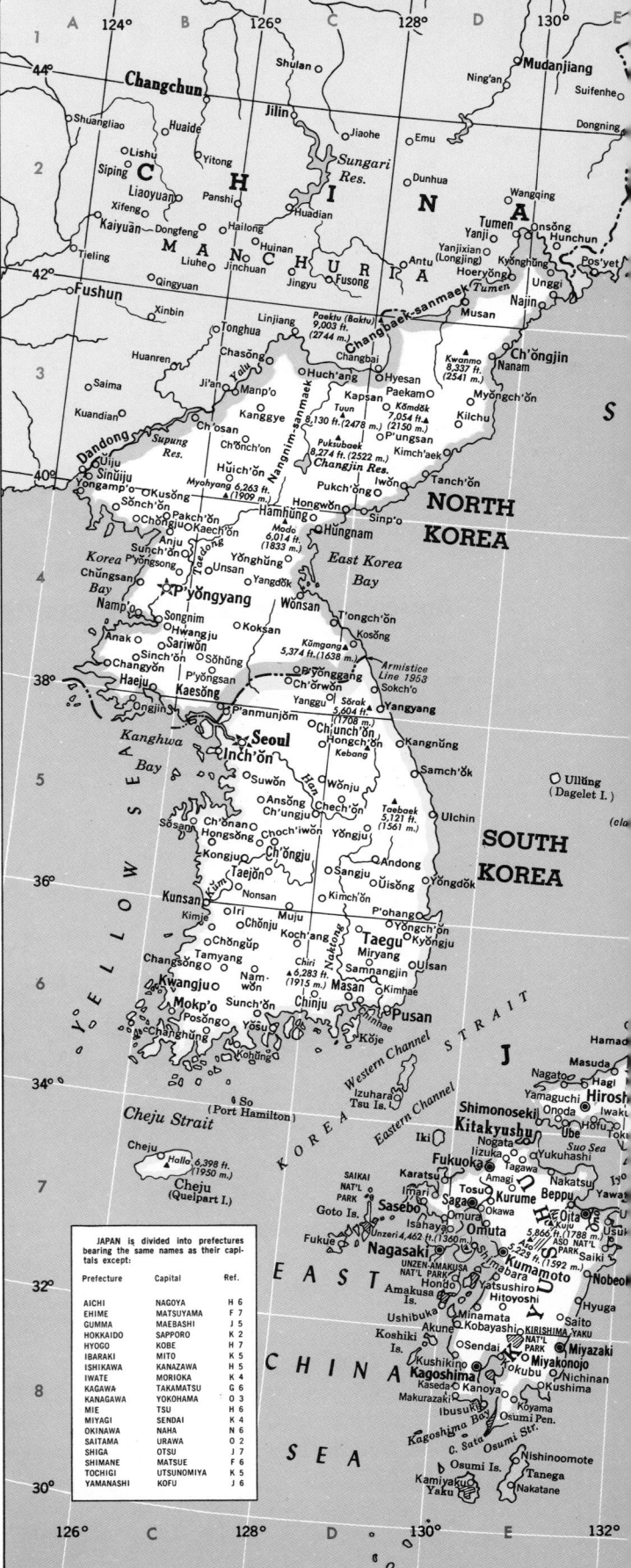

JAPAN is divided into prefectures bearing the same names as their capitals except:

Prefecture	Capital	Ref.
AICHI	NAGOYA	H 6
EHIME	MATSUYAMA	F 7
GUMMA	MAEBASHI	J 5
HOKKAIDO	SAPPORO	K 2
HYOGO	KOBE	H 7
IBARAKI	MITO	K 5
ISHIKAWA	KANAZAWA	H 5
IWATE	MORIOKA	K 4
KAGAWA	TAKAMATSU	G 6
KANAGAWA	YOKOHAMA	O 3
MIE	TSU	H 6
MIYAGI	SENDAI	K 4
OKINAWA	NAHA	N 6
SAITAMA	URAWA	O 2
SHIGA	OTSU	J 7
SHIMANE	MATSUE	F 6
TOCHIGI	UTSUNOMIYA	K 5
YAMANASHI	KOFU	J 6

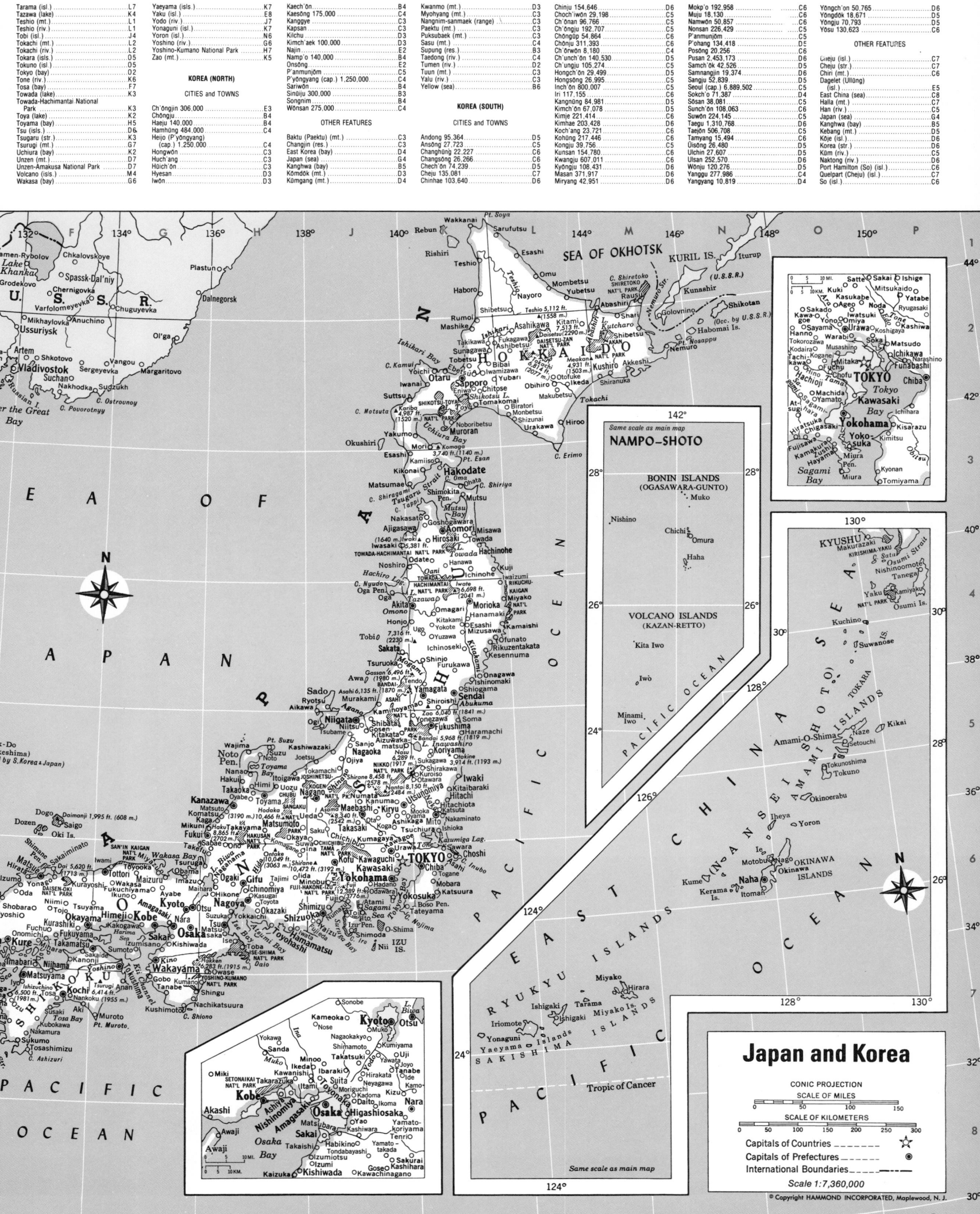

Japan and Korea

CONIC PROJECTION

SCALE OF MILES

SCALE OF KILOMETERS

Capitals of Countries _____ ☆
Capitals of Prefectures _____ ◉
International Boundaries _____

Scale 1:7,360,000

© Copyright HAMMOND INCORPORATED, Maplewood, N.J.

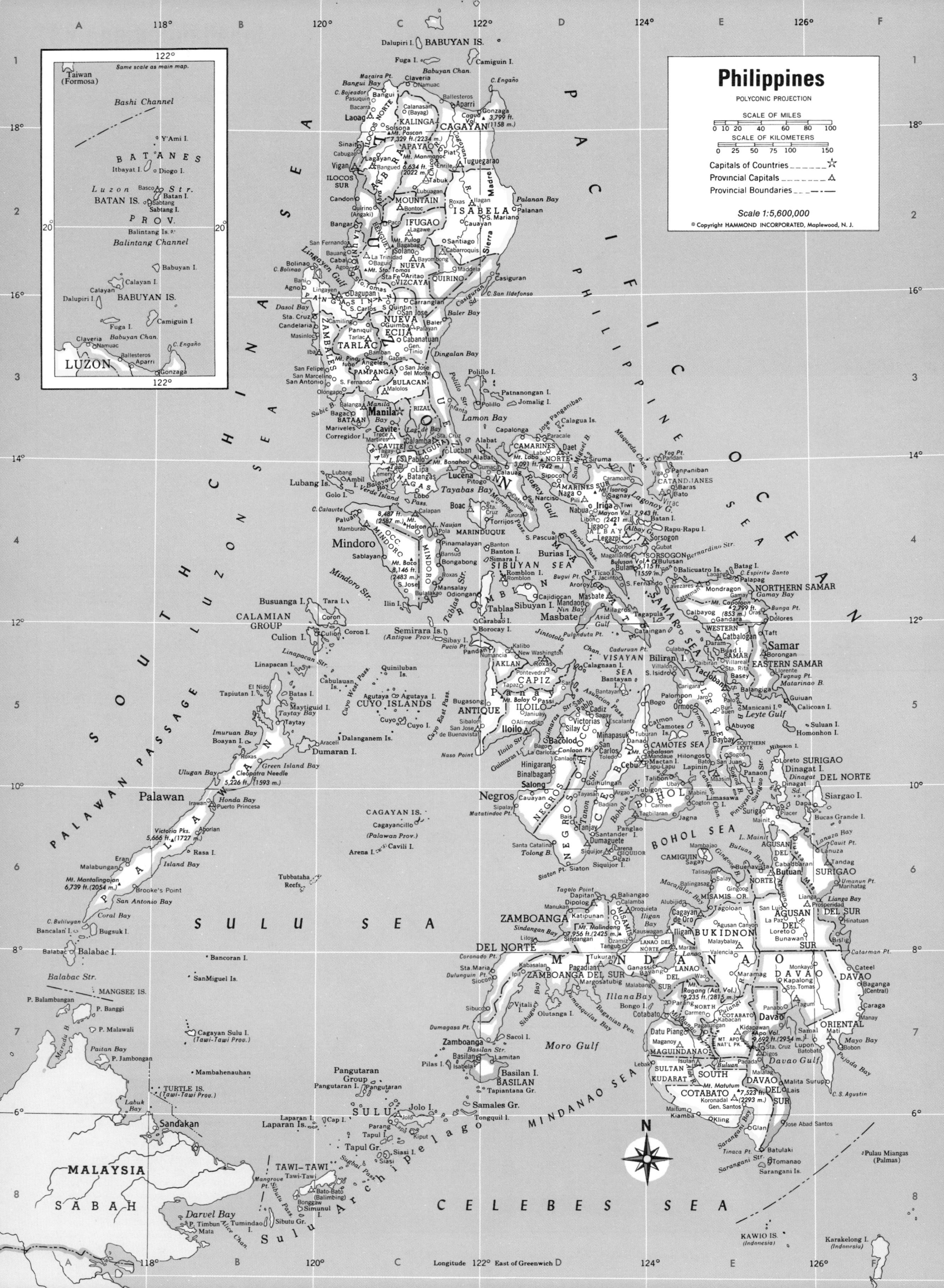

Philippines

POLYCONIC PROJECTION

SCALE OF MILES

0 10 20 40 60 80 100

SCALE OF KILOMETERS

0 25 50 75 100 150

Capitals of Countries ☆
Provincial Capitals △
Provincial Boundaries

Scale 1:5,600,000

© Copyright HAMMOND INCORPORATED, Maplewood, N. J.

Taiwan (Formosa)

Bashi Channel

Same scale as main map.

B A T A N E S

Luzon Str.

BATAN IS.

P R O V.

Balintang Is.

Balintang Channel

BABUYAN IS.

LUZON

Longitude 122° East of Greenwich

Philippines 83

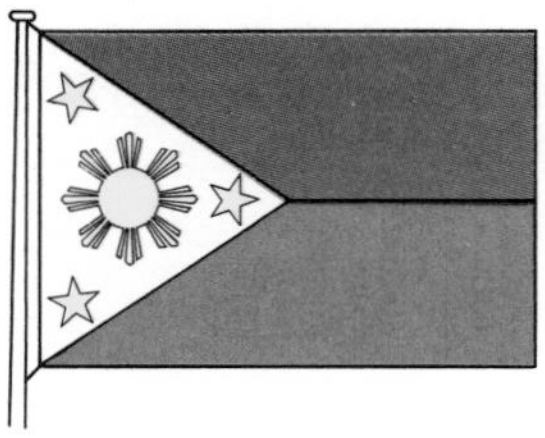

AREA 115,707 sq. mi. (299,681 sq. km.)
POPULATION 47,914,017
CAPITAL Manila
LARGEST CITY Manila
HIGHEST POINT Apo 9,692 ft. (2,954 m.)
MONETARY UNIT piso
MAJOR LANGUAGES Pilipino (Tagalog), English, Spanish, Bisayan, Ilocano, Bikol
MAJOR RELIGIONS Roman Catholicism, Islam, Protestantism, tribal religions

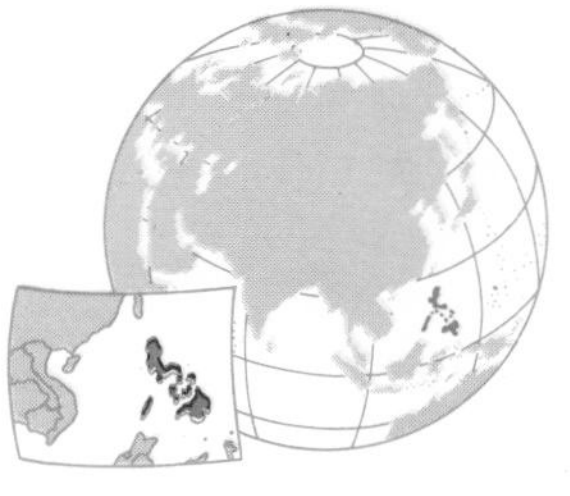

PROVINCES

Abra 168,196 C2
Agusan del Norte 366,721 E6
Agusan del Sur 260,576 E6
Aklan 325,491 D5
Albay 803,274 D4
Antique 344,905 D5
Basilan 199,029 D7
Bataan 321,860 C3
Batanes 12,111 A2
Batangas 1,173,767 C4
Benguet 355,577 C2
Bohol 805,924 E6
Bukidnon 630,128 E6
Bulacan 1,095,963 C3
Cagayan 712,029 C1
Camarines Norte 307,995 D3
Camarines Sur 1,100,044 D4
Camiguin 57,128 E6
Capiz 492,766 D5
Catanduanes 175,657 E4
Cavite 771,796 C3
Cebu 2,090,317 D5
Davao del Norte 692,654 E7
Davao del Sur 1,134,436 E7
Davao Oriental 341,586 F7
Eastern Samar 321,477 E5
Ifugao 111,403 C2
Ilocos Norte 393,485 C1
Ilocos Sur 443,591 C2
Iloilo 1,432,000 D5
Isabela 870,389 C2
Kalinga-Apayao 190,118 C1
Laguna 972,730 C3
Lanao del Norte 429,260 E6
Lanao del Sur 405,627 E7
La Union 453,211 C2
Leyte 1,302,377 E5
Maguindanao 542,104 E7
Manila 5,924,563 C3
Marinduque 178,725 C4
Masbate 550,444 D4
Misamis Occidental 391,013 D6
Misamis Oriental 694,423 E6
Mountain 103,052 C2
National Capital Region (Manila) 5,924,563 C3
Negros Occidental 1,936,770 D6
Negros Oriental 822,923 D6
North Cotabato 549,521 E7
Northern Samar 383,245 E4
Nueva Ecija 1,069,406 C3
Nueva Vizcaya 240,962 C2
Occidental Mindoro 222,025 C4
Oriental Mindoro 446,857 C4
Palawan 370,991 B6
Pampanga 1,175,314 C3
Pangasinan 1,636,520 C3
Quezon 1,129,138 C3
Quirino 83,232 C2
Rizal 552,312 C3
Romblon 193,190 D4
Siquijor 70,161 D6
Sorsogon 499,614 E4
South Cotabato 768,321 E7
Southern Leyte 256,581 E5
Sultan Kudarat 285,459 E7
Sulu 317,876 C7
Surigao del Norte 346,491 F5
Surigao del Sur 373,705 F6
Tarlac 687,980 C3
Tawi-Tawi 187,403 B8
Western Samar 509,073 E5
Zambales 443,859 C3
Zamboanga del Norte 583,550 D6
Zamboanga del Sur 1,178,700 D7

CITIES and TOWNS

Angeles 185,995 C3
Aparri 14,597 C1
Bacolod 266,604 D5
Bago 103,166 D5
Baguio 118,611 C2
Bais 49,301 D6
Balanga 1,298 C3
Baler• 14,632 C3
Balimbing (Bato-Bato) 3,880 C8
Bangued 10,482 C2
Bantayan 11,771 D5
Basco• 3,757 A2
Basilan 171,266 C7
Batangas 143,554 C4
Bato-Bato 3,880 C8
Baybay 11,989 E5
Bayombong 11,697 C2
Binalbagan 17,456 D5
Bislig 26,625 F6
Boac 3,497 C4
Bogo 11,069 E5
Bontoc 3,336 C2
Bulan 19,716 D4
Burauen 12,172 E5
Butuan 172,404 E6
Cabanatuan 138,297 C3
Cabarroquis C2
Cadiz 128,839 D5
Cagayan de Oro 228,409 E6
Calamba, Laguna 22,750 C3
Calapan 11,376 C4
Calbayog 110,938 E4
Camiling 12,996 C3
Canlaon 28,785 D5
Carigara 11,824 E5
Catarman 13,018 E4
Catbalogan 18,413 E5
Catmon• 14,837 E5
Cavite 87,813 C3
Cebu 489,208 D5
Cotabato 88,486 D7
Daet 23,739 D3
Dagupan 98,362 C2
Danao 56,957 D5
Dapitan 54,698 D6
Davao 611,311 E7
Digos 17,334 E7
Dipolog 61,928 D6
Dumaguete 63,411 D6
Escalante 16,324 D5
Ganassi• 13,227 D7
Gapan 11,958 C3
General Santos 146,556 E7
Gingoog 81,098 E6
Gubat 11,369 E4
Guimba 10,077 C3
Gumaca 9,459 D4
Hinigaran 10,864 D5
Iba 4,486 B3
Ilagan 11,494 C2
Iligan 165,742 E6
Iloilo 244,211 D5
Iriga 66,117 D4
Isabela 12,879 C7
Isulan 10,075 E7
Jolo 46,586 C8
Jose Panganiban 9,970 D3
Kalibo 10,564 D5
Kauswagan• 12,316 E6
Kidapawan 11,344 E7
Koronadal 14,003 E7
La Carlota 42,651 D5
Lagawe 3,038 C2
Lais 15,209 E7
Laoag 69,648 C1
Lapu-Lapu 98,860 E5
La Trinidad• 18,551 C2
Lazi• 14,875 D6
Legazpi 100,488 D4
Lianga 12,689 E6
Lingayen 15,333 C2
Lipa 121,162 C4
Loreto, Agusan del Sur• 13,057 E6
Lucban 18,466 C3
Lucena 107,872 C4
Maasin 12,661 E5
Maganoy 1,648 E7
Mainit 3,559 E6
Malabang 9,244 D7
Malaybalay 10,193 E6
Malita 9,705 E7
Malolos 73,996 C3
Mandaue 110,665 E5
Manila (cap.) 1,626,249 C3
Marawi 53,198 E6
Mariveles 4,502 C3
Masbate 17,749 D4
Mati 16,186 F7
Mondragon• 14,974 E4
Naga 90,712 D4
Olongapo 156,312 C3
Ormoc 104,912 E5
Oroquieta 47,176 D6
Ozamiz 78,036 D6
Padada• 14,402 E7
Pagadian 80,519 D7
Palayan 14,959 C3
Paniqui 11,789 C3
Parang, Sulu• 21,115 C8
Prosperidad 3,043 F6
Puerto Princesa 59,347 B6
Romblon 4,241 D4
Roxas, Capiz 81,183 D5
Roxas, Isabela 9,849 C2
Sabiayan• 18,256 C4
Sagay, Negros Occ. 36,855 D5
Sagnay• 16,968 D4
Salong 35,137 D5
San Antonio 13,270 B3
San Carlos, Negros Occ. 93,268 D5
San Carlos, Pangasinan 101,254 C3
San Fernando, La Union 11,084 C2
San Fernando, Pampanga 84,362 C3
San Isidro• 23,569 E5
San Jose, Nueva Ecija 64,250 C3
San Jose, Occ. Mindoro 10,388 C4
San Mariano• 20,227 D2
San Pablo, Laguna 131,686 C3
Santa Cruz, Davao del Sur 9,787 E7
Santa Cruz, Laguna 47,114 C3
Santa Rita• 20,713 E5
Santiago• 49,688 C2
Siasi 9,930 C8
Silay 104,018 D5
Sindangan 10,965 D6
Sipalay• 34,771 D6
Sipocot• 38,153 D4
Siquijor 766 D6
Solano 14,274 C2
Solsona• 12,803 C1
Sorsogon 19,008 E4
Surigao 78,235 E6
Tacloban 102,609 E5
Tagaytay 16,312 C3
Tagbilaran 42,275 E6
Tagum 17,161 E7
Tangub 44,903 D6
Tanjay 12,676 D6
Tarlac 23,547 C3
Toledo 91,618 D5
Tuguegarao 14,116 C2
Tukuran• 19,274 D7
Victorias 13,416 D5
Vigan 30,252 C2
Virac 10,314 E4
Zamboanga 344,275 C7

OTHER FEATURES

Abra (riv.) C2
Agusan (riv.) E6
Agutaya (isl.) C5
Alabat (isl.) D3
Ambil (isl.) C4
Apo (vol.) E7
Asid (gulf) D4
Babuyan (isl.) B2
Baganian (pen.) D7
Balabac (isl.) A7
Balayan (bay) C4
Balicuatro (isls.) E4
Balintang (chan.) A2
Baloy (mt.) D5
Bancalan (isl.) A6
Bantayan (isl.) D5
Banton (isl.) D4
Bashi (chan.) A1
Basilan (isl.) D7
Batag (isl.) E4
Batan, Albay (isl.) E4
Batan, Batanes (isl.) B2
Batan (isls.) A2
Batas (isl.) B5
Bay, Laguna de (lake) C3
Biliran (isl.) E5
Bohol (isl.) E6
Bojeador (cape) C1
Bongo (isl.) D7
Borocay (isl.) D5
Buad (isl.) E5
Bucas Grande (isl.) F6
Bugsuk (isl.) A6
Buliluyan (cape) A6
Bunga (pt.) E4
Burias (isl.) D4
Busuanga (isl.) B4
Cabalasan (mt.) E5
Cabulauan (isls.) C5
Cagayan (isls.) C6
Cagayan (riv.) C2
Cagayan Sulu (isl.) B7
Cagua (vol.) D1
Calagnaan (isl.) D5
Calagua (isls.) D3
Calamian Group (isls.) B4

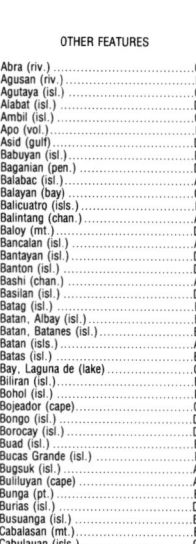

Topography

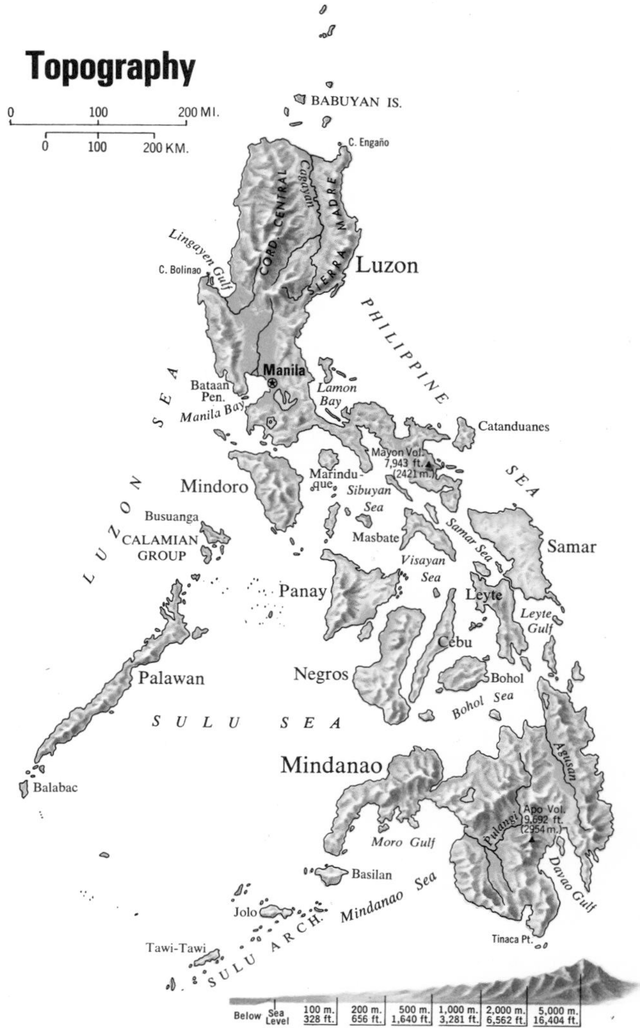
0 100 200 MI.
0 100 200 KM.
BABUYAN IS.
C. Engaño
Lingayen Gulf
C. Bolinao
CORD. CENTRAL
SIERRA MADRE
Cagayan
Luzon
PHILIPPINE
Bataan Pen.
Manila
Manila Bay
Lamon Bay
Catanduanes
Mayon Vol. 7,943 ft. (2421 m.)
SEA
Mindoro
Marinduque
Sibuyan Sea
Busuanga
CALAMIAN GROUP
Masbate
Samar Sea
Samar
LUZON
Visayan Sea
Panay
Leyte
Leyte Gulf
Cebu
Palawan
Negros
Bohol
Bohol Sea
SULU SEA
Mindanao
Agusan
Balabac
Apo Vol. 9,692 ft. (2954 m.)
Pulangi
Moro Gulf
Davao Gulf
Basilan
Jolo
Mindanao Sea
Tinaca Pt.
Tawi-Tawi
SULU ARCH.
Below Sea Level 100 m. 328 ft. 200 m. 656 ft. 500 m. 1,640 ft. 1,000 m. 3,281 ft. 2,000 m. 6,562 ft. 5,000 m. 16,404 ft.

Agriculture, Industry and Resources

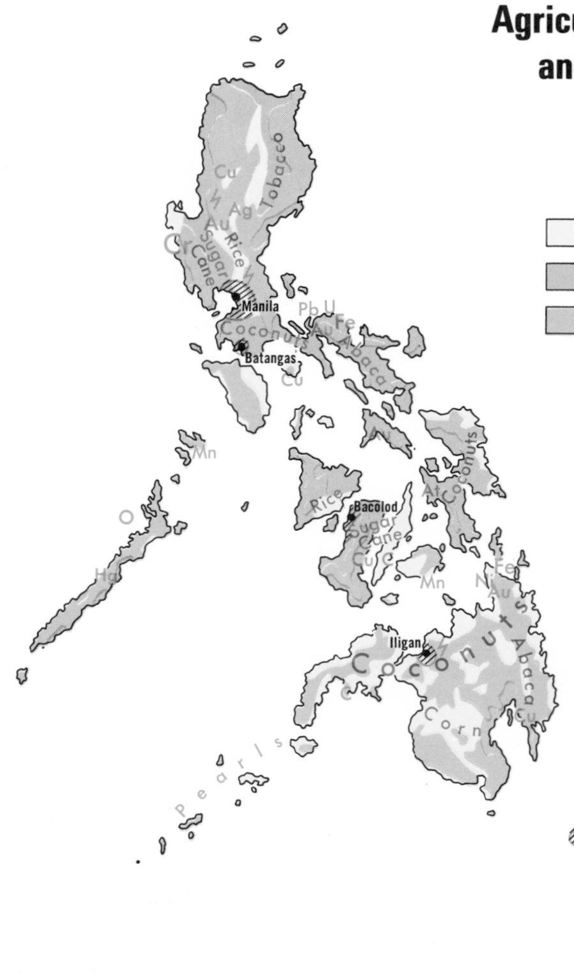
Tobacco
Cu
Au
Ag
Rice
Sugar Cane
Manila
Pb
Fe
Coconuts
Batangas
Abaca
Cu
Mn
Rice
Bacolod
Sugar Cane
Coconuts
Mn
Iligan
Coconuts
Abaca
Corn
Pearls

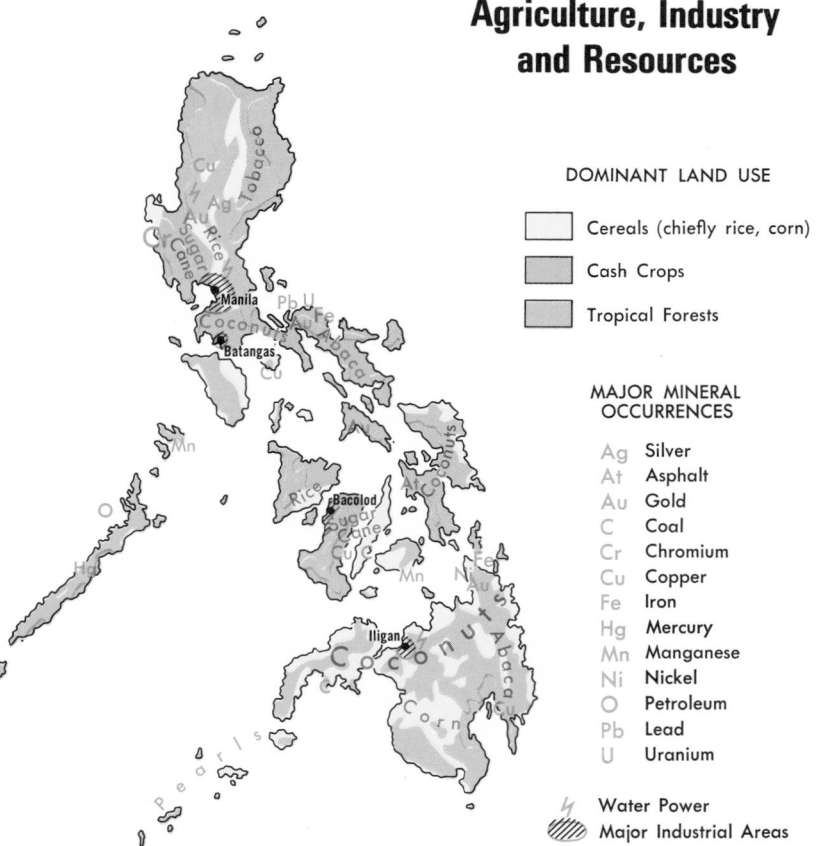

DOMINANT LAND USE

- Cereals (chiefly rice, corn)
- Cash Crops
- Tropical Forests

MAJOR MINERAL OCCURRENCES

- Ag Silver
- At Asphalt
- Au Gold
- C Coal
- Cr Chromium
- Cu Copper
- Fe Iron
- Hg Mercury
- Mn Manganese
- Ni Nickel
- O Petroleum
- Pb Lead
- U Uranium

- Water Power
- Major Industrial Areas

Calayan (isl.) A2
Calicoan (isl.) E5
Camiguin, Cagayan (isl.) B3
Camiguin, Camiguin (isl.) E6
Camotes (isls.) E5
Camotes (sea) E5
Canigao (chan.) E5
Canlaon (peak) D5
Capotoan (mt.) E4
Carabao (isl.) D4
Catanduanes (isl.) E4
Cebu (isl.) D5
Celebes (sea) D8
Cleopatra Needle (mt.) B5
Coron (isl.) C5
Culion (isl.) B5
Cuyo (isl.) C5
Cuyo (isls.) C5
Dalanganem (isls.) C5
Daram (isl.) E5
Davao (gulf) E7
Dinagat (isl.) E5
Diuata (mts.) E6
Dumanquilas (bay) D7
Dumaran (isl.) C5
Engaño (cape) D1
Espiritu Santo (cape) E4
Fuga (isl.) A3
Golo (isl.) C4
Guimaras (isl.) D5
Halcon (mt.) C4
Hibuson (isl.) E5
Homonhon (isl.) E5
Honda (bay) B6
Iligan (bay) E6
Ilin (isl.) C4
Illana (bay) D7
Imuruan (bay) B5
Island (bay) B6
Itbayat (isl.) A2
Jintotolo (chan.) D5
Jolo (isl.) C7
Jomalig (isl.) D3
Lagonoy (gulf) E4
Lamon (bay) C3
Lanao (lake) E7
Laparan (isls.) B8
Lapinin (isl.) E5
Leyte (gulf) E5
Leyte (isl.) E5
Limasawa (isl.) E6
Linapacan (isl.) B5
Lingayen (gulf) C2
Lubang (isls.) B4
Luzon (isl.) C3
Luzon (str.) A2
Macajalar (bay) E6
Mactan (isl.) E5
Malindang (mt.) D6
Mangsee (isls.) A7
Manicani (isl.) E5
Manila (bay) C3
Mantalingajan (mt.) A6
Maqueda (chan.) D3
Maraira (pt.) C1
Marinduque (isl.) C4
Masbate (isl.) D4
Mayon (vol.) D4
Maytiguid (isl.) B5
Mindanao (isl.) D7
Mindanao (riv.) E7
Mindoro (isl.) C4
Mindoro (str.) C4
Mompog (passage) D4
Moro (gulf) D7
Mount Apo National Park E7
Naso (pt.) C5
Negros (isl.) D6
Olutanga (isl.) D7
Pacsan (mt.) C2
Palawan (isl.) B6
Palawan (passage) A6
Panaon (isl.) E5
Panay (isl.) D5
Panglao (isl.) D6
Pangutaran (isl.) C7
Pangutaran Group (isls.) C7
Patnanongan (isl.) D3
Philippine (sea) D3
Pilas (isl.) C7
Pinatubo (mt.) C3
Polillo (isl.) C3
Pujada (bay) F7
Pulangi (riv.) E7
Quiniluban (isls.) C5
Ragang (vol.) E7
Ragay (gulf) D4
Rapu-Rapu (isl.) E4
Romblon (isl.) D4
Sabtang (isl.) B2
Sacol (isl.) D7
Samal (isl.) E7
Samales Group (isls.) D7
Samar (isl.) E5
Samar (sea) E4
San Agustin (cape) F7
San Bernardino (str.) E4
San Miguel (bay) D3
San Pedro (bay) E5
Santo Tomas (mt.) C2
Sarangani (isls.) E8
Semirara (isls.) C5
Siargao (isl.) F6
Siasi (isl.) C8
Sibay (isl.) C5
Sibuguey (bay) D7
Sibutu Group (isls.) B8
Sibuyan (isl.) D4
Sibuyan (sea) D4
Sierra Madre (mts.) D2
Simara (isl.) D4
Simunul (isl.) B8
Siquijor (isl.) D6
South China (sea) B3
Subic (bay) C3
Sulu (arch.) B8
Sulu (sea) B6
Suluan (isl.) F5
Taal (lake) C4
Tablas (isl.) D4
Tablas (str.) C4
Tagapula (isl.) E4
Tagolo (pt.) D6
Tanon (str.) D6
Tapiantana Group (isls.) D7
Tapul (isl.) C8
Tapul Group (isls.) C8
Tara (isl.) C4
Tawi-Tawi (isl.) B8
Tayabas (bay) C4
Ticao (isl.) D4
Tinaca (pt.) E8
Tongquil (isl.) D8
Tumindao (isl.) B8
Turtle (isls.) B7
Verde Island (passage) C4
Victoria (peaks) B6
Visayan (sea) D5
Vitali (isl.) D7

•Population of municipality.

BRUNEI

CITIES and TOWNS

Bandar Seri Begawan 36,987 .... E 4

INDONESIA

CITIES and TOWNS

Agats K7
Ambon (Amboina) 79,636 .... H6
Amurang G5
Baa G8
Bagansiapiapi C5
Balikpapan 137,340 .... F6
Banda Aceh 53,668 .... A4
Bandung 1,201,730 .... H2
Bangil⊙ 49,438 .... K2
Bangkalan⊙ 41,639 .... K2
Banjarmasin 281,673 .... E6
Bantul⊙ 40,585 .... J2
Banyumas J2
Banyuwangi⊙ 76,596 .... L2
Barabai⊙ 33,688 .... F6
Barus⊙ 46,120 .... B5
Batang⊙ 69,577 .... J2
Batavia (Jakarta) (cap.) 4,576,009 .... H1
Baturaja⊙ 48,350 .... C6
Bekasi⊙ 123,264 .... H2
Belawan B5
Bengkalis⊙ 14,072 .... C5
Bengkayang⊙ 15,404 .... E5
Bengkulu 31,866 .... C6
Beo H5
Biak K6
Binjai 59,882 .... B5
Bitung⊙ 59,507 .... H5
Blitar 67,856 .... K2
Blora⊙ 67,853 .... K2
Bogor 195,882 .... H2
Bojonegoro⊙ 74,241 .... J2
Bondowoso⊙ 50,317 .... L2
Bonthain⊙ 30,377 .... F7
Brebes⊙ 87,918 .... H2
Bukittinggi 63,132 .... B6
Bula J6
Bumiayu⊙ 65,403 .... H2
Ciamis⊙ 105,434 .... H2
Cianjur⊙ 132,058 .... H2
Cijulang⊙ 44,487 .... H2
Cilacap⊙ 118,815 .... H2
Cimahi⊙ 157,222 .... H2
Cirebon 178,529 .... H2
Curup⊙ 71,965 .... C6
Demak⊙ 57,676 .... J2
Demta L6
Denpasar⊙ 98,005 .... E7
Dili H7
Djakarta (Jakarta) (cap.) 4,576,009 .... H1
Djambi (Jambi) 158,559 .... C6
Djokjakarta (Yogyakarta) 342,267 .... J2
Dobo J7
Dompu⊙ 14,103 .... F7
Donggala F6
Fakfak J6
Galela⊙ 11,554 .... H5
Garut⊙ 93,340 .... H2
Gorontalo 82,320 .... G5
Gresik⊙ 48,561 .... K2
Hollandia (Jayapura)⊙ 45,786 .... K6
Indramayu⊙ 69,441 .... H2
Jailolo⊙ 17,243 .... H5
Jakarta (cap.) 4,576,009 .... H1
Jambi 158,559 .... C6
Jayapura⊙ 45,786 .... L6
Jember⊙ 115,201 .... K2
Jeneponto⊙ 6,883 .... F7
Jepara⊙ 75,124 .... J2
Jogjakarta (Yogyakarta) 342,267 .... J2
Jombang⊙ 80,643 .... K2
Kaimana J6
Kayuagung⊙ 37,319 .... D6
Kalianda⊙ 42,609 .... D7
Kampung Baru (Tolitoli)⊙ 10,071 .... G5
Karangasem⊙ 15,177 .... F7
Kebumen⊙ 81,571 .... J2
Kediri 178,865 .... K2
Kendal⊙ 32,544 .... J2
Kendari⊙ 28,628 .... G6
Kendawangan D6
Kepi K7
Ketapang E6
Klaten⊙ 58,870 .... J2
Kokonau K6
Kolaka⊙ 10,384 .... G6
Kolonodale G6
Kotaagung⊙ 20,154 .... C7
Kotabaru⊙ 23,443 .... F6
Kotawaringin E6
Kragan⊙ 33,389 .... K2
Krawang⊙ 99,552 .... H2
Kudus⊙ 79,186 .... J2
Kumai E6
Kumai⊙ 13,564 .... E6
Kuningan⊙ 105,255 .... H2
Kupang⊙ 49,354 .... G8
Kutaraja (Banda Aceh) 53,668 .... A4
Kutoarjo⊙ 52,989 .... J2
Labuha H6
Labuhan⊙ 34,274 .... G2
Lahat⊙ 48,136 .... C6
Laiwui H6
Lamongan⊙ 38,897 .... K2
Langsa⊙ 58,060 .... B5
Larantuka G7
Lawang⊙ 59,071 .... K2
Lekitobi G6
Longnawan F5
Lubuklinggau⊙ 43,011 .... C6
Lubuksikaping⊙ 24,244 .... B5
Lumajang⊙ 79,641 .... K2
Madiun 136,147 .... K2
Majalengka⊙ 80,999 .... H2
Majene F6
Magelang 110,308 .... J2
Magetan⊙ 59,507 .... K2
Makassar (Ujung Pandang) 434,766 .... F7
Malang 422,428 .... K2
Malili G6
Malinau⊙ 14,130 .... F5
Mamuju⊙ 17,345 .... F6
Manado 169,684 .... G5
Marabahan E6
Martapura⊙ 55,011 .... F6
Masamba⊙ 16,571 .... G6
Mataram⊙ 46,846 .... F7
Maumere G7
Medan 635,562 .... B5
Menggala⊙ 20,878 .... D6
Merauke⊙ 21,366 .... K7
Mindiptana L7
Mojokerto 60,013 .... K2
Muarabungo⊙ 26,304 .... C6
Muntok⊙ 31,719 .... D6
Nangapinoh⊙ 19,983 .... E6
Negara⊙ 65,762 .... E7
Ngabang⊙ 33,190 .... D5
Pacitan⊙ 51,993 .... J2
Padang 196,339 .... B6
Padangpanjang 30,711 .... B6
Padangsidempuan⊙ 134,611 .... B5
Painan C6
Pakanbaru 145,030 .... C5
Palangkaraya 27,132 .... E6
Palaumerak⊙ 58,655 .... G1
Paleleh⊙ 7,603 .... G5
Palembang 582,961 .... D6
Palu F6
Pamangkat⊙ 62,402 .... D5
Pamekasan⊙ 55,409 .... L2
Pameungpeuk⊙ 41,449 .... H2
Panarukan⊙ 37,482 .... K2
Pandeglang⊙ 35,550 .... G1
Pangkalanberandan⊙ 60,299 .... B5
Pangkalpinang 74,733 .... D6
Pare⊙ 107,806 .... K2
Parepare 72,538 .... F6
Pariaman⊙ 44,428 .... B6
Pasuruan 75,266 .... K2
Pati⊙ 75,397 .... J2
Payakumbuh 63,388 .... C6
Pekalongan 111,537 .... J2
Pemalang⊙ 110,206 .... J2
Pematangsiantar 129,232 .... B5
Perabumulih⊙ 88,031 .... C6
Pinrang F6
Plaju D6
Ponorogo⊙ 58,321 .... J2
Pontianak 217,555 .... D6
Poso G6
Prapat⊙ 7,723 .... B5
Praya⊙ 89,266 .... F7
Probolinggo 82,008 .... K2
Purbolinggo⊙ 41,031 .... J2
Purwakarta⊙ 93,016 .... H2
Purwodadi⊙ 75,713 .... J2
Purwokerto⊙ 125,464 .... H2
Purworejo⊙ 28,663 .... J2
Putussibau⊙ 12,408 .... E5
Raha G6
Rangkasbitung⊙ 78,685 .... G2
Rembang⊙ 33,610 .... K2
Rengat⊙ 33,559 .... C6
Ruteng⊙ 12,294 .... G7
Sabang, Celebes F5
Sabang, Weh 17,625 .... B4
Salatiga 69,831 .... J2
Samarinda 137,521 .... F6
Sambas⊙ 48,253 .... D5
Samboja F6
Sampang⊙ 60,136 .... K2
Sampit E6
Sanana H6
Sanggau⊙ 7,040 .... E5
Sangkulirang⊙ 8,769 .... F5
Saonek J6
Saparua H6
Sarmi K6
Saumlaki J7
Sawahlunto 12,427 .... C6
Seba G8
Semarang 646,590 .... J2
Semitau⊙ 7,165 .... E5
Serang⊙ 79,675 .... G1
Serui K6
Siaksriinderapura C5
Sibolga 42,223 .... B5
Sidoharjo⊙ 59,942 .... K2
Sigli⊙ 10,623 .... B4
Sinabang B5
Sindangbarang⊙ 70,603 .... D7
Singaraja F7
Singkang F6
Singkawang⊙ 93,650 .... D5
Sintang⊙ 24,842 .... E5
Situbondo⊙ 36,094 .... L2
Solo (Surakarta) 414,285 .... J2
Solok 24,771 .... C6
Sorong⊙ 23,763 .... J6
Sragen⊙ 50,515 .... J2
Subang⊙ 35,077 .... H2
Sukabumi 96,242 .... H2
Sukadana⊙ 9,741 .... E6
Sumbawa Besar F7
Sumedang H2
Sumenep⊙ 46,659 .... L2
Sungaipenuh C6
Surabaya 1,556,255 .... K2
Surakarta 414,285 .... J2
Takalar F7
Takingeun B5
Talangbetutu C6
Tanahgrogot F6
Tanahmerah K7
Tangerang G1
Tanjungbalai 33,604 .... C5
Tanjungkarang 198,986 .... C7
Tanjungpandan⊙ 61,225 .... D6
Tanjungpriok⊙ 147,824 .... H1
Tanjungpura⊙ 30,992 .... B5
Tanjungselor F5
Tarakan⊙ 31,118 .... F5
Tasikmalaya⊙ 135,919 .... H2
Tebingtinggi 30,314 .... B5
Tegal 105,752 .... J2
Telukbayur C6
Temanggung⊙ 85,492 .... J2
Tenggarong⊙ 15,081 .... F6
Tepa H7
Terempa D5
Ternate⊙ 34,539 .... H5
Tjilatjap (Cilacap)⊙ 118,815 .... H2
Tjirebon (Cirebon) 178,529 .... H2
Tolitoli⊙ 10,071 .... G5
Tondano⊙ 35,978 .... H5
Trenggalek⊙ 49,065 .... K2
Tuban⊙ 54,212 .... K2
Tulungagung⊙ 53,880 .... K2
Turen⊙ 76,018 .... K2
Ujung Pandang 434,766 .... F7
Wahai H6
Wajabula H5
Wasior K6
Watampone G6
Weda H5
Wonogiri⊙ 56,435 .... J2
Wonosobo⊙ 47,650 .... J2
Wonreli H7
Yogyakarta 342,267 .... J2

OTHER FEATURES

Alas (str.) F7
Anambas (isls.) D5
Arafura (sea) J8
Aru (isls.) K7
Asahan (riv.) B5
Babar (isl.) H7
Bali (isl.) F7
Bali (sea) F7
Banda (sea) H7
Banggai (arch.) G6
Bangka (isl.) D6
Banyak (isls.) B5
Barisan (mts.) C6
Barito (riv.) E6
Batu (isls.) B6
Bawean (isl.) K1
Belitung (Billiton) (isl.) D6
Benggala (str.) A4
Berau (bay) J6
Biak (isl.) K6
Billiton (isl.) D6
Binongko (isl.) G7
Bone (gulf) G7
Borneo (isl.) E5
Bosch, van den (cape) J6
Bungalaut (chan.) B6
Bunguran (Great Natuna) (isl.) D5
Buru (isl.) H6
Butung (isl.) G6
Celebes (Sulawesi) (isl.) G5
Celebes (sea) G5
Cenderawasih (bay) K6
Damar (isl.) H7
Dampier (str.) J6
Digul (riv.) K7
Doberai (pen.) J6
Enggano (isl.) C7
Ewab (Kai) (isls.) J7
Flores (isl.) G7
Flores (sea) F7
Frederik Hendrik (Kolepom) (isl.) K7
Gebe (isl.) H6
Geelvink (Cenderawasih) (bay) K6
Gorong (isl.) J6
Great Kai (isl.) J7
Halmahera (isl.) H5
Irian Jaya (reg.) J6
Jambuair (cape) B4
Jamursba (cape) J5
Java (head) C7
Java (isl.) J2
Java (sea) D6
Jaya, Puncak (mt.) K6
Jayawijaya (range) K6
Jemaja (isl.) D5
Kabaena (isl.) G7
Kai (isls.) J7
Kalao (isl.) G7
Kalaotoa (isl.) G5
Kalimantan (reg.) E5
Kangean (isl.) F7
Kapuas (riv.) D6
Karakelong (isl.) H5
Karimata (arch.) D6
Karimunjawa (isls.) J1
Kerinci (mt.) C6
Kisar (isl.) H7
Komodo (isl.) F7
Krakatau (Rakata) (isl.) C7
Laut (isl.) F6
Leuser (mt.) B5
Lingga (arch.) D5
Lingga (isl.) D6
Lombok (isl.) F7
Madura (isl.) K2
Mahakam (riv.) F6
Makassar (str.) F6
Malacca (str.) C5
Mamberamo (riv.) K6
Maoke (mts.) K6
Mapia (isls.) J5
Mentawai (isls.) B6
Misool (isl.) J6
Molucca (sea) H6
Moluccas (isls.) H6
Morotai (isl.) H5
Muli (str.) K7
Müller (mts.) E5
Muna (isl.) G7
Musi (riv.) C6
Natuna (isls.) D5
Ngunju (cape) F8
Nias (isl.) B5
Numfoor (isl.) J6
Obi (isls.) H6
Ombai (str.) H7
Pantar (isl.) G7
Perkam (cape) K6
Puting, Borneo (cape) E6
Puting, Sumatra (cape) C7
Raja Ampat Group (isls.) H6
Rakata (isl.) C7
Rantekombola (mt.) F6
Raya (mt.) E6
Riau (arch.) C5
Rokan (riv.) C5
Roti (isl.) G8
Salawati (isl.) J6
Sangihe (isl.) H5
Sangihe (isls.) G5
Sawu (isls.) G8
Sawu (sea) G7
Schouten (isls.) K6
Schwaner (mts.) E6
Sebuku (bay) F5
Selatan (cape) E6
Selayar (isl.) G7
Semeru (mt.) K2
Siau (isl.) H5
Siberut (str.) B6
Simeulue (isl.) A5
Singkep (isl.) D6
Sipura (isl.) B6
Slamet (mt.) J2
Sorikmerapi (mt.) B5
South Natuna (isls.) D5
Sudirman (range) K6
Sula (isls.) H6
Sulawesi (isl.) G6
Sumatra (isl.) B5
Sumba (isl.) F7
Sumba (str.) F7
Sumbawa (isl.) F7
Sunda (str.) C7
Tahulandang (isl.) H5
Talaud (isls.) H5
Taliabu (isl.) G6
Tambelan (isls.) D5
Tanimbar (isls.) J7
Tariku (riv.) K6
Tidore (isl.) H5
Timor (reg.) H7
Timor (sea) H7
Toba (lake) B5
Tolo (gulf) G6
Tomini (gulf) G6
Tukangbesi (isls.) G7
Vals (cape) K7
Vogelkop (Doberai) (pen.) J6
Waigeo (isl.) J5
Wakde (isl.) K6
Wangiwangi (isl.) G7
We (isl.) B4
Wetar (isl.) H7

Topography

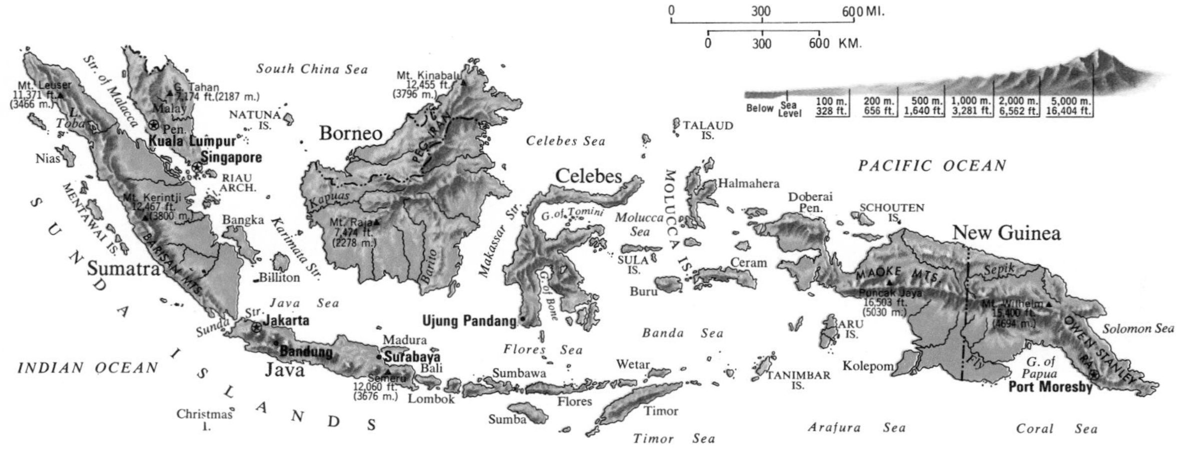

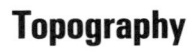

Agriculture, Industry and Resources

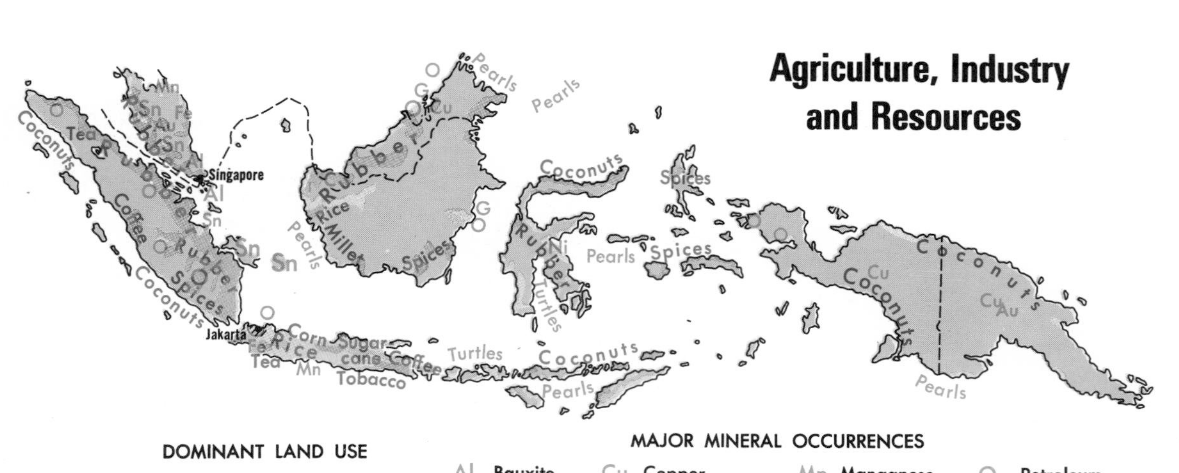

DOMINANT LAND USE

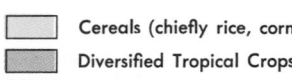

- Cereals (chiefly rice, corn)
- Diversified Tropical Crops
- Forests

MAJOR MINERAL OCCURRENCES

Al	Bauxite	Cu	Copper	Mn	Manganese	O	Petroleum
Au	Gold	Fe	Iron Ore	Ni	Nickel	Sn	Tin
C	Coal	G	Natural Gas				

Major Industrial Areas

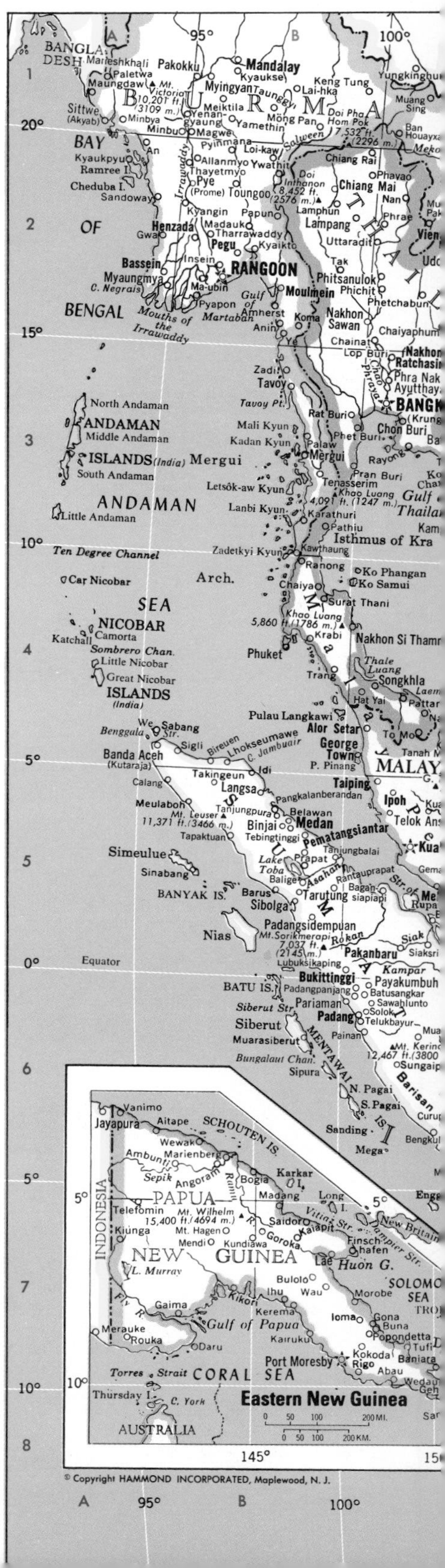

Yapen (isl.) K6

MALAYSIA ★

STATES

North Borneo (Sabah) 1,002,608 ...F3
Sabah 1,002,608 ....F4
Sarawak 1,294,753 ....E5

CITIES and TOWNS

Beaufort 2,709 ....F4
Bintulu 4,424 ....E5
Kampong Sibuti E5
Kapit 1,929 ....E5
Keningau 2,037 ....F4
Kota Kinabalu 40,939 ....E5
Kuching 63,535 ....E5
Kudat 5,089 ....F4
Labuan 7,216 ....E4
Lahad Datu 5,169 ....F4
Marudi 4,700 ....E5
Miri 35,702 ....E5
Mukah 1,717 ....F4
Papar 1,855 ....F4
Ranau 2,024 ....F4
Sandakan 42,413 ....F4
Semporna 3,371 ....F5
Serian 2,209 ....E5
Sibu 50,635 ....E5
Simanggang 8,445 ....E5
Tawau 24,247 ....F5
Weston F4

OTHER FEATURES

Balambangan (isl.) F4
Banggi (isl.) F4

Iran (mts.) E5
Kinabalu (mt.) F4
Labuan (isl.) E4
Labuk (bay) F4
Rajang (riv.) E5
Sirik (cape) E5

PAPUA NEW GUINEA

CITIES and TOWNS

Abau C7
Aitape 3,366 ....B6
Ambuntic 989 ....B6
Angoram 1,830 ....B6
Baniara C7
Bogiac 678 ....B6
Bulolo 6,801 ....C7
Buna C7
Daru 7,149 ....C7
Finschhafen B7
Gaima B7
Gehua C7
Gona C7
Goroka 18,797 ....C7
Ioma B7
Kairuku C7
Kerema 3,354 ....C7
Kikori 670 ....C7
Kiungao 1,113 ....C7
Kokoda C7
Kundiawa 4,298 ....B7
Lae 61,682 ....B7
Madang 21,332 ....B7
Mendi 4,131 ....B7
Morobe C7
Mount Hagen 13,642 ....B7
Popondetta 6,343 ....C7

Port Moresby (cap.) 122,761 ..B7
Rigo C7
Saidor B7
Samarai 1,948 ....C8
Tufi C7
Vanimo 3,051 ....B6
Wau 2,374 ....B7
Wewak 19,554 ....B6

OTHER FEATURES

Dampier (str.) C7
D'Entrecasteaux (isls.) C7
Fly (riv.) A7
Huon (gulf) B7
Karkar (isl.) B6
Kiriwina (isl.) B7
Long (isl.) B7
Louisiade (arch.) C8
Milne (bay) C8
Misima (isl.) C8
New Britain (isl.) B7
Ramu (riv.) B7
Rossel (isl.) D8
Schouten (isls.) B6
Sepik (riv.) B6
Solomon (sea) B7
Tagula (isl.) C8
Torres (str.) C7
Trobriand (isls.) C7
Vitiaz (str.) C7
Woodlark (isl.) C7

○ Population of district.
◎ Population of sub-district or division.
★ See page 74 for other Malaysian entries.

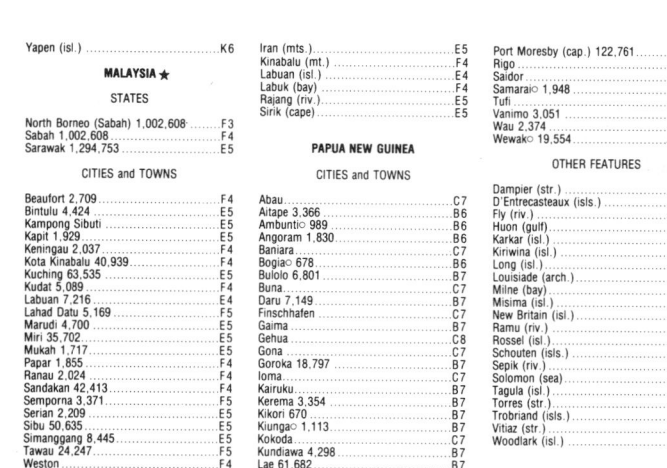

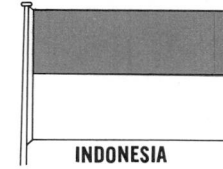

INDONESIA

PAPUA NEW GUINEA

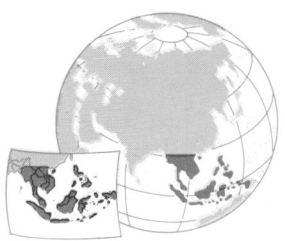

INDONESIA

AREA 788,430 sq. mi. (2,042,034 sq. km.)
POPULATION 147,383,075
CAPITAL Jakarta
LARGEST CITY Jakarta
HIGHEST POINT Puncak Jaya 16,503 ft. (5,030 m.)
MONETARY UNIT rupiah
MAJOR LANGUAGES Bahasa Indonesia, Indonesian and Papuan languages, English
MAJOR RELIGIONS Islam, tribal religions, Christianity, Hinduism

PAPUA NEW GUINEA

AREA 183,540 sq. mi. (475,369 sq. km.)
POPULATION 3,006,799
CAPITAL Port Moresby
LARGEST CITY Port Moresby
HIGHEST POINT Mt. Wilhelm 15,400 ft. (4,694 m.)
MONETARY UNIT kina
MAJOR LANGUAGES pidgin English, Hiri Motu, English
MAJOR RELIGIONS Tribal religions, Christianity

BRUNEI

AREA 2,226 sq. mi. (5,765 sq. km.)
POPULATION 212,840
CAPITAL Bandar Seri Begawan

Java

0   25   50   75 MI.
0   25   50   75 KM.

Southeast Asia

LAMBERT AZIMUTHAL EQUAL-AREA PROJECTION

SCALE OF MILES
0   100   200   300   400   500   600

SCALE OF KILOMETERS
0   100   200   300   400   500   600

Capitals of Countries ....☆
Administrative Center ....◉
International Boundaries ....
Other Boundaries ....

Scale 1:19,000,000

FIJI

AREA 7,055 sq. mi. (18,272 sq. km.)
POPULATION 588,068
CAPITAL Suva
LARGEST CITY Suva
HIGHEST POINT Tomaniivi 4,341 ft. (1,323 m.)
MONETARY UNIT Fijian dollar
MAJOR LANGUAGES Fijian, Hindi, English
MAJOR RELIGIONS Protestantism, Hinduism

KIRIBATI

AREA 291 sq. mi. (754 sq. km.)
POPULATION 56,213
CAPITAL Bairiki (Tarawa)
HIGHEST POINT (on Banaba I.) 285 ft. (87 m.)
MONETARY UNIT Australian dollar
MAJOR LANGUAGES I-Kiribati, English
MAJOR RELIGIONS Protestantism, Roman Catholicism

NAURU

AREA 7.7 sq. mi. (20 sq. km.)
POPULATION 7,254
CAPITAL Yaren (district)
MONETARY UNIT Australian dollar
MAJOR LANGUAGES Nauruan, English
MAJOR RELIGION Protestantism

SOLOMON ISLANDS

AREA 11,500 sq. mi. (29,785 sq. km.)
POPULATION 221,000
CAPITAL Honiara
HIGHEST POINT Mount Popomanatseu 7,647 ft. (2,331 m.)
MONETARY UNIT Solomon Islands dollar
MAJOR LANGUAGES English, pidgin English, Melanesian dialects
MAJOR RELIGIONS Tribal religions, Protestantism, Roman Catholicism

TONGA

AREA 270 sq. mi. (699 sq. km.)
POPULATION 90,128
CAPITAL Nuku'alofa
LARGEST CITY Nuku'alofa
HIGHEST POINT 3,389 ft. (1,033 m.)
MONETARY UNIT pa'anga
MAJOR LANGUAGES Tongan, English
MAJOR RELIGION Protestantism

TUVALU

AREA 9.78 sq. mi. (25.33 sq. km.)
POPULATION 7,349
CAPITAL Fongafale (Funafuti)
HIGHEST POINT 15 ft. (4.6 m.)
MONETARY UNIT Australian dollar
MAJOR LANGUAGES English, Tuvaluan
MAJOR RELIGION Protestantism

Abaiang (atoll) 3,296	H5	
Abemama (atoll) 2,300	H5	
Adamstown (cap.), Pitcairn Is. 61	N8	
Admiralty (isls.)	E6	
Agana (cap.), Guam 881	E4	
Agrihan (isl.)	E4	
Ahau 117	H7	
Ailinglapalap (atoll)	G5	
Ailuk (atoll)	H4	
Aitutaki (atoll) 2,423	L7	
Alamagan (isl.)	E4	
Alofi (cap.), Niue 957	K7	
Alotau 4,310	E7	
Amanu (atoll)	N7	
Ambrym (isl.) 6,324	G7	
American Samoa 32,395	J7	
Anaa (atoll) 444	M7	
Anatahan (isl.)	E4	
Aneityum (Anatom) (isl.) 464	H8	
Angaur (isl.)	D5	
Apataki (atoll)	M7	
Apia (cap.), W. Samoa 32,099	J7	
Arafura (sea)	D6	
Arno (atoll)	H5	
Arorae (atoll) 1,626	H6	
Asuncion (isl.)	E4	
Atafu (atoll) 577	J6	
Atiu (isl.) 1,312	L8	
Auki 1,926	G6	
Austral (isls.) 5,208	L8	
Australia 13,548,448	C8	
Babelthuap (isl.)	D5	
Bairiki (cap.), Kiribati 1,777	H5	
Baker (isl.)	J5	
Banaba (isl.) 2,314	G6	
Banks (isls.) 3,158	G7	
Bass (isls.)	M8	
Belau (Palau) 12,177	D5	
Belep (isls.) 624	G7	
Bellona (reefs)	G8	
Beru (atoll) 2,318	H6	
Bikar (atoll)	H4	
Bikini (atoll)	G4	
Bismarck (arch.) 314,308	E6	
Bonin (isls.) 1,507	E3	
Bora-Bora (isl.) 2,572	L7	
Bougainville (isl.) 128,890	F6	
Bounty (isls.)	H10	
Bourail 3,149	G8	
Buka (isl.) 1,517	F6	
Butaritari (atoll) 2,971	H5	
Canberra (cap.), Australia 197,622	F9	
Canton (isl.)	J6	
Capitol Hill (cap.), No. Marianas 1,245	E4	
Caroline (isl.)	M7	
Caroline (isls.)	E5	
Chesterfield (isls.)	F7	
Chichi (isl.) 1,507	E3	
Choiseul (isl.) 10,349	F6	
Christmas (isl.) 674	L5	
Cook (isls.) 18,128	L7	
Coral (sea)	F7	
Danger (Pukapuka) (atoll) 785	K7	
Daru 7,149	E6	
D'Entrecasteaux (isls.)	F6	
Disappointment (isls.) 373	N7	
Ducie (isl.)	O8	
Duke of Gloucester (isls.)	M8	
Easter (isl.) 1,598	Q8	
Eauripik (atoll)	E5	
Ebon (atoll)	G5	
Efate (isl.) 18,038	G7	
Eiao (isl.)	M6	
Elato (atoll)	E5	
Enderbury (isl.)	J6	
Enewetak (Eniwetok) (atoll)	G4	
Erromanga (isl.) 945	H7	
Espiritu Santo (isl.) 16,220	G7	
Fais (isl.)	E5	
Fakaofo (atoll) 654	J6	
Fakarava (atoll)	M7	
Fanning (isl.) 340	L5	
Faraulep (atoll)	E5	
Fatu Hiva (isl.)	N7	
Fatuhiva (isl.) 386	N7	
Fiji 588,068	L7	
Flint (isl.)	L7	
Fongafale (cap.), Tuvalu	H6	
French Polynesia 137,382	L8	
Funafuti 2,120	H6	
Futuna (Hoorn) (isls.) 3,173	J7	
Gaferut (isl.)	E5	
Gambier (isls.) 556	N8	
Gardner (isl.)	J6	
Gilbert (isls.) 47,711	H6	
Greenwich (Kapingamarangi) (atoll)	F5	
Guadalcanal (isl.) 46,619	F7	
Guam (isl.) 105,821	E4	
Ha'apa Group (isls.) 10,812	J8	
Haha (isl.)	E3	
Hall (isls.)	F5	
Hao (atoll)	N7	
Hawaiian (isls.) 769,913	J3	
Henderson (isl.)	O8	
Hikueru (atoll)	M7	
Hivaoa (isl.) 1,159	N6	
Honiara (cap.), Solomon Is. 14,942	F6	
Hoorn (isls.) 3,173	J7	
Howland (isl.)	J5	
Huahine (isl.) 3,140	L7	
Huon (gulf)	E6	
Huon (isls.)	G7	
Ifalik (atoll)	E5	
Iwo (isl.)	E3	
Jaluit (atoll)	G5	
Jarvis (isl.)	K6	
Johnston (atoll) 339	K4	
Kadavu (Kandavu) (isl.) 8,699	H7	
Kanton (Canton) (isl.)	J6	
Kapingamarangi (atoll)	F5	
Kavieng 4,556	E6	
Kermadec (isls.) 11	J8	
Kieta 3,445	F6	
Kili (isl.)	G5	
Kimbe 4,680	F6	
Kingman (reef)	K5	
Kiribati 57,500	J6	
Kita Iwo (isl.)	D3	

Kingman (reef)	K5	
Kiribati 57,500	J6	
Kita Iwo (isl.)	D3	
Malden (isl.)	L6	
Malekula (isl.) 15,931	G7	
Maloelap (atoll)	H5	
Mangaia (isl.) 1,530	L8	
Mangareva (isl.) 556	N8	
Manihiki (atoll) 266	K7	
Manra (Sydney) (isl.)	K6	
Manua (isls.) 1,740	K7	
Manus (atoll)	K7	
Manus (isl.) 25,844	E6	
Marcus (isl.)	F3	
Maré (isl.) 4,156	G8	
Maria (isl.)	L8	
Marianas, Northern 16,862	E4	
Mariana Trench	E4	
Marquesas (isls.) 5,419	N6	
Marshall Islands 31,042	G4	
Marutea (atoll)	N8	
Mata Utu (cap.), Wallis and Futuna 558	J7	
Mauke (isl.) 711	L8	
Mehetia (isl.)	M7	
Melanesia (reg.)	E5	
Merir (isl.)	D5	
Micronesia (reg.)	E4	
Micronesia, Federated States of 73,755	F5	
Midway (isls.) 526	J3	
Mili (atoll)	H5	
Minami Iwo (isl.)	D3	
Minerva (reefs)	J8	
Mitiaro, Cook Is. 305	L7	
Moen (isl.)	F5	
Mokil (atoll)	G5	

Moorea (isl.) 5,788	L7	
Morane (isl.)	N8	
Mururoa (atoll)	M8	
Nadi 6,938	H7	
Namonuito (atoll)	E5	
Namorik (atoll)	G5	
Nanumea (atoll) 844	H6	
Napier □ 50,164	H9	
Nassau (isl.) 123	K7	
Nauru 7,254	G6	
Ndeni (isl.) 4,854	G7	
Neiafu 3,307	J7	
New Britain (isl.) 222,759	F6	
New Caledonia (isl.) 118,715	G8	
New Caledonia 133,233	G8	
New Georgia (isl.) 16,472	F6	
New Hanover (Lavongai) (isl.)	F6	
New Hebrides (Vanuatu) 112,596	G7	
New Ireland (isl.) 65,705	F6	
New Zealand 3,167,357	G9	
Ngatik (atoll)	F5	
Ngulu (atoll)	D5	
Nikumaroro (Gardner) (isl.)	J6	
Ninigo Group (isls.)	D6	
Niuafo'ou (isl.) 678	J7	
Niuatoputapu (isl.) 1,650	J7	
Niue (isl.) 3,843	K7	
Nomoi (isls.) 866	F5	
Nonouti (atoll) 2,223	H6	
Norfolk Island (terr.) 2,180	G8	
Northern Marianas 168,621	E4	
North Pacific (ocean)	F4	
Nouméa (cap.), New Caled. 56,078	G8	

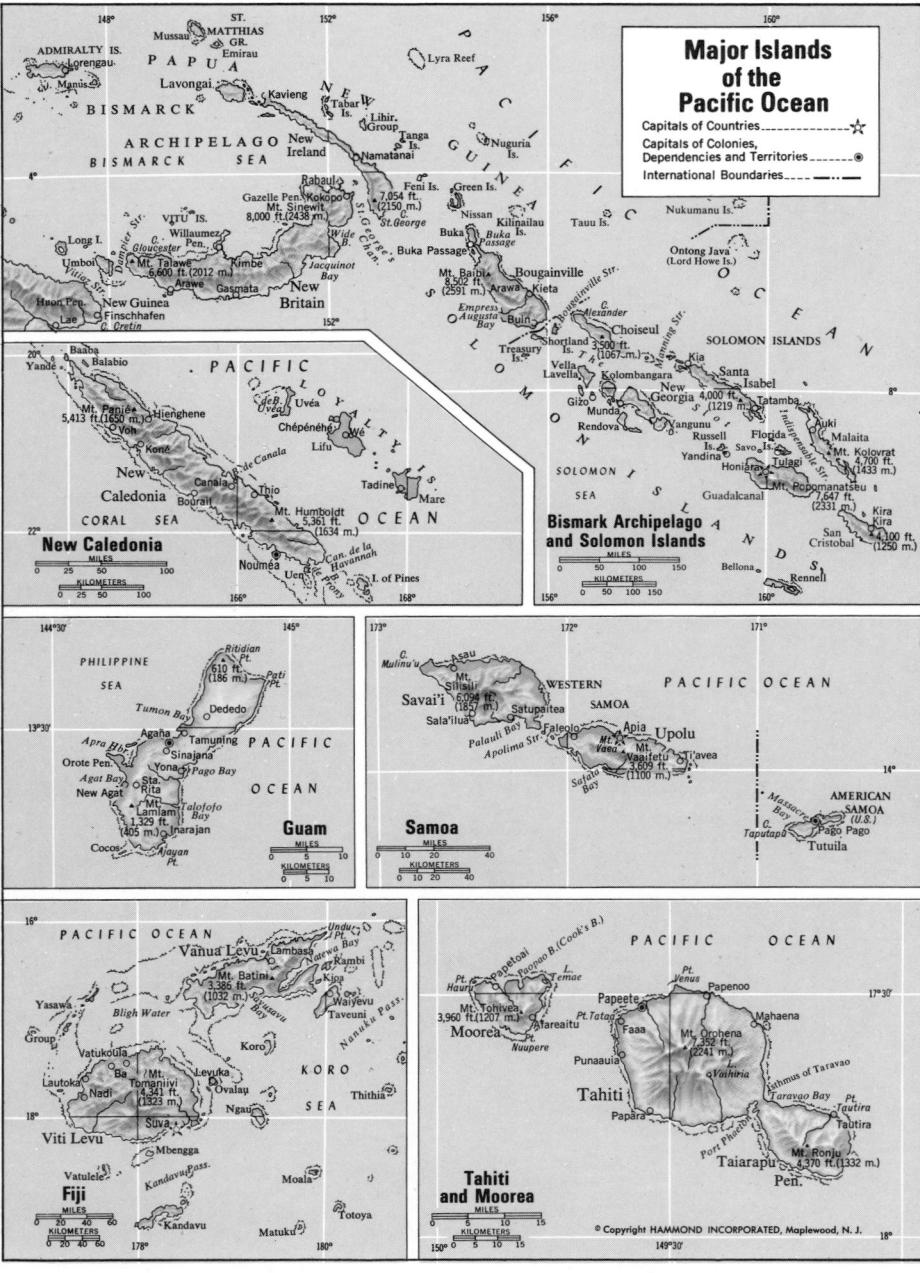

Major Islands of the Pacific Ocean

Capitals of Countries .... ☆
Capitals of Colonies, Dependencies and Territories ...... ◉
International Boundaries ..... _._._._

New Caledonia

Bismark Archipelago and Solomon Islands

Guam

Samoa

Fiji

Tahiti and Moorea

© Copyright HAMMOND INCORPORATED, Maplewood, N. J.

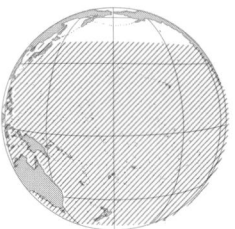

Nouméa□ 74,335 ....G8	Polynesia (reg.) K7	Santa Isabel (isl.) 10,420 ....G6
Nui (atoll) 603 ....H6	Ponape 6,343 ....F5	Sarigan (isl.) E4
Nuku'alofa (cap.), Tonga 18,356 ....J8	Popondetta 6,343 ....E6	Satawal (isl.) E5
Nukuhiva (isl.) 1,484 ....M6	Port Moresby (cap.), Papua N.G. 122,761 ....E6	Savai'i (isl.) 42,218 ....J7
Nukulaelae (atoll) 347 ....H6	Pukapuka (atoll) 785 ....K7	Senyavin (isls.) F5
Nukumanu (atoll) 368 ....F6	Puka-Puka (atoll) 95 ....N7	Society (isls.) 117,703 ....L7
Nukuoro (atoll) D5	Pulap (atoll) E5	Solomon (isls.) F6
Ocean (Banaba) (isl.) 2,314 ....G6	Pulo Anna (isl.) D5	Solomon Islands 221,000 ....G6
Oeno (isl.) O8	Puluwat (atoll) E5	Solomon (sea) F6
Onotoa (atoll) 1,997 ....H6	Rabaul 14,973 ....F6	Sonsorol (isl.) D5
Ontong Java (atoll) 1,082 ....G6	Raiatea (isl.) 2,517 ....L7	Sorol (atoll) D5
Oroluk (atoll) F5	Raivavae (isl.) 1,023 ....M8	South Pacific (ocean) H8
Orona (Hull) (isl.) J6	Rakahanga (atoll) 283 ....K7	Starbuck (isl.) L6
Pacific Islands, Terr. of the 133,836 ....F5	Rangiroa (atoll) M7	Suva (cap.), Fiji 63,628 ....H7
Pagan (isl.) E4	Raoul (isl.) J8	Suva□ 117,827 ....H7
Pago Pago (cap.), Amer. Samoa 3,058 ....J7	Rapa (isl.) 398 ....M8	Suwarrow (atoll) 1 ....K7
Palau (Belau) 12,177 ....D5	Rapa Nui (Easter) (isl.) 1,598 ....Q8	Swains (isl.) 29 ....K7
Palmerston (atoll) 56 ....K7	Raraka (atoll) M7	Sydney (isl.) K6
Palmyra (atoll) K5	Raroia (atoll) M7	Tabiang 38 ....H6
Pangai 1,472 ....J7	Rarotonga (isl.) 9,802 ....K8	Tabiteuea (atoll) 3,942 ....H6
Papeete (cap.) Fr. Poly. 22,967 ....M7	Ratak Chain (isls.) G5	Tahaa (isl.) 3,513 ....L7
Papeete□ 51,987 ....M7	Reao (atoll) 424 ....N7	Tahiti (isl.) 95,604 ....L7
Papua (gulf) E6	Rennell (isl.) 1,132 ....F7	Takaroa (atoll) 337 ....M7
Papua New Guinea 3,006,799 ....E6	Rimatara (isl.) 813 ....L8	Tanna (isl.) 15,715 ....H7
Parece Vela (isl.) D3	Rongelap (atoll) G4	Tasman (sea) G9
Peleliu (isl.) D5	Rota (isl.) 1,274 ....E4	Taongi (atoll) G4
Penrhyn (Tongareva) (atoll) 531 ....L6	Rotuma (isl.) 2,805 ....H7	Tarawa (atoll) 17,129 ....H5
Phoenix (isls.) J6	Rururtu (isl.) 1,555 ....L8	Taveuni (isl.) H7
Pines (isl.) 1,095 ....G8	Saipan (isl.) 14,585 ....E4	Tematangi (isl.) M8
Pingelap (atoll) G5	Sala y Gómez (isl.) P8	Tetiaroa (atoll) M7
Pitcairn (isl.) 61 ....O8	Samarai 1,948 ....E7	Tikopia (isl.) 1,115 ....G7
	Samoa (isls.) J7	Tinian (isl.) 899 ....E4
	San Cristobal (isl.) 11,212 ....G7	Tobi (isl.) 64 ....D5
	Santa Cruz (isls.) 5,421 ....G6	Tokelau (isls.) 1,575 ....J6
		Tonga 90,128 ....J8
		Tongareva (atoll) 531 ....L6
		Tongatapu (isls.) 57,130 ....J8

VANUATU

AREA 5,700 sq. mi. (14,763 sq. km.)
POPULATION 112,596
CAPITAL Vila
HIGHEST POINT Mt. Tabwemasana 6,165 ft. (1,879 m.)
MONETARY UNIT vatu
MAJOR LANGUAGES Bislama, English, French
MAJOR RELIGIONS Christian, animist

WESTERN SAMOA

AREA 1,133 sq. mi. (2,934 sq. km.)
POPULATION 151,983
CAPITAL Apia
LARGEST CITY Apia
HIGHEST POINT Mt. Silisili 6,094 ft. (1,857 m.)
MONETARY UNIT tala
MAJOR LANGUAGES Samoan, English
MAJOR RELIGIONS Protestantism, Roman Catholicism

Torres (isls.) 325 ....G7	Uturoa 2,517 ....L7	Wallis (isls.) 6,019 ....J7
Torres (strait) E7	Uvéa (isl.) 2,777 ....G7	Wallis and Futuna 9,192 ....J7
Trobriand (isls.) F6	Vahitahi (atoll) N7	Washington (isl.) 458 ....L5
Truk (isls.) F5	Vaitupu (atoll) 1,273 ....H6	Wau 2,374 ....E6
Tuamotu (arch.) 9,052 ....M7	Vanikoro (isl.) 267 ....G7	Wellington (cap.), N. Zealand□ 327,414 ....H10
Tubuai (isl.) 1,419 ....M8	Vanimo 3,051 ....E6	Western Samoa 151,983 ....J7
Tubuai (Austral) (isls.) 5,208 ....M8	Vanua Levu (isl.) 103,122 ....H7	Wewak 19,554 ....E6
Tureia (atoll) N8	Vanuatu 112,596 ....G7	Woleai (atoll) E5
Tutuila (isl.) 30,626 ....J7	Vava'u Group (isls.) 15,065 ....J7	Wotje (atoll) H5
Tuvalu 7,349 ....H6	Vila (cap.), Vanuatu 4,729 ....G7	Yap (isl) D5
Uahuka 350 ....N6	Vila□ 14,797 ....G7	
Uapou (isl.) 1,563 ....M6	Viti Levu (isl.) 445,422 ....H7	
Ujelang (atoll) F5	Volcano (isls.) E3	
Ulithi (atoll) D4	Vostok (isl.) L7	
Upolu 109,765 ....J7	Wake (isl.) G4	

*City and suburbs.
○Population of sub-district or division.
□Population of urban area.

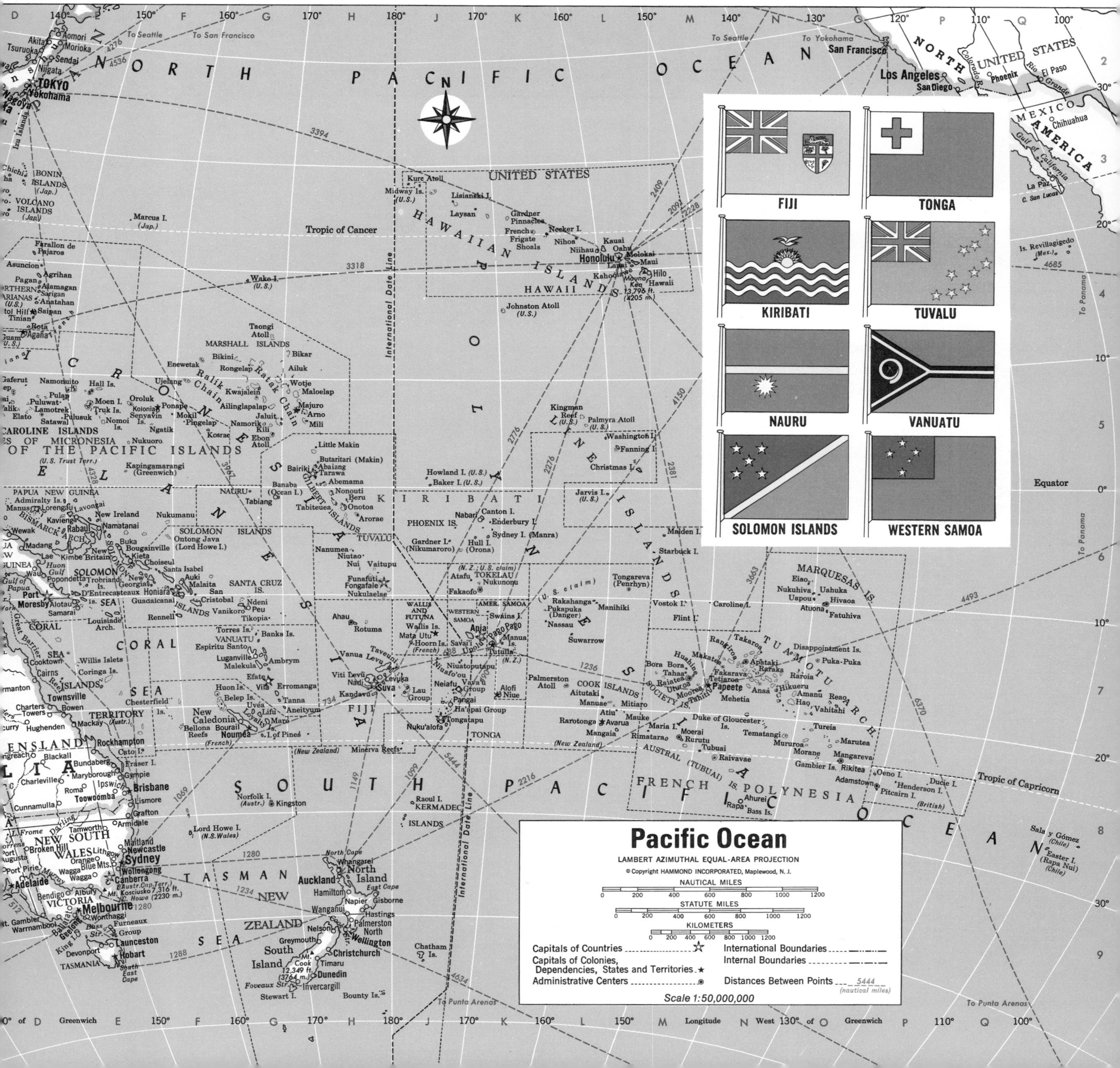

Flags

FIJI TONGA KIRIBATI TUVALU NAURU VANUATU SOLOMON ISLANDS WESTERN SAMOA

Pacific Ocean

LAMBERT AZIMUTHAL EQUAL-AREA PROJECTION
© Copyright HAMMOND INCORPORATED, Maplewood, N.J.

NAUTICAL MILES
0 200 400 600 800 1000 1200

STATUTE MILES
0 200 400 600 800 1000 1200

KILOMETERS
0 200 400 600 800 1000 1200

Capitals of Countries ....☆
Capitals of Colonies, Dependencies, States and Territories ....★
Administrative Centers ....●
International Boundaries ....
Internal Boundaries ....
Distances Between Points ....5444 (nautical miles)

Scale 1:50,000,000

Australia
CONIC PROJECTION

MILES
0 50 100   200   300   400   500
KILOMETERS
0 50 100 200   300   400   500

Capital of Country .... ⊛   State & Territorial Capitals .... ⊛
International Boundaries .... _____   State & Territorial Boundaries ...... _____

Scale 1:19,000,000

© Copyright HAMMOND INCORPORATED, Maplewood, N.J.

AREA 2,966,136 sq. mi. (7,682,300 sq. km.)
POPULATION 13,548,448
CAPITAL Canberra
LARGEST CITY Sydney
HIGHEST POINT Mt. Kosciusko 7,310 ft.
(2,228 m.)
LOWEST POINT Lake Eyre -39 ft. (-12 m.)
MONETARY UNIT Australian dollar
MAJOR LANGUAGE English
MAJOR RELIGIONS Protestantism,
Roman Catholicism

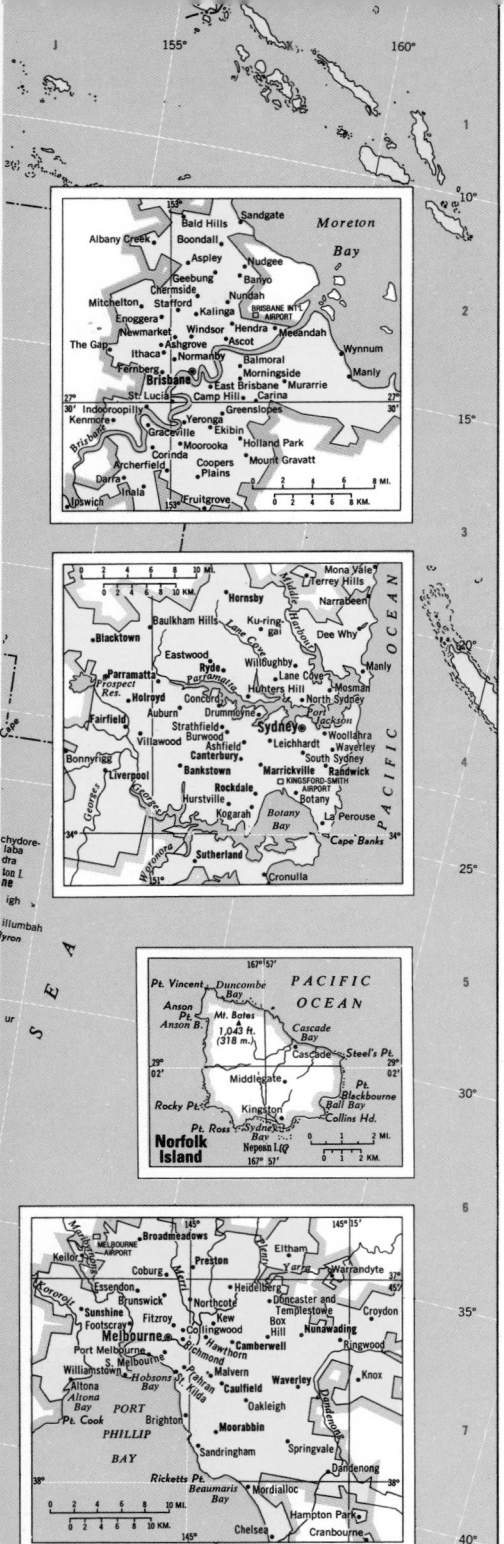

Population Distribution

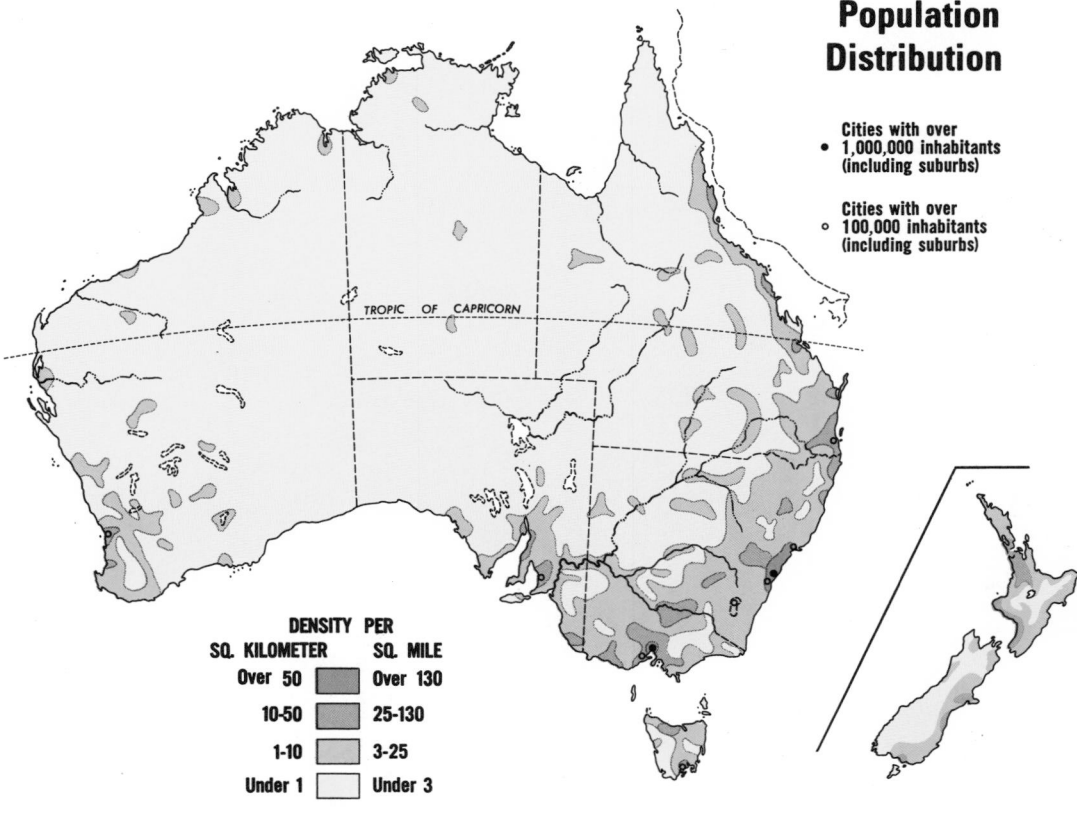

Cities with over
● 1,000,000 inhabitants
(including suburbs)

Cities with over
○ 100,000 inhabitants
(including suburbs)

DENSITY PER	
SQ. KILOMETER	SQ. MILE
Over 50	Over 130
10-50	25-130
1-10	3-25
Under 1	Under 3

Vegetation

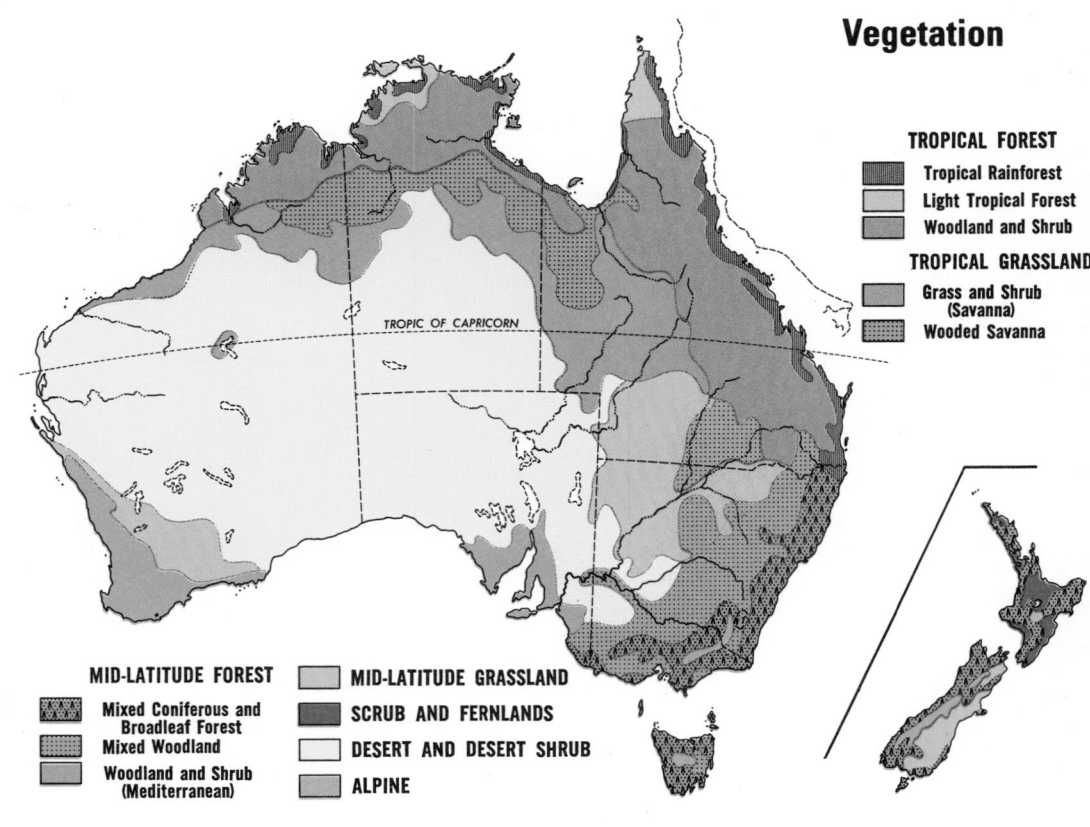

TROPICAL FOREST
Tropical Rainforest
Light Tropical Forest
Woodland and Shrub

TROPICAL GRASSLAND
Grass and Shrub (Savanna)
Wooded Savanna

MID-LATITUDE FOREST
Mixed Coniferous and Broadleaf Forest
Mixed Woodland
Woodland and Shrub (Mediterranean)

MID-LATITUDE GRASSLAND
SCRUB AND FERNLANDS
DESERT AND DESERT SHRUB
ALPINE

Average January Temperature

Darwin 83°
Cairns 81°
Derby 88°
Onslow 85°
Alice Springs 82°
Brisbane 77°
Kalgoorlie 78°
Broken Hill 79°
Perth 74°
Adelaide 72°
Sydney 70°
Albany 63°
Melbourne 67°
Hobart 62°

Tropic of Capricorn

FAHRENHEIT	CELSIUS
Over 86°	Over 30°
68° to 86°	20° to 30°
50° to 68°	10° to 20°
32° to 50°	0° to 10°
Under 32°	Under 0°

Auckland 66°
Dunedin 60°

• Sydney 70° Average January temperature in degrees Fahrenheit at selected stations

Average July Temperature

Darwin 76°
Cairns 70°
Derby 72°
Onslow 63°
Alice Springs 52°
Brisbane 59°
Broken Hill 51°
Kalgoorlie 52°
Perth 55°
Adelaide 52°
Sydney 54°
Albany 53°
Melbourne 49°
Hobart 46°

Tropic of Capricorn

FAHRENHEIT	CELSIUS
Over 68°	20° to 30°
50° to 68°	10° to 20°
32° to 50°	0° to 10°
Under 32°	Under 0°

Auckland 52°
Dunedin 43°

• Sydney 54° Average July temperature in degrees Fahrenheit at selected stations

Rainfall

Thursday Island 66
Darwin 60
Cairns 86
Derby 23
Tennant Creek 15
Cloncurry 19
Mackay 63
Onslow 12
Alice Springs 12
William Creek 5
Brisbane 45
Geraldton 19
Broken Hill 9
Kalgoorlie 9
Perth 36
Adelaide 20
Albury 28
Sydney 47
Albany 37
Melbourne 26
Hobart 25

Tropic of Capricorn

AVERAGE ANNUAL RAINFALL

INCHES	CENTIMETERS
Over 80	Over 200
60 to 80	150 to 200
40 to 60	100 to 150
20 to 40	50 to 100
10 to 20	25 to 50
Under 10	Under 25

Auckland 48
Hokitika 116
Wellington 48
Dunedin 36

• Sydney 47 Average annual rainfall in inches at selected stations

DOMINANT LAND USE

- Cereals (chiefly wheat), Livestock
- Dairy, Truck Farming
- Cash Crops, Horticulture, Fruit
- Pasture Livestock
- Range Livestock
- Forests
- Nonagricultural Land

MAJOR MINERAL OCCURRENCES

Ab	Asbestos	Na	Salt
Ag	Silver	Ni	Nickel
Al	Bauxite	O	Petroleum
Au	Gold	Op	Opals
C	Coal	P	Phosphates
Cu	Copper	Pb	Lead
D	Diamonds	S	Sulfur, Pyrites
Fe	Iron Ore	Sb	Antimony
G	Natural Gas	Sn	Tin
Gp	Gypsum	Ti	Titanium
Lg	Lignite	U	Uranium
Ls	Limestone	W	Tungsten
Mg	Magnesium	Zn	Zinc
Mi	Mica	Zr	Zirconium
Mn	Manganese		

⚡ Water Power

▨ Major Industrial Areas

Agriculture, Industry and Resources

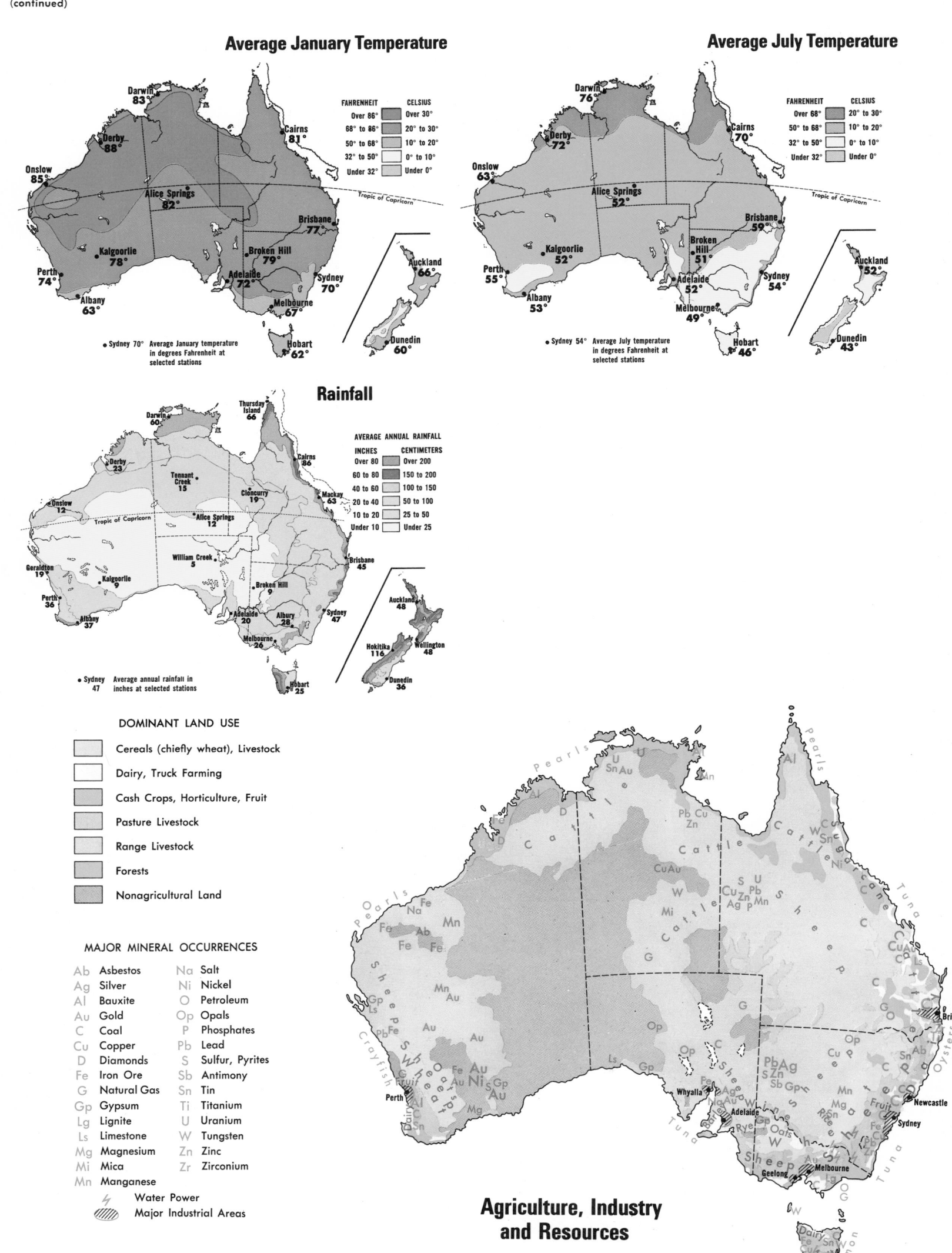

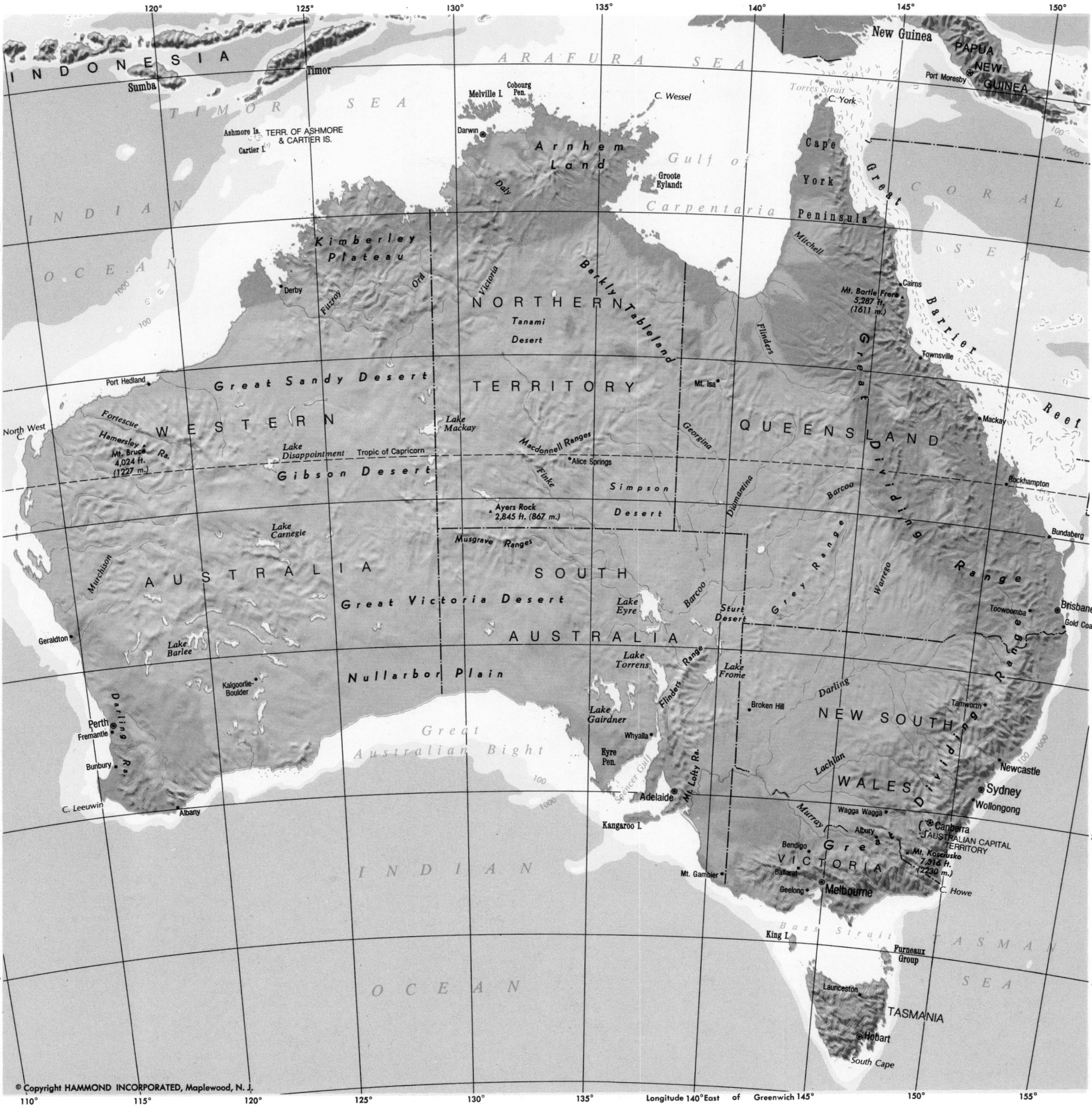

110° 120° 125° 130° 135° 140° 145° 150°

INDONESIA

ARAFURA SEA

New Guinea

PAPUA NEW GUINEA

Timor

Sumba

10°   Port Moresby   10°

TIMOR SEA

Melville I.
Cobourg Pen.

C. Wessel

Ashmore Is. TERR. OF ASHMORE & CARTIER IS.
Cartier I.

Darwin

Gulf of

Cape York

INDIAN

Arnhem Land

Groote Eylandt

Carpentaria

C. York

CORAL

Torres Strait

15°   15°

Kimberley Plateau

Daly

OCEAN

Victoria

NORTHERN

Barkly Tableland

Mitchell

Mt. Bartle Frere 5,287 ft. (1611 m.)

Cairns

Derby

Fitzroy

Ord

Great

Townsville

Barrier

20°   20°

Port Hedland

Great Sandy Desert

TERRITORY

Tanami Desert

Mt. Isa

QUEENSLAND

Mackay

Reef

North West C.

Fortescue

WESTERN

Lake Mackay

Hamersley Ra.
Mt. Bruce 4,024 ft. (1227 m.)

Lake Disappointment   Tropic of Capricorn

Gibson Desert

Macdonnell Ranges

Alice Springs

Finke

Georgina

Flinders

Diamantina

Barcoo

Rockhampton

25°   25°

Lake Carnegie

AUSTRALIA

Ayers Rock 2,845 ft. (867 m.)

Simpson Desert

Sturt Desert

Bundaberg

Musgrave   Ranges

SOUTH

Grey Range

Warrego

Toowoomba

Brisbane
Gold Coast

Geraldton

Murchison

Great Victoria Desert

Lake Eyre

Barcoo

Range

Lake Barlee

AUSTRALIA

30°   30°

Kalgoorlie-Boulder

Nullarbor Plain

Lake Torrens

Lake Gairdner

Lake Frome

Darling

Broken Hill

NEW SOUTH

Tamworth

Perth
Fremantle

Darling R.

Whyalla

Flinders Range

Mt. Lofty Ra.

WALES

Lachlan

Newcastle

Bunbury

Great

Eyre Pen.

Sydney

C. Leeuwin

Australian   Bight

Wollongong

Albany

Adelaide

Murray

Wagga Wagga

Albury

Canberra
AUSTRALIAN CAPITAL TERRITORY

35°   35°

Kangaroo I.

INDIAN

Bendigo

Great

Mt. Kosciusko 7,316 ft. (2230 m.)

Mt. Gambier

VICTORIA

Ballarat

C. Howe

OCEAN

Geelong

Melbourne

King I.

Bass Strait

Furneaux Group

TASMAN

40°   40°

Launceston

TASMANIA

SEA

Hobart

South Cape

© Copyright HAMMOND INCORPORATED, Maplewood, N.J.

Longitude 140° East of Greenwich 145°

110° 115° 120° 125° 130° 135° 140° 145° 150° 155°

Vegetation/Relief

SCALE OF MILES
0 100 200 300 400 500 600

SCALE OF KILOMETERS
0 100 200 300 400 500 600

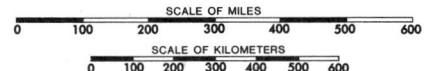

Capital of Country..............................⊛

State and Territorial Capitals.................◉

International Boundaries.......................

State and Territorial Boundaries..............

Depths in Fathoms

Forest
Woodland and Scrub
Grassland
Forest and Grassland
Cropland
Desert
Tundra and Alpine
Ice and Snow
Grassland and Scrub
Scrub and Fernlands

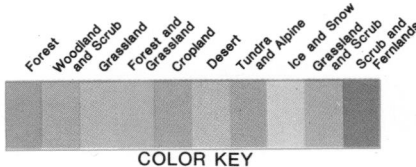

COLOR KEY

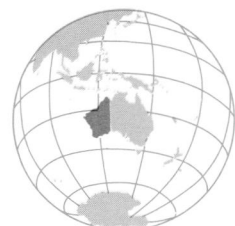

AREA 975,096 sq. mi.
(2,525,500 sq. km.)
POPULATION 1,169,800
CAPITAL Perth
LARGEST CITY Perth
HIGHEST POINT Mt. Bruce 4,024 ft.
(1,227 m.)

Topography

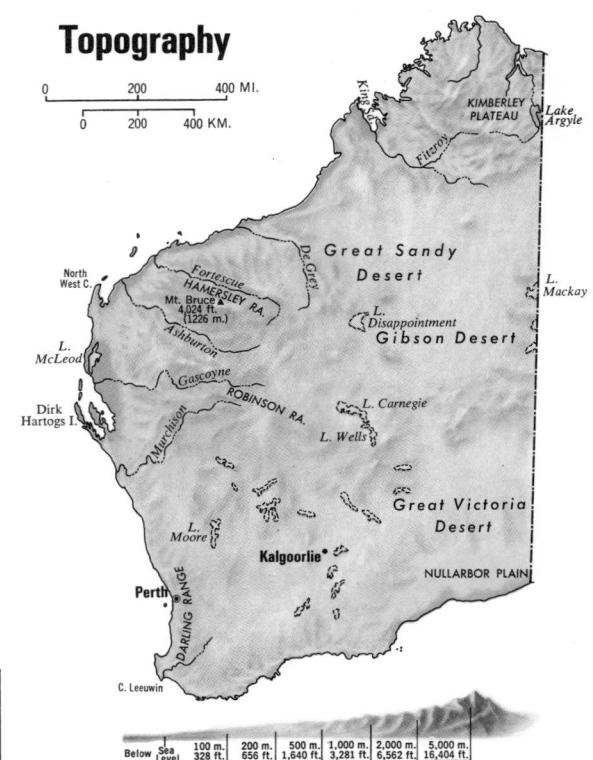

0   200   400 MI.
0   200   400 KM.

Below Sea Level	100 m. 328 ft.	200 m. 656 ft.	500 m. 1,640 ft.	1,000 m. 3,281 ft.	2,000 m. 6,562 ft.	5,000 m. 16,404 ft.

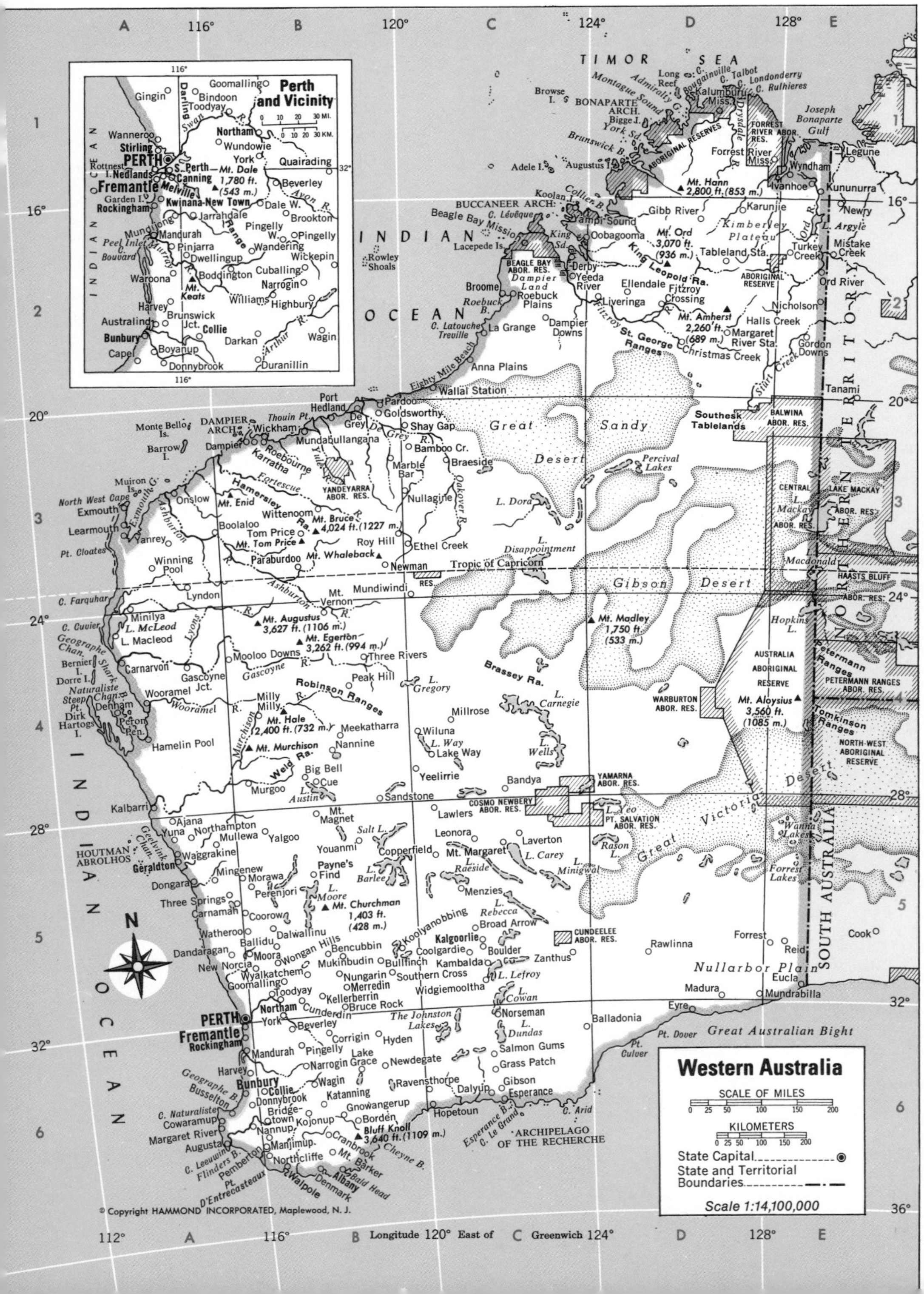

CITIES and TOWNS

Albany 13,696 ....B6
Australind 832 ....A2
Beverley 755 ....B1
Boulder-Kalgoorlie 19,041....C5
Bridgetown 1,316 ....B6
Broome 2,920 ....C2
Brunswick Junction 893 ....A2
Bunbury 19,513 ....A2
Busselton 5,550 ....A6
Canning 43,337 ....A1
Capel 669 ....A2
Carnarvon 5,341 ....A4
Collie 6,771 ....B2
Coolgardie 643 ....C5
Corrigin 853 ....B6
Cuballing⊙ 624 ....B2
Cunderdin 756 ....B5
Dalwallinu 683 ....B5
Dampier 2,727 ....B3

Dandaragan⊙ 1,725 ....A5
Denmark 786 ....B6
Derby 2,411 ....C2
Donnybrook 1,008 ....A2
Esperance 5,262 ....C6
Exmouth 2,336 ....A3
Fremantle 23,497 ....A1
Geraldton 18,773 ....A5
Gnowangerup 892 ....B6
Goldsworthy 989 ....B3
Goomalling 644 ....B1
Halls Creek 767 ....D2
Harvey 2,418 ....A2
Kalbarri 695 ....A4
Kalgoorlie 9,067 ....C5
Kalgoorlie-Boulder 19,041 ....C5
Kambalda 4,784 ....C5
Karratha 4,243 ....B3
Katanning 4,162 ....B6
Kellerberrin 1,198 ....B5
Kojonup 944 ....B6
Kununurra 1,540 ....E2

Kwinana New Town 10,981 A1
Lake Grace 616 ....B6
Laverton 848 ....C5
Learmonth A3
Mandurah 7,050 ....A2
Manjimup 3,734 ....B6
Margaret River 701 ....B6
Meekatharra 829 ....B4
Melville 54,384 ....A1
Merredin 3,661 ....B5
Moora 1,545 ....B5
Morawa 814 ....B5
Mount Barker 1,562 ....B6
Mullewa 933 ....A5
Narrogin 4,812 ....B6
Nedlands 20,974 ....A1
Newman 4,672 ....B4
Norseman 929 ....C6
Northam 6,866 ....B1
Northampton 703 ....A5
Onslow 220 ....A3
Paraburdoo 2,402 ....B3

Pardoo B3
Pemberton 777 ....A6
Perth (cap.) 87,598 ....A1
Perth‡ 731,275 ....A1
Pingelly 978 ....B2
Pinjarra 1,196 ....A2
Port Hedland 11,144 ....B3
Quairading 808 ....B1
Rockingham 17,693 ....A2
Roebourne 1,368 ....B3
Shay Gap 856 ....C3
Southern Cross 880 ....B5
South Perth 30,388 ....A1
Stirling 162,313 ....A1
Three Springs 605 ....A5
Tom Price 3,193 ....B3
Wagin 1,658 ....B2
Wanneroo 4,319 ....A1
Waroona 1,160 ....A2
Wickham 2,312 ....B3
Wiluna⊙ 879 ....C4
Wittenoom 962 ....B3
Wongan Hills 888 ....B5
Wundowie 969 ....B1
Wyndham 1,383 ....E1
Yampi Sound C2
York 1,108 ....B1

OTHER FEATURES

Adele (isl.) C1
Admiralty (gulf) D1
Aloysius (mt.) E4
Amherst (mt.) D2
Argyle (lake) E2
Arid (cape) C6
Arthur (riv.) B2
Ashburton (riv.) A3
Augustus (isl.) D1
Augustus (mt.) A4
Austin (lake) B4

Australia Aboriginal Res. E4
Avon (riv.) A1
Bald (head) B6
Balwina Aboriginal Res. E3
Barlee (lake) B5
Barrow (isl.) A3
Beaglebay Aboriginal Res. C2
Bernier (isl.) A4
Bigge (isl.) D1
Bluff Knoll (mt.) B6
Bonaparte (arch.) D1
Bougainville (cape) D1
Bouvard (cape) A2
Brassey (range) C4
Browse (isl.) C1
Bruce (mt.) B3
Brunswick (bay) D1
Buccaneer (arch.) C2
Carey (lake) C5
Carnegie (lake) C4
Central Aboriginal Res. E3
Cheyne (bay) B6
Churchman (mt.) B5
Cloates (pt.) A3
Collier (range) C1
Cosmo Newbery Aboriginal Res. C5
Cowan (lake) C5
Culver (pt.) D6
Cundeelee Aboriginal Res. C5
Cuvier (cape) A4
Dale (mt.) B1
Dampier (arch.) B3
Dampier Land (reg.) C2
Darling (range) A1
De Grey (riv.) B3
D'Entrecasteaux (pt.) A6
Dirk Hartogs (isl.) A4
Disappointment (lake) C3
Dora (lake) C3
Dorre (isl.) A4
Dover (pt.) D6
Drysdale (riv.) D1
Dundas (lake) C6
Egerton (mt.) B4
Eighty Mile (beach) C2
Enid (mt.) B3
Esperance (bay) C6
Exmouth (gulf) A3
Farquhar (cape) A3
Fitzroy (riv.) D2
Flinders (bay) A6
Forrest River Aboriginal Res. E1
Fortescue (riv.) B3
Garden (isl.) A1
Gascoyne (riv.) B4
Geelvink (chan.) A5
Geographe (bay) A6
Geographe (chan.) A4
Gibson (des.) D3
Great Australian (bight) E6
Great Sandy (des.) C3
Great Victoria (des.) D5
Gregory (lake) C4
Hale (mt.) B4
Hamersley (range) B3
Hann (mt.) D1
Hopkins (lake) E4
Houtman Abrolhos (isls.) A5
Indian Ocean A5
Johnston, The (lks.) C6
Joseph Bonaparte (gulf) E1
Keats (mt.) A2

Kimberley (plat.) D2
King (sound) C2
King Leopold (range) D2
Koolan (isl.) C1
Lacepede (isls.) C2
Latouche Treville (cape) C2
Leeuwin (cape) A6
Lefroy (lake) C5
Le Grand (cape) C6
Lévêque (cape) C2
Londonderry (cape) D1
Long (reef) D1
Lyons (riv.) A4
Macdonald (lake) E3
Mackay (lake) E3
Madley (mt.) D4
McLeod (lake) A4
Minigwal (lake) C5
Montague (sound) D1
Monte Bello (isls.) A3
Moore (lake) B5
Muiron (isls.) A3
Murchison (mt.) B4
Murchison (riv.) B4
Murray (riv.) A2
Naturaliste (cape) A6
Naturaliste (chan.) A4
North West (cape) A3
North-West Aboriginal Res. D4
Nullarbor (plain) D5
Oakover (riv.) C3
Ord (mt.) D1
Ord (riv.) E2
Peel (inlet) A2
Percival (lks.) D3
Peron (pen.) A4
Petermann (ranges) E4
Point Salvation Aboriginal Res. D5
Raeside (lake) C5
Rason (lake) D5
Rebecca (lake) C5
Recherche (arch.) C6
Robinson (ranges) B4
Roebuck (bay) C2
Rottnest (isl.) A1
Rowley (shoals) B2
Rulhieres (cape) D1
Saint George (ranges) D2
Salt (lake) B5
Shark (bay) A4
Southesk Tablelands D3
Steep (pt.) A4
Sturt (creek) D2
Swan (riv.) A1
Talbot (cape) D1
Thouin (pt.) B3
Timor (sea) D1
Tomkinson (ranges) E4
Wanna (lake) E5
Warburton Aboriginal Res. D4
Way (lake) C4
Weld (range) B4
Wells (lake) C4
Whaleback (mt.) B3
Wooramel (riv.) A4
Yamarna Aboriginal Res. D4
Yeo (lake) D5
York (sound) D1
Yule (riv.) B3

⊙Population of district.
‡Population of met. area.

© Copyright HAMMOND INCORPORATED, Maplewood, N.J.

Western Australia

SCALE OF MILES
0 25 50 100 150 200

KILOMETERS
0 25 50 100 150 200

State Capital ...... ◉
State and Territorial Boundaries ...... ——

Scale 1:14,100,000

Perth and Vicinity

0 10 20 30 MI.
0 10 20 30 KM.

CITIES and TOWNS

Adelaide River	B2
Alexandria	E5
Alice Springs 14,149	D7
Alyangula 988	E2
Angas Downs	C8
Angurugu 700	E3
Anthony Lagoon	D4
Areyonga 291	C8
Argadargada	E6
Aritunga	D7
Avon Downs	E5
Bamyili-Beswick 675	C3
Banka Banka	C5
Barrow Creek	D6
Batchelor	B2
Bathurst Island 895	B1
Birdum	C3
Birrimbah	C3
Birrindudu	A5
Borroloola 370	E4
Bundooma	D8
Burramurra	E6
Charlotte Waters	D8
Coniston	C7
Coolibah	B3
Creswell Downs	E4
Crocker Island Mission 244	C1
Daly River 430	B2
Daly Waters	C4
Darwin (cap.) 39,193	B2
Docker River 275	A8
Epenarra	D6
Erldunda	C8
Eva Downs	D5
Ewaninga	D7
Goulburn Island 243	C1
Gove (Nhulunbuy) 3,553	E2
Harts Range	D7
Hatches Creek	D6
Helen Srings	C5
Hermannsburg 694	C7
Hooker Creek 616	B5
Humpty Doo	B2
Juno	C5
Katherine 3,127	B3
Kildurk	A4
Koolpinyah	B2
Kulgera	C8
Kurundi	D6
Larrimah	C3
Legune	A3
Limbunya	B4
Lucy Creek	E7
Mainoru	C3
Maningimbi 660	C2
Mataranka	C3
Milingimbi 677	D2
Mistake Creek	A4
Montejinnie	C4
Mount Cavenagh	C8
Mount Doreen	B7
Murray Downs	D6
Napperby	C7
Newcastle Waters	C4
Nhulunbuy 3,553	E2
Numbulwar 378	D3
Oenpelli 508	C2
O. T. Downs	D4
Papunya 455	B7
Plenty River Mine	D7
Port Keats 882	A3
Powell Creek	C5
Rankine Store	E5
Robinson River	E4
Rockhampton Downs	D5
Rodinga	D8
Roper River 357	D3
Rum Jungle	B2
Santa Teresa 579	D8
Soudan	E6
Stirling Station	C6
Tanami	A5
Tarlton Downs	E7
Tea Tree Well	C7
Tempe Downs	C8
Tennant Creek 2,236	C5
The Granites	B6
Ucharonidge	D4
Umbakumba 371	E3
Umbeara	C8
Urapunga	D3
Utopia	D7
Victoria River Downs	B4
Warrego	C5
Wave Hill	B4
White Quartz Hill	D7
Willeroo	B3
Willowra	C6
Wollogorang	F4
Yambah	C7
Yirrkala 647	E2
Yuendumu 460	B7

OTHER FEATURES

Amadeus (lake)	B8
Arafura (sea)	D1
Arnhem Land (reg.)	D2
Arnhem Land Aboriginal Res.	C2
Arnold (riv.)	D3
Ayers Rock Nat'l Park	B8
Barkly Tableland	D4
Bathurst (isl.)	A1
Beagle (gulf)	A2
Beatrice (cape)	E3
Bennett (lake)	B7
Beswick Aboriginal Res.	C3
Bickerton (isl.)	E2
Blaze (pt.)	A2
Boucaut (bay)	D1
Carpentaria (gulf)	E3
Central Wedge (mt.)	C7
Clarence (str.)	B2
Cobourg (pen.)	C1
Conner (mt.)	B8
Croker (cape)	C1
Daly (riv.)	B2
Daly River Aboriginal Res.	A2
Davenport (mt.)	B7
Dobbie (mt.)	E7
Drummond (mt.)	E5
Dry (riv.)	C3
Dundas (str.)	B1
East Alligator (riv.)	C2
Ehrenberg (range)	B7
Elcho (isl.)	D1
Ewing (mt.)	E7
Fitzmaurice (riv.)	B3
Flora (riv.)	B3
Ford (cape)	A2
Georgina (riv.)	E6
Goulburn (isls.)	C1
Grey (mt.)	D2
Groote Eylandt (isl.)	E3
Haasts Bluff Aboriginal Res.	B8
Hale (riv.)	D8
Hanson (riv.)	C6
Hay (cape)	A3
Hay (dry riv.)	E7
Hogarth (mt.)	E6
Hopkins (lake)	A8
Joseph Bonaparte (gulf)	A3
Katherine (riv.)	C3
Lake MacKay Aboriginal Res.	A6
Lander (riv.)	C6
Leisler (mt.)	A7
Limmen (bight)	D3
Limmen Bight (riv.)	D4
Macdonald (lake)	B7
Macdonnell (ranges)	C7
MacKay (lake)	A7
Mann (riv.)	D2
Marshall (riv.)	D7
Melville (bay)	E2
Melville (isl.)	B1
Mount Olga Nat'l Park	B8
Murchison (range)	D6
Napier (mt.)	A4
Neale (lake)	A8
Newcastle (creek)	C4
Nicholson (riv.)	E5
Old Marsh Bed	C4
Olga (mt.)	B8
Peron (isls.)	A2
Petermann (ranges)	A8
Petermann Ranges Aboriginal Res.	A8
Port Darwin (inlet)	B2
Ranken (riv.)	E6
Robinson (riv.)	E4
Roper (riv.)	C3
Rose (riv.)	D2
Sandover (riv.)	D6
Simpson (des.)	E8
Singleton (mt.)	B7
Sir Edward Pellew Group (isls.)	E3
South Alligator (riv.)	C2
Stanley (mt.)	B7
Stewart (cape)	D1
Stirling (creek)	A4
Sturt (plain)	C4
Sylvester (lake)	D5
Tanami (des.)	C5
Timor (sea)	A2
Todd (riv.)	D8
Vanderlin (isl.)	E3
Van Diemen (cape)	A1
Van Diemen (gulf)	B1
Victoria (riv.)	B3
Wagait Aboriginal Res.	B2
Warwick (chan.)	E3
Wessel (isls.)	E1
West Baines (riv.)	A4
White (lake)	A6
Winnecke (creek)	B5
Woods (lake)	C4
Ziel (mt.)	C7

AREA 519,768 sq. mi. (1,346,200 sq. km.)
POPULATION 97,090
CAPITAL Darwin
LARGEST CITY Darwin
HIGHEST POINT Mt. Ziel 4,955 ft. (1,510 m.)

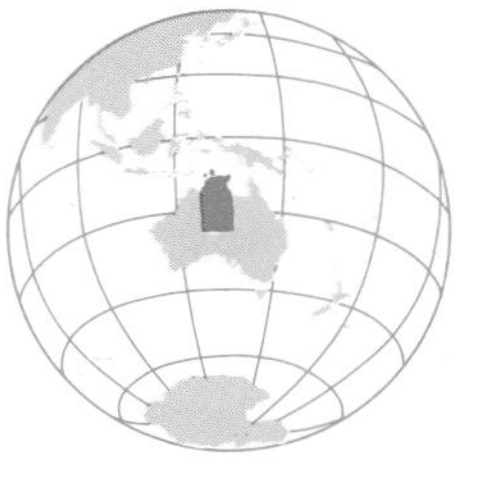

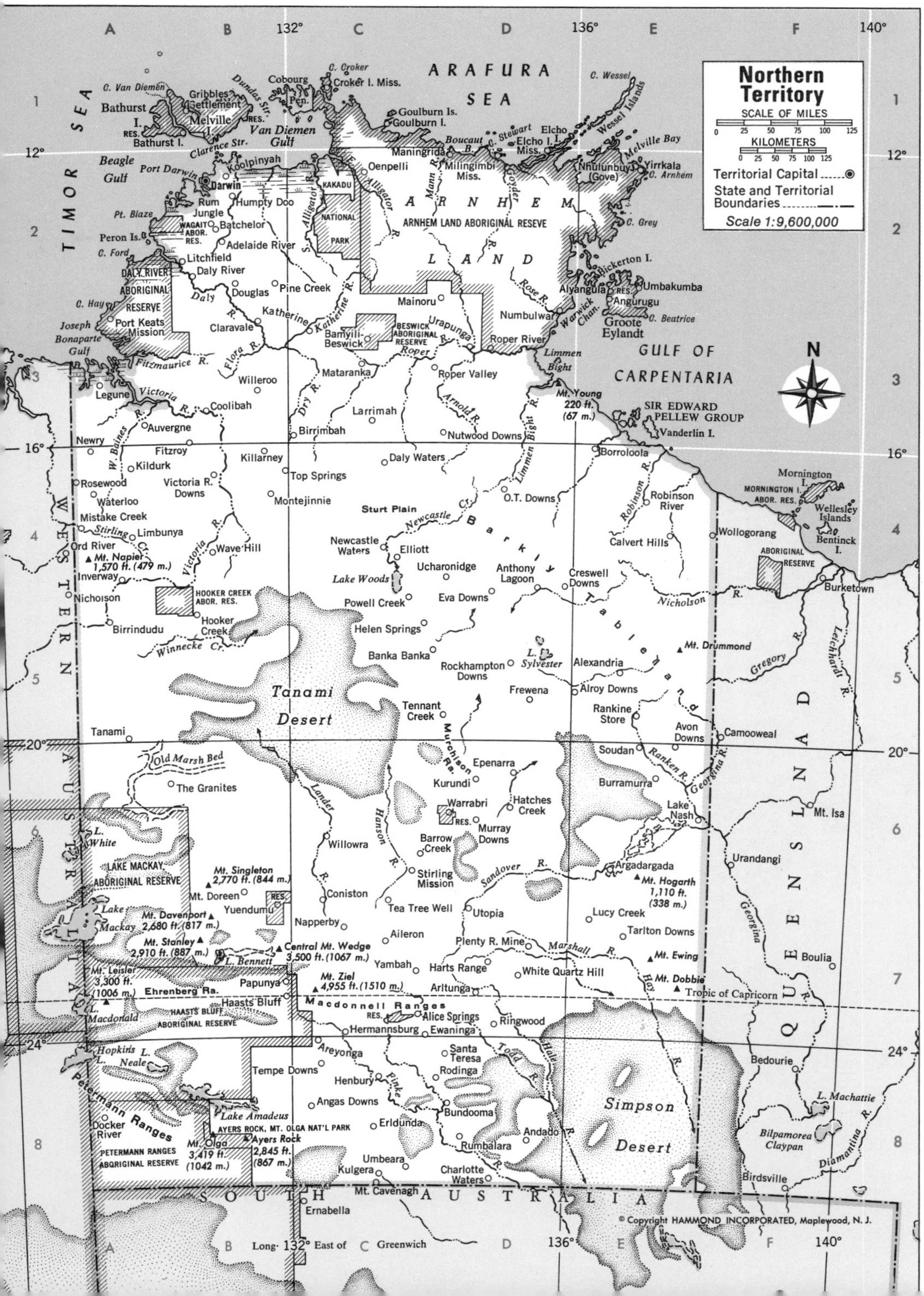

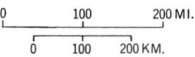

Northern Territory

SCALE OF MILES
0 25 50 75 100 125
KILOMETERS
0 25 50 75 100 125
Territorial Capital ......◉
State and Territorial Boundaries ......
Scale 1:9,600,000

Topography

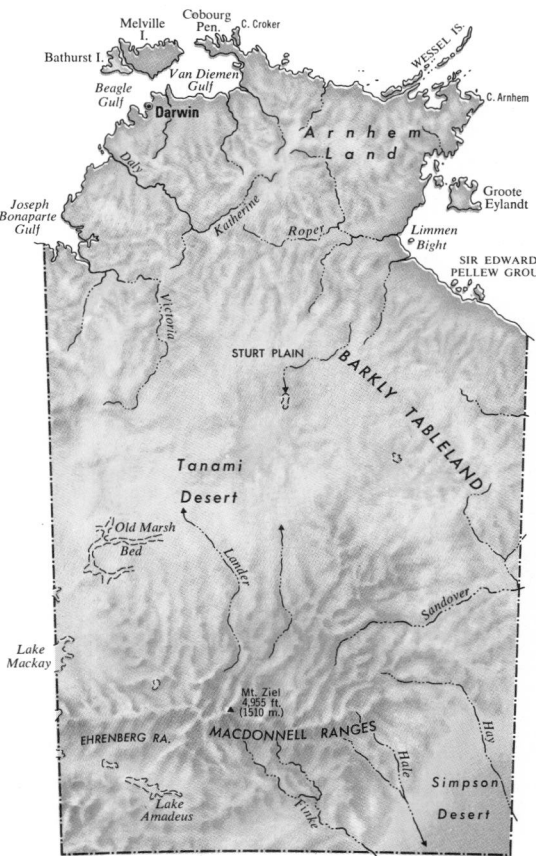

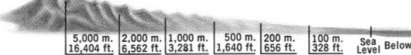

5,000 m. / 16,404 ft.   2,000 m. / 6,562 ft.   1,000 m. / 3,281 ft.   500 m. / 1,640 ft.   200 m. / 656 ft.   100 m. / 328 ft.   Sea Level   Below

© Copyright HAMMOND INCORPORATED, Maplewood, N.J.

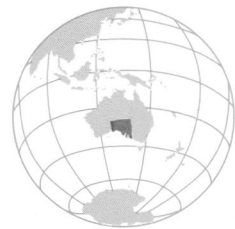

AREA 379,922 sq. mi. (984,000 sq. km.)
POPULATION 1,261,600
CAPITAL Adelaide
LARGEST CITY Adelaide
HIGHEST POINT Mt. Woodroffe 4,970 ft.
(1,515 m.)

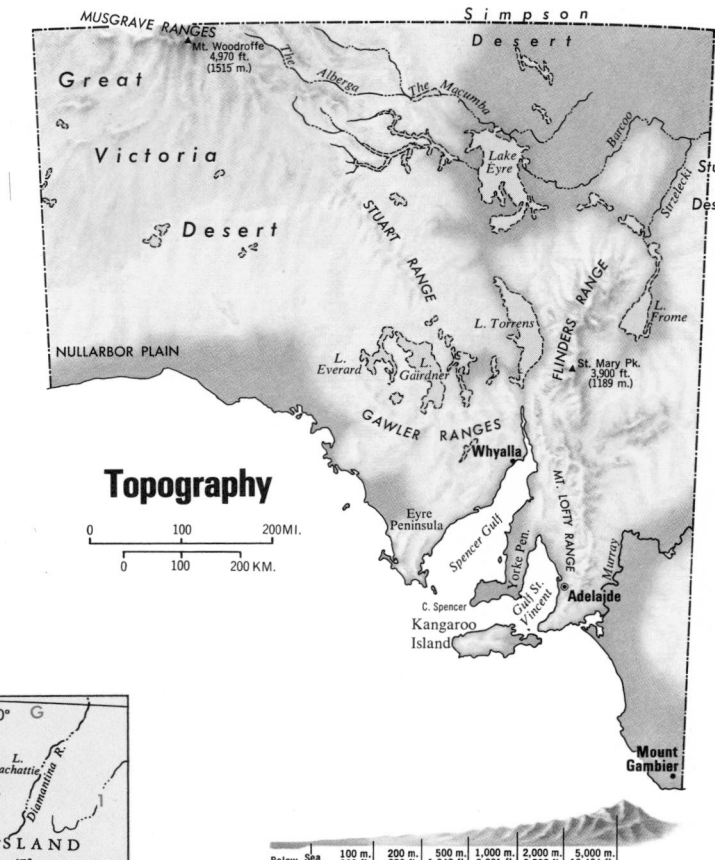

Topography

0 100 200 MI.
0 100 200 KM.

Below Sea Level | 100 m. 328 ft. | 200 m. 656 ft. | 500 m. 1,640 ft. | 1,000 m. 3,281 ft. | 2,000 m. 6,562 ft. | 5,000 m. 16,404 ft.

CITIES and TOWNS

Adelaide (cap.)‡ 857,196 ....B6
Andamooka 420 ....E4
Angaston 1,734 ....F6
Balaklava 1,237 ....F6
Barmera 1,946 ....G6
Berri 2,890 ....G6
Bordertown 1,983 ....G7
Brighton 21,407 ....A8
Burnside 38,461 ....B8
Burra 1,201 ....F5
Campbelltown 41,252 ....B7
Ceduna 2,327 ....D5
Clare 2,260 ....F5
Cleve 804 ....E5
Coober Pedy 1,903 ....D3
Cowell 627 ....E5
Crafters-Bridgewater 6,600 ..B8
Crystal Brook 1,410 ....E5
Cummins 761 ....D6

Elizabeth 33,721 ....B7
Elliston⊙ 1,268 ....D5
Enfield 73,505 ....B7
Gawler 8,596 ....B6
Gladstone 802 ....F5
Glenelg 14,413 ....A8
Hahndorf 937 ....B8
Hindmarsh 8,691 ....A7
Iron Knob 691 ....E5
Jamestown 1,215 ....F5
Kadina 2,849 ....E5
Kapunda 1,362 ....F6
Keith 1,191 ....G7
Kensington and Norwood
9,651 ....B8
Kimba 819 ....E5
Kingscote 1,121 ....E6
Kingston 1,250 ....G7
Laura 472 ....F5
Leigh Creek 999 ....F4
Lobethal 1,422 ....C7
Loxton 2,786 ....G6

Maitland 1,017 ....E6
Mannum 2,137 ....F6
Marion 67,283 ....A8
Meningie 736 ....F6
Millicent 5,471 ....F7
Minlaton 822 ....E6
Mitcham 59,887 ....B8
Moonta 1,379 ....E5
Mount Barker 3,204 ....C8
Mount Gambier 17,858 ....G7
Murray Bridge 7,476 ....F6
Nairne 594 ....C8
Nangwarry 863 ....G7
Naracoorte 4,571 ....G7
Nuriootpa 2,808 ....F6
Ororroo 631 ....F5
Payneham 17,545 ....B7
Penola 1,254 ....G7
Peterborough 2,760 ....F5
Pinnaroo 758 ....G6
Port Adelaide 36,024 ....A7
Port Augusta 13,092 ....E5

Port Broughton 654 ....F5
Port Lincoln 9,809 ....E6
Port Pirie 15,005 ....E5
Prospect 19,485 ....B7
Quorn 1,048 ....F5
Radium Hill G5
Renmark 6,247 ....G5
Robe 490 ....F7
Salisbury 77,477 ....B7
Snowtown 511 ....E5
Stirling North 1,028 ....E5
Strathalbyn 1,701 ....F6
Streaky Bay 1,008 ....D5
Tailem Bend 1,999 ....F6
Tanunda 2,254 ....C6
Tea Tree Gully 56,050 ....B7
Thebarton 10,315 ....A7
Tumby Bay 900 ....D6
Unley 37,016 ....B8
Victor Harbor 4,279 ....F6
Waikerie 1,611 ....F6
Wallaroo 1,969 ....E5
West Torrens 47,992 ....A8
Whyalla 33,389 ....E5
Williamstown 475 ....C7
Willunga 537 ....F6
Woodside 724 ....C8
Woodville 75,276 ....A7
Womera 2,958 ....B3
Wudinna 507 ....D5
Yorketown 679 ....E6

OTHER FEATURES

Acraman (lake) D5
Alberga The, (riv.) D2
Alexandrina (lake) F6
Anxious (bay) D5
Arckaringa (creek) D2
Barcoo (creek) F3
Barossa (res.) C6
Birksgate (range) A2
Blanche (lake) F7
Brady (mt.) D3
Cadibarrawirracanna (lake) D3
Callabonna (lake) F3
Catastrophe (cape) D6
Coffin (bay) D6
Coffin Bay (pen.) D6
Coopers (Barcoo) (creek) ..F3
Coorong, The (lag.) F6
Dey Dey (lake) B3
Encounter (bay) F6
Everard (lake) D4
Everard (ranges) C2
Eyre (pen.) D6
Eyre North (lake) E3
Eyre South (lake) E3
Finke (riv.) C1
Flinders (range) F4
Frome (lake) G4
Gairdner (lake) D4
Gawler (ranges) E5
Gawler (riv.) B6
Gilles (lake) E5
Goyders (lag.) F2
Great Australian (bight) A5
Great Victoria (des.) B3
Gregory (lake) F3

Hack (mt.) F4
Hamilton, The (riv.) D2
Harris (lake) D4
Head of Bight (bay) B4
Indian Ocean E7
Investigator (str.) E6
Investigator Group (isls.)....D5
Island (lag.) E4
Jaffa (cape) F7
Kangaroo (isl.) E7
Lacepede (bay) F7
Little Para (riv.) B7
Lofty (mt.) B8
Macfarlane (lake) E5
Macumba (riv.) E2
Maurice (lake) B3
Meramangye (lake) C3
Morris (mt.) B2
Mount Bold (res.) B8
Murray (riv.) F6
Musgrave (ranges) B2
Neales, The (riv.) E3
Neptune (isls.) D6
Northumberland (cape) F8
Nukey Bluff (mt.) D5
Nullarbor (plain) A4
Nurrari (lkes) B3
Nuyts (arch.) C5
Nuyts (cape) C5
Onkaparinga (riv.) B8
Peera Peera Poolanna (lake) F2
Saint Mary (peak) F5
Saint Vincent (gulf) F6
Serpentine (lkes) A3
Simpson (des.) E1
Sir Joseph Banks Group
(isls.) E6
South Para (riv.) C7
Spencer (cape) E6
Spencer (gulf) E6
Stevenson, The (riv.) D2
Streaky (bay) C5
Strzelecki (creek) G3
Stuart (range) D3
Sturt (des.) G3
Sturt (riv.) B8
The Alberga (riv.) D2
The Coorong (lag.) F6
The Hamilton (riv.) D2
The Macumba (riv.) E2
The Neales (riv.) E3
The Stevenson (riv.) D2
The Warburton (riv.) F2
Thistle (isl.) E6
Torrens (lake) E4
Torrens (riv.) B8
Warburton The, (riv.) F2
Warren (res.) C7
Whidbey (isls.) D6
Wilkinson (lkes) C3
Wilson Bluff (prom.) A4
Woodroffe (mt.) B2
Yalata Aboriginal Res. B4
Yarle (lkes) B4
Yorke (pen.) E6

⊙Population of district.
‡Population of met. area.

Adelaide and Vicinity

0 4 8 12 MI.
0 4 8 12 KM.

South Australia

SCALE OF MILES
0 25 50 75 100 125 150
KILOMETERS
0 25 50 75 100 125 150

State Capital .... ⊚
State and Territorial
Boundaries............ — · —
Scale 1:9,790,000

© Copyright HAMMOND INCORPORATED, Maplewood, N.J.

128° A 132° B C 136° D Longitude East of E Greenwich F 140° G

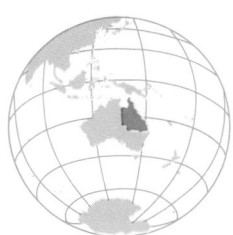

CITIES and TOWNS

Ascot 4,606................E2
Atherton 3,611............C3
Ayr 8,606.................C3
Beaudesert 4,029.........E6
Biloela 4,586............D5
Blackwater 4,638.........D4
Bowen 6,707..............D3
Brisbane (cap.) 696,740..D2
Brisbane‡ 892,987........D2
Bundaberg 31,189.........D5
Cairns 39,305............C3
Caloundra 10,602.........E5
Camp Hill 9,961..........E3
Charleville 3,802........C5
Charters Towers 7,914....C4
Chermside 7,666..........D2
Coopers Plains 5,017.....D3
Corinda 4,132............D3
Dalby 8,997..............D5
East Brisbane 5,506......E3
Emerald 3,161............C4
Gatton 3,986.............E5
Geebung 5,585............D2
Gladstone 18,591.........D4
Gold Coast 87,510........D6
Goondiwindi 3,741........D6
Greenslopes 7,349........E3
Gympie 11,205............E5
Hervey Bay 9,150.........E5
Holland Park 7,708.......E3
Home Hill 3,330..........C3
Inala 20,037.............D3
Indooroopilly 8,534......D3
Ingham 5,868.............C3
Innisfail 7,933..........C3
Ipswich 69,242...........E5
Kingaroy 5,088...........D5
Longreach 3,354..........B4
Mackay 31,522............D4
Mareeba 5,776............C3
Maroochydore-Mooloolaba 10,283...........E5
Maryborough 21,527.......E5
Mary Kathleen 811........A4
Mitchelton 6,115.........D2
Moorooka 9,639...........D3
Moranbah 4,053...........C9
Mount Isa 25,377.........A4
Mount Morgan 3,246.......D4
Nambour 7,435............E5
Newmarket 3,955..........E2
Nundah 7,590.............E2
Redcliffe 39,073.........E5
Rockhampton 50,132.......D4
Roma 5,898...............D5
Sandgate 7,204...........D2
Stafford 7,303...........D2
Stanthorpe 3,927.........D6
Tewantin-Noosa 5,834.....E5
Toowoomba 63,956.........D5
Townsville 78,653........C3
Warwick 9,169............D6
Weipa 2,876..............B2
Windsor 6,363............D2
Wynnum 11,497............E5
Yeppoon 5,575............D4
Yeronga 4,813............D3

OTHER FEATURES

Albatross (bay)..........B2
Alice (riv.).............C4
Archer (riv.)............B2
Balonne (riv.)...........D6
Banks (isl.).............B1
Barcoo (creek)...........B5
Barkly Tableland.........A4
Bartle Frere (mt.).......C3
Beal (range).............B5
Belyando (riv.)..........C4
Bentinck (isl.)..........A3
Bigge (range)............D5
Bowling Green (cape).....C3
Bramble (bay)............E2
Brisbane (riv.)..........E2
Brisbane Airport.........E2
Broad (sound)............D4
Bulimba (creek)..........E3
Bulloo (lake)............B6
Bulloo (riv.)............B6
Bunker Group (isls.).....E4
Burdekin (riv.)..........C3
Cabbage Tree (creek).....D2
Cape York (pen.).........B3
Capricorn (chan.)........D4
Capricorn Group (isls.)..E4
Carnarvon (range)........D5
Carpentaria (gulf).......A2
Caryapundy (swamp).......B6
Clarke (range)...........C4
Cloncurry (riv.).........B4
Coleman (riv.)...........B2
Comet (riv.).............D5
Condamine (riv.).........D5
Coopers (Barcoo) (creek).B5
Coral (sea)..............C1
Culgoa (riv.)............C6
Cumberland (isls.).......D4
Curtis (isl.)............D4
Darling Downs............D5
Dawson (riv.)............D5
Diamantina (riv.)........B4
Direction (cape).........B2
Downfall (creek).........D2

Drummond (range).........C5
Duifken (pt.)............B2
Endeavour (str.).........B1
Enoggera (creek).........D2
Fitzroy (riv.)...........D4
Flattery (cape)..........C2
Flinders (riv.)..........B3
Fraser (isl.)............E5
Galilee (lake)...........C4
Georgina (riv.)..........A4
Gilbert (riv.)...........B3
Great Dividing (range)...C4
Great Sandy (Fraser) (isl.)..E5

Gregory (range)..........B3
Gregory (riv.)...........A3
Grenville (cape).........B1
Grey (range).............B5
Halifax (bay)............C3
Hamilton (riv.)..........B4
Hervey (bay).............E5
Hinchinbrook (isl.)......C3
Holroyd (riv.)...........B2
Hook (isl.)..............D4
Isaacs (riv.)............D4
Kedron (brook)...........D2
Keerweer (cape)..........B2

AREA 666,872 sq. mi. (1,727,200 sq. km.)
POPULATION 2,111,700
CAPITAL Brisbane
LARGEST CITY Brisbane
HIGHEST POINT Mt. Bartle Frere 5,287 ft. (1,611 m.)

Topography

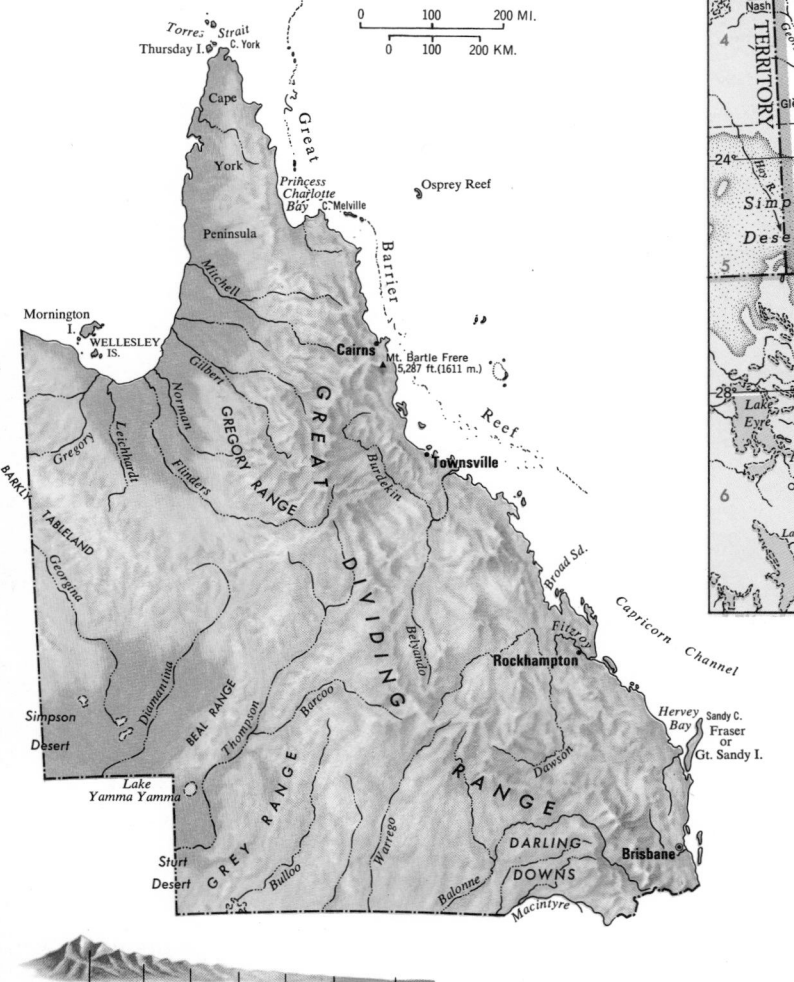

Leichhardt (range)........C4
Leichhardt (riv.).........A3
Machattie (lake)..........B5
Macintyre (riv.)..........D6
Manifold (cape)...........D4
Maranoa (riv.)............C5
Mary (riv.)...............E5
McIlwraith (range)........B2
Melville (cape)...........C2
Mitchell (riv.)...........B2
Moonah (riv.).............A4
Moreton (bay).............E5
Moreton (isl.)............E5
Mornington (isl.).........A3
Nicholson (riv.)..........A3
Nogoa (riv.)..............C5
Norman (creek)............D3
Norman (riv.).............B3
Normandy (riv.)...........C2
Northern Peninsula Aboriginal Res..........B1
Northumberland (isls.)....D4

Oxley (creek).............D3
Palmer (riv.).............B2
Paroo (riv.)..............C6
Peak (range)..............C4
Pera (creek)..............B2
Prince of Wales (isl.)....B2
Princess Charlotte (bay)..C2
Sandy (cape)..............E5
Selwyn (range)............B4
Sidmouth (cape)...........C2
Simpson (des.)............A5
Staaten (riv.)............B3
Sturt (des.)..............B3
Suttor (riv.).............C4
Swain (reefs).............E4
Thompson (riv.)...........B5
Torres (str.).............B1
Trinity (bay).............C3
Tully (falls).............C3
Warrego (range)...........C5
Warrego (riv.)............C5
Wellesley (isls.).........A3

Whitsunday (isl.).........D4
Wide (bay)................E5
Willies (range)...........C6
Wilson (riv.).............B5
Yamma Yamma (lake)........B5
York (cape)...............B1

CORAL SEA ISLANDS TERR.

PHYSICAL FEATURES

Bougainville (reef).......C2
Flinders (reefs)..........D3
Great Barrier (reef)......C2
Herald (cays).............D3
Holmes (reef).............C3
Marion (reef).............C2
Osprey (reef).............C2
Saumarez (reef)...........E4

‡Population of met. area.

© Copyright HAMMOND INCORPORATED, Maplewood, N. J.

AUSTRALIAN CAPITAL TERRITORY

CITIES and TOWNS

Canberra (cap.),
 Australia 196,538 .... E4
Canberra‡ 197,622 .... E4
Jervis Bay F4

OTHER FEATURES

St. Georges (Head) F4

NEW SOUTH WALES

CITIES and TOWNS

Aberdeen 1,133	F3
Adelong 766	D4
Albert	D3
Albury 31,954	D5
Alstonville 1,457	G1
Ardlethan 675	D4
Armidale 19,711	F2
Ashfield 42,322	J3
Ashford 692	F1
Ashley	E1
Auburn 47,556	J3
Avondale 1,929	F3
Baan Baa	E2
Ballina 7,323	G1
Balpunga	A3
Balranald 1,396	B4
Bangalow 568	G1
Bankstown 155,843	J3
Baradine 754	E2
Bargo 669	F4
Barham 1,108	C4
Barraba 1,947	F2
Barringun	C1
Baryulgil	G1
Batemans Bay 3,463	F4
Bathurst 18,589	E3
Batlow 1,374	E4
Baulkham Hills 21,182	H3
Bega 4,253	E5
Bellata	E1
Bellbird-Cessnock 16,256	F3
Bellingen 1,398	G2
Belmore	J3
Bemboka	E5
Benanee	B4
Bendemeer	F2
Berrigan 952	C4
Berry 1,132	F4
Bibbenluke 1,808	E5
Bigga	E4
Binda	E4
Bingara 1,295	F1
Binnaway 612	E2
Birriwa	E3
Blacktown 159,734	H3
Blayney 2,535	E3
Blue Mountains 45,798	F3
Bobadah	D3
Bogan Gate	D3
Boggabri 973	F2
Bomaderry-Nowra 15,496	F4
Bombala 1,474	E5
Bonnyrigg	H3
Booligal	C3
Boomi 2,301	E1
Boorooban	C4
Boorowa 1,192	E4
Botany 35,739	J4
Bourke 3,534	D2
Bowral 6,283	F4
Bowraville 801	G2
Braidwood 989	E4
Branxton-Greta 2,485	F3
Bredbo	E4
Brewarrina 1,386	D1
Bribbaree	D3
Brisbane Water 54,819	F3
Broken Hill 27,647	A3
Browning	E4
Brunswick Heads 1,402	G1
Budgewoi Lake 15,748	F3
Bugaldie	E2
Bulahdelah 986	G3
Bundanoon 843	F4
Bungendore 601	E4
Burcher	D3
Burns	A3
Burraboi	C4
Burta	A3
Burwood 29,045	J3
Byrock	D2
Byron Bay 2,525	G1
Camden 7,644	F4
Camden Haven 2,168	G2
Campbelltown 52,299	F4
Canbelego	D2
Canowindra 1,743	E3

NEW SOUTH WALES

AREA 309,498 sq. mi.
(801,600 sq. km.)
POPULATION 4,914,300
CAPITAL Sydney
LARGEST CITY Sydney
HIGHEST POINT Mt. Kosciusko
7,310 ft. (2,228 m.)

VICTORIA

AREA 87,876 sq. mi.
(227,600 sq. km.)
POPULATION 3,746,000
CAPITAL Melbourne
LARGEST CITY Melbourne
HIGHEST POINT Mt. Bogong
6,508 ft. (1,984 m.)

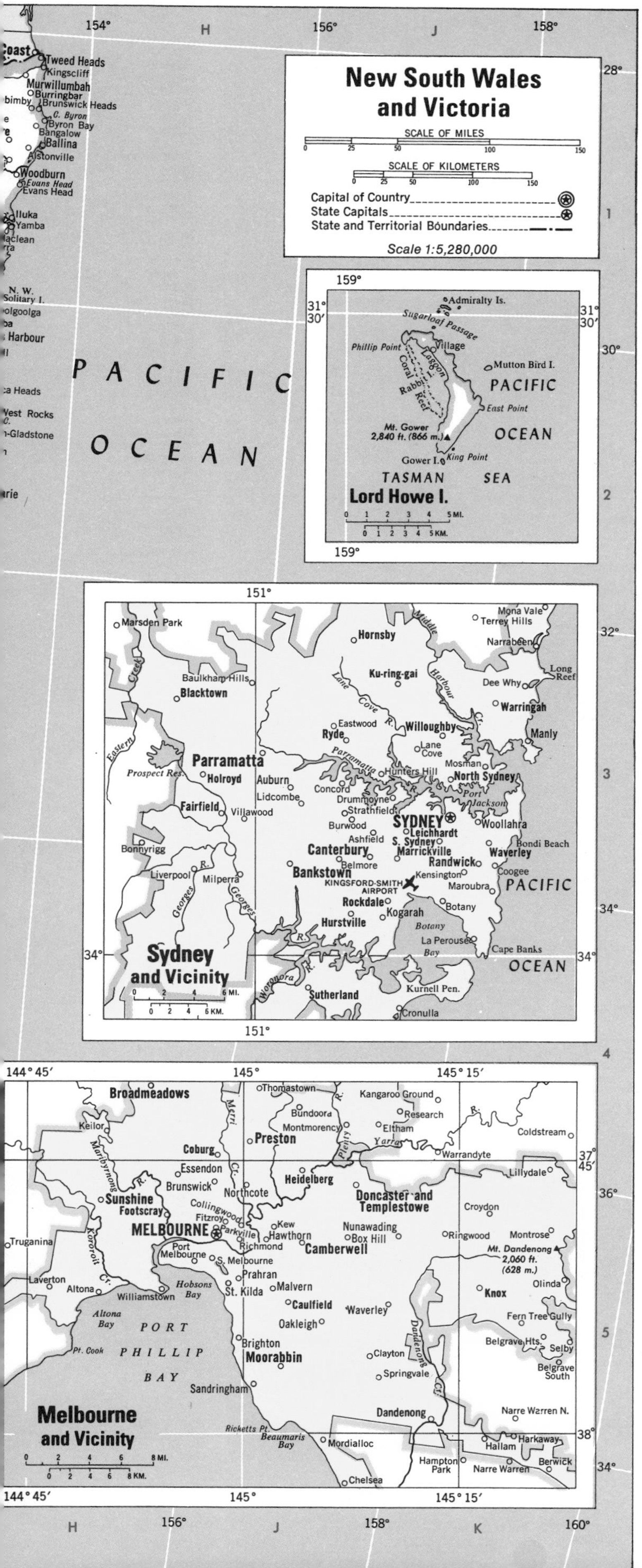

Topography

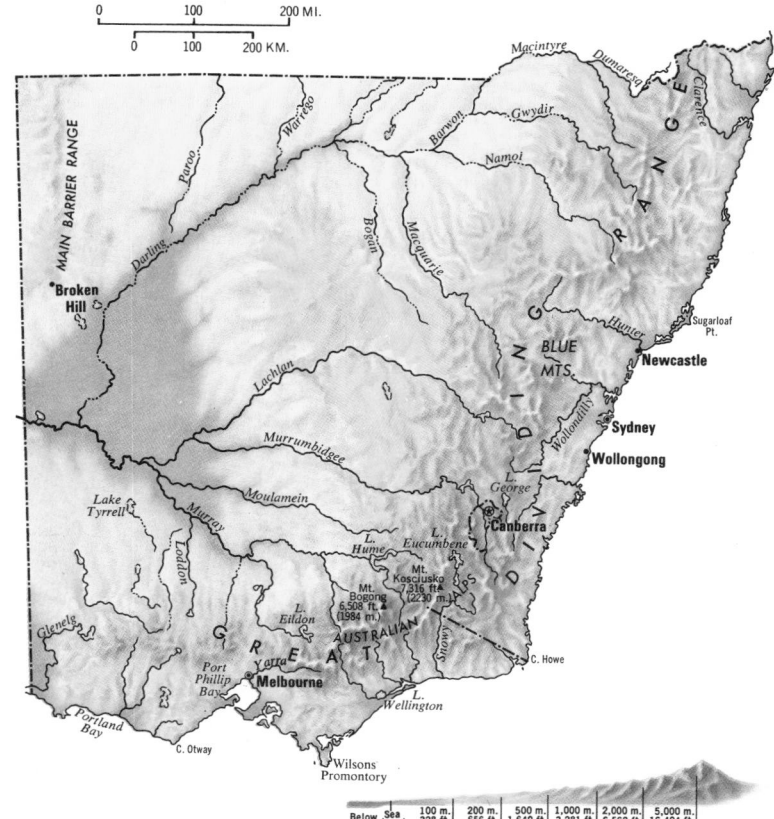

Below Sea Level	100 m. 328 ft.	200 m. 656 ft.	500 m. 1,640 ft.	1,000 m. 3,281 ft.	2,000 m. 6,562 ft.	5,000 m. 16,404 ft.

(continued on following page)

New South Wales and Victoria

SCALE OF MILES
0   25   50   75   100   125   150

SCALE OF KILOMETERS
0   25   50   75   100   125   150

Capital of Country
State Capitals
State and Territorial Boundaries

Scale 1:5,280,000

Lord Howe I.

Sydney and Vicinity

Melbourne and Vicinity

Terrigal-Wamberal 7,453 ....F3
The Entrance 20,107 ....F3
The Rock 656 ....D4
Thurloo Downs B1
Tibbita C4
Tiltagara C2
Tingha 868 ....F1
Tocumwal 1,131 ....C4
Tongo B2
Torrowangee A2
Trangie 1,016 ....D3
Tumbarumba 1,499 ....D4
Tumut 5,569 ....E4
Ulladulla 4,271 ....F4
Uralla 1,940 ....F2
Urunga 1,601 ....G2
Village J2
Villawood H3
Wagga Wagga 32,984 ....D4
Walcha 1,665 ....F2
Walgett 2,253 ....E2
Wallerawang 1,658 ....F3
Wangi-Rathmines 3,539 ....F3
Warialda 1,264 ....F1
Warragamba 1,535 ....F3
Warren 2,077 ....D2
Wauchope 3,525 ....G2
Waverley 61,693 ....K3
Waverley Downs B1
Wee Waa 1,904 ....E2
Wellington 5,395 ....E3
Wentworth 1,136 ....B4
Werris Creek 1,999 ....F2
West Wyalong 3,534 ....D3
Wetuppa B4
Whyjonta B1
Wilcannia 1,023 ....B2
Willoughby 51,541 ....J3
Wingham 3,435 ....G2
Wollongong 165,086 ....F4
Wollongong* 197,127 ....F4
Woodburn 610 ....G1
Woolgoolga 1,601 ....G2
Woollahra 53,259 ....K3
Wyong 3,679 ....F3
Yallock C3
Yalpunga A1
Yamba 1,649 ....G1
Yancannia B2
Yantara B1
Yass 4,247 ....E4
Yenda 667 ....D4
Young 6,459 ....E4

OTHER FEATURES

Admiralty (isls.) J1
Ana Branch, Darling (riv.) A3
Australian Alps (mts.) D5
Bancannia (lake) A2
Banks (isl.) K4
Baradine (creek) E2
Barrington Tops (mt.) F2
Barwon (riv.) D2
Birrie (riv.) D1
Blowering (res.) E4
Blue (mts.) F3
Bogan (riv.) D2
Bokhara (riv.) D1
Bondi (beach) K3
Botany (bay) J4
Brewster (lake) D3
Broken (bay) F3
Burrinjuck (res.) E4
Byron (cape) G1
Carpertee (riv.) F3
Caryapundy (swamp) B1
Castlereagh (riv.) E2
Cawndilla (lake) A3
Clarence (riv.) G1
Colo (riv.) F3
Cowal (lake) D3
Crowdy (head) G2
Crowl (creek) C2
Culgoa (riv.) D1
Cuttaburra (creek) C1
Darling (riv.) B3
Dumaresq (riv.) F1
East (pt.) J2
Eastern (creek) H3
Eucumbene (lake) E5
Evans (head) G1
George (lake) E4
Georges (riv.) H4
Gower (isl.) J2
Gower (mt.) J2
Great Dividing (range) E3
Green (cape) F5
Gunderbooka (ranges) C2
Gwydir (riv.) E1
Horton (riv.) F2
Howe (cape) F5
Hume (res.) D4
Hunter (riv.) F3
Innes (lake) G2
Irrara (creek) C1
Jindabyne (lake) E5
King (pt.) J2
Kingsford-Smith Airport J4
Kosciusko (mt.) E5
Kulkyne (creek) C1
Kurnell (pen.) J4

Lachlan (range) C3
Lachlan (riv.) C3
Lane Cove (riv.) J3
Liverpool (range) F2
Long Reef (pt.) K3
Lord Howe (isl.) J2
Macintyre (riv.) E1
Macquarie (lake) F3
Macquarie (riv.) D2
Main Barrier (range) A2
Manning (riv.) F2
Marra (creek) D2
Marrowie (creek) C3
Marthaguy (creek) D2
McPherson (range) G1
Medgun (creek) E1
Menindee (lake) B3
Middle Harbour (creek) J3
Monaro (range) E5
Moomin (creek) E1
Moonie (riv.) E1
Moulamein (creek) C4
Mount Royal (range) F2
Murray (riv.) A4
Murrumbidgee (riv.) C4
Mutton Bird (isl.) J2
Myall (lake) G3
Namoi (riv.) E2
Narran (lake) D1
Narran (riv.) D1
Nedgera (creek) E2
New England (range) F1
Nymboida (riv.) G1
Ottleys (creek) F1
Paroo (chan.) B2
Paroo (riv.) C1
Parramatta (riv.) J3
Peery (lake) B2
Phillip (pt.) J2
Pian (creek) E1
Pitarpunga (lake) B4
Plomer (pt.) G2
Poopeloe (lake) C2
Popilta (lake) A3
Port Jackson (inlet) J3
Port Stephens (inlet) G3
Prospect (res.) H3
Rabbit (isl.) J2
Richmond (range) G1
Richmond (riv.) G1
Riverina (reg.) C4
Robe (riv.) A2
Round, The (mt.) G2
Salt, The (lake) B2
Severn (riv.) F1
Shoalhaven (riv.) E4

Smoky (cape) G2
Snowy (mts.) E5
Snowy (riv.) E5
Solitary (isl.) G1
Stony (ranges) B2
Sturt (mt.) A1
Sugarloaf (passage) J1
Sugarloaf (pt.) G3
Talyawalka (creek) B2
Talyawalka Ana Branch, Darling
  (riv.) B3
Tandou (lake) A3
Tasman (sea) F5
The Round (mt.) G2
The Salt (lake) B2
Timbarra (riv.) G1
Tongo (lake) B2
Travellers (lake) B3
Tuggerah (lake) F3
Twofold (bay) F5
Urana (lake) D4
Victoria (lake) A3
Wallis (lake) G3
Warrego (riv.) C1
Whalan (creek) E1
Willandra Billabong (creek) C3
Wollondilly (riv.) F4
Wongalarra (creek) C2
Woronora (riv.) J4
Wyangala (res.) E3
Yanko (creek) C4
Yantara (lake) B1

VICTORIA

CITIES and TOWNS

Alexandra 1,808 ....C5
Altona 30,272 ....H5
Apollo Bay 978 ....B6
Ararat 8,288 ....B5
Avoca 992 ....B5
Bacchus Marsh 4,956 ....C5
Bairnsdale 9,130 ....D5
Ballarat 37,863 ....C5
Ballarat☐ 60,737 ....C5
Beaufort 1,219 ....B5
Beechworth 3,241 ....D5
Belgrave Heights J5
Belgrave South K5
Benalla 8,300 ....D5
Bendigo 32,573 ....C5
Bendigo☐ 50,169 ....C5
Berwick 25,616 ....K6
Birchip 945 ....B4

Boort 878 ....B5
Box Hill 50,280 ....J5
Bright 1,240 ....D5
Brighton 35,783 ....J5
Broadford 1,567 ....C5
Broadmeadows 108,744 ....H4
Brunswick 46,192 ....H5
Bruthen 568 ....D5
Bundoora J4
Camberwell 89,865 ....J5
Camperdown 3,596 ....C6
Casterton 2,163 ....A5
Castlemaine 7,583 ....C5
Caulfield 73,630 ....J5
Charlton 1,358 ....B5
Chelsea 26,357 ....J5
Churchill 3,509 ....D6
Clunes 726 ....C5
Cobden 1,418 ....B6
Cobram 3,378 ....C4
Coburg 58,379 ....H5
Cohuna 2,132 ....C4
Colac 10,431 ....B6
Coldstream K4
Coleraine 1,289 ....A5
Collingwood 16,645 ....J5
Corryong 1,406 ....D5
Craigieburn 2,491 ....C5
Cranbourne 5,162 ....C6
Creswick 2,033 ....B5
Croydon 33,474 ....K5
Dandenong 48,444 ....K5
Darby D6
Daylesford 2,913 ....C5
Dimboola 1,706 ....B5
Donald 1,627 ....B5
Doncaster and
  Templestowe 82,090 ....J5
Drouin 3,100 ....C6
Dunolly 621 ....C5
Eaglehawk 6,447 ....C5
Echuca 7,873 ....C5
Edenhope 916 ....A5
Eildon 796 ....C5
Eltham 28,631 ....J4
Essendon 51,133 ....H5
Euroa 2,713 ....C5
Fitzroy 20,451 ....H5
Footscray 51,774 ....H5
Geelong 15,727 ....C6
Geelong☐ 122,080 ....C5
Geelong West 15,978 ....C6
Hamilton 9,504 ....B5
Hampton Park 3,316 ....K6
Harkaway K6
Hawthorn 32,505 ....J5

Healesville 3,709 ....C5
Heathcote 1,076 ....C5
Heidelberg 66,108 ....J5
Heyfield 1,699 ....D6
Heywood 1,193 ....A6
Hopetoun 867 ....B4
Horsham 11,647 ....B5
Inglewood 745 ....C5
Inverloch 1,459 ....C6
Kaniva⊙ 1,949 ....A5
Keilor 70,597 ....H5
Kerang 4,022 ....B4
Kew 29,683 ....J5
Kilmore 1,517 ....C5
Knox 74,456 ....K5
Koondrook B4
Koroit 1,408 ....B6
Korumburra 2,795 ....D6
Kyabram 5,122 ....C5
Kyneton 3,694 ....C5
Lakes Entrance 3,023 ....E5
Lara 1,573 ....C6
Leongatha 3,586 ....C6
Lillydale 50,858 ....J4
Maffra 3,836 ....D5
Maldon 946 ....C5
Mallacoota 572 ....E5
Malvern 45,566 ....J5
Mansfield 1,919 ....D5
Maryborough 7,569 ....B5
Melbourne (cap.) 64,970 ....H5
Melbourne‡ 2,479,225 ....H5
Melton⊙ 13,856 ....C5
Merbein 1,727 ....A4
Mildura 14,417 ....A4
Minyip 561 ....B5
Moe 15,345 ....D6
Montmorency J4
Montrose K5
Moorabbin 103,059 ....J5
Mordialloc 28,615 ....J5
Morea A5
Mornington 20,206 ....C6
Mortlake 1,138 ....B5
Morwell 16,094 ....D5
Mount Beauty 1,492 ....D5
Murtoa 1,003 ....B5
Myrtleford 2,810 ....C5
Nagambie 1,075 ....C5
Narre Warren North 603 ....K5
Nathalia 1,220 ....C4
Newtown 10,797 ....C6
Nhill 2,124 ....A5
Northcote 54,881 ....J5
Numurkah 2,658 ....C5
Nunawading 94,325 ....J5

Oakleigh 54,532 ....J5
Olinda K5
Omeo⊙ 1,605 ....D5
Orbost 2,789 ....E5
Ouyen 1,609 ....B4
Port Fairy 2,399 ....B6
Portland 6,368 ....A6
Port Melbourne 9,356 ....H5
Prahran 48,462 ....J5
Preston 88,384 ....J4
Queenscliff 2,993 ....C6
Rainbow 693 ....B4
Red Cliffs 2,254 ....A4
Richmond 26,179 ....J5
Ringwood 37,085 ....K5
Robinvale 1,654 ....A4
Rochester 2,205 ....C5
Rushworth 955 ....C5
Rutherglen 1,325 ....C5
Saint Arnaud 2,786 ....B5
Saint Kilda 52,154 ....J5
Sale 12,111 ....D6
Sandringham 32,698 ....J5
Sea Lake 986 ....B4
Sebastopol 5,941 ....B5
Selby K5
Seymour 6,240 ....C5
Shepparton 25,848 ....C5
South Barwon 32,411 ....C6
South Melbourne 21,334 ....J5
Springvale 72,474 ....J5
Stawell 6,150 ....B5
Sunbury 8,243 ....C5
Sunshine 88,167 ....H5
Swan Hill 7,857 ....B4
Tallangatta 924 ....D5
Tatura 2,630 ....C5
Templestowe and
  Doncaster 82,090 ....J5
Terang 2,183 ....B5
Thomastown J4
Tongala 928 ....C5
Traralgon 15,089 ....D6
Wangaratta 16,157 ....C5
Warburton 1,753 ....C5
Warracknabeal 2,775 ....B5
Warragul 7,442 ....C6
Warrandyte 3,711 ....J4
Warrnambool 20,195 ....B6
Waverley 117,144 ....H5
Wedderburn 801 ....B5
Whittlesea 48,039 ....C5
Williamstown 26,348 ....H5
Winchelsea‡ 3,858 ....B6
Wodonga 15,733 ....D5
Wonthaggi 4,021 ....C6
Woodend 1,404 ....C5
Wycheproof 964 ....B5
Yallourn 1,825 ....D6
Yarram 2,125 ....D6
Yarrawonga 3,293 ....C5
Yea 1,052 ....C5

OTHER FEATURES

Altona (bay) H5
Australian Alps (mts.) D5
Avoca (riv.) B5
Barry (mts.) D5
Beaumaris (bay) J6
Bogong (mt.) D5
Bridgewater (cape) A6
Buller (mt.) D5
Campaspe (riv.) C5
Cook (pt.) H5
Corangamite (lake) B6
Corner (inlet) D6
Dandenong (creek) K5
Dandenong (mt.) K5
Difficult (mt.) B5
Discovery (bay) A6
Eildon (lake) C5
French (isl.), 66 ....C6
Gippsland (reg.) D6
Glenelg (riv.) A5
Goulburn (riv.) C5
Hindmarsh (lake) A5
Hobsons (bay) H5
Hopkins (riv.) B5
Hume (lake) D4
Indian Ocean B6
Kororoit (creek) H5
Loddon (riv.) B5
Maribyrnong (riv.) H5
Mitchell (riv.) D5
Mitta Mitta (riv.) D5
Mornington (pen.) C6
Mount Emu (creek) B5
Murray (riv.) A4
Nelson (cape) A6
Ninety Mile (beach) D6
Otway (cape) B6
Ovens (riv.) D5
Phillip (isl.), 2,273 ....C6
Plenty (riv.) J4
Portland (bay) A6
Port Phillip (bay) C6
Ricketts (pt.) J6
Rocklands (res.) A5
Snake (isl.) D6
South East (pt.) D6
Tamboritha (mt.) D5
Tasman (sea) F5
Tyrrell (lake) B4
Venus (bay) C6
Waranga (res.) C5
Waratah (bay) C6
Wellington (lake) D6
Western Port (inlet) D6
Wilsons (prom.) D6
Wimmera (riv.) A5
Yarra (riv.) C5

*City and suburbs.
⊙Population of district.
‡Population of met. area.
☐Population of urban area.

Irrigation Areas and Artesian Basins in Australia

Permanent Rivers
Non-Permanent Rivers
Flowing Water Bores
Major Dams
Major Irrigation and Other Water Supply Areas
Basins Where Artesian Water Is Generally Available

Prepared from Atlas of Australian Resources.

Topography

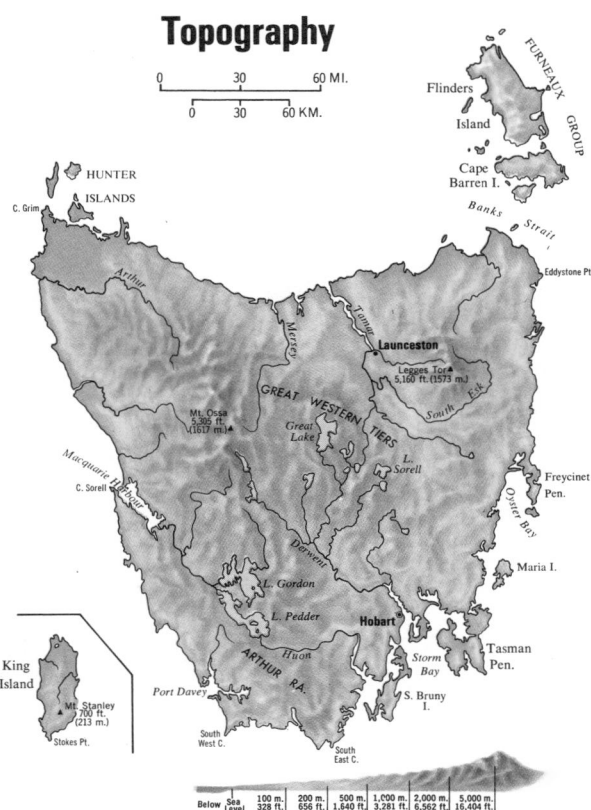

0   30   60 MI.
0   30   60 KM.

| Below Sea Level | 100 m. 328 ft. | 200 m. 656 ft. | 500 m. 1,640 ft. | 1,000 m. 3,281 ft. | 2,000 m. 6,562 ft. | 5,000 m. 16,404 ft. |

AREA 26,178 sq. mi. (67,800 sq. km.)
POPULATION 402,866
CAPITAL Hobart
LARGEST CITY Hobart
HIGHEST POINT Mt. Ossa 5,305 ft.
(1,617 m.)

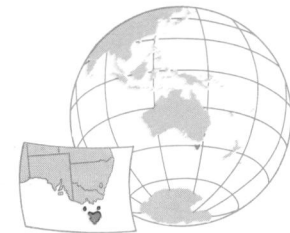

Great (lake) C3
Great Western Tiers (mts.) C3
Grim (cape) A2
Hartz (mt.) C5
Hibbs (pt.) B4
High Rocky (pt.) B4
Hogan Group (isls.) D1
Hummock (isl.) D2
Hunter (isl.) A2
Hunter (isls.) B2
Huon (riv.) C5
Indian Ocean A4
Kent Group (isls.) D1
King (isl.) A1
King (riv.) B4
King William (lake) C4
Lake (riv.) D3
Legges Tor (mt.) D3
Leven (riv.) B3
Lodi (cape) E3
Lofty (range) B3
Long (pt.) E3

Low Rocky (pt.) B4
Lyell (mt.) B4
Maatsuyker (isls.) C5
Macquarie (harb.) B4
Macquarie (riv.) D3
Maria (isl.) E4
Marion (bay) E4
Mersey (riv.) C3
Munro (mt.) E2
Naturaliste (cape) E2
Nive (riv.) C4
Norfolk (bay) D4
North (pt.) E1
North Bruny (isl.) D5
North Esk (riv.) D3
Ossa (mt.) C3
Ouse (riv.) C4
Oyster (bay) E4
Pedder (lake) B4
Peron (cape) E4
Phoques (bay) A1
Picton (mt.) C5

Pieman (riv.) B3
Pillar (cape) E5
Port Davey (inlet) B5
Portland (cape) D2
Ramsey (mt.) B3
Raoul (cape) D5
Reid (rocks) B1
Ringarooma (bay) D2
Robbins (isl.) B2
Rocky (isl.) B2
Saint Clair (lake) C4
Saint Helens (pt.) E3
Saint Vincent (cape) B5
Sandy (cape) A3
Savage (riv.) B3
Schouten (isl.) E4
Sorell (cape) B4
Sorell (lake) D4
South (cape) C5
South Bruny (isl.) D5
South East (cape) C5
South Esk (riv.) D3

South West (cape) B5
Stanley (mt.) A1
Stokes (pt.) A1
Stony (head) C2
Storm (bay) D5
Strzelecki (mt.) D2
Swan (isl.) E2
Tamar (riv.) D3
Tasman (head) D5
Tasman (pen.) E5
Tasman (sea) E4
Three Hummock (isl.) B2
Tooms (lake) D4
Vansittart (isl.) E2
Walker (isl.) B2
Waterhouse (isl.) D2
West (pt.) A2
West Sister (isl.) D1
Wickham (cape) A1

‡Population of met. area.

CITIES and TOWNS

Adventure Bay D5
Bagdad D4
Barrington C3
Beaconsfield 936 ....C3
Beauty Point 1,012 ....C3
Bell Bay B2
Boat Harbour B2
Bridgewater 2,750 ....D4
Bridport 725 ....D3
Brighton 4,927 ....D4
Burnie 19,465 ....B3
Bushy Park C4
Cambridge D4
Campbell Town 936 ....D3
Chudleigh C3
Colebrook D4
Conara Junction D3
Cornwall E3
Cranbrook D4
Cressy 621 ....C3
Currie 861 ....A1
Cygnet 720 ....C5
Deloraine 1,843 ....C3
Derwent Bridge C4
Devonport 19,399 ....C3
Egg Lagoon A1
Ellendale C4
Elliott B3
Emita D2
Evandale 529 ....D3
Flowerdale B2
Franklin 530 ....C5
Geeveston 900 ....C5
George Town 5,296 ....C3
Glenorchy 42,437 ....D4
Grassy 718 ....B1
Gravelly Beach 522 ....C3
Hadspen 619 ....D3
Hobart (cap.) 50,384 ....D4
Hobart‡ 131,524 ....D4
Huonville-Ranelagh 1,340 .....C5
Kingston 6,259 ....D4
Latrobe 2,375 ....C3
Lauderdale 1,881 ....D4
Launceston 32,953 ....C3
Launceston‡ 63,386 ....C3
Longford 1,785 ....C3
Maydena 537 ....C4
New Norfolk 6,679 ....C4
Oatlands 553 ....D4
Penguin 2,502 ....C3
Perth 1,141 ....D3
Port Sorell 772 ....C3
Queenstown 4,520 ....B4
Railton 926 ....C3
Rosebery 2,534 ....B3
Saint Helens 817 ....E3
Saint Marys 677 ....E3
Savage River 1,186 ....B3
Scottsdale 1,815 ....D3

Sheffield 833 ....C3
Smithton 3,235 ....A2
Snug 668 ....D5
Sorell-Midway Point 2,183 ....D4
Stanley 650 ....B2
Strathgordon 912 ....C4
Temma A3
Triabunna 881 ....D4
Ulverstone 8,793 ....C3
Westbury 1,006 ....C3
Wynyard 4,348 ....B3
Zeehan 1,754 ....B3

OTHER FEATURES

Anderson (bay) D2
Anne (mt.) C4
Anser Group (isls.) C1
Arthur (lake) D4
Arthur (range) C5
Arthur (riv.) B3
Babel (isls.) E1
Banks (str.) D2
Barn Bluff (mt.) B3
Barren (cape) E2
Bass (str.) C1
Bathurst (harb.) C5
Cape Barren (isl.) E2
Chappell (isls.) D2
Circular (head) B2
Clarke (isl.) E2
Clyde (riv.) D4
Cox (bight) C5
Cradle (mt.) B3
Cradle Mt. Lake St. Clair Nat'l
    Park B3
Crescent (lake) D4
Curtis Group (isls.) C1
D'Aguilar (range) B4
Davey (riv.) B4
Deal (isl.) D1
Dee (riv.) C4
Denison (range) C4
D'Entrecasteaux (chan.) D5
Derwent (riv.) C4
East Sister (isl.) E1
Echo (lake) C4
Eddystone (pt.) E2
Elliott (bay) B5
Fires (pt.) D1
Flinders (isl.) D1
Florence (riv.) B4
Forestier (cape) E4
Forestier (pen.) E4
Forth (riv.) C3
Frankland (cape) D1
Frankland (range) B4
Franklin (riv.) B4
Frenchmans Cap (mt.) B4
Freycinet (pen.) E4
Furneaux Group (isls.) E1
Gordon (lake) C4
Gordon (riv.) B4

Tasmania

MILES
0   10   20   30
KILOMETERS
0 10 20 30

State Capital ....◉
State Boundaries ....____

Scale 1:3,000,000

© Copyright HAMMOND INCORPORATED, Maplewood, N. J.

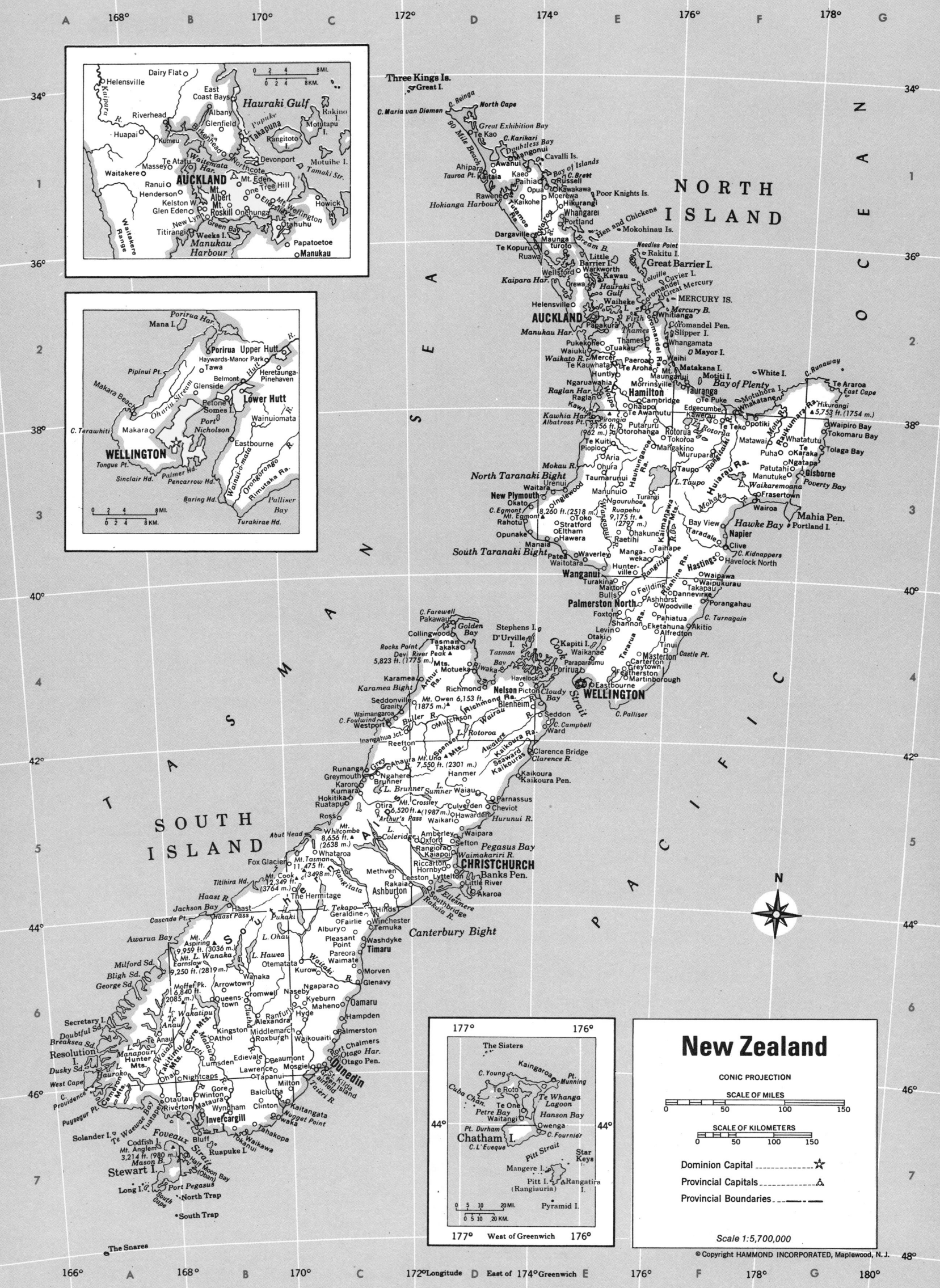

New Zealand

CONIC PROJECTION

SCALE OF MILES

0   50   100   150

SCALE OF KILOMETERS

0   50   100   150

Dominion Capital .... ☆

Provincial Capitals .... △

Provincial Boundaries ....

Scale 1:5,700,000

© Copyright HAMMOND INCORPORATED, Maplewood, N.J.

Topography

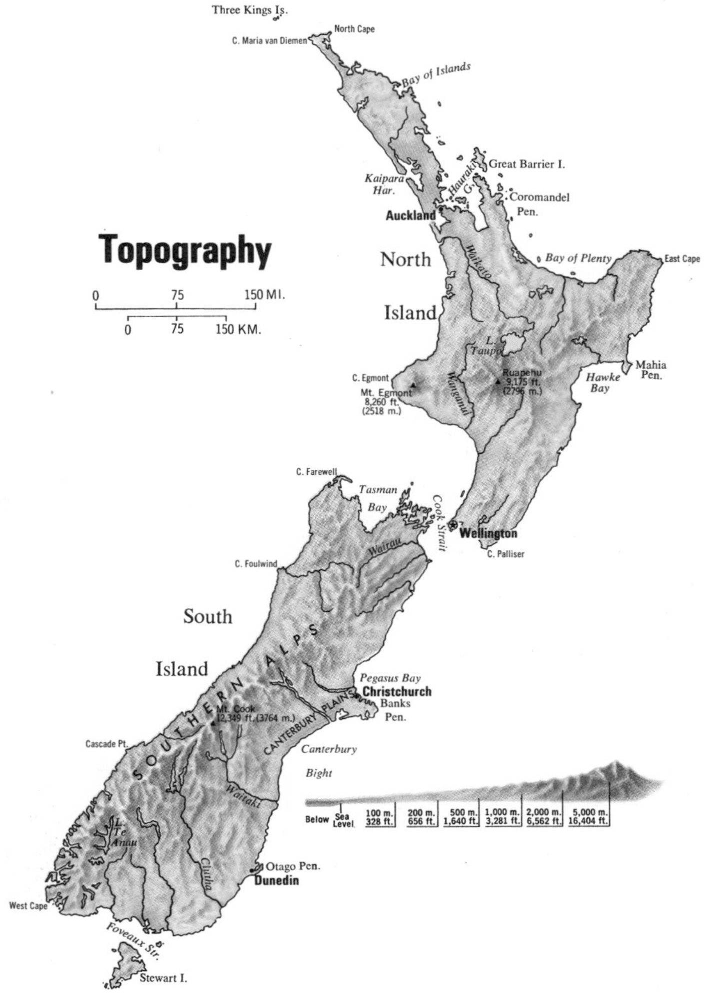
Three Kings Is.
North Cape
C. Maria van Diemen
Bay of Islands
Great Barrier I.
Kaipara Har.
Hauraki G.
Coromandel Pen.
Auckland
North Island
Bay of Plenty
East Cape
Waikato
L. Taupo
Ruapehu 9,175 ft. (2796 m.)
C. Egmont
Mt. Egmont 8,260 ft. (2518 m.)
Wanganui
Hawke Bay
Mahia Pen.
0 75 150 MI.
0 75 150 KM.
C. Farewell
Tasman Bay
Cook Strait
Wellington
C. Palliser
C. Foulwind
Wairau
South Island
SOUTHERN ALPS
Pegasus Bay
Christchurch
Banks Pen.
Mt. Cook 12,349 ft. (3764 m.)
CANTERBURY PLAINS
Canterbury Bight
Cascade Pt.
Waitaki
Clutha
Otago Pen.
Dunedin
West Cape
Foveaux Str.
Stewart I.
Below Sea Level
100 m. 328 ft.
200 m. 656 ft.
500 m. 1,640 ft.
1,000 m. 3,281 ft.
2,000 m. 6,562 ft.
5,000 m. 16,404 ft.

AREA 103,736 sq. mi. (268,676 sq. km.)
POPULATION 3,167,357
CAPITAL Wellington
LARGEST CITY Auckland
HIGHEST POINT Mt. Cook 12,349 ft. (3,764 m.)
MONETARY UNIT New Zealand dollar
MAJOR LANGUAGES English, Maori
MAJOR RELIGIONS Protestantism, Roman Catholicism

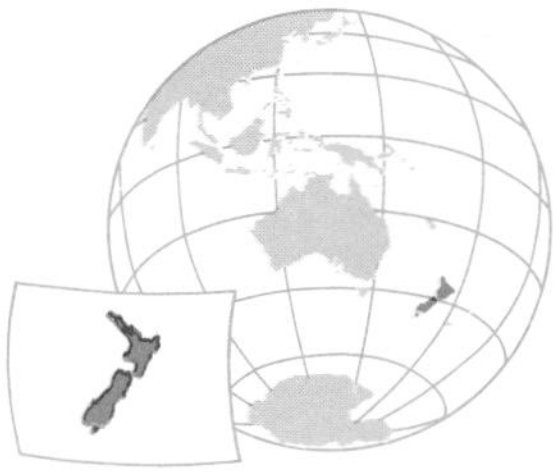

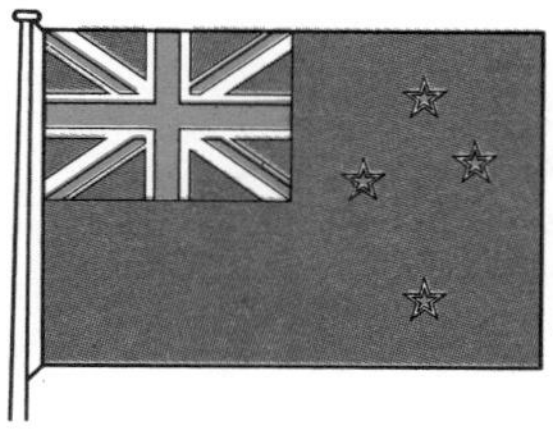

CITIES and TOWNS

Alexandra 4,137	B6
Ashburton 14,225	C5
Auckland 150,708	B1
Auckland□ 742,786	B1
Balclutha 4,740	B7
Birkenhead 19,683	B1
Blenheim 17,156	D4
Bluff 3,016	B7
Cambridge 7,841	E2
Carterton 3,985	E4
Christchurch 171,987	D5
Christchurch□ 295,296	D5
Clive 4,216	F3
Dannevirke 5,638	F4
Dargaville 4,559	D1
Devonport 11,003	C1
Dunedin 82,546	C6
Dunedin□ 113,222	C6
Eastbourne 4,779	B3
East Coast Bays 23,490	B1
Ellerslie 5,574	C1
Feilding 10,893	E4
Gisborne 29,698	G3
Gisborne□ 31,790	G3
Glen Eden 8,370	B1
Glenfield 17,746	B1
Gore 9,179	B7
Green Bay	B1
Green Island 6,979	C7
Greymouth 8,282	C5
Hamilton 87,968	E2
Hamilton□ 94,777	E2
Hastings 33,960	F3
Hastings□ 50,814	F3
Havelock North 8,348	F3
Hawera 8,506	E3
Henderson 7,076	B1
Heretaunga-Pinehaven 5,849	C2
Hokitika 3,530	C5
Hornby 8,679	D5
Howick 13,949	C1
Huntly 5,559	E2
Hutt (Upper and Lower)□ 115,604	B2
Invercargill 49,738	B7
Invercargill□ 53,762	B7
Kaiapoi 4,746	D5
Kaikohe 3,567	D1
Kaitaia 4,243	D1
Kawerau 7,743	F3
Kelston West	B1
Kumeu 3,125	B1
Levin 14,759	E4
Lower Hutt 64,553	B2
Lyttelton 3,327	D5
Mangonui 459	D1
Manukau 139,059	C1
Marton 4,910	E4
Massey 8,318	B1
Masterton 19,460	E4
Morrinsville 4,783	E2
Mosgiel 9,289	C6
Motueka 4,384	D4
Mount Albert 28,131	B1
Mount Eden 19,815	B1
Mount Maunganui 10,103	E2
Mount Roskill 34,645	B1
Mount Wellington 20,533	C1
Napier 46,994	F3
Napier□ 50,164	F3
Nelson 32,793	D4
New Lynn 10,466	B1
New Plymouth 37,711	D3
New Plymouth□ 43,914	D3
Ngaruawahia 4,385	E2
Northcote 9,921	B1
Oamaru 13,480	C6
Oban (Half Moon Bay) 333	B7
Onehunga 16,655	B1
One Tree Hill 11,711	B1
Orewa 4,328	E2
Otahuhu 10,558	C1
Otaki 4,202	E4
Paeroa 3,796	E2
Palmerston North 57,931	E4
Palmerston North□ 63,873	E4
Papakura 21,452	E2
Papatoetoe 22,864	C1
Petone 8,883	B2
Picton 3,276	D4
Pinehaven (Heretaunga-Pinehaven) 5,849	C2
Porirua 42,833	B2
Port Chalmers 3,123	C6
Pukekohe 8,770	E2
Putaruru 4,442	E3
Queenstown 3,133	B6
Rangiora 5,991	D5
Riccarton 7,280	D5
Richmond 6,587	D4
Rotorua 37,229	F3
Rotorua□ 46,650	F3
Saint Kilda 6,542	C7
Stratford 5,444	E3
Takapuna 62,220	B1
Taradale 4,747	F3
Taumarunui 6,479	E3
Taupo 12,898	F3
Tauranga 33,672	F2
Tauranga□ 48,153	F2
Tawa 12,297	B2
Te Aroha 3,202	E2
Te Atatu 16,393	B1
Te Awamutu 7,619	E3
Te Kuiti 4,840	E3
Temuka 3,711	C6
Te Puke 3,810	F2
Thames 6,769	E2
The Hermitage	C5
Timaru 29,267	C6
Timaru□ 29,958	C6
Titirangi 8,227	B1
Tokoroa 18,635	F3
Turangi 5,496	E3
Upper Hutt 30,616	B2
Waihi 3,415	E2
Waikanae 4,184	E4
Waimate 3,378	C6
Wainuiomata 19,318	B3
Waipara 292	D5
Waipukurau 3,632	F4
Wairoa 5,466	F3
Waitangi 251	D7
Waitara 6,036	E3
Waiuku 3,494	E2
Wanaka 1,178	B6
Wanganui 37,307	E3
Wanganui□ 39,679	E3
Wellington (cap.) 139,566	A3
Wellington□ 327,414	A3
Westport 4,988	C4
Whakatane 11,542	F2
Whangarei 34,981	E1
Whangarei□ 39,069	E1

OTHER FEATURES

Abut (head)	B5
Albatross (pt.)	E3
Anglem (mt.)	A7
Arthur (range)	D4
Arthur's (pass)	C5
Aspiring (mt.)	B6
Awarua (bay)	A6
Awatere (riv.)	D5
Banks (pen.)	D5
Baring (head)	B3
Bligh (sound)	A6
Bonpland (mt.)	A6
Breaksea (sound)	A6
Bream (bay)	E1
Brett (cape)	E1
Brunner (lake)	C5
Buller (riv.)	D4
Cameron (mts.)	A7
Campbell (cape)	E4
Canterbury (bight)	D6
Cascade (pt.)	B6
Castle, (pt.)	F4
Cavalli (isls.)	E1
Chatham (isl.)	D7
Chatham (isls.)	D7
Clarence (riv.)	E5
Cloudy (bay)	E4
Clutha (riv.)	B6
Codfish (isl.)	A7
Coleridge (lake)	C5
Colville (cape)	E2
Cook (mt.)	C5
Cook (str.)	E4
Coromandel (pen.)	F2
Coromandel (range)	E2
Crossley (mt.)	D5
Cuba (chan.)	D7
Cuvier (isl.)	E2
Devil River (peak)	D4
Doubtful (sound)	A6
Doubtless (bay)	D1
Durham (pt.)	D7
D'Urville (isl.)	D4
Dusky (sound)	A6
Earnslaw (mt.)	B6
East (cape)	G2
Egmont (cape)	D3
Egmont (mt.)	D3
Ellesmere (lake)	D5
Eyre (mts.)	B6
Farewell (cape)	D4
Foulwind (cape)	C4
Fournier (cape)	E7
Foveaux (str.)	A7
George (sound)	A6
Golden (bay)	D4
Great (isl.)	D1
Great Barrier (isl.)	E2
Great Exhibition (bay)	D1
Great Mercury (isl.)	F2
Grey (riv.)	C5
Haast (pass)	B6
Haast (riv.)	B5
Hanson (bay)	E7
Hauhungaroa (range)	E3
Hauraki (gulf)	C1
Hauroko (lake)	A6
Hawea (lake)	B6
Hawke (bay)	F3
Hen and Chickens (isls.)	E1
Hikurangi (mt.)	G2
Hokianga (harb.)	D1
Huiarau (range)	F3
Hunter (mts.)	A6
Hurunui (riv.)	D5
Hutt (riv.)	C2
Islands (bay)	E1
Jackson (bay)	B5
Kaikoura (range)	D5
Kaikoura (pen.)	E5
Kaimanawa (range)	E3
Kaipara (harb.)	D2
Kaipara (riv.)	A1
Kapiti (isl.)	E4
Karamea (bight)	C4
Karikari (cape)	D1
Kawau (isl.)	E2
Kawhia (harb.)	E3
Kidnappers (cape)	F3
L'Eveque (cape)	D7
Little Barrier (isl.)	E2
Long (isl.)	A7
Mahia (pen.)	G3
Mana (isl.)	B2
Manapouri (lake)	A6
Mangere (isl.)	E7
Manukau (harb.)	B1
Maria van Diemen (cape)	D1
Mason (bay)	A7
Matakana (isl.)	F2
Mataura (riv.)	B6
Mavora (mt.)	B6
Mayor (isl.)	F2
Mercury (bay)	F2
Mercury (isls.)	F2
Milford (sound)	A6
Moffet (peak)	B6
Mohaka (riv.)	F3
Mokau (riv.)	E3
Mokohinau (isl.)	E1
Motiti (isl.)	F2
Motu (riv.)	F3
Motuhora (isl.)	F2
Motuihe (isl.)	C1
Motutapu (isl.)	C1
Munning (pt.)	E7
Needles (pt.)	E2
Ngauruhoe (mt.)	E3
Nicholson Port, (inlet)	B3
Ninety Mile (beach)	D1
North (cape)	D1
North (isl.)	F1
North Taranaki, (bight)	D3
North Trap (isl.)	B7
Nugget (pt.)	C7
Ohariu (stream)	B2
Ohau (lake)	B6
Oreti (riv.)	B6
Orongorongo (riv.)	B3
Otago (harb.)	C6
Otago (pen.)	C6
Owen (mt.)	D4
Palliser (bay)	C3
Palliser (cape)	E4
Palmer (head)	B3
Pegasus (bay)	D5
Pegasus Port (inlet)	B7
Pencarrow (head)	B3
Petre (bay)	D7
Pipinui (pt.)	B2
Pirongia (mt.)	E3
Pitt (isl.)	E7
Pitt (str.)	E7
Plenty (bay)	F2
Poor Knights (isls.)	E1
Porirua (harb.)	B2
Portland (isl.)	G3
Port Nicholson (inlet)	B3
Port Pegasus (inlet)	B7
Poverty (bay)	G3
Providence (cape)	A7
Pukaki (lake)	B6
Pupuke (lake)	B1
Puysegur (pt.)	A7
Pyramid (isl.)	E7
Raglan (harb.)	E2
Rakaia (riv.)	C5
Rakino (isl.)	C1
Rakitu (isl.)	E2
Rangatira (isl.)	E7
Rangiauria (Pitt) (isl.)	E7
Rangitaiki (riv.)	F3
Rangitata (riv.)	C5
Rangitikei (riv.)	E3
Rangitoto (isl.)	C1
Raukumara (range)	F3
Reinga (cape)	D1
Resolution (isl.)	A6
Richmond (range)	D4
Rimutaka (range)	B3
Rocks (pt.)	C4
Rotoroa (lake)	D4
Rotorua (lake)	F3
Ruahine (range)	F4
Ruapehu (mt.)	E3
Ruapuke (isl.)	B7
Ruñaway (cape)	G2
Seaward Kaikouras (range)	D5
Secretary (isl.)	A6
Sinclair (head)	A3
Sisters The, (isls.)	D6
Slipper (isl.)	F2
Snares The (isls.)	A7
Solander (isl.)	A7
Somes (isl.)	B2
South (cape)	A7
South (isl.)	B5
Southern Alps (range)	C5
South Taranaki (bight)	D3
South Trap (isl.)	B7
Spenser (mts.)	D5
Star Keys (isls.)	E7
Stephens (isl.)	D4
Stewart (isl.)	A7
Sumner (lake)	D5
Taieri (riv.)	C7
Takitimu (mts.)	A6
Tamaki (str.)	C1
Tararua (range)	E4
Tasman (bay)	D4
Tasman (mt.)	C5
Tasman (mts.)	D4
Tasman (sea)	B4
Taupo (lake)	F3
Tauroa (pt.)	D1
Te Anau (lake)	A6
Tekapo (lake)	C5
Terawhiti (cape)	A3
Te Waewae (bay)	A7
Te Whanga (mts.)	E7
Thames (firth)	E2
Three Kings (isls.)	D1
Titihira, (head)	B5
Tongue (pt.)	A3
Turakirae (head)	B3
Turnagain (cape)	F4
Tutamoe (range)	D1
Una (mt.)	D5
Waiau (riv.)	A6
Waiheke (isl.)	E2
Waikaremoana (lake)	F3
Waikato (riv.)	E2
Waimakariri (riv.)	D5
Wainui-o-mata (riv.)	B3
Waipa (riv.)	E2
Wairau (riv.)	D4
Wairoa (riv.)	E1
Waitakere (range)	A1
Waitaki (riv.)	C6
Waitemata (harb.)	B1
Wakatipu (lake)	B6
Wanaka (lake)	B6
Wanganui (riv.)	E3
Weeks (isl.)	B1
West (cape)	A6
Whitcombe (mt.)	C5
White (isl.)	F2
Young (cape)	D7

□Population of urban area.

Agriculture, Industry and Resources

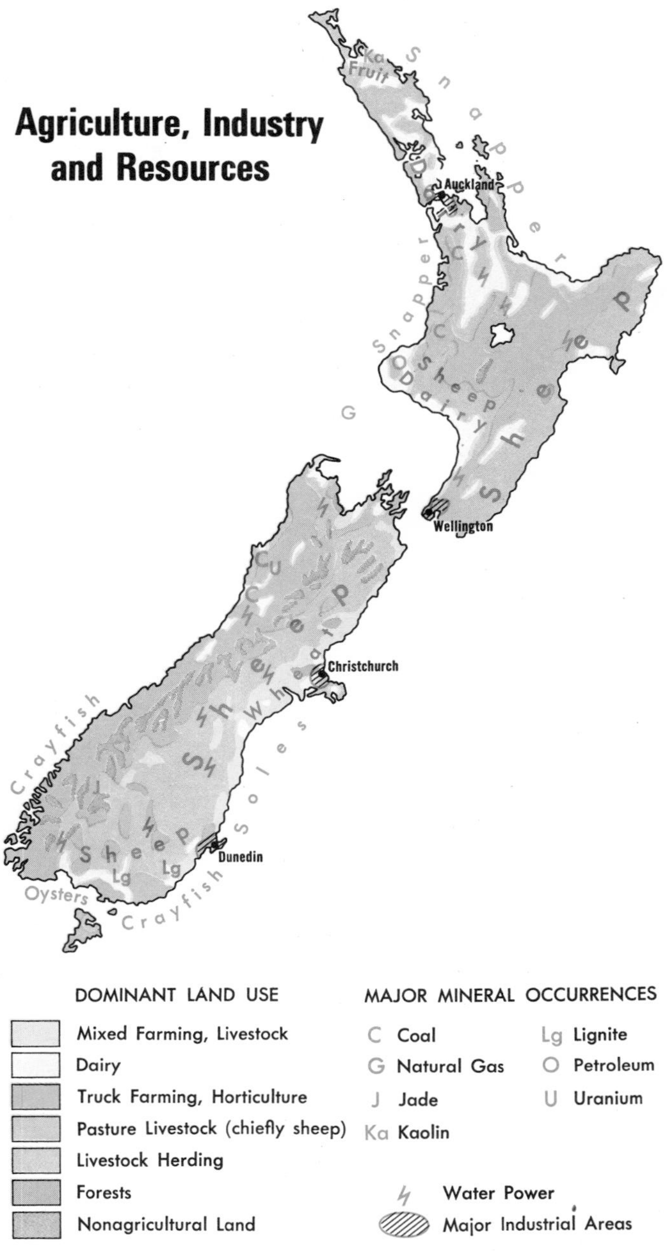
Fruit
Snapper
Auckland
Sheep
Dairy
Wellington
Christchurch
Wheat
Crayfish
Soles
Dunedin
Oysters
DOMINANT LAND USE
Mixed Farming, Livestock
Dairy
Truck Farming, Horticulture
Pasture Livestock (chiefly sheep)
Livestock Herding
Forests
Nonagricultural Land
MAJOR MINERAL OCCURRENCES
C Coal
G Natural Gas
J Jade
Ka Kaolin
Lg Lignite
O Petroleum
U Uranium
Water Power
Major Industrial Areas

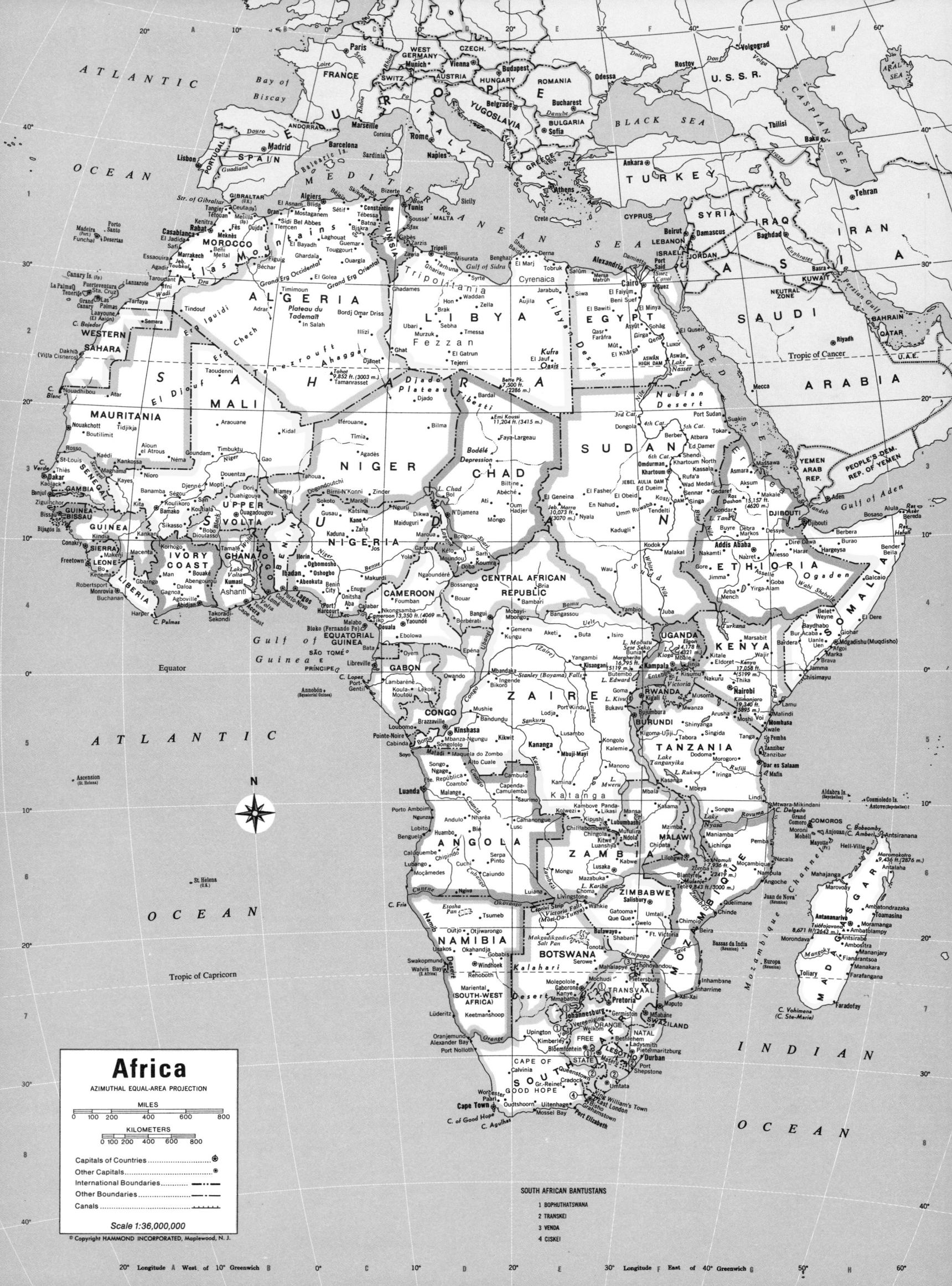

Africa

AZIMUTHAL EQUAL-AREA PROJECTION

MILES
0 100 200   400   600   800

KILOMETERS
0 100 200   400   600   800

Capitals of Countries .... ⊛
Other Capitals .... ⊛
International Boundaries .... — ·· —
Other Boundaries .... — · —
Canals ....

Scale 1:36,000,000

© Copyright HAMMOND INCORPORATED, Maplewood, N.J.

SOUTH AFRICAN BANTUSTANS

1 BOPHUTHATSWANA
2 TRANSKEI
3 VENDA
4 CISKEI

20° Longitude A West of 10° Greenwich   B   0°   C   10°   D   20°   E   30° Longitude F East of 40° Greenwich   G   50°   H   60°

AFRICA
AREA 11,707,000 sq. mi. (30,321,130 sq. km.)
POPULATION 469,000,000
LARGEST CITY Cairo
HIGHEST POINT Kilimanjaro 19,340 ft. (5,895 m.)
LOWEST POINT Lake Assal, Djibouti -512 ft. (-156 m.)

Population Distribution

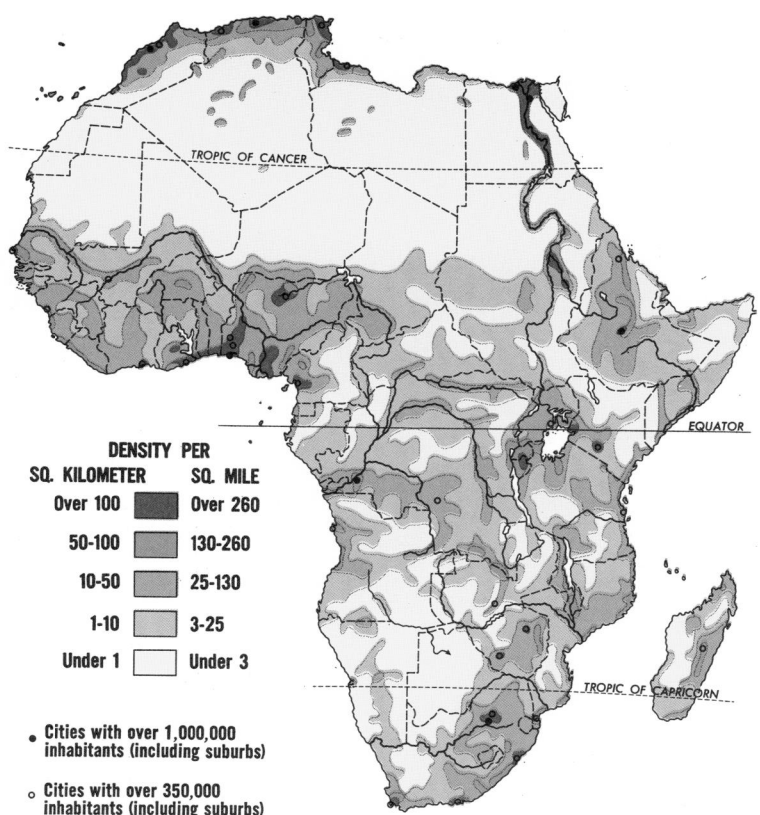

DENSITY PER

SQ. KILOMETER	SQ. MILE
Over 100	Over 260
50-100	130-260
10-50	25-130
1-10	3-25
Under 1	Under 3

• Cities with over 1,000,000 inhabitants (including suburbs)

o Cities with over 350,000 inhabitants (including suburbs)

Vegetation

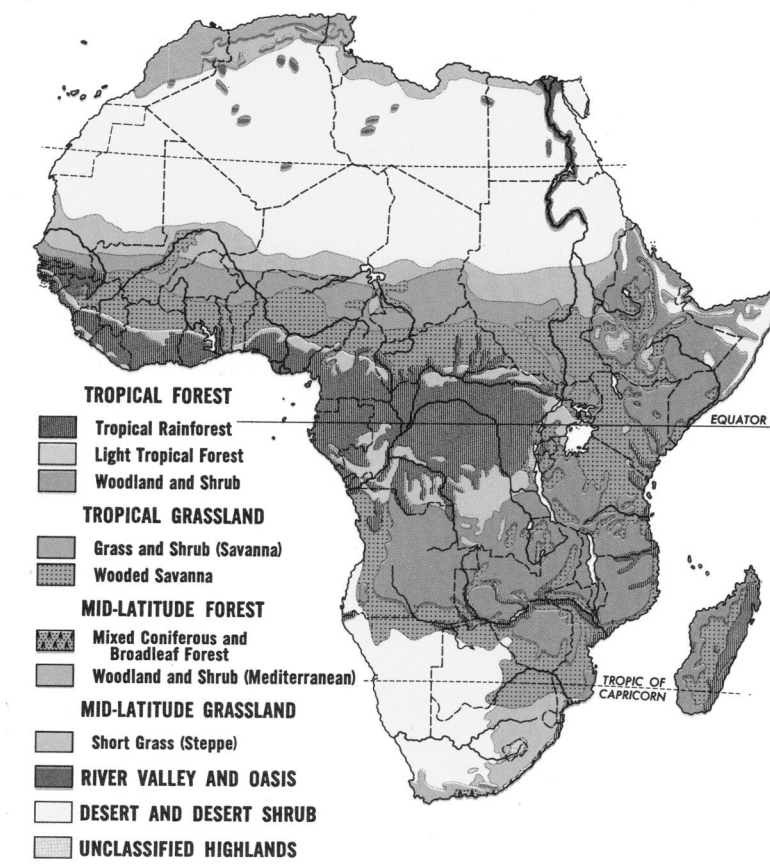

TROPICAL FOREST
- Tropical Rainforest
- Light Tropical Forest
- Woodland and Shrub

TROPICAL GRASSLAND
- Grass and Shrub (Savanna)
- Wooded Savanna

MID-LATITUDE FOREST
- Mixed Coniferous and Broadleaf Forest
- Woodland and Shrub (Mediterranean)

MID-LATITUDE GRASSLAND
- Short Grass (Steppe)

RIVER VALLEY AND OASIS

DESERT AND DESERT SHRUB

UNCLASSIFIED HIGHLANDS

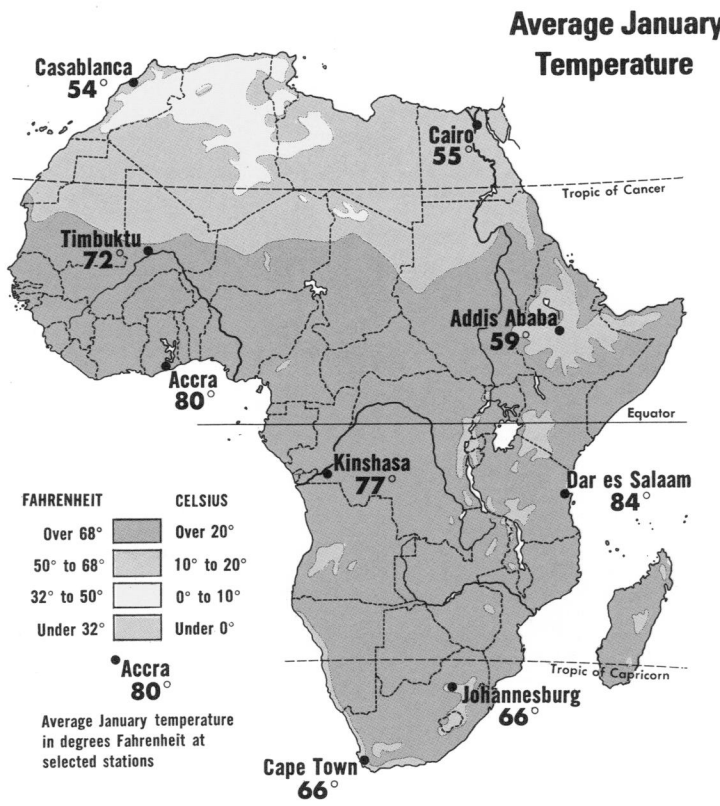

Average January Temperature

Casablanca 54°

Cairo 55°

Tropic of Cancer

Timbuktu 72°

Addis Ababa 59°

Accra 80°

Equator

Kinshasa 77°

Dar es Salaam 84°

FAHRENHEIT	CELSIUS
Over 68°	Over 20°
50° to 68°	10° to 20°
32° to 50°	0° to 10°
Under 32°	Under 0°

Accra 80°

Johannesburg 66°

Tropic of Capricorn

Cape Town 66°

Average January temperature in degrees Fahrenheit at selected stations

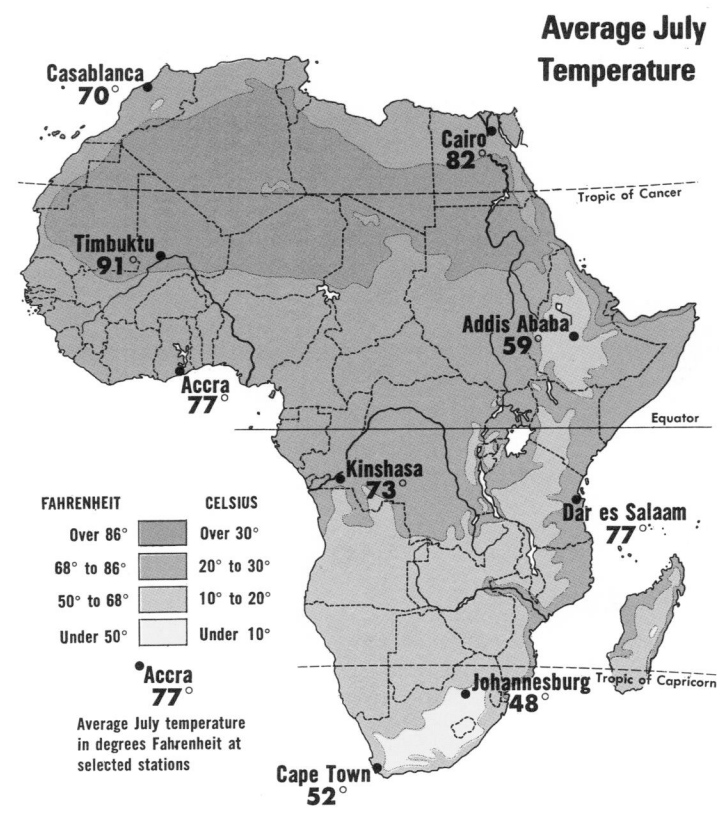

Average July Temperature

Casablanca 70°

Cairo 82°

Tropic of Cancer

Timbuktu 91°

Addis Ababa 59°

Accra 77°

Equator

Kinshasa 73°

Dar es Salaam 77°

FAHRENHEIT	CELSIUS
Over 86°	Over 30°
68° to 86°	20° to 30°
50° to 68°	10° to 20°
Under 50°	Under 10°

Accra 77°

Johannesburg 48°

Tropic of Capricorn

Cape Town 52°

Average July temperature in degrees Fahrenheit at selected stations

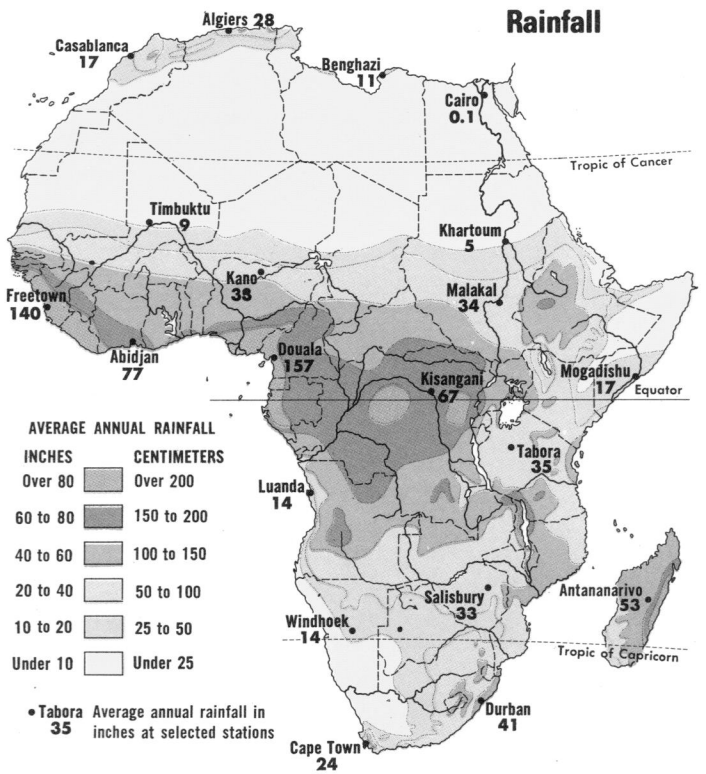

Rainfall

Algiers 28

Casablanca 17

Benghazi 11

Cairo 0.1

Tropic of Cancer

Timbuktu 9

Khartoum 5

Kano 38

Malakal 34

Freetown 140

Abidjan 77

Douala 157

Kisangani 67

Mogadishu 17

Equator

Luanda 14

Tabora 35

AVERAGE ANNUAL RAINFALL	
INCHES	CENTIMETERS
Over 80	Over 200
60 to 80	150 to 200
40 to 60	100 to 150
20 to 40	50 to 100
10 to 20	25 to 50
Under 10	Under 25

Salisbury 33

Antananarivo 53

Windhoek 14

Tropic of Capricorn

Durban 41

Cape Town 24

Tabora 35 Average annual rainfall in inches at selected stations

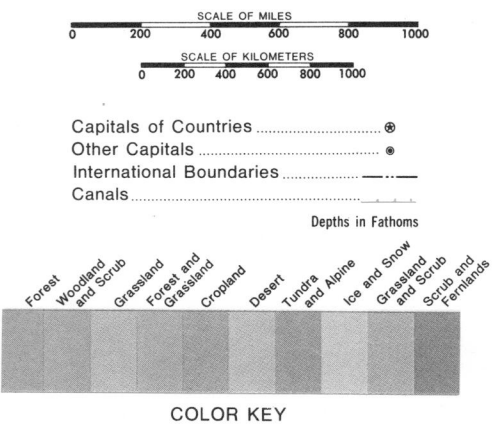

Vegetation/Relief

SCALE OF MILES
0   200   400   600   800   1000

SCALE OF KILOMETERS
0   200   400   600   800   1000

Capitals of Countries .... ⊛
Other Capitals .... ⊛
International Boundaries .... —·—
Canals ....

Depths in Fathoms

Forest | Woodland and Scrub | Grassland | Forest and Grassland | Cropland | Desert | Tundra and Alpine | Ice and Snow | Grassland and Scrub | Scrub and Fernlands

COLOR KEY

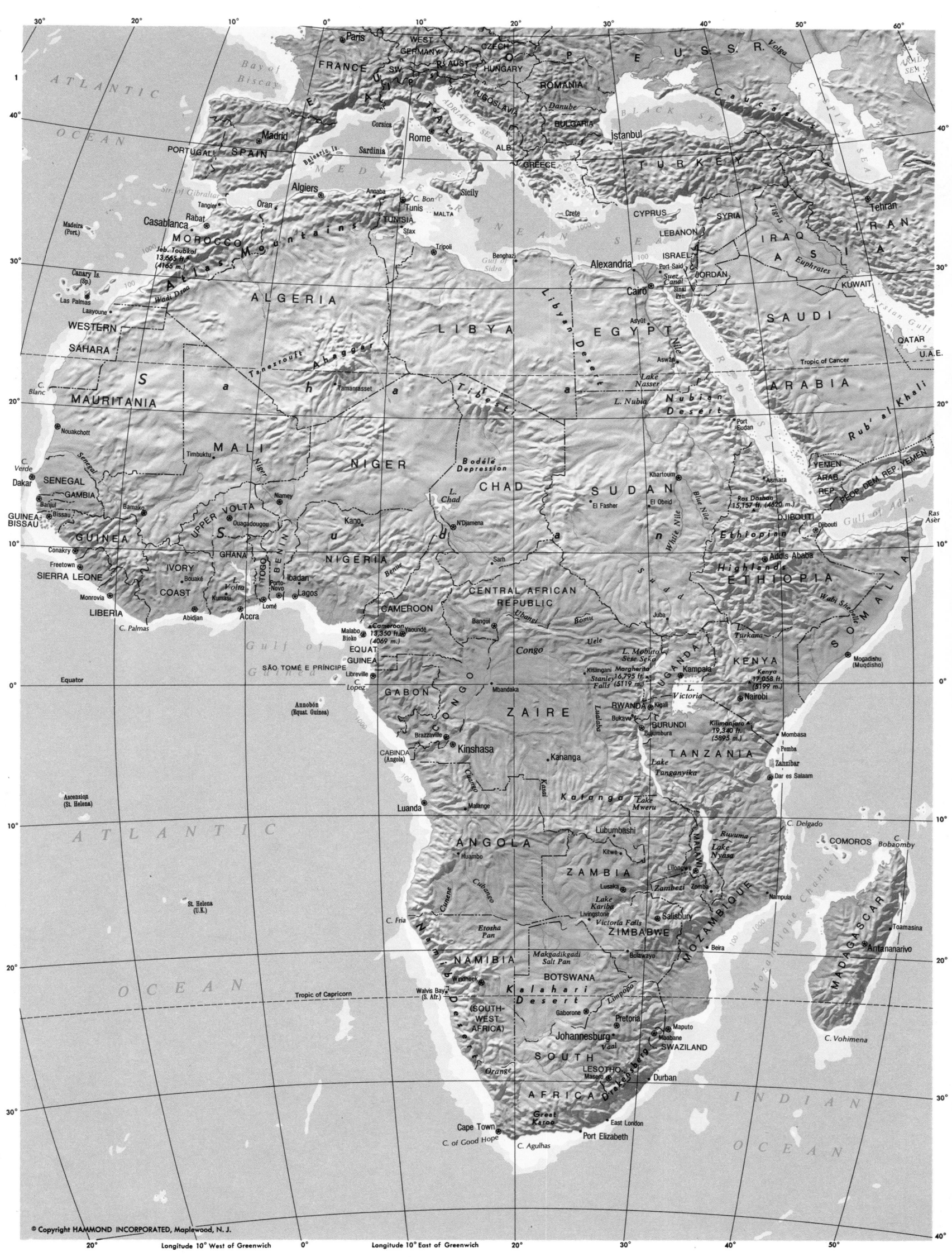

Longitude 10° West of Greenwich

Longitude 10° East of Greenwich

Western Africa

CONIC EQUAL-AREA PROJECTION

SCALE OF MILES

0 100 200 400

SCALE OF KILOMETERS

0 100 200 400

Capitals of Countries ____☆____ International Boundaries _____

Other Capitals _____◉ Internal Boundaries ___ ___

Scale 1:15,200,000

© Copyright HAMMOND INCORPORATED, Maplewood, N.J.

Cape Verde

0 25 50 75 100 Ml.

0 25 50 75 100 KM.

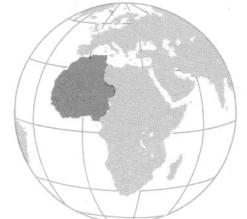

ALGERIA

AREA 919,591 sq. mi. (2,381,740 sq. km.)
POPULATION 17,422,000
CAPITAL Algiers
LARGEST CITY Algiers
HIGHEST POINT Tahat 9,852 ft. (3,003 m.)
MONETARY UNIT Algerian dinar
MAJOR LANGUAGES Arabic, Berber, French
MAJOR RELIGION Islam

BENIN

AREA 43,483 sq. mi. (112,620 sq. km.)
POPULATION 3,338,240
CAPITAL Porto-Novo
LARGEST CITY Cotonou
HIGHEST POINT Atakora Mts. 2,083 ft. (635 m.)
MONETARY UNIT CFA franc
MAJOR LANGUAGES Fon, Somba, Yoruba, Bariba, French, Mina, Dendi
MAJOR RELIGIONS Tribal religions, Islam, Roman Catholicism

CAPE VERDE

AREA 1,557 sq. mi. (4,033 sq. km.)
POPULATION 324,000
CAPITAL Praia
LARGEST CITY Praia
HIGHEST POINT 9,281 ft. (2,829 m.)
MONETARY UNIT Cape Verde escudo
MAJOR LANGUAGE Portuguese
MAJOR RELIGION Roman Catholicism

GAMBIA

AREA 4,127 sq. mi. (10,689 sq. km.)
POPULATION 601,000
CAPITAL Banjul
LARGEST CITY Banjul
HIGHEST POINT 100 ft. (30 m.)
MONETARY UNIT dalasi
MAJOR LANGUAGES Mandingo, Fulani, Wolof, English, Malinke
MAJOR RELIGIONS Islam, tribal religions, Christianity

GHANA

AREA 92,099 sq. mi. (238,536 sq. km.)
POPULATION 11,450,000
CAPITAL Accra
LARGEST CITY Accra
HIGHEST POINT Togo Hills 2,900 ft. (884 m.)
MONETARY UNIT cedi
MAJOR LANGUAGES Twi, Fante, Dagbani, Ewe, Ga, English, Hausa, Akan
MAJOR RELIGIONS Tribal religions, Christianity, Islam

GUINEA

AREA 94,925 sq. mi. (245,856 sq. km.)
POPULATION 5,143,284
CAPITAL Conakry
LARGEST CITY Conakry
HIGHEST POINT Nimba Mts. 6,070 ft. (1,850 m.)
MONETARY UNIT syli
MAJOR LANGUAGES Fulani, Mandingo, Susu, French
MAJOR RELIGIONS Islam, tribal religions

GUINEA-BISSAU

AREA 13,948 sq. mi. (36,125 sq. km.)
POPULATION 777,214
CAPITAL Bissau
LARGEST CITY Bissau
HIGHEST POINT 689 ft. (210 m.)
MONETARY UNIT Guinea-Bissau escudo
MAJOR LANGUAGES Balante, Fulani, Crioulo, Mandingo, Portuguese
MAJOR RELIGIONS Islam, tribal religions, Roman Catholicism

IVORY COAST

AREA 124,504 sq. mi. (322,465 sq. km.)
POPULATION 7,920,000
CAPITAL Abidjan
LARGEST CITY Abidjan
HIGHEST POINT 5,745 ft. (1,751 m.)
MONETARY UNIT CFA franc
MAJOR LANGUAGES Bale, Bete, Senufu, French, Dioula
MAJOR RELIGIONS Tribal religions, Islam

LIBERIA

AREA 43,000 sq. mi. (111,370 sq. km.)
POPULATION 1,873,000
CAPITAL Monrovia
LARGEST CITY Monrovia
HIGHEST POINT Wutivi 5,584 ft. (1,702 m.)
MONETARY UNIT Liberian dollar
MAJOR LANGUAGES Kru, Kpelle, Bassa, Vai, English
MAJOR RELIGIONS Christianity, tribal religions, Islam

MALI

AREA 464,873 sq. mi. (1,204,021 sq. km.)
POPULATION 6,906,000
CAPITAL Bamako
LARGEST CITY Bamako
HIGHEST POINT Hombori Mts. 3,789 ft. (1,155 m.)
MONETARY UNIT Mali franc
MAJOR LANGUAGES Bambara, Senufu, Fulani, Soninke, French
MAJOR RELIGIONS Islam, tribal religions

MAURITANIA

AREA 419,229 sq. mi. (1,085,803 sq. km.)
POPULATION 1,634,000
CAPITAL Nouakchott
LARGEST CITY Nouakchott
HIGHEST POINT 2,972 ft. (906 m.)
MONETARY UNIT ouguiya
MAJOR LANGUAGES Arabic, Wolof, Tukolor, French
MAJOR RELIGION Islam

MOROCCO

AREA 172,414 sq. mi. (446,550 sq. km.)
POPULATION 20,242,000
CAPITAL Rabat
LARGEST CITY Casablanca
HIGHEST POINT Jeb. Toubkal 13,665 ft. (4,165 m.)
MONETARY UNIT dirham
MAJOR LANGUAGES Arabic, Berber, French
MAJOR RELIGIONS Islam, Judaism, Christianity

NIGER

AREA 489,189 sq. mi. (1,267,000 sq. km.)
POPULATION 5,098,427
CAPITAL Niamey
LARGEST CITY Niamey
HIGHEST POINT Banguezane 6,234 ft. (1,900 m.)
MONETARY UNIT CFA franc
MAJOR LANGUAGES Hausa, Songhai, Fulani, French, Tamashek, Djerma
MAJOR RELIGIONS Islam, tribal religions

NIGERIA

AREA 357,000 sq. mi. (924,630 sq. km.)
POPULATION 82,643,000
CAPITAL Lagos
LARGEST CITY Lagos
HIGHEST POINT Dimlang 6,700 ft. (2,042 m.)
MONETARY UNIT naira
MAJOR LANGUAGES Hausa, Yoruba, Ibo, Ijaw, Fulani, Tiv, Kanuri, Ibibio, English, Edo
MAJOR RELIGIONS Islam, Christianity, tribal religions

SÃO TOMÉ E PRÍNCIPE

AREA 372 sq. mi. (963 sq. km.)
POPULATION 85,000
CAPITAL São Tomé
LARGEST CITY São Tomé
HIGHEST POINT Pico 6,640 ft. (2,024 m.)
MONETARY UNIT dobra
MAJOR LANGUAGES Bantu languages, Portuguese
MAJOR RELIGIONS Tribal religions, Roman Catholicism

SENEGAL

AREA 75,954 sq. mi. (196,720 sq. km.)
POPULATION 5,508,000
CAPITAL Dakar
LARGEST CITY Dakar
HIGHEST POINT Futa Jallon 1,640 ft. (500 m.)
MONETARY UNIT CFA franc
MAJOR LANGUAGES Wolof, Peul (Fulani), French, Mende, Mandingo, Dida
MAJOR RELIGIONS Islam, tribal religions, Roman Catholicism

SIERRA LEONE

AREA 27,925 sq. mi. (72,325 sq. km.)
POPULATION 3,470,000
CAPITAL Freetown
LARGEST CITY Freetown
HIGHEST POINT Loma Mts. 6,390 ft. (1,947 m.)
MONETARY UNIT leone
MAJOR LANGUAGES Mende, Temne, Vai, English, Krio (pidgin)
MAJOR RELIGIONS Tribal religions, Islam, Christianity

TOGO

AREA 21,622 sq. mi. (56,000 sq. km.)
POPULATION 2,472,000
CAPITAL Lomé
LARGEST CITY Lomé
HIGHEST POINT Agou 3,445 ft. (1,050 m.)
MONETARY UNIT CFA franc
MAJOR LANGUAGES Ewe, French, Twi, Hausa
MAJOR RELIGIONS Tribal religions, Roman Catholicism, Islam

TUNISIA

AREA 63,378 sq. mi. (164,149 sq. km.)
POPULATION 6,367,000
CAPITAL Tunis
LARGEST CITY Tunis
HIGHEST POINT Jeb. Chambi 5,066 ft. (1,544 m.)
MONETARY UNIT Tunisian dinar
MAJOR LANGUAGES Arabic, French
MAJOR RELIGION Islam

UPPER VOLTA

AREA 105,869 sq. mi. (274,200 sq. km.)
POPULATION 6,908,000
CAPITAL Ouagadougou
LARGEST CITY Ouagadougou
HIGHEST POINT 2,352 ft. (717 m.)
MONETARY UNIT CFA franc
MAJOR LANGUAGES Mossi, Lobi, French, Samo, Gourounsi
MAJOR RELIGIONS Islam, tribal religions, Roman Catholicism

WESTERN SAHARA

AREA 102,703 sq. mi. (266,000 sq. km.)
POPULATION 76,425
HIGHEST POINT 2,700 ft. (823 m.)
MAJOR LANGUAGE Arabic
MAJOR RELIGION Islam

Topography

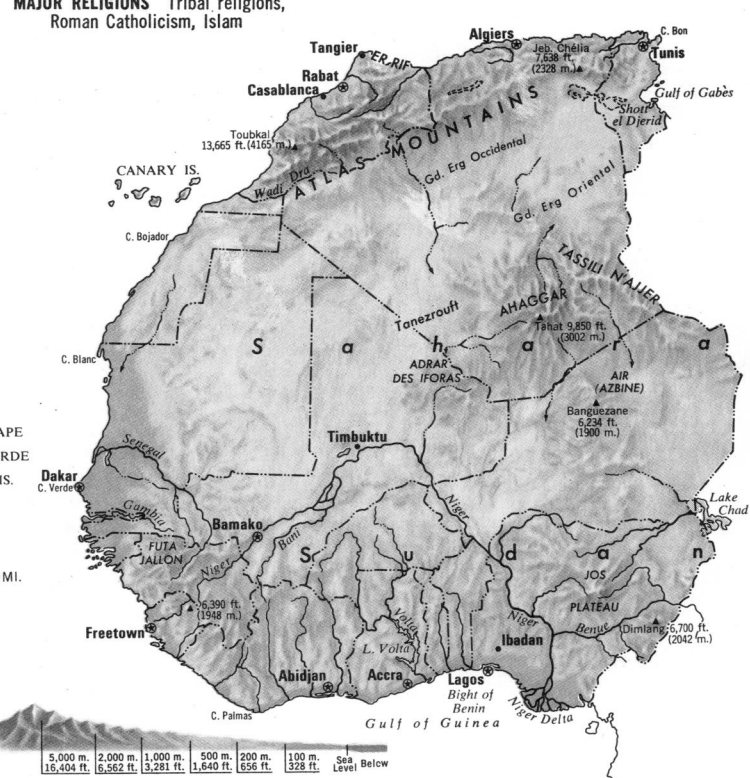

(continued)

ALGERIA

CITIES and TOWNS

Abadla 12,200 D2
Adrar 22,800 D3
Aïn Beïda 26,976 F1
Aïn Sefra 22,400 D2
Aïn Temouchent 42,000 D1
Algiers (cap.) 1,365,400 E1
Amguid F3
Annaba 255,900 F1
Aoulef 17,200 E3
Arak E3
Batna 112,100 F1
Béchar 72,800 D2
Bejaïa 89,500 F1
Beni Abbès 5,000 D2
Beni Ounif 7,500 D2
Beni Saf 30,700 D1
Berga E3
Bidon 5 (Poste Maurice Cordier) E4
Biskra 90,500 F2
Blida 160,900 E1
Bône (Annaba) 255,900 F1
Bordj Bou Arreridj 65,000 E1
Bordj Fly Sainte Marie D3
Bordj Omar Driss 1,900 F3
Boufarik 50,000 E1
Bougie (Béjaïa) 89,500 F1
Bou Saâda 50,000 E1
Brezina 10,000 E2
Charouine D3
Chenachane D3
Cherchell 36,800 E1
Constantine 335,100 F1
Deldoul E3
Dellys 29,700 E1
Djanet 5,300 F4
Djelfa 51,000 E2
Djemaa 34,600 F2
Edjeleh F3
El Abiod Sidi Cheikh 15,300 E2
El Asnam 106,100 E1
El Bayadh 38,500 E2
El Djezair (Algiers) (cap.) 1,365,400 E1
El Goléa 24,400 E2
El Oued 72,100 F2
Fort Lallemand F2
Fort MacMahon E3
Fort Miribel E3
Fort Tarat F3
Ghardaïa 70,500 E2
Ghazaouet 25,900 D2
Guelma 60,100 F1
Guemar F2
Guerara 22,300 E2
Guerzim D3
Hassi Messaoud F2
Hassi R'Mel E2
Idelès F4
Igli 3,400 D2
Illizi 4,600 F3
In Amenas 4,200 F3
In Amguel E4
In Eker F4
In Guezzam F5
In Rhar E3
In Salah 18,800 E3
Jijel 49,800 F1
Kenadsa 7,600 D2
Kerzaz 2,900 D3
Khemis Miliana 57,800 E1
Ksar el Boukhari 41,200 E1
Laghouat 59,200 E2
Mascara 62,300 D1
Mecheria 22,600 D2
Médéa 72,300 E1
Metlili Chaamba 21,300 E2
Miliana 36,400 E1
Mohammadia 53,700 D1
Mostaganem 101,600 D1
M'Sila 49,100 E1
Oran 491,900 D1
Orléansville (El Asnam) 106,100 E1
Ouallene E4
Ouargla 77,400 F2
Ouled Djellal 22,700 F2
Philippeville (Skikda) 107,700 F1
Poste Maurice Cortier E4
Poste Weygand D4
Reggane 11,300 D3
Relizane 60,000 E1
Saïda 62,100 E2
Sbaa D3
Sétif 144,200 F1
Sidi Bel-Abbes 116,000 D1
Silet E4
Skikda 107,700 F1
Souk Ahras 60,200 F1
Tabelbala 3,100 D3
Taghit 3,500 D2
Tamanrasset 23,200 F4
Tamentit D3
Taourirt E3
Tébessa 67,200 F1
Temacine F2
Ténès 30,100 E1
Tiaret 62,900 E1
Tiguentourine F3
Timgad 9,800 F1
Timimoun 20,500 E3
Tindouf 6,500 C3
Tinjoub C3
Tin-Zaouatene E5
Tizi Ouzou 73,100 E1
Tlemcen 109,400 D2
Touggourt 75,600 F2
Zaouiet Kounta 13,800 D3

OTHER FEATURES

Adrar des Iforas (plat.) E5
Ahaggar (range) F4
Anaï (well) G4
Aouinet Bel Egrâ (well) C3
Atlas (mts.) E2
Aurès (lag.) F1
Azzel Mati, Sebkha (lake) E3
Bougaroun (cape) F1
Chech, Erg (des.) D3
Chelia (mt.) F1
Chelif (riv.) E1
Chergui, Chott Ech (salt lake) E2
Gourara (oasis) E3
Grand Erg Occidental (des.) E2
Grand Erg Oriental (des.) F2
Guir Hamada (des.) D2
High Plateaus (ranges) D2
Iguidi, Erg (des.) C3
In Ezzane (well) G4
Irharhar, Wadi (dry riv.) F3
Issaouane Erg (des.) F3
Kabylia (reg.) E1
Mediterranean (sea) E1
Medjerda (riv.) F1
Melrhir, Chott (salt lake) F2
Mouydir (mts.) E3
Mya, Wadi (dry riv.) E2
M'zab (oasis) E2
Raoui, Erg er (des.) D3
Rhir, Wadi (dry riv.) F2
Sahara (des.) E4
Saharan Atlas (ranges) E2
Saoura, Wadi (dry riv.) D3
Souf (oasis) F2
Tademaït, Plateau du (plat.) E3
Tafassasset, Wadi (dry riv.) F4
Tahat (mt.) F4
Tamanrasset, Wadi (dry riv.) E4
Tanezrouft (des.) E4
Tassili N'Ahagger (plat.) E4
Tassili N'Ajjer (plat.) F3
Tidikelt (oasis) E3
Timmissao (well) E4
Tindouf, Sebkha de (salt lake) C3
Tinrhert, Hamada de (des.) F3
Tni Haïa (well) D4
Touat (oasis) E3
Touila (well) C3

BENIN

CITIES and TOWNS

Abomey 38,000 E7
Cotonou 178,000 E7
Djougou E7
Grand-Popo E7
Kandi E6
Lokossa 6,000 E7
Malanville E6
Natitingou 49,000 E6
Nikki E7
Ouidah E7
Parakou 21,000 E7
Porto-Novo (cap.) 104,000 E7
Savalou E7
Savé E7

OTHER FEATURES

Atakora (mts.) E6
Benin (bight) E8
Guinea (gulf) E8
Mono (riv.) E7
Niger (riv.) E6
Ouémé (riv.) E7
Slave Coast (reg.) E7
Sudan (reg.) E6

CAPE VERDE

CITIES and TOWNS

Mindelo 28,797 A7
Praia (cap.) 21,494 B8
Ribeira Grande 1,892 B7
Sal Rei 1,296 B8
Santa Maria 956 B8

OTHER FEATURES

Boa Vista (isl.) B8
Brava (isl.) B8
Fogo (isl.) B8
Maio (isl.) B8
Sal (isl.) B7
Santa Luzia (isl.) B8
Santo Antão (isl.) A7
São Nicolau (isl.) B8
São Tiago (isl.) B8
São Vicente (isl.) B7

GAMBIA

CITIES and TOWNS

Basse Santa Su 2,899 B6
Bathurst (cap.) 39,476 A6
Brikama 9,483 A6
Georgetown 2,510 A6

OTHER FEATURES

Gambia (riv.) B6

GHANA

CITIES and TOWNS

Accra (cap.) 564,194 D7
Accra* 738,498 D7
Ada 4,285 E7
Akuse 3,791 E7
Attebubu 6,630 D7
Awaso 5,449 D7
Axim 8,107 D8
Bawku 20,567 D6
Bekwai 11,287 D7
Berekum 14,296 D7
Bole 4,772 D7
Bolgatanga 18,896 D6
Cape Coast 51,653 D7
Daboya 1,872 D7
Damongo 7,760 D7
Dunkwa 15,437 D7
Elmina 11,401 D8
Enchi 4,382 D7
Gambaga 3,730 D6
Gyasikan 6,403 D7
Half Assini 5,429 D8
Ho 24,199 E7
Keta 14,446 E7
Kete Krachi 5,097 E7
Kintampo 7,149 D7
Koforidua 46,235 D7
Kpandu 12,842 D7
Kumasi 260,286 D7
Kumasi* 345,117 D7
Lawra 2,709 D6
Mampong 13,895 D7
Mpraeso 5,908 D7
Navrongo D6
Nsawam 25,518 D7
Nsuta 3,854 D7
Obuasi 31,005 D7
Oda 20,957 D7
Prestea 15,143 D7
Salaga 6,413 D7
Sekondi 33,713 D8
Sekondi-Takoradi* 160,868 D8
Sunyani 23,780 D7
Takoradi 58,161 D8
Tamale 83,653 D7
Tarkwa 14,702 D7
Tema 60,767 E7
Tumu 4,366 D6
Wa 21,374 D6
Wenchi 13,836 D7
Wiawso 5,558 D7
Winneba 30,778 D7
Yapei 1,203 D7
Yendi 22,072 D7

OTHER FEATURES

Ashanti (reg.) D7
Benin (bight) E8
Black Volta (riv.) D6
Gold Coast (reg.) D8
Guinea (gulf) E8
Oti (riv.) E7
Red Volta (riv.) D6
Saint Paul (cape) E7
Three Points (cape) D8
Volta (lake) D7
Volta (riv.) E7
White Volta (riv.) D6

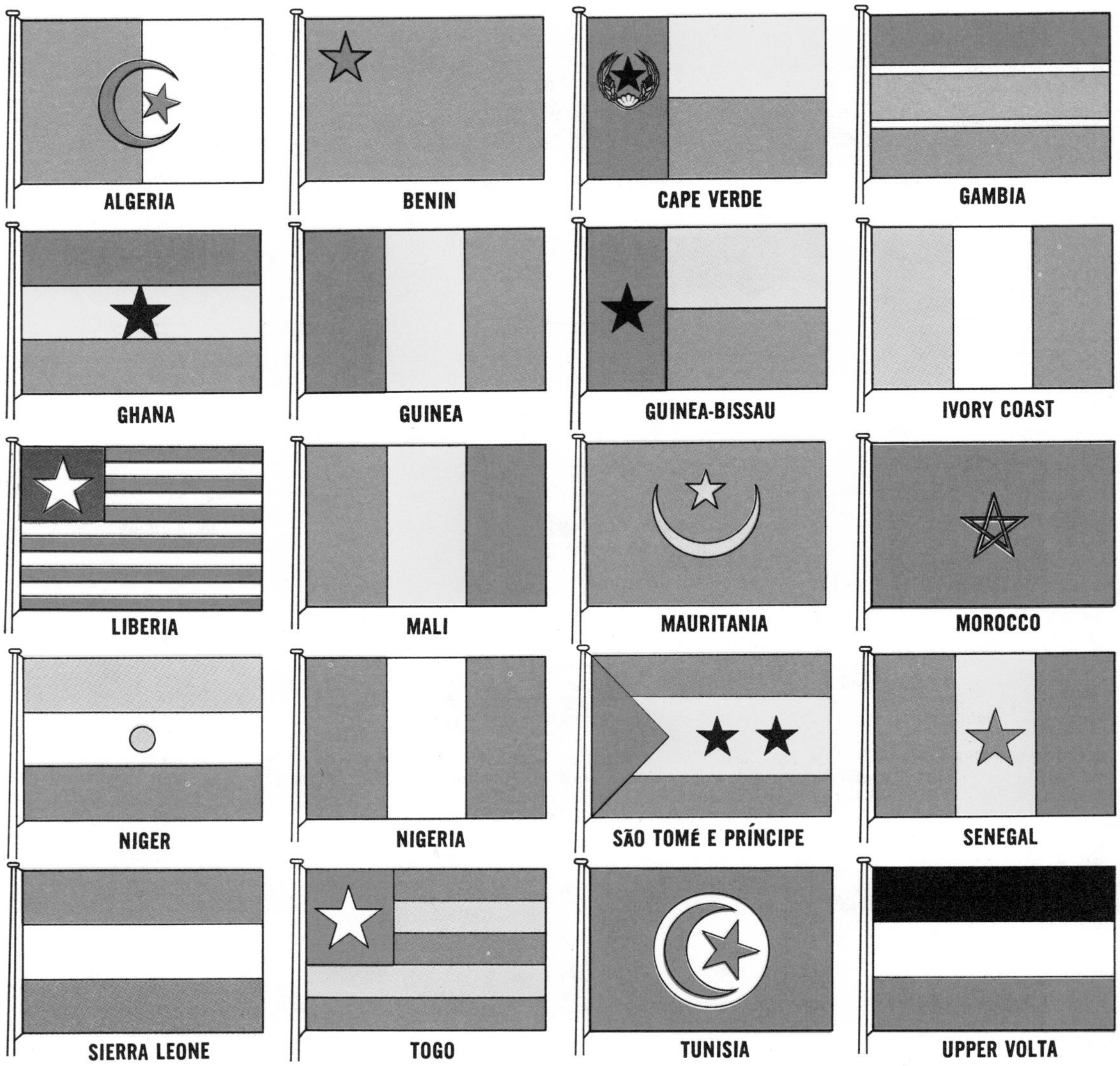

GUINEA

CITIES and TOWNS

Beyla C7
Boffa B6
Boké B6
Conakry (cap.)* 525,671 B7
Dabola B6
Dalaba B6
Dinguiraye B6
Dubréka B7
Faranah B6
Forécariah B7
Fria B6
Gaoual B6
Guéckédou B7
Kamsar B6
Kankan 85,310 C6
Kérouané C7
Kindia 79,861 B6
Kissidougou B7
Koundara 6,000 B6
Kouroussa C6
Labé 79,670 B6
Macenta C7
Mali B6
Mamou B6
N'Zérékoré 23,000 C7
Sangaredyi B6
Siguiri C6
Télimélé 12,000 B6
Tougué B6
Victoria B6

OTHER FEATURES

Bafing (riv.) B6
Bakoy (riv.) B6
Futa Jallon (lag.) B6
Los (isls.) B7
Milo (riv.) C7
Moa (riv.) B7
Niger (riv.) C6
Nimba (lag.) C7
Verga (cape) B6

GUINEA-BISSAU

CITIES and TOWNS

Bissau (cap.) 109,486 A6
Bolama○ 9,133 A6
Buba○ 6,706 B6
Bubaque○ 8,441 A6
Cacheu○ 15,194 A6

OTHER FEATURES

Bijagós (isls.) A6

IVORY COAST

CITIES and TOWNS

Abengourou 31,239 D7
Abidjan (cap.) 685,828 D7
Aboisso 14,272 D7
Agboville 27,192 D7
Bingerville 18,218 D7
Bondoukou 19,111 D7
Bouaflé 15,917 C7
Bouaké 173,248 D7
Bouna 5,787 D7
Boundiali 9,869 C7
Dabakala 3,272 D7
Dabou 23,870 D7
Daloa 60,958 C7
Danané 19,872 C7
Dimbokro 30,986 D7
Divo 37,896 C7
Ferkessédougou 25,307 D7
Fresco 1,865 C7
Gagnoa 42,362 C7
Grand-Bassam 25,808 D7
Grand-Lahou 4,070 C8
Guiglo 10,441 C7
Issia 11,143 C7
Katiola 21,559 C7
Kong 2,551 D7
Korhogo 47,657 C7
Man 50,315 C7
Mankono 6,570 C7
Odienné 13,864 C7
Port-Bouet 72,616 D7
San Pedro 27,616 C8
Sassandra 9,404 C8
Séguéla 12,587 C7
Sinfra 16,399 C7
Tabou 7,255 C8
Touba 5,256 C7
Toumodi 12,983 D7

OTHER FEATURES

Aby (lag.) D8
Bagoé (riv.) C6
Bandama (riv.) C7
Baoulé (riv.) C6
Black Volta (riv.) D6
Cavally (riv.) C7
Comoé (riv.) D7
Ebrié (lag.) D8
Guinea (gulf) E8
Ivory Coast (reg.) C8
Kossou, Lac de (lake) C7
Nimba (lag.) C7
Sassandra (riv.) C7

LIBERIA

CITIES and TOWNS

Buchanan 23,999 B7
Gbarnga 6,896 C7
Grand Cess C8
Greenville 8,462 C8
Harbel 11,445 B7
Harper 10,627 C8
Kolahun C7
Marshall B7
Monrovia (cap.) 166,507 B7
Plahn C7
River Cess 2,041 C7
Robertsport 2,562 B7
Sasstown C8
Tapeta 3,927 C7
Tchien 6,094 C7
Tubmanburg 14,089 B7

OTHER FEATURES

Bong (range) B7
Cavalla (riv.) C7
Cestos (riv.) C7
Grain Coast (reg.) B8
Kru Coast (reg.) C8
Mano (riv.) B7
Mount (cape) B7
Nimba (lag.) C7
Palmas (cape) C8
Roberts Field Int'l Airport C7

MALI

CITIES and TOWNS

Anéfis E5
Ansongo 3,485 E5
Araouane D5
Bafoulabé 2,163 B6
Bamako (cap.) 404,022 C6
Bamba D5
Banamba 6,776 C6
Bandiagara 8,920 D6
Bankass 3,229 D6
Bou Djebeha D5
Bougouni 17,246 C6
Bourem 4,538 E5
Dioila 4,953 C6
Dire 8,941 D5
Djenné 10,251 D6
Douentza 6,746 D6
Gao 30,714 E5
Goundam 10,262 D5
Gourma-Rharous 4,671 D5
Hombori D5
Kadiolo 3,991 C6
Kangaba 3,184 C6
Kati 24,991 C6
Kayes 44,736 B6
Ké-Macina 5,426 C6
Kéniéba 4,510 B6
Kerchoual E5
Kidal 3,308 E5
Kita 17,538 C6
Kolokani 8,923 C6
Kolondiéba 5,882 C6
Koulikoro 16,376 C6
Kourouba B6
Koutiala 27,497 C6
Mabrouk D5
Ménaka 3,693 E5
Mopti 53,885 D6
Nampala C5
Nara 6,091 C5
Niafunké 6,399 D5
Niono 12,290 C6
Nioro 11,617 C5
San 22,962 D6
Satadougou B6
Ségou 64,890 C6
Sikasso 47,030 C6
Sokolo C6
Taoudenni D4
Ténenkou 4,708 C6
Tessalit E4
Timbuktu (Tombouctou) 20,483 D5
Toukoto C6
Yanfolila 3,809 C6
Yelimané 1,481 B5
Yorosso 2,390 C6

OTHER FEATURES

Achourat (well) D4
Adrar des Iforas (plat.) E5
Asselar (well) D5
Azaouad (reg.) D5
Azaouak (dry riv.) E5
Bafing (riv.) B6
Bagoé (riv.) C6
Bakoy (riv.) B6
Bani (riv.) C6
Baoulé (dry riv.) C6
Baoulé (riv.) C6
Bir Ounane (well) D4
Chech, Erg (des.) D4
Debo (lake) D5
El Mraiti (well) D5
Faguibine (lake) D5
Falémé (riv.) B6
Haricha Hamada (des.) D4
Hombori (mts.) D5
In Dagouber (well) D4
Macina (depr.) D6
Niger (riv.) D5
Oum el Asel (well) D4
Sahara (des.) D4
Sekkane, Erg (des.) D4
Senegal (riv.) B5
Sudan (reg.) D6
Tadjnout Hagguerete (well) D4
Terhazza (ruins) C4
Tilemsi (valley) E5
Toufourine (well) C4

MAURITANIA

CITIES and TOWNS

Aïoun el Atrous C5
Akjoujt 8,044 B5
Akreïjit C5
Aleg 6,415 B5
Atar 16,326 B4
Bassikounou C5
Bir Mogreïn B3
Boutilimit 7,261 B5
Bogué 8,056 B5
Chinguetti B4
Fderik (Fort-Gouraud) 2,160 B4
Kaédi 20,848 B5
Kankossa B5
Kiffa 10,629 B5
Maghama B5
M'Bout B5
Méderdra A5
Néma 8,232 C5
Nouakchott (cap.) 134,986 A5
Nouadhibou 21,961 A4
Ouadane B4
Oualata C5
Oujaf C5
Oujeft B4
Rosso 16,466 A5
Sélibaby 5,994 B5
Tamchakett B5
Tamsagout C4
Tazadit B4
Tichitt C5
Tidjikja 7,870 B5
Timbédra 5,317 C5
Zouîrât 17,474 B4

OTHER FEATURES

Adafer (reg.) B5
Adrar (reg.) B4
Affolé (reg.) B5
Agueraktem (well) C4
Aïn ben Tili (well) C3
Arguin (bay) A4
Assaba (reg.) B5
Atoui, Wadi (dry riv.) B4
Ben Guerdane (well) B3
Bir el Khzaim (well) C4
Blanc (cape) A4
Brakna (reg.) B5
Chegga (well) C3
Djouf, El (des.) C4
El Mrayer (well) C4
El Mreïti (well) C4
Gorgol (reg.) B5
Hodh (reg.) C5
Iguidi, Erg (des.) C3
Inchiri (reg.) A5
Koumbi Saleh (ruins) C5
Lévrier (bay) A4
Makteïr (des.) B4
Meraia (reg.) C5
Mirik (Timiris) (cape) A5
Ouarane (reg.) B4
Sahara (des.) C4
Senegal (riv.) B5
Tagant (reg.) B5
Tidra (isl.) A5
Timiris (cape) A5
Touila (well) C3
Trarza (reg.) A5

MOROCCO

CITIES and TOWNS

Agadir 61,192 C2
Al Hoceima 18,686 D1
Asilah 14,074 C1
Azemmour 17,182 C2
Azrou 20,756 C2
Beni Mellal 53,826 C2
Berguent 3,356 D2
Bou Arfa D2
Bou Izakarn 2,342 C3
Boujad 18,838 C2
Casablanca 1,506,373 C2
Chechaouene 15,362 D1
Dar-el-Beida (Casablanca) 1,506,373 C2
El Jadida 55,501 C2
El Kelaa des Srarhna 17,163 C2
Erfoud 5,400 D2
Essaouira 30,061 B2
Fédala (Mohammedia) 70,392 C2
Fès (Fez) 325,327 D2
Figuig 13,660 D2
Goulmima 4,056 C2
Inezgane 11,495 C2
Ifni 13,650 B3

Jerada 30,633 ..... D2
Kenitra 139,206 ..... C2
Khenifra 25,526 ..... C2
Khouribga 73,667 ..... C2
Ksar el Kebir 48,262 ..... C2
Ksar es Souk 16,775 ..... D2
Larache 45,710 ..... C1
Marrakech 332,741 ..... C2
Mazagan (El Jadida) 55,501 ..... C2
Meknès 248,369 ..... C2
Mogador (Essaouira) 30,061 ..... B2
Mohammedia 70,392 ..... C2
Nador 32,490 ..... D1
Ouarzazate 11,142 ..... C2
Oued Zem 33,323 ..... C2
Ouezzane 33,267 ..... C2
Oujda 175,532 ..... D2
Petitjean (Sidi-Kacem) 26,831 ..... C2
Port-Lyautey (Kenitra) 139,206 ..... C2
Rabat (cap.) 367,620 ..... C2
Safi 129,113 ..... C2
Saïdia D2
Salé 155,557 ..... C2
Sefrou 28,607 ..... D2
Settat 42,325 ..... C2
Sidi Kacem 26,831 ..... C2
Tagounite C3
Tangier (Tanger) 187,894 ..... C1
Tan-Tan 10,772 ..... B3
Taourirt 15,580 ..... D2
Taouz D2
Tarfaya 1,104 ..... B3
Taroudannt 22,272 ..... C2
Taza 55,157 ..... D2
Tendrara D2
Tétouan 139,105 ..... C1
Tiznit 11,391 ..... B3
Youssoufia 22,435 ..... C2
Zagora 5,306 ..... C2

OTHER FEATURES

Anti-Atlas (ranges) C3
Atlas (mts.) C2
Bani, Jebel (mts.) C3
Beddouza, Ras (cape) C2
Dra, Wadi (dry riv.) C3
Er Rif (range) D2
Gibraltar (str.) C1
High Atlas (ranges) C2
Juby (cape) B3
Mediterranean (sea) D1
Middle Atlas (ranges) C2
Moulouya (riv.) D2
Rhéris, Wadi (dry riv.) D2
Rhir (cape) B2
Rif, Er (range) D2
Sarhro, Jebel (mts.) C2
Sebou (riv.) C2
Sim (cape) B2
Toubkal, Jebel (mt.) C2
Ziz, Wadi (dry riv.) D2

NIGER

CITIES and TOWNS

Agadès 11,000 ..... F5
Arhli (Arlit) F4
Bilma G5
Birni-N'Konni 10,000 ..... E6
Bosso G6
Chirfa G4
Dakoro F6
Dessa E6
Diffa G6
Djado G4
Dogondoutchi 9,000 ..... E6
Dosso E6
Fachi G5
Filingué 10,000 ..... E6
Gangara F6
Gaya 5,000 ..... E6
Gouré G6
Iférouane F5
Illéla 9,000 ..... F6
In-Gall F5
Madama G4
Madaoua F6
Magaria F6
Mainé-Soroa G6
Maradi 45,852 ..... F6
N'Guigmi G6
Niamey (cap.) 225,314 ..... E6
Ouallam E6
Say E6
Tahoua 31,265 ..... F6
Tanout F6
Téra 8,000 ..... E6
Tessaoua 5,000 ..... F6
Tillabéry E6
Tîmia F4
Zinder 58,436 ..... F6

OTHER FEATURES

Achégour (well) G5
Agadem (well) G5
Aïr (mts.) F5
Anaye (well) G5
Assakarai (dry riv.) F5
Azaoua (reg.) E5
Azbine (Aïr) (mts.) F5
Bagam (well) F5
Banguezane (mt.) F5
Bedouaram (well) G5
Chad (lake) G6
Dallol Bosso (dry riv.) E6
Dillia (dry riv.) G5
Djado (plat.) G4
El War (well) G4
In Azaoua (well) F4
Komadugu Yobe (riv.) G6
Mantas (well) F5
Niger (riv.) E6
Sahara (des.) F4
Sudan (reg.) F6
Tafassasset, Wadi (dry riv.) F4
Talak (reg.) E5
Ténéré (des.) G5
Timboulaga (well) F5
Tummo (El War) (well) G4
Zoo Baba (well) G5

NIGERIA

STATES

Anambra 2,300,000 ..... F7
Bauchi 2,496,329 ..... F6
Bendel 2,336,000 ..... F7
Benue 2,641,496 ..... F7
Borno 2,853,553 ..... G6
Cross River 3,633,582 ..... F7
Gongola 1,585,200 ..... G7
Imo 5,000,000 ..... F7
Kaduna 4,098,303 ..... F6
Kano 5,775,000 ..... F6
Kwara 1,600,600 ..... E7
Lagos 1,100,000 ..... E7
Niger 2,900,000 ..... F7
Ogun 1,448,966 ..... E7
Ondo 2,727,676 ..... F7
Oyo 5,208,884 ..... E7
Plateau 1,367,450 ..... F7
Rivers 1,544,314 ..... F8
Sokoto 1,367,450 ..... F6

CITIES and TOWNS

Aba 177,000 ..... F7
Abeokuta 253,000 ..... E7
Abuja F7
Ado 213,000 ..... E7
Afikpo F7
Aku F7
Akure F7
Argungu E6
Asaba F7
Azare G6
Baga G6
Bama G6
Baro F7
Bauchi F6
Benin City 136,000 ..... F7
Bida F7
Birnin Kebbi E6
Biu G6
Bonny F8
Brass F8
Burutu F7
Calabar 103,000 ..... F7
Deba Habe G6
Degema F8
Dikwa G6
Donga G7
Ede 182,000 ..... E7
Eha Amufu F7
Enugu 187,000 ..... F7
Forcados E7
Funtua F6
Gashaka G7
Gbogo F7
Geidam G6
Gombe G6
Gumel F6
Gummi F6
Gusau F6
Gwadabawa F6
Hadejia G6
Ibadan 847,000 ..... E7
Ibi F7
Ife 176,000 ..... E7
Ijebu-Ode E7
Ikeja E7
Ikom F7
Ilesha 224,000 ..... E7
Ilorin 282,000 ..... E7
Isa F6
Iseyin 115,083 ..... E7
Iwo 214,000 ..... E7
Jalingo G7
Jebba E7
Jega E6
Jos F7
Kabba F7
Kaduna 202,000 ..... F6
Kaiama E7
Kalmalo F6
Kano 399,000 ..... F6
Katsina 109,424 ..... F6
Katsina Ala F7
Kaura Namoda F6
Keffi F7
Koko F7
Kontagora F6
Kukawa G6
Kumo G7
Kuta F7
Lafia F7
Lafiagi F7
Lagos (cap.) 1,060,848 ..... E7
Laro E7
Lere F7
Lokoja F7
Maiduguri 189,000 ..... G6
Maigatari F6
Makurdi F7
Minna F7
Mubi G6
Nasarawa F7
New Bussa E6
Nguru G6
Nnewi F7
Nsukka F7
Offa E7
Ogbomosho 432,000 ..... E7
Ogoja F7
Okene F7
Ondo F7
Onitsha 220,000 ..... F7
Oron F8
Oshogbo 282,000 ..... F7
Owerri F7
Owo F7
Oyo 152,000 ..... E7
Pankshin F7
Panyam F7
Port Harcourt 242,000 ..... F8
Ringim F6
Sapele F7
Shaki E7
Shendam F7
Sokoto F6
Toungo G7
Uromi F7
Vom F7
Wamba F7
Warri F7
Wukari F7
Yan G7
Yelwa F6
Yola G7
Zaria 224,000 ..... F6
Zungeru F7

OTHER FEATURES

Adamawa (reg.) G7
Benin (bight) E8
Benue (riv.) F7
Biafra (bight) F8
Biu (plat.) G6
Bonny (bight) F8
Chad (lake) G6
Cross (riv.) F7
Dimlang (mt.) G7
Donga (riv.) G7
Foge (isl.) E6
Gongola (riv.) G6
Guinea (gulf) E8
Hadejia (riv.) F6
Jos (plat.) F7
Kaduna (riv.) F7
Kainji (res.) E6
Kebbi (riv.) E6
Komadugu Yobe (riv.) G6
Niger (delta) F8
Niger (riv.) F7
Osse (riv.) F7
Slave Coast (reg.) E7
Sokoto (riv.) F6
Sudan (reg.) F6

PORTUGAL-Madeira

CITIES and TOWNS

Funchal (cap.) 38,340 ..... A2

OTHER FEATURES

Desertas (isls.) A2
Madeira (isl.) A2
Pôrto Santo (isl.) A2
Salvage (isls.) A2

SÃO TOMÉ E PRINCIPE

CITIES and TOWNS

Santo António 1,618 ..... F8
São Tomé (cap.) 7,681 ..... F8

OTHER FEATURES

Guinea (gulf) E8
Príncipe (isl.) F8
São Tomé (isl.) F8

SENEGAL

CITIES and TOWNS

Bakel 6,339 ..... B6
Bignona 14,537 ..... A6
Dagana 10,506 ..... A5
Dakar (cap.) 798,792 ..... A6
Diourbel 50,618 ..... A6
Kaolack 106,899 ..... A6
Kédougou 7,575 ..... B6
Kaffrine 11,211 ..... A6
Kolda 19,302 ..... B6
Linguère 7,890 ..... B5
Louga 35,063 ..... A5
Matam 10,002 ..... B5
M'Bour 37,663 ..... A6
Nioro-du-Rip 7,824 ..... A6
Podor 6,914 ..... B5
Richard Toll A5
Rufisque A6
Saint-Louis 88,404 ..... A5
Sedhiou 9,421 ..... A6
Tambacounda 25,147 ..... B6
Thiès 117,333 ..... A5
Tivaouane 17,351 ..... A5
Touba A6
Yarboutenda B6
Ziguinchor 72,726 ..... A6

OTHER FEATURES

Casamance (riv.) A6
Falémé (riv.) B6
Ferlo (reg.) B6
Gambia (riv.) B6
Senegal (riv.) B5
Verde (cape) A6

SIERRA LEONE

CITIES and TOWNS

Bo 42,216 ..... B7
Bonthe 6,230 ..... B7
Freetown (cap.) 274,000 ..... B7
Kabala 4,610 ..... B7
Kambia 3,700 ..... B7
Kenema 33,880 ..... B7
Lungi 2,170 ..... B7
Marampa B7
Makeni 28,684 ..... B7
Moyamba 4,564 ..... B7
Pendembu 2,696 ..... B7
Pepel 3,793 ..... B7
Port Loko 5,809 ..... B7
Pujehun 1 ..... B7

OTHER FEATURES

Loma, Mansa (lag.) B7
Mano (riv.) B7
Moa (riv.) B7
Sherbro (isl.) B7
Yawri (bay) B7

SPAIN-Canary Islands, Ceuta and Melilla

CITIES and TOWNS

Arrecife 21,310 ..... B3
Ceuta 60,639 ..... C1
La Laguna A3
Las Palmas de Gran Canaria 260,368 ..... B3
Melilla 64,942 ..... D1
Santa Cruz de la Palma 10,393 ..... A3
Santa Cruz de Tenerife 74,910 ..... A3

OTHER FEATURES

Canary (isls.) A3
Fuerteventura (isl.) B3
Gomera (isl.) A3
Grand Canary (isl.) A3
Hierro (isl.) A3
Lanzarote (isl.) B3
La Palma (isl.) A3
Tenerife (isl.) A3

TOGO

CITIES and TOWNS

Aného (Anécho) 10,889 ..... E7
Atakpamé 17,440 ..... E7
Dapaong 10,100 ..... E6
Kpalimé 19,801 ..... E7
Kpémé 3,600 ..... E7
Lama-Kara 9,400 ..... E7
Lomé (cap.) 148,443 ..... E7
Mango 9,600 ..... E6
Sokodé 29,623 ..... E7

OTHER FEATURES

Benin (bight) E8
Guinea (gulf) E8
Mono (riv.) E7
Oti (riv.) E7
Slave Coast (reg.) E7

TUNISIA

CITIES and TOWNS

Béja 39,226 ..... F1
Ben Gardane 6,593 ..... G2
Bizerte 62,856 ..... F1
Burj al Hattaba F2
El Borma F2
El Djem 10,666 ..... G1
El Kef 27,939 ..... F1
Gabès 40,585 ..... F2
Gafsa 42,225 ..... F2
Halq el Oued 41,912 ..... G1
Jendouba 18,127 ..... F1
Kairouan 54,546 ..... F1
Kalaa-Kebira 23,508 ..... F1
Kasserine 22,594 ..... F1
La Goulette (Halq el Oued) 41,912 ..... G1
La Skhirra 4,565 ..... G2
Le Kef (El Kef) 27,939 ..... F1
Mahdia 25,711 ..... G1
Mareth 2,185 ..... F2
Mateur 19,645 ..... F1
Médenine 15,826 ..... F2
Menzel Bourguiba 42,111 ..... F1
Menzel Temime 18,857 ..... G1
Moknine 26,035 ..... G1
Monastir 26,759 ..... G1
Msaken 33,559 ..... G1
Nabeul 30,476 ..... G1
Nefta 12,476 ..... F2
Remada 6,100 ..... F2
Sbeitla 8,039 ..... F1
Sfax 171,297 ..... G2
Sousse 69,530 ..... G1
Tabarka 3,140 ..... F1
Tatahouine 10,399 ..... G2
Tozeur 16,772 ..... F2
Tunis (cap.) 550,404 ..... G1
Tunis* 873,515 ..... G1
Zarzis 14,420 ..... G2

OTHER FEATURES

Abiad, Ras el (Blanc) (cape) G1
Blanc (cape) G1
Bon (cape) G1
Chambi, Jebel (mt.) F2
Djerba (isl.) G2
Djerid, Shott el (salt lake) F2
Gabès (gulf) G2
Grand Erg Oriental (des.) F2
Hammamet (gulf) G1
Jefara (reg.) G2
Kerkennah (isls.) G2
Mediterranean (sea) F1
Medjerda (riv.) F1
Tib, Ras el (Bon) (cape) G1
Tunis (gulf) G1

UPPER VOLTA

CITIES and TOWNS

Aribinda D6
Banfora 12,358 ..... D6
Batié D7
Bobo Dioulasso 115,063 ..... D6
Bogandé E6
Dédougou D6
Diapaga E6
Diébougou D6
Djibo D6
Dori D6
Fada-N'Gourma 12,000 ..... E6
Gaoua D6
Houndé D6
Kaya 18,000 ..... D6
Koudougou 36,838 ..... D6
Koupela D6
Léo D6
Ouagadougou (cap.) 172,661 ..... D6
Ouahigouya 25,690 ..... D6
Pama E6
Po D6
Tenkodogo E6
Tougan D6
Yako D6
Zabré D6

OTHER FEATURES

Black Volta (riv.) D6
Comoé (riv.) D7
Oti (riv.) E7
Red Volta (riv.) D6
Sudan (reg.) D6
White Volta (riv.) D6

WESTERN SAHARA

CITIES and TOWNS

Dakhla 6,554 ..... A4
El Aaiún (Laayoune) 24,519 ..... B3
Semara 2,655 ..... B3
Villa Cisneros (Dakhla) 6,554 ..... A4

OTHER FEATURES

Atoui, Wadi (dry riv.) B4
Ausert (well) B4
Barbas (cape) A4
Bir Ganduz (well) A4
Bir Nzaran (well) B4
Blanc (cape) A4
Bojador (cape) B3
Durnford (pt.) A4
Guelta de Zemmur (well) B3
Saguia el Hamra (dry riv.) B3
Tichlá (well) B4

*City and suburbs.
○Population of sub-district or division.

Agriculture, Industry and Resources

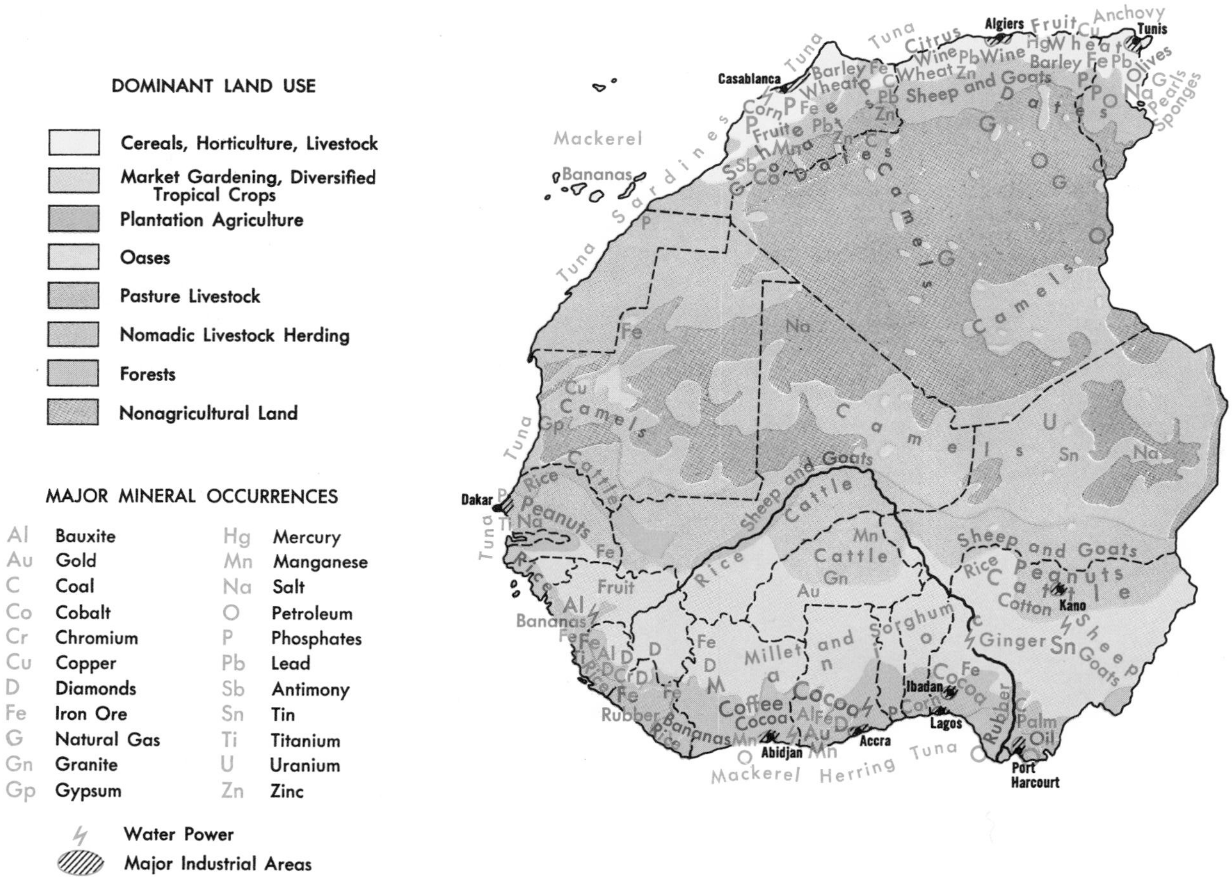
DOMINANT LAND USE
Cereals, Horticulture, Livestock
Market Gardening, Diversified Tropical Crops
Plantation Agriculture
Oases
Pasture Livestock
Nomadic Livestock Herding
Forests
Nonagricultural Land
MAJOR MINERAL OCCURRENCES
Al Bauxite
Au Gold
C Coal
Co Cobalt
Cr Chromium
Cu Copper
D Diamonds
Fe Iron Ore
G Natural Gas
Gn Granite
Gp Gypsum
Hg Mercury
Mn Manganese
Na Salt
O Petroleum
P Phosphates
Pb Lead
Sb Antimony
Sn Tin
Ti Titanium
U Uranium
Zn Zinc
Water Power
Major Industrial Areas
Algiers
Tunis
Casablanca
Dakar
Kano
Ibadan
Lagos
Accra
Abidjan
Port Harcourt
Tuna
Citrus
Fruit
Anchovy
Wine
Wheat
Barley
Olives
Pearls
Sponges
Sheep and Goats
Dates
Mackerel
Bananas
Sardines
Camels
Cattle
Rice
Peanuts
Sheep and Cattle
Millet and Sorghum
Cocoa
Coffee
Rubber
Palm Oil
Ginger
Cotton
Herring

LIBYA

EGYPT

CHAD

SUDAN

ETHIOPIA

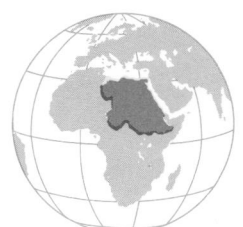

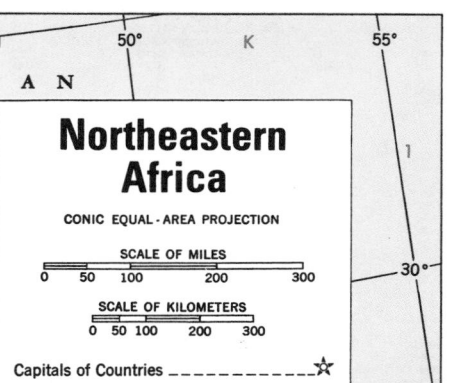

LIBYA
AREA 679,358 sq. mi. (1,759,537 sq. km.)
POPULATION 2,856,000
CAPITAL Tripoli
LARGEST CITY Tripoli
HIGHEST POINT Bette Pk. 7,500 ft. (2,286 m.)
MONETARY UNIT Libyan dinar
MAJOR LANGUAGES Arabic, Berber
MAJOR RELIGION Islam

EGYPT
AREA 386,659 sq. mi. (1,001,447 sq. km.)
POPULATION 41,572,000
CAPITAL Cairo
LARGEST CITY Cairo
HIGHEST POINT Jeb. Katherina 8,651 ft. (2,637 m.)
MONETARY UNIT Egyptian pound
MAJOR LANGUAGE Arabic
MAJOR RELIGIONS Islam, Coptic Christianity

CHAD
AREA 495,752 sq. mi. (1,283,998 sq. km.)
POPULATION 4,309,000
CAPITAL N'Djamena
LARGEST CITY N'Djamena
HIGHEST POINT Emi Koussi 11,204 ft. (3,415 m.)
MONETARY UNIT CFA franc
MAJOR LANGUAGES Arabic,-Bagirmi, French, Sara, Massa, Moudang
MAJOR RELIGIONS Islam, tribal religions

SUDAN
AREA 967,494 sq. mi. (2,505,809 sq. km.)
POPULATION 18,691,000
CAPITAL Khartoum
LARGEST CITY Khartoum
HIGHEST POINT Jeb. Marra 10,073 ft. (3,070 m.)
MONETARY UNIT Sudanese pound
MAJOR LANGUAGES Arabic, Dinka, Nubian, Beja, Nuer
MAJOR RELIGIONS Islam, tribal religions

ETHIOPIA
AREA 471,776 sq. mi. (1,221,900 sq. km.)
POPULATION 31,065,000
CAPITAL Addis Ababa
LARGEST CITY Addis Ababa
HIGHEST POINT Ras Dashan 15,157 ft. (4,620 m.)
MONETARY UNIT birr
MAJOR LANGUAGES Amharic, Gallinya, Tigrinya, Somali, Sidamo, Arabic, Ge'ez
MAJOR RELIGIONS Coptic Christianity, Islam

DJIBOUTI
AREA 8,880 sq. mi. (23,000 sq. km.)
POPULATION 386,000
CAPITAL Djibouti
LARGEST CITY Djibouti
HIGHEST POINT Moussa Ali 6,768 ft. (2,063 m.)
MONETARY UNIT Djibouti franc
MAJOR LANGUAGES Arabic, Somali, Afar, French
MAJOR RELIGIONS Islam, Roman Catholicism

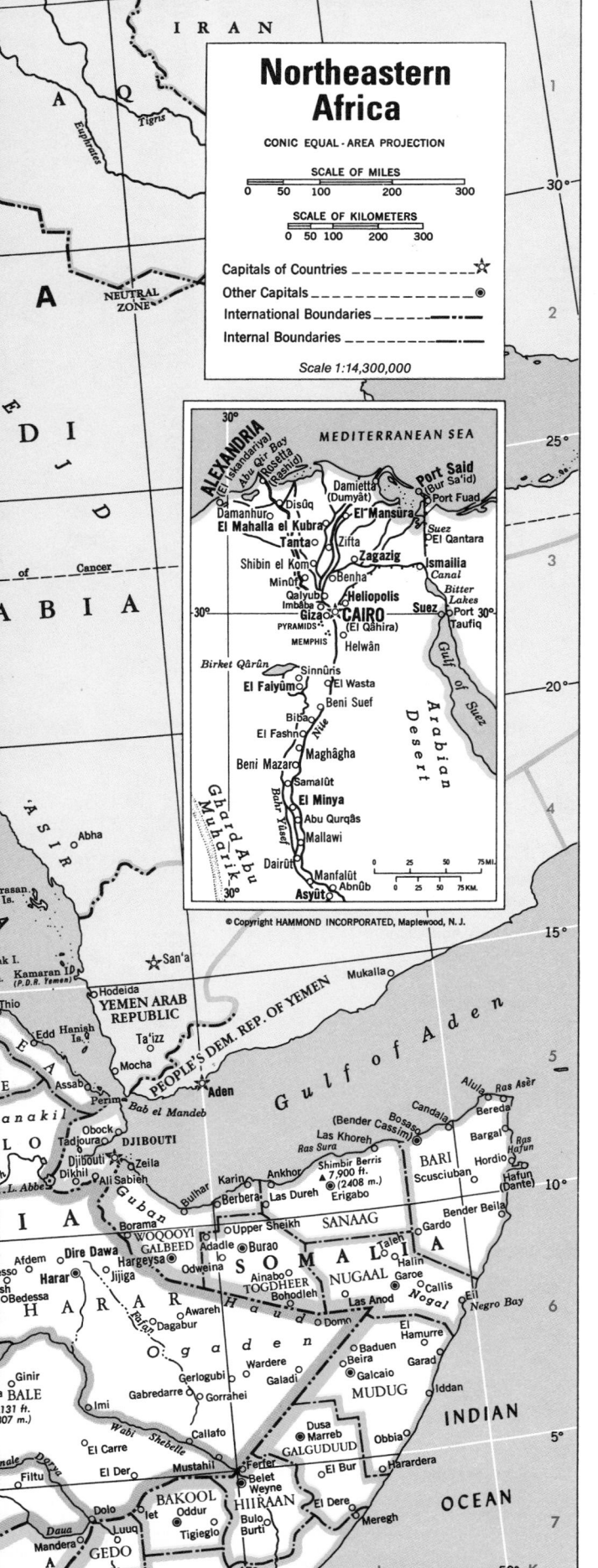

CHAD

CITIES and TOWNS

Abéché 28,100	D5
Abou Dela	C5
Adré	D5
Ain-Galakka	C4
Am-Dam	D5
Am-Timan 4,200	D5
Arada	C4
Ati 7,500	C5
Baïbokoum 5,500	C6
Bardaï	C3
Biltine 3,900	D5
Bitkine 5,000	C5
Bokoro 6,500	C5
Bol 2,500	B5
Bongor 14,300	C5
Bousso 4,500	C5
Doba 13,300	C6
Fada	D4
Faya-Largeau 6,800	C4
Fianga 10,000	C6
Gouro	C4
Goz Belda	D5
Guéréda	D5
Ham	C5

Haraz	C5
Iriba	D4
Kélo 16,800	C6
Koro Toro	C4
Koumra 17,000	C6
Kouno	C6
Kyabé 5,000	C6
Lal 10,400	C6
Léré	B6
Madadi	D4
Mangueigne	D5
Mao 4,900	C5
Massakory	C5
Massénya	C5
Melfi	C5
Mogororo	D5
Moïssala 5,100	C6
Mongo 8,300	C5
Moundou 39,600	C6
Moussoro 7,700	C5
N'Djamena (cap.) 179,000	C5
Nokou	B5
Oum Chalouba	D4
Oum Hadjer 5,600	C5
Oumianga-Kébir	D4
Pala 13,200	B6
Rig Rig	B5
Sarh 43,700	C6
Wour	C3
Yarda	C4

Yebbi-Bou	C3
Ziguei	C5
Zouar	C3

OTHER FEATURES

Azoum, Bahr	D5
Baguirmi (reg.)	C5
Bahr el Ghazal (dry riv.)	C5
Batha (riv.)	C5
Bodélé (depr.)	C4
Borku 72	C4
Chad (lake)	B5
Domar (dry riv.)	C4
Emi Koussi (mt.)	C4
Ennedi (plat.)	D4
Fittri (lake)	C5
Haouach, Wadi (dry riv.)	C5
Jef Jef es Seghin (plat.)	D3
Kanem (reg.)	C5
Logone (riv.)	C5
Maro (dry riv.)	C5
Mbéré (riv.)	C6
Mourdi (depr.)	D4
Ouham (riv.)	C6
Pendé (riv.)	C6
Sahara (des.)	C3
Salamat, Bahr (riv.)	C6
Sara (riv.)	C6
Shari (riv.)	C5

Sudan (reg.)	C5
Tibesti (mts.)	C3
Wadai (reg.)	D5

DJIBOUTI

CITIES and TOWNS

Ali Sabieh	H5
Dikhil	H5
Djibouti (cap.) 96,000	H5
Obock	H5
Tadjoura	H5

OTHER FEATURES

Abbe (lake)	H5
Aden (gulf)	J5
Bab el Mandeb (str.)	H5

EGYPT

CITIES and TOWNS

Abnûb 39,343	J4
Abu Qurqâs	J4
Akhmim 53,234	F2
Alexandria 2,318,655	J2

(continued on following page)

Topography

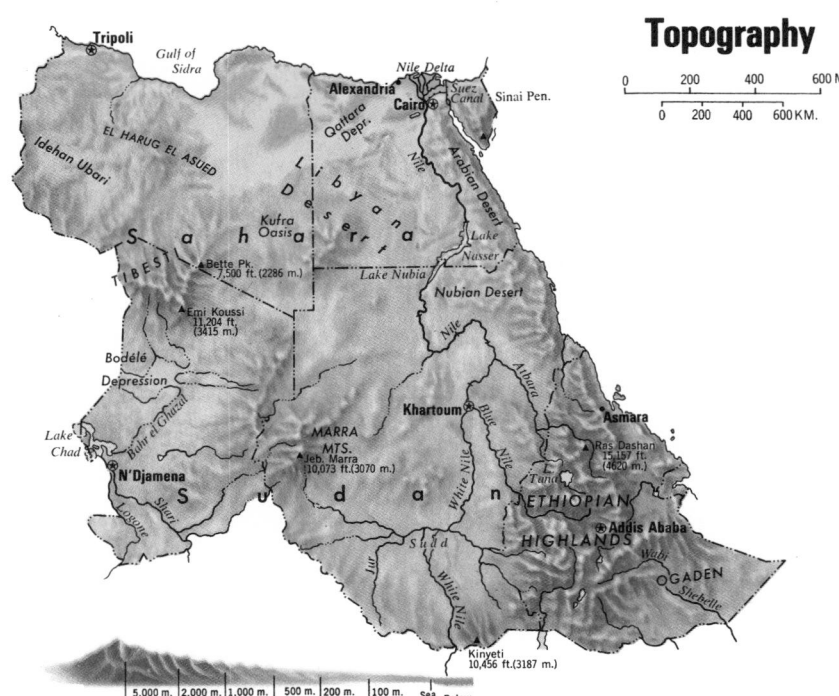

112 Northeastern Africa

(continued)

Aswân 144,377 F3
Asyût 213,983 J4
Bâris F3
Benha 88,992 J3
Beni Mazar 39,373 J4
Beni Suef 118,148 J3
Biba 33,074 J4
Bûlaq F2
Bur Sai'd (Port Said) 262,620 K2
Cairo (cap.) 5,084,463 J3
Dahab F2
Dairût 31,624 J4
Damanhur 188,927 J3
Damietta 93,546 J3
Disûq 58,650 J3
Dumyât (Damietta) 93,546 J3
Dûsh F3
El A'lamein E1
El A'rish F1
El Bawiti E2
El Faiyûm 167,081 J3
El Fashn 33,506 J4
El Hammam 6,588 E1
El Iskandariya (Alexandria) 2,318,655 J2
El Karnak F2
El Khârga 26,375 F2
El Mahalla el Kubra 292,853 J3
El Mansûra 257,866 K3
El Minya 146,423 J4
El Qâhira (Cairo) (cap.) 5,084,463 J3
El Qantara 919 K3
El Qasr E2
El Quseir 12,297 F2
El Tûr F2
El Wasta 17,659 J3
Gemsa F2
Girga 51,110 F2
Giza 1,246,713 J3
Heliopolis J3
Helwân J3
Hurghada F2
Idfu 34,858 F3
Imbâba J3
Ismailia 145,978 K3
Isna 34,186 F2
Karnak (El Karnak) F2
Kôm Ombo 44,531 F3
Luxor 92,748 F2
Maghâgha 40,802 J4
Mallawi 74,256 J4
Manfalût 41,126 J4
Mersâ Matrûh 27,857 E1
Minûf 55,131 J3
Mût 8,032 E2
Nuweiba F2
Port Fuad K3
Port Safâga F2
Port Said 262,620 K2
Port Taufiq K3
Qalyub 62,739 J3
Qasr Farâfra E2
Qena 94,013 F2
Ras Ghârib F2
Rashid (Rosetta) 42,962 J2
Rudeis F2
Salûm 4,161 E1
Samalût 48,146 J4
Shibin el Kom 102,844 J3
Sidi Barrani 1,574 E1
Sinnûris 42,022 J3
Siwa 4,999 E2
Sohâg 101,758 F2
Suez 194,001 K3
Tahta 45,242 F2
Tanta 284,636 J3
Zagazig 202,637 K3
Zifta 50,410 J3

OTHER FEATURES

Abu Qir (bay) J2
Abydos (ruins) F2
A'llaqi, Wadi (dry riv.) F3
A'qaba (gulf) G2
Arabian (des.) F2
Aswân (dam) F3
Aswân High (dam) F3
Bahariya (oasis) E2
Bahr Yusef (stream) J4
Bânâs, Ras (cape) G3
Berenice (ruins) F3
Birket Qârûn (lake) J3
Bir Taba (well) F2
Bitter (lkes) K3
Dakhla (oasis) E2
Eastern (Arabian) (des.) F2
El Sollum (gulf) E1
Farâfra (oasis) E2
Foul (bay) G3
Ghard Abu Muharik (des.) J4
Gilf Kebir (plat.) E3
Great Sand Sea (des.) D2
Katherina, Jebel (mt.) F2
Khârga (oasis) F2
Libyan (des.) E2
Libyan (plat.) E1
Mediterranean (sea) E1
Memphis (ruins) J3
Muhammad, Ras (cape) F2
Nasser (lake) F3
Nile (riv.) F2
Pyramids (ruins) J3
Qattara (depr.) E2
Red (sea) G3
Sahara (des.) E3
Sinai (mt.) F2
Sinai (pen.) F2
Siwa (oasis) E2
Suez (canal) K3
Suez (gulf) F2
Tiran (str.) F2
U'weinat, Jebel (mt.) E3

ETHIOPIA

PROVINCES

Arusi 852,900 G6
Bale 707,800 H6
Begemdir 1,355,800 G5
Eritrea 1,947,600 G4
Gamu-Gofa 698,800 G6
Gojjam 1,750,100 G5
Harar 3,359,200 H6
Ilubabor 688,800 F6
Kaffa 1,693,000 G6
Shoa 5,369,500 G6
Sidamo 2,479,800 G7
Tigre 1,828,900 H5
Wallaga 1,269,100 G6
Wallo 2,459,900 H5

CITIES and TOWNS

Addis Ababa (cap.) 1,196,300 G6
Addis Alam 5,500 G6
Adigrat 9,400 G5
Adi Ugri 12,800 G5
Adwa 16,400 G5
Afdem H6
Agordat G4
Aksum 12,800 G5
Ankober H6
Arba Mench 7,660 G6
Asmara 393,800 G4
Asosa F5
Assab 16,000 H5
Asselle 19,390 G6
Awareh H6
Awash H6
Axum (Aksum) 12,800 G5
Bahir Dar 25,100 G5
Burei G6
Burye G5
Callafo H6
Chilga G5
Dagabur H6
Dallol G5
Dangila G5
Debra Birhan 16,700 G6
Debra Markos 30,260 G5
Debra Tabor 8,700 G5
Dembidollo 7,600 F6
Dessye 49,750 G5
Dilla 13,800 G6
Dire Dawa 63,700 H6
Dolo H7
Domo J6
Edd H5
El Carre H6
El Der H6
Filtu H6
Gabredarre H6
Galadi J6
Gambela F6
Gardula 5,800 G6
Gedo G6
Gerlogubi H6
Ghimbi 8,300 G6
Ginir H6
Goba 13,500 H6
Gondar 38,600 G5
Gore 8,500 G6
Gorrahei H6
Harar 48,440 H6
Harkiko G4
Hosseina 8,500 G6
Imi H6
Jijiga 8,000 H6
Jimma 47,360 G6
Jiran G6
Karkabat G4
Keren G4
Kibre Mengist 8,300 G6
Lalibela G5
Magdala G5
Maji G6
Makale 30,780 G5
Massawa 19,800 G4
Mega G7
Mendi G6
Mersa Fatma H5
Metamma G5
Miesso H6
Mizan Teferi G6
Moyale G7
Murle G6
Mustahil H6
Nakamti 18,310 G6
Nakfa G4
Nazret 42,900 G6
Negelli 8,800 G6
Nejo G6
Saio (Dembidollo) 7,600 F6
Soddu 11,900 G6
Sokota G5
Tessenei G4
Thio H5
Tori F6
Umm Hajar G5
Waka G6
Waldia 9,600 G5
Wardere J6
Wolta G6
Yaballo G6
Yirga Alam 14,500 G6
Zula G4

OTHER FEATURES

Abay (riv.) G5
Abaya (lake) G6
Akobo (riv.) F6
Assale (lake) H5
Atbara (riv.) G5
Awash (riv.) H5
Bale (mt.) G6
Baraka (riv.) G4
Baro (riv.) G6
Billate (riv.) G6
Blue Nile (Abay) (riv.) G5
Buri (pen.) H4
Chamo (lake) G6
Dahlak (arch.) H4
Dahlak (isl.) H4
Danakil (reg.) H5
Dawa (riv.) G7
Fafan (riv.) H6
Ganale Dorya (riv.) H6
Gash Mareb (riv.) G5
Gughe (mt.) G6
Haud (reg.) J6
Kasar, Ras (cape) G4
Ogaden (reg.) H6
Omo (riv.) G6
Ras Dashan (mt.) G5
Red (sea) H4
Rudolf (Turkana) (lake) G7
Simen (mts.) G5
Stefanie (lake) G7
Takkaze (riv.) G5
Tana (lake) G5
Tisisat (fall) G5
Turkana (lake) G7
Wabi (riv.) H6
Wabi Shebelle (riv.) H6
Zwai (lake) G6

LIBYA

CITIES and TOWNS

Ajedabia○ 53,170 D1
Aujila○ 6,695 D2
Baida○ 59,765 D1
Barce (El Marj)○ 55,444 D1
Benghazi (cap.)○ 286,943 C1
Beni Ulid○ 19,113 B1
Berken B2
Brak○ 12,507 B2
Bu Ngem C1
Cyrene (Shahat)○ 17,157 D1
Derj○ 2,152 B1
Derna○ 44,145 D1
Edri B2
El Abiar○ 17,685 D1
El Agheila C1
El Azizia○ 34,077 B1
El Bardi○ 4,330 D1
El Barkat○ 2,139 B3
El Fogaha C2
El Gatrun B3
El Gezira D2
El Jauf○ 6,481 D3
El Marj○ 55,444 D1
El' Uweinat B2
Es Sidr○ 706 C1
Ez Zuetina○ 7,256 D1
Ghadames○ 6,172 A2
Gharian○ 65,224 B1
Ghat○ 6,924 B3
Ghemines○ 4,313 C1
Homs○ 66,890 B1
Hon○ 2,766 C2
Jaghbub (Jarabub)○ 1,436 D2
Jalo D2
Jarabub○ 1,436 D2
Marada○ 3,201 C2
Marsa el Brega○ 2,618 D1
Marsa el Hariga○ 5,043 D1
Mekili D1
Misurata○ 102,439 C1
Mizda○ 11,472 B1
Murzuk○ 22,185 B2
Nalut○ 23,535 B1
Ras Lanuf○ 1,990 C1
Sabratha○ 30,836 B1
Sebha○ 35,879 B2
Shahat○ 17,157 D1
Sinawen○ 1,549 B1
Sokna○ 3,757 C2
Soluk○ 6,501 D1
Susa D1
Syrte○ 22,797 C1
Tarhuna○ 52,657 B1
Tejerri B3
Tesawa B2
Tmessa C2
Tobruk○ 58,384 D1
Tokra○ 10,714 D1
Traghen B2
Tripoli (cap.)○ 550,438 B1
Ubari○ 19,132 B2
Umm el Abid C2
Waddan○ 5,347 C2
Wau el Kebir C2
Zawia○ 72,092 B1
Zella○ 4,835 C2
Zliten○ 58,981 C1
Zuila C2
Zwara○ 15,078 B1

OTHER FEATURES

Ain Zueiya (well) D3
Akhdar, Jebel (mts.) D1
A'mir, Ras (cape) D1
Barqa (Cyrenaica) (reg.) D1
Ben Ghnema, Jebel (mts.) C2
Bette (peak) C3
Bey el Kebir, Wadi (dry riv.) B1
Bir Hakeim (ruins) D1
Bishiara (well) D3
Bomba (gulf) D1
Buzeima (well) D3
Calansho Sand Sea (des.) D2
Calansho, Serir (des.) D2
Cyrenaica (reg.) D1
Fezzan (reg.) B2
Great Sand Sea (des.) D2
Harug el Asued, El (mts.) C2
Homra, Hamada el (des.) B2
Hosenofu (well) D3
Idehan Ubari (des.) B2
Idehan Murzuk (des.) B3
Jalo (oasis) D2
Jefara (reg.) B1
Jef Jef es Seghir (plat.) C2
Jofra (oasis) C2
Kufra (oasis) D3
Leptis Magna (ruins) B1
Libyan (des.) D2
Libyan (plat.) D1
Mediterranean (sea) C1
Nefusa, Jebel (mts.) B1
Rebiana○ (oasis) D3
Rebiana Sand Sea (des.) D3
Sahara (des.) C3
Sarra (well) D3
Shati, Wadi esh (dry riv.) B2
Sidra (gulf) C1
Soda, Jebel es (mts.) C2
Tazerbo○ (oasis) D2
Tibesti, Serir (des.) C3
Tinghert Hamada (Tinrhert) (des.) B2
Tripolitania (reg.) B1
U'weinat, Jebel (mt.) E3
Zelten, Jebel (mts.) D2

SUDAN

PROVINCES

Bahr El Ghazal 813,000 E6
Blue Nile 216,000 F5
Darfur, Northern 1,013,000 D5
Darfur, Southern 1,160,000 E5
El Buheyrat 574,000 E6
El Gezira 1,775,000 F5
Equatoria, Eastern 507,000 F6
Equatoria, Western 251,000 E6
Junglei 202,000 F6
Kassala 1,113,000 F4
Khartoum 1,160,000 F4
Kordofan, Northern 1,266,000 E5
Kordofan, Southern 951,000 E5
Nile 552,000 F4
Northern 416,000 E3
Red Sea 446,000 G4
Upper Nile 621,000 F6
White Nile 1,122,000 F5

CITIES and TOWNS

A'bri F3
Abu Hamed F4
Abu Matariq E5
Abu Zabad E5
Abwong F6
Adarama G4
Adok F6
Akasha F3
Akobo F6
Amadi F6
A'qiq G4
Argo F4
Aroma G4
Atbara 66,000 F4
Aweil E6
Ayod F6
Babanusa E5
Bara E5
Bentiu E6
Berber F4
Bor F6
Bo River Post E6
Buram E5
Damazin (Ed Damazin) 12,000 F5
Deim Zubeir E6
Delgo F3
Derudeb G4
Dilling E5
Dongola 6,000 F4
Dungunab G3
Ed Dae'in E5
Ed Damer 17,000 F4
Ed Damazin 12,000 F5
Ed Debba F4
Ed Dueim 27,000 F5
El Abbasiya F5
El Fasher 52,000 E5
El Fifi D5
El Geneina 33,000 D5
El Geteina F5
El Hilla E5
El Khandaq E4
El Managil F5
El Obeid 90,000 E5
El Odaiya E5
En Nahud 23,000 E5
Er Rahad F5
Er Roseires F5
Famaka F5
Fangak F6
Fashoda (Kodok) F6
Gabras E5
Gallabat G5
Gebeit Mine G3
Gedaref 92,000 G5
Gogrial E6
Goz Regeb G4
Haiya Junction G4
Halaib G3
Heiban F5
Jonglei F6
Juba 57,000 F7
Kadugli 18,000 E5
Kafia Kingi D6
Kajok E6
Kaka F5
Kapoeta F7
Karima F4
Karora G4
Kassala 99,000 G4
Kerma F4
Khartoum (cap.) 334,000 F4
Khartoum North 151,000 F4
Khashm el Girba G5
Kodok F6
Kongor F6
Korti F4
Kosti 57,000 F5
Kubbum D5
Kurmuk F5
Kutum D5
Lado F6
Loka F7
Malakal 35,000 F6
Maridi E7
Marsa Oseif G3
Melut F5
Merowe F4
Meshra er Req E6
Mongalla F6
Muglad E5
Muhammad Qol G3
Musmar G4
Nagishot F7
Nasir F6
Nimule F7
Nyala 60,000 E5
Nyamlell E6
Nyerol F6
Omdurman 299,000 F4
Opari F7
Pibor Post F6
Port Sudan 133,000 G4
Qalae'n Nahl F5
Raga E6
Rashad F5
Rejaf F7
Renk F5
Rufaa' F5
Rumbek 17,000 E6
Sennar F5
Shambe F6
Shendi F4
Shereik F4
Showak G5
Singa F5
Sinkat G4
Sodiri E5
Suakin G4
Suki F5
Tali Post F6
Talodi F5
Tambura E6
Tendelti F5
Tokar G4
Tombe F6
Tonga F6
Tonj E6
Torit F7
Towot F6
Trinkitat G4
Umm Keddada E5
Umm Ruwaba F5
Wadi Halfa F3
Wad Medani 107,000 F5
Wankai E6
Wau 53,000 E6
Yambio 7,000 E7
Yei F7
Yirol F6
Zalingei D5

OTHER FEATURES

Abu Dara, Ras (cape) G3
Abu Habl, Wadi (dry riv.) F5
Abu Shagara, Ras (cape) G3
Abu Tabari (well) E4
Adda (riv.) D6
Akobo (riv.) F6
A'mur, Wadi (dry riv.) G4
Asoteriba, Jebel (mt.) G3
Atbara (riv.) G4
Bahr Azoum (riv.) D5
Bahr el A'rab (riv.) E6
Bahr ez Zeraf (riv.) F6
Baraka (riv.) G4
Blue Nile (riv.) F5
Dar Hamid (reg.) F5
Dar Masalit (reg.) D5
Dinder (riv.) F5
El A'trun (oasis) E4
Fifth Cataract F4
Fourth Cataract F4
Gabgaba, Wadi (dry riv.) F3
Gezira, El (reg.) F5
Ghalla, Wadi el (dry riv.) E5
Hadarba, Ras (cape) G3
Howar, Wadi (dry riv.) E4
Ibra, Wadi (dry riv.) D5
Jebel Abyad (plat.) E4
Jebel Aulia (dam) F4
Jur (riv.) E6
Kasar, Ras (cape) G4
Kinyeti (mt.) F7
Laqiya U'mran (well) E3
Libyan (des.) E3
Lol (dry riv.) E6
Lotagipi Swamp (plain) F6
Marra, Jebel (mt.) D5
Meroe (ruins) F4
Milk, Wadi el (dry riv.) E4
Muqaddam, Wadi (dry riv.) F4
Napata (ruins) F4
Naqa (ruins) F4
Nile (riv.) F4
Nuba (mts.) E5
Nubia (lake) F3
Nubian (des.) F3
Nukheila (oasis) E4
Nuri (ruins) F4
Oda, Jebel (mt.) G3
Pibor (riv.) F6
Red (sea) G3
Sahara (des.) E3
Second Cataract F3
Selima (oasis) E3
Sennar (dam) F5
Setit (riv.) G5
Sixth Cataract F4
Sobat (riv.) F6
Suakin (arch.) G4
Sudan (reg.) E5
Sudd (swamp) F6
Sue (riv.) E6
Third Cataract E4
U'weinat, Jebel (mt.) E3
White Nile (riv.) F5

○Population of sub-district or division.

Agriculture, Industry and Resources

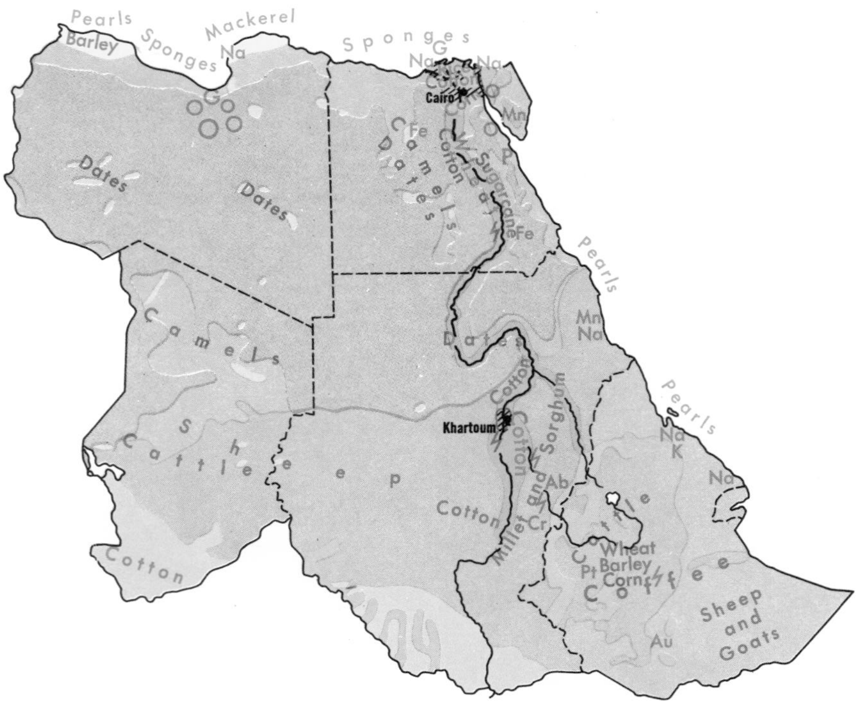

DOMINANT LAND USE

- Cereals, Horticulture, Livestock
- Cash Crops, Mixed Cereals
- Cotton, Cereals
- Market Gardening, Diversified Tropical Crops
- Plantation Agriculture
- Oases
- Pasture Livestock
- Nomadic Livestock Herding
- Forests
- Nonagricultural Land

MAJOR MINERAL OCCURRENCES

Ab	Asbestos	Mn	Manganese
Au	Gold	Na	Salt
Cr	Chromium	O	Petroleum
Fe	Iron Ore	P	Phosphates
G	Natural Gas	Pt	Platinum
K	Potash		

Water Power

Major Industrial Areas

ANGOLA

AREA 481,351 sq. mi. (1,246,700 sq. km.)
POPULATION 7,078,000
CAPITAL Luanda
LARGEST CITY Luanda
HIGHEST POINT Mt. Moco 8,593 ft. (2,620 m.)
MONETARY UNIT kwanza
MAJOR LANGUAGES Mbundu, Kongo, Lunda, Portuguese
MAJOR RELIGIONS Tribal religions, Roman Catholicism

BURUNDI

AREA 10,747 sq. mi. (27,835 sq. km.)
POPULATION 4,021,910
CAPITAL Bujumbura
LARGEST CITY Bujumbura
HIGHEST POINT 8,858 ft. (2,700 m.)
MONETARY UNIT Burundi franc
MAJOR LANGUAGES Kirundi, French, Swahili
MAJOR RELIGIONS Tribal religions, Roman Catholicism, Islam

CAMEROON

AREA 183,568 sq. mi. (475,441 sq. km.)
POPULATION 8,503,000
CAPITAL Yaoundé
LARGEST CITY Douala
HIGHEST POINT Cameroon 13,350 ft. (4,069 m.)
MONETARY UNIT CFA tranc
MAJOR LANGUAGES Fang, Bamileke, Fulani, Duala, French, English
MAJOR RELIGIONS Tribal religions, Christianity, Islam

CENTRAL AFRICAN REP.

AREA 242,000 sq. mi. (626,780 sq. km.)
POPULATION 2,284,000
CAPITAL Bangui
LARGEST CITY Bangui
HIGHEST POINT Gao 4,659 ft. (1,420 m.)
MONETARY UNIT CFA franc
MAJOR LANGUAGES Banda, Gbaya, Sangho, French
MAJOR RELIGIONS Tribal religions, Christianity, Islam

CONGO

AREA 132,046 sq. mi. (342,000 sq. km.)
POPULATION 1,537,000
CAPITAL Brazzaville
LARGEST CITY Brazzaville
HIGHEST POINT Leketi Mts. 3,412 ft. (1,040 m.)
MONETARY UNIT CFA franc
MAJOR LANGUAGES Kikongo, Bateke, Lingala, French
MAJOR RELIGIONS Christianity, tribal religions, Islam

EQUATORIAL GUINEA

AREA 10,831 sq. mi. (28,052 sq. km.)
POPULATION 244,000
CAPITAL Malabo
LARGEST CITY Malabo
HIGHEST POINT 9,868 ft. (3,008 m.)
MONETARY UNIT ekuele
MAJOR LANGUAGES Fang, Bubi, Spanish
MAJOR RELIGIONS Tribal religions, Christianity

GABON

AREA 103,346 sq. mi. (267,666 sq. km.)
POPULATION 551,000
CAPITAL Libreville
LARGEST CITY Libreville
HIGHEST POINT Ibounzi 5,165 ft. (1,574 m.)
MONETARY UNIT CFA franc
MAJOR LANGUAGES Fang and other Bantu languages, French
MAJOR RELIGIONS Tribal religions, Christianity, Islam

KENYA

AREA 224,960 sq. mi. (582,646 sq. km.)
POPULATION 15,327,061
CAPITAL Nairobi
LARGEST CITY Nairobi
HIGHEST POINT Kenya 17,058 ft. (5,199 m.)
MONETARY UNIT Kenya shilling
MAJOR LANGUAGES Kikuyu, Luo, Kavirondo, Kamba, Swahili, English
MAJOR RELIGIONS Tribal religions, Christianity, Hinduism, Islam

MALAWI

AREA 45,747 sq. mi. (118,485 sq. km.)
POPULATION 5,968,000
CAPITAL Lilongwe
LARGEST CITY Blantyre
HIGHEST POINT Mulanje 9,843 ft. (3,000 m.)
MONETARY UNIT Malawi kwacha
MAJOR LANGUAGES Chichewa, Yao, English, Nyanja, Tumbuka, Tonga, Ngoni
MAJOR RELIGIONS Tribal religions, Islam, Christianity

RWANDA

AREA 10,169 sq. mi. (26,337 sq. km.)
POPULATION 4,819,317
CAPITAL Kigali
LARGEST CITY Kigali
HIGHEST POINT Karisimbi 14,780 ft. (4,505 m.)
MONETARY UNIT Rwanda franc
MAJOR LANGUAGES Kinyarwanda, French, Swahili
MAJOR RELIGIONS Tribal religions, Roman Catholicism, Islam

SOMALIA

AREA 246,200 sq. mi. (637,658 sq. km.)
POPULATION 3,645,000
CAPITAL Mogadishu
LARGEST CITY Mogadishu
HIGHEST POINT Surud Ad 7,900 ft. (2,408 m.)
MONETARY UNIT Somali shilling
MAJOR LANGUAGES Somali, Arabic, Italian, English
MAJOR RELIGION Islam

TANZANIA

AREA 363,708 sq. mi. (942,003 sq. km.)
POPULATION 17,527,560
CAPITAL Dar es Salaam
LARGEST CITY Dar es Salaam
HIGHEST POINT Kilimanjaro 19,340 ft. (5,895 m.)
MONETARY UNIT Tanzanian shilling
MAJOR LANGUAGES Nyamwezi-Sukuma, Swahili, English
MAJOR RELIGIONS Tribal religions, Christianity, Islam

UGANDA

AREA 91,076 sq. mi. (235,887 sq. km.)
POPULATION 12,630,076
CAPITAL Kampala
LARGEST CITY Kampala
HIGHEST POINT Margherita 16,795 ft. (5,119 m.)
MONETARY UNIT Ugandan shilling
MAJOR LANGUAGES Luganda, Acholi, Teso, Nyoro, Soga, Nkole, English, Swahili
MAJOR RELIGIONS Tribal religions, Christianity, Islam

ZAIRE

AREA 905,063 sq. mi. (2,344,113 sq. km.)
POPULATION 28,291,000
CAPITAL Kinshasa
LARGEST CITY Kinshasa
HIGHEST POINT Margherita 16,795 ft. (5,119 m.)
MONETARY UNIT zaire
MAJOR LANGUAGES Tshiluba, Mongo, Kikongo, Kingwana, Zande, Lingala, Swahili, French
MAJOR RELIGIONS Tribal religions, Christianity

ZAMBIA

AREA 290,586 sq. mi. (752,618 sq. km.)
POPULATION 5,679,808
CAPITAL Lusaka
LARGEST CITY Lusaka
HIGHEST POINT Sunzu 6,782 ft. (2,067 m.)
MONETARY UNIT Zambian kwacha
MAJOR LANGUAGES Bemba, Tonga, Lozi, Luvale, Nyanja, English
MAJOR RELIGIONS Tribal religions

ANGOLA

DISTRICTS

Bengo 68,885	B5
Benguela 474,897	C6
Bié 650,337	C6
Cabinda 80,857	B5
Cuando Cubango 112,073	C7
Cuanza-Norte 298,062	B5
Cuanza-Sul 458,592	C6
Cunene 147,394	C7
Huambo 837,627	C6
Hulla 497,470	B7
Luanda 491,704	B5
Lunda Norte 210,000	C5
Lunda Sul 98,000	D5
Malange 558,630	C6
Moçâmedes 53,058	B7
Moxico 213,119	D6
Uíge 386,037	B5
Zaire 41,766	B5

CITIES and TOWNS

Alto Chicapa	C6
Alto Cuale	C5
Ambriz	B5
Andulo	C6
Bala dos Tigres	B7
Baia Farta	B6
Balombo	B6
Bela Vista	B6
Bembe	B5
Benguela 40,996	B6
Bié 18,941	C6
Caála 8,894	C6
Cabinda 21,124	B5
Caconda	B6
Cacuso	C7
Caiundo	C7
Calulo	B6
Caluquembe	C6
Camacupa 5,740	C6
Camanongue	D6
Cambulo	C5
Cangamba	C6
Capelongo	C6
Capenda-Camulemba	C5
Cassai	D6
Cassamba	D6
Catete	B5
Catumbela	B6
Caúngula	C5
Caxito	B5
Cazombo	D6
Cela 2,784	B6
Chiange	B7
Chinguar	C6
Chipindo	C6
Chitado	B7
Chitembo	C6
Coambo	C5
Cuango	C5
Cuchi	C6
Cuilo	C5
Cuito-Cuanavale	C7
Cuma	B6
Damba	B5
Dirico	D7
Dombe Grande	B6
Dondo	B5

Duque de Bragança	C5
Folgares	C6
Forte República	C5
Foz do Cunene	B7
Gabela 6,930	B6
Gambos	B6
Golungo Alto	B5
Huambo 61,885	C6
Iona	B7
Kassinga	C7
Lobito 59,528	B6
Lóvua	D5
Luacano	D6
Luachimo	D5
Luanda (cap.) 475,328	B5
Lubango 31,674	B6
Lucira	B6
Luiana	D7
Lukapa	D5

Macondo	D6
Malange 31,599	C5
Maquela do Zombo	C5
Massango (Forte República)	C5
Mavinga	D7
Mbanza Congo 4,002	B5
Moçâmedes 12,076	B7
Menongue 3,023	C7
Mucope	B7
Mucusso	D7
Munhango	C6
Muxima	B5
Nana Candundo	D6
Ndalatando 7,342	B5
N'gage 2,548	C5
Ngiva	C7
Ngunza 7,911	B6
Nharêa	C6
Noqui	B5
Nova Chaves	D6

Nova Gaia	C5
Nzeto	B5
Oncócua	D5
Porto Alexandre 8,235	B7
Porto Amboim	C6
Quela	C6
Quibala	C5
Quibaxe	B5
Quinzau	B5
Sanza Pombo	B5
São Nicolau	B6
Saurimo 12,901	D5
Songo	B5
Soyo	B5
Ulge 11,972	C5
Vila Guilherme Capelo	B5
Vila Nova de Seles	B6
Xangongo	C7

OTHER FEATURES

Bero (riv.)	B7
Chicapa (riv.)	D5
Chiumbe (riv.)	D5
Congo (riv.)	C4
Coporolo (riv.)	B6
Cuando (riv.)	C7
Cuango (riv.)	C5
Cuanza (riv.)	C5
Cubango (riv.)	C7
Cuito (riv.)	C7
Cunene (riv.)	B7
Cunene (riv.)	B7
Cuvo (riv.)	B6
Kasai (riv.)	C5
Kwilu (riv.)	C5
Loange (riv.)	C5
Loge (riv.)	B5
Lungwebungu (riv.)	D6
Matala (dam)	B6

M'Bridge (riv.)	B5
Moco (mt.)	C6
Negro (cape)	B7
Palmeirinhas (pt.)	B5
Ruacana Falls (dam)	B7
Santa Maria (cape)	D6
Zambezi (riv.)	D6

BURUNDI

CITIES and TOWNS

Bujumbura (cap.) 141,040	E4
Bururi 7,800	E4
Gitega 19,500	F4

OTHER FEATURES

Ruzizi (riv.)	E4

Tanganyika (lake)	E5

CAMEROON

CITIES and TOWNS

Abong-Mbang 6,000	B3
Ambam 4,000	B3
Bafia 12,000	B3
Bafoussam 62,239	B2
Bali	A2
Bamenda 48,111	B2
Banyo	B2
Batouri 7,000	B3
Bélabo	B3
Bengbis	B3
Bertoua 10,000	B2
Bétaré-Oya	B2
Bonabéri	A3

ANGOLA

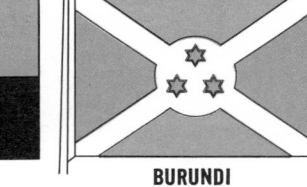

BURUNDI

CAMEROON

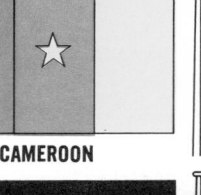

CENTRAL AFRICAN REP.

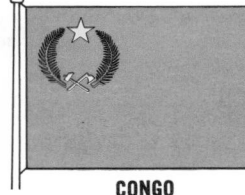

CONGO

EQUATORIAL GUINEA

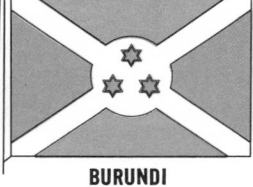

GABON

KENYA

MALAWI

RWANDA

SOMALIA

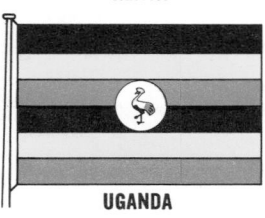

TANZANIA

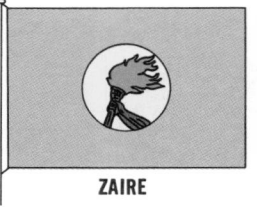

UGANDA

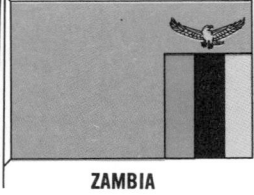

ZAIRE

ZAMBIA

(continued on following page)

Buea 24,584	A3	Kontcha	B2	Nanga-Eboko	B3
Campo	B3	Kousséri 7,000	B1	Ngaoundéré 38,992	B2
Djoum	B3	Kribi 5,000	A3	Nkambe	A3
Douala 458,426	B3	Kumba 44,175	A3	Nkongsamba 71,298	B2
Doumé	B3	Kumbo 10,000	B2	Poli	B2
Dschang 20,000	A2	Lomié	B3	Rey Bouba	B2
Ebolowa 24,000	B3	Makari	B1	Sangmélima 12,000	B3
Edéa 25,493	B3	Mamfé 10,000	A3	Tcholliré	B2
Eséka 10,000	B3	Maroua 67,187	B1	Tibati	B2
Essé	B3	Mbalmayo 22,106	B3	Tignère	B2
Fort-Foureau (Kousseri) 7,000	B1	Meiganga 6,000	B2	Tiko 11,000	A3
Foumban 33,944	B2	Mokolo 7,000	B1	Victoria 27,016	A3
Garoua 63,900	B2	Moloundou	C3	Wum 13,000	A3
Guidder 10,000	B1	Monatélé	B3	Yabassi 10,000	B3
Kaélé 17,000	B1	Mora 6,000	B1	Yagoua 11,000	B1

Yaoundé (cap.) 313,706	B3
Yokadouma 6,000	B3
Yoko	B2

OTHER FEATURES

Adamawa (reg.)	B2
Benué (riv.)	A2
Biafra (bight)	A3
Cameroon (mt.)	A3
Cross (riv.)	A3
Dja (riv.)	B3
Donga (riv.)	A2
Ivindo (riv.)	B3
Kadei (riv.)	C3

Logone (riv.)	C2
Lom (riv.)	B2
Mbéré (riv.)	B2
Mbakou (res.)	B2
Sanaga (riv.)	B3
Sanga (riv.)	C3

CENTRAL AFRICAN REPUBLIC

CITIES and TOWNS

Alindao 12,295	D2
Baboua 3,999	C2
Bakia	E2

Bambari 31,285	D2
Bangassou 21,773	D3
Bangui (cap.) 279,792	C3
Batangafo 12,543	C2
Berbérati 27,285	C3
Birao 3,317	D1
Bocaranga 6,202	C2
Boda 5,771	C3
Bossangoa 25,150	C2
Bossembele 5,091	C3
Bouali	C3
Bouar 29,528	C2
Bouca 8,874	C2
Boula	C2

Bozoum 13,573	C2
Bria 14,786	D3
Carnot 17,863	C3
Damara 2,556	C3
Dekoa 7,663	C2
Gaza	C3
Goubere	D3
Grimari 7,308	C2
Ippy 10,816	D3
Kaga Bandoro 11,876	C2
Kaka	D2
Kembe 5,051	D3
Kouango 2,602	D3
Kouki	C2

(continued on following page)

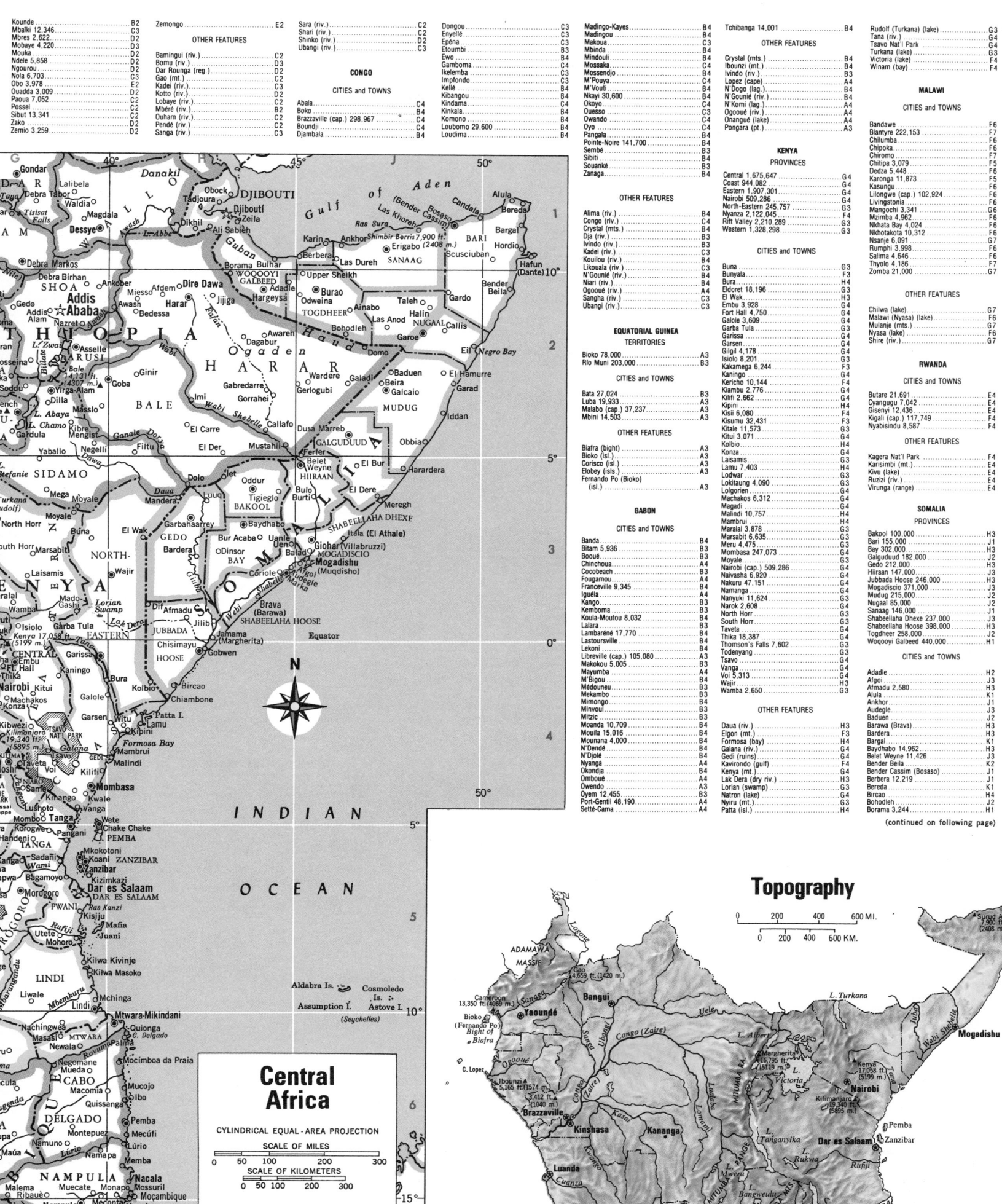

Central Africa

CYLINDRICAL EQUAL-AREA PROJECTION

SCALE OF MILES
0 50 100   200   300

SCALE OF KILOMETERS
0 50 100   200   300

Capitals of Countries ___☆
Other Capitals ___◉
International Boundaries ___
Internal Boundaries ___

Scale 1:13,800,000

© Copyright HAMMOND INCORPORATED, Maplewood, N.J.

Topography

0 200 400 600 MI.
0 200 400 600 KM.

Below Sea Level | 100 m. 328 ft. | 200 m. 656 ft. | 500 m. 1,640 ft. | 1,000 m. 3,281 ft. | 2,000 m. 6,562 ft. | 5,000 m. 16,404 ft.

(continued)

Bosaso J1
Brava 6,167 H3
Bulhar H1
Bulo Burti 5,247 J3
Bur Acaba H3
Burao 12,617 J2
Callis J2
Candala J1
Chisimayu 17,872 H4
Chiambone H4
Coriole 4,341 H3
Dante (Hafun) K1
Dif H3
Dinsor H3
Dusa Marreb J2
Eil J2
El Athale (Itala) J3
El Bur J3
El Dere J3
El Hamurre J2
Erigabo 4,279 J1
Ferfer J2
Galcaio J2
Garad J2
Garbahaarrey H3
Gardo J2
Garoe J2
Giohar 13,156 J3
Gobwen H4
Hafun K1
Halin J2
Harardera J3
Hargeysa 40,254 H2
Hordio K1
Iddan J2
Iet H3
Itala J3
Jamama 5,408 H3
Jilib 3,232 H3
Karin J1
Kismayu (Chisimayu) 17,872 H4
Las Dureh J1
Luuq H3
Margherita (Jamama) H3
Marka (Merka) 17,708 H3
Mogadishu (cap.) 371,000 J3
Muqdisho (Mogadishu) (cap.) 371,000 J3
Obbia J2
Oddur H3
Taleh J2
Uanle Uen H3
Upper Sheikh J2
Villabruzzi (Johar) J3
Zeila 1,226 H1

OTHER FEATURES

Aden (gulf) J1
Asèr, Ras (cape) K1
Giuba (riv.) H3
Guban (reg.) H1
Hafun, Ras (cape) K1
Haud (plat.) J2
Lak Dera (dry riv.) H3
Negro (bay) J2
Nogal (reg.) J2
Shimbir Berris (mt.) J1
Sura, Ras (cape) J1
Surud Ad (mt.) J1
Webi Shabelle (riv.) H3

TANZANIA

REGIONS

Arusha 928,478 G4
Dodoma 971,921 G5
Iringa 922,801 G5
Kigoma 648,950 F4
Kilimanjaro 902,394 G4
Lindi 527,902 G5
Mara 723,295 F4
Mbeya 1,080,241 F5
Morogoro 939,190 G5
Mtwara 771,726 G5
Mwanza 1,443,418 F4
Pemba 205,870 H5
Pwani (Coast) 516,949 G5
Rukwa 451,897 F5
Ruvuma 564,113 G6
Shinyanga 1,323,482 F4
Singida 614,030 F5
Tabora 818,049 F5
Tanga 1,088,592 G5
Zanzibar Mjini 143,616 G5
Zanzibar Shambani North 77,424 G5
Zanzibar Shambani South 52,325 G5
Ziwa Magharibi (West Lake) 1,009,379 F4

CITIES and TOWNS

Arusha 55,281 G4
Babati G4
Bagamoyo 5,112 G5
Bukoba 20,430 F4
Chake Chake 4,862 H5
Dar es Salaam (cap.) 757,346 G5
Dodoma 45,703 G5
Geita 3,066 F4
Handeni G5
Ifakara G5
Iringa 57,182 G5
Itigi F5
Kahama 3,211 F4
Kaliua F5
Kanga G5
Karema F5
Kasanga F5
Kasulu F4
Kibara F4
Kibaya G5
Kibondo F4
Kigoma-Ujiji 50,044 E4
Kilosa 4,458 G5
Kilwa Kivinje 2,790 G5
Kilwa Masoko G5
Kinyangiri G4
Kipili F5
Kisiju G5
Kitunda F5
Kizimkazi G5
Kondoa 4,514 G4
Kongwa G5
Korogwe 6,675 G5
Lindi 27,308 G5
Liuli F6
Liwale G5
Longido G4
Mahenge G5
Makumbako G5
Manda F6
Manyoni G5
Masasi G6
Mbamba Bay G6
Mbeya 76,606 F5
Mbulu G4
Mchinga H5
Mohoro G5
Mombo G4
Morogoro 61,890 G5
Moshi 52,223 G4
Mpanda F5
Mtakuja F5
Mtwara-Mikindani 48,510 H6
Murongo F4
Musoma 32,658 F4
Muwale F5
Mwadui 7,383 F4
Mwanza 110,611 F4
Mwaya F5
Mwesi F5
Nachingwea 3,751 G6
Newala G6
Ngara F4
Njombe F5
Pangani 2,955 G5
Rungwa F5
Sadani G5
Same G4
Sekenke F4
Shinyanga 21,703 F4
Singida 29,252 F4
Songea 17,954 G6
Sumbawanga 28,586 F5
Tabora 67,392 F5
Tanga 103,409 G4
Tukuyu 4,089 F5
Tunduru G6
Urambo F4
Utete G5
Uvinza F5
Wete 8,469 G4
Zanzibar 110,669 G5

OTHER FEATURES

Eyasi (lake) F4
Great Ruaha (riv.) G5
Juani (isl.) G5
Kalambo (falls) F5
Kanzi (cape) G5
Kilimanjaro (mt.) G4
Kilombero (riv.) G5
Mafia (isl.) H5
Manyara (lake) G4
Masai (steppe) G4
Mbarangandu (riv.) G5
Mbemkuru (riv.) G5
Meru (mt.) G4
Mikumi Nat'l Park G5
Natron (lake) G4
Ngorongoro (crater) F4
Njombe (riv.) F5
Nyasa (lake) F6
Olduvai Gorge (canyon) G4
Pangani (riv.) G4
Pemba (isl.) H5
Rovuma (riv.) G6
Rufiji (riv.) G5
Ruaha Nat'l Park F5
Rukwa (lake) F5
Rungwa (riv.) F5
Rungwe (mt.) F5
Serengeti Nat'l Park F4
Tanganyika (lake) E5
Tarangire Nat'l Park G4
Victoria (lake) F4
Wami (riv.) G5
Wembere (riv.) F4
Zanzibar (isl.) G5

UGANDA

CITIES and TOWNS

Arua 10,837 F3
Atura F3
Butiaba 261 F3
Entebbe 21,096 F4
Fort Portal 7,947 F3
Gulu 18,170 F3
Hoima 2,339 F3
Jinja 52,509 F3
Kabale 8,234 E4
Kampala (cap.) 478,895 F3
Kasese 7,213 F3
Kilembe F3
Kitgum 3,242 F3
Lira 7,340 F3
Masaka 12,987 F4
Masindi 2,100 F3
Mbale 23,544 F3
Mbarara 16,078 F4
Moroto 5,488 F3
Moyo 2,656 F3
Mubende 6,004 F3
Rhino Camp 198 F3
Soroti 8,130 F3
Tororo 15,977 F3

OTHER FEATURES

Albert (Mobuto Sese Seko) (lake) F3
Edward (lake) E4
Elgon (mt.) F3
George (lake) F4
Kabarega Nat'l Park F3
Kidepo Nat'l Park F3
Kioga (lake) F3
Margherita (mt.) E3
Mobuto Sese Seko (lake) F3
Murchison (falls) F3
Owen Falls (dam) F3
Ruwenzori (range) E3
Sese (isls.) F4
Victoria (lake) F4
Virunga Nat'l Park F4
Virunga (range) E4

ZAIRE

PROVINCES

Bandundu 2,600,556 C4
Bas-Zaïre 1,504,361 B4
Equateur 2,431,812 D3
Haut-Zaïre 3,356,419 E3
Kasai-Occidental 2,433,861 D4
Kasai-Oriental 1,872,231 D5
Kinshasa 1,323,039 C4
Kivu 3,361,883 E4
Shaba 2,753,714 E5

CITIES and TOWNS

Aba 7,600 F3
Abumombazi D3
Aketi 17,200 D3
Andoma E3
Ango E3
Ankoro E5
Bagata C4
Balangala D3
Bambesa E3
Bambili E3
Banalia E3
Banana B5
Bandundu 74,467 C4
Baraka E4
Basankusu C3
Basoko 9,100 D3
Basongo D4
Befale D3
Bena-Dibele D4
Beni 22,800 E3
Bikoro C4
Boende 12,800 D4
Bokote D4
Bokungu D4
Bolobo 10,300 C4
Bolomba 7,200 C3
Boma 61,100 B5
Bomboma C3
Bomongo C3
Bondo 10,000 D3
Bongandanga 12,900 D3
Bosobolo 11,100 D3
Budjala C3
Bukama E5
Bukavu 134,861 E4
Bulungu 16,300 C4
Bumba 34,700 D3
Bunia 28,800 E3
Bunkeya 5,100 E6
Businga 11,000 D3
Busu-Djanoa D3
Buta 19,800 D3
Butembo 27,800 E3
Dekese D4
Demba 22,000 D5
Dibaya 11,400 D5
Dibaya-Lubue 7,900 C4
Dilolo 14,000 D6
Dimbelenge D5
Djolu D3
Djugu F3
Dongo C3
Doruma E3
Dungu 9,100 E3
Etoile E6
Faradje 10,400 E3
Feshi C5
Fizi E4
Gandajika 60,100 D5
Gemena 37,300 D3
Goma 48,600 E4
Gungu C5
Idiofa C4
Ikela D4
Ilebo 32,200 D4
Imese C3
Ingende C4
Inongo 14,800 C4
Irumu 9,300 E3
Isangi D3
Isiro 49,300 E3
Kabalo 22,600 E5
Kabambare E4
Kabare 12,600 E4
Kabinda 60,500 D5
Kabongo 6,500 E5
Kahemba C5
Kalehe E4
Kalemie 62,300 E5
Kalima 27,500 E4
Kama 17,700 E4
Kambove 18,900 E6
Kamina 56,300 D5
Kampene 14,600 E4
Kananga 428,960 D5
Kanda-Kanda D5
Kaniama D5
Kapanga D5
Kasaji D6
Kasangulu 11,900 C4
Kasenga E6
Kasenyi E3
Kasese E4
Kasongo 37,800 E4
Kasongo-Lunda C5
Katako-Kombe D4
Katenga E5
Kazumba D5
Kenge 17,500 C4
Kiambi E5
Kibombo E4
Kikwit 111,960 C5
Kilembe C5
Kilwa E5
Kilo E3
Kinda D5
Kiniama E6
Kinshasa (cap.) 1,323,039 C4
Kipushi 32,900 E6
Kiri C4
Kirundu E4
Kisangani 229,596 E3
Kole, Kasai-Oriental D4
Kole, Haut-Zaïre E3
Kolwezi 81,600 E6
Komba D3
Kongolo 14,800 E5
Kungu C3
Kutu 10,000 C4
Kwamouth C4
Libenge 12,500 C3
Likasi, Panda- 146,394 E6
Likati D3
Lisala D3
Lodja 20,300 D4
Lokolama D4
Lomela D4
Loto D4
Luashi D6
Lubefu D4
Lubero E4
Lubudi 6,000 E5
Lubumbashi 318,000 E6
Lubutu E4
Luebo 21,800 D5
Luishia E6
Luiza D5
Lukolela, Equateur C4
Lukolela, Kasai-Oriental D5
Lukula 9,400 B5
Luozi 7,000 B5
Lusambo 13,100 D4
Makanza C3
Malemba-Nkulu E5
Mambasa 7,400 E3
Mangai 15,200 C4
Manono 44,500 E5
Masi-Manimba 6,300 C4
Masisi E4
Matadi 110,436 B5
Mbandaka 107,910 C3
Mbanza-Ngungu 55,800 C5
Mbuji-Mayi 256,154 D5
Mitwaba E5
Moanda 6,400 B5
Mobayi-Mbongo D3
Moliro E5
Monga D3
Monkoto D4
Mulongo E5
Mungbere E3
Mushie 13,700 C4
Mutshatsha D6
Muyumba E5
Mwadingusha E6
Mwanza E5
Mweka 24,900 D4
Mwene-Ditu 71,200 D5
Mwenga E4
Niangara 9,200 E3
Niemba E5
Nyunzu 11,300 E5
Opala D4
Oshwe C4
Panda-Likasi 146,394 E6
Pangi E4
Penge D5
Poko E3
Popokabaka C5
Port Kindu 42,800 E4
Punia E4
Pweto E5
Rutshuru E4
Sakania E6
Sampwe E5
Sandoa D5
Seke-Banza B5
Sentery 24,300 E5
Shabunda 6,900 E4
Songololo 4,600 B5
Tenke E6
Titule E3
Tshela 10,700 B4
Tshikapa 38,900 D5
Tshofa D5
Ubundu 6,300 E4
Uvira 15,900 E4
Virunga 21,900 E5
Waka D3
Walikale E4
Wamba 11,500 E3
Watsa 21,300 E3
Yahuma D3
Yakoma D3
Yangambi 22,600 D3
Zongo C3

OTHER FEATURES

Albert (Mobuto Sese Seko) (lake) F3
Aruwimi (riv.) E3
Bomu (riv.) D3
Boyama (Stanley) (falls) D3
Chicapa (riv.) D5
Congo (riv.) C4
Edward (lake) E4
Elila (riv.) E4
Fimi (riv.) C4
Garamba Nat'l Park E3
Giri (riv.) C3
Itimbiri (riv.) D3
Ituri (for.) E3
Karisimbi (mt.) E4
Kasai (riv.) C4
Kivu (lake) E4
Kwa (riv.) C4
Kwango (riv.) C5
Kwilu (riv.) C5
Lindi (riv.) E3
Livingstone (falls) B5
Loange (riv.) C5
Lokoro (riv.) C4
Lomami (riv.) D4
Lomela (riv.) D4
Lowa (riv.) E4
Lua (riv.) C3
Lualaba (riv.) E4
Luapula (riv.) E6
Lubilash (riv.) D5
Lufira (riv.) E5
Luilaka (riv.) C4
Lukenie (riv.) D4
Lukuga (riv.) E5
Lulua (riv.) D5
Luvua (riv.) E5
Mai-Ndombe (lake) C4
Malebo (Stanley Pool) (lake) C4
Margherita (mt.) E3
Marungu (mts.) E5
Mobuto Sese Seko (lake) F3
Mweru (lake) E5
Ruwenzori (range) E3
Ruzizi (riv.) E4
Salonga Nat'l Park D4
Sankuru (riv.) D4
Stanley (falls) D3
Stanley Pool (lake) C4
Tanganyika (lake) E5
Tshuapa (riv.) D4
Tumba (lake) C4
Ubangi (riv.) C3
Uele (riv.) E3
Ulindi (riv.) E4
Upemba (lake) E5
Upemba Nat'l Park E5
Virunga (range) E4
Virunga Nat'l Park E4
Zaire (Congo) (riv.) C4

ZAMBIA

CITIES and TOWNS

Abercorn (Mbala) 11,179 F5
Bancroft (Chililabombwe) 61,928 E6
Broken Hill (Kabwe) 143,635 E6
Chibwe E6
Chilanga 12,503 E7
Chililabombwe 61,928 E6
Chingola 145,869 E6
Chinsali 4,211 F6
Chipata 32,291 F6
Choma 17,943 E7
Fort Rosebery (Mansa) 34,801 E6
Isoka 6,832 F6
Kabompo 5,357 D6
Kabwe 143,635 E6
Kafue 29,794 E7
Kalabo 7,398 D6
Kalomo 5,878 E7
Kaoma 6,731 D6
Kapiri Mposhi 13,677 E6
Kasama 38,093 F6
Kasempa 3,063 E6
Kataba D7
Kawambwa 7,235 E5
Kitwe 314,794 E6
Lealui D6
Livingstone 71,987 E7
Luanshya 132,164 E6
Lundazi 4,083 F6
Lusaka (cap.) 538,469 E7
Luwingu 3,763 E6
Mansa 34,801 E6
Mazabuka 29,602 E7
Mbala 11,179 F5
Mkushi 4,104 E6
Mongu 24,919 D7
Monze 13,141 E7
Mpika 25,880 F6
Mporokoso 6,008 F5
Mpulungu 6,354 F5
Mufulira 149,778 E6
Mulobezi 2,589 E7
Mumbwa 7,570 E6
Mwinilunga 3,169 D6
Nakonde 4,599 F5
Namwala 3,008 E7
Ndola 282,439 E6
Petauke 7,531 F6
Senanga 7,204 D7
Serenje 6,008 F6
Sesheke 3,500 D7
Solwezi 15,032 E6
Zambezi 8,166 D6

OTHER FEATURES

Bangweulu (lake) F6
Barotseland (reg.) D7
Chambeshi (riv.) F6
Cuando (riv.) D7
Dongwe (riv.) D6
Kabompo (riv.) D6
Kafue (riv.) E7
Kafue Nat'l Park E6
Kalambo (falls) F5
Kariba (dam) E7
Kariba (lake) E7
Luangwa (riv.) F6
Luapula (riv.) E6
Lungwebungu (riv.) D6
Mosi-Oa-Tunya (Victoria) (falls) E7
Mulungushi (dam) E6
Mweru (lake) E5
Sunzu (mt.) F5
Tanganyika (lake) E5
Victoria (falls) E7
Zambezi (riv.) D7

Agriculture, Industry and Resources

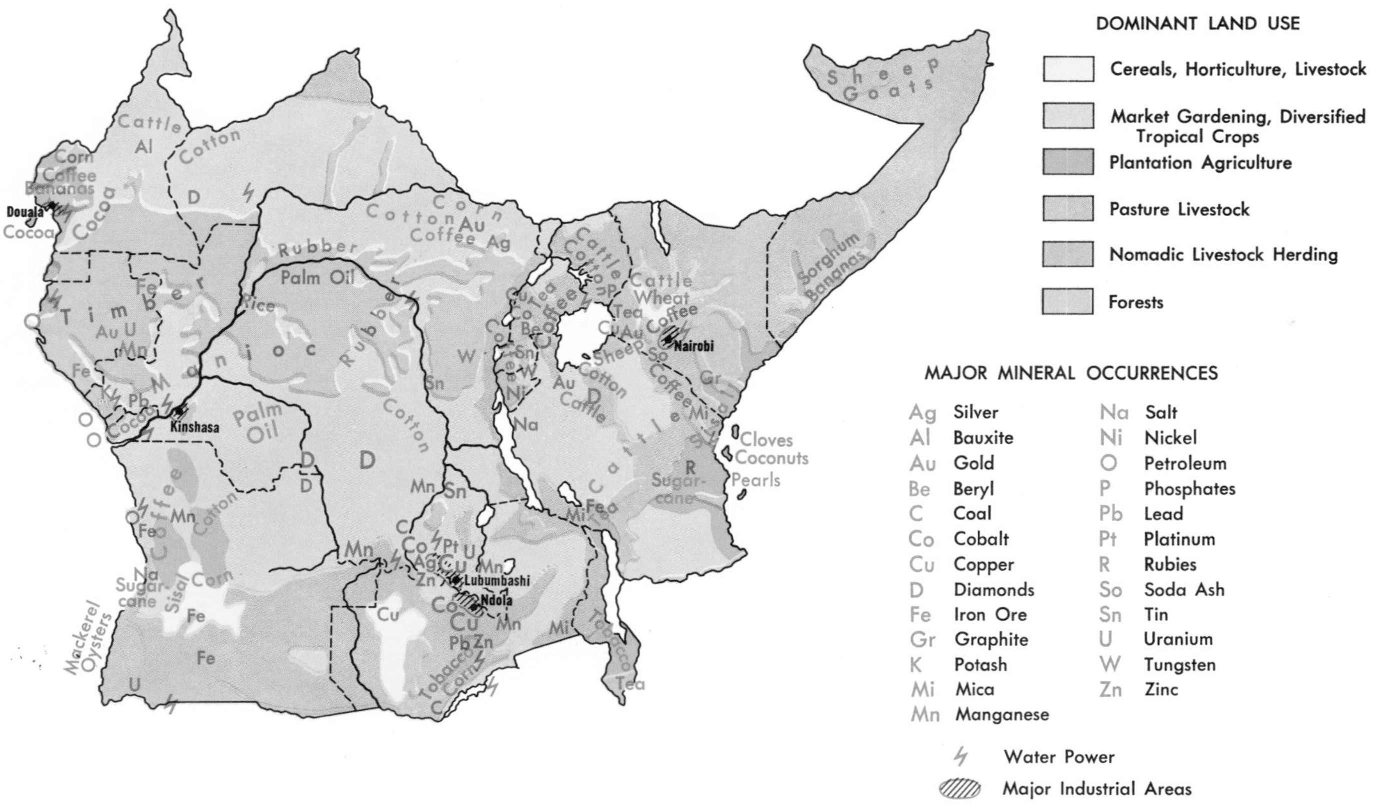

Douala
Cocoa
Cattle
Al
Cotton
Corn
Coffee
Bananas
Timber
Palm Oil
Rubber
Manioc
Kinshasa
Nairobi
Lubumbashi
Ndola
Sheep
Goats
Sorghum
Bananas
Cloves
Coconuts
Pearls
Sugar-cane
Mackerel
Oysters
Tea
Tobacco
DOMINANT LAND USE
Cereals, Horticulture, Livestock
Market Gardening, Diversified Tropical Crops
Plantation Agriculture
Pasture Livestock
Nomadic Livestock Herding
Forests
MAJOR MINERAL OCCURRENCES
Ag Silver
Al Bauxite
Au Gold
Be Beryl
C Coal
Co Cobalt
Cu Copper
D Diamonds
Fe Iron Ore
Gr Graphite
K Potash
Mi Mica
Mn Manganese
Na Salt
Ni Nickel
O Petroleum
P Phosphates
Pb Lead
Pt Platinum
R Rubies
So Soda Ash
Sn Tin
U Uranium
W Tungsten
Zn Zinc
Water Power
Major Industrial Areas

NAMIBIA (SOUTH-WEST AFRICA)

AREA 317,827 sq. mi. (823,172 sq. km.)
POPULATION 1,200,000
CAPITAL Windhoek
LARGEST CITY Windhoek
HIGHEST POINT Brandberg 8,550 ft. (2,606 m.)
MONETARY UNIT rand
MAJOR LANGUAGES Ovambo, Hottentot, Herero, Afrikaans, English
MAJOR RELIGIONS Tribal religions, Protestantism

SOUTH AFRICA

AREA 455,318 sq. mi. (1,179,274 sq. km.)
POPULATION 23,771,970
CAPITALS Cape Town, Pretoria
LARGEST CITY Johannesburg
HIGHEST POINT Injasuti 11,182 ft. (3,408 m.)
MONETARY UNIT rand
MAJOR LANGUAGES Afrikaans, English, Xhosa, Zulu, Sesotho
MAJOR RELIGIONS Protestantism, Roman Catholicism, Islam, Hinduism, tribal religions

LESOTHO

AREA 11,720 sq. mi. (30,355 sq. km.)
POPULATION 1,339,000
CAPITAL Maseru
LARGEST CITY Maseru
HIGHEST POINT 11,425 ft. (3,482 m.)
MONETARY UNIT loti
MAJOR LANGUAGES Sesotho, English
MAJOR RELIGIONS Tribal religions, Christianity

BOTSWANA

AREA 224,764 sq. mi. (582,139 sq. km.)
POPULATION 819,000
CAPITAL Gaborone
LARGEST CITY Francistown
HIGHEST POINT Tsodilo Hill 5,922 ft. (1,805 m.)
MONETARY UNIT pula
MAJOR LANGUAGES Setswana, Shona, Bushman, English, Afrikaans
MAJOR RELIGIONS Tribal religions, Protestantism

MOZAMBIQUE

AREA 303,769 sq. mi. (786,762 sq. km.)
POPULATION 12,130,000
CAPITAL Maputo
LARGEST CITY Maputo
HIGHEST POINT Mt. Binga 7,992 ft. (2,436 m.)
MONETARY UNIT metical
MAJOR LANGUAGES Makua, Thonga, Shona, Portuguese
MAJOR RELIGIONS Tribal religions, Roman Catholicism, Islam

SWAZILAND

AREA 6,705 sq. mi. (17,366 sq. km.)
POPULATION 547,000
CAPITAL Mbabane
LARGEST CITY Manzini
HIGHEST POINT Emlembe 6,109 ft. (1,862 m.)
MONETARY UNIT lilangeni
MAJOR LANGUAGES siSwati, English
MAJOR RELIGIONS Tribal religions, Christianity

ZIMBABWE

AREA 150,803 sq. mi. (390,580 sq. km.)
POPULATION 7,360,000
CAPITAL Salisbury
LARGEST CITY Salisbury
HIGHEST POINT Mt. Inyangani 8,517 ft. (2,596 m.)
MONETARY UNIT Zimbabwe dollar
MAJOR LANGUAGES English, Shona, Ndebele
MAJOR RELIGIONS Tribal religions, Protestantism

MADAGASCAR

AREA 226,657 sq. mi. (587,041 sq. km.)
POPULATION 8,742,000
CAPITAL Antananarivo
LARGEST CITY Antananarivo
HIGHEST POINT Maromokotro 9,436 ft. (2,876 m.)
MONETARY UNIT Madagascar franc
MAJOR LANGUAGES Malagasy, French
MAJOR RELIGIONS Tribal religions, Roman Catholicism, Protestantism

COMOROS

AREA 719 sq. mi. (1,862 sq. km.)
POPULATION 290,000
CAPITAL Moroni
LARGEST CITY Moroni
HIGHEST POINT Karthala 7,746 ft. (2,361 m.)
MONETARY UNIT CFA franc
MAJOR LANGUAGES Arabic, French, Swahili
MAJOR RELIGION Islam

MAURITIUS

AREA 790 sq. mi. (2,046 sq. km.)
POPULATION 959,000
CAPITAL Port Louis
LARGEST CITY Port Louis
HIGHEST POINT 2,711 ft. (826 m.)
MONETARY UNIT Mauritian rupee
MAJOR LANGUAGES English, French, French Creole, Hindi, Urdu
MAJOR RELIGIONS Hinduism, Christianity, Islam

SEYCHELLES

AREA 145 sq. mi. (375 sq. km.)
POPULATION 63,000
CAPITAL Victoria
LARGEST CITY Victoria
HIGHEST POINT Morne Seychellois 2,993 ft. (912 m.)
MONETARY UNIT Seychellois rupee
MAJOR LANGUAGES English, French, Creole
MAJOR RELIGION Roman Catholicism

REUNION

AREA 969 sq. mi. (2,510 sq. km.)
POPULATION 491,000
CAPITAL St-Denis

MAYOTTE

AREA 144 sq. mi. (373 sq. km.)
POPULATION 47,300
CAPITAL Dzaoudzi

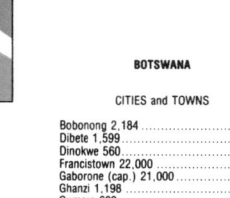

ZIMBABWE **BOTSWANA** **SOUTH AFRICA** **LESOTHO** **SWAZILAND**

MOZAMBIQUE **COMOROS** **MADAGASCAR** **MAURITIUS** **SEYCHELLES**

Agriculture, Industry and Resources

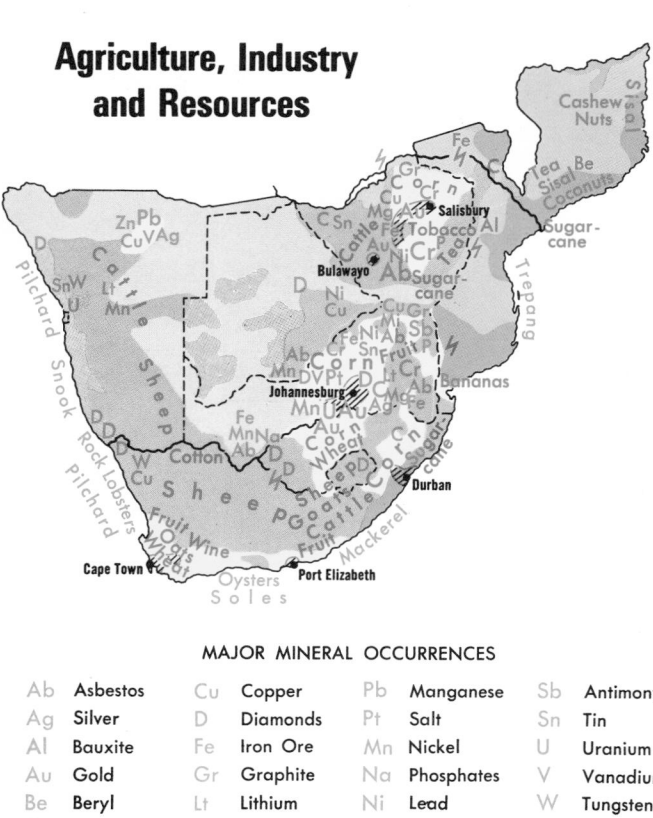

DOMINANT LAND USE

	Cereals, Horticulture, Livestock
	Market Gardening, Diversified Tropical Crops
	Plantation Agriculture
	Pasture Livestock
	Nomadic Livestock Herding
	Forests
	Nonagricultural Land

MAJOR MINERAL OCCURRENCES

Ab	Asbestos	Cu	Copper	Pb	Manganese	Sb	Antimony
Ag	Silver	D	Diamonds	Pt	Salt	Sn	Tin
Al	Bauxite	Fe	Iron Ore	Mn	Nickel	U	Uranium
Au	Gold	Gr	Graphite	Na	Phosphates	V	Vanadium
Be	Beryl	Lt	Lithium	Ni	Lead	W	Tungsten
C	Coal	Mg	Magnesium	P	Platinum	Zn	Zinc
Cr	Chromium	Mi	Mica				

⚡ Water Power

▨ Major Industrial Areas

(continued on following page)

Topography

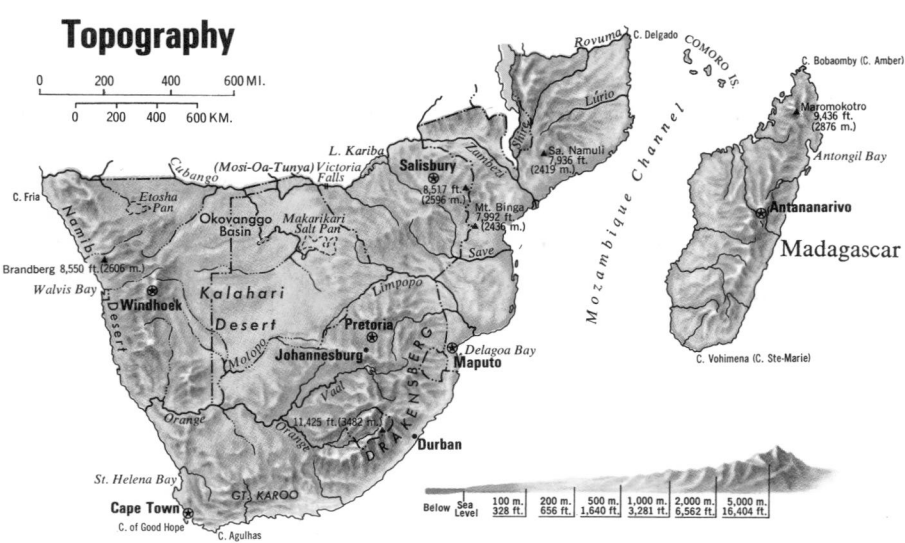

0   200   400   600 MI.
0   200   400   600 KM.

Below Sea Level	100 m. 328 ft.	200 m. 656 ft.	500 m. 1,640 ft.	1,000 m. 3,281 ft.	2,000 m. 6,562 ft.	5,000 m. 16,404 ft.

Southern Africa

CONIC PROJECTION

SCALE OF MILES
0   50   100   200   300

SCALE OF KILOMETERS
0   50 100   200   300

Capitals of Countries ....☆
Other Capitals ....◉
International Boundaries ....
Internal Boundaries ....
Scale 1:14,500,000

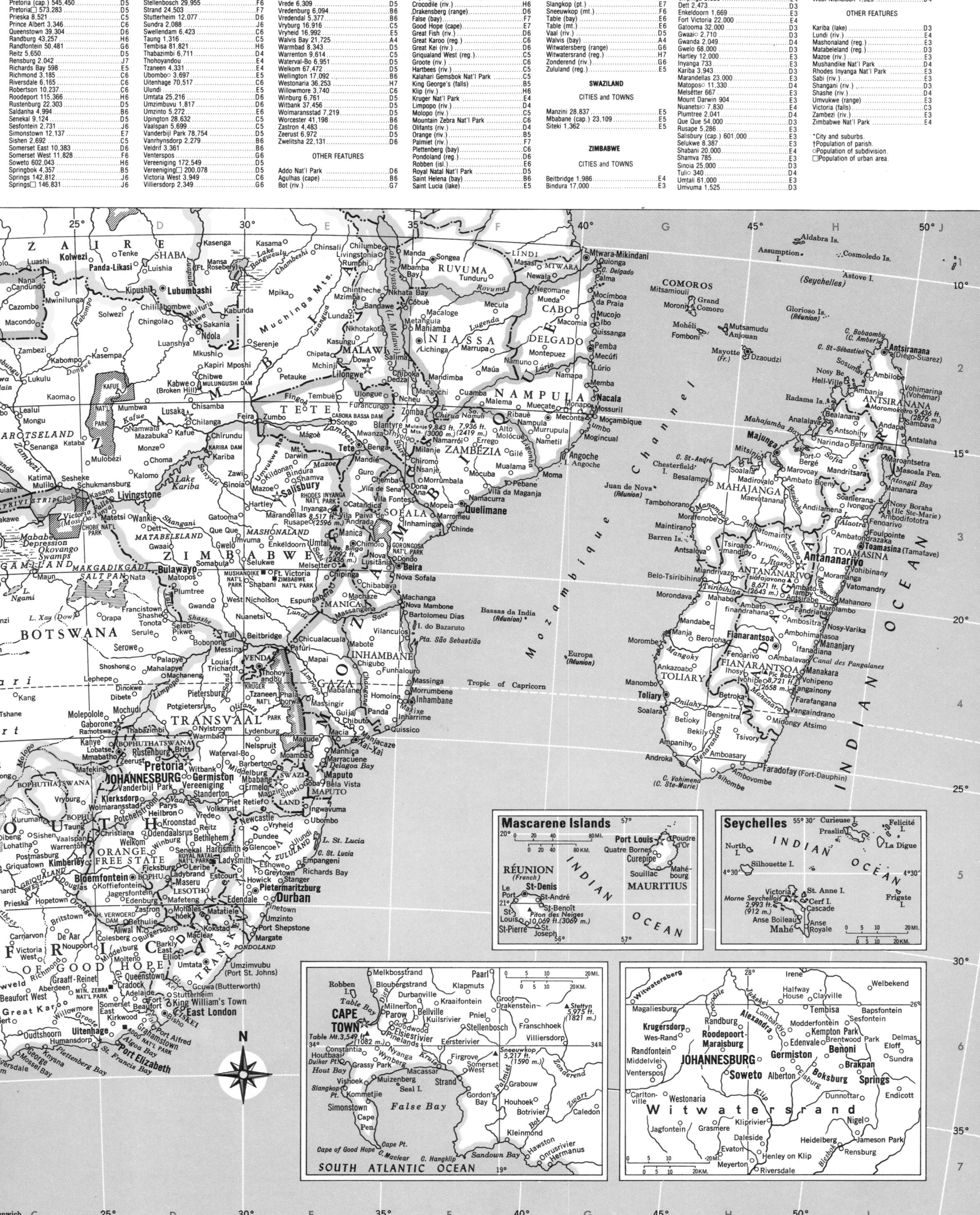

Population Distribution

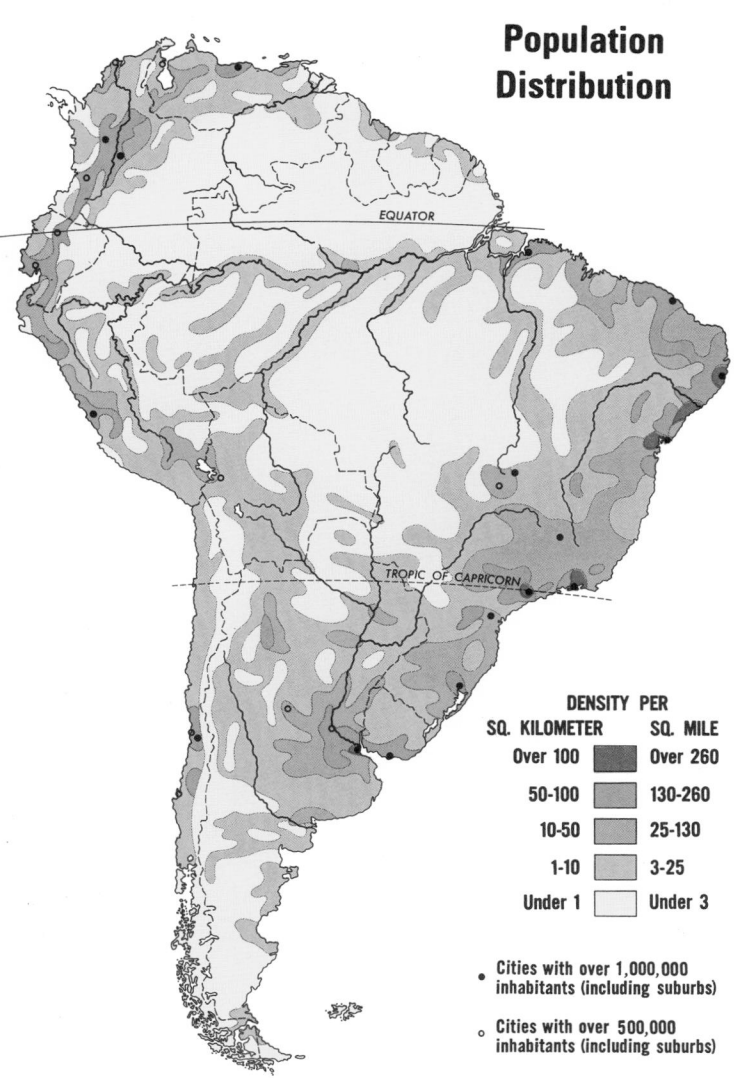

AREA 6,875,000 sq. mi. (17,806,250 sq. km.)
POPULATION 245,000,000
LARGEST CITY São Paulo
HIGHEST POINT Cerro Aconcagua 22,831 ft. (6,959 m.)
LOWEST POINT Salina Grande -131 ft. (-40 m.)

Vegetation

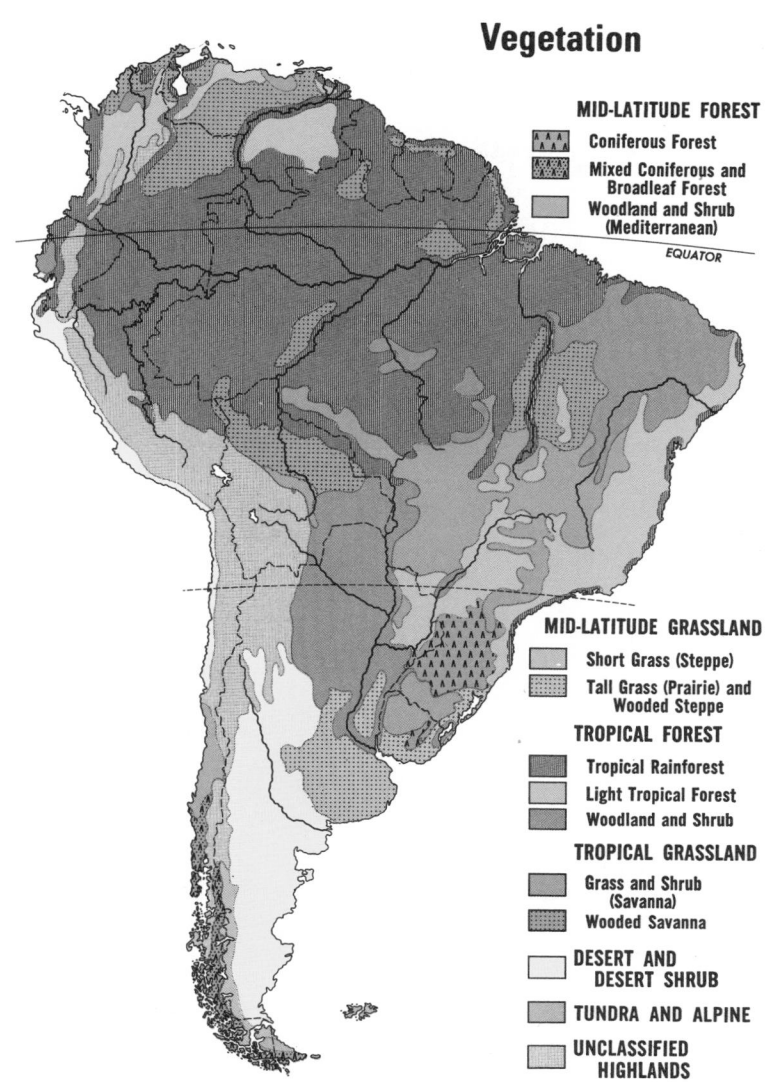

MID-LATITUDE FOREST
Coniferous Forest
Mixed Coniferous and Broadleaf Forest
Woodland and Shrub (Mediterranean)

MID-LATITUDE GRASSLAND
Short Grass (Steppe)
Tall Grass (Prairie) and Wooded Steppe

TROPICAL FOREST
Tropical Rainforest
Light Tropical Forest
Woodland and Shrub

TROPICAL GRASSLAND
Grass and Shrub (Savanna)
Wooded Savanna

DESERT AND DESERT SHRUB

TUNDRA AND ALPINE

UNCLASSIFIED HIGHLANDS

DENSITY PER

SQ. KILOMETER	SQ. MILE
Over 100	Over 260
50-100	130-260
10-50	25-130
1-10	3-25
Under 1	Under 3

• Cities with over 1,000,000 inhabitants (including suburbs)

○ Cities with over 500,000 inhabitants (including suburbs)

Average January Temperature

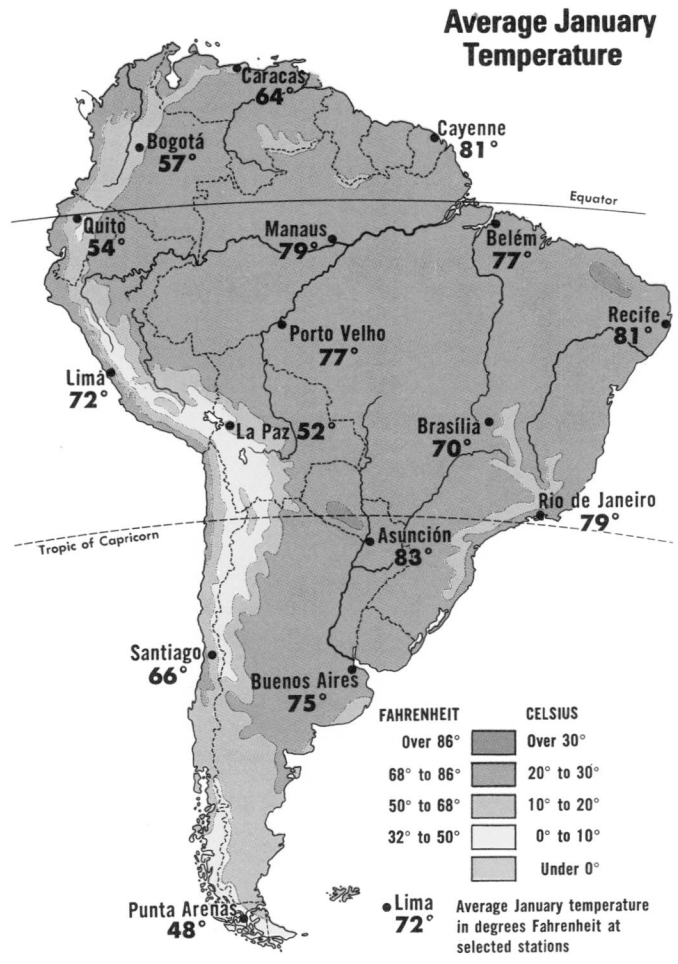

Caracas 64°
Cayenne 81°
Bogotá 57°
Equator
Quito 54°
Manaus 79°
Belém 77°
Porto Velho 77°
Recife 81°
Lima 72°
La Paz 52°
Brasília 70°
Rio de Janeiro 79°
Tropic of Capricorn
Asunción 83°
Santiago 66°
Buenos Aires 75°
Punta Arenas 48°

FAHRENHEIT	CELSIUS
Over 86°	Over 30°
68° to 86°	20° to 30°
50° to 68°	10° to 20°
32° to 50°	0° to 10°
	Under 0°

• Lima 72°   Average January temperature in degrees Fahrenheit at selected stations

Average July Temperature

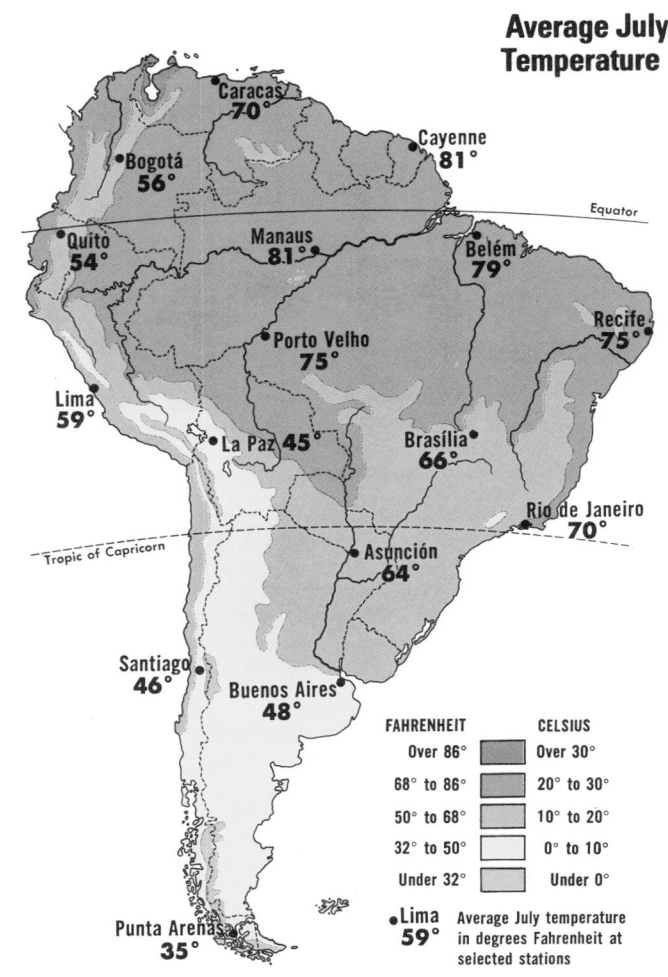

Caracas 70°
Cayenne 81°
Bogotá 56°
Equator
Quito 54°
Manaus 81°
Belém 79°
Porto Velho 75°
Recife 75°
Lima 59°
La Paz 45°
Brasília 66°
Rio de Janeiro 70°
Tropic of Capricorn
Asunción 64°
Santiago 46°
Buenos Aires 48°
Punta Arenas 35°

FAHRENHEIT	CELSIUS
Over 86°	Over 30°
68° to 86°	20° to 30°
50° to 68°	10° to 20°
32° to 50°	0° to 10°
Under 32°	Under 0°

• Lima 59°   Average July temperature in degrees Fahrenheit at selected stations

Rainfall

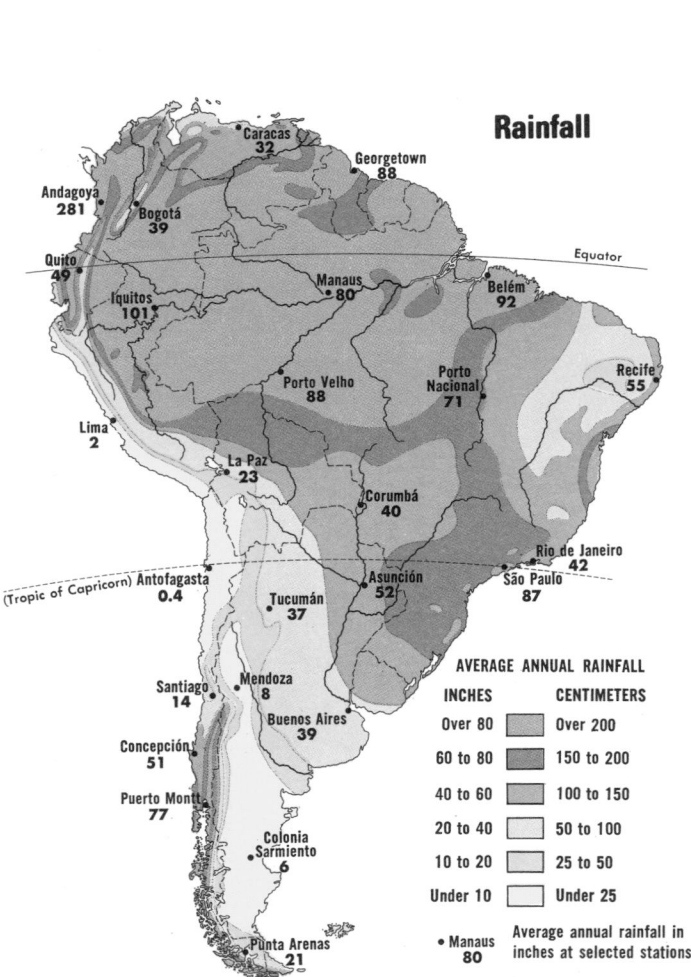

Caracas 32
Georgetown 88
Andagoya 281
Bogotá 39
Equator
Quito 49
Manaus 80
Belém 92
Iquitos 101
Porto Velho 88
Porto Nacional 71
Recife 55
Lima 2
La Paz 23
Corumbá 40
Rio de Janeiro 42
(Tropic of Capricorn) Antofagasta 0.4
Tucumán 37
Asunción 52
São Paulo 87
Santiago 14
Mendoza 8
Buenos Aires 39
Concepción 51
Puerto Montt 77
Colonia Sarmiento 6
Punta Arenas 21

AVERAGE ANNUAL RAINFALL

INCHES	CENTIMETERS
Over 80	Over 200
60 to 80	150 to 200
40 to 60	100 to 150
20 to 40	50 to 100
10 to 20	25 to 50
Under 10	Under 25

• Manaus 80   Average annual rainfall in inches at selected stations

Vegetation/Relief

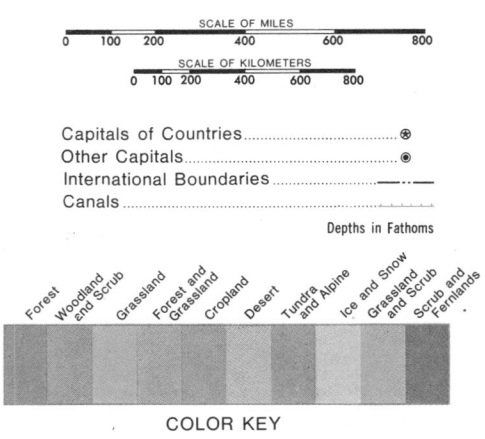

SCALE OF MILES
0 100 200 400 600 800

SCALE OF KILOMETERS
0 100 200 400 600 800

Capitals of Countries................⊛
Other Capitals.........................⊚
International Boundaries...........—··—
Canals...................................

Depths in Fathoms

Forest | Woodland and Scrub | Grassland | Forest and Grassland | Cropland | Desert | Tundra and Alpine | Ice and Snow | Grassland and Scrub | Scrub and Fernlands

COLOR KEY

STATES

Amazonas (terr.) 21,696......E5
Anzoátegui 506,297......F3
Apure 164,705......D4
Aragua 543,170......E3
Barinas 231,046......D3
Bolívar 391,665......F7
Carabobo 659,339......D2
Cojedes 94,351......D3
Delta Amacuro (terr.) 48,139......H3
Dependencias
Federales (terr.) 463......E2
Distrito Federal 1,860,637......E2
Falcón 407,957......D2
Guárico 318,905......E3
Lara 671,410......C2
Mérida 347,095......C3
Miranda 856,272......E2
Monagas 298,239......G3
Nueva Esparta 118,830......G2
Portuguesa 297,047......D3
Sucre 469,004......G2
Táchira 511,346......C4
Trujillo 381,334......C3
Yaracuy 223,545......D2
Zulia 1,299,030......B2

CITIES and TOWNS

Acarigua 56,743......D3
Achaguas 4,633......D4
Adícora 707......D2
Aguada Grande 2,901......D2
Agua Fría......D2
Agua Linda......E5
Aguasay 1,752......G3
Altagracia 11,116......C2
Altagracia de Orituco 18,717......E3
Amuay......D2
Aracua 29,487......F3
Aparurén......G5
Apurito 740......D4
Aragua de Barcelona 9,107......F3
Aragua de Maturín 4,051......G3
Araure 22,466......D3
Aricagua 231......C3
Arichuna 1,204......E4
Aripao 296......F4
Arismendi 1,257......D3
Aroa 5,418......D2
Atapirire 337......F3
Bachaquero......D2
Baragua 659......D2
Barbacoas 2,513......E3
Barcelona 78,201......F2
Barinas 56,329......C3
Barinitas 9,644......C3
Barquisimeto 330,815......D2
Barrancas, Barinas 4,489......C3
Barrancas, Monagas 5,738......G3
Betijoque 5,851......C3
Biruaca 2,266......E4
Biscucuy 6,114......D3
Bobare 1,204......D2
Bobures 2,468......C3
Boca de Aroa 2,756......D2
Boca del Mangle......D2
Boca del Pao 403......F3
Bocono 15,915......C3
Borbón......F4
Borojó 423......C2
Bruzual 941......D4
Buena Vista, Anzoátegui......F3
Buena Vista, Apure......D4
Buena Vista, Falcón 944......D2
Cabimas 118,037......C2
Cabruta 1,927......E4
Cabudare 14,593......D3
Cabure 1,673......C2
Cachipo......G3
Cacuri......F5
Cagua 29,601......E3
Caicara 6,092......C3
Caicara de Orinoco 6,867......E4
Calabozo 37,282......E3
Caldera 1,927......C3
Camaguán 4,143......E3
Camatagua 3,335......E3
Campo Claro 1,832......G2
Candelaria......E3
Cantaura 15,839......F3
Capatárida 1,375......C2
Capibara......E6
Carabobo, Bolívar......H4
Carabobo, Carabobo......D3
Caracas (cap.) 1,035,499......E2
Caracas* 2,183,935......E2
Carache 3,966......C3
Carapa 119......D2
Corozo Pando......E3
Cúa 9,953......E2
Cubiro 1,988......D3
Cuchivero......F4
Cumaná 119,751......G2
Cumanacoa 9,179......G2
Cunaviche 795......E4
Curiapo......H3
Dabajuro 4,516......C2
Delicias 1,616......B4
Democracia......E6
Dolores 1,454......D3
Duaca 7,519......D2
Ejido 11,170......C3
El Almacén......H4
El Amparo de Apure 2,015......D4
El Baúl 1,715......D3
El Callao 4,270......G4
El Calvario 384......E3
El Chaparro 3,768......F3
El Cristo......G4
El Dorado 1,888......H4
El Empedrado 1,788......C3
El Guapo 1,231......F2
El Manteco 1,962......H4
El Miamo 335......H4
Elorza 3,184......D4
El Oso......H5
Cachipo......G3
Carache 3,966......C3
Carapa 119......D2
Cariaco 6,549......G2
Caribén......E4
Cariben 4,729......C3
Caripito 19,053......G2
Caripe......G2
Carirubana 15,701......C2
Carmelo 2,556......C3
Carora 36,115......C2
Carrasquero 2,193......B2
Carúpano 50,935......G2
Casanay 4,985......G2
Casigua, Falcón 460......C2
Casigua, Zulia 3,665......B3
Caucagua 6,218......C3
Cazorla 700......E3
Chaguaramas 2,636......E3
Chichirivche 3,236......D2
Chivacoa 19,210......D3
Choroní 534......E2
Churuguara 6,636......C2
Ciudad Bolívar 103,728......G3
Ciudad Bolivia 4,864......C3
Ciudad de Nutrias 769......D3
Ciudad Guayana 143,540......H3
Ciudad Ojeda 83,083......C2
Ciudad Piar 3,965......G4
Clarines 2,099......F3
Cojoro......C2
Colón......E6
Comunidad......E6
Coporito......H3
Coro 68,701......D2
Guárico 3,259......D3
Guariquén 619......G2
Guasdualito 7,793......C4
Guasimal 582......G2
Guasipati 4,807......H4
Guayabal, Amazonas......E6
Guayabal, Guárico 1,403......E3
Güiria 13,905......G2
Guri......G4
Guzmán Blanco......E6
Higuerote 5,008......E2
Icabarú......B4
Independencia 4,897......B4
Irapa 4,470......G2
Juangriego 6,062......G2
Judibana......C2
Jusepín......G3
Kavanayen......G5
La Aduana......D3
La Asunción 6,381......G2
La Canoa......E3
La Ceiba, Apure......C3
La Ceiba, Trujillo 212......C3
La Concepción 13,885......B2
La Esmeralda......F6
La Esperanza......H3
La Fría 8,134......B3
La Grita 9,954......C3
La Guaira 20,344......E2
Lagunetas......C3
Lagunillas......C2
El Palmar 2,758......G4
El Pao, Anzoátegui 761......F3
El Pao, Bolívar 1,259......G3
El Pao, Cojedes 1,715......D3
El Perú......H4
El Pilar 3,278......G2
El Rastro 903......D3
El Roque......E2
El Samán de Apure 1,399......C4
El Socorro......E3
El Sombrero 8,373......E3
El Tigre 49,801......F3
El Tocuyo 19,351......C3
El Toro......H3
El Vigía 20,970......C3
El Vínculo......D1
El Yagual 699......D4
Encontrados 5,607......B3
Esperanza......E3
Espino 559......F3
Garcitas......C3
Guacara 35,111......D2
Guachara 577......D4
Guadarrama 334......D3
Guaina......G5
Guana......G5
Guanare 34,148......D3
Guanarito 3,150......D3
Guanoco......F2
Guanta 9,017......F2
Guardatinajas 1,206......E3
Guarero......B2

La Horqueta G3
La Inglesa G3
La Leona G3
La Luz 672 .... D3
La Margarita H3
La Paragua 1,676 .... G4
Las Bonitas 343 .... F4
Las Lajitas F4
Las Mercedes 6,739 .... E3
Las Piedras, Falcón C2
Las Piedras, Zulia 4,583 .... B2
Las Trincheras F4
Las Vegas 3,212 .... D3
La Tigra H4
La Trinidad 129 .... D3
La Trinidad de Arauca D4
La Trinidad de Orichuna 665 .... D4
La Unión 713 .... E3
La Urbana 661 .... E4
La Vela de Coro 7,172 .... D2
La Victoria, Apure 689 .... D4
La Victoria, Apure C4
La Victoria, Aragua 40,731 .... E2
Libertad, Barinas 2,072 .... D3
Libertad, Cojedes 1,919 .... D3
Los Castillos G3
Los Taques 1,160 .... C2
Los Teques 63,106 .... E2
Macareo Santo Niño H3
Machiques 18,898 .... B3
Macuro 1,122 .... H2
Macuto 11,704 .... E2

Maiquetía 59,238 .... E2
Mantecal, Apure 1,136 .... D4
Mantecal, Bolívar F4
Mapararí 1,376 .... D2
Mapire 1,195 .... F4
Maporal 249 .... C4
Maracaibo 651,574 .... C2
Maracay 255,134 .... E2
Marigüitar 5,645 .... G2
Maripa 913 .... F4
Maroa 408 .... E6
Matu F4
Maturín 98,188 .... G3
Mene de Mauroa 4,336 .... C2
Mene Grande 11,498 .... C3
Mérida 74,214 .... C3
Mesa Bolívar 956 .... C3
Mirimire 3,424 .... D2
Moitaco 458 .... F4
Morganito E5
Morón 19,451 .... D2
Mucuchachí 472 .... C3
Mucuchíes 1,625 .... C3
Naricual 1,047 .... F2
Nirgua 11,918 .... D2
Nuevo Mamo G3
Obispos 1,140 .... D3
Ocumare de la Costa 2,840 .... E2
Ocumare del Tuy 24,229 .... E2
Onoto 1,991 .... F3
Ortiz 1,793 .... E3
Ospino 3,544 .... D3
Palmarejo C2
Palmarito, Apure 926 .... D4
Palmarito, Guárico F3
Palmarito, Mérida 988 .... C3
Papelón 774 .... D3
Paraguaipoa 3,850 .... C2
Paraíso de
  Chabasquén 2,094 .... D3
Pariaguán 8,173 .... F3
Parmana F4
Pedernales G3
Pedregal 1,317 .... C2
Peraitepuí H5
Piacoa H3
Pimichín E6
Píritu, Anzoátegui 2,479 .... F2
Píritu, Falcón 1,186 .... D2
Píritu, Portuguesa 8,128 .... D3
Platanal F6
Porlamar 31,985 .... G2
Pozuelos 45,391 .... F2
Pregonero 3,598 .... C3
Pueblo Hondo B3
Pueblo Nuevo 3,426 .... D1
Puerto Ayacucho 10,417 .... E5
Puerto Cabello 72,103 .... E2
Puerto Cumarebo 10,064 .... D2
Puerto de Nutrias 675 .... D3
Puerto Hierro H2
Puerto La Cruz 63,276 .... F2
Puerto Miranda E4
Puerto Páez 954 .... E4
Puerto Píritu 3,495 .... F2
Punta Cardón 18,182 .... C2
Punta de Mata 7,777 .... G3
Punta de Piedras 2,826 .... F2
Punto Fijo 5,548 .... D2
Puruey F4
Puruname E6
Quibor 12,216 .... D3
Quiriquire 7,304 .... G3
Quisiro 1,383 .... C2
Río Caribe 8,963 .... G2
Río Chico 4,491 .... F2
Río Claro 2,460 .... D3
Río Tocuyo 916 .... C2
Rosario B2
Rubio 19,156 .... B4
Sabaneta, Barinas 4,680 .... D3
Sabaneta, Falcón 650 .... D2
Samariapo E5
San Antonio, Amazonas E6
San Antonio, Monagas 4,235 .... G2
San Antonio, Zulia C3
San Antonio de Caparo 289 .... C4
San Antonio del
  Táchira 20,342 .... B4
San Antonio de Tabasca G3
Sanare 6,717 .... D3
San Carlos, Cojedes 21,029 .... D3
San Carlos, Zulia 749 .... C2

San Carlos del Zulia 26,762 .... C3
San Carlos de Río Negro 515 .... E7
San Casimiro 4,843 .... E3
San Cristóbal 151,717 .... B4
San Diego de Cabrutica 432 .... F3
San Felipe, Yaracuy 43,801 .... D2
San Felipe, Zulia B3
San Félix 379 .... C2
San Fernando de Apure 38,960 .... E4
San Fernando de Atabapo 1,537 .... E5
San Francisco, Lara 861 .... C2
San Ignacio B2
San José, Amazonas E5
San José, Zulia 4,498 .... B3
San José de Amacuro H3
San José de Areocuar 985 .... G2
San José de Guanipa 22,530 .... G3
San José de la Costa D2
San José de Río
  Chico 3,600 .... F2
San José de Tiznados 666 .... E3
San Juan de Colón B3
San Juan de las Galdonas 1,196 .... G2
San Juan de los Cayos 1,692 .... D2
San Juan de los Morros 38,265 .... E3
San Juan de Manapiare E5
San Juan de Payara 1,018 .... E4
San Lorenzo, Falcón 716 .... D2
San Lorenzo, Zulia C3
San Luis 1,405 .... D2
San Mateo 2,424 .... F3
San Mauricio E3
San Pedro de las Bocas G4
San Rafael 10,910 .... C2
San Rafael de Atamaica 635 .... E4
San Rafael de Orituco 1,378 .... E3
San Sebastián 5,582 .... E2
San Simón del Cocuy E3
Santa Ana, Anzoátegui 3,558 .... F3
Santa Ana, Táchira 5,116 .... B4
Santa Bárbara, Amazonas E6
Santa Bárbara, Barinas 6,155 .... C4
Santa Bárbara, Monagas 2,034 .... G3
Santa Bárbara, Zulia C3
Santa Catalina, Barinas 1,077 .... D4
Santa Catalina, Delta
  Amacuro H3
Santa Cruz C3
Santa Cruz de Bucaral 2,904 .... D2
Santa Cruz del Zulia 4,221 .... B3
Santa Cruz de Mara 5,773 .... C2
Santa Cruz de Orinoco 513 .... F3
Santa Elena 608 .... H5
Santa Inés,
  Anzoátegui 1,049 .... F3
Santa Inés, Barinas 391 .... C3
Santa Isabel F7
Santa Lucía 619 .... D3
Santa María, Bolívar G3
Santa María de Erebató F5
Santa María de Ipire 3,307 .... F3
Santa María del Orinoco E4
Santa Rita, Guárico E3
Santa Rita, Zulia 15,668 .... C2
Santa Rosa, Anzoátegui 954 .... F3

Santa Rosa, Apure D4
Santa Rosa, Barinas 1,514 .... D3
Santa Rosa de Amanadona E7
Santa Rosalía 513 .... F4
Santa Teresa 10,220 .... E2
San Timoteo 3,635 .... C3
San Tomé F3
San Vicente, Amazonas E5
San Vicente, Apure 365 .... D4
Sarare 4,236 .... D3
Seboruco 2,616 .... B3
Simaraña G5
Sinamaica B2
Siquisique 3,821 .... D2
Solano E6

Soledad 7,108 .... G3
Sucre 608 .... D3
Suripa D4
Tamatama F6
Táriba 15,683 .... B4
Temblador 5,380 .... G3
Tia Juana C2
Timotes 3,229 .... C3
Tinaco 7,263 .... D3
Tinaquillo 12,015 .... D3
Tocópero 1,033 .... D2
Tocuyo de la Costa 4,023 .... D2
Torunos 739 .... C3
Tovar 12,814 .... C3
Trujillo 25,921 .... C3

Tucacas 4,780 .... D2
Tucupido 9,522 .... F3
Tucupita 21,417 .... H3
Tumeremo 5,036 .... H4
Tupí 88 .... D2
Turén D3
Turiamo E2
Turmero 43,832 .... E2
Upata 22,793 .... G3
Urachiche 4,759 .... D2
Uracoa 1,165 .... G3
Urica 1,881 .... F3
Urimán G5
Urumaco 829 .... C2
Uruyén G5
Uverito 468 .... F3
Valencia 367,171 .... E2
Valera 76,740 .... C3
Valle de Guanape 3,468 .... F3
Valle de la Pascua 36,809 .... F3
Vara de María C4
Villa Bruzual 14,003 .... D3
Villa de Cura 27,832 .... E2
Villa Frontado 1,600 .... G2
Yaguaraparo 3,931 .... G2
Yaritagua 21,363 .... D2
Yavita E6
Yerichaña F5
Yoco 2,196 .... G2
Zanja de Lira E3
Zaraza 15,480 .... F3
Zuata 914 .... F3

OTHER FEATURES

Amacuro (riv.) H4
Angel (fall) G5
Aponguao (riv.) H5
Apure (riv.) E4
Arauca (riv.) E4
Arichuna (riv.) D4
Aro (riv.) F4
Atabapo (riv.) E6
Auyantepui (mt.) G5
Baria (riv.) E7
Bolívar, Cerro (mt.) G4
Bolívar, Pico (peak) C3
Canagua (riv.) C3
Caño Capure (riv.) H3
Caño Macareo (riv.) H3
Caño Mánamo (riv.) G3
Capanaparo (riv.) E4
Caparo (riv.) C4
Caroní (riv.) G4
Carrao (riv.) G5
Caruai (riv.) H5
Casiquiare, Brazo (riv.) E6
Catatumbo (riv.) B3
Caura (riv.) F5
Chicanán (riv.) H4
Chimantá-tepuí (mt.) G5
Chivapure (riv.) E4
Cinaruco (riv.) D4
Coche (isl.) F2
Codera (cape) F2
Cojedes (riv.) D3
Cuao (riv.) E5
Cubagua (isl.) F2
Cuchivero (riv.) F4
Cuquenán (riv.) H5
Curutú (riv.) G5
Cuyuni (riv.) H4
Delgado Chalbaud, Cerro (mt.) G6
Dragons Mouth (str.) H2
Duida, Cerro (mt.) F6
Erebato (riv.) F5
Gran Sabana, La (plain) G5
Guainía (riv.) E6
Guampí, Sierra de (mts.) F4

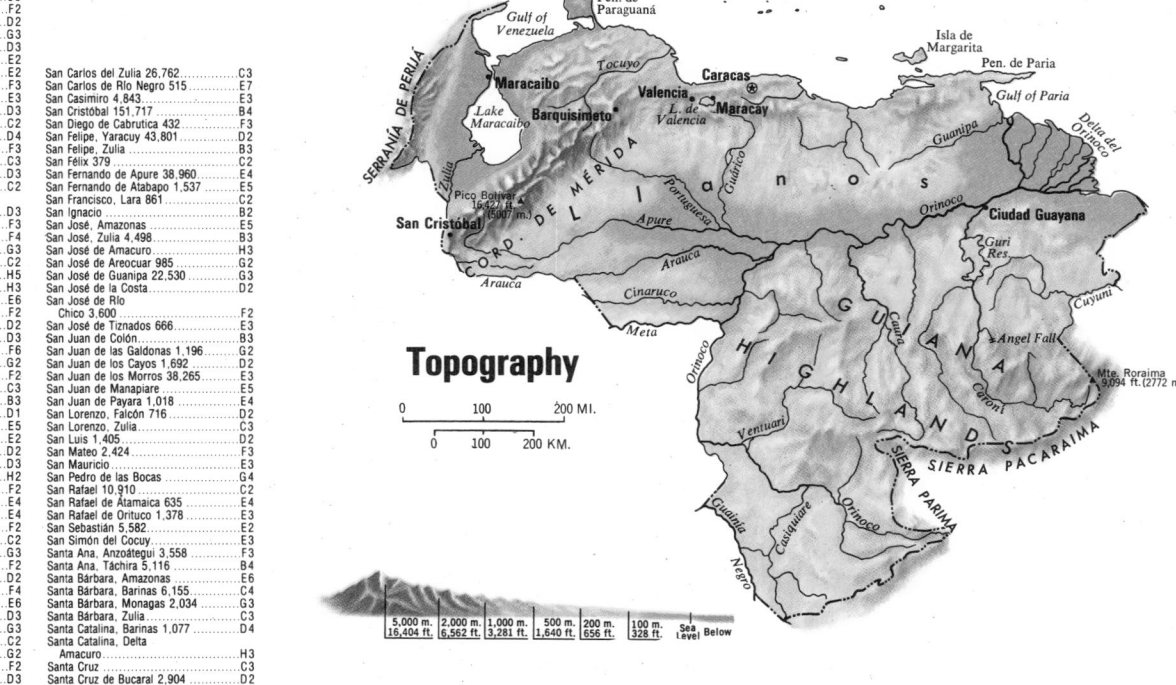

Guanare (riv.) D3
Guanare Viejo (riv.) D3
Guanipa (riv.) G3
Guárico (res.) E3
Guárico (riv.) E3
Guayapo, Serranía (mts.) E5
Güere (riv.) F3
Guri (res.) G4
Icabarú (riv.) G5
Imataca, Serranía (mts.) H4
Imeri, Sierra (mts.) F7
La Blanquilla (isl.) F2
La Gran Sabana (plain) G5
La Orchila (isl.) F2
Las Aves (isls.) E2
La Tortuga (isl.) F2
Los Hermanos (isls.) F2
Los Monjes (isls.) C1
Los Roques (isls.) E2
Los Testigos (isls.) G2
Macanao (pen.) F2
Maigualida, Sierra (range) F4
Manapire (riv.) E3
Maracaibo (lake) C3
Margarita (isl.) F2
Mavaca (riv.) F6
Médanos (isth.) D2
Merevari (riv.) F5
Mérida, Cordillera de
  (range) C3
Meta (riv.) E4
Morichal Largo (riv.) G3
Neblina (Phelps) (peak) E7
Negro (riv.) E7
Nuria, Sierra de (mts.) H4
Ocamo (riv.) F6
Orinoco (delta) H3
Orinoco (riv.) G3
Orituco (riv.) E3
Pacaraima, Sierra (mts.) G5
Pao (riv.) D3
Pao (riv.) F3
Paragua (riv.) G4
Paraguaná (pen.) C1
Paria (gulf) H2
Paria (pen.) G2
Parima, Sierra (mts.) F6
Perijá, Sierra de (mts.) B2
Phelps (peak) E7
Portuguesa (riv.) D3
Roraima (mt.) H5
Salto Angel (fall) G5
Sarare (riv.) C4
Serpents Mouth (passage) H3
Siapa (riv.) E7
Sipapo (riv.) E5
Suapure (riv.) E4
Suripá (riv.) C4
Tapirapecó, Sierra (mts.) F7
Tigre (riv.) G3
Tocuco (riv.) B3
Tocuyo (riv.) D2
Tramán-tepuí (mt.) G5
Triste (gulf) D2
Turagua, Serranía (mts.) F4
Tuy (riv.) E2
Unare (riv.) F3
Valencia (lake) E2
Venamo, Cerro (mt.) H4
Venamo (riv.) H4
Venezuela (gulf) C2
Ventuari (riv.) E5
Votamo (riv.) F6
Yatua (riv.) E7
Yuruari (riv.) H4
Zuata (riv.) F3
Zulia (riv.) B3

*City and suburbs

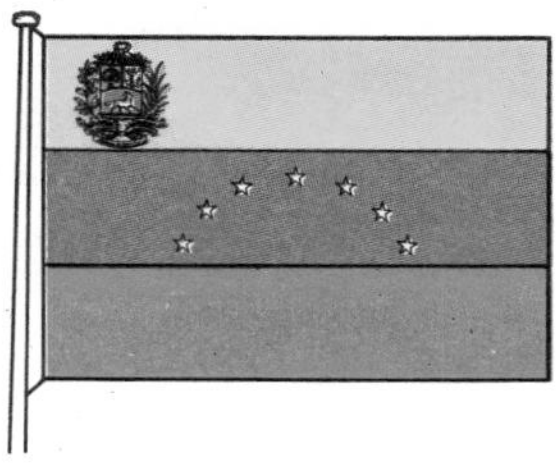

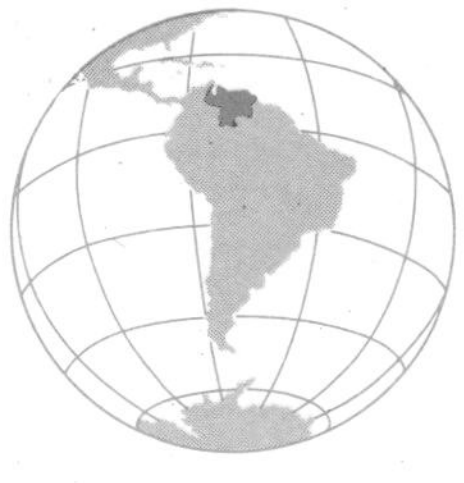

AREA 352,143 sq. mi. (912,050 sq. km.)
POPULATION 13,913,000
CAPITAL Caracas
LARGEST CITY Caracas
HIGHEST POINT Pico Bolívar 16,427 ft. (5,007 m.)
MONETARY UNIT Bolívar
MAJOR LANGUAGE Spanish
MAJOR RELIGION Roman Catholicism

Topography

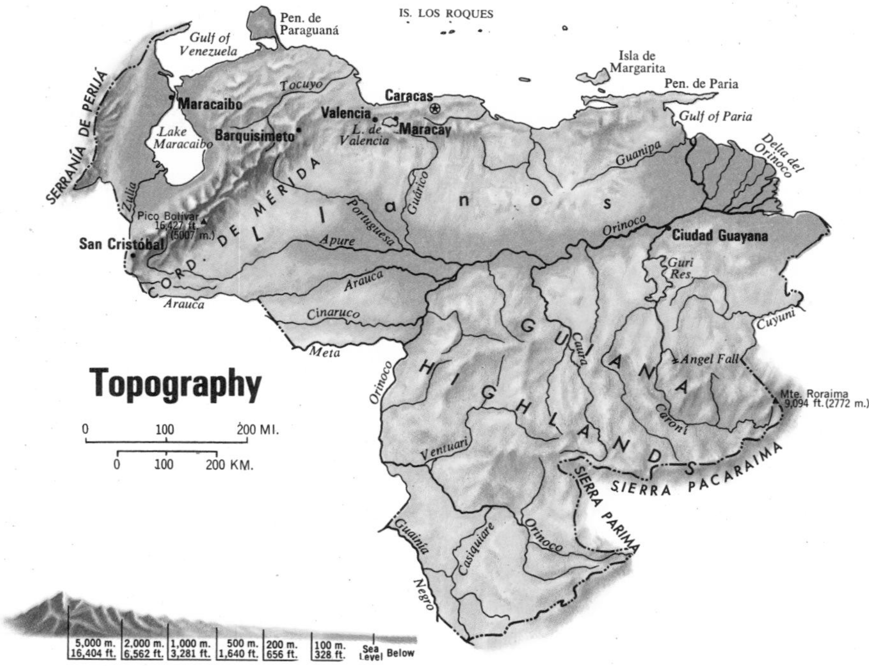
Pen. de Paraguaná
IS. LOS ROQUES
Gulf of Venezuela
Isla de Margarita
Pen. de Paria
Gulf of Paria
Delta del Orinoco
Maracaibo
Caracas
Valencia
Maracay
Barquisimeto
Lake Maracaibo
L. de Valencia
SERRANÍA DE PERIJÁ
CORD. DE MÉRIDA
Pico Bolívar 16,427 ft. (5007 m.)
San Cristóbal
Llanos
Ciudad Guayana
Guri Res.
Angel Fall
Mte. Roraima 9,094 ft. (2772 m.)
GUIANA HIGHLANDS
SIERRA PACARAIMA
SIERRA PARIMA
Orinoco
Apure
Arauca
Meta
Cinaruco
Caura
Caroni
Cuyuni
Ventuari
Casiquiare
Guainía
Negro
0 100 200 MI.
0 100 200 KM.
5,000 m. 16,404 ft.
2,000 m. 6,562 ft.
1,000 m. 3,281 ft.
500 m. 1,640 ft.
200 m. 656 ft.
100 m. 328 ft.
Sea Level
Below

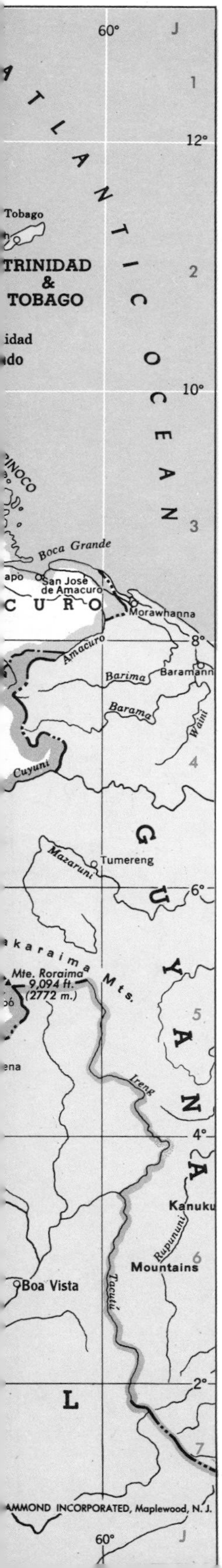
60°
J
ATLANTIC OCEAN
12°
Tobago
TRINIDAD & TOBAGO
10°
Boca Grande
San José de Amacuro
Morawhanna
8°
Amacuro
Barima
Baramanni
Waini
Cuyuni
Mazaruni
Tumereng
6°
GUYANA
Mte. Roraima 9,094 ft. (2772 m.)
Ireng
4°
Kanuku Mountains
Rupununi
Takutu
Boa Vista
2°
L
HAMMOND INCORPORATED, Maplewood, N.J.

Agriculture, Industry and Resources

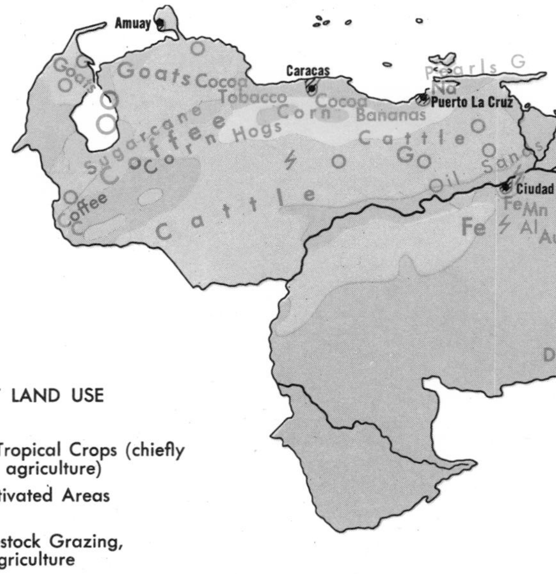
Amuay
Caracas
Puerto La Cruz
Ciudad Guayana
Goats
Cocoa
Tobacco
Sugarcane
Coffee
Corn
Hogs
Cattle
Bananas
Pearls
Oil Sands
Fe
Mn
Al
Au
D

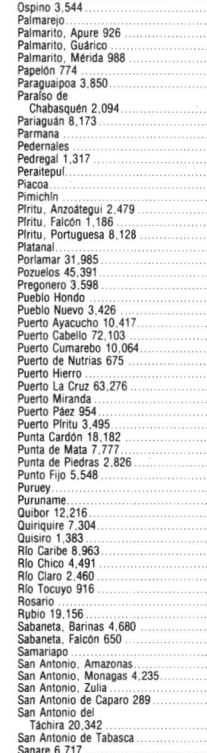

MAJOR MINERAL OCCURRENCES

- Al Bauxite
- Au Gold
- C Coal
- D Diamonds
- Fe Iron Ore
- G Natural Gas
- Mn Manganese
- Na Salt
- O Petroleum

- Water Power
- Major Industrial Areas

DOMINANT LAND USE

- Diversified Tropical Crops (chiefly plantation agriculture)
- Upland Cultivated Areas
- Upland Livestock Grazing, Limited Agriculture
- Extensive Livestock Ranching
- Forests

Colombia

MERCATOR PROJECTION

SCALE OF MILES

0 25 50 75 100 125 150

SCALE OF KILOMETERS

0 25 50 75 100 125 150

Capitals of Countries .... ☆
Other Capitals .... ●
International Boundaries ____ ___ ___
Other Boundaries _____
Canals _____

Scale 1:6,800,000

INTENDENCIA DE
SAN ANDRÉS Y PROVIDENCIA
Same scale as main map

© Copyright HAMMOND INCORPORATED, Maplewood, N.J.

INTERNAL DIVISIONS

Amazonas (comm.) 6,825 ... D8
Antioquia (dept.) 2,976,153 ... B4
Arauca (inten.) 19,884 ... E4
Atlántico (dept.) 958,560 ... C2
Bolívar (dept.) 802,407 ... C3
Boyacá (dept.) 1,084,766 ... D5
Caldas (dept.) 700,954 ... C5
Caquetá (inten.) 57,103 ... C7
Casanare (inten.) ... B3
Cauca (dept.) 603,894 ... B6
César (dept.) 339,843 ... D3
Chocó (dept.) 201,915 ... B4
Córdoba (dept.) 645,478 ... C3
Cundinamarca (dept.) 1,106,626 ... C5
Distrito Especial 2,855,065 ... C5
Guainía (comm.) 1,792 ... F6
Guajira, La (dept.) 180,520 ... D2
Huila (dept.) 469,834 ... C6
La Guajira (dept.) 180,520 ... D2
Magdalena (dept.) 536,122 ... C3
Meta (dept.) 245,176 ... D6
Nariño (dept.) 807,112 ... B7
Norte de Santander (dept.) 693,298 ... D3
Putumayo (inten.) 22,916 ... C7
Quindío (dept.) 321,677 ... C5
Risaralda (dept.) 452,626 ... B5
San Andrés y Providencia (inten.) 22,719 ... B10
Santander (dept.) 1,130,977 ... D4
Sucre (dept.) 354,412 ... C3
Tolima (dept.) 903,520 ... C5
Valle del Cauca (dept.) 2,204,722 ... B6
Vaupés (comm.) 6,923 ... E7
Vichada (comm.) 2,172 ... F5

CITIES and TOWNS

Acacías 9,238 ... D6
Acandí 2,358 ... B3
Agrado 2,771 ... C6
Aguachica 16,771 ... D3
Aguadas 9,995 ... C5
Agua de Dios 9,689 ... C5
Agustín Codazzi 21,932 ... D3
Aipe 3,794 ... C6
Algeciras 5,022 ... C6
Almaguer 1,518 ... B7
Amalfi 6,494 ... C4
Andes 14,957 ... C5
Anserma 15,559 ... B5
Antioquia 6,841 ... B4
Anzá 647 ... C4
Aracataca 7,511 ... D2
Arauca 7,613 ... E4
Arauquita 1,096 ... E4
Arjona 20,571 ... C2
Armenia 135,615 ... B5
Armero 19,567 ... C5
Ayapel 7,475 ... C3
Bagadó 1,575 ... B5
Baranoa 18,397 ... C2
Baraya 2,581 ... C6
Barbacoas 4,653 ... A7
Barbosa 7,960 ... D5
Barichara 2,548 ... D4
Barrancabermeja 87,191 ... C4
Barrancas 2,979 ... D2
Barranco de Loba 2,215 ... C3
Barranquilla 661,009 ... C2
Belén de los Andaquíes 2,190 ... C7
Bello 115,119 ... C4
Bogotá (cap.) 2,696,270 ... D5
Bogotá* 2,855,065 ... D5
Bolívar, Antioquia 13,259 ... C5
Bucaramanga 291,661 ... D4
Buenaventura 115,770 ... B6
Buesaco 2,763 ... B7
Buga 71,016 ... B6
Cáceres 7,154 ... C4
Caicedonia 23,567 ... C5
Calamar, Bolívar 5,867 ... C2
Calarcá 29,349 ... C5
Cali 898,253 ... B6
Campoalegre 11,799 ... C6
Campo de la Cruz 13,137 ... C2
Cañasgordas 3,900 ... B4
Cartagena 292,512 ... C2
Cartago 69,154 ... B5
Caucasia 19,348 ... C4
Cereté 18,788 ... C3
Cerro de San Antonio 3,394 ... C2
Chaparral 14,546 ... C6
Chimichaqua 6,382 ... D3
Chinácota 4,478 ... D4
Chinchiná 24,891 ... C5
Chinú 10,023 ... C3
Chiquinquirá 21,727 ... C5
Chiriguaná 6,611 ... D3
Ciénaga 42,546 ... C2
Ciénaga de Oro 10,607 ... C3
Cisneros 7,226 ... C4
Colombia 2,903 ... C6
Colón 1,306 ... B7
Condoto 4,798 ... B5
Contratación 3,057 ... D4
Convención 7,545 ... D3
Corinto 6,933 ... B6
Corozal 17,419 ... C3
Cravo Norte 771 ... F4
Cúcuta 219,772 ... D4
Cumbal 2,891 ... B7
Dabeiba 7,600 ... B4
Dagua 5,392 ... B6
Duitama 36,551 ... D5
El Banco 20,756 ... D3
El Carmen, Chocó 1,879 ... B5
El Carmen, Norte de Santander 2,362 ... D3
El Carmen de Bolívar 23,392 ... C3
El Cerrito 17,357 ... B6
El Cocuy 2,740 ... D4
El Tambo 2,179 ... B6
Envigado 63,584 ... C4
Espinal 32,475 ... C5
Facatativá 27,892 ... C5
Florencia 31,817 ... C7
Fonseca 9,988 ... D2
Fresno 8,141 ... C5
Fundación 17,497 ... C2
Fusagasugá 25,456 ... C5
Gachalá 1,364 ... D5
Gamarra 5,071 ... D3
Garzón 13,783 ... C6
Gigante 4,880 ... C6
Girardot 59,165 ... C5
Gramalote 2,880 ... D4
Guamal, Magdalena 4,986 ... C3
Guamal, Meta 2,854 ... D6
Guapí 5,005 ... B6
Guateque 6,032 ... D5
Honda 21,506 ... C5
Ibagué 176,223 ... C5
Inírida 1,792 ... F6
Ipiales 30,871 ... B7
Iscuandé 561 ... A6
Istmina 5,575 ... B5
Itagüí 96,972 ... C4
Ituango 5,561 ... C4
Juradó 935 ... B4
La Cruz 4,353 ... B7
La Dorada 30,962 ... C5
La Gloria 2,632 ... D3
La Palma 5,430 ... C5
La Plata 8,047 ... C6
La Unión 5,392 ... B7
Leticia 6,285 ... F10
Líbano 19,132 ... C5
Lorica 18,251 ... C3
Los Andes 1,414 ... B7
Magangué 34,396 ... C3
Maicao 21,645 ... D2
Majagual 2,329 ... C3
Málaga 10,645 ... D4

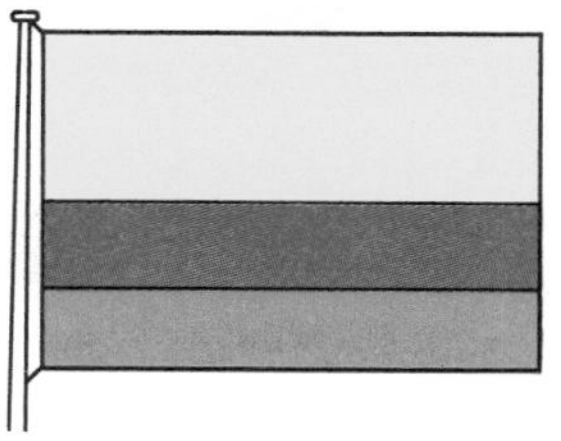

Maní 951 ... D5
Manizales 199,904 ... C5
Matanza 1,211 ... D4
Medellín 1,070,924 ... C4
Medina 1,436 ... D5
Mercaderes 3,877 ... B7
Miraflores, Boyacá 3,584 ... D5
Miraflores, Vaupés 536 ... D7
Miranda 6,439 ... B6
Mitú 1,637 ... E7
Mocoa 6,221 ... B7
Mompós 14,076 ... C3
Moniquirá 5,711 ... D5
Montería 89,583 ... B3
Morichal ... E6
Mosquera 594 ... A6
Murindó 485 ... B4
Muzo 1,823 ... D5
Natagaima 7,772 ... C6
Neiva 105,476 ... C6
Nóvita 802 ... B5
Nunchía 437 ... D5
Nuquí 1,115 ... B5
Ocaña 38,352 ... D3
Orocué 1,011 ... E5
Ortega 5,150 ... C6
Pacho 6,786 ... C5
Páez 2,098 ... C6
Paipa 4,260 ... D5
Palmira 140,481 ... B6
Pamplona 31,817 ... D4
Pasto 119,339 ... B7
Patía 5,306 ... B6
Paz de Ariporo 2,584 ... E5
Paz de Río 3,464 ... D4
Pedraza 1,872 ... C2
Pereira 174,128 ... C5
Piedecuesta 17,308 ... D4
Piendamó 5,046 ... B6
Pitalito 15,049 ... B7
Pivijay 10,172 ... C2
Planeta Rica 12,932 ... C3
Plato 18,589 ... C3
Popayán 77,669 ... B6
Pore 389 ... D5
Pradera 15,732 ... B6
Puente Nacional 4,317 ... D5
Puerto Asís 6,364 ... B7
Puerto Berrío 19,579 ... C4
Puerto Carreño 2,172 ... G4
Puerto Colombia 9,255 ... C2
Puerto Escondido 1,368 ... B3
Puerto Leguízamo 3,179 ... C8
Puerto López, Meta 4,948 ... D5
Puerto Murillo ... G4
Puerto Mutis ... B4
Puerto Nare ... D7
Puerto Paulina ... D7
Puerto Rico, Caquetá 4,853 ... C7
Puerto Rondón 1,010 ... E4
Puerto Salgar 6,396 ... C5
Puerto Tejada 18,315 ... B6

AREA 439,513 sq. mi. (1,138,339 sq. km.)
POPULATION 27,520,000
CAPITAL Bogotá
LARGEST CITY Bogotá
HIGHEST POINT Pico Cristóbal Colón 19,029 ft. (5,800 m.)
MONETARY UNIT Colombian peso
MAJOR LANGUAGE Spanish
MAJOR RELIGION Roman Catholicism

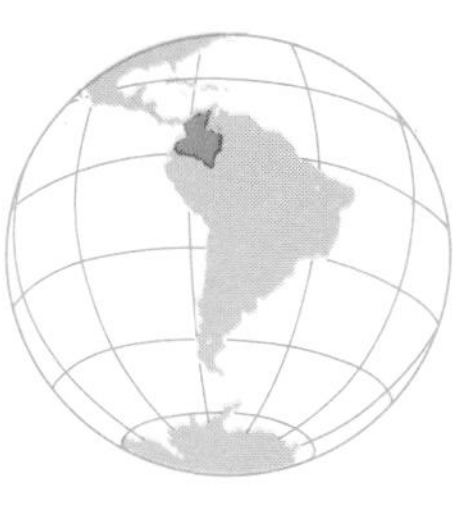

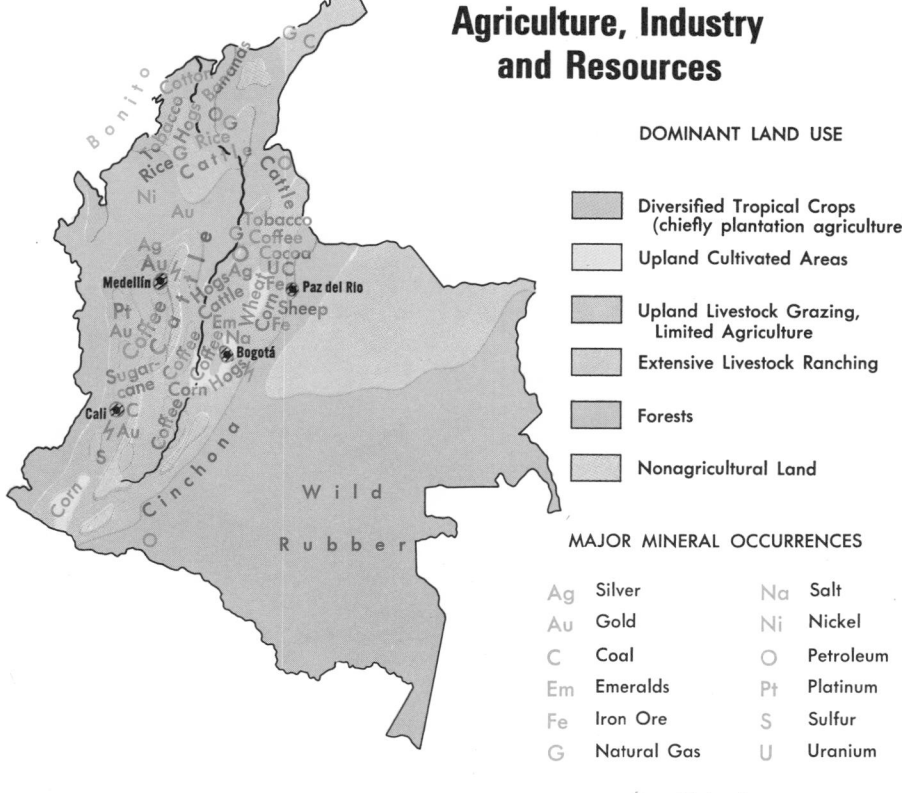

Agriculture, Industry and Resources

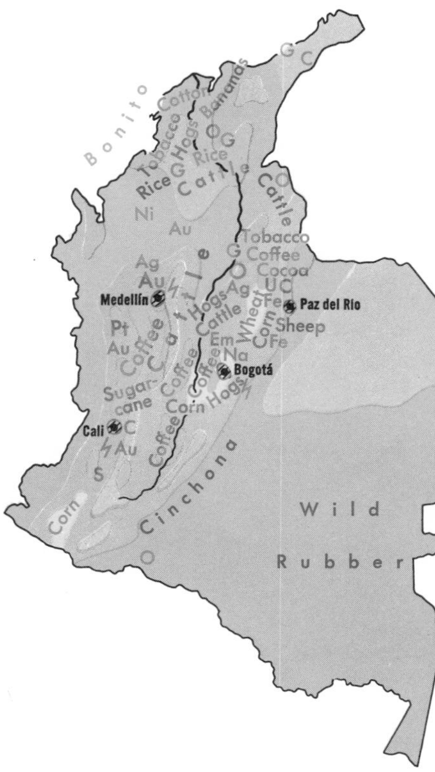
Bonito
Medellín
Paz del Río
Bogotá
Cali
Cinchona
Wild Rubber

DOMINANT LAND USE

- Diversified Tropical Crops (chiefly plantation agriculture)
- Upland Cultivated Areas
- Upland Livestock Grazing, Limited Agriculture
- Extensive Livestock Ranching
- Forests
- Nonagricultural Land

MAJOR MINERAL OCCURRENCES

Ag	Silver	Na	Salt
Au	Gold	Ni	Nickel
C	Coal	O	Petroleum
Em	Emeralds	Pt	Platinum
Fe	Iron Ore	S	Sulfur
G	Natural Gas	U	Uranium

Water Power
Major Industrial Areas

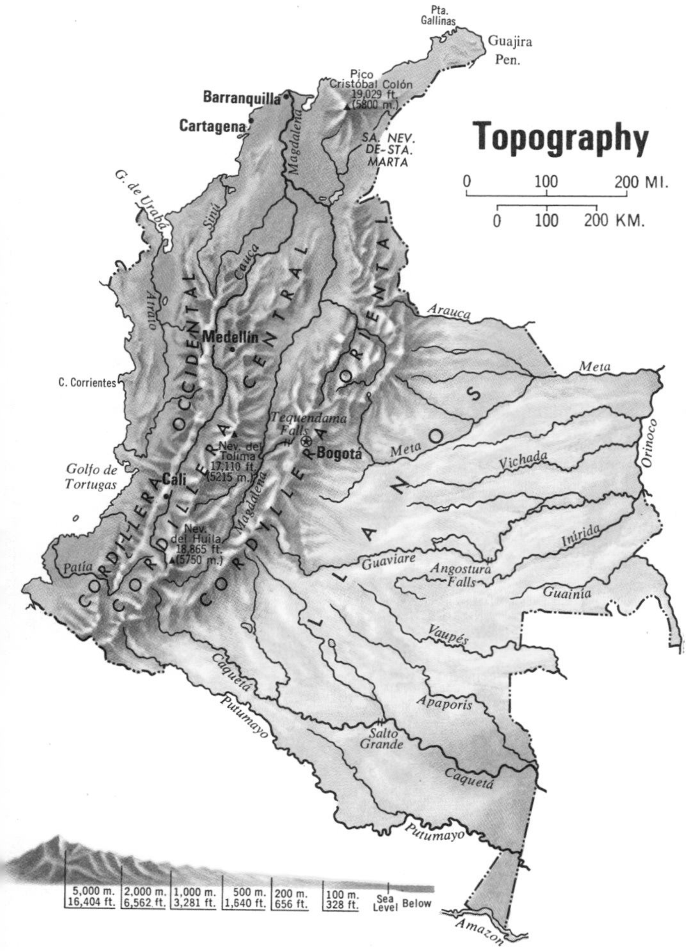
Topography
0 100 200 MI.
0 100 200 KM.
Pta. Gallinas
Guajira Pen.
Pico Cristóbal Colón 19,029 ft. (5800 m.)
Barranquilla
Cartagena
SA. NEV. DE STA. MARTA
G. de Urabá
Sinú
Cauca
Magdalena
Atrato
Medellín
C. Corrientes
Arauca
Meta
Orinoco
Tequendama Falls
Nev. del Tolima 17,110 ft. (5215 m.)
Bogotá
Vichada
Golfo de Tortugas
Cali
Nev. del Huila 18,865 ft. (5750 m.)
Patía
CORDILLERA OCCIDENTAL
CORDILLERA CENTRAL
CORDILLERA ORIENTAL
LLANOS
Guaviare
Angostura Falls
Inírida
Guainía
Vaupés
Caquetá
Apaporis
Putumayo
Salto Grande
Amazon
5,000 m. 16,404 ft.
2,000 m. 6,562 ft.
1,000 m. 3,281 ft.
500 m. 1,640 ft.
200 m. 656 ft.
100 m. 328 ft.
Sea Level
Below

Puerto Wilches 5,282 ... D4
Pupiales 2,723 ... B7
Purificación 8,164 ... C6
Quibdó 28,040 ... B5
Remedios 4,681 ... C4
Remolino 3,408 ... C2
Restrepo 2,704 ... D5
Ricaurte 1,205 ... A7
Río de Oro 2,985 ... D3
Riohacha 19,604 ... D2
Rionegro, Antioquia 22,654 ... C4
Rionegro, Santander 3,491 ... D4
Riosucio, Caldas 11,619 ... C5
Riosucio, Chocó 2,184 ... B4
Roberto Payán 445 ... A7
Robles 5,422 ... D2
Rovira 5,105 ... C5
Sabanalarga 26,542 ... C2
Sácama 69 ... D4
Sahagún 18,717 ... C3
Salamina 12,136 ... C5
Salazar 2,791 ... D4
Samaniego 4,790 ... B7
San Agustín 4,532 ... B7
San Andrés, Antioquia 2,003 ... C4
San Andrés, San Andrés y Providencia 14,428 ... A9
San Antero 7,129 ... C3
Sandoná 7,222 ... B7
San Francisco 1,654 ... B7
San Gil 21,679 ... D4
San Jacinto 13,459 ... C3
San José del Guaviare 4,138 ... D6
San Juan del César 9,468 ... D2
San Marcos 10,415 ... C3
San Martín 8,281 ... D6
San Onofre 7,899 ... C3
San Pablo 3,662 ... B7
San Roque 4,972 ... C4
Santa Bárbara 11,848 ... C5
Santa Marta 102,484 ... D2
Santander 13,625 ... B6
Santa Rosa de Cabal 28,368 ... C5
Santa Rosa de Osos 8,593 ... C4
San Vicente del Caguán 3,182 ... C6
Sardinata 3,726 ... D3
Segovia 10,000 ... C4
Sevilla 31,143 ... C5
Sibundoy 2,853 ... B7
Silvia 3,045 ... B6
Simití 3,062 ... C4
Sincé 11,909 ... C3
Sincelejo 68,797 ... C3
Sipí 153 ... B5
Sitionuevo 5,919 ... C2
Soatá 4,294 ... D4
Socorro 15,596 ... D4
Sogamoso 48,891 ... D5
Soledad 64,469 ... C2
Sonsón 15,990 ... C5
Sopetrán 5,223 ... C4
Tadó 3,102 ... B5
Támara 947 ... D5
Tame 4,811 ... E4
Tibaná 1,100 ... D5
Tierralta 7,950 ... C3
Timaná 4,262 ... C7
Timbío 4,755 ... B6
Timbiquí 1,048 ... B6
Toledo 2,942 ... D4
Tolú 9,118 ... C3
Trinidad 729 ... E5
Tuluá 86,736 ... B5
Tumaco 38,742 ... A7
Tunja 51,620 ... D5
Túquerres 12,058 ... B7
Turbaco 19,360 ... C2
Turbo 16,070 ... B3
Ubaté 7,716 ... D5
Uribia 2,193 ... D2
Urrao 8,577 ... B4
Valdivia 4,318 ... C4
Valledupar 87,425 ... D2
Vélez 8,241 ... D4
Venadillo 8,383 ... C5
Villanueva 9,836 ... D2
Villa Rosario 8,668 ... D4
Villavicencio 82,869 ... D5
Villeta 6,507 ... C5
Yarumal 21,333 ... C4
Yopal 5,851 ... D5
Yumbo 28,011 ... B6
Zapatoca 6,258 ... D4
Zaragoza 9,660 ... C4
Zarzal 21,370 ... B5
Zipaquirá 25,413 ... D5

OTHER FEATURES

Abibe, Serranía de, (mts.) ... B3
Aguarico, (riv.) ... B7
Aguja, La, (cape) ... C2
Albuquerque, (cays) ... A10
Alicia, (bank) ... B8
Alto Ritacuva, (mt.) ... D4
Amazon, (riv.) ... E9
Ancón de Sardinas, (bay) ... A7
Angostura, (falls) ... E6
Apaporis, (riv.) ... F8
Araracuara, Cerros de, (mts.) ... E7
Arauca, (riv.) ... E4
Ariari, (riv.) ... D6
Ariguaní, (riv.) ... D3
Ariporo, (riv.) ... E4
Atabapo, (riv.) ... G6
Atrato, (riv.) ... B4
Augusta, (cape) ... C2
Ayapel, Serranía de, (mts.) ... C4
Bajo Nuevo, (shoal) ... C8
Barú, (isl.) ... C2
Baudó, Serranía de, (mts.) ... B5
Baudó, (riv.) ... B5
Bita, (riv.) ... F5
Buenaventura, (bay) ... B6
Caguán, (riv.) ... C7
Cahuinari, (riv.) ... E8
Caquetá, (riv.) ... E8
Caraparaná, (riv.) ... D8
Casanare, (riv.) ... E4
Catatumbo, (riv.) ... D3
Cauca, (riv.) ... C4
Cazueleja, Cerro, (mt.) ... C6
Central, Cordillera, (range) ... C5
César, (riv.) ... D2
Chaira, Laguna, (lake) ... C7
Chamusa, Sierra, (mts.) ... C6
Charambirá, (pt.) ... B5
Chicamocha, (riv.) ... D4
Chiribiquete, Sierra de, (mts.) ... D7
Cinaruco, (riv.) ... F4
Chocó, (bay) ... B6
Cocuy, Sierra Nevada del, (mts.) ... D4
Coredó (Humboldt), (bay) ... B4
Corrientes, (cape) ... B5
Courtown (Este Sudeste), (cays) ... A10
Cravo Norte, (riv.) ... E4
Cravo Sur, (riv.) ... E5
Cristóbal Colón, Pico, (peak) ... D2
Cuemaní, (riv.) ... D7
Cupica, (gulf) ... B4
Cuquiari, (riv.) ... E7
Cusachón, (isl.) ... D1
Cusiana, (riv.) ... D5
Espada, (pt.) ... E1
Este Sudeste, (cays) ... A10
Fuerte, (isl.) ... B3
Gallinas, (pt.) ... E1
Gorgona, (isl.) ... A6
Grande, (isl.) ... B4
Grande, Salto, (falls) ... D8
Guainía, (riv.) ... F6
Guajira, (pen.) ... E1
Guapi, (bay) ... A6
Guaviare, (riv.) ... F6
Guayabero, (riv.) ... D6
Huila, Nevado del, (mt.) ... C6
Humboldt, (bay) ... B4
Igara-Paraná, (riv.) ... D8
Inírida, (riv.) ... F6
Isana, (riv.) ... F7
La Aguja, (cape) ... C2
La Macarena, Serranía de, (mts.) ... D6
La Vela, (cape) ... D1
Lebrija, (riv.) ... D4
Llanos, (plains) ... D5
Losada, (riv.) ... C6
Macarena, Serranía de La, (mts.) ... D6
Magdalena, (riv.) ... C3
Manacacías, (riv.) ... D6
Mapiripán, Laguna, (lake) ... E6
Marzo, (pt.) ... B4
Mesai, (riv.) ... D7
Meta, (riv.) ... E5
Metica, (riv.) ... D6
Mira, (riv.) ... A7
Miritiparaná, (riv.) ... E8
Morrosquillo, (gulf) ... C3
Muco, (riv.) ... E5
Naipo, (isl.) ... F6
Nechí, (riv.) ... C4
Negro, (riv.) ... G7
Occidental, Cordillera, (range) ... B5
Oriental, Cordillera, (range) ... D5
Orinoco, (riv.) ... G5
Orteguaza, (riv.) ... C7
Papunáua, (riv.) ... E6
Papurí, (riv.) ... F7
Patía, (riv.) ... B6
Pauto, (riv.) ... E5
Perijá, Serranía de, (mts.) ... D2
Providencia, (isl.) ... B9
Puracé, (vol.) ... B6
Putumayo, (riv.) ... E9
Quitasueño, (bank) ... A8
Roca que Vela, (cay) ... B8
Roncador, (cays) ... B9
Saldaña, (riv.) ... C6
Salto Grande, (falls) ... D8
San Andrés, (isl.) ... A10
San Bernardo, (isls.) ... C3
San Jorge, (riv.) ... C3
San Juan, (riv.) ... B5
San Miguel, (riv.) ... B7
Santa Catalina, (isl.) ... A9
Santa Marta, Sierra Nevada de, (range) ... D2
Serrana, (bank) ... B9
Serranilla, (bank) ... B8
Sinú, (riv.) ... B3
Sogamoso, (riv.) ... D4
Solano, (pt.) ... B4
Suárez, (riv.) ... D4
Sucio, (riv.) ... B4
Taraíra, (riv.) ... F8
Tequendama, (falls) ... C5
Tibugá, (gulf) ... B5
Tolima, Nevada del, (mt.) ... C5
Tomo, (riv.) ... F5
Tortugas, (gulf) ... B6
Tota, Laguna de, (lake) ... D5
Truandó, (riv.) ... B4
Tumaco, Rada de, (bay) ... A6
Tunahí, Sierra, (mts.) ... E7
Upía, (riv.) ... D5
Urabá, (gulf) ... B3
Uva, Laguna, (lake) ... E6
Uva, (riv.) ... E6
Vaupés, (riv.) ... E7
Vela, La, (cape) ... D1
Vela, Roca que, (cay) ... B8
Vichada, (riv.) ... F5
Vigía, (cay) ... A10
Yarí, (riv.) ... D8
Zapatosa, Ciénaga de, (swamp) ... D3

*City and suburbs.

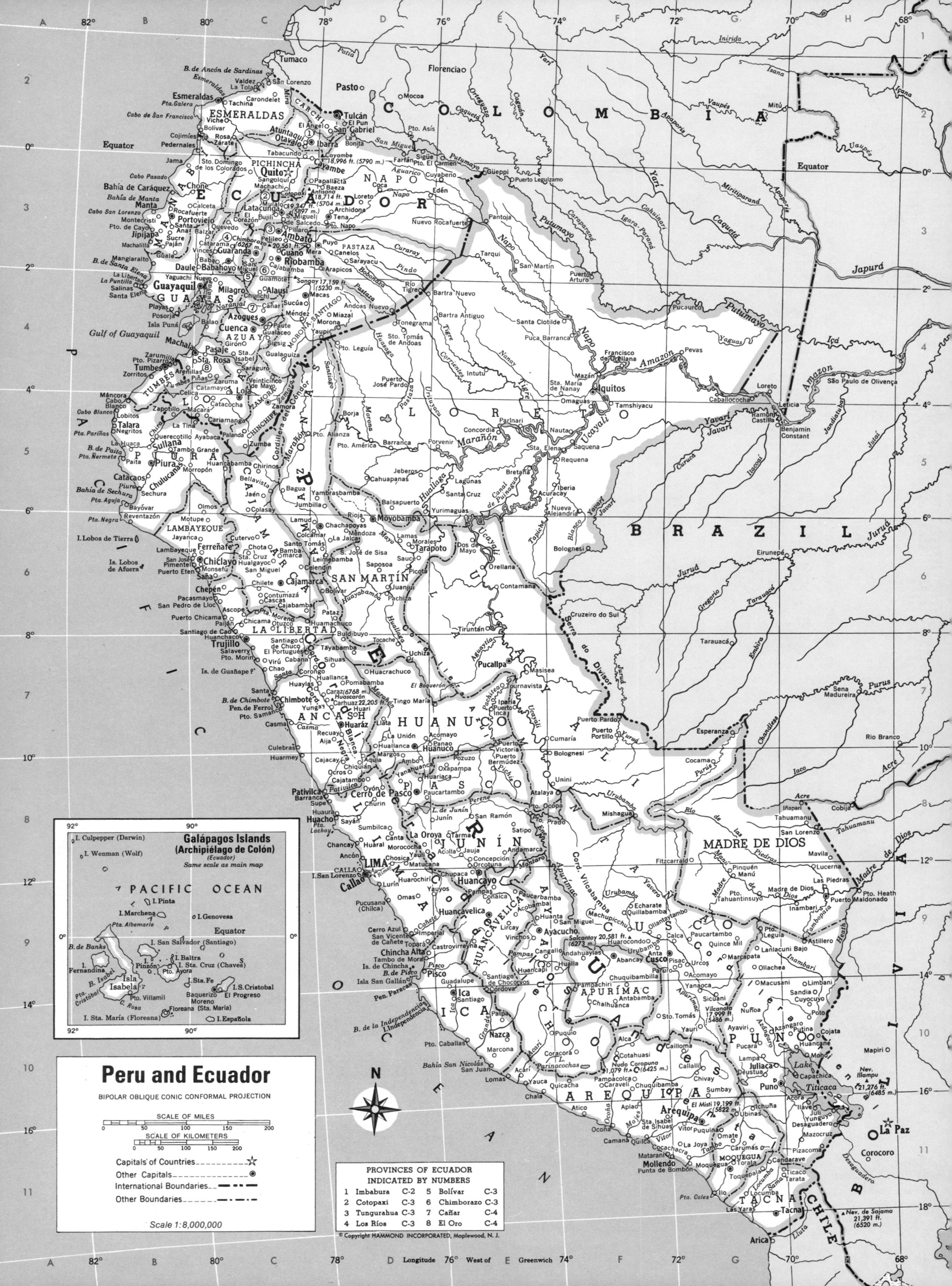

Peru and Ecuador

BIPOLAR OBLIQUE CONIC CONFORMAL PROJECTION

SCALE OF MILES

0   50   100   150   200

SCALE OF KILOMETERS

0   50   100   150   200

Capitals of Countries _____ ☆

Other Capitals _____ ◉

International Boundaries _____

Other Boundaries _____

Scale 1:8,000,000

Galápagos Islands
(Archipiélago de Colón)
(Ecuador)
Same scale as main map

PACIFIC OCEAN

PROVINCES OF ECUADOR
INDICATED BY NUMBERS

1 Imbabura	C-2	5 Bolívar	C-3
2 Cotopaxi	C-3	6 Chimborazo	C-3
3 Tungurahua	C-3	7 Cañar	C-4
4 Los Ríos	C-3	8 El Oro	C-4

© Copyright HAMMOND INCORPORATED, Maplewood, N.J.

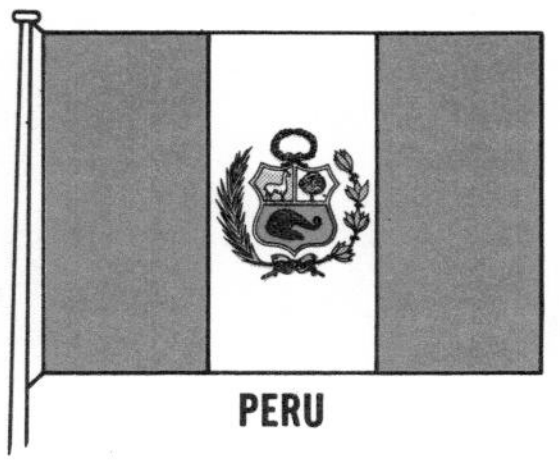

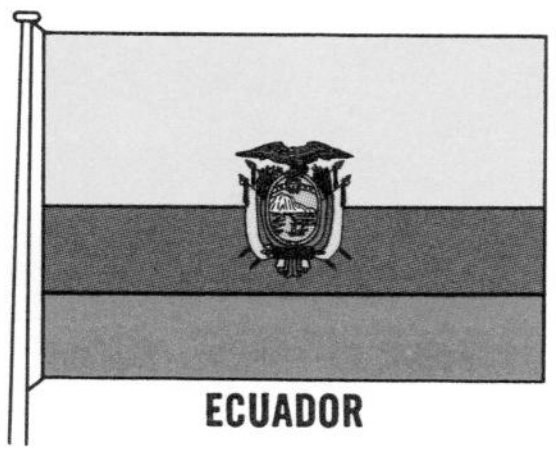

PERU

AREA 496,222 sq. mi. (1,285,215 sq. km.)
POPULATION 17,031,221
CAPITAL Lima
LARGEST CITY Lima
HIGHEST POINT Huascarán 22,205 ft. (6,768 m.)
MONETARY UNIT sol
MAJOR LANGUAGES Spanish, Quechua, Aymara
MAJOR RELIGION Roman Catholicism

ECUADOR

AREA 109,483 sq. mi. (283,561 sq. km.)
POPULATION 8,354,000
CAPITAL Quito
LARGEST CITY Guayaquil
HIGHEST POINT Chimborazo 20,561 ft. (6,267 m.)
MONETARY UNIT sucre
MAJOR LANGUAGES Spanish, Quechua
MAJOR RELIGION Roman Catholicism

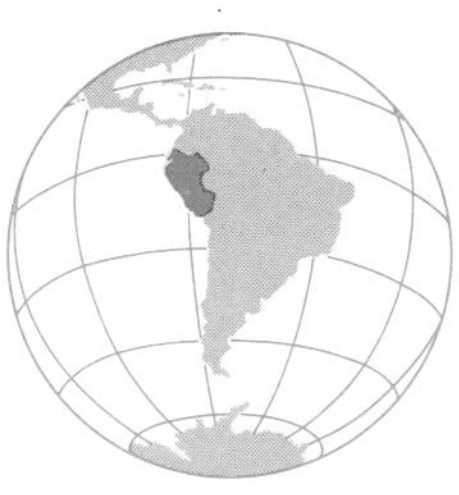

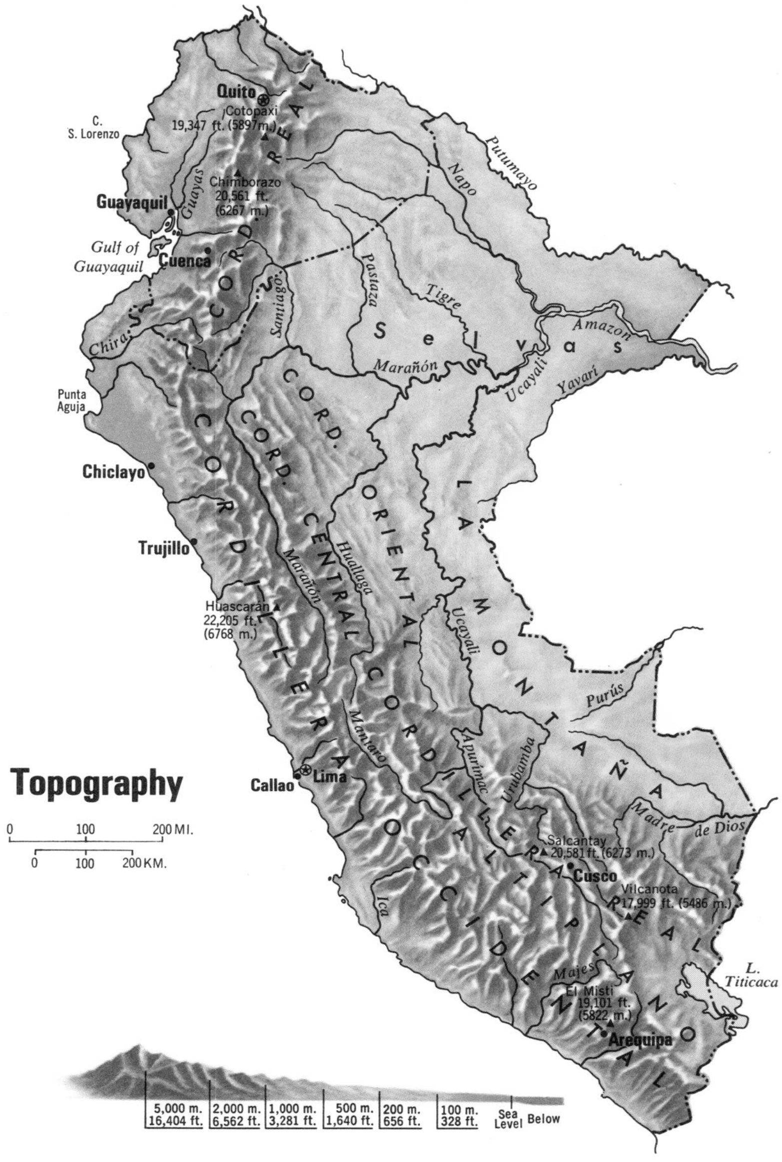

PERU

DEPARTMENTS

Amazonas 196,469 ... C5
Ancash 726,665 ... D7
Apurímac 307,805 ... F10
Arequipa 530,528 ... F10
Ayacucho 459,747 ... E9
Cajamarca 916,331 ... C6
Callao (prov.) 315,605 ... D9
Cuzco 712,918 ... F9
Huancavelica 331,155 ... E9
Huánuco 420,764 ... D7
Ica 357,973 ... E10
Junín 691,130 ... E8
La Libertad 806,368 ... C6
Lambayeque 515,363 ... B6
Lima 3,485,411 ... D8
Loreto 339,298 ... E5
Madre de Dios 21,968 ... G8
Moquegua 74,573 ... G11
Pasco 176,750 ... E8
Piura 854,668 ... B5
Puno 779,594 ... G10
San Martín 224,310 ... D6
Tacna 95,263 ... G11
Tumbes 75,399 ... B4
Ucayali 155,637 ... E6

CITIES and TOWNS

Abancay 12,172 ... F9
Acarí 4,364 ... E10
Acobamba 2,069 ... E9
Acolla 5,061 ... E8
Acomayo, Cuzco 1,795 ... G9
Acomayo, Huánuco 734 ... E7
Acora 1,510 ... H11
Acuracay 1,025 ... F5
Aija 2,027 ... D7
Alca 698 ... F10
Ambo 2,006 ... D8
Ancón 5,761 ... D8
Andahuaylas 4,912 ... F9
Andamarca 243 ... E8
Anta 2,797 ... F9
Antabamba 1,962 ... F10
Aplao 1,561 ... F11
Aquia 1,014 ... D8
Arequipa 304,653 ... G11
Arequipa⊙ ... 72
Ascope 9,438 ... C6
Astillero ... H9
Atalaya 2,132 ... E8
Atico 3,053 ... F11
Ayabaca 4,292 ... C5
Ayacucho 43,304 ... F9
Ayaviri 9,719 ... G10
Azángaro 6,565 ... H10
Bagua 4,907 ... C5
Balsapuerto 121 ... D5
Bambamarca 5,045 ... C6
Barranca, Lima 23,399 ... C8
Barranca, Loreto 222 ... D5
Bartra Antiguo ... E4
Bartra Nuevo ... E4
Bayóvar ... B5
Bellavista 23,666 ... C5
Bolívar 1,083 ... D6
Bolognesi ... F6
Bolognesi 553 ... F8
Borja 220 ... D5
Bretaña 757 ... E5
Buldibuyo 509 ... D7
Caballococha 1,827 ... G4
Cabana 1,981 ... C7
Cabo Blanco ... B5
Cahuapanas 194 ... D5
Cailloma 1,905 ... G10
Cajabamba 5,851 ... C6
Cajacay 667 ... D8
Cajamarca 37,608 ... C6
Cajatambo 3,811 ... D8
Calca 4,457 ... G9
Callalli 465 ... G10
Callao 296,220 ... D9
Camaná 10,121 ... F11
Candarave 1,009 ... G11
Cangallo 1,536 ... E9
Canta 2,439 ... D8
Capachica 271 ... H10
Carás 5,214 ... D7
Caravelí 2,002 ... F10
Carhuás 2,386 ... D7
Carumás 3,138 ... G11
Cascas 2,511 ... C6
Casma 9,037 ... C7
Castrovirreyna 1,501 ... E9
Catacaos 19,155 ... B5
Celendín 7,957 ... D6
Cerro Azul 2,022 ... D9
Cerro de Pasco 47,178 ... D8
Chachapoyas 10,418 ... D6
Chala 1,335 ... E10
Chalhuanca 3,544 ... F10
Chancay 20,034 ... D8
Chao ... C7
Chepén 23,562 ... C6
Chicama 10,087 ... C6
Chiclayo 189,685 ... C6
Chilca (Pucusana) 2,397 ... D9
Chilete 1,297 ... C6
Chimbote 159,045 ... C7
Chincha Alta 28,785 ... D9
Chiquián 3,841 ... D8
Chirinos 863 ... C5
Chivay 2,448 ... G10
Chosica ... D8
Chota 6,430 ... C6
Chulucanas 26,278 ... B5
Chupaca 2,875 ... E9
Chuquibamba 3,044 ... F10
Chuquibambilla 1,733 ... F9
Churín 1,303 ... D8
Cocachacra 2,682 ... G11
Cocama ... G8
Cojata 658 ... H10
Colasay 747 ... C5
Colcamar 1,578 ... D6
Conaica 2,058 ... E9
Concepción 5,864 ... E8
Concordia 304 ... E5
Contamana 5,088 ... E6
Contumazá 2,632 ... C6
Coracora 4,508 ... F10
Córdova 567 ... E10
Corongo 1,619 ... D7
Cotahuasi 2,308 ... F10
Culebras ... C7
Cumaría ... F7
Cutervo 5,856 ... C6
Cuyocuyo 896 ... H10
Cuzco 120,881 ... F9
Desaguadero 1,467 ... H11
Deustua 392 ... G10
Dos de Mayo 1,948 ... E6
Echarate 229 ... F9
El Portugués ... C7
Esperanza 240 ... G7
Ferreñafe 16,251 ... C6
Fitzcarrald ... G8
Francisco de Orellana 511 ... F4
Guadalupe 5,484 ... E9
Güeppi ... E3
Huacho 36,697 ... D8
Huacrachuco 1,604 ... D7
Hualgayoc 1,018 ... C6
Hualla 4,027 ... F9
Huallanca, Ancash 953 ... D7
Huallanca, Huánuco ... D7
Huamachuco 7,368 ... D6
Huancabamba 4,427 ... C5
Huancané 5,187 ... H10
Huancapi 2,646 ... E9
Huancavelica 15,916 ... E9
Huancayo 115,693 ... E9
Huanchaco 2,641 ... C7
Huanta 7,729 ... E9
Huánuco 41,123 ... E7
Huaral 20,331 ... D8
Huaráz 29,719 ... D7
Huari 2,461 ... D7
Huariaca 3,427 ... E8
Huarmey 11,818 ... C8
Huarochirí⊙ 2,446 ... D9
Huarocondo 2,790 ... F9
Huaura⊙ 11,209 ... D8
Huaylas 1,066 ... C7
Iberia 518 ... F5
Ica 73,883 ... E10
Ichuña 180 ... G11
Ilave 6,832 ... H11
Ilo 21,551 ... G11
Imperial⊙ 14,571 ... D9
Inambari 190 ... H9
Iñapari 86 ... H8
Intutu 743 ... E4
Iparia 284 ... E7
Iquitos 111,327 ... F4
Jaén 13,912 ... C5
Jauja 13,936 ... E8
Jayanca 5,694 ... B6
Jeberos 1,626 ... D5
Juanjuí 6,386 ... D6
Juli 5,398 ... H11
Juliaca 38,475 ... G10
Jumbilla 1,146 ... C5
Junín 8,282 ... E8
Lagunas 4,584 ... E5
La Huaca 2,006 ... B5
La Jalca 1,944 ... D6
La Joya 2,412 ... G11
Lamas 6,553 ... D6
Lambayeque 18,167 ... B6
Lampa 3,852 ... G10
Lamud 2,897 ... C6
Lanlacuni Bajo 77 ... G9
La Oroya 25,908 ... D8
Las Piedras ... H9
Las Yaras 289 ... G11
La Tina ... B5
La Unión 2,524 ... D7
Leimebamba 1,327 ... D6
Lima 354,292 ... D8
Lima* 2,386,374 ... D8
Limbani 389 ... H10
Lircay 2,268 ... E9
Llata 2,266 ... D7
Lobitos 2,488 ... B5
Locumba 260 ... G11
Lomas 240 ... E10
Lucerna ... H9
Lurín⊙ 12,789 ... D9
Machupicchu 235 ... F9
Macusani 2,790 ... G10
Madre de Dios ... G9
Máncora 3,896 ... B5
Manú ... G9
Marcapata 380 ... G9
Marcona 8,218 ... E10
Margos 1,235 ... D8
Masisea 1,791 ... E7
Matarani ... F11
Matucana 2,643 ... D8
Mavila ... H8
Mazán 947 ... F4
Mazocruz 2,369 ... H11
Mendoza 1,272 ... D6
Mishagua ... F8
Moho 2,028 ... H10
Mollendo 15,573 ... F11
Monsefú 14,255 ... C6
Moquegua 16,959 ... G11
Morales 3,274 ... D6
Morococha 6,145 ... D8
Morropón 5,643 ... C5
Motupe 6,753 ... C6
Moyobamba 10,004 ... D6
Nauta 3,768 ... F5
Nazca 21,025 ... E10
Negritos 18,024 ... B5
Nueva Alejandría 56 ... F5
Nuñoa 3,001 ... G10
Ocoña 3,039 ... F11
Ocros 1,061 ... D8
Ollachea 1,000 ... G9
Ollantaytambo 1,240 ... F9
Olmos 4,066 ... C5
Omaguas ... F5
Omas 277 ... D9
Omate 887 ... G11
Orcotuna 3,286 ... E8
Orellana 1,550 ... E6
Otuzco 8,410 ... C6
Oxapampa 4,338 ... E8
Oyón 5,798 ... D8
Pacasmayo 15,381 ... C6
Pachiza 683 ... D6
Paiján 10,321 ... C6
Paita 14,875 ... B5
Palpa 2,935 ... E10
Pampachiri 452 ... F10
Pampacolca 2,046 ... F10
Pampas 2,123 ... E9
Panao 1,455 ... E7
Pantoja 204 ... E3
Paramonga ... C8
Parinari 138 ... E5
Paruro 1,746 ... F9
Pataz 450 ... D6
Paucarbamba 636 ... E9
Paucartambo, Cuzco 2,055 ... G9
Paucartambo, Pasco 2,172 ... E8
Pevas 1,347 ... G4
Picota 2,265 ... D6
Pimentel 7,742 ... B6
Pinquén ... G9
Pisac 1,182 ... G9
Pisco 41,429 ... D9
Piura 126,702 ... B5
Pizacoma 220 ... H11
Pomabamba 2,802 ... D7
Porvenir ... E5
Poto 161 ... H10
Pozuzo 260 ... E8
Puca Barranca ... E4
Pucallpa 57,525 ... E7
Pucará 1,252 ... G10
Pucaurco 632 ... G4
Pucusana 2,397 ... D9
Puerto Alianza ... D5
Puerto América 144 ... D5
Puerto Bermúdez 366 ... E8
Puerto Chicama 4,741 ... C6
Puerto Eten 8,932 ... B6
Puerto Leguía, Loreto ... D4
Puerto Leguía, Puno ... G9
Puerto Maldonado 6,419 ... H9
Puerto Morín ... C7
Puerto Ocopa 1,492 ... E8
Puerto Pardo ... F7
Puerto Pizarro ... B4
Puerto Portillo ... F7
Puerto Prado 265 ... E8
Puerto Samanco 1,795 ... C7
Puerto Tahuantinsuyo ... G9
Puerto Victoria ... E7
Puno 41,166 ... G10
Punta de Bombón 3,907 ... F11
Punta Moreno ... C6
Puquina 1,087 ... G11
Puquio 8,691 ... F10
Putina 4,581 ... H10
Querecotillo 8,008 ... B5
Quicacha 615 ... F10
Quilca 199 ... F11
Quillabamba 10,857 ... F9
Quince Mil ... G9
Ramón Castilla 1,327 ... G5
Recuay 2,169 ... D7
Requena 7,300 ... F5
Reventazón ... B6
Rioja 6,066 ... D6
Salaverry 5,316 ... C7
Saña 26,933 ... C6
Sandia 1,752 ... H10
San José 3,480 ... B6
San José de Sisa 4,147 ... D6
San Juan ... E10
San Lorenzo 120 ... H8
San Martín ... E3
San Miguel, Ayacucho 1,084 ... F9
San Miguel, Cajamarca 3,800 ... C6
San Pedro de Lloc 9,326 ... C6
San Ramón 4,646 ... E8
Santa 13,956 ... C7
Santa Clotilde 863 ... E4
Santa Cruz, Cajamarca 2,846 ... C6
Santa Cruz, Loreto 602 ... E5
Santa Elena 400 ... F5
Santa Isabel de Sihuas 116 ... F11
Santa María de Nanay 251 ... F4
Santiago 3,624 ... E10
Santiago de Cao 18,635 ... C6
Santiago de Chocorvos 407 ... E9
Santiago de Chuco ... C7
Santo Tomás, Amazonas 1,039 ... C6
Santo Tomás, Cuzco 2,095 ... G10
Santo Tomás de Andoas 122 ... D4
San Vicente de Cañete 8,751 ... D9
Saposoa 4,339 ... D6
Saquena 2,281 ... F5
Satipo 5,944 ... E8
Sauce 1,726 ... D6
Sayán 4,052 ... D8
Sechura 6,174 ... B5
Sicuani 12,956 ... G10
Sihuas 1,509 ... D7
Sullana 60,112 ... B5
Sumbilca 1,724 ... D8
Supe 15,623 ... D8
Tacna 55,752 ... G11
Tahuamanu 120 ... H8
Talara 29,884 ... B5
Tambo de Mora 2,717 ... D9
Tambo Grande 7,184 ... B5
Tamshiyacu 2,220 ... F5
Tarapoto 21,260 ... D6
Tarata 2,808 ... H11
Tarma 28,100 ... E8
Tarqui ... E3
Tayabamba 1,786 ... D7
Ticaco 963 ... H11
Tingo María 20,320 ... D7
Tiruntán 743 ... E6
Tocache 3,503 ... D7
Tonegrama ... D4
Topará ... D9
Toquepala ... G11
Torata 1,732 ... G11
Tournavista ... E7
Trujillo 241,882 ... C7
Tumbes 32,972 ... B4
Ubinas 384 ... G11
Uchiza 1,999 ... D7
Unini ... F8
Urcos 3,180 ... G9
Urubamba 3,504 ... F9
Vinchos 768 ... E9
Virú 3,205 ... C7
Vitor 200 ... G11
Yambrasbamba 360 ... D5
Yanahuanca 6,278 ... D8
Yanaoca 1,090 ... G10
Yauca 2,043 ... E10
Yauli 1,962 ... D8
Yauri 4,066 ... G10
Yauyos 1,845 ... E9
Yunguyo 4,360 ... H11
Yurimaguas 17,414 ... E5
Zarumilla 5,083 ... B4
Zorritos 3,796 ... B4

OTHER FEATURES

Acarí (riv.) ... E10
Aguaytía (riv.) ... E7
Aguja (pt.) ... B5
Amazon (riv.) ... F4
Andes, Cordillera de los (mts.) ... F10
Apurímac (riv.) ... F9
Azángaro (riv.) ... G10
Azul, Cordillera (mts.) ... E7
Blanca, Cordillera (mts.) ... D7
Blanco (cape) ... B5
Blanco (riv.) ... F6
Boquerón, El (pass) ... E7
Cañete (riv.) ... D9
Casma (riv.) ... C7
Chimbote (bay) ... C7
Chincha (isls.) ... D9
Coles (pt.) ... G11
Cóndor, Cordillera del (range) ... C5
Coropuna, Nudo (mt.) ... F10
Corrientes (riv.) ... E4
El Boquerón (pass) ... E7
El Misti (mt.) ... G11
Ene (riv.) ... E8
Ferrol (pen.) ... C7
Grande (riv.) ... E10
Guañape (isls.) ... C7
Heath (riv.) ... H9
Huallaga (riv.) ... D5
Huasaga (riv.) ... D4
Huascarán (mt.) ... D7
Huayabamba (riv.) ... D6
Ica (riv.) ... E10
Inambari (riv.) ... H9
Independencia (bay) ... D10
Independencia (isl.) ... D10
Junín (lake) ... E8
Juruá (riv.) ... F7
Lachay (pt.) ... D8
Lobos de Afuera (isls.) ... B6
Lobos de Tierra (isl.) ... B6
Locumba (riv.) ... G11
Madre de Dios (riv.) ... G9
Majes (riv.) ... F11
Mantaro (riv.) ... E8
Manú (riv.) ... G8
Marañón (riv.) ... E5
Mayo (riv.) ... D6
Misti, El (mt.) ... G11
Montaña, La (reg.) ... F8
Morona (riv.) ... D5
Nanay (riv.) ... E4
Napo (riv.) ... F4
Negra, Cordillera (mts.) ... D7
Negra (pt.) ... B6
Ñermete (pt.) ... B5
Occidental, Cordillera (range) ... F10
Ocoña (riv.) ... F11
Oriental, Cordillera (range) ... H10
Pachitea (riv.) ... E7
Paita (bay) ... B5
Pampas (riv.) ... E9
Paracas (pen.) ... D9
Parinacochas (lake) ... F10
Pariñas (pt.) ... B5
Pastaza (riv.) ... D5
Pativilca (riv.) ... D8
Perené (riv.) ... E8
Pichis (riv.) ... E8
Piedras, Las (riv.) ... G8
Pisco (bay) ... D9
Pisco (riv.) ... D9
Piura (riv.) ... B5
Puinagua, Canal de (riv.) ... E5
Purús (riv.) ... G8
Putumayo (riv.) ... G4
Rímac (riv.) ... D9
Salcantay (mt.) ... F9
Sama (riv.) ... G11
San Gallán (isl.) ... D9
San Lorenzo (isl.) ... D9
San Nicolás (bay) ... E10
Santa (riv.) ... C7
Santiago (riv.) ... D4
Sechura (bay) ... B5
Tahuamanu (riv.) ... H8
Tambo (riv.) ... G11
Tambopata (riv.) ... H9
Tapiche (riv.) ... E6
Tigre (riv.) ... E4
Titicaca (lake) ... H10
Tumbes (riv.) ... B4
Ucayali (riv.) ... F5

(continued on following page)

Agriculture, Industry and Resources

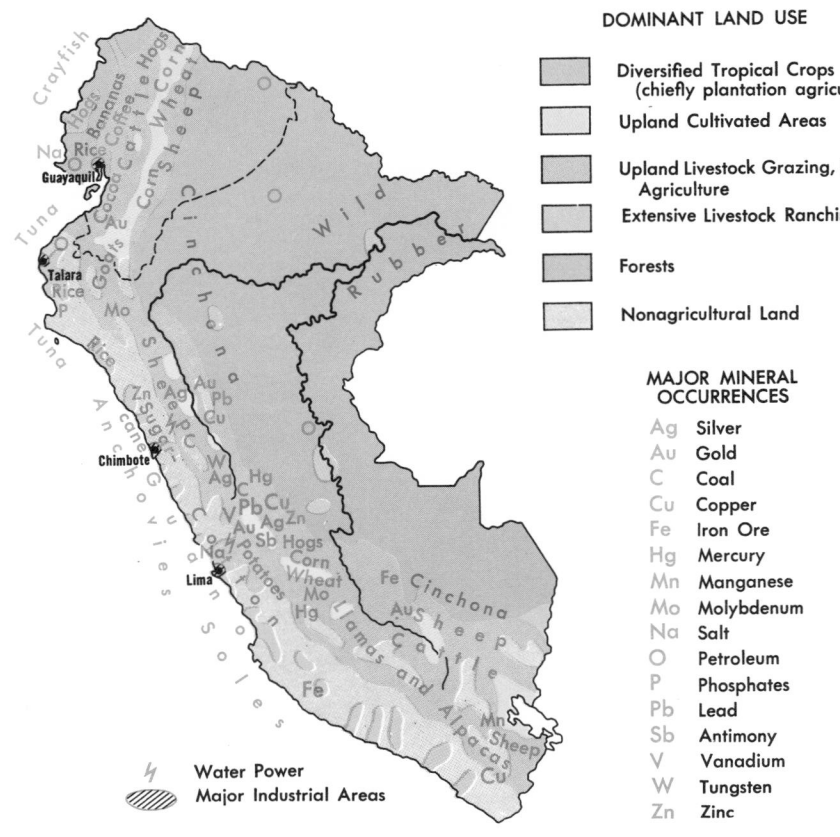

DOMINANT LAND USE

- Diversified Tropical Crops (chiefly plantation agriculture)
- Upland Cultivated Areas
- Upland Livestock Grazing, Limited Agriculture
- Extensive Livestock Ranching
- Forests
- Nonagricultural Land

Water Power
Major Industrial Areas

MAJOR MINERAL OCCURRENCES

Ag	Silver
Au	Gold
C	Coal
Cu	Copper
Fe	Iron Ore
Hg	Mercury
Mn	Manganese
Mo	Molybdenum
Na	Salt
O	Petroleum
P	Phosphates
Pb	Lead
Sb	Antimony
V	Vanadium
W	Tungsten
Zn	Zinc

Agriculture, Industry and Resources

DOMINANT LAND USE

- Diversified Tropical Crops (chiefly plantation agriculture)
- Extensive Livestock Ranching
- Forests

MAJOR MINERAL OCCURRENCES

Al	Bauxite
Au	Gold
D	Diamonds
Mn	Manganese

Water Power

* City and suburbs
○ Population of district.

GUYANA
AREA 83,000 sq. mi. (214,970 sq. km.)
POPULATION 820,000
CAPITAL Georgetown
LARGEST CITY Georgetown
HIGHEST POINT Mt. Roraima 9,094 ft. (2,772 m.)
MONETARY UNIT Guyana dollar
MAJOR LANGUAGES English, Hindi
MAJOR RELIGIONS Christianity, Hinduism, Islam

SURINAME
AREA 55,144 sq. mi. (142,823 sq. km.)
POPULATION 352,041
CAPITAL Paramaribo
LARGEST CITY Paramaribo
HIGHEST POINT Julianatop 4,200 ft. (1,280 m.)
MONETARY UNIT Suriname guilder
MAJOR LANGUAGES Dutch, Hindi, Indonesian
MAJOR RELIGIONS Christianity, Islam, Hinduism

FRENCH GUIANA
AREA 35,135 sq. mi. (91,000 sq. km.)
POPULATION 64,000
CAPITAL Cayenne
LARGEST CITY Cayenne
HIGHEST POINT 2,723 ft. (830 m.)
MONETARY UNIT French franc
MAJOR LANGUAGE French
MAJOR RELIGIONS Roman Catholicism, Protestantism

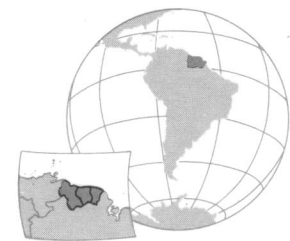

GUYANA

Courantyne (riv.)	C3
Cuyuni (riv.)	B2
Demerara (riv.)	B3
Enwarak (mt.)	B3
Essequibo (riv.)	B3
Great (fall)	B3
Ireng (riv.)	B3
Kaieteur (fall)	B3
Kamaria (falls)	B2
Kuyuwini (riv.)	B4
Kwitaro (riv.)	B4
Leguan (isl.)	B2
Marudi (mts.)	B5
Mazaruni (mts.)	A2
Moruka (riv.)	B2
New (riv.)	C4
Pakaraima (mts.)	A3
Playa (pt.)	B1
Pomeroon (riv.)	B2
Potaro (riv.)	B2
Puruni (riv.)	B2
Roraima (mt.)	A3
Rupununi (riv.)	B4
Sororieng (mt.)	B2
Surwakwima (fall)	A2
Takutu (riv.)	B4
Venamo (mt.)	A3
Waini (riv.)	B2
Wenamu (riv.)	A2

SURINAME
DISTRICTS

Brokopondo 17,763	D4
Commewijne 18,740	D3
Coronie 3,251	C3
Marowijne 25,911	D4
Nickerie 35,178	C3
Para 16,635	D3
Paramaribo 102,297	D2
Saramacca 13,554	C3
Suriname 151,585	D3

CITIES and TOWNS

Ajoewa	C4
Alalapadu	C4
Albina 1,000	D3
Asidonhoppo	D4
Berg en Dal	D3
Bitagron	C3
Brokopondo	D3
Burnside	C3
Calcutta 1,100	C3
Cottica	D4
Domburg 1,200	D3
Groningen 600	D2
Huwelijkszorg	C2
Kwakoegron	D3
Lelydorp 300	D3
Majoli	D4
Mariënburg 3,500	D2
Moengo 2,100	D3
Nieuw-Amsterdam 1,400	D3
Nieuw-Nickerie 7,400	C2
Onverwacht	D3
Paramaribo (cap.) 102,297	D2
Paranam	D3
Totness 1,300	C3
Wageningen 800	C3
Zanderij	D3

OTHER FEATURES

Bakhuys (mts.)	C3
Coeroeni (riv.)	C4
Commewijne (riv.)	D3
Coppename (riv.)	C3
Corantijn (riv.)	C3
Cottica (riv.)	D3
Eilerts de Haan (mts.)	C4
Frederik Willem IV (falls)	C4
Julianatop (mt.)	C4
Kayser (mts.)	C4
Lely (mts.)	D3
Litani (riv.)	D4
Marowijne (riv.)	D3
Nickerie (riv.)	C3
Orange (mts.)	D4
Saramacca (riv.)	C3
Sipaliwini (riv.)	C4
Suriname (riv.)	D3
Tapanahoni (riv.)	D4
Toekomstig (res.)	C3
Van Blommestein (lake)	D3
Wilhelmina (mts.)	C4

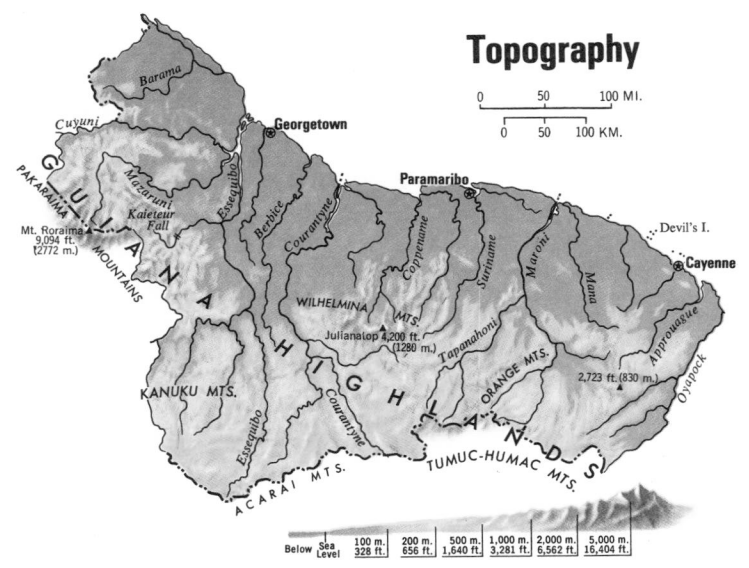

Topography

0 50 100 MI.

0 50 100 KM.

Below Sea Level	100 m. 328 ft.	200 m. 656 ft.	500 m. 1,640 ft.	1,000 m. 3,281 ft.	2,000 m. 6,562 ft.	5,000 m. 16,404 ft.

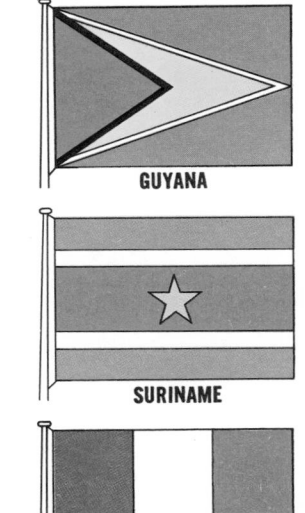

GUYANA

SURINAME

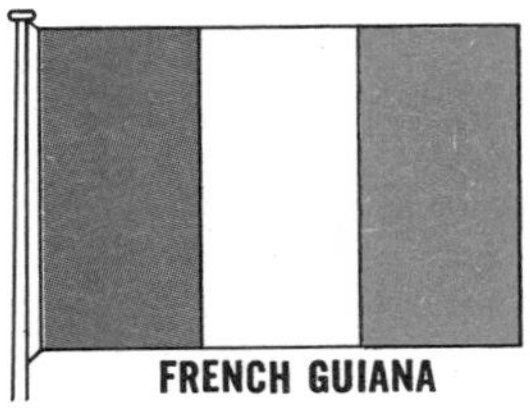

FRENCH GUIANA

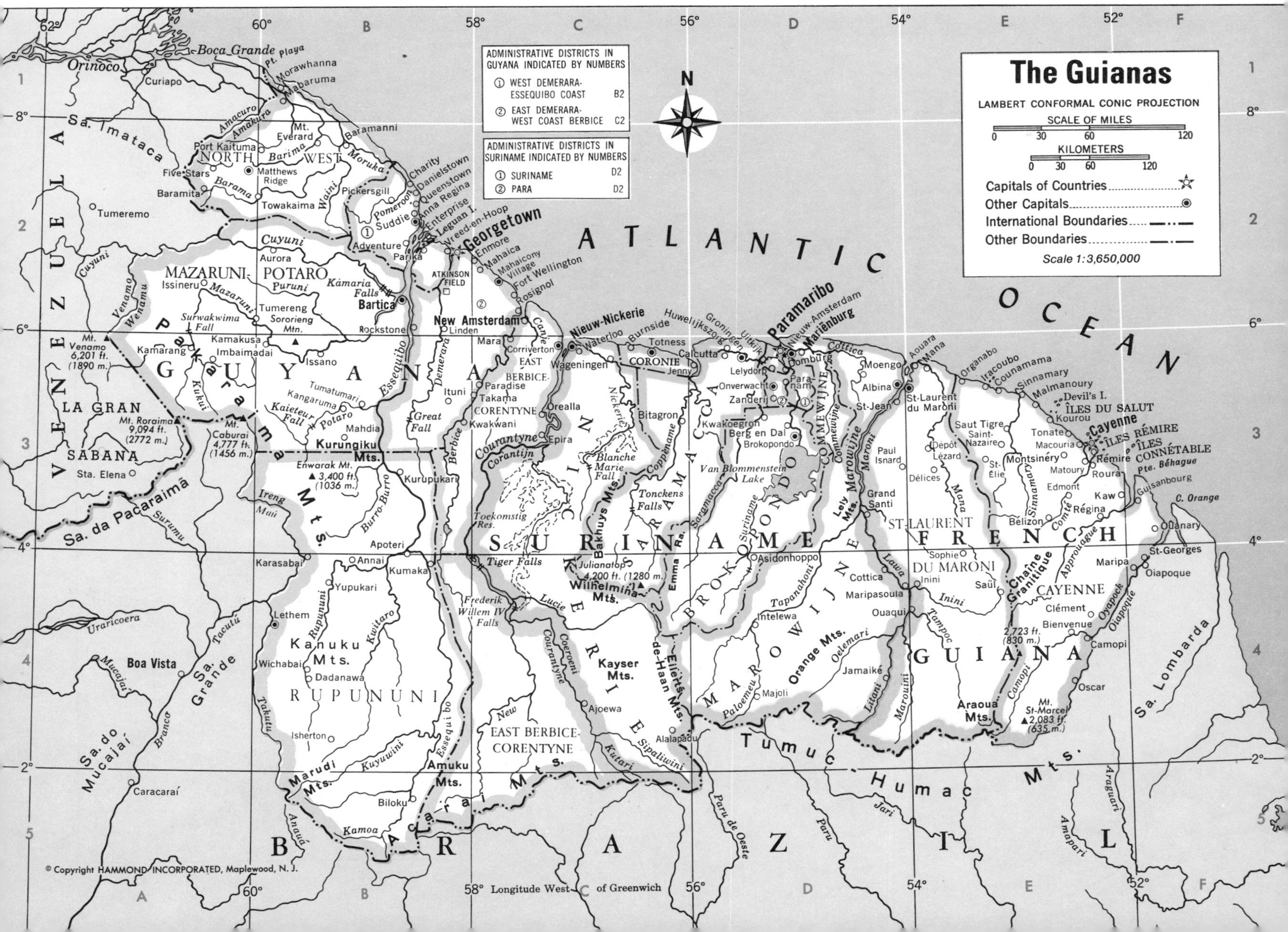

The Guianas
LAMBERT CONFORMAL CONIC PROJECTION

SCALE OF MILES
0 30 60 120

KILOMETERS
0 30 60 120

Capitals of Countries ⭐
Other Capitals ◉
International Boundaries ——·——
Other Boundaries ————

Scale 1:3,650,000

ADMINISTRATIVE DISTRICTS IN GUYANA INDICATED BY NUMBERS
① WEST DEMERARA-ESSEQUIBO COAST B2
② EAST DEMERARA-WEST COAST BERBICE C2

ADMINISTRATIVE DISTRICTS IN SURINAME INDICATED BY NUMBERS
① SURINAME D2
② PARA D2

58° Longitude West of Greenwich

Brazil

BIPOLAR OBLIQUE CONIC CONFORMAL PROJECTION

SCALE OF MILES

KILOMETERS

Capitals of Countries .... ⊛
State Capitals .... ◉
International Boundaries .... –·–·–
State Boundaries .... ——

Scale 1:14,700,000

© Copyright HAMMOND INCORPORATED, Maplewood, N.J.

Brazil
Western Part

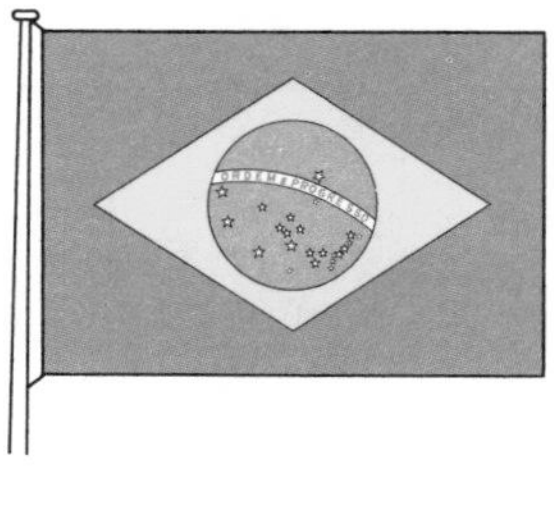

STATES and TERRITORIES

Acre 216,200 ... G10
Alagoas 1,589,605 ... G5
Amapá (terr.) 114,687 ... D2
Amazonas 955,394 ... G9
Bahia 7,508,779 ... F6
Ceará 4,366,970 ... G4
Espírito Santo 1,600,305 ... F7
Federal District 538,351 ... E6
Goiás 2,941,107 ... D6
Maranhão 2,997,576 ... E4
Mato Grosso 1,600,494 ... B6
Mato Grosso do Sul ... C7
Minas Gerais 11,497,574 ... E7
Pará 2,161,316 ... C4
Paraíba 2,384,615 ... G4
Paraná 6,936,743 ... D9
Pernambuco 5,166,554 ... G5
Piauí 1,680,954 ... F4
Rio de Janeiro 4,746,848 ... F8
Rio Grande do Norte 1,552,158 ... G4
Rio Grande do Sul 6,670,382 ... C10
Rondônia (terr.) 113,659 ... H10
Roraima (terr.) 40,915 ... H8
Santa Catarina 2,903,360 ... D9
São Paulo 17,775,889 ... D8
Sergipe 901,618 ... G5

AREA 3,284,426 sq. mi. (8,506,663 sq. km.)
POPULATION 119,024,600
CAPITAL Brasília
LARGEST CITY São Paulo (greater)
HIGHEST POINT Pico da Neblina 9,889 ft. (3,014 m.)
MONETARY UNIT cruzeiro
MAJOR LANGUAGE Portuguese
MAJOR RELIGION Roman Catholicism

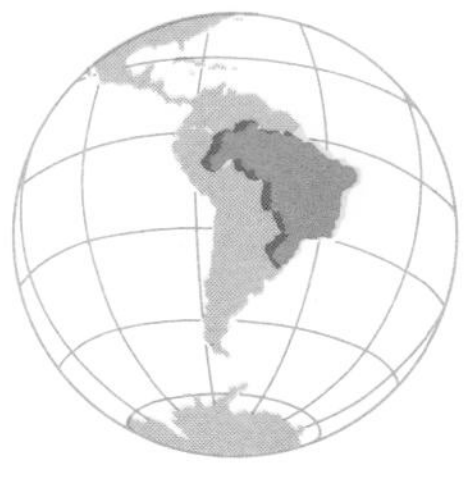

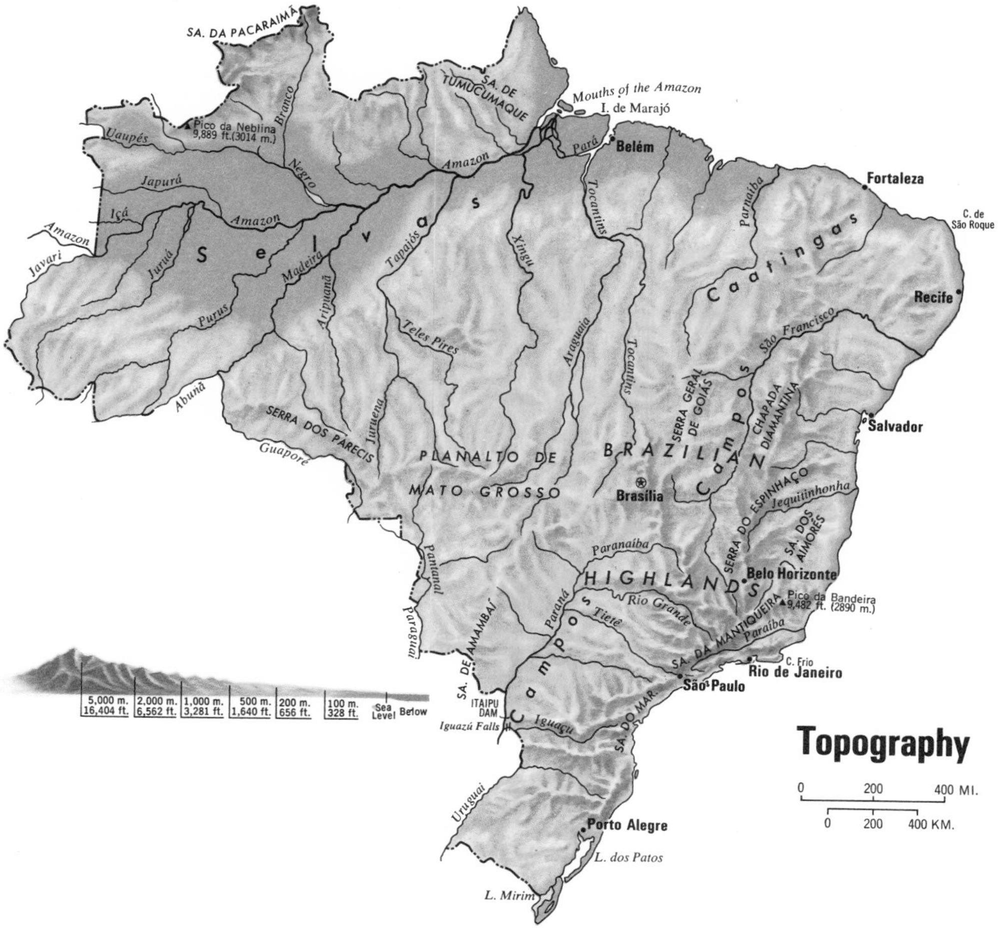

Topography

CITIES and TOWNS

Abaeté 11,174 ... E7
Abaetetuba 19,197 ... D3
Acaraú 4,699 ... F3
Acopiara 6,159 ... G4
Acorizal 770 ... C6
Açu 13,268 ... G4
Afuá 699 ... D3
Agudos 11,901 ... *B3
Alagoa Grande 12,741 ... H4
Alagoinhas 53,891 ... G6
Alcobaça 2,257 ... G7
Alegre 8,312 ... *F2
Alegrete 45,522 ... B10
Além Paraíba 21,758 ... *E2
Alenquer 10,825 ... C3
Alfenas 20,806 ... *D2
Altamira 5,741 ... C3
Alto Araguaia 3,176 ... C7
Alto Parnaíba 1,249 ... E5
Altos 9,734 ... F4
Amambaí 4,400 ... C8
Amapá 1,923 ... D2
Amarante 4,410 ... F4
Amargosa 7,634 ... F6
Americana 62,387 ... *C3
Amparo 19,349 ... *C3
Anápolis 89,405 ... D7
Anchieta 2,022 ... F8
Andaraí 2,243 ... F6
Andradina 43,465 ... D8
Andrelândia 5,952 ... *D2
Angicos 4,683 ... G4
Angra dos Reis 16,513 ... *D3
Anicuns 5,259 ... D7
Antonina 10,737 ... *B4
Aparecida 23,136 ... *D3
Apiaí 3,748 ... *B4
Aquidauana 16,534 ... C8
Aracaju 179,512 ... G5
Aracati 14,509 ... G4
Araçatuba 85,660 ... *A2
Araçuaí 9,180 ... F7
Araguacema 1,715 ... D5
Araguaiana 1,026 ... C6
Araguari 48,702 ... D7
Araioses 3,655 ... F3
Araranguá 12,261 ... D10
Araraquara 82,607 ... *B2
Araras 40,945 ... *C3
Arari 5,550 ... E3
Araxá 31,498 ... E7
Arcoverde 33,308 ... G5
Areia Branca 10,778 ... G4
Aripuanã 89 ... A5
Arraias 1,911 ... E6
Assis 45,531 ... *A3
Aurora 4,972 ... G4
Avaré 29,878 ... *B3
Bacabal, Maranhão 29,251 ... E4
Bacabal, Pará ... B4
Bagé 57,036 ... C10
Bahia (Salvador) 1,501,209 ... G6
Baião 2,441 ... D3
Baixo Guandu 11,558 ... F7
Balsas 7,017 ... E4
Bambuí 10,867 ... *C2
Barão de Cocais 8,178 ... *E1
Barbacena 57,766 ... *E2
Barcelos 821 ... H9
Bariri 11,532 ... *B3
Barra 8,774 ... F5
Barra do Bugres 948 ... B6
Barra do Corda 9,528 ... E4
Barra do Piraí 42,713 ... *E3
Barra Mansa 75,006 ... *D3
Barras 5,776 ... F4
Barreiras 9,855 ... E6
Barreirinha 951 ... B3
Barreirinhas 3,422 ... F3
Barreiros 17,347 ... H5
Barretos 53,050 ... *B2
Batalha 2,143 ... F3
Batatais 21,061 ... *C2
Baturité 8,799 ... G4
Bauru 120,178 ... *B3
Bebedouro 28,824 ... *B2
Bela Vista, Mato Grosso 10,563 ... C8
Bela Vista de Goiás 3,429 ... D7
Belém 934,330 ... E3
Belém‡ 1,000,357 ... E3
Belmonte 7,072 ... G6
Belo Horizonte 1,774,712 ... *D1
Belo Horizonte* 2,534,576 ... *D1
Belterra ... C3
Beneditinos 1,378 ... F4
Benjamin Constant 4,469 ... G9
Bento Gonçalves 18,879 ... C10
Bertolínia 1,121 ... F4
Betim 17,571 ... *D2
Bicas 8,463 ... *E2
Birigui 27,154 ... *A2
Blumenau 85,942 ... D9
Boa Esperança 12,093 ... *D2
Boa Nova ... B5
Boa Vista 16,720 ... H8
Boca do Acre 4,007 ... G10
Bocaiúva 9,417 ... E7
Bom Conselho 10,973 ... G5
Bom Despacho 18,783 ... *D1
Bom Jesus 2,347 ... E5
Bom Jesus da Lapa 12,213 ... F6
Bom Retiro 1,857 ... D10
Bom Sucesso 7,846 ... *D2
Borba 2,274 ... H9
Bragança 16,642 ... E3
Bragança Paulista 39,573 ... *C3
Brasiléia 2,665 ... G10
Brasília (cap.) 1,176,748 ... E6
Brasília de Minas 5,988 ... F7
Brejo 4,438 ... F3
Breves 4,023 ... D3
Brumado 15,416 ... F6
Brusque 32,427 ... D9
Buri 3,295 ... *B3
Buriti 1,868 ... F3
Buriti Alegre 6,192 ... D7
Buriti dos Lopes 2,702 ... F3
Cabedelo 12,811 ... H4
Cabo Frio 25,211 ... *F3
Caçador 18,129 ... D9
Caçapava 24,626 ... *D3
Caçapava do Sul 9,528 ... C10
Cáceres 16,102 ... B7
Cachoeira 11,464 ... G6
Cachoeira do Arari 3,280 ... D3
Cachoeira do Sul 50,001 ... C10
Cachoeiro de Itapemirim 58,968 ... G8
Caeté 18,524 ... *E1
Caetité 6,667 ... F6
Cafelândia 7,527 ... *B2
Caiapônia 4,399 ... C7
Caicó 24,594 ... G4
Cajazeiras 24,079 ... G4
Cajuru 6,960 ... *C2
Caldas Novas 2,636 ... D7
Camaquã 19,771 ... C10
Cambará 11,097 ... *A3
Cambuí 5,665 ... *C3
Cametá 7,965 ... D3
Camocim 12,068 ... F3
Campanha 6,500 ... *D2
Campina Grande 163,206 ... G4
Campinas 328,629 ... *C3
Campo Belo 20,174 ... *D2
Campo Florido 1,758 ... *B1
Campo Formoso 5,033 ... F5
Campo Grande 130,792 ... C8
Campo Largo 15,415 ... *B4
Campo Maior 18,413 ... F4
Campos 153,310 ... *F2
Campos Altos 5,803 ... *C1
Cananéia 1,791 ... *C4
Canavieiras 11,680 ... G6
Cândido Mendes 1,710 ... E3
Canguaretama 6,538 ... H4
Canindé 11,420 ... G4
Canoas 148,798 ... D10
Canoinhas 13,864 ... D9
Cantagalo 5,004 ... *E3
Canto do Buriti 3,224 ... F5
Canutama 1,317 ... G9
Capanema 15,616 ... E3
Capela 5,687 ... G5
Capão Bonito 10,691 ... *B4
Caraguatatuba 10,755 ... *D3
Carandaí 5,779 ... *E2
Carangola 14,924 ... *E2
Caratinga 28,119 ... *E1
Carauari 2,386 ... G9
Caraúbas 4,454 ... G4
Caravelas 3,650 ... G7
Carazinho 28,363 ... C10
Carinhanha 3,079 ... E6
Carolina 8,653 ... E4
Caruaru 101,006 ... G5
Carutapera 2,811 ... E3
Casa Branca 11,660 ... *C2
Casa Nova 2,382 ... F5
Cascavel 5,216 ... G4
Cássia 8,616 ... *C2
Castanhal 24,815 ... E3
Castelo 7,734 ... F8
Castelo do Piauí 4,504 ... F4
Castro 11,887 ... *B4
Castro Alves 9,618 ... G6
Cataguases 32,515 ... *E2
Catalão 15,223 ... D7
Catanduva 48,446 ... *B2
Catolé do Rocha 9,119 ... G4
Catrimani ... H9
Caxambu 13,382 ... *D2
Caxias 31,089 ... F4
Caxias do Sul 107,487 ... D10
Ceará (Fortaleza) 1,308,859 ... G3
Ceará-Mirim 12,880 ... H4
Ceres 11,288 ... D6
Cêrro Azul 1,251 ... *B4
Chapecó 18,576 ... C9
Chaves 431 ... D3
Cícero Dantas 4,092 ... G5
Clevelândia do Norte 826 ... D2
Coari 8,880 ... H9
Codajás 2,397 ... H9
Codó 19,564 ... E4
Colatina 46,012 ... F7
Colinas 4,425 ... F4
Conceição da Barra 4,125 ... G7
Conceição do Araguaia 4,969 ... D5
Concórdia 9,220 ... D9
Conde 3,627 ... G5
Conselheiro Lafaiete 44,894 ... *E2
Corinto 15,554 ... E7
Cornélio Procópio 25,021 ... D8
Coroatá 11,926 ... F3
Coromandel 6,955 ... E7
Corrente 3,354 ... E5
Correntina 2,930 ... E6
Corumbá 48,607 ... B7
Coxim 4,088 ... C7
Crateús 25,022 ... F4
Crato 36,836 ... G4
Criciúma 50,430 ... D10
Cristalina 5,638 ... E7
Cruz Alta 43,568 ... C10
Cruzeiro 42,366 ... *D3
Cruzeiro do Sul 8,426 ... G10
Cubatão 37,255 ... *C3
Cuiabá 83,621 ... C6
Curaçá 1,453 ... G5
Curitiba 1,025,979 ... *B4
Curitiba‡ 1,441,743 ... *B4
Currais Novos 15,858 ... G4
Curuçá 4,372 ... E3
Cururupu 8,544 ... E3
Curvelo 30,225 ... E7
Diamantina 17,551 ... F7
Diamantino 1,264 ... B6
Dianópolis 2,698 ... E5
Divinópolis 69,872 ... *D2
Dois Córregos 8,970 ... *B3
Dom Pedrito 20,522 ... C10
Dores do Indaiá 12,511 ... E7
Dourados 25,977 ... C8
Duque de Caxias 256,582 ... *E3
Eirunepé 3,979 ... G10
Eldorado 1,951 ... *B4
Entre Rios ... C4
Erexim 32,426 ... C9
Erval 1,955 ... C11
Esperança 10,364 ... G4
Esplanada 5,483 ... G5
Estância 20,265 ... G5
Exu 3,627 ... G4
Fagundes ... C4
Faro 1,795 ... B3
Feijó 2,178 ... G10
Feira de Santana 127,105 ... G5
Fernandópolis 27,772 ... *A2
Ferreira Gomes ... D2
Ferros 2,864 ... F7
Flores 2,445 ... G4
Floriano 26,791 ... F4
Florianópolis 115,665 ... E9
Fonte Boa 2,021 ... G9
Formiga 28,719 ... *D2
Formosa 12,255 ... E6
Fortaleza 1,308,859 ... G3
Fortaleza‡ 1,581,457 ... G3
Foz do Iguaçu 18,605 ... C9
Franca 86,852 ... *C2
Fronteiras 2,344 ... F4
Frutal 16,937 ... *B2
Garanhuns 49,579 ... G5
Garça 21,871 ... *B3
Gilbués 573 ... E5
Goiana 24,403 ... H4
Goiandira 3,517 ... E7
Goiânia 362,152 ... D7
Goiás 10,316 ... D6
Governador Valadares 125,174 ... F7
Gradaús ... D4
Grajaú 3,972 ... E4
Granja 6,667 ... F3
Guaçuí 8,984 ... *F2
Guajará-Mirim 10,823 ... H10
Guarapuava 14,419 ... C9
Guaratinguetá 55,069 ... *D3
Guarujá 30,741 ... *C4
Guarulhos 221,639 ... *C3
Guaxupé 17,319 ... *C2
Guimarães 1,994 ... E3
Guiratinga 5,768 ... C7
Gurupá 1,319 ... D3
Gurupi 14,108 ... D5
Humaitá 1,175 ... H10
Ibaiti 6,969 ... *A3
Ibiá 10,102 ... E7
Ibicaraí 15,087 ... G6
Ibipetuba 3,422 ... F5
Ibitinga 14,667 ... *B2
Icó 7,707 ... G4
Igarapava 12,398 ... *C2
Igarapé-Miri 5,690 ... D3
Iguape 8,895 ... *C4
Iguatu 27,851 ... G4
Ijuí 31,879 ... C10
Ilhéus 58,529 ... G6
Imbituba 9,550 ... D10
Imbituva 4,151 ... *A4
Imperatriz 34,709 ... E4
Independencia ... C6
Inhumas 16,626 ... D7
Ipameri 11,572 ... E7
Ipu 8,989 ... F4
Irati 14,820 ... *A4
Itabaiana, Paraíba 14,148 ... H4
Itabaiana, Sergipe 16,425 ... G5
Itaberaba 16,003 ... F6
Itabira 40,143 ... F7
Itabirito 17,469 ... *E2
Itabuna 89,928 ... G6
Itacoatiara 15,881 ... B3
Itaguatins 925 ... D4
Itaí 3,869 ... *B3
Itaituba 2,780 ... C4
Itajaí 54,135 ... D9
Itajubá 42,485 ... *D3
Itamarandiba 2,878 ... F7
Itanhaem 12,278 ... *C4
Itapecerica 8,757 ... *D2
Itapecuru-Mirim 6,224 ... F3
Itapemirim 6,918 ... F8
Itaperuna 26,508 ... *F2
Itapetinga 30,578 ... G6
Itapetininga 42,331 ... *B3
Itapeva 24,240 ... *B3
Itapicuru 1,227 ... G5
Itapipoca 11,902 ... G3
Itapira 25,357 ... *C3
Itapiranga 677 ... B3
Itápolis 9,372 ... *B2
Itaporanga 6,758 ... G4
Itaqui 17,262 ... B10
Itararé 15,696 ... *B4
Itariri 1,751 ... *C4
Itatiba 20,765 ... *C3
Itaúna 32,731 ... *D2
Itu 35,907 ... *C3
Ituaçu 1,558 ... F6
Ituberá 4,833 ... G6
Ituiutaba 46,784 ... D7
Itumbiara 29,917 ... D7
Itupiranga 1,421 ... D4
Iturama 5,204 ... *A1
Ituverava 17,013 ... *C2
Jaboatão 52,537 ... H5
Jaboticabal 29,019 ... *B2
Jacareí 48,684 ... *D3
Jacaréacanga ... B4
Jacarezinho 19,161 ... *A3
Jacobina 18,892 ... F5
Jacupiranga 3,706 ... *B4
Jaguaquara 7,613 ... F6
Jaguarão 16,541 ... C11
Jaguariaíva 7,213 ... *B4
Jaicós 1,760 ... F4
Januária 13,605 ... E6
Japurá 129 ... G9
Jardim 3,119 ... G4
Jataí 26,708 ... D7
Jaú 40,989 ... *B3
Jequié 62,341 ... F6
Jequitinhonha 8,763 ... F7
Jeremoabo 4,952 ... G5
Jerumenha 1,016 ... F4
Joaçaba 11,870 ... D9
João Pessoa 197,398 ... H4
João Pinheiro 8,654 ... E7
Joaquim Távora 4,330 ... *B3
Joinvile 77,760 ... D9
Juazeiro 36,273 ... G5
Juazeiro do Norte 79,796 ... F4
Juiz de Fora 218,832 ... *E2
Jundiaí 145,785 ... *C3
Juruena ... B6
Juruti 3,063 ... B3
Lábrea 3,017 ... G10
Lages 82,325 ... D9
Laguna 16,916 ... D10
Lambari 8,211 ... *D2
Lapa 9,502 ... D9
Laranjeiras do Sul 4,831 ... C9
Lavras 35,489 ... *D2
Leme 23,508 ... *C3
Lençóis 2,272 ... F6
Leopoldina 21,142 ... *E2
Lima Duarte 5,474 ... *E2
Limeira 77,243 ... *C3
Limoeiro 30,726 ... H4
Limoeiro do Norte 6,179 ... G4
Linhares 25,188 ... F7
Lins 38,080 ... *B2
Londrina 156,670 ... D8
Lorena 39,655 ... *D3
Luís Correia 2,170 ... F3
Luz 7,061 ... *D1
Luziânia 9,132 ... E7
Luzilândia 4,155 ... F3
Macaé 29,348 ... *F3
Macaíba 9,935 ... H4
Macapá 51,563 ... D2
Macau 18,853 ... G4
Macaúbas 2,956 ... F6
Maceió 242,867 ... H5
Machado 11,119 ... *C2
Mafra 19,312 ... D9
Magé 19,618 ... *E3
Maloca ... C4
Mamanguape 12,138 ... H4
Manacapuru 5,113 ... H9
Manaus 248,118 ... H9
Manga 2,586 ... E6
Manhuaçu 15,300 ... *E2
Manhumirim 9,638 ... *E2
Manicoré 2,274 ... H9
Marabá 14,593 ... D4
Maracaju 3,410 ... C8
Maragogipe 12,769 ... G6
Maranguape 12,746 ... G3
Marapanim 3,717 ... E3
Marechal Deodoro 5,508 ... H5
Mariana 7,466 ... *E2
Marília 73,165 ... *A3
Maringá 51,620 ... D8
Maruim 6,238 ... G5
Massapê 5,927 ... G3
Mata de São João 12,402 ... G6
Mato Grosso 828 ... B6
Maués 6,011 ... B3
Mazagão 970 ... D3
Miguel Alves 2,214 ... F4
Mimoso do Sul 5,861 ... *F2
Minas Novas 2,213 ... F7
Mineiros 9,836 ... C7
Miracema 12,756 ... *E2
Mirador 973 ... E4
Miranda 3,398 ... C8
Mirassol 16,559 ... *B2
Mocajuba 2,359 ... D3
Mococa 21,082 ... *C2
Mogi das Cruzes 90,330 ... *C3
Mogi-Mirim 28,408 ... *C3
Monte Alegre 6,008 ... C3
Monte Alegre de Minas 5,697 ... D7
Monte Aprazível 8,616 ... *A2
Monte Azul 5,962 ... F6
Monte Dourado 10,000 ... C2
Monteiro 8,699 ... G4
Montenegro 21,497 ... D10
Monte Real ... A5
Monte Santo 2,387 ... G5
Montes Claros 81,572 ... E7
Morrinhos 2,797 ... D7
Morro do Chapéu 3,560 ... F5
Morros 2,153 ... F3
Mossoró 77,251 ... G4
Mucugê 540 ... F6
Mucuri 966 ... G7
Mundo Novo 3,493 ... F5
Munguba 5,000 ... C2
Muqui 4,515 ... F8
Muriaé 34,118 ... *E2
Muzambinho 7,198 ... *C2
Nanuque 34,714 ... F7
Natal 250,787 ... H4
Natividade 1,345 ... E5
Nazaré 16,285 ... G6
Neópolis 7,250 ... G5
Nioaque 3,035 ... C8
Niquelândia 2,193 ... D6
Niterói 291,970 ... *E3
Nossa Senhora do Livramento 933 ... B6
Nova Cruz 8,533 ... H4
Nova Era 9,241 ... *E1
Nova Friburgo 65,732 ... *E3
Nova Granada 5,383 ... *B2
Nova Iguaçu 331,457 ... *E3
Nova Iorque 1,358 ... E4
Nova Lima 27,386 ... *E2
Nova Russas 7,080 ... F4
Novo Hamburgo 81,248 ... D10
Novo Horizonte 13,088 ... *B2
Óbidos 8,657 ... C3
Oeiras 9,626 ... F4
Olímpia 19,571 ... *B2
Olinda 187,553 ... H4
Oliveira 18,557 ... *D2
Oriximiná 6,774 ... C3
Orlândia 15,135 ... *C2
Orleães 3,881 ... D10
Ourinhos 40,733 ... *B3
Ouro Fino 9,122 ... *C3
Ouro Preto 24,050 ... *E2
Palmares 31,281 ... H5
Palmas 9,385 ... C9
Palmeira 7,888 ... *B4
Palmeira das Missões 14,146 ... C9
Pará (Belém) 934,330 ... E3
Paracatu 17,453 ... E7
Pará de Minas 24,071 ... *D1
Paraguaçu Paulista 13,318 ... D8
Paraíba do Sul 9,933 ... *E3
Paranã 1,020 ... E6
Paranaíba 8,410 ... D7

(continued on following page)

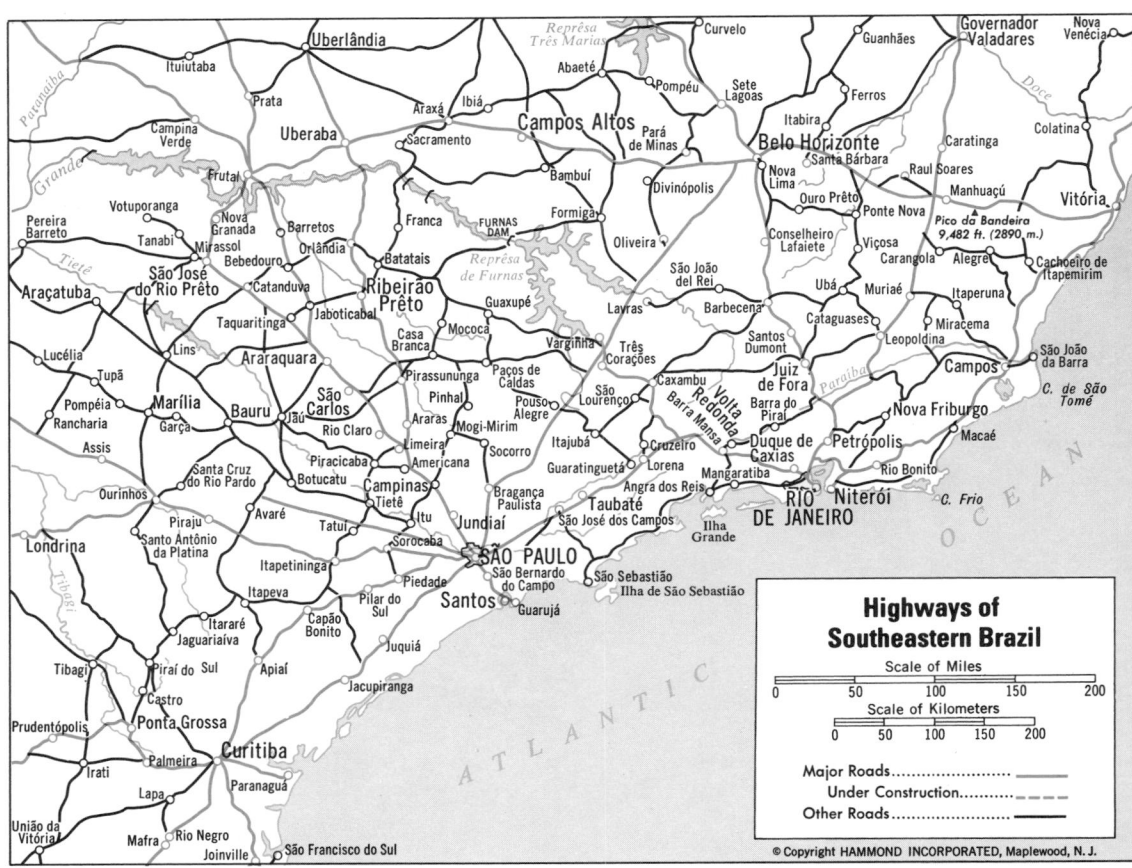

Highways of Southeastern Brazil

Scale of Miles
0   50   100   150   200

Scale of Kilometers
0   50   100   150   200

Major Roads ....
Under Construction ....
Other Roads ....

© Copyright HAMMOND INCORPORATED, Maplewood, N.J.

Agriculture, Industry and Resources

DOMINANT LAND USE

- Diversified Tropical Crops (chiefly plantation agriculture)
- Wheat, Corn, Livestock
- Intensive Livestock Ranching
- Extensive Livestock Ranching
- Forests

MAJOR MINERAL OCCURRENCES

Ab	Asbestos	Fe	Iron Ore	P	Phosphates
Al	Bauxite	Gr	Graphite	Pb	Lead
Au	Gold	Lt	Lithium	Q	Quartz Crystal
Be	Beryl	Mi	Mica	Sn	Tin
C	Coal	Mg	Magnesium	Ti	Titanium
Cr	Chromium	Mn	Manganese	U	Uranium
Cu	Copper	Ni	Nickel	W	Tungsten
D	Diamonds	O	Petroleum	Zn	Zinc

⚡ Water Power

▨ Major Industrial Areas

†Population of metropolitan area.
*Preceding reference indicates that the name will be found on S.E. Brazil Map, page 135.

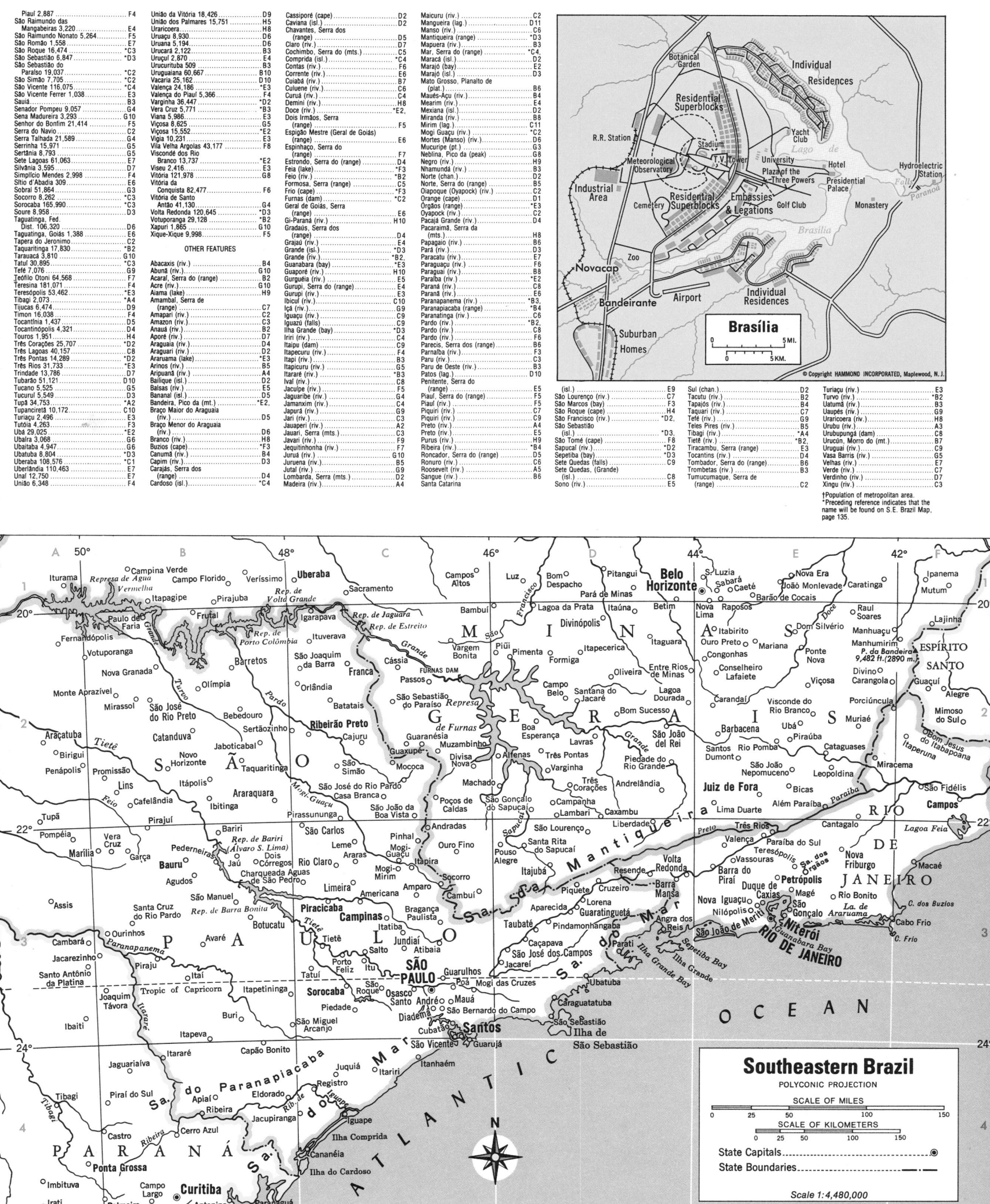

Brasília

0 — 5 MI.
0 — 5 KM.

© Copyright HAMMOND INCORPORATED, Maplewood, N.J.

Southeastern Brazil

POLYCONIC PROJECTION

SCALE OF MILES
0   25   50   100   150

SCALE OF KILOMETERS
0   25   50   100   150

State Capitals .... ◉
State Boundaries ....

Scale 1:4,480,000

© Copyright HAMMOND INCORPORATED, Maplewood, N.J.

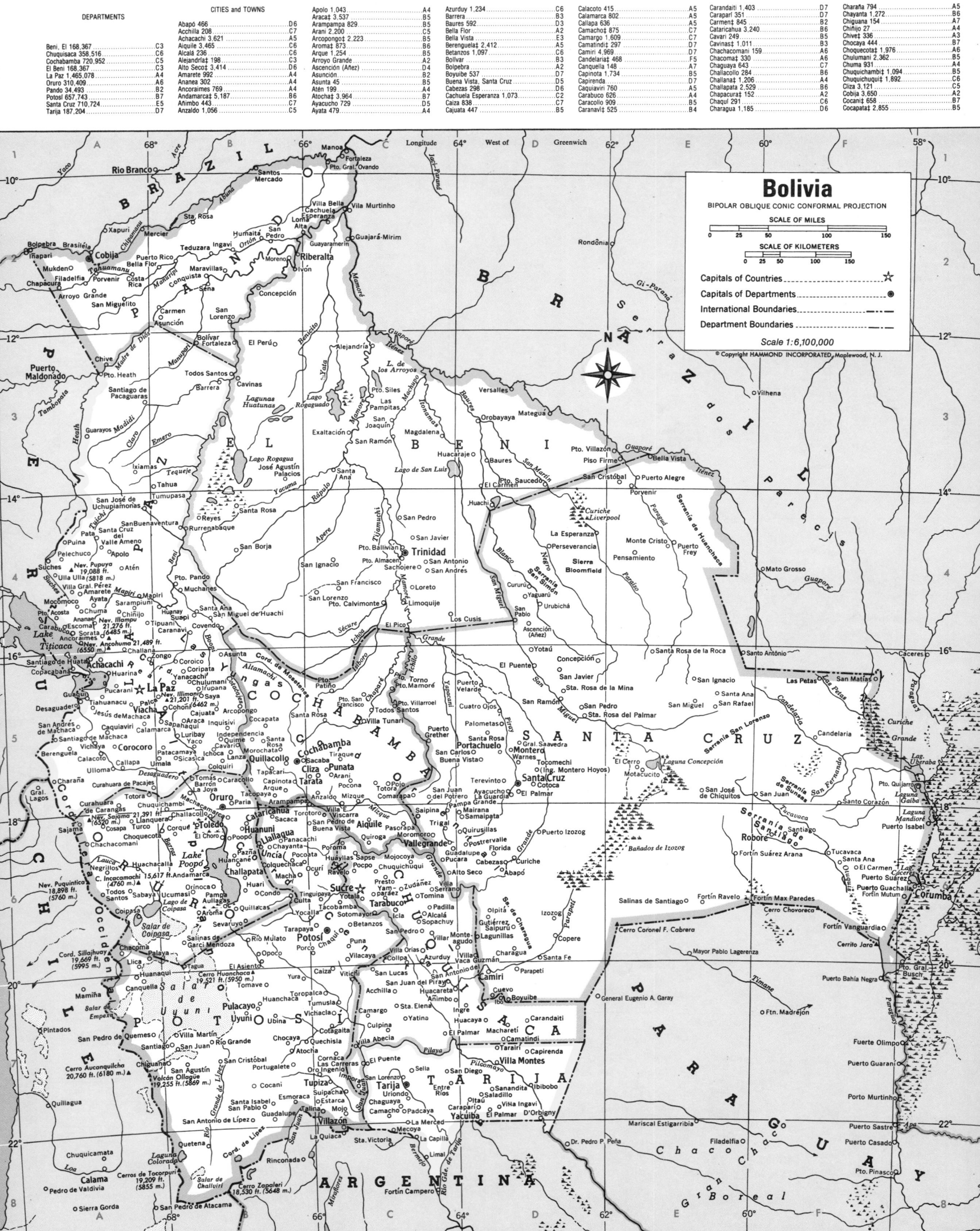

Cochabamba 204,684 C5
Cohoni 890 B5
Coipasa‡ 202 A6
Collpa 481 C6
Colquechaca 1,070 B6
Colquiri 806 B5
Comarapa 1,096 C5
Concepción, El Beni‡ 61 B2
Concepción, Santa Cruz 1,056 D5
Condo‡ 5,525 B6
Conquista‡ 1,162 B2
Copacabana 1,981 A5
Copere D6
Coripata 1,647 B5
Cornaca 264 C7
Corocoro 4,431 A5
Coroico 2,235 B5
Corque 423 B6
Cosapa 297 A6
Costa Rica‡ 43 A2
Cotagaita 1,353 C7
Cotoca 915 D5
Covendo 71 B4
Cuatro Ojos‡ 465 D5
Cuevo 902 D7
Culpina 981 C7
Culta‡ 4,412 B6
Curahuara de Carangas 235 A5
Curahuara de Pacajes 510 A5
Curiche 257 D6
Cururú D4
Desaguadero 201 A5
D'Orbigny‡ 214 D7
El Asiento B6
El Carmen, El Beni 232 D3
El Carmen, Santa Cruz F6
El Cerro 117 E5
El Choro 224 B6
El Palmar, Chuquisaca‡ 772 D7
El Palmar, Santa Cruz 437 D5
El Palmar, Tarija 832 D7
El Perú B3
El Pico C4
El Puente, Santa Cruz‡ 1,185 D5
El Puente, Tarija‡ 1,310 C7
Entre Ríos 1,011 C7
Escoma 220 A4
Esmoraca‡ 1,137 B7
Estarca‡ 2,331 C7
Exaltación, El Beni 405 C3
Filadelfia‡ 942 A2
Florida, Santa Cruz 128 D6
Fortaleza‡ 765 B3
Fortaleza C1
Fortín Campero‡ 87 C8
Fortín Max Paredes F6
Fortín Mutum F6
Fortín Ravelo E6
Fortín Suárez Arana F6
Fortín Vanguardia F6
General Saavedra 1,006 D5
Guadalupe, Potosí 71 B7
Guadalupe, Santa Cruz 2,355 C6
Guaqui 2,266 A5
Guayaramerín 1,470 C2
Huacaraje 673 D3
Huacareta 239 C7
Huacaya 229 D7
Huachacalla 801 A6
Huachi D4
Huanaqui 359 A7
Huanay 574 B4
Huancané 148 B6
Huanchaca B7
Huanuni 5,696 B6
Huari 1,070 B6
Huarina 1,151 A5
Huayllas 206 C6
Humaitá‡ 429 B2
Ibibobo D7
Ibo D7
Ichoca 591 B5
Icla 196 C6
Impora 274 C7
Independencia 1,742 B5
Ingavi‡ 111 B2
Ingeniero Montero Hoyos (Tocomechi) 575 D5
Ingre 162 D7
Inquisivi 530 B5
Irupana 1,937 B5
Itaú 102 D7
Ivón‡ 772 C2
Ixiamas 292 A3
Izozog‡ 2,759 D6
Jesús de Machaca 529 A5
José Agustín Palacios‡ 2,273 B3
La Capilla‡ 1,870 C8
La Esmeralda D8
La Esperanza D4
La Guardia 470 D5
Lagunillas 840 D6
La Joya 401 B5
La Merced‡ 688 C8
Lanza 526 B5
La Paz (cap.) 635,283 B5
Las Carreras 155 C7
Las Pampitas‡ 71 C3
Las Petas‡ 383 F5
Limal‡ 524 C8
Limoquije C4
Llallagua 6,719 B6
Llanquera 613 A6
Llica 560 A6
Loma Alta B2
Loreto 589 C4
Los Cusis D4
Luribay 392 B5
Macha 1,050 B6
Machacamarca 1,746 B5
Macharetí‡ 1,164 D7
Magdalena 1,724 C3
Mairana 508 D6
Manoa C1
Mapiri 289 B4
Maravillas B2
Mateguá 38 D3
Mecoya‡ 585 C8
Mercier‡ 272 B2
Mizque 870 C5
Mocomoco 977 A4
Mojo 469 C7
Mojocoya 498 C6
Monteagudo 971 D6
Monte Cristo E4
Montero 2,713 D5
Moreno B2
Morochata 461 B5
Moromoro 556 C6
Motacucito‡ 585 E5
Muchanes B4
Mukden‡ 84 A2
Negrillos 85 A6
Ocurí 1,531 C6
Opoco B6
Orinoca‡ 2,380 B6
Orobayaya‡ 1,132 D3
Oro Ingenio‡ 945 C7
Oruro 124,213 B5
Padcaya 324 C7
Padilla 2,462 C6
Palaya 300 A6
Palca 887 A5
Palometas‡ 3,453 D5
Pampa Aullagas‡ 1,834 B6
Pampa Grande 727 D5
Panacachi 952 B6
Paria 335 B5
Pasorapa 1,016 C6
Pata 122 A4
Patacamaya 1,278 B5
Pazña 671 B6
Pelechuco 873 A4
Pensamiento E4
Perseverancia D4
Piso Firme D3
Pocoata 859 B6
Pocona 518 C5
Pocpo‡ 2,791 C6
Pojo 1,047 C5
Poopó 736 B6
Porco 817 B6
Poroma 171 C6
Portachuelo 2,456 D5
Portugalete‡ 1,590 B7
Porvenir, Pando‡ 846 A2
Porvenir, Santa Cruz E4
Postrervalle 750 D6
Potosí 77,397 C6
Presto 725 C6
Pucara 762 C6
Pucarani 1,041 A5
Puerto Acosta 1,302 A4
Puerto Alegre E3
Puerto Almacén 358 C4
Puerto Ballivián C4
Puerto Calvimonte C4
Puerto Frey E4
Puerto General Ovando 50
Puerto Grether C5
Puerto Guachalla F6
Puerto Heath‡ 570 A3
Puerto Isabel F6
Puerto Izozog D6
Puerto Mamoré C5
Puerto Pando B4
Puerto Patiño C5
Puerto Quijarro G5
Puerto Rico‡ 539 B2
Puerto San Francisco C5
Puerto Saucedo D3
Puerto Siles 357 C3
Puerto Suárez 1,159 F6
Puerto Torno C5
Puerto Velarde D5
Puerto Villarroel C5
Puerto Villazón D3
Puina A4
Pulacayo 7,984 B7
Puna 852 C6
Punata 5,014 C5
Quechisla 171 C7
Queteña 183 B8
Quillacas 1,170 B6
Quillacollo 9,123 B5
Quime 1,256 B5
Quiroga‡ 3,467 C6
Quirusillas 433 D6
Ravelo 907 C6
Reyes 1,404 B4
Riberalta 6,549 C2
Río Grande 281 B7
Río Mulato 381 B6
Roboré 3,715 F6
Rurrenabaque 1,225 B4
Sabaya 649 A6
Sacaba 2,752 C5
Sacaca 1,778 B6
Sachojere 401 C4
Saipina 573 C6
Sajama 231 A6
Saladillo‡ 1,315 D7
Salinas de Garci Mendoza 335 B6
Salinas de Santiago E6
Samaipata 1,656 D6
San Agustín‡ 810 B7
Sanandita 379 D7
San Andrés 399 C4
San Andrés de Machaca 101 A5
San Antonio, El Beni 436 C4
San Antonio de Lípez‡ 177 B7
San Antonio del Parapetí 497 D7
San Borja 708 B4
San Buenaventura 307 A4
San Carlos 570 D5
San Cristóbal, Potosí‡ 1,200 B7
San Cristóbal, Santa Cruz E3
San Diego‡ 773 D7
San Francisco, El Beni 185 C4
San Ignacio, El Beni 1,757 C4
San Ignacio, Santa Cruz 1,819 E5
San Javier, El Beni 233 C4
San Javier, Santa Cruz 564 D5
San Joaquín 1,959 C3
San José de Chiquitos 1,933 E5
San José de Uchupiamonas 277 A4
San Juan, Potosí 131 B7
San Juan, Santa Cruz‡ 1,482 F5
San Juan del Piray 541 C7
San Juan del Potrero 263 C5
San Lorenzo, El Beni 496 C4
San Lorenzo, Pando‡ 317 B2
San Lorenzo, Tarija 785 C7
San Lucas 925 C7
San Matías 887 F5
San Miguel 502 E5
San Miguel de Huachi 25 B4
San Miguelito A2
San Pablo, Potosí 11 B7
San Pablo, Santa Cruz D4
San Pedro, Chuquisaca 182 C6
San Pedro, El Beni 262 C4
San Pedro, Pando‡ 312 B2
San Pedro, Santa Cruz 80 D5
San Pedro de Buena Vista 1,094 C6
San Pedro de Quemes‡ 290 A7
San Rafael‡ 1,282 E5
San Ramón, El Beni 1,161 C3
San Ramón, Santa Cruz 379 D5
Santa Ana, El Beni 2,225 C3
Santa Ana, La Paz 171 B4
Santa Ana, Santa Cruz 275 E5
Santa Ana, Santa Cruz 663 F6
Santa Cruz, Santa Cruz 254,682 D5
Santa Cruz del Valle Ameno 442 A4
Santa Elena‡ 4,474 C7
Santa Fe D6
Santa Isabel‡ 323 B7
Santa Rosa, Cochabamba‡ 942 B5
Santa Rosa, Cochabamba‡ 276 C5
Santa Rosa, El Beni 765 B4
Santa Rosa, Pando‡ 105 B2
Santa Rosa, Santa Cruz 995 D5
Santa Rosa de la Mina 99 D5
Santa Rosa de la Roca 101 E5
Santa Rosa del Palmar 441 E5
Santiago, Potosí 172 A7
Santiago, Santa Cruz 765 F6
Santiago de Huata 948 A5
Santiago de Machaca 218 A5
Santiago de Pacaguaras A3
Santo Corazón‡ 963 F5
Santos Mercado B1
Sapahaqui 55 B5
Sapse‡ 89 C6
Sarampiuni 138 A4
Saya 339 B5
Sella C7
Sena‡ 660 B2
Sevaruyo 475 B6
Sicasica 1,486 B5
Sopachuy 713 C6
Sorata 2,087 A4
Sotomayor 510 C6
Suapi‡ 1,750 B4
Suches‡ 231 A4
Sucre (cap.) 63,625 C6
Suipacha‡ 2,701 C7
Tacobamba‡ 6,933 C6
Tacopaya 795 B5
Tagua B6
Tahua B3
Talina 122 B7
Tapacarí 980 B5
Tarabuco 2,833 C6
Tarairí‡ 394 D7
Tarapaya 357 B6
Tarata 3,016 C5
Tarija 38,916 C7
Teduzara‡ 271 B2
Terevinto‡ 3,790 D5
Tiahuanacu 1,227 A5
Tinguipaya 766 C6
Tipuani‡ 1,216 B4
Tiraque 1,390 C5
Tocomechi 575 D5
Todos Santos, Cochabamba 408 C5
Todos Santos, La Paz B3
Todos Santos, Oruro 68 A6
Toledo 3,273 B6
Tomás Barrón 1,852 B5
Tomave 201 B7
Tomina 708 C6
Toropalca‡ 199 B7
Torotoro 1,233 C6
Totora, Cochabamba C5
Totora, Oruro A5
Trigal 749 C6
Trinidad, El Beni 27,487 C4
Trinidad, Pando‡ 332 B2
Tucavaca F6
Tumupasa 349 B4
Tumusla‡ 526 C7
Tupiza 8,248 C7
Turco 131 A6
Ubina‡ 462 B7
Ucumasi‡ 1,040 B6
Ulla Ulla 52 A4
Ulloma 116 A5
Umala 481 B5
Uncía 4,507 B6
Uriondo 860 C7
Urubichá 1,369 D4
Uyuni 6,968 B7
Vallegrande 5,094 C6
Versalles 83 D3
Viacha 6,607 A5
Vichacla 317 C7
Vichaya 422 A5
Vilacaya 200 C6
Villa Abecia 539 C7
Villa Bella 88 C2
Villa E. Viscarra 658 C6
Villa General Pérez 802 A4
Villa Ingavi 122 D7
Villa Martín 543 B7
Villa Montes 3,105 D7
Villa Orías 404 C6
Villar 322 C6
Villa Serrano 1,570 C6
Villa Tunari 510 C5
Villa Vaca Guzmán 699 D6
Villazón 6,261 C7
Vitichi 1,515 C7
Warnes 1,571 D5
Yaco 835 B5
Yacuiba 5,027 D7
Yaguarú D4
Yamparaéz 725 C6
Yanacachi‡ 1,964 B5
Yatina‡ 1,850 C7
Yocalla‡ 1,814 B6
Yotala 1,554 C6
Yotaú D5
Yura 136 B7
Zongo 141 B5
Zudáñez 1,868 C6

AREA 424,163 sq. mi. (1,098,582 sq. km.)
POPULATION 5,600,000
CAPITALS La Paz, Sucre
LARGEST CITY La Paz
HIGHEST POINT Nevada Ancohuma 21,489 ft. (6,550 m.)
MONETARY UNIT Bolivian peso
MAJOR LANGUAGES Spanish, Quechua, Aymara
MAJOR RELIGION Roman Catholicism

Topography

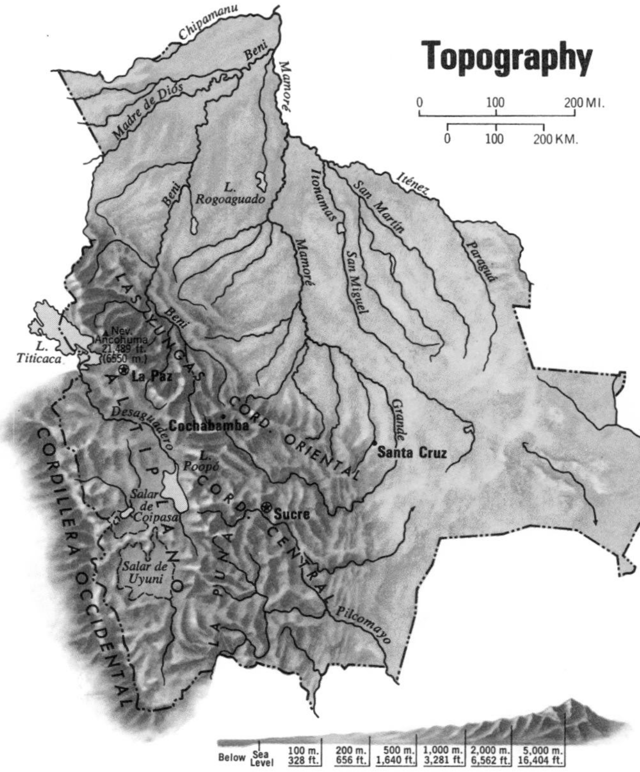
0 100 200 MI.
0 100 200 KM.
Chipamanu
Beni
Mamoré
Madre de Diós
Beni
L. Rogoaguado
Itonamas
San Martín
Iténez
Paraguá
Mamoré
San Miguel
Beni
Nev. Ancohuma 21,489 ft. (6550 m.)
L. Titicaca
La Paz
Desaguadero
Cochabamba
CORD. ORIENTAL
Grande
Santa Cruz
L. Poopó
Salar de Coipasa
Sucre
Salar de Uyuni
CORDILLERA OCCIDENTAL
Pilcomayo
Below Sea Level 100 m. 328 ft. 200 m. 656 ft. 500 m. 1,640 ft. 1,000 m. 3,281 ft. 2,000 m. 6,562 ft. 5,000 m. 16,404 ft.

OTHER FEATURES

Abuná (riv.) B2
Altamachi (riv.) B5
Ancohuma, Nevada (mt.) A4
Apere (riv.) C4
Arroyas, Los (lake) C3
Barras (riv.) B6
Baures (riv.) D3
Beni (riv.) B3
Benicito (riv.) C3
Bermejo (riv.) C8
Blanco (riv.) D4
Bloomfield, Sierra (mts.) D4
Boopi (riv.) B4
Cáceres (lag.) G6
Candelaria (riv.) F5
Capitán Ustarés, Cerro (mt.) E6
Central, Cordillera (range) C6
Challviri (salt dep.) B8
Chaparé (riv.) C5
Charagua, Sierra de (mts.) D6
Chipamanu (riv.) A2
Chovoreca, Cerro (mt.) F6
Claro (riv.) A3
Coipasa (lake) B6
Coipasa (salt dep.) A6
Colorada (lag.) A8
Concepción (lag.) E5
Coronel F. Gabrera E6
Cotacajes (riv.) B5
Desaguadero (riv.) B5
Emero (riv.) B3
Empexa (salt dep.) A7
Gaiba (lag.) F5
Grande (marsh) F5
Grande (riv.) C4
Grande (riv.) C6
Grande de Lípez (riv.) B7
Guaporé (riv.) C3
Heath (riv.) A3
Huanchaca, Cerro (mt.) B7
Huanchaca, Serranía de (mts.) E4
Huatunas (lag.) B3
Ichilo (riv.) C5
Ichoa (riv.) C4
Illampu, Nevada (mt.) A4
Illimani, Nevada (mt.) B5
Incacamachi, Cerro (mt.) A6
Isiboro (riv.) C5
Iténez (Guaporé) (riv.) C3
Itonamas (riv.) C3
Izozog (swamp) E6
Jara, Cerrito (mt.) F6
Las Yungas (reg.) B5
Lauca (riv.) A6
Lípez, Cordillera de (range) B8
Liverpool (swamp) D4
Machupo (riv.) C3
Madidi (riv.) A3
Madre de Diós (riv.) A3
Mamoré (riv.) C2
Mandioré (lag.) F6
Manuripi (riv.) B2
Mizque (riv.) C6
Mosetenes, Cordillera de (range) B5
Negro (riv.) D4
Occidental, Cordillera (range) A6
Ollagüe (vol.) B7
Oriental, Cordillera (range) C5
Ortón (riv.) B2
Otuquis (riv.) F6
Paraguá (riv.) E4
Paraguay (riv.) F7
Parapetí (riv.) D6
Petas, Las (riv.) F5
Pilaya (riv.) C7
Pilcomayo (riv.) D7
Piray (riv.) D5
Poopó (lake) B6
Pupuya, Nevada (mt.) A4
Puquintica, Nevada (mt.) A6
Rápulo (riv.) C4
Real, Cordillera (range) A5
Rogagua (lake) B3
Rogoaguado (lake) C3
Sajama, Nevada (mt.) A6
San Fernando (riv.) F5
San Juan (riv.) C7
San Lorenzo, Serranía (mts.) E5
San Luis (lake) C3
San Martín (riv.) D3
San Miguel (riv.) D4
San Simón, Serranía (mts.) D4
Santiago, Serranía de (mts.) F6
Sécure (riv.) C4
Sillajhuay, Cordillera (mt.) A6
Suches (riv.) A4
Sunsas, Serranía de (mts.) F5
Tahuamanu (riv.) A2
Tarija, Río Grande de (riv.) C8
Tequeje (riv.) B3
Tijamuchi (riv.) C4
Titicaca (lake) A4
Tocorpuri, Cerros de (mt.) A8
Tucavaca (riv.) F6
Tuichi (riv.) A4
Uberaba (lag.) G5
Uyuni (salt dep.) B7
Yacuma (riv.) B3
Yapacaní (riv.) C5
Yata (riv.) C3
Yungas, Las (reg.) B5
Zapaleri, Cerro (mt.) B8

‡Population of canton.

Agriculture, Industry and Resources

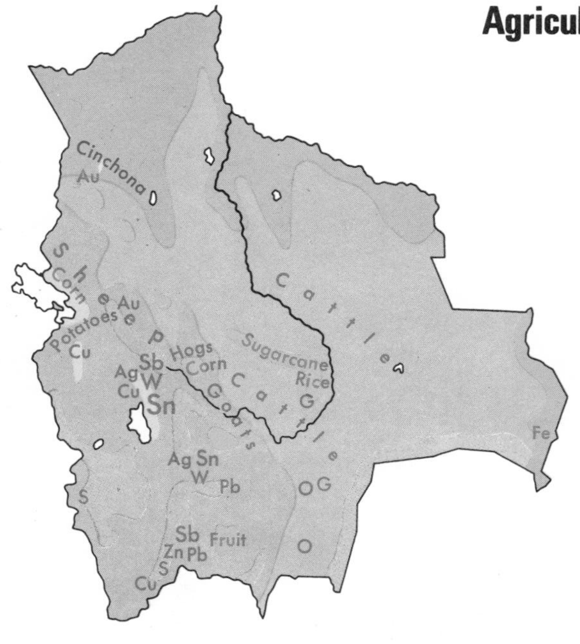
Cinchona
Au
Sheep
Corn
Au
Potatoes
Cu
Ag
Sb
W
Cu
Sn
Hogs
Corn
Sugarcane
Rice
Cattle
Goats
Cattle
Fe
Ag Sn
W
Pb
O G
S
Sb
Fruit
Zn Pb
S
Cu
O

DOMINANT LAND USE

- Diversified Tropical Crops (chiefly plantation agriculture)
- Upland Cultivated Areas
- Upland Livestock Grazing, Limited Agriculture
- Extensive Livestock Ranching
- Forests
- Nonagricultural Land

MAJOR MINERAL OCCURRENCES

Ag	Silver	G	Natural Gas	Sb	Antimony
Au	Gold	O	Petroleum	Sn	Tin
Cu	Copper	Pb	Lead	W	Tungsten
Fe	Iron Ore	S	Sulfur	Zn	Zinc

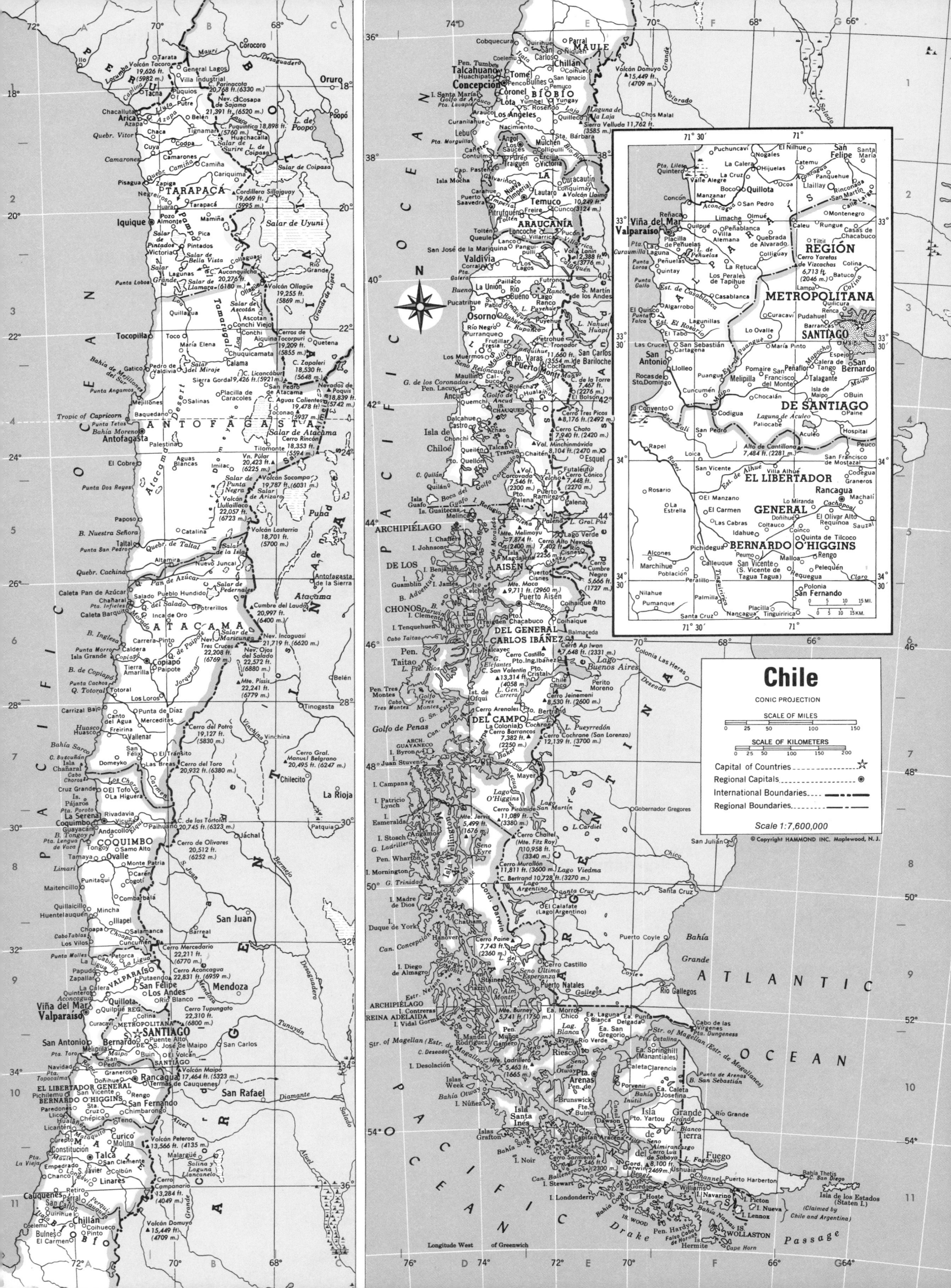

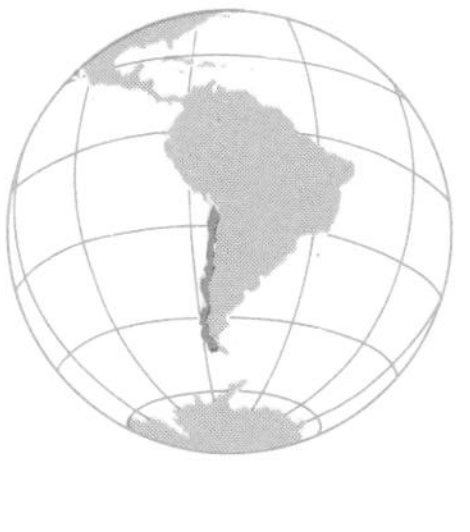

AREA 292,257 sq. mi. (756,946 sq. km.)
POPULATION 11,198,789
CAPITAL Santiago
LARGEST CITY Santiago
HIGHEST POINT Ojos del Salado 22,572 ft. (6,880 m.)
MONETARY UNIT Chilean escudo
MAJOR LANGUAGE Spanish
MAJOR RELIGION Roman Catholicism

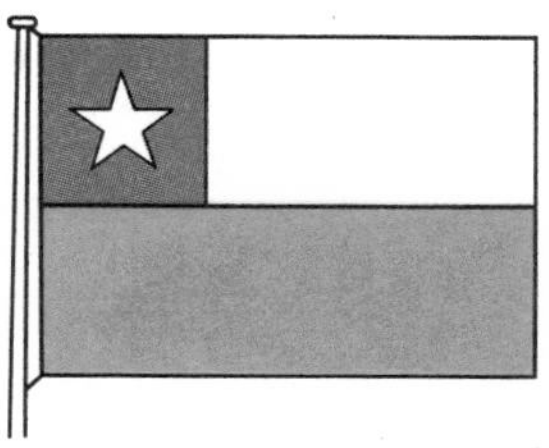

Topography

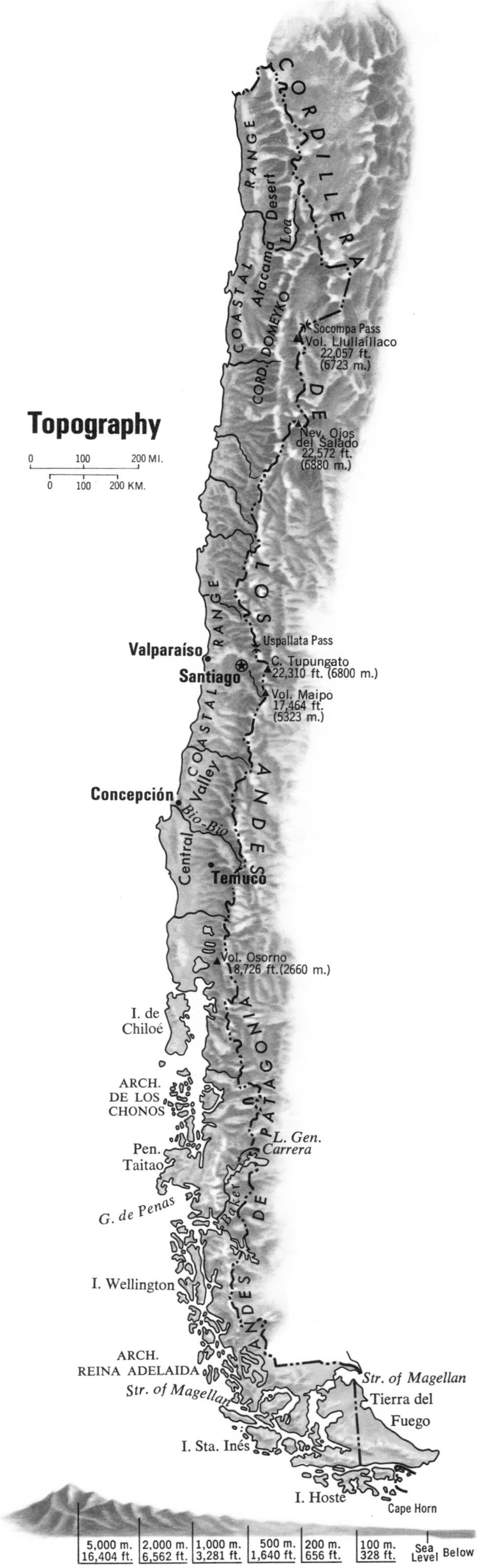
0 100 200 MI.
0 100 200 KM.
CORDILLERA DE LOS ANDES
COASTAL RANGE
Atacama Desert
Loa
CORD. DOMEYKO
Socompa Pass
Vol. Llullaillaco 22,057 ft. (6723 m.)
Nev. Ojos del Salado 22,572 ft. (6880 m.)
Valparaíso
Santiago
Uspallata Pass
C. Tupungato 22,310 ft. (6800 m.)
Vol. Maipo 17,464 ft. (5323 m.)
Central Valley
Concepción
Bío-Bío
Temuco
Vol. Osorno 8,726 ft. (2660 m.)
I. de Chiloé
ARCH. DE LOS CHONOS
Pen. Taitao
L. Gen. Carrera
G. de Penas
Baker
ANDES DE PATAGONIA
I. Wellington
ARCH. REINA ADELAIDA
Str. of Magellan
Tierra del Fuego
I. Sta. Inés
I. Hoste
Cape Horn
5,000 m. 16,404 ft.
2,000 m. 6,562 ft.
1,000 m. 3,281 ft.
500 m. 1,640 ft.
200 m. 656 ft.
100 m. 328 ft.
Sea Level
Below

REGIONS

Aconcagua A9
Aisén del General Carlos Ibáñez del Campo E6
Antofagasta B4
Atacama B6
Bíobío E1
Coquimbo A8
El Libertador General Bernardo O'Higgins A10
La Araucanía E2
Los Lagos D3
Magallanes E10
Maule A11
Santiago, Región Metropolitana de (Santiago Metropolitan Region) A9
Tarapacá B2
Valparaíso A9

CITIES and TOWNS

Achao† 11,501 D4
Aguas Blancas† 203 B4
Algarrobo† 3,941 F3
Ancud 11,900 D4
Andacollo 6,000 A8
Angol 23,500 D1
Antofagasta 125,100 A4
Arauco 5,400 D1
Arica 87,700 A1
Ascotán B3
Baquedano A4
Barrancas† 184,241 G3
Batuco G3
Belén† 925 B1
Boco F2
Buin 11,800 G4
Bulnes 6,900 E1
Cabildo 5,800 A9
Calama 45,900 B3
Calbuco† 21,673 D4
Caldera† 3,268 A6
Calera de Tango† 6,198 G4
Caleta Barquito A6
Caleta Clarencia E10
Caleta Pan de Azúcar A5
Caleu G2
Calle Larga† 7,172 G2
Calleuque F5
Camarones B2
Camiña B2
Cañete 7,900 D2
Canto del Agua A7
Capitán Pastene D2
Carahue† 12,733 D2
Carén A8
Cariquima B2
Carrera Pinto B6
Carrizal Bajo A7
Cartagena† 7,124 F3
Casablanca 5,500 F3
Castro 11,200 D4
Catalina† 1,637 B5
Catemu† 8,728 G2
Cauquenes 20,200 A11
Cerro Castillo† 537 E9
Cerro Manantiales F10
Chaca B1
Chacabuco G2
Chacalluta A1
Chaitén† 4,067 E4
Chañaral† 36,949 A6
Chanco† 12,433 A11
Chépica† 11,199 A10
Chile Chico E6
Chillán 87,600 A11
Chimbarongo 5,300 A10
Choapa A9
Chocalán F4
Chonchi† 8,911 D4
Chuquicamata 22,100 B3
Cobquecura† 6,298 D1
Cochamó† 5,042 E3
Codegua† 6,757 G4
Codigua F4
Codpa† 950 B1
Coelemu 5,400 D1
Cogotí A8
Coihaique 16,100 E6
Coihaique Alto E6
Coihueco† 17,276 A11
Coinco† 4,942 G5
Colbún† 12,924 A11
Colina 7,400 G3
Collaguasi B3
Colliguay F3
Collipulli 7,200 E2
Coltauco† 11,857 F5
Combarbalá† 17,332 A8
Concepción 178,200 D1
Conchi B3
Conchi Viejo B3
Concón F2
Constitución 11,500 A11
Contulmo† 13,987 D2
Copiapó 45,200 B6
Coquimbo 52,700 A8
Coronel 37,300 D1
Corral† 5,533 D3
Cruz Grande A7
Cunco† 18,836 E2
Cuncumén, Coquimbo A9
Cuncumén, Santiago F4
Curacautín 9,800 E2
Curacaví 5,800 G3
Curanilahue 13,200 D1
Curepto† 13,020 A10
Curicó 41,300 A10
Cuya B2
Dalcahue† 7,084 D4
Domeiko A7
Doñihue† 8,837 G5
El Carmen, Ñuble† 13,226 A11
El Carmen, O'Higgins F5
El Cobre A4
El Convento F4
El Manzano F5
El Monte 7,000 G4
El Ñilhue G2
El Quisco† 2,152 E3
El Tabo† 2,180 F3
El Tofo A7
El Tránsito B7
El Volcán B10
Empedrado† 7,887 A11
Ercilla† 8,061 E2
Espejo G3
Estancia Caleta Josefina† 1,042 F10
Estancia Laguna Blanca E9
Estancia Morro Chico† 785 E9
Estancia Punta Delgada E9
Estancia San Gregorio† 1,156 E9
Estancia Springhill (Cerro Manantiales) F10
Freire† 23,313 E2
Freirina† 5,523 A7
Fresia† 15,359 D3
Frutillar† 12,721 D3
Fuerte Bulnes E10
Futaleufú† 2,366 E4
Futrono† 7,109 E3
Galvarino† 9,495 D2
Gatico A4
General Lagos† 810 B1
Graneros 8,900 G5
Guayacán A8
Hijuelas† 7,128 F2
Hospital G4
Huachipato D1
Hualaihué E4
Hualañé† 6,912 A10
Huara† 1,934 B2
Huasco† 4,971 A7
Huentelauquén A8
Illapel 12,200 A8
Imilac B4
Inca de Oro 1,406 B6
Iquique 64,500 A2
Isla de Maipo† 12,903 G4
La Calera 24,600 F2
La Cruz† 8,907 F2
La Estrella† 3,707 F5
Lago Ranco† 12,767 E3
Lago Verde E5
Lagunas† 5,653 B3
Lagunillas F3
La Higuera† 6,991 A7
La Laguna F2
La Ligua 7,500 A9
Lampa† 10,220 G3
Lanco 5,200 D2
La Retuca F3
Las Breas B7
Las Cabras† 12,119 F5
Las Cruces F3
La Serena 61,900 A8
La Unión 15,200 D3
Lautaro 11,900 E2
Lebu 12,500 D1
Licantén† 6,354 A10
Limache 15,200 F2
Linares 37,900 A11
Llay-Llay 9,700 G2
Llico A10
Llolleo F4
Loica F4
Lo Miranda G5
Loncoche† 17,539 D2
Longaví† 15,909 A11
Lonquimay† 9,524 E2
Lo Ovalle F3
Los Andes 23,500 B9
Los Ángeles 49,500 D1
Los Lagos† 14,934 D3
Los Loros B6
Los Muermos† 9,296 D3
Los Perales de Tapihue F3
Los Sauces† 7,613 D2
Los Vilos† 10,453 A9
Lota 48,100 D1
Machalí 5,800 G5
Maipú† 117,872 G3
Maitencillo A8
Malloa† 9,742 G5
Mamiña B2
Manzanar F2
Marchigüe† 4,451 F5
María Elena 5,900 B3
María Pinto† 5,980 G3
Maullín† 14,544 D4
Mayer E7
Mejillones† 3,333 A4
Melinca D5
Melipilla 23,900 F4
Merceditas B7
Mincha† 11,329 A8
Molina 9,400 A10
Montenegro G2
Monte Patria† 18,927 A8
Mulchén 13,700 E1
Nacimiento† 17,651 D1
Nancagua† 11,076 F6
Navidad† 6,618 A10
Negreiros† 1,144 B2
Nilahue E6
Ñiquén† 13,640 E1
Nogales† 18,529 F2
Nueva Imperial 8,000 D2
Nuevo Juncal B5
Ocoa G2
Olivar Alto† 5,414 G5
Olmué† 8,804 F2
Osorno 68,800 D3
Ollagüe B3
Ovalle 31,700 A8
Paihuano† 6,048 B8
Paillaco 5,200 D3
Paine† 21,876 G4
Paipote B6
Palena† 2,508 E5
Palestina B4
Paliocabe (Payocabe) F4
Palmilla† 7,965 F6
Panguipulli 5,700 E2
Panquehue† 4,230 G2
Paposo A5
Papudo† 2,594 A9
Paredones† 7,404 A10
Parral 17,000 A11
Pedro de Valdivia 6,200 B4
Pelequén G5
Pemuco† 7,577 E1
Peñablanca F2
Peñaflor 15,500 G4
Penco† 33,962 D1
Peñuelas F3
Petorca† 8,343 A9
Petrohué E3
Peuco G4
Peumo† 11,308 F5
Pica† 1,487 B2
Pichidegua† 13,550 F5
Pichilemu† 8,042 A10
Pintados B2
Pinto† 8,687 A11
Pisagua† 1,880 A2
Pitrufquén 7,800 D2
Placilla† 6,441 F6
Placilla de Caracoles B4
Placilla de Peñuelas F2
Población F5
Polonia G6
Pomaire F4
Porvenir† 3,600 E10
Potrerillos 5,800 B6
Pozo Almonte† 1,798 B2
Puangue F4
Pucatrihue D3
Puchuncaví† 7,542 F2
Pucón† 16,872 E2
Pudahuel G3
Pueblo Hundido 6,200 B6
Puente Alto 65,100 B10
Puerto Aisén 7,100 E6
Puerto Bertrand E7
Puerto Chacabuco D6
Puerto Cisnes† 2,800 E5
Puerto Ingeniero Ibáñez† 1,900 E6
Puerto Montt 62,700 E4
Puerto Natales 11,500 E9
Puerto Palena D5
Puerto Quellón† 7,734 D4
Puerto Varas 10,900 E3
Puerto Williams† 949 F11
Pumanque† 3,137 F6
Punitaqui† 16,167 A8
Punta Arenas 61,800 E10
Punta de Díaz B7
Puquios B1
Purén† 11,604 D2
Purranque 5,900 D3
Putaendo† 12,806 A9
Putre† 855 B1
Puyehue E3
Quebrada de Alvarado F2
Queilén† 6,055 D4
Quemchi† 6,707 D4
Queule D2
Quilicura 8,100 G3
Quillagua B3
Quillaicillo A8
Quilleco† 16,043 E1
Quillota 36,500 F2
Quilpué 40,600 F2
Quinta de Tilcoco† 6,513 G5
Quintay F3
Quintero 9,900 F2
Quirihue† 11,178 E1
Rancagua 86,500 G5
Rapel F4
Reñaca F2
Renca† 67,168 G3
Rengo 12,400 G5
Requegua G5
Requínoa† 10,730 G5
Retiro† 15,146 A11
Rinconada San Martín† 4,118 G2
Río Blanco B9
Río Bueno 9,600 D3
Río Cisnes E5
Río Negro 5,100 D3
Río Verde† 554 E10
Rivadavia A7
Rocas de Santo Domingo† 4,114 F4
Rolecha D4
Rosario† 3,383 F5
Rungue G2
Salado A6
Salamanca† 18,741 A9
Salinas B4
Samo Alto† 5,689 A8
San Antonio 46,700 F3
San Bernardo† 117,766 G4
San Carlos 17,000 E1
San Clemente† 23,273 A11
San Felipe 26,100 G2
San Félix A7
San Fernando 23,600 G6
San Francisco de Mostazal† 11,439 G4
San Ignacio† 13,523 E1
San Javier 10,800 A11
San José de la Mariquina D2
San José de Maipo† 9,601 B10
San Pablo† 7,978 D3
San Pedro, Santiago† 8,255 F4
San Pedro, Valparaíso F2
San Pedro de Atacama C4
San Rosendo† 14,337 E1
Santa Bárbara† 14,345 E1
Santa Cruz 8,600 F6
Santa María† 8,162 G2
Santiago (cap.) 2,728,600 G3
Santiago* 3,691,548 G3
San Vicente F4
San Vicente (San Vicente de Tagua)† 28,333 F5
Sauzal G5
Sierra Gorda† 8,805 B4
Talagante 16,500 G4
Talca 94,400 A11
Talcahuano 148,300 D1
Taltal 6,400 A5
Tamaya A8
Tarapacá B2
Temuco 110,300 E2
Teno† 17,675 A10
Termas de Cauquenes B10
Tierra Amarilla† 7,899 A6
Tignamar B1
Tilomonte B4
Tiltil† 9,198 G2
Tinguiririca G6
Toco† 8,734 B3
Toconao C4
Tocopilla 22,000 A3
Toltén† 16,265 D2
Tomé 29,600 D1
Tongoy A8
Totoral A6
Traiguén 11,400 D2
Valdivia 82,300 D3
Valle Alegre F2
Vallenar 26,800 A7
Valparaíso 250,400 E2
Victoria, Malleco 16,500 D2
Victoria, Tarapacá A3
Vicuña 5,100 A8
Villa Alemana 29,600 F2
Villa Alhué† 5,078 G4
Villa Industrial B1
Villarrica 13,000 E2
Viña del Mar 182,000 F2
Yumbel† 21,858 E1
Yungay† 10,725 E1
Zapallar† 2,894 A9
Zapiga B2

OTHER FEATURES

Aconcagua (riv.) F2
Aculeo (lag.) G4
Adventure (bay) D5
Aguas Calientes, Cerro (mt.) C4
Alhué, Estero de (riv.) F4
Almeida, Sierra (mts.) C4
Almirantazgo (bay) F11
Almirante Montt (gulf) D9
Alto de Cantillana (mt.) G4
Alto Nevado, Cerro (mt.) E5
Ancud (gulf) D4
Andes, Cordillera de los (mts.) C5,E
Angamos (isl.) D8
Angamos (pt.) A4
Ap Iwan, Cerro (mt.) E6
Arauco (gulf) D1
Arenales, Cerro (mt.) D7
Ascotán, Salar de (salt dep.) B3
Atacama (des.) B4
Atacama, Salar de (salt dep.) C4
Aucanquilcha, Cerro (mt.) B3
Azapa, Quebrada (riv.) B1
Baker (riv.) D7
Ballenero (chan.) E11
Barrancos, Cerro (mt.) D7
Bascuñán (cape) A7
Beagle (chan.) E11
Bella Vista, Salar de (salt dep.) B3
Benjamín (isl.) D5
Bertrand, Cerro (mt.) D8
Bío-Bío (riv.) E2
Blanca (lag.) E10
Blanco (lake) F10
Bravo (riv.) D7
Brunswick (pen.) E10
Bueno (riv.) D3
Buenos Aires (lake) E6
Burney (mt.) D9
Byron (isl.) D7
Cachapoal (riv.) G5
Cachina, Quebrada (riv.) A5
Cachos (pt.) A6
Calafquén (lake) E3
Camarones (riv.) A2
Camiña, Quebrada (riv.) B2
Campana (isl.) D7
Campanario, Cerro (mt.) A10
Cantillana, Alto de (mt.) G4
Capitán Aracena (isl.) E10
Carmen (riv.) B7
Casablanca, Estero de (riv.) F3
Castillo, Cerro (mt.) E6
Catalina (pt.) F10
Chaffers (isl.) D5
Chaltel, Cerro (mt.) E8
Chañaral (isl.) A7
Chatham (isl.) D9
Chato, Cerro (mt.) E4
Chauques (isls.) D4
Cheap (chan.) D7
Chiloé (isl.) D4
Choapa (riv.) A9
Chonos (arch.) D6

(continued on following page)

Agriculture, Industry and Resources

DOMINANT LAND USE

- Cereals, Livestock
- Mediterranean Agriculture (cereals, fruit, livestock)
- Pasture Livestock
- Extensive Livestock Ranching
- Limited Seasonal Grazing
- Forests
- Nonagricultural Land

MAJOR MINERAL OCCURRENCES

Ag	Silver	Hg	Mercury
Au	Gold	Id	Iodine
C	Coal	Mn	Manganese
Cu	Copper	Mo	Molybdenum
Fe	Iron Ore	N	Nitrates
G	Natural Gas	Na	Salt
Gp	Gypsum	O	Petroleum
		S	Sulfur

⚡ Water Power   ▧ Major Industrial Areas

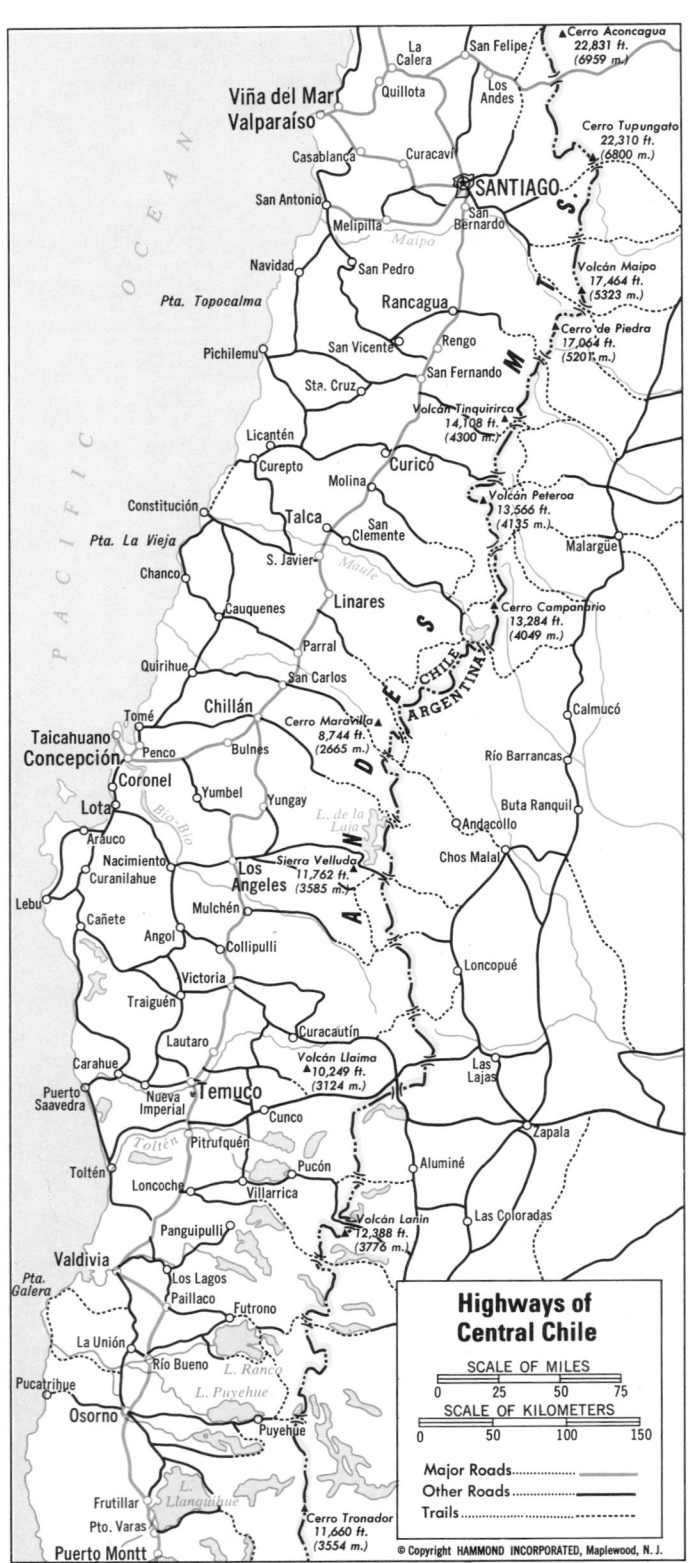

Highways of Central Chile

SCALE OF MILES
0   25   50   75

SCALE OF KILOMETERS
0   50   100   150

Major Roads
Other Roads
Trails

© Copyright HAMMOND INCORPORATED, Maplewood, N. J.

PROVINCES

Buenos Aires 10,796,036 D4
Catamarca 206,204 C2
Chaco 692,410 D2
Chubut 262,196 C5
Córdoba 2,407,135 D3
Corrientes 657,716 E2
Distrito Federal 2,908,001 H7
Entre Ríos 902,241 E3
Formosa 292,479 D1
Jujuy 408,514 C1
La Pampa 207,132 C4
La Rioja 163,342 C2
Mendoza 1,187,305 C4
Misiones 579,579 F2
Neuquén 241,904 C4
Río Negro 383,896 C5
Salta 662,369 D1
San Juan 469,973 C3
San Luis 212,837 C3
Santa Cruz 114,479 C6
Santa Fe 2,457,188 D3
Santiago del Estero 652,318 D2
Tierra del Fuego, Antártida, e Islas d 29,066 C7
Tucumán 968,066 C2

CITIES and TOWNS

Abra Pampa 2,091 C1
Acevedo 1,263 F6
Acuña G5
Adolfo Alsina 6,323 D4
Aguaray 5,069 D1
Aguilares 11,924 C2
Aimogasta 4,134 C2
Alberti 5,792 G7
Alcaraz 1,518 G5
Alcorta 4,996 F6
Alejandra 1,381 F5
Algarrobo del´guila C4
Allen 9,380 C4
Alpachiri 1,374 D4
Alta Gracia 24,371 D3
Aluminé 1,098 B4
Alvear 2,258 E2
Ameghino 3,195 D3
Añatuya 11,918 D2
Andacollo B4
Andalgalá 5,687 C2
Antofagasta de la Sierra C2
Apóstoles 8,111 E2
Arrecifes 13,503 F7
Arribeños 2,286 F7
Arroyo Seco 11,969 F6
Ascensión 2,888 F7
Avellaneda 337,538 G7
Ayacucho 12,046 E4
Azul 36,023 E4
Bahía Blanca 182,158 D4
Bahía Bustamante C6
Bahía Thetis C7
Baigorrita 1,426 F7
Balcarce 26,461 E4
Balnearia 4,502 D3
Bandera 1,920 D2
Baradero 16,026 G6
Barrancas 29,107 F6
Barranqueras E2
Barreal C3
Basavibaso 7,338 G6
Belén 6,152 C2
Bella Vista, Corrientes 10,554 E2
Bella Vista, Tucumán 7,013 D2
Bell Ville 22,528 D3
Bernardo de Irigoyen 1,206 F2
Bernasconi 1,563 D4
Bolívar 18,643 D4
Bovril 2,988 G5
Bragado 23,366 F7
Buena Esperanza 1,192 C3
Buenos Aires (cap.) 2,908,001 H7
Buenos Aires* 9,749,000 H7
Bustinza F6
Buta-Ranquil C4
Cabo Vírgenes C7
Cachi 1,018 C2
Cafayate 3,365 C2
Calafate B7
Calchaquí 4,362 F5
Caleta Olivia 13,366 C6
Caleufú 1,081 C4
Camarones C5
Campana 33,919 G6
Cañada de Gómez 20,611 F6
Canals 6,331 D3
Captain Bermúdez F6
Cañuelas 10,390 G7
Carabelas 1,029 F6
Carcarañá 8,201 F6
Carlos Casares 10,775 F7
Carlos Tejedor 3,555 D4
Carmen de Areco 6,556 F7
Carmen de Patagones 10,587 D5
Casilda 19,240 F6
Castelli, Buenos Aires 3,658 H7
Castelli, Chaco D2
Catamarca 64,410 C2
Catriló 1,697 D4
Caucete 10,719 C3
Cayasta 1,554 F5
Cayastacito F5
Ceres 9,108 D2
Chabás 3,812 F6
Chacabuco 23,660 F7
Chajarí 10,720 G5
Chamical 4,634 C3
Charadai D2
Charata 7,975 D2
Chascomús 17,103 H7
Chepes 4,108 C3
Chicoana 1,274 C2
Chilecito 11,234 C2
Chivilcoy 37,190 F7
Choele-Choel 3,510 C4
Chos-Malal 2,545 C4
Chumbicha 2,118 C2
Cinco Saltos 11,122 C4
Cipolletti 23,768 C4
Clorinda 16,125 E2
Colón, Buenos Aires 12,530 F6
Colón, Entre Ríos 10,122 G6
Colonia Elisa 1,047 E2
Colonia Josefa D4
Colonia Las Heras 2,151 C6
Comandante Fontana 2,752 D2
Comandante Luis Piedrabuena 2,586 C6
Comodoro Rivadavia 72,906 C6
Concepción, Corrientes 2,679 E2
Concepción, Tucumán 20,694 C2
Concepción de la Sierra 2,457 E2

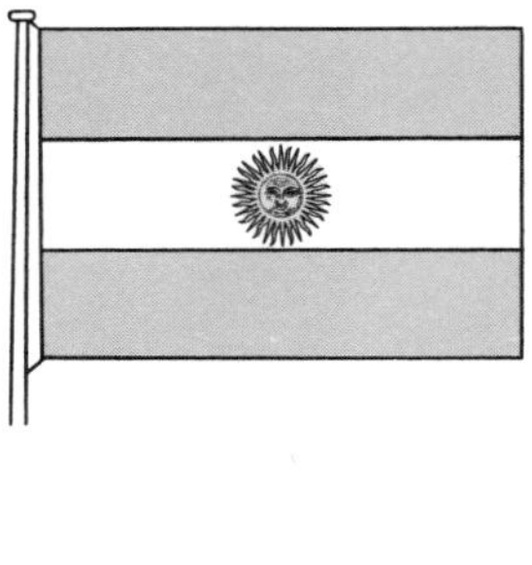

AREA 1,072,070 sq. mi. (2,776,661 sq. km.)
POPULATION 27,862,771
CAPITAL Buenos Aires
LARGEST CITY Buenos Aires
HIGHEST POINT Cerro Aconcagua 22,831 ft. (6,959 m.)
MONETARY UNIT Argentine peso
MAJOR LANGUAGE Spanish
MAJOR RELIGION Roman Catholicism

Agriculture, Industry and Resources

DOMINANT LAND USE

- Wheat, Livestock
- Wheat, Corn, Livestock
- Diversified Tropical Crops (chiefly plantation agriculture)
- Truck Farming, Horticulture, Special Crops
- Intensive Livestock Ranching
- Upland Livestock Grazing, Limited Agriculture
- Extensive Livestock Ranching
- Forests
- Nonagricultural Land

MAJOR MINERAL OCCURRENCES

Ag	Silver	O	Petroleum
Be	Beryl	Pb	Lead
C	Coal	S	Sulfur
Cu	Copper	Sn	Tin
Fe	Iron Ore	U	Uranium
G	Natural Gas	W	Tungsten
Mn	Manganese	Zn	Zinc
Na	Salt		

Water Power
Major Industrial Areas

Concepción del Uruguay 38,967 G6
Concordia 72,136 G5
Constanza G6
Copacabana C2
Córdoba 790,508 D3
Coronda 9,100 F6
Coronel Bogado 1,432 F6
Coronel Brandsen 7,688 H7
Coronel Dorrego 10,448 D4
Coronel Moldes 1,617 C2
Coronel Pringles 16,228 D4
Coronel Suárez 14,570 D4
Coronel Vidal 3,746 E4
Corral de Bustos 7,296 D3
Corrientes 136,924 E2
Cosquín 11,436 D3
Coto D2
Crespo 7,615 F6
Cruz del Eje 23,401 C3
Cuadro Nacional 1,690 C3
Cuchillo-Có D4
Curuzú Cuatiá 20,636 G5
Cutral-Có 19,404 C4
Daireaux 6,614 D4
Deán Funes 15,592 D3
Del Valle F7
Diamante 12,686 F6
Díaz 1,311 F6
Doblas 1,231 D4
Dolavon 1,281 C5
Dolores 17,414 E4
Domínguez G6
Dudignac 2,377 F7
Eduardo Castex 3,739 D4
El Bolsón 2,678 B5
El Chorro D1
El Cuy C4
Eldorado 14,057 F2
El Huecu B4
Elisa F5
El Maitén B5
El Milagro 1,824 C3
Elortondo 4,026 F6
El Pintado D1
El Piquete D1
El Quebrachal D2
Embarcación 7,207 D1
Emilio Ayarza 1,050 F7
Empedrado 4,269 E2
Enrique Carbó G6
Ensenada 31,586 H7
Escobar 36,278 G7
Esperanza 17,636 F5
Espinillo 1,249 E2
Esquel 13,771 B5
Esquina 6,931 G5
Facundo C6
Famatina 1,204 C2
Federación 4,876 G5
Felipe Yofré G4
Fernández 4,800 D2
Fiambalá 1,119 C2
Firmat 11,127 F6
Formosa 61,071 E2
Fortín Olmos F4
French 1,109 F7
Frías 12,421 D2
Gaiman 1,702 C5
Gálvez 12,195 F6
Gan Gan C5
Gastre C5
General Acha 6,270 C4
General Alvear, Buenos Aires 4,875 F7
General Alvear, Mendoza 17,277 C3
General Arenales 2,855 F7
General Belgrano 9,213 G7
General Campos 1,475 G5
General Conesa 3,117 C5
General Galarza C6
General Güemes 11,159 D1
General Guido 1,073 E4
General José de San Martín 9,588 E2
General Juan Madariaga 10,280 E4
General La Madrid 5,523 D4
General Las Heras 4,972 G7
General Lavalle 1,103 E4
General O'Brien 1,771 F7
General Paz 4,327 H7
General Pico 21,897 D4
General Ramírez 4,439 F6
General Roca 29,320 C4
General San Martín 1,883 D4
General San Martín G4
General Viamonte 8,896 F7
General Villegas 8,884 D4
Gobernador Crespo 2,527 F5
Gobernador Gregores 1,139 C6
Gobernador Mansilla 1,050 G6
Godoy Cruz 112,481 C3
Gorchs G7
Goya 39,367 G4
Gualeguay 20,401 G6
Gualeguaychú 40,661 G6
Guandacol 1,073 C2
Guardia Mitre D5
Hale F7
Hasenkamp 1,950 F5
Helvecia 2,948 F5
Hernandarias 2,735 F5
Hernández 1,035 F6
Hernando 7,370 D3
Herradura E2
Herrera D2
Huanqueros F5
Huinca Renancó 6,181 D3
Humahuaca 2,918 C1
Humberto 3,903 F5
Ibarreta 2,578 D2
Ibicuy 3,073 G6
Icaño, Catamarca C2
Icaño, Santiago del Estero 1,528 D2
Ingeniero Huergo 2,226 C4
Ingeniero Jacobacci 3,233 C5
Ingeniero Luiggi 2,113 D4
Intendente Alvear 2,534 D4
Itatí 2,327 E2
Ituzaingó 2,429 E2
Jáchal 6,815 C3
Jesús María 14,163 D3
Joaquín V. González 4,351 D2
José de San Martín 1,313 B5
José M. Micheo G7
Juárez 11,329 D4
Jujuy 82,637 C1
Juncal F6
Junín 59,020 F7
Junín de los Andes 3,870 B4
La Banda 33,032 D2
Laboulaye 13,537 D3
La Carlota D3
La Clarita G5
La Cruz 3,069 E2
La Cumbre 4,790 C3
La Esperanza B7
La Falda 10,551 D3
La Gallareta 2,261 F5
Lago Blanco B6
Laguna Paiva 11,196 F5
La Merced 2,087 C2
Lanús 449,824 H7
La Paz, Entre Ríos 12,299 G5
La Paz, Mendoza 3,533 C3
La Pelada F5
La Plata 478,666 H7
Laprida 6,802 D4
La Quiaca 6,034 C1
La Rioja 46,090 C2
Larroque 2,138 F5
Las Flores 15,655 E4
Las Lajas 1,300 B4
Las Lomitas 3,490 D1
Las Palmas 2,805 E2
Las Parejas 4,880 F6
Las Plumas C5
Las Rosas 8,708 F6
Las Termas D2
Las Varillas 8,608 D3
La Toma 3,113 C3
Lavalle G4
Leleque B5
Lezama 3,118 H7
Lincoln 17,391 F7
Lobería 9,923 E4
Lobos 13,677 G7
Lomas de Zamora 410,806 G7
Loncopué 1,078 B4
Lucas González 3,085 G6
Luján 38,393 G7
Lules 6,044 C2
Macachín 1,701 D4
Maciel 3,849 F6
Magdalena 5,398 H7
Maipú 6,997 E4
Makallé 1,286 E2
Malabrigo 2,791 F4
Malargüe 5,462 C4
Maquinchao 1,495 C5
Marcos Juárez 16,533 D3
Mar del Plata 302,282 E4
Margarita 1,740 F5
Mariano I. Loza 1,186 G4
Máximo Paz 2,653 F6
Mburucuya 2,533 E2
Médanos, Buenos Aires 4,112 D4
Médanos, Entre Ríos G6
Media Agua 1,870 C3
Melincué 2,130 F6
Mendoza 470,896 C3
Mercedes, Buenos Aires 39,760 G7
Mercedes, Corrientes 18,476 G4
Mercedes, San Luis 40,052 C3
Merlo 184,843 G7
Metán 14,615 D2
Miguel Riglos 1,344 D4
Miramar 10,512 E4
Moisés Ville 2,959 E5
Monte Caseros 14,306 G5
Monte Comán 2,350 C3
Monte Quemado 4,046 D2
Monteros 11,872 C2

(continued on following page)

Morón 485,983 ... G7
Morteros 9,669 ... D3
Navarro 5,973 ... G7
Necochea 39,868 ... E4
Nelson 2,902 ... F5
Neuquén 43,070 ... C4
Nogoyá 128,777 ... F6
Norberto de la Riestra 2,089 ... B5
Norquinco ... B5
Norumbega ...
Nueve de Julio 19,762 ... F7
Oberá 16,994 ... F2
Olavarría 52,453 ... D4
Oliva 7,799 ... D3
Olta 1,241 ... C3
Ordoqui ... F7
Palo Santo 1,984 ... C2
Pampa de las Salinas ... C3
Pampa del Infierno 1,293 ... D2
Paraná 127,635 ... F5
Paso de Indios ... C5
Paso de Los Libres 17,341 ... F3
Paso Flores ... C5
Patquía ... C3
Pedernal ... G5
Pedro Díaz Colodrero ... G5
Pedro Luro 2,641 ... D4
Pehuajó 21,078 ... D4
Pellegrini 2,974 ... D4
Pergamino 56,078 ... F6
Perito Moreno 1,793 ... B6
Perugorría 1,133 ... G4
Peyrano 2,005 ... F6
Pico Truncado 6,021 ... C6
Pigüé 8,703 ... D4
Pilar 3,520 ... H7
Pipinas 1,226 ... H7
Pirané 4,210 ... E2
Plaza Huincul 4,714 ... B4
Pomán 1,156 ... C2
Posadas 97,514 ... E2
Pozo Hondo ... D2
Presidencia de la Plaza 3,834 ... D2
Presidencia Roque Sáenz
  Peña 38,620 ... D2
Puán 3,406 ... D4
Puelches ... C4
Puelén ... C4
Puente del Inca ... B3
Puerto Coig ... C7
Puerto Deseado 3,735 ... C7
Puerto Harberton ... C7
Puerto Iguazú 3,001 ... F2
Puerto Madryn 6,115 ... C5
Puerto Rico ... D1
Punta Alta 36,805 ... D4
Punta Medanosa ... C6
Quebracho Coto ... D2
Quemú-Quemú 2,423 ... D4
Quequén 9,299 ... E4
Quimilí 4,076 ... D2
Quines 2,853 ... C3
Quiroga 1,839 ... F7
Quitilipi 7,232 ... D2
Rafaela 43,695 ... F5
Raíces ... G6
Ramallo 6,704 ... F6
Rauch 8,689 ... E4
Rawson, Buenos Aires 1,987 ... F7
Rawson, Chubut 7,229 ... D5

Reconquista 25,333 ... F4
Recreo 2,806 ... E2
Resistencia 142,848 ... E2
Rinconada ... C1
Río Colorado, La Pampa ... D4
Río Colorado, Río
  Negro 5,670 ... D4
Río Cuarto 88,852 ... D3
Río Gallegos 27,833 ... C7
Río Grande ... C7
Río Segundo 9,587 ... D3
Río Tercero 21,907 ... D3
Rivadavia, Mendoza 13,072 ... C3
Rivadavia, Salta ... D1
Rivadavia, San Juan 22,683 ... C3
Rojas 10,074 ... F6
Roldán 6,126 ... F6
Romang 3,134 ... F4
Roque Pérez 4,377 ... G7
Rosario 806,942 ... F6
Rosario de la Frontera 9,075 ... D2
Rosario de Lerma 6,268 ... C1
Rosario del Tala 8,005 ... G6
Rufino 14,138 ... E3
Saladillo 5,468 ... E2
Saladillo 13,817 ... G7
Salliqueló 4,566 ... D4
Salta 176,216 ... C1
Salto 14,551 ... F7
San Antonio de Areco 10,788 ... G7
San Antonio de los
  Cobres 1,947 ... C1
San Antonio Oeste 6,566 ... C5
San Carlos, Mendoza 1,463 ... C3
San Carlos, Santa Fe 5,973 ... F5
San Carlos de Bariloche 26,799 ... B5
San Cayetano 6,025 ... E4
San Cristóbal 11,825 ... F5
San Fernando 113,249 ... G7
San Francisco,
  Córdoba 48,896 ... D3
San Francisco, San Luis 1,952 ... C3
San Genaro 2,230 ... F6
San Ignacio 2,332 ... C2
San Isidro ... G7
San Jaime de la frontera 2,517 ... G5
San Javier, Río Negro ... D5
San Javier, Santa Fe 5,585 ... F5
San José de Feliciano 3,884 ... G5
San Juan 217,514 ... C3
San Julián 3,589 ... C6
San Justo 11,085 ... F5
San Lorenzo 56,487 ... F6
San Luis 50,771 ... C3
San Martín 24,300 ... C3
San Martín de los
  Andes 5,960 ... C5
San Miguel 1,540 ... E2
San Miguel del Monte 5,768 ... G7
San Miguel de
  Tucumán 366,392 ... D2
San Nicolás 64,730 ... F6
San Pedro, Buenos Aires 23,365 ... F6
San Pedro, Jujuy 25,265 ... D1
San Rafael 58,237 ... C3
San Ramon de la Nva.
  Orán 20,212 ... D1
San Salvador 4,529 ... G5
San Sebastián ... C7
Santa Cruz 1,448 ... C7
Santa Elena 11,525 ... F5

Santa Fe 244,655 ... F5
Santa Lucía, Buenos
  Aires 1,817 ... F6
Santa Lucía,
  Corrientes 3,738 ... E2
Santa María 3,736 ... C2
Santa Rosa, Córdoba 3,488 ... D3
Santa Rosa, La Pampa 33,649 ... D4
Santa Rosa, San Luis 2,609 ... C3
Santa Victoria ... D1
Santiago del Estero 105,127 ... D2
Santo Tomé,
  Corrientes 11,058 ... F2
Santo Tomé, Santa Fe 23,572 ... F5
San Urbano ... F6
Sarmiento 5,555 ... B6
Sauce 4,134 ... G5
Sauce de Luna 1,161 ... G5
Seguí 2,232 ... F6
Selva 1,575 ... D2
Sierra Colorada ... C5
Sierra Grande ... C5
Soledad ... F5
Stroeder 2,206 ... D5
Suipacha 4,002 ... G7
Sumampa 2,334 ... D2
Sunchales 10,393 ... F5
Suncho Corral 3,597 ... D2
Susques ... C1
Tamberías ... C3
Tandil 65,876 ... E4
Tapalqué 4,769 ... E4
Tartagal 23,696 ... D1
Tecka ... B5
Telsen ... C5
Tigre 146,451 ... G7
Tilcara 2,226 ... C1
Tinogasta 6,313 ... C2
Tintina 2,215 ... D2
Toay 2,191 ... D4
Tornquist 3,054 ... D4
Tostado 7,921 ... D2
Trelew 22,547 ... D5
Trenel 1,847 ... D4
Trenque Lauquen 18,169 ... D4
Tres Arroyos 37,991 ... D4
Trevelin 1,214 ... B5
Tunuyán 10,813 ... C3
Urdinarrain 4,577 ... G6
Ushuaia 5,373 ... C7
Valcheta 1,776 ... C5
Valdés ... C3
Vedia 5,139 ... F7
Veinticinco de Mayo 16,678 ... F7
Veintiocho de Noviembre 5,168 ... B7
Venado Tuerto 35,677 ... D3
Vera 10,664 ... D2
Vergara ... H7
Verónica 4,938 ... H7
Viale 4,411 ... F5
Vicente López 285,178 ... G7
Victoria 17,046 ... F6
Victorica 3,184 ... D4
Vicuña Mackenna 4,594 ... D3
Viedma 12,888 ... D5
Vieytes ... H7
Villa Ana 1,208 ... E2
Villa 'ngela 17,091 ... D2
Villa Atamisqui ... D2
Villa Atuel 2,783 ... C3

Villa Cañas 6,206 ... F6
Villa Clara 1,736 ... G5
Villa Constitución 25,148 ... F6
Villa Diego ... F6
Villa del Rosario 8,060 ... D3
Villa de María 1,343 ... D2
Villa Dolores 19,010 ... C3
Villa Elisa 3,227 ... G6
Villa Federal 6,917 ... G5
Villa General Ramírez 4,439 ... F6
Villa General Roca ... C3
Villaguay 15,591 ... G5
Villa Guillermina 2,237 ... F4
Villa Huidobro 3,280 ... D3
Villa Krause ... C3
Villa Mantero ... G6
Villa María 56,087 ... D3
Villa María Grande 3,431 ... F5
Villa Nueva 3,533 ... D3
Villa Ocampo 8,104 ... F4
Villa Regina 10,965 ... C4
Villa San Agustín 1,795 ... C3
Villa San José 4,046 ... G6
Villa San Martín 4,013 ... D2
Villa Unión 1,789 ... C2
Vinchina 1,491 ... C2
Zapala 11,385 ... B4
Zárate 54,772 ... F6
Zavalla 2,887 ... F6

OTHER FEATURES

Aconcagua, Cerro (mt.) ... C3
Andes, Cordillera de los
  (mts.) ... C2
Argentino (lake) ... B7
Arizaro, Salar de (salt dep.) ... C2
Arrecifes (riv.) ... G6
Atacama, Puna de (reg.) ... C1
Atuel (riv.) ... C4
Barrancas (riv.) ... G5
Bermejo (riv.) ... E2
Blanca (bay) ... D4
Brazo Sur, Pilcomayo (riv.) ... E1
Buenos Aires (lake) ... B6
Campanario, Cerro (mt.) ... C4
Chaco Austral (reg.) ... D2
Chaco Central (reg.) ... D1
Chato, Cerro (mt.) ... B5
Chico (riv.) ... C6
Chico (riv.) ... C6
Chubut (riv.) ... C5
Colhué Huapi (lake) ... C6
Colorado (riv.) ... D4
Cónico, Cerro (mt.) ... B5
Corrientes (riv.) ... E2
Coyle (riv.) ... C7
Deseado (riv.) ... C6
Desaguadero (riv.) ... C3
Diamante (riv.) ... C3
Domuyo (vol.) ... B4
Dos Bahías (cape) ... D5
Dulce (riv.) ... D2
Dungeness (pt.) ... C7
El Chocón (res.) ... C4
Estados, Los (isl.) ... D7
Fagnano (lake) ... C7
Famatina, Sierra de (mts.) ... C2
Feliciano (riv.) ... G5

Flores, Las (riv.) ... G7
Gallegos (riv.) ... B7
General Manuel Belgrano, Cerro
  (mt.) ... C2
Gran Chaco (reg.) ... D1
Grande (bay) ... C7
Grande (falls) ... E3
Grande (riv.) ... C4
Grande de Tierra del Fuego
  (isl.) ... C7
Gualeguay (riv.) ... G5
Guayquiraró (riv.) ... F5
Iguazú (falls) ... F2
Iguazú Nat'l Park ... E2
Incahuasi, Cerro de (mt.) ... C2
Lanín (vol.) ... B4
Lanín Nat'l Park ... B4
Lechiguanas (isls.) ... G6
Lennox (isl.) ... C8
Limay (riv.) ... C4
Llancanelo (lag.) ... C4
Llullaillaco (mt.) ... C1
Magallanes (Magellan) (str.) ... C8
Maipo (vol.) ... C3
Mar Chiquita (lake) ... D3
Martín García (isl.) ... H6
Mendoza (riv.) ... C3
Mercedario, Cerro (mt.) ... B3
Mogotes (pt.) ... E4
Montemayor (plat.) ... C6
Muralión, Cerro (mt.) ... B6
Nahuel Huapi (lake) ... B5
Nahuel Huapi Nat'l Park ... B5
Negro (riv.) ... D4
Neuquén (riv.) ... C4
Ninfas (pt.) ... D5
Norte (pt.) ... D5
Norte del Cabo San Antonio
  (pt.) ... E4
Nuevo (gulf) ... D5
Ojos del Salado, Cerro (mt.) ... C2
Olivares, Cerro de (mt.) ... B3
Pampa de la Tres Hermanas
  (plain) ... C6
Pampas (plain) ... D4
Paraná (riv.) ... E2
Patagonia (reg.) ... B5
Peteroa (vol.) ... B4
Pilcomayo (riv.) ... E1
Pissis (mt.) ... C2
Plata, Río de la (est.) ... E4
Pueyrredón (lake) ... B6
Puna de Atacama (reg.) ... C2
Quinto (riv.) ... D3
Rincón, Cerro (mt.) ... C1
Saladillo (riv.) ... D3
Salado (riv.) ... C4
Salado (riv.) ... H7

Salado del Norte (riv.) ... D2
Salí (riv.) ... C2
Salto (riv.) ... F7
Samborombón (bay) ... E4
San Antonio (cape) ... E4
San Diego (cape) ... D7
San Jorge (gulf) ... C6
San Juan (riv.) ... C3
San Lorenzo, Cerro (mt.) ... B6
San Martín (lake) ... B6
San Matías (gulf) ... D5
Santa Cruz (riv.) ... B7
Senguerr (riv.) ... B6
Staten (Los Estados) (isl.) ... D7
Sur del Cabo San Antonio
  (pt.) ... E4
Tarija (riv.) ... D1
Tercero (riv.) ... D3
Teuco (riv.) ... D1
Tierra del Fuego, Grande de
  (isl.) ... C7
Toro, Cerro del (mt.) ... B2
Tres Puntas (cape) ... C7
Trinidad (riv.) ... B5
Tronador (mt.) ... B5
Tunuyán (riv.) ... C3
Tupungato, Cerro (mt.) ... B3
Uruguay (riv.) ... E3
Valdés (pen.) ... D5
Vallimanca (riv.) ... D4
Viedma (lake) ... B6
Zapaleri, Cerro (mt.) ... C1

*City and suburbs

Topography

Pilcomayo · Bermejo · GRAN CHACO · Paraguay · Paraná · Iguassú Falls · Socompa Pass · Salado del N. · Uruguay · San Miguel de Tucumán · Salinas Grandes · SAS. DE CÓRDOBA · Córdoba · C. Aconcagua 22,831 ft (6959 m.) · Uspallata Pass · Mendoza · Salado · Rosario · Buenos Aires · Río de la Plata · C. San Antonio · CORDILLERA DE LOS ANDES · PAMPAS · Colorado · Negro · B. Blanca · G. San Matías · Pen. Valdés · ANDES DE PATAGONIA · Chubut · G. San Jorge · C. Tres Puntas · Deseado · PATAGONIA · Str. of Magellan · Tierra del Fuego

0 150 300 MI.
0 150 300 KM.

5,000 m. 16,404 ft. | 2,000 m. 6,562 ft. | 1,000 m. 3,281 ft. | 500 m. 1,640 ft. | 200 m. 656 ft. | 100 m. 328 ft. | Sea Level | Below

Highways of Central Argentina

San Carlos · Jesús María · Rafaela · Constitución · Concordia · Salto · Córdoba · V. del Rosario · San Francisco · Bovril · Santa Fe · Paraná · Alta Gracia · Las Varas · Sastre · Villaguay · V. Dolores · Río Tercero · Gálvez · Crespo · Viale · Villa María · Diamante · Nogoyá · Colón · Paysandú · Bell Ville · Victoria · Basavilbaso · Algorta · D. Vélez · Marcos Juárez · Concepción del Uruguay · Young · Río Cuarto · S. Victoria · Rosario · Gualeguaychú · Sampacho · Cda. de Gómez · Casilda · Gualeguay · Fray Bentos · Mercedes · Durazno · José Batlle y Ordóñez · La Carlota · Isla Verde · Firmat · San Nicolás · Palmitas · Trinidad · Mercedes · Vicuña Mac Kenna · Peyrano · San Pedro · Dolores · Sarandí Grande · Cerro Colorado · Pérgamino · Constanza · Nva. Palmira · Cardona · Laboulaye · Rufino · Colón · Rojas · Arrecifes · Campana · Carmelo · J. L. Lacaze · San José de Mayo · Tala · Aiguá · V. Valeria · Vedia · Junín · Chacabuco · Salto · Colonia · BUENOS AIRES · Minas · San Carlos · Huinca Renancó · Gral. Pinto · Lincoln · Mercedes · Luján · Lanús · Libertad · Maldonado · Punta del Este · Realicó · Chivilcoy · Navarro · La Plata · MONTEVIDEO · Nueva Galia · Rivadavia · Gral. Villegas · Lobos · Magdalena · Alta Italia · Carlos Tejedor · 9 de Julio · Bragado · Cnel. Brandsen · Pta. Piedras · E. Castex · Gral. Pico · Pehuajó · 25 de Mayo · Saladillo · Roque Pérez · Chascomús · Gral. Belgrano · Trenque Lauquen · C. Casares · Del Valle · Las Flores · Pila · Bahía Samborombón · Victorica · Winifreda · Bolívar · Tapalqué · Real Audiencia · Dolores · Pta. Norte del C. San Antonio · Santa Rosa · Catriló · Tres Lomas · Castelli · Gral. Lavalle · Cereales · Guaminí · Gral. La Madrid · Azul · Rauch · Maipú · Gral. Conesa · Gral. Acha · Macachín · A. Alsina · Olavarría · Ayacucho · Gral. Madariaga · Bernasconi · Puán · Pigüé · Guatraché · Tandil · Juárez · Cnel. Vidal · Gral. Acha (no) · Tornquist · Cnel. Pringles · González Chaves · Lobería · Balcarce · Mar del Plata · Villa Iris · Tres Picos · Irene · Tres Arroyos · San Germán · Cnel. Dorrego · Conetonas · Necochea · Pichi Mahuida · Médanos · Bahía Blanca · Colorado · Río Colorado · Choele-Choel

MILES
0   25   50   75
KILOMETERS
0   50   100   150

Major Roads..........
Other Roads..........

© HAMMOND INCORPORATED, Maplewood, N.J.

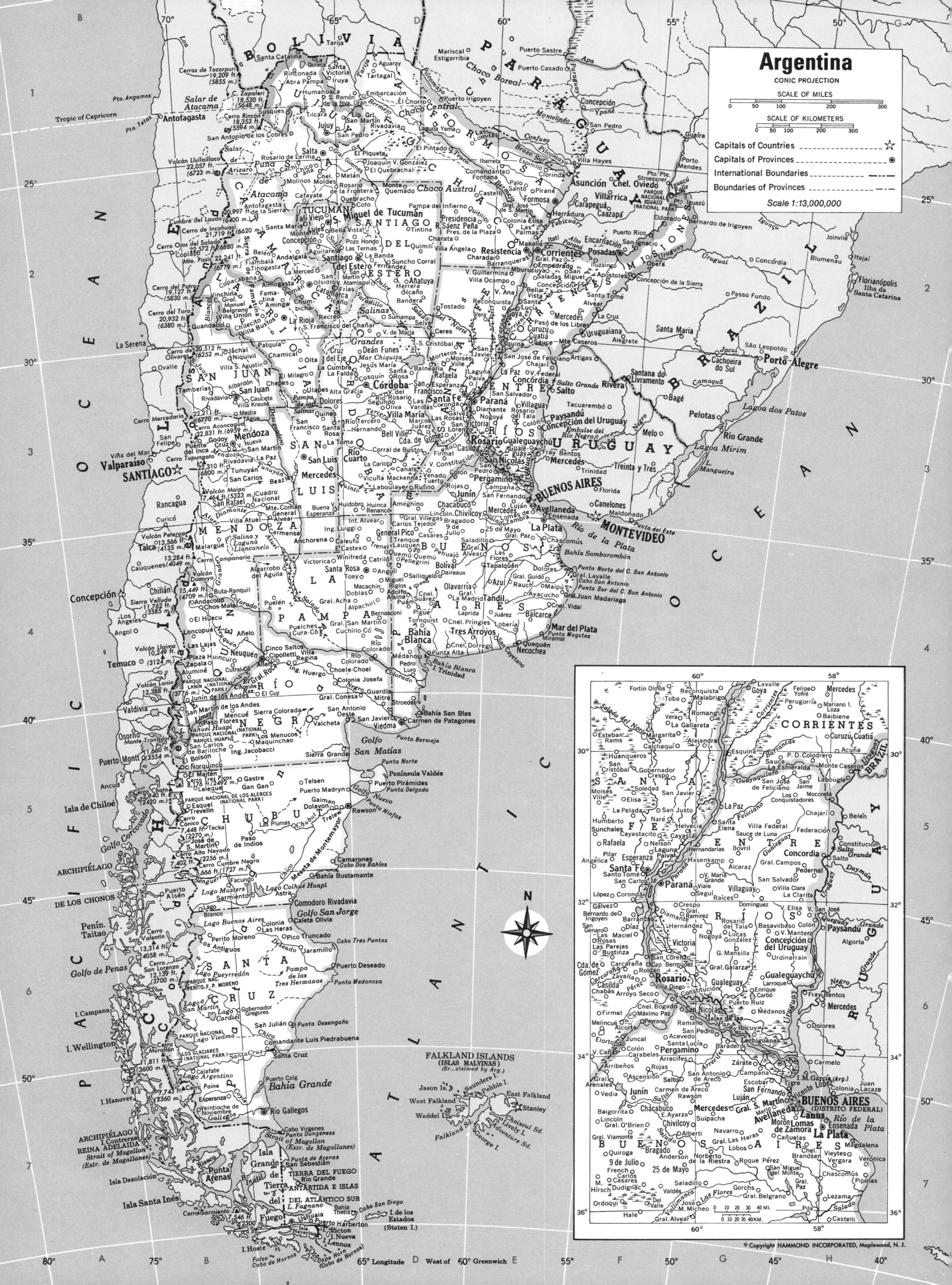

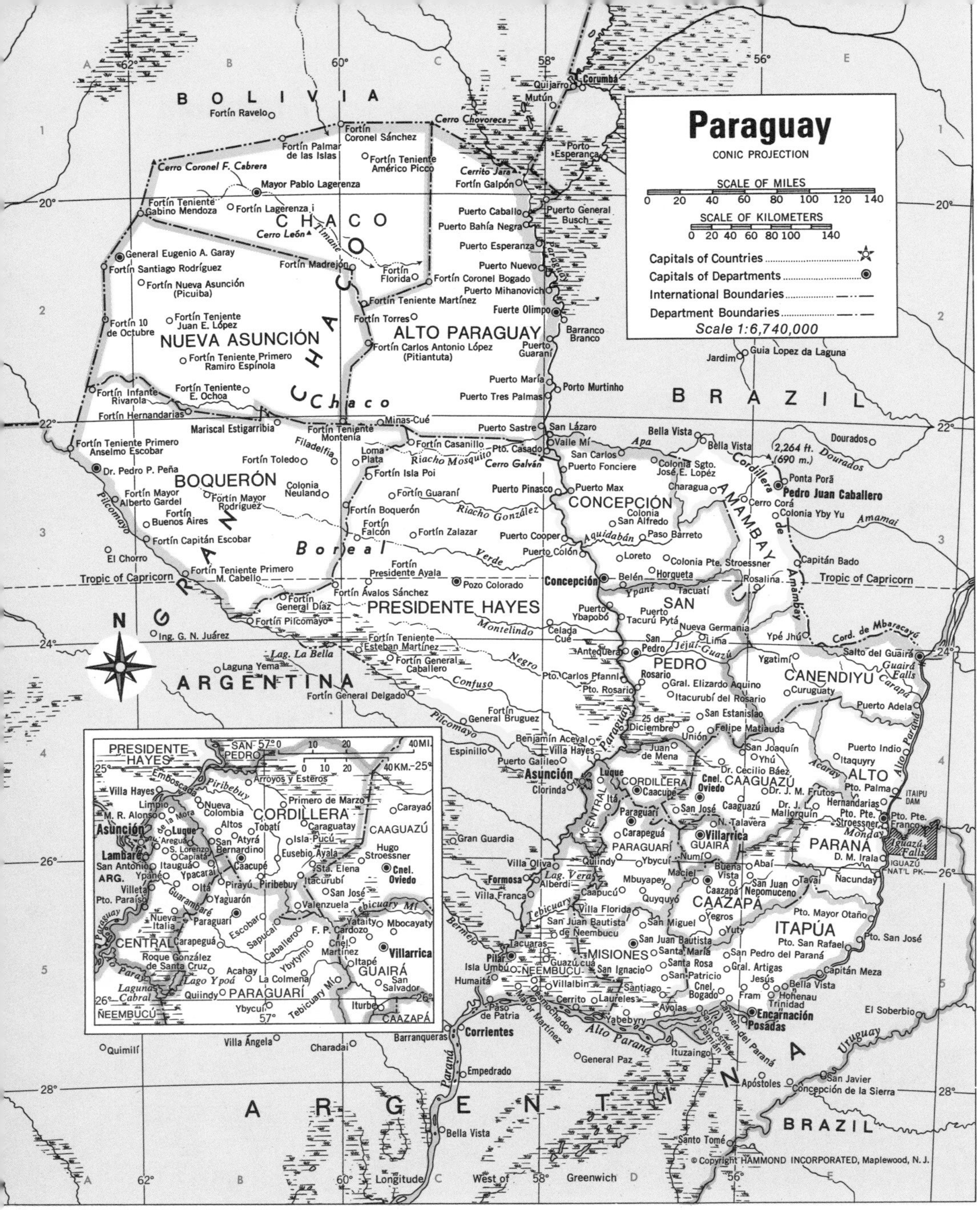

Paraguay

CONIC PROJECTION

SCALE OF MILES

0 20 40 60 80 100 120 140

SCALE OF KILOMETERS

0 20 40 60 80 100 120 140

Capitals of Countries .... ★
Capitals of Departments .... ◉
International Boundaries ....
Department Boundaries ....

Scale 1:6,740,000

© Copyright HAMMOND INCORPORATED, Maplewood, N.J.

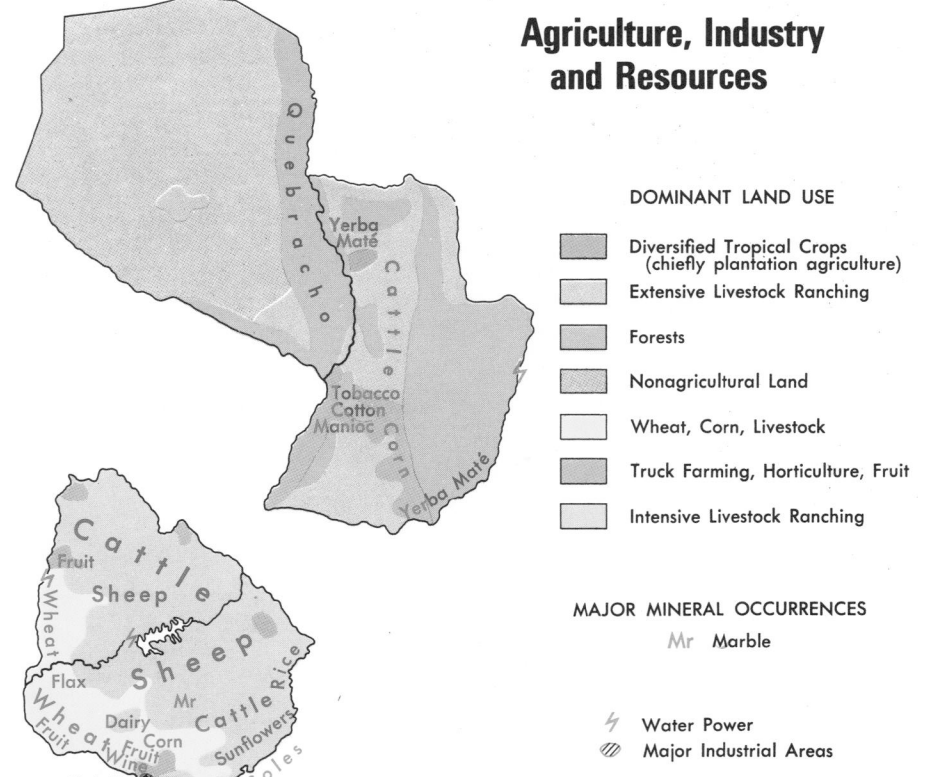

Agriculture, Industry and Resources

DOMINANT LAND USE

Diversified Tropical Crops (chiefly plantation agriculture)

Extensive Livestock Ranching

Forests

Nonagricultural Land

Wheat, Corn, Livestock

Truck Farming, Horticulture, Fruit

Intensive Livestock Ranching

MAJOR MINERAL OCCURRENCES

Mr Marble

⚡ Water Power

▨ Major Industrial Areas

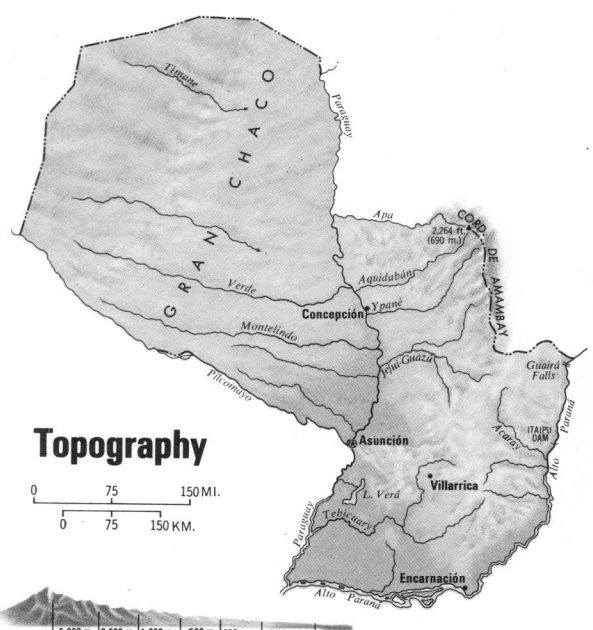

Topography

0 75 150 MI.

0 75 150 KM.

5,000 m. 2,000 m. 1,000 m. 500 m. 200 m. 100 m. Sea Level Below
16,404 ft. 6,562 ft. 3,281 ft. 1,640 ft. 656 ft. 328 ft.

URUGUAY
DEPARTMENTS

Artigas 52,843................B1
Canelones 258,195..........D5
Cerro Largo 71,023..........E3
Colonia 105,350.............B5
Durazno 53,635..............C4
Flores 23,530...............C4
Florida 63,987..............D4
Lavalleja 65,823............D4
Maldonado 61,259............E5
Montevideo 1,202,757........B3
Paysandú 88,029.............B3
Río Negro 46,861............B3
Rivera 77,086...............D2
Rocha 55,097................E4
Salto 92,183................B2
San José 79,563.............C5
Soriano 77,906..............B4
Tacuarembó 76,964...........D3
Treinta y Tres 43,419.......E4

CITIES and TOWNS

Aceguá 930...................E2
Achar 606....................C3
Agraciada 638................A4
Aguas Corrientes 992.........A6
Aigua 2,470..................E5
Algorta 1,372................B3
Artigas 29,256...............C1
Atlántida 2,268..............C6
Balneario El Tesoro..........E5
Balneario La Barra...........E5
Balneario Solís 288..........D5
Baltasar Brum 1,753..........B1
Belén 2,129..................B1
Bella Unión 7,778............B1
Bernabé Rivera 540...........B1
Blanquillo 1,053.............D3
Cañada Nieto 503.............B4
Canelones 15,938.............B6
Cardal 847...................D4
Cardona 4,126................C4
Cardozo 143..................C4
Carlos Reyles 961............C4
Carmelo 13,631...............A4
Carmen 2,318.................D4
Carrasco....................
Castillos 6,446..............F5
Casupá 2,265.................D4
Cebollatí 1,233..............F4
Cerrillos 1,690..............A6
Cerro Chato, Treinta y
  Tres 1,850.................D4
Chamizo 486..................D5
Chuy 4,472...................F4
Colón, Lavalleja 367.........E4
Colonia 16,895...............B5
Colonia Lavalleja...........
Colonia Rossel y Rius 130....D4
Colonia Valdense 2,113.......B5
Conchillas 748...............A5
Constitución 3,217...........A2
Costa Azul 453...............B5
Cufré 430....................B5
Cuñapirú.....................C2
Curtina 723..................C3
Diez y Nueve (19) de Abril 308...E4
Diez y Ocho (18) de
  Julio 742..................F4
Dolores 12,771...............A4
Durazno 25,811...............C4
Egaña 667....................C4
Empalme Olmos 2,084..........B6
Estación Atlántida 1,845.....B6
Estación Migues 241..........C6
Florida 25,030...............D4
Fortaleza de Santa Teresa....F5
Fraile Muerto 2,468..........E3
Fray Bentos 19,569...........A4
Fray Marcos 1,573............D5
Garzón 258...................E5
General Enrique
  Martínez 973...............F4
Goñi 278.....................C4
Grecco 447...................B3
Guichón 4,720................B3
Ituzaingó 717................A6
Javier de Viana 286..........C1
Joanicó 692..................B6
Joaquín Suárez,
  Canelones 3,517...........B6
José Batlle y
  Ordóñez 2,044.............D4
José Enrique Rodó 1,334......C4
José Pedro Varela 3,541......E4
Juan L. Lacaze 11,133........B5
Julio María Sanz............
La Bolsa....................C1
La Coronilla 571............F4
La Cruz 633.................C4
La Cuchilla.................C4
La Floresta................C7
La Lata.....................E2
La Paloma 1,558.............F5
La Paz, Canelones 14,402....B6
La Paz, Colonia.............B5
La Pedrera 116..............F5
Lascano 6,043...............E4
Las Flores 403..............E5
La Sierra...................E5
Las Piedras 53,983..........B6
Las Toscas 893..............E3
Libertad 6,071..............C5
Lorenzo Geyres 474..........B3

Mal Abrigo 209..............C5
Maldonado 22,159............D6
Mariscala 1,393.............E5
Mazangano...................E3
Melo 38,260.................E3
Mercedes 34,667.............B4
Merinos 403.................B3
Miguelete 533...............B5
Migues 2,183................C6
Minas 35,433................D5
Minas de Corrales 2,518.....D2
Montes 2,217................D5
Montevideo (cap.) 1,173,254...B7
Nico Pérez..................D4
Nueva Helvecia 8,598........B5
Nueva Palmira 6,934.........A4
Nuevo Berlín 1,970..........A3
Ombúes de Lavalle 1,689.....B4
Ombúes de Oribe.............C4
Palmitas 1,332..............B4
Pan de Azúcar 4,862.........D5
Pando 16,184................B6
Paso de la Laguna, Salto....B2
Paso de la Laguna,
  Tacuarembó................D3
Paso de León................B1
Paso del Borracho...........D2
Paso del Cerro 317..........C3
Paso de los Toros 13,178....C3
Paso Potrero................C2
Paysandú 62,412.............A3
Peralta.....................C3
Piedra Sola 233.............C3
Piedras Coloradas 487.......B3
Piñera 261..................C3
Pintado, Artigas............C1
Pirarajá 774................E4
Piriápolis 5,221............D5
Porvenir 705................B3
Progreso 8,257..............B6
Pueblo del Sauce............E4
Pueblo Nuevo................B2
Punta del Este 6,914........E5
Quebracho 1,514.............B2
Reboledo 373................D4
Río Branco 5,697............F3
Rivera 49,013...............D1
Rocha 21,612................E5
Rodríguez 1,575.............C5
Rosario 8,302...............B5
Salto 72,94.................B2
San Antonio, Canelones 1,122...B6
San Bautista 1,472..........B6
San Carlos 16,883...........E5
San Gregorio, San José......C4
San Gregorio,
  Tacuarembó 2,892..........D3
San Jacinto 2,292...........C6
San Javier 1,583............A3
San José de Mayo 28,427.....C5
San Ramón 6,570.............D5
San Servando................B4
Santa Catalina 885..........B4
Santa Clara de Olimar 2,867...D3
Santa Lucía 14,101..........B6
Santa Rosa 2,736............B6
Santiago Vázquez 1,323......B7
Sarandí del Yi 6,326........D4
Sarandí de Navarro 259......B3
Sarandí Grande 3,986........D4
Sauce, Canelones 3,942......B6
Sauce del Yi................D4
Saucedo.....................C3
Sequeira....................C1
Solís 356...................D5
Solís de Mataojo 1,763......D5
Soriano 1,125...............A4
Tacuarembó 34,152...........D3
Tala 3,611..................D5
Tambores 1,534..............C2
Toledo 3,127................B6
Tomás Gomensoro 2,105.......C1
Totoral.....................C3
Tranqueras 3,922............D2
Treinta y Tres 25,757.......E4
Tres Bocas..................B2
Tres Islas..................E3
Trinidad 17,598.............C4
Tupambaé 1,039..............E3
Unión.......................E4
Valentines 153..............E4
Veinticinco (25) de
  Agosto 1,891..............A6
Veinticinco (25) de Mayo 1,744...C5
Velázquez 1,042.............E5
Vergara 2,822...............E2
Vichadero 1,989.............E2
Villa Darwin 507............B4
Villa del Cerro.............A7
Young 11,080................B3
Zapicán 764.................E4
Zapucay.....................D2

OTHER FEATURES

Aiguá (riv.)................E4
Alferez (riv.)..............E5
Arapey Chico (riv.).........B1
Arapey Grande (riv.)........B1
Belén (range)...............C1
Bonete (dam)................C3
Brava (pt.).................B7
Cañas (range)...............D2
Caraguatá (riv.)............D3
Castillos (lag.)............F5
Cebollatí (riv.)............F4
Cordobés (riv.).............D3

PARAGUAY

AREA 157,047 sq. mi. (406,752 sq. km.)
POPULATION 2,973,000
CAPITAL Asunción
LARGEST CITY Asunción
HIGHEST POINT Amambay Range
  2,264 ft. (690 m.)
MONETARY UNIT guaraní
MAJOR LANGUAGES Spanish, Guaraní
MAJOR RELIGION Roman Catholicism

Cuareim (riv.)..............B1
Cuñapirú, Arroyo (riv.).....D2
Daymán (range)..............B2
Daymán (riv.)...............B2
Durazno, Grande del (range)...C4
Espinillo (pt.).............A7
Este (pt.)..................E5
Flores (isl.)...............D5
Garzón (lag.)...............E5
Grande (range)..............C4
Grande, Arroyo (riv.).......B4
Grande Inferior (range).....B4
Haedo (range)...............C2
India Muerta (riv.).........E5
José Ignacio (lag.).........E5
Lobos (isl.)................E6
Maciel, Arroyo (riv.).......B4
Merín (lag.)................F3
Mirador Nacional (mt.)......D5
Negra (range)...............F5
Negra (range)...............E2
Negro (riv.)................C3
Negro, Arroyo (riv.)........B3
Olimar Grande (riv.)........E4

URUGUAY

AREA 72,172 sq. mi. (186,925 sq. km.)
POPULATION 2,899,000
CAPITAL Montevideo
LARGEST CITY Montevideo
HIGHEST POINT Mirador Nacional 1,644 ft.
  (501 m.)
MONETARY UNIT Uruguayan peso
MAJOR LANGUAGE Spanish
MAJOR RELIGION Roman Catholicism

Pando (riv.)................B6
Parao (riv.)................E3
Plata, La (riv.)............B5
Polonio (cape)..............F5
Quequay Chico (riv.)........B3
Quequay Grande (riv.).......B3
Río Negro (res.)............D3
Rocha (lag.)................F4
Salto Grande (falls)........A2
San José (riv.).............C5
San Miguel (swamp)..........F4
San Salvador (riv.).........B4
Santa Ana (range)...........D2
Santa Lucía (riv.)..........D5
Santa Lucía Chico (riv.)....D4
Santa María (cape)..........F5
Sauce (lag.)................D5
Sopas, Arroyo (riv.)........C2
Tacuarembó (riv.)...........D3
Tacuarí (riv.)..............E3
Tigre (isl.)................A3
Uruguay (riv.)..............A3
Yaguarón (riv.).............F3
Yi (riv.)...................B4

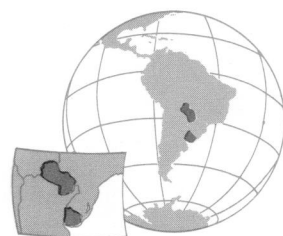

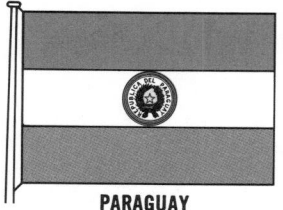
PARAGUAY

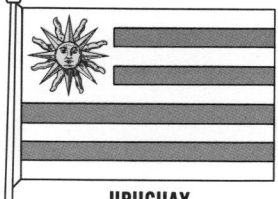
URUGUAY

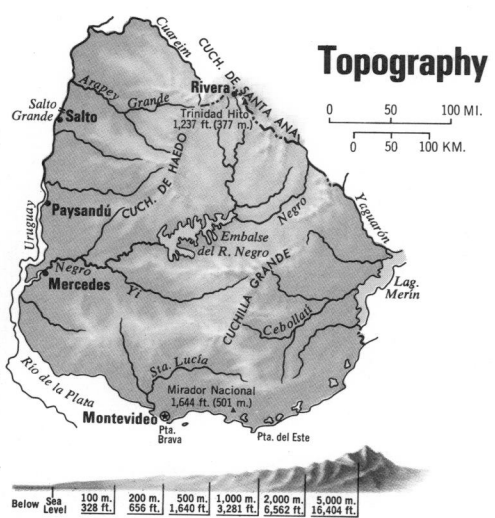

Topography

0   50   100 MI.
0   50   100 KM.

Mirador Nacional
1,644 ft. (501 m.)

Below Sea Level	100 m. 328 ft.	200 m. 656 ft.	500 m. 1,640 ft.	1,000 m. 3,281 ft.	2,000 m. 6,562 ft.	5,000 m. 16,404 ft.

Uruguay

CONIC PROJECTION

SCALE OF MILES
0   20   40   60

SCALE OF KILOMETERS
0   20   40   60

Capitals of Countries .... ☆
Department Capitals .... ●
International Boundaries ....
Department Boundaries ....

Scale 1:3,800,000

© Copyright HAMMOND INCORPORATED, Maplewood, N.J.

North America

LAMBERT AZIMUTHAL EQUAL-AREA PROJECTION

MILES
0   100 200   400   600   800

KILOMETERS
0 100 200 400   600   800

Capitals of Countries .... ◉
Other Capitals .... ◎
International Boundaries .... — · — · —
Other Boundaries .... — — — —

Scale 1:36,600,000

© Copyright HAMMOND INCORPORATED, Maplewood, N.J.

Population Distribution

AREA 9,363,000 sq. mi.
(24,250,170 sq. km.)
POPULATION 370,000,000
LARGEST CITY New York
HIGHEST POINT Mt. McKinley 20,320 ft.
(6,194 m.)
LOWEST POINT Death Valley -282 ft.
(-86 m.)

Vegetation

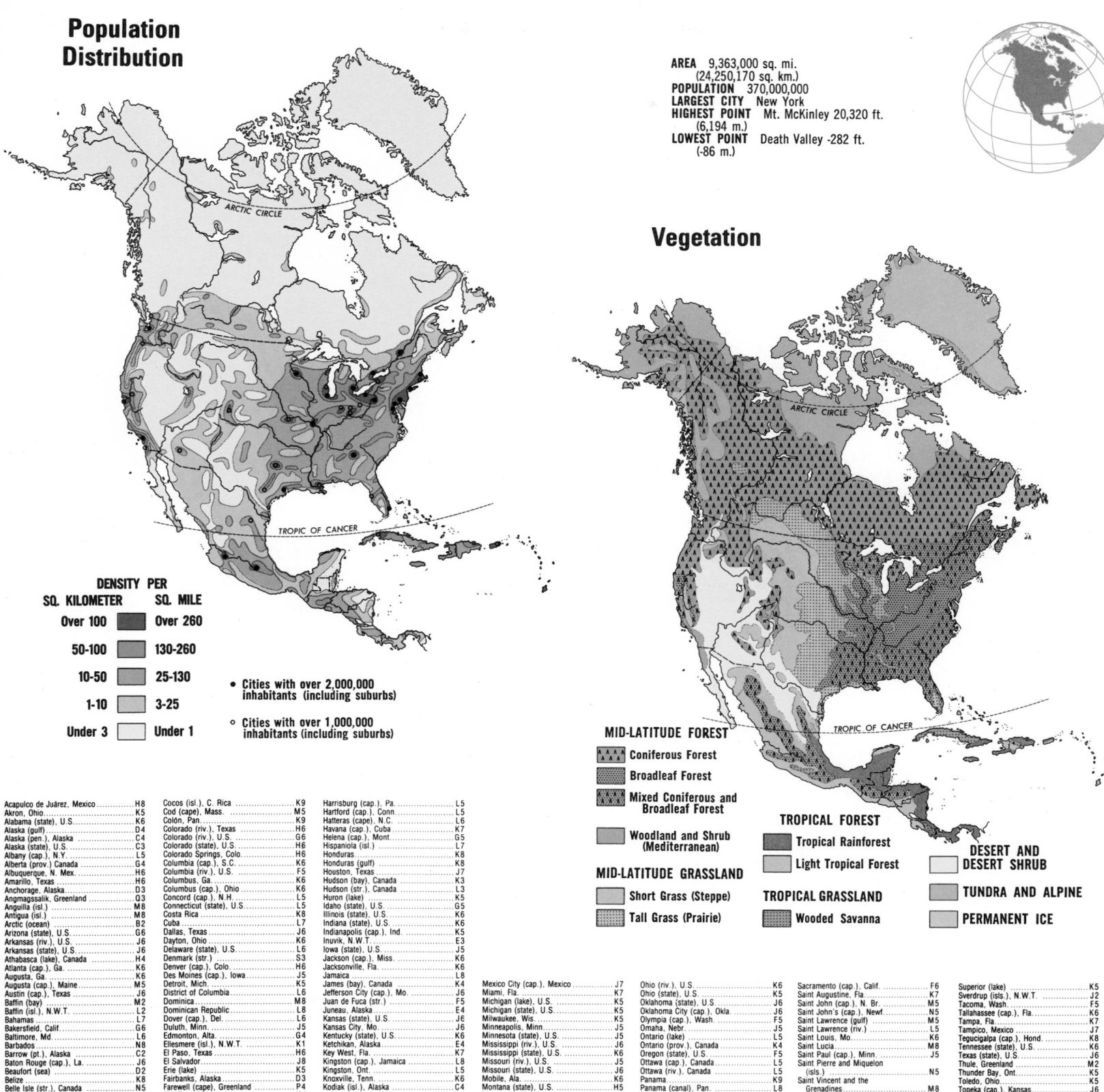

ARCTIC CIRCLE

TROPIC OF CANCER

DENSITY PER

SQ. KILOMETER	SQ. MILE
Over 100	Over 260
50-100	130-260
10-50	25-130
1-10	3-25
Under 3	Under 1

• Cities with over 2,000,000 inhabitants (including suburbs)

○ Cities with over 1,000,000 inhabitants (including suburbs)

MID-LATITUDE FOREST
Coniferous Forest
Broadleaf Forest
Mixed Coniferous and Broadleaf Forest
Woodland and Shrub (Mediterranean)

MID-LATITUDE GRASSLAND
Short Grass (Steppe)
Tall Grass (Prairie)

TROPICAL FOREST
Tropical Rainforest
Light Tropical Forest

TROPICAL GRASSLAND
Wooded Savanna

DESERT AND DESERT SHRUB

TUNDRA AND ALPINE

PERMANENT ICE

Average January Temperature

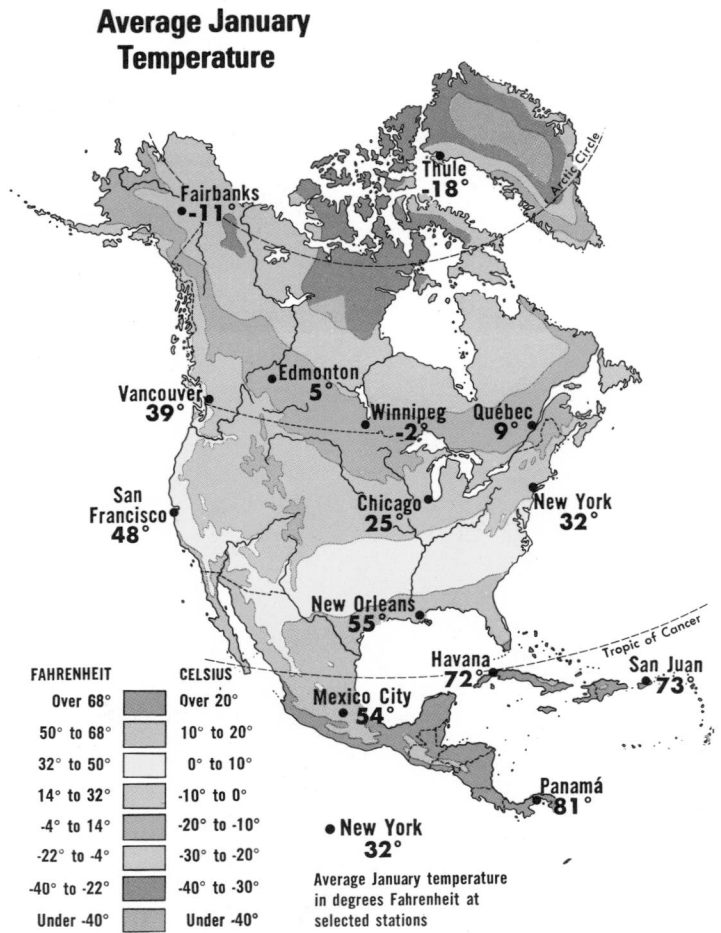

FAHRENHEIT		CELSIUS
Over 68°		Over 20°
50° to 68°		10° to 20°
32° to 50°		0° to 10°
14° to 32°		-10° to 0°
-4° to 14°		-20° to -10°
-22° to -4°		-30° to -20°
-40° to -22°		-40° to -30°
Under -40°		Under -40°

● New York
32°

Average January temperature in degrees Fahrenheit at selected stations

Average July Temperature

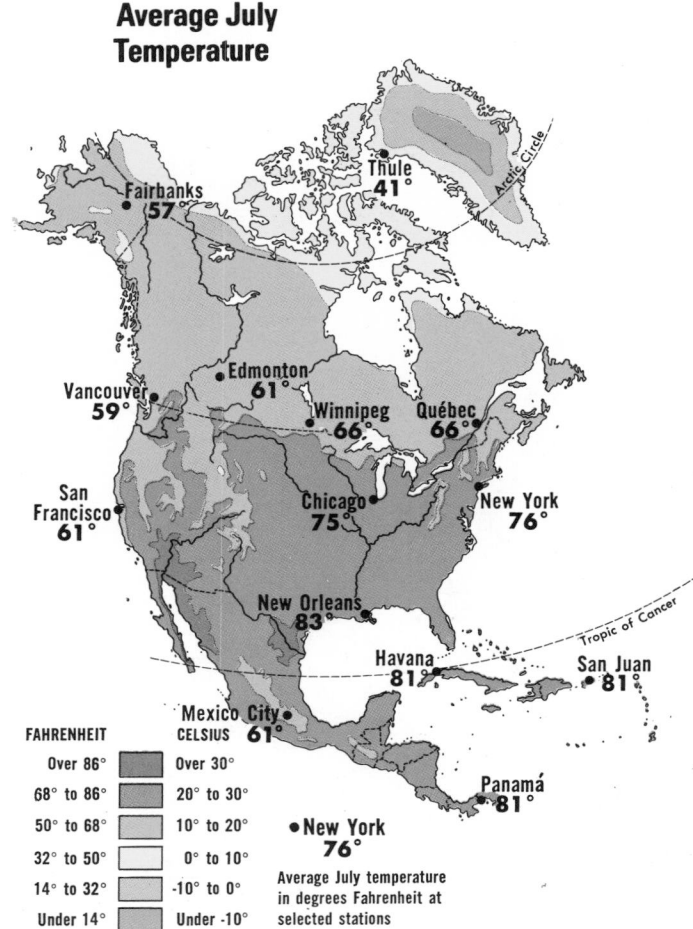

FAHRENHEIT		CELSIUS
Over 86°		Over 30°
68° to 86°		20° to 30°
50° to 68°		10° to 20°
32° to 50°		0° to 10°
14° to 32°		-10° to 0°
Under 14°		Under -10°

● New York
76°

Average July temperature in degrees Fahrenheit at selected stations

Rainfall

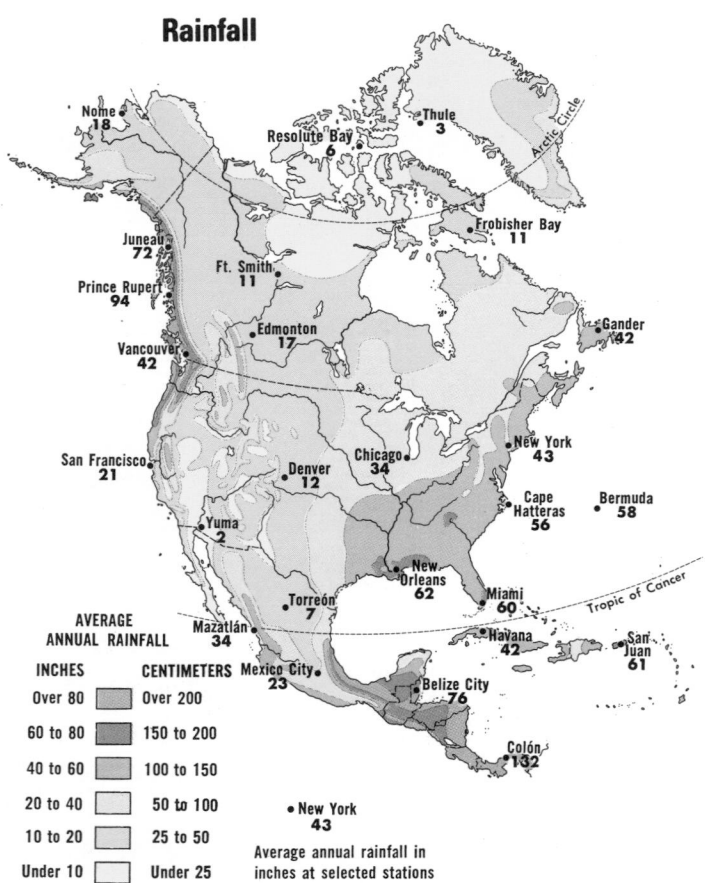

AVERAGE ANNUAL RAINFALL

INCHES		CENTIMETERS
Over 80		Over 200
60 to 80		150 to 200
40 to 60		100 to 150
20 to 40		50 to 100
10 to 20		25 to 50
Under 10		Under 25

● New York
43

Average annual rainfall in inches at selected stations

Vegetation/Relief

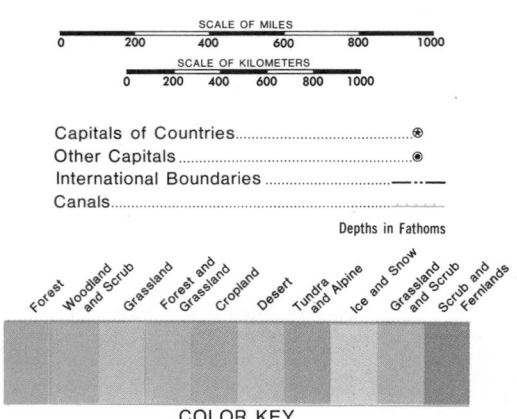

SCALE OF MILES
0   200   400   600   800   1000

SCALE OF KILOMETERS
0   200   400   600   800   1000

Capitals of Countries.................................⊛
Other Capitals...⊛
International Boundaries ....—--—
Canals...

Depths in Fathoms

Forest | Woodland and Scrub | Grassland | Forest and Grassland | Cropland | Desert | Tundra and Alpine | Ice and Snow | Grassland and Scrub | Scrub and Fernlands

COLOR KEY

Longitude 90° West of Greenwich

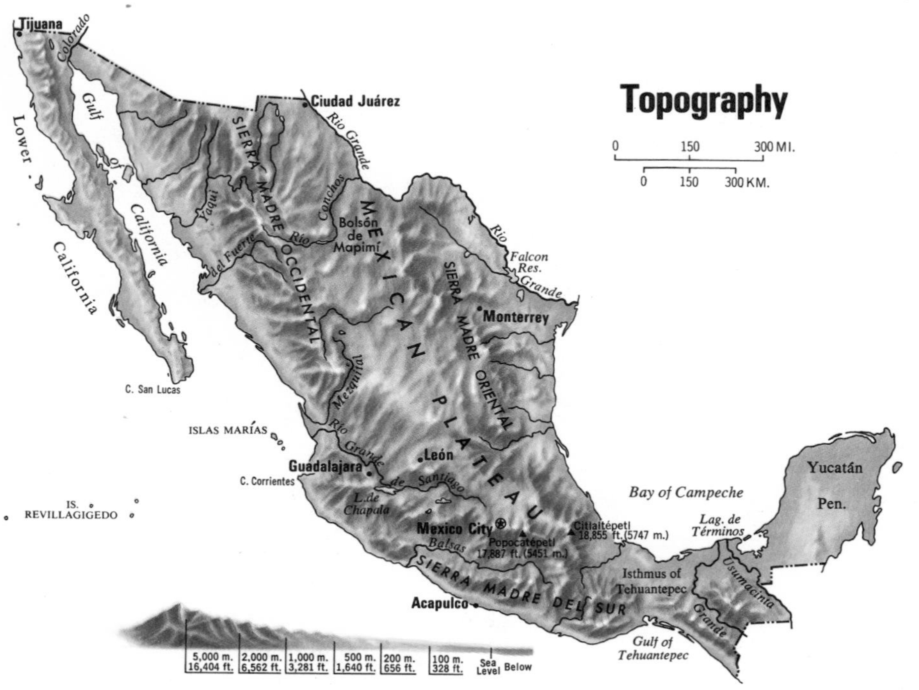

STATES

Aguascalientes 504,300 .... H6
Baja California 1,227,400 .... B1
Baja California Sur 221,000 .... C3
Campeche 371,800 .... O7
Chiapas 2,097,500 .... N8
Chihuahua 1,935,100 .... F2
Coahuila 1,561,000 .... H3
Colima 339,400 .... G7
Distrito Federal 9,377,300 .... L1
Durango 1,160,300 .... G4
Guanajuato 3,045,600 .... J6
Guerrero 2,174,200 .... J8
Hidalgo 1,518,200 .... K6
Jalisco 4,296,500 .... H6
México 7,542,300 .... K7
Michoacán 3,049,400 .... H7
Morelos 931,400 .... K7
Nayarit 729,500 .... G6
Nuevo León 2,463,500 .... K4
Oaxaca 2,517,500 .... L8
Puebla 3,285,300 .... L7
Querétaro 730,900 .... J6
Quintana Roo 209,900 .... P7
San Luis Potosí 1,669,900 .... J5
Sinaloa 1,882,200 .... F4
Sonora 1,498,100 .... D2
Tabasco 1,150,000 .... N7
Tamaulipas 1,924,900 .... K4
Tlaxcala 548,500 .... N1
Veracruz 5,263,800 .... L7
Yucatán 1,034,300 .... P6
Zacatecas 1,144,700 .... H5

CITIES and TOWNS

Acala 11,483 .... N8
Acámbaro 32,257 .... J7
Acaponeta 11,844 .... G5
Acapulco de Juárez 309,254 .... K8
Acatlán de Osorio 7,624 .... K7
Acatzingo de Hidalgo 6,905 .... N2
Acayucan 21,173 .... M8
Aconchi 1,596 .... D2
Actopan, Hidalgo 11,037 .... K6
Actopan, Veracruz 2,265 .... Q1
Agua Dulce 21,060 .... M7
Agualeguas 2,502 .... J3
Agua Prieta 20,754 .... E1
Aguascalientes 181,277 .... H6
Aguililla 5,715 .... H7
Ahome 4,182 .... E4
Ahuacatitlán 6,436 .... L1
Ahuacatlán 5,350 .... G6
Ahumada 6,466 .... F1
Ajalpan 8,238 .... L7
Alamo 9,954 .... L6
Álamos 4,269 .... E3
Aldama, Chihuahua 6,047 .... G2
Aldama, Tamaulipas 3,033 .... L5
Aljojuca 3,204 .... O1
Allende, Coahuila 11,076 .... J2
Allende, Nuevo León 9,914 .... J4
Almoloya del Río 3,714 .... K1
Altamira 6,053 .... L5
Altar 2,519 .... D1
Altepexi 6,661 .... L7
Alto Lucero 3,698 .... P1
Altotonga 6,754 .... P1
Alvarado 15,592 .... M7
Amatlán de los Reyes 3,664 .... P2
Amealco 2,960 .... K6
Ameca 21,018 .... H6
Amecameca de Juárez 16,276 .... L1
Amozoc de Mota 9,203 .... N2
Anáhuac, Chihuahua 10,886 .... F2
Anáhuac, Nuevo León 8,168 .... J3
Angostura 2,663 .... E4
Antiguo Morelos 1,569 .... K5
Apan 13,705 .... M1
Apatzingán de la Constitución 44,849 .... H7
Apizaco 21,189 .... N1
Aquiles Serdán 2,565 .... G2
Aramberri 1,786 .... J5
Arandas 18,934 .... H6
Arcelia 10,024 .... J7
Ario de Rosales 8,774 .... J7
Arizpe 1,736 .... D1
Armería 10,616 .... G7
Arriaga 13,193 .... N8
Arteaga 5,324 .... H7
Ascensión 4,104 .... E1
Asunción Nochixtlán 3,235 .... L8
Atlixco 41,967 .... M2
Atotonilco el Alto 16,271 .... H6
Atoyac de Álvarez 8,874 .... J8
Autlán de Navarro 20,398 .... G7
Axochiapan 8,283 .... M2
Ayutla de los Libres 3,618 .... K8
Azcapotzalco 534,554 .... L1
Azoyú 3,446 .... K8
Bacadéhuachi 1,514 .... E2
Bacalar 2,121 .... P7
Bachíniva 1,809 .... F2
Bácum 2,668 .... D3
Bahía Tortugas 1,457 .... B3
Balancán de Domínguez 3,669 .... O8
Bamoa 5,866 .... E4
Banderilla 3,488 .... P1
Baviácora 2,049 .... E2
Benjamín Hill 5,366 .... D1
Bernardino de Sahagún 12,327 .... M1
Boca del Río 2,354 .... Q2
Bolonchén de Rejón 2,342 .... O7
Buenaventura 3,924 .... F2
Burgos 673 .... K4
Cabo San Lucas 1,534 .... E5
Cacahoatán 5,079 .... N9
Cadereyta Jiménez 13,586 .... K4
Calkiní 6,870 .... O6
Calnali 3,318 .... K6
Calpulálpan 8,659 .... M1
Calvillo 6,453 .... H6
Campeche 69,506 .... O7
Cananea 17,518 .... D1
Canatlán 5,983 .... G4
Cancún 326 .... Q6
Candela 1,689 .... J3
Candelaria 1,982 .... O7
Cañitas de Felipe Pescador 4,885 .... H5
Capulhuac de Mirafuentes 8,289 .... K1
Carbo 2,804 .... D2
Cárdenas, San Luis Potosí 12,020 .... K6
Cárdenas, Tabasco 15,643 .... N8
Carichic 1,520 .... F2
Castaños 8,996 .... J3
Catemaco 11,786 .... M7
Ceballos 2,937 .... H3
Cedral 4,057 .... J5
Celaya 79,977 .... J6
Celestún 1,490 .... O6
Cerritos 10,421 .... J5
Cerro Azul 20,259 .... L6
Chahuites 5,218 .... M8
Chalchihuites 1,894 .... G5
Chalco de Díaz Covarrubias 12,172 .... M1
Champotón 6,606 .... O7
Charcas 10,491 .... J5
Chetumal 23,685 .... Q7
Chiapa de Corzo 8,571 .... N8
Chiautempan 12,327 .... N1
Chietla 4,602 .... M2
Chignahuapan 3,805 .... N1
Chihuahua 327,313 .... F2
Chilapa de Álvarez 9,204 .... K8
Chilpancingo de los Bravos 36,193 .... K8
China, Nuevo León 4,958 .... K4
Chocomán 5,114 .... P2
Choix 2,503 .... E3
Cholula de Rivadavia 15,399 .... M1
Cihuatlán 9,451 .... G7
Cintalapa de Figueroa 12,036 .... N8
Ciudad Acuña (Villa Acuña) 30,276 .... J2
Ciudad Altamirano 8,694 .... J7
Ciudad Camargo, Chihuahua 24,030 .... G3
Ciudad Camargo, Tamaulipas 5,953 .... K3
Ciudad del Carmen 34,656 .... N7
Ciudad Delicias 52,446 .... G2
Ciudad del Maíz 5,241 .... K5
Ciudad de Río Grande 11,651 .... H5
Ciudad Guerrero 3,110 .... F2
Ciudad Guzmán 48,166 .... H7
Ciudad Hidalgo, Chiapas 4,105 .... N9
Ciudad Hidalgo, Michoacán 24,692 .... J7
Ciudad Juárez 424,135 .... F1
Ciudad Lerdo 19,803 .... H4
Ciudad Madero 115,302 .... L5
Ciudad Mante 51,247 .... K5
Ciudad Mendoza 18,696 .... O2
Ciudad Miguel Alemán 11,259 .... K3
Ciudad Obregón 144,795 .... E3
Ciudad Río Bravo 39,018 .... K4
Ciudad Satélite 35,083 .... L1
Ciudad Serdán 9,581 .... O2
Ciudad Valles 47,587 .... K5
Ciudad Victoria 83,897 .... K5
Coalcomán de Matamoros 4,875 .... H7
Coatepec 21,542 .... P1
Coatetelco 5,268 .... L2
Coatzacoalcos 69,753 .... M7
Coatzingo 3,038 .... N2
Cocorit 4,478 .... E3
Colima 58,450 .... H7
Colón 3,346 .... K6
Colotlán 6,135 .... H5
Comala 5,592 .... H7
Comalcalco 14,963 .... N7
Comitán de Domínguez 21,249 .... O8
Compostela 9,801 .... G6
Concepción del Oro 8,144 .... J4
Concordia 3,947 .... G5
Contla 7,517 .... N1
Copala 3,783 .... K8
Coquimatlán 6,212 .... G7
Córdoba 78,495 .... P2
Cosalá 2,279 .... F4
Cosamaloapan de Carpio 19,766 .... M7
Cosautlán de Carvajal 2,039 .... P1
Coscomatepec de Bravo 6,023 .... P2
Cosío 2,680 .... H5
Costa Rica 11,795 .... F4
Cotija de la Paz 9,178 .... H7
Coyoacán 339,446 .... L1
Coyotepec 8,888 .... L1
Coyuca de Benítez 6,328 .... J8
Coyuca de Catalán 2,926 .... J7
Coyutla 3,726 .... L6
Cozumel 5,858 .... Q6
Creel 2,449 .... E3
Cuatrociénagas de Carranza 5,523 .... H3
Cuauhtémoc 26,598 .... F2
Cuautepec de Hinojosa 5,501 .... K6
Cuautitlán de Romero Rubio 11,439 .... L1
Cuautla Morelos 13,946 .... L2
Cuencamé de Ceniceros 3,774 .... H4
Cuernavaca 239,813 .... L2
Cuicatlán 2,733 .... L8
Cuitlahuac 4,813 .... P2
Culiacán 228,001 .... F4
Cumpas 2,395 .... E1
Cunduacán 4,397 .... N7
Dimas 2,194 .... F5
Doctor Arroyo 4,290 .... K5
Dolores Hidalgo de la Independencia Naci 16,849 .... J6
Durango 182,633 .... G1
Dzibalchén 1,917 .... P7
Dzidzantún 7,064 .... P6
Dzitbalché 4,393 .... P6
Ebano 17,489 .... K5
Ecatepec de Morelos 11,899 .... L1
Ejutla de Crespo 5,263 .... L8
Eldorado 8,115 .... E4
El Fuerte 7,179 .... E3
El Porvenir 3,030 .... G1
El Potosí 2,032 .... J4
El Salto 7,818 .... G5
El Zacatón 2,686 .... J5
Empalme 24,927 .... D2
Encarnación de Díaz 10,474 .... H6
Ensenada 77,687 .... A1
Escalón 2,998 .... G3
Escarcega 7,248 .... O7
Escuinapa de Hidalgo 16,442 .... G5
Escuintla 4,111 .... N9
Esperanza, Puebla 4,258 .... O2
Esperanza, Sonora 11,762 .... E3
Espita 5,394 .... Q6
Esqueda 1,458 .... E1
Etchojoa 4,398 .... E3
Ezequiel Montes 3,139 .... K6
Fortín de las Flores 9,358 .... P2
Francisco I. Madero 12,613 .... H4
Fresnillo de González Echererría 44,475 .... H5
Frontera 10,066 .... N7
Galeana, Nuevo León 3,429 .... J4
General Bravo 2,894 .... K4
General Cepeda 3,486 .... J4
General Terán 5,354 .... K4
Gómez Farías 3,030 .... F2
Gómez Palacio 79,650 .... G4
González 6,440 .... K5
Guadalajara 1,478,383 .... H6
Guadalajara* 2,343,034 .... H6
Guadalupe, Nuevo León 51,899 .... K4
Guadalupe, Zacatecas 13,246 .... H5
Guadalupe Bravo 3,333 .... F1
Guadalupe Victoria, Durango 7,931 .... H4
Guadalupe Victoria, Puebla 3,946 .... O1
Guamúchil 17,151 .... E4
Guanajuato 36,809 .... J6
Guasave 26,080 .... E4
Guaymas 57,492 .... D3
Gustavo Díaz Ordaz 10,154 .... K3
Gutiérrez Zamora 9,099 .... L6
Halachó 4,804 .... O6
Hecelchakán 4,279 .... O6
Hermosillo 232,691 .... D2
Heroica Caborca 20,771 .... C1
Heroica Nogales 52,108 .... D1
Hidalgo, Tamaulipas 2,450 .... K4
Hidalgo del Parral (Parral) 57,619 .... G3
Hopelchén 3,699 .... P7
Huajuapan de León 13,822 .... L8
Huamantla 15,565 .... N1
Huaquechula 2,294 .... M2
Huatabampo 18,506 .... D3
Huatusco de Chicuellar 9,501 .... P2
Huauchinango 16,826 .... L6
Huautla de Jiménez 6,132 .... L7
Huehuetlán el Chico 2,667 .... M2
Huejotzingo 8,552 .... M1
Huejutla 6,854 .... K6
Huetamo 9,333 .... J7
Hueyotlipan de Hidalgo 2,353 .... M1
Huimanguillo 7,075 .... N8
Huitzilán 3,573 .... O1
Huitzuco de los Figueroa 9,406 .... K7
Huixcolotla 4,039 .... N2
Huixtepec 5,927 .... L8
Huixtla 15,737 .... N9
Hunucmá 8,020 .... O6
Ignacio de la Llave 3,962 .... Q2
Iguala de la Independencia 45,355 .... K7
Imuris 1,958 .... D1
Irapuato 135,596 .... J6
Isla Mujeres 2,663 .... Q6
Isla, Veracruz 8,075 .... M7
Ixmiquilpan 6,048 .... K6
Ixtapa J8
Ixtapalapa 522,095 .... L1
Ixtenco 5,035 .... N1
Ixtepec 14,025 .... M8
Ixtlán del Río 10,986 .... G6
Izamal 9,749 .... P6
Izúcar de Matamoros 21,164 .... M2
Jala 4,535 .... G6
Jalacingo 3,427 .... P1
Jalapa Enríquez 161,352 .... P1
Jalpa 9,904 .... H6
Jalpa de Méndez 4,785 .... N7
Jalpan 1,878 .... K6
Jáltipan de Morelos 15,170 .... M8
Jantetelco 2,015 .... L2
Jaumave 3,072 .... K5
Jerez de García Salinas 20,325 .... H5
Jico 7,269 .... P1
Jilotepec de Abasolo 4,252 .... K7
Jiménez, Chihuahua 18,095 .... G3
Joachín 3,918 .... Q2
Jojutla de Juárez 14,438 .... L2
Jonacatepec 3,868 .... M2
Jonuta 2,746 .... N7
José Cardel 5,396 .... Q1
Juan Aldama 9,667 .... H4
Juchipila 6,328 .... H6
Juchitán de Zaragoza 30,218 .... M8
Kantunilkin 1,970 .... Q6
La Barca 18,055 .... H6
La Barra de Navidad 1,829 .... G7
La Concordia 3,559 .... N9
La Cruz, Sinaloa 4,218 .... F5
Lagos de Moreno 33,782 .... J6
La Huerta 4,328 .... G7
La Paz, Baja California Sur 46,011 .... D5
La Paz, San Luis Potosí 3,735 .... J5
La Piedad Cavadas 34,963 .... H6
Las Choapas 20,166 .... M7
Las Hadas G7
Las Nieves 2,262 .... G3
Las Rosas 7,658 .... N8
León 468,887 .... J6
Lerdo de Tejada 11,628 .... M8
Lerma 4,158 .... O7
Libres 4,830 .... O1
Linares 24,456 .... K4
Llera de Canales 3,564 .... K5
Loma Bonita 15,804 .... M7
Loreto, Baja California 2,570 .... D4
Loreto, Zacatecas 7,132 .... J5
Los Mochis 67,953 .... E4
Los Reyes de Salgado 19,452 .... H7
Macuspana 12,293 .... N8
Madera 9,759 .... F2
Magdalena de Kino 10,281 .... D1
Maltrata 5,457 .... O2
Manzanillo 20,777 .... G7
Mapastepec 5,907 .... N9
Mapimí 2,737 .... G4
Martínez de la Torre 17,203 .... L6
Mascota 5,674 .... G6
Matamoros, Coahuila 15,125 .... H4
Matamoros, Tamaulipas 165,124 .... L4
Matehuala 28,799 .... J5
Matías Romero 13,200 .... M8
Maxcanú 6,505 .... O6
Mazatlán 147,010 .... F5
Melchor Múzquiz 18,868 .... H3
Melchor Ocampo del Balsas 4,766 .... H8
Meoquí 12,308 .... G2
Mérida 233,912 .... P6
Metepec 4,625 .... M2
Metlatonoc 1,870 .... K8
Mexicali 317,228 .... B1
Mexico City (cap.) 9,377,300 .... L1
Mexico City* 13,993,866 .... L1
Miacatlán 3,980 .... K2
Mier 5,636 .... K3
Miguel Auza 9,303 .... H4
Minatitlán 68,397 .... M8
Mineral del Monte 8,887 .... K6
Miquihuana 1,971 .... J5
Misantla 8,799 .... P1
Miahuatlán de Porfirio Díaz 5,714 .... L8
Mocorito 3,993 .... F4
Moctezuma, San Luis Potosí 1,734 .... J5
Moctezuma, Sonora 2,700 .... E2
Monclova 78,134 .... J3
Montemorelos 18,642 .... K4
Monterrey 1,006,221 .... J4
Monterrey* 1,923,402 .... J4
Morelia 199,099 .... J7
Morelos 4,241 .... J2
Morelos Cañada 2,288 .... O2
Moroleón 25,620 .... J6
Motozintla de Mendoza 4,682 .... N9
Motul de Felipe Carillo Puerto 12,949 .... P6
Muna 5,491 .... P6
Naco 3,580 .... D1
Nacozari 2,976 .... E1
Nadadores 2,461 .... H3
Naica 7,190 .... G2
Namiquipa 4,875 .... F2
Nanacamilpa 6,356 .... M1
Naolinco de Victoria 4,365 .... P1
Naranjos 14,732 .... L6
Naucalpan de Juárez 9,425 .... L1
Nautla 1,935 .... L6
Nava 4,097 .... J2
Navojoa 43,817 .... E3
Navolato 12,799 .... E4
Nazas 2,881 .... G4
Netzahualcóyotl 580,436 .... L1
Nieves 3,966 .... H5
Nochistlán 8,780 .... H6
Nogales 14,254 .... P2
Nombre de Dios 3,188 .... G5
Nopalucan de la Granja 3,002 .... O1
Nueva Casas Grandes 20,023 .... F1
Nueva Ciudad Guerrero 3,300 .... K3
Nueva Italia de Ruiz 14,718 .... J7
Nueva Rosita 34,706 .... J2
Nuevo Ideal 5,252 .... G4
Nuevo Laredo 184,622 .... J3
Oaxaca de Juárez 114,948 .... L8
Ocampo, Coahuila 1,613 .... H3
Ocampo, Tamaulipas 4,801 .... K5
Ocosingo 2,946 .... O8
Ocotlán 35,361 .... H6
Ocotlán de Morelos 5,882 .... L8
Ojinaga 12,757 .... G2
Ojocaliente 7,582 .... H5
Ometepec 7,342 .... K8
Oriental 6,009 .... O1
Orizaba 105,150 .... P2
Otumba de Gómez Farías 3,198 .... M1
Oxkutzcab 8,182 .... P6
Ozuluama 2,851 .... L6
Ozumba de Alzate 6,876 .... M1
Pachuca de Soto 83,892 .... K6
Padilla 4,581 .... K5
Palenque 2,595 .... O8
Palizada 2,332 .... O7
Palomas 2,129 .... F1

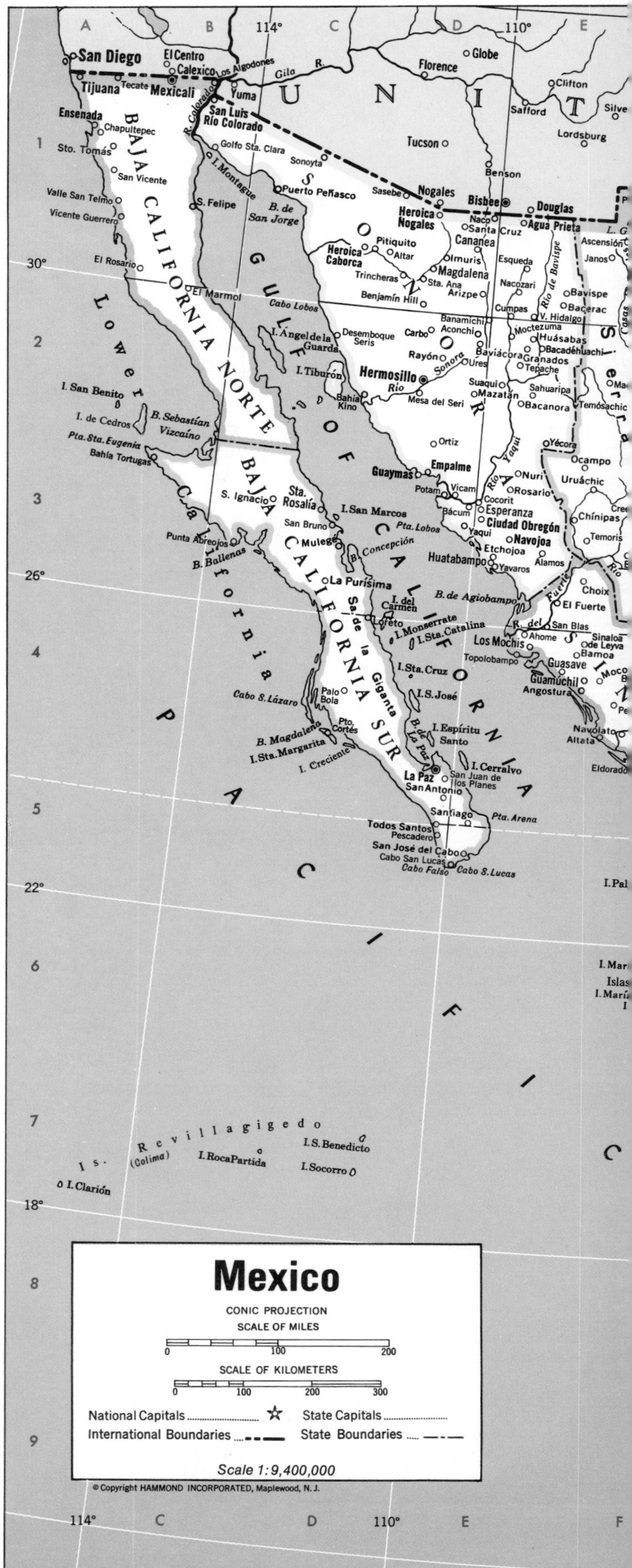

(continued on following page)

AREA 761,601 sq. mi. (1,972,546 sq. km.)
POPULATION 67,395,826
CAPITAL Mexico City
LARGEST CITY Mexico City
HIGHEST POINT Citlaltépetl 18,855 ft. (5,747 m.)
MONETARY UNIT Mexican peso
MAJOR LANGUAGE Spanish
MAJOR RELIGION Roman Catholicism

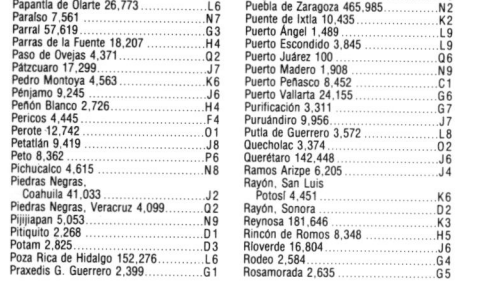

States Indicated by Numbers

1 Tlaxcala	6 Querétaro
2 Morelos	7 Guanajuato
3 Distrito Federal	8 Aguascalientes
4 México	9 Nayarit
5 Hidalgo	10 Colima

Index (continued)

Rosario, Sinaloa 10,276 ..... G5
Rosario, Sonora 1,887 ..... E3
Ruiz 8,954 ..... G6
Sabancuy 1,819 ..... O7
Sabinas 20,538 ..... J3
Sabinas Hidalgo 17,439 ..... J3
Sahuaripa 4,710 ..... E2
Sahuayo de Díaz 28,727 ..... H7
Sain Alto 3,628 ..... H5
Salamanca 61,039 ..... J6
Salina Cruz 22,004 ..... M9
Salinas 7,471 ..... J5
Saltillo 200,712 ..... J4
Salvatierra 18,975 ..... J6
San Andrés Tuxtla 24,267 ..... M7
San Blas, Nayarit 3,443 ..... G6
San Blas, Sinaloa 6,222 ..... E3
San Buenaventura 9,188 ..... J3
San Carlos, Coahuila 1,960 ..... J2
San Cristóbal de las
  Casas 25,700 ..... N8
San Felipe, Baja
  California 160 ..... B1
San Felipe, Guanajuato 10,129 ..... J6
San Fernando,
  Tamaulipas 27,656 ..... L4
San Francisco del Oro 12,116 ..... F3
San Francisco del
  Rincón 27,079 ..... H6
San Gabriel Chilac 6,707 ..... K7
San Ignacio, Sinaloa 1,804 ..... F5
San Jerónimo de
  Juárez 5,204 ..... J8
San José del Cabo 2,571 ..... D5
San Juan 15,422 ..... K6
San Juan de los Lagos 19,570 ..... H6
San Juan Xiutetelco 3,306 ..... O1
San Luis de la Paz 12,654 ..... J6
San Luis del Cordero 2,203 ..... H4
San Luis Potosí 271,123 ..... J5
San Luis Río Colorado 49,990 ..... B1
San Marcos 5,861 ..... K8
San Martín de las
  Pirámides 4,575 ..... M1
San Martín Texmelucan 23,355 ..... M1
San Miguel de Allende 24,286 ..... J6
San Nicolás de los
  Garza 28,803 ..... J3
San Pedro de las
  Colonias 26,882 ..... H4
San Pedro Pochutla 4,395 ..... L9
San Rafael 8,974 ..... O1
San Salvador el Seco 7,729 ..... O1
Santa Ana 7,020 ..... D1
Santa Ana Chiautempan
  (Chiautempan) 12,327 ..... N1
Santa Bárbara 16,978 ..... F3
Santa Clara 3,449 ..... H4
Santa María del Oro 4,231 ..... G3
Santa María del Río 4,972 ..... J6
Santa María del Tule 1,674 ..... L8
Santander Jiménez 3,586 ..... K4
Santa Rosalía 7,356 ..... C3
Santiago Ixcuintla 17,321 ..... G6
Santiago Jamiltepec 5,280 ..... K8
Santiago Juxtlahuaca 2,923 ..... K8
Santiago Miahuatlán 4,917 ..... O2
Santiago Papasquiaro 6,636 ..... F4
Santiago Pinotepa
  Nacional 9,382 ..... K8
Santiago Tuxtla 9,426 ..... M7
Saucillo 8,467 ..... G2
Sayula 14,333 ..... H7
Sayula de Alemán 4,896 ..... M8
Seybaplaya 4,439 ..... O7
Silao 31,825 ..... J6
Simojovel de Allende 3,779 ..... N8
Sinaloa de Leyva 1,998 ..... E4
Soledad de Doblado 6,612 ..... L7
Soledad Díez

Gutiérrez 9,622 ..... J5
Sombrerete 11,077 ..... H5
Sonoyta 2,463 ..... C1
Sotuta 3,772 ..... P6
Tabasco 3,197 ..... H6
Tacámbaro de Codallos 9,695 ..... J7
Tacotalpa 2,019 ..... N8
Tala 15,744 ..... G6
Talpa de Allende 4,264 ..... G6
Tamazulapan del Progreso 2,870 ..... L1
Tamazunchale 12,302 ..... K6
Tamiahua 6,264 ..... L6
Tampico 212,188 ..... L5
Tamuín 7,251 ..... K6
Tantoyuca 11,902 ..... L6
Tapachula 60,620 ..... N9
Taxco de Alarcón 27,089 ..... K7
Tayoltita 2,697 ..... G4
Teapa 6,534 ..... N8
Tecamachalco 3,319 ..... O2
Tecate 14,738 ..... A1
Tecomán 31,625 ..... H8
Tecpan de Galeana 8,095 ..... J8
Tecuala 12,461 ..... G5
Tehuacán 47,497 ..... L7
Tehuantepec 16,179 ..... M8
Tekax de Álaro
  Obregón 10,326 ..... P6
Teloloapan 10,335 ..... J7
Temax 4,915 ..... P6
Temósachic 1,738 ..... E2
Tenabo 3,278 ..... P6
Tenancingo de Degollado 12,807 ..... K7
Tenango de Río Blanco 12,302 ..... O2
Tenosique de Pino
  Suárez 11,393 ..... O8
Teocaltiche 13,745 ..... H6
Teocelo 4,572 ..... P1
Teotihuacán de Arista 2,238 ..... L1
Teotitlán del Camino 3,106 ..... L8
Tepache 1,591 ..... E2
Tepalcingo 5,968 ..... M2
Tepatitlán de Morelos 29,292 ..... H6
Tepeaca 7,466 ..... N2
Tepeapulco 7,027 ..... M1
Tepehuanes 2,531 ..... G4
Tepeji del Río 10,365 ..... L1
Tepexi de Rodríguez 2,618 ..... N2
Tepic 108,924 ..... G6
Tepoztlán 6,851 ..... L1
Tequixquitla 4,825 ..... O1
Terán 5,215 ..... N1
Terrenate 1,515 ..... N1
Texcoco de Mora 18,044 ..... M1
Teziutlán 23,948 ..... O1
Tezonapa 3,506 ..... P2
Tezontepec 2,762 ..... M1
Ticul 14,341 ..... P6
Tierra Blanca 22,727 ..... L7
Tila 2,633 ..... N8
Tijuana 363,154 ..... A1
Tixtla de Guerrero 10,334 ..... K8
Tizayuca 5,262 ..... L1
Tizimín 18,343 ..... Q6
Tlachichuca 3,721 ..... O1
Tlacolula de Matamoros 8,300 ..... L8
Tlacotepec de Mejía 1,595 ..... P1
Tlahualilo de Zaragoza 8,951 ..... H3
Tlalancaneca 5,090 ..... M1
Tlalixcoyan 3,211 ..... Q2
Tlalmanalco de
  Velázquez 5,744 ..... L1
Tlalnepantla de
  Comonfort 45,575 ..... L1
Tlalpan 130,719 ..... L1
Tlaltenango de Sánchez
  Román 7,698 ..... H6
Tlaltizapán 6,384 ..... L2
Tlapacoyan 13,172 ..... P1
Tlapa de Comonfort 6,676 ..... K8

Tlaquepaque 59,760 ..... G6
Tlatlauquitepec 4,272 ..... O1
Tlaquiltenango 8,625 ..... L2
Tlaxcala de Xicotencatl 9,972 ..... M1
Tlaxco 4,969 ..... N1
Tlaxiaco 4,477 ..... L8
Tochimilco 3,538 ..... L1
Tochimilco 3,190 ..... M2
Todos Santos 2,400 ..... D5
Toluca de Lerdo 136,092 ..... K7
Tomatlán 2,695 ..... G6
Tonalá 15,611 ..... N8
Topolobampo 4,685 ..... E4
Torreón 244,309 ..... H4
Tula, Tamaulipas 5,407 ..... K5

Tula de Allende 10,720 ..... K6
Tulancingo 35,799 ..... K7
Tulcingo del Valle 2,983 ..... M2
Tultepec 8,321 ..... L1
Tuxpan, Jalisco 14,693 ..... H7
Tuxpan, Nayarit 20,322 ..... G6
Tuxpan de Rodríguez
  Cano 33,901 ..... L6
Tuxtepec 17,701 ..... L7
Tuxtla Gutiérrez 66,851 ..... N8
Tzucabab 4,876 ..... P7
Umán 8,371 ..... P6
Unión de Tula 6,399 ..... G7
Unión Hidalgo 8,658 ..... M8
Ures 3,681 ..... D2

Úrsulo Galván 2,637 ..... Q1
Uruapan del Progreso 108,124 ..... H7
Valladolid 14,663 ..... P6
Valle de Cos 1,850 ..... H5
Valle de Allende 4,973 ..... G3
Valle de Bravo 7,628 ..... J7
Valle Hermoso 19,278 ..... L4
Vanegas 2,042 ..... J5
Venado 2,790 ..... J5
Venustiano Carranza 23,624 ..... N8
Vicam 4,104 ..... D3
Vicente Guerrero,
  Durango 8,451 ..... G5
Víctor Rosales 7,629 ..... H5
Viesca 2,923 ..... H4

Villa Acuña 30,276 ..... J2
Villa Cuauhtémoc 6,611 ..... L5
Villa de Cos 1,850 ..... H5
Villa de Guadalupe
  Hidalgo 88,537 ..... L1
Villa Frontera 25,761 ..... J3
Villa García 2,765 ..... J5
Villahermosa 133,181 ..... N8
Villa Hidalgo, Sonora 2,126 ..... E1
Villaldama 2,350 ..... J3
Villa Matamoros 1,998 ..... G3
Villanueva 5,895 ..... H5
Villa Unión, Coahuila 4,058 ..... J2
Villa Unión, Durango 4,042 ..... F5
Villa Unión, Sinaloa 6,789 ..... F5
Villa Vicente Guerrero 18,280 ..... N1
Xaltocan 2,524 ..... N1
Xicoténcatl 6,374 ..... K5
Xicotepec de Juárez 12,656 ..... L6
Xochihuehuetlán 3,268 ..... K8
Xochimilco 116,493 ..... L1
Xochitlán 3,312 ..... N2
Yajalón 4,506 ..... N8
Yaqui 8,061 ..... D3
Yautepec 13,952 ..... L2
Yavaros 1,959 ..... E3
Yécora E2
Yecuatla 2,816 ..... P1
Yehualtepec 2,558 ..... O2
Zaachila 7,270 ..... L8
Zacapu 31,989 ..... J7
Zacatepec 16,839 ..... L2
Zacatecas 50,251 ..... H5
Zacatelco 14,117 ..... N1
Zacatlán 7,909 ..... N1
Zacoalco de Torres 11,343 ..... H6
Zamora de Hidalgo 5,775 ..... H7
Zaragoza, Coahuila 6,797 ..... J2
Zaragoza, Chihuahua 3,984 ..... F1
Zaragoza, Puebla 4,754 ..... O1
Zempoala 5,064 ..... Q1
Zihuatanejo 4,879 ..... J8
Zimatlán de Álvarez 5,746 ..... L8
Zitácuaro 36,911 ..... J7
Zongolica 2,378 ..... P2
Zumpango de Ocampo 12,923 ..... L1
Zumpango del Río 8,162 ..... J8

Falcón (res.) K3
Falso (cape) D5
Roca Partida (isl.) F3
Giganta, Sierra de la (mts.) D3
Grande (riv.) G2
Grande (riv.) J4
Grande de Santiago (riv.) G6
Grijalva (riv.) N7
Guzmán (lake) F1
Herrero (pt.) Q7
Hondo (riv.) Q7
Jesús María (reef) L4
La Boquilla (res.) G3
La Paz (bay) D4
Lobos (cape) D2
Lobos (pt.) L6
Lower California (pen.) C3
Madre (lag.) L4
Madre del Sur, Sierra (mts.) K8
Madre Occidental, Sierra
  (mts.) E2
Madre Oriental, Sierra (mts.) J4
Magdalena (bay) C4
Maldonado (pt.) K8
Mapimí (depr.) G3
María Cleofas (isl.) F6
María Madre (isl.) F6
María Magdalena (isl.) F6
Mexico (gulf) N7
Mezquital (riv.) G5
Mita (pt.) G6
Mitla (ruin) M8
Moctezuma (riv.) K6
Monserrate (isl.) D3
Montague (isl.) B1
Muerto, Mar (lag.) N9
Nauhcampatépetl (mt.) O2
Nayarit, Sierra (mts.) G5
Nazas (riv.) G4
Nuevo, Bajo (reef) Q5
Orizaba (Citlaltépetl)
  (mt.) O2
Palenque (ruin) O8
Palmito de la Virgen
  (isl.) F5
Palmito del Verde (isl.) F5
Pánuco (riv.) K5
Paricutín (vol.) H7
Pátzcuaro (lake) H7
Pérez (isl.) P5
Petacalco (bay) J8
Popocatépetl (mt.) M1
Ramos (riv.) G4
Revillagigedo (isls.) C7
Sabinas (riv.) J3
San Antonio (res.) L4
San Benedicto (isl.) C7
San Benito (isl.) B2
San Jorge (bay) C1
San José (isl.) D3
San Lázaro (cape) C4
San Lucas (cape) E5
San Marcos (isl.) D3
San Rafael (reef) L4
Santa Ana (reef) N7
Santa Catalina (isl.) D3
Santa Cruz (isl.) D4
Santa Eugenia (pt.) B3
Santa Margarita (isl.) C4
Santa María (lake) F1
Santa María (riv.) F1
Santiaguillo (lake) G4
Sebastián Vizcaíno (bay) B2
Socorro (isl.) C7
Sonora (riv.) D2
Superior (lag.) M9
Teacapán (inlet) F5
Tehuantepec (gulf) M9
Tehuantepec (isth.) M8
Teotihuacán (ruin) M1
Términos (lag.) O7
Tiburón (isl.) C2
Triángulo Este (isl.) N6
Triángulo Oeste (isl.) N6
Tula (riv.) L1
Urique (riv.) G2
Usumacinta (riv.) O8
Uxmal (ruin) P6
Valsequillo (res.) N2
Verde (riv.) H6
Verde (isl.) L8
Yaqui (riv.) E2

OTHER FEATURES

Agiobampo (bay) E3
Aguanaval (riv.) H4
Amistad (res.) J2
Ángel de la Guarda (isl.) C2
Antigua (riv.) Q1
Arena (pt.) E5
Arenas (cay) O5
Atoyac (riv.) N2
Atoyac (riv.) Q2
Babía (riv.) J2
Bacalar (lake) P7
Ballenas (bay) C3
Balsas (riv.) J7
Banderas (bay) G6
Bavispe, Río de (riv.) E1
Blanco (riv.) Q2
Bravo (Grande) (riv.) J2
Burro (mts.) J2
California (gulf) D3
Campeche (bank) O6
Campeche (bay) N7
Candelaria (riv.) O8
Carmen (isl.) D3
Casas Grandes (riv.) F1
Catoche (pt.) Q6
Cedros (isl.) B2
Cerralvo (isl.) E4
Chamela (bay) G7
Chapala (lake) H6
Chetumal (bay) P8
Chichén-Itzá (ruin) P6
Citlaltépetl (mt.) O2
Clarión (isl.) B7
Colorado (riv.) B1
Conchos (riv.) G2
Corrientes (cape) F6
Coyuca (riv.) O1
Creciente (isl.) C4
Cuitzeo (lake) J7
Delgada (pt.) L7
Dzibalchaltún (ruin) P6
El Azúcar (res.) K3
Espíritu Santo (isl.) D4

*City and suburbs.

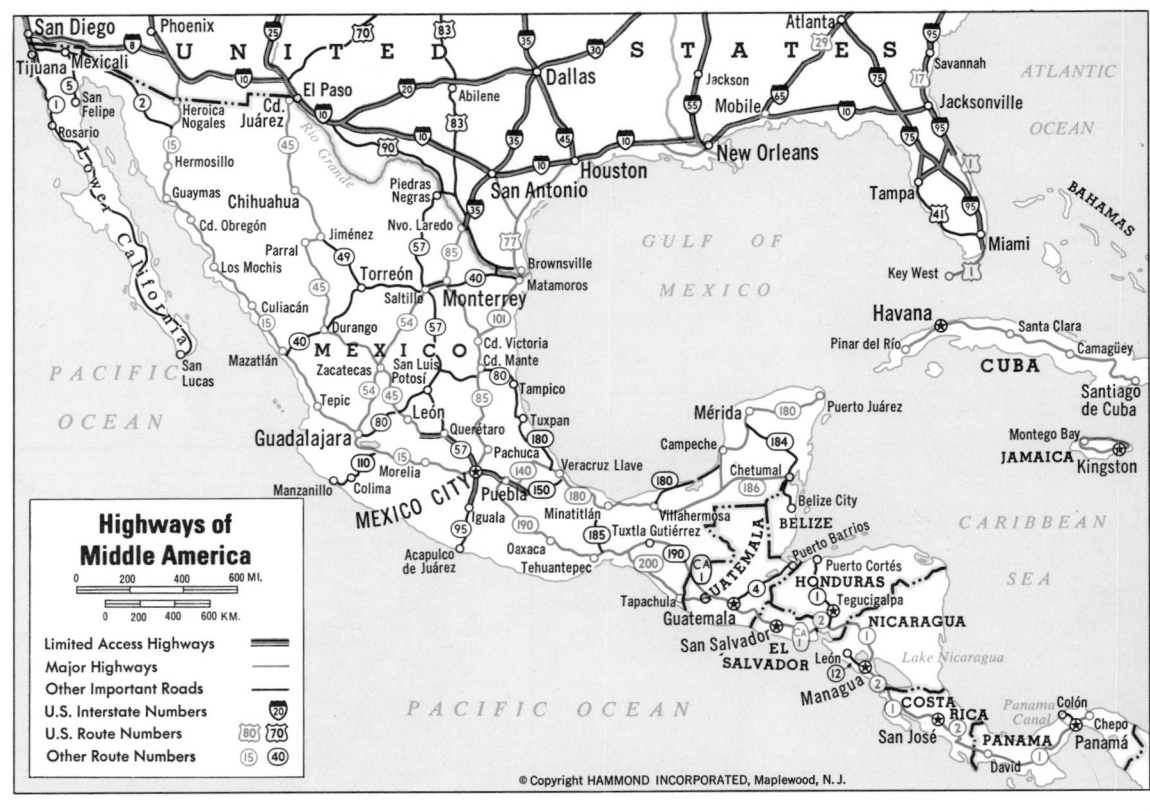

Highways of Middle America

| 0 | 200 | 400 | 600 MI. |
| 0 | 200 | 400 | 600 KM. |

Limited Access Highways
Major Highways
Other Important Roads
U.S. Interstate Numbers
U.S. Route Numbers
Other Route Numbers

© Copyright HAMMOND INCORPORATED, Maplewood, N.J.

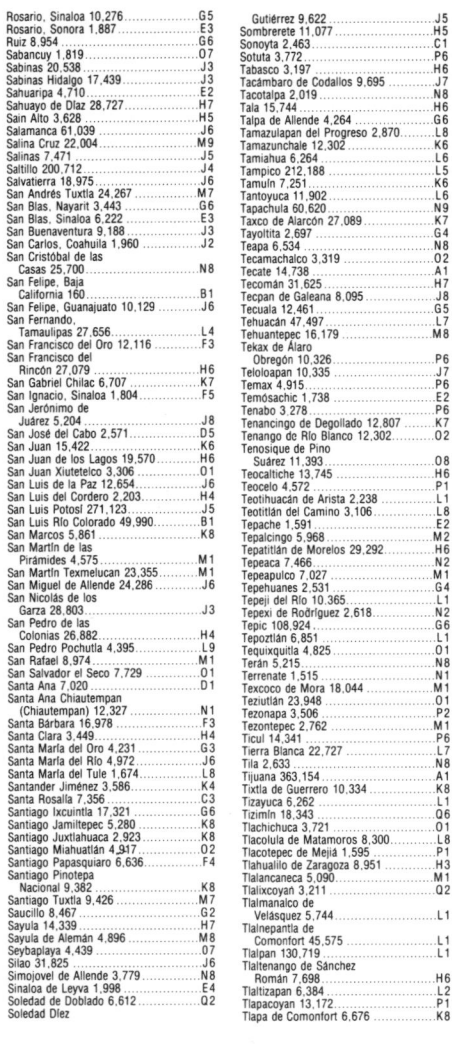

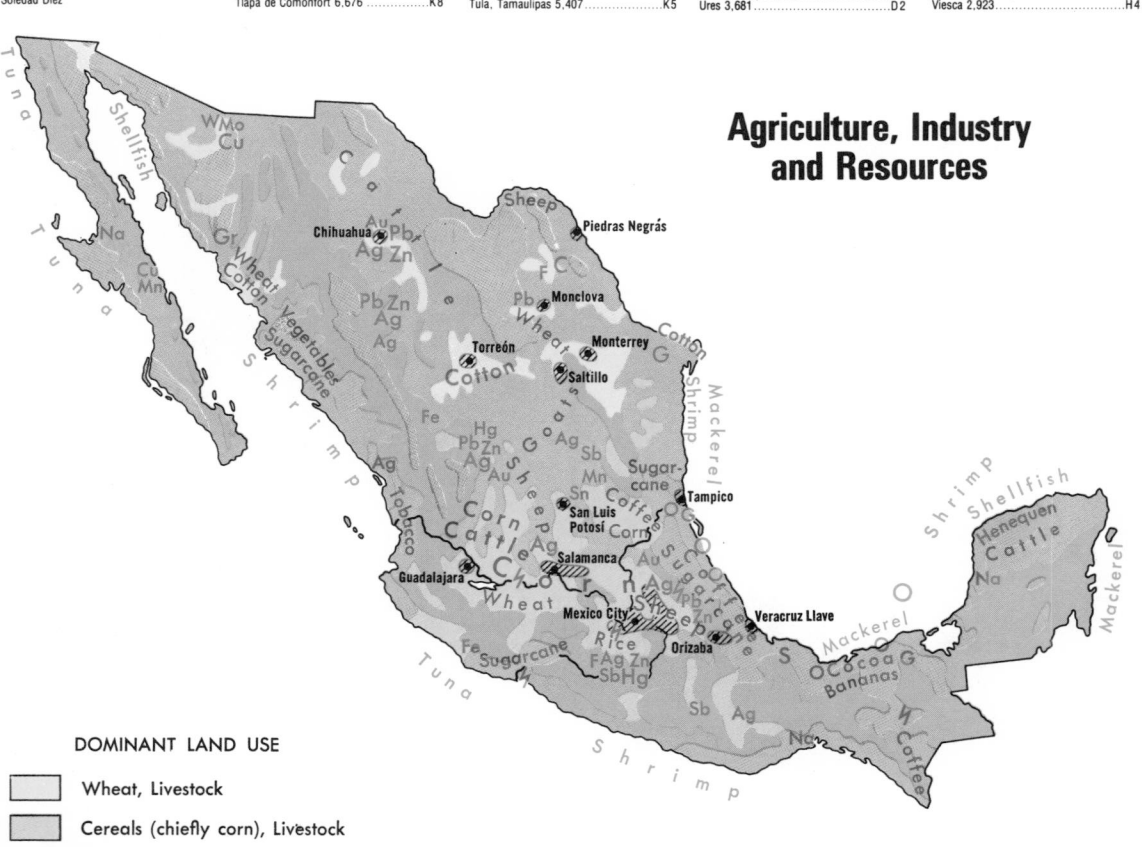

Agriculture, Industry and Resources

DOMINANT LAND USE

Wheat, Livestock
Cereals (chiefly corn), Livestock
Diversified Tropical Cash Crops
Cotton, Mixed Cereals
Livestock, Limited Agriculture
Range Livestock
Forests
Nonagricultural Land

Water Power
Major Industrial Areas

MAJOR MINERAL OCCURRENCES

Ag Silver
Au Gold
C Coal
Cu Copper
F Fluorspar
Fe Iron Ore

G Natural Gas
Gr Graphite
Hg Mercury
Mn Manganese
Mo Molybdenum
Na Salt

O Petroleum
Pb Lead
S Sulfur
Sb Antimony
Sn Tin
W Tungsten
Zn Zinc

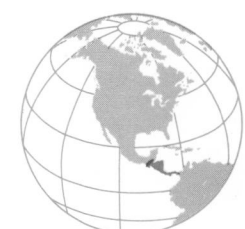

GUATEMALA

AREA 42,042 sq. mi. (108,889 sq. km.)
POPULATION 7,262,419
CAPITAL Guatemala
LARGEST CITY Guatemala
HIGHEST POINT Tajumulco 13,845 ft. (4,220 m.)
MONETARY UNIT quetzal
MAJOR LANGUAGES Spanish, Quiché
MAJOR RELIGION Roman Catholicism

BELIZE

AREA 8,867 sq. mi. (22,966 sq. km.)
POPULATION 144,857
CAPITAL Belmopan
LARGEST CITY Belize City
HIGHEST POINT Victoria Peak 3,681 ft. (1,122 m.)
MONETARY UNIT Belize dollar
MAJOR LANGUAGES English, Spanish, Mayan
MAJOR RELIGIONS Roman Catholicism, Protestantism

EL SALVADOR

AREA 8,260 sq. mi. (21,393 sq. km.)
POPULATION 4,813,000
CAPITAL San Salvador
LARGEST CITY San Salvador
HIGHEST POINT Santa Ana 7,825 ft. (2,385 m.)
MONETARY UNIT colón
MAJOR LANGUAGE Spanish
MAJOR RELIGION Roman Catholicism

HONDURAS

AREA 43,277 sq. mi. (112,087 sq. km.)
POPULATION 3,691,000
CAPITAL Tegucigalpa
LARGEST CITY Tegucigalpa
HIGHEST POINT Las Minas 9,347 ft. (2,849 m.)
MONETARY UNIT lempira
MAJOR LANGUAGE Spanish
MAJOR RELIGION Roman Catholicism

NICARAGUA

AREA 45,698 sq. mi. (118,358 sq. km.)
POPULATION 2,703,000
CAPITAL Managua
LARGEST CITY Managua
HIGHEST POINT Cerro Mocotón 6,913 ft. (2,107 m.)
MONETARY UNIT córdoba
MAJOR LANGUAGE Spanish
MAJOR RELIGION Roman Catholicism

COSTA RICA

AREA 19,575 sq. mi. (50,700 sq. km.)
POPULATION 2,245,000
CAPITAL San José
LARGEST CITY San José
HIGHEST POINT Chirripó Grande 12,530 ft. (3,819 m.)
MONETARY UNIT colón
MAJOR LANGUAGE Spanish
MAJOR RELIGION Roman Catholicism

PANAMA

AREA 29,761 sq. mi. (77,082 sq. km.)
POPULATION 1,830,175
CAPITAL Panamá
LARGEST CITY Panamá
HIGHEST POINT Vol. Baru 11,401 ft. (3,475 m.)
MONETARY UNIT balboa
MAJOR LANGUAGE Spanish
MAJOR RELIGION Roman Catholicism

Agriculture, Industry and Resources

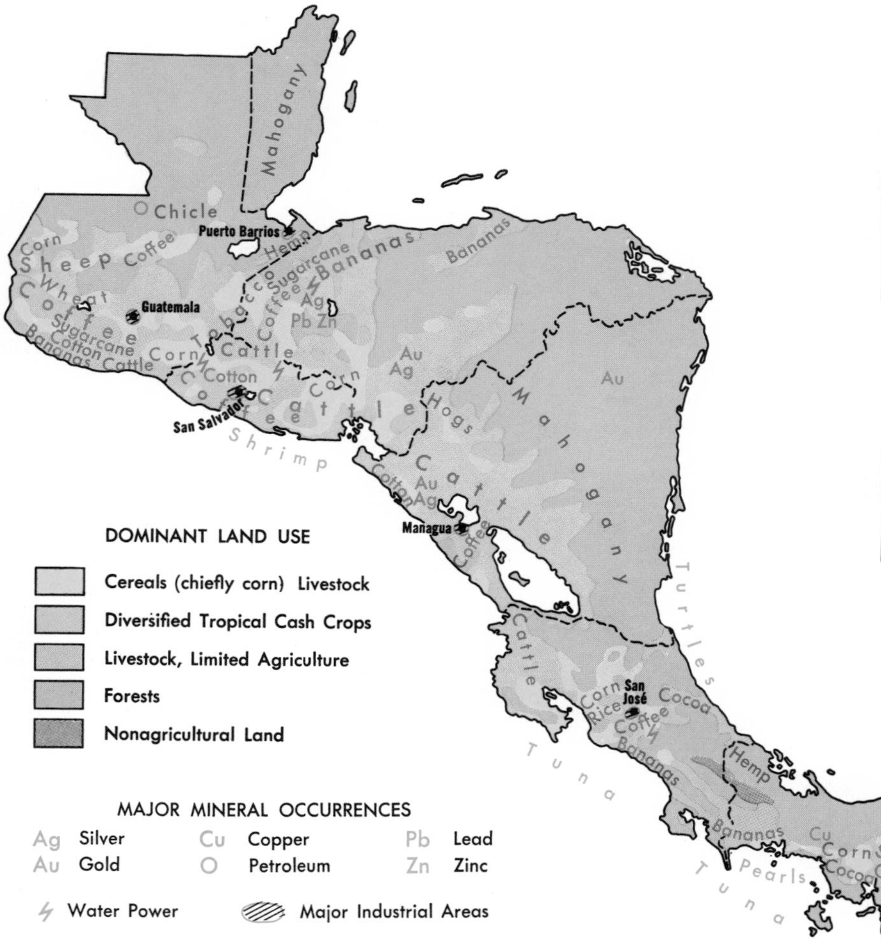
Puerto Barrios
Guatemala
San Salvador
Managua
San José
Colón
Panamá
Chicle
Mahogany
Bananas
Sheep
Coffee
Wheat
Sugarcane
Cotton
Cattle
Corn
Tobacco
Hemp
Ag
Pb Zn
Au
Hogs
Shrimp
Turtles
Rice
Cocoa
Tuna
Pearls
Cu
DOMINANT LAND USE
Cereals (chiefly corn) Livestock
Diversified Tropical Cash Crops
Livestock, Limited Agriculture
Forests
Nonagricultural Land
MAJOR MINERAL OCCURRENCES
Ag Silver
Au Gold
Cu Copper
O Petroleum
Pb Lead
Zn Zinc
Water Power
Major Industrial Areas

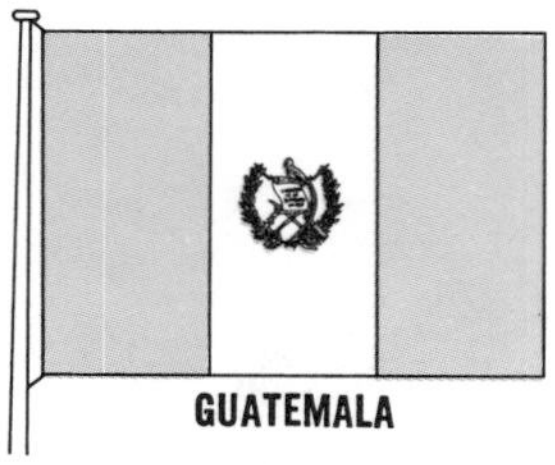

GUATEMALA

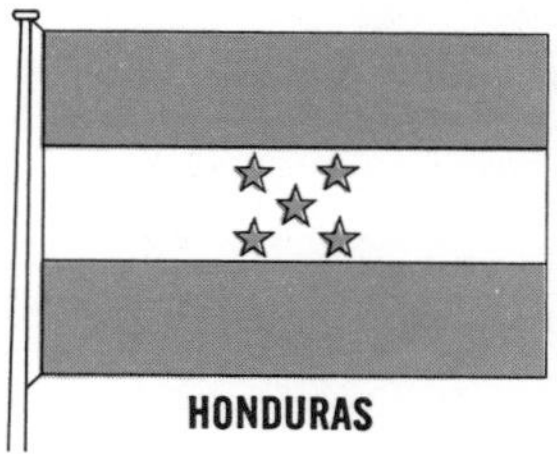

HONDURAS

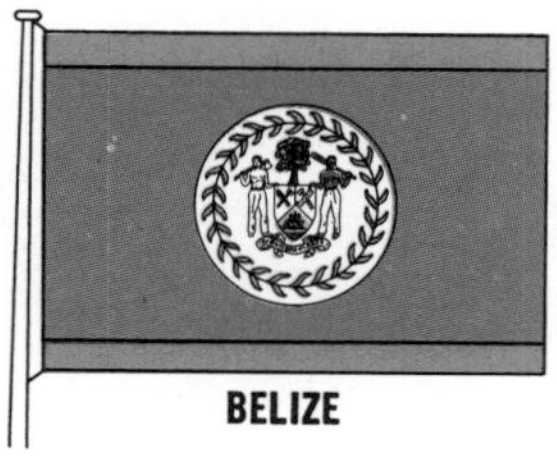

BELIZE

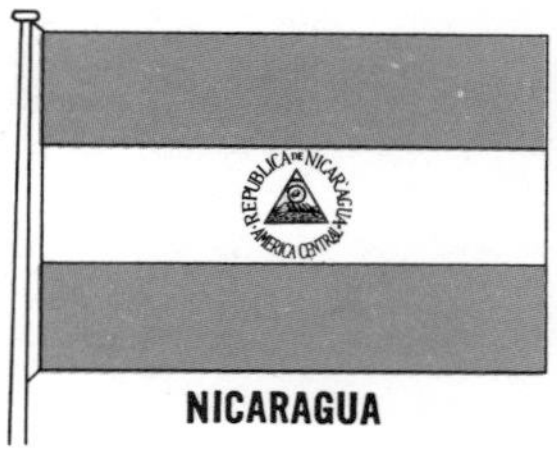

NICARAGUA

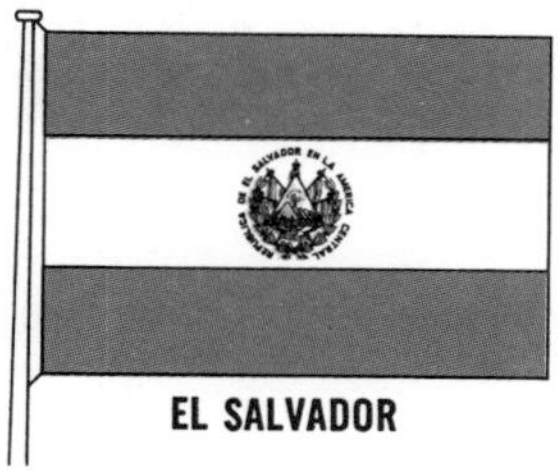

EL SALVADOR

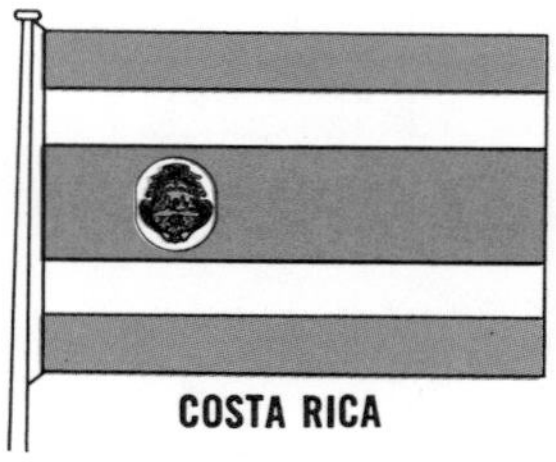

COSTA RICA

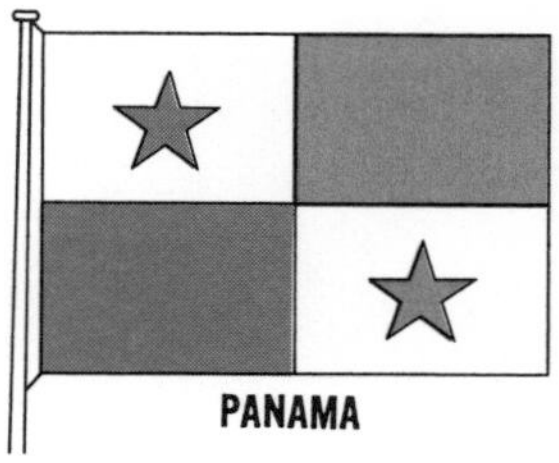

PANAMA

BELIZE

CITIES and TOWNS

Belize City 39,887 .... C2
Belize City* 50,925 .... C2
Belmopan (cap.) 2,932 .... C2
Corozal Town 6,862 .... C1
Hattieville 904 .... C2
Libertad 856 .... C1
Orange Walk Town 8,441 .... C1
Punta Gorda 2,219 .... C2
San Ignacio 5,606 .... C2
Stann Creek Town 6,627 .... C2

OTHER FEATURES

Ambergris (cay) D1
Belize (riv.) C2
Bokel (cay) D2
Glover (reef) D2
Half Moon (cay) D2
Hondo (riv.) C1
Honduras (gulf) D2
Mauger (cay) D2
New (riv.) C2
Saint Georges (cay) D2
Sarstún (riv.) C3
Turneffe (isls.) D2

COSTA RICA

CITIES and TOWNS

Alajuela 33,122 .... E6
Atenas 1,728 .... E6
Bagaces 2,129 .... E5
Boruca⊙ 1,892 .... F6
Buenos Aires⊙ 302 .... F6
Cañas 6,053 .... E5
Cartago 21,753 .... F6
Ciudad Quesada 9,754 .... E5
Esparta 4,699 .... E5
Filadelfia 2,958 .... E5
Golfito 6,962 .... F6
Grecia 8,355 .... E5
Guácimo 1,168 .... F5
Guápiles 3,524 .... F5
Heredia 22,700 .... E5
Las Juntas 1,129 .... E5
Liberia 10,802 .... E5
Limón 29,621 .... F6
Miramar 1,673 .... E5
Nicoya 7,474 .... E5
Orotina 3,170 .... E6
Palmares 3,083 .... F6
Paralso 8,446 .... F6
Puerto Cortés 2,070 .... F6
Puntarenas 26,331 .... E6
Quepos 2,155 .... E6
San José (cap.) 215,441 .... F5
San José* 391,107 .... F5
San Marcos 917 .... E6
San Ramón 9,245 .... E5
Santa Cruz 5,777 .... E5
Santo Domingo 5,148 .... F6
Siquirres 4,361 .... F5
Turrialba 12,151 .... F6

(continued on following page)

(continued)

OTHER FEATURES

Blanca (pt.) F5
Blanco (cape) E6
Blanco (peak) F6
Burica (pt.) F6
Cahuita (pt.) F6
Caño (isl.) F6
Carreta (pt.) F6
Chirripó Grande (mt.) F6
Coronada (bay) F6
Cuilapa Miravalles (vol.) E5
Dulce (gulf) F6
Góngora (mt.) E5
Guionos (pt.) E6
Irazú (mt.) F6
Judas (pt.) E6
Llerena (pt.) F6
Matapalo (cape) F6
Nicoya (gulf) E6
Nicoya (pen.) E6
Papagayo (gulf) E5
Salinas (bay) D5
San Juan (riv.) E5
Santa Elena (cape) D5
Talamanca (range) F6
Velas (cape) D5

EL SALVADOR

CITIES and TOWNS

Acajutla 8,598 ..... B4
Ahuachapán 17,242 ..... B4
Atiquizaya 7,035 ..... C3
Chalatenango 7,633 ..... C3
Chinameca 6,303 ..... C4
Cojutepeque 20,615 ..... C4
Estanzuelas 2,548 ..... C4
Ilobasco 6,572 ..... C4
Intipucá 3,469 ..... D4
Jucuarán 1,443 ..... C4
La Libertad C4
La Palma 1,998 ..... C3
La Unión 17,207 ..... D4
Metapán 7,704 ..... C3
Nueva San Salvador 35,106 ..... C4
Puerto de la Concordia C4
San Francisco Gotera 4,725 ..... C4
San Miguel 59,304 ..... D4
San Salvador (cap.) 337,171 ..... C4
Santa Ana 96,306 ..... C4
Santa Rosa de Lima 5,707 ..... D4
San Vicente 18,872 ..... C4
Sensuntepeque 7,226 ..... C4
Sonsonate 33,562 ..... C4
Suchitoto 5,540 ..... C4
Texistepeque 1,722 ..... C3
Usulután 19,616 ..... C4
Zacatecoluca 15,718 ..... C4

OTHER FEATURES

Fonseca (gulf) D4
Güija (lake) C3
Lempa (riv.) C4
Remedios (pt.) B4
Santa Ana (mt.) C4

GUATEMALA

CITIES and TOWNS

Amatitlán 15,251 ..... B3
Antigua 17,994 ..... B3
Asunción Mita 7,477 ..... C3
Cahabón 1,344 ..... C3
Chajul 4,329 ..... B3
Champerico 5,722 ..... A3
Chichicastenango 2,635 ..... B3
Chimaltenango 12,860 ..... B3
Chiquimula 16,126 ..... C3
Coatepeque 15,979 ..... A3
Cobán 11,418 ..... B3
Comalapa 10,980 ..... B3
Cubulco 2,021 ..... B3
Cuilapa 4,287 ..... B3
Cuilco 862 ..... B3
Dolores 973 ..... C2
El Estor 2,324 ..... C3
El Progreso 4,009 ..... B3
Escuintla 33,205 ..... B3
Flores 1,477 ..... C2
Gualán 5,169 ..... C3
Guatemala (cap.) 700,538 ..... B3
Huehuetenango 12,570 ..... B3
Ipala 3,386 ..... C3
Iztapa 1,237 ..... B4
Jacaltenango 4,517 ..... B3
Jalapa 13,788 ..... B3
Jutiapa 8,210 ..... B3
La Gomera 2,394 ..... B3
La Libertad 908 ..... B2
Livingston 2,898 ..... C3
Los Amates 1,383 ..... C3
Masagua 1,178 ..... B3
Mazatenango 23,285 ..... B3
Momostenango 5,210 ..... B3
Morales 2,113 ..... C3
Ocós 741 ..... A3
Panzós 1,643 ..... C3
Puerto Barrios 22,598 ..... C3
Quezaltenango 53,021 ..... B3
Quezaltepeque 2,222 ..... C3
Rabinal 4,625 ..... B3
Retalhuleu 19,060 ..... B3
Río Hondo 1,416 ..... C3
Sacapulas 1,439 ..... B3
Salamá 5,529 ..... B3
San Andrés 1,066 ..... B2
San Felipe 3,210 ..... B3
San José 9,402 ..... B4
San Luis 1,136 ..... C2
San Luis Jilotepeque 6,055 ..... C3
San Marcos 5,700 ..... B3
San Martín Jilotepeque 3,770 ..... B3
San Mateo Ixtatán 1,834 ..... B3
San Pedro Carchá 4,465 ..... B3
Santa Cruz del Quiché 7,651 ..... B3
Santa Rosa de Lima 1,161 ..... B3
Sololá 3,960 ..... B3
Tacaná 1,280 ..... A3
Tejutla 1,205 ..... B3
Tikal C2
Totonicapán 8,568 ..... B3
Zacapa 12,688 ..... C3

OTHER FEATURES

Atitlán (lake) B3
Atitlán (vol.) B3
Azul (riv.) C2
Chixoy (riv.) B2
Güija (lake) C3
Honduras (gulf) D2
Izabal (lake) C3
Minas (mts.) C3
Motagua (riv.) C3
Pasión (riv.) B2
Petén-Itzá (lake) B2
San Pedro (riv.) B2
Sarstún (riv.) C3
Tacaná (vol.) A3
Tajumulco (vol.) B3
Tres Puntas (cape) C3
Usumacinta (riv.) B2

HONDURAS

CITIES and TOWNS

Amapala 2,274 ..... D4
Brus Laguna 933 ..... E3
Catacamas 9,134 ..... E3
Cedros 917 ..... D3
Choloma 961 ..... C3
Choluteca 26,152 ..... D4
Comayagua 15,941 ..... D3
Corquín 2,629 ..... C3
Danlí 10,825 ..... D3
El Dulce Nombre 1,297 ..... E3

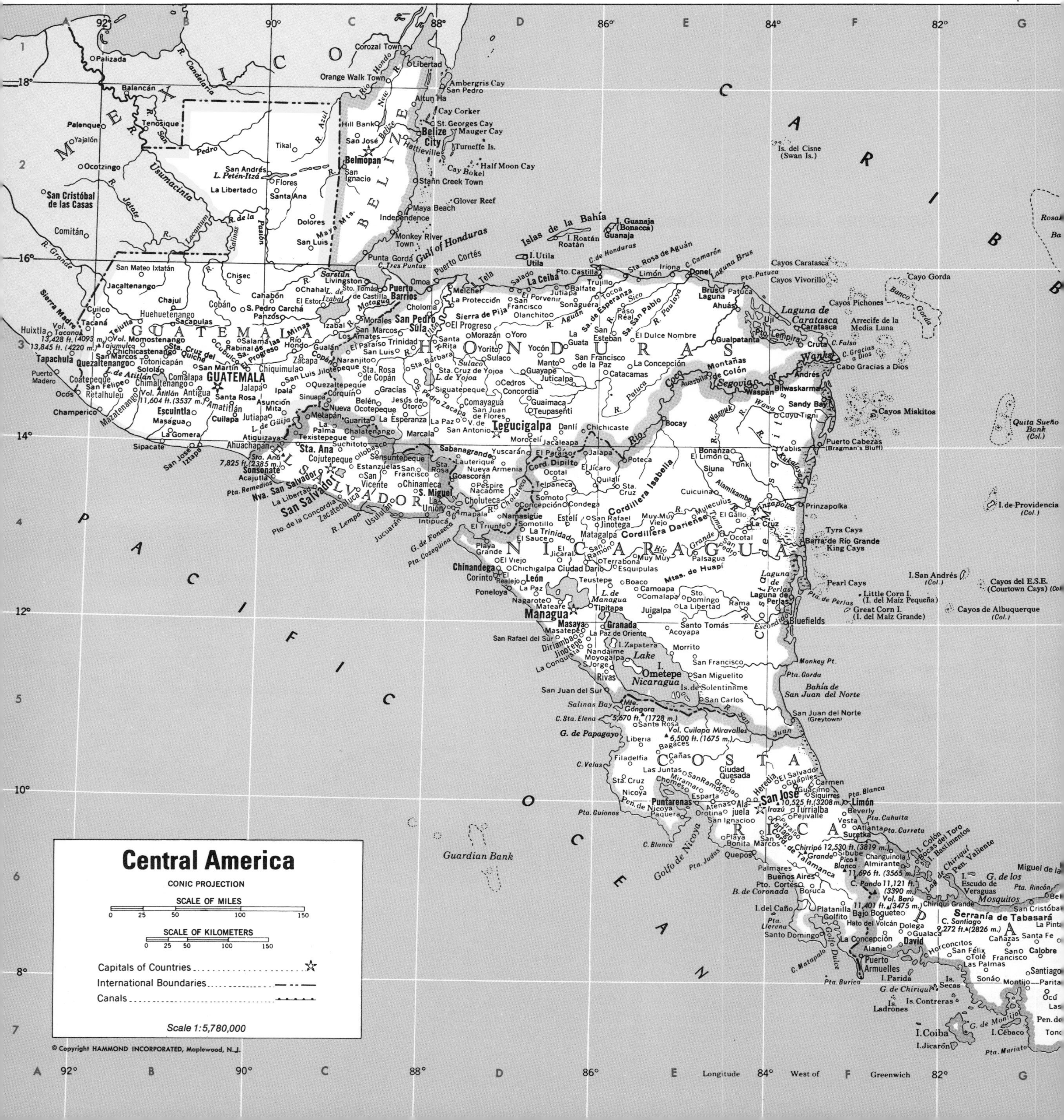

Central America
CONIC PROJECTION
SCALE OF MILES
0 25 50 100 150
SCALE OF KILOMETERS
0 25 50 100 150
Capitals of Countries
International Boundaries
Canals
Scale 1:5,780,000
MEXICO
BELIZE
GUATEMALA
HONDURAS
EL SALVADOR
NICARAGUA
COSTA RICA
CARIBBEAN SEA
PACIFIC OCEAN
Longitude 84° West of Greenwich

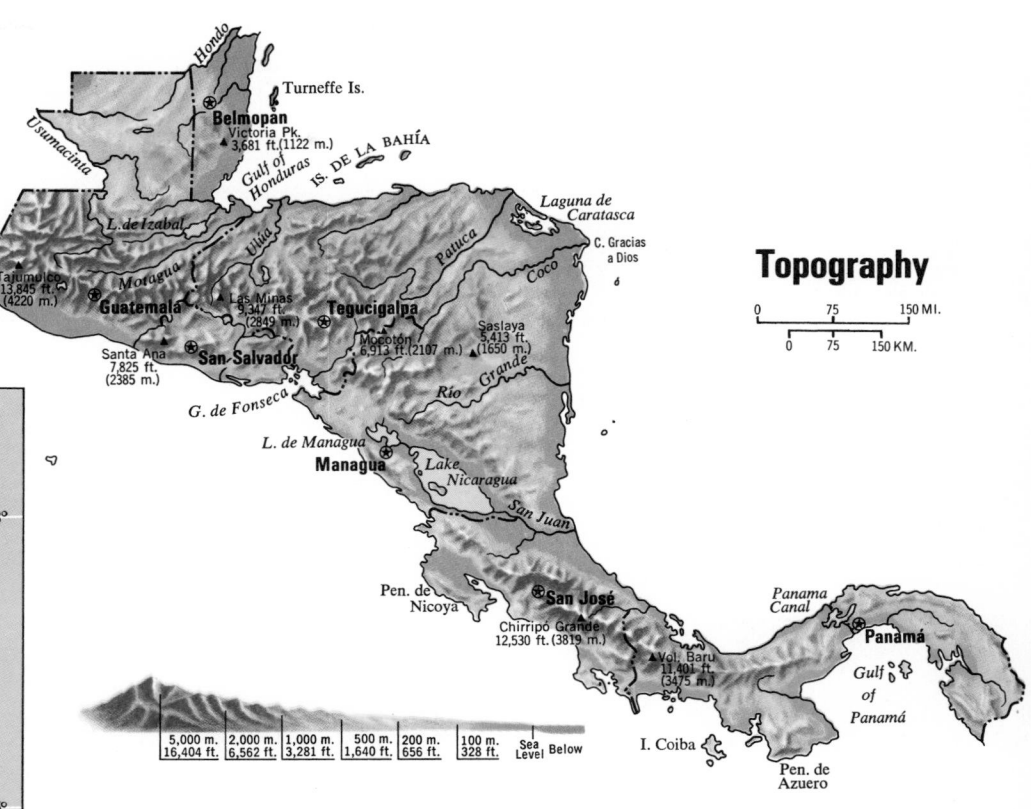

Topography

0 75 150 MI.
0 75 150 KM.

5,000 m. 16,404 ft.	2,000 m. 6,562 ft.	1,000 m. 3,281 ft.	500 m. 1,640 ft.	200 m. 656 ft.	100 m. 328 ft.	Sea Level	Below

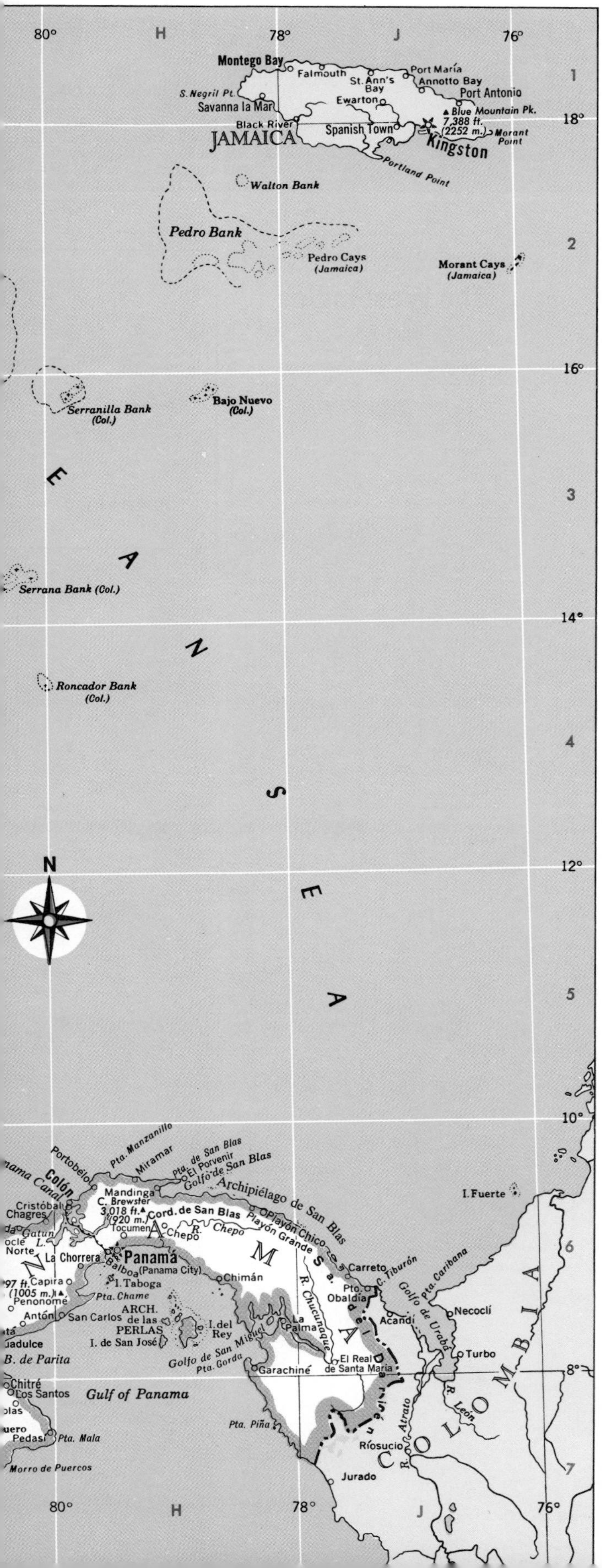

*City and suburbs.
⊙Population of sub-district or division.
⊙Population of district.

CUBA 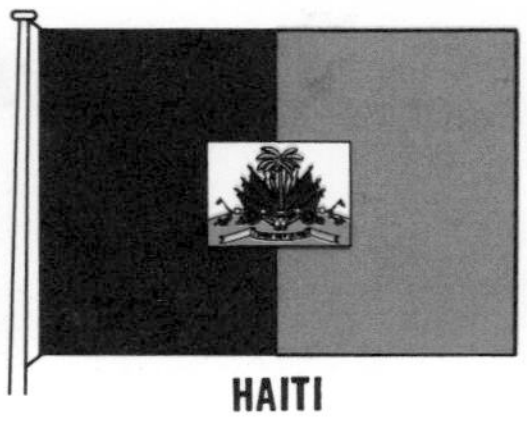 HAITI  DOMINICAN REPUBLIC  JAMAICA 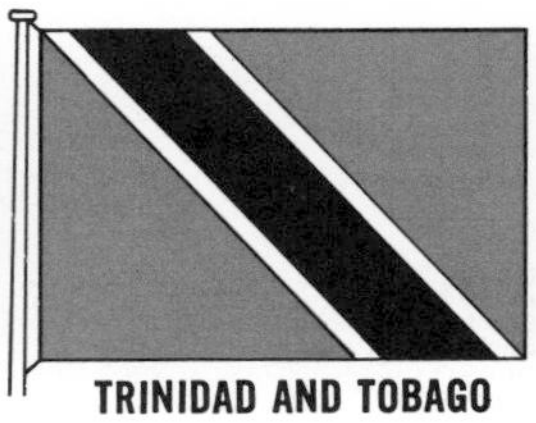 TRINIDAD AND TOBAGO  BARBADOS

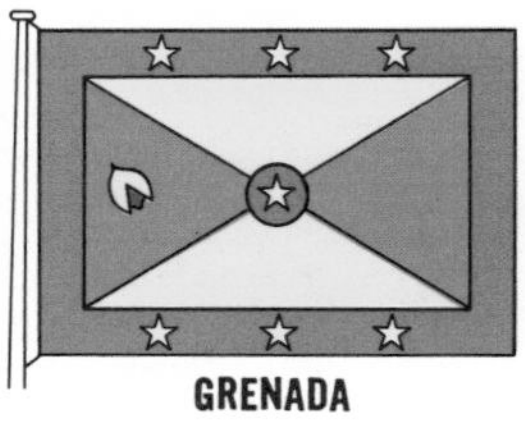

GRENADA 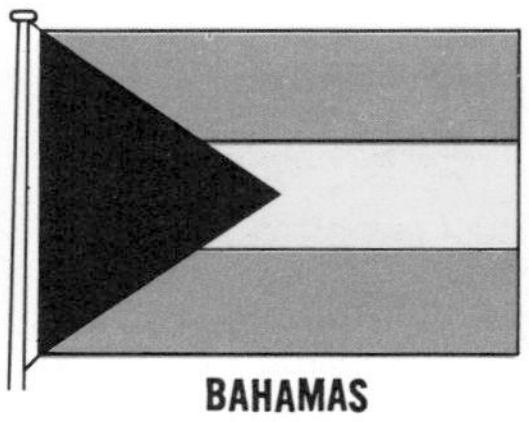 BAHAMAS  DOMINICA  ST. LUCIA  ST. VINC. & GRENS.  ANTIGUA AND BARBUDA

CUBA
AREA 44,206 sq. mi. (114,494 sq. km.)
POPULATION 9,706,369
CAPITAL Havana
LARGEST CITY Havana
HIGHEST POINT Pico Turquino
6,561 ft. (2,000 m.)
MONETARY UNIT Cuban peso
MAJOR LANGUAGE Spanish
MAJOR RELIGION Roman Catholicism

HAITI
AREA 10,694 sq. mi. (27,697 sq. km.)
POPULATION 5,009,000
CAPITAL Port-au-Prince
LARGEST CITY Port-au-Prince
HIGHEST POINT Pic La Selle 8,793 ft.
(2,680 m.)
MONETARY UNIT gourde
MAJOR LANGUAGES Creole French, French
MAJOR RELIGION Roman Catholicism

DOMINICAN REPUBLIC
AREA 18,704 sq. mi. (48,443 sq. km.)
POPULATION 5,431,000
CAPITAL Santo Domingo
LARGEST CITY Santo Domingo
HIGHEST POINT Pico Duarte
10,417 ft. (3,175 m.)
MONETARY UNIT Dominican peso
MAJOR LANGUAGE Spanish
MAJOR RELIGION Roman Catholicism

JAMAICA
AREA 4,411 sq. mi. (11,424 sq. km.)
POPULATION 2,161,000
CAPITAL Kingston
LARGEST CITY Kingston
HIGHEST POINT Blue Mountain Peak
7,402 ft. (2,256 m.)
MONETARY UNIT Jamaican dollar
MAJOR LANGUAGE English
MAJOR RELIGIONS Protestantism,
Roman Catholicism

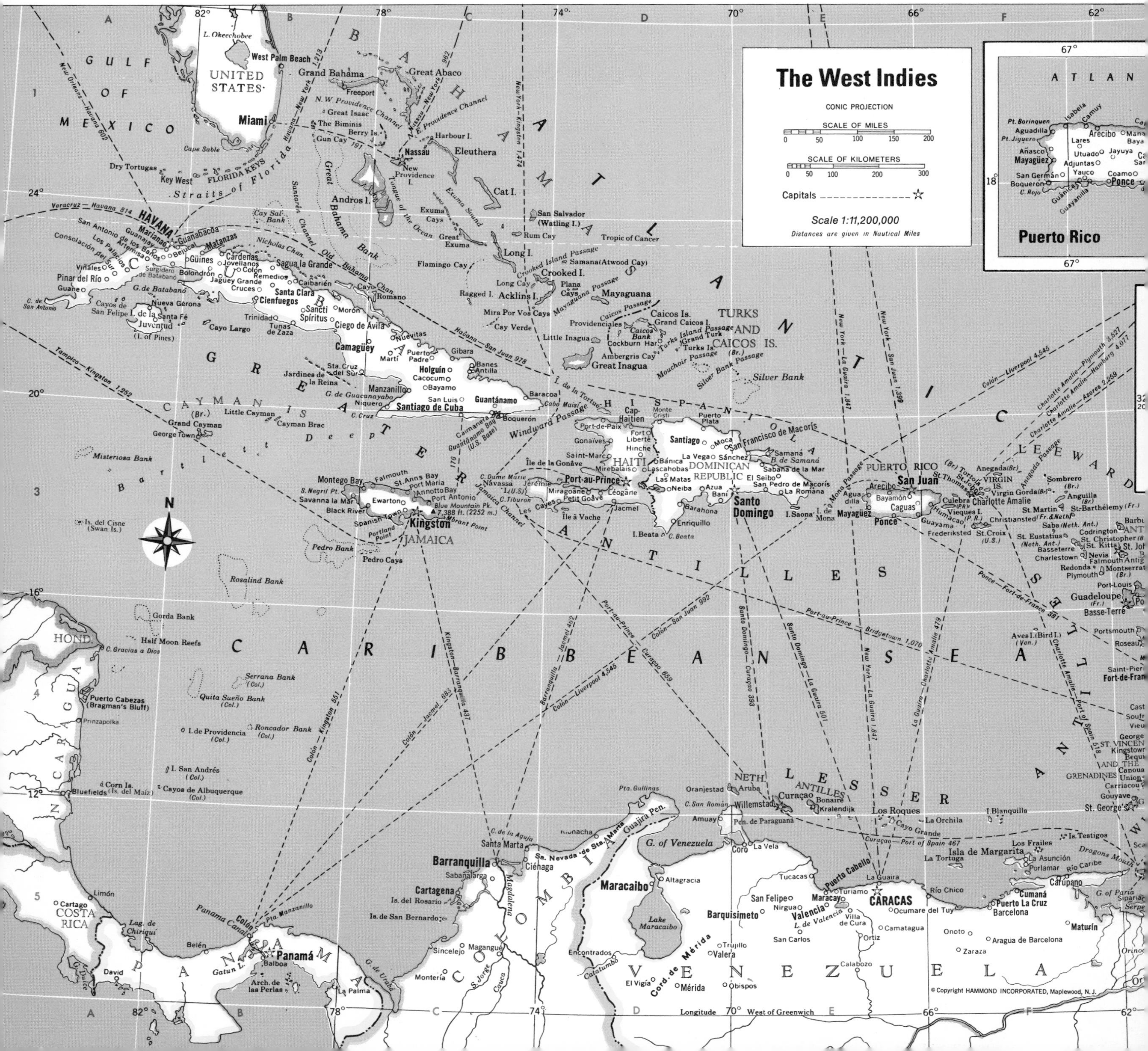

The West Indies
CONIC PROJECTION

SCALE OF MILES
0 50 100 150 200

SCALE OF KILOMETERS
0 50 100 200 300

Capitals ------------- ☆

Scale 1:11,200,000
Distances are given in Nautical Miles

© Copyright HAMMOND INCORPORATED, Maplewood, N.J.

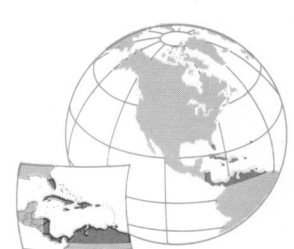

TRINIDAD AND TOBAGO

AREA 1,980 sq. mi. (5,128 sq. km.)
POPULATION 1,067,108
CAPITAL Port of Spain
LARGEST CITY Port of Spain
HIGHEST POINT Mt. Aripo 3,084 ft. (940 m.)
MONETARY UNIT Trinidad and Tobago dollar
MAJOR LANGUAGES English, Hindi
MAJOR RELIGIONS Roman Catholicism, Protestantism, Hinduism, Islam

BARBADOS

AREA 166 sq. mi. (430 sq. km.)
POPULATION 249,000
CAPITAL Bridgetown
LARGEST CITY Bridgetown
HIGHEST POINT Mt. Hillaby 1,104 ft. (336 m.)
MONETARY UNIT Barbadian dollar
MAJOR LANGUAGE English
MAJOR RELIGION Protestantism

GRENADA

AREA 133 sq. mi. (344 sq. km.)
POPULATION 110,000
CAPITAL St. George's
LARGEST CITY St. George's
HIGHEST POINT Mt. St. Catherine 2,757 ft. (840 m.)
MONETARY UNIT East Caribbean dollar
MAJOR LANGUAGES English, French patois
MAJOR RELIGIONS Roman Catholicism, Protestantism

BAHAMAS

AREA 5,382 sq. mi. (13,939 sq. km.)
POPULATION 223,455
CAPITAL Nassau
LARGEST CITY Nassau
HIGHEST POINT Mt. Alvernia 206 ft. (63 m.)
MONETARY UNIT Bahamian dollar
MAJOR LANGUAGE English
MAJOR RELIGIONS Roman Catholicism, Protestantism

DOMINICA

AREA 290 sq. mi. (751 sq. km.)
POPULATION 74,089
CAPITAL Roseau
HIGHEST POINT Morne Diablotin 4,747 ft. (1,447 m.)
MONETARY UNIT Dominican dollar
MAJOR LANGUAGES English, French patois
MAJOR RELIGIONS Roman Catholicism, Protestantism

SAINT LUCIA

AREA 238 sq. mi. (616 sq. km.)
POPULATION 115,783
CAPITAL Castries
HIGHEST POINT Mt. Gimie 3,117 ft. (950 m.)
MONETARY UNIT East Caribbean dollar
MAJOR LANGUAGES English, French patois
MAJOR RELIGIONS Roman Catholicism, Protestantism

SAINT VINCENT AND THE GRENADINES

AREA 150 sq. mi. (388 sq. km.)
POPULATION 124,000
CAPITAL Kingstown
HIGHEST POINT Soufrière 4,000 ft. (1,219 m.)
MONETARY UNIT East Caribbean dollar
MAJOR LANGUAGE English
MAJOR RELIGIONS Protestantism, Roman Catholicism

Anegada
San Juan
Road Town
Tortola
Virgin Gorda
Jost Van Dyke
St. Thomas
Culebra (P.R.)
Charlotte Amalie
St. John
Vieques
Vieques I. (P.R.)
VIRGIN IS.
Christiansted
Frederiksted
St. Croix
North Rocks
N.E. Breakers
Ledge Flats
St. George's I.
St. George
St. Davids I.
Castle Harbour
Harrington Sound
Ireland I.
Somerset I.
Great Sound
Hamilton
Bermuda Islands
Bermuda I.
Speightstown
Bridgetown
BARBADOS
St. Vincent
ST. LUCIA
Martinique (Fr.)
Tobago
TRINIDAD AND TOBAGO
Sangre Grande
San Fernando
Trinidad

BERMUDA

AREA 21 sq. mi. (54 sq. km.)
POPULATION 67,761
CAPITAL Hamilton
MONETARY UNIT Bermuda dollar
MAJOR LANGUAGE English
MAJOR RELIGION Protestantism

PUERTO RICO

AREA 3,515 sq. mi. (9,104 sq. km.)
POPULATION 3,186,076
CAPITAL San Juan
MONETARY UNIT U.S. dollar
MAJOR LANGUAGES Spanish, English
MAJOR RELIGION Roman Catholicism

NETHERLANDS ANTILLES

AREA 390 sq. mi. (1,010 sq. km.)
POPULATION 246,000
CAPITAL Willemstad
MONETARY UNIT Antilles guilder
MAJOR LANGUAGES Dutch, Papiamento, English
MAJOR RELIGIONS Roman Catholicism, Protestantism

ANTIGUA AND BARBUDA

AREA 171 sq. mi. (443 sq. km.)
POPULATION 72,000
CAPITAL St. John's
HIGHEST POINT Boggy Peak 1,319 ft. (402 m.)
MONETARY UNIT East Caribbean dollar
MAJOR LANGUAGE English
MAJOR RELIGION Protestantism

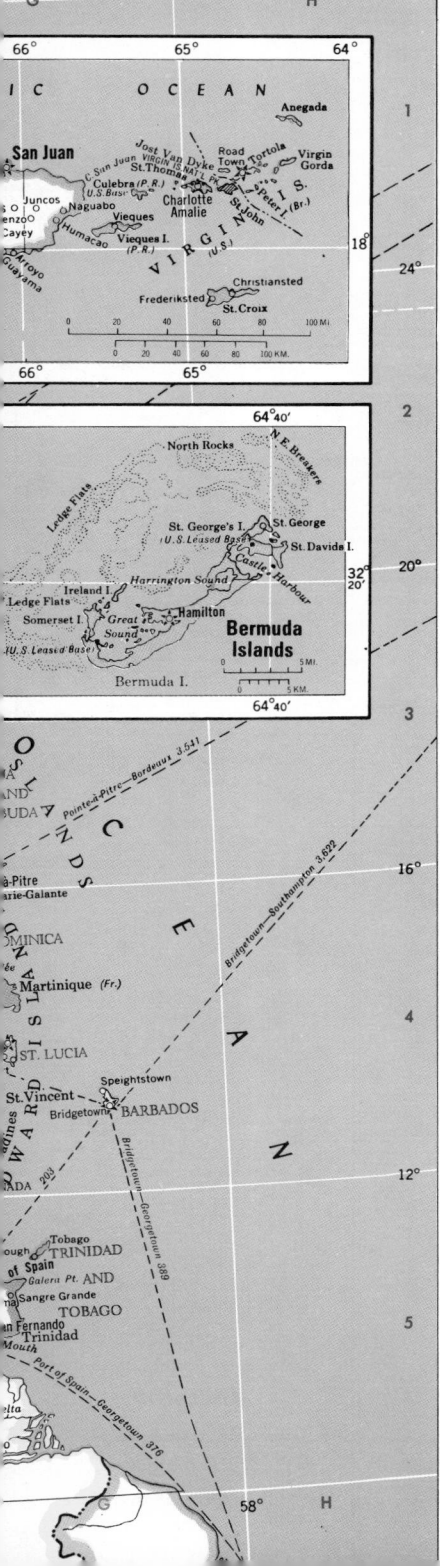

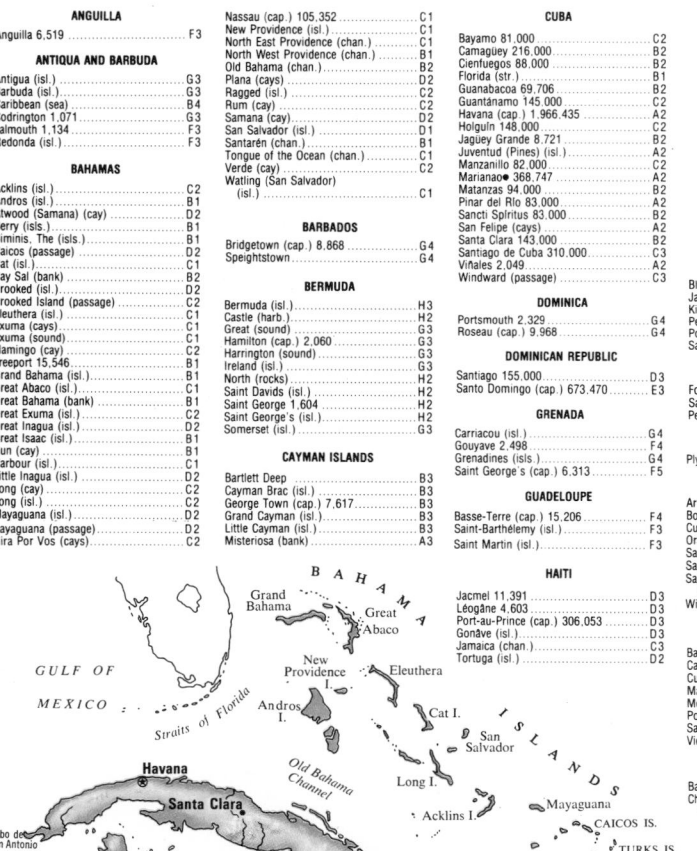

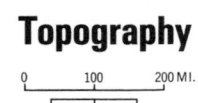

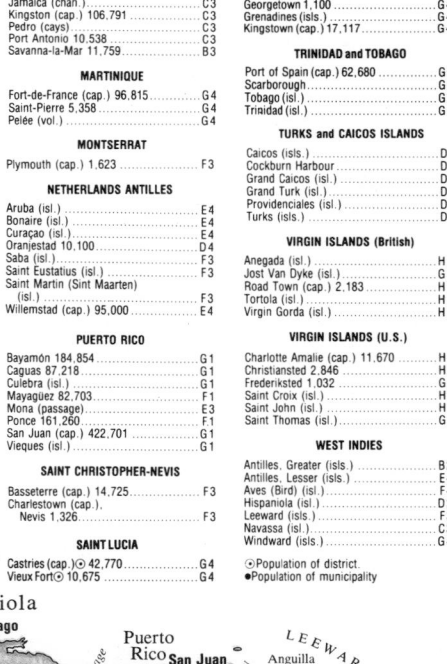

ANGUILLA

Anguilla 6,519 ..... F3

ANTIQUA AND BARBUDA

Antigua (isl.) G3
Barbuda (isl.) G3
Caribbean (sea) B4
Codrington 1,071 ..... G3
Falmouth 1,134 ..... F3
Redonda (isl.) F3

BAHAMAS

Acklins (isl.) C2
Andros (isl.) B1
Atwood (Samana) (cay) D2
Berry (isls.) B1
Biminis, The (isls.) B1
Caicos (passage) D2
Cat (isl.) C1
Cay Sal (bank) B2
Crooked (isl.) D2
Crooked Island (passage) C2
Eleuthera (isl.) C1
Exuma (cays) C1
Exuma (sound) C1
Flamingo (cay) C2
Freeport 15,546 ..... B1
Grand Bahama (isl.) B1
Great Abaco (isl.) C1
Great Bahama (bank) B1
Great Exuma (isl.) C2
Great Inagua (isl.) D2
Great Isaac (isl.) B1
Gun (cay) B1
Harbour (isl.) C1
Little Inagua (isl.) D2
Long (cay) C2
Long (isl.) C2
Mayaguana (isl.) D2
Mayaguana (passage) D2
Mira Por Vos (cays) C2
Nassau (cap.) 105,352 ..... C1
New Providence (isl.) C1
North East Providence (chan.) C1
North West Providence (chan.) B1
Old Bahama (chan.) B2
Plana (cays) D2
Ragged (isl.) C2
Rum (cay) C2
Samana (cay) D2
San Salvador (isl.) D1
Santarén (chan.) B1
Tongue of the Ocean (chan.) C1
Verde (cay) C2
Watling (San Salvador) (isl.) C1

BARBADOS

Bridgetown (cap.) 8,868 ..... G4
Speightstown G4

BERMUDA

Bermuda (isl.) H3
Castle (harb.) H2
Great (sound) G3
Hamilton (cap.) 2,060 ..... G3
Harrington (sound) G3
Ireland (isl.) G3
North (rocks) H2
Saint Davids (isl.) H2
Saint George 1,604 ..... H2
Saint George's (isl.) H2
Somerset (isl.) G3

CAYMAN ISLANDS

Bartlett Deep B3
Cayman Brac (isl.) B3
George Town (cap.) 7,617 ..... B3
Grand Cayman (isl.) B3
Little Cayman (isl.) B3
Misteriosa (bank) A3

CUBA

Bayamo 81,000 ..... C2
Camagüey 216,000 ..... B2
Cienfuegos 88,000 ..... B2
Florida (str.) B1
Guanabacoa 69,706 ..... B2
Guantánamo 145,000 ..... C2
Havana (cap.) 1,966,435 ..... A2
Holguín 148,000 ..... C2
Jagüey Grande 8,721 ..... B2
Juventud (Pines) (isl.) A2
Manzanillo 82,000 ..... C2
Marianao● 368,747 ..... A2
Matanzas 94,000 ..... B2
Pinar del Río 83,000 ..... A2
Sancti Spíritus 83,000 ..... B2
San Felipe (cays) A2
Santa Clara 143,000 ..... B2
Santiago de Cuba 310,000 ..... C3
Viñales 2,049 ..... A2
Windward (passage) C3

DOMINICA

Portsmouth 2,329 ..... G4
Roseau (cap.) 9,968 ..... G4

DOMINICAN REPUBLIC

Santiago 155,000 ..... D3
Santo Domingo (cap.) 673,470 ..... E3

GRENADA

Carriacou (isl.) G4
Gouyave 2,498 ..... F4
Grenadines (isls.) G4
Saint George's (cap.) 6,313 ..... F5

GUADELOUPE

Basse-Terre (cap.) 15,206 ..... F4
Saint-Barthélemy (isl.) F3
Saint Martin (isl.) F3

HAITI

Jacmel 11,391 ..... D3
Léogâne 4,603 ..... D3
Port-au-Prince (cap.) 306,053 ..... D3
Gonâve (isl.) D3
Jamaica (chan.) C3
Tortuga (isl.) D2

JAMAICA

Blue Mountain (peak) C3
Jamaica (chan.) C3
Kingston (cap.) 106,791 ..... C3
Pedro (cays) C3
Port Antonio 10,538 ..... C3
Savanna-la-Mar 11,759 ..... B3

MARTINIQUE

Fort-de-France (cap.) 96,815 ..... G4
Saint-Pierre 5,358 ..... G4
Pelée (vol.) G4

MONTSERRAT

Plymouth (cap.) 1,623 ..... F3

NETHERLANDS ANTILLES

Aruba (isl.) E4
Bonaire (isl.) E4
Curaçao (isl.) E4
Oranjestad 10,100 ..... D4
Saba (isl.) F3
Saint Eustatius (isl.) F3
Saint Martin (Sint Maarten) (isl.) F3
Willemstad (cap.) 95,000 ..... E4

PUERTO RICO

Bayamón 184,854 ..... G1
Caguas 87,218 ..... G1
Culebra (isl.) G1
Mayagüez 82,703 ..... F1
Mona (passage) E3
Ponce 161,260 ..... F1
San Juan (cap.) 422,701 ..... G1
Vieques (isl.) G1

SAINT CHRISTOPHER-NEVIS

Basseterre (cap.) 14,725 ..... F3
Charlestown (cap.), Nevis 1,326 ..... F3

SAINT LUCIA

Castries (cap.)⊙ 42,770 ..... G4
Vieux Fort⊙ 10,675 ..... G4

SAINT VINCENT and THE GRENADINES

Bequia (isl.) G4
Georgetown 1,100 ..... G4
Grenadines (isls.) G4
Kingstown (cap.) 17,117 ..... G4

TRINIDAD and TOBAGO

Port of Spain (cap.) 62,680 ..... G5
Scarborough G5
Tobago (isl.) G5
Trinidad (isl.) G5

TURKS and CAICOS ISLANDS

Caicos (isls.) D2
Cockburn Harbour D2
Grand Caicos (isl.) D2
Grand Turk (isl.) D2
Providenciales (isl.) D2
Turks (isls.) D2

VIRGIN ISLANDS (British)

Anegada (isl.) H1
Jost Van Dyke (isl.) G1
Road Town (cap.) 2,183 ..... H1
Tortola (isl.) H1
Virgin Gorda (isl.) H1

VIRGIN ISLANDS (U.S.)

Charlotte Amalie (cap.) 11,670 ..... H1
Christiansted 2,846 ..... H2
Frederiksted 1,032 ..... G2
Saint Croix (isl.) H2
Saint John (isl.) H1
Saint Thomas (isl.) G1

WEST INDIES

Antilles, Greater (isls.) B2
Antilles, Lesser (isls.) E4
Aves (Bird) (isl.) F4
Hispaniola (isl.) D2
Leeward (isls.) F3
Navassa (isl.) C3
Windward (isls.) G4

⊙Population of district.
●Population of municipality

Topography
0 100 200 MI.
0 100 200 KM.
BAHAMA ISLANDS
Grand Bahama
Great Abaco
New Providence I.
Eleuthera
Andros I.
Cat I.
San Salvador
Long I.
Acklins I.
Mayaguana
CAICOS IS.
TURKS IS.
Great Inagua
GULF OF MEXICO
Straits of Florida
Old Bahama Channel
Havana
Santa Clara
Cabo de San Antonio
I. de la Juventud
Cuba
Holguín
Cabo Maisí
SIERRA MAESTRA
Pico Turquino 6,561 ft. (1200 m.)
Windward Passage
CAYMAN IS.
GREATER ANTILLES
Jamaica
Kingston
Blue Mtn. Pk. 7,402 ft. (2256 m.)
Jamaica Channel
Hispaniola
Santiago
Pico Duarte 10,417 ft. (3175 m.)
Port-au-Prince
Santo Domingo
Mona Passage
Puerto Rico
San Juan
VIRGIN IS.
St. Croix
Anguilla
Barbuda
Nevis
Antigua
Guadeloupe
Dominica
Martinique
St. Lucia
Barbados
St. Vincent
Grenada
Tobago
Trinidad
LEEWARD ISLANDS
WINDWARD ISLANDS
CARIBBEAN SEA
LESSER ANTILLES
NETH. ANTILLES
Aruba
Curaçao
Bonaire
I. de Margarita
Below Sea Level
100 m. 328 ft.
200 m. 656 ft.
500 m. 1,640 ft.
1,000 m. 3,281 ft.
2,000 m. 6,562 ft.
5,000 m. 16,404 ft.

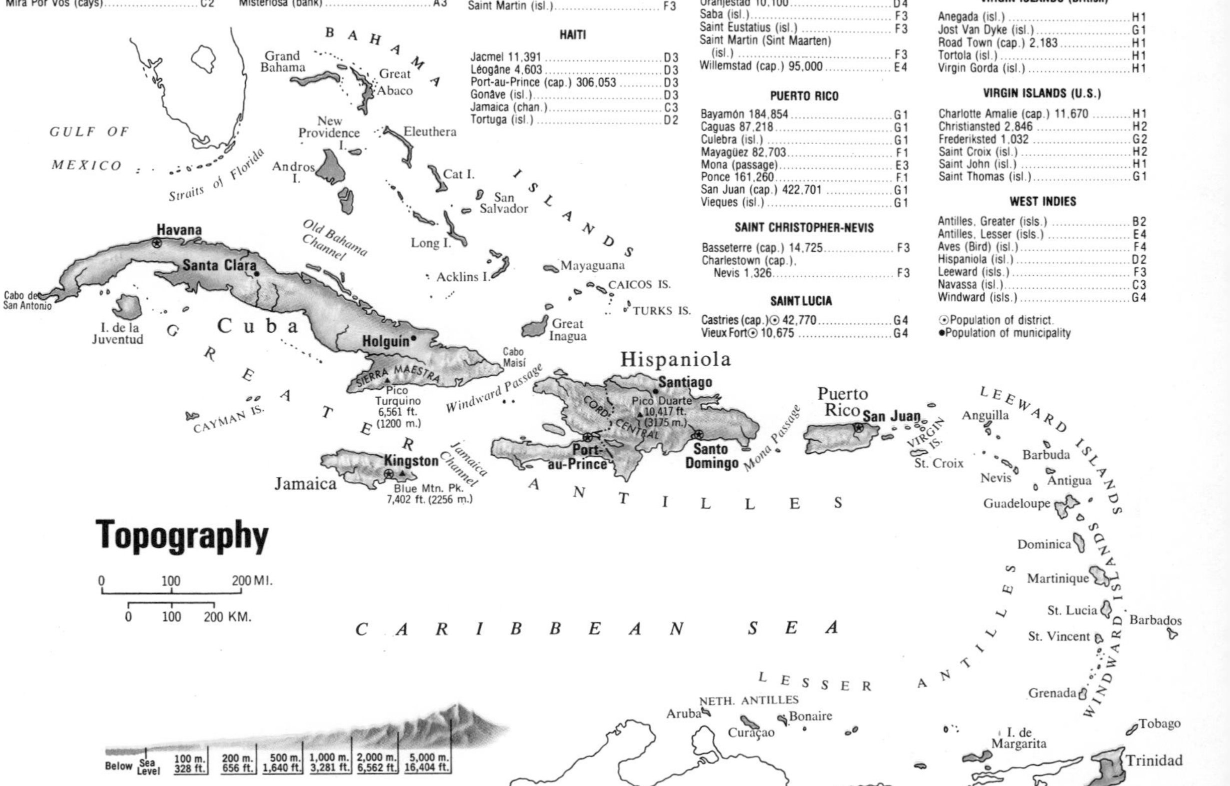

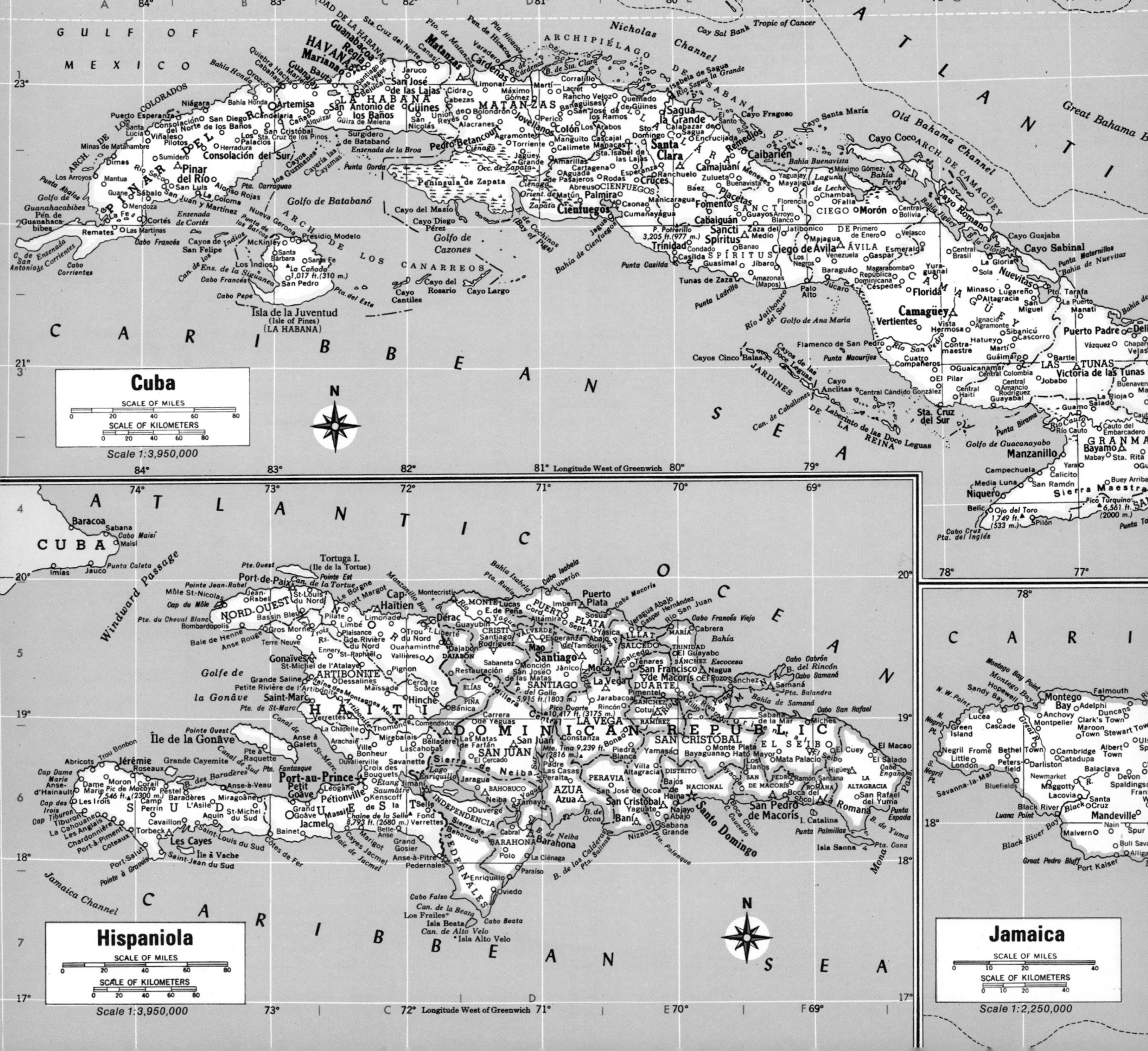

Cauto (riv.) H3
Cayamas (cays) C2
Cazones (gulf) C2
Cienfuegos (bay) D2
Cinco Balas (cays) E3
Cochinos (bay) D2
Coco (cay) G1
Colorados, Los (arch.) A1
Corrientes (cape) A2
Corrientes (inlet) A2
Cortés (inlet) B2
Cristal, Sierra del (mts.) J3
Cruz (cape) G4
Diego Pérez (cay) C2
Doce Leguas (cays) F3
Este (pt.) C3
Fragoso (cay) F1
Francés (cape) A2
Francés (cape) B2
Gloria (bay) G2
Gorda (pt.) C2
Gran Piedra (mt.) J4
Guacanayabo (gulf) G4
Guajaba (cay) G2
Guanahacabibes (gulf) A2
Guanahacabibes (pen.) A2
Guantánamo (bay) J4
Guantánamo Bay U.S. Nav. Reserve K4
Guarico (pt.) K3
Guzmanes (cays) B2
Hicacos (pen.) D1
Hicacos (pt.) D1
Honda (bay) B1
Indios (chan.) B2
Inglés (pt.) G4
Jardines de la Reina (arch.) F3
Jatibonico del Sur (riv.) F3
Jigüey (bay) G2
Juventud, (Isla de la) (Pines) 30,103 B3
Laberinto de las Doce Leguas (cays) F3
Ladrillo (pt.) E3
Largo (cay) D2
Leche (lag.) F2
Los Barcos (pt.) B2
Los Canarreos (arch.) C2
Los Colorados (arch.) A1
Lucrecia (cape) J3
Macurijes (pt.) F3
Maestra, Sierra (mts.) H4
Maisí (cape) K4
Malagueta (bay) H3
Mangle (pt.) J3
Masío (cay) C2
Matanzas (bay) D1
Maternillos (pt.) H2
Mexico (gulf) A1
Nicholas (chan.) E1
Nipe (bay) J3
Nuevitas (bay) H2
Ojo del Toro (mt.) G4
Old Bahama (chan.) G1
Pepe (cape) B3
Perros (bay) G2
Pigs (Cochinos) (bay) D2
Pines (Isla de la Juventud) (isl.) B3
Potrerillo (peak) E2
Purial, Sierra de (mts.) K4
Quemado (pt.) K4
Romano (cay) G2
Rosario (cay) C2
Sabana (arch.) E1
Sabinal (cay) H2
Sagua la Grande (riv.) E1
San Antonio (cape) A2
San Felipe (cays) B2
San Pedro (riv.) G3
Santa Clara (bay) D1
Santa María (cay) F1
Siguanea (bay) B2
Tabacal (pt.) H4
Toa, Cuchillas de (mts.) K4
Tortuguilla (pt.) K4
Turquino (peak) H4
Zapata (pen.) C2
Zapata Occidental (swamp) D2
Zapata Oriental (swamp) D2

DOMINICAN REPUBLIC

PROVINCES

Azua 86,850 D6
Bahoruco 67,025 D6
Barahona 111,115 D6
Dajabón 52,695 D5
Distrito Nacional 817,645 E6
Duarte 201,795 E5
El Seibo 132,480 F6
Espaillat 138,265 E5
Independencia 32,525 D6
La Altagracia 86,070 F6
La Estrelleta 54,495 C5
La Romana 56,980 F6
La Vega 293,730 D6
María Trinidad Sánchez 95,635 E5
Montecristi 69,605 D5
Pedernales 12,625 D7
Peravia 129,335 E6
Puerto Plata 189,490 D5
Salcedo 88,415 E5
Samaná 53,015 E5
Sánchez Ramírez 106,775 E5
San Cristóbal 323,535 E6
San Juan 190,905 D6
San Pedro de Macorís 105,405 F6
Santiago 387,255 D5
Santiago Rodríguez 47,490 D5
Valverde 75,250 D5

CITIES and TOWNS

Altamira 1,907 D5
Azua 13,880 D6
Bajos de Haina 11,180 E6
Baní 23,530 E6
Bánica 1,294 D5
Barahona 37,260 D6
Bayaguana 2,975 E6
Boca Chica E6
Boca del Soco F6
Bonao 22,020 E6
Cabral 5,549 D6
Cabrera 1,920 E5
Carrera de Yeguas D6
Castillo 3,220 E5
Cayacoa E6
Comendador 4,296 C6
Constanza 5,128 D6
Cotuí 7,653 E5
Dajabón 6,030 D5
Duvergé 7,793 D6
El Cercado 3,348 D6
El Cuey F6
El Macao F6
El Pozo E5
El Salado F6
El Seibo 9,101 F6
Enriquillo 4,071 D7
Esperanza 10,530 D5
Gaspar Hernández 2,182 E5
Guayubín 1,407 D5
Hato Mayor 10,135 F6
Higüey 17,995 F6
Imbert 4,440 D5
Jánico 1,110 D5
Jarabacoa 6,317 E5
Jaragua 4,904 D6
Jimaní 2,248 C6
La Ciénaga D6
La Romana 36,720 F6
Las Matas de Farfán 8,001 D6
La Vega 31,060 E5
Los Llanos 1,840 F6
Lucas E. de Peña D5
Luperón 2,046 D5
Mao 25,660 D5
Mata Palacio F6
Miches 4,498 F6
Moca 24,195 D5
Monción 2,007 D5
Montecristi 8,312 C5
Monte Plata 3,672 E6
Nagua 13,740 E5
Najayo Abajo E6
Neiba 9,785 D6
Nizao 3,007 E6
Oviedo 2,139 D7
Padre Las Casas 4,776 D6
Paraíso 2,660 D7
Pedernales 5,539 C7
Piedra Blanca E6
Pimentel 5,823 E5
Polo D6
Puerto Plata 32,105 D5
Ramón Santana 965 F6
Restauración 1,969 D5
Rincón E5
Río San Juan 2,755 E5
Sabana de la Mar 6,849 F5
Sabana Grande 1,965 E6
Sabaneta 6,619 D5
Salcedo 8,919 E5
Samaná 4,541 F5
Sánchez 16,193 E5
San Cristóbal 26,930 E6
San Francisco de Macorís 44,620 E5
San José de las Matas 2,691 D5
San José de Ocoa 10,243 E6
San Juan 32,965 D6
San Pedro de Macorís 43,010 F6
San Rafael del Yuma 1,835 F6
Santiago 155,000 D5
Santo Domingo (cap.) 673,470 E6
Sosúa 3,521 E5
Tamayo 3,840 D6
Tamboril 4,299 D5
Tenares E5
Valverde D5
Veragua Abajo E5
Villa Altagracia 11,900 E6
Villa Riva 2,162 E5
Yaguate 1,872 E6
Yamasá 2,701 E6
Yásica Abajo E5

OTHER FEATURES

Alto Velo (chan.) C7
Alto Velo (isl.) D7
Bahoruco, Sierra de (mts.) D6
Balandra (pt.) F5
Beata (cape) D7
Beata (chan.) C7
Beata (isl.) C7
Cabrón (cape) F5
Calderas (bay) D6
Cana (pt.) F6
Catalina (isl.) F6
Caucedo (cape) E6
Central, Cordillera (range) D5
Duarte (peak) D5
Engaño (cape) F6
Enriquillo (lake) C6
Escocesa (bay) E5
Espada (pt.) F6
Falso (cape) C7
Frailes, Los (isl.) C7
Francés Viejo (cape) E5
Gallo (mt.) D5
Isabela (bay) D5
Isabela (cape) D5
Los Frailes (isl.) C7
Macorís (cape) E5
Manzanillo (bay) C5
Mona (passage) F6
Neiba (bay) D6
Neiba, Sierra de (mts.) D6
Noires (mts.) C5
Ocoa (bay) D6
Oriental, Cordillera (range) F6
Palenque (pt.) E6
Palmillas (pt.) F6
Rincón (bay) F5
Rucia (pt.) D5
Salinas (pt.) E6
Samaná (bay) F5
Samaná (cape) F5
San Rafael (cape) F5
Saona (isl.) F6
Septentrional, Cordillera (range) D5
Tina (mt.) D6
Yaque del Norte (riv.) D5
Yaque del Sur (riv.) D6
Yuma (bay) F6
Yuna (riv.) E5

HAITI

DEPARTMENTS

Artibonite 755,760 C5
Nord 699,886 C5
Nord-Ouest 216,504 B5
Ouest 1,669,691 C6
Sud 972,787 A6

CITIES and TOWNS

Abricots 1,226 A6
Anse à Galets B6
Anse-à-Pitre 696 C6
Anse-à-Veau 1,253 B6
Anse-d'Hainault 3,680 A6
Anse Rouge 1,230 B5
Aquin 2,173 B6
Arcahaie 2,498 C6
Baie de Henne 661 B5
Bainet 1,509 B6
Baradères 1,083 B6
Bassin Bleu 616 B5
Belladère 2,207 C6
Belle-Anse 1,985 C6
Bombardopolis 940 B5
Camp Perrin 1,091 A6
Cap-Haïtien 46,217 C5
Cavaillon 988 A6
Cayes Jacmel 712 C6
Cerca la Source 1,262 C5
Chardonnière 2,156 A6
Corail 1,733 A6
Coteaux 1,426 A6
Côtes de Fer 1,023 B6
Croix des Bouquets 3,958 C6
Dame Marie 4,038 A6
Dérac 761 C5
Dessalines 3,842 C5
Duvalierville 1,378 C6
Ennery 974 C5
Fort Liberté 2,982 C5
Gonaïves 29,261 B5
Grand Goâve 2,277 B6
Grand Gosier 359 C6
Grande Rivière du Nord 5,285 C5
Grande Saline 1,020 B5
Gros Morne 3,257 B5
Hinche 8,462 C5
Jacmel 11,391 C6
Jean-Rabel 2,019 B5
Jérémie 17,624 A6
Kènscoff 2,287 C6
La Cahouane 519 A6
La Chapelle 793 C5
Lascahobas 3,132 C6
L'Asile 585 B6
Le Borgne 2,273 C5
Léogâne 4,603 C6
Les Anglais 1,808 A6
Les Cayes 22,065 B6
Les Irois 2,024 A6
Limbé 6,502 C5
Limonade 1,793 C5
Maïssade 2,280 C5
Marigot 1,814 C6
Miragoâne 3,570 B6
Mirebalais 3,952 C6
Môle Saint Nicolas 771 B5
Moron 2,367 A6
Ouanaminthe 5,320 C5
Pestel 820 A6
Pétionville 35,257 C6
Petit Goâve 8,779 B6
Petite Rivière de l'Artibonite 8,462 B5
Pignon 3,069 C5
Pilate 2,155 C5
Plaisance 1,859 C5
Pointe à Raquette B6
Port-à-Piment 3,280 A6
Port-au-Prince (cap.) 306,053 C6
Port-de-Paix 13,913 B5
Port Margot 2,673 C5
Port-Salut 1,034 A6
Roseaux 689 A6
Saint-Jean du Sud 401 B6
Saint-Louis du Nord 5,642 B5
Saint-Louis du Sud 1,039 B6
Saint-Marc 17,263 B5
Saint-Michel de l'Atalaye 4,636 C5
Saint-Michel du Sud 621 B6
Saint-Raphaël 2,691 C5
Savanette 834 C6
Terre Neuve 776 B5
Thomonde 1,911 C6
Tiburon 1,494 A6
Torbeck 797 A6
Trou Bonbon 658 A6
Trou du Nord 5,367 C5
Vallières 400 C5
Verrettes 2,448 C5
Ville Bonheur 1,866 C6

OTHER FEATURES

Artibonite (riv.) C5
Baradères (bay) B6
Cheval Blanc (pt.) B5
Dame Marie (cape) A6
Est (pt.) C4
Fantasque (pt.) B6
Gonâve (gulf) B5
Gonâve (isl.) B6
Grande Cayemite (isl.) B6
Gravois (pt.) A7
Irois (cape) A6
Jean-Rabel (pt.) B5
Macaya (mt.) A6
Manzanillo (bay) C5
Môle (cape) B5
Noires (mts.) C5
Ouest (pt.) B4
Ouest (pt.) B6
Saint-Marc (pt.) B5
Saint-Marc (chan.) B6
Saumâtre (lake) C6
Selle (peak) C6
Sud (chan.) B6
Tiburon (cape) A6
Tortue (chan.) C5
Tortue (Tortuga) (isl.) C4
Tortuga (isl.) C4
Trois-Rivières (riv.) B5
Vache (isl.) B6
Windward (passage) A5

JAMAICA

CITIES and TOWNS

Adelphi 1,649 H5
Albany J6
Albert Town H6
Alexandria 1,213 J6
Alley J7
Alligator Pond H6
Anchovy 2,558 H5
Annotto Bay K6
Balaclava 1,553 H6
Bamboo 2,971 J6
Bath K6
Bethel Town G6
Black River 2,701 H6
Bluefields G6
Bog Walk J6
Bowden K6
Browns Town 5,479 J6
Buff Bay K6
Bull Savanna-Junction 5,110 H6
Cambridge 2,449 H6
Cascade G6
Castleton J6
Catadupa H6
Chapelton J6
Christiana H6
Claremont 2,212 J6
Clark's Town H6
Darliston H6
Devon H6
Discovery Bay 1,814 J5
Duncans H5
Ewarton J6
Falmouth 3,937 H5
Four Paths J6
Frankfield H6
Frome G6
Gayle J6
Golden Grove K6
Green Island G6
Hayes J6
Highgate J6
Hope Bay K6
Hopewell G5
Kingston (cap.) 106,791 K6
Kingston* 516,865 J7
Lacovia 2,478 H6
Linstead J6
Lionel Town J7
Little London G6
Long Bay K6
Lucea 3,635 G5
Maggotty 1,753 H6
Malvern 1,316 H6
Manchioneal K6
Mandeville 14,421 H6
Maroon Town 2,717 H6
May Pen 26,074 J6
Moneague 1,963 J6
Montego Bay 43,521 H5
Montpelier H6
Moore Town K6
Morant Bay 7,465 K7
Nain 1,830 H6
Negril G6
Newmarket 1,793 H6
Ocho Rios 5,851 J6
Old England H6
Old Harbour J6
Old Harbour Bay J6
Oracabessa J5
Petersfield G6
Port Antonio 10,538 K6
Port Kaiser H7
Port Maria 5,259 J6
Port Morant K6
Port Rhoades H5
Port Royal J6
Porus H6
Richmond J6
Rio Bueno H5
Riversdale J6
Runaway Bay 1,116 J5
Saint Ann's Bay 7,101 J5
Saint Margaret's Bay K6
Sandy Bay G5
Santa Cruz 2,050 H6
Savanna-la-Mar 11,759 G6
Spaldings H6
Spanish Town 40,731 J6
Spur Tree H6
Stewart Town H6
Trinity Ville K6
Trout Hall J6
Ulster Spring H6
Williamsfield H6
Yallahs K6

OTHER FEATURES

Black (riv.) H6
Black River (bay) G6
Blue (mts.) J6
Blue Mountain (peak) K6
Galina (pt.) J6
Grande (riv.) K6
Great (riv.) H6
Great Pedro Bluff (prom.) H6
Long (bay) H7
Luana (pt.) G6
Minho (riv.) J6
Montego (bay) G5
Montego Bay (pt.) G5
North East (pt.) K6
North Negril (pt.) G6
North West (pt.) G5
Old Harbour (bay) J6
Portland (pt.) J7
Sir John's (peak) K6
South East (pt.) K6
South Negril (pt.) G6

*City and suburbs.
•Population of municipality.
*City and suburbs.

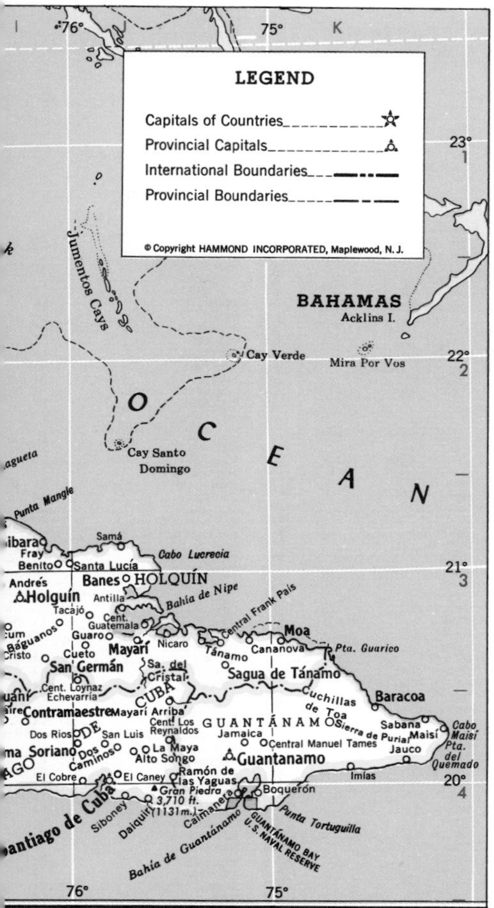
LEGEND
Capitals of Countries
Provincial Capitals
International Boundaries
Provincial Boundaries
© Copyright HAMMOND INCORPORATED, Maplewood, N. J.
BAHAMAS
Acklins I.
Mira Por Vos
Cay Santo Domingo
Jumentos Cays
O C E A N
Holguín
Banes
Mayarí
Moa
Sagua de Tánamo
Baracoa
Guantánamo
Santiago de Cuba
Longitude West of Greenwich

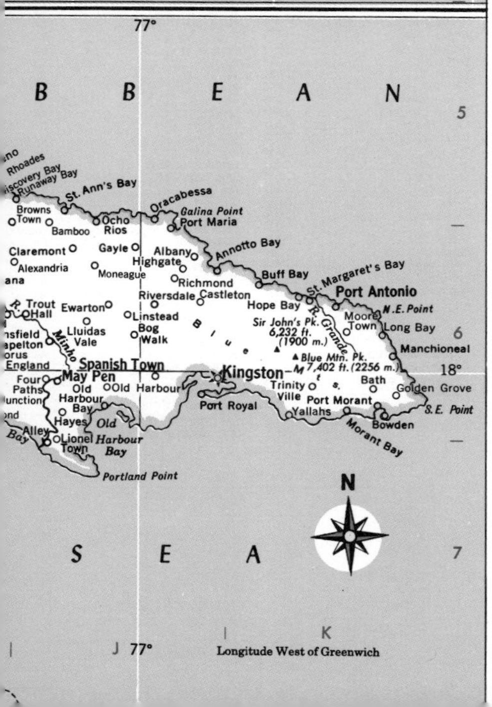
B B E A N
S E A
Montego Bay
St. Ann's Bay
Ocho Rios
Oracabessa
Port Maria
Annotto Bay
Buff Bay
Port Antonio
Spanish Town
Kingston
May Pen
Port Royal
Morant Bay
Longitude West of Greenwich

Agriculture, Industry and Resources

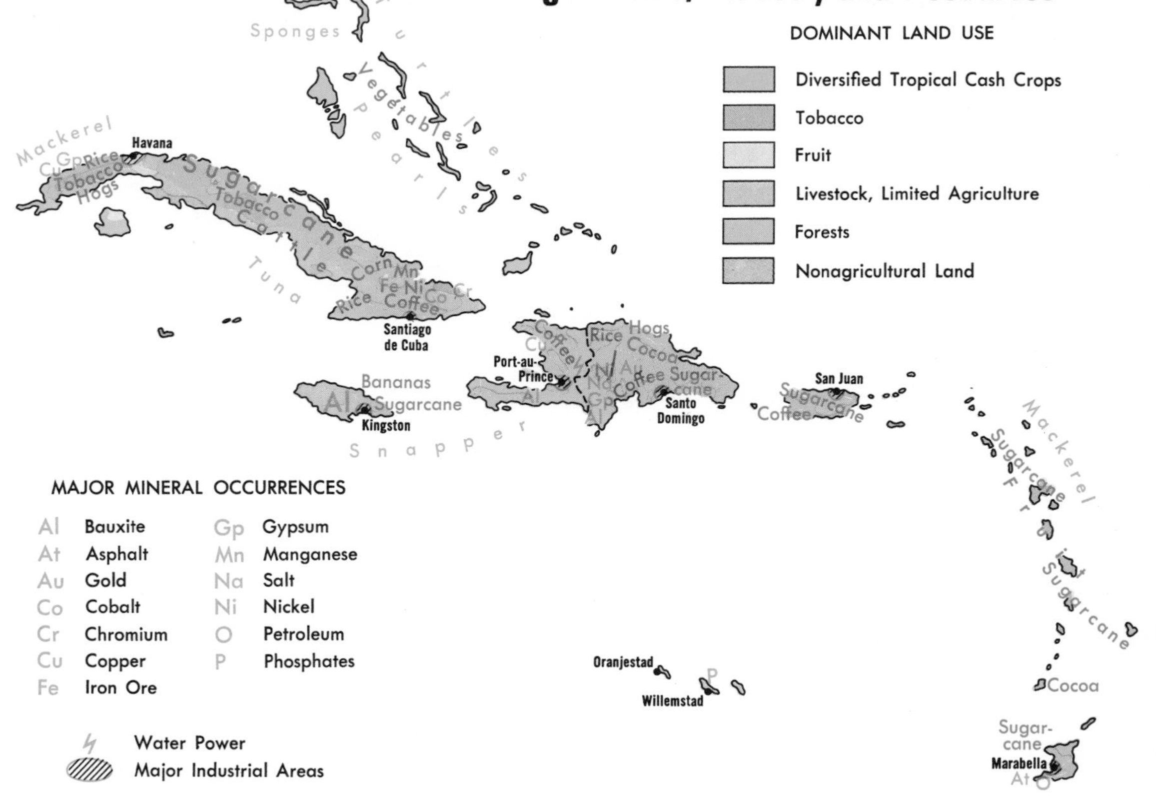
DOMINANT LAND USE
Diversified Tropical Cash Crops
Tobacco
Fruit
Livestock, Limited Agriculture
Forests
Nonagricultural Land
MAJOR MINERAL OCCURRENCES
Al Bauxite
At Asphalt
Au Gold
Co Cobalt
Cr Chromium
Cu Copper
Fe Iron Ore
Gp Gypsum
Mn Manganese
Na Salt
Ni Nickel
O Petroleum
P Phosphates
Water Power
Major Industrial Areas
Havana
Santiago de Cuba
Port-au-Prince
Santo Domingo
Kingston
San Juan
Oranjestad
Willemstad
Marabella

PUERTO RICO

DISTRICTS

Aguadilla ... A1
Arecibo ... C1
Bayamón ... D1
Guayama ... D2
Humacao ... E2
Mayagüez ... B2
Ponce ... C2
San Juan ... D1

CITIES and TOWNS

Adjuntas 5,184 ... B2
Aguada 5,028 ... A1
Aguadilla 20,879 ... A1
Aguas Buenas 3,769 ... E2
Aibonito 9,369 ... D2
Añasco 5,340 ... A1
Ángeles• 2,802 ... B2
Arecibo 48,586 ... B1
Arroyo 8,486 ... E3
Arus ... C3
Bahomamey ... A1
Bajadero ... C1
Barceloneta 4,498 ... C1
Barranquitas 3,613 ... D2
Bayamón 184,854 ... D1
Boquerón• 1,427 ... A3
Cabo Rojo 10,254 ... A2
Caguas 87,218 ... E2
Caguas‡ 173,929 ... E2
Camuy 3,832 ... B1
Carolina 147,100 ... E1
Cataño 26,318 ... D1
Cayey 23,315 ... D2
Ceiba 4,964 ... F2
Central Aguirre ... D3
Ciales 3,590 ... C1
Cidra 6,065 ... D2
Coamo 12,834 ... D2
Comerlo 5,751 ... D2
Coquí ... D3
Corozal 5,891 ... D1
Corral Viejo ... C2
Coto Laurel• 5,084 ... C2
Culebra 937 ... G1
Dewey (Culebra) 937 ... G1
Dorado 10,204 ... D1
Ensenada ... B3
Esperanza ... G2
Fajardo 26,845 ... F1
Guánica 9,627 ... B3
Guayama 21,044 ... E3
Guayanilla 6,191 ... B3
Guaynabo 65,091 ... D1
Gurabo 7,646 ... E2
Hatillo 5,039 ... B1
Hato Rey ... E1
Hormigüeros 11,991 ... A2
Humacao 19,135 ... E2
Isabela 12,097 ... A1
Isabel Segunda 2,322 ... G2
Jayuya 3,577 ... C2
Jobos ... D3
Juana Dlaz 10,496 ... C2
Juncos 7,898 ... E2
Lajas 4,267 ... A2
Lares 5,178 ... B2
Las Marias 801 ... B2
Las Piedras 4,878 ... E2
Levittown ... D1
Lolza 3,942 ... E1
Lolza Aldea ... E1
Luquillo 4,536 ... F1
Manatí 17,254 ... C1
Maricao 1,403 ... B2
Maunabo 2,992 ... E3
Mayagüez 82,703 ... A2
Mayagüez‡ 132,814 ... A2
Moca 3,890 ... A1
Morovis 2,636 ... D1
Naguabo 4,140 ... F2
Naranjito 2,845 ... D1
Orocovis 1,257 ... C2
Palmer ... F1
Palo Seco ... D1
Parguera ... A3
Patillas 3,148 ... E2
Peñuelas 3,471 ... B2
Playa de Fajardo ... F1
Playa de Humacao ... F2
Ponce 161,260 ... C3
Ponce‡ 8,252,420 ... C3
Puerto Nuevo ... D1
Puerto Real (Playa de Fajardo) ... F1
Punta Santiago (Playa de Humacao)• 1,912 ... F2
Quebradillas 3,787 ... B1
Rincón 1,702 ... A1
Rlo Blanco ... F2
Rlo Grande 12,068 ... E1
Rlo Piedras ... E1
Rosario ... A2
Sabana Grande 7,368 ... B2
Sabana Seca ... D1
Salinas 6,240 ... D3
San Antonio ... A1
San Germán 13,093 ... A2
San Juan (cap.) 422,701 ... E1
San Juan‡ 1,083,664 ... E1
San Lorenzo 8,886 ... E2
San Sebastián 10,792 ... B1
Santa Isabel 6,965 ... C3
Santurce ... E1
Tallaboa ... B3
Toa Alta 4,419 ... D1
Toa Baja 1,979 ... D1
Trujillo Alto 41,097 ... E1
Utuado 11,049 ... B2
Vega Alta 10,554 ... D1
Vega Baja 18,020 ... D1
Vieques (Isabel Segunda) 2,322 ... G2
Villalba 3,468 ... C2
Yabucoa 6,782 ... E2
Yauco 14,598 ... B2

OTHER FEATURES

Aguadilla (bay) ... A1
Algarrobo (pt.) ... A2
Añasco (bay) ... A1
Arenas (pt.) ... F2
Bauta (riv.) ... C2
Bayamón (riv.) ... D1
Boquerón (bay) ... A3
Borinquen (pt.) ... A1
Cabullones (pt.) ... C3
Caja de Muertos (isl.) ... C3
Camuy (riv.) ... B1
Candelero (pt.) ... F2
Canóvanas (riv.) ... E1
Caonillas (lake) ... C2
Carite (lake) ... E2
Carralzo (lake) ... E1
Cayey, Sierra de (mts.) ... D2
Central, Cordillera (range) ... C2
Cerro Gordo (pt.) ... D1
Coamo (res.) ... D3
Coamo (riv.) ... D3
Culebra (isl.) ... G1
Culebrinas (riv.) ... A1
Culebrita (isl.) ... G2
El Toro (mt.) ... F2
El Yunque (mt.) ... F1
Este (pt.) ... G2
Fajardo (riv.) ... F1
Figuras (pt.) ... E3
Fosforescente (bay) ... A3
Grande de Añasco (riv.) ... B2
Grande de Arecibo (riv.) ... C1
Grande de Lolza (riv.) ... E1
Grande de Manatí (riv.) ... C1
Guajataca (lake) ... B1
Guanajibo (pt.) ... A2
Guanajibo (riv.) ... A2
Guánica (lake) ... B3
Guaniquilla (pt.) ... A2
Guayabal (lake) ... C2
Guayanés (pt.) ... F2
Guayanés (riv.) ... E2
Guayanilla (bay) ... B3
Guayo (lake) ... B2
Guilarte (mt.) ... B2
Honda (bay) ... F2
Humacao (riv.) ... E2
Jacaguas (riv.) ... C2
Jaicoa, Cordillera (mts.) ... B1
Jiguero (pt.) ... A1
Jobos (bay) ... D3
La Bandera (pt.) ... F1
Lima (pt.) ... F2
Lobo (cay) ... G1
Luquillo, Sierra de (mts.) ... E2
Manglillo (pt.) ... B3
Mayagüez (bay) ... A2
Miquillo (pt.) ... F1
Molinos (pt.) ... G1
Mona (passage) ... A2
Negra (pt.) ... G2
Nigua (riv.) ... D2
Ola Grande (pt.) ... D3
Palmas Altas (pt.) ... C1
Patillas (lake) ... E2
Peñón (pt.) ... B1
Petrona (pt.) ... D3
Pirata (mt.) ... F2
Plata (riv.) ... D2
Puerca (pt.) ... F2
Puerto Medio Mundo (bay) ... F2
Puerto Nuevo (pt.) ... C1
Punta, Cerro de (mt.) ... C2
Ramey A.F.B. ... A1
Rincón (bay) ... D3
Rojo (cape) ... A3
Roosevelt Road Naval Res. ... F2
Salinas (pt.) ... D1
San José (lag.) ... E1
San Juan, Cabezas de (prom.) ... F1
San Juan Nat'l Hist. Site ... D1
Sardina (pt.) ... A1
Soldado (pt.) ... G2
Sucia (bay) ... A3
Tanamá (riv.) ... B1
Toro, El (mt.) ... F2
Torrecilla (lag.) ... E1
Tortuguero (lag.) ... D1
Tuna (pt.) ... E3
Vacla Talega (pt.) ... E1
Viento (pt.) ... E3
Vieques (isl.) ... G2
Vieques (passage) ... F2
Vieques (sound) ... G2
Yagüez (riv.) ... A2
Yauco (lake) ... B2
Yeguas (pt.) ... F3

ANTIGUA
Total Population, 72,000

CITIES and TOWNS

All Saints 1,796 ... E11
Cedar Grove 1,460 ... E11
Falmouth 1,134 ... E11
Freetown 1,250 ... E11
Jennings 1,370 ... D11
Johnsons Point 725 ... D11
Liberta 2,394 ... E11
Old Road 1,244 ... D11
Parham 1,570 ... E11
Saint John's (cap.) 21,814 ... E11

OTHER FEATURES

Antigua (isl.) ... E11
Boggy (peak) ... D11
Boon (pt.) ... E11
Green (isl.) ... E11
Guiana (isl.) ... E11
Long (isl.) ... E11
Saint John's (harb.) ... C11
Standfast (pt.) ... E11
Willoughby (bay) ... E11

BARBADOS

CITIES and TOWNS

Bathsheba ... B8
Belleplaine ... B8
Bridgetown (cap.) 8,868 ... B9
Carlton ... B8
Cave Hill ... B9
Checker Hall ... B8
Codrington ... B8
Crab Hill ... B8
Crane ... C9
Drax Hall ... B8
Ellerton ... B9
Greenland ... B8
Holetown ... B8
Kendal ... B8
Lodge Hill ... B8
Marchfield ... B9
Mount Standfast ... B8
Oistins ... B9
Portland ... B8
Rose Hill ... B8
Rouen ... B9
Saint Lawrence ... B9
Saint Martins ... C9
Scarboro ... B9
Seawell ... B9
Six Mens ... B8
Speightstown ... B8
Spring Hall ... B8
Welchman Hall ... B8

OTHER FEATURES

Carlisle (bay) ... B9
Hillaby (mt.) ... B8
Long (bay) ... B9
North (pt.) ... B8
Oistins (bay) ... B9
Pelican (isl.) ... B9
Ragged (pt.) ... C8
Sam Lord's Castle ... C9
South (pt.) ... B9

DOMINICA

CITIES and TOWNS

Barroui 1,480 ... E6
Castle Bruce 1,975 ... F6
Coulihaut 1,735 ... E6
Delice ... F7
Grand Bay 3,152 ... F7
Laudat 366 ... E6
Mahout 2,095 ... E6
Marigot 3,183 ... F6
Petit Soufrière ... F6
Portsmouth 2,329 ... E5
Rosalie ... F6
Roseau (cap.) 9,968 ... E7
Roseau* 16,035 ... E7
Saint Joseph 2,643 ... E6
Salybia ... F6
Soufrière ... E7
Vieille Case ... E5
Wesley 2,002 ... F5

OTHER FEATURES

Capuchin (cape) ... E5
Carib Reserve ... F6
Clyde (riv.) ... F6
Crumpton (pt.) ... F5
Diablotin, Morne (mt.) ... E6
Dominica (passage) ... E5
Douglas (bay) ... E5
Grand (bay) ... F7
Jaquet (pt.) ... E5
Layou (riv.) ... E6
Martinique (passage) ... E7
Micotrin (mt.) ... F6
Pagoua (bay) ... F6
Prince Rupert (bay) ... E5
Roseau (riv.) ... E7
Scotts (head) ... E7
Soufrière (bay) ... E7
Trois Pitons, Morne (mt.) ... E6

GRENADA

CITIES and TOWNS

Crochu ... D8
Gouyave 2,498 ... C8
Grand Anse ... C9
Grand Roy ... C8
Grenville 1,723 ... D8
Hermitage ... D8
La Taste ... D8
Marquis ... D8
Mount Tivoli ... D8
Providence ... D9
Saint George's (cap.) 6,313 ... C9
Saint George's* 29,860 ... C9
Sauteurs 6,055 ... D8
Union ... D8
Victoria 1,673 ... D8
Woburn ... C9
Woodford ... C8

OTHER FEATURES

Bedford (pt.) ... D8
David (pt.) ... D8
Great Bacolet (pt.) ... D8
Green (isl.) ... D8
Grenville (bay) ... D8
Gros (pt.) ... C8
Halifax (harb.) ... C8
Irvin's (bay) ... D8
Les Tantes (isls.) ... D7
Molinière (pt.) ... C8
Prickly (pt.) ... C9
Ronde (isl.) ... D7
Saint Catherine (mt.) ... D8
Saline (pt.) ... C9
Sinai (mt.) ... D8
Telescope (pt.) ... D8

GUADELOUPE
Total Population, 319,000

CITIES and TOWNS

Anse-Bertrand 2,236 ... A5
Baie-Mahault 2,576 ... A6
Baillif 2,214 ... A7
Bananier ... A7
Basse-Terre (cap.) 15,206 ... A7
Bouillante 1,882 ... A6
Bourg-des-Saintes 1,039 ... A7
Capesterre 6,857 ... A7
Capesterre, Marie-Galante 931 ... B7
Deshaies 736 ... A6
Ferry ... A6
Gosier 5,111 ... B6
Gourbeyre 2,822 ... A7
Goyave 1,301 ... A6
Grand-Bourg 3,332 ... B7
Grippon ... B6
Lamentin 1,849 ... A6
Les Abymes 10,202 ... B6
Morne-à-l'Eau 9,384 ... A6
Moule 8,636 ... B6
Petit-Bourg 3,631 ... A6
Petit-Canal 1,874 ... A6
Pigeon ... A6
Pointe-à-Pitre 23,750 ... B6
Pointe-Noire 2,128 ... A6
Port-Louis 5,069 ... B5
Saint-Claude 3,858 ... A7
Sainte-Anne 3,660 ... B6
Sainte-Marguerite ... B6
Sainte-Marie ... A6
Sainte-Rose 3,312 ... A6
Saint-François 3,151 ... B6
Saint-Louis 1,378 ... B7
Trois-Rivières 1,669 ... A7
Vieux-Fort 1,120 ... B7
Vieux-Habitants 1,927 ... A7

OTHER FEATURES

Allègre (pt.) ... A6
Antigues (pt.) ... A5
Basse-Terre (isl.) ... A6
Châteaux (pt.) ... B6
Constant, Morne (hill) ... B7
Désirade, La (isl.) ... B6
Fajou (isl.) ... A6
Grand Cul-de-Sac Marin (bay) ... A6
Grande-Terre ... B6
Grande Vigie ... B5
Grand-Îlet (isl.) ... A7
Guadeloupe (isl.) ... B6
Guadeloupe (passage) ... A5
Guadeloupe Nat'l Park ... A6
Kahouanne (isl.) ... A6
Marie-Galante (isl.) ... B7
Nord (pt.) ... B7
Nord-Est (bay) ... B6
Petit Cul-de-Sac Marin (bay) ... A6
Petite-Terre (isls.) ... B6
Saintes (chan.) ... A7
Saintes (isls.) ... A7
Salée (riv.) ... A6
Sans Toucher (mt.) ... A6
Soufrière (mt.) ... A7
Terre-de-Bas (isl.) ... A7
Terre-de-Haut (isl.) ... A7
Vieux-Fort (pt.) ... A7

MARTINIQUE
Total Population, 308,000

CITIES and TOWNS

Ajoupa-Bouillon 1,515 ... C5
Basse-Pointe 2,329 ... C5
Bellefontaine 1,240 ... C6
Case-Pilote 1,609 ... C6
Ducos 1,809 ... D6
Fond-Lahaye ... C6
Fond-Saint-Denis 931 ... C6
Fort-de-France (cap.) 96,815 ... C6
Fort-Desaix ... D6
Grande' Rivière 1,219 ... C5
Gros-Morne 1,326 ... D6
La Trinité 4,230 ... D6
Le Carbet 2,446 ... C6
Le Diamant 598 ... D7
Le François 3,288 ... D6
Le Lamentin 7,198 ... D6
Le Lorrain 1,808 ... D6
Le Marin 2,725 ... D7
Le Morne-Rouge 3,036 ... C5
Le Morne-Vert 413 ... C6
Le Prêcheur 1,710 ... C5
Le Robert 2,377 ... D6
Le Saint-Esprlt 2,842 ... D6
Les Anse-d' Arlets 794 ... C7
Les Trois-Îlets 1,302 ... D6
Le Vauclin 3,534 ... D6
Macouba 1,113 ... C5
Marigot 1,816 ... D5
Rivière-Pilote 1,653 ... D7
Rivière-Salée 1,837 ... D7
Sainte-Anne 957 ... D7
Sainte-Luce 1,299 ... D7
Sainte-Marie 3,751 ... D5
Saint-Joseph 2,040 ... D6
Saint-Pierre 5,358 ... C6
Schoelcher 13,792 ... C6
Vert-Pré ... D6

OTHER FEATURES

Cabet, Pitons du (mt.) ... C6
Cabrits (isl.) ... D7
Caravelle (pen.) ... D6
Cul-de-Sac du Marin (bay) ... D7
Diable (pt.) ... D5
Diamant, Rocher du (isl.) ... C7
Ferré (cape) ... E7
Fort-de-France (bay) ... C6
Galion (bay) ... D6
Lézarde (riv.) ... D6
Long (isl.) ... D6
Lorrain (riv.) ... D5
Martinique (passage) ... C5
Pelée (vol.) ... C5
Pilote (riv.) ... D7
Ramièrs (isl.) ... C6
Ramville (isl.) ... D6
Robert (harb.) ... D6
Rose (pt.) ... D6
Saint-Martin (cape) ... C5
Saint-Pierre (bay) ... C6
Salines (pt.) ... D7
Salomon (pt.) ... C7
Vauclin (mt.) ... D6

NETHERLANDS ANTILLES

CITIES and TOWNS

Aresji ... D9
Ascension ... F8
Bacuna ... E8
Balashi ... E10
Boven Bolivia ... E8
Bubali ... D10
Bushiribana ... E10
Dokterstuin ... F8
Druif ... D10
Emmastad ... F9
Entrejo ... E8
Fontein ... E8
Fuik ... G9
Groot Sint Joris ... G9
Hato ... G8
Kralendijk (cap.), Bonaire 2,500 ... E8
Lago ... E10
Lagoen ... F8
Montanja di Reij ... G9
New Port ... G9
Noord di Salinja ... E8
Onima ... E8
Oranjestad (cap.), Aruba 10,100 ... D10
Otrabanda ... F9
Patrick ... F8
Rincon ... E8
Rooi⊙ 1,989 ... E8
Santa Barbara ... G9
Santa Catharina ... G9
Savaneta ... E10
Savonet ... F8
Sint Anna ... D10
Sint Jan ... D8
Sint Kruis ... F8
Sint Martha ... F8
Sint Michiel ... F9
Sint Nicolaas ... E10
Sint Willebrordus ... F8
Terra Corra ... E8
Westpunt, Aruba ... D10
Westpunt, Curaçao ... F8
Willemstad (cap.) 95,000 ... F9
Willemstad* 130,000 ... F9

OTHER FEATURES

Aruba (isl.) ... E9
Basora (pt.) ... E10
Bonaire (isl.) ... E9
Bullen (bay) ... F8
Caracas (bay) ... G9
Curaçao (isl.) ... G7
Goto (lake) ... D8
Jamanota (mt.) ... E10
Kanon (pt.) ... G9
Klein Bonaire (isl.) ... E8
Kudarebe (pt.) ... D9
Lac (bay) ... D9
Lacre (pt.) ... E9
Malmok (mt.) ... E8
Noord (pt.) ... D8
Noord (pt.) ... F8
Paarden (bay) ... D10
Palm (beach) ... D10
Pekelmeer (lake) ... E9
Piscadera (bay) ... F9
Schottegat (bay) ... G9
Sint Anna (bay) ... F9
Sint Christoffel (mt.) ... F8
Sint Joris (bay) ... G9
Slag (bay) ... D8
Vierkant (pt.) ... E8

SAINT CHRISTOPHER, and NEVIS
Total Population, 44,404

CITIES and TOWNS

Basseterre (cap.) 14,725 ... C10
Cayon ... C10
Charlestown 1,326 ... C11
Cotton Ground 471 ... C11
Dieppe Bay ... C10
Frigate ... C10
Gingerland ... D11
Golden Rock ... C10
Newcastle ... D11
Old Road Town ... C10
Sadlers Village ... C10
Sandy Point 862 ... C10
Tabernacle ... C10

OTHER FEATURES

Brimstone (hill) ... C10
Dogwood (pt.) ... D11
Fort (pt.) ... C11
Great Salt (pond) ... D10
Heldens (pt.) ... C10
Horse Shoe (pt.) ... C11
Misery (mt.) ... C10
Monkey (hill) ... C10
Muddy (pt.) ... C10
Narrows, The (str.) ... D11
Nevis (isl.) ... D11
Nevis (peak) ... D11
North Friars (bay) ... D10
Palmetto (pt.) ... C10
Pinney's (beach) ... D11
Saint Christopher (isl.) ... D10
Saint Kitts (Saint Christopher) (isl.) ... D10
South Friars (bay) ... C10

SAINT LUCIA

CITIES and TOWNS

Anse la Raye⊙ 5,007 ... F6
Canaries⊙ 2,075 ... G6
Castries (cap.)⊙ 42,770 ... G6
Choc ... G5
Choiseul⊙ 6,382 ... F7
Dauphin ... G5
Dennery⊙ 9,654 ... G6
Gros Islet⊙ 10,329 ... G5
Laborie⊙ 6,944 ... G7
Marigot ... G6
Marquis ... G6
Micoud⊙ 12,264 ... G6
Praslin ... G6
Soufrière⊙ 7,456 ... F6
Vieux Fort⊙ 10,675 ... G7

OTHER FEATURES

Beaumont (pt.) ... F6
Canaries, Piton (mt.) ... G6
Cannelles (pt.) ... G7
Cannelles (riv.) ... G6
Cap (pt.) ... G5
Choc (bay) ... G5
Fond d'Or (bay) ... G6
Gimie (mt.) ... G6
Grand Caille (pt.) ... F6
Grand Cul de Sac (riv.) ... G6
Gros Islet (bay) ... G5
Gros Piton (mt.) ... G6
La Sorcière (mt.) ... G6
Maria (isls.) ... G7
Ministre (pt.) ... G7
Moule à Chique (cape) ... G7
Petit Piton (mt.) ... G6
Pigeon (isl.) ... G5
Port Castries (harb.) ... G6
Port Praslin (bay) ... G6
Roseau (riv.) ... G6
Saint Lucia (chan.) ... G5
Saint Vincent (chan.) ... G7
Savannes (bay) ... G7
Sorcière, La (mt.) ... G6
Soufrière (bay) ... F6
Vierge (pt.) ... G6
Vieux Fort (riv.) ... G6

SAINT VINCENT & THE GRENADINES

CITIES and TOWNS

Barrouallie 1,298 ... A9
Calliaqua 627 ... A9
Camden Park ... A9
Chateaubelair 237 ... A8
Colonarie ... A9
Georgetown 1,100 ... A8
Kingstown (cap.) 17,117 ... A9
Kingstown* 23,330 ... A9
Layou 1,147 ... A9
Orange Hill ... A8
Wallibu ... A8

OTHER FEATURES

Colonarie (pt.) ... A9
Cumberland (bay) ... A8
Dark (head) ... A8
De Volet (pt.) ... A8
Espagnol (pt.) ... A8
Greathead (bay) ... A9
Kingstown (bay) ... A9
Owia (bay) ... A8
Porter (pt.) ... A8
Richmond (peak) ... A8
Saint Andrew (mt.) ... A9
Saint Vincent (passage) ... A8
Soufrière (mt.) ... A8
Yambou (head) ... A9

TRINIDAD and TOBAGO

CITIES and TOWNS

Arima 11,636 ... B10
Arouca ... B10
Basse Terre ... B11
Biche ... B10
Blanchisseuse ... B10
California ... A11
Carapichaima ... B10
Caroni ... B10
Cedros ... A11
Chaguanas ... B10
Chaguaramas ... A10
Couva ... B10
Cunapo ... B10
Débé ... B11
Ecclesville ... B11
Flanagin Town ... B10
Fullarton ... A11
Fyzabad ... A11
Gran Couva ... B11
Grande Rivière ... B10
Guaico ... B10
Guayaguayare ... B11
La Brea ... A11
La Lune ... B11
Marabella ... A11
Matelot ... B10
Matura ... B10
Mayaro ... B11
Moruga ... B11
Mucurapo ... A10
Nestor ... B10
Palo Seco ... A11
Peñal ... B11
Piarco ... B10
Point Fortin ... A11
Port-of-Spain (cap.) 62,680 ... A10
Princes Town ... B11
Redhead ... B10
Rio Claro ... B11
Sadhoowa ... B11
Saint Joseph ... B10
Saint Joseph ... B11
San Fernando 36,870 ... A11
San Francique ... A11
Sangre Grande 8,286 ... B10
San Juan ... A10
Sans Souci ... B10
Siparia 6,154 ... B11
Tabaquite ... B11
Tableland ... B11
Tacarigua ... B10
Talparo ... B10
Toco ... B10
Tunapuna ... B10
Upper Manzanilla ... B10
Valencia ... B10
Waterloo ... A10

OTHER FEATURES

Aripo, El Cerro del (mt.) ... B10
Boca Grande (passage) ... A10
Casa Cruz (cape) ... B11
Chacachacare (isl.) ... A10
Chupara (pt.) ... B10
Cocos (bay) ... B10
Dragons Mouth (str.) ... A10
El Tucuche (mt.) ... B10
Erin (bay) ... A11
Erin (pt.) ... A11
Galeota (pt.) ... B11
Galera (pt.) ... C10
Guapo (bay) ... A11
Guatuaro (pt.) ... B11
Icacos (pt.) ... A11
Maracas (bay) ...
Matura (bay) ... B10
Mayaro (bay) ... B11
Monos (isl.) ... A10
Nariva (swamp) ... B10
Oropuche (riv.) ... B10
Ortoire (riv.) ... B11
Paria (gulf) ... A11
Pitch (lake) ... A11
Serpents Mouth (passage) ... A11
Tamana (mt.) ... B10
Trinidad (isl.) ... A9

VIRGIN ISLANDS (Br.)

CITIES and TOWNS

Road Town (cap.) 2,183 ... D3
West End ... C4

OTHER FEATURES

Flanagan (passage) ... D4
Frenchman (cay) ... C4
Great Thatch (isl.) ... C4
Great Tobago (isl.) ... B3
Jost Van Dyke (isl.) ... C3
Little Tobago (isl.) ... B3
Narrows, The (str.) ... C4
Norman (isl.) ... D4
Peter (isl.) ... D4
Road (bay) ... D3
Sage (mt.) ... D4
Sir Francis Drake (chan.) ... D4
Tortola (isl.) ... D3

VIRGIN ISLANDS (U.S.)

CITIES and TOWNS

Bethlehem ... E4
Canebay ... E3
Charlotte Amalie (cap.) 11,670 ... B4
Christiansted 2,846 ... F4
Cruz Bay 1,930 ... C4
Diamond ... F4
Eastend ... D4
Emmaus ... C4
Fredensdal ... F4
Frederiksted 1,032 ... E4
Grove Place ... E4
Kingshill ... F4
Longford ... F4
Negro Bay ... E4

OTHER FEATURES

Altona (lag.) ... F4
Annaly (bay) ... E3
Baron Bluff (prom.) ... E3
Bordeaux (mt.) ... C4
Brass (isls.) ... A4
Buck (isl.) ... G3
Buck Island (chan.) ... F3
Buck Island Reef Nat'l Mon. ... G3
Butler (bay) ... E4
Caneel (bay) ... B4
Capella (isls.) ... B5
Christiansted Nat'l Hist. Site ... F4
Coral (bay) ... C4
Crown (mt.) ... A4
Dutch Cap (cay) ... A4
Eagle (mt.) ... E4
East (pt.) ... G4
Flanagan (passage) ... D4
Flat (cays) ... A4
Grass (pt.) ... G4
Great (pond) ... F4
Great Pond (bay) ... F4
Green (cay) ... F4
Hams Bluff (prom.) ... E3
Hans Lollik (isls.) ... B4
Hassel (isl.) ... B4
Jersey (bay) ... B4
Krause (chan.) ... F4
Leeward (passage) ... B4
Long (pt.) ... B4
Long (pt.) ... E4
Lovango (cay) ... C4
Magens (bay) ... B4
Maho (bay) ... C4
Narrows, The (str.) ... C4
Nulliberg (mt.) ... B4
Perseverance (bay) ... A4
Picara (pt.) ... B4
Pillsbury (sound) ... B4
Privateer (pt.) ... D4
Pull (pt.) ... F3
Ram (head) ... C5
Red (pt.) ... D4
Reef (bay) ... C4
Saba (isl.) ... A4
Saint Croix (isl.) ... G4
Saint James (isls.) ... B4
Saint John (isl.) ... C4
Saint Thomas (harb.) ... B4
Saint Thomas (isl.) ... A4
Salt (cay) ... A4
Salt (riv.) ... F4
Salt River (bay) ... F3
Sandy (pt.) ... D4
Savana (isl.) ... A4
Southwest (cape) ... E4
Tague (bay) ... G4
Thatch (cay) ... B4
Turner Hole (bay) ... G4
U.S. Nav. Air Sta. ... A4
Vagthus (pt.) ... F4
Virgin (str.) ... A4
Virgin Isls. Nat'l Park ... C4
Water (isl.) ... A4
Westend Saltpond (lag.) ... E4

⊙Population of district.
• Population of municipality.
*City and suburbs.
‡ Population of metropolitan area.

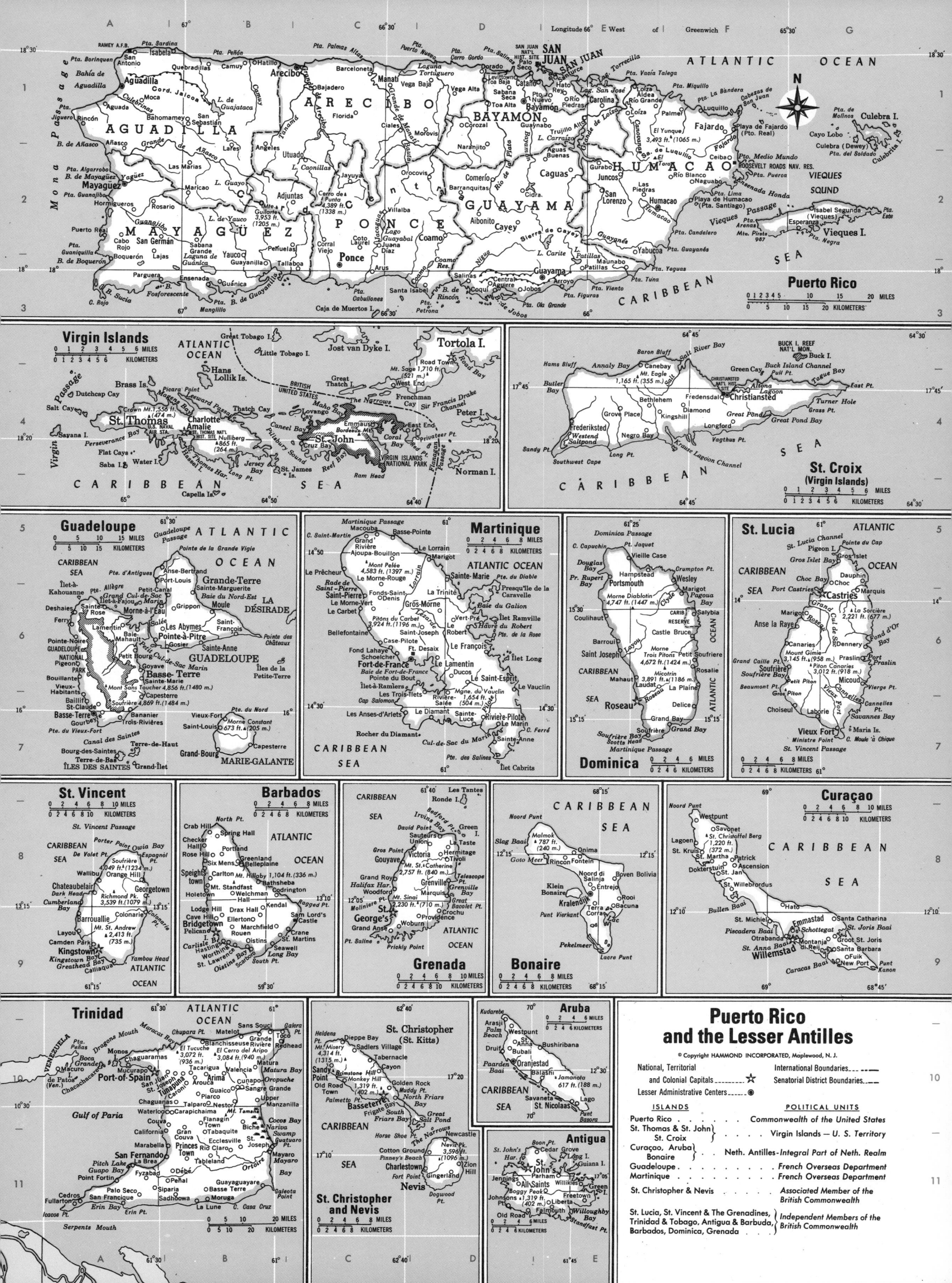

Puerto Rico and the Lesser Antilles

© Copyright HAMMOND INCORPORATED, Maplewood, N.J.

National, Territorial and Colonial Capitals ★	International Boundaries
Lesser Administrative Centers ◉	Senatorial District Boundaries

ISLANDS	POLITICAL UNITS
Puerto Rico	Commonwealth of the United States
St. Thomas & St. John }	Virgin Islands — U. S. Territory
St. Croix	
Curaçao, Aruba }	Neth. Antilles-Integral Part of Neth. Realm
Bonaire	
Guadeloupe	French Overseas Department
Martinique	French Overseas Department
St. Christopher & Nevis	Associated Member of the British Commonwealth
St. Lucia, St. Vincent & The Grenadines, Trinidad & Tobago, Antigua & Barbuda, Barbados, Dominica, Grenada	Independent Members of the British Commonwealth

Puerto Rico

Virgin Islands

St. Croix (Virgin Islands)

Guadeloupe

Martinique

Dominica

St. Lucia

St. Vincent

Barbados

Grenada

Bonaire

Curaçao

Trinidad

St. Christopher (St. Kitts)

St. Christopher and Nevis

Aruba

Antigua

Canada

CONIC PROJECTION

SCALE OF MILES
0 50 100   200   300

SCALE OF KILOMETERS
0 50 100 200 300 400 500

Capitals of Countries .... ☆
Provincial & Territorial Capitals .... △
International Boundaries ....
Provincial Boundaries ....

Scale 1:19,600,000

© Copyright HAMMOND INCORPORATED, Maplewood, N.J.

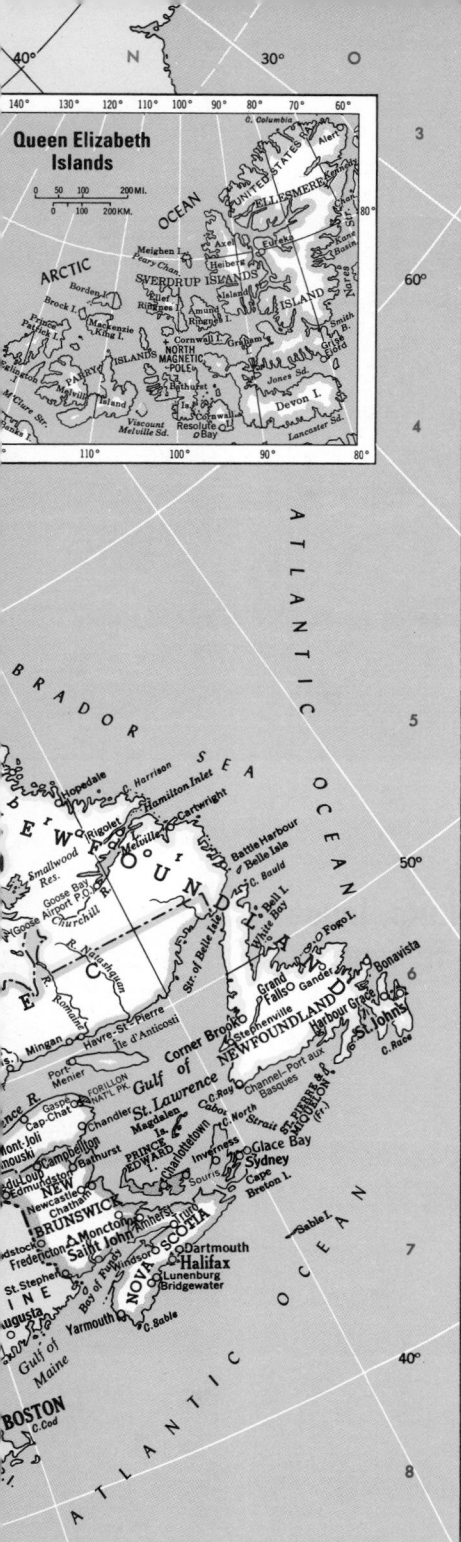

AREA 3,851,787 sq. mi. (9,976,139 sq. km.)
POPULATION 24,105,163
CAPITAL Ottawa
LARGEST CITY Montréal
HIGHEST POINT Mt. Logan 19,524 ft. (5,951 m.)
MONETARY UNIT Canadian dollar
MAJOR LANGUAGES English, French
MAJOR RELIGIONS Protestantism, Roman Catholicism

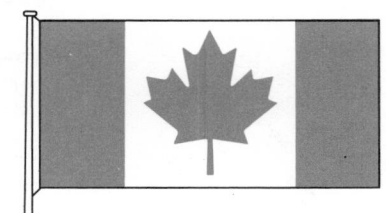

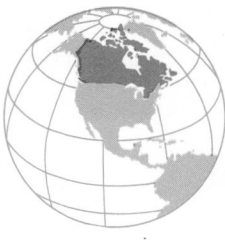

Population Distribution

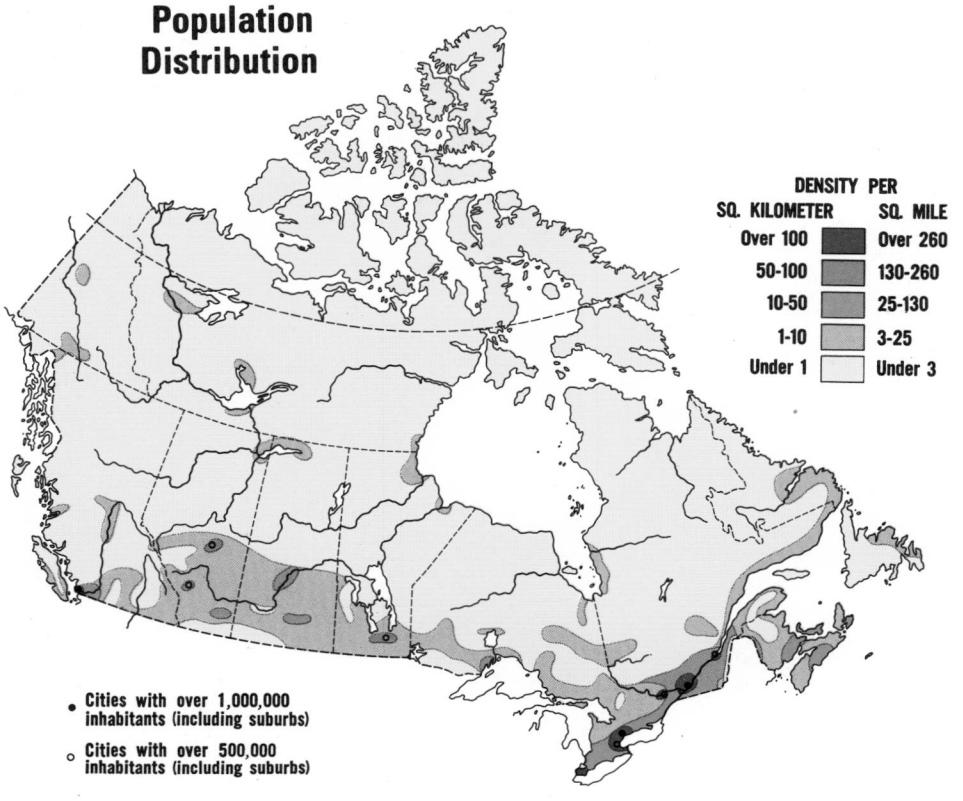

DENSITY PER

SQ. KILOMETER	SQ. MILE
Over 100	Over 260
50-100	130-260
10-50	25-130
1-10	3-25
Under 1	Under 3

● Cities with over 1,000,000 inhabitants (including suburbs)

○ Cities with over 500,000 inhabitants (including suburbs)

Vegetation

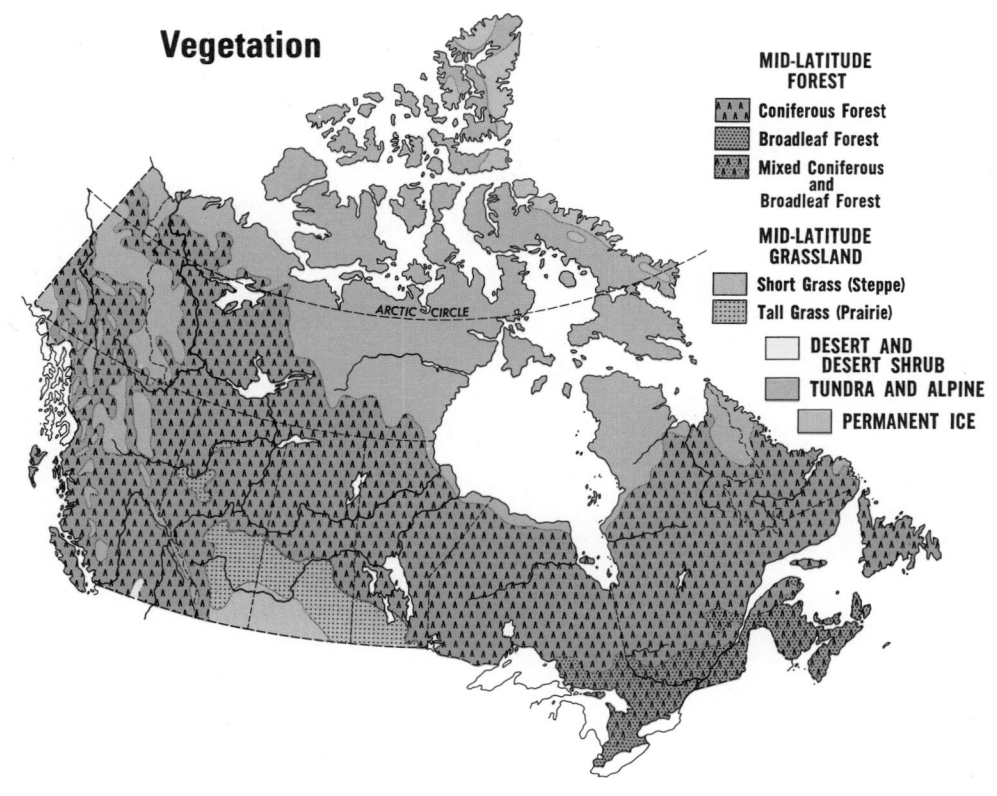

MID-LATITUDE FOREST
Coniferous Forest
Broadleaf Forest
Mixed Coniferous and Broadleaf Forest

MID-LATITUDE GRASSLAND
Short Grass (Steppe)
Tall Grass (Prairie)

DESERT AND DESERT SHRUB
TUNDRA AND ALPINE
PERMANENT ICE

Average January Temperature

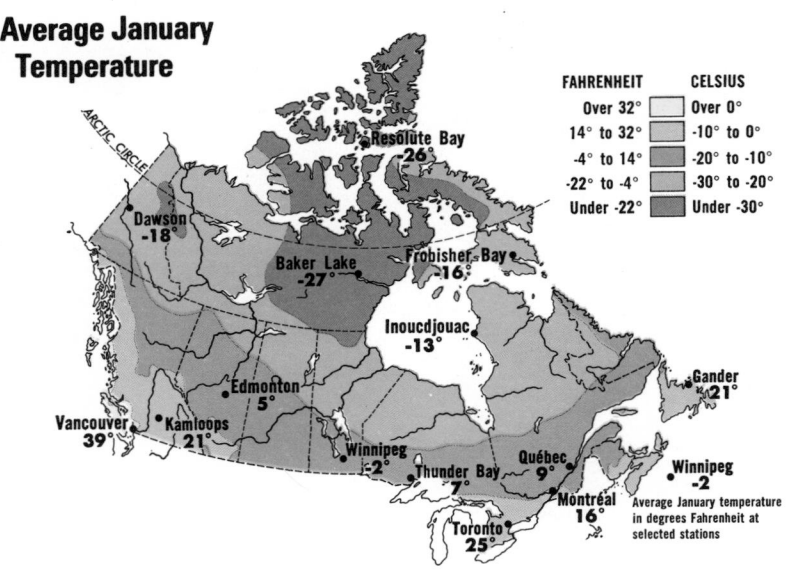

FAHRENHEIT	CELSIUS
Over 32°	Over 0°
14° to 32°	-10° to 0°
-4° to 14°	-20° to -10°
-22° to -4°	-30° to -20°
Under -22°	Under -30°

Resolute Bay 26°
Dawson -18°
Baker Lake -27°
Frobisher Bay -16°
Inoucdjouac -13°
Gander 21°
Edmonton 5°
Vancouver 39°
Kamloops 21°
Winnipeg -2°
Thunder Bay 7°
Québec 9°
Montréal 16°
Toronto 25°

Winnipeg -2
Average January temperature in degrees Fahrenheit at selected stations

ARCTIC CIRCLE

Average July Temperature

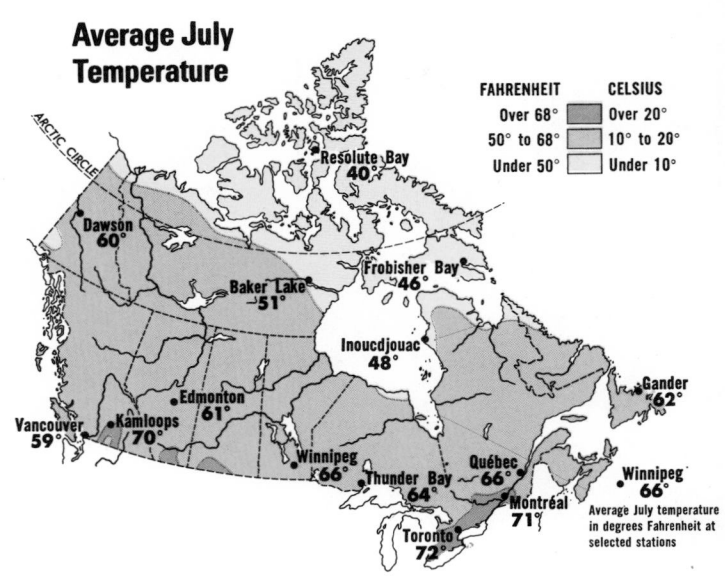

FAHRENHEIT	CELSIUS
Over 68°	Over 20°
50° to 68°	10° to 20°
Under 50°	Under 10°

Resolute Bay 40°
Dawson 60°
Baker Lake 51°
Frobisher Bay 46°
Inoucdjouac 48°
Gander 62°
Edmonton 61°
Vancouver 59°
Kamloops 70°
Winnipeg 66°
Thunder Bay 64°
Québec 66°
Montréal 71°
Toronto 72°

Winnipeg 66°
Average July temperature in degrees Fahrenheit at selected stations

ARCTIC CIRCLE

Agriculture, Industry and Resources

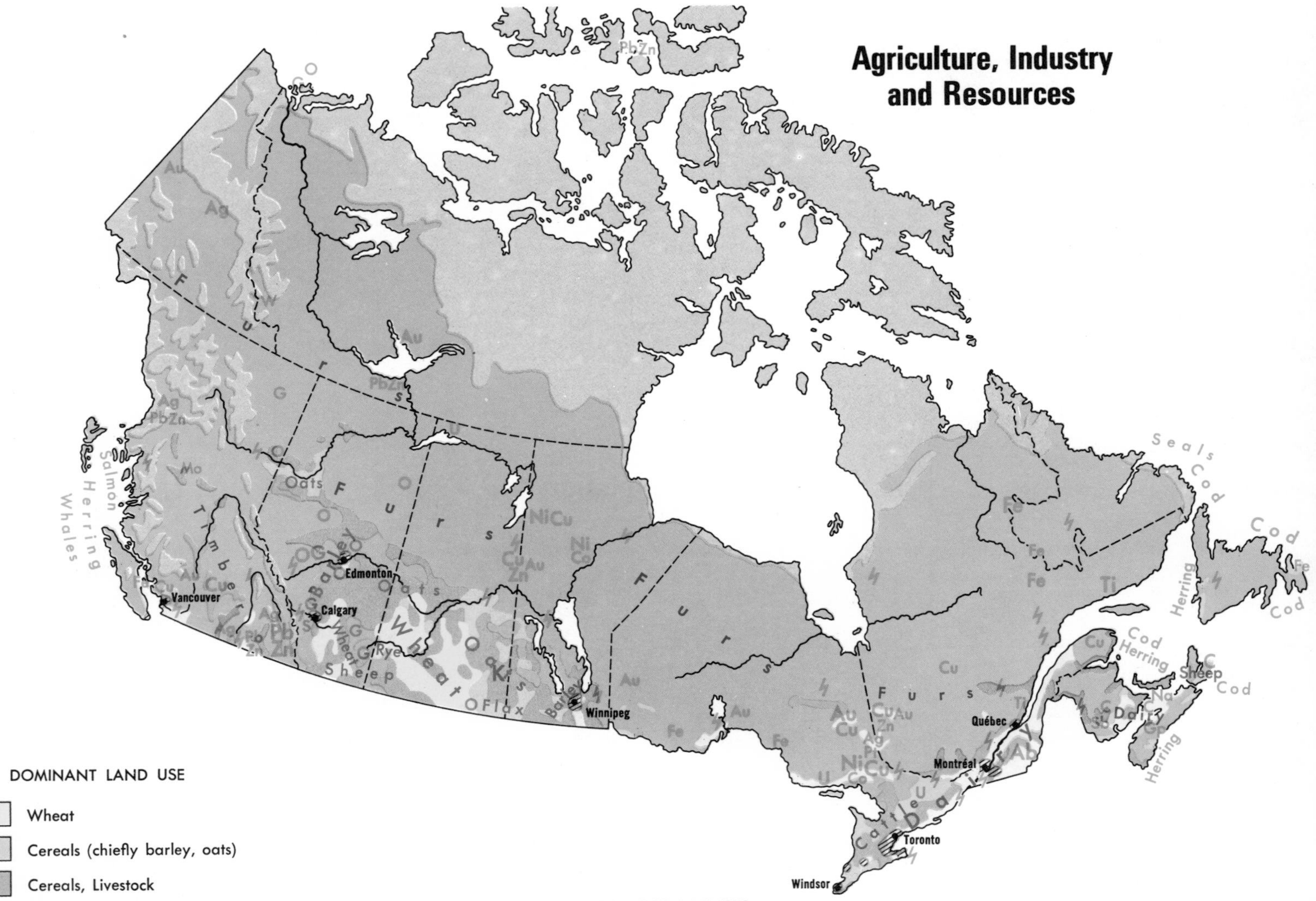

DOMINANT LAND USE

- Wheat
- Cereals (chiefly barley, oats)
- Cereals, Livestock
- General Farming, Livestock
- Dairy
- Fruit, Vegetables
- Pasture Livestock
- Range Livestock
- Forests
- Nonagricultural Land

MAJOR MINERAL OCCURRENCES

Ab	Asbestos	Fe	Iron Ore	Ni	Nickel
Ag	Silver	G	Natural Gas	O	Petroleum
Au	Gold	Gp	Gypsum	Pb	Lead
C	Coal	K	Potash	Pt	Platinum
Co	Cobalt	Mo	Molybdenum	S	Sulfur
Cu	Copper	Na	Salt		

Sb	Antimony
Ti	Titanium
U	Uranium
W	Tungsten
Zn	Zinc

⚡ Water Power

▨ Major Industrial Areas

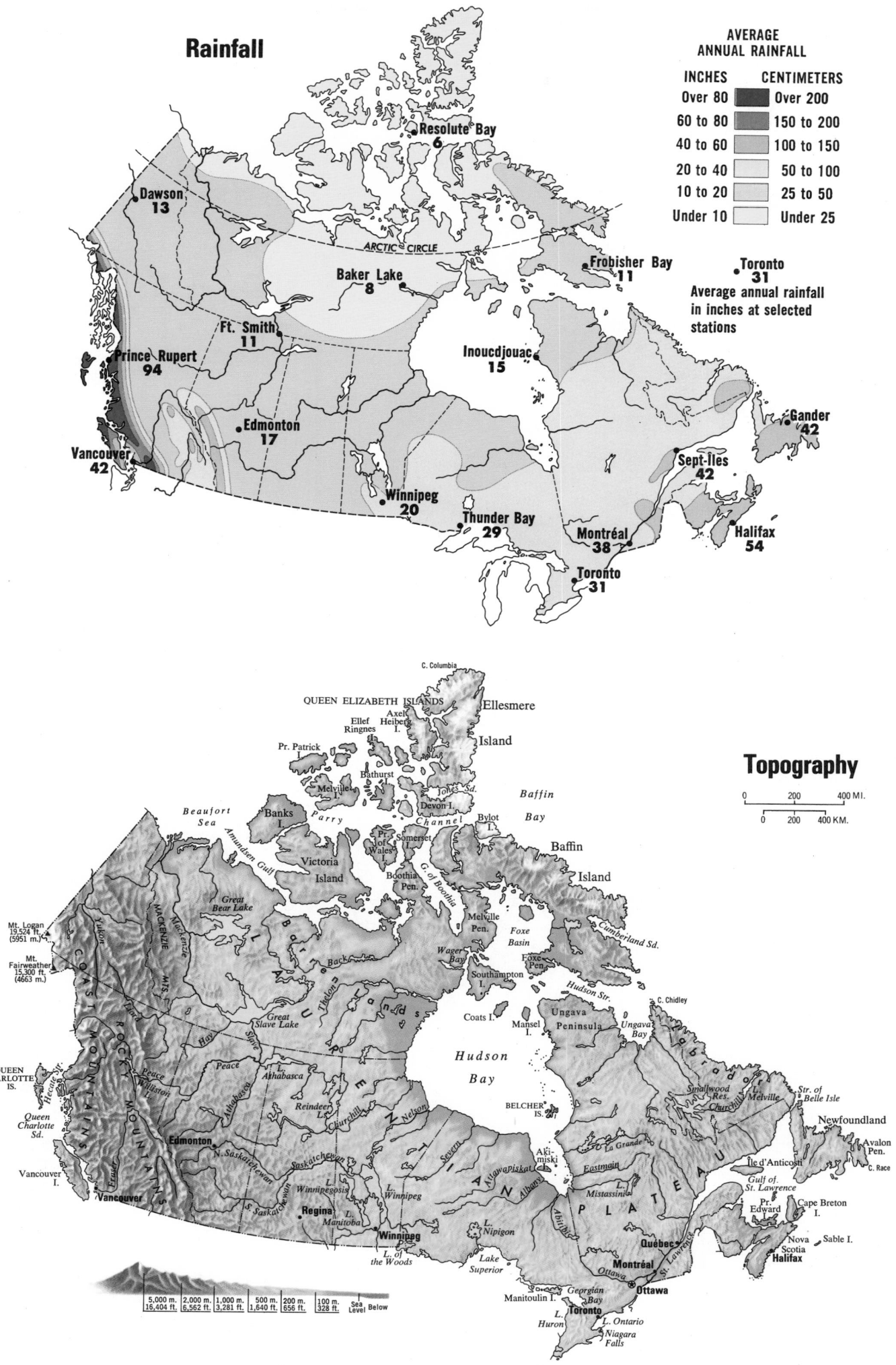

Rainfall

AVERAGE
ANNUAL RAINFALL

INCHES	CENTIMETERS
Over 80	Over 200
60 to 80	150 to 200
40 to 60	100 to 150
20 to 40	50 to 100
10 to 20	25 to 50
Under 10	Under 25

Toronto
31
Average annual rainfall
in inches at selected
stations

Resolute Bay 6
Dawson 13
Frobisher Bay 11
Baker Lake 8
Ft. Smith 11
Inoucdjouac 15
Prince Rupert 94
Edmonton 17
Gander 42
Vancouver 42
Sept-Îles 42
Winnipeg 20
Thunder Bay 29
Montréal 38
Halifax 54
Toronto 31

Topography

0   200   400 MI.
0   200   400 KM.

5,000 m. 2,000 m. 1,000 m. 500 m. 200 m. 100 m. Sea Level Below
16,404 ft. 6,562 ft. 3,281 ft. 1,640 ft. 656 ft. 328 ft.

Newfoundland
including Labrador

SCALE

| 0 | 25 | 50 | 100 | 150 MI. |
| 0 | 25 | 50 | 100 | 150 KM. |

Capitals of Provinces .... ⊛
Provincial Boundaries .... — ·· — ·· —
Provincial Boundary according to
Imperial Privy Council decision, 1927 .... - - - -

Scale 1:5,200,000

LABRADOR SEA

ATLANTIC OCEAN

QUÉBEC

NEW BRUNSWICK

PRINCE EDWARD ISLAND

MAGDALEN ISLANDS (Quebec)

Gulf of St. Lawrence

ST PIERRE & MIQUELON (Fr.)

Newfoundland

ST. JOHN'S

© Copyright HAMMOND INCORPORATED, Maplewood, N.J.

NEWFOUNDLAND

CITIES and TOWNS

Argentia 68 C2
Arnold's Cove 1,160 C2
Avondale 937 D2
Badger 1,160 C4
Badger's Quay 649 D4
Baie Verte 2,528 C4
Battle Harbour C3
Bay Bulls 1,104 D2
Bay de Verde 749 D2
Bay Roberts 4,072 D2
Birchy Bay 646 D4
Bishop's Falls 4,504 C4
Blackhead Road 1,840 D2
Blaketown 537 D2
Bloomfield 677 D2
Bonavista 4,299 D2
Botwood 4,554 C4
Brigus 912 D2
Burgeo 2,474 C4
Burin 2,892 C4
Burnt Islands 914 C4
Campbellton 757 D4
Cape Broyle 711 D2
Carbonear 5,026 D2
Carmanville 911 D4
Cartwright 675 C3
Catalina 1,129 D2
Channel-Port aux Basques 6,187 C4
Chapel Arm 712 D2
Churchill Falls 930 B3
Clarenville 2,807 C2
Clarke's Beach 997 D2
Colliers 840 D2
Conception Harbour 910 D2
Corner Brook 25,198 C4
Cow Head 650 C3
Cox's Cove 1,004 C4
Creston 768 C2
Cupids 750 D2
Daniel's Harbour 579 C3
Dark Cove 1,418 D4
Deer Lake 4,546 C4
Dildo 858 D2
Dunville 1,909 D2
Durrell 1,137 D4
Eastport 567 D1
Elliston 540 D2
Embree 855 C4
Englee 989 C3
Ferryland 656 D2
Flat Rock 743 D2
Fleur de Lys 694 C3
Fogo 1,103 D4
Fortune 2,406 C4
Fox Harbour 627 D2
Gander 9,301 D4
Garnish 678 C4
Gaultois 588 C4
Glenwood 1,128 D4
Glovertown 2,176 C1
Goose Bay-Happy Valley 8,075 B3
Goulds 3,317 D2
Grand Bank 3,802 C4
Grand Falls 8,729 C4
Green's Harbour 705 D2
Hampden 780 C4
Happy Valley-Goose Bay 8,075 B3
Harbour Breton 2,317 C4
Harbour Grace 2,937 D2
Harbour Main 992 D2
Hare Bay 1,598 D4
Head of Bay d'Espoir 560 C4
Heart's Content 634 D2
Heart's Delight 590 D2
Hermitage 675 C4
Holyrood 1,610 D2
Hopedale 447 B2
Isle aux Morts 1,270 C4
Jerseyside 1,024 B3
Joe Batt's Arm 821 D4
King's Point 770 C4
Kippens 1,267 C4
Labrador City 12,012 A3
Lamaline 543 C4
Lark Harbour 771 C4
La Scie 1,256 C4
Lawn 1,025 C4
Lethbridge 736 D2
Lewisporte 3,782 C4
Little Catalina 736 D2
Lourdes 987 C4
Lumsden 597 D4
Main Brook 551 C3
Marystown 5,915 D4
Middle Arm 555 C4
Milltown 748 C4
Mount Pearl 10,193 D2
Musgrave Harbour 1,530 D4
Musgravetown 641 C2
Nain 812 B2
New Harbour 779 D2
Norman's Cove 842 D2
Norris Arm 1,342 C4
Norris Point 1,065 C4
North West River 1,022 B3
Old Perlican 626 D2
Paradise 2,131 D2
Parson's Pond 544 C3
Pasadena 1,850 C4
Peterview 1,099 C4
Petty Harbour 824 D2
Placentia 2,209 C2
Point Leamington 882 C4
Port au Choix 1,141 C3
Port au Port 660 C4
Port Blandford 815 C2
Port Hope Simpson 548 C3
Port Saunders 691 C3
Portugal Cove 1,527 D2
Port Union 678 D2
Pouch Cove 1,543 D2
Ramea 1,226 C4
Rigolet 238 C3
Robert's Arm 1,064 C4
Rocky Harbour 1,267 C4
Roddickton 1,234 C3
Rose Blanche 766 C4
Saint Alban's 2,040 C4
Saint Anthony 2,987 C3
Saint Bride's 578 C2
Saint George's 1,976 C4
Saint John's (cap.) 86,576 D2
Saint Lawrence 2,258 C4
Saint Lunaire-Griquet 921 C3
Saint Phillips 807 D2
Saint Vincent's 604 C2
Salmon Cove 733 D2
Seal Cove 774 C4
Shoal Harbour 1,009 C2
South Brook, Green Bay dist. 828 C4
Southern Harbour 759 C2
South River 598 D2
Spaniard's Bay 1,568 D2
Springdale 3,513 C4
Stephenville 10,284 C4
Stephenville Crossing 2,207 C4
Summerford 1,099 C4
Sunnyside 726 D2
Terrenceville 764 D4
Torbay 2,908 D2
Trepassey 1,427 D2
Trinity 559 D2
Trout River 784 C4
Twillingate 1,404 C4
Upper Island Cove 1,851 D2
Victoria 1,767 D2
Wabana 4,824 D2
Wabush 3,769 A3
Wesleyville 1,167 D4
Whitbourne 1,268 D2
Windsor 6,349 C4
Winterton 796 D2
Witless Bay 888 D2

OTHER FEATURES

Adlatok, (bay) B2
Adlavik, (isls.) C2
Aguanus, (riv.) B3
Alexis, (riv.) C3
Anaktalik Brook, (riv.) B2
Andre, (lake) A3
Anguille, (cape) C4
Annieopscotch, (mts.) C4
Ashuanipi, (lake) A3
Ashuanipi, (riv.) A3
Assigny, (lake) A3
Astray, (lake) A3
Atikonak, (lake) B3
Attikamagen, (lake) A3
Avalon, (pen.) D2
Avayalik, (isls.) B1
Baccalieu, (isl.) D2
Backway, The, (inlet) C3
Ballard, (cape) D2
Barachois Pond Prov. Park C4
Bauld, (cape) C3
Beaver, (riv.) B3
Bell, (isl.) C3
Bell, (isl.) D2
Belle Isle, (isl.) C3
Belle Isle, (str.) C3
Benedict, (mt.) C3
Big, (bay) B2
Big, (isl.) B3
Big, (riv.) B2
Biscay Bay, (riv.) D2
Bishops Mitre, (mt.) B2
Blackhead, (bay) D2
Black River, (pond) C2
Bluff, (cape) C3
Bonaventure, (cape) D2
Bonavista, (bay) D1
Bonavista, (cape) D1
Bonne, (bay) C4
Branch, (riv.) C2
Broyle, (cape) D2
Brunette, (isl.) C4
Bull, (isl.) D2
Bull Arm, (inlet) D2
Bulldog, (isl.) C3
Burin, (pen.) C4
Burnt, (lake) B3
Butter Pot Prov. Park D2
Byron, (bay) C3
Cabot, (lake) B2
Cabot, (str.) B4
Canada, (bay) C3
Chance Cove, (cape) D2
Chidley, (cape) B1
Churchill, (falls) B3
Churchill, (riv.) B3
Cirque, (mt.) B2
Clode, (sound) D2
Cod, (isl.) B2
Conception, (bay) D2
Deep, (inlet) B2
Deer, (harb.) D2
Disappointment, (lake) B3
Dog, (isl.) B3
Dominion, (lake) B3
Double Mer, (lake) C3
Dyke, (lake) A3
Eagle, (riv.) C3
Eclipse, (harb.) B2
Eliot, (mt.) B2
Espoir, (bay) C4
Exploits, (riv.) C4
Ferolle, (pt.) C3
Ferryland, (cape) D2
Fig, (riv.) B3
Fleur-de-May, (lake) B3
Flowers, (bay) B2
Fogo, (isl.) D4
Fonteneau, (lake) B3
Fortune, (bay) C4
Four, (peaks) B2
Franks, (pond) D2
Fraser, (riv.) B2
Freels, (cape) D3
Funk, (isl.) D4
Gander, (lake) D4
Gander, (riv.) D4
George, (isl.) C3
Gilbert, (riv.) C3
Glover, (isl.) C4
Goose, (riv.) B3
Grady, (isl.) C3
Grand, (lake) B3
Grand, (lake) C4
Grates, (pt.) D2
Great Burnt, (lake) C4
Great Colinet, (isl.) D2
Grey, (isls.) C3
Groais, (isl.) C3
Gros Morne, (mt.) C4
Gros Morne Nat'l Park C4
Groswater, (bay) C3
Gulch, (cape) B2
Gull, (isl.) D2
Gull Island, (pt.) D2
Hamilton, (inlet) C3
Hamilton, (sound) D4
Hare, (bay) C3
Harp, (lake) B2
Harrison, (cape) C3
Hawke, (isl.) C3
Hawke, (hills) D2
Hawke, (riv.) C3
Hebron, (fjord) B2
Hermitage, (bay) C4
Holyrood, (bay) D2
Holyrood, (pond) D2
Home, (isl.) B1
Hope, (lake) B3
Horse, (isls.) C3
Horse Chops, (head) D2
Humber, (riv.) C4
Huntingdon, (isl.) C3
Iglosiatik, (isl.) B2
Ingornachoix, (bay) C3
Iona, (isls.) C2
Ireland's Eye, (isl.) D2
Ironbound, (isls.) C2
Islands, (bay) C2
Islands, (bay) C4
Jeanette, (bay) C3
Joseph, (lake) B3
Kaipokok, (bay) B2
Kaipokok, (riv.) B3
Kakkiviak, (cape) B1
Kanairiktok, (riv.) B3
Kaumajet, (mts.) B2
Kenamu, (riv.) B3
Kiglapait, (cape) B2
Kiglapait, (mts.) B2
Kikiktaksoak, (isl.) B2
Kikkertavak, (isl.) B2
Kingurutik, (mesa) B2
Knox, (lake) A3
Kogaluk, (riv.) B2
Labrador, (reg.) B2
Labrador, (sea) C2
Lady, (pond) D2
La Manche Valley Prov. Park D2
La Poile, (bay) C4
Lewis Hill, (mt.) C4
Little Mecatina, (riv.) B3
Little Trout River, (pond) C4
Long, (isl.) C2
Long, (isl.) D2
Long, (lake) B3
Long, (lake) A3
Long, (pt.) C4
Long Range, (mts.) C4
Lozeau, (lake) B3
Mabille, (lake) B3
Maccles, (lake) C1
Main Topsail, (mt.) C4
Makkovik, (cape) C2
McLelan, (str.) B1
McPhadyen, (riv.) A3
Mealy, (lake) C3
Meelpaeg, (lake) C4
Melville, (lake) C3
Menihek, (lkes) A3
Menistouc, (lake) A3
Merasheen, (isl.) C2
Merrifield, (bay) B2
Metchin, (riv.) B3
Michael, (lake) C3
Minipi, (lake) B3
Minipi, (riv.) B3
Mistaken, (pt.) D2
Mistastin, (lake) B2
Mistastin, (riv.) B2
Mistinippi, (lake) B3
Mobile Big, (pond) D2
Mugford, (cape) B2
Nachvak, (fjord) B2
Nanuktok, (isls.) C2
Napaktok, (bay) B2
Naskaupi, (riv.) B3
Natashquan, (riv.) B3
Natashquan-Est, (riv.) B3
Newfoundland, (isl.) C4
Newman, (sound) D2
New World, (isl.) C4
Nipishish, (lake) B3
Norman, (cape) C3
North, (riv.) B2
North, (riv.) C3
North Aulatsivik, (isl.) B2
North West Arm, (inlet) D2
North West Brook, (riv.) D2
North West Gander, (riv.) C4
Notakwanon, (riv.) B2
Notre Dame, (bay) C4
Nunaksaluk, (isl.) B2
Okak, (bay) B2
Okak, (isls.) B2
Ossokmanuan, (res.) B3
Paradise, (riv.) C3
Partridge, (bay) C3
Partridge, (pt.) C3
Paul, (isl.) B2
Peter's, (riv.) D2
Petitsikapau, (lake) A3
Pine, (cape) D2
Pinware, (riv.) C3
Pistolet, (bay) C3
Placentia, (bay) C2
Placentia, (sound) C2
Poissons, (riv.) A3
Ponds, (isl.) C3
Porcupine, (cape) C3
Port au Port, (bay) C4
Port au Port, (pen.) C4
Portland Creek, (pond) C3
Port Manvers, (harb.) B2
Race, (cape) D2
Ragged, (isls.) C2
Ramah, (bay) B2
Ramea, (isls.) C4
Random, (isl.) D2
Random, (sound) D2
Ray, (cape) C4
Red, (isl.) C2
Red Indian, (lake) C4
Red Wine, (riv.) B3
Riche, (pt.) C3
River of Ponds, (lake) C3
Rocky, (bay) C3
Rocky, (riv.) D2
Romaine, (riv.) B3
Round, (pond) C4
Ryans, (bay) B2
Saglek, (bay) B2
Saglek, (fjord) B2
Saint Augustin, (riv.) C3
Saint Francis, (cape) D2
Saint George, (cape) C4
Saint George's, (bay) C4
Saint Gregory, (cape) C4
Saint John, (bay) C3
Saint John, (cape) C3
Saint John, (isl.) C3
Saint Lawrence, (gulf) B4
Saint Lewis, (cape) C3
Saint Lewis, (riv.) C3
Saint Mary's, (bay) C2
Saint Mary's, (cape) C2
Saint Michaels, (bay) C3
Saint Paul, (riv.) C3
Salmonier, (riv.) D2
Sand Hill, (riv.) C3
Sandwich, (bay) C3
Sandy, (lake) C4
Seahorse, (lake) A3
Seal, (lake) B3
Senécal, (lake) B3
Seven Islands, (bay) B2
Shabogamo, (lake) A3
Shapio, (lake) B3
Shoal, (bay) D2
Sims, (lake) A3
Smallwood, (res.) B3
Smith, (sound) D2
Snegamook, (lake) B3
South Aulatsivik, (isl.) B2
South West, (brook) C2
South West Arm, (inlet) D2
South West Gander, (riv.) C4
South Wolf, (isl.) C3
Spear, (cape) D2
Squires Mem. Park C4
Stony, (isl.) C3
Swale, (isl.) D1
Table, (bay) C3
Tasisuak, (lake) B2
Ten Mile, (lake) C3
Terra Nova, (riv.) C2
Terra Nova Nat'l Park D2
Territok, (cape) B2
Thoresby, (mt.) B2
Tickle, (bay) D2
Torbay, (pt.) D2
Torngat, (mts.) B2
Trespassey, (bay) D2
Trinity, (bay) D2
Tunungayualok, (isl.) B2
Turnavik, (isls.) C2
Ugjoktok, (bay) B2
Uivak, (cape) B2
Ukasiksalik, (isl.) B2
Umiakovik, (lake) B2
Victoria, (lake) C4
Voisey, (bay) B2
Wade, (lake) A3
Watchman, (isl.) B2
Webb, (bay) B2
White, (bay) C3
White Bear, (isl.) B2
White Bear, (lake) C4
White Bear, (riv.) C4
White Handkerchief, (cape) B2
Winokapau, (lake) B3
Woods, (lake) B3

SAINT PIERRE AND MIQUELON

CITIES and TOWNS

Saint-Pierre (cap.) 5,232 C4

OTHER FEATURES

Miquelon, (isl.) C4
Saint Pierre, (isl.) C4

AREA 156,184 sq. mi. (404,517 sq. km.)
POPULATION 561,996
CAPITAL St. John's
LARGEST CITY St. John's
HIGHEST POINT in Torngat Mountains 5,420 ft. (1,652 m.)
SETTLED IN 1610
ADMITTED TO CONFEDERATION 1949
PROVINCIAL FLOWER Pitcher Plant

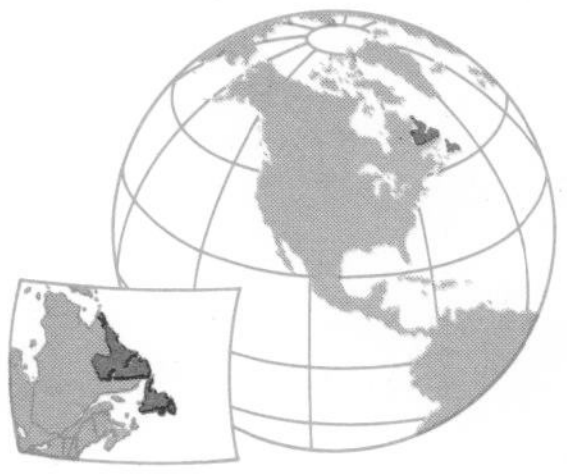

Agriculture, Industry and Resources

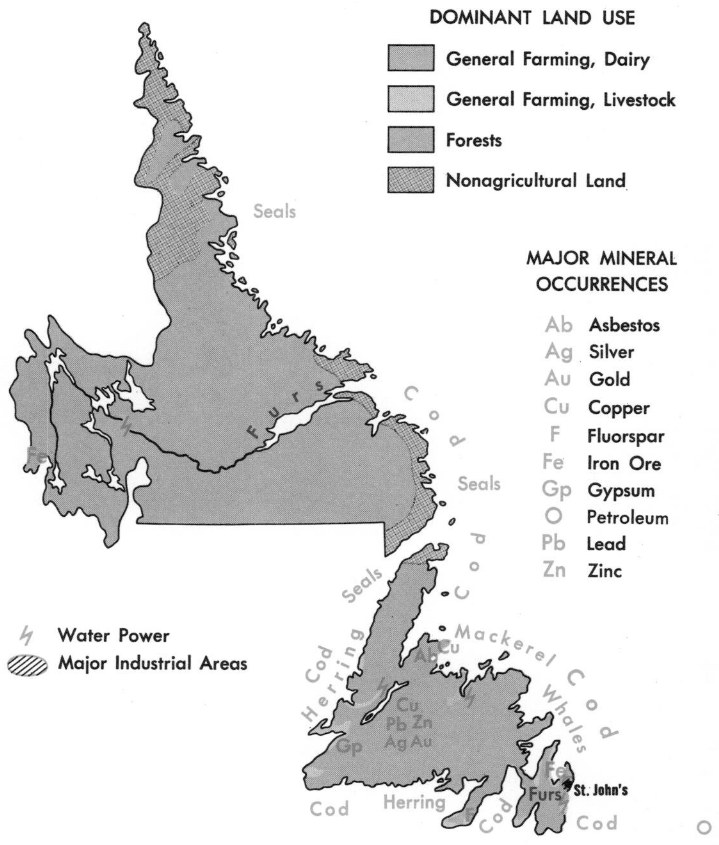
DOMINANT LAND USE
General Farming, Dairy
General Farming, Livestock
Forests
Nonagricultural Land
MAJOR MINERAL OCCURRENCES
Ab Asbestos
Ag Silver
Au Gold
Cu Copper
F Fluorspar
Fe Iron Ore
Gp Gypsum
Petroleum
Pb Lead
Zn Zinc
Water Power
Major Industrial Areas
Seals
Furs
Cod
Mackerel
Whales
Herring
St. John's

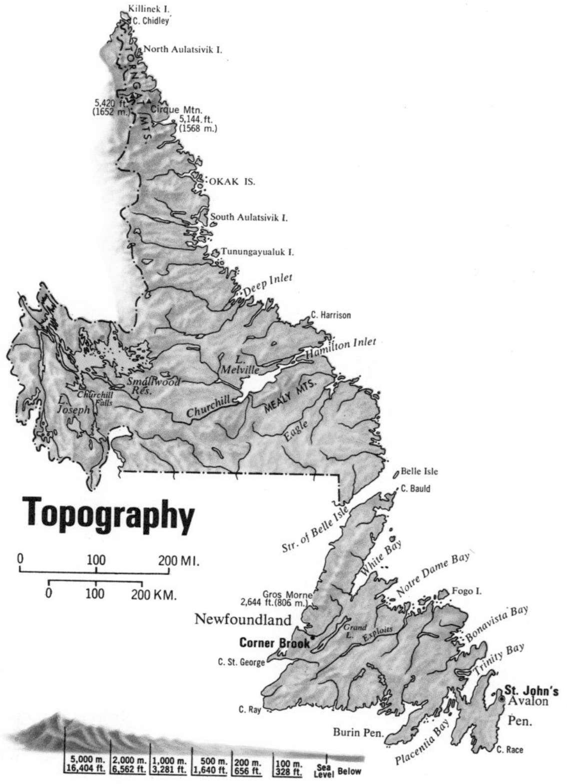
Topography
Killinek I.
C. Chidley
North Aulatsivik I.
5,420 ft. (1652 m.)
Cirque Mtn.
5,144 ft. (1568 m.)
OKAK IS.
South Aulatsivik I.
Tunungayualuk I.
Deep Inlet
C. Harrison
Hamilton Inlet
L. Melville
Smallwood Res.
Churchill Falls
Joseph
Churchill
MEALY MTS.
Eagle
Belle Isle
C. Bauld
Str. of Belle Isle
White Bay
Notre Dame Bay
Fogo I.
Gros Morne 2,644 ft. (806 m.)
Newfoundland
Corner Brook
C. St. George
Exploits
Bonavista Bay
Trinity Bay
St. John's
Avalon Pen.
C. Ray
Burin Pen.
Placentia Bay
C. Race
0 100 200 MI.
0 100 200 KM.
5,000 m. 16,404 ft.
2,000 m. 6,562 ft.
1,000 m. 3,281 ft.
500 m. 1,640 ft.
200 m. 656 ft.
100 m. 328 ft.
Sea Level
Below

NOVA SCOTIA

COUNTIES

Annapolis 23,208	C4
Antigonish 17,573	F3
Cape Breton 128,229	H3
Colchester 41,771	E3
Cumberland 35,914	D3
Digby 20,932	C4
Guysborough 12,825	F3
Halifax 278,531	E4
Hants 32,383	D4
Inverness 21,773	H2
Kings 47,977	D4
Lunenburg 42,388	D4
Pictou 49,076	F3
Queens 12,947	C4
Richmond 12,447	H3
Shelburne 16,970	C5
Victoria 8,417	H2
Yarmouth 25,210	C5

CITIES and TOWNS

Alder Point	H2
Aldershot	D3
Amherst⊙ 10,263	D3
Annapolis Royal⊙ 738	C4
Antigonish⊙ 5,442	F3
Arichat⊙ 893	H3
Baddeck⊙ 943	H2
Bear River 716	C4
Beaverbank 1,294	E4
Berwick 1,701	D4
Bible Hill 4,266	E3
Bridgetown 1,037	C4
Bridgewater 6,010	D4
Brookfield 892	E3
Brooklyn 1,179	D4
Cambridge Station 922	D3
Canso 1,173	H3
Cape North 136	H2
Centreville, Kings 736	D4
Chester 1,121	D4
Chéticamp 1,027	G2
Church Point 377	B4
Clark's Harbour 1,077	C5
Dartmouth 65,341	E4
Digby⊙ 2,542	C4
Dominion 2,938	J2
Donkin 1,087	J2
Echo Lake 1,048	E4
Elmsdale 944	E4
Elmsvale 132	E3
Enfield 1,234	E4
Fall River 1,060	E4
Falmouth 1,017	D4
Florence 2,111	H2
Glace Bay 21,836	J2
Guysborough⊙ 514	G3
Halifax (cap.)⊙ 117,882	E4
Hantsport 1,423	D4
Harrietsfield 949	E4
Herring Cove 1,363	E4
Hilden 1,076	E3
Ingonish 407	H2
Inverness 1,980	G2
Judique 770	G3
Kentville⊙ 5,056	D3
Kingston 1,562	D4
Lakeside 1,831	E4
Lantz 769	E4
Liverpool⊙ 3,336	D4
Lockeport 1,030	C5
Louisbourg 1,519	J3
Louisdale 1,026	H3
Lower West Pubnico 778	C5
Lunenburg⊙ 3,024	D4
Mahone Bay 1,236	D4
Meteghan 761	B4
Middleton 1,823	C4
Milton 1,918	C4
Mira Road 1,496	H2
Mulgrave 1,206	G3
New Germany 910	D4
New Glasgow 10,672	F3
New Minas 2,873	D3
New Victoria 1,345	H2
New Waterford 9,223	J2
North Sydney 8,319	H2
Oxford 1,498	E3
Parrsboro 1,857	D3
Petit-de-Grat 762	H3
Pictou⊙ 4,588	F3
Porters Lake 991	E4
Port Hastings 719	G3
Port Hawkesbury 4,008	G3
Port Hood 769	G2
Port Morien 763	J2
Port Williams 993	D3
Pugwash 746	E3
Reserve Mines 2,394	H2
River Hébert 861	D3
Sackville 14,590	E4
Saint Peters 705	H3
Salmon River, Colchester 1,889	E3
Scotchtown 2,086	J2
Sheet Harbour 762	F4
Shelburne⊙ 2,511	C5
Springhill 5,220	D3
Stellarton 5,366	F3
Stewiacke 1,174	E3
Sydney⊙ 30 645	H2
Sydney Mines 8,965	H2
Sydney River 2,468	H2
Terence Bay 1,087	E4
Thorburn 965	F3
Three Mile Plains 950	D4
Timberlea 1,657	E4
Trenton 3,224	F3
Truro⊙ 12,840	E3
Waterville 1,215	D3
Waverley 1,142	E4
Wedgeport 797	C5
Western Shore 1,242	D4
Westmount 2,080	H2
Westville 4,251	F3
Wileville 890	D4
Windsor⊙ 3,702	D3
Wolfville 3,073	D3
Yarmouth⊙ 7,801	B5

OTHER FEATURES

Advocate, (bay)	D3
Ainslie, (lake)	G2
Amet, (sound)	E3
Andrew, (isl.)	H3
Annapolis, (basin)	C4
Annapolis, (riv.)	C4
Antigonish, (harb.)	G3
Argos, (cape)	G3
Aspy, (bay)	H2
Avon, (riv.)	D4
Baccaro, (pt.)	C5
Baddeck, (riv.)	H2
Barachois, (pt.)	C5
Barren, (isl.)	H2
Barrington, (bay)	C5
Bedford, (basin)	E4
Berry, (head)	D4
Boularderie, (isl.)	H2
Bras d'Or, (lake)	H3
Breton, (cape)	J3
Brier, (isl.)	B4
Canso, (cape)	H3
Canso, (str.)	G3
Cap d'Or, (cape)	D3

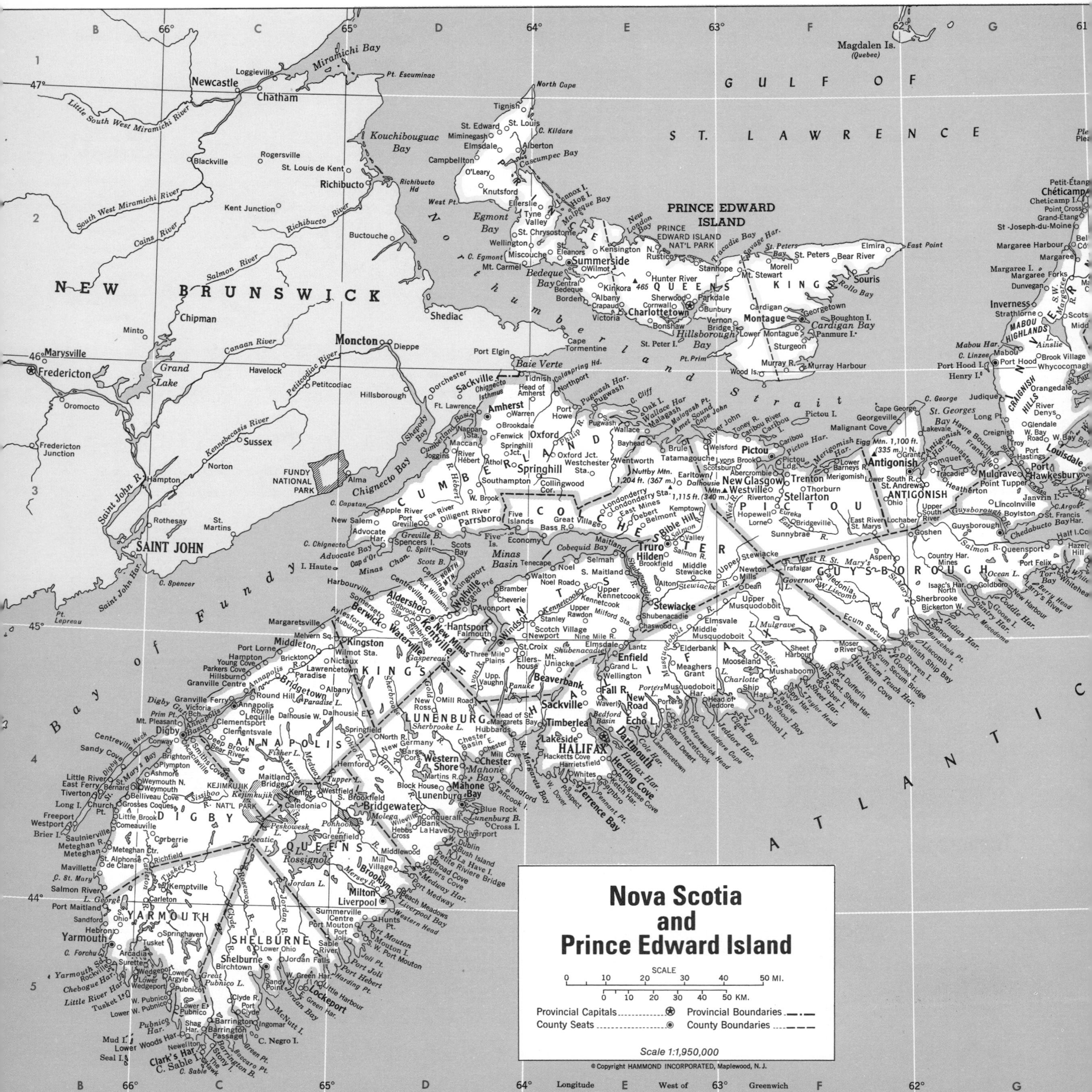

Nova Scotia and Prince Edward Island

SCALE

0 10 20 30 40 50 MI.

0 10 20 30 40 50 KM.

Provincial Capitals	⊛
County Seats	⊙
Provincial Boundaries	—·—·—
County Boundaries	———

Scale 1:1,950,000

Cape Breton (isl.) J2	Craignish (hills) G3
Cape Breton Highlands Nat'l Park H2	Cross (isl.) D4
	Cumberland (basin) D3
Cape Negro (isl.) C5	Dalhousie (mt.) E3
Cape Sable (isl.) C5	Dauphin (cape) H2
Capstan (cape) D3	Digby Gut (chan.) C4
Caribou (riv.) F3	Digby Neck (pen.) B4
Carleton (riv.) C4	East (bay) H3
Charlotte (lake) F4	East (riv.) F3
Chebogue (harb.) B5	East Bay (hills) H3
Chedabucto (bay) G3	Egmont (cape) H2
Chéticamp (isl.) G2	Eigg (mt.) F3
Chignecto (bay) D3	Fisher (lake) C4
Chignecto (cape) D3	Five (isls.) D3
Chignecto (isth.) D3	Forchu (harb.) H3
Clam (bay) F4	Forchu (bay) B5
Cliff (cape) E3	Framboise Cove (bay) H3
Clyde (riv.) C5	Fundy (bay) C3
Cobequid (bay) E3	Gabarus (bay) H3
Coddle (harb.) G3	Gabarus (cape) J3
Coldspring (head) E3	Gaspereau (lake) D4
Cole (harb.) E4	George (cape) G3
Country (harb.) G3	George (lake) B5

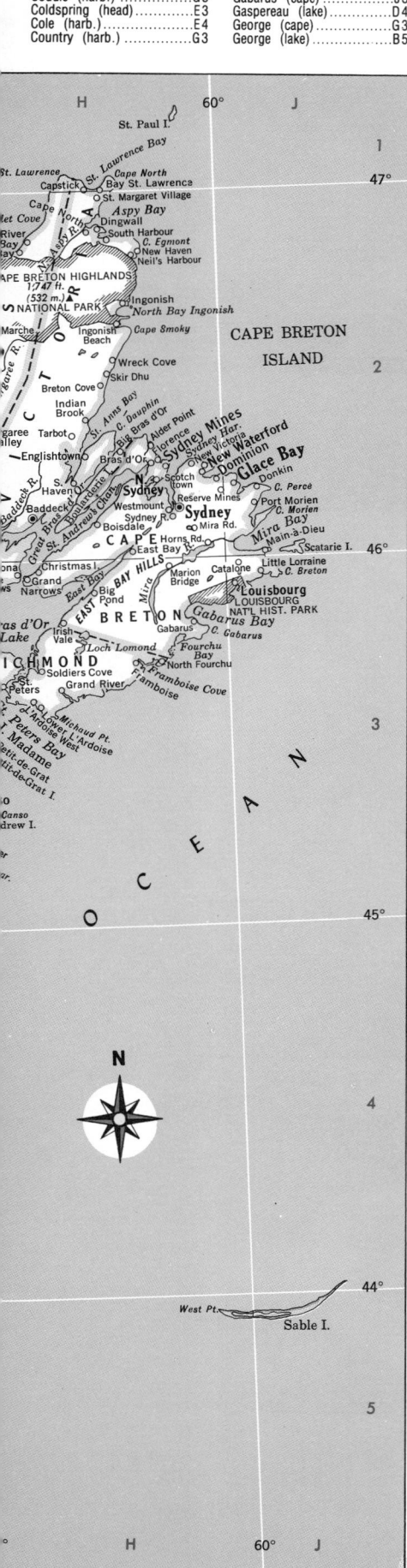

PRINCE EDWARD ISLAND

AREA 2,184 sq. mi. (5,657 sq. km.)
POPULATION 121,328
CAPITAL Charlottetown
LARGEST CITY Charlottetown
HIGHEST POINT 465 ft. (142 m.)
SETTLED IN 1720
ADMITTED TO CONFEDERATION 1873
PROVINCIAL FLOWER Lady's Slipper

NOVA SCOTIA

AREA 21,425 sq. mi. (55,491 sq. km.)
POPULATION 837,789
CAPITAL Halifax
LARGEST CITY Halifax
HIGHEST POINT Cape Breton Highlands 1,747 ft. (532 m.)
SETTLED IN 1605
ADMITTED TO CONFEDERATION 1867
PROVINCIAL FLOWER Trailing Arbutus or Mayflower

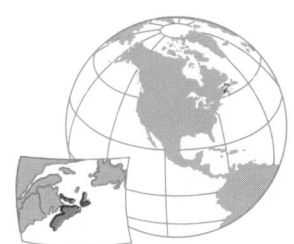

Topography

0   30   60 MI.

0   30   60 KM.

Below Sea Level	100 m. 328 ft.	200 m. 656 ft.	500 m. 1,640 ft.	1,000 m. 3,281 ft.	2,000 m. 6,562 ft.	5,000 m. 16,404 ft.

Agriculture, Industry and Resources

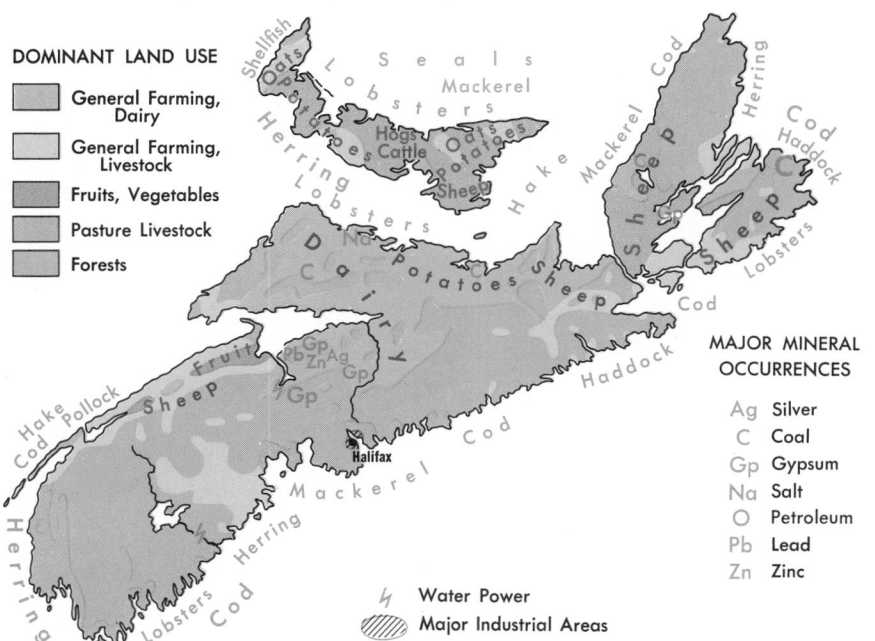

DOMINANT LAND USE

- General Farming, Dairy
- General Farming, Livestock
- Fruits, Vegetables
- Pasture Livestock
- Forests

MAJOR MINERAL OCCURRENCES

Ag   Silver
C   Coal
Gp   Gypsum
Na   Salt
O   Petroleum
Pb   Lead
Zn   Zinc

⚡ Water Power
▨ Major Industrial Areas

COUNTIES

Albert 22,159 ....F3
Carleton 24,561 ....C2
Charlotte 25,423 ....C3
Gloucester 81,025 ....E1
Kent 28,987 ....E2
King's 43,588 ....E3
Madawaska 34,892 ....B1
Northumberland 53,894 ....D2
Queen's 12,720 ....D3
Restigouche 40,620 ....C1
Saint John 90,103 ....D3
Sunbury 21,190 ....D3
Victoria 20,932 ....C1
Westmorland 105,725 ....F2
York 71,431 ....C3

CITIES and TOWNS

Acadie Siding 88 ....E2
Acadieville 179 ....E2
Adamsville 119 ....E2
Albert Mines 102 ....F3
Alcida 148 ....E1
Aldouane 488 ....E2
Allardville 529 ....E1
Alma 334 ....F3

Anagance 100 ....E3
Anse-Bleue 490 ....E1
Apohaqui 354 ....E3
Argyle 46 ....C2
Armstrong Brook 231 ....E1
Arthurette 199 ....C2
Astle 180 ....D2
Atholville 1,862 ....D1
Aulac 109 ....F3
Back Bay 393 ....D3
Baie-Sainte-Anne 701 ....F1
Baie-Verte 168 ....F2
Bairdsville 70 ....C2
Baker Brook 499 ....B1
Balmoral 1,722 ....D1
Barachois 588 ....F2
Barnaby River E2
Barnettville 123 ....E2
Bartibog Bridge 129 ....E2
Bas-Caraquet 1,728 ....F1
Bass River 99 ....E2
Bath 882 ....C2
Bathurst☉ 16,301 ....E1
Bathurst Mines 34 ....E1
Bayfield 105 ....G2
Bayside 180 ....C3
Beaubois 68 ....E1
Beaver Brook Station 132 .....E1
Beaver Harbour 302 ....D3

Beechwood 123 ....C2
Beersville 41 ....E2
Belledune 747 ....E1
Bellefleur 95 ....C1
Bellefond 205 ....D1
Belleisle Creek 168 ....E3
Benjamin 77 ....D1
Ben Lomond 418 ....E3
Benton 101 ....C3
Beresford 3,199 ....E1
Berry Mills 148 ....E2
Bertrand 1,203 ....E1
Berwick 138 ....E3
Black Point 124 ....D1
Black River 96 ....E3
Black River Bridge E2
Blacks Harbour 1,619 ....D3
Blackville 924 ....D2
Blissfield 127 ....D2
Bloomfield Ridge 184 ....D2
Bloomfield Station 94 ....E3
Bocabec 29 ....C3
Boiestown 326 ....D2
Bonny River D3
Bossé 178 ....B1
Bourgeois 214 ....F2
Brantville 984 ....E1
Breau-Village 277 ....F2
Brest 116 ....C2
Brewers Mills 373 ....C2

Bridgedale F3
Briggs Corner 74 ....E2
Bristol 860 ....C2
Brockway 70 ....C3
Browns Flat 263 ....D3
Buctouche 2,556 ....F2
Burnsville 157 ....E1
Burton☉ 294 ....D3
Burtts Corner 429 ....D2
Cambridge-Narrows 406 ....E3
Campbellton 9,282 ....D1
Canaan 84 ....E2
Canaan Forks 67 ....E2
Canaan Road 80 ....E2
Canterbury 501 ....C3
Cap-Bateau 433 ....F1
Cape Tormentine 239 ....G2
Cap Lumière 255 ....F2
Cap-Pelé 2,287 ....F2
Caraquet 3,950 ....F1
Carlingford 203 ....C2
Carlisle 40 ....C2
Caron Brook 118 ....B1
Carrolls Crossing 109 ....D2
Castalia 126 ....D4
Central Blissville 100 ....D3
Centre-Saint-Simon 365 ....E1
Centreville 606 ....C2
Chance Harbour 203 ....D3
Charlo 1,302 ....D1

Chatham 7,601 ....E1
Chatham Head 1,196 ....E1
Chipman 1,999 ....E2
Clair 792 ....B1
Clarendon 63 ....D3
Cliffordvale 85 ....C2
Clifton 140 ....E2
Coal Branch 93 ....E2
Coal Creek 40 ....E2
Cocagne 325 ....F2
Cocagne Cape 245 ....F2
Codys 124 ....E3
Coldstream 182 ....C2
Coles Island 150 ....E3
College Bridge 590 ....F2
Collette 212 ....E1
Connell 70 ....C2
Connors 82 ....B1
Cork 70 ....D3
Cornhill 167 ....E3
Coughlan 183 ....E2
Cross Creek 216 ....D2
Cumberland Bay 217 ....E2
Dalhousie☉ 5,640 ....D1
Dalhousie Junction 123 ....D1
Darlington 624 ....D1
Daulnay 533 ....E1
Dawsonville 234 ....C1
Debec 226 ....C2

Dipper Harbour 162 ....D3
Doaktown 1,022 ....D2
Dorchester☉ 1,125 ....F3
Dorchester Crossing 568 ......F2
Douglas Harbour 55 ....D3
Douglastown 1,032 ....E1
Drummond 675 ....C1
Duguayville 358 ....E1
Dumbarton 40 ....C3
Dumfries 98 ....C3
Dupuis Corner 269 ....F2
Durham Bridge 255 ....D2
Edmundston☉ 12,710 ....B1
Eel River Bridge 348 ....E1
Eel River Crossing 811 ....D1
Elgin 275 ....E3
Enniskillen 50 ....D3
Escuminac 210 ....F1
Evandale 58 ....D3
Evangeline 373 ....F1
Everett 56 ....C1
Fairfield 198 ....C2
Fairhaven 137 ....C4
Fairisle 569 ....E1
Fairvale 3,258 ....E3
Ferry Road 291 ....E1
Fielding 173 ....C2
Five Fingers 157 ....C1
Flatlands 250 ....D1
Florenceville 768 ....C2

Fontaine 13 ....F2
Forest City 40 ....C3
Fosterville 84 ....C3
Four Falls 79 ....C2
Fredericton (cap.)☉ 45,248 ...D3
Fredericton Junction 630 .....D3
Gagetown☉ 655 ....D3
Gardner Creek 40 ....E3
Geary 892 ....D3
Germantown 27 ....F3
Gillespie 63 ....C1
Glassville 114 ....C2
Glencoe 142 ....C1
Glenlivet 273 ....D1
Gloucester Junction 33 ....E1
Gondola Point 1,846 ....E3
Grafton 409 ....C2
Grand Bay 2,947 ....D3
Grande-Anse 765 ....E1
Grand Falls 6,223 ....C1
Grand Falls Hill 93 ....C1
Grand Harbour 527 ....D4
Gray Rapids 273 ....E2
Hammondvale 77 ....E3
Hampstead 100 ....D3
Hampton☉ 2,641 ....E3
Harcourt 119 ....E2
Hardwicke 96 ....E1
Hardwood Ridge 173 ....D2
Hartland 974 ....C2

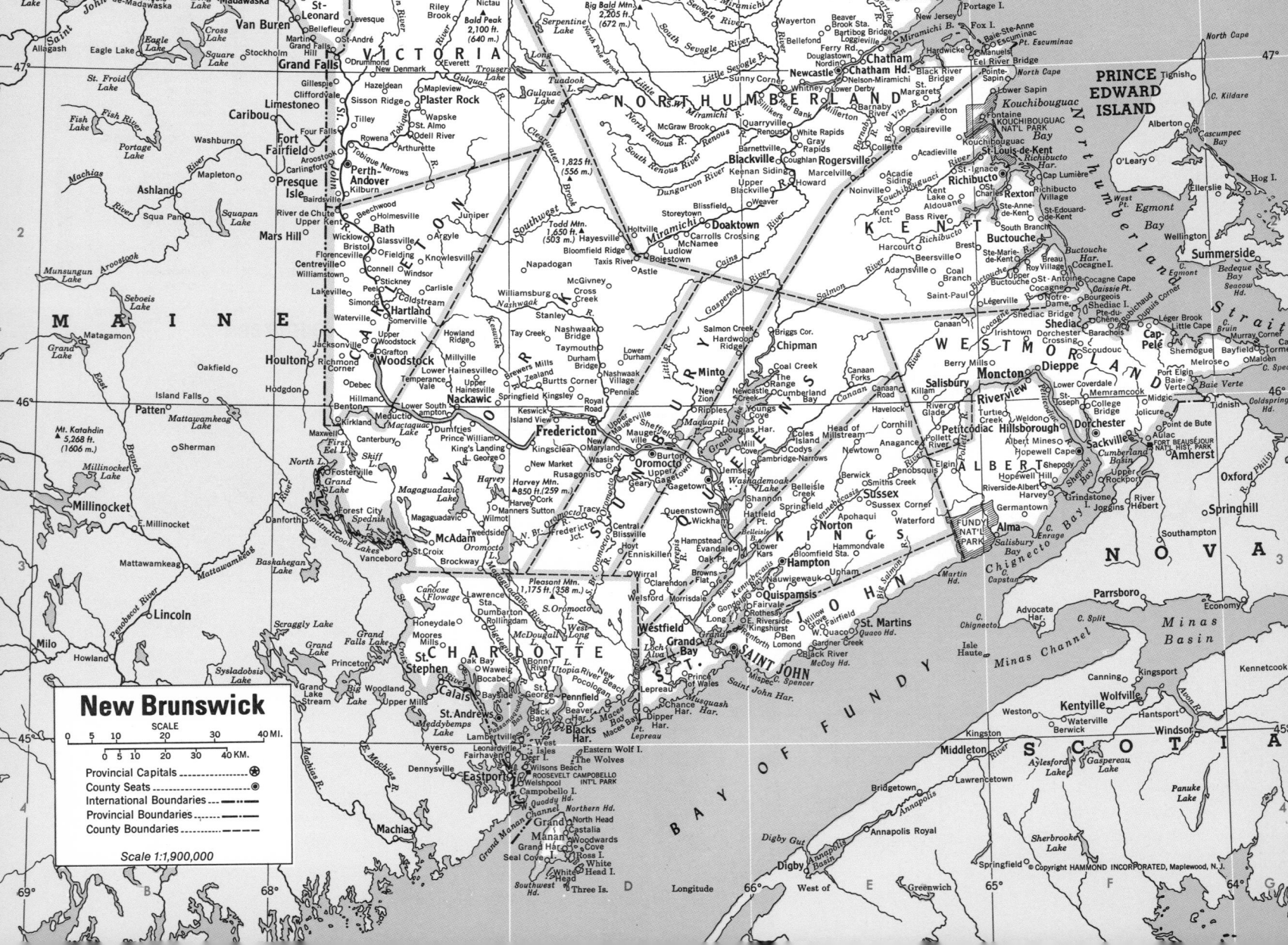

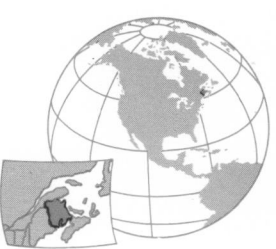

AREA 28,354 sq. mi. (73,437 sq. km.)
POPULATION 688,926
CAPITAL Fredericton
LARGEST CITY Saint John
HIGHEST POINT Mt. Carleton 2,690 ft. (820 m.)
SETTLED IN 1611
ADMITTED TO CONFEDERATION 1867
PROVINCIAL FLOWER Purple Violet

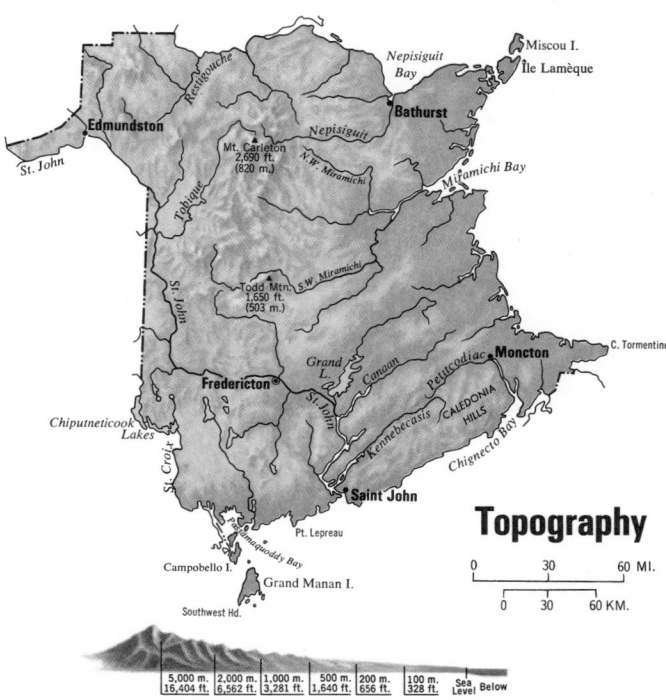

Topography

Agriculture, Industry and Resources

DOMINANT LAND USE

- Cereals, Livestock
- Dairy
- Potatoes
- General Farming, Livestock
- Pasture Livestock
- Forests

MAJOR MINERAL OCCURRENCES

Ag Silver   Pb Lead
C Coal   Sb Antimony
Cu Copper   Zn Zinc

⚡ Water Power
▨ Major Industrial Areas

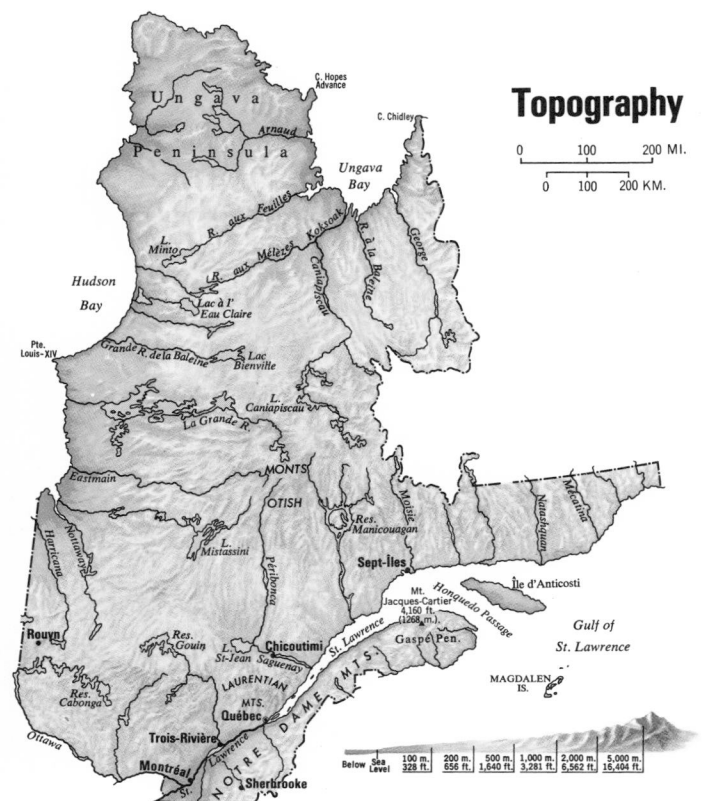

Topography

0 100 200 MI.
0 100 200 KM.

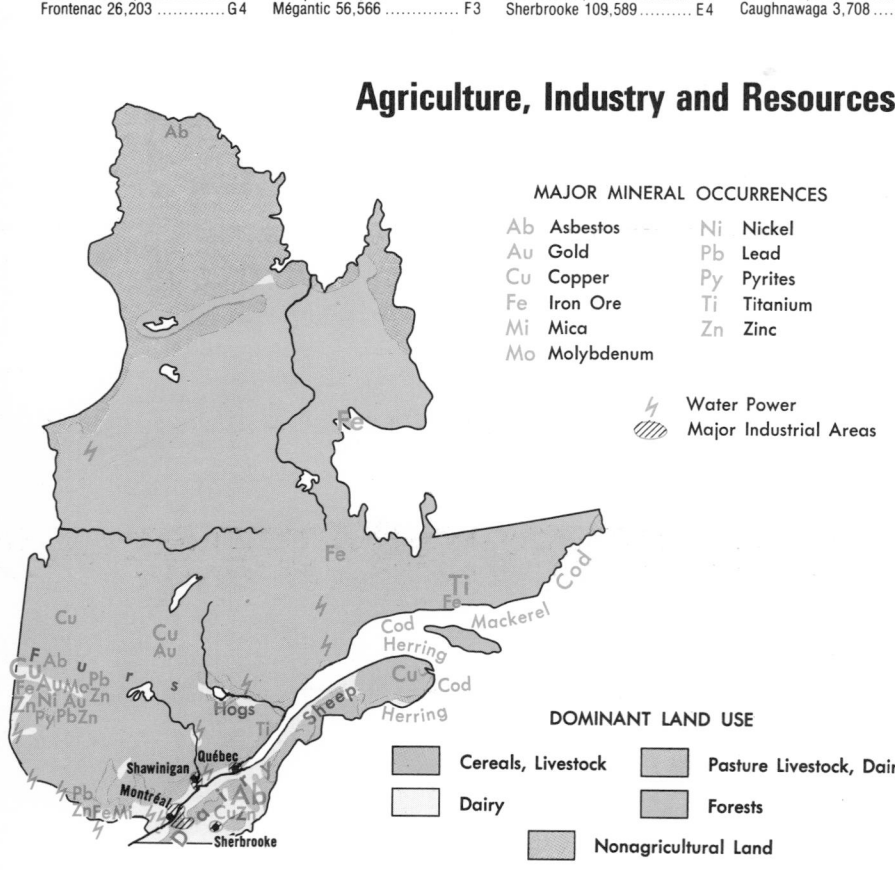

Agriculture, Industry and Resources

MAJOR MINERAL OCCURRENCES

Ab	Asbestos	Ni	Nickel
Au	Gold	Pb	Lead
Cu	Copper	Py	Pyrites
Fe	Iron Ore	Ti	Titanium
Mi	Mica	Zn	Zinc
Mo	Molybdenum		

⚡ Water Power
▨ Major Industrial Areas

DOMINANT LAND USE

- Cereals, Livestock
- Dairy
- Pasture Livestock, Dairy
- Forests
- Nonagricultural Land

COUNTIES

Argenteuil 31,654 .... C4
Arthabaska 54,176 .... E4
Bagot 24,791 .... E4
Beauce 67,083 .... G3
Beauharnois 53,026 .... C4
Bellechasse 22,908 .... G3
Berthier 28,465 .... C3
Bonaventure 40,724 .... C2
Brome 16,410 .... E4
Chambly 286,130 .... J4
Champlain 114,078 .... E2
Charlevoix-Est 17,085 .... G2
Charlevoix-Ouest 13,601 .... G2
Châteauguay 57,252 .... D4
Chicoutimi 165,853 .... G1
Compton 20,512 .... G4
Deux-Montagnes 58,568 .... C4
Dorchester 32,396 .... G3
Drummond 66,122 .... E4
Frontenac 26,203 .... G4
Gaspé-Est 40,720 .... D1
Gaspé-Ouest 19,238 .... C1
Gatineau 52,193 .... B3
Hull 134,518 .... B4
Huntingdon 16,653 .... C4
Iberville 21,296 .... D4
Île-de-Montréal 1,869,641 .... H4
Île-Jésus 246,243 .... H4
Joliette 55,524 .... C3
Kamouraska 27,740 .... H2
Labelle 31,065 .... B3
Lac-Saint-Jean-Est 45,558 .... F1
Lac-Saint-Jean-Ouest 57,556 .... E1
L'Assomption 84,967 .... D4
Lévis 75,916 .... J3
L'Islet 22,223 .... G2
Lotbinière 27,780 .... F3
Maskinongé 20,879 .... D3
Matane 28,954 .... B1
Matapédia 24,063 .... B2
Mégantic 56,566 .... F3
Missisquoi 34,853 .... D4
Montcalm 23,534 .... C3
Montmagny 26,622 .... G3
Montmorency No. 1 20,712 .... F2
Montmorency No. 2 5,869 .... G3
Napierville 12,595 .... D4
Nicolet 31,102 .... E3
Papineau 36,275 .... B4
Pontiac 20,559 .... A3
Portneuf 51,643 .... E3
Québec 449,633 .... F3
Richelieu 49,944 .... D4
Richmond 39,895 .... E4
Rimouski 64,768 .... J1
Rouville 15,916 .... D4
Saguenay 115,736 .... H1
Saint-Hyacinthe 52,417 .... D4
Saint-Jean 50,587 .... D4
Saint-Maurice 106,023 .... D3
Shefford 65,528 .... E4
Sherbrooke 109,589 .... E4

Soulanges 13,254 .... C4
Stanstead 36,737 .... F4
Témiscouata 52,871 .... J2
Terrebonne 164,502 .... H4
Vaudreuil 44,257 .... C4
Verchères 49,298 .... J4
Wolfe 15,254 .... F4
Yamaska 14,490 .... E3

CITIES and TOWNS

Acton Vale 4,326 .... E4
Albanel 889 .... E1
Alma⊙ 25,638 .... F1
Amqui⊙ 3,949 .... B2
Ancienne-Lorette 11,694 .... H3
Angers B4
Anjou 36,596 .... H4
Annaville 586 .... E3
Armagh 966 .... G3
Arthabaska⊙ 5,907 .... F3
Arvida F1
Asbestos 9,075 .... F4
Ascot Corner 895 .... F4
Ayer's Cliff⊙ 873 .... E4
Aylmer 25,714 .... B4
Baie-Comeau 11,911 .... A1
Baie-des-Sables 588 .... A1
Baie-d'Urfé 3,955 .... G4
Baie-Saint-Paul⊙ 4,062 .... G2
Baie-Trinité 802 .... B1
Beaconsfield 20,417 .... H4
Beauceville 4,276 .... G3
Beauharnois⊙ 7,665 .... D4
Beaumont 635 .... F3
Beauport 55,539 .... J3
Beaupré 2,821 .... G2
Bécancour⊙ 9,043 .... E3
Bedford⊙ 3,010 .... E4
Beebe Plain 1,155 .... E4
Bélair 10,716 .... H3
Beloeil 15,913 .... D4
Bernierville 2,182 .... F3
Berthier-en-Bas 576 .... G3
Berthierville⊙ 4,249 .... D3
Bic 2,670 .... J1
Biencourt 818 .... J2
Black Lake 4,051 .... F3
Blainville 12,517 .... H4
Boischatel 2,279 .... J3
Bois-des-Filion 4,346 .... H4
Bolduc 1,593 .... G4
Bonaventure 1,195 .... C2
Boucherville 25,530 .... J4
Boulanger 953 .... E1
Bromont 2,505 .... E4
Bromptonville 2,992 .... F4
Brossard 37,641 .... H4
Brownsburg 3,114 .... C4
Buckingham 14,328 .... B4
Cabano 3,193 .... J2
Cacouna 1,083 .... H2
Calumet 708 .... C4
Candiac 7,166 .... J4
Cap-à-l'Aigle 712 .... G2
Cap-Chat 3,617 .... B1
Cap-de-la-Madeleine 32,126 .... E3
Cap-des-Rosiers 691 .... D1
Cap-Saint-Ignace 1,312 .... G2
Cap-Santé⊙ 1,312 .... F3
Carignan 3,585 .... J4
Carleton 2,538 .... C2
Caughnawaga 3,708 .... H4

Causapscal 2,743 .... B2
Chambly 11,815 .... J4
Chambord 1,058 .... E1
Champlain 548 .... E3
Chandler 4,011 .... D2
Charette 538 .... D3
Charlemagne 4,025 .... H4
Charlesbourg 63,147 .... J3
Charny 6,416 .... J3
Châteauguay 36,329 .... H4
Château-Centre H4
Château-Richer⊙ 3,075 .... F3
Chénéville 699 .... B4
Chicoutimi⊙ 57,737 .... G1
Chicoutimi-Nord F1
Chute-aux-Outardes 2,103 .... A1
Clermont 3,518 .... G2
Cloridorme 553 .... D1
Coaticook 6,392 .... F4
Coleraine 1,485 .... F4
Compton 584 .... F4
Contrecoeur D4
Cookshire⊙ 1,453 .... F4
Coteau-du-Lac 1,248 .... C4
Coteau-Landing⊙ 1,106 .... C4
Côte-Saint-Luc 25,721 .... H4
Courcelles 677 .... G4
Courville J3
Cowansville 11,902 .... E4
Crabtree 1,942 .... D4
Danville 2,367 .... E4
Daveluyville 1,321 .... E3
Deauville 804 .... E4
Dégelis 3,304 .... J2
Delisle 1,249 .... F1
Delson 4,241 .... H4
Desbiens 1,673 .... E1
Deschambault 1,018 .... E3
Deschênes B4
Deux-Montagnes 8,957 .... H4
Didyme 759 .... E1
Disraëli 3,306 .... F4
Dixville 534 .... F4
Dolbeau 8,451 .... E1
Dollard-des-Ormeaux 36,837 .... H4
Donnacona 5,800 .... F3
Dorion 5,843 .... C4
Dorval 19,131 .... H4
Douville D4
Drummondville⊙ 29,286 .... E4
Drummondville-Nord 2,298 .... E4
Drummondville-Sud 9,420 .... E4
Dunham 2,505 .... E4
Durham-Sud 1,040 .... E4
East Angus 4,417 .... F4
East Broughton 1,371 .... F3
East Broughton Station 1,191 .... F3
Eastman 557 .... E4
Escoumins 2,324 .... H1
Farnham 6,476 .... E4
Ferme-Neuve 2,113 .... B3
Forestville 1,819 .... H1
Frampton 759 .... G3
Francoeur 1,389 .... F3
Gaspé 16,842 .... D1
Gatineau 73,479 .... B4
Giffard J3
Girardville 1,035 .... E1
Godbout 593 .... B1
Gracefield 927 .... A3
Granby 37,132 .... E4
Grande-Rivière 4,390 .... D2
Grandes-Bergeronnes 779 .... H1
Grande-Vallée 632 .... D1
Grand'Mère 15,999 .... E3
Greenfield Park 18,430 .... J4
Grenville 1,517 .... C4
Gros-Morne 584 .... C1
Hampstead 7,562 .... H4
Ham-Sud⊙ 67 .... F4
Hauterive 14,724 .... A1
Hébertville 1,520 .... F1
Hébertville-Station 1,362 .... F1
Hemmingford 763 .... D4
Henryville 590 .... D4
Howick 660 .... D4
Huberdeau 679 .... C4
Hudson 4,480 .... C4
Hull⊙ 61,039 .... B4
Huntingdon⊙ 3,098 .... C4
Iberville⊙ 8,897 .... D4
Île-Bizard 2,985 .... H4
Île-Perrot 5,272 .... G4
Inverness⊙ 365 .... F3
Joliette⊙ 18,118 .... D3
Jonquière 60,691 .... F1
Kingsey Falls 601 .... E4
Kirkland 7,476 .... H4
La Baie 20,116 .... G1
La Baie-de-Shawinigan 632 .... E3
Labelle 2,007 .... C3
Lac-Alouette 738 .... D4
Lac-au-Saumon 1,309 .... B2
Lac-aux-Sables 818 .... E3
Lac-Beauport F3
Lac-Bouchette 1,685 .... E1
Lac-Carré 687 .... C3
Lac-des-Aigles 787 .... J2
Lac-des-Écorces 638 .... B3
Lac-Drolet 1,015 .... G4
Lac-Etchemin 2,746 .... G3
Lachenaie 7,118 .... D4
Lachine 41,503 .... H4
Lachute⊙ 11,928 .... C4
Lacolle 1,193 .... D4
Lac-Mégantic⊙ 6,457 .... G4
Lac-Saint-Charles 3,285 .... H3
La Durantaye 763 .... G3
Lafontaine 4,442 .... C4
La Guadeloupe 1,804 .... F4
Lambton 777 .... F4
Lamartine 675 .... G2
L'Ange-Gardien 1,838 .... F3
Langlais 1,197 .... F1
L'Annonciation 2,186 .... C3

Lanoraie 1,362 .... D4
La Pérade 1,032 .... E3
La Pêche 4,662 .... B4
La Pocatière 4,319 .... H2
La Prairie⊙ 9,173 .... J4
La Providence E4
La Rédemption 808 .... B2
Larouche 549 .... F1
La Salle 76,713 .... H4
L'Ascension, Lac-St-Jean E. 1,090 .... F1
L'Assomption⊙ 4,832 .... D4
La Station-du-Coteau 869 .... C4
Laterrière 693 .... F1
La Trinité-des-Monts 592 .... J1
La Tuque 12,067 .... E2
Laurentides 1,804 .... D4
Laurier-Station 1,260 .... F3
Laurierville 867 .... F3
Lauzon 12,663 .... J3
Laval 246,243 .... H4
Lavaltrie 1,473 .... D4
Lawrenceville 528 .... E4
Le Moyne 7,202 .... J4
Lennoxville 3,682 .... F4
L'Épiphanie 2,912 .... D4
Léry 2,201 .... H4
Les Becquets 577 .... E3
Les Éboulements 1,190 .... G2
Les Méchins 1,049 .... B1
Lévis 17,819 .... J3
Linière 1,176 .... G3
L'Islet 1,113 .... G2
L'Islet-sur-Mer 817 .... G2

L'Isle-Verte 1,201 .... G1
Longueuil 122,429 .... J4
Loretteville⊙ 14,767 .... H3
Lorraine 5,388 .... H4
Louiseville⊙ 3,993 .... E3
Lucerne 8,000 .... B4
Luceville 1,513 .... J1
Lyster 811 .... F3
Magog 13,290 .... E4
Maniwaki⊙ 5,969 .... B3
Manseau 656 .... E3
Mansonville 590 .... E4
Maple Grove 1,857 .... H4
bmarbleton 551 .... F4
Maria 1,016 .... C2
Marieville⊙ 4,853 .... D4
Marsoui 541 .... C1
Mascouche 14,266 .... H4
Maskinongé 1,001 .... E3
Masson B4
Massueville E4
Matane⊙ 12,726 .... B1
Matapédia 581 .... B2
Melocheville 1,660 .... C4
Mercier 4,957 .... H4
Metabetchouan 3,016 .... F1
Mirabel⊙ 13,486 .... H4
Mistassini 5,473 .... E1
Montauban 903 .... E3
Mont-Carmel 852 .... H2
Montcerf 587 .... A3
Montebello 1,276 .... B4
Mont-Joli 6,508 .... J1
Mont-Laurier⊙ 8,565 .... B3

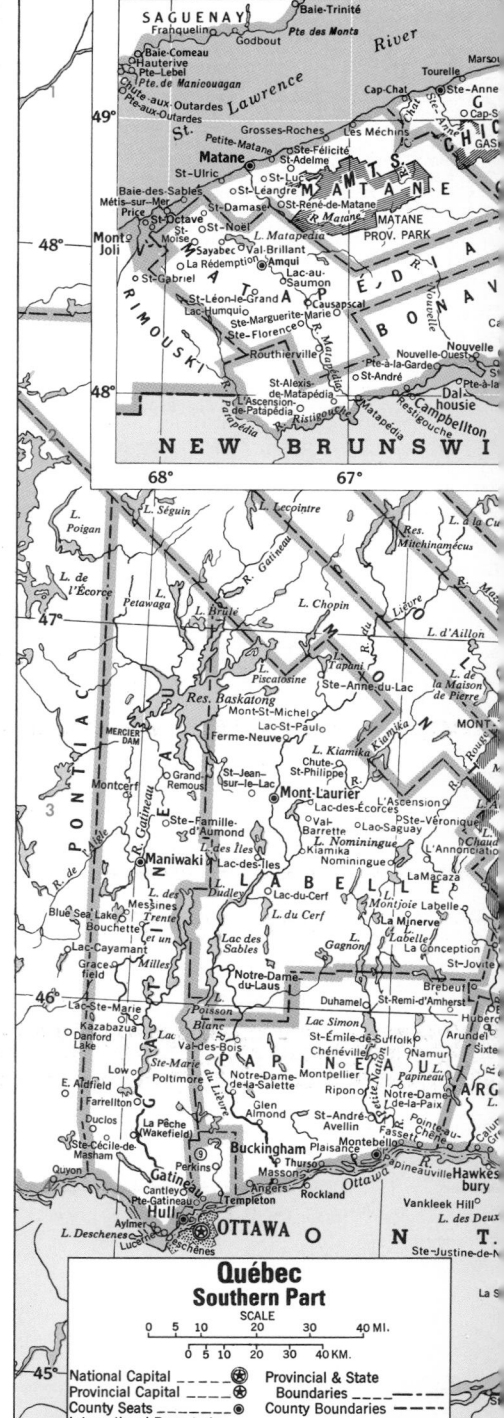

Québec
Southern Part

SCALE
0 5 10 20 30 40 MI.
0 5 10 20 30 40 KM.

National Capital ⊛
Provincial Capital ⊕
County Seats ⊙
International Boundaries
Provincial & State Boundaries
County Boundaries

Scale 1:2,250,000

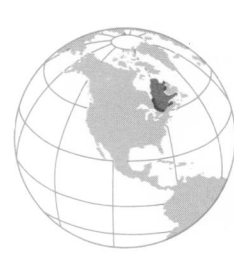

Montmagny⊙ 12,326 .... G3
Montréal⊙ 1,080,546 .... H4
Montréal-Est 4,372 .... J4
Montréal-Nord 97,250 .... H4
Mont-Rolland 1,591 .... C4
Mont-Royal 20,514 .... H4
Mont-Saint-Hilaire 7,688 .... D4
Murdochville 3,704 .... C1
Napierville⊙ 2,166 .... D4
Neuville 918 .... F3
New Carlisle⊙ 1,403 .... D2
Newport 558 .... D2
New Richmond 4,295 .... C2
Nicolet 4,818 .... E3
Nominingue 757 .... B3
Normandin 1,874 .... E1
North Hatley 788 .... F4
Notre-Dame-de-la-Doré 1,119 .... E1
Notre-Dame-des-Anges 903 .... E3
Notre-Dame-des-Laurentides H3
Notre-Dame-des-Prairies 5,714 .... D3
Notre-Dame-du-Bon-Conseil 1,023 .... E4
Notre-Dame-du-Lac⊙ 2,153 .... J2
Nouvelle 682 .... C2
Oka 1,483 .... C4
Omerville 1,308 .... E4
Ormstown 1,503 .... D4
Orsainville H3
Otterburn Park 4,159 .... D4
Outremont 27,089 .... H4
Pabos 1,018 .... D2
Pabos-Mills 1,512 .... D2
Packington 700 .... J2
Papineauville⊙ 1,509 .... C4
Paspébiac 1,807 .... D2
Percé⊙ 5,198 .... D1
Perkins 3,551 .... B4
Petit Cap 1,028 .... D1
Petite-Matane 920 .... B1
Petit-Saguenay (Saint-François-d'Assis 680 .... G1
Pierrefonds 35,402 .... H4
Pierreville 1,311 .... E3
Pincourt 7,892 .... D4
Plaisance 634 .... B4
Plessisville 7,238 .... F3
Pohénégamooke 3,627 .... H2
Pointe-à-la-Croix 1,515 .... C2
Pointe-au-Pic 1,066 .... G2
Pointe-aux-Outardes 968 .... A1
Pointe-aux-Trembles 35,618 .... J4
Pointe-Claire 25,917 .... H4
Pointe-du-Lac 2,737 .... E3
Pointe-Gatineau B4
Pointe-Lebel 1,302 .... A1
Pont-Rouge 3,342 .... F3
Port-Alfred G1
Portneuf 1,320 .... F3
Price 2,461 .... A1
Princeville 3,852 .... F3
Proulxville 608 .... E3
Québec (cap.) 177,082 .... H3
Quyon A4
Rawdon 2,808 .... D3
Repentigny 26,698 .... J4
Richelieu 1,755 .... D4
Richmond⊙ 4,021 .... E4
Rigaud 2,203 .... C4
Rimouski⊙ 27,897 .... J1
Rimouski-Est 2,328 .... J1
Rivière-à-Pierre 604 .... E3
Rivière-au-Renard 1,772 .... D1
Rivière-du-Loup⊙ 13,103 .... H2
Rivière-du-Moulin G1
Rivière-Éternité 709 .... G1
Rivière-Portneuf 959 .... H1
Robertsonville 1,666 .... F3
Roberval⊙ 8,543 .... E1
Rock Forest 652 .... F4
Rock Island 1,230 .... E4
Rosemère 7,112 .... H4
Rougemont 933 .... D4
Roxboro 7,106 .... H4
Roxton Falls 1,215 .... E4
Saint-Adelme 738 .... B1
Saint-Adelphe 1,220 .... E3
Saint-Adolphe-d'Howard 1,315 .... C4
Saint-Agapitville 1,672 .... F3
Saint-Aimé-des-Lacs 805 .... G2
Saint-Alban 726 .... E3
Saint-Alexandre-de-Kamouraska 966 .... H2
Saint-Alexis-des-Monts 1,815 .... D3
Saint-Amable 1,557 .... J4
Saint-Ambroise 3,169 .... F1
Saint-Anaclet 1,009 .... J1
Saint-André-Avellin 1,088 .... B4
Saint-André-Est 1,206 .... C4
Saint-Anselme 1,735 .... F3
Saint-Antoine 6,872 .... H4
Saint-Aubert 881 .... G2
Saint-Augustin-de-Québec 3,904 .... E3
Saint-Basile-le-Grand 5,843 .... J4
Saint-Basile-Sud 1,649 .... F3
Saint-Benjamin 1,072 .... G3
Saint-Bernard 562 .... F3
Saint-Boniface-de-Shawinigan 2,680 .... D3
Saint-Bruno 2,259 .... F1
Saint-Bruno-de-Montarville 21,272 .... J4
Saint-Camille-de-Bellechasse 1,235 .... G3
Saint-Casimir 1,184 .... E3
Saint-Césaire 2,701 .... D4
Saint-Charles, Bellechasse 1,027 .... G3
Saint-Charles-de-Mandeville 847 .... D3
Saint-Charles-Garnier 558 .... J1
Saint-Chrysostome 1,065 .... D4
Saint-Côme 839 .... D3
Saint-Constant 7,659 .... H4
Saint-Cyprien 791 .... J2
Saint-Cyrille 1,059 .... E4
Saint-Damien-de-Buckland 1,676 .... G3
Saint-David 4,386 .... J3
Saint-David-de-Falardeau 1,692 .... F1

AREA 594,857 sq. mi. (1,540,680 sq. km.)
POPULATION 6,377,518
CAPITAL Québec
LARGEST CITY Montréal
HIGHEST POINT Mont D'Iberville 5,420 ft. (1,652 m.)
SETTLED IN 1608
ADMITTED TO CONFEDERATION 1867
PROVINCIAL FLOWER White Garden Lily

Saint-Denis 888 .... D4
Saint-Dominique 1,772 .... E4
Saint-Donat-de-Montcal 1,460 .... C3
Sainte-Adèle 4,186 .... C4
Sainte-Agathe 727 .... F3
Sainte-Agathe-des-Monts 5,435 .... C3
Sainte-Agnes-de-Charlevoix 551 .... G2
Sainte-Anne-de-Beaupré 3,284 .... F2
Sainte-Anne-de-Bellevue 3,738 .... H4
Sainte-Anne-des-Monts⊙ 5,945 .... C1
Sainte-Anne-des-Plaines 2,329 .... H4
Sainte-Aurélie 1,103 .... G3
Sainte-Blandine 1,008 .... J1
Sainte-Catherine 901 .... F3
Sainte-Claire 1,528 .... G3
Sainte-Croix⊙ 1,719 .... F3
Sainte-Émélie-de-l'Énergie 558 .... D3
Sainte-Félicité 762 .... B1
Sainte-Foy 71,237 .... H3
Sainte-Françoise 647 .... H1
Sainte-Geneviève 2,869 .... H4
Sainte-Geneviève-de-Batiscan⊙ 412 .... E3
Sainte-Hedwidge-de-Roberval 966 .... E1
Sainte-Hélène-de-Kamouraska 658 .... H2
Sainte-Hénédine⊙ 561 .... F3
Sainte-Julie-de-Verchères 8,666 .... J4
Sainte-Julienne⊙ 809 .... D4
Sainte-Justine 1,116 .... G3
Saint-Éleuthère 1,033 .... H2
Saint-Élie 601 .... E3
Sainte-Louise 851 .... G2
Saint-Elzéar 643 .... F3
Saint-Elzéar-de-Bonaventure 617 .... C2
Sainte-Marie, Beauce 4,462 .... G3
Sainte-Martine⊙ 1,957 .... D4
Saint-Émile 4,205 .... H3
Sainte-Monique, Lac-St-Jean-E. 596 .... F1
Sainte-Perpétue-de-L'Islet 1,269 .... H2
Saint-Éphrem-de-Tring 880 .... G3

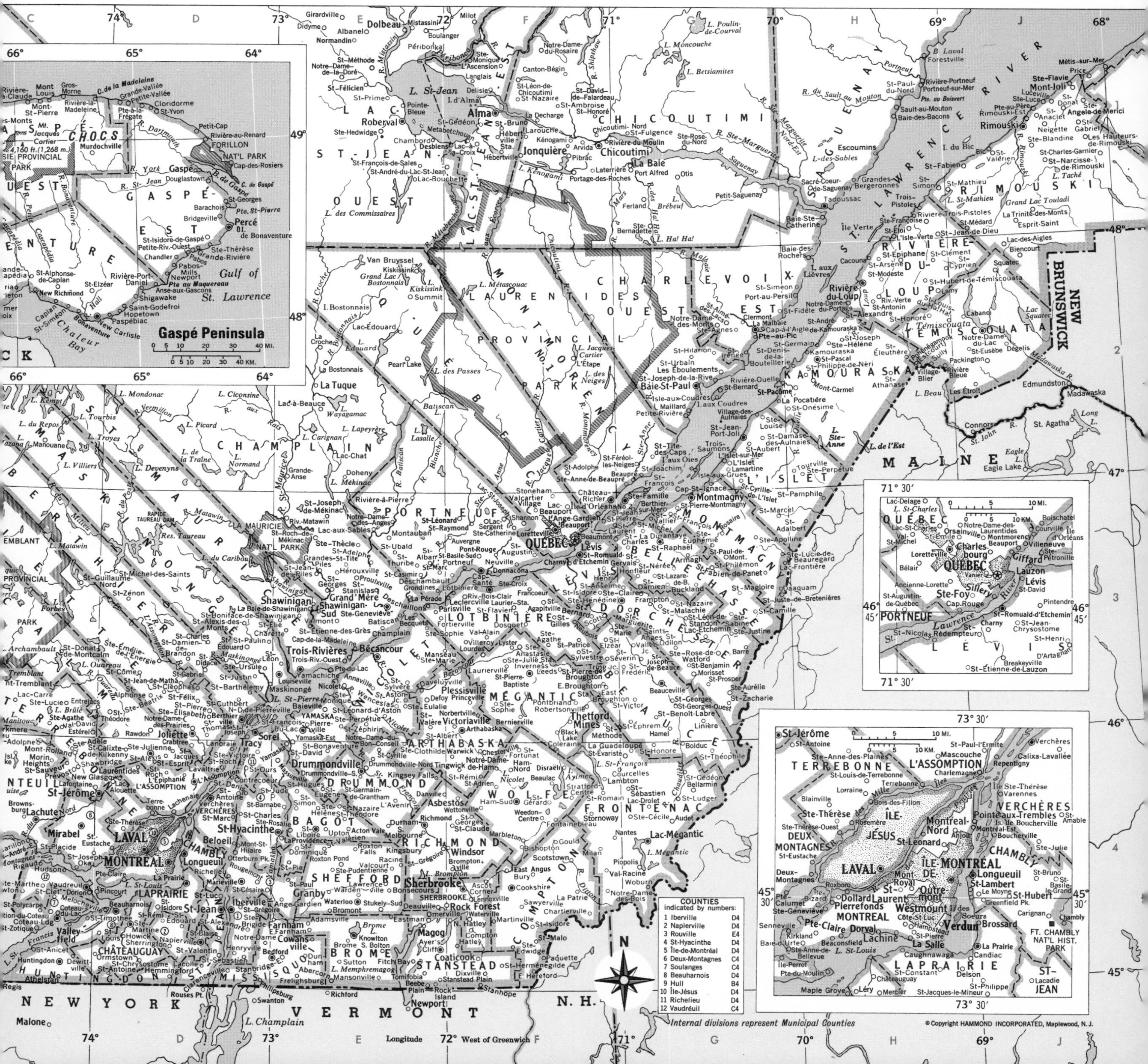
Gaspé Peninsula
Gulf of St. Lawrence
Chaleur Bay
NEW BRUNSWICK
MAINE
NEW YORK
VERMONT
N.H.
QUÉBEC
Montréal
Trois-Rivières
Sherbrooke
Chicoutimi
Rimouski
COUNTIES indicated by numbers:
1 Iberville D4
2 Napierville D4
3 Rouville E4
4 St-Hyacinthe D4
5 Île-de-Montréal D4
6 Deux-Montagnes C4
7 Soulanges C4
8 Beauharnois D4
9 Hull B4
10 Île-Jésus D4
11 Richelieu D4
12 Vaudreuil C4
Internal divisions represent Municipal Counties
Longitude 72° West of Greenwich
© Copyright HAMMOND INCORPORATED, Maplewood, N. J.

Sainte-Pudentienne 802 ...E4
Saint-Esprit 948 ...D4
Sainte-Thècle 1,761 ...E3
Sainte-Thérèse 17,479 ...H4
Saint-Étienne-de-Grès 728 ...E3
Saint-Eustache 21,248 ...H4
Saint-Évariste-de-Forsyth 787 ...F4
Saint-Fabien 1,458 ...J1
Saint-Félicien 4,985 ...E1
Saint-Félix-de-Valois 1,495 ...D3
Saint-Flavien 693 ...F3
Saint-Fulgence 966 ...G1
Saint-François-d'Assise 680 ...G1
Saint-François-de-Sales 803 ...E1
Saint-François-du-Lac⊙ 971 ...E3
Saint-Gabriel 3,271 ...D3
Saint-Gédéon, Frontenac 1,292 ...G4
Saint-Gédéon, Lac-St-Jean-E. 697 ...F1
Saint-Georges, Beauce 8,605 ...G3
Saint-Georges, Champlain 2,707 ...E3
Saint-Georges-Ouest 6,478 ...G3
Saint-Germain-de-Grantham 1,289 ...E4
Saint-Gervais 780 ...G3
Saint-Gilles 905 ...F3
Saint-Grégoire-de-Greenlay 622 ...E4
Saint-Henri ...J3
Saint-Honoré, Beauce 1,115 ...G4
Saint-Honoré, Chicoutimi 1,546 ...F1
Saint-Honoré-de-Témiscouata 539 ...H2
Saint-Hubert 49,706 ...J4
Saint-Hubert-de-Témiscouata 539 ...J2
Saint-Hyacinthe⊙ 37,500 ...D4
Saint-Isidore 768 ...F3
Saint-Isidore-de-Laprairie 846 ...D4
Saint-Jacques 2,095 ...D4
Saint-Jacques-le-Mineur 1,086 ...H4
Saint-Jean⊙ 34,363 ...D4
Saint-Jean-Chrysostome 3,606 ...J3
Saint-Jean-de-Dieu 1,261 ...J1
Saint-Jean-de-Matha 947 ...D3
Saint-Jean-Port-Joli⊙ 1,844 ...G2
Saint-Jérôme, Terrebonne⊙ 25,175 ...H4
Saint-Joachim 943 ...G2

Saint-Joseph-de-Beauce 3,213 ...G3
Saint-Joseph-de-Sorel 2,811 ...D3
Saint-Jovite 3,595 ...C3
Saint-Lambert 20,318 ...J4
Saint-Laurent 64,404 ...H4
Saint-Lazare 558 ...G3
Saint-Léonard 78,452 ...H4
Saint-Léonard-d'Aston 1,049 ...E3
Saint-Léonard-de-Portneuf 555 ...F3
Saint-Léon-de-Standon 855 ...G3
Saint-Léon-le-Grand 1,325 ...B2
Saint-Liboire⊙ 648 ...E4
Saint-Louis-de-Terrebonne 8,479 ...H4
Saint-Louis-du-Ha Ha 672 ...H2
Saint-Luc 7,103 ...D4
Saint-Luc-de-Matane 609 ...B1
Saint-Marc-des-Carrières 2,625 ...E3
Saint-Méthode-de-Frontenac 898 ...F3
Saint-Michel-de-Bellechasse 960 ...G3
Saint-Michel-des-Saints 1,966 ...D3
Saint-Nazaire-de-Chicoutimi 938 ...F1
Saint-Nérée 907 ...G3
Saint-Noël 777 ...B1
Saint-Odilon 697 ...G3
Saint-Omer 569 ...C2
Saint-Ours 742 ...D4
Saint-Pacôme 1,167 ...G2
Saint-Pamphile 3,450 ...H3
Saint-Pascal⊙ 2,552 ...H2
Saint-Paul 544 ...E4
Saint-Paul-de-Montminy 691 ...G3
Saint-Paulin 734 ...D3
Saint-Paul-l'Ermite 6,107 ...J3
Saint-Petronille 801 ...J3
Saint-Philippe-de-Néri 732 ...H2
Saint-Pie 1,720 ...D4
Saint-Pierre, Île-de-Mont. 6,039 ...H4
Saint-Pierre, Joliette 679 ...D3
Saint-Pierre-d'Orléans 619 ...G3
Saint-Polycarpe 540 ...C4
Saint-Prime 2,266 ...E1
Saint-Prosper-de-Dorchester 1,878 ...G3
Saint-Raphaël 1,328 ...G3
Saint-Raymond 3,742 ...F3
Saint-Rédempteur 3,031 ...J3
Saint-Régis ...C4

Saint-Rémi 4,866 ...D4
Saint-Roch-de-l'Achigan 1,052 ...D4
Saint-Roch-de-Richelieu 614 ...D4
Saint-Romuald-d'Etchemin 9,160 ...J3
Saint-Sauveur-des-Monts 1,999 ...C4
Saint-Siméon 1,163 ...G1
Saint-Siméon-de-Bonaventure 650 ...C2
Saint-Simon 675 ...H1
Saint-Thomas-de-Joliette 577 ...D3
Saint-Timothée 1,927 ...C4
Saint-Tite 3,128 ...E3
Saint-Tite-des-Caps 609 ...G2
Saint-Ubald ...E3
Saint-Ulric 804 ...B1
Saint-Urbain-de-Charlevoix 1,076 ...G2
Saint-Victor 1,044 ...G3
Saint-Zacharie 1,300 ...G3
Saint-Zotique 1,519 ...C4
Sault-au-Mouton 914 ...H1
Sawyerville 878 ...F4
Sayabec 1,818 ...B2
Scotstown 827 ...F4
Scott-Jonction 571 ...F3
Senneville 1,333 ...G4
Shawbridge 831 ...C4
Shawinigan 24,921 ...E3
Shawinigan-Sud 11,155 ...E3
Shawville 1,724 ...A4
Sherbrooke⊙ 76,804 ...E4
Sillery 13,580 ...J3
Sorel⊙ 19,666 ...D4
Squatec 920 ...J2
Stanstead Plain 1,163 ...F4
Sully 833 ...H2
Sutton 1,655 ...E4
Tadoussac⊙ 998 ...H1
Terrebonne 11,204 ...H4
Thetford Mines 20,874 ...F3
Thurso 3,066 ...B4
Tourville 669 ...H2
Tracy 12,284 ...D3
Tring-Jonction 1,248 ...F3
Trois-Pistoles 4,554 ...H1
Trois-Rivières 52,518 ...E3
Trois-Rivières-Ouest 10,564 ...E3
Upton 822 ...E4
Val-Brillant 677 ...B1
Valcourt 2,566 ...E4
Val-David 2,073 ...C3
Vallée-Jonction 1,288 ...G3
Valleyfield 29,716 ...C4

Vanier 10,683 ...J3
Varennes 6,469 ...J4
Vaudreuil⊙ 5,630 ...C4
Verchères 3,586 ...J4
Verdun 68,013 ...H4
Victoriaville 21,825 ...F3
Villeneuve ...J3
Warwick 2,865 ...F4
Waterloo⊙ 4,746 ...E4
Waterville 1,458 ...E4
Weedon-Centre 1,264 ...F4
Westmount 22,153 ...H4
Windsor 5,637 ...E4
Woburn 542 ...G4
Wottonville 700 ...E4
Yamachiche⊙ 1,202 ...E3

OTHER FEATURES

Alma (isl.) ...F1
Aylmer (lake) ...F4
Baskatong (res.) ...B3
Batiscan (riv.) ...E2
Bécancour (riv.) ...F3
Bonaventure (isl.) ...D1
Bonaventure (riv.) ...C1
Brome (lake) ...E4
Brompton (lake) ...E4
Cascapédia (riv.) ...C1
Chaleur (bay) ...C1
Champlain (lake) ...D4
Chaudière (riv.) ...G4
Chic-Chocs (mts.) ...C1
Chicoutimi (riv.) ...F2
Coudres (isl.) ...G2
Deschênes (lake) ...A4
Deux Montagnes (lake) ...H4
Ditton (riv.) ...F4
Forillon Nat'l Park ...D1
Fort Chambly Nat'l Hist. Park ...J4
Gaspé (bay) ...D1
Gaspé (cape) ...D1
Gaspé (pt.) ...D2
Gaspésie Prov. Park ...C1
Gatineau (riv.) ...B3
Îles (lake) ...B3
Jacques-Cartier (mt.) ...C1
Jacques-Cartier (riv.) ...F2
Kénogami (lake) ...F1
Kiamika (lake) ...B3
La Maurice Nat'l Park ...D3
Laurentides Prov. Park ...F2
Lièvre (riv.) ...B4
Lièvres (isl.) ...H2
Maskinongé (riv.) ...D3

Matane (riv.) ...B1
Matane Prov. Park ...B1
Matapédia (riv.) ...C2
Mégantic (lake) ...G4
Memphremagog (lake) ...E4
Mercier (dam) ...A3
Métabetchouane (riv.) ...F1
Mille Îles (riv.) ...H4
Montmorency (riv.) ...F2
Mont-Tremblant Prov. Park ...C3
Nicolet (riv.) ...E3
Nominingue (lake) ...B3
Nord (riv.) ...C4
Orléans (isl.) ...G3
Ottawa (riv.) ...B4
Ouareau (riv.) ...D3
Patapédia (riv.) ...B2
Péribonca (riv.) ...F1
Petite Nation (riv.) ...B4
Prairies (riv.) ...H4
Rimouski (riv.) ...J1
Ristigouche (riv.) ...B2
Saguenay (riv.) ...G1
Sainte-Anne (riv.) ...F3
Sainte-Anne (riv.) ...G2
Saint-François (lake) ...F4
Saint-François (riv.) ...E4
Saint-Jean (lake) ...E1
Saint Lawrence (gulf) ...D2
Saint Lawrence (riv.) ...H1
Saint-Louis (lake) ...H4
Saint-Maurice (riv.) ...E2
Saint-Pierre (lake) ...E3
Shawinigan (riv.) ...E3
Shipshaw (riv.) ...F1
Soeurs (isl.) ...H4
Témiscouata (lake) ...H2
Tremblant (lake) ...C3
Trente et un Milles (lake) ...B3
Verte (isl.) ...H1
Yamaska (riv.) ...E4
York (riv.) ...D1

QUÉBEC, NORTHERN

INTERNAL DIVISIONS

Abitibi (county) 88,229 ...B2
Abitibi (terr.) ...B3
Berthier (county) 28,465 ...D3
Bonaventure (county) 40,724 ...D3
Champlain (county) 114,078 ...C3
Charlevoix-Est (county) 17,065 ...C3

Charlevoix-Ouest (county) 13,601 ...C3
Chicoutimi (county) 165,859 ...C2
Gaspé-Est (county) 40,720 ...E3
Gaspé-Ouest (county) 19,238 ...D3
Gatineau (county) 52,193 ...B3
Joliette (county) 55,524 ...B3
Lac-Saint-Jean-Est (county) 45,558 ...C3
Lac-Saint-Jean-Ouest (county) 57,556 ...C2
Maskinongé (county) 20,879 ...C3
Matane (county) 28,954 ...D3
Matapédia (county) 24,063 ...D3
Mistassini (terr.) ...B2
Montcalm (county) 23,534 ...B3
Montmorency No. I (county) 20,712 ...C3
Nouveau-Québec (terr.) 38,982 ...E1
Pontiac (county) 20,559 ...B3
Portneuf (county) 51,643 ...C3
Québec (county) 449,633 ...C3
Rimouski (county) 64,768 ...D3
Saguenay (county) 115,736 ...D3
Saint-Maurice (county) 106,023 ...C3
Témiscamingue (county) 52,871 ...B3

CITIES and TOWNS

Alma⊙ 25,638 ...C3
Amos⊙ 9,213 ...B3
Baie-Comeau 11,911 ...D3
Baie-du-Poste ...C2
Chibougamau 10,536 ...C3
Chicoutimi⊙ 57,737 ...C3
Gaspé 16,842 ...E3
Hauterive 14,724 ...D3
Jonquière 60,691 ...C3
La Tuque 12,067 ...C3
Lévis 17,819 ...D3
Manicouagan ...D2
Matane⊙ 12,726 ...D3
Mistassini (Baie-du-Poste) ...C2
Montmagny⊙ 12,326 ...C3
New Carlisle⊙ 1,403 ...E3
Noranda 9,809 ...B3
Nouveau-Comptoir ...B2
Percé⊙ 5,198 ...E3
Port-Cartier-Ouest 1,171 ...D3
Port-Menier⊙ 438 ...E3
Povungnituk ...E1
Québec (cap.)⊙ 177,082 ...C3
Rimouski⊙ 27,897 ...D3

Rivière-au-Tonnerre ...D2
Rivière-du-Loup⊙ 13,103 ...D3
Rouyn 17,678 ...B3
Sept-Îles 30,617 ...D2
Seven Islands (Sept-Îles) 30,617 ...D2
Shawinigan 24,921 ...C3
Tadoussac⊙ 998 ...C3
Val d'Or 19,915 ...B3
Ville-Marie⊙ 2,274 ...B3

OTHER FEATURES

Allard (lake) ...E2
Anticosti (isl.) ...E3
Baleine, Grand Rivière de la (riv.) ...B1
Bell (riv.) ...B3
Betsiamites (riv.) ...C2
Bienville (lake) ...B2
Broadback (riv.) ...B2
Cabonga (res.) ...B3
Caniapiscau (riv.) ...D1
Eastmain (riv.) ...B2
Eau Claire (lake) ...C1
Feuilles (riv.) ...C1
Gaspésie Prov. Park ...D3
George (riv.) ...F2
Gouin (res.) ...C3
Grande Rivière, La (riv.) ...B2
Honguedo (passage) ...E3
Hudson (bay) ...A1
Hudson (str.) ...F1
Jacques-Cartier (passage) ...E3
James (bay) ...A2
Koksoak (riv.) ...D1
Laurentides Prov. Park ...C3
Louis-XIV (pt.) ...B2
Manicouagan (res.) ...D2
Minto (lake) ...D1
Mistassini (riv.) ...C3
Mistassini (lake) ...C2
Moisie (riv.) ...D2
Mont-Tremblant Prov. Park ...C3
Natashquan (riv.) ...E2
Nottaway (riv.) ...B2
Nouveau-Québec (crater) ...F1
Otish (mts.) ...C3
Ottawa (riv.) ...B3
Péribonca (riv.) ...C2
Plétipi (lake) ...C2
Saguenay (riv.) ...C3
Saint-Jean (lake) ...C3
Saint Lawrence (gulf) ...E3
Saint Lawrence (riv.) ...D3
Ungava (pen.) ...E1

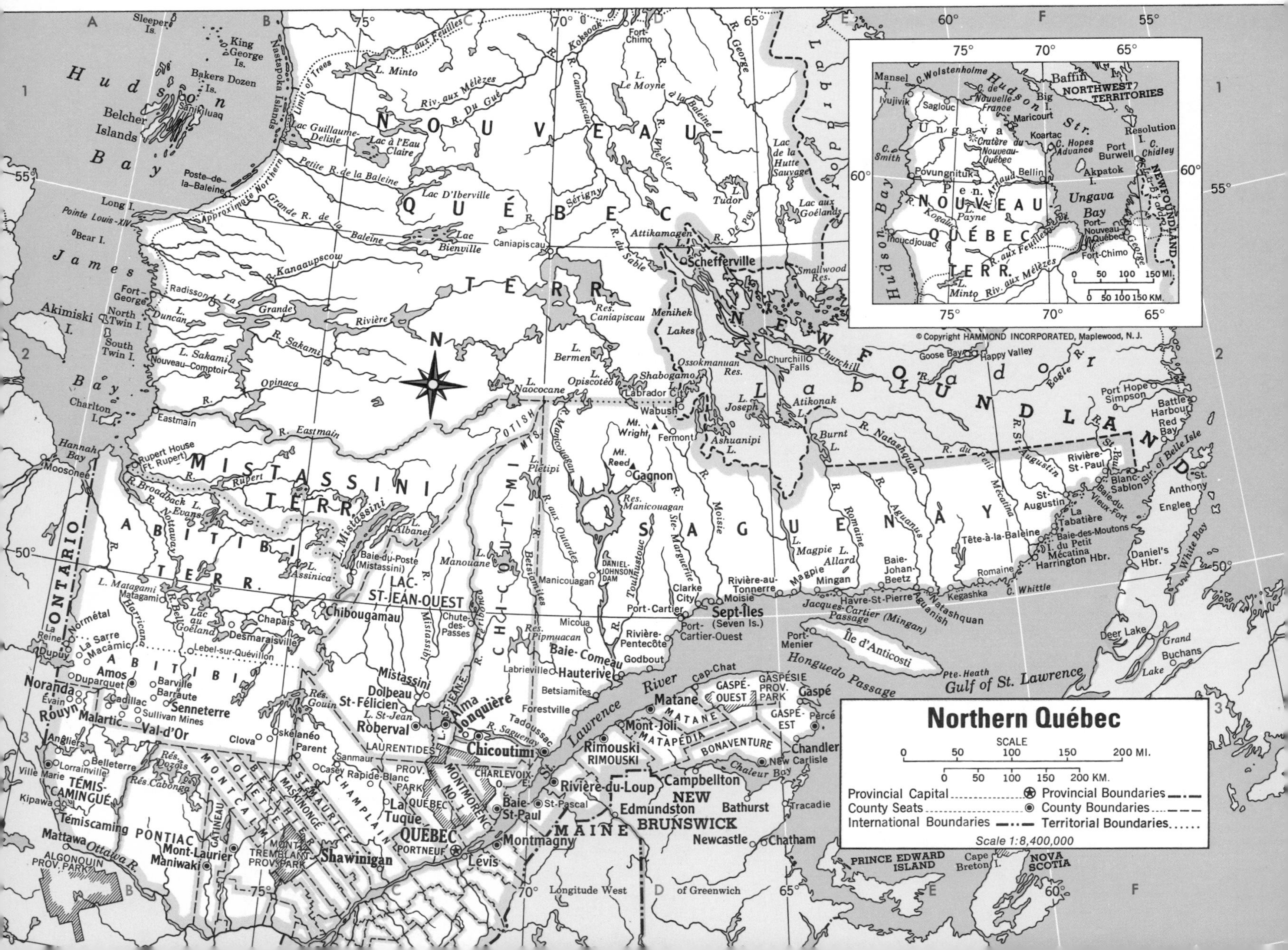

© Copyright HAMMOND INCORPORATED, Maplewood, N.J.

Northern Québec

SCALE
0   50   100   150   200 MI.
0   50   100   150   200 KM.

Provincial Capital ....⊛   Provincial Boundaries ___ _ ___
County Seats ....⊙   County Boundaries ____
International Boundaries ___ · ___   Territorial Boundaries ....

Scale 1:8,400,000

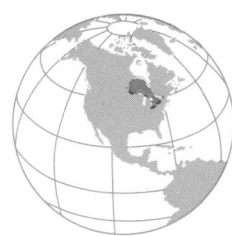

ONTARIO, NORTHERN

INTERNAL DIVISIONS

Algoma (terr. dist.) 122,883 D3
Cochrane (terr. dist.) 96,825 D2
Kenora (terr. dist.) 57,980 C2
Manitoulin (terr. dist.) 10,893 D3
Nipissing (terr. dist.) 81,739 E3
Parry Sound (terr. dist.) 32,654 E3
Rainy River (terr. dist.) 24,768 B3
Renfrew (county) 89,099 E3
Sudbury (reg. munic.) 167,705 D3
Sudbury (terr. dist.) 27,287 D3
Thunder Bay (terr. dist.) 150,647 C3
Timiskaming (terr. dist.) 43,760 D3

CITIES and TOWNS

Chalk River 1,095 E3
Fort Albany D2
Huntsville 11,123 E3
Kapuskasing 12,676 D3
Kenora⊙ 10,565 B3
Kirkland Lake 13,567 D3
Moose Factory 554 D2
Moosonee 1,349 D2
Nickel Centre 13,157 D3
North Bay⊙ 51,639 E3
Pembroke⊙ 14,927 E3
Sault Sainte Marie⊙ 81,048 D3
Sudbury 97,604 D3
Thunder Bay⊙ 111,476 C3
Timmins 44,747 D3
Valley East 19,591 D3
Walden 10,453 D3

OTHER FEATURES

Abitibi (lake) E3
Abitibi (riv.) D2
Albany (riv.) C2
Algonquin Prov. Park E3
Asheweig (riv.) C2
Attawapiskat (lake) C2
Attawapiskat (riv.) C2
Basswood (lake) B3
Berens (riv.) A2
Big Trout (lake) B2
Black Duck (riv.) C1
Bloodvein (riv.) A2
Caribou (isl.) C3
Cobham (riv.) A2
Eabamet (lake) C2
Ekwan (riv.) C2
English (riv.) B2
Fawn (riv.) C2
Finger (lake) B2
Georgian (bay) D3
Hannah (bay) D2
Henrietta Maria (cape) D1
Hudson (bay) D1
Huron (lake) D3
James (bay) D2
Kapiskau (riv.) D2
Kapuskasing (riv.) D3
Kenogami (riv.) C2
Kesagami (lake) E2
Lake of the Woods (lake) B3
Lake Superior Prov. Park D3
Little Current (riv.) C2
Long (lake) C3
Manitoulin (isl.) D3
Mattagami (riv.) D3
Michipicoten (isl.) C3
Mille Lacs (lake) B3
Missinaibi (lake) D3
Missinaibi (riv.) D2
Missisa (lake) D2
Nipigon (lake) C3
Nipissing (lake) E3
North (chan.) D3
North Caribou (lake) B2
Nungesser (lake) B2
Ogidaki (mt.) D3
Ogoki (riv.) C2
Opazatika (riv.) D3
Opinnagau (riv.) D2
Otoskwin (riv.) B2
Ottawa (riv.) E3
Pipestone (riv.) B2
Polar Bear Prov. Park D2
Pukaskwa Prov. Park C3
Quetico Prov. Park B3
Rainy (lake) B3
Red (lake) B2
Sachigo (riv.) B2
Saganaga (lake) B3
Saint Ignace (isl.) C3
Saint Joseph (lake) B2
Sandy (lake) B2
Savant (lake) B2
Seine (riv.) B3
Seul (lake) B2
Severn (lake) B2
Severn (riv.) B2
Shamattawa (riv.) C2
Shibogama (lake) C2
Sibley Prov. Park C3
Slate (isls.) C3
Stout (lake) B2
Superior (lake) C3
Sutton (lake) D2
Sutton (riv.) D2
Timagami (lake) D3
Timiskaming (lake) E3
Trout (lake) B2
Wabuk (pt.) D1
Winisk (lake) C2
Winisk (riv.) C2
Winnipeg (riv.) A2
Woods (lake) B3

ONTARIO

INTERNAL DIVISIONS

Algoma (terr. dist.) 122,883 J5
Brant (county) 99,950 D4
Bruce (county) 57,472 C3
Cochrane (terr. dist.) 96,825 J4
Dufferin (county) 28,528 D3
Dundas (county) 18,507 J2
Durham (reg. munic.) 247,473 F3
Elgin (county) 69,092 C5
Essex (county) 310,362 B5
Frontenac (county) 108,052 H3
Glengarry (county) 19,270 K2
Grenville (county) 26,025 J3
Grey (county) 72,176 D3
Haldimand-Norfolk (reg. munic.) 89,252 E5
Haliburton (county) 10,795 F2
Halton (reg. munic.) 128,497 E4
Hamilton-Wentworth (reg. munic.) 409,490 D4
Hastings (county) 105,837 G3
Huron (county) 56,007 C4
Kenora (terr. dist.) 57,980 G5
Kent (county) 106,130 B5
Lambton (county) 120,576 B5
Lanark (county) 44,197 H3
Leeds (county) 52,579 H3
Lennox and Addington (county) 32,633 G3
Manitoulin (terr. dist.) 10,893 B2
Middlesex (county) 303,745 C4
Muskoka (dist. munic.) 36,691 E3
Niagara (reg. munic.) 365,438 E4
Nipissing (terr. dist.) 81,739 F2
Northumberland (county) 64,441 G3
Ottawa-Carleton (reg. munic.) 520,533 J2
Oxford (county) 85,337 D4
Parry Sound (terr. dist.) 32,654 D2
Peel (reg. munic.) 375,910 E4
Perth (county) 66,279 C4
Peterborough (county) 99,930 F3
Prescott (county) 29,100 K2
Prince Edward (county) 22,559 G3
Rainy River (terr. dist.) 24,768 G5
Renfrew (county) 89,099 G2
Russell (county) 19,735 J2
Simcoe (county) 210,691 E3
Stormont (county) 61,173 K2
Sudbury (reg. munic.) 167,705 K6
Sudbury (terr. dist.) 27,287 J5
Thunder Bay (terr. dist.) 150,647 H5
Timiskaming (terr. dist.) 43,760 K5
Toronto (metro. munic.) 2,124,291 K4
Victoria (county) 43,543 F3
Waterloo (reg. munic.) 289,129 D4
Wellington (county) 123,736 D4
York (reg. munic.) 203,915 E4

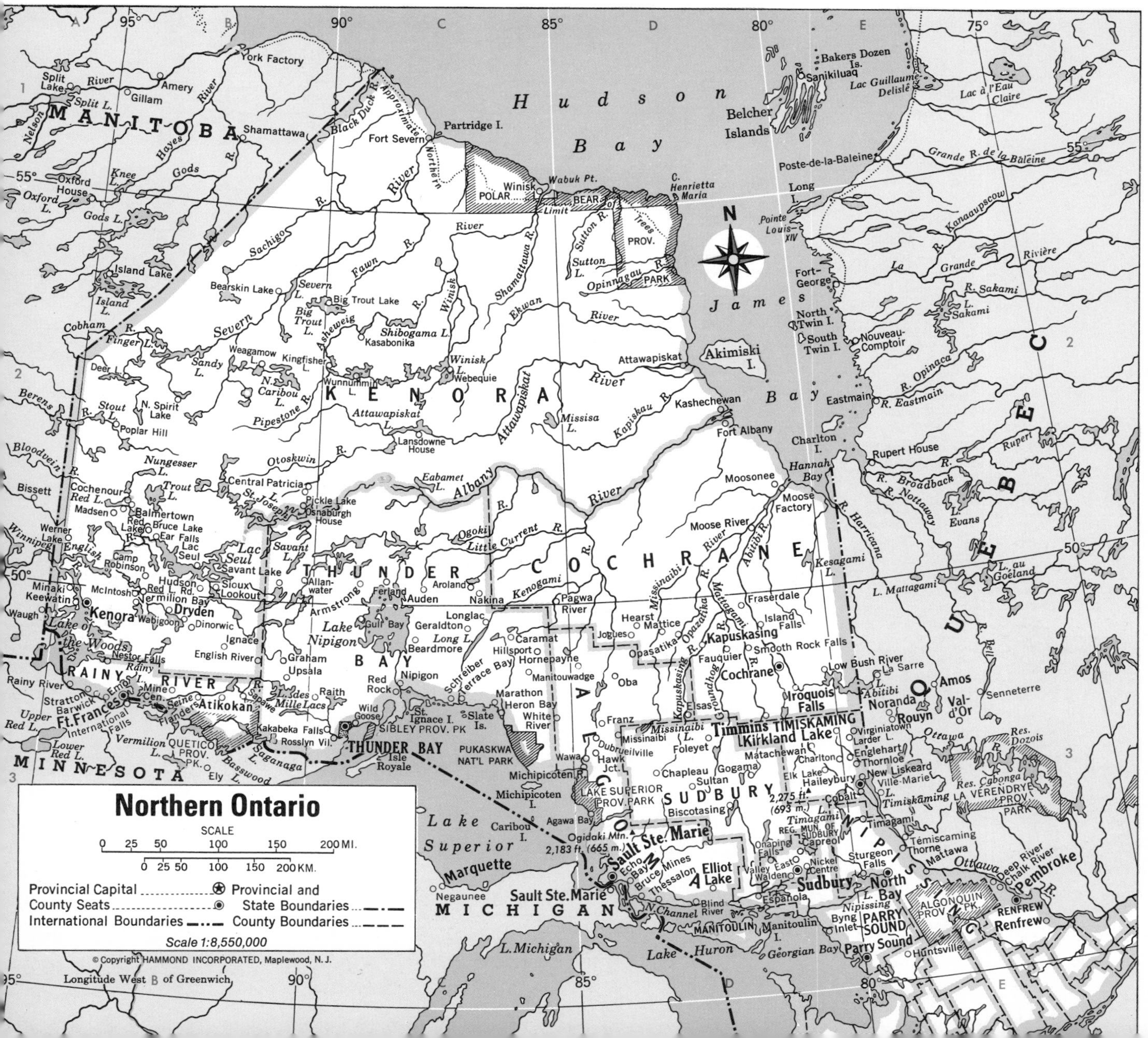

AREA 412,580 sq. mi. (1,068,582 sq. km.)
POPULATION 8,551,733
CAPITAL Toronto
LARGEST CITY Toronto
HIGHEST POINT in Timiskaming Dist. 2,275 ft. (693 m.)
SETTLED IN 1749
ADMITTED TO CONFEDERATION 1867
PROVINCIAL FLOWER White Trillium

CITIES and TOWNS

Ailsa Craig 701 C4
Ajax 20,774 E4
Alban 351 D1
Alcona Beach 861 E3
Alexandria 3,498 K2
Alfred 1,105 K2
Alliston 4,155 E3
Alma 271 D4
Almonte 3,693 H2
Alvinston 672 B5
Amherstburg 5,566 A5
Amherst View 5,295 H3
Ancaster 14,255 D4
Angus 3,494 E3
Apple Hill 271 K2
Apsley 281 F3
Arkona 458 C4
Armstrong 323 H4
Arnprior 6,111 H2
Arthur 1,660 D4
Astorville 373 E1
Athens 1,054 J3
Atherley 367 E3
Atikokan 5,668 G5
Atwood 720 D4
Aurora 14,249 J3
Avonmore 300 K2
Aylmer 5,125 C5
Ayr 1,331 D4
Ayton 450 D3
Baden 824 D4
Bala 536 E2
Bancroft 2,332 G2
Barrie⊙ 34,389 E3
Barry's Bay 1,256 G2
Batawa 484 G3
Bath 762 H3
Bayfield 549 C4
Bayside 3,356 G3
Beachburg 649 H2
Beachville 988 D4
Beardmore 656 H5
Beaverton 1,737 E3
Beeton 1,604 E3
Belle River 3,254 B5
Belleville⊙ 35,311 G3
Belmont 739 C5
Bethany 314 F3
Bewdley 475 F3
Binbrook 465 E4
Blackstock 767 F3
Blenheim 3,804 C5
Blind River 3,142 J5
Bloomfield 756 G4
Blyth 866 C4
Bobcaygeon 1,562 F3
Bonfield 722 E1
Bothwell 899 C5
Bourget 949 J2
Bracebridge⊙ 8,428 E2
Bradford 5,080 E3
Braeside 538 H2
Brampton⊙ 103,459 J4
Brantford⊙ 66,950 D4
Bridgenorth 1,368 F3
Brigden 548 B5
Brighton 3,199 G3
Brights Grove 1,113 B4
Britt 468 D2
Brockville⊙ 19,903 J3
Bruce Mines 517 J5
Brussels 1,043 C4
Burford 1,051 D4
Burgessville 289 D4
Burk's Falls 871 E2
Burlington 104,314 E4
Cache Bay 691 D1
Caesarea 547 F3
Calabogie 289 H2
Caledon 22,434 E4
Callander 1,058 E1
Cambridge 72,383 D4
Campbellford 3,487 G3
Cannington 1,419 E3
Capreol 4,089 K5
Caramat 382 H5
Cardinal 1,867 J3
Carleton Place 5,256 H2
Carlisle 565 D4
Carlsbad Springs 478 J2
Carp 681 H2
Cartier 673 J5
Casselman 1,422 J2
Castleton 326 F3
Cedar Springs 281 B5
Chalk River 1,095 G1
Chapleau 3,253 J5
Charing Cross 441 B5
Chatham⊙ 38,685 B5
Chatsworth 394 D3
Cherry Valley 273 G4
Chesley 1,839 C3
Chesterville 1,324 J2
Chute-à-Blondeau 350 K2
City View J2
Clarence Creek 395 J2
Clarksburg 481 D3
Clifford 641 D4
Clinton 3,151 C4
Cobalt 2,056 K5
Cobden 1,025 H2
Coboconk 377 F3
Cobourg⊙ 11,421 F4
Cochrane⊙ 4,974 K5
Codes Corner 407 H3
Colborne 1,724 G4
Colchester 990 B6
Coldwater 803 E3
Collingwood 11,114 D3
Collins Bay 6,897 H3
Comber 649 B5
Consecon 363 G3
Cookstown 874 E3
Cornwall⊙ 46,121 K2
Corunna 3,723 B5
Cottam 514 B5
Courtland 602 D5
Coverdale 1,573 F4
Crediton 439 C4
Creemore 1,089 D3
Crysler 490 J2
Cumberland 550 J2
Cumberland Beach 686 E3
Dashwood 434 C4
Deep River 5,565 G1
Delaware 346 C5
Delhi 3,929 D5
Delta 310 H3
Denbigh 294 G2
Deseronto 1,893 G3
Dorchester 2,756 C5
Douglas 291 H2
Drayton 801 D4
Dresden 2,484 B5
Drumbo 397 D4
Dryden 6,799 G4
Dublin 282 C4
Dubreuilville 818 J5
Dundalk 1,165 D3
Dundas 19,179 D4
Dunnville 11,642 E5
Durham 2,501 D3
Dutton 1,036 C5
Earlton 1,008 K5
East York 106,950 J4
Echo Bay 745 J5
Eden Mills 332 D4
Eganville 1,328 G2
Egmondville 429 C4
Elgin 292 H3
Elk Lake 564 K5
Elliot Lake 8,849 B1
Elmira 7,034 D4
Elmvale 1,176 E3
Elmwood 423 C3
Elora 2,589 D4
Embro 800 C4
Embrun 1,763 J2
Emeryville B5
Emo 792 F5
Englehart 1,767 K5
Enterprise 295 H3
Erieau 453 C5
Erin 2,007 D4
Espanola 5,926 J5
Essex 5,577 B5
Etobicoke 297,109 J4
Everett 438 E3
Exeter 3,494 C4
Fauquier 620 J5
Fenelon Falls 1,637 F3
Fergus 6,001 D4
Field 568 E1
Finch 407 J2
Fingal 345 C5
Fitzroy Harbour 431 H2
Flesherton 568 D3
Foleyet 538 J5
Fordwich 412 C4
Forest 2,557 C4
Formosa 395 C3
Fort Erie 24,031 E5
Fort Frances⊙ 9,325 F5
Foxboro 560 G3
Frankford 1,851 G3
Fraserdale 385 J5
Freelton 310 D4
Gananoque 5,103 H3
Garden Village 265 E1
Geraldton 3,127 H5
Glencoe 1,818 C5
Glen Miller 605 G3
Glen Robertson 312 K2
Glen Walter 662 K2
Goderich⊙ 7,385 C4
Gogama 702 J5

(continued on following page)

Northern Ontario
SCALE
0 25 50 100 150 200 MI.
0 25 50 100 150 200 KM.
Provincial Capital ⊛ Provincial and State Boundaries
County Seats ⊙
International Boundaries County Boundaries
Scale 1:8,550,000
© Copyright HAMMOND INCORPORATED, Maplewood, N.J.
Longitude West B of Greenwich

Gore Bay⊙ 767 ....B2	Hudson 565 ....G4	Lambeth 2,876 ....C5	Manotick 1,410 ....J2	Moose Creek 382 ....K2	Oakville 68,950⊙ E4	Plattsville 498 ....D4
Gorrie 424 ....C4	Huntsville 11,123 ....E2	Lanark 803 ....H2	Marathon 2,250 ....H5	Morpeth 305 ....C5	Oakwood 382 ....F3	Point Edward 2,524 ....B4
Grafton 402 ....G4	Huron Park 1,341 ....C4	Lancaster 540 ....K2	Markdale 1,361 ....D3	Morrisburg 2,188 ....J3	Odessa 877 ....H3	Pontypool 497 ....F3
Grand Bend 750 ....C4	Ignace 515 ....G5	Langton 421 ....D5	Markham 56,206 ....K4	Mount Albert 909 ....E3	Oil Springs 618 ....B5	Port Burwell 726 ....D5
Grand Valley 1,096 ....D4	Ilderton 330 ....C4	Lansdowne 542 ....H3	Markstay 521 ....D1	Mount Brydges 1,573 ....C4	Omemee 790 ....F3	Port Carling 628 ....E2
Granton 313 ....C4	Ingersoll 8,198 ....C4	Larder Lake 1,238 ....K5	Marmora 1,323 ....G3	Mount Elgin 289 ....D5	Onaping Falls 6,776 ....J5	Port Colborne 20,536 ....E5
Greely 509 ....J2	Ingleside 1,106 ....J3	Latchford 457 ....J5	Martintown 366 ....K2	Mount Forest 3,376 ....D4	Opasatika 798 ....J5	Port Elgin 5,069 ....C3
Green Valley 478 ....K2	Innerkip 655 ....D4	Lefroy 534 ....E3	Massey 1,345 ....C1	Mount Hope 687 ....E4	Orangeville⊙ 12,021 ....D4	Port Hope 9,788 ....F4
Grimsby 15,567 ....E4	Inverhuron 275 ....C3	Limoges 616 ....J2	Matachewan 619 ....J5	Mount Pleasant 545 ....D4	Orillia 24,412 ....E3	Port Lambton 716 ....B5
Guelph⊙ 67,538 ....D4	Iron Bridge 790 ....A1	Lincoln 14,460 ....E4	Matheson 703 ....K5	Munster 1,119 ....J2	Orleans 4,316 ....J2	Portland 282 ....H3
Haileybury⊙ 4,939 ....K5	Iroquois 1,278 ....J3	Linden Beach 484 ....B6	Mattawa 2,849 ....F1	Nairn 457 ....C1	Osgoode 984 ....J2	Port McNicoll 1,522 ....E3
Haldimand 16,375 ....E5	Iroquois Falls 6,887 ....J5	Lindsay⊙ 13,062 ....F3	Mattice 816 ....J5	Nakina 602 ....H4	Oshawa 107,023⊙ F4	Port Perry 3,917 ....F3
Haliburton 1,124 ....F2	Jasper 374 ....H3	Linwood 455 ....D4	Maxville 852 ....K2	Nanticoke 19,489 ....E5	Ottawa (cap.), Canada⊙	Port Rowan 806 ....D5
Halton Hills 34,477 ....E4	Johnstown 560 ....J3	Lion's Head 500 ....C2	Maynooth 281 ....G2	Napanee⊙ 4,844 ....G3	304,462 ....J2	Port Stanley 1,707 ....C5
Hamilton⊙ 312,003 ....E4	Kakabeka Falls 367 ....G5	Listowel 5,126 ....D4	McGregor 810 ....B5	Neustadt 543 ....D3	Otterville 785 ....D5	Pottageville 298 ....J2
Hanover 5,691 ....C3	Kaladar 262 ....H3	Little Britain 359 ....F3	McKerrow 323 ....C1	Newburgh 628 ....H3	Owen Sound⊙ 19,525 ....D3	Powassan 1,238 ....E1
Harriston 1,872 ....D4	Kanata 6,304 ....J2	Little Current 1,476 ....C1	Meaford 4,319 ....D3	Newbury 388 ....C4	Paincourt 403 ....B5	Prescott⊙ 4,975 ....J3
Harrow 1,936 ....B5	Kapuskasing 12,676 ....J5	London⊙ 240,392 ....C4	Melbourne 339 ....C4	Newcastle 31,928 ....F4	Painswick 785 ....E3	Princeton 480 ....D4
Harrowsmith 533 ....H3	Kars 409 ....J2	Longlac 1,923 ....H5	Merlin 722 ....B5	New Hamburg 3,628 ....D4	Paisley 1,033 ....C3	Rainy River 1,092 ....F5
Harwood 262 ....F3	Kearney 285 ....E2	Long Sault 1,096 ....K2	Merrickville 932 ....J2	Newington 278 ....J3	Pakenham 1,322 ....H2	Ramore 335 ....K5
Hastings 990 ....G3	Keene 275 ....F3	L'Orignal 1,380 ....K2	Metcalfe 681 ....J2	New Liskeard 5,601 ....K5	Palmerston 1,961 ....D4	Rayside-Balfour 16,035 ....J5
Havelock 1,250 ....G3	Keewatin 1,954 ....F5	Lucan 1,377 ....C4	Midhurst 626 ....E3	Newmarket⊙ 24,795 ....E3	Paris 6,173 ....D4	Red Rock 1,244 ....H5
Hawkesbury 9,789 ....K2	Kemptville 2,544 ....J2	Lucknow 1,127 ....C4	Midland 11,568 ....E3	Niagara Falls 69,423 ....E4	Parkhill 1,300 ....C4	Renfrew 8,617 ....H2
Hawkstone 309 ....E3	Kenora⊙ 10,565 ....F4	Lyn 562 ....J3	Mildmay 990 ....C3	Niagara-on-the-Lake 12,485 ....E4	Parry Sound⊙ 5,501 ....E2	Richards Landing 313 ....J5
Hawk Junction 363 ....J5	Keswick 1,217 ....E3	Lynden 457 ....D4	Milford Bay 320 ....E2	Nickel Centre 13,157 ....D1	Pefferlaw 750 ....E3	Richmond 2,667 ....J2
Hearst 5,195 ....J5	Killaloe Station 699 ....G2	Lynhurst 429 ....C5	Milbank 383 ....D4	Nipigon 2,724 ....H5	Pelham 10,071 ....E4	Richmond Hill 34,716 ....J4
Hensall 993 ....C4	Killarney 445 ....C2	Macdiarmid 444 ....H5	Millbrook 898 ....F3	Nobel 291 ....D2	Pembroke⊙ 14,927 ....G2	Ridgetown 3,100 ....C5
Hepworth 377 ....C3	Kincardine 4,182 ....C3	MacGregor's Bay 885 ....C2	Milton⊙ 20,756 ....E4	Nobleton 1,537 ....J2	Penetanguishene 6,221 ....D3	Ripley 577 ....C3
Heyden 316 ....J5	King City 2,182 ....J4	MacTier 690 ....E2	Milverton 1,393 ....D4	Noelville 665 ....D1	Perkinsfield 342 ....E3	Rockcliffe Park 2,117 ....J2
Highgate 418 ....C5	Kingston⊙ 56,032 ....H3	Madawaska 288 ....F2	Mindemoya 402 ....B2	North Bay⊙ 51,639 ....E1	Perth⊙ 5,675 ....H3	Rockland 3,930 ....J2
Hillsburgh 819 ....D4	Kingsville 4,692 ....B6	Madoc 1,363 ....G3	Minden⊙ 590 ....F2	North Brook 409 ....H3	Petawawa 5,815 ....G2	Rockwood 959 ....D4
Hillsdale 274 ....E3	Kinmount 270 ....F3	Maitland 584 ....J3	Mississauga 250,017 ....J4	North Gower 825 ....J2	Peterborough⊙ 59,683 ....F3	Rodney 983 ....C5
Holland Landing 1,782 ....E3	Kirkland Lake 13,567 ....K5	Mallorytown 290 ....J3	Mitchell 2,742 ....C4	North York 558,398 ....J4	Petrolia 4,393 ....B5	Rolphton 290 ....G1
Honey Harbour 289 ....D2	Kitchener⊙ 131,870 ....D4	Manitouwadge 3,551 ....H5	Monkton 550 ....C4	Norwich 1,891 ....D5	Pickering 27,879 ....K4	Rosseau 260 ....E2
Hornepayne 1,694 ....J5	Komoka 812 ....C5	Manitowaning 373 ....C2	Moonbeam 925 ....J5	Norwood 1,243 ....G3	Picton⊙ 4,649 ....G3	Rosslyn Village 320 ....G5
	Lakefield 2,240 ....F3		Moorefield 304 ....D4	Nottawa 326 ....D3	Plantagenet 919 ....K2	Russell 857 ....J2

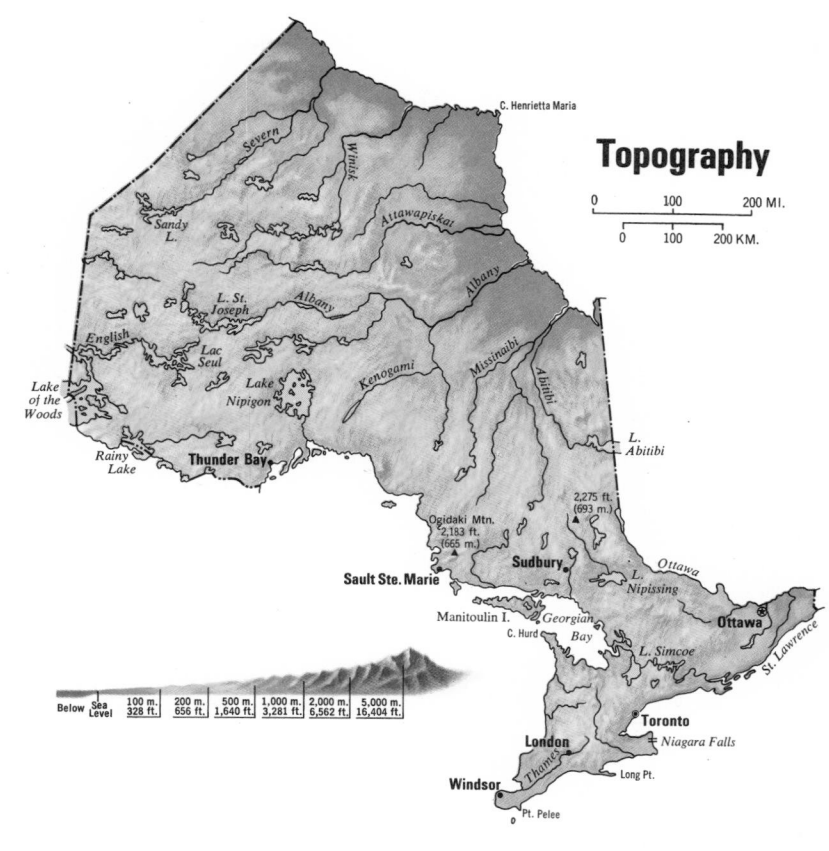

Topography

0   100   200 MI.

0   100   200 KM.

C. Henrietta Maria

L. St. Joseph

Sandy L.

Severn

Winisk

Attawapiskat

Albany

Lac Seul

Lake Nipigon

English

Kenogami

Missinaibi

Abitibi

L. Abitibi

Lake of the Woods

Rainy Lake

Thunder Bay

2,275 ft. (693 m.)

Ogidaki Mtn. 2,183 ft. (665 m.)

Sault Ste. Marie

Sudbury

Ottawa R.

L. Nipissing

Ottawa

Manitoulin I.

C. Hurd

Georgian Bay

L. Simcoe

St. Lawrence

Toronto

London

Niagara Falls

Thames

Long Pt.

Windsor

Pt. Pelee

| Below Sea Level | 100 m. 328 ft. | 200 m. 656 ft. | 500 m. 1,640 ft. | 1,000 m. 3,281 ft. | 2,000 m. 6,562 ft. | 5,000 m. 16,404 ft. |

Ontario
Southern Part

SCALE

0 10 20 30 40 50 MI.

0 10 20 30 40 50 KM.

National Capital ....⊛
Provincial Capital ....⊛
County Seats ....⊙
International Boundaries ...

Provincial & State Boundaries ...
County Boundaries ...
Canals ...

Scale 1:2,620,000

Agriculture, Industry and Resources

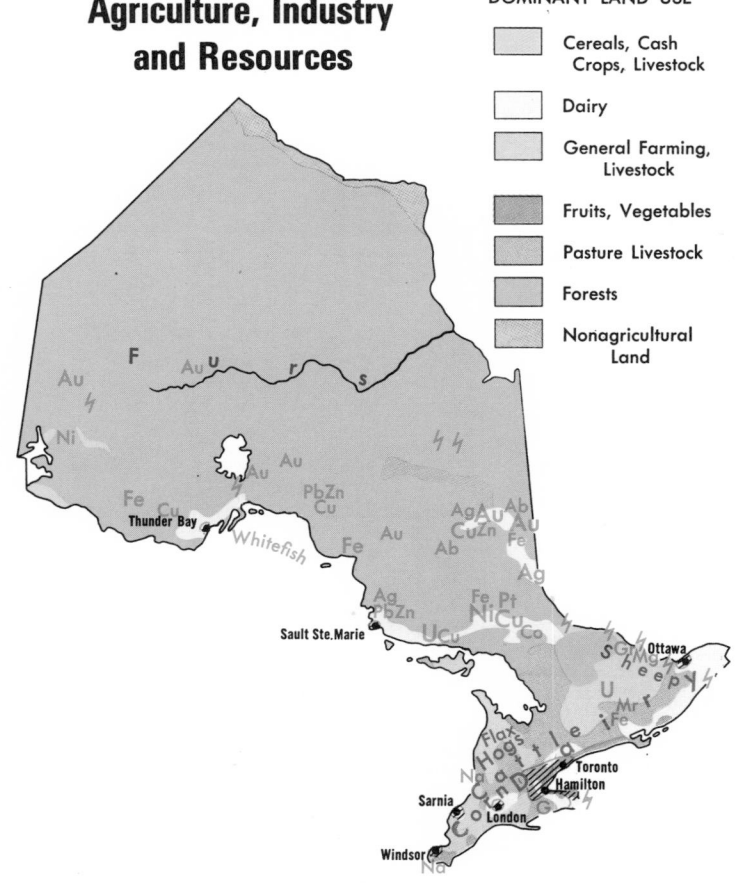

DOMINANT LAND USE

Cereals, Cash Crops, Livestock

Dairy

General Farming, Livestock

Fruits, Vegetables

Pasture Livestock

Forests

Nonagricultural Land

MAJOR MINERAL OCCURRENCES

Ab	Asbestos	Mg	Magnesium
Ag	Silver	Mr	Marble
Au	Gold	Na	Salt
Co	Cobalt	Ni	Nickel
Cu	Copper	Pb	Lead
Fe	Iron Ore	Pt	Platinum
G	Natural Gas	U	Uranium
Gr	Graphite	Zn	Zinc

⚡ Water Power

▨ Major Industrial Areas

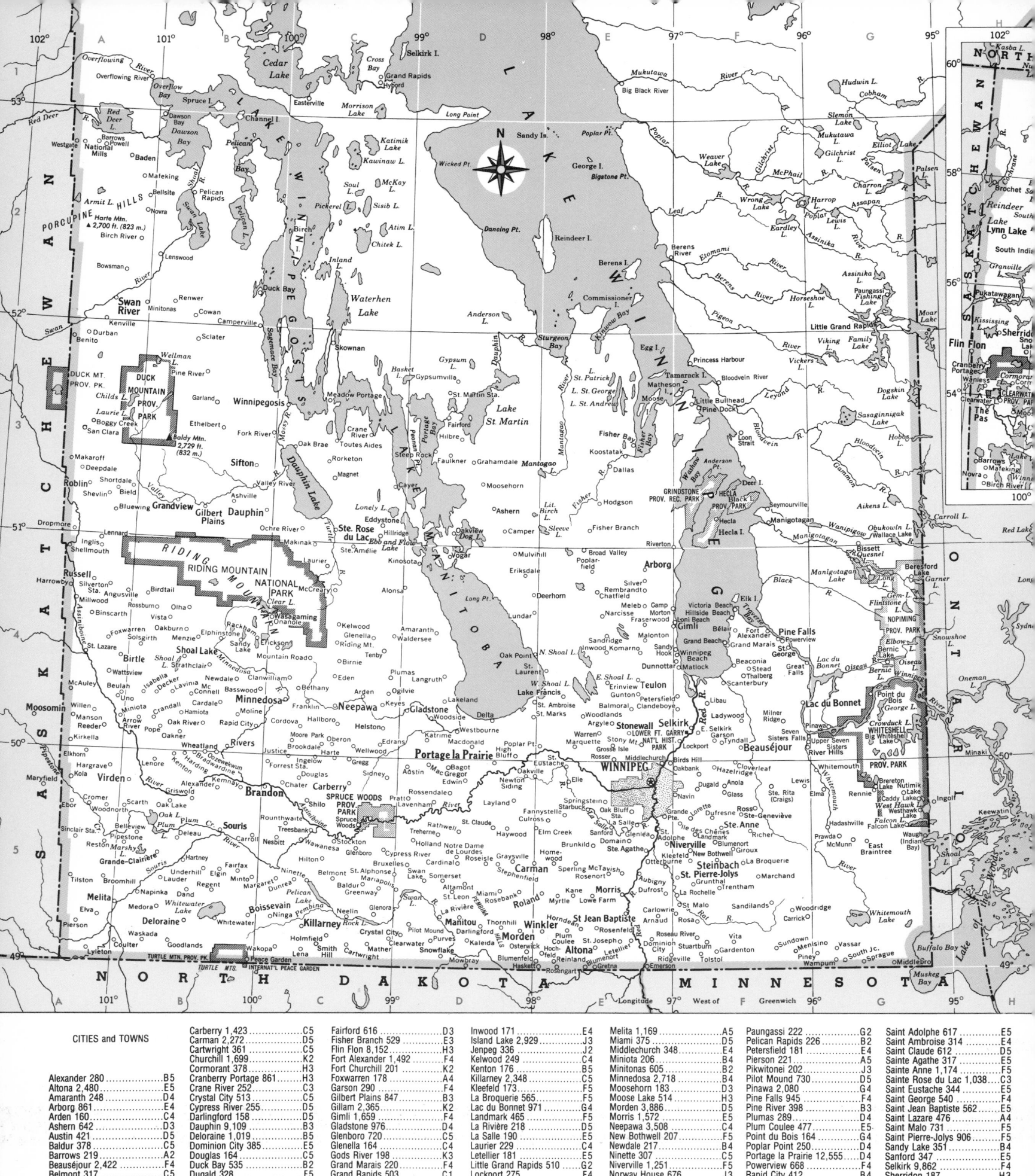

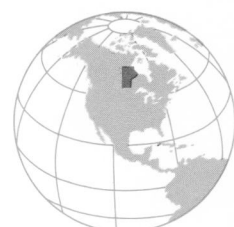

Manitoba
Northern Part

0 40 80 120 MI.
0 40 80 120 KM.

HUDSON BAY

Manitoba
Southern Part

SCALE

0 5 10 20   40   60 MI.
0 5 10 20   40   60 KM.

Provincial Capital ....⊛
International Boundaries — ·· — ··
Provincial Boundaries — · — ·

Scale 1:2,340,000

© Copyright HAMMOND INCORPORATED, Maplewood, N.J.

Swan Lake 338 ....D5
Swan River 3,443 ....A2
Teulon 873 ....E4
The Pas 6,602 ....H3
Thicket Portage 255 ....J3
Thompson 17,291 ....J2
Treherne 706 ....D5
Tyndall 411 ....F4
Virden 2,936 ....A5
Vita 213 ....F5
Wabowden 847 ....J3
Wanless 252 ....H3
Warren 302 ....E4
Waskada 257 ....B5
Wawanesa 487 ....C5
Whitemouth 314 ....G5
Whitewater 885 ....B5
Winkler 3,749 ....E5
Winnipeg (cap.) 560,874 ....E5
Winnipeg Beach 582 ....F4
Winnipegosis 893 ....B3
Woodridge 175 ....G5
York Landing 198 ....J2

OTHER FEATURES

Aikens (lake) G3
Anderson (lake) D2
Anderson, (pt.) F3
Armit (lake) A2
Assapan (riv.) G2
Assiniboine (riv.) C5
Assinika (lake) G2
Assinika (riv.) G2
Atim (lake) C2
Baldy (mt.) B3
Baralzon (lake) J1
Basket (lake) C3
Beaverhill (lake) J3
Berens (isl.) F2
Berens (riv.) F2
Bernic (lake) G4
Big Sand (lake) H2
Bigstone (lake) J3
Bigstone (pt.) E2
Bigstone (riv.) J3
Birch (isl.) C3
Black (isl.) F3
Black (riv.) F3
Bloodvein (riv.) F4
Bonnet (lake) G4
Buffalo (bay) G5
Burntwood (riv.) J2
Caribou (riv.) J1
Carroll (lake) G3
Cedar (lake) B1
Channel (isl.) B2
Charron (lake) G2
Childs (lake) A3
Chitek (lake) C2
Churchill (cape) K2
Churchill (riv.) J2
Clear (lake) C4
Clearwater Lake Prov. Park H3
Cobham (riv.) G1
Cochrane (riv.) H2
Commissioner (isl.) E2
Cormorant (lake) H3
Cross (bay) C1
Cross (lake) J3
Crowduck (lake) G4
Dancing (pt.) D2
Dauphin (lake) C3
Dauphin (riv.) D3
Dawson (bay) B2
Dog (lake) D3
Dogskin (lake) G3
Duck Mountain Prov. Park ...B3

Eardley (lake) F2
East Shoal (lake) E4
Ebb and Flow (lake) C3
Egg (isl.) E3
Elbow (lake) G4
Elk (isl.) F4
Elliot (lake) G2
Etawney (lake) J2
Etomami (riv.) F2
Falcon (lake) G5
Family (lake) G3
Fisher (bay) E3
Fisher (riv.) E3
Fishing (lake) G4
Flintstone (lake) G4
Fox (riv.) K2
Gammon (riv.) G3
Garner (lake) G4
Gem (lake) E4
George (isl.) G4
George (lake) G4
Gilchrist (creek) F2
Gilchrist (lake) G2
Gods (lake) K3
Gods (riv.) K3
Granville (lake) H2
Grass (riv.) J3
Grass River Prov. Park J3
Grindstone Prov. Rec. Park F3
Gunisao (lake) J3
Gypsum (lake) D3
Harrop (lake) G2
Harte (mt.) A2
Hayes (riv.) K3
Hecla (isl.) F3
Hecla Prov. Park F3
Hobbs (lake) G3
Horseshoe (lake) G2
Hubbart (pt.) H3
Hudson (bay) K2
Hudwin (lake) G1
Inland (lake) C2
International Peace Garden ..B5
Island (lake) K2
Katimik (lake) C2
Kawinaw (lake) C2
Kinwow (bay) E2
Kississing (lake) H2
Knee, (lake) J3
Lake of the Woods (lake) ...H5
La Salle (riv.) E5
Laurie (lake) A3
Leaf (riv.) F2
Lewis (lake) G2
Leyond (riv.) F3
Little Birch (lake) E3
Lonely (lake) C3
Long (lake) G4
Long (pt.) D1
Long (pt.) D4

Manigotagan (lake) G4
Manigotagan (riv.) G3
Manitoba (lake) D4
Mantagao (lake) E3
Mantagao (riv.) E3
Mantagao (riv.) E3
Marshy (lake) B5
McKay (lake) C2
McPhail (riv.) F2
Minnedosa (riv.) B4
Moar (lake) G2
Molson (lake) J3
Moose (isl.) B3
Morrison (lake) C1
Mossy (riv.) C3
Mukutawa (riv.) E1
Muskeg (bay) G6
Nejanilini (lake) J1
Nelson (riv.) J2
Nopiming Prov. Park G4
Northern Indian (lake) J2
North Knife (lake) J2
North Seal (riv.) H2
North Shoal (lake) E4
Nueltin (lake) H1
Oak (lake) B5
Obukowin (lake) G3
Oiseau (lake) G4
Oiseau (riv.) G4
Overflow (bay) A1
Overflowing (riv.) A1
Owl (riv.) K2
Oxford (lake) J3
Paint (lake) J2
Palsen (riv.) G2
Pelican (bay) B2
Pelican (lake) B2
Pelican (lake) C5
Pembina (hills) D5
Pembina (riv.) C5
Peonan (pt.) D3
Pickerel (lake) C2
Pigeon (riv.) F2
Pipestone (creek) A5
Plum (creek) B5
Plum (lake) B5
Poplar (pt.) E2
Poplar (riv.) E2
Porcupine (hills) A2
Portage (bay) D3
Punk (isl.) F3
Quesnel (lake) G4
Rat (riv.) F5
Red (riv.) F4
Red Deer (lake) A2
Red Deer (riv.) A2
Reindeer (isl.) E2
Reindeer (lake) H2
Riding (mt.) B4
Riding Mountain Nat'l Park ..B4
Rock (lake) C5

Ross (isl.) J3
Sagemace (bay) B3
Saint Andrew (lake) E3
Saint George (lake) E3
Saint Martin (lake) D3
Saint Patrick (lake) E3
Sale (riv.) E5
Sandy (isls.) D2
Sasaginnigak (lake) G3
Seal (riv.) J2
Selkirk (isl.) C1
Setting (lake) H3
Shoal (lake) B4
Shoal (lake) G5
Shoal (riv.) B2
Sipiwesk (lake) J3
Sisib (lake) C3
Sleeve (lake) E3
Slemon (lake) G1
Snowshoe (lake) G4
Soul (lake) C2
Souris (riv.) B5
Southern Indian (lake) H2
South Knife (riv.) J2
South Seal (riv.) J2
Split (lake) J2
Spruce (isl.) B1
Spruce Woods Prov. Park ..C5
Stevenson (lake) B2
Sturgeon (bay) B2
Swan (lake) B2
Swan (lake) D5
Swan (riv.) A3
Tadoule (lake) J2
Tamarack (lake) F3
Tatnam (cape) K2
Traverse (bay) F4
Turtle (mts.) B5
Turtle (riv.) B5
Turtle Mountain Prov. Park B5
Valley (riv.) B3
Vickers (lake) F3
Viking (lake) G3
Wanipigow (riv.) G3
Washow (bay) F3
Waterhen (lake) C2
Weaver (lake) F2
Wellman (lake) B3
West Hawk (lake) G5
West Shoal (lake) E4
Whitemouth (lake) G5
Whitemouth (riv.) G5
Whiteshell Prov. Park G4
Whitewater (lake) B5
Wicked (pt.) D2
Winnipeg (lake) E2
Winnipeg (riv.) G4
Winnipegosis (lake) C2
Woods (lake) H5
Wrong (lake) F2

AREA 250,999 sq. mi. (650,087 sq. km.)
POPULATION 1,017,323
CAPITAL Winnipeg
LARGEST CITY Winnipeg
HIGHEST POINT Baldy Mtn. 2,729 ft. (832 m.)
SETTLED IN 1812
ADMITTED TO CONFEDERATION 1870
PROVINCIAL FLOWER Prairie Crocus

Topography

0 75 150 MI.
0 75 150 KM.

Below Sea Level | 100 m. 328 ft. | 200 m. 656 ft. | 500 m. 1,640 ft. | 1,000 m. 3,281 ft. | 2,000 m. 6,562 ft. | 5,000 m. 16,404 ft.

Agriculture, Industry and Resources

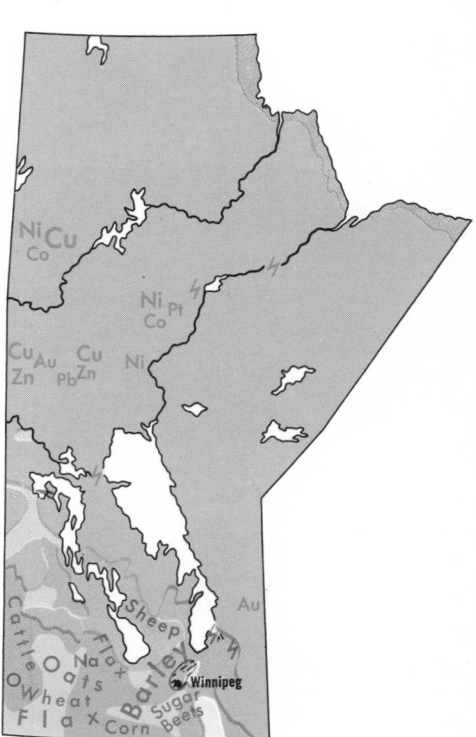

DOMINANT LAND USE

- Cereals (chiefly barley, oats)
- Cereals, Livestock
- Dairy
- Livestock
- Forests
- Nonagricultural Land

MAJOR MINERAL OCCURRENCES

Au Gold
Co Cobalt
Cu Copper
Na Salt
Ni Nickel
O Petroleum
Pb Lead
Pt Platinum
Zn Zinc

⚡ Water Power
▨ Major Industrial Areas

Topography

0 60 120 MI.
0 60 120 KM.

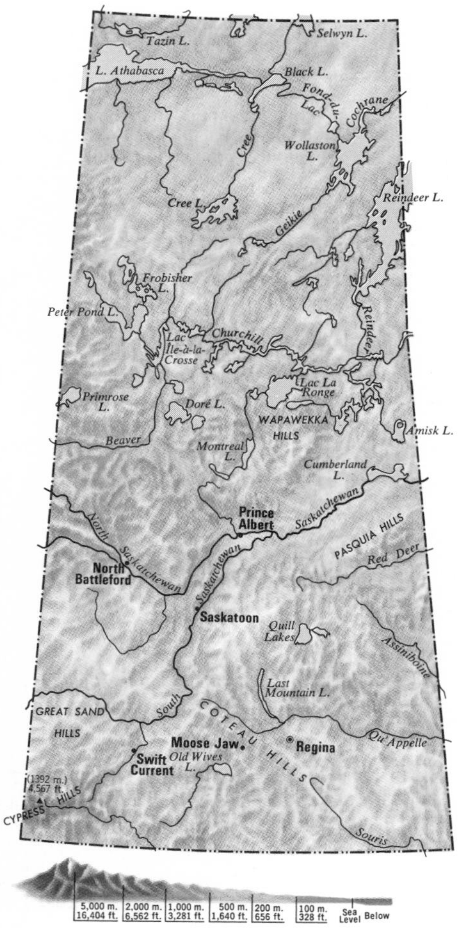
Tazin L.
Selwyn L.
L. Athabasca
Black L.
Wollaston L.
Cree L.
Reindeer L.
Frobisher L.
Peter Pond L.
Churchill
Lac Île-à-la-Crosse
Lac La Ronge
Primrose L.
Doré L.
WAPAWEKKA HILLS
Amisk L.
Beaver
Montreal L.
Cumberland L.
Prince Albert
North Battleford
Saskatoon
Quill Lakes
PASQUIA HILLS
Red Deer
Assiniboine
Last Mountain L.
GREAT SAND HILLS
COTEAU HILLS
Moose Jaw
Regina
Swift Current
Old Wives L.
Qu'Appelle
Souris
CYPRESS HILLS
5,000 m. 16,404 ft.
2,000 m. 6,562 ft.
1,000 m. 3,281 ft.
500 m. 1,640 ft.
200 m. 656 ft.
100 m. 328 ft.
Sea Level
Below

CITIES and TOWNS

Abbey 259 ..... C5
Aberdeen 373 ..... E3
Abernethy 299 ..... H5
Air Ronge 348 ..... M3
Alameda 319 ..... J6
Alida 163 ..... K6
Allan 720 ..... E4
Alsask 734 ..... B4
Aneroid 153 ..... D6
Annaheim 187 ..... G3
Antelope 150 ..... C5
Arborfield 400 ..... H2
Archerwill 272 ..... H3
Arcola 547 ..... J6
Asquith 416 ..... D3
Assiniboia 2,738 ..... E6
Avonlea 415 ..... G5
Aylsham 153 ..... H2
Balcarres 729 ..... H5
Balgonie 715 ..... G5
Batoche E3
Battleford 2,569 ..... C3
Beauval 518 ..... L3
Beechy 344 ..... D5
Bellevue 145 ..... F3
Bengough 603 ..... F6
Bethune 317 ..... F5
Bienfait 807 ..... J6
Biggar 2,491 ..... C3
Big River 827 ..... D2
Birch Hills 752 ..... F3
Bjorkdale 248 ..... H3
Blaine Lake 631 ..... D3
Borden 195 ..... D3
Bredenbury 441 ..... K5
Broadview 861 ..... J5
Brock 183 ..... C4
Broderick 135 ..... E4
Bruno 762 ..... F3
Buchanan 434 ..... J4
Buffalo Narrows 837 ..... L3
Burstall 548 ..... B5
Cabri 631 ..... C5
Cadillac 203 ..... D6
Calder 158 ..... K4
Cando 144 ..... C3
Canoe Lake 155 ..... L3
Canora 2,689 ..... J4
Carievale 245 ..... K6
Carlyle 1,057 ..... J6
Carnduff 1,071 ..... K6
Carrot River 1,020 ..... H2
Central Butte 518 ..... E5
Ceylon 259 ..... G6
Chaplin 382 ..... E5
Chitek Lake 172 ..... D2
Choiceland 535 ..... G2
Christopher Lake 193 ..... F2
Churchbridge 928 ..... J5
Climax 277 ..... C6
Cochin 221 ..... C2
Codette 214 ..... H2
Coleville 398 ..... B4
Colonsay 542 ..... F4
Connaught Heights 162 ..... G3
Conquest 265 ..... D4
Consul 160 ..... B6
Coronach 386 ..... F6
Craik 543 ..... F4
Craven 185 ..... G5
Creelman 178 ..... H6
Creighton 1,746 ..... N4
Crooked River 155 ..... H3
Cudworth 907 ..... F3
Cumberland House 796 ..... J2
Cupar 611 ..... G5
Cut Knife 530 ..... B3
Dalmeny 602 ..... E3
Davidson 1,092 ..... E4
Debden 381 ..... E2
Delisle 783 ..... D4
Delmas 153 ..... C3
Denare Beach 308 ..... M4
Denzil 230 ..... B3
Deschambault Lake 372 ..... M3
Dinsmore 398 ..... D4
Dodsland 312 ..... C4
Domremy 188 ..... F3
Dorintosh 159 ..... L4
Drake 251 ..... G4
Dubuc 142 ..... J5
Duck Lake 683 ..... E3
Dundurn 409 ..... E4
Dysart 236 ..... H5
Earl Grey 242 ..... G5
Eastend 771 ..... C6
Eatonia 553 ..... B4
Ebenezer 155 ..... J4
Edam 348 ..... C2
Edenwold 134 ..... G5
Elbow 286 ..... E4
Elfros 213 ..... H4
Elrose 614 ..... D4
Elstow 146 ..... E4
Endeavour 220 ..... J3
Englefeld 258 ..... G3
Esterhazy 2,894 ..... K5
Estevan 8,847 ..... J6
Eston 1,354 ..... C4
Eyebrow 198 ..... E5
Fillmore 350 ..... H6
Fleming 164 ..... K5
Flin Flon 408 ..... N4
Foam Lake 1,387 ..... H4
Fond du Lac 449 ..... L2
Fort Qu'Appelle 1,764 ..... H5
Fox Valley 429 ..... B5
Francis 150 ..... H5
Frobisher 187 ..... J6
Frontier 385 ..... C6
Gainsborough 311 ..... K6
Gerald 139 ..... K5
Glaslyn 383 ..... C2
Glenavon 295 ..... J5
Glen Ewen 143 ..... K6
Goodeve 134 ..... H4
Goodsoil 217 ..... L4
Govan 323 ..... G4
Gravelbourg 1,326 ..... E6
Grayson 260 ..... J5
Green Acres 165 ..... F2
Green Lake 616 ..... L4
Grenfell 1,363 ..... J5
Guernsey 222 ..... F4
Gull Lake 1,053 ..... C5
Hafford 515 ..... D3
Hague 530 ..... E3
Hanley 446 ..... E4
Harris 233 ..... D4
Hawarden 133 ..... E4
Hepburn 352 ..... E3
Herbert 986 ..... D5
Hodgeville 332 ..... E5
Holdfast 312 ..... F5
Hudson Bay 2,280 ..... J3
Humboldt 4,265 ..... F3
Hyas 190 ..... J4
Île-à-la-Crosse 821 ..... L3
Imperial 456 ..... F4
Indian Head 1,720 ..... H5
Invermay 397 ..... J4
Ituna 910 ..... H4
Jansen 209 ..... G4
Kamsack 2,726 ..... K4
Kelliher 411 ..... H4
Kelvington 1,053 ..... H3
Kenaston 352 ..... E4
Kennedy 241 ..... J5
Kenosee Park 135 ..... J6
Kerrobert 1,100 ..... C4
Killaly 137 ..... J5
Kincaid 245 ..... D6
Kindersley 3,523 ..... B4
Kinistino 763 ..... F3
Kipling 949 ..... J5
Kisbey 252 ..... J6
Kuroki 145 ..... H4
Kyle 499 ..... C5
Lafleche 639 ..... E6
Laird 201 ..... E3
Lake Lenore 385 ..... G3
La Loche 1,651 ..... L3
Lampman 720 ..... J6
Lancer 171 ..... C5
Landis 285 ..... C3
Lang 189 ..... G6
Langenburg 1,197 ..... K5
Langham 729 ..... E3
Lanigan 1,646 ..... F4
La Ronge 1,714 ..... L3
Lashburn 517 ..... B2
Leader 1,160 ..... B5
Leask 446 ..... E2
Lebret 268 ..... H5
Lemberg 417 ..... H5
Leoville 404 ..... D2
Leroy 436 ..... G4
Lestock 414 ..... G4
Limerick 166 ..... E6
Lintlaw 225 ..... H3
Lipton 353 ..... H5
Lloydminster 4,493 ..... A2
Loon Lake 365 ..... B1
Loreburn 224 ..... E4
Lucky Lake 340 ..... D5
Lumsden 1,116 ..... G5
Luseland 682 ..... B3
Macdowall 146 ..... E2
Macklin 873 ..... A3
MacNutt 141 ..... K4
Macoun 163 ..... H6
Maidstone 747 ..... B2
Major 150 ..... B4
Manitou Beach 136 ..... F4
Mankota 406 ..... D6
Manor 348 ..... K6
Maple Creek 2,330 ..... B6
Marcelin 273 ..... E3
Margo 178 ..... H4
Marsden 211 ..... B3
Marshall 326 ..... B2
Martensville 960 ..... E3
Maryfield 408 ..... K6
Maymont 172 ..... D3
McLean 184 ..... G5
Meacham 184 ..... F3
Meadow Lake 3,662 ..... C1
Meath Park 298 ..... F2
Medstead 197 ..... C2
Melfort 5,141 ..... G3
Melville 5,149 ..... J5
Meota 248 ..... C2
Mervin 174 ..... C2
Midale 572 ..... H6
Middle Lake 270 ..... F3
Milden 234 ..... D4
Milestone 511 ..... G5
Minton 159 ..... G6
Mistatim 139 ..... H3
Molanosa 248 ..... M4
Montmartre 534 ..... H5
Montreal Lake 306 ..... F1
Moose Jaw 32,581 ..... F5
Moosomin 2,449 ..... K5
Morse 435 ..... D5
Mortlach 278 ..... E5
Mossbank 444 ..... E6
Muenster 333 ..... F3
Naicam 739 ..... G3
Neilburg 369 ..... B3
Neudorf 394 ..... J5
Neuhorst 146 ..... E3
Nipawin 4,317 ..... H2
Nokomis 535 ..... F4
Norquay 520 ..... J4
North Battleford 13,158 ..... C3
North Portal 157 ..... J6
Odessa 203 ..... H5
Ogema 432 ..... G6
Ormiston 144 ..... F6
Osler 225 ..... E3
Outlook 1,687 ..... E4
Oxbow 1,221 ..... J6
Paddockwood 179 ..... F2
Pangman 208 ..... G6
Paradise Hill 395 ..... B2
Patuanak 136 ..... L3
Paynton 186 ..... B2
Pelican Narrows 212 ..... N3
Pelly 354 ..... K4
Pennant 216 ..... C5
Pense 356 ..... G5
Perdue 393 ..... D3
Pierceland 358 ..... K4
Pilot Butte 585 ..... G5
Pine House 528 ..... M3
Plenty 193 ..... C4
Plunkett 139 ..... F4
Ponteix 760 ..... D6
Porcupine Plain 935 ..... H3
Preeceville 1,170 ..... J4
Prelate 337 ..... B5
Prince Albert 28,631 ..... F2
Prud'homme 239 ..... F3
Punnichy 400 ..... G4
Qu'Appelle 551 ..... H5
Quill Lake 534 ..... G3
Quinton 189 ..... G4
Rabbit Lake 166 ..... D2
Radisson 432 ..... D3
Radville 1,008 ..... G6
Rama 163 ..... H4
Raymore 562 ..... G4
Redvers 843 ..... K6
Regina (cap.) 149,593 ..... G5
Regina Beach 488 ..... F5
Reserve 187 ..... J3
Rhein 284 ..... J4
Richmound 174 ..... B5
Ridgedale 147 ..... H2
Riverhurst 182 ..... E5
Rocanville 872 ..... K5
Rockglen 508 ..... F6
Rosetown 2,551 ..... D4
Rose Valley 534 ..... H3
Rosthern 1,604 ..... E3
Rouleau 380 ..... G5
Saint Benedict 164 ..... F3
Saint Brieux 362 ..... G3
Saint Gregor 144 ..... G3
Saint Louis 394 ..... F3
Saint Philips 636 ..... K4
Saint Walburg 718 ..... B2
Saltcoats 488 ..... J4
Sandy Bay 555 ..... N3
Saskatoon 133,750 ..... E3
Sceptre 204 ..... B5
Scott 209 ..... C3
Sedley 289 ..... H5
Semans 343 ..... G4
Shaunavon 2,183 ..... C6
Sheho 311 ..... H4
Shellbrook 1,098 ..... E2
Shell Lake 217 ..... D2
Simmie 174 ..... C6
Simpson 223 ..... F4
Sintaluta 213 ..... H5
Smeaton 275 ..... G2
Southey 604 ..... G5
Spalding 375 ..... G3
Speers 135 ..... D3
Spiritwood 841 ..... D2
Springside 474 ..... J4
Spy Hill 351 ..... K5
Squaw Rapids 1,024 ..... H2
Star City 539 ..... G3
Stenen 182 ..... J4
Stockholm 329 ..... J5
Stony Rapids 526 ..... M2
Storthoaks 152 ..... K6
Stoughton 705 ..... J6
Strasbourg 812 ..... G4
Sturgis 705 ..... J4
Swift Current 14,264 ..... D5
Tantallon 186 ..... K5
Theodore 463 ..... J4
Tisdale 3,026 ..... H3
Togo 197 ..... K4
Tompkins 274 ..... C5
Torquay 344 ..... H6
Tramping Lake 200 ..... B3
Tugaske 179 ..... E5
Turnor Lake 190 ..... L3
Turtleford 442 ..... B2
Unity 2,244 ..... B3
Uranium City 1,765 ..... L2
Val Marie 253 ..... D6
Vanguard 286 ..... D6
Vanscoy 276 ..... D4
Veregin 140 ..... K4
Vibank 305 ..... H5
Viscount 424 ..... F4
Vonda 311 ..... F3
Wadena 1,377 ..... H4
Wakaw 1,031 ..... F3
Waldeck 196 ..... D5
Waldheim 647 ..... E3
Wapella 453 ..... K5
Warman 1,117 ..... E3
Waskesiu Lake 176 ..... E2
Watrous 1,520 ..... F4
Watson 940 ..... G3
Wawota 619 ..... J6
Weekes 166 ..... J3
Weirdale 160 ..... F2
Weldon 272 ..... F2
Welwyn 180 ..... K5
Weyburn 8,892 ..... H6
White City 340 ..... G5
White Fox 380 ..... H2
Whitewood 1,072 ..... J5
Wilcox 175 ..... G5
Wilkie 1,604 ..... C3
Willow Bunch 417 ..... F6
Windthorst 215 ..... J5
Wiseton 201 ..... D4
Wishart 238 ..... H4
Wollaston Lake 263 ..... N2
Wolseley 883 ..... H5
Wymark 148 ..... D5
Wynyard 2,045 ..... G4
Yarbo 139 ..... K5
Yellow Creek 166 ..... F3
Yellow Grass 461 ..... H6
Yorkton 14,119 ..... J4
Young 495 ..... F4
Zealandia 150 ..... D4
Zenon Park 313 ..... H2

OTHER FEATURES

Allan (hills) E4
Amisk (lake) M4
Antelope (lake) C5
Antler (riv.) K6
Arm (riv.) F5
Assiniboine (riv.) J3
Athabasca (lake) L2
Bad (lake) C4
Bad (hills) C4
Basin (lake) F3
Batoche Nat'l Hist. Site E3
Battle (creek) B6
Battle (riv.) B3
Bear (hills) C4
Beaver (hills) H4
Beaver (riv.) L4
Beaverlodge (lake) L2
Big Muddy (lake) G6
Bigstick (lake) B5
Birch (lake) C2
Bitter (lake) B5
Black (lake) M2

Agriculture, Industry and Resources

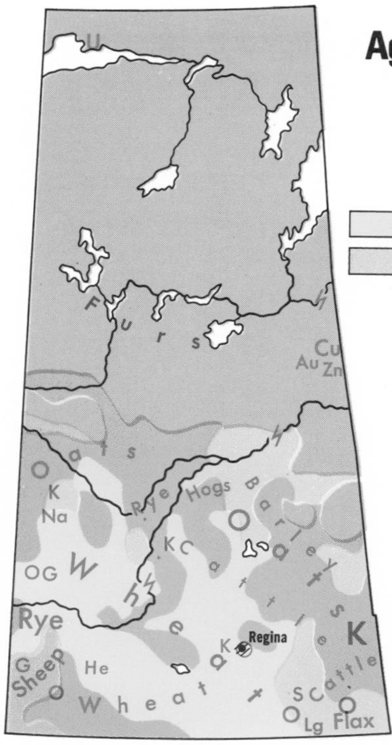
Furs
Cu
Au Zn
Oats
Rye
Hogs
Barley
Na
K
OG
Wheat
Cattle
Regina
Sheep
He
Lg
Flax

DOMINANT LAND USE

- Wheat
- Cereals (chiefly barley, oats)
- Cereals, Livestock
- Livestock
- Forests

MAJOR MINERAL OCCURRENCES

Au	Gold	Na	Salt
Cu	Copper	O	Petroleum
G	Natural Gas	S	Sulfur
He	Helium	U	Uranium
K	Potash	Zn	Zinc
Lg	Lignite		

Water Power
Major Industrial Areas

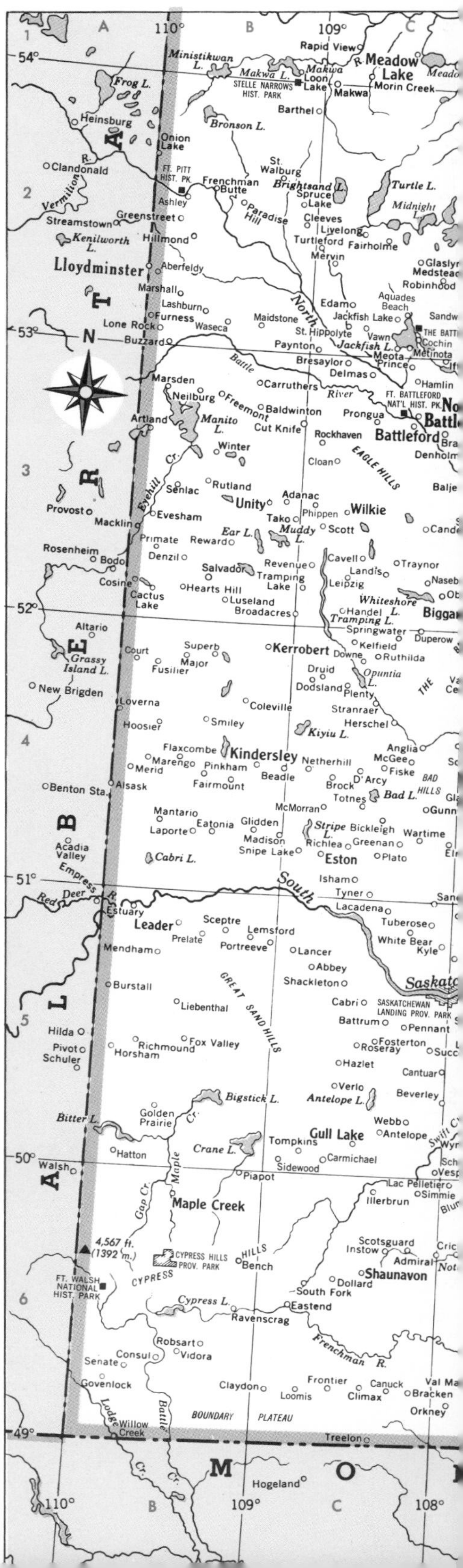
110°
109°
108°
54°
53°
52°
51°
50°
49°
Meadow Lake
Makwa L.
Loon Lake
STELLE NARROWS HIST. PARK
Frog L.
Lloydminster
North Battleford
Battleford
Kindersley
Leader
Maple Creek
Shaunavon
CYPRESS HILLS PROV. PARK
FT. WALSH NATIONAL HIST. PARK
Gull Lake
Kerrobert
Unity
Wilkie
ALBERTA
MONTANA
4,567 ft. (1392 m.)
Cypress L.
Frenchman R.
South Saskatchewan
GREAT SAND HILLS
Bigstick L.
Bitter L.
Crane L.
Eagle Hills

Boundary (plat.) B6
Brightsand (lake)............B2
Bronson (lake) B2
Buffalo Pound Prov. Park.....F5
Cabri (lake) B4
Cactus (hills)...................F5
Candle (lake)...................F2
Cannington Manon Hist. Park J6
Canoe (lake) L3
Carrot (riv.) J2
Chaplin (lake)...................E5
Chipman (riv.) M2
Chitek (lake) D2
Churchill (riv.) M3
Clearwater (riv.) L3
Cochrane (riv.) N2
Coteau (hills) D4
Cowan (lake) D2
Crane (lake).....................B5
Crean (lake) E1
Cree (lake) L3
Cree (riv.) M2
Cumberland (lake) J1
Cypress (hills)..................B6
Cypress (lake) B6
Cypress Hills Prov. Park.......B6
Danielson Prov. Park E4
Delaronde (lake)...............E1
Diefenbaker (lake).............E4
Doré (lake) L3
Douglas Prov. Park E4
Duck Lake Hist. Park..........E3
Duck Mountain Prov. Park ...K4
Eagle (hills) C3
Eaglehill (creek) D4
Ear (lake).........................B3
Echo Valley Prov. Park G5
Etomami (riv.) J3
Eyebrow (lake) E5
Eyehill (creek) B3
Fife (lake) E6
File (hills) H5
Fir (riv.) J2
Fond du Lac (riv.) M2
Forrest (lake) L3
Fort Battleford Nat'l Hist. Park C3
Fort Carlton Hist. Park E3
Fort Pitt Hist. Park B2
Fort Walsh Nat'l Hist. Park...A6
Foster (riv.) M3
Frenchman (riv.) C6
Frobisher (lake) L3
Gap (creek) B6
Gardiner (dam)..................D4
Geikie (riv.) M3
Good Spirit (lake) J4
Goodspirit Lake Prov. Park ...J4
Great Sand (hills) B5
Green (lake) D1
Greenwater Lake Prov. Park H3
Haultain (riv.) L3
Île-à-la-Crosse (lake) L3
Ironspring (creek) G3
Jackfish (lake)...................C2
Katepwa Prov. Park...........H5
Kingsmere (lake) E1
Kiyiu (lake).......................C4
Lac La Ronge Prov. Park....M3
Lanigan (creek).................F4
Last Mountain (lake)..........F4
Leaf (lake) J2
Leech (lake) J4
Lenore (lake) G3
Little Manitou (lake) F4
Lodge (creek) B6
Long (creek).....................H6
Loon (creek).....................G4
Makwa (lake) B1
Makwa (riv.) B1
Manito (lake) B3
Maple (creek)...................B5
McFarlane (riv.) L2
Meadow (lake) C1
Meadow Lake Prov. Park.....K4
Meeting (lake) D2
Midnight (lake) C2
Ministikwan (lake) B1
Missouri Coteau (hills) F5
Montreal (lake) F1
Moose (mt.) J6
Moose Jaw (riv.) G5
Moose Mountain (creek) J6
Moose Mountain Prov. Park J6
Mossy (riv.) H1
Muddy (lake) B3
Mudjatik (riv.) L3
Nipawin Prov. Park............G1
North Saskatchewan (riv.) D3
Notukeu (creek) D6
Oldman (riv.) L2
Old Wives (lake) E5
Opuntia (lake) C4
Overflowing (riv.) K2
Pasquia (hills) J2
Pasquia (riv.)...................K2
Pelican (lake) E5
Peter Pond (lake) L3
Pheasant (hills)................J5
Pine Lake Prov. Park.........E4
Pinto (creek) D6
Pipestone (creek) K6
Pipestone (riv.).................L2
Ponass (lkes)....................H3
Poplar (riv.).....................E6
Porcupine (hills) K3
Primrose (lake).................L3
Primrose Lake Air Weapons Range..............................L3
Prince Albert Nat'l Park.......E1
Qu'Appelle (riv.) J5
Quill (lkes) G4
Red Deer (riv.) A5
Red Deer (riv.) K3
Reindeer (lake) N3
Reindeer (riv.) M3
Riou (lake) M2
Rivers (lake) F6

AREA 251,699 sq. mi. (651,900 sq. km.)
POPULATION 957,025
CAPITAL Regina
LARGEST CITY Regina
HIGHEST POINT Cypress Hills 4,567 ft. (1,392 m.)
SETTLED IN 1774
ADMITTED TO CONFEDERATION 1905
PROVINCIAL FLOWER Prairie Lily

Ronge, La (lake) M3
Rowans Ravine Prov. Park ...F4
St. Victor Petroglyths Hist. Park E6
Saskatchewan (riv.) H2
Saskatchewan Landing Prov. Park C5
Saskeram (riv.) K2
Scott (lake).......................M2
Selwyn (lake) M2
Souris (riv.) H6
South Saskatchewan (riv.) C5
Steele Narrows Hist. Park....B2
Stripe (lake) C4
Sturgeon (riv.) E2
Swan (riv.) J3
Swift Current (creek).........D5
Tazin (lake) L2
The Battlefords Prov. Park ...C2
Thickwood (hills) D2
Thunder (hills)..................L4
Tobin (lake) H2
Torch (riv.) H2
Touchwood (hills) G4
Tramping (lake) C3
Trout (riv.) L3
Turtle (lake) C2
Twelvemile (lake) E6
Vermilion (hills) E5
Wapawekka (hills)............M4
Waskana (creek) G5
Waskesiu (lake) E2
Wathaman (riv.) M3
Weed (hills) J5
White Fox (riv.) G2
White Gull (creek) G2
Whiteshore (lake) C3
Whiteswan (lkes) F1
William (riv.) L2
Willow Bunch (lake) F6
Witchekan (lake) D2
Wollaston (lake) N2
Wood (mt.) E6
Wood (riv.) E6
Wood Mountain Hist. Park ...E6

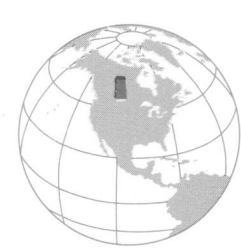

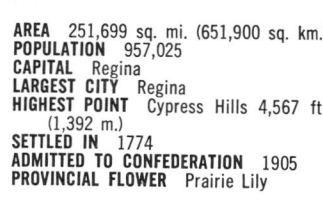

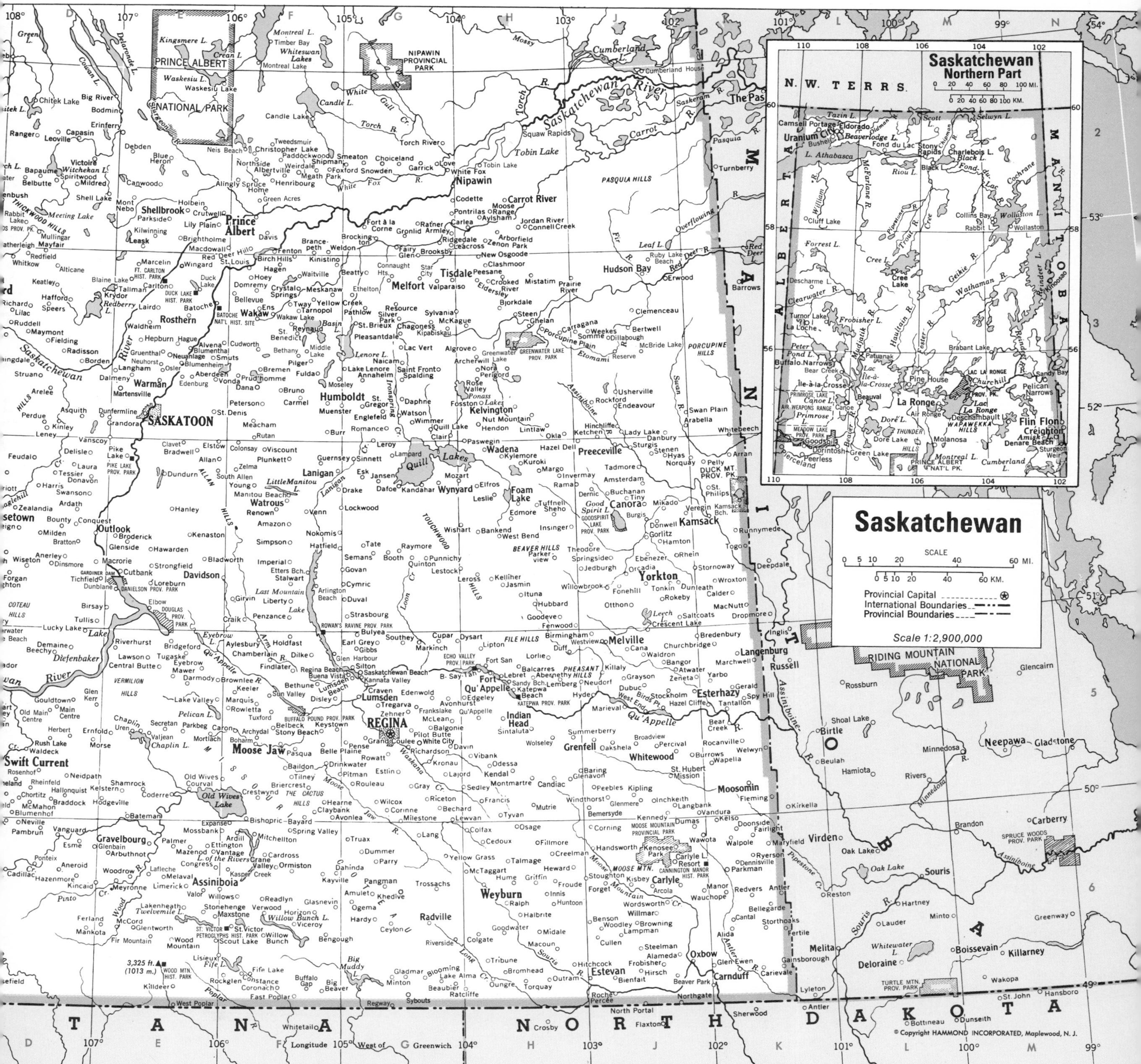

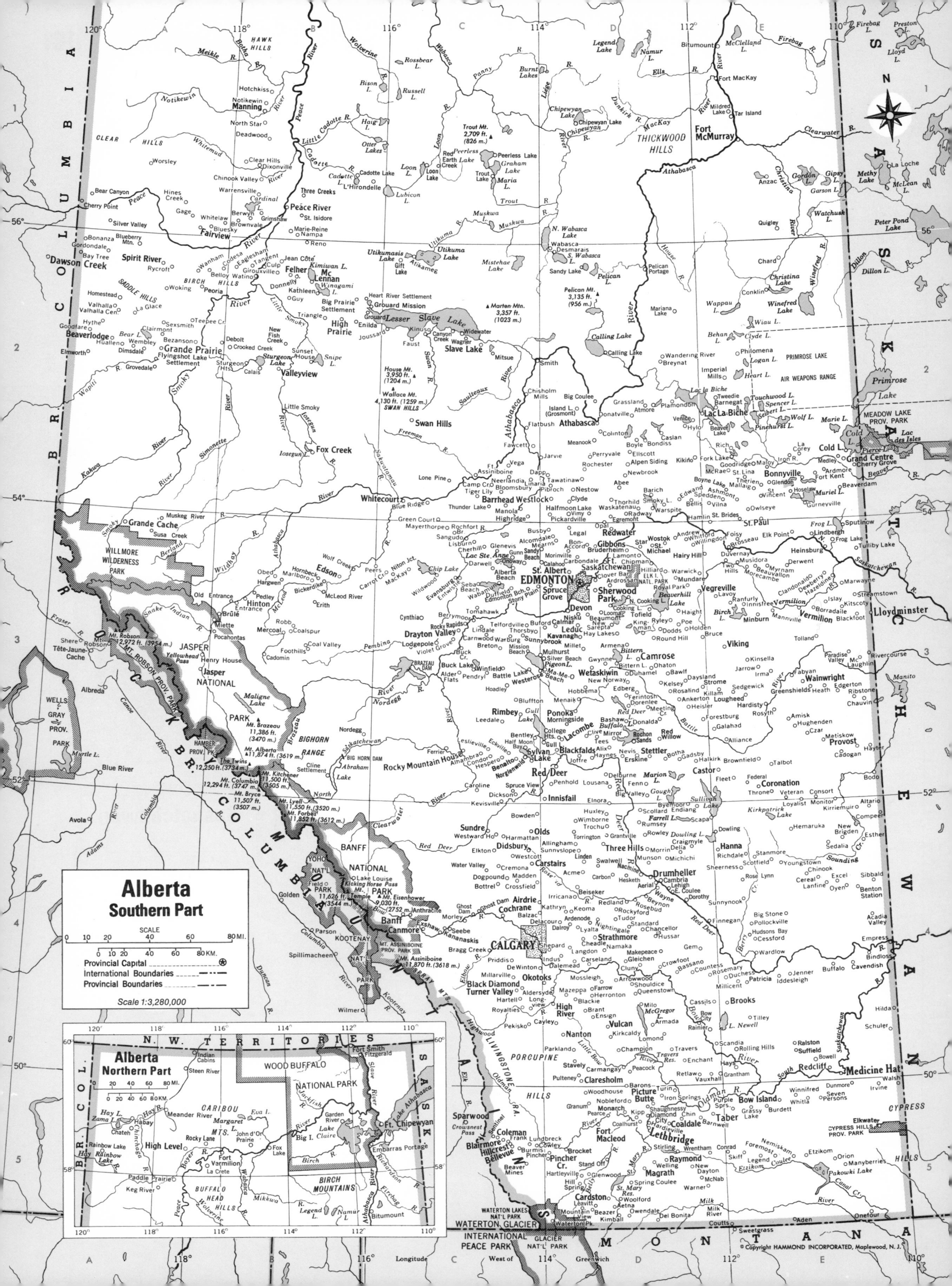

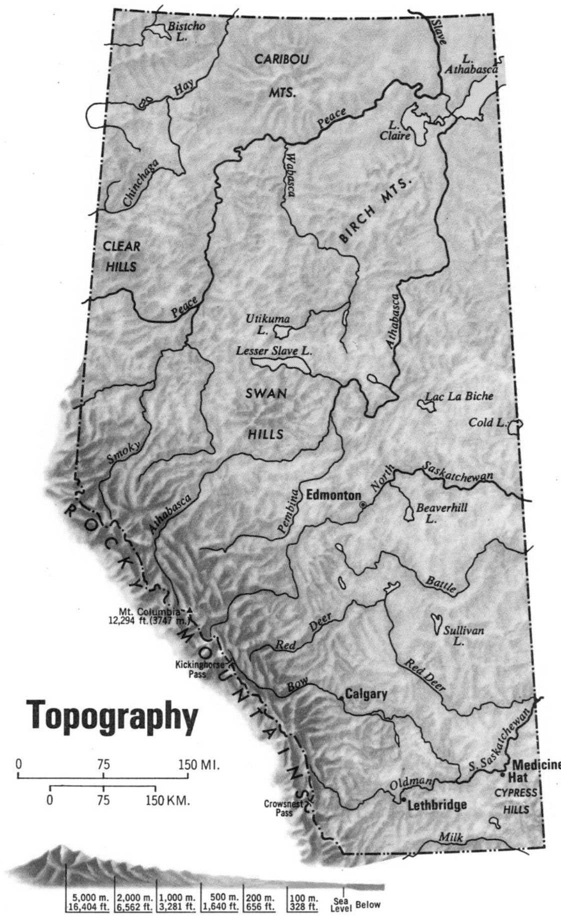
Bistcho L.
CARIBOU MTS.
Hay
L. Athabasca
Slave
Peace
L. Claire
Chinchaga
Wabasca
BIRCH MTS.
CLEAR HILLS
Peace
Utikuma L.
Lesser Slave L.
Athabasca
SWAN HILLS
Lac La Biche
Cold L.
Smoky
North Saskatchewan
Edmonton
Pembina
Beaverhill L.
Athabasca
ROCKY MOUNTAINS
Battle
Mt. Columbia 12,294 ft. (3747 m.)
Sullivan L.
Red Deer
Kickinghorse Pass
Bow
Calgary
Red Deer
S. Saskatchewan
Medicine Hat
Oldman
CYPRESS HILLS
Crowsnest Pass
Lethbridge
Milk
0 75 150 MI.
0 75 150 KM.
5,000 m. 16,404 ft.
2,000 m. 6,562 ft.
1,000 m. 3,281 ft.
500 m. 1,640 ft.
200 m. 656 ft.
100 m. 328 ft.
Sea Level
Below

Topography

AREA 255,285 sq. mi. (661,185 sq. km.)
POPULATION 2,207,856
CAPITAL Edmonton
LARGEST CITY Edmonton
HIGHEST POINT Mt. Columbia 12,294 ft. (3,747 m.)
SETTLED IN 1861
ADMITTED TO CONFEDERATION 1905
PROVINCIAL FLOWER Wild Rose

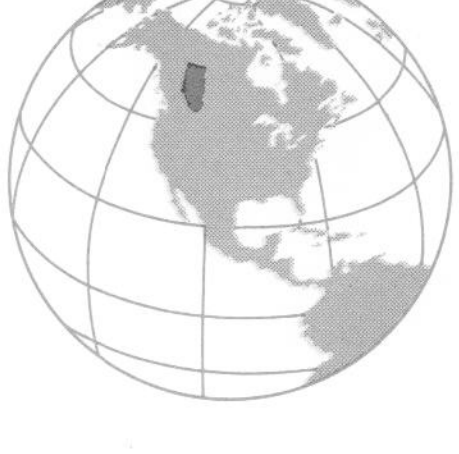

CITIES and TOWNS

Acme 351 D4
Airdrie 1,408 C4
Alberta Beach 432 C3
Alix 669 D3
Alliance 228 E3
Andrew 486 D3
Ardmore 238 E2
Athabasca 1,759 D2
Banff 3,410 C4
Barons 283 D4
Barrhead 2,944 C2
Bashaw 773 D3
Bassano 999 D4
Beaumont 851 D3
Beaverlodge 1,332 A2
Beiseker 486 D4
Bellevue 1,186 C5
Bentley 730 C3
Berwyn 433 B1
Big Valley 344 D3
Black Diamond 1,242 C4
Blackfalds 1,024 D3
Blackie 223 D4
Blairmore 2,321 C5
Bon Accord 882 D3
Bonnyville 2,885 E2
Bowden 661 C4
Bow Island 1,296 E5
Boyle 576 D2
Bragg Creek 384 C4
Breton 424 C3
Brocket 405 D5
Brooks 6,339 E4
Bruce 93 E3
Bruderheim 484 D3
Burdett 214 E5
Calgary 469,917 C4
Calmar 872 D3
Camrose 10,104 D3
Canmore 1,927 C4
Carbon 435 D4
Cardston 3,043 D5
Carmangay 263 D4
Caroline 385 C3
Carstairs 1,059 D4
Castor 1,207 D3
Cereal 231 E4
Champion 300 D4
Chateh 400 A5
Chauvin 296 E3
Chipman 296 D3
Clairmont 599 A2
Claresholm 3,276 D4
Clive 254 D3
Clyde 312 D2
Coaldale 3,654 D5
Coalhurst 473 D5
Cochrane 1,450 C4
Cold Lake 1,317 E2
Coleman 1,543 C5
College Heights 332 D3
Consort 609 E3
Cooking Lake 237 D3
Coronation 1,198 E3
Coutts 387 D5
Cowley 284 C5
Cremona 227 C4
Crossfield 777 C4
Daysland 615 D3
Delburne 417 D3
Delia 232 D4
Devon 2,786 D3
Didsbury 2,153 C4
Donnelly 278 B2
Drayton Valley 4,303 C3
Drumheller 6,154 D4
Duchess 343 E4
Eaglesham 229 B2
East Coulée 261 D4
Eckville 774 C3
Edgerton 324 E3
Edmonton (cap.) 461,361 D3
Edmonton Beach 243 C3
Edson 4,038 B3
Elk Point 807 E3
Elkton 226 C4
Elnora 211 D3
Empress 238 E4
Entwistle 380 C3
Erskine 234 D3
Evansburg 671 C3
Exshaw 389 C4
Fairview 2,248 A1
Falher 1,120 B2
Faust 298 C2
Foremost 534 E5
Forestburg 808 E3
Fort Assiniboine 185 C2
Fort Chipewyan 1,179 C5
Fort Macleod 3,067 D5
Fort McMurray 15,424 E1
Fort Saskatchewan 8,304 D3
Fort Vermilion 729 B5
Fox Creek 1,625 B2
Fox Lake 482 B5
Gibbons 1,093 D3
Gift Lake 432 C2
Girouxville 303 B2
Gleichen 339 D4
Glendon 370 E2
Grand Centre 2,780 E2
Grande Cache 4,116 A3
Grande Prairie 17,626 A2
Granum 413 D5
Grimshaw 1,665 B1
Grouard Mission 213 C2
Gunn 223 C3
Hanna 2,627 E4
Hardieville 546 D5
Hardisty 534 E3
Hay Lakes 236 D3
High Level 1,562 A5
High Prairie 2,281 B2
High River 3,598 D4
Hillcrest 653 C5
Hines Creek 503 A1
Hinton 6,731 B3
Holden 393 D3
Hughenden 236 E3
Hythe 460 A2
Innisfail 2,897 D3
Innisfree 265 E3
Irma 428 E3
Irricana 264 D4
Irvine 221 E5
Jasper 3,404 B3
John d'Or Prairie 326 B5
Joussard 270 B2
Killam 887 E3
Kinuso 305 C2
Kitscoty 391 E3
Lac La Biche 1,954 E2
Lacombe 3,888 D3
La Crete 349 B5
Lake Louise 140 B4
Lamont 997 D3
Leduc 8,576 D3
Legal 874 D3
Lethbridge 46,752 D5
Linden 296 D4
Lloydminster 5,818 E3
Lougheed 213 E3
Magrath 1,315 D5
Mallaig 339 E2
Manning 1,050 B1
Mannville 681 E3
Marwayne 376 E3
Mayerthorpe 1,018 C3
McLennan 1,133 B2
Medicine Hat 32,811 E4
Midlandvale 449 D4
Milk River 814 D5
Millet 762 D3
Mirror 335 D3
Morinville 2,097 D3
Morrin 230 D4
Mundare 555 D3
Myrnam 396 E3
Nacmine 330 D4
Nampa 286 B1
Nanton 1,152 D4
New Norway 276 D3
New Sarepta 237 D3
Nobleford 417 D5
Okotoks 1,795 C4
Olds 3,658 D4
Onoway 444 C3
Oyen 962 E4
Peace River 4,840 B1
Penhold 773 D3
Picture Butte 1,164 D5
Pincher Creek 3,448 D5
Plamondon 228 D2
Pollockville 29 E4
Ponoka 4,636 D3
Provost 1,532 E3
Rainbow Lake 434 A5
Ralston 465 E4
Raymond 2,290 D5
Redcliff 3,006 E4
Red Deer 32,184 D3
Redwater 1,493 D3
Rimbey 1,452 C3
Rockyford 276 D4
Rocky Mountain House 3,432 C3
Rosemary 273 E4
Rycroft 533 A2
Ryley 432 D3
Saint Albert 24,129 D3
Saint Paul 4,337 E3
Sangudo 409 C3
Sedgewick 825 E3
Sexsmith 770 A2
Shaughnessy 299 D5
Sherwood Park 26,534 D3
Slave Lake 3,561 C2
Smith 353 D2
Smoky Lake 925 D2
Spirit River 1,020 A2
Spruce Grove 6,907 D3
Standard 305 D4
Stavely 432 D4
Stettler 4,182 D3
Stirling 543 D5
Stony Plain 2,717 C3
Strathmore 1,561 D4
Strome 227 E3
Sundre 1,099 C4
Swan Hills 2,012 C2
Sylvan Lake 1,837 C3
Taber 5,296 E5
Thorhild 533 D2
Thorsby 657 C3
Three Hills 1,564 D4
Tilley 329 E4
Tofield 1,120 D3
Trochu 752 D4
Turner Valley 1,132 C4
Two Hills 943 E3
Valleyview 1,716 B2
Vauxhall 954 D4
Vegreville 4,158 E3
Vermilion 3,182 E3
Veteran 279 E3
Viking 1,217 E3
Vilna 348 E2
Vulcan 1,442 D4
Wabamun 581 C3
Wabasca 528 D2
Wainwright 3,890 E3
Wanham 225 A2
Warburg 408 C3
Warner 434 D5
Waskatenau 271 D2
Wayne 255 D4
Wembley 507 A2
Westlock 3,721 C2
Wetaskiwin 6,754 D3
Whitecourt 3,878 C2
Wildwood 360 C3
Willingdon 308 E3
Youngstown 272 E4

OTHER FEATURES

Abraham (lake) B3
Alberta (mt.) B3
Assiniboine (mt.) C4
Athabasca (lake) C5
Athabasca (riv.) D1
Banff Nat'l Park 3,849 B4
Battle (riv.) D3
Bear (lake) A2
Beaver (riv.) E2
Beaverhill (lake) D3
Behan (lake) E2
Belly (riv.) D5
Berland (riv.) A3
Berry (creek) E4
Biche (lake) E2
Big (isl.) B5
Big Horn (dam) B3
Bighorn (range) B3
Birch (hills) A2
Birch (lake) E3
Birch (mts.) B5
Birch (riv.) B5
Bison (lake) B1
Bittern (lake) D3
Botha (riv.) B1
Bow (riv.) D4
Boyer (riv.) A5
Brazeau (dam) C3
Brazeau (mt.) B3
Brazeau (riv.) B3
Buffalo (lake) D3
Buffalo Head (hills) B5
Burnt (lkes) C1
Cadotte (lake) B1
Cadotte (riv.) B1
Calling (lake) D2
Canal (creek) E5
Cardinal (lake) B1
Caribou (mts.) B5
Chinchaga (riv.) A5
Chip (lake) C3
Chipewyan (lake) D1
Chipewyan (riv.) D1
Christina (lake) E2
Christina (riv.) E1
Claire (lake) B5
Clear (hills) A1
Clearwater (riv.) C4
Clearwater (riv.) E1
Clyde (lake) E2
Cold (lake) E2
Columbia (mt.) B3
Crowsnest (pass) C5
Cypress (hills) E5
Cypress Hills Prov. Park E5
Dillon (riv.) E2
Dowling (lake) D4
Dunkirk (riv.) D1
Eisenhower (mt.) C4
Elbow (riv.) C4
Elk Island Nat'l Park 33 D3
Ells (riv.) D1
Etzikom Coulee (riv.) E5
Eva (lake) B5
Farrell (lake) D4
Firebag (riv.) E1
Forbes (mt.) B4
Freeman (riv.) C2
Frog (lake) E3
Garson (lake) E1
Gipsy (lake) E1
Gordon (lake) E1
Gough (lake) D3
Graham (lake) C1
Gull (lake) C3
Haig (lake) B1
Hawk (hills) B1
Hay (lake) A5
Hay (riv.) A5
Heart (lake) E2
Highwood (riv.) C4
House (mt.) C2
House (riv.) D2
Iosegun (lake) B2
Iosegun (riv.) B2
Jackfish (riv.) B5
Jasper Nat'l Park 3,602 A3
Kakwa (riv.) A2
Kickinghorse (pass) B4
Kimiwan (lake) B2
Kirkpatrick (lake) E4
Kitchener (mt.) B3
Legend (lake) D1
Lesser Slave (lake) C2
Liége (riv.) D1
Little Bow (riv.) D4
Little Cadotte (riv.) B1
Little Smoky (riv.) B2
Livingstone (range) C4
Logan (lake) E2
Loon (lake) C1
Loon (riv.) C1
Lubicon (lake) C1
Lyell (mt.) B4
MacKay (riv.) D1
Maligne (lake) B3
Margaret (lake) B5
Marie (lake) E2
Marion (lake) D3
Marten (mt.) C2
McClelland (lake) E1
McGregor (lake) D4
McLeod (riv.) B3
Meikle (riv.) A1
Mikkwa (riv.) B5
Milk (riv.) D5
Mistehae (lake) C2
Muriel (lake) E2
Muskwa (lake) C1
Muskwa (riv.) C1
Namur (lake) D1
Newell (lake) E4
Nordegg (riv.) C3
North Saskatchewan (riv.) E3
North Wabasca (lake) D1
Notikewin (riv.) A1
Oldman (riv.) D5
Otter (lkes) B1
Pakowki (lake) E5
Panny (riv.) C1
Peace (riv.) B1
Peerless (lake) C1
Pelican (lake) D2
Pelican (mt.) D2
Pelican (mts.) D2
Pembina (riv.) C3
Pigeon (lake) D3
Pinehurst (lake) E2
Porcupine (hills) C4
Primrose (lake) E2
Rainbow (lake) A5
Red Deer (lake) D3
Red Deer (riv.) D4
Richardson (riv.) C5
Rocky (mts.) C4
Rosebud (riv.) D4
Rossbear (lake) C1
Russell (lake) C1
Saddle (hills) A2
Sainte Anne (lake) C3
Saint Mary (res.) D5
Saint Mary (riv.) D5
Sakwatamau (riv.) C2
Saulteaux (riv.) C2
Seibert (lake) E2
Simonette (riv.) A2
Slave (riv.) C5
Smoky (riv.) A2
Snake Indian (riv.) A3
Snipe (lake) B2
Sounding (creek) E4
South Saskatchewan (riv.) E4
South Wabasca (lake) D2
Spencer (lake) E2
Spray (mts.) C4
Sturgeon (lake) B2
Sullivan (lake) D3
Swan (hills) C2
Swan (riv.) C2
Temple (mt.) B4
The Twins (mt.) B3
Thickwood (hills) D1
Touchwood (lake) E2
Travers (res.) D4
Trout (mt.) C1
Trout (riv.) C1
Utikuma (lake) C2
Utikuma (riv.) C1
Utikumasis (lake) C2
Vermilion (riv.) E3
Wabasca (riv.) C1
Wallace (mt.) C2
Wapiti (riv.) A2
Wappau (lake) E2
Watchusk (lake) E1
Waterton-Glacier Int'l Peace Park 194 C5
Waterton Lakes Nat'l Park 194 C5
Whitemud (riv.) A1
Wiau (lake) E2
Wildhay (riv.) B3
Willmore Wilderness Prov. Park A3
Winagami (lake) B2
Winefred (lake) E2
Winefred (riv.) E2
Wolf (lake) E2
Wolverine (riv.) B1
Wood Buffalo Nat'l Park 199 B5
Yellowhead (pass) A3
Zama (lake) A5

Agriculture, Industry and Resources

DOMINANT LAND USE

- Wheat
- Cereals (chiefly barley, oats)
- Cereals, Livestock
- Dairy
- Pasture Livestock
- Range Livestock
- Forests
- Nonagricultural Land

MAJOR MINERAL OCCURRENCES

- C Coal
- G Natural Gas
- Na Salt
- O Petroleum
- S Sulfur

- Water Power
- Major Industrial Areas

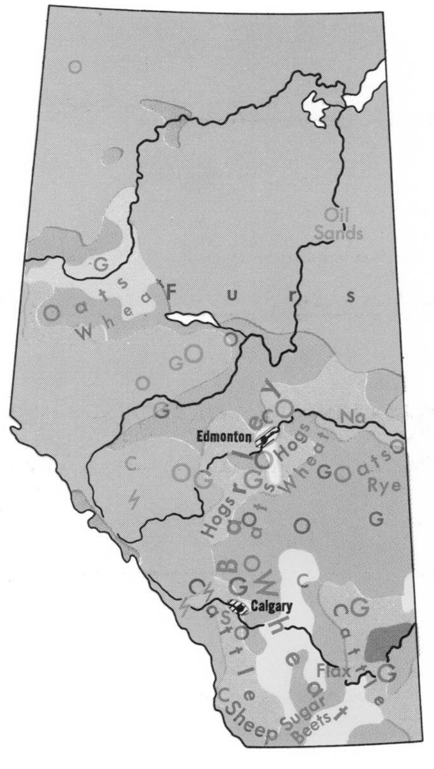
Oil Sands
Furs
Oats
Wheat
Edmonton
Hogs
Wheat
Oats
Rye
Na
Calgary
Cattle
Sheep
Sugar Beets
Flax

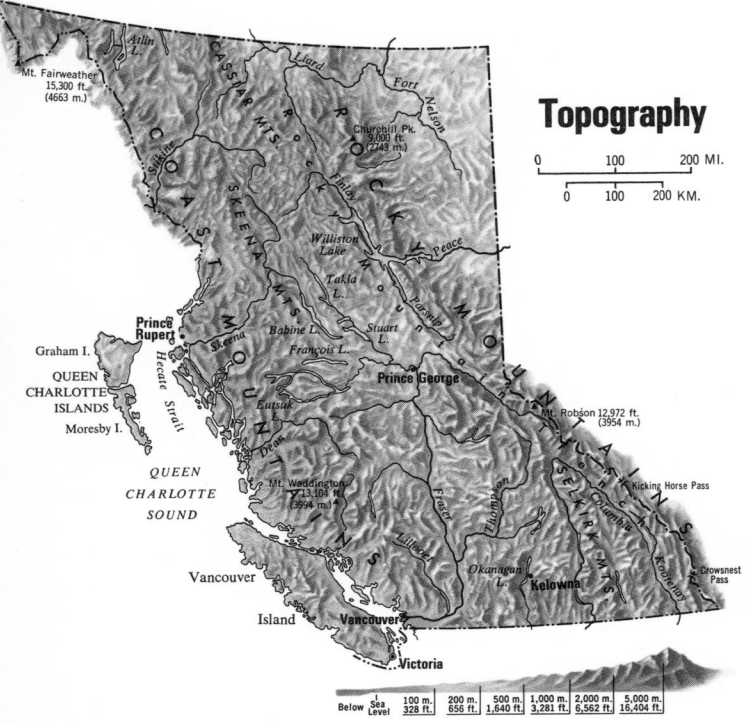

Topography

0   100   200 MI.

0   100   200 KM.

Below Sea Level	100 m. 328 ft.	200 m. 656 ft.	500 m. 1,640 ft.	1,000 m. 3,281 ft.	2,000 m. 6,562 ft.	5,000 m. 16,404 ft.

CITIES and TOWNS

Abbotsford 9,507 ....L3
Alert Bay 605 ....D5
Armstrong 2,260 ....H5
Ashcroft 2,032 ....G5
Barrière 835 ....H4
Bear Lake 431 ....F3
Big Eddy 833 ....H4
Blueberry Creek 660 ....J5
Blue River 425 ....H4
Boston Bar 602 ....G5
Brackendale 1,410 ....F5
Britannia Beach 431 ....K2
Burnaby● 131,599 ....K3
Burns Lake 1,433 ....D3
Cache Creek 1,050 ....G5
Campbell River 11,781● E5
Canal Flats 832 ....K5
Cassiar 801 ....K2
Castlegar 6,255 ....J5

Central Saanich● 7,413 ......K3
Chase 1,425 ....H5
Chemainus 2,129 ....J3
Cherry Creek 496 ....G5
Chetwynd 1,487 ....G2
Chilliwack 8,634 ....M3
Clearbrook 4,849 ....L3
Clearwater 766 ....G4
Clinton 808 ....G4
Coldstream● 4,995 ....H5
Comox 5,359 ....H2
Coquitlam● 55,464 ....K3
Courtenay 7,733 ....E5
Cranbrook 13,510 ....K5
Creston 3,552 ....J5
Crofton 1,143 ....J3
Cultus Lake 470 ....M3
Cumberland 1,697 ....E5
Dawson Creek 10,528 ....G2
Delta● 64,492 ....K3
Duncan 4,106 ....J3
East Kelowna 607 ....H5
Edgewater 424 ....J5
Elkford 1,873 ....K5

Enderby 1,482 ....H5
Erickson 1,008 ....J5
Errington 466 ....J3
Falkland 456 ....H5
Fernie 4,608 ....K5
Fort Fraser 443 ....E3
Fort Langley 2,072 ....L3
Fort Nelson 2,916 ....M2
Fort Saint James 2,110 ....E3
Fort Saint John 8,947 ....G2
Fraser Lake 1,430 ....E3
Fraser Mills● 663 ....K3
Fruitvale 1,481 ....J5
Gabriola 1,169 ....J3
Galiano 480 ....K3
Ganges 444 ....K3
Gibsons 2,074 ....K3
Gillies Bay 560 ....H2
Golden 3,282 ....J4
Gold River 1,942 ....D5
Grand Forks 3,096 ....H6
Granisle 1,210 ....D3
Greenwood 931 ....H5

Haney 2,441 ....L3
Harrison Hot Springs 572 ..M3
Hatzic 1,140 ....L3
Hedley 480 ....G5
Holberg 421 ....C5
Honeymoon Bay 501 ....J3
Hope 2,963 ....M3
Hornby Island 411 ....H2
Houston 1,266 ....D3
Hudson Hope 981 ....F2
Invermere 1,194 ....J5
Kaleden 789 ....H5
Kamloops 58,311● G5
Kaslo 756 ....J5
Kelowna 51,955 ....H5
Kent● 2,924 ....M3
Keremeos 702 ....H5
Kimberley 7,111 ....K5
Kitimat 11,791 ....C3
Ladysmith 4,004 ....J3
Lake Cowichan 2,369 ....J3
Langley 10,123 ....L3
Lantzville 813 ....J3
Lillooet 2,218 ....G5
Lion's Bay 785 ....K3
Logan Lake 1,388 ....G5
Lumby 1,081 ....H5
Lytton 468 ....G5
Mackenzie● 5,338 ....F2
Mackenzie 5,266 ....F2
Maple Bay 578 ....K3
Maple Ridge● 29,462 ....L3
Masset 1,563 ....B3
Matsqui● 31,178 ....L3
Mayne 480 ....K3
McBride 619 ....G3
Merritt 5,680 ....G5
Metchosin 517 ....K4
Mica Creek 738 ....H4
Midway 589 ....H6
Mill Bay 566 ....K3
Mission● 14,997 ....L3
Mission City 8,278 ....L3
Montrose 1,197 ....J5
Nakusp 1,416 ....J5
Nanaimo 40,336 ....J3
Naramata 741 ....H5
Nelson 9,235 ....J5
New Denver 668 ....J5
New Hazelton 742 ....D2
New Westminster 33,393 ..L3
Nootka D5
North Cowichan 15,956 ..J3
North Pender Island 709 ..K3
North Saanich● 4,697 ....K3
North Vancouver● 63,471 ..K3
Oak Bay● 17,658 ....K4
Ocean Falls 985 ....D4
Okanagan Falls 874 ....H5
Okanagan Landing 825 ..H5
Old Barkerville 9 ....G4
Oliver 1,641 ....H5
One Hundred Mile House 1,584 ....G4
Osoyoos 2,100 ....H5
Oyama 460 ....H5
Parksville 3,187 ....J3
Peachland 2,225● G5
Penticton 21,344 ....H5
Pitt Meadows● 4,689 ....L3
Port Alberni 19,585 ....H3

Port Alice 1,497 ....D5
Port Clements 409 ....B3
Port Coquitlam 23,926 ..L3
Port Edward 1,189 ....B3
Port Hammond 1,353 ....L3
Port Hardy● 3,653 ....D5
Port McNeill 1,480 ....D5
Port Moody 11,649 ....L3
Pouce-Coupé 776 ....G2
Powell River● 13,694 ....E5
Prince George 59,929 ....F3
Prince Rupert 14,754 ....B3
Princeton 3,132 ....G5
Qualicum Beach 1,724 ....G5
Queen Charlotte 727 ....A3
Quesnel 7,637 ....F4
Revelstoke 4,615 ....J5
Richmond● 80,034 ....K3
Roberts Creek 711 ....J3
Robson 1,044 ....J5
Rossland 3,716 ....H6
Royston 635 ....H2
Rutland 1,283 ....H5
Saanich● 73,383 ....K3
Salmo 1,089 ....J5
Salmon Arm● 9,391 ....H5
Salmon Arm 1,876 ....H5
Saltair 1,339 ....J3
Sandspit 598 ....B3
Sardis 1,430 ....M3
Saseenos 772 ....J3
Savona 609 ....G5
Sechelt 822 ....J2
Shoreacres 426 ....J5
Sicamous 809 ....H5
Sidney 6,732 ....K3
Slocan Park 446 ....J5
Smithers 3,783 ....D3
Sointula 546 ....D5
Sooke 650 ....J4
South Hazelton 578 ....D2
South Wellington 606 ....J3
Spallumcheen 3,378 ....H5
Sparwood 3,081 ....K5
Sproat Lake 408 ....H3
Squamish 1,611 ....F5
Stewart● 1,382 ....C2
Summerland● 6,724 ....G5
Surrey● 116,497 ....K3
Tahsis 1,663 ....D5
Taylor 649 ....G2
Telkwa 967 ....D3
Terrace● 10,251 ....C3
Terrace 7,576 ....C3
Thornhill 3,938 ....C3
Tofino 612 ....E5
Trail 9,976 ....J6
Ucluelet 1,180 ....E6
Union Bay 513 ....H2
Valemount 878 ....H4
Vananda 407 ....E5
Vancouver 410,188 ....K3
Vancouver (Greater)● 1,085,242 ....K3
Vanderhoof 1,990 ....E3
Vavenby 845 ....H4
Vernon 17,546 ....H5
Victoria (cap.) 62,551 ....K4
Victoria‡ 230,592 ....K4
Warfield 1,957 ....J5
Wasa 403 ....K5
Westbank 1,067 ....H5
West Vancouver● 37,144 ..K3
Westwold 451 ....G5
Whistler 531 ....F5
White Rock 12,497 ....K3
Williams Lake 6,199 ....F4
Wilson Creek 417 ....J2
Windermere 635 ....K5
Winfield 1,033 ....H5
Winlaw 444 ....J5
Woss Lake 408 ....D5
Wynndel 528 ....J5
Yarrow 1,070 ....M3
Youbou 1,064 ....J3

OTHER FEATURES

Adams (lake) H4
Adams (riv.) H4
Alberni (inlet) H3
Alsek (riv.) H1
Aristazabal (isl.) C4
Assiniboine (mt.) K5
Atlin (lake) J1
Azure (lake) G4
Babine (lake) E3
Babine (riv.) D2
Banks (isl.) B3
Barkley (sound) E6
Beale (cape) E6
Bear (lake) D2
Beatton (riv.) G1
Bella Coola (riv.) D4
Bell-Irving (riv.) C2
Bennett, W.A.C. (dam) ..F2
Birkenhead Lake Prov. Park F5
Bowron Lake Prov. Park ..G3
Bowser (lake) C2
Brooks (pen.) D5
Browning Entrance (str.) ..B3
Bryce (mt.) J4
Bugaboo Glacier Prov. Park J5
Bulkley (riv.) D2
Burke (chan.) D4
Burnaby (isl.) B4
Bute (inlet) E5
Caamaño (sound) C4
Calvert (isl.) C4
Canim (lake) G4
Canoe (riv.) H4
Cariboo (mts.) G3
Carpenter (lake) F5
Carp Lake Prov. Park F3
Cassiar (mts.) K2
Castle (mt.) A2
Cathedral Prov. Park H5

Charlotte (lake) E4
Chatham (sound) B3
Chehalis L3
Chilcotin (riv.) E4
Chilko (lake) F4
Chilko (riv.) E4
Chilkoot (pass) J1
Chuchi (lake) E2
Churchill (peak) L2
Clayoquot (sound) D5
Clearwater (lake) G4
Clearwater (riv.) G4
Coast (mts.) D3
Columbia (lake) K5
Columbia (mt.) J4
Columbia (riv.) H5
Cook (cape) C5
Cowichan (lake) J3
Crowsnest (pass) K5
Cypress Prov. Park K3
Dean (chan.) D4
Dean (riv.) D4
Dease (lake) K2
Dease (riv.) K2
Devils Thumb (mt.) A1
Dixon Entrance (chan.) ..A3
Douglas (chan.) C3
Duncan (riv.) J5
Dundas (isl.) B3
Elk (riv.) K5
Elk Lakes Prov. Park K5
Eutsuk (lake) D3
Fairweather (mt.) H1

Finlay (riv.) E1
Fitzhugh (sound) D4
Flathead (riv.) K6
Flores (isl.) D5
Fontas (riv.) M2
Forbes (mt.) J4
Fort Nelson (riv.) M2
François (lake) D3
Fraser (lake) E3
Fraser (riv.) F4
Fraser Reach (chan.) C3
Galiano (isl.) K3
Gardner (canal) C3
Garibaldi Prov. Park F5
Georgia (str.) J3
Germansen (lake) E2
Gil (isl.) C3
Glacier Nat'l Park J4
Golden Ears Prov. Park ..L3
Gordon (riv.) H3
Graham (isl.) A3
Graham Reach (chan.) ..C3
Grenville (chan.) C3
Halfway (riv.) H4
Hamber Prov. Park H4
Harrison (lake) M2
Hawkesbury (isl.) C3
Hazelton (mts.) C2
Hecate (str.) B3
Hobson (lake) H4
Homathko (riv.) E4
Horsefly (lake) G4
Howe (sound) K2

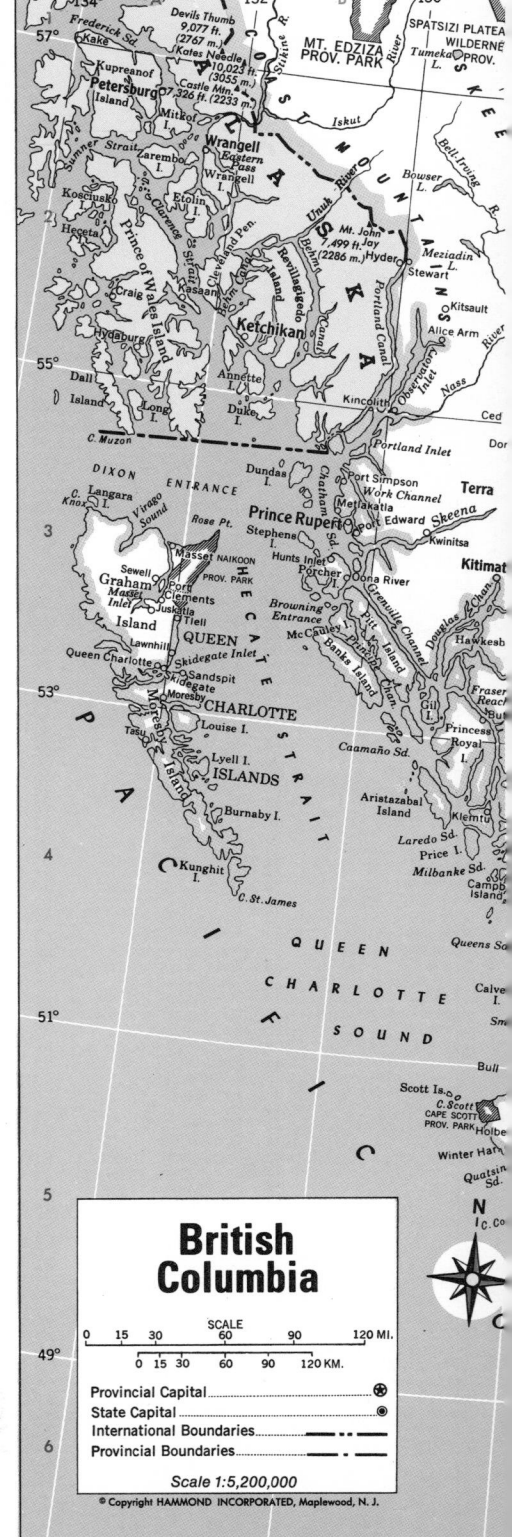

Agriculture, Industry and Resources

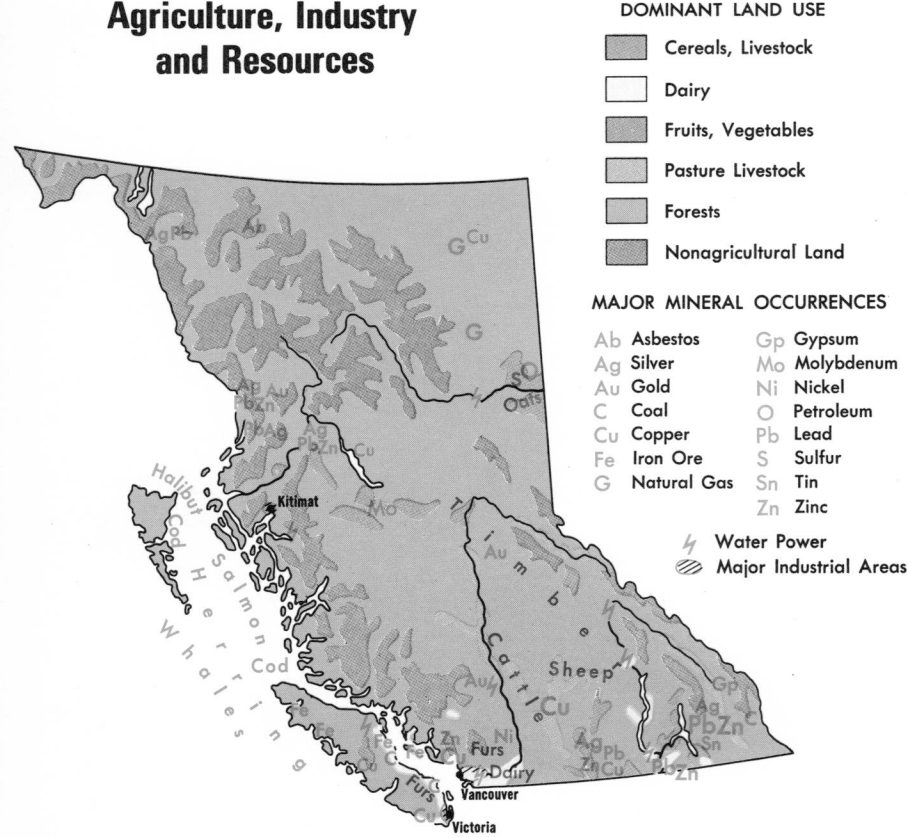

DOMINANT LAND USE

- Cereals, Livestock
- Dairy
- Fruits, Vegetables
- Pasture Livestock
- Forests
- Nonagricultural Land

MAJOR MINERAL OCCURRENCES

Ab	Asbestos	Gp	Gypsum
Ag	Silver	Mo	Molybdenum
Au	Gold	Ni	Nickel
C	Coal	O	Petroleum
Cu	Copper	Pb	Lead
Fe	Iron Ore	S	Sulfur
G	Natural Gas	Sn	Tin
		Zn	Zinc

⚡ Water Power

〰 Major Industrial Areas

British Columbia

SCALE

0   15   30   60   90   120 MI.

0   15 30   60   90   120 KM.

Provincial Capital ....⊛
State Capital ....◉
International Boundaries ..._ _ _ _
Provincial Boundaries ......_ · _ · _

Scale 1:5,200,000

© Copyright HAMMOND INCORPORATED, Maplewood, N.J.

Hunter (isl.) C4
Inklin (riv.) J2
Inzana (lake) E3
Isaac (lake) G3
Iskut (riv.) B2
Jervis (inlet) E5
John Jay (mt.) B2
Johnstone (str.) D5
Juan de Fuca (str.) J4
Kates Needle (mt.) A1
Kechika (riv.) L2
Kenney (dam) E3
Kettle (riv.) H5
Kicking Horse (pass) J4
King (isl.) D4
Kiskatinaw (riv.) G2
Klinaklini (riv.) E4
Kloch (lake) E2
Knight (inlet) E5
Knox (cape) A3
Kokanee Glacier Prov. Park J5
Koocanusa (lake) K6
Kootenay (lake) J5
Kootenay (riv.) K5
Kootenay Nat'l Park J4
Kotcho (lake) M2
Kotcho (riv.) M2
Kunghit (isl.) B4
Kyuquot (sound) D5
Langara (isl.) A3
Laredo (sound) C4
Liard (riv.) L2
Lillooet (riv.) F5
Louise (isl.) B4
Lower Arrow (lake) H5
Lyell (isl.) B4
Lyell (mt.) J4
Mabel (lake) H5
Mahood (lake) G4
Malaspina (str.) J2
Manning Prov. Park G5
Masset (inlet) A3
McCauley (isl.) B3
McGregor (riv.) G3
Meziadin (lake) C2
Milbanke (sound) C4
Moberly (lake) F2
Monashee (mts.) H4
Moresby (isl.) B4
Morice (lake) D3
Morice (riv.) D3
Mount Assiniboine Prov. Park K5
Mount Edziza Prov. Park and Rec. Area B1
Mount Revelstoke Nat'l Park H4
Mount Robson Prov. Park H3
Muncho Lake Prov. Park L2
Murray (riv.) G3
Murtle (lake) H4
Muskwa (riv.) M2
Nanika (dam) D3
Nanika (lake) D3
Nass (riv.) C2
Nation (riv.) F2
Nechako (riv.) E3
Nitinat (lake) H3
Nootka (isl.) D5
Nootka (sound) D5
North Thompson (riv.) G4
Observatory (inlet) C2
Okanagan (lake) H5
Okanagan Mtn. Prov. Park G5
Okanogan (riv.) H6
Omineca (mts.) E2
Omineca (riv.) E2
Ootsa (lake) D3
Owikeno (lake) D4
Pacific Rim Nat'l Park E6
Parsnip (riv.) F3
Peace (riv.) G2
Pend Oreille (riv.) J6
Petitot (riv.) M2
Pinchi (lake) E3
Pine (riv.) G2
Pitt (isl.) C3
Pitt (lake) L2
Porcher (isl.) B3
Portland (canal) B2
Portland (inlet) C3
Price (isl.) C4
Princess Royal (isl.) C3
Principe (chan.) C3
Prophet (riv.) M2
Purcell (mts.) J5
Quatsino (sound) C5
Queen Charlotte (isls.) B3
Queen Charlotte (sound) C4
Queen Charlotte (str.) D5
Queens (sound) C4
Quesnel (lake) G4
Quesnel (riv.) F4
Rivers (inlet) D4
Robson (mt.) H3
Rocky (mts.) F2
Roderick (isl.) C4
Rose (pt.) B3
Saint James (cape) B4
Salmon (riv.) F3
Salmon Arm (inlet) J2
San Juan (riv.) J3
Schoen Lake Prov. Park E5
Scott (cape) C5
Scott (isls.) C5
Sechelt (inlet) J2
Sechelt (pen.) J2
Selkirk (mts.) J4
Seymour (inlet) D4
Sheslay (riv.) J2
Shuswap (lake) H4
Sikanni Chief (riv.) F1
Silver Star Prov. Park H5
Sir Sandford (mt.) H4
Skagit (riv.) G6
Skeena (mts.) C2
Skeena (riv.) C3
Skidegate (inlet) B3
Slocan (lake) J5
Smith (sound) C4
South Bentinck Arm (inlet) D4
Stave (lake) L3
Stephens (isl.) B3
Stikine (riv.) B1

AREA 366,253 sq. mi. (948,596 sq. km.)
POPULATION 2,716,301
CAPITAL Victoria
LARGEST CITY Vancouver
HIGHEST POINT Mt. Fairweather 15,300 ft. (4,663 m.)
SETTLED IN 1806
ADMITTED TO CONFEDERATION 1871
PROVINCIAL FLOWER Dogwood

Stone Mountain Prov. Park L2
Strathcona Prov. Park E5
Stuart (lake) E3
Sustut (riv.) D2
Tagish (lake) J1
Tahtsa (lake) D3
Takla (lake) D2
Taku (riv.) J2
Tatlatui (lake) D2
Tatlayoko (lake) E4
Tchentlo (lake) E2
Teslin (lake) K1
Tetachuck (lake) E3
Texada (isl.) J2
Tezzeron (lake) E3
Thompson (riv.) G5
Three Guardsmen (mt.) J1
Thutade (lake) D2
Tiedemann (mt.) E4
Toad (riv.) L2
Toba (inlet) E5
Tochcha (lake) E3
Top Of The World Prov. Park K5
Trembleur (lake) E3
Troitsa (lake) D3
Tumeka (lake) C1
Turnagain (riv.) K2
Tuya (riv.) K2
Tweedsmuir Prov. Park D3
Unuk (riv.) B2
Upper Arrow (lake) H5
Valdes (isl.) K3
Vancouver (isl.) D5
Virago (sound) A3
Waddington (mt.) E4
Wapiti (riv.) H3
Wells Gray Prov. Park H4
West Road (riv.) E3
Whitesail (lake) D3
Williston (lake) F2
Work (chan.) C3
Yellowhead (pass) H4
Yoho Nat'l Park J4

•Population of municipality.

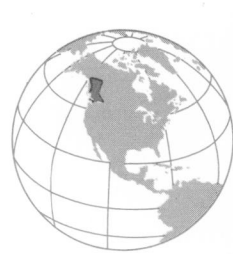

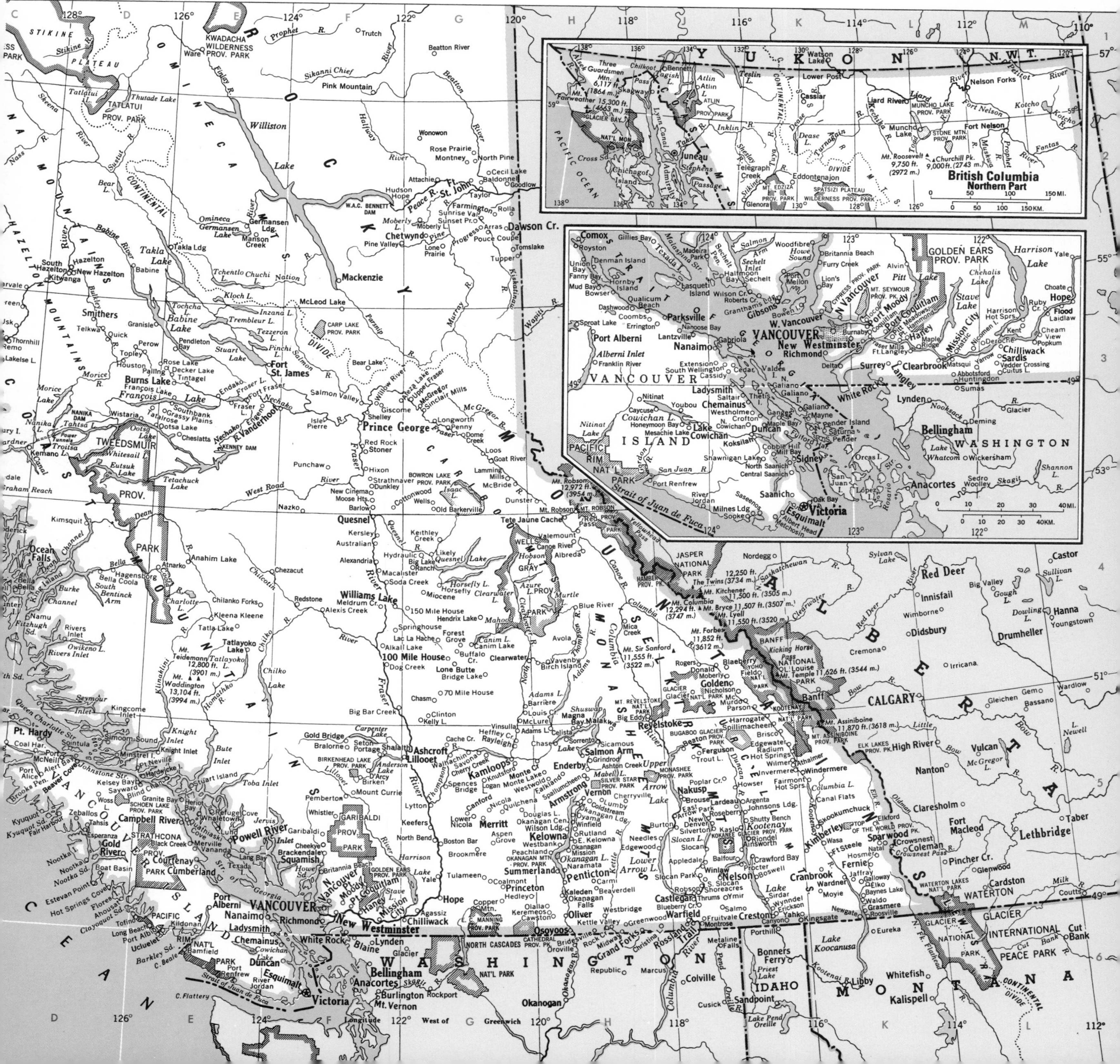

NORTHWEST TERRITORIES

DISTRICTS

Baffin 7,180 ....K2
Fort Smith 24,268 ....G3
Inuvik 7,183 ....F3
Keewatin 3,978 ....J3

CITIES and TOWNS

Aklavik 781 ....E3
Alert M1
Amadjuak L3
Arctic Bay 388 ....K2
Arctic Red River 120 ......E3
Baker Lake 856 ....J3
Bathurst Inlet 20 ....H3
Bay Chimo 39 ....H3
Bell Rock 1 ....G3
Broughton Island 351 .....M3
Buffalo River Junction 12 ...G3
Cambridge Bay 612 ....H3
Cape Dorset 677 ....L3
Cape Dyer M3
Cape Smith 147 ....L3
Chesterfield Inlet 241 .....K3
Clyde 348 ....M2
Colville Lake 56 ....F3
Coppermine 755 ....G3
Coral Harbour 414 ....K3
Detah G3
Dory Point 8 ....G3
Enterprise 82 ....G3
Eskimo Point 835 ....J3
Fort Franklin 422 ....F3
Fort Good Hope 440 ....F3
Fort Liard 296 ....F3
Fort McPherson 704 ....E3
Fort Norman 230 ....F3
Fort Providence 598 ....G3
Fort Resolution 497 ....G3
Fort Simpson 1,136 ....F3
Fort Smith 2,288 ....G4
Frobisher Bay 2,320 ......M3
Gjoa Haven 416 ....J3
Grise Fiord 120 ....K2
Hall Beach 288 ....K3
Hay River 3,268 ....G3
Holman Island 263 ....G2
Igloolik 675 ....K3
Inuvik 3,116 ....E3
Isachsen H2
Jean-Marie River 62 ....F3
Kakisa 40 ....G3
Kipisa 32 ....M3
Lac la Martre 212 ....G3
Lake Harbour 233 ....L3
Mould Bay F2
Nahanni Butte 90 ....F3
Nanisivik K2
Norman Wells 364 ....F3
Pangnirtung 807 ....M3
Paulatuk 127 ....F3
Pelly Bay 246 ....K3
Pine Point 1,915 ....G3
Pond Inlet 500 ....L2
Port Burwell 94 ....M3
Port Radium 51 ....G3
Rae-Edzo 1,158 ....G3
Rae Lake 163 ....G3
Rankin Inlet 852 ....J3
Reliance H3
Repulse Bay 264 ....K3
Resolution Island 8 ....M3

Rocher River 38 ....G3
Sachs Harbour 162 ....F2
Salt River 5 ....G3
Sawmill Bay G3
Snare Lake G3
Snowdrift 222 ....G3
Spence Bay 439 ....J3
Trout Lake 57 ....F3
Tuktoyaktuk 590 ....E3
Tungsten 227 ....F3
Whale Cove 177 ....J3
Wrigley 142 ....F3
Yellowknife (cap.) 8,256 ....G3

OTHER FEATURES

Aberdeen (lake) J3
Adair (cape) L2
Adelaide (pen.) J3
Admiralty (inlet) K2
Air Force (isl.) L3
Akpatok (isl.) M3
Albert Edward (bay) H3
Alert (pt.) K1
Amadjuak (lake) L3
Amund Ringnes (isl.) J2
Amundsen (gulf) F2
Anderson (riv.) F3
Angijak (isl.) M3
Angikuni (lake) J3
Archer (fiord) M1
Arctic Red (riv.) E3
Artillery (lake) H3
Aston (bay) J2
Atkinson (pt.) E2
Auyuittuq Nat'l Park M3
Axel Heiberg (isl.) J2
Aylmer (lake) H3
Bache (pen.) L2
Back (riv.) J3
Baffin (bay) M2
Baffin (isl.) L2
Baillie (isls.) F2
Baird (pen.) L3
Baker (lake) J3
Ballantyne (str.) G2
Banks (isl.) F2
Barbeau (peak) L1
Baring (cape) G3
Barrow (str.) J2
Bathurst (cape) F2
Bathurst (inlet) H3
Bathurst (isl.) J2
Beaufort (sea) D2
Boothia (gulf) K3
Boothia (pen.) J2
Borden (isl.) G2
Borden (pen.) K2
Brodeur (pen.) K2
Bruce (mts.) L2
Buchan (gulf) L2
Burnside (riv.) G3
Byam Martin (chan.) H2
Byam Martin (isl.) H2
Bylot (isl.) L2
Camsell (riv.) G3
Challenger (mts.) L1
Chantrey (inlet) J3
Chesterfield (inlet) J3
Chidley (cape) M3
Clinton-Colden (lake) H3
Clyde (inlet) M2
Coats (isl.) K3
Coburg (isl.) L2
Columbia (cape) M1

Colville (lake) F3
Committee (bay) K3
Contwoyto (lake) H3
Coppermine (riv.) G3
Cornwall (isl.) J2
Cornwallis (isl.) J2
Coronation (gulf) G3
Croker (bay) K2
Crown Prince Frederik (isl.) K3
Cumberland (pen.) M3
Cumberland (sound) M3
Davis (str.) M3
Dease (str.) H3
Denmark (bay) H2
Devon (isl.) K2
Dolphin and Union (str.) G3
Dubawnt (lake) H3
Dubawnt (riv.) H3
Dundas (pen.) G2
Dyer (cape) M3
Eclipse (sound) L2
Eglinton (isl.) F2
Ellef Ringnes (isl.) H2
Ellesmere (isl.) K2
Ennadai (lake) H3
Eskimo (lkes) E3
Eureka (sound) K2
Evans (str.) K3
Exeter (sound) M3
Fisher (str.) K3
Fosheim (pen.) K1
Foxe (basin) L3
Foxe (chan.) K3
Foxe (pen.) L3
Franklin (bay) F2
Franklin (mts.) F3
Franklin (str.) J2
Frobisher (bay) M3
Frozen (str.) K3
Fury and Hecla (str.) K3
Gabriel (str.) M3
Garry (lake) H3
Gods Mercy (bay) K3
Great Bear (lake) F3
Great Bear (riv.) F3
Great Slave (lake) G3
Greely (fjord) K1
Grinnell (pen.) J2
Hadley (bay) H2
Hall (basin) M1
Hall (pen.) M3
Hayes (riv.) J3
Hazen (lake) L1
Hazen (str.) G2
Henik (lkes) J3
Henry Kater (cape) M3
Home (bay) M3
Hood (riv.) G3
Horn (mts.) G3
Hornaday (riv.) F3
Horton (riv.) F3
Hottah (lake) G3
Hudson (bay) K3
Hudson (str.) L3
Isachsen (cape) H2
James Ross (str.) J3
Jenny Lind (isl.) H3
Jens Munk (isl.) K3
Jones (sound) K2
Kaminuriak (lake) J3
Kane (basin) L2
Kasba (lake) H3
Kazan (riv.) H3
Keele (riv.) F3
Keith Arm (inlet) F3

Kellett (cape) F2
Kellett (str.) G2
Kennedy (chan.) M1
Kent (pen.) H3
King Christian (isl.) H2
King William (isl.) J3
Lady Ann (str.) K2
La Martre (lake) G3
Lancaster (sound) K2
Lands End (cape) F2
Larsen (sound) J2
Liard (riv.) F4
Lincoln (sea) M1
Liverpool (bay) E2
Lockhart (riv.) H3
Lougheed (isl.) H2
Lyon (inlet) K3
MacKay (lake) G3
Mackenzie (bay) E3
Mackenzie (mts.) E3
Mackenzie (riv.) F3
Mackenzie King (isl.) G2
Macmillan (pass) F3
Maguse (lake) J3
Makinson (inlet) L2
Mansel (isl.) K3
Marian (lake) G3
Markham (inlet) L1

McLeod (bay) G3
M'Clintock (chan.) H2
M'Clure (str.) G2
McTavish Arm (inlet) G3
Meighen (isl.) H1
Melville (isl.) G2
Melville (pen.) K3
Mercy (cape) M3
Mills (lake) G3
Minto (inlet) G2
Mistake (bay) J3
Nahanni Nat'l Park F3
Nansen (sound) J1
Nares (str.) L2
Navy Board (inlet) K2
Nettilling (lake) L3
Nonacho (lake) H3
North Arm (inlet) G3
North Magnetic Pole H2
Norwegian (bay) J2
Nottingham (isl.) L3
Nueltin (lake) H3
Ommanney (bay) H2
Padloping (isl.) M3
Parry (bay) K3
Parry (chan.) G2
Parry (isls.) G2
Parry (pen.) F2

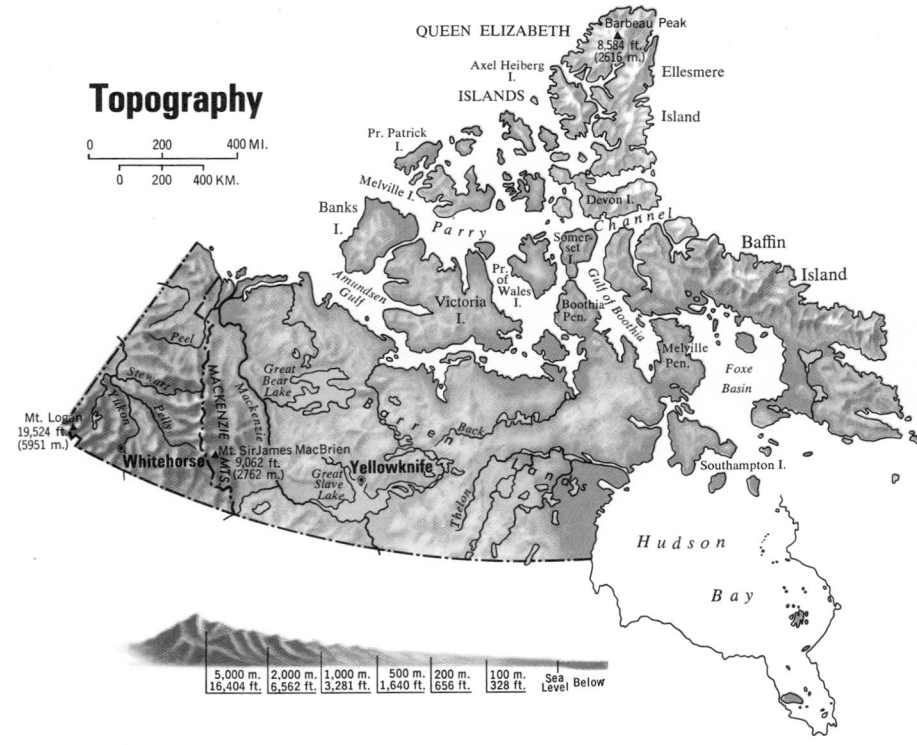

Topography

0 200 400 MI.

0 200 400 KM.

QUEEN ELIZABETH

Barbeau Peak
8,584 ft.
(2616 m.)

Axel Heiberg
I.

Ellesmere
Island

ISLANDS

Pr. Patrick
I.

Melville I.

Devon I.

Banks
I.

Parry   Channel

Somerset
I.

Baffin

Island

Amundsen
Gulf

Victoria
I.

Pr. of
Wales I.

Boothia
Pen.

Gulf of Boothia

Great
Bear
Lake

Melville
Pen.

Peel

Stewart

M A C K E N Z I E

Mackenzie

Baffin

Back

Foxe
Basin

Melville
Pen.

Falls

Mt. Logan
19,524 ft.
(5951 m.)

Whitehorse

Mt. Sir James MacBrien
9,062 ft.
(2762 m.)

Great
Slave
Lake

Yellowknife

Thelon

Southampton I.

Hudson

Bay

5,000 m. | 2,000 m. | 1,000 m. | 500 m. | 200 m. | 100 m. | Sea
16,404 ft. | 6,562 ft. | 3,281 ft. | 1,640 ft. | 656 ft. | 328 ft. | Level Below

Agriculture, Industry and Resources

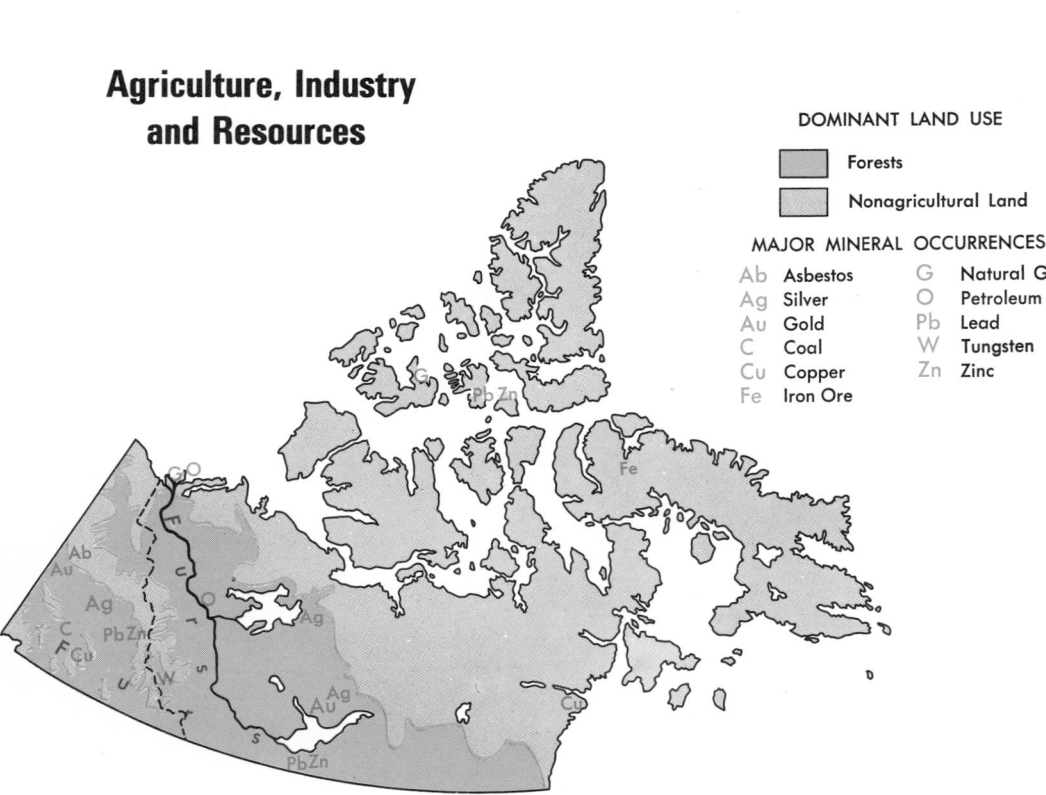

DOMINANT LAND USE

Forests

Nonagricultural Land

MAJOR MINERAL OCCURRENCES

Ab Asbestos
Ag Silver
Au Gold
C   Coal
Cu Copper
Fe Iron Ore

G   Natural Gas
O   Petroleum
Pb Lead
W   Tungsten
Zn Zinc

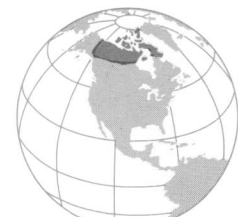

Peary (chan.)	H2	Selwyn (lake)	H4
Peel (sound)	J2	Sherman (inlet)	J3
Pelly (bay)	J3	Simpson (pen.)	K3
Penny (str.)	J2	Sir James MacBrien (mt.)	F3
Point (lake)	G3	Slave (riv.)	G3
Pond (inlet)	L2	Smith (bay)	L2
Prince Albert (pen.)	G2	Smith (cape)	L3
Prince Albert (sound)	G2	Smith (sound)	L2
Prince Charles (isl.)	L3	Snare (riv.)	G3
Prince Gustav Adolf (sea)	H2	Snowbird (lake)	H3
Prince of Wales (isl.)	J2	Somerset (isl.)	J2
Prince of Wales (str.)	G2	South (bay)	K3
Prince Patrick (isl.)	F2	Southampton (isl.)	K3
Prince Regent (inlet)	J2	South Nahanni (riv.)	F3
Queen Elizabeth (isls.)	H1	Stallworthy (cape)	J1
Queen Maud (gulf)	H3	Steensby (inlet)	L2
Queens (chan.)	J2	Stefansson (isl.)	H2
Raanes (pen.)	K2	Sverdrup (chan.)	J1
Rae (isth.)	K3	Sverdrup (isls.)	J2
Rae (riv.)	G3	Talbot (inlet)	L2
Rae (str.)	J3	Taltson (riv.)	G3
Ramparts (riv.)	E3	Tathlina (lake)	F3
Resolution	M3	Tha-anne (riv.)	J3
Richard Collinson (inlet)	G2	Thelon (riv.)	H3
Richards (isl.)	E3	Thlewiaza (riv.)	J3
Richardson (mts.)	E3	Trout (lake)	F3
Robeson (chan.)	M1	Ungava (bay)	M4
Roes Welcome (sound)	K3	Vansittart (isl.)	K3
Royal Geographical Society (isls.)	J3	Victoria (isl.)	G2
Russell (isl.)	J2	Victoria (str.)	H3
Sabine (pen.)	H2	Viscount Melville (sound)	G2
Salisbury (isl.)	L3	Wager (bay)	K3
Seahorse (pt.)	L3	Wales (isl.)	K3
		Walsingham (cape)	M3

YUKON TERRITORY

AREA 207,075 sq. mi.
(536,324 sq. km.)
POPULATION 22,684
CAPITAL Whitehorse
LARGEST CITY Whitehorse
HIGHEST POINT Mt. Logan 19,524 ft.
(5,951 m.)
SETTLED IN 1897
ADMITTED TO CONFEDERATION 1898
PROVINCIAL FLOWER Fireweed

NORTHWEST TERRITORIES

AREA 1,304,896 sq. mi. (3,379,683 sq. km.)
POPULATION 44,684
CAPITAL Yellowknife
LARGEST CITY Yellowknife
HIGHEST POINT Mt. Sir James MacBrien
9,062 ft. (2,762 m.)
SETTLED IN 1800
ADMITTED TO CONFEDERATION 1870
PROVINCIAL FLOWER Mountain Avens

Wellington (chan.)	J2	Carmacks 346	E3	Rock Creek 43	E3
Wholdaia (lake)	H3	Champagne	E3	Ross River 371	E3
Winter (harb.)	H2	Clinton Creek 191	D3	Stewart Crossing 39	E3
Wollaston (pen.)	G3	Cowley 13	E3	Stewart River 3	D3
Wood Buffalo Nat'l Park	G3	Dawson 838	E3	Swift River 33	E3
Wynniatt (bay)	G2	Destruction Bay 72	E3	Tagish 4	E3
Yathkyed (lake)	J3	Elsa 456	E3	Teslin 241	E3
Yellowknife (riv.)	G3	Faro 1,544	E3	Tuchitua Lake 10	F3
		Haines Junction 268	E3	Upper Liard 106	F3
YUKON TERRITORY		Johnson's Crossing 34	E3	Watson Lake 808	E3
		Keno Hill 70	E3	Whitehorse (cap.) 13,311	E3
CITIES and TOWNS		Koidern	D3		
Beaver Creek 123	D3	Mayo 448	E3	**OTHER FEATURES**	
Burwash Landing 71	E3	Old Crow 221	E3		
Carcross 175	E3	Pelly Crossing 135	E3		

Alsek (riv.)	E3	Mayo (lake)	E3
British (mts.)	D3	Ogilvie (mts.)	E3
Cassiar (mts.)	E3	Peel (riv.)	E3
Frances (lake)	E3	Pelly (mts.)	E3
Herschel (isl.)	D3	Pelly (riv.)	E3
Hess (riv.)	E3	Porcupine (riv.)	E3
Hyland (riv.)	F3	Richardson (mts.)	E3
Keele (peak)	E3	Rocky (mts.)	F4
Klondike (riv.)	E3	Saint Elias (mt.)	D3
Kluane (lake)	E3	Saint Elias (mts.)	D3
Kluane Nat'l Park	E3	Selwyn (mts.)	E3
Logan (mt.)	D3	Stewart (riv.)	E3
Mackenzie (bay)	E3	Teslin (riv.)	E3
Mackenzie (mts.)	E3	White (riv.)	D3
Macmillan (riv.)	E3	Yukon (riv.)	E3

Yukon and Northwest Territories

SCALE
0   50   100   200   300 MI.
0 50 100   200   300 KM.

Territorial Capitals ⊛
International Boundaries
Provincial & Territorial Boundaries
District Boundaries

Scale 1:14,000,000

© Copyright HAMMOND INCORPORATED, Maplewood, N.J.

All islands in Hudson and James Bays lie within the District of Keewatin.

Longitude West of Greenwich

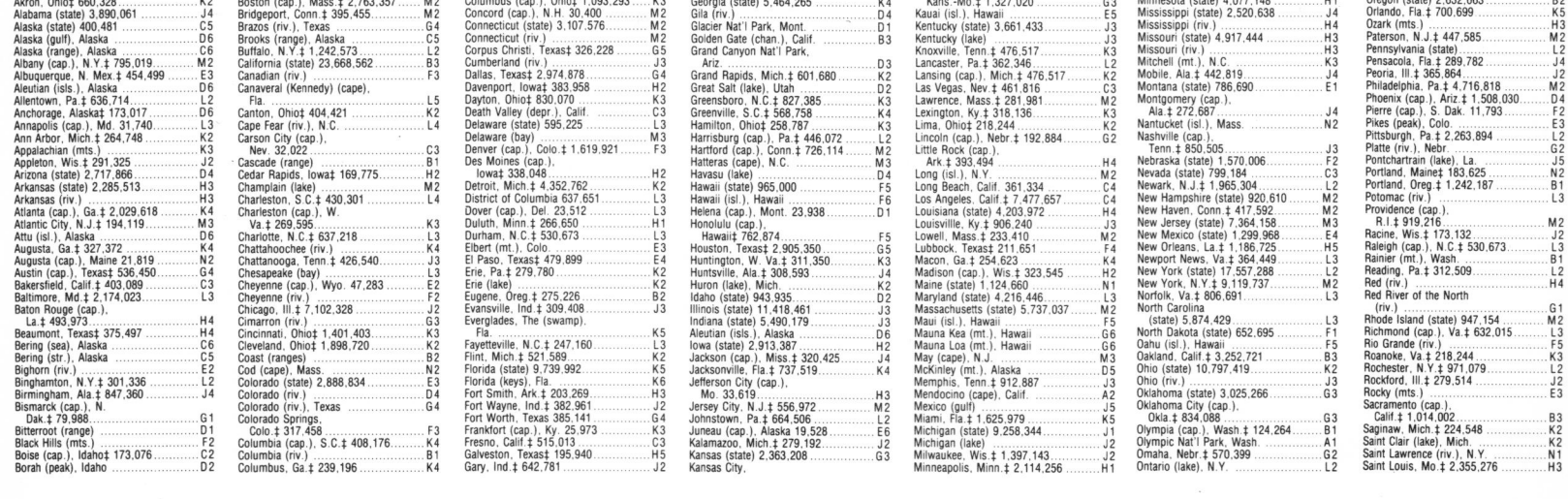

Akron, Ohio‡ 660,328 ...... K2
Alabama (state) 3,890,061 ...... J4
Alaska (state) 400,481 ...... C5
Alaska (gulf), Alaska D6
Alaska (range), Alaska C6
Albany (cap.), N.Y.‡ 795,019 ...... M2
Albuquerque, N. Mex ‡ 454,499 ...... E3
Aleutian (isl.), Alaska D6
Allentown, Pa.‡ 636,714 ...... L2
Anchorage, Alaska‡ 173,017 ...... D6
Annapolis (cap.), Md. 31,740 ...... L3
Ann Arbor, Mich.‡ 264,748 ...... K2
Appalachian (mts.) K3
Appleton, Wis.‡ 291,325 ...... J2
Arizona (state) 2,717,866 ...... D4
Arkansas (state) 2,285,513 ...... H3
Arkansas (riv.) H3
Atlanta (cap.), Ga.‡ 2,029,618 ...... K4
Atlantic City, N.J.‡ 194,119 ...... M3
Attu (isl.), Alaska D6
Augusta, Ga.‡ 327,372 ...... K4
Augusta (cap.), Maine 21,819 ...... N2
Austin (cap.), Texas‡ 536,450 ...... G4
Bakersfield, Calif.‡ 403,089 ...... C3
Baltimore, Md.‡ 2,174,023 ...... L3
Baton Rouge (cap.), La.‡ 493,973 ...... H4
Beaumont, Texas‡ 375,497 ...... H4
Bering (sea), Alaska C6
Bering (str.), Alaska C5
Bighorn (riv.) E2
Binghamton, N.Y.‡ 301,336 ...... L2
Birmingham, Ala.‡ 847,360 ...... J4
Bismarck (cap.), Dak.‡ 79,988 ...... G1
Bitterroot (range) D2
Black Hills (mts.) F2
Boise (cap.), Idaho‡ 173,076 ...... C2
Borah (peak), Idaho D2

Boston (cap.), Mass.‡ 2,763,357 ...... M2
Bridgeport, Conn.‡ 395,455 ...... M2
Brooks (range), Alaska C5
Brazos (riv.), Texas G4
Buffalo, N.Y.‡ 1,242,573 ...... L2
Cumberland (riv.) J3
Canadian (riv.) F3
California (state) 23,668,562 ...... B3
Canaveral (Kennedy) (cape), Fla. L5
Canton, Ohio‡ 404,421 ...... K2
Cape Fear (riv.), N.C. L4
Carson City (cap.), Nev. 32,022 ...... C3
Cascade (range) B2
Cedar Rapids, Iowa‡ 169,775 ...... H2
Champlain (lake) M2
Charleston, S.C.‡ 430,301 ...... L4
Charleston (cap.), W. K3
Charlotte, N.C.‡ 637,218 ...... K3
Chattahoochee (riv.) J4
Chattanooga, Tenn.‡ 426,540 ...... J3
Chesapeake (bay) L3
Cheyenne (cap.), Wyo.‡ 47,283 ...... E2
Cheyenne (riv.) F2
Cimarron (riv.) G3
Cincinnati, Ohio‡ 1,401,403 ...... J3
Cleveland, Ohio‡ 1,898,720 ...... K2
Coast (ranges) B2
Cod (cape), Mass. N2
Colorado (state) 2,888,834 ...... E3
Colorado (riv.) D4
Colorado (riv.), Texas G4
Columbia (cap.), S.C.‡ 408,176 ...... K4
Columbia (riv.) B1
Columbus, Ga.‡ 239,196 ...... K4

Columbus (cap.), Ohio‡ 1,093,293 ...... K3
Concord (cap.), N.H. 30,400 ...... M2
Connecticut (state) 3,107,576 ...... M2
Connecticut (riv.) M2
Corpus Christi, Texas‡ 326,228 ...... G5
Cumberland (riv.) ......
Dallas, Texas‡ 2,974,878 ...... G4
Davenport, Iowa‡ 383,958 ...... H2
Dayton, Ohio‡ 830,070 ...... J3
Death Valley (depr.), Calif. C3
Delaware (state) 595,225 ...... L3
Delaware (bay) M3
Denver (cap.), Colo.‡ 1,619,921 ...... F3
Des Moines (cap.), Iowa‡ 338,048 ...... H2
Detroit, Mich.‡ 4,352,762 ...... K2
District of Columbia 637,651 ...... L3
Dover (cap.), Del. 23,512 ...... L3
Duluth, Minn.‡ 266,650 ...... H1
Durham, N.C.‡ 530,673 ...... L3
El Paso, Texas‡ 479,899 ...... E4
Elbert (mt.), Colo. E3
Erie, Pa.‡ 279,780 ...... K2
Erie (lake) K2
Eugene, Oreg.‡ 275,226 ...... B2
Evansville, Ind.‡ 309,408 ...... J3
Everglades, The (swamp), Fla. K5
Fayetteville, N.C.‡ 247,160 ...... L3
Flint, Mich.‡ 521,589 ...... K2
Florida (state) 9,739,992 ...... K5
Florida (keys), Fla. K6
Fort Smith, Ark.‡ 203,269 ...... H3
Fort Wayne, Ind.‡ 382,961 ...... J2
Fort Worth, Texas 385,141 ...... G4
Frankfort (cap.), Ky. 25,973 ...... J3
Fresno, Calif.‡ 515,013 ...... C3
Galveston, Texas‡ 195,940 ...... H5
Gary, Ind.‡ 642,781 ...... J2

Georgia (state) 5,464,265 ...... K4
Gila (riv.) D4
Glacier Nat'l Park, Mont. D1
Golden Gate (chan.), Calif. B3
Grand Canyon Nat'l Park, Ariz. D3
Grand Rapids, Mich.‡ 601,680 ...... J2
Great Salt (lake), Utah D2
Greensboro, N.C.‡ 827,385 ...... K3
Greenville, S.C.‡ 568,758 ...... K4
Hamilton, Ohio‡ 258,787 ...... K3
Harrisburg (cap.), Pa.‡ 446,072 ...... L2
Hartford (cap.), Conn.‡ 726,114 ...... M2
Hatteras (cape), N.C. L3
Havasu (lake) D4
Hawaii (state) 965,000 ...... F5
Hawaii (isl.), Hawaii F6
Helena (cap.), Mont. 23,938 ...... D1
Honolulu (cap.), Hawaii‡ 762,874 ...... F5
Houston, Texas‡ 2,905,350 ...... G5
Huntington, W. Va.‡ 311,350 ...... K3
Huntsville, Ala.‡ 308,593 ...... J4
Huron (lake), Mich. K2
Idaho (state) 943,935 ...... D2
Illinois (state) 11,418,461 ...... J3
Indiana (state) 5,490,179 ...... J3
Iowa (state) 2,913,387 ...... H2
Jackson (cap.), Miss.‡ 320,425 ...... J4
Jacksonville, Fla.‡ 737,519 ...... K4
Jefferson City (cap.), Mo. 33,619 ...... H3

Kans.-Mo.‡ 1,327,020 ...... G3
Kauai (isl.), Hawaii E5
Kentucky (state) 3,661,433 ...... J3
Kentucky (lake) J3
Knoxville, Tenn.‡ 476,517 ...... K3
Lancaster, Pa.‡ 362,346 ...... L2
Lansing (cap.), Mich.‡ 476,517 ...... J2
Las Vegas, Nev.‡ 461,816 ...... C3
Lawrence, Mass.‡ 281,981 ...... M2
Lexington, Ky.‡ 318,136 ...... J3
Lima, Ohio‡ 218,244 ...... K2
Lincoln (cap.), Nebr.‡ 192,884 ...... G2
Little Rock (cap.), Ark.‡ 393,494 ...... H4
Long (isl.), N.Y. M2
Long Beach, Calif. 361,334 ...... C4
Los Angeles, Calif.‡ 7,477,657 ...... C4
Louisiana (state) 4,203,972 ...... H4
Louisville, Ky.‡ 906,240 ...... J3
Lowell, Mass.‡ 233,410 ...... M2
Lubbock, Texas‡ 211,651 ...... F4
Macon, Ga.‡ 254,623 ...... K4
Madison (cap.), Wis.‡ 323,545 ...... J2
Maine (state) 1,124,660 ...... N1
Maryland (state) 4,216,446 ...... L3
Massachusetts (state) 5,737,037 ...... M2
Maui (isl.), Hawaii F5
Mauna Kea (mt.), Hawaii F6
Mauna Loa (mt.), Hawaii F6
May (cape), N.J. M3
McKinley (mt.), Alaska C5
Memphis, Tenn.‡ 912,887 ...... J3
Mexico (gulf) J5
Miami, Fla.‡ 1,625,979 ...... K5
Michigan (state) 9,258,344 ...... J2
Michigan (lake) J2
Milwaukee, Wis.‡ 1,397,143 ...... J2
Minneapolis, Minn.‡ 2,114,256 ...... H1

Minnesota (state) 4,077,148 ...... H1
Mississippi (state) 2,520,638 ...... J4
Mississippi (riv.) H4
Missouri (state) 4,917,444 ...... H3
Missouri (riv.) ......
Mitchell (mt.), N.C. K3
Mobile, Ala.‡ 442,819 ...... J4
Montana (state) 786,690 ...... E1
Montgomery (cap.), Ala.‡ 272,687 ...... J4
Nantucket (isl.), Mass. N2
Nashville (cap.), Tenn.‡ 850,505 ...... J3
Nebraska (state) 1,570,006 ...... F2
Nevada (state) 799,184 ...... C3
Newark, N.J.‡ 1,965,304 ...... L2
New Hampshire (state) 920,610 ...... M2
New Haven, Conn.‡ 417,592 ...... M2
New Jersey (state) 7,364,158 ...... M3
New Mexico (state) 1,299,968 ...... E4
New Orleans, La.‡ 1,186,725 ...... H5
Newport News, Va.‡ 364,449 ...... L3
New York (state) 17,557,288 ...... L2
New York, N.Y.‡ 9,119,737 ...... M2
Norfolk, Va.‡ 806,691 ...... L3
North Carolina (state) 5,874,429 ...... L3
North Dakota (state) 652,695 ...... F1
Oahu (isl.), Hawaii F5
Oakland, Calif.‡ 3,252,721 ...... B3
Ohio (state) 10,797,419 ...... J3
Ohio (riv.) J3
Oklahoma (state) 3,025,266 ...... G3
Oklahoma City (cap.), Okla.‡ 834,088 ...... G3
Olympia (cap.), Wash.‡ 124,264 ...... B1
Omaha, Nebr.‡ 570,399 ...... G2
Ontario (lake), N.Y. L2

Oregon (state) 2,632,663 ...... B2
Orlando, Fla.‡ 700,699 ...... K5
Ozark (mts.) H3
Paterson, N.J.‡ 447,585 ...... M2
Pennsylvania (state) L2
Pensacola, Fla.‡ 289,782 ...... J4
Peoria, Ill.‡ 365,864 ...... J2
Philadelphia, Pa.‡ 4,716,818 ...... M2
Phoenix (cap.), Ariz.‡ 1,508,030 ...... D4
Pierre (cap.), S. Dak. 11,793 ...... F2
Pikes (peak), Colo. E3
Pittsburgh, Pa.‡ 2,263,894 ...... L2
Platte (riv.), Nebr. G2
Pontchartrain (lake), La. J5
Portland, Maine‡ 183,625 ...... N2
Portland, Oreg.‡ 1,242,187 ...... B1
Potomac (riv.) ......
Providence (cap.), R.I.‡ 919,216 ...... M2
Racine, Wis.‡ 173,132 ...... J2
Raleigh (cap.), N.C.‡ 530,673 ...... L3
Rainier (mt.), Wash. B1
Reading, Pa.‡ 312,509 ...... L2
Red (riv.) ......
Red River of the North (riv.) G1
Rhode Island (state) 947,154 ...... M2
Richmond (cap.), Va.‡ 632,015 ...... L3
Rio Grande (riv.) F5
Roanoke, Va.‡ 218,244 ...... K3
Rochester, N.Y.‡ 971,079 ...... L2
Rockford, Ill.‡ 279,514 ...... J2
Rocky (mts.) E3
Sacramento (cap.), Calif.‡ 1,014,002 ...... B3
Saginaw, Mich.‡ 224,548 ...... K2
Saint Clair (lake), Mich. K2
Saint Lawrence (riv.), N.Y. N1
Saint Louis, Mo.‡ 2,355,276 ...... H3

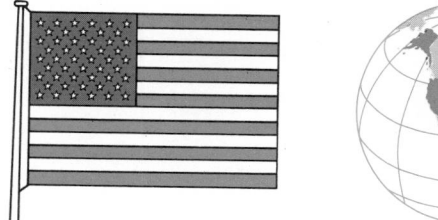

AREA 3,623,420 sq. mi.
(9,384,658 sq. km.)
POPULATION 226,504,825
CAPITAL Washington
LARGEST CITY New York
HIGHEST POINT Mt. McKinley 20,320 ft.
(6,194 m.)
MONETARY UNIT U.S. dollar
MAJOR LANGUAGE English
MAJOR RELIGIONS Protestantism,
Roman Catholicism, Judaism

Population Distribution

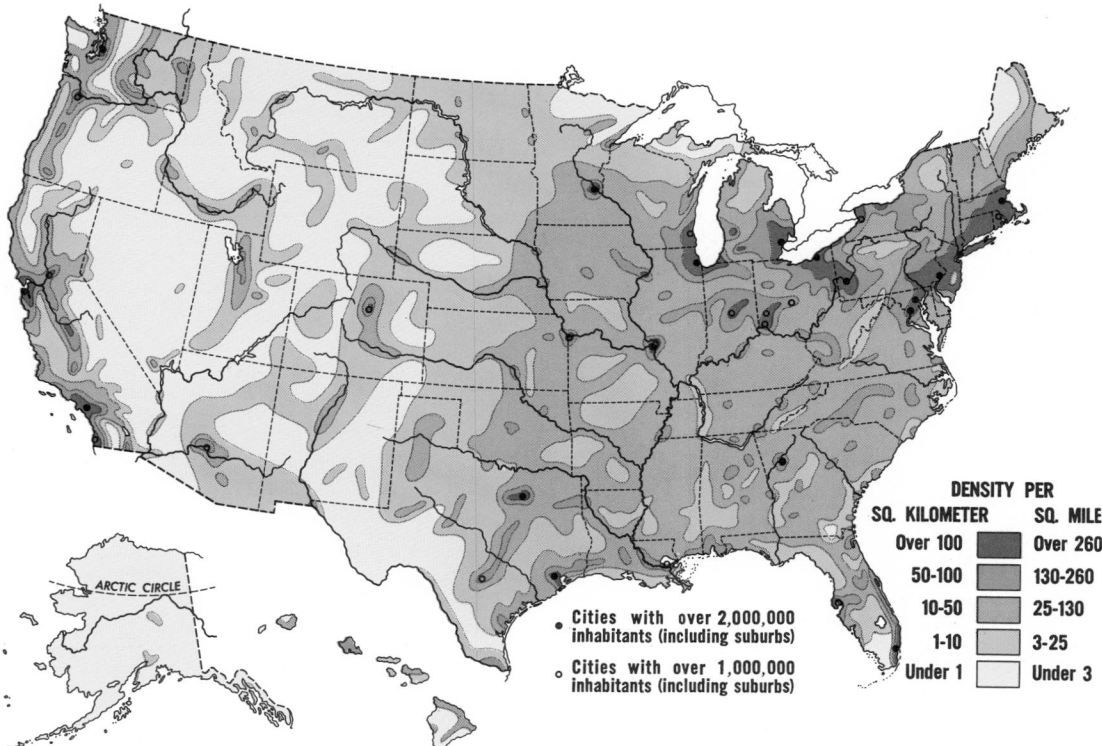

DENSITY PER

SQ. KILOMETER	SQ. MILE
Over 100	Over 260
50-100	130-260
10-50	25-130
1-10	3-25
Under 1	Under 3

• Cities with over 2,000,000 inhabitants (including suburbs)
○ Cities with over 1,000,000 inhabitants (including suburbs)

Vegetation

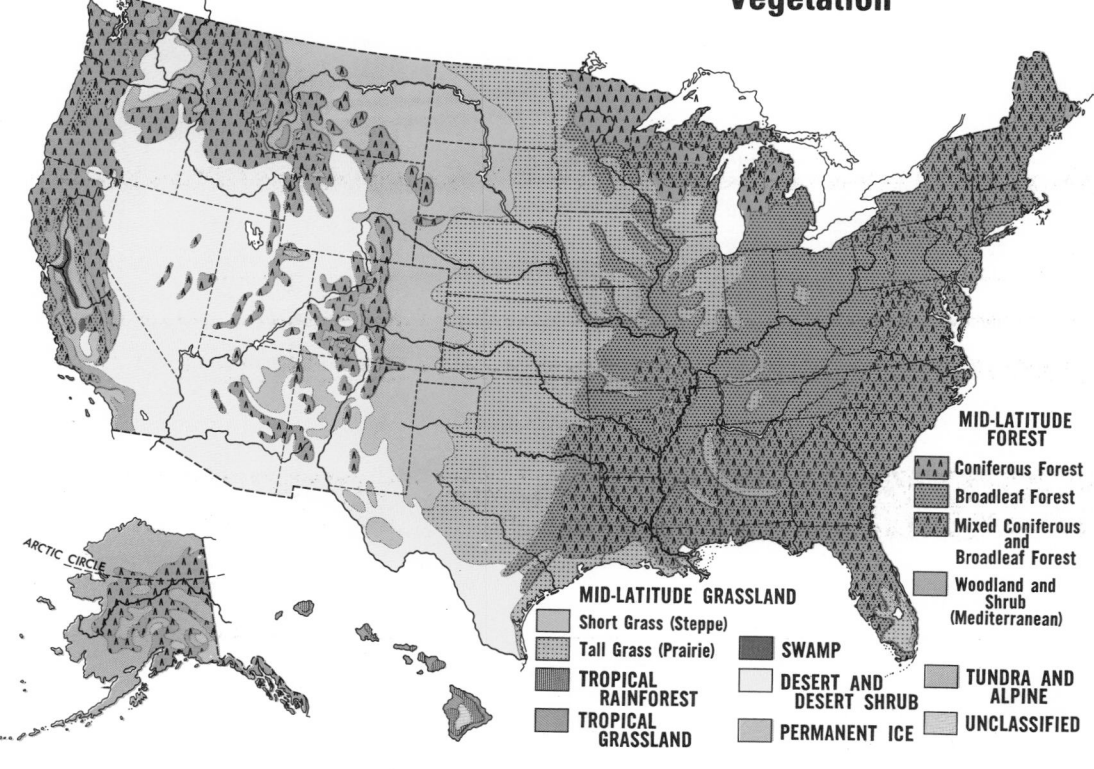

MID-LATITUDE FOREST
Coniferous Forest
Broadleaf Forest
Mixed Coniferous and Broadleaf Forest
Woodland and Shrub (Mediterranean)

MID-LATITUDE GRASSLAND
Short Grass (Steppe)
Tall Grass (Prairie)

SWAMP
DESERT AND DESERT SHRUB
PERMANENT ICE

TROPICAL RAINFOREST
TROPICAL GRASSLAND

TUNDRA AND ALPINE
UNCLASSIFIED

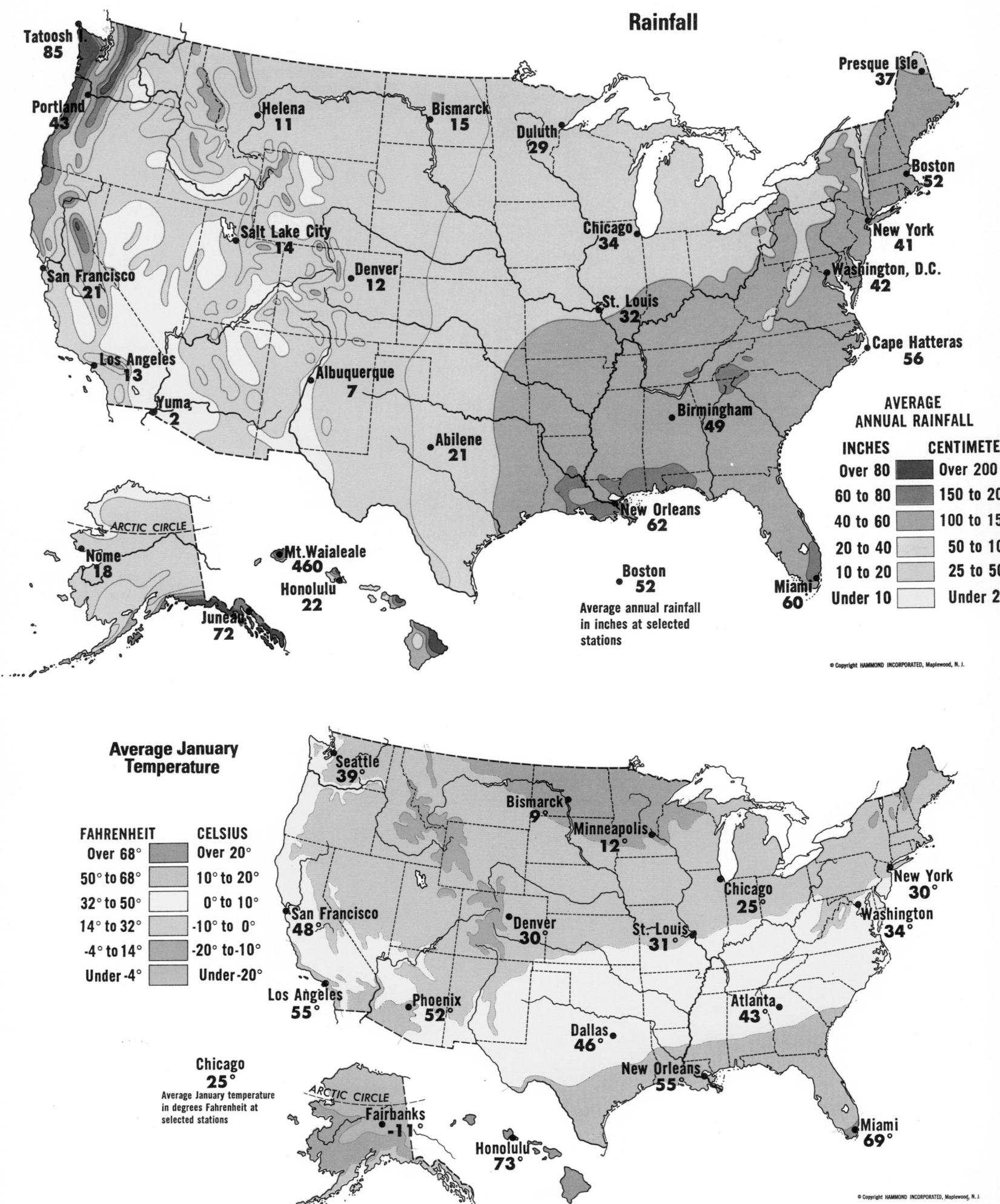

Rainfall

Tatoosh I.
85

Portland
43

Helena
11

Bismarck
15

Duluth
29

Presque Isle
37

Boston
52

Chicago
34

New York
41

Salt Lake City
14

Denver
12

St. Louis
32

Washington, D.C.
42

San Francisco
21

Los Angeles
13

Albuquerque
7

Yuma
2

Abilene
21

Birmingham
49

Cape Hatteras
56

New Orleans
62

Miami
60

Nome
18

Mt.Waialeale
460

Honolulu
22

Juneau
72

Boston
52

Average annual rainfall
in inches at selected
stations

**AVERAGE
ANNUAL RAINFALL**

INCHES	CENTIMETER
Over 80	Over 200
60 to 80	150 to 200
40 to 60	100 to 150
20 to 40	50 to 100
10 to 20	25 to 50
Under 10	Under 25

© Copyright HAMMOND INCORPORATED, Maplewood, N. J.

Average January Temperature

FAHRENHEIT	CELSIUS
Over 68°	Over 20°
50° to 68°	10° to 20°
32° to 50°	0° to 10°
14° to 32°	-10° to 0°
-4° to 14°	-20° to -10°
Under -4°	Under -20°

Seattle
39°

Bismarck
9°

Minneapolis
12°

New York
30°

Chicago
25°

Washington
34°

San Francisco
48°

Denver
30°

St. Louis
31°

Los Angeles
55°

Phoenix
52°

Dallas
46°

Atlanta
43°

New Orleans
55°

Chicago
25°

Average January temperature
in degrees Fahrenheit at
selected stations

ARCTIC CIRCLE

Fairbanks
-11°

Honolulu
73°

Miami
69°

© Copyright HAMMOND INCORPORATED, Maplewood, N. J.

Topography

200 0 200 400 MI.
0 200 400 KM.

PACIFIC OCEAN

C. Flattery
Seattle
COAST RANGE
Mt. Rainier 14,410 ft. (4392 m.)
Mt. St. Helens 8,364 ft. (2549 m.)
CASCADE RANGE
COLUMBIA PLATEAU
Columbia
Snake
BITTERROOT RANGE
ROCKY
Missouri
Yellowstone
Fort Peck Lake
GREAT
Rainy
Lake Superior
Keweenaw Pen.
Lake Sakakawea
Wisconsin
Lake Huron
Lake Michigan
St. Lawrence
Gulf of Maine
Boston
C. Cod

SIERRA NEVADA
Great Basin
Great Salt Lake
MOUNTAINS
N. Platte
Platte
PLAINS
Lake Oahe
James
Minneapolis
Milwaukee
Chicago
Detroit
Lake Erie
Cleveland
Lake Ontario
Niagara Falls
L. Champlain
New York
Philadelphia
Long Island

San Francisco
Central Valley
Sacramento
Mt. Whitney 14,494 ft. (4418 m.)
Pt. Conception
SANTA BARBARA IS.
Mojave Desert
Los Angeles
San Diego
L. Mead
Lake Powell
Grand Canyon
PLATEAU
Colorado
Phoenix
Gila
COLORADO
Denver 14,431 ft. (4399 m.)
Mt. Elbert
Arkansas
Colorado
Rio Grande
LLANO ESTACADO
Pecos
EDWARDS PLATEAU
Brazos
Colorado
Houston
Des Moines
Illinois
Kansas City
Missouri
St. Louis
OZARK PLATEAU
Indianapolis
Ohio
Washington
Wabash
ALLEGHENY MTS.
APPALACHIAN MOUNTAINS
Mt. Mitchell 6,684 ft. (2037 m.)
Chesapeake Bay
C. Hatteras
ATLANTIC
OCEAN

Memphis
Tennessee
Wheeler L.
Chattahoochee
Atlanta
Savannah
PIEDMONT
C. Fear
Dallas
Red
Mississippi
New Orleans
Mississippi Delta
GULF COASTAL PLAIN
ATLANTIC COASTAL PLAIN
Jacksonville
C. Canaveral
Okeechobee
The Everglades
Miami
FLORIDA KEYS

Gulf of Mexico

ARCTIC OCEAN
0 200 400 MI.
0 200 400 KM.
BROOKS RA.
St. Lawrence I.
Bering Str.
Yukon
Tanana
Mt. McKinley 20,320 ft. (6194 m.)
Anchorage
Alaska Ra.
BERING SEA
Gulf of Alaska
Kodiak I.
ALEXANDER ARCHIPELAGO
Aleutian Islands

Kauai
HAWAIIAN ISLANDS
Oahu
Honolulu
Molokai
Maui
PACIFIC OCEAN
0 50 100 MI.
0 50 100 KM.
Mauna Kea 13,976 ft. (4260 m.)
Hawaii

5,000 m. 16,404 ft. | 2,000 m. 6,562 ft. | 1,000 m. 3,281 ft. | 500 m. 1,640 ft. | 200 m. 656 ft. | 100 m. 328 ft. | Sea Level | Below

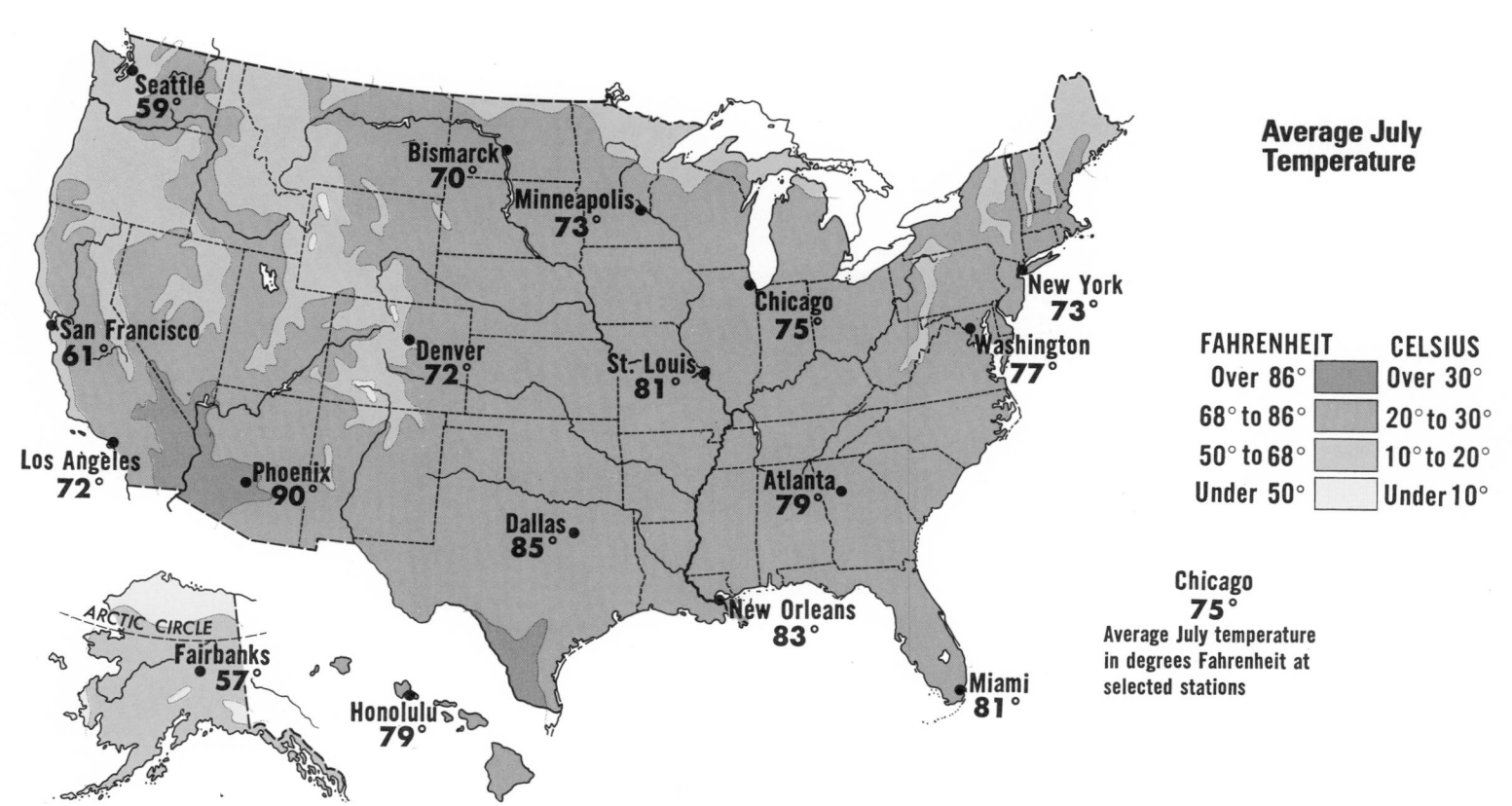

Average July Temperature

Seattle 59°
Bismarck 70°
Minneapolis 73°
San Francisco 61°
Denver 72°
St. Louis 81°
Chicago 75°
New York 73°
Washington 77°
Los Angeles 72°
Phoenix 90°
Dallas 85°
Atlanta 79°
New Orleans 83°
Miami 81°
Fairbanks 57°
ARCTIC CIRCLE
Honolulu 79°

FAHRENHEIT — CELSIUS
Over 86° — Over 30°
68° to 86° — 20° to 30°
50° to 68° — 10° to 20°
Under 50° — Under 10°

Chicago
75°
Average July temperature in degrees Fahrenheit at selected stations

United States Standard Time Zones

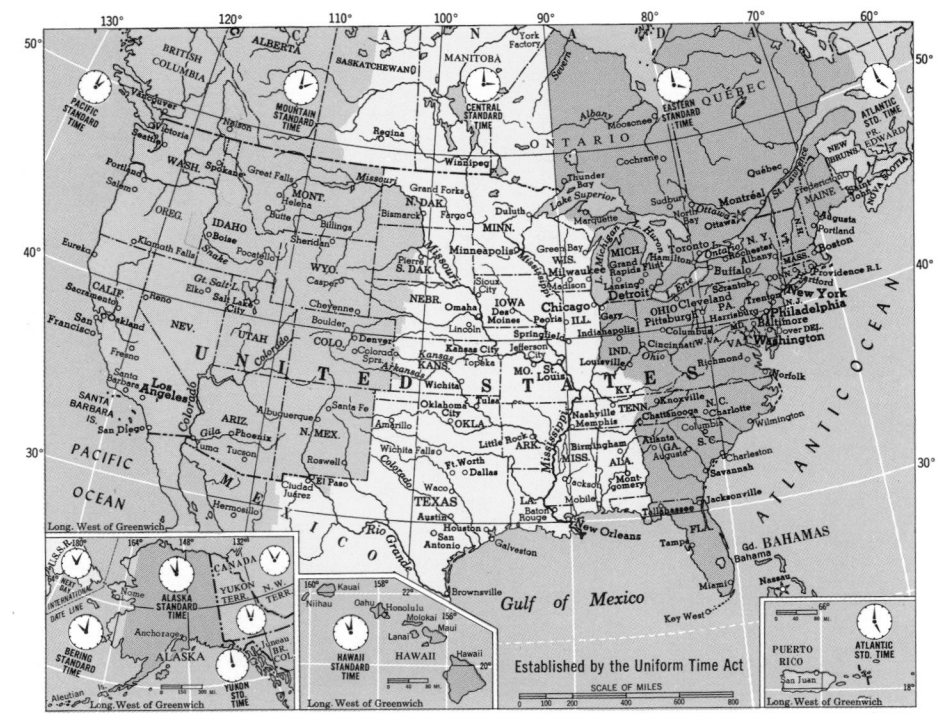

PACIFIC STANDARD TIME
MOUNTAIN STANDARD TIME
CENTRAL STANDARD TIME
EASTERN STANDARD TIME
ATLANTIC STD. TIME
ALASKA STANDARD TIME
BERING STANDARD TIME
YUKON STD. TIME
HAWAII STANDARD TIME
ATLANTIC STD. TIME
PACIFIC OCEAN
ATLANTIC OCEAN
Gulf of Mexico
UNITED STATES
ONTARIO
QUÉBEC
MANITOBA
SASKATCHEWAN
ALBERTA
BRITISH COLUMBIA
ALASKA
HAWAII
PUERTO RICO
Gd. BAHAMAS
Established by the Uniform Time Act
SCALE OF MILES
Long. West of Greenwich

Agriculture, Industry and Resources

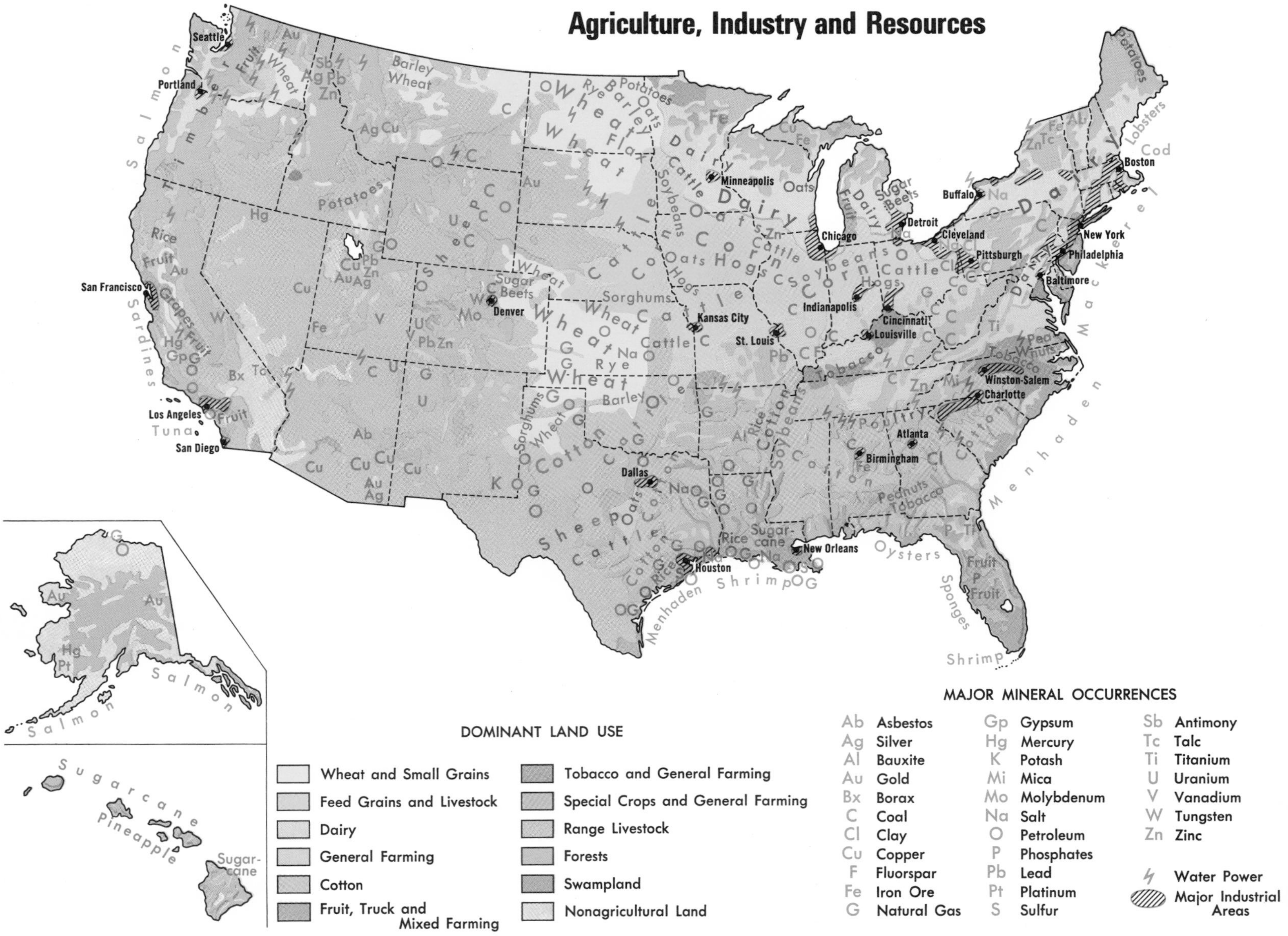

DOMINANT LAND USE
Wheat and Small Grains
Feed Grains and Livestock
Dairy
General Farming
Cotton
Fruit, Truck and Mixed Farming
Tobacco and General Farming
Special Crops and General Farming
Range Livestock
Forests
Swampland
Nonagricultural Land
MAJOR MINERAL OCCURRENCES
Ab Asbestos
Ag Silver
Al Bauxite
Au Gold
Bx Borax
C Coal
Cl Clay
Cu Copper
F Fluorspar
Fe Iron Ore
G Natural Gas
Gp Gypsum
Hg Mercury
K Potash
Mi Mica
Mo Molybdenum
Na Salt
O Petroleum
P Phosphates
Pb Lead
Pt Platinum
S Sulfur
Sb Antimony
Tc Talc
Ti Titanium
U Uranium
V Vanadium
W Tungsten
Zn Zinc
Water Power
Major Industrial Areas
Seattle
Portland
San Francisco
Los Angeles
San Diego
Denver
Minneapolis
Kansas City
St. Louis
Dallas
Houston
New Orleans
Chicago
Detroit
Indianapolis
Cincinnati
Louisville
Birmingham
Atlanta
Charlotte
Winston-Salem
Cleveland
Pittsburgh
Buffalo
Boston
New York
Philadelphia
Baltimore

AREA 51,705 sq. mi. (133,916 sq. km.)
POPULATION 3,893,888
CAPITAL Montgomery
LARGEST CITY Birmingham
HIGHEST POINT Cheaha Mtn. 2,407 ft. (734 m.)
SETTLED IN 1702
ADMITTED TO UNION December 14, 1819
POPULAR NAME Heart of Dixie; Cotton State; Yellowhammer State
STATE FLOWER Camellia
STATE BIRD Yellowhammer

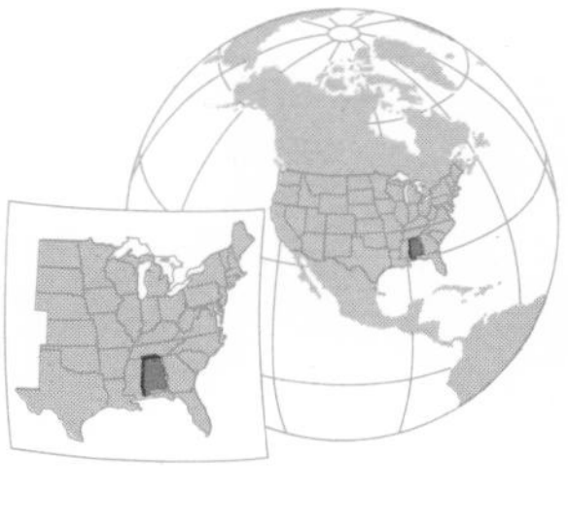

COUNTIES

Autauga 32,259 E5
Baldwin 78,556 C9
Barbour 24,756 H7
Bibb 15,723 D5
Blount 36,459 E2
Bullock 10,596 G6
Butler 21,680 E7
Calhoun 119,761 G3
Chambers 39,191 H5
Cherokee 18,760 G2
Chilton 30,612 E5
Choctaw 16,839 B6
Clarke 27,702 C7
Clay 13,703 G4
Cleburne 12,595 G3
Coffee 38,533 G8
Colbert 54,519 C1
Conecuh 15,884 E8
Coosa 11,377 F5
Covington 36,850 F8
Crenshaw 14,110 F7
Cullman 61,642 E2
Dale 47,821 G8
Dallas 53,981 D6
De Kalb 53,658 G2
Elmore 43,390 F5
Escambia 38,440 D8
Etowah 103,057 F2
Fayette 18,809 C3
Franklin 28,350 C2
Geneva 24,253 G8
Greene 11,021 C5
Hale 15,604 C5
Henry 15,302 H7
Houston 74,632 H8
Jackson 51,407 F1
Jefferson 671,324 E3
Lamar 16,453 B3
Lauderdale 80,546 C1
Lawrence 30,170 D1
Lee 76,283 H5
Limestone 46,005 E1
Lowndes 13,253 E6
Macon 26,829 G6
Madison 196,966 E1
Marengo 25,047 C6
Marion 30,041 C2
Marshall 65,622 F2
Mobile 364,980 B9
Monroe 22,651 D7
Montgomery 197,038 F6
Morgan 90,231 E2
Perry 15,012 D5
Pickens 21,481 B4
Pike 28,050 G7
Randolph 20,075 H4
Russell 47,356 H6
Saint Clair 41,205 F3
Shelby 66,298 E4
Sumter 16,908 B5
Talladega 73,826 F4
Tallapoosa 38,676 G5
Tuscaloosa 137,541 C4
Walker 68,660 D3
Washington 16,821 B8
Wilcox 14,755 D7
Winston 21,953 D2

CITIES and TOWNS

Zip Name/Pop. Key

36310 Abbeville⊙ 3,155 H7
35440 Abernant 405 D4
35005 Adamsville 2,498 D3
35540 Addison 746 D2
35006 Adger 400 D4
35441 Akron 604 C5
35007 Alabaster 7,079 E4
35950 Albertville 12,039 F2
†35115 Aldrich 500 E4
35010 Alexander City 13,807 G5
36250 Alexandria 600 G3
35442 Aliceville 3,207 B4
35013 Allgood 387 F3
36501 Alma 500 C8
35952 Altoona 928 F2
36420 Andalusia⊙ 10,415 E8
35610 Anderson 405 D1
36201 Anniston⊙ 29,523 G3
Anniston‡ 116,936 G3
35016 Arab 5,967 E2
35805 Ardmore 1,096 E1
†35173 Argo 600 E3
36311 Ariton 844 G7
35033 Arkadelphia 150 E3
35541 Arley 276 D2
†35035 Ashby 500 E4
36312 Ashford 2,165 H8
36251 Ashland⊙ 2,052 G4
35953 Ashville⊙ 1,489 F3
35611 Athens⊙ 14,558 E1
36503 Atmore 8,789 C8
35954 Attalla 7,737 F2
36830 Auburn 28,471 H5
36003 Autaugaville 843 E6
†36312 Avon 433 H8
36505 Axis 500 B9
†36420 Babbie 553 F8
35019 Baileyton 396 E2
36005 Banks 160 G7
†36532 Barnwell 700 C10
36507 Bay Minette⊙ 7,455 C9
36509 Bayou La Batre 2,005 B10
35543 Bear Creek 353 C2
36425 Beatrice 558 D7
35544 Beaverton 360 B3
†35653 Belgreen 500 C2
35545 Belk 308 C3
36901 Bellamy 700 B6
35615 Belle Mina 675 E1
36313 Bellwood 400 G8
36785 Benton 74 E6
35546 Berry 916 C3
35020 Bessemer 31,729 D4
†36872 Beulah 500 H5
36006 Billingsley 106 E5
*35201 Birmingham⊙ 284,413 D3
Birmingham‡ 847,360 D3
36314 Black 156 G8
35031 Blountsville 1,509 E2
36201 Blue Mountain 284 G3
†36017 Blue Springs 112 G7
35957 Boaz 7,151 F2
35443 Boligee 164 C5
35032 Bon Air 118 F4
36511 Bon Secour 850 C10
†35120 Branchville 365 F3
36009 Brantley 1,151 F7
35034 Brent 2,862 D5
36426 Brewton⊙ 6,680 D8
35740 Bridgeport 2,974 G1
35020 Brighton 5,308 D4
35548 Brilliant 871 C2
35036 Brookside 1,409 E3
35444 Brookwood 492 D4
36010 Brundidge 3,213 G7
36725 Burkville 250 E6
36431 Burnt Corn 60 D7
36904 Butler⊙ 1,882 B6
†36767 Cahaba 75 D6
35040 Calera 2,035 E4
†36047 Calhoun 950 F6
36513 Calvert 600 B8
36726 Camden⊙ 2,406 D7
36850 Camp Hill 1,628 G5
†36502 Canoe 560 D8
†36726 Canton Bend 300 D6
35549 Carbon Hill 2,452 D3
35041 Cardiff 140 E3
†36420 Carolina 203 E8
35447 Carrollton⊙ 1,104 B4
†36023 Carrville 820 G5
†36548 Carson 400 C8
36432 Castleberry 847 D8
35959 Cedar Bluff 1,129 G2
35960 Centre⊙ 2,351 G2
35042 Centreville⊙ 2,504 D5
36518 Chatom⊙ 1,122 B8
35043 Chelsea 600 E4
35616 Cherokee 1,589 C1
36611 Chickasaw 7,402 B9
35044 Childersburg 5,084 F4
36254 Choccolocco 500 G3
36905 Choctaw 600 B6
†36550 Chrysler 400 C8
36521 Chunchula 700 B9
36522 Citronelle 2,841 B8
35045 Clanton⊙ 5,832 E5
†36322 Clayhatchee 560 G8
36015 Clayton⊙ 1,589 G7
35049 Cleveland 487 E3
36017 Clio 1,224 G7
35449 Coaling 400 D4
36523 Coden 600 B10
36318 Coffee Springs 339 G8
36524 Coffeeville 448 B7
35452 Coker 800 C4
35961 Collinsville 1,383 G2
36319 Columbia 881 H8
35051 Columbiana⊙ 2,655 E4
36020 Coosada 980 F5
35550 Cordova 3,123 D3
35453 Cottondale 500 D4
36320 Cottonwood 1,352 H8
†35172 County Line 199 E3
†36467 County Line 124 F8
35618 Courtland 456 D1
36321 Cowarts 418 H8
36435 Coy 950 D7
36525 Creola 1,652 B9
36906 Cromwell 650 B6
35962 Crossville 1,222 G2
36907 Cuba 486 B6
35055 Cullman⊙ 13,084 E2
36852 Cusseta 650 H5
36853 Dadeville⊙ 3,263 G5
36322 Daleville 4,250 G8
36526 Daphne 3,406 C9
36528 Dauphin Island 950 B10
36256 Daviston 334 G4
36731 Dayton 113 C6
*35601 Decatur⊙ 42,002 D1
36257 De Armanville 350 G3
36732 Demopolis 7,678 C6
35552 Detroit 326 B2
35062 Dora 2,327 D3
*36303 Dothan⊙ 48,750 H8
35553 Double Springs⊙ 1,057 D2
35964 Douglas 116 F2
36028 Dozier 494 F7
35744 Dutton 276 G1
36426 East Brewton 3,012 E8
36024 Eclectic 1,124 F5
36261 Edwardsville 207 H3
36323 Elba⊙ 4,355 F8
36530 Elberta 491 C10
35554 Eldridge 230 C3
35620 Elkmont 429 E1
36025 Elmore 600 F5
35458 Elrod 746 C4
35063 Empire 600 D3
36330 Enterprise 18,033 G8
35460 Epes 399 B5
35461 Ethelsville 95 B4
36027 Eufaula 12,097 H7
†36340 Eunola 169 G8
35462 Eutaw⊙ 2,444 C5
35621 Eva 185 E2
36401 Evergreen⊙ 4,171 E8
36439 Excel 385 D8
35746 Fackler 250 G1
36854 Fairfax 3,776 H5
35064 Fairfield 13,242 E4
36532 Fairhope 7,286 C10
35208 Fairview 450 E2
35622 Falkville 1,310 E2
36738 Faunsdale 174 C6
35555 Fayette⊙ 5,287 C3
36855 Five Points 197 H4
35966 Flat Rock 750 G1
†35601 Flint City 673 D1
36441 Flomaton 1,882 D8
36442 Florala 2,165 F8
*35630 Florence⊙ 37,029 C1
Florence‡ 135,023 C1
36535 Foley 4,003 C10
35214 Forestdale 10,814 E3
36740 Forkland 429 C5
36031 Fort Davis 500 G6
36032 Fort Deposit 1,519 E7
36856 Fort Mitchell 900 H6
35967 Fort Payne⊙ 11,485 G2
35463 Fosters 400 C4
36444 Franklin 133 G6
36445 Frisco City 1,424 D8
36539 Fruitdale 500 B8
36262 Fruithurst 239 G3
36446 Fulton 606 C7
35068 Fultondale 6,217 E3
35971 Fyffe 1,305 G2
*35901 Gadsden⊙ 47,565 G2
Gadsden‡ 103,057 G2
35464 Gainesville 207 B5
35972 Gallant 475 F2
36038 Gantt 314 E8
35070 Garden City 655 E2
35071 Gardendale 7,928 E3
35973 Gaylesville 192 G2
†35459 Geiger 200 B5
36340 Geneva⊙ 4,866 G8
36033 Georgiana 1,993 E7
35974 Geraldine 911 G2
36908 Gilbertown 218 B7
35559 Glen Allen 312 C3
35905 Glencoe 4,648 G3
36034 Glenwood 341 F7
†35010 Goldville 89 G4
†36024 Good Hope 1,442 E2
35072 Goodwater 1,895 F4
35466 Gordo 2,112 C4
36343 Gordon 362 H8
†35580 Gorgas 500 D3
36035 Goshen 365 F7
†36482 Gosport 500 C7
36541 Grand Bay 3,185 B10
35747 Grant 632 F1
35073 Graysville 2,642 D3
35074 Green Pond 750 D4
36744 Greensboro⊙ 3,248 C5
36037 Greenville⊙ 7,807 E7
†36350 Grimes 298 H8
36451 Grove Hill⊙ 1,912 C7
35563 Guin 2,418 C3
36542 Gulf Shores 1,349 C10
35976 Guntersville⊙ 7,041 F2
35748 Gurley 735 F1
†35563 Gu-Win 266 C3
35564 Hackleburg 883 C2
†36319 Haleburg 106 H8
35565 Haleyville 5,306 C2

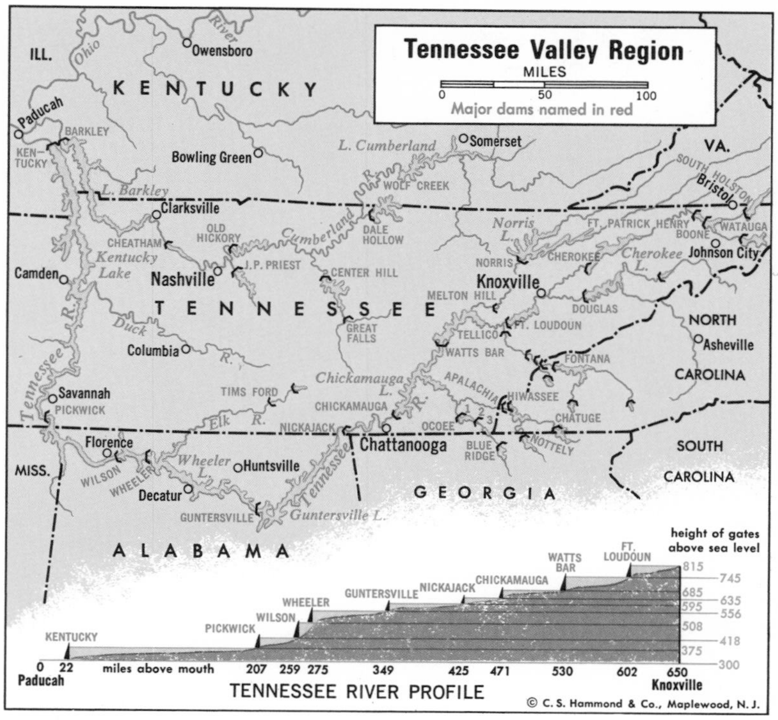

35570 Hamilton⊙ 5,093 C2
†35989 Hammondville 369 G1
35077 Hanceville 2,220 E2
36039 Hardaway 600 G6
35078 Harpersville 934 F4
36344 Hartford 2,647 G8
35640 Hartselle 8,858 E2
36858 Hatchechubbee 840 H6
†35672 Hatton 950 D1
35079 Hayden 268 E3
36040 Hayneville⊙ 592 E6
35750 Hazel Green 1,503 E1
36345 Headland 3,327 H8
†36558 Healing Springs 100 B7
†36420 Heath 354 F8
36264 Heflin⊙ 3,014 G3
35080 Helena 2,130 E4
35978 Henagar 1,188 G1
35979 Higdon 925 G1
†35013 Highland Lake 210 F3
35643 Hillsboro 278 D1
†36201 Hobson City 1,268 G3
35571 Hodges 250 C2
35903 Hokes Bluff 3,216 G3
35082 Hollins 500 F4
35083 Holly Pond 493 E2
35752 Hollywood 1,110 G1
35209 Homewood 21,412 E4
†35216 Hoover 19,792 E4
36043 Hope Hull 975 F6
†36467 Horn Hill 186 F8
35020 Hueytown 13,478 D4
*35801 Huntsville⊙ 142,513 E1
Huntsville‡ 308,593 E1
36860 Hurtsboro 752 H6
35981 Ider 698 G1
35210 Irondale 6,510 E3
36545 Jackson 6,073 C8
36861 Jacksons Gap 800 G5
36265 Jacksonville 9,735 G3
35501 Jasper⊙ 11,894 D3
35085 Jemison 1,828 E5
35573 Kansas 267 C3
35574 Kennedy 604 B3
35645 Killen 747 D1
35091 Kimberly 1,043 E3
†36301 Kinsey 1,239 H8
36453 Kinston 604 F8
36862 Lafayette⊙ 3,647 H5
†35986 Lakeview 441 G2
36863 Lanett 6,897 H5
36864 Langdale 2,034 H5
†35768 Larkinsville 425 F1
36911 Lavaca 500 B6
35094 Leeds 8,638 E3
35983 Leesburg 116 G2
35646 Leighton 1,218 D1
36548 Leroy 699 B8
35647 Lester 117 D1
†36322 Level Plains 867 G8
35648 Lexington 884 D1
†36420 Libertyville 141 F8
35096 Lincoln 2,081 F3
36748 Linden⊙ 2,773 C6
36266 Lineville 2,257 G4
35020 Lipscomb 3,741 E4
36912 Lisman 638 B6
†36876 Little Shawmut 2,793 H5
†35653 Littleville 1,262 C1
35470 Livingston⊙ 3,187 B5
36865 Loachapoka 335 G5
36455 Lockhart 547 F8
35097 Locust Fork 488 E3
†35137 Longview 475 E4
36048 Louisville 791 G7
36751 Lower Peach Tree 926 C7
36752 Lowndesboro 207 E6
36551 Loxley 804 C9
36049 Luverne⊙ 2,639 F7
35575 Lynn 554 C2
35758 Madison 4,057 E1
36348 Madrid 172 H8
36555 Magnolia Springs 800 C10
36349 Malvern 558 G8
36750 Maplesville 754 E5
35112 Margaret 757 F3
36756 Marion⊙ 4,467 D5
35114 Maylene 500 E4
35111 McCalla 657 E4
36552 McCullough 500 D8
36553 McIntosh 319 B8
36456 McKenzie 605 E7
†35442 Memphis 95 B4
35984 Mentone 476 G1
35759 Meridianville 1,403 F1
35228 Midfield 6,203 E4
36350 Midland City 1,903 H8
36053 Midway 593 H6
†35150 Mignon 2,054 F4
36054 Millbrook 3,101 F6
35576 Millport 1,287 B3
36558 Millry 956 B7
36761 Minter 450 D6
*36601 Mobile⊙ 200,452 B9
Mobile‡ 442,819 B9
36460 Monroeville⊙ 5,674 D7
†35804 Monrovia 500 E1
35115 Montevallo 3,965 E4
*36101 Montgomery (cap.)⊙ 178,857 F6
Montgomery‡ 272,687 F6
36559 Montrose 750 C9
†35125 Moody 1,840 F3
35649 Mooresville 58 E1
35116 Morris 623 E3
35650 Moulton⊙ 3,197 D2
35474 Moundville 1,310 C5
†35957 Mountainboro 266 F2
35223 Mountain Brook 19,718 E4
36560 Mount Vernon 1,038 B8
36268 Munford 700 F3
35660 Muscle Shoals 8,911 C1
36763 Myrtlewood 252 C6
36764 Nanafalia 500 B6
36303 Napier Field 493 H8
35578 Nauvoo 259 D3
†35049 Nectar 367 E3
36765 Newbern 307 C5
36351 New Brockton 1,392 G8
35760 New Hope 1,546 F1
35761 New Market 680 F1
†35010 New Site 340 G4
36352 Newton 1,540 G8
36353 Newville 814 H8
35086 North Johns 243 D4
35476 Northport 14,291 C4
36866 Notasulga 876 G5
35006 Oak Grove 638 F4
36766 Oak Hill 63 D7
35579 Oakman 770 D3
35120 Odenville 724 F3
36271 Ohatchee 860 G3
35121 Oneonta⊙ 4,824 E3
†36467 Onycha 147 F8
36801 Opelika⊙ 21,896 H5
36467 Opp 7,204 F8
36561 Orange Beach 600 C10
36767 Orrville 349 D6
35763 Owens Cross Roads 804 E1
36203 Oxford 8,939 G3
36360 Ozark⊙ 13,188 G8
35764 Paint Rock 221 F1
35580 Parrish 1,583 D3
35124 Pelham 6,759 E4
35125 Pell City⊙ 6,616 F3
36916 Pennington 355 B6
36562 Perdido 500 C8
36471 Peterman 600 D7
36062 Petrey 93 F7
36867 Phenix City⊙ 26,928 H6
35581 Phil Campbell 1,549 C2
†35447 Pickensville 132 B4
36272 Piedmont 5,544 G3
36371 Pinckard 771 G8
36768 Pine Apple 298 E7
36769 Pine Hill 510 C7
35765 Pisgah 699 G1
36758 Plantersville 650 E5
35127 Pleasant Grove 7,102 D4
36564 Point Clear 1,812 C10
†36441 Pollard 144 D8

(continued on following page)

Agriculture, Industry and Resources

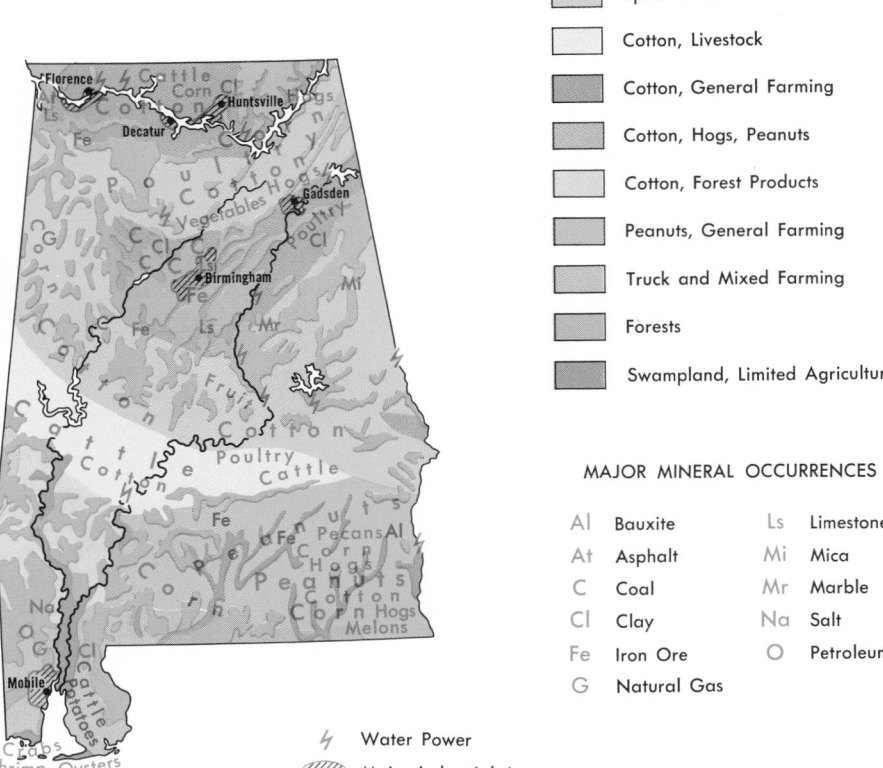

DOMINANT LAND USE

- Specialized Cotton
- Cotton, Livestock
- Cotton, General Farming
- Cotton, Hogs, Peanuts
- Cotton, Forest Products
- Peanuts, General Farming
- Truck and Mixed Farming
- Forests
- Swampland, Limited Agriculture

MAJOR MINERAL OCCURRENCES

Al	Bauxite	Ls	Limestone
At	Asphalt	Mi	Mica
C	Coal	Mr	Marble
Cl	Clay	Na	Salt
Fe	Iron Ore	O	Petroleum
G	Natural Gas		

⚡ Water Power

▨ Major Industrial Areas

Topography

0   30   60 MI.

0   30   60 KM.

Below Sea Level | 100 m. 328 ft. | 200 m. 656 ft. | 500 m. 1,640 ft. | 1,000 m. 3,281 ft. | 2,000 m. 6,562 ft. | 5,000 m. 16,404 ft.

Alabama

SCALE
0 5 10   20   30   40 MI.
0 5 10   20   30   40 KM.

State Capitals .... ⊛
County Seats .... ⊙
Major Limited Access Hwys. _____

Scale 1:1,930,000

© Copyright HAMMOND INCORPORATED, Maplewood, N.J.

SENATORIAL DISTRICTS

Central H2
Northwestern E2
South Central G3
Southeastern L3

CITIES and TOWNS

Zip Name/Pop. Key
†99609 Akolmiut (Kasigluk) 641.. F2
99554 Alakanuk 522 .... E2
*99501 Anchorage⊙ 174,431... B1
Anchorage‡ 174,431...... B1
†99760 Anderson 517 .... H2
99723 Barrow 2,207 .... G1
99559 Bethel 3,576 .... F2
99704 Clear 504 .... J2
99701 College 4,043 .... J1
99574 Cordova 1,879 .... D1
99921 Craig 527 .... M2
99737 Delta Junction 945 ...... J2
99576 Dillingham 1,563 .... G3
†99685 Dutch Harbor 250 ...... E4
99581 Emanguk (Emmonak) 567 E2
99701 Fairbanks⊙ 22,645 ...... J2
99740 Fort Yukon 619 .... J1
99741 Galena 765 .... G2
99588 Glennallen 511 .... D1
99827 Haines 993 .... M1
99603 Homer 2,209 .... B2
99829 Hoonah 680 .... M1

99604 Hooper Bay 627 .... E2
99801 Juneau (cap.) ⊙ 19,528. N1
99830 Kake 555 .... M1
99609 Kasigluk 641 .... F2
99611 Kenai 4,324 .... B1
99901 Ketchikan 7,198 .... N2
99615 Kodiak 4,756 .... H3
99752 Kotzebue 2,054 .... F1
†99901 Mountain Point 396 ... N2
99632 Mountain Village 583 .. E2
99926 Metlakatla 1,056 .... N2
99762 Nome⊙ 2,301 .... E2
99763 Noorvik 492 .... F1
99645 Palmer 2,141 .... C1
99833 Petersburg 2,821 .... N2
99660 Saint Paul Island 551 .. D3
99661 Sand Point 625 .... G3
99664 Seward 1,843 .... C1
99835 Sitka 7,803 .... M1
99840 Skagway 768 .... M1
99669 Soldotna 2,320 .... B1
99503 Spenard C1
99672 Sterling 919 .... B1
99780 Tok 589 .... K2
99684 Unalakleet 623 .... G2
99685 Unalaska 1,322 .... E4
99686 Valdez 3,079 .... D1
99929 Wrangell 2,184 .... N2
99689 Yakutat 449 .... L3

OTHER FEATURES

Adak (isl.) L4
Admiralty (isl.) M1

Afognak (isl.) H3
Agattu (isl.) J3
Akutan (isl.) E4
Alaska (gulf) K3
Alaska (range) H2
Aleutian (isls.) J4
Aleutian (range) G3
Alexander (arch.) L1
Amchitka (isl.) K4
Amlia (passage) L4
Amukta (isl.) D4
Andreanof (isls.) L4
Atka (isl.) L4
Attu (isl.) J3
Baird (mts.) F1
Baranof (isl.) M1
Barrow (pt.) G1
Bear (mt.) K2
Beaufort (sea) K1
Becharof (lake) G3
Bering (glac.) K2
Bering (sea) D2
Bering (str.) E1
Blackburn (mt.) K2
Bona (mt.) K2
Bristol (bay) F3
British (mts.) K1
Brooks (range) G1
Chandalar (riv.) J1
Chatham (str.) M1
Chichagof (isl.) M1
Chignik (bay) G3
Chilkoot (pass) M1
Chirikof (isl.) G3

Chitina (riv.) K2
Christian (sound) M2
Chugash (mts.) C1
Chukchi (sea) E1
Clarence (str.) N2
Clark (lake) H2
Coast (mts.) N1
Columbia (glac.) C1
Colville (riv.) G1
Constantine (cape) G3
Cook (inlet) B1
Cook (mt.) K2
Copper (riv.) J2
Cordova (bay) M2
Coronation (isl.) M2
Cross (sound) L1
Dease (inlet) H1
Decision (cape) M2
Denali Nat'l Park H2
Devils Paw (mt.) N1
Dixon Entrance (chan.) M2
Douglas (mt.) H3
Dry (bay) L3
Eielson A.F.B. 5,232 .... J2
Elmendorf A.F.B. B1
Endicott (mts.) H1
Etolin (isl.) N2
Fairweather (cape) L1
Fairweather (mt.) L1
Firth (riv.) K1
Foraker (mt.) H2
Fort Davis E2
Fort Greely 1,635 .... J2
Fort Richardson C1

Fort Wainwright J1
Four Mountains (isls.) E4
Fox (isls.) E4
Frederick (sound) N1
Gates of the Arctic Nat'l
Park H1
Glacier (bay) M1
Glacier Bay Nat'l Park M1
Goodhope (bay) F1
Great Sitkin (isl.) L4
Guyot (glac.) K2
Hagemeister (isl.) F3
Halkett (cape) H1
Hall (isl.) D2
Harding Icefield H1
Harrison (bay) H1
Hayes (mt.) J2
Hazen (bay) E2
Hinchinbrook (isl.) D1
Hoonah (sound) M1
Hope (pt.) E1
Howard (pass) G1
Icy (bay) K3
Icy (cape) H1
Icy (pt.) L1
Icy (str.) M1
Iliamna (lake) G3
Iliamna (vol.) H2
Innoko (riv.) G2
Kachemak (bay) B2
Kanaga (isl.) K3
Kates Needle (mt.) N1
Katmai (vol.) H3
Katmai Nat'l Park H3

Kayak (isl.) K3
Kenai (lake) C1
Kenai (mt.) C2
Kenai (pen.) C2
Kenai Fjords Nat'l Park H3
Kennedy Entrance (str.) H3
King (isl.) E1
Kiska (isl.) J4
Kiska (vol.) J4
Klondike Gold Rush Nat'l Hist.
Park N1
Knight (isl.) N1
Knik Arm (inlet) B1
Kobuk (riv.) G1
Kobuk Valley Nat'l Park G1
Kodiak (isl.) H3
Kotzebue (sound) F1
Koyukuk (riv.) G1
Krusenstern (cape) F1
Kuiu (isl.) M2
Kuskokwim (bay) F3
Kuskokwim (mts.) G2
Kuskokwim (riv.) G2
Kvichak (bay) G3
Lake Clark Nat'l Park H2
Lisburne (cape) E1
Little Diomede (isl.) E1
Little Sitkin (isl.) K4
Lynn Canal (inlet) M1
Makushin (vol.) E4
Malaspina (glac.) K3
Marcus Baker (mt.) C1
Marmot (isl.) H3
Matanuska (riv.) C1

Agriculture, Industry and Resources

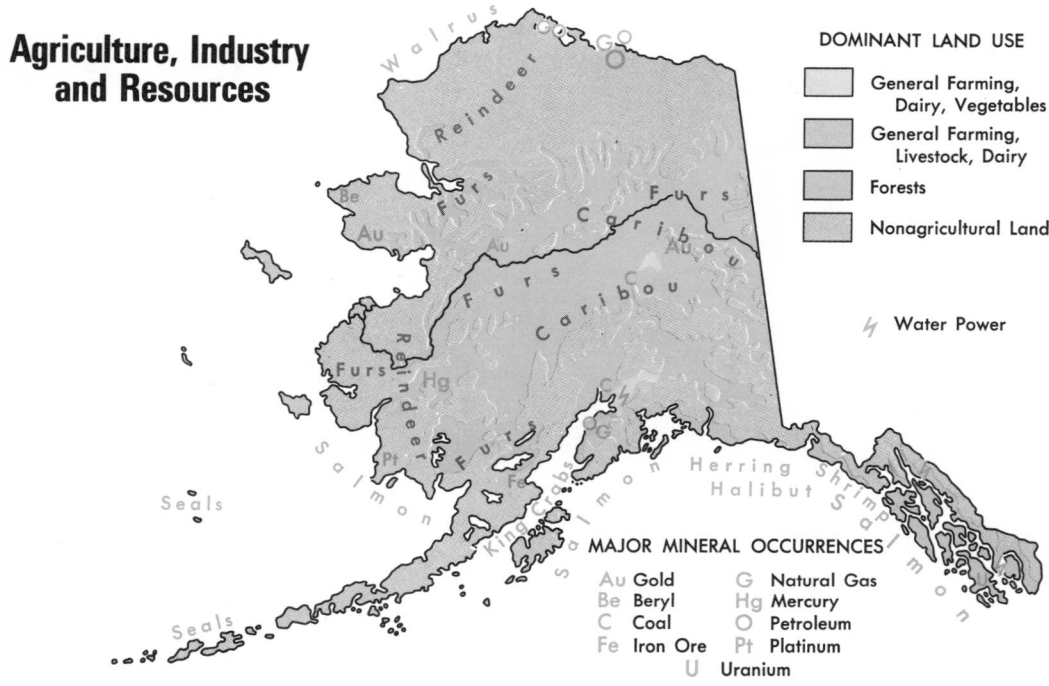

DOMINANT LAND USE

General Farming, Dairy, Vegetables
General Farming, Livestock, Dairy
Forests
Nonagricultural Land

⚡ Water Power

MAJOR MINERAL OCCURRENCES

Au	Gold	G	Natural Gas
Be	Beryl	Hg	Mercury
C	Coal	O	Petroleum
Fe	Iron Ore	Pt	Platinum
U	Uranium		

Topography

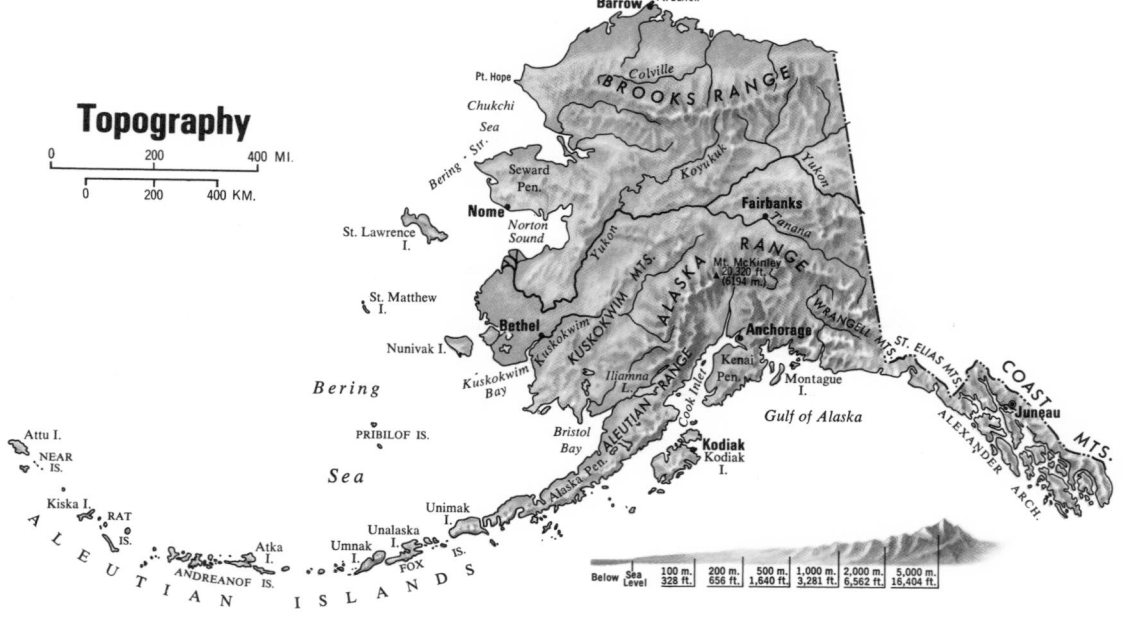

0   200   400 MI.
0   200   400 KM.

Below Sea Level / Sea Level | 100 m. 328 ft. | 200 m. 656 ft. | 500 m. 1,640 ft. | 1,000 m. 3,281 ft. | 2,000 m. 6,562 ft. | 5,000 m. 16,404 ft.

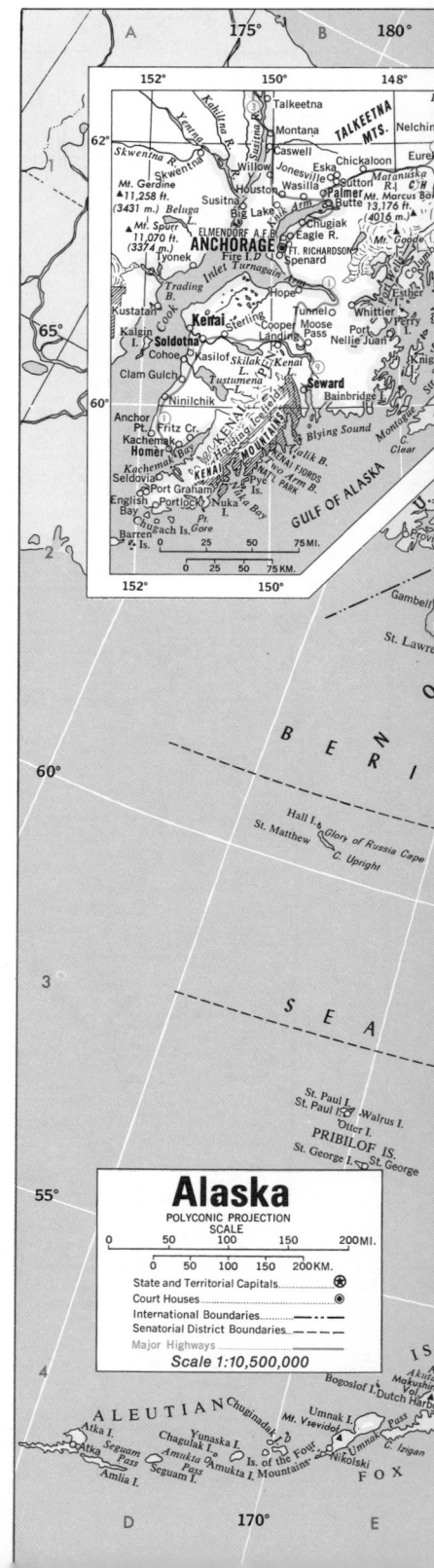

Alaska

POLYCONIC PROJECTION

SCALE

0   50   100   150   200 MI.
0   50   100   150   200 KM.

State and Territorial Capitals......... ⊛
Court Houses.......................... ⊛
International Boundaries..............
Senatorial District Boundaries........
Major Highways.......................

Scale 1:10,500,000

McKinley (mt.) H2
Meade (riv.) G1
Mendenhall (cape) E3
Mentasta (pass) K2
Merrill (pass) H2
Michelson (mt.) K1
Middleton (isl.) J3
Misty Fjords Nat'l Mon. N2
Mitkof (isl.) M1
Montague (isl.) D1
Muir (glac.) M1
Mulchatna (riv.) G2
Muzon (cape) M2
Naknek (lake) G3
Near (isls.) H3
Nelson (isl.) E2
Newenham (cape) F3
Noatak (riv.) F1
Norton (bay) F2
Norton (sound) E2
Nowitna (riv.) H2
Nuka (bay) C2
Nunivak (isl.) E3
Nushagak (riv.) G2
Nuyakuk (lake) F3
Ommaney (cape) M2
Otter (isl.) D3
Pastol (bay) F2
Pavlof (bay) F3
Pavlof (vol.) F3
Philip Smith (mts.) J1
Porcupine (riv.) K1
Port Clarence (inlet) E1
Port Heiden (inlet) G3

Portland Canal (inlet) N2
Port Moller (inlet) F3
Port Wells (inlet) C1
Pribilof (isls.) D3
Prince of Wales (cape) E1
Prince of Wales (isl.) N2
Prince William (sound) D1
Prudhoe (bay) J1
Rat (isl.) K4
Redoubt (vol.) H2
Revillagigedo (chan.) N2
Revillagigedo (isl.) N2
Romanzof (cape) E2
Sagavanirktok (riv.) J1
Saint Elias (cape) K3
Saint Elias (mts.) L2
Saint George (isl.) D3
Saint Lawrence (isl.) D2
Saint Matthew (isl.) D2
Saint Paul (isl.) D3
Salisbury (sound) M1
Sanak (isl.) F4
Sanford (mt.) K2
Schwatka (mts.) G1
Seguam (isl.) D4
Selawik (lake) F1
Semichi (isls.) J3
Semidi (isls.) G3
Semisopochnoi (isl.) K4
Seward (pen.) E1
Seymour (canal) N1
Sheenjek (riv.) K1
Shelikof (str.) H3
Shemya (isl.) J3

Shishaldin (vol.) E4
Shumagin (isls.) G4
Shuyak (isl.) H3
Sitka (sound) M1
Sitka Nat'l Hist. Park M1
Sitkinak (str.) H3
Skilak (lake) C1
Skwentna (riv.) A1
Smith (bay) H1
Spencer (cape) L1
Stephens (passage) N1
Stevenson Entrance (str.) .. H3
Stikine (riv.) N2
Stikine (str.) N2
Stony (riv.) G2
Stuart (isl.) F2
Suemez (isl.) M2
Sumner (str.) M2
Susitna (riv.) B1
Sutwik (isl.) G3
Taku (glac.) N1
Taku (riv.) N1
Talkeetna (mts.) J2
Tanaga (isl.) K4
Tanaga (vol.) K4
Tanana (riv.) J2
Taylor (mts.) G2
Tazlina (lake) D1
Tazlina (riv.) D1
Teshekpuk (lake) H1
Tigalda (isl.) F4
Tikchik (lkes.) G2
Togiak (bay) F3
Tugidak (isl.) G3

Turnagain Arm (inlet) B1
Tustumena (lake) C1
Two Arm (bay) C2
Ugashik (lkes.) G3
Umnak (isl.) E4
Umnak (passage) E4
Unalaska (isl.) E4
Unga (isl.) F3
Unimak (isl.) F4
Unimak (passage) F4
Utukok (riv.) F1
Valley of Ten Thousand Smokes . G3
Vancouver (mt.) L2
Veniaminof (crater) F3
Vsevidof (mt.) E4
Walrus (isl.) G1
Walrus (isl.) G3
Waring (mts.) G1
West Point (mt.) K2
White (pass) N1
White (riv.) K1
White Mountains Nat'l Rec. Area . J1
Witherspoon (mt.) C1
Wrangell (cape) H3
Wrangell (isl.) N2
Wrangell (mts.) K2
Wrangell-St. Elias Nat'l Park ... K2
Yakobi (isl.) M1
Yakutat (bay) K3
Yentna (riv.) A1
Yukon (riv.) F2

⊙ Court House
‡ Population of metropolitan area.
† Zip of nearest p.o.
* Multiple zips.

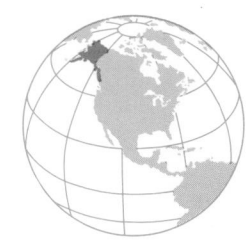

AREA 591,004 sq. mi. (1,530,700 sq. km.)
POPULATION 401,851
CAPITAL Juneau
LARGEST CITY Anchorage
HIGHEST POINT Mt. McKinley 20,320 ft. (6194 m.)
SETTLED IN 1801
ADMITTED TO UNION January 3, 1959
POPULAR NAME Great Land; Last Frontier
STATE FLOWER Forget-me-not
STATE BIRD Willow Ptarmigan

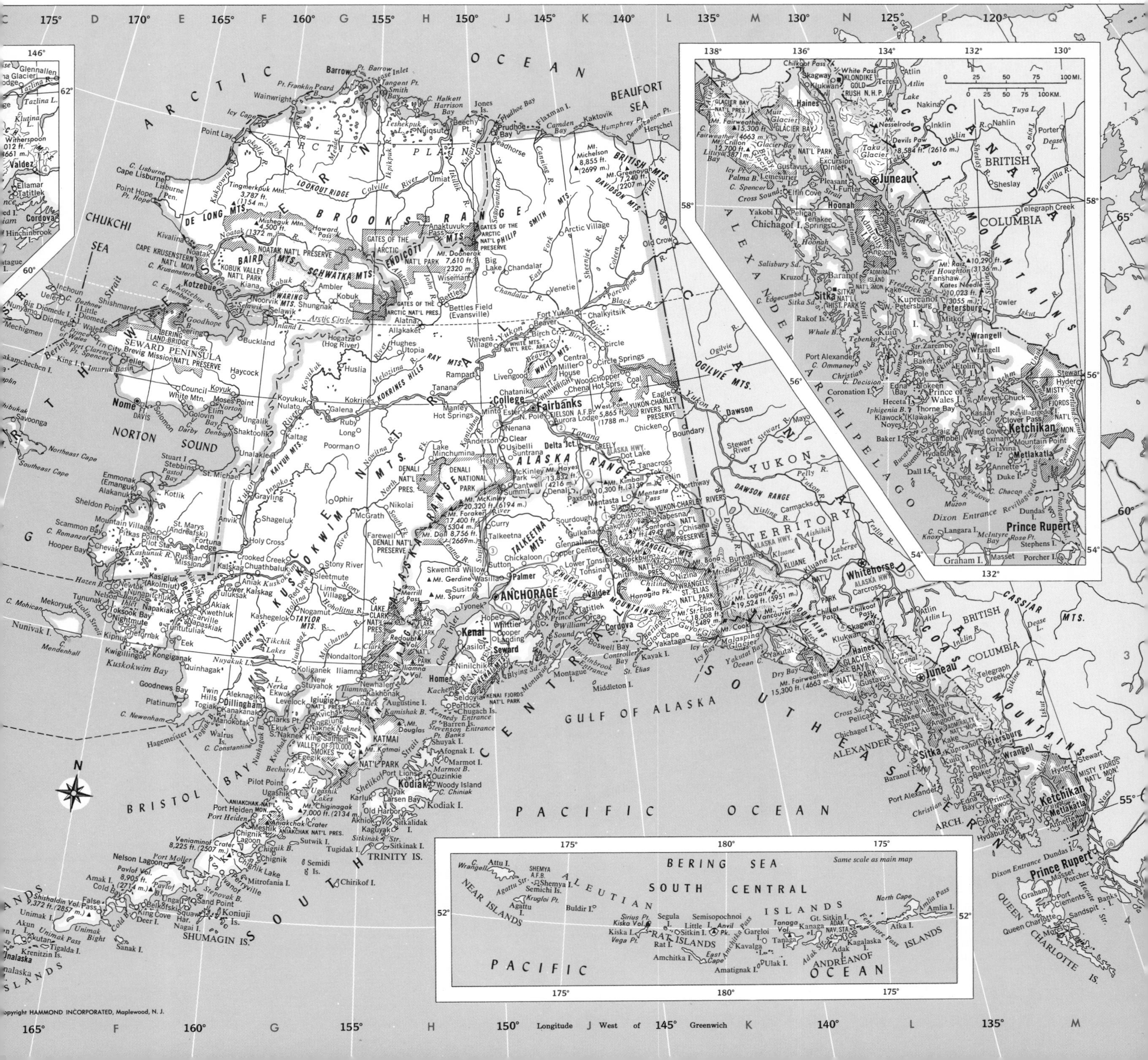

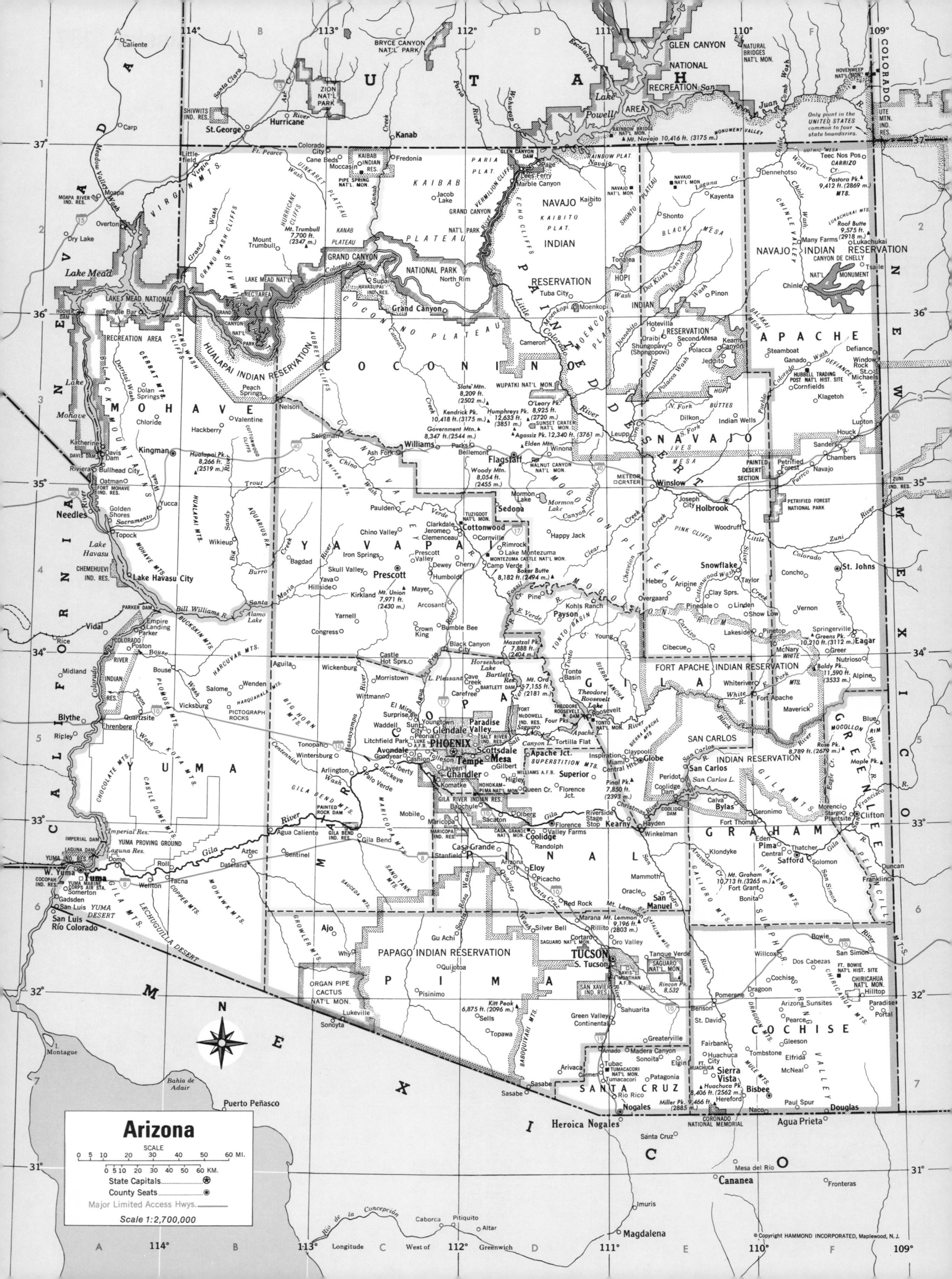

Arizona

SCALE

0 5 10   20   30   40   50   60 MI.

0 5 10 20 30 40 50 60 KM.

State Capitals.................... ✪

County Seats...................... ◉

Major Limited Access Hwys. _____

Scale 1:2,700,000

© Copyright HAMMOND INCORPORATED, Maplewood, N.J.

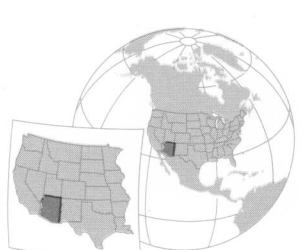

AREA 114,000 sq. mi. (295,260 sq. km.)
POPULATION 2,718,425
CAPITAL Phoenix
LARGEST CITY Phoenix
HIGHEST POINT Humphreys Pk. 12,633 ft.
(3851 m.)
SETTLED IN 1752
ADMITTED TO UNION February 14, 1912
POPULAR NAME Grand Canyon State
STATE FLOWER Saguaro Cactus Blossom
STATE BIRD Cactus Wren

Agriculture, Industry and Resources

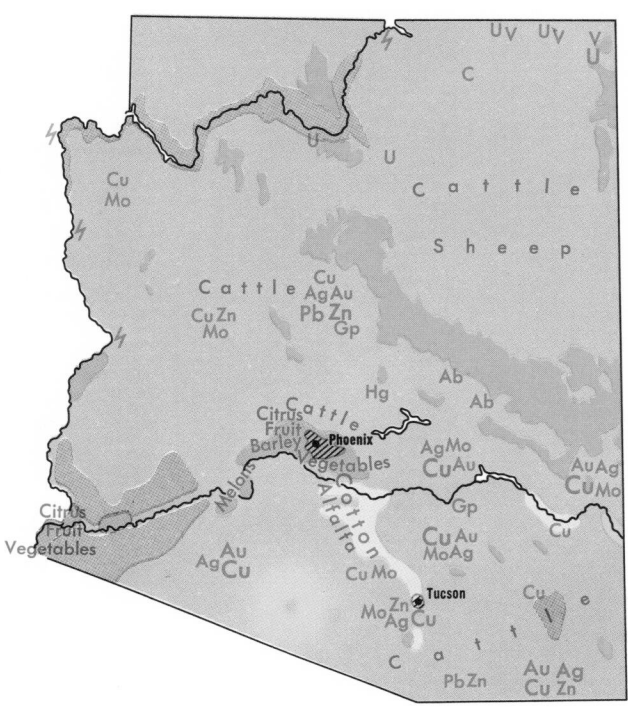

MAJOR MINERAL OCCURRENCES

Ab	Asbestos	Cu	Copper	Pb	Lead
Ag	Silver	Gp	Gypsum	U	Uranium
Au	Gold	Hg	Mercury	V	Vanadium
C	Coal	Mo	Molybdenum	Zn	Zinc

DOMINANT LAND USE

Fruit, Truck and Mixed Farming

Cotton and Alfalfa

General Farming, Livestock, Special Crops

Range Livestock

Forests

Nonagricultural Land

⚡ Water Power

▨ Major Industrial Areas

COUNTIES

Apache 52,108 ....F3
Cochise 85,686 ....F7
Coconino 75,008 ....C3
Gila 37,080 ....E5
Graham 22,862 ....E6
Greenlee 11,406 ....F5
Maricopa 1,509,052 ....C5
Mohave 55,865 ....A3
Navajo 67,629 ....E3
Pima 531,443 ....D6
Pinal 90,918 ....D6
Santa Cruz 20,459 ....E7
Yavapai 68,145 ....C4
Yuma 90,554 ....A5

CITIES and TOWNS

Zip	Name/Pop.	Key
†85333	Agua Caliente 60	B6
85320	Aguila 900	B5
85321	Ajo 5,189	C6
85920	Alpine 450	F5
85640	Amado 75	D7
85220	Apache Junction 9,935	D5
†85901	Aripine 25	E4
85601	Arivaca 400	D7
85223	Arizona City 825	D6
85625	Arizona Sunsites 825	F7
85322	Arlington 950	C5
86320	Ash Fork 800	C3

85323 Avondale 8,168 ....C5
†85333 Aztec 20 ....B6
86321 Bagdad 2,331 ....B4
85221 Bapchule 400 ....D5
86015 Bellemont 210 ....D3
85602 Benson 4,190 ....E7
85603 Bisbee⊙ 7,154 ....F7
85324 Black Canyon City 600 .....C4
85922 Blue 50 ....F5
†85643 Bonita 20 ....E6
85325 Bouse 500 ....A5
85605 Bowie 600 ....F6
85326 Buckeye 3,434 ....C5
86430 Bullhead
    City-Riviera 10,364 ......A3
†86301 Bumble Bee 15 ....C4
85530 Bylas 1,175 ....E5
†85530 Calva 10 ....E5
86020 Cameron 600 ....D3
86322 Camp Verde 1,125 ....D4
†86022 Cane Beds 30 ....B2
85331 Carefree 986 ....C5
†85640 Carmen 200 ....D7
85222 Casa Grande 14,971 ....D6
85329 Cashion 3,014 ....C5
†85342 Castle Hot Springs 50 .....C5
85331 Cave Creek 1,589 ....D5
85531 Central 300 ....F6
†85501 Central Heights-Midland
    City 2,791 ....E5
86502 Chambers 500 ....F3
85224 Chandler 29,673 ....D5
†86327 Cherry 20 ....C4
86503 Chinle 2,815 ....F2

86323 Chino Valley 2,858 ....C4
86431 Chloride 225 ....A3
†85292 Christmas 201 ....E5
85911 Cibecue 100 ....E4
86324 Clarkdale 1,512 ....C4
85532 Claypool 2,362 ....E5
†85934 Clay Springs 500 ....E4
†86326 Clemenceau 300 ....C4
85533 Clifton⊙ 4,245 ....F5
85606 Cochise 150 ....F6
86021 Colorado City 350 ....B2
85924 Concho 100 ....F4
85332 Congress 800 ....C4
†85640 Continental 250 ....D7
85228 Coolidge 6,851 ....D6
†85542 Coolidge Dam 42 ....E5
†86505 Cornfields 200 ....F3
86325 Cornville 425 ....D4
85230 Cortaro 375 ....D6
86326 Cottonwood 4,550 ....D4
86333 Crown King 100 ....C4
85333 Dateland 100 ....B6
†86430 Davis Dam 125 ....A3
86327 Dewey 100 ....C4
†86047 Dilkon 90 ....E3
86441 Dolan Springs 870 ....A3
85364 Dome 48 ....A6
†85643 Dos Cabezas 30 ....F6
85607 Douglas 13,058 ....F7
85609 Dragoon 150 ....F6
85534 Duncan 603 ....F6
85925 Eagar 2,791 ....F4
85535 Eden 89 ....F6
85334 Ehrenburg 93 ....A5

(continued on following page)

Topography

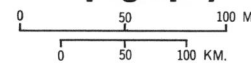

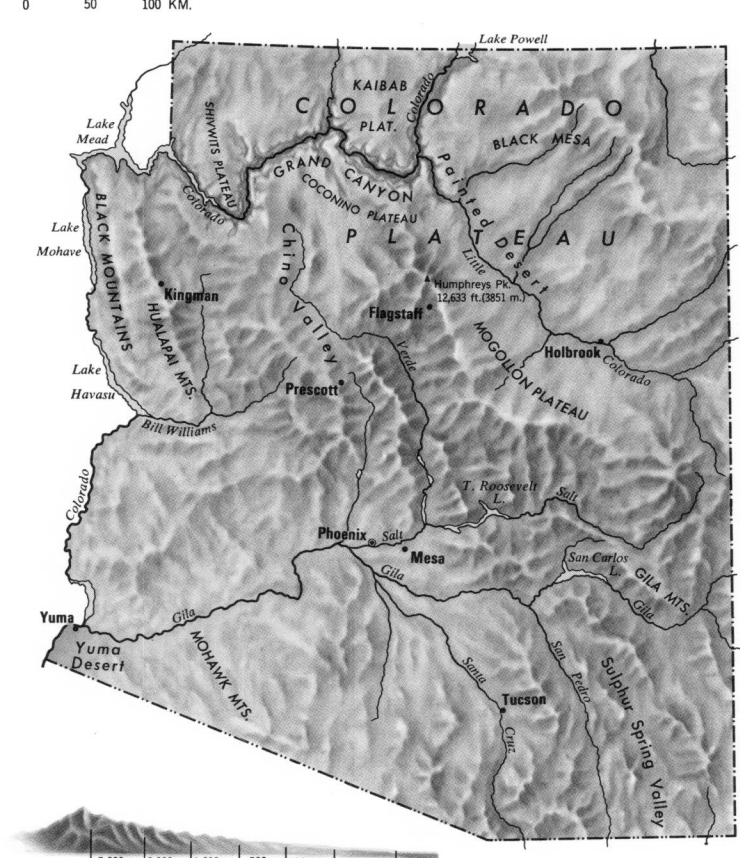

†85617 Elfrida 700 .... F7
†85637 Elgin 525 .... E7
85335 El Mirage 4,307 .... C5
85231 Eloy 6,240 .... D6
85612 Fairbank 100 .... E7
86001 Flagstaff⊙ 34,743 .... D3
85232 Florence⊙ 3,391 .... D5
†85220 Florence Junction 35 .... D5
85926 Fort Apache 500 .... F5
86504 Fort Defiance 3,431 .... F3
85643 Fort Grant 240 .... E6
85536 Fort Thomas 450 .... E5
85534 Franklin 300 .... F6
86022 Fredonia 1,040 .... C2
85336 Gadsden 250 .... A6
86505 Ganado 816 .... F3
†85536 Geronimo 25 .... F5
85337 Gila Bend 1,585 .... C6
85234 Gilbert 5,717 .... D5
†85617 Gleeson 15 .... F7
*85301 Glendale 97,172 .... C5
85501 Globe⊙ 6,886 .... E5
85323 Goodyear 2,747 .... C5
86023 Grand Canyon 1,348 .... C2
†85637 Greaterville 15 .... E7
85614 Green Valley 7,999 .... D7
85927 Greer 385 .... F4
†85634 Gu Achi 339 .... C6
86411 Hackberry 250 .... B3
86024 Happy Jack 50 .... D4
85235 Hayden 1,205 .... E5
85928 Heber 750 .... E4
85615 Hereford 10 .... E7
85236 Higley 500 .... D5
†86301 Hillside 100 .... B4
†85632 Hilltop 9 .... F6
86025 Holbrook⊙ 5,785 .... E4
86030 Hotevilla 3,009 .... E3
86506 Houck 900 .... F3
85616 Huachuca City 1,661 .... E7
86329 Humboldt 787 .... C4
86031 Indian Wells 150 .... E3
85537 Inspiration 500 .... D5
86330 Iron Springs 175 .... C4
86051 Jacob Lake 16 .... C2
†86025 Jeddito 20 .... E3
86331 Jerome 420 .... C4
86032 Joseph City 650 .... E4
86053 Kaibito 275 .... D2
†86430 Katherine 102 .... A3
86033 Kayenta 3,343 .... E2
86034 Keams Canyon 400 .... E3
85237 Kearny 2,646 .... E5
86401 Kingman⊙ 9,257 .... A3
86332 Kirkland 100 .... C4
†86505 Klagetoh 200 .... F3
85643 Klondyke 86 .... E6
85538 Kohls Ranch 100 .... D4
†85339 Komatke 300 .... C5
86403 Lake Havasu City 15,909 .... A4
86342 Lake Montezuma 900 .... D4
85929 Lakeside 1,333 .... E4
85339 Laveen 800 .... C5
†86036 Lees Ferry 10 .... D2
86035 Leupp 150 .... E3
†85326 Liberty 150 .... C5
†85901 Linden 50 .... E4
85340 Litchfield Park 3,657 .... C5
86432 Littlefield 40 .... B2
86507 Lukachukai 1,049 .... F2
85341 Lukeville 50 .... C7
86508 Lupton 250 .... F3
†85637 Madera Canyon 75 .... E7
85618 Mammoth 1,906 .... E6
86538 Many Farms 1,364 .... F2
85238 Marana 1,674 .... D6
86036 Marble Canyon 6 .... D2
85239 Maricopa 750 .... C5
†85920 Maverick 50 .... F5
86333 Mayer 810 .... C4
85930 McNary 1,320 .... F4
85617 McNeal 100 .... F7
*85201 Mesa 152,453 .... D5
85539 Miami 2,716 .... E5
†85239 Mobile 100 .... C5
†86022 Moccasin 150 .... C2
†86045 Moenkopi D2
85540 Morenci 2,736 .... F5
86038 Mormon Lake 20 .... D4
85342 Morristown 400 .... C5
85619 Mount Lemmon 400 .... E6
†84770 Mount Trumbull 14 .... B2
85620 Naco 750 .... E7
86509 Navajo 100 .... F3
†86434 Nelson 39 .... B3
85621 Nogales⊙ 15,683 .... E7
86052 North Rim 50 .... C2
85932 Nutrioso 500 .... F5
86433 Oatman 175 .... A3
†85247 Olberg 65 .... D5
85623 Oracle 2,484 .... E6
86039 Oraibi 600 .... E3
†85704 Oro Valley 1,489 .... E6
85933 Overgaard 750 .... E4
86040 Page 4,907 .... D2
85343 Palo Verde 500 .... C5
†85632 Paradise 15 .... F7
85253 Paradise Valley 11,085 .... D5
85344 Parker 2,542 .... A4
86018 Parks 175 .... C3
85624 Patagonia 980 .... E7
86334 Paulden 350 .... C4
†85607 Paul Spur 34 .... F7
85541 Payson 5,068 .... D4
86434 Peach Springs 900 .... B3
85625 Pearce 700 .... F7
85345 Peoria 12,307 .... C5
85542 Peridot 950 .... E5
86028 Petrified Forest 80 .... F3
*85001 Phoenix (cap.)⊙ 789,704 .... C5
Phoenix‡ 1,508,030 .... C5
85241 Picacho 850 .... D6
85543 Pima 1,599 .... F6
85544 Pine 800 .... D4
85934 Pinedale 400 .... E4
85935 Pinetop 1,527 .... F4
86510 Pinon 100 .... E2
85634 Pisinimo 187 .... C6
†85540 Plantsite F5
86042 Polacca 500 .... E3
85627 Pomerene 365 .... E6
85632 Portal 72 .... F7
85371 Poston 500 .... A4
86301 Prescott⊙ 20,055 .... C4
†86301 Prescott Valley 2,284 .... C4
85346 Quartzsite 255 .... A5
85242 Queen Creek 600 .... D5
†85634 Quijotoa 200 .... C6
85243 Randolph 350 .... D6
85245 Red Rock 250 .... D6
85246 Rillito 400 .... D6
86335 Rimrock 217 .... D4
85237 Riverside Stage Stop 418 .... D5
86440 Riviera-Bullhead City 10,364 .... A3
85347 Roll 700 .... A6
85545 Roosevelt 125 .... D5
85247 Sacaton 1,951 .... D5
85546 Safford⊙ 7,010 .... F6
85629 Sahuarita 200 .... E7
85630 Saint David 800 .... E7
85936 Saint Johns⊙ 3,368 .... F4
86511 Saint Michaels 250 .... F3
85348 Salome 800 .... B5
85550 San Carlos 2,668 .... E5
86512 Sanders 900 .... F3
85349 San Luis 1,946 .... A6
85631 San Manuel 5,443 .... E6
85632 San Simon 400 .... F6
85633 Sasabe 50 .... D7
*85251 Scottsdale 88,622 .... D5
86043 Second Mesa 450 .... E3
86336 Sedona 5,368 .... D4
86337 Seligman 510 .... B3
85634 Sells 1,864 .... D7
†85333 Sentinel 40 .... B6
86054 Shonto 700 .... E2
85901 Show Low 4,298 .... F4
†86043 Shungopavy (Shongopovi) 570 .... E3
85635 Sierra Vista 24,937 .... E7
85270 Silver Bell 900 .... D6
86338 Skull Valley 250 .... C4
85937 Snowflake 3,510 .... E4
85551 Solomon 700 .... F6
85350 Somerton 5,761 .... A6
85637 Sonoita 220 .... E7
85713 South Tucson 6,554 .... D6
85938 Springerville 1,452 .... F4
85272 Stanfield 150 .... C6
†85540 Stargo 1,038 .... F5
†86505 Steamboat 100 .... F3
*85351 Sun City 40,505 .... C5
86435 Supai 350 .... C2
85273 Superior 4,600 .... D5
85345 Surprise 3,723 .... C5
85352 Tacna 950 .... B6
†85701 Tanque Verde 850 .... E6
85939 Taylor 1,915 .... E4
86514 Teec Nos Pos 550 .... F2
*85282 Tempe 106,743 .... D5
86443 Temple Bar 84 .... A2
85552 Thatcher 3,374 .... F6
85353 Tolleson 4,433 .... C5
85638 Tombstone 1,632 .... F7
86044 Tonalea 125 .... E2
85354 Tonopah 54 .... B5
85553 Tonto Basin 250 .... D5
85639 Topawa 500 .... D7
86436 Topock 325 .... A4
85290 Tortilla Flat 37 .... D5
85640 Tubac 140 .... E7
86045 Tuba City 5,045 .... D2
*85701 Tucson⊙ 330,537 .... D6
Tucson‡ 531,263 .... D6
85640 Tumacacori 100 .... D7
85641 Vail 175 .... E6
86437 Valentine 120 .... B3
85291 Valley Farms 240 .... D6
85940 Vernon 75 .... F4
†85348 Vicksburg 16 .... B5
85355 Waddell 100 .... C5
85356 Wellton 911 .... A6
85357 Wenden 400 .... B5
85941 Whiteriver 2,256 .... E5
85321 Why 65 .... C6
85358 Wickenburg 3,535 .... C5
85360 Wikieup 150 .... B4
85643 Willcox 3,243 .... F6
86046 Williams 2,266 .... C3
86515 Window Rock 2,230 .... F3
85292 Winkelman 1,060 .... E6
†86001 Winona 25 .... D3
86047 Winslow 7,921 .... E3
†85322 Wintersburg 400 .... B5
85361 Wittmann 600 .... C5
85942 Woodruff 280 .... E4
85362 Yarnell 800 .... C4
†86301 Yava 40 .... C4
85554 Young 500 .... D4
85363 Youngtown 2,254 .... C5
86438 Yucca 250 .... A4
85364 Yuma⊙ 42,481 .... A6

OTHER FEATURES

Agassiz (peak) D3
Agua Fria (riv.) C5
Alamo (lake) B4
Apache (lake) D5
Aquarius (range) B4
Aravaipa (creek) E6
Aubrey (cliffs) B3
Baboquivari (mts.) D7
Baker Butte (mt.) D4
Balakai (mesa) F3
Baldy (peak) F5
Bartlett (dam) D5
Bartlett (res.) D5
Big Chino Wash (dry riv.) C3
Big Horn (mts.) B5
Big Sandy (riv.) B4
Bill Williams (riv.) B4
Black (mesa) E2
Black (mts.) A3
Black (riv.) E5
Blue (riv.) F5
Bouse Wash (dry riv.) A4
Buckskin (mts.) B4
Burro (creek) B4
Canyon (lake) D5
Canyon de Chelly Nat'l Mon. F2
Carrizo (creek) E4
Carrizo (mts.) G2
Casa Grande Ruins Nat'l Mon. D6
Castle Dome (mts.) A5
Cataract (creek) C3
Centennial Wash (dry riv.) B5
Cerbat (mts.) A3
Cherry (creek) E4
Chevelon (creek) E4
Chinle (creek) F2
Chinle (valley) F2
Chinle Wash (dry riv.) F2
Chino (valley) C3
Chiricahua (mts.) F6
Chiricahua Nat'l Mon. F6
Chocolate (mts.) A5
Clear (creek) D4
Coconino (plat.) C3
Cocopah Ind. Res. 355 .... A6
Colorado (riv.) A5
Colorado River Ind. Res. 6,640 .... A5
Coolidge (dam) E5
Copper (mts.) B6
Corn (creek) E3
Coronado Nat'l Memorial E7
Cottonwood (cliffs) B3
Cottonwood Wash (dry riv.) E4
Davis (dam) A3
Davis-Monthan A.F.B. 6,279 .... E6
Defiance (plat.) F3
Detrital Wash (dry riv.) A3
Diablo (canyon) D4
Dinnebito Wash (dry riv.) E3
Dot Klish (canyon) E2
Dragoon (mts.) F7
Eagle (creek) F5
East Verde (riv.) D4
Echo (cliffs) D2
Elden (mt.) D3
Fort Apache Ind. Res. 7,774 .... E5
Fort Bowie Nat'l Hist. Site F6
Fort Huachuca E7
Fort McDowell Ind. Res. 349 .... D5
Fort Mohave Ind. Res. 183 .... A4
Fort Pearce Wash (dry riv.) B2
Fossil (creek) D4
Four Peaks (mt.) D5
Galiuro (mts.) E6
Gila (mts.) A6
Gila (mts.) F5
Gila (riv.) B6
Gila Bend (mts.) B5
Gila Bend Ind. Res. 353 .... C6
Gila River Ind. Res. 7,445 .... C5
Glen Canyon (dam) D2
Glen Canyon Nat'l Rec. Area D1
Gothic (mesa) F2
Government (mt.) C3
Graham (mt.) F6
Grand Canyon Nat'l Park C2
Grand Wash (butte) B2
Grand Wash (riv.) B2
Greens (peak) F4
Growler (mts.) B6
Harcuvar (mts.) B5
Harquahala (mts.) B5
Hassayampa (riv.) C5
Havasu (lake) A4
Havasupai Ind. Res. 282 .... C2
Hohokam Pima Nat'l Mon. D5
Hoover (dam) A2
Hopi (buttes) E3
Hopi Ind. Res. 6,896 .... E2
Horseshoe (lake) D5
Huachuca (peak) E7
Hualapai (mts.) B4
Hualapai (peak) B3
Hualapai Ind. Res. 849 .... B3
Hubbell Trading Post Nat'l Hist. Site F3
Humphreys (peak) D3
Hurricane (cliffs) B2
Imperial (res.) A6
Ives (mesa) E3
Juniper (mts.) C3
Kaibab (plat.) C2
Kaibab Ind. Res. 173 .... C2
Kaibito (plat.) D2
Kanab (creek) C2
Kanab (plat.) C2
Kellogg (mt.) E6
Kendrick (peak) D3
Kitt (peak) D7
Kofa (mts.) B5
Laguna (creek) E2
Laguna (res.) A6
Lake Mead Nat'l Rec. Area A2
Lechuguilla (des.) A6
Lemmon (mt.) E6
Little Colorado (riv.) D3
Lukachukai (mts.) F2
Luke A.F.B. 3,515 .... C5
Maple (peak) F5
Marble Canyon Nat'l Mon. D2
Maricopa (mts.) C5
Maricopa Ind. Res. 397 .... C6
Mazatzal (peak) D4
Mead (lake) A2
Meteor (crater) E3
Miller (peak) E7
Moencopi (plat.) D3
Moenkopi Wash (dry riv.) D2
Mogollon (plat.) D4
Mogollon Rim (cliffs) D4
Mohave (lake) A3
Mohave (mts.) A4
Mohawk (mts.) B6
Montezuma Castle Nat'l Mon. D4
Mormon (lake) D4
Mule (mts.) E7
Navajo (creek) D2
Navajo Ind. Res. 76,173 .... D2
Navajo Nat'l Mon. E2
Navajo Ord. Depot D3
O'Leary (peak) D3
Oraibi Wash (dry riv.) E3
Ord (mt.) D5
Organ Pipe Cactus Nat'l Mon. C6
Painted (des.) D2
Painted Desert Section (Petrified Forest F3
Painted Rock (dam) C5
Papago Ind. Res. 7,171 .... C6
Paria (plat.) D2
Paria (riv.) D1
Parker (dam) A4
Pastora (peak) F2
Peloncillo (mts.) F6
Petrified Forest Nat'l Park F4
Pictograph (rocks) B5
Pinal (peak) E5
Pinaleno (mts.) F6
Pink (cliffs) E4
Pipe Spring Nat'l Mon. C2
Pleasant (lake) C5
Plomosa (mts.) A5
Polacca Wash (dry riv.) E3
Powell (lake) E1
Pueblo Colorado Wash (dry riv.) F3
Puerco (riv.) F3
Quajote Wash (dry riv.) D6
Rainbow (plat.) D2
Rincon (peak) E6
Roof Butte (mt.) F2
Rose (peak) F5
Sacramento Wash (dry riv.) A4
Saguaro (lake) D5
Saguaro Nat'l Mon. E6
Salt (riv.) D5
Salt River Ind. Res. 4,089 .... D5
San Carlos (lake) E5
San Carlos (riv.) E5
San Carlos Ind. Res. 6,104 .... E5
Sand Tank (mt.) C6
San Francisco (riv.) F5
San Pedro (riv.) E6
San Simon (riv.) F6
Santa Catalina (mts.) E6
Santa Cruz (riv.) D6
Santa Maria (riv.) B4
Santa Rosa Wash (dry riv.) D6
San Xavier Ind. Res. 875 .... D6
Sauceda (mts.) C6
Shivwits (plat.) B2
Shonto (plat.) E2
Sierra Ancha (mts.) D5
Sierra Apache (mts.) E5
Silver (creek) E4
Slate (mt.) D3
Sulphur Spring (valley) F6
Sunset Crater Nat'l Mon. D3
Superstition (mts.) D5
Theodore Roosevelt (lake) D5
Tonto (creek) D4
Tonto Nat'l Mon. D5
Trout (creek) B3
Trumbull (mt.) B2
Tumacacori Nat'l Mon. E7
Tuzigoot Nat'l Mon. D4
Tyson Wash (dry riv.) A5
Uinkaret (plat.) B2
Union (mt.) C4
Verde (riv.) D5
Vermilion (cliffs) D2
Virgin (mts.) B2
Walker (creek) F2
Walnut Canyon Nat'l Mon. D3
White (riv.) E5
Williams A.F.B. 3,435 .... D5
Woody (mt.) D3
Wupatki Nat'l Mon. D3
Yuma (des.) A6
Yuma Proving Ground 1,098 .... A6
Zuni (riv.) F4

⊙County seat.
‡Population of metropolitan area.
† Zip of nearest p.o. * Multiple zips.

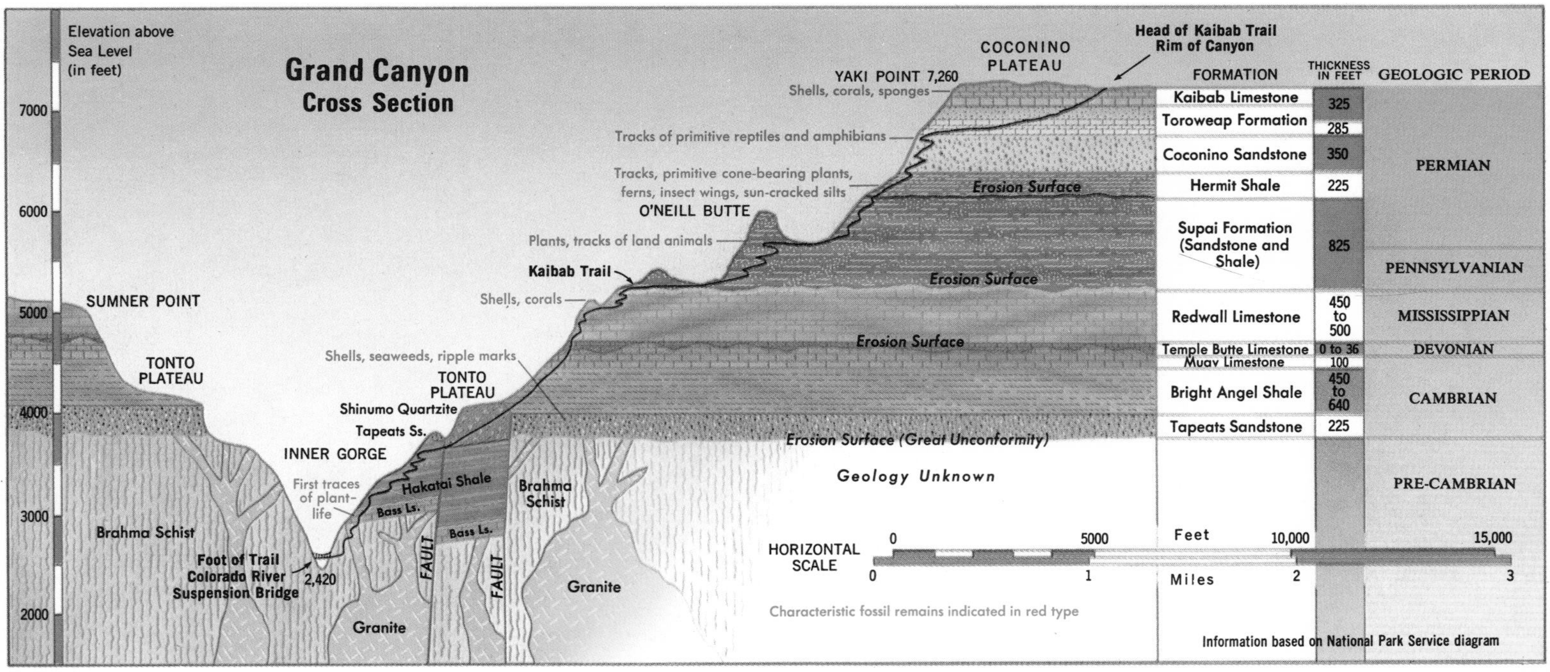
Grand Canyon Cross Section
Elevation above Sea Level (in feet)
7000
6000
5000
4000
3000
2000
SUMNER POINT
TONTO PLATEAU
Brahma Schist
INNER GORGE
First traces of plant-life
Foot of Trail Colorado River Suspension Bridge
2,420
Granite
Shells, seaweeds, ripple marks
TONTO PLATEAU
Shinumo Quartzite
Tapeats Ss.
Hakatai Shale
Bass Ls.
FAULT
Brahma Schist
Granite
Shells, corals
Kaibab Trail
Plants, tracks of land animals
O'NEILL BUTTE
Tracks, primitive cone-bearing plants, ferns, insect wings, sun-cracked silts
Tracks of primitive reptiles and amphibians
YAKI POINT 7,260
Shells, corals, sponges
COCONINO PLATEAU
Head of Kaibab Trail Rim of Canyon
Erosion Surface
Erosion Surface
Erosion Surface
Erosion Surface (Great Unconformity)
Geology Unknown
FORMATION
THICKNESS IN FEET
GEOLOGIC PERIOD
Kaibab Limestone 325
Toroweap Formation 285
Coconino Sandstone 350
Hermit Shale 225
PERMIAN
Supai Formation (Sandstone and Shale) 825
PENNSYLVANIAN
Redwall Limestone 450 to 500
MISSISSIPPIAN
Temple Butte Limestone 0 to 36
DEVONIAN
Muav Limestone 100
Bright Angel Shale 450 to 640
Tapeats Sandstone 225
CAMBRIAN
PRE-CAMBRIAN
HORIZONTAL SCALE
0 5000 Feet 10,000 15,000
0 1 Miles 2 3
Characteristic fossil remains indicated in red type
Information based on National Park Service diagram

AREA 53,187 sq. mi. (137,754 sq. km.)
POPULATION 2,286,435
CAPITAL Little Rock
LARGEST CITY Little Rock
HIGHEST POINT Magazine Mtn. 2,753 ft. (839 m.)
SETTLED IN 1685
ADMITTED TO UNION June 15, 1836
POPULAR NAME Land of Opportunity
STATE FLOWER Apple Blossom
STATE BIRD Mockingbird

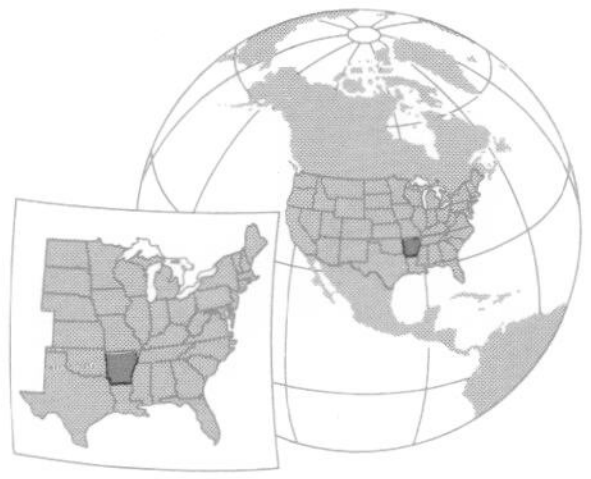

COUNTIES

Arkansas 24,175 ....H5
Ashley 26,538 ....G7
Baxter 27,409.......F1
Benton 78,115.......B1
Boone 26,067.......D1
Bradley 13,803 ....F7
Calhoun 6,079 ....E6
Carroll 16,203 ....C1
Chicot 17,793.......H7
Clark 23,326 ....D5
Clay 20,616 ....K1
Cleburne 16,909.......F2
Cleveland 7,868 ....F6
Columbia 26,644 ....D7
Conway 19,505.......E3
Craighead 63,239 ....J2
Crawford 36,892 ....B2
Crittenden 49,499 ....K3
Cross 20,434 ....J3
Dallas 10,515 ....E6
Desha 19,760.......H6
Drew 17,910.......G6
Faulkner 46,192 ....F3
Franklin 14,705.......C2
Fulton 9,975 ....G1
Garland 70,531 ....D4
Grant 13,008.......F5
Greene 30,744.......J1
Hempstead 23,635.......C6
Hot Spring 26,819 ....E5
Howard 13,459.......C5
Independence 30,147 ....G2
Izard 10,768 ....G1
Jackson 21,646 ....H2
Jefferson 90,718 ....G5
Johnson 17,423.......C2
Lafayette 10,213.......C7
Lawrence 18,447.......H1
Lee 15,539 ....J4
Lincoln 13,369.......G6
Little River 13,952 ....B6
Logan 20,144.......C3
Lonoke 34,518 ....G4
Madison 11,373 ....C1
Marion 11,334.......E1
Miller 37,766.......C7
Mississippi 59,517.......K2
Monroe 14,052.......H4
Montgomery 7,771 ....C4
Nevada 11,097 ....D6
Newton 7,756.......D2
Ouachita 30,541 ....E6
Perry 7,266 ....E4
Phillips 34,772.......J5
Pike 10,373 ....C5
Poinsett 27,032.......J2
Polk 17,007 ....B5
Pope 39,021 ....D3
Prairie 10,140.......G4
Pulaski 340,613 ....F4
Randolph 16,834.......H1
Saint Francis 30,858.......J3
Saline 53,161 ....E4
Scott 9,685.......B4
Searcy 8,847.......E2
Sebastian 95,172.......B3
Sevier 14,060.......B6
Sharp 14,607 ....G1
Stone 9,022.......F2
Union 48,573 ....E7
Van Buren 13,357 ....E2
Washington 100,494 ....B2
White 50,835 ....G3
Woodruff 11,222.......H3
Yell 17,026.......D3

CITIES and TOWNS

Zip *Name/Pop.* *Key*

72001 Adona 230 ....E3
72002 Alexander 223 ....F4
72410 Alicia 246.......H2
72820 Alix 225.......C3
†72046 Allport 295 ....G4
72921 Alma 2,755 ....B3
72003 Almyra 294.......H5
72611 Alpena 344 ....D1
72004 Altheimer 1,231 ....G5
72821 Altus 441 ....C3
72005 Amagon 126.......H2
71921 Amity 859 ....D5
71922 Antoine 194.......D5
71923 Arkadelphia⊙ 10,005 ....D5
71630 Arkansas City⊙ 668.......H6
72310 Armorel 500 ....L2
71822 Ashdown⊙ 4,218 ....B6
72513 Ash Flat⊙ 524 ....G1
72823 Atkins 3,002 ....E3
72311 Aubrey 267.......J4
72006 Augusta⊙ 3,496.......H3
72007 Austin 269 ....G4
72711 Avoca 256.......B1
72010 Bald Knob 2,756.......G3
71631 Banks 216.......F6
72922 Barber 35.......B3
72923 Barling 3,761 ....B3
72313 Bassett 243 ....K2
72924 Bates B4
72501 Batesville⊙ 8,263 ....G2
72411 Bay 1,605 ....J2
71720 Bearden 1,191.......E6
72613 Beaver.......C1
72012 Beebe 3,599 ....G3
72014 Beedeville 183 ....H3
†72712 Bella Vista 2,589.......B1
†72601 Bellefonte 393 ....D1
72824 Belleville 571 ....D3
71823 Ben Lomond 155 ....B6
72015 Benton⊙ 17,717.......E4
72712 Bentonville⊙ 8,756 ....B1
72615 Bergman 320 ....E1
72616 Berryville⊙ 2,966.......C1
†72764 Bethel Heights 296 ....B1
72016 Bigelow 373.......E3
72617 Big Flat 150.......F1
72413 Biggers 363.......J1
72017 Biscoe 486 ....H4
72414 Black Oak 309.......K2
72415 Black Rock 848 ....H1
†71960 Black Springs 92.......C5
71825 Blevins 314 ....C6
65611 Blue Eye 43.......D1
72826 Blue Mountain 112 ....C3
71722 Bluff City 292.......D6
72315 Blytheville⊙ 23,844 ....L2
†71858 Bodcaw 197.......D6
†72901 Bonanza 553.......B3
72416 Bono 967.......J2
72927 Booneville⊙ 3,718 ....C3
72020 Bradford 950.......G3
71826 Bradley 790 ....C7
72928 Branch 353.......C3
72021 Brinkley 4,909.......H4
72417 Brookland 840.......J2
72022 Bryant 2,682.......F4
71827 Buckner 436 ....D7
72619 Bull Shoals 1,312.......E1
72321 Burdette 328.......L2
72023 Cabot 4,806.......F4
72322 Caldwell 283 ....J3
71828 Cale 110 ....D6
72519 Calico Rock 1,046 ....F1
71724 Calion 638.......E7
71701 Camden⊙ 15,356 ....E6
†72201 Cammack Village 920 ....E4
†72473 Campbell Station 297 ....H2
72419 Caraway 1,165 ....K2
72024 Carlisle 2,567 ....G4
71725 Carthage 568 ....E5
72025 Casa 179 ....D3
72421 Cash 285 ....J2
72026 Casscoe 297 ....H4
†72951 Caulksville 234 ....C3
72521 Cave City 1,634 ....G2
72718 Cave Springs 429.......B1
72932 Cedarville 375 ....B2
72719 Centerton 425 ....B1
72829 Centerville 300.......D3
†72923 Central City 339 ....B3
72933 Charleston⊙ 1,748.......B3
†72525 Cherokee Village-Hidden Valley 4,058.......G1
72324 Cherry Valley 729.......J3
72934 Chester 139.......B2
71726 Chidester 342.......D6
72029 Clarendon⊙ 2,361 ....H4
72325 Clarkedale 300.......K3
72830 Clarksville⊙ 5,237.......D3
72031 Clinton⊙ 1,284 ....F2
72832 Coal Hill 859.......C3
72476 College City 432.......J1
72326 Colt 378 ....J3
71831 Columbus 265.......C6
72523 Concord 234.......G2
72032 Conway⊙ 20,375.......F3
72524 Cord 250 ....H2
72422 Corning⊙ 3,650 ....J1
72626 Cotter 920.......E1
72036 Cotton Plant 1,323 ....H3
71937 Cove 391 ....B5
72037 Coy 183 ....G4
72327 Crawfordsville 685 ....K3
71635 Crossett 6,706.......G7
71728 Curtis 300.......D6
72526 Cushman 556.......G2
†71950 Daisy 177 ....C5
72039 Damascus 307 ....F3
72833 Danville⊙ 1,698 ....D3
72834 Dardanelle⊙ 3,621 ....D3
72424 Datto 112.......J1
72722 Decatur 1,013 ....A1
72425 Delaplaine 161.......J1
71940 Delight 431.......C5
72426 Dell 310.......K2
†72821 Denning 238 ....C3
71832 De Queen⊙ 4,594.......B5
71638 Dermott 4,731.......H7
72040 Des Arc⊙ 2,001 ....G4
72041 De Valls Bluff⊙ 738.......H4
72042 De Witt⊙ 3,928 ....H5
72644 Diamond City 650 ....E1
72043 Diaz 1,192 ....H2
71833 Dierks 1,249.......B5
71941 Donaldson 300 ....E5
72837 Dover 948.......D3
71639 Dumas 6,091 ....H6
72935 Dyer 608 ....B3
72330 Dyess 446.......K2
72331 Earle 3,517.......K3
71701 East Camden 632 ....E6
72332 Edmondson 344 ....K3
72333 Elaine 991 ....J5
71730 El Dorado⊙ 25,270 ....E7
72727 Elkins 579 ....C1
72728 Elm Springs 781 ....B1
71740 Emerson 444 ....D7
71835 Emmet 475 ....D6
72046 England 3,081 ....G4
72047 Enola 186 ....F3
71640 Eudora 3,840 ....H7
72632 Eureka Springs⊙ 1,989 ....C1
72532 Evening Shade 397 ....G1
72633 Everton 134 ....E1
72730 Farmington 1,283.......B1
72701 Fayetteville⊙ 36,608 ....B1
Fayetteville-Springdale 07 ....B1
†71747 Felsenthal 220 ....F7
72429 Fisher 302.......J2
72634 Flippin 1,072.......E1
71742 Fordyce⊙ 5,175 ....F6
71836 Foreman 1,377 ....B6
72335 Forrest City⊙ 13,803 ....J3
*72901 Fort Smith⊙ 71,626 ....B3
Fort Smith‡ 203,269.......B3
71837 Fouke 614 ....C7
71642 Fountain Hill 352.......G7
†72016 Fourche 51 ....E4
72536 Franklin 253.......G1
72017 Fredonia (Biscoe) 486.......H4
71942 Friendship 163.......E5
71838 Fulton 326.......C6
72732 Garfield 187 ....C1
71839 Garland 660.......C7
72052 Garner 216.......G3
72635 Gassville 859 ....F1
72733 Gateway 75 ....B1
71840 Genoa 350 ....C7
72734 Gentry 1,468.......A1
72636 Gilbert 43.......E2
72055 Gillett 927 ....H5
71841 Gillham 252 ....B5
72339 Gilmore 503.......K3
71943 Glenwood 1,402 ....C5
72340 Goodwin 225 ....J4
†72315 Gosnell 3,215.......K2
71643 Gould 1,671 ....G6
71644 Grady 488 ....G5
71944 Grannis 349.......B5
72838 Gravelly 300 ....C4
72736 Gravette 1,218.......B1
72058 Greenbrier 1,423.......F3
72638 Green Forest 1,609.......D1
72737 Greenland 622.......B1
72430 Greenway 317 ....K1
72936 Greenwood⊙ 3,317 ....B3
†72067 Greers Ferry 558 ....F2
72060 Griffithville 254 ....G3
72431 Grubbs 546 ....H2
72540 Guion 177.......G2
†71923 Gum Springs 255.......D5
71743 Gurdon 2,707 ....D6
72061 Guy 209 ....F3
72937 Hackett 505 ....B3
†71638 Halley.......H6
71646 Hamburg⊙ 3,394 ....G7
71744 Hampton⊙ 1,627.......F6
72542 Hardy 643 ....H1
71745 Harrell 302 ....F7
72432 Harrisburg⊙ 1,921 ....J2
72601 Harrison⊙ 9,567 ....D1
72938 Hartford 613 ....B3
72840 Hartman 517.......C3
†72015 Haskell 1,074 ....E4
71945 Hatfield 410 ....B5
72842 Havana 352 ....D3
72341 Haynes 359 ....J4
72064 Hazen 1,636 ....G4
72543 Heber Springs⊙ 4,589 .....G2
72843 Hector 449 ....E3
72342 Helena⊙ 9,598 ....J4
72065 Hensley 500.......F4
71647 Hermitage 378.......F7
72347 Hickory Ridge 478.......J3
72067 Higden 45 ....F2
72068 Higginson 333.......G3
†72734 Highfill 92 ....B1
72738 Hindsville C1
72069 Holly Grove 754.......H4
†72958 Hon 250 ....B4
71801 Hope⊙ 10,290.......C6
71842 Horatio 989 ....B3
72512 Horseshoe Bend 1,909 .....G1
71901 Hot Springs National Park⊙ 35,781 ....D4
72070 Houston 183.......E3

(continued on following page)

Agriculture, Industry and Resources

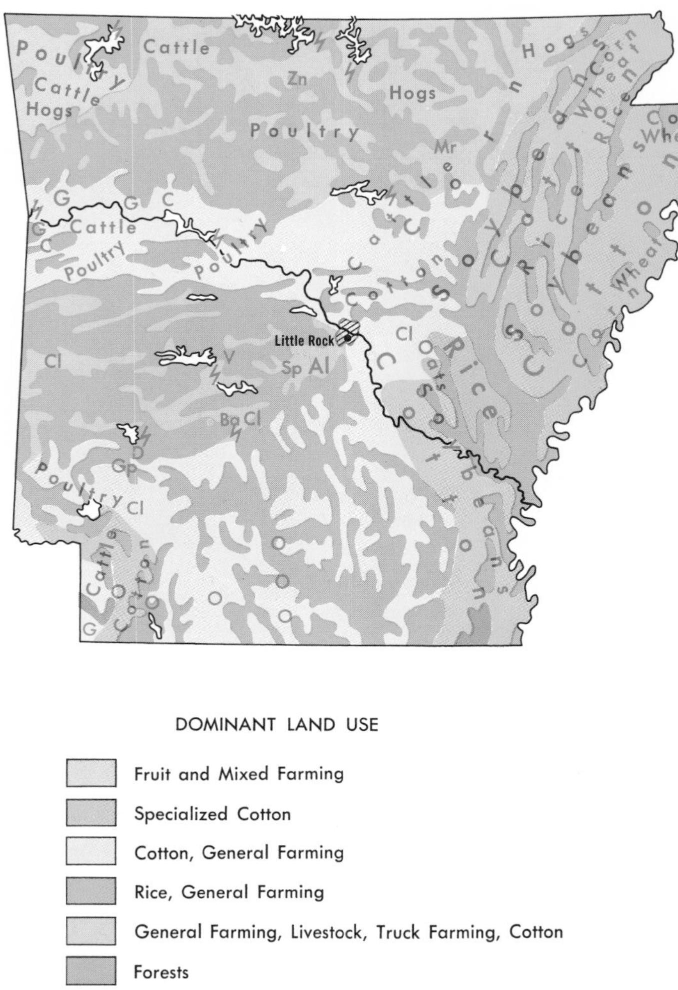

DOMINANT LAND USE

- Fruit and Mixed Farming
- Specialized Cotton
- Cotton, General Farming
- Rice, General Farming
- General Farming, Livestock, Truck Farming, Cotton
- Forests
- Swampland, Limited Agriculture

MAJOR MINERAL OCCURRENCES

Al	Bauxite	Gp	Gypsum
Ba	Barite	Mr	Marble
C	Coal	O	Petroleum
Cl	Clay	Sp	Soapstone
D	Diamonds	V	Vanadium
G	Natural Gas	Zn	Zinc
ϟ	Water Power	▨	Major Industrial Areas

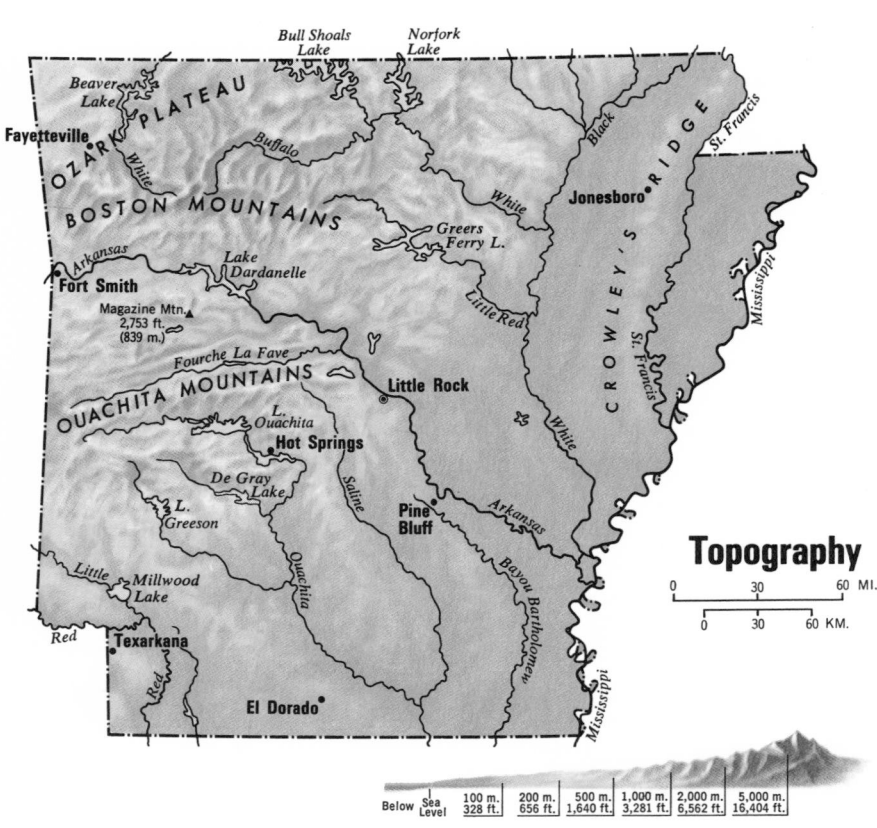

Topography

0   30   60 MI.
0   30   60 KM.

Below Sea Level | 100 m. 328 ft. | 200 m. 656 ft. | 500 m. 1,640 ft. | 1,000 m. 3,281 ft. | 2,000 m. 6,562 ft. | 5,000 m. 16,404 ft.

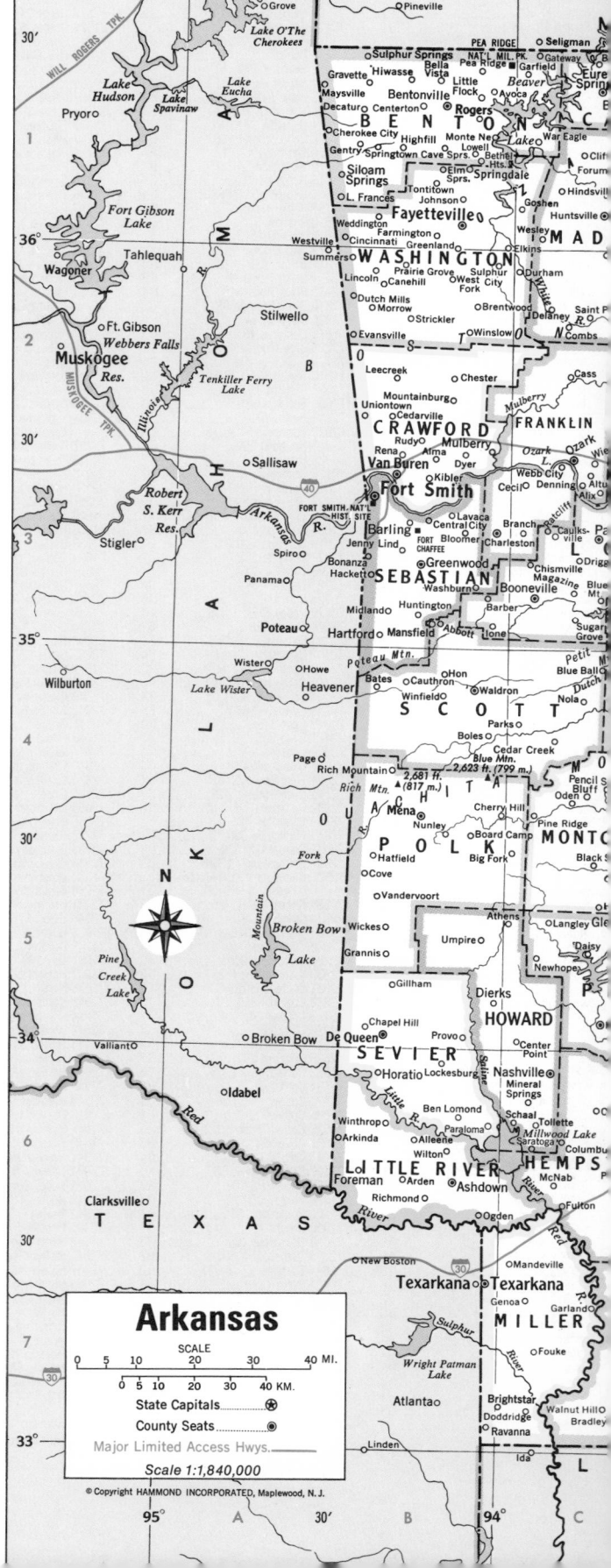

Arkansas

SCALE
0 5 10   20   30   40 MI.
0 5 10   20   30   40 KM.
State Capitals ....⊛
County Seats ....⊙
Major Limited Access Hwys. _____
Scale 1:1,840,000
© Copyright HAMMOND INCORPORATED, Maplewood, N.J.

71764 Stephens 1,366 ....E7
72159 Steprock 600 ....G3
72469 Strawberry 280 ....H2
71765 Strong 785 ....F7
72160 Stuttgart⊙ 10,941 ....H4
72865 Subiaco 744 ....C3
72470 Success 223 ....J1
72579 Sulphur Rock 316 ....H2
72768 Sulphur Springs 496 ......B1
72677 Summit 506 ....E1
72471 Swifton 859 ....H2
71861 Taylor 657 ....D7
75502 Texarkana⊙ 21,459 ....C7
　　　 Texarkana‡ 127,019 ....C7
71766 Thornton 711 ....F6
72166 Tichnor 350 ....H5
71670 Tillar 280 ....H6
71767 Tinsman 112 ....F6
71851 Tollette 407 ....C6

72770 Tontitown 615 ....B1
72167 Traskwood 459 ....E5
72472 Trumann 6,405 ....J2
72168 Tucker 375 ....G5
72473 Tuckerman 2,078 ....H2
†72015 Tull 281 ....E5
72169 Tupelo 248 ....H3
72384 Turrell 1,041 ....K3
72386 Tyronza 777 ....K3
72170 Ulm 201 ....H4
72955 Uniontown 600 ....B2
71768 Urbana 500 ....E7
72682 Valley Springs 190 ....D1
72956 Van Buren⊙ 12,020 ....B3
71972 Vandervoort 98 ....B4
72370 Victoria 175 ....K2
72173 Vilonia 736 ....F3
†72002 Vimy Ridge 600 ....F4
72583 Viola 362 ....G1

72433 Hoxie 2,961 ....H1
72348 Hughes 1,919 ....J4
72072 Humnoke 442 ....G4
72073 Humphrey 872 ....G5
72074 Hunter 170 ....H3
72940 Huntington 662 ....B3
72740 Huntsville⊙ 1,394 ......C1
71747 Huttig 976 ....F7
72434 Imboden 661 ....H1
72075 Jacksonport 288 ....H2
72076 Jacksonville 27,589 ...F4
†72501 Jamestown G2
72641 Jasper⊙ 519 ....D1
72079 Jefferson 250 ....F5
71650 Jerome 54 ....G7
72080 Jerusalem 300 ....E3
71949 Jessieville 350 ....D4
72741 Johnson 519 ....B1
72350 Joiner 725 ....K3
72401 Jonesboro⊙ 31,530 ...J2
72081 Judsonia 2,025 ....G3
71749 Junction City 813 .....E7
72351 Keiser 962 ....K2
72082 Kensett 1,751 ....G3
72083 Keo 208 ....G4
†72956 Kibler 798 ....B3
71652 Kingsland 320 ....F6
71950 Kirby 800 ....C5
72435 Knobel 503 ....J1
72845 Knoxville 264 ....D3
72436 Lafe 215 ....J1
72437 Lake City⊙ 1,842 ......K2
72642 Lakeview 512 ....E1
†72389 Lake View 609 ....J5
71653 Lake Village⊙ 3,088 ...H7
72846 Lamar 708 ....D3
72941 Lavaca 1,092 ....B3
71750 Lawson 250 ....F7
72438 Leachville 1,882 ....K2
72644 Lead Hill 247 ....D1
72084 Leola 481 ....E5
72354 Lepanto 1,964 ....K2
72645 Leslie 501 ....E2
72085 Letona 231 ....G3
71845 Lewisville⊙ 1,476 .....C7
72355 Lexa 500 ....J4
72744 Lincoln 1,422 ....B2
†72712 Little Flock 663 ....B1
*72201 Little Rock
　　　　(cap.)⊙ 158,461 ....F4
　　　 Little Rock-North Little
　　　 Rock‡ 393,494 ....F4
71846 Lockesburg 616 ....B6
72847 London 859 ....D3
72086 Lonoke⊙ 4,128 ....G4
72087 Lonsdale 117 ....E4
71751 Louann 282 ....E7
72745 Lowell 1,078 ....B1
†72856 Lurton 38 ....D2
72358 Luxora 1,739 ....K2
72440 Lynn 345 ....H2
72359 Madison 1,238 ....J4
72943 Magazine 799 ....C3
72553 Magness 196 ....H2
71753 Magnolia⊙ 11,909 ....D7
72104 Malvern⊙ 10,163 ......E5
72554 Mammoth Spring 1,158 ...G1
72442 Manila 2,553 ....K2
72944 Mansfield 1,000 ....B3
72360 Marianna⊙ 6,220 .....J4
†72395 Marie 287 ....K2
72364 Marion⊙ 2,996 ....K3

72365 Marked Tree 3,201 ...K2
72443 Marmaduke 1,168 ....K1
72650 Marshall⊙ 1,595 ....E2
72366 Marvell 1,724 ....J4
72106 Mayflower 1,381 ......F4
72444 Maynard 381 ....J1
71847 McCaskill 87 ....C6
72101 McCrory 1,942 ....H3
72441 McDougal 239 ....K1
71654 McGehee 5,671 ....H6
71752 McNeil 725 ....D7
72102 McRae 641 ....G3
72556 Melbourne⊙ 1,619 ...G1
72367 Mellwood 250 ....H5
71953 Mena⊙ 5,154 ....B4
72107 Menifee 368 ....E3
72945 Midland 286 ....B3
71851 Mineral Springs 936 ...C6
72245 Minturn 169 ....H2
†71639 Mitchellville 618 .....H6
72447 Monette 1,165 ....K2
72108 Monroe 250 ....H4
71655 Monticello⊙ 8,259 ...G6
71658 Montrose 641 ....H7
*72501 Moorefield 129 ....G2
72368 Moro 327 ....H4
72110 Morrilton⊙ 7,355 .....E3
71659 Moscow 325 ....G5
72946 Mountainburg 595 ...B2
72653 Mountain Home⊙ 8,066 ...F1
71956 Mountain Pine 1,068 ...D4
72560 Mountain View⊙ 2,147 ...F2
71758 Mount Holly 250 ......E7
71957 Mount Ida⊙ 1,023 ....C4
72561 Mount Pleasant 438 ...G2
72111 Mount Vernon 157 ...F3
72947 Mulberry 1,444 ....B2
71958 Murfreesboro⊙ 1,883 ...C5
71852 Nashville⊙ 4,554 .....C6
72562 Newark 1,128 ....H2
72851 New Blaine 200 ....D3
71959 Newhope 300 ....C5
72112 Newport⊙ 8,339 ....H2
72461 Nimmons 112 ....K1
†71601 Noble Lake 250 ....G5
72658 Norfork 399 ....F1
71960 Norman 539 ....C5
71759 Norphlet 756 ....E7
†72801 Norristown 625 ....D3
71635 North Crossett 3,513 ...G7
*72114 North Little Rock 64,288 ...F4
72660 Oak Grove 265 ....C1
†71801 Oakhaven 72 ....C6
71961 Oden 186 ....C4
71853 Ogden 334 ....B6
72564 Oil Trough 280 ....G2
72449 O'Kean 291 ....J1
71962 Okolona 200 ....D5
72853 Ola 1,121 ....D3
72662 Omaha 191 ....D1
†72110 Oppelo 486 ....E3
72370 Osceola⊙ 8,881 ....K2
72565 Oxford 520 ....G1
71855 Ozan 111 ....C6
72949 Ozark⊙ 3,597 ....C3
72372 Palestine 976 ....J4
72121 Pangburn 673 ....G3
72450 Paragould⊙ 15,248 ...J1
72855 Paris⊙ 3,991 ....C3
71661 Parkdale 471 ....H7
72373 Parkin 2,035 ....J3
72950 Parks 600 ....B4

†71801 Patmos 88 ....C7
72123 Patterson 567 ....H3
72453 Peach Orchard 243 ...J1
71964 Pearcy 400 ....D5
72751 Pea Ridge 1,488 ......B1
†72104 Perla 149 ....E5
72125 Perry 254 ....E3
71801 Perrytown 282 ....C6
72126 Perryville⊙ 1,058 .....E3
71654 Piggott⊙ 3,762 ....K1
*71601 Pine Bluff⊙ 56,636 ...F5
　　　 Pine Bluff‡ 90,718 .....F5
†72847 Piney 2,283 ....D3
72857 Plainview 752 ....D4
72568 Pleasant Plains 267 ...G2
72127 Plumerville 785 ....E3
72455 Pocahontas⊙ 5,995 ...H1
72456 Pollard 298 ....K1
72374 Poplar Grove 300 ....J4
72457 Portia 480 ....H1
71663 Portland 701 ....H7
72858 Pottsville 564 ....D3
72458 Powhatan 49 ....H1
72128 Poyen 329 ....E5
72753 Prairie Grove 1,708 ...B2
72129 Prattsville 317 ....F5
71857 Prescott⊙ 4,103 ......D6
72672 Pyatt 217 ....E1
72131 Quitman 556 ....F3
72951 Ratcliff 197 ....C3
†72333 Ratio 250 ....J5
72459 Ravenden 338 ....H1
72460 Ravenden Springs 230 ...H1
71726 Reader 127 ....D6
72461 Rector 2,336 ....K1
72132 Redfield 745 ....F5
71670 Reed 395 ....H6
72462 Reyno 521 ....J1
71665 Rison⊙ 1,325 ....F6
†72014 Rockport 231 ....E5
72134 Roe 136 ....H4
72756 Rogers 17,429 ....B1
†72355 Rondo 330 ....J4
72137 Rose Bud 202 ....F3
71858 Rosston 274 ....D6
72952 Rudy 79 ....B2
72139 Russell 232 ....G3
72801 Russellville⊙ 14,031 ...D3
72140 Saint Charles 199 ....H5
72464 Saint Francis 266 ....K1
72760 Saint Paul 198 ....C2
72576 Salem⊙ 1,424 ....G1
†72658 Salesville 406 ....F1
72863 Scranton 244 ....C3
72143 Searcy⊙ 13,612 ....G3
72465 Sedgwick 205 ....J2
†72103 Shannon Hills 1,656 ...F4
72150 Sheridan⊙ 3,042 ......F5
72152 Sherrill 161 ....F5
72116 Sherwood 10,406 ....F4
72153 Shirley 354 ....F2
72577 Sidney 270 ....G1
72761 Siloam Springs 7,940 ...B1
71762 Smackover 2,453 .....E7
72466 Smithville 113 ....H1
†71658 Snyder 700 ....G7
71763 Sparkman 622 ....E6
72764 Springdale 23,458 ...B1
　　　 Springdale-Fayetteville‡
　　　 177,850 ....B1
71860 Stamps 2,859 ....D7
71667 Star City⊙ 2,066 .....G6

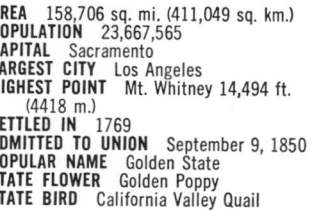

COUNTIES

Alameda 1,105,379 D6
Alpine 1,097 F5
Amador 19,314 E5
Butte 143,851 D4
Calaveras 20,710 E5
Colusa 12,791 C4
Contra Costa 656,380 D6
Del Norte 18,217 B2
El Dorado 85,812 E5
Fresno 514,229 E7
Glenn 21,350 C4
Humboldt 108,514 B3
Imperial 92,110 K10
Inyo 17,895 H7
Kern 403,089 G8
Kings 73,738 G8
Lake 36,366 C4
Lassen 21,661 E3
Los Angeles 7,477,503 G9
Madera 63,116 F6
Marin 222,592 C5
Mariposa 11,108 E6
Mendocino 66,738 B4
Merced 134,558 E6
Modoc 8,610 E2
Mono 8,577 F5
Monterey 290,444 D7
Napa 99,199 C5
Nevada 51,645 E4
Orange 1,932,709 H10
Placer 117,247 E4
Plumas 17,340 E4
Riverside 663,199 J10
Sacramento 783,381 D5
San Benito 25,005 D7
San Bernardino 895,016 J9
San Diego 1,861,846 J10
San Francisco (city county) 678,974 J2
San Joaquin 347,342 D6
San Luis Obispo 155,435 E8
San Mateo 587,329 C3
Santa Barbara 298,694 E9
Santa Clara 1,295,071 D6
Santa Cruz 188,141 C6
Shasta 115,715 C3
Sierra 3,073 E4
Siskiyou 39,732 C2
Solano 235,203 D5
Sonoma 299,681 C5
Stanislaus 265,900 D6
Sutter 52,246 D4
Tehama 38,888 C3
Trinity 11,858 B3
Tulare 245,738 G7
Tuolumne 33,928 F5
Ventura 529,174 F9
Yolo 113,374 D5
Yuba 49,733 D4

CITIES and TOWNS

Zip *Name/Pop.* *Key*

94501 Alameda 63,852 J2
94507 Alamo 8,505 K2
94706 Albany 15,130 J2
*91801 Alhambra 64,615 C10
92001 Alpine 5,368 J11
91001 Altadena 40,983 C10
96101 Alturas⊙ 3,025 E2
†95116 Alum Rock 16,890 L3
*92801 Anaheim 219,494 D11
Anaheim-Santa Ana-Garden Grove‡ 1,931,570 D11
96007 Anderson 7,381 C3
95222 Angels Camp 2,302 E5
94508 Angwin 3,526 C5
94509 Antioch 42,683 L1
92307 Apple Valley 14,305 H9
95003 Aptos 7,039 K4
91006 Arcadia 45,994 C10
95521 Arcata 12,850 A3
95825 Arden-Arcade 87,570 B8
93420 Arroyo Grande 11,290 E8
90701 Artesia 14,301 C11
93203 Arvin 6,863 G8
†94577 Ashland 13,983 K2
95413 Asti 75 C5
93422 Atascadero 16,232 E8
94025 Atherton 7,797 K3
95301 Atwater 17,530 E6
95603 Auburn⊙ 7,540 C8
90704 Avalon 2,022 G10
93204 Avenal 4,137 E8
91702 Azusa 29,380 D10
*93301 Bakersfield⊙ 105,735 G8
Bakersfield‡ 403,089 G8
91706 Baldwin Park 50,554 D10
92220 Banning 14,020 J10
92311 Barstow 17,690 H9
†93402 Baywood Park-Los Osos 10,933 E8
92223 Beaumont 6,818 J10
90201 Bell 25,450 C11
90706 Bellflower 53,441 C11
90201 Bell Gardens 34,117 C11
94002 Belmont 24,505 J3
94510 Benicia 15,376 K1
95005 Ben Lomond 7,238 K4
*94701 Berkeley 103,328 J2
*90210 Beverly Hills 32,367 B10
92315 Big Bear Lake J9
93920 Big Sur 500 D7
93514 Bishop 3,333 G6
92316 Bloomington 18,888 E10
92225 Blythe 6,805 L10
94923 Bodega Bay 800 B5
93516 Boron 2,040 H8
92004 Borrego Springs 1,405 J10
95006 Boulder Creek 5,662 J4
92227 Brawley 14,946 K11
92621 Brea 27,913 D11
94513 Brentwood 4,434 L2
93517 Bridgeport⊙ 525 F5
94005 Brisbane 2,969 J2
95605 Broderick-Bryte 10,194 B8
*90622 Buena Park 64,165 D11
*91501 Burbank 84,625 C10
94010 Burlingame 26,173 J2
96013 Burney 3,187 D3
92231 Calexico 14,412 K11
93505 California City 2,743 H8
94515 Calistoga 3,879 C5
93745 Calwa 6,640 F7
93010 Camarillo 37,797 F9
95008 Campbell 26,910 K3
*91303 Canoga Park B10
92624 Capistrano Beach 6,168 H10
95010 Capitola 9,095 K4
92007 Cardiff-by-the-Sea 10,054 H10
92008 Carlsbad 35,490 H10
93923 Carmel 4,707 D7
93924 Carmel Valley 4,013 D7
95608 Carmichael 43,108 C8
93013 Carpinteria 10,835 F9
90745 Carson 81,221 C11
94546 Castro Valley 44,011 K2
95012 Castroville 4,396 D7
92234 Cathedral City 4,130 J10
96019 Central Valley 3,424 C3
95307 Ceres 13,281 D6
†90701 Cerritos 53,020 C11
†94541 Cherryland 9,425 K2
95926 Chico 26,603 D4
Chico‡ 143,851 D4
†93555 China Lake 4,275 H8
95309 Chinese Camp 150 E6
91710 Chino 40,165 D10
93610 Chowchilla 5,122 E6
*92010 Chula Vista 83,927 J11
95610 Citrus Heights 85,911 C8
91711 Claremont 30,950 D10
95425 Cloverdale 3,989 B5
93612 Clovis 33,021 F7
92236 Coachella 9,129 J10
93210 Coalinga 6,593 E7
95713 Colfax 981 E4
92324 Colton 15,201 E10
95932 Colusa⊙ 4,075 C4
90040 Commerce 10,509 C10
*90220 Compton 81,286 C11
*94520 Concord 103,255 K1
93212 Corcoran 6,454 F7
96021 Corning 4,745 C4
91720 Corona 37,791 E11
92118 Coronado 18,790 H11
94925 Corte Madera 8,074 J2
*92626 Costa Mesa 82,562 D11
94928 Cotati 3,346 C5
*91722 Covina 33,751 D10
95531 Crescent City⊙ 3,075 A2
92325 Crestline 6,715 H9
90201 Cudahy 17,984 C11
90230 Culver City 38,139 B10
95014 Cupertino 34,265 K3
93615 Cutler 3,149 F7
90630 Cypress 40,391 D11
*94014 Daly City 78,519 H2
92629 Dana Point 10,602 H10
94526 Danville 26,446 K2
95616 Davis 36,640 B8
93215 Delano 16,491 F8
95315 Delhi 2,832 E6
92014 Del Mar 5,017 H11
92240 Desert Hot Springs 5,941 J9
93618 Dinuba 9,907 F7
95620 Dixon 7,541 B9
93620 Dos Palos 3,121 E6
*90240 Downey 82,602 C11
95936 Downieville⊙ 500 E4

AREA 158,706 sq. mi. (411,049 sq. km.)
POPULATION 23,667,565
CAPITAL Sacramento
LARGEST CITY Los Angeles
HIGHEST POINT Mt. Whitney 14,494 ft. (4418 m.)
SETTLED IN 1769
ADMITTED TO UNION September 9, 1850
POPULAR NAME Golden State
STATE FLOWER Golden Poppy
STATE BIRD California Valley Quail

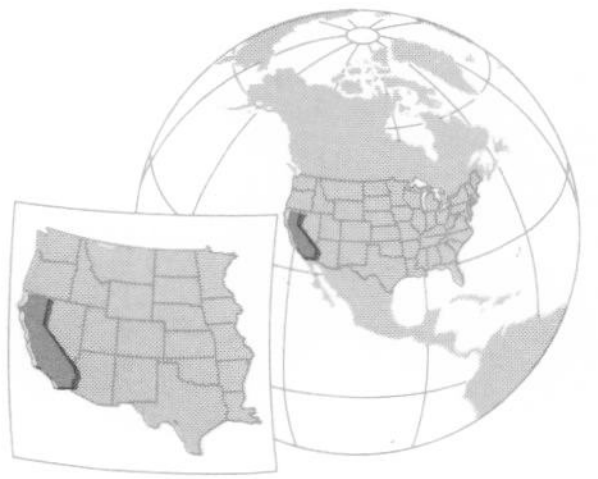

91010 Duarte 16,766 D10
94566 Dublin 13,496 K2
93219 Earlimart 4,578 F8
90022 East Los Angeles 100,017 C10
*92020 El Cajon 73,892 J11
92243 El Centro⊙ 23,996 K11
94530 El Cerrito 22,731 J2
95630 El Dorado Hills 3,453 C8
94018 El Granada 3,582 H3
95624 Elk Grove 10,959 B9
*91731 El Monte 79,494 D10
†93030 El Rio 5,674 F9
90245 El Segundo 13,752 B11
92630 El Toro 38,153 E11
94608 Emeryville 3,714 J2
92024 Encinitas 10,796 H10
91316 Encino B10
93930 Escalon 3,127 E6
*92025 Escondido 64,355 J10
95501 Eureka⊙ 24,153 A3
93221 Exeter 5,606 F7
94930 Fairfax 7,391 H1
94533 Fairfield⊙ 58,099 K1
95628 Fair Oaks 22,602 C8
92028 Fallbrook 14,041 H10
93223 Farmersville 5,544 F7
95018 Felton 4,564 K4
93015 Fillmore 9,602 G9
93622 Firebaugh 3,740 E7
95828 Florin 16,523 B8
95630 Folsom 11,003 C8
92335 Fontana 37,107 E10
†93268 Ford City 3,392 F8
95437 Fort Bragg 5,019 B4
†95421 Fort Ross 30 B5
95540 Fortuna 7,591 A3
94404 Foster City 23,287 J2
92708 Fountain Valley 55,080 D11
95019 Freedom 6,416 L4
*94536 Fremont 131,945 K3
*93706 Fresno⊙ 217,289 F7
Fresno‡ 515,013 F7
*92631 Fullerton 102,034 D11
95632 Galt 5,514 C9
*90747 Gardena 45,165 C11
*92640 Garden Grove 123,307 D11
95020 Gilroy 21,641 D6
92509 Glen Avon Heights 8,444 E10
*91201 Glendale 139,060 C10
91740 Glendora 38,500 D10
93926 Gonzales 2,891 D7
91344 Granada Hills B10
92324 Grand Terrace 8,498 E10
95945 Grass Valley 6,697 D4
93308 Greenacres 5,381 F8
93927 Greenfield 4,181 D7
95948 Gridley 3,982 D4
93433 Grover City 8,827 E8
93434 Guadalupe 3,629 E9
95322 Gustine 3,142 D6
94019 Half Moon Bay 7,282 H3
93230 Hanford⊙ 20,958 F7
90250 Hawthorne 56,447 C11
*94541 Hayward 94,342 K2
95448 Healdsburg 7,217 B5
92343 Hemet 22,454 H10
94547 Hercules 5,963 J1
90254 Hermosa Beach 18,070 B11
92345 Hesperia 13,540 H9
92346 Highland 10,908 H9
94010 Hillsborough 10,372 J2
95023 Hollister⊙ 11,488 D7
90028 Hollywood C10
92250 Holtville 4,399 K11
†91720 Home Gardens 5,783 E11
95326 Hughson 2,943 E6
*92646 Huntington Beach 170,505 C11
90255 Huntington Park 46,223 C11
92251 Imperial 3,451 K11
92032 Imperial Beach 22,689 H11
93526 Independence⊙ 748 H7
92201 Indio 21,611 J10
*90301 Inglewood 94,245 B11
92713 Irvine 62,134 D11
95642 Jackson⊙ 2,331 C9
†94701 Kensington 5,342 J2
93600 Kerman 4,002 E7
93930 King City 5,495 D7
93631 Kingsburg 5,115 F7
91011 La Canada 20,153 C10
91214 La Crescenta-Montrose 16,531 C10
94549 Lafayette 20,879 K2
*92651 Laguna Beach 17,901 G10
92653 Laguna Hills 33,600 D11
92677 Laguna Niguel 12,237 H10
90631 La Habra 45,232 D11
92037 La Jolla H11
92352 Lake Arrowhead 6,272 H9
92330 Lake Elsinore 5,982 F11
93240 Lake Isabella 3,428 G8
95453 Lakeport⊙ 3,675 C4
*90712 Lakewood 74,654 C11
92041 La Mesa 50,308 H11
90638 La Mirada 40,986 D11
93241 Lamont 9,616 G8
93534 Lancaster 48,027 G9
*91744 La Puente 30,882 D10
94939 Larkspur 11,064 H1
95330 Lathrop 3,717 D6
91750 La Verne 23,508 D10
90260 Lawndale 23,460 B11
92045 Lemon Grove 20,780 J11
93245 Lemoore 8,832 F7
†92311 Lenwood 2,974 H9
92024 Leucadia 9,478 H10
95648 Lincoln 4,132 B8
†95901 Linda 10,225 D4
93247 Lindsay 6,924 F7
95953 Live Oak 3,103 D4
†95073 Live Oak 11,482 K4
94550 Livermore 48,349 L2
95334 Livingston 5,326 E6
95240 Lodi 35,221 C9
92354 Loma Linda 10,694 F10
90717 Lomita 18,807 C11
93436 Lompoc 26,267 E9
*90801 Long Beach 361,334 C11
90720 Los Alamitos 11,529 D11
94022 Los Altos 25,769 K3
94022 Los Altos Hills 7,421 J3
*90001 Los Angeles⊙ 2,966,850 C10
Los Angeles-Long Beach‡ 7,477,657 C10
93635 Los Banos 10,341 E6
95030 Los Gatos 26,906 K4
†93402 Los Osos-Baywood Park 10,933 E8
90262 Lynwood 48,548 C11
93637 Madera⊙ 21,732 E7
90265 Malibu B10
93546 Mammoth Lakes 3,929 E6
90266 Manhattan Beach 31,542 B11
95336 Manteca 24,925 D6
93933 Marina 20,647 D7
95338 Mariposa⊙ 1,150 F6
94553 Martinez⊙ 22,582 K1
95901 Marysville⊙ 9,898 D4
90201 Maywood 21,810 C10
93250 McFarland 5,151 F8
93023 Meiners Oaks-Mira Monte 9,512 F9
93640 Mendota 5,038 E7
94025 Menlo Park 26,369 J3
95340 Merced⊙ 36,499 E6
94030 Millbrae 20,058 J2
94941 Mill Valley 12,967 H2
95035 Milpitas 37,820 L3
91752 Mira Loma 8,707 E10
92691 Mission Viejo 50,666 D11
*95350 Modesto⊙ 106,602 D6
Modesto‡ 265,902 D6
93501 Mojave 2,886 G8
91016 Monrovia 30,531 D10
91763 Montclair 22,628 D10
90640 Montebello 52,929 C10
93940 Monterey 27,558 D7
91754 Monterey Park 54,338 C10
95030 Monte Sereno 3,434 K4
91214 Montrose-La Crescenta 16,531 C10
93021 Moorpark 4,030 G9
94556 Moraga 15,014 K2
95037 Morgan Hill 17,060 L4
93442 Morro Bay 9,064 D8
*94042 Mountain View 58,655 K3
96067 Mount Shasta 2,837 C5
92405 Muscoy 6,188 E10
94558 Napa⊙ 50,879 C5
92050 National City 48,772 J11
92363 Needles 4,120 L9
95959 Nevada City⊙ 2,431 D4
94560 Newark 32,126 K3
91321 Newhall 12,029 G9
95360 Newman 2,785 D6
*92660 Newport Beach 62,556 D11
93444 Nipomo 5,247 E8
91760 Norco 21,126 E11
95660 North Highlands 37,825 B8
*91601 North Hollywood B10
90650 Norwalk 85,286 C11
94947 Novato 43,916 H1
95361 Oakdale 8,474 E6
*94601 Oakland⊙ 339,337 J2
93022 Oak View 4,671 F9
93445 Oceano 4,478 E8
92054 Oceanside 76,698 H10
93308 Oildale 23,382 F8
93023 Ojai 6,816 F9
*91761 Ontario 88,820 D10
†95060 Opal Cliffs 5,041 K4
*92666 Orange 91,450 D11
93646 Orange Cove 4,026 F7
94563 Orinda 16,825 J2
95963 Orland 4,031 C4
93647 Orosi 4,076 F7
95965 Oroville⊙ 8,683 D4
93030 Oxnard 108,195 F9
Oxnard-Simi Valley-Ventura‡ 529,899 F9
94553 Pacheco-Vine Hill 6,129 K1
94044 Pacifica 36,866 H2
93950 Pacific Grove 15,755 C7
93550 Palmdale 12,277 G9
92260 Palm Desert 11,801 J10
92262 Palm Springs 32,366 J10
*94301 Palo Alto 55,225 K3
90274 Palos Verdes Estates 14,376 B11
95969 Paradise 22,571 D4
90723 Paramount 36,407 C11
93648 Parlier 2,902 F7
*91101 Pasadena 118,072 C10
93446 Paso Robles 9,163 E8
95363 Patterson 3,908 D6
93953 Pebble Beach C7
92370 Perris 6,827 F11
94952 Petaluma 33,834 H1
90660 Pico Rivera 53,387 C10
94611 Piedmont 10,498 J2
94564 Pinole 14,253 J1
93449 Pismo Beach 5,364 E8
94565 Pittsburg 33,034 L1
92670 Placentia 35,041 D11
95667 Placerville⊙ 6,739 C8
94523 Pleasant Hill 25,124 K2
94566 Pleasanton 35,160 L2
*91766 Pomona 92,742 D10
93257 Porterville 19,707 G7
93041 Port Hueneme 17,803 F9
94025 Portola Valley 3,939 J3
92064 Poway 32,263 J11
93534 Quartz Hill 7,421 G9
95971 Quincy⊙ 4,451 E4
92065 Ramona 8,173 J10
95670 Rancho Cordova 42,881 C8
91730 Rancho Cucamonga 55,250 E10
92270 Rancho Mirage 6,281 J10
90274 Rancho Palos Verdes 36,577 B11
92067 Rancho Santa Fe 4,014 H10
96080 Red Bluff⊙ 9,490 C3
96001 Redding⊙ 41,995 C3
Redding○ 80
92373 Redlands 43,619 H9
*90277 Redondo Beach 57,102 B11
*94061 Redwood City⊙ 54,951 J3
93654 Reedley 11,071 F7
92376 Rialto 37,474 E10
*94801 Richmond 74,676 J1
93555 Ridgecrest 15,929 H8
95562 Rio Dell 2,687 A3
95673 Rio Linda 7,359 B8
94571 Rio Vista 3,142 L1
95366 Ripon 3,509 D6
95367 Riverbank 5,695 E6
*92501 Riverside⊙ 170,591 E11
Riverside-San Bernardino-Ontario‡ 1,557,080 E11
95677 Rocklin 7,344 B8
94572 Rodeo 8,286 J1
94928 Rohnert Park 22,965 C5
90274 Rolling Hills 2,049 B11
90274 Rolling Hills Estates 7,701 B11
91770 Rosemead 42,604 C10
95678 Roseville 24,347 B8
94957 Ross 2,801 H1
92509 Rubidoux 17,048 E10

(continued on following page)

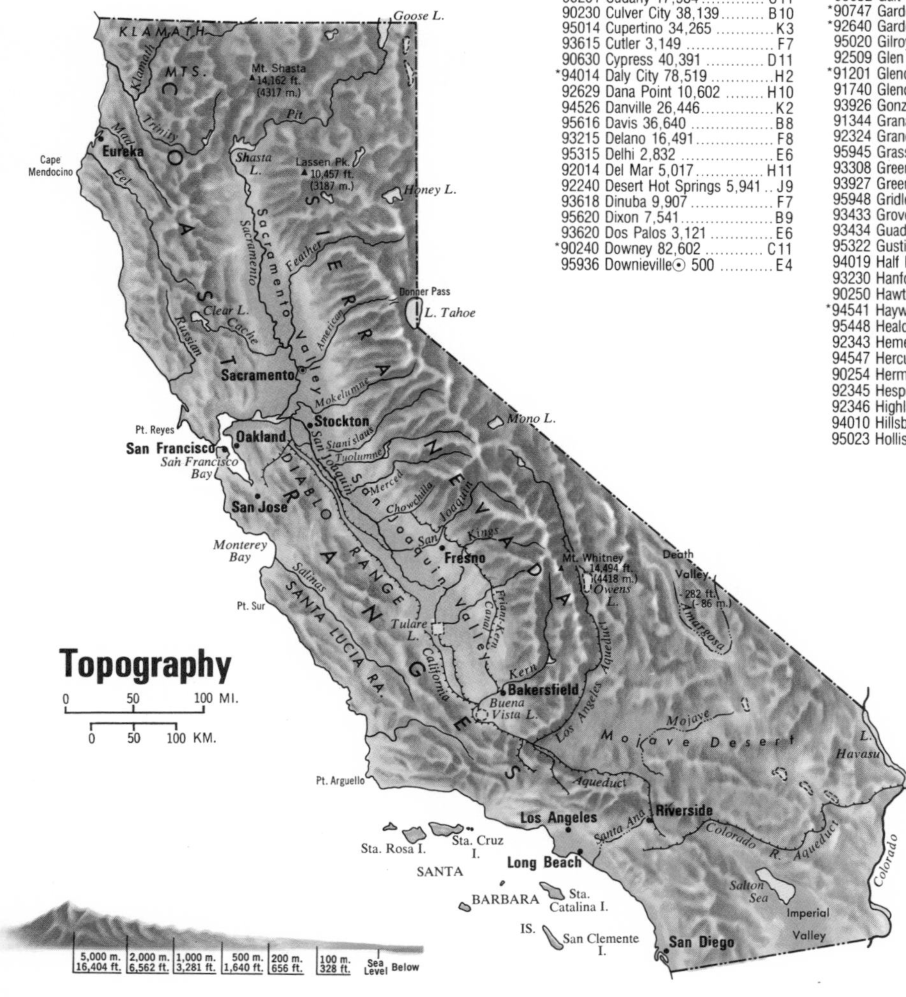
Topography
0 50 100 MI.
0 50 100 KM.
KLAMATH
MTS.
Goose L.
Mt. Shasta 14,162 ft. (4317 m.)
Pit
Cape Mendocino
Eureka
Shasta L.
Lassen Pk. 10,457 ft. (3187 m.)
Honey L.
Sacramento
Feather
Donner Pass
L. Tahoe
Clear L.
Sacramento
Oakland
Stockton
Pt. Reyes
San Francisco
San Francisco Bay
San Jose
Mono L.
Monterey Bay
Fresno
Mt. Whitney 14,494 ft. (4418 m.)
Death Valley
-282 ft. (-86 m.)
Pt. Sur
Tulare L.
Bakersfield
Buena Vista L.
Mojave Desert
Havasu
Pt. Arguello
Los Angeles
Riverside
Sta. Rosa I.
Sta. Cruz I.
Long Beach
SANTA BARBARA IS.
Sta. Catalina I.
San Clemente I.
San Diego
Salton Sea
Imperial Valley
Colorado
SIERRA NEVADA
DIABLO RANGE
SANTA LUCIA RA.
5,000 m. 16,404 ft.
2,000 m. 6,562 ft.
1,000 m. 3,281 ft.
500 m. 1,640 ft.
200 m. 656 ft.
100 m. 328 ft.
Sea Level
Below

*95801 Sacramento (cap.)⊙ 275,741 B8
Sacramento‡ 1,014,002 B8
94574 Saint Helena 4,898 C5
93901 Salinas⊙ 80,479 D7
Salinas-Seaside-Monterey‡ 290,444 D7
95249 San Andreas⊙ 1,912 E5
94960 San Anselmo 12,067 H1
*92401 San Bernardino⊙ 118,794 E10
94066 San Bruno 35,417 J2
94070 San Carlos 24,710 J3
92672 San Clemente 27,325 H10
*92101 San Diego⊙ 875,538 H11
San Diego‡ 1,861,846 H11
91773 San Dimas 24,014 D10
*91340 San Fernando 17,731 C10
*94101 San Francisco⊙ 678,974 H2
San Francisco-Oakland‡ 3,252,721 H2
*91775 San Gabriel 30,072 C10
93657 Sanger 12,542 F7
92383 San Jacinto 7,098 H10
*95101 San Jose⊙ 629,546 L3
San Jose‡ 1,295,071 L3
†92691 San Juan Capistrano 18,959 H10
*94577 San Leandro 63,952 J2
94580 San Lorenzo 20,545 K2
93401 San Luis Obispo⊙ 34,252 E8
92069 San Marcos 17,479 H10
91108 San Marino 13,307 D10
*94401 San Mateo 77,640 J3
94806 San Pablo 19,750 J1
94964 San Quentin 450 H1
*94901 San Rafael⊙ 44,700 J1
94583 San Ramon 22,356 K2
93452 San Simeon 350 D8
*92701 Santa Ana⊙ 204,023 D11
*93101 Santa Barbara⊙ 74,414 F9
Santa Barbara-Santa Maria-Lompoc‡ 298,660 F9
*95050 Santa Clara 87,700 K3
*95060 Santa Cruz⊙ 41,483 K4
Santa Cruz‡ 188,141 K4
90670 Santa Fe Springs 14,520 C11
93454 Santa Maria 39,685 E9
*90401 Santa Monica 88,314 B10
93060 Santa Paula 20,552 F9
*95401 Santa Rosa⊙ 83,320 C5
Santa Rosa‡ 299,827 C5
92071 Santee 47,080 J11
95070 Saratoga 29,261 K4
94965 Sausalito 7,338 H2
95060 Scotts Valley 6,891 K4
90740 Seal Beach 25,975 C11
93955 Seaside 36,567 D7
95472 Sebastopol 5,595 C5
93662 Selma 10,942 F7
93263 Shafter 7,010 F8
96125 Sierra City 500 E4
91024 Sierra Madre 10,837 D10
†90806 Signal Hill 5,734 C11
*93065 Simi Valley 77,500 G9
92075 Solana Beach 13,047 H11
93960 Soledad 5,928 D7
93463 Solvang 3,091 E9
95476 Sonoma 6,054 C5
95370 Sonora⊙ 3,247 E6
95073 Soquel 6,212 K4
91733 South El Monte 16,623 C10
90280 South Gate 66,784 C11
95705 South Lake Tahoe 20,681 F5
†95965 South Oroville 7,246 D4
91030 South Pasadena 22,681 C10
94080 South San Francisco 49,393 J2
94305 Stanford 11,045 J3
90680 Stanton 23,723 D11
*95201 Stockton⊙ 149,779 D6
Stockton‡ 347,342 D6
94585 Suisun City 11,087 K1
92381 Sun City 8,460 F11
92388 Sunnymead 11,554 F11
*94086 Sunnyvale 106,618 K3
96130 Susanville⊙ 6,520 E3
95685 Sutter Creek 1,705 C9
93268 Taft 5,316 F8
95730 Tahoe City E4
93561 Tehachapi 4,126 G8
91780 Temple City 28,972 D10
†95965 Thermalito 4,961 D4
*91360 Thousand Oaks 77,072 G9
92276 Thousand Palms 1,718 J10
94920 Tiburon 6,685 J2
90290 Topanga B10
*90501 Torrance 129,881 C11
95376 Tracy 18,428 D6
93274 Tulare 22,526 F7
95380 Turlock 26,287 E6
92680 Tustin 32,317 D11
92277 Twentynine Palms 7,465 K9
†95060 Twin Lakes 4,502 K4
95482 Ukiah⊙ 12,035 B4
94587 Union City 39,406 K2
91786 Upland 47,647 E10
95688 Vacaville 43,367 D5
91355 Valencia 12,163 G9
94590 Vallejo 80,303 J1
Vallejo-Fairfield-Napa‡ 334,402 J1
*91401 Van Nuys B10
90291 Venice B11
*93001 Ventura⊙ 74,393 F9
92392 Victorville 14,220 H9
92667 Villa Park 7,137 D11
93277 Visalia⊙ 49,729 F7
Visalia-Tulare-Porterville‡ 245,738 F7
92083 Vista 35,834 H10
91789 Walnut 12,478 D10
*94595 Walnut Creek 53,643 K2
93280 Wasco 9,613 F8
95386 Waterford 2,683 E6
95076 Watsonville 23,663 D7
96093 Weaverville⊙ 2,787 B3
96094 Weed 2,879 C2
*91790 West Covina 80,291 D10
†90069 West Hollywood 35,703 B10
90025 West Los Angeles B10
92683 Westminster 71,133 D11
†90047 Westmont 27,916 C11
†94565 West Pittsburg 8,773 K1
95691 West Sacramento 10,875 B8
*90601 Whittier 69,717 D11
95490 Willits 4,008 B4
95988 Willows⊙ 4,777 C4
*90744 Wilmington C11
95388 Winton 4,995 E6
93286 Woodlake 4,343 G7
95695 Woodland⊙ 30,235 B8
*91364 Woodland Hills B10
94062 Woodside 5,291 J3
95697 Yolo 600 B8
92686 Yorba Linda 28,254 D11
94599 Yountville 2,893 C5
96097 Yreka⊙ 5,916 C2
95991 Yuba City⊙ 18,736 D4
Yuba City‡ 101,979 D4
92399 Yucaipa 23,345 J9
92284 Yucca Valley 8,294 J9

OTHER FEATURES

Agua Caliente Ind. Res. J10
Alameda (creek) K3
Alamo (riv.) K10
Alcatraz (isl.) J2
Alkali (lkes) E2
All American (canal) K11
Almanor (lake) D3
Amargosa (range) J7
Amargosa (riv.) J7
American (riv.) C8
Anacapa (isl.) F10
Angel (isl.) J2
Ano Nuevo (pt.) J4
Arena (pt.) B5
Arguello (pt.) E9
Argus (range) H7
Arroyo del Valle (dry riv.) L3
Arroyo Hondo (dry riv.) L3
Arroyo Mocho (dry riv.) L2
Arroyo Seco (dry riv.) K10
Beale A.F.B. D4
Berryessa (lake) D5
Bethany (res.) L2
Big Sage (res.) E2
Black Butte (lake) C4
Bodega (bay) B5
Bonita (pt.) H2
Bristol (lake) K9
Buchon (pt.) D8
Buena Vista (lake) F8
Cabrillo Nat'l Mon. H11
Cachuma (lake) F9
Cadiz (lake) K9
Cahuilla Ind. Res. J10
Calaveras (res.) L3
California Aqueduct E7
Camanche (res.) C9
Camp Pendleton 10,017 H10
Campo Ind. Res. J11
Capitan Grande Ind. Res. J11
Cascade (range) D1
Castle A.F.B. E6
Channel Islands Nat'l Park E11
China Lake Naval Weapons Center H8
Chemehuevi Valley Ind. Res. L9
Chocolate (mts.) K10
Clair Engle (lake) C3
Clear (lake) C4
Clear Lake (res.) D2
Coachella (canal) K10
Coast (ranges) D7
Colorado (riv.) L8
Colorado River Aqueduct K10
Colorado River Ind. Res. L10
Conception (pt.) E9
Cooper (pt.) D7
Copco (lake) C2
Cosumnes (riv.) C9
Cottonwood (creek) C3
Coyote (res.) L4
Crowley (lake) G6
Crystal Springs (res.) J3
Cuyama (riv.) E8
Cuyapaipe Ind. Res. J11
Danby (lake) K9
Death (valley) H7
Death Valley Nat'l Mon. H7
Delgada (pt.) A3
Del Valle (lake) L3
Devils Postpile Nat'l Mon. F6
Donner (pass) E4
Dume (pt.) G10
Duxbury (pt.) H2
Eagle (lake) E3
Eagle (peak) E2
Eagle Crags (mt.) J8
Edison (lake) F6
Edwards A.F.B. 8,554 H9
Eel (riv.) B4
Elsinore (lake) E11
El Toro Marine Air Sta. 7,632 D11
Estero (bay) D8
Estero (pt.) D8
Estrella (riv.) E8
Eugene O'Neill Nat'l Hist. Site K2
Farallon (isls.) B6
Farallons, The (gulf) H2
Feather (riv.) D4
Florence (lake) G6
Folsom (lake) C8
Fort Bidwell Ind. Res. E2
Fort Hunter Liggett D8
Fort Independence Ind. Res. G7
Fort MacArthur C11
Fort Mohave Ind. Res. L9
Fort Ord D7
Fort Point Nat'l Hist. Site J2
Freel (peak) F5
Fremont (peak) H8
Fresno (riv.) E7
Friant-Kern (canal) F8
General Grant Grove Section (King's Canyon) G7
George A.F.B. 7,061 H9
Golden Gate (chan.) H2
Golden Gate Nat'l Rec. Area H2
Goose (lake) E1
Grapevine (mts.) H7
Grizzly (bay) K1
Guadalupe (riv.) K3
Haiwee H7
Hamilton (mt.) L3
Hat (peak) E2
Havasu (lake) L9
Hetch Hetchy (res.) F6
Hoffman (mt.) D2
Honey (lake) E3
Hoopa Valley Ind. Res. A2
Humboldt (bay) A3
Imperial (res.) L10
Imperial (valley) K10
Ingalls (mt.) E3
Inyo (mts.) G6
Iron Gate (res.) C2
Isabella (lake) G8
John Muir Nat'l Hist. Site K1
Joshua Tree Nat'l Mon. J10
Kern (riv.) G8
Kings (riv.) F7
Kings Canyon Nat'l Park G7
Klamath (riv.) B2
Laguna (res.) L11
La Jolla Ind. Res. J10
Lassen (peak) D3
Lassen Volcanic Nat'l Park D3
Lava Beds Nat'l Mon. D2
Lemoore N.A.S. 5,888 F7
Leroy Anderson (res.) L4
Lopez (pt.) D7
Los Angeles Aqueduct G8
Los Coyotes Ind. Res. J10
Lost (riv.) D1
Lower Alkali (lake) E2
Lower Klamath (lake) D2
Mad (riv.) B3
Manzanita Ind. Res. J11
March A.F.B. 3,607 E11
Mare Island Navy Yard J1
Mather A.F.B. 5,245 C8
Mathews (lake) E11
McClellan A.F.B. B8
McClure (lake) E6
Mendocino (cape) A3
Merced (riv.) E6
Middle Alkali (lake) E2
Mill (creek) D3
Millerton (lake) F6
Moffett Nav. Air Sta. K3
Mojave (des.) H9
Mojave (riv.) J9
Mokelumne (riv.) C9
Mono (lake) G5
Monterey (bay) K4
Moon (lake) E2
Morongo Ind. Res. J10
Mountain Meadows (res.) E3
Muir Woods Nat'l Mon. H2
Nacimiento (riv.) D8
Navarro (riv.) B4
Nevada, Sierra (mts.) E4
New (riv.) K11
Norton A.F.B. F10
Noyo (riv.) B4
Oakland Army Base J2
Old (riv.) L1
Oroville (lake) D4
Owens (lake) H7
Owens (peak) H8
Owens (riv.) G6
Oxnard A.F.B. F9
Paiute Ind. Res. G6
Pala Ind. Res. H10
Palomar (mt.) J10
Panamint (range) H7
Panamint (valley) H7
Pescadero (pt.) J3
Piedras Blancas (pt.) D8
Pillar (pt.) H3
Pillsbury (lake) C4
Pine (creek) D3
Pine Flat (lake) F7
Pinnacles Nat'l Mon. D7
Pit (riv.) D2
Point Mugu Pacific Missile Test Center F9
Point Reyes Nat'l Seashore H1
Presidio J2
Providence (mts.) K8
Punta Gorda (pt.) A3
Quartz (peak) L11
Railroad Canyon (res.) E11
Redwood Nat'l Park A2
Reyes (pt.) B6
Rogers (lake) H9
Rosamond (lake) G9
Round Valley Ind. Res. B4
Russian (riv.) B4
Sacramento (riv.) D5
Sacramento Army Depot B8
Saint George (pt.) A2
Salinas (riv.) D7
Salmon (riv.) B2
Salton Sea (lake) K10
San Andreas (lake) H2
San Antonio (lake) E8
San Benito (riv.) D7
San Bernardino (mts.) J10
San Clemente (isl.) G11
San Diego (bay) H11
San Francisco (bay) J2
San Gabriel (res.) D10
San Joaquin (riv.) E6
San Joaquin (valley) D6
San Lorenzo (riv.) K4
San Luis (res.) E7
San Martin (cape) D8
San Miguel (isl.) E9
San Nicolas (isl.) F10
San Pablo (bay) J1
San Pedro (bay) C11
Santa Ana (riv.) E11
Santa Barbara (chan.) E9
Santa Barbara (isl.) G10
Santa Barbara (isls.) F10
Santa Catalina (gulf) G11
Santa Catalina (isl.) G10
Santa Cruz (chan.) F10
Santa Cruz (isl.) F10
Santa Maria (riv.) E9
Santa Monica (bay) B11
Santa Rosa (isl.) E10
Santa Rosa Ind. Res. J10
Santa Ynez (riv.) E9
Santa Ysabel Ind. Res. J10
Searles (lake) H8
Sequoia Nat'l Park G7
Sharpe Army Depot D6
Shasta (lake) C3
Shasta (mt.) C2
Shasta (riv.) C2
Sierra Army Depot E3
Sierra Nevada (mts.) E4
Siskiyou (mts.) C2
Smith (riv.) A2
Soda (lake) K8
South Bay Aqueduct L2
South Cow (creek) C3
Stony Gorge (res.) C4
Suisun (bay) K1
Sur (pt.) D7
Tahoe (lake) F4
Tamalpais (mt.) H1
Tehachapi (mts.) G9
Telescope (peak) H7
Tomales (pt.) B5
Torres Martinez Ind. Res. J10
Travis A.F.B. L1
Trinidad (head) A2
Trinity (riv.) B3
Truckee (riv.) F4
Tulare (lake) F7
Tule (lake) D2
Tule River Ind. Res. G7
Twentynine Palms Marine Base 7,079 J9
Twitchell (res.) E9
Upper Alkali (lake) E2
Vandenberg A.F.B. 8,136 E9
Vizcaino (cape) B4
Walnut (creek) K1
Wheeler (peak) F5
Whipple (mts.) L9
Whiskeytown-Shasta-Trinity Nat'l Rec. Area C3
Whitney (mt.) G7
Willow (creek) E3
Wilson (mt.) D10
Yosemite Nat'l Park F6
Yuba (riv.) D4
Yuma Ind. Res. L11

⊙County seat.
‡Population of metropolitan area.
† Zip of nearest p.o. * Multiple zips.

Agriculture, Industry and Resources

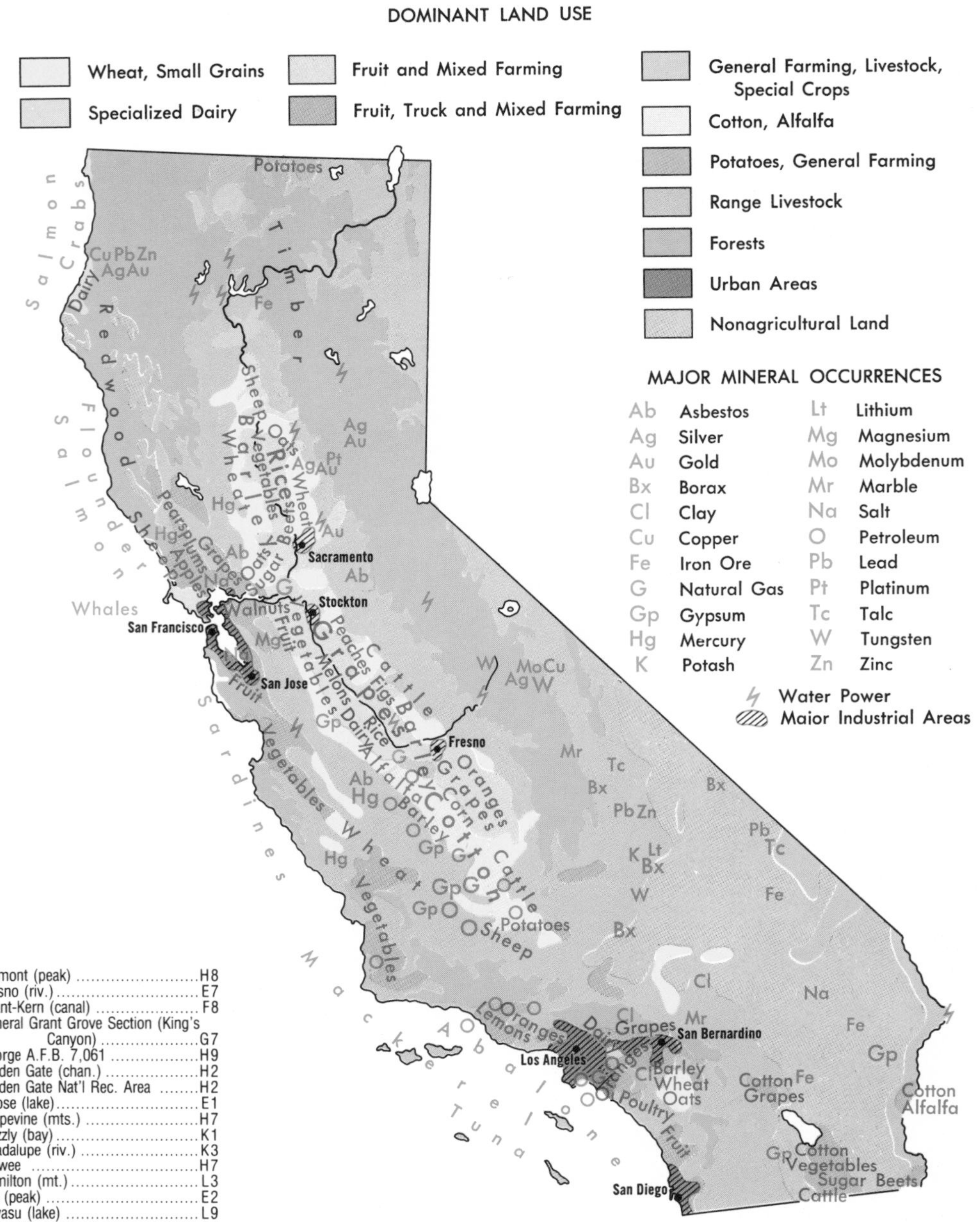
DOMINANT LAND USE
Wheat, Small Grains
Specialized Dairy
Fruit and Mixed Farming
Fruit, Truck and Mixed Farming
General Farming, Livestock, Special Crops
Cotton, Alfalfa
Potatoes, General Farming
Range Livestock
Forests
Urban Areas
Nonagricultural Land
MAJOR MINERAL OCCURRENCES
Ab Asbestos
Ag Silver
Au Gold
Bx Borax
Cl Clay
Cu Copper
Fe Iron Ore
G Natural Gas
Gp Gypsum
Hg Mercury
K Potash
Lt Lithium
Mg Magnesium
Mo Molybdenum
Mr Marble
Na Salt
O Petroleum
Pb Lead
Pt Platinum
Tc Talc
W Tungsten
Zn Zinc
Water Power
Major Industrial Areas
Sacramento
Stockton
San Francisco
San Jose
Fresno
San Bernardino
Los Angeles
San Diego

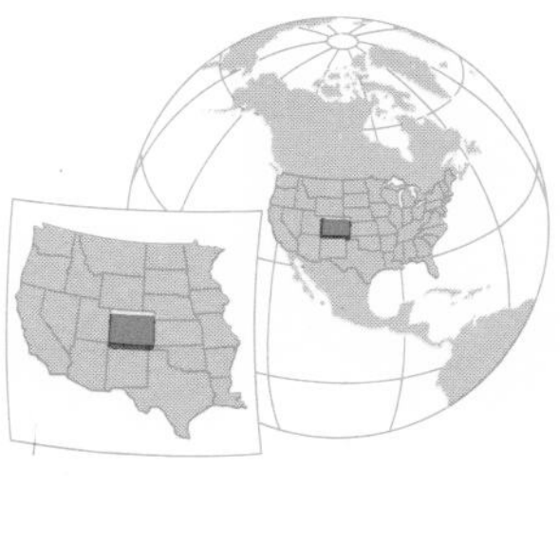

AREA 104,091 sq. mi. (269,596 sq. km.)
POPULATION 2,889,735
CAPITAL Denver
LARGEST CITY Denver
HIGHEST POINT Mt. Elbert 14,433 ft. (4399 m.)
SETTLED IN 1858
ADMITTED TO UNION August 1, 1876
POPULAR NAME Centennial State
STATE FLOWER Rocky Mountain Columbine
STATE BIRD Lark Bunting

COUNTIES

Adams 245,944 .... L3
Alamosa 11,799 .... H7
Arapahoe 293,621 .... L3
Archuleta 3,664 .... E8
Baca 5,419 .... O8
Bent 5,945 .... N7
Boulder 189,625 .... J2
Chaffee 13,227 .... G5
Cheyenne 2,153 .... O5
Clear Creek 7,308 .... H3
Conejos 7,794 .... G8
Costilla 3,071 .... J8
Crowley 2,988 .... M6
Custer 1,528 .... J6
Delta 21,225 .... D5
Denver 492,365 .... K3
Dolores 1,658 .... C7
Douglas 25,153 .... K4
Eagle 13,320 .... F3
Elbert 6,850 .... L4
El Paso 309,424 .... K5
Fremont 28,676 .... J5
Garfield 22,514 .... C3
Gilpin 2,441 .... H3
Grand 7,475 .... G2
Gunnison 10,689 .... E5
Hinsdale 408 .... E7
Huerfano 6,440 .... K7
Jackson 1,863 .... G1
Jefferson 371,741 .... J3
Kiowa 1,936 .... O6
Kit Carson 7,599 .... O4
Lake 8,830 .... G4
La Plata 27,195 .... D8
Larimer 149,184 .... H1
Las Animas 14,897 .... L8
Lincoln 4,663 .... M5
Logan 19,800 .... N1
Mesa 81,530 .... B5
Mineral 804 .... F7
Moffat 13,133 .... C1
Montezuma 16,510 .... B8
Montrose 24,352 .... C6
Morgan 22,513 .... M2
Otero 22,567 .... M7
Ouray 1,925 .... D6
Park 5,333 .... H4
Phillips 4,542 .... P1
Pitkin 10,338 .... F4
Prowers 13,070 .... P7
Pueblo 125,972 .... K6
Rio Blanco 6,255 .... C3
Rio Grande 10,511 .... G7
Routt 13,404 .... E1
Saguache 3,935 .... G6
San Juan 833 .... D7
San Miguel 3,192 .... C6
Sedgwick 3,266 .... P1
Summit 8,848 .... G3
Teller 8,034 .... J5
Washington 5,304 .... N3
Weld 123,438 .... L1
Yuma 9,682 .... P2

CITIES and TOWNS

Zip Name/Pop. Key

80101 Agate 90 .... M4
81020 Aguilar 624 .... K8
80720 Akron⊙ 1,716 .... N2
81101 Alamosa⊙ 6,830 .... H8
80510 Allenspark 200 .... J2
80420 Alma 132 .... G4
81210 Almont 135 .... F5
80721 Amherst 85 .... P1
80801 Anton 55 .... N3
81120 Antonito 1,103 .... H8
80802 Arapahoe 300 .... P5
81021 Arlington 37 .... N6
80804 Arriba 236 .... N4
†81323 Arriola 56 .... B8
*80001 Arvada 84,576 .... J3
81611 Aspen⊙ 3,678 .... F4
80722 Atwood 100 .... N1
80610 Ault 1,056 .... K1
*80010 Aurora 158,588 .... K3
81410 Austin D5
81620 Avon 640 .... F3
81022 Avondale 750 .... L6
80421 Bailey 150 .... H4
†80624 Barnesville 20 .... L2
81621 Basalt 529 .... E4
81122 Bayfield 724 .... D8
81411 Bedrock 45 .... B6
†80758 Beecher Island 5 .... P3
80512 Bellvue 250 .... J1
80102 Bennett 942 .... L3
80513 Berthoud 2,362 .... J2
†80438 Berthoud Pass 40 .... H3
80805 Bethune 149 .... P4
81023 Beulah 650 .... K6
80908 Black Forest 3,372 .... K4
80422 Black Hawk 232 .... J3
81123 Blanca 252 .... H8
†80424 Blue River 230 .... G4
†81155 Bonanza 8 .... G6
81024 Boncarbo 200 .... K8
80423 Bond 65 .... F3
81025 Boone 431 .... L6
*80301 Boulder⊙ 76,685 .... J2
†81428 Bowie 18 .... D5
80821 Boyero 12 .... N5
81026 Brandon 30 .... P6
81027 Branson 73 .... M8
80424 Breckenridge⊙ 818 .... G4
80611 Briggsdale 85 .... L1
80601 Brighton⊙ 12,773 .... K3
81028 Bristol 200 .... P6
†81212 Brookside 178 .... J6
80020 Broomfield 20,730 .... J3
80723 Brush 4,082 .... M2
†80742 Buckingham 5 .... L1
81211 Buena Vista 2,075 .... G5
80425 Buffalo Creek 150 .... J4
80807 Burlington⊙ 3,107 .... P4
80426 Burns 100 .... F3
80103 Byers 490 .... L3
81320 Cahone 200 .... B7
80808 Calhan 541 .... L4
81029 Campo 185 .... O8
81212 Canon City⊙ 13,037 .... J6
81124 Capulin 600 .... G8
81623 Carbondale 2,084 .... E4
80612 Carr 49 .... K1
80909 Cascade 950 .... K5
80104 Castle Rock⊙ 3,921 .... K4
81413 Cedaredge 1,184 .... D5
81125 Center 1,630 .... G7
80427 Central City⊙ 329 .... J3
81126 Chama 239 .... J8
81030 Cheraw 233 .... N6
80810 Cheyenne Wells⊙ 950 .... P5
81127 Chimney Rock 76 .... E8
81031 Chivington 20 .... O6
81128 Chromo 115 .... F8
81220 Cimarron 50 .... D6
80428 Clark 20 .... F1
81520 Clifton 5,223 .... C4
80429 Climax 975 .... G4
81221 Coal Creek 190 .... J6
81222 Coaldale 153 .... H6
80430 Coalmont 50 .... F1
81032 Cokedale 90 .... K8
81624 Collbran 344 .... C4
†81401 Colona 54 .... D6
81019 Colorado City 411 .... K6
*80901 Colorado Springs⊙ 214,821 .... K5
Colorado Springs‡ 317,458 K5
†80428 Columbine 12 .... E1
80022 Commerce City 16,234 .... K3
80432 Como 30 .... H4
81129 Conejos⊙ 200 .... G8
80812 Cope 110 .... O3
†80611 Cornish 15 .... L2
81321 Cortez⊙ 7,095 .... B8
81223 Cotopaxi 250 .... H6
80434 Cowdrey 80 .... G1
81625 Craig⊙ 8,133 .... D2
81415 Crawford 268 .... D5
81130 Creede⊙ 610 .... E7
81224 Crested Butte 959 .... E5
81131 Crestone 54 .... H7
80813 Cripple Creek⊙ 655 .... J5
80726 Crook 177 .... O1
81033 Crowley 192 .... M6
81055 Cuchara 43 .... J8
80514 Dacono 2,321 .... K2
†80728 Dailey 20 .... O1
81630 De Beque 279 .... C4
†80135 Deckers 4 .... J4
80105 Deer Trail 463 .... M3
†81059 Delhi 10 .... M7
81132 Del Norte⊙ 1,709 .... G7
81416 Delta⊙ 3,931 .... D5
*80201 Denver (cap.)⊙ 492,365 .... K3
Denver‡ 1,619,921 .... K3
†81054 Deora 2 .... O7
80435 Dillon 337 .... H3
81610 Dinosaur 313 .... B2
80814 Divide 700 .... J5
81323 Dolores 802 .... C8
81324 Dove Creek⊙ 826 .... A7
†81239 Doyleville 75 .... F6
80515 Drake 300 .... J2
81301 Durango⊙ 11,649 .... D8
81036 Eads⊙ 878 .... O6
81631 Eagle⊙ 950 .... F3
80615 Eaton 1,932 .... K1
80727 Eckley 262 .... P2
80214 Edgewater 4,766 .... J3
81632 Edwards 250 .... F3
81325 Egnar 50 .... B7
80106 Elbert 200 .... L4
†80466 Eldora 100 .... H3
80107 Elizabeth 789 .... K4
81633 Elk Springs 18 .... C2
80438 Empire 423 .... H3
†80110 Englewood 30,021 .... K3
80516 Erie 1,254 .... K2
80517 Estes Park 2,703 .... J2
†81433 Eureka 25 .... D7
80620 Evans 5,063 .... K2
80439 Evergreen 6,376 .... J3
80440 Fairplay⊙ 421 .... H4
81037 Farisita 116 .... J7
†80221 Federal Heights 7,846 .... J3
80520 Firestone 1,204 .... K2
†80810 Firstview 6 .... O5
80815 Flagler 550 .... N4
80728 Fleming 388 .... O1
81226 Florence 2,987 .... J6
80816 Florissant 130 .... J5
80521 Fort Collins⊙ 65,092 .... J1
Fort Collins‡ 149,184 .... J1
81133 Fort Garland 700 .... J8
80621 Fort Lupton 4,251 .... K2
81038 Fort Lyon 500 .... N6
80701 Fort Morgan⊙ 8,768 .... M2
80817 Fountain 8,324 .... K5
81039 Fowler 1,227 .... L6
80441 Foxton 12 .... J4
80116 Franktown 200 .... K4
80442 Fraser 470 .... H3
80530 Frederick 855 .... K2
80820 Freshwater (Guffey) 24 .... H5
80443 Frisco 1,221 .... G3
81521 Fruita 2,810 .... B4
80622 Galeton 200 .... K1
81134 Garcia 75 .... J8
81040 Gardner 100 .... J7
81227 Garfield 30 .... G5
81522 Gateway 350 .... B5
80818 Genoa 165 .... N4
80444 Georgetown⊙ 830 .... H3
80623 Gilcrest 1,025 .... K2
80624 Gill 250 .... L2
81634 Gilman 160 .... G3
81523 Glade Park 100 .... B5
†80485 Glendevey 50 .... H1
80532 Glen Haven 110 .... H2
81601 Glenwood Springs⊙ 4,637 E4
80401 Golden⊙ 12,237 .... J3
†80653 Goodrich 85 .... M2
†80480 Gould 12 .... G2
81041 Granada 557 .... P6
80446 Granby 963 .... H2
81501 Grand Junction⊙ 27,956 .... B4
80447 Grand Lake 382 .... H2
81228 Granite 47 .... G4
80448 Grant 50 .... H4
80631 Greeley⊙ 53,006 .... K2
Greeley‡ 123,438 .... K2
†80118 Greenland 21 .... K4
80819 Green Mountain Falls 607 .... K5
†81640 Greystone 2 .... B1
80729 Grover 158 .... L1
80820 Guffey 24 .... H5
81042 Gulnare 6 .... K8
81230 Gunnison⊙ 5,785 .... E5
81637 Gypsum 743 .... F3
80730 Hale 4 .... P3
81638 Hamilton 100 .... D2
81043 Hartman 122 .... P6
80449 Hartsel 69 .... H4
81044 Hasty 150 .... O6
81045 Haswell 126 .... N6
80731 Haxtun 1,014 .... O1
81639 Hayden 1,720 .... E2
80732 Hereford 50 .... L1
81326 Hesperus 250 .... C8
80733 Hillrose 213 .... N2
81232 Hillside 79 .... H6
81046 Hoehne 400 .... L8
81047 Holly 969 .... P6
80734 Holyoke⊙ 2,092 .... P1
81136 Hooper 71 .... H7
81419 Hotchkiss 849 .... D5
80451 Hot Sulphur Springs⊙ 405 .... H2
81233 Howard 200 .... H6
80641 Hoyt 60 .... L2
80642 Hudson 698 .... K2
80821 Hugo⊙ 776 .... N4
80533 Hygiene 450 .... J2
80452 Idaho Springs 2,077 .... H3
80735 Idalia 125 .... P3
81137 Ignacio 667 .... D8
80736 Iliff 218 .... N1
80455 Jamestown 223 .... J2
†81082 Jansen 267 .... K8
81138 Jaroso 50 .... H8
80456 Jefferson 50 .... H4
80822 Joes 100 .... O3
80534 Johnstown 1,535 .... K2
80737 Julesburg⊙ 1,528 .... P1
80823 Karval 51 .... N5
80643 Keenesburg 541 .... L2
†80729 Keota 4 .... L1
80644 Kersey 913 .... L2
81049 Kim 100 .... N8
80117 Kiowa⊙ 206 .... L4
80824 Kirk 30 .... P3
80825 Kit Carson 278 .... O5
80459 Kremmling 1,296 .... G2
†80832 Kutch 2 .... M5
80026 Lafayette 8,935 .... K3
†81132 La Garita 10 .... G7
80739 Laird 105 .... P2
81140 La Jara 858 .... H8
81050 La Junta⊙ 8,388 .... M7
81235 Lake City⊙ 206 .... E6
80827 Lake George 500 .... J5
80215 Lakewood 113,808 .... J3
81052 Lamar⊙ 7,713 .... O6
80535 Laporte 950 .... J1
80118 Larkspur 141 .... K4
80645 La Salle 1,929 .... K2
81054 Las Animas⊙ 2,818 .... N6
†81151 Lasauces 150 .... H8
†81153 Lavalley 237 .... J8
81055 La Veta 611 .... J8
†80452 Lawson 108 .... H3
†81625 Lay 40 .... D2
81420 Lazear 60 .... D5
80461 Leadville⊙ 3,879 .... G4
†81323 Lebanon 50 .... B8
81327 Lewis 150 .... B8
80828 Limon 1,805 .... M4
†81212 Lincoln Park 2,984 .... J6
80740 Lindon 60 .... N3
*80120 Littleton⊙ 28,631 .... K3
80536 Livermore 150 .... J1
†80601 Lochbuie 895 .... K2
†80701 Log Lane Village 709 .... M2
81524 Loma 265 .... B4
80501 Longmont 42,942 .... J2
†80135 Longview 10 .... J4
80027 Louisville 5,593 .... J3
80131 Louviers 300 .... K4
80537 Loveland 30,244 .... J2
80646 Lucerne 135 .... K2
†81054 Lycan 4 .... P7
80540 Lyons 1,137 .... J2
81525 Mack 380 .... B4
81421 Maher 75 .... D5
†80461 Malta 200 .... G4
81141 Manassa 945 .... H8
81328 Mancos 870 .... C8
80829 Manitou Springs 4,475 .... J5
81058 Manzanola 459 .... M6
†81623 Marble 30 .... E4
81329 Marvel 176 .... C8
80541 Masonville 200 .... J2
†80649 Masters 50 .... L2
80830 Matheson 120 .... M4
81640 Maybell 130 .... C2
81057 McClave 125 .... O6
80463 McCoy 62 .... F3
80542 Mead 356 .... K2
81641 Meeker⊙ 2,356 .... D2
81642 Meredith 47 .... F4
80741 Merino 255 .... N2
81005 Mesa 120 .... C4
81330 Mesa Verde National Park 45 .... C8
81142 Mesita 70 .... H8
80543 Milliken 1,506 .... K2
80477 Milner 196 .... F2
81645 Minturn 1,060 .... G3

(continued on following page)

Agriculture, Industry and Resources

DOMINANT LAND USE

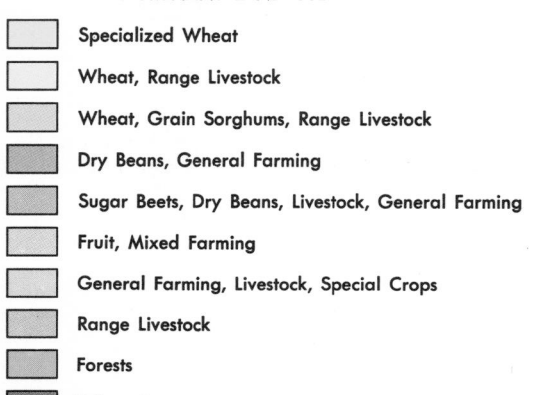

- Specialized Wheat
- Wheat, Range Livestock
- Wheat, Grain Sorghums, Range Livestock
- Dry Beans, General Farming
- Sugar Beets, Dry Beans, Livestock, General Farming
- Fruit, Mixed Farming
- General Farming, Livestock, Special Crops
- Range Livestock
- Forests
- Urban Areas
- Nonagricultural Land

MAJOR MINERAL OCCURRENCES

Ag	Silver	Mi	Mica
Au	Gold	Mo	Molybdenum
Be	Beryl	Mr	Marble
C	Coal	O	Petroleum
Cl	Clay	Pb	Lead
Cu	Copper	U	Uranium
F	Fluorspar	V	Vanadium
Fe	Iron Ore	W	Tungsten
G	Natural Gas	Zn	Zinc

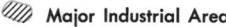

Water Power
Major Industrial Areas

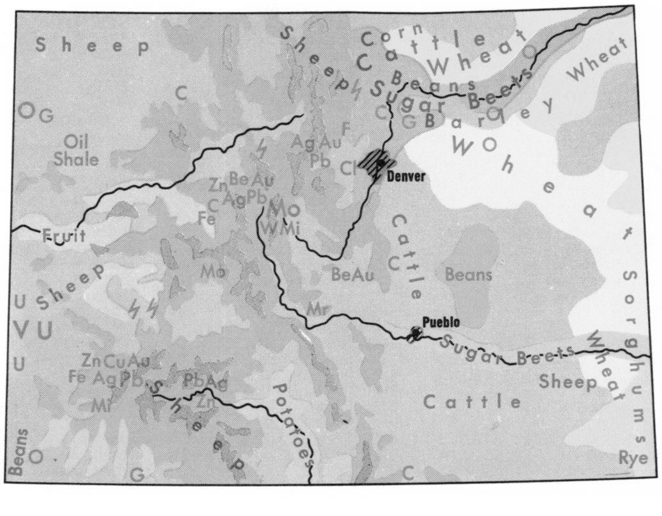

Topography

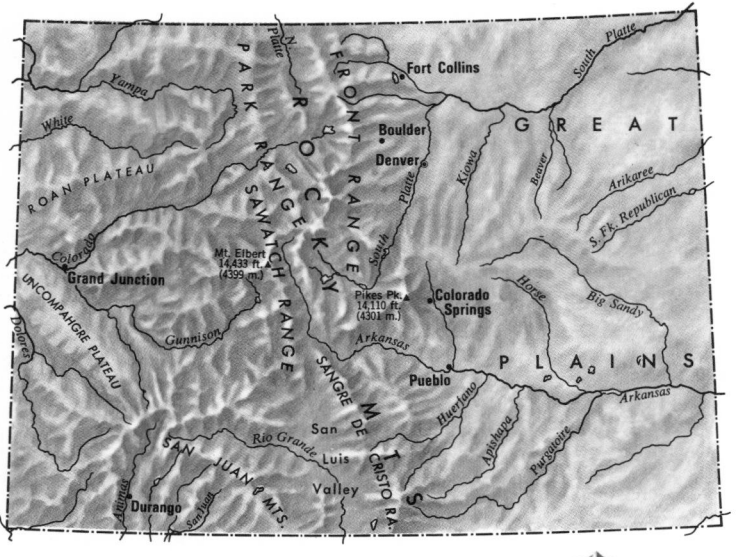

Below Sea Level | 100 m. 328 ft. | 200 m. 656 ft. | 500 m. 1,640 ft. | 1,000 m. 3,281 ft. | 2,000 m. 6,562 ft. | 5,000 m. 16,404 ft.

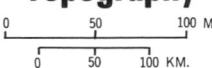

Colorado
SCALE
0 5 10 20 30 40MI.
0 5 10 20 30 40KM.
State Capitals.... ⊛ County Seats....◎
Major Limited Access Hwys. ――――
Scale 1:2,200,000

© Copyright HAMMOND INCORPORATED, Maplewood, N.J.

81646 Molina 200	D4
81144 Monte Vista 3,902	G7
†80435 Montezuma 6	H3
81401 Montrose◎ 8,722	D6
80132 Monument 690	K4
80465 Morrison 478	J3
81146 Mosca 100	H7
81236 Nathrop 150	H5
81422 Naturita 819	B6
80466 Nederland 1,212	H3
81647 New Castle 563	E3
80742 New Raymer 80	M1
†81054 Niniaview 2	N7
80544 Niwot 500	J2
†81022 North Avondale 110	L6
80233 Northglenn 29,847	K3
†81050 North La Junta 1,076	N7
81423 Norwood 478	C6
81424 Nucla 1,027	B6
80648 Nunn 295	K1
80467 Oak Creek 929	F2
81237 Ohio 100	F5
81425 Olathe 1,262	D5
81062 Olney Springs 253	M6
81426 Ophir 38	D7
80649 Orchard 79	L2
†81501 Orchard Mesa 4,876	C4
81063 Ordway◎ 1,135	M6
†81120 Ortiz 163	H8
80743 Otis 534	O2
81427 Ouray◎ 684	D6
80744 Ovid 439	P1
80745 Padroni 100	N1
†81147 Pagosa Junction 15	E8
†81147 Pagosa Springs◎ 1,331	E8
81526 Palisade 1,551	C4
80133 Palmer Lake 1,130	J4
80746 Paoli 81	P1
81428 Paonia 1,425	D5
81635 Parachute 338	C4
81429 Paradox 250	B6
†81212 Parkdale 21	H6
80134 Parker 200	K4
81239 Parlin 100	F6
80468 Parshall 80	G2
80747 Peetz 220	N1
81240 Penrose 500	K6
80831 Peyton 250	K4
80469 Phippsburg 300	F2
80650 Pierce 878	K1
80470 Pine 100	J4
80471 Pinecliffe 375	J3
†81001 Pinon 50	K6
81241 Pitkin 59	F5
81430 Placerville 50	D6
†81624 Plateau City 35	D4
†80743 Platner 30	N2
80651 Platteville 1,662	K2
81331 Pleasant View 300	B7
81242 Poncha Springs 321	G6
†81226 Portland 17	K6
†81427 Portland	D6
81243 Powderhorn 100	E6
81064 Pritchett 183	O8
†80736 Proctor 25	N1
81065 Pryor 50	K8
*81001 Pueblo‡ 101,686	K6
Pueblo‡ 125,972	K6
80472 Radium 22	G3
80832 Ramah 119	L4
80473 Rand 50	G2
81648 Rangely 2,113	B2

80473 Rand 50	G2
81648 Rangely 2,113	B2
80742 Raymer (New Raymer) 80	M1
81649 Red Cliff 409	G4
80545 Red Feather Lakes 150	H1
†81326 Red Mesa 100	C8
†81623 Redstone 115	E4
81431 Redvale 300	B6
81066 Red Wing 200	J7
81332 Rico 76	C7
81432 Ridgway 369	D6
81650 Rifle 3,215	D3
†81650 Rio Blanco	C3
81244 Rockvale 338	J6
81067 Rocky Ford 4,804	M6
80652 Roggen 100	L2
81148 Romeo 308	G8
80833 Rush 40	L5
81069 Rye 232	K7
81149 Saguache◎ 656	G6
†81236 Saint Elmo 75	G5
81201 Salida◎ 44,870	H6
81150 San Acacio 50	J8
81151 Sanford 687	H8
81069 San Isabel 8	K7
81152 San Luis◎ 842	J8
81153 San Pablo 150	J8
81248 Sargents 31	F6
81430 Sawpit 41	D7
80911 Security-Widefield 18,768	K5
80135 Sedalia 200	K4
80749 Sedgwick 258	O1
81070 Segundo 200	K8
80834 Seibert 180	O4
80546 Severance 102	K1
80475 Shawnee 100	H4
†80110 Sheridan 5,377	J3
81071 Sheridan Lake 87	P6
81652 Silt 923	D4
81249 Silver Cliff 280	J6
80476 Silver Plume 140	H3
80498 Silverthorne 989	G3
81433 Silverton◎ 794	D7
80835 Simla 494	M4
81653 Slater 10	E1
81654 Snowmass 999	E4
80750 Snyder 200	M2
81434 Somerset 200	E5
81154 South Fork 500	F7
81073 Springfield◎ 1,657	O8
80477 Starkville 127	L8
†80477 Steamboat Springs◎ 5,098	F2
80751 Sterling◎ 11,385	N1
80754 Stoneham 35	M1
81075 Stonington 27	P8
80136 Strasburg 1,005	L3
80836 Stratton 705	O4
81076 Sugar City 306	M6
†81077 Sunbeam 19	C1
†80027 Superior 208	J3
81077 Swink 668	M7
81435 Telluride◎ 1,047	D7
†80461 Tennessee Pass 5	G4
81250 Texas Creek 80	H6
†81082 Thatcher 50	L7
80229 Thornton 40,343	K3
†81137 Tiffany 24	D8
†81034 Timpas 25	M7
†81210 Tincup 8	F5
80479 Toponas 55	F2

81334 Towaoc 300	B8
81080 Towner 61	P6
81081 Trinchera 30	M8
81082 Trinidad◎ 9,663	L8
†80864 Truckton 10	L5
81251 Twin Lakes 40	G4
81084 Two Buttes 84	P7
†81059 Tyrone 9	L8
81436 Uravan 500	B6
†81064 Utleyville 2	O8
81657 Vail 2,261	G3
†81082 Valdez 12	K8
80755 Vernon 50	P3
81087 Victor 265	J5
81087 Vilas 118	P8
81155 Villa Grove 37	G6
81088 Villegreen 6	M8
†81001 Vineland 100	K6
80548 Virginia Dale 2	J1
80861 Vona 94	O4
†81130 Wagon Wheel Gap 20	F7
80480 Walden◎ 947	G1
81089 Walsenburg◎ 3,945	K7
81090 Walsh 884	P8
80481 Ward 129	H2
80653 Weldona 200	M2
80549 Wellington 1,215	K1
81252 Westcliffe◎ 324	H6
†80135 Westcreek 2	J4
80030 Westminster 50,211	J3
81091 Weston 150	K8
81253 Wetmore 150	J6
80033 Wheat Ridge 30,293	J3
81527 Whitewater 300	C5
80654 Wiggins 531	L2
80862 Wild Horse 13	N5
81092 Wiley 425	O6
†81226 Williamsburg 72	J6
80550 Windsor 4,277	J2
80482 Winter Park 480	H3
81655 Wolcott 30	F3
80863 Woodland Park 2,634	J4
80757 Woodrow 24	M3
81656 Woody Creek 400	F4
80758 Wray◎ 2,131	P2
80483 Yampa 472	F2
81335 Yellow Jacket 115	B7
80864 Yoder 25	L5
80759 Yuma 2,824	O2

OTHER FEATURES

Adams (mt.)	H6
Adobe Creek (res.)	N6
Air Force Academy 8,655	K5
Alamosa (creek)	G8
Alva B. Adams (tunnel)	H2
Animas (riv.)	D8
Antero (mt.)	G5
Antero (res.)	H5
Antora (peak)	G6
Apishapa (riv.)	L8
Arapaho Nat'l Rec. Area	G2
Arapahoe (peak)	H2
Arikaree (riv.)	O3
Arkansas (riv.)	P6
Arkansas Divide (mts.)	L4
Baker (mt.)	H2
Bald (mt.)	H4
Bear (creek)	P8
Beaver (creek)	M3
Bennett (peak)	G7

Bent's Old Fort Nat'l Hist. Site	M6
Big Grizzly (creek)	G1
Big Sandy (creek)	N4
Big Thompson (riv.)	H2
Bijou (creek)	L3
Black Canyon of the Gunnison Nat'l Mon.	D5
Black Squirrel (creek)	L5
Blanca (peak)	H7
Blue (mt.)	B2
Blue (riv.)	G3
Blue Mesa (res.)	E6
Bonny (res.)	P3
Box Elder (creek)	K4
Cache la Poudre (riv.)	H1
Cameron (peak)	H1
Camp Hale	G4
Carbon (peak)	E5
Castle (peak)	F5
Cebolla (creek)	E6
Chacuaco (creek)	M8
Cheesman (lake)	J4
Clay (creek)	O7

Cochetopa (creek)	F6
Colorado (riv.)	A5
Colorado Nat'l Mon.	B4
Conejos (peak)	G8
Conejos (riv.)	G8
Crestone (peak)	H7
Crow (creek)	L1
Culebra (peak)	J8
Culebra (riv.)	H8
Curecanti Nat'l Rec. Area	F6
Del Norte (peak)	F7
De Weese (plat.)	J6
Dinosaur Nat'l Mon.	B2
Disappointment (creek)	B7
Dolores (riv.)	B5
Douglas (creek)	B3
Eagle (riv.)	E3
Elbert (mt.)	G4
El Diente (peak)	C7
Eleven Mile Canyon (res.)	H5
Elk (riv.)	F1
Empire (res.)	L2
Ent A.F.B.	K5
Ethel (mt.)	F1

Evans (mt.)	H3
Florissant Fossil Beds Nat'l Mon.	J5
Fort Carson 19,399	K5
Fountain (creek)	K5
Frenchman (creek)	P1
Frenchman, North Fork (creek)	O1
Frenchman, South Fork (creek)	O1
Front (range)	H1
Gore (range)	G3
Graham (peak)	G2
Granby (lake)	G2
Great Sand Dunes Nat'l Mon.	H7
Green (riv.)	A2
Green Mountain (res.)	G3
Gunnison (riv.)	C5
Gunnison (tunnel)	D5
Gunnison, North Fork (riv.)	D5
Hale, Camp	G4
Handies (peak)	E7
Harvard (mt.)	G5
Hermosa (peak)	D7
Hesperus (mt.)	C8
Holy Cross (mt.)	F4

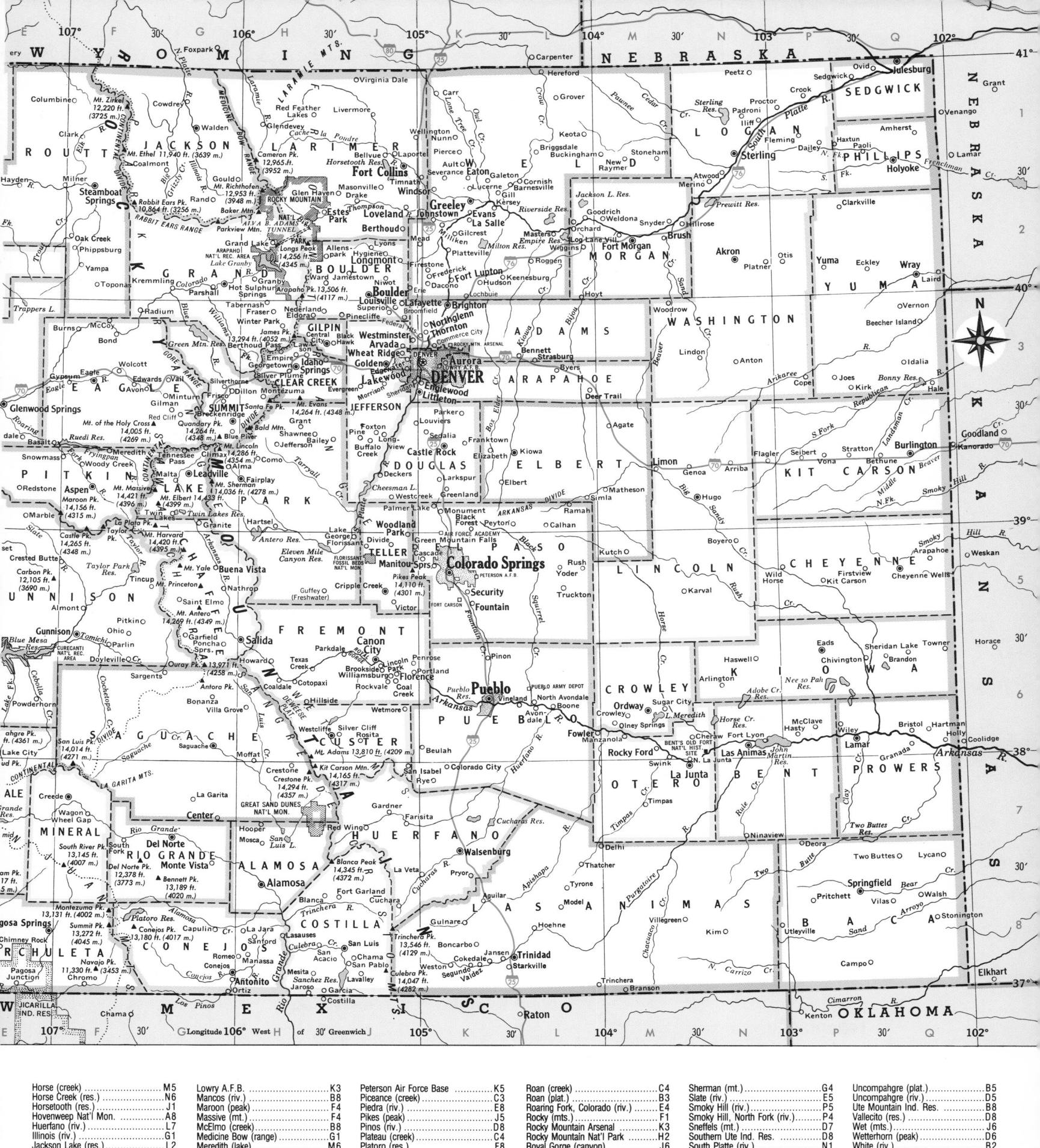

Connecticut

SCALE

0   5   10   15 MI.

0   5   10   15 KM.

State Capitals .... ⊛

Major Limited Access Hwys. ―――

Scale 1:610,000

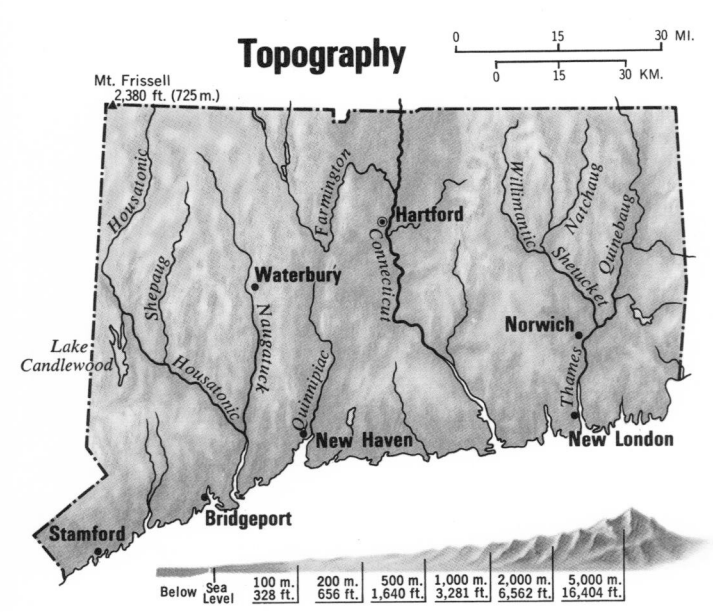

Topography

Mt. Frissell
2,380 ft. (725 m.)

0   15   30 MI.

0   15   30 KM.

| Below Sea Level | 100 m. 328 ft. | 200 m. 656 ft. | 500 m. 1,640 ft. | 1,000 m. 3,281 ft. | 2,000 m. 6,562 ft. | 5,000 m. 16,404 ft. |

COUNTIES

Fairfield 807,143 .... B3
Hartford 807,766 .... D1
Litchfield 156,769 .... B1
Middlesex 129,017 .... E3
New Haven 761,337 .... D3
New London 238,409 .... G2
Tolland 114,823 .... F1
Windham 92,312 .... H1

CITIES and TOWNS

Zip	Name/Pop.	Key
06230	Abington 600	G1
06231	Amston 900	F2
06232	Andover○ 2,144	F2
06401	Ansonia 19,039	C3
06278	Ashford○ 3,221	G1
06278	Ashford P.O.	
	(Warrenville) 500	G1
†06241	Attawaugan 400	H1
06001	Avon○ 11,201	D1
06001	Avon 1,434	D1
06233	Ballouville 800	H1
06330	Baltic	G2
06750	Bantam 860	B2
†06063	Barkhamsted○ 2,935	D1
†06423	Bashan 90	F2
06403	Beacon Falls○ 3,995	C3
06037	Berlin○ 15,121	E2
†06501	Bethany○ 4,330	C3
06801	Bethel○ 16,004	B3
06801	Bethel 8,755	B3
06751	Bethlehem○ 2,573	C2
06751	Bethlehem 1,762	C2
06002	Bloomfield○ 18,608	E1
06112	Blue Hills	E1
06040	Bolton○ 3,951	F1
06404	Botsford 400	C3
†06829	Branchville 600	B3
06405	Branford○ 23,363	D3
06405	Branford 5,438	D3
*06601	Bridgeport 142,546	C4
	Bridgeport‡ 395,455	C4
06752	Bridgewater○ 1,563	B2
06010	Bristol 57,370	D2
	Bristol‡ 73,762	D2
06016	Broad Brook	E1
06804	Brookfield○ 12,872	B3
06234	Brooklyn○ 5,691	H1
06013	Burlington○ 5,660	D1
06830	Byram	A4
06018	Canaan○ 1,002	B1
06018	Canaan 1,160	B1
†06897	Cannondale 400	B4
06331	Canterbury○ 3,426	H2
06019	Canton○ 7,635	D1
06019	Canton 1,680	D1
06409	Centerbrook 800	F3
06332	Central Village 950	H2
06235	Chaplin○ 1,793	G1
06410	Cheshire○ 21,788	D2
06410	Cheshire 5,722	D2
06412	Chester○ 3,068	F3
06412	Chester 1,388	F3
06413	Clinton○ 11,195	E3
06413	Clinton 3,168	E3
06414	Cobalt 700	E2
06415	Colchester○ 7,761	F2
06415	Colchester 3,190	F2
06021	Colebrook○ 1,221	C1
06022	Collinsville 2,555	D1
06237	Columbia○ 3,386	F2
06753	Cornwall○ 1,288	B1
06807	Cos Cob	A4
06238	Coventry○ 8,895	F1
06416	Cromwell○ 10,265	E2
06810	Danbury 60,470	B3
	Danbury‡ 146,405	B3
06239	Danielson 4,553	H1
06820	Darien○ 18,892	B4
06241	Dayville	H1
06417	Deep River○ 3,994	F3
06417	Deep River 2,495	F3
06418	Derby 12,346	C3
06422	Durham○ 5,143	E3
06422	Durham 2,641	E3
06023	East Berlin 950	E2
†06239	East Brooklyn 1,251	H1
06024	East Canaan 800	B1
06242	Eastford○ 1,028	G1
06025	East Glastonbury 300	E1
06026	East Granby○ 4,102	E1
06423	East Haddam○ 5,621	F3
06424	East Hampton○ 8,572	E2

AREA 5,018 sq. mi. (12,997 sq. km.)
POPULATION 3,107,576
CAPITAL Hartford
LARGEST CITY Bridgeport
HIGHEST POINT Mt. Frissell (S. Slope) 2,380 ft. (725 m.)
SETTLED IN 1635
ADMITTED TO UNION January 9, 1788
POPULAR NAME Constitution State; Nutmeg State
STATE FLOWER Mountain Laurel
STATE BIRD Robin

06351 Lisbon 3,279	G2
06759 Litchfield○ 7,605	C2
06759 Litchfield 1,489	C2
†06378 Lords Point 500	H3
06443 Madison 14,031	E3
06443 Madison 2,069	E3
06040 Manchester○ 49,761	E1
06040 Manchester 31,058	E1
†06250 Mansfield○ 20,634	F1
06250 Mansfield Center 1,043	G1
06777 Marble Dale 300	B2
06444 Marion 900	D2
06447 Marlborough○ 4,746	F2
06447 Marlborough 1,039	F2
†06382 Massapeag 350	G3
06252 Mechanicsville 425	H1
06450 Meriden 57,118	D2
Meriden‡ 57,118	D2
06762 Middlebury○ 5,995	C2
06455 Middlefield○ 3,796	E2
06456 Middle Haddam 325	E2
06457 Middletown 39,040	E2
06460 Milford 49,101	C4
06467 Milldale 975	D2
†06759 Milton 600	C1
06468 Monroe○ 14,010	C3
06468 Monroe P.O. (Stepney)	B3
06353 Montville○ 16,455	G3
06353 Montville 1,711	G3
06469 Moodus 1,179	F2
06354 Moosup 3,308	H2
06763 Morris○ 1,899	C2
06355 Mystic 2,333	H3
06770 Naugatuck 26,456	C3
*06050 New Britain 73,840	E2
New Britain‡ 142,241	E2
06840 New Canaan○ 17,931	B4
06810 New Fairfield○ 11,260	B3
06057 New Hartford○ 4,884	C1
06057 New Hartford 1,310	C1
*06501 New Haven 126,109	D3
New Haven-West Haven‡ 417,592	D3
06111 Newington 28,841	E2
06320 New London 28,842	G3
New London-Norwich‡ 248,554	G3
06776 New Milford 19,420	B2
06776 New Milford 5,186	B2
06777 New Preston 1,209	B2
06470 Newtown○ 19,107	B3
06470 Newtown 2,022	B3
06357 Niantic 3,151	G3
06340 Noank 1,406	G3
06058 Norfolk○ 2,156	C1
06471 North Branford 11,554	E3
06778 Northfield 600	C2
06254 North Franklin 500	G2
06060 North Granby 450	D1
06255 North Grosvenor Dale 1,856	H1
†06437 North Guilford	E3
06473 North Haven 22,080	D3
06359 North Stonington 4,219	H3
06256 North Windham 200	G1
*06850 Norwalk 77,767	B4
06360 Norwich 38,074	G2
06370 Oakdale 608	G3
06779 Oakville 8,737	C2
06371 Old Lyme○ 6,159	F3

06372 Old Mystic 600	H3
06475 Old Saybrook○ 9,287	F3
06475 Old Saybrook 1,857	F3
06373 Oneco 550	H2
06477 Orange○ 13,237	C3
06483 Oxford○ 6,634	C3
06379 Pawcatuck 5,216	H3
06781 Pequabuck 642	C2
06061 Pine Meadow 400	D1
†06405 Pine Orchard 300	D3
06374 Plainfield○ 12,774	H2
06374 Plainfield 2,799	H2
06062 Plainville○ 16,401	D2
06063 Pleasant Valley 300	C1
†06385 Pleasure Beach 1,356	G3
06782 Plymouth○ 10,732	C2
06254 Pomfret 2,775	H1
†06340 Poquonock Bridge 2,549	G3
06480 Portland○ 8,383	E2
06480 Portland 5,914	E2
06712 Prospect○ 6,807	D2
06260 Putnam○ 8,580	H1
06260 Putnam 6,855	H1
06375 Quaker Hill 2,052	G3
06262 Quinebaug 1,088	H1
06875 Redding○ 7,272	B3
06876 Redding Ridge 550	B3
06877 Ridgefield○ 20,120	B3
06877 Ridgefield 6,066	B3
06065 Riverton 250	D1
06481 Rockfall 900	E2
†06066 Rockville	F1
06067 Rocky Hill 14,559	E2
06263 Rogers 650	H1
06783 Roxbury 1,468	B2
†06415 Salem○ 2,335	F3
06068 Salisbury○ 3,896	B1
06264 Scotland 1,072	G2
06483 Seymour○ 13,434	C3
06069 Sharon○ 2,623	B1
06484 Shelton 31,314	C3
06784 Sherman○ 2,281	B2
06070 Simsbury○ 21,161	D1
06070 Simsbury 5,488	D1
06071 Somers○ 8,473	F1
06071 Somers 1,643	F1
06072 Somersville 750	F1
06487 South Britain 390	B3
06488 Southbury○ 14,156	C3
†06238 South Coventry (Coventry) 3,769	F1
06073 South Glastonbury	E2
06489 Southington○ 36,879	D2
06785 South Kent 450	B2
06265 South Willington 450	F1
06266 South Windham 1,399	G2
06074 South Windsor○ 17,198	E1
06267 South Woodstock 1,319	G1
06075 Stafford 9,268	F1
06076 Stafford Springs 3,392	F1
06077 Staffordville 500	G1
*06901 Stamford 102,453	A4
Stamford‡ 198,854	A4
†06468 Stepney	B3
06377 Sterling 1,791	H2
06491 Stevenson 300	C3
06378 Stonington○ 16,220	H3
06378 Stonington 1,228	H3
06268 Storrs 11,394	F1
06497 Stratford 50,541	C4

06078 Suffield○ 9,294	E1
06078 Suffield 1,122	E1
06079 Taconic 400	B1
06380 Taftville	G2
06081 Tariffville 1,324	D1
06786 Terryville 5,234	C2
06787 Thomaston○ 6,276	C2
06277 Thompson○ 8,141	H1
†06082 Thompsonville	E1
06084 Tolland○ 9,694	F1
06790 Torrington 30,987	C1
06611 Trumbull○ 32,989	C4
06382 Uncasville 1,597	G3
†06076 Union 546	G1
06066 Vernon○ 27,974	F1
06383 Versailles 540	G2
06384 Voluntown○ 1,637	H2
06492 Wallingford 37,274	D3
06492 Wallingford 17,821	D3
06754 Warren○ 1,027	B2
†06278 Warrenville 500	G1
06793 Washington○ 3,657	B2
06794 Washington Depot 900	B2
*06701 Waterbury 103,266	C2
Waterbury‡ 228,178	C2
06385 Waterford○ 17,843	G3
06385 Waterford 2,736	G3
06795 Watertown○ 19,489	C2
06089 Weatogue 2,249	D1
06498 Westbrook○ 5,216	F3
06498 Westbrook 2,035	F3
06796 West Cornwall 425	B1
06090 West Granby 567	D1
06107 West Hartford 61,301	D1
06516 West Haven 53,184	D3
06388 West Mystic 3,364	H3
06883 Weston○ 8,284	B4
06880 Westport○ 25,290	B4
06896 West Redding 500	B3
06092 West Simsbury 2,140	D1
06109 Wethersfield 26,013	E2
06517 Whitneyville	D3
06226 Willimantic 14,652	G2
†06279 Willington○ 4,694	F1
06897 Wilton○ 15,351	B4
06094 Winchester○ 10,841	C1
06094 Winchester Center 350	C1
06280 Windham○ 21,062	G2
06095 Windsor○ 25,204	E1
06095 Windsor 17,517	E1
06096 Windsor Locks○ 12,190	E1
06097 Windsorville 450	E1
06098 Winsted 8,092	C1
†06417 Winthrop 750	E3
06716 Wolcott○ 13,008	D2
†06515 Woodbridge○ 7,761	D3
06798 Woodbury○ 6,942	C2
06798 Woodbury 1,290	C2
†06460 Woodmont 1,797	D4
06281 Woodstock○ 5,117	H1

OTHER FEATURES

Aspetuck (riv.)	B4
Bantam (lake)	C2
Barkhamsted (res.)	D1
Bear (mt.)	B1
Byram (riv.)	A4
Candlewood (lake)	A2
Coast Guard Academy	G3

Colebrook River (lake)	C1
Congamond (lkes.)	E1
Connecticut (riv.)	E2
Dennis (hill)	C1
Easton (res.)	B3
Eight Mile (riv.)	F3
Farmington (riv.)	D1
French (riv.)	H1
Frissell (mt.)	B1
Gaillard (lake)	D3
Gardner (lake)	G2
Hammonasset (pt.)	E3
Hammonasset (res.)	E3
Haystack (mt.)	C1
Highland (lake)	C1
Hockanum (riv.)	E1
Hop (riv.)	F1
Housatonic (riv.)	B3
Lillinonah (lake)	B3
Little (riv.)	G2
Long Island (sound)	C4
Mad (riv.)	C2
Mashapaug (lake)	G1
Mason (lake)	H3
Mattabesset (riv.)	E2
Mianus (riv.)	A4
Mohawk (mt.)	B1
Moosup (riv.)	H2
Mount Hope (riv.)	G1
Mudge (pond)	B1
Mystic (riv.)	H3
Natchaug (riv.)	G1
Naugatuck (riv.)	C3
Nepaug (res.)	C1
Niantic (riv.)	G3
Norwalk (riv.)	B4
Pachaug (pond)	H2
Pawcatuck (riv.)	H3
Pequabuck (riv.)	C2
Pequonnock (riv.)	C3
Pocotopaug (lake)	E2
Quaddick (res.)	H1
Quinebaug (riv.)	H2
Quinnipiac (riv.)	D3
Rippowam (riv.)	A4
Sachem (head)	E4
Salmon (brook)	D1
Salmon (riv.)	F2
Saugatuck (riv.)	B3
Scantic (riv.)	E1
Shenipsit (lake)	F1
Shepaug (riv.)	B2
Shetucket (riv.)	G2
Silvermine (riv.)	B4
Spectacle (lkes.)	B2
Still (riv.)	B3
Still (riv.)	C1
Talcott (range)	D1
Thames (riv.)	G3
Thomaston (res.)	C2
Titicus (res.)	A3
Trap Falls (res.)	C3
Twin (lkes.)	B1
Wamgumbaug (lake)	B4
Waramaug (lake)	B2
West Rock Ridge (hills)	D3
Willimantic (riv.)	F1
Wononskopomuc (lake)	B1
Yantic (riv.)	G2

‡Population of metropolitan area.
○Population of town or township.
† Zip of nearest p.o. * Multiple zips.

Agriculture, Industry and Resources

DOMINANT LAND USE

Specialized Dairy

Dairy, Poultry, Mixed Farming

Forests

Urban Areas

MAJOR MINERAL OCCURRENCES

Cl Clay   Mi Mica

Major Industrial Areas

Bottom-left index:

06424 East Hampton 2,152	E2
06108 East Hartford○ 52,563	E1
06027 East Hartland 900	D1
06512 East Haven○ 25,028	D3
06243 East Killingly 900	H1
06333 East Lyme○ 13,870	G3
†06763 East Morris 800	C2
06612 Easton○ 5,962	B4
†06088 East Windsor○ 8,925	E1
06028 East Windsor Hill 500	E1
06244 East Woodstock 400	H1
06029 Ellington○ 9,711	F1
06082 Enfield○ 42,695	E1
06082 Enfield 8,151	E1
06426 Essex○ 5,078	F3
06426 Essex 2,501	F3
06245 Fabyan 600	H1
06430 Fairfield 54,849	B4
06031 Falls Village 600	B1
06032 Farmington 16,407	D2
06334 Fitchville 400	G2
†06254 Franklin 1,592	G2
06335 Gales Ferry 1,191	G3
06755 Gaylordsville 960	A2
06829 Georgetown 1,834	B4
06336 Gilman 350	G2
06337 Glasgo 450	H2
06033 Glastonbury○ 24,327	E2
06033 Glastonbury 7,049	E2
06756 Goshen 1,706	C1
06035 Granby○ 7,956	D1
06035 Granby 1,912	D1

06830 Greenwich○ 59,578	A4
06246 Grosvenor Dale 700	H1
06340 Groton○ 41,062	G3
06340 Groton 10,086	G3
06437 Guilford○ 17,375	E3
06437 Guilford 2,555	E3
06438 Haddam○ 6,383	E3
06439 Hadlyme 450	F3
06514 Hamden○ 51,071	D3
06247 Hampton○ 1,322	G1
06350 Hanover 500	G2
*06101 Hartford (cap.) 136,392	E1
Hartford‡ 726,114	E1
†06091 Hartland○ 1,416	D1
06791 Harwinton○ 4,889	C1
06791 Harwinton 3,293	C1
06440 Hawleyville 600	B3
06082 Hazardville 5,436	E1
06248 Hebron○ 5,453	F2
06441 Higganum 1,660	E2
†06040 Highland Park 500	F1
06351 Jewett City 3,294	H2
06037 Kensington 7,502	D2
06757 Kent○ 2,505	B2
†06241 Killingly○ 14,519	H1
†06413 Killingworth○ 3,976	E3
†06424 Lake Pocotopaug 2,137	E2
06758 Lakeside 350	B2
06249 Lebanon○ 4,762	G2
06339 Ledyard○ 13,735	G3
†06437 Leetes Island 500	E3
†06039 Lime Rock 350	B1

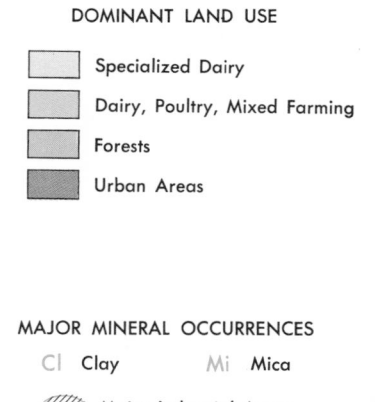

Florida

AREA 58,664 sq. mi. (151,940 sq. km.)
POPULATION 9,746,342
CAPITAL Tallahassee
LARGEST CITY Jacksonville
HIGHEST POINT (Walton County) 345 ft. (105 m.)
SETTLED IN 1565
ADMITTED TO UNION March 3, 1845
POPULAR NAME Sunshine State; Peninsula State
STATE FLOWER Orange Blossom
STATE BIRD Mockingbird

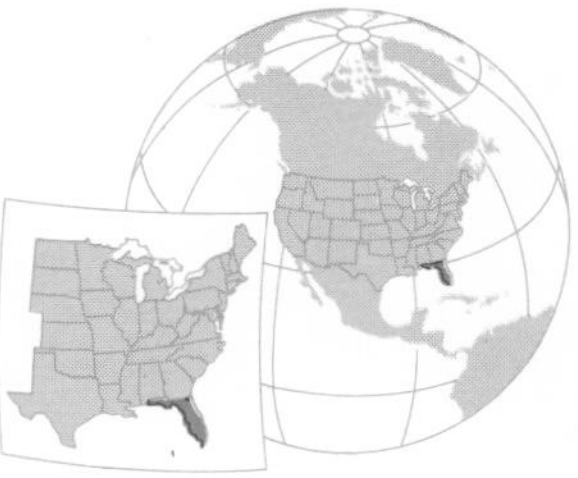

Topography

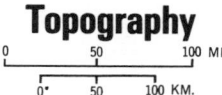

COUNTIES

Alachua 151,348 ... D2
Baker 15,289 ... D1
Bay 97,740 ... C6
Bradford 20,023 ... D2
Brevard 272,959 ... F3
Broward 101,820 ... F5
Calhoun 9,294 ... D6
Charlotte 58,460 ... E5
Citrus 54,703 ... D3
Clay 67,052 ... E2
Collier 85,791 ... E5
Columbia 35,399 ... D1
Dade 1,625,781 ... F6
De Soto 19,039 ... E4
Dixie 7,751 ... C2
Duval 571,003 ... E1
Escambia 233,794 ... B6
Flagler 10,913 ... E2
Franklin 7,661 ... B2
Gadsden 41,565 ... B1
Gilchrist 5,767 ... D2
Glades 5,992 ... E5
Gulf 10,658 ... D7
Hamilton 8,761 ... D1
Hardee 19,379 ... E4
Hendry 18,599 ... E5
Hernando 44,4693
Highlands 47,526 ... E4
Hillsborough 646,960 ... D4
Holmes 14,723 ... C5
Indian River 59,896 ... F4
Jackson 39,154 ... D5
Jefferson 10,703 ... C1
Lafayette 4,035 ... C2
Lake 104,870 ... E3
Lee 205,266 ... E5
Leon 148,655 ... B1
Levy 19,870 ... D2
Liberty 4,260 ... B1
Madison 14,894 ... C1
Manatee 148,442 ... D4
Marion 122,488 ... D2
Martin 64,014 ... F4
Monroe 63,188 ... E7
Nassau 32,894 ... E1
Okaloosa 109,920 ... C6
Okeechobee 20,264 ... F4
Orange 471,016 ... E3
Osceola 49,287 ... E3
Palm Beach 576,863 ... F5
Pasco 193,643 ... D3
Pinellas 728,531 ... D4
Polk 321,652 ... E4
Putnam 50,549 ... E2
Saint Johns 51,303 ... E2
Saint Lucie 87,182 ... F4
Santa Rosa 55,988 ... B6
Sarasota 202,251 ... D4
Seminole 179,752 ... E3
Sumter 24,272 ... D3
Suwannee 22,287 ... C1
Taylor 16,532 ... C1
Union 10,166 ... D1
Volusia 258,762 ... E2
Wakulla 10,887 ... B1
Walton 21,300 ... C6
Washington 14,509 ... C6

CITIES and TOWNS

Zip *Name/Pop.* *Key*

32615 Alachua 3,561 ... D2
32420 Alford 548 ... D6
32701 Altamonte Springs 22,028 . E3
32421 Altha 478 ... A1
33820 Alturas 900 ... E4
33501 Anna Maria 1,537 ... D4
32320 Apalachicola⊙ 2,565 ... A2
33570 Apollo Beach 4,014 ... C3
32703 Apopka 6,019 ... E3
33821 Arcadia⊙ 6,002 ... E4
32618 Archer 1,230 ... D2
33502 Aripeka 450 ... D3
32705 Astatula 755 ... E3
32233 Atlantic Beach 7,847 ... E1
33823 Auburndale 6,501 ... E3
33825 Avon Park 8,026 ... E4
32807 Azalea Park 8,301 ... E3
32530 Bagdad 1,479 ... B6
32234 Baldwin 1,526 ... E1
†33101 Bal Harbour 2,973 ... C4
33830 Bartow⊙ 14,780 ... E4
32423 Bascom 134 ... A1
†33101 Bay Harbor Islands 4,869 .. B4
†32786 Bay Lake 74 ... E3
33504 Bay Pines 5,757 ... B3
33507 Bayshore Gardens 14,945 .. D4
†33578 Bee Ridge 3,313 ... D4
32619 Bell 227 ... D2
33540 Belleair 3,673 ... B2
†33540 Belleair Beach 1,643 ... B2
33540 Belleair Bluffs 2,522 ... B3
†33540 Belleair Shores 80 ... B3
33430 Belle Glade 16,535 ... F5
†33430 Belle Glade Camp 1,645 ... F5
†32801 Belle Isle 2,848 ... E3
32620 Belleview 1,913 ... D2
†32036 Beverly Beach 217 ... E2
33152 Biscayne Park 3,088 ... B4
†32801 Bithlo 3,143 ... E3
32424 Blountstown⊙ 2,632 ... A1
33921 Boca Grande 900 ... D5
*33432 Boca Raton 49,505 ... F5
32425 Bonifay⊙ 2,534 ... C5
33923 Bonita Springs 5,435 ... E5
33834 Bowling Green 2,310 ... E4
*33435 Boynton Beach 35,624 ... F5
*33506 Bradenton⊙ 30,170 ... D4
Bradenton‡ 148,442 ... D4
33510 Bradenton Beach 1,595 ... D4
33835 Bradley 1,108 ... D4
33511 Brandon 41,826 ... D4
32008 Branford 622 ... D2
†33435 Briny Breezes 387 ... G5
32321 Bristol⊙ 1,044 ... B1
†33314 Broadview Park 6,022 ... B4
32621 Bronson⊙ 853 ... D2
32622 Brooker 429 ... D2
33512 Brooksville⊙ 5,582 ... D3
†33311 Browardale 7,409 ... B4
32010 Bunnell⊙ 1,816 ... E2
33513 Bushnell⊙ 983 ... D3
32011 Callahan 869 ... E1
32401 Calloway 7,154 ... D6
32426 Campbellton 336 ... D5
32624 Candler 275 ... E2
32920 Cape Canaveral 5,733 ... F3
33904 Cape Coral 32,103 ... E5
33055 Carol City 47,349 ... B4
Carrabelle 1,304 ... B2
32427 Caryville 633 ... C6
32707 Casselberry 15,247 ... E3
†32401 Cedar Grove 1,104 ... D6
32625 Cedar Key 700 ... C2
33514 Center Hill 751 ... D3
32535 Century 495 ... B5
†33950 Charlotte Harbor 2,084 ... E5
32324 Chattahoochee 5,332 ... B1
32626 Chiefland 1,986 ... D2
32428 Chipley⊙ 3,330 ... D6
†32548 Cinco Bayou 202 ... B6
*33515 Clearwater⊙ 85,528 ... B2
32711 Clermont 5,461 ... E3
†33950 Cleveland 2,417 ... E5
33440 Clewiston 5,219 ... E5
32922 Cocoa 16,096 ... F3
32931 Cocoa Beach 10,926 ... F3
†33060 Coconut Creek 6,288 ... F5
33521 Coleman 1,022 ... D3
33328 Cooper City 10,140 ... B4
†33559 Coral Cove 2,042 ... D4
33134 Coral Gables 43,241 ... B5
33060 Coral Springs 37,349 ... F5
33522 Cortez 3,821 ... D4
32431 Cottondale 1,056 ... D6
32327 Crawfordville⊙ 1,110 ... B1
32012 Crescent City 1,722 ... E2
32536 Crestview⊙ 7,617 ... C6
32628 Cross City⊙ 2,154 ... C2
32629 Crystal River 2,778 ... D3
33157 Cutler Ridge 20,886 ... F6
33880 Cypress Gardens 8,043 ... E3
†33472 Cypress Quarters 1,479 ... F4
33525 Dade City⊙ 4,923 ... D3
33004 Dania 11,811.B4
33837 Davenport 1,509 ... E3
33314 Davie 20,877 ... B4
*32014 Daytona Beach 54,176 ... F2
Daytona Beach‡ 258,762 .. F2
32016 Daytona Beach Shores 1,324 ... F2
32713 De Bary 4,980 ... E3
33441 Deerfield Beach 39,193 ... F5
32433 De Funiak Springs⊙ 5,563 C6
32720 De Land⊙ 15,354 ... E2
32028 De Leon Springs 1,669 ... E2
*33444 Delray Beach 34,325 ... F5
32725 Deltona 15,710 ... E3
32541 Destin 3,672 ... C6
33527 Dover 2,354 ... D4
33838 Dundee 2,227 ... E3
33528 Dunedin 30,203 ... B2
32630 Dunnellon 1,427 ... D2
33839 Eagle Lake 1,678 ... E4
†33601 East Lake-Orient Park 5,612 ... C2
†33940 East Naples 12,127 ... E5
32031 East Palatka 1,613 ... E2
32328 Eastpoint 1,246 ... B2
32751 Eatonville 2,185 ... E3
32437 Ebro 233 ... C6
32032 Edgewater 6,726 ... F3
†32801 Edgewood 1,034 ... E3
†33614 Egypt Lake 11,932 ... C2
33531 Elfers 11,396 ... D3
†33101 El Portal 1,819 ... B4
33533 Englewood 9,633 ... D5
32504 Ensley 14,422 ... B6
32425 Esto 304 ... C5
32726 Eustis 9,453 ... E3
33929 Everglades City 524 ... E6
32634 Fairfield 450 ... D2
†32693 Fanning Springs (Suwannee Riv.) 314 ... D2
32948 Fellsmere 1,161 ... F4
32034 Fernandina Beach⊙ 7,224 . E1
32922 Five Points 1,691 ... D1
32036 Flagler Beach 2,208 ... E2
32636 Floral City 1,181 ... D3
33034 Florida City 6,174 ... F6
†32960 Florida Ridge 4,988 ... F4
†33472 Fort Drum 70 ... F4
*33301 Fort Lauderdale⊙ 153,279. C4
Fort Lauderdale-Hollywood‡ 1,014,043 .. C4
33841 Fort Meade 5,546 ... E4
*33901 Fort Myers⊙ 36,638 ... E5
Fort Myers-Cape Coral‡ 205,266 ... E5
33931 Fort Myers Beach 5,753 ... E5
33842 Fort Ogden 900 ... E4
*33450 Fort Pierce⊙ 33,802 ... F4
32548 Fort Walton Beach 20,829 . C6
Fort Walton Beach‡ 109,920 ... C6
32038 Fort White 386 ... D2
32438 Fountain 900 ... D6
32439 Freeport 669 ... C6
33843 Frostproof 2,995 ... E4
32731 Fruitland Park 2,259 ... D3
33578 Fruitville 3,070 ... D4
*32601 Gainesville⊙ 81,371 ... D2
Gainesville‡ 151,348 ... D2
32732 Geneva 1,120 ... E3
33534 Gibsonton 7,219 ... C3
32960 Gifford 6,240 ... F4
32040 Glen Saint Mary 462 ... D1
†33160 Golden Beach 612 ... C4
33999 Golden Gate 4,327 ... E5
†33444 Golf 110 ... F5
32560 Gonzalez 6,084 ... B6
33933 Goodland 600 ... E6
†32502 Goulding 5,352 ... B6
33170 Goulds 7,078 ... F6
32440 Graceville 2,918 ... D5
32442 Grand Ridge 591 ... A1
33463 Greenacres City 8,843 ... F5
32043 Green Cove Springs⊙ 4,154 ... E2
32330 Greensboro 562 ... B1
32331 Greenville 1,096 ... C1
32443 Greenwood 577 ... A1
32332 Gretna 1,448 ... B1
33533 Grove City 1,932 ... D5
32736 Groveland 1,992 ... E3
32561 Gulf Breeze 5,478 ... B6
33737 Gulfport 11,180 ... B3
†33444 Gulf Stream 475 ... F5
†33301 Hacienda Village 126 ... B4
33844 Haines City 10,799 ... E3
33009 Hallandale 36,517 ... B4
32044 Hampton 466 ... D2
33440 Harlem 2,669 ... F5
32045 Hastings 636 ... E2
32333 Havana 2,782 ... B1
32640 Hawthorne 1,303 ... D2
32642 Hernando 1,653 ... D3
*33010 Hialeah 145,254 ... B4
†33010 Hialeah Gardens 2,700 ... B4
33431 Highland Beach 2,030 ... F5
33846 Highland City 1,555 ... E4
32401 Highland Park 184 ... E4
32643 High Springs 2,491 ... D2
32405 Hiland Park 4,763 ... C6
†33827 Hillcrest Heights 177 ... E4
32046 Hilliard 1,869 ... E1
†33060 Hillsboro Beach 1,554 ... F5
33455 Hobe Sound 6,822 ... F4
32047 Hollister 980 ... E2
32017 Holly Hill 9,953 ... E2
*33020 Hollywood 121,323 ... B4
33509 Holmes Beach 4,023 ... D4
*33030 Homestead 20,668 ... F6
32646 Homosassa 1,426 ... D3
32648 Horseshoe Beach 304 ... C2
32334 Hosford 750 ... B1
32737 Howey In The Hills 626 ... E3
33568 Hudson 5,799 ... D3
†33460 Hypoluxo 573 ... F5
33934 Immokalee 11,038 ... E5
32903 Indialantic 2,883 ... F3
†33139 Indian Creek 103 ... B4
†32901 Indian Harbour Beach 5,967 ... F3
32960 Indian River Shores 1,254 . F4
33535 Indian Rocks Beach 3,717 . B3
†33535 Indian Shores 984 ... B3
33456 Indiantown 3,383 ... F4
32649 Inglis 1,173 ... D2
32048 Interlachen 848 ... E2
32650 Inverness⊙ 4,095 ... D3
33036 Islamorada 1,441 ... F7
†33101 Islandia 12 ... F6
*32201 Jacksonville⊙ 540,920 ... E1
Jacksonville‡ 737,519 ... E1
32250 Jacksonville Beach 15,462 . E1
†33568 Jasmine Estates 11,995 ... D3
32052 Jasper⊙ 2,093 ... D1
32565 Jay 633 ... B5
32053 Jennings 749 ... C1
33457 Jensen Beach 6,639 ... F4
†32901 June Park 4,051 ... F3
†33404 Juno Beach 1,142 ... F5
33458 Jupiter 9,868 ... F5
†33455 Jupiter Island 364 ... F4
33849 Kathleen 1,866 ... D3
33156 Kendall 73,758 ... B5
33709 Kenneth City 4,344 ... B3
33149 Key Biscayne 6,313 ... B5
33051 Key Colony Beach 977 ... F7
33037 Key Largo 7,447 ... F6
32656 Keystone Heights 1,056 ... E2
33040 Key West⊙ 24,382 ... E7
32741 Kissimmee⊙ 15,487 ... E3
33935 La Belle⊙ 2,287 ... E5
33537 Lacoochee 1,720 ... D3
32658 La Crosse 170 ... D2
32659 Lady Lake 1,193 ... E3
33850 Lake Alfred 3,134 ... E3
†32830 Lake Buena Vista 98 ... E3
32054 Lake Butler⊙ 1,830 ... D1
†33601 Lake Carroll 13,012 ... C2
32055 Lake City⊙ 9,257 ... D1
32744 Lake Helen 2,047 ... E3
*33801 Lakeland 47,406 ... D3
Lakeland-Winter Haven‡ 321,652 ... D3
†33612 Lake Magdalene 13,331 ... D3
32746 Lake Mary 2,853 ... E3
33403 Lake Park 6,909 ... F5
33852 Lake Placid 963 ... E4
33853 Lake Wales 8,466 ... E4
*33460 Lake Worth 27,048 ... G5
33539 Land O'Lakes 4,515 ... D3
33462 Lantana 8,048 ... F5
*33540 Largo 58,977 ... B3
33308 Lauderdale-by-the-Sea 2,639 ... C3
†33313 Lauderdale Lakes 25,426 ... B3
33313 Lauderhill 37,271 ... B3
33545 Laurel 6,368 ... D4
32567 Laurel Hill 610 ... C5
32058 Lawtey 692 ... D1
†33050 Layton 88 ... F7
†33301 Lazy Lake 31 ... B3
32059 Lee 297 ... C1
32748 Leesburg 13,191 ... E3
33936 Lehigh Acres 9,604 ... E5
33033 Leisure City 17,905 ... F6
†33614 Leto 9,003 ... C2
33064 Lighthouse Point 11,488 ... F5
32060 Live Oak⊙ 6,732 ... D1
32662 Lochloosa 450 ... E2
33548 Longboat Key 4,843 ... D4
32750 Longwood 10,029 ... E3
33549 Lutz 5,555 ... D3
32444 Lynn Haven 6,239 ... C6
32063 Macclenny⊙ 3,851 ... D1

(continued on following page)

Agriculture, Industry and Resources

DOMINANT LAND USE

Fruit, Truck & Mixed Farming

Truck & Mixed Farming

Truck Farming

Cotton, Tobacco, Hogs, Peanuts

Peanuts, General Farming

General Farming, Forest Products, Truck Farming, Cotton

Livestock Grazing

Forests

Swampland, Limited Agriculture

Urban Areas

Nonagricultural Land

MAJOR MINERAL OCCURRENCES

Cl Clay
Ls Limestone
O Petroleum
P Phosphates
Pe Peat
Ti Titanium
Zr Zirconium

⚡ Water Power   ▨ Major Industrial Areas

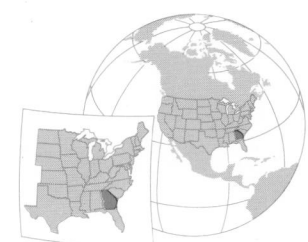

AREA 58,910 sq. mi. (152,577 sq. km.)
POPULATION 5,463,105
CAPITAL Atlanta
LARGEST CITY Atlanta
HIGHEST POINT Brasstown Bald 4,784 ft.
(1458 m.)
SETTLED IN 1733
ADMITTED TO UNION January 2, 1788
POPULAR NAME Empire State of the South;
Peach State
STATE FLOWER Cherokee Rose
STATE BIRD Brown Thrasher

COUNTIES

Appling 15,565	H7
Atkinson 6,141	G8
Bacon 9,379	G7
Baker 3,808	D8
Baldwin 34,686	F4
Banks 8,702	E2
Barrow 21,293	E2
Bartow 40,760	C2
Ben Hill 16,000	F7
Berrien 13,525	F8
Bibb 151,085	E5
Bleckley 10,767	F6
Brantley 8,701	J8
Brooks 15,255	E9
Bryan 10,175	K6
Bulloch 35,785	J4
Burke 19,349	J4
Butts 13,665	E4
Calhoun 5,717	C7
Camden 13,371	J9
Candler 7,518	H6
Carroll 56,346	B3
Catoosa 36,991	B1
Charlton 7,343	H9
Chatham 202,226	K6
Chattahoochee 21,732	C6
Chattooga 21,856	B1
Cherokee 51,699	D2
Clarke 74,498	F3
Clay 3,553	B7
Clayton 150,357	D3
Clinch 6,660	G9
Cobb 297,694	C3
Coffee 26,894	G8
Colquitt 35,376	E8
Columbia 40,118	H3
Cook 13,490	F8
Coweta 39,268	C4
Crawford 7,684	E5
Crisp 19,489	E7
Dade 12,318	A1
Dawson 4,774	D2
Decatur 25,495	C9
De Kalb 483,024	D3
Dodge 16,955	F6
Dooly 10,826	E6
Dougherty 100,978	D7
Douglas 54,573	C3
Early 13,158	C8
Echols 2,297	G9
Effingham 18,327	K6
Elbert 18,758	G2
Emanuel 20,795	H5
Evans 8,428	J6
Fannin 14,748	D1
Fayette 29,043	C4
Floyd 79,800	B2
Forsyth 27,958	D2
Franklin 15,185	F2
Fulton 589,904	D3
Gilmer 11,110	D1
Glascock 2,382	G4
Glynn 54,981	J8
Gordon 30,070	C2
Grady 19,845	D9
Greene 11,391	F3
Gwinnett 166,903	D2
Habersham 25,020	E1
Hall 75,649	E2
Hancock 9,466	G4
Haralson 18,422	B3
Harris 15,464	C5
Hart 18,585	G2
Heard 6,520	B4
Henry 36,309	D4
Houston 77,605	E6
Irwin 8,988	F7
Jackson 25,343	E2
Jasper 7,553	E4
Jeff Davis 11,473	G7
Jefferson 18,403	H4
Jenkins 8,841	J5
Johnson 8,660	G5
Jones 16,579	E5
Lamar 12,215	D4
Lanier 5,654	F8
Laurens 36,990	G6
Lee 11,684	D7
Liberty 37,583	J7
Lincoln 6,949	H3
Long 4,524	J7
Lowndes 67,972	F9
Lumpkin 10,762	D1
Macon 14,003	D6
Madison 17,747	F2
Marion 5,297	C6
McDuffie 18,546	H4
McIntosh 8,046	K7
Meriwether 21,229	C4
Miller 7,038	C8
Mitchell 21,114	D8
Monroe 14,610	E4
Montgomery 7,011	G6
Morgan 11,572	F3
Murray 19,685	C1
Muscogee 170,108	C6
Newton 34,489	E3
Oconee 12,427	F3
Oglethorpe 8,929	F3
Paulding 26,042	C3
Peach 19,151	E5
Pickens 11,652	D2
Pierce 11,897	H8
Pike 8,937	D4
Polk 32,386	B3
Pulaski 8,950	E6
Putnam 10,295	F4
Quitman 2,357	B7
Rabun 10,466	F1
Randolph 9,599	C7
Richmond 181,629	H4
Rockdale 36,747	D3
Schley 3,433	D6
Screven 14,043	J5
Seminole 9,057	C9
Spalding 47,899	D4
Stephens 21,763	F1
Stewart 5,896	C6
Sumter 29,360	D6
Talbot 6,536	C5
Taliaferro 2,032	G3
Tattnall 18,134	J6
Taylor 7,902	D5
Telfair 11,445	G7
Terrell 12,017	D7
Thomas 38,098	E9
Tift 32,862	E7
Toombs 22,592	H6
Towns 5,638	E1
Treutlen 6,087	G6
Troup 50,003	B4
Turner 9,510	E7
Twiggs 9,354	F5
Union 9,390	E1
Upson 25,998	D5
Walker 56,470	B1
Walton 31,211	E3
Ware 37,180	H8
Warren 6,583	G4
Washington 18,842	G4
Wayne 20,750	J7
Webster 2,341	C6
Wheeler 5,155	G6
White 10,120	E1
Whitfield 65,780	B1
Wilcox 7,682	F7
Wilkes 10,951	G3
Wilkinson 10,368	F5
Worth 18,064	E8

CITIES and TOWNS

Zip	Name/Pop.	Key
31001	Abbeville⊙ 985	F7
30101	Acworth 3,648	C2
30103	Adairsville 1,739	C2
31620	Adel⊙ 5,592	F8
31002	Adrian 756	G5
30410	Ailey 579	G6
30411	Alamo⊙ 993	G6
31622	Alapaha 771	F8
*31701	Albany⊙ 74,550	D7
	Albany‡ 112,456	D7
†30204	Aldora 139	D4
31301	Allenhurst 606	J7
31003	Allentown 321	F5
31510	Alma⊙ 3,819	G7
30201	Alpharetta 3,128	D2
30412	Alston 111	H6
30510	Alto 618	E2
†30161	Alto Park	B2
31512	Ambrose 360	G7
31709	Americus⊙ 16,120	D6
31711	Andersonville 267	D6
30802	Appling⊙ 150	H3
31712	Arabi 376	E7
30104	Aragon 855	B2
†30549	Arcade 223	E2
†31520	Arco	J8
31623	Argyle 206	G8
31713	Arlington 1,572	C8
30619	Arnoldsville 187	F3
31714	Ashburn⊙ 4,766	E7
*30601	Athens⊙ 42,549	F3
	Athens‡ 130,015	F3
*30301	Atlanta (cap.)⊙ 425,022	K1
	Atlanta‡ 2,029,618	K1
31715	Attapulgus 623	D9
30203	Auburn 692	E2
*30901	Augusta⊙ 47,532	J4
	Augusta‡ 327,372	J4
30001	Austell 3,939	J1
†30557	Avalon 200	F1
30803	Avera 248	G4
30002	Avondale Estates 1,313	L1
31716	Baconton 763	D8
31717	Bainbridge⊙ 10,553	C9
30511	Baldwin 1,080	E2
30107	Ball Ground 640	D2
30204	Barnesville⊙ 4,887	D4
31625	Barney 146	E8
30413	Bartow 357	G5
31720	Barwick 413	E9
31513	Baxley⊙ 3,586	H7
†31554	Beach	G8
30404	Bellville 173	H6
31721	Benevolence 138	C7
†30136	Berkeley Lake 503	D3
31722	Berlin 538	E8
30620	Bethlehem 281	E3
30621	Bishop 172	F3
31516	Blackshear⊙ 3,222	H8
30512	Blairsville⊙ 530	E1
31723	Blakely⊙ 5,880	C8
31302	Bloomingdale 1,855	K6
30513	Blue Ridge⊙ 1,376	D1
31724	Bluffton 132	C7
30805	Blythe 367	H4
30622	Bogart 819	E3
31626	Boston 1,424	E9
30623	Bostwick 357	E3
30108	Bowdon 1,743	B3
30516	Bowersville 318	G2
30624	Bowman 890	G2
30517	Braselton 308	E2
†30153	Braswell 282	C3
30110	Bremen 3,966	B3
31725	Brinson 274	C9
31726	Bronwood 524	D7
30415	Brooklet 1,035	J6
30205	Brooks 199	D4
31519	Broxton 1,117	G7
31520	Brunswick⊙ 17,605	K8
30113	Buchanan⊙ 1,019	B3
30625	Buckhead 219	F3
31803	Buena Vista⊙ 1,544	C6
30518	Buford 6,578	D2
31006	Butler⊙ 1,959	D5
31007	Byromville 567	E6
31008	Byron 1,661	E5
31009	Cadwell 353	G6
31728	Cairo⊙ 8,777	D9
30701	Calhoun⊙ 5,335	C1
30807	Camak 283	G4
31730	Camilla⊙ 5,414	D8
30520	Canon 704	F2
30114	Canton⊙ 3,601	C2
30203	Carl 239	E3
30627	Carlton 291	F2
30521	Carnesville⊙ 465	F2
30117	Carrollton⊙ 14,078	C3
30120	Cartersville⊙ 9,247	C2
30124	Cave Spring 883	B2
31627	Cecil 280	F8
30125	Cedartown⊙ 8,619	B2
†30601	Center 330	F2
31028	Centerville 2,622	E5
†30217	Centralhatchee 240	B4
†31816	Chalybeate Springs 265	C5
30341	Chamblee 7,137	K1
30705	Chatsworth⊙ 2,493	C1
31011	Chauncey 350	F6
31012	Chester 409	F6
30707	Chickamauga 2,232	B1
30523	Clarkesville⊙ 1,348	F1
30021	Clarkston 4,539	L1
31724	Claxton⊙ 2,694	J6
30525	Clayton⊙ 1,838	F1
30527	Clermont 300	E2
30528	Cleveland⊙ 1,578	E1
31734	Climax 407	D9
31735	Cobb	E7
30420	Cobbtown 494	H6
31014	Cochran⊙ 5,121	F6
30710	Cohutta 407	C1
30628	Colbert 498	F2
31736	Coleman 164	C7
30337	College Park 24,632	K2
30421	Collins 639	H6
31737	Colquitt⊙ 2,065	C8
*31901	Columbus⊙ 169,441	C6
	Columbus‡ 239,196	C6
30629	Comer 930	F2
30529	Commerce 4,092	E2
30206	Concord 317	D4
*30207	Conyers⊙ 6,567	D3
31738	Coolidge 736	E8
31015	Cordele⊙ 11,184	E7
30531	Cornelia 3,203	E1
31739	Cotton 122	D8
30209	Covington⊙ 10,586	E3
30711	Crandall	C1
30630	Crawford 498	F3
30631	Crawfordville⊙ 594	G3
†31771	Crosland	E8
31016	Culloden 281	D5
30130	Cumming⊙ 2,094	D2
31805	Cusseta⊙ 1,218	C6
31740	Cuthbert⊙ 4,340	C7
30211	Dacula 1,577	E3
30533	Dahlonega⊙ 2,844	D1
30423	Daisy 174	J6
30132	Dallas⊙ 2,440	C3
30721	Dalton⊙ 20,743	C1
31741	Damascus 403	C8
30633	Danielsville⊙ 354	F2
31017	Danville 529	F5
31305	Darien⊙ 1,731	K8
31601	Dasher 659	F9
31018	Davisboro 433	G5
31742	Dawson⊙ 5,699	D7
30534	Dawsonville⊙ 342	D2
30808	Dearing 539	H4
*30030	Decatur⊙ 18,404	K1
†31501	Deenwood	H8
31082	Deepstep 120	G4
30535	Demorest 1,130	F1
31532	Denton 286	G7
31743	De Soto 248	D7
31019	Dexter 527	G6
30537	Dillard 238	F1
31629	Dixie 259	E9
†31520	Dock Junction (Arco)	J8
31744	Doerun 1,062	E8
31745	Donalsonville⊙ 3,320	C8
30340	Doraville 7,414	K1
31533	Douglas⊙ 10,980	G7
*30133	Douglasville⊙ 7,641	C3
31021	Dublin⊙ 16,083	G5
31022	Dudley 425	F5
30136	Duluth 2,956	D2
31630	Du Pont 267	G9
†31830	Durand 206	C5
31021	East Dublin 2,916	G5
30539	East Ellijay 469	C1

(continued on following page)

Agriculture, Industry and Resources

DOMINANT LAND USE

- Specialized Cotton
- Cotton, General Farming
- Cotton, Tobacco, Hogs, Peanuts
- Peanuts, General Farming
- General Farming, Livestock, Fruit, Tobacco
- General Farming, Forest Products, Cotton, Truck Farming
- Forests
- Swampland, Limited Agriculture
- Urban Areas

MAJOR MINERAL OCCURRENCES

- Al Bauxite
- Ba Barite
- C Coal
- Cl Clay
- Fe Iron Ore
- Gn Granite
- Mi Mica
- Mn Manganese
- Mr Marble
- Sl Slate
- Tc Talc
- Ti Titanium

⚡ Water Power   Major Industrial Areas

†31046 East Juliette E4
31023 Eastman⊙ 5,330 F6
†30263 East Newnan C4
30344 East Point 37,486 K2
†30677 Eastville E3
31024 Eatonton⊙ 4,833 F4
31307 Eden 990 K6
31746 Edison 1,128 C7
30635 Elberton⊙ 5,686 G2
31806 Ellaville⊙ 1,684 D6
31747 Ellenton 277 E8
31807 Ellerslie 700 C5
30540 Ellijay⊙ 1,507 C1
30137 Emerson 1,110 C2
31749 Enigma 574 F8
†30217 Ephesus 184 B4
30724 Eton 301 C1
†30120 Euharlee 477 C2
30809 Evans H3
30212 Experiment D4
30213 Fairburn 3,466 J2
30139 Fairmount 842 C2
30214 Fayetteville⊙ 2,715 C4
†31071 Finleyson 101 F6
31750 Fitzgerald⊙ 10,187 F7
†31313 Flemington 440 K7
30216 Flovilla 458 E4
30542 Flowery Branch 755 E2
31537 Folkston⊙ 2,243 H9
30050 Forest Park 18,782 K2
31029 Forsyth⊙ 4,624 E4
31751 Fort Gaines⊙ 1,260 C7
30742 Fort Oglethorpe 5,443 B1
31030 Fort Valley⊙ 9,000 E5
30217 Franklin⊙ 711 B4
30639 Franklin Springs 797 F2
31753 Funston 337 E8
30501 Gainesville⊙ 15,280 E2
31408 Garden City 6,895 K6
30425 Garfield 222 H5
30218 Gay 175 C4
31810 Geneva 232 C5
31754 Georgetown⊙ 935 B7
30810 Gibson⊙ 730 G4
30426 Girard 225 J4
30427 Glennville 4,144 J7
30428 Glenwood 824 L1
30641 Good Hope 200 E3
31031 Gordon 2,768 F5
30220 Grantville 1,110 C4
31032 Gray⊙ 2,145 F4
30221 Grayson 464 E3
30726 Graysville 193 B1
30642 Greensboro⊙ 2,985 F3
30222 Greenville⊙ 1,213 C4
30223 Griffin⊙ 20,728 D4
30813 Grovetown 3,491 H4
31312 Guyton 749 K6
31033 Haddock 800 F4
30429 Hagan 880 J6
31632 Hahira 1,534 F9
31811 Hamilton⊙ 506 C5
30228 Hampton 2,059 D4
30354 Hapeville 6,166 K2
30229 Haralson 123 C4
31034 Hardwick F4
30814 Harlem 1,485 H4
31035 Harrison 456 G5
30643 Hartwell⊙ 4,855 G2
31036 Hawkinsville⊙ 4,372 E6
31539 Hazlehurst⊙ 4,249 G7
30545 Helen 265 E1
31037 Helena 1,390 G6
30815 Hephzibah 1,452 H4
30546 Hiawassee⊙ 491 E1
†30410 Higgston 152 G6
30467 Hilltonia 515 J5
31313 Hinesville⊙ 11,309 J7
30141 Hiram 711 C3
31542 Hoboken 514 H8
30230 Hogansville 3,362 C4
30142 Holly Springs 687 D2
†31537 Homeland 683 H9
30547 Homer⊙ 734 F2
31634 Homerville⊙ 3,112 G8
30548 Hoschton 490 E2
30646 Hull 188 F2
31041 Ideal 619 D6
30647 Ila 287 F2
†30705 Industrial City 1,054 C1
31759 Iron City 367 C8
31042 Irwinton⊙ 841 F5
†31031 Ivey 455 F5
30233 Jackson⊙ 4,133 E4
31544 Jacksonville 206 G7
31761 Jakin 194 C8
30143 Jasper⊙ 1,556 D2
30549 Jefferson⊙ 1,820 F2
31044 Jeffersonville⊙ 1,473 F5
30234 Jenkinsburg 360 E4
30235 Jersey 201 E3
31545 Jesup⊙ 9,418 J7
30236 Jonesboro⊙ 4,132 D4
31812 Junction City 254 C5
30144 Kennesaw 5,095 C2
31548 Kingsland 2,008 J9
30145 Kingston 733 C2
31049 Kite 328 G5
31050 Knoxville⊙ 75 E5
30728 La Fayette⊙ 6,517 B1
30240 La Grange⊙ 24,204 B4
30252 Lake 2,963 D3
31635 Lakeland⊙ 2,647 F8
31636 Lake Park 448 F9
30553 Lavonia 2,024 F2
30245 Lawrenceville⊙ 8,928 D3
31762 Leary 783 C8
30146 Lebanon 800 D2
31763 Leesburg⊙ 1,301 D7
31637 Lenox 965 F8
31764 Leslie 470 D7
30648 Lexington⊙ 278 F3
30247 Lilburn 3,765 D3
31051 Lilly 202 E6
†30286 Lincoln Park D5
30817 Lincolnton⊙ 1,406 G3
30147 Lindale B2
†30728 Linwood 417 B1
30058 Lithonia 2,637 D3
30248 Locust Grove 1,479 D4
30249 Loganville 1,841 E3
30433 Lollie G6
†30230 Lone Oak 119 C4
†30741 Lookout Mountain 1,505 B1
30434 Louisville⊙ 2,823 H4
30250 Lovejoy 205 D4
31316 Ludowici⊙ 1,286 J7
30554 Lula 857 E2
31549 Lumber City 1,426 G7
31815 Lumpkin⊙ 1,335 C6
30251 Luthersville 597 C4
30730 Lyerly 482 B2
30436 Lyons⊙ 4,203 H6
30059 Mableton J1
*31201 Macon⊙ 116,860 E5
Macon‡ 254,623 E5
30650 Madison⊙ 2,954 F3
30438 Manassas 116 H6
31816 Manchester 4,796 C5
30255 Mansfield 435 E4
*30060 Marietta⊙ 30,805 J1
31057 Marshallville 1,540 D6
30557 Martin 305 F2
30671 Maxeys 205 F3
30558 Maysville 619 E2
30555 McCaysville 1,219 D1
30253 McDonough⊙ 2,778 D4
31054 McIntyre 386 F5
31055 McRae⊙ 3,409 G6
30256 Meansville 303 D4
30040 Mechanicsville L1
31765 Meigs 1,231 D8
30731 Menlo 611 B2
†31792 Metcalf E9
30439 Metter⊙ 3,531 H6
30441 Midville 670 H5
31320 Midway 457 K7
31060 Milan 1,115 G6
31061 Milledgeville⊙ 12,176 F4
30442 Millen⊙ 3,988 J5
30257 Milner 320 D4
30207 Milstead D3
30559 Mineral Bluff 130 D1
30820 Mitchell 214 G4
30258 Molena 379 D4
30655 Monroe⊙ 8,854 E3
31063 Montezuma 4,830 E6
31064 Monticello⊙ 2,382 E4
31065 Montrose 170 F5
30259 Moreland 358 C4
31766 Morgan⊙ 364 C7
30560 Morganton 263 D1
30260 Morrow 3,791 K2
31638 Morven 471 E9
31768 Moultrie⊙ 15,708 E8
30562 Mountain City 701 F1
†30075 Mountain Park 378 D2
30563 Mount Airy 670 F1
30149 Mount Berry B2
30445 Mount Vernon⊙ 1,737 G6
30261 Mountville 168 C4
30150 Mount Zion 445 B3
31553 Nahunta⊙ 951 H8
31639 Nashville⊙ 4,831 F8
31641 Naylor 228 F9
30151 Nelson 562 D2
30262 Newborn 391 E3
30446 Newington 402 J5
30263 Newnan⊙ 11,449 C4
31770 Newton⊙ 711 D8
31554 Nicholls 1,114 G7
30565 Nicholson 491 F2
*30071 Norcross 3,317 D3
31771 Norman Park 757 E8
†30645 North High Shoals 256 F3
30821 Norwood 306 G4
30448 Nunez 168 H5
31772 Oakfield 113 E7
30732 Oakman 150 C1
31903 Oak Park 256 H6
30566 Oakwood 723 E2
31773 Ochlocknee 627 E9
31774 Ocilla⊙ 3,436 F7
31067 Oconee 306 G5
†30222 Odessadale 142 C5
31555 Odum 401 H7
31406 Oglethorpe⊙ 1,305 D6
30449 Oliver 239 J5
31821 Omaha 169 C6
31775 Omega 996 E8
30266 Orchard Hill 162 D4
30267 Oxford 1,750 E3
30268 Palmetto 2,086 C3
31777 Parrott 222 D7
31557 Patterson 763 H8
31778 Pavo 830 E9
†31201 Payne 196 E5
30269 Peachtree City 6,429 C4
31642 Pearson⊙ 1,827 G8
31779 Pelham 4,306 D8
31321 Pembroke⊙ 1,400 J6
30567 Pendergrass 302 E2
31069 Perry⊙ 9,453 E6
†31794 Phillipsburg E8
31070 Pinehurst 431 E6
30072 Pine Lake 901 D3
31822 Pine Mountain 984 C5
†31312 Pineora 387 K6
†31728 Pine Park D9
31071 Pineview 564 F6
31072 Pitts 384 E7
31073 Plainfield 128 F6
31780 Plains 651 D6
30733 Plainville 281 C2
31322 Pooler 2,543 K6
30450 Portal 694 J5
30270 Porterdale 1,451 E3
31407 Port Wentworth 3,947 K6
31781 Poulan 818 E8
30073 Powder Springs 3,381 C3
31824 Preston⊙ 429 C6
30451 Pulaski 257 J6
31643 Quitman⊙ 5,188 E9
30734 Ranger 171 C2
31645 Ray City 658 F8
30660 Rayle 177 G3
31783 Rebecca 272 E7
30453 Reidsville⊙ 2,296 H6
31601 Remerton 443 F9
31075 Rentz 337 G6
†30518 Rest Haven 231 E2
31076 Reynolds 1,298 D5
31077 Rhine 590 F7
31323 Riceboro 216 K7
31825 Richland 1,802 C6
31324 Richmond Hill 1,177 K7
†31018 Riddleville 154 G5
31326 Rincon 1,988 K6
30736 Ringgold⊙ 1,821 B1
*30274 Riverdale 7,121 K2
†31768 Riverside 99 E8
†30759 Riverside B2
31078 Roberta 859 D5
31079 Rochelle 1,626 F7
30153 Rockmart 3,645 B2
30455 Rocky Ford 223 J5
30161 Rome⊙ 29,654 B2
30170 Roopville 229 B4
30741 Rossville 3,851 B1
*30075 Roswell 23,337 D2
30662 Royston 2,404 F2
†30680 Russell 378 E3
30663 Rutledge 694 E3
31558 Saint Marys 3,596 J9
31522 Saint Simons Island K8
31784 Sale City 336 D8
31082 Sandersville⊙ 6,137 G5
†20436 Santa Claus 167 H6
30456 Sardis 1,180 J5
30275 Sargent 800 C4
31785 Sasser 407 D7
*31401 Savannah⊙ 141,634 L6
Savannah‡ 230,728 L6
31083 Scotland 222 G6
31095 Scott 139 G5
31560 Screven 872 H7
30276 Senoia 900 C4
31084 Seville 209 E7
31085 Shady Dale 155 E4
30172 Shannon B2
30664 Sharon 140 G3
30277 Sharpsburg 194 C4
31786 Shellman 1,254 C7
31826 Shiloh 392 C5
30665 Siloam 446 F3
31787 Smithville 867 D7
30080 Smyrna 20,312 K1
30278 Snellville 8,514 D3
30279 Social Circle 2,591 E3
30457 Soperton⊙ 2,981 G6
31647 Sparks 1,353 F8
31087 Sparta⊙ 1,754 F4
31329 Springfield⊙ 1,075 K6
†30705 Spring Place 246 C1
30823 Stapleton 388 H4
31648 Statenville⊙ 700 G9
30458 Statesboro⊙ 14,866 J6
30666 Statham 1,101 E3
30464 Stillmore 527 H6
30281 Stockbridge 2,103 D3
*30083 Stone Mountain 4,867 D3
†30518 Sugar Hill 2,473 E2
30746 Sugar Valley C1
30466 Summertown 215 H5
30747 Summerville⊙ 4,878 B2
31789 Sumner 213 E7
30284 Sunny Side 338 D4
31563 Surrency 368 H7
30174 Suwanee 1,026 D2
30401 Swainsboro⊙ 7,602 H5
31790 Sycamore 474 E7
30467 Sylvania⊙ 3,352 J5
31791 Sylvester⊙ 5,860 E7
31827 Talbotton⊙ 1,140 C5
30176 Tallapoosa 2,647 B3
30573 Tallulah Falls 162 F1
30575 Talmo E2
30470 Tarrytown 145 H6
30178 Taylorsville 266 C2
30179 Temple 1,520 B3
31089 Tennille 1,709 G5
30285 The Rock 78 D5
30286 Thomaston⊙ 9,682 D5
31792 Thomasville⊙ 18,463 E9
30824 Thomson⊙ 7,001 H4
†31404 Thunderbolt 2,165 K6
31794 Tifton⊙ 13,749 F8
30576 Tiger 299 F1
30668 Tignall 733 G3
30577 Toccoa⊙ 9,104 F1
31090 Toomsboro 673 F5
30752 Trenton⊙ 1,636 A1
30753 Trion 1,732 B1
30755 Tunnel Hill 867 C1
30289 Turin 260 C4
30471 Twin City 1,402 H5
31328 Tybee Island 2,240 L6
30290 Tyrone 1,038 C4
31795 Ty Ty 618 E8
31091 Unadilla 1,566 E6
30291 Union City 4,780 J2
30669 Union Point 1,750 F3
†31794 Unionville F8
30473 Uvalda 646 H6
31601 Valdosta⊙ 37,596 F9
30672 Vanna F2
†30153 Van Wert 303 B3
30756 Varnell 288 C1
†31401 Vernonburg 178 K7
30474 Vidalia 10,393 H6
†30830 Vidette H4
31092 Vienna⊙ 2,886 E6
30180 Villa Rica 3,420 C3
30182 Waco 471 B3
30477 Wadley 2,438 H5
30183 Waleska 450 D2
†30209 Walnut Grove 387 E3
31333 Walthourville 905 J7
31830 Warm Springs 425 C5
31093 Warner Robins 39,893 E5
30828 Warrenton⊙ 2,172 G4
31796 Warwick 488 E7
30673 Washington⊙ 4,662 G3
30677 Watkinsville⊙ 1,240 E3
31831 Waverly Hall 913 C5
31501 Waycross⊙ 19,371 H8
30830 Waynesboro⊙ 5,760 J4
31832 Weston 109 C7
31833 West Point 4,294 B5
31797 Whigham 507 D9
30184 White 501 C2
31568 White Oak 450 J8
30678 White Plains 231 F4
30185 Whitesburg 775 B4
31650 Willacoochee 1,166 G8
30292 Williamson 250 D4
31410 Wilmington Island L7
30680 Winder⊙ 6,705 E3
31406 Windsor Forest K7
30683 Winterville 621 F3
31569 Woodbine⊙ 910 J9
30293 Woodbury 1,738 C5
31836 Woodland 664 D5
30188 Woodstock 2,699 D2
30670 Woodville 455 F3
30833 Wrens 2,415 H4
31096 Wrightsville⊙ 2,526 G5
31097 Yatesville 390 D5
30582 Young Harris 687 E1
30295 Zebulon⊙ 995 D4

OTHER FEATURES

Alapaha (riv.) F7
Allatoona (lake) C2
Altamaha (riv.) H7
Andersonville Nat'l Hist. Site D6
Atlanta Nav. Air Sta. J1
Banks (lake) F9
Bartletts Ferry (dam) B5
Blackshear (lake) E7
Blue Ridge (mts.) D1
Brasstown Bald (mt.) E1
Burton (lake) E1
Carters (lake) C1
Chattahoochee (riv.) B8
Chattahoochee River Nat'l Rec. Area K1
Chattooga (riv.) A2
Chattooga (riv.) F1
Chatuge (lake) E1
Chickamauga and Chattanooga Nat'l Mil. Park B1
Clark Hill (lake) H3
Coosa (riv.) A2
Coosawattee (riv.) C1
Cumberland (isl.) K9
Cumberland Island Nat'l Seashore K9
Dobbins A.F.B. J1
Doboy (sound) K8
Etowah (riv.) C2
Eufaula (Walter F. George Res.) (lake) B7
Flint (riv.) D8
Fort Benning B6
Fort Frederica Nat'l Mon. K8
Fort Gordon H4
Fort McPherson K1
Fort Pulaski Nat'l Mon. L6
Fort Stewart J7
Goat Rock (lake) B5
Harding (lake) B5
Hartwell (lake) G2
Jekyll (isl.) K8
Kennesaw Mtn. Nat'l Battlefield Park J1
Lawson A.A.F. B6
Martin Luther King, Jr., Nat'l Hist. Site K1
Moody A.F.B. F9
Nottely (lake) D1
Ochlockonee (riv.) C10
Ocmulgee (riv.) E5
Ocmulgee Nat'l Mon. F5
Oconee (riv.) F5
Ogeechee (riv.) J5
Okefenokee (swamp) H9
Oliver (lake) B5
Oostanaula (riv.) B2
Ossabaw (sound) K7
Rabun (lake) E1
Robins A.F.B. F5
Saint Andrew (sound) K9
Saint Catherines (isl.) K7
Saint Marys (riv.) J9
Saint Simons K8
Sapelo (isl.) K8
Satilla (riv.) G8
Savannah (riv.) K5
Sea (isls.) K9
Seminole (lake) B9
Sidney Lanier (lake) D2
Sinclair (lake) F4
Skidaway (isl.) L7
Springer (mt.) D1
Suwannee (riv.) G10
Tugaloo (riv.) F1
Walter F. George (res.) B7
Wassaw (sound) L7
Weiss (lake) A2
West Point (lake) B4

⊙County seat.
‡Population of metropolitan area.
† Zip of nearest p.o. * Multiple zips.

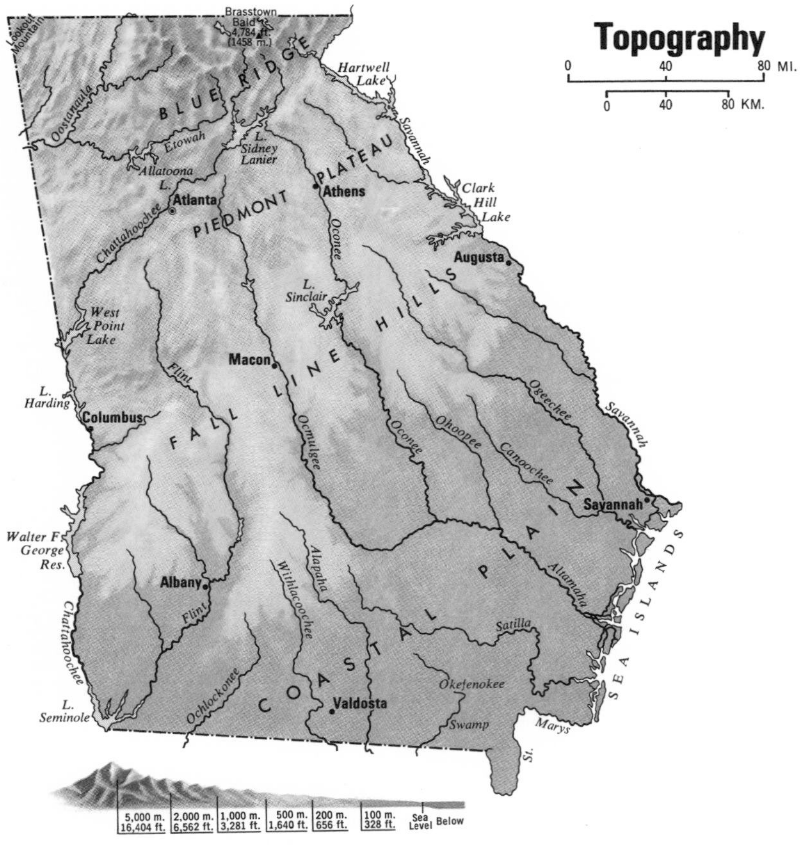
Topography
0 40 80 MI.
0 40 80 KM.
Brasstown Bald 4,784 ft. (1458 m.)
Lookout Mountain
BLUE RIDGE
Hartwell Lake
Oostanaula
Etowah
L. Sidney Lanier
Allatoona L.
Savannah
Atlanta
PIEDMONT PLATEAU
Athens
Clark Hill Lake
Chattahoochee
Oconee
Augusta
L. Sinclair
West Point Lake
Macon
FALL LINE HILLS
Flint
L. Harding
Columbus
Ocmulgee
Ogeechee
Ohoopee
Canoochee
Savannah
Walter F. George Res.
Albany
Alapaha
Withlacoochee
COASTAL PLAIN
Altamaha
Satilla
SEA ISLANDS
L. Seminole
Ochlockonee
Valdosta
Okefenokee Swamp
St. Marys
5,000 m. 16,404 ft.
2,000 m. 6,562 ft.
1,000 m. 3,281 ft.
500 m. 1,640 ft.
200 m. 656 ft.
100 m. 328 ft.
Sea Level
Below

Georgia

SCALE
0 5 10   20   30   40 MI.
0 5 10   20   30   40 KM.

State Capitals .... ⊛
County Seats .... ◉
Major Limited Access Hwys. ....

Scale 1:2,210,000

© Copyright HAMMOND INCORPORATED, Maplewood, N.J.

COUNTIES

Hawaii 92,053 .... K7
Honolulu 762,565 .... D3
Kalawao 144 .... G1
Kauai 39,082 .... A1
Maui 70,847 .... J1

CITIES and TOWNS

Zip	Name/Pop.	Key

96701 Aiea 32,879 .... B3
96821 Aina Haina F2
  Ala Moana 96,820 .... C4
96703 Anahola 915 .... C1
†96706 Barbers Point 1,373 ...... E2
96704 Captain Cook 2,008 .... G5
96705 Eleele 580 .... C2
96706 Ewa 2,637 .... A4
96706 Ewa Beach 14,369 .... A4
†96701 Foster Village B3
96714 Haena 200 .... C1
96708 Haiku 619 .... J2
96710 Hakalau J4
†96711 Halawa, Hawaii 50 .... G3
96748 Halawa, Molokai 15 .... H1
†96701 Halawa Heights B3
96712 Haleiwa 2,412 .... E1
†96718 Halfway House 150 .... H6
96787 Haliimaile 741 .... J2
†96713 Hamoa 35 .... K2
96713 Hana 643 .... K2
96714 Hanalei 483 .... C1
96715 Hanamaulu 3,227 .... C1
96716 Hanapepe 1,417 .... C2
96717 Hauula 2,997 .... E1
96825 Hawaii Kai F2
96718 Hawaii Nat'l Park 250 ... J6
96719 Hawi 795 .... G3
96824 Hickam Housing 4,425 ... B4
96720 Hilo⊙ 35,269 .... J5
96725 Holualoa 1,243 .... G5
96726 Honaunau 950 .... G6
96727 Honokaa 1,936 .... H4
†96761 Honokahua 309 .... H1
*96801 Honolulu (cap.)⊙ 365,048 C4
  Honolulu‡ 762,874 .... C4
96728 Honomu 559 .... J4
96729 Hoolehua G1
†96706 Iroquois Point 3,915 ..... A4
96730 Kaaawa 959 .... F1
†96761 Kaanapali 541 .... H2
96793 Kahakuloa 75 .... J1
96801 Kahala D5
96744 Kahaluu 2,925 .... E2
96731 Kahuku 935 .... E1
96732 Kahului 12,978 .... J2
96740 Kailua (Kailua Kona),
  Hawaii 4,751 .... F5
96734 Kailua, Oahu 35,812 .... F2
96740 Kailua Kona 4,751 .... F5
†96750 Kainaliu 512 .... G5
96741 Kalaheo 2,500 .... C2
96742 Kalaupapa⊙ 170 .... G1
96754 Kalihiwai 40 .... C1
†96748 Kaluaaha 20 .... H1
96743 Kamuela 1,179 .... G3
96744 Kaneohe 29,919 .... F2
96746 Kapaa 4,467 .... D1
96755 Kapaau 612 .... G3
96817 Kapalama C4
96747 Kaumakani 888 .... C2
96748 Kaunakakai 2,231 ...... G1
96708 Kaupakulua 600 .... K2
96743 Kaupo 65 .... K2
96743 Kawaihae 50 .... G4
†96712 Kawailoa 200 .... E1
96749 Keaau 775 .... J5
96750 Kealakekua 1,033 ...... G5
96751 Kealia, Kauai 300 ...... D1
†96708 Keanae 280 .... K2
96752 Kekaha 3,260 .... C2
96753 Kihei 5,644 .... J2
96754 Kilauea 895 .... C1
†96713 Kipahulu 75 .... K2
96713 Koali 60 .... K2
96755 Kohala (Kapaau) 612 ... G3
†96708 Kokomo 500 .... K2
96756 Koloa 1,457 .... C2
†96756 Koloa Landing C2
96757 Kualapuu 502 .... G1
†96775 Kukaiau 75 .... H4
96727 Kukuihaele 332 .... H3
96790 Kula 800 .... J2
96759 Kunia 550 .... E2
96760 Kurtistown 900 .... J5
96761 Lahaina 6,095 .... H2
96762 Laie 4,643 .... E1
96763 Lanai City 2,092 ...... H2
96764 Laupahoehoe 500 ..... J4
96765 Lawai 950 .... C2
96766 Lihue⊙ 4,000 .... C2
†96779 Lower Paia 1,500 ...... J1
96719 Mahukona 2 .... G3
96792 Maili 5,026 .... D2
96792 Makaha 6,582 .... D2
96706 Makakilo 7,691 .... E2
96768 Makawao 2,900 .... K2
96769 Makaweli 500 .... B2
96790 Makena 100 .... J2
96822 Makiki C4
96770 Maunaloa 633 .... G1
96744 Maunawili 5,239 ...... F2
96789 Mililani Town 21,365 .. E2
96828 Moiliili C4
†96734 Mokapu 11,615 .... F2
96771 Mountainview 540 .... J5
96772 Naalehu 1,168 .... H7
†96713 Nahiku 50 .... K2
96792 Nanakuli 8,185 .... D2
†96761 Napili-Honokowai 2,446 .. H1
96773 Ninole 75 .... J4
†96781 Onomea 10 .... J4
96774 Ookala 401 .... J4
96775 Paauhau 350 .... H4
96776 Paauilo 755 .... H4
96777 Pahala 1,619 .... H6
96778 Pahoa 923 .... J5
96779 Paia J2
96780 Papaaloa J4
96781 Papaikou 1,567 .... J5
†96781 Paukaa 544 .... J5
†96708 Pauwela 468 .... K2
96708 Peahi 308 .... K2
96782 Pearl City 42,575 .... B3
96783 Pepeekeo J4
96756 Poipu 685 .... C2
†96714 Princeville 500 ...... C1
96766 Puhi 991 .... C2
96788 Pukalani 3,950 ...... J2
†96748 Pukoo 50 .... H1
†96713 Puuiki 75 .... K2
96784 Puunene 572 .... J2
†96801 Puunui C4
96786 Schofield Barracks 18,851 .. E2
96779 Spreckelsville 350 .... J1
†96708 Ulumalu 201 .... K2
96776 Umikoa 25 .... H4
96785 Volcano 400 .... J6
96786 Wahiawa 16,911 ...... E2
†96788 Waiakoa J2
96816 Waialae D4
†96731 Waialee 50 .... E1
96748 Waialua, Molokai 30 .. H1
96791 Waialua, Oahu 4,051 .. E1
96792 Waianae 7,941 .... D2
†96793 Waihee 413 .... J2
†96793 Waikapu 698 .... J2
96815 Waikiki C4
†96748 Wailau 20 .... H1
†96710 Wailea, Hawaii 150 .. J4
96790 Wailea, Maui 1,124 .. J2
96746 Wailua 1,587 .... D2
96793 Wailuku⊙ 10,260 ...... J2
96795 Waimanalo 3,562 ..... F2
†96795 Waimanalo Bch. 4,161 .. F2
†96743 Waimea (Kamuela),
  Hawaii 1,179 .... G3
96796 Waimea, Kauai 1,569 .. B2
96720 Wainaku 1,045 .... J5
†96714 Wainiha 175 .... C1
96797 Waipahu 29,139 ...... A3
†96786 Waipio Acres 4,091 .. E2
†96786 Whitmore Village 2,318.. E1

OTHER FEATURES

Alalakeiki (chan.) J3
Alenuihaha (chan.) E7

Topography

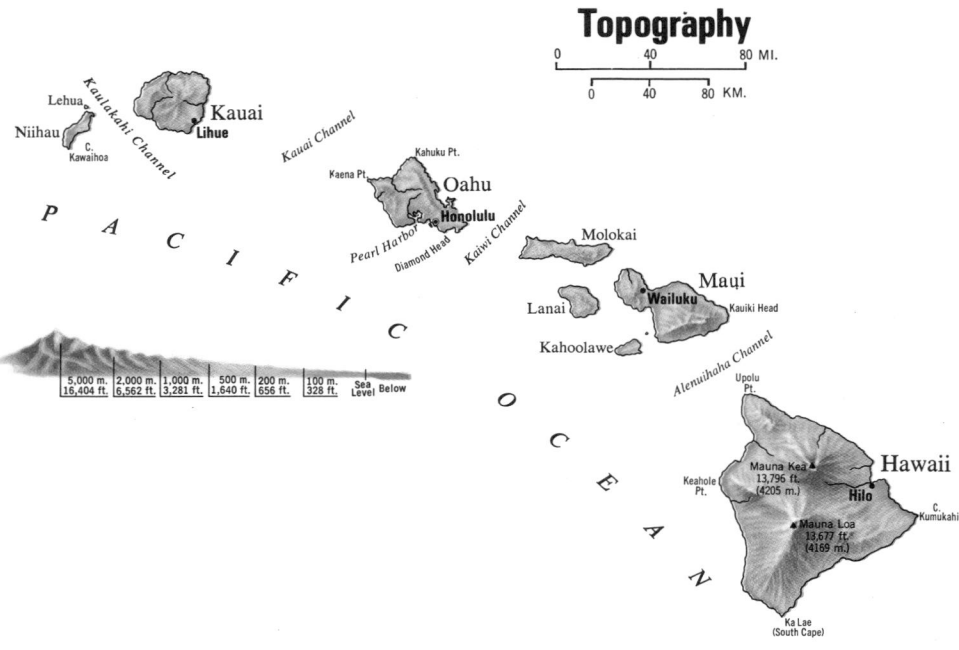

Agriculture, Industry and Resources

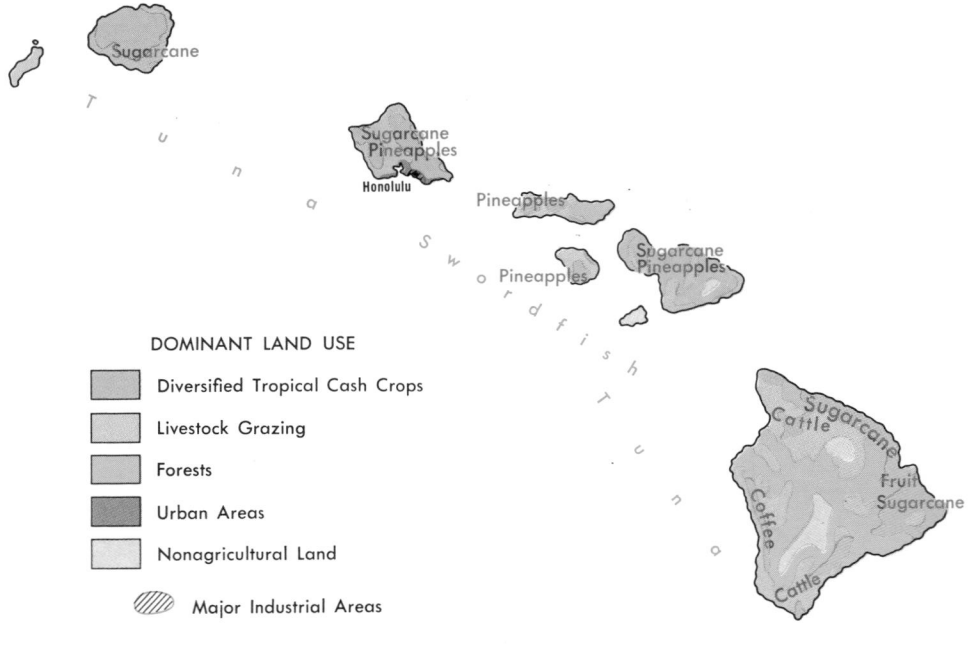

DOMINANT LAND USE

- Diversified Tropical Cash Crops
- Livestock Grazing
- Forests
- Urban Areas
- Nonagricultural Land
- Major Industrial Areas

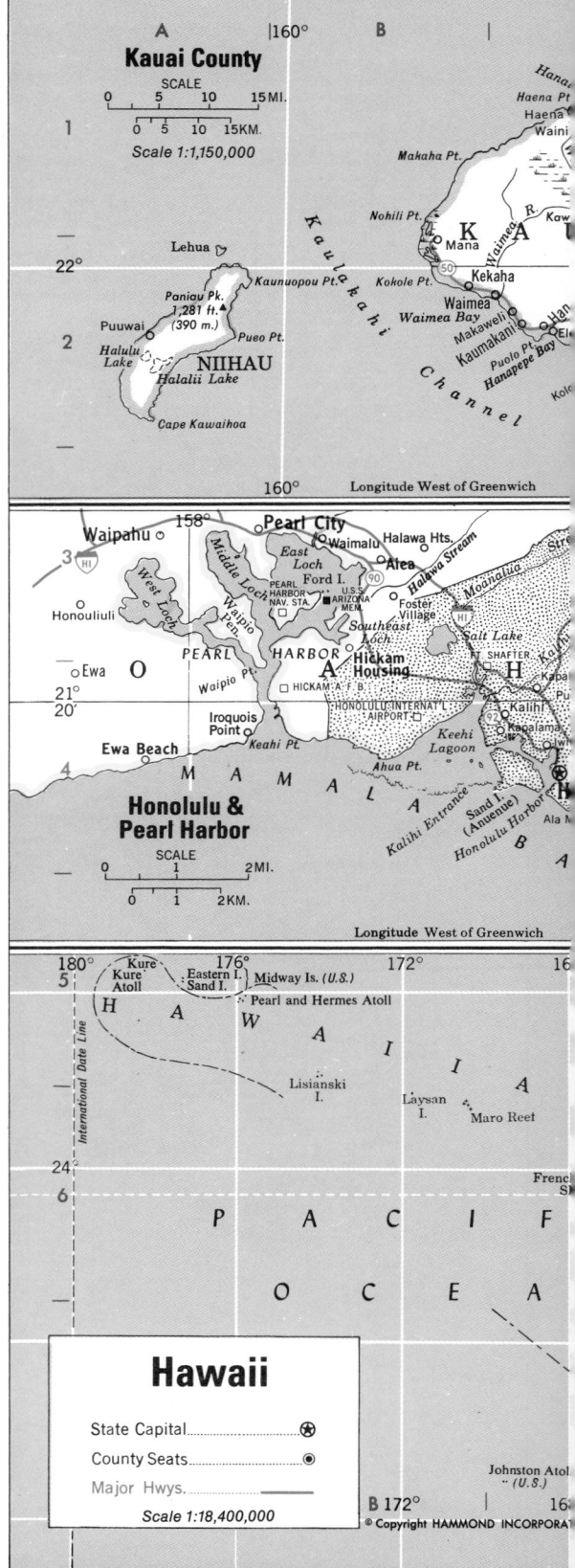

Kauai County

SCALE
0 5 10 15 MI.
0 5 10 15 KM.
Scale 1:1,150,000

Honolulu & Pearl Harbor

SCALE
0 1 2 MI.
0 1 2 KM.

Longitude West of Greenwich

Hawaii

State Capital .... ✪
County Seats .... ⊙
Major Hwys.
Scale 1:18,400,000

© Copyright HAMMOND INCORPORATED

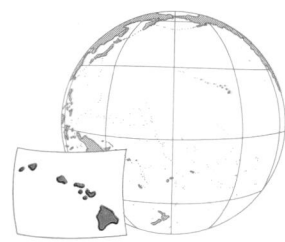

Anuenue (Sand) (isl.)................C4
Auau (chan.)............................H2
Barbers Point Nav. Air Sta.......E2
Diamond (head)........................C5
East Loch (inlet)......................B3
Ford (isl.)................................B3
Fort Shafter............................C3
French Frigate (shoals)............C6
Gardner Pinnacles (isls.).........C6
Halalii (lake)............................A2
Halawa (bay)...........................H1
Haleakala (crater)....................K2
Haleakala Nat'l Park................K2
Hawaii (isl.)............................H5
Hawaii Volcanoes Nat'l Park....H6
Hickam A.F.B...........................B4
Hilo (bay)................................J5
Honolulu Int'l Airport................B4
Honolulu (harb.)......................C4
Ilio (pt.)..................................G1
Kaala (mt.)...............................D1
Kahala (pt.)..............................D1
Kahana (bay)............................F1
Kaiwi (chan.)...........................E6
Ka Lae (cape)..........................G7
Kalaupapa Nat'l Hist. Park......H1
Kalohi (chan.)..........................G1
Kaloko-Honokohau Nat'l Hist.
  Park......................................F6
Kamakou (peak).......................H1

Kanapou (bay).........................J3
Kaneohe Bay U.S.M.C. Air
  Station..................................F2
Kau (des.)...............................J6
Kauai (chan.)...........................E6
Kauai (isl.)..............................C1
Kauiki (head)...........................K2
Kaula (isl.)..............................D6
Kaulakahi (chan.).....................B2
Kawaihae (bay)........................G4
Kawaihoa (cape)......................A2
Kawaikini (peak)......................C1
Keahi (pt.)...............................A4
Kealaikahiki (chan.)..................H3
Kealakekua (bay)......................F6
Keanapapa (pt.).......................G2
Keehi (lag.).............................B4
Kiholo (bay)............................F4
Kilauea (crater).......................H6
Kohala (mts.)...........................G4
Koko (head)............................F2
Konahuanui (peaks)..................C4
Koolau (range).........................E2
Kumukahi (cape)......................K5
Kure (atoll).............................A5
Kure (isl.)...............................A5
Laau (pt.)................................G1
Lanai (isl.)...............................H2
Lanaihale (mt.).........................H2
Laysan (isl.)............................B5

Lisianski (isl.)..........................B5
Lua Makika (mt.).......................J3
Maalaea (bay)..........................J2
Makaha (pt.).............................B1
Makahuena (pt.).......................C2
Makapuu (pt.)...........................F2
Mamala (bay)...........................B4
Manana (isl.)............................F2
Maro (reef)..............................C6
Maui (isl.)................................J2
Mauna Kea (mt.)......................H4
Mauna Loa (mt.).......................G6
Middle Loch (inlet)...................A3
Moanalua (stream)....................B3
Mokapu (pen.)..........................F2
Mokolii (isl.)............................F2
Mokuaweoweo (crater).............H6
Molokai (isl.)...........................G1
Molokini (isl.)..........................J2
Nawiliwili (bay)........................D2
Necker (isl.)............................D6
Nihoa (isl.)..............................D6
Niihau (isl.)..............................A2
Oahu (isl.)...............................E2
Pailolo (chan.)..........................H1
Palolo (stream)........................D4
Paniau (peak)...........................A2
Pearl (harb.)............................A3
Pearl and Hermes (atoll)..........B5
Pearl Harbor Naval Sta.............B3
Punchbowl (hill).......................C4

Puolo (pt.)...............................C2
Puuhonua O Honaunau Nat'l Hist.
  Park......................................F6
Puu Keahiakahoe (mt.).............D3
Puukohola Heiau Nat'l Hist.
  Site......................................G4
Puu Kukui (mt.).......................J2
Red Hill (mt.)...........................K2
Roundtop (mt.).........................C4
Salt (lake)...............................B3
Sand (isl.)...............................B4
South (Ka Lae) (cape)..............G7
Southeast Loch (inlet)..............B3
Sugarloaf (hill).........................C4
Tantalus (mt.)..........................D4
Upolu (pt.)..............................G3
U.S.S. Arizona Memorial...........B3
Waialeale (mt.)........................C1
Waikiki (beach)........................C4
Wailuku (riv.)...........................J5
Waimea (bay)...........................B2
Waimea (riv.)...........................C2
Wainiha (riv.)...........................C1
Waipio (bay)............................H3
Waipio (pen.)...........................A3
Waipio (pt.).............................A4
West Loch (inlet)......................A3
Wheeler A.F.B.........................E1

⊙County seat.
‡Population of metropolitan area.
† Zip of nearest p.o   * Multiple zips.

AREA 6,471 sq. mi. (16,760 sq. km.)
POPULATION 964,691
CAPITAL Honolulu
LARGEST CITY Honolulu
HIGHEST POINT Mauna Kea 13,796 ft. (4205 m.)
SETTLED IN —
ADMITTED TO UNION August 21, 1959
POPULAR NAME Aloha State
STATE FLOWER Hibiscus
STATE BIRD Nene (Hawaiian Goose)

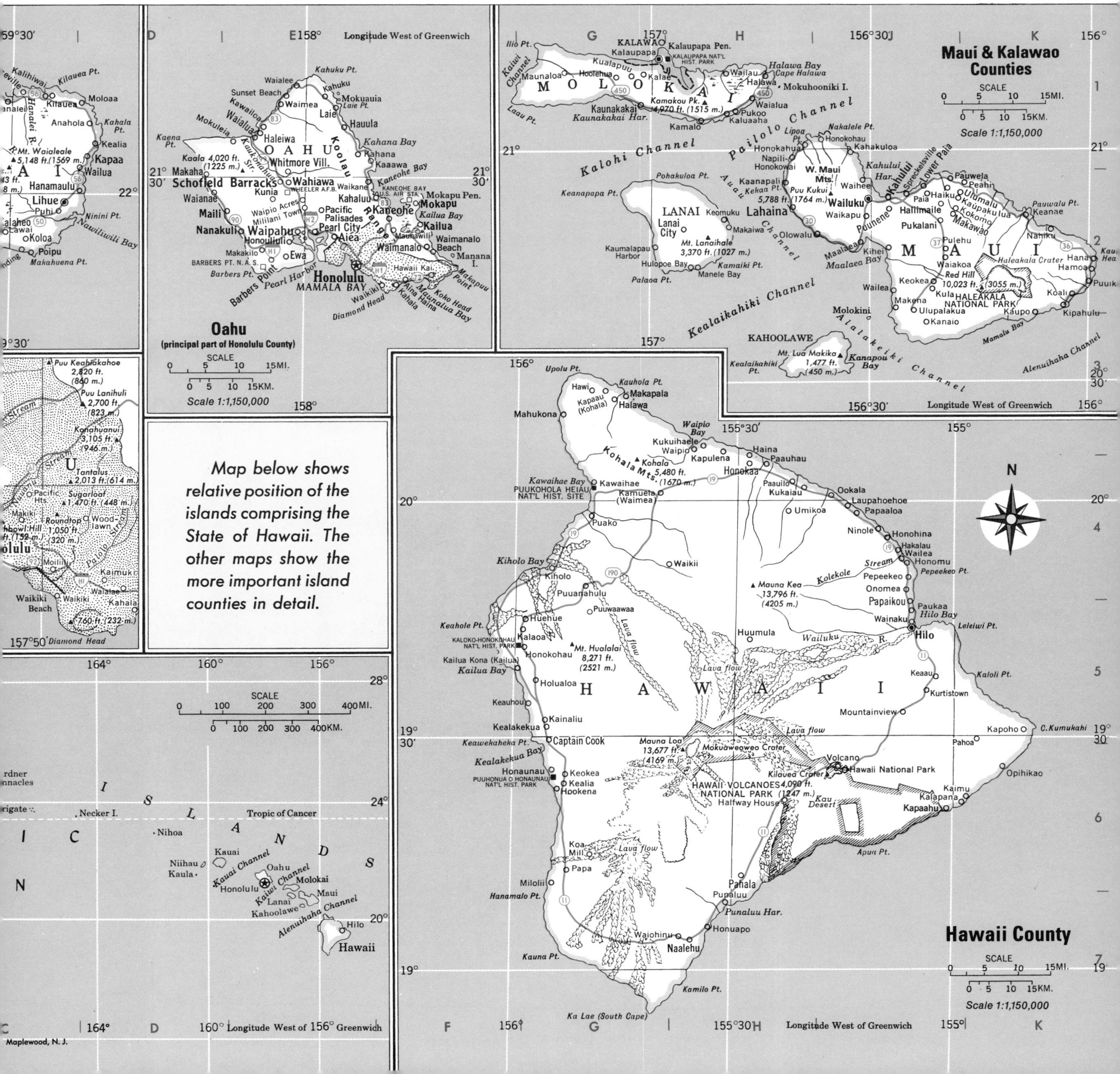

Oahu
(principal part of Honolulu County)
Scale 1:1,150,000

Maui & Kalawao Counties
Scale 1:1,150,000

Hawaii County
Scale 1:1,150,000

Map below shows relative position of the islands comprising the State of Hawaii. The other maps show the more important island counties in detail.

Maplewood, N.J.

AREA 83,564 sq. mi. (216,431 sq. km.)
POPULATION 944,038
CAPITAL Boise
LARGEST CITY Boise
HIGHEST POINT Borah Pk. 12,662 ft. (3859 m.)
SETTLED IN 1842
ADMITTED TO UNION July 3, 1890
POPULAR NAME Gem State
STATE FLOWER Syringa
STATE BIRD Mountain Bluebird

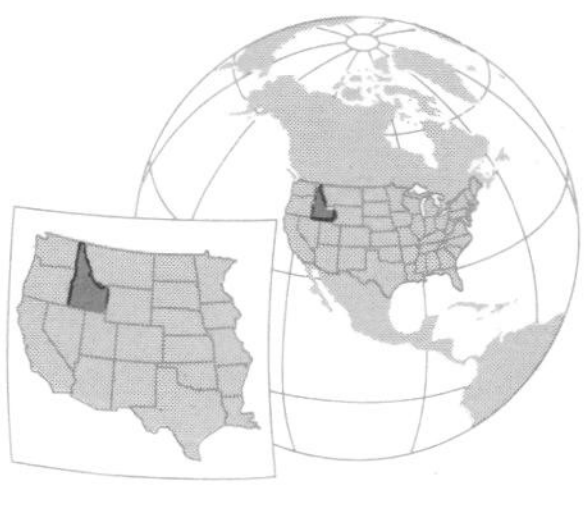

COUNTIES

Ada 173,036 B6
Adams 3,347 B5
Bannock 65,421 F7
Bear Lake 6,931 G7
Benewah 8,292 B2
Bingham 36,489 F6
Blaine 9,841 D6
Boise 2,999 C6
Bonner 24,163 B1
Bonneville 65,980 G6
Boundary 7,289 B1
Butte 3,342 E6
Camas 818 D6
Canyon 83,756 B6
Caribou 8,695 G7
Cassia 19,427 E7
Clark 798 F5
Clearwater 10,390 C3
Custer 3,385 D5
Elmore 21,565 C6
Franklin 8,895 G7
Fremont 10,813 G5
Gem 11,972 B6
Gooding 11,874 D6
Idaho 14,769 C4
Jefferson 15,304 F6
Jerome 14,840 D7
Kootenai 59,770 B2
Latah 28,749 B3
Lemhi 7,460 D4
Lewis 4,118 B3
Lincoln 3,436 D6
Madison 19,480 G6
Minidoka 19,718 E7
Nez Perce 33,220 B3
Oneida 3,258 F7
Owyhee 8,272 B7
Payette 15,825 B5
Power 6,844 F7
Shoshone 19,226 B2
Teton 2,897 G6
Twin Falls 52,927 D7
Valley 5,604 C5
Washington 8,803 B5

CITIES and TOWNS

Zip *Name/Pop.* *Key*

83210 Aberdeen 1,528 F7
83350 Acequia 100 E7
83311 Albion 286 E7
83211 American Falls⊙ 3,626 E7
†83401 Ammon 4,669 G6
83213 Arco⊙ 1,241 E6
83214 Arimo 338 F7
83420 Ashton 1,219 G5
83801 Athol 312 B2
83217 Bancroft 505 G7
83218 Basalt 414 F6
83313 Bellevue 1,016 D6
83221 Blackfoot⊙ 10,065 F6
83314 Bliss 208 D7
83223 Bloomington 212 G7
*83701 Boise (cap.)⊙ 102,160 B6
Boise‡ 173,036 B6
83805 Bonners Ferry⊙ 1,906 B1
83806 Bovill 289 B3
83316 Buhl 3,629 D7
83318 Burley⊙ 8,761 E7
83213 Butte City 93 E6
83605 Caldwell⊙ 17,699 B6
83610 Cambridge 428 B5
83611 Cascade⊙ 945 C5
83321 Castleford 191 C7
83226 Challis⊙ 758 D5
†83851 Chatcolet 181 B2
83202 Chubbuck 7,052 F7
83811 Clark Fork 449 B1
83227 Clayton 43 D5
83228 Clifton 208 F7
83814 Coeur d'Alene⊙ 20,054 B2
83522 Cottonwood 941 B3
83612 Council⊙ 917 B5
83523 Craigmont 617 B3
†83622 Crouch 69 B5
83524 Culdesac 261 B3
†83814 Dalton Gardens 1,795 B2
83232 Dayton 368 F7
83823 Deary 539 B3
83323 Declo 276 E7
83324 Dietrich 101 D7
83615 Donnelly 139 B5
83234 Downey 645 F7
83422 Driggs⊙ 727 G6
83423 Dubois⊙ 413 F5
83616 Eagle 2,620 B6
†83836 East Hope 258 B1
83325 Eden 355 D7
83827 Elk River 265 B3
83617 Emmett⊙ 4,605 B6
83327 Fairfield⊙ 404 D6
83526 Ferdinand 144 B3
†83814 Fernan Lake 178 B2
83328 Filer 1,645 D7
83236 Firth 460 F6
83203 Fort Hall 750 F6
83237 Franklin 423 G7
83619 Fruitland 2,456 B6
†83704 Garden City 4,571 B6
83832 Genesee 791 B3
83239 Georgetown 544 G7
83623 Glenns Ferry 1,374 C7
83330 Gooding⊙ 2,949 D7
83241 Grace 1,216 G7
83624 Grand View 366 B7
83530 Grangeville⊙ 3,666 B4
83626 Greenleaf 663 B6
83332 Hagerman 602 D7
83333 Hailey⊙ 2,109 D6
83425 Hamer 93 F6
83334 Hansen 1,078 D7
83833 Harrison 260 B2
†83854 Hauser 305 A2
†83835 Hayden 2,586 B2
83835 Hayden Lake 273 B2
83335 Hazelton 496 E7
83336 Heyburn 2,889 E7
†83301 Hollister 167 D7
83628 Homedale 2,078 A6
83836 Hope 106 B1
83629 Horseshoe Bend 700 B6
†83854 Huetter 65 B2
83631 Idaho City⊙ 300 C6
*83401 Idaho Falls⊙ 39,590 F6
83245 Inkom 830 F7
83427 Iona 1,072 G6
83428 Irwin 113 G6
83429 Island Park 154 G5
83338 Jerome⊙ 6,891 D7
83535 Juliaetta 522 B3
83536 Kamiah 1,478 B3
83837 Kellogg 3,417 B2
83537 Kendrick 395 B3
83340 Ketchum 2,200 D6
83341 Kimberly 2,307 D7
83539 Kooskia 784 C3
83840 Kootenai 280 B1
83634 Kuna 1,767 B6
83540 Lapwai 1,043 B3
83246 Lava Hot Springs 467 F7
83464 Leadore 114 E5
83501 Lewiston⊙ 27,986 A3
83431 Lewisville 502 F6
83251 Mackay 541 E6
83252 Malad City⊙ 1,915 F7
83342 Malta 196 E7
83639 Marsing 786 B6
83638 McCall 2,188 C5
83250 McCammon 770 F7
83641 Melba 276 B6
83434 Menan 605 F6
83642 Meridian 6,658 B6
83644 Middleton 1,901 B6
83645 Midvale 205 B5
83343 Minidoka 101 E7
83254 Montpelier 3,107 G7
83255 Moore 210 E6
83843 Moscow⊙ 16,513 B3
83647 Mountain Home⊙ 7,540 C6
83845 Moyie Springs 386 B1
†83450 Mud Lake 243 F6
83846 Mullan 1,269 C2
83650 Murphy⊙ 200 B6
83344 Murtaugh 114 D7
83651 Nampa 25,112 B6
83436 Newdale 329 G6
83654 New Meadows 576 B4
83655 New Plymouth 1,186 B6
83543 Nezperce⊙ 517 B3
83656 Notus 437 B6
83346 Oakley 663 D7
†99156 Oldtown 257 A1
†83855 Onaway 254 B3
83544 Orofino⊙ 3,711 B3
83849 Osburn 2,220 B2
†83263 Oxford 66 F7
83261 Paris⊙ 707 G7
83438 Parker 262 G6
83660 Parma 1,820 B6
83347 Paul 940 E7
83661 Payette⊙ 5,448 B5
83545 Peck 209 B3
83546 Pierce 1,060 C3
83850 Pinehurst 2,183 B2
83851 Plummer 634 B2
*83201 Pocatello⊙ 46,340 F7
83852 Ponderay 399 B1
83854 Post Falls 5,736 A2
83855 Potlatch 819 A3
83263 Preston⊙ 3,759 G7
83856 Priest River 1,639 A1
83858 Rathdrum 1,369 A2
83548 Reubens 87 B3
83440 Rexburg⊙ 11,559 G6
83349 Richfield 357 D6
83442 Rigby⊙ 2,624 F6
83549 Riggins 527 B4
83443 Ririe 555 G6
83444 Roberts 466 F6
83271 Rockland 283 F7
83350 Rupert⊙ 5,476 E7
83445 Saint Anthony⊙ 3,212 G6
83272 Saint Charles 211 G7
83861 Saint Maries⊙ 2,794 B2
83467 Salmon⊙ 3,308 D4
83864 Sandpoint⊙ 4,460 B1
83274 Shelley 3,300 F6
83352 Shoshone⊙ 1,242 D7
†83650 Silver City 1 B6
83868 Smelterville 776 B2
83276 Soda Springs⊙ 4,051 G7
83869 Spirit Lake 834 A2
83278 Stanley 99 D5
83552 Stites 253 C3
83448 Sugar City 1,022 G6
83353 Sun Valley 545 D6
83449 Swan Valley 135 G6
83870 Tensed 113 B2
83451 Teton 559 G6
83452 Tetonia 191 G6
83871 Troy 820 B3
83301 Twin Falls⊙ 26,209 D7
83454 Ucon 833 F6
83455 Victor 323 G6
83873 Wallace⊙ 1,736 C2
†83837 Wardner 423 B2
83553 Weippe 828 C3
83672 Weiser⊙ 4,771 B5
83355 Wendell 1,974 D7
83286 Weston 310 F7
83554 White Bird 154 B4
83676 Wilder 1,260 A6
83555 Winchester 343 B3
83876 Worley 206 B2

OTHER FEATURES

Albeni Falls (dam) B1
Albion (mts.) E7
Allan (mt.) D4
American Falls (res.) F6
Anderson Ranch (res.) C6
Antelope (creek) E6
Arrowrock (res.) C6
Auger (falls) D7
Badger (peak) E7
Bald (mt.) D5
Bannock (creek) F7
Bannock (peak) F7
Bannock (range) F7
Bargamin (creek) C4
Battle (creek) B7
Bear (lake) G7
Bear (riv.) G7
Beaver (creek) F5
Beaverhead (mts.) E4
Big (creek) C4
Big Boulder (creek) B7
Big Elk (peak) G6
Big Hole (mts.) G6
Big Lost (riv.) E6
Big Southern (butte) E6
Big Wood (riv.) D6
Birch (creek) F5
Birch Creek (valley) E5
Bitterroot (range) D3
Blackfoot (res.) G7
Black Pine (mts.) E7
Blue Nose (mt.) D4
Boise (mts.) B6
Boise (riv.) B6
Borah (peak) E5
Boulder (mts.) D6
Brownlee (dam) B5
Bruneau (riv.) C7
Camas (creek) D5
Camas (creek) D6
Camas (creek) F5
Canyon (creek) C6
Cape Horn (mt.) C5
Caribou (mt.) G6
Caribou (range) G6
Cascade (res.) C5
Castle (creek) B7
Castle (peak) D5
Cedar Creek (peak) E7
Cedar Creek (res.) D7
Centennial (mts.) F5
Clearwater (mts.) C3
Clearwater (riv.) B3
Coeur d'Alene (lake) B2
Coeur d'Alene (mts.) C2
Coeur d'Alene (riv.) B2
Cottonwood (butte) C4
Craig (mts.) B4
Crane Creek (res.) B5
Craters of the Moon Nat'l Mon. E6
Deadwood (res.) C5
Deep (creek) B7
Deep (creek) F7
Deep Creek (mts.) F7
Diamond (peak) E5
Dworshak (res.) C3
East Sister (peak) C2
Eighteen Mile (peak) E5
Fish Creek (res.) E6
Fort Hall Ind. Res. F6
Goldstone (mt.) E4
Goose (creek) E7
Goose Creek (mts.) E7
Grand Canyon of the Snake River (canyon) B4
Grays (lake) G6
Grays Lake Outlet (creek) G6
Greylock (mt.) C6
Hayden (lake) B2
Hells (canyon) B4
Hells Canyon Nat'l Rec. Area B4
Henrys (lake) G5
Henrys Fork, Snake (riv.) G5
Hunter (peak) D3
Hyndman (peak) D6
Indian (creek) C5
Island Park (res.) G5
Jarbidge (riv.) C7
Johnson (creek) C5
Jordan (creek) A7
Kootenai (riv.) C1
Lemhi (pass) E5
Lemhi (range) E5
Lemhi (riv.) E5
Little Lost (riv.) E5
Little Owyhee (riv.) B7
Little Salmon (riv.) B4
Little Weiser (riv.) B5
Little Wood (riv.) D6
Lochsa (riv.) C3
Lolo (creek) C3
Lolo (pass) D3
Lone Pine (peak) D5
Lookout (mt.) D5
Lookout (mt.) F5
Lost River (range) E5
Lost Trail (pass) E4
Lowell (lake) B6
Lower Goose Creek (res.) D7
Lower Granite (lake) A3
Lucky Peak (lake) B6
Mackay (res.) E6
Magic (res.) D6
Malad (riv.) F7
Marsh (creek) F7
McGuire (mt.) D4
Meade (peak) G7
Meadow (creek) C4
Medicine Lodge (creek) F5
Middle Fork (peak) D5
Monument (peak) B4
Moose (creek) D3
Mores (creek) C6
Mormon (mt.) D4
Mountain Home (res.) C6
Mountain Home A.F.B. 6,403 C6
Moyie (riv.) B1
Mud (lake) F6
National Reactor Testing Sta. (U.S.A.E.C.) F6
Nez Perce Nat'l Hist. Park B-C3
North Fork (riv.) B7
Norton (peak) D6
Orofino (creek) C3
Owyhee (mts.) B6
Owyhee, East Fork (riv.) B7
Oxbow (dam) B5
Pack (riv.) B1
Pahsimeroi (riv.) E5
Palisades (res.) G6
Palouse (riv.) B3
Panther (creek) D4
Payette (lake) C4
Payette (mts.) B5
Payette (riv.) B6
Peale (mts.) G7
Pend Oreille (lake) B1
Pend Oreille (mt.) B1
Pend Oreille (riv.) A1
Pilot (peak) C4
Pilot (peak) C6
Pilot Knob (mt.) C4
Pinyon (peak) C5
Pioneer (mts.) D6
Portneuf (res.) F7
Pot (mt.) C3
Potlatch (riv.) B3
Priest (lake) B1
Priest (riv.) B1
Purcell (mts.) B1
Pyramid (peak) E4
Raft (riv.) E7
Rainbow (mt.) C4
Ranger (peak) D3
Rays (lake) F6
Red (riv.) C4
Redfish (lake) D5
Reynolds (creek) B6
Rhodes (peak) D3
Rocky (mts.) D1
Rocky Ridge (mt.) C3
Ryan (peak) D6
Saddle (mt.) D3
Saddle (mt.) F6
Sailor (creek) C7
Saint Joe (riv.) B2
Saint Maries (riv.) B2
Salmon (falls) C7
Salmon (riv.) B4
Salmon Falls (creek) D7
Salmon Falls Creek (res.) D7
Salmon River (mts.) C5
Sawtooth (range) C6
Sawtooth Nat'l Rec. Area D5
Secesh (riv.) C4
Selkirk (mts.) B1
Selway (riv.) C3
Seven Devils (mts.) B4
Shoshone (falls) D7
Sleeping Deer (mt.) D5
Smith (creek) B1
Smoky (mts.) D6
Snake (riv.) A3
Snake River (plain) D7
Snake River (range) G6
Spirit (lake) B2
Squaw (creek) B5
Squaw (peak) D4
Steamboat (mt.) C4
Steel (mt.) C6
Strike, C.J. (res.) C7
Sublett (mts.) E7
Sunset (peak) E6
Taylor (mt.) D5
Teton (riv.) G6
Thompson (peak) C5
Trinity (mt.) C6
Trout (creek) B1
Twin (falls) D7
Twin Peaks (mt.) D5
Walcott (lake) E7
Wasatch (range) G7
Waugh (mt.) D4
Weiser (riv.) B5
Western Shoshone Ind. Res. B7
White Knob (mts.) E6
Wickahoney (creek) C7
Willow (creek) G6
Wilson Lake (res.) D7
Yankee Fork, Salmon (riv.) D5
Yellowstone Nat'l Park G5

⊙County seat.
‡Population of metropolitan area.
† Zip of nearest p.o.
* Multiple zips.

Agriculture, Industry and Resources

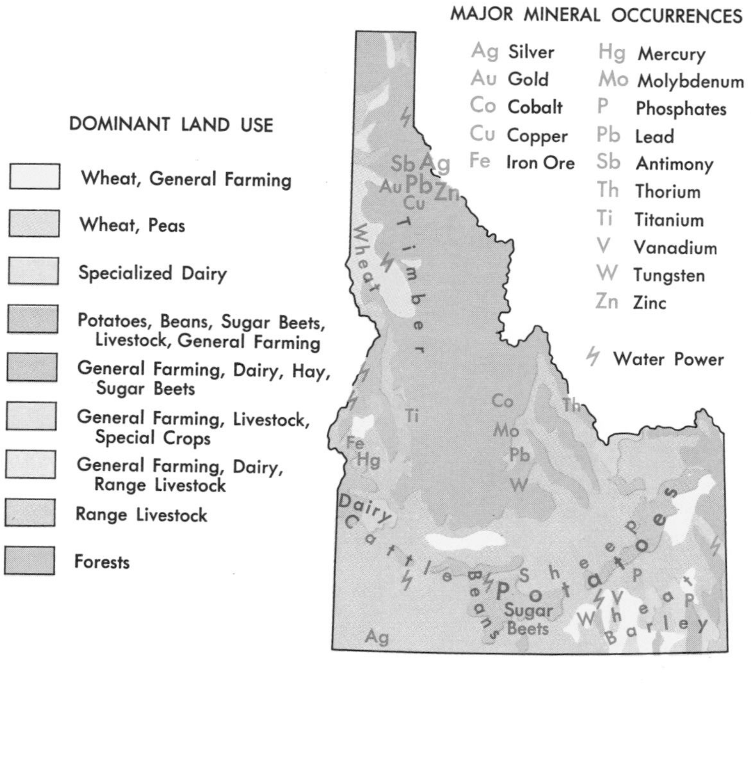
MAJOR MINERAL OCCURRENCES
Ag Silver
Au Gold
Co Cobalt
Cu Copper
Fe Iron Ore
Hg Mercury
Mo Molybdenum
P Phosphates
Pb Lead
Sb Antimony
Th Thorium
Ti Titanium
V Vanadium
W Tungsten
Zn Zinc
Water Power
DOMINANT LAND USE
Wheat, General Farming
Wheat, Peas
Specialized Dairy
Potatoes, Beans, Sugar Beets, Livestock, General Farming
General Farming, Dairy, Hay, Sugar Beets
General Farming, Livestock, Special Crops
General Farming, Dairy, Range Livestock
Range Livestock
Forests
Wheat
Timber
Dairy
Cattle
Sheep
Potatoes
Beans
Sugar Beets
Wheat
Barley

AREA 56,345 sq. mi. (145,934 sq. km.)
POPULATION 11,426,596
CAPITAL Springfield
LARGEST CITY Chicago
HIGHEST POINT Charles Mound 1,235 ft. (376 m.)
SETTLED IN 1720
ADMITTED TO UNION December 3, 1818
POPULAR NAME Prairie State; Land of Lincoln
STATE FLOWER Native Violet
STATE BIRD Cardinal

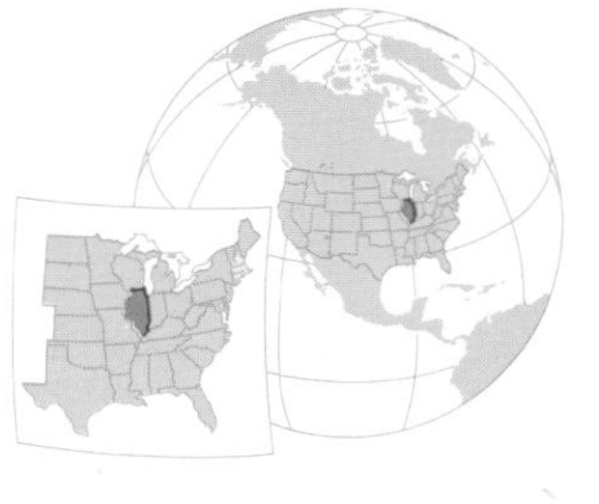

COUNTIES

Adams 71,622 .... B4
Alexander 12,264 .... D6
Bond 16,224 .... D5
Boone 28,630 .... E1
Brown 5,411 .... C4
Bureau 39,114 .... D2
Calhoun 5,867 .... C4
Carroll 18,779 .... D1
Cass 15,084 .... C4
Champaign 168,392 .... E3
Christian 36,446 .... D4
Clark 16,913 .... F4
Clay 15,283 .... E5
Clinton 32,617 .... D5
Coles 52,260 .... E4
Cook 5,253,655 .... F2
Crawford 20,818 .... F4
Cumberland 11,062 .... E4
De Kalb 74,624 .... E2
De Witt 18,108 .... E3
Douglas 19,774 .... E4
Du Page 658,835 .... E2
Edgar 21,725 .... F4
Edwards 7,961 .... E5
Effingham 30,944 .... E4
Fayette 22,167 .... D4
Ford 15,265 .... E3
Franklin 43,201 .... E5
Fulton 43,687 .... C3
Gallatin 7,590 .... E6
Greene 16,661 .... C4
Grundy 30,582 .... E2
Hamilton 9,172 .... E5
Hancock 23,877 .... B3
Hardin 5,383 .... E6
Henderson 9,114 .... C3
Henry 57,968 .... C2
Iroquois 32,976 .... F3
Jackson 61,522 .... D6
Jasper 11,318 .... E4
Jefferson 36,354 .... E5
Jersey 20,538 .... C4
Jo Daviess 23,520 .... C1
Johnson 9,624 .... E6
Kane 278,405 .... E2
Kankakee 102,926 .... F2
Kendall 37,202 .... E2
Knox 61,607 .... C3
Lake 440,372 .... E1
La Salle 112,033 .... E2
Lawrence 17,807 .... F5
Lee 36,328 .... D2
Livingston 41,381 .... E3
Logan 31,802 .... D3
Macon 131,375 .... E4
Macoupin 49,384 .... D4
Madison 247,691 .... D5
Marion 43,523 .... E5
Marshall 14,479 .... D2
Mason 19,492 .... D3
Massac 14,990 .... E6
McDonough 37,467 .... C3
McHenry 147,897 .... E1
McLean 119,149 .... E3
Menard 11,700 .... D3
Mercer 19,286 .... C2
Monroe 20,117 .... C5
Montgomery 31,686 .... D4
Morgan 37,502 .... C4
Moultrie 14,546 .... E4
Ogle 46,338 .... D1
Peoria 200,466 .... D3
Perry 21,714 .... D5
Piatt 16,581 .... E4
Pike 18,896 .... C4
Pope 4,404 .... E6
Pulaski 8,840 .... D6
Putnam 6,085 .... D2
Randolph 35,652 .... D5
Richland 17,587 .... E5
Rock Island 165,968 .... C2
Saint Clair 267,531 .... D5
Saline 28,448 .... E6
Sangamon 176,089 .... D4
Schuyler 8,365 .... C3
Scott 6,142 .... C4
Shelby 23,923 .... E4
Stark 7,389 .... D2
Stephenson 49,536 .... D1
Tazewell 132,078 .... D3
Union 17,765 .... D6
Vermilion 95,222 .... F3
Wabash 13,713 .... F5
Warren 21,943 .... C3
Washington 15,472 .... D5
Wayne 18,059 .... E5
White 17,864 .... E5
Whiteside 65,970 .... D2
Will 324,460 .... F2
Williamson 56,538 .... E6
Winnebago 250,884 .... D1
Woodford 33,320 .... D3

CITIES and TOWNS

Zip *Name/Pop.* *Key*

61410 Abingdon 4,210 .... C3
60101 Addison 29,826 .... B5
61230 Albany 1,014 .... C2
62806 Albion⊙ 2,285 .... E5
61231 Aledo⊙ 3,881 .... C2
61412 Alexis 1,076 .... C2
60102 Algonquin 5,834 .... E1
62207 Alorton 2,237 .... B2
61413 Alpha 815 .... C2
†60658 Alsip 17,134 .... B6
62411 Altamont 2,389 .... E4
62002 Alton 34,171 .... A2
61310 Amboy 2,377 .... D2
61232 Andalusia 1,238 .... C2
62906 Anna 5,408 .... D6
61234 Annawan 908 .... C2
60002 Antioch 4,419 .... E1
61910 Arcola 2,714 .... E4
62501 Argenta 994 .... E4
*60004 Arlington Heights 66,116 .... B5
61911 Arthur 2,122 .... E4
60911 Ashkum 735 .... E3
62612 Ashland 1,351 .... C4
62808 Ashley 658 .... D5
61912 Ashmore 883 .... F4
61006 Ashton 1,140 .... D2
62510 Assumption 1,283 .... E4
61501 Astoria 1,370 .... C3
62613 Athens 1,371 .... D4
61235 Atkinson 1,138 .... C2
61723 Atlanta 1,807 .... D3
61913 Atwood 1,464 .... E4
62615 Auburn 3,616 .... D4
62311 Augusta 764 .... C3
*60504 Aurora 81,293 .... E2
62907 Ava 811 .... D6
62216 Aviston 846 .... D5
61415 Avon 1,019 .... C3
†60015 Bannockburn 1,316 .... B5
60010 Barrington 9,029 .... A5
†60010 Barrington Hills 3,631 .... A5
62312 Barry 1,487 .... B4
60103 Bartlett 13,254 .... A5
61607 Bartonville 6,137 .... D3
60510 Batavia 12,574 .... E2
62618 Beardstown 6,338 .... C3
62219 Beckemeyer 1,119 .... D5
60401 Beecher 2,024 .... F2
*62220 Belleville⊙ 41,580 .... B3
60104 Bellwood 19,811 .... B5
61008 Belvidere⊙ 15,176 .... E1
61813 Bement 1,770 .... E4
62009 Benld 1,638 .... D4
60106 Bensenville 16,124 .... B5
62812 Benton⊙ 7,778 .... E6
60162 Berkeley 5,467 .... B5
60402 Berwyn 46,849 .... B6
62010 Bethalto 8,630 .... B2
61914 Bethany 1,550 .... E4
61420 Blandinsville 886 .... C3
60108 Bloomingdale 12,659 .... A5
61701 Bloomington⊙ 44,189 .... D3
Bloomington-Normal‡ 119,149 .... D3
60406 Blue Island 21,855 .... B6
62513 Blue Mound 1,338 .... D4
62621 Bluffs 821 .... C4
60439 Bolingbrook 37,261 .... A6
60914 Bourbonnais 13,280 .... F2
60407 Braceville 721 .... E2
61421 Bradford 924 .... D2
60915 Bradley 11,008 .... F2
60408 Braidwood 3,429 .... E2
62230 Breese 3,516 .... D5
62417 Bridgeport 2,281 .... F5
60455 Bridgeview 14,155 .... B6
62012 Brighton 2,364 .... C4
61517 Brimfield 890 .... D3
60153 Broadview 8,618 .... B6
60513 Brookfield 19,395 .... B6
†62059 Brooklyn (Lovejoy) 1,233 .... A2
62910 Brookport 1,128 .... E6
61314 Buda 668 .... D2
†60090 Buffalo Grove 22,230 .... B5
62014 Bunker Hill 1,700 .... D4
60459 Burbank 28,462 .... B6
†60601 Burnham 4,030 .... C6
†60558 Burr Ridge 3,833 .... B6
61422 Bushnell 3,811 .... C3
61010 Byron 2,035 .... D1
62206 Cahokia 18,904 .... A3
62914 Cairo⊙ 5,931 .... D6
60409 Calumet City 39,697 .... C6
†60643 Calumet Park 8,788 .... C6
62915 Cambria 1,090 .... D6
61238 Cambridge⊙ 2,217 .... C2
62320 Camp Point 1,285 .... B3
61520 Canton 14,626 .... C3
61239 Carbon Cliff 1,578 .... C2
62901 Carbondale 26,414 .... D6
62626 Carlinville⊙ 5,439 .... D4
62231 Carlyle⊙ 3,388 .... D5
62821 Carmi⊙ 6,264 .... E5
†60187 Carol Stream 15,472 .... A5
60110 Carpentersville 23,272 .... E1
62917 Carrier Mills 2,268 .... E6
62016 Carrollton⊙ 2,816 .... C4
62918 Carterville 3,445 .... D6
62321 Carthage⊙ 2,978 .... B3
60013 Cary 6,640 .... E1
62420 Casey 3,026 .... F4
62232 Caseyville 4,308 .... B2
61817 Catlin 2,226 .... F3
61013 Cedarville 766 .... D1
†62801 Central City 1,505 .... D5
62801 Centralia 15,126 .... D5
62206 Centreville 9,747 .... B3
61818 Cerro Gordo 1,553 .... E4
61820 Champaign 58,133 .... E3
Champaign-Urbana-Rantoul‡ 168,392 .... E3
62627 Chandlerville 842 .... C3
60410 Channahon 3,734 .... E2
61920 Charleston⊙ 19,355 .... E4
62629 Chatham 5,597 .... D4
60921 Chatsworth 1,187 .... E3
60922 Chebanse 1,191 .... F3
61726 Chenoa 1,847 .... E3
61016 Cherry Valley 946 .... D1
62233 Chester⊙ 8,401 .... D6
*60601 Chicago⊙ 3,005,072 .... C5
Chicago‡ 7,102,328 .... C5
60411 Chicago Heights 37,026 .... C6
60415 Chicago Ridge 13,473 .... B6
61523 Chillicothe 6,176 .... D3
61924 Chrisman 1,413 .... F4
62822 Christopher 3,086 .... D6
60650 Cicero 61,232 .... B5
60924 Cissna Park 825 .... F3
60514 Clarendon Hills 6,870 .... B6
62824 Clay City 1,038 .... E5
62324 Clayton 889 .... B3
60927 Clifton 1,390 .... F3
61727 Clinton⊙ 8,014 .... E3
60416 Coal City 3,028 .... E2
61240 Coal Valley 3,800 .... C2
62920 Cobden 1,210 .... D6
62017 Coffeen 842 .... D4
62326 Colchester 1,729 .... C3
61728 Colfax 920 .... E3
62234 Collinsville 19,613 .... B2
61241 Colona 2,172 .... C2
62236 Columbia 4,269 .... C5
60112 Cortland 1,019 .... E2
62018 Cottage Hills B2
62237 Coulterville 1,118 .... D5
†60525 Countryside 6,538 .... B6
62922 Creal Springs 845 .... E6
60431 Crest Hill 9,252 .... E2
†60445 Crestwood 10,852 .... B6
60417 Crete 5,417 .... F2
61611 Creve Coeur 6,851 .... D3
62827 Crossville 944 .... F5
60014 Crystal Lake 18,590 .... E1
61427 Cuba 1,648 .... C3
62330 Dallas City 1,408 .... B3
61320 Dalzell 824 .... D2
61732 Danvers 921 .... D3
61832 Danville⊙ 38,985 .... F3
†60559 Darien 14,536 .... B6
*62521 Decatur⊙ 94,081 .... E4
Decatur‡ 131,375 .... E4
60015 Deerfield 17,430 .... B5
†60010 Deer Park 1,368 .... A5
60115 De Kalb 33,099 .... E2
61734 Delavan 1,973 .... D3
61322 Depue 1,873 .... D2
62924 De Soto 1,589 .... D6
*60016 Des Plaines 53,568 .... B5
62530 Divernon 1,081 .... D4
†60469 Dixmoor 4,175 .... C6
61021 Dixon⊙ 15,701 .... D2
60419 Dolton 24,766 .... C6
62926 Dongola 886 .... D6
60515 Downers Grove 42,572 .... A6
60118 Dundee (East and West Dundee) 6,169 .... E1
61525 Dunlap 824 .... D3
62239 Dupo 3,039 .... A3
62832 Du Quoin 6,594 .... D5
61024 Durand 1,073 .... D1
60420 Dwight 4,146 .... E2
60518 Earlville 1,382 .... E2
62024 East Alton 7,096 .... A2
†60411 East Chicago Heights 5,347 .... C6
61025 East Dubuque 2,194 .... C1
†60118 East Dundee (Dundee) 2,618 .... E1
61430 East Galesburg 928 .... C3
†60429 East Hazelcrest 1,362 .... C6
61244 East Moline 20,907 .... C2
61611 East Peoria 22,385 .... D3
*62201 East Saint Louis 55,200 .... A2
62531 Edinburg 1,231 .... D4
62025 Edwardsville⊙ 12,480 .... B2
62401 Effingham⊙ 11,270 .... E4
60119 Elburn 1,224 .... E2
62930 Eldorado 5,198 .... E6
60120 Elgin 63,981 .... E1
61028 Elizabeth 772 .... C1
62931 Elizabethtown⊙ 478 .... E6
60007 Elk Grove Village 28,907 .... B5
62932 Elkville 973 .... D6
60126 Elmhurst 44,276 .... B5
61529 Elmwood 2,117 .... D3
60635 Elmwood Park 24,016 .... B5
61738 El Paso 2,676 .... D3
62028 Elsah 990 .... C5
60421 Elwood 814 .... E2
62933 Energy 1,138 .... E6
62835 Enfield 890 .... E5
62934 Equality 831 .... E6
61250 Erie 1,725 .... C2
61530 Eureka⊙ 4,306 .... D3
*60201 Evanston 73,706 .... B5
62242 Evansville 863 .... D5
60642 Evergreen Park 22,260 .... B6
61739 Fairbury 3,544 .... E3
62837 Fairfield⊙ 5,954 .... E5
†62201 Fairmont City 2,313 .... B2
61841 Fairmount 851 .... F3
62208 Fairview Heights 12,414 .... B3
61842 Farmer City 2,252 .... E3
61531 Farmington 3,118 .... C3
62534 Findlay 868 .... E4
61843 Fisher 1,572 .... E3
61740 Flanagan 978 .... E3
62839 Flora 5,379 .... E5
60422 Flossmoor 8,423 .... B6
60130 Forest Park 15,177 .... B5
†60402 Forest View 764 .... B6
61741 Forrest 1,246 .... E3
61030 Forreston 1,384 .... D1
60020 Fox Lake 6,831 .... A4
60021 Fox River Grove 2,515 .... A5
60423 Frankfort 4,357 .... B6
61031 Franklin Grove 965 .... D2
60131 Franklin Park 17,507 .... B5
62243 Freeburg 2,989 .... D5
61032 Freeport⊙ 26,266 .... D1
61252 Fulton 3,936 .... C2
62935 Galatia 1,042 .... E6
61036 Galena⊙ 3,876 .... C1
61401 Galesburg⊙ 35,305 .... C3
61434 Galva 3,185 .... D2
60424 Gardner 1,322 .... E2
61254 Geneseo 6,373 .... C2
60134 Geneva⊙ 9,881 .... E2
60135 Genoa 3,276 .... E1
61846 Georgetown 4,220 .... F4
62245 Germantown 1,191 .... D5
60936 Gibson City 3,498 .... E3
61847 Gifford 848 .... E3
62033 Gillespie 3,740 .... D4
60938 Gilman 1,913 .... E3
62640 Girard 2,246 .... D4
61533 Glasford 1,201 .... D3
62034 Glen Carbon 5,197 .... B2
60022 Glencoe 9,200 .... B5
†60108 Glendale Heights 23,163 .... A5
60137 Glen Ellyn 23,717 .... A5
60025 Glenview 32,060 .... B5
60425 Glenwood 10,538 .... C6
62035 Godfrey A2
62938 Golconda⊙ 960 .... E6
62939 Goreville 978 .... E6
62037 Grafton 1,024 .... C5
62942 Grand Tower 748 .... D6
†62701 Grandview 1,794 .... D4
62040 Granite City 36,815 .... A2
60940 Grant Park 1,038 .... F2
61326 Granville 1,537 .... D2
60030 Grayslake 5,260 .... B4
62844 Grayville 2,313 .... B4
62044 Greenfield 1,090 .... C4
†60048 Green Oaks 1,415 .... B4
†61241 Green Rock 3,324 .... C2
62428 Greenup 1,655 .... E4
61534 Green Valley 768 .... D3
62642 Greenview 830 .... D3
62246 Greenville⊙ 5,271 .... D5
61744 Gridley 1,246 .... E3
62340 Griggsville 1,301 .... C4
60031 Gurnee 7,179 .... B4
62341 Hamilton 3,509 .... B3
60140 Hampshire 1,735 .... E1
61256 Hampton 1,873 .... C2
61536 Hanna City 1,361 .... D3
61041 Hanover 1,069 .... C1
60103 Hanover Park 28,719 .... A5
62047 Hardin⊙ 1,107 .... C4
62946 Harrisburg⊙ 10,410 .... E6
62537 Harristown 1,456 .... D4
62048 Hartford 1,887 .... A2
60033 Harvard 5,126 .... E1
60426 Harvey 35,810 .... B6
60656 Harwood Heights 8,228 .... B5
62644 Havana⊙ 4,277 .... D3
†60047 Hawthorn Woods 1,658 .... B5
60429 Hazel Crest 13,973 .... B6
60034 Hebron 786 .... E1
†61832 Hegeler 1,853 .... F3
61327 Hennepin⊙ 716 .... D2
61537 Henry 2,740 .... D2
62948 Herrin 10,708 .... E6
60941 Herscher 1,214 .... E2
61745 Heyworth 1,598 .... E3
60457 Hickory Hills 13,778 .... B6
62249 Highland 7,122 .... D5
60035 Highland Park 30,611 .... B5
60040 Highwood 5,452 .... B5
62049 Hillsboro⊙ 4,408 .... D4
60162 Hillside 8,279 .... B5
60520 Hinckley 1,447 .... E2
60521 Hinsdale 16,726 .... B6
60525 Hodgkins 2,005 .... B6
60195 Hoffman Estates 37,272 .... A5
61849 Homer 1,279 .... F3
60456 Hometown 5,324 .... B6
60430 Homewood 19,724 .... B6
60942 Hoopeston 6,411 .... F3
61747 Hohedale 913 .... D3
61748 Hudson 929 .... E3

(continued on following page)

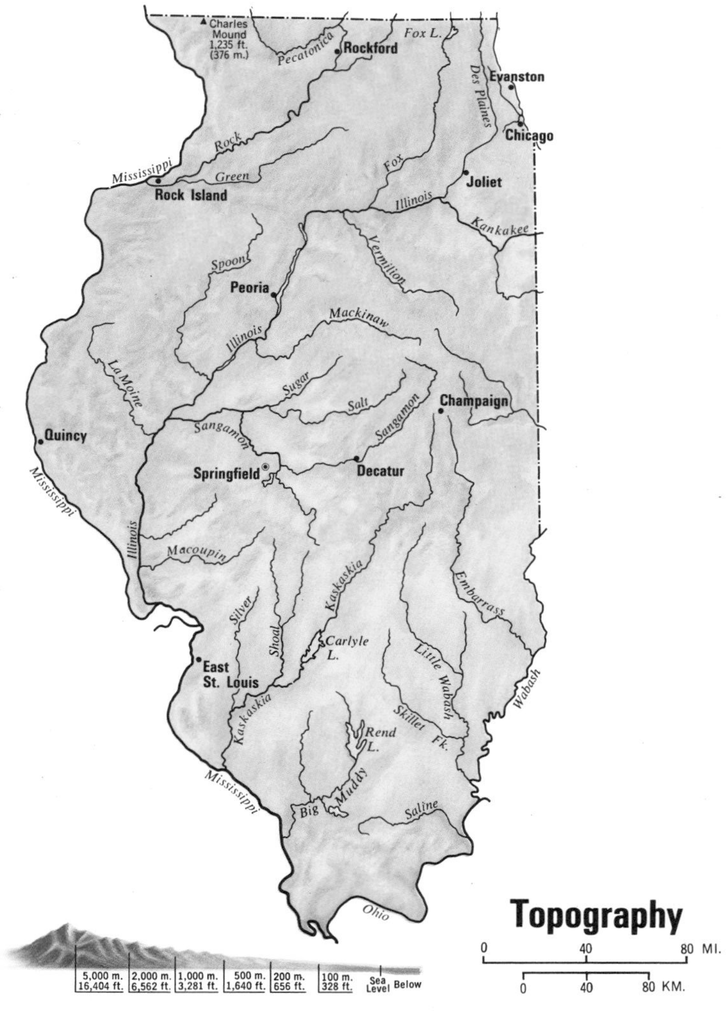
Charles Mound 1,235 ft. (376 m.)
Pecatonica
Rockford
Fox L.
Des Plaines
Evanston
Chicago
Rock
Mississippi
Green
Rock Island
Fox
Joliet
Illinois
Kankakee
Vermilion
Spoon
Peoria
Mackinaw
Illinois
La Moine
Sugar
Salt
Champaign
Sangamon
Quincy
Sangamon
Springfield
Decatur
Mississippi
Illinois
Macoupin
Embarrass
Silver
Shoal
Kaskaskia
Carlyle L.
Little Wabash
East St. Louis
Kaskaskia
Wabash
Skillet Fk.
Rend L.
Mississippi
Big Muddy
Saline
Ohio
Topography
0 40 80 MI.
0 40 80 KM.
5,000 m. 16,404 ft.
2,000 m. 6,562 ft.
1,000 m. 3,281 ft.
500 m. 1,640 ft.
200 m. 656 ft.
100 m. 328 ft.
Sea Level
Below

Agriculture, Industry and Resources

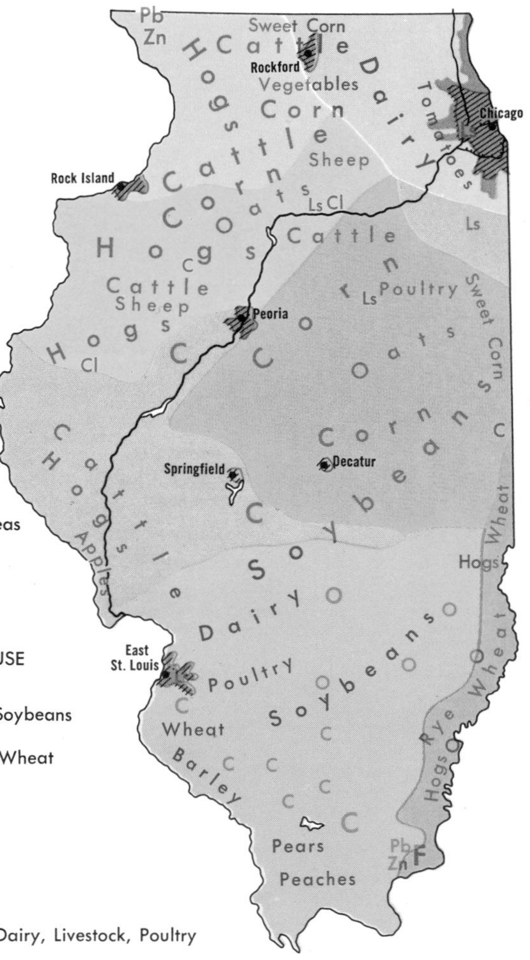

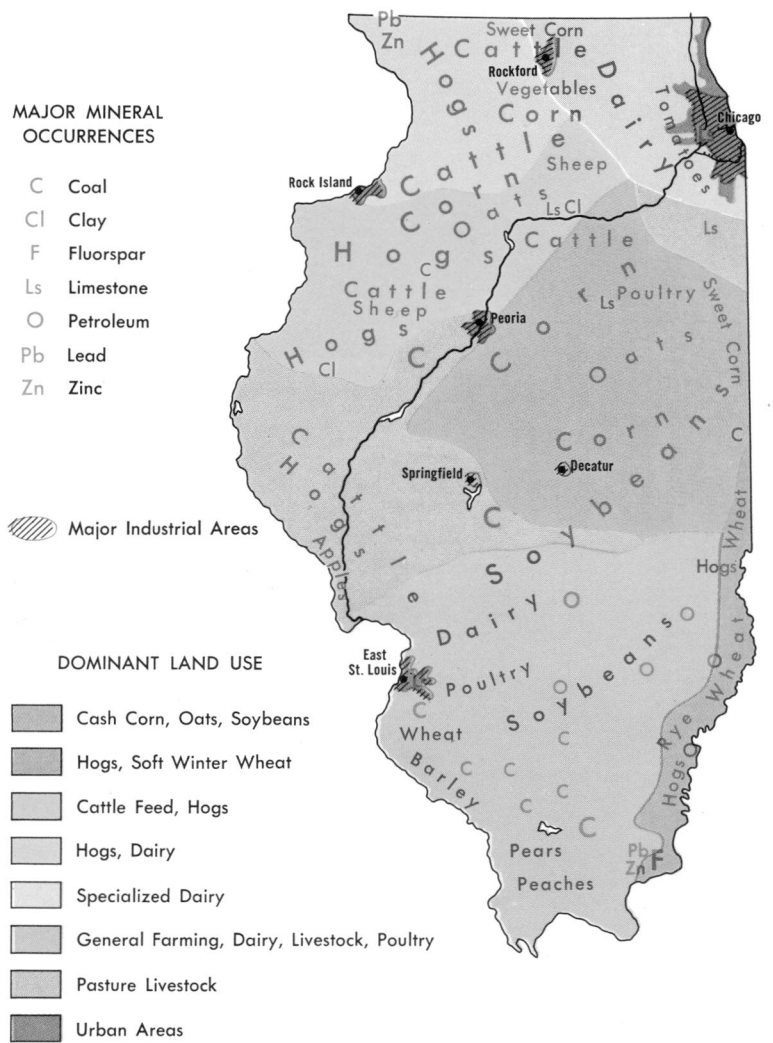

MAJOR MINERAL OCCURRENCES

C Coal
Cl Clay
F Fluorspar
Ls Limestone
O Petroleum
Pb Lead
Zn Zinc

Major Industrial Areas

DOMINANT LAND USE

Cash Corn, Oats, Soybeans
Hogs, Soft Winter Wheat
Cattle Feed, Hogs
Hogs, Dairy
Specialized Dairy
General Farming, Dairy, Livestock, Poultry
Pasture Livestock
Urban Areas

60142 Huntley 1,646 .... E1
62949 Hurst 938 .... D6
62539 Illiopolis 1,118 .... D4
†60067 Inverness 4,046 .... A5
62848 Irvington 789 .... D5
60042 Island Lake 2,293 .... A4
60143 Itasca 7,129 .... B5
62650 Jacksonville⊙ 20,284 .... C4
†62701 Jerome 1,374 .... D4
62052 Jerseyville⊙ 7,506 .... C4
62436 Jewett 230 .... E4
62951 Johnston City 3,873 .... E6
*60431 Joliet⊙ 77,956 .... E2
62952 Jonesboro⊙ 1,842 .... D6
†60458 Justice 10,552 .... B6
60901 Kankakee⊙ 30,141 .... F2
Kankakee‡ 102,926 .... F2
61933 Kansas 791 .... F4
†63673 Kaskaskia 33 .... C6
61442 Keithsburg 936 .... B2
60043 Kenilworth 2,708 .... B5
61443 Kewanee 14,508 .... C2
†60069 Kildeer 1,609 .... A5
62540 Kincaid 1,591 .... D4
62854 Kinmundy 945 .... E5
60146 Kirkland 1,155 .... E1
61447 Kirkwood 1,008 .... C3
61448 Knoxville 3,432 .... C3
61540 Lacon⊙ 2,135 .... D2
61329 Ladd 1,337 .... D2
60525 La Grange 15,445 .... B6
60525 La Grange Park 13,359 .... B5
61450 La Harpe 1,471 .... C3
†60010 Lake Barrington 2,320 .... A5
60044 Lake Bluff 4,434 .... B4
†60002 Lake Catherine 1,335 .... E1
60045 Lake Forest 15,245 .... B4
†60102 Lake in the Hills 5,651 .... E1
60046 Lake Villa 1,462 .... A4
62438 Lakewood 1,254 .... E4
60047 Lake Zurich 8,225 .... A5
61330 La Moille 734 .... D2
61046 Lanark 1,483 .... D1
60438 Lansing 29,039 .... C6
61301 La Salle 10,347 .... E2
62439 Lawrenceville⊙ 5,652 .... F5
62254 Lebanon 3,245 .... D5
60531 Leland 775 .... E2
60439 Lemont 5,640 .... B6
61048 Lena 2,295 .... D1
61752 Le Roy 2,870 .... E3
61542 Lewistown⊙ 2,758 .... C3
61753 Lexington 1,806 .... E3
60048 Libertyville 16,520 .... B4
62656 Lincoln⊙ 16,327 .... D3
†60015 Lincolnshire 4,151 .... B5
†60645 Lincolnwood 11,921 .... B5
†60046 Lindenhurst 6,220 .... B4
60532 Lisle 13,625 .... A6
62056 Litchfield 7,204 .... D4
62058 Livingston 949 .... D5
62661 Loami 770 .... D4
60441 Lockport 9,170 .... B6
60148 Lombard 36,897 .... B5
60047 Long Grove 2,013 .... B5
62858 Louisville⊙ 1,166 .... E5
62059 Lovejoy 1,233 .... A2
61111 Loves Park 13,192 .... E1
61937 Lovington 1,313 .... E4
61261 Lyndon 777 .... D2
†60411 Lynwood 4,195 .... C6
60534 Lyons 9,925 .... B6
61755 Mackinaw 1,354 .... D3
61455 Macomb⊙ 19,863 .... C3
62544 Macon 1,300 .... E4
62060 Madison 5,915 .... A2
61853 Mahomet 1,986 .... E3
60150 Malta 995 .... E2
60442 Manhattan 1,944 .... F2
61546 Manito 1,869 .... D3
61854 Mansfield 921 .... E3
60950 Manteno 3,155 .... F2
60152 Marengo 4,361 .... E1
62061 Marine 957 .... D5
62959 Marion⊙ 14,031 .... E6
62257 Marissa 2,568 .... D5
60426 Markham 15,172 .... B6
61756 Maroa 1,760 .... E3
†61554 Marquette Heights 3,386 .... D3
61341 Marseilles 4,766 .... E2
62441 Marshall⊙ 3,655 .... F4
62442 Martinsville 1,298 .... F4
62062 Maryville 1,937 .... B2
62258 Mascoutah 4,962 .... D5
62664 Mason City 2,719 .... D3
61263 Matherville 793 .... C2
60443 Matteson 10,223 .... B6
61938 Mattoon 19,055 .... E4
60153 Maywood 27,998 .... B5
60444 Mazon 828 .... E2
60050 McHenry 10,908 .... E1
†60050 McHenry Shores 1,041 .... E1
61754 McLean 836 .... D3
62859 McLeansboro⊙ 2,960 .... E5
†62010 Meadowbrook 1,082 .... B2
*60160 Melrose Park 20,735 .... B5
62351 Mendon 979 .... B3
61342 Mendota 7,134 .... D2
62665 Meredosia 1,272 .... C4
†60601 Merrionette Park 2,054 .... B6
61548 Metamora 2,482 .... D3
62960 Metropolis⊙ 7,171 .... E6
60445 Midlothian 14,274 .... B6
61264 Milan 6,264 .... C2
60953 Milford 1,716 .... F3
61051 Milledgeville 1,209 .... D1
62260 Millstadt 2,736 .... B3
61759 Minier 1,261 .... D3
61760 Minonk 2,039 .... D3
60447 Minooka 1,565 .... E2
60448 Mokena 4,578 .... B6
61265 Moline 46,278 .... C2
60954 Momence 3,297 .... F2
60449 Monee 993 .... F2
61462 Monmouth⊙ 10,706 .... C3
60538 Montgomery 3,369 .... E2
61856 Monticello⊙ 4,753 .... E3
60450 Morris⊙ 8,833 .... E2
61270 Morrison⊙ 4,605 .... C2
62546 Morrisonville 1,208 .... D4
61550 Morton 14,178 .... D3
60053 Morton Grove 23,747 .... B5
62963 Mound City⊙ 1,102 .... D6
62964 Mounds 1,669 .... D6
62863 Mount Carmel⊙ 8,908 .... F5
61053 Mount Carroll⊙ 1,936 .... D1
61054 Mount Morris 2,989 .... D1
62069 Mount Olive 2,357 .... D4
60056 Mount Prospect 52,634 .... B5
62548 Mount Pulaski 1,783 .... D3
62353 Mount Sterling⊙ 2,186 .... C4
62864 Mount Vernon⊙ 17,193 .... E5
62549 Mount Zion 4,563 .... E4
62550 Moweaqua 1,922 .... E4
60060 Mundelein 17,053 .... A4
62966 Murphysboro⊙ 9,866 .... D6
60540 Naperville 42,601 .... A6
62263 Nashville⊙ 3,186 .... D5
62354 Nauvoo 1,133 .... B3
62447 Neoga 1,736 .... E4
60541 Newark 798 .... E2
62264 New Athens 1,937 .... D5
62265 New Baden 2,476 .... D5
62670 New Berlin 834 .... D4
61272 New Boston 731 .... B2
60451 New Lenox 5,792 .... B6
61942 Newman 1,079 .... B6
62448 Newton⊙ 3,186 .... E5
61465 New Windsor 863 .... C2
62551 Niantic 761 .... D4
60648 Niles 30,363 .... B5
62868 Noble 832 .... E5
62075 Nokomis 2,656 .... D4
61761 Normal 35,672 .... E3
†60656 Norridge 16,483 .... B5
62869 Norris City 1,515 .... E6
60542 North Aurora 5,205 .... E2
†60010 North Barrington 1,475 .... A5
60062 Northbrook 30,778 .... B5
60064 North Chicago 38,774 .... B4
60093 Northfield 5,807 .... B5
60164 Northlake 12,166 .... B5
†61111 North Park 15,806 .... D1
†61554 North Pekin 1,824 .... D3
60546 North Riverside 6,764 .... B5
†61373 North Utica (Utica) 1,067 .... E2
60521 Oak Brook 6,641 .... B6
†60181 Oakbrook Terrace 2,285 .... B5
60452 Oak Forest 26,096 .... B6
61943 Oakland 1,035 .... F4
*60453 Oak Lawn 60,590 .... B6
*60303 Oak Park 54,887 .... B5
61858 Oakwood 1,627 .... F3
62449 Oblong 1,840 .... F5
60460 Odell 1,083 .... E2
62870 Odin 1,285 .... D5
62269 O'Fallon 12,241 .... B2
61859 Ogden 818 .... F3
61348 Oglesby 3,979 .... D2
62271 Okawville 1,337 .... D5
62450 Olney⊙ 9,026 .... E5
60461 Olympia Fields 4,146 .... B6
60955 Onarga 1,269 .... F3
61467 Oneida 765 .... C2
61469 Oquawka⊙ 1,533 .... C3
62554 Oreana 999 .... E4
61061 Oregon⊙ 3,559 .... D1
61273 Orion 2,013 .... C2
60462 Orland Park 23,045 .... B6
60543 Oswego 3,021 .... E2
61350 Ottawa⊙ 18,166 .... E2
60067 Palatine 32,166 .... B5
62451 Palestine 1,718 .... F4
62674 Palmyra 864 .... C4
60463 Palos Heights 11,096 .... B6
60465 Palos Hills 16,654 .... B6
60464 Palos Park 3,150 .... B6
62557 Pana 6,040 .... D4
61944 Paris⊙ 9,885 .... F4
†60085 Park City 3,673 .... B4
60466 Park Forest 26,222 .... B6
60466 Park Forest South 6,245 .... F2
60068 Park Ridge 38,704 .... B5
62558 Pawnee 2,577 .... D4
61353 Pawpaw 839 .... E2
60957 Paxton⊙ 4,258 .... E3
62360 Payson 1,065 .... B4
61063 Pecatonica 1,732 .... D1
61554 Pekin⊙ 33,967 .... D3
*61601 Peoria⊙ 124,160 .... D3
Peoria‡ 365,864 .... D3
61614 Peoria Heights 7,453 .... D3
60468 Peotone 2,832 .... F2
62272 Percy 1,053 .... D5
61354 Peru 10,886 .... D2
62675 Petersburg⊙ 2,419 .... D4
61864 Philo 973 .... E3
†60426 Phoenix 2,850 .... C6
62274 Pinckneyville⊙ 3,319 .... D5
60959 Piper City 905 .... E3
62363 Pittsfield⊙ 4,170 .... C4
60544 Plainfield 3,767 .... A6
60545 Plano 4,875 .... E2
62366 Pleasant Hill 1,112 .... C4
62275 Pocahontas 866 .... D5
61074 Polo 2,643 .... D1
61764 Pontiac⊙ 11,227 .... E3
†62040 Pontoon Beach 3,336 .... A2
61065 Poplar Grove 818 .... E1
61275 Port Byron 1,289 .... C2
60469 Posen 4,642 .... B6
61865 Potomac 874 .... F3
61470 Prairie City 580 .... C3
61356 Princeton⊙ 7,342 .... D2
61559 Princeville 1,712 .... D3
61277 Prophetstown 2,141 .... D2
60070 Prospect Heights 11,808 .... B5
62301 Quincy⊙ 42,554 .... B4
62080 Ramsey 1,058 .... D4
60960 Rankin 727 .... F3
61866 Rantoul 20,161 .... E3
61278 Rapids City 1,058 .... C2
62560 Raymond 957 .... D4
62278 Red Bud 2,850 .... D5
60071 Richmond 1,068 .... E1
60471 Richton Park 9,403 .... B6
61870 Ridge Farm 1,096 .... F4
62979 Ridgway 1,245 .... E6
60627 Riverdale 13,233 .... C6
60305 River Forest 12,392 .... B5
60171 River Grove 10,368 .... B5
60546 Riverside 9,236 .... B6
62561 Riverton 2,783 .... D4
†60015 Riverwoods 2,804 .... B5
61561 Roanoke 2,001 .... D3
60472 Robbins 8,853 .... B6
62454 Robinson⊙ 7,285 .... F5
61068 Rochelle 8,982 .... D2
62563 Rochester 2,488 .... D4
60436 Rockdale 1,913 .... E2
61071 Rock Falls 10,633 .... D2
*61101 Rockford⊙ 139,712 .... D1
Rockford‡ 279,514 .... D1
61201 Rock Island⊙ 46,928 .... C2
Rock Island-Moline-
Davenport‡ 383,958 .... C2
61072 Rockton 2,313 .... E1
60008 Rolling Meadows 20,167 .... A5
61562 Rome 2,744 .... D3
60441 Romeoville 15,519 .... B6
62082 Roodhouse 2,364 .... C4
61073 Roscoe 1,388 .... D1
60172 Roselle 16,948 .... A5
60018 Rosemont 4,137 .... B5
61473 Roseville 1,254 .... C3
†62024 Rosewood Heights 5,085 .... B2
62982 Rosiclare 1,441 .... E6
60963 Rossville 1,363 .... F3
60673 Round Lake 2,644 .... A4
†60673 Round Lake Beach 12,921 .... A4
†60673 Round Lake Heights 1,192 .... E1
†60673 Round Lake Park 4,032 .... A4
62084 Roxana 1,587 .... B2
62983 Royalton 1,320 .... D6
62681 Rushville⊙ 3,348 .... C3
60964 Saint Anne 1,421 .... F2
60174 Saint Charles 17,492 .... E2
61563 Saint David 786 .... C3
62458 Saint Elmo 1,611 .... E4
62460 Saint Francisville 1,040 .... F5
62281 Saint Jacob 792 .... D5
61873 Saint Joseph 1,900 .... E3
62881 Salem⊙ 7,813 .... E5
62882 Sandoval 1,734 .... D5
60548 Sandwich 5,244 .... E2
62682 San Jose 784 .... D3
60411 Sauk Village 10,906 .... C6
61074 Savanna 4,529 .... C1
61874 Savoy 2,126 .... E3
61770 Saybrook 882 .... E3
60194 Schaumburg 53,305 .... A5
60176 Schiller Park 11,458 .... B5
61360 Seneca 2,098 .... E2
62884 Sesser 2,238 .... D5
60550 Shabbona 851 .... E2
61078 Shannon 938 .... D1
62984 Shawneetown⊙ 1,841 .... E6
61361 Sheffield 1,130 .... D2
62565 Shelbyville⊙ 5,259 .... E4
60966 Sheldon 1,215 .... F3
62684 Sherman 1,501 .... D4
61281 Sherrard 811 .... C2
†62220 Shiloh 1,045 .... B3
60435 Shorewood 4,714 .... E2
61877 Sidney 886 .... E3
61282 Silvis 7,130 .... C2
*60076 Skokie 60,278 .... B5
†60118 Sleepy Hollow 2,000 .... E1
62285 Smithton 1,447 .... C5
60552 Somonauk 1,344 .... E2
†60010 South Barrington 1,168 .... A5
61080 South Beloit 4,088 .... E1
60411 South Chicago
Heights 3,932 .... C6
60177 South Elgin 5,970 .... E2
60473 South Holland 24,977 .... C6
†62650 South Jacksonville 3,382 .... C4
61564 South Pekin 1,243 .... D3
62087 South Roxana 2,286 .... B2
60474 South Wilmington 747 .... E2
62286 Sparta 4,957 .... D5
*62701 Springfield (cap.)⊙
100,054 .... D4
Springfield‡ 187,789 .... D4
61362 Spring Valley 5,822 .... D2
61774 Stanford 720 .... D3
62088 Staunton 4,744 .... D5
62288 Steeleville 2,240 .... D6
60475 Steger 9,269 .... F2
61081 Sterling 16,281 .... D2
62463 Stewardson 745 .... E4
60402 Stickney 5,893 .... B6
61084 Stillman Valley 961 .... D1
61085 Stockton 1,872 .... C1
†60160 Stone Park 4,273 .... B5
62567 Stonington 1,184 .... D4
60103 Streamwood 23,456 .... A5
61364 Streator 14,795 .... E2
61480 Stronghurst 865 .... C3
60554 Sugar Grove 1,366 .... E2
61951 Sullivan⊙ 4,526 .... E4
60501 Summit-Argo 10,110 .... B6
62466 Sumner 1,238 .... F5
†60050 Sunnyside 1,432 .... A4
62221 Swansea 5,347 .... B3
60178 Sycamore⊙ 9,219 .... E2
62888 Tamaroa 885 .... D5
62988 Tamms 826 .... D6
61283 Tampico 966 .... D2
62568 Taylorville⊙ 11,386 .... D4
62467 Teutopolis 1,414 .... E4
62689 Thayer 759 .... D4
61878 Thomasboro 1,242 .... E3
61285 Thomson 911 .... C2
60476 Thornton 3,024 .... C6
62292 Tilden 1,025 .... D5
†61832 Tilton 2,405 .... F3
60477 Tinley Park 26,171 .... B6
61368 Tiskilwa 990 .... D2
62468 Toledo⊙ 1,284 .... E4
61880 Tolono 2,434 .... E3
61369 Toluca 1,471 .... D2
61483 Toulon⊙ 1,390 .... D2
†60010 Tower Lakes 1,177 .... A4
61568 Tremont 2,096 .... D3
62293 Trenton 2,504 .... D5
62294 Troy 3,772 .... B2
61953 Tuscola⊙ 3,839 .... E4
61801 Urbana⊙ 35,978 .... E3
61373 Utica 1,067 .... E2
62891 Valier 729 .... D5
†60120 Valley View 2,112 .... E2
62295 Valmeyer 898 .... C5
62471 Vandalia⊙ 5,338 .... D5
62090 Venice 3,480 .... A2
61484 Vermont 885 .... C3
60061 Vernon Hills 9,827 .... B4
62995 Vienna⊙ 1,420 .... E6
61956 Villa Grove 2,707 .... E4
60181 Villa Park 23,185 .... B5
61486 Viola 1,144 .... C2
62690 Virden 3,899 .... D4
62691 Virginia⊙ 1,825 .... C4
60083 Wadsworth 1,104 .... B4
61376 Walnut 1,513 .... D2
†62801 Wamac 1,665 .... D5
61777 Wapella 768 .... E3
61087 Warren 1,595 .... C1
62573 Warrensburg 1,372 .... D4
60555 Warrenville 7,519 .... A6
62379 Warsaw 1,842 .... B3
61570 Washburn 1,206 .... D3
61571 Washington 10,364 .... D3
62204 Washington Park 8,223 .... B2
61488 Wataga 996 .... C2
62298 Waterloo⊙ 4,646 .... C5
60556 Waterman 943 .... E2
60970 Watseka⊙ 5,543 .... F3
60084 Wauconda 5,688 .... A4
60085 Waukegan⊙ 67,653 .... B4
62692 Waverly 1,537 .... D4
60184 Wayne 940 .... E2
62895 Wayne City 1,132 .... E5
61377 Wenona 1,025 .... E2
60153 Westchester 17,730 .... B5
60185 West Chicago 12,550 .... A5
†60118 West Dundee
(Dundee) 3,551 .... E1
60558 Western Springs 12,876 .... B6
62474 Westfield 733 .... F4
62896 West Frankfort 9,437 .... E6
†60462 Westhaven 2,784 .... B6
60559 Westmont 16,718 .... B6
62476 West Salem 1,145 .... F5
61883 Westville 3,573 .... F3
60187 Wheaton⊙ 43,043 .... A5
60090 Wheeling 23,266 .... B5
62092 White Hall 2,935 .... C4
62693 Williamsville 996 .... D4
†60521 Willowbrook 4,953 .... B6
60480 Willow Springs 4,147 .... B6
60091 Wilmette 28,229 .... B5
60481 Wilmington 4,424 .... E2
62694 Winchester⊙ 1,716 .... C4
61957 Windsor 1,228 .... E4
†61465 Windsor (New
Windsor) 863 .... C2
60190 Winfield 4,422 .... A5
61088 Winnebago 1,644 .... D1
60093 Winnetka 12,772 .... B5
60096 Winthrop Harbor 5,431 .... F1
62094 Witt 1,205 .... D4
60191 Wood Dale 11,251 .... B5
61490 Woodhull 901 .... C2
†60517 Woodridge 22,561 .... B6
62095 Wood River 12,446 .... B2
60098 Woodstock⊙ 11,725 .... E1
62097 Worden 953 .... B2
60482 Worth 11,592 .... B6
61379 Wyanet 1,069 .... D2
61491 Wyoming 1,614 .... D2
61572 Yates City 860 .... C3
60560 Yorkville⊙ 3,422 .... E2
62999 Zeigler 1,858 .... D6
60099 Zion 17,861 .... F1

OTHER FEATURES

Apple (creek) C4
Apple (riv.) C1
Argonne Nat'l Laboratory B6
Big Bureau (riv.) D2
Big Muddy (riv.) D6
Bonpas (creek) F5
Cache (riv.) D6
Calumet (lake) C6
Carlyle (lake) D5
Chanute A.F.B. E3
Charles Mound (hill) C1
Chicago Portage Nat'l Hist. Site B6
Crab Orchard (lake) E6
Des Plaines (riv.) A6
Du Page (riv.) E2
Edwards (riv.) C2
Embarras (riv.) E4
Fort Sheridan B5
Fox (lake) A4
Fox (riv.) E2
Fox (riv.) E5
Glenview Nav. Air. Sta. B5
Granite City Army Depot A2
Great Lakes Nav. Trng. Ctr. B4
Green (riv.) D2
Henderson (riv.) C2
Illinois (riv.) C4
Illinois - Mississippi (canal) C2
Iroquois (riv.) F3
Kankakee (riv.) F2
Kaskaskia (riv.) E4
La Moine (riv.) C3
Little Wabash (riv.) E5
Mackinaw (riv.) E3
Macoupin (riv.) C4
Michigan (lake) F1
Mississippi (riv.) C5
O'Hare Field-Chicago International
Airport B5
Ohio (riv.) E6
Plum (riv.) C1
Pope (creek) C2
Rend (lake) E5
Rock (creek) D2
Rock (riv.) C2
Rock Island Arsenal C2
Saline (riv.) E6
Salt (creek) D3
Sangamon (riv.) C3
Savanna Army Depot C1
Scott A.F.B. 8,648 .... B3
Shelbyville (lake) E4
Spoon (riv.) C3
Wabash (riv.) F5

⊙County seat.
‡Population of metropolitan area.
† Zip of nearest p.o. * Multiple zips.

AREA 36,185 sq. mi. (93,719 sq. km.)
POPULATION 5,490,260
CAPITAL Indianapolis
LARGEST CITY Indianapolis
HIGHEST POINT 1,257 ft. (383 m.) (Wayne County)
SETTLED IN 1730
ADMITTED TO UNION December 11, 1816
POPULAR NAME Hoosier State
STATE FLOWER Peony
STATE BIRD Cardinal

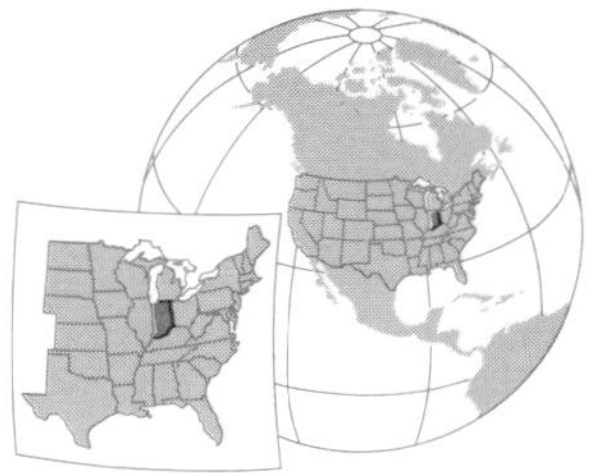

COUNTIES

Adams 29,619 H3
Allen 294,335 G2
Bartholomew 65,088 F6
Benton 10,218 C3
Blackford 15,570 G4
Boone 36,446 E4
Brown 12,377 E6
Carroll 19,722 D3
Cass 40,936 E3
Clark 88,838 F8
Clay 24,862 C6
Clinton 31,545 E4
Crawford 9,820 E8
Daviess 27,836 C7
Dearborn 34,291 H6
Decatur 23,841 G6
De Kalb 33,606 H2
Delaware 128,587 G4
Dubois 34,238 D8
Elkhart 137,330 F1
Fayette 28,272 G5
Floyd 61,169 F8
Fountain 19,033 C4
Franklin 19,612 G6
Fulton 19,335 E2
Gibson 33,156 B8
Grant 80,934 F3
Greene 30,416 D6
Hamilton 82,027 E4
Hancock 43,939 F5
Harrison 27,276 E8
Hendricks 69,804 D5
Henry 53,336 G5
Howard 86,896 E4
Huntington 35,596 G3
Jackson 36,523 E7
Jasper 26,138 C2
Jay 23,239 G4
Jefferson 30,419 G7
Jennings 22,854 F7
Johnson 77,240 E6
Knox 41,838 C7
Kosciusko 59,555 F2
Lagrange 25,550 G1
Lake 522,965 C2
LaPorte 108,632 D1
Lawrence 4,272 E7
Madison 139,336 F4
Marion 765,233 E5
Marshall 39,155 E2
Martin 11,001 D7
Miami 39,820 E3
Monroe 98,785 D6
Montgomery 35,501 D4
Morgan 51,999 E6
Newton 14,844 C3
Noble 35,443 G2
Ohio 5,114 H7
Orange 18,677 E7
Owen 15,841 D6
Parke 16,372 C5
Perry 19,346 D8
Pike 13,465 C8
Porter 119,816 C2
Posey 26,414 B8
Pulaski 13,258 D2
Putnam 29,163 D5
Randolph 29,997 G4
Ripley 24,398 G6
Rush 19,604 G5
Saint Joseph 241,617 E1
Scott 20,422 F7
Shelby 39,887 F5
Spencer 19,361 C9
Starke 21,997 D2
Steuben 24,694 G1
Sullivan 21,107 C6
Switzerland 7,153 G7
Tippecanoe 121,702 D4
Tipton 16,819 E4
Union 6,860 H5
Vanderburgh 167,515 B8
Vermillion 18,229 C5
Vigo 112,385 C6
Wabash 36,640 F3
Warren 8,976 C4
Warrick 41,474 C8
Washington 21,932 E7
Wayne 76,058 G5
Wells 25,401 G3
White 23,867 D3
Whitley 26,215 F2

CITIES and TOWNS

Zip *Name/Pop.* *Key*

47240 Adams 250 F6
†46947 Adamsboro 325 E3
46102 Advance 559 D5
46910 Akron 1,045 E2
47320 Albany 2,625 G4
46701 Albion⊙ 1,637 G2
†47283 Alert 102 F6
46001 Alexandria 6,028 F4
†46738 Altona 263 G2
47917 Ambia 274 C4
46911 Amboy 450 F3
†46131 Amity 200 E6
46103 Amo 444 D5
*46011 Anderson⊙ 64,695 F4
Anderson‡ 139,336 F4
†47024 Andersonville 225 G5
46702 Andrews 1,243 F3
46703 Angola⊙ 5,486 G1
46030 Arcadia 1,801 E4
46704 Arcola 300 G2
†46624 Ardmore 800 E1
46501 Argos 1,547 E2
46104 Arlington 500 F5
46705 Ashley 841 G1
46031 Atlanta 657 E4
47918 Attica 3,841 C4
46502 Atwood 300 F2
46706 Auburn⊙ 8,122 G2
47001 Aurora 3,816 H6
47102 Austin 4,857 F7
46710 Avilla 1,272 G2
47420 Avoca 400 D7
46105 Bainbridge 644 D5
46106 Bargersville 1,647 E5
47006 Batesville 4,152 G6
47920 Battle Ground 812 D3
47421 Bedford⊙ 14,410 E7
46107 Beech Grove 13,196 E5
†46526 Benton 220 F2
46711 Berne 3,300 H3
†46111 Bethany 127 E5
46301 Beverly Shores 864 C1
47512 Bicknell 4,713 C7
46713 Bippus 300 F3
47513 Birdseye 533 D8
†46406 Black Oak C1
47831 Blanford 500 B5
47138 Blocher 400 F7
47424 Bloomfield⊙ 2,705 D6
47832 Bloomingdale 409 C5
47401 Bloomington⊙ 52,044 D6
Bloomington‡ 98,387 D6
†47360 Blountsville 213 G4
†46176 Blue Ridge 219 F5
46714 Bluffton⊙ 8,705 G3
46110 Boggstown 200 F5
46302 Boone Grove 220 C2
47601 Boonville⊙ 6,300 C8
47106 Borden 384 F8
47324 Boston 189 H5
47921 Boswell 810 C3
46504 Bourbon 1,522 E2
47833 Bowling Green 200 D6
47107 Bradford 350 E8
47834 Brazil⊙ 7,852 C5
46506 Bremen 3,565 E2
47836 Bridgeton 250 C5
†45030 Bright 450 H6
46720 Brimfield 292 G2
46913 Bringhurst 275 E3
46507 Bristol 1,203 F1
47922 Brook 926 C3
46111 Brooklyn 889 E5
†47250 Brooksburg 132 G7
47923 Brookston 1,701 D3
47012 Brookville⊙ 2,874 G6
46112 Brownsburg 6,242 E5
47220 Brownstown⊙ 2,704 F7
47325 Brownsville 250 H5
47516 Bruceville 646 C7
47326 Bryant 277 G3
47924 Buck Creek 225 D4
47647 Buckskin 200 C8
47925 Buffalo 500 D3
46914 Bunker Hill 984 E3
46508 Burket 260 F2
46915 Burlington 680 E4
47926 Burnettsville 496 D3
47222 Burney 300 F6
†46401 Burns Harbor 920 C1
46916 Burrows 250 E3
46721 Butler 2,509 H2
47223 Butlerville 300 F6
†46371 Byron 200 C5
†47362 Cadiz 180 G5
47327 Cambridge City 2,407 G5
46917 Camden 618 D3
47108 Campbellsburg 695 E7
47224 Canaan 90 G7
47519 Cannelburg 152 C7
47520 Cannelton⊙ 2,373 D9
47837 Carbon 307 C5
47838 Carlisle 717 C7
46032 Carmel 18,272 E5
46114 Cartersburg 300 E5
46115 Carthage 886 F5
47927 Cates 125 C4
47928 Cayuga 1,258 C5
47016 Cedar Grove 217 H6
46303 Cedar Lake 8,754 C2
47521 Celestine 150 D8
†47842 Centenary 150 B5
†46901 Center 310 E4
47840 Centerpoint 242 C6
46116 Centerton 250 E5
47330 Centerville 2,284 H5
47929 Chalmers 554 D3
47610 Chandler 3,043 C8
47111 Charlestown 5,596 F8
46117 Charlottesville 300 F5
†47138 Chelsea 200 F7
46017 Chesterfield 2,701 F4
46304 Chesterton 8,531 D1
47611 Chrisney 537 C8
46723 Churubusco 1,638 G2
46034 Cicero 2,557 E4
47225 Clarksburg 300 G6
47930 Clarks Hill 653 D4
47130 Clarksville 15,164 F8
47841 Clay City 883 C6
46510 Claypool 464 F2
46118 Clayton 703 D5
47426 Clear Creek 200 E6
†46737 Clear Lake 301 H1
47226 Clifford 310 F6
47842 Clinton 5,267 C5
46120 Cloverdale 1,357 D5
†47834 Cloverland 175 C6
47427 Coal City 225 D6
47845 Coalmont 450 C6
46121 Coatesville 474 D5
47931 Colburn 300 D3
46035 Colfax 823 D4
47978 Collegeville 1,059 C3
46725 Columbia City⊙ 5,091 G2
47201 Columbus⊙ 30,614 E6
47331 Connersville⊙ 17,023 G5
46919 Converse 1,279 F3
47228 Cortland 175 F7
46730 Corunna 304 G2
47112 Corydon⊙ 2,724 E8
47932 Covington⊙ 2,883 C4
†47302 Cowan 428 G4
47114 Crandall 176 E8
47522 Crane D7
47933 Crawfordsville⊙ 13,325 D4
46732 Cromwell 458 F2
47229 Crothersville 1,747 F7
46307 Crown Point⊙ 16,455 C2
46511 Culver 1,601 E2
46229 Cumberland 3,375 E5
47612 Cynthiana 874 B8
47523 Dale 1,693 D8
47334 Daleville F4
47847 Dana 803 C5
46122 Danville⊙ 4,220 D5
47940 Darlington 811 D4
47618 Darmstadt 1,280 B8
47941 Dayton 781 D4
46733 Decatur⊙ 8,649 H3
47524 Decker 256 B7
†46917 Deer Creek 250 E3
46923 Delphi⊙ 3,042 D3
46310 Demotte 2,559 C2
46926 Denver 589 E3
47230 Deputy 200 F7
47302 Desoto 385 G4
47018 Dillsboro 1,038 G6
46513 Donaldson 320 E2
†47118 Doolittle Mills 200 D8
47335 Dublin 979 G5
47525 Dubois 550 D8
47848 Dugger 1,118 C6
†46304 Dune Acres 291 C1
47336 Dunkirk 3,180 G4
†46514 Dunlap 5,397 F1
47337 Dunreith 184 F5
47231 Dupont 392 G7
46311 Dyer 9,555 C1
†46074 Eagletown 306 E4
47942 Earl Park 469 C3
46312 East Chicago 39,786 C1
47019 East Enterprise 250 H7
†47370 East Germantown (Pershing) 438 G5
47338 Eaton 1,804 G4
47116 Eckerty 108 D8
47339 Economy 237 G5
†46011 Edgewood 2,215 F4
46124 Edinburgh 4,856 E6
47528 Edwardsport 459 C7
†47150 Edwardsville 700 F8
47613 Elberfeld 640 C8
47117 Elizabeth 178 F8
47232 Elizabethtown 603 F6
46514 Elkhart 41,305 F1
Elkhart‡ 137,330 F1
47429 Ellettsville 3,328 D6
47529 Elnora 756 C7
†47018 Elrod 200 G6
†47901 Elston 500 D4
46036 Elwood 10,867 F4
46125 Eminence 200 D5
47118 English⊙ 633 E8
46524 Etna Green 522 E2
†47928 Eugene 400 B5
*47701 Evansville⊙ 130,496 C9
Evansville‡ 309,408 C9
†47331 Everton 500 G5
46126 Fairland 950 F5
46928 Fairmount 3,286 F4
†47842 Fairview Park 1,545 C5
47850 Farmersburg 1,240 C6
47340 Farmland 1,560 G4
†47421 Fayetteville 180 D7
47532 Ferdinand 2,192 D8
46128 Fillmore 550 D5
46129 Finly 400 F5
46038 Fishers 2,008 E5
47234 Flat Rock 323 F6
46929 Flora 2,303 E3
47119 Floyds Knobs 500 F8
47851 Fontanet 325 C5
46039 Forest 400 E4
47648 Fort Branch 2,504 B8
46040 Fortville 2,787 F5
*46801 Fort Wayne⊙ 172,028 G2
Fort Wayne‡ 382,961 G2
47341 Fountain City 839 H5
46130 Fountaintown 225 F5
47944 Fowler⊙ 2,319 C3
46930 Fowlerton 300 F4
47946 Francesville 944 D3
47649 Francisco 612 B8
46041 Frankfort⊙ 15,168 E4
46131 Franklin⊙ 11,563 E6
46044 Frankton 2,080 F4
47120 Fredericksburg 233 E8
47431 Freedom 100 D6
47535 Freelandville 600 C7
47235 Freetown 600 E7
46737 Fremont 1,180 H1
47432 French Lick 2,265 D7
46931 Fulton 393 E3
†47119 Galena 1,186 F8
46932 Galveston 1,822 E3
46738 Garrett 4,751 G2
*46401 Gary 151,953 C1
Gary-Hammond-East Chicago‡ 642,781 C1
46933 Gas City 6,370 F4
47342 Gaston 1,150 G4
46740 Geneva 1,430 H3
47537 Gentryville 299 C8
47122 Georgetown 1,494 F8
46133 Glenwood 370 G5
†47567 Glezen 300 C8
46045 Goldsmith 235 E4

(continued on following page)

Agriculture, Industry and Resources

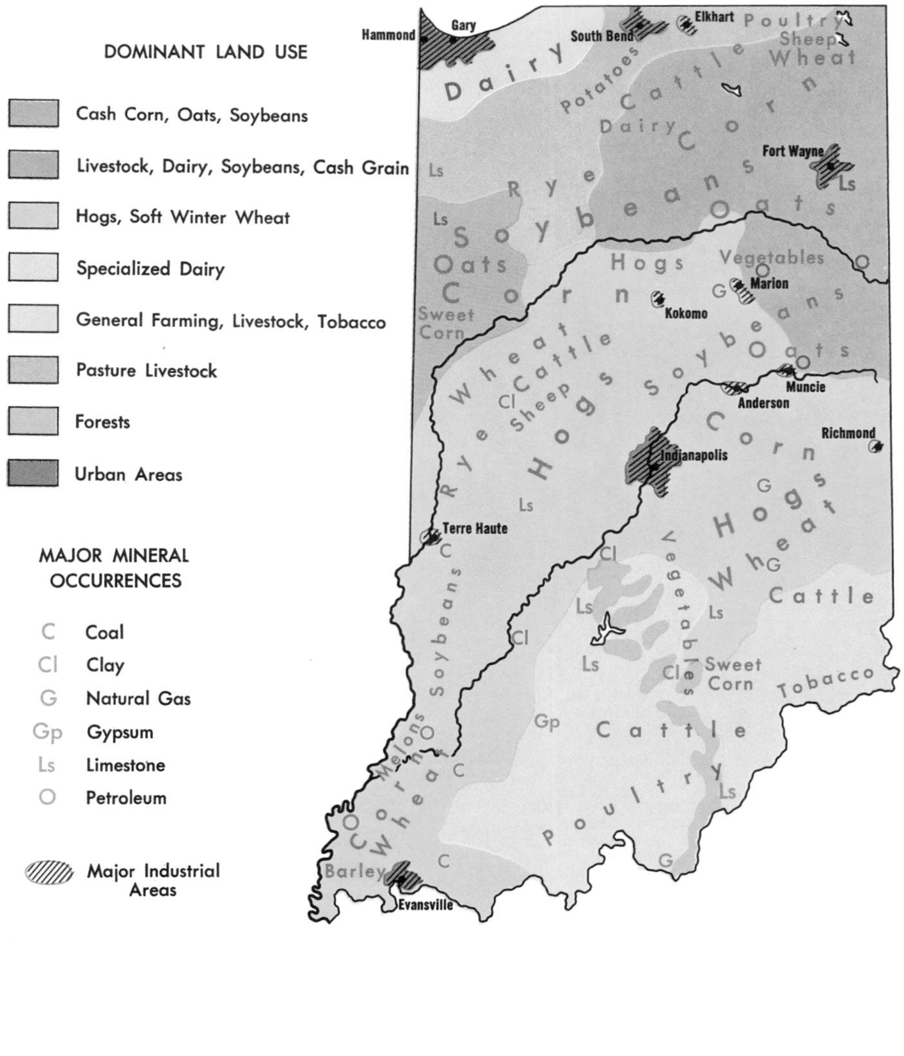
DOMINANT LAND USE
Cash Corn, Oats, Soybeans
Livestock, Dairy, Soybeans, Cash Grain
Hogs, Soft Winter Wheat
Specialized Dairy
General Farming, Livestock, Tobacco
Pasture Livestock
Forests
Urban Areas
MAJOR MINERAL OCCURRENCES
C Coal
Cl Clay
G Natural Gas
Gp Gypsum
Ls Limestone
O Petroleum
Major Industrial Areas
Hammond
Gary
South Bend
Elkhart
Fort Wayne
Marion
Kokomo
Anderson
Muncie
Richmond
Indianapolis
Terre Haute
Evansville
Poultry
Sheep
Wheat
Dairy
Potatoes
Cattle
Corn
Rye
Soybeans
Oats
Hogs
Vegetables
Sweet Corn
Tobacco
Melons
Barley

47948 Goodland 1,200 C3
46526 Goshen⊙ 19,665 F1
47433 Gosport 729 D6
46741 Grabill 658 H2
47615 Grandview 670 C9
46530 Granger 350 E1
46135 Greencastle⊙ 8,403 D5
†47025 Greendale 3,795 H6
46140 Greenfield⊙ 11,299 F5
47344 Greensboro 175 G5
47240 Greensburg⊙ 9,254 G6
47345 Greens Fork 426 H5
46936 Greentown 2,265 E4
47124 Greenville 537 F8
46142 Greenwood 19,327 E5
47616 Griffin 192 B8
46319 Griffith 17,026 C1
46144 Gwynneville 250 F5
47346 Hagerstown 1,950 G5
46742 Hamilton 587 H1
46532 Hamlet 738 D2
*46320 Hammond 93,714 B1
46340 Hanna 550 D2
47243 Hanover 4,054 F7
47125 Hardinsburg 298 E8
46743 Harlan 840 H2
47853 Harmony 613 C5
47434 Harrodsburg 400 D6
47348 Hartford City⊙ 7,622 G4
47244 Hartsville 379 F6
47617 Hatfield 800 C9
47639 Haubstadt 1,389 B8
†47546 Haysville 600 D8
47640 Hazleton 368 B8
46341 Hebron 2,696 C2
47436 Heltonville 400 E7
46937 Hemlock 300 F4
47126 Henryville 1,132 F7
46322 Highland 25,935 B1
47949 Hillsboro 561 C4
47854 Hillsdale 500 C5
46745 Hoagland 600 H3
46342 Hobart 22,987 C1
46047 Hobbs 200 F4
47541 Holland 683 C8
47023 Holton 487 G6
46146 Homer 235 F5
47246 Hope 2,185 F6
†46069 Hortonville 240 E4
46746 Howe 800 G1
46747 Hudson 447 G1
46552 Hudson Lake 1,347 D1
46748 Huntertown 1,265 G2
47542 Huntingburg 5,376 D8
46750 Huntington⊙ 16,202 G3
†46064 Huntsville 120 G4
47437 Huron 250 D7
47855 Hymera 1,054 C6
47950 Idaville 655 D3
*46201 Indianapolis (cap.)⊙
700,807 E5
Indianapolis‡ 1,166,929 E5
†46601 Indian Village 151 E1
46048 Ingalls 909 F5
47545 Ireland 600 C8
46147 Jamestown 924 D5
47438 Jasonville 2,497 C6
47546 Jasper⊙ 9,097 D8
47130 Jeffersonville⊙ 21,220 F8
†47565 Johnson 100 B8
†46074 Jolietville 300 E4
46938 Jonesboro 2,279 F4
47247 Jonesville 213 F6
46049 Kempton 410 E4
46755 Kendallville 7,299 G2
47351 Kennard 441 G5
47951 Kentland⊙ 1,936 C3
46939 Kewanna 711 E2
46759 Keystone 204 G3
46760 Kimmell 250 F2
47952 Kingman 566 C5
46345 Kingsbury 329 D1
46346 Kingsford Heights 1,618 D2
46050 Kirklin 662 E4
46148 Knightstown 2,325 F5
47857 Knightsville 763 C5
46534 Knox⊙ 3,674 D2
46901 Kokomo⊙ 47,808 E4
Kokomo‡ 103,715 E4
†46574 Koontz Lake 1,436 D2
46347 Kouts 1,619 C2
46348 La Crosse 713 D2
47954 Ladoga 1,151 D5
*47901 Lafayette⊙ 43,011 D4
Lafayette-West Lafayette‡
121,702 D4
46940 La Fontaine 946 F3
46761 Lagrange⊙ 2,164 F1
46941 Lagro 549 F3
†46157 Lake Hart 231 E5
†46703 Lake James 400 H1
46943 Laketon 500 F3
46349 Lake Village 900 C2
46536 Lakeville 629 E1
46944 Landess 150 F3
47136 Lanesville 570 E8
46763 Laotto 361 G2
46537 Lapaz 651 E2
46051 Lapel 1,881 F4
46350 LaPorte⊙ 21,796 D1
46764 Larwill 286 F2
47024 Laurel 819 G6
46226 Lawrence 25,591 E5
47025 Lawrenceburg⊙ 4,403 H6
47137 Leavenworth 356 E8
46052 Lebanon⊙ 11,456 D4
46538 Leesburg 629 F2
46945 Leiters Ford 280 E2
46765 Leo 500 G2
47551 Leopold 175 D8
46355 Leroy 400 C2
†47240 Letts 247 F6
47352 Lewisville 577 G5
47138 Lexington F7
47353 Liberty⊙ 1,844 H5
46766 Liberty Center 275 G3
46946 Liberty Mills 200 F2

46767 Ligonier 3,134 F2
47955 Linden 700 D4
46769 Linn Grove 175 H3
47441 Linton 6,315 C6
†46755 Lisbon 200 G2
47139 Little York 150 F7
46149 Lizton 456 D5
46947 Logansport⊙ 17,731 E3
†46360 Long Beach 2,262 D1
47553 Loogootee 3,100 D7
47354 Losantville 306 G4
46356 Lowell 5,827 C2
46950 Lucerne 135 E3
†46601 Lydick E1
†47874 Lyford 400 C5
47355 Lynn 1,250 H4
47619 Lynnville 566 C8
47443 Lyons 782 C7
46951 Macy 282 E3
47250 Madison⊙ 12,472 G7
47555 Magnet 75 D8
†47001 Manchester 250 H6
46150 Manilla 350 F5
†47872 Mansfield 200 C5
†47443 Marco 150 C7
47140 Marengo 892 E8
47556 Mariah Hill 300 D8
†46176 Marietta 234 F6
46952 Marion⊙ 35,874 F3
46770 Markle 975 G3
46056 Markleville 427 F5
47859 Marshall 413 C5
46151 Martinsville⊙ 11,311 D6
46957 Matthews 745 F4
46154 Maxwell 300 F5
46055 McCordsville 600 F5
47860 Mecca 482 C5
47957 Medaryville 731 D2
47260 Medora 853 E7
47958 Mellott 294 C4
47143 Memphis 300 F8
46539 Mentone 973 E2
47861 Merom 360 B6
46410 Merrillville 27,677 C2
47030 Metamora 350 G6
†46703 Metz 200 H1
46958 Mexico 850 E3
46959 Miami 350 E3
†49117 Michiana Shores 464 D1
46360 Michigan City 36,850 C1
46057 Michigantown 453 E4
46540 Middlebury 1,665 F1
47356 Middletown 2,978 F4
47445 Midland 250 C6
47031 Milan 1,566 G6
46542 Milford 1,153 F2
†47240 Milford 177 F6
46543 Millersburg 809 F1
47261 Millhousen 214 G6
47145 Milltown 1,006 E8
†47362 Millville 275 G5
46156 Milroy 750 G6
47357 Milton 729 G5
46544 Mishawaka 40,201 E1
47446 Mitchell 4,641 E7
47358 Modoc 243 G4
46771 Mongo 225 G1
47959 Monon 1,540 D3
46772 Monroe 739 H3
47557 Monroe City 569 C7
46773 Monroeville 1,372 H3
46157 Monrovia 800 E5
46960 Monterey 236 D2
47862 Montezuma 1,352 C5
47558 Montgomery 390 C7
47960 Monticello⊙ 5,162 D3
47962 Montmorenci 300 D4
47359 Montpelier 1,995 G3
47360 Mooreland 479 G5
47032 Moores Hill 566 G6
46158 Mooresville 5,349 E5
46160 Morgantown 897 E6
47963 Morocco 1,348 C3
47033 Morris 350 G6
46161 Morristown 989 F5
†47327 Mount Auburn 192 G5
47964 Mount Ayr 207 C3
47361 Mount Summit 357 G4
47620 Mount Vernon⊙ 7,656 B9
46058 Mulberry 1,225 D4
*47302 Muncie⊙ 77,216 G4
Muncie‡ G4
46321 Munster 20,671 B1
47147 Nabb 150 F7
47034 Napoleon 246 G6
46550 Nappanee 4,694 F2
47448 Nashville⊙ 705 E6
†47421 Needmore 200 E7
47150 New Albany⊙ 37,103 F8
47449 Newberry 246 C7
47630 Newburgh 2,906 C9
46552 New Carlisle 1,439 E1
47362 New Castle⊙ 20,056 G5
†46342 New Chicago 3,284 C1
47863 New Goshen 500 B5
47631 New Harmony 945 B8
46774 New Haven 6,714 H2
47366 New Lisbon 300 G5
†46979 New London 200 E4
47965 New Market 608 D5
46163 New Palestine 749 F5
46553 New Paris 1,062 F2
†47165 New Pekin 1,125 F7
47263 New Point 296 G6
47966 Newport⊙ 704 C5
†47106 New Providence
(Borden) 384 F8
47967 New Richmond 403 D4
47968 New Ross 306 D5
†46173 New Salem 200 G5
47161 New Salisbury 350 E8
47632 Newtonville 136 D8
47969 Newtown 277 C4
47035 New Trenton 200 H6
47162 New Washington 800 F7
46961 New Waverly 162 E3
46184 New Whiteland 4,502 E5

†46122 New Winchester 180 D5
46060 Noblesville⊙ 12,056 F4
46366 North Judson 1,653 D2
46554 North Liberty 1,211 E1
46962 North Manchester 5,998 F3
46165 North Salem 581 D5
47805 North Terre Haute C5
47265 North Vernon 5,768 F6
46555 North Webster 709 F2
†47960 Norway 300 D3
46556 Notre Dame E1
†47331 Nulltown 235 G5
46965 Oakford 285 E4
47660 Oakland City 3,301 C8
47561 Oaktown 776 C7
47367 Oakville 220 G4
47562 Odon 1,463 C7
†46401 Ogden Dunes 1,489 C1
47036 Oldenburg 770 G6
47451 Oolitic 1,495 E7
†47343 Orange 200 G5
46063 Orestes 539 F4
46776 Orland 424 G1
47452 Orleans 2,161 D7
46561 Osceola 1,990 E1
47037 Osgood 1,554 G6
46777 Ossian 1,945 G3
46367 Otis 250 D1
47163 Otisco 425 F7
47970 Otterbein 1,118 C4
47564 Otwell 600 C8
47453 Owensburg 785 D7
47665 Owensville 1,261 B8
47971 Oxford 1,327 C3
†46508 Palestine 800 F2
47164 Palmyra 692 E8
47454 Paoli⊙ 3,637 E7
46166 Paragon 538 D6
47368 Parker City 1,414 G4
47666 Patoka 832 B8
47455 Patricksburg 250 D6
47038 Patriot 265 H7
47865 Paxton 200 C6
47165 Pekin 950 E7
46064 Pendleton 2,130 F5
47369 Pennville 805 G4
†46011 Perkinsville 175 F4
47974 Perrysville 532 C4
47370 Pershing 438 G5
†46975 Pershing 425 E2
46970 Peru⊙ 13,764 E3
47567 Petersburg⊙ 2,987 C7
46778 Petroleum 212 G3
46562 Pierceton 1,086 F2
47866 Pimento 150 C6
†46350 Pine Lake 1,676 D1
47975 Pine Village 257 C4
46167 Pittsboro 891 D5
†46923 Pittsburg 175 D3
46168 Plainfield 9,191 E5
47568 Plainville 556 C7
46779 Pleasant Lake 800 H1
46563 Plymouth⊙ 7,693 E2
47868 Poland 230 C6
46781 Poneto 250 G3
46368 Portage 27,409 C1
46304 Porter 2,988 C1
47371 Portland⊙ 7,074 H4
47633 Poseyville 1,247 B8
†46360 Pottawattamie Park 284 C1
47869 Prairie Creek 275 C6
47870 Prairieton 200 C6
46782 Preble 150 H3
†46164 Princes Lakes 937 E6
47670 Princeton⊙ 8,976 B8
46170 Putnamville 250 D6
47456 Quincy 250 D6
47573 Ragsdale 135 C7
46737 Ray 200 H1
†47274 Reddington 400 F6
46171 Reelsville 210 D5
47977 Remington 1,268 C3
47978 Rensselaer⊙ 4,944 C3
47980 Reynolds 632 D3
47634 Richland 500 C9
47374 Richmond⊙ 41,349 H5
47380 Ridgeville 933 G4
47871 Riley 269 C6
47040 Rising Sun⊙ 2,478 H7
46172 Roachdale 958 D5
46974 Roann 548 F3
46783 Roanoke 891 G3
46975 Rochester⊙ 5,050 E2
46977 Rockfield 300 D3
47635 Rockport⊙ 2,590 C9
47872 Rockville⊙ 2,785 C5
46371 Rolling Prairie 550 D1
47574 Rome 50 D9
46784 Rome City 1,319 G1
47981 Romney 250 D4
47874 Rosedale 744 C5
†46601 Roseland 832 E1
†46310 Roselawn 200 C2
46065 Rossville 1,148 D4
46978 Royal Center 908 E3
†47302 Royerton 300 G4
46173 Rushville⊙ 6,113 G5
46175 Russellville 376 D5
46975 Russiaville 973 E4
47575 Saint Anthony 470 D8
47875 Saint Bernice 500 C5
46785 Saint Joe 546 H2
46383 Saint John 3,974 C2
46373 Saint Leon 515 H6
47876 Saint Mary-of-
the-Woods 920 B6
†46556 Saint Marys E1
47577 Saint Meinrad 910 D8
47272 Saint Paul 976 F6
†47012 Saint Peter 175 H6
†47620 Saint Philip 400 B9
†47638 Saint Wendel 250 B8
47167 Salem⊙ 5,290 E7
47578 Sandborn 576 C7
†47401 Sanders 65 E6
46374 San Pierre 325 D2
47579 Santa Claus 514 D8

47382 Saratoga 338 H4
†47283 Sardinia 133 F6
46375 Schererville 13,209 C2
46376 Schneider 364 C2
47580 Schnellville 250 D8
47273 Scipio 200 F6
46066 Scircleville 125 E4
47170 Scottsburg⊙ 5,068 F7
47878 Seelyville 1,374 C6
47172 Sellersburg 3,211 F8
47383 Selma 1,056 G4
47274 Seymour 15,050 F7
46068 Sharpsville 617 E4
47879 Shelburn 1,259 C6
46377 Shelby 700 C2
46176 Shelbyville⊙ 14,989 F6
47880 Shepardsville 325 B5
46069 Sheridan 2,200 E4
†47338 Shideler 275 G4
46565 Shipshewana 466 F1
47384 Shirley 919 F5
†46797 Shirley City (Woodburn)
1,002 H2
47581 Shoals⊙ 967 D7
46566 Sidney 194 F2
46982 Silver Lake 576 F2
46983 Sims 250 F3
†46142 Smith Valley E5
47458 Smithville 500 D6
46984 Somerset 350 F3
47683 Somerville 340 C8
*46601 South Bend⊙ 109,727 E1
South Bend‡ 280,772 E1
46786 South Milford 270 G1
†46201 Southport 2,266 E5
46787 South Whitley 1,575 F2
†47355 Spartanburg 201 H4
47172 Speed 800 F8
46224 Speedway 12,641 E5
†47808 Spelterville 200 C5
47460 Spencer⊙ 2,732 D6
46788 Spencerville 400 G2
47385 Spiceland 940 F5
†47374 Spring Grove 469 H5
†46140 Spring Lake 236 F5
47386 Springport 221 G4
47462 Springville 279 D7
47584 Spurgeon 250 C8
47463 Stanford 200 D6
46985 Star City 351 D3
47982 State Line 233 C4
47861 Staunton 607 C6
47585 Stendal 175 C8
47636 Stewartsville 225 B8
46180 Stilesville 350 D5
46351 Stillwell 225 D1
47464 Stinesville 227 D6
47983 Stockwell 310 D4
47387 Straughn 331 G5
46789 Stroh 350 G1
47882 Sullivan⊙ 4,774 C6
47388 Sulphur Springs 345 G4
46379 Sumava Resorts 300 C2
46070 Summitville 1,085 F4
47041 Sunman 924 G6
46987 Sweetser 944 F3
47465 Switz City 300 C6
46567 Syracuse 2,579 F2
47280 Taylorsville 1,247 F6
47586 Tell City 8,704 D9
47637 Tennyson 331 C8
*47801 Terre Haute⊙ 61,125 C6
Terre Haute‡ 176,583 C6
46381 Thayer 350 C2
46071 Thorntown 1,468 D4
†46975 Tiosa 100 E2
46570 Tippecanoe 320 E2
46072 Tipton⊙ 5,004 E4
46571 Topeka 876 F1
†46360 Town of Pines 962 D1
46181 Trafalgar 466 E6
†46360 Trail Creek 2,581 D1
†46725 Tri Lakes 1,356 G2
47588 Troy 550 D9
46988 Twelve Mile 240 E3
46572 Tyner 245 E2
47177 Underwood 550 F7
47390 Union City 3,908 H4
46791 Uniondale 303 G3
46382 Union Mills 650 D2
47468 Unionville 225 E6
47884 Universal 428 C5
46989 Upland 3,335 F4
46990 Urbana 400 F3
†47130 Utica 501 F8
47281 Vallonia 550 E7
46383 Valparaiso⊙ 22,247 C2
46991 Van Buren 935 F3
47987 Veedersburg 2,261 C4
47590 Velpen 375 C8
47282 Vernon⊙ 329 F7
47042 Versailles⊙ 1,560 G6
47043 Vevay⊙ 1,343 G7
†47441 Vicksburg 175 C6
†47170 Vienna 175 F7
47591 Vincennes⊙ 20,857 C7
46992 Wabash⊙ 12,985 F3
47638 Wadesville 450 B8
46573 Wakarusa 1,281 F1
46182 Waldron 850 F6
†47201 Walesboro 214 F6
46574 Walkerton 2,051 E2
†46802 Wallen 945 G2
46994 Walton 1,202 E3
46390 Wanatah 879 D2
46792 Warren 1,254 G3
46580 Warsaw⊙ 10,647 F2
47501 Washington⊙ 11,325 C7
46793 Waterloo 1,951 G2
†47130 Watson 200 F8
47989 Waveland 559 D5
46794 Wawaka 320 F2
47990 Waynetown 915 C4
47392 Webster 350 H5
47469 West Baden Springs 796 D7
†47353 West College Corner 614 H5
46074 Westfield 2,783 E4

Topography

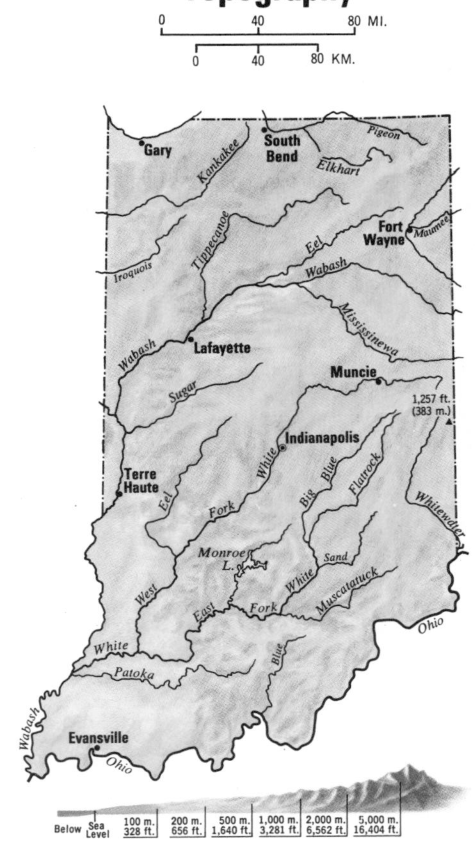

†45030 West Harrison 328 H6
47906 West Lafayette 21,247 D4
47991 West Lebanon 946 C4
46995 West Middleton 327 E4
47596 Westphalia 300 C7
47992 Westpoint 375 C4
47283 Westport 1,450 F6
47885 West Terre Haute 2,806 B6
46391 Westville 2,887 D1
46392 Wheatfield 755 C2
47597 Wheatland 532 C7
46393 Wheeler 540 C1
†47342 Wheeling 180 G4
46184 Whiteland 1,956 E5
46075 Whitestown 497 E5
46394 Whiting 5,630 C1
46186 Wilkinson 493 F5
47470 Williams 350 D7
47993 Williamsport⊙ 1,747 C4
46996 Winamac⊙ 2,370 D2
47394 Winchester⊙ 5,659 G4
46076 Windfall 911 F4
47994 Wingate 373 C4
46590 Winona Lake 2,827 F2
47598 Winslow 1,017 C8
47995 Wolcott 923 C3
46795 Wolcottville 890 G1
46796 Wolflake 230 F2
46797 Woodburn 1,002 H2
†46624 Woodland 400 E1
47471 Worthington 1,574 C6
46595 Wyatt 250 E1
†47630 Yankeetown 250 C9
46798 Yoder 250 G3
47396 Yorktown 3,945 G4
46998 Young America 259 E3
†47808 Youngstown 350 C6
46799 Zanesville 575 G3
46077 Zionsville 3,948 E5

OTHER FEATURES

Anderson (riv.) D8
Bass (lake) D2
Beanblossom (creek) D6
Big (creek) B8
Big Blue (riv.) F5
Big Pine (creek) C3
Big Raccoon (creek) C5
Big Walnut (creek) D5
Blue (riv.) E8
Brookville (lake) G6
Buck (creek) E8
Busseron (creek) C7
Camp (creek) E6
Cedar (creek) G2
Clifty (creek) F6
Coal (creek) C4
Crooked (creek) D2
Cypress (pond) B8
Deer (creek) E3
Deer (creek) D5
Eagle (creek) E4
Eel (riv.) C6
Eel (riv.) F3
Elkhart (riv.) F1
Fawn (riv.) G1
Flatrock (creek) F5
Fort Benjamin Harrison E5
Freeman (lake) D3
Geist (res.) F5
George Rogers Clark Nat'l Hist.
Park B7
Graham (creek) F7
Grissom A.F.B. 4,676 E3
Huntington (lake) F3
Indian (creek) E8
Indian (creek) D6
Indiana Dunes Nat'l Lakeshore C1
Iroquois (riv.) B3
Jefferson Proving Ground G7
Kankakee (riv.) C2
Lemon (lake) E6
Lincoln Boyhood Nat'l Mem. C8
Little (riv.) G3
Little Elkhart (riv.) F1
Little Pigeon (creek) C9
Little Vermilion (riv.) B5
Lost (riv.) D7
Maria (creek) C7
Maumee (riv.) H2
Maxinkuckee (lake) E2
Michigan (lake) C1
Mill (creek) D5
Mississinewa (lake) F3
Mississinewa (riv.) F3
Monroe (lake) E6
Morse (res.) E4
Muscatatuck (riv.) E7
Ohio (riv.) B9
Patoka (riv.) C8
Pigeon (creek) C8
Pigeon (riv.) F1
Pipe (creek) F4
Prairie (creek) C7
Richland (creek) D6
Saint Joseph (riv.) E1
Saint Joseph (riv.) H2
Saint Marys (lake) H3
Saint Marys (riv.) H3
Salamonie (lake) F3
Salamonie (riv.) G4
Salt (creek) E6
Sand (creek) F6
Shafer (lake) D3
Silver (creek) F8
Sugar (creek) C5
Sugar (creek) F5
Sugar (creek) B3
Tippecanoe (riv.) E2
Vermilion (riv.) B4
Vernon Fork (creek) F7
Wabash (riv.) B7
Wawasee (lake) F2
White (riv.) B8
White, East Fork (riv.) C7
White, West Fork (riv.) C7
Whitewater (riv.) H6
Wildcat (creek) E4

⊙County seat.
‡Population of metropolitan area.
† Zip of nearest p.o. * Multiple zips.

COUNTIES

Adair 9,509 .... E6	Clinton 57,122 .... M5	Ida 8,908 .... C4
Adams 5,731 .... D6	Crawford 18,935 .... C4	Iowa 15,429 .... J5
Allamakee 15,108 .... L2	Dallas 29,513 .... E5	Jackson 22,503 .... M4
Appanoose 15,511 .... H7	Davis 9,104 .... J7	Jasper 36,425 .... G5
Audubon 8,559 .... D5	Decatur 9,794 .... F7	Jefferson 16,316 .... K6
Benton 23,649 .... J4	Delaware 18,933 .... L4	Johnson 81,717 .... K5
Black Hawk 137,961 ..... J4	Des Moines 46,203 ...... L7	Jones 20,401 .... L4
Boone 26,184 .... F5	Dickinson 15,629 .... C2	Keokuk 12,921 .... J6
Bremer 24,820 .... J3	Dubuque 93,745 .... M4	Kossuth 21,891 .... E2
Buchanan 22,900 .... K4	Emmet 13,336 .... D2	Lee 43,106 .... L7
Buena Vista 20,774 ...... C3	Fayette 25,488 .... K3	Linn 169,775 .... K4
Butler 17,668 .... H3	Floyd 19,597 .... H2	Louisa 12,055 .... L6
Calhoun 13,542 .... D4	Franklin 13,036 .... G3	Lucas 10,313 .... G6
Carroll 22,951 .... D4	Fremont 9,401 .... B7	Lyon 12,896 .... A2
Cass 16,932 .... D6	Greene 12,119 .... E5	Madison 12,597 .... E6
Cedar 18,635 .... L5	Grundy 14,366 .... H4	Mahaska 22,867 .... H6
Cerro Gordo 48,458 ..... G2	Guthrie 11,983 .... D5	Marion 29,669 .... G6
Cherokee 16,238 .... B3	Hamilton 17,862 .... F4	Marshall 41,652 .... G4
Chickasaw 15,437 .... J2	Hancock 13,833 .... F2	Mills 13,406 .... B6
Clarke 8,612 .... F6	Hardin 21,776 .... G4	Mitchell 12,329 .... H2
Clay 19,576 .... C2	Harrison 16,348 .... B5	Monona 11,692 .... B4
Clayton 21,098 .... L3	Henry 18,890 .... L6	Monroe 9,209 .... H7
	Howard 11,114 .... J2	Montgomery 13,413 ..... C6
	Humboldt 12,246 .... E3	Muscatine 40,436 .... L5

O'Brien 16,972 .... B2	Winnebago 13,010 .... F2
Osceola 8,371 .... B2	Winneshiek 21,876 .... K2
Page 19,063 .... C7	Woodbury 100,884 .... B4
Palo Alto 12,721 .... D2	Worth 9,075 .... G2
Plymouth 24,743 .... A3	Wright 16,319 .... F3
Pocahontas 11,369 ...... D3	
Polk 303,170 .... F5	
Pottawattamie 86,561 .. B6	
Poweshiek 19,306 .... H5	
Ringgold 6,112 .... E7	
Sac 14,118 .... C4	
Scott 160,022 .... M5	
Shelby 15,043 .... C5	
Sioux 30,813 .... A2	
Story 72,326 .... G4	
Tama 19,533 .... H4	
Taylor 8,353 .... D7	
Union 13,858 .... E7	
Van Buren 8,626 .... K7	
Wapello 40,241 .... J6	
Warren 34,878 .... F6	
Washington 20,141 ...... K6	
Wayne 8,199 .... G7	
Webster 45,953 .... E4	

CITIES and TOWNS

Zip	Name/Pop.	Key
50601	Ackley 1,900	G3
50002	Adair 883	D6
50003	Adel⊙ 2,846	E5
50830	Afton 985	E6
52530	Agency 657	J7
52201	Ainsworth 547	K6
51001	Akron 1,517	A3
52531	Albia⊙ 4,184	H6
50005	Albion 739	H4
52202	Alburnett 411	K4
50006	Alden 953	G4
50511	Algona⊙ 6,289	E2
50007	Alleman 307	F5
50008	Allerton 670	G7

Zip	Name/Pop.	Key
50602	Allison⊙ 1,132	H3
51002	Alta 1,720	C3
50603	Alta Vista 314	J2
51003	Alton 986	A3
50009	Altoona 5,764	G5
51230	Alvord 246	A2
52203	Amana 300	K5
50010	Ames 45,775	F4
52205	Anamosa⊙ 4,958	L4
52030	Andrew 349	M4
50020	Anita 1,153	D6
50021	Ankeny 15,429	F5
51004	Anthon 687	B4
50604	Aplington 1,027	H3
51430	Arcadia 454	C4
50606	Arlington 498	K3
51431	Arthur 288	C4
†52001	Asbury 2,017	M4
52720	Atalissa 360	L5
52206	Atkins 678	K4
50022	Atlantic⊙ 7,789	D6

51433 Auburn 320 ....D4
50025 Audubon⊙ 2,841.......D5
51005 Aurelia 1,143.........C3
50607 Aurora 248..............K3
51521 Avoca 1,650............C6
50515 Ayrshire 243...........D2
50516 Badger 653.............E3
50026 Bagley 370.............E5
50517 Bancroft 1,082.........E2
50027 Barnes City 266........H6
52533 Batavia 525............J7
51006 Battle Creek 919.......B4
50028 Baxter 951.............G5
50029 Bayard 637.............D5
52534 Beacon 530.............H6
50833 Bedford⊙ 1,692.........D7
52208 Belle Plaine 2,903.....J5
52031 Bellevue 2,450.........M4
50421 Belmond 2,505..........F3
52721 Bennett 458............L5
50032 Berwick 600............G5
52722 Bettendorf 27,381......N5
52535 Birmingham 410.........K7
50034 Blairsburg 288.........F4

52209 Blairstown 695.........J5
52536 Blakesburg 404.........H7
51523 Blencoe 247............A5
50836 Blockton 280...........D7
52537 Bloomfield⊙ 2,849......J7
52726 Blue Grass 1,377.......M5
50519 Bode 406...............E3
52620 Bonaparte 489..........K7
50035 Bondurant 1,283........G5
50036 Boone⊙ 12,602..........F4
50040 Boxholm 267............E4
51234 Boyden 708.............B2
52210 Brandon 337............K4
51436 Breda 502..............C4
50837 Bridgewater 233........D6
52540 Brighton 804...........K6
50611 Bristow 252............H3
50423 Britt 2,185............F2
51007 Bronson 289............A4
52211 Brooklyn 1,509.........J5
52728 Buffalo 1,569..........M6
50424 Buffalo Center 1,233...F2
52601 Burlington⊙ 29,529.....L7
50522 Burt 689...............E2

AREA 56,275 sq. mi. (145,752 sq. km.)
POPULATION 2,913,808
CAPITAL Des Moines
LARGEST CITY Des Moines
HIGHEST POINT (Osceola Co.) 1670 ft. (509 m.)
SETTLED IN 1788
ADMITTED TO UNION December 28, 1846
POPULAR NAME Hawkeye State
STATE FLOWER Wild Rose
STATE BIRD Eastern Goldfinch

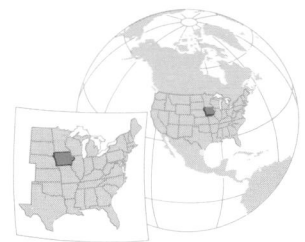

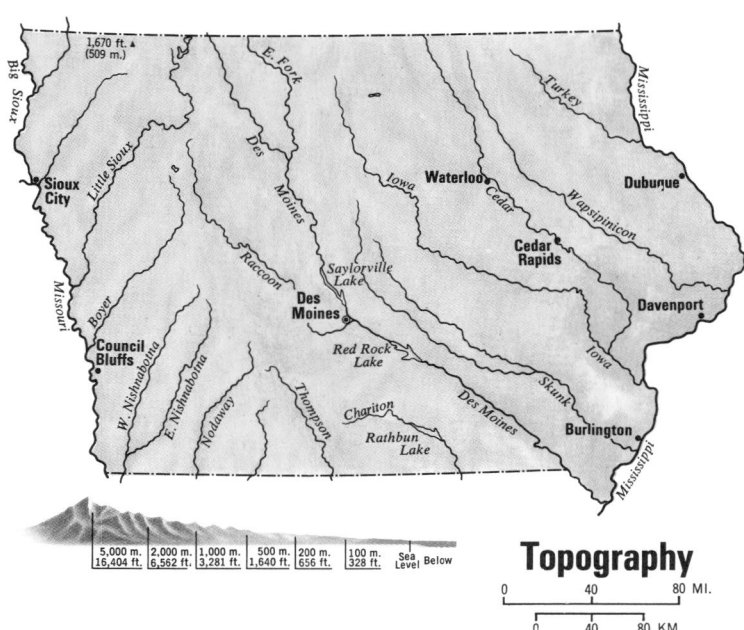

Topography

50044 Bussey 579.................H6
52729 Calamus 452................M5
50523 Callender 446..............E4
52132 Calmar 1,053...............K2
52730 Camanche 4,725.............N5
50046 Cambridge 732..............G5
52542 Cantril 299................J7
50047 Carlisle 3,073.............G6
51401 Carroll⊙ 9,705.............D4
51525 Carson 716.................C6
†68101 Carter Lake 3,438.........B6
52033 Cascade 1,912..............L4
50048 Casey 473..................D5
50613 Cedar Falls 36,322.........H3
*52401 Cedar Rapids⊙ 110,243......K5
  Cedar Rapids‡ 169,775.....K5
52213 Center Point 1,591.........K4
52544 Centerville⊙ 6,558.........H7
52214 Central City 1,067.........K4
50049 Chariton⊙ 4,987............G6
50616 Charles City⊙ 8,778........H2
52731 Charlotte 442..............M5
52215 Chelsea 376................J5
51012 Cherokee⊙ 7,004............B3
50050 Churdan 540................D4
52549 Cincinnati 598.............G7
52216 Clarence 1,001.............M5
51632 Clarinda⊙ 5,458............C7
50525 Clarion⊙ 3,060.............F3
50619 Clarksville 1,424..........H3
50840 Clearfield 433.............D7
50428 Clear Lake 7,458...........G2
51014 Cleghorn 275...............B3
52135 Clermont 602...............K3
52732 Clinton⊙ 32,828............N5
50318 Clive 6,064................F5
52217 Clutier 249................J4
52218 Coggon 639.................L4
51636 Coin 316...................C7
52035 Colesburg 463..............L3
50054 Colfax 2,234...............G5
51637 College Springs 307........C7
50055 Collins 451................G5
50056 Colo 808...................G4
52737 Columbus City 367..........L6
52738 Columbus Junction 1,429....L6
52739 Conesville 301.............L6
50631 Conrad 1,133...............H4
52220 Conroy 250.................J5
50058 Coon Rapids 1,448..........D5
52241 Coralville 7,687...........K5
50841 Corning⊙ 1,939.............D7
51016 Correctionville 935........B4
50430 Corwith 480................F3
50060 Corydon⊙ 1,818.............G7
50431 Coulter 264................G3
51501 Council Bluffs⊙ 56,449.....B6
52621 Crawfordsville 290.........K6
51526 Crescent 547...............B6
52136 Cresco⊙ 3,860..............J2
50801 Creston⊙ 8,429.............E6
50432 Crystal Lake 314...........F2
50843 Cumberland 351.............D6

51018 Cushing 270................B4
50529 Dakota City⊙ 1,072.........E3
50062 Dallas 451.................G6
50063 Dallas Center 1,360........E5
51019 Danbury 492................B4
52623 Danville 994...............L7
*52801 Davenport⊙ 103,264.........M5
  Davenport-Rock
  Island-Moline‡ 383.958 M5
50065 Davis City 327.............F7
50530 Dayton 941.................E4
52101 Decorah⊙ 7,991.............K2
52222 Deep River 323.............J5
51527 Dedham 321.................D5
52223 Delhi 511..................L4
51441 Deloit 345.................C4
52550 Delta 482..................J6
51442 Denison⊙ 6,675.............C4
52624 Denmark 480................L7
50622 Denver 1,647...............J3
*50301 Des Moines
  (cap.)⊙ 191,003...........G5
  Des Moines‡ 338,048.......G5
50069 De Soto 1,035..............E5
50623 Dewar 230..................J3
52742 De Witt 4,512..............N5
50070 Dexter 678.................E5
50845 Diagonal 362...............E7
51333 Dickens 289................C2
50624 Dike 987...................H4
52745 Dixon 312..................M5
52746 Donahue 289................M5
52625 Donnellson 972.............K7
51235 Doon 537...................A2
52551 Douds 425..................J7
51528 Dow City 616...............B5
50071 Dows 771...................F3
52001 Dubuque⊙ 62,321............M3
  Dubuque‡ 93,745...........M3
50625 Dumont 815.................H3
50532 Duncombe 504...............E4
50626 Dunkerton 718..............J3
51529 Dunlap 1,374...............B5
52747 Durant 1,583...............M5
52040 Dyersville 3,825...........L3
52224 Dysart 1,355...............J4
50533 Eagle Grove 4,324..........F3
50072 Earlham 1,140..............E6
51530 Earling 520................C5
52041 Earlville 844..............L4
50535 Early 670..................C4
52553 Eddyville 1,116............H6
52042 Edgewood 900...............K3
52554 Eldon 1,255................J7
50627 Eldora⊙ 3,063..............G4
52748 Eldridge 3,279.............M5
52141 Elgin 702..................K3
52043 Elkader⊙ 1,688.............L3
50073 Elkhart 256................F5
51531 Elk Horn 746...............C5
†50700 Elk Run Heights 1,186......J4
51532 Elliott 493................C6

50075 Ellsworth 480..............F4
50628 Elma 714...................J2
52227 Ely 425....................K5
51533 Emerson 502................C6
50536 Emmetsburg⊙ 4,621..........D2
52045 Epworth 1,380..............M4
51638 Essex 1,001................C7
51334 Estherville⊙ 7,518.........D2
50707 Evansdale 4,798............J4
51338 Everly 796.................C2
50076 Exira 978..................D5
50629 Fairbank 980...............K3
52228 Fairfax 683................K5
52556 Fairfield⊙ 9,428...........J6
52046 Farley 1,287...............L4
52047 Farmersburg 276............L3
52626 Farmington 869.............K7
50538 Farnhamville 461...........D4
51639 Farragut 603...............C7
52142 Fayette 1,515..............K3
50539 Fenton 394.................E2
50434 Fertile 372................G2
50435 Floyd 408..................H2
50540 Fonda 863..................D3
50846 Fontanelle 805.............E6
50436 Forest City⊙ 4,270.........F2
52144 Fort Atkinson 374..........J2
50501 Fort Dodge⊙ 29,423.........E3
52627 Fort Madison⊙ 13,520.......L7
51340 Fostoria 261...............C2
50630 Fredericksburg 1,075.......J3
50631 Fredericka 223.............J3
52561 Fremont 730................H6
52749 Fruitland 461..............L6
51020 Galva 420..................C3
50103 Garden Grove 297...........F7
52049 Garnavillo 723.............L3
50438 Garner⊙ 2,908..............F2
52229 Garrison 411...............J4
50632 Garwin 626.................H4
51237 George 1,241...............B2
50105 Gilbert 805................F5
50634 Gilbertville 740...........J4
50106 Gilman 642.................H5
50541 Gilmore City 626...........D3
50635 Gladbrook 970..............H4
51534 Glenwood⊙ 5,280............B6
51443 Glidden 1,076..............D4
50542 Goldfield 789..............F3
52750 Goose Lake 274.............N5
50543 Gowrie 1,089...............E4
51342 Graettinger 923............D2
50440 Grafton 255................G2
50107 Grand Junction 970.........E4
52751 Grand Mound 674............M5
52752 Grandview 473..............L6
50109 Granger 619................F5
51022 Granville 336..............B3
50848 Gravity 245................D7
52050 Greeley 313................L3
50636 Greene 1,332...............H3
50849 Greenfield⊙ 2,243..........E6
50111 Grimes 1,973...............F5
50112 Grinnell 8,868.............H5

(continued on following page)

Agriculture, Industry and Resources

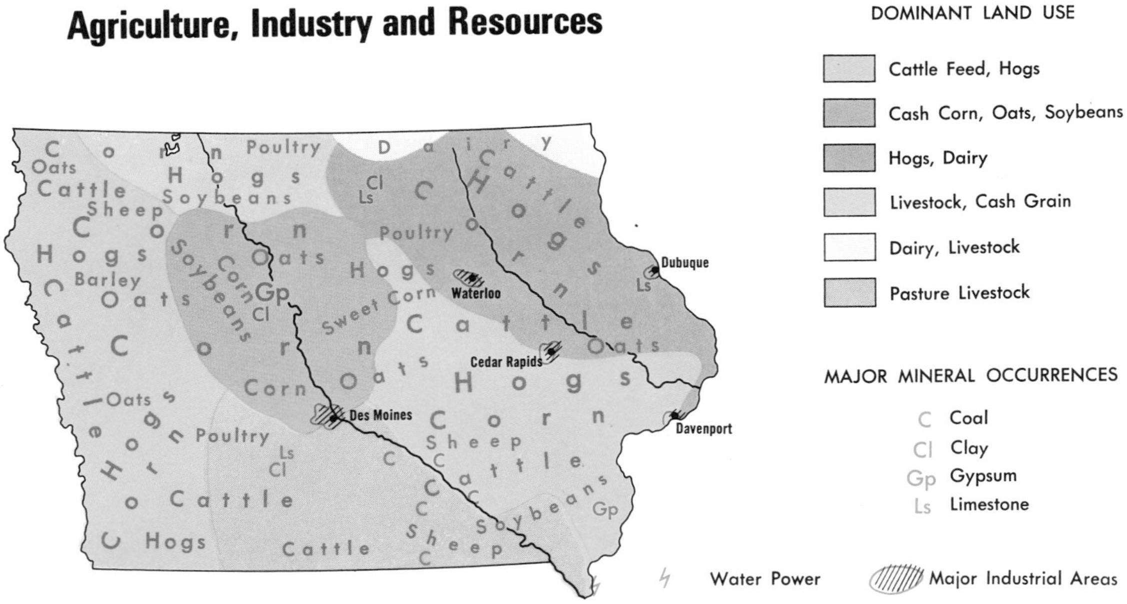

DOMINANT LAND USE
Cattle Feed, Hogs
Cash Corn, Oats, Soybeans
Hogs, Dairy
Livestock, Cash Grain
Dairy, Livestock
Pasture Livestock
MAJOR MINERAL OCCURRENCES
C Coal
Cl Clay
Gp Gypsum
Ls Limestone
Water Power
Major Industrial Areas
Dubuque
Waterloo
Cedar Rapids
Des Moines
Davenport

51535 Griswold 1,176 .... C6
50638 Grundy Center⊙ 2,880 .... H4
50115 Guthrie Center⊙ 1,713 .... D5
52052 Guttenberg 2,428 .... L3
51640 Hamburg 1,597 .... B7
50441 Hampton⊙ 4,630 .... G3
51536 Hancock 254 .... C6
50544 Harcourt 347 .... E4
51537 Harlan⊙ 5,357 .... C5
52146 Harpers Ferry 258 .... L2
50118 Hartford 761 .... G6
51346 Hartley 1,700 .... C2
50119 Harvey 275 .... H6
50546 Havelock 279 .... D3
51023 Hawarden 2,722 .... A2
52147 Hawkeye 512 .... J3
50641 Hazleton 877 .... K3
52563 Hedrick 847 .... J6
51541 Henderson 236 .... B6
52233 Hiawatha 4,825 .... K4
52235 Hills 547 .... K5
52630 Hillsboro 208 .... K7
51024 Hinton 659 .... A3
50642 Holland 278 .... H4
51025 Holstein 1,477 .... B4
52053 Holy Cross 310 .... L3
52237 Hopkinton 774 .... L4
51026 Hornick 239 .... A4
51238 Hospers 655 .... B2
50122 Hubbard 852 .... G4
50643 Hudson 2,267 .... H4
51239 Hull 1,714 .... A2
50548 Humboldt 4,794 .... E3
50123 Humeston 671 .... G7
50124 Huxley 1,884 .... F5
51445 Ida Grove⊙ 2,285 .... B4
50644 Independence⊙ 6,392 .... K4
50125 Indianola⊙ 10,843 .... F6
51240 Inwood 755 .... A2
50645 Ionia 350 .... J2
52240 Iowa City⊙ 50,508 .... L5
Iowa City○‡ 81,717 .... L5
50126 Iowa Falls 6,174 .... G3
51027 Ireton 588 .... A3
51446 Irwin 427 .... C5
50128 Jamaica 275 .... E5
50647 Janesville 840 .... J3
50129 Jefferson⊙ 4,854 .... E4
50648 Jesup 2,343 .... J4
50130 Jewell 1,145 .... F4
50131 Johnston 2,617 .... F5
52247 Kalona 1,862 .... K6
50447 Kanawha 756 .... F3
50133 Kellerton 278 .... E7
50134 Kelley 237 .... F5
50135 Kellogg 654 .... H5
50448 Kensett 360 .... G2
52632 Keokuk⊙ 13,536 .... L8
52565 Keosauqua⊙ 1,003 .... J7
52248 Keota 1,034 .... K6
50136 Keswick 300 .... J6
52249 Keystone 618 .... J5
51543 Kimballton 362 .... D5
51028 Kingsley 1,209 .... A3
51448 Kiron 317 .... C4
50449 Klemme 620 .... F3
50138 Knoxville⊙ 8,143 .... G6
50139 Lacona 376 .... G6
52251 Ladora 289 .... J5
51449 Lake City 2,006 .... D4
50450 Lake Mills 2,281 .... F2
51347 Lake Park 1,123 .... C2
50588 Lakeside 589 .... C3
51450 Lake View 1,291 .... C4
50451 Lakota 330 .... E2
50140 Lamoni 2,705 .... E7
50650 Lamont 554 .... K3
52054 La Motte 322 .... M4
52151 Lansing 1,181 .... L2
50651 La Porte City 2,324 .... J4
51241 Larchwood 701 .... A2
50452 Latimer 441 .... G3
50141 Laurel 278 .... H5
50554 Laurens 1,606 .... D3
52154 Lawler 534 .... J2
51030 Lawton 447 .... A4
52753 Le Claire 2,899 .... N5
50142 Le Grand 921 .... H5
50557 Lehigh 654 .... E4
50453 Leland 274 .... F2
51031 Le Mars⊙ 8,276 .... A3
50851 Lenox 1,338 .... D7
50144 Leon⊙ 2,094 .... F7
51242 Lester 274 .... A2
52754 Letts 473 .... L6
51544 Lewis 497 .... C6
52567 Libertyville 281 .... K7
52155 Lime Springs 476 .... J2
50146 Linden 264 .... E5
50147 Lineville 319 .... G7
52253 Lisbon 1,458 .... L5
50148 Liscomb 296 .... H4
51243 Little Rock 490 .... B2
51545 Little Sioux 251 .... B5
50558 Livermore 490 .... E3
52635 Lockridge 271 .... K7
51546 Logan⊙ 1,540 .... B5
51453 Lohrville 521 .... D4
52755 Lone Tree 1,014 .... L6
52756 Long Grove 596 .... M5
50149 Lorimor 405 .... E6
52254 Lost Nation 524 .... M5
50150 Lovilia 637 .... H6
52255 Lowden 717 .... L5
52757 Low Moor 346 .... N5
52156 Luana 246 .... K2
50151 Lucas 292 .... G6
50560 Lu Verne 418 .... E3
52056 Luxemburg 271 .... L3
50153 Lynnville 406 .... H5
50561 Lytton 377 .... D4
51549 Macedonia 279 .... C6
50156 Madrid 2,281 .... F5
50157 Malcom 418 .... H5
50562 Mallard 407 .... D3
51551 Malvern 1,244 .... B7
52057 Manchester⊙ 4,942 .... L3
51454 Manilla 1,020 .... C5
50456 Manly 1,496 .... G2
51455 Manning 1,609 .... C5
50563 Manson 1,924 .... D3
51034 Mapleton 1,495 .... B4
52060 Maquoketa⊙ 6,313 .... M4
50565 Marathon 442 .... C3
50653 Marble Rock 419 .... H3
51035 Marcus 1,206 .... B3
52301 Marengo⊙ 2,308 .... J5
52302 Marion 19,474 .... K4
52158 Marquette 528 .... L2
50158 Marshalltown⊙ 26,938 .... G4
52305 Martelle 316 .... L4
50160 Martensdale 438 .... F6
50401 Mason City⊙ 30,144 .... G2
50853 Massena 518 .... D6
51036 Maurice 288 .... A3
50161 Maxwell 783 .... G5
50655 Maynard 561 .... K3
50154 McCallsburg 304 .... G4
52758 McCausland 381 .... M5
52157 McGregor 945 .... L2
52306 Mechanicsville 1,166 .... L5
52637 Mediapolis 1,685 .... L6
50162 Melbourne 732 .... G5
50163 Melcher 953 .... G6
51350 Melvin 277 .... B2
50164 Menlo 410 .... E5
51037 Meriden 233 .... B3
51038 Merrill 737 .... A3
50457 Meservey 324 .... G3
52307 Middle 335 .... K5
52638 Middletown 487 .... L7
52064 Miles 398 .... N4
51351 Milford 2,076 .... C2
50166 Milo 778 .... G6
52570 Milton 567 .... J7
50167 Minburn 390 .... E5
51553 Minden 419 .... C6
50168 Mingo 303 .... G5
51555 Missouri Valley 3,107 .... B5
50169 Mitchellville 1,530 .... G5
51556 Modale 373 .... B5
51557 Mondamin 423 .... B5
52159 Monona 1,530 .... L2
50170 Monroe 1,875 .... G5
50171 Montezuma⊙ 1,485 .... H5
52310 Monticello 3,641 .... L4
50173 Montour 387 .... H5
52759 Montpelier 250 .... M6
52639 Montrose 1,038 .... L7
51558 Moorhead 264 .... B5
50566 Moorland 257 .... E4
52571 Moravia 706 .... H7
52640 Morning Sun 959 .... L6
52760 Moscow 350 .... L5
52572 Moulton 762 .... H7
50854 Mount Ayr⊙ 1,938 .... E7
52641 Mount Pleasant⊙ 7,322 .... L7
52314 Mount Vernon 3,325 .... K5
51039 Moville 1,273 .... A4
50174 Murray 703 .... F6
52761 Muscatine⊙ 23,467 .... L6
52574 Mystic 665 .... H7
50658 Nashua 1,846 .... J3
51559 Neola 839 .... B6
50201 Nevada⊙ 5,912 .... G5
52160 New Albin 609 .... L2
50568 Newell 913 .... D3
52315 Newhall 899 .... K5
50660 New Hartford 764 .... H3
52645 New London 2,043 .... L7
51646 New Market 554 .... D7
50206 New Providence 249 .... G4
50207 New Sharon 1,225 .... H6
50208 Newton⊙ 15,292 .... H5
52065 New Vienna 430 .... L3
50210 New Virginia 512 .... F6
52766 Nichols 375 .... L6
50458 Nora Springs 1,572 .... H2
52316 North English 990 .... J5
52317 North Liberty 2,046 .... K5
50459 Northwood⊙ 2,193 .... G2
50211 Norwalk 2,676 .... F6
52318 Norway 633 .... K5
52319 Oakdale 300 .... K5
51560 Oakland 1,552 .... C6
52646 Oakville 470 .... L6
51354 Ocheyedan 599 .... B2
51458 Odebolt 1,299 .... C4
50662 Oelwein 7,564 .... K3
50212 Ogden 1,953 .... E4
51355 Okoboji 559 .... C2
52320 Olin 735 .... L5
52576 Ollie 232 .... J6
51040 Onawa⊙ 3,283 .... A4
51041 Orange City⊙ 4,588 .... A2
50858 Orient 416 .... E6
†51360 Orleans 546 .... C2
50461 Osage⊙ 3,718 .... H2
50213 Osceola⊙ 3,750 .... F6
52577 Oskaloosa⊙ 10,984 .... H6
52161 Ossian 829 .... K2
50569 Otho 692 .... E4
52501 Ottumwa⊙ 27,381 .... J6
52322 Oxford 676 .... K5
52323 Oxford Junction 600 .... M4
51561 Pacific Junction 511 .... B6
50571 Palmer 288 .... D3
52324 Palo 529 .... K4
51562 Panama 229 .... B5
50216 Panora 1,211 .... E5
50665 Parkersburg 1,968 .... H3
52325 Parnell 234 .... J5
50217 Paton 291 .... E4
51046 Paullina 1,224 .... B3
50219 Pella 8,349 .... H6
50220 Perry 7,053 .... E5
50221 Pershing 325 .... G6
51563 Persia 355 .... B5
51047 Peterson 470 .... C3
51048 Pierson 408 .... B3
51564 Pisgah 307 .... B5
50666 Plainfield 469 .... J3
50225 Pleasantville 1,531 .... G6
50464 Plymouth 463 .... G2
50574 Pocahontas⊙ 2,352 .... D3
50226 Polk City 1,658 .... F5
50575 Pomeroy 895 .... D3
51565 Portsmouth 240 .... C5
52162 Postville 1,475 .... K2
50228 Prairie City 1,278 .... G5
50859 Prescott 349 .... D6
52069 Preston 1,120 .... N4
Primghar⊙ 1,050 .... B2
52768 Princeton 965 .... N5
52163 Protivin 368 .... J2
52584 Pulaski 267 .... J7
52326 Quasqueton 599 .... K4
51049 Quimby 424 .... B3
50230 Radcliffe 593 .... G4
50465 Rake 283 .... F2
50667 Raymond 655 .... J4
50668 Readlyn 858 .... J3
50232 Reasnor 277 .... G5
50233 Redfield 959 .... E5
51566 Red Oak⊙ 6,810 .... C6
50669 Reinbeck 1,808 .... H4
50576 Rembrandt 291 .... C3
51050 Remsen 1,592 .... B3
50577 Renwick 410 .... E3
50234 Rhodes 367 .... G5
50466 Riceville 919 .... H2
52585 Richland 600 .... K6
52165 Ridgeway 308 .... K2
50578 Ringsted 557 .... D2
50235 Rippey 304 .... E5
†52722 Riverdale 462 .... N5
52327 Riverside 826 .... K6
51650 Riverton 342 .... B7
52328 Robins 726 .... K4
50468 Rockford 1,012 .... H2
51246 Rock Rapids⊙ 2,693 .... A2
51247 Rock Valley 2,706 .... A2
50469 Rockwell 1,039 .... G3
50579 Rockwell City⊙ 2,276 .... D4
50236 Roland 1,005 .... F4
50581 Rolfe 796 .... D3
50470 Rowan 259 .... F3
52329 Rowley 275 .... K4
51357 Royal 522 .... C2
50471 Rudd 460 .... H2
50237 Runnells 377 .... G5
50238 Russell 593 .... G7
51358 Ruthven 769 .... D2
52330 Ryan 390 .... K4
52070 Sabula 824 .... N4
50583 Sac City⊙ 3,000 .... C4
†52001 Sageville 291 .... M3
50472 Saint Ansgar 1,100 .... H2
50240 Saint Charles 507 .... F6
52649 Salem 463 .... K7
51052 Salix 429 .... A4
51248 Sanborn 1,398 .... B2
51053 Schaller 832 .... C4
51461 Schleswig 868 .... B4
51462 Scranton 748 .... D4
51054 Sergeant Bluff 2,416 .... A4
52590 Seymour 1,036 .... G7
50475 Sheffield 1,224 .... G3
51570 Shelby 665 .... C5
50243 Sheldahl 315 .... F5
51201 Sheldon 5,003 .... B2
50670 Shell Rock 1,478 .... H3
52332 Shellsburg 771 .... K4
51601 Shenandoah 6,274 .... C7
†52401 Shueyville 287 .... K5
51249 Sibley⊙ 3,051 .... B2
51652 Sidney⊙ 1,308 .... B7
52591 Sigourney⊙ 2,330 .... J6
51571 Silver City 291 .... B6
51250 Sioux Center 4,588 .... A2
*51101 Sioux City⊙ 82,003 .... A3
Sioux City‡ 117,457 .... A3
50585 Sioux Rapids 897 .... C3
50244 Slater 1,312 .... F5
51055 Sloan 978 .... A4
51056 Smithland 282 .... B4
51572 Soldier 257 .... B5
52333 Solon 969 .... L5
51301 Spencer⊙ 11,726 .... C2
52168 Spillville 415 .... J2
51360 Spirit Lake⊙ 3,976 .... C2
52336 Springville 1,165 .... L4
50476 Stacyville 538 .... H2
50246 Stanhope 492 .... F4
51573 Stanton 747 .... C7
52337 Stanwood 705 .... L5
50247 State Center 1,292 .... G5
50672 Steamboat Rock 387 .... G4
52651 Stockport 272 .... K7
52769 Stockton 240 .... M5
50588 Storm Lake⊙ 8,814 .... C3
50248 Story City 2,762 .... F4
50249 Stratford 806 .... F4
52076 Strawberry Point 1,463 .... K3
50250 Stuart 1,650 .... E6
50251 Sully 828 .... H5
50674 Sumner 2,335 .... J3
51058 Sutherland 897 .... B3
50590 Swea City 813 .... E2
52338 Swisher 654 .... K5
51653 Tabor 1,088 .... B7
52339 Tama 2,968 .... H5
51463 Templeton 319 .... D5
51364 Terril 420 .... C2
50478 Thompson 668 .... F2
50479 Thornton 442 .... G3
52340 Tiffin 413 .... K5
52772 Tipton⊙ 3,055 .... L5
50480 Titonka 607 .... E2
52342 Toledo⊙ 2,445 .... H4
50675 Traer 1,703 .... J4
51575 Treynor 981 .... B6
50676 Tripoli 1,280 .... J3
50257 Truro 407 .... F6
51576 Underwood 448 .... B6
50258 Union 515 .... G4
†52240 University Heights 1,069 .... K5
52595 University Park 645 .... H6
52345 Urbana 574 .... K4
50322 Urbandale 17,869 .... F5
51060 Ute 479 .... B4
51465 Vail 490 .... C4
52346 Van Horne 682 .... J4
50261 Van Meter 747 .... E5
50262 Van Wert 245 .... F7
50482 Ventura 614 .... F2
52347 Victor 1,046 .... J5
50864 Villisca 1,434 .... C7
52349 Vinton⊙ 5,040 .... J4
52077 Volga 310 .... L3
52169 Wadena 230 .... K3
†51360 Wahpeton 372 .... C2
52773 Walcott 1,425 .... M5
52351 Walford 285 .... K5
52352 Walker 733 .... K4
51365 Wallingford 256 .... D2
51466 Wall Lake 892 .... C4
51577 Walnut 897 .... C6
52653 Wapello⊙ 2,011 .... L6
52353 Washington⊙ 6,584 .... K6
51061 Washta 320 .... B3
*50701 Waterloo⊙ 75,985 .... J4
Waterloo-Cedar Falls‡ 137,961 .... J4
52171 Waucoma 308 .... J2
50263 Waukee 2,227 .... F5
52172 Waukon⊙ 3,983 .... L2
50677 Waverly⊙ 8,444 .... J3
52654 Wayland 720 .... K6
52356 Wellman 1,125 .... K6
50680 Wellsburg 761 .... H4
50483 Wesley 598 .... E2
50597 West Bend 941 .... D3
52358 West Branch 1,867 .... L5
52655 West Burlington 3,371 .... L7
50318 West Des Moines 21,894 .... F5
50681 Westgate 263 .... K3
52776 West Liberty 2,723 .... L5
†51351 West Okoboji 435 .... C2
52656 West Point 1,133 .... K7
51467 Westside 387 .... C4
52175 West Union⊙ 2,783 .... K3
50268 What Cheer 803 .... J6
52777 Wheatland 840 .... M5
51063 Whiting 734 .... A4
50598 Whittemore 647 .... E2
50271 Williams 410 .... F3
52361 Williamsburg 2,033 .... J5
52778 Wilton 2,502 .... M5
50311 Windsor Heights 5,474 .... F5
52659 Winfield 1,042 .... L6
50273 Winterset⊙ 4,021 .... E6
50682 Winthrop 767 .... K4
50484 Woden 287 .... F2
51579 Woodbine 1,463 .... B5
50276 Woodward 1,212 .... E5
50599 Woolstock 235 .... F3
52078 Worthington 432 .... L4
52362 Wyoming 702 .... L4
50277 Yale 299 .... E5
50278 Zearing 630 .... G4

OTHER FEATURES

Big Sioux (riv.) A3
Boyer (riv.) B5
Cedar (riv.) K4
Chariton (riv.) G7
Clear (lake) G2
Eagle (lake) F2
East Nishnabotna (riv.) C6
Effigy Mounds Nat'l Mon. L2
Five Island (lake) D2
Floyd (riv.) A3
Herbert Hoover Nat'l Hist. Site L5
Iowa (riv.) H4
Little Sioux (riv.) B3
Lost Island (lake) D2
Mississippi (riv.) L7
Missouri (riv.) A4
Nodaway (riv.) D7
Palo Alto (lake) D2
Platte (riv.) D8
Raccoon (riv.) D4
Rathbun (lake) G7
Red Rock (lake) G6
Rock (riv.) A2
Sac and Fox Ind. Res. H5
Saylorville (lake) F5
Skunk (riv.) K6
Spirit (lake) C2
Storm (lake) C3
Thompson (riv.) E7
Trumbull (lake) C2
Turkey (riv.) K2
Upper Iowa (riv.) K2
Wapsipinicon (riv.) J3
West Nishnabotna (riv.) C6

⊙County seat.
‡Population of metropolitan area.
† Zip of nearest p.o. * Multiple zips.

AREA 82,277 sq. mi. (213,097 sq. km.)
POPULATION 2,364,236
CAPITAL Topeka
LARGEST CITY Wichita
HIGHEST POINT Mt. Sunflower 4,039 ft. (1231 m.)
SETTLED IN 1831
ADMITTED TO UNION January 29, 1861
POPULAR NAME Sunflower State
STATE FLOWER Sunflower
STATE BIRD Western Meadowlark

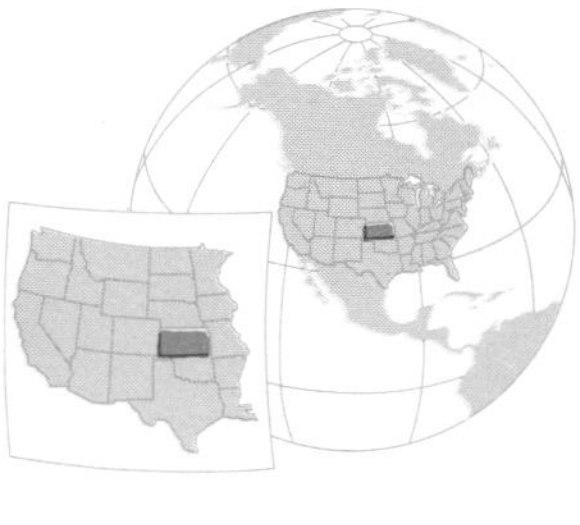

Agriculture, Industry and Resources

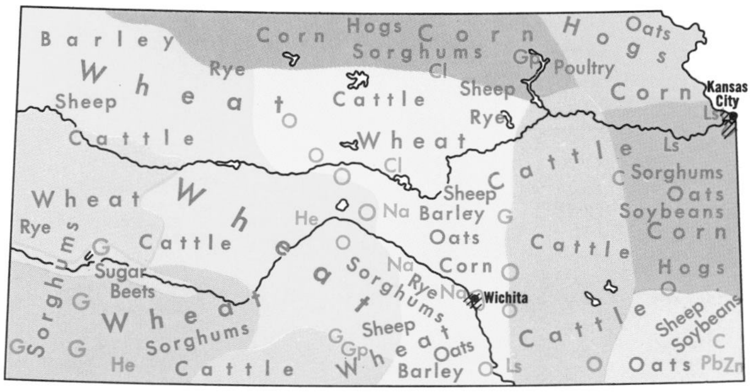

DOMINANT LAND USE

- Specialized Wheat
- Wheat, General Farming
- Wheat, Range Livestock
- Wheat, Grain Sorghums, Range Livestock
- Cattle Feed, Hogs
- Livestock, Cash Grain
- Livestock, Cash Grain, Dairy
- General Farming, Livestock, Cash Grain
- General Farming, Livestock, Special Crops
- Range Livestock

MAJOR MINERAL OCCURRENCES

C	Coal	Ls	Limestone
Cl	Clay	Na	Salt
G	Natural Gas	O	Petroleum
Gp	Gypsum	Pb	Lead
He	Helium	Zn	Zinc

Major Industrial Areas

COUNTIES

Allen 15,654	G4
Anderson 8,749	G3
Atchison 18,397	G2
Barber 6,548	D4
Barton 31,343	D3
Bourbon 15,969	H4
Brown 11,955	G2
Butler 44,782	F4
Chase 3,309	F3
Chautauqua 5,016	F4
Cherokee 22,304	H4
Cheyenne 3,678	A2
Clark 2,599	C4
Clay 9,802	E2
Cloud 12,494	E2
Coffey 9,370	G3
Comanche 2,554	C4
Cowley 36,824	F4
Crawford 37,916	H4
Decatur 4,509	B2
Dickinson 20,175	E3
Doniphan 9,268	G2
Douglas 67,640	G3
Edwards 4,271	C4
Elk 3,918	F4
Ellis 26,098	C3
Ellsworth 6,640	D3
Finney 23,825	B3
Ford 24,315	C4
Franklin 22,062	G3
Geary 29,852	F3
Gove 3,726	B3
Graham 3,995	C2
Grant 6,977	A4
Gray 5,138	B4
Greeley 1,845	A3
Greenwood 8,764	F4
Hamilton 2,514	A3
Harper 7,778	D4
Harvey 30,531	E3
Haskell 3,814	B4
Hodgeman 2,269	C3
Jackson 11,644	G2
Jefferson 15,207	G2
Jewell 5,241	D2
Johnson 270,269	H3
Kearny 3,435	A3
Kingman 8,960	D4
Kiowa 4,046	C4
Labette 25,682	G4
Lane 2,472	B3
Leavenworth 54,809	G2
Lincoln 4,145	D2
Linn 8,234	H3
Logan 3,478	A3
Lyon 35,108	F3
Marion 13,522	E3
Marshall 12,787	F2
McPherson 26,855	E3
Meade 4,788	B4
Miami 21,618	H3
Mitchell 8,117	D2
Montgomery 42,281	G4
Morris 6,419	F3
Morton 3,454	A4
Nemaha 11,211	F2
Neosho 18,967	G4
Ness 4,498	C3
Norton 6,689	C2
Osage 15,319	G3
Osborne 5,959	D2
Ottawa 5,971	E2
Pawnee 8,065	C3
Phillips 7,406	C2
Pottawatomie 14,782	F2
Pratt 10,275	D4
Rawlins 4,105	A2
Reno 64,983	D4
Republic 7,569	E2
Rice 11,900	D3
Riley 63,505	F2
Rooks 7,006	C2
Rush 4,516	C3
Russell 8,868	D3
Saline 48,905	E3
Scott 5,782	B3
Sedgwick 367,088	E4
Seward 17,071	B4
Shawnee 154,916	G2
Sheridan 3,544	B2
Sherman 7,759	A2
Smith 5,947	D2
Stafford 5,694	D3
Stanton 2,339	A4
Stevens 4,736	A4
Sumner 24,928	E4
Thomas 8,451	A2
Trego 4,165	C3
Wabaunsee 6,867	F3
Wallace 2,045	A3
Washington 8,543	E2
Wichita 3,041	A3
Wilson 12,128	G4
Woodson 4,600	G4
Wyandotte 172,335	H2

CITIES and TOWNS

Zip	Name/Pop.	Key
67510	Abbyville 123	D4
67410	Abilene⊙ 6,572	E3
66830	Admire 158	F3
66930	Agenda 106	E2
67621	Agra 321	C2
67511	Albert 236	C3
67512	Alden 214	D3
67513	Alexander 116	C3
66833	Allen 205	F3
66401	Alma⊙ 925	F2
67622	Almena 517	C2
67330	Altamont 1,054	G4
66834	Alta Vista 430	F3
67623	Alton 135	D2
66710	Altoona 564	G4
66835	Americus 915	F3
67001	Andale 538	E4
67002	Andover 2,801	E4
67003	Anthony⊙ 2,661	D4
66711	Arcadia 460	H4
67004	Argonia 587	E4
67005	Arkansas City 13,201	E4
67514	Arlington 631	D4
66712	Arma 1,676	H4
67831	Ashland⊙ 1,096	C4
67416	Assaria 414	E3
66002	Atchison⊙ 11,407	G2
66932	Athol 90	D2
67008	Atlanta 256	F4
67009	Attica 730	D4
67730	Atwood⊙ 1,665	B2
66402	Auburn 890	G3
67010	Augusta 6,968	F4
67417	Aurora 130	E2
66403	Axtell 470	F2
66404	Baileyville 130	F2
66006	Baldwin City 2,829	G3
67418	Barnard 163	D2
66933	Barnes 257	F2
67332	Bartlett 163	G4
66007	Basehor 1,483	G2
†66749	Bassett 31	G4
66713	Baxter Springs 4,730	H4
67516	Bazine 385	C3
66406	Beattie 316	F2
67013	Belle Plaine 1,706	E4
66935	Belleville⊙ 2,805	E2
67420	Beloit⊙ 4,367	D2
67519	Belpre 154	C4
66407	Belvue 212	F2
66714	Benedict 111	G4
67422	Bennington 579	E2
67016	Bentley 311	E4
67017	Benton 609	E4
66408	Bern 220	F2
67423	Beverly 171	E2
67731	Bird City 546	A2
67520	Bison 279	C3
66010	Blue Mound 319	H3
66411	Blue Rapids 1,280	F2
67018	Bluff City 95	E4
67625	Bogue 197	C2
66012	Bonner Springs 6,266	H2
67732	Brewster 327	A2
66716	Bronson 414	H4
67425	Brookville 259	E3
67521	Brownell 92	C3
67834	Bucklin 786	C4
66717	Buffalo 386	G4
67522	Buhler 1,188	E3
67626	Bunker Hill 124	D3
67019	Burden 518	F4
67523	Burdett 275	C3
66413	Burlingame 1,239	G3
66839	Burlington⊙ 2,901	G3
66840	Burns 224	F3
66936	Burr Oak 366	D2
67020	Burrton 976	E3
66841	Bushong 62	F3
67427	Bushton 388	D3
67021	Byers 47	D4
67022	Caldwell 1,401	E4
67023	Cambridge 113	F4
67333	Caney 2,284	G4
67428	Canton 926	E3
66414	Carbondale 1,518	G3
67429	Carlton 49	E3
66842	Cassoday 122	F3
67430	Cawker City 640	D2
67628	Cedar 53	D2
66843	Cedar Point 66	F3
67024	Cedar Vale 848	F4
66415	Centralia 486	F2
66720	Chanute 10,506	G4
67431	Chapman 1,255	E3
67524	Chase 753	D3
67334	Chautauqua 156	F4
67025	Cheney 1,404	E4
66724	Cherokee 775	H4
67335	Cherryvale 2,769	G4
67336	Chetopa 1,751	G4
67835	Cimarron⊙ 1,491	B4
66416	Circleville 164	G2
67525	Claflin 764	D3
67432	Clay Center⊙ 4,948	E2
67629	Clayton 102	B2
67026	Clearwater 1,684	E4
66937	Clifton 695	E2
67027	Climax 81	F4
66938	Clyde 909	E2
67028	Coats 153	D4
67337	Coffeyville 15,185	G4
67701	Colby⊙ 5,544	A2
67029	Coldwater⊙ 989	C4
67631	Collyer 151	B2
66015	Colony 474	G3
66725	Columbus⊙ 3,426	H4
67030	Colwich 935	E4
66901	Concordia⊙ 6,847	E2
67031	Conway Springs 1,313	E4
67836	Coolidge 82	A3
67837	Copeland 323	B4
66417	Corning 158	F2
66845	Cottonwood Falls⊙ 954	F3
66846	Council Grove⊙ 2,381	F3
66939	Courtland 377	E2
66727	Coyville 98	G4
66940	Cuba 286	E2
†67124	Cullison 154	D4
67435	Culver 167	E3
67035	Cunningham 540	D4
67632	Damar 204	C2
67036	Danville 71	E4
67340	Dearing 475	G4
67838	Deerfield 538	A4
66418	Delia 181	G2
67436	Delphos 570	E2
66419	Denison 231	G2
66017	Denton 156	G2
67037	Derby 9,786	E4
66018	De Soto 2,061	H3
67038	Dexter 366	F4
67839	Dighton⊙ 1,390	B3
67801	Dodge City⊙ 18,001	B4
67634	Dorrance 220	D3
67039	Douglass 1,450	F4
67437	Downs 1,324	D2
67635	Dresden 84	B2
66848	Dunlap 82	F3
67438	Durham 130	E3
66849	Dwight 320	F3
†66720	Earlton 79	G4
†67201	Eastborough 854	E4
66020	Easton 460	G2
66021	Edgerton 1,214	H3
67636	Edmond 56	C2
67342	Edna 537	G4
66113	Edwardsville 3,364	H2
66023	Effingham 634	G2
67041	Elbing 175	E3
67042	El Dorado⊙ 10,510	F4
†67361	Elgin 139	F4
67344	Elk City 404	G4
67345	Elk Falls 151	F4
67950	Elkhart⊙ 2,243	A4
67526	Ellinwood 2,508	D3
67637	Ellis 2,062	C3
67439	Ellsworth⊙ 2,465	D3
66850	Elmdale 109	F3
66732	Elsmore 104	G4
66024	Elwood 1,275	H2
66422	Emmett 223	F2
66801	Emporia⊙ 25,287	F3
67840	Englewood 111	C4
67841	Ensign 209	B4
67441	Enterprise 839	E3
66733	Erie⊙ 1,415	G4
66941	Esbon 234	D2
66423	Eskridge 603	F3
66025	Eudora 2,934	G3
67045	Eureka⊙ 3,425	F4
66424	Everest 331	G2
66425	Fairview 258	G2
†66101	Fairway 4,619	H2
67047	Fall River 173	G4
66851	Florence 729	E3
66026	Fontana 173	H3
67842	Ford 272	C4
66942	Formoso 166	D2
67843	Fort Dodge 400	C4
66027	Fort Leavenworth	H2
66701	Fort Scott⊙ 8,893	H4
67844	Fowler 592	B4
66427	Frankfort 1,038	F2
66735	Franklin 400	H4
66736	Fredonia⊙ 3,047	G4
67049	Freeport 12	E4
66762	Frontenac 2,586	H4
66738	Fulton 194	H4
66739	Galena 3,587	H4
66740	Galesburg 181	G4
67443	Galva 651	E3
67846	Garden City⊙ 18,256	B4
67050	Garden Plain 775	E4
66030	Gardner 2,392	H3
67529	Garfield 277	C3
66032	Garnett⊙ 3,310	G3
66742	Gas 543	G4
67638	Gaylord 203	D2
67734	Gem 101	B2
67444	Geneseo 496	D3
67051	Geuda Springs 217	E4
66743	Girard⊙ 2,888	H4
67639	Glade 131	C2
67445	Glasco 710	E2
67446	Glen Elder 491	D2
67052	Goddard 1,427	E4
67053	Goessel 421	E3
66428	Goff 196	G2
67735	Goodland⊙ 5,708	A2
67640	Gorham 355	D3
67736	Gove⊙ 148	B3
67737	Grainfield 417	B2
†66441	Grandview Plaza 1,189	F2
66429	Grantville 220	G2
67530	Great Bend⊙ 16,608	D3
66033	Greeley 405	G3
67447	Green 155	E2
66943	Greenleaf 462	E2
67054	Greensburg⊙ 1,885	C4
67346	Grenola 335	F4
66852	Gridley 404	G3
67738	Grinnell 410	B2
67448	Gypsum 423	E3
66944	Haddam 239	E2
67056	Halstead 1,994	E4
66853	Hamilton 363	F4
66945	Hanover 802	F2
67849	Hanston 257	C3
67057	Hardtner 336	D4
67058	Harper 1,823	D4
66854	Hartford 551	F3
66431	Harveyville 280	F3
67347	Havana 169	G4
67543	Haven 1,125	E4
66432	Havensville 183	F2
67059	Haviland 770	C4

(continued on following page)

67601 Hays⊙ 16,301 ....C3	67545 Hudson 157 ....D3	66039 Kincaid 192 ....G3	67073 Lehigh 189 ....E3	66053 Louisburg 1,744 ....H3	67745 McDonald 239 ....A2
67060 Haysville 8,006 ....E4	67951 Hugoton⊙ 3,165 ....A4	67068 Kingman⊙ 3,563 ....D4	66215 Lenexa 18,639 ....H2	66650 Louisville 207 ....F2	66501 McFarland 242 ....F2
67850 Healy 275 ....B3	66748 Humboldt 2,230 ....G4	67547 Kiowa 1,409 ....C4	67645 Lenora 444 ....C2	67648 Lucas 524 ....D2	66054 McLouth 700 ....G2
67061 Hazelton 143 ....D4	67452 Hunter 135 ....D2	67070 Kiowa 1,409 ....D4	67074 Leon 667 ....F4	67549 Luray 295 ....D2	67460 McPherson⊙ 11,753 ....E3
66746 Hepler 165 ....H4	66038 Huron 107 ....G2	67644 Kirwin 249 ....C2	66448 Leona 73 ....G2	67451 Lyndon⊙ 1,132 ....G3	67864 Meade⊙ 1,777 ....B4
67449 Herington 2,930 ....E3	67501 Hutchinson⊙ 40,284 ....D3	67859 Kismet 368 ....B4	66449 Leonardville 437 ....F2	67554 Lyons⊙ 4,134 ....D3	67104 Medicine Lodge⊙ 2,384 ....D4
67739 Herndon 220 ....B2	67301 Independence⊙ 10,598 ....G4	67350 Labette 123 ....G4	67861 Leoti⊙ 1,869 ....A3	67557 Macksville 546 ....D4	66510 Melvern 481 ....G3
67062 Hesston 3,013 ....E3	67853 Ingalls 274 ....B4	66040 La Cygne 1,025 ....H3	67552 Lewis 551 ....C4	66860 Madison 1,099 ....F3	67746 Menlo 42 ....B2
66434 Hiawatha⊙ 3,702 ....G2	67546 Inman 947 ....E3	66751 La Harpe 687 ....G4	67901 Liberal⊙ 14,911 ....A4	66955 Mahaska 119 ....E2	66512 Meriden 707 ....G2
†67880 Hickock 68 ....A4	66749 Iola⊙ 6,938 ....G4	67860 Lakin⊙ 1,823 ....A4	67351 Liberty 174 ....G4	67101 Maize 1,294 ....E4	66203 Merriam 10,794 ....H3
66035 Highland 954 ....G2	67065 Isabel 137 ....D4	66041 Lancaster 274 ....G2	67553 Liebenthal 163 ....C3	67463 Manchester 98 ....E2	67105 Milan 135 ....E4
67642 Hill City⊙ 2,028 ....C2	67066 Iuka 235 ....D4	66042 Lane 249 ....G3	66755 Lincolnville 235 ....F3	66502 Manhattan⊙ 32,644 ....F2	66055 Mildred 64 ....G4
67063 Hillsboro 2,717 ....E3	66948 Jamestown 440 ....E2	67549 Langdon 84 ....D3	67456 Lincolnville 235 ....F3	66956 Mankato⊙ 1,205 ....D2	66514 Milford 465 ....F2
67544 Hoisington 3,678 ....D3	67643 Jennings 194 ....B2	66043 Lansing 5,307 ....H2	67456 Lindsborg 3,155 ....E3	67862 Manter 205 ....A4	67466 Miltonvale 588 ....E2
67851 Holcomb 816 ....B3	67854 Jetmore⊙ 862 ....B3	67550 Larned⊙ 4,811 ....C3	66953 Linn 483 ....E2	66507 Maple Hill 381 ....F2	67467 Minneapolis⊙ 2,075 ....E2
66946 Hollenberg 57 ....F2	66949 Jewell 589 ....D2	67072 Latham 148 ....F4	66052 Linwood 343 ....G2	66754 Mapleton 121 ....H3	67865 Minneola 712 ....C4
66436 Holton⊙ 3,132 ....G2	67855 Johnson⊙ 1,244 ....A4	66044 Lawrence⊙ 52,738 ....G3	67457 Little River 529 ....E3	66861 Marion⊙ 1,951 ....F3	66205 Mission 8,643 ....H2
67450 Holyrood 567 ....D3	66441 Junction City⊙ 19,305 ....F2	Lawrence‡ 67,640 ....H2	67646 Logan 720 ....C2	67464 Marquette 639 ....E3	67353 Moline 553 ....F4
67451 Hope 468 ....E3	67454 Kanopolis 729 ....D3	66048 Leavenworth⊙ 33,656 ....H2	67458 Longford 109 ....E2	66508 Marysville⊙ 3,670 ....F2	67867 Montezuma 730 ....B4
†67439 Horace 137 ....A3	67741 Kanorado 207 ....A2	66206 Leawood 13,360 ....H2	67647 Long Island 187 ....C2	66682 Matfield Green 71 ....F3	66755 Moran 543 ....G4
66439 Horton 2,130 ....G2	*66101 Kansas City⊙ 161,148 ....H2	66952 Lebanon 440 ....D2	67352 Longton 396 ....F4	66509 Mayetta 287 ....G2	67468 Morganville 261 ....E2
67349 Howard⊙ 1,295 ....F4	Kansas City‡ 1,327,020 ....H2	66856 Lebo 966 ....G3	67459 Lorraine 157 ....D3	67103 Mayfield 120 ....E4	66550 Morland 223 ....B2
67740 Hoxie⊙ 1,462 ....B2	67067 Kechi 288 ....E4	66050 Lecompton 576 ....G2	66859 Lost Springs 94 ....E3	67556 McCracken 292 ....C3	66515 Morrill 336 ....G2
66440 Hoyt 536 ....G2	66951 Kensington 681 ....C2			66754 McCune 528 ....G4	66958 Morrowville 180 ....E2

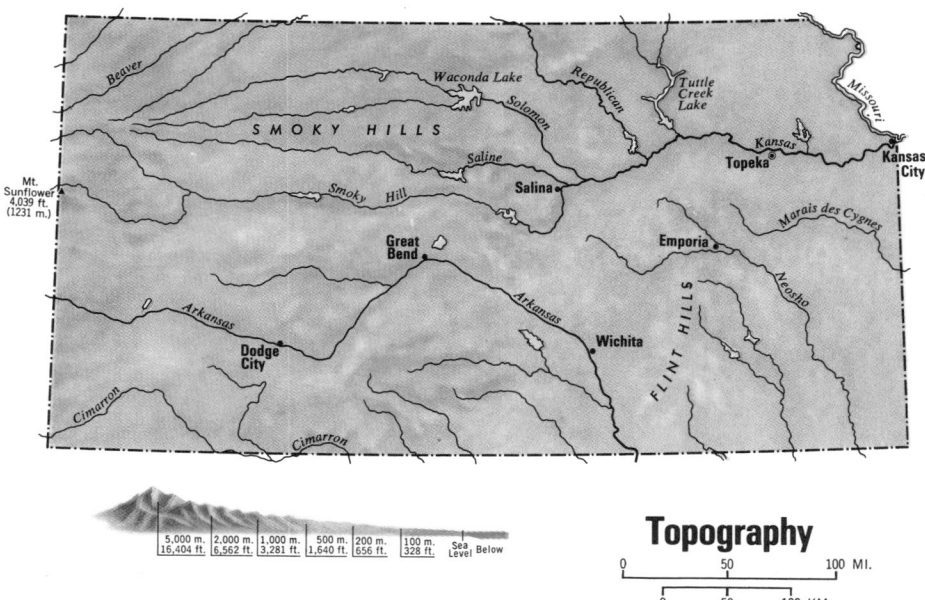

Topography

KENTUCKY

COUNTIES

Adair 15,233 .... L6
Allen 14,128 .... J7
Anderson 12,567 .... M5
Ballard 8,798 .... C6
Barren 34,009 .... K7
Bath 10,025 .... O4
Bell 34,330 .... O7
Boone 45,842 .... M3
Bourbon 19,405 .... N4
Boyd 55,513 .... R4
Boyle 25,066 .... M5
Bracken 7,738 .... N3
Breathitt 17,004 .... P5
Breckinridge 16,861 .... H5
Bullitt 43,346 .... K5
Butler 11,064 .... H6
Caldwell 13,473 .... F6
Calloway 30,031 .... E7
Campbell 83,317 .... N3
Carlisle 5,487 .... C7
Carroll 9,270 .... L3
Carter 25,060 .... P4
Casey 14,818 .... M6
Christian 66,878 .... F7
Clark 28,322 .... N4
Clay 22,752 .... O6
Clinton 9,321 .... L7
Crittenden 9,207 .... E6
Cumberland 7,289 .... L7
Daviess 85,949 .... G5
Edmonson 9,962 .... J6
Elliott 6,908 .... P4
Estill 14,495 .... O5
Fayette 204,165 .... N4
Fleming 12,323 .... O4
Floyd 48,764 .... R5
Franklin 41,830 .... M4
Fulton 8,971 .... C7
Gallatin 4,842 .... M3
Garrard 10,853 .... M5
Grant 13,308 .... M3
Graves 34,049 .... D7
Grayson 20,854 .... J5
Green 11,043 .... K6
Greenup 39,132 .... R3
Hancock 7,742 .... H5
Hardin 88,917 .... K5
Harlan 41,889 .... P7
Harrison 15,166 .... N4
Hart 15,402 .... K6
Henderson 40,849 .... F5
Henry 12,740 .... L4
Hickman 6,065 .... C7
Hopkins 46,174 .... F6
Jackson 11,996 .... N6
Jefferson 684,565 .... K4
Jessamine 26,065 .... M5
Johnson 24,432 .... R5
Kenton 137,058 .... M3
Knott 17,940 .... R6
Knox 30,239 .... O7
Larue 11,922 .... K5
Laurel 38,982 .... N6
Lawrence 14,121 .... R4
Lee 7,754 .... O5
Leslie 14,882 .... P6
Letcher 30,687 .... R6
Lewis 14,545 .... P3
Lincoln 19,053 .... M6
Livingston 9,219 .... E6
Logan 24,138 .... H7
Lyon 6,490 .... E6
Madison 53,352 .... N5
Magoffin 13,515 .... P5
Marion 17,910 .... L5
Marshall 25,637 .... E7
Martin 13,925 .... R5
Mason 17,765 .... O3
McCracken 61,310 .... D6
McCreary 15,634 .... N7
McLean 10,090 .... G5
Meade 22,854 .... J5
Menifee 5,117 .... O5
Mercer 19,011 .... M5
Metcalfe 9,484 .... K7
Monroe 12,353 .... K7
Montgomery 20,046 .... O4
Morgan 12,103 .... P5
Muhlenberg 32,238 .... G6
Nelson 27,584 .... K5
Nicholas 7,157 .... N4
Ohio 21,765 .... H6
Oldham 27,795 .... L4
Owen 8,924 .... M3
Owsley 5,709 .... O6
Pendleton 10,989 .... N3
Perry 33,763 .... P6
Pike 81,123 .... S6
Powell 11,101 .... O5
Pulaski 45,803 .... M6
Robertson 2,265 .... N3
Rockcastle 13,973 .... N6
Rowan 19,049 .... P4
Russell 13,708 .... L7
Scott 21,813 .... M4
Shelby 23,328 .... L4
Simpson 14,673 .... H7
Spencer 5,929 .... L4
Taylor 21,178 .... L6
Todd 11,874 .... G7
Trigg 9,384 .... F7
Trimble 6,253 .... L3
Union 17,821 .... F5
Warren 71,828 .... H6
Washington 10,764 .... L5
Wayne 17,022 .... M7
Webster 14,832 .... F5
Whitley 33,396 .... N7
Wolfe 6,698 .... O5
Woodford 17,778 .... M4

CITIES and TOWNS

Zip *Name/Pop.* *Key*

42202 Adairville 1,105 .... H7
42602 Albany⊙ 2,083 .... L7
41001 Alexandria⊙ 4,735 .... N3
41601 Allen 338 .... R5
42204 Allensville 170 .... G7
40223 Anchorage 1,726 .... L2
41101 Ashland 27,064 .... R4
Ashland-Huntington‡ 311,350 .... R4
42206 Auburn 1,467 .... H7
†40201 Audubon Park 1,571 .... J2
41002 Augusta 1,455 .... N3
41602 Auxier 900 .... R5
†40222 Bancroft 725 .... K1
41603 Banner 950 .... R5
†40201 Barbourmeade 1,038 .... K1
40906 Barbourville⊙ 3,333 .... O7
40004 Bardstown⊙ 6,155 .... L5
42023 Bardwell⊙ 988 .... D7
42024 Barlow 746 .... D6
41311 Beattyville⊙ 1,068 .... O5
42320 Beaver Dam 3,185 .... H6
40006 Bedford⊙ 835 .... L3
40359 Beechwood Village 1,462 .... K2
†40201 Bellemeade 918 .... L2
41073 Bellevue 7,678 .... S1
40807 Benham 936 .... R7
42025 Benton⊙ 3,700 .... E7
40403 Berea 8,226 .... N5
41003 Berry 287 .... N3
41605 Betsy Layne 975 .... R5
41124 Blaine 358 .... R4
40008 Bloomfield 954 .... L5
†40201 Blue Ridge Manor 465 .... L2
42713 Bonnieville 372 .... K6
†40403 Boone 300 .... N5
41314 Booneville⊙ 191 .... O6
42101 Bowling Green⊙ 40,450 .... H7
40009 Bradfordsville 331 .... L6
40108 Brandenburg⊙ 1,831 .... J4
†42025 Briensburg E7
†40201 Broadfields 311 .... K2
40409 Brodhead 686 .... N6
†41016 Bromley 844 .... S2
40109 Brooks 1,344 .... K4
41004 Brooksville⊙ 680 .... N3
†40201 Brownsboro Farm 790 .... L1
42210 Brownsville⊙ 674 .... J6
40218 Buechel 6,709 .... K2
40310 Burgin 1,008 .... M5
42717 Burkesville⊙ 2,051 .... L7
41005 Burlington⊙ 500 .... R2
42519 Burnside 775 .... M6
41006 Butler 663 .... N3
42211 Cadiz⊙ 1,661 .... F7
42327 Calhoun⊙ 1,080 .... G5
41007 California 135 .... N3
42029 Calvert City 2,388 .... E6
†40337 Camargo 1,301 .... K4
40011 Campbellsburg 714 .... L3
42718 Campbellsville⊙ 8,715 .... L6
41301 Campton⊙ 486 .... O5
42721 Caneyville 642 .... J6
40311 Carlisle⊙ 1,757 .... N4
41008 Carrollton⊙ 3,967 .... L3
42030 Carrsville 99 .... E6
†42459 Caseyville 43 .... E5
41129 Catlettsburg⊙ 3,005 .... R4
42127 Cave City 2,098 .... K6
†41522 Cedarville 81 .... S6
42328 Centertown 462 .... G6
42330 Central City 5,214 .... G6
42726 Clarkson 666 .... J6
42404 Clay 1,356 .... F6
40312 Clay City 1,276 .... O5
40313 Clearfield 1,250 .... P4
42031 Clinton⊙ 1,720 .... D7
40111 Cloverport 1,585 .... H5
†41501 Coal Run 348 .... R5
41076 Cold Spring 2,117 .... T2
42728 Columbia⊙ 3,710 .... L6
42032 Columbus 296 .... C7
41729 Combs 900 .... P6
41131 Concord 67 .... P3
40701 Corbin 8,075 .... N7
41010 Corinth 258 .... M3
42406 Corydon 874 .... F5
*41011 Covington 49,563 .... S2
40419 Crab Orchard 843 .... M6
†41016 Crescent Springs 1,951 .... R2
†41076 Crestview 528 .... S2
†41017 Crestview Hills 1,408 .... R2
40014 Crestwood 531 .... L4
41030 Crittenden 597 .... M3
42217 Crofton 823 .... G6
40823 Cumberland 3,712 .... R6
41031 Cynthiana⊙ 5,881 .... N4
40422 Danville⊙ 12,942 .... M5
42408 Dawson Springs 3,275 .... F6
41074 Dayton 6,979 .... T1
†40201 Devondale 1,164 .... K2
42036 Dexter E7
42409 Dixon⊙ 533 .... F5
†40243 Douglass Hills 4,384 .... L2
41034 Dover 305 .... O3
42337 Drakesboro 798 .... H6
41035 Dry Ridge 1,250 .... M3
42037 Dycusburg 64 .... E6
42410 Earlington 2,011 .... F6
42038 Eddyville⊙ 1,949 .... E6
†41017 Edgewood 7,230 .... S2
42129 Edmonton⊙ 1,401 .... K7
40117 Ekron 239 .... J5
42701 Elizabethtown⊙ 15,380 .... K5
41522 Elkhorn City 1,446 .... S6
42220 Elkton⊙ 1,815 .... G7
†41018 Elsmere 7,203 .... R2
40019 Eminence 2,260 .... L4
40826 Eolia 875 .... R6
41018 Erlanger 14,433 .... R2
40827 Essie 650 .... P6
42567 Eubank 207 .... M6
40828 Evarts 1,234 .... P7
41039 Ewing 144 .... O4
40118 Fairdale 7,315 .... K4
40020 Fairfield 169 .... L5
†41101 Fairview 198 .... S2
41040 Falmouth⊙ 2,482 .... N3
41524 Fedscreek 950 .... S6
42533 Ferguson 1,009 .... M6
†40222 Fincastle 804 .... L1
41139 Flatwoods 8,354 .... R4
41816 Fleming-Neon 1,195 .... R6
41041 Flemingsburg⊙ 2,835 .... O4
41042 Florence 15,586 .... R2
42343 Fordsville 561 .... H5
41527 Forest Hills 502 .... L2
40121 Fort Knox 31,055 .... K5
41017 Fort Mitchell 7,297 .... S2
41075 Fort Thomas 16,012 .... S2
†41011 Fort Wright 4,481 .... S2
41043 Foster 80 .... N3
42133 Fountain Run 340 .... K7
40601 Frankfort (cap.)⊙ 25,973 .... M4
42134 Franklin⊙ 7,738 .... J7
42411 Fredonia 535 .... E6
40322 Frenchburg⊙ 550 .... O5
†41175 Fullerton 950 .... P3
42041 Fulton 3,137 .... D7
42140 Gamaliel 456 .... K7
40324 Georgetown⊙ 10,972 .... M4
41044 Germantown 347 .... O3
41045 Ghent 439 .... L3
42044 Gilbertsville E7
42141 Glasgow⊙ 12,958 .... J7
41046 Glencoe 354 .... M3
†40222 Glenview 212 .... K1
†40222 Goose Creek 394 .... L1
42045 Grand Rivers 428 .... E7
†41005 Grant 150 .... M3
40327 Gratz 124 .... M4
†40201 Graymoor 1,167 .... K1
41143 Grayson⊙ 3,423 .... R4
42743 Greensburg⊙ 2,377 .... K6
41144 Greenup⊙ 1,386 .... R3
42345 Greenville⊙ 4,631 .... G6
42234 Guthrie 1,361 .... G7
42413 Hanson 485 .... G6
42048 Hardin 545 .... E7
40143 Hardinsburg⊙ 2,211 .... H5
41531 Hardy 900 .... S5
40831 Harlan⊙ 3,024 .... P7
40330 Harrodsburg⊙ 7,265 .... M5
42347 Hartford⊙ 2,512 .... H6
42348 Hawesville⊙ 1,036 .... H5
41701 Hazard⊙ 5,371 .... P6
42049 Hazel 465 .... E7
40949 Heidrick 400 .... O7
42420 Henderson⊙ 24,834 .... F5
42050 Hickman⊙ 2,894 .... C7
42051 Hickory D7
41076 Highland Heights 4,435 .... T2
41822 Hindman⊙ 876 .... R6
42152 Hiseville 349 .... K6
42748 Hodgenville⊙ 2,531 .... K5
†40228 Hollow Creek 1,023 .... K4
†41018 Hopeful Heights R2
42240 Hopkinsville⊙ 27,318 .... F7
42749 Horse Cave 2,045 .... K6
†40201 Houston Acres 608 .... K2
40437 Hustonville 339 .... M6
41749 Hyden⊙ 488 .... P6
41051 Independence⊙ 7,998 .... M3
†40201 Indian Hills 787 .... K1
41224 Inez⊙ 413 .... S5
40336 Irvine⊙ 2,889 .... O5
40146 Irvington 1,409 .... J5
42350 Island 532 .... G6
41642 Ivel 850 .... R5
41339 Jackson⊙ 2,651 .... P5
42629 Jamestown⊙ 1,441 .... L7
40299 Jeffersontown 15,795 .... L2
40337 Jeffersonville 1,528 .... O5
41537 Jenkins 3,271 .... R6
40440 Junction City 2,045 .... M5
40737 Keavy 900 .... N6
†41011 Kenton Vale 145 .... S2
42053 Kevil 382 .... D6
†40201 Kingsley 464 .... K2
42055 Kuttawa 560 .... E6
42056 La Center 1,044 .... C6
41643 Lackey R6
42254 La Fayette 160 .... F7
40031 La Grange⊙ 2,971 .... L4
†41017 Lakeside Park 3,038 .... R2
40444 Lancaster⊙ 3,365 .... M5
40342 Lawrenceburg⊙ 5,167 .... M4
40033 Lebanon⊙ 6,590 .... L5
40150 Lebanon Junction 1,581 .... K5
42754 Leitchfield⊙ 4,533 .... J6
42256 Lewisburg 972 .... G6
42351 Lewisport 1,832 .... H5
*40501 Lexington⊙ 204,165 .... N4
Lexington‡ 318,136 .... N4
42539 Liberty⊙ 2,206 .... M6
42352 Livermore 1,672 .... G5
40445 Livingston 334 .... N6
40036 Lockport 84 .... M4
40741 London⊙ 4,002 .... N6
42001 Lone Oak 443 .... D6
40037 Loretto 954 .... L5
41230 Louisa⊙ 1,832 .... R4
*40201 Louisville⊙ 298,840 .... J2
Louisville‡ 906,240 .... J2
40854 Loyall 1,210 .... P7
41016 Ludlow 4,959 .... S2
40855 Lynch 1,614 .... R7
†40201 Lynnview 1,157 .... K4
40040 Mackville 229 .... L5
42431 Madisonville⊙ 16,979 .... F6
40962 Manchester⊙ 1,838 .... O6
42064 Marion⊙ 3,392 .... E6
41649 Martin 827 .... R5
42066 Mayfield⊙ 10,705 .... D7
41056 Maysville⊙ 7,983 .... O3
41543 McAndrews 975 .... S5
42354 McHenry 582 .... H6
40447 McKee⊙ 759 .... O6
41835 McRoberts 1,106 .... R6
†40201 Meadow Vale 1,008 .... L1
41059 Melbourne 628 .... T2
†41060 Mentor 169 .... N3
40965 Middlesboro 12,251 .... O7
40243 Middletown 414 .... L2
40347 Midway 1,445 .... M4
40348 Millersburg 987 .... N4
40045 Milton 718 .... L3
†40201 Minor Lane Heights 1,882 .... K4
†40359 Monterey 186 .... M4
42633 Monticello⊙ 5,677 .... M7
†40223 Moorland 513 .... L2
40351 Morehead⊙ 7,789 .... P4
42437 Morganfield⊙ 3,781 .... E5
42261 Morgantown⊙ 2,000 .... H6
42440 Mortons Gap 1,201 .... F6
41064 Mount Olivet⊙ 346 .... N3
†40437 Mount Salem 50 .... M6
40353 Mount Sterling⊙ 5,820 .... N4
40456 Mount Vernon⊙ 2,334 .... N6
40047 Mount Washington 3,997 .... K4
41548 Mouthcard 900 .... S6
40155 Muldraugh 1,752 .... J5
42765 Munfordville⊙ 1,783 .... J6
42071 Murray⊙ 14,248 .... E7
42441 Nebo 269 .... F6
41840 Neon-Fleming 1,195 .... R6
40050 New Castle⊙ 832 .... L4
40051 New Haven 926 .... K5
*41071 Newport 21,587 .... S2
40356 Nicholasville⊙ 10,319 .... N5
†40201 Northfield 906 .... K1
40357 North Middletown 637 .... N4
42442 Nortonville 1,336 .... G6
42262 Oak Grove 2,088 .... G7
42159 Oakland 264 .... J6
41238 Oil Springs 900 .... P5
40219 Okolona 20,039 .... K4
41164 Olive Hill 2,539 .... P4
42301 Owensboro⊙ 54,450 .... G5
Owensboro‡ 85,949 .... G5
40359 Owenton⊙ 1,341 .... M3
40360 Owingsville⊙ 1,419 .... O4
42001 Paducah⊙ 29,315 .... D6
41240 Paintsville⊙ 3,815 .... R5
40361 Paris⊙ 7,935 .... N4
42160 Park City 614 .... J6
†41011 Park Hills 3,500 .... S2
†40201 Parkway Village 754 .... J2
42266 Pembroke 636 .... G7
40468 Perryville 841 .... M5
40056 Pewee Valley 982 .... L4
41553 Phelps 1,126 .... S6
41501 Pikeville⊙ 4,756 .... S6
42635 Pine Knot 1,389 .... M7
40977 Pineville⊙ 2,599 .... O7
†40201 Plantation 969 .... K1
40258 Pleasure Ridge Park 27,332 .... J4
40057 Pleasureville 837 .... L4
†42101 Plum Springs 393 .... J7
42367 Powderly 848 .... G6
41653 Prestonsburg⊙ 4,011 .... R5
†41008 Prestonville 205 .... L3
42445 Princeton⊙ 7,073 .... F6
40059 Prospect 1,981 .... K4
42450 Providence 4,434 .... F6
41169 Raceland 1,970 .... R3
40160 Radcliff 14,519 .... K5
40472 Ravenna 793 .... O5
40475 Richmond⊙ 21,705 .... N5
†40222 Riverwood 435 .... K1
42273 Rochester 289 .... H6

Agriculture, Industry and Resources

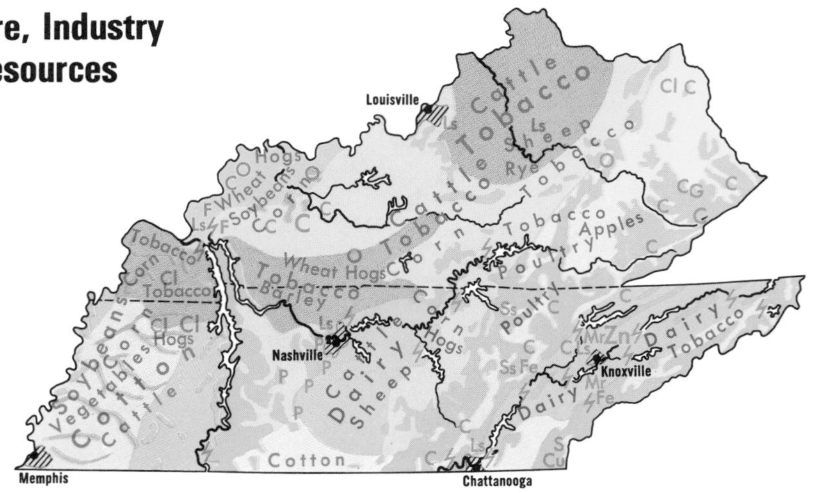

DOMINANT LAND USE

- Hogs, Soft Winter Wheat
- Tobacco, General Farming
- General Farming, Livestock, Tobacco
- General Farming, Livestock, Dairy
- General Farming, Livestock, Fruit, Tobacco
- Specialized Cotton
- Cotton, General Farming
- Cotton, Livestock
- Forests
- Swampland, Limited Agriculture

MAJOR MINERAL OCCURRENCES

C	Coal	G	Natural Gas	P	Phosphates
Cl	Clay	Ls	Limestone	S	Pyrites
Cu	Copper	Mr	Marble	Ss	Sandstone
F	Fluorspar	O	Petroleum	Zn	Zinc
Fe	Iron Ore				

Water Power

Major Industrial Areas

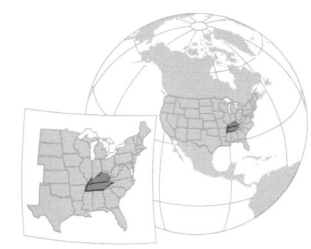

KENTUCKY

AREA 40,409 sq. mi. (104,659 sq. km.)
POPULATION 3,660,257
CAPITAL Frankfort
LARGEST CITY Louisville
HIGHEST POINT Black Mtn. 4,145 ft. (1263 m.)
SETTLED IN 1774
ADMITTED TO UNION June 1, 1792
POPULAR NAME Bluegrass State
STATE FLOWER Goldenrod
STATE BIRD Cardinal

TENNESSEE

AREA 42,144 sq. mi. (109,153 sq. km.)
POPULATION 4,591,120
CAPITAL Nashville
LARGEST CITY Memphis
HIGHEST POINT Clingmans Dome 6,643 ft. (2025 m.)
SETTLED IN 1757
ADMITTED TO UNION June 1, 1796
POPULAR NAME Volunteer State
STATE FLOWER Iris
STATE BIRD Mockingbird

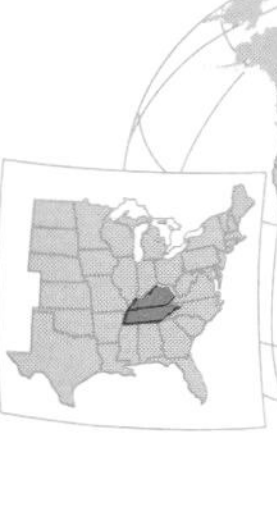

42369 Rockport 511 .... H6
†40201 Rolling Fields 731 .... K2
†40201 Rolling Hills 1,122 .... L1
41169 Russell 3,824 .... R3
42642 Russell Springs 1,831 .... L6
42276 Russellville⊙ 7,520 .... H7
†41015 Ryland Heights 252 .... M3
42372 Sacramento 538 .... G6
40370 Sadieville 253 .... M4
42453 Saint Charles 405 .... F6
40207 Saint Matthews 13,519 .... K2
†40201 Saint Regis Park 1,735 .... K2
42078 Salem 833 .... E6
40371 Salt Lick 347 .... O4
41465 Salyersville⊙ 1,352 .... P5
41083 Sanders 332 .... M3
41171 Sandy Hook⊙ 627 .... P4
41056 Sardis 198 .... O3
42553 Science Hill 655 .... M6
42164 Scottsville⊙ 4,278 .... J7
42455 Sebree 1,516 .... F5
†40201 Seneca Gardens 748 .... K2
40983 Sextons Creek 975 .... O6
40374 Sharpsburg 339 .... O4
40065 Shelbyville⊙ 5,329 .... L4
40165 Shepherdsville⊙ 4,454 .... K4
40216 Shively 16,819 .... K4
41085 Silver Grove 1,260 .... T2
40067 Simpsonville 642 .... L4
42456 Slaughters 269 .... F6
41764 Smilax 987 .... P6
40068 Smithfield 137 .... L4
42081 Smithland⊙ 512 .... E6
42171 Smiths Grove 767 .... J6
42501 Somerset⊙ 10,649 .... M6
42776 Sonora 416 .... K5
42374 South Carrollton 262 .... G6
41071 Southgate 2,833 .... T2
41174 South Portsmouth 900 .... P3
41175 South Shore 1,525 .... R3
25661 South Williamson 1,016 .... S5
41086 Sparta 192 .... M3
42458 Spottsville 914 .... G5
40069 Springfield⊙ 3,179 .... L5
†40201 Springlee 498 .... K2
40379 Stamping Ground 562 .... M4
40484 Stanford⊙ 2,764 .... M5
40380 Stanton⊙ 2,691 .... O5
42647 Stearns 1,557 .... N7
41567 Stone 900 .... S5
†40201 Strathmoor Village 466 .... J2
42459 Sturgis 2,293 .... F5
†41011 Taylor Mill 4,509 .... S2
40071 Taylorsville⊙ 801 .... L4
†40222 Thornhill 233 .... K1
41189 Tollesboro 808 .... O3
42167 Tompkinsville⊙ 4,366 .... K7
42286 Trenton 465 .... G7
41091 Union 601 .... M3
42461 Uniontown 1,169 .... F5
42784 Upton 731 .... K6
40272 Valley Station 24,474 .... K4
41179 Vanceburg⊙ 1,939 .... P3
41265 Van Lear 2,035 .... R5
†40828 Verda 1,133 .... P7
40383 Versailles⊙ 6,427 .... M4
41773 Vicco 456 .... P6
†41017 Villa Hills 4,402 .... R2
40175 Vine Grove 3,583 .... K5
†41063 Visalia 198 .... N3
40873 Wallins Creek 459 .... O7
41094 Walton 1,651 .... M3
41095 Warsaw⊙ 1,328 .... M3
41096 Washington 624 .... O3
42085 Water Valley 395 .... D7
42462 Waverly 434 .... F5
42167 Wayland 601 .... R6
41667 Weeksbury 850 .... R6
†40201 Wellington 653 .... K2
†40218 West Buechel 1,205 .... K2
41472 West Liberty⊙ 1,381 .... P5
40177 West Point 1,339 .... J4
†42501 West Somerset 850 .... M6
41101 Westwood 5,973 .... R4
†40207 Westwood 826 .... L1
42463 Wheatcroft 325 .... F5
41669 Wheelwright 865 .... R6
41390 Whick 280 .... P6
42464 White Plains 859 .... G6
41858 Whitesburg⊙ 1,525 .... R6
42378 Whitesville 788 .... H5
42653 Whitley City⊙ 1,683 .... N7
42087 Wickliffe⊙ 1,034 .... C7
†41071 Wilders 633 .... S2
40769 Williamsburg⊙ 5,560 .... N7
41097 Williamstown⊙ 2,502 .... M3
40078 Willisburg 235 .... L5
40390 Wilmore 3,787 .... M5
40391 Winchester⊙ 15,216 .... N5
†40201 Windy Hills 2,214 .... K1
42087 Wingo 606 .... D7
40771 Woodbine 900 .... N7
42170 Woodburn 330 .... J7
†40201 Woodland Hills 839 .... L2
†42001 Woodlawn-Oakdale 4,722 .... D6
†41071 Woodlawn 331 .... T2
†40201 Woodlawn Park 1,052 .... K2
41183 Worthington 1,948 .... R3
41098 Worthville 272 .... L3
41144 Wurtland 1,301 .... R3

OTHER FEATURES

Abraham Lincoln Birthplace Nat'l Hist. Site K5
Barkley (dam) E6
Barkley (lake) F7
Barren (riv.) H6
Barren River (lake) J7
Beech Fork (riv.) L5
Big Sandy (riv.) R4
Black (mt.) R7
Buckhorn (lake) O6
Chaplin (riv.) L5
Clarks, East Fork (riv.) E7
Cove Run (lake) O4
Cumberland (lake) M7
Cumberland (mt.) P7
Cumberland (riv.) K8
Cumberland Gap Nat'l Hist. Park P7
Dale Hollow (lake) L7
Dewey (lake) R5
Dix (riv.) M5
Drakes (creek) J7
Dry (creek) R3
Eagle (creek) M3
Fishtrap (lake) S6
Fort Campbell G7
Grayson (lake) P4
Green (riv.) G6
Green River (lake) L6
Herrington (lake) M5
Hinkston (creek) N4
Kentucky (dam) E7
Kentucky (lake) E8
Kentucky (riv.) M3
Land Between The Lakes Rec. Area E7
Laurel River (lake) N6
Lexington Blue Grass Army Depot N5
Licking (riv.) N3
Mammoth Cave Nat'l Park J6
Mayfield (creek) C7
Mississippi (riv.) A10
Mud (riv.) H7
Nolin (lake) K6
Nolin (riv.) J6
Obion (creek) C7
Ohio (riv.) F5
Paint Lick (riv.) M5
Panther (creek) G5
Pine (mt.) O7
Pond (riv.) G6
Red (riv.) O5
Red (riv.) G7
Rockcastle (riv.) N6
Rolling Fork (riv.) L5
Rough (riv.) H5
Rough River (lake) J5
Salt (riv.) K5
Tennessee (riv.) D6
Tradewater (riv.) F6
Tug Fork (riv.) S5

TENNESSEE

COUNTIES

Anderson 67,346 .... N8
Bedford 27,916 .... J9
Benton 14,901 .... E8
Bledsoe 9,478 .... L9
Blount 77,770 .... O9
Bradley 67,547 .... M10
Campbell 34,923 .... N8
Cannon 10,234 .... J9
Carroll 28,285 .... E9
Carter 50,205 .... S8
Cheatham 21,616 .... G8
Chester 12,727 .... D10
Claiborne 24,595 .... O8
Clay 7,676 .... K7
Cocke 28,792 .... P9
Coffee 38,311 .... J9
Crockett 14,941 .... C9
Cumberland 28,676 .... L9
Davidson 477,811 .... H8
Decatur 10,857 .... E9
De Kalb 13,589 .... K9
Dickson 30,037 .... G8
Dyer 34,663 .... C8
Fayette 25,305 .... C10
Fentress 14,826 .... M8
Franklin 31,983 .... J10
Gibson 49,467 .... D9
Giles 24,625 .... G10
Grainger 16,751 .... O8
Greene 54,422 .... R8
Grundy 13,787 .... K10
Hamblen 49,300 .... P8
Hamilton 287,740 .... L10
Hancock 6,887 .... P7
Hardeman 23,873 .... C10
Hardin 22,280 .... E10
Hawkins 43,751 .... P8
Haywood 20,318 .... C9
Henderson 21,390 .... E9
Henry 28,656 .... E8
Hickman 15,151 .... G9
Houston 6,871 .... F8
Humphreys 15,957 .... F8
Jackson 9,398 .... K8
Jefferson 31,284 .... P8
Johnson 13,745 .... T7
Knox 319,694 .... O9
Lake 7,455 .... B8
Lauderdale 24,555 .... B9
Lawrence 34,110 .... G10
Lewis 9,700 .... F9
Lincoln 26,483 .... H10
Loudon 28,553 .... N9
Macon 15,700 .... J7
Madison 74,546 .... D9
Marion 24,416 .... K10
Marshall 19,698 .... H10
Maury 51,095 .... G9
McMinn 41,878 .... M10
McNairy 22,525 .... D10
Meigs 7,431 .... M9
Monroe 28,700 .... N10
Montgomery 83,342 .... G8
Moore 4,510 .... J10
Morgan 16,604 .... M8
Obion 32,781 .... C8
Overton 17,575 .... L8
Perry 6,111 .... F9
Pickett 4,358 .... M7
Polk 13,602 .... N10
Putnam 47,690 .... K8
Rhea 24,235 .... M9
Roane 48,425 .... M9
Robertson 37,021 .... H7
Rutherford 84,058 .... J9
Scott 19,259 .... M8
Sequatchie 8,605 .... L10
Sevier 41,418 .... O9
Shelby 777,113 .... B10
Smith 14,935 .... J8
Stewart 8,665 .... F7
Sullivan 143,968 .... S7
Sumner 85,790 .... J8
Tipton 32,930 .... B9
Trousdale 6,137 .... J8
Unicoi 16,362 .... S8
Union 11,707 .... O8
Van Buren 4,728 .... L9
Warren 32,653 .... K9
Washington 88,755 .... R8
Wayne 13,946 .... F10
Weakley 32,896 .... D8
White 19,567 .... L9
Williamson 58,108 .... H9
Wilson 56,064 .... J8

CITIES and TOWNS

Zip *Name/Pop.* *Key*

†38301 Adair 70 .... D9
37010 Adams 600 .... G7
38310 Adamsville 1,453 .... E10
38001 Alamo⊙ 2,615 .... C9
37701 Alcoa 6,870 .... N9
37012 Alexandria 689 .... J8
38501 Algood 2,406 .... K8
38504 Allardt 654 .... M8
37301 Altamont⊙ 679 .... K10
38449 Ardmore 835 .... H10
38002 Arlington 1,778 .... B10
37015 Ashland City⊙ 2,329 .... G8
37303 Athens⊙ 12,080 .... M10
38004 Atoka 691 .... B10
38220 Atwood 1,143 .... D9
37016 Auburntown 204 .... J9
37743 Baileyton 333 .... R8
†37650 Banner Hill 2,913 .... R8
38134 Bartlett 17,170 .... B10
38544 Baxter 1,411 .... K8
37305 Beersheba Springs 643 .... K10
37020 Bell Buckle 450 .... J9
37205 Belle Meade 3,182 .... H8
38006 Bells 1,571 .... C9
37307 Benton⊙ 1,115 .... M10
†37201 Berry Hill 1,113 .... H8
†37027 Berry's Chapel 2,703 .... H9
38315 Bethel Springs 873 .... D10
38221 Big Sandy 650 .... E8
37709 Blaine 1,147 .... O8
37660 Bloomingdale 12,088 .... R7
37617 Blountville⊙ 2,554 .... S7
37618 Bluff City 1,121 .... S8
38008 Bolivar⊙ 6,597 .... C10
38010 Braden 293 .... B10
38316 Bradford 1,146 .... D8
37027 Brentwood 9,431 .... H8
37710 Briceville 850 .... N8
38011 Brighton 976 .... B10
37620 Bristol 23,986 .... S7
38012 Brownsville⊙ 9,307 .... C9
38317 Bruceton 1,579 .... E8
37711 Bulls Gap 821 .... P8
38015 Burlison 386 .... B9
37029 Burns 777 .... G8
38549 Byrdstown⊙ 884 .... L7
37309 Calhoun 590 .... M10
38320 Camden⊙ 3,279 .... E8
37030 Carthage⊙ 2,672 .... K8
37714 Caryville 2,039 .... N8
37032 Cedar Hill 420 .... H7
38551 Celina⊙ 1,580 .... K7
†37110 Centertown 300 .... K9
37033 Centerville⊙ 2,824 .... G9
37034 Chapel Hill 861 .... H9
37310 Charleston 756 .... M10
37036 Charlotte⊙ 788 .... G8
*37401 Chattanooga⊙ 169,558 .... K10
Chattanooga‡ 426,540 .... K10
37642 Church Hill 4,110 .... R7
38324 Clarksburg 400 .... E9
37040 Clarksville⊙ 54,777 .... G7
Clarksville‡ 150,220 .... G7
37311 Cleveland⊙ 26,415 .... M10
38425 Clifton 773 .... F10
37716 Clinton⊙ 5,245 .... N8
37313 Coalmont 625 .... K10
37315 Collegedale 4,607 .... M10
38017 Collierville 7,839 .... B10
38450 Collinwood 1,064 .... F10
37663 Colonial Heights 6,744 .... R8
38401 Columbia⊙ 26,571 .... G9
37720 Concord 8,569 .... N9
38501 Cookeville⊙ 20,535 .... L8
37317 Copperhill 418 .... N10
37047 Cornersville 722 .... H10
38224 Cottage Grove 117 .... E8
38326 Counce 975 .... E10
38019 Covington⊙ 6,065 .... B9
37318 Cowan 1,790 .... K10
37723 Crab Orchard 1,065 .... M9
37049 Cross Plains 655 .... H7
38555 Crossville⊙ 6,394 .... L9
37050 Cumberland City 276 .... F8
37724 Cumberland Gap 263 .... O8
37725 Dandridge⊙ 1,383 .... O8
37321 Dayton⊙ 5,913 .... L9
37322 Decatur⊙ 1,069 .... M9
38329 Decaturville⊙ 1,004 .... E9
37324 Decherd 2,233 .... J10
38391 Denmark 51 .... D9
37055 Dickson 7,040 .... G8
37058 Dover⊙ 1,197 .... F8
37059 Dowelltown 341 .... K8
38559 Doyle 344 .... K9
38225 Dresden⊙ 2,256 .... D8
37326 Ducktown 583 .... N10
37327 Dunlap⊙ 3,681 .... L10
38330 Dyer 2,419 .... D8
38024 Dyersburg⊙ 15,856 .... C8
†37801 Eagleton Village 5,331 .... O9
37060 Eagleville 444 .... H9
37412 East Ridge 21,236 .... L11
†38367 Eastview 552 .... D10
37643 Elizabethton⊙ 12,431 .... S8
38455 Elkton 540 .... H10
38029 Ellendale 850 .... B10
37329 Englewood 1,840 .... M10
38332 Enville 287 .... E10
37061 Erin⊙ 1,614 .... F8
37650 Erwin⊙ 4,739 .... S8
37330 Estill Springs 1,324 .... J10
38456 Ethridge 548 .... G10
37331 Etowah 3,758 .... M10
37062 Fairview 3,648 .... G9
37656 Fall Branch 1,340 .... R8
37334 Fayetteville⊙ 7,559 .... H10
38334 Finger 245 .... D10
38030 Finley 1,014 .... B8
†37201 Forest Hills 4,516 .... H8
37064 Franklin⊙ 12,407 .... H9
38034 Friendship 763 .... C9
37737 Friendsville 694 .... N9
38337 Gadsden 683 .... D9
38562 Gainesboro⊙ 1,119 .... K8
37066 Gallatin⊙ 17,191 .... H8
38036 Gallaway 804 .... B10
†38019 Garland 301 .... B9
38037 Gates 729 .... C9
37738 Gatlinburg 3,210 .... O9
38138 Germantown 21,482 .... B10
38338 Gibson 458 .... D9
†38015 Gilt Edge 142 .... B9
38229 Gleason 1,335 .... D8
37072 Goodlettsville 8,327 .... H8
38563 Gordonsville 893 .... K8
38039 Grand Junction 360 .... C10
37338 Graysville 1,380 .... L10
37742 Greenback 546 .... N9
37073 Greenbrier 3,180 .... H8
37743 Greeneville⊙ 14,097 .... R8
38230 Greenfield 2,109 .... D8
37339 Gruetli 910 .... K10
38040 Halls 2,444 .... C9
37658 Hampton 2,236 .... S8
37748 Harriman 8,303 .... M9
37341 Harrison 6,206 .... L10
37752 Harrogate-Shawanee 2,530 .... O8
37074 Hartsville⊙ 2,674 .... J8
38340 Henderson⊙ 4,449 .... D10
37075 Hendersonville 26,561 .... H8
38041 Henning 638 .... B9
38231 Henry 295 .... E8
38042 Hickory Valley 252 .... C10
38462 Hohenwald⊙ 3,922 .... F9
38342 Hollow Rock 955 .... E8
38232 Hornbeak 452 .... C8
38044 Hornsby 401 .... D10
38343 Humboldt 10,209 .... D9
38344 Huntingdon⊙ 3,962 .... E8
37345 Huntland 983 .... J10
37756 Huntsville⊙ 519 .... N8
37078 Hurricane Mills 850 .... F9
38463 Iron City 482 .... F10
37757 Jacksboro⊙ 1,722 .... N8
38301 Jackson⊙ 49,131 .... D9
38556 Jamestown⊙ 2,364 .... M8
37347 Jasper⊙ 2,633 .... K10
37760 Jefferson City 5,612 .... P8
37762 Jellico 2,798 .... N7
37601 Johnson City 39,753 .... S8
Johnson City-Kingsport-Bristol‡ 433,638 .... S8
37659 Jonesboro⊙ 2,829 .... R8
37921 Karns 1,173 .... N9
38233 Kenton 1,551 .... C8
†37347 Kimball 1,220 .... K10
*37660 Kingsport 32,027 .... R7
37763 Kingston⊙ 4,441 .... N9
37082 Kingston Springs 1,017 .... G8
*37901 Knoxville⊙ 175,045 .... O9
Knoxville‡ 476,517 .... O9
37083 Lafayette⊙ 3,808 .... J7
37766 La Follette 8,198 .... N8
38046 La Grange 185 .... C10
37769 Lake City 2,335 .... N8
†38134 Lakeland 612 .... B10
†37379 Lakesite 651 .... L10
†37138 Lakewood 2,325 .... H8
37086 La Vergne 5,495 .... H9
38464 Lawrenceburg⊙ 10,184 .... G10
37087 Lebanon⊙ 11,872 .... J8
37771 Lenoir City 5,446 .... N9
37091 Lewisburg⊙ 8,760 .... H10
38351 Lexington⊙ 5,934 .... E9
37095 Liberty 365 .... K8
37096 Linden⊙ 1,087 .... F9
38570 Livingston⊙ 3,372 .... L8
37097 Lobelville 993 .... F9
37350 Lookout Mountain 1,886 .... L11
38469 Loretto 1,612 .... G10
37774 Loudon⊙ 3,943 .... N9
37779 Luttrell 962 .... O8
37352 Lynchburg⊙ 668 .... J10
38472 Lynnville 383 .... G10
37354 Madisonville⊙ 2,884 .... N9
37355 Manchester⊙ 7,250 .... J10
38237 Martin 8,898 .... D8
37801 Maryville⊙ 17,480 .... O9
37806 Mascot 2,203 .... O8
38049 Mason 471 .... B10
38050 Maury City 989 .... C9
37807 Maynardville⊙ 924 .... O8
37101 McEwen 1,352 .... F8
38201 McKenzie 5,405 .... E8
38235 McLemoresville 311 .... D9
37110 McMinnville⊙ 10,683 .... K9
38355 Medina 687 .... D9
38356 Medon 169 .... D10
*38101 Memphis⊙ 646,174 .... B10
Memphis‡ 912,887 .... B10
38357 Michie 530 .... E10
38052 Middleton 596 .... D10
38358 Milan 8,083 .... D9
38359 Milledgeville 392 .... E10
38053 Millington 20,236 .... B10
38473 Minor Hill 564 .... G10
37119 Mitchellville 209 .... J7
37356 Monteagle 1,126 .... K10
38574 Monterey 2,610 .... L8
37357 Morrison 587 .... K9
†37660 Morrison City 2,032 .... R7
37814 Morristown⊙ 19,683 .... P8
38057 Moscow 499 .... C10
37818 Mosheim 1,539 .... R8
37683 Mountain City⊙ 2,125 .... T8
37642 Mount Carmel 3,764 .... R8
37122 Mount Juliet 2,879 .... H8
38474 Mount Pleasant 3,375 .... G9
38058 Munford 2,336 .... B10
37130 Murfreesboro⊙ 32,845 .... J9
*37201 Nashville (cap.)⊙ 455,651 .... H8
Nashville-Davidson‡ 850,505 .... H8
38059 Newbern 2,794 .... C8
†37380 New Hope 681 .... K11
37134 New Johnsonville 1,824 .... E8
37820 New Market 1,216 .... O8
37821 Newport⊙ 7,580 .... P9
37825 New Tazewell 1,677 .... O8
37826 Niota 765 .... M9
37360 Normandy 118 .... J10
37828 Norris 1,374 .... N8
37829 Oakdale 323 .... M9
†37201 Oak Hill 4,609 .... H8
38060 Oakland 472 .... B10
37830 Oak Ridge 27,662 .... N8
38240 Obion 1,282 .... C8
37840 Oliver Springs 3,659 .... N8
37841 Oneida 3,717 .... N7
37363 Ooltewah 950 .... M10
†37660 Orebank 1,284 .... R7
37141 Orlinda 382 .... H7
35740 Orme 181 .... K10
37365 Palmer 1,027 .... K10
38242 Paris⊙ 10,728 .... E8
37843 Parrottsville 118 .... P8
38363 Parsons 2,422 .... E9
37143 Pegram 1,081 .... H8
37144 Petersburg 681 .... H10
37845 Petros 1,286 .... M8
37846 Philadelphia 507 .... M9
37863 Pigeon Forge 1,822 .... O9
37367 Pikeville⊙ 2,085 .... L9
†38017 Piperton 746 .... B10
†37738 Pittman Center 488 .... P9
38578 Pleasant Hill 371 .... L9
37148 Portland 4,030 .... H7
37849 Powell 7,220 .... N8
†37397 Powells Crossroads 918 .... L10
38478 Pulaski⊙ 7,184 .... G10
38251 Puryear 624 .... E8
38367 Ramer 429 .... D10
37415 Red Bank 13,299 .... L10
37150 Red Boiling Springs 1,173 .... K7
†37641 Rheatown R8
†37380 Richard City 87 .... K11
38080 Ridgely 1,932 .... B8
†37401 Ridgeside 417 .... L10
37152 Ridgetop 1,225 .... H8
38063 Ripley⊙ 6,366 .... B9
38253 Rives 386 .... C8
37687 Roan Mountain 1,108 .... S8
37853 Rockford 567 .... O9
37854 Rockwood 5,767 .... M9
37857 Rogersville⊙ 4,368 .... P8
38053 Rosemark 950 .... B10
38066 Rossville 379 .... B10
37860 Russellville 1,069 .... P8
38369 Rutherford 1,378 .... C8
37861 Rutledge⊙ 1,058 .... P8
38481 Saint Joseph 897 .... G10
37373 Sale Creek 900 .... L10
38370 Saltillo 434 .... E10
38254 Samburg 465 .... C8
38371 Sardis 301 .... E10
38067 Saulsbury 156 .... C10
38372 Savannah⊙ 6,992 .... E10
38374 Scotts Hill 668 .... E10
38375 Selmer⊙ 3,979 .... D10
37862 Sevierville⊙ 4,556 .... P9
37375 Sewanee 2,298 .... K10
38255 Sharon 1,134 .... D8
37160 Shelbyville⊙ 13,530 .... H10
37376 Sherwood 900 .... K10
37377 Signal Mountain 5,818 .... L10
38377 Silerton 100 .... D10
37165 Slayden 69 .... G8
37166 Smithville⊙ 3,839 .... K9
37167 Smyrna 8,839 .... H9
37869 Sneedville⊙ 1,110 .... P7
37319 Soddy-Daisy 8,388 .... L10
38068 Somerville⊙ 2,264 .... C10
†37030 South Carthage 1,004 .... K8
†37311 South Cleveland 4,360 .... M10
†37716 South Clinton 1,671 .... N8
†42041 South Fulton 2,735 .... D8
37380 South Pittsburg 3,636 .... K10
37171 Southside 800 .... G8
38583 Sparta⊙ 4,864 .... K9
38585 Spencer⊙ 1,126 .... L9
37381 Spring City 1,951 .... M9
37172 Springfield⊙ 10,814 .... H8
37174 Spring Hill 989 .... H9
38069 Stanton 540 .... C10
38379 Stantonville 271 .... E10
†37660 Sullivan Gardens 2,513 .... R8
38483 Summertown 850 .... G10
37873 Surgoinsville 1,536 .... R8
37874 Sweetwater 4,725 .... N9
37877 Talbott 975 .... P8
37879 Tazewell⊙ 2,090 .... O8
37385 Tellico Plains 698 .... N10
37178 Tennessee Ridge 1,325 .... F8
38079 Tiptonville⊙ 2,438 .... B8
38381 Toone 355 .... D10
37882 Townsend 351 .... O9
37387 Tracy City 1,356 .... K10
38382 Trenton⊙ 4,601 .... D9
38258 Trezevant 921 .... D8
38259 Trimble 722 .... C8
38260 Troy 1,093 .... C8
37388 Tullahoma 15,800 .... J10
37743 Tusculum 1,242 .... R8
38261 Union City⊙ 10,436 .... C8
37181 Vanleer 401 .... G8
†37397 Victoria 800 .... K10
37394 Viola 149 .... K9

(continued on following page)

37885 Vonore 528 ....N9
†37377 Walden 1,293 ....L10
37887 Wartburg⊙ 761 ....M8
37183 Wartrace 540 ....J9
37694 Watauga 376 ....S8
37184 Watertown 1,300 ....J8
37185 Waverly⊙ 4,405 ....F8
38485 Waynesboro⊙ 2,109 ....F10
38074 Western Institute 850 ...C10
37186 Westmoreland 1,754 ......J7
37187 White Bluff 2,055 ....G8
37188 White House 2,225 ....H8
37890 White Pine 1,900 ....P8
38075 Whiteville 1,270 ....C10
37397 Whitwell 1,783 ....K10
38076 Williston 395 ....C10
37398 Winchester⊙ 5,821 ....J10
37190 Woodbury⊙ 2,160 ....J9
38271 Woodland Mills 526 ......C8
38389 Yorkville 272 ....C8

OTHER FEATURES

Andrew Johnson Nat'l Hist. Site ..R8
Appalachian (mts.) M10
Bald (mts.) R9
Barkley (lake) F7
Big Sandy (riv.) E9
Boone (lake) S8
Buffalo (riv.) F9
Caney Fork (riv.) L9
Center Hill (lake) K9
Cheatham (dam) H8
Cheatham (lake) H8
Cherokee (dam) P8
Cherokee (lake) P8
Chickamauga (dam) L10
Chickamauga (lake) L10
Chilhowee (mt.) O9
Clinch (riv.) N9
Clingmans Dome (mt.) P10
Collins (riv.) K9
Conasauga (riv.) M11
Cordell Hull (res.) K8
Cumberland (plat.) L9
Cumberland (riv.) K9
Cumberland Gap Nat'l Hist. Park ...O7
Dale Hollow (lake) L7
Douglas (lake) P9
Duck (riv.) F9
Elk (riv.) H10
Emory (riv.) M8
Forked Deer (riv.) C9
Fort Campbell G7
Fort Donelson Nat'l Mil. Park F8
Fort Loudoun (lake) N9
French Broad (riv.) P9
Great Falls (dam) K9
Great Smoky (mts.) P9
Great Smoky Mountains Nat'l
  Park P9
Green (riv.) F10
Guyot (mt.) P9
Harpeth (riv.) G8
Hatchie (riv.) B9
Hiwassee (riv.) O10
Holston (riv.) O8
Iron (mts.) S8
Kentucky (lake) E8
Land Between The Lakes Rec.
  Area E7
Lick (creek) R8
Little Tennessee (riv.) N10
Looosahatchie (riv.) B10
Melton Hill (lake) N9
Memphis Naval Air Sta. B10
Meriwether Lewis Park, Natchez Trace
  Pkwy. G10
Mississippi (riv.) A10
Nolichucky (riv.) R8
Norris (dam) N8
Norris (lake) O8
Obed (riv.) M8
Obion (riv.) C8
Ocoee (riv.) M10
Old Hickory (dam) H8
Old Hickory (lake) J8
Pickwick (lake) E11
Powell (riv.) P8
Priest, J. Percy (lake) J8
Red (riv.) G7
Reelfoot (lake) C8
Richland (creek) G10
Rutherford Fork, Obion (riv.) ..D8
Sequatchie (riv.) L10
Sewart A.F.B. J8
Shiloh Nat'l Mil. Park E10
Shoal (creek) F10
South Holston (lake) S7
Stone (riv.) T8
Stones (riv.) H9
Stones River Nat'l Battlefield ...H9
Sulphur Fork, Red (riv.) H8
Tellico (riv.) N10
Tennessee (riv.) E10
Tims Ford (lake) J10
Unaka (mts.) S8
Unicoi (mts.) N10
Watauga (lake) T8
Watts Bar (dam) M9
Watts Bar (lake) M9
Whiteoak (creek) F8
Wolf (riv.) B10
Woods (res.) J10
Yellow (creek) F8

⊙County seat.
‡Population of metropolitan area.
† Zip of nearest p.o.
* Multiple zips.

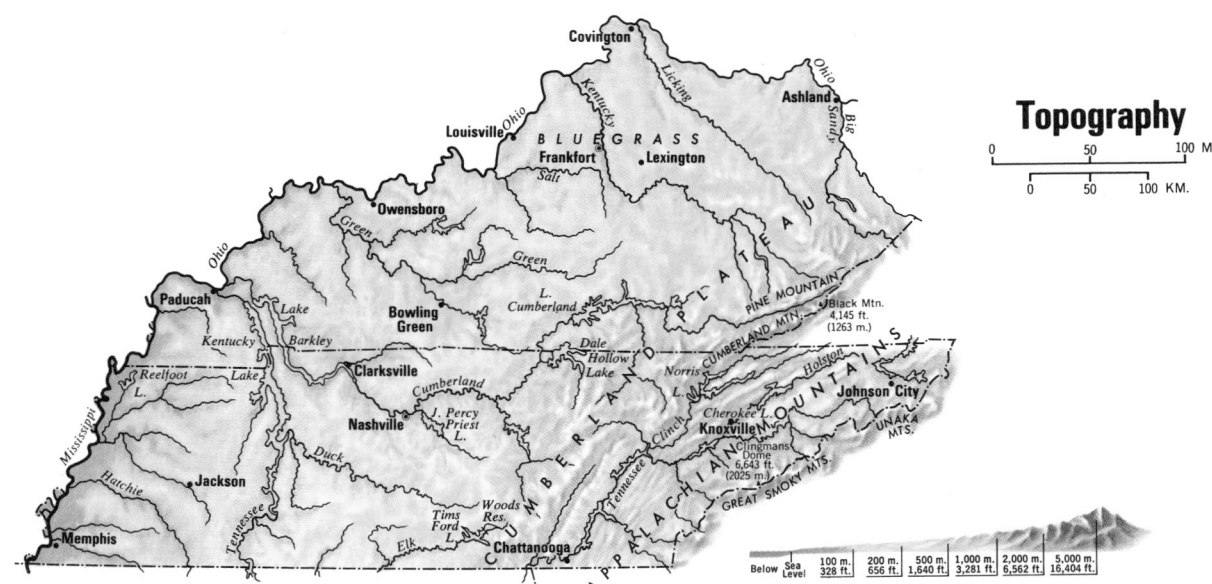

Topography

| Below Sea Level | 100 m. 328 ft. | 200 m. 656 ft. | 500 m. 1,640 ft. | 1,000 m. 3,281 ft. | 2,000 m. 6,562 ft. | 5,000 m. 16,404 ft. |

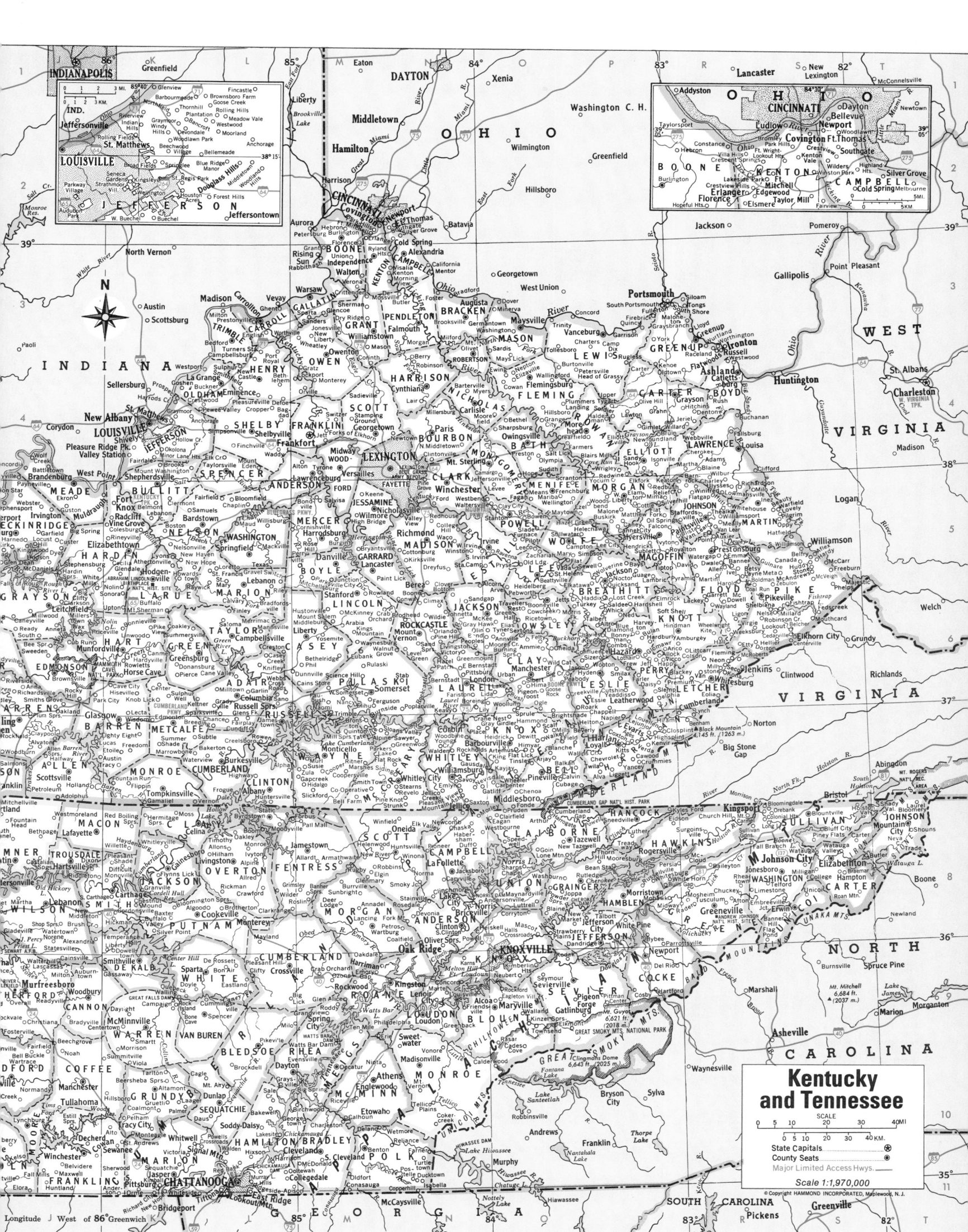

Kentucky and Tennessee

SCALE

0 5 10 20 30 40 MI

0 5 10 20 30 40 KM.

State Capitals ⊛

County Seats ◉

Major Limited Access Hwys.

Scale 1:1,970,000

© Copyright HAMMOND INCORPORATED, Maplewood, N.J.

Topography

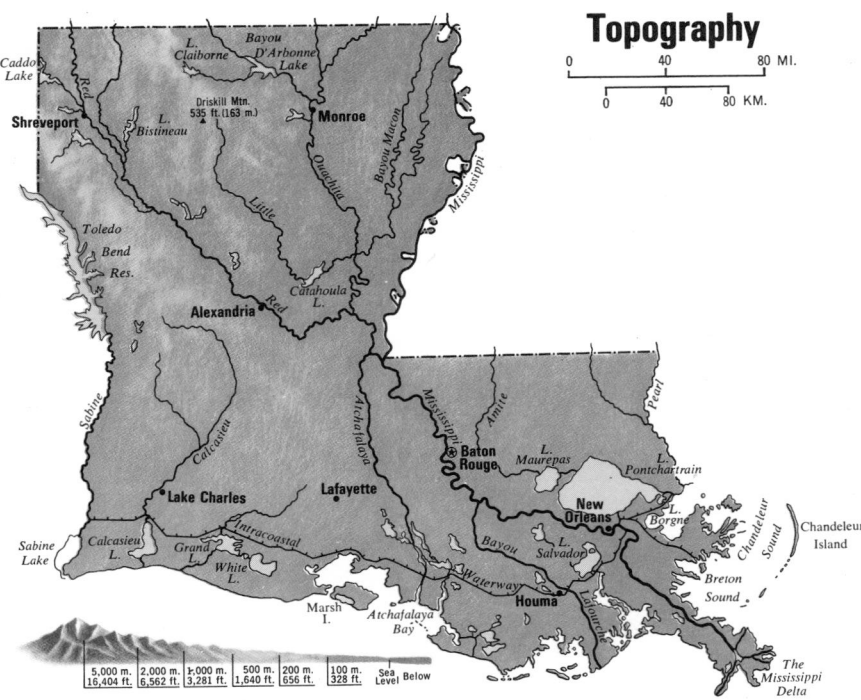

0 40 80 MI.
0 40 80 KM.

Driskill Mtn. 535 ft. (163 m.)

Shreveport
Monroe
L. Claiborne
Bayou D'Arbonne Lake
Caddo Lake
Red
L. Bistineau
Toledo Bend Res.
Ouachita
Little
Bayou Macon
Mississippi
Catahoula L.
Alexandria
Red
Sabine
Calcasieu
Lake Charles
Lafayette
Intracoastal
Sabine Lake
Calcasieu L.
White L.
Grand L.
Marsh I.
Atchafalaya Bay
Atchafalaya
Waterway
Bayou
Baton Rouge
L. Maurepas
L. Pontchartrain
New Orleans
L. Salvador
L. Borgne
Amite
Pearl
Houma
The Mississippi Delta
Chandeleur Sound
Chandeleur Island
Breton Sound

5,000 m. 16,404 ft. | 2,000 m. 6,562 ft. | 1,000 m. 3,281 ft. | 500 m. 1,640 ft. | 200 m. 656 ft. | 100 m. 328 ft. | Sea Level | Below

PARISHES

Acadia 56,427 ....F6
Allen 21,390 ....E5
Ascension 50,068 ....J6
Assumption 22,084 ....H7
Avoyelles 41,393 ....G4
Beauregard 29,692 ....D5
Bienville 16,387 ....D2
Bossier 80,721 ....C1
Caddo 252,358 ....C1
Calcasieu 167,223 ....D6
Caldwell 10,761 ....F2
Cameron 9,336 ....D7
Catahoula 12,287 ....G3
Claiborne 17,095 ....D1
Concordia 22,981 ....G4
De Soto 25,727 ....C2
East Baton Rouge 366,191 .....K1
East Carroll 11,772 ....H1
East Feliciana 19,015 ....H5
Evangeline 33,343 ....F5
Franklin 24,141 ....G2
Grant 16,703 ....E3
Iberia 63,752 ....G7
Iberville 32,159 ....H6
Jackson 17,321 ....E2
Jefferson 454,592 ....K7
Jefferson Davis 32,168 ....E6
Lafayette 150,017 ....F6
Lafourche 82,483 ....K7
La Salle 17,004 ....F3
Lincoln 39,763 ....E1
Livingston 58,806 ....L2
Madison 15,975 ....H2
Morehouse 34,803 ....G1
Natchitoches 39,863 ....D3
Orleans 557,515 ....L6
Ouachita 139,241 ....F2
Plaquemines 26,049 ....L8
Pointe Coupee 24,045 ....G5
Rapides 135,282 ....E4
Red River 10,433 ....D2
Richland 22,187 ....G2
Sabine 25,280 ....C3
Saint Bernard 64,097 ....L7
Saint Charles 37,259 ....K7
Saint Helena 9,827 ....J5
Saint James 21,495 ....L3
Saint John the Baptist 31,924 .M3
Saint Landry 84,128 ....F5
Saint Martin 40,214 ....G6
Saint Mary 64,253 ....H7
Saint Tammany 110,869 ....L6
Tangipahoa 80,698 ....K5
Tensas 8,525 ....H2
Terrebonne 94,393 ....J8
Union 21,167 ....F1
Vermilion 48,458 ....F7
Vernon 53,475 ....D4
Washington 44,207 ....K5
Webster 43,631 ....D1
West Baton Rouge 19,086 .....H6
West Carroll 12,922 ....H1
West Feliciana 12,186 ....H5
Winn 17,253 ....E3

CITIES and TOWNS

Zip	Name/Pop.	Key
70510	Abbeville⊙ 12,391	F7
70420	Abita Springs 1,072	L6
71316	Acme 235	G4
70710	Addis 1,320	J2
71401	Aimwell 55	G3
70421	Akers 150	N2

70711	Albany 857	M1
71301	Alexandria⊙ 51,565	E4
	Alexandria‡ 151,985	E4
†70458	Alton 500	L6
70340	Amelia 3,617	H7
70422	Amite⊙ 4,301	K5
71403	Anacoco 820	D4
70426	Angie 311	L5
70712	Angola 600	G5
70032	Arabi 10,248	P4
71001	Arcadia⊙ 3,403	E1
71218	Archibald 425	G2
70512	Arnaudville 1,679	G6
71002	Ashland 307	D2
71003	Athens 419	E1
71404	Atlanta 127	E3
70513	Avery Island 500	G7
70714	Baker 12,865	K1
71405	Ball 3,405	F4
†70401	Baptist 150	M1
70036	Barataria 1,123	K7
70515	Basile 2,635	E5
71219	Baskin 286	G2
71220	Bastrop⊙ 15,527	G1
70715	Batchelor 500	G5
*70801	Baton Rouge (cap.)⊙ 219,419	K2
	Baton Rouge‡ 493,973	K2
†70360	Bayou Cane 15,723	J7
†70380	Bayou Vista 5,805	H7
71004	Belcher 436	C1
70630	Bell City 400	D6
70037	Belle Chasse 5,412	O4
71406	Belmont 350	C3
71407	Bentley 120	E3
71006	Benton⊙ 1,864	C1
†70558	Bermuda 50	D3
71222	Bernice 1,956	E1
70342	Berwick 4,466	H7
71007	Bethany 300	B2
71008	Bienville 249	D2
71009	Blanchard 1,128	C1
70427	Bogalusa 16,976	L5
†71064	Bolinger 200	C1
71223	Bonita 503	G1
71320	Bordelonville 350	G4
70343	Bourg 2,073	J7
71409	Boyce 1,198	E4
70040	Braithwaite 350	P4
70516	Branch 200	F6
70517	Breaux Bridge 5,922	G6
70718	Brittany 475	L3
70518	Broussard 2,923	F6
70719	Brusly 1,762	J2
71014	Bryceland 94	E2
71321	Buckeye 280	F4
71322	Bunkie 5,364	F5
70041	Buras-Triumph 4,137	L8
70519	Cade 175	G6
71225	Calhoun 380	F2
71410	Calvin 263	E3
70631	Cameron⊙ 1,736	D7
71411	Campti 1,069	D3
†70584	Cankton 303	F6
70520	Carencro 3,712	G6
70042	Carlisle 975	L7
70721	Carville 1,037	K3
71115	Caspiana 50	C2
71016	Castor 195	D2
70522	Centerville 600	H7
70043	Chalmette⊙ 33,847	P4
†70767	Chamberlin 20	J1
71324	Chase 200	G2
70524	Chataignier 431	F5

71226	Chatham 714	F2
70344	Chauvin 3,338	J8
71325	Cheneyville 865	F4
71412	Chopin 175	E4
71227	Choudrant 809	F1
70525	Church Point 4,599	F6
71414	Clarence 612	E3
71415	Clarks 931	F2
71326	Clayton 1,204	H3
70722	Clinton⊙ 1,919	J5
71416	Cloutierville 100	E3
71417	Colfax⊙ 1,680	E3
71229	Collinston 439	G1
71418	Columbia⊙ 687	F2
70723	Convent⊙ 400	L3
71419	Converse 449	C3
†71107	Cooper Road	C1
71327	Cottonport 1,911	F5
71018	Cotton Valley 1,445	D1
71019	Coushatta⊙ 2,084	D2
70433	Covington⊙ 7,892	K5
†70510	Cow Island 200	F7
†70656	Cravens 200	E5
71020	Creston 135	E3
70526	Crowley⊙ 16,036	F6
71230	Crowville 400	G2
71021	Cullen 1,869	D1
70345	Cut Off 5,049	K7
71420	Cypress 55	D3
70046	Davant 600	L7
70528	Delcambre 2,216	G7
71232	Delhi 3,290	H2
71233	Delta 295	J2
70726	Denham Springs 8,563	L2
70633	De Quincy 3,966	D6
70634	De Ridder⊙ 11,057	D5
71421	Derry 75	E3
70030	Des Allemands 2,920	N4
70047	Destrehan 2,382	N4
†71055	Dixie Inn 453	D1
71422	Dodson 469	E2
70346	Donaldsonville⊙ 7,901	K3
70352	Donner 500	J7
71234	Downsville 213	F1
71023	Doyline 801	D1
70637	Dry Creek 300	D5
71423	Dry Prong 526	E3
71235	Dubach 1,161	E1
71024	Dubberly 421	D1
70353	Dulac 675	J8
71236	Dunn 225	G2
70728	Duplessis 500	K2
70529	Duson 1,253	F6
†71247	East Hodge 439	E2
71025	East Point 100	D2
71330	Echo 525	F4
70049	Edgard⊙ 400	M3
†71019	Edgefield 312	D2
71331	Effie 300	F4
70638	Elizabeth 454	E5
71424	Elmer 200	E4
71051	Elm Grove 100	C2
70532	Elton 1,450	E6
71425	Enterprise 375	G3
71332	Eola 47	F5
71237	Epps 672	G1
70533	Erath 2,133	F7
71238	Eros 158	F2
70534	Estherwood 691	F6
70730	Ethel 250	H5
70535	Eunice 12,479	F6
70639	Evans 500	D5
71333	Evergreen 272	F5
71240	Fairbanks 300	F1
71241	Farmerville⊙ 3,768	F1
70640	Fenton 491	E6

(continued)

Louisiana

SCALE
0 5 10 20 30 40 MI.
0 5 10 20 30 40 KM.

State Capitals .... ⊛
Parish Seats .... ⊙
Canals ....
Major Limited Access Hwys. ....

Scale 1:2,000,000

AREA 47,752 sq. mi. (123,678 sq. km.)
POPULATION 4,206,312
CAPITAL Baton Rouge
LARGEST CITY New Orleans
HIGHEST POINT Driskill Mtn. 535 ft. (163 m.)
SETTLED IN 1699
ADMITTED TO UNION April 30, 1812
POPULAR NAME Pelican State
STATE FLOWER Magnolia
STATE BIRD Eastern Brown Pelican

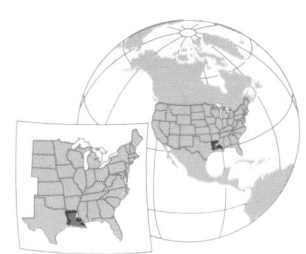

New Orleans, Baton Rouge and Vicinity

© Copyright HAMMOND INCORPORATED, Maplewood, N.J.

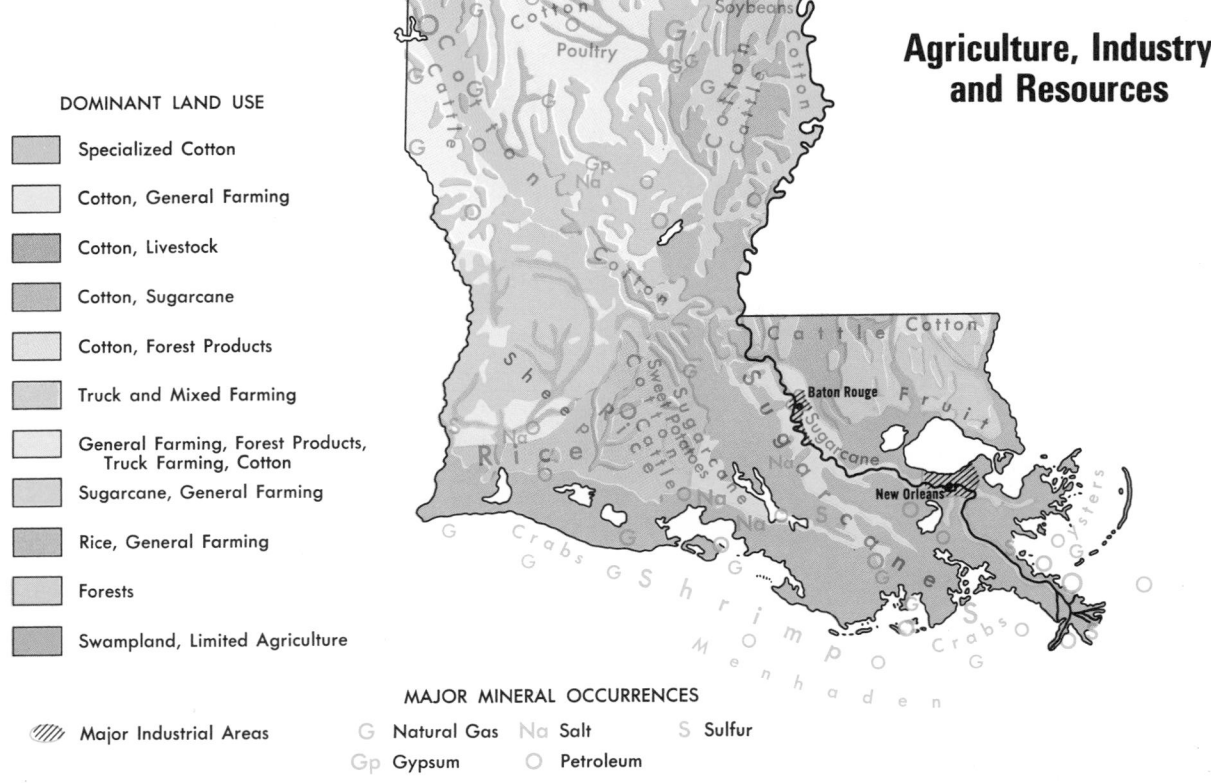

Agriculture, Industry and Resources

DOMINANT LAND USE

- Specialized Cotton
- Cotton, General Farming
- Cotton, Livestock
- Cotton, Sugarcane
- Cotton, Forest Products
- Truck and Mixed Farming
- General Farming, Forest Products, Truck Farming, Cotton
- Sugarcane, General Farming
- Rice, General Farming
- Forests
- Swampland, Limited Agriculture

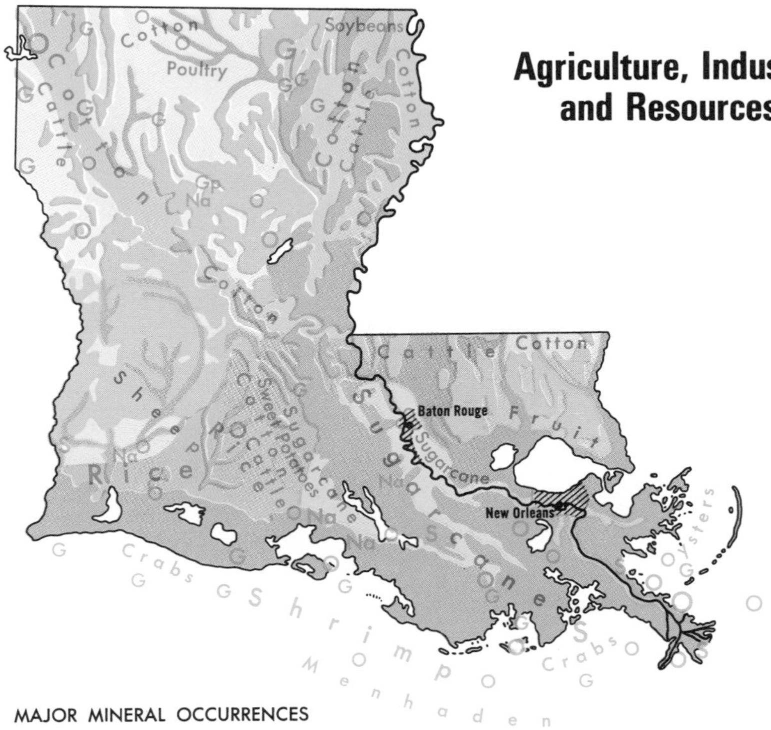

Major Industrial Areas

MAJOR MINERAL OCCURRENCES
G Natural Gas
Na Salt
S Sulfur
Gp Gypsum
O Petroleum

71334 Ferriday 4,472 G3
71426 Fisher 325 D4
71427 Flatwoods 360 E4
71428 Flora 300 D3
71429 Florien 964 D4
70436 Fluker 400 K5
70437 Folsom 319 K5
70732 Fordoche 676 G5
71242 Forest 299 H1
71430 Forest Hill 494 E4
70538 Franklin⊙ 9,584 G7
70438 Franklinton⊙ 4,119 K5
70733 French Settlement 761 L2
†71447 Galbraith 30 E4
70354 Galliano 5,159 K8
70540 Garden City 225 H7
70051 Garyville 2,856 M3
71432 Georgetown 381 F3
70355 Gheens 350 K7
71028 Gibsland 1,354 E1
71336 Gilbert 800 G2
71029 Gilliam 244 C1
71244 Girard 150 G2
71433 Glenmora 1,479 E5
71030 Gloster 780 C2
70736 Glynn 700 H5
70357 Golden Meadow 2,282 K8
71031 Goldonna 526 D2
70737 Gonzales 7,287 L2
†70079 Good Hope 500 N3
†71342 Good Pine-Trout 1,033 F3
71434 Gorum 150 E4
71338 Goudeau 25 G5
71245 Grambling 4,226 E1
70052 Gramercy 3,211 M3
71032 Grand Cane 252 C2
70541 Grand Coteau 1,165 G6
70358 Grand Isle 1,982 L8
70644 Grant 225 E5
71435 Grayson 564 F2
70441 Greensburg⊙ 662 J5
70739 Greenwell Springs 350 K1
71033 Greenwood 1,043 B2
70053 Gretna⊙ 20,615 O4
70740 Grosse Tete 749 G6
70542 Gueydan 1,695 E6
70057 Hahnville⊙ 2,947 N4
71034 Hall Summit 276 D2
70401 Hammond 15,043 N1
71035 Hanna 138 D3
70123 Harahan 11,384 O4
71340 Harrisonburg⊙ 610 G3
70058 Harvey 22,709 O4
71037 Haughton 1,510 C1
†71446 Hawthorn 400 D4
70646 Hayes 600 E6
71038 Haynesville 3,454 D1
71039 Heflin 279 D2
†70517 Henderson 1,560 G6
71341 Hessmer 743 F4
70743 Hester 250 L3
71437 Hicks 379 E4
71438 Hineston 400 E4
71247 Hodge 708 E2
70744 Holden 600 M1
71248 Holly Ridge 100 G2
71040 Homer⊙ 4,307 D1
71439 Hornbeck 470 D4
71043 Hosston 480 C1
70360 Houma⊙ 32,602 J7
70746 Iberville 367 K2
71044 Ida 306 C1
70443 Independence 1,684 M1
70747 Innis 200 G5
70543 Iota 1,326 E6
70647 Iowa 2,437 D6
†70427 Isabel 550 K5
70748 Jackson 3,133 H5
71045 Jamestown 131 D2
70544 Jeanerette 6,511 G7
†70067 Jean Lafitte 936 K7
70121 Jefferson 15,550 O4
71342 Jena⊙ 4,375 F3
70546 Jennings⊙ 12,401 E6
71249 Jigger 300 G2
71250 Jones 350 G1
71251 Jonesboro⊙ 5,061 E2
71343 Jonesville 2,828 G3
71749 Junction City 727 E1
70548 Kaplan 5,016 F6
71046 Keatchie 342 C2
71441 Kelly 325 F3
70062 Kenner 66,382 N4
70444 Kentwood 2,667 J5
71253 Kilbourne 286 H1
†70462 Killian 611 M2
70066 Killona 950 M3
70648 Kinder 2,603 E6
70371 Kraemer 350 M4
70750 Krotz Springs 1,374 G5
71443 Kurthwood 65 D4
70372 Labadieville 2,138 K4
71444 Lacamp 150 E4
70650 Lacassine 400 E6
70445 Lacombe 5,146 L6
*70501 Lafayette⊙ 81,961 F6
Lafayette‡ 150,017 F6
70067 Lafitte 1,312 K7
70549 Lake Arthur 3,615 E6
*70601 Lake Charles⊙ 75,226 D6
Lake Charles‡ 167,048 D6
70752 Lakeland 800 H5
71254 Lake Providence⊙ 6,361 H1
70068 La Place 16,112 N3
70373 Larose 5,234 K7
71344 Larto 500 G4
70550 Lawtell 1,014 F5
71445 Leander 145 E4
71345 Lebeau 200 F5
70651 Le Blanc 400 E5
71346 Lecompte 1,661 F4
71446 Leesville⊙ 9,054 D4
71447 Lena 300 E4
70551 Leonville 1,143 G6
†71008 Liberty Hill 50 E2
71348 Libuse 500 F4
71256 Lillie 172 E1
71257 Linville 150 F1
71048 Lisbon 138 E1
70754 Livingston⊙ 1,260 L1
70755 Livonia 980 G5
†70767 Lobdell 200 J1
70374 Lockport 2,424 K7
71049 Logansport 1,565 C3
71448 Longleaf 80 E4
71050 Longstreet 281 B2
70652 Longville 300 D5
70446 Loranger 250 N1
70552 Loreauville 860 G6
70756 Lottie 400 G5
†71008 Lucky 370 E2
70070 Luling 4,006 N4
70071 Lutcher 4,730 L3
70447 Madisonville 799 K6
70554 Mamou 3,194 F5
70448 Mandeville 6,076 L6
71259 Mangham 867 G2
71052 Mansfield⊙ 6,485 C2
71350 Mansura 2,074 G4
71449 Many⊙ 3,988 C3
70757 Maringouin 1,291 G6
71260 Marion 989 F1
71351 Marksville⊙ 5,113 G4
70072 Marrero 36,548 O4
†71019 Martin 584 D2
70555 Maurice 478 F6
†71433 McNary 240 E5
71346 Meeker 50 F4
71451 Melder 150 E4
71452 Melrose 500 E3
71353 Melville 1,764 G5
70556 Mermentau 771 E6
71261 Mer Rouge 802 G1
70653 Merryville 1,286 D5
*70001 Metairie 164,160 O4
70557 Midland 560 F6
70558 Milton 450 F6
†70070 Mimosa Park 3,737 N4
71055 Minden⊙ 15,074 D1
71059 Mira 354 C1
71453 Mitchell 155 C3
70376 Modeste 225 K3
*71201 Monroe⊙ 57,597 F1
Monroe‡ 139,241 F1
71454 Montgomery 843 E3
†70422 Montpelier 219 M1
71060 Mooringsport 911 B1
71354 Mora 427 E4
71355 Moreauville 853 G4
70380 Morgan City 16,114 H7
70759 Morganza 846 G5
71356 Morrow 600 F5
70559 Morse 835 F6
71262 Mound 40 H2
70450 Mount Hermon 170 K5
†71028 Mount Lebanon 105 D2
70390 Napoleonville⊙ 829 K4
70451 Natalbany 900 N1
71456 Natchez 527 D3
71457 Natchitoches⊙ 16,664 D3
71460 Negreet 400 C4
71357 Newellton 1,726 H2
70560 New Iberia⊙ 32,766 G6
71461 Newllano 2,213 D4
*70101 New Orleans⊙ 557,927 O4
New Orleans‡ 1,186,725 O4
70760 New Roads⊙ 3,924 G5
70078 New Sarpy 2,249 N4
71462 Noble 194 C3
70079 Norco 4,416 N3
†71247 North Hodge 573 E2
70761 Norwood 421 H5
71463 Oakdale 7,155 E5
71263 Oak Grove⊙ 2,214 H1
71264 Oak Ridge 257 G1
70655 Oberlin⊙ 1,764 E5
71061 Oil City 1,323 C1
71465 Olla 1,603 F3
70570 Opelousas⊙ 18,903 G5
70762 Oscar 650 H5
71466 Otis 400 E4
70391 Paincourtville 2,004 K3
71358 Palmetto 327 G5
70582 Parks 545 G6
70392 Patterson 4,693 H7
70452 Pearl River 1,693 L6
71063 Pelican 250 C3
70575 Perry 230 F7
70081 Pilottown 175 M8
70453 Pine Grove 570 J5
70576 Pine Prairie 734 E5
71360 Pineville 12,034 F4
71266 Pioneer 221 H1
70656 Pitkin 600 E5
71064 Plain Dealing 1,213 C1
70764 Plaquemine⊙ 7,521 J2
70393 Plattenville 205 K4
71362 Plaucheville 196 G5
71065 Pleasant Hill 776 C3
70082 Pointe a la Hache⊙ 750 L7
71467 Pollock 399 F3
70454 Ponchatoula 5,469 N2
70767 Port Allen⊙ 6,114 J2
70577 Port Barre 2,625 G5
70083 Port Sulphur 3,318 L8
†70726 Port Vincent 450 L2
71066 Powhatan 279 D3
71468 Provencal 695 D3
71268 Quitman 231 E2
70394 Raceland 6,302 J7
70578 Rayne 9,066 F6
71269 Rayville⊙ 4,610 G2
70580 Reddell 500 F5
70658 Reeves 199 D5
70084 Reserve 7,288 M3
†71218 Richmond 505 H2
†71201 Richwood 1,223 F2
†71334 Ridgecrest 895 G3
71068 Ringgold 1,655 D2
†70427 Rio 400 L5
70581 Roanoke 800 E6
71469 Robeline 238 D3
71069 Rodessa 337 B1
71364 Rosa 300 G5
70772 Rosedale 658 G6
70456 Roseland 1,346 J5
70659 Rosepine 953 D5
71365 Ruby 400 F4
71270 Ruston⊙ 20,585 E1
70457 Saint Benedict 190 K5
70775 Saint
Francisville⊙ 1,471 H5
71366 Saint Joseph⊙ 1,687 H3
71367 Saint Landry 550 F5
70582 Saint Martinville⊙ 7,965 G6
71471 Saint Maurice 560 E3
71070 Saline 293 E2
71071 Sarepta 831 D1
70807 Scotlandville 15,113 J1
70583 Scott 2,239 F6
†70764 Seymourville 2,891 J2
71072 Shongaloo 163 D1
*71101 Shreveport⊙ 205,820 C2
Shreveport‡ 376,646 C2
71073 Sibley 1,211 D1
71368 Sicily Island 691 G3
71472 Sieper 226 E4
71473 Sikes 226 F2
71369 Simmesport 2,293 G5
71474 Simpson 534 D4
71275 Simsboro 553 E1
70660 Singer 250 D5
71475 Slagle 650 D4
70777 Slaughter 729 H5
70458 Slidell 26,718 L6
71276 Sondheimer 225 H1
70778 Sorrento 1,197 L3
†71052 South Mansfield 1,463 C3
71277 Spearsville 181 E1
71278 Spencer 50 F1
70462 Springfield 424 M2
71075 Springhill 6,516 D1
†71049 Stanley 151 C3
71280 Sterlington 1,400 F1
71078 Stonewall 1,175 C2
70662 Sugartown 375 D5
70663 Sulphur 19,709 D6
70463 Sun 404 L5
70584 Sunset 2,300 F6
70464 Talisheek 315 L5
71282 Tallulah⊙ 11,634 H2
70465 Tangipahoa 493 J5
71080 Taylor 500 D1
71476 Temple 250 E4
71285 Terry 50 H1
†70053 Terry Town 23,548 O4
70397 Theriot 450 J8
70301 Thibodaux⊙ 15,810 J7
70466 Tickfaw 571 M1
71286 Transylvania 400 H1
71081 Trees 327 B1
†70041 Triumph-Buras 4,137 L8
71371 Trout-Good Pine 1,033 F3
71479 Tullos 776 F3
70782 Tunica 500 G5
70585 Turkey Creek 366 F5
71480 Urania 849 F3
70090 Vacherie 2,169 L3
70467 Varnado 249 L5
71481 Verda 100 E3
71373 Vidalia⊙ 5,936 G3
†71270 Vienna 519 E1
70586 Ville Platte⊙ 9,201 F5
70668 Vinton 3,631 C6
70092 Violet 11,678 P4
71082 Vivian 4,146 B1
†71418 Vixen 40 F2
70784 Wakefield 400 H5
†70433 Waldheim 25 L5
70785 Walker 2,957 L1
71289 Warden 130 H1
70589 Washington 1,266 G5
71375 Waterproof 1,339 H3
70786 Watson 800 L1
70591 Welsh 3,515 E6
70669 Westlake 5,246 D6
71291 West Monroe 14,993 F1
70094 Westwego 12,663 O4
70787 Weyanoke 500 H5
70788 White Castle 2,160 J3
†71371 White Sulphur Springs 50 F3
71376 Whiteville 150 F5
71377 Wildsville 800 G3
†70040 Wills Point 150 L7
70789 Wilson 656 H5
71483 Winnfield⊙ 7,311 E3
71295 Winnsboro⊙ 5,921 G2
71378 Wisner 1,424 G3
71485 Woodworth 412 E4
70592 Youngsville 1,053 G6
70791 Zachary 7,297 K1
†71371 Zenoria 76 F3
†71409 Zimmerman 20 E4
71486 Zwolle 2,602 C3

OTHER FEATURES

Allemands (lake) M4
Alligator (pt.) L6
Amite (riv.) L2
Anacoco (lake) D4
Atchafalaya (bay) H8
Atchafalaya (riv.) G6
Barataria (bay) L8
Barataria (passage) L8
Barksdale A.F.B. C2
Bayou D'Arbonne (lake) F1
Bird (isl.) M8
Bistineau (lake) D2
Black (lake) D3
Black Lake (bayou) D1
Boeuf (lake) J7
Boeuf (riv.) G1
Bonnet Carré Spillway and
Floodway N3
Borgne (lake) L7
Boudreau (bay) M7
Boudreaux (lake) J8
Breton (isls.) M8
Breton (sound) M7
Bundick (lake) D5
Caddo (lake) B1
Caillou (bay) J8
Calcasieu (lake) D7
Calcasieu (passage) D7
Calcasieu (riv.) E5
Catahoula (lake) F4
Cataouatche (lake) N4
Cat Island (chan.) M6
Cat Island (passage) J8
Chandeleur (isls.) N7
Chandeleur (sound) M7
Chenier (lake) F2
Chicot (pt.) M7
Claiborne (lake) E1
Clear (lake) D3
Cocodrie (lake) E5
Cotile (lake) E4
Cross (lake) C2
Curlew (isls.) M7
Dernieres (isls.) J8
Door (pt.) M6
Driskill (mt.) E2
Drum (bay) M7
East (bay) M8
East Cote Blanche (bay) G7
Edwards (lake) C2
Eloi (bay) M7
England A.F.B. E4
Fields (lake) J7
Fort Polk 14,142 D4
Free Mason (isls.) M7
Garden Island (bay) M8
Grand (lake) E7
Grand (lake) H8
Grand Terre (isls.) L8
Iatt (lake) E3
Jean Lafitte Nat'l Hist. Park P4
Lafourche (bayou) K8
Little (riv.) F3
Louisiana (pt.) C7
Macon (bayou) H1
Main (passage) M8
Manchac (passage) N2
Marsh (isl.) G7
Maurepas (lake) M2
Mermentau (riv.) E7
Mexico (gulf) F8
Mississippi (delta) M8
Mississippi (riv.) H3
Mississippi (sound) M6
Mississippi River Gulf Outlet
(canal) L7
Mozambique (pt.) M7
Mud (lake) D7
Naval Air Sta. O4
North (isls.) M7
North (pass) N8
North (pt.) M7
Northeast (pass) M8
Ouachita (riv.) F1
Palourde (lake) H7
Pearl (riv.) L5
Point au Fer (isl.) H8
Point au Fer (pt.) H8
Pontchartrain (lake) O3
Pontchartrain Causeway O3
Raccoon (pt.) H8
Red (riv.) G4
Sabine (lake) C7
Sabine (passage) C7
Sabine (riv.) C5
Saline (lake) E3
Salvador (lake) K7
Smithport (lake) C2
South (pass) M8
South (pt.) G8
Southeast (pass) M8
Southwest (pass) L8
Tangipahoa (riv.) N1
Tensas (riv.) G3
Terrebonne (bay) J8
Tickfaw (riv.) M1
Timbalier (bay) K8
Timbalier (isl.) K8
Toledo Bend (res.) C3
Turkey Creek (lake) G3
Vermilion (bay) F7
Vernon (lake) D4
Verret (lake) H7
Wallace (lake) C2
West (bay) M8
West Cote Blanche (bay) G7
White (lake) E7

⊙Parish seat.
‡Population of metropolitan area.
† Zip of nearest p.o. * Multiple zips.

AREA 33,265 sq. mi. (86,156 sq. km.)
POPULATION 1,125,027
CAPITAL Augusta
LARGEST POINT Portland
HIGHEST POINT Katahdin 5,268 ft. (1606 m.)
SETTLED IN 1624
ADMITTED TO UNION March 15, 1820
POPULAR NAME Pine Tree State
STATE FLOWER White Pine Cone & Tassel
STATE BIRD Chickadee

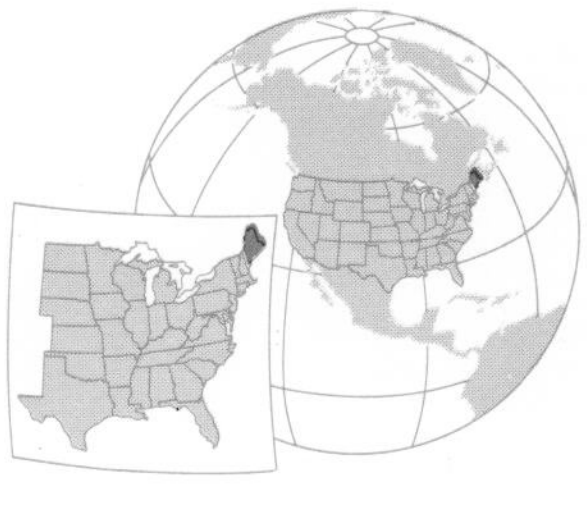

COUNTIES

Androscoggin 99,657 ... C7
Aroostook 91,331 ... F2
Cumberland 215,789 ... C8
Franklin 27,098 ... B5
Hancock 41,781 ... G6
Kennebec 109,889 ... D7
Knox 32,941 ... E7
Lincoln 25,691 ... D7
Oxford 48,968 ... B7
Penobscot 137,015 ... F5
Piscataquis 17,634 ... E4
Sagadahoc 28,795 ... D7
Somerset 45,028 ... C4
Waldo 28,414 ... E6
Washington 34,963 ... H6
York 139,666 ... B9

CITIES and TOWNS

Zip *Name/Pop.* *Key*

04406 Abbot Village○ 576 ... D5
04001 Acton○ 1,228 ... B8
04606 Addison○ 1,061 ... H6
04910 Albion○ 1,551 ... E6
†04610 Alexander○ 385 ... H5
04002 Alfred○ 1,890 ... B9
†04774 Allagash○ 448 ... F1
†04938 Allens Mills 100 ... C6
04535 Alna○ 425 ... D7
†04468 Alton○ 468 ... F5
†04408 Amherst○ 203 ... G6
04216 Andover○ 850 ... B6
04911 Anson○ 2,226 ... D6
†04862 Appleton○ 818 ... E7
†04468 Argyle 225 ... F5
04732 Ashland○ 1,865 ... G2
04607 Ashville 36 ... G7
04912 Athens○ 802 ... D6
†04426 Atkinson○ 306 ... E5
04608 Atlantic 120 ... G7
04210 Auburn⊙ 23,128 ... C7
04330 Augusta (cap.)⊙ 21,819 ... D7
04408 Aurora○ 110 ... G6
04003 Bailey Island 500 ... D8
†04497 Bancroft○ 61 ... H4
04401 Bangor⊙ 31,643 ... F6
Bangor‡ 83,919 ... F6
04609 Bar Harbor○ 4,124 ... G7
04609 Bar Harbor 2,685 ... G7
†04619 Baring○ 308 ... J5
04004 Bar Mills 800 ... C8
04653 Bass Harbor 450 ... G7
04530 Bath⊙ 10,246 ... D8
†04915 Bayside ... F7
04611 Beals○ 695 ... H7
†04622 Beddington○ 36 ... H6
04915 Belfast⊙ 6,243 ... F7
04917 Belgrade○ 2,043 ... D7
†04915 Belmont○ 520 ... E7
04733 Benedicta○ 225 ... G4
†04937 Benton○ 2,188 ... D6
03901 Berwick○ 4,149 ... B9
03901 Berwick 2,378 ... B9
04217 Bethel○ 2,340 ... B7
04005 Biddeford 19,638 ... B9
04920 Bingham○ 1,184 ... D5
04920 Bingham 1,074 ... D5
04613 Birch Harbor 300 ... H7
04734 Blaine○ 922 ... H2
04734 Blaine-Mars Hill 1,921 ... H2
04614 Blue Hill○ 1,644 ... F7
04615 Blue Hill Falls 135 ... F7
04537 Boothbay○ 2,308 ... D8
04538 Boothbay Harbor 2,207 ... D8
04008 Bowdoinham○ 1,828 ... D7
†04481 Bowerbank○ 27 ... E5
04410 Bradford○ 888 ... F5
†04410 Bradford Center 105 ... F5
04411 Bradley○ 1,149 ... F6
04412 Brewer 9,017 ... F6
04735 Bridgewater○ 742 ... H3
04009 Bridgton○ 3,528 ... B7
04009 Bridgton 1,639 ... B7
†04990 Brighton○ 74 ... D5
04539 Bristol○ 2,095 ... D8
04616 Brooklin○ 619 ... F7
04921 Brooks○ 804 ... E6
04617 Brooksville○ 753 ... F7
04413 Brookton 175 ... H4
04010 Brownfield○ 767 ... B8
04414 Brownville○ 1,545 ... E5
04011 Brunswick○ 17,366 ... C8
04011 Brunswick 10,990 ... C8
04219 Bryant Pond 600 ... B7
†04232 Buckfield○ 1,333 ... C7
04618 Bucks Harbor 300 ... J6
04416 Bucksport○ 4,345 ... F6
04416 Bucksport 2,853 ... F6
04540 Burkettville 120 ... E7
04417 Burlington○ 322 ... G5
04922 Burnham○ 951 ... E6
†04093 Buxton○ 5,775 ... C8
†04275 Byron○ 114 ... B6
04619 Calais 4,262 ... J5
04923 Cambridge○ 445 ... E5
04843 Camden○ 4,584 ... F7
04843 Camden 3,743 ... F7
04924 Canaan○ 1,189 ... D6
04221 Canton○ 831 ... C7
03902 Cape Neddick 850 ... B9
04014 Cape Porpoise 500 ... C9
04736 Caribou 9,916 ... G2
04419 Carmel○ 1,695 ... E6
†04947 Carrabassett Valley○ 107 ... C5
†04487 Carroll○ 175 ... G5
†04224 Carthage○ 438 ... C6
†04465 Cary○ 229 ... H4
04015 Casco○ 2,243 ... B7
04421 Castine○ 1,304 ... F7
†04941 Center Montville 16 ... E7
†04623 Centerville○ 28 ... H6
†04757 Chapman○ 406 ... G2
04422 Charleston○ 1,037 ... F5
†04666 Charlotte○ 300 ... J5
04017 Chebeague Island 900 ... C8
†04345 Chelsea○ 2,522 ... D7
04622 Cherryfield○ 983 ... H6
†04458 Chester○ 434 ... F5
†04938 Chesterville○ 869 ... C6
†04478 Chesuncook 6 ... D3
04926 China○ 2,918 ... E7
†04239 Chisholm 1,796 ... C7
†04428 Clifton○ 462 ... G6
04927 Clinton○ 2,696 ... D6
04927 Clinton 1,305 ... D6
†04623 Columbia○ 275 ... H6
04623 Columbia Falls○ 517 ... H6
†04638 Cooper○ 105 ... H6
04624 Corea 375 ... H7
04928 Corinna○ 1,887 ... E6
04020 Cornish○ 1,047 ... B8
†04976 Cornville○ 838 ... D6
04625 Cranberry Isles○ 198 ... G7
†04610 Crawford○ 86 ... H5
†04015 Crescent Lake 325 ... C7
†04851 Criehaven 5 ... F8
04738 Crouseville 450 ... G2
†04747 Crystal○ 349 ... G4
04021 Cumberland Center○ 5,284 ... C8
04021 Cumberland Center 2,015 ... C8
04563 Cushing○ 795 ... E7
04626 Cutler○ 726 ... J6
04543 Damariscotta○ 1,493 ... E7
04543 Damariscotta-Newcastle 1,411 ... E7
04424 Danforth○ 826 ... H4
†04622 Deblois○ 44 ... H6
†04429 Dedham○ 841 ... F6
04627 Deer Isle○ 1,492 ... F7
04022 Denmark○ 672 ... B8
04628 Dennysville○ 296 ... J6
04929 Detroit○ 744 ... E6
04930 Dexter○ 4,286 ... E5
04930 Dexter 3,118 ... E5
04224 Dixfield○ 2,389 ... C6
04224 Dixfield 1,725 ... C6
04932 Dixmont○ 812 ... E6
04426 Dover-Foxcroft○ 4,323 ... E5
04426 Dover-Foxcroft⊙ 2,974 ... E5
†04426 Dover South Mills 54 ... E5
04342 Dresden○ 998 ... D7
†04747 Dyer Brook○ 275 ... G3
04739 Eagle Lake○ 1,019 ... F1
04226 East Andover 250 ... B6
04544 East Boothbay 800 ... D8
04427 East Corinth 525 ... F5
04227 East Dixfield 250 ... C6
04429 East Holden 600 ... F6
04027 East Lebanon 950 ... B9
04228 East Livermore 500 ... C7
04630 East Machias○ 1,233 ... J6
04430 East Millinocket○ 2,372 ... F4
04430 East Millinocket 2,361 ... F4
04740 Easton○ 1,305 ... H2
04028 East Parsonfield 400 ... B8
04229 East Peru 200 ... C7
†04210 East Poland 200 ... C7
04631 Eastport 1,982 ... K6
04231 East Stoneham 300 ... B7
†04607 East Sullivan 496 ... G6
†04220 East Sumner 120 ... C7
†04862 East Union 75 ... E7
†04428 Eddington○ 1,769 ... F6
†04556 Edgecomb○ 841 ... D8
03903 Eliot○ 4,948 ... B9
04605 Ellsworth⊙ 5,179 ... F6
04031 Emery Mills 100 ... B8
04433 Enfield○ 1,397 ... F5
04434 Etna○ 758 ... E6
04936 Eustis○ 582 ... B5
04435 Exeter○ 823 ... E6
†04938 Fairbanks 400 ... C6
04937 Fairfield○ 6,113 ... D6
04937 Fairfield 3,169 ... D6
04105 Falmouth○ 6,853 ... C8
04105 Falmouth 1,655 ... C8
†04345 Farmingdale○ 2,535 ... D7
†04345 Farmingdale 2,014 ... D7
04938 Farmington○ 6,730 ... C6
04938 Farmington⊙ 3,583 ... C6
04940 Farmington Falls 500 ... C6
†04349 Fayette○ 812 ... C7
04546 Five Islands 225 ... D8
04742 Fort Fairfield○ 4,376 ... H2
04742 Fort Fairfield 2,282 ... H2
04743 Fort Kent○ 4,826 ... F1
04743 Fort Kent 2,375 ... F1
04744 Fort Kent Mills 200 ... F1
04438 Frankfort○ 783 ... F6
04634 Franklin○ 979 ... G6
04941 Freedom○ 458 ... E7
04032 Freeport○ 5,863 ... C8
04032 Freeport 1,906 ... C8
04635 Frenchboro○ 43 ... G7
04745 Frenchville○ 1,450 ... G1
04547 Friendship○ 1,000 ... E7
04037 Fryeburg○ 2,715 ... A7
04037 Fryeburg 1,644 ... A7
04345 Gardiner 6,485 ... D7
04939 Garland○ 718 ... E5
04548 Georgetown○ 735 ... D8
†04217 Gilead○ 191 ... B7
†04401 Glenburn○ 2,319 ... F6
04846 Glen Cove 250 ... E7
04038 Gorham○ 10,101 ... C8
04038 Gorham 4,052 ... C8
†04607 Gouldsboro○ 1,574 ... H7
04746 Grand Isle○ 719 ... G1
04637 Grand Lake Stream○ 198 ... H5
04039 Gray○ 4,344 ... C8
†04408 Great Pond○ 45 ... G6
04236 Greene○ 3,037 ... C7
04441 Greenville○ 1,839 ... D5
04441 Greenville 1,640 ... D5
04442 Greenville Junction 650 ... D5
04443 Guilford○ 1,793 ... E5
04443 Guilford 1,235 ... E5
04347 Hallowell 2,502 ... D7
†04785 Hamlin○ 340 ... H1
04444 Hampden○ 5,250 ... F6
04444 Hampden 3,538 ... F6
04445 Hampden Highlands 950 ... F6
04640 Hancock○ 1,409 ... G6
04237 Hanover○ 256 ... B7
04942 Harmony○ 755 ... D6
†04011 Harpswell○ 3,796 ... D8
04643 Harrington○ 859 ... H6
04040 Harrison○ 1,667 ... B7
†04221 Hartford○ 480 ... C7
04943 Hartland○ 1,669 ... D6
04943 Hartland 1,041 ... D6
04446 Haynesville○ 169 ... G4
04238 Hebron○ 665 ... C7
†04401 Hermon○ 3,170 ... F6
04944 Hinckley 140 ... D6
04041 Hiram○ 1,067 ... B8
†04730 Hodgdon○ 1,084 ... H3
04042 Hollis Center○ 2,892 ... B8
04847 Hope○ 730 ... E7
04730 Houlton○ 6,766 ... H3
04730 Houlton⊙ 5,730 ... H3
04448 Howland○ 1,602 ... F5
04448 Howland 1,502 ... F5
04449 Hudson○ 797 ... F5
04644 Hulls Cove 200 ... G7
04747 Island Falls○ 981 ... G3
04645 Isle Au Haut○ 57 ... F7
04848 Islesboro○ 521 ... F7
04945 Jackman○ 1,003 ... C4
†04630 Jacksonville 200 ... J6
04239 Jay○ 5,080 ... C7
04348 Jefferson○ 1,616 ... D7
04648 Jonesboro○ 553 ... J6
04649 Jonesport○ 1,512 ... H6
04649 Jonesport 1,050 ... H6
04450 Kenduskeag○ 1,210 ... E6
04043 Kennebunk○ 6,621 ... B9
04043 Kennebunk 3,294 ... B9
†04043 Kennebunk Beach 200 ... C9
04046 Kennebunkport○ 2,952 ... C9
04046 Kennebunkport 1,685 ... C9
04349 Kents Hill 300 ... D7
04947 Kingfield○ 1,083 ... C6
04451 Kingman 281 ... G4
†04990 Kingsbury○ 4 ... D5
03904 Kittery○ 9,314 ... B9
03904 Kittery 5,465 ... B9
03905 Kittery Point 1,260 ... B9
†04986 Knox○ 558 ... E6
04453 La Grange○ 509 ... F5
†04463 Lake View○ 20 ... F5
†04605 Lamoine○ 953 ... G7
04455 Lee○ 688 ... G5
†04263 Leeds○ 1,463 ... C7
04456 Levant○ 1,117 ... F6
04240 Lewiston 40,481 ... C7
Lewiston-Auburn‡ 72,378 ... C7
04949 Liberty○ 694 ... E7
04749 Lille 300 ... G1
04048 Limerick○ 1,356 ... B8
04750 Limestone○ 8,719 ... H2
04750 Limestone 1,334 ... H2
04049 Limington○ 2,203 ... B8
04457 Lincoln○ 5,066 ... G5
04457 Lincoln 3,524 ... G5
04849 Lincolnville○ 1,414 ... E7
04850 Lincolnville Center 200 ... E7
†04730 Linneus○ 752 ... H3
04250 Lisbon○ 8,769 ... C7
04250 Lisbon-Lisbon Center 1,865 ... C7
04252 Lisbon Falls 4,370 ... D7
04350 Litchfield○ 1,954 ... D7
†04627 Little Deer Isle 475 ... F7
04082 Little Falls-South Windham 1,366 ... C8
†04760 Littleton○ 1,009 ... H3
04253 Livermore○ 1,826 ... C7
04254 Livermore Falls○ 3,572 ... C7
04254 Livermore Falls 2,441 ... C7
04255 Locke Mills 600 ... B7
04051 Lovell○ 767 ... B7
†04433 Lowell○ 194 ... F5
04652 Lubec○ 2,045 ... K6
†04730 Ludlow○ 403 ... G3
04654 Machias○ 2,458 ... J6
04654 Machias⊙ 1,277 ... J6
04655 Machiasport○ 1,108 ... H6
†04451 Macwahoc○ 126 ... G4
04756 Madawaska○ 5,282 ... G1
04756 Madawaska 4,165 ... G1
04950 Madison○ 4,367 ... D6
04950 Madison 2,788 ... D6
†04966 Madrid○ 178 ... B6
†04942 Mainstream 100 ... D6
04351 Manchester○ 1,949 ... D7
04757 Mapleton○ 1,895 ... G2
04758 Mars Hill○ 1,892 ... H2
04758 Mars Hill-Blaine 1,921 ... H2
04759 Masardis○ 328 ... G3
04851 Matinicus 66 ... F8
04459 Mattawamkeag○ 1,000 ... G5
04256 Mechanic Falls○ 2,616 ... C7
04256 Mechanic Falls 2,198 ... C7
04657 Meddybemps○ 110 ... J5
†04453 Medford○ 163 ... F5
†04453 Medford Center 100 ... F5
04460 Medway○ 1,871 ... G4
04957 Mercer○ 448 ... D6
04257 Mexico○ 3,698 ... B6
04257 Mexico 3,207 ... B6
†04216 Middledam 10 ... B6
04658 Milbridge○ 1,306 ... H6
04461 Milford○ 2,160 ... F6
04461 Milford 1,688 ... F6
04462 Millinocket○ 7,567 ... F4

(continued on following page)

Agriculture, Industry and Resources

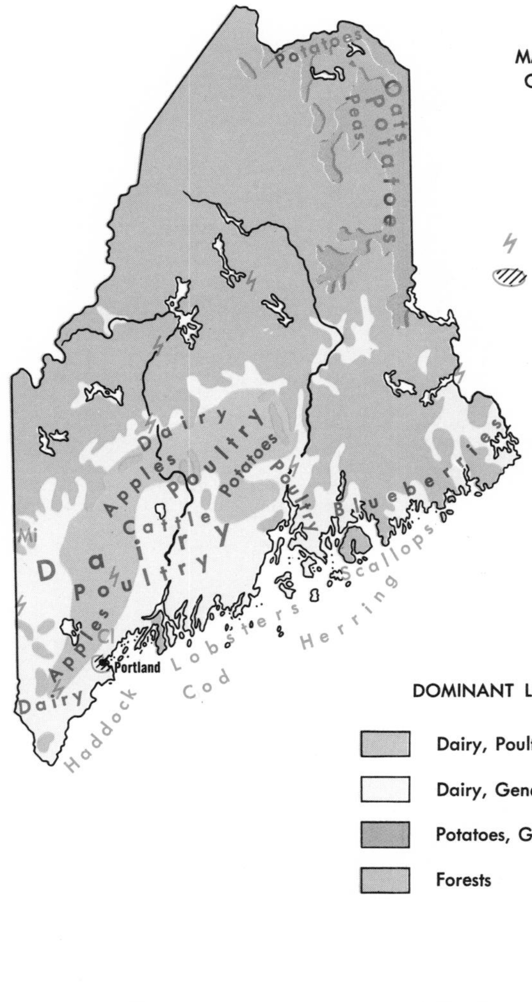

MAJOR MINERAL OCCURRENCES

Cl Clay
Mi Mica

Water Power
Major Industrial Areas

DOMINANT LAND USE

Dairy, Poultry, Mixed Farming
Dairy, General Farming
Potatoes, General Farming
Forests

(continued)

04463 Milo○ 2,624 F5
04463 Milo 2,255 F5
04258 Minot○ 1,631 C7
04659 Minturn 150 G7
†04776 Monarda 100 G4
04852 Monhegan○ 109 E8
04259 Monmouth○ 2,888 D7
04951 Monroe○ 657 E6
04464 Monson○ 804 E5
04760 Monticello○ 950 H3
†04941 Montville○ 631 E7
04054 Moody 500 B9
†04478 Moosehead 6 D4
†04945 Moose River○ 252 C4
04952 Morrill○ 506 E7
04660 Mount Desert○ 2,063 G7
04352 Mount Vernon○ 1,021 D7
04055 Naples○ 1,833 B8
04552 Newagen 100 D8
†04445 Newburgh○ 1,228 F6
04553 Newcastle○ 1,227 D7
04553 Newcastle-Damariscotta 1,411 E7
04056 Newfield○ 644 B8
04260 New Gloucester○ 3,180 C8
04554 New Harbor 850 E8
04761 New Limerick○ 513 G3
04953 Newport○ 2,755 E6
04953 Newport 1,748 E6
04954 New Portland○ 651 C6
04261 Newry○ 235 B6
04955 New Sharon○ 969 C6
04762 New Sweden○ 737 G2
04956 New Vineyard○ 607 C6
04555 Nobleboro○ 1,154 D7
†04462 Norcross 13 F4
04957 Norridgewock○ 2,552 D6
04957 Norridgewock 1,318 D6
04958 North Anson 950 D6
03906 North Berwick○ 2,878 B9
03906 North Berwick 1,436 B9
04057 North Bridgton 300 B7
†04938 North Chesterville 50 C6
†04441 North East Carry 2 D4
04662 Northeast Harbor 800 G7
†04654 Northfield○ 88 H6
04853 North Haven○ 373 F7
04262 North Jay 800 C6
†04254 North Livermore 250 C7
04961 North New Portland 500 D6
†04476 North Penobscot 246 F7
†04849 Northport○ 958 E7
†04274 North Raymond 225 C8
04266 North Turner 350 C7
04962 North Vassalboro 950 D7
04267 North Waterford 390 B7
04062 North Windham 5,492 C8
†04219 North Woodstock 75 B7
†04096 North Yarmouth○ 1,919 C8
04268 Norway○ 4,042 B7
04268 Norway 2,653 B7
†04268 Norway Lake 75 B7
04763 Oakfield○ 847 G3
04963 Oakland○ 5,162 D6
04963 Oakland 3,387 D6
04063 Ocean Park 200 C9
03907 Ogunquit 1,492 B9
04064 Old Orchard Beach○ 6,291 C9
04064 Old Orchard Beach 6,023 C9
04468 Old Town 8,422 F6
04964 Oquossoc 150 B6
04471 Orient○ 97 H4
04472 Orland○ 1,645 F6
04473 Orono○ 10,578 F6
04473 Orono 9,891 F6
04474 Orrington○ 3,244 F6
04066 Orrs Island 600 D8
†04270 Otisfield○ 897 B7
04665 Otter Creek 260 G7
04854 Owls Head○ 1,633 F7
04764 Oxbow○ 84 G3
04270 Oxford○ 3,143 B7
04354 Palermo○ 760 E7
04965 Palmyra○ 1,485 E6
04271 Paris○ 4,168 B7
†04443 Parkman○ 621 D5
04475 Passadumkeag○ 430 F5
04765 Patten○ 1,368 F4
04765 Patten 1,057 F4
04558 Pemaquid 200 E8
04666 Pembroke○ 920 J6
04476 Penobscot○ 1,104 F7
04766 Perham○ 437 G2
04667 Perry○ 737 J6
04272 Peru○ 1,564 C6
04966 Phillips○ 1,092 C6
04562 Phippsburg○ 1,527 D8
04967 Pittsfield○ 4,125 E6
04967 Pittsfield 3,117 E6
†04345 Pittston○ 2,267 D7
04767 Plaisted 125 F1
†04925 Pleasant Pond 18 D5
04969 Plymouth○ 811 E6
04273 Poland○ 3,578 C7
04562 Popham Beach 40 D8
04768 Portage○ 562 G2
04855 Port Clyde 400 E8
04068 Porter○ 1,222 B8
*04101 Portland⊙ 61,572 C8
Portland‡ 183,625 C8
04069 Pownal○ 1,189 C8
†04487 Prentiss○ 205 G5
04769 Presque Isle 11,172 H2
04668 Princeton○ 994 H5
†04981 Prospect○ 511 F6
04669 Prospect Harbor 445 H7
04770 Quimby 50 F2
†04345 Randolph○ 1,834 D7
04970 Rangeley○ 1,023 B6
04071 Raymond○ 2,251 B8
04355 Readfield○ 1,943 D7
04357 Richmond○ 2,627 D7
04357 Richmond 1,578 D7
†04262 Riley 50 C6
†04930 Ripley○ 439 E5
04671 Robbinston○ 492 J5
†04734 Robinsons 160 H3
04841 Rockland⊙ 7,919 E7
04856 Rockport○ 2,749 F7
04478 Rockwood 265 D4
†04957 Rome○ 627 D6
†04654 Roque Bluffs○ 244 H6
04564 Round Pond 400 E8
04275 Roxbury○ 373 B6
04276 Rumford○ 8,240 B6
04276 Rumford 6,256 B6
04279 Rumford Point 320 B6
04280 Sabattus○ 3,081 C7
04280 Sabattus 1,234 C7
04072 Saco 12,921 C8
04772 Saint Agatha○ 1,035 G1
04971 Saint Albans○ 1,400 E6
04773 Saint David 915 G1
04774 Saint Francis○ 839 E1
04857 Saint George○ 1,948 E7
†04743 Saint John○ 322 F1
†04983 Salem 125 C6
†04009 Sandy Creek 132 B7
04972 Sandy Point 350 F7
04073 Sanford○ 18,020 B9
04073 Sanford 10,268 B9
04479 Sangerville○ 1,219 E5
†04417 Saponac 8 G5
04074 Scarborough○ 11,347 C8
04074 Scarborough 2,280 C8
04674 Seal Cove 215 G7
04675 Seal Harbor 500 G7
04973 Searsmont○ 782 E7
04974 Searsport○ 2,309 F7
04974 Searsport 1,348 F7
04075 Sebago Lake 800 B8
04481 Sebec○ 469 E5
04484 Seboeis○ 53 F5
†04478 Seboomook 3 D4
04676 Sedgwick○ 795 F7
04076 Shapleigh○ 1,370 B8
04975 Shawmut 500 D6
04775 Sheridan 300 F2
†04777 Sherman○ 1,021 G4
04777 Sherman Station 650 F4
04485 Shirley Mills○ 242 D5
†04330 Sidney○ 2,052 D7
04779 Sinclair 264 G1
04976 Skowhegan○ 8,098 D6
04976 Skowhegan⊙ 6,517 D6
04567 Small Point 22 D8
04978 Smithfield○ 748 D6
04780 Smyrna Mills○ 354 G3
04979 Solon○ 827 D6
†04341 Somerville○ 377 D7
†04660 Somesville (Mount Desert) 150 G7
04677 Sorrento○ 276 G7
03908 South Berwick○ 4,046 B9
†04009 South Bridgton 373 B8
04568 South Bristol○ 800 D8
04077 South Casco 750 B8
†03903 South Eliot 1,681 B9
†04928 South Exeter 100 E6
04080 South Hiram 350 B8
†04862 South Hope 200 E7
†04453 South La Grange 150 F5
†04259 South Monmouth 400 D7
04281 South Paris⊙ 2,128 C7
†04538 Southport○ 598 D8
04106 South Portland 22,712 C8
04858 South Thomaston○ 1,064 E7
†04864 South Union 50 E7
04081 South Waterford 300 B7
04679 Southwest Harbor○ 1,855 G7
04679 Southwest Harbor 1,052 G7
04082 South Windham (Little Falls-South Windham 1,366 C8
04487 Springfield○ 443 G5
04083 Springvale 2,940 B9
04782 Stacyville○ 554 F4
04084 Standish○ 5,946 B8
†04980 Starks○ 440 D6
04488 Stetson○ 618 E6
04680 Steuben○ 970 H6
04489 Stillwater 700 F6
04783 Stockholm○ 319 G1
04981 Stockton Springs○ 1,230 F7
04681 Stonington○ 1,273 F7
†04058 Stow○ 186 A7
04982 Stratton 600 B5
04983 Strong○ 1,506 C6
†04689 Sullivan○ 967 G6
†04292 Sumner○ 613 C7
04232 Sumner-East Sumner C7
04683 Sunset 165 F7
†04627 Sunshine 100 G7
04684 Surry○ 894 F7
04685 Swans Island○ 337 G7
†04915 Swanville○ 873 E6
†04040 Sweden○ 163 B7
04984 Temple○ 518 C6
04860 Tenants Harbor 900 E8
04861 Thomaston○ 2,900 E7
04861 Thomaston 2,348 E7
04986 Thorndike○ 603 E6
04490 Topsfield○ 240 H5
04086 Topsham○ 6,431 D8
04086 Topsham 4,657 D8
†04653 Tremont○ 1,222 G7
†04605 Trenton○ 718 G7
04571 Trevett 400 D8
04987 Troy○ 701 E6
04282 Turner○ 3,539 C7
04862 Union○ 1,569 E7
04988 Unity○ 1,431 E6
†04293 Upper Dam 2 B6
04784 Upper Frenchville 405 G1
04261 Upton○ 65 B6
04785 Van Buren○ 3,557 G1
04785 Van Buren 3,282 G1
04491 Vanceboro○ 256 J4
04989 Vassalboro○ 3,410 D7
04401 Veazie○ 1,610 F6
04360 Vienna○ 454 D6
04863 Vinalhaven○ 1,211 F7
04492 Waite○ 130 H5
†04915 Waldo○ 495 E7
04572 Waldoboro○ 3,985 E7
04572 Waldoboro 1,195 E7
†04605 Waltham○ 186 G6
04864 Warren○ 2,566 E7
04786 Washburn○ 2,028 G2
04786 Washburn 1,221 G2
04574 Washington○ 954 E7
04087 Waterboro○ 2,943 B8
04088 Waterford○ 951 B7
04901 Waterville 17,779 D6
04284 Wayne○ 680 D7
04285 Weld○ 435 C6
04990 Wellington○ 287 D5
04090 Wells○ 8,211 B9
04686 Wesley○ 140 H6
†04530 West Bath○ 1,309 D8
04092 Westbrook 14,976 C8
04493 West Enfield 609 F5
04787 Westfield○ 647 G2
04985 West Forks○ 72 D5
†04649 West Jonesport 400 H6
04094 West Kennebunk 750 B9
†04938 West Mills 75 C6
04288 West Minot 400 C7
04095 West Newfield 300 B8
04424 Weston○ 155 H4
04289 West Paris○ 1,390 B7
04290 West Peru 700 C7
04291 West Poland 250 C7
04074 West Scarborough 500 C8
04690 West Tremont 250 G7
04362 Whitefield○ 1,606 D7
04691 Whiting○ 335 J6
04692 Whitneyville○ 264 H6
†04443 Willimantic○ 164 E5
04293 Wilsons Mills 50 B6
04294 Wilton○ 4,382 C6
04294 Wilton 2,262 C6
04363 Windsor○ 1,702 D7
04495 Winn○ 503 G5
†04901 Winslow○ 8,057 D6
†04901 Winslow 5,903 D6
04693 Winter Harbor○ 1,120 G7
04496 Winterport○ 2,675 F6
04496 Winterport 1,126 F6
04788 Winterville○ 235 F2
04364 Winthrop○ 5,889 C7
04364 Winthrop 3,264 C7
04578 Wiscasset○ 2,832 D7
04694 Woodland○ 1,363 H5
04579 Woolwich○ 2,156 D8
04497 Wytopitlock 130 G4
04096 Yarmouth○ 6,585 C8
04096 Yarmouth 2,981 C8
03909 York○ 8,465 B9
03909 York 4,530 B9
03910 York Beach 900 B9
03911 York Harbor 950 B9

OTHER FEATURES

Abraham (mt.) C5
Acadia Nat'l Park G7
Allagash (lake) D3
Allagash (riv.) E2
Androscoggin (riv.) C7
Aroostook (riv.) G2
Atteam (pond) C4
Baker (lake) D3
Baskahegan (lake) H5
Bear (riv.) B6
Big (brook) E2
Big (lake) H5
Big Black (riv.) D2
Bigelow (bight) C9
Big Spencer (mt.) E4
Black (pond) D3
Blue (mt.) C6
Blue Hill (bay) G7
Bog (lake) H6
Brassua (lake) D4
Casco (bay) C8
Cathance (lake) J6
Caucomgomoc (lake) D3
Center (pond) E5
Chamberlain (lake) E3
Chemquasabamticook (lake) D3
Chesuncook (lake) E3
Chiputneticook (lakes) H4
Clayton (lake) D2
Clifford (lake) H5
Cold Stream (pond) G5
Crawford (lake) H5
Cross (isl.) J6
Cross (lake) G1
Cupsuptic (riv.) B5
Dead (riv.) C5
Deer (isl.) F7
Duck (isls.) G7
Eagle (lake) E3
Eagle (lake) F1
East Machias (riv.) H6
East Musquash (lake) H5
Elizabeth (cape) C8
Ellis (pond) B6
Ellis (riv.) B6
Embden (pond) D6
Endless (lake) F5
Englishman (bay) J6
Eskutassis (pond) G5
Fifth (lake) H5
Fish (riv.) F2
Fish River (lake) F2
Flagstaff (lake) C5
Fourth (lake) H5
Frenchman (bay) G7
Gardner (lake) J6
Georges (isls.) E8
Graham (lake) G6
Grand (lake) H4
Grand Falls (lake) H5
Grand Lake Seboeis (lake) F3
Grand Manan (chan.) K6
Great Moose (lake) D6
Great Wass (isl.) J7
Green (isl.) F8
Harrington (lake) E4
Haut (isl.) G7
Indian Pond (lake) D4
Islesboro (isl.) F7
Jo-Mary (lakes) E4
Katahdin (mt.) F4
Kennebec (riv.) D7
Kezar (lake) B7
Kezar (pond) B7
Kingsbury (pond) D5
Little Black (riv.) E1
Little Madawaska (riv.) G2
Lobster (lake) E4
Long (lake) B7
Long (lake) E2
Long (lake) G1
Long (pond) C4
Long (pond) D6
Long (pond) E5
Long Falls (dam) C5
Longfellow (mts.) B6
Loon (lake) D3
Loring A.F.B. 6,572 H2
Lower Roach (pond) E4
Lower Sysladobsis (lake) G5
Machias (bay) J6
Machias (riv.) F2
Machias (riv.) H6
Machias Seal (isl.) J7
Madagascal (pond) G5
Marshall (isl.) G7
Matinicus Rock (isl.) F8
Mattamiscontis (lake) F4
Mattawamkeag (lake) G4
Mattawamkeag (riv.) G4
Meddybemps (lake) J5
Metinic (isl.) E8
Millinocket (lake) F4
Millinocket (lake) F3
Molunkus (lake) G4
Monhegan (isl.) E8
Moose (pond) B7
Moose (riv.) D4
Moosehead (lake) D4
Mooseleuk (stream) F2
Mooselookmeguntic (lake) B6
Mopang (lake) H6
Mount Desert (isl.) G7
Mount Desert Rock (isl.) G8
Moxie (lake) D5
Munsungan (lake) E3
Muscongus (bay) E8
Musquacook (lakes) E2
Nahmakanta (lake) E4
Nicatous (lake) G5
Nollesemic (lake) F4
Old (stream) H6
Onawa (lake) E5
Parlin (pond) C4
Parmachenee (lake) B5
Passamaquoddy (bay) J5
Passamaquoddy Ind. Res. J6
Pemadumcook (lake) E4
Penobscot (bay) F7
Penobscot (lake) C4
Penobscot (riv.) F5
Penobscot Ind. Res. F6
Pierce (pond) C5
Piscataqua (riv.) B9
Piscataquis (riv.) E5
Pleasant (lake) E3
Pleasant (lake) G3
Pleasant (lake) H5
Pleasant (riv.) H6
Pocomoonshine (lake) H5
Portage (lake) F2
Presque Isle A.F.B. G2
Priestly (lake) E2
Pushaw (lake) F6
Ragged (isl.) F8
Ragged (lake) E4
Rainbow (lake) E4
Rangeley (lake) B6
Richardson (lakes) B6
Rocky (lake) J6
Round (pond) E2
Rowe (lake) F2
Saco (riv.) B8
Saint Croix (riv.) J5
Saint Croix Isl. Nat'l Mon. J5
Saint Francis (riv.) E1
Saint Froid (lake) F2
Saint John (pond) D3
Saint John (riv.) G1
Salmon Falls (riv.) B9
Sandy (riv.) C6
Schoodic (lake) F5
Scraggly (lake) F3
Scraggly (lake) H5
Seal (isl.) F8
Sebago (lake) B8
Sebasticook (lake) E6
Seboeis (lake) F5
Seboeis (riv.) F3
Seboomook (lake) D4
Shallow (lake) E3
Small (cape) D8
Sourdnahunk (lake) F3
Spencer (pond) D4
Spencer (stream) C5
Spider (lake) E3
Squa Pan (lake) G2
Square (lake) G1
Sunday (riv.) B6
Swift (riv.) B6
Sysladobsis, Lower (lake) G5
Third (lake) H5
Twin (lakes) F4
Umbagog (lake) A6
Umcalcus (lake) G3
Umsaskis (lake) E2
Union, West Branch (riv.) G6
Vinalhaven (isl.) F7
Wassataquoik (stream) F4
Webb (lake) C6
Webster (brook) E3
West Grand (lake) H5
West Musquash (lake) H5
West Quoddy (head) K6
Wilson E5
Winnecook (lake) E6
Wooden Ball (isl.) F8
Wyman (lake) C5
Wytopitlock (lake) G4

⊙County seat.
‡Population of metropolitan area.
○Population of town or township.
† Zip of nearest p.o.
* Multiple zips.

Topography

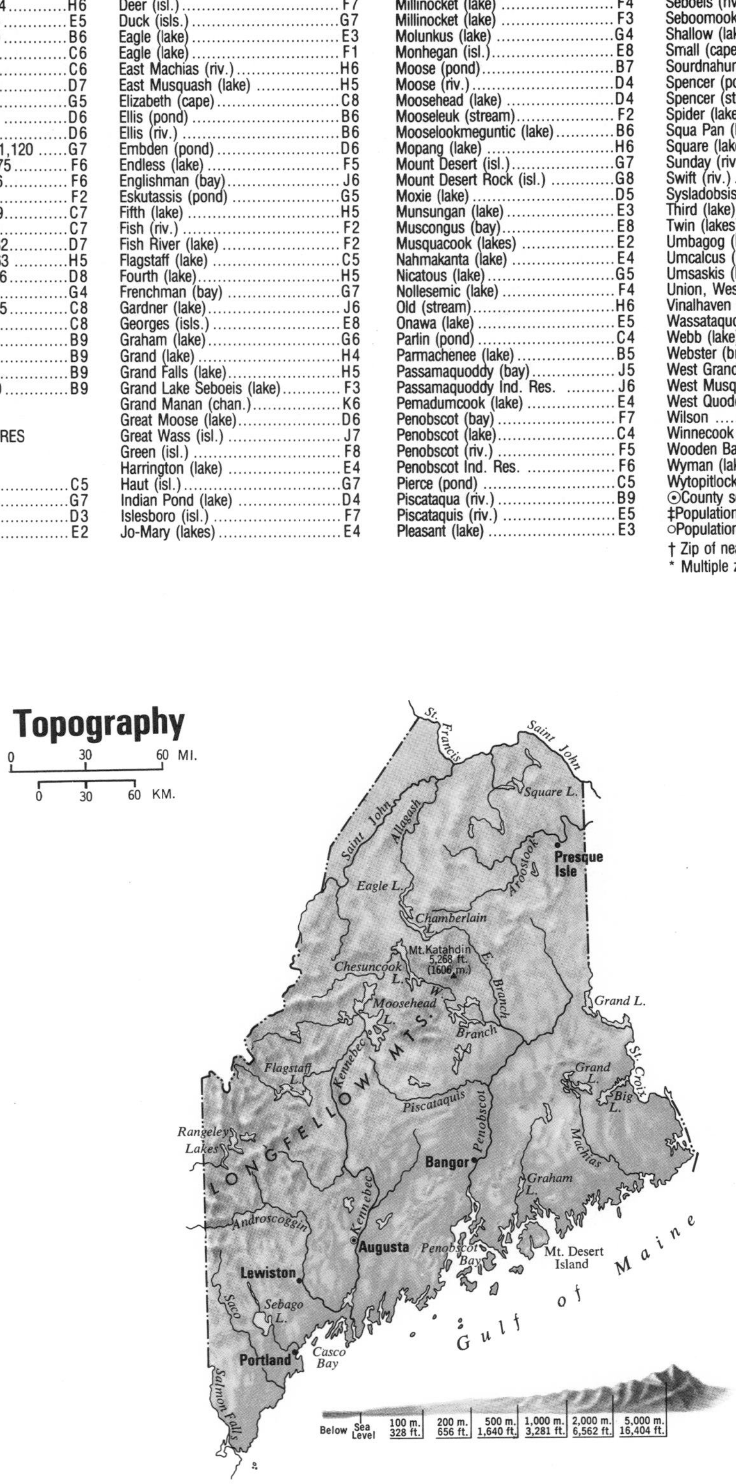
0 30 60 MI.
0 30 60 KM.
St. Francis
Saint John
Square L.
Saint John
Allagash
Aroostook
Presque Isle
Eagle L.
Chamberlain
Mt. Katahdin 5,268 ft. (1606 m.)
Chesuncook L.
E. Branch
Moosehead L.
W. Branch
Grand L.
Flagstaff L.
Kennebec
LONGFELLOW MTS.
Piscataquis
Penobscot
Grand L.
Big L.
St. Croix
Rangeley Lakes
Machias
Bangor
Graham L.
Androscoggin
Kennebec
Augusta
Penobscot Bay
Mt. Desert Island
Gulf of Maine
Lewiston
Saco
Sebago L.
Portland
Casco Bay
Salmon Falls
Below Sea Level
100 m. 328 ft.
200 m. 656 ft.
500 m. 1,640 ft.
1,000 m. 3,281 ft.
2,000 m. 6,562 ft.
5,000 m. 16,404 ft.

MARYLAND

COUNTIES

Allegany 80,548 .... C2
Anne Arundel 370,775 ...... M4
Baltimore 655,615 .... M3
Baltimore (city county) 786,775 . M3
Calvert 34,638 .... M6
Caroline 23,143 .... P5
Carroll 96,356 .... K2
Cecil 60,430 .... P2
Charles 72,751 .... K6
Dorchester 30,623 .... O7
Frederick 114,792 .... J3
Garrett 26,498 .... A2
Harford 145,930 .... N2
Howard 118,572 .... L4
Kent 16,695 .... O3
Montgomery 579,053 .... J4
Prince Georges 665,071 ..... L5
Queen Annes 25,508 .... P4
Saint Marys 59,895 .... M7
Somerset 19,188 .... R8
Talbot 25,604 .... O5
Washington 113,086 .... G2
Wicomico 64,540 .... R7
Worcester 30,889 .... S8

CITIES and TOWNS

Zip	Name/Pop.	Key

21001 Aberdeen 11,533 .... O2
21009 Abingdon 500 .... N3
21520 Accident 246 .... A2
20607 Accokeek 3,894 .... L6
*21401 Annapolis (cap.) ⊙ 31,740 M5
20701 Annapolis Junction 775 .... M4
20608 Aquasco 950 .... L6
†21227 Arbutus 20,163 .... M4
†20785 Ardmore 500 .... G4
Aspen Hill 47,455 .... K4
*21201 Baltimore 786,775 .... M3
Baltimore‡ 2,174,023 .... M3
20610 Barstow 500 .... M6
21521 Barton 617 .... B2
21014 Bel Air ⊙ 7,814 .... N2
20611 Bel Alton 800 .... L7
20705 Beltsville 12,760 .... G3
20612 Benedict 850 .... M6
21811 Berlin 2,162 .... T7
†20740 Berwyn Heights 3,135 .. G4
*20014 Bethesda 62,736 .... E4
21609 Bethlehem 500 .... P6
21610 Betterton 356 .... O3
20710 Bladensburg 7,691 ...... G4
21523 Bloomington 486 .... B3
21713 Boonsboro 1,908 .... H2
†20027 Boulevard Heights 500 .. F5
20715 Bowie 33,695 .... L4
21612 Bozman 700 .... N5
20613 Brandywine 1,319 ...... L6
20722 Brentwood 2,988 .... F4
21225 Brooklyn 11,508 .... M4
†21659 Brookview 78 .... P6
21716 Brunswick 4,572 .... H3
21717 Buckeystown 400 ...... J3
21718 Burkittsville 202 .... H3
20618 Bushwood 750 .... L7
20731 Cabin
John-Brookmont 5,135 . E4
20619 California 5,770 .... M7
†20705 Calverton 7,649 .... L4
21613 Cambridge ⊙ 11,703 ... O6
20748 Camp Springs 16,118 ... G6
21401 Cape Saint Claire 6,022 . N4
20743 Capitol Heights 3,271 ... G5
21024 Cardiff 475 .... N2
†20028 Carmody Hills-Pepper Mill
Village 5,571 .... G5
†21034 Castleton 750 .... N2
†21788 Catoctin Furnace 516 .. J2
21228 Catonsville 33,208 ..... M3
21720 Cavetown 1,533 .... H2
21913 Cecilton 508 .... P3
21617 Centreville ⊙ 2,018 .... O4
21816 Chance 600 .... P8
21914 Charlestown 720 .... P2
20622 Charlotte Hall 1,901 ... M7
21027 Chase 900 .... N3
20623 Cheltenham 950 .... L6
20732 Chesapeake Beach 1,408 . N6
21915 Chesapeake City 899 ... P2
21619 Chester 950 .... N5
21620 Chestertown ⊙ 3,300 .. O4
20785 Cheverly 5,751 .... G4
20815 Chevy Chase 12,232 ... E4
†20015 Chevy Chase Section
Four 3,189 .... E4
20783 Chillum 32,775 .... F4
21622 Church Creek 124 ..... O6
21623 Church Hill 319 .... O4
21028 Churchville 500 .... N2
20734 Clarksburg 400 .... J4
21029 Clarksville 500 .... L4
21722 Clear Spring 477 ...... G2
20624 Clements 800 .... L7
20735 Clinton 16,438 .... G6
21030 Cockeysville 17,013 .. M3
20904 Colesville 14,359 ..... K4
20740 College Park 23,614 .. G4
†20722 Colmar Manor 1,286 .. F4
20626 Coltons Point 600 .... M8
21043 Columbia 52,518 ...... L4
20627 Compton 500 .... M7
21723 Cooksville 497 .... K3
†20027 Coral Hills 11,602 .... G5
21524 Corriganville 1,020 ... C2
†20722 Cottage City 1,122 ... F4
†20611 Cox Station (Bel
Alton) 800 .... L7
21502 Cresaptown 4,645 .... C2
21817 Crisfield 2,924 .... P9
21114 Crofton 12,009 .... M4
21032 Crownsville 500 ...... M4
21502 Cumberland ⊙ 25,933 . D2
Cumberland‡ 107,782 .. D2

20750 Damascus 4,129 .... K3
20628 Dameron 759 .... N8
21034 Darlington 850 .... N2
†20760 Darnestown 950 .... J4
20751 Deale 3,008 .... M5
21821 Deal Island 800 .... P8
21550 Deer Park 486 .... A3
†20784 Defense Heights G4
21875 Delmar 1,232 .... R7
21629 Denton ⊙ 1,927 .... P5
20855 Derwood 413 .... K4
20753 Dickerson 530 .... J4
20747 District Heights 6,799 .... G5
20630 Drayden 400 .... N8
21222 Dundalk 71,293 .... N3
†20608 Eagle Harbor 45 .... M6
21631 East New Market 230 ..... P6
21601 Easton ⊙ 7,536 .... O5
21528 Eckhart Mines 1,333 ...... C2
21822 Eden 800 .... R7
†21219 Edgemere 9,078 .... N4
†21040 Edgewood 19,455 .... N3
†21784 Eldersburg 4,959 .... L3

†21659 Eldorado 93 .... P6
21920 Elk Mills 550 .... P2
21901 Elk Neck 700 .... P2
21921 Elkton ⊙ 6,468 .... P2
21529 Ellerslie 950 .... C2
21043 Ellicott City 21,784 .... L3
21727 Emmitsburg 1,552 .... J2
21221 Essex 39,614 .... N3
21824 Ewell 595 .... O9
20027 Fairmount Heights 1,616 .. G5
21047 Fallston 5,572 .... N2
21632 Federalsburg 1,952 .... P6
21061 Ferndale 14,314 .... M4
21048 Finksburg 950 .... L3
21634 Fishing Creek 595 .... N7
21530 Flintstone 400 .... D2
†20001 Forest Heights 2,999 ..... F5
21050 Forest Hill 450 .... N2
†20028 Forestville 16,401 .... G5
20022 Fort Foote 700 .... F6
20744 Fort Washington L6
†21740 Fountain Head 1,745 ..... G2
21760 Foxville 175 .... H2
21701 Frederick ⊙ 28,086 .... J3

21053 Freeland 500 .... M2
20758 Friendship 600 .... M6
21531 Friendsville 511 .... A2
21532 Frostburg 7,715 .... C2
21826 Fruitland 2,694 .... R7
21734 Funkstown 1,103 .... H2
20760 Gaithersburg 26,424 ...... K4
21635 Galena 374 .... P3
†19973 Galestown 142 .... P6
20765 Galesville 600 .... M5
†20148 Gamber 950 .... L3
21054 Gambrills 460 .... M4
20766 Garrett Park 1,178 .... E3
21055 Garrison 950 .... L3
20767 Germantown 9,721 .... J4
21636 Goldsboro 188 .... P4
†21163 Granite 950 .... L3
21536 Grantsville 498 .... B2
21638 Grasonville 1,910 .... O5
20770 Greenbelt 17,332 .... G4

21122 Green Haven 6,577 .... M4
21639 Greensboro 1,253 .... P5
21740 Hagerstown ⊙ 34,132 .... G2
Hagerstown‡ 113,086 ... G2
†21740 Halfway 8,659 .... G2
21074 Hampstead 1,293 .... L2
21750 Hancock 1,887 .... F2
21201 Hanover 500 .... M4
21077 Harmans 400 .... M4
21830 Havre de Grace 8,763 .... N2
21640 Henderson 156 .... P4
†21111 Hereford 680 .... M2
21753 Highfield-Cascade 1,096 . J2
21401 Highland Beach 8 .... M5
†20903 Hillandale 9,686 .... G4
†20031 Hillcrest Heights 17,021 . F5
20768 Glen Echo 229 .... E4
21641 Hillsboro 180 .... P5
20636 Hollywood 500 .... M7
20637 Huntingtown 450 .... M6
21643 Hurlock 1,690 .... P6
*20780 Hyattsville 12,709 ...... F4
20640 Indian Head 1,381 ..... K6

†20685 Island Creek 400 .... M7
21084 Jarrettsville 1,485 .... M2
†21085 Joppatowne 11,348 .... N3
21756 Keedysville 476 .... H3
†20901 Kemp Mill F3
20795 Kensington 1,822 .... E4
21087 Kingsville 2,824 .... N3
21538 Kitzmiller 387 .... B3
21758 Knoxville 500 .... H3
20785 Landover 5,374 .... G4
20784 Landover Hills 1,428 ... G4
20787 Langley Park 14,038 ... F4
20801 Lanham-Seabrook 15,814 . G4
21227 Lansdowne-Baltimore
Highlands 16,759 .... M3
20646 La Plata ⊙ 2,484 .... L5
21502 Le Gore 500 .... G5
*20810 Laurel 12,103 .... L4
21502 La Vale-Narrows
Park 5,523 .... C2
20760 Laytonsville 195 .... K4
21761 Le Gore 500 .... J2
†21740 Leitersburg 350 .... H2
20650 Leonardtown ⊙ 1,448 .. M7

(continued)

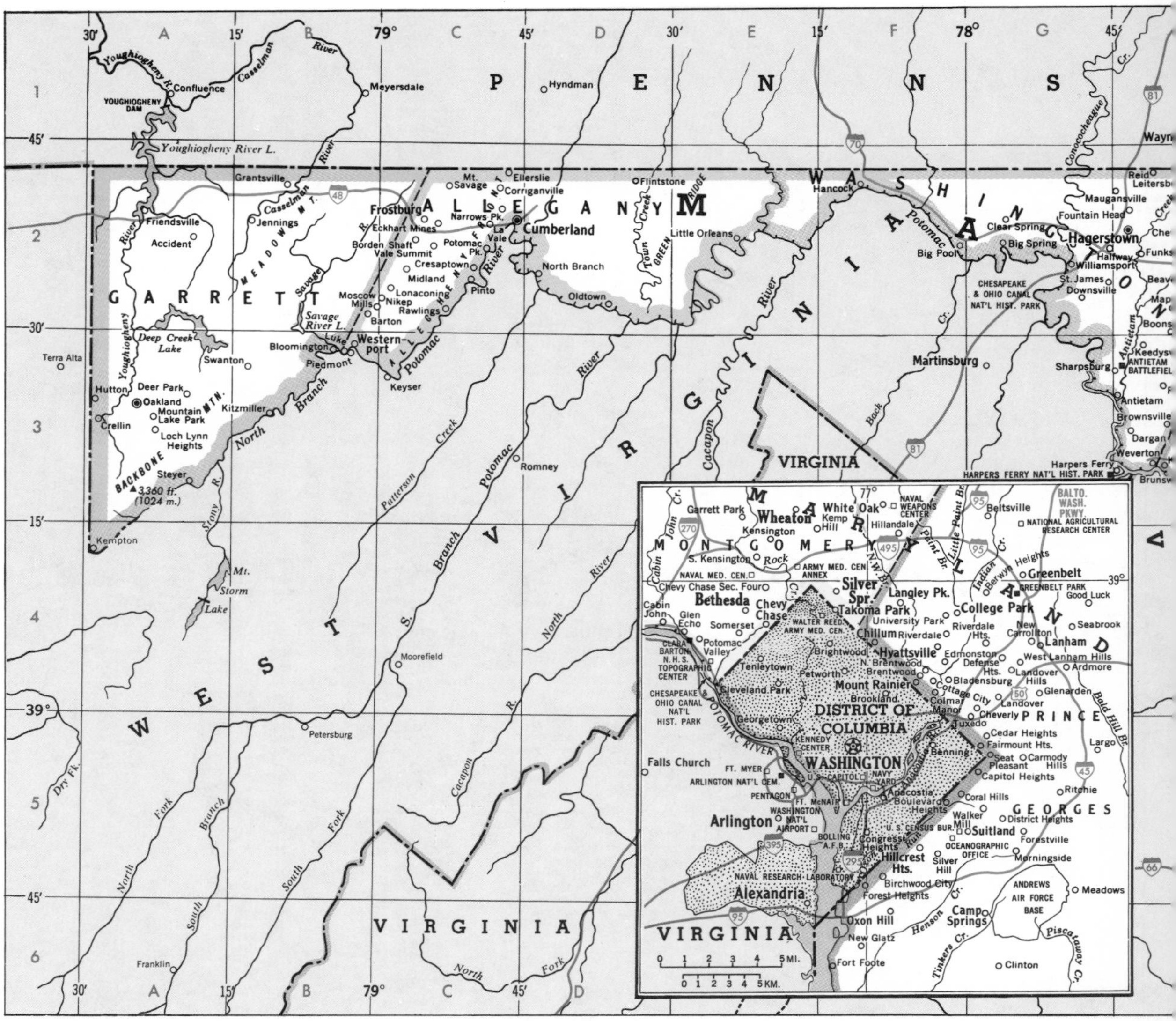

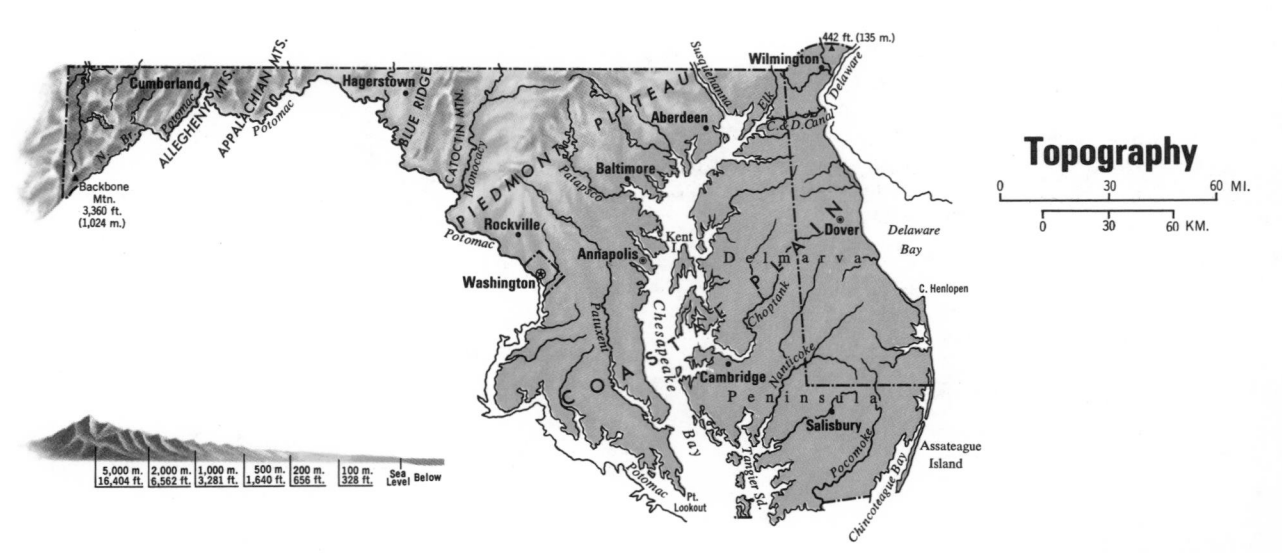

Topography

0   30   60 MI.

0   30   60 KM.

5,000 m.   2,000 m.   1,000 m.   500 m.   200 m.   100 m.   Sea   Below
16,404 ft. 6,562 ft. 3,281 ft. 1,640 ft. 656 ft. 328 ft. Level

MARYLAND

AREA   10,460 sq. mi. (27,091 sq. km.)
POPULATION   4,216,975
CAPITAL   Annapolis
LARGEST CITY   Baltimore
HIGHEST POINT   Backbone Mtn. 3,360 ft.
   (1024 m.)
SETTLED IN   1634
ADMITTED TO UNION   April 28, 1788
POPULAR NAME   Old Line State; Free State
STATE FLOWER   Black-eyed Susan
STATE BIRD   Baltimore Oriole

DELAWARE

AREA   2,044 sq. mi. (5,294 sq. km.)
POPULATION   594,317
CAPITAL   Dover
LARGEST CITY   Wilmington
HIGHEST POINT   Ebright Road 442 ft. (135 m.)
SETTLED IN   1627
ADMITTED TO UNION   December 7, 1787
POPULAR NAME   First State; Diamond State
STATE FLOWER   Peach Blossom
STATE BIRD   Blue Hen Chicken

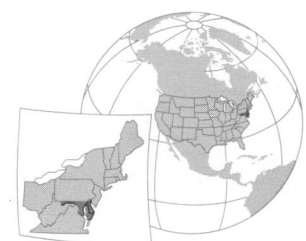

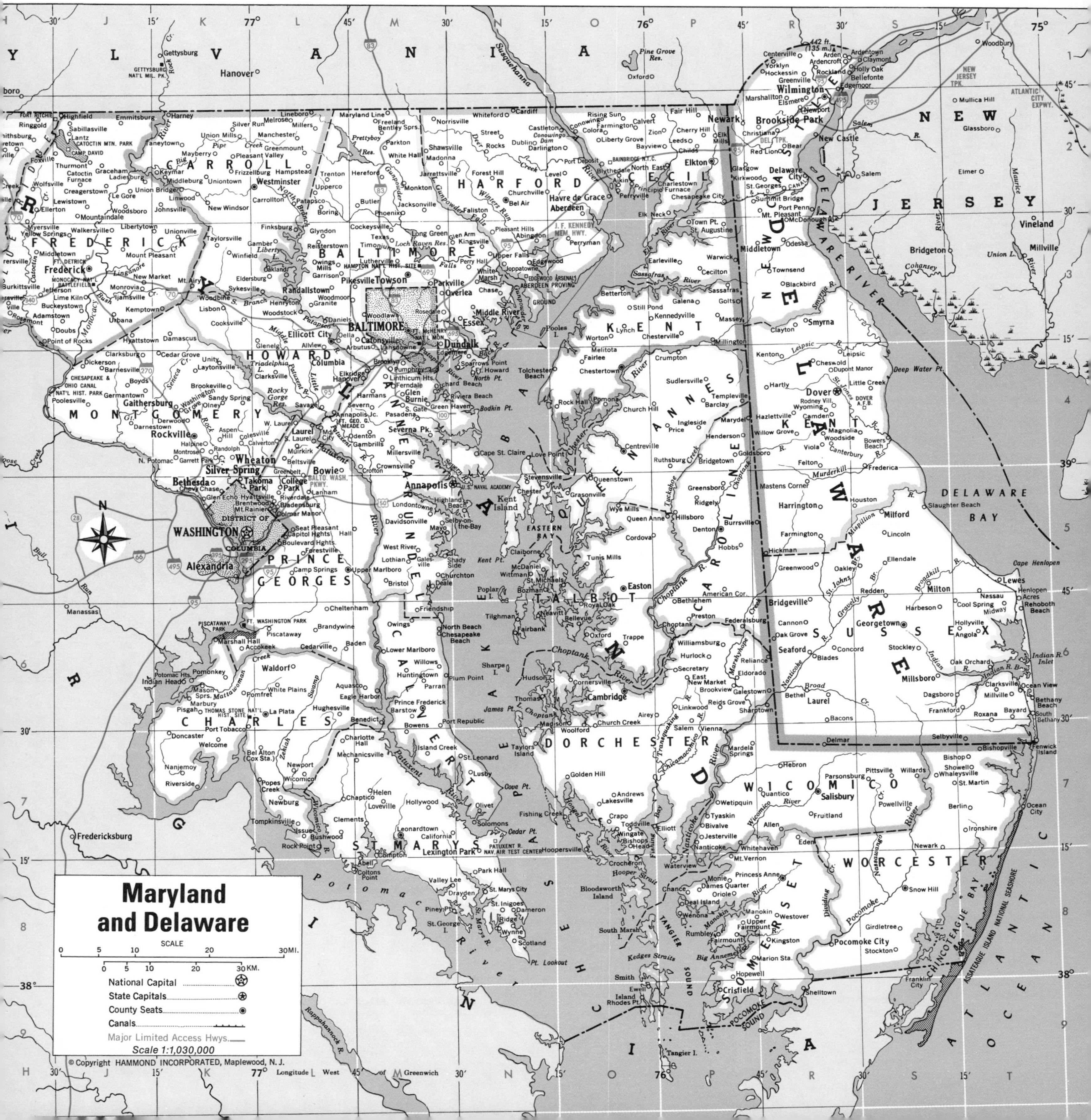

Maryland and Delaware

SCALE
0   5   10   20   30 MI.
0   5   10   20   30 KM.

National Capital .... ⊛
State Capitals .... ✪
County Seats .... ◉
Canals
Major Limited Access Hwys.
Scale 1:1,030,000

© Copyright HAMMOND INCORPORATED, Maplewood, N.J.

(continued)

21701 Lewistown 600 J2
20653 Lexington Park 10,361 M7
21762 Libertytown 400 J3
21090 Linthicum Heights 7,457 M4
21766 Little Orleans 600 E2
†21550 Loch Lynn Heights 503 A3
21539 Lonaconing 1,420 C2
†21035 Londontowne 6,052 M4
21092 Long Green 1,626 M3
20656 Loveville 600 M7
21540 Luke 329 B3
21093 Lutherville-Timonium 16,871 M3
21648 Madison 350 O6
21102 Manchester 1,830 L2
20658 Marbury 1,189 K6
21837 Mardela Springs 320 P7
21838 Marion Station 400 R8
†20616 Marshall Hall 325 K6
21649 Marydel 152 P4
†21113 Maryland City 6,949 L4
21767 Maugansville 1,707 H2
21106 Mayo 2,795 M5
20659 Mechanicsville 784 M7
21220 Middle River 26,756 N3
21769 Middletown 1,748 J3
21542 Midland 601 C2
21108 Millersville 380 M4
21651 Millington 546 P3
†20028 Morningside 1,395 G5
†21701 Mountaindale 400 J2
21550 Mountain Lake Park 1,597 A3
21771 Mount Airy 2,450 K3
†21701 Mount Pleasant 400 J3
20822 Mount Rainier 7,361 F4
21545 Mount Savage 1,640 C2
†21853 Mount Vernon 900 P8
†20705 Muirkirk 950 L4
21773 Myersville 432 H3
21840 Nanticoke 450 P7
†21502 Narrows Park-La Vale 5,523 C2
21841 Newark 900 S7
20664 Newburg 550 L7
20784 New Carrollton 12,632 G4
21774 New Market 306 J3
21776 New Windsor 799 K2
20831 North Beach 1,504 N6
†20722 North Brentwood 580 F4
21901 North East 1,469 P2
†20854 North Potomac K4
21550 Oakland⊙ 1,994 A3
†21784 Oakland 2,242 L3
21842 Ocean City 4,946 T7
21113 Odenton 13,270 M4
†21228 Oella 600 L3
20832 Olney 13,026 K4
21206 Overlea 12,965 N3
20836 Owings 700 M6
21117 Owings Mills 9,526 L3
21654 Oxford 754 O6
20745 Oxon Hill 36,267 F6
20667 Park Hall 775 N8
21234 Parkville 35,159 M3
21122 Pasadena 7,439 M4
21128 Perry Hall 13,455 N3
21130 Perryman 1,819 O3
21903 Perryville 2,018 O2
21208 Pikesville 22,555 M3
20674 Piney Point 950 M8
†20735 Piscataway 500 L6
20640 Pisgah 650 K6
21850 Pittsville 519 S7
†21087 Pleasant Hills 2,790 N3
21851 Pocomoke City 3,558 R8
20675 Pomfret 600 L6
†20640 Pomonkey 410 K6
20837 Poolesville 3,428 J4
21904 Port Deposit 664 O2
20677 Port Tobacco 40 K6
20640 Potomac Heights 2,456 K6
†21502 Potomac Park-Bowling Green 2,275 C2
21852 Powellville 400 S7
21655 Preston 498 P6
20678 Prince Frederick⊙ 1,805 M6
21853 Princess Anne⊙ 1,499 P8
†21090 Pumphrey 5,666 M4
21657 Queen Anne 259 O5
21658 Queenstown 491 O5
21133 Randallstown 25,927 L3
21557 Rawlings 500 C2
21136 Reisterstown 19,385 L3
20680 Ridge 550 N8
21660 Ridgely 933 P5
21911 Rising Sun 1,160 O2
†20027 Ritchie 950 G5
†20840 Riverdale Heights G4
†21061 Riviera Beach 8,812 N4
21661 Rock Hall 1,511 O4
†21084 Rocks 450 N2
*20850 Rockville⊙ 43,811 K4
21779 Rohrersville 525 H3
21237 Rosedale 19,956 M3
†21758 Rosemont 305 H3
21662 Royal Oak 600 O6
21780 Sabillasville 450 J2
20684 Saint Inigoes 750 N8
21663 Saint Michaels 1,301 N5
21801 Salisbury⊙ 16,429 R7
20860 Sandy Spring-Ashton 2,659 K4
20863 Savage-Guilford 2,928 L4
20687 Scotland 475 N8
20801 Seabrook-Lanham 15,814 G4
20027 Seat Pleasant 5,217 G5
21664 Secretary 487 P6
†21037 Selby-on-the-Bay 3,125 N5
21144 Severn 20,147 M4
21146 Severna Park 21,253 M4
20867 Shady Side 2,877 M5
21782 Sharpsburg 721 G3
21861 Sharptown 654 R6
20023 Silver Hill-Suitland 32,164 F5
†21157 Silver Run 350 K2
*20901 Silver Spring 72,893 F4
21783 Smithsburg 833 H2
21863 Snow Hill⊙ 2,192 S8
†20015 Somerset 1,101 E4
†21113 South Gate 24,185 M4
†20795 South Kensington 9,344 E4
†20810 South Laurel 18,034 L4
21219 Sparrows Point N4
21666 Stevensville 500 N5
21667 Still Pond 350 O3
21864 Stockton 400 S8
21668 Sudlersville 443 P4
†20746 Suitland-Silver Hill 32,164 F5
21784 Sykesville 1,712 K3
20912 Takoma Park 16,231 F4
21787 Taneytown 2,618 K2
21669 Taylors Island 400 N7
21670 Templeville 96 P4
21788 Thurmont 2,934 J2
21671 Tilghman 979 N6
21093 Timonium-Lutherville 16,871 M3
21672 Toddville 500 O7
21204 Towson⊙ 51,083 M3
21673 Trappe 739 O6
†20780 Tuxedo 500 G5
21791 Union Bridge 927 K2
†20740 University Park 2,536 F4
21155 Upperco 500 L2
21867 Upper Fairmount 500 P8
21156 Upper Falls 550 N3
20870 Upper Marlboro⊙ 828 M5
20692 Valley Lee 600 M8
21869 Vienna 300 P7
20601 Waldorf 9,782 L6
†20023 Walker Mill 10,651 F5
21793 Walkersville 2,212 J3
21912 Warwick 550 P3
20880 Washington Grove 527 K4
20693 Welcome 438 K7
21562 Westernport 2,706 B3
†20784 West Lanham Hills 350 G4
21157 Westminster⊙ 8,808 L2
21871 Westover 450 R8
20902 Wheaton-Glenmont 48,598 E3
21160 Whiteford 500 N2
21161 White Hall 360 M2
21162 White Marsh 500 N3
†20901 White Oak 13,700 F3
20695 White Plains 5,167 L6
21874 Willards 540 S7
21795 Williamsport 2,153 G2
21676 Wittman 544 N5
21797 Woodbine 872 K3
21798 Woodsboro 506 J2
21163 Woodstock 700 L3
21677 Woolford 330 O7
21679 Wye Mills 315 O5
†20680 Wynne 450 N8
†21701 Yellow Springs 940 H3

OTHER FEATURES

Aberdeen Proving Ground 5,722 N3
Allegheny Front (mts.) C2
Andrews A.F.B. 10,064 G5
Antietam (creek) H2
Antietam Nat'l Battlefield H3
Army Chemical Center O3
Back (riv.) N4
Backbone (mt.) A3
Bainbridge N.T.C. O2
Bald Hill Branch (riv.) G4
Big Annemessex (riv.) P8
Big Pipe (creek) K2
Bloodsworth (isl.) O8
Blue Ridge (mts.) H3
Bodkin (pt.) N4
Bush (creek) J3
Cabin John (creek) E4
Camp David J2
Casselman (riv.) B2
Catoctin (creek) H3
Catoctin Mt. Park J2
Cedar (pt.) N7
Census Bureau F5
Chesapeake (bay) N7
Chesapeake and Delaware (canal) R2
Chesapeake and Ohio Canal Nat'l Hist. Park J4
Chester (riv.) O4
Chicamacomico (riv.) P7
Chincoteague (bay) S8
Choptank (riv.) O6
Clara Barton Nat'l Hist. Site E4
Conococheague (creek) G1
Conowingo (dam) O2
Cove (pt.) N7
Deep Creek (lake) A3
Deer (creek) N2
Dividing (creek) N8
Eastern (bay) N5
Elk (riv.) P3
Fishing (bay) O7
Fort Detrick J3
Fort George G. Meade 14,083 L4
Fort McHenry Nat'l Mon. M3
Fort Ritchie 1,754 H2
Fort Washington Park L6
Great Seneca (creek) J4
Greenbelt Park G4
Green Ridge (mts.) E2
Gunpowder (riv.) N3
Gunpowder Falls (creek) M2
Hampton Nat'l Hist. Site M3
Harpers Ferry Nat'l Hist. Park G3
Henson (creek) F6
Honga (riv.) O7
Hooper (str.) O8
Indian (creek) G4
James (pt.) N6
Kedges (strs) O8
Kent (isl.) N5
Kent (pt.) N5
Liberty (lake) L3
Linganore (creek) J3
Little Choptank (riv.) N6
Little Gunpowder Falls (creek) M2
Little Paint Branch (riv.) F4
Little Patuxent (riv.) L4
Loch Raven (res.) M3
Lookout (pt.) N8
Manokin (riv.) P8
Marshyhope (creek) P6
Mattawoman (creek) K6
Meadow (mt.) B2
Middle Patuxent (riv.) L3
Monocacy (riv.) J3
Monocacy Nat'l Battlefield J3
Nanticoke (riv.) P7
Nassawango (creek) S8
National Agricultural Research Center G3
Naval Academy, U.S. 5,367 N5
Naval Medical Center E4
Naval Weapons Center F3
North (pt.) N4
Oceanographic Office F5
Oxon Run (riv.) F5
Paint Branch (riv.) F4
Patapsco (riv.) M4
Patuxent (riv.) M7
Patuxent River Nav. Air Test Ctr. N7
Piscataway (creek) G6
Piscataway Park K6
Pocomoke (riv.) S8
Pocomoke (sound) P9
Pooles (isl.) O3
Poplar (isl.) N5
Potomac (riv.) M8
Prettyboy (res.) M2
Rock (creek) K4
Rocky Gorge (res.) L4
Saint George (isl.) M8
Saint Marys (riv.) N8
Sassafras (riv.) P3
Savage (riv.) B2
Savage River (lake) B2
Severn (riv.) N4
Sharps (isl.) N6
Smith (isl.) O8
South Marsh (isl.) O8
Susquehanna (riv.) N1
Tangier (sound) P8
Thomas Stone Nat'l Hist. Site K6
Tinkers (creek) F6
Topographic Center E4
Town (creek) E2
Transquaking (riv.) P7
Triadelphia (lake) L4
Tuckahoe (creek) P5
Walter Reed Army Med. Ctr. Annex E4
Wicomico (riv.) L7
Wicomico (riv.) R7
Winters Run (creek) N2
Youghiogheny (riv.) A3
Youghiogheny River (lake) A2
Zekiah Swamp (riv.) L7

DELAWARE

COUNTIES

Kent 98,219 R4
New Castle 398,115 R2
Sussex 97,983 S6

CITIES and TOWNS

Zip Name/Pop. Key
†19801 Arden 516 R1
†19810 Ardencroft 267 R1
†19810 Ardentown 307 S1
19809 Bellefonte 1,279 S1
19930 Bethany Beach 330 T6
19931 Bethel 197 R6
†19973 Blades 664 R6
†19962 Bowers Beach 198 S4
19933 Bridgeville 1,238 R6
19711 Brookside 15,255 R2
19934 Camden 1,757 R4
†19801 Centerville 800 R1
19936 Cheswold 269 R4
†19711 Christiana 500 R2
19937 Clarksville 350 T6
19703 Claymont 10,022 S1
19938 Clayton 1,216 R3
19930 Dagsboro 344 S6
19706 Delaware City 1,858 R2
19940 Delmar 948 R7
19901 Dover (cap.)⊙ 23,507 R4
†19901 Dupont Manor 1,059 R4
†19801 Edgemoor 7,397 S1
19941 Ellendale 361 S5
†19801 Elsmere 6,493 R2
19942 Farmington 141 R5
19943 Felton 547 R4
19944 Fenwick Island 114 T7
19945 Frankford 828 S6
19946 Frederica 864 S4
19947 Georgetown⊙ 1,710 S6
†19711 Glasgow 350 R2
19950 Greenwood 578 R5
19952 Harrington 2,405 R5
†19971 Henlopen Acres 176 T6
19707 Hockessin 950 R1
†19801 Holly Oak S1
19954 Houston 357 S5
19955 Kenton 243 R4
19708 Kirkwood 350 R2
19956 Laurel 3,052 R6
†19901 Leipsic 228 S4
19958 Lewes 2,197 T5
19960 Lincoln 757 S5
19961 Little Creek 230 S4
19962 Magnolia 197 R4
19709 Middletown 2,946 R3
19963 Milford 5,366 S5
19966 Millsboro 1,233 S6
19967 Millville 178 T6
19968 Milton 1,359 S5
19711 Newark 25,247 P2
19720 New Castle 4,907 R2
19804 Newport 1,167 R2
†19966 Oak Orchard 350 T6
19970 Ocean View 495 T6
19730 Odessa 384 R3
19971 Rehoboth Beach 1,730 T6
19901 Rodney Village 1,753 R4
19733 Saint Georges 450 R2
19973 Seaford 5,256 R6
19975 Selbyville 1,251 S7
†19963 Slaughter Beach 121 S5
19977 Smyrna 4,750 R3
†19930 South Bethany 115 T6
19734 Townsend 386 R3
19979 Viola 167 R4
*19801 Wilmington⊙ 70,195 R2
Wilmington‡ 524,108 R2
19980 Woodside 248 R4
19934 Wyoming 960 R4
19736 Yorklyn 600 R1

OTHER FEATURES

Broad (creek) R6
Broadkill (riv.) S5
Chesapeake and Delaware (canal) R2
Choptank (riv.) P5
Deep Water (pt.) S4
Delaware (bay) T5
Delaware (riv.) R3
Dover A.F.B. 4,391 S4
Henlopen (cape) T5
Indian (riv.) S6
Indian River (bay) T6
Indian River (inlet) T6
Leipsic (riv.) R4
Mispillion (riv.) S5
Murderkill (riv.) R5
Nanticoke (riv.) R6
Saint Jones (riv.) R4
Smyrna (res.) R3

DISTRICT OF COLUMBIA

CITIES and TOWNS

Zip Name/Pop. Key
20007 Georgetown E5
*20001 Washington, D.C. (cap.), U.S. 638,432 F5
Washington‡ 3,060,240 F5

OTHER FEATURES

Anacostia (riv.) F5
Bolling A.F.B. E5
Fort Lesley J. McNair E5
Kennedy Center A5
Naval Yard F5
U.S. Capitol F5
Walter Reed Army Med. Ctr. E4

⊙County seat.
‡Population of metropolitan area.
† Zip of nearest p.o.
* Multiple zips.

Agriculture, Industry and Resources

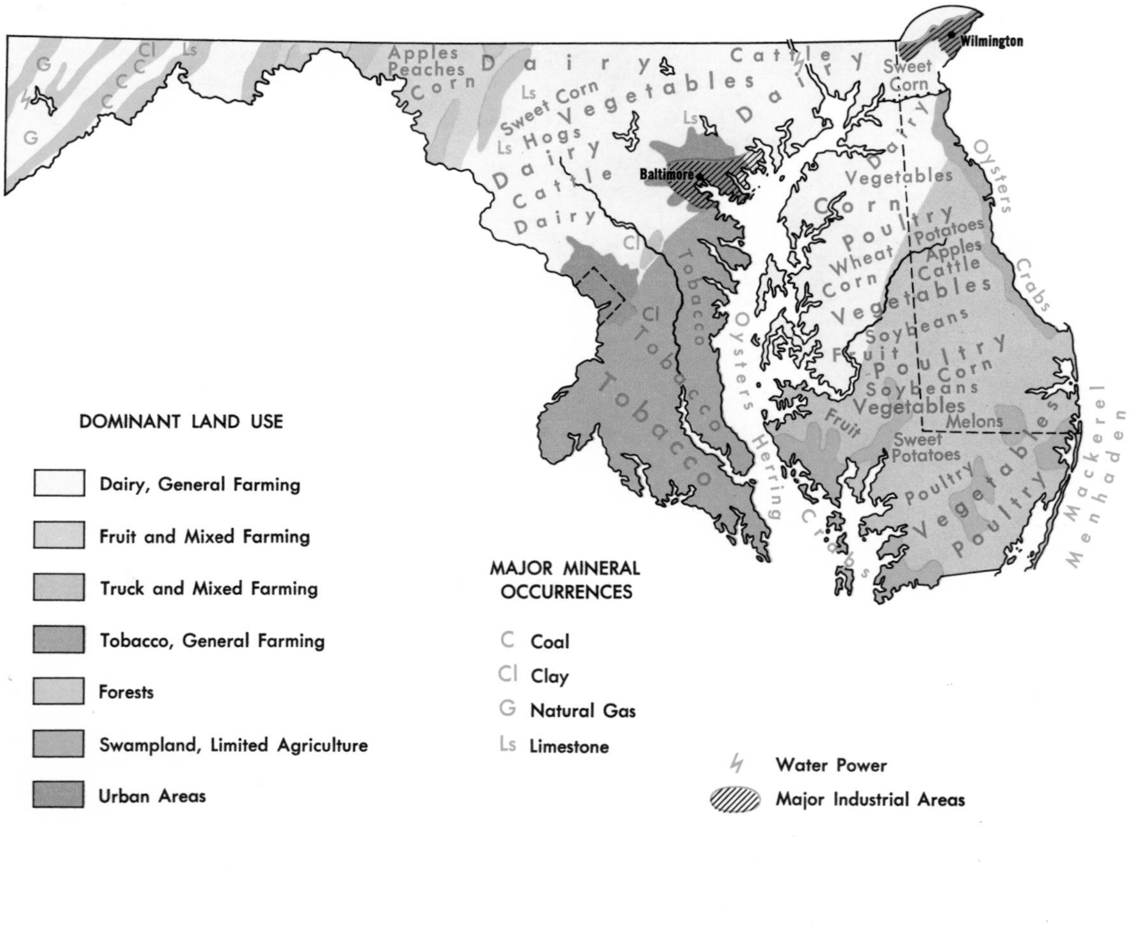
Wilmington
Baltimore
Apples
Peaches
Corn
Dairy
Cattle
Vegetables
Sweet Corn
Hogs
Poultry
Potatoes
Wheat
Tobacco
Soybeans
Fruit
Melons
Sweet Potatoes
Oysters
Crabs
Herring
Mackerel
Menhaden
DOMINANT LAND USE
Dairy, General Farming
Fruit and Mixed Farming
Truck and Mixed Farming
Tobacco, General Farming
Forests
Swampland, Limited Agriculture
Urban Areas
MAJOR MINERAL OCCURRENCES
C Coal
Cl Clay
G Natural Gas
Ls Limestone
Water Power
Major Industrial Areas

MASSACHUSETTS

AREA 8,284 sq. mi. (21,456 sq. km.)
POPULATION 5,737,037
CAPITAL Boston
LARGEST CITY Boston
HIGHEST POINT Mt. Greylock 3,491 ft. (1064 m.)
SETTLED IN 1620
ADMITTED TO UNION February 6, 1788
POPULAR NAME Bay State; Old Colony
STATE FLOWER Mayflower
STATE BIRD Chickadee

RHODE ISLAND

AREA 1,212 sq. mi. (3,139 sq. km.)
POPULATION 947,154
CAPITAL Providence
LARGEST CITY Providence
HIGHEST POINT Jerimoth Hill 812 ft. (247 m.)
SETTLED IN 1636
ADMITTED TO UNION May 29, 1790
POPULAR NAME Little Rhody; Ocean State
STATE FLOWER Violet
STATE BIRD Rhode Island Red

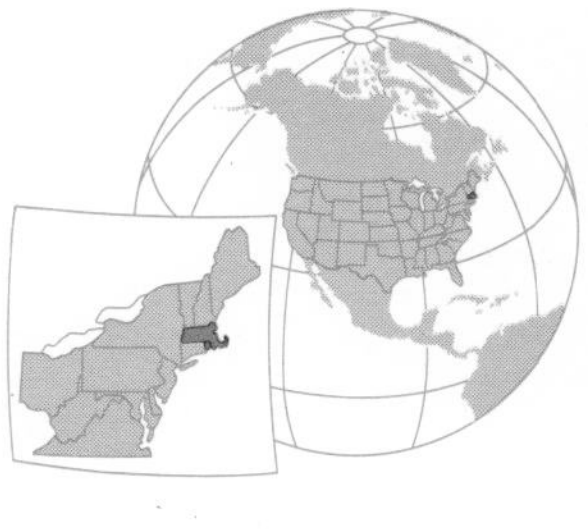

Agriculture, Industry and Resources

DOMINANT LAND USE

- Specialized Dairy
- Dairy, Poultry, Mixed Farming
- Forests
- Urban Areas

MAJOR MINERAL OCCURRENCES

Gn Granite

Water Power

Major Industrial Areas

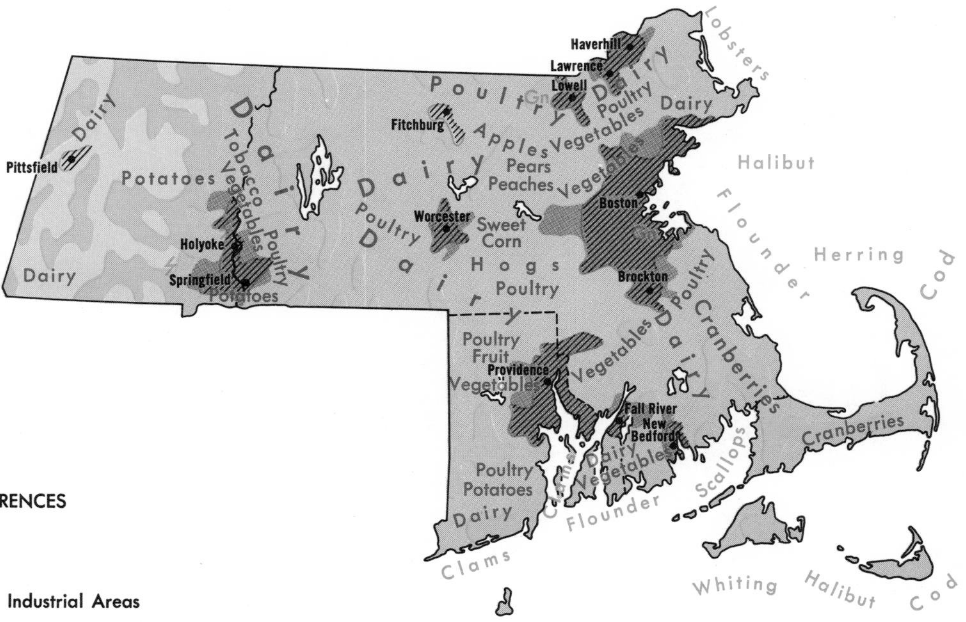

MASSACHUSETTS

COUNTIES

Barnstable 147,925 ... N6
Berkshire 145,110 ... B3
Bristol 474,641 ... K5
Dukes 8,942 ... M7
Essex 633,632 ... L2
Franklin 64,317 ... D2
Hampden 443,018 ... D4
Hampshire 138,813 ... D3
Middlesex 1,367,034 ... J3
Nantucket 5,087 ... O7
Norfolk 606,587 ... K4
Plymouth 405,437 ... L5
Suffolk 650,142 ... K3
Worcester 646,352 ... G3

CITIES and TOWNS

Zip Name/Pop. Key

02351 Abington○ 13,517 ... L4
01720 Acton○ 17,544 ... J3
02743 Acushnet○ 8,704 ... L6
01220 Adams○ 10,381 ... B2
01220 Adams 6,857 ... B2
01001 Agawam○ 26,271 ... D4
†01261 Alford○ 394 ... A4
01913 Amesbury○ 13,971 ... L1
01913 Amesbury 12,236 ... L1
01002 Amherst○ 33,229 ... E3
01002 Amherst 17,773 ... E3
01810 Andover○ 26,370 ... K2
01810 Andover 8,445 ... K2
02174 Arlington○ 48,219 ... C6
01430 Ashburnham○ 4,075 ... G2
01430 Ashburnham 900 ... G2
01431 Ashby○ 2,311 ... G2
01330 Ashfield○ 1,458 ... C2
01721 Ashland○ 9,165 ... J3
01331 Athol○ 10,634 ... F2
01331 Athol 8,708 ... F2
02703 Attleboro 34,196 ... J5
01501 Auburn○ 14,845 ... G4
02322 Avon○ 5,026 ... K4
*01432 Ayer○ 6,993 ... H2
*01432 Ayer 3,165 ... H2
01436 Baldwinville 1,709 ... F2
02630 Barnstable○ 30,898 ... N6
02630 Barnstable⊙ 2,033 ... N6
01005 Barre○ 4,102 ... F3
01005 Barre 1,136 ... F3
01223 Becket○ 1,339 ... B3
01730 Bedford○ 13,067 ... B6
01007 Belchertown○ 8,339 ... E3
01007 Belchertown 2,531 ... E3
02019 Bellingham○ 14,300 ... J4
02019 Bellingham 4,454 ... J4
02178 Belmont○ 26,100 ... C6
†02780 Berkley○ 2,731 ... K5
01503 Berlin○ 2,215 ... H3
01337 Bernardston○ 1,750 ... D2
01915 Beverly 37,655 ... E5
01821 Billerica○ 36,727 ... J2
01504 Blackstone○ 6,570 ... H4
01008 Blandford○ 1,038 ... C4
01740 Bolton○ 2,530 ... H3
01009 Bondsville 1,906 ... E4
*02101 Boston (cap.)⊙ 562,994 ... D7
Boston‡ 2,763,357 ... D7
02532 Bourne○ 13,874 ... M6
02532 Bourne 2,678 ... M6
01719 Boxborough○ 3,126 ... H3
01921 Boxford○ 5,374 ... L2
01921 Boxford 1,841 ... L2
01505 Boylston○ 3,470 ... H3
02184 Braintree○ 36,337 ... D8
02020 Brant Rock-Ocean Bluff 4,055 ... M4
02631 Brewster○ 5,226 ... O5
02631 Brewster 1,744 ... O5
02324 Bridgewater○ 17,202 ... K5
02324 Bridgewater 6,781 ... K5
01010 Brimfield○ 2,318 ... F4
*C2401 Brockton 95,172 ... K4
Brockton‡ 169,374 ... K4
01506 Brookfield○ 2,397 ... F4
01506 Brookfield 1,037 ... F4
02146 Brookline○ 55,062 ... C7
01338 Buckland○ 1,864 ... C2
01803 Burlington○ 23,486 ... C5
02532 Buzzards Bay 3,375 ... M5
02138 Cambridge⊙ 95,322 ... C7
02021 Canton○ 18,182 ... C8
01741 Carlisle○ 3,306 ... J2
02330 Carver○ 6,988 ... M5
02632 Centerville 3,640 ... N6
01339 Charlemont○ 1,149 ... C2
01507 Charlton○ 6,719 ... F4
02633 Chatham○ 6,071 ... P6
02633 Chatham 1,922 ... P6
01824 Chelmsford○ 31,174 ... J2
02150 Chelsea 25,431 ... D6
01225 Cheshire○ 3,124 ... B2
01011 Chester○ 1,123 ... C3
01012 Chesterfield○ 1,000 ... C3
*01013 Chicopee 55,112 ... D4
02535 Chilmark○ 489 ... M7
†02054 Clicquot-Millis 3,777 ... A8
01510 Clinton○ 12,771 ... H3
01778 Cochituate 6,126 ... A7
02025 Cohasset○ 7,174 ... F7
01340 Colrain○ 1,552 ... D2
01742 Concord○ 16,293 ... B6
01341 Conway○ 1,213 ... D2
†01772 Cordaville 1,384 ... H3
01026 Cummington○ 657 ... C3
01226 Dalton○ 6,797 ... B3
01923 Danvers○ 24,100 ... D5
02714 Dartmouth○ 23,966 ... K6
02026 Dedham⊙○ 25,298 ... C7
01342 Deerfield○ 4,517 ... D2
02638 Dennis○ 12,360 ... O5
02639 Dennis Port 2,570 ... O6
02715 Dighton○ 5,352 ... K5
†02122 Dorchester ... D7
†01516 Douglas○ 3,730 ... H4
02030 Dover○ 4,703 ... B7
02030 Dover 2,051 ... B7
01826 Dracut○ 21,249 ... J2
01570 Dudley○ 8,717 ... G4
01827 Dunstable○ 1,671 ... J2
02332 Duxbury○ 11,807 ... M4
02332 Duxbury 1,685 ... M4
02333 East Bridgewater○ 9,945 ... L4
01515 East Brookfield○ 1,955 ... G4
01515 East Brookfield 1,443 ... G4
01516 East Douglas 1,683 ... G4
02536 East Falmouth (Teaticket) 5,181 ... M6
02642 Eastham○ 3,472 ... O5
01027 Easthampton○ 15,580 ... D3
01028 East Longmeadow○ 12,905 E4
02334 Easton○ 16,623 ... K4
01437 East Pepperell 2,212 ... H2
02539 Edgartown○ 2,204 ... M7
02539 Edgartown⊙ 1,138 ... M7
01344 Erving○ 1,326 ... E2
01929 Essex○ 2,998 ... L2
01929 Essex 1,490 ... L2
02149 Everett 37,195 ... D6
02719 Fairhaven○ 15,759 ... L6
*02720 Fall River 92,574 ... K6
Fall River‡ 176,831 ... K6
*02540 Falmouth○ 23,640 ... M6
*02540 Falmouth 5,720 ... M6
01518 Fiskdale 1,859 ... F4
01420 Fitchburg⊙ 39,580 ... G2
Fitchburg-Leominster‡ 99,957 ... G2
†01247 Florida○ 730 ... B2
02035 Foxboro○ 14,148 ... J4
02035 Foxboro 5,697 ... J4
01701 Framingham○ 65,113 ... A7
02038 Franklin○ 18,217 ... J4
02038 Franklin 9,296 ... J4
01440 Gardner 17,900 ... G2
†02535 Gay Head○ 220 ... L7
01833 Georgetown○ 5,687 ... L2
01031 Gilbertville 1,029 ... F3
†01376 Gill○ 1,259 ... D2
01930 Gloucester 27,768 ... M2
01032 Goshen○ 651 ... C3
01519 Grafton○ 11,238 ... H4
01033 Granby○ 5,380 ... E3
01033 Granby 1,302 ... E3
01034 Granville○ 1,204 ... C4
01230 Great Barrington○ 7,405 ... A4
01230 Great Barrington 3,150 ... A4
01301 Greenfield○ 18,436 ... D2
01301 Greenfield⊙ 14,198 ... D2
02041 Green Harbor 2,002 ... M4
01450 Groton○ 6,154 ... H2
01450 Groton 1,264 ... H2
01830 Groveland○ 5,040 ... L1
01035 Hadley○ 4,125 ... D3
02338 Halifax○ 5,513 ... L5
01936 Hamilton○ 6,960 ... L2
01036 Hampden○ 4,745 ... E4
01237 Hancock○ 643 ... A2
02339 Hanover○ 11,358 ... L4
02341 Hanson○ 8,617 ... L4
02341 Hanson 2,120 ... L4
01037 Hardwick○ 2,272 ... F3
01451 Harvard○ 12,170 ... H2
02645 Harwich○ 8,971 ... O6
02645 Harwich 4,399 ... O6
01038 Hatfield○ 3,045 ... D3
01038 Hatfield 1,251 ... D3
01830 Haverhill 46,865 ... K1
01346 Heath○ 482 ... C2
02043 Hingham○ 20,339 ... E8
02043 Hingham 5,742 ... E8
01235 Hinsdale○ 1,707 ... B3
02343 Holbrook○ 11,140 ... D8
01520 Holden○ 13,336 ... G3
†01550 Holland○ 1,589 ... F4
01746 Holliston○ 12,622 ... A8
01040 Holyoke 44,678 ... D4
01747 Hopedale○ 3,905 ... H4
01747 Hopedale 2,810 ... H4
01748 Hopkinton○ 7,114 ... J4
01748 Hopkinton 2,542 ... J4
01236 Housatonic 1,314 ... A3
01452 Hubbardston○ 1,797 ... F3
01749 Hudson○ 16,408 ... H3
01749 Hudson 14,156 ... H3
02045 Hull○ 9,714 ... E7
01050 Huntington○ 1,804 ... C4
02601 Hyannis 9,118 ... N6
01938 Ipswich○ 11,158 ... L2
01938 Ipswich 4,548 ... L2
02364 Kingston○ 7,362 ... M5
02364 Kingston 4,405 ... M5
02346 Lakeville○ 5,931 ... L5
02346 Lakeville 1,948 ... L5
01523 Lancaster○ 6,334 ... H3
01237 Lanesboro○ 3,131 ... A2
*01840 Lawrence⊙ 63,175 ... K2
Lawrence-Haverhill‡ 281,981 ... K2
01238 Lee○ 6,247 ... B3
01238 Lee 2,140 ... B3
01524 Leicester○ 9,446 ... G4
01240 Lenox○ 6,523 ... A3
01240 Lenox 2,668 ... A3
01453 Leominster 34,508 ... G2
01054 Leverett○ 1,471 ... E3
02173 Lexington○ 29,479 ... B6
†01301 Leyden○ 498 ... D2
01773 Lincoln○ 7,098 ... B6
01460 Littleton○ 6,970 ... H2
†01460 Littleton Common 3,109 ... J2
01106 Longmeadow○ 16,301 ... D4
*01850 Lowell⊙ 92,418 ... J2
Lowell‡ 233,410 ... J2
01056 Ludlow○ 18,150 ... E4
01462 Lunenburg○ 8,405 ... H2
01462 Lunenburg 1,789 ... H2
*01901 Lynn 78,471 ... D6
01940 Lynnfield○ 11,267 ... D5
02148 Malden 53,386 ... D6
01944 Manchester○ 5,424 ... F5
02048 Mansfield○ 13,453 ... J4
02048 Mansfield 6,786 ... J4
01945 Marblehead○ 20,126 ... E7
02738 Marion○ 3,932 ... L6
02738 Marion 1,438 ... L6
01752 Marlborough 30,617 ... H3
02050 Marshfield○ 20,916 ... M4
02050 Marshfield 4,421 ... M4
02051 Marshfield Hills 2,308 ... M4
02649 Mashpee○ 3,700 ... M6
02739 Mattapoisett○ 5,597 ... L6
02739 Mattapoisett 3,159 ... L6
01754 Maynard○ 9,590 ... J3
02052 Medfield○ 10,220 ... B8
02052 Medfield 6,108 ... B8
02155 Medford 58,076 ... C6
02053 Medway○ 8,447 ... J4
02176 Melrose 30,055 ... D6
01756 Mendon○ 3,108 ... H4
01860 Merrimac○ 4,451 ... L1
01844 Methuen○ 36,701 ... K2
02346 Middleboro○ 16,404 ... L5
02346 Middleboro 7,012 ... L5
01243 Middlefield○ 385 ... B3
01949 Middleton○ 4,135 ... K2
01757 Milford○ 23,390 ... H4
01757 Milford 21,730 ... H4
01527 Millbury○ 11,808 ... H4
01349 Millers Falls 1,101 ... E2
02054 Millis○ 6,908 ... A8
02054 Millis-Clicquot 3,777 ... A8
01529 Millville○ 1,693 ... H4
02186 Milton○ 25,860 ... D7
01057 Monson○ 7,315 ... E4
01057 Monson 2,167 ... E4
01351 Montague○ 8,011 ... E2
01245 Monterey○ 818 ... B4
†12517 Mount Washington○ 93 ... A4
01908 Nahant○ 3,947 ... E6
02554 Nantucket○ 5,087 ... O7
02554 Nantucket⊙ 3,229 ... O7
01760 Natick○ 29,461 ... A7
02192 Needham○ 27,901 ... B7
*02740 New Bedford⊙ 98,478 ... K6
New Bedford‡ 169,425 ... K6
01531 New Braintree○ 671 ... F3
01950 Newbury○ 4,529 ... L1
01950 Newburyport⊙ 15,900 ... L1
†01230 New Marlborough○ 1,160 ... B4
01355 New Salem○ 688 ... E2
†02158 Newton 83,622 ... C7
02056 Norfolk○ 6,363 ... J4
01247 North Adams 18,063 ... B2
01059 North Amherst 5,616 ... E3
01060 Northampton⊙ 29,286 ... D3
01845 North Andover○ 20,129 ... K2
*02760 North Attleboro○ 21,095 ... J5
01532 Northborough○ 10,568 ... H3
01532 Northborough 5,670 ... H3
01534 Northbridge○ 12,246 ... H4
01535 North Brookfield○ 4,150 ... F3
01535 North Brookfield 2,543 ... F3
02764 North Dighton 1,174 ... K5
02651 North Eastham 1,318 ... O5
01360 Northfield○ 2,386 ... E2
01360 Northfield 1,182 ... E2
02358 North Pembroke 2,215 ... M4
02360 North Plymouth 3,250 ... L5
01864 North Reading○ 11,455 ... C5
02060 North Scituate 5,221 ... F8
02766 Norton○ 12,690 ... K5
02766 Norton 2,035 ... K5
02061 Norwell○ 9,182 ... F8
02062 Norwood○ 29,711 ... B8
02557 Oak Bluffs○ 1,984 ... M7
02557 Oak Bluffs 1,124 ... M7
01068 Oakham○ 994 ... F3
02065 Ocean Bluff-Brant Rock 4,055 ... M4
†01566 Old Sturbridge Village 500 ... F4
02558 Onset 1,493 ... M6
01364 Orange○ 6,844 ... E2
01364 Orange 3,942 ... E2
02653 Orleans○ 5,306 ... O5
02653 Orleans 1,811 ... O5
02655 Osterville 1,799 ... N6
01253 Otis○ 963 ... B4
01540 Oxford○ 11,680 ... G4
01540 Oxford 6,369 ... G4
01069 Palmer○ 11,389 ... E4
01069 Palmer 3,854 ... E4
01612 Paxton○ 3,762 ... G3
01960 Peabody 45,976 ... E5
†01002 Pelham○ 1,112 ... E3
02359 Pembroke○ 13,487 ... L4
01463 Pepperell○ 8,061 ... H2
01463 Pepperell 2,076 ... H2
01366 Petersham○ 1,024 ... F3
†01331 Phillipston○ 953 ... F2
01866 Pinehurst 6,588 ... B5
01201 Pittsfield⊙ 51,974 ... A3
Pittsfield‡ 90,505 ... A3
01070 Plainfield○ 425 ... C2
02762 Plainville○ 5,857 ... J4
02360 Plymouth○ 35,913 ... M5
02360 Plymouth⊙ 7,232 ... M5
02367 Plympton○ 1,974 ... L5
01541 Princeton○ 2,425 ... G3
02657 Provincetown○ 3,536 ... O4
02657 Provincetown 3,372 ... O4
02169 Quincy 84,743 ... D7
02368 Randolph○ 28,218 ... D8
02767 Raynham○ 9,085 ... K5
02768 Raynham Center 3,776 ... K5
01867 Reading○ 22,678 ... C5
02769 Rehoboth○ 7,570 ... K5
02151 Revere 42,423 ... D6

(continued on following page)

01266 West Stockbridge○ 1,280 ...A3
02575 West Tisbury○ 1,010.......M7
01587 West Upton-Upton 2,184...H4
02576 West Wareham 1,837.......L5
02090 Westwood 13,212 ....B8
02673 West Yarmouth 3,852 ....N6
02188 Weymouth 55,601 ....D8
01093 Whately 1,341 ....D3
01588 Whitinsville 5,379 ....H4
02382 Whitman 13,534 ....L4
01095 Wilbraham 12,053 ....E4
01095 Wilbraham 3,379 ....E4
01096 Williamsburg○ 2,237 .....C3
01267 Williamstown 8,741 ....B2
01267 Williamstown 4,798 ....B2
01887 Wilmington○ 17,471 ......C5
01475 Winchendon 7,019 ....F2
01475 Winchendon 4,030 ....F2
01890 Winchester○ 20,701 ......C6
01270 Windsor 598 ....B2

02152 Winthrop○ 19,294 ....D6
01801 Woburn 36,626 ....C6
02543 Woods Hole 1,080 ....M6
*01601 Worcester○ 161,799 .....H3
      Worcester‡ 372,940 ....H3
01098 Worthington○ 932 ....C3
02093 Wrentham 7,580 ....J4
      Yarmouth 18,449 ....O6
02675 Yarmouth Port 2,490 .....N6

OTHER FEATURES

Adams Nat'l Hist. Site D7
Agawam (riv.) M5
Allerton (pt.) E7
Ann (cape) M2
Ashmere (lake) B3
Assabet (riv.) H3
Assawompset (pond) L5
Bachelor (brook) D3

Berkshire (hills) B4
Big (pond) B4
Bigelow (bight) M1
Blackstone (riv.) G3
Blue (hills) C8
Boston (bay) E6
Boston (harb.) D7
Boston Nat'l Hist. Park D6
Brewster (isls.) E7
Buel (lake) A4
Buzzards (bay) L7
Cambridge (res.) B6
Cape Cod (bay) N5
Cape Cod (canal) N5
Cape Cod Nat'l Seashore P5
Chappaquiddick (isl.) N7
Charles (riv.) C7
Chicopee (riv.) C3
Cobble Mountain (res.) C4
Cochituate (lake) A7

Cod (cape) O4
Concord (riv.) J2
Congamond (lkes) D4
Connecticut (riv.) D2
Cuttyhunk (isl.) L7
Deer (isl.) E7
East (pt.) E6
East Chop (pt.) M7
Eastern (pt.) M2
Elizabeth (isls.) L7
Everett (mt.) A4
Falls (riv.) D2
Fort Rodman L6
Fresh (pond) C6
Gammon (pt.) N6
Gay Head (prom.) L7
Grace (mt.) E2
Great (pt.) O7
Green (riv.) B2
Greylock (mt.) B2
Gurnet (pt.) M4
Hingham (bay) E7
Holyoke (range) D3
Hoosac (mts.) B2
Hoosic (riv.) A1
Housatonic (riv.) A4
Ipswich (riv.) L2
John F. Kennedy Nat'l Hist.
      Site C7
Knightville (res.) C3
Laurence G. Hanscom Field ...B6
Little (riv.) C4
Logan Internat'l Airport D7
Long (isl.) E7
Long (pt.) O4
Long (pond) L5
Lowell Nat'l Hist. Park J2
Maine (gulf) M2
Manhan (riv.) D4
Manomet (pt.) N5
Marblehead (neck) F6
Martha's Vineyard (isl.) M7
Massachusetts (bay) M4
Merrimack (riv.) K1
Mill (riv.) C3
Mill (riv.) D3
Millers (riv.) E2
Minute Man Nat'l Hist. Park ...B6
Mishaum (pt.) L6
Monomonac (lake) G2
Monomoy (isl.) O6
Monomoy (pt.) O6
Mount Hope (bay) K6
Muskeget (chan.) N7
Muskeget (isl.) N7
Mystic (lake) C6
Mystic (riv.) C6
Nahant (bay) E6
Nantucket (isl.) O8
Nantucket (sound) N6
Nashawena (isl.) L7
Nashua (riv.) H3
Naushon (isl.) L7
Neponset (riv.) C8
Nomans Land (isl.) L7
Nonamesset (isl.) M6
North (pt.) D2
North (riv.) L4
Onota (lake) A3
Otis (res.) B4

Otis A.F.B. M6
Pasque (isl.) L7
Plum (isl.) L2
Plymouth (bay) M5
Poge (cape) N7
Pontoosuc (lake) A3
Quabbin (res.) E3
Quaboag (riv.) F4
Quincy (bay) D7
Quinebaug (riv.) F4
Race (pt.) N4
Salem Maritime Nat'l Hist.
      Site E5
Saugus Iron Works Nat'l Hist.
      Site D6
Shawsheen (riv.) K2
Silver (lake) L4
South (riv.) D2
Springfield Armory Nat'l Hist.
      Site D4
Squibnocket (pt.) M7
Stillwater (res.) G3
Sudbury (res.) H3
Sudbury (riv.) A6
Swift (riv.) E4
Taconic (mts.) A2
Taunton (riv.) K5
Thompson (isl.) D7
Toby (mt.) E3
Tom (mt.) D4
Tuckernuck (isl.) N7
Vineyard (sound) L7
Wachusett (mt.) G3
Wachusett (res.) G3
Walden (pond) A6
Ware (riv.) F3
Watuppa (pond) K6
Webster (lake) G4
Wellfleet (harb.) O5
West (riv.) H4
West Branch, Farmington
      (riv.) B4
West Chop (pt.) M7
Westfield (riv.) C3
Westover A.F.B. D4
Weweantic (riv.) L5
Whitman (riv.) G2
Winter I. Coast Guard Air Sta. ...E5

RHODE ISLAND

COUNTIES

Bristol 46,942 ....J6
Kent 154,163 ....H6
Newport 81,383 ....K6
Providence 571,349 ....H5
Washington 93,317 ....H7

CITIES and TOWNS

Zip	Name/Pop.	Key
02804	Ashaway 1,747	G7
02806	Barrington 16,174	J6
02807	Block Island 620	H8
02808	Bradford 1,354	H7
02809	Bristol○○ 20,128	J6
02863	Central Falls 16,995	J5
02816	Coventry 27,065	H6
02910	Cranston 71,992	J5
02818	East Greenwich○ 10,211	H6
02914	East Providence 50,980	J5

02822 Exeter○ 4,453 ....H6
02825 Foster○ 3,370 ....H5
02828 Greenville 7,516 ....H5
02830 Harrisville 1,224 ....H5
02832 Hope Valley 1,414 ......H6
02833 Hopkinton○ 6,406 ......H7
02835 Jamestown 4,040 ....J6
02835 Jamestown 2,156 ....J6
02881 Kingston 5,479 ....H7
02837 Little Compton○ 3,085 .K6
02840 Middletown 17,216 .....J6
02882 Narragansett 12,088 ...J7
02882 Narragansett 3,342 .....J7
02840 Newport○ 29,259 ....J7
†02807 New Shoreham (Block
      Island)○ 620 ....H8
02852 North Kingstown○
      21,938 ....J6
02908 North Providence○
      29,188 ....J5
02859 Pascoag 3,807 ....H5
*02860 Pawtucket 71,204 ....J5
02883 Peace
      Dale-Wakefield 6,474 ..J7
02871 Portsmouth○ 14,257 ..J6
*02901 Providence
      (cap.)○○ 156,804 ....H5
      Providence-Warwick-
      Pawtucket‡ 919,216 ..H5
02878 Tiverton 13,526 ....K6
02878 Tiverton 7,653 ....K6
†02864 Valley Falls 10,892 ...J5
*02879 Wakefield-Peace
      Dale 6,474 ....J7
02885 Warren○ 10,640 ....J6
*02886 Warwick 87,123 ......J6
02891 Westerly○ 18,580 ......G7
02891 Westerly○ 14,093 ......G7
02893 West Warwick 27,026 .H6
02895 Woonsocket○ 45,914 ..J4

OTHER FEATURES

Black Rock (pt.) H8
Block (isl.) H8
Block Island (sound) J7
Brenton (pt.) J7
Conanicut (isl.) J6
Dickens (pt.) H8
Durfee (hill) G5
Grace (pt.) H8
Jerimoth (hill) G5
Judith (pt.) J7
Mount Hope (bay) K6
Narragansett (bay) J6
Noyes (pt.) H7
Pawcatuck (riv.) G7
Prudence (isl.) J6
Rhode Island (isl.) J6
Rhode Island (sound) J7
Roger Williams Nat'l Mem. ..J5
Sakonnet (pt.) K7
Sakonnet (riv.) K7
Sandy (pt.) H8
Scituate (res.) H5
Stillwater (res.) C2
Touro Synagogue Nat'l Hist.
      Site J7
Watch Hill (pt.) G7

○County seat (Shire town).
‡Population of metropolitan area.
○Population of town or township.
† Zip of nearest p.o.   * Multiple zips.

Massachusetts and Rhode Island

SCALE
0 5 10 15 20MI.
0 5 10 15 20KM.

State Capitals ....⊛
County Seats (Shire Towns) ....◉
Canals ....
Major Limited Access Hwys. ....

Scale 1:970,000

© Copyright HAMMOND INCORPORATED, Maplewood, N.J.

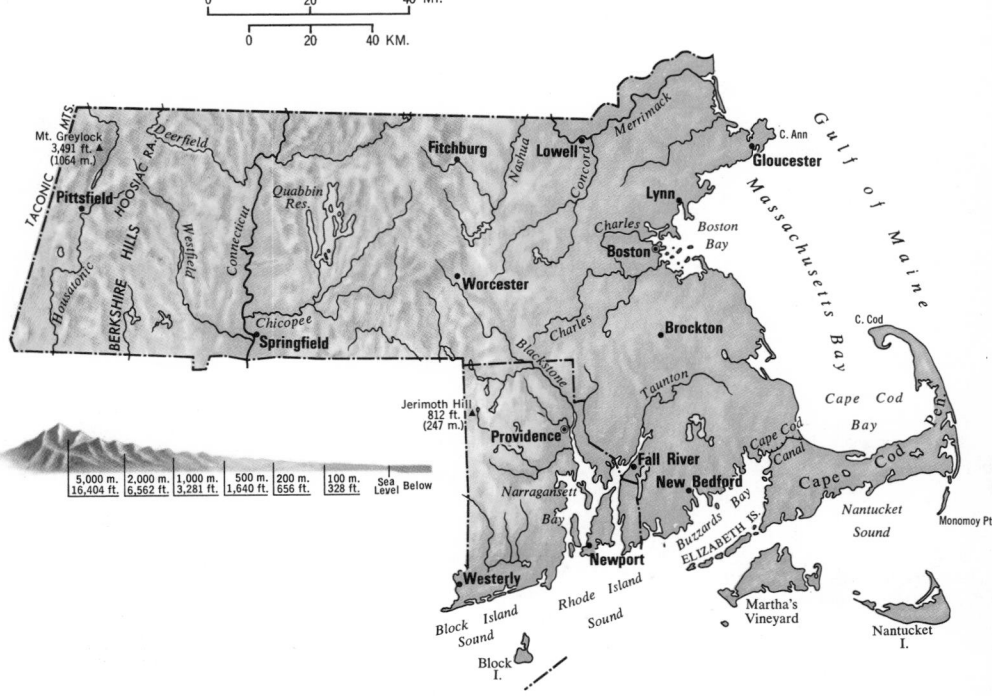

Topography

0   20   40 MI.
0   20   40 KM.

Mt. Greylock 3,491 ft. (1064 m.)

Jerimoth Hill 812 ft. (247 m.)

| 5,000 m. 16,404 ft. | 2,000 m. 6,562 ft. | 1,000 m. 3,281 ft. | 500 m. 1,640 ft. | 200 m. 656 ft. | 100 m. 328 ft. | Sea Level | Below |

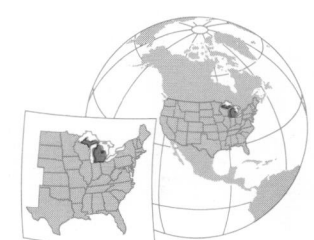

AREA 58,527 sq. mi. (151,585 sq. km.)
POPULATION 9,262,078
CAPITAL Lansing
LARGEST CITY Detroit
HIGHEST POINT Mt. Curwood 1,980 ft. (604 m.)
SETTLED IN 1650
ADMITTED TO UNION January 26, 1837
POPULAR NAME Wolverine State
STATE FLOWER Apple Blossom
STATE BIRD Robin

Topography

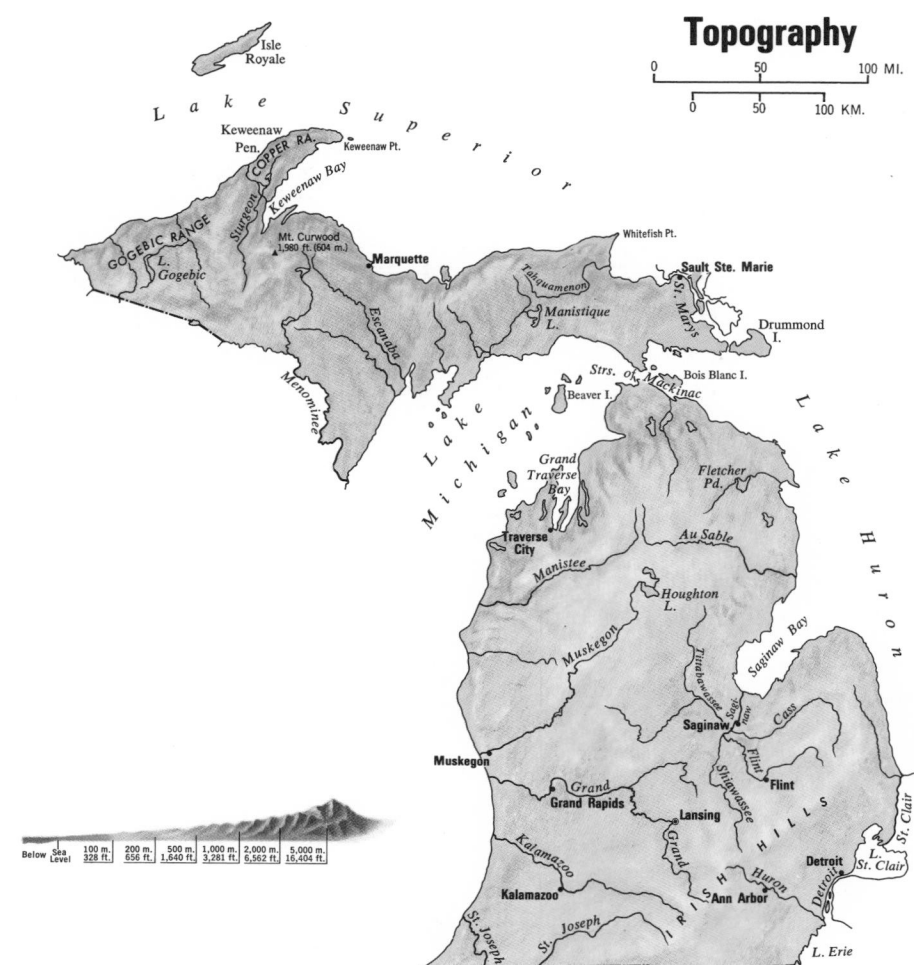

COUNTIES

Alcona 9,740	F4
Alger 9,225	C2
Allegan 81,555	D6
Alpena 32,315	F4
Antrim 16,194	D3
Arenac 14,706	F4
Baraga 8,484	A2
Barry 45,781	D6
Bay 119,881	E5
Benzie 11,205	C4
Berrien 171,276	C7
Branch 40,188	D7
Calhoun 141,557	D6
Cass 49,499	C7
Charlevoix 19,907	D3
Cheboygan 20,649	E3
Chippewa 29,029	E2
Clare 23,822	E5
Clinton 55,893	E6
Crawford 9,465	E4
Delta 38,947	C2
Dickinson 25,341	B2
Eaton 88,337	E6
Emmet 22,992	E3
Genesee 450,449	F5
Gladwin 19,957	E4
Gogebic 19,686	F2
Grand Traverse 54,899	D4
Gratiot 40,448	E5
Hillsdale 42,071	E7
Houghton 37,872	G1
Huron 36,459	F5
Ingham 275,520	E6
Ionia 51,815	D6
Iosco 28,349	F4
Iron 13,635	G2
Isabella 54,110	E5
Jackson 151,495	E6
Kalamazoo 212,378	D6
Kalkaska 10,952	D4
Kent 444,506	D5
Keweenaw 1,963	A1
Lake 7,711	D5
Lapeer 70,038	F5
Leelanau 14,007	D4
Lenawee 89,948	E7
Livingston 100,289	F6
Luce 6,659	D2
Mackinac 10,178	D2
Macomb 694,600	G6
Manistee 23,019	C4
Marquette 74,101	B2
Mason 26,365	C4
Mecosta 36,961	D5
Menominee 26,201	B3
Midland 73,578	E5
Missaukee 10,009	D4
Monroe 134,659	F7
Montcalm 47,555	D5
Montmorency 7,492	E3
Muskegon 157,589	C5
Newaygo 34,917	D5
Oakland 1,011,793	F6
Oceana 22,002	C5
Ogemaw 16,436	E4
Ontonagon 9,861	F1
Osceola 18,928	D5
Oscoda 6,858	E4
Otsego 14,993	E3
Ottawa 157,174	C6
Presque Isle 14,267	F3
Roscommon 16,374	E4
Saginaw 228,059	E5
Saint Clair 138,802	G6
Saint Joseph 56,083	D7
Sanilac 40,789	G5
Schoolcraft 8,575	C2
Shiawassee 71,140	E6
Tuscola 56,961	F5
Van Buren 66,814	C6
Washtenaw 264,748	F6
Wayne 2,337,891	F6
Wexford 25,102	D4

CITIES and TOWNS

Zip	Name/Pop.	Key
49220	Addison 655	E7
49221	Adrian⊙ 21,186	F7
48701	Akron 538	F5
†48763	Alabaster 46	F4
49224	Albion 11,059	E6
48001	Algonac 4,412	G6
49010	Allegan⊙ 4,576	D6
48101	Allen Park 34,196	B7
48801	Alma 9,652	E5
48003	Almont 1,857	F6
49707	Alpena⊙ 12,214	F3
*48103	Ann Arbor⊙ 107,966	F6
	Ann Arbor‡ 264,748	F6
48005	Armada 1,392	G6
48806	Ashley 570	E5
49011	Athens 960	D6
49709	Atlanta⊙ 475	E3
48611	Auburn 1,921	F5
48703	Au Gres 768	F4
49012	Augusta 913	D6
†48750	Au Sable 1,240	F4
48413	Bad Axe⊙ 3,184	G5
49304	Baldwin⊙ 674	D5
48414	Bancroft 618	E6
49013	Bangor 2,001	C6
49908	Baraga 1,055	G1
49101	Baroda 627	C7
*49014	Battle Creek 35,724	D6
	Battle Creek‡ 187,338	D6
48706	Bay City⊙ 41,593	F5
	Bay City‡ 119,881	F5
48612	Beaverton 1,025	E5
†49423	Beechwood 2,333	C6
48809	Belding 5,634	D5
49615	Bellaire⊙ 1,063	D4
48111	Belleville 3,366	F6
49021	Bellevue 1,289	E6
49022	Benton Harbor 14,707	C6
	Benton Harbor‡ 171,276	C6
†49022	Benton Heights 6,787	C6
48072	Berkley 18,637	B6
49103	Berrien Springs 2,042	C7
49911	Bessemer⊙ 2,553	F2
49617	Beulah⊙ 454	C4
†48010	Beverly Hills 11,598	B6
49307	Big Rapids⊙ 14,361	D5
48415	Birch Run 1,196	F5
*48008	Birmingham 21,689	B6
49228	Blissfield 3,107	F7
48013	Bloomfield Hills 3,985	B6
49026	Bloomingdale 537	C6
49712	Boyne City 3,348	E3
48615	Breckenridge 1,495	E5
49106	Bridgman 2,235	C7
48116	Brighton 4,268	F6
48229	Britton 693	F7
49028	Bronson 2,271	D7
49230	Brooklyn 1,110	E6
48416	Brown City 1,163	G5
49107	Buchanan 5,142	C7
49030	Burr Oak 853	D7
48507	Burton 29,976	F6
48418	Byron 689	E6
49601	Cadillac⊙ 10,199	D4
49316	Caledonia 722	D6
49913	Calumet 1,013	A1
48014	Capac 1,377	G5
48117	Carleton 2,786	F6
48723	Caro⊙ 4,317	F5
48724	Carrollton 7,482	E5
48811	Carson City 1,229	E5
48419	Carsonville 622	G5
48725	Caseville 851	F5
49915	Caspian 1,038	G2
48726	Cass City 2,258	F5
49031	Cassopolis⊙ 1,933	C7
49233	Cement City 539	E6
49015	Center Line 9,293	B6
49622	Central Lake 895	D3
49032	Centreville⊙ 1,202	D7
49720	Charlevoix⊙ 3,519	D3
48813	Charlotte⊙ 8,251	E6
49721	Cheboygan⊙ 5,106	E3
48118	Chelsea 3,816	E6
48616	Chesaning 2,656	E5
48617	Clare 3,300	E5
48016	Clarkston 968	F6
48017	Clawson 15,103	B6
49034	Climax 619	D6
49236	Clinton 2,342	F6
48420	Clio 2,669	F5
49036	Coldwater⊙ 9,461	D7
48618	Coleman 1,429	E5
49038	Coloma 1,833	C6
49040	Colon 1,190	D7
48421	Columbiaville 953	F5
49041	Comstock⊙ 11,162	D6
49237	Concord 900	E6
49042	Constantine 1,680	D7
49404	Coopersville 2,889	C5
48817	Corunna⊙ 3,206	E6
48422	Croswell 2,073	G5
49920	Crystal Falls⊙ 1,965	A2
49508	Cutlerville 8,256	D6
48423	Davison 6,087	F5
*48120	Dearborn 90,660	B7
48127	Dearborn Heights 67,706	B7
49045	Decatur 1,915	C6
48427	Deckerville 887	G5
49238	Deerfield 957	F7
*48201	Detroit⊙ 1,203,339	B7
	Detroit‡ 4,352,762	B7
48820	De Witt 3,165	E6
48130	Dexter 1,524	F6
48821	Dimondale 1,008	E6
49406	Douglas 948	C6
49047	Dowagiac 6,307	C6
48820	Drayton Plains	F6
49726	Drummond Island◇ 746	F3
48428	Dryden 650	F6
48131	Dundee 2,575	F7
48429	Durand 4,241	E6
49924	Eagle River⊙ 20	A1
48021	East Detroit 38,280	B6
†49506	East Grand Rapids 10,914	D6
49727	East Jordan 2,185	D3
†49801	East Kingsford	A3
48823	East Lansing 51,392	E6
48730	East Tawas 2,584	F4
†49001	Eastwood 7,186	D6
48827	Eaton Rapids 4,510	E6
49111	Eau Claire 573	C6
48229	Ecorse 14,447	B7
48829	Edmore 1,176	E5
49112	Edwardsburg 1,135	C7
49628	Elberta 556	C4
49629	Elk Rapids 1,504	D4
48731	Elkton 953	F5
48831	Elsie 1,022	E5
49829	Escanaba⊙ 14,355	C3
48732	Essexville 4,378	F5
49631	Evart 1,945	D5
48733	Fairgrove 691	F5
49022	Fair Plain 8,289	C6
*48024	Farmington 11,022	F6
48024	Farmington Hills 58,056	F6
48622	Farwell 804	E5
49408	Fennville 934	C6
48430	Fenton 8,098	F6
48220	Ferndale 26,227	B6
49409	Ferrysburg 2,440	C5
48134	Flat Rock 6,853	F6
*48501	Flint⊙ 159,611	F5
	Flint‡ 521,589	F5
48433	Flushing 8,624	F5
48835	Fowler 1,021	E5
48836	Fowlerville 2,289	F6
48734	Frankenmuth 3,753	F5
49635	Frankfort 1,603	C4
48025	Franklin 2,864	B6
48026	Fraser 14,560	B6
48623	Freeland 1,364	E5
49412	Fremont 3,672	D5
49415	Fruitport 1,143	C6
49053	Galesburg 1,822	D6
49113	Galien 692	C7
48135	Garden City 35,640	F6
48730	Garden⊙ 664	F4
49735	Gaylord⊙ 3,011	E3
48173	Gibraltar 4,458	F6
49837	Gladstone 4,533	C3
48624	Gladwin⊙ 2,479	E5
49055	Gobles 816	D6
48438	Goodrich 795	F6
48439	Grand Blanc 6,848	F6
49417	Grand Haven⊙ 11,763	C5
48837	Grand Ledge 6,920	E6
*49501	Grand Rapids⊙ 181,843	D5
	Grand Rapids‡ 601,680	D5
49418	Grandville 12,412	D6
49327	Grant 683	D5
49240	Grass Lake 962	E6
49738	Grayling⊙ 1,792	E4
48838	Greenville 8,019	D5
48138	Grosse Ile 9,320	B7
48236	Grosse Pointe 5,901	B7
†48236	Grosse Pointe Farms 10,551	B7
†48236	Grosse Pointe Park 13,639	B7
†48236	Grosse Pointe Shores 3,122	B6
†48236	Grosse Pointe Woods 18,886	B6
48841	Gwinn 1,408	B2
48212	Hamtramck 21,300	B7
49930	Hancock 5,122	G1
48441	Harbor Beach 2,000	G5
49740	Harbor Springs 1,567	D3
48225	Harper Woods 16,361	B6
48625	Harrison⊙ 1,700	E4
48740	Harrisville⊙ 559	F4
49420	Hart⊙ 1,888	C5
49057	Hartford 2,493	C6
48840	Haslett 7,025	E6
49058	Hastings⊙ 6,418	D6
48030	Hazel Park 20,914	B6
48626	Hemlock 1,362	E5
49421	Hesperia 876	D5
48203	Highland Park 27,909	B6
49242	Hillsdale⊙ 7,432	E7
49423	Holland 26,281	C6
48842	Holt 10,097	E6
49245	Homer 1,791	E6
49931	Houghton⊙ 7,512	G1
48629	Houghton Lake 2,449	E4
48630	Houghton Lake Heights	E4
49329	Howard City 1,118	D5
48843	Howell⊙ 6,976	E6
49934	Hubbell 1,278	A1
49247	Hudson 2,545	E7
49426	Hudsonville 4,844	D6
48444	Imlay City 2,495	F5
48141	Inkster 35,190	B7
49643	Interlochen 600	D4
48846	Ionia⊙ 5,920	D6
49801	Iron Mountain⊙ 8,341	B3
49935	Iron River 2,426	G2
49938	Ironwood 7,741	F2
49849	Ishpeming 7,538	B2
48847	Ithaca⊙ 2,950	E5
*49201	Jackson⊙ 39,739	E6
	Jackson‡ 151,495	E6
49428	Jenison 16,330	D6
49250	Jonesville 2,172	E6
*49001	Kalamazoo⊙ 79,722	D6
	Kalamazoo-Portage‡ 279,192	D6
49646	Kalkaska⊙ 1,654	D4
48030	Keego Harbor 3,083	F6
49330	Kent City 860	D5
49508	Kentwood 30,438	D6
48445	Kinde 600	G5
49801	Kingsford 5,290	A3
49649	Kingsley 664	D4
48848	Laingsburg 1,145	E6
49651	Lake City⊙ 863	D4
49945	Lake Linden 1,181	A1
†49039	Lake Michigan Beach 2,001	C6
48849	Lake Odessa 2,171	D6
48035	Lake Orion 2,907	F6
48850	Lakeview 1,139	D5
†49440	Lakewood Club 695	C5
48144	Lambertville 6,341	F7
49946	L'Anse⊙ 2,500	G1
*48901	Lansing (cap.) 130,414	E6
	Lansing-East Lansing‡ 468,482	E6
48446	Lapeer⊙ 6,198	F5
49913	Laurium 2,678	A1
49064	Lawrence 903	C6
49654	Leland⊙ 776	D3
48449	Lennon 600	E5
49251	Leslie 2,110	E6
48450	Lexington 765	G5
48742	Lincoln 361	F4
48146	Lincoln Park 45,105	B7
48451	Linden 2,174	F5
49252	Litchfield 1,353	E6
*48150	Livonia 104,814	F6
49331	Lowell 3,707	D6
49431	Ludington⊙ 8,937	C5

(continued on following page)

48157 Luna Pier 1,443 F7
48851 Lyons 708 E6
49757 Mackinac Island 479 E3
49701 Mackinaw City 820 E3
48071 Madison Heights 35,375 B6
49659 Mancelona 1,432 E4
48158 Manchester 1,686 E6
49660 Manistee⊙ 7,566 C4
49854 Manistique⊙ 3,962 C3
49663 Manton 1,212 D4
48853 Maple Rapids 683 E5
49067 Marcellus 1,134 D6
48039 Marine City 4,414 G6
49665 Marion 816 D4
48453 Marlette 1,761 G5
49855 Marquette⊙ 23,288 B2
49068 Marshall⊙ 7,201 E6
49070 Martin 447 D6
48040 Marysville 7,345 G6
48854 Mason⊙ 6,019 E6
49071 Mattawan 2,143 D6
48744 Mayville 958 F5
49657 McBain 519 D4
48122 Melvindale 12,322 B7
48041 Memphis 1,171 G6
49072 Mendon 951 D7
49858 Menominee⊙ 10,099 B3
48637 Merrill 851 E5
48455 Metamora 552 F6
49254 Michigan Center 5,244 E6
49333 Middleville 1,797 D6
48640 Midland⊙ 37,250 E5
48160 Milan 4,182 F6
48042 Milford 5,041 F6
48746 Millington 1,237 F5
48647 Mio⊙ 975 E4
48161 Monroe⊙ 23,531 F7
49437 Montague 2,332 C5
48457 Montrose 1,706 F5
49256 Morenci 2,110 E7
49336 Morley 507 D5
48857 Morrice 733 E6
48043 Mount Clemens⊙ 18,806 G6
48458 Mount Morris 3,246 F5
48858 Mount Pleasant⊙ 23,746 E5
48860 Muir 698 D5
48861 Mulliken 550 E6
49862 Munising⊙ 3,083 C2
*49440 Muskegon⊙ 40,823 C5
Muskegon-Norton Shores-Muskegon Heights‡ 179,591 C5
49444 Muskegon Heights 14,611 C5
49261 Napoleon 1,400 E6
49073 Nashville 1,628 D6
49866 Negaunee 5,189 B2
49337 Newaygo 1,271 D5
48047 New Baltimore 5,439 G6
49868 Newberry⊙ 2,120 D2
48164 New Boston 1,200 F6
49117 New Buffalo 2,821 C7
48048 New Haven 1,871 G6
48460 New Lothrop 646 F5
49120 Niles 13,115 C7
49262 North Adams 565 E7
48461 North Branch 896 F5
49445 North Muskegon 4,024 C5
49670 Northport 611 D3
48167 Northville 5,698 F6
†49441 Norton Shores 22,025 C5
49870 Norway 2,919 B3
48050 Novi 22,525 F6
48237 Oak Park 31,537 B6
48864 Okemos 8,882 E6
49076 Olivet 1,604 E6
49765 Onaway 1,084 E3
49675 Onekama 582 C4
49265 Onsted 670 E6
49953 Ontonagon⊙ 2,182 F1
48033 Orchard Lake 1,798 F6
48462 Ortonville 1,190 F6
48750 Oscoda 2,431 F4
48463 Otisville 682 F5
49078 Otsego 3,802 D6
48866 Ovid 1,712 E5
48867 Owosso 16,455 E5
48051 Oxford 2,746 F6
49004 Parchment 1,817 D6
49269 Parma 873 E6
49079 Paw Paw⊙ 3,211 D6
†49038 Paw Paw Lake 4,193 C6
48052 Pearl Beach 3,430 G6
48466 Peck 606 G5
49769 Pellston 565 E3
49449 Pentwater 1,165 C5
48872 Perry 2,051 E6
49270 Petersburg 1,222 F7
49770 Petoskey⊙ 6,097 E3
48755 Pigeon 1,247 F5
48169 Pinckney 1,390 F6
48650 Pinconning 1,430 F5
49080 Plainwell 3,751 D6
48069 Pleasant Ridge 3,217 B6
*48170 Plymouth 9,986 F6
*48053 Pontiac⊙ 76,715 F6
49081 Portage 38,157 D6
48467 Port Austin 839 F4
48060 Port Huron⊙ 33,981 G6
48875 Portland 3,963 E6
48469 Port Sanilac 598 G5
49776 Posen 270 F3
48876 Potterville 1,502 E6
49082 Quincy 1,569 E7
49959 Ramsay F2
49451 Ravenna 951 D5
49274 Reading 1,203 E7
49677 Reed City⊙ 2,221 D5
48757 Reese 1,645 F5
48062 Richmond 3,536 G6
48218 River Rouge 12,912 B7
48192 Riverview 14,569 B7
48063 Rochester 7,203 F6
49341 Rockford 3,324 D5
48173 Rockwood 3,346 F6
49779 Rogers City⊙ 3,923 F3
48065 Romeo 3,509 F6
48174 Romulus 24,857 F6
49444 Roosevelt Park 4,015 C5
48653 Roscommon⊙ 834 E4
48654 Rose City 661 E4
48066 Roseville 54,311 B6
49452 Rothbury 522 C5
*48067 Royal Oak 70,893 B6
*48601 Saginaw⊙ 77,508 F5
Saginaw‡ 228,059 F5
48655 Saint Charles 2,276 E5
48079 Saint Clair 4,780 G6
*48080 Saint Clair Shores 76,210 B6
49781 Saint Ignace⊙ 2,632 E3
48879 Saint Johns⊙ 7,376 E6
49085 Saint Joseph⊙ 9,622 C6
48880 Saint Louis 4,107 E5
48176 Saline 6,483 F6
48471 Sandusky⊙ 2,216 G5
48657 Sanford 864 E5
48881 Saranac 1,421 D6
49453 Saugatuck 1,079 C6
49783 Sault Sainte Marie⊙ 14,448 E2
49087 Schoolcraft 1,359 D6
49454 Scottville 1,241 C5
48759 Sebewaing 2,046 F5
49455 Shelby 1,624 C5
48883 Shepherd 1,534 E5
48884 Sheridan 664 D5
†49085 Shoreham 742 C6
†49125 Shorewood 1,735 C7
*48034 Southfield 75,568 F6
48195 Southgate 32,058 F6
49090 South Haven 5,943 C6
48178 South Lyon 5,214 F6
†48161 South Monroe 4,232 F7
49963 South Range 861 G1
48179 South Rockwood 1,353 F7
†48060 Sparlingville 1,718 G6
49345 Sparta 3,373 D5
49283 Spring Arbor 2,101 E6
49015 Springfield 5,917 D6
49456 Spring Lake 2,731 C5
49284 Springport 675 E6
49964 Stambaugh 1,442 G2
48658 Standish⊙ 1,264 F5
48888 Stanton⊙ 1,315 D5
49887 Stephenson 967 B3
48659 Sterling 457 E4
48077 Sterling Heights 108,999 B6
49127 Stevensville 1,268 C6
49285 Stockbridge 1,213 E6
49091 Sturgis 9,468 D7
48890 Sunfield 591 D6
49682 Suttons Bay 504 D3
48473 Swartz Creek 5,013 F6
†48053 Sylvan Lake 1,949 F6
48763 Tawas City⊙ 1,967 F4
48180 Taylor 77,568 B7
49286 Tecumseh 7,320 E7
49092 Tekonsha 755 E6
49128 Three Oaks 1,774 C7
49093 Three Rivers 7,015 D7
49684 Traverse City⊙ 15,516 D4
48183 Trenton 22,762 B7
*48084 Troy 67,102 B6
48475 Ubly 862 G5
49094 Union City 1,667 D6
49129 Union Pier 1,039 C7
48767 Unionville 578 F5
*48087 Utica 5,282 F6
49095 Vandalia 447 D7
49795 Vanderbilt 525 E3
48768 Vassar 2,727 F5
49096 Vermontville 832 E6
48476 Vernon 1,008 F6
49097 Vicksburg 2,224 D6
49968 Wakefield 2,591 F2
49288 Waldron 570 E7
49504 Walker 15,088 D6
48088 Walled Lake 4,748 F6
*48089 Warren 161,134 B6
49098 Watervliet 1,867 C6
49348 Wayland 2,023 D6
48184 Wayne 21,159 F6
48892 Webberville 1,535 E6
49894 Wells B3
48661 West Branch⊙ 1,785 E4
48185 Westland 84,603 F6
48894 Westphalia 896 E6
49349 White Cloud⊙ 1,101 D5
49461 Whitehall 2,856 C5
49099 White Pigeon 1,478 D7
49971 White Pine 1,142 F1
48189 Whitmore Lake 2,920 F6
48770 Whittemore 438 F4
48895 Williamston 2,981 E6
48096 Wixom 6,705 F6
†49440 Wolf Lake 3,876 D5
49799 Wolverine 364 E3
†48183 Woodhaven 10,902 F6
48897 Woodland 431 D6
48192 Wyandotte 34,006 B7
49509 Wyoming 59,616 D6
48097 Yale 1,814 G5
48197 Ypsilanti 24,031 F6
49464 Zeeland 4,764 D6
†48601 Zilwaukee 2,201 F5

OTHER FEATURES

Abbaye (pt.) B2
Au Sable (pt.) C2
Au Sable (pt.) F4
Au Sable (riv.) E4
Au Train (bay) C2
Bad (riv.) E5
Barques (pt.) C3
Beaver (isl.) D3
Beaver (lake) F4
Belle (riv.) G6
Bete Grise (bay) B1
Betsy (riv.) D2
Big Bay (pt.) B2
Big Bay de Noc (bay) C3
Big Iron (riv.) F1
Big Sable (pt.) C4
Big Sable (riv.) C4
Big Star (lake) C5
Black (lake) E3
Black (riv.) E3
Black (riv.) G5
Blake (pt.) E1
Boardman (riv.) D4
Bois Blanc (isl.) E3
Bond Falls (res.) G2
Brevoort (lake) D3
Brule (riv.) A3
Burt (lake) E3
Cass (riv.) F5
Cedar (lake) F4
Charlevoix (lake) D3
Chippewa (riv.) E5
Crisp (pt.) D2
Crystal (lake) C4
Curwood (mt.) A2
Dead (riv.) B2
Deer (riv.) A2
De Tour (passage) E3
Detour (pt.) C3
Detroit (riv.) B7
Drummond (isl.) F2
Duck (lake) F4
Elk (lake) D4
Erie (lake) G7
Escanaba (riv.) B2
False Detour (chan.) F3
Fawn (riv.) D7
Fence (riv.) A2
Firesteel (riv.) G1
Fletcher (pond) F4
Flint (riv.) F5
Ford (riv.) B2
Forty Mile (pt.) F3
Fourteen Mile (pt.) F1
Garden (isl.) D3
Garden (pen.) C3
Glen (lake) C4
Gogebic (lake) F2
Good Harbor (bay) D3
Government (peak) F1
Grand (isl.) C2
Grand (lake) F3
Grand (riv.) D6
Grand Traverse (bay) D3
Granite (pt.) B2
Green (bay) B4
Gun (lake) D6
Hamlin (lake) C4
Higgins (lake) E4
High (isl.) D3
Hog (isl.) D3
Houghton (lake) E4
Hubbard (lake) F4
Huron (bay) A2
Huron (lake) G4
Huron (riv.) F6
Huron River (pt.) B2
Independence (lake) B2
Indian (lake) C2
Isle Royale Nat'l Park E1
Kalamazoo (riv.) C6
Keweenaw (bay) A1
Keweenaw (pt.) B1
K.I. Sawyer A.F.B. 7,345 B2
L'Anse Ind. Res. A2
Laughing Fish (pt.) B2
Leelanau (lake) D4
Light House (pt.) D3
Little Bay de Noc (bay) B3
Little Girl (pt.) E1
Little Sable (pt.) C5
Little Summer (isl.) C3
Little Traverse (bay) D3
Long (lake) F3
Lookingglass (riv.) E6
Mackinac (isl.) E3
Mackinac (str.) E3
Manistee (riv.) C4
Manistique (lake) D2
Manistique (riv.) C2
Manitou (isl.) B1
Maple (riv.) E5
Margrethe (lake) E4
Marquette (isl.) E3
Maumee (bay) F7
Menominee (riv.) B3
Michigamme (lake) A2
Michigamme (res.) B2
Michigamme (riv.) A2
Michigan (lake) B5
Mill (creek) G5
Millecoquins (lake) D2
Misery (bay) G1
Misery (riv.) G1
Montreal (riv.) F1
Mullett (lake) E3
Munuscong (lake) E2
Muskegon (riv.) C5
Neebish (isl.) E2
Net (riv.) G2
Ninemile (pt.) E3
North (chan.) F2
North (pt.) F3
North Fox (isl.) D3
North Manitou (isl.) C3
Oak (pt.) F5
Ontonagon (riv.) G1
Ontonagon Ind. Res. F1
Otsego (lake) E4
Paint (riv.) A2
Paradise (lake) E3
Passage (isl.) E1
Patterson (pt.) D3
Paw Paw (riv.) C6
Peninsula (pt.) C3
Perch (lake) G2
Perch (riv.) G2
Pere Marquette (riv.) D5
Pictured Rocks (cliff) C2
Pictured Rocks Nat'l Lakeshore C2
Pigeon (riv.) D7
Pigeon (riv.) E3
Pine (lake) F4
Pine (riv.) D4
Pine (riv.) E5
Platte (lake) C4
Porcupine (mts.) F1
Potagannissing (bay) F2
Poverty (isl.) C3
Prairie (riv.) D7
Presque Isle (riv.) F1
Rabbit (riv.) D6
Raisin (riv.) F7
Rapid (riv.) B2
Reedsburg (res.) E4
Rifle (riv.) E4
Royale (isl.) E1
Saginaw (bay) F5
Saginaw (riv.) F5
Saint Clair (lake) G6
Saint Clair (riv.) G6
Saint Joseph (riv.) C7
Saint Martin (bay) E3
Saint Martin (isl.) C3
Saint Marys (riv.) E2
Salt (pt.) E2
Sand (pt.) F5
Seul Choix (pt.) D3
Shiawassee (riv.) E5
Siskiwit (bay) E1
Sleeping Bear Dunes Nat'l Lakeshore C4
South (bay) C2
South (chan.) E3
South (pt.) F4
South Fox (isl.) D3
South Manitou (isl.) C3
Sturgeon (riv.) C2
Sugar (isl.) E2
Summer (isl.) C3
Superior (lake) C2
Tahquamenon (falls) D2
Tahquamenon (riv.) D2
Tawas (lake) F4
Tawas (pt.) F4
Thunder (bay) F4
Thunder Bay (riv.) F3
Tittabawassee (riv.) E5
Torch (lake) D3
Traverse (isl.) A1
Traverse (pt.) A1
Turtle (lake) F4
Two Hearted (riv.) D2
Vieux Desert (lake) G2
Walloon (lake) E3
White (riv.) C5
Whitefish (bay) E2
Whitefish (pt.) E2
Whitefish (riv.) C2
Wood (isl.) C2
Wurtsmith A.F.B. 5,166 F4
Yellow Dog (riv.) B2

⊙County seat.
‡Population of metropolitan area.
○Population of township.
† Zip of nearest p.o. * Multiple zips.

Agriculture, Industry and Resources

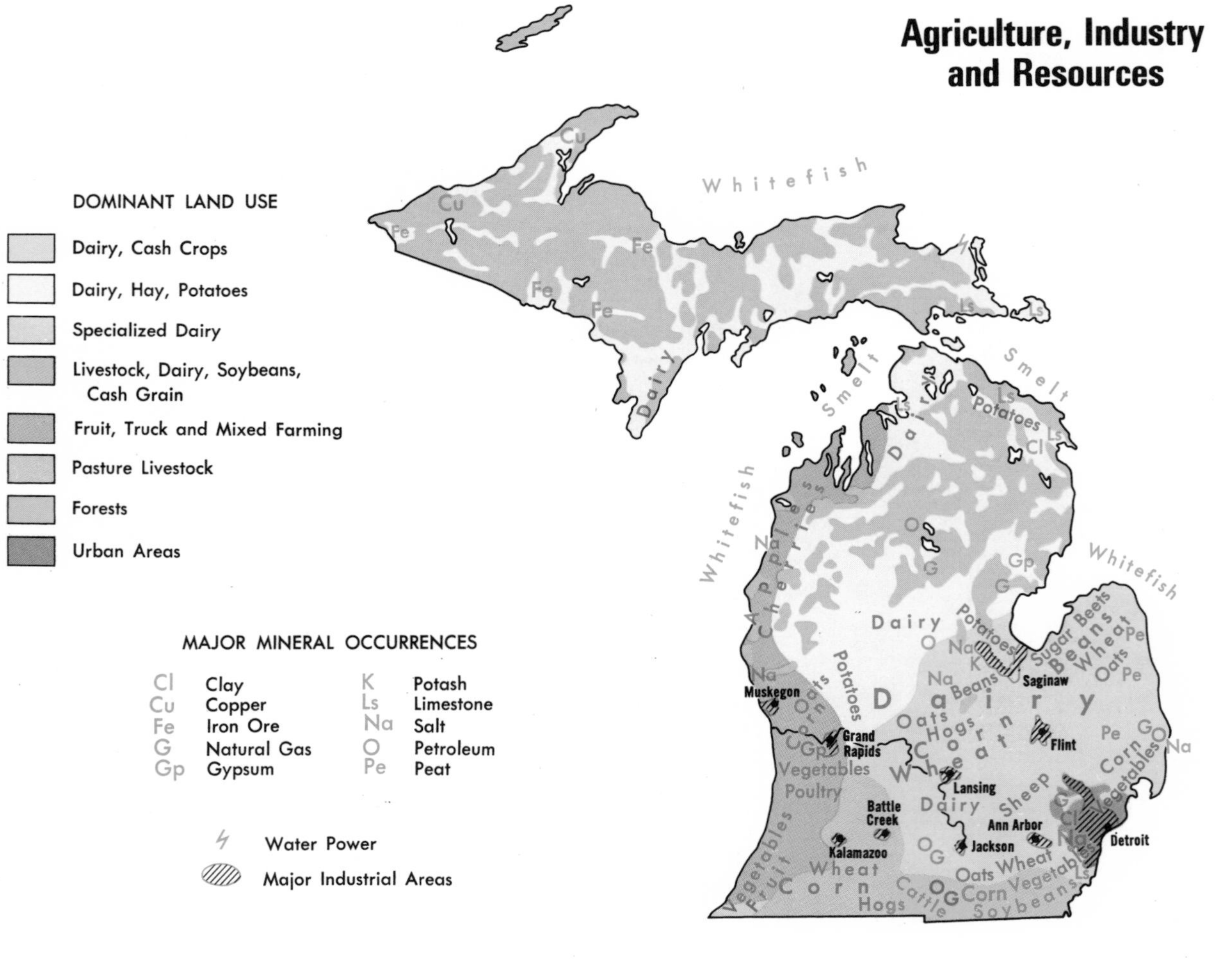
DOMINANT LAND USE
Dairy, Cash Crops
Dairy, Hay, Potatoes
Specialized Dairy
Livestock, Dairy, Soybeans, Cash Grain
Fruit, Truck and Mixed Farming
Pasture Livestock
Forests
Urban Areas
MAJOR MINERAL OCCURRENCES
Cl Clay
Cu Copper
Fe Iron Ore
G Natural Gas
Gp Gypsum
K Potash
Ls Limestone
Na Salt
O Petroleum
Pe Peat
Water Power
Major Industrial Areas
Whitefish
Smelt
Dairy
Potatoes
Cherries
Apples
Beans
Sugar Beets
Wheat
Oats
Hogs
Corn
Sheep
Vegetables
Poultry
Fruit
Cattle
Soybeans
Muskegon
Grand Rapids
Saginaw
Flint
Lansing
Battle Creek
Kalamazoo
Jackson
Ann Arbor
Detroit

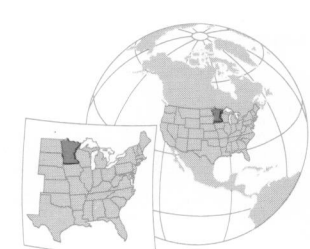

AREA 84,402 sq. mi. (218,601 sq. km.)
POPULATION 4,075,970
CAPITAL St. Paul
LARGEST CITY Minneapolis
HIGHEST POINT Eagle Mtn. 2,301 ft. (701 m.)
SETTLED IN 1805
ADMITTED TO UNION May 11, 1858
POPULAR NAME North Star State; Gopher State
STATE FLOWER Pink & White Lady's-Slipper
STATE BIRD Common Loon

COUNTIES

Name/Pop.	Key
Aitkin 13,404	E4
Anoka 195,998	E5
Becker 29,336	C4
Beltrami 30,982	C2
Benton 25,187	D5
Big Stone 7,716	B5
Blue Earth 52,314	D6
Brown 28,645	D6
Carlton 29,936	F4
Carver 37,046	E6
Cass 21,050	D4
Chippewa 14,941	C5
Chisago 25,717	F5
Clay 49,327	B4
Clearwater 8,761	C3
Cook 4,092	H3
Cottonwood 14,854	C6
Crow Wing 41,722	D4
Dakota 194,279	E6
Dodge 14,773	F7
Douglas 27,839	C5
Faribault 19,714	D7
Fillmore 21,930	F7
Freeborn 36,329	E7
Goodhue 38,749	F6
Grant 7,171	B5
Hennepin 941,411	E5
Houston 18,382	G7
Hubbard 14,098	D3
Isanti 23,600	E5
Itasca 43,069	E3
Jackson 13,690	C7
Kanabec 12,161	E5
Kandiyohi 36,763	C5
Kittson 6,672	B2
Koochiching 17,571	E2
Lac qui Parle 10,592	B6
Lake 13,043	G3
Lake of the Woods 3,764	D2
Le Sueur 23,434	E6
Lincoln 8,207	B6
Lyon 25,207	C6
Mahnomen 5,535	C3
Marshall 13,027	B2
Martin 24,687	D7
McLeod 29,657	D6
Meeker 20,594	D5
Mille Lacs 18,430	E5
Morrison 29,311	D4
Mower 40,390	F7
Murray 11,507	C6
Nicollet 26,929	D6
Nobles 21,840	C7
Norman 9,379	B3
Olmsted 92,006	F7
Otter Tail 51,937	C4
Pennington 15,258	B2
Pine 19,871	F4
Pipestone 11,690	B6
Polk 34,844	B3
Pope 11,657	C5
Ramsey 459,784	E5
Red Lake 5,471	B3
Redwood 19,341	C6
Renville 20,401	C6
Rice 46,087	E6
Rock 10,703	B7
Roseau 12,574	C2
Saint Louis 222,229	F3
Scott 43,784	E6
Sherburne 29,908	E5
Sibley 15,448	D6
Stearns 108,161	D5
Steele 30,328	E7
Stevens 11,322	B5
Swift 12,920	C5
Todd 24,991	D4
Traverse 5,542	B5
Wabasha 19,335	F6
Wadena 14,192	D4
Waseca 18,448	E6
Washington 113,571	F5
Watonwan 12,361	D7
Wilkin 8,454	B4
Winona 46,256	G6
Wright 58,681	D5
Yellow Medicine 13,653	B6

CITIES and TOWNS

Zip	Name/Pop.	Key
56510	Ada⊙ 1,971	B3
55909	Adams 797	F7
56110	Adrian 1,336	C7
55001	Afton 2,550	F6
56430	Ah-Gwah-Ching 400	D3
56431	Aitkin⊙ 1,770	E4
56433	Akeley 486	D3
56307	Albany 1,569	D5
56207	Alberta 145	B5
56007	Albert Lea⊙ 19,200	E7
55301	Albertville 564	E5
56009	Alden 687	E7
56308	Alexandria⊙ 7,608	C5
56111	Alpha 180	D7
55910	Altura 354	G6
56710	Alvarado 385	B2
56010	Amboy 606	D7
†55303	Andover 9,387	E5
55302	Annandale 1,568	D5
55303	Anoka⊙ 15,634	E5
56208	Appleton 1,842	C5
†55124	Apple Valley 21,818	G6
56713	Argyle 741	B2
55307	Arlington 1,779	D6
56309	Ashby 486	C4
55704	Askov 350	F4
56209	Atwater 1,128	D5
56511	Audubon 383	C4
55705	Aurora 2,670	F3
55912	Austin⊙ 23,020	E7
56114	Avoca 201	C7
56310	Avon 804	D5
55706	Babbitt 2,435	G3
56435	Backus 255	D4
56714	Badger 320	B2
56621	Bagley⊙ 1,321	C3
56115	Balaton 752	C6
56514	Barnesville 2,207	B4
55707	Barnum 464	F4
56311	Barrett 388	B5
56515	Battle Lake 708	C4
56623	Baudette⊙ 1,170	D2
†56401	Baxter 2,625	D4
55003	Bayport 2,932	F5
56211	Beardsley 344	B5
55601	Beaver Bay 283	G3
56116	Beaver Creek 260	B7
55308	Becker 601	E5
56312	Belgrade 805	C5
†55027	Bellechester 220	F6
56011	Belle Plaine 2,754	E6
56212	Bellingham 290	B5
56214	Belview 438	C6
56601	Bemidji⊙ 10,949	D3
56626	Bena 153	D3
56215	Benson⊙ 3,656	C5
56437	Bertha 510	C4
55005	Bethel 272	E5
56117	Bigelow 249	C7
56627	Big Falls 490	E2
56628	Bigfork 457	E3
55309	Big Lake 2,210	E5
56118	Bingham Lake 222	C7
55310	Bird Island 1,372	D6
55708	Biwabik 1,428	F3
56630	Blackduck 653	D3
†55433	Blaine 28,558	G5
56216	Blomkest 200	D6
55917	Blooming Prairie 1,969	E7
55420	Bloomington 81,831	G6
56013	Blue Earth⊙ 4,132	D7
56518	Bluffton 206	C4
56519	Borup 160	B3
55709	Bovey 813	E3
56314	Bowlus 276	D5
56218	Boyd 329	C6
55006	Braham 1,015	E5
56401	Brainerd⊙ 11,489	D4
†55056	Branch 1,866	F5
56315	Brandon 473	C5
56520	Breckenridge⊙ 3,909	B4
†56472	Breezy Point 384	D4
56119	Brewster 559	C7
56014	Bricelyn 487	E7
55429	Brooklyn Center 31,230	G5
†55444	Brooklyn Park 43,332	G5
56715	Brooks 173	B3
56316	Brooten 647	C5
56438	Browerville 693	D4
55918	Brownsdale 691	F7
56219	Browns Valley 887	B5
55919	Brownsville 418	G7
55312	Brownton 697	D6
56317	Buckman 171	D5
55313	Buffalo⊙ 4,560	E5
55314	Buffalo Lake 782	D6
55713	Buhl 1,284	F3
55337	Burnsville 35,674	E6
56318	Burtrum 177	D5
56120	Butterfield 634	D7
55920	Byron 1,715	F6
55921	Caledonia⊙ 2,691	G7
56521	Callaway 238	C3
55716	Calumet 469	E3
55008	Cambridge⊙ 3,287	E5
56522	Campbell 286	B4
56220	Canby 2,143	B6
55009	Cannon Falls 2,653	F6
55922	Canton 386	F7
56319	Carlos 364	C5
55718	Carlton⊙ 862	F4
55315	Carver 642	E6
56633	Cass Lake 1,001	D3
55012	Center City⊙ 458	F5
†55038	Centerville 734	E5
56121	Ceylon 543	D7
55316	Champlin 9,006	G5
56122	Chandler 344	C7
55317	Chanhassen 6,359	F6
55318	Chaska⊙ 8,346	F6
55923	Chatfield 2,055	F7
55013	Chisago City 1,634	E5
55719	Chisholm 5,930	E3
56221	Chokio 559	B5
55014	Circle Pines 3,321	G5
56222	Clara City 1,574	C6
55924	Claremont 591	E6
56440	Clarissa 663	C4
56223	Clarkfield 1,171	C6
56016	Clarks Grove 620	E7
56634	Clearbrook 579	C3
55319	Clear Lake 266	E5
55320	Clearwater 379	D5
56224	Clements 227	D6
56017	Cleveland 699	E6
56523	Climax 273	B3
56225	Clinton 622	B5
56226	Clontarf 196	C5
55720	Cloquet 11,142	F4
†55068	Coates 207	E6
55321	Cokato 2,056	D5
56320	Cold Spring 2,294	D5
55722	Coleraine 1,116	E3
55322	Cologne 545	E6
55421	Columbia Heights 20,029	G5
56019	Comfrey 548	D6
56020	Conger 183	E7
55723	Cook 800	F3
55433	Coon Rapids 35,826	G5
†55340	Corcoran 4,252	F5
56228	Cosmos 571	D6
55016	Cottage Grove 18,994	F6
56229	Cottonwood 924	C6
56021	Courtland 399	D6
55726	Cromwell 229	F4
56716	Crookston⊙ 8,628	B3
56441	Crosby 2,218	D4
56442	Crosslake 1,064	E4
†55428	Crystal 25,543	G5
55323	Crystal Bay (Orono) 6,845	F5
56123	Currie 359	C6
56323	Cyrus 334	C5
55925	Dakota 350	G7
56324	Dalton 248	C4
56230	Danube 590	C6
56231	Danvers 152	C5
56022	Darfur 139	D6
55324	Darwin 282	D5
55325	Dassel 1,066	D5
56232	Dawson 1,901	B6
55327	Dayton 4,070	E5
55391	Deephaven 3,716	G5
56527	Deer Creek 392	C4
56636	Deer River 907	E3
56444	Deerwood 580	E4
56233	De Graff 179	C5
55328	Delano 2,480	E5
56023	Delavan 262	D7
†55110	Dellwood 751	F5
56528	Dent 167	C4
56501	Detroit Lakes⊙ 7,106	C4
55926	Dexter 279	F7
56529	Dilworth 2,585	B4
55927	Dodge Center 1,816	F6
56235	Donnelly 317	B5
55929	Dover 312	F7
*55801	Duluth⊙ 92,811	F4
	Duluth-Superior‡ 266,650	F4
56236	Dumont 173	B5
55019	Dundas 422	E6
56127	Dunnell 216	D7
55111	Eagan 20,700	G6
56446	Eagle Bend 593	D4
56024	Eagle Lake 1,470	E6
†55005	East Bethel 6,626	E5
56721	East Grand Forks 8,537	B3
†56401	East Gull Lake 586	D4
56025	Easton 283	E7
56237	Echo 334	C6
55344	Eden Prairie 16,263	G6
55329	Eden Valley 763	D5
56128	Edgerton 1,123	B7
55424	Edina 46,073	G5
55931	Eitzen 226	G7
†55910	Elba 198	F6
56531	Elbow Lake⊙ 1,358	B5
55932	Elgin 667	F6
56533	Elizabeth 195	B4
55020	Elko 274	E6
55330	Elk River⊙ 6,785	E5
56026	Ellendale 555	E7
56129	Ellsworth 629	C7
56027	Elmore 882	D7
56325	Elrosa 214	C5
55731	Ely 4,820	G3
56028	Elysian 454	E6
56447	Emily 588	E4
56029	Emmons 465	E7
56534	Erhard 194	B4
56535	Erskine 585	B3
56326	Evansville 571	C4
55734	Eveleth 5,042	F3
55331	Excelsior 2,523	E6
55934	Eyota 1,244	F7
55332	Fairfax 1,405	D6
56031	Fairmont⊙ 11,506	D7
55113	Falcon Heights 5,291	G5
55021	Faribault⊙ 16,241	E6
55024	Farmington 4,370	E6
56641	Federal Dam 192	D3
56536	Felton 264	B3
56537	Fergus Falls⊙ 12,519	B4
56540	Fertile 869	B3
56448	Fifty Lakes 263	D4
55735	Finlayson 202	F4
56723	Fisher 453	B3
56328	Flensburg 256	D5
55736	Floodwood 648	E4
56329	Foley⊙ 1,606	D5
†56308	Forada 191	C5
55025	Forest Lake 4,596	F5
56330	Foreston 283	E5
56542	Fosston 1,599	C3
55935	Fountain 327	F7
56543	Foxhome 161	B4
55333	Franklin 512	D6
56544	Frazee 1,284	C4
56032	Freeborn 323	E7
56331	Freeport 563	D5
55432	Fridley 30,228	G5
56033	Frost 293	D7
56131	Fulda 1,308	C7
56332	Garfield 284	C5
56450	Garrison 174	E4
56132	Garvin 172	C6
56545	Gary 241	B3
55334	Gaylord⊙ 1,933	D6
56035	Geneva 417	E7
56239	Ghent 356	C6
55335	Gibbon 787	D6
55741	Gilbert 2,721	F3
56333	Gilman 156	E5
55336	Glencoe⊙ 4,396	D6
56036	Glenville 851	E7
56334	Glenwood⊙ 2,523	C5
56547	Glyndon 882	B4
55427	Golden Valley 22,775	G5
56644	Gonvick 362	C3
55027	Goodhue 657	F6
56725	Goodridge 191	C2
56037	Good Thunder 560	D6
55027	Goodview 2,567	G6
56240	Graceville 780	B5
56039	Granada 377	D7
55604	Grand Marais⊙ 1,289	G2
55936	Grand Meadow 965	F7
55744	Grand Rapids⊙ 7,934	E3
56241	Granite Falls⊙ 3,451	C6
55030	Grasston 123	E5
56726	Greenbush 817	B2
†55373	Greenfield 1,391	F5
55338	Green Isle 357	E6
56335	Greenwald 259	D5
56336	Grey Eagle 338	D5
56243	Grove City 596	D5
56727	Grygla 216	C2
56452	Hackensack 285	D4
56728	Hallock⊙ 1,405	A2
56548	Halstad 690	B3
55339	Hamburg 475	D6
55340	Hamel 2,623	F5
55304	Ham Lake 7,832	E5
55938	Hammond 178	F6
55031	Hampton 299	E6
56244	Hancock 877	C5
56245	Hanley Falls 265	C6
55341	Hanover 647	E5
56041	Hanska 429	D6
56134	Hardwick 279	B7
55939	Harmony 1,133	F7
55032	Harris 678	F5
56042	Hartland 322	E7
55033	Hastings⊙ 12,827	F6
56549	Hawley 1,634	B4
55940	Hayfield 1,243	F7
56043	Hayward 294	E7
55342	Hector 1,252	D6
56044	Henderson 739	E6
56136	Hendricks 737	B6
56550	Hendrum 336	B3
56551	Henning 832	C4
56248	Herman 600	B5
†55811	Hermantown 6,759	F4
56137	Heron Lake 783	C7
56453	Hewitt 299	C4
55746	Hibbing 21,193	F3
55748	Hill City 533	E4
56138	Hills 598	B7
55037	Hinckley 963	E4
56552	Hitterdal 253	B4

(continued on following page)

Agriculture, Industry and Resources

DOMINANT LAND USE

- Wheat, General Farming
- Dairy, Livestock
- Dairy, Hay, Potatoes
- Cattle Feed, Hogs
- Livestock, Cash Grain
- Forests
- Swampland, Limited Agriculture
- Urban Areas

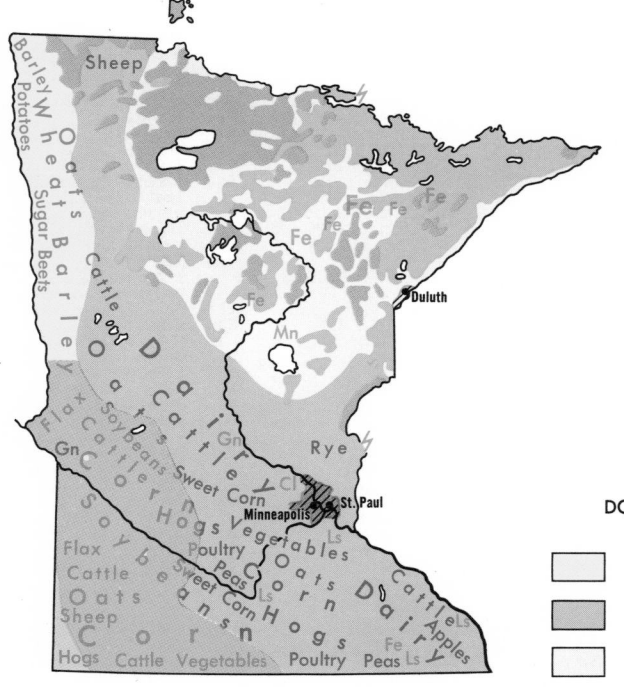

MAJOR MINERAL OCCURRENCES

- Cl Clay
- Fe Iron Ore
- Gn Granite
- Ls Limestone
- Mn Manganese
- Water Power
- Major Industrial Areas

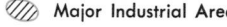

56339 Hoffman 631 C5
55941 Hokah 686 G7
56340 Holdingford 635 D5
56139 Holland 234 B6
56045 Hollandale 290 E7
56249 Holloway 142 C5
55343 Hopkins 15,336 G5
55943 Houston 1,057 G7
55349 Howard Lake 1,240 D5
55750 Hoyt Lakes 3,186 F3
55038 Hugo 3,771 E5
55350 Hutchinson 9,244 D6
†55359 Independence 2,640 F5
56649 International Falls⊙ 5,611 E2
55075 Inver Grove Heights 17,171 E6
56141 Iona 248 C7
56455 Ironton 537 D4
55040 Isanti 858 E5
56342 Isle 573 E4
56142 Ivanhoe⊙ 761 B6
56143 Jackson⊙ 3,797 C7
56048 Janesville 1,897 E6
56144 Jasper 731 B7
56145 Jeffers 437 C6
56456 Jenkins 219 D4
55352 Jordan 2,663 E6
56251 Kandiyohi 447 D5
56732 Karlstad 934 B2
56050 Kasota 739 D6
55944 Kasson 2,827 F6
55753 Keewatin 1,443 E3
56650 Kelliher 324 D3
55945 Kellogg 440 G6
55754 Kelly Lake 900 F3
56733 Kennedy 405 B2
56343 Kensington 331 C5
55946 Kenyon 1,529 E6
56252 Kerkhoven 761 C5
56051 Kiester 670 E7
56052 Kilkenny 177 E6
55353 Kimball 651 D5
55758 Kinney 447 F3
55947 La Crescent 3,674 G7
56054 Lafayette 507 D6
56149 Lake Benton 869 B6
56734 Lake Bronson 298 B2
55041 Lake City 4,505 F6
56055 Lake Crystal 2,078 D6
55042 Lake Elmo 5,296 F6
56150 Lakefield 1,845 C7
†55398 Lake Fremont (Zimmerman) 1,074 E5
55043 Lakeland 1,812 F6
56253 Lake Lillian 329 C6
56554 Lake Park 716 B4
†55043 Lake Saint Croix Beach 1,176 F6
†56401 Lake Shore 583 D4
55044 Lakeville 14,790 E6
56151 Lake Wilson 380 B7
56152 Lamberton 1,032 C6
56735 Lancaster 368 B2
55949 Lanesboro 923 G7
56461 Laporte 160 D3
†55744 La Prairie 536 E3
56344 Lastrup 150 D4
†55101 Lauderdale 1,985 G5
56057 Le Center⊙ 1,967 E6
55951 Le Roy 930 F7
55354 Lester Prairie 1,229 D6
56058 Le Sueur 3,763 E6
55952 Lewiston 1,226 G7
56060 Lewisville 273 D7
†55014 Lexington 2,150 G5
†55050 Lilydale 417 G5
55045 Lindstrom 1,972 F5
†55038 Lino Lakes 4,966 G5
56155 Lismore 276 B7
55355 Litchfield⊙ 5,904 D5
56345 Little Falls⊙ 7,250 D5
56653 Littlefork 918 E2
†56334 Long Beach 263 C5
55356 Long Lake 1,747 F5
56347 Long Prairie⊙ 2,859 D5
56655 Longville 191 D4
55046 Lonsdale 1,160 E6
55357 Loretto 297 F5
56349 Lowry 283 C5
56255 Lucan 262 C6
56156 Luverne⊙ 4,568 B7
55953 Lyle 576 F7
56157 Lynd 304 C6
55954 Mabel 861 G7
56062 Madelia 2,130 D6
56256 Madison⊙ 2,212 B5
56063 Madison Lake 592 E6
56158 Magnolia 234 B7
56557 Mahnomen⊙ 1,283 C3
55115 Mahtomedi 3,851 F5
56001 Mankato⊙ 28,651 E6
55955 Mantorville⊙ 705 F6
†55369 Maple Grove 20,525 G5
55358 Maple Lake 1,132 D5
55359 Maple Plain 1,421 F5
56065 Mapleton 1,516 E7
†55912 Mapleview 253 E7
55109 Maplewood 26,990 G5
55764 Marble 757 E3
56257 Marietta 279 B5
55047 Marine on Saint Croix 543 F5
56258 Marshall⊙ 11,161 C6
55360 Mayer 388 E6
56260 Maynard 428 C6
55956 Mazeppa 680 F6
55760 McGregor 447 E4
56556 McIntosh 681 C3
55761 McKinley 230 F3
55049 Medford 775 E6
55441 Medicine Lake 419 G5
†55340 Medina (Hamel) 2,623 F5
†56352 Meire Grove 174 C5
56352 Melrose 2,409 D5
56464 Menahga 980 C4
55050 Mendota 219 G5
†55050 Mendota Heights 7,288 G6
56736 Mentor 219 B3
56737 Middle River 349 B2
†55033 Miesville 179 F6
56262 Milan 417 C5
55957 Millville 186 F6
56263 Milroy 242 C6
56354 Miltona 187 C4
*55401 Minneapolis⊙ 370,951 G5
Minneapolis-Saint Paul‡ 2,114,256 G5
56264 Minneota 1,470 C6
55959 Minnesota City 265 G6
56068 Minnesota Lake 744 E7
55343 Minnetonka 38,683 G5
†55364 Minnetrista 3,236 F5
56265 Montevideo⊙ 5,845 C6
56069 Montgomery 2,349 E6
55362 Monticello 2,830 E5
55363 Montrose 762 E5
56560 Moorhead⊙ 29,998 B4
Moorhead-Fargo‡ 137,574 B4
55767 Moose Lake 1,408 F4
55051 Mora⊙ 2,890 E5
56266 Morgan 975 D6
56267 Morris⊙ 5,367 C5
55052 Morristown 639 E6
56270 Morton 549 C6
56466 Motley 444 D4
55364 Mound 9,280 E6
†55112 Mounds View 12,593 G5
55768 Mountain Iron 4,134 F3
56159 Mountain Lake 2,277 D7
56271 Murdock 343 C5
55769 Nashwauk 1,419 E3
56355 Nelson 209 C5
55053 Nerstrand 255 E6
56467 Nevis 332 D4
55366 New Auburn 331 D6
55112 New Brighton 23,269 G5
56738 Newfolden 384 B2
55367 New Germany 347 E6
†55428 New Hope 23,087 G5
56273 New London 812 C5
55054 New Market 286 E6
56356 New Munich 302 D5
55055 Newport 3,323 F6
56071 New Prague 2,952 E6
56072 New Richland 1,263 E7
56073 New Ulm⊙ 13,755 D6
56567 New York Mills 972 C4
56074 Nicollet 709 D6
56568 Nielsville 145 B3
56468 Nisswa 1,407 D4
55056 North Branch 1,597 F5
55057 Northfield 12,562 E6
56001 North Mankato 9,145 D6
†55101 North Oaks 2,846 G5
56661 Northome 312 D3
56275 North Redwood 206 D6
56075 Northrop 269 D7
55109 North Saint Paul 11,921 G5
55368 Norwood 1,219 E6
†55109 Oakdale 12,123 E5
56276 Odessa 177 B5
56160 Odin 134 D7
56569 Ogema 215 C3
56358 Ogilvie 423 E5
56161 Okabena 263 C7
56742 Oklee 536 C3
56277 Olivia⊙ 2,802 C6
56359 Onamia 691 E4
56162 Ormsby 181 D7
†55323 Orono 6,845 F5
55960 Oronoco 574 F6
55771 Orr 294 F2
56278 Ortonville⊙ 2,550 B5
56360 Osakis 1,355 C5
56744 Oslo 379 A2
55369 Osseo 2,974 G5
55961 Ostrander 293 F7
56571 Ottertail 239 C4
55060 Owatonna⊙ 18,632 E6
56469 Palisade 155 E4
56361 Parkers Prairie 917 C4
56470 Park Rapids⊙ 2,976 D4
56362 Paynesville 2,140 D5
56363 Pease 174 E5
†56472 Pelican Lakes (Breezy Point) 384 D4
56572 Pelican Rapids 1,867 E4
56078 Pemberton 208 E7
56279 Pennock 410 C5
56472 Pequot Lakes 681 D4
56573 Perham 2,086 C4
55962 Peterson 291 G7
†56364 Pierz 1,018 D5
56473 Pillager 341 D4
55063 Pine City⊙ 2,489 F5
55963 Pine Island 1,986 F6
56474 Pine River 881 D4
56164 Pipestone⊙ 4,887 B7
55964 Plainview 2,416 F6
55370 Plato 390 D6
56748 Plummer 353 B3
†55441 Plymouth 31,615 G5
56280 Porter 211 B6
55965 Preston⊙ 1,478 F7
55371 Princeton 3,146 E5
56281 Prinsburg 557 C6
55372 Prior Lake 7,284 E6
55810 Proctor 3,180 F4
55967 Racine 285 F7
56475 Randall 527 D4
55065 Randolph 351 E6
56668 Ranier 237 E2
56282 Raymond 723 C5
56750 Red Lake Falls⊙ 1,732 B3
55066 Red Wing⊙ 13,736 F6
56283 Redwood Falls⊙ 5,210 C6
56672 Remer 356 E3
56284 Renville 1,493 C6
56166 Revere 158 C6
56367 Rice 499 D5
55423 Richfield 37,851 G6
56368 Richmond 867 D5
55422 Robbinsdale 14,422 G5
55901 Rochester⊙ 57,890 F6
Rochester‡ 91,971 F6
55067 Rock Creek 890 F5
55373 Rockford 2,408 F5
56369 Rockville 597 D5
55374 Rogers 652 E5
55969 Rollingstone 528 G6
56371 Roscoe 154 D5
56751 Roseau⊙ 2,272 C2
55970 Rose Creek 371 F7
55068 Rosemount 5,083 E6
55113 Roseville 35,820 G5
56579 Rothsay 476 B4
56167 Round Lake 480 C7
56373 Royalton 660 D5
55069 Rush City 1,198 F5
55971 Rushford 1,478 G7
56168 Rushmore 387 C7
56169 Russell 412 C6
56170 Ruthton 328 B6
55778 Rutledge 185 F4
56580 Sabin 446 B4
56285 Sacred Heart 666 C6
55414 Saint Anthony 7,981 G5
55375 Saint Bonifacius 857 F5
55972 Saint Charles 2,184 F7
56080 Saint Clair 655 E6
56301 Saint Cloud⊙ 42,566 D5
Saint Cloud‡ 163,256 D5
55070 Saint Francis 1,184 E5
56554 Saint Hilaire 388 B2
56081 Saint James⊙ 4,346 D7
56374 Saint Joseph 2,994 D5
55426 Saint Louis Park 42,931 G5
56376 Saint Martin 220 D5
55376 Saint Michael 1,519 E5
*55101 Saint Paul (cap.)⊙ 270,230 G6
Saint Paul-Minneapolis‡ 2,114,256 G5
55071 Saint Paul Park 4,864 G6
56082 Saint Peter⊙ 9,056 E6
56375 Saint Stephen 453 D5
56755 Saint Vincent 141 A2
56083 Sanborn 518 C6
55072 Sandstone 1,594 F4
56377 Sartell 3,427 D5
56378 Sauk Centre 3,709 D5
56379 Sauk Rapids 5,793 D5
55378 Savage 3,954 G6
†55720 Scanlon 1,050 F4
56477 Sebeka 774 C4
55074 Shafer 180 F5
55379 Shakopee⊙ 9,941 F6
56581 Shelly 276 B3
56171 Sherburn 1,275 D7
56676 Shevlin 193 C3
†55112 Shoreview 17,300 G5
†55331 Shorewood 4,646 F5
55614 Silver Bay 2,917 G3
55381 Silver Lake 698 D6
†56001 Skyline 399 D6
56172 Slayton⊙ 2,420 C7
56085 Sleepy Eye 3,581 D6
†56345 Sobieski 219 D5
55382 South Haven 205 D5
56679 South International Falls 2,806 E2
55075 South Saint Paul 21,235 G6
56288 Spicer 909 C5
56087 Springfield 2,303 C6
55974 Spring Grove 1,275 G7
†55432 Spring Lake Park 6,477 E5
55384 Spring Park 1,465 F5
55975 Spring Valley 2,616 F7
56681 Squaw Lake 162 D3
55079 Stacy 996 E5
56479 Staples 2,887 D4
56381 Starbuck 1,224 C5
56173 Steen 153 B7
56757 Stephen 898 A2
55385 Stewart 616 D6
55976 Stewartville 3,925 F7
55082 Stillwater⊙ 12,290 F5
55988 Stockton 517 G6
56174 Storden 341 C6
56758 Strandquist 136 B2
55783 Sturgeon Lake 222 F4
†55075 Sunfish Lake 344 E6
56382 Swanville 295 D5
55786 Taconite 331 E3
56291 Taunton 177 B6
55084 Taylors Falls 623 F5
56683 Tenstrike 159 D3
56701 Thief River Falls⊙ 9,105 B2
†56319 Thomson 152 F4
†55331 Tonka Bay 1,354 F5
55790 Tower 640 F3
56175 Tracy 2,478 C6
56176 Trimont 805 D7
56088 Truman 1,392 D7
56089 Twin Lakes 210 E7
56584 Twin Valley 907 B3
55616 Two Harbors⊙ 4,039 G3
56178 Tyler 1,353 B6
56585 Ulen 514 B3
56586 Underwood 332 C4
56384 Upsala 400 D5
55979 Utica 249 G7
†55101 Vadnais Heights 5,111 G5
56587 Vergas 287 C4
55085 Vermillion 438 F6
56481 Verndale 504 C4
56090 Vernon Center 365 D7
56292 Vesta 360 C6
55386 Victoria 1,425 F6
56385 Villard 275 C5
55792 Virginia 11,056 F3
55981 Wabasha⊙ 2,372 G6
56293 Wabasso 745 C6
55387 Waconia 2,638 E6
56482 Wadena⊙ 4,699 C4
56386 Wahkon 271 E4
56387 Waite Park 3,496 D5
56091 Waldorf 249 E7
56484 Walker⊙ 970 D3
56180 Walnut Grove 753 C6
55982 Waltham 176 F7
55983 Wanamingo 717 F6
55743 Warba 150 E3
56762 Warren⊙ 2,105 B2
56763 Warroad 1,216 C2
56093 Waseca⊙ 8,219 E6
55388 Watertown 1,818 E6
56096 Waterville 1,717 E6
55389 Watkins 757 D5
56295 Watson 238 C5
56589 Waubun 390 C3
55390 Waverly 470 E5
55391 Wayzata 3,621 G5
56181 Welcome 855 D7
56097 Wells 2,777 E7
56590 Wendell 216 B4
56183 Westbrook 978 C6
55985 West Concord 762 F6
55118 West Saint Paul 18,527 G5
56296 Wheaton⊙ 1,969 B5
55110 White Bear Lake 22,538 G5
55090 Willernie 654 G5
56686 Williams 217 D2
56201 Willmar⊙ 15,895 C5
55795 Willow River 303 F4
56185 Wilmont 380 C7
56687 Wilton 176 C3
56101 Windom⊙ 4,666 C7
56592 Winger 200 B3
56098 Winnebago 1,869 D7
55987 Winona⊙ 25,075 G6
55395 Winsted 1,522 D6
55396 Winthrop 1,376 D6
55796 Winton 276 G3
56594 Wolverton 177 B4
†55798 Woodbury 10,297 F6
56297 Wood Lake 420 C6
56186 Woodstock 180 B7
56187 Worthington⊙ 10,243 C7
55797 Wrenshall 333 F4
55798 Wright 162 E4
55990 Wykoff 482 F7
55092 Wyoming 1,559 F5
55397 Young America 1,237 E6
55398 Zimmerman 1,074 E5
55991 Zumbro Falls 208 F6
55992 Zumbrota 2,129 F6

OTHER FEATURES

Ash (riv.) F2
Bald Eagle (lake) G3
Basswood (lake) E2
Battle (riv.) D3
Baudette (riv.) D2
Bear (riv.) E3
Bemidji (lake) D3
Benton (lake) B6
Big Fork (riv.) E2
Big Sandy (lake) E4
Big Stone (lake) B5
Birch (lake) G3
Black (riv.) D2
Blue Earth (riv.) D7
Bois de Sioux (riv.) B4
Bowstring (lake) E3
Buffalo (riv.) B4
Burntside (lake) F3
Cass (lake) D3
Cedar (riv.) F7
Chippewa (riv.) C5
Christina (lake) C4
Clearwater (riv.) C3
Cloquet (riv.) F4
Cobb (riv.) E7
Cottonwood (riv.) C6
Crooked (creek) F4
Crooked (lake) G2
Crow (riv.) F5
Crow Wing (riv.) D4
Cuyuna (range) D4
Dead (lake) C4
Deer (lake) E3
Des Moines (riv.) C7
Eagle (mt.) G2
East Swan (riv.) F3
Elbow (lake) C3
Emily (lake) D4
Fond du Lac Ind. Res. F4
Grand Portage Ind. Res. G2
Grand Portage Nat'l Mon. G2
Green (lake) D5
Greenwood (lake) G3
Gull (lake) D4
Heron (lake) C7
Hill (riv.) C3
Independence (lake) F5
Isabella (lake) G3
Itasca (lake) C3
Kabetogama (lake) E2
Kanaranzi (creek) C7
Kettle (riv.) F4
Knife (lake) G2
La Croix (lake) F2
Lac qui Parle (lake) C5
Lac qui Parle (riv.) B6
Lake of the Woods (lake) D1
Leaf (riv.) C4
Leech (lake) D3
Leech Lake Ind. Res. D3
Lida (lake) C4
Little Fork (riv.) E2
Little Rock (creek) C7
Long (lake) D4
Long (lake) F3
Long Prairie (riv.) D4
Lost (riv.) C3
Lower Red (lake) C3
Maple (lake) B3
Maple (riv.) E7
Marsh (lake) B5
Mary (lake) C5
Mesabi (range) E3
Middle (riv.) B2
Mille Lac Ind. Res. E4
Mille Lacs (lake) E4
Miltona (lake) C4
Minneapolis-Saint Paul Airport G5
Minnesota (riv.) E6
Minnetonka (lake) F5
Minnewaska (lake) C5
Misquah (hills) F2
Mississippi (riv.) D4
Moose (riv.) C2
Mud (lake) C2
Mud (riv.) C2
Muskeg (bay) C2
Mustinka (riv.) B5
Nemadji (riv.) F4
Nett (lake) E2
Nett Lake Ind. Res. E2
North (lake) F1
Otter Tail (lake) C4
Otter Tail (riv.) B4
Partridge (riv.) G3
Pelican (lake) C4
Pelican (lake) D4
Pelican (lake) F2
Pelican (riv.) B4
Pelican (riv.) F2
Pepin (lake) F6
Pigeon (riv.) G2
Pike (riv.) F3
Pipestone Nat'l Mon. B6
Pokegama (lake) E3
Pomme de Terre (riv.) C5
Poplar (riv.) C3
Prairie (riv.) E3
Rainy (lake) E2
Rainy (riv.) D2
Rapid (riv.) D2
Redeye (riv.) D4
Red Lake (riv.) B2
Red Lake Ind. Res. C2
Red River of the North (riv.) A2
Redwood (riv.) C6
Reno (lake) C5
Rice (lake) E4
Rock (riv.) B7
Root (riv.) G7
Roseau (riv.) B2
Rum (riv.) E5
Saganaga (lake) H2
Saint Croix (riv.) F5
Saint Louis (riv.) F4
Sand (creek) F5
Sand Hill (riv.) B3
Sarah (lake) F5
Schoolcraft (riv.) C3
Shakopee (creek) C5
Shell (riv.) C4
Shetek (lake) C6
Sleepy Eye (creek) C6
Snake (riv.) A2
Snake (riv.) E4
South Fowl (lake) G1
Star (lake) C4
Sturgeon (riv.) F3
Superior (lake) G3
Swan (lake) D6
Tamarac (riv.) A2
Tamarack (riv.) D2
Thief (lake) C2
Thief (riv.) B2
Traverse (lake) B5
Trout (lake) F2
Two Rivers (riv.) A1
Upper Red (lake) D2
Vermilion (lake) F3
Vermilion (range) F3
Vermilion (riv.) F2
Voyageurs Nat'l Park F2
Wabatawangang (lake) D3
West Swan (riv.) F3
White Earth Ind. Res. C3
Whiteface (riv.) F3
Whitefish (lake) D4
White Iron (lake) G3
Wild Rice (lake) F4
Wild Rice (riv.) B3
Willow (riv.) E4
Winnibigoshish (lake) D3
Woods (lake) D1
Zumbro (riv.) F6

⊙County seat.
‡Population of metropolitan area.
† Zip of nearest p.o. * Multiple zips.

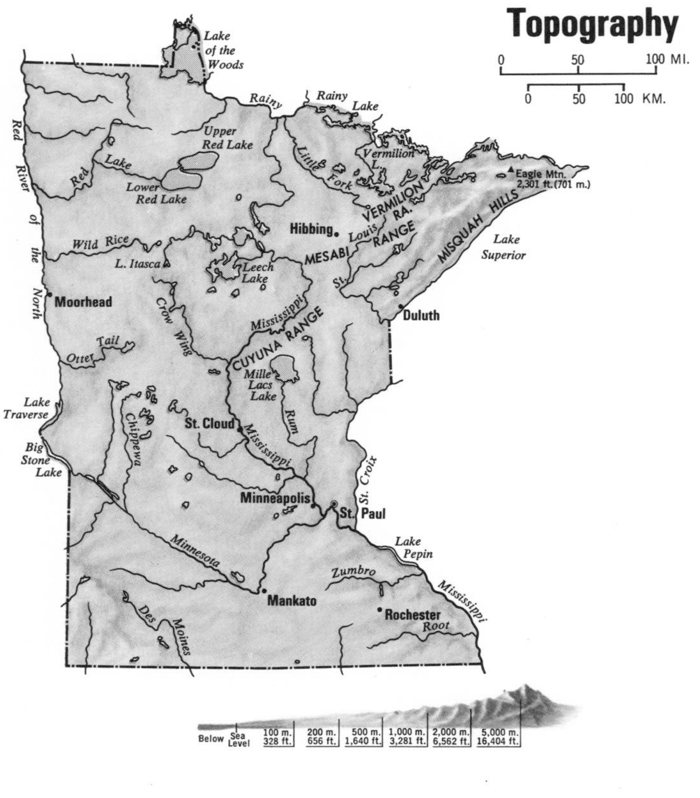
Topography
0 50 100 MI.
0 50 100 KM.
Lake of the Woods
Rainy
Rainy Lake
Upper Red Lake
Red Lake
Lower Red Lake
Red River of the North
Vermilion
Little Fork
Eagle Mtn. 2,301 ft. (701 m.)
VERMILION RA.
MISQUAH HILLS
Hibbing
Louis
MESABI RANGE
St.
Lake Superior
Wild Rice
L. Itasca
Leech Lake
Moorhead
Crow Wing
Mississippi
CUYUNA RANGE
Duluth
Otter Tail
Mille Lacs Lake
Lake Traverse
Chippewa
St. Cloud
Rum
Big Stone Lake
Mississippi
St. Croix
Minneapolis
St. Paul
Lake Pepin
Minnesota
Zumbro
Mississippi
Mankato
Rochester
Root
Des Moines
Below Sea Level
100 m. 328 ft.
200 m. 656 ft.
500 m. 1,640 ft.
1,000 m. 3,281 ft.
2,000 m. 6,562 ft.
5,000 m. 16,404 ft.

Minnesota

SCALE

0 5 10 20 30 40 50 MI.

0 5 10 20 30 40 50 KM.

State Capitals .... ⊛

County Seats .... ⊗

Major Limited Access Hwys. ———

Scale 1:2,300,000

Northeastern Part of Minnesota

Same scale as main map

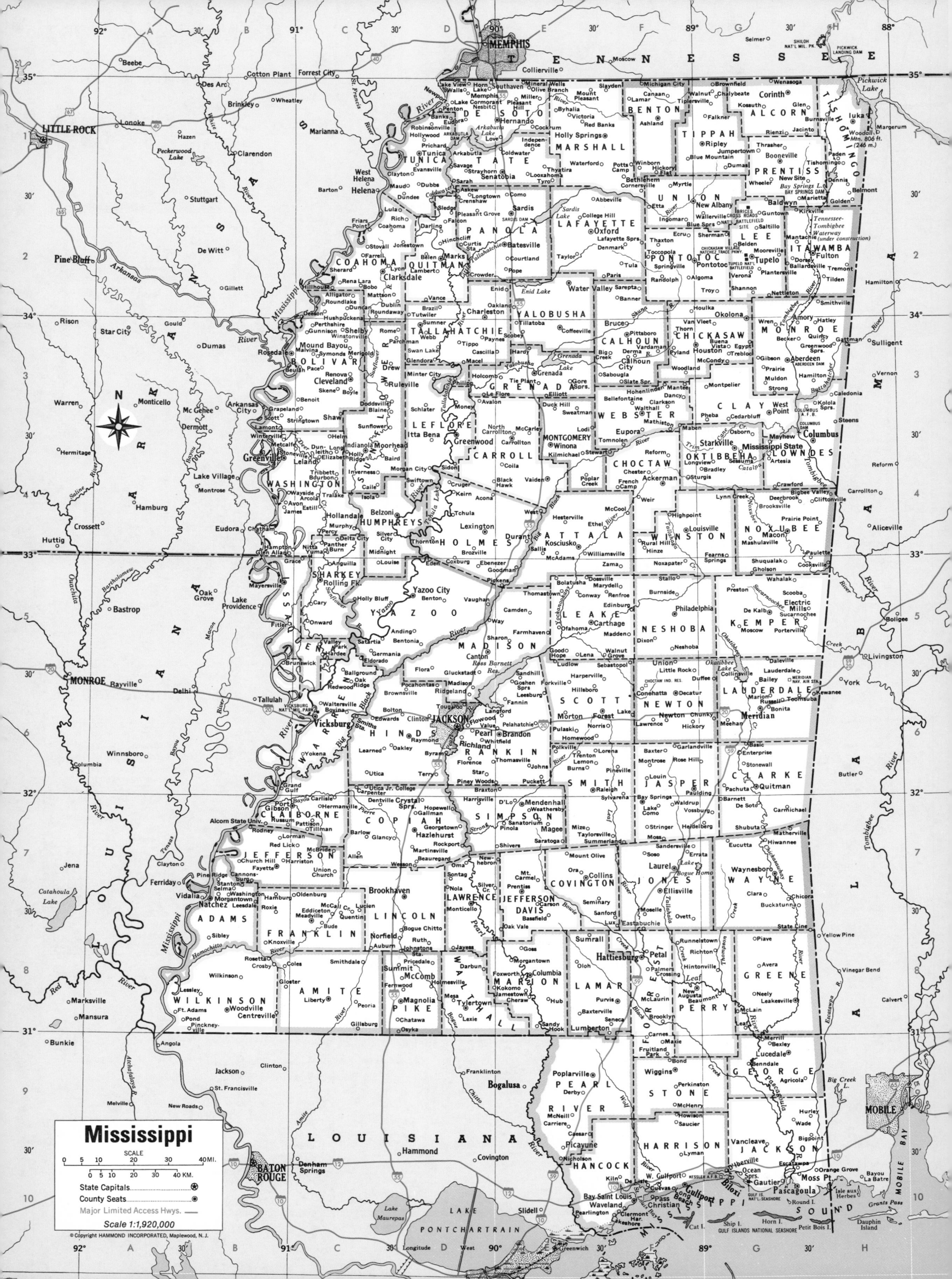

COUNTIES

Adams 38,035 B8
Alcorn 33,036 G1
Amite 13,369 C8
Attala 19,865 E4
Benton 8,153 F1
Bolivar 45,965 C3
Calhoun 15,664 F3
Carroll 9,776 E4
Chickasaw 17,853 G3
Choctaw 8,996 F4
Claiborne 12,279 C7
Clarke 16,945 G6
Clay 21,082 G3
Coahoma 36,918 C2
Copiah 26,503 D7
Covington 15,927 E7
De Soto 53,930 E1
Forrest 66,018 F8
Franklin 8,208 C8
George 15,297 G9
Greene 9,827 G8
Grenada 21,043 E3
Hancock 24,537 E10
Harrison 157,665 F10
Hinds 250,998 D6
Holmes 22,970 D4
Humphreys 13,931 C4
Issaquena 2,513 B5
Itawamba 20,518 H2
Jackson 118,015 G9
Jasper 17,265 F6
Jefferson 9,181 B7
Jefferson Davis 13,846 E7
Jones 61,912 F7
Kemper 10,148 G5
Lafayette 31,030 E2
Lamar 23,821 E8
Lauderdale 77,285 G6
Lawrence 12,518 D7
Leake 18,790 E5
Lee 57,061 G2
Leflore 41,525 D3
Lincoln 30,174 D8
Lowndes 57,304 H4
Madison 41,613 D5
Marion 25,708 E8
Marshall 29,296 E1
Monroe 36,404 H3
Montgomery 13,366 E4
Neshoba 23,789 F5
Newton 19,944 F6
Noxubee 13,212 G4
Oktibbeha 36,018 G4
Panola 28,164 E2
Pearl River 33,795 E9
Perry 9,864 G8
Pike 36,173 D8
Pontotoc 20,918 F2
Prentiss 24,025 G1
Quitman 12,636 D2
Rankin 69,427 E6
Scott 24,556 E6
Sharkey 7,964 C5
Simpson 23,441 E7
Smith 15,077 E6
Stone 9,716 F9
Sunflower 34,844 C3
Tallahatchie 17,157 D3
Tate 20,119 E1
Tippah 18,739 G1
Tishomingo 18,434 H1
Tunica 9,652 D1
Union 21,741 F2
Walthall 13,761 D8
Warren 51,627 C6
Washington 72,344 C4
Wayne 19,135 G7
Webster 10,300 F3
Wilkinson 10,021 B8
Winston 19,474 F4
Yalobusha 13,139 E2
Yazoo 27,349 D5

CITIES and TOWNS

Zip Name/Pop. Key

38601 Abbeville 448 F2
39730 Aberdeen⊙ 7,184 H3
39735 Ackerman⊙ 1,567 F4
39096 Alcorn State University B7
38820 Algoma 175 G2
†39083 Allen 15 C7
38720 Alligator 256 C2
38821 Amory 7,307 H3
38721 Anguilla 950 C5
38722 Arcola 588 C4
38602 Arkabutla 400 D1
39736 Artesia 526 G4
38603 Ashland⊙ 532 F1
38604 Askew 300 D1
†39664 Auburn 500 C8
38912 Avalon 100 D3
38723 Avon 400 B4
39320 Bailey 320 G6
38724 Baird 150 C4
38824 Baldwyn 3,427 G2
†39156 Ballground 30 C5
38913 Banner 120 F2
†39083 Barlow 20 C7
†39330 Basic 60 G6
39421 Bassfield 325 E8
38606 Batesville⊙ 4,692 E2
†39343 Baxter 75 F6
†39455 Baxterville 100 E8
39520 Bay Saint Louis⊙ 7,891 F10
39422 Bay Springs⊙ 1,884 F7
39423 Beaumont 1,112 G8
†39191 Beauregard 185 D7
38825 Becker 350 G3
38826 Belden 241 G2
38609 Belen 400 D2
39737 Bellefontaine 400 F3
38827 Belmont 1,420 H1
39038 Belzoni⊙ 2,982 C4
†39450 Benndale 500 G9
38725 Benoit 499 C3
39039 Benton 350 D5
39040 Bentonia 518 D5
†38659 Bethlehem 210 F1
38726 Beulah 431 B3
39738 Bigbee Valley 370 H4
38914 Big Creek 146 F3
†39567 Bigpoint 350 H9
*39530 Biloxi 49,311 G10
Biloxi-Gulfport‡ 191,918 G10
†38917 Black Hawk 41 E4
38727 Blaine 75 C3
38610 Blue Mountain 867 G1
38828 Blue Springs 131 G2
†38614 Bobo 200 C2
39629 Bogue Chitto 575 D8
39041 Bolton 664 D6
39550 Bond 350 F9
†39301 Bonita 300 G6
38829 Booneville⊙ 6,199 G1
†38756 Bourbon 200 C4
†39180 Bovina 50 C6
38730 Boyle 888 C3
39042 Brandon⊙ 9,626 E6
39044 Braxton 172 D6
38963 Brazil 229 D2
39601 Brookhaven⊙ 10,800 C7
39425 Brooklyn 450 F8
39739 Brooksville 1,038 G4
†38683 Brownfield 125 G1
38915 Bruce 2,208 F3
39322 Buckatunna 500 G7
39630 Bude 1,092 C8
38833 Burnsville 889 H1
38611 Byhalia 757 E1
†39205 Byram 250 D6
†38754 Caile 30 C4
39740 Caledonia 497 H3
38916 Calhoun City 2,033 F3
39045 Camden 150 E5
38612 Canaan 200 F1
39046 Canton⊙ 11,116 D5
39049 Carlisle 425 C7
†39360 Carmichael 75 G7
39050 Carpenter 200 C6
39426 Carriere 900 E9
38917 Carrollton⊙ 338 E4
39427 Carson 400 E7
39051 Carthage⊙ 3,453 E5
39054 Cary 470 C5
38920 Cascilla 230 D3
39741 Cedarbluff 175 G3
39631 Centreville 1,844 B8
38684 Chalybeate 350 G1
38921 Charleston⊙ 2,878 D2
39632 Chatawa 300 D8
38731 Chatham 150 B4
39323 Chunky 277 G6
39055 Church Hill 350 B7
39324 Clara 275 G7
38614 Clarksdale⊙ 21,137 D2
39551 Clermont Harbor 550 F10
38732 Cleveland⊙ 14,524 C3
39056 Clinton 14,660 D6
38617 Coahoma 350 C2
†38632 Cockrum 150 E1
38922 Coffeeville⊙ 1,129 E3
38923 Coila 75 E4
38618 Coldwater 1,505 E1
†39638 Coles 150 C8
†38655 College Hill 150 E2
39428 Collins⊙ 2,131 E7
39325 Collinsville 700 G6
39429 Columbia⊙ 7,733 E8
39701 Columbus⊙ 27,383 H3
38619 Como 1,378 E1
39057 Conehatta 200 F6
†39051 Conway 25 E5
38834 Corinth⊙ 13,839 G1
†38659 Cornersville 65 F1
38620 Courtland 381 E2
†39095 Coxburg 300 D5
39743 Crawford 495 G4
38621 Crenshaw 1,019 D2
39633 Crosby 349 B8
38622 Crowder 789 D2
38924 Cruger 540 D4
39059 Crystal Springs 4,902 D7
†38606 Curtis Station 350 D2
39326 Daleville 210 G5
†39643 Darbun 100 D8
38623 Darling 275 D2
39327 Decatur⊙ 1,148 F6
†39739 Deerbrook 30 G4
39328 De Kalb⊙ 1,159 G5
†39571 De Lisle 450 F10
39061 Delta City 310 C4
†38655 Denmark 40 E2
38838 Dennis 150 H1
†39059 Dentville 175 C7
†39470 Derby 298 E9
38839 Derma 793 F3
†39532 D'Iberville 13,369 G10
39062 D'Lo 463 E7
38736 Doddsville 232 C3
38737 Drew 2,528 C3
38739 Dublin 100 C2
38925 Duck Hill 706 E3
†39337 Duffee 175 G6
38625 Dumas 312 G1
38740 Duncan 501 C2
38626 Dundee 600 D1
39063 Durant 2,889 E4
39436 Eastabuchie 200 F8
39064 Ebenezer 200 D5
38841 Ecru 687 F2
39634 Eddiceton 65 C8
39065 Eden 150 D5
39066 Edwards 1,515 C6
†39156 Eldorado 20 C5
39329 Electric Mills 100 G5
38742 Elizabeth 500 C4
38926 Elliott 200 E3
39437 Ellisville⊙ 4,652 F7
38927 Enid E2
39067 Enterprise 607 G6
†39440 Errata 85 F7
39552 Escatawpa 5,367 G10
39067 Ethel 486 F4
38627 Etta 75 F2
39744 Eupora 2,048 F3
†38676 Evansville 60 D1
38628 Falcon 260 D2
38629 Falkner 251 G1
38630 Farrell 300 C2
39069 Fayette⊙ 2,033 B7
39635 Fernwood 500 D8
39070 Fitler 175 B5
39071 Flora 1,507 D5
39073 Florence 1,111 D6
†39201 Flowood 943 D6
39074 Forest⊙ 5,229 F6
39076 Forkville 185 E6
39636 Fort Adams 75 B8
39483 Foxworth 800 E8
39745 French Camp 306 F4
38631 Friars Point 1,400 C2
39577 Fruitland Park 75 F9
38843 Fulton⊙ 3,238 H2
39077 Gallman D7
38844 Gattman 151 H3
39553 Gautier 8,917 G10
39078 Georgetown 343 D7
†39354 Gholson 50 G5
†39083 Glancy 25 C7
38846 Glen 100 H1
38744 Glen Allan 650 B4
38928 Glendora 220 D3
39638 Gloster 1,726 B8
†39110 Gluckstadt 150 D5
38847 Golden 292 H2
39079 Goodman 1,285 E5
38929 Gore Springs 125 E3
38745 Grace 325 C5
†38725 Grapeland 200 B3
38701 Greenville⊙ 40,613 B4
38930 Greenwood⊙ 20,115 D4
38848 Greenwood Springs 170 H3
38901 Grenada⊙ 12,641 E3
*39501 Gulfport⊙ 39,676 F10
38746 Gunnison 708 C3
38849 Guntown 359 G2
†39661 Hamburg 150 B7
39746 Hamilton 500 H3
†38901 Hardy 45 E3
39080 Harperville 200 E6
39081 Harriston 500 C7
39082 Harrisville 500 D7
†38821 Hatley 497 H3
39401 Hattiesburg⊙ 40,829 F8
39083 Hazlehurst⊙ 4,437 D7
39439 Heidelberg 1,098 F7
39086 Hermanville 750 C7
38632 Hernando⊙ 2,969 E1
†39192 Hesterville 25 E4
39332 Hickory 670 F6
38633 Hickory Flat 458 F1
39087 Hillsboro 800 E6
†38646 Hinchcliff 60 D2
†39462 Hintonville 300 F8
†39108 Hinze 30 F4
†39751 Hohenlinden 96 F3
38940 Holcomb 50 D3
38748 Hollandale 4,336 C4
39088 Holly Bluff 700 C5
38749 Holly Ridge 350 C4
38635 Holly Springs⊙ 7,285 E1
†38676 Hollywood 80 D1
†39648 Holmesville 50 D8
38637 Horn Lake 4,326 D1
38850 Houlka 710 G2
38851 Houston⊙ 3,747 G3
†39574 Howison 300 F9
†39429 Hub 80 E8
39555 Hurley 500 H9
†38774 Hushpuckena 60 C2
38638 Independence 150 E1
38751 Indianola⊙ 8,221 C4
†38652 Ingomar 150 F2
38753 Inverness 1,034 C4
38754 Isola 834 C4
38941 Itta Bena 2,904 D4
38852 Iuka⊙ 2,846 H1
†38865 Jacinto 65 H1
*39201 Jackson (cap.)⊙ 202,895 D6
Jackson‡ 320,425 D6
39641 Jayess 200 D8
38639 Jonestown 1,231 D2
†38829 Jumpertown 472 G1
†38924 Keirn 3 D4
†39364 Kewanee 250 H6
39747 Kilmichael 906 E4
39556 Kiln 800 F10
†39661 Knoxville 65 B8
39643 Kokomo 250 E8
†39740 Kolola Springs 100 H3
39090 Kosciusko⊙ 7,415 E4
38834 Kossuth 190 G1
38640 Lafayette Springs 80 F2
39092 Lake 524 F6
38641 Lake Cormorant 300 D1
39558 Lakeshore 550 F10
38642 Lamar 200 F1
38643 Lambert 1,624 D2
38755 Lamont 400 B3
39335 Lauderdale 600 G5
39440 Laurel⊙ 21,897 F7
39336 Lawrence 250 F6
39450 Leaf 250 G8
39451 Leakesville⊙ 1,120 G8
39093 Learned 113 C6
38756 Leland 6,667 C4
39094 Lena 231 E5
†39667 Lexie 40 D8
39095 Lexington⊙ 2,628 D4
39645 Liberty⊙ 669 C8
39337 Little Rock 70 F5
39560 Long Beach 7,967 F10
†39759 Longview 800 G4
39096 Lorman 350 B7
39338 Louin 338 F6
39097 Louise 400 C5
39339 Louisville⊙ 7,323 G4
†38632 Love 50 D1

AREA 47,689 sq. mi. (123,515 sq. km.)
POPULATION 2,520,638
CAPITAL Jackson
LARGEST CITY Jackson
HIGHEST POINT Woodall Mtn. 806 ft. (246 m.)
SETTLED IN 1716
ADMITTED TO UNION December 10, 1817
POPULAR NAME Magnolia State
STATE FLOWER Magnolia
STATE BIRD Mockingbird

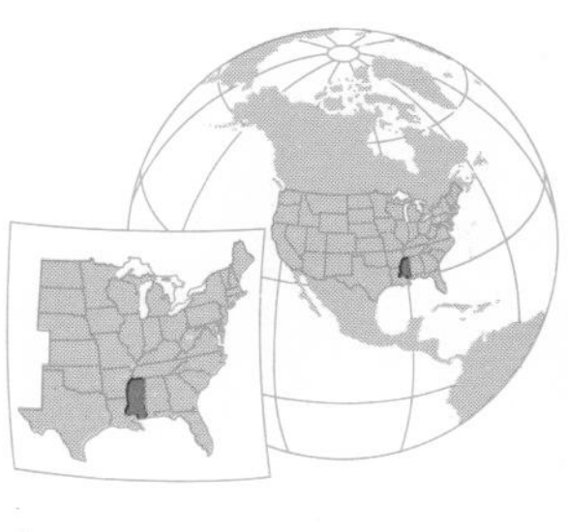

Topography

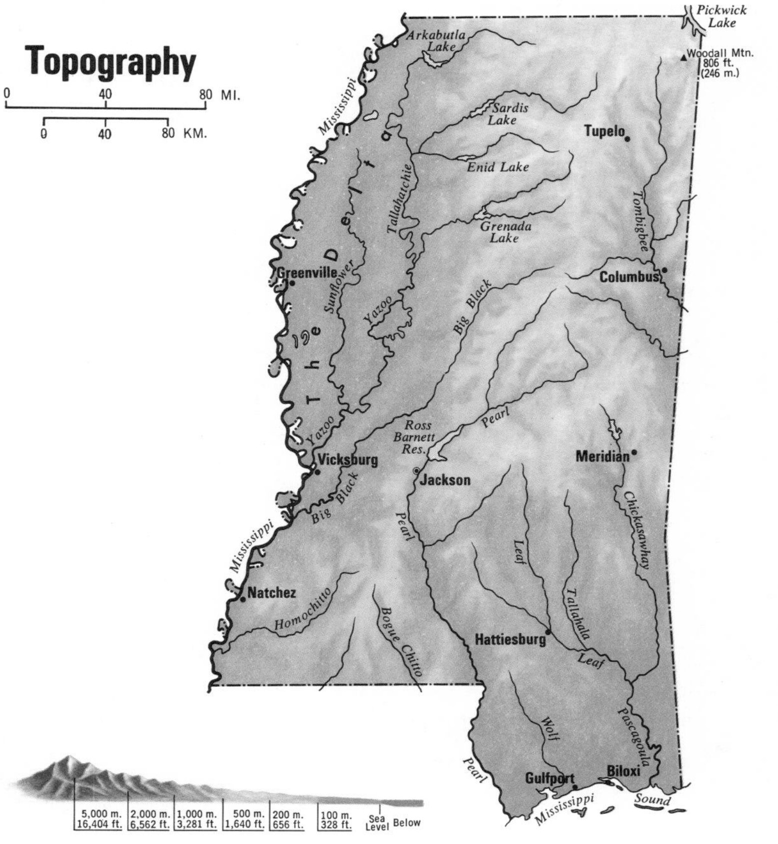

39452 Lucedale⊙ 2,429 G9
39646 Lucien 75 C7
39098 Ludlow 350 E5
38644 Lula 394 C2
39455 Lumberton 2,217 E8
†39501 Lyman 500 F10
†39739 Lynn Creek 20 G4
38645 Lyon 531 D2
39750 Maben 855 F3
39341 Macon⊙ 2,396 G4
39109 Madden 450 F5
39110 Madison 2,241 D6
39111 Magee 3,497 E7
39652 Magnolia⊙ 2,461 D8
†38769 Malvina 100 C3
38855 Mantachie 732 H2
39751 Mantee 158 F3
38856 Marietta 298 H2
39342 Marion 771 G6
38646 Marks⊙ 2,260 D2
†39083 Martinsville 30 D7
†39051 Marydell 99 F5
39752 Mathiston 632 F3
38758 Mattson 200 C2
†39458 Maxie 233 F9
39113 Mayersville⊙ 378 B5
39753 Mayhew 150 G4
39107 McAdams 350 E4
†39144 McBride 2 C7
39647 McCall Creek 250 C7
38943 McCarley 250 E3
39648 McComb 12,331 D8
38854 McCondy 150 G3
39108 McCool 203 F4
39561 McHenry 660 F9
39456 McLain 688 G8
39457 McNeill 800 E9
39653 Meadville⊙ 575 C8
39114 Mendenhall⊙ 2,533 E7
39301 Meridian⊙ 46,577 G6
38759 Merigold 574 C3
†39667 Mesa 30 D8
38760 Metcalfe 952 B4
38647 Michigan City 350 F1
39115 Midnight 500 C4
38648 Mineral Wells 250 E1
38944 Minter City 150 D3
39762 Mississippi State G4
39116 Mize 363 E7
38945 Money 350 D3
39654 Monticello⊙ 1,834 D7
39754 Montpelier 175 G3
†39338 Montrose 120 F6
38857 Mooreville 200 G2
38761 Moorhead 2,358 C4
38946 Morgan City 319 D4
39484 Morgantown 325 E8
†39120 Morgantown 3,445 B7
39117 Morton 3,303 E6
†39328 Moscow 30 G5
39459 Moselle 525 F8
39460 Moss 65 F7
39563 Moss Point 18,998 G10
38762 Mound Bayou 2,917 C3
†39474 Mount Carmel 30 E7
39119 Mount Olive 993 E7
38649 Mount Pleasant 250 E1
38650 Myrtle 402 F1
39120 Natchez⊙ 22,015 B7
39461 Neely 270 G8
38651 Nesbit 366 D1
39365 Neshoba 250 F5
38858 Nettleton 1,911 G2
38652 New Albany⊙ 7,072 G2
39462 New Augusta⊙ 589 F8
39140 Newhebron 470 D7
38850 New Houlka (Houlka) 710 G2
38859 New Site 100 H1
39345 Newton 3,708 F6
39463 Nicholson 400 E10
38763 Nitta Yuma 150 C4
†39629 Norfield 75 C8
38947 North Carrollton 859 E3
39346 Noxapater 516 F5
38948 Oakland 540 E2
†39154 Oakley 133 D6
39656 Oak Vale E8
39564 Ocean Springs 14,504 G10
39141 Ofahoma 350 E5
38860 Okolona⊙ 3,409 G2
38654 Olive Branch 2,067 E1
†39482 Oloh 93 E8
†39654 Oma 200 D7
†39501 Orange Grove 13,476 H10
39657 Osyka 581 D8
39464 Ovett 600 F8
38655 Oxford⊙ 9,882 F2
38764 Pace 519 C3
39347 Pachuta 256 G6
38861 Paden 119 H1
†39401 Palmers Crossing 2,765 F8
38765 Panther Burn 300 C4
38738 Parchman 200 D3
38949 Paris 253 F2
39567 Pascagoula⊙ 29,318 G10
Pascagoula-Moss Point‡ 118,015 G10
39571 Pass Christian 5,014 F10
39144 Pattison 540 C7
39348 Paulding⊙ 630 F6
39349 Paulette 230 H4
†38920 Paynes 100 D3
39028 Pearl 18,580 D6
39572 Pearlington 500 E10
39145 Pelahatchie 1,445 E6
39573 Perkinston 950 F9
†38746 Perthshire 25 C3
39465 Petal 8,476 F8
39755 Pheba 280 G3
39350 Philadelphia⊙ 6,434 F5
38950 Philipp 975 D3
†39476 Piave 150 G8
39466 Picayune 10,361 E9
39146 Pickens 1,386 E5
39148 Piney Woods 450 D6
39149 Pinola E7

(continued on following page)

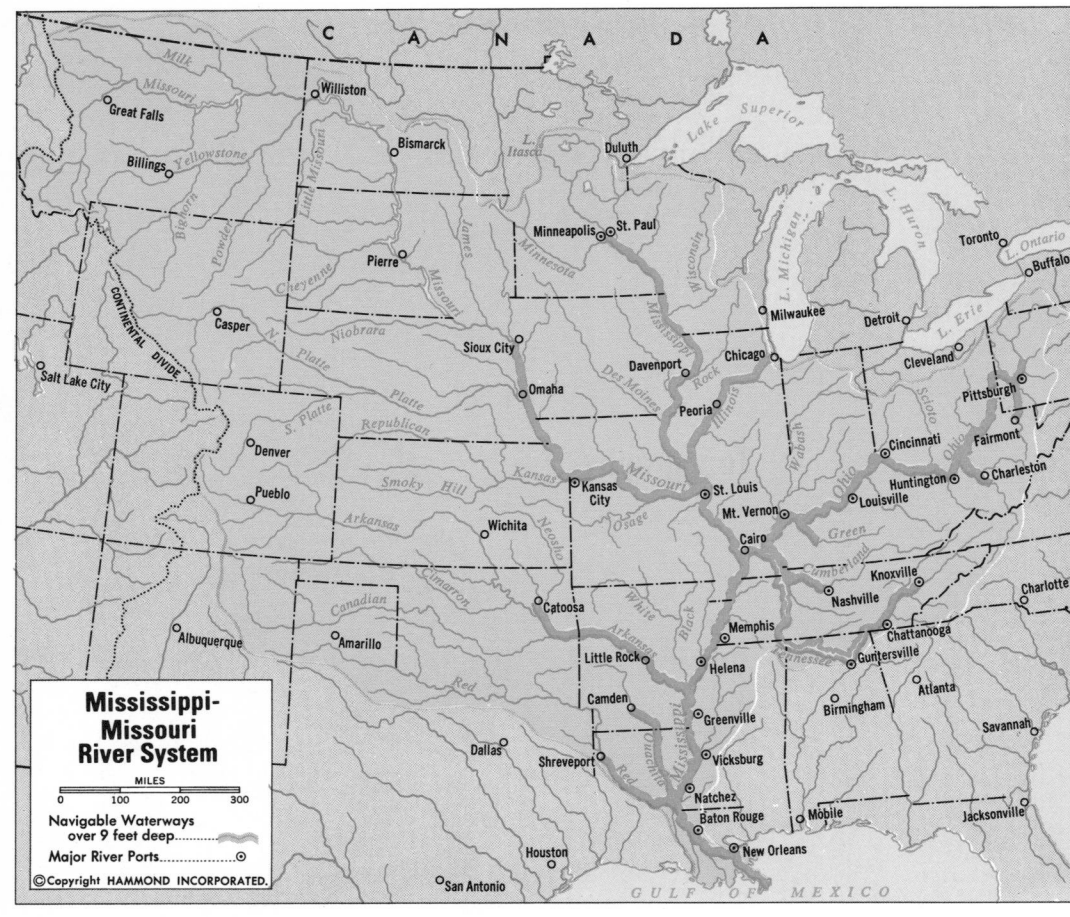

Mississippi-Missouri River System

MILES
0   100   200   300

Navigable Waterways over 9 feet deep..........
Major River Ports..........⊙
©Copyright HAMMOND INCORPORATED.

Agriculture, Industry and Resources

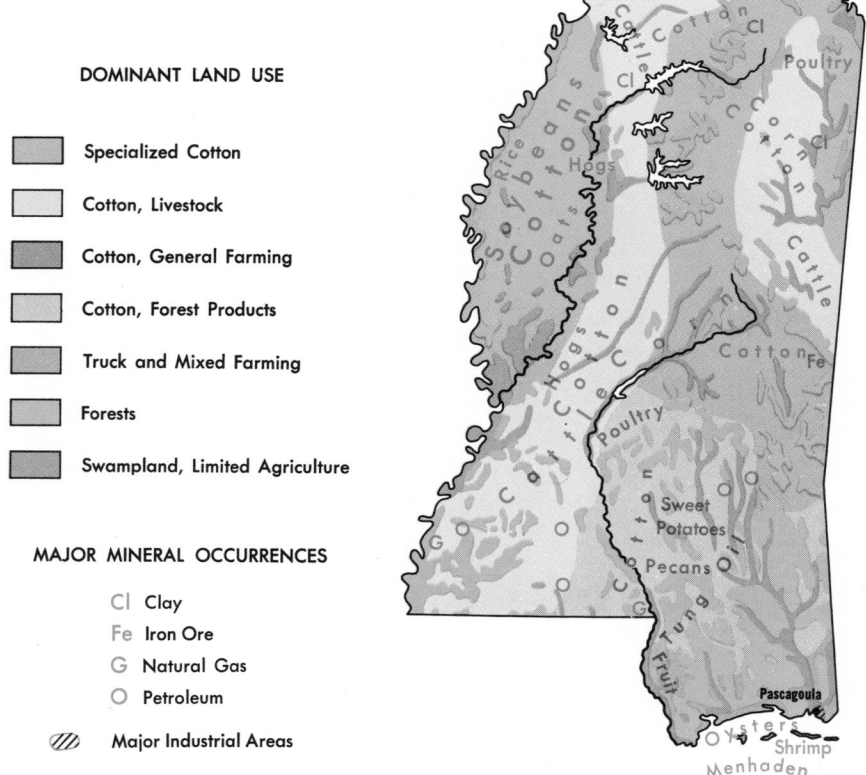

DOMINANT LAND USE

▨	Specialized Cotton
▧	Cotton, Livestock
▨	Cotton, General Farming
▨	Cotton, Forest Products
▨	Truck and Mixed Farming
▨	Forests
▨	Swampland, Limited Agriculture

MAJOR MINERAL OCCURRENCES

Cl Clay
Fe Iron Ore
G   Natural Gas
O   Petroleum
▨   Major Industrial Areas

38951 Pittsboro⊙ 269 ....F3
38862 Plantersville 920 ....G2
38657 Pleasant Grove 100 ....D2
†38651 Pleasant Hill 400 ....E1
39072 Pocahontas 80 ....D6
39118 Polkville 129 ....E6
38863 Pontotoc⊙ 4,723 ....G2
38568 Pope 208 ....E2
39470 Poplarville⊙ 2,562 ....E9
39352 Porterville 150 ....G5
39150 Port Gibson⊙ 2,371 ....B7
38659 Potts Camp 525 ....F1
39756 Prairie G3
39353 Prairie Point 150 ....H4
39474 Prentiss⊙ 1,465 ....E7
39354 Preston 500 ....G5
†39666 Pricedale 400 ....D8
†38676 Prichard 50 ....D1
39151 Puckett 279 ....E6
39152 Pulaski 108 ....E6
39475 Purvis⊙ 2,256 ....F8
39647 Quentin 40 ....C8
39355 Quitman⊙ 2,632 ....G6
39153 Raleigh⊙ 998 ....F6
38864 Randolph F2
39154 Raymond⊙ 1,967 ....D6
38661 Red Banks 350 ....F1
†39096 Red Lick 100 ....B7
39156 Redwood 80 ....C6
39757 Reform 100 ....F4
38767 Rena Lara 350 ....C2
†39051 Renfroe 32 ....F5
†38732 Renova 659 ....C3
38662 Rich 72 ....D2
†39218 Richland 3,955 ....D6
39476 Richton 1,205 ....G8
39157 Ridgeland 5,461 ....D6
38865 Rienzi 423 ....G1
38663 Ripley⊙ 4,271 ....G1
38664 Robinsonville 285 ....D1
†39083 Rockport 30 ....D7
†39096 Rodney 100 ....B7
39159 Rolling Fork⊙ 2,590 ....C5
38768 Rome C3
38769 Rosedale⊙ 2,793 ....B3
39356 Rose Hill 500 ....F6
†39633 Rosetta 120 ....B8
39661 Roxie 591 ....B8
38771 Ruleville 3,332 ....D3
†39108 Rural Hill 25 ....E4
†39150 Russum 200 ....B7
39662 Ruth 400 ....D8
39160 Sallis 211 ....E4
38866 Saltillo 1,271 ....G2
39112 Sanatorium 400 ....E7
39477 Sandersville 800 ....F7
39161 Sandhill 100 ....E5
39478 Sandy Hook 70 ....E8
*39479 Sanford 150 ....F8
38665 Sarah 150 ....D1
38666 Sardis⊙ 2,278 ....D1
38867 Sarepta 120 ....F2
39162 Satartia 73 ....C5
39574 Saucier 100 ....F9
38667 Savage 100 ....D1
38952 Schlater 429 ....D3
38953 Scobey 100 ....E3
39358 Scooba 511 ....G5
38772 Scott 400 ....B3
39359 Sebastopol 314 ....F5
39479 Seminary 327 ....E7
38668 Senatobia⊙ 5,013 ....E1
39758 Sessums 150 ....G4
38868 Shannon 680 ....G2
39163 Sharon 200 ....E5
38773 Shaw 2,461 ....C3
38774 Shelby 2,540 ....C3
38669 Sherard 150 ....C2
38869 Sherman 499 ....G2
39164 Shivers 100 ....E7
39360 Shubuta 626 ....G7
39361 Shuqualak 554 ....G5
39165 Sibley 350 ....B8
38954 Sidon 450 ....D4
39166 Silver City 378 ....C4
39663 Silver Creek 272 ....D7
38775 Skene 250 ....C3
38955 Slate Spring 102 ....F3
38670 Sledge 699 ....D2
39664 Smithdale 200 ....C8
38870 Smithville 866 ....H2
39665 Sontag 200 ....D7
39480 Soso 434 ....F7
38671 Southaven 16,071 ....E1
39167 Star 600 ....D6
39759 Starkville⊙ 15,169 ....G4
39362 State Line 484 ....G8
39766 Steens 125 ....H3
39767 Stewart 350 ....F4
38776 Stoneville 250 ....C4
39363 Stonewall 1,345 ....G6
38672 Stovall 50 ....C2
†38665 Strayhorn 275 ....D1
39481 Stringer 350 ....F7
38777 Stringtown 300 ....C3
39769 Sturgis 269 ....G4
39666 Summit 1,753 ....D8
38957 Sumner⊙ 452 ....C3
39482 Sumrall 1,197 ....E8
38778 Sunflower 1,027 ....C3
38958 Swan Lake 325 ....D3
38959 Swiftown 320 ....D4
39153 Sylvarena 102 ....F6
38673 Taylor 301 ....E2
39168 Taylorsville 1,387 ....F7
39769 Terry 655 ....D6
38871 Thaxton 404 ....F2
39171 Thomastown 400 ....E5
†39073 Thomasville 50 ....E6
39172 Thornton 135 ....D4
†38829 Thrasher 100 ....G1
38960 Tie Plant 500 ....E3
38961 Tillatoba 106 ....E3
†39150 Tillman 65 ....C7
38674 Tiplersville 100 ....G1
38962 Tippo 200 ....D3

38873 Tishomingo 387 ....H1
38874 Toccopola 184 ....F2
39770 Tomnolen 200 ....F4
39364 Toomsuba 500 ....G6
39174 Tougaloo 800 ....D6
38757 Tralake 200 ....C4
38875 Trebloc 100 ....G3
38876 Tremont 379 ....H2
38779 Tribbett 100 ....C4
38675 Tula 140 ....F2
38676 Tunica⊙ 1,361 ....D1
38801 Tupelo⊙ 23,905 ....G2
38963 Tutwiler 1,174 ....D2
39667 Tylertown⊙ 1,976 ....D8
39365 Union 1,931 ....F5
39668 Union Church 75 ....C7
39175 Utica 865 ....C6
39175 Utica Junior College 40 ....C6
39177 Vaiden⊙ 924 ....E4
39177 Valley Park 400 ....C5
39178 Value 327 ....D6
38964 Vance 200 ....D2
†39564 Vancleave 1,330 ....G9
38851 Van Vleet 400 ....G3
38878 Vardaman 1,009 ....F3
39179 Vaughan 210 ....D5
38879 Verona 2,497 ....G2
39180 Vicksburg⊙ 25,434 ....C6
38679 Victoria 800 ....E1
39366 Vossburg 300 ....F7
†39567 Wade 800 ....G9
38780 Wahalak 92 ....G5
38680 Walls 50 ....D1
38683 Walnut 513 ....G1
39189 Walnut Grove 439 ....F5
39771 Walthall⊙ 206 ....F3
39190 Washington 250 ....B7
38685 Waterford 400 ....E1
38965 Water Valley⊙ 4,147 ....E2
39576 Waveland 4,186 ....F10
39367 Waynesboro⊙ 5,349 ....G7
38780 Wayside 500 ....C4
39114 Weathersby D7
38966 Webb 782 ....D3
39772 Weir 553 ....F4
†38834 Wenasoga 175 ....G1
39191 Wesson 1,313 ....D7
39192 West 253 ....E4
†39501 West Gulfport (North Gulfport) 6,660 ....F10
39773 West Point⊙ 8,811 ....G3
38880 Wheeler 600 ....G1
39193 Whitfield 900 ....E6
39577 Wiggins⊙ 3,205 ....F9
†38659 Winborn 70 ....F1
38967 Winona⊙ 6,177 ....E4
38781 Winstonville 486 ....C3
38782 Winterville 200 ....B4
39776 Woodland 135 ....F3
†39730 Wren 150 ....G3
39669 Woodville⊙ 1,512 ....B8
39194 Yazoo City⊙ 12,092 ....D5
†39090 Zama 100 ....F5

OTHER FEATURES

Amite (riv.) C9
Arkabutla (lake) D1
Big Black (riv.) C6
Black (creek) F8
Bogue Chitto (riv.) D8
Bogue Homo (lake) E7
Bowie (creek) E7
Brices Cross Roads Nat'l Battlefield Site G2
Buttahatchee (riv.) H3
Cat (isl.) F10
Catalpa (creek) E7
Chickasaw Village, Natchez Trace Pkwy. G2
Chickasawhay (riv.) G7
Coldwater (riv.) D1
Columbus A.F.B. 3,650 ....H3
Deer (creek) C4
Enid (lake) E2
Grenada (lake) E3
Gulf Islands Nat'l Seashore G10
Homochitto (riv.) B8
Horn (isl.) G10
Keesler A.F.B. G10
Leaf (riv.) F8
Little Tallahatchie (riv.) D2
Meridian Naval Air Sta. G5
Mississippi (riv.) A8
Mississippi (sound) G10
Noxubee (riv.) G4
Okatibbee (lake) G5
Pascagoula (riv.) G9
Pearl (riv.) D8
Petit Bois (isl.) H10
Pickwick (lake) H1
Pierre (bayou) C7
Ross Barnett (res.) D6
Round (isl.) G10
Saint Louis (bay) F10
Sardis (lake) E2
Ship (isl.) G10
Skuna (riv.) F2
Strong (riv.) D7
Sucarnoochee (creek) G5
Sunflower (riv.) C5
Tallahaga (creek) F4
Tallahala (creek) F7
Tallahatchie (riv.) D2
Tchula (creek) D4
Tennessee-Tombigbee Waterway H2
Thompson (creek) G8
Tombigbee (riv.) H4
Trim Cane (creek) G3
Tupelo Nat'l Battlefield G2
Vicksburg Nat'l Mil. Park C6
Wolf (riv.) F9
Woodall (mt.) H1
Yalobusha (riv.) E3
Yazoo (riv.) C5
Yockanookany (riv.) E5

⊙County seat.
‡Population of metropolitan area.
† Zip of nearest p.o.   * Multiple zips.

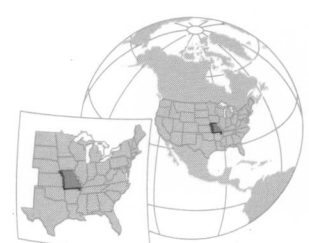

AREA 69,697 sq. mi. (180,515 sq. km.)
POPULATION 4,916,759
CAPITAL Jefferson City
LARGEST CITY St. Louis
HIGHEST POINT Taum Sauk Mtn. 1,772 ft.
(540 m.)
SETTLED IN 1764
ADMITTED TO UNION August 10, 1821
POPULAR NAME Show Me State
STATE FLOWER Hawthorn
STATE BIRD Bluebird

COUNTIES

Adair 24,870 .... G2
Andrew 13,980 .... C3
Atchison 8,605 .... B2
Audrain 26,458 .... J4
Barry 24,408 .... E9
Barton 11,292 .... D7
Bates 15,873 .... D6
Benton 12,183 .... F6
Bollinger 10,301 .... M8
Boone 100,376 .... H4
Buchanan 87,888 .... C3
Butler 37,693 .... M9
Caldwell 8,660 .... E3
Callaway 32,252 .... J5
Camden 20,017 .... G6
Cape Girardeau 58,837 ... N8
Carroll 12,131 .... F4
Carter 5,428 .... L9
Cass 51,029 .... D5
Cedar 11,894 .... E7
Chariton 10,489 .... F3
Christian 22,402 .... F9
Clark 8,493 .... J2
Clay 136,488 .... D4
Clinton 15,916 .... D3
Cole 56,663 .... H6
Cooper 14,643 .... G5
Crawford 18,300 .... K7
Dade 7,383 .... E8
Dallas 12,096 .... F7
Daviess 8,905 .... E3
De Kalb 8,222 .... D3
Dent 14,517 .... J7
Douglas 11,594 .... G9
Dunklin 36,324 .... M10
Franklin 71,233 .... K6
Gasconade 13,181 .... J6
Gentry 7,887 .... D2
Greene 185,302 .... F8
Grundy 11,959 .... E2
Harrison 9,890 .... E2
Henry 19,672 .... E6
Hickory 6,367 .... F7
Holt 6,882 .... B2
Howard 10,008 .... G4
Howell 28,807 .... J9
Iron 11,084 .... L7
Jackson 629,266 .... R5
Jasper 86,958 .... D8
Jefferson 146,183 .... L6
Johnson 39,059 .... E5
Knox 5,508 .... H2
Laclede 24,323 .... G7
Lafayette 29,925 .... E4
Lawrence 28,973 .... E8
Lewis 10,901 .... J2
Lincoln 22,193 .... L4
Linn 15,495 .... F3
Livingston 15,739 .... E3
Macon 16,313 .... G3
Madison 10,725 .... M8
Maries 7,551 .... J6
Marion 28,638 .... J3
McDonald 14,917 .... D9
Mercer 4,685 .... E2
Miller 18,532 .... H6
Mississippi 15,726 .... O9
Moniteau 12,068 .... G5
Monroe 9,716 .... H3
Montgomery 11,537 ..... K5
Morgan 13,807 .... G6
New Madrid 22,945 ...... N9
Newton 40,555 .... D9
Nodaway 21,996 .... C2
Oregon 10,238 .... K9
Osage 12,014 .... J6
Ozark 7,961 .... H9
Pemiscot 24,987 .... N10
Perry 16,784 .... N7
Pettis 36,378 .... F5
Phelps 33,633 .... J7
Pike 17,568 .... K4
Platte 46,341 .... C4
Polk 18,822 .... F7
Pulaski 42,011 .... H7
Putnam 6,092 .... F2
Ralls 8,984 .... J3
Randolph 25,460 .... G3
Ray 21,378 .... E4
Reynolds 7,230 .... L8
Ripley 12,458 .... L9
Saint Charles 144,107 .. M2
Saint Clair 8,622 .... E6
Sainte Genevieve 15,180 . M7
Saint Francois 42,600 .. M7
Saint Louis 973,896 ..... O3
Saint Louis (city county) 453,085 ... P3
Saline 24,919 .... F4
Schuyler 4,979 .... G2
Scotland 5,415 .... H2
Scott 39,647 .... N8
Shannon 7,885 .... K8
Shelby 7,826 .... H3
Stoddard 29,009 .... N9
Stone 15,587 .... F9
Sullivan 7,434 .... F2

Taney 20,467 .... F9
Texas 21,070 .... J8
Vernon 19,806 .... D7
Warren 14,900 .... K5
Washington 17,983 ...... L7
Wayne 11,277 .... L8
Webster 20,414 .... G8
Worth 3,008 .... D2
Wright 16,188 .... H8

CITIES and TOWNS

Zip .... Name/Pop. .... Key

64720 Adrian 1,484 .... D6
64730 Advance 1,054 .... N8
63123 Affton 23,181 .... P4
64401 Agency 419 .... C3
64830 Alba 474 .... D8
64402 Albany⊙ 2,152 .... D2
63430 Alexandria 417 .... K2
64001 Alma 445 .... E4
65606 Alton⊙ 721 .... K9
64421 Amazonia 314 .... C3
64723 Amsterdam 231 .... D6
64831 Anderson 1,237 .... D9
63620 Annapolis 370 .... L8
63820 Anniston 320 .... O9
64724 Appleton City 1,257 ... D6
63821 Arbyrd 704 .... M10
63621 Arcadia 683 .... L7
64725 Archie 753 .... D5
65230 Armstrong 360 .... G4
63010 Arnold 19,141 .... M6
65604 Ash Grove 1,157 ...... E8
65010 Ashland 1,021 .... H5
63530 Atlanta 441 .... H3
63332 Augusta 308 .... L5
65605 Aurora 6,437 .... E9
65231 Auxvasse 858 .... J4
†64501 Country Club
        Village 1,234 .... C3
64437 Craig 379 .... B2
65633 Crane 1,185 .... E9
64739 Creighton 301 .... D6
†63126 Crestwood 12,815 .... O3
63141 Creve Coeur 11,757 ... O2
65452 Crocker 979 .... H7
63019 Crystal City 3,618 .... M6

64633 Carrollton⊙ 4,700 ..... E4
64835 Carterville 1,973 ...... D8
63830 Carthage⊙ 11,104 ..... D8
63830 Caruthersville⊙ 7,958 . N10
65625 Cassville⊙ 2,091 ...... E9
65022 Cedar City 427 .... H5
63436 Center 669 .... J3
65023 Centertown 304 ...... H5
63633 Centerville⊙ 241 ..... L8
65240 Centralia 3,537 .... H4
65024 Chamois 546 .... J5
†63101 Charlack 1,537 .... P2
63834 Charleston⊙ 5,230 ... O9
64733 Chilhowee 349 .... E5
64601 Chillicothe⊙ 9,089 ... E3
63437 Clarence 1,147 .... H3
65243 Clark 304 .... H4
65025 Clarksburg 352 .... G5
64430 Clarksdale 278 .... D3
†63017 Clarkson Valley 1,435 . N3
63336 Clarksville 585 .... K4
63837 Clarkton 1,228 .... M10
†64119 Claycomo 1,671 ...... P5
63105 Clayton⊙ 14,273 ..... P3
64734 Cleveland 485 .... C5
65631 Clever 551 .... F8
64735 Clinton⊙ 8,366 ...... E6
65325 Cole Camp 1,022 .... F6
65201 Columbia⊙ 62,061 ... H5
        Columbia‡ 100,376 .. H5
†63128 Concord 20,896 ...... P4
64020 Concordia 2,129 ..... E5
65632 Conway 601 .... G7
†63101 Cool Valley 2,084 .... P2
63839 Cooter 479 .... N10
64021 Corder 483 .... E4
63846 Essex 545 .... N9
63601 Esther 1,038 .... M7
63025 Eureka 3,862 .... M4
63440 Ewing 400 .... J2
64024 Excelsior Springs 10,424 . R4
65037 Fairfax 835 .... B2
64446 Fairfax 835 .... B2
65647 Exeter 588 .... D9
65648 Fair Grove 863 ...... F8
65649 Fair Play 384 .... E7

†63101 Crystal Lake Park 496 .. O3
65453 Cuba 2,120 .... K6
63339 Curryville 323 .... K4
64439 Dearborn 547 .... C3
64740 Deepwater 475 ...... E6
64440 De Kalb 245 .... C3
†63135 Dellwood 6,200 ..... R2
63744 Delta 524 .... N8
63636 Des Arc 237 .... L8
63601 Desloge 3,481 ...... M7
63020 De Soto 5,993 ...... L6
63131 Des Peres 8,254 .... O3
63841 Dexter 7,043 .... N9
64840 Diamond 766 .... D9
65459 Dixon 1,402 .... H6
63935 Doniphan⊙ 1,921 ... L9
†65550 Doolittle 701 .... J7
63536 Downing 462 .... H2
64742 Drexel 908 .... C6
64841 Duenweg 703 .... D8
64801 Duquesne 1,252 .... D8
64442 Eagleville 364 ...... D2
64443 Easton 313 .... C3
63845 East Prairie 3,713 .. O9
64444 Edgerton 584 .... C3
63537 Edina⊙ 1,520 .... H2
63101 Edmundson 1,374 .. O2
65026 Eldon 4,342 .... G6
64744 El Dorado Springs 3,868 . E7
63638 Ellington 1,215 .... L8
†63011 Ellisville 6,233 .... M3
63937 Elsinore 362 .... L9
63343 Elsberry 1,272 .... L4
63639 Elvins 1,548 .... L7
65466 Eminence⊙ 614 .... K8
63344 Eolia 401 .... L4
64029 Grain Valley 1,327 . S6
64844 Granby 1,908 ...... D9
64030 Grandview 24,502 . P6
64456 Grant City⊙ 1,068 . D2
†63155 Grantwood Village 1,002 . O4
65037 Gravois Mills G6
65661 Greenfield⊙ 1,394 . E8
65332 Green Ridge 488 ... F5
63546 Greentop 538 ...... H2

63345 Farber 503 .... J4
63640 Farmington⊙ 8,270 ... M7
65248 Fayette⊙ 2,983 ...... G4
63026 Fenton 2,417 .... O4
†63135 Ferguson 24,740 .... P2
64163 Ferrelview 447 ...... O4
63028 Festus 7,574 .... M6
64449 Fillmore 265 .... C2
63940 Fisk 450 .... M9
63601 Flat River 4,443 ... M7
64451 Forest City 387 ... B3
65653 Forsyth⊙ 1,010 ... F9
63441 Frankford 443 .... K4
63645 Fredericktown⊙ 4,036 . M7
65035 Freeburg 554 ..... J6
64746 Freeman 485 ..... C5
†63101 Frontenac 3,654 .. O3
65251 Fulton⊙ 11,046 .. J5
65655 Gainesville⊙ 707 . G9
65656 Galena⊙ 423 ..... F9
64640 Gallatin⊙ 2,063 . E3
64641 Galt 323 .... F2
63037 Gerald 921 .... K6
63848 Gideon 1,240 .... N10
64642 Gilman City 414 . D2
65254 Glasgow 1,336 .. G4
†64068 Glenaire 541 .... R5
63122 Glendale 6,035 .. P3
64748 Golden City 900 . D8
63843 Goodman 1,030 . C9
63543 Gorin H2
64454 Gower 1,276 ..... C3

63944 Greenville⊙ 393 .... M8
64034 Greenwood 1,315 ... R6
64643 Hale 529 .... F3
65255 Hallsville 624 ...... H4
64644 Hamilton 1,582 .... E3
†63101 Hanley Hills 2,439 . P2
63401 Hannibal 18,811 .. K3
64035 Hardin 688 .... E4
64701 Harrisonville⊙ 6,372 . D5
65667 Hartville⊙ 576 .... G8
63945 Harviell M9
63349 Hawk Point 386 .. K5
63851 Hayti 3,964 .... N10
†63851 Hayti Heights 1,023 . N10
†63736 Haywood City 425 . N9
*63042 Hazelwood 12,935 . P2
64036 Henrietta 424 ...... E4
63048 Herculaneum 2,293 . M6
65041 Hermann 2,695 ... K5
65668 Hermitage⊙ 384 .. F7
65257 Higbee 817 .... H4
64037 Higginsville 4,595 . E4
63350 High Hill 254 ..... K5
63050 Hillsboro⊙ 1,508 . L6
†63101 Hillsdale 2,247 ... R2
63852 Holcomb 632 ..... N10
64040 Holden 2,195 ..... E5
63853 Holland 295 ...... N10
65672 Hollister 1,439 ... F9
64048 Holt 276 .... D4
65043 Holts Summit 2,540 . H6
†63879 Homestown 306 .. N10
64461 Hopkins 634 ...... C2
63855 Hornersville 704 .. M10
65483 Houston⊙ 2,157 .. J8
65333 Houstonia 327 ... F5
64152 Houston Lake 280 . O5
†63869 Howardville 536 .. N9
65674 Humansville 907 . E7
64752 Hume 315 .... C6
63443 Hunnewell 235 ... J3
†63101 Huntleigh 428 .... O3
65259 Huntsville⊙ 1,657 . H4
63547 Hurdland 227 .... H2
65486 Iberia 852 .... H6
63754 Illmo 1,368 .... O8

(continued on following page)

Agriculture, Industry and Resources

DOMINANT LAND USE

- Cattle Feed, Hogs
- Livestock, Cash Grain, Dairy
- Pasture Livestock
- Specialized Cotton
- General Farming, Dairy, Livestock, Poultry
- General Farming, Livestock, Truck Farming, Cotton
- Fruit and Mixed Farming
- Forests
- Urban Areas

MAJOR MINERAL OCCURRENCES

Ag	Silver	G	Natural Gas
Ba	Barite	Ls	Limestone
C	Coal	Mr	Marble
Cl	Clay	Pb	Lead
Cu	Copper	Zn	Zinc
Fe	Iron Ore		

⚡ Water Power   ▨ Major Industrial Areas

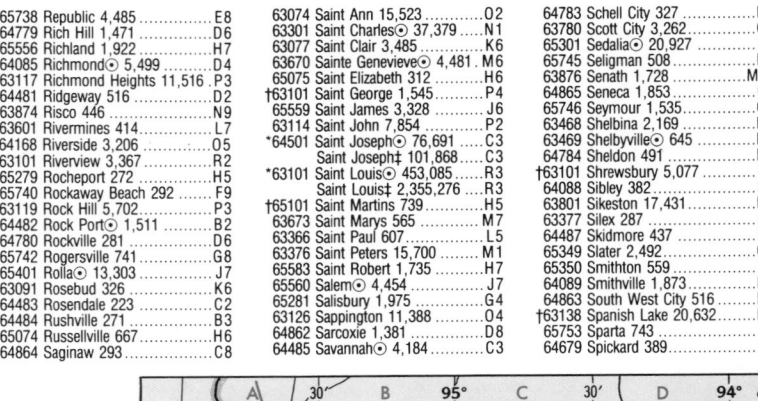

*64050 Independence⊙ 111,806...R5	63762 Lutesville 865...M8	65714 Nixa 2,662...F8	65738 Republic 4,485...E8
63648 Irondale 349...L7	63552 Macon⊙ 5,680...H3	64854 Noel 1,161...D9	64779 Rich Hill 1,471...D6
†64801 Iron Gates 314...C8	65263 Madison 656...H4	64668 Norborne 931...E4	65556 Richland 1,922...H7
63650 Ironton 1,743...L7	64466 Maitland 415...B2	63121 Normandy 5,174...P3	64085 Richmond⊙ 5,499...D4
63755 Jackson⊙ 7,827...N8	63863 Malden 6,096...M9	64116 North Kansas City 4,507...P5	63117 Richmond Heights 11,516...P3
64648 Jamesport 651...E3	65339 Malta Bend 292...F4	†64152 Northmoor 506...P5	64481 Ridgeway 516...D2
65046 Jamestown 317...G5	63011 Manchester 6,191...O3	65717 Norwood 391...H8	63874 Risco 446...N9
64755 Jasper 1,012...D8	65704 Mansfield 1,423...G8	63559 Novinger 626...G2	†63601 Rivermines 414...L7
65101 Jefferson City (cap.)⊙ 33,619...H5	63143 Maplewood 10,960...P3	64075 Oak Grove 4,067...S6	64168 Riverside 3,206...O5
63136 Jennings 17,026...R2	63764 Marble Hill⊙ 601...N8	†63080 Oak Grove 386...K6	†63101 Riverview 3,367...R2
63351 Jonesburg 614...K5	65705 Marionville 1,920...E8	†63101 Oakland 1,728...P3	65279 Rocheport 1,090...H5
64801 Joplin 39,023...C8	†63101 Marlborough 2,012...P3	63769 Oak Ridge 252...N7	65740 Rockaway Beach 292...F9
Joplin‡ 127,513...C8	63655 Marquand 397...M8	†64116 Oakwood 497...P5	†63119 Rock Hill 5,702...P3
†63645 Junction City 238...M7	65340 Marshall⊙ 12,781...F4	63401 Oakwood 227...P5	64482 Rock Port 1,511...B2
63445 Kahoka⊙ 2,101...J2	65706 Marshfield⊙ 3,871...G8	64076 Odessa 3,088...E5	64780 Rockville 281...D6
*64101 Kansas City 448,159...P5	63866 Marston 742...N9	63369 Old Monroe 272...L5	65742 Rogersville 741...G8
Kansas City‡ 1,327,020...P5	63357 Marthasville 543...L5	63124 Olivette 7,985...O2	65401 Rolla⊙ 13,303...J7
64060 Kearney 1,433...D4	65264 Martinsburg 309...J4	63050 Olympian Village 774...M6	63091 Rosebud 326...K6
63758 Kelso 455...O8	63043 Maryland Heights 5,676...O2	63771 Oran 1,266...N8	64483 Rosendale 223...C2
63857 Kennett⊙ 10,145...M10	64468 Maryville⊙ 9,558...C2	64473 Oregon⊙ 901...B2	64484 Rushville 271...B3
65261 Keytesville⊙ 689...G4	64469 Maysville⊙ 1,187...D3	64855 Oronogo 525...D8	65074 Russellville 667...H6
64649 Kidder 265...D3	64071 Mayview 291...E4	64077 Orrick 922...D4	64864 Saginaw 293...C8
65686 Kimberling City 1,285...F9	64659 Meadville 416...F3	65065 Osage Beach 1,992...G6	63074 Saint Ann 15,523...O2
64463 King City 1,063...D2	63555 Memphis⊙ 2,105...H2	64474 Osborn 381...D3	63301 Saint Charles⊙ 37,379...N1
64650 Kingston⊙ 280...E3	64660 Mendon 252...F3	65348 Osceola⊙ 841...E6	63077 Saint Clair 3,485...K6
64061 Kingsville 365...D5	64661 Mercer 442...F2	65348 Otterville 472...G5	63670 Sainte Genevieve⊙ 4,481...M6
63140 Kinloch 4,455...P2	65058 Meta 336...H6	63114 Overland 19,620...O2	65075 Saint Elizabeth 312...H6
63501 Kirksville⊙ 17,167...H2	65265 Mexico⊙ 12,276...J4	65066 Owensville 2,241...K6	†63101 Saint George 1,545...P3
63122 Kirkwood 27,987...O3	63359 Middletown 268...J4	65721 Ozark⊙ 2,980...F8	63114 Saint John 7,854...P2
65336 Knob Noster 2,040...F5	63556 Milan⊙ 1,947...F2	†63101 Pagedale 4,542...P2	*64501 Saint Joseph⊙ 76,691...C3
63446 Knox City 281...H2	65707 Miller 795...E8	63461 Palmyra⊙ 3,469...J3	Saint Joseph‡ 101,868...C3
63447 La Belle 845...J2	63952 Mill Spring 257...L8	65275 Paris⊙ 1,598...J4	*63101 Saint Louis⊙ 453,085...R3
64651 Laclede 445...F3	64769 Mindenmines 318...C8	64152 Parkville 1,997...O5	Saint Louis‡ 2,355,276...R3
63352 Laddonia 726...J4	†63801 Miner 1,182...N9	64130 Parkway 254...L6	†65101 Saint Martins 739...H5
†63124 Ladue 9,376...P3	64072 Missouri City 343...R5	63870 Parma 1,081...N9	63673 Saint Marys 565...M7
63448 La Grange 1,217...K2	65270 Moberly 13,418...G4	64670 Pattonsburg 502...D2	63366 Saint Paul 607...L5
64063 Lake Lotawana 1,875...R6	65059 Mokane 293...J5	64078 Peculiar 1,571...D5	63376 Saint Peters 15,700...M1
65049 Lake Ozark 427...G6	†63101 Moline Acres 2,774...R2	63462 Perry 836...J4	65583 Saint Robert 1,735...H7
†63336 Lake Saint Louis 3,843...L5	65708 Monett 6,148...E9	63775 Perryville⊙ 7,343...N7	65560 Salem⊙ 4,454...J7
†63101 Lakeshire 1,593...P4	63456 Monroe City 2,557...J3	63070 Pevely 2,732...M6	65281 Salisbury 1,975...G4
†64015 Lake Tapawingo 925...R6	63361 Montgomery City⊙ 2,101...K5	64476 Pickering 215...C2	63126 Sappington 11,388...O4
†64152 Lake Waukomis 1,050...P5	63457 Monticello⊙ 134...J2	63957 Piedmont 2,359...L8	64862 Sarcoxie 1,381...D8
64034 Lake Winnebago 681...R6	64770 Montrose 498...E6	65723 Pierce City 1,391...E8	64485 Savannah⊙ 4,184...C3
64759 Lamar⊙ 4,053...D8	63868 Morehouse 1,220...N9	65276 Pilot Grove 745...G5	
65337 La Monte 1,054...F5	63767 Morley 745...N8	63663 Pilot Knob 722...L7	
64847 Lanagan 440...C9	65710 Morrisville 331...F8	63120 Pine Lawn 6,662...R2	
63548 Lancaster⊙ 855...H1	64073 Mosby 284...R4	64856 Pineville⊙ 504...D9	
63549 La Plata 1,423...H2	63362 Moscow Mills 484...K5	64079 Platte City 2,114...C4	
64652 Laredo 340...E2	64760 Mound City 1,447...B2	†64152 Platte Woods 467...O5	
64760 Latour 84...D5	64062 Lawson 1,688...D4	64477 Plattsburg⊙ 2,095...D3	
64062 Lawson 1,688...D4	63653 Leadwood 1,371...L7	64080 Pleasant Hill 3,301...D5	
†63640 Leadington 238...M7	65711 Mountain Grove 3,974...H8	65725 Pleasant Hope 354...F8	
63653 Leadwood 1,371...L7	65548 Mountain View 1,664...J8	64836 Pleasant Valley 1,545...R5	
65535 Leasburg 304...K6	64665 Mount Moriah 162...E2	64671 Polo 583...D3	
65536 Lebanon⊙ 9,507...G7	65712 Mount Vernon⊙ 3,341...E8	63901 Poplar Bluff⊙ 17,139...L9	
64063 Lee's Summit 28,741...R6	†63088 Murphy 8,121...O4	63373 Portage Des Sioux 488...M5	
64761 Leeton 604...E5	64074 Napoleon 214...E4	63873 Portageville 3,470...N10	
63125 Lemay 35,424...R4	63953 Naylor 602...L9	63664 Potosi⊙ 2,528...L7	
64066 Levasy 235...R4	63954 Neelyville 474...M9	65068 Prairie Home 279...G5	
63452 Lewistown 502...J2	65347 Nelson 248...F4	64673 Princeton⊙ 1,264...E2	
64067 Lexington⊙ 5,063...E4	64850 Neosho⊙ 9,493...D9	64857 Purcell 322...D8	
64762 Liberal 701...D7	64772 Nevada⊙ 9,044...D7	64674 Purdin 243...F3	
64068 Liberty⊙ 16,251...R5	65063 New Bloomfield 519...J5	65734 Purdy 928...E9	
65542 Licking 1,272...J8	65550 Newburg 743...J7	63960 Puxico 833...M9	
63862 Lilbourn 1,463...N9	63558 New Cambria 246...G3	63561 Queen City 783...H2	
65338 Lincoln 819...F6	63363 New Florence 731...K5	63961 Qulin 545...M9	
65051 Linn⊙ 1,211...J5	65274 New Franklin 1,228...G4	†64101 Randolph 91...P5	
65052 Linn Creek 242...G6	†63736 New Hamburg...O8	64479 Ravenwood 436...C2	
64653 Linneus⊙ 421...F3	64471 New Hampton 358...D2	65555 Raymondville 388...J8	
65682 Lockwood 971...E8	63068 New Haven 1,541...K5	64083 Raymore 3,154...D5	
64070 Lone Jack 420...S6	63459 New London⊙ 1,161...K3	64133 Raytown 31,759...P6	
63353 Louisiana 4,261...K4	63869 New Madrid⊙ 3,204...O9	65737 Reeds Spring 461...F9	
64763 Lowry City 676...E6	65713 Niangua 376...G8		

64783 Schell City 327...D6	
63780 Scott City 3,262...O8	
65301 Sedalia⊙ 20,927...F5	
65745 Seligman 508...D9	
63876 Senath 1,728...M10	
64865 Seneca 1,853...C9	
65746 Seymour 1,535...G8	
63468 Shelbina 2,169...H3	
63469 Shelbyville⊙ 645...H3	
64784 Sheldon 491...D7	
†63101 Shrewsbury 5,077...P3	
64088 Sibley 382...S5	
63801 Sikeston 17,431...N8	
63377 Silex 287...K4	
64487 Skidmore 437...C2	
65349 Slater 2,492...G5	
63080 Smithton 559...F5	
64089 Smithville 1,873...O4	
64863 South West City 516...D9	
†63138 Spanish Lake 20,632...R1	
65753 Sparta 743...F9	
64679 Spickard 389...F2	

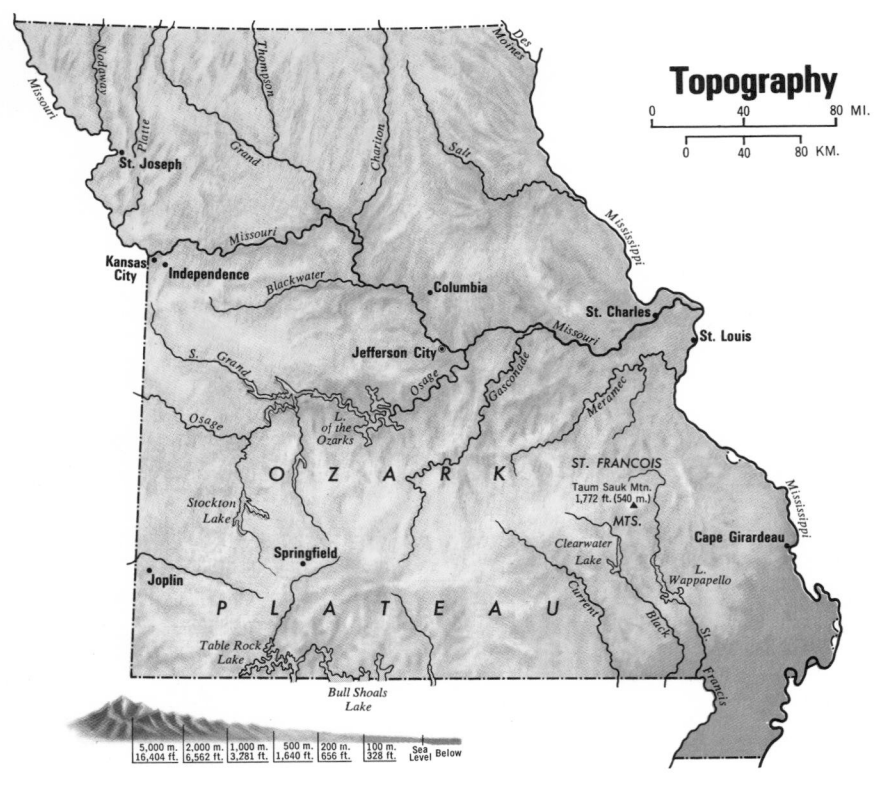

Topography

5,000 m. 16,404 ft. | 2,000 m. 6,562 ft. | 1,000 m. 3,281 ft. | 500 m. 1,640 ft. | 200 m. 656 ft. | 100 m. 328 ft. | Sea Level | Below

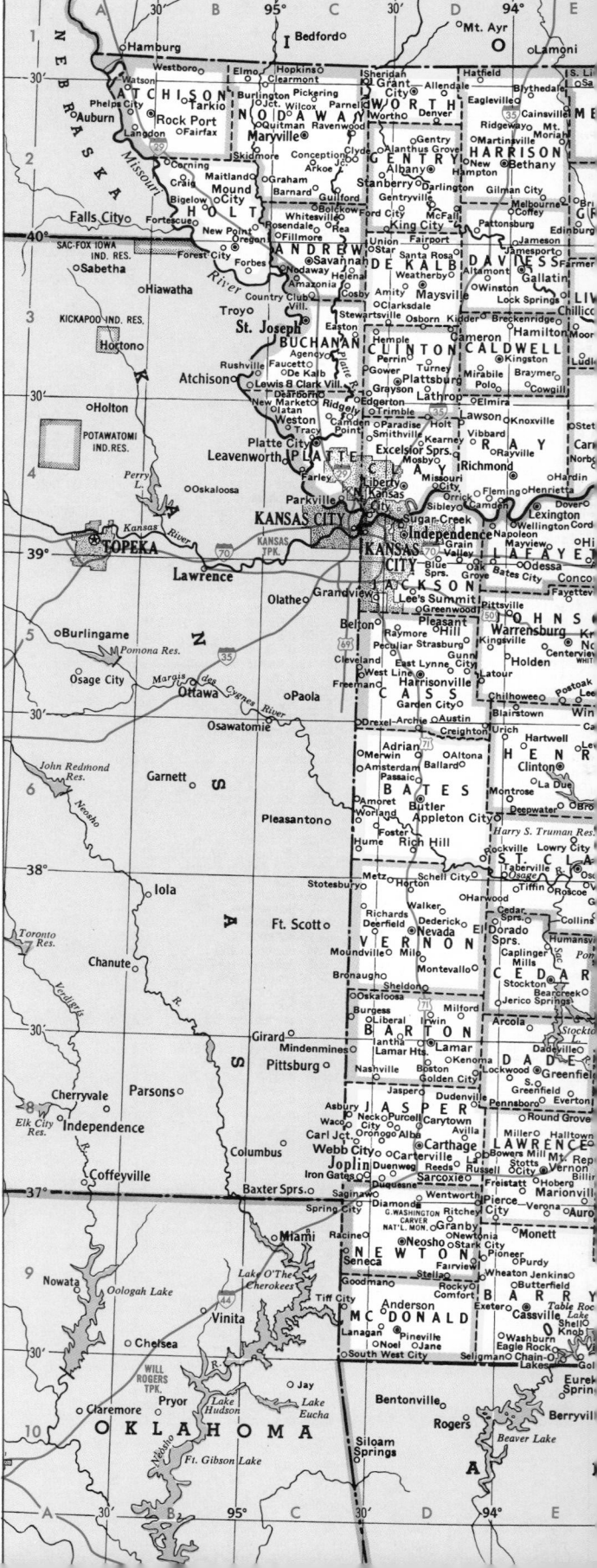

Agriculture, Industry and Resources

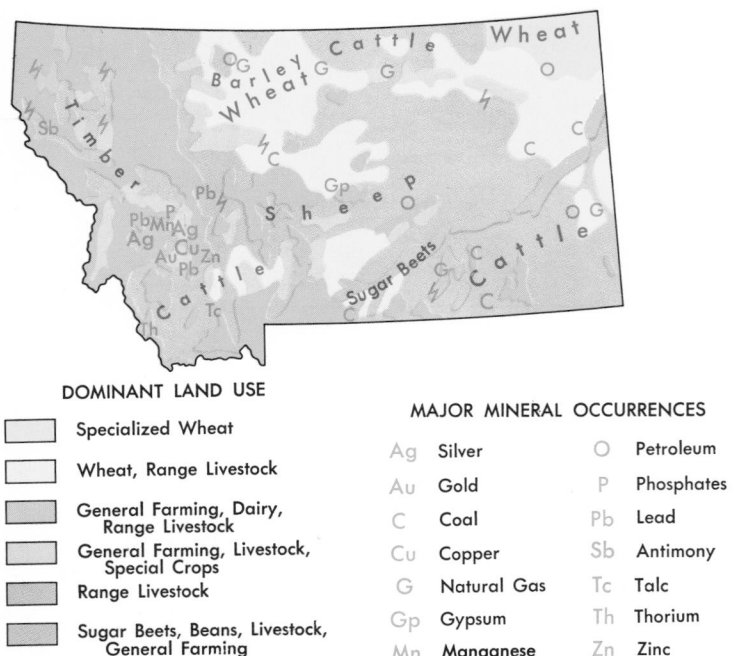

DOMINANT LAND USE

- Specialized Wheat
- Wheat, Range Livestock
- General Farming, Dairy, Range Livestock
- General Farming, Livestock, Special Crops
- Range Livestock
- Sugar Beets, Beans, Livestock, General Farming
- Forests

MAJOR MINERAL OCCURRENCES

Ag	Silver	O	Petroleum
Au	Gold	P	Phosphates
C	Coal	Pb	Lead
Cu	Copper	Sb	Antimony
G	Natural Gas	Tc	Talc
Gp	Gypsum	Th	Thorium
Mn	Manganese	Zn	Zinc

⚡ Water Power

COUNTIES

Beaverhead 8,186 ....C5
Big Horn 11,096 ....J5
Blaine 6,999 ....G2
Broadwater 3,267 ....E4
Carbon 8,099 ....G5
Carter 1,799 ....M5
Cascade 80,696 ....E3
Chouteau 6,092 ....F3
Custer 13,109 ....L4
Daniels 2,835 ....L2
Dawson 11,805 ....M3
Deer Lodge 12,518 ....C5
Fallon 3,763 ....M4
Fergus 13,076 ....G3
Flathead 51,966 ....B2
Gallatin 42,865 ....E5
Garfield 1,656 ....J3
Glacier 10,628 ....C2
Golden Valley 1,026 ....G4
Granite 2,700 ....C4
Hill 17,985 ....F2
Jefferson 7,029 ....D4
Judith Basin 2,646 ....F4
Lake 19,056 ....B3
Lewis and Clark 43,039 ....D3
Liberty 2,329 ....E2
Lincoln 17,752 ....A2
Madison 5,448 ....D5
McCone 2,702 ....L3
Meagher 2,154 ....F4
Mineral 3,675 ....B3
Missoula 76,016 ....C3
Musselshell 4,428 ....H4
Park 12,869 ....F5
Petroleum 655 ....H3
Phillips 5,367 ....J2
Pondera 6,731 ....D2
Powder River 2,520 ....L5
Powell 6,958 ....D4
Prairie 1,836 ....L4
Ravalli 12,493 ....B4
Richland 12,243 ....M3
Roosevelt 10,467 ....L2
Rosebud 9,899 ....K4
Sanders 8,675 ....A3
Sheridan 5,414 ....M2
Silver Bow 38,092 ....D5
Stillwater 5,598 ....G5
Sweet Grass 3,216 ....G5
Teton 6,491 ....D3
Toole 5,559 ....E2
Treasure 981 ....J4
Valley 10,250 ....K2
Wheatland 2,359 ....G4
Wibaux 1,476 ....M4
Yellowstone 108,035 ....H4
Yellowstone Nat'l Park 275 ....F6

CITIES and TOWNS

Zip	Name/Pop.	Key
59001	Absarokee 830	G5
59820	Alberton 368	B3
59710	Alder 120	D5
†59741	Amsterdam 130	E5
59711	Anaconda-Deer Lodge County⊙ 12,518	C4
59312	Angela 50	K4
59211	Antelope 83	M2
59821	Arlee 200	B3
59003	Ashland 600	K5
59410	Augusta 497	D3
59713	Avon 125	D4
59411	Babb 150	C2
59313	Baker⊙ 2,354	M4
59006	Ballantine 380	J5
†59725	Bannack 2	C5
59613	Basin 350	D4
59007	Bearcreek 61	G5
59008	Belfry 300	H5
59714	Belgrade 2,336	E5
59412	Belt 825	E3
59314	Biddle 28	L5
59910	Big Arm 250	B3
59911	Bigfork 1,080	C2
59520	Big Sandy 835	G2
59011	Big Timber⊙ 1,690	G5
*59101	Billings⊙ 66,842	H5
	Billings‡ 108,035	H5
59012	Birney 100	K5
59414	Black Eagle 1,500	E3
59415	Blackfoot 100	D2
59823	Bonner-West Riverside 1,742	C4
59632	Boulder⊙ 1,441	E4
59521	Box Elder 300	F2
59715	Bozeman⊙ 21,645	E5
59416	Brady 450	E2
59014	Bridger 724	H5
59317	Broadus⊙ 712	L5
59015	Broadview 120	H4
59213	Brockton 374	M2
59417	Browning 1,226	C2
59016	Busby 700	J5
59701	Butte-Silver Bow County⊙ 37,205	D5
59720	Cameron 150	D5
59633	Canyon Creek 100	D4
†59347	Cartersville 115	K4
59824	Charlo 250	B3
59522	Chester⊙ 963	E2
59523	Chinook⊙ 1,660	G2
59422	Choteau⊙ 1,798	D3
59215	Circle⊙ 931	L3
59018	Clyde Park 283	F5
†59351	Coalwood 2	L5
59322	Cohagen 12	K3
59323	Colstrip 1,476	K5
59912	Columbia Falls 3,112	B2
59019	Columbus⊙ 1,439	G5
59826	Condon 300	C3
59827	Conner 420	C4
59425	Conrad⊙ 3,074	D2
59020	Cooke City 120	G5
59913	Coram 450	C2
59828	Corvallis 500	C4
59217	Crane 163	M3
59022	Crow Agency 975	J5
59218	Culbertson 887	M2
59024	Custer 300	J4
59427	Cut Bank⊙ 3,688	D2
59829	Darby 581	B4
59914	Dayton 140	B3
59830	De Borgia 300	A3
59025	Decker 150	K5
59722	Deer Lodge⊙ 4,023	D4
59430	Denton 356	G3

Montana

State Capitals	⊛
County Seats	⊙
Major Limited Access Hwys.	—

Scale 1:3,450,000

© Copyright HAMMOND INCORPORATED, Maplewood, N.J.

Topography

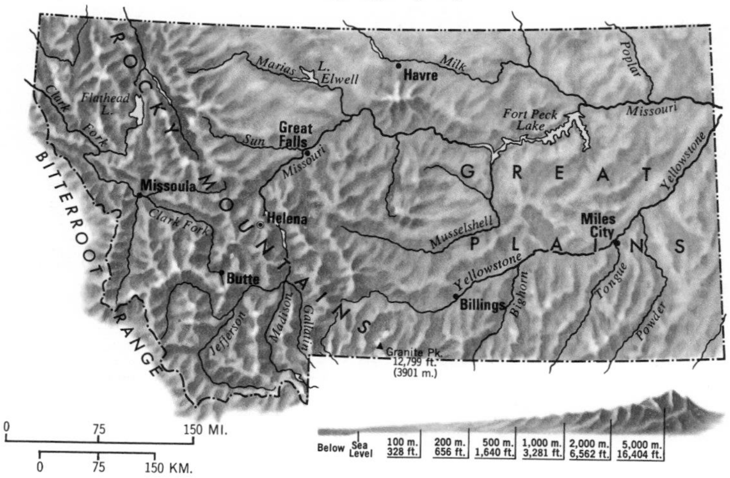

ROCKY MOUNTAINS
BITTERROOT RANGE
GREAT PLAINS
Marias
L. Elwell
Havre
Milk
Poplar
Flathead L.
Great Falls
Sun
Fort Peck Lake
Missouri
Missoula
Clark Fork
Helena
Butte
Musselshell
Miles City
Yellowstone
Billings
Bighorn
Tongue
Powder
Jefferson
Madison
Gallatin
Granite Pk. 12,799 ft. (3901 m.)
0 75 150 MI.
0 75 150 KM.
Below Sea Level
100 m. 328 ft.
200 m. 656 ft.
500 m. 1,640 ft.
1,000 m. 3,281 ft.
2,000 m. 6,562 ft.
5,000 m. 16,404 ft.

AREA 147,046 sq. mi. (380,849 sq. km.)
POPULATION 786,690
CAPITAL Helena
LARGEST CITY Billings
HIGHEST POINT Granite Pk. 12,799 ft. (3901 m.)
SETTLED IN 1809
ADMITTED TO UNION November 8, 1889
POPULAR NAME Treasure State; Big Sky Country
STATE FLOWER Bitterroot
STATE BIRD Western Meadowlark

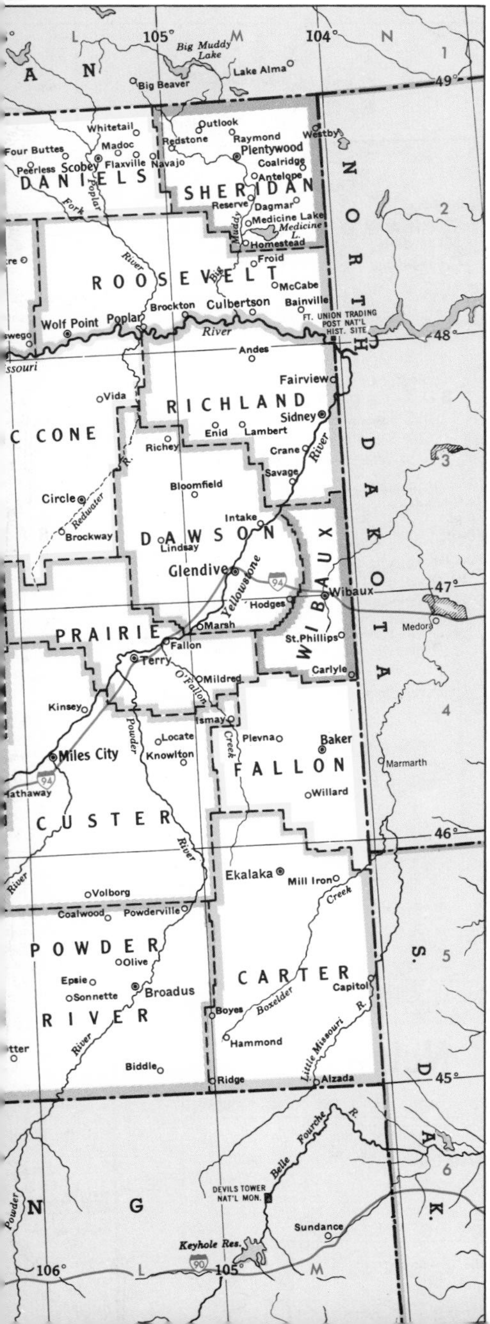

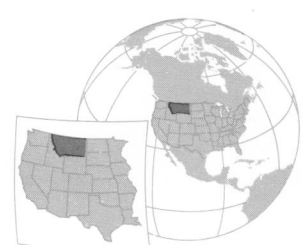

59725 Dillon⊙ 3,976 ..... D5
59727 Divide 275 ..... D5
59831 Dixon 550 ..... B3
59524 Dodson 158 ..... H2
59832 Drummond 414 ..... D4
59432 Dupuyer 105 ..... D2
59433 Dutton 359 ..... E3
59434 East Glacier Park 475 ..... C2
59635 East Helena 1,647 ..... E4
59026 Edgar 220 ..... H5
59324 Ekalaka⊙ 620 ..... M5
59728 Elliston 250 ..... D4
59915 Elmo 250 ..... B3
59729 Ennis 660 ..... E5
59917 Eureka 1,119 ..... B2
59436 Fairfield 650 ..... D3
59221 Fairview 1,366 ..... M3
59326 Fallon 225 ..... L4
59222 Flaxville 142 ..... L2
59833 Florence 700 ..... B4
59441 Forestgrove 100 ..... H3
59327 Forsyth⊙ 2,553 ..... K4
†59526 Fort Belknap 185 ..... H2
59442 Fort Benton⊙ 1,693 ..... F3
59918 Fortine 250 ..... A2
59223 Fort Peck 456 ..... K2
59443 Fort Shaw 200 ..... E3
†59075 Fort Smith 300 ..... J5
59225 Frazer 200 ..... K2
59834 Frenchtown 300 ..... B3
59226 Froid 323 ..... M2
59029 Fromberg 469 ..... H5
59444 Galata 100 ..... E2
59730 Gallatin Gateway 600 ..... E5
59030 Gardiner 600 ..... F5
59731 Garrison 300 ..... D4
59031 Garryowen 200 ..... J5
59446 Geraldine 305 ..... F3
59447 Geyser 125 ..... F3
59525 Gildford 250 ..... F2
59230 Glasgow⊙ 4,455 ..... K2
59330 Glendive⊙ 5,978 ..... M3
59733 Goldcreek 100 ..... D4
59835 Grantsdale 500 ..... B4
59032 Grass Range 139 ..... H3
59401 Great Falls⊙ 56,725 ..... E3
Great Falls‡ 80,696 ..... E3
59836 Greenough 120 ..... C4
59837 Hall 130 ..... C4
59840 Hamilton⊙ 2,661 ..... B4
59034 Hardin⊙ 3,300 ..... J5
59526 Harlem 1,023 ..... H2
59036 Harlowton⊙ 1,181 ..... F4
59735 Harrison 94 ..... E5
59842 Haugan 90 ..... A3
59501 Havre⊙ 10,891 ..... G2
59527 Hays 400 ..... H2
59448 Heart Butte 300 ..... C2
59601 Helena (cap.)⊙ 23,938 ..... E4
59843 Helmville 250 ..... C4
59450 Highwood 150 ..... F3
59528 Hingham 186 ..... F2
59241 Hinsdale 260 ..... K2
59452 Hobson 261 ..... G4
59845 Hot Springs 601 ..... B3
59919 Hungry Horse 700 ..... C2
59037 Huntley 250 ..... H5
59846 Huson 97 ..... B3
59038 Hysham⊙ 449 ..... J4
59530 Inverness 150 ..... F2
59336 Ismay 31 ..... M4
59736 Jackson 210 ..... C5
59638 Jefferson City 162 ..... E4
59041 Joliet 580 ..... G5
59531 Joplin 300 ..... F2
59337 Jordan⊙ 485 ..... J3
59453 Judith Gap 213 ..... G4
59901 Kalispell⊙ 10,648 ..... B2
59454 Kevin 208 ..... D2
59920 Kila 350 ..... B2
59338 Kinsey 100 ..... L4
†59072 Klein 250 ..... H4
59532 Kremlin 304 ..... F2
59922 Lakeside 663 ..... B2
59243 Lambert 203 ..... M3
59043 Lame Deer 460 ..... K5
59044 Laurel 5,481 ..... H5
59046 Lavina 164 ..... H4
59457 Lewistown⊙ 7,104 ..... G3
59923 Libby⊙ 2,748 ..... A2
59739 Lima 272 ..... D6
59639 Lincoln 473 ..... D4
59047 Livingston⊙ 6,994 ..... F5
59050 Lodge Grass 771 ..... J5
†59524 Lodge Pole 292 ..... H2
59847 Lolo 2,418 ..... B4
†59847 Lolo Hot Springs 25 ..... B4
59460 Loma 200 ..... F3
59225 Lustre 25 ..... K2
59538 Malta⊙ 2,367 ..... J2
59741 Manhattan 988 ..... E5
59925 Marion 450 ..... B2
59052 McLeod 150 ..... G5
59247 Medicine Lake 408 ..... M2
59743 Melrose 350 ..... D5
59054 Melstone 238 ..... H4
59055 Melville 100 ..... F4
59301 Miles City⊙ 9,602 ..... L4
59851 Milltown 300 ..... C4
*59801 Missoula⊙ 33,388 ..... C4
59463 Monarch 120 ..... F3
59464 Moore 229 ..... G4
59059 Musselshell 117 ..... H4
59248 Nashua 495 ..... K2
59465 Neihart 91 ..... F4
†59501 North Havre 1,230 ..... G2
59853 Noxon 800 ..... A3
59927 Olney 200 ..... B2
59250 Opheim 210 ..... K2
59252 Outlook 122 ..... M2
59854 Ovando 300 ..... C3
59855 Pablo 500 ..... B3
59856 Paradise 400 ..... B3
59063 Park City 800 ..... H5
59253 Peerless 110 ..... L2
59467 Pendroy 100 ..... D2
59858 Philipsburg⊙ 1,138 ..... C4
59859 Plains 1,116 ..... B3
59254 Plentywood⊙ 2,476 ..... M2
59344 Plevna 191 ..... M4
59860 Polson⊙ 2,798 ..... B3
59064 Pompeys Pillar 300 ..... J5
59747 Pony 130 ..... E5
59255 Poplar 995 ..... L2
59468 Power 159 ..... E3
59929 Proctor 150 ..... B3
59066 Pryor 146 ..... H5
59641 Radersburg 104 ..... E4
59863 Ravalli 150 ..... B3
59068 Red Lodge⊙ 1,896 ..... G5
59069 Reedpoint 160 ..... G5
59258 Reserve 80 ..... M2
59930 Rexford 130 ..... A2
59259 Richey 417 ..... L3
59642 Ringling 102 ..... F4
59070 Roberts 312 ..... G5
59931 Rollins 200 ..... B3
59864 Ronan 1,530 ..... C3
59347 Rosebud 259 ..... K4
59072 Roundup⊙ 2,119 ..... H4
59471 Roy 200 ..... H3
59540 Rudyard 450 ..... F2
59074 Ryegate⊙ 273 ..... G4
59261 Saco 252 ..... J2
59865 Saint Ignatius 877 ..... C3
59866 Saint Regis 500 ..... A3
59075 Saint Xavier 200 ..... J5
59867 Saltese 90 ..... A3
59472 Sand Coulee 600 ..... E3
59473 Santa Rita 120 ..... D2
59262 Savage 300 ..... M3
59263 Scobey⊙ 1,382 ..... L2
59868 Seeley Lake 900 ..... C3
59474 Shelby⊙ 3,142 ..... E2
59079 Shepherd 200 ..... H5
59749 Sheridan 646 ..... D5
59270 Sidney⊙ 5,726 ..... M3
59751 Silver Star 125 ..... D5
59477 Simms 200 ..... E3
59932 Somers 700 ..... B2
59479 Stanford⊙ 595 ..... F3
59870 Stevensville 1,207 ..... C4
59480 Stockett 500 ..... E3
59933 Stryker 96 ..... B2
59871 Sula 200 ..... B5
59482 Sunburst 476 ..... E2
59483 Sun River 300 ..... E3
59872 Superior⊙ 1,054 ..... B3
59911 Swan Lake 100 ..... C3
59484 Sweetgrass 250 ..... E2
59349 Terry⊙ 929 ..... L4
59873 Thompson Falls⊙ 1,478 ..... A3
59752 Three Forks 1,247 ..... E5
59644 Townsend⊙ 1,587 ..... E4
59874 Trout Creek 300 ..... A3
59935 Troy 1,088 ..... A2
59542 Turner 150 ..... H2
59754 Twin Bridges 437 ..... D5
59085 Twodot 285 ..... F4
59485 Ulm 450 ..... E3
59486 Valier 640 ..... D2
59487 Vaughn 2,270 ..... E3
59875 Victor 700 ..... B4
59755 Virginia City⊙ 192 ..... E5
59351 Volborg 125 ..... L5
59701 Walkerville 887 ..... D4
59756 Warmsprings 500 ..... D4
59275 Westby 291 ..... M2
59936 West Glacier 150 ..... C2
59758 West Yellowstone 735 ..... E6
59937 Whitefish 3,703 ..... B2
59759 Whitehall 1,030 ..... D5
59645 White Sulphur Springs⊙ 1,302 ..... E4
59276 Whitetail 150 ..... L2
59544 Whitewater 100 ..... J2
59353 Wibaux⊙ 782 ..... M3
59760 Willow Creek 150 ..... E5
59086 Wilsall 250 ..... F5
59489 Winifred 155 ..... G3
59087 Winnett⊙ 207 ..... H4
59647 Winston 120 ..... E4
59761 Wisdom 140 ..... C5
59762 Wise River 150 ..... C5
59648 Wolf Creek 500 ..... D3
59201 Wolf Point⊙ 3,074 ..... L2
59088 Worden 600 ..... H5
59089 Wyola 350 ..... J5

OTHER FEATURES

Absaroka (range) F5
Allen (mt.) C2
Arrow (creek) F3
Ashley (lake) B2
Battle (creek) G1
Bearhat (mt.) C2
Bearpaw (mts.) G2
Beartooth (mts.) G5
Beaver (creek) J2
Beaverhead (riv.) D5
Benton (lake) E3
Big (lake) G5
Big Belt (mts.) E4
Big Dry (creek) K3
Big Hole (riv.) C5
Big Hole Nat'l Battlefield C5
Bighorn (lake) H5
Bighorn (riv.) J5
Bighorn Canyon Nat'l Rec. Area H5
Big Muddy (riv.) M2
Big Porcupine (creek) J4
Birch (creek) D2
Birch Creek (res.) D2
Bitterroot (range) B4
Bitterroot (riv.) B4
Blackfeet Ind. Res. D2
Blackfoot (riv.) C4
Blackmore (mt.) F5
Bowdoin (lake) J2
Boxelder (creek) H3
Boxelder (creek) M5
Bynum (res.) D2
Cabinet (mts.) A2
Canyon Ferry (lake) E4
Clark Canyon (res.) D6
Clark Fork (riv.) A3
Clarks Fork, Yellowstone (riv.) G6
Cottonwood (creek) E2
Cow (creek) G2
Crazy (peak) F4
Crow Ind. Res. H5
Custer Battlefield Nat'l Mon. J5
Cut Bank (creek) D2
Douglas (mt.) F5
Earthquake (lake) E6
Electric (peak) F6
Elwell (lake) E2
Emigrant (peak) F5
Ennis (lake) E5
Flathead (lake) C3
Flathead (riv.) B2
Flathead, North Fork (riv.) B2
Flathead, South Fork (riv.) C3
Flathead Ind. Res. B3
Flatwillow (creek) H4
Fort Belknap Ind. Res. H2
Fort Peck (lake) K3
Fort Union Trading Post Nat'l Hist. Site N2
Frances (lake) D2
Freezeout (lake) D3
Frenchman (riv.) J1
Fresno (res.) F2
Gallatin (peak) E5
Gallatin (riv.) E5
Georgetown (lake) C4
Gibson (res.) D3
Glacier Nat'l Park C2
Granite (peak) F5
Grant-Kohrs Ranch Nat'l Hist. Site D4
Hauser (lake) E4
Haystack (peak) A3
Hebgen (lake) E6
Helena (lake) E4
Holter (lake) D4
Hungry Horse (res.) C2
Hurricane (mt.) D2
Hyalite (peak) E5
Jackson (mt.) C2
Jefferson (riv.) D5
Judith (riv.) G3
Koocanusa (lake) A2
Kootenai (riv.) A2
Lemhi (pass) C6
Lewis (range) C2
Lima (res.) D6
Little Bighorn (riv.) J5
Little Bitterroot (lake) B2
Little Dry (creek) K3
Little Missouri (riv.) M5
Lockhart (mt.) D3
Lodge (creek) G1
Lolo (pass) B4
Lone (mt.) E5
Lost Trail (pass) B5
Lower Red Rock (lake) E6
Lower Saint Mary (lake) C2
Madison (riv.) E5
Malmstrom A.F.B. 6,675 ..... E3
Marias (riv.) D2
Martinsdale (res.) F4
Mary Ronan (lake) B3
McDonald (lake) B2
McGloughlin (peak) C4
McGregor (lake) B3
Medicine (lake) M2
Milk (riv.) J2
Mission (range) C3
Missouri (riv.) L3
Musselshell (riv.) J3
Nelson (res.) J2
Ninepipe (res.) C3
Northern Cheyenne Indian Reservation K5
O'Fallon (creek) L4
Pishkun (res.) D3
Poplar (riv.) L2
Porcupine (creek) K2
Powder (riv.) L4
Purcell (mts.) A2
Railley (mt.) C3
Red Rock (lkes) E6
Red Rock (riv.) D6
Redwater (riv.) L3
Rock (creek) C4
Rocky (mts.) D4
Rocky Boy's Ind. Res. G2
Rosebud (creek) K4
Ruby (riv.) D5
Ruby River (res.) D5
Sage (creek) F2
Saint Mary (lake) C2
Saint Mary (riv.) C1
Sandy (creek) F2
Sheep (mt.) C2
Shields (riv.) F4
Siyeh (mt.) C2
Smith (riv.) E3
Sphinx (mt.) E5
Stillwater (riv.) G5
Stimson (mt.) C2
Sun (riv.) D3
Swan (lake) C3
Teton (riv.) E3
Tongue (riv.) K5
Upper Red Rock (lake) E6
Ward (peak) A3
Waterton-Glacier Int'l Peace Park C2
Whitefish (lake) B2
Willow (creek) E2
Willow Creek (res.) D3
Yellowstone (riv.) M3
Yellowstone National Park F6

⊙County seat.
‡Population of metropolitan area.
† Zip or nearest p.o. * Multiple zips.

COUNTIES

Adams 30,656 F4
Antelope 8,675 F2
Arthur 513 C3
Banner 918 A3
Blaine 867 E3
Boone 7,391 F3
Box Butte 13,696 A2
Boyd 3,331 F2
Brown 4,377 E2
Buffalo 34,797 E4
Burt 8,813 H3
Butler 9,330 G3
Cass 20,297 H4
Cedar 11,375 G2
Chase 4,758 C4
Cherry 6,758 C2
Cheyenne 10,057 A3
Clay 8,106 F4
Colfax 9,890 G3
Cuming 11,664 H3
Custer 13,877 E3
Dakota 16,573 H2
Dawes 9,609 A2
Dawson 22,304 E4
Deuel 2,462 B3
Dixon 7,137 H2
Dodge 35,847 H3
Douglas 397,038 H3
Dundy 2,861 C4
Fillmore 7,920 G4
Franklin 4,377 F4
Frontier 3,647 D4
Furnas 6,486 E4
Gage 24,456 H4
Garden 2,802 B3
Garfield 2,363 F3
Gosper 2,140 E4
Grant 877 C3
Greeley 3,462 F3
Hall 47,690 F4
Hamilton 9,301 F4
Harlan 4,292 E4
Hayes 1,356 C4
Hitchcock 4,079 C4
Holt 13,552 F2
Hooker 990 C3
Howard 6,773 F3
Jefferson 9,817 G4
Johnson 5,285 H4
Kearney 7,053 F4
Keith 9,364 C3
Keya Paha 1,301 E2
Kimball 4,882 A3
Knox 11,457 G2
Lancaster 192,884 H4
Lincoln 36,455 D4
Logan 983 D3
Loup 859 E3
Madison 31,382 G3
McPherson 593 C3
Merrick 8,945 F3
Morrill 6,085 A3
Nance 4,740 F3
Nemaha 8,367 J4
Nuckolls 6,726 F4
Otoe 15,183 H4
Pawnee 3,937 H4
Perkins 3,637 C4
Phelps 9,769 E4
Pierce 8,481 G2
Platte 28,852 G3
Polk 6,320 G3
Red Willow 12,615 D4
Richardson 11,315 J4
Rock 2,383 E2
Saline 13,131 G4
Sarpy 86,015 H3
Saunders 18,716 H3
Scotts Bluff 38,344 A3
Seward 15,789 G4
Sheridan 7,544 B2
Sherman 4,226 F3
Sioux 1,845 A2
Stanton 6,549 G3
Thayer 7,582 G4
Thomas 973 D3
Thurston 7,186 H2
Valley 5,633 E3
Washington 15,508 H3
Wayne 9,858 G2
Webster 4,858 F4
Wheeler 1,060 F3
York 14,798 G4

CITIES and TOWNS

Zip	Name/Pop.	Key
68301	Adams 395	H4
69210	Ainsworth⊙ 2,256	D2
68620	Albion⊙ 1,997	F3
68810	Alda 601	F4
68710	Allen 390	H2
69301	Alliance⊙ 9,920	A2
68920	Alma⊙ 1,369	E4
68304	Alvo 144	H4
68812	Amherst 269	E4
68814	Ansley 644	E3
68922	Arapahoe 1,107	E4
68815	Arcadia 412	F3
68002	Arlington 1,117	H3
69120	Arnold 813	D3
69121	Arthur⊙ 124	C3
68003	Ashland 2,274	H3
68713	Atkinson 1,521	E2
68305	Auburn⊙ 3,482	J4
68818	Aurora⊙ 3,717	F4
68924	Axtell 602	E4
68004	Bancroft 552	H2
68622	Bartlett⊙ 144	F3
69020	Bartley 342	D4
68714	Bassett⊙ 1,009	E2
68715	Battle Creek 948	G3
69334	Bayard 1,435	A3
68310	Beatrice⊙ 12,891	H4
68926	Beaver City⊙ 775	E4
68313	Beaver Crossing 458	G4
68716	Beemer 853	H3
68005	Bellevue 21,813	J3
68624	Bellwood 407	G3
69021	Benkelman⊙ 1,235	C4
68317	Bennet 523	H4
68007	Bennington 631	H3
68927	Bertrand 775	E4
69122	Big Springs 505	B3
68928	Bladen 298	F4
68008	Blair⊙ 6,418	H3
68718	Bloomfield 1,393	G2
68930	Blue Hill 883	F4
68318	Blue Springs 521	H4
68010	Boys Town 622	H3
68319	Bradshaw 373	G4
69123	Brady 377	D3
68821	Brewster⊙ 46	D3
69336	Bridgeport⊙ 1,668	A3
68822	Broken Bow⊙ 3,979	E3
69127	Brule 438	C3
68322	Bruning 330	G4
68823	Burwell⊙ 1,383	E3
68722	Butte⊙ 529	F2
68824	Cairo 737	F3
68825	Callaway 579	D3
69022	Cambridge 1,206	D4
68932	Campbell 441	F4
68015	Cedar Bluffs 632	H3
68016	Cedar Creek 311	H3
68627	Cedar Rapids 447	F3
68724	Center⊙ 123	G2
68826	Central City⊙ 3,083	F3
68017	Ceresco 836	H3
69337	Chadron⊙ 5,933	B2
68725	Chambers 390	F2
68827	Chapman 349	F3
69129	Chappell⊙ 1,095	B3
68327	Chester 435	G4
68628	Clarks 445	G3
68629	Clarkson 817	G3
68328	Clatonia 273	H4
68933	Clay Center⊙ 962	F4
68726	Clearwater 409	F2
†69343	Clinton 80	B2
68727	Coleridge 673	G2
68601	Columbus⊙ 17,328	G3
68329	Cook 341	H4
68331	Cortland 403	H4
69130	Cozad 4,453	E4
69339	Crawford 1,315	A2
68729	Creighton 1,341	G2
68333	Crete 4,872	G4
68730	Crofton 948	G2
69024	Culbertson 767	C4
69025	Curtis 1,014	D4
68731	Dakota City⊙ 1,440	H2
69131	Dalton 345	B3
68831	Dannebrog 356	F3
68335	Davenport 445	G4
68632	David City⊙ 2,514	G3
68020	Decatur 723	H2
68340	Deshler 997	G4
68341	De Witt 642	G4
68342	Diller 311	H4
69133	Dix 275	A3
68633	Dodge 815	H3
68832	Doniphan 696	F4
68343	Dorchester 611	G4
68634	Duncan 410	G3
68347	Eagle 832	H4
68935	Edgar 705	F4
68636	Elgin 807	F3
68022	Elkhorn 1,344	H3
68836	Elm Creek 862	E4
68349	Elmwood 598	H4
68937	Elwood⊙ 716	E4
68733	Emerson 874	H2
68350	Endicott 198	G4
69028	Eustis 460	D4
68735	Ewing 520	F2
68351	Exeter 807	G4
68352	Fairbury⊙ 4,885	G4
68938	Fairfield 543	G4
68354	Fairmont 767	G4
68355	Falls City⊙ 5,374	J4
69029	Farnam 268	D4
68358	Firth 384	H4
68023	Fort Calhoun 641	J3
68939	Franklin⊙ 1,167	E4
68025	Fremont⊙ 23,979	H3
68359	Friend 1,079	G4
68638	Fullerton⊙ 1,506	F3
68361	Geneva⊙ 2,400	G4
68640	Genoa 1,090	G3
69341	Gering⊙ 7,760	A3
68840	Gibbon 1,531	F4
68841	Giltner 400	F4
68941	Glenvil 363	F4
69343	Gordon 2,167	B2
69138	Gothenburg 3,479	D4
68801	Grand Island⊙ 33,180	F4
69140	Grant⊙ 1,270	C4
68842	Greeley⊙ 597	F3
68366	Greenwood 587	H3
68367	Gresham 320	G3
68028	Gretna 1,609	H3
68942	Guide Rock 344	F4
68738	Hadar 286	G2
68368	Hallam 290	H4
68843	Hampton 419	G4
69346	Harrison⊙ 361	A2
68739	Hartington⊙ 1,730	G2
68944	Harvard 1,217	F4
68901	Hastings⊙ 23,045	F4
69032	Hayes Center⊙ 231	C4
69347	Hay Springs 794	B2
68370	Hebron⊙ 1,906	G4
69348	Hemingford 1,023	A2
68371	Henderson 1,072	G4
68029	Herman 340	H3
69143	Hershey 633	D3
68372	Hickman 687	H4
68947	Hildreth 394	E4
68948	Holbrook 297	D4
68949	Holdrege⊙ 5,624	E4
68030	Homer 564	H2
68031	Hooper 932	H3
68740	Hoskins 306	G2
68641	Howells 677	H3
68376	Humboldt 1,176	J4
68642	Humphrey 799	G3
69350	Hyannis⊙ 336	C3
69033	Imperial⊙ 1,941	C4
69034	Indianola 856	D4
68743	Jackson 287	H2
68378	Johnson 341	J4
68955	Juniata 703	F4
68847	Kearney⊙ 21,158	E4
68956	Kenesaw 854	F4
68034	Kennard 372	H3
69145	Kimball⊙ 3,120	A3
69035	Lamar 60	C4
68745	Laurel 1,031	G2
†68046	La Vista 9,588	J3
68957	Lawrence 350	F4
68643	Leigh 509	G3
69147	Lewellen 368	B3
68850	Lexington⊙ 7,040	E4
*68501	Lincoln (cap.)⊙ 171,932	H4
	Lincoln‡ 192,884	H4
68644	Lindsay 383	G3
69149	Lodgepole 413	B3
69217	Long Pine 521	E2
68958	Loomis 447	E4
68037	Louisville 1,022	H3
68853	Loup City⊙ 1,368	E3
69352	Lyman 551	A3
68746	Lynch 357	F2
68038	Lyons 1,214	H3
68748	Madison⊙ 1,950	G3
69150	Madrid 284	C4
68402	Malcolm 355	H4
68854	Marquette 303	G4
69151	Maxwell 410	D3
69038	Maywood 332	D4
69001	McCook⊙ 8,404	D4
68401	McCool Junction 404	G4
68041	Mead 506	H3
68752	Meadow Grove 400	G2
68856	Merna 389	E3
68405	Milford 2,108	H4
68406	Milligan 332	G4
69356	Minatare 969	A3
68959	Minden⊙ 2,939	F4
69357	Mitchell 1,956	A3
68647	Monroe 294	G3
69358	Morrill 1,097	A3
69152	Mullen⊙ 720	C2
68409	Murray 465	J4
68410	Nebraska City⊙ 7,127	J4
68413	Nehawka 270	H4
68756	Neligh⊙ 1,893	G2
68961	Nelson⊙ 733	F4
68757	Newcastle 348	H2
68758	Newman Grove 930	G3
68760	Niobrara 419	G2
68962	Nora 24	G4
68701	Norfolk 19,449	G2
68649	North Bend 1,368	H3
68859	North Loup 405	F3
69101	North Platte⊙ 24,509	D3
68761	Oakdale 410	F2
68045	Oakland 1,393	H3
68415	Odell 322	H4
69153	Ogallala⊙ 5,638	C3
*68101	Omaha⊙ 313,911	J3
	Omaha‡ 570,399	J3
68763	O'Neill⊙ 4,049	F2
68764	Orchard 482	F2
68862	Ord⊙ 2,658	F3
68966	Orleans 527	E4
68651	Osceola⊙ 975	G3
69154	Oshkosh⊙ 1,057	B3
68765	Osmond 871	G2
68863	Overton 633	E4
68967	Oxford 1,109	E4
69040	Palisade 401	C4
68864	Palmer 487	F3
68418	Palmyra 512	H4
68046	Papillion⊙ 6,399	J3
68420	Pawnee City⊙ 1,156	H4
69155	Paxton 568	C3
68047	Pender⊙ 1,318	H2
68421	Peru 998	J4
68652	Petersburg 381	G3
68865	Phillips 405	F4
68767	Pierce⊙ 1,535	G2
68768	Pilger 400	G2
68769	Plainview 1,483	G2
68653	Platte Center 367	G3
68048	Plattsmouth⊙ 6,295	J3
68866	Pleasanton 349	E4
68424	Plymouth 506	G4
68654	Polk 440	G3
68770	Ponca⊙ 1,057	H2
68867	Poole	F4
69156	Potter 369	A3
68050	Prague 285	H3
68127	Ralston 5,143	J3
68771	Randolph 1,106	G2
68869	Ravenna 1,296	F4
68970	Red Cloud⊙ 1,300	F4
68658	Rising City 392	G3
69360	Rushville⊙ 1,217	B2
68660	Saint Edward 891	G3
68873	Saint Paul⊙ 2,094	F3
†68760	Santee 388	G2
68874	Sargent 828	E3
68661	Schuyler⊙ 4,151	G3
68875	Scotia 349	F3
69361	Scottsbluff 14,156	A3
68057	Scribner 1,011	H3
68434	Seward⊙ 5,713	H4
68662	Shelby 724	G3
68876	Shelton 1,046	F4
68436	Shickley 413	G4
69162	Sidney⊙ 6,010	B3
68663	Silver Creek 496	G3
68664	Snyder 387	H3
68776	South Sioux City 9,339	H2
68665	Spalding 645	F3
68777	Spencer 596	F2
68059	Springfield 782	H3
68778	Springview⊙ 326	E2
68779	Stanton⊙ 1,603	G3
68439	Staplehurst 306	G4
69163	Stapleton⊙ 340	D3
68442	Stella 289	J4
68443	Sterling 526	H4
69042	Stockville⊙ 45	D4
69043	Stratton 499	C4
68666	Stromsburg 1,290	G3
68780	Stuart 641	E2
68978	Superior 2,502	F4
69165	Sutherland 1,238	C3
68979	Sutton 1,416	G4
68446	Syracuse 1,638	H4
68447	Table Rock 393	H4

Agriculture, Industry and Resources

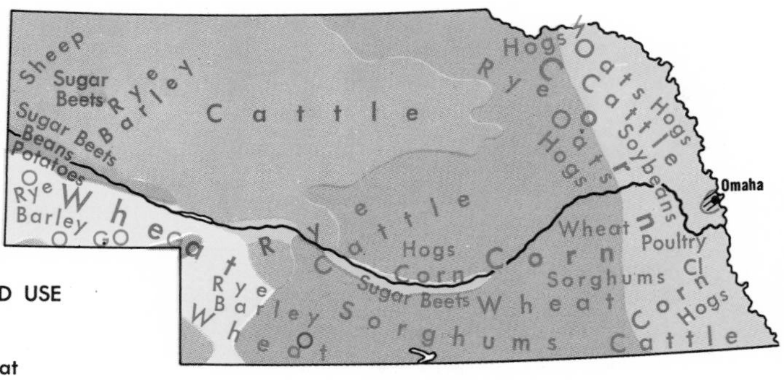

Sheep
Sugar Beets
Rye
Barley
Cattle
Sugar Beets
Beans
Potatoes
Rye
Barley
Wheat
Hogs
Oats
Corn
Soybeans
Omaha
Poultry
Sorghums
Cl

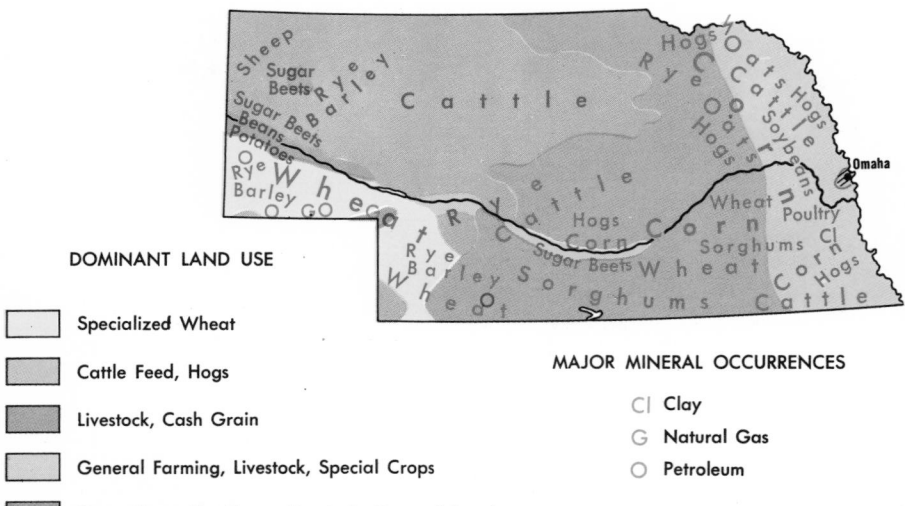

DOMINANT LAND USE

- Specialized Wheat
- Cattle Feed, Hogs
- Livestock, Cash Grain
- General Farming, Livestock, Special Crops
- Sugar Beets, Dry Beans, Livestock, General Farming
- Range Livestock

MAJOR MINERAL OCCURRENCES

- Cl Clay
- G Natural Gas
- O Petroleum
- Water Power
- Major Industrial Areas

104°
103°
102°
PINE RIDGE IND. RES.
S O U
Pine Ridge
Whiteclay
Chadron
Whitney
D A W E S
Gordon
Rushville
Clinton
Hay Springs
Harrison
Crawford
Fort Robinson
S I O U X
Marsland
Box Butte Res.
Niobrara
Agate
AGATE FOSSIL BEDS NAT'L MON.
S H E R I D A N
Hemingford
B O X B U T T E
Berea
Alliance
W Y O M I N G
Antioch
Lakeside
Ellsworth
Bingham
Ashby
Henry
Lake Alice
Morrill
Lyman
Mitchell
Lake Minatare
S C O T T S B L U F F
Scottsbluff
Terrytown
Gering
Minatare
Melbeta
McGrew
Angora
SCOTTS BLUFF NAT'L MON.
M O R R I L L
Bayard
Swan Lake
Crescent Lake
CHIMNEY ROCK NAT'L HIST. SITE
Northport
Bridgeport
Pumpkin
Harrisburg
Broadwater
Redington
B A N N E R
G A R D E N
Lisco
Oshkosh
Dalton
Gurley
C H E Y E N N E
Lewellen
Bushnell
Kimball
Dix
Potter
Sidney
Sunol
Lodgepole
K I M B A L L
D E U E L
Chappell
Big Springs
Brule
Lake C. W. McConaughy
5,426 ft. (1,654 m.)
Julesburg
Sterling Res.
C O L O R A D O
Sterling
Holyoke
Grant
Brandon
Venango
Lamar
Champion
Wray
Haigler
Benkelman
Parks
Nebraska
SCALE
0 5 10 20 30 40 50 60 MI.
0 5 10 20 30 40 50 60 KM.
State Capitals
County Seats
Major Limited Access Hwys.
Scale 1:2,400,000
© Copyright HAMMOND

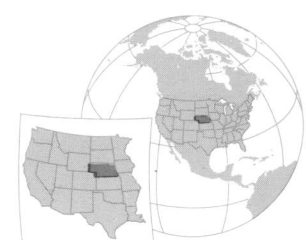

AREA 77,355 sq. mi. (200,349 sq. km.)
POPULATION 1,569,825
CAPITAL Lincoln
LARGEST CITY Omaha
HIGHEST POINT (Kimball Co.) 5,246 ft. (1654 m.)
SETTLED IN 1847
ADMITTED TO UNION March 1, 1867
POPULAR NAME Cornhusker State
STATE FLOWER Goldenrod
STATE BIRD Western Meadowlark

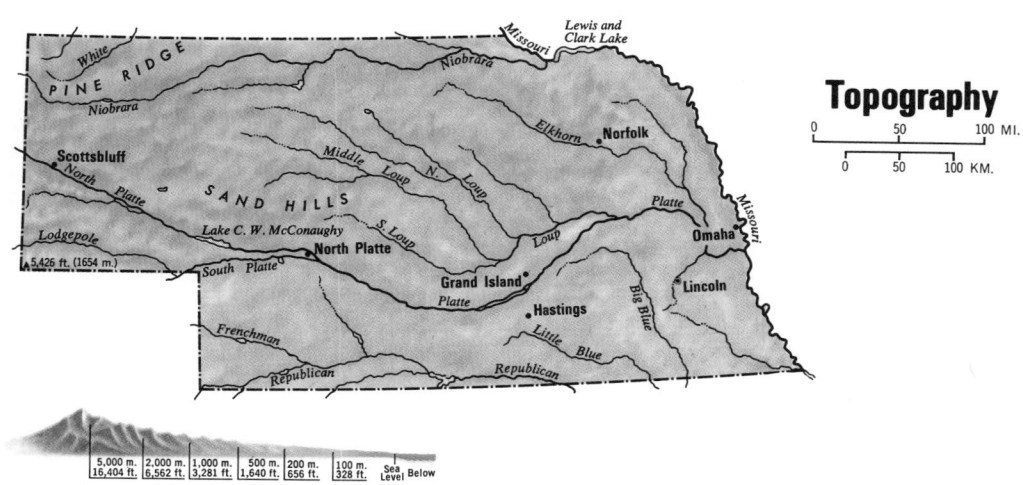

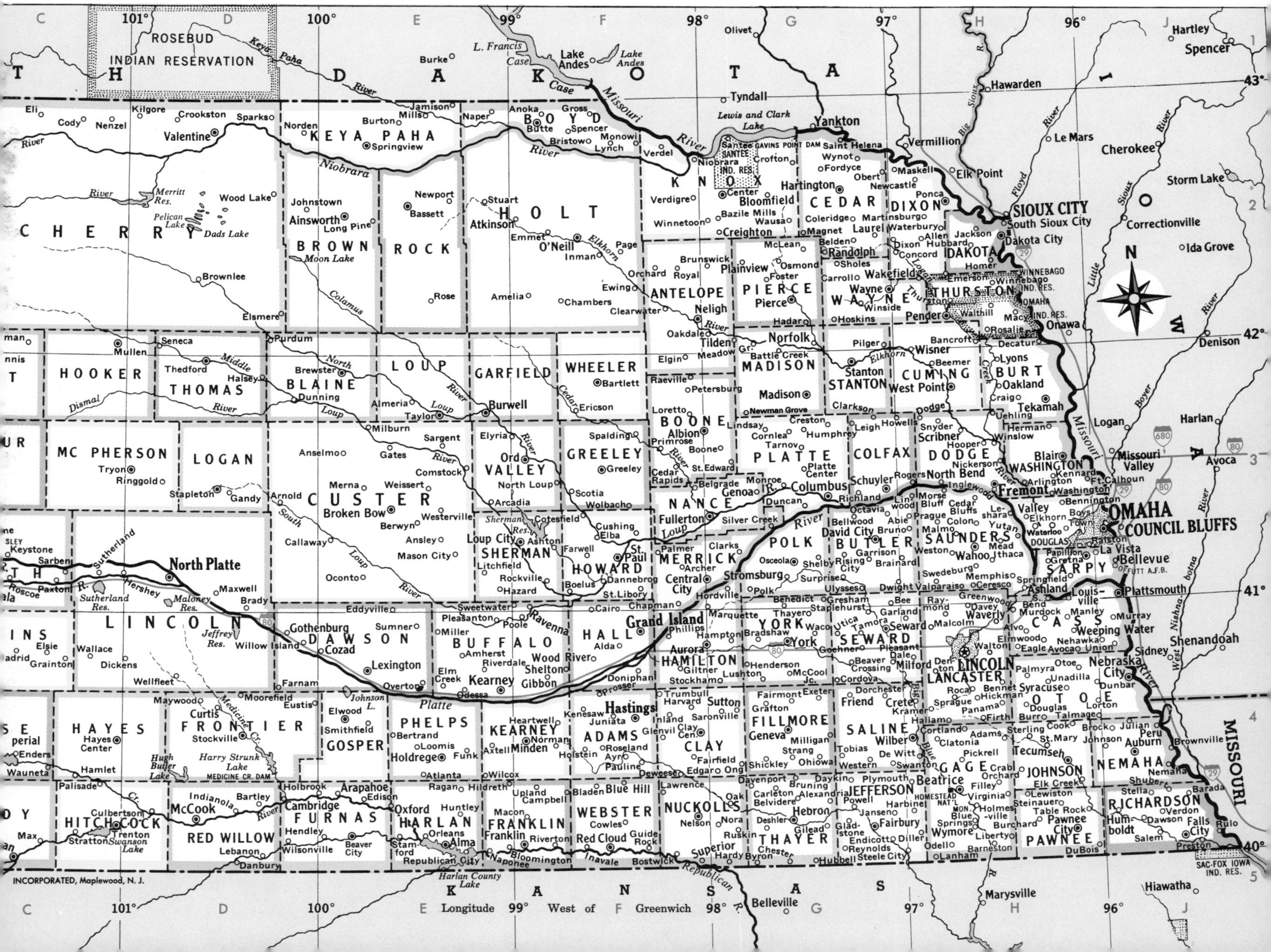

Topography

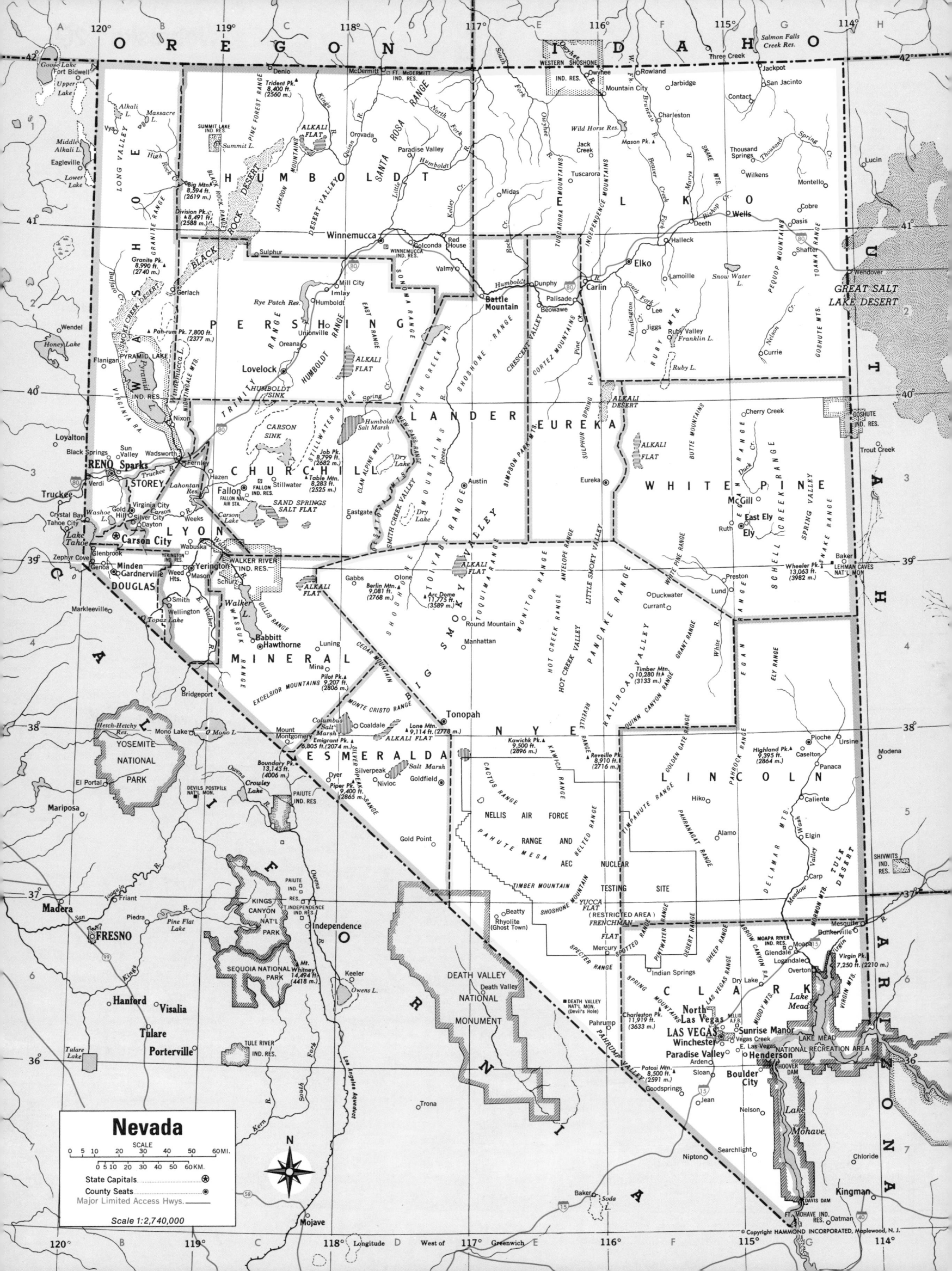

AREA 110,561 sq. mi. (286,353 sq. km.)
POPULATION 800,493
CAPITAL Carson City
LARGEST CITY Las Vegas
HIGHEST POINT Boundary Pk. 13,143 ft. (4006 m.)
SETTLED IN 1850
ADMITTED TO UNION October 31, 1864
POPULAR NAME Silver State; Sagebrush State
STATE FLOWER Sagebrush
STATE BIRD Mountain Bluebird

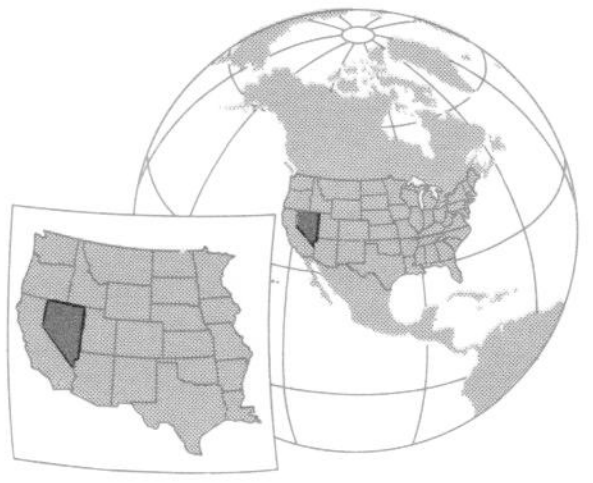

Agriculture, Industry and Resources

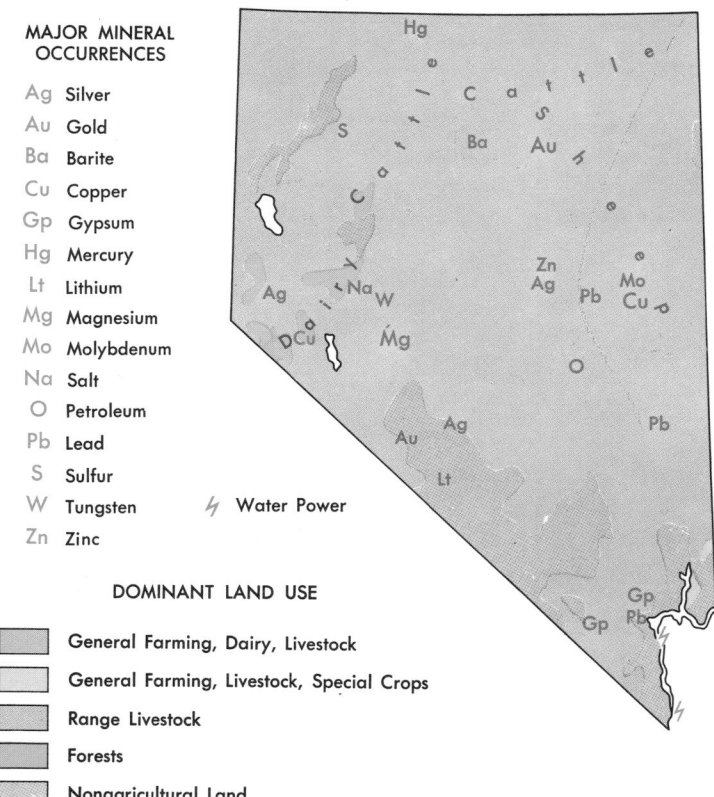

MAJOR MINERAL OCCURRENCES

- Ag Silver
- Au Gold
- Ba Barite
- Cu Copper
- Gp Gypsum
- Hg Mercury
- Lt Lithium
- Mg Magnesium
- Mo Molybdenum
- Na Salt
- O Petroleum
- Pb Lead
- S Sulfur
- W Tungsten
- Zn Zinc
- Water Power

DOMINANT LAND USE

- General Farming, Dairy, Livestock
- General Farming, Livestock, Special Crops
- Range Livestock
- Forests
- Nonagricultural Land

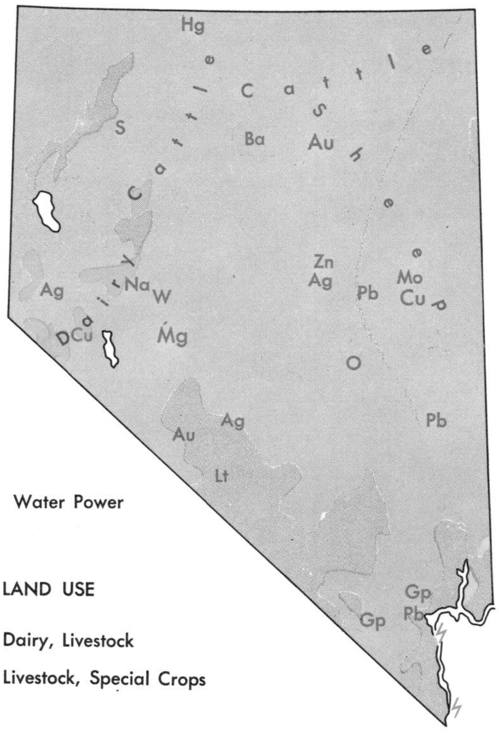

Hg
Cattle
Dairy Cattle
Sheep
S
Ba
Au
Ag
Na
W
Cu
Mg
Zn
Ag
Pb
Mo
Cu
O
Ag
Au
Lt
Pb
Gp
Pb
Gp

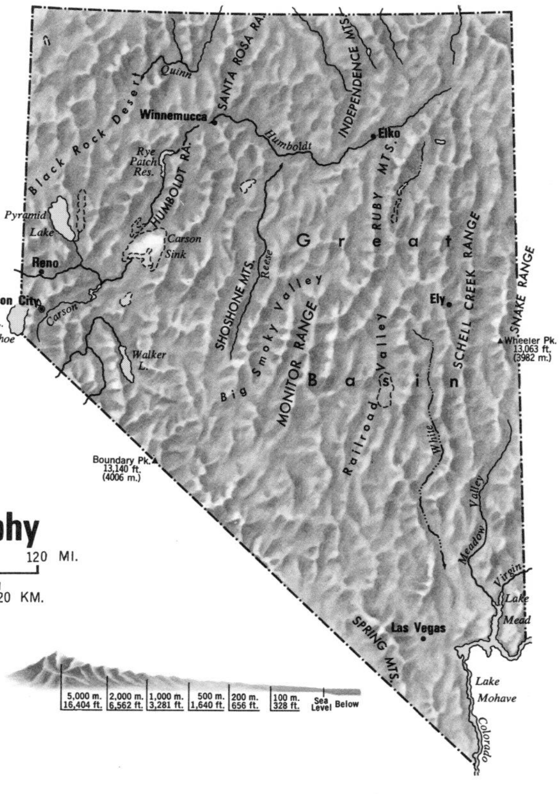

Quinn
SANTA ROSA RA.
INDEPENDENCE MTS.
Black Rock Desert
Winnemucca
Humboldt
Elko
Rye Patch Res.
HUMBOLDT RA.
RUBY MTS.
Pyramid Lake
Carson Sink
Great Basin
Reno
Carson City
L. Tahoe
SHOSHONE MTS.
Reese
Big Smoky Valley
MONITOR RANGE
Railroad Valley
White
SCHELL CREEK RANGE
SNAKE RANGE
Ely
Wheeler Pk. 13,063 ft. (3982 m.)
Walker L.
Boundary Pk. 13,140 ft. (4006 m.)
Meadow Valley
SPRING MTS.
Las Vegas
Virgin
Lake Mead
Lake Mohave
Colorado
5,000 m. 16,404 ft.
2,000 m. 6,562 ft.
1,000 m. 3,281 ft.
500 m. 1,640 ft.
200 m. 656 ft.
100 m. 328 ft.
Sea Level
Below

Topography

0 60 120 MI.
0 60 120 KM.

COUNTIES

Carson City (city) 32,022	B3
Churchill 13,917	C3
Clark 463,087	F6
Douglas 19,421	B4
Elko 17,269	F1
Esmeralda 777	D5
Eureka 1,198	E3
Humboldt 9,434	C1
Lander 4,076	D3
Lincoln 3,732	F5
Lyon 13,594	B3
Mineral 6,217	C4
Nye 9,048	E4
Pershing 3,408	C2
Storey 1,503	B3
Washoe 193,623	B2
White Pine 8,167	F3

CITIES and TOWNS

Zip	*Name/Pop.*	*Key*
89001	Alamo 300	F5
89310	Austin⊙ 300	E3
89416	Babbitt	C4
89311	Baker 140	G3
89820	Battle Mountain 2,749	E2
89003	Beatty 600	E6
89821	Beowawe 77	E2
†89508	Black Springs 180	B3
89005	Boulder City 9,590	G7
89007	Bunkerville 300	G6
89008	Caliente 982	G5
89822	Carlin 1,232	E2
†89008	Carp 30	G5
89701	Carson City (cap.) 32,022	B3
†89043	Caselton	G5
†89301	Cherry Creek 80	G3
89402	Crystal Bay 6,225	A3
89403	Dayton 350	B3
89823	Deeth 125	F1
89404	Denio 35	C1
89314	Duckwater 80	F4
89010	Dyer 56	C5
89315	East Ely	G3
89112	East Las Vegas 6,449	F6
89801	Elko⊙ 8,758	F2
89301	Ely⊙ 4,882	G3
89316	Eureka⊙ 300	E3
89406	Fallon⊙ 4,262	C3
89408	Fernley 750	B3
89409	Gabbs 811	D4
89410	Gardnerville 1,610	B4
89411	Genoa 254	B4
89412	Gerlach 400	B2
89413	Glenbrook 800	B3
89414	Golconda 275	D2
89013	Goldfield⊙ 500	D5
89019	Goodsprings 80	F7
89824	Halleck 68	F2
89415	Hawthorne⊙ 3,741	C4
89417	Hazen 76	C3
89015	Henderson 24,363	G6
89017	Hiko 210	F5
†89418	Humboldt 14	C2
89418	Imlay 250	C2
89018	Indian Springs 500	F6
†89310	Ione 20	D4
†89834	Jack Creek	E1
89825	Jackpot 400	G1
89826	Jarbidge 11	F1
89019	Jean 125	F7
89828	Lamoille 100	F2
*89101	Las Vegas⊙ 164,674	F6
	Las Vegas‡ 461,816	F6
89829	Lee 125	F2
89021	Logandale 410	G6
89419	Lovelock⊙ 1,680	C2
89317	Lund 380	F4
89420	Luning 90	C4
89022	Manhattan 93	E4
†89447	Mason 200	B4
89421	McDermitt 240	D1
89318	McGill 1,419	G3
89023	Mercury 900	E6
89024	Mesquite 500	G6
89422	Mina 450	C4
89423	Minden⊙ 1,029	B4
89025	Moapa 275	G6
89830	Montello 100	G1
89831	Mountain City 100	F1
†89046	Nelson 75	G7
89424	Nixon 400	B3
89030	North Las Vegas 42,739	F6
89425	Orovada 200	D1
89040	Overton 1,111	G6
89041	Pahrump 400	E6
89042	Panaca 650	G5
89119	Paradise Valley 84,818	F6
89426	Paradise Valley 115	D1
89043	Pioche⊙ 850	G5
*89501	Reno⊙ 100,756	B3
	Reno‡ 193,623	B3
†89003	Rhyolite (Ghost Town) 8	E6
89045	Round Mountain 400	E4
89833	Ruby Valley 150	F2
89319	Ruth 455	F3
89427	Schurz 800	C4
89046	Searchlight 500	F7
89428	Silver City 150	B3
89047	Silverpeak 100	D5
89430	Smith 200	B4
89431	Sparks 40,780	B3
†89406	Stillwater 150	C3
†89445	Sulphur	C2
†89110	Sunrise Manor 44,155	F6
†89431	Sun Valley 8,822	B3
†89835	Thousand Springs	G1
89049	Tonopah⊙ 1,952	D4
89834	Tuscarora 24	E1
89438	Valmy 200	D2
89121	Vegas Creek	G6
89440	Virginia City⊙ 750	B3
89442	Wadsworth 400	B3
89443	Weed Heights 8	B4
89444	Wellington 505	B4
89835	Wells 1,218	G1
†89109	Winchester 19,728	F6
89445	Winnemucca⊙ 4,140	D2
89447	Yerington⊙ 2,021	B4
89448	Zephyr Cove 1,316	A3

OTHER FEATURES

Alkali (lake)	B1
Antelope (range)	E3
Arc Dome (mt.)	D4
Arrow Canyon (range)	G6
Beaver Creek Fork, Humboldt (riv.)	F1
Belted (range)	E5
Berlin (mt.)	D4
Big (mt.)	B1
Big Smoky (valley)	D4
Bishop (creek)	F1
Black Rock (des.)	B2
Black Rock (range)	B1
Boundary (peak)	C5
Buffalo (creek)	B2
Butte (mts.)	F3
Cactus (range)	E5
Carson (lake)	C3
Carson (riv.)	B3
Carson (sink)	C3
Cedar (mt.)	D4
Charleston (peak)	F6
Clan Alpine (mts.)	D3
Columbus Salt (marsh)	C4
Cortez (mts.)	E2
Crescent (valley)	E2
Davis (dam)	G7
Death Valley Nat'l Mon.	E6
Delamar (mts.)	G5
Desatoya (mts.)	D3
Desert (range)	F6
Desert (valley)	C1
Devil's Hole (Death Valley Nat'l Mon.)	E6
Division (peak)	B1
Duck (creek)	G3
East (range)	D2
East Walker (riv.)	B4
Egan (range)	G4
Ely (range)	G4
Emigrant (peak)	C5
Excelsior (mts.)	C4
Fallon Ind. Res.	C3
Fallon Nav. Air Sta.	C3
Fish Creek (mts.)	D2
Fort McDermitt Ind. Res.	D1
Fort Mohave Ind. Res.	G7
Franklin (lake)	F2
Frenchman Flat (basin)	F6
Gillis (range)	C4
Golden Gate (range)	F5
Goshute (mts.)	G2
Goshute Ind. Res.	G3
Granite (peak)	B2
Granite (range)	B2
Grant (range)	F4
Great Salt Lake (des.)	H2
High Rock (creek)	B1
Highland (peak)	G5
Hoover (dam)	G7
Hot Creek (range)	E4
Hot Creek (valley)	E4
Humboldt (range)	C2
Humboldt (riv.)	E2
Humboldt (sink)	C2
Humboldt Salt (marsh)	D3
Huntington (creek)	F2
Independence (mts.)	E1
Jackson (mts.)	C1
Job (peak)	C3
Kawich (peak)	E5
Kawich (range)	E5
Kelley (creek)	D1
Kings (riv.)	C1
Lahontan (res.)	B3
Lake Mead Nat'l Rec. Area	G6
Las Vegas (range)	F6
Lehman Caves Nat'l Mon.	G4
Little Humboldt (riv.)	D1
Little Smoky (valley)	E4
Lone (mt.)	D4
Long (valley)	B1
Marys (riv.)	F1
Mason (peak)	F1
Massacre (lake)	B1
Mead (lake)	G6
Meadow Valley Wash (riv.)	G5
Moapa River Ind. Res.	G6
Mohave (lake)	G7
Monitor (range)	E4
Monte Cristo (range)	D4
Mormon (mts.)	G5
Muddy (mts.)	G6
Nellis A.F.B. 7,476	F6
Nellis Air Force Range and AEC Nuclear Testing Site	E5
Nelson (creek)	G2
New Pass (range)	D3
Nightingale (mts.)	B2
Owyhee (riv.)	E1
Pahranagat (range)	F5
Pahrock (range)	F5
Pah-rum (peak)	B2
Pahrump (valley)	F6
Pahute (mesa)	E5
Pancake (range)	F4
Pequop (mts.)	G2
Pilot (peak)	C4
Pine (creek)	E2
Pine Forest (range)	C1
Pintwater (range)	F6
Piper (peak)	D5
Potosi (mt.)	F7
Pyramid (lake)	B2
Pyramid Lake Ind. Res.	B2
Quinn (riv.)	D1
Quinn Canyon (range)	F4
Railroad (valley)	F4
Reese (riv.)	D3
Reveille (peak)	E5
Reveille (range)	E4
Ruby (lake)	F2
Ruby (mts.)	F2
Rye Patch (res.)	C2
Sand Springs (salt flat)	C3
Santa Rosa (range)	D1
Schell Creek (range)	G3
Sheep (range)	F6
Shoshone (mt.)	E6
Shoshone (mts.)	D3
Shoshone (range)	E2
Silver Peak (range)	D5
Simpson Park (mts.)	E3
Smith Creek (valley)	D3
Smoke Creek (des.)	B2
Snake (mts.)	F1
Snake (range)	G3
Snow Water (lake)	G2
Sonoma (range)	D2
Specter (range)	E6
Spotted (range)	F6
Spring (creek)	D2
Spring (mts.)	F6
Spring (valley)	G3
Stillwater (range)	C3
Sulphur Spring (range)	E3
Summit (lake)	C1
Summit Lake Ind. Res.	B1
Table (mt.)	C3
Tahoe (lake)	B3
Thousand Spring (creek)	G1
Timber (mt.)	F4
Timber (mt.)	E5
Timpahute (range)	F5
Toana (range)	G2
Toiyabe (range)	D3
Topaz (lake)	B4
Toquima (range)	E4
Trident (peak)	C1
Trinity (range)	C2
Truckee (riv.)	B3
Tule (des.)	G5
Tuscarora (mts.)	E1
Virgin (mts.)	G6
Virgin (peak)	G6
Virgin (riv.)	G6
Virginia (range)	B3
Walker (lake)	C4
Walker (riv.)	C3
Walker River Ind. Res.	C3
Washoe (lake)	B3
Wassuk (range)	C4
Western Shoshone Ind. Res.	E1
Wheeler (peak)	G4
White (riv.)	F4
White Pine (range)	F3
Wild Horse (res.)	E1
Winnemucca (lake)	B2
Winnemucca Ind. Res.	D2
Yerington Ind. Res.	B3
Yucca Flat (basin)	E6

⊙County seat.
‡Population of metropolitan area.
† Zip of nearest p.o.
* Multiple zips.

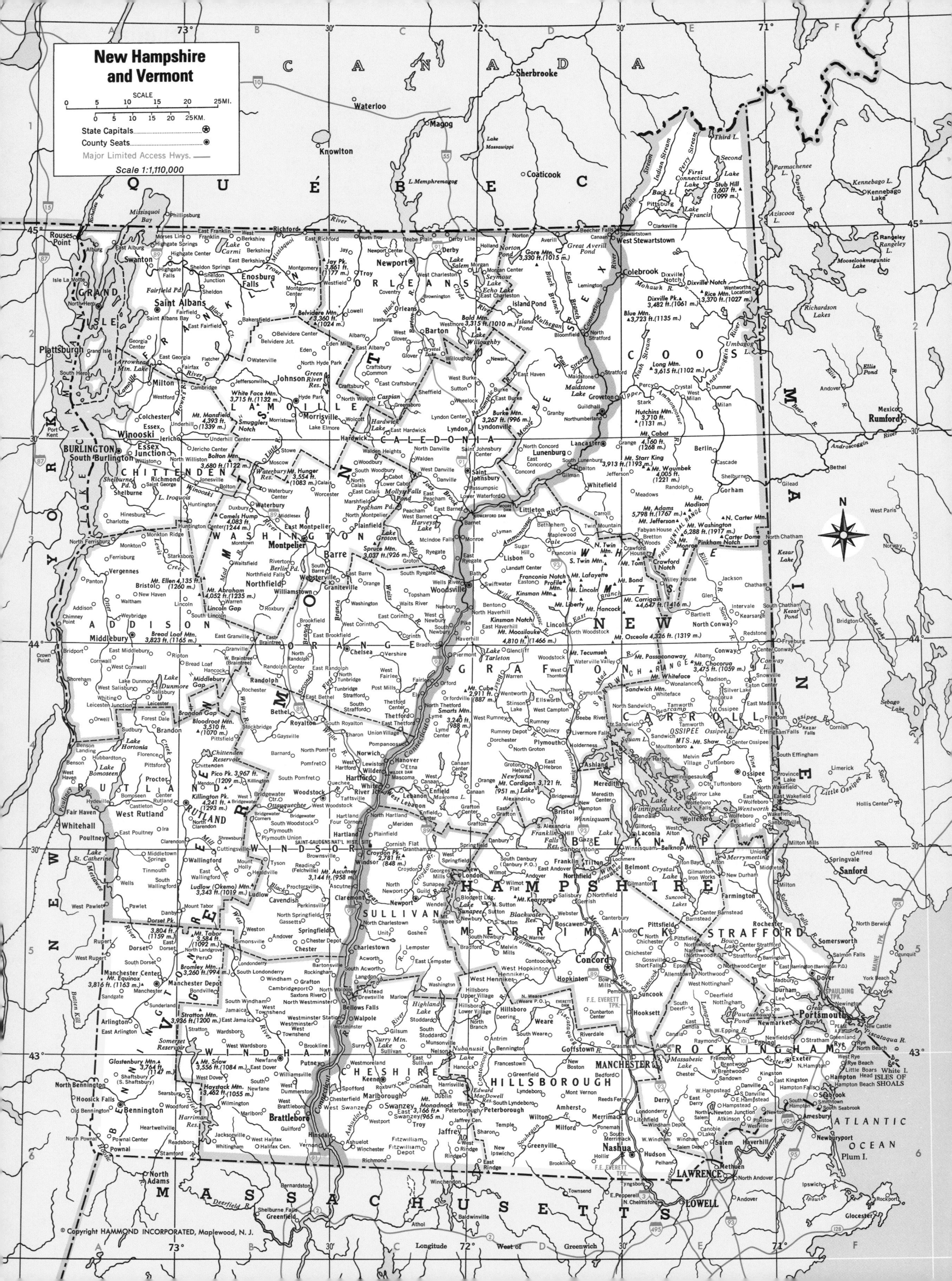

New Hampshire
and Vermont

SCALE

0 5 10 15 20 25MI.

0 5 10 15 20 25KM.

State Capitals .... ⊛

County Seats .... ⊙

Major Limited Access Hwys. ———

Scale 1:1,110,000

NEW HAMPSHIRE
AREA 9,279 sq. mi. (24,033 sq. km.)
POPULATION 920,610
CAPITAL Concord
LARGEST CITY Manchester
HIGHEST POINT Mt. Washington 6,288 ft. (1917 m.)
SETTLED IN 1623
ADMITTED TO UNION June 21, 1788
POPULAR NAME Granite State
STATE FLOWER Purple Lilac
STATE BIRD Purple Finch

VERMONT
AREA 9,614 sq. mi. (24,900 sq. km.)
POPULATION 511,456
CAPITAL Montpelier
LARGEST CITY Burlington
HIGHEST POINT Mt. Mansfield 4,393 ft. (1339 m.)
SETTLED IN 1764
ADMITTED TO UNION March 4, 1791
POPULAR NAME Green Mountain State
STATE FLOWER Red Clover
STATE BIRD Hermit Thrush

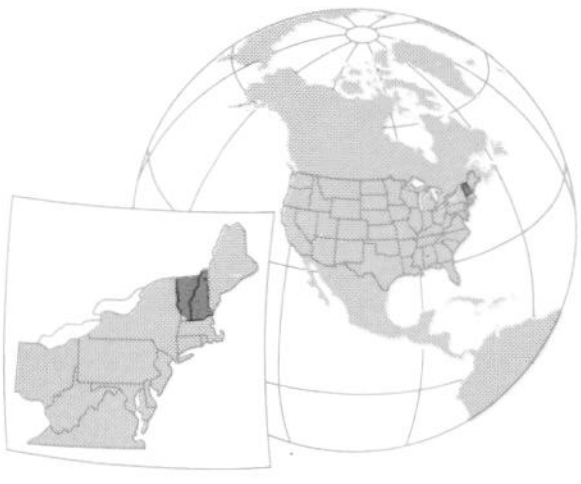

Topography

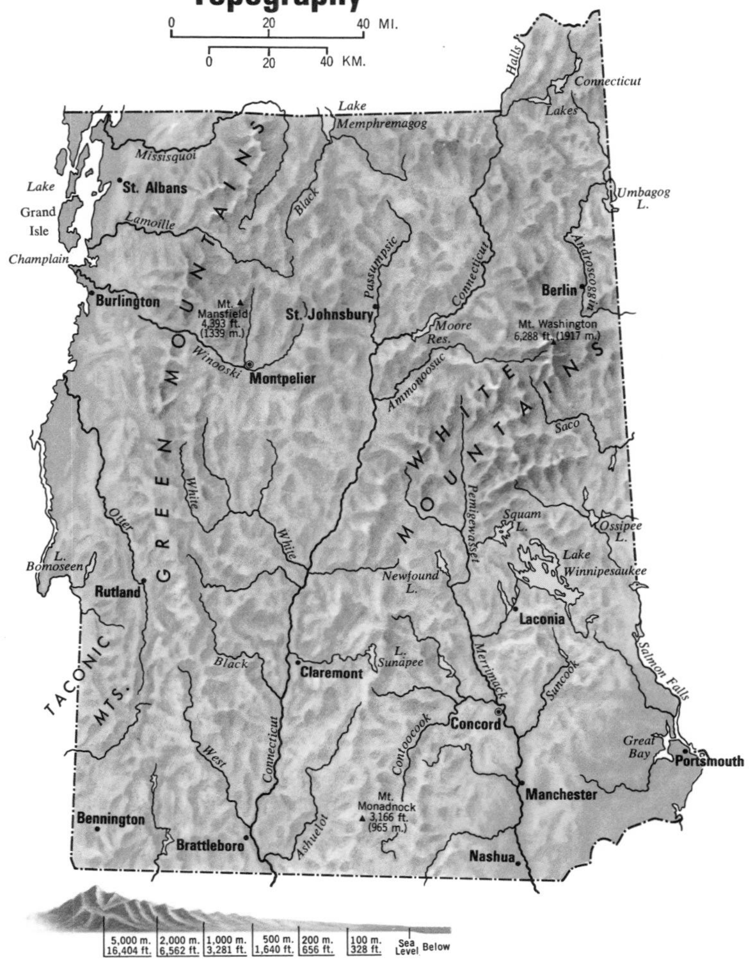

NEW HAMPSHIRE

COUNTIES

Belknap 42,884 D4
Carroll 27,931 E4
Cheshire 62,116 C6
Coos 35,147 E2
Grafton 65,806 D4
Hillsborough 276,608 D6
Merrimack 98,302 D5
Rockingham 190,345 E5
Strafford 85,408 E5
Sullivan 36,063 C5

CITIES and TOWNS

Zip Name/Pop. Key

03601 Acworth○ 590 C5
†03864 Albany○ 383 E4
†03222 Alexandria○ 706 D4
†03275 Allenstown○ 4,398 E5
03602 Alstead○ 1,461 C5
03809 Alton○ 2,440 E5
03810 Alton Bay 500 E5
03031 Amherst○ 8,243 D6
03216 Andover○ 1,587 D5
03440 Antrim○ 2,208 D5
03440 Antrim 1,142 D5
03217 Ashland○ 1,807 D4
03217 Ashland 1,479 D4
03441 Ashuelot 810 C6
03811 Atkinson○ 4,397 E6
03032 Auburn○ 2,883 E5
03218 Barnstead○ 2,292 E5
†03825 Barrington○ 4,404 F5
03812 Bartlett○ 1,566 E3
03740 Bath○ 761 D3
03102 Bedford○ 9,481 D6
03220 Belmont○ 4,026 E5
03442 Bennington○ 890 D5
†03785 Benton○ 333 D3
03570 Berlin 13,084 E3
03574 Bethlehem○ 1,784 D3
03301 Boscawen○ 3,435 D5
03221 Bradford○ 1,115 D5
†03833 Brentwood○ 2,004 E6
†03222 Bridgewater○ 606 D4
03222 Bristol○ 2,198 D4
03222 Bristol 1,258 D4
†03872 Brookfield○ 385 E4
03033 Brookline○ 1,766 D6
03223 Campton○ 1,694 D4
03741 Canaan○ 2,456 C4
03034 Candia○ 2,989 E5
03224 Canterbury○ 1,410 D5
†03595 Carroll○ 647 D3
03813 Center Conway 558 E4
03226 Center Harbor○ 808 E4
03814 Center Ossipee 800 E4
03603 Charlestown○ 4,417 C5
03603 Charlestown 1,294 C5
†04037 Chatham○ 189 E3
03036 Chester○ 2,006 E6
03443 Chesterfield○ 2,561 C6
†03258 Chichester○ 1,492 E5
03817 Chocorua 575 E4
03743 Claremont 14,557 C5
†05902 Clarksville○ 262 E1
03576 Colebrook○ 2,459 E2
03576 Colebrook 1,131 E2
03301 Concord (cap.)⊙ 30,400 D5
03229 Contoocook 1,499 D5
03818 Conway○ 7,158 E4
03818 Conway 1,781 E4
03746 Cornish Flat 450 C4
†03753 Croydon○ 457 C5
†03598 Dalton○ 672 D3
03230 Danbury○ 680 D4
03819 Danville○ 1,318 E6
03037 Deerfield○ 1,979 E5
†03244 Deering○ 1,041 D5
03038 Derry○ 18,875 E6
03038 Derry 12,248 E6
†03266 Dorchester○ 244 D4
03820 Dover⊙ 22,377 F5
03444 Dublin○ 1,303 C6
†03588 Dummer○ 390 E2
†03301 Dunbarton○ 1,174 D5
03824 Durham○ 10,652 F5
03824 Durham 8,448 F5
03231 East Andover 500 D5
03826 East Hampstead 900 E6
03827 East Kingston○ 1,135 F6
†03580 Easton○ 124 D3
03446 East Swanzey 500 C6
03832 Eaton (Eaton Center)○ 256 E4
†03264 Ellsworth○ 53 D4
03748 Enfield○ 3,175 C4
03748 Enfield 1,581 C4
03042 Epping○ 3,460 E5
03042 Epping 1,384 E5
03234 Epsom○ 2,743 E5
03579 Errol○ 313 E2
03750 Etna 550 C4
03833 Exeter○ 11,024 F6
03833 Exeter⊙ 8,947 F6
03835 Farmington○ 4,630 E5
03835 Farmington 3,284 E5
03447 Fitzwilliam○ 1,795 C6
03043 Francestown○ 830 D6
03580 Franconia○ 743 D3
03235 Franklin 7,901 D5
03836 Freedom○ 720 E4
03044 Fremont○ 1,333 E6
†03246 Gilford○ 4,841 E5
03237 Gilmanton○ 1,941 E5
03448 Gilsum○ 652 C5
03838 Glen 600 E3
03045 Goffstown○ 11,315 D5
03581 Gorham○ 3,322 E3
03581 Gorham 2,180 E3
03752 Goshen○ 549 C5
03240 Grafton○ 739 D4
03753 Grantham○ 704 C5
03047 Greenfield○ 972 D6
03840 Greenland○ 2,129 F5
03048 Greenville○ 1,988 D6
03048 Greenville 1,447 D6
†03241 Groton○ 255 D4
03582 Groveton 1,389 D2
03754 Guild 500 C5
03841 Hampstead○ 3,785 E6
03842 Hampton○ 10,493 F6
03842 Hampton 6,779 F6
03844 Hampton Falls○ 1,372 F6
03449 Hancock○ 1,193 C6
03755 Hanover○ 9,119 C4
03755 Hanover 6,861 C4
03450 Harrisville○ 860 C6
03765 Haverhill○ 3,445 C3
03241 Hebron○ 349 D4
03242 Henniker○ 3,246 D5
03242 Henniker 1,538 D5
03243 Hill○ 736 D4
03244 Hillsboro○ 3,437 D5
03244 Hillsboro 1,797 D5
03451 Hinsdale○ 3,631 C6
03451 Hinsdale 1,546 C6
03245 Holderness○ 1,586 D4
03049 Hollis○ 4,679 D6
03106 Hooksett○ 7,303 E5
03106 Hooksett 1,868 E5
03301 Hopkinton○ 3,861 D5
03051 Hudson○ 14,022 E6
03051 Hudson 6,248 E6
03845 Intervale 725 E3
03846 Jackson○ 642 E3
03452 Jaffrey○ 4,349 C6
03452 Jaffrey 2,684 C6
03583 Jefferson○ 803 D3
03431 Keene⊙ 21,449 C6
03848 Kingston○ 4,111 E6
03246 Laconia⊙ 15,575 E4
03584 Lancaster○ 3,401 D3
03584 Lancaster⊙ 2,134 D3
†03585 Landaff○ 266 D3
†03602 Langdon○ 437 C5
03766 Lebanon 11,134 C4
†03857 Lee○ 2,111 F5
03606 Lempster○ 637 C5
03251 Lincoln○ 1,313 D3
03585 Lisbon○ 1,517 D3
03585 Lisbon 1,151 D3
†03051 Litchfield○ 4,150 E6
03561 Littleton○ 5,558 D3
03561 Littleton 4,480 D3
03053 Londonderry○ 13,598 E6
03301 Loudon○ 2,454 E5
†03585 Lyman○ 281 D3
03768 Lyme○ 1,289 C4
†03082 Lyndeborough○ 1,070 D6
†03820 Madbury○ 987 F5
03849 Madison○ 1,051 E4
*03101 Manchester 90,936 E6
Manchester‡ 160,767 E6
03455 Marlborough○ 1,846 C6
03455 Marlborough 1,184 C6
03456 Marlow○ 542 C5
03850 Melvin Village 450 E4
03253 Meredith○ 4,646 D4
03253 Meredith 1,202 D4
03770 Meriden 800 C4
03054 Merrimack○ 15,406 D6
†03887 Middleton○ 734 E5
03588 Milan○ 1,013 E2
03055 Milford○ 8,685 D6
03055 Milford 6,269 D6
03851 Milton○ 2,438 F5
03852 Milton Mills 450 F4
03771 Monroe○ 619 C3
03057 Mont Vernon○ 1,444 D6
03254 Moultonboro○ 2,206 E4
03060 Nashua⊙ 67,865 D6
Nashua‡ 114,221 D6
†03457 Nelson○ 442 C5
03070 New Boston○ 1,928 D6
03255 Newbury○ 961 C5
03854 New Castle○ 936 F5
03855 New Durham○ 1,183 E5
03856 Newfields○ 817 F5
03256 New Hampton○ 1,249 D4
†03801 Newington○ 716 F5
03071 New Ipswich○ 2,433 D6
03257 New London○ 2,935 D5
03257 New London 1,335 D5
03857 Newmarket○ 4,290 F5
03857 Newmarket 3,749 F5
03773 Newport○ 6,229 C5
03773 Newport⊙ 4,388 C5
03858 Newton○ 3,068 E6
03859 Newton Junction 450 E6
03860 North Conway 2,104 E3
†03276 Northfield○ 3,051 D5
†03276 Northfield-Tilton 2,574 D5
03862 North Hampton○ 3,425 F6
03590 North Stratford 600 D2
†03582 Northumberland○ 2,520 D2
03261 Northwood○ 2,175 E5
03262 North Woodstock 750 D3
03290 Nottingham○ 1,952 E5
†03741 Orange○ 197 D4
03777 Orford○ 928 C4
03864 Ossipee 2,465 E4
03076 Pelham○ 8,090 E6
†03275 Pembroke○ 4,861 E5
03458 Peterborough○ 4,895 D6
03458 Peterborough 2,568 D6
03779 Piermont○ 507 C4
03592 Pittsburg○ 780 E1
03263 Pittsfield○ 2,889 E5
03263 Pittsfield 1,584 E5
03781 Plainfield○ 1,749 C4
03865 Plaistow○ 5,609 E6
03264 Plymouth○ 5,094 D4
03264 Plymouth 3,628 D4
03801 Portsmouth 26,254 F5
Portsmouth-Dover-Rochester‡ 163,880 F5
03593 Randolph○ 274 E3
03077 Raymond○ 5,453 E5
03077 Raymond 1,192 E5
†03470 Richmond○ 518 C6
03461 Rindge○ 3,375 C6
03867 Rochester 21,560 E5
†03431 Roxbury○ 190 C6
03266 Rumney○ 1,212 D4
03870 Rye○ 4,508 F5
03871 Rye Beach 600 F6
03079 Salem○ 24,124 E6
03268 Salisbury○ 781 D5
03269 Sanbornton○ 1,679 D5
03872 Sanbornville 750 F4
03873 Sandown○ 2,057 E6
03270 Sandwich○ 905 E4
03874 Seabrook○ 5,917 F6
†03458 Sharon○ 184 D6
†03581 Shelburne○ 318 E3
03878 Somersworth 10,350 F5
†01913 South Hampton○ 660 F6
03462 Spofford 750 C6
†03284 Springfield○ 532 C4
†03582 Stark○ 470 E2
†03576 Stewartstown○ 943 E2
03464 Stoddard○ 482 C5
03884 Strafford○ 1,663 E5
†03590 Stratford○ 989 D2
03885 Stratham○ 2,507 F5
03585 Sugar Hill○ 397 D3
†03445 Sullivan○ 585 C5
03782 Sunapee○ 2,312 C5
03275 Suncook 4,698 D5
03431 Surry○ 656 C5
†03260 Sutton○ 1,091 D5
†03431 Swanzey○ 5,183 C6
03886 Tamworth○ 1,672 E4
03084 Temple○ 692 D6
†03285 Thornton○ 952 D4
03276 Tilton○ 3,387 D5
03276 Tilton-Northfield 2,574 D5
03465 Troy○ 2,131 C6
03465 Troy 1,318 C6
†03816 Tuftonboro○ 1,500 E4
03595 Twin Mountain 500 D3
†03743 Unity○ 1,092 C5
†03872 Wakefield○ 2,237 F4
03608 Walpole○ 3,188 C5
03278 Warner○ 1,963 D5
03279 Warren○ 650 D4
03280 Washington○ 411 C5
03223 Waterville Valley○ 180 D4
03281 Weare○ 3,232 D5
†03301 Webster○ 1,095 D5
03282 Wentworth○ 527 D4
†03579 Wentworths Location○ 49 E2
†03242 West Henniker 500 D5
03784 West Lebanon C4
03467 Westmoreland○ 1,452 C6
03597 West Stewartstown 700 E2
03469 West Swanzey 1,022 C6
03865 Westville 750 E6
03598 Whitefield○ 1,681 D3
03598 Whitefield 1,005 D3
†03287 Wilmot○ 725 D5
03287 Wilmot Flat 450 D5
03086 Wilton○ 2,669 D6
03086 Wilton 1,310 D6
03470 Winchester○ 3,465 C6
03470 Winchester 1,732 C6
03087 Windham○ 5,664 E6
03289 Winnisquam 500 E5
03894 Wolfeboro○ 3,968 E4
03894 Wolfeboro 2,271 E4
03896 Wolfeboro Falls 600 E4
03293 Woodstock○ 1,008 D4
03785 Woodsville⊙ 1,195 C3

OTHER FEATURES

Adams (mt.) E3
Ammonoosuc (riv.) D3
Androscoggin (riv.) E2
Ashuelot (riv.) C6
Back (lake) E1
Baker (riv.) D4
Bearcamp (riv.) E4
Beaver (brook) E6
Belknap (mt.) E5
Blackwater (res.) D5
Blue (mt.) E2
Bond (mt.) E3
Bow (lake) E5
Cabot (mt.) E2
Cannon (mt.) D3
Cardigan (mt.) D4
Carrigain (mt.) E3
Carter Dome (mt.) E3
Chocorua (mt.) E4
Cocheco (riv.) E5
Cold (riv.) C5
Comerford (dam) D3
Connecticut (riv.) B6
Contoocook (riv.) D6
Conway (lake) E4
Crawford Notch (pass) E3
Croydon (peak) C5
Croydon Branch, Sugar (riv.) C5
Crystal (lake) E5
Cube (mt.) D4
Dixville (peak) E2
Dixville Notch (pass) E2
Edward MacDowell (res.) D6
Ellis (riv.) E3
Everett (dam) D5
Exeter (riv.) E6
First Connecticut (lake) E1
Francis (lake) E1
Franconia Notch (pass) D3
Franklin Falls (res.) D4
Gale (riv.) D3
Great (bay) F5
Halls (stream) E1
Hancock (mt.) D3
Highland (lake) C5
Hutchins (mt.) E2
Indian (stream) E1
Jefferson (mt.) E3
Kearsarge (mt.) D5
Kinsman (mt.) D3
Kinsman Notch (pass) D3
Lafayette (mt.) D3
Lamprey (riv.) E5
Liberty (mt.) D3
Lincoln (mt.) D3
Long (mt.) E2
Mad (riv.) D4
Madison (mt.) E3
Mascoma (lake) C4
Massabesic (lake) E6
Merrimack (riv.) D5
Merrymeeting (lake) E5
Mohawk (riv.) E2
Monadnock (mt.) C6
Monroe (mt.) E3
Moore (dam) D3
Moore (res.) D3
Moosilauke (mt.) D3
Nash (stream) E2
Newfound (lake) D4
North Carter (mt.) E3
North Twin (mt.) D3
Nubanusit (lake) C5
Osceola (mt.) E3
Ossipee (lake) E4
Ossipee (mts.) E4
Ossipee (riv.) F4
Passaconaway (mt.) E4
Pawtuckaway (pond) E5
Pease A.F.B. F5
Pemigewasset (riv.) D4
Perry (stream) E1
Pine (riv.) E4
Pinkham Notch (pass) E3
Piscataqua (riv.) F5
Piscataquog (riv.) D5
Presidential (range) E3
Rice (mt.) E2
Saco (riv.) E3
Saint-Gaudens Nat'l Hist. Site B4
Salmon Falls (riv.) F5

(continued on following page)

Agriculture, Industry and Resources

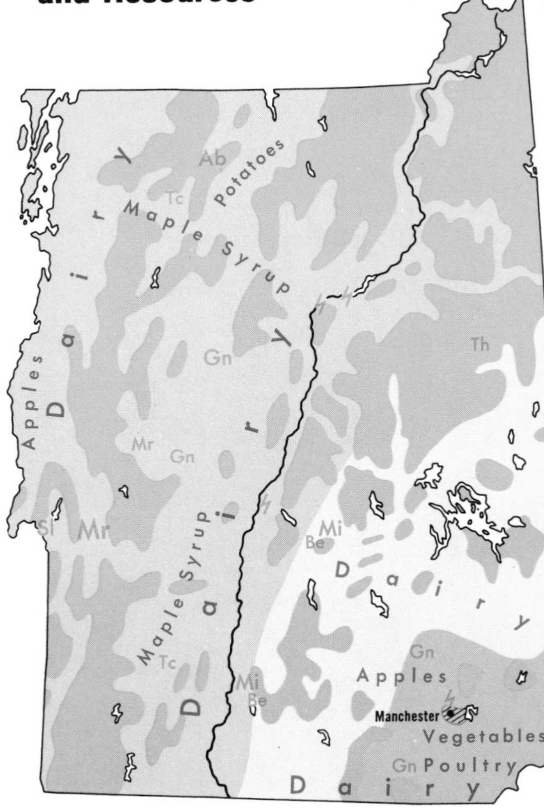

DOMINANT LAND USE

- Specialized Dairy
- Dairy, General Farming
- Dairy, Poultry, Mixed Farming
- Forests

- Water Power
- Major Industrial Areas

MAJOR MINERAL OCCURRENCES

Ab	Asbestos	Mr	Marble
Be	Beryl	Sl	Slate
Gn	Granite	Tc	Talc
Mi	Mica	Th	Thorium

Sandwich (mt.)	E4
Sandwich (range)	E4
Second (lake)	E1
Shaw (mt.)	E4
Shoals (isls.)	F6
Smarts (mt.)	C4
Souhegan (riv.)	D6
South Twin (mt.)	D3
Squam (lake)	E4
Starr King (mt.)	E3
Stub Hill (mt.)	E1
Sugar (riv.)	C5
Sunapee (lake)	C5
Suncook (lkes)	E5
Suncook (riv.)	E5
Surry Mountain (lake)	C5
Tarleton (lake)	D4
Tecumseh (mt.)	D4
Third (lake)	E1
Tom (mt.)	E3
Umbagog (lake)	E2
Upper Ammonoosuc (riv.)	E2
Warner (riv.)	D5
Washington (mt.)	E3
Waumbek (mt.)	E3
Wentworth (lake)	E4
White (isl.)	F6
White (mts.)	E3
Whiteface (mt.)	E4
Wild Ammonoosuc (riv.)	D3
Wilder (dam)	C4
Winnipesaukee (lake)	E4
Winnipesaukee (riv.)	D5
Winnisquam (lake)	D4

VERMONT

COUNTIES

Addison 29,406	A3
Bennington 33,345	A6
Caledonia 25,808	C2
Chittenden 115,534	A3
Essex 6,313	D2
Franklin 34,788	B2
Grand Isle 4,613	A2
Lamoille 16,767	B2
Orange 22,739	C3
Orleans 23,440	C2
Rutland 58,347	A4
Washington 52,393	B3
Windham 36,933	B5
Windsor 51,030	B4

CITIES and TOWNS

Zip	*Name/Pop.*	*Key*
05820	Albany○ 705	C2
05440	Alburg○ 1,352	A2
05440	Alburg 496	A2
†05143	Andover○ 350	B5
05250	Arlington○ 2,184	A5
05250	Arlington 1,309	A5
05441	Bakersfield○ 852	B2
05031	Barnard○ 790	B4
05821	Barnet○ 1,338	C3
05641	Barre 9,824	C3
05641	Barre○ 7,090	C3
05822	Barton○ 2,990	C2
05822	Barton 1,062	C2
05823	Beebe Plain 500	C2
05902	Beecher Falls 950	D2
05101	Bellows Falls 3,456	C5
05442	Belvidere○ 218	B2
05201	Bennington○ 15,815	A6
05201	Bennington⊙ 9,349	A6
05731	Benson○ 739	A4
†05476	Berkshire○ 1,116	B2
05032	Bethel○ 1,715	B4
05032	Bethel 1,016	B4
†03590	Bloomfield○ 188	D2
†05466	Bolton○ 715	B3
05732	Bomoseen 700	A4
05340	Bondville 500	B5
05033	Bradford○ 2,191	C3
05033	Bradford 831	C3
†05669	Braintree○ 1,065	B4
05733	Brandon○ 4,194	A4
05733	Brandon 1,925	A4
05301	Brattleboro○ 11,886	B6
05301	Brattleboro 8,596	B6
05034	Bridgewater○ 867	B4
05734	Bridport○ 997	A4
05443	Bristol○ 3,293	A3
05443	Bristol 1,793	A3
05036	Brookfield○ 959	B3
†05345	Brookline○ 310	B5
†05860	Brownington○ 708	C2
†05871	Burke○ 1,385	D2
05401	Burlington⊙ 37,712	A3
	Burlington‡ 114,070	A3
05647	Cabot○ 958	C3
05647	Cabot 259	C3
05648	Calais○ 1,207	B3
05444	Cambridge○ 2,019	B2
05444	Cambridge 217	B2
05903	Canaan○ 1,196	D2
05735	Castleton○ 3,637	A4
05142	Cavendish○ 1,355	B5
05736	Center Rutland 465	A4
05445	Charlotte○ 2,561	A3
05038	Chelsea 1,091	C4
05143	Chester○ 2,791	B5
05143	Chester-Chester Depot 1,267	B5
05737	Chittenden○ 927	B4
†05759	Clarendon○ 2,372	A4
05446	Colchester○ 12,629	A2
05824	Concord○ 1,125	D3
05039	Corinth○ 904	C3
†05753	Cornwall○ 993	A4
05825	Coventry○ 674	C2
05826	Craftsbury○ 844	C2
05739	Danby○ 992	A5
05828	Danville○ 1,705	C3
05829	Derby○ 4,222	C2
05829	Derby (Derby Center) 598	C2
05830	Derby Line 874	C2
05251	Dorset○ 1,648	A5
†05676	Duxbury○ 877	B3
05252	East Arlington 600	A5
05649	East Barre-Graniteville 2,172	C3
05253	East Dorset 550	A5
05837	East Haven○ 280	D2
05740	East Middlebury 550	A4
05651	East Montpelier○ 2,205	B3
05741	East Poultney 450	A4
05742	East Wallingford 500	B5
05652	Eden○ 612	B2
05450	Enosburg Falls 1,207	B2
05451	Essex○ 14,392	A2
05452	Essex Junction 7,033	A3
05454	Fairfax○ 1,805	B2
05455	Fairfield○ 1,493	B2
05743	Fair Haven○ 2,819	A4
05743	Fair Haven 2,363	A4
05045	Fairlee○ 770	C4
05456	Ferrisburg○ 2,117	A3
†05444	Fletcher○ 626	B2
05745	Forest Dale 500	A4
05457	Franklin○ 1,006	B2
†05478	Georgia○ 2,818	A2
05904	Gilman 600	D3
05839	Glover○ 843	C2
05146	Grafton○ 604	B5
05840	Granby○ 70	D2
05458	Grand Isle○ 1,238	A2
05654	Graniteville-East Barre 2,172	C3
05747	Granville○ 288	B4
05841	Greensboro○ 677	C2
05046	Groton○ 667	C3
05905	Guildhall 202	D2
†05301	Guilford○ 1,532	B6
†05358	Halifax○ 488	B6
05748	Hancock○ 334	B4
05843	Hardwick○ 2,613	C2
05843	Hardwick 1,476	C2
05047	Hartford○ 7,963	C4
05048	Hartland○ 2,396	C4
†05459	Highgate○ 2,493	B2
05461	Hinesburg○ 2,690	A3
†05830	Holland○ 473	D2
05749	Hubbardton○ 490	A4
05462	Huntington○ 1,161	B3
05655	Hyde Park○ 2,021	B2
05655	Hyde Park⊙ 475	B2
05750	Hydeville 500	A4
†05777	Ira○ 354	A4
05845	Irasburg○ 870	C2
05846	Island Pond 1,216	D2
05463	Isle La Motte○ 393	A2
05342	Jacksonville 252	B6
05343	Jamaica○ 681	B5
†05859	Jay○ 302	C2
05464	Jeffersonville 491	B2
05465	Jericho○ 3,575	A2
05465	Jericho 1,340	A2
05656	Johnson○ 2,581	B2
05656	Johnson 1,393	B2
05751	Killington 700	B4
†05752	Leicester○ 803	A4
†03576	Lemington○ 108	D2
†05443	Lincoln○ 870	B3
05148	Londonderry○ 1,510	B5
05847	Lowell○ 573	C2
05149	Ludlow○ 2,414	B5
05149	Ludlow 1,352	B5
05906	Lunenburg○ 1,138	D3
05849	Lyndon○ 4,924	C2
05850	Lyndon Center	C2
05851	Lyndonville 1,401	D2
†05905	Maidstone○ 100	D2
05254	Manchester○ 3,261	A5
05254	Manchester⊙ 563	A5
05255	Manchester Center 1,719	A5
05344	Marlboro○ 695	B6
05658	Marshfield○ 1,267	C3
05658	Marshfield 301	C3
†05701	Mendon○ 1,056	B4
05753	Middlebury○ 7,574	A3
05753	Middlebury⊙ 5,591	A3
†05602	Middlesex○ 1,235	B3
05757	Middletown Springs○ 603	A5
05468	Milton○ 6,829	A2
05468	Milton 1,411	A2
05469	Monkton○ 1,201	A3
05470	Montgomery○ 681	B2
05471	Montgomery Center 400	B2
05602	Montpelier (cap.)⊙ 8,241	B3
05660	Moretown○ 1,221	B3
05853	Morgan○ 460	D2
†05661	Morristown○ 4,448	B2
05661	Morrisville 2,074	B2
05758	Mount Holly○ 938	B5
†05739	Mount Tabor○ 211	B5
†05871	Newark○ 280	D2
05051	Newbury○ 1,699	C3
05051	Newbury 425	C3
05345	Newfane○ 1,129	B6
05345	Newfane⊙ 119	B6
05472	New Haven○ 1,217	A3
05855	Newport○ 1,319	C2
05855	Newport⊙ 4,756	C2
05257	North Bennington 1,685	A6
05663	Northfield○ 5,435	B3
05663	Northfield 2,033	B3
05664	Northfield Falls 600	B3
05052	North Hartland 500	C4
05474	North Hero 442	A2
05665	North Hyde Park 450	B2
05053	North Pomfret 400	B4
05260	North Pownal 700	A6
05150	North Springfield	B5
05859	North Troy 717	C2
†05101	North Westminster 310	B5
05907	Norton○ 184	D2
05055	Norwich○ 2,398	C4
†05201	Old Bennington 353	A6
†05649	Orange○ 752	C3
05860	Orleans 983	C2
05760	Orwell○ 901	A4
†05491	Panton○ 537	A3
05761	Pawlet○ 1,244	A5
05862	Peacham○ 531	C3
05151	Perkinsville 187	B5
05152	Peru○ 312	B5
05762	Pittsfield○ 396	B4
05763	Pittsford○ 2,590	A4
05763	Pittsford 666	A4
05667	Plainfield○ 1,249	C3
05667	Plainfield 599	C3
05056	Plymouth○ 405	B4
†05067	Pomfret○ 856	B4
05058	Post Mills 500	C4
05764	Poultney○ 3,196	A4
05764	Poultney 1,554	A4
05261	Pownal○ 3,269	A6
05765	Proctor○ 1,998	A4
05153	Proctorsville 481	B5
05346	Putney○ 1,850	B6
05059	Quechee 900	C4
05060	Randolph○ 4,689	B4
05060	Randolph 2,217	B4
05062	Reading○ 647	B5
05350	Readsboro○ 638	B6
05350	Readsboro 402	B6
05476	Richford○ 2,206	B2
05476	Richford 1,471	B2
05477	Richmond○ 3,159	A3
05477	Richmond 865	A3
05766	Ripton○ 327	A4
05767	Rochester○ 1,054	B4
†05101	Rockingham○ 5,538	B5
05669	Roxbury○ 452	B3
†05068	Royalton○ 2,100	B4
05768	Rupert○ 605	A5
05701	Rutland○ 3,300	B4
05701	Rutland⊙ 18,436	B4
05042	Ryegate○ 1,000	C3
05478	Saint Albans○ 3,555	A2
05478	Saint Albans⊙ 7,308	A2
†05401	Saint George○ 677	A2
05819	Saint Johnsbury○ 7,938	D3
05819	Saint Johnsbury⊙ 7,150	D3
05863	Saint Johnsbury Center 400	D3
05769	Salisbury○ 881	A4
†05250	Sandgate○ 234	A5
05154	Saxtons River 593	B5
†05363	Searsburg○ 72	A6
05262	Shaftsbury○ 3,001	A6
05065	Sharon○ 828	C4
05866	Sheffield○ 435	C2
05482	Shelburne○ 5,000	A3
05483	Sheldon○ 1,618	B2
05770	Shoreham○ 972	A4
†05738	Shrewsbury○ 866	B4
05670	South Barre 1,301	B3
05401	South Burlington 10,679	A3
05486	South Hero○ 1,188	A2
05155	South Londonderry 500	B5
05068	South Royalton 700	C4
05069	South Ryegate 400	C3
05156	Springfield○ 10,190	B5
05156	Springfield 5,603	B5
05352	Stamford○ 773	A6
05487	Starksboro○ 1,336	A3
05772	Stockbridge○ 508	B4
05672	Stowe○ 2,991	B3
05672	Stowe 531	B3
05072	Strafford○ 731	C4
†05360	Stratton○ 122	B5
†05733	Sudbury○ 380	A4
†05250	Sunderland○ 768	A5
05867	Sutton○ 667	C2
05488	Swanton○ 5,141	A2
05488	Swanton 2,520	A2
05074	Thetford○ 2,188	C4
†05773	Tinmouth○ 406	A5
05076	Topsham○ 767	C3
05353	Townshend○ 849	B5
05868	Troy○ 1,498	C2
05077	Tunbridge○ 925	C4
05489	Underhill○ 2,172	B2
05490	Underhill Center 575	B2
05491	Vergennes 2,273	A3
05354	Vernon○ 1,175	B6
05079	Vershire○ 442	C4
05673	Waitsfield○ 1,300	B3
†05873	Walden○ 575	C3
05773	Wallingford○ 1,893	B5
05773	Wallingford 1,141	B5
†05491	Waltham○ 394	A3
05355	Wardsboro○ 505	B5
05674	Warren○ 956	B3
05675	Washington○ 855	C3
05676	Waterbury○ 4,465	B3
05676	Waterbury 1,892	B3
05492	Waterville○ 470	B2
05678	Websterville 700	B3
05774	Wells○ 815	A5
05081	Wells River 396	C3
05301	West Brattleboro 2,795	B6
05871	West Burke 338	C2
05356	West Dover 550	B6
05083	West Fairlee○ 427	C4
05874	Westfield○ 418	C2
05494	Westford○ 1,413	A2
05875	West Glover	C2
†05743	West Haven○ 253	A4
05158	Westminster○ 2,493	C5
05158	Westminster 319	C5
†05860	Westmore○ 257	C2
05161	Weston○ 627	B5
05777	West Rutland○ 2,351	A4
05777	West Rutland 2,169	A4
05359	West Townshend 500	B5
†05753	Weybridge○ 667	A3
†05851	Wheelock○ 444	C2
05001	White River Junction 2,582	C4
05778	Whiting○ 379	A4
05361	Whitingham○ 1,043	B6
05088	Wilder 1,461	C4
05679	Williamstown○ 2,284	B3
05495	Williston○ 3,843	A3
05363	Wilmington○ 1,808	B6
†05359	Windham○ 223	B5
05089	Windsor○ 4,084	C5
05089	Windsor 3,478	C5
05404	Winooski 6,318	A2
05680	Wolcott○ 986	C2
05681	Woodbury○ 573	C3
†05201	Woodford○ 314	A6
05091	Woodstock○ 3,214	B4
05091	Woodstock⊙ 1,178	B4
05682	Worcester○ 727	B3

OTHER FEATURES

Abraham (mt.)	B3
Arrowhead Mountain (lake)	A2
Ascutney (mt.)	C5
Bald (mt.)	D2
Barton (riv.)	C2
Batten Kill (riv.)	A5
Belvidere (mt.)	B2
Black (riv.)	B5
Black (riv.)	C2
Bloodroot (mt.)	B4
Bolton (mt.)	B3
Bomoseen (lake)	A4
Brandon Gap (pass)	B4
Bread Loaf (mt.)	A3
Bromley (mt.)	B5
Brown's (riv.)	A2
Burke (mt.)	D2
Camels Hump (mt.)	B3
Carmi (lake)	B2
Caspian (lake)	C2
Champlain (lake)	A2
Chittenden (res.)	B4
Clyde (riv.)	C2
Comerford (dam)	D3
Connecticut (riv.)	C4
Crystal (lake)	C2
Dorset (peak)	A5
Dunmore (lake)	A4
Echo (lake)	D2
Ellen (mt.)	B3
Equinox (mt.)	A5
Fairfield (pond)	A2
Glastenbury (mt.)	A6
Gore (mt.)	D2
Green (mts.)	B4
Green River (res.)	B2
Groton (lake)	C3
Hardwick (lake)	C2
Harriman (res.)	B6
Harveys (lake)	C3
Haystack (mt.)	B6
Hoosic (riv.)	A6
Hortonia (lake)	A4
Hunger (mt.)	B3
Iroquois (lake)	A3
Island (pond)	D2
Jay (peak)	B2
Joes (brook)	C3
Killington (peak)	B4
Lamoille (riv.)	A2
Lewis (creek)	A3
Lincoln Gap (pass)	B3
Little (riv.)	B3
Mad (riv.)	B3
Maidstone (lake)	D2
Mansfield (mt.)	B2
Memphremagog (lake)	C1
Mettawee (riv.)	A5
Middlebury Gap (pass)	B4
Mill (riv.)	B4
Missisquoi (riv.)	B2
Mollys Falls (pond)	C3
Moore (dam)	D3
Moore (res.)	D3
Moose (riv.)	D2
Norton (pond)	D2
Nulhegan (riv.)	D2
Ottauquechee (riv.)	B4
Otter (creek)	A3
Passumpsic (riv.)	D2
Pico (peak)	B4
Poultney (riv.)	A4
Saint Catherine (lake)	A5
Salem (lake)	C2
Seymour (lake)	D2
Shelburne (pond)	A3
Smugglers Notch (pass)	B2
Snow (mt.)	B6
Somerset (res.)	A5
Spruce (mt.)	C3
Stratton (mt.)	B5
Tabor (mt.)	B5
Trout (riv.)	B2
Waits (riv.)	C3
Waterbury (res.)	B3
Wells (riv.)	C3
West (riv.)	B5
White (riv.)	C4
White Face (mt.)	B2
Wilder (dam)	C4
Willoughby (lake)	D2
Winooski (riv.)	B3

⊙County seat.
‡Population of metropolitan area.
○Population of town or township.
† Zip of nearest p.o. * Multiple zips.

AREA 7,787 sq. mi. (20,168 sq. km.)
POPULATION 7,364,823
CAPITAL Trenton
LARGEST CITY Newark
HIGHEST POINT High Point 1,803 ft. (550 m.)
SETTLED IN 1617
ADMITTED TO UNION December 18, 1787
POPULAR NAME Garden State
STATE FLOWER Purple Violet
STATE BIRD Eastern Goldfinch

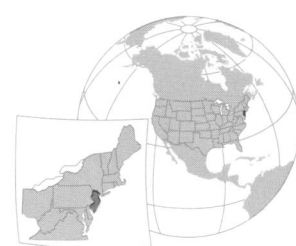

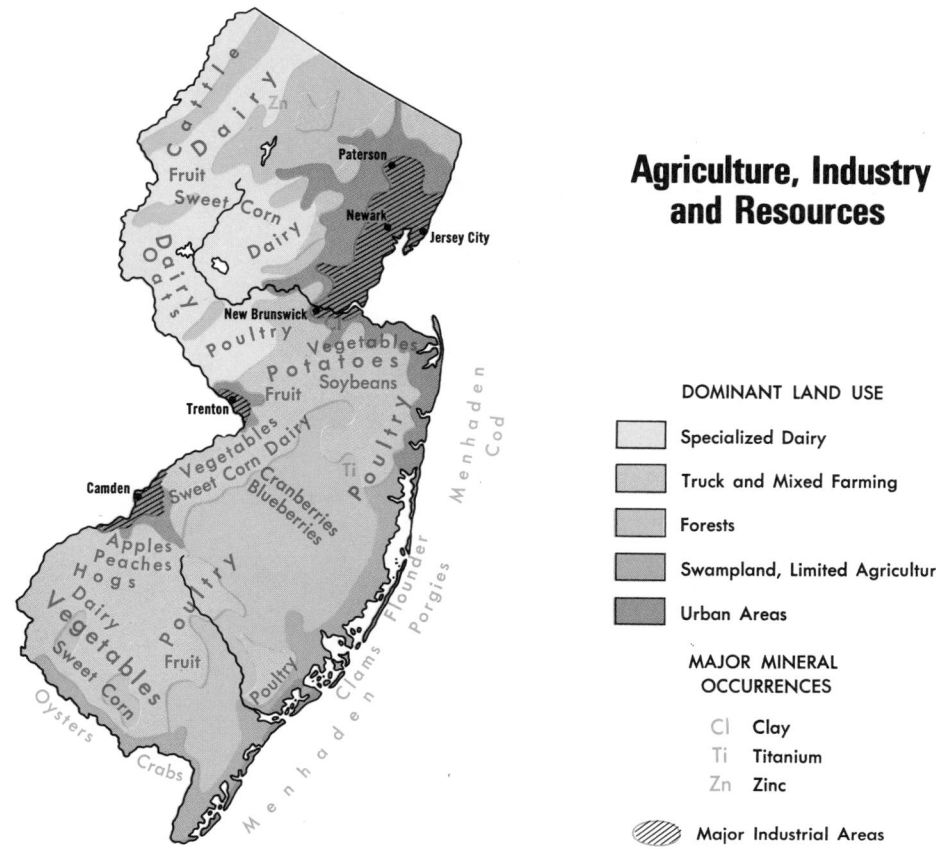

Agriculture, Industry and Resources

DOMINANT LAND USE

Specialized Dairy

Truck and Mixed Farming

Forests

Swampland, Limited Agriculture

Urban Areas

MAJOR MINERAL OCCURRENCES

Cl   Clay

Ti   Titanium

Zn   Zinc

Major Industrial Areas

The Urban Northeast

Urbanized Areas

● Places with more than 10,000 inhabitants

● Places with 5,000-10,000 inhabitants

● Places with 2,500-5,000 inhabitants

© Copyright HAMMOND INCORPORATED, Maplewood, N.J.

COUNTIES

Name	Pop.	Key
Atlantic	194,119	D5
Bergen	845,385	E2
Burlington	362,542	D4
Camden	471,650	D4
Cape May	82,266	D5
Cumberland	132,866	C5
Essex	851,116	E2
Gloucester	199,917	C4
Hudson	556,972	E2
Hunterdon	87,361	D2
Mercer	307,863	D3
Middlesex	595,893	E3
Monmouth	503,173	E3
Morris	407,630	D2
Ocean	346,038	E4
Passaic	447,585	E1
Salem	64,676	C4
Somerset	203,129	D2
Sussex	116,119	D1
Union	504,094	E2
Warren	84,429	C2

CITIES and TOWNS

Zip	Name/Pop.	Key
08201	Absecon 6,859	D5
07820	Allamuchy 600	D2
07401	Allendale 5,901	B1
07711	Allenhurst 912	F3
08501	Allentown 1,962	D3
08720	Allenwood	E3
08001	Alloway 1,370	C4
08865	Alpha 2,644	C2
07620	Alpine 1,549	C1
07821	Andover 892	D2
08801	Annandale 1,040	D2
07712	Asbury Park 17,015	F3
	Asbury Park-Long Branch‡ 503,173	F3
†08033	Ashland	B3
08004	Atco	D4
*08401	Atlantic City 40,199	E5
	Atlantic City‡ 194,119	E5
07716	Atlantic Highlands 4,950	F3
08106	Audubon 9,533	B3
†08106	Audubon Park 1,274	B3
08202	Avalon 2,162	D5
07001	Avenel	E2
07717	Avon By The Sea 2,337	F3
08005	Barnegat 1,012	E4
08006	Barnegat Light 619	E4
08007	Barrington 7,418	B3
07920	Basking Ridge	D2
08742	Bay Head 1,340	E3
07002	Bayonne 65,047	B2
08008	Beach Haven 1,714	E4
08722	Beachwood 7,687	E4
07921	Bedminster◌ 2,469	D2
08502	Belle Mead	D3
07109	Belleville 35,367	B2
08031	Bellmawr 13,721	B3
07719	Belmar 6,771	E3
07823	Belvidere◉ 2,475	C2
07621	Bergenfield 25,568	C1
07922	Berkeley Heights◌ 12,549	E2
08009	Berlin 5,786	D4
07924	Bernardsville 6,715	D2
08010	Beverly 2,919	D3
08012	Blackwood 5,219	C4
07825	Blairstown◌ 4,360	C2
07003	Bloomfield 47,792	B2
07403	Bloomingdale 7,867	E1
08804	Bloomsbury 864	C2
07603	Bogota 8,344	B2
07005	Boonton 8,620	E2
08505	Bordentown 4,441	D3
08805	Bound Brook 9,710	D2
07720	Bradley Beach 4,772	F3
07826	Branchville 870	D1
08723	Breton Woods	E3
08723	Brick◌ 53,629	E3
08014	Bridgeport 750	C4
08302	Bridgeton◉ 18,795	C5
08807	Bridgewater◌ 29,175	D2
08730	Brielle 4,068	E3
08203	Brigantine 8,318	E5
08030	Brooklawn 2,133	B3
08015	Browns Mills 10,568	D4
07828	Budd Lake 6,523	D2
08310	Buena 3,642	D4
08016	Burlington 10,246	D3
07405	Butler 7,616	E2
07830	Califon 1,023	D2
*08101	Camden◉ 84,910	B3
†08701	Candlewood 6,750	E4
08204	Cape May 4,853	D6
08210	Cape May Court House◉ 3,597	D5
07072	Carlstadt 6,166	B2
08069	Carneys Point 7,574	C4
07008	Carteret 20,598	E2
07009	Cedar Grove◌ 12,600	B2
†08723	Cedarwood Park	E3
07928	Chatham 8,537	E2
08019	Chatsworth 700	D4
08879	Cheesequake	E3
*08034	Cherry Hill◌ 68,785	B3
†08089	Chesilhurst 1,590	D4
07930	Chester 1,433	D2
†08505	Chesterfield◌ 3,867	D3
†08077	Cinnaminson◌ 16,072	B3
07066	Clark◌ 16,699	A3
08020	Clarksboro	C4
08510	Clarksburg 800	E3
08312	Clayton 6,013	C4
08021	Clementon 5,764	D4
07010	Cliffside Park 21,464	C2
07721	Cliffwood	E3
*07011	Clifton 74,388	B2
08809	Clinton 1,910	D2
07624	Closter 8,164	C1
08108	Collingswood 15,838	B3
08213	Cologne 800	D4
07722	Colts Neck 950	E3
07832	Columbia 600	C2
08022	Columbus 800	D3
07961	Convent Station	E2
†08270	Corbin City 254	D5
†07821	Cranberry Lake 500	D2
08512	Cranbury 1,255	E3
07016	Cranford◌ 24,573	E2
07626	Cresskill 7,609	C1
08515	Crosswicks 265	D3
07723	Deal 1,952	F3
08023	Deepwater 800	C4
08110	Delair	B3
08075	Delanco◌ 3,730	D3
08075	Delran◌ 14,811	B3
07627	Demarest 4,963	C1
08214	Dennisville 890	D5
07834	Denville◌ 14,380	E2
08096	Deptford◌ 23,473	B4
08317	Dorothy 900	D5
07801	Dover 14,681	D2
07628	Dumont 18,334	C1
08812	Dunellen 6,593	D2
08816	East Brunswick◌ 37,711	E3
07936	East Hanover◌ 9,319	E2
07734	East Keansburg	E3
08873	East Millstone 950	D3
†07100	East Newark 1,923	B2
*07017	East Orange 77,690	B2
07073	East Rutherford 7,849	B2
07724	Eatontown 12,703	E3
07020	Edgewater 4,628	C2
†08010	Edgewater Park◌ 9,273	D3
*08817	Edison◌ 70,193	E2
08215	Egg Harbor City 4,618	D4
07740	Elberon	F3
*07201	Elizabeth◉ 106,201	B2
08318	Elmer 1,569	C4
†07407	Elmwood Park 18,377	B2
08217	Elwood 1,538	D4
07630	Emerson 7,793	B1
*07631	Englewood 23,701	C2
07632	Englewood Cliffs 5,698	C2
07726	Englishtown 976	E3
07021	Essex Fells 2,363	B2
08319	Estell Manor 848	D5
08025	Ewan 610	C4
07006	Fairfield◌ 7,987	A2
07701	Fair Haven 5,679	E3
07410	Fair Lawn 32,229	B1
08320	Fairton 1,107	C5
07022	Fairview 10,519	C2
07023	Fanwood 7,767	E2
07931	Far Hills 677	D2
07727	Farmingdale 1,348	E3
†08505	Fieldsboro 597	D3
07836	Flanders	D2
08822	Flemington◌ 4,132	D2
08518	Florence-Roebling 7,677	D3
07932	Florham Park 9,359	E2
†08037	Folsom 1,892	D4
08863	Fords	E2
08731	Forked River 900	E4
07024	Fort Lee 32,449	C2
07416	Franklin 4,486	D1
07417	Franklin Lakes 8,769	B1
†08823	Franklin Park◌ 31,358	D3
08322	Franklinville	C4
07728	Freehold◉ 10,020	E3
08825	Frenchtown 1,573	C2
07026	Garfield 26,803	B2
07027	Garwood 4,752	E2
08026	Gibbsboro 2,510	B4
	Gibbstown	C4
†08753	Gilford Park 6,528	E4
07933	Gillette	E2
08028	Glassboro 14,574	C4
08029	Glendora 5,632	B4
08826	Glen Gardner 834	D2
07028	Glen Ridge 7,855	B2
07452	Glen Rock 11,497	B1
08030	Gloucester City 13,121	B3
07435	Green Pond 800	E1
07935	Green Village 800	D2
08323	Greenwich◌ 973	C5
08032	Grenloch 700	C4

(continued on following page)

07093 Guttenberg 7,340 C2
*07601 Hackensack⊙ 36,039 B2
07840 Hackettstown 8,850 D2
08033 Haddonfield 12,337 B3
08035 Haddon Heights 8,361 B3
08036 Hainesport○ 3,236 D4
07508 Haledon 6,607 B1
07419 Hamburg 1,832 D1
08690 Hamilton Square-
Mercerville 25,446 D3
08037 Hammonton 12,298 D4
08827 Hampton 1,614 D2
07640 Harrington Park 4,532 C1
07029 Harrison 12,242 B2
†08057 Hartford 650 D4
08008 Harvey Cedars 363 E4
07604 Hasbrouck Heights 12,166 B2
07641 Haworth 3,509 C1
07507 Hawthorne 18,200 B2
07730 Hazlet 23,013 E3
08828 Helmetta 955 E3
07421 Hewitt 950 E1
08829 High Bridge 3,435 D2
07422 Highland Lakes 2,888 E1
08904 Highland Park 13,396 D2
07732 Highlands 5,187 F3
08520 Hightstown 4,581 D3
07642 Hillsdale 10,495 B1
07205 Hillside○ 21,440 B2
†08083 Hi-Nella 1,250 B4
07030 Hoboken 42,460 C2
07423 Ho Ho Kus 4,129 B1
07733 Holmdel○ 8,447 E3
07843 Hopatcong 15,531 D2
07844 Hope 310 D2
08525 Hopewell 2,001 D3
07731 Howell○ 25,065 E3
†07712 Interlaken 1,037 E3
07845 Ironia D2
07111 Irvington 61,493 B2
08830 Iselin E2
08732 Island Heights 1,575 E4
08527 Jackson○ 25,644 E3
08831 Jamesburg 4,114 E3
*07301 Jersey City⊙ 223,532 B2
Jersey City‡ 556,972 B2
07734 Keansburg 10,613 E3
07032 Kearny 35,735 B2
08824 Kendall Park 7,419 D3
07033 Kenilworth 8,221 E2
07735 Keyport 7,413 E3
08528 Kingston D3
07405 Kinnelon 7,770 E2
07848 Lafayette 900 D1
07034 Lake Hiawatha E2
07849 Lake Hopatcong D2
08733 Lakehurst 2,908 E3
†07871 Lake Mohawk 8,498 D1
08701 Lakewood 22,863 E3
08530 Lambertville 4,044 D3
07850 Landing D2
08734 Lanoka Harbor E4
08021 Laurel Springs 2,249 B4
08879 Laurence Harbor 6,737 E3
08735 Lavallette 2,072 E4
08045 Lawnside 3,042 B3
08648 Lawrenceville 19,724 D3
08833 Lebanon 820 D2
07852 Ledgewood D2
08327 Leesburg 700 D5
07737 Leonardo E3
07605 Leonia 8,027 C2
07938 Liberty Corner D2
07035 Lincoln Park 8,806 A1
07738 Lincroft E3
07036 Linden 37,836 A3
08021 Lindenwold 18,196 B4
08221 Linwood 6,144 D5
07424 Little Falls○ 11,496 B2
07643 Little Ferry 9,399 B2
07739 Little Silver 5,548 F3
07039 Livingston○ 28,040 E2
07644 Lodi 23,956 B2
07740 Long Branch 29,819 F3
Long Branch-Asbury Park‡
503,173 F3
08403 Longport 1,249 D5
07853 Long Valley 1,682 D2
08048 Lumberton 600 D4
07071 Lyndhurst○ 20,326 B2
07939 Lyons D2
07940 Madison 15,357 E2
08049 Magnolia 4,881 B3
07430 Mahwah○ 12,127 E1
08328 Malaga 950 C4
08050 Manahawkin 1,469 E4
08736 Manasquan 5,354 E3
08738 Mantoloking 433 E3
08051 Mantua○ 9,193 C4
08835 Manville 11,278 D2
08052 Maple Shade○ 20,525 B3
07040 Maplewood○ 22,950 E2
08402 Margate City 9,179 E5
07746 Marlboro○ 17,560 E3
08053 Marlton 9,411 D4
08223 Marmora 650 D5
08836 Martinsville D2
07747 Matawan 8,837 E3
08330 Mays Landing⊙ 2,054 D5
07607 Maywood 9,895 B2
07428 McAfee 800 D1
†08232 McKee City 950 D5
08055 Medford D4
08055 Medford Lakes 4,958 D4
07945 Mendham 4,899 D2
08837 Menlo Park E2
08619 Mercerville-Hamilton
Square 25,446 D3
08109 Merchantville 3,972 B3
08840 Metuchen 13,762 E2
08846 Middlesex 13,480 E2
07748 Middletown○ 62,574 E3
07432 Midland Park 7,381 B1
08848 Milford 1,368 C2
07041 Millburn○ 19,543 E2
07946 Millington 975 D2
†08876 Millstone 530 D2

08850 Milltown 7,136 E3
08332 Millville 24,815 C5
†07801 Mine Hill○ 3,325 D2
08342 Mizpah 900 D5
07750 Monmouth Beach 3,318 F3
08852 Monmouth Junction 2,579 D3
07434 Monroe○ 15,858 E3
*07042 Montclair 38,321 B2
07645 Montvale 7,318 B1
07045 Montville○ 14,290 E2
†07070 Moonachie 2,706 B2
08057 Moorestown 13,695 B3
07950 Morris Plains 5,305 D2
07960 Morristown⊙ 16,614 D2
07046 Mountain Lakes 4,153 E2
07092 Mountainside 7,118 E2
07856 Mount Arlington 4,251 D2
08059 Mount Ephraim 4,863 B3
07970 Mount Freedom D2
08060 Mount Holly 10,818 D4
†08054 Mount Laurel○ 17,614 D4
†07828 Mount Olive○ 18,748 D2
08061 Mount Royal 900 C4
08062 Mullica Hill 1,050 C4
08087 Mystic Islands 4,929 E4
08063 National Park 3,552 B3
07752 Navesink E3
07753 Neptune○ 28,366 E3
07753 Neptune City 5,276 E3
07857 Netcong 3,557 D2
*07101 Newark⊙ 329,248 B2
Newark‡ 1,965,304 B2
*08901 New Brunswick⊙ 41,442 E3
New Brunswick-Perth
Amboy-Sayreville‡
595,893 E3
08533 New Egypt 2,111 E3
08344 Newfield 1,563 D4
07435 Newfoundland 900 D1
08224 New Gretna 800 E4
07646 New Milford 16,876 B1
07974 New Providence 12,426 E2
07860 Newton⊙ 7,748 D1
08346 Newtonville 950 D4
07976 New Vernon D2
07032 North Arlington 16,587 B2
07047 North Bergen○ 47,019 B2
08876 North Branch 610 D2
08902 North Brunswick○ 22,220 D3
†07006 North Caldwell 5,832 B2
08204 North Cape May 4,029 C6
08225 Northfield 7,795 D5
07508 North Haledon 8,177 B1
07060 North Plainfield 19,108 E2
07647 Northvale 5,046 F1
08260 North Wildwood 4,714 D6
07648 Norwood 4,413 C1
07110 Nutley 28,998 B2
07755 Oakhurst E3
07436 Oakland 13,443 B1
08107 Oaklyn 4,223 B3
08226 Ocean City 13,949 D5
08740 Ocean Gate 1,385 E4
07756 Ocean Grove F3
07757 Oceanport 5,888 F3
07439 Ogdensburg 2,737 D1
08857 Old Bridge 21,815 E3
07675 Old Tappan 4,168 C1
07649 Oradell 8,658 B1
*07050 Orange 31,136 B2
08723 Osbornsville E3
07863 Oxford 1,587 C2
07470 Packanack Lake B1
07650 Palisades Park 13,732 C2
08065 Palmyra 7,085 B3
07652 Paramus 26,474 B1
07656 Park Ridge 8,515 B1
07054 Parsippany-Troy
Hills○ 49,868 E2
07055 Passaic 52,463 E2
*07501 Paterson⊙ 137,970 B2
Paterson-Clifton-Passaic‡
447,585 B2
08066 Paulsboro 6,944 C4
07977 Peapack-Gladstone 2,038 D2
08067 Pedricktown C4
08068 Pemberton 1,198 D4
08534 Pennington 2,109 D3
08110 Pennsauken○ 33,775 B3
08069 Penns Grove 5,760 C4
08070 Pennsville 12,467 C4
07440 Pequannock○ 13,776 B1
*08861 Perth Amboy 38,951 E2
08865 Phillipsburg 16,647 C2
08741 Pine Beach 1,796 E4
07058 Pine Brook E2
08021 Pine Hill 8,684 D4
08854 Piscataway○ 42,223 D2
0807; Pitman 9,744 C4
*07060 Plainfield 45,555 E2
08536 Plainsboro D3
08232 Pleasantville 13,435 D5
08742 Point Pleasant 17,747 E3
08742 Point Pleasant Beach
5,415 E3
08240 Pomona 2,358 D5
07442 Pompton Lakes 10,660 A1
07444 Pompton Plains B1
07758 Port Monmouth E3
†07850 Port Morris 616 D2
07865 Port Murray 250 D2
08349 Port Norris 1,730 C5
08241 Port Republic 837 D4
08540 Princeton 12,035 D3
08550 Princeton Junction 2,419 D3
†07885 Prospect Park 5,142 B1
08072 Quinton 750 C4
*07065 Rahway 26,723 E2
†08054 Ramblewood 6,475 D4
07446 Ramsey 12,899 B1
†07801 Randolph○ 17,828 D2
08869 Raritan 6,128 D2
07701 Red Bank 12,031 E3
07657 Ridgefield 10,294 B2
07660 Ridgefield Park 12,738 B2
*07450 Ridgewood 25,208 B1
08551 Ringoes 682 D3

07456 Ringwood 12,625 E1
08242 Rio Grande 2,016 D5
07457 Riverdale 2,530 A1
07661 River Edge 11,111 B1
08075 Riverside○ 7,941 B3
08077 Riverton 3,068 B3
07675 River Vale○ 9,489 B1
07662 Rochelle Park○ 5,603 B2
07866 Rockaway 6,852 D2
07647 Rockleigh 192 C1
08553 Rocky Hill 717 D3
08554 Roebling-Florence 7,677 D3
08555 Roosevelt 835 E3
07068 Roseland 5,330 A2
07203 Roselle 20,641 B2
07204 Roselle Park 13,377 A2
08352 Rosenhayn 950 C5
†07876 Roxbury○ 18,878 D2
07760 Rumson 7,623 F3
08078 Runnemede 9,461 B3
*07070 Rutherford 19,068 B2
07662 Saddle Brook○ 14,084 B1
07458 Saddle River 2,763 B1
08079 Salem⊙ 6,959 C4
08872 Sayreville 29,969 E3
07076 Scotch Plains○ 20,774 E2
07760 Sea Bright 1,812 F3
08302 Seabrook 1,411 C5
08750 Sea Girt 2,650 E3
08243 Sea Isle City 2,644 D5
08751 Seaside Heights 1,802 E4
08752 Seaside Park 1,795 E4
07094 Secaucus 13,719 B2
07077 Sewaren E2
08080 Sewell C4
08353 Shiloh 604 C5
08008 Ship Bottom 1,427 E4
07078 Short Hills E2
07701 Shrewsbury 2,962 E3
08081 Sicklerville D4
08558 Skillman D3
08201 Smithville 70 E5
08083 Somerdale 5,900 B4
08244 Somers Point 10,330 D5
08876 Somerville⊙ 11,973 D2
08879 South Amboy 8,322 E3
†07719 South Belmar 1,566 E3
08880 South Bound Brook 4,331 E2
†08852 South Brunswick○ 17,127 E3
07079 South Orange○ 15,864 A2
07080 South Plainfield 20,521 E2
08882 South River 14,361 E3
08753 South Toms River 3,954 E4
07871 Sparta○ 13,333 D1
08884 Spotswood 7,840 E3
07081 Springfield○ 13,955 E2
07762 Spring Lake 4,215 F3
†07762 Spring Lake Heights 5,424 E3
07874 Stanhope 3,638 D2
08886 Stewartsville 950 C2
07980 Stirling E2
07460 Stockholm D1
08559 Stockton 643 D3
08247 Stone Harbor 1,187 D5
08084 Stratford 8,005 B4
†07747 Strathmore E3
07876 Succasunna 10,931 D2
07901 Summit 21,071 E2
08008 Surf City 1,571 E4
07461 Sussex 2,418 D1
08085 Swedesboro 2,031 C4
07878 Tabor E2
07666 Teaneck○ 39,007 B2
07670 Tenafly 13,552 C1
07608 Teterboro 19 B2
08086 Thorofare B4
08887 Three Bridges 750 D2
07724 Tinton Falls 7,740 E3
08753 Toms River⊙ 7,465 E4
07512 Totowa 11,448 B1
07082 Towaco E2
*08601 Trenton (cap.)⊙ 92,124 D3
Trenton‡ 307,863 D3
08087 Tuckerton 2,472 E4
07083 Union○ 50,184 A2
07735 Union Beach 6,354 E3
07087 Union City 55,593 C2
†07421 Upper Greenwood
Lake 2,734 E1
†07458 Upper Saddle River 7,958 B1
08406 Ventnor City 11,704 E5
07462 Vernon 800 E1
07044 Verona 14,166 B2
08251 Villas 5,909 D5
08088 Vincentown 900 D4
08360 Vineland 53,753 C5
Vineland-Millville-Bridgeton‡
132,866 C5
†08043 Voorhees○ 12,919 B3
07463 Waldwick 10,802 B1
07719 Wall○ 18,952 E3
07057 Wallington 10,741 B2
†07712 Wanamassa E3
07465 Wanaque 10,025 B1
08758 Waretown 1,175 E4
†07060 Warren○ 9,805 D2
07882 Washington 6,429 D2
07060 Watchung 5,290 E2
07470 Wayne○ 46,474 A1
07087 Weehawken○ 13,168 C2
08090 Wenonah 2,303 C4
07006 West Caldwell 11,407 A2
†08204 West Cape May 1,091 D6
08092 West Creek 827 E4
†08086 West Deptford○ 18,002 B3
*07090 Westfield 30,447 E2
07764 West Long Branch 7,380 F3
07480 West Milford 950 E1
08108 Westmont 15,875 B3
07093 West New York 39,194 C2
07052 West Orange 39,510 A2
07424 West Paterson 11,293 B2
08628 West Trenton D3
08093 Westville 4,786 B3
†08260 West Wildwood 360 D6
07675 Westwood 10,714 B1
07885 Wharton 5,485 D2

Topography

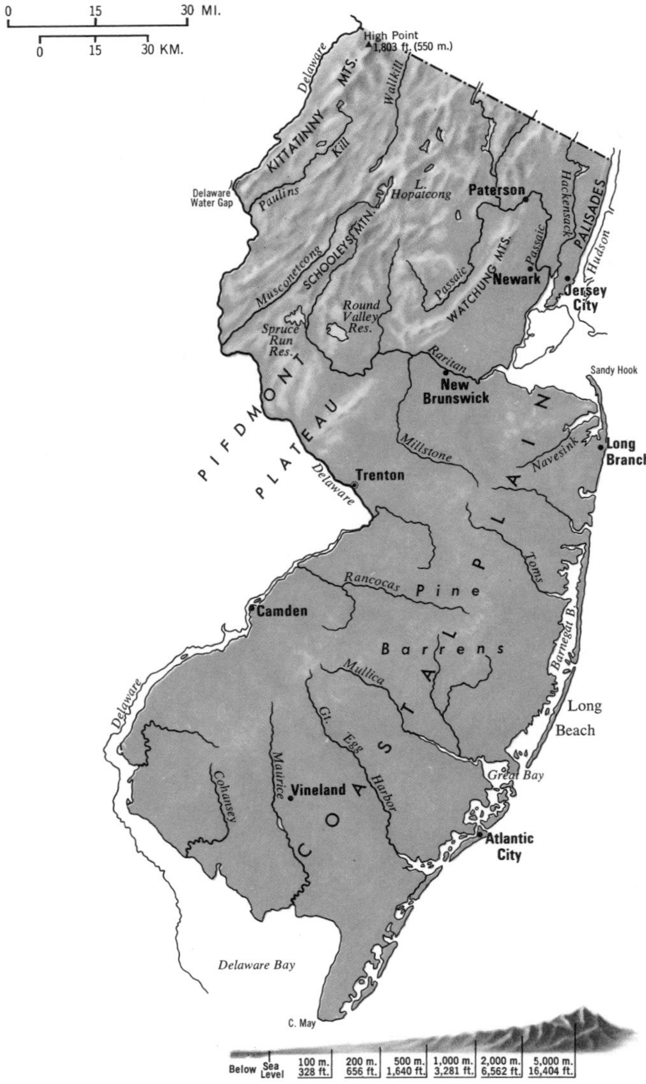

07981 Whippany E2
08889 White House Station D2
†07866 White Meadow Lake 8,429 D2
08252 Whitesboro 1,583 D5
07765 Wickatunk 950 E3
08260 Wildwood 4,913 D6
08260 Wildwood Crest 4,149 D6
08094 Williamstown 5,768 D4
08046 Willingboro○ 39,912 D3
†07036 Winfield○ 1,785 B2
08270 Woodbine 2,809 D5
07095 Woodbridge○ 90,074 E2
08096 Woodbury⊙ 10,353 B4
08097 Woodbury Heights 3,460 B4
07675 Woodcliff Lake 5,644 B1
†08107 Wood-Lynne 2,578 B3
†07885 Woodport D2
07075 Wood-Ridge 7,929 B2
08098 Woodstown 3,250 C4
08562 Wrightstown 3,031 D3
07481 Wyckoff○ 15,500 B1
08620 Yardville 9,414 D3

OTHER FEATURES

Absecon (inlet) E5
Alloways (creek) C4
Arthur Kill (str.) B3
Atlantic Highlands (ridge) E3
Barnegat (bay) E4
Batsto (riv.) D4
Bayonne Military Ocean Terminal B2
Beach Haven (inlet) E4
Beaver (brook) C2
Ben Davis (pt.) C5
Big Flat (brook) D1
Big Timber (creek) C4
Boonton (res.) E2
Brigantine (inlet) E5
Budd (lake) D2
Canistear (res.) E1
Cedar (creek) E4
Clinton (res.) E1
Cohansey (riv.) C5
Cold Spring (inlet) D6
Cooper (riv.) B3
Corson (inlet) D5
Crosswicks (creek) D3
Culvers (lake) D1
Delaware (bay) C5
Delaware (riv.) D3
Delaware Water Gap Nat'l Rec.
Area C1
Earle Naval Weapons Sta. E3
Echo (lake) E1
Edison Nat'l Hist. Site A2
Egg Island (pt.) C5
Fort Dix 14,297 D3
Fort Hancock F3
Fort Monmouth E3
Gateway Nat'l Rec. Area E2
Great (bay) E4
Great Egg Harbor (inlet) E5
Greenwood (lake) E1
Hackensack (riv.) C1
Hereford (inlet) D5
High Point (mt.) D1
Hopatcong (lake) D2
Hudson (riv.) C1
Island (beach) E4
Kill Van Kull (str.) B2
Kittatinny (mts.) D1
Lakehurst Naval Air Engineering
Center E3
Lamington (riv.) D2
Landing (creek) D4
Little Egg (harb.) E4
Lockatong (creek) C3
Long (beach) E4
Long Beach (isl.) E4
Lower New York (bay) E2
Manasquan (riv.) E3
Manumuskin (riv.) D5
Maurice (riv.) C4
May (cape) C6
McGuire A.F.B. 7,853 D3
Metedeconk (riv.) E3
Mill (creek) E4
Millstone (riv.) D3
Mohawk (lake) D1
Morristown Nat'l Hist. Park D2
Mullica (riv.) D4
Musconetcong (riv.) C2
Navesink (riv.) E3
Newark (bay) B2
Oak Ridge (res.) D1
Oldmans (creek) C4
Oradell (res.) B1
Oswego (riv.) E4
Owassa (lake) D1
Palisades C1
Passaic (riv.) E2
Paulins Kill (riv.) D1
Pennsauken (creek) B3
Pequest (riv.) D2
Picatinny Arsenal D2
Pohatcong (creek) C2
Pompton (lake) B1
Raccoon (creek) C4
Ramapo (riv.) E1
Rancocas (creek) D3
Raritan (bay) E3
Raritan (riv.) D2
Ridgeway Branch, Toms (riv.) E3
Round Valley (res.) D2
Saddle (riv.) B1
Salem (riv.) C4
Sandy Hook (spit) F3
Shoal Branch, Wading (riv.) D4
Spruce Run (res.) D2
Statue of Liberty Nat'l Mon. B2
Stony (brook) D3
Stow (creek) C5
Swartswood (lake) D1
Tappan (lake) C1
The Narrows (str.) E2
Toms (riv.) E3
Townsend (inlet) D5
Tuckahoe (riv.) D5
Union (lake) C5
Upper New York (bay) B2
Wading (riv.) D4
Wallkill (riv.) D1
Wanaque (res.) E1
Wawayanda (lake) E1

⊙County seat.
‡Population of metropolitan area.
○Population of town or township.
† Zip of nearest p.o. * Multiple zips.

New Jersey

SCALE

0   5   10   15   20 MI.

0   5   10   15   20 KM.

State Capitals .... ⊛

County Seats .... ⊙

Canals ....

Major Limited Access Hwys. _____

Scale 1:930,000

© Copyright HAMMOND INCORPORATED, Maplewood, N.J.

COUNTIES

Bernalillo 419,700 ....C4
Catron 2,720 ....A4
Chaves 51,103 ....E5
Cibola B3
Colfax 13,667 ....E2
Curry 42,019 ....F4
De Baca 2,454 ....E5
Dona Ana 96,340 ....C6
Eddy 47,855 ....F6
Grant 26,204 ....A5
Guadalupe 4,496 ....E3
Harding 1,090 ....F3
Hidalgo 6,049 ....A7
Lea 55,993 ....F6
Lincoln 10,997 ....D5

Los Alamos 17,599 ....C3
Luna 15,585 ....B6
McKinley 56,449 ....A3
Mora 4,205 ....E3
Otero 44,665 ....D6
Quay 10,577 ....F3
Rio Arriba 29,282 ....B2
Roosevelt 15,695 ....F4
Sandoval 34,799 ....C3
San Juan 81,433 ....A2
San Miguel
   22,751 ....D3
Santa Fe 75,360 ....C3
Sierra 8,454 ....B5
Socorro 12,566 ....C5
Torrance 7,491 ....D4
Union 4,725 ....F2
Valencia 61,115 ....C4

CITIES and TOWNS

Zip	Name/Pop.	Key
87510	Abiquiu 500	C2
†87034	Acoma 150	B4
*87034	Acomita (Pueblo of Acoma) 975	B3
88310	Alamogordo⊙ 24,024	C6
*87101	Albuquerque⊙ 331,767	C3
	Albuquerque‡ 454,499	C3
87511	Alcalde 975	C2
87001	Algodones 195	C3
88312	Alto 285	D5
87512	Amalia 200	D2
88021	Anthony 3,285	C6
87711	Anton Chico 400	D4
87930	Arrey 367	B6
87513	Arroyo Hondo 400	D2

87514	Arroyo Seco 500	D2
88210	Artesia 10,385	E6
87410	Aztec⊙ 5,512	B2
88023	Bayard 3,036	A6
87002	Belen 5,617	C4
88314	Bent 294	D5
88024	Berino 600	C6
87004	Bernalillo⊙ 3,012	C3
87412	Blanco 200	B2
87413	Bloomfield 4,881	A2
87005	Bluewater 300	A3
87006	Bosque (Bosque Farms) 3,353	C4
87712	Buena Vista 178	D3
87515	Canjilon 380	C2
87516	Canones 300	C2
88316	Capitan 762	D5
88414	Capulin 100	F2
88220	Carlsbad⊙ 25,496	E6

88301	Carrizozo⊙ 1,222	D5
87007	Casa Blanca 560	B4
88113	Causey 81	F5
87518	Cebolla 100	C2
87008	Cedar Crest 600	C3
†87410	Cedar Hill 145	B2
88026	Central 1,968	A6
87010	Cerrillos 500	D3
87519	Cerro 400	D2
87713	Chacon 310	D2
87520	Chama 1,090	C2
88027	Chamberino 700	C6
87521	Chamisal 642	D2
87522	Chimayo 1,993	D2
87714	Cimarron 888	E2
88316	Capitan 762	D5
88415	Clayton⊙ 2,968	F2
88230	Cleveland 450	D2
88028	Cliff 600	A6
88317	Cloudcroft 521	D6

88101	Clovis⊙ 31,194	F4
†87041	Cochiti 983	C3
88029	Columbus 414	B7
88416	Conchas Dam 240	E3
87523	Cordova 750	D2
88318	Corona 236	D4
87048	Corrales 2,791	C3
87524	Costilla 400	D2
87313	Crownpoint 1,134	A3
87013	Cuba 609	C2
87014	Cubero 300	B3
87821	Datil 150	B4
88030	Deming⊙ 9,964	A6
87933	Derry 175	B6
88418	Des Moines 178	F2
88230	Dexter 882	E5
87527	Dixon 800	D2
88032	Dona Ana 800	C6
†86504	Crystal 200	A2

88115 Dora 168 .... F5
87528 Dulce 1,648 .... B2
87718 Eagle Nest 202 .... D2
88116 Elida 202 .... F5
87529 El Prado 200 .... D2
87530 El Rito 475 .... C2
87531 Embudo 400 .... C2
88321 Encino 155 .... D4
87532 Espanola 6,803 .... C3
87016 Estancia⊙ 830 .... D4
88231 Eunice 2,970 .... F6
88033 Fairacres 700 .... C6
87401 Farmington 31,222 .... A2
†88041 Fierro 200 .... A6
87415 Flora Vista 500 .... A2
88118 Floyd 146 .... F4
88419 Folsom 73 .... F2
88036 Fort Bayard 400 .... A6
88323 Fort Stanton 80 .... D5
88119 Fort Sumner⊙ 1,421 .... E4
87316 Fort Wingate 800 .... A3
87416 Fruitland 800 .... A2
†87540 Galisteo 125 .... D3
87017 Gallina 420 .... C2
87301 Gallup⊙ 18,167 .... A3
87317 Gamerco 800 .... A3
87936 Garfield 600 .... B6
88038 Gila 350 .... A6
88324 Glencoe 125 .... D5
88039 Glenwood 220 .... A5
87535 Glorieta 300 .... D3
88120 Grady 122 .... F4
87020 Grants 11,439 .... B3
88424 Grenville 39 .... F2
87722 Guadalupita 300 .... D2
88232 Hagerman 936 .... E5
88041 Hanover 300 .... A6
87937 Hatch 1,028 .... B6
87537 Hernandez 500 .... C2
88325 High Rolls-Mountain Park 555 .... D5
88042 Hillsboro 175 .... B6
88240 Hobbs 29,153 .... F6
87723 Holman 400 .... D2
88336 Hondo 425 .... D5
88250 Hope 111 .... E6
87901 Hot Springs (Truth or Consequences)⊙ 5,219 .... B5
88121 House 117 .... F4
88043 Hurley 1,616 .... A6
87022 Isleta 1,246 .... C4
88252 Jal 2,675 .... F6
87023 Jarales 700 .... C4
87024 Jemez Pueblo 1,503 .... C3
87025 Jemez Springs 316 .... C3
87417 Kirtland 2,358 .... A2
87026 Laguna 900 .... B3
87027 La Jara 210 .... B2
88253 Lake Arthur 327 .... E5
88337 La Luz 1,194 .... C6
87539 La Madera 200 .... C2
88044 La Mesa 900 .... C6
87418 La Plata 150 .... A2
88001 Las Cruces⊙ 45,086 .... C6
Las Cruces‡ 96,340 .... C6
87701 Las Vegas⊙ 14,322 .... D3
87725 Ledoux 300 .... D3
87823 Lemitar 800 .... B4
88338 Lincoln 100 .... D5
87543 Llano 325 .... D2
88255 Loco Hills 375 .... F6
88426 Logan 735 .... F3
88045 Lordsburg⊙ 3,195 .... A6
87544 Los Alamos⊙ 11,039 .... C3
87031 Los Lunas⊙ 3,525 .... C4
†87101 Los Ranchos De Albuquerque 2,702 .... C3
88256 Loving 1,355 .... E6
88260 Lovington⊙ 9,727 .... F6
87547 Lumberton 175 .... C2
87824 Luna 200 .... A5
87825 Magdalena 1,022 .... B4
88263 Malaga 300 .... E6
87728 Maxwell 316 .... E2
88339 Mayhill 300 .... D6
†79901 Meadow Vista 3,377 .... C7
88124 Melrose 649 .... F4
87319 Mentmore 315 .... A3
88340 Mescalero 1,259 .... D5
88046 Mesilla 2,029 .... C6
88047 Mesilla Park C6
88048 Mesquite 500 .... C6
87320 Mexican Springs 150 .... A3
87729 Miami 112 .... E2
87021 Milan 3,747 .... B3
88049 Mimbres 300 .... B6
87731 Montezuma 250 .... D3
87939 Monticello 125 .... B5
88265 Monument 300 .... F6
87732 Mora⊙ D3
87035 Moriarty 1,276 .... D4
87733 Mosquero⊙ 197 .... F3
87036 Mountainair 1,170 .... C4
†87501 Nambe 1,017 .... D3
88430 Nara Visa 250 .... F3
87328 Navajo 920 .... A3
†87325 Newcomb 500 .... A2
87038 New Laguna 250 .... B4
88266 Oil Center 236 .... F6
87549 Ojo Caliente 600 .... D2
87735 Ojo Feliz 133 .... E2
87550 Ojo Sarco 380 .... D2
88052 Organ 300 .... C6
87040 Paguate 500 .... B3
87552 Pecos 885 .... D3
87041 Pena Blanca 700 .... C3
87553 Penasco 860 .... D2
87042 Peralta 400 .... C4
88343 Picacho 100 .... D5
88053 Pinos Altos 250 .... A6
87044 Ponderosa 300 .... C3
88130 Portales⊙ 9,940 .... F4
87045 Prewitt 300 .... B3
88432 Puerto de Luna 175 .... E4
87829 Quemado 450 .... A4
87556 Questa 1,202 .... D2
88054 Radium Springs 150 .... B6
87736 Rainsville 350 .... D2
87321 Ramah 574 .... A3
87557 Ranches of Taos 1,411 .... D2
87740 Raton⊙ 8,225 .... E2
87558 Red River 332 .... D2
87322 Rehoboth 200 .... A3
87830 Reserve⊙ 439 .... A5
87560 Ribera 84 .... D3
87940 Rincon 300 .... C6
87124 Rio Rancho 9,985 .... C3
87561 Rodarte 650 .... D2
88201 Roswell⊙ 39,676 .... E5
87562 Rowe 290 .... D3
87743 Roy 381 .... E3
88345 Ruidoso 4,260 .... D5
88346 Ruidoso Downs 949 .... D5
87941 Salem 400 .... B6
87831 San Acacia 286 .... B4
87832 San Antonio 359 .... B5
87564 San Cristobal 350 .... D2
87047 Sandia Park 450 .... C3
†87001 San Felipe Pueblo 1,465 .... C3
†87501 San Ildefonso 232 .... C3
88434 San Jon 341 .... F3
87565 San Jose 150 .... D3
87566 San Juan Pueblo 870 .... C2
88041 San Lorenzo 200 .... B6
87050 San Mateo 200 .... B3
88058 San Miguel 400 .... C6
88348 San Patricio 300 .... D5
87051 San Rafael 300 .... A3
87567 Santa Cruz 754 .... D2
87501 Santa Fe (cap.)⊙ 48,953 .... C3
†88041 Santa Rita 600 .... B6
88435 Santa Rosa⊙ 2,469 .... E4
87052 Santo Domingo Pueblo 2,082 .... C3
87053 San Ysidro 199 .... C3
87745 Sapello 600 .... D3
87055 Seboyeta 125 .... B3
87568 Sena 150 .... D3
87569 Serafina 225 .... D3
87420 Shiprock 7,237 .... A2
88061 Silver City⊙ 9,887 .... A6
87801 Socorro⊙ 7,173 .... C4
†87565 Soham 104 .... D3
87747 Springer 1,657 .... E2
87057 Tajique 145 .... C4
87571 Taos⊙ 3,369 .... D2
†87571 Taos Pueblo 900 .... D2
88267 Tatum 896 .... F5
87574 Tesuque 1,014 .... C3
88135 Texico 958 .... F4
87323 Thoreau 1,099 .... A3
87575 Tierra Amarilla⊙ 850 .... C2
87059 Tijeras 311 .... C3
87324 Toadlena 200 .... A2
87325 Tohatchi 1,011 .... A3
87060 Tome 500 .... C4
87577 Tres Piedras 200 .... D2
87578 Truchas 275 .... D2
†87701 Trujillo 148 .... E3
87901 Truth or Consequences⊙ 5,219 .... B5
88401 Tucumcari⊙ 6,765 .... F3
88352 Tularosa 2,536 .... C5
88003 University Park 4,353 .... C6
87579 Vadito 400 .... D2
88072 Vado 325 .... C6
87580 Valdez 300 .... D2
†87031 Valencia 500 .... C4
87581 Vallecitos 450 .... C2
88073 Vanadium 150 .... A6
88353 Vaughn 737 .... D4
87582 Velarde 950 .... C2
87583 Villanueva 500 .... D3
†88055 Virden 246 .... A6
87752 Wagon Mound 416 .... E2
87421 Waterflow 475 .... A2
87753 Watrous 175 .... D3
87544 White Rock 6,560 .... C3
88002 White Sands Missile Range 3,120 .... C6
87063 Willard 166 .... D4
87942 Williamsburg 433 .... B5
88136 Yeso 200 .... E4
87064 Youngsville 125 .... C2
†87053 Zia Pueblo 500 .... C3
87327 Zuni 5,551 .... A3

AREA 121,593 sq. mi. (314,926 sq. km.)
POPULATION 1,302,981
CAPITAL Santa Fe
LARGEST CITY Albuquerque
HIGHEST POINT Wheeler Pk. 13,161 ft. (4011 m.)
SETTLED IN 1605
ADMITTED TO UNION January 6, 1912
POPULAR NAME Land of Enchantment
STATE FLOWER Yucca
STATE BIRD Road Runner

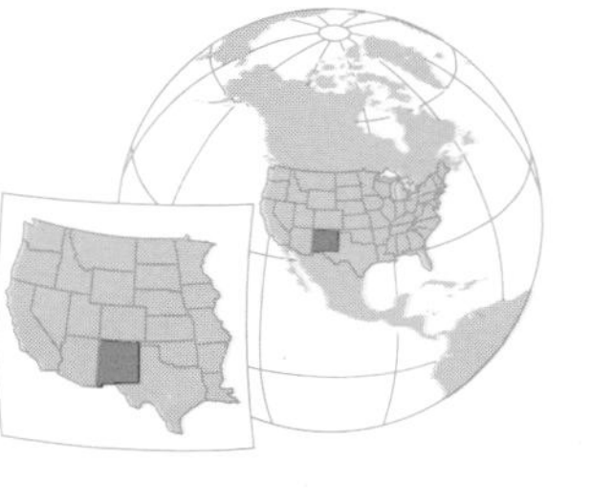

OTHER FEATURES

Abiquiu (res.) C2
Alamosa (riv.) B5
Animas (riv.) B1
Avalon (res.) E6
Aztec Ruins Nat'l Mon. A2
Baldy (peak) D3
Bandelier Nat'l Mon. C3
Big Burro (mts.) A6
Black (mt.) A6
Black (range) B5
Blanco (creek) F4
Bluewater (creek) B4
Bluewater (creek) D6
Bluewater (lake) A3
Boulder (lake) C2
Brazos (peak) C2
Burford (lake) C2
Caballo (res.) B6
Canadian (riv.) F3
Cannon A.F.B. 3,798 .... F4
Canyon Blanco (creek) B2
Capitan (mts.) D5
Capitan (peak) D5
Capulin Mountain Nat'l Mon. E2
Carlsbad Caverns Nat'l Park E6
Carrizo (creek) F2
Chaco (mesa) B3
Chaco (riv.) A2
Chaco Culture Nat'l Hist. Park B2
Chico Arroyo (creek) B3
Chivato (mesa) B3
Chupadera (mesa) C5
Chuska (mts.) A2
Cimarron (riv.) E2
Colorado, Arroyo (riv.) B4
Compañero, Arroyo (creek) B2
Conchas (lake) E3
Conchas (riv.) E3
Cookes (range) B6
Corrumpa (creek) F2
Costilla (peak) D2
Cuchillo Negro (creek) B5
Cuervo (creek) E3
Dark Canyon (creek) E6
Datil (mts.) B4
Dry Cimarron (riv.) F2
Eagle Nest (lake) D2
Elephant Butte (res.) B5
El Morro Nat'l Mon. A3
El Rito (riv.) C2
Fifteenmile Arroyo (creek) D4
Florida (mts.) B7
Fort Bliss Mil. Res. C6
Fort Union Nat'l Mon. E3
Gallinas (mts.) B4
Gallinas (riv.) E3
Gila (riv.) A6
Gila Cliff Dwellings Nat'l Mon. A5
Grouse (mt.) A5
Guadalupe (mts.) D6
Hatchet (mts.) A7
Holloman A.F.B. 7,245 .... C6
Hueco (mts.) D6
Jemez (riv.) C3
Jemez Canyon (res.) C3
Jicarilla Ind. Res. B2
Jornada del Muerto (valley) C5
Kirtland A.F.B. C3
Ladron (mts.) B4
La Plata (riv.) A1
Largo, Cañon (creek) B2
Las Animas (creek) B5
Llano Estacado (Staked) (plain) F5
Lucero (lake) C6
Macho, Arroyo del (creek) D5
Magdalena (mts.) B4
Manzano (mts.) C4
Manzano (peak) C4
McMillan (lake) E6
Mescalero (ridge) F6
Mescalero (valley) F5
Mescalero Apache Ind. Res. D5
Mimbres (mts.) B6
Mimbres (riv.) B6
Mogollon (mts.) A5
Mogollon Baldy (peak) A5
Montosa (mesa) E3
Mora (riv.) E3
Nacimiento (mts.) C3
Nacimiento (peak) C2
Navajo (res.) B2
Navajo Ind. Res. A2
North Truchas (peak) D3
Ocate (creek) E2
O'Keeffe Nat'l Hist. Site C2
Oscura (mts.) C5
Osha (peak) C4
Padilla (creek) D5
Pajarito (creek) A2
Pecos (riv.) E5
Pecos Nat'l Mon. D3
Peloncillo (mts.) A6
Perro (mts.) D4
Pinos, Rio de los (riv.) B2
Pintada Arroyo (creek) E4
Playas (lake) A7
Potrillo (mts.) B7
Pueblo Ind. Res. B4
Pueblo Ind. Res. D3
Pueblo Ind. Res. C4
Pueblo Ind. Res. D2
Puerco (riv.) A3
Red Bluff (lake) E7
Revuelto (creek) F3
Rio Brazos (riv.) C2
Rio Chama (riv.) C2
Rio Felix (riv.) E5
Rio Grande (riv.) C5
Rio Hondo (riv.) E5
Rio Penasco (riv.) E6
Rio Puerco (riv.) C4
Rio Salado (riv.) B4
Rocky (mts.) C1
Sacramento (mts.) D6
Salinas Nat'l Mon. C4
Salt (creek) E5
Salt (lake) F4
San Agustin (plains) B5
San Andres (mts.) C6
San Antonio (peak) C2
Sandia (peak) C3
San Francisco (riv.) A5
Sangre de Cristo (mts.) D3
San Jose (riv.) B3
San Juan (riv.) B2
San Mateo (mts.) B5
Seven Rivers (riv.) E6
Ship Rock (peak) A2
Sierra Blanca (peak) C5
Staked (Llano Estacado) (plain) F5
Sumner (lake) E4
Taylor (mt.) B3
Tecolote (creek) D3
Tequesquite (creek) E2
Thompson (peak) D3
Tierra Blanca (creek) B6
Tramperos (creek) F2
Tularosa (valley) C6
Ute (creek) F3
Ute (peak) D2
Ute (res.) F3
Ute Mountain Ind. Res. A1
Vermejo (riv.) E2
Wheeler (peak) D2
White Sands (des.) C5
White Sands Missile Range C5
White Sands Nat'l Mon. C6
Whitewater Baldy (mt.) A5
Wingate Army Depot A3
Yeso (creek) E4
Zuni (mts.) A3
Zuni (riv.) A3
Zuni Ind. Res. A3

⊙County seat.
‡Population of metropolitan area.
† Zip of nearest p.o. * Multiple zips.

Topography

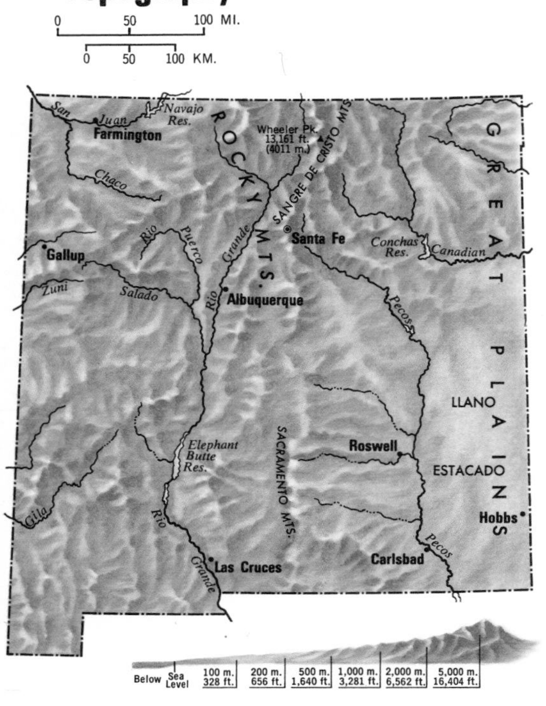

0 50 100 MI.
0 50 100 KM.
San Juan
Navajo Res.
Farmington
Wheeler Pk. 13,161 ft. (4011 m.)
SANGRE DE CRISTO MTS.
ROCKY MTS.
GREAT PLAINS
Chaco
Rio Puerco
Rio Grande
Santa Fe
Conchas Res.
Canadian
Gallup
Zuni
Salado
Albuquerque
Pecos
LLANO
ESTACADO
Elephant Butte Res.
SACRAMENTO MTS.
Roswell
Gila
Hobbs
Carlsbad
Las Cruces
Below Sea Level
100 m. 328 ft.
200 m. 656 ft.
500 m. 1,640 ft.
1,000 m. 3,281 ft.
2,000 m. 6,562 ft.
5,000 m. 16,404 ft.

Agriculture, Industry and Resources

DOMINANT LAND USE

- Wheat, Grain Sorghums, Range Livestock
- General Farming, Livestock, Special Crops
- General Farming, Livestock, Cash Grain
- Dry Beans, General Farming
- Cotton, Forest Products
- Range Livestock
- Forests
- Nonagricultural Land

MAJOR MINERAL OCCURRENCES

Ag	Silver	Gp	Gypsum	U	Uranium
Au	Gold	K	Potash	V	Vanadium
C	Coal	Mo	Molybdenum	Zn	Zinc
Cu	Copper	Mr	Marble	O	Petroleum
G	Natural Gas	Na	Salt	Pb	Lead

ϟ Water Power

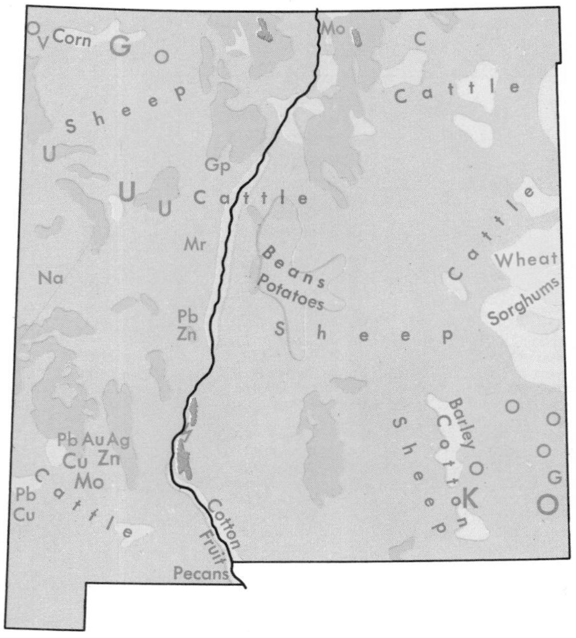

Corn
Sheep
Cattle
Wheat
Sorghums
Beans
Potatoes
Sheep
Barley
Cattle
Sheep
Cotton
Fruit
Pecans
Gp
Mr
Na
Pb Zn
Pb Au Ag
Cu Zn
Mo
Pb
Cu
Mo
K

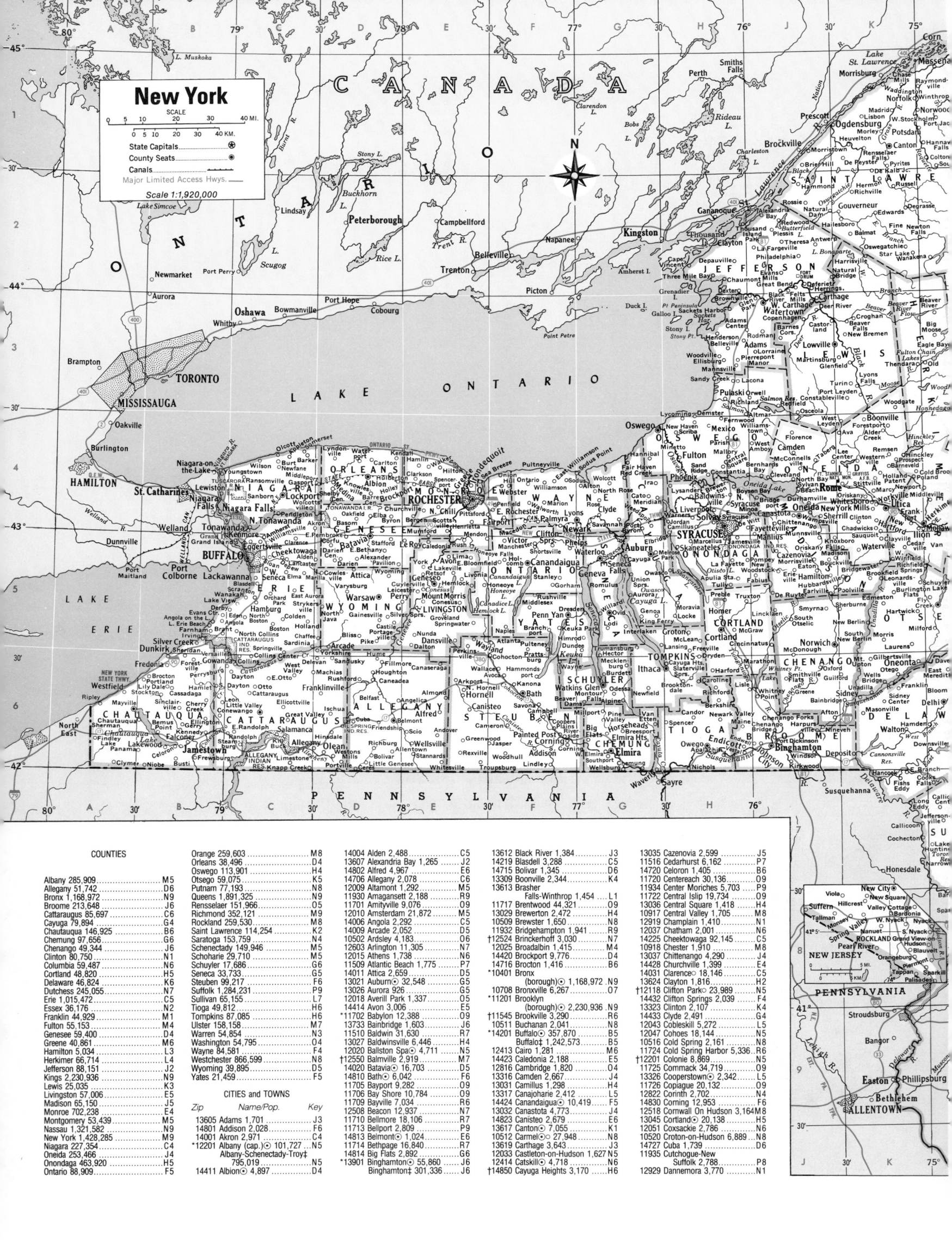

New York

SCALE

0 5 10 20 30 40 MI.
0 5 10 20 30 40 KM.

State Capitals .... ⊛
County Seats .... ⊙
Canals ....
Major Limited Access Hwys. ____
Scale 1:1,920,000

COUNTIES

Albany 285,909	M5
Allegany 51,742	D6
Bronx 1,168,972	N9
Broome 213,648	J6
Cattaraugus 85,697	C6
Cayuga 79,894	G4
Chautauqua 146,925	B6
Chemung 97,656	G6
Chenango 49,344	J6
Clinton 80,750	N1
Columbia 59,487	N6
Cortland 48,820	H5
Delaware 46,824	K6
Dutchess 245,055	N7
Erie 1,015,472	C5
Essex 36,176	N2
Franklin 44,929	M1
Fulton 55,153	M4
Genesee 59,400	D4
Greene 40,861	M6
Hamilton 5,034	L3
Herkimer 66,714	L4
Jefferson 88,151	J2
Kings 2,230,936	N9
Lewis 25,035	K3
Livingston 57,006	E5
Madison 65,150	J5
Monroe 702,238	E4
Montgomery 53,439	M5
Nassau 1,321,582	N9
New York 1,428,285	N9
Niagara 227,354	C4
Oneida 253,466	J4
Onondaga 463,920	H5
Ontario 88,909	F5
Orange 259,603	M8
Orleans 38,496	D4
Oswego 113,901	H4
Otsego 59,075	K5
Putnam 77,193	N8
Queens 1,891,325	N9
Rensselaer 151,966	O5
Richmond 352,121	M9
Rockland 259,530	M8
Saint Lawrence 114,254	K2
Saratoga 153,759	N4
Schenectady 149,946	M5
Schoharie 29,710	M5
Schuyler 17,686	G5
Seneca 33,733	G5
Steuben 99,217	F6
Suffolk 1,284,231	N9
Sullivan 65,155	L7
Tioga 49,812	H6
Tompkins 87,085	H6
Ulster 158,158	M7
Warren 54,854	N3
Washington 54,795	N4
Wayne 84,581	F4
Westchester 866,599	N8
Wyoming 39,895	D5
Yates 21,459	F5

CITIES and TOWNS

Zip	Name/Pop.	Key
13605	Adams 1,701	J3
14801	Addison 2,028	F6
14001	Akron 2,971	C4
14411	Albion⊙ 4,897	D4
*12201	Albany (cap.)⊙ 101,727	M5
	Albany-Schenectady-Troy‡ 795,019	M5
14004	Alden 2,488	C5
13607	Alexandria Bay 1,265	J2
14802	Alfred 4,967	E6
14706	Allegany 2,078	C6
12009	Altamont 1,292	M5
11930	Amagansett 2,188	R9
11701	Amityville 9,076	O9
12010	Amsterdam 21,872	M5
14006	Angola 2,292	D5
14009	Arcade 2,052	D5
10502	Ardsley 4,183	O5
12603	Arlington 11,305	N7
12015	Athens 1,738	N6
11509	Atlantic Beach 1,775	P7
14011	Attica 2,659	D5
13021	Auburn⊙ 32,548	G5
13026	Aurora 926	G5
12018	Averill Park 1,337	O5
14414	Avon 3,006	E5
*11702	Babylon 12,388	O9
13733	Bainbridge 1,603	J6
11510	Baldwin 31,630	R7
13027	Baldwinsville 6,446	H4
12020	Ballston Spa⊙ 4,711	N5
*12550	Balmville 2,919	M7
14020	Batavia⊙ 16,703	D4
14810	Bath⊙ 6,042	F6
11705	Bayport 9,282	O9
11706	Bay Shore 10,784	O9
11709	Bayville 7,034	R6
12508	Beacon 12,937	N7
11710	Bellmore 18,106	R7
11713	Bellport 2,809	P9
14813	Belmont⊙ 1,024	E6
11714	Bethpage 16,840	R7
14814	Big Flats 2,892	G6
*13901	Binghamton⊙ 55,860	J6
	Binghamton‡ 301,336	J6
*14850	Cayuga Heights 3,170	H6
13612	Black River 1,384	J3
14219	Blasdell 3,288	C5
14715	Bolivar 1,345	D6
12803	Boonville 2,344	K4
13613	Brasher Falls-Winthrop 1,454	L1
11717	Brentwood 44,321	O9
13029	Brewerton 2,472	H4
10509	Brewster 1,650	N8
11932	Bridgehampton 1,941	R9
†12524	Brinckerhoff 3,030	N7
12025	Broadalbin 1,415	M4
14420	Brockport 9,776	D4
14716	Brocton 1,416	B6
*10401	Bronx (borough)⊙ 1,168,972	N9
10708	Bronxville 6,267	O7
*11201	Brooklyn (borough)⊙ 2,230,936	N9
†11545	Brookville 3,290	R6
10511	Buchanan 2,041	N8
*14201	Buffalo⊙ 357,870	B5
	Buffalo‡ 1,242,573	B5
12413	Cairo 1,281	M6
14423	Caledonia 2,188	E5
12816	Cambridge 1,820	O4
13316	Camden 2,667	J4
13031	Camillus 1,298	H4
13317	Canajoharie 2,412	L5
14424	Canandaigua⊙ 10,419	F5
13032	Canastota 4,773	J4
14823	Canisteo 2,679	E6
13617	Canton⊙ 7,055	K1
10512	Carmel⊙ 27,948	N8
13619	Carthage 3,643	J3
12033	Castleton-on-Hudson 1,627	N5
12414	Catskill⊙ 4,718	M6
*14850	Cayuga Heights 3,170	H6
13035	Cazenovia 2,599	J5
11516	Cedarhurst 6,162	P7
14720	Celoron 1,405	B6
11720	Centereach 30,136	O9
11934	Center Moriches 5,703	P9
11722	Central Islip 19,734	O9
13036	Central Square 1,418	H4
10917	Central Valley 1,705	M8
12919	Champlain 1,410	N1
12037	Chatham 2,001	N6
14225	Cheektowaga 92,145	C5
10918	Chester 1,910	M8
13037	Chittenango 4,290	J4
14428	Churchville 1,399	E4
14031	Clarence 18,146	C5
13624	Clayton 1,816	H2
†12118	Clifton Park 23,989	N5
14432	Clifton Springs 2,039	F4
13323	Clinton 2,107	K4
14433	Clyde 2,491	G4
12043	Cobleskill 4,533	L5
12047	Cohoes 18,144	N5
10516	Cold Spring 2,161	N8
11724	Cold Spring Harbor 5,336	R6
†12201	Colonie 8,869	O4
11725	Commack 34,719	O9
13326	Cooperstown⊙ 2,342	L5
11726	Copiague 20,132	O9
12822	Corinth 2,702	N4
14830	Corning 12,953	F6
12518	Cornwall On Hudson 3,164	M8
13045	Cortland⊙ 20,138	H5
12051	Coxsackie 2,786	N6
10520	Croton-on-Hudson 6,889	N8
14727	Cuba 1,739	D6
11935	Cutchogue-New Suffolk 2,788	P8
12929	Dannemora 3,770	N1

AREA 49,108 sq. mi. (127,190 sq. km.)
POPULATION 17,558,072
CAPITAL Albany
LARGEST CITY New York
HIGHEST POINT Mt. Marcy 5,344 ft. (1629 m.)
SETTLED IN 1614
ADMITTED TO UNION July 26, 1788
POPULAR NAME Empire State
STATE FLOWER Rose
STATE BIRD Bluebird

Topography

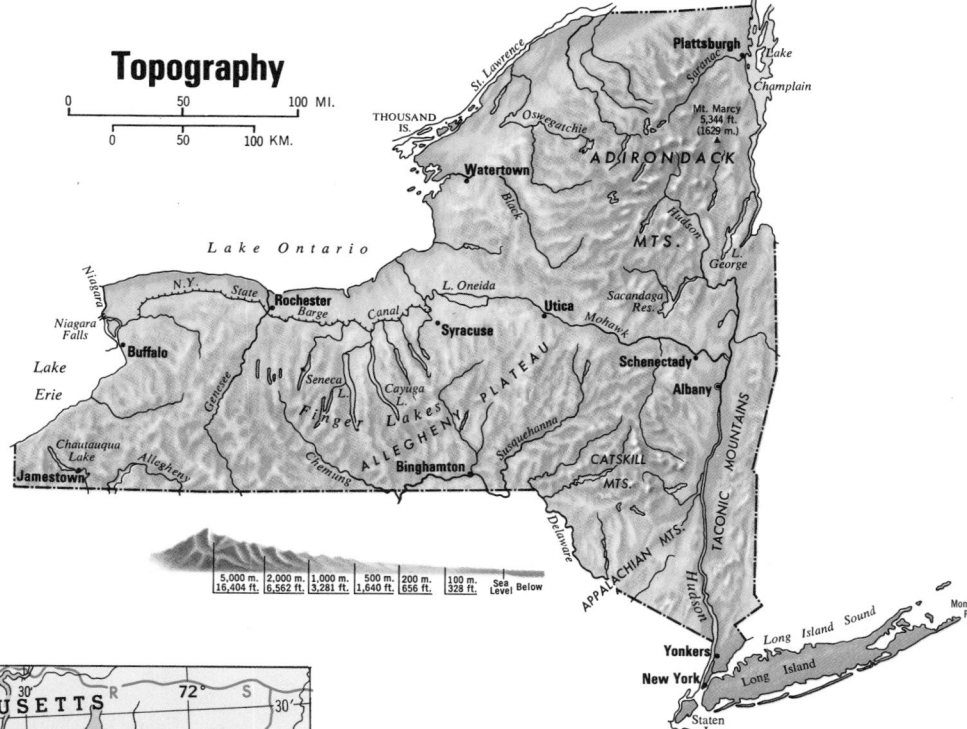

0   50   100 MI.

0   50   100 KM.

5,000 m.	2,000 m.	1,000 m.	500 m.	200 m.	100 m.	Sea
16,404 ft.	6,562 ft.	3,281 ft.	1,640 ft.	656 ft.	328 ft.	Level Below

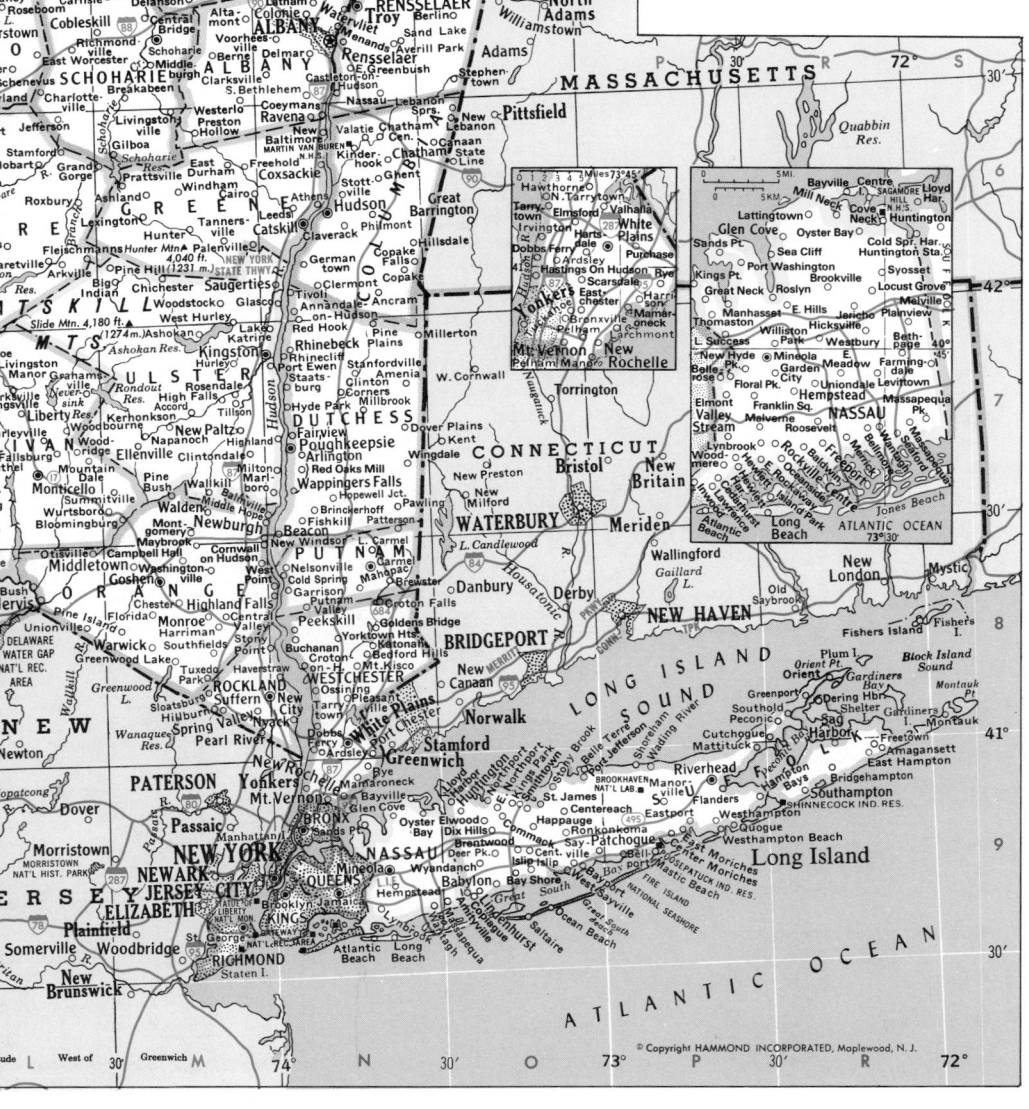

© Copyright HAMMOND INCORPORATED, Maplewood, N.J.

14437 Dansville 4,979	E5
11729 Deer Park 30,394	O9
13753 Delhi⊙ 3,374	L6
12054 Delmar 8,423	N5
14043 Depew 19,819	C5
13754 Deposit 1,897	K6
13214 DeWitt 9,024	H4
11746 Dix Hills 26,693	O9
10522 Dobbs Ferry 10,053	O6
13329 Dolgeville 2,602	L4
12522 Dover Plains 1,753	O7
14837 Dundee 1,556	F5
14048 Dunkirk 15,310	B5
14052 East Aurora 6,803	C5
10709 Eastchester 20,305	P6
11937 East Hampton 1,886	R9
†11576 East Hills 7,160	R7
11554 East Meadow 39,317	R7
11731 East Northport 20,187	O9
14445 East Rochester 7,596	F4
11518 East Rockaway 10,917	R7
13057 East Syracuse 3,412	H4
14057 Eden 3,000	C5
14058 Elba 750	D4
12932 Elizabethtown⊙ 659	N2
12428 Ellenville 4,405	M7
14059 Elma 2,459	C5
*14901 Elmira⊙ 35,327	G6
Elmira‡ 97,656	G6
14903 Elmira Heights 4,279	G6
11003 Elmont 27,592	P7
10523 Elmsford 3,361	O6
11731 Elwood 11,847	O9
13760 Endicott 14,457	H6
13760 Endwell 13,745	H6
14450 Fairport 5,970	F4
†12601 Fairview 5,852	N7
14733 Falconer 2,778	B6
11735 Farmingdale 7,946	R7
13066 Fayetteville 4,709	J4
†12801 Fernwood 3,640	N4
12524 Fishkill 1,555	N7
†11901 Flanders-Riverside 5,400	P9
*11001 Floral Park 16,805	P7
10921 Florida 1,947	M8
12068 Fonda⊙ 1,006	M5
12937 Fort Covington⊙ 1,804	M1
12828 Fort Edward 3,561	N4
13339 Fort Plain 2,555	L5
13340 Frankfort 2,995	K4
11010 Franklin Square 29,051	R7
14737 Franklinville 1,887	D6
14063 Fredonia 11,126	B6
11520 Freeport 38,272	R7
14738 Frewsburg 1,908	B6
14739 Friendship 1,461	D6
13069 Fulton 13,312	H4
11530 Garden City 22,927	R7
14067 Gasport 1,339	C4
14454 Geneseo⊙ 6,746	E5

14456 Geneva 15,133	G5
11542 Glen Cove 24,618	R6
12801 Glens Falls 15,897	N4
Glens Falls‡ 109,649	N4
12078 Gloversville 17,836	M4
10526 Golden's Bridge 1,367	N8
10924 Goshen⊙ 4,874	M8
13642 Gouverneur 4,285	K2
14070 Gowanda 2,713	B6
12832 Granville 2,696	O4
*11020 Great Neck 9,168	P6
14616 Greece 16,177	E4
13778 Greene 1,747	J6
12183 Green Island 2,696	N5
11944 Greenport 2,273	P8
12834 Greenwich 1,955	O4
10925 Greenwood Lake 2,809	M8
13073 Groton 2,313	H5
12835 Hadley-Lake Luzerne 1,988	N4
12086 Hagaman 1,331	M5
14075 Hamburg 10,582	C5
13346 Hamilton 3,725	J5
11946 Hampton Bays 7,256	R9
13783 Hancock 1,526	K7
10528 Harrison 23,046	P6
10530 Hartsdale 10,216	P6
10706 Hastings On Hudson 8,573	O6
11787 Hauppauge 20,960	O9
10927 Haverstraw 8,800	M8
10532 Hawthorne 5,010	O6
*11550 Hempstead 40,404	R7
13350 Herkimer⊙ 8,383	L4
11557 Hewlett 6,986	P7
†11557 Hewlett Harbor 1,331	P7
11801 Hicksville 43,245	R7
12528 Highland 3,967	M7
10928 Highland Falls 4,187	M8
10931 Hillburn 926	M8
†10977 Hillcrest 5,733	K8
14468 Hilton 4,151	E4
14080 Holland 1,347	C5
14470 Holley 1,882	D4
13077 Homer 3,635	H5
14472 Honeoye Falls 2,410	F5
12090 Hoosick Falls 3,609	O5
12533 Hopewell Junction 1,754	N7
14843 Hornell 10,234	E6
14845 Horseheads 7,348	G6
14744 Houghton 1,604	D6
12534 Hudson⊙ 7,986	N6
12839 Hudson Falls⊙ 7,419	O4
11743 Huntington 21,727	R6
11746 Huntington Station 28,769	R6
12443 Hurley 4,892	M7
12538 Hyde Park 2,550	N6
13357 Ilion 9,450	K5
11696 Inwood 8,228	P7
14617 Irondequoit 57,648	E4
10533 Irvington 5,774	O6
11558 Island Park 4,847	R7

(continued on following page)

(continued)

11751 Islip 13,438 ... O9
14850 Ithaca⊙ 28,732 ... G6
*11401 Jamaica⊙ ... N9
14701 Jamestown 35,775 ... B6
11753 Jericho 12,739 ... R6
13790 Johnson City 17,126 ... J6
12095 Johnstown⊙ 9,360 ... M4
13080 Jordan 1,371 ... H4
12944 Keeseville 2,025 ... O2
14271 Kenmore 18,474 ... C5
12446 Kerhonkson 1,646 ... M7
12106 Kinderhook 1,377 ... N6
11754 Kings Park 16,131 ... O9
11024 Kings Point 5,234 ... P6
12401 Kingston⊙ 24,481 ... M7
14218 Lackawanna 22,701 ... B5
10512 Lake Carmel 7,295 ... N8
†14006 Lake Erie Beach 4,625 ... B5
12845 Lake George⊙ 1,047 ... N4
12449 Lake Katrine 2,011 ... M7
12846 Lake Luzerne-Hadley 1,988 N4
12946 Lake Placid 2,490 ... N2
12108 Lake Pleasant⊙ 700 ... M4
11040 Lake Success 2,396 ... P7
14750 Lakewood 3,941 ... B6
14086 Lancaster 13,056 ... C5
14882 Lansing 3,039 ... H5
10538 Larchmont 6,308 ... P7
12110 Latham 11,182 ... N5
†11560 Lattingtown 1,749 ... R6
11559 Lawrence 6,175 ... P7
14482 Le Roy 4,900 ... E5
11756 Levittown 57,045 ... R7
14092 Lewiston 3,326 ... B4
12754 Liberty 4,293 ... L7
14485 Lima 2,025 ... E5
11757 Lindenhurst 26,919 ... O9
13365 Little Falls 6,156 ... L4
14755 Little Valley⊙ 1,203 ... C6
13088 Liverpool 2,849 ... H4
12758 Livingston Manor 1,436 ... L7
†11743 Lloyd Harbor 3,405 ... R6
14094 Lockport⊙ 24,844 ... C4
†11791 Locust Grove 9,670 ... R6
11561 Long Beach 34,073 ... R7
13367 Lowville⊙ 3,364 ... J3
11563 Lynbrook 20,424 ... P7
14489 Lyons⊙ 4,160 ... F4
14502 Macedon 1,400 ... F4
10541 Mahopac 7,681 ... N8
12953 Malone⊙ 7,668 ... M1
11565 Malverne 9,262 ... R7
10543 Mamaroneck 17,616 ... P7
14504 Manchester 1,698 ... F5
11030 Manhasset 8,485 ... P7
*10001 Manhattan (borough) 1,428,285 ... M9
13104 Manlius 5,241 ... J5
13108 Marcellus 1,870 ... H5
12542 Marlboro 2,275 ... M7
11758 Massapequa 24,454 ... R7
11762 Massapequa Park 19,779 ... R7
13662 Massena 12,851 ... L1
11950 Mastic Beach 8,318 ... P9
11952 Mattituck 3,923 ... P9
12543 Maybrook 2,007 ... M8
14757 Mayville⊙ 1,626 ... A6
12118 Mechanicville 5,500 ... N5
14103 Medina 6,392 ... D4
†13021 Melrose Park 2,171 ... G5
11746 Melville 8,139 ... O9
†12201 Menands 4,012 ... N5
11566 Merrick 24,478 ... R7
13114 Mexico 1,621 ... H4
12122 Middleburgh 1,358 ... M5
12550 Middle Hope 3,229 ... M7
14105 Middleport 1,995 ... C4
10940 Middletown 21,454 ... L8
†12020 Milton 2,063 ... N4
11501 Mineola⊙ 20,757 ... R7
13115 Minetto 1,629 ... H4
12956 Mineville-Witherbee 1,925 ... O2
13116 Minoa 3,640 ... H4
13407 Mohawk 2,956 ... L4
10950 Monroe 5,996 ... M8
10952 Monsey 12,380 ... J8
12549 Montgomery 2,316 ... M7
12701 Monticello⊙ 6,306 ... L7
14865 Montour Falls 1,791 ... G6
13118 Moravia 1,582 ... H5
12962 Morrisonville 1,721 ... N1
13408 Morrisville 2,707 ... J5
10549 Mount Kisco 8,025 ... N8
14510 Mount Morris 3,039 ... E5
*10550 Mount Vernon 66,713 ... O7
10954 Nanuet 12,578 ... K8
12123 Nassau 1,285 ... N5
Nassau-Suffolk‡ 2,605,813 R7
14513 Newark 10,017 ... G4
13411 New Berlin 1,392 ... K5
12550 Newburgh 23,438 ... M7
Newburgh-Middletown‡ 259,603 ... M7
10956 New City⊙ 35,859 ... K8
14108 Newfane 3,120 ... C4
13413 New Hartford 2,313 ... K4
11040 New Hyde Park 9,801 ... P7
12561 New Paltz 4,938 ... M7
*10801 New Rochelle 70,794 ... P7
†10901 New Square 1,750 ... K8
12550 New Windsor 7,812 ... N8
*10001 New York⊙ 7,071,639 ... M9
New York‡ 9,119,737 ... M9
13417 New York Mills 3,549 ... K4
*14301 Niagara Falls 71,384 ... C4
†12301 Niskayuna 5,223 ... N5
13667 Norfolk 1,599 ... K1
14110 North Boston 2,743 ... C5
14111 North Collins 1,496 ... C5
11768 Northport 7,651 ... O9
13212 North Syracuse 7,970 ... H4
10591 North Tarrytown 7,994 ... O6
14120 North Tonawanda 35,760 ... C4
12134 Northville 1,304 ... M4
13815 Norwich⊙ 8,082 ... J5
13668 Norwood 1,902 ... L1
10960 Nyack 6,428 ... K8
14125 Oakfield 1,791 ... D4
11572 Oceanside 33,639 ... R7
13669 Ogdensburg 12,375 ... K1
14126 Olcott 1,571 ... C4
14760 Olean 18,207 ... D6
13421 Oneida 10,810 ... J4
13820 Oneonta 14,933 ... K6
14127 Orchard Park 3,671 ... C5
13424 Oriskany 1,680 ... K4
10562 Ossining 20,196 ... N8
13126 Oswego⊙ 19,793 ... G4
14521 Ovid⊙ 666 ... G5
13827 Owego⊙ 4,364 ... H6
13830 Oxford 1,765 ... J6
11771 Oyster Bay 6,497 ... R6
14870 Painted Post 2,196 ... F6
14522 Palmyra 3,729 ... F4
11772 Patchogue 11,291 ... P9
12564 Pawling 1,996 ... N7
10965 Pearl River 15,893 ... K8
10566 Peekskill 18,236 ... N8
10803 Pelham 6,848 ... O7
†10803 Pelham Manor 6,130 ... O7
14527 Penn Yan⊙ 5,242 ... F5
14530 Perry 4,198 ... D5
12972 Peru 1,716 ... N1
14532 Phelps 2,004 ... F5
12565 Philmont 1,539 ... N6
13135 Phoenix 2,357 ... H4
10968 Piermont 2,269 ... K8
12567 Pine Plains 1,303 ... N7
14534 Pittsford 1,568 ... E4
11803 Plainview 28,037 ... R7
12901 Plattsburgh⊙ 21,057 ... O1
10570 Pleasantville 6,749 ... N8
13140 Port Byron 1,400 ... G4
10573 Port Chester 23,565 ... P7
†13901 Port Dickinson 1,974 ... J6
12466 Port Ewen 2,813 ... N7
12974 Port Henry 1,450 ... O2
11777 Port Jefferson 6,731 ... P9
12771 Port Jervis 8,699 ... L8
11050 Port Washington 14,521 ... R6
13676 Potsdam 10,635 ... K1
*12601 Poughkeepsie⊙ 29,757 ... N7
Poughkeepsie‡ 245,055 ... N7
14873 Prattsburg○ 1,657 ... F5
13142 Pulaski 2,415 ... H3
10579 Putnam Valley○ 8,994 ... N8
*11101 Queens (borough) 1,891,325 ... N9
14772 Randolph 1,398 ... C6
14131 Ransomville 1,401 ... C4
12143 Ravena 3,091 ... N6
12571 Red Hook 1,692 ... N7
†12601 Red Oaks Mill 5,236 ... N7
12144 Rensselaer 9,047 ... N5
12572 Rhinebeck 2,542 ... N7
13439 Richfield Springs 1,561 ... K5
*10301 Richmond (Staten Island) (borough) 352,121 ... M9
11901 Riverhead⊙ 6,339 ... P9
*14601 Rochester⊙ 241,741 ... E4
Rochester‡ 971,879 ... E4
*11570 Rockville Centre 25,412 ... R7
13440 Rome 43,826 ... J4
11575 Roosevelt 14,109 ... R7
11576 Roslyn 2,134 ... R6
12979 Rouses Point 2,266 ... O1
10580 Rye 15,083 ... P6
11963 Sag Harbor 2,581 ... R8
11780 Saint James 12,122 ... O9
13452 Saint Johnsville 1,974 ... L5
14779 Salamanca 6,890 ... C6
†13132 Sand Ridge 1,293 ... H4
†11050 Sands Point 2,742 ... P6
12983 Saranac Lake 5,578 ... M2
12866 Saratoga Springs 23,906 ... N4
12477 Saugerties 3,882 ... M6
13146 Savannah○ 1,905 ... G4
11782 Sayville 12,013 ... O9
10583 Scarsdale 17,650 ... P6
*12301 Schenectady⊙ 67,972 ... M5
12157 Schoharie⊙ 1,016 ... M5
12871 Schuylerville 1,256 ... N4
12302 Scotia 7,280 ... N5
14546 Scottsville 1,789 ... E4
11579 Sea Cliff 5,364 ... R6
11783 Seaford 16,117 ... R7
13148 Seneca Falls 7,466 ... G5
13460 Sherburne 1,561 ... K5
13461 Sherrill 2,830 ... J4
14548 Shortsville 1,669 ... F5
13838 Sidney 4,861 ... K6
14136 Silver Creek 3,088 ... B5
13152 Skaneateles 2,789 ... H5
†14201 Sloan 4,529 ... C5
10974 Sloatsburg 3,154 ... M8
11787 Smithtown 30,906 ... O9
14551 Sodus 1,790 ... G4
14555 Sodus Point 1,334 ... G4
13209 Solvay 7,140 ... H4
11968 Southampton 4,000 ... R9
12779 South Fallsburg 2,196 ... L7
†12801 South Glens Falls 3,714 ... N4
†10960 South Nyack 3,602 ... K8
11971 Southold 4,770 ... P8
†14901 Southport 8,329 ... G6
14559 Spencerport 3,424 ... E4
10977 Spring Valley 20,537 ... K8
14141 Springville 4,285 ... C5
*10301 Staten Island (borough) 352,121 ... M9
12170 Stillwater 1,572 ... N5
11790 Stony Brook 16,155 ... O9
10980 Stony Point 8,686 ... M8
12172 Stottville 1,387 ... N6
10901 Suffern 10,794 ... J8
11791 Syosset 9,818 ... R6
*13201 Syracuse⊙ 170,105 ... H4
Syracuse‡ 642,375 ... H4
10983 Tappan 8,267 ... K8
10591 Tarrytown 10,648 ... O6
†11020 Thomaston 2,684 ... P7
12883 Ticonderoga 2,938 ... N3
12486 Tillson 1,529 ... M7
14150 Tonawanda 18,693 ... B4
*12180 Troy⊙ 56,638 ... N5
14886 Trumansburg 1,722 ... G5
10707 Tuckahoe 6,076 ... O7
12986 Tupper Lake 4,478 ... M2
13849 Unadilla 1,367 ... K6
11553 Uniondale 20,016 ... R7
*13501 Utica⊙ 75,632 ... K4
Utica-Rome‡ 320,180 ... K4
12184 Valatie 1,492 ... N6
10989 Valley Cottage 8,214 ... K8
*11580 Valley Stream 35,769 ... P7
13850 Vestal○ 27,238 ... H6
14564 Victor 2,370 ... F5
†10901 Viola 5,340 ... J8
12186 Voorheesville 3,320 ... M5
12586 Walden 5,659 ... M7
12589 Wallkill 2,064 ... M7
13856 Walton 3,329 ... K6
13163 Wampsville⊙ 569 ... J4
11793 Wantagh 19,817 ... R7
12590 Wappingers Falls 5,110 ... N7
12885 Warrensburg 2,834 ... N3
14569 Warsaw⊙ 3,619 ... D5
10990 Warwick 4,320 ... M8
10992 Washingtonville 2,380 ... M8
12188 Waterford 2,405 ... N5
13165 Waterloo⊙ 5,303 ... G5
13601 Watertown⊙ 27,861 ... J3
13480 Waterville 1,672 ... K5
12189 Watervliet 11,354 ... N5
14891 Watkins Glen⊙ 2,440 ... G6
14892 Waverly 4,738 ... G7
14572 Wayland 1,846 ... E5
14580 Webster 5,499 ... F4
13166 Weedsport 1,952 ... G4
14895 Wellsville 5,769 ... E6
11590 Westbury 13,871 ... R7
†13619 West Carthage 1,824 ... J3
†14901 West Elmira 5,485 ... G6
14787 Westfield 3,446 ... A6
†12801 West Glens Falls 5,331 ... N4
11977 Westhampton 2,774 ... P9
11978 Westhampton Beach 1,629 P9
12491 West Hurley 2,382 ... M6
10994 West Nyack 8,553 ... K8
14788 Westons Mills 1,837 ... D6
10996 West Point 8,105 ... M8
11796 West Sayville 8,185 ... O9
14224 West Seneca 51,210 ... C5
12887 Whitehall 3,241 ... O3
*10601 White Plains⊙ 46,999 ... P6
13492 Whitesboro 4,460 ... K4
14588 Willard 1,339 ... G5
14589 Williamson 1,768 ... F4
14221 Williamsville 6,017 ... C5
11596 Williston Park 8,216 ... R7
13865 Windsor 1,155 ... J6
13697 Winthrop-Brasher Falls 1,454 ... L1
12998 Witherbee-Mineville 1,925 ... N2
14590 Wolcott 1,496 ... G4
11598 Woodmere 17,205 ... P7
12498 Woodstock 2,280 ... M6
12790 Wurtsboro 1,128 ... L7
11798 Wyandanch 13,215 ... N9
*10701 Yonkers 195,351 ... O6
10598 Yorktown Heights 7,696 ... N8
13495 Yorkville 3,115 ... K4
14174 Youngstown 2,191 ... C4

OTHER FEATURES

Adirondack (mts.) ... M3
Algonquin (peak) ... M2
Allegany Ind. Res. 1,243 ... C6
Allegheny (res.) ... C7
Allegheny (riv.) ... C6
Ashokan (res.) ... M7
Ausable (riv.) ... N2
Batten Kill (riv.) ... O4
Beaver (riv.) ... K3
Big Moose (lake) ... L3
Black (lake) ... J1
Black (riv.) ... K3
Block Island (sound) ... S8
Blue Mountain (lake) ... M3
Bonaparte (lake) ... K2
Brandreth (lake) ... L3
Brant (lake) ... N3
Brookhaven Nat'l Lab. ... P9
Butterfield (lake) ... J2
Canandaigua (lake) ... F5
Canisteo (riv.) ... F6
Cannonsville (res.) ... K6
Catskill (mts.) ... L6
Cattaraugus (creek) ... C6
Cattaraugus Ind. Res. 1,994 ... C5
Cayuga (lake) ... G5
Champlain (lake) ... O1
Chateaugay, Upper (lake) ... M1
Chautauqua (lake) ... A6
Chazy (lake) ... N1
Chenango (riv.) ... J6
Cohocton (riv.) ... F6
Conesus (lake) ... E5
Conewango (creek) ... B6
Cranberry (lake) ... L2
Deer (riv.) ... J3
Deer (riv.) ... L1
Delaware (riv.) ... K7
East (riv.) ... N9
Erie (lake) ... A5
Fire Island Nat'l Seashore ... P9
Fishers (isl.) ... S8
Forked (lake) ... L3
Fort Drum ... J2
Fort Niagara ... C4
Fort Stanwix Nat'l Mon. ... J4
Fulton Chain (lkes) ... K3
Galloo (isl.) ... H3
Gardiners (bay) ... R8
Gardiners (isl.) ... R8
Gateway Nat'l Rec. Area ... M9
Genesee (riv.) ... E5
George (lake) ... N4
Grand (isl.) ... B5
Grass (riv.) ... K1
Great Sacandaga (lake) ... M4
Great South (bay) ... O9
Great South (beach) ... O9
Greenwood (lake) ... M8
Grenadier (isl.) ... H2
Griffiss A.F.B. ... K4
Haystack (mt.) ... N2
Hemlock (lake) ... E5
Hinckley (res.) ... K4
Honeoye (lake) ... F5
Honnedaga (lake) ... L3
Hudson (riv.) ... N7
Hunter (mt.) ... M6
Indian (lake) ... M3
Jones (beach) ... R7
Keuka (lake) ... F5
Lila (lake) ... L2
Little Tupper (lake) ... L2
Long (isl.) ... P9
Long (lake) ... M2
Long Island (sound) ... P9
Manhattan (isl.) ... M9
Marcy (mt.) ... N2
Martin Van Buren Nat'l Hist. Site ... N6
Meacham (lake) ... M1
Mohawk (riv.) ... L5
Montauk (pt.) ... S8
Moose (riv.) ... K3
Neversink (res.) ... L7
New York State Barge (canal) ... C4
Niagara (riv.) ... B4
Oil Spring Ind. Res. 6 ... D6
Oneida (lake) ... J4
Onondaga Ind. Res. 596 ... H5
Ontario (lake) ... F3
Orient (pt.) ... R8
Oswegatchie (riv.) ... K2
Oswego (riv.) ... H4
Otisco (lake) ... H5
Otsego (lake) ... L5
Otselic (riv.) ... J5
Owasco (lake) ... G5
Peconic (bay) ... R9
Peninsula (pt.) ... H3
Pepacton (res.) ... L6
Piseco (lake) ... M4
Placid (lake) ... N2
Plattsburgh A.F.B. 5,905 ... N1
Pleasant (lake) ... M4
Plum (isl.) ... R8
Poosepatuck Ind. Res. 203 ... P9
Raquette (lake) ... L3
Rondout (res.) ... M7
Round (lake) ... L2
Sacandaga (lake) ... L3
Sackets (harb.) ... H3
Sagamore Hill Nat'l Hist. Site ... R6
Saint Lawrence (lake) ... K1
Saint Lawrence (riv.) ... J2
Saint Regis (riv.) ... L1
Saint Regis Ind. Res. 1,802 ... M1
Salmon (res.) ... J3
Salmon (riv.) ... H3
Salmon (riv.) ... M1
Saranac (lkes) ... M2
Saranac (riv.) ... N1
Saratoga (lake) ... N4
Saratoga Nat'l Hist. Park ... N4
Schoharie (res.) ... M6
Schroon (lake) ... N3
Seneca (lake) ... G5
Seneca (riv.) ... G5
Shelter (isl.) ... R8
Shinnecock Ind. Res. 297 ... R9
Silver (lake) ... N1
Skaneateles (lake) ... H5
Skylight (mt.) ... M2
Slide (mt.) ... L6
Staten (isl.) ... M9
Statue of Liberty Nat'l Mon. ... M9
Stony (isl.) ... H3
Stony (pt.) ... H3
Susquehanna (riv.) ... H6
Thousand (isls.) ... H2
Tioughnioga (riv.) ... H6
Titus (lake) ... M1
Tomhannock (res.) ... O5
Tonawanda Ind. Res. 467 ... D4
Toronto (res.) ... L7
Tupper (lake) ... M2
Tuscarora Ind. Res. 921 ... B4
Unadilla (riv.) ... K5
Upper Chateaugay (lake) ... M1
Valcour (isl.) ... N1
Wallkill (riv.) ... L8
Whiteface (mt.) ... N2
Whitney Point (lake) ... J6
Woodhull (lake) ... L3

⊙County seat.
‡Population of metropolitan area.
○Population of town or township.
† Zip of nearest p.o. * Multiple zips.

Agriculture, Industry and Resources

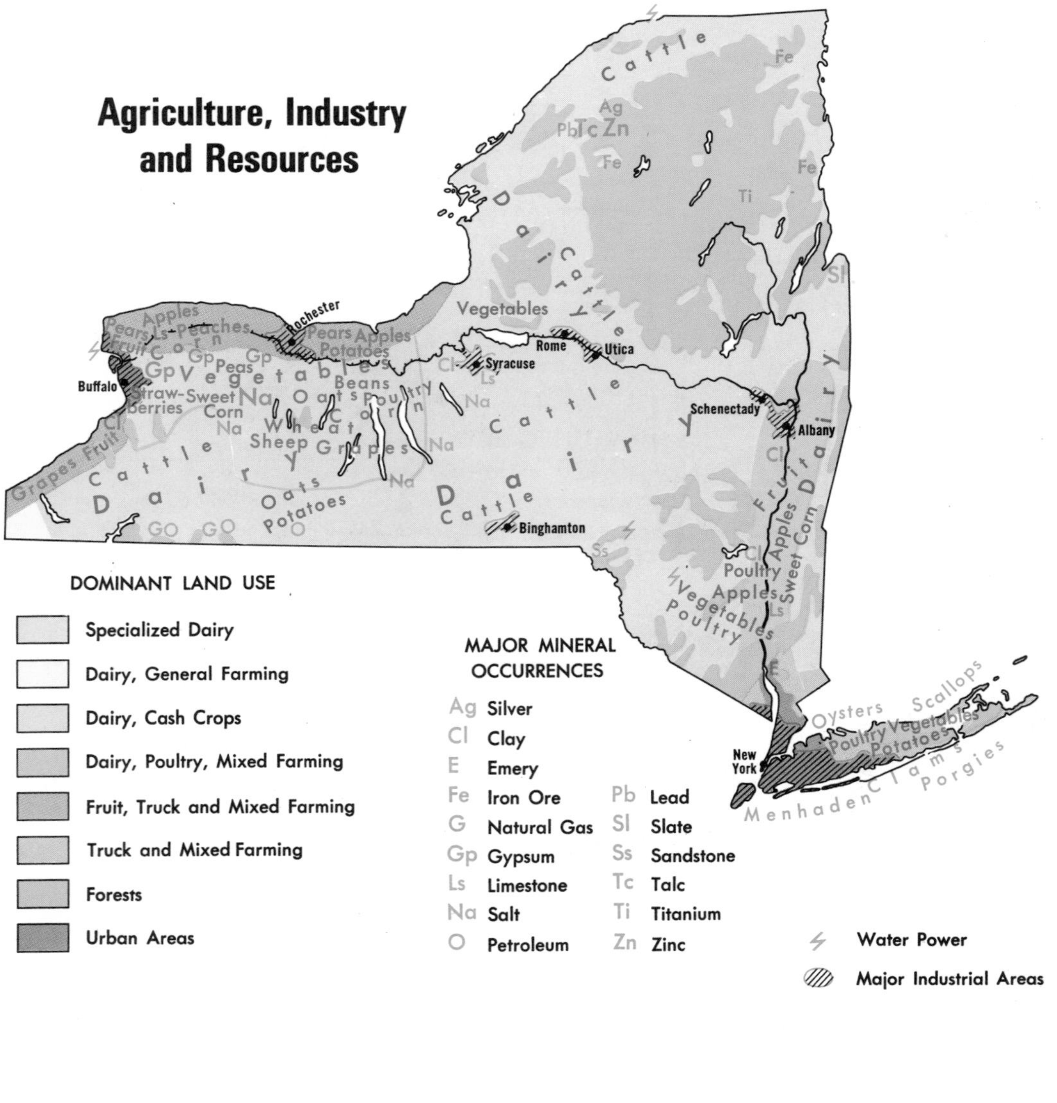
Cattle
Fe
Ag
Pb Tc Zn
Fe
Ti
Dairy
Cattle
Vegetables
Rochester
Apples
Pears Peaches
Fruit
Corn
Pears Apples
Potatoes
Rome
Utica
Syracuse
Buffalo
Gp Vegetables
Peas
Straw-Sweet Berries
Corn
Na
Oats
Beans
Poultry
Wheat
Sheep
Grapes
Cattle
Dairy
Schenectady
Albany
Grapes Fruit
Cattle
Dairy
Oats
Potatoes
Dairy
Cattle
Binghamton
Fruit
Apples
Sweet Corn
Poultry
Apples
Vegetables
Poultry
Oysters
Scallops
Poultry Vegetables
Potatoes
Clams
Menhaden
Porgies
New York
DOMINANT LAND USE
Specialized Dairy
Dairy, General Farming
Dairy, Cash Crops
Dairy, Poultry, Mixed Farming
Fruit, Truck and Mixed Farming
Truck and Mixed Farming
Forests
Urban Areas
MAJOR MINERAL OCCURRENCES
Ag Silver
Cl Clay
E Emery
Fe Iron Ore
G Natural Gas
Gp Gypsum
Ls Limestone
Na Salt
O Petroleum
Pb Lead
Sl Slate
Ss Sandstone
Tc Talc
Ti Titanium
Zn Zinc
Water Power
Major Industrial Areas

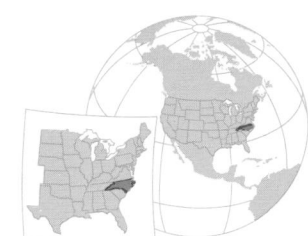

AREA 52,669 sq. mi. (136,413 sq. km.)
POPULATION 5,881,813
CAPITAL Raleigh
LARGEST CITY Charlotte
HIGHEST POINT Mt. Mitchell 6,684 ft. (2037 m.)
SETTLED IN 1650
ADMITTED TO UNION November 21, 1789
POPULAR NAME Tarheel State
STATE FLOWER Flowering Dogwood
STATE BIRD Cardinal

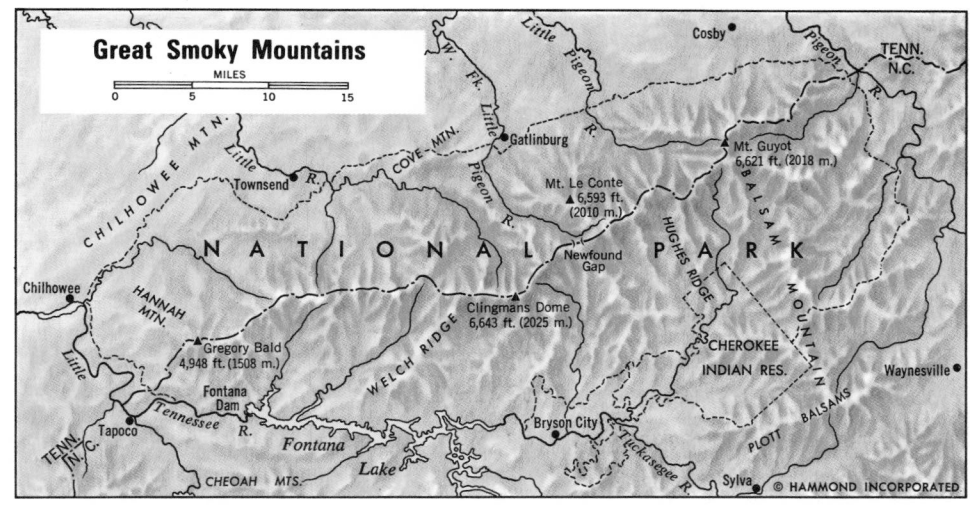

Great Smoky Mountains

© HAMMOND INCORPORATED

COUNTIES

Alamance 99,319	L3
Alexander 24,999	G3
Alleghany 9,587	G1
Anson 25,649	J4
Ashe 22,325	F2
Avery 14,409	F2
Beaufort 40,355	R4
Bertie 21,024	P2
Bladen 30,491	M5
Brunswick 35,777	N6
Buncombe 160,934	D3
Burke 72,504	F3
Cabarrus 85,895	H4
Caldwell 67,746	F3
Camden 5,829	S2
Carteret 41,092	R5
Caswell 20,705	L2
Catawba 105,208	G3
Chatham 33,415	L3
Cherokee 18,933	A4
Chowan 12,558	R2
Clay 6,619	B4
Cleveland 83,435	F4
Columbus 51,037	M6
Craven 71,043	P4
Cumberland 247,160	M4
Currituck 11,089	S2
Dare 13,377	T3
Davidson 113,162	J3
Davie 24,599	H3
Duplin 40,952	O5
Durham 152,785	M3
Edgecombe 55,988	O3
Forsyth 243,683	J2
Franklin 30,055	N2
Gaston 162,568	G4
Gates 8,875	R2
Graham 7,217	B4
Granville 34,043	M2
Greene 16,117	O3
Guilford 317,154	K3
Halifax 55,286	O2
Harnett 59,570	M4
Haywood 46,495	C3
Henderson 58,580	D4
Hertford 23,368	P2
Hoke 20,383	L4
Hyde 5,873	S3
Iredell 82,538	H3
Jackson 25,811	C4
Johnston 70,599	N4
Jones 9,705	P4

Lee 36,718	L4
Lenoir 59,819	O4
Lincoln 42,372	G3
Macon 20,178	B4
Madison 16,827	D3
Martin 25,948	P3
McDowell 35,135	E3
Mecklenburg 404,270	H4
Mitchell 14,428	E2
Montgomery 22,469	K4
Moore 50,505	L4
Nash 67,153	O2
New Hanover 103,471	O6
Northampton 22,584	P2
Onslow 112,784	P5
Orange 77,055	L2
Pamlico 10,398	R4
Pasquotank 28,462	S2
Pender 22,215	O5
Perquimans 9,486	S2
Person 29,164	M2
Pitt 90,146	P3
Polk 12,984	E4
Randolph 91,728	K3
Richmond 45,481	K4
Robeson 101,610	L5
Rockingham 83,426	K2
Rowan 99,186	H3
Rutherford 53,787	E4
Sampson 49,687	N4
Scotland 32,273	L5
Stanly 48,517	J4
Stokes 33,086	J2
Surry 59,449	H2
Swain 10,283	B3
Transylvania 23,417	D4
Tyrrell 3,975	S3
Union 70,380	H4
Vance 36,748	N2
Wake 301,327	M3
Warren 16,232	N2
Washington 14,801	R3
Watauga 31,666	F2
Wayne 97,054	N4
Wilkes 58,657	G2
Wilson 63,132	O3
Yadkin 28,439	H2
Yancey 14,934	E3

CITIES and TOWNS

Zip	Name/Pop.	Key
28315	Aberdeen 1,945	L4
27910	Ahoskie 4,887	P2
27201	Alamance 320	K2
28001	Albemarle⊙ 15,110	J4
†28043	Alexander Mills 643	F4
28509	Alliance 616	R4
28702	Almond 140	B4
28901	Andrews 1,621	B4
27501	Angier 1,709	M4
28007	Ansonville 794	J4
27502	Apex 2,847	M3
28510	Arapahoe 467	R4
27263	Archdale 5,326	K3
†28642	Arlington 872	H2
28420	Ash 150	N6
27203	Asheboro⊙ 15,252	K3
	Asheville‡ 177,761	D3
†27983	Askewville 227	R2
28421	Atkinson 298	N5
28512	Atlantic Beach 941	R5
27805	Aulander 1,214	P2
27806	Aurora 698	R4
28318	Autryville 228	M4
27915	Avon 500	U4
28513	Ayden 4,361	P4
27916	Aydlett 205	T2
28009	Badin 1,514	J4
27807	Bailey 685	N3
28705	Bakersville⊙ 373	E2
28706	Balfour 1,772	E4
28707	Balsam 200	C4
28604	Banner Elk 1,087	F2
27813	Black Creek 523	O3
28711	Black Mountain 4,083	E3
27008	Barber 155	H3
†28739	Barker Heights 1,267	D4
28710	Bat Cave 450	E4
28808	Bath 207	R4
27809	Battleboro 632	O2
28515	Bayboro⊙ 759	R4
†27892	Beargrass 82	P3
28516	Beaufort⊙ 3,826	R5
27810	Belhaven 2,430	R3
27811	Bellarthur 350	O3
28012	Belmont 4,607	H4
†28451	Belville 102	N6
†28090	Belwood 613	F4
27208	Bennett 254	K3
27504	Benson 2,792	N4
28016	Bessemer City 4,787	G4
27812	Bethel 1,825	P3
28518	Beulaville 1,060	O5
†28803	Biltmore Forest 1,499	E3
27209	Biscoe 1,334	K4
28711	Black Mountain 4,083	E3
28320	Bladenboro 1,428	M5
27212	Blanch 200	L2
28605	Blowing Rock 1,337	F2
28092	Boger City 2,252	G4
28461	Boiling Spring Lakes 998	N7
28017	Boiling Springs 2,381	F4
28422	Bolivia 252	N6
28423	Bolton 563	N6
27213	Bonlee 300	L3
28606	Boomer 250	G2
28607	Boone⊙ 10,191	F2
27011	Boonville 1,028	H2
28322	Bowdens 200	N4
28712	Brevard⊙ 5,323	D4
28519	Bridgeton 461	R4
27505	Broadway 908	L4
†28601	Brookford 467	G3
28424	Brunswick 223	M6
28713	Bryson City⊙ 1,556	C4
27506	Buies Creek 1,939	M4
27507	Bullock 525	M2
27508	Bunn 505	N3
28425	Burgaw⊙ 1,738	N5
27215	Burlington 37,266	K2
	Burlington‡ 99,136	F2
28714	Burnsville⊙ 1,452	E3
27509	Burton 4,240	M2
27312	Bynum 350	L3
†29566	Calabash 128	M7
28325	Calypso 689	N4
27921	Camden⊙ 300	S2
28326	Cameron 225	L4
27229	Candor 868	K4
28716	Canton 4,631	D3
†28584	Cape Carteret 944	P5
28428	Carolina Beach 2,000	O6
27510	Carrboro 7,336	L3
28327	Carthage⊙ 925	K4
27511	Cary 21,763	M3
28020	Casar 346	F3
28717	Cashiers 553	C4
28429	Castle Hayne 1,087	O6
†28461	Caswell Beach 110	N7
28609	Catawba 523	G3
27230	Cedar Falls 400	K3
27231	Cedar Grove 250	L2
28520	Cedar Island 310	S5
†27549	Centerville 135	N2
28430	Cerro Gordo 295	M6
28431	Chadbourn 1,975	M6
†28445	Chadwick Acres 15	P6
27514	Chapel Hill 32,421	L3
*28201	Charlotte⊙ 314,447	H4
	Charlotte-Gastonia‡ 637,218	H4
28021	Cherryville 4,844	G4
28023	China Grove 2,081	H3
28521	Chinquapin 280	O5
27817	Chocowinity 644	P4
28610	Claremont 880	G3
28433	Clarkton 664	M6
27520	Clayton 4,091	N3
27012	Clemmons 7,401	J2
27013	Cleveland 595	H3
28328	Clinton⊙ 7,552	N5
28721	Clyde 1,008	D3
27521	Coats 1,385	M4
27922	Cofield 465	R2
27924	Colerain 284	R2
27925	Columbia⊙ 758	S3
28722	Columbus⊙ 727	E4
28522	Comfort 325	O5
27818	Como 89	P1
28025	Concord⊙ 16,942	H4
27819	Conetoe 215	O3
28613	Conover 4,245	G3
27820	Conway 678	P2
27014	Cooleemee 1,448	H3
28031	Cornelius 1,460	H4
27927	Corolla 158	T2
28523	Cove City 500	P4
28032	Cramerton 1,869	G4
27522	Creedmoor 1,641	M2
27928	Creswell 426	S3
27852	Crisp 435	O3
28616	Crossnore 297	F2
28331	Cumberland 400	M5
27237	Cumnock 200	L3
27929	Currituck⊙ 700	T2
28034	Dallas 3,340	G4
27016	Danbury⊙ 140	J2
28036	Davidson 3,241	H4
28524	Davis 612	R5
27239	Denton 949	J3
28725	Dillsboro 179	C4
27017	Dobson⊙ 1,222	H2
†28801	Dortches 885	O2
28526	Dover 600	P4
28619	Drexel 1,392	F3
28332	Dublin 477	M5
28334	Dunn 8,962	M4
*27701	Durham⊙ 100,538	M2
	Durham-Raleigh‡ 530,673	M2
27242	Eagle Springs 280	K4
28038	Earl 206	F4
†28434	East Arcadia 461	N6
27018	East Bend 602	H2
28726	East Flat Rock 3,365	E4
†28723	East Laport 150	C4
28352	East Laurinburg 536	L5
†28752	East Marion 1,851	F3
28039	East Spencer 2,150	J3
27288	Eden 15,672	K1
27932	Edenton⊙ 5,357	R2
27909	Elizabeth City⊙ 14,004	S2
28337	Elizabethtown⊙ 3,551	M5
28621	Elkin 2,858	H2
28622	Elk Park 535	E2
28040	Ellenboro 560	F4
28338	Ellerbe 1,415	K4
27822	Elm City 1,561	O3
27244	Elon College 2,873	L2
†28557	Emerald Isle 865	P5
27823	Enfield 2,995	O2
28728	Enka 5,567	D3
28339	Erwin 2,828	M4
27247	Ether 425	K4
27935	Eure 300	R2
27825	Everetts 213	P3
27830	Eureka 303	O3
28438	Evergreen 310	M6
28439	Fair Bluff 1,095	M6
27826	Fairfield 900	S3
28340	Fairmont 2,658	L6
28341	Faison 636	N4
28041	Faith 552	J3

(continued on following page)

Agriculture, Industry and Resources

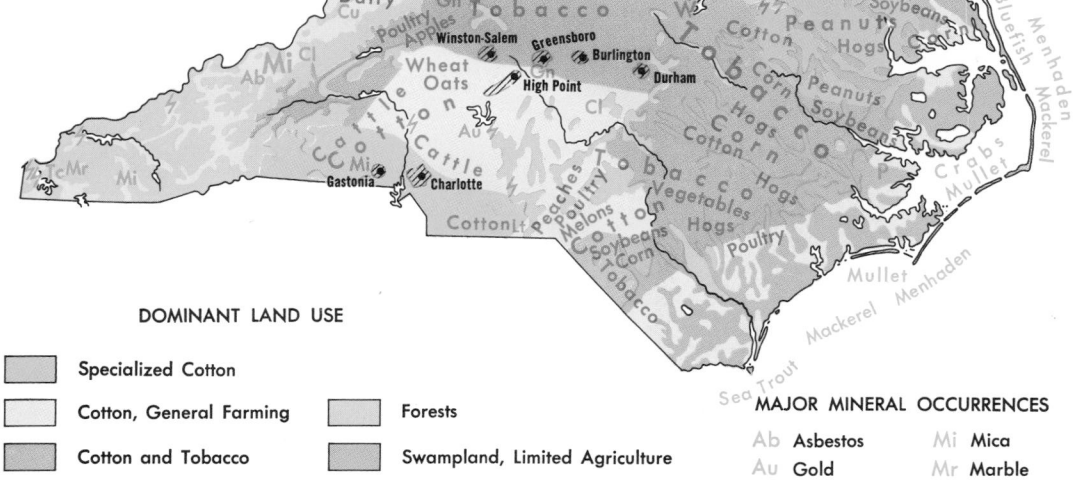

DOMINANT LAND USE

- Specialized Cotton
- Cotton, General Farming
- Cotton and Tobacco
- Tobacco, General Farming
- Peanuts, General Farming
- General Farming, Livestock, Fruit, Tobacco
- General Farming, Truck Farming, Tobacco, Livestock
- Forests
- Swampland, Limited Agriculture
- Nonagricultural Land

⚡ Water Power
▨ Major Industrial Areas

MAJOR MINERAL OCCURRENCES

Ab	Asbestos		Mi	Mica
Au	Gold		Mr	Marble
Cl	Clay		P	Phosphates
Cu	Copper		Tc	Talc
Gn	Granite		W	Tungsten
Lt	Lithium			

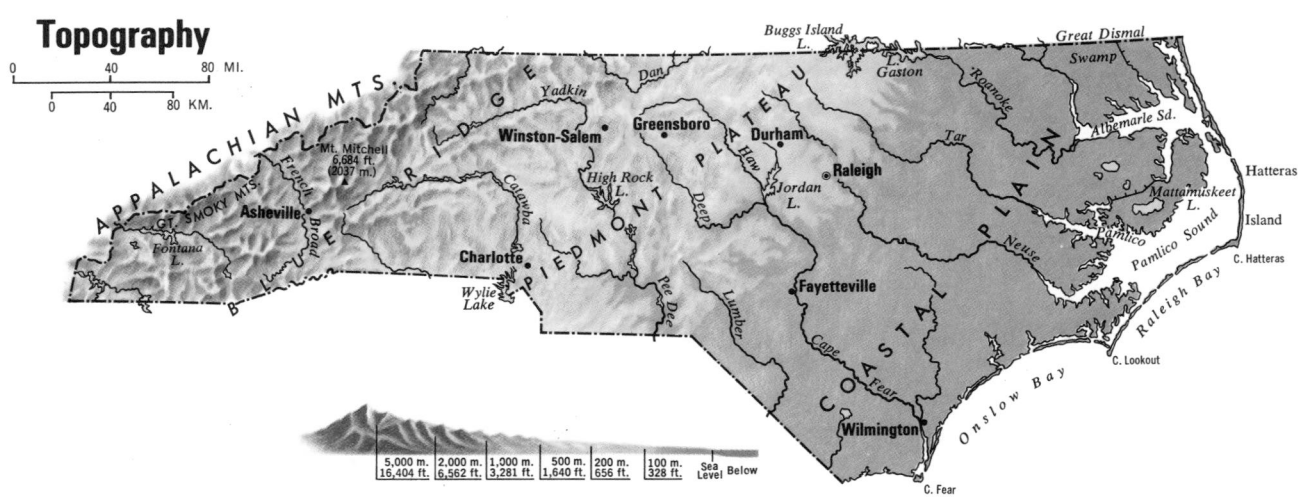

Topography

0   40   80 MI.

0   40   80 KM.

5,000 m. 16,404 ft. 2,000 m. 6,562 ft. 1,000 m. 3,281 ft. 500 m. 1,640 ft. 200 m. 656 ft. 100 m. 328 ft. Sea Level Below

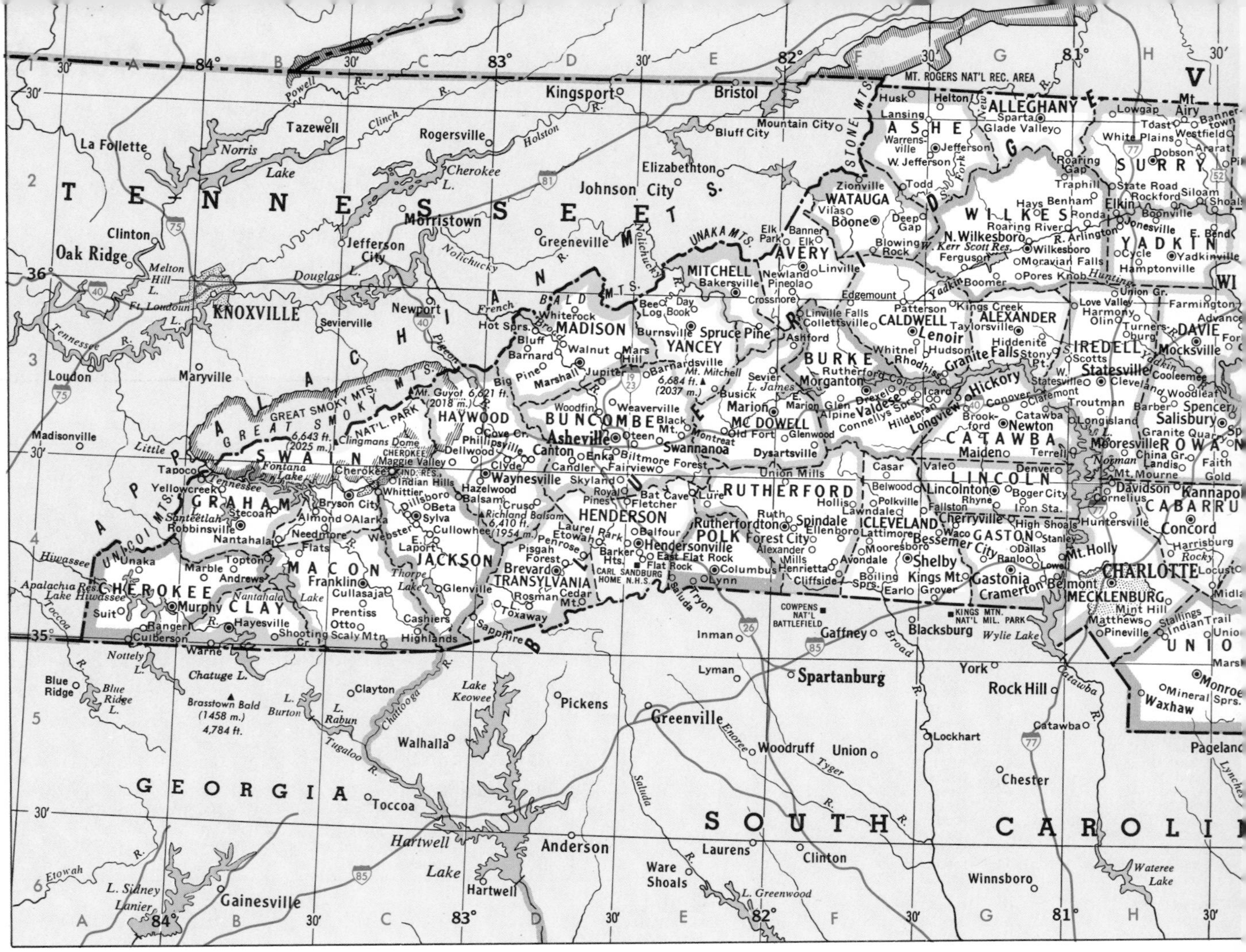

North Carolina

SCALE
0 5 10   20   30   40   50 MI.
0 5 10 20 30 40 50 KM.

State Capitals.........................⊛
County Seats...........................⊙
Canals.................................
Major Limited Access Hwys.

Scale 1:2,070,000

© Copyright HAMMOND INCORPORATED, Maplewood, N.J.

†28302 Rockfish 200............L5	†27530 South Goldsboro 2,531...N4	28560 Trent Woods 1,177.........P4	Wilmington‡ 139,238............N6	Clingmans Dome (mt.)............C3	Neuse (riv.)....................R5
28379 Rockingham⊙ 8,300........K5	28461 Southport⊙ 2,824.........N7	28166 Troutman 1,360............H3	27893 Wilson⊙ 34,424............O3	Contentnea (creek).............N3	New (riv.)......................O5
28138 Rockwell 1,339...........J3	†27890 South Weldon 1,801......O2	28571 Troy⊙ 2,702...............K4	27983 Windsor⊙ 2,126............P2	Core (banks)...................S5	New, South Fork (riv.)..........G2
27801 Rocky Mount 41,283.......O3	28675 Sparta⊙ 1,687............G1	28782 Tryon 1,796...............E4	27985 Winfall 634...............S2	Core (sound)...................S5	New River (inlet)...............O5
27571 Rolesville 381...........N3	27881 Speed 95.................P3	28393 Turkey 417...............N4	28174 Wingate 2,615............J5	Corncake (inlet)...............O7	Nolichucky (riv.)...............E2
28670 Ronda 457................H2	28159 Spencer 2,938............H3	27980 Tyner 264................S2	*27101 Winston-Salem 131,885...J2	Croatan (sound)................T3	Norman (lake)...................H3
27970 Roper 795................P3	28160 Spindale 4,246...........F4	†27203 Ulah 546...............K3	28590 Winterville 2,052........P3	Currituck (sound)..............T2	North East Cape Fear (riv.)....O4
28382 Roseboro 1,227...........N5	27882 Spring Hope 1,254........N3	28689 Union Grove 614..........H2	27986 Winton⊙ 825..............P2	Dan (riv.).....................L1	Ocracoke (inlet)...............T5
28458 Rose Hill 1,508..........N4	28390 Spring Lake 6,273........M4	28890 Valdese 3,364............F3	27594 Wise 550.................N2	Deep (riv.)....................K3	Ocracoke (isl.)................T4
28772 Rosman 512...............D4	27882 Spruce Pine 2,282........E3	28586 Vanceboro 833............P4	28804 Woodfin 3,260............D3	Dismal (Great) (swamp).........S1	Onslow (bay)...................P6
28383 Rowland 1,841............L5	27355 Staley 204...............K3	28587 Vandemere 335............R4	27897 Woodland 861.............P2	Drum (inlet)...................S5	Oregon (inlet).................U3
27573 Roxboro⊙ 7,532...........M2	†28079 Stallings 1,826.........H4	28394 Vass 828................L4	27054 Woodleaf 550.............H3	Fear (cape)....................O7	Pamlico (riv.).................R4
27872 Roxobel 278..............P2	28163 Stanfield 463............J4	28169 Waco 322.................G4	27378 Worthville 350...........H3	Fishing (creek)................O2	Pamlico (sound)................S4
27326 Ruffin 680...............K2	28164 Stanley 2,341............G4	28395 Wade 474................M4	28480 Wrightsville Beach 2,910..O6	Fontana (lake).................B4	Pee Dee (riv.).................J4
27045 Rural Hall 1,336.........J2	†27045 Stanleyville 5,039......J2	28170 Wadesboro⊙ 4,206.........J5	27055 Yadkinville⊙ 2,216.......H2	Fort Bragg 37,834..............M4	Phelps (lake)..................S3
†28139 Ruth 381...............E4	27883 Stantonsburg 920.........O3	28396 Wagram 617..............L5	27379 Yanceyville⊙ 1,511.......L2	Fort Raleigh Nat'l Hist. Site..T3	Pigeon (riv.)..................C3
28671 Rutherford College 1,108..F3	27356 Star 816.................J4	27587 Wake Forest 3,780........M3	†28461 Yaupon Beach 569.......N7	French Broad (riv.)............D3	Pope A.F.B.....................L4
28139 Rutherfordton⊙ 3,434.....E4	28677 Statesville⊙ 18,622......H3	28466 Wallace 2,903............N5	27596 Youngsville 486..........N2	Gaston (res.)..................O2	Portsmouth (isl.)..............T5
28384 Saint Pauls 1,639........M5	28391 Stedman 723..............M4	27373 Wallburg 300.............H3	27597 Zebulon 2,055............N3	Great (lake)...................P5	Pungo (lake)...................S3
28385 Salemburg 742............N4	28582 Stella 700...............P5	27052 Walnut Cove 1,147........J2	28698 Zionville 525............F2	Great Dismal (swamp)...........S1	Pungo (riv.)...................R4
28144 Salisbury⊙ 22,677‡.......H3	27581 Stem 222.................M2	27888 Walstonburg 181..........O3		Great Smoky (mts.).............B3	Raleigh (bay)..................S5
Salisbury-Concord‡	27884 Stokes 450...............P3	27981 Wanchese 1,105...........T3	OTHER FEATURES	Great Smoky Mts. Nat'l Park....B3	Richland Balsam (mt.)..........D4
185,081..............H3	27357 Stokesdale 1,070.........K2	28909 Warne 200...............B5		Green (swamp)..................N6	Roanoke (isl.).................T3
28773 Saluda 607...............E4	27048 Stoneville 1,054.........K2	27589 Warrenton⊙ 908..........N2	Albemarle (sound)..............S2	Guyot (mt.)....................C3	Roanoke (riv.).................P2
27972 Salvo 150................U3	28583 Stonewall 360............R4	28398 Warsaw 2,910............N4	Alligator (lake)..............S3	Hatteras (cape)................U4	Rocky (riv.)...................H4
27330 Sanford⊙ 14,773..........L4	28678 Stony Point 1,150........G3	28173 Waxhaw 1,208............H5	Alligator (river).............S3	Hatteras (inlet)...............T4	Santeetlah (lake)..............B4
28774 Sapphire 350............D4	27582 Stovall 417.............M2	28786 Waynesville⊙ 6,765.......D4	Angola (swamp)................O5	Hatteras (isl.)................U4	Seymour Johnson A.F.B..........N4
27340 Saxapahaw 500...........L3	†28579 Straits 151............R5	28787 Weaverville 1,495........D3	Apalachia (lake)..............A4	High Rock (lake)...............J3	Six Run (creek)................N4
28775 Scaly Mountain 100.......C4	27978 Stumpy Point 250.........T3	28888 Webster 200.............C4	Appalachian (mts.)............D2	Hiwassee (lake)................A4	Smith (isl.)...................N7
27874 Scotland Neck 2,834......P2	28906 Suit 350................A4	27909 Weeksville 500..........T3	Ashe (isl.)...................P6	Hiwassee (riv.)................A4	South (riv.)...................M5
28699 Scotts 500...............H2	27358 Summerfield 1,680........K2	27374 Welcome 3,243...........J3	Bald (mts.)...................D3	Holly Shelter (swamp).........O6	South Yadkin (riv.)............H3
27875 Scranton 250.............S4	27979 Sunbury 400.............R2	27890 Weldon 1,844............O2	Black (riv.)..................N5	Hunting (riv.)................H2	Stone (mts.)...................F2
27876 Seaboard 687.............O1	28459 Surf City 421...........O6	27591 Wendell 2,222...........N3	Blue Ridge (mts.).............E3	Hyco (riv.)...................L2	Sunny Point Mil. Ocean Term....O6
27341 Seagrove 294.............K3	28778 Swannanoa 5,586..........E3	27375 Wentworth⊙ 150..........K2	Bodie (isl.)..................T2	James (riv.)..................E3	Tar (riv.).....................O3
27576 Selma 4,762..............N3	27885 Swanquarter⊙ 550.........S4	27053 Westfield 450...........H2	Broad (riv.)..................E4	Jordan, B. Everett (lake).....M3	Thorpe (lake)..................C4
27343 Semora 500...............L2	28584 Swansboro 976............P5	28694 West Jefferson 822......F2	Buggs Island (lake)...........M1	Kerr, W. Scott (res.).........G2	Tillery (lake).................J4
28578 Seven Springs 166........O4	28779 Sylva⊙ 1,699............C4	†28389 Whispering Pines 1,160..L4	Camp Lejeune Marine Corps	Lanes (creek).................J5	Trent (riv.)...................P4
27877 Severn 309...............P2	28463 Tabor City 2,710.........M6	27891 Whitakers 924...........O2	Base 30,764.................P5	Little (riv.).................N3	Unaka (mts.)...................A4
28459 Shallotte 680............N7	27886 Tarboro⊙ 8,634..........P3	28337 White Lake 968..........N5	Cape Fear (riv.)..............M5	Little (riv.).................L4	Unicoi (mts.)..................A4
27878 Sharpsburg 997...........O3	28392 Tar Heel 118............M5	27031 White Plains 200........H2	Cape Hatteras Nat'l Seashore..T4	Little Pee Dee (riv.).........L6	Waccamaw (lake)................N6
27973 Shawboro 300.............S2	28681 Taylorsville⊙ 1,103......G3	28472 Whiteville⊙ 5,565........M6	Carl Sandburg Home Nat'l Hist.	Little Tennessee (riv.).......B4	Waccamaw (riv.)................M7
28150 Shelby⊙ 15,310...........D4	28464 Teachey 373.............N5	28789 Whittier 200............C4	Site.......................D4	Long (lake)...................P5	Whiteoak (swamp)...............P5
27344 Siler City 4,446.........L3	27360 Thomasville 14,144.......J3	28697 Wilkesboro⊙ 2,335........G2	Catawba (lake)................G4	Lookout (cape)................S5	W. Scott Kerr (res.)...........G2
27879 Simpson 407..............N3	27583 Tarheel 500.............M2	†27530 Williamsboro 59........M2	Catawba (riv.)................H5	Lumber (riv.).................L6	Wright Brothers Nat'l Mem......T3
27880 Sims 192.................N3	27887 Tillery 400.............O2	27892 Williamston⊙ 6,159.......P3	Catfish (lake)................P5	Mattamuskeet (lake)...........S3	Yadkin (riv.)..................J3
27577 Smithfield⊙ 7,288........N3	27049 Toast 2,339.............H2	28401 Wilmington⊙ 44,000.......N6	Chatuge (lake)................B5	Meherrin (riv.)...............P1	
28579 Smyrna 291...............R5	28445 Topsail Beach 264........O6		Cherokee Ind. Res.............C3	Mitchell (mt.)................E3	⊙County seat.
28580 Snow Hill⊙ 1,374.........O4	28685 Traphill 500............H2		Cherry Point Marine Air Sta...R5	Moores Creek Nat'l Battlefield..N6	‡Population of metropolitan area.
27350 Sophia 350...............H3			Chowan (riv.).................R2	Nantahala (lake)..............B4	† Zip of nearest p.o.
28387 Southern Pines 8,620.....L4					* Multiple zips.

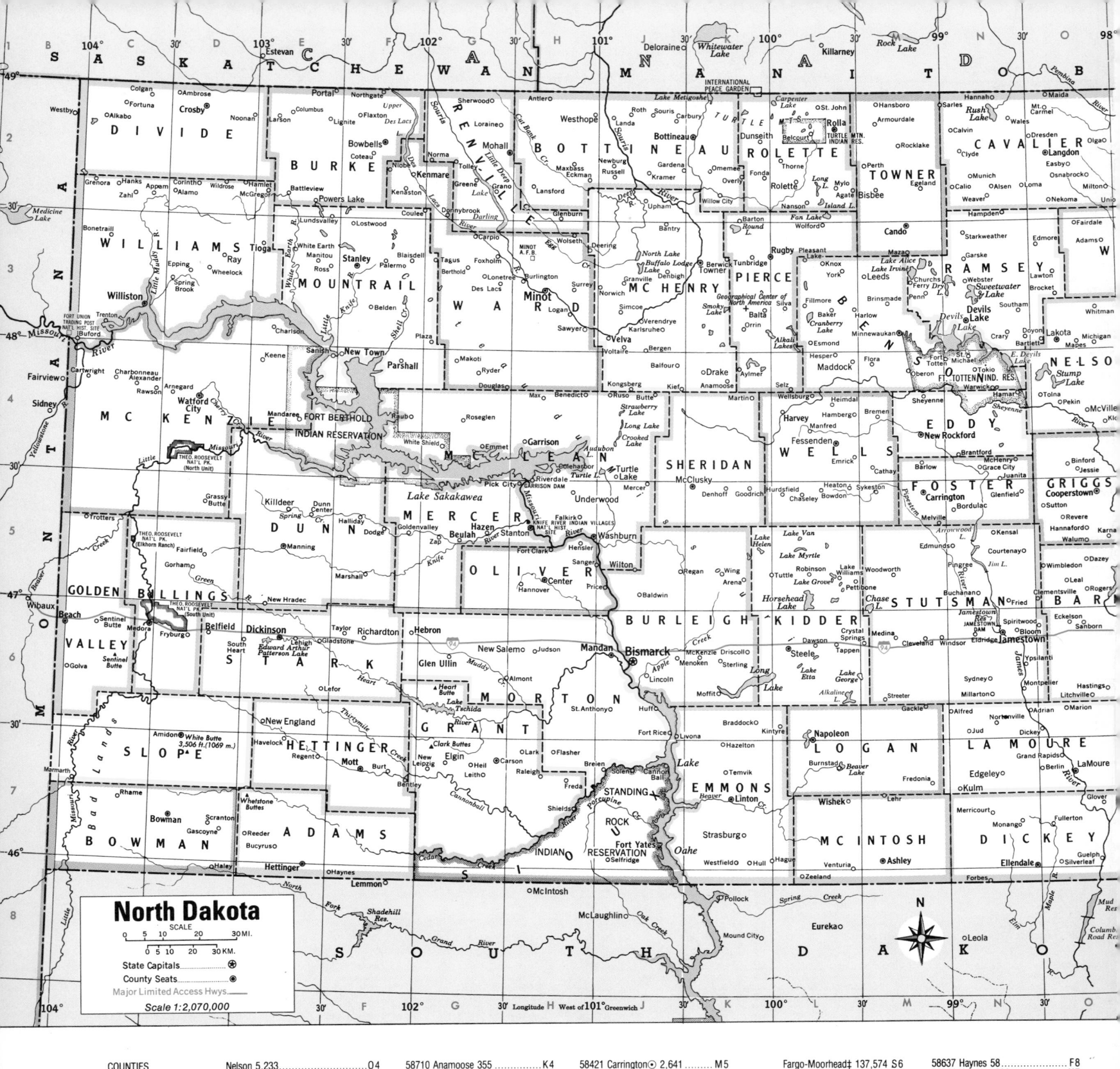

North Dakota

SCALE
0 5 10 20 30 MI.
0 5 10 20 30 KM.

State Capitals .... ⊛
County Seats .... ⊙
Major Limited Access Hwys

Scale 1:2,070,000

COUNTIES

County	Key
Adams 3,584	F7
Barnes 13,960	O5
Benson 7,944	M3
Billings 1,138	D5
Bottineau 9,239	J2
Bowman 4,229	C7
Burke 3,822	E2
Burleigh 54,811	J6
Cass 88,247	R5
Cavalier 7,636	N2
Dickey 7,207	N7
Divide 3,494	C2
Dunn 4,627	E5
Eddy 3,554	N4
Emmons 5,877	K7
Foster 4,611	N5
Golden Valley 2,391	C5
Grand Forks 66,100	P3
Grant 4,274	G6
Griggs 3,714	O5
Hettinger 4,275	E7
Kidder 3,833	L6
LaMoure 6,473	N7
Logan 3,493	L7
McHenry 7,858	J3
McIntosh 4,800	L7
McKenzie 7,132	D4
McLean 12,383	G4
Mercer 9,404	G5
Morton 25,177	H6
Mountrail 7,679	E3
Nelson 5,233	O4
Oliver 2,495	H5
Pembina 10,399	P2
Pierce 6,166	K3
Ramsey 13,048	N3
Ransom 6,698	P7
Renville 3,608	G2
Richland 19,207	R7
Rolette 12,177	L2
Sargent 5,512	P7
Sheridan 2,819	K4
Sioux 3,620	H7
Slope 1,157	C7
Stark 23,697	E6
Steele 3,106	P4
Stutsman 24,154	M5
Towner 4,052	M2
Traill 9,624	R5
Walsh 15,371	P3
Ward 58,392	G3
Wells 6,979	L4
Williams 22,237	C3

CITIES and TOWNS

Zip	Name/Pop.	Key
58001	Abercrombie 260	S7
58210	Adams 303	O3
58831	Alexander 358	C4
58003	Alice 62	P6
58833	Ambrose 60	D2
58004	Amenia 93	R6
58620	Amidon⊙ 43	D7
58710	Anamoose 355	K4
58212	Aneta 341	P4
58213	Ardoch 78	R3
58835	Arnegard 193	D4
58006	Arthur 445	R5
58413	Ashley⊙ 1,192	M7
58007	Ayr 42	P4
58712	Balfour 51	J4
58008	Barney 70	S7
58216	Bathgate 67	P2
58621	Beach⊙ 1,381	C6
58316	Belcourt 1,803	L2
58622	Belfield 1,274	D6
58716	Benedict 68	H4
58415	Berlin 71	O7
58718	Berthold 485	G3
58523	Beulah 2,908	G5
58317	Bisbee 257	M2
58501	Bismarck (cap.)⊙ 44,485	J6
58318	Bottineau⊙ 2,829	J2
58721	Bowbells⊙ 587	F2
58623	Bowman⊙ 2,071	D7
58320	Brinsmade 54	M3
58321	Brocket 74	O3
58722	Burlington 762	H3
58218	Buxton 336	R4
58322	Calio 61	N2
58323	Calvin 61	N2
58324	Cando⊙ 1,496	M3
†58241	Canton (Hensel) 68	P2
58725	Carpio 244	G3
58421	Carrington⊙ 2,641	M5
58529	Carson⊙ 469	H7
58012	Casselton 1,661	R6
58422	Cathay 66	M4
58530	Center⊙ 900	H5
58013	Cayuga 75	P7
58016	Clifford 51	R5
58017	Cogswell 227	P7
58425	Cooperstown⊙ 1,308	O5
58727	Columbus 325	E2
58730	Crosby⊙ 1,469	D2
58222	Crystal 256	P2
58021	Davenport 195	R6
58731	Deering 93	J3
58301	Devils Lake⊙ 7,442	N3
58431	Dickey 74	N6
58601	Dickinson⊙ 15,924	E6
58736	Drake 479	K4
58225	Drayton 1,082	R2
58329	Dunseith 625	K2
58024	Dwight 72	S7
58433	Edgeley 843	N7
58227	Edinburg 300	P3
58330	Edmore 416	O3
58533	Elgin 659	G7
58436	Ellendale⊙ 1,967	N7
58228	Emerado 596	R4
58027	Enderlin 1,151	P6
58332	Esmond 337	L3
58229	Fairdale 87	O3
58030	Fairmount 480	S7
58102	Fargo 61,383	S6
	Fargo-Moorhead‡ 137,574	S6
58438	Fessenden⊙ 761	L4
58230	Finley⊙ 718	P4
58535	Flasher 410	H7
58439	Forbes 84	N8
58231	Fordville 326	P3
58032	Forman⊙ 529	P7
58033	Fort Ransom 99	P6
58844	Fortuna 98	C2
58538	Fort Yates⊙ 771	J7
58440	Fredonia 82	M7
58442	Gackle 456	M6
58739	Gardena 66	J2
58036	Gardner 94	R5
58540	Garrison 1,830	H4
58235	Gilby 283	R3
58630	Gladstone 317	F6
58631	Glen Ullin 1,125	G6
58541	Goldenvalley 287	F5
58444	Goodrich 288	K5
58237	Grafton⊙ 5,293	P3
58201	Grand Forks⊙ 43,765	R4
	Grand Forks‡ 100,944	R4
58741	Granville 281	J3
58845	Grenora 362	C2
58040	Gwinner 725	P7
58636	Halliday 355	F5
58041	Hankinson 1,158	S7
58341	Harvey 2,527	L4
58042	Harwood 326	S6
58240	Hatton 787	R4
58637	Haynes 58	F8
58544	Hazelton 266	K7
58545	Hazen 2,365	G5
58638	Hebron 1,078	G6
58639	Hettinger⊙ 1,739	E8
58045	Hillsboro⊙ 1,600	S5
58243	Hoople 350	P2
58046	Hope 406	P5
58047	Horace 494	S6
58048	Hunter 369	R5
58244	Inkster 135	P3
58401	Jamestown⊙ 16,280	N6
58744	Karlsruhe 164	J3
58746	Kenmare 1,456	G2
58640	Killdeer 790	E5
58051	Kindred 568	R6
58343	Knox 69	N3
58748	Kramer 84	J2
58456	Kulm 570	N7
58344	Lakota⊙ 963	O3
58458	LaMoure⊙ 1,077	O7
58749	Landa 62	J2
58249	Langdon⊙ 2,335	O2
58750	Lansford 294	H2
58251	Larimore 1,524	P4
58459	Leal 45	O5
58346	Leeds 678	M3
58460	Lehr 254	M7
58551	Leith 59	G7
58052	Leonard 289	R6
58053	Lidgerwood 971	R7
58752	Lignite 332	F2

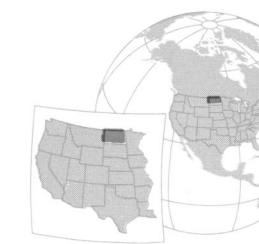

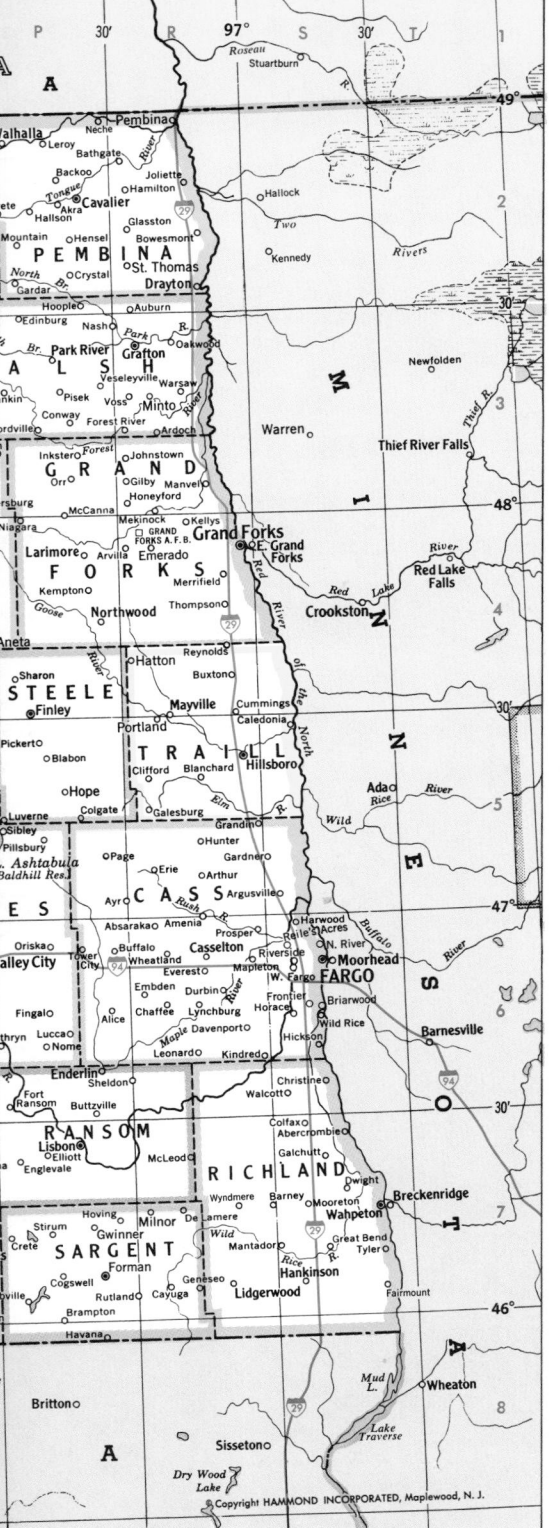

58276 Saint Thomas 528 ....R2
58780 Sanish E4
58781 Sawyer 417 ....H3
58653 Scranton 415 ....D7
58568 Selfridge 273 ....J7
58654 Sentinel Butte 86 ......C6
58068 Sheldon 173 ....P6
58782 Sherwood 294 ....G2
58374 Sheyenne 307 ....M4
58655 South Heart 294 ....D6
58850 Spring Brook 52 ....D3
58784 Stanley⊙ 1,631 ....F3
58571 Stanton⊙ 623 ....H5
58482 Steele⊙ 796 ....L6
58573 Strasburg 623 ....K7
58483 Streeter 264 ....M6
58785 Surrey 999 ....H3
58487 Tappen 271 ....L6
58656 Taylor 239 ....F6
58278 Thompson 785 ....R4
58852 Tioga 1,597 ....E3
58380 Tolna 241 ....O4
58071 Tower City 293 ....P6
58788 Towner⊙ 867 ....K3
58575 Turtle Lake 802 ......J4
58576 Underwood 1,329 ......H5
58072 Valley City⊙ 7,774 ...P6
58790 Velva 1,101 ....J3
58792 Voltaire 65 ....J3
58075 Wahpeton⊙ 9,064 ......S7
58281 Wales 74 ....N2
58282 Walhalla 1,429 ....P2
58577 Washburn⊙ 1,767 ......J5
58854 Watford City⊙ 2,119 ..D4
58078 West Fargo 10,099 ....S6
58793 Westhope 741 ....H2
58794 White Earth 98 ....E3
58795 Wildrose 214 ....D2
58801 Williston⊙ 13,336 ....C3
58834 Willow City 329 ......K2
58579 Wilton 950 ....J5
58492 Wimbledon 330 ....O5
58495 Wishek 1,345 ....L7
58385 Wolford 76 ....L3
58081 Wyndmere 550 ....R7
58386 York 69 ....L3
58580 Zap 511 ....G5
58581 Zeeland 253 ....L8

OTHER FEATURES

Alkali (lkes) L3
Alkaline (lake) L6
Apple (creek) J6
Arrowwood (lake) N5
Ashtabula (lake) P5
Audubon (lake) H4
Bad Lands (reg.) C7
Baldhill (Ashtabula) (res.) ...P5
Bear (creek) O7
Beaver (creek) B5
Beaver (creek) K7
Beaver (creek) L7
Buffalo Lodge (lake) J3
Cannonball (riv.) G7
Carpenter (lake) L2
Cedar (creek) G7
Chase (lake) M5
Cherry (creek) D4
Clark (buttes) G7
Coteau du Missouri (plain) G3
Cranberry (lake) L3
Crooked (lake) J4
Cut Bank (creek) H2
Darling (lake) G2
Deep (riv.) J1
Des Lacs (riv.) G3
Devils (lake) N3
Dry (lake) M3
East Devils (lake) N4
Egg (creek) H3
Elm (riv.) N8
Elm (riv.) R5
Etta (lake) L6

Fan (lake) L2
Forest (lake) P3
Fort Berthold Ind. Res. E4
Fort Totten Ind. Res. N4
Fort Union Trading Post Nat'l Hist.
  Site B3
Garrison (dam) H5
George (lake) L6
Goose (riv.) P4
Grand, North Fork (riv.) E8
Grand Forks A.F.B. 9,390 ......R4
Green (riv.) D5
Grove (lake) L5
Heart (butte) G6
Heart (riv.) F6
Helen (lake) K5
Horsehead (lake) L5
International Peace Garden K1
Irvine (lake) M3
Island (lake) L2
James (riv.) N6
Jamestown (res.) N6
Jim (lake) N5
Knife (riv.) H5
Knife R. Indian Villages Nat'l Hist.
  Site H5
Little Deep (creek) G2
Little Knife (riv.) F3

Little Missouri (riv.) D4
Little Muddy (riv.) C3
Long (lake) J4
Long (lake) K6
Long (lake) L2
Maple (riv.) O8
Maple (riv.) R6
Metigoshe (lake) K2
Minot A.F.B. 9,880 ....H3
Missouri (riv.) H5
Muddy (creek) G6
Myrtle (lake) L5
North (lake) J3
Oahe (lake) J7
Oak (creek) J8
Park (riv.) R3
Patterson, Edward A. (lake) ...E6
Pembina (riv.) O1
Pipestem (riv.) M5
Porcupine (creek) J7
Red River of the North (riv.) .S4
Round (lake) K3
Rush (lake) N2
Rush (lake) R5
Sakakawea (lake) G5
Sentinel (butte) C6
Shell (creek) F3
Sheyenne (riv.) O6

Smoky (lake) K3
Souris (riv.) J2
Spring (creek) E5
Standing Rock Ind. Res. J7
Strawberry (lake) J4
Stump (lake) O4
Sweetwater (lake) N3
Theodore Roosevelt Nat'l Mem. Park
  ....C5, D4,D6
Thirty Mile (creek) F6
Tongue (riv.) P2
Tschida (lake) G6
Turtle (lake) H4
Turtle (mts.) K2
Turtle Mountain Ind. Res. L2
Upper Des Lacs (lake) F2
Van (lake) L5
Whetstone (buttes) E7
White (butte) D7
White Butte (mt.) D7
White Earth (riv.) E3
Wild Rice (riv.) R7
Yellowstone (riv.) B4

⊙County seat.
‡Population of metropolitan area.
† Zip of nearest p.o.
* Multiple zips.

AREA, POPULATION, ETC.

AREA 70,702 sq. mi. (183,118 sq. km.)
POPULATION 652,717
CAPITAL Bismarck
LARGEST CITY Fargo
HIGHEST POINT White Butte 3,506 ft.
  (1069 m.)
SETTLED IN 1780
ADMITTED TO UNION November 2, 1889
POPULAR NAME Flickertail State; Sioux
  State
STATE FLOWER Wild Prairie Rose
STATE BIRD Western Meadowlark

Topography

| 5,000 m. 16,404 ft. | 2,000 m. 6,562 ft. | 1,000 m. 3,281 ft. | 500 m. 1,640 ft. | 200 m. 656 ft. | 100 m. 328 ft. | Sea Level | Below |

0   50   100 MI.
0   50   100 KM.

†58501 Lincoln 656 ....J6
58552 Linton⊙ 1,561 ....K7
58054 Lisbon⊙ 2,283 ....P7
58461 Litchville 251 ....O6
58056 Luverne 65 ....P5
58348 Maddock 677 ....L4
58554 Mandan 15,513 ....J6
58642 Manning⊙ 75 ....E5
58058 Mantador 76 ....R7
58256 Manvel 308 ....R3
58059 Mapleton 306 ....R6
58643 Marmarth 190 ....B7
58759 Max 317 ....H4
58257 Mayville 2,255 ....R4
58463 McClusky⊙ 658 ....K4
58254 McVille 626 ....O4
58467 Medina 521 ....M6
58645 Medora⊙ 94 ....C6
58259 Michigan 502 ....O3
58060 Milnor 716 ....R7
58351 Minnewaukan⊙ 461 ....M3
58701 Minot⊙ 32,843 ....H3
58261 Minto 592 ....R3
58761 Mohall⊙ 1,049 ....G2
58471 Monango 59 ....N7
58645 Montpelier 96 ....N6
58646 Mott⊙ 1,315 ....F7
58352 Munich 300 ....N2
58561 Napoleon⊙ 1,103 ....L6
58265 Neche 471 ....P2
58562 New Leipzig 352 ....G7
58356 New Rockford 1,791 .....N4

58563 New Salem 1,081 ....G6
58763 New Town 1,335 ....F4
58266 Niagara 76 ....P4
58062 Nome 67 ....P6
58765 Noonan 283 ....D2
58267 Northwood 1,240 ....P4
58474 Oakes 2,112 ....O7
58063 Oriska 125 ....P6
58064 Page 329 ....P5
58769 Palermo 86 ....F3
58270 Park River 1,844 ......P3
58770 Parshall 1,059 ....F4
58271 Pembina 673 ....R2
58476 Pingree 88 ....N5
58772 Portal 238 ....E2
58274 Portland 627 ....R5
58773 Powers Lake 466 ....E2
58849 Ray 766 ....D3
58649 Reeder 355 ....E7
58477 Regan 71 ....K5
58650 Regent 297 ....E7
58275 Reynolds 309 ....R4
58651 Rhame 222 ....C7
58652 Richardton 699 ....F6
†58078 Riverside 465 ....S6
58365 Rocklake 287 ....M2
58479 Rogers 68 ....O5
58366 Rolette 667 ....L2
58367 Rolla⊙ 1,538 ....L2
58368 Rugby⊙ 3,335 ....L3
58067 Rutland 250 ....P7
58369 Saint John 401 ....L2

Agriculture, Industry and Resources

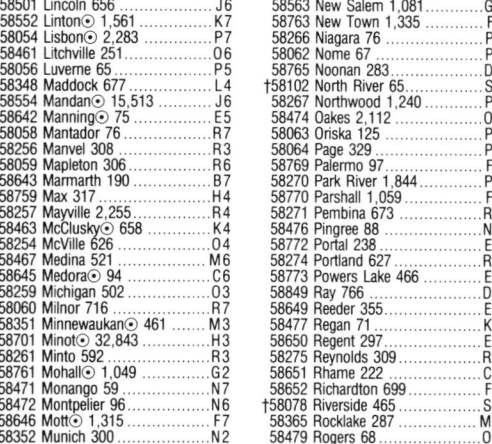

DOMINANT LAND USE

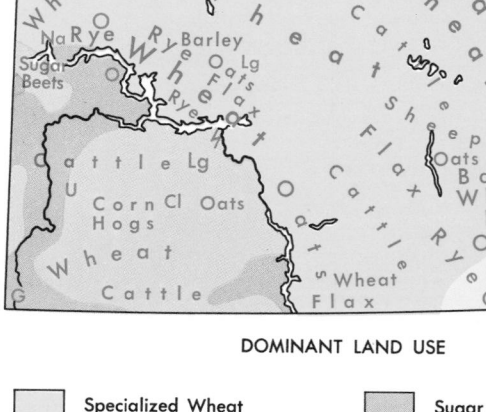

▢ Specialized Wheat	▢ Sugar Beets, Dry Beans, Livestock, General Farming
▢ Wheat, General Farming	▢ Range Livestock
▢ Wheat, Range Livestock	
▢ Livestock, Cash Grain	⚡ Water Power

MAJOR MINERAL OCCURRENCES

Cl Clay
G Natural Gas
Lg Lignite
Na Salt
O Petroleum
U Uranium

© Copyright HAMMOND INCORPORATED, Maplewood, N.J.

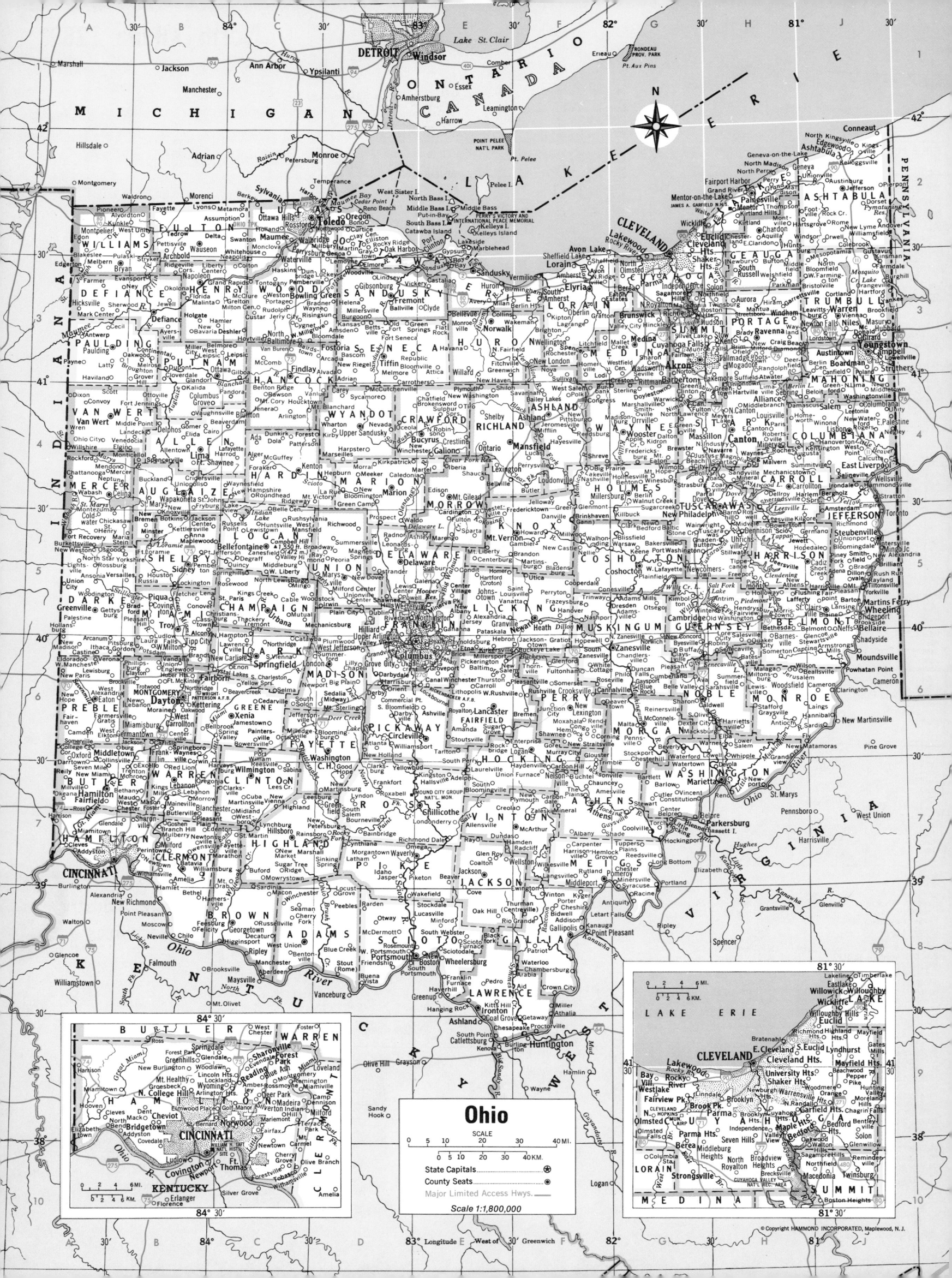

Ohio

SCALE

0 5 10   20   30   40 MI.

0 5 10   20   30   40KM.

State Capitals........................⊛
County Seats.........................◉
Major Limited Access Hwys._____

Scale 1:1,800,000

© Copyright HAMMOND INCORPORATED, Maplewood, N.J.

AREA 41,330 sq. mi. (107,045 sq. km.)
POPULATION 10,797,624
CAPITAL Columbus
LARGEST CITY Cleveland
HIGHEST POINT Campbell Hill 1,550 ft. (472 m.)
SETTLED IN 1788
ADMITTED TO UNION March 1, 1803
POPULAR NAME Buckeye State
STATE FLOWER Scarlet Carnation
STATE BIRD Cardinal

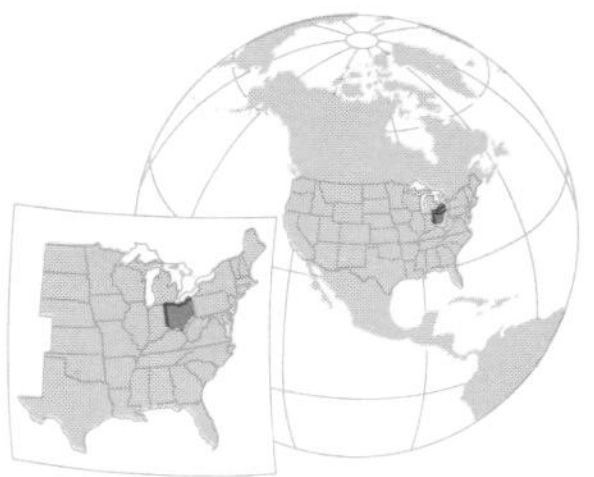

Topography

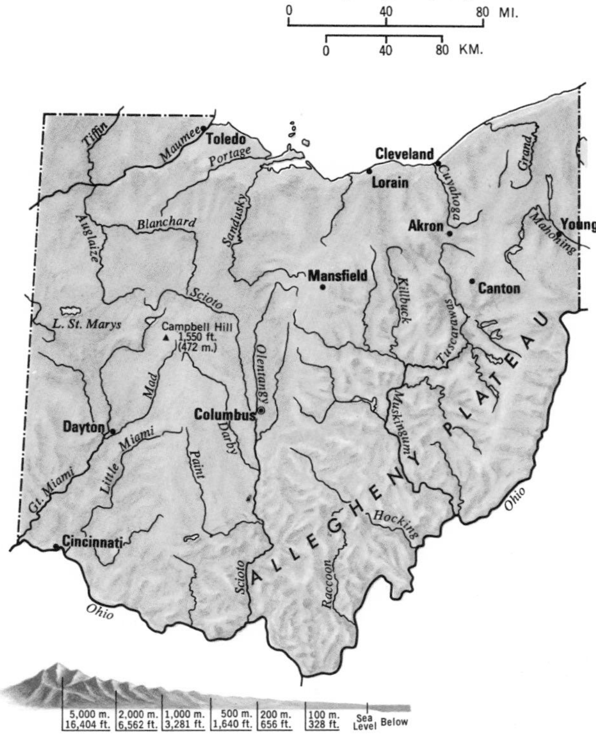
0 40 80 MI.
0 40 80 KM.
Toledo
Cleveland
Lorain
Akron
Youngstown
Mansfield
Canton
Campbell Hill 1,550 ft. (472 m.)
Columbus
Dayton
Cincinnati
Tiffin
Maumee
Portage
Blanchard
Auglaize
Sandusky
Cuyahoga
Grand
Mahoning
Scioto
L. St. Marys
Killbuck
Tuscarawas
Olentangy
Mad
Muskingum
Darby
Little Miami
Paint
Gt. Miami
Hocking
Raccoon
Ohio
ALLEGHENY PLATEAU
5,000 m. 16,404 ft.
2,000 m. 6,562 ft.
1,000 m. 3,281 ft.
500 m. 1,640 ft.
200 m. 656 ft.
100 m. 328 ft.
Sea Level
Below

COUNTIES

Adams 24,328 .... D8
Allen 112,241 .... B4
Ashland 46,178 .... F4
Ashtabula 104,215 .... J2
Athens 56,399 .... F7
Auglaize 42,554 .... B4
Belmont 82,569 .... J5
Brown 31,920 .... C8
Butler 258,787 .... A7
Carroll 25,598 .... H4
Champaign 33,649 .... C5
Clark 150,236 .... C6
Clermont 128,483 .... B7
Clinton 34,603 .... C7
Columbiana 113,572 .... J4
Coshocton 36,024 .... G5
Crawford 50,075 .... E4
Cuyahoga 1,498,400 .... G3
Darke 55,096 .... A5
Defiance 39,987 .... A3
Delaware 53,840 .... D5
Erie 79,655 .... E3
Fairfield 93,678 .... E6
Fayette 27,467 .... D6
Franklin 869,126 .... E5
Fulton 37,751 .... B2
Gallia 30,098 .... F8
Geauga 74,474 .... H3
Greene 129,769 .... C6
Guernsey 42,024 .... H5
Hamilton 873,224 .... A7
Hancock 64,581 .... C3
Hardin 32,719 .... C4
Harrison 18,152 .... H5
Henry 28,383 .... B3
Highland 33,477 .... C7
Hocking 24,304 .... F6
Holmes 29,416 .... G4
Huron 54,608 .... E3
Jackson 30,592 .... E7
Jefferson 91,564 .... J5
Knox 46,304 .... F5
Lake 212,801 .... H2
Lawrence 63,849 .... E8
Licking 120,981 .... F5
Logan 39,155 .... C5
Lorain 274,909 .... F3
Lucas 471,741 .... C2
Madison 33,004 .... D6
Mahoning 289,487 .... J4
Marion 67,974 .... D4
Medina 113,150 .... G3
Meigs 23,641 .... F7
Mercer 38,334 .... A4
Miami 90,381 .... B5
Monroe 17,382 .... H6
Montgomery 571,697 .... B6
Morgan 14,241 .... G6
Morrow 26,480 .... E4
Muskingum 83,340 .... G5
Noble 11,310 .... G6
Ottawa 40,076 .... D2
Paulding 21,302 .... A3
Perry 31,032 .... F6
Pickaway 43,662 .... D6
Pike 22,802 .... D7
Portage 135,856 .... H3
Preble 38,223 .... A6
Putnam 32,991 .... B3
Richland 131,205 .... E4
Ross 65,004 .... D7
Sandusky 63,267 .... D3
Scioto 84,545 .... D8
Seneca 61,901 .... D3
Shelby 43,089 .... B5
Stark 378,823 .... H4
Summit 524,472 .... G3
Trumbull 241,863 .... J3
Tuscarawas 84,614 .... H5
Union 29,536 .... D5
Van Wert 30,458 .... A4
Vinton 11,584 .... E7
Warren 99,276 .... B7
Washington 64,266 .... H7
Wayne 97,408 .... G4
Williams 36,369 .... A2
Wood 107,372 .... C3
Wyandot 22,651 .... D4

CITIES and TOWNS

Zip Name/Pop. Key

45101 Aberdeen 1,566 .... C8
45810 Ada 5,669 .... C4
45001 Addyston 1,195 .... B9
43101 Adelphi 472 .... E7
43901 Adena 1,062 .... J5
*44301 Akron⊙ 237,177 .... G3
Akron‡ 660,328 .... G3
45710 Albany 905 .... F7
43001 Alexandria 489 .... E5
45812 Alger 992 .... C4
44601 Alliance 24,315 .... H4
43102 Amanda 720 .... E6
†45201 Amberley 3,442 .... C9
45102 Amelia 1,108 .... D10
44001 Amherst 10,638 .... F3
43903 Amsterdam 783 .... J5
44003 Andover 1,205 .... J2
45302 Anna 1,038 .... B5
45303 Ansonia 1,267 .... A5
45813 Antwerp 1,765 .... A3
44606 Apple Creek 741 .... G4
44804 Arcadia 580 .... D3
45304 Arcanum 2,002 .... A6
43502 Archbold 3,318 .... B2
45814 Arlington 1,187 .... C4
†45201 Arlington Heights 1,082 .... C9
44805 Ashland⊙ 20,326 .... F4
43003 Ashley 1,057 .... E5
44004 Ashtabula 23,449 .... J2
43103 Ashville 2,046 .... E6
45701 Athens⊙ 19,743 .... F7
44807 Attica 865 .... E3
44201 Atwater 975 .... H3
44202 Aurora 8,177 .... H3
44010 Austinburg 900 .... J2
44515 Austintown 33,636 .... J3
44011 Avon 7,241 .... F3
44012 Avon Lake 13,222 .... F2
†43512 Ayersville 950 .... B3
†44805 Bailey Lakes 397 .... F4
45612 Bainbridge 1,042 .... D7
43804 Baltic 563 .... G5
43105 Baltimore 2,689 .... E6
44203 Barberton 29,751 .... G4
43713 Barnesville 4,633 .... H6
43905 Barton 1,039 .... J5
45103 Batavia⊙ 1,896 .... B7
†44870 Bay View 804 .... E3
44140 Bay Village 17,846 .... G9
44608 Beach City 1,083 .... G4
44122 Beachwood 9,983 .... J9
43716 Beallsville 601 .... J6
45808 Beaverdam 492 .... C4
44146 Bedford 15,056 .... H9
†44146 Bedford Heights 13,214 .... J9
43906 Bellaire 8,241 .... J5
45305 Bellbrook 5,174 .... C6
43310 Belle Center 930 .... C4
43311 Bellefontaine⊙ 11,888 .... C5
44811 Bellevue 8,187 .... E3
44813 Bellville 1,714 .... E4
43718 Belmont 714 .... J5
44609 Beloit 1,093 .... J4
45714 Belpre 7,193 .... G7
44017 Berea 19,567 .... G10
43908 Bergholz 914 .... J4
44814 Berlin Heights 756 .... F3
45106 Bethel 2,231 .... B8
43719 Bethesda 1,429 .... H5
44815 Bettsville 752 .... D3
45715 Beverly 1,471 .... G6
43209 Bexley 13,405 .... E6
45107 Blanchester 3,202 .... B7
44817 Bloomdale 744 .... D3
43106 Bloomingburg 869 .... D6
44818 Bloomville 1,019 .... D3
†45242 Blue Ash 9,506 .... C9
45817 Bluffton 3,310 .... C4
44512 Boardman 39,161 .... J3
44612 Bolivar 989 .... G4
†44264 Boston Heights 781 .... J10
45306 Botkins 1,372 .... B5
44695 Bowerston 487 .... H5
43402 Bowling Green⊙ 25,728 .... C3
45308 Bradford 2,166 .... B5
43406 Bradner 1,175 .... C3
44211 Brady Lake 470 .... H3
†44101 Bratenahl 1,485 .... H9
44141 Brecksville 10,132 .... H10
43107 Bremen 1,432 .... F6
44613 Brewster 2,321 .... G4
43912 Bridgeport 2,642 .... J5
†45211 Bridgetown 11,460 .... B9
43913 Brilliant 1,751 .... J5
†44240 Brimfield 3,161 .... H3
44402 Bristolville 900 .... J3
†44141 Broadview Heights 10,920 .... H10
44403 Brookfield 1,527 .... J3
44144 Brooklyn 12,342 .... H9
†44131 Brooklyn Heights 1,653 .... H9
44142 Brook Park 26,195 .... G9
†43912 Brookside 887 .... J5
45309 Brookville 4,322 .... B6
44212 Brunswick 28,104 .... G3
43506 Bryan⊙ 7,879 .... A3
45716 Buchtel 585 .... F7
43008 Buckeye Lake F6
44820 Bucyrus⊙ 13,433 .... E4
†45680 Burlington 900 .... F9
44021 Burton 1,401 .... H3
44822 Butler 991 .... F4
43723 Byesville 2,572 .... G6
43907 Cadiz⊙ 4,058 .... J5
45820 Cairo 596 .... B4
43920 Calcutta 1,121 .... J4
43724 Caldwell⊙ 1,935 .... G6
43314 Caledonia 759 .... D4
43725 Cambridge⊙ 13,573 .... G5
45311 Camden 1,971 .... A6
44405 Campbell 11,619 .... J3
45111 Camp Dennison 625 .... D9
44614 Canal Fulton 3,481 .... H4
43110 Canal Winchester 2,749 .... E6
44406 Canfield 5,535 .... J3
*44701 Canton⊙ 93,077 .... H4
Canton‡ 404,421 .... H4
43315 Cardington 1,665 .... E5
43316 Carey 3,674 .... D4
45005 Carlisle 4,276 .... B6
43112 Carroll 641 .... E6
44615 Carrollton⊙ 3,065 .... J4
44824 Castalia 973 .... E3
45314 Cedarville 2,799 .... C6
45822 Celina⊙ 9,137 .... A4
43011 Centerburg 1,275 .... E5
45459 Centerville 18,886 .... B6
44022 Chagrin Falls 4,335 .... J9
†45631 Chambersburg F8
44024 Chardon⊙ 4,434 .... H2
45719 Chauncey 1,050 .... F7
†45202 Cherry Grove 850 .... C10
45619 Chesapeake 1,370 .... E9
44026 Chesterland 2,301 .... H2
†45211 Cheviot 9,888 .... B9
45601 Chillicothe⊙ 23,420 .... E7
45389 Christiansburg 593 .... C5
*45201 Cincinnati⊙ 385,457 .... B9
Cincinnati‡ 1,401,403 .... B9
43113 Circleville⊙ 11,700 .... D6
43915 Clarington 558 .... J6
43115 Clarksburg 483 .... D7
45113 Clarksville 525 .... C7
45315 Clayton 752 .... B6
*44101 Cleveland⊙ 573,822 .... H9
Cleveland‡ 1,898,720 .... H9
44118 Cleveland Heights 56,438 .... H9
45002 Cleves 2,094 .... B9
44216 Clinton 1,277 .... G4
43410 Clyde 5,489 .... E3
†45638 Coal Grove 2,602 .... E9
45621 Coalton 639 .... E7
45828 Coldwater 4,220 .... A5
†44034 Colebrook 700 .... J2
44028 Columbia Station 518 .... G10
44408 Columbiana 4,987 .... J4
*43201 Columbus (cap.)⊙ 565,032 .... E6
Columbus‡ 1,093,293 .... E6
45830 Columbus Grove 2,313 .... B4
43811 Conesville 451 .... G5
44030 Conneaut 13,835 .... J2
45831 Continental 1,179 .... B3
45832 Convoy 1,140 .... A4
45723 Coolville 649 .... G7
43730 Corning 789 .... F6
44410 Cortland 5,011 .... J3
43812 Coshocton⊙ 13,405 .... G5
†45238 Covedale 5,830 .... B10
45318 Covington 2,610 .... B5
†44429 Craig Beach 1,657 .... H3
44827 Crestline 5,406 .... E4
44217 Creston 1,828 .... G3
45806 Cridersville 1,843 .... B4
43731 Crooksville 2,766 .... F6
45623 Crown City 513 .... F8
†45341 Crystal Lakes 1,463 .... C6
*44221 Cuyahoga Falls 43,890 .... G3
†44101 Cuyahoga Heights 739 .... H9
43413 Cygnet 646 .... C3
44618 Dalton 1,357 .... G4
43014 Danville 1,127 .... F5
†43123 Darbydale 825 .... D6
*45401 Dayton⊙ 193,444 .... B6
Dayton‡ 830,070 .... B6
44411 Deerfield 800 .... H3
45236 Deer Park 6,745 .... C9
43512 Defiance⊙ 16,810 .... B3
43318 Degraff 1,358 .... C5
43015 Delaware⊙ 18,780 .... E5
45833 Delphos 7,314 .... B4
43515 Delta 2,831 .... B2
44621 Dennison 3,398 .... H5
†45202 Dent 800 .... B9
43516 Deshler 1,870 .... C3
45750 Devola 2,708 .... H7
43917 Dillonvale 912 .... J5
44622 Dover 11,782 .... G4
44230 Doylestown 2,493 .... G4
43821 Dresden 1,646 .... G5
43017 Dublin 3,855 .... D5
43734 Duncan Falls 900 .... G6
45836 Dunkirk 954 .... C4
44730 East Canton 1,721 .... H4
44112 East Cleveland 36,957 .... H9
†44094 Eastlake 22,104 .... J8
43920 East Liverpool 16,687 .... J4
44413 East Palestine 5,306 .... J4
44626 East Sparta 868 .... H4
45320 Eaton⊙ 6,839 .... A6
†44035 Eaton Estates 1,806 .... G3
43517 Edgerton 1,813 .... A3
†44004 Edgewood 3,099 .... J2
43320 Edison 504 .... E4
43518 Edon 947 .... A2
45321 Eldorado 509 .... A6
45807 Elida 1,349 .... B4
43416 Elmore 1,271 .... D3
45216 Elmwood Place 2,840 .... B9
*44035 Elyria⊙ 57,538 .... F3
45322 Englewood 11,329 .... B6
45323 Enon 2,597 .... C6
44117 Euclid 59,999 .... J9
†45201 Evendale 1,954 .... C9
45042 Excello 900 .... B7
45324 Fairborn 29,702 .... B6
†45201 Fairfax 2,222 .... C9
45014 Fairfield 30,777 .... A7
44313 Fairlawn 6,100 .... G3
44077 Fairport Harbor 3,357 .... H2
44126 Fairview Park 19,311 .... G9
45325 Farmersville 950 .... A6
43521 Fayette 1,222 .... B2
45120 Felicity 929 .... B8
45840 Findlay⊙ 35,594 .... C3
45326 Fletcher 498 .... B5
43977 Flushing 1,266 .... J5
45843 Forest 1,633 .... C4
45405 Forest Park 18,675 .... B9
45230 Forestville 950 .... C10
45844 Fort Jennings 538 .... B4
45845 Fort Loramie 977 .... B5
†45426 Fort McKinley B6
45846 Fort Recovery 1,370 .... A5
†45801 Fort Shawnee 4,541 .... B4
44830 Fostoria 15,743 .... D3
45628 Frankfort 1,008 .... D7
45005 Franklin 10,711 .... B6
45629 Franklin Furnace 1,093 .... E8
43822 Frazeysburg 1,025 .... F5
44627 Fredericksburg 511 .... G4
43019 Fredericktown 2,299 .... F5
43973 Freeport 525 .... H5
43420 Fremont⊙ 17,834 .... D3
45630 Friendship 900 .... D8
43230 Gahanna 18,001 .... E5
44833 Galion 12,391 .... E4
45631 Gallipolis⊙ 5,576 .... F8
43022 Gambier 2,056 .... F5
44125 Garfield Heights 34,938 .... J9
44231 Garrettsville 1,769 .... H3
44040 Gates Mills 2,236 .... J9
44041 Geneva 6,655 .... J2
44043 Geneva-on-the-Lake 1,634 .... H2
43430 Genoa 2,213 .... D2
45121 Georgetown⊙ 3,467 .... C8
45327 Germantown 5,015 .... B6
45328 Gettysburg 545 .... A5
43431 Gibsonburg 2,479 .... D3
44420 Girard 12,517 .... J3
45848 Glandorf 746 .... B3
45246 Glendale 2,368 .... C9
†44139 Glenwillow 492 .... J10
45732 Glouster 2,211 .... F6
44629 Gnadenhutten 1,320 .... G5
†45201 Golf Manor 4,317 .... C9
45122 Goshen B7
44044 Grafton 2,231 .... F3
43522 Grand Rapids 962 .... C3
44045 Grand River 412 .... H2
†43212 Grandview Heights 7,420 .... D6
43023 Granville 3,851 .... E5
45330 Gratis 809 .... A6
43322 Green Camp 475 .... D4
45123 Greenfield 5,150 .... D7
45218 Greenhills 4,927 .... B9
44232 Greensburg 950 .... G4
44836 Green Springs 1,568 .... E3
44630 Greentown 300 .... H4
45331 Greenville⊙ 12,999 .... A5
44837 Greenwich 1,458 .... E3
43123 Grove City 16,816 .... D6
43125 Groveport 3,286 .... E6
45849 Grover Hill 486 .... B3
45634 Hamden 1,010 .... F7
45130 Hamersville 688 .... C8
*45011 Hamilton⊙ 63,189 .... A7
Hamilton-Middletown‡ 258,787 .... A7
43524 Hamler 625 .... B3
43931 Hannibal 550 .... J6
†43055 Hanover 926 .... F5
43126 Harrisburg 363 .... D6
45030 Harrison 5,855 .... A9
45850 Harrod 506 .... C4
†44085 Hartsgrove 200 .... J2
44632 Hartville 1,772 .... H4
43525 Haskins 568 .... C3
43127 Haydenville 395 .... F7
44838 Hayesville 518 .... F4
43055 Heath 6,969 .... F5
43025 Hebron 2,035 .... E6
43526 Hicksville 3,929 .... A3
†44143 Highland Heights 5,739 .... J9
43026 Hilliard 8,008 .... D5
45133 Hillsboro⊙ 6,356 .... C7
44234 Hiram 1,360 .... H3
43527 Holgate 1,315 .... B3
43528 Holland 1,048 .... C2
45033 Hooven 550 .... A9
43976 Hopedale 857 .... J5
44425 Hubbard 9,245 .... J3
45424 Huber Heights 35,480 .... B6
44236 Hudson 4,615 .... H3
†44022 Hunting Valley 786 .... J9
44839 Huron 7,123 .... E3
44131 Independence 6,607 .... H9
†45201 Indian Hill 5,521 .... C9
43932 Irondale 535 .... J4
45638 Ironton⊙ 14,290 .... E8
45640 Jackson⊙ 6,675 .... E7
45334 Jackson Center 1,310 .... B5
45740 Jacksonville 651 .... F7
45335 Jamestown 1,702 .... C6
44047 Jefferson⊙ 2,952 .... J2
†43162 Jefferson (West Jefferson) 4,448 .... D6
43128 Jeffersonville 1,252 .... C6
44840 Jeromesville 582 .... F4
43437 Jerry City 512 .... C3
43986 Jewett 972 .... H5
43031 Johnstown 3,158 .... E5
43748 Junction City 754 .... F6
45853 Kalida 1,019 .... B4
44240 Kent 26,164 .... H3
43326 Kenton⊙ 8,605 .... C4
45429 Kettering 61,186 .... B6
44637 Killbuck 937 .... G5
45034 Kings Mills 500 .... B7
45644 Kingston 1,208 .... E7
44048 Kingsville J2
44428 Kinsman 900 .... J3
43033 Kirkersville 626 .... E6
†44094 Kirtland 5,969 .... H2
43951 Lafferty 855 .... H5
44050 Lagrange 1,258 .... F3
44250 Lakemore 2,744 .... H3
43440 Lakeside 850 .... E2
43331 Lakeview 1,089 .... C4
44107 Lakewood 61,963 .... G9
43130 Lancaster⊙ 34,953 .... E6
43934 Lansing 950 .... J5
43332 La Rue 861 .... D4
43135 Laurelville 591 .... E7
†45501 Lawrenceville 307 .... C6
45036 Lebanon⊙ 9,636 .... B7
45135 Leesburg 1,019 .... D7
44431 Leetonia 2,121 .... J4
45856 Leipsic 2,171 .... C3
45338 Lewisburg 1,450 .... A6
44904 Lexington 3,823 .... E4
43532 Liberty Center 1,111 .... B3
*45801 Lima⊙ 47,381 .... B4
Lima‡ 218,244 .... B4
†45201 Lincoln Heights 5,259 .... C9
43442 Lindsey 571 .... D3
44432 Lisbon⊙ 3,159 .... J4
44253 Litchfield 650 .... F3
43136 Lithopolis 652 .... E6
45742 Little Hocking 800 .... G7
45215 Lockland 4,292 .... C9
44254 Lodi 2,942 .... F3
43138 Logan⊙ 6,557 .... F6
43140 London⊙ 6,958 .... C6
*44052 Lorain 75,416 .... F3
Lorain-Elyria‡ 274,909 .... F3
†44481 Lordstown 3,280 .... J3
44842 Loudonville 2,945 .... F4
44641 Louisville 7,996 .... H4
45140 Loveland 9,106 .... D9
45744 Lowell 729 .... H6
44436 Lowellville 1,558 .... J3
44843 Lucas 753 .... F4
45648 Lucasville 3,349 .... E8
43443 Luckey 895 .... D3
45142 Lynchburg 1,205 .... C7
44124 Lyndhurst 18,092 .... J9
43533 Lyons 596 .... B2
44056 Macedonia 6,571 .... J10
†45202 Mack B9
45243 Madeira 9,341 .... C9
44057 Madison 2,291 .... H2
44643 Magnolia 986 .... H4
43758 Malta 956 .... G6
44644 Malvern 1,032 .... H4
45144 Manchester 2,313 .... C8
*44901 Mansfield⊙ 53,927 .... F4
Mansfield‡ 131,205 .... F4
44255 Mantua 1,041 .... H3
44137 Maple Heights 29,735 .... H9
†43440 Marblehead 679 .... E2
45860 Maria Stein 950 .... A5

(continued on following page)

Agriculture, Industry and Resources

DOMINANT LAND USE

- Hogs, Soft Winter Wheat
- Livestock, Dairy, Soybeans, Cash Grain
- Dairy, General Farming
- General Farming, Livestock, Tobacco
- Fruit, Truck and Mixed Farming
- Forests
- Urban Areas

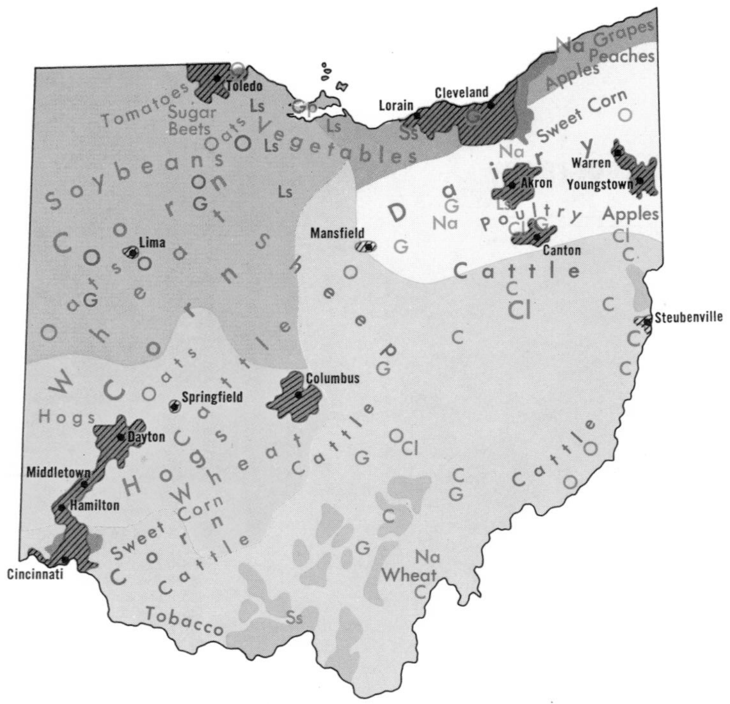

Toledo
Lorain
Cleveland
Warren
Youngstown
Akron
Canton
Mansfield
Lima
Steubenville
Columbus
Springfield
Dayton
Middletown
Hamilton
Cincinnati
Tomatoes
Sugar Beets
Oats
Vegetables
Grapes
Peaches
Apples
Sweet Corn
Dairy
Poultry
Apples
Soybeans
Corn
Oats
Hogs
Cattle
Sheep
Wheat
Sweet Corn
Tobacco

MAJOR MINERAL OCCURRENCES

- C Coal
- Cl Clay
- G Natural Gas
- Gp Gypsum
- Ls Limestone
- Na Salt
- O Petroleum
- Ss Sandstone
- Major Industrial Areas

45227 Mariemont 3,295 C9
45750 Marietta⊙ 16,467 G7
43302 Marion⊙ 37,040 D4
44645 Marshallville 788 G4
43935 Martins Ferry 9,331 J5
45146 Martinsville 539 C7
43040 Marysville⊙ 7,414 D5
45040 Mason 8,692 B7
44646 Massillon 30,557 H4
44438 Masury 1,836 J3
†45069 Maud 800 B7
43537 Maumee 15,747 C2
44124 Mayfield 3,577 J9
44124 Mayfield Heights 21,550 J9
45651 McArthur⊙ 1,912 F7
43534 McClure 694 C3
45858 McComb 1,608 C3
43756 McConnelsville⊙ 2,018 G6
44437 McDonald 3,744 J3
45859 McGuffey 646 C4
43044 Mechanicsburg 1,792 D5
44256 Medina⊙ 15,268 G3
45862 Mendon 749 A4
44060 Mentor 42,065 H2
44060 Mentor-on-the-Lake 7,919 G2
43540 Metamora 556 C2
45342 Miamisburg 15,304 B6
45041 Miamitown 800 A9
44652 Middlebranch 300 H4
†44017 Middleburg Heights 16,218 G10
44062 Middlefield 1,997 H3
45863 Middle Point 709 B4
45760 Middleport 2,971 F7
45042 Middletown 43,719 A6
44653 Midvale 654 H5
44846 Milan 1,569 E3
45150 Milford 5,232 D9
43045 Milford Center 764 D5
43447 Millbury 955 D2
44654 Millersburg⊙ 3,247 F4
43046 Millersport 844 E6
†45011 Millville 809 A7
44656 Mineral City 884 H4
44657 Minerva 4,549 H4
†43201 Minerva Park 1,618 E5
43938 Mingo Junction 4,834 J5
45865 Minster 2,557 B5
44260 Mogadore 4,190 H3
45050 Monroe 4,256 B7
44847 Monroeville 1,329 E3
45242 Montgomery 10,088 C9
43543 Montpelier 4,431 A2
†45439 Moraine 5,325 B6
†44022 Moreland Hills 3,083 J9
45152 Morrow 1,254 B7
43338 Mount Gilead⊙ 2,911 E4
45231 Mount Healthy 7,562 B9
45154 Mount Orab 1,573 C7
43939 Mount Pleasant 616 J5
43143 Mount Sterling 1,623 D6
43050 Mount Vernon⊙ 14,323 E5
43340 Mount Victory 667 D4
44262 Munroe Falls 4,731 H3
43144 Murray City 579 F6
43545 Napoleon⊙ 8,614 B3
44662 Navarre 1,343 H4
43940 Neffs 1,106 J5
44441 Negley 917 J4
45764 Nelsonville 4,567 F7
44849 Nevada 945 D4
43055 Newark⊙ 41,200 F5
Newark‡ 120,981 F5
45662 New Boston 3,188 E8
45869 New Bremen 2,393 B5
†44101 Newburgh Heights 2,678 H9
†45201 New Burlington 900 B9
45344 New Carlisle 6,498 C6
43832 Newcomerstown 3,986 G5
43762 New Concord 1,860 G6
43145 New Holland 783 D6
45871 New Knoxville 760 B5
45345 New Lebanon 4,501 B6
43764 New Lexington⊙ 5,179 F6
44851 New London 2,449 F3
45346 New Madison 1,008 A6
45767 New Matamoras J6
45011 New Miami 2,980 A7
44442 New Middletown 2,195 J4
45347 New Paris 1,709 A6
44663 New Philadelphia⊙ 16,883 G5
45768 Newport 975 H7
45157 New Richmond 2,769 B8
43766 New Straitsville 937 F6
44444 Newton Falls 4,960 J3
45244 Newtown 1,817 C10
45159 New Vienna 1,133 C7
44854 New Washington 1,213 E4
44445 New Waterford 1,314 J4
44446 Niles 23,088 J3
45872 North Baltimore 3,127 C3
45052 North Bend 546 B9
44450 North Bloomfield 650 J3
44720 North Canton 14,228 H4
45239 North College Hill 11,114 B9
44855 North Fairfield 525 E3
44067 Northfield 3,913 J10
44707 North Industry H4
44068 North Kingsville 2,939 J2
43060 North Lewisburg 1,072 C5
44452 North Lima 800 J4
†44057 North Madison 8,741 H2
44070 North Olmsted 36,486 G9
†44081 North Perry 897 H2
†44101 North Randall 1,054 H9
45414 Northridge 9,720 B6
44039 North Ridgeville 21,522 F3
44133 North Royalton 17,671 H10
†43619 Northwood 5,495 D2
†43701 North Zanesville 2,166 G6
44203 Norton 12,242 G3
44857 Norwalk⊙ 14,358 E3
45212 Norwood 26,342 C9
43449 Oak Harbor 2,678 D2
45656 Oak Hill 1,713 E8
†45419 Oakwood 9,372 B6
†44146 Oakwood 3,786 H9
45873 Oakwood 886 B3
44074 Oberlin 8,660 F3
†43201 Obetz 3,095 E6
45874 Ohio City 881 A4
44138 Olmsted Falls 5,868 G9
44862 Ontario 4,123 E4
†44101 Orange 2,376 J9
43616 Oregon 18,675 D2
44667 Orrville 7,511 G4
44076 Orwell 1,067 J2
45875 Ottawa⊙ 3,874 B3
†43601 Ottawa Hills 4,065 C2
45876 Ottoville 833 B4
45160 Owensville 858 B7
45056 Oxford 17,655 A6
44077 Painesville⊙ 16,391 H2
45877 Pandora 977 C4
44080 Parkman 600 H3
44129 Parma 92,548 H9
†44130 Parma Heights 23,112 G9
43062 Pataskala 2,284 E5
45879 Paulding⊙ 2,754 A3
45880 Payne 1,399 A3
45660 Peebles 1,790 D8
43450 Pemberville 1,321 C3
44264 Peninsula 604 G3
†44124 Pepper Pike 6,177 J9
44081 Perry 961 H2
43551 Perrysburg 10,215 C2
44864 Perrysville 836 F4
45354 Phillipsburg 705 B6
43771 Philo 799 G6
43147 Pickerington 3,917 E6
45661 Piketon 1,726 E7
43554 Pioneer 1,133 A2
45356 Piqua 20,480 B5
43064 Plain City 2,102 D5
43772 Pleasant City 481 G6
45359 Pleasant Hill 1,051 B5
43148 Pleasantville 780 F6
44865 Plymouth 1,939 E4
44514 Poland 3,084 J3
45769 Pomeroy⊙ 2,728 G7
43452 Port Clinton⊙ 7,223 E2
45770 Portland 150 G7
45662 Portsmouth⊙ 25,943 D8
43837 Port Washington 622 G5
43942 Powhatan Point 2,181 J6
45669 Proctorville 975 F9
43342 Prospect 1,159 D5
43456 Put-in-Bay 146 E2
43773 Quaker City 698 H6
43343 Quincy 633 C5
45771 Racine 908 G8
44265 Randolph 900 H3
44266 Ravenna⊙ 11,987 H3
43943 Rayland 566 J5
45215 Reading 12,843 C9
†44202 Reminderville 1,960 J10
†45202 Remington 600 C9
45773 Reno 576 H7
†43412 Reno Beach D2
44867 Republic 656 D3
43068 Reynoldsburg 20,661 E6
44286 Richfield 3,437 G3
43944 Richmond 624 J5
†44045 Richmond (Grand River) 412 H2
45673 Richmond Dale 950 E7
44143 Richmond Heights 10,095 H9
43344 Richwood 2,181 D5
45674 Rio Grande 864 F8
45167 Ripley 2,174 C8
43457 Risingsun 698 C3
44270 Rittman 6,063 G4
†43085 Riverlea 528 D5
44670 Robertsville 600 H4
44084 Rock Creek 652 J2
45882 Rockford 1,245 A4
44116 Rocky River 21,084 G9
44085 Rome 210 J2
44272 Rootstown 900 H3
†45662 Rosemount 1,747 D8
43777 Roseville 1,915 F6
45061 Ross 2,767 B9
43460 Rossford 5,978 C2
45236 Rossmoyne C9
†43943 Rush Run 560 J5
43347 Rushsylvania 610 C5
43348 Russells Point 1,156 C5
45775 Rutland 635 F7
45169 Sabina 2,799 C7
†44067 Sagamore Hills J10
45217 Saint Bernard 5,396 B9
43950 Saint Clairsville⊙ 5,452 J5
45883 Saint Henry 1,596 A5
45885 Saint Marys 8,414 B4
43072 Saint Paris 1,742 C5
44460 Salem 12,869 J4
43945 Salineville 1,629 J4
44870 Sandusky⊙ 31,360 E3
44671 Sandyville 500 H4
45171 Sardinia 826 C7
43946 Sardis 865 J6
43988 Scio 1,003 H5
†45662 Sciotodale 1,191 E8
45679 Seaman 1,039 C8
44672 Sebring 5,078 H4
†44131 Seven Hills 13,650 H9
45062 Seven Mile 841 A7
44273 Seville 1,568 G3
43947 Shadyside 4,315 J6
44120 Shaker Heights 32,487 H9
45241 Sharonville 10,108 C9
43782 Shawnee 924 F6
†44052 Sheffield 1,886 F3
44054 Sheffield Lake 10,484 F3
44875 Shelby 9,646 E4
43556 Sherwood 915 A3
44878 Shiloh 857 E4
44676 Shreve 1,608 F4
45365 Sidney⊙ 17,657 B5
†44221 Silver Lake 2,915 G3
†45201 Silverton 6,172 C9
43948 Smithfield 1,308 J5
44677 Smithville 1,467 G4
44139 Solon 14,341 J9
43783 Somerset 1,432 F6
†44001 South Amherst 1,848 F3
†43103 South Bloomfield 934 D6
45368 South Charleston 1,682 C6
44121 South Euclid 25,713 H9
45065 South Lebanon 2,700 B7
45680 South Point 3,918 E9
†44022 South Russell 2,784 H3
45369 South Vienna 464 C6
45682 South Webster 886 E8
43701 South Zanesville 1,739 F6
44275 Spencer 764 F3
45887 Spencerville 2,184 B4
45066 Springboro 4,962 B6
45246 Springdale 10,111 B9
*45501 Springfield⊙ 72,563 C6
Springfield‡ 183,885 C6
45370 Spring Valley 541 C6
44276 Sterling 600 G4
43952 Steubenville⊙ 26,400 J5
Steubenville-Weirton‡ 163,099 J5
43787 Stockport 558 G6
43154 Stoutsville 537 E6
44224 Stow 25,303 H3
44680 Strasburg 2,091 G4
44240 Streetsboro 9,055 H3
44136 Strongsville 28,577 G10
44471 Struthers 13,624 J3
43557 Stryker 1,423 B3
†44260 Suffield 650 H3
44681 Sugarcreek 1,966 G5
43074 Sunbury 2,101 E5
43558 Swanton 3,424 C2
44882 Sycamore 1,059 D4
43560 Sylvania 15,527 C2
45779 Syracuse 946 G7
44278 Tallmadge 15,269 H3
†43771 Taylorsville (Philo) 799 G6
45174 Terrace Park 2,044 D9
45780 The Plains 2,044 F7
43076 Thornville 838 F6
44883 Tiffin⊙ 19,549 D3
43963 Tiltonsville 1,750 J5
†44094 Timberlake 885 J8
45371 Tipp City 5,595 B6
†45245 Tobasco 950 C10
*43601 Toledo⊙ 354,635 D2
Toledo‡ 791,599 D2
43964 Toronto 6,934 J5
45067 Trenton 6,401 B7
45782 Trimble 579 F7
45426 Trotwood 7,802 B6
45373 Troy⊙ 19,086 B5
44682 Tuscarawas 917 H5
44087 Twinsburg 7,632 J10
44683 Uhrichsville 6,130 H5
45322 Union 5,219 B6
†47390 Union City 1,716 A5
44685 Uniontown 875 H4
44118 University Heights 15,401 H9
43221 Upper Arlington 35,648 D6
43351 Upper Sandusky⊙ 5,967 D4
43078 Urbana⊙ 10,762 C5
†43123 Urbancrest 880 D6
43080 Utica 2,238 F5
†43201 Valley View 730 D6
†44101 Valleyview 1,576 H9
45377 Vandalia 13,161 B6
45890 Vanlue 390 C4
45891 Van Wert⊙ 11,035 A4
44089 Vermilion 11,012 F3
45378 Verona 571 A6
45380 Versailles 2,384 A5
44473 Vienna 900 J3
44281 Wadsworth 15,166 G3
†44094 Waite Hill 529 H2
45687 Wakefield 300 E8
44889 Wakeman 906 F3
43465 Walbridge 2,900 C2
44687 Walnut Creek 550 G4
†44146 Walton Hills 2,199 J10
45895 Wapakoneta⊙ 8,402 B4
45785 Warner 250 H6
*44481 Warren⊙ 56,629 J3
44128 Warrensville Heights 16,565 H9
43844 Warsaw 765 G5
43160 Washington Court House⊙ 12,682 D6
44490 Washingtonville 865 J4
45786 Waterford 600 G6
43566 Waterville 3,884 C3
43567 Wauseon⊙ 6,173 B2
45690 Waverly⊙ 4,603 D7
43466 Wayne 894 C3
44688 Waynesburg 1,160 H4
45896 Waynesfield 826 C4
45068 Waynesville 1,796 B6
44090 Wellington 4,146 F3
45692 Wellston 6,016 F7
43968 Wellsville 5,095 J4
45381 West Alexandria 1,313 A6
45449 West Carrollton 13,148 B6
43081 Westerville 23,414 D5
44491 West Farmington 563 J3
44251 Westfield Center 791 G3
43162 West Jefferson 4,448 D6
43845 West Lafayette 2,225 G5
44145 Westlake 19,483 G9
43357 West Liberty 1,653 C5
43358 West Mansfield 716 C5
45383 West Milton 4,119 B6
43569 Weston 1,708 C3
†45662 West Portsmouth 4,095 D8
44287 West Salem 1,357 F4
45693 West Union⊙ 2,791 C8
43570 West Unity 1,639 B2
45694 Wheelersburg 4,796 E8
43213 Whitehall 21,299 E6
43571 Whitehouse 2,137 C2
44092 Wickliffe 16,790 J9
44890 Willard 5,720 E3
45176 Williamsburg 1,952 B7
44093 Williamsfield 950 J2
43164 Williamsport 792 D6
44094 Willoughby 19,329 J8
†44094 Willoughby Hills 8,612 J9
44094 Willowick 17,834 J8
45898 Willshire 564 A4
45177 Wilmington⊙ 10,431 C7
45697 Winchester 1,080 C8
44288 Windham 3,721 H3
43952 Wintersville 4,724 J5
45245 Withamsville 975 C10
†45201 Woodlawn 2,715 C9
†44101 Woodmere 877 J9
43793 Woodsfield⊙ 3,145 H6
43469 Woodville 2,050 D3
44691 Wooster⊙ 19,289 G4
43085 Worthington 15,016 E5
45215 Wyoming 8,282 C9
45385 Xenia⊙ 24,653 C6
45387 Yellow Springs 4,077 C6
43971 Yorkville 1,447 J5
*44501 Youngstown⊙ 115,436 J3
Youngstown-Warren‡ 531,350 J3
43701 Zanesville⊙ 28,655 G6
44697 Zoar 264 H4
44698 Zoarville 125 H4

OTHER FEATURES

Atwood (lake) H4
Auglaize (riv.) B4
Berlin (lake) H4
Big Walnut (creek) E5
Black (riv.) F3
Black Fork, Mohican (riv.) F4
Blanchard (riv.) C4
Blennerhassett (isl.) G7
Buckeye (lake) F6
Campbell (hill) C5
Captina (creek) J6
Cedar (pt.) D2
Chagrin (riv.) J8
Clear Fork (res.) E4
Clear Fork, Mohican (riv.) F4
Clendening (lake) H5
Cleveland-Hopkins Mun. Airport G9
Cuyahoga (riv.) H10
Darby (creek) D5
Deer (creek) D6
Delaware (lake) E5
Dillon (lake) F5
Dover (lake) H4
Duck (creek) H6
Erie (lake) H1
Eufaula (res.) L4
Grand (riv.) H2
Great Miami (riv.) A7
Hocking (riv.) F7
Hoover (res.) E5
Huron (riv.) E3
Indian (lake) C5
James A. Garfield Nat'l Hist. Site G2
Kelleys (isl.) E2
Keystone (res.) K2
Killbuck (creek) G4
Kokosing (riv.) E5
Leesville (lake) H5
Licking (riv.) F5
Little Beaver (creek) J4
Little Miami (riv.) B6
Little Miami, East Fork (riv.) C7
Little Muskingum (riv.) H6
Loramie (lake) B5
Mad (riv.) C6
Maumee (bay) D2
Maumee (riv.) A3
Middle Bass (isl.) E2
Mohican (riv.) F4
Mosquito Creek (lake) J3
Mound City Group Nat'l Mon. E7
Muskingum (riv.) G6
North Bass (isl.) E2
Ohio (riv.) B8
Ohio Brush (creek) D8
Olentangy (riv.) D4
Paint (creek) D7
Perry's Victory and Int'l Peace Mem. E2
Piedmont (lake) H5
Portage (riv.) D3
Pymatuning (res.) J2
Raccoon (creek) F8
Rattlesnake (creek) C7
Rickenbacker Air Force Base 1,763 E6
Rocky (riv.) G9
Rocky, West Branch (riv.) G10
Rocky Fork (lake) D7
Saint Joseph (riv.) A3
Saint Marys (lake) A4
Saint Marys (riv.) A4
Salt Fork (creek) H5
Sandusky (bay) E3
Sandusky (riv.) D3
Scioto (riv.) D8
Senecaville (lake) H6
Sevenmile (creek) A6
South Bass (isl.) E2
Stillwater (riv.) B5
Symmes (creek) F8
Tappan (lake) H5
Tiffin (riv.) B3
Tuscarawas (riv.) H5
Vermilion (riv.) F3
Wabash (riv.) A5
West Sister (isl.) D2
Whiteoak (creek) C7
William H. Taft Nat'l Hist. Site C10
Wills (creek) G5
Wills Creek (lake) G5
Wright-Patterson Air Force Base 9,155 B6
Yellow (creek) J4

⊙County seat.
‡Population of metropolitan area.
† Zip of nearest p.o. * Multiple zips.

AREA 69,956 sq. mi. (181,186 sq. km.)
POPULATION 3,025,290
CAPITAL Oklahoma City
LARGEST CITY Oklahoma City
HIGHEST POINT Black Mesa 4,973 ft. (1516 m.)
SETTLED IN 1889
ADMITTED TO UNION November 16, 1907
POPULAR NAME Sooner State
STATE FLOWER Mistletoe
STATE BIRD Scissor-tailed Flycatcher

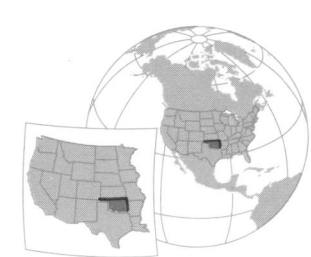

COUNTIES

Adair 18,575 .....S3
Alfalfa 7,077 .....K1
Atoka 12,748 .....O6
Beaver 6,806 .....E1
Beckham 19,243 .....G4
Blaine 13,443 .....K3
Bryan 30,535 .....O7
Caddo 30,905 .....K4
Canadian 56,452 .....K3
Carter 43,610 .....M6
Cherokee 30,684 .....R3
Choctaw 17,203 .....P6
Cimarron 3,648 .....A1
Cleveland 133,173 .....M4
Coal 6,041 .....O5
Comanche 112,456 .....K5
Cotton 7,338 .....K6
Craig 15,014 .....R1
Creek 59,016 .....O3
Custer 25,995 .....H3
Delaware 23,946 .....S2
Dewey 5,922 .....H2
Ellis 5,596 .....G2
Garfield 62,820 .....L2
Garvin 27,856 .....M5
Grady 39,490 .....L5
Grant 6,518 .....L1
Greer 7,028 .....G5
Harmon 4,519 .....G5
Harper 4,715 .....G1
Haskell 11,010 .....R4
Hughes 14,338 .....O4
Jackson 30,356 .....H5
Jefferson 8,183 .....L6
Johnston 10,356 .....N6
Kay 49,852 .....M1
Kingfisher 14,187 .....L3
Kiowa 12,711 .....J5
Latimer 9,840 .....R5
Le Flore 40,698 .....S5
Lincoln 26,601 .....N3
Logan 26,881 .....M3
Love 7,469 .....M7
Major 8,772 .....K2
Marshall 10,550 .....N6
Mayes 32,261 .....R2
McClain 20,291 .....L5

McCurtain 36,151 .....S6
McIntosh 15,562 .....P4
Murray 12,147 .....M6
Muskogee 66,939 .....R3
Noble 11,573 .....M2
Nowata 11,486 .....P1
Okfuskee 11,125 .....O3
Oklahoma 568,933 .....M3
Okmulgee 39,169 .....P3
Osage 39,327 .....O1
Ottawa 32,870 .....S1
Pawnee 15,310 .....N2
Payne 62,435 .....N2
Pittsburg 40,524 .....P5
Pontotoc 32,598 .....N5
Pottawatomie 55,239 .....N4
Pushmataha 11,773 .....R6
Roger Mills 4,799 .....G3
Rogers 46,436 .....P2
Seminole 27,473 .....N4
Sequoyah 30,749 .....S3
Stephens 43,419 .....L6
Texas 17,727 .....C1
Tillman 12,398 .....J6
Tulsa 470,593 .....P2
Wagoner 41,801 .....P3
Washington 48,113 .....P1
Washita 13,798 .....J4
Woods 10,923 .....J1
Woodward 21,172 .....H2

CITIES and TOWNS

Zip | Name/Pop. | Key
74720 Achille 480 .....O7
74820 Ada⊙ 15,902 .....N5
74330 Adair 508 .....R2
73901 Adams 150 .....D1
73520 Addington 141 .....L6
74431 Afton 1,174 .....S1
74824 Agra 354 .....N3
74721 Albany 65 .....O7
73001 Albert 100 .....K4
74521 Albion 165 .....R5
74522 Alderson 366 .....P5
73002 Alex 769 .....L5
73716 Aline 313 .....K1
74825 Allen 998 .....O5
73521 Altus⊙ 23,101 .....H5

73717 Alva⊙ 6,416 .....J1
73004 Amber 416 .....L4
73718 Ames 314 .....K2
73719 Amorita 66 .....K1
73005 Anadarko⊙ 6,378 .....K4
73006 Apache 1,560 .....K5
73620 Arapaho⊙ 851 .....H3
73401 Ardmore⊙ 23,689 .....M6
74901 Arkoma 2,175 .....T4
73832 Arnett⊙ 714 .....G2
74826 Asher 659 .....N5
73524 Ashland 72 .....O5
74525 Atoka⊙ 3,409 .....O6
74827 Atwood 225 .....O5
74001 Avant 461 .....O2
†73860 Avard 51 .....J1
73930 Baker 70 .....D1
74002 Barnsdall 1,501 .....O1
†74965 Baron 300 .....S3
74003 Bartlesville⊙ 34,568 .....O1
74722 Battiest 250 .....S6
73932 Beaver⊙ 1,939 .....F1
74421 Beggs 1,428 .....P3
†74966 Bengal 300 .....R5
74723 Bennington 302 .....P7
74331 Bernice 318 .....S1
73622 Bessie 245 .....H4
73008 Bethany 22,130 .....L3
74724 Bethel 350 .....S6
†74801 Bethel Acres 2,314 .....M4
74332 Big Cabin 252 .....R1
74630 Billings 632 .....M1
73009 Binger 791 .....K4
73720 Bison 103 .....L2
74008 Bixby 6,969 .....P3
74058 Blackburn 114 .....N2
74631 Blackwell 8,400 .....M1
73526 Blair 1,092 .....H5
73010 Blanchard 1,688 .....L4
74528 Blanco 215 .....P5
74521 Blocker 135 .....P4
†74701 Blue 150 .....O7
74333 Bluejacket 247 .....R1
73933 Boise City⊙ 1,761 .....B1
74726 Bokchito 628 .....O6
74930 Bokoshe 556 .....S4
74829 Boley 423 .....O4
74727 Boswell 702 .....P6

74830 Bowlegs 522 .....N4
74009 Bowring 115 .....O1
74422 Boynton 518 .....P3
73011 Bradley 284 .....L5
74423 Braggs 351 .....R3
74632 Braman 355 .....M1
73012 Bray 591 .....L5
73721 Breckinridge 261 .....L2
†73047 Bridgeport 115 .....K3
74010 Bristow 4,702 .....O3
74012 Broken Arrow 35,761 .....P2
74728 Broken Bow 3,965 .....S7
74530 Bromide 180 .....N6
†74873 Brooksville 46 .....M4
†74447 Bryant 74 .....P4
73834 Buffalo⊙ 1,381 .....G1
74931 Bunch 64 .....S3
74633 Burbank 161 .....N1
73722 Burlington 206 .....K1
73430 Burneyville 150 .....M7
73624 Burns Flat 2,431 .....H4
73625 Butler 388 .....H3
74831 Byars 353 .....N5
†74820 Byng 833 .....N5
73723 Byron 67 .....K1
73527 Cache 1,661 .....J5
74729 Caddo 923 .....O6
74730 Calera 1,390 .....O7
73014 Calumet 469 .....K3
74531 Calvin 315 .....O5
73835 Camargo 264 .....H2
74932 Cameron 365 .....T4
74425 Canadian 279 .....P4
74533 Caney 147 .....O6
73724 Canton 854 .....J2
73626 Carmen 676 .....H4
73725 Capron 54 .....J1
73726 Carmen 365 .....J1
73015 Carnegie 2,016 .....J4
74832 Carney 622 .....N3
73727 Carrier 259 .....K2
73627 Carter 367 .....H4
74934 Cartersville 79 .....S4
73016 Cashion 547 .....L3
74833 Castle 130 .....O4
74015 Catoosa 1,561 .....P2
73017 Cement 884 .....K5

74534 Centrahoma 166 .....O5
74834 Chandler⊙ 2,926 .....N3
73528 Chattanooga 403 .....J6
74426 Checotah 3,454 .....R4
74016 Chelsea 1,754 .....P1
73728 Cherokee⊙ 2,105 .....K1
73838 Chester 104 .....J2
73628 Cheyenne⊙ 1,207 .....G3
73018 Chickasha⊙ 15,828 .....L4
74635 Chilocco 400 .....M1
73020 Choctaw 7,520 .....M3
74337 Chouteau 1,559 .....R2
†74965 Christie 375 .....S3
73111 Cimarron L3
74017 Claremore⊙ 12,085 .....R2
74535 Clarita 72 .....O6
74536 Clayton 833 .....R5
74835 Clearview 250 .....O4
73729 Cleo Springs 514 .....K2
74020 Cleveland 2,972 .....O2
73601 Clinton 8,796 .....H3
74538 Coalgate⊙ 2,001 .....O5
74733 Colbert 1,122 .....O7
74338 Colcord 530 .....S2
†73010 Cole 309 .....L5
73432 Coleman 200 .....O6
74021 Collinsville 3,556 .....P2
73021 Colony 185 .....J4
73529 Comanche 1,937 .....L6
74339 Commerce 2,556 .....R1
73022 Concho 300 .....L3
†73041 Cooperton 31 .....J5
74022 Copan 960 .....O1
73632 Cordell⊙ 3,301 .....H4
73024 Corn 542 .....J4
†73456 Cornish 115 .....L6
74428 Council Hill 141 .....P3
73025 Countyline 550 .....L6
73730 Covington 715 .....L2
74429 Coweta 4,554 .....P3
73027 Coyle 345 .....M3
73638 Crawford 53 .....G3
73028 Crescent 1,651 .....L3
74837 Cromwell 337 .....N4
74430 Crowder 431 .....P4
†73446 Cumberland 100 .....N6
74023 Cushing 7,720 .....N3
73639 Custer City 530 .....J3
73029 Cyril 1,220 .....K5
73731 Dacoma 226 .....J1
74838 Dale 160 .....M4
74026 Davenport 974 .....N3
73530 Davidson 501 .....J6
73030 Davis 2,782 .....M5
74636 Deer Creek 174 .....L1
74027 Delaware 544 .....P1
73115 Del City 28,523 .....L4
74028 Depew 682 .....O3
73531 Devol 186 .....J6
74431 Dewar 1,048 .....P4
74029 Dewey 3,545 .....P1
73031 Dibble 348 .....L4
†73401 Dickson 996 .....M6
73641 Dill City 649 .....H4
74340 Disney 464 .....S2
73032 Dougherty 210 .....M6
73733 Douglas 89 .....L2
74341 Douthat 30 .....S1
73734 Dover 570 .....L3
73735 Drummond 482 .....L2
74030 Drumright 3,162 .....N3
73533 Duncan⊙ 22,517 .....L5
74701 Durant⊙ 11,972 .....O6
73642 Durham 30 .....G3
74839 Dustin 498 .....O4
74734 Eagletown 650 .....S6
73033 Eakly 452 .....K4
74840 Earlsboro 266 .....N4
†73352 East Duke 484 .....H5
73034 Edmond 34,637 .....M3
73537 Eldorado 688 .....G6
73538 Elgin 1,003 .....K5
73644 Elk City 9,579 .....G4
73539 Elmer 131 .....H6
73035 Elmore City 582 .....M5
73935 Elmwood 300 .....F1
73036 El Reno⊙ 15,486 .....K3
†73529 Empire City 13 .....L6
73701 Enid⊙ 50,363 .....L2
73645 Erick 1,375 .....G4
74342 Eucha 210 .....S2
74432 Eufaula⊙ 3,159 .....P4
74637 Fairfax 1,949 .....N1
74343 Fairland 1,073 .....S1
73736 Fairmont 419 .....L2
†74080 Fair Oaks 346 .....P2
73737 Fairview⊙ 3,370 .....J2
†74881 Fallis 22 .....M3
74935 Fanshawe 416 .....S5
73840 Fargo 409 .....G2
73540 Faxon 140 .....J6
73646 Fay 140 .....J3
73937 Felt 120 .....A1
74543 Finley 350 .....R6
74842 Fittstown 500 .....N5

74843 Fitzhugh 150 .....N5
†73569 Fleetwood 12 .....L7
73541 Fletcher 1,074 .....K5
74652 Foraker 34 .....O1
†73101 Forest Park 1,148 .....M3
73938 Forgan 611 .....E1
73038 Fort Cobb 760 .....K4
74434 Fort Gibson 2,477 .....R3
73841 Fort Supply 559 .....G1
74735 Fort Towson 789 .....R7
73647 Foss 188 .....H4
73039 Foster 100 .....M5
73435 Fox 400 .....M6
74031 Foyil 191 .....R2
74844 Francis 365 .....N5
73542 Frederick⊙ 6,153 .....H6
73842 Freedom 339 .....H1
73843 Gage 667 .....G2
74936 Gans 346 .....S4
73738 Garber 1,215 .....M2
74736 Garvin 162 .....S7
73844 Gate 146 .....F1
73040 Geary 1,700 .....K3
73436 Gene Autry 178 .....N6
73543 Geronimo 726 .....K6
†74531 Gerty 149 .....O5
74032 Glencoe 490 .....M2
74033 Glenpool 2,706 .....P3
74737 Golden 300 .....S6
†73093 Goldsby 603 .....L4
73739 Goltry 305 .....K1
†74740 Goodwater 240 .....S7
73939 Goodwell 1,186 .....C1
74435 Gore 445 .....R3
73041 Gotebo 457 .....J4
73544 Gould 318 .....G5
74545 Gowen 75 .....R5
74042 Gracemont 503 .....K4
73545 Grady 85 .....L6
73437 Graham 200 .....M6
†74652 Grainola 67 .....N1
73546 Grandfield 1,445 .....J6
†74349 Grand Lake Towne 36 .....S1
73547 Granite 1,617 .....H5
†74437 Grayson 150 .....P3
73043 Greenfield 233 .....K3
74344 Grove 3,378 .....S1
73044 Guthrie⊙ 10,312 .....M3
73942 Guymon⊙ 8,492 .....D1
74546 Haileyville 832 .....P5
74034 Hallett 186 .....N2
†73069 Hall Park 577 .....M4
73650 Hammon 866 .....H3
74845 Hanna 157 .....P4
74846 Harden City 250 .....N5
73944 Hardesty 243 .....D1
73832 Harmon 27 .....G2
73045 Harrah 2,897 .....M4
†74740 Harris 192 .....S7
74547 Hartshorne 2,380 .....R5
74436 Haskell 1,953 .....P3
73548 Hastings 246 .....K6
74740 Haworth 341 .....S7
73549 Headrick 223 .....H5
73438 Healdton 3,769 .....M6
74937 Heavener 2,776 .....S5
73741 Helena 710 .....K1
74741 Hendrix 106 .....O7
73046 Hennepin 300 .....M5
73742 Hennessey 2,287 .....L2
74437 Henryetta 6,432 .....O4
†73086 Hickory 95 .....N5
73743 Hillsdale 110 .....K1
73047 Hinton 1,432 .....K4
73744 Hitchcock 172 .....K3
74438 Hitchita 126 .....P4
73651 Hobart⊙ 4,735 .....J5
74439 Hoffman 407 .....P4
74848 Holdenville⊙ 5,469 .....O4
73550 Hollis⊙ 2,958 .....G5
73551 Hollister 82 .....J6
74035 Hominy 3,130 .....O2
74549 Honobia 80 .....R5
73945 Hooker 1,788 .....D1
†74366 Hoot Owl 3 .....R2
73746 Hopeton 42 .....J1
74940 Howe 562 .....S5
74440 Hoyt 160 .....R4
74743 Hugo⊙ 7,172 .....P7
74441 Hulbert 633 .....R3
74640 Hunter 276 .....L1
74745 Idabel⊙ 7,622 .....S7
73552 Indiahoma 364 .....J5
74442 Indianola 254 .....P4
74036 Inola 1,550 .....P2
73747 Isabella 113 .....K2
74346 Jay⊙ 2,100 .....S2
†73759 Jefferson 92 .....L1
74037 Jenks 5,876 .....P2
74038 Jennings 395 .....N2
73749 Jet 352 .....K1
73049 Jones 2,270 .....M3
74547 Kansas 491 .....S2
74641 Kaw City 283 .....N1
74039 Kellyville 960 .....O3

(continued on following page)

Agriculture, Industry and Resources

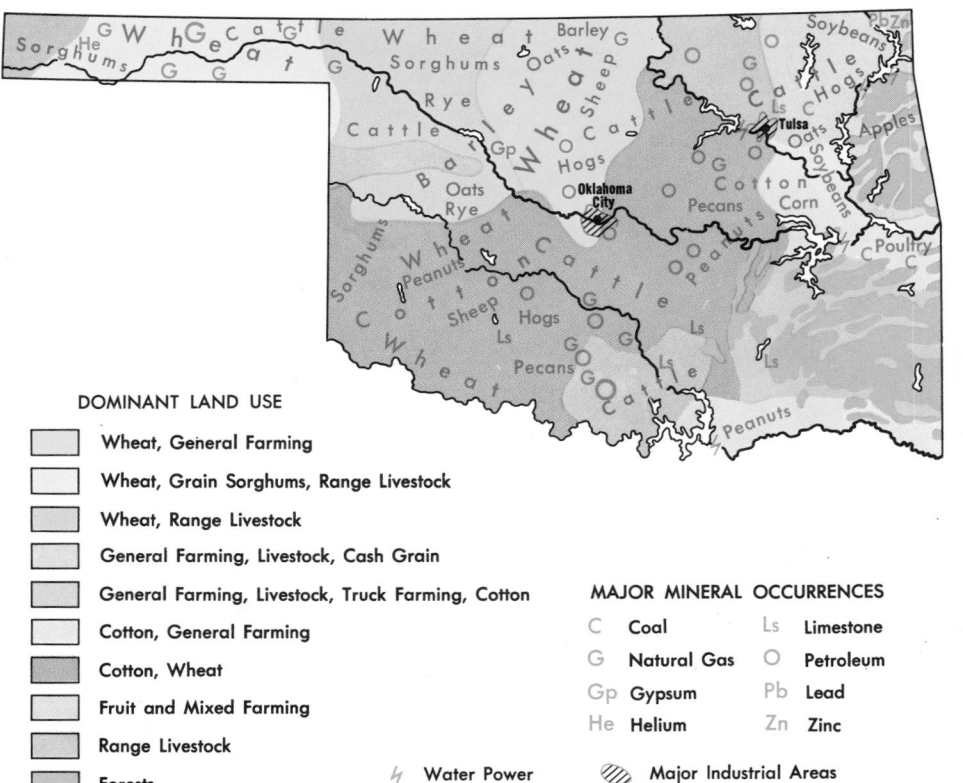

DOMINANT LAND USE

- Wheat, General Farming
- Wheat, Grain Sorghums, Range Livestock
- Wheat, Range Livestock
- General Farming, Livestock, Cash Grain
- General Farming, Livestock, Truck Farming, Cotton
- Cotton, General Farming
- Cotton, Wheat
- Fruit and Mixed Farming
- Range Livestock
- Forests

MAJOR MINERAL OCCURRENCES

C	Coal	Ls	Limestone
G	Natural Gas	O	Petroleum
Gp	Gypsum	Pb	Lead
He	Helium	Zn	Zinc

⚡ Water Power   ▨ Major Industrial Areas

Oklahoma

SCALE
0 5 10 20 30 40 MI.
0 5 10 20 30 40 KM.

State Capitals ..... ⊛
County Seats ..... ⊙
Major Limited Access Hwys.

Scale 1:2,040,000

© Copyright HAMMOND INCORPORATED, Maplewood, N.J.

COLORADO · KANSAS · NEW MEXICO · TEXAS

Black Mesa 4,973 ft. (1516 m.)

Kenton · Wheeless · Boise City · Keyes · Felt · Griggs · Clayton · Stratford · Dalhart · Nara Visa

CIMARRON · TEXAS · BEAVER · HARPER · WOODWARD · ELLIS · ROGER MILLS · BECKHAM · GREER · HARMON · JACKSON

Elkhart · Tyrone · Liberal · Englewood · Hooker · Baker · Forgan · Knowles · Gate · Buffalo · Selman · Rosston
Eva · Optima · Turpin · Beaver · Laverne · May
Guymon · Goodwell · Hardesty · Boyd · Balko · Elmwood · Logan · Ft. Supply · Woodward · Tangier
Texhoma · Adams · Ft. Supply Lake
Coldwater · Perryton · Follett · Fargo · Arnett · Harmon · Vici
Spearman · Lipscomb · Sharon · Mutual · Shattuck
Higgins · Durham · Crawford · Leedey
Borger · Canadian · Miami · Washita · Reydon · Cheyenne · Strong City · Hammon · Foss Res.
Pampa · Wheeler · Grimes · Berlin · Sweetwater · Elk City · Canute
Shamrock · Texola · Erick · Delhi · Carter · North · Mayfield · Sayre · Burns Flat · Dill City
Willow · Brinkman · Reed · Granite · Mangum · Altus Res.
Wellington · Vinson · Gould · Duke · Hester · Blair · Martha
Childress · Hollis · Altus · Olustee · Eldorado · Elmer · Hess
Quanah · Prairie · Dog · Town · Paducah · Chillicothe · Crowell · Vernon · Quanah · Seymour

Topography

Black Mesa 4,973 ft. (1516 m.)

Enid · Stillwater · Tulsa · Muskogee · Oklahoma City · Lawton · Ardmore

Keystone Lake · Kaw L. · Oologah L. · Lake O' the Cherokees · Ft. Gibson · Lake Hudson · Eufaula Lake · Lake Texoma

BOSTON MTS. · OUACHITA MTS. · WICHITA MTS.

Rivers: Cimarron, North Canadian, Canadian, Arkansas, Washita, Red, N. Fork Red, Salt Fork

5,000 m. 16,404 ft. / 2,000 m. 6,562 ft. / 1,000 m. 3,281 ft. / 500 m. 1,640 ft. / 200 m. 656 ft. / 100 m. 328 ft. / Sea Level / Below

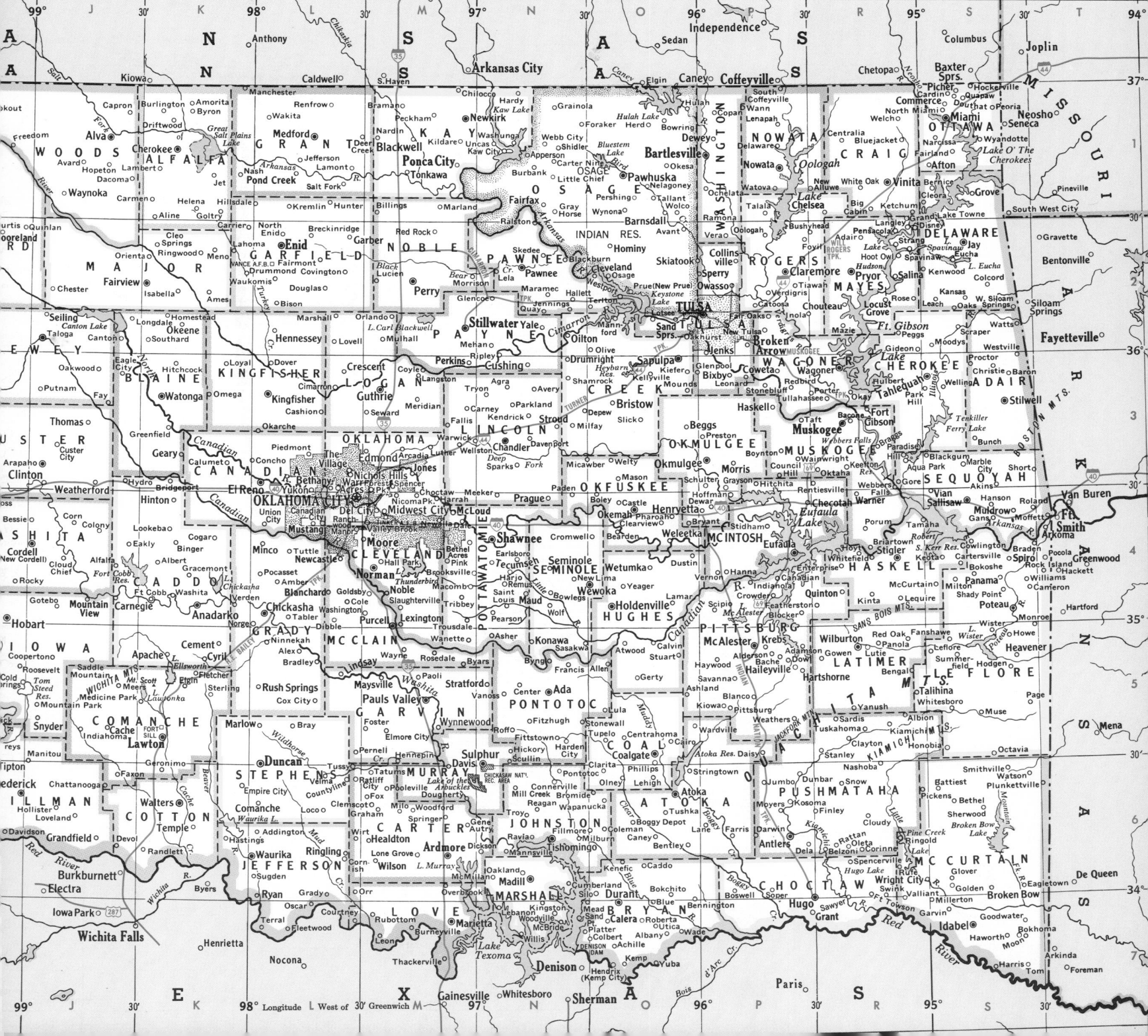

290 Oregon

COUNTIES

Baker 16,134 .... K3
Benton 68,211 .... D3
Clackamas 241,911 .... E2
Clatsop 32,489 .... D1
Columbia 35,646 .... D2
Coos 64,047 .... C4
Crook 13,091 .... G3
Curry 16,992 .... C5
Deschutes 62,142 .... F4
Douglas 93,748 .... D4
Gilliam 2,057 .... G2
Grant 8,210 .... J3
Harney 8,314 .... H4
Hood River 15,835 .... F2
Jackson 132,456 .... E5
Jefferson 11,599 .... F3
Josephine 58,855 .... D5
Klamath 59,117 .... F5
Lake 7,532 .... G5
Lane 275,226 .... E4
Lincoln 35,264 .... D3
Linn 89,495 .... E3

Malheur 26,896 .... K4
Marion 204,692 .... E3
Morrow 7,519 .... H2
Multnomah 562,640 .... E2
Polk 45,203 .... D3
Sherman 2,172 .... G2
Tillamook 21,164 .... D2
Umatilla 58,861 .... J2
Union 23,921 .... J2
Wallowa 7,273 .... K2
Wasco 21,732 .... F2
Washington 245,860 .... D2
Wheeler 1,513 .... G3
Yamhill 55,332 .... D2

CITIES and TOWNS

Zip   Name/Pop.   Key
†97330 Adair Village 589 ....D3
97810 Adams 240 ....J2
97620 Adel 24 ....H5
97901 Adrian 162 ....K4
†97365 Agate Beach 975 ....C3
97406 Agness 30 ....C5
97321 Albany⊙ 26,678 ....D3
97407 Allegany 300 ....D4
97005 Aloha 28,353 ....A2
97324 Alsea 125 ....D3
†97601 Altamont 19,805 ....F5
97409 Alvadore 800 ....D3
97101 Amity 1,092 ....D2
97001 Antelope 39 ....F3
97530 Applegate 150 ....D5
97458 Arago 200 ....C4
97812 Athena 965 ....J2
97520 Ashland 14,943 ....E5
97103 Astoria⊙ 9,998 ....D1
97813 Athena 965 ....J2
97325 Aumsville 1,432 ....E3
97002 Aurora 523 ....B2
†97814 Baker⊙ 9,471 ....K3
†97378 Ballston 120 ....D2
97411 Bandon 2,311 ....C4
97106 Banks 489 ....A1
†97013 Barlow 105 ....B2

†97009 Barton 100 ....B2
†97136 Bar View 170 ....C2
†97420 Barview 1,462 ....C4
97817 Bates 56 ....J3
97107 Bay City 986 ....D2
97621 Beatty 350 ....F5
97108 Beaver 350 ....D2
97004 Beavercreek 708 ....B2
97005 Beaverton 30,582 ....A2
97701 Bend⊙ 17,263 ....F3
†97058 Biggs 50 ....G2
97412 Blachly 80 ....D3
†97108 Blaine 38 ....D2
97326 Blodgett 250 ....D3
97413 Blue River 318 ....E3
97622 Bly 800 ....F5
97818 Boardman 1,261 ......H2
97623 Bonanza 270 ....F5
97008 Bonneville 80 ....E2
97009 Boring 150 ....E2
97010 Bridal Veil 20 ......E2
†97458 Bridge 200 ....D4
†97136 Brighton 150 ....C2
97001 Brightwood 200 .....E2

†97414 Broadbent 400 ....C4
97903 Brogan 130 ....K3
97415 Brookings 3,384 ....C5
97305 Brooks 490 ....A3
†97524 Brownsboro 150 ....E5
97327 Brownsville 1,261 .....E3
97351 Buena Vista 130 ......D3
97420 Bunker Hill 1,555 ....C4
97720 Burns⊙ 3,579 ....H4
97522 Butte Falls 428 .....E5
†97002 Butteville 20 ....A2
97109 Buxton 450 ....D2
97416 Camas Valley 750 ....D4
97730 Camp Sherman 350 ...F3
†97493 Canary 23 ....D3
97013 Canby 7,659 ....B2
97110 Cannon Beach 1,187 ..D2
97820 Canyon City⊙ 639 ...J3
97417 Canyonville 1,288 ..D5
97111 Carlton 1,302 ....D2
97014 Cascade Locks 838 ..E2
97329 Cascadia 250 ....E3
97523 Cave Junction 1,023 .D5
97821 Cayuse 200 ....J2

97225 Cedar Hills 9,619 ....A2
†97005 Cedar Mill 900 ....A2
†97058 Celilo 50 ....G2
97502 Central Point 6,357 .....D5
97420 Charleston 500 ....C4
97306 Chemawa 400 ....A3
97731 Chemult 800 ....F4
†97058 Chenoweth 2,820 ....F2
†97119 Cherry Grove 350 ......D2
†97055 Cherryville 75 ....E2
97419 Cheshire 300 ....D3
97624 Chiloquin 778 ....F5
97015 Clackamas B2
97016 Clatskanie 1,648 ....D1
97112 Cloverdale 260 ......D2
97401 Coburg 699 ....D3
97017 Colton 305 ....B3
97018 Columbia City 678 ..D2
97823 Condon⊙ 783 ....G2
97420 Coos Bay 14,424 ...C4
97424 Coquille⊙ 4,481 ..C4
97113 Cornelius 4,462 ...A2
†97330 Corvallis⊙ 40,960 .D3
97424 Cottage Grove 7,148 .D4

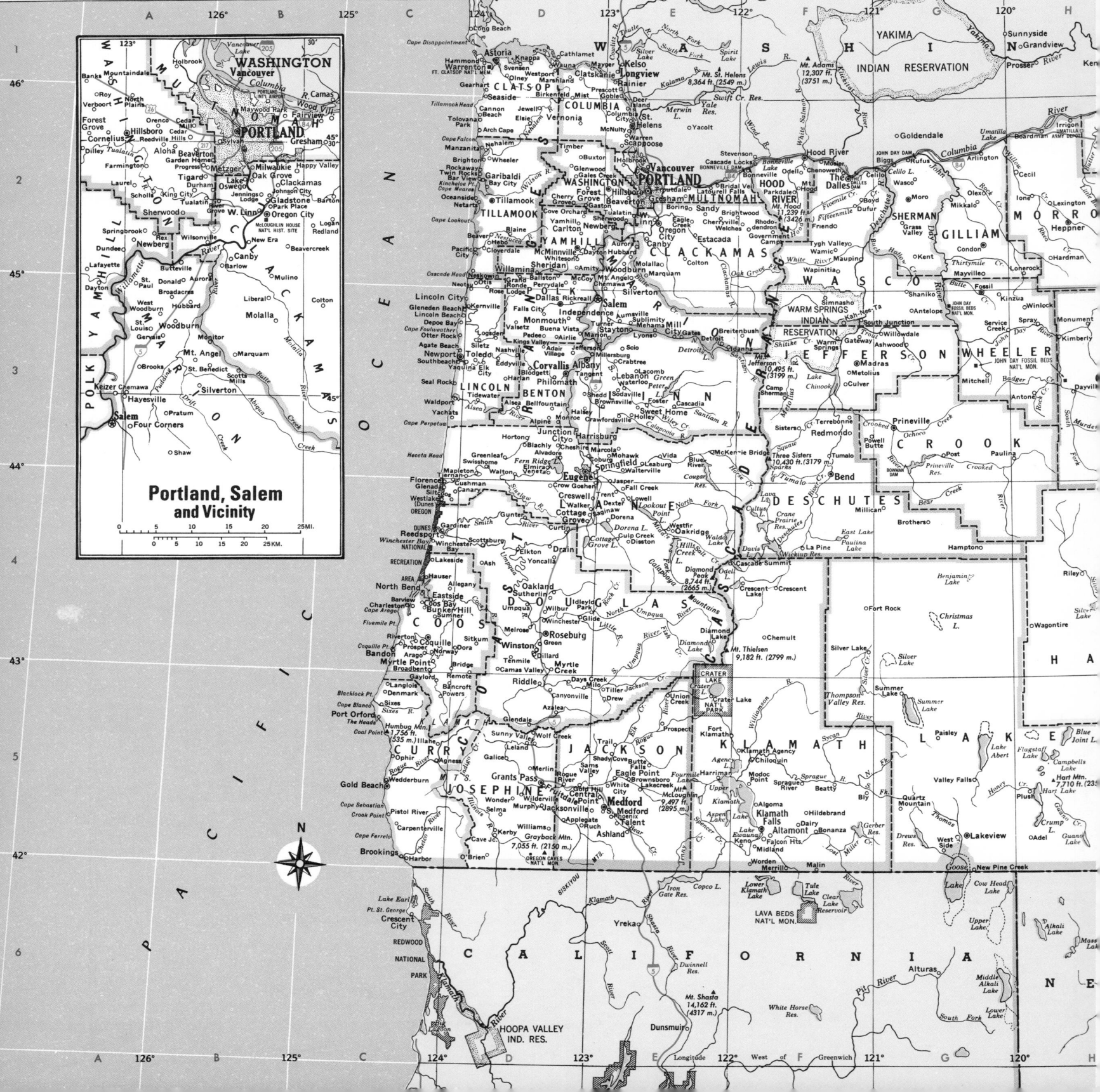

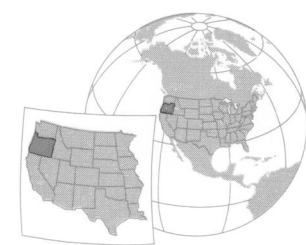

AREA 97,073 sq. mi. (251,419 sq. km.)
POPULATION 2,633,149
CAPITAL Salem
LARGEST CITY Portland
HIGHEST POINT Mt. Hood 11,239 ft. (3426 m.)
SETTLED IN 1810
ADMITTED TO UNION February 14, 1859
POPULAR NAME Beaver State
STATE FLOWER Oregon Grape
STATE BIRD Western Meadowlark

Topography

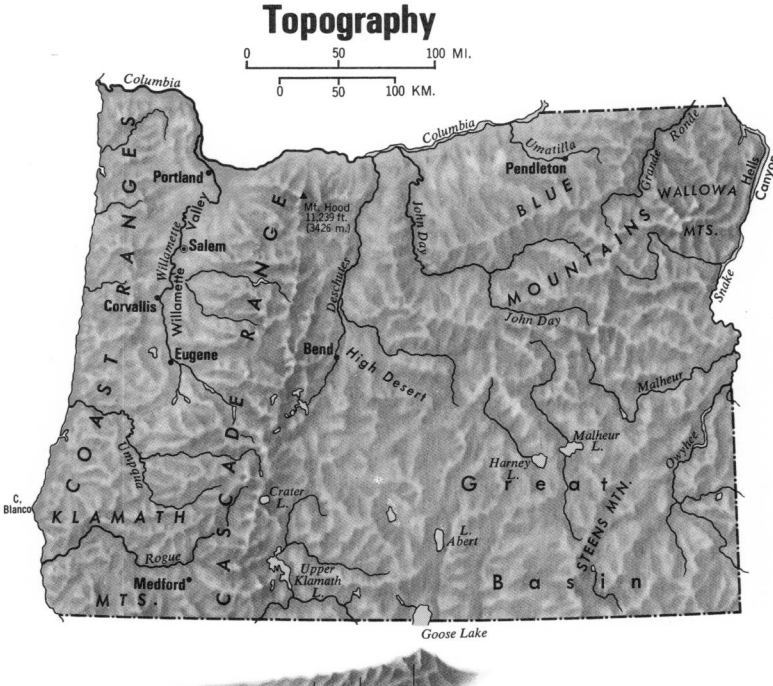

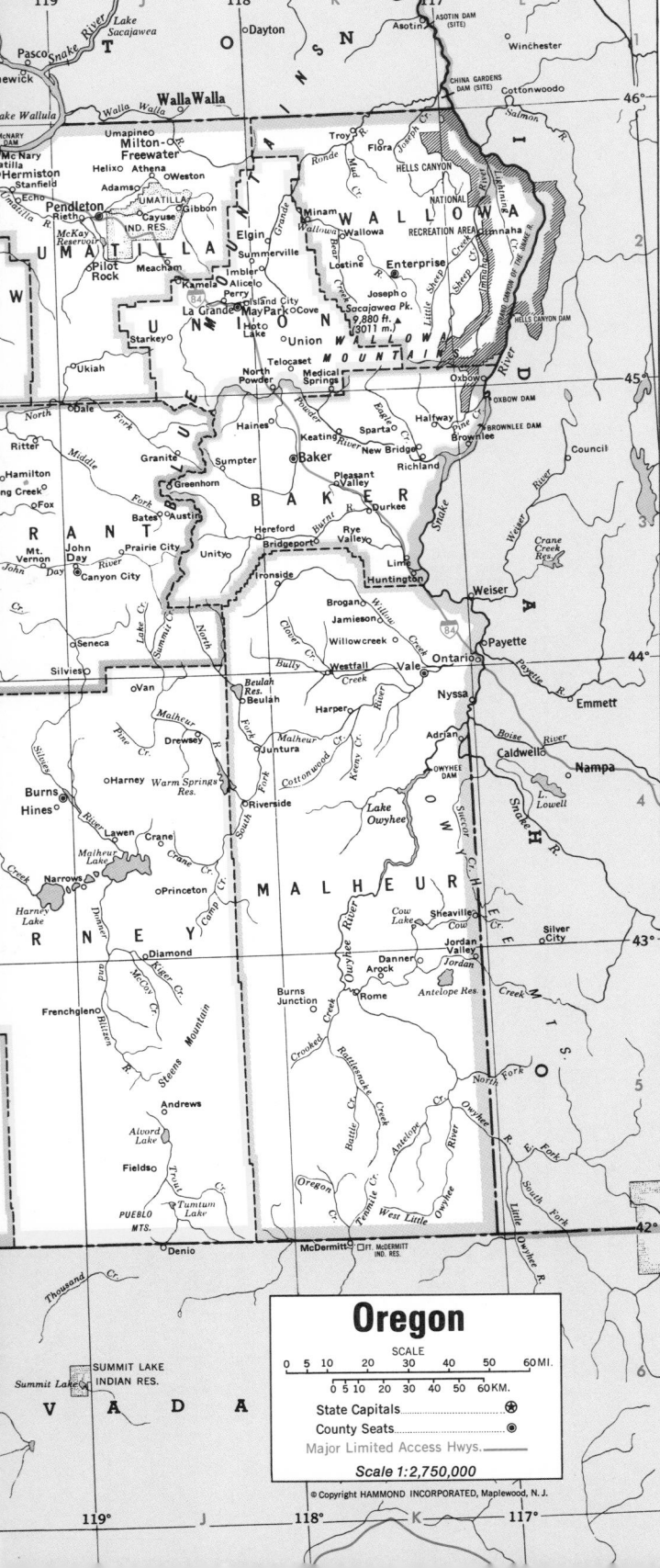

Oregon

SCALE

0 5 10 20 30 40 50 60 MI.

0 5 10 20 30 40 50 60 KM.

State Capitals .... ☉
County Seats .... ☉

Major Limited Access Hwys. ——————

Scale 1:2,750,000

© Copyright HAMMOND INCORPORATED, Maplewood, N.J.

Agriculture, Industry and Resources

DOMINANT LAND USE

- Specialized Wheat
- Wheat, Peas
- Specialized Dairy
- Dairy, Poultry, Mixed Farming
- Fruit and Mixed Farming
- Potatoes, General Farming
- General Farming, Dairy, Hay, Sugar Beets
- General Farming, Livestock, Special Crops
- Range Livestock
- Forests
- Nonagricultural Land

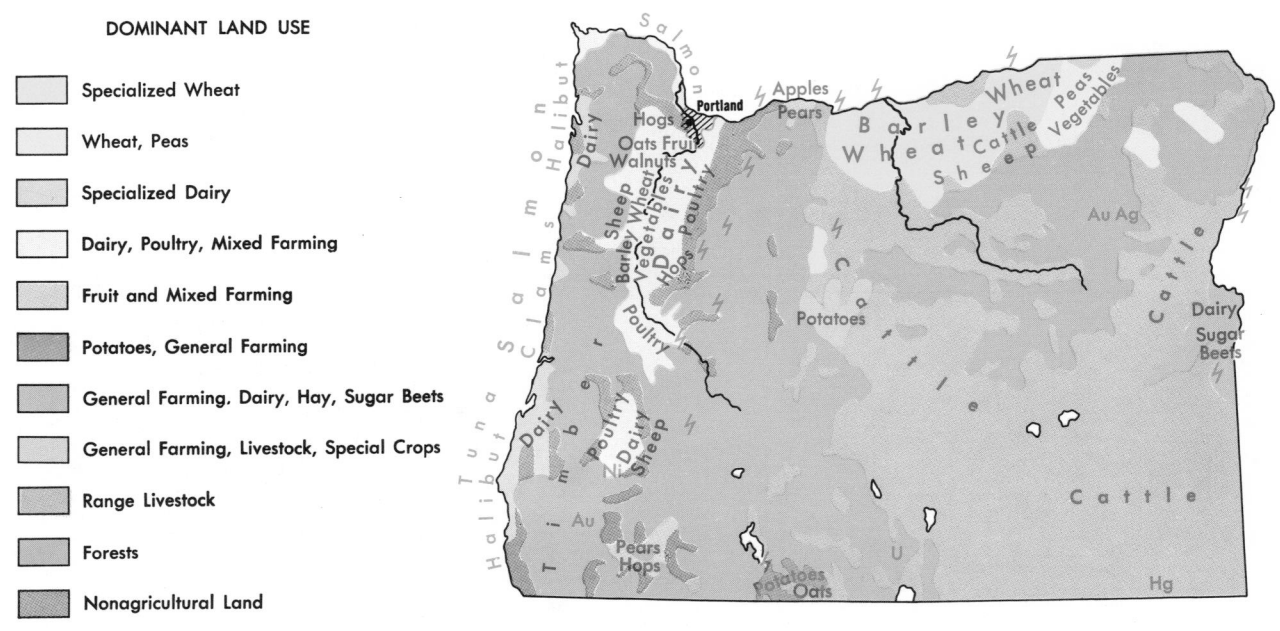

MAJOR MINERAL OCCURRENCES

Ag	Silver	Hg	Mercury
Au	Gold	Ni	Nickel
	U	Uranium	

⚡ Water Power
▨ Major Industrial Areas

†97005 Reedville 850	A2	
97870 Richland 181	K3	
97371 Rickreall 700	D3	
97469 Riddle 1,265	D5	
†97801 Rieth 300	J2	
97758 Riley 100	H4	
†97223 River Grove 314	B2	
†97423 Riverton 150	C4	
97136 Rockaway 906	C2	
97537 Rogue River 1,308	D5	
97470 Roseburg⊙ 16,644	D4	
97372 Rose Lodge 300	D3	
†97106 Roy 200	A2	
97050 Rufus 352	G2	
97472 Saginaw 150	E4	
97051 Saint Helens⊙ 7,064	E2	
†97026 Saint Louis 102	A3	
97137 Saint Paul 312	A3	
*97301 Salem (cap.)⊙ 89,233	A3	
Salem‡ 249,895	A3	
†97525 Sams Valley 100	E5	
97055 Sandy 2,905	E2	
97056 Scappoose 3,213	E2	
97374 Scio 579	E3	
97473 Scottsburg 300	D4	
97375 Scotts Mills 249	B3	
97376 Seal Rock 430	C3	
97138 Seaside 5,193	D2	
97538 Selma 150	D5	
97873 Seneca 285	J3	
97539 Shady Cove 1,097	E5	
97057 Shaniko 30	G3	
†97325 Shaw 800	A3	
97377 Shedd 850	D3	
97378 Sheridan 2,249	D2	
97140 Sherwood 2,386	A2	
97380 Siletz 1,001	D3	
97638 Silver Lake 200	F4	
97381 Silverton 5,168	B3	
97759 Sisters 696	F3	
97476 Sixes 300	C5	
†97355 Sodaville 171	E3	
97366 Southbeach 300	C3	
†97501 South Medford 2,898	E5	
97639 Sprague River 200	F5	
97874 Spray 155	H3	
†97132 Springbrook 500	A2	
97477 Springfield 41,621	E3	
97875 Stanfield 1,568	H2	
97383 Stayton 4,396	E3	
97385 Sublimity 1,077	E3	
97876 Summerville 143	K2	
†97420 Sumner 100	C4	
97877 Sumpter 133	J3	
97478 Sunny Valley 159	D5	
97479 Sutherlin 4,560	D4	
†97103 Svensen 950	D1	
97386 Sweet Home 6,921	E3	
97480 Swisshome 350	D3	
†97201 Sylvan	B2	

97540 Talent 2,577	E5	
97389 Tangent 478	D3	
97481 Tenmile 500	D4	
97760 Terrebonne 521	F3	
97058 The Dalles⊙ 10,820	F2	
97223 Tigard 14,286	A2	
97141 Tillamook⊙ 3,981	D2	
97484 Tiller 300	E5	
97144 Timber 175	D2	
97391 Toledo 3,151	D3	
97145 Tolovana Park 165	C2	
97541 Trail 350	E5	
†97431 Trent 100	E4	
97060 Troutdale 5,908	E2	
97062 Tualatin 7,483	A2	
†97701 Tumalo 500	F3	
97392 Turner 1,116	E3	
†97136 Twin Rocks 450	C2	
97063 Tygh Valley 663	F2	
97880 Ukiah 249	J2	
97881 Umapine 100	J2	
97882 Umatilla 3,199	H2	
97486 Umpqua 705	D4	
97883 Union 2,062	K2	
97884 Unity 115	J3	
97918 Vale⊙ 1,558	K4	
97393 Valsetz 320	D3	
97487 Veneta 2,449	D3	
†97116 Verboort 280	A2	
97064 Vernonia 1,785	D2	
97488 Vida 300	E3	
97394 Waldport 1,274	C3	
97885 Wallowa 847	K2	
97489 Walterville 250	E3	
97490 Walton 300	D3	
97063 Wamic 255	F2	
97761 Warm Springs 550	F3	
97053 Warren 700	E2	
97146 Warrenton 2,493	C1	
97065 Wasco 415	G2	
†97355 Waterloo 221	E3	
97491 Wedderburn 700	C5	
†97067 Welches 100	E2	
97492 Westfir 312	E4	
97493 Westlake 1,124	C4	
97068 West Linn 12,956	B2	
97886 Weston 719	J2	
97016 Westport 400	D1	
†97071 West Woodburn 600	A3	
97147 Wheeler 319	D2	
97503 White City 5,445	E5	
†97128 Whiteson 100	D2	
97494 Wilbur 476	D4	
97543 Wilderville 600	D5	
97396 Willamina 1,749	D2	
97544 Williams 750	D5	
97070 Wilsonville 2,920	A2	
97495 Winchester 900	D4	
97467 Winchester Bay 535	C4	
97496 Winston 3,359	D4	

97497 Wolf Creek 500	D5	
97071 Woodburn 11,196	A3	
†97060 Wood Village 2,253	B2	
97498 Yachats 482	C3	
97148 Yamhill 690	D2	
†97365 Yaquina 175	C3	
97499 Yoncalla 805	D4	

OTHER FEATURES

Abert (lake)	G5
Abiqua (creek)	B3
Agency (lake)	E5
Alsea (riv.)	D3
Alvord (lake)	J5
Antelope (creek)	K5
Arago (cape)	C4
Aspen (lake)	E5
Badger (creek)	H3
Battle (creek)	K5
Bear (creek)	E5
Bear (creek)	K2
Bear (creek)	G4
Benjamin (lake)	G4
Beulah (res.)	J4
Blacklock (pt.)	C5
Blanco (cape)	C5
Blue (mts.)	J3
Bonneville (dam)	E2
Brownlee (dam)	L3
Buck Hollow (creek)	G2
Bully (creek)	K3
Burnt (riv.)	K3
Butte (creek)	G2
Butte (creek)	B3
Butter (creek)	H2
Calapooia (riv.)	E3
Calapooya (mts.)	E4
Camp (creek)	J4
Campbells (lake)	H5
Cascade (head)	C2
Cascade (range)	E4
Celilo (lake)	G2
Chetco (riv.)	C5
Clackamas (riv.)	E2
Clover (creek)	K3
Coal (pt.)	C5
Coast (ranges)	D5
Columbia (riv.)	G2
Coos (riv.)	D4
Coquille (pt.)	C4
Cottage Grove (lake)	E4
Cottonwood (creek)	K4
Cougar (res.)	E3
Cow (creek)	K4
Crane (creek)	J4
Crane Prairie (res.)	F4
Crater (lake)	E5

Crater Lake Nat'l Park	E5
Crook (pt.)	C5
Crooked (creek)	K5
Crooked (riv.)	G3
Cultus (lake)	F4
Dalles, The (dam)	F2
Davis (lake)	F4
Deschutes (riv.)	G2
Detroit (lake)	E3
Diamond (lake)	E4
Donner and Blitzen (riv.)	J4
Dorena (lake)	E4
Drews (res.)	G5
Drift (creek)	B3
Eagle (creek)	K3
East (lake)	F4
Elk (creek)	E5
Ewauna (lake)	F5
Falcon (cape)	C2
Fern Ridge (lake)	D3
Ferrelo (cape)	C5
Fifteenmile (creek)	F2
Fish (creek)	E4
Fivemile (creek)	F2
Fivemile (pt.)	C4
Flagstaff (lake)	H5
Fort Clatsop Nat'l Mem.	C1
Foulweather (cape)	C3
Fourmile (lake)	E5
Gerber (res.)	F5
Goose (lake)	G5
Grand Canyon, Snake R. (canyon)	L2
Grande Ronde (riv.)	K2
Green Peter (lake)	E3
Guano (creek)	H5
Guano (lake)	H5
Harney (lake)	H4
Hart (lake)	H5
Hart (mt.)	H5
Heads, The (prom.)	C5
Heceta (cape)	C3
Hells Canyon (dam)	L2
Hells Canyon Nat'l Rec. Area	K2
Hills Creek (lake)	E4
Honey (creek)	G5
Hood (mt.)	F2
Hood (riv.)	F2
Horse (creek)	F3
Illinois (riv.)	D5
Imnaha (riv.)	L2
Indigo (creek)	D5
Jackson (creek)	J5
Jefferson (mt.)	F3
Jenny (creek)	E5
John Day (dam)	G2
John Day (riv.)	G2
John Day Fossil Beds Nat'l Mon.	G3
Jordan (creek)	K5
Joseph (creek)	K2
Keeny (creek)	K4

Kiger (creek)	J5
Kincheloe (pt.)	C2
Klamath (mts.)	C5
Lake (creek)	J3
Lava (lake)	F4
Lightning (creek)	L2
Little (riv.)	E4
Little Butter (creek)	H3
Little Sheep (creek)	K2
Lookout (cape)	C2
Lookout Point (lake)	E4
Lost (riv.)	F5
Malheur (lake)	J4
Malheur (riv.)	J4
McCoy (creek)	J5
McKay (res.)	J2
McKenzie, South Fork (riv.)	E3
McLoughlin (mt.)	E5
McLoughlin House Nat'l Hist. Site	B2
McNary (dam)	H2
Meares (cape)	C2
Metolius (riv.)	F3
Miller (creek)	F2
Molalla (riv.)	B3
Mud (creek)	K2
Murderers (creek)	H3
Nehalem (riv.)	D2
Nestucca (riv.)	D2
North Santiam (riv.)	E4
North Umpqua (riv.)	E4
Oak Grove Fork, Clackamas (riv.)	F2
Ochoco (creek)	G3
Odell (lake)	F4
Oregon (creek)	K5
Oregon Caves Nat'l Mon.	D5
Oregon Dunes Nat'l Rec. Area	C4
Owyhee (dam)	K4
Owyhee (lake)	K4
Owyhee (mts.)	K4
Owyhee (riv.)	K5
Owyhee, North Fork (riv.)	K5
Oxbow (dam)	L3
Paulina (lake)	F4
Perpetua (cape)	C3
Pine (creek)	L3
Pine (creek)	K3
Portland Int'l Airport	B2
Powder (riv.)	K3
Prineville (res.)	G3
Pudding (riv.)	A3
Pueblo (mts.)	J5
Rattlesnake (creek)	K5
Rhea (creek)	H2
Rock (creek)	E4
Rock (creek)	H2
Rock (creek)	G2
Rogue (riv.)	D5
Salt (creek)	E4
Sebastian (cape)	C5

Sheep (creek)	L2
Shitike (creek)	F3
Silver (creek)	F4
Silver (creek)	H4
Silver (creek)	J3
Silver (lake)	G4
Silver (lake)	H4
Silvies (riv.)	H4
Siskiyou (mts.)	D6
Siuslaw (riv.)	D4
Sixes (riv.)	C5
Smith (riv.)	D4
Snake (riv.)	K3
South Santiam (riv.)	E3
South Umpqua (riv.)	E4
Sparks (lake)	F3
Spencer (creek)	E5
Sprague (riv.)	F5
Squaw (creek)	F3
Steens (mt.)	J5
Succor (creek)	K4
Summer (lake)	G5
Summit (creek)	J3
Sycan (riv.)	F5
Tenmile (creek)	K5
The Dalles (dam)	F2
Thielsen (mt.)	F4
Thirtymile (creek)	G2
Thomas (creek)	G5
Three Sisters (mt.)	F3
Tillamook (head)	C2
Trout (creek)	J5
Trout (creek)	F3
Tualatin (riv.)	A2
Tumalo (creek)	F3
Tumtum (lake)	J5
Umatilla (lake)	G2
Umatilla (riv.)	H2
Umatilla Army Depot	H2
Umatilla Ind. Res.	J2
Umpqua (riv.)	D4
Upper Klamath (lake)	E5
Waldo (lake)	E4
Walla Walla (riv.)	J1
Wallowa (mts.)	K2
Wallowa (riv.)	K2
Wallula (lake)	H1
Warm Springs (res.)	J4
Warm Springs Ind. Res.	F3
White (riv.)	F2
Wickiup (res.)	F4
Wiley (creek)	E3
Willamette (riv.)	A3
Willamette, Middle Fork (riv.)	E4
Williamson (riv.)	F5
Willow (creek)	H2
Willow (creek)	K3
Wilson (riv.)	D2
Winchester (bay)	C4
⊙ County seat.	
‡Population of metropolitan area.	
† Zip of nearest p.o. * Multiple zips.	

DOMINANT LAND USE

- Specialized Dairy
- Dairy, General Farming
- Fruit and Mixed Farming
- Fruit, Truck and Mixed Farming
- General Farming, Livestock, Tobacco
- General Farming, Livestock, Fruit, Tobacco
- Forests
- Urban Areas

AREA 45,308 sq. mi. (117,348 sq. km.)
POPULATION 11,863,895
CAPITAL Harrisburg
LARGEST CITY Philadelphia
HIGHEST POINT Mt. Davis 3,213 ft. (979 m.)
SETTLED IN 1682
ADMITTED TO UNION December 12, 1787
POPULAR NAME Keystone State
STATE FLOWER Mountain Laurel
STATE BIRD Ruffed Grouse

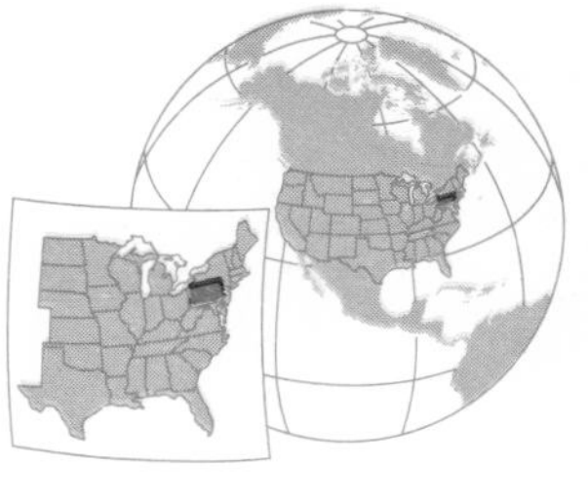

MAJOR MINERAL OCCURRENCES

C	Coal	G	Natural Gas	Sl	Slate
Cl	Clay	Ls	Limestone	Ss	Sandstone
Co	Cobalt	O	Petroleum	Zn	Zinc
Fe	Iron Ore				

Water Power
Major Industrial Areas

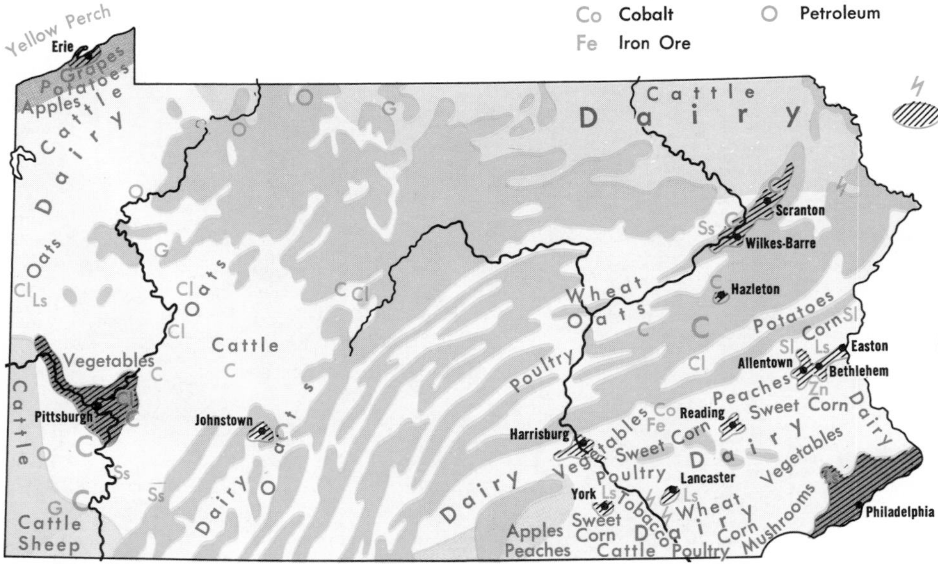

Agriculture, Industry and Resources

COUNTIES

Adams 68,292 .... H6
Allegheny 1,450,085 .... B5
Armstrong 77,768 .... D4
Beaver 204,441 .... B4
Bedford 46,784 .... E6
Berks 312,509 .... K5
Blair 136,621 .... F4
Bradford 62,919 .... J2
Bucks 479,211 .... M5
Butler 147,912 .... C4
Cambria 183,263 .... E4
Cameron 6,674 .... F3
Carbon 53,285 .... L4
Centre 112,760 .... G4
Chester 316,660 .... L6
Clarion 43,362 .... D3
Clearfield 83,578 .... F3
Clinton 38,971 .... G3
Columbia 61,967 .... K3
Crawford 88,869 .... B2
Cumberland 178,541 .... H5
Dauphin 232,317 .... J5
Delaware 555,007 .... M6
Elk 38,338 .... E3
Erie 279,780 .... B2
Fayette 159,417 .... C6
Forest 5,072 .... D2
Franklin 113,629 .... G6
Fulton 12,842 .... F6
Greene 40,476 .... B6
Huntingdon 42,253 .... F5
Indiana 92,281 .... D4
Jefferson 48,303 .... D3
Juniata 19,188 .... H4
Lackawanna 227,908 .... L3
Lancaster 362,346 .... K5
Lawrence 107,150 .... B4
Lebanon 108,582 .... K5
Lehigh 272,349 .... L4
Luzerne 343,079 .... L3
Lycoming 118,416 .... H3
McKean 50,635 .... E2
Mercer 128,299 .... B3
Mifflin 46,908 .... G4
Monroe 69,409 .... M3
Montgomery 643,621 .... M5
Montour 16,675 .... J3
Northampton 225,418 .... M4
Northumberland 100,381 .... J4
Perry 35,718 .... H5
Philadelphia (city county) 1,688,210 .... M6
Pike 18,271 .... M3
Potter 17,726 .... G2
Schuylkill 160,630 .... K4
Snyder 33,584 .... H4
Somerset 81,243 .... D6
Sullivan 6,349 .... J3
Susquehanna 37,876 .... L2
Tioga 40,973 .... H2
Union 32,870 .... H4
Venango 64,444 .... C3
Warren 47,449 .... D2
Washington 217,074 .... B5
Wayne 35,237 .... M2
Westmoreland 392,294 .... D5
Wyoming 26,433 .... K2
York 312,963 .... J6

CITIES and TOWNS

Zip *Name/Pop.* *Key*

19001 Abington○ 59,084 .... M5
19501 Adamstown 1,119 .... K5
17501 Akron 3,471 .... K5
16401 Albion 1,818 .... B2
18011 Alburtis 1,428 .... L5
†19018 Aldan 4,671 .... M7
15001 Aliquippa 17,094 .... B4
*18101 Allentown⊙ 103,758 .... L4
Allentown-Bethlehem-Easton‡ 636,714 .... L4
15101 Allison Park 10,000 .... C4
*16601 Altoona 57,078 .... F4
Altoona‡ 136,621 .... F4
19002 Ambler 6,628 .... M5
15003 Ambridge 9,575 .... B4
17003 Annville 4,493 .... J5
15613 Apollo 2,212 .... C4
18403 Archbald 6,295 .... F6
19003 Ardmore M6
15068 Arnold 6,853 .... C4
17921 Ashland 4,235 .... K4
18706 Ashley 3,512 .... E7
15215 Aspinwall 3,284 .... C6
18810 Athens 3,622 .... K2
17851 Atlas 1,162 .... K4
15202 Avalon 6,240 .... B6
15312 Avella 900 .... B5
17721 Avis 1,718 .... H3
18641 Avoca 3,536 .... F7
19311 Avondale 891 .... L6
15618 Avonmore 1,234 .... C4
15005 Baden 5,318 .... B4
19004 Bala-Cynwyd N6
†15208 Baldwin 24,598 .... B7
19503 Bally 1,051 .... L5
18013 Bangor 5,006 .... M4
15714 Barnesboro 2,741 .... E4
18014 Bath 1,953 .... M4
15009 Beaver⊙ 5,441 .... B4
15921 Beaverdale 1,187 .... E5
15010 Beaver Falls 12,525 .... B4
18216 Beaver Meadows 1,078 .... L4
15522 Bedford⊙ 3,326 .... F5
16823 Bellefonte⊙ 6,300 .... G4
15012 Belle Vernon 1,489 .... C5
17004 Belleville 1,689 .... G4
15202 Bellevue 10,128 .... B6
16617 Bellwood 2,114 .... F4
†15202 Ben Avon 2,314 .... B6
15314 Bentleyville 2,525 .... B5
15530 Berlin 1,999 .... E6
19506 Bernville 798 .... K5
18603 Berwick 11,850 .... K3
19312 Berwyn 5,246 .... L5
16112 Bessemer 1,293 .... B4
15102 Bethel Park 34,755 .... B7
*18015 Bethlehem 70,419 .... M4
19508 Birdsboro 3,481 .... L5
15716 Black Lick 1,313 .... D4
15717 Blairsville 4,166 .... D5
18447 Blakely 7,438 .... F6
15238 Blawnox 1,653 .... C6
17068 Bloomfield (New Bloomfield)⊙ 1,109 .... H5
17815 Bloomsburg⊙ 11,717 .... J3
16912 Blossburg 1,757 .... H2
16827 Boalsburg 2,295 .... G4
15315 Bobtown 1,008 .... B6
17007 Boiling Springs 2,223 .... H5
15923 Bolivar 706 .... D5
15531 Boswell 1,480 .... E5
18030 Bowmanstown 1,078 .... L4
19512 Boyertown 3,979 .... L5
15014 Brackenridge 4,297 .... C4
15104 Braddock 5,634 .... C7
16701 Bradford 11,211 .... E2
15227 Brentwood 11,907 .... B7
19405 Bridgeport 4,843 .... M5
15017 Bridgeville 6,154 .... B5
19007 Bristol 10,867 .... N5
19007 Bristol○ 58,733 .... N5
15824 Brockway 2,376 .... E3
19015 Brookhaven 7,912 .... M7
15825 Brookville⊙ 4,568 .... D3
19008 Broomall M6
15417 Brownsville 4,043 .... C5
19010 Bryn Mawr M5
15021 Burgettstown 1,867 .... A5
17009 Burnham 2,457 .... H4
16001 Butler⊙ 17,026 .... C4
15924 Cairnbrook 1,081 .... E5
15419 California 5,703 .... C5
16403 Cambridge Springs 2,102 .... C2
17011 Camp Hill 8,422 .... H5
15317 Canonsburg 10,459 .... B5
17724 Canton 1,959 .... J2
18407 Carbondale 11,255 .... L2
17013 Carlisle⊙ 18,314 .... H5
15106 Carnegie 10,099 .... B7
15722 Carrolltown 1,395 .... E4
15234 Castle Shannon 10,164 .... B7
18032 Catasauqua 6,711 .... M4
17820 Catawissa 1,568 .... K4
16404 Centerville 4,207 .... B6
15926 Central City 1,496 .... E5
17927 Centralia 1,017 .... K4
16828 Centre Hall 1,233 .... G4
18914 Chalfont 2,802 .... M5
17201 Chambersburg⊙ 16,174 .... G6
15022 Charleroi 5,717 .... C5
19012 Cheltenham○ 35,509 .... M5
*19013 Chester 45,794 .... L7
19017 Chester Heights 1,302 .... L7
†16866 Chester Hill 1,054 .... F4
15024 Cheswick 2,336 .... C6
16025 Chicora 1,192 .... C4
17509 Christiana 1,183 .... K6
†15235 Churchill 4,285 .... C7
15025 Clairton 12,188 .... C7
16214 Clarion⊙ 6,664 .... D3
†18411 Clarks Green 1,862 .... F6
18411 Clarks Summit 5,272 .... F6
16625 Claysburg 1,346 .... F5
15323 Claysville 1,029 .... B5
16830 Clearfield⊙ 7,580 .... F3
19018 Clifton Heights 7,320 .... M7
15728 Clymer 1,761 .... E4
18218 Coaldale 2,762 .... L4
19320 Coatesville 10,698 .... L5
16314 Cochranton 1,240 .... B2
19426 Collegeville 3,406 .... M5
19023 Collingdale 9,539 .... N7
17512 Columbia 10,466 .... K5
15927 Colver 1,165 .... E4
†19023 Colwyn 2,851 .... N7
15425 Connellsville 10,319 .... C5
19428 Conshohocken 8,475 .... M5
15027 Conway 2,747 .... B4
18219 Conyngham 2,242 .... K3
18036 Coopersburg 2,595 .... M5
18037 Coplay 3,130 .... L4
15108 Coraopolis 7,308 .... B4
17016 Cornwall 2,653 .... K5
16407 Corry 7,149 .... C2
16915 Coudersport⊙ 2,791 .... G2
15624 Crabtree 900 .... D5
15205 Crafton 7,623 .... B7
16630 Cresson 2,184 .... E5
17929 Cressona 1,810 .... K4
16833 Curwensville 3,116 .... E4
†15901 Dale 1,906 .... E5
18612 Dallas 2,679 .... E7
17313 Dallastown 3,949 .... J6
18414 Dalton 1,383 .... L2
17821 Danville⊙ 5,239 .... J4
19023 Darby 11,513 .... M7
18327 Delaware Water Gap 597 .... M4
15626 Delmont 2,159 .... D5
17517 Denver 2,018 .... K5
15627 Derry 3,072 .... D5
18519 Dickson City 6,699 .... F7
17019 Dillsburg 1,733 .... J5
15033 Donora 7,524 .... C5
15216 Dormont 11,275 .... B7
17315 Dover 1,910 .... J6
19335 Downingtown 7,650 .... L5
18901 Doylestown⊙ 8,717 .... M5
15034 Dravosburg 2,511 .... C7
19026 Drexel Hill M6
18221 Drifton 1,786 .... L3
18917 Dublin 1,565 .... M5
15801 DuBois 9,290 .... E3
†17701 Duboistown 1,218 .... H3
15431 Dunbar 1,369 .... C6
17020 Duncannon 1,645 .... H5
16635 Duncansville 1,355 .... F5
18512 Dunmore 16,781 .... F7
18641 Dupont 3,460 .... F7
15110 Duquesne 10,094 .... C7
18642 Duryea 5,415 .... F7
17316 East Berlin 1,054 .... J6
†18603 East Berwick 2,324 .... K3
16028 East Brady 1,153 .... C3
15909 East Conemaugh 2,128 .... E5
†17701 East Faxon 3,951 .... J3
18041 East Greenville 2,456 .... L5
†19050 East Lansdowne 2,806 .... M7
18042 Easton⊙ 26,027 .... M4
17520 East Petersburg 3,600 .... K5
18301 East Stroudsburg 8,039 .... M4
†15301 East Washington 2,241 .... B5
15931 Ebensburg⊙ 4,096 .... E5
†15005 Economy 9,538 .... B4
†19013 Eddystone 2,555 .... M7
†15218 Edgewood 4,382 .... B7
†15143 Edgeworth 1,738 .... B4
16412 Edinboro 6,324 .... B2
18704 Edwardsville 5,729 .... E7
16731 Eldred 965 .... F2
15037 Elizabeth 1,892 .... C5
17022 Elizabethtown 8,233 .... J5
17023 Elizabethville 1,531 .... J4
16920 Elkland 1,974 .... H1
15331 Ellsworth 1,228 .... B5
16117 Ellwood City 9,998 .... B4
17824 Elysburg 1,447 .... K4
17318 Emigsville 2,413 .... J5
16373 Emlenton 807 .... C3
18049 Emmaus 11,001 .... M4
15834 Emporium⊙ 2,837 .... F2
15202 Emsworth 3,074 .... B6
17025 Enola J5
17522 Ephrata 11,095 .... K5
*16501 Erie⊙ 119,123 .... B1
Erie‡ 279,780 .... B1
17815 Espy 1,571 .... K4
15223 Etna 4,534 .... B6
16033 Evans City 2,299 .... B4
15537 Everett 1,828 .... F5
15631 Everson 1,032 .... C5
15632 Export 1,143 .... C5
15436 Fairchance 2,106 .... C6
19030 Fairless Hills 16,000 .... N5
16415 Fairview 1,855 .... B1
15840 Falls Creek 1,208 .... E3
16121 Farrell 8,645 .... A3
17222 Fayetteville 3,202 .... G6
18921 Ferndale 2,204 .... E5
19522 Fleetwood 3,422 .... L5
†17745 Flemington 1,416 .... G3
19032 Folcroft 8,231 .... M7
16226 Ford City 3,923 .... D4
18421 Forest City 1,924 .... L2
†15221 Forest Hills 8,198 .... C7
18704 Forty Fort 5,590 .... F7
†18015 Fountain Hill 4,805 .... L4
†15238 Fox Chapel 5,049 .... C6
17931 Frackville 5,308 .... K4
16323 Franklin⊙ 8,146 .... C3
†16335 Fredericksburg 1,202 .... B2
15333 Fredericktown 1,052 .... C6
15042 Freedom 2,272 .... B4
18224 Freeland 4,285 .... L3
†18017 Freemansburg 1,879 .... M4
16229 Freeport 2,381 .... C4
16922 Galeton 1,462 .... G2
16641 Gallitzin 2,315 .... E4
†17701 Garden View 2,777 .... H3
15904 Geistown 3,304 .... E5
17325 Gettysburg⊙ 7,194 .... H6
17934 Gilberton 1,096 .... K4
16417 Girard 2,615 .... B2
17935 Girardville 2,268 .... K4
15045 Glassport 6,242 .... C7
18617 Glen Lyon 2,352 .... E7
19036 Glenolden 7,633 .... M7
17327 Glen Rock 1,662 .... J6
19038 Glenside M5
15634 Grapeville C5
18821 Great Bend 740 .... L2
17225 Greencastle 3,679 .... G6
15601 Greensburg⊙ 17,558 .... D5
15242 Greentree 5,722 .... B7
16125 Greenville 7,730 .... B3
16127 Grove City 8,162 .... B3
17032 Halifax 909 .... J5
17406 Hallam 1,428 .... J6
18822 Hallstead 1,280 .... L2
19526 Hamburg 4,011 .... L4
17331 Hanover 14,890 .... J6
16037 Harmony 1,334 .... B4
*17101 Harrisburg (cap.)⊙ 53,264 .... H5
Harrisburg‡ 446,072 .... H5
16038 Harrisville 1,033 .... B3
18618 Harveys Lake 2,318 .... E7
16646 Hastings 1,574 .... E4
19040 Hatboro 7,579 .... M5
19440 Hatfield 2,533 .... M5
19041 Haverford○ 52,349 .... M6
19083 Havertown M6
16840 Hawk Run 1,960 .... F4
18428 Hawley 1,181 .... M3
18201 Hazleton 27,318 .... L4
15106 Heidelberg 1,606 .... B7
17406 Hellam (Hallam) 1,428 .... J6
18055 Hellertown 6,025 .... M4
17033 Hershey 13,249 .... J5
†17044 Highland Park 1,879 .... H4
17034 Highspire 2,959 .... J5
16648 Hollidaysburg⊙ 5,892 .... F5
15748 Homer City 2,248 .... D4
15120 Homestead 5,092 .... B7
18431 Honesdale⊙ 5,128 .... M2
19344 Honey Brook 1,164 .... L5
15936 Hooversville 863 .... E5
15445 Hopwood 2,420 .... C6
15342 Houston 1,568 .... B5
16651 Houtzdale 1,222 .... F4
†18640 Hughestown 1,783 .... F7
17737 Hughesville 2,174 .... J3
17036 Hummelstown 4,267 .... J5
16652 Huntingdon⊙ 7,042 .... G5
16843 Hyde 1,791 .... F4
15545 Hyndman 1,106 .... E6
15126 Imperial 3,207 .... B5
15701 Indiana⊙ 16,051 .... D4
15052 Industry 2,417 .... B4
†15205 Ingram 4,346 .... B7
15642 Irwin 4,995 .... C5
17407 Jacobus 1,396 .... J6
15644 Jeannette 13,106 .... C5
†15025 Jefferson 8,643 .... B7
19046 Jenkintown 4,942 .... M5
18433 Jermyn 2,411 .... L2
15937 Jerome 1,196 .... D5
17740 Jersey Shore 4,631 .... H3
18434 Jessup 4,974 .... F6
18229 Jim Thorpe⊙ 5,263 .... L4
15845 Johnsonburg 3,938 .... E3
*15901 Johnstown 35,496 .... D5
Johnstown‡ 264,506 .... D5
16735 Kane 4,916 .... E2
†19607 Kenhorst 3,187 .... L5
19348 Kennett Square 4,715 .... L6
18704 Kingston 15,681 .... F7
16201 Kittanning⊙ 5,432 .... D4
16232 Knox 1,364 .... C3
16136 Koppel 1,146 .... B4
17834 Kulpmont 3,675 .... J4
19530 Kutztown 4,040 .... L4
16423 Lake City 2,384 .... B1
*17601 Lancaster⊙ 54,725 .... K5
Lancaster‡ 362,346 .... K5

(continued on following page)

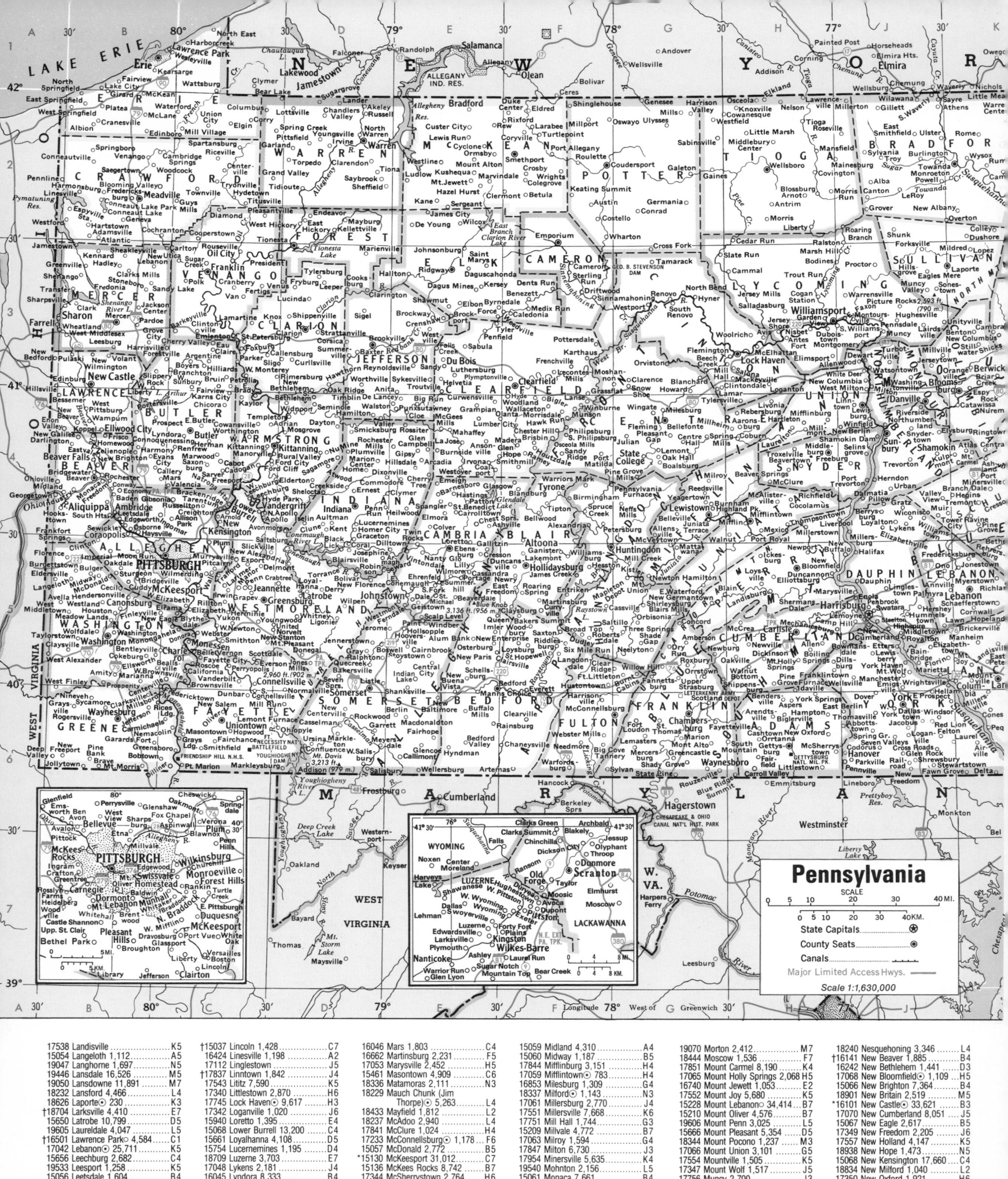

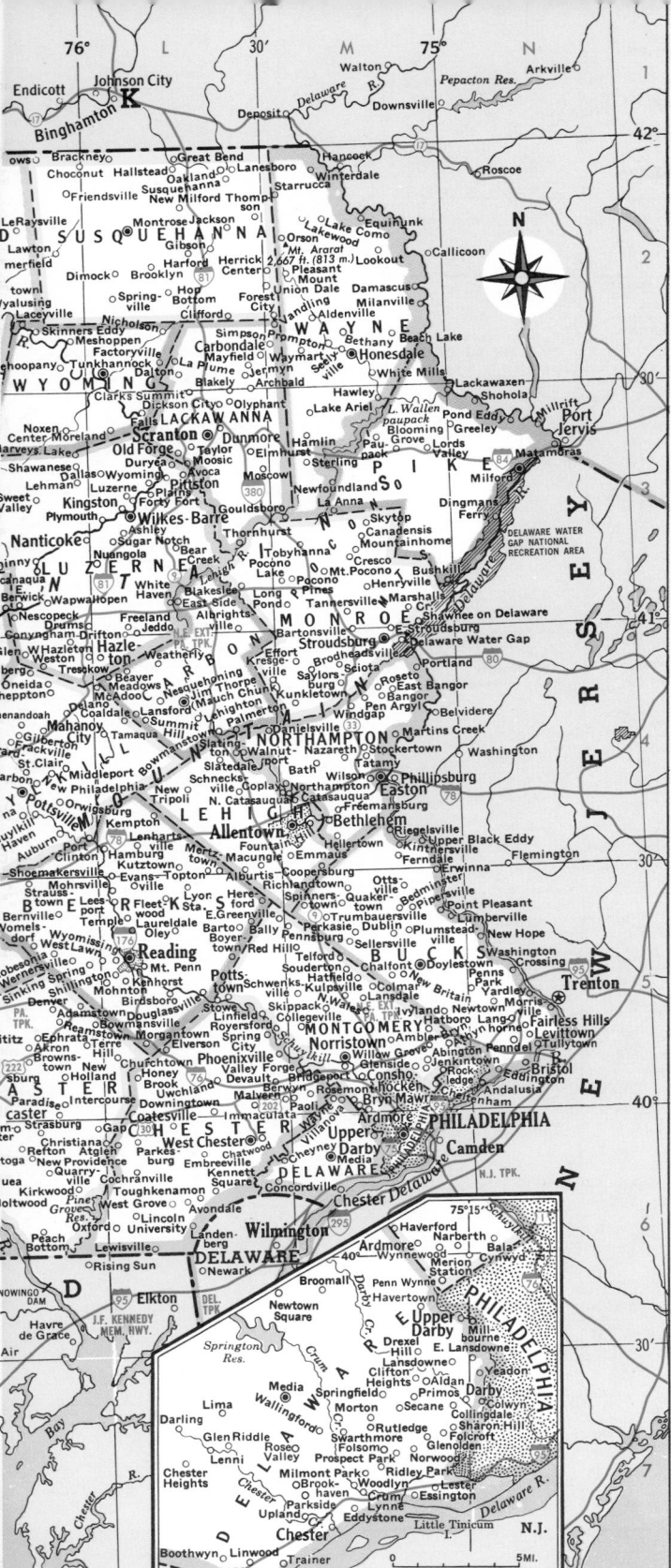

16823 Pleasant Gap 1,859	G4
15236 Pleasant Hills 9,676	B7
16341 Pleasantville 1,099	C2
15239 Plum 25,390	C5
18651 Plymouth 7,605	E7
15474 Point Marion 1,642	C6
16342 Polk 1,884	C3
15946 Portage 3,510	E5
16743 Port Allegany 2,593	F2
17965 Port Carbon 2,576	K4
†15133 Port Vue 5,316	C7
19464 Pottstown 22,729	L5
17901 Pottsville‡ 18,195	K4
19076 Prospect Park 6,593	M7
15767 Punxsutawney 7,479	E4
18951 Quakertown 8,867	M5
17566 Quarryville 1,558	K6
†15104 Rankin 2,892	C7
*19601 Reading 78,686	L5
Reading‡ 312,509	L5
17567 Reamstown 1,308	K5
18076 Red Hill 1,727	L5
17356 Red Lion 5,824	J6
17084 Reedsville 1,023	G4
17764 Renovo 1,812	G3
15851 Reynoldsville 3,016	D3
17087 Richland 1,470	K5
18955 Richlandtown 1,180	M5
15853 Ridgway 5,604	E3
19078 Ridley Park 7,889	M7
18077 Riegelsville 993	M4
16248 Rimersburg 1,096	D3
17868 Riverside 2,266	J4
16673 Roaring Spring 2,962	F5
19551 Robesonia 1,748	K5
15074 Rochester 4,759	B4
†19101 Rockledge 2,538	M5
15557 Rockwood 1,058	D6
15477 Roscoe 1,123	C5
18013 Roseto 1,484	M4
†19065 Rose Valley 1,038	L7
19078 Rouzerville 1,371	G6
19468 Royersford 4,243	L5
16249 Rural Valley 1,033	D4
15076 Russellton 1,878	C4
17970 Saint Clair 4,037	K4
15857 Saint Marys 6,417	E3
15951 Saint Michael 1,445	E5
15681 Saltsburg 964	C4
†15801 Sandy 1,835	E3
16056 Saxonburg 1,336	C4
18840 Sayre 6,951	K2
†15963 Scalp Level 1,186	E5
17972 Schuylkill Haven 5,977	K4
19473 Schwenksville 1,041	L5
15683 Scottdale 5,833	C5
*18501 Scranton⊙ 88,117	F7
Scranton (Northeast Pa.)‡ 640,396	F7
17870 Selinsgrove 5,227	J4
18960 Sellersville 3,143	M5
15143 Sewickley 4,778	B4
18872 Shamokin 10,357	J4
17876 Shamokin Dam 1,622	J4
16146 Sharon 19,057	B3
Sharon‡ 128,299	B3
19079 Sharon Hill 6,221	N7
15215 Sharpsburg 4,351	B6
16150 Sharpsville 5,375	A3
16347 Sheffield 1,471	D2
17976 Shenandoah 7,589	K4
18655 Shickshinny 1,192	K3
19607 Shillington 5,601	K5
16748 Shinglehouse 1,197	F2
17257 Shippensburg 5,261	H5
19555 Shoemakersville 1,391	K4
17361 Shrewsbury 2,688	J6
19608 Sinking Spring 2,617	K5
18080 Slatington 4,277	L4
15684 Slickville 1,178	C5
16057 Slippery Rock 3,047	B3
16749 Smethport 1,797	F2
15478 Smithfield 1,084	C6
15501 Somerset⊙ 6,474	D6
18964 Souderton 6,657	M5
15425 South Connellsville 2,296	C6
15956 South Fork 1,401	E5
†18840 South Waverly 1,176	J2

17701 South Williamsport 6,581	J3
15775 Spangler 2,399	E4
19475 Spring City 3,389	L5
15144 Springdale 4,418	C6
19064 Springfield 25,326	M7
17362 Spring Grove 1,832	J6
16801 State College 36,130	G4
State College‡ 112,760	G4
17263 State Line 1,253	H6
17113 Steelton 6,484	J5
17363 Stewartstown 1,072	K6
16153 Stoneboro 1,177	B3
19464 Stowe 3,860	L5
17579 Strasburg 1,999	K6
18360 Stroudsburg⊙ 5,148	M4
15082 Sturgeon 1,312	B7
†16323 Sugar Creek 5,954	C3
18706 Sugar Notch 1,191	E7
18250 Summit Hill 3,418	L4
17801 Sunbury⊙ 12,292	J4
18847 Susquehanna 1,994	L2
19081 Swarthmore 5,950	M7
†17111 Swatara⊙ 18,796	J5
15218 Swissvale 11,345	C7
18704 Swoyersville 5,795	E7
15865 Sykesville 1,537	E3
18252 Tamaqua 8,843	L4
15084 Tarentum 6,419	C4
18517 Taylor 7,246	F7
17980 Telford 3,507	M5
19560 Temple 1,486	L5
17581 Terre Hill 1,217	L5
18512 Throop 4,166	F7
16351 Tidioute 844	D2
16353 Tionesta⊙ 659	C2
16684 Tipton 1,348	F4
16354 Titusville 6,884	C2
19562 Topton 1,818	L5
19374 Toughkenamon 1,111	L6
18848 Towanda⊙ 3,526	J2
17980 Tower City 1,667	J4
15085 Trafford 3,662	C5
†19013 Trainer 2,056	L7
17981 Tremont 1,796	K4
18254 Tresckow 1,128	K4
17881 Trevorton 2,192	J4
16947 Troy 1,381	J2
19007 Tullytown 2,007	N5
15145 Turtle Creek 6,959	C7
16686 Tyrone 6,346	F4
16438 Union City 3,623	C2
15401 Uniontown⊙ 14,510	C6
†19013 Upland 3,458	L7
*19082 Upper Darby⊙ 84,054	M6
15241 Upper Saint Claire⊙ 19,023	B7
19481 Valley Forge 400	L5
17983 Valley View 1,722	J4
15690 Vandergrift 6,823	C4
15147 Verona 3,179	C6
15132 Versailles 2,150	C7
19085 Villanova 1	M6
18088 Walnutport 2,007	L4
16365 Warren⊙ 12,146	D2
15301 Washington⊙ 18,363	B5
16441 Waterford 1,568	C2
17777 Watsontown 2,366	J3
19087 Wayne	M6
17268 Waynesboro 9,726	G6
15370 Waynesburg⊙ 4,482	B6
18255 Weatherly 2,891	L4
16901 Wellsboro⊙ 3,805	H1
19565 Wernersville 1,811	K5
16510 Wesleyville 3,998	C1
15417 West Brownsville 1,433	C5
19380 West Chester⊙ 17,435	L6
16950 Westfield 1,268	H2
19390 West Grove 1,820	L6
18201 West Hazleton 4,871	K4
†16201 West Kittanning 1,591	C4
16159 West Middlesex 1,064	B3
15122 West Mifflin 26,279	C7
†15905 Westmont 6,113	D5
15089 West Newton 3,387	C5
16160 West Pittsburg 1,133	B4
18643 West Pittston 5,980	F7
15229 West View 7,648	B6

18644 West Wyoming 3,288	E7
†17401 West York 4,526	J6
15120 Whitaker 1,615	C7
†15234 Whitehall 15,206	B7
18661 White Haven 1,921	L3
15131 White Oak 9,480	C7
17097 Wiconisco 1,321	J4
*18701 Wilkes-Barre⊙ 51,551	F7
15221 Wilkinsburg 23,669	C7
16693 Williamsburg 1,400	F5
17701 Williamsport⊙ 33,401	H3
Williamsport‡ 118,416	H3
17098 Williamstown 1,664	J4
19090 Willow Grove	M5
15148 Wilmerding 2,421	C5
15025 Wilson 7,564	M4
15963 Windber 5,585	E5
18091 Windgap 2,651	M4
19567 Womelsdorf 1,827	K5
19094 Woodlyn	M7
17368 Wrightsville 2,365	J5
18644 Wyoming 3,655	E7
19610 Wyomissing 6,551	L5
19067 Yardley 2,533	N5
17099 Yeagertown 1,305	G4
*17401 York⊙ 44,619	J6
York‡ 381,255	J6
16371 Youngsville 2,006	D2
15697 Youngwood 3,749	D5
16063 Zelienople 3,502	B4

OTHER FEATURES

Allegheny (res.)	E2
Allegheny (riv.)	D2
Allegheny Front (mts.)	E5
Appalachian (mts.)	H4
Ararat (mt.)	M2
Arthur (lake)	C4
Beaver (riv.)	B4
Blue (mt.)	G5
Blue Knob (mt.)	E5
Casselman (riv.)	D6
Clarion (riv.)	D3
Conemaugh (riv.)	D5
Conemaugh River (lake)	D4
Conewango (creek)	D1
Davis (mt.)	D6
Delaware (riv.)	N3
Delaware Water Gap Nat'l Rec. Area	N3
Erie (lake)	B1
Fort Necessity Nat'l Battlefield	C6
George B. Stevenson (dam)	G3
Gettysburg Nat'l Mil. Park	H6
Glendale (lake)	F4
Juniata (riv.)	G5
Laurel Hill (mt.)	D5
Lehigh (riv.)	L3
Letterkenny Army Depot	G6
Licking (creek)	F6
Little Tinicum (isl.)	M7
Lycoming (creek)	H3
Monongahela (riv.)	C6
North (mt.)	K3
Ohio (riv.)	A4
Oil (creek)	C2
Pine (creek)	H2
Pine Grove (res.)	L5
Pocono (mts.)	M3
Pymatuning (res.)	A2
Redbank (creek)	E3
Schuylkill (riv.)	L5
Shenango River (lake)	B3
Sinnemahoning (creek)	F3
South (mt.)	H6
Susquehanna (riv.)	K6
Tioga (riv.)	H1
Tionesta Creek (lake)	D3
Towanda (creek)	J2
Tuscarora (mt.)	G5
Wallenpaupack (lake)	M3
Youghiogheny River (lake)	D6

⊙County seat.
‡Population of metropolitan area.
⊙Population of town or township.
† Zip of nearest p.o. * Multiple zips.

Topography

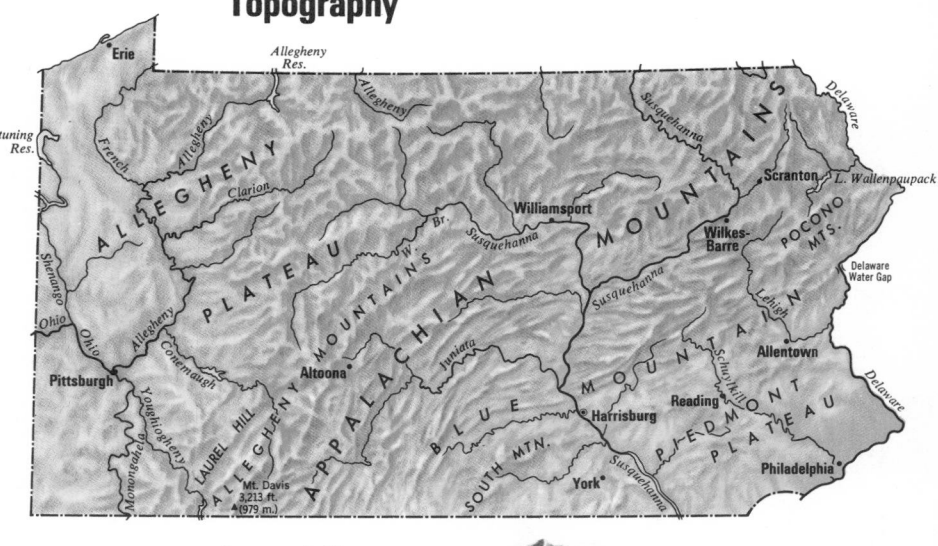

5,000 m. 16,404 ft.	2,000 m. 6,562 ft.	1,000 m. 3,281 ft.	500 m. 1,640 ft.	200 m. 656 ft.	100 m. 328 ft.	Sea Level Below

18067 Northampton 8,240	M4
15673 North Apollo 1,487	D4
15104 North Braddock 8,711	C7
†18032 North Catasauqua 2,554	L4
16428 North East 4,568	C1
17857 Northumberland 3,636	J4
19454 North Wales 3,391	M5
†16365 North Warren 1,232	D2
15074 Norvelt 2,541	D5
19074 Norwood 6,647	M7
15071 Oakdale 1,955	B5
15139 Oakmont 7,039	C6
†15059 Ohioville 4,217	B4
16301 Oil City 13,881	C3
18518 Old Forge 9,304	F7
15472 Oliver 3,777	C6
18447 Olyphant 5,204	F7
17961 Orwigsburg 2,700	K4
16666 Osceola Mills 1,466	F4
19363 Oxford 3,633	K6
†15963 Paint 1,177	E5
18071 Palmerton 5,455	L4
17078 Palmyra 7,228	J5
19301 Paoli 5,277	M5

17562 Paradise 1,107	K5
19365 Parkesburg 2,578	L6
†19013 Parkside 2,464	M7
†17331 Parkville 5,009	J6
16668 Patton 2,441	E4
18072 Pen Argyl 3,388	M4
17103 Penbrook 3,006	J5
19047 Penndel 2,703	N5
18073 Pennsburg 2,339	M5
†17331 Pennville 1,398	J6
†19151 Penn Wynne	M6
18944 Perkasie 5,241	M5
15473 Perryopolis 2,139	C5
*19101 Philadelphia⊙ 1,688,210	N6
Philadelphia‡ 4,716,818	N6
16866 Philipsburg 3,533	F4
19460 Phoenixville 14,165	L5
17963 Pine Grove 2,244	K4
16868 Pine Grove Mills 1,030	G4
15140 Pitcairn 4,175	C5
*15201 Pittsburgh⊙ 423,938	B7
Pittsburgh‡ 2,263,894	B7
†18640 Pittston 9,930	F7
†18701 Plains 5,455	F7

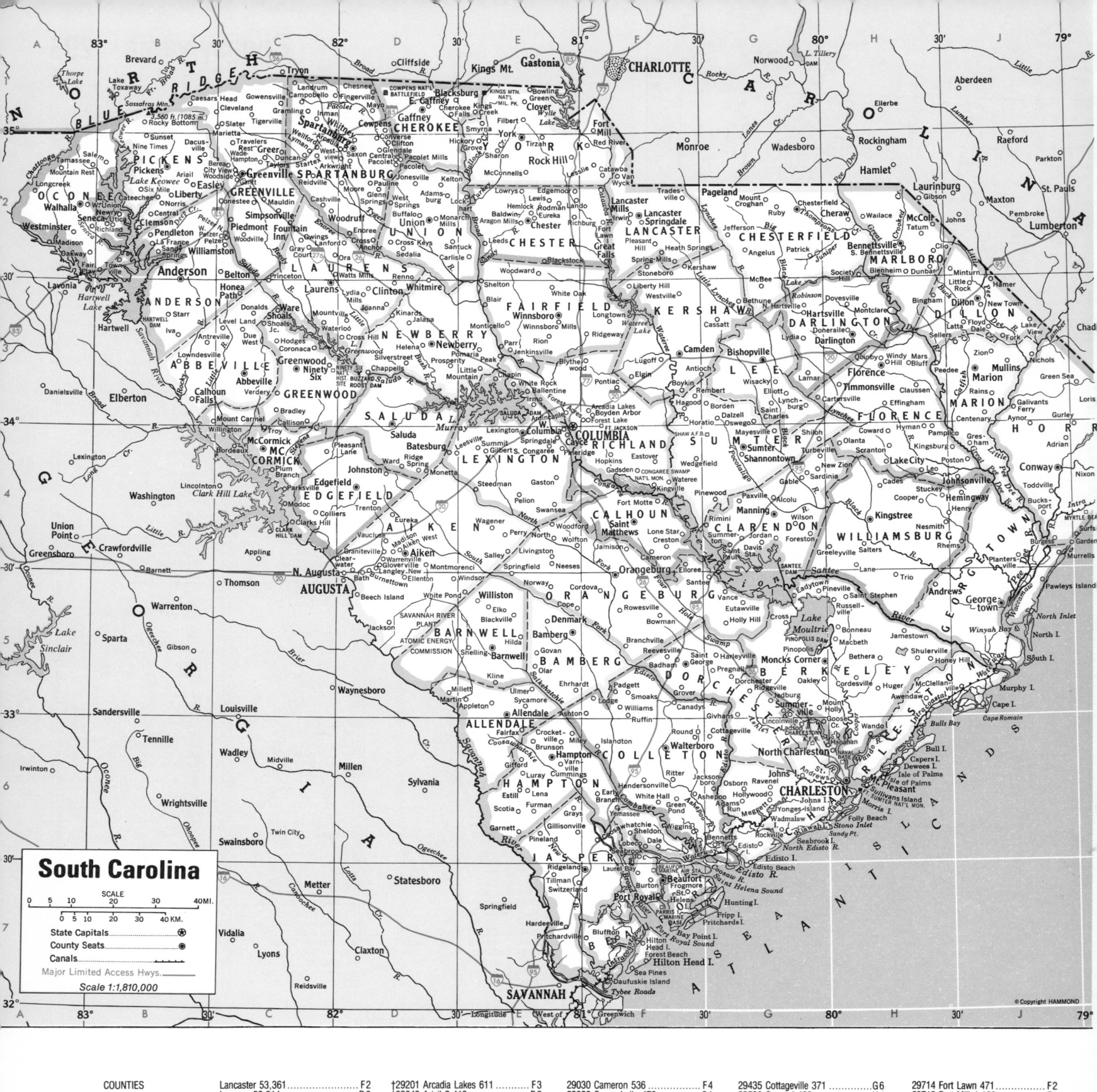

COUNTIES

Abbeville 22,627	B3
Aiken 105,625	D4
Allendale 10,700	E6
Anderson 133,235	B2
Bamberg 18,118	E5
Barnwell 19,868	E5
Beaufort 65,364	F7
Berkeley 94,727	G5
Calhoun 12,206	F4
Charleston 276,974	H6
Cherokee 40,983	D1
Chester 30,148	E2
Chesterfield 38,161	G2
Clarendon 27,464	G4
Colleton 31,776	F6
Darlington 62,717	H3
Dillon 31,083	J3
Dorchester 58,761	G5
Edgefield 17,528	D4
Fairfield 20,700	E3
Florence 110,163	H3
Georgetown 42,461	J5
Greenville 287,913	C2
Greenwood 57,847	C3
Hampton 18,159	E6
Horry 101,419	J4
Jasper 14,504	E6
Kershaw 39,015	F3

Lancaster 53,361	F2
Laurens 52,214	D2
Lee 18,929	G3
Lexington 140,353	E4
Marion 34,179	J3
Marlboro 31,634	H2
McCormick 7,797	C4
Newberry 31,242	D3
Oconee 48,611	A2
Orangeburg 82,276	F5
Pickens 79,292	B2
Richland 269,735	F4
Saluda 16,150	D3
Spartanburg 201,861	D2
Sumter 88,243	G4
Union 30,764	D2
Williamsburg 38,226	H4
York 106,720	E2

CITIES and TOWNS

Zip	Name/Pop.	Key
29620	Abbeville⊙ 5,833	C3
29801	Aiken⊙ 14,978	D4
†29801	Aiken West 3,083	D4
29810	Allendale⊙ 4,400	E5
*29621	Anderson⊙ 27,965	B2
	Anderson‡ 133,235	B2
29510	Andrews 3,129	H5
29320	Arcadia 2,088	C2
†29201	Arcadia Lakes 611	F3
†29640	Ariail 2,419	B2
†29301	Arkwright 2,623	C2
†29582	Atlantic Beach 289	K4
29511	Aynor 643	J3
29003	Bamberg⊙ 3,672	E5
29812	Barnwell⊙ 5,572	E5
29006	Batesburg 4,023	D4
29816	Bath 2,242	D5
29902	Beaufort⊙ 8,634	F7
29627	Belton 5,312	C2
29512	Bennettsville⊙ 8,774	H2
29611	Berea 13,164	C2
29009	Bethune 481	G3
29010	Bishopville⊙ 3,429	G3
29702	Blacksburg 1,873	D1
29817	Blackville 2,840	E5
29516	Bonheim 202	H2
29910	Bluffton 541	F7
29016	Blythewood 92	F3
29431	Bonneau 401	H5
29018	Bowman 1,137	F5
29432	Branchville 1,769	F5
29911	Brunson 590	E6
29527	Bucksport 1,125	J4
29321	Buffalo 1,641	D2
29628	Calhoun Falls 2,491	B3
29020	Camden⊙ 7,462	F3

Zip	Name/Pop.	Key
29030	Cameron 536	F4
29322	Campobello 472	C1
29031	Carlisle 503	D2
29169	Cayce 11,701	E4
29519	Centenary 700	J3
29630	Central 1,914	B2
†29372	Central Pacolet 315	D2
29036	Chapin 311	E3
29037	Chappells 109	D3
*29401	Charleston⊙ 69,510	G6
	Charleston-North	
	Charleston‡ 430,301	G6
29520	Cheraw 5,654	H2
29323	Chesnee 1,069	D1
29706	Chester⊙ 6,820	E2
29709	Chesterfield⊙ 1,432	G2
29611	City View 1,662	C2
29822	Clearwater 3,967	D4
29631	Clemson 8,118	B2
29635	Cleveland 800	C1
29324	Clifton 950	D2
29325	Clinton 8,596	D3
29525	Clio 1,031	H2
29710	Clover 3,451	E1
*29201	Columbia (cap.)⊙ 100,385	F4
	Columbia‡ 408,176	F4
29329	Converse 1,173	D2
†29834	Burnettown 359	D5
29526	Conway⊙ 10,240	J4
29038	Cope 167	F5
29039	Cordova 202	F5

Zip	Name/Pop.	Key
29435	Cottageville 371	G6
29530	Coward 428	H4
29330	Cowpens 2,023	D1
29332	Cross Hill 604	D3
29532	Darlington⊙ 7,989	H3
29042	Denmark 4,434	E5
29536	Dillon⊙ 7,060	J3
29638	Donalds 366	C3
†29532	Doneraile 1,276	H3
29639	Due West 1,366	C3
29334	Duncan 1,259	C2
29640	Easley⊙ 14,264	B2
†29340	East Gaffney 4,092	D1
29044	Eastover 899	F4
29824	Edgefield⊙ 2,713	C4
†29438	Edisto Beach 193	G7
29438	Edisto Island 900	G6
29081	Ehrhardt 353	E5
29045	Elgin 595	F3
29826	Elko 329	E5
29047	Elloree 909	F4
29335	Enoree 1,107	D2
29918	Estill 2,308	E6
†29706	Eureka 1,627	D2
29048	Eutawville 615	G5
29827	Fairfax 2,154	E6
29501	Florence⊙ 29,176	H3
	Florence‡ 110,163	H3
29439	Folly Beach 1,478	H6
29206	Forest Acres 6,071	E3

Zip	Name/Pop.	Key
29714	Fort Lawn 471	F2
29715	Fort Mill 4,162	F1
29050	Fort Motte 700	F4
29644	Fountain Inn 4,226	C2
29921	Furman 348	E6
29340	Gaffney⊙ 13,453	D1
†29609	Gantt 13,719	C2
29053	Gaston 960	E4
29440	Georgetown⊙ 10,144	J5
29923	Gifford 385	E6
29054	Gilbert 211	E4
29346	Glendale 1,049	D2
29828	Gloverville 2,619	D4
29445	Goose Creek 17,811	H6
†29843	Govan 109	E5
29645	Gray Court 988	C2
29055	Great Falls 2,601	F2
29056	Greeleyville 593	H4
*29601	Greenville⊙ 58,242	C2
	Greenville-Spartanburg‡ 568,758	C2
29646	Greenwood⊙ 21,613	C3
29651	Greer 10,525	C2
29924	Hampton⊙ 3,143	E6
29410	Hanahan 13,224	H6
29927	Hardeville 1,250	E7
29448	Harleyville 606	G5
29550	Hartsville 7,631	G3
29058	Heath Springs 979	F2

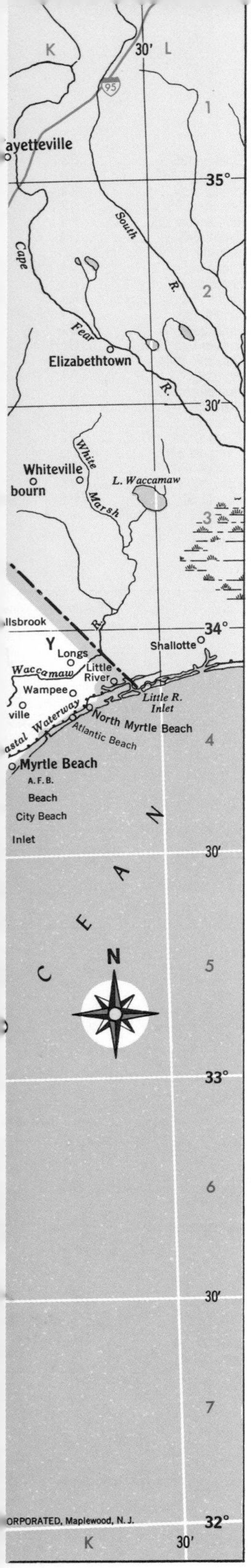
ayetteville
Cape Fear R.
South R.
Elizabethtown
Whiteville
L. Waccamaw
White Marsh
Shallotte
Longs
Little River
Wampee
Little R. Inlet
North Myrtle Beach
Atlantic Beach
Myrtle Beach
A.F.B.
Beach
City Beach
Inlet
N
ORPORATED, Maplewood, N. J.

Agriculture, Industry and Resources

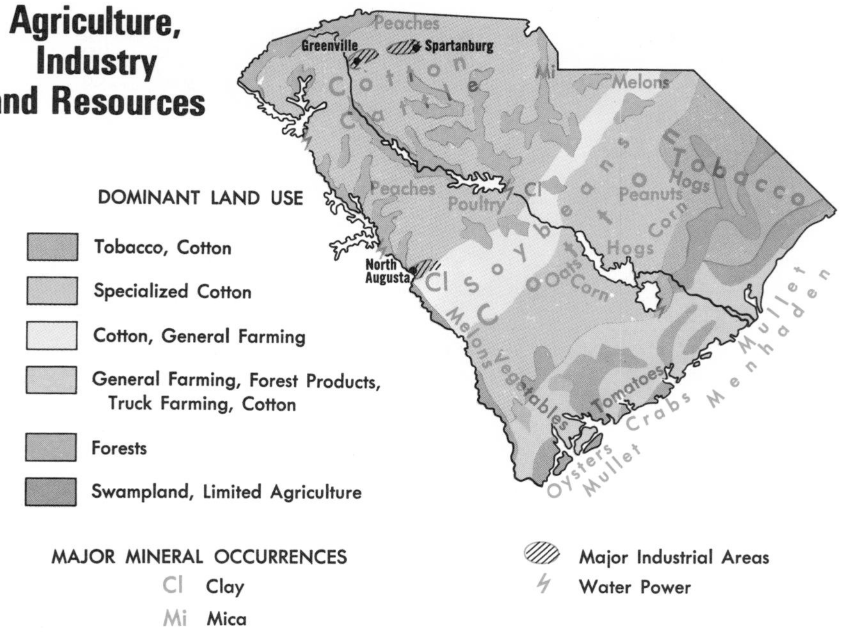
Greenville
Spartanburg
North Augusta
Peaches
Cotton
Cattle
Melons
Tobacco
Hogs
Peanuts
Corn
Poultry
Soybeans
Oats
Vegetables
Tomatoes
Oysters
Mullet
Crabs
Menhaden
DOMINANT LAND USE
Tobacco, Cotton
Specialized Cotton
Cotton, General Farming
General Farming, Forest Products, Truck Farming, Cotton
Forests
Swampland, Limited Agriculture
MAJOR MINERAL OCCURRENCES
Cl Clay
Mi Mica
Major Industrial Areas
Water Power

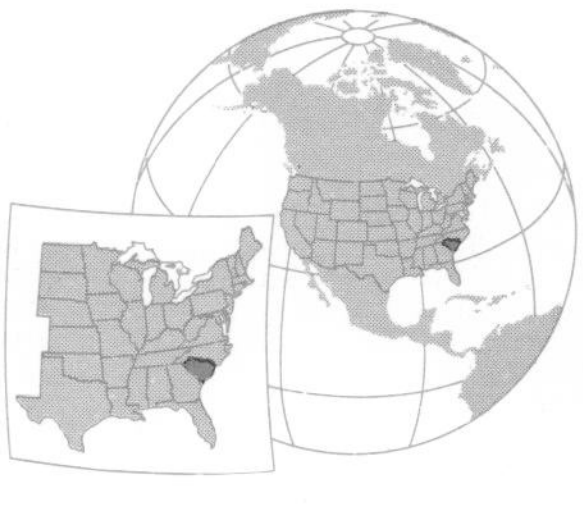

AREA 31,113 sq. mi. (80,583 sq. km.)
POPULATION 3,121,833
CAPITAL Columbia
LARGEST CITY Columbia
HIGHEST POINT Sassafras Mtn. 3,560 ft. (1085 m.)
SETTLED IN 1670
ADMITTED TO UNION May 23, 1788
POPULAR NAME Palmetto State
STATE FLOWER Carolina (Yellow) Jessamine
STATE BIRD Carolina Wren

29554	Hemingway 853	J4
†29706	Hemlock (Eureka) 1,627	E2
29717	Hickory Grove 344	E2
29813	Hilda 355	E5
29928	Hilton Head Island 11,344	F7
29653	Hodges 154	C3
29059	Holly Hill 1,785	G5
29449	Hollywood 729	G6
29654	Honea Path 4,114	C3
29349	Inman 1,554	C1
29063	Irmo 3,957	E3
†29720	Irwin 1,373	F2
29451	Isle of Palms 3,421	H6
29655	Iva 1,369	B3
29831	Jackson 1,771	D5
29453	Jamestown 193	H5
†29483	Jedburg 900	G5
29718	Jefferson 651	G2
29351	Joanna 1,839	D3
29555	Johnsonville 1,421	J4
29832	Johnston 2,624	D4
29353	Jonesville 1,201	D2
29067	Kershaw 1,993	G2
29556	Kingstree⊙ 4,147	H4
29814	Kline 315	E5
29456	Ladson 13,246	G6
29560	Lake City 6,731	H4
29563	Lake View 939	J3
29069	Lamar 1,333	G3
29720	Lancaster⊙ 9,703	F2
†29720	Lancaster Mills 2,096	F2
29356	Landrum 2,141	C1
29564	Lane 554	H5
29834	Langley 1,714	D4
29565	Latta 1,804	J3
29902	Laurel Bay 5,238	F7
29360	Laurens⊙ 10,587	C3
29070	Leesville 2,296	E4
†29730	Lesslie 1,102	E2
29072	Lexington⊙ 2,131	E4
29657	Liberty 3,167	B2
†29483	Lincolnville 808	G6
29075	Little Mountain 282	E3
29076	Livingston 166	E4
29364	Lockhart 85	E2
29082	Lodge 145	F5
29569	Loris 2,193	K3
29659	Lowndesville 197	B3
†29706	Lowrys 225	E2
29078	Lugoff 2,939	F3
29932	Luray 149	E6
29325	Lydia Mills 925	D3
29365	Lyman 1,067	C2
29080	Lynchburg 534	G3
†29829	Madison 1,150	D4
29102	Manning⊙ 4,746	G4
29661	Marietta-Slater 1,834	C1
29571	Marion⊙ 7,700	J3
29662	Mauldin 8,143	C2
29104	Mayesville 663	G4
29101	McBee 774	G3
29458	McClellanville 436	H5
29570	McColl 2,677	H2
29726	McConnells 171	E2
29835	McCormick⊙ 1,725	C4
29460	Meggett 249	G6
†29379	Monarch Mills 2,353	D2
29461	Moncks Corner⊙ 3,699	G5
29105	Monetta 167	D4
29840	Mount Carmel 182	C3
29727	Mount Croghan 146	G2
29464	Mount Pleasant 14,209	H6
29574	Mullins 6,068	J3
29576	Murrells Inlet 2,410	K4
29577	Myrtle Beach 18,446	K4
29107	Neeses 557	E4
29108	Newberry⊙ 9,866	D3
29809	New Ellenton 2,628	D5
†29536	New Town 950	J3
29581	Nichols 606	J3
29666	Ninety Six 2,249	C3
29667	Norris 903	B2
29112	North 1,304	E4
29841	North Augusta 13,593	C5
29406	North Charleston 62,534	G6
†29550	North Hartsville 2,650	G3
29582	North Myrtle Beach 3,960	K4
29113	Norway 518	E5
29114	Olanta 699	H4
29843	Olar 381	E5
29115	Orangeburg⊙ 14,933	F4
29372	Pacolet 1,556	D2
29373	Pacolet Mills 1,051	D2
29728	Pageland 2,720	G2
29583	Pamplico 1,213	H4
29844	Parksville 157	C4
29584	Patrick 375	G2
29102	Paxville 244	G4
29122	Peak 82	E3
29123	Pelion 213	E4
29669	Pelzer 130	B2
29670	Pendleton 3,154	B2
29124	Perry 273	E4
29671	Pickens⊙ 3,199	B2
29673	Piedmont 2,992	C2
29934	Pineland 800	E6
†29169	Pineridge 1,287	E4
29468	Pineville 900	H5
29125	Pinewood 689	G4
29469	Pinopolis 788	G5
29845	Plum Branch 73	C4
29126	Pomaria 271	E3
29935	Port Royal 2,977	F7
29127	Prosperity 803	D3
†29501	Quinby 952	H3
29470	Ravenel 1,655	G6
29471	Reevesville 241	F5
29729	Richburg 269	E2
29936	Ridgeland⊙ 1,143	E7
29129	Ridge Spring 969	D4
29472	Ridgeville 603	G5
29130	Ridgeway 343	F3
29730	Rock Hill 35,344	E2
	Rock Hill‡ 106,720	E2
29133	Rowesville 388	F5
29741	Ruby 256	G2
29407	Saint Andrews 9,908	G6
29477	Saint George⊙ 2,134	F5
29135	Saint Matthews⊙ 2,496	F4
29479	Saint Stephen 1,850	H5
29676	Salem 194	A2
29137	Salley 584	E4
29138	Saluda⊙ 2,752	D4
29142	Santee 612	F5
†29301	Saxon 4,383	D2
29939	Scotia 72	E6
29591	Scranton 861	H4
29592	Sellers 388	H3
29678	Seneca 7,436	A2
29742	Sharon 323	E2
29145	Silverstreet 200	D3
29681	Simpsonville 9,037	C2
29682	Six Mile 470	B2
29683	Slater-Marietta 1,834	C1
29481	Smoaks 165	F5
29743	Smyrna 47	E1
†29812	Snelling 111	E5
29593	Society Hill 848	H2
†29512	South Bennettsville 1,065	H2
†29169	South Congaree 2,113	E4
*29301	Spartanburg⊙ 43,826	C1
29169	Springdale 2,985	E4
†29720	Springdale 2,570	F2
29146	Springfield 604	E4
†29067	Spring Mills 1,419	F2
29684	Starr 241	B3
29377	Startex 1,006	C2
29554	Stuckey 222	H4
29482	Sullivans Island 1,867	H6
29148	Summerton 1,173	G4
29483	Summerville 6,706	G5
†29054	Summit 172	E4
29150	Sumter⊙ 24,890	G4
29577	Surfside Beach 2,522	K4
29160	Swansea 888	E4
29846	Sycamore 261	E5
29594	Tatum 101	H2
29687	Taylors 15,801	C2
29688	Tigerville 975	C1
29161	Timmonsville 2,112	H3
29690	Travelers Rest 3,017	C2
29847	Trenton 404	D4
29848	Troy 705	C4
29162	Turbeville 549	G4
29849	Ulmer 91	E5
29379	Union⊙ 10,523	D2
†29678	Utica 1,501	B2
29163	Vance 89	G5
29944	Varnville 1,948	E6
†29607	Wade-Hampton 20,180	C2
29164	Wagener 903	E4
29691	Walhalla⊙ 3,977	A2
29488	Walterboro⊙ 6,209	F6
29166	Ward 98	D4
29692	Ware Shoals 2,370	C3
29851	Warrenville 1,029	D4
29384	Waterloo 200	C3
†29360	Watts Mills 1,324	D2
29385	Wellford 2,143	C2
29169	West Columbia 10,409	E4
29693	Westminster 3,114	A2
29669	West Pelzer 944	B2
29696	West Union 300	B2
†29301	Westview 1,999	C2
29178	Whitmire 2,038	D3
29303	Whitney 4,052	D1
29493	Williams 205	F5
29697	Williamston 4,310	B2
29853	Williston 3,173	E5
29856	Windsor 55	E5
†29501	Windy Hill 1,622	H3
29180	Winnsboro⊙ 2,919	E3
†29180	Winnsboro Mills 1,890	E3
†29112	Woodford 206	E4
29388	Woodruff 5,171	D2
29945	Yemassee 789	F6
29745	York⊙ 6,412	E1

OTHER FEATURES

Ashepoo (riv.)	F6
Ashley (riv.)	G6
Bay Point (isl.)	F7
Beaufort Marine Air Sta.	F7
Big Black (creek)	G2
Black (riv.)	H4
Blue Ridge (mts.)	B1
Broad (riv.)	E2
Broad (riv.)	F7
Buck (creek)	J3
Bull (isl.)	H6
Bullock (creek)	E2
Bulls (bay)	H6
Bush (riv.)	D3
Buzzard Roost (dam)	D3
Cape (isl.)	J5
Capers (isl.)	H6
Catawba (riv.)	F2
Catfish (creek)	J3
Charleston A.F.B.	G6
Chattooga (riv.)	A2
Clark Hill (dam)	C4
Clark Hill (lake)	C4
Combahee (riv.)	F6
Congaree (riv.)	F4
Congaree Nat'l Mon.	F4
Cooper (riv.)	H6
Coosaw (riv.)	G7
Coosawhatchie (riv.)	E6
Cowpens Nat'l Battlefield	D1
Crooked (creek)	H2
Deep (creek)	B2
Dewees (isl.)	H6
Donaldson A.F.B.	C2
Edisto (isl.)	G6
Edisto (riv.)	G7
Enoree (riv.)	C2
Fort Jackson	F4
Fort Sumter Nat'l Mon.	H6
Four Hole Swamp (creek)	F5
Fripp (isl.)	G7
Great Pee Dee (riv.)	J4
Greenwood (lake)	D3
Hartwell (dam)	B3
Hartwell (lake)	A3
Hilton Head (isl.)	F7
Hunting (isl.)	G7
Intracoastal Waterway	H5
James (isl.)	H6
Johns (isl.)	G6
Juniper (creek)	H2
Keowee (lake)	B2
Keowee (riv.)	B2
Kiawah (isl.)	G6
Kings Mountain Nat'l Mil. Park	E1
Little (riv.)	C3
Little (riv.)	D3
Little Lynches (riv.)	G3
Little Pee Dee (riv.)	J4
Little River (inlet)	L4
Lumber (riv.)	J3
Lynches (riv.)	H3
Marion (lake)	G5
Morris (isl.)	H6
Moultrie (lake)	G5
Murphy (isl.)	J5
Murray (lake)	D4
Myrtle Beach A.F.B.	K4
Naval Base	H6
New (riv.)	E6
Ninety Six Nat'l Hist. Site	C3
North (inlet)	J5
North (isl.)	J5
North Edisto (riv.)	G6
Pacolet (riv.)	D1
Palms, Isle of (isl.)	H6
Parris Island Marine Base	F7
Pee Dee (riv.)	H2
Pinopolis (dam)	G5
Pocotaligo (riv.)	G4
Port Royal (sound)	F7
Pritchards (isl.)	G7
Reedy (riv.)	C2
Robinson (lake)	G3
Romain (cape)	J6
Saint Helena (isl.)	F7
Saint Helena (sound)	G7
Salkehatchie (riv.)	E5
Saluda (riv.)	D3
Sandy (pt.)	H6
Sandy (riv.)	E2
Santee (dam)	G4
Santee (riv.)	H5
Sassafras (mt.)	B1
Savannah (riv.)	E6
Savannah River Plant Atomic Energy Commission	D5
Sea (isls.)	G7
Seabrook (isl.)	G6
Seneca (riv.)	B2
Shaw A.F.B. 6,939	F4
South (isl.)	J5
Stevens (creek)	C4
Stono (inlet)	H6
Thompsons (creek)	G2
Tugaloo (riv.)	A2
Turkey (creek)	E2
Tybee Roads (chan.)	F7
Tyger (riv.)	D2
Waccamaw (riv.)	J5
Wadmalaw (isl.)	G6
Wando (riv.)	H6
Wateree (lake)	F3
Wateree (riv.)	F3
Winyah (bay)	J5
Wylie (lake)	E1

⊙County seat.
‡Population of metropolitan area.
† Zip of nearest p.o. * Multiple zips.

Topography

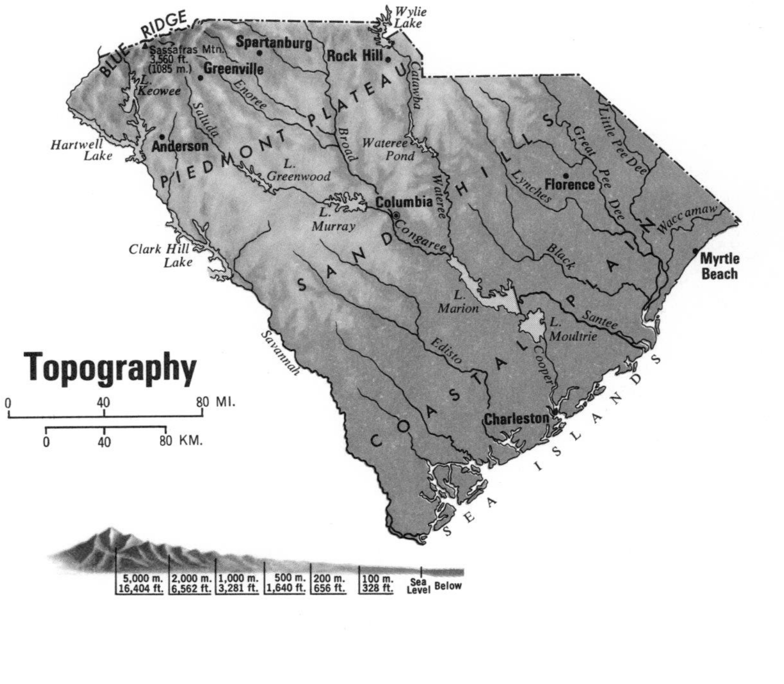
BLUE RIDGE
Sassafras Mtn. 3,560 ft. (1085 m.)
Wylie Lake
Spartanburg
Greenville
Rock Hill
L. Keowee
Hartwell Lake
Anderson
PIEDMONT PLATEAU
Enoree
Saluda
Broad
Catawba
Wateree Pond
L. Greenwood
Columbia
Congaree
L. Murray
Clark Hill Lake
SAND HILLS
Florence
Little Pee Dee
Great Pee Dee
Lynches
Black
Waccamaw
Myrtle Beach
L. Marion
L. Moultrie
Santee
Edisto
Cooper
Savannah
COASTAL PLAIN
Charleston
SEA ISLANDS
0 40 80 MI.
0 40 80 KM.
5,000 m. 16,404 ft.
2,000 m. 6,562 ft.
1,000 m. 3,281 ft.
500 m. 1,640 ft.
200 m. 656 ft.
100 m. 328 ft.
Sea Level
Below

COUNTIES

Aurora 3,628	M6
Beadle 19,195	N5
Bennett 3,044	F7
Bon Homme 8,059	O7
Brookings 24,332	R5
Brown 36,962	N2
Brule 5,245	L6
Buffalo 1,795	L5
Butte 8,372	B4
Campbell 2,243	J2
Charles Mix 9,680	M7
Clark 4,894	O4
Clay 13,689	P8
Codington 20,885	P4
Corson 5,196	G2
Custer 6,000	B6
Davison 17,820	N6
Day 8,133	O3
Deuel 5,289	R4
Dewey 5,366	G3
Douglas 4,181	N7
Edmunds 5,159	L3
Fall River 8,439	B7
Faulk 3,327	L3
Grant 9,013	R3
Gregory 6,015	L7
Haakon 2,794	F5
Hamlin 5,261	P4
Hand 4,948	L4
Hanson 3,415	O6
Harding 1,700	B2
Hughes 14,220	J5
Hutchinson 9,350	O7
Hyde 2,069	K4
Jackson 3,437	F6
Jerauld 2,929	M5
Jones 1,463	H6
Kingsbury 6,679	P5
Lake 10,724	P5
Lawrence 18,339	B5
Lincoln 13,942	R7
Lyman 3,864	J6
Marshall 5,404	O2
McCook 6,444	P6
McPherson 4,027	L2
Meade 20,717	D5
Mellette 2,249	H6
Miner 3,739	O5
Minnehaha 109,435	R6
Moody 6,692	R5
Pennington 70,361	C6
Perkins 4,700	D3
Potter 3,674	J3
Roberts 10,911	P2
Sanborn 3,213	N5
Shannon 11,323	D7
Spink 9,201	N4
Stanley 2,533	H5
Sully 1,990	J4
Todd 7,328	H7
Tripp 7,268	K7
Turner 9,255	P7
Union 10,938	R8
Walworth 7,011	J3

CITIES and TOWNS

Zip	Name/Pop.	Key
	Yankton 18,952	P7
	Ziebach 2,308	F4
57401	Aberdeen⊙ 25,851	M3
57310	Academy 10	M7
57520	Agar 139	J4
57420	Akaska 49	J3
57210	Albee 23	S3
57001	Alcester 885	R7
57311	Alexandria⊙ 588	O6
57714	Allen 300	F7
57312	Alpena 288	N5
57211	Altamont 58	R4
57421	Amherst 75	O2
57422	Andover 139	O3
57715	Ardmore 16	B7
57212	Arlington 991	P5
57313	Armour⊙ 819	N7
57423	Artas 43	K2
57314	Artesian 227	O6
57424	Ashton 154	N3
57213	Astoria 154	S4
57425	Athol 38	M3
57002	Aurora 507	R5
57315	Avon 576	N8
57214	Badger 99	P5
57003	Baltic 679	R6
57316	Bancroft 41	O4
57426	Barnard 65	N2
57716	Batesland 163	E7
57427	Bath 175	N3
57717	Belle Fourche⊙ 4,692	B4
57521	Belvidere 80	G6
57215	Bemis 37	R4
57004	Beresford 1,865	R7
57216	Big Stone City 672	S3
†57310	Bijou Hills 12	L6
57620	Bison⊙ 457	E2
57718	Black Hawk 1,608	C5
57522	Blunt 424	J4
57317	Bonesteel 358	M7
57428	Bowdle 644	K3
57719	Box Elder 3,186	D5
57217	Bradley 135	O3
57005	Brandon 2,589	R6
57218	Brandt 129	R4
57429	Brentford 91	N3
57319	Bridgewater 653	P6
57219	Bristol 445	O3
57430	Britton⊙ 1,590	O2
†57350	Broadland 49	N4
57006	Brookings⊙ 14,951	R5
57220	Bruce 254	R5
57221	Bryant 388	P4
57720	Buffalo⊙ 453	B2
57722	Buffalo Gap 186	C6
57621	Bullhead 400	G2
57010	Burbank 92	R8
57523	Burke⊙ 859	L7
†57276	Bushnell 76	R5
57222	Butler 22	O3
57724	Camp Crook 100	B2
57012	Canistota 626	P6
57321	Canova 194	O6
57013	Canton⊙ 2,886	R7
57725	Caputa 50	D5

(continued on following page)

AREA 77,116 sq. mi. (199,730 sq. km.)
POPULATION 690,768
CAPITAL Pierre
LARGEST CITY Sioux Falls
HIGHEST POINT Harney Pk. 7,242 ft. (2207 m.)
SETTLED IN 1856
ADMITTED TO UNION November 2, 1889
POPULAR NAME Coyote State; Sunshine State
STATE FLOWER Pasqueflower
STATE BIRD Ring-necked Pheasant

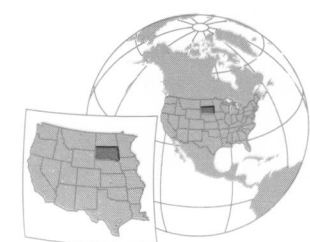

Topography

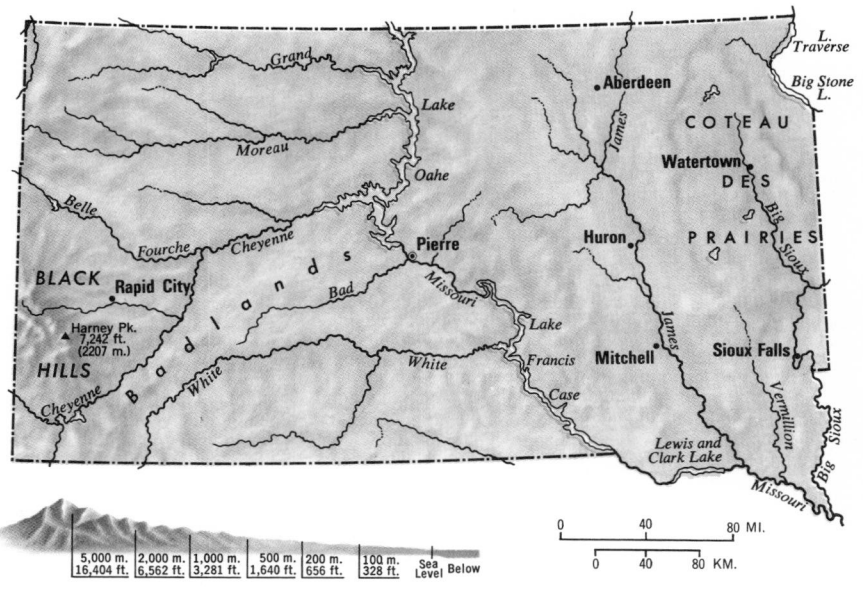

5,000 m.	2,000 m.	1,000 m.	500 m.	200 m.	100 m.	Sea
16,404 ft.	6,562 ft.	3,281 ft.	1,640 ft.	656 ft.	328 ft.	Level	Below

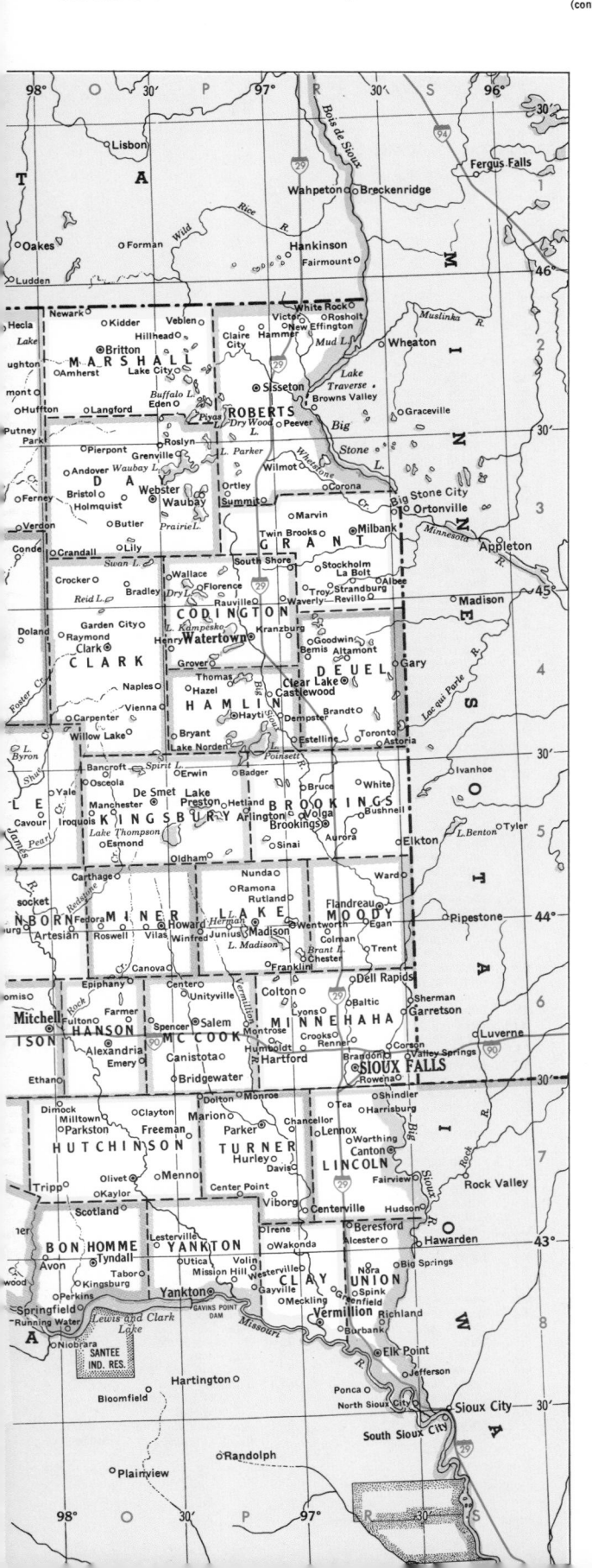

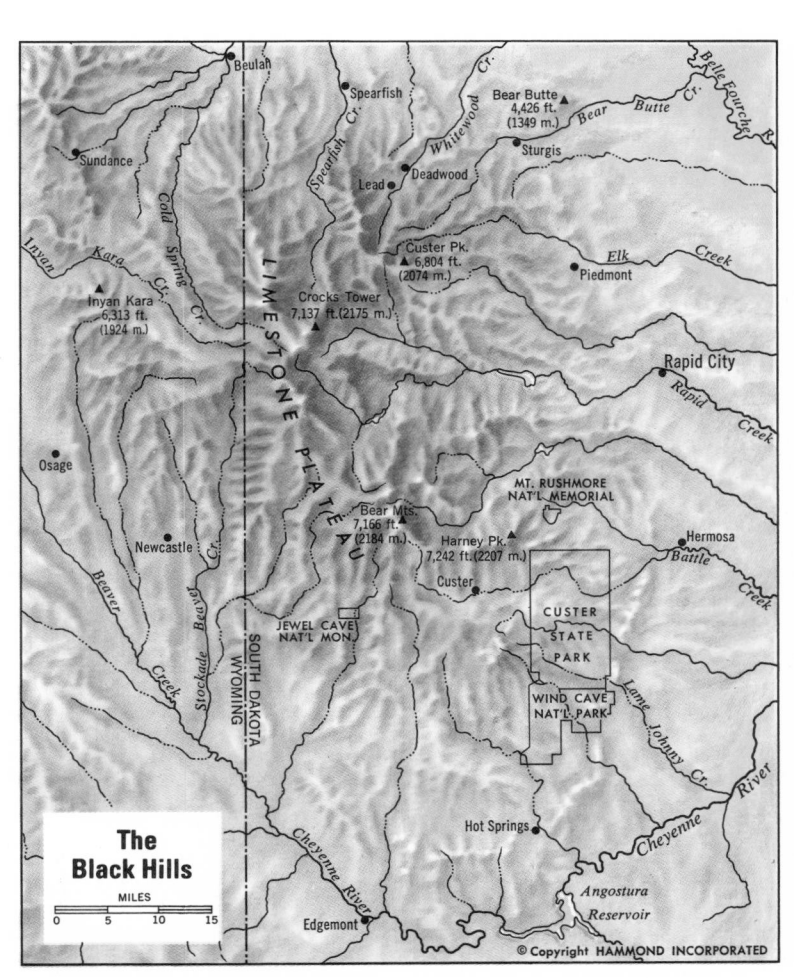

The Black Hills

MILES
0   5   10   15

© Copyright HAMMOND INCORPORATED

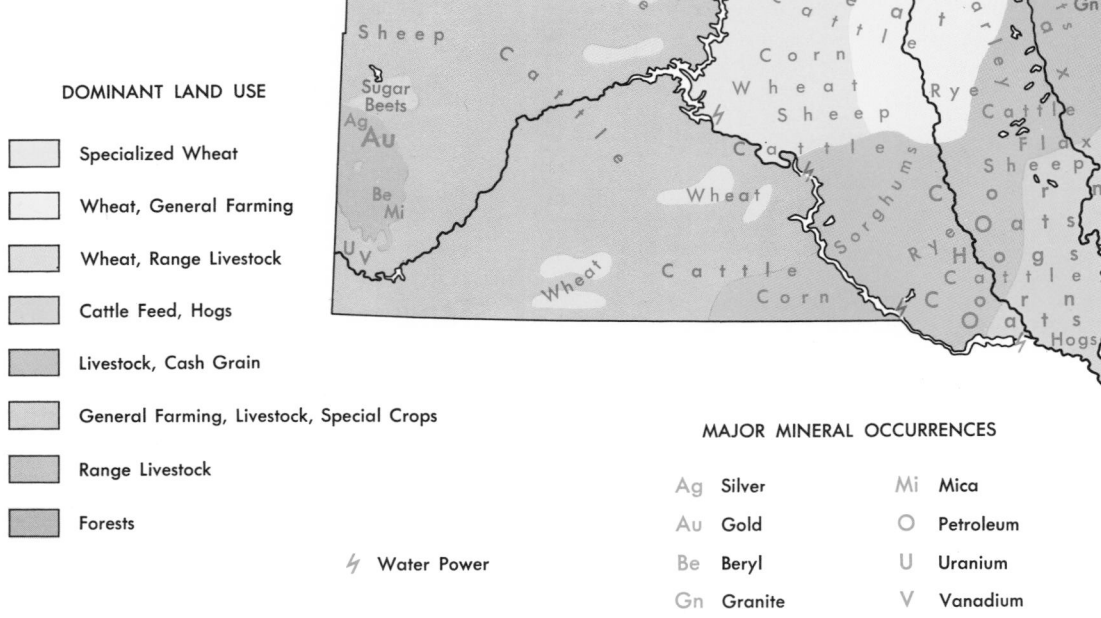

Agriculture, Industry and Resources

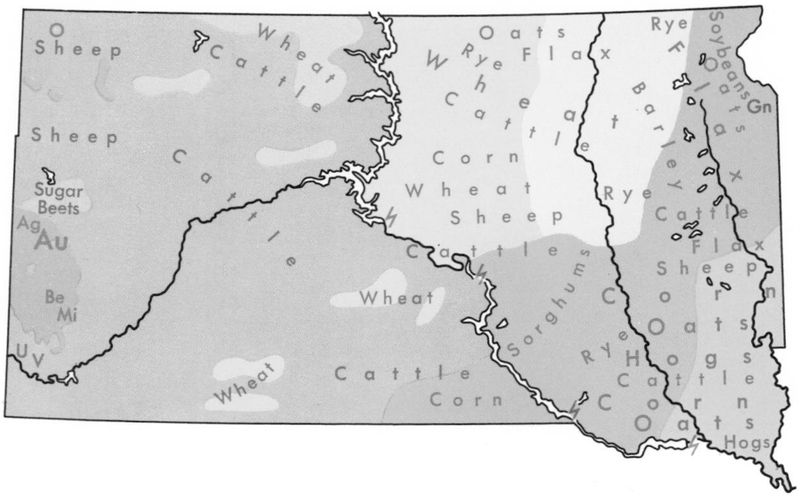

DOMINANT LAND USE

- Specialized Wheat
- Wheat, General Farming
- Wheat, Range Livestock
- Cattle Feed, Hogs
- Livestock, Cash Grain
- General Farming, Livestock, Special Crops
- Range Livestock
- Forests

Water Power

MAJOR MINERAL OCCURRENCES

Ag Silver
Au Gold
Be Beryl
Gn Granite
Mi Mica
O Petroleum
U Uranium
V Vanadium

57235 Florence 190 ... P3
57338 Forestburg 100 ... N5
57532 Fort Pierre⊙ 1,789 ... H5
57339 Fort Thompson 750 ... L5
57440 Frankfort 209 ... N4
57441 Frederick 307 ... N2
57029 Freeman 1,462 ... O7
57742 Fruitdale 88 ... B4
57340 Fulton 108 ... O6
57341 Gannvalley⊙ 70 ... L5
57236 Garden City 104 ... O4
57030 Garretson 963 ... S6
57237 Gary 354 ... S4
57031 Gayville 407 ... P8
57342 Geddes 303 ... M7
57442 Gettysburg⊙ 1,623 ... K3
57629 Glad Valley 75 ... F3
57630 Glencross 150 ... H3
57631 Glenham 169 ... J2
57238 Goodwin 139 ... R4
57533 Gregory 1,503 ... L7
57239 Grenville 119 ... O3
57445 Groton 1,230 ... N3
57534 Hamill 25 ... K6
57032 Harrisburg 558 ... R7
57344 Harrison 89 ... M7
57536 Harrold 196 ... K4
57033 Hartford 1,207 ... P6
57537 Hayes 25 ... H5
57241 Hayti⊙ 371 ... P4
57242 Hazel 94 ... P4
57446 Hecla 435 ... N2
57243 Henry 217 ... P4
57743 Hereford 50 ... D5
57744 Hermosa 251 ... C6
57632 Herreid 570 ... K2
57538 Herrick 115 ... L7
57244 Hetland 66 ... P5
57345 Highmore⊙ 1,055 ... L4
57745 Hill City 535 ... B6
†57437 Hillsview 9 ... L2
57348 Hitchcock 132 ... M4
57540 Holabird 30 ... K4
†57274 Holmquist 25 ... O3
57448 Hosmer 385 ... L2
57747 Hot Springs⊙ 4,742 ... C7
57449 Houghton 80 ... N2
57450 Hoven 615 ... K3
57349 Howard⊙ 1,169 ... P5
57748 Howes 4 ... E4
57034 Hudson 388 ... R7
57035 Humboldt 487 ... P6
57036 Hurley 419 ... P7
57350 Huron⊙ 13,000 ... N5
57541 Ideal 250 ... K6
57750 Interior 62 ... F6
57542 Iona 4 ... L6
57451 Ipswich⊙ 1,153 ... L3
57037 Irene 523 ... P7
57353 Iroquois 348 ... O5
57633 Isabel 332 ... G3
57452 Java 261 ... K3
57038 Jefferson 592 ... S8
57543 Kadoka⊙ 832 ... F6
57354 Kaylor 120 ... O7
57634 Keldron 17 ... F2
57544 Kennebec⊙ 334 ... K6
57545 Keyapaha 4 ... J7
57751 Keystone 295 ... C6
57355 Kimball 752 ... M6
57245 Kranzburg 136 ... R4
57752 Kyle 600 ... E7
57246 La Bolt 94 ... R3
57356 Lake Andes⊙ 1,029 ... M7
57247 Lake City 46 ... O2
57248 Lake Norden 417 ... P4
57249 Lake Preston 789 ... P5
57358 Lane 83 ... N5
57454 Langford 307 ... O2
57636 Lantry 200 ... G3
57754 Lead 4,330 ... B5
57455 Lebanon 129 ... K3
57638 Lemmon 1,871 ... E2
57039 Lennox 1,827 ... R7
57456 Leola⊙ 645 ... M2
57040 Lesterville 156 ... O7
57359 Letcher 221 ... N6
57250 Lily 38 ... O3
57639 Little Eagle 150 ... H2
57640 Lodgepole 20 ... D2
57457 Longlake 117 ... L2
57547 Longvalley 15 ... F7
57360 Loomis 55 ... N6
†57472 Lowry 22 ... K3
†57471 Loyalton 6 ... L3
57755 Ludlow 10 ... C2
57041 Lyons 100 ... R6
57042 Madison⊙ 6,210 ... P6
57643 Mahto 9 ... H2
57756 Manderson 450 ... D7
57460 Mansfield 120 ... N3
57757 Marcus 5 ... E4
57043 Marion 830 ... P7
57551 Martin⊙ 1,018 ... F7
57361 Marty 250 ... N8
57251 Marvin 52 ... R3
57641 McIntosh⊙ 418 ... G2
57642 McLaughlin 754 ... H2
57644 Meadow 21 ... E2
57044 Meckling 108 ... R8
57461 Mellette 192 ... N3
57045 Menno 793 ... P7
57552 Midland 277 ... G5
57252 Milbank⊙ 4,120 ... R3
57553 Milesville 6 ... F5
57554 Millboro 12 ... K7
57362 Miller⊙ 1,931 ... L4
57462 Mina 29 ... M3
57463 Miranda 30 ... M4
57555 Mission 748 ... H7
57046 Mission Hill 197 ... P8
57557 Mission Ridge 46 ... H4
57301 Mitchell⊙ 13,916 ... N6
57601 Mobridge 4,174 ... J2
57047 Monroe 170 ... P7
57048 Montrose 396 ... P6
57645 Morristown 127 ... F2
57558 Mosher 9 ... J7
57646 Mound City⊙ 111 ... K2
57363 Mount Vernon 402 ... N6
57758 Mud Butte 3 ... D4
57559 Murdo⊙ 723 ... H6
†57271 Naples 45 ... O4
57759 Nemo 42 ... B5
57255 New Effington 261 ... R2
57760 Newell 638 ... C4
57364 New Holland 125 ... M7
57761 New Underwood 517 ... D5
†57584 New Witten 134 ... K7
57762 Nisland 216 ... C4
57560 Norris 25 ... G7
†57625 North Eagle Butte 1,354 ... G3
57049 North Sioux City 1,992 ... R8
57465 Northville 138 ... M3
57050 Nunda 60 ... P5
57365 Oacoma 289 ... L6
57763 Oelrichs 124 ... C7
57764 Oglala 475 ... D7
57562 Okaton 30 ... H6
57563 Okreek 500 ... J7
57051 Oldham 222 ... P5
57052 Olivet⊙ 96 ... O7
57466 Onaka 70 ... L3
57564 Onida⊙ 851 ... K4
57765 Opal 5 ... D4
57766 Oral 60 ... C7
57467 Orient 87 ... L4
57256 Ortley 80 ... P3
57565 Ottumwa 3 ... G5
57767 Owanka 18 ... D5
57647 Parade 2 ... G3
57053 Parker⊙ 999 ... P7
57366 Parkston 1,545 ... O7
57566 Parmelee 600 ... G7
57257 Peever 232 ... R2
57567 Philip⊙ 1,088 ... F5
57367 Pickstown 225 ... M7
57769 Piedmont 500 ... C5
57468 Pierpont 184 ... O3
57501 Pierre (cap.)⊙ 11,973 ... J5
57770 Pine Ridge 3,059 ... E7
57771 Plainview 2 ... E4
57368 Plankinton⊙ 644 ... N6
57369 Platte 1,334 ... M7
57648 Pollock 355 ... J2
57772 Porcupine 260 ... E7
57649 Prairie City 50 ... D2
57568 Presho 760 ... J6
57773 Pringle 105 ... B6
57774 Provo 60 ... B7
57370 Pukwana 234 ... L6
57775 Quinn 80 ... E5
57650 Ralph 12 ... C2
57054 Ramona 241 ... P5
57701 Rapid City⊙ 46,492 ... C5
Rapid City‡ 90,850 ... C5
57357 Ravinia 88 ... N7
57258 Raymond 106 ... O4
57469 Redfield⊙ 3,027 ... N4
57776 Redig 50 ... C3
57777 Redowl 10 ... D4
57371 Ree Heights 88 ... L4
57569 Reliance 190 ... K6
57055 Renner 320 ... R6
57651 Reva 8 ... C2
57259 Revillo 158 ... R3
57652 Ridgeview 75 ... H3
†57701 Rockerville 28 ... C6
57470 Rockham 52 ... M4
57471 Roscoe 370 ... L3
57570 Rosebud 900 ... H7
57260 Rosholt 446 ... R2
57261 Roslyn 261 ... P2
57372 Roswell 19 ... O6
57056 Rowena 100 ... R6
57057 Rutland 30 ... P5
57571 Saint Charles 25 ... L7
57572 Saint Francis 766 ... H7
57373 Saint Lawrence 223 ... M4
57779 Saint Onge 250 ... B4
57058 Salem⊙ 1,486 ... P6
57780 Scenic 26 ... D6
57059 Scotland 1,022 ... O7
57472 Selby⊙ 884 ... J3
57473 Seneca 103 ... L3
57060 Sherman 100 ... S6
57781 Silver City 31 ... B5
57061 Sinai 129 ... P5
*57101 Sioux Falls⊙ 81,343 ... R6
Sioux Falls‡ 109,435 ... R6
57262 Sisseton⊙ 2,789 ... R2
57782 Smithwick 50 ... C7
57654 Sorum 2 ... D3
57263 South Shore 241 ... P3
57783 Spearfish 5,251 ... B5
57374 Spencer 380 ... O6
†57010 Spink 75 ... R8
57062 Springfield 1,377 ... N8
57346 Stephan 30 ... K5
57375 Stickney 409 ... M6
57264 Stockholm 95 ... R3
57784 Stoneville 20 ... D4
†57359 Storla 19 ... M6
57265 Strandburg 79 ... R3
57474 Stratford 82 ... N3
57785 Sturgis⊙ 5,184 ... B5
57266 Summit 290 ... P3
57063 Tabor 460 ... O8
†57433 Tacoma Park 20 ... N2
57064 Tea 729 ... R7
†57242 Thomas 12 ... P4
†57638 Thunder Hawk 26 ... F2
†57769 Tilford 75 ... C5
57656 Timber Lake⊙ 660 ... H3
57475 Tolstoy 97 ... K3
57268 Toronto 236 ... R4
57657 Trail City 68 ... H3
57065 Trent 197 ... R6
57376 Tripp 804 ... N7
†57754 Trojan 40 ... B5
†57265 Troy 18 ... R3
57476 Tulare 238 ... N4
57477 Turton 101 ... N3
57574 Tuthill 75 ... G7
57269 Twin Brooks 87 ... R3
57066 Tyndall⊙ 1,253 ... O8
57787 Union Center 63 ... D4
†57058 Unityville 20 ... P6
57067 Utica 100 ... P8
57788 Vale 160 ... C4
57068 Valley Springs 801 ... S6
†57381 Vayland 3 ... M5
57270 Veblen 368 ... P2
57478 Verdon 7 ... N3
57069 Vermillion⊙ 10,136 ... R8
57575 Vetal 19 ... G7
57070 Viborg 812 ... P7
†57260 Victor 9 ... R2
57271 Vienna 90 ... O4
†57349 Vilas 28 ... O6
†57701 Villa Ranchaero 1,666 ... C5
57379 Virgil 37 ... N5
57576 Vivian 95 ... J6
57071 Volga 1,221 ... R5
57072 Volin 156 ... P8
57380 Wagner 1,453 ... N7
57073 Wakonda 383 ... P7
57658 Wakpala 500 ... H2
57659 Walker 12 ... G2
57790 Wall 770 ... E6
57272 Wallace 90 ... P3
57577 Wanblee 550 ... F6
57074 Ward 43 ... R5
57479 Warner 322 ... M3
57791 Wasta 99 ... D5
57660 Watauga 50 ... F2
57201 Watertown⊙ 15,649 ... P4
57273 Waubay 675 ... P3
57202 Waverly 30 ... R3
57274 Webster⊙ 2,417 ... P3
57480 Wecota 30 ... L3
57075 Wentworth 193 ... R6
57381 Wessington 327 ... M5
57382 Wessington Springs⊙ 1,203 ... M5
†57069 Westerville 21 ... P8
57481 Westport 122 ... M2
57482 Wetonka 22 ... M2
57578 Wewela 6 ... K7
57276 White 474 ... R5
†57638 White Butte 21 ... E2
57661 Whitehorse 196 ... H3
57383 White Lake 414 ... M6
57792 White Owl 6 ... E4
57579 White River⊙ 561 ... H6
†57260 White Rock 10 ... R2
57793 Whitewood 821 ... B5
57278 Willow Lake 375 ... O4
57279 Wilmot 507 ... R3
57076 Winfred 81 ... P6
57580 Winner⊙ 3,472 ... K7
57584 Witten 134 ... J7
57384 Wolsey 437 ... N5
57585 Wood 134 ... J6
57385 Woonsocket⊙ 799 ... N5
57077 Worthing 388 ... R7
57794 Wounded Knee 376 ... D7
57386 Yale 136 ... O5
57078 Yankton⊙ 12,011 ... P8
57483 Zell 60 ... M4
57795 Zeona 2 ... D3

OTHER FEATURES

Aeber (creek) ... G4
Andes (lake) ... N7
Angostura (res.) ... B7
Antelope (creek) ... D3
Bad (riv.) ... G5
Badlands Nat'l Mon. ... E6
Battle (creek) ... C6
Bear in the Lodge (creek) ... F6
Beaver (creek) ... A6
Belle Fourche (res.) ... B4
Belle Fourche (riv.) ... C4
Big Bend (dam) ... K5
Big Sioux (riv.) ... S7
Big Stone (lake) ... R3
Black Hills (mts.) ... B5
Black Pine (creek) ... G6
Bois de Sioux (riv.) ... R1
Boxelder (creek) ... D5
Brant (lake) ... R6
Buffalo (creek) ... F6
Buffalo (lake) ... P2
Bull (creek) ... C2
Bull (creek) ... K6
Byron (lake) ... N4
Cain (creek) ... N5
Cherry (creek) ... F4
Cherry (creek) ... F5
Cheyenne (riv.) ... F4
Cheyenne River Ind. Res. ... F4
Choteau (creek) ... N7
Columbia Road (res.) ... N2
Cottonwood (creek) ... E5
Cottonwood (lake) ... M4
Crazy Horse Mon. ... B6
Crow (creek) ... A4
Crow Creek Ind. Res. ... L5
Dog Ear (creek) ... K6
Dry (creek) ... G4
Dry (lake) ... P3
Dry Wood (lake) ... P2
Elk (creek) ... C5
Ellsworth A.F.B. 4,766 ... C5
Elm (creek) ... D4
Elm (riv.) ... M2
Firesteel (creek) ... N6
Flint Rock (creek) ... E3
Fort Randall (dam) ... N7
Foster (creek) ... N4
Francis Case (lake) ... L7
French (creek) ... C6
Gavins Point (dam) ... P8
Geographical Center of U.S. ... B4
Grand (riv.) ... F2
Harney (peak) ... B6
Hat (creek) ... B7
Hell Canyon (creek) ... B6
Herman (lake) ... P5
Horsehead (creek) ... C7
Indian (creek) ... B4
James (riv.) ... N5
Jewel Cave Nat'l Mon. ... B6
Kampeska (lake) ... P4
Keya Paha (riv.) ... K7
Lame Johnny (creek) ... C6
Lewis and Clark (lake) ... O8
Little Missouri (riv.) ... B1
Little Moreau (riv.) ... G3
Little White (riv.) ... H7
Long (lake) ... L2
Lower Brule Ind. Res. ... K5
Madison (lake) ... P6
Maple (riv.) ... M1
Medicine (creek) ... J6
Medicine Knoll (creek) ... J5
Minnechaduza (creek) ... H7
Minnesota (riv.) ... S3
Missouri (riv.) ... P8
Mitchell (creek) ... G5
Moreau (riv.) ... G3
Mount Rushmore Nat'l Mem. ... B6
Mud (creek) ... N3
Mud (lake) ... R2
Mud Lake (res.) ... N2
Nasty (creek) ... C2
Oahe (dam) ... J5
Oahe (lake) ... J1
Oak (creek) ... H2
Oak (creek) ... J6
Okobojo (creek) ... J4
Old Lodge (creek) ... K6
Owl (creek) ... B4
Parker (lake) ... P3
Pearl (creek) ... N5
Pine Ridge Ind. Res. ... D7
Piyas (lake) ... P2
Platte (lake) ... M6
Pleasant Valley (creek) ... B6
Poinsett (lake) ... P4
Ponca (creek) ... L7
Prairie (lake) ... P3
Rabbit (creek) ... E3
Red (lake) ... L6
Red Owl (creek) ... E4
Red Scaffold (creek) ... F4
Redstone (creek) ... O5
Redwater (creek) ... A4
Reid (lake) ... O3
Rock (creek) ... O6
Rosebud Ind. Res. ... H7
Sand (creek) ... C2
Sand (creek) ... M5
Shadehill (res.) ... E2
Sharpe (lake) ... J5
Shue (creek) ... N5
Smith (creek) ... L6
Snake (creek) ... F4
Snake (creek) ... F5
Snake (creek) ... M3
Spirit (lake) ... O4
Spring (creek) ... C6
Spring (creek) ... J2
Squaw (creek) ... B3
Sulphur (creek) ... D4
Swan (creek) ... J3
Swan (lake) ... O3
Swan (lake) ... K3
Thompson (lake) ... O5
Thunder (creek) ... N4
Thunder Butte (creek) ... E3
Traverse (lake) ... R2
Turtle (creek) ... M4
Vermillion (riv.) ... P6
Virgin (creek) ... H3
Waubay (lake) ... O3
Whetstone (creek) ... R3
White (lake) ... M6
White (riv.) ... D7
Whitewood (creek) ... B4
Willow (creek) ... C4
Wind Cave Nat'l Park ... B6
Wolf (creek) ... L4
Wounded Knee (creek) ... E7

⊙County seat.
‡Population of metropolitan area.
† Zip of nearest p.o. * Multiple zips.

COUNTIES

Anderson 38,381 .... J6
Andrews 13,323 .... B5
Angelina 64,172 .... K6
Aransas 14,260 .... H10
Archer 7,266 .... F4
Armstrong 1,994 .... C3
Atascosa 25,055 .... F9
Austin 17,726 .... H8
Bailey 8,168 .... B3
Bandera 7,084 .... E8
Bastrop 24,726 .... G7
Baylor 4,919 .... E4
Bee 26,030 .... G9
Bell 157,820 .... G6
Bexar 988,798 .... F8
Blanco 4,681 .... F8
Borden 859 .... C5
Bosque 13,401 .... G6
Bowie 75,301 .... K4
Brazoria 169,587 .... J8
Brazos 93,588 .... H7
Brewster 7,573 .... A8
Briscoe 2,579 .... C3
Brooks 8,428 .... F11
Brown 33,057 .... F6
Burleson 12,313 .... H7
Burnet 17,803 .... F7
Caldwell 23,637 .... G8
Calhoun 19,574 .... H9
Callahan 10,992 .... E5
Cameron 209,727 .... G11
Camp 9,275 .... K5
Carson 6,672 .... C2
Cass 29,430 .... K4
Castro 10,556 .... B3
Chambers 18,538 .... K8
Cherokee 38,127 .... J6
Childress 6,950 .... D3
Clay 9,582 .... F4
Cochran 4,825 .... B4
Coke 3,196 .... D6
Coleman 10,439 .... E6
Collin 144,576 .... H4
Collingsworth 4,648 .... D3
Colorado 18,823 .... H8
Comal 36,446 .... F8
Comanche 12,617 .... F5
Concho 2,915 .... E6
Cooke 27,656 .... G4
Coryell 56,767 .... G6
Cottle 2,947 .... D3
Crane 4,600 .... B6
Crockett 4,608 .... C7
Crosby 8,859 .... C4
Culberson 3,315 .... C11
Dallam 6,531 .... B1
Dallas 1,556,390 .... H5
Dawson 16,184 .... C5
Deaf Smith 21,165 .... B3
Delta 4,839 .... J4
Denton 143,126 .... G4
De Witt 18,903 .... G9
Dickens 3,539 .... D4
Dimmit 11,367 .... E9
Donley 4,075 .... D2
Duval 12,517 .... F10
Eastland 19,480 .... F5
Ector 115,374 .... B6
Edwards 2,033 .... D7
Ellis 59,743 .... H5
El Paso 479,899 .... A10
Erath 22,560 .... F5
Falls 17,946 .... H6
Fannin 24,285 .... H4
Fayette 18,832 .... H8
Fisher 5,891 .... D5
Floyd 9,834 .... C3
Foard 2,158 .... E3
Fort Bend 130,846 .... J8
Franklin 6,893 .... J4
Freestone 14,830 .... H6
Frio 13,785 .... E9
Gaines 13,150 .... B5
Galveston 195,940 .... K8
Garza 5,336 .... C4
Gillespie 13,532 .... F7
Glasscock 1,304 .... C6
Goliad 5,193 .... G9
Gonzales 15,949 .... G8
Gray 26,386 .... D2
Grayson 89,796 .... H4
Gregg 99,495 .... K5
Grimes 13,580 .... J7
Guadalupe 46,708 .... G8
Hale 37,592 .... C3
Hall 5,594 .... D3
Hamilton 8,297 .... F6
Hansford 6,209 .... C1
Hardeman 6,368 .... E3
Hardin 40,721 .... K7
Harris 2,409,547 .... J8
Harrison 52,265 .... K5
Hartley 3,987 .... B2
Haskell 7,725 .... E4
Hays 40,594 .... F7
Hemphill 5,304 .... D2
Henderson 42,606 .... J5
Hidalgo 283,323 .... F11
Hill 25,024 .... G5
Hockley 23,230 .... B4
Hood 17,714 .... G5
Hopkins 25,247 .... J4
Houston 22,299 .... J6
Howard 33,142 .... C5
Hudspeth 2,728 .... B10
Hunt 55,248 .... H4
Hutchinson 26,304 .... C2
Irion 1,386 .... C6
Jack 7,408 .... F4
Jackson 13,352 .... H9
Jasper 30,781 .... K7
Jeff Davis 1,647 .... C11
Jefferson 250,938 .... K8
Jim Hogg 5,168 .... F11
Jim Wells 36,498 .... F10
Johnson 67,649 .... G5
Jones 17,268 .... E5
Karnes 13,593 .... G9
Kaufman 39,029 .... H5
Kendall 10,635 .... F8
Kenedy 543 .... G11
Kent 1,145 .... D4
Kerr 28,780 .... E7
Kimble 4,063 .... E7
King 425 .... D4
Kinney 2,279 .... D8
Kleberg 33,358 .... G10
Knox 5,329 .... E4
Lamar 42,156 .... J4
Lamb 18,669 .... B3
Lampasas 12,005 .... F6
La Salle 5,514 .... E9
Lavaca 19,004 .... H8
Lee 10,952 .... H7
Leon 9,594 .... J6
Liberty 47,088 .... K7
Limestone 20,224 .... H6
Lipscomb 3,766 .... D1
Live Oak 9,606 .... F9
Llano 10,144 .... F7
Loving 91 .... A6
Lubbock 211,651 .... C4
Lynn 8,605 .... C4
Madison 10,649 .... J6
Marion 10,360 .... K5
Martin 4,684 .... C5
Mason 3,683 .... E7
Matagorda 37,828 .... H9
Maverick 31,398 .... D9
McCulloch 8,735 .... E6
McLennan 170,755 .... G6
McMullen 789 .... F9
Medina 23,164 .... E8
Menard 2,346 .... E7
Midland 82,636 .... B6
Milam 22,732 .... H7
Mills 4,477 .... F6
Mitchell 9,088 .... D5
Montague 17,410 .... G4
Montgomery 128,487 .... J7
Moore 16,575 .... C2
Morris 14,629 .... K4
Motley 1,950 .... D3
Nacogdoches 46,786 .... K6
Navarro 35,323 .... H5
Newton 13,254 .... L7
Nolan 17,359 .... D5
Nueces 268,215 .... G10
Ochiltree 9,588 .... D1
Oldham 2,283 .... B2
Orange 83,838 .... L7
Palo Pinto 24,062 .... F5
Panola 20,724 .... K5
Parker 44,609 .... G5
Parmer 11,038 .... B3
Pecos 14,618 .... B7
Polk 24,407 .... K7
Potter 98,637 .... C2
Presidio 5,188 .... C12
Rains 4,839 .... J5
Randall 75,062 .... C2
Reagan 4,135 .... C6
Real 2,469 .... E8
Red River 16,101 .... J4
Reeves 15,801 .... D11
Refugio 9,289 .... G9
Roberts 1,187 .... D2
Robertson 14,653 .... H6
Rockwall 14,528 .... H5
Runnels 11,872 .... E6
Rusk 41,382 .... K5
Sabine 8,702 .... L6
San Augustine 8,785 .... K6
San Jacinto 11,434 .... J7
San Patricio 58,013 .... G10
San Saba 6,204 .... F6
Schleicher 2,820 .... D7
Scurry 18,192 .... D5
Shackelford 3,915 .... E5
Shelby 23,084 .... K6
Sherman 3,174 .... C1
Smith 128,366 .... J5
Somervell 4,154 .... G5
Starr 27,266 .... F11
Stephens 9,926 .... F5
Sterling 1,206 .... C6
Stonewall 2,406 .... D4
Sutton 5,130 .... D7
Swisher 9,723 .... C3
Tarrant 860,880 .... G5
Taylor 110,932 .... E5
Terrell 1,595 .... B7
Terry 14,581 .... B4
Throckmorton 2,053 .... E4
Titus 21,442 .... K4
Tom Green 84,784 .... D6
Travis 419,573 .... G7
Trinity 9,450 .... J6
Tyler 16,223 .... K7
Upshur 28,595 .... K5
Upton 4,619 .... B6
Uvalde 22,441 .... E8
Val Verde 35,910 .... C8
Van Zandt 31,426 .... J5
Victoria 68,807 .... H9
Walker 41,789 .... J7
Waller 19,798 .... J8
Ward 13,976 .... A6
Washington 21,998 .... H7
Webb 99,258 .... E10
Wharton 40,242 .... H8
Wheeler 7,137 .... D2
Wichita 121,082 .... F3
Wilbarger 15,931 .... E3
Willacy 17,495 .... G11
Williamson 76,507 .... G7
Wilson 16,756 .... F8
Winkler 9,944 .... A6
Wise 26,575 .... G4
Wood 24,697 .... J5
Yoakum 8,299 .... B4
Young 19,083 .... F4
Zapata 6,628 .... E11
Zavala 11,666 .... E9

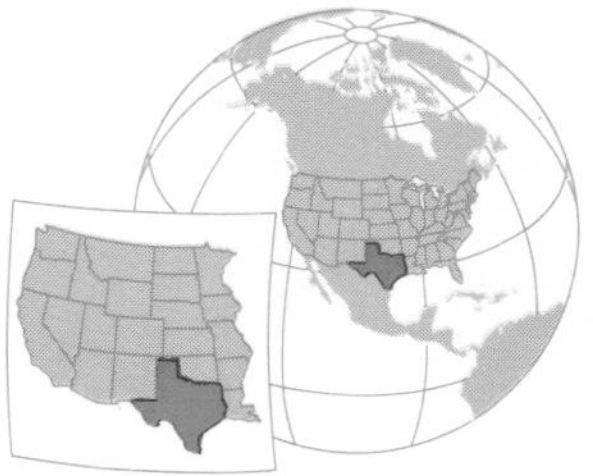

AREA 266,807 sq. mi. (691,030 sq. km.)
POPULATION 14,229,288
CAPITAL Austin
LARGEST CITY Houston
HIGHEST POINT Guadalupe Pk. 8,749 ft. (2667 m.)
SETTLED IN 1686
ADMITTED TO UNION December 29, 1845
POPULAR NAME Lone Star State
STATE FLOWER Bluebonnet
STATE BIRD Mockingbird

CITIES and TOWNS

Zip Name/Pop. Key

*79601 Abilene⊙ 98,315 .... E5
Abilene‡ 139,192 .... E5
78516 Alamo 5,831 .... F11
78209 Alamo Heights 6,252 .... K10
76430 Albany⊙ 2,450 .... E5
78332 Alice⊙ 20,961 .... F10
75002 Allen 8,314 .... H1
79830 Alpine⊙ 5,465 .... D12
77511 Alvin 16,515 .... J3
*79101 Amarillo⊙ 149,230 .... C2
Amarillo‡ 173,699 .... C2
77514 Anahuac⊙ 1,840 .... K8
77830 Anderson⊙ 500 .... J7
79714 Andrews⊙ 11,061 .... B5
77515 Angleton⊙ 13,929 .... J8
79501 Anson⊙ 2,831 .... E5
78336 Aransas Pass 7,173 .... G10
76351 Archer City⊙ 1,862 .... F4
*76010 Arlington 160,123 .... F2
79502 Aspermont⊙ 1,357 .... D4
75751 Athens⊙ 10,197 .... J5
75551 Atlanta 6,272 .... K4
*78701 Austin (cap.)⊙ 345,496 .... G7
Austin‡ 536,450 .... G7
76020 Azle 5,822 .... E2
77518 Bacliff 4,851 .... K2
79504 Baird⊙ 1,696 .... E5
75180 Balch Springs 13,746 .... H2
†78201 Balcones Heights 2,511 .... J10
76821 Ballinger⊙ 4,207 .... E6
78003 Bandera⊙ 947 .... F8
77532 Barrett 3,183 .... K1
78602 Bastrop⊙ 3,789 .... G7
77414 Bay City⊙ 17,837 .... H9
77520 Baytown 56,923 .... L2
*77701 Beaumont⊙ 118,102 .... K7
Beaumont-Port Arthur-Orange‡ 375,497 K7
76021 Bedford 20,821 .... F2
78102 Beeville⊙ 14,574 .... G9
77401 Bellaire 14,950 .... J2
76704 Bellmead 7,569 .... H6
77418 Bellville⊙ 2,860 .... H8
76513 Belton⊙ 10,660 .... G7
76126 Benbrook 13,579 .... E2
79505 Benjamin⊙ 257 .... E4
76932 Big Lake⊙ 3,404 .... C6
79720 Big Spring⊙ 24,804 .... C5
78006 Boerne⊙ 3,229 .... J10
75418 Bonham⊙ 7,338 .... H4
79007 Borger 15,837 .... C2
77557 Boston⊙ 400 .... K4
76230 Bowie 5,610 .... G4
78832 Brackettville⊙ 1,676 .... D8
76825 Brady⊙ 5,969 .... E6
77422 Brazoria 3,025 .... J9
76024 Breckenridge⊙ 6,921 .... F5
77833 Brenham⊙ 10,966 .... H7
77611 Bridge City 7,667 .... L7
79316 Brownfield⊙ 10,387 .... B4
*78520 Brownsville⊙ 84,997 .... G12
Brownsville-Harlingen-San Benito‡ 209,680 .... G12
76801 Brownwood⊙ 19,396 .... F6
77801 Bryan⊙ 44,337 .... H7
Bryan-College Station‡ 93,588 .... H7
76354 Burkburnett 10,668 .... F3
76028 Burleson 11,734 .... F3
78611 Burnet⊙ 3,410 .... F7
77836 Caldwell⊙ 2,953 .... H7
76520 Cameron⊙ 5,721 .... H7
79014 Canadian⊙ 3,491 .... D2
75103 Canton⊙ 2,845 .... J5
79015 Canyon⊙ 10,724 .... C3
78834 Carrizo Springs⊙ 6,886 .... E9
*75006 Carrollton 40,595 .... G2
75633 Carthage⊙ 6,447 .... K5
†78213 Castle Hills 4,773 .... J10
75104 Cedar Hill 6,849 .... G3
75935 Center⊙ 5,827 .... K6
75833 Centerville⊙ 799 .... H6
77530 Channelview 17,471 .... K1
79018 Channing⊙ 304 .... B2
79201 Childress⊙ 5,817 .... D3
76437 Cisco 4,517 .... E5
79226 Clarendon⊙ 2,220 .... C3
75426 Clarksville⊙ 4,917 .... K4
79019 Claude⊙ 1,112 .... C2
†77565 Clear Lake Shores 755 .... K2
76031 Cleburne⊙ 19,218 .... G5
77327 Cleveland 5,977 .... K7
77531 Clute 9,577 .... J9
77331 Coldspring⊙ 569 .... J7
76834 Coleman⊙ 5,960 .... E6
77840 College Station 37,272 .... H7
76034 Colleyville 6,700 .... F2
79512 Colorado City⊙ 5,405 .... C5
78934 Columbus⊙ 3,923 .... H8
76442 Comanche⊙ 4,075 .... F6
75428 Commerce 8,136 .... J4
*77301 Conroe⊙ 18,034 .... J7
78109 Converse 5,150 .... K11
75432 Cooper⊙ 2,338 .... J4
76522 Copperas Cove 19,469 .... G6
*78401 Corpus Christi⊙ 231,999 .... G10
Corpus Christi‡ 326,228 .... G10
75110 Corsicana⊙ 21,712 .... H5
78014 Cotulla⊙ 3,912 .... E9
79731 Crane⊙ 3,622 .... B6
75835 Crockett⊙ 7,405 .... J6
79322 Crosbyton⊙ 2,289 .... C4
79227 Crowell⊙ 1,509 .... E4
76036 Crowley 5,852 .... E3
78839 Crystal City⊙ 8,334 .... E9
77954 Cuero⊙ 7,124 .... G8
75638 Daingerfield⊙ 3,030 .... K4
79022 Dalhart⊙ 6,854 .... B1
*75201 Dallas⊙ 904,078 .... G2
Dallas-Ft. Worth‡ 2,974,878 .... G2
77535 Dayton 4,908 .... J7
76234 Decatur⊙ 4,104 .... G4
77536 Deer Park 22,648 .... K2
76444 De Leon 2,478 .... F5
78840 Del Rio⊙ 30,034 .... D8
75020 Denison 23,884 .... H4
76201 Denton⊙ 48,063 .... G4

(continued on following page)

DOMINANT LAND USE

- Wheat, Grain Sorghums, Range Livestock
- Cotton, Wheat
- Specialized Cotton
- Cotton, General Farming
- Cotton, Forest Products
- Cotton, Range Livestock
- Rice, General Farming
- Peanuts, General Farming
- General Farming, Livestock, Cash Grain
- General Farming, Forest Products, Truck Farming, Cotton
- Fruit, Truck and Mixed Farming
- Range Livestock
- Forests
- Swampland, Limited Agriculture
- Nonagricultural Land
- Urban Areas

MAJOR MINERAL OCCURRENCES

At	Asphalt	He	Helium
Cl	Clay	Ls	Limestone
Fe	Iron Ore	Na	Salt
G	Natural Gas	O	Petroleum
Gn	Granite	S	Sulfur
Gp	Gypsum	Tc	Talc
Gr	Graphite	U	Uranium

Water Power

Major Industrial Areas

Agriculture, Industry and Resources

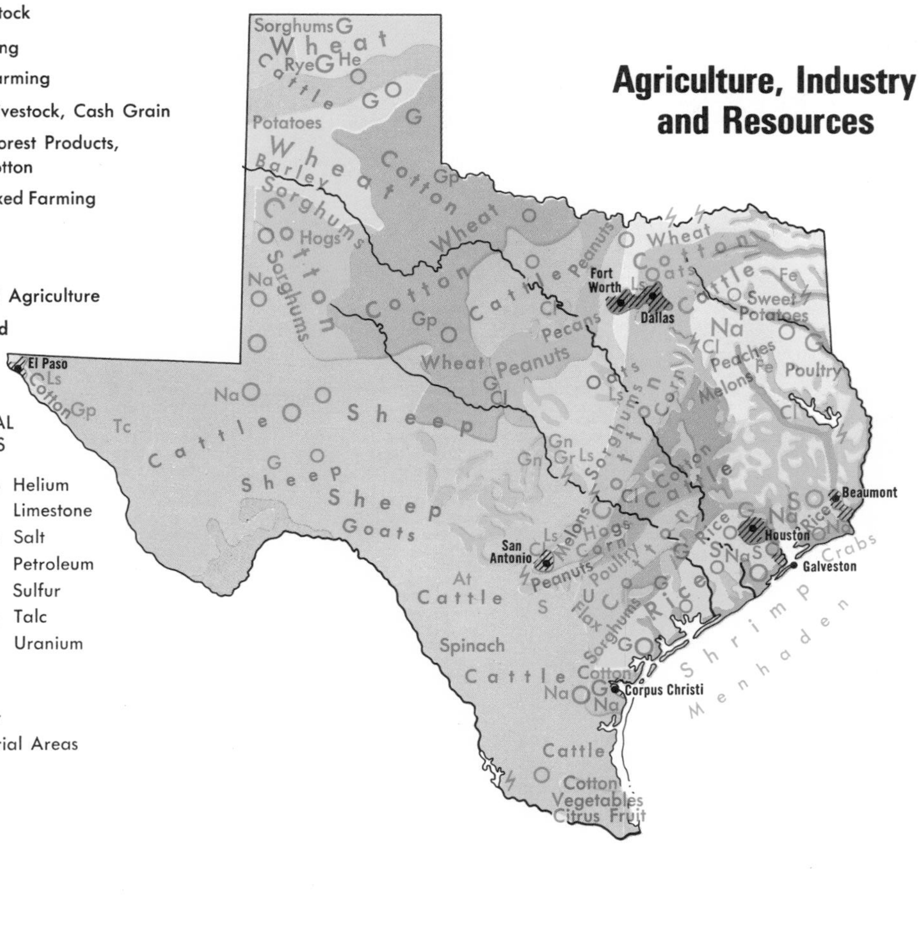

79323 Denver City 4,704 .... B4
75115 De Soto 15,538 .... G3
78016 Devine 3,756 .... E8
75941 Diboll 5,227 .... K6
79229 Dickens⊙ 409 .... D4
77539 Dickinson 7,505 .... K3
79027 Dimmitt⊙ 5,019 .... B3
78537 Donna 9,952 .... F11
79029 Dumas⊙ 12,194 .... C2
75116 Duncanville 27,781 .... G3
78852 Eagle Pass⊙ 21,407 .... D9
76448 Eastland⊙ 3,747 .... F5
78539 Edinburg⊙ 24,075 .... F11
77957 Edna⊙ 5,650 .... H9
77437 El Campo 10,462 .... H8
76936 Eldorado⊙ 2,061 .... D7
78621 Elgin 4,535 .... G7
*79901 El Paso⊙ 425,259 .... A10
El Paso‡ 479,899 .... A10
78543 Elsa 5,061 .... G11
75440 Emory⊙ 813 .... J5
75119 Ennis 12,110 .... H5
76039 Euless 24,002 .... F2
76140 Everman 5,387 .... F3
79838 Fabens 4,285 .... B10
75840 Fairfield⊙ 3,505 .... H6
78355 Falfurrias⊙ 6,103 .... F10
75234 Farmers Branch 24,863 .... G2
79325 Farwell⊙ 1,354 .... A3
78114 Floresville⊙ 4,381 .... K11
†75067 Flower Mound 4,402 .... F1
79235 Floydada⊙ 4,193 .... C3
†76119 Forest Hill 11,684 .... F2
79734 Fort Davis⊙ 900 .... D11
79735 Fort Stockton⊙ 8,688 .... A7
*76101 Fort Worth⊙ 385,164 .... F2
77856 Franklin⊙ 1,349 .... H7
78624 Fredericksburg⊙ 6,412 .... E7
76842 Fredonia 50 .... E7
77541 Freeport 13,444 .... J9
77546 Friendswood 10,719 .... J2
79035 Friona 3,809 .... B3
75034 Frisco 3,499 .... H4
79738 Gail⊙ 171 .... C5
76240 Gainesville⊙ 14,081 .... G4
77547 Galena Park 9,879 .... J1
*77550 Galveston⊙ 61,902 .... L3
Galveston-Texas City‡ 195,940 .... L3
79739 Garden City⊙ 350 .... C6
*75040 Garland 138,857 .... H2
76528 Gatesville⊙ 6,260 .... G6
78626 Georgetown⊙ 9,468 .... G7
78022 George West⊙ 2,627 .... F9
78942 Giddings⊙ 3,950 .... H7
75644 Gilmer⊙ 5,167 .... J5
75647 Gladewater 6,548 .... K5
76043 Glen Rose⊙ 2,075 .... G5
76844 Goldthwaite⊙ 1,783 .... F6
77963 Goliad⊙ 1,990 .... G9
78629 Gonzales⊙ 7,152 .... G8
76046 Graham⊙ 9,170 .... F4
76048 Granbury⊙ 3,332 .... G5
*75050 Grand Prairie 71,462 .... G2
76051 Grapevine 11,801 .... F2
75401 Greenville⊙ 22,161 .... H4
76642 Groesbeck⊙ 3,373 .... H6
77619 Groves 17,090 .... L8
75845 Groveton⊙ 1,262 .... J7
79236 Guthrie⊙ 170 .... D4
77964 Hallettsville⊙ 2,865 .... G8
76117 Haltom City 29,014 .... F2
76531 Hamilton⊙ 3,189 .... G6
78550 Harlingen 43,543 .... G11
79521 Haskell⊙ 3,782 .... E4
77859 Hearne 5,418 .... H7
78361 Hebbronville⊙ 4,684 .... F10
75948 Hemphill⊙ 1,353 .... L6
77445 Hempstead⊙ 3,456 .... J7
75652 Henderson⊙ 11,473 .... K5
76365 Henrietta⊙ 3,149 .... F4
79045 Hereford⊙ 15,853 .... B3
†75201 Highland Park 8,909 .... G2
77562 Highlands 6,467 .... K1
76645 Hillsboro⊙ 7,397 .... G5
77563 Hitchcock 6,655 .... K3
78861 Hondo⊙ 6,057 .... E8
*77001 Houston⊙ 1,595,138 .... J2
Houston‡ 2,905,350 .... J2
*77338 Humble 6,729 .... J7
†77001 Hunters Creek Village 4,215 .... J1
77340 Huntsville⊙ 23,936 .... J7
76053 Hurst 31,420 .... F2
76367 Iowa Park 6,184 .... F4
*75061 Irving 109,943 .... G2
77029 Jacinto City 8,953 .... J1
76056 Jacksboro⊙ 4,000 .... F4
75766 Jacksonville 12,264 .... J5
75951 Jasper⊙ 6,959 .... L7
79528 Jayton⊙ 638 .... D4
75657 Jefferson⊙ 2,643 .... K5
†77001 Jersey Village 4,084 .... J1
78636 Johnson City⊙ 872 .... F7
78026 Jourdanton⊙ 2,743 .... F9
76849 Junction⊙ 2,593 .... E7
78118 Karnes City⊙ 3,296 .... G9
77450 Katy 5,660 .... J8
75142 Kaufman⊙ 4,658 .... H5
76248 Keller 4,156 .... F2
78119 Kenedy 4,356 .... G9
79745 Kermit⊙ 8,015 .... B6
78028 Kerrville⊙ 15,276 .... E7
75662 Kilgore 11,006 .... K5
76541 Killeen 46,296 .... G6
Killeen-Temple‡ 214,656 ... G6
78363 Kingsville⊙ 28,808 .... G10
†78109 Kirby 6,435 .... K11
77625 Kountze⊙ 2,716 .... K7
78945 La Grange⊙ 3,768 .... G8
77566 Lake Jackson 19,102 .... J8
76135 Lake Worth 4,394 .... E2
77568 La Marque 15,372 .... K3
79331 Lamesa⊙ 11,790 .... C5
76550 Lampasas⊙ 6,165 .... F6
*75146 Lancaster 14,807 .... G3
77571 La Porte 14,062 .... K2
*78040 Laredo⊙ 91,449 .... E10
Laredo‡ 99,258 .... E10
77573 League City 16,578 .... K2
78873 Leakey⊙ 468 .... E8
†78201 Leon Valley 9,088 .... J10
79336 Levelland⊙ 13,809 .... B4
*75067 Lewisville 24,273 .... G1
77575 Liberty⊙ 7,945 .... K7
75563 Linden⊙ 2,443 .... K4
79056 Lipscomb⊙ 52 .... D1
79339 Littlefield⊙ 7,409 .... B4
†78201 Live Oak 8,183 .... K10
77351 Livingston⊙ 4,928 .... K7
78643 Llano⊙ 3,071 .... F7
78644 Lockhart⊙ 7,953 .... G8
79241 Lockney 2,334 .... C3
*75601 Longview⊙ 62,762 .... K5
Longview-Marshall‡ 151,752 .... K5
*79401 Lubbock⊙ 173,979 .... C4
Lubbock‡ 211,651 .... C4
75901 Lufkin⊙ 28,562 .... K6
78648 Luling 5,039 .... G8
77864 Madisonville⊙ 3,660 .... J7
76063 Mansfield 8,092 .... F3
77578 Manvel 3,549 .... J3
79843 Marfa⊙ 2,466 .... C12
76661 Marlin⊙ 7,099 .... H6
75670 Marshall⊙ 24,921 .... K5
76856 Mason⊙ 2,153 .... E7
79244 Matador⊙ 1,052 .... D3
78368 Mathis 5,667 .... G9
78501 McAllen 66,281 .... F11
McAllen-Pharr-Edinburg‡ 283,229 .... F11
76657 McGregor 4,513 .... G6
75069 McKinney⊙ 16,256 .... H4
†77520 McNair K1
79245 Memphis⊙ 3,352 .... D3
76859 Menard⊙ 1,697 .... E7
79754 Mentone⊙ 50 .... D10
78570 Mercedes 11,851 .... F12
76665 Meridian⊙ 1,330 .... G6
76941 Mertzon⊙ 687 .... C6
*75149 Mesquite 67,053 .... H2
76667 Mexia 7,094 .... H6
79059 Miami⊙ 813 .... D2
*79701 Midland⊙ 70,525 .... C6
Midland‡ 82,636 .... C6
76065 Midlothian 3,219 .... G5
75773 Mineola 4,346 .... J5
76067 Mineral Wells 14,468 .... F5
78572 Mission 22,653 .... F11
77459 Missouri City 24,533 .... J2
79756 Monahans⊙ 8,397 .... B6
76251 Montague⊙ 1,253 .... G4
79346 Morton⊙ 2,674 .... B4
75455 Mount Pleasant⊙ 11,003 .. K4
75457 Mount Vernon⊙ 2,025 .... J4
79347 Muleshoe⊙ 4,842 .... B3
75961 Nacogdoches⊙ 27,149 .... J6
†77598 Nassau Bay 4,526 .... K2
77868 Navasota 5,971 .... J7
77627 Nederland 16,855 .... K8
75570 New Boston 4,628 .... K4
78130 New Braunfels⊙ 22,402 . K10
75966 Newton⊙ 1,620 .... L7
76118 North Richland Hills 30,592 .... F2
79760 Odessa⊙ 90,027 .... B6
Odessa‡ 115,374 .... B6
76374 Olney 4,060 .... F4
77630 Orange⊙ 23,628 .... L7
76943 Ozona⊙ 3,766 .... C7
79248 Paducah⊙ 2,216 .... D4
76866 Paint Rock⊙ 256 .... E6
77465 Palacios 4,667 .... H9
75801 Palestine⊙ 15,948 .... J6
76072 Palo Pinto⊙ 350 .... F5
79065 Pampa⊙ 21,396 .... D2
79068 Panhandle⊙ 2,226 .... C2
75460 Paris⊙ 25,498 .... J4
*77501 Pasadena 112,560 .... J2
77581 Pearland 13,248 .... J2
78061 Pearsall⊙ 7,383 .... E9
79772 Pecos⊙ 12,855 .... D10
79070 Perryton⊙ 7,991 .... D1
78577 Pharr 21,381 .... F11
75686 Pittsburg⊙ 4,245 .... J4
79355 Plains⊙ 1,457 .... B4
79072 Plainview⊙ 22,187 .... C3
75074 Plano 72,331 .... G1
78064 Pleasanton 6,346 .... F9
77640 Port Arthur 61,251 .... K8
78578 Port Isabel 3,769 .... G11
78374 Portland 12,023 .... G10
77979 Port Lavaca⊙ 10,911 .... H9
77651 Port Neches 13,944 .... K7
79356 Post⊙ 3,961 .... C4
78065 Poteet 3,086 .... F8
77445 Prairie View 3,993 .... J7
79845 Presidio 1,723 .... C12
79252 Quanah⊙ 3,890 .... E3
76470 Ranger 3,142 .... F5
79778 Rankin⊙ 1,216 .... B6
78580 Raymondville⊙ 9,493 .... G11
78377 Refugio⊙ 3,898 .... G9
75080 Richardson 72,496 .... G2
76118 Richland Hills 7,977 .... F2
77469 Richmond⊙ 9,692 .... J8
78582 Rio Grande City⊙ 8,930 .. F11
77019 River Oaks 6,890 .... E2
76945 Robert Lee⊙ 1,202 .... D6
78380 Robstown 12,100 .... G10
79543 Roby⊙ 814 .... D5
76567 Rockdale 5,611 .... G7
78382 Rockport⊙ 3,686 .... H9
78880 Rocksprings⊙ 1,317 .... D8
75087 Rockwall⊙ 5,939 .... H5
78584 Roma-Los Saenz 3,384 .... E11
77471 Rosenberg 17,995 .... J8
78664 Round Rock 12,740 .... G7
75088 Rowlett 7,522 .... H2
75785 Rusk⊙ 4,681 .... J6
76179 Saginaw 5,736 .... E2
*76901 San Angelo⊙ 73,240 .... D6
San Angelo‡ 84,784 .... D6

Topography
0 90 180 MI.
0 90 180 KM.
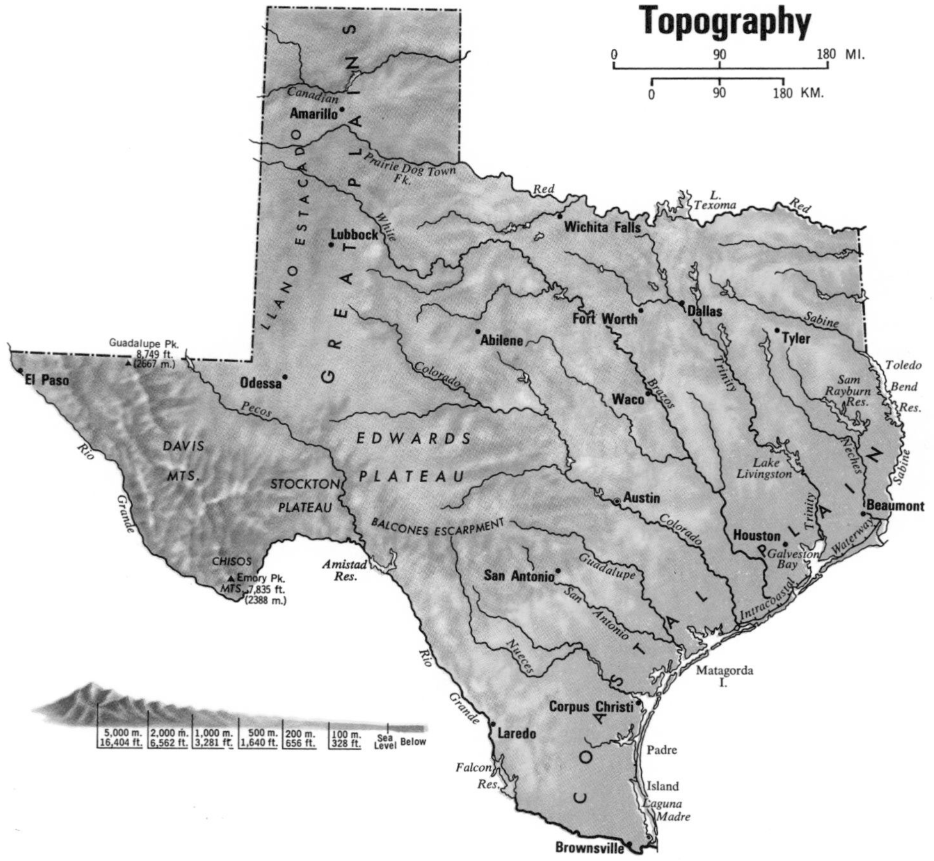
Amarillo
Canadian
LLANO ESTACADO
GREAT PLAINS
Prairie Dog Town Fk.
Red
Lubbock
White
Wichita Falls
L. Texoma
Red
Fort Worth
Dallas
Abilene
Tyler
Sabine
Toledo Bend Res.
Sam Rayburn Res.
Guadalupe Pk. 8,749 ft. (2667 m.)
El Paso
Odessa
Pecos
Colorado
Brazos
Trinity
Waco
Neches
Lake Livingston
Beaumont
DAVIS MTS.
EDWARDS PLATEAU
STOCKTON PLATEAU
Rio Grande
BALCONES ESCARPMENT
Austin
Houston
Galveston Bay
Intracoastal Waterway
San Antonio
Guadalupe
CHISOS MTS.
Emory Pk. 7,835 ft. (2388 m.)
Amistad Res.
Nueces
COASTAL PLAIN
Matagorda I.
Corpus Christi
Laredo
Padre Island
Laguna Madre
Falcon Res.
Brownsville
5,000 m. 16,404 ft.
2,000 m. 6,562 ft.
1,000 m. 3,281 ft.
500 m. 1,640 ft.
200 m. 656 ft.
100 m. 328 ft.
Sea Level
Below

*78201 San Antonio⊙ 786,023 .... J11
San Antonio‡ 1,071,954 .. J11
75972 San Augustine⊙ 2,930 .... K6
78586 San Benito 17,988 .... G12
79848 Sanderson⊙ 1,241 .... B7
78384 San Diego⊙ 5,225 .... F10
76266 Sanger 2,574 .... G4
78589 San Juan 7,608 .... F11
78666 San Marcos⊙ 23,420 .... F8
76877 San Saba⊙ 2,847 .... F6
†76101 Sansom Park Village 3,921 E2
†77510 Santa Fe 6,172 .... K3
78385 Sarita⊙ 200 .... G10
78154 Schertz 7,262 .... K10
77586 Seabrook 4,670 .... K2
75159 Seagoville 7,304 .... H3
77474 Sealy 3,875 .... H8
78155 Seguin⊙ 17,854 .... G8
79360 Seminole⊙ 6,080 .... B5
†78357 Seven Sisters 2 .... F9
76380 Seymour⊙ 3,657 .... E4
75090 Sherman⊙ 30,413 .... H4
Sherman-Denison‡ 89,796 H4
79851 Sierra Blanca⊙ 800 .... B11
77656 Silsbee 7,684 .... K7
79257 Silverton⊙ 918 .... C3
78387 Sinton⊙ 6,044 .... G9
79364 Slaton 6,804 .... C4
78957 Smithville 3,470 .... G7
79549 Snyder⊙ 12,705 .... D5
76950 Sonora⊙ 3,856 .... D7
77587 South Houston 13,293 .... J2
79081 Spearman⊙ 3,413 .... C1
*77373 Spring J7
†77001 Spring Valley 3,353 .... J1
77477 Stafford 4,755 .... J2
79553 Stamford 4,542 .... E5
79782 Stanton⊙ 2,314 .... C5
76401 Stephenville⊙ 11,881 .... F5
76951 Sterling City⊙ 915 .... D6
79083 Stinnett⊙ 2,222 .... C2
79084 Stratford⊙ 1,917 .... C1
77478 Sugar Land 8,826 .... J8
75482 Sulphur Springs⊙ 12,804 . J4
77480 Sweeny 3,538 .... J8
79556 Sweetwater⊙ 12,242 .... D5
78390 Taft 3,686 .... G9
79373 Tahoka⊙ 3,262 .... C4
76574 Taylor 10,619 .... G7
†77586 Taylor Lake Village 3,669 .. K2
75860 Teague 3,390 .... H6
76501 Temple 42,354 .... G6
79852 Terlingua 100 .... D12
75160 Terrell 13,269 .... H5
†78201 Terrell Hills 4,644 .... K11
*75501 Texarkana 31,271 .... L4
Texarkana, Tex.-Texarkana, Ark.‡ 27,019 .... L4
77590 Texas City 41,403 .... K3
73949 Texhoma 358 .... C1
The Colony 11,586 .... G1
76083 Throckmorton⊙ 1,174 .... F4
78072 Tilden⊙ 450 .... F9
77375 Tomball 3,996 .... J7
75862 Trinity 2,620 .... J7
79088 Tulia⊙ 5,033 .... C3
*75701 Tyler⊙ 70,508 .... J5
Tyler‡ 128,366 .... J5
78148 Universal City 10,720 .... K10
†75205 University Park 22,254 .... G2
78801 Uvalde⊙ 14,178 .... E8
75095 Van Alstyne 1,860 .... H4
79855 Van Horn⊙ 2,772 .... C11
79092 Vega⊙ 900 .... B2
76384 Vernon⊙ 12,695 .... E3
77901 Victoria⊙ 50,695 .... H9
Victoria‡ 68,807 .... H9
77662 Vidor 11,834 .... L7
*76701 Waco⊙ 101,261 .... G6
Waco‡ 170,755 .... G6
75501 Wake Village 3,865 .... K4
75165 Waxahachie⊙ 14,624 .... H5
76086 Weatherford⊙ 12,049 .... G5
79095 Wellington⊙ 3,043 .... D3
78596 Weslaco 19,331 .... F11
77486 West Columbia 4,109 .... J8
77630 West Orange 4,610 .... L7
†77005 West University Place 12,010 .... J2
†76101 Westworth 3,651 .... E2
77488 Wharton⊙ 9,033 .... J8
79096 Wheeler⊙ 1,584 .... D2
75693 White Oak 4,415 .... K5
76273 Whitesboro 3,197 .... H4
76108 White Settlement 13,508 ... E2
*76301 Wichita Falls⊙ 94,201 .... F4
Wichita Falls‡ 130,664 .... F4
†78201 Windcrest 5,332 .... K11
75494 Winnsboro 3,458 .... J5
79567 Winters 3,061 .... E6
75979 Woodville⊙ 2,821 .... K7
75098 Wylie 3,152 .... H1
78076 Zapata⊙ 3,831 .... E11

OTHER FEATURES

Amistad (res.) C8
Amistad Nat'l Rec. Area D8
Angelina (riv.) K6
Apache (mts.) C11
Aransas (passage) H10
Arlington (lake) F2
Baffin (bay) G10
Balcones Escarpment (plat.) E8
Beals (creek) C5
Benbrook (lake) E3
Bergstrom A.F.B. G7
Big Bend Nat'l Park A8
Bolivar (pen.) K8
Brazos (riv.) H7
Brownwood (lake) E6
Buchanan (lake) F7
Buck (creek) D3
Caddo (lake) L5
Canadian (riv.) D1
Carrizo (creek) A1
Carswell A.F.B. E2
Cathedral (mt.) D12
Cavallo (passage) H9
Cedar (lake) B5
Cerro Alto (mt.) B10
Chamizal Nat'l Mem. A10
Chase N.A.S. G9
Chinati (mts.) C12
Chinati (peak) C12
Chisos (mts.) A8
Cibolo (creek) K11
Clear Fork, Brazos (riv.) D5
Coldwater (creek) B1
Colorado (riv.) F7
Copano (bay) G9
Corpus Christi (lake) F9
Corpus Christi N.A.S. G10
Cottonwood Draw (dry riv.) C10
Davis (mts.) C11
Deep (creek) C5
Delaware (creek) C10
Delaware (mts.) C10
Denison (dam) H4
Devils (riv.) D7
Diablo, Sierra (mts.) C10
Double Mountain Fork, Brazos (riv.) C4
Dyess A.F.B. D5
Eagle (peak) C11
Eagle Mountain (lake) E1
Edwards (plat.) C7
Elephant (mt.) D12
Ellington A.F.B. K2
Elm Fork, Trinity (riv.) G2
Emory (peak) A8
Falcon (res.) E11
Finlay (mts.) B10
Fort Bliss 12,687 .... A10
Fort Davis Nat'l Hist. Site D11
Fort Hood 31,250 .... G6
Frio (riv.) E8
Galveston (bay) L2
Galveston (isl.) K3
Glass (mts.) A7
Goodfellow A.F.B. D6
Grapevine (lake) F2
Guadalupe (mts.) C10
Guadalupe (peak) B10
Guadalupe (riv.) G8
Guadalupe Mts. Nat'l Park C10
Houston (lake) J8
Houston Ship (chan.) K2
Howard (creek) C7
Hubbard Creek (lake) F5
Hueco (mts.) B10
Intracoastal Waterway J9
Johnson Draw (dry riv.) C7
Kelly A.F.B. J11
Kemp (lake) E4
Kingsville N.A.S. G10
Kiowa (creek) D1
Lackland A.F.B. 14,459 .... J11
Lake Meredith Nat'l Rec. Area C2
Lampasas (riv.) G6
Laughlin A.F.B. 2,994 .... D8
Lavon (lake) H1
Leon (riv.) F6
Livermore (mt.) C11
Livingston (lake) K7
Llano (riv.) D7
Llano Estacado (plain) B4
Locke (mt.) D11
Los Olmos (creek) D11
Los Olmos (creek) F11
Lyndon B. Johnson Nat'l Hist. Site F7
Lyndon B. Johnson Space Ctr. K2
Madre (lag.) G11
Maravillas (creek) A7
Matagorda (bay) H9
Matagorda (isl.) H9
Matagorda (pen.) J9
Matagorda Isl. Bombing and Gunnery Range H9
Medina (lake) E8
Medina (riv.) J11
Mexico (gulf) K9
Middle Concho (riv.) C6
Mountain Creek (lake) G2
Mustang (creek) A1
Mustang (isl.) G10
Mustang Draw (dry riv.) B5
Navasota (riv.) H7
Navidad (riv.) H8
Neches (riv.) K6
North Concho (riv.) C6
North Pease (riv.) D3
Nueces (riv.) F9
Padre (isl.) G10
Padre Island Nat'l Seashore G11
Palo Duro (creek) B2
Palo Duro (creek) C1
Pease (riv.) D3
Pecos (riv.) C7
Pedernales (riv.) F7
Possum Kingdom (lake) F5
Prairie Dog Town Fork, Red (riv.) ... C3
Quitman (mts.) B11
Red (riv.) F3
Red Bluff (lake) A6
Reese A.F.B. 1,934 .... B4
Rio Grande (riv.) D9
Rita Blanca (creek) B2
Sabine (riv.) L7
Salt Fork, Red (riv.) D3
Sam Rayburn (res.) K6
San Antonio (bay) H9
San Antonio (mt.) B10
San Antonio Missions Nat'l Hist. Park J11
San Francisco (creek) B8
San Luis (passage) K8
San Martine Draw (dry riv.) C11
San Saba (riv.) D7
Santa Isabel (creek) E10
Santiago (mts.) A8
Santiago (peak) D12
Sheppard A.F.B. F3
Sierra Diablo (mts.) C10
Sierra Vieja (mts.) C11
Staked (Llano Estacado) (plain) B4
Stamford (lake) E4
Stockton (plat.) B7
Sulphur (riv.) J4
Sulphur Draw (dry riv.) B4
Sulphur Springs (creek) B4
Tenmile (creek) G3
Terlingua (creek) D12
Texoma (lake) H3
Tierra Blanca (creek) B3
Toledo Bend (res.) L6
Toyah (creek) D11
Toyah (lake) A6
Travis (lake) G7
Trinity (bay) L2
Trinity (riv.) H5
Trinity, West Fork (riv.) G2
Trujillo (creek) A2
Vieja, Sierra (mts.) C11
Walnut (creek) F3
Washita (riv.) D2
West (bay) K3
White (riv.) C3
White River (lake) C4
White Rock (creek) G2
Wichita (riv.) F4
Wolf (creek) D1
Worth (lake) E2

⊙County seat.
‡Population of metropolitan area.
† Zip of nearest p.o. * Multiple zips.

Texas

Scale 1:4,600,000

State Capitals ⊛
County Seats ⊙
Major Limited Access Hwys. ——

© Copyright Hammond Incorporated, Maplewood, N.J.

Western Part of Texas
Same scale as main map

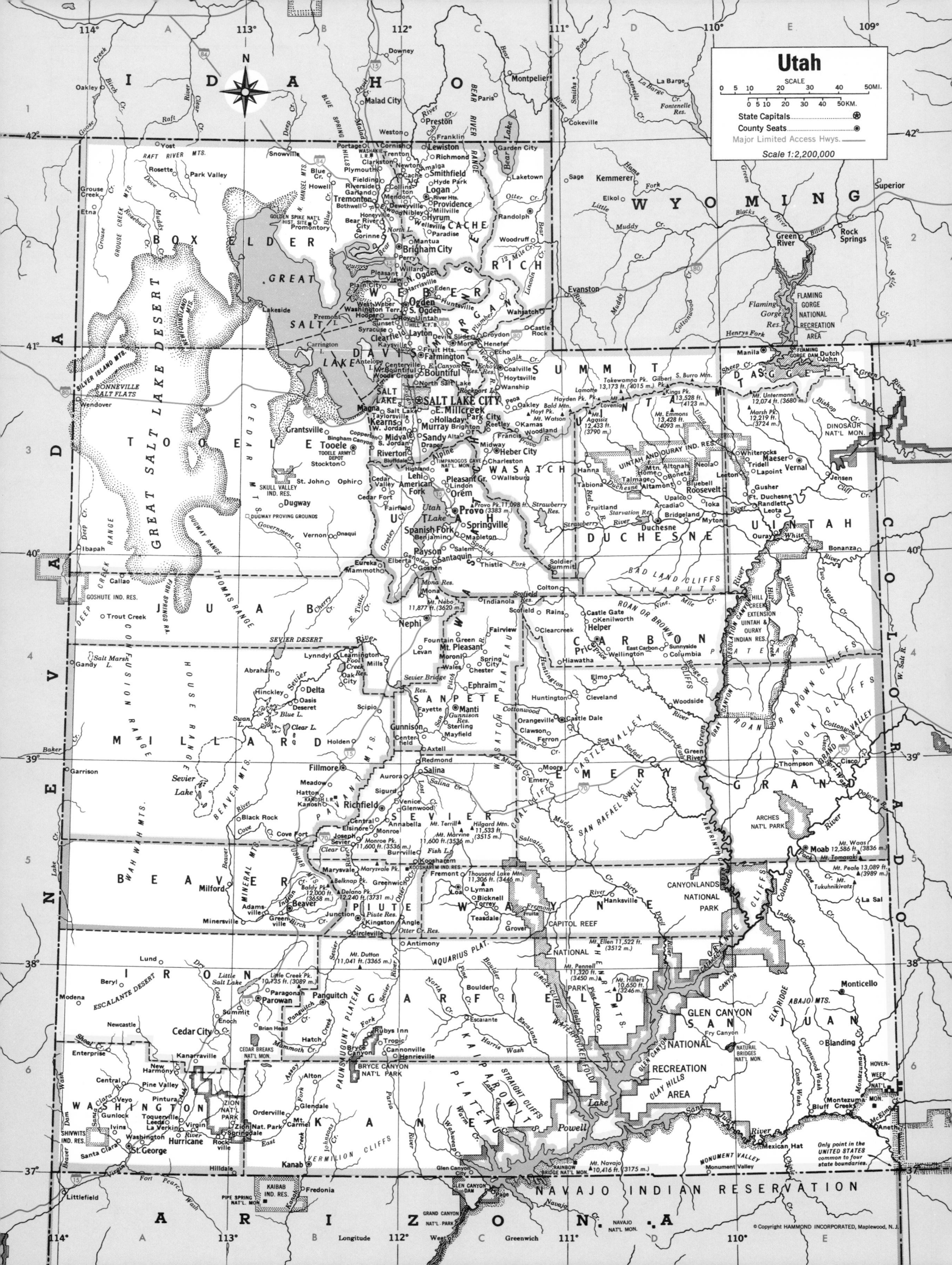

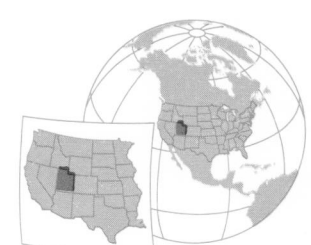

AREA 84,899 sq. mi. (219,888 sq. km.)
POPULATION 1,461,037
CAPITAL Salt Lake City
LARGEST CITY Salt Lake City
HIGHEST POINT Kings Pk. 13,528 ft. (4123 m.)
SETTLED IN 1847
ADMITTED TO UNION January 4, 1896
POPULAR NAME Beehive State
STATE FLOWER Sego Lily
STATE BIRD Sea Gull

COUNTIES

Beaver 4,378 ....A5
Box Elder 33,222 ....A2
Cache 57,176 ....C2
Carbon 22,179 ....D4
Daggett 769 ....E3
Davis 146,540 ....B3
Duchesne 12,565 ....D3
Emery 11,451 ....D4
Garfield 3,673 ....C6
Grand 8,241 ....E5
Iron 17,349 ....A6
Juab 5,530 ....A4
Kane 4,024 ....B6
Millard 8,970 ....A4
Morgan 4,917 ....C2
Piute 1,329 ....B5
Rich 2,100 ....C2
Salt Lake 619,066 ....B3
San Juan 12,253 ....E6
Sanpete 14,620 ....C4
Sevier 14,727 ....C5
Summit 10,198 ....D3
Tooele 26,033 ....A3
Uintah 20,506 ....E3
Utah 218,106 ....C3
Wasatch 8,523 ....C3
Washington 26,065 ....A6
Wayne 1,911 ....C5
Weber 144,616 ....B2

CITIES and TOWNS

Zip	Name/Pop.	Key
†84003	Alpine 2,649	C3
84003	American Fork 12,693	C3
84713	Beaver⊙ 1,792	B5
84511	Blanding 3,118	E6
†84065	Bluffdale 1,300	B3
84010	Bountiful 32,877	C3
84302	Brigham City⊙ 15,596	C2
†84101	Brighton 150	C3
84513	Castle Dale⊙ 1,910	D4
84720	Cedar City 10,972	A6
84014	Centerville 8,069	C3
84015	Clearfield 17,982	B2
84017	Coalville⊙ 1,031	C3
84624	Delta 1,930	B4
84020	Draper 5,521	C3
84021	Duchesne⊙ 1,677	D3
84022	Dugway 1,646	B3
84520	East Carbon 1,942	D4
84109	East Millcreek 24,150	C3
84627	Ephraim 2,810	C4
84025	Farmington⊙ 4,691	C3
84523	Ferron 1,718	C4
84631	Fillmore⊙ 2,083	B5
†84037	Fruit Heights 2,728	C2
84312	Garland 1,405	B2
84029	Grantsville 4,419	B3
84525	Green River 1,048	D4
84634	Gunnison 1,255	C4
†84401	Harrisville 1,371	C2
84032	Heber City⊙ 4,362	C3
84526	Helper 2,724	D4
†84043	Highland 2,435	C3
†84767	Hildale 1,009	A6
84117	Holladay 22,189	C3
84528	Huntington 2,316	C4
84737	Hurricane 2,361	A6
84318	Hyde Park 1,495	C2
84319	Hyrum 3,952	C2
84740	Junction⊙ 151	B5
84036	Kamas 1,064	C3
84741	Kanab⊙ 2,148	B6
84037	Kaysville 9,811	B2
84118	Kearns 21,353	B3
84745	La Verkin 1,174	A6
84041	Layton 22,862	C2
84043	Lehi 6,848	C3
84320	Lewiston 1,438	C2
†84062	Lindon 2,796	C3
84747	Loa⊙ 364	C5
84321	Logan⊙ 26,844	C2
†84078	Maeser 2,216	E3
84044	Magna 13,138	B3
84046	Manila⊙ 272	E3
84642	Manti⊙ 2,080	C4
†84663	Mapleton 2,726	C3
84531	Mexican Hat 250	E6
84047	Midvale 10,146	B3
84049	Midway 1,194	C3
84751	Milford 1,293	A5
84532	Moab⊙ 5,333	E5
84754	Monroe 1,476	B5
84535	Monticello⊙ 1,929	E6
84050	Morgan⊙ 1,896	C2
84646	Moroni 1,086	C4
84647	Mount Pleasant 2,049	C4
84107	Murray 25,750	C3
84648	Nephi⊙ 3,285	C4
†84321	Nibley 1,036	C2
†84404	North Ogden 9,309	C2
†84010	North Salt Lake 5,548	C3
*84401	Ogden⊙ 64,407	C2
	Ogden-Salt Lake City‡ 936,255	C4
84537	Orangeville 1,309	C4
84057	Orem 52,399	C3
	Orem-Provo‡ 218,106	C3
84759	Panguitch⊙ 1,343	B6
84060	Park City 2,823	C3
84761	Parowan⊙ 1,836	B6
84651	Payson 8,246	C3
†84302	Perry 1,084	C2
†84401	Plain City 2,379	C2
84062	Pleasant Grove 10,833	C3
†84401	Pleasant View 3,983	C2
84501	Price⊙ 9,086	D4
84332	Providence 2,675	C2
84601	Provo⊙ 74,108	C3
	Provo-Orem‡ 218,106	C3
84064	Randolph⊙ 659	C2
84701	Richfield⊙ 5,482	B5
84333	Richmond 1,705	C2
†84321	River Heights 1,211	C2
84065	Riverton 7,293	B3
84066	Roosevelt 3,842	D3
84067	Roy 19,694	C2
	Saint George⊙ 11,350	A6
84653	Salem 2,233	C3
84654	Salina 1,992	C5
*84101	Salt Lake City (cap)⊙ 163,697	C3
	Salt Lake City-Ogden‡ 936,255	C3
*84070	Sandy 52,210	C3
84765	Santa Clara 1,091	A6
84655	Santaquin 2,175	C4
84335	Smithfield 4,993	C2
†84065	South Jordan 7,492	B3
†84403	South Ogden 11,366	C2
84115	South Salt Lake 9,884	C3
84660	Spanish Fork 9,825	C3
84663	Springville 12,101	C3
†84015	Sunset 5,733	B2
†84041	Syracuse 3,702	B2
†84101	Taylorsville 17,448	B3
84074	Tooele⊙ 14,335	B3
84337	Tremonton 3,464	B2
84078	Vernal⊙ 6,600	E3
84780	Washington 3,092	A6
†84403	Washington Terrace 8,212	B2
84542	Wellington 1,406	D4
84339	Wellsville 1,952	C2
84083	Wendover 1,099	A3
†84087	West Bountiful 3,556	B3
84084	West Jordan 27,192	B3
84340	Willard 1,241	C2
84087	Woods Cross 4,263	B3

OTHER FEATURES

Abajo (mts.) E6
Agassiz (mt.) D3
Antelope (isl.) B3
Aquarius (plat.) C5
Arches Nat'l Park E5
Assay (creek) B6
Bad Land (cliffs) D4
Baldy (peak) B5
Bear (lake) C2
Bear (riv.) B2
Beaver (mts.) A5
Beaver (riv.) A5
Beaver Dam Wash (creek) A6
Birch (creek) B5
Blue (creek) B2
Bonneville (salt flats) A3
Book (cliffs) E4
Brown (Roan) (cliffs) E4
Bryce Canyon Nat'l Park B6
Canyonlands Nat'l Park D5
Capitol Reef Nat'l Park D4
Castle (valley) D4
Cedar (mts.) B3
Cedar Breaks Nat'l Mon. B6
Chalk (creek) C3
Chinle (creek) E6
Clear (lake) B4
Cliff (creek) E3
Coal (cliffs) C5
Colorado (riv.) E5
Confusion (range) A4
Cottonwood (creek) C4
Cub (creek) C1
Deep (creek) B1
Deep Creek (range) A4
Delano (peak) B5
Desolation (canyon) E4
Dinosaur Nat'l Mon. E3
Dirty Devil (riv.) D5
Dolores (riv.) E5
Dry Coal (creek) A6
Duchesne (riv.) D3
Dugway (range) A3
Dugway Proving Grounds B3
Dutton (mt.) B5
East Canyon (res.) C3
Echo (res.) C3
Elk (ridge) E6
Ellen (mt.) D5
Emmons (mt.) D3
Escalante (des.) A6
Escalante (riv.) C6
Fish (lake) C5
Fish Springs (range) A4
Flaming Gorge (res.) E3
Flaming Gorge Nat'l Rec. Area ...E2
Fool Creek (res.) B4
Fremont (isl.) B2
Fremont (riv.) C5
Glen Canyon Nat'l Rec. Area D6
Golden Spike Nat'l Hist. Site B2
Goshute Ind. Res. A4
Government (creek) B3
Gray (canyon) D4
Great Salt (lake) B2
Great Salt Lake (des.) A3
Greeley (creek) B3
Green (riv.) D4
Grouse (creek) A2
Grouse Creek (mts.) A2
Gunnison (res.) C4
Henry (mts.) D6
Hilgard (mt.) C5
Hill (creek) E4
Hill A.F.B. C2
Hill Creek Ext., Uintah and Ouray Ind. Res. E4
Hillers (mt.) D6
House (range) A4
Hovenweep Nat'l Mon. E6
Huntington (creek) C4
Indian (creek) B5
Jordan (riv.) C3
Kaiparowits (plat.) C6
Kanab (creek) B7
Kanosh Ind. Res. B5
Kings (peak) D3
Koosharem Ind. Res. C5
Little Creek (peak) B6
Little Salt (lake) A6
Malad (riv.) B1
Marsh (peak) E3
Marvine (mt.) C5
Mineral (mts.) B5
Mona (res.) C4
Monroe (peak) B5
Montezuma (creek) E6
Monument (valley) D6
Muddy (creek) C4
Natural Bridges Nat'l Mon. E6
Navajo (mt.) D6
Navajo Ind. Res. D7
Nebo (mt.) C4
Newfoundland (mts.) A2
Nine Mile (creek) D4
North (lake) B2
Orange (cliffs) D5
Otter (creek) C5
Otter Creek (res.) C5
Paria (riv.) B6
Paunsaugunt (plat.) B6
Pavant (mts.) B5
Peale (mt.) E5
Pennell (mt.) D6
Piute (res.) B5
Plumber (creek) C2
Powell (lake) D6
Price (riv.) D4
Provo (peak) C3
Provo (riv.) C3
Raft River (mts.) A2
Rainbow Bridge Nat'l Mon. C6
Roan (cliffs) E4
Rockport (lake) C3
Salvation (creek) C5
San Juan (riv.) D6
San Pitch (riv.) C4
San Rafael (riv.) D4
San Rafael Swell (mts.) D5
Santa Clara (riv.) A6
Sevier (des.) B4
Sevier (lake) A5
Sevier (riv.) B4
Sevier Bridge (res.) C4
Shivwits Ind. Res. A6
Silver Island (mts.) A3
Skull Valley Ind. Res. B3
Spanish Fork (riv.) C3
Strait (cliffs) C6
Strawberry (riv.) C3
Strawberry (riv.) D3
Swan (lake) B4
Tavaputs (plat.) D4
Thomas (range) A4
Thousand Lake (mt.) C5
Timpanogos Cave Nat'l Mon. C3
Tokewamna (mt.) D3
Tooele Army Depot B3
Two Water (creek) E4
Uinta (mts.) D3
Uinta (riv.) D3
Uintah and Ouray Ind. Res. D3
Utah (lake) C3
Virgin (riv.) A6
Waas (mt.) E5
Wah Wah (mts.) A5
Wahweap (creek) C6
Wasatch (range) C3
Washakie Ind. Res. B2
Waterpocket Fold (cliffs) D6
Weber (riv.) C3
White (riv.) E3
Willow (creek) E4
Zion Nat'l Park A6

⊙County seat.
‡Population of metropolitan area.
† Zip of nearest p.o.
* Multiple zips.

Agriculture, Industry and Resources

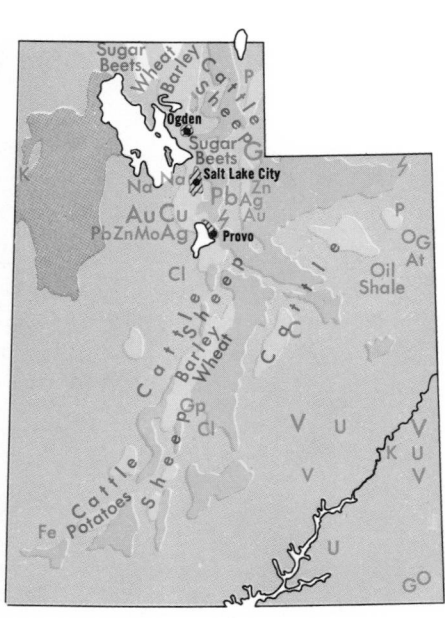

DOMINANT LAND USE

Wheat, General Farming

General Farming, Livestock, Special Crops

Range Livestock

Forests

Nonagricultural Land

MAJOR MINERAL OCCURRENCES

Ag Silver
At Asphalt
Au Gold
C Coal
Cl Clay
Cu Copper

Fe Iron Ore
G Natural Gas
Gp Gypsum
K Potash
Mo Molybdenum
Na Salt

O Petroleum
P Phosphates
Pb Lead
U Uranium
V Vanadium
Zn Zinc

⚡ Water Power
▨ Major Industrial Areas

Topography

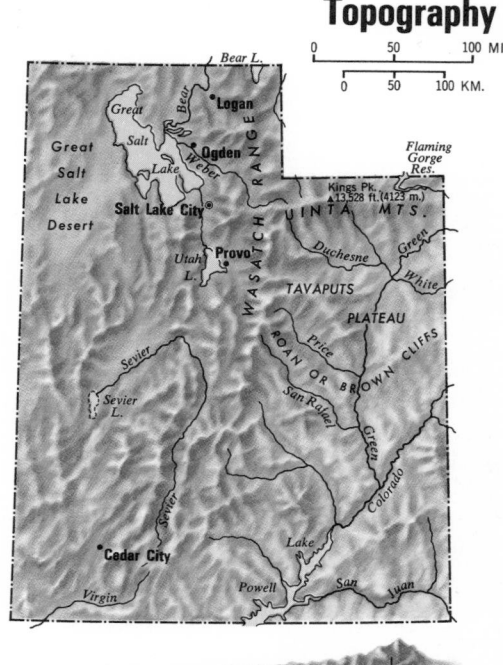

Topography

0   40   80 MI.
0   40   80 KM.

5,000 m. 2,000 m. 1,000 m. 500 m. 200 m. 100 m. Sea
16,404 ft. 6,562 ft. 3,281 ft. 1,640 ft. 656 ft. 328 ft. Level Below

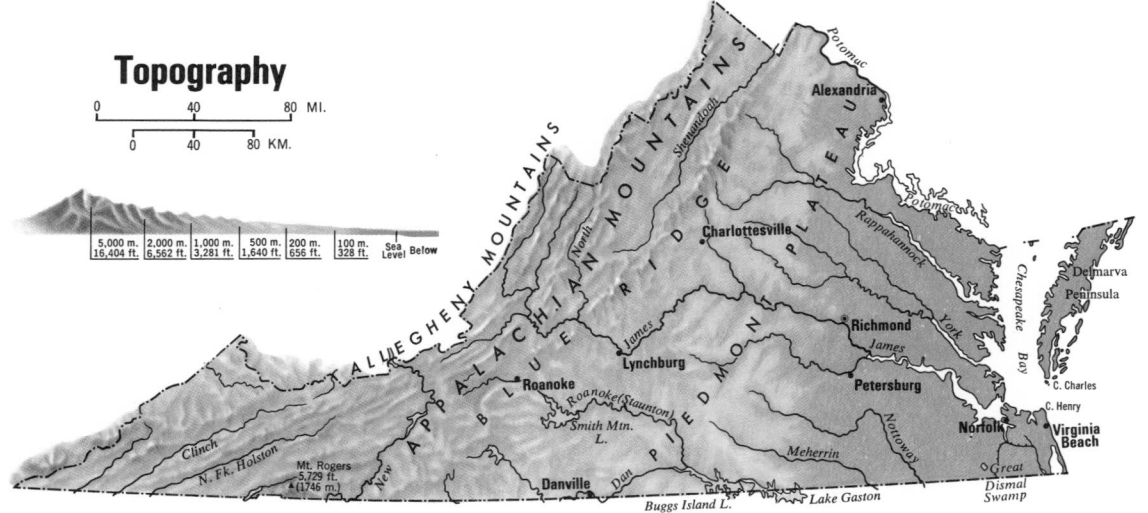

*22901 Charlottesville		
(I.C.) 39,916	M4	
Charlottesville‡ 113,568	M4	
23924 Chase City 2,749	M7	
24531 Chatham⊙ 1,390	K7	
23316 Cheriton 695	R6	
*23320 Chesapeake (I.C.)		
114,486	R7	
23831 Chester 11,728	O6	
23832 Chesterfield⊙ 950	N6	
22623 Chester Gap 400	M3	
24319 Chilhowie 1,269	E6	
23336 Chincoteague 1,607	T5	
24073 Christiansburg⊙ 10,345	H6	
23032 Church View 200	P5	
23899 Claremont 380	P6	
23927 Clarksville 1,468	L7	
†23061 Clay Bank 200	P6	
†23139 Clayville 200	N6	
22624 Clear Brook 300	M2	
24225 Cleveland 360	D7	
24422 Clifton Forge		
(I.C.) 5,046	J5	
24321 Clinchburg 250	E7	
24226 Clinchco 900	D6	
24244 Clinchport 89	C7	
24228 Clintwood⊙ 1,369	D6	
24534 Clover 215	K7	
24077 Cloverdale 850	J6	
24535 Cluster Springs 350	L7	
23035 Cobbs Creek 700	P6	
24230 Coeburn 2,625	D7	
24536 Coleman Falls 250	K6	
†24450 Collierstown 300	J5	
24078 Collinsville 7,517	J7	
22443 Colonial Beach 2,474	P4	
23834 Colonial Heights		
(I.C.) 16,509	O6	
23038 Columbia 111	M5	
24538 Concord 500	K6	
23837 Courtland⊙ 976	O7	
22931 Covesville 475	L5	
24426 Covington (I.C.)⊙		
9,063	J5	
24430 Craigsville 845	J4	
23930 Crewe 2,325	M6	
24431 Crimora 450	L4	
24322 Cripple Creek 200	F7	
24323 Crockett 200	F7	
22932 Crozet 2,553	L4	
23039 Crozier 300	N5	
24539 Crystal Hill 475	L7	
23934 Cullen 725	L6	
22701 Culpeper⊙ 6,621	M4	
23040 Cumberland⊙ 300	M6	
22448 Dahlgren 950	O4	
22193 Dale City 33,127	O3	
24083 Daleville 450	J6	
24236 Damascus 1,330	E7	
24237 Dante 1,083	D7	
*24540 Danville (I.C.) 45,642	J7	
Danville‡ 111,789	J7	

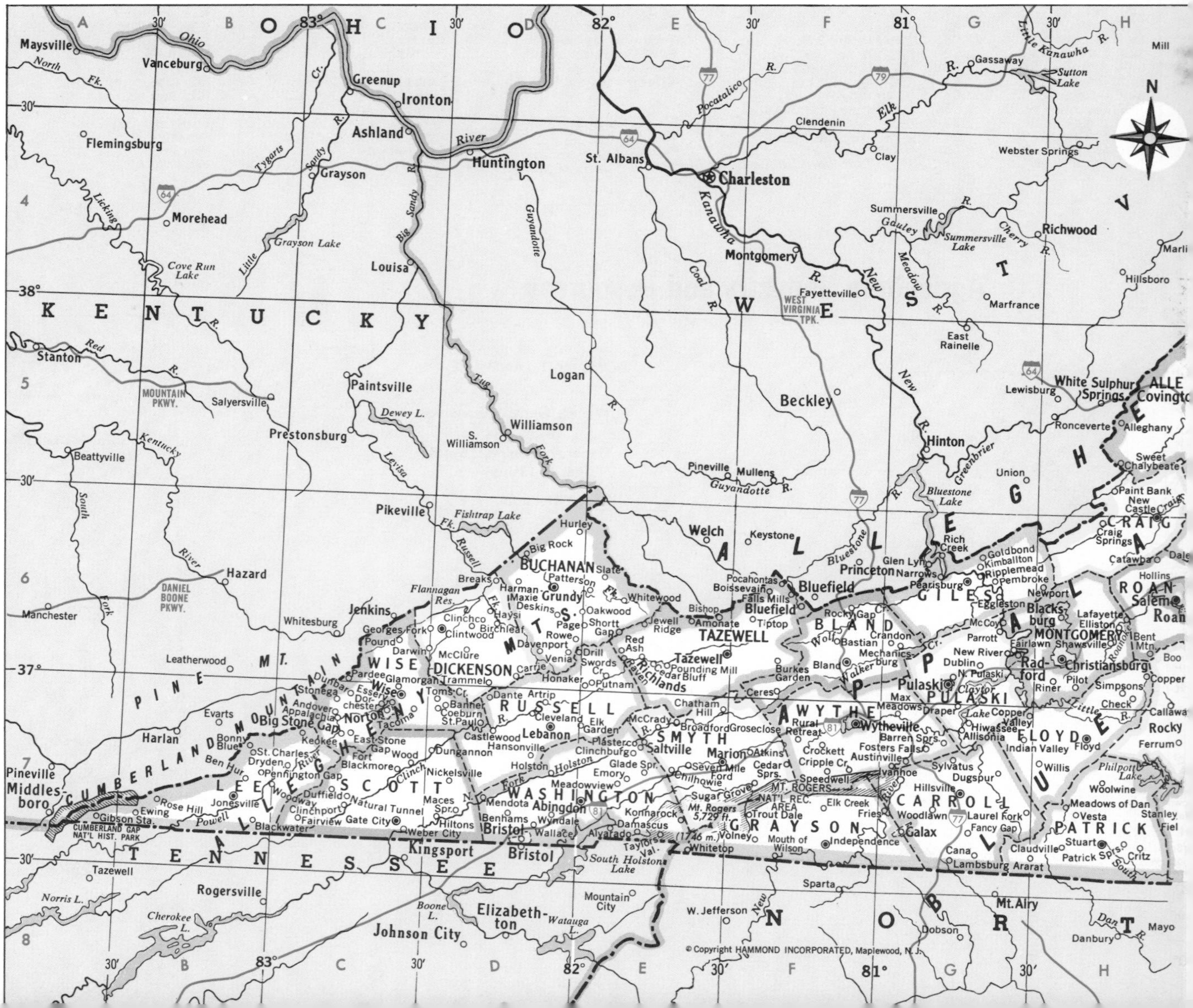

COUNTIES

Accomack 31,268 .... S5
Albemarle 55,783 .... L5
Alleghany 14,333 .... H5
Amelia 8,405 .... M6
Amherst 29,122 .... K5
Appomattox 11,971 .... L6
Arlington 152,599 .... S2
Augusta 53,732 .... K4
Bath 5,860 .... J4
Bedford 34,927 .... J6
Bland 6,349 .... F6
Botetourt 23,270 .... J5
Brunswick 15,632 .... N7
Buchanan 37,989 .... D6
Buckingham 11,751 .... L5
Campbell 45,424 .... K6
Caroline 17,904 .... O4
Carroll 27,270 .... G7
Charles City 6,692 .... O6
Charlotte 12,266 .... L6
Chesterfield 141,372 .... N6
Clarke 9,965 .... M2
Craig 3,948 .... H6
Culpeper 22,620 .... M3
Cumberland 7,881 .... M6
Dickenson 19,806 .... D6
Dinwiddie 22,602 .... N6
Essex 8,864 .... P5
Fairfax 596,901 .... O3
Fauquier 35,889 .... N3
Floyd 11,563 .... H7
Fluvanna 10,244 .... M5
Franklin 35,740 .... J6
Frederick 34,150 .... M2
Giles 17,810 .... G6
Gloucester 20,107 .... P6
Goochland 11,761 .... N5
Grayson 16,579 .... F7
Greene 7,625 .... M4
Greensville 10,903 .... N7
Halifax 30,599 .... L7
Hanover 50,398 .... N5
Henrico 180,735 .... O6
Henry 57,654 .... J7
Highland 2,937 .... J4
Isle of Wight 21,603 .... P7
James City 22,763 .... P6
King and Queen 5,968 .... P5
King George 10,543 .... O4
King William 9,334 .... O5
Lancaster 10,129 .... R5
Lee 25,956 .... B7
Loudoun 57,427 .... N2
Louisa 17,825 .... N5
Lunenburg 12,124 .... M7
Madison 10,232 .... M4
Mathews 7,995 .... R6
Mecklenburg 29,444 .... M7
Middlesex 7,719 .... R5
Montgomery 63,516 .... H6
Nelson 12,204 .... L5
New Kent 8,781 .... P5
Northampton 14,625 .... S6
Northumberland 9,828 .... R5
Nottoway 14,666 .... M6
Orange 18,063 .... M4
Page 19,401 .... M3
Patrick 17,647 .... H7
Pittsylvania 66,147 .... K7
Powhatan 13,062 .... N5
Prince Edward 16,456 .... M6
Prince George 25,733 .... O6
Prince William 144,703 .... O3
Pulaski 35,229 .... G6
Rappahannock 6,093 .... M3
Richmond 6,952 .... P5
Roanoke 72,945 .... H6
Rockbridge 17,911 .... K5
Rockingham 57,038 .... L4
Russell 31,761 .... D7
Scott 25,068 .... C7
Shenandoah 27,559 .... L3
Smyth 33,366 .... E7
Southampton 18,731 .... O7
Spotsylvania 34,435 .... N4
Stafford 40,470 .... O4
Surry 6,046 .... P6
Sussex 10,874 .... O7
Tazewell 50,511 .... E6
Warren 21,200 .... M3

Washington 46,487 .... D7
Westmoreland 14,041 .... P4
Wise 43,863 .... C6
Wythe 25,522 .... F7
York 35,463 .... P6

CITIES and TOWNS

Zip   Name/Pop.   Key

24210 Abingdon⊙ 4,318 .... D7
23301 Accomac⊙ 522 .... S5
23001 Achilles 525 .... R6
22920 Afton 350 .... L4
23821 Alberta 394 .... N7
24411 Augusta Springs 600 .... K4
24312 Austinville 750 .... F7
24054 Axton 540 .... J7
22041 Bailey's
   Crossroads 12,564 .... S3
24230 Banner 327 .... D7
22923 Barboursville 600 .... M4
24055 Bassett 2,034 .... J7
24314 Bastian 600 .... F6
22924 Batesville 575 .... L5
23015 Beaverdam 500 .... N5
24523 Bedford (I.C.)⊙ 5,991 .... J6
23306 Belle Haven 589 .... S5
22610 Bentonville 500 .... M3
22611 Berryville⊙ 1,752 .... M2
24526 Big Island 500 .... K5
24603 Big Rock 900 .... D6
24219 Big Stone Gap 4,748 .... C7
24220 Birchleaf 650 .... D6
23307 Birdsnest 736 .... S6
24604 Bishop 600 .... E6
24060 Blacksburg 30,638 .... H6

23004 Arvonia 500 .... M5
22011 Ashburn 345 .... O2
23005 Ashland 4,640 .... N5
24311 Atkins 1,352 .... F7
*22301 Alexandria (I.C.) 103,217 .... S3
24310 Allisonia 325 .... G7
24517 Altavista 3,849 .... K6
24520 Alton 500 .... K7
23002 Amelia Court House⊙ 500 .... N6
24521 Amherst⊙ 1,135 .... K5
22003 Annandale 49,524 .... S3
24216 Appalachia 2,418 .... C7
24522 Appomattox⊙ 1,345 .... L6
24053 Ararat 500 .... G7
*22201 Arlington⊙ 152,599 .... T3
22922 Arrington 500 .... L5

23824 Blackstone 3,624 .... N6
24527 Blairs 500 .... K7
24315 Bland⊙ 950 .... F6
23308 Bloxom 407 .... S5
24605 Bluefield 5,946 .... F6
24064 Blue Ridge 2,347 .... J6
24606 Boissevain 975 .... F6
23235 Bon Air 16,224 .... N5
24065 Boones Mill 344 .... J6
22713 Boston 400 .... M3
22227 Bowling Green⊙ 665 .... O4
22620 Boyce 401 .... M2
23917 Boydton⊙ 486 .... M7
23827 Boykins 791 .... O7
22714 Brandy Station 400 .... N4
22812 Bridgewater 3,289 .... K4
24201 Bristol (I.C.)⊙ 19,042 .... D7
24316 Broadford 500 .... E7
22815 Broadway 1,234 .... L3
23920 Brodnax 492 .... N7
22430 Brooke 245 .... O4
24528 Brookneal 1,454 .... L6
24415 Brownsburg 300 .... K5
22610 Browntown 300 .... M3
22622 Brucetown 250 .... M2
23923 Charlotte Court
   House⊙ 568 .... L6

23921 Buckingham⊙ 200 .... L5
24416 Buena Vista
   (I.C.) 6,717 .... K5
24529 Buffalo Junction 300 .... L7
22015 Burke 33,835 .... R3
24608 Burkes Garden 267 .... F6
23922 Burkeville 606 .... M6
22435 Callao 500 .... P5
24067 Callaway 225 .... H7
22016 Calverton 500 .... N3
23310 Cape Charles 1,512 .... R6
23313 Capeville 325 .... R6
23829 Capron 238 .... O7
23315 Carrsville 300 .... P7
23830 Carson 500 .... O6
22017 Casanova 370 .... N3
24069 Cascade 835 .... J7
24224 Castlewood 2,420 .... D7
24070 Catawba 350 .... H6
22019 Catlett 500 .... N3
24609 Cedar Bluff 1,550 .... E6
22437 Center Cross 360 .... P5
†22401 Chancellorsville 40 .... N4
22021 Chantilly 500 .... O3
23030 Charles City⊙ 5 .... O6

© Copyright HAMMOND INCORPORATED, Maplewood, N.J.

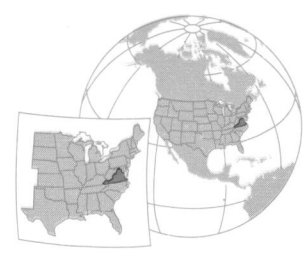

AREA 40,767 sq. mi. (105,587 sq. km.)
POPULATION 5,346,818
CAPITAL Richmond
LARGEST CITY Norfolk
HIGHEST POINT Mt. Rogers 5,729 ft. (1746 m.)
SETTLED IN 1607
ADMITTED TO UNION June 26, 1788
POPULAR NAME Old Dominion
STATE FLOWER Dogwood
STATE BIRD Cardinal

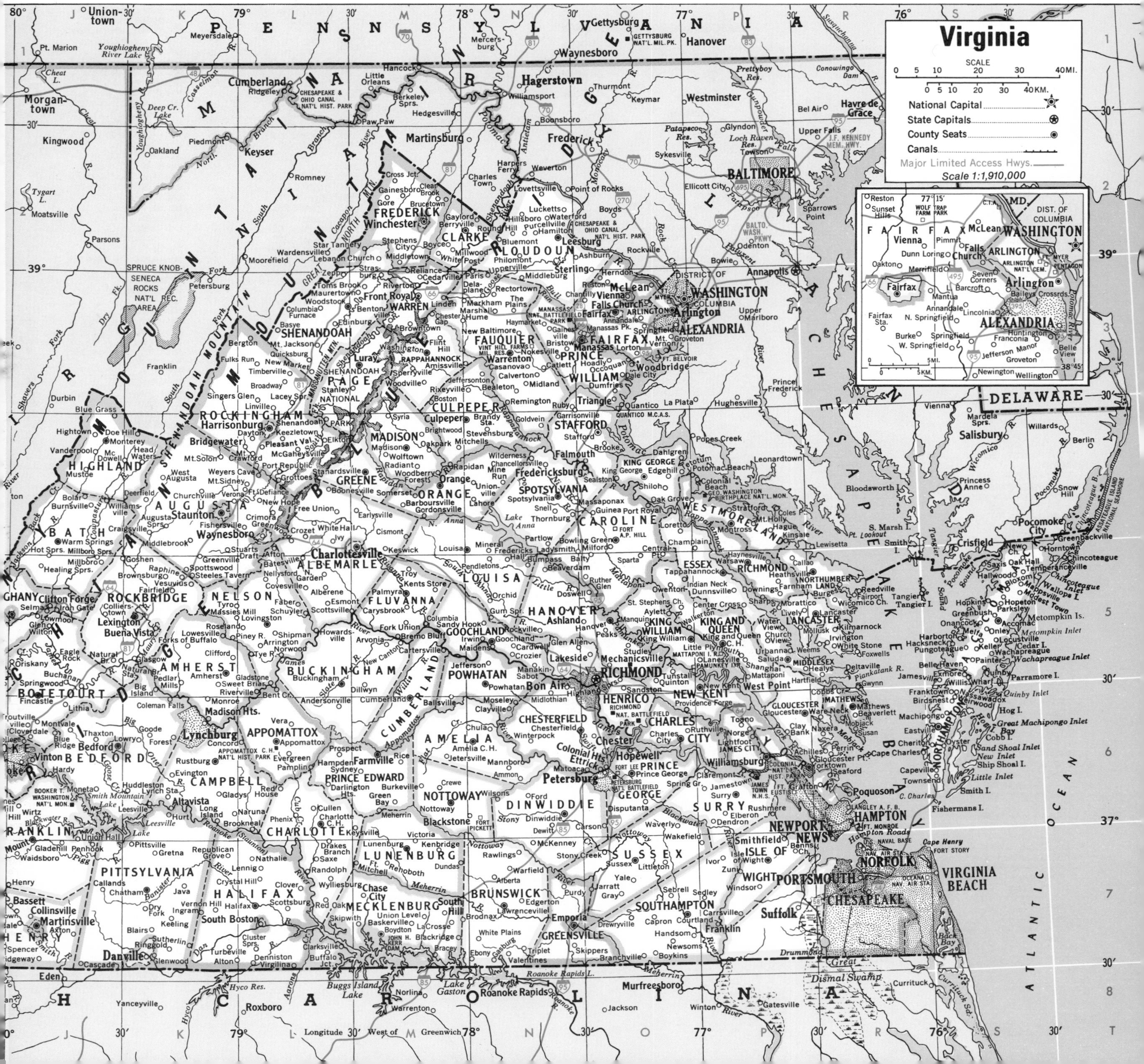

(continued on following page)

Virginia

SCALE
0 5 10   20   30   40 MI.
0 5 10   20   30   40 KM.

National Capital ★
State Capitals ⊛
County Seats ⊙
Canals

Major Limited Access Hwys.
Scale 1:1,910,000

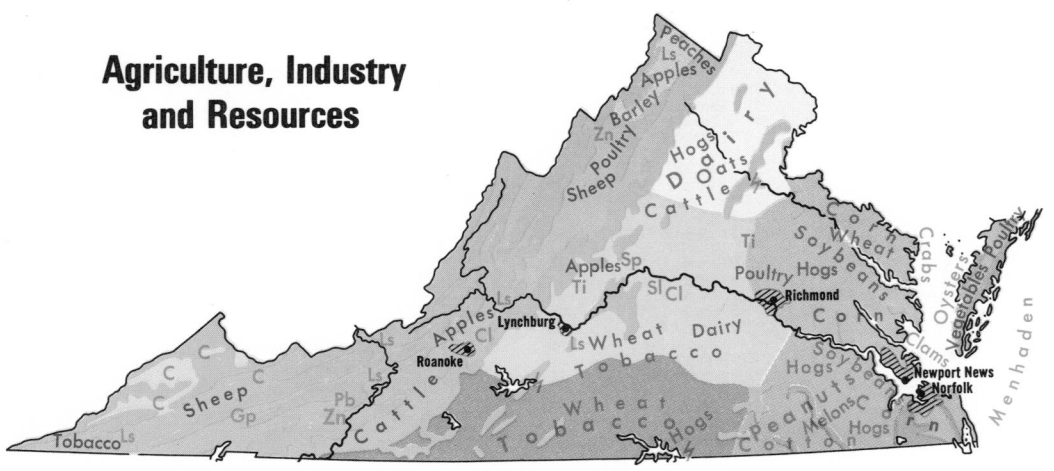

Agriculture, Industry and Resources

DOMINANT LAND USE

- Dairy, General Farming
- General Farming, Livestock, Dairy
- General Farming, Livestock, Tobacco
- General Farming, Livestock, Fruit, Tobacco
- General Farming, Truck Farming, Tobacco, Livestock
- Tobacco, General Farming
- Peanuts, General Farming
- Fruit and Mixed Farming
- Truck and Mixed Farming
- Forests
- Swampland, Limited Agriculture

MAJOR MINERAL OCCURRENCES

C	Coal	Sl	Slate
Cl	Clay	Sp	Soapstone
Gp	Gypsum	Ti	Titanium
Ls	Limestone	Zn	Zinc
Pb	Lead		

⚡ Water Power
▨ Major Industrial Areas

AREA 68,139 sq. mi. (176,480 sq. km.)
POPULATION 4,132,180
CAPITAL Olympia
LARGEST CITY Seattle
HIGHEST POINT Mt. Rainier 14,410 ft. (4392 m.)
SETTLED IN 1811
ADMITTED TO UNION November 11, 1889
POPULAR NAME Evergreen State
STATE FLOWER Western Rhododendron
STATE BIRD Willow Goldfinch

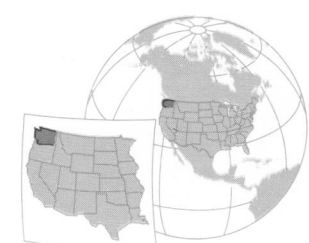

COUNTIES

Adams 13,267 ....G3
Asotin 16,823 ....H4
Benton 109,444 ....F4
Chelan 45,061 ....E3
Clallam 51,648 ....B2
Clark 192,227 ....C5
Columbia 4,057 ....H4
Cowlitz 79,548 ....C4
Douglas 22,144 ....F3
Ferry 5,811 ....G2
Franklin 35,025 ....G4
Garfield 2,468 ....H4
Grant 48,522 ....F3
Grays Harbor 66,314 ....B3
Island 44,048 ....C2
Jefferson 15,965 ....B3
King 1,269,749 ....D3
Kitsap 147,152 ....C3
Kittitas 24,877 ....E3
Klickitat 15,822 ....E5
Lewis 56,028 ....C4
Lincoln 9,604 ....G3
Mason 31,184 ....B3
Okanogan 30,639 ....F2
Pacific 17,237 ....B4
Pend Oreille 8,580 ....H2
Pierce 485,667 ....C3
San Juan 7,838 ....C2
Skagit 64,138 ....D2
Skamania 7,919 ....D5
Snohomish 337,720 ....D2
Spokane 341,835 ....H3
Stevens 28,979 ....H2
Thurston 124,264 ....C4
Wahkiakum 3,832 ....B4
Walla Walla 47,435 ....G4
Whatcom 106,701 ....D2
Whitman 40,103 ....H4
Yakima 172,508 ....E4

CITIES and TOWNS

Zip	Name/Pop.	Key
98520	Aberdeen 18,739	B3
98220	Acme 500	C2
99001	Airway Heights 1,730	H3
99102	Albion 631	H4
†98328	Alder 300	C4
98002	Algona 1,467	C3
98524	Allyn 850	C3
99103	Almira 330	G3
98526	Amanda Park 495	A3
98221	Anacortes 9,013	C2
98601	Amboy 480	C5
98603	Ariel 386	C5
98223	Arlington 3,282	C2
98304	Ashford 300	C4
99402	Asotin⊙ 943	H4
98002	Auburn 26,417	C3
98110	Bainbridge Island-Winslow (Winslow) 2,196	A2
98604	Battle Ground 2,774	C5
†98004	Beaux Arts Village 328	B2
98305	Beaver 450	A2
98528	Belfair 500	C3
*98004	Bellevue 73,903	B2
98225	Bellingham⊙ 45,794	C2
	Bellingham‡ 106,701	C2
99320	Benton City 1,980	F4
98605	Bingen 644	D5
98010	Black Diamond 1,170	C3
98230	Blaine 2,363	C2
†98390	Bonney Lake 5,328	C3
98011	Bothell 7,943	B1
98310	Bremerton 36,208	A2
	Bremerton‡ 146,609	A2
98812	Brewster 1,337	F2
98813	Bridgeport 1,174	F3
†98036	Brier 2,915	C3
98320	Brinnon 500	B3
†98101	Bryn Mawr-Skyway 11,754	B2
98321	Buckley 3,143	C3
98530	Bucoda 519	C4
98921	Buena 500	E4
98166	Burien 23,189	A2
98233	Burlington 3,894	C2
98013	Burton 650	C3
98607	Camas 5,681	C5
98323	Carbonado 456	D3
98324	Carlsborg 500	B2
98814	Carlton 410	F2
98014	Carnation 913	D3
98610	Carson 500	D5
98815	Cashmere 2,240	E3
98611	Castle Rock 2,162	B4
98612	Cathlamet⊙ 635	B4
98531	Centralia 11,555	C4
98520	Central Park 2,709	B3
98532	Chehalis⊙ 6,100	C4
98816	Chelan 2,802	E3
99004	Cheney 7,630	H3
99109	Chewelah 1,888	H2
98614	Chinook 928	B4
98326	Clallam Bay 600	A2
99403	Clarkston 6,903	H4
98235	Clearlake 750	C2
98922	Cle Elum 1,773	E3
98236	Clinton 900	C3
†98004	Clyde Hill 3,229	B2
†98055	Coalfield 500	C3
99111	Colfax⊙ 2,780	H4
99324	College Place 5,771	G4
99113	Colton 307	H4
†98632	Columbia Heights 2,515	C4
99114	Colville⊙ 4,510	H2
98819	Conconully 157	F2
98237	Concrete 592	D2
99326	Connell 1,981	G4
98535	Copalis Beach 600	A3
98536	Copalis Crossing 500	B3
98537	Cosmopolis 1,575	B3
98115	Coulee City 510	F3
99116	Coulee Dam 1,412	G3
98239	Coupeville⊙ 1,006	C2
99117	Creston 309	G3
99119	Cusick 246	H2
98240	Custer 300	C2
98617	Dallesport 600	D5
98241	Darrington 1,064	D2
99122	Davenport⊙ 1,559	G3
99328	Dayton⊙ 2,565	H4
98243	Deer Harbor 400	B2
99006	Deer Park 2,140	H3
98188	Des Moines 7,378	B2
99213	Dishman 10,169	H3
99329	Dixie 210	G4
98821	Dryden 500	E3
†98382	Dungeness 675	B2
98327	Du Pont 559	C3
98019	Duvall 729	D3
98245	Eastsound 800	B2
98801	East Wenatchee 1,640	E3
98328	Eatonville 998	C4
98020	Edmonds 27,679	C3
98926	Ellensburg⊙ 11,752	E3
98541	Elma 2,720	B4
99124	Elmer City 312	G2
99125	Endicott 290	H4
†98310	Enetai 2,638	A2
98822	Entiat 445	E3
98022	Enumclaw 5,427	D3
98823	Ephrata⊙ 5,359	F3
98310	Erlands Point 1,254	A2
98201	Everett⊙ 54,413	C3
98247	Everson 898	C2
99012	Fairfield 582	H3
†98901	Fairview-Sumach 2,788	E4
98024	Fall City 1,528	D3
99128	Farmington 176	H3
98248	Ferndale 3,855	C2
98424	Fife 1,823	C3
98466	Fircrest 5,477	C3
†98531	Fords Prairie 2,582	B4
98331	Forks 3,060	A3
99014	Four Lakes 500	H3
98250	Friday Harbor⊙ 1,200	B2
†98901	Fruitvale 3,967	E4
99130	Garfield 599	H3
†99362	Garrett 1,134	G4
98824	George 261	F3
98335	Gig Harbor 2,429	C3
98336	Glenoma 500	C4
98619	Glenwood 626	D4
98251	Gold Bar 794	D3
98620	Goldendale⊙ 3,575	E5
98337	Gorst 750	A2
99133	Grand Coulee 1,180	G3
98930	Grandview 5,615	E4
98932	Granger 1,812	E4
98252	Granite Falls 911	D2
98547	Grayland 750	A4
98621	Grays River 350	B4
98253	Greenbank 600	C2
98339	Hadlock-Irondale 1,752	C2
98255	Hamilton 268	D2
†98366	Harper 300	A2
98933	Harrah 343	E4
99134	Harrington 507	G3
99135	Hartline 165	F3
99332	Hatton 81	G4
98025	Hobart 500	D3
98548	Hoodsport 500	B3
98550	Hoquiam 9,719	A3
†98004	Hunts Point 480	B2
98624	Ilwaco 604	A4
98256	Index 147	D3
98342	Indianola 800	A1
99139	Ione 594	H2
98027	Issaquah 5,536	C3
98343	Joyce 375	B2
98033	Juanita 17,232	B1
99335	Kahlotus 203	G4
98625	Kalama 1,216	C4
98344	Kapowsin 500	C4
98626	Kelso⊙ 11,129	C4
98028	Kenmore 7,281	B1
99336	Kennewick 34,397	F4
98031	Kent 23,152	C3
98141	Kettle Falls 1,087	H2
98345	Keyport 900	A2
98346	Kingston 950	C3
98033	Kirkland 18,779	H3
98934	Kittitas 782	E4
98628	Klickitat 750	D5
†98832	Krupp (Marlin) 83	F3
98629	La Center 439	C5
98503	Lacey 13,940	C3
98257	La Conner 633	C2
99143	Lacrosse 373	H4
†98101	Lake Forest Park 2,485	B1
98258	Lake Stevens 1,660	D3
98017	Lamont 101	H3
98260	Langley 650	C2
98350	La Push 500	A3
99018	Latah 155	H3
98826	Leavenworth 1,522	E3
99019	Liberty Lake 1,599	J3
98555	Lilliwaup 75	B3
99341	Lind 567	G4
98556	Littlerock 850	B4
98631	Long Beach 1,199	A4
98351	Longbranch 640	C3
98632	Longview 31,052	B4
99148	Loon Lake 500	H2
98262	Lummi Island 675	C2
98635	Lyle 580	D5
98263	Lyman 285	D2
98264	Lynden 4,022	C2
98036	Lynnwood 22,641	C3
98935	Mabton 1,248	E4
99149	Malden 200	H3
98829	Malott 350	F2
98353	Manchester 400	A2
98830	Mansfield 315	F3
98266	Maple Falls 300	D2
98038	Maple Valley 900	C3
99151	Marcus 174	H2
98268	Marietta-Alderwood 2,324	C2
98832	Marlin 83	F3
98270	Marysville 5,080	C2
99344	Mattawa 299	F4
98557	McCleary 1,419	B3
99022	Medical Lake 3,600	H3
98039	Medina 3,220	B2
98040	Mercer Island (city) 21,522	B2
99343	Mesa 278	G4
99152	Metaline 190	H2
99153	Metaline Falls 296	H2
†99210	Millwood 1,717	H3
98354	Milton 3,162	C3
98355	Mineral 550	C4
98562	Moclips 500	A3
98836	Monitor 650	E3
98272	Monroe 2,869	D3
98563	Montesano⊙ 3,247	B4
98356	Morton 1,264	C4
98837	Moses Lake 10,629	F3
98564	Mossyrock 463	C4
98043	Mountlake Terrace 16,534	B1
98273	Mount Vernon⊙ 13,009	C2
98936	Moxee City 687	E4
98275	Mukilteo 1,426	C3
98937	Naches 644	E4
98565	Napavine 611	C4
98638	Naselle 500	B4
†98310	Navy Yard City 2,594	A2
98357	Neah Bay 800	A2
99155	Nespelem 284	G2
†98283	Newhalem 350	D2
99156	Newport⊙ 1,665	H2
†98501	Nisqually 500	C3
98276	Nooksack 429	C2
98358	Nordland 706	C2
†98100	Normandy Park 4,268	A2
98045	North Bend 1,701	D3
98639	North Bonneville 394	C5
99157	Northport 368	H2
98158	Oakesdale 444	H3
98277	Oak Harbor 12,271	C2
98568	Oakville 537	B4
98569	Ocean City 350	A3
98640	Ocean Park 918	A4
98551	Ocean Shores 1,692	A3
†98520	Ocosta 369	B4
99159	Odessa 1,009	G3
98840	Okanogan⊙ 2,302	F2
98359	Olalla 500	A2
*98501	Olympia (cap.)⊙ 27,447	C3
	Olympia‡ 124,264	C3
98841	Omak 4,007	F2
98570	Onalaska 600	C4
99214	Opportunity 21,241	H3
98662	Orchards 8,828	C5
98844	Oroville 1,483	F2
98360	Orting 1,787	C3
99344	Othello 4,454	F4
99027	Otis Orchards-East Farms 4,597	H3
98938	Outlook 300	E4
98047	Pacific 2,261	C3
98571	Pacific Beach 900	A3
98361	Packwood 800	D4
99161	Palouse 1,005	H4
98939	Parker 500	E4
98444	Parkland 23,355	C3
99301	Pasco⊙ 18,425	F4
98846	Pateros 555	F2
98572	Pe Ell 617	B4
98847	Peshastin 500	E3
98281	Point Roberts 500	B2
99347	Pomeroy⊙ 1,716	H4
98362	Port Angeles⊙ 17,311	B2
†98101	Port Blakely 600	A2
98366	Port Orchard⊙ 4,787	A2
98368	Port Townsend⊙ 6,067	C2
†98584	Potlach 100	B3
98370	Poulsbo 3,453	A1
98348	Prescott 341	G4
98050	Preston 500	D3
99350	Prosser⊙ 3,896	F4
99163	Pullman 23,579	H4
98376	Puyallup 18,251	C3
98376	Quilcene 900	B3
98575	Quinault 450	B3
98848	Quincy 3,525	F3
98576	Rainier 891	C4

(continued on following page)

Agriculture, Industry and Resources

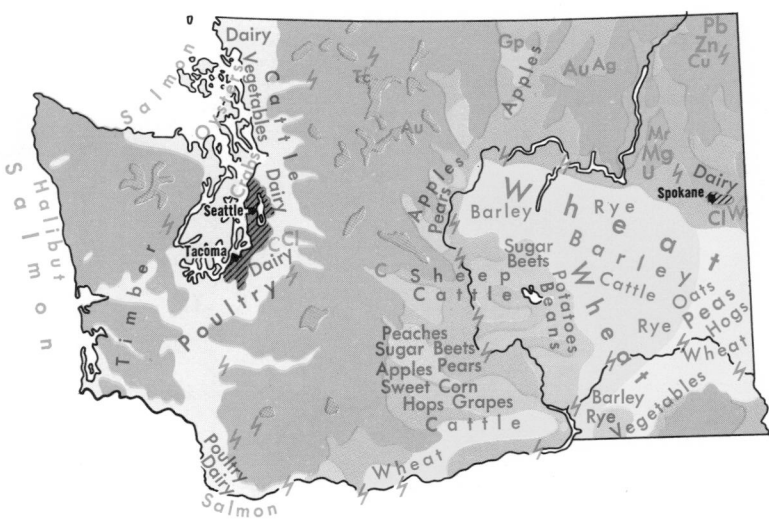

DOMINANT LAND USE

- Specialized Wheat
- Wheat, Peas
- Dairy, Poultry, Mixed Farming
- Fruit and Mixed Farming
- General Farming, Dairy, Range Livestock
- General Farming, Livestock, Special Crops
- Range Livestock
- Forests
- Urban Areas
- Nonagricultural Land

MAJOR MINERAL OCCURRENCES

Ag	Silver	Mr	Marble
Au	Gold	Pb	Lead
C	Coal	Tc	Talc
Cl	Clay	U	Uranium
Cu	Copper	W	Tungsten
Gp	Gypsum	Zn	Zinc
Mg	Magnesium		

⚡ Water Power

▨ Major Industrial Areas

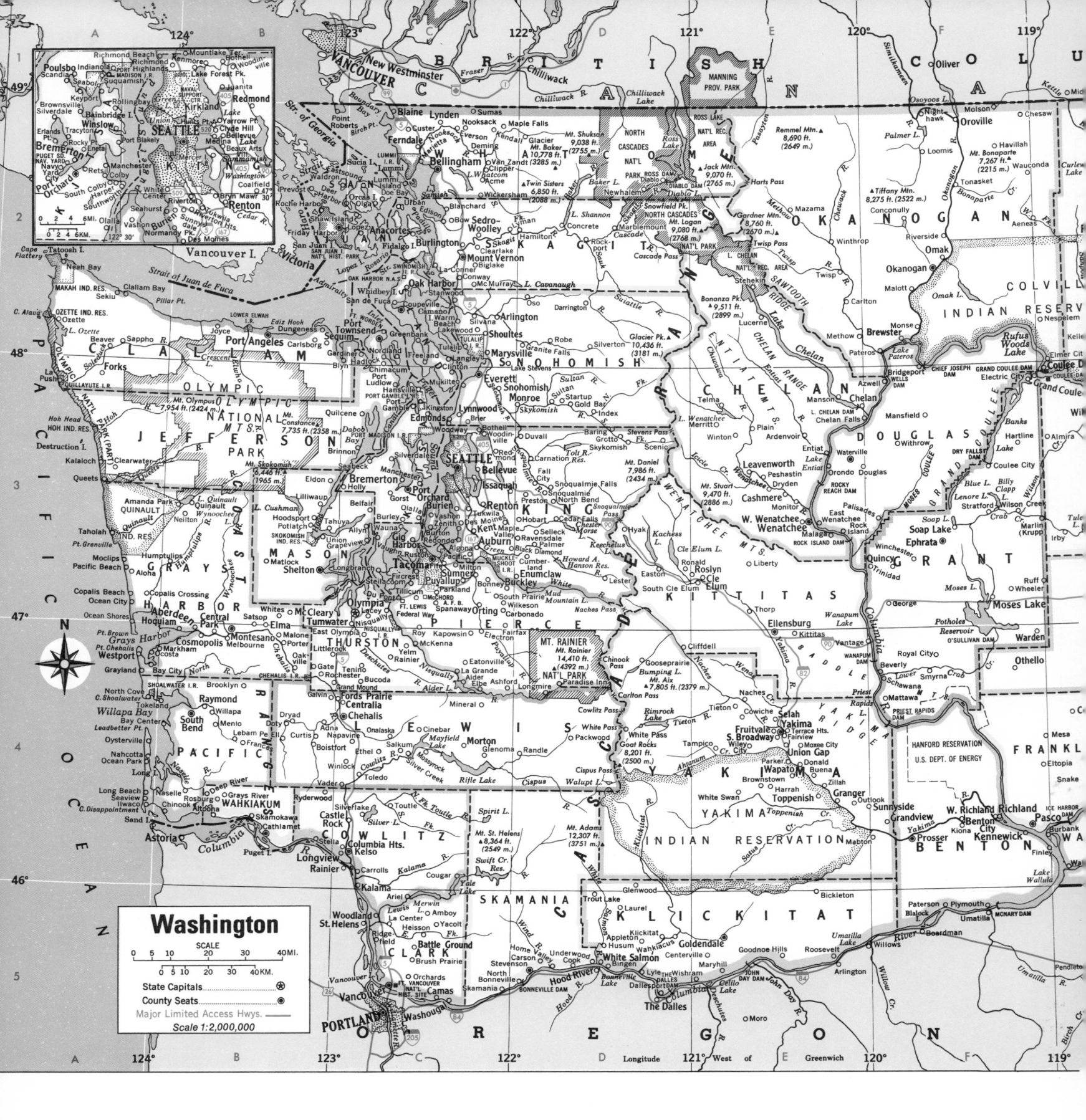

Washington

SCALE
```
0  5  10    20      30    40MI.
0  5  10    20      30    40KM.
```
State Capitals..................⊛
County Seats....................◉
Major Limited Access Hwys.━━━
Scale 1:2,000,000

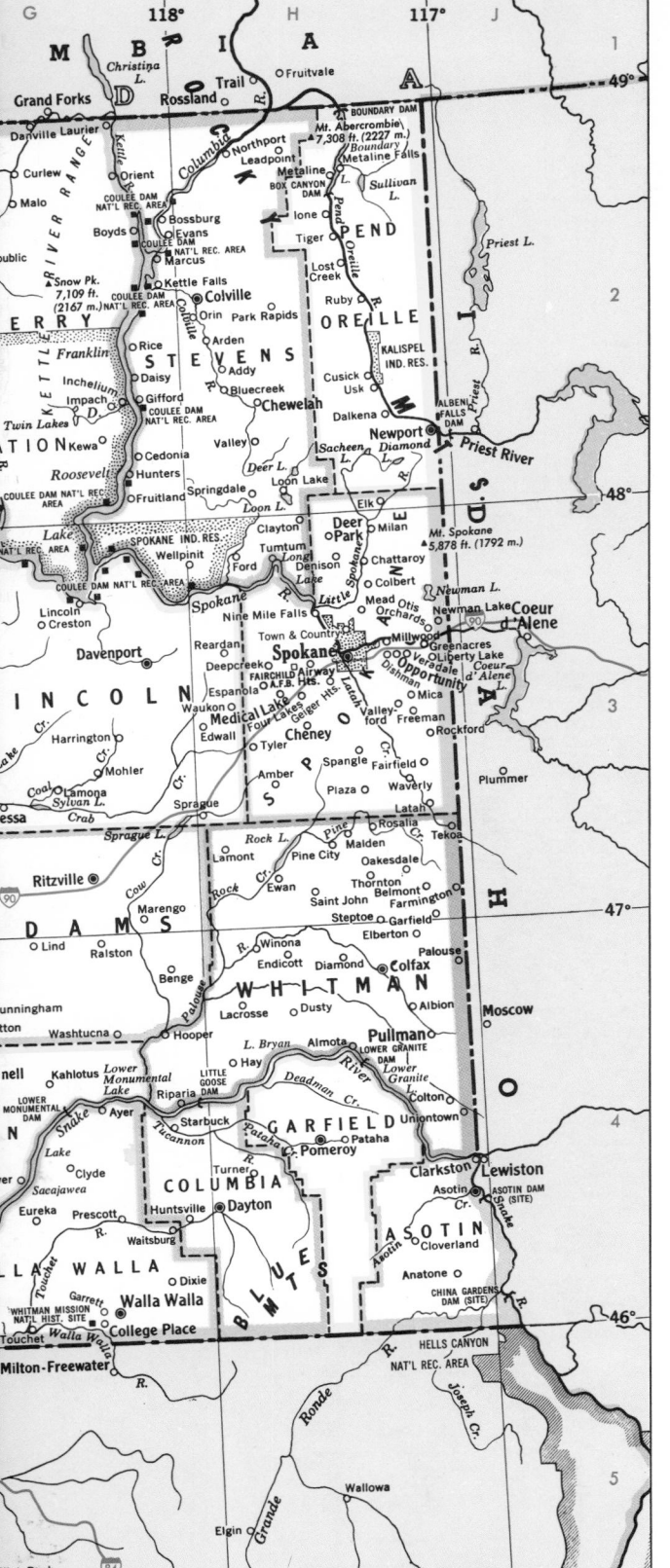

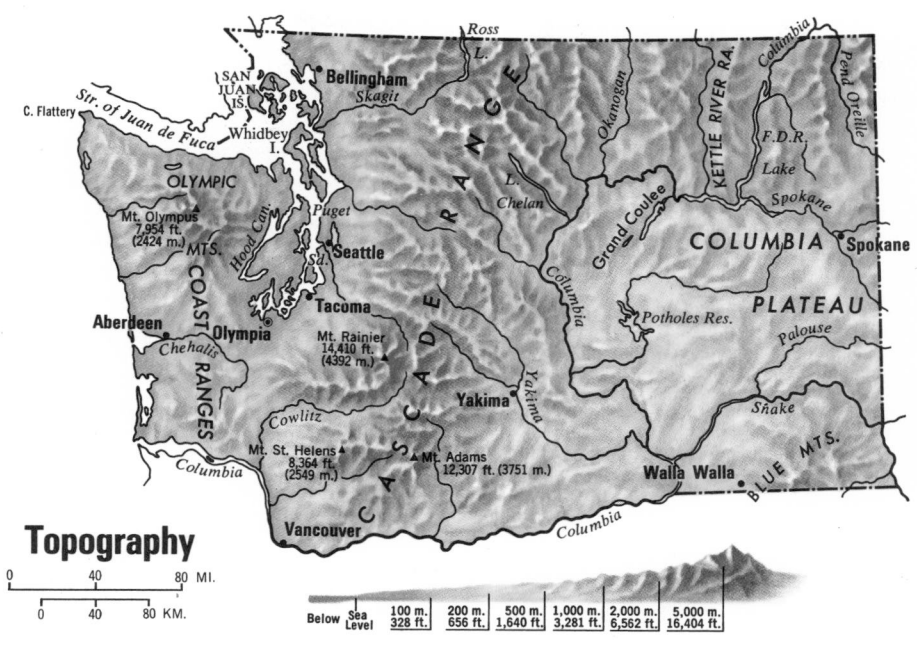

Topography

0   40   80 MI.

0   40   80 KM.

Below Sea Level	100 m. 328 ft.	200 m. 656 ft.	500 m. 1,640 ft.	1,000 m. 3,281 ft.	2,000 m. 6,562 ft.	5,000 m. 16,404 ft.

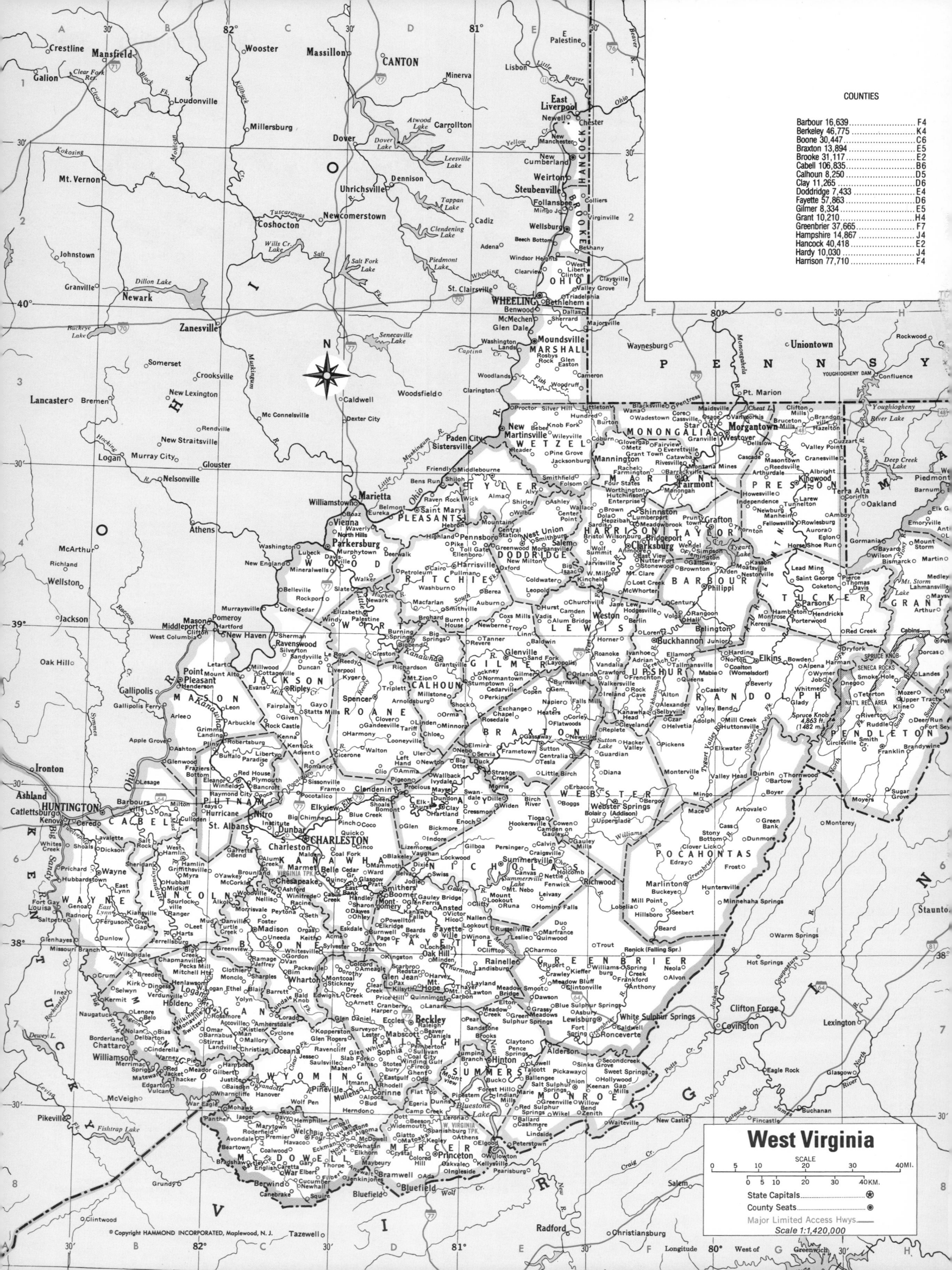

West Virginia

COUNTIES

Barbour 16,639		F4
Berkeley 46,775		K4
Boone 30,447		C6
Braxton 13,894		E5
Brooke 31,117		E2
Cabell 106,835		B6
Calhoun 8,250		D5
Clay 11,265		D6
Doddridge 7,433		E4
Fayette 57,863		D6
Gilmer 8,334		E5
Grant 10,210		H4
Greenbrier 37,665		F7
Hampshire 14,867		J4
Hancock 40,418		E2
Hardy 10,030		J4
Harrison 77,710		F4

SCALE
0   5   10   20   30   40 MI.

0   5 10   20   30   40 KM.

⊛ State Capitals
◉ County Seats
Major Limited Access Hwys

Scale 1:1,420,000

© Copyright HAMMOND INCORPORATED, Maplewood, N.J.

Longitude 80° West of G Greenwich 30'

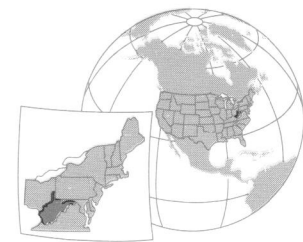

AREA 24,231 sq. mi. (62,758 sq. km.)
POPULATION 1,950,279
CAPITAL Charleston
LARGEST CITY Charleston
HIGHEST POINT Spruce Knob 4,863 ft. (1482 m.)
SETTLED IN 1774
ADMITTED TO UNION June 20, 1863
POPULAR NAME Mountain State
STATE FLOWER Big Rhododendron
STATE BIRD Cardinal

Counties (left columns)

County	Pop.	Key
Jackson	25,794	C5
Jefferson	30,302	L4
Kanawha	231,414	C6
Lewis	18,813	E4
Lincoln	23,675	B6
Logan	50,679	C7
Marion	65,789	F4
Marshall	41,608	E3
Mason	27,045	B5
McDowell	49,899	C8
Mercer	73,942	D8
Mineral	27,234	J4
Mingo	37,336	B7
Monongalia	75,024	F3
Monroe	12,873	E7
Morgan	10,711	K3
Nicholas	28,126	E6
Ohio	61,389	E2
Pendleton	7,910	H5
Pleasants	8,236	D4
Pocahontas	9,919	F6
Preston	30,460	G4
Putnam	38,181	C6
Raleigh	86,821	D7
Randolph	28,734	G5
Ritchie	11,442	D4
Roane	15,952	D5
Summers	15,875	E7
Taylor	16,584	F4
Tucker	8,675	F4
Tyler	11,320	E4
Upshur	23,427	F5
Wayne	46,021	B6
Webster	12,245	F6
Wetzel	21,874	E3
Wirt	4,922	D4
Wood	93,648	D4
Wyoming	35,993	C7

CITIES and TOWNS

Zip	Name/Pop.	Key
25606	Accoville 975	C7
†26288	Addison (Webster Springs)⊙ 939	F6
26210	Adrian 510	F5
26519	Albright 357	G3
24910	Alderson 1,375	E7
24807	Algoma 200	D8
25501	Alkol 500	C6
26320	Alma 197	E4
24710	Alpoca 200	D7
26321	Alum Bridge 150	E4
25003	Alum Creek 900	C6
26322	Alvy 150	E4
25004	Ameagle 230	D7
25005	Amma 200	D5
25607	Amherstdale 1,075	C7
24808	Anawalt 652	D8

Zip	Name/Pop.	Key
26323	Anmoore 865	F4
25812	Ansted 1,952	D6
25502	Apple Grove 900	B5
24915	Arbovale 610	G6
26816	Arthur 350	H4
26520	Arthurdale 1,063	G3
24916	Asbury 280	E7
24809	Asco 175	C8
25009	Ashford 400	C6
25503	Ashton 259	B5
24712	Athens 1,147	E8
26325	Auburn 116	E4
26704	Augusta 750	J4
26705	Aurora 250	G4
24811	Avondale 250	C8
25608	Baisden 500	C7
26801	Baker 200	J4
25410	Bakerton 125	L4
25010	Bald Knob 356	C7
26326	Baldwin 92	E5
25011	Bancroft 528	C5
25504	Barboursville 2,871	B6
25609	Barnabus 750	C7
26559	Barrackville 1,815	F3
25013	Barrett 950	C7
24813	Bartley 900	C8
24920	Bartow 500	G5
†25411	Bath (Berkeley Springs)⊙ 789	K3
26707	Bayard 540	H4
25014	Beards Fork 400	D6
25813	Beaver (Glen Hedrick) 1,122	D7
25801	Beckley⊙ 20,492	D7
26030	Beech Bottom 507	E2
24714	Beeson 300	D8
26250	Belington 2,038	F4
25015	Belle 1,621	C6
26133	Belleville 105	C4
26134	Belmont 887	D4
26656	Belva 275	D6
26135	Bens Run 85	D4
26031	Benwood 1,994	E2
26298	Bergoo 220	F6
25411	Berkeley Springs (Bath)⊙ 789	K3
24815	Berwind 615	C8
26032	Bethany 1,336	E2
†26003	Bethlehem 3,045	E2
26253	Beverly 475	G5
25019	Bickmore 300	D6
26136	Bigbend 120	D5
25302	Big Chimney 450	C6
25505	Big Creek 500	B7
26137	Big Springs 485	D5
25021	Bim 500	C7
26610	Birch River 650	E6
26521	Blacksville 248	F3
25022	Blair 800	C7
26817	Bloomery 200	K4
25026	Blue Creek 500	D6
24701	Bluefield 16,060	D8
26288	Bolair 450	F6
†25425	Bolivar 672	L4
25030	Bomont 170	D6
25031	Boomer 1,051	D6
24817	Bradshaw 1,002	C8
24715	Bramwell 989	D8
26523	Brandonville 92	G3
26802	Brandywine 300	H5
25666	Breeden 600	B7
26330	Bridgeport 6,604	F4
26138	Brohard 80	D4
25957	Brooks 196	E7
26334	Brownton 400	F4
26525	Bruceton Mills 296	G3
24924	Buckeye 125	F6
26201	Buckhannon⊙ 6,820	F5
24716	Bud 400	D7
25033	Buffalo 1,034	C5
25413	Bunker Hill 600	K4
26710	Burlington 300	J4
26335	Burnsville 531	E5
26336	Burnt House 175	D4
26562	Burton 200	F3
25035	Cabin Creek 900	C6
26337	Cairo 428	D4
24925	Caldwell 795	F7
26660	Calvin 400	E6
26208	Camden on Gauley 236	E6
26033	Cameron 1,474	E3
24819	Canebrake 300	C8
26662	Canvas 300	E6
26711	Capon Bridge 191	K4
26823	Capon Springs 580	K4
25037	Carbon 300	D6
24821	Carbon 650	C8
24927	Cass 148	G6
26527	Cassville 800	F3
25039	Cedar Grove 1,479	D6
26339	Center Point 250	E4
26612	Centralia 100	E5
26340	Central Station 200	E4
26214	Century 150	F4
25507	Ceredo 2,255	B6
25508	Chapmanville 1,164	B7

Zip	Name/Pop.	Key
*25301	Charleston (cap.)⊙ 63,968	C6
	Charleston‡ 269,595	C6
25414	Charles Town⊙ 2,857	L4
25958	Charmco 800	E6
25667	Chattaroy 1,383	B7
25418	Cherry Run 120	L3
*25301	Chesapeake 2,364	C6
26034	Chester 3,297	E1
26301	Clarksburg⊙ 22,371	F4
25043	Clay⊙ 940	D5
25044	Clear Creek 300	D7
†26003	Clearview 740	E2
25045	Clendenin 1,373	D5
26215	Cleveland 74	F5
25822	Clifftop 100	D6
25237	Clifton 325	B5
24928	Clintonville 250	E7
25046	Clio 300	D5
25047	Clothier 900	C7
25823	Coal City 2,324	D7
25306	Coal Fork 2,775	C6
26257	Coalton 306	G5
24824	Coalwood 650	C8
25048	Colcord 600	D7
26035	Colliers 864	E2
26615	Copen 50	E5
25826	Corinne 900	D7
25051	Costa 250	C6
25239	Cottageville 300	C5
25509	Cove Gap 650	B6
26206	Cowen 723	E6
26342	Coxs Mills 250	E4
26205	Craigsville 1,562	E6
25828	Cranberry 315	D7
24931	Crawley 395	E7
25669	Crum 500	B7
24826	Cucumber 274	C8
25510	Culloden 2,931	B6
24827	Cyclone 500	C7
26036	Dallas 450	E2
25832	Daniels 1,959	D7
25053	Danville 727	C6
†25422	Darkesville 150	L4
26260	Davis 979	H4
24828	Davy 882	C8
25054	Dawes 800	D6
24932	Dawson 300	D7
25670	Delbarton 981	B7
26531	Dellslow 300	G3
26217	Diana 300	F5
26617	Dille 300	E6
25671	Dingess 600	B7
25059	Dixie 985	D6
25060	Dorothy 400	D7
24721	Dott 100	D8
25062	Dry Creek 441	D7
25063	Duck 500	E5
25064	Dunbar 9,285	C6
26434	Dunmore 280	G6
26264	Durbin 379	G5
25067	East Bank 1,155	D6
25835	Eastgulf 300	D7
25512	East Lynn 150	B6
25836	Eccles 1,162	C7
24829	Eckman 750	C8
25672	Edgarton 415	B7
26716	Eglon 70	G4
24830	Elbert 400	C8
25070	Eleanor 1,282	C5
26143	Elizabeth⊙ 856	D4
26717	Elk Garden 291	H4
26241	Elkins⊙ 8,536	G5
25071	Elkview 1,161	C6
26267	Ellamore 250	F5
26346	Ellenboro 357	D4
25965	Elton 200	E7
24832	English 500	C8
26568	Enterprise 1,110	F4
25075	Eskdale 400	D6
25076	Ethel 450	C7
26144	Eureka 125	D4
25241	Evans 400	C5
26533	Everettville 175	F3
26554	Fairmont⊙ 23,863	F3
26570	Fairview 759	F3
†24966	Falling Spring (Renick) 240	F6
26571	Farmington 583	F3
25840	Fayetteville⊙ 2,366	D6
26202	Fenwick 500	E6
24835	Filbert 130	D8
26818	Fisher 400	J4
26621	Flatwoods 600	E5
26347	Flemington 452	F4
26037	Follansbee 3,994	E2
26348	Folsom 360	E4
24935	Forest Hill 314	E7
26719	Fort Ashby 1,205	J4
25514	Fort Gay 886	A6
26806	Fort Seybert 200	H5
24936	Fort Spring 250	E7
25081	Foster 500	C6

Zip	Name/Pop.	Key
26572	Four States 500	F4
26071	Frame 76	C5
26623	Frametown 150	E5
26807	Franklin⊙ 780	H5
25082	Fraziers Bottom 250	B5
26219	Frenchton 102	F5
26146	Friendly 242	D3
25515	Gallipolis Ferry 325	B5
26349	Galloway 500	F4
25243	Gandeeville 150	D5
24941	Gap Mills 300	E7
24836	Gary 2,233	C8
26624	Gassaway 1,225	E5
25085	Gauley Bridge 1,177	D6
26240	Gauley Mills 165	E6
25244	Gay 300	C5
25420	Gerrardstown 240	K4
25843	Ghent 500	D7
25621	Gilbert 757	C7
26671	Gilboa 500	E6
26350	Gilmer 110	E5
26268	Glady 175	G5
25086	Glasgow 1,031	D6
25088	Glen 175	D6
26038	Glen Dale 1,875	E3
26039	Glen Easton 100	E3
25090	Glen Ferris 200	D6
25421	Glengary 250	K4
†25813	Glen Hedrick (Beaver) 1,122	D7
25846	Glen Jean	D7
25848	Glen Rogers 500	D7
26351	Glenville⊙ 2,155	E5
25849	Glen White 300	D7
25520	Glenwood 400	B5
†26585	Glovergap 100	F3
25093	Gordon 300	C7
26720	Gormania 100	H4
26354	Grafton⊙ 6,845	G4
26147	Grantsville⊙ 788	D5
26574	Grant Town 987	F3
26534	Granville 992	F3
24943	Grassy Meadows 100	E7
25422	Great Cacapon 750	K3
24944	Green Bank 115	G6
25966	Green Sulphur Springs 225	E7
24945	Greenville 125	E7
26360	Greenwood 750	E4
25095	Grimms Landing 350	B5
26221	Guardian 175	F5
26222	Hacker Valley 440	F5
25423	Halltown 375	L4
26269	Hambleton 403	G4
25523	Hamlin⊙ 1,219	B6
25623	Hampden 300	C7
25424	Hancock 175	K3
25102	Handley 633	D6
†26250	Harding 100	G5
26270	Harman 181	G5
25246	Harmony 600	D5
25851	Harper 400	D7
25425	Harpers Ferry 361	L4
26362	Harrisville⊙ 1,673	E4
25247	Hartford 556	C4
25524	Harts 400	B6
25852	Harvey 300	C7
24841	Havaco 350	C8
26627	Heaters 440	E5
25427	Hedgesville 217	K3
26224	Helvetia 130	F5
24842	Hemphill 700	C8
25106	Henderson 604	B5
26271	Hendricks 390	G4
25624	Henlawson 900	B7
26369	Hepzibah 600	F4
24726	Herndon 500	D7
25854	Hico 750	D6
24946	Hillsboro 276	F6
25951	Hinton⊙ 4,622	E7
25625	Holden 2,036	B7
26372	Horner 125	F5
26769	Horse Shoe Run 500	G4
†25506	Hubball 145	B6
26575	Hundred 485	F3
*25701	Huntington⊙ 63,684	A6
	Huntington-Ashland‡ 311,350	A6
25526	Hurricane 3,751	C6
26273	Huttonsville 242	G5
24844	Iaeger 833	C8
26374	Independence 200	G4
24949	Indian Mills 150	E7
25111	Indore 300	D6
25112	Institute	C6
25428	Inwood 1,159	K4
24847	Itmann 600	D7
25113	Ivydale 800	D5
26377	Jacksonburg 400	E3
26378	Jane Lew 406	F4
25114	Jeffrey 900	C7
24848	Jenkinjones 750	C8
24849	Jesse 400	C7
26674	Jodie 440	D7
25969	Jumping Branch 700	E7
26824	Junction 75	J4

(continued on following page)

Agriculture, Industry and Resources

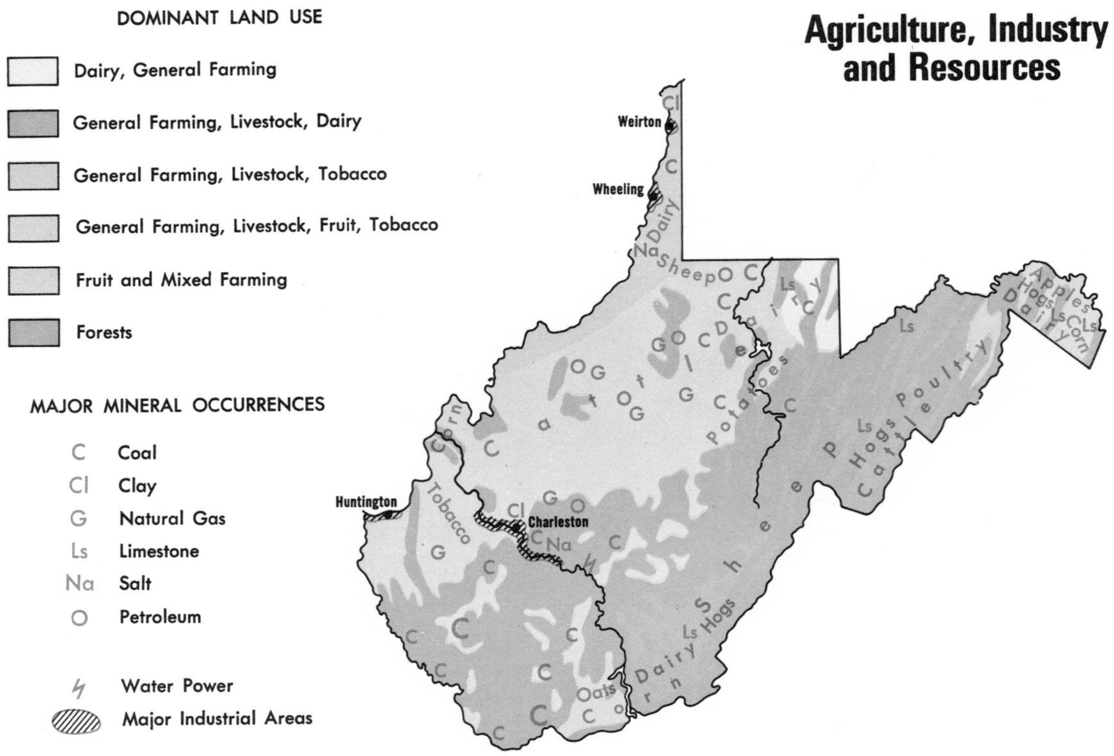
DOMINANT LAND USE
Dairy, General Farming
General Farming, Livestock, Dairy
General Farming, Livestock, Tobacco
General Farming, Livestock, Fruit, Tobacco
Fruit and Mixed Farming
Forests
MAJOR MINERAL OCCURRENCES
C Coal
Cl Clay
G Natural Gas
Ls Limestone
Na Salt
O Petroleum
Water Power
Major Industrial Areas
Weirton
Wheeling
Huntington
Charleston
Dairy
Sheep
Cattle
Potatoes
Corn
Tobacco
Hogs
Poultry
Apples
Oats

26275 Junior 591 ....G5
24851 Justice 600 ....C7
25115 Kanawha Falls 105 ....D6
25430 Kearneysville 250 ....L4
24731 Kegley 900 ....D8
24732 Kellysville 165 ....E8
25248 Kenna 150 ....C5
25530 Kenova 4,454 ....A6
25249 Kentuck 200 ....C5
25674 Kermit 705 ....B7
26726 Keyser⊙ 6,569 ....J4
24852 Keystone 902 ....D8
24950 Kieffer 135 ....E7
25859 Kilsyth 200 ....D7
24853 Kimball 871 ....C8
25120 Kingston 189 ....D7
26537 Kingwood⊙ 2,877 ....G4
26729 Kirby 110 ....J4
25628 Kistler 200 ....C7
26579 Knob Fork 106 ....E3
24854 Kopperston 700 ....C7
26731 Lahmansville 200 ....H4
25860 Lanark 559 ....D7
25629 Landville 400 ....C7
25535 Lavalette 600 ....B6
25863 Lawton 100 ....E7
25864 Layland 500 ....E7
†26430 Layopolis (Sand Fork) 280 ....E5
25251 Left Hand 700 ....D5
26676 Leivasy 200 ....E6
25676 Lenore 800 ....B7
25123 Leon 228 ....C5
25971 Lerona 550 ....D8
25537 Lesage 600 ....B5
25972 Leslie 350 ....E6
25865 Lester 626 ....D7
25253 Letart 350 ....C5
25431 Levels 180 ....J4
24901 Lewisburg⊙ 3,065 ....E7
26384 Linn 165 ....E4
26629 Little Birch 400 ....E5
26581 Littleton 335 ....F3
25125 Lizemores 400 ....D6
25866 Lochgelly 250 ....D6
25258 Lockney 190 ....E5
25601 Logan⊙ 3,029 ....B7
25630 Lorado 400 ....C7
†26201 Lorentz 200 ....F4
26810 Lost City 130 ....J5
26385 Lost Creek 604 ....F4
26811 Lost River 500 ....J5
†26101 Lubeck 1,356 ....C4
26386 Lumberport 939 ....F4
25631 Lundale 525 ....C7
25870 Maben 450 ....D7
26278 Mabie 550 ....F5
25871 Mabscott 1,668 ....D7
26148 Macfarlan 436 ....D4
25130 Madison⊙ 3,228 ....C6
26541 Maidsville 500 ....F3
25306 Malden 900 ....C6
25634 Mallory 1,330 ....C7
25132 Mammoth 563 ....D6
25635 Man 1,333 ....C7
26582 Mannington 3,036 ....F3
25975 Marfrance 225 ....E6
24954 Marlinton⊙ 1,352 ....F6
25315 Marmet 2,196 ....C6
25401 Martinsburg⊙ 13,063 ....K4
25260 Mason 1,432 ....B4
26542 Masontown 1,052 ....G3

25678 Matewan 822 ....B7
24736 Matoaka 613 ....D8
24861 Maybeury 300 ....D8
26833 Maysville 150 ....H4
24858 McDowell 500 ....D8
26040 McMechen 2,402 ....E3
26401 McWhorter 150 ....F4
24958 Meadow Bluff 250 ....E7
25976 Meadow Bridge 530 ....E7
26404 Meadowbrook 500 ....F4
25977 Meadow Creek 300 ....E7
26585 Metz 150 ....F3
26149 Middlebourne⊙ 941 ....E3
25540 Midkiff 650 ....B6
26280 Mill Creek 801 ....G5
24959 Mill Point 148 ....F6
25261 Millstone 850 ....D5
25262 Millwood 800 ....C5
25541 Milton 2,178 ....B6
25879 Minden 800 ....D7
26150 Mineralwells 325 ....C4
26281 Mingo 350 ....F5
25263 Minnora 500 ....D5
26405 Moatsville 150 ....G4
25636 Monaville 950 ....B7
26554 Monongah 1,132 ....F4
26586 Montana Mines 200 ....F3
25135 Montcoal 150 ....D7
26282 Monterville 250 ....F5
25136 Montgomery 3,104 ....D6
26283 Montrose 129 ....G4
26836 Moorefield⊙ 2,257 ....J4
26505 Morgantown⊙ 27,605 ....G3
25542 Morrisvale 450 ....C6
26041 Moundsville⊙ 12,419 ....E3
26407 Mountain 200 ....E4
25264 Mount Alto 200 ....C5
25139 Mount Carbon 450 ....D7
26408 Mount Clare 950 ....F4
25637 Mount Gay 4,366 ....C7
25880 Mount Hope 1,849 ....D7
26678 Mount Lookout 500 ....E6
26679 Mount Nebo 535 ....E6
26739 Mount Storm 500 ....H4
25882 Mullens 2,919 ....D7
26680 Nallen 250 ....E6
26631 Napier 158 ....E5
25685 Naugatuck 500 ....B7
25141 Nebo 200 ....D5
25142 Nellis 600 ....C6
24961 Neola 300 ....F7
26681 Nettie 500 ....E6
26410 Newburg 418 ....G4
26047 New Cumberland⊙ 1,752 ....E2
26050 Newell 2,032 ....E1
26154 New England 335 ....C4
24866 Newhall 400 ....C8
25265 New Haven 1,723 ....C5
26056 New Manchester 800 ....E1
26155 New Martinsville⊙ 7,109 ....E3
25266 Newton 390 ....D5
26632 Newville 160 ....E5
25143 Nitro 8,074 ....C6
25687 Nolan 250 ....B7
25267 Normantown 112 ....E5
24868 Northfork 1,105 ....D8
†26101 North Hills 940 ....D4
26285 Norton 400 ....G5
26301 Nutter Fort 2,078 ....F4
25901 Oak Hill 7,120 ....D6
24739 Oakvale 208 ....D8
24870 Oceana 2,143 ....C7

25902 Odd 500 ....D7
25147 Ohley 450 ....D6
25638 Omar 900 ....C7
26886 Onego 400 ....H5
25148 Orgas 500 ....C6
26412 Orlando 700 ....E5
25268 Orma D5
26543 Osage 285 ....F3
25151 Packsville 225 ....C7
26159 Paden City 3,671 ....D3
25152 Page 600 ....D6
26160 Palestine 110 ....D4
24872 Panther 450 ....C8
26101 Parkersburg⊙ 39,967 ....D4
Parkersburg-Marietta‡ 162,836 ....D4
26287 Parsons⊙ 1,937 ....G4
26746 Patterson Creek 157 ....J3
25434 Paw Paw 644 ....K3
25904 Pax 274 ....D7
†25955 Pear 100 ....E7
25547 Pecks Mill 350 ....B7
25905 Pemberton 300 ....D7
24962 Pence Springs 300 ....E7
26415 Pennsboro 1,652 ....E4
26544 Pentress 250 ....F3
26847 Petersburg⊙ 2,084 ....H5
24963 Peterstown 648 ....E8
25154 Peytona 175 ....C6
26416 Philippi⊙ 3,194 ....G4
24964 Pickaway 225 ....E7
26230 Pickens 240 ....F5
25689 Pie 250 ....B7
26750 Piedmont 1,491 ....H4
25156 Pinch 800 ....D6
26419 Pine Grove 767 ....E3
24874 Pineville⊙ 1,140 ....C7
25158 Pliny 900 ....B5
25159 Poca 1,142 ....C6
†25301 Pocotalico 2,420 ....C6
25550 Point Pleasant⊙ 5,682 ....B5
25437 Points 250 ....J4
25161 Powellton 1,339 ....D6
24877 Powhatan 400 ....D8
25162 Pratt 821 ....D6
24878 Premier 400 ....C8
†25880 Price Hill 175 ....D7
25555 Prichard 500 ....A6
24740 Princeton⊙ 7,493 ....D8
25164 Procious 600 ....D5
26055 Proctor 350 ....E3
26421 Pullman 196 ....D4
26852 Purgitsville 450 ....J4
25045 Quick 400 ....D6
†25015 Quincy 150 ....C6
25981 Quinwood 460 ....E6
26587 Rachel 550 ....F3
25165 Racine 725 ....C6
25556 Radnor 300 ....A6
25962 Rainelle 1,983 ....E7
25911 Raleigh 900 ....D7
25166 Ramage 350 ....C7
25557 Ranger 300 ....B6
25438 Ranson 2,471 ....L4
25913 Ravencliff 350 ....C7
26164 Ravenswood 4,126 ....C5
26167 Reader 950 ....E3
26289 Red Creek 125 ....H4
25168 Red House 600 ....C5
25692 Red Jacket 850 ....B7
26547 Reedsville 564 ....G3
25270 Reedy 338 ....D5

24966 Renick 240 ....F6
25915 Rhodell 472 ....D7
26261 Richwood 3,568 ....F6
26753 Ridgeley 994 ....J3
25440 Ridgeway 200 ....K4
26755 Rio 140 ....J4
25271 Ripley⊙ 3,464 ....C5
25441 Rippon 500 ....L4
26588 Rivesville 1,327 ....F3
26234 Rock Cave 400 ....F5
24881 Roderfield 900 ....C8
26757 Romney⊙ 2,094 ....J4
24970 Ronceverte 2,312 ....F7
26636 Rosedale 400 ....E5
25643 Rossmore 200 ....C7
26425 Rowlesburg 966 ....G4
26688 Runa 150 ....E6
25984 Rupert 1,276 ....E7
26689 Russellville 280 ....E6
25177 Saint Albans 12,402 ....C6
26290 Saint George 150 ....G4
26170 Saint Marys⊙ 2,219 ....D4
26426 Salem 2,706 ....E4
25559 Salt Rock 350 ....B6
26430 Sand Fork 280 ....E5
25985 Sandstone 300 ....E7
25275 Sandyville 500 ....C5
25876 Saulsville 250 ....C7
25917 Scarbro 800 ....D7
24975 Seebert 100 ....F6
25181 Seth 950 ....C6
26761 Shanks 500 ....J4
25182 Sharon 450 ....D6
25183 Sharples 250 ....C7
25443 Shepherdstown 1,791 ....L4
26173 Sherman 104 ....C5
26431 Shinnston 3,059 ....F4
26434 Shirley 275 ....E4
25562 Shoals 150 ....B6
26638 Shock 200 ....D5
†26164 Silverton 250 ....C5
26435 Simpson 250 ....F4
24976 Sinks Grove 156 ....F7
25320 Sissonville 450 ....C5
26175 Sistersville 2,367 ....D3
25920 Slab Fork 210 ....D7
25444 Slanesville 250 ....K4
26436 Smithburg 130 ....E4
25186 Smithers 1,482 ....D6
26437 Smithfield 278 ....E4
26178 Smithville 200 ....D4
24977 Smoot 300 ....E7
25921 Sophia 1,216 ....D7
25303 South Charleston 15,968 ....C6
25922 Spanishburg 550 ....D8
25276 Spencer⊙ 2,799 ....D5
25693 Sprigg 225 ....B7
26763 Springfield 250 ....J4
25565 Spurlockville 250 ....B6
24884 Squire 900 ....C8
26505 Star City 1,464 ....F3
25279 Statts Mills 400 ....C5
25188 Stickney 150 ....D7
25645 Stirrat 250 ....C7
26301 Stonewood 2,058 ....F4
24979 Stony Bottom 50 ....F6
25280 Stumptown 125 ....E5
26651 Summersville⊙ 2,972 ....E6
25446 Summit Point 455 ....K4
25932 Surveyor 300 ....D7
26601 Sutton⊙ 1,192 ....E5
26690 Swiss 500 ....D6

25647 Switzer 1,034 ....B7
25193 Sylvester 256 ....C6
24981 Talcott 800 ....E7
26237 Tallmansville 140 ....F5
26179 Tanner 375 ....E5
26764 Terra Alta 1,946 ....H4
26640 Tesla 300 ....E5
25694 Thacker 525 ....B7
26292 Thomas 747 ....H4
26440 Thornton 200 ....G4
24888 Thorpe 600 ....D8
26765 Three Churches 350 ....J4
25936 Thurmond 67 ....D7
26691 Tioga 825 ....E6
26059 Triadelphia 1,461 ....E2
26443 Troy 110 ....E4
26444 Tunnelton 510 ....G4
25203 Turtle Creek 566 ....C6
25205 Uneeda 700 ....C6
25447 Unger 300 ....K4
24983 Union⊙ 743 ....E7
26266 Upperglade 750 ....F6
26866 Upper Tract 155 ....H5
26445 Vadis 130 ....E4
26293 Valley Bend 950 ....F5
26060 Valley Grove 597 ....E2
26294 Valley Head 900 ....G5
25206 Van 800 ....C7
25696 Varney 750 ....B7
25649 Verdunville 950 ....B7
25938 Victor 500 ....D6
26105 Vienna 11,618 ....D4
24891 Vivian 500 ....D8
26238 Volga 125 ....F4
25697 Vulcan 130 ....B7
26589 Wadestown 300 ....F3
24984 Waiteville 230 ....F8
26180 Walker 100 ....D4
26448 Wallace 325 ....E4
25286 Walton 550 ....D5
26590 Wana 150 ....F3
24892 War 2,158 ....C8
26851 Wardensville 241 ....J4
26181 Washington 450 ....C4
26184 Waverly 500 ....D4
25570 Wayne⊙ 1,495 ....B6
26288 Webster Springs⊙ 939 ....F6
26062 Weirton 25,371 ....E2
Weirton-Steubenville‡ 163,099 ....E2
24801 Welch⊙ 3,885 ....C8
26070 Wellsburg⊙ 3,963 ....E2
25287 West Columbia 245 ....B5
25571 West Hamlin 643 ....B6
26074 West Liberty 744 ....E2
25601 West Logan 630 ....C7
26451 West Milford 510 ....F4
26452 Weston⊙ 6,250 ....F4
26505 Westover 4,884 ....G3
26456 West Union⊙ 1,090 ....E4
25651 Wharncliffe 900 ....C7
25208 Wharton 450 ....C7
26003 Wheeling⊙ 43,070 ....E2
Wheeling‡ 185,566 ....E2
24986 White Sulphur Springs 3,371 ....F7
25209 Whitesville 689 ....C6
26296 Whitmer 400 ....G5
25211 Widen 230 ....E6
26767 Wiley Ford 1,224 ....J3
26186 Wileyville 175 ....E3
25653 Wilkinson 975 ....B7

24991 Williamsburg 350 ....F7
25661 Williamson⊙ 5,219 ....B7
26187 Williamstown 3,095 ....C4
26461 Wilsonburg 350 ....F4
25699 Wilsondale 250 ....B7
26075 Windsor Heights 800 ....E2
25213 Winfield⊙ 329 ....C5
25214 Winifrede 750 ....C6
25942 Winona 250 ....E6
26462 Wolf Summit 750 ....F4
†26257 Womelsdorf (Coalton) 306 ....G5
25572 Woodville 300 ....C6
26591 Worthington 329 ....F4
25573 Yawkey 985 ....C6
26865 Yellow Spring 280 ....J4
25654 Yolyn 400 ....C7

OTHER FEATURES

Big Sandy (riv.) A6
Bluestone (lake) E7
Buckhannon (riv.) F5
Cacapon (riv.) J4
Cheat (riv.) G3
Cherry (riv.) E6
Chesapeake and Ohio Canal Nat'l Hist. Pa J3
Clear Fork, Guyandotte (riv.) C7
Coal (riv.) C6
Dry Fork (riv.) C8
Dry Fork (riv.) G5
East Lynn (lake) B6
Elk (riv.) D6
Fish (creek) E3
Gauley (riv.) D6
Greenbrier (riv.) F6
Guyandotte (riv.) B6
Harpers Ferry Nat'l Hist. Park L4
Hughes (riv.) D4
Kanawha (riv.) C5
Little Kanawha (riv.) D5
Meadow (riv.) E6
Mill (creek) C5
Monongahela (riv.) G3
Mount Storm (lake) H4
Mud (riv.) B6
New (riv.) E7
North (riv.) J4
Ohio (riv.) B5
Patterson (creek) J4
Pigeon (creek) B7
Pocatalico (riv.) C5
Pond Fork (riv.) C6
Potomac (riv.) L3
Potts (creek) F7
Reedy (creek) D5
Shavers Fork (riv.) G5
Shenandoah (riv.) K4
Spruce Knob (mt.) G5
Spruce Knob-Seneca Rocks Nat'l Rec. Area H5
Stony (riv.) H4
Summersville (lake) E6
Sutton (lake) F5
Tug Fork (riv.) B7
Twelvepole (creek) A6
Tygart (lake) G4
Tygart Valley (riv.) F5
West Fork (riv.) E5
Williams (riv.) F6

⊙County seat.
‡Population of metropolitan area.
† Zip of nearest p.o. * Multiple zips.

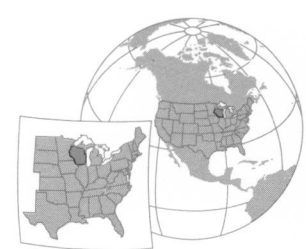

AREA 56,153 sq. mi. (145,436 sq. km.)
POPULATION 4,705,521
CAPITAL Madison
LARGEST CITY Milwaukee
HIGHEST POINT Timms Hill 1,951 ft. (595 m.)
SETTLED IN 1670
ADMITTED TO UNION May 29, 1848
POPULAR NAME Badger State
STATE FLOWER Wood Violet
STATE BIRD Robin

COUNTIES

Adams 13,457 ... G7
Ashland 16,783 ... E3
Barron 38,730 ... C5
Bayfield 13,822 ... D3
Brown 175,280 ... L7
Buffalo 14,309 ... C7
Burnett 12,340 ... B4
Calumet 30,867 ... K7
Chippewa 52,127 ... D5
Clark 32,910 ... E6
Columbia 43,222 ... H9
Crawford 16,556 ... E9
Dane 323,545 ... H9
Dodge 75,064 ... J9
Door 25,029 ... M6
Douglas 44,421 ... C3
Dunn 34,314 ... C6
Eau Claire 78,805 ... D6
Florence 4,172 ... K4
Fond du Lac 88,964 ... K8
Forest 9,044 ... J4
Grant 51,736 ... E10
Green 30,012 ... G10
Green Lake 18,370 ... H8
Iowa 19,802 ... F9
Iron 6,730 ... F3
Jackson 16,831 ... E7
Jefferson 66,152 ... J9
Juneau 21,039 ... F8
Kenosha 123,137 ... K10
Kewaunee 19,539 ... L6
La Crosse 91,056 ... D8
Lafayette 17,412 ... F10
Langlade 19,978 ... H5
Lincoln 26,555 ... G5
Manitowoc 82,918 ... L7
Marathon 111,270 ... G6
Marinette 39,314 ... K5
Marquette 11,672 ... H8
Menominee 3,373 ... J5
Milwaukee 964,988 ... L9
Monroe 35,074 ... E8
Oconto 28,947 ... K6
Oneida 31,216 ... G4
Outagamie 128,799 ... K7
Ozaukee 66,981 ... L9
Pepin 7,477 ... C6
Pierce 31,149 ... B6
Polk 32,351 ... B5
Portage 57,420 ... G6
Price 15,788 ... F4
Racine 173,132 ... K10
Richland 17,476 ... F9
Rock 139,420 ... H10
Rusk 15,589 ... D5
Saint Croix 43,262 ... B5
Sauk 43,469 ... G9
Sawyer 12,843 ... D4
Shawano 35,928 ... J6
Sheboygan 100,935 ... L8
Taylor 18,817 ... E5
Trempealeau 26,158 ... D7
Vernon 25,642 ... E8
Vilas 16,535 ... G3
Walworth 71,507 ... J10
Washburn 13,174 ... C4
Washington 84,848 ... K9
Waukesha 280,080 ... K9
Waupaca 42,831 ... J6
Waushara 18,526 ... H7
Winnebago 131,722 ... J8
Wood 72,799 ... F7

CITIES and TOWNS

Zip *Name/Pop.* *Key*

54405 Abbotsford 1,901 ... F6
53910 Adams 1,744 ... G8
53001 Adell 545 ... L8
53501 Afton 225 ... H10
53502 Albany 1,051 ... G10
†53534 Albion 300 ... H10
54201 Algoma 3,656 ... M6
53002 Allenton 915 ... K9
†54301 Allouez 14,882 ... L7
54610 Alma⊙ 876 ... C7
54611 Alma Center 454 ... E7
54805 Almena 526 ... B5
54909 Almond 477 ... G7
54720 Altoona 4,393 ... C6
54102 Amberg 875 ... K5
54001 Amery 2,404 ... B5
54406 Amherst 701 ... H7
54407 Amherst Junction 225 ... H7
54408 Aniwa 273 ... H6
54409 Antigo⊙ 8,653 ... H5
54911 Appleton⊙ 58,913 ... J7
Appleton-Oshkosh‡ 291,325 J7
†54568 Arbor Vitae 900 ... G4
54612 Arcadia 2,109 ... D7
53503 Arena 451 ... G9
54511 Argonne 600 ... J4
53504 Argyle 720 ... G10
54721 Arkansaw 400 ... B6
53911 Arlington 440 ... H9
54103 Armstrong Creek 615 ... K4
54410 Arpin 361 ... G6
53003 Ashippun 750 ... H1
54806 Ashland⊙ 9,115 ... E2
54304 Ashwaubenon 14,486 ... K7
54411 Athens 988 ... G5
54412 Auburndale 641 ... F6
54722 Augusta 1,560 ... D6
53506 Avoca 505 ... F9
†53520 Avon 120 ... H10
54413 Babcock 250 ... F7
53801 Bagley 317 ... D10
54202 Baileys Harbor 250 ... M5
54002 Baldwin 1,620 ... B6
54810 Balsam Lake⊙ 749 ... B5
54921 Bancroft 355 ... G7
54614 Bangor 1,012 ... E8
53913 Baraboo⊙ 8,081 ... G9
†54873 Barnes 225 ... D3
53507 Barneveld 579 ... F10
54812 Barron⊙ 2,595 ... C5
†53001 Batavia 125 ... K8
54723 Bay City 543 ... B6
54814 Bayfield 778 ... E2
†53201 Bayside 4,724 ... M1
54922 Bear Creek 454 ... J6
53916 Beaver Dam 14,149 ... J9
53802 Beetown 150 ... E10
53004 Belgium 892 ... L8
†54631 Bell Center 124 ... E9
53508 Belleville 1,302 ... G10
53510 Belmont 826 ... F10
53511 Beloit 35,207 ... H10
53803 Benton 983 ... F10
54923 Berlin 5,478 ... H8
†54410 Bethel 210 ... F6
†54440 Bevent 200 ... H6
53103 Big Bend 1,345 ... K2
54926 Big Falls 107 ... H6
54817 Birchwood 437 ... C4
54414 Birnamwood 688 ... H6
†54494 Biron 698 ... G7
54106 Black Creek 1,097 ... K7
53515 Black Earth 1,145 ... G9
54615 Black River Falls⊙ 3,434 ... E7
†54541 Blackwell 550 ... J4
54616 Blair 1,142 ... D7
53516 Blanchardville 803 ... G10
54617 Bloom City 167 ... E8
54724 Bloomer 3,342 ... D5
53804 Bloomington 743 ... E10
53517 Blue Mounds 387 ... G9
53518 Blue River 412 ... E9
†53581 Boaz 161 ... E9
†53105 Bohners Lake 1,507 ... K10
54107 Bonduel 1,160 ... K6
53805 Boscobel 2,662 ... E9
54512 Boulder Junction 780 ... G3
54416 Bowler 339 ... J6
54725 Boyceville 862 ... C5
54726 Boyd 660 ... E6
54203 Branch 300 ... L7
53919 Brandon 862 ... J8
54513 Brantwood 500 ... F4
53920 Briggsville 250 ... H8
54110 Brillion 2,907 ... L7
53520 Brodhead 3,153 ... G10
54417 Brokaw 298 ... G5
53005 Brookfield 34,035 ... K1
53521 Brooklyn 627 ... H10
53209 Brown Deer 12,921 ... L1
†53105 Brown's Lake 1,648 ... K3
53006 Brownsville 433 ... J8
53522 Browntown 284 ... G10
54819 Bruce 905 ... D5
54820 Brule 335 ... C2
54204 Brussels 500 ... L6
†54622 Buffalo 894 ... C7
53105 Burlington 8,385 ... K10
53922 Burnett 260 ... J9
53007 Butler 2,059 ... K1
54514 Butternut 438 ... E3
53009 Byron 40 ... K8
54821 Cable 227 ... D3
54727 Cadott 1,247 ... D6
53923 Cambria 680 ... H8
53523 Cambridge 844 ... H9
54822 Cameron 1,115 ... C5
†53019 Campbellsport 1,740 ... K8
54618 Camp Douglas 589 ... F8
53109 Camp Lake 2,060 ... K10
54823 Canton 100 ... C5
54928 Caroline 450 ... J6
53011 Cascade 615 ... K8
54205 Casco 484 ... L6
54619 Cashton 827 ... E8
53806 Cassville 1,270 ... E10
54620 Cataract 200 ... E7
54515 Catawba 205 ... E4
54206 Cato 85 ... L7
53924 Cazenovia 259 ... F8
54111 Cecil 445 ... K6
53012 Cedarburg 9,005 ... L9
53013 Cedar Grove 1,420 ... L8
54824 Centuria 711 ... A5
54621 Chaseburg 279 ... D8
54419 Chelsea 120 ... F5
†53029 Chenequa 532 ... J1
54728 Chetek 1,931 ... C5
54420 Chili 185 ... F6
53014 Chilton⊙ 2,965 ... K7
54729 Chippewa Falls⊙ 12,270 ... D6
54004 Clayton 425 ... B5
54005 Clear Lake 899 ... B5
53015 Cleveland 1,270 ... L8
53525 Clinton 1,751 ... J10
54929 Clintonville 4,567 ... J6
53016 Clyman 317 ... J9
53526 Cobb 409 ... F10
54622 Cochrane 512 ... C7
54421 Colby 1,496 ... F6
54112 Coleman 852 ... L5
54730 Colfax 1,149 ... C6
54930 Coloma 367 ... H7
53925 Columbus 4,049 ... H9
54113 Combined Locks 2,573 ... K7
†53147 Como 1,376 ... K10
54519 Conover 480 ... H3
54731 Conrath 86 ... E5
54623 Coon Valley 758 ... E8
54732 Cornell 1,583 ... D5
54827 Cornucopia 250 ... D2
54520 Crandon⊙ 1,969 ... H4
54114 Crivitz 1,041 ... L5
53528 Cross Plains 2,156 ... G9
53807 Cuba City 2,129 ... F10
53110 Cudahy 19,547 ... M2
54829 Cumberland 1,983 ... C4
54422 Curtiss 127 ... F6
54006 Cushing 150 ... A4
54931 Dale 410 ... J7
54733 Dallas 477 ... C5
53926 Dalton 300 ... H8
53529 Dane 518 ... G9
53114 Darien 1,152 ... J10
53530 Darlington⊙ 2,300 ... F10
53531 Deerfield 1,466 ... H9
54007 Deer Park 232 ... B5
53532 De Forest 3,367 ... H9
53018 Delafield 4,083 ... J1
53115 Delavan 5,684 ... J10
†53115 Delavan Lake 2,082 ... J10
†54856 Delta 35 ... D3
54208 Denmark 1,475 ... L7
54115 De Pere 14,892 ... K7
†54663 De Soto 318 ... D9
†54014 Diamond Bluff 100 ... A6
53808 Dickeyville 1,156 ... E10
54625 Dodge 185 ... D7
53533 Dodgeville⊙ 3,458 ... F10
54425 Dorchester 613 ... F5
53118 Dousman 1,153 ... J1
54734 Downing 242 ... B5
54735 Downsville 200 ... C6
53928 Doylestown 294 ... H9
54009 Dresser 670 ... A5
54832 Drummond 200 ... D3
54736 Durand⊙ 2,047 ... C6
53119 Eagle 1,008 ... H2
54521 Eagle River⊙ 1,326 ... H4
54626 Eastman 371 ... D9
53120 East Troy 2,385 ... J2
54701 Eau Claire⊙ 51,509 ... D6
Eau Claire‡ 130,507 ... D6
53019 Eden 534 ... K8
54426 Edgar 1,194 ... G6
53534 Edgerton 4,335 ... H10
54209 Egg Harbor 238 ... M5
54427 Eland 230 ... H6
54428 Elcho 500 ... H5
54429 Elderon 191 ... H6
54932 Eldorado 200 ... J8
54738 Eleva 593 ... D6
53020 Elkhart Lake 1,054 ... L8
53121 Elkhorn⊙ 4,605 ... J10
54739 Elk Mound 737 ... C6
54210 Ellison Bay 112 ... M5
54011 Ellsworth⊙ 2,143 ... A6
53122 Elm Grove 6,735 ... K1
54740 Elmwood 885 ... B6
†53401 Elmwood Park 483 ... M3
53929 Elroy 1,504 ... F8
54430 Elton 150 ... J5
54933 Embarrass 496 ... J6
53930 Endeavor 335 ... G8
54211 Ephraim 319 ... M5
54627 Ettrick 462 ... D7
53536 Evansville 2,835 ... H10
54835 Exeland 219 ... D4
54741 Fairchild 577 ... D6
53931 Fair Water 310 ... J8
54742 Fall Creek 1,148 ... D6
53932 Fall River 850 ... H9
†54840 Falun 95 ... A4
54120 Fence 200 ... K4
53809 Fennimore 2,212 ... E9
54431 Fenwood 165 ... F6
54628 Ferryville 227 ... D9
54524 Fifield 310 ... F4
54212 Fish Creek 119 ... M5
54121 Florence⊙ 780 ... K4
54935 Fond du Lac⊙ 35,863 ... K8
53125 Fontana 1,764 ... J10
53537 Footville 794 ... H10
54123 Forest Junction 140 ... K7
54213 Forestville 455 ... L6
53538 Fort Atkinson 9,785 ... J10
54629 Fountain City 963 ... C7
54836 Foxboro 360 ... B2
53933 Fox Lake 1,373 ... J8
†53117 Fox Point 7,649 ... M1
54214 Francis Creek 589 ... L7
53132 Franklin 16,871 ... L2
54837 Frederic 1,039 ... B4
53021 Fredonia 1,437 ... L8
54940 Fremont 510 ... J7
53934 Friendship⊙ 744 ... G8
53935 Friesland 267 ... H8
54630 Galesville 1,239 ... D7
54631 Gays Mills 627 ... E9
53127 Genesee Depot 350 ... J2
54632 Genoa 283 ... D8
53128 Genoa City 1,202 ... K11
53022 Germantown 10,729 ... K1
54124 Gillett 1,356 ... K6
54433 Gilman 436 ... E5
54743 Gilmanton 300 ... C7
54435 Gleason 200 ... G5
53023 Glenbeulah 423 ... L8
†53209 Glendale 13,882 ... M1
54526 Glen Flora 83 ... E4
53810 Glen Haven 160 ... E10
54013 Glenwood City 950 ... B5
54527 Glidden 940 ... E3
54125 Goodman 875 ... K4
54838 Gordon 600 ... C3
53540 Gotham 250 ... F9
53024 Grafton 8,381 ... L9
53936 Grand Marsh 725 ... G8
54839 Grand View 447 ... D3
54436 Granton 399 ... E6
54840 Grantsburg⊙ 1,153 ... A4
53541 Gratiot 280 ... F10
*54301 Green Bay⊙ 87,899 ... K6
Green Bay‡ 175,280 ... K6
53129 Greendale 16,928 ... L2
53220 Greenfield 31,467 ... L2
54941 Green Lake⊙ 1,208 ... H8
54126 Greenleaf 300 ... L7
54942 Greenville 900 ... J7
54437 Greenwood 1,124 ... E6
54128 Gresham 534 ... J6
54014 Hager City 110 ... A6
53130 Hales Corners 7,110 ... K2
54015 Hammond 991 ... A6
54943 Hancock 419 ... G7
54529 Harshaw 87 ... G4
53027 Hartford 7,046 ... K9
53029 Hartland 5,559 ... J1
54440 Hatley 300 ... H6
54841 Haugen 251 ... C4
54530 Hawkins 407 ... E4
54842 Hawthorne 200 ... C3
54843 Hayward⊙ 1,698 ... D3
53811 Hazel Green 1,282 ... F11
54531 Hazelhurst 630 ... G4
†53538 Hebron 450 ... J10
53137 Helenville 300 ... J10
54844 Herbster 100 ... D2
54441 Hewitt 470 ... F6
53543 Highland 860 ... F9
54129 Hilbert 1,176 ... K7
†54511 Hiles 350 ... J4

(continued on following page)

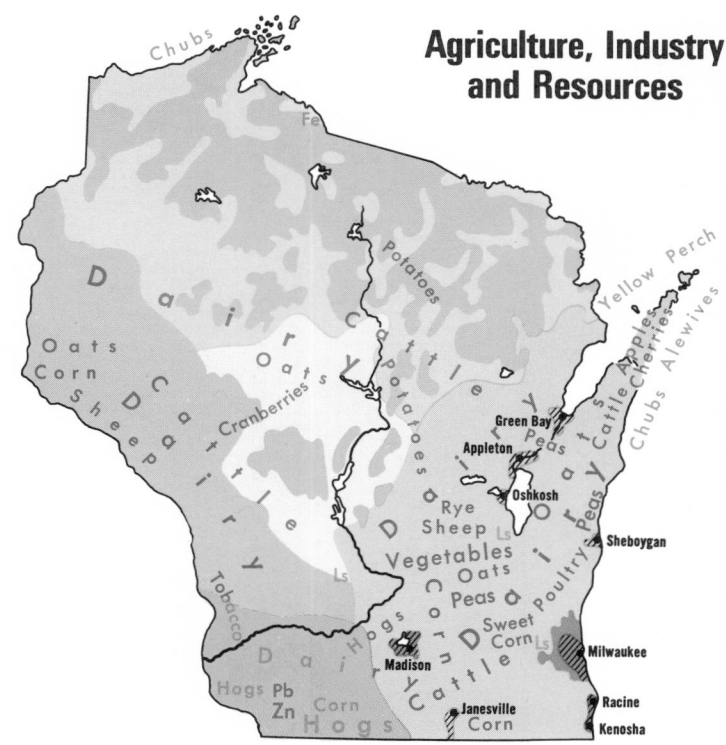

Agriculture, Industry and Resources

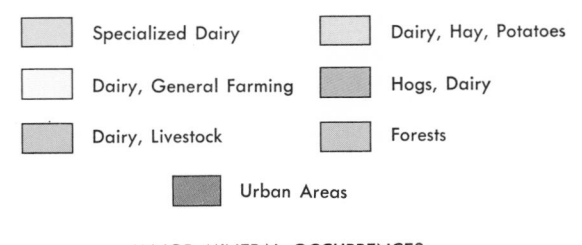

DOMINANT LAND USE

Specialized Dairy
Dairy, Hay, Potatoes
Dairy, General Farming
Hogs, Dairy
Dairy, Livestock
Forests
Urban Areas

MAJOR MINERAL OCCURRENCES

Fe Iron Ore
Pb Lead
Ls Limestone
Zn Zinc

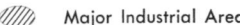

Major Industrial Areas

54634 Hillsboro 1,263 ... F8
53031 Hingham 250 ... K8
54635 Hixton 364 ... E7
54745 Holcombe 200 ... D5
53544 Hollandale 271 ... G10
54636 Holmen 2,411 ... D8
53138 Honey Creek 300 ... J3
53032 Horicon 3,584 ... J9
54944 Hortonville 2,016 ... J7
†55082 Houlton 915 ... A5
54303 Howard 8,240 ... K6
53081 Howards Grove-Millersville 1,838 ... L8
53033 Hubertus 600 ... K1
54016 Hudson⊙ 5,434 ... A6
54746 Humbird 190 ... E6
54534 Hurley⊙ 2,015 ... F3
53034 Hustisford 874 ... J9
54637 Hustler 170 ... F8
54747 Independence 1,180 ... D7
54945 Iola 957 ... H6
54536 Iron Belt 300 ... F3
53035 Iron Ridge 766 ... K9
54847 Iron River 878 ... D2
†53941 Ironton 206 ... F8
53036 Ixonia 525 ... H1
53037 Jackson 1,817 ... K9
†54235 Jacksonport 150 ... M6
53545 Janesville⊙ 51,071 ... H10
Janesville-Beloit‡ 139,420 ... H10
53549 Jefferson⊙ 5,647 ... J10
54748 Jim Falls 100 ... D5
53038 Johnson Creek 1,136 ... J9
53550 Juda 500 ... H10
54443 Junction City 523 ... G6
53039 Juneau⊙ 2,045 ... J9
53139 Kansasville 150 ... L3
54130 Kaukauna 11,310 ... K7
†53050 Kekoskee 224 ... J8
54215 Kellnersville 369 ... L7
54638 Kendall 486 ... F8
54537 Kennan 194 ... F5
*53140 Kenosha⊙ 77,685 ... M3
Kenosha‡ 123,137 ... M3
54135 Keshena⊙ 980 ... J6
53040 Kewaskum 2,381 ... K8
54216 Kewaunee⊙ 2,801 ... M7
53042 Kiel 3,083 ... L8
53812 Kieler 800 ... E10
54136 Kimberly 5,881 ... K7
53939 Kingston 328 ... H8
54749 Knapp 419 ... B6
†54455 Knowlton 127 ... G6
53044 Kohler 1,651 ... L8
53147 Krakow 345 ... K6
54538 Lac du Flambeau 500 ... G4
†53066 Lac La Belle 289 ... H1
54601 La Crosse⊙ 48,347 ... D8
La Crosse‡ 91,056 ... D8
54848 Ladysmith⊙ 3,826 ... D5
54639 La Farge 746 ... E8
53940 Lake Delton 1,158 ... G8
53147 Lake Geneva 5,612 ... K10
53551 Lake Mills 3,670 ... H9
54849 Lake Nebagamon 780 ... C3
54539 Lake Tomahawk 600 ... H4
†54494 Lake Wazeecha 2,176 ... G7
†54729 Lake Wissota 1,788 ... D6
54138 Lakewood 425 ... K5
53813 Lancaster⊙ 4,076 ... E10
54540 Land O'Lakes 786 ... H3
53046 Lannon 987 ... K1
53941 La Valle 412 ... F8
53047 Lebanon 250 ... H1
54139 Lena 585 ... K6
†54656 Leon 100 ... E8
54948 Leopolis 200 ... J6
54851 Lewis 200 ... B4
53942 Limeridge 191 ... F9
53553 Linden 395 ... F10
54140 Little Chute 7,907 ... K7
53554 Livingston 642 ... E10
53555 Lodi 1,959 ... G9
53943 Loganville 239 ... F9
†54970 Lohrville 336 ... H7
53048 Lomira 1,446 ... J8
53556 Lone Rock 577 ... F9
54542 Long Lake 150 ... J4
53557 Lowell 326 ... J9
54446 Loyal 1,252 ... E6
54447 Lublin 142 ... E5
54853 Luck 997 ... B4
54217 Luxemburg 1,040 ... L6
53944 Lyndon Station 375 ... F8
54640 Lynxville 174 ... D9
53148 Lyons 550 ... K10
*53701 Madison (cap.)⊙ 170,616 ... H9
Madison‡ 323,545 ... H9
54750 Maiden Rock 172 ... B6
54949 Manawa 1,205 ... J7
54220 Manitowoc⊙ 32,547 ... L7
54226 Maplewood 200 ... M6
54448 Marathon 1,552 ... G6
54855 Marengo 130 ... E3
54227 Maribel 363 ... L7
54143 Marinette⊙ 11,965 ... L5
54950 Marion 1,348 ... J6
53946 Markesan 1,446 ... J8
53947 Marquette 204 ... H8
53559 Marshall 2,363 ... H9
54449 Marshfield 18,290 ... F6
54856 Mason 102 ... D3
54450 Mattoon 382 ... J5
53948 Mauston⊙ 3,284 ... F8
53050 Mayville 4,333 ... K9
53560 Mazomanie 1,248 ... G9
53558 McFarland 3,783 ... H10
54543 McNaughton 450 ... H4
54451 Medford⊙ 4,035 ... F5
54546 Mellen 1,046 ... E3
54642 Melrose 507 ... E7
54619 Melvina 117 ... E8
54952 Menasha 14,728 ... J7
53051 Menomonee Falls 27,845 ... K1
54751 Menomonie⊙ 12,769 ... C6
53092 Mequon 16,193 ... L1
54452 Merrill⊙ 9,578 ... G5

54754 Merrillan 587 ... E7
53561 Merrimac 365 ... G9
53056 Merton 1,045 ... K1
53562 Middleton 11,848 ... G9
54857 Mikana 200 ... C4
54453 Milan 153 ... F6
†53038 Milford 35 ... J9
54454 Milladore 250 ... G6
54643 Millston 110 ... E7
54858 Milltown 732 ... B4
53563 Milton 4,092 ... J10
*53201 Milwaukee⊙ 636,236 ... M1
Milwaukee‡ 1,397,143 ... M1
54644 Mindoro 200 ... D7
53565 Mineral Point 2,259 ... F10
54548 Minocqua 950 ... G4
54859 Minong 557 ... C3
54228 Mishicot 1,503 ... L7
54755 Mondovi 2,545 ... C6
54549 Monico 250 ... H4
53716 Monona 8,809 ... H9
53566 Monroe⊙ 10,027 ... G10
53949 Montello⊙ 1,273 ... H8
53569 Montfort 616 ... E10
53570 Monticello 1,021 ... G10
54550 Montreal 887 ... F3
53571 Morrisonville 375 ... G9
54455 Mosinee 3,015 ... G6
54149 Mountain 250 ... K5
53057 Mount Calvary 585 ... K8
53816 Mount Hope 197 ... D10
53572 Mount Horeb 3,251 ... G10
54645 Mount Sterling 223 ... D9
†53572 Mount Vernon 138 ... G10
53149 Mukwonago 4,014 ... J2
53573 Muscoda 1,331 ... F9
53150 Muskego 15,277 ... K2
53058 Nashotah 513 ... J1
54646 Necedah 773 ... F7
54956 Neenah 22,432 ... J7
54456 Neillsville⊙ 2,780 ... E6
54457 Nekoosa 2,519 ... G7
54756 Nelson 389 ... C7
54458 Nelsonville 199 ... H7
54150 Neopit 1,065 ... J6
53059 Neosho 575 ... J9
54960 Neshkoro 386 ... H8
54551 Newald 375 ... J4
54757 New Auburn 466 ... D5
53151 New Berlin 30,529 ... K2
53060 Newburg 783 ... K9
†61075 New Diggings 65 ... F10
54229 New Franken 150 ... L6
53574 New Glarus 1,763 ... G10
53061 New Holstein 3,412 ... K8
53950 New Lisbon 1,390 ... F8
54961 New London 6,210 ... J7
54017 New Richmond 4,306 ... A5
54151 Niagara 2,079 ... K4
54152 Nichols 267 ... K6
†53401 North Bay 219 ... M3
†54935 North Fond du Lac 3,844 ... J8
53951 North Freedom 616 ... G9
†54016 North Hudson 2,218 ... A5
53064 North Lake 400 ... J1
53217 North Shore 14,930 ... M1
54648 Norwalk 517 ... E8
53154 Oak Creek 16,932 ... M2
54649 Oakdale 150 ... F8
53065 Oakfield 990 ... J8
53066 Oconomowoc 9,909 ... H1
†53066 Oconomowoc Lake 524 ... H1
54153 Oconto⊙ 4,505 ... L6
54154 Oconto Falls 2,500 ... K6
54962 Ogdensburg 214 ... J7
54459 Ogema 238 ... F5
53069 Okauchee 3,958 ... J1
†53555 Okee 250 ... H9
†54880 Oliver 253 ... B2
54963 Omro 2,763 ... J7
54650 Onalaska 9,249 ... D8
54155 Oneida 900 ... K7
54651 Ontario 398 ... E8
53070 Oostburg 1,647 ... L8
53575 Oregon 3,876 ... H10
53576 Orfordville 1,143 ... H10
54020 Osceola 1,581 ... A5
54901 Oshkosh⊙ 49,620 ... J8
54758 Osseo 1,474 ... D6
54460 Owen 998 ... F6
53952 Oxford 432 ... H8
53953 Packwaukee 271 ... G8
†53168 Paddock Lake 2,207 ... K10
53156 Palmyra 1,515 ... H2
53954 Pardeeville 1,594 ... H8
54552 Park Falls 3,192 ... F4
†54481 Park Ridge 643 ... H6
53817 Patch Grove 259 ... D10
53157 Pell Lake 1,826 ... K10
54553 Pence 234 ... F3
54759 Pepin 890 ... B7
54157 Peshtigo 2,807 ... L5
53072 Pewaukee 4,637 ... K1
54554 Phelps 950 ... H3
54555 Phillips⊙ 1,522 ... E4
54464 Phlox 150 ... J5
54465 Pickerel 107 ... J5
54760 Pigeon Falls 338 ... D7
54466 Pittsville 810 ... F7
53577 Plain 676 ... F9
54966 Plainfield 813 ... G7
†53017 Plat 120 ... K1
53818 Platteville 9,580 ... F10
53158 Pleasant Prairie 950 ... L10
54467 Plover 5,310 ... G7
54761 Plum City 505 ... B6
53073 Plymouth 6,027 ... L8
†54423 Polonia 200 ... H6
54864 Poplar 569 ... C2
53901 Portage⊙ 7,896 ... G8
54469 Port Edwards 2,077 ... G7
53074 Port Washington⊙ 8,612 ... L9
54865 Port Wing 290 ... D2
53820 Potosi 736 ... E10
54160 Potter 330 ... K7
54161 Pound 407 ... L5
53955 Poynette 1,447 ... G9

54967 Poy Sippi 425 ... J7
53821 Prairie du Chien⊙ 5,859 ... D9
53578 Prairie du Sac 2,145 ... G9
54762 Prairie Farm 387 ... C5
54556 Prentice 605 ... F4
54021 Prescott 2,654 ... A6
54968 Princeton 1,479 ... H8
54162 Pulaski 1,875 ... K6
54164 Pulcifer 35 ... K6
*53401 Racine⊙ 85,725 ... M3
Racine‡ 173,132 ... M3
54867 Radisson 280 ... D4
53956 Randolph 1,691 ... H8
53075 Random Lake 1,287 ... K8
†53126 Raymond 300 ... L2
54652 Readstown 396 ... E9
54970 Redgranite 976 ... J7
53959 Reedsburg 5,038 ... G8
54230 Reedsville 1,134 ... L7
53579 Reeseville 649 ... J9
53580 Rewey 233 ... F10
54501 Rhinelander⊙ 7,873 ... H4
54470 Rib Lake 945 ... F5
54868 Rice Lake 7,691 ... C5
53581 Richland Center⊙ 4,997 ... F9
54763 Ridgeland 300 ... B5
53582 Ridgeway 503 ... F10
53960 Rio 785 ... H9
54971 Ripon 7,111 ... J8
54022 River Falls 9,019 ... A6
†53201 River Hills 1,642 ... M1
54023 Roberts 833 ... A6
53167 Rochester 746 ... K3
†53523 Rockdale 200 ... J10
53077 Rockfield 200 ... L1
54653 Rockland 383 ... D8
53961 Rock Springs 426 ... F8
†53178 Rome 200 ... H1
54974 Rosendale 725 ... J8
54473 Rosholt 520 ... H6
54474 Rothschild 3,338 ... G6
†53583 Roxbury 260 ... G9
54475 Rudolph 392 ... G7
†54751 Rusk 40 ... C6
53079 Saint Cloud 560 ... K8
54024 Saint Croix Falls 1,497 ... A5
†53207 Saint Francis 10,042 ... M2
†54601 Saint Joseph Ridge 450 ... D8
54232 Saint Nazianz 738 ... L7
54765 Sand Creek 225 ... C5
53583 Sauk City 2,703 ... G9
53080 Saukville 3,494 ... L9
54559 Saxon 375 ... F3
54977 Scandinavia 292 ... H7
54476 Schofield 2,226 ... H6
†54843 Seeley 68 ... D3
54654 Seneca 235 ... E9
53584 Sextonville 225 ... F9
54165 Seymour 2,530 ... K6
53585 Sharon 1,280 ... J11
54166 Shawano⊙ 7,013 ... J6
53081 Sheboygan⊙ 48,085 ... L8
Sheboygan‡ 100,935 ... L8
53085 Sheboygan Falls 5,253 ... L8
54766 Sheldon 292 ... D5
54871 Shell Lake⊙ 1,135 ... C4
54169 Sherwood 372 ... K7
54170 Shiocton 805 ... K7
53211 Shorewood 14,327 ... M1
†53701 Shorewood Hills 1,837 ... G9
53586 Shullsburg 1,484 ... F10
53170 Silver Lake 1,598 ... K10
54872 Siren 896 ... B4
54234 Sister Bay 564 ... M5
53086 Slinger 1,612 ... K9
54655 Soldiers Grove 622 ... E9
54873 Solon Springs 590 ... C3
54025 Somerset 860 ... A5
53172 South Milwaukee 21,069 ... M2
53587 South Wayne 495 ... G10
54656 Sparta⊙ 6,934 ... E8
54479 Spencer 1,754 ... F6
54801 Spooner 2,365 ... B4
53588 Spring Green 1,265 ... G9
54767 Spring Valley 982 ... B6
54768 Stanley 2,095 ... E6
54026 Star Prairie 420 ... A5
54480 Stetsonville 487 ... F5
54657 Steuben 175 ... E9
54481 Stevens Point⊙ 22,970 ... G7
54172 Stiles 300 ... L6
53825 Stitzer 190 ... E10
53088 Stockbridge 567 ... K7
54769 Stockholm 104 ... B7
54658 Stoddard 762 ... D8
54876 Stone Lake 210 ... C4
53589 Stoughton 7,589 ... H10
54484 Stratford 1,385 ... F6
54770 Strum 944 ... D6
54235 Sturgeon Bay⊙ 8,847 ... M6
53177 Sturtevant 4,130 ... M3
54173 Suamico 900 ... K6
53178 Sullivan 434 ... H1
54485 Summit Lake 250 ... H5
53590 Sun Prairie 12,931 ... H9
54880 Superior⊙ 29,571 ... C2
Superior-Duluth‡ 266,650 ... C2
†54880 Superior Village 580 ... B2
54174 Suring 581 ... K5
53089 Sussex 3,482 ... K1
53090 Taycheedah 350 ... K8
54659 Taylor 411 ... E7
†53820 Tennyson 476 ... E10
53091 Theresa 766 ... K8
53092 Thiensville 3,341 ... L1
54771 Thorp 1,635 ... E6
54562 Three Lakes 950 ... H4
54486 Tigerton 865 ... H6
54240 Tisch Mills 315 ... L7
54660 Tomah 7,204 ... F8
54487 Tomahawk 3,527 ... G5
54563 Tony 146 ... E5
54888 Trego 280 ... C4
54661 Trempealeau 956 ... C8
54662 Tunnel City 200 ... E7
54889 Turtle Lake 762 ... B5
53181 Twin Lakes 3,474 ... K11

Topography

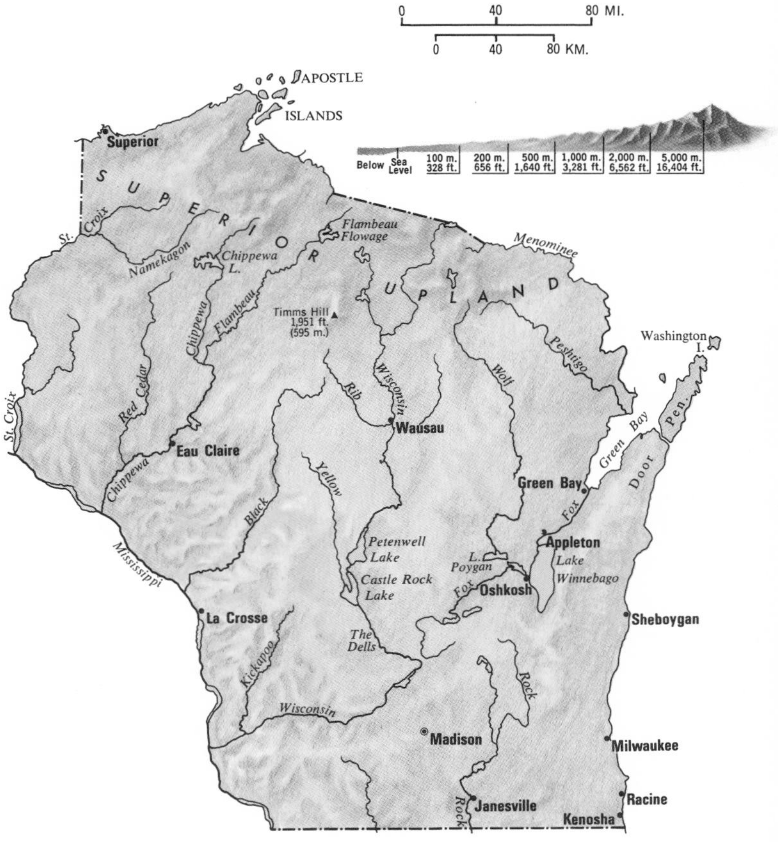

54241 Two Rivers 13,354 ... M7
53962 Union Center 216 ... F8
53182 Union Grove 3,517 ... L3
54488 Unity 418 ... F6
54245 Valders 984 ... L7
53593 Verona 3,336 ... G9
54489 Vesper 554 ... F7
54664 Viola 696 ... E8
54665 Viroqua⊙ 3,716 ... D8
54566 Wabeno 800 ... J5
53093 Waldo 416 ... L8
53183 Wales 1,992 ... J1
53184 Walworth 1,607 ... J10
54666 Warrens 300 ... E7
54890 Wascott 70 ... C3
54891 Washburn⊙ 2,080 ... D2
54246 Washington Island 550 ... M5
53185 Waterford 2,051 ... K3
53594 Waterloo 2,393 ... J9
53094 Watertown 18,113 ... J9
53021 Waubeka 450 ... L9
53186 Waukesha⊙ 50,365 ... K1
53597 Waunakee 3,866 ... G9
54981 Waupaca⊙ 4,472 ... H7
53963 Waupun 8,132 ... J8
54401 Wausau⊙ 32,426 ... G6
Wausau‡ 111,270 ... G6
54177 Wausaukee 648 ... K5
54982 Wautoma⊙ 1,629 ... H7
53226 Wauwatosa 51,308 ... L1
53826 Wauzeka 580 ... E9
†54126 Wayside 140 ... L7
54893 Webster 610 ... B4
53214 West Allis 63,982 ... L1
†53913 West Baraboo 846 ... G9
53095 West Bend⊙ 21,484 ... K9
54490 Westboro 750 ... F5
54667 Westby 1,797 ... E8
53964 Westfield 1,033 ... H8
†53201 West Milwaukee 3,535 ... L1
†54476 Weston 8,775 ... G6
54669 West Salem 3,276 ... D8
54983 Weyauwega 1,549 ... H7
54895 Weyerhaeuser 313 ... D5
54772 Wheeler 231 ... C5
54773 Whitehall⊙ 1,530 ... D7
54491 White Lake 309 ... J5
54247 Whitelaw 649 ... L7
53190 Whitewater 11,520 ... J10
†54481 Whiting 2,050 ... H7
54984 Wild Rose 741 ... H7
53191 Williams Bay 1,763 ... J10
54027 Wilson 155 ... B6
54670 Wilton 465 ... F8
54567 Winchester 300 ... G3
53185 Wind Lake 900 ... K2
†53401 Wind Point 1,695 ... M2
53598 Windsor 827 ... H9
54985 Winnebago 1,433 ... J8
54986 Winneconne 1,935 ... J7
54896 Winter 376 ... E4
53965 Wisconsin Dells 2,521 ... G8
54494 Wisconsin Rapids⊙ 17,995 ... G7

54498 Withee 509 ... E6
54499 Wittenberg 997 ... H6
53968 Wonewoc 842 ... F8
53827 Woodman 116 ... E9
54568 Woodruff 850 ... G4
54028 Woodville 725 ... B6
54180 Wrightstown 1,169 ... K7
54671 Wyeville 163 ... F7
53969 Wyocena 548 ... H9
54182 Zachow 135 ... K6

OTHER FEATURES

Apostle (isls.) ... F2
Apostle Islands Nat'l Lakeshore ... E1
Apple (riv.) ... A5
Bad River Ind. Res. ... E2
Bardon (lake) ... C3
Bear (isl.) ... E1
Beaver Dam (lake) ... J9
Beulah (lake) ... J2
Big Eau Pleine (res.) ... G6
Big Muskego (lake) ... L2
Big Rib (riv.) ... G5
Black (riv.) ... E7
Butternut (lake) ... J4
Castle Rock (lake) ... G8
Cat (isl.) ... E1
Chambers (isl.) ... M5
Chequamegon (bay) ... E2
Chetac (lake) ... D4
Chippewa (lake) ... D4
Chippewa (riv.) ... B7
Clam (lake) ... B4
Clam (riv.) ... A4
Dells, The (valley) ... G8
Denoon (lake) ... K2
Du Bay (lake) ... G6
Eagle (lake) ... H2
Eagle (lake) ... K3
Eau Claire (riv.) ... D6
Flambeau (riv.) ... E4
Flambeau Flowage (res.) ... F3
Fox (riv.) ... K2
Fox (riv.) ... K7
General Mitchell Field ... M2
Geneva (lake) ... K10
Golden (lake) ... H1
Green (bay) ... L6
Grindstone (lake) ... C4
Holcombe Flowage (res.) ... D5
Jump (riv.) ... E5
Kegonsa (lake) ... H10
Kickapoo (riv.) ... E9
Koshkonong (lake) ... H10
La Belle (lake) ... H1
Lac Court Oreilles Ind. Res. ... D4
Lac du Flambeau Ind. Res. ... G3
Long (lake) ... C4
Madeline (isl.) ... E2
Mendota (lake) ... H9
Menominee (riv.) ... L5
Metonga (lake) ... J4

Michigan (isl.) ... F2
Michigan (lake) ... M9
Mississippi (riv.) ... D10
Montreal (riv.) ... F2
Moose (lake) ... E3
Moose (lake) ... F3
Nagawicka (lake) ... J1
Namekagon (lake) ... D3
Namekagon (riv.) ... C3
North (lake) ... J1
Oak (isl.) ... E2
Oconomowoc (lake) ... H1
Oconto (riv.) ... K5
Okauchee (lake) ... J1
Outer (isl.) ... F1
Owen (lake) ... D3
Pecatonica (riv.) ... H11
Pelican (lake) ... H4
Pepin (lake) ... B7
Peshtigo (riv.) ... K5
Petenwell (lake) ... G7
Pewaukee (lake) ... K1
Phantom (lake) ... J2
Pine (lake) ... J1
Porte des Morts (str.) ... N5
Poygan (lake) ... J7
Puckaway (lake) ... H8
Red Cedar (riv.) ... C5
Red Cliff Ind. Res. ... E2
Rib (mt.) ... G6
Rock (riv.) ... J9
Round (lake) ... F4
Round (lake) ... D3
Saint Croix (lake) ... A6
Saint Croix (riv.) ... A4
Saint Croix Flowage (res.) ... C3
Saint Louis (riv.) ... A2
Sand (isl.) ... D2
Shawano (lake) ... K6
Shell (lake) ... C4
Spider (lake) ... D3
Stockbridge Ind. Res. ... J6
Stockton (isl.) ... F2
Sugar (riv.) ... H10
Sugarbush Hill (mt.) ... J4
Superior (lake) ... F1
Thunder (lake) ... H4
Tichigan (lake) ... K2
Timms Hill (mt.) ... F5
Trempealeau (riv.) ... C7
Trout (lake) ... G3
Vieux Desert (lake) ... J3
Washington (isl.) ... M5
Willow (res.) ... F4
Wind (lake) ... K2
Winnebago (lake) ... K7
Wisconsin (riv.) ... E9
Wolf (riv.) ... J5
Yellow (lake) ... B4
Yellow (riv.) ... F7

⊙County seat.
‡Population of metropolitan area.
† Zip of nearest p.o. * Multiple zips.

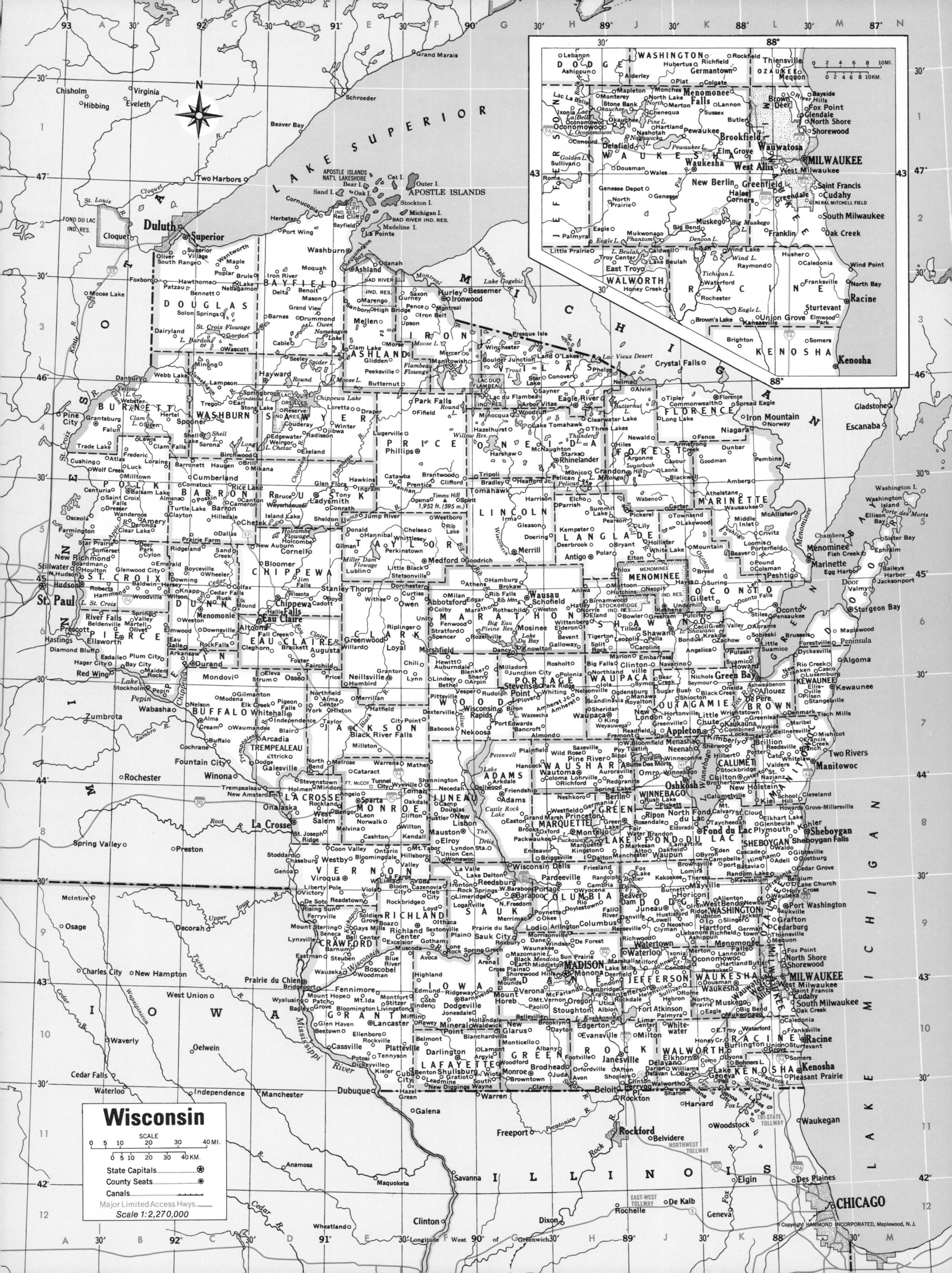

Wisconsin

SCALE
0 5 10   20   30   40 MI.

0 5 10   20   30   40 KM.

State Capitals..............⊛
County Seats...............◉
Canals.........................⊥⊥⊥

Major Limited Access Hwys
Scale 1:2,270,000

Copyright HAMMOND INCORPORATED, Maplewood, N.J.

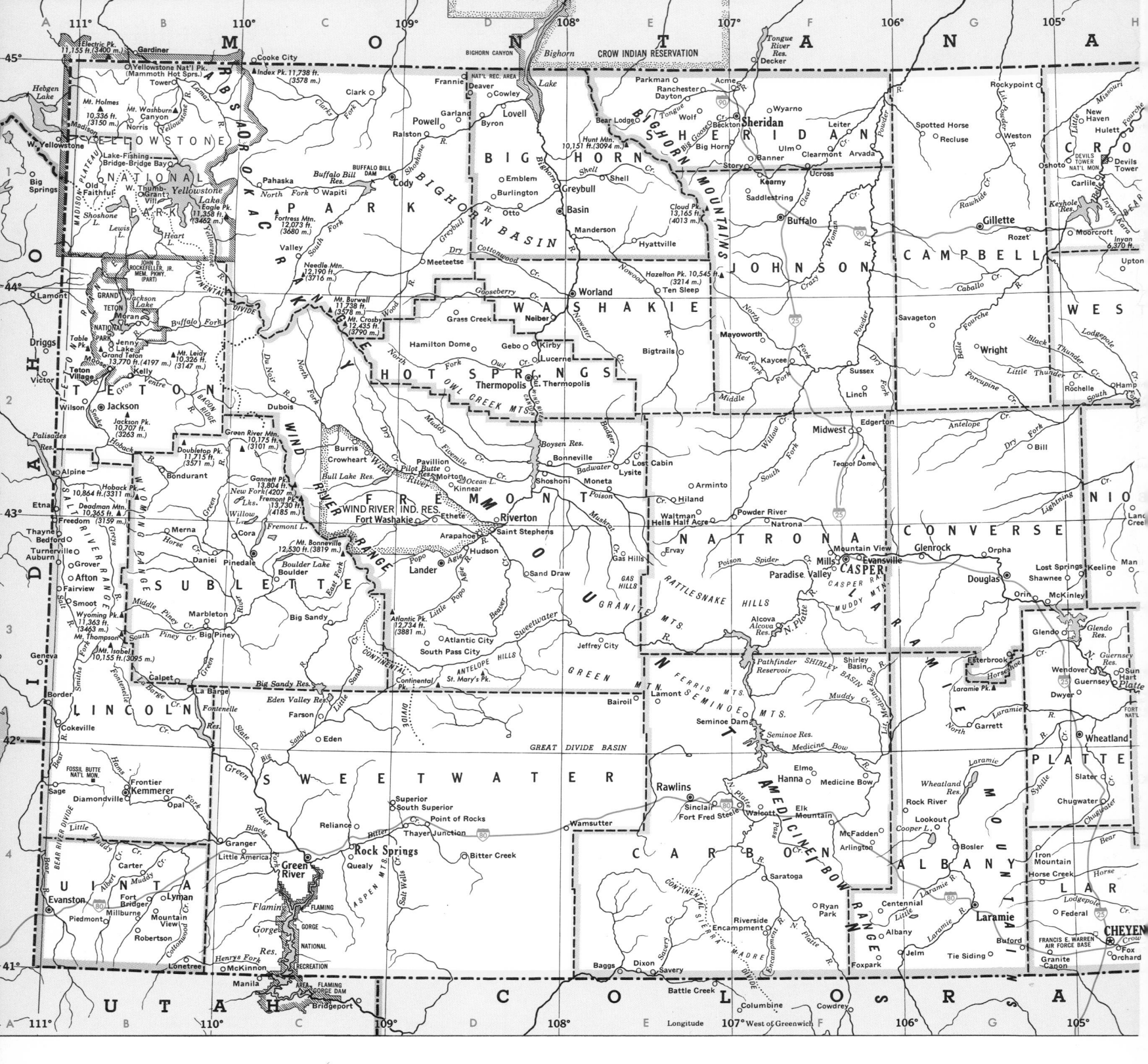

Agriculture, Industry and Resources

DOMINANT LAND USE

Specialized Wheat

Specialized Dairy

General Farming, Livestock, Special Crops

Sugar Beets, Dry Beans, Livestock, General Farming

Range Livestock

Forests

Nonagricultural Land

MAJOR MINERAL OCCURRENCES

C Coal
Cl Clay
Fe Iron Ore
G Natural Gas
O Petroleum
P Phosphates
So Soda Ash
U Uranium
V Vanadium
⚡ Water Power

COUNTIES

Albany 29,062	G4
Big Horn 11,896	E1
Campbell 24,367	G1
Carbon 21,896	F4
Converse 14,069	G3
Crook 5,308	H1
Fremont 38,992	D2
Goshen 12,040	H4
Hot Springs 5,710	D2
Johnson 6,700	F1
Laramie 68,649	H4
Lincoln 12,177	B3
Natrona 71,856	F3
Niobrara 2,924	H2
Park 21,639	C1
Platte 11,975	H4
Sheridan 25,048	F1
Sublette 4,548	C3
Sweetwater 41,723	D4
Teton 9,355	B2
Uinta 13,021	B4
Washakie 9,496	E2
Weston 7,106	H2

CITIES and TOWNS

Zip Name/Pop.	Key
83110 Afton 1,481	B3
82050 Albin 128	H4
82620 Alcova 275	F3

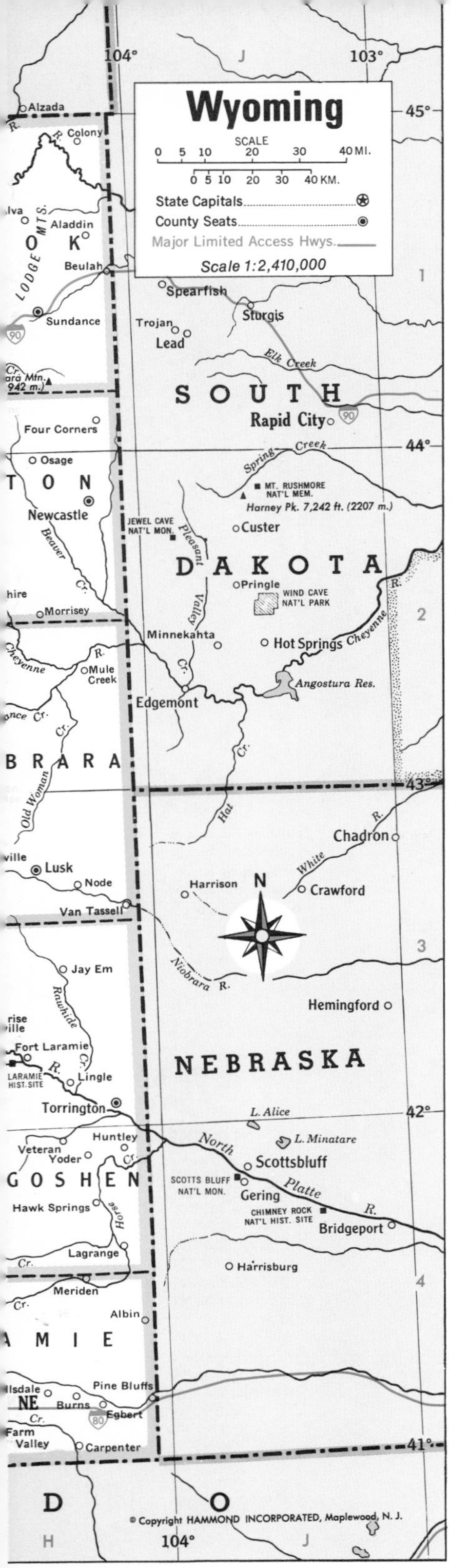
Wyoming
SCALE
0 5 10 20 30 40 MI.
0 5 10 20 30 40 KM.
State Capitals
County Seats
Major Limited Access Hwys.
Scale 1:2,410,000
104°
103°
45°
44°
43°
42°
41°
SOUTH
DAKOTA
NEBRASKA
Rapid City
Sturgis
Lead
Spearfish
Belle Fourche
Custer
Hot Springs
Edgemont
Chadron
Crawford
Harrison
Lusk
Van Tassell
Torrington
Scottsbluff
Gering
Bridgeport
Harrisburg
Pine Bluffs
Carpenter
Beulah
Sundance
Newcastle
JEWEL CAVE NAT'L MON.
WIND CAVE NAT'L PARK
MT. RUSHMORE NAT'L MEM.
Harney Pk. 7,242 ft. (2207 m.)
SCOTTS BLUFF NAT'L MON.
CHIMNEY ROCK NAT'L HIST. SITE
Angostura Res.
L. Alice
L. Minatare
© Copyright HAMMOND INCORPORATED, Maplewood, N. J.

AREA 97,809 sq. mi. (253,325 sq. km.)
POPULATION 469,557
CAPITAL Cheyenne
LARGEST CITY Casper
HIGHEST POINT Gannett Pk. 13,804 ft. (4207 m.)
SETTLED IN 1834
ADMITTED TO UNION July 10, 1890
POPULAR NAME Equality State
STATE FLOWER Indian Paintbrush
STATE BIRD Meadowlark

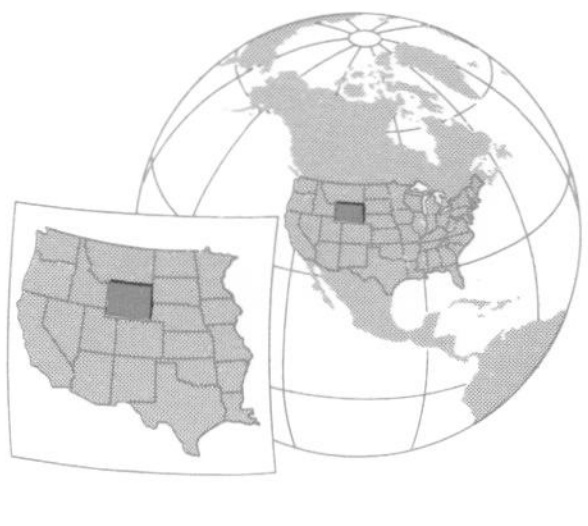

Topography

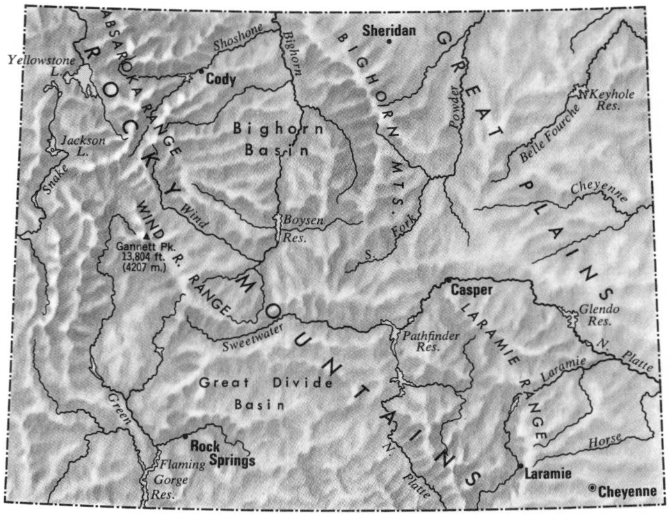
0 50 100 MI.
0 50 100 KM.
Yellowstone L.
Jackson L.
Cody
Sheridan
BIGHORN MTS.
GREAT PLAINS
Bighorn Basin
Boysen Res.
Keyhole Res.
Gannett Pk. 13,804 ft. (4207 m.)
WIND R. RANGE
ROCKY MOUNTAINS
Casper
Glendo Res.
Pathfinder Res.
LARAMIE RANGE
Great Divide Basin
Rock Springs
Flaming Gorge Res.
Laramie
Cheyenne

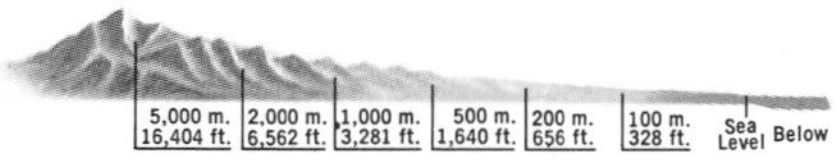
5,000 m. 16,404 ft.
2,000 m. 6,562 ft.
1,000 m. 3,281 ft.
500 m. 1,640 ft.
200 m. 656 ft.
100 m. 328 ft.
Sea Level
Below

82510 Arapahoe 682 .... D3
83111 Auburn 360 .... A3
82321 Baggs 433 .... E4
82322 Bairoil 300 .... E3
82410 Basin⊙ 1,349 .... E1
†82801 Beckton 110 .... E1
83112 Bedford 350 .... A3
82712 Beulah 184 .... H1
82833 Big Horn 350 .... E1
83113 Big Piney 530 .... B3
82051 Bosler 195 .... G4
82834 Buffalo⊙ 3,799 .... F1
82411 Burlington 300 .... D1
82053 Burns 268 .... H4
82412 Byron 633 .... D1
82601 Casper⊙ 51,016 .... F3
82055 Centennial 140 .... F4
82001 Cheyenne (cap.)⊙ 47,283 . H4
82210 Chugwater 282 .... H4
82835 Clearmont 191 .... F1
82414 Cody⊙ 6,790 .... D1
83114 Cokeville 515 .... B3
82420 Cowley 455 .... D1
82512 Crowheart 200 .... C2
83115 Daniel 130 .... B3
82836 Dayton 701 .... E1
82421 Deaver 178 .... D1
83116 Diamondville 1,000 .... B4
82323 Dixon 82 .... E4
82633 Douglas⊙ 6,030 .... G3
82513 Dubois 1,067 .... C2
†82443 East Thermopolis 359 .... D2
82926 Eden 198 .... C3
82635 Edgerton 510 .... F2
82324 Elk Mountain 338 .... F4
82325 Encampment 611 .... F4
83118 Etna 200 .... A2
82930 Evanston⊙ 6,421 .... B4
82636 Evansville 2,335 .... F3
83119 Fairview 150 .... B3
82932 Farson 350 .... C3
82933 Fort Bridger 300 .... B4
82212 Fort Laramie 356 .... H3
82514 Fort Washakie 400 .... C2
†82001 Fox Farm 2,850 .... H4
82423 Frannie 138 .... D1
83120 Freedom 400 .... B3
83121 Frontier 150 .... B4
82501 Gas Hills 150 .... E3
82716 Gillette⊙ 12,134 .... G1
82213 Glendo 367 .... G3
82637 Glenrock 2,736 .... G3
82934 Granger 177 .... C4
82425 Grass Creek 152 .... D2
82935 Green River⊙ 12,807 .... C4
82426 Greybull 2,277 .... E1
83122 Grover 425 .... B3
82214 Guernsey 1,512 .... H3
82327 Hanna 2,288 .... F4
82215 Hartville 149 .... H3
82060 Hillsdale 160 .... H4
82061 Horse Creek 225 .... G4
82515 Hudson 514 .... D3
82720 Hulett 291 .... H1
83001 Jackson⊙ 4,511 .... B2
82310 Jeffrey City 1,882 .... E3
82639 Kaycee 271 .... F2
83011 Kelly 100 .... B2
83101 Kemmerer⊙ 3,273 .... B4
82516 Kinnear 145 .... D2
82430 Kirby 129 .... D2
83123 La Barge 302 .... B3
82221 Lagrange 232 .... H4
82520 Lander⊙ 7,867 .... D3
82070 Laramie⊙ 24,410 .... G4
82640 Linch 187 .... F2
82223 Lingle 475 .... H3
82929 Little America 175 .... C4
†82642 Lost Cabin 25 .... E2
82224 Lost Springs 9 .... G3
82431 Lovell 2,447 .... D1
†82443 Lucerne 240 .... D2
82225 Lusk⊙ 1,650 .... H3
82937 Lyman 2,284 .... B4
82642 Lysite 175 .... E2
†82190 Mammoth Hot Springs
(Yellowstone Nat'l Park 350 .... B1
82432 Manderson 174 .... E1
82227 Manville 94 .... H3
†83113 Marbleton 537 .... B3
82938 McKinnon 135 .... C4
82329 Medicine Bow 953 .... F4
82433 Meeteetse 512 .... D1
82643 Midwest 638 .... F2
82644 Mills 2,139 .... F3
82721 Moorcroft 1,014 .... H1
83012 Moose 150 .... B2
83013 Moran 200 .... B2
†82601 Mountain View F3
82939 Mountain View 628 .... B4
82701 Newcastle⊙ 3,596 .... H2
82190 Old Faithful 75 .... B1
†82001 Orchard Valley 3,327 .... H4
82723 Osage 500 .... H2
†82601 Paradise Valley F3
82523 Pavillion 287 .... D2
82082 Pine Bluffs 1,077 .... H4
82941 Pinedale⊙ 1,066 .... C3
82942 Point of Rocks 425 .... D4
82435 Powell 5,310 .... D1
82839 Ranchester 655 .... E1
82301 Rawlins⊙ 11,547 .... E4
82725 Recluse 225 .... G1
82943 Reliance 325 .... C4
†82325 Riverside 55 .... F4
82501 Riverton 9,247 .... D2
82944 Robertson 142 .... B4
82083 Rock River 415 .... G4
82901 Rock Springs 19,458 .... C4
82331 Saratoga 2,410 .... F4
82801 Sheridan⊙ 15,146 .... F1
82615 Shirley Basin 400 .... F3
82649 Shoshoni 879 .... D2
82334 Sinclair 586 .... E4
83126 Smoot 310 .... B3
†82945 South Superior 586 .... D4
82842 Story 637 .... F1
82729 Sundance⊙ 1,087 .... H1
82945 Superior 500 .... D4
82442 Ten Sleep 407 .... E1
83127 Thayne 256 .... A3
82443 Thermopolis⊙ 3,852 .... D2
82240 Torrington⊙ 5,441 .... H3
82730 Upton 1,193 .... H1
82242 Van Tassell 10 .... H3
82335 Walcott 200 .... F4
82336 Wamsutter 681 .... E4
82201 Wheatland⊙ 5,816 .... H3
83014 Wilson 480 .... B2
82401 Worland⊙ 6,391 .... E1
82732 Wright 1,117 .... G2
82190 Yellowstone Nat'l Pk. 350 .. B1
82244 Yoder 110 .... H4

OTHER FEATURES

Absaroka (range) C1
Antelope (creek) G2
Antelope (hills) D3
Aspen (mts.) C4
Atlantic (peak) D3
Badwater (creek) E2
Bear (creek) H4
Bear (riv.) B4
Bear Lodge (mts.) H1
Bear River Divide (mts.) B4
Beaver (creek) D3
Beaver (creek) H2
Belle Fourche (riv.) H1
Big Goose (creek) E1
Bighorn (basin) D1
Bighorn (lake) D1
Bighorn (mts.) E1
Bighorn (riv.) D1
Bighorn Canyon Nat'l Rec. Area D1
Big Sandy (riv.) C3
Bitter (creek) C4
Blacks Fork, Green (riv.) C4
Black Thunder (creek) G2
Bonneville (mt.) C3
Boysen (res.) D2
Buffalo Bill (dam) C1
Buffalo Bill (res.) C1
Buffalo Fork, Snake (riv.) B2
Burwell (mt.) C2
Caballo (creek) G1
Casper (range) F3
Cheyenne (riv.) H2
Chugwater (creek) H4
Clarks Fork (riv.) C1
Clear (creek) F1
Cloud (peak) E1
Cottonwood (creek) B4
Crazy Woman (creek) F1
Crosby (mt.) C2
Crow (creek) H4
Deadman (mt.) B2
Devils Tower Nat'l Mon. H1
Doubletop (peak) B2
Dry (creek) C2
Dry Cottonwood (creek) D1
Eagle (peak) B1
Fivemile (creek) D2
Flaming Gorge (res.) C4
Flaming Gorge Nat'l Rec. Area C4
Fontenelle (creek) B3
Fontenelle (res.) B3
Fort Laramie Nat'l Hist. Site H3
Fortress (mt.) C1
Fossil Butte Nat'l Mon. B4
Francis E. Warren A.F.B. 3,627 .... G4
Fremont (lake) C3
Fremont (peak) C2
Gannett (peak) C2
Gas (hills) E3
Glendo (res.) H3
Gooseberry (creek) D1
Grand Teton (mt.) B2
Grand Teton Nat'l Park B2
Granite (mts.) E3
Great Divide (basin) E3
Green (mt.) E3
Green (riv.) C4
Green, East Fork (riv.) C3
Green River (mt.) C2
Greybull (riv.) D1
Greys (riv.) B3
Gros Ventre (riv.) B2
Guernsey (res.) H3
Hams Fork (riv.) B4
Hazelton (peak) E1
Henrys Fork, Green (riv.) C4
Hoback (peak) B2
Hoback (riv.) B2
Holmes (mt.) B1
Horse (creek) H4
Horseshoe (creek) G3
Hunt (mt.) E1
Index (peak) C1
Inyan Kara (creek) H1
Inyan Kara (mt.) H1
Isabel (mt.) B3
Jackson (lake) B2
Jackson (peak) B2
John D. Rockefeller, Jr., Mem.
Pkwy. B1
Keyhole (res.) H1
Lamar (riv.) B1
Lance (creek) H2
Laramie (mts.) G3
Laramie (peak) G3
Laramie (riv.) G4
Leidy (mt.) B2
Lewis (lake) B1
Lightning (creek) G2
Little Missouri (riv.) H1
Little Muddy (creek) B4
Little Powder (riv.) G1
Little Sandy (creek) C3
Little Thunder (creek) G2
Lodgepole (creek) H2
Lodgepole (creek) H4
Madison (plat.) B1
Medicine Bow (range) F4
Medicine Bow (riv.) F3
Middle Piney (creek) B3
Muddy (creek) D2
Muskrat (creek) E2
Needle (mt.) C1
Niobrara (riv.) J3
North Laramie (riv.) G3
North Platte (riv.) H3
Nowater (creek) E2
Nowood (riv.) E1
Owl, North Fork (creek) D2
Owl Creek (mts.) D2
Palisades (res.) A2
Pass (creek) F4
Pathfinder (res.) F3
Poison (creek) E2
Poison Spider (creek) F3
Popo Agie (riv.) D3
Powder (riv.) F2
Rattlesnake (range) E3
Rawhide (creek) G1
Rawhide (creek) H3
Rocky (mts.) C1
Salt (riv.) B3
Salt River (range) B3
Salt Wells (creek) D4
Seminoe (mts.) E3
Seminoe (res.) F3
Shell (creek) E1
Shirley (basin) F3
Shoshone (lake) B1
Shoshone (riv.) D1
Sierra Madre (mts.) E4
Slate (creek) C3
Smiths Fork (riv.) B3
Snake (riv.) B2
South Cheyenne (riv.) H2
South Piney (creek) B3
Sweetwater (riv.) D3
Sybille (creek) G4
Teapot Dome (mt.) F2
Teton (range) B2
Tongue (riv.) E1
Washburn (mt.) B1
Wheatland (res.) G4
Willow (creek) F2
Wind (riv.) C2
Wind River (canyon) D2
Wind River (range) C2
Wind River Ind. Res. C2
Wood (riv.) C2
Wyoming (peak) B3
Wyoming (range) B2
Yellowstone (lake) B1
Yellowstone (riv.) B1
Yellowstone Nat'l Park B1

⊙County seat.
† Zip of nearest p.o. * Multiple zips.

Acquisitions of Territory

The United States in 1783 comprised the thirteen original states and included lands acquired by conquest during the Revolution and by the Treaty of 1783.

Rank by Area

Rank by Population

YEAR OF ADMISSION TO THE UNION

DELAWARE ☆	1787
PENNSYLVANIA ☆	
NEW JERSEY ☆	
GEORGIA ☆	1788
CONNECTICUT ☆	
MASSACHUSETTS ☆	
MARYLAND ☆	
SOUTH CAROLINA ☆	
NEW HAMPSHIRE ☆	
VIRGINIA ☆	
NEW YORK ☆	1789
NORTH CAROLINA ☆	1790
RHODE ISLAND ☆	1791
VERMONT ☆	1792
KENTUCKY ☆	
TENNESSEE ☆	1796
OHIO ☆	1803
LOUISIANA ☆	1812
INDIANA ☆	1816
MISSISSIPPI ☆	1817
ILLINOIS ☆	1818
ALABAMA ☆	1819
MAINE ☆	1820
MISSOURI ☆	1821

☆ HAWAII 1959
☆ ALASKA

☆ ARIZONA 1912
☆ NEW MEXICO

☆ OKLAHOMA 1907

NORTH DAKOTA ☆
SOUTH DAKOTA ☆
MONTANA ☆
UTAH ☆ IDAHO ☆ WASHINGTON ☆
WYOMING ☆ 1889 1890

WEST VIRGINIA
MINNESOTA
KANSAS
NEVADA
OREGON
CALIFORNIA
WISCONSIN
IOWA
FLORIDA
TEXAS
ARKANSAS
MICHIGAN

COLORADO ☆ 1876
NEBRASKA ☆

1896   1867 1864 1861 1858   1848 1845
         1863 1859   1850 1846
                                          1836
                                          1837

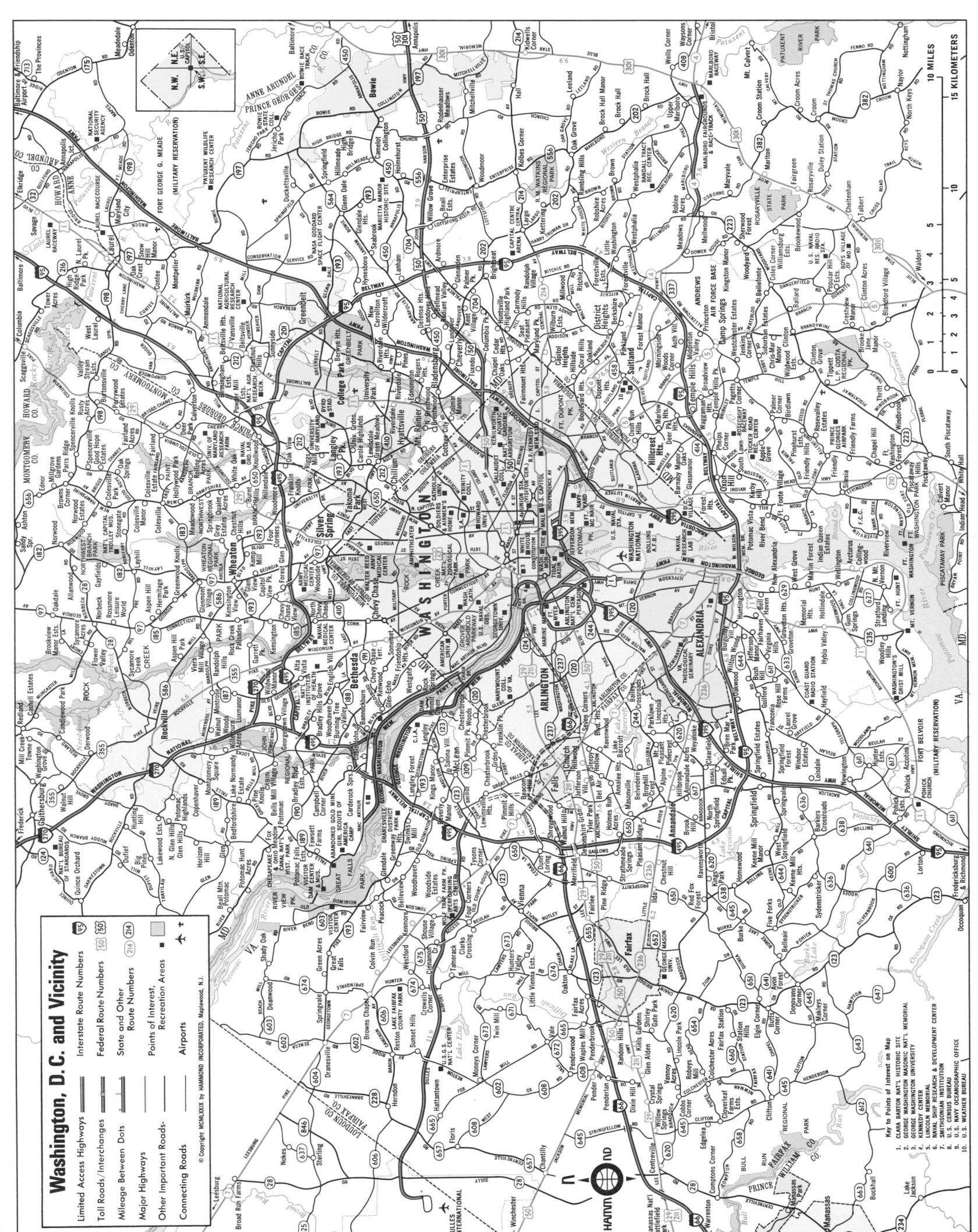

Washington, D.C. and Vicinity

Interstate Route Numbers

Federal Route Numbers

State and Other Route Numbers

Points of Interest, Recreation Areas

Airports

Limited Access Highways

Toll Roads/Interchanges

Mileage Between Dots

Major Highways

Other Important Roads

Connecting Roads

© Copyright MCMLXXIX by HAMMOND INCORPORATED, Maplewood, N.J.

Key to Points of Interest on Map
1. CLARA BARTON NAT'L HISTORIC SITE
2. GEORGE WASHINGTON MASONIC NAT'L MEMORIAL
3. GEORGE WASHINGTON UNIVERSITY
4. KENNEDY CENTER
5. LINCOLN MEMORIAL
6. NAVAL SHIP RESEARCH & DEVELOPMENT CENTER
7. SMITHSONIAN INSTITUTION
8. U.S. CENSUS BUREAU
9. U.S. NAVY OCEANOGRAPHIC OFFICE
10. U.S. WEATHER BUREAU

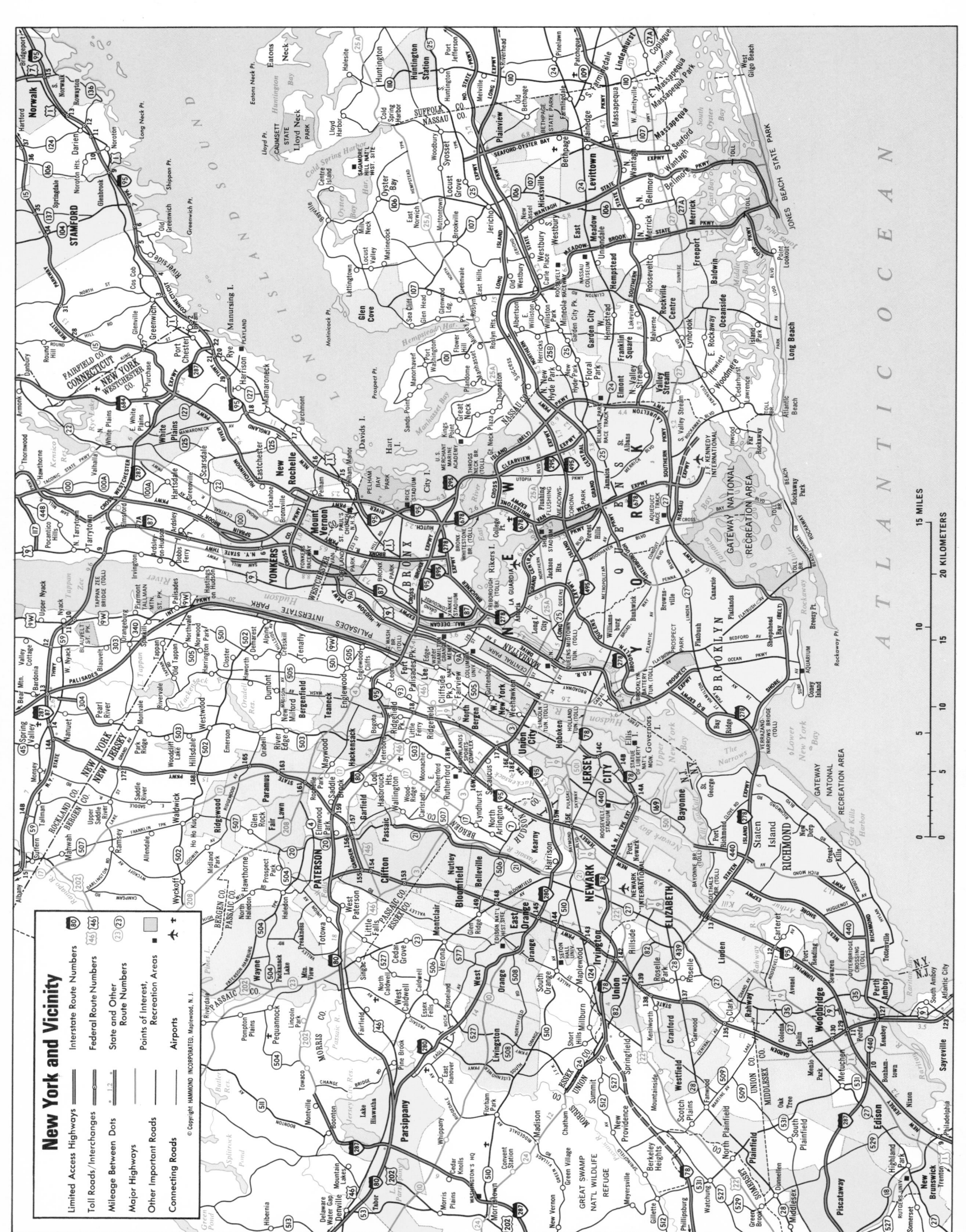

New York and Vicinity

Limited Access Highways

Toll Roads/Interchanges

Mileage Between Dots

Major Highways

Other Important Roads

Connecting Roads

Interstate Route Numbers

Federal Route Numbers

State and Other Route Numbers

Points of Interest, Recreation Areas

Airports

© Copyright HAMMOND INCORPORATED, Maplewood, N.J.

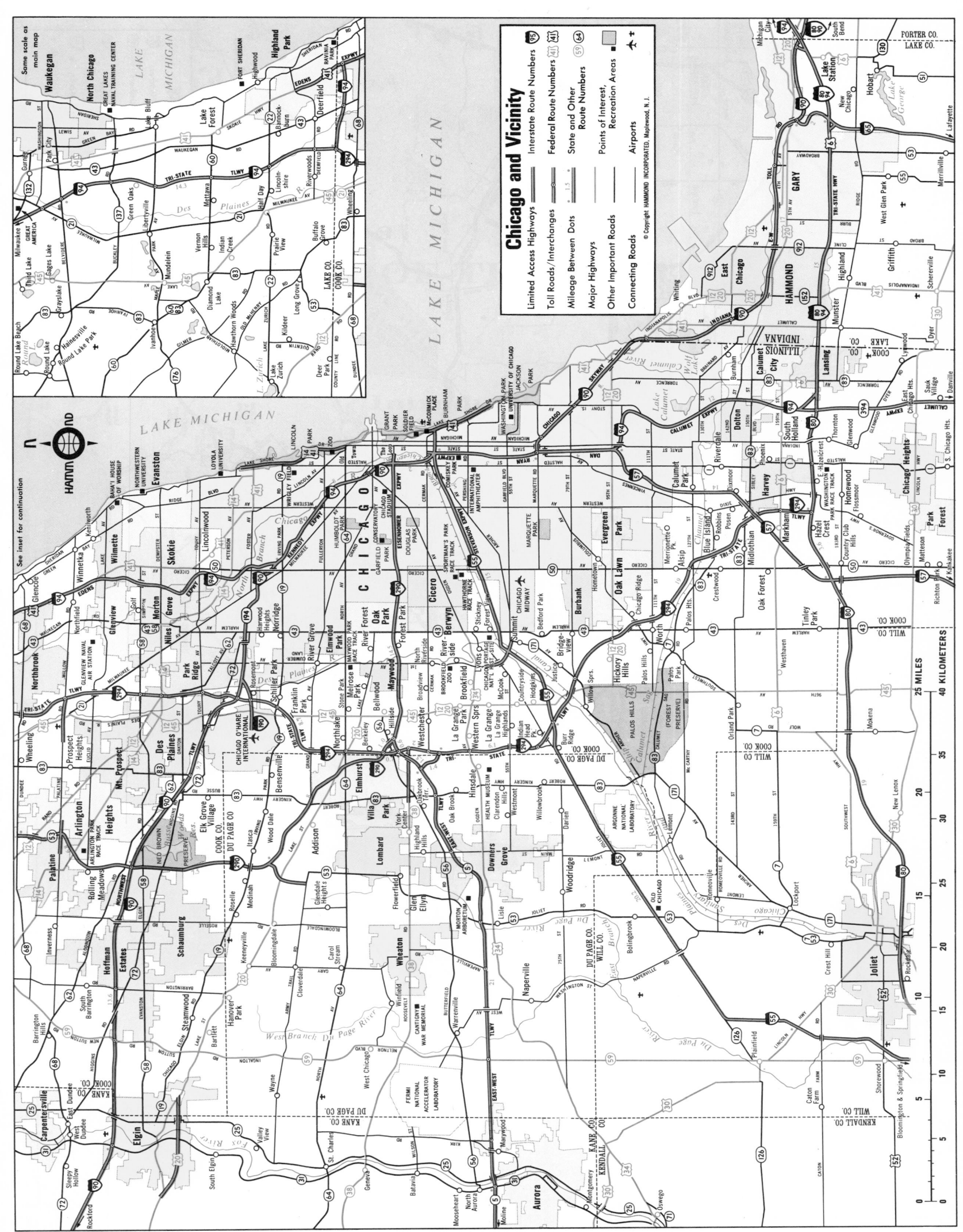

A

Villeurbanne, France, 28
Villingen-Schwenningen, W. Ger., 22
Villupuram, India, 68
Vilna (Vilnius), U.S.S.R., 53
Vilvoorde, Belg., 27
Vilyuy (range), U.S.S.R., 48
Vilyuy (riv.), U.S.S.R., 48
Viña del Mar, Chile, 138
Vinalhaven (isl.), Maine, 243
Vinaroz, Spain, 33
Vincennes (bay), Antarc., 5
Vincennes, France, 28
Vincennes, Ind., 227
Vinces, Ecuador, 128
Vindelälven (riv.), Sweden, 18
Vindhya (range), India, 68
Vineland, N.J., 273
Vineyard (sound), Mass., 249
Vinh, Vietnam, 72
Vinh Long, Vietnam, 72
Vinita, Okla., 288
Vinkovci, Yugo., 45
Vinnitsa, U.S.S.R., 52
Vinton, Iowa, 229
Vinton, La., 238
Vinton, Va., 307
Viqueque, Indon., 85
Virac, Phil., 82
Viramgam, India, 68
Virden, Ill., 222
Virden, Manitoba, 179
Virgin (riv.), U.S., 266, 304
Virgin Gorda (isl.), Virgin Is. (Br.), 156, 161
Virginia, Minn., 255
Virginia (state), U.S., 307
Virginia Beach, Va., 307
Virginia City, Mont., 262
Virginia City, Nev., 266
Virgin Islands (Br.), 156, 161
Virgin Islands (U.S.), 156, 161
Virgin Islands Nat'l Park, Virgin Is. (U.S.), 161
Virochey, Cambodia, 72
Viroqua, Wis., 317
Virovitica, Yugo., 45
Virunga (range), Africa, 115
Virunga, Zaire, 115
Vis (isl.), Yugo., 45
Visakhapatnam, India, 68
Visalia, Calif., 204
Visayan (sea), Phil., 82
Visby, Sweden, 18
Visconde do Rio Branco, Brazil, 135
Viscount Melville (sound), N.W. Terr., 187
Viseu, Portugal, 33
Vişeul de Sus, Romania, 45
Vishoek, S. Africa, 118
Visnagar, India, 68
Visp, Switz., 39
Vista, Calif., 204
Vistula (riv.), Poland, 47
Vitebsk, U.S.S.R., 52
Viterbo (prov.), Italy, 34
Viterbo, Italy, 34
Viti Levu (isl.), Fiji, 87
Vitim (riv.), U.S.S.R., 48
Vitória, Brazil, 132
Vitoria, Spain, 33
Vitória da Conquista, Brazil, 132
Vitória de Santo Antão, Brazil, 132
Vitry, France, 28
Vittoria, Italy, 34
Vittorio Veneto, Italy, 34
Vivian, La., 238
Vizagapatam (Visakhapatnam), India, 68
Vizcaya (prov.), Spain, 33
Vizianagaram, India, 68
Vlaardingen, Neth., 27
Vladimir, U.S.S.R., 52
Vladivostok, U.S.S.R., 48
Vlissingen (Flushing), Neth., 27
Vlorë, Alb., 45
Vltava (riv.), Czech., 41
Vöcklabruck, Austria, 41
Vogelkop (Doberai) (pen.), Indon., 85
Vogelsberg (mt.), W. Ger., 22
Voghera, Italy, 34
Vohimarina (Vohémar), Madagascar, 118
Vohimena (cape), Madagascar, 118
Vohipeno, Madagascar, 118
Voi, Kenya, 115
Voiron, France, 28
Vojens, Den., 21
Vojmsjön (lake), Sweden, 18
Vojvodina (aut. prov.), Yugo., 45
Volcano (isls.), Japan, 81
Volendam-Edam, Neth., 27
Volga (riv.), U.S.S.R., 52
Volga-Don (canal), U.S.S.R., 52
Volgodonsk, U.S.S.R., 52
Volgograd, U.S.S.R., 52
Volkhov, U.S.S.R., 52
Völklingen, W. Ger., 22
Volksrust, S. Africa, 118
Vologda, U.S.S.R., 52
Vólos, Greece, 45
Vol'sk, U.S.S.R., 52
Volta (lake), Ghana, 106
Volta (riv.), Ghana, 106
Volta Redonda, Brazil, 135
Volturno (riv.), Italy, 34
Vólvi (lake), Greece, 45
Volyn Oblast, U.S.S.R., 52
Volzhsk, U.S.S.R., 52
Volzhskiy, U.S.S.R., 52
Voorne (isl.), Neth., 27
Vopnafjördhur (fjord), Iceland, 21
Voralberg (prov.), Austria, 41
Vorderrhein (riv.), Switz., 39
Vordingborg, Den., 21
Vorgod (riv.), Den., 21
Vorkuta, U.S.S.R., 52
Voronezh, U.S.S.R., 52
Voroshilovgrad, U.S.S.R., 52
Vorskla (riv.), U.S.S.R., 52
Võru, U.S.S.R., 53
Vosges (dept.), France, 28
Vosges (mts.), France, 28
Voskresensk, U.S.S.R., 52
Vostok (isl.), Kiribati, 87
Votkinsk, U.S.S.R., 52
Votuporanga, Brazil, 135
Voyageurs Nat'l Park, Minn., 255
Voy-Vozh, U.S.S.R., 52
Voznesensk, U.S.S.R., 52
Vranje, Yugo., 45
Vratsa, Bulg., 45
Vrbas, Yugo., 45
Vrede, S. Africa, 118
Vreed-en-Hoop, Guyana, 131
Vršac, Yugo., 45
Vryburg, S. Africa, 118
Vryheid, S. Africa, 118
Vsetín, Czech., 41
Vught, Neth., 27
Vukovar, Yugo., 45
Vulcan, Alberta, 182
Vulcano (isl.), Italy, 34
Vung Tau, Vietnam, 72
Vyatka (riv.), U.S.S.R., 52
Vyaz'ma, U.S.S.R., 52
Vyborg, U.S.S.R., 52
Vychegda (riv.), U.S.S.R., 52
Východočeský (reg.), Czech., 41
Východoslovenský (reg.), Czech., 41
Vyksa, U.S.S.R., 52
Vym' (riv.), U.S.S.R., 52
Vyshniy Volochek, U.S.S.R., 52
Vysoké Tatry, Czech., 41

W

Wa, Ghana, 106
Waal (riv.), Neth., 27
Wabana, Newf., 166
Wabasca (riv.), Alberta, 182
Wabash, Ind., 227
Wabash (riv.), U.S., 227
Wabasha, Minn., 255
Wąbrzeźno, Poland, 47
Wabush, Newf., 166
Waccamaw (lake), N.C., 281
Waco, Texas, 303
Wadai (reg.), Chad, 111
Waddan, Libya, 111
Waddenzee (sound), Neth., 27
Waddington (mt.), Br. Col., 184
Wade-Hampton, S.C., 296
Wadena, Minn., 255
Wadena, Sask., 181
Wädenswil, Switz., 39
Wadesboro, N.C., 281
Wadi es Sir, Jordan, 65
Wadi Halfa, Sudan, 111
Wadi Musa, Jordan, 65
Wadmalaw (isl.), S.C., 296
Wad Medani, Sudan, 111
Wadsworth, Ohio, 284
Wageningen, Neth., 27
Wager (bay), N.W. Terr., 187
Wagga Wagga, N.S. Wales, 97
Wagin, W. Australia, 92
Wagoner, Okla., 288
Wągrowiec, Poland, 47
Wahiawa, Hawaii, 218
Wahoo, Nebr., 264
Wahpeton, N. Dak., 283
Wai, Poulo (isls.), Vietnam, 72
Waialua, Hawaii, 218
Waianae, Hawaii, 218
Waiau (riv.), N. Zealand, 100
Waidhofen, Austria, 41
Waigeo (isl.), Indon., 85
Waihi, N. Zealand, 100
Waikanae, N. Zealand, 100
Waikato (riv.), N. Zealand, 100
Waikiki (beach), Hawaii, 218
Wailuku, Hawaii, 218
Waimanalo, Hawaii, 218
Waimate, N. Zealand, 100
Waimea (bay), Hawaii, 218
Wainuiomata, N. Zealand, 100
Wainwright, Alberta, 182
Waipawa, N. Zealand, 100
Waipio (pen.), Hawaii, 218
Wairau (riv.), N. Zealand, 100
Wairoa, N. Zealand, 100
Waitaki (riv.), N. Zealand, 100
Waitara, N. Zealand, 100
Wajir, Kenya, 115
Wakasa (bay), Japan, 81
Wakatipu (lake), N. Zealand, 100
Wakaw, Sask., 181
Wakayama (pref.), Japan, 81
Wakayama, Japan, 81
Wake (isl.), Pacific, 87
WaKeeney, Kans., 232
Wakefield, England, 13
Wakefield, Mass., 249
Wakefield, Mich., 250
Wakefield, R.I., 249
Wake Forest, N.C., 281
Wakema, Burma, 72
Wakkanai, Japan, 81
Wałbrzych, Poland, 47
Walcha, N.S. Wales, 97
Walchensee (lake), W. Ger., 22
Walcheren (isl.), Neth., 27
Wałcz, Poland, 47
Wald, Switz., 39
Walden, N.Y., 276
Walden, Ontario, 175
Waldwick, N.J., 273
Walensee (lake), Switz., 39
Wales, U.K., 13
Walgett, N.S. Wales, 97
Walhalla, S.C., 296
Walker, Mich., 250
Walker (lake), Nev., 266
Walkerton, Ontario, 177
Walkerville, Mont., 262
Wall, N.J., 273
Wallace, Idaho, 220
Wallaceburg, Ontario, 177
Wallaga (prov.), Ethiopia, 111
Wallaroo, S. Australia, 94
Wallasey, England, 10
Walla Walla, Wash., 310
Walled Lake, Mich., 250
Wallerawang, N.S. Wales, 97
Wallingford, Conn., 210
Wallington, N.J., 273
Wallis (isls.), Wallis & Futuna, 87
Wallis and Futuna, 87
Wallo (prov.), Ethiopia, 111
Wallowa (mts.), Oreg., 291
Wallsend, England, 13
Wallula (lake), U.S., 291, 310
Walney, Isle of (isl.), England, 13
Walnut Canyon Nat'l Mon., Ariz., 198
Walnut Creek, Calif., 204
Walnut Ridge, Ark., 203
Walsall, England, 10
Walsenburg, Colo., 208
Walsrode, W. Ger., 22
Walterboro, S.C., 296
Walters, Okla., 288
Waltershausen, E. Ger., 22
Waltham, Mass., 249
Waltham Forest, England, 10
Waltham Holy Cross, England, 10
Walton, N.Y., 276
Walton and Weybridge, England, 10
Walvis Bay, S. Africa, 118
Wamba, Zaire, 115
Wanaka (lake), N. Zealand, 100
Wanamassa, N.J., 273
Wanaque, N.J., 273
Wanaque (res.), N.J., 273
Wandel (sea), Greenl., 4
Wandsworth, England, 10
Wanganui, N. Zealand, 100
Wangaratta, Victoria, 97
Wangen im Allgäu, W. Ger., 22
Wangiwangi (isl.), Indon., 85
Wankie, Zimbabwe, 118
Wanks (Coco) (riv.), Cent. Amer., 154
Wanne-Eickel, W. Ger., 22
Wanneroo, W. Australia, 92
Wantagh, N.Y., 276
Wanxian (Wanhsien), China, 77
Wapakoneta, Ohio, 284
Wapato, Wash., 310
Wapawekka (hills), Sask., 181
Wappingers Falls, N.Y., 276
War, W. Va., 313
Waramaug (lake), Conn., 210
Waranga (res.), Victoria, 97
Warangal, India, 68
Waratah (bay), Victoria, 97
Warburton, The (riv.), S. Australia, 94
Warburton, Victoria, 97
Wardere, Ethiopia, 111
Wardha, India, 68
Ware, England, 13
Ware, Mass., 249
Wareham, Mass., 249
Waren, E. Ger., 22
Warendorf, W. Ger., 22
Ware Shoals, S.C., 296
Warfield, Br. Col., 184
Warialda, N.S. Wales, 97
Warin Chamrap, Thai., 72
Warley, England, 10
Warmbad, Namibia, 118
Warmbad, S. Africa, 118
Warner Robins, Ga., 217
Warnes, Bolivia, 136
Warooná, W. Australia, 92
Warracknabeal, Victoria, 97
Warr Acres, Okla., 288
Warragamba, N.S. Wales, 97
Warragul, Victoria, 97
Warrego (riv.), Australia, 95, 97
Warren, Ark., 203
Warren, Mich., 250
Warren, N.S. Wales, 97
Warren, Ohio, 284
Warren, Pa., 294
Warren, R.I., 249
Warrenpoint, N. Ireland, 17
Warrensburg, Mo., 261
Warrensville Hts., Ohio, 284
Warrenton, S. Africa, 118
Warrenton, Va., 307
Warri, Nigeria, 106
Warrington, England, 10
Warrington, Fla., 212
Warrnambool, Victoria, 97
Warroad, Minn., 255
Warsaw, Ind., 227
Warsaw, N.Y., 276
Warsaw (prov.), Poland, 47
Warsaw (cap.), Poland, 47
Warta (riv.), Poland, 47
Warwick, England, 13
Warwick, N.Y., 276
Warwick, Queensland, 95
Warwick, R.I., 249
Warwickshire (co.), England, 13
Wasatch (range), U.S., 220, 304
Wasco, Calif., 204
Waseca, Minn., 255
Wash, The (bay), England, 13
Washburn (mt.), Wyo., 319
Washington, Ga., 217
Washington (isl.), Kiribati, 87
Washington, Ill., 222
Washington, Ind., 227
Washington, Iowa, 229
Washington, Mo., 261
Washington (mt.), N.H., 268
Washington, N.J., 273
Washington, N.C., 281
Washington, Pa., 294
Washington (state), U.S., 310
Washington, D.C. (cap.), U.S., 245
Washington (lake), Wash., 310
Washington (isl.), Wis., 317
Washington C.H., Ohio, 284
Washington Park, Ill., 222
Washington Terrace, Utah, 304
Washita (riv.), Texas, 303
Washoe (lake), Nev., 266
Washougal, Wash., 310
Wasit (gov.), Iraq, 66
Waspán, Nicaragua, 154
Wasserbillig, Lux., 27
Wassuk (range), Nev., 266
Watauga (lake), Tenn., 237
Watch Hill (pt.), R.I., 249
Watchung, N.J., 273
Waterbury, Conn., 210
Waterbury, Vt., 268
Wateree (riv.), S.C., 296
Waterford, Conn., 210
Waterford (co.), Ireland, 17
Waterford, Ireland, 17
Waterford, N.Y., 276
Waterhen (lake), Manitoba, 179
Waterloo, Belg., 27
Waterloo, Ill., 222
Waterloo, Iowa, 229
Waterloo, N.Y., 276
Waterloo, Ontario, 177
Waterloo, Québec, 172
Watermael-Boitsfort, Belg., 27
Waterton-Glacier Int'l Peace Park, N. Amer., 182, 262
Waterton Lakes Nat'l Park, Alberta, 182
Watertown, Conn., 210
Watertown, Mass., 249
Watertown, N.Y., 276
Watertown, S. Dak., 298
Watertown, Wis., 317
Water Valley, Miss., 256
Waterville, Maine, 243
Watervliet, N.Y., 276
Waterways, Alberta, 182
Watford, England, 10
Watford City, N. Dak., 283
Watkins Glen, N.Y., 276
Watling (San Salvador) (isl.), Bahamas, 156
Watonga, Okla., 288
Watrous, Sask., 181
Watsa, Zaire, 115
Watseka, Ill., 222
Watson, Sask., 181
Watson Lake, Yukon, 187
Watsonville, Calif., 204
Watts Bar (lake), Tenn., 237
Wattwil, Switz., 39
Watzmann (mt.), W. Ger., 22
Wau, Papua N.G., 85
Wau, Sudan, 111
Wauchope, N.S. Wales, 97
Wauchula, Fla., 212
Wauconda, Ill., 222
Waukegan, Ill., 222
Waukesha, Wis., 317
Waukon, Iowa, 229
Waupaca, Wis., 317
Waupun, Wis., 317
Wausau, Wis., 317
Wauseon, Ohio, 284
Wauwatosa, Wis., 317
Waverley, N.S. Wales, 97
Waverley, Victoria, 97
Waverly, Iowa, 229
Waverly, N.Y., 276
Waverly, Ohio, 284
Waverly, Tenn., 237
Wawa, Ontario, 175
Waxahachie, Texas, 303
Waycross, Ga., 217
Wayne, Mich., 250
Wayne, Nebr., 264
Wayne, N.J., 273
Wayne, Pa., 294
Waynesboro, Ga., 217
Waynesboro, Miss., 256
Waynesboro, Pa., 294
Waynesboro, Va., 307
Waynesville, N.C., 281
Wayzata, Minn., 255
We (isl.), Indon., 85
Wear (riv.), England, 13
Weatherford, Okla., 288
Weatherford, Texas, 303
Weatherly, Pa., 294
Webb City, Mo., 261
Webster, Mass., 249
Webster, N.Y., 276
Webster, S. Dak., 298
Webster Groves, Mo., 261
Weddell (sea), Antarc., 5
Wedel, W. Ger., 22
Weed, Calif., 204
Weehawken, N.J., 273
Weert, Neth., 27
Weesp, Neth., 27
Wee Waa, N.S. Wales, 97
Weida, E. Ger., 22
Weiden in der Oberpfalz, W. Ger., 22
Weifang, China, 77
Weihai, China, 77
Wei He (riv.), China, 77
Weilheim im Oberbayern, W. Ger., 22
Weimar, E. Ger., 22
Weinfelden, Switz., 39
Weingarten, W. Ger., 22
Weinheim, W. Ger., 22
Weipa, Queensland, 95
Weirton, W. Va., 313
Weiser, Idaho, 220
Weissenburg im Bayern, W. Ger., 22
Weissenfels, E. Ger., 22
Weissensee, E. Ger., 22
Weissenstein (mts.), Switz., 39
Weisshorn (mt.), Switz., 39
Weisswasser, E. Ger., 22
Weiz, Austria, 41
Wejh, Saudi Arabia, 59
Wejherowo, Poland, 47
Welch, W. Va., 313
Welkom, S. Africa, 118
Welland, Ontario, 177
Welland (canal), Ontario, 177
Wellesley, Mass., 249
Wellesley (isls.), Queensland, 95
Wellingborough, England, 13
Wellington (isl), Chile, 138
Wellington, England, 13
Wellington, Kans., 232
Wellington, N.S. Wales, 97
Wellington (cap.), N. Zealand, 100
Wellington, Ohio, 284
Wellington, S. Africa, 118
Wellington, Texas, 303
Wells, Minn., 255
Wells, Nev., 266
Wells (lake), W. Australia, 92
Wellsboro, Pa., 294
Wellsburg, W. Va., 313
Wellsford, N. Zealand, 100
Wellston, Mo., 261
Wellston, Ohio, 284
Wellsville, N.Y., 276
Wellsville, Ohio, 284
Wels, Austria, 41
Welsh, La., 238
Welshpool, Wales, 13
Welwyn, England, 13
Wemmel, Belg., 27
Wenatchee, Wash., 310
Wenatchee (riv.), Wash., 310
Wenchi, Ghana, 106
Wentworth, N.S. Wales, 97
Wentzville, Mo., 261
Wen Xian, China, 77
Wenzhou (Wenchow), China, 77
Werdau, E. Ger., 22
Wernigerode, E. Ger., 22
Werra (riv.), Ger., 22
Werris Creek, N.S. Wales, 97
Wertheim, W. Ger., 22
Wervik, Belg., 27
Wesel, W. Ger., 22
Weser (riv.), W. Ger., 22
Weslaco, Texas, 303
Wesley, Dominica, 161
Wesleyville, Newf., 166
Wesleyville, Pa., 294
Wessel (cape), N. Terr., 93
Wessel (isls.), N. Terr., 93
Wessington Springs, S. Dak., 298
West (cape), N. Zealand, 100
West Allis, Wis., 317
West Azerbaijan (prov.), Iran, 66
West Bank, 65
West Bend, Wis., 317
West Bengal (state), India, 68
Westborough, Mass., 249
West Bridgewater, Mass., 249
West Bromwich, England, 10
Westbrook, Maine, 243
West Burlington, Iowa, 229
Westbury, N.Y., 276
Westbury, Tasmania, 99
West Caldwell, N.J., 273
West Carrollton, Ohio, 284
Westchester, Ill., 222
West Chester, Pa., 294
West Chicago, Ill., 222
West Columbia, S.C., 296
West Columbia, Texas, 303
West Covina, Calif., 204
West Demerara-Essequibo Coast (dist.), Guyana, 131
West Des Moines, Iowa, 229
West Elmira, N.Y., 276
West End, Virgin Is. (Br.), 161
Westerly, R.I., 249
Western (prov.), Kenya, 115
Western Australia (state), Australia, 92
Western Dvina (riv.), U.S.S.R., 52
Western Ghats (mts.), India, 68
Westernport, Md., 245
Western Port (inlet), Victoria, 97
Western Sahara, 106
Western Samar (prov.), Phil., 82
Western Samoa, 87
Western Sprs., Ill., 222
Westerstede, W. Ger., 22
Westerville, Ohio, 284
Westerwald (for.), W. Ger., 22
West Fargo, N. Dak., 283
Westfield, Mass., 249
Westfield, N.J., 273
Westfield, N.Y., 276
West Flanders (prov.), Belg., 27
West Frankfort, Ill., 222
West Frisian (isls.), Neth., 27
West Germany (Federal Republic), 22
West Glamorgan (co.), Wales, 13
West Glens Falls, N.Y., 276
West Hartford, Conn., 210
West Haven, Conn., 210
West Hazleton, Pa., 294
West Helena, Ark., 203
West Hollywood, Calif., 204
West Indies (area), Scotland, 15
West Indies, 156
West Jefferson, Ohio, 284
West Jordan, Utah, 304
West Kilbride, Scotland, 15
West Lafayette, Ind., 227
Westlake, La., 238
Westlake, Ohio, 284
Westland, Mich., 250
West Lebanon, N.H., 268
West Linn, Oreg., 291
Westlock, Alberta, 182
West Los Angeles, Calif., 204
West Lothian (trad. co.), Scotland, 15
West Malaysia (reg.), Malaysia, 72
Westmeath (co.), Ireland, 17
West Memphis, Ark., 203
West Miami, Fla., 212
West Midlands (co.), England, 13
West Mifflin, Pa., 294
West Milton, Ohio, 284
West Milwaukee, Wis., 317
Westminster, Calif., 204
Westminster, Colo., 208
Westminster, England, 10
Westminster, Md., 245
West Monroe, La., 238
Westmont, Ill., 222
Westmont, Pa., 294
Westmount, Québec, 172
West Mystic, Conn., 210
West Newton, Pa., 294
West New York, N.J., 273
West Nicholson, Zimbabwe, 118
Weston, W. Va., 313
Westonaria, S. Africa, 118
Weston-super-Mare, England, 13
West Orange, N.J., 273
West Orange, Texas, 303
Westover, W. Va., 313
Westover A.F.B., Mass., 249
West Palm Beach, Fla., 212
West Paterson, N.J., 273
West Pensacola, Fla., 212
West Pittsburg, Calif., 204
West Plains, Mo., 261
West Point, Ga., 217
West Point, Miss., 256
West Point, Nebr., 264
West Point, N.Y., 276
Westport, Conn., 210
Westport, Ireland, 17
Westport, Mass., 249
Westport, N. Zealand, 100
West Portsmouth, Ohio, 284
West Quoddy (head), Maine, 243
Westray (isl.), Scotland, 15
West Sacramento, Calif., 204
West St. Paul, Minn., 255
West Seneca, N.Y., 276
West Springfield, Mass., 249
West Sussex (co.), England, 13
West Swanzey, N.H., 268
West Terre Haute, Ind., 227
West Torrens, S. Australia, 94
West Trenton, N.J., 273
West Union, Iowa, 229
West University Place, Texas, 303
West Vancouver, Br. Col., 184
West View, Pa., 294
Westville, Ill., 222
Westville, N.J., 273
Westville, Nova Scotia, 169
West Virginia (state), U.S., 313
West Warwick, R.I., 249
Westwego, La., 238
West Wenatchee, Wash., 310
Westwood, Ky., 237
Westwood, N.J., 273
Westwood Lakes, Fla., 212
Westworth, Texas, 303
West Wyalong, N.S. Wales, 97
West York, Pa., 294
West Yorkshire (co.), England, 13
Wetar (isl.), Indon., 85
Wetaskiwin, Alberta, 182
Wete, Tanz., 115
Wethersfield, Conn., 210
Wetteren, Belg., 27
Wetterhorn (mt.), Switz., 39
Wettingen, Switz., 39
Wetumpka, Ala., 195
Wetzikon, Switz., 39
Wetzlar, W. Ger., 22
Wewak, Papua N.G., 85
Wewoka, Okla., 288
Wexford (co.), Ireland, 17
Wexford, Ireland, 17
Weyburn, Sask., 181
Weymouth, Mass., 249
Weymouth and Melcombe Regis, England, 13
Whaleback (mt.), W. Australia, 92
Whaley Bridge, England, 10
Whalsay (isl.), Scotland, 15
Whangarei, N. Zealand, 100
Wharfe (riv.), England, 13
Wharton, N.J., 273
Wharton, Texas, 303
Wheatland, Wyo., 319
Wheatley, Ontario, 177
Wheaton, Ill., 222
Wheaton, Md., 245
Wheaton, Minn., 255
Wheat Ridge, Colo., 208
Wheeler (dam), Ala., 195
Wheeler (peak), Nev., 266
Wheeler (peak), N. Mex., 274
Wheeler A.F.B., Hawaii, 218
Wheelersburg, Ohio, 284
Wheeling, Ill., 222
Wheeling, W. Va., 313
Whidbey (isl.), Wash., 310
Whippany, N.J., 273
Whiskeytown-Shasta-Trinity Nat'l Rec. Area, Calif., 204
Whitburn, Scotland, 15
Whitby, England, 13
Whitby, Ontario, 177
Whitchurch-Stouffville, Ontario, 177
Whitcombe (mt.), N. Zealand, 100
White (riv.), Ind., 227
White (lake), La., 238
White (bay), Newf., 166
White (mts.), N.H., 268
White (isl.), N. Zealand, 100
White (sea), U.S.S.R., 52
White (riv.), U.S., 203, 261
White (riv.), Vt., 268
White Bear (lake), Minn., 255
White Bear (lake), Newf., 166
White Carpathians (mts.), Czech., 41
White Center, Wash., 310
Whitecourt, Alberta, 182
White Elster (riv.), E. Ger., 22
Whitefish (bay), Mich., 250
Whitefish, Mont., 262
White Hall, Ill., 222
Whitehall, Mich., 250
Whitehall, N.Y., 276
Whitehall, Ohio, 284
Whitehall, Pa., 294
Whitehaven, England, 13
White Head (isl.), New Bruns., 170
Whitehead, N. Ireland, 17
Whitehorse (cap.), Yukon, 187
White Nile (riv.), Africa, 111
White Nile (prov.), Sudan, 111
White Oak, Pa., 294
White Plains, N.Y., 276
White River, Ontario, 177
White River Jct., Vt., 268
White Rock, Br. Col., 184
White Russian S.S.R., U.S.S.R., 52
White Sands Missile Range, N. Mex., 274
White Sands Nat'l Mon., N. Mex., 274
Whitesboro, N.Y., 276
White Settlement, Texas, 303
White Sulphur Springs, Mont., 262
White Sulphur Springs, W. Va., 313
Whiteville, N.C., 281
White Volta (riv.), Africa, 106
Whitewater (lake), Manitoba, 179
Whitewater, Wis., 317
Whiting, Ind., 227
Whitinsville, Mass., 249
Whitley Bay, England, 13
Whitman, Mass., 249
Whitman Mission Nat'l Hist. Site, Wash., 310
Whitmire, S.C., 296
Whitney (mt.), Calif., 204
Whitney, S.C., 296
Whitneyville, Conn., 210
Whitsunday (isl.), Queensland, 95
Whittier, Alaska, 196
Whittier, Calif., 204
Wholdaia (lake), N.W. Terr., 187
Whyalla, S. Australia, 94
Wiarton, Ontario, 177
Wiawso, Ghana, 106
Wichita, Kans., 232
Wichita (mts.), Okla., 288
Wichita Falls, Texas, 303
Wick, Scotland, 15
Wickenburg, Ariz., 198
Wickham (cape), Tasmania, 99
Wickiup (res.), Oreg., 291
Wickliffe, Ohio, 284
Wicklow (co.), Ireland, 17
Wicklow, Ireland, 17
Wicklow (mts.), Ireland, 17
Wicomico (riv.), Md., 245
Widnes, England, 10
Wieliczka, Poland, 47
Wieluń, Poland, 47
Wien (Vienna) (cap.), Austria, 41
Wiener Neustadt, Austria, 41
Wieringermeer (polder), Neth., 27
Wiesbaden, W. Ger., 22
Wigan, England, 10
Wight, Isle of (isl.), England, 13
Wigston, England, 13
Wigtown (trad. co.), Scotland, 15
Wigtown (bay), Scotland, 15
Wil, Switz., 39
Wildhorn (mt.), Switz., 39
Wildspitze (mt.), Austria, 41
Wildwood, N.J., 273
Wildwood Crest, N.J., 273
Wilhelm II Coast (reg.), Antarc., 5
Wilhelmina (canal), Neth., 27
Wilhelmina (mts.), Suriname, 131
Wilhelm-Pieck-Stadt, E. Ger., 22
Wilhelmshaven, W. Ger., 22
Wilkes-Barre, Pa., 294
Wilkes Land (reg.), Antarc., 5
Wilkie, Sask., 181
Wilkinsburg, Pa., 294
Willamette (riv.), Oreg., 291
Willard, Ohio, 284
Willcox, Ariz., 198
Willebroek, Belg., 27
Willems (canal), Neth., 27
Willemstad (cap.), Neth. Antilles, 161
William (riv.), Sask., 181
William H. Taft Nat'l Hist. Site, Ohio, 284
Williams, Ariz., 198
Williamsburg, Ky., 237
Williamsburg, Va., 307
Williams Lake, Br. Col., 184
Williamson, W. Va., 313
Williamsport, Pa., 294
Williamston, N.C., 281
Williamston, S.C., 296
Williamstown, Mass., 249
Williamstown, N.J., 273
Williamstown, Victoria, 97
Williamstown, W. Va., 313
Williamsville, N.Y., 276
Willikies, Ant. & Bar., 161
Willimantic, Conn., 210
Willingboro, N.J., 273
Williston (lake), Br. Col., 184
Williston, N. Dak., 283
Williston, S.C., 296
Williston Park, N.Y., 276
Willits, Calif., 204
Willmar, Minn., 255
Willmore Wilderness Prov. Park, Alberta, 182
Willoughby, N.S. Wales, 97
Willoughby, Ohio, 284
Willoughby (lake), Vt., 268
Willoughby Hills, Ohio, 284
Willow, Alaska, 196
Willow Bunch, Sask., 181
Willow Grove, Pa., 294
Willowick, Ohio, 284
Willows, Calif., 204
Wilmerding, Pa., 294
Wilmette, Ill., 222
Wilmington, Calif., 204
Wilmington, Del., 245
Wilmington, Ill., 222
Wilmington, N.C., 281
Wilmington, Ohio, 284
Wilmore, Ky., 237
Wilmslow, England, 10
Wilson (mt.), Calif., 204
Wilson, N.C., 281
Wilson, Pa., 294
Wilsons (prom.), Victoria, 97
Wilson's Creek Nat'l Battlefield, Mo., 261
Wilton, Conn., 210
Wilton Manors, Fla., 212
Wiltshire (co.), England, 13
Wiltz, Lux., 27
Wimmera (riv.), Victoria, 97
Winchelsea, Victoria, 97
Winchendon, Mass., 249
Winchester, England, 13
Winchester, Ind., 227
Winchester, Ky. 237
Winchester, Mass., 249
Winchester, Nev., 266
Winchester, Tenn., 237
Winchester, Va., 307
Windber, Pa., 294
Wind Cave Nat'l Park, S. Dak., 298
Winder, Ga., 217
Windermere, England, 13
Windham, Conn., 210
Windham, Ohio, 284
Windhoek (cap.), Namibia, 118
Windisch, Switz., 39
Windom, Minn., 255
Window Rock, Ariz., 198
Wind River (range), Wyo., 319
Windsor, Conn., 210
Windsor, New, England, 13
Windsor, Mo., 261
Windsor, Newf., 166
Windsor, Nova Scotia, 169
Windsor, Ontario, 177
Windsor, Québec, 172
Windsor, Queensland, 95
Windsor, Vt., 268
Windsor Hts., Iowa, 229
Windward (isls.), W. Indies, 156
Windward (passage), W. Indies, 156
Winefred (lake), Alberta, 182
Winfield, Ala., 195
Winfield, Kans., 232
Winfield, N.J., 273
Wingham, N.S. Wales, 97
Wingham, Ontario, 177
Winisk (riv.), Ontario, 177
Winkelman, Ariz., 198
Winkler, Manitoba, 179
Winneba, Ghana, 106
Winnebago (lake), Wis., 317
Winnemucca, Nev., 266
Winnemucca (lake), Nev., 266
Winner, S. Dak., 298
Winnetka, Ill., 222
Winnfield, La., 238
Winnibigoshish (lake), Minn., 255
Winnipeg (cap.), Manitoba, 179
Winnipeg (lake), Manitoba, 179
Winnipegosis, Manitoba, 179
Winnipesaukee (lake), N.H., 268
Winnsboro, La., 238
Winnsboro, S.C., 296
Winnsboro, Texas, 303
Winona, Minn., 255
Winona, Miss., 256
Winooski, Vt., 268
Winooski (riv.), Vt., 268
Winschoten, Neth., 27
Winsford, England, 10
Winslow, Ariz., 198
Winslow, Maine, 243
Winsted, Conn., 210
Winston-Salem, N.C., 281
Winter Haven, Fla., 212
Winter Park, Fla., 212
Winters, Texas, 303
Winterset, Iowa, 229
Wintersville, Ohio, 284
Winterswijk, Neth., 27
Winterthur, Switz., 39
Winthrop, Mass., 249
Winthrop Harbor, Ill., 222
Winton, N. Zealand, 100
Winyah (bay), S.C., 296
Wirral, England, 10
Wisbech, England, 13
Wisconsin (state), U.S., 317
Wisconsin (riv.), Wis., 317
Wisconsin Dells, Wis., 317
Wisconsin Rapids, Wis., 317
Wise, Va., 307
Wisła (Vistula) (riv.), Poland, 47
Wismar, E. Ger., 22
Witbank, S. Africa, 118
Witham (riv.), England, 13
Withamsville, Ohio, 284
Withlacoochee (riv.), Fla., 212
Witten, W. Ger., 22
Wittenberg, E. Ger., 22
Wittenberge, E. Ger., 22
Wittenoom, W. Australia, 92
Witu, Kenya, 115
Witvlei, Namibia, 118
Witwatersrand (reg.), S. Africa, 118
Włocławek, Poland, 47
Woburn, Mass., 249
Wodonga, Victoria, 97
Woerden, Neth., 27
Wohlen, Switz., 39
Woking, England, 10
Wokingham, England, 13
Woleai (atoll), Micronesia, 87
Wolf (riv.), Tenn., 237
Wolfenbüttel, W. Ger., 22
Wolf Lake, Mich., 250
Wolf Point, Mont., 262
Wolfsberg, Austria, 41
Wolfsburg, W. Ger., 22
Wolfville, Nova Scotia, 169
Wolgast, E. Ger., 22
Wolin (isl.), Poland, 47
Wollaston (isl.), Chile, 138
Wollaston (lake), Sask., 181
Wollongong, N.S. Wales, 97
Wolmaransstad, S. Africa, 118
Wołomin, Poland, 47
Wolseley, Sask., 181
Wolstenholme (cape), Québec, 174
Woluwe-Saint-Lambert, Belg., 27
Woluwe-Saint-Pierre, Belg., 27
Wolverhampton, England, 10
Wombwell, England, 13
Wŏnju, S. Korea, 81
Wonogiri, Indon., 85
Wonosobo, Indon., 85
Wŏnsan, N. Korea, 81
Wonthaggi, Victoria, 97
Woodall (mt.), Miss., 256
Woodbine, N.J., 273
Woodbridge, N.J., 273
Wood Buffalo Nat'l Park, Canada, 182, 187
Woodburn, Oreg., 291
Woodbury, Conn., 210
Woodbury, N.J., 273
Woodcliff Lake, N.J., 273
Wood Dale, Ill., 222
Woodend, Victoria, 97
Woodlake, Calif., 204
Woodland, Calif., 204
Woodland Hills, Calif., 204
Woodlands, Sing., 72
Woodlark (isl.), Papua N.G., 85
Woodlawn, Ohio, 284
Woodlyn, Pa., 294
Wood-Lynne, N.J., 273
Woodmere, N.Y., 276
Woodmont, Conn., 210
Woodridge, Ill., 222
Wood-Ridge, N.J., 273
Wood River, Ill., 222
Woodroffe (mt.), S. Australia, 94
Woodruff, S.C., 296
Woods (lake), N. Amer., 179, 255
Woods (lake), N. Terr., 93
Woodsfield, Ohio, 284
Woods Hole, Mass., 249
Woodside, Calif., 204
Woodson Terrace, Mo., 261
Woodstock, Ill., 222
Woodstock, New Bruns., 170
Woodstock, N.Y., 276
Woodstock, Ontario, 177
Woodstock, Vt., 268
Woodstown, N.J., 273
Woodville, N. Zealand, 100
Woodville, S. Australia, 94
Woodward, Okla., 288
Woody Point, Newf., 166
Woolgoolga, N.S. Wales, 97
Woollahra, N.S. Wales, 97
Woomera, S. Australia, 94
Woonsocket, R.I., 249
Woonsocket, S. Dak., 298

GEOGRAPHICAL TERMS

A. = Arabic Burm. = Burmese Camb. = Cambodian Ch. = Chinese Czech. = Czechoslovakian Dan. = Danish Du. = Dutch Finn. = Finnish Fr. = French Ger. = German Ice. = Icelandic It. = Italian Jap. = Japanese Mong. = Mongol Nor. = Norwegian Per. = Persian Port. = Portuguese Russ. = Russian Sp. = Spanish Sw. = Swedish Turk. = Turkish

Å	Nor., Sw.	Stream
Aas	Dan., Nor	Hills
Abajo	Sp	Lower
Ada, Adasi	Turk	Island
Altipiano	It	Plateau
Altiplano	Sp	Plateau
Alv, Alf, Elf	Sw	River
Arrecife	Sp	Reef
Asa	Nor., Sw	Hill
Asaga	Turk	Lower
Austral	Sp	Southern
Baai	Du	Bay
Bab	Arabic	Gate or Strait
Bahia	Sp	Bay
Bahr	Arabic	Marsh, Lake, Sea, River
Baia	Port	Bay
Baie	Fr	Bay, Gulf
Baizo	Port	Low
Bakke	Dan	Hill
Bana	Jap	Cape
Bañados	Sp	Marshes
Band	Per	Mt. Range
Bandao	Ch	Peninsula
Bandar	Per	Harbor
Barra	Sp	Reef
Bel	Turk	Pass
Belt	Ger	Strait
Ben	Gaelic	Mountain
Bera	Du	Mountain
Berg	Ger., Du	Mountain
Bir	Arabic	Well
Boca	Sp	Gulf, Inlet
Boğhaz	Turk	Strait
Bolshoi, Bolshaya	Russ	Big
Bolson	Sp	Depression
Bong	Korean	Mountain
Boreal	Sp	Northern
Breen	Nor	Glacier
Bro	Dan., Nor., Sw.	Bridge
Bucht	Ger	Bay
Bugt	Dan	Bay
Bukhta	Russ	Bay
Bukit	Malay	Hill, Mountain
Bukt	Nor., Sw	Bay, Gulf
Burnu, Burun	Turk	Cape, Point
By	Dan., Nor., Sw	Town
Cabo	Port., Sp	Cape
Campos	Port	Plains
Canal	Port., Sp	Channel
Cap, Capo	Fr., It	Cape
Cataratas	Sp	Falls
Catena	It	Mt. Range
Catingas	Port.	Open Woodlands
Cayos	Sp	Islands
Central, Centrale	Fr., It	Middle
Cerrito, Cerro	Sp	Hill
Cerros	Sp	Hills, Mountains
Chai	Turk	River
Chott	Arabic	Salt Lake
Ciénaga	Sp	Swamp
Ciudad	Sp	City
Col	Fr	Pass
Cordillera	Sp	Mt. Range, Mts.
Côte	Fr	Coast
Csatoria	Magyar	Canal
Cuchilla	Sp	Mt. Range
Curiche	Sp	Swamp
Dağ, Daği	Turk	Mountain, Peak
Dağlari	Turk	Mt. Range
Dal	Nor., Sw	Valley
Dar	Arabic	Land
Dar'ya	Russ	River
Daryacheh	Per	Marshy Lake
Dasht	Per	Desert, Plain
Deniz, Denizi	Turk	Sea, Lake
Desierto	Sp	Desert
Détroit	Fr	Strait
Djeziret	Arabic, Turk	Island
Do	Korean	Island
Doi	Thai	Mountain
Eiland	Du	Island
Elv	Dan., Nor	River
Embalse	Sp	Reservoir
Emi	Berber	Mountain
Erg	Arabic	Dune, Desert
Eski	Turk	Old
Est, Este	Fr., Port., Sp	East
Estero	Sp	Estuary, Creek
Estrecho, Estreito	Sp., Port	Strait
Etang	Fr	Pond, Lagoon, Lake
Feng	Ch	Mountain
Fiume	It	River
Fjäll	Sw	Mountain
Fjeld, Fjell	Nor	Hills, Mountain
Fjord	Dan., Nor., Sw	Fiord
Fleuve	Fr	River
Fljót	Ice	Stream
Fluss	Ger	River
Fors	Sw	Waterfall
Fos, Foss	Dan., Nor	Waterfall
Gamla	Nor	Old
Gamle	Dan	Old
Gata	Jap	Lake
Gawa	Jap	River
Gebel	Arabic	Mountain
Gebergte	Du	Mt. Range
Gebirge	Ger	Mt. Range
Gobi	Mongol	Desert
Goe	Jap	Pass
Gol	Mongol, Turk	Lake, Stream
Golf	Ger., Du	Gulf
Golfe	Fr	Gulf
Golfo	Sp., It., Port	Gulf
Gölü	Turk	Lake
Gora	Russ	Mountain
Grand, Grande	Fr., Sp	Big
Groot	Du	Big
Gross	Ger	Big
Grosso	It., Port	Big
Guba	Russ	Bay, Gulf
Gunto	Jap	Archipelago
Gunung	Malay	Mountain
Hai	Ch	Sea
Haixia	Ch	Strait
Halbinsel	Ger	Peninsula
Hamáda, Hammada	Arabic.	Rocky Plateau
Hamn	Sw	Harbor
Hamún	Per	Marsh
Hanto	Jap	Peninsula
Has, Hassi	Arabic	Well
Hav	Dan., Nor., Sw	Sea, Ocean
Havet	Nor	Bay
Havn	Dan., Nor	Harbor
Havre	Fr	Harbor
He	Ch	River, Stream
Higashi, Higasi	Jap	East
Hochebene	Ger	Plateau
Hoek	Du	Cape
Hoku	Jap	North
Holm	Dan., Nor., Sw	Island
Hory	Czech	Mountains
Hoved	Dan., Nor	Cape, Promontory
Hu	Ch	Lake
Huang	Ch	Yellow
Huk	Dan., Nor., Sw	Point
Hus, Huus	Dan., Nor., Sw	House
Idehan	Arabic	Desert
Ile	Fr	Island
Ilet	Fr	Islet
Ilot	Fr	Islet
Indre	Dan., Nor	Inner
Inferieur, Inferiore	Fr., It	Lower
Inner, Inre	Sw	Inner
Insel	Ger	Island
Irmak	Turk	River
Isla	Sp	Island
Isola	It	Island
Jabal, Jebel	Arabic	Mountains
Järvi	Finn	Lake
Jaure	Sw	Lake
Jiang	Ch	River, Stream
Jima	Jap	Island
Joki	Finn	River
Kaap	Du	Cape
Kabir, Kebir	Arabic	Big
Kai	Jap	Sea
Kaikyo	Jap	Strait
Kami	Turk	Upper
Kanaal	Du	Canal
Kanal	Russ., Ger	Canal, Channel
Kao	Thai	Mountain
Kap, Kapp	Nor., Sw., Ice	Cape
Kaupunki	Finn	Town
Kawa	Jap	River
Khao	Thai	Mountain
Khrebet	Russ	Mt. Range
Kita	Jap	North
Klein	Du., Ger	Small
Klint	Dan	Promontory
Kô	Jap	Lake
Ko	Thai	Island
Koh	Camb., Khmer	Island
Kop	Du	Peak, Head
Köping	Sw	Market, Borough
Körfez, Körfezi	Turk	Gulf
Kosa	Russ	Spit
Kosui	Jap	Lake
Kraal	Du	Native Village
Kuchuk	Turk	Small
Kuh, Kuhha	Per	Mt. Range, Mts.
Kul	Sinkiang Turki	Lake
Kum	Turk	Desert
Kuro	Jap	Black
Laag	Du	Low
Lac	Fr	Lake
Lago	Port., Sp., It	Lake
Lagoa	Port	Lagoon
Laguna	Sp	Lagoon
Lagune	Fr	Lagoon
Lahti	Finn	Bay, Bight
Län	Sw	County
Liedao	Ch	Islands, Archipelago
Lilla	Sw	Small
Lille	Dan., Nor	Small
Ling	Ch	Mountain
Llanos	Sp	Plains
Mae Nam	Thai	River
Mali, Malaya	Russ	Small
Man	Korean	Bay
Mar	Sp., Port	Sea
Mare	It	Sea
Medio	Sp	Middle
Meer	Du	Lake
Meer	Ger	Sea
Mer	Fr	Sea
Meridionale	It	Southern
Meseta	Sp	Plateau
Middelst, Midden	Du	Middle
Minami	Jap	Southern
Mis	Russ	Cape
Misaki	Jap	Cape
Mittel	Ger	Middle
Mont	Fr	Mountain
Montagne	Fr	Mountain
Montaña	Sp	Mountains
Monte	Sp., It., Port.	Mountain
More	Russ	Sea
Mörön	Mong	Stream
Morro	Port., Sp	Mountain, Promontory
Morue	Fr	Hill
Moyen	Fr	Middle
Muang	Siamese	Town
Mui	Vietnamese	Cape, Point
Mys	Russ	Cape
Nada	Jap	Sea
Naka	Jap	Middle
Nam	Burm., Lao	River
Namakzar	Per	Salt Waste
Nan	Jap	South
Nes	Nor	Cape, Point
Nevado	Sp	Snow-covered Peak
Nieder	Ger	Lower
Nishi, Nisi	Jap	West
Nizhni, Nizhnyaya	Russ	Lower
Njarga	Finn	Peninsula, Promontory
Nong	Thai	Lake
Noord	Du	North
Nord	Fr., Ger	North
Norte	Sp., It., Port	North
Nos	Russ	Cape
Novi, Novaya	Russ	New
Nur, Nuur	Ch., Mong	Lake
Nuruu	Mong	Mountains
Nusa	Malay	Island
Ny, Nya	Nor., Sw	New
O	Jap	Big
ö	Nor., Sw	Island
Ober	Ger	Upper
Occidental, Occidentale	Sp., It	Western
Odde	Dan	Point
Oeste	Port	West
Ooster	Du	Eastern
Opper, Over	Du	Upper
Oriental	Sp., Fr	Eastern
Orientale	It	Eastern
Orta	Turk	Middle
Ost	Ger	East
Ostrov	Russ	Island
Ouest	Fr	West
öy	Nor	Island
Ozero	Russ	Lake
Pampa	Sp	Plain
Pas	Fr	Channel, Strait
Paso	Sp	Pass
Passo	It., Port	Pass
Peña	Sp	Rock, Mountain
Pendi	Ch	Basin
Penisola	It	Peninsula
Pequeño	Sp	Small
Pereval	Russ	Pass
Peski	Russ	Desert
Petit, Petite	Fr	Small
Phu	Lao, Annamese	Mtn.
Pic	Fr	Mountain
Piccolo	It	Small
Pico	Port., Sp	Mountain, Peak
Pik	Russ	Mountain, Peak
Piton	Fr	Mountain, Peak
Planalto	Port	Plateau
Plato	Russ	Plateau
Pointe	Fr	Point
Poluostrov	Russ	Peninsula
Ponta	Port	Point
Presa	Sp	Reservoir
Presqu'île	Fr	Peninsula
Proliv	Russ	Strait
Pulou, Pulo	Malay	Island
Punt	Du	Point
Punta	Sp., It., Port	Point
Qiryat	Hebrew	City, Settlement
Qum	Turk	Desert
Qundao	Ch	Islands
Rada	Sp	Inlet
Rade	Fr	Bay, Inlet
Ras	Arabic	Cape
Reka	Russ	River
Retto	Jap	Archipelago
Ria	Sp	Estuary
Río	Sp	River
Rivier, Rivière	Du., Fr	River
Rud	Per	River
Sai	Jap	West
Saki	Jap	Cape
Salar, Salina	Sp	Salt Deposit
Salto	Sp., Port	Falls
San	Jap., Korean	Hill
Sanmaek	Korean	Mt. Range
Schiereiland	Du	Peninsula
Se	Camb., Khmer	River
See	Ger	Sea, Lake
Selvas	Sp., Port	Woods, Forest
Seno	Sp	Bay, Gulf
Serra	Port	Mts.
Serranía	Sp	Mts.
Seto	Jap	Strait
Settentrionale	It	Northern
Severni, Severnaya	Russ	North
Shamo	Ch	Desert
Shan	Ch., Jap	Hill, Mts.
Shankou	Ch	Pass
Shatt	Arabic	River
Shima	Jap	Island
Shimo	Jap	Lower
Shin	Jap	Land
Shiro	Jap	White
Shoto	Jap	Islands
Si	Ch	West
Sierra	Sp	Mt. Range, Mts.
Sjö	Nor., Sw	Lake, Sea
Sok, Suk, Souk	Arabic	Market
Song	Annamese	River
Sopka	Russ	Volcano
Spitze	Ger	Mt. Peak
Sredni, Srednyaya	Russ	Middle
Stad	Dan., Nor., Sw	City
Stari, Staraya	Russ	Old
Step	Russ	Treeless Plain
Straat	Du	Strait
Strasse	Ger	Strait
Stretto	It	Strait
Ström	Dan., Nor., Sw	Sound
Stung	Camb., Khmer	River
Su	Turk	River
Sud, Süd	Sp., Fr., Ger	South
Suido	Jap	Strait, Channel
Sul	Port	South
Sund	Dan., Nor., Sw.	Sound
Sungei	Malay	River
Supérieur	Fr	Upper
Superior, Superiore	Sp., It	Upper
Sur	Sp	South
Suyu	Turk	River
Ta	Ch	Big
Tafelland	Du	Plateau
Tagh	Turk	Mt. Range
Take	Jap	Peak, Ridge
Takht	Arabic	Lower
Tal	Ger	Valley
Tanjung	Malay	Cape, Point
Tell	Arabic	Hill
Thale	Thai	Sea, Lake
Tind	Nor	Peak
Tö	Jap	East
To	Jap	Island
Toge	Jap	Pass
Trask	Finn	Lake
Tugh	Somali	Dry River
Ujung	Malay	Point
Umi	Jap	Bay
Unter	Ger	Lower
Ura	Jap	Inlet
Uul	Mong	Mountain
Val	Fr	Valley
Vatn	Nor	Lake
Vecchio	It	Old
Veld	Du	Plain, Field
Velho	Port	Old
Verkhni	Russ	Upper
Vesi	Finn	Lake
Viejo	Sp	Old
Vik	Nor., Sw	Bay
Vishni, Vishnyaya	Russ	High
Vodokhranilishche	Russ	Reservoir
Volcán	Sp	Volcano
Vostochni, Vostochnaya	Russ	East, Eastern
Wadi	Arabic	Dry River
Wald	Ger	Forest
Wan	Jap	Bay
Westersch	Du	Western
Wüste	Ger	Desert
Yama	Jap	Mountain
Yug, Yuzhni, Yuzhnaya	Russ	South, Southern
Zaki	Jap	Cape
Zaliv	Russ	Bay, Gulf
Zangbo	Tibetan	River, Stream
Zapadni, Zapadnaya	Russ	Western
Zee	Du	Sea
Zemlya	Russ	Land
Zizhiqu	Ch	Autonomous Region
Zuid	Du	South

Between Principal Cities in the United States

FROM/TO	Albuquerque, N. Mex.	Atlanta, Ga.	Baltimore, Md.	Boise, Idaho	Boston, Mass.	Brownsville, Tex.	Buffalo, N. Y.	Chicago, Ill.	Cincinnati, Ohio	Cleveland, Ohio	Denver, Colo.	Des Moines, Iowa	Detroit, Mich.	El Paso, Tex.	Fargo, N. Dak.
Albuquerque, N. Mex.	....	1273	1670	774	1967	838	1577	1126	1248	1417	332	833	1360	228	968
Atlanta, Ga.	1273	....	575	1830	933	960	695	583	368	550	1208	738	595	1293	1112
Baltimore, Md.	1670	575	....	2055	358	1525	273	603	423	305	1505	913	398	1750	1143
Boise, Idaho	774	1830	2055	....	2266	1610	1872	1453	1663	1754	637	1155	1671	969	975
Boston, Mass.	1967	933	358	2266	....	1881	398	849	737	550	1766	1159	613	2067	1304
Brownsville, Tex.	838	960	1525	1610	1881	....	1575	1234	1184	1402	1047	1102	1398	682	1445
Buffalo, N. Y.	1577	695	273	1872	398	1575	....	454	392	175	1368	762	218	1690	923
Chicago, Ill.	1126	583	603	1453	849	1234	454	....	249	307	918	310	236	1249	571
Cincinnati, Ohio	1248	368	423	1663	737	1184	392	249	....	218	1090	509	234	1333	818
Cleveland, Ohio	1417	550	305	1754	550	1402	175	307	218	....	1223	617	94	1521	838
Denver, Colo.	332	1208	1505	637	1766	1047	1368	918	1090	1223	....	607	1153	554	642
Des Moines, Iowa	833	738	913	1155	1159	1102	762	310	509	617	607	....	545	980	397
Detroit, Mich.	1360	595	398	1671	613	1398	218	236	234	94	1153	545	....	1475	745
El Paso, Tex.	228	1293	1750	969	2067	682	1690	1249	1333	1521	554	980	1475	....	1161
Fargo, N. Dak.	968	1112	1143	975	1304	1445	923	571	818	838	642	397	745	1161	....
Fort Worth, Tex.	561	750	1239	1263	1574	471	1221	820	839	1046	643	640	1018	543	973
Galveston, Tex.	803	688	1245	1538	1598	287	1289	954	897	1116	925	851	1111	723	1218
Hastings, Nebr.	588	901	1154	934	1415	1013	1019	566	742	871	353	256	800	757	440
Hot Springs, Ark.	773	498	964	1384	1302	650	956	585	569	787	749	488	761	802	875
Houghton, Mich.	1252	947	808	1367	922	1543	560	367	589	518	970	458	427	1422	393
Jacksonville, Fla.	1492	286	682	2098	1015	1025	880	861	628	768	1468	1024	832	1481	1400
Kansas City, Mo.	717	675	962	1158	1250	923	862	413	541	700	555	180	643	836	548
Los Angeles, Calif.	663	1935	2313	663	2590	1370	2195	1741	1892	2044	828	1433	1976	702	1426
Louisville, Ky.	1174	317	498	1623	823	1093	483	268	92	309	1035	477	315	1253	818
Memphis, Tenn.	938	335	792	1506	1133	777	802	481	410	627	878	485	621	978	882
Miami, Fla.	1710	610	958	2368	1258	1100	1184	1190	957	1088	1732	1338	1156	1662	1721
Minneapolis, Minn.	980	905	948	1140	1125	1335	733	356	603	632	699	235	542	1156	219
Missoula, Mont.	895	1790	1947	252	2124	1706	1740	1348	1578	1640	670	1074	1552	1115	819
Nashville, Tenn.	1117	218	597	1631	941	952	626	394	239	456	1018	523	468	1169	900
New Orleans, La.	1030	427	1001	1713	1359	536	1087	831	708	922	1079	825	938	986	1221
New York, N. Y.	1810	747	170	2153	188	1695	291	711	568	404	1628	1023	483	1902	1213
Norfolk, Va.	1696	507	167	2137	467	1465	435	696	474	429	1562	983	522	1755	1258
Oklahoma, Okla.	518	753	1173	1138	1490	659	1117	689	755	946	503	469	905	578	786
Omaha, Nebr.	718	815	1026	1044	1280	1061	883	432	620	738	485	122	666	875	390
Philadelphia, Pa.	1748	663	90	2113	268	1614	278	664	501	343	575	972	444	1834	1186
Phoenix, Ariz.	330	1592	2002	733	2295	1023	1904	1451	1578	1745	585	1154	1685	347	1225
Pittsburgh, Pa.	1498	520	194	1863	478	1424	178	411	258	115	1320	718	208	1592	952
Portland, Me.	2015	1022	446	2282	100	1961	438	892	802	603	1803	1197	657	2126	1313
Portland, Oreg.	1107	2172	2367	349	2553	1944	2167	1765	1987	2063	985	1479	1975	1286	1248
Richmond, Va.	1628	470	128	2060	471	1428	375	618	399	353	1488	905	445	1695	1180
St. Louis, Mo.	938	467	731	1389	1036	975	662	259	308	490	793	270	452	1033	658
Salt Lake City, Utah	483	1580	1858	292	2099	1317	1701	1260	1450	1567	372	952	1490	689	865
San Francisco, Calif.	893	2133	2451	516	2696	1675	2298	1855	2037	2163	946	1547	2087	993	1447
Schenectady, N. Y.	1823	840	278	2120	150	1770	249	702	605	408	1618	1012	467	1930	1157
Seattle, Wash.	1178	2180	2341	405	2508	2015	2130	1743	1974	2035	1020	1470	1945	1373	1206
Shreveport, La.	764	548	1064	1433	1410	510	1080	725	688	904	799	624	891	752	1002
Spokane, Wash.	1028	1960	2110	290	2279	1852	1900	1514	1746	1804	827	1243	1715	1238	976
Springfield, Mass.	1889	863	282	2196	79	1805	325	774	659	473	1692	1085	540	1990	1240
Vermillion, S. Dak.	742	917	1083	973	1314	1161	916	479	694	785	468	187	705	920	284
Washington, D. C.	1648	542	33	2045	392	1493	290	594	403	303	1490	895	397	1726	1141

FROM/TO	Fort Worth, Tex.	Galveston, Tex.	Hastings, Nebr.	Hot Springs, Ark.	Houghton, Mich.	Jacksonville, Fla.	Kansas City, Mo.	Los Angeles, Calif.	Louisville, Ky.	Memphis, Tenn.	Miami, Fla.	Minneapolis, Minn.	Missoula, Mont.	Nashville, Tenn.	New Orleans, La.
Albuquerque, N. Mex.	561	803	588	773	1252	1492	717	663	1174	938	1710	980	895	1117	1030
Atlanta, Ga.	750	688	901	498	947	286	675	1935	317	335	610	905	1790	218	427
Baltimore, Md.	1239	1245	1154	964	808	682	962	2313	498	792	958	948	1947	597	1001
Boise, Idaho	1263	1538	934	1384	1367	2098	1158	663	1623	1506	2368	1140	252	1631	1713
Boston, Mass.	1574	1598	1415	1302	922	1015	1250	2590	823	1133	1258	1125	2124	941	1359
Brownsville, Tex.	471	287	1013	650	1543	1025	923	1370	1093	777	1100	1335	1706	952	536
Buffalo, N. Y.	1221	1289	1019	956	560	880	862	2195	483	802	1184	733	1740	626	1087
Chicago, Ill.	820	954	566	585	367	861	413	1741	268	481	1190	356	1348	394	831
Cincinnati, Ohio	839	897	742	569	589	628	541	1892	92	410	957	603	1578	239	708
Cleveland, Ohio	1046	1116	871	787	518	768	700	2044	309	627	1088	632	1640	456	922
Denver, Colo.	643	925	353	749	970	1468	555	828	1035	878	1732	699	670	1018	1079
Des Moines, Iowa	640	851	256	488	458	1024	180	1433	477	485	1338	235	1074	523	825
Detroit, Mich.	1018	1111	800	761	427	832	643	1976	315	621	1156	542	1552	468	938
El Paso, Tex.	543	723	757	802	1422	1481	836	702	1253	978	1662	1156	1115	1169	986
Fargo, N. Dak.	973	1218	440	875	393	1400	548	1426	818	882	1721	219	819	900	1221
Fort Worth, Tex.	....	283	544	273	1093	943	460	1212	751	448	1150	870	1312	643	470
Galveston, Tex.	283	....	808	375	1277	799	677	1423	807	492	941	1087	1595	666	288
Hastings, Nebr.	544	808	....	513	666	1178	226	1177	693	591	1468	399	891	697	870
Hot Springs, Ark.	273	375	513	....	901	728	326	1437	480	176	983	722	1385	370	358
Houghton, Mich.	1093	1277	666	901	....	1216	633	1787	636	830	1545	272	1208	760	1187
Jacksonville, Fla.	943	799	1178	728	1216	....	952	2153	595	591	328	1192	2070	502	511
Kansas City, Mo.	460	677	226	326	633	952	....	1352	480	370	1247	413	1117	472	678
Los Angeles, Calif.	1212	1423	1177	1437	1787	2153	1352	....	1825	1602	2355	1522	910	1777	1675
Louisville, Ky.	751	807	693	480	636	595	480	1825	....	319	923	605	1550	153	623
Memphis, Tenn.	448	492	591	176	830	591	370	1602	319	....	878	700	1483	195	358
Miami, Fla.	1150	941	1468	983	1545	328	1247	2355	923	878	....	1516	2359	821	681
Minneapolis, Minn.	870	1087	399	722	272	1192	413	1522	605	700	1516	....	1010	695	1050
Missoula, Mont.	1312	1595	891	1385	1208	2070	1117	910	1550	1483	2359	1010	....	1582	1733
Nashville, Tenn.	643	666	697	370	760	502	472	1777	153	195	821	695	1582	....	470
New Orleans, La.	470	288	870	358	1187	511	678	1675	623	358	681	1050	1733	470	....
New York, N. Y.	1398	1415	1275	1125	849	838	1097	2446	650	953	1095	1019	2030	758	1173
Norfolk, Va.	1226	1195	1216	955	946	548	1009	2352	528	778	802	1047	2045	586	932
Oklahoma, Okla.	188	456	357	260	926	988	293	1182	675	422	1233	692	1162	602	575
Omaha, Nebr.	590	828	135	490	547	1098	165	1312	579	529	1402	291	978	604	845
Philadelphia, Pa.	1324	1335	1222	1051	827	758	1037	2388	580	878	1023	985	1997	683	1090
Phoenix, Ariz.	858	1065	901	1094	1550	1800	1045	357	1512	1264	1998	1279	932	1445	1318
Pittsburgh, Pa.	1097	1140	967	825	530	703	784	2135	345	660	1014	745	1754	472	923
Portland, Me.	1642	1678	1454	1371	924	1113	1300	2631	892	1205	1357	1145	2133	1015	1445
Portland, Oreg.	1612	1885	1271	1733	1638	2442	1397	825	1953	1852	2716	1435	430	1970	2063
Richmond, Va.	1170	1154	1142	897	870	953	937	2283	457	722	831	968	1967	526	899
St. Louis, Mo.	568	697	455	325	591	755	238	1585	242	242	1067	464	1331	253	599
Salt Lake City, Utah	977	1249	708	1116	1242	1840	922	577	1400	1250	2098	988	435	1390	1433
San Francisco, Calif.	1454	1693	1297	1648	1833	2375	1500	345	1983	1800	2603	1585	762	1958	1923
Schenectady, N. Y.	1445	1487	1267	1175	776	960	1107	2445	695	1010	1229	975	1978	820	1259
Seattle, Wash.	1658	1938	1288	1759	1588	2450	1505	956	1945	1867	2740	1403	395	1973	2098
Shreveport, La.	209	233	615	142	1043	733	326	1420	598	279	950	859	1457	470	280
Spokane, Wash.	1470	1753	1061	1552	1360	2239	1286	939	1720	1652	2528	1173	170	1752	1898
Springfield, Mass.	1495	1524	1340	1224	860	957	1173	2515	745	1055	1210	1056	2060	863	1287
Vermillion, S. Dak.	689	938	167	605	510	1203	280	1291	663	642	1510	238	887	704	960
Washington, D. C.	1210	1214	1139	936	813	647	943	2295	473	763	927	936	1940	567	968

FROM/TO	New York, N. Y.	Norfolk, Va.	Oklahoma, Okla.	Omaha, Nebr.	Philadelphia, Pa.	Phoenix, Ariz.	Pittsburgh, Pa.	Portland, Me.
Albuquerque, N. Mex.	1810	1696	518	718	1748	330	1498	2015
Atlanta, Ga.	747	507	753	815	663	1592	520	1022
Baltimore, Md.	170	167	1173	1026	90	2002	194	446
Boise, Idaho	2153	2137	1138	1044	2113	733	1863	2282
Boston, Mass.	188	467	1490	1280	268	2295	478	100
Brownsville, Tex.	1695	1465	659	1061	1614	1023	1424	1961
Buffalo, N. Y.	291	435	1117	883	278	1904	178	438
Chicago, Ill.	711	696	689	432	664	1451	411	892
Cincinnati, Ohio	568	474	755	620	501	1578	258	802
Cleveland, Ohio	404	429	946	738	343	1745	115	603
Denver, Colo.	1628	1562	503	485	1575	585	1320	1803
Des Moines, Iowa	1023	983	469	122	972	1154	718	1197
Detroit, Mich.	483	522	905	666	444	1685	208	657
El Paso, Tex.	1902	1755	578	875	1834	347	1592	2126
Fargo, N. Dak.	1213	1258	786	390	1186	1225	952	1313
Fort Worth, Tex.	1398	1226	188	590	1324	858	1097	1642
Galveston, Tex.	1415	1195	456	828	1336	1065	1140	1078
Hastings, Nebr.	1275	1216	357	135	1222	901	967	1454
Hot Springs, Ark.	1125	955	260	490	1051	1094	825	1371
Houghton, Mich.	849	946	926	547	827	1550	630	924
Jacksonville, Fla.	838	548	988	1098	758	1800	703	1113
Kansas City, Mo.	1097	1009	293	165	1037	1045	784	1300
Los Angeles, Calif.	2446	2352	1182	1312	2388	357	2135	2631
Louisville, Ky.	650	528	675	579	580	1512	345	892
Memphis, Tenn.	953	778	422	529	878	1264	660	1205
Miami, Fla.	1095	802	1233	1402	1023	1998	1014	1357
Minneapolis, Minn.	1019	1047	692	291	985	1279	745	1145
Missoula, Mont.	2030	2045	1162	978	1997	932	1754	2133
Nashville, Tenn.	758	586	602	604	683	1445	472	1015
New Orleans, La.	1173	932	575	845	1090	1318	923	1445
New York, N. Y.	....	293	1324	1144	83	2142	313	277
Norfolk, Va.	293	....	1186	1095	220	2027	316	565
Oklahoma, Okla.	1324	1186	....	405	1256	843	1013	1550
Omaha, Nebr.	1144	1095	405	....	1094	1032	837	1318
Philadelphia, Pa.	83	220	1256	1094	....	2079	254	360
Phoenix, Ariz.	2142	2027	843	1032	2079	....	1829	2345
Pittsburgh, Pa.	313	316	1013	837	254	1829	....	545
Portland, Me.	277	565	1550	1318	360	2345	545	....
Portland, Oreg.	2455	2458	1488	1373	2419	1007	2174	2563
Richmond, Va.	287	79	1122	1020	205	1960	242	565
St. Louis, Mo.	873	771	456	352	808	1270	561	1094
Salt Lake City, Utah	1972	1925	862	833	1923	504	1670	2127
San Francisco, Calif.	2568	2510	1386	1425	2518	652	2264	2725
Schenectady, N. Y.	142	426	1354	1133	205	2152	350	197
Seattle, Wash.	2419	2440	1523	1372	2388	1112	2145	2513
Shreveport, La.	1230	1037	297	617	1153	1067	939	1484
Spokane, Wash.	2190	2211	1324	1149	2159	1020	1918	2285
Springfield, Mass.	120	411	1412	1205	201	2220	400	159
Vermillion, S. Dak.	1189	1166	502	115	1143	1043	891	1345
Washington, D. C.	204	145	1150	1012	122	1980	188	480

Between Principal Cities of Europe

	Amsterdam	Athens	Baku	Barcelona	Belgrade	Berlin	Brussels	Bucharest	Budapest	Cologne	Copenhagen	Istanbul	Dresden	Dublin	Frankfort
Amsterdam	....	1340	2218	770	875	365	105	1100	710	128	381	1360	385	468	228
Athens	1340	....	1395	1160	500	1112	1292	460	698	1200	1320	350	1022	1765	1113
Baku	2218	1395	....	2427	1487	1867	2240	1220	1562	2127	1980	1070	1837	2490	2055
Barcelona	770	1160	2427	....	998	925	658	1210	924	692	1085	1380	860	919	665
Belgrade	875	500	1487	998	....	618	850	295	205	750	840	502	530	1327	652
Berlin	365	1112	1867	925	618	....	401	798	425	300	225	1068	95	815	268
Brussels	105	1292	2240	658	850	401	....	1110	700	110	475	1345	407	480	198
Bucharest	1100	460	1220	1210	295	798	1110	....	295	982	970	272	725	1560	890
Budapest	710	698	1562	924	205	425	700	295	....	590	629	650	345	1176	504
Cologne	128	1200	2127	692	750	300	110	982	590	....	400	1240	292	585	93
Copenhagen	381	1320	1960	1085	840	225	475	970	629	400	....	1240	315	768	412
Istanbul	1360	350	1070	1380	502	1068	1345	272	650	1240	1240	....	995	1830	1150
Dresden	385	1022	1837	860	530	95	407	725	345	292	315	995	....	852	236
Dublin	468	1765	2490	919	1327	815	480	1560	1176	585	768	1830	852	....	671
Frankfort	228	1113	2055	665	652	268	198	890	504	93	412	1150	236	671	....
Hamburg	232	1250	2020	910	760	165	301	950	572	228	180	1222	238	668	250
Leningrad	1090	1535	1570	1740	1165	815	1175	1080	965	1090	708	1292	885	1440	1075
Lisbon	1140	1770	3050	610	1555	1410	998	1842	1515	1126	1520	2005	1380	1015	1160
London	220	1476	2435	707	1040	575	202	1285	900	308	590	1540	592	300	392
Lyon	458	1100	2238	327	752	601	352	1025	680	370	760	1238	540	720	350
Madrid	912	1463	2742	316	1235	1149	807	1518	1214	875	1272	1690	1100	902	888
Marseilles	627	1025	2238	211	750	730	521	1020	718	528	906	1205	655	875	492
Milan	517	900	2028	450	540	570	435	819	476	390	720	1030	435	880	323
Moscow	1325	1388	1175	1852	1160	995	1392	920	965	1285	970	1180	1200	1728	1240
Munich	415	925	1912	648	475	310	372	725	350	282	520	975	227	855	193
Oslo	568	1610	2118	1330	1112	520	672	1245	920	635	303	1505	620	786	675
Paris	257	1300	2335	518	890	540	170	1152	770	250	634	1390	523	480	295
Riga	820	1310	1590	1440	855	520	900	870	685	805	453	1115	585	1210	780
Rome	808	650	1900	530	440	730	730	700	500	675	948	840	630	1175	698
Sofia	1073	335	1360	1072	231	810	945	194	395	945	1010	315	730	1525	860
Stockholm	695	1495	1862	1410	1005	503	793	1080	820	722	330	1340	598	1010	730
Toulouse	625	1215	2425	156	930	815	515	1210	883	875	962	1400	762	761	560
Warsaw	673	990	1555	1150	510	320	720	580	342	602	415	852	325	1130	550
Vienna	580	795	1700	830	300	322	568	520	128	460	538	790	235	1040	370
Zurich	375	1000	2050	513	590	410	312	855	498	259	595	1090	342	768	193

	Hamburg	Leningrad	Lisbon	London	Lyon	Madrid	Marseilles	Milan	Moscow	Munich	Oslo	Paris	Riga	Rome	Sofia	Stockholm	Toulouse	Warsaw	Vienna	Zurich
Amsterdam	232	1090	1140	220	458	912	627	517	1325	415	568	257	820	808	1073	695	625	673	580	375
Athens	1250	1535	1770	1476	1100	1463	1025	900	1388	925	1610	1300	1310	650	335	1495	1215	990	795	1000
Baku	2020	1570	3050	2435	2238	2742	2238	2028	1175	1912	2118	2335	1590	1900	1360	1862	2425	1555	1700	2050
Barcelona	910	1740	610	707	327	316	211	450	1852	648	1330	518	1440	530	1072	1410	156	1150	830	513
Belgrade	760	1165	1555	1040	752	1235	750	540	1160	475	1112	890	855	440	231	1005	930	510	300	590
Berlin	165	815	1410	575	601	1149	730	570	995	310	520	540	520	730	810	503	815	320	322	410
Brussels	301	1175	998	202	352	807	521	435	1392	372	672	170	900	730	945	793	515	720	568	312
Bucharest	950	1080	1842	1285	1025	1518	1020	819	920	725	1245	1152	870	700	194	1080	1210	580	520	855
Budapest	572	965	1515	900	680	1214	718	476	965	350	920	770	685	500	395	820	883	342	128	498
Cologne	228	1090	1126	308	370	875	528	390	1285	282	635	250	805	675	945	722	875	602	460	259
Copenhagen	180	708	1520	590	760	1272	906	720	970	520	303	634	453	948	1010	330	962	415	538	595
Istanbul	1222	1292	2005	1540	1238	1690	1205	1030	1180	975	1505	1390	1115	840	315	1340	1400	852	790	1090
Dresden	238	885	1380	592	540	1100	655	435	1200	227	620	523	585	630	730	598	762	325	235	342
Dublin	668	1440	1015	300	720	902	875	880	1728	855	786	480	1210	1175	1525	1010	761	1130	1040	768
Frankfort	250	1075	1160	392	350	888	492	323	1240	193	675	295	780	698	860	730	560	550	370	193
Hamburg	....	880	1301	448	580	1098	730	570	1100	378	445	459	600	810	954	502	780	462	460	432
Leningrad	880	....	2235	1300	1420	1980	1540	1315	391	1100	670	1335	300	1440	1218	435	1635	640	975	1225
Lisbon	1301	2235	....	975	850	313	810	1350	430	1208	1690	890	1940	1150	1685	1848	640	1700	1415	1058
London	448	1300	975	....	455	777	620	595	1540	526	720	210	1035	890	1235	885	550	890	762	480
Lyon	580	1420	850	455	....	577	170	210	1560	352	1005	248	1122	462	928	1080	228	850	562	206
Madrid	1098	1980	313	777	557	....	394	728	2120	910	1474	645	1670	840	1385	1598	344	1410	1110	765
Marseilles	730	1540	810	620	170	394	....	238	1642	445	1165	410	1238	372	895	1225	196	950	620	318
Milan	570	1315	1350	595	210	728	238	....	1408	215	1000	400	1010	295	715	1020	400	705	385	137
Moscow	1100	391	430	1540	1560	2120	1642	1408	....	1220	1030	1538	520	1462	1100	770	1770	710	1028	1350
Munich	378	1100	1208	526	352	910	445	215	1220	....	810	425	800	430	672	811	570	500	222	158
Oslo	445	670	1690	720	1005	1474	1165	1000	1030	810	....	830	531	1242	1295	267	1140	653	835	869
Paris	459	1335	890	210	248	645	410	400	1538	425	830	....	1050	690	1080	950	431	845	770	295
Riga	600	300	1940	1035	1122	1670	1238	1010	520	800	531	1050	....	1155	985	276	1335	350	685	930
Rome	810	1440	1150	890	462	840	372	295	1462	430	1242	690	1155	....	545	1220	569	810	470	421
Sofia	954	1218	1685	1235	928	1385	895	715	1100	672	1295	1080	985	545	....	1170	1080	662	500	780
Stockholm	502	435	1848	885	1080	1598	1225	1020	770	811	267	950	276	1220	1170	....	1281	500	770	908
Toulouse	780	1635	640	550	228	344	196	400	1770	570	1140	431	1335	569	1080	1281	....	1062	725	425
Warsaw	462	640	1700	890	850	1410	950	705	710	500	653	845	350	810	662	500	1062	....	345	640
Vienna	460	975	1415	762	562	1110	620	385	1028	222	835	770	685	470	500	770	725	345	....	365
Zurich	432	1225	1058	480	206	765	318	137	1350	158	869	295	930	421	780	908	425	640	365	....

Portland, Oreg.	Richmond, Va.	St. Louis, Mo.	Salt Lake City, Utah	San Francisco, Calif.	Schenectady, N. Y.	Seattle, Wash.	Shreveport, La.	Spokane, Wash.	Springfield, Mass.	Vermillion, S. Dak.	Washington, D.
1107	1628	938	483	893	1823	1178	764	1028	1889	742	1648
2172	470	467	1580	2133	840	2180	548	1960	863	917	542
2367	128	731	1858	2451	278	2341	1064	2110	282	1083	33
349	2060	1389	292	516	2120	405	1433	290	2196	973	2045
2553	471	1036	2099	2696	150	2508	1410	2279	79	1314	392
1944	1428	975	1317	1675	1770	2015	510	1852	1805	1161	1493
2167	375	662	1701	2298	249	2130	1080	1900	325	916	290
1765	618	259	1260	1855	702	1743	725	1514	774	479	594
1987	399	308	1450	2037	605	1974	688	1746	659	694	403
2063	353	490	1567	2163	408	2035	904	1804	478	785	303
985	1488	793	372	946	1618	1020	799	827	1692	468	1490
1479	905	270	952	1547	1012	1470	624	1243	1085	187	895
1975	445	452	1490	2087	467	1945	891	1715	540	705	397
1286	1695	1033	689	993	1930	1373	752	1238	1990	920	1726
1248	1180	658	865	1447	1157	1206	1002	976	1240	284	1141
1612	1170	568	977	1454	1445	1658	209	1470	1495	689	1210
1885	1154	697	1249	1693	1487	1938	233	1753	1524	938	1214
1271	1142	455	708	1297	1267	1288	615	1061	1340	167	1139
1733	897	325	1116	1648	1175	1759	142	1552	1224	605	936
1638	870	591	1242	1833	776	1588	1043	1360	860	510	813
2442	953	755	1840	2375	960	2450	733	2239	957	1203	647
1397	937	238	922	1500	1107	1505	326	1286	1173	280	943
825	2283	1585	577	345	2445	956	1420	939	2515	1291	2295
1953	457	242	1400	1983	695	1945	598	1720	745	663	473
1852	722	242	1250	1800	1010	1867	279	1652	1055	642	763
2716	831	1067	2098	2603	1229	2740	950	2528	1210	1510	927
1435	968	464	988	1585	975	1403	859	1173	1056	238	936
430	1967	1331	435	762	1978	395	1457	170	2060	887	1940
1970	526	253	1390	1958	820	1973	470	1752	863	704	567
2063	899	599	1433	1923	1259	2098	280	1898	1287	960	968
2455	287	873	1972	2568	142	2419	1230	2190	120	1189	204
2458	79	771	1925	2510	426	2440	1037	2211	411	1166	145
1488	1122	456	862	1386	1354	1523	297	1324	1412	502	1150
1373	1020	352	833	1425	1133	1372	617	1149	1205	115	1012
2419	205	808	1923	2518	205	2388	1153	2159	201	1143	122
1007	1960	1270	504	652	2152	1112	1067	1020	2220	1043	1980
2174	242	561	1670	2264	350	2145	939	1918	400	891	188
2563	565	1094	2127	2725	197	2513	1484	2285	159	1345	480
....	2381	1723	636	536	2405	143	1783	295	2488	1293	2360
2381	....	699	1850	2436	406	2362	985	2133	407	1089	96
1723	699	....	1158	1738	898	1722	466	1500	958	450	710
636	1850	1158	....	592	1950	697	1155	548	2027	785	1845
536	2436	1738	592	....	2548	680	1655	730	2625	1383	2437
2405	406	898	1950	2548	....	2363	1290	2139	86	1165	313
143	2362	1722	697	680	2363	....	1820	229	2445	1282	2335
1783	985	466	1155	1655	1290	1820	....	1621	1333	726	1035
295	2133	1500	548	730	2139	229	1621	....	2216	1055	2105
2488	407	958	2027	2625	86	2445	1333	2216	....	1242	321
1293	1089	450	785	1383	1165	1282	726	1055	1242	....	1073
2360	96	710	1845	2437	313	2335	1035	2105	321	1073	....

TABLES OF AIRLINE DISTANCES

All Distances in Statute Miles

Between Representative Cities of the United States and Latin America

New York to	Miles	San Francisco to	Miles	Seattle to	Miles	Washington to	Miles
Buenos Aires	5,295	Buenos Aires	6,487	Buenos Aires	6,956	Buenos Aires	5,205
Bogota	2,474	Bogota	3,863	Bogota	4,166	Bogota	2,344
Caracas	2,100	Caracas	3,900	Caracas	4,100	Caracas	2,040
Guatemala City	2,060	Guatemala City	2,525	Guatemala City	2,930	Guatemala City	1,835
Havana	1,302	Havana	2,600	Havana	2,805	Havana	1,110
La Paz	3,905	La Paz	5,080	La Paz	5,110	La Paz	3,780
Panama	2,211	Panama	3,349	Panama	3,680	Panama	2,020
Para	3,281	Para	5,430	Para	5,550	Para	3,270
Managua	2,100	Managua	2,860	Managua	3,240	Managua	1,920
Rio de Janeiro	4,810	Rio de Janeiro	6,655	Rio de Janeiro	6,945	Rio de Janeiro	4,710
San Jose	2,200	San Jose	3,070	San Jose	3,430	San Jose	2,030
Santiago	5,134	Santiago	5,960	Santiago	6,466	Santiago	4,965
Tampico	1,880	Tampico	1,790	Tampico	2,200	Tampico	1,665

Chicago to	Miles	Denver to	Miles	Los Angeles to	Miles	New Orleans to	Miles
Buenos Aires	5,598	Buenos Aires	5,935	Buenos Aires	6,148	Buenos Aires	4,902
Bogota	2,691	Bogota	3,100	Bogota	3,515	Bogota	1,996
Caracas	2,480	Caracas	3,105	Caracas	3,610	Caracas	1,990
Guatemala City	1,870	Guatemala City	1,935	Guatemala City	2,190	Guatemala City	1,050
Havana	1,315	Havana	1,760	Havana	2,320	Havana	672
La Paz	4,130	La Paz	4,445	La Paz	4,805	La Paz	3,480
Panama	2,320	Panama	2,620	Panama	3,025	Panama	1,600
Para	3,820	Para	4,580	Para	5,110	Para	3,470
Managua	2,060	Managua	2,230	Managua	2,540	Managua	1,250
Rio de Janeiro	5,320	Rio de Janeiro	5,900	Rio de Janeiro	6,330	Rio de Janeiro	4,798
San Jose	2,100	San Jose	2,420	San Jose	2,725	San Jose	1,425
Santiago	5,320	Santiago	5,495	Santiago	5,595	Santiago	4,553
Tampico	1,460	Tampico	1,240	Tampico	1,470	Tampico	720

Between Principal Cities of the World

FROM/TO	Azores	Bagdad	Berlin	Bombay	Buenos Aires	Callao	Cairo	Cape Town	Chicago	Istanbul
Azores	....	3906	2148	5930	5385	4825	3325	5670	3305	2880
Bagdad	3906	....	2040	2022	8215	8618	785	4923	6490	1085
Berlin	2148	2040	....	3947	7411	6937	1823	5949	4458	1068
Bombay	5930	2022	3947	....	9380	10530	2698	5133	8144	3043
Buenos Aires	5385	8215	7411	9380	....	1982	7428	4332	5598	7638
Callao	4825	8618	6937	10530	1982	....	7870	6195	3765	7666
Cairo	3325	785	1823	2698	7428	7870	....	4476	6231	780
Cape Town	5670	4923	5949	5133	4332	6195	4476	....	8551	5210
Chicago	3305	6490	4458	8144	5598	3765	6231	8551	....	5530
Istanbul	2880	1085	1068	3043	7638	7666	780	5210	5530	....
Guam	8985	6380	7158	4831	10516	9760	7175	8918	7510	7015
Honolulu	7421	8445	7384	8172	7653	5993	8925	11655	4315	8200
Juneau	4715	6180	4638	6992	7964	5806	6352	10382	2310	5665
London	1562	2568	575	4526	6919	6376	2218	5975	4015	1540
Los Angeles	5034	7695	5849	8810	6148	4155	7675	10165	1741	6895
Melbourne	12190	8150	9992	6140	7336	8196	8720	6510	9837	9189
Mexico City	4584	8155	6119	9818	4609	2619	7807	8620	1690	7160
Montreal	2548	5814	3776	7582	5619	3954	5502	7975	750	4825
New Orleans	3718	7212	5182	8952	4902	2990	6862	8390	827	6220
New York	2604	6066	4026	7875	5295	3633	5701	7845	727	5060
Panama	3918	7807	5902	9832	3319	1450	7230	7090	2320	6797
Paris	1617	2385	540	4391	6891	6455	2020	5762	4219	1390
Rio de Janeiro	4312	7012	6246	8438	1230	2400	6242	3850	5320	6420
San Francisco	5114	7521	5744	8523	6487	4500	7554	10340	1875	6770
Santiago	5718	8876	7842	10127	731	1548	8100	5080	5325	8230
Seattle	4720	6848	5121	7830	6956	4964	6915	10305	1753	6124
Shanghai	7324	4468	5323	3219	12295	10760	5290	8179	7155	5084
Singapore	8338	4443	6226	2425	9940	11700	5152	6025	9475	5440
Tokyo	7370	5242	5623	4247	11601	9740	6005	9234	6410	5649
Wellington	11475	9782	11384	7752	6341	6696	10360	7149	8465	10790

FROM/TO	Guam	Honolulu	Juneau	London	Los Angeles	Melbourne	Mexico City	Montreal	New Orleans	New York
Azores	8985	7421	4715	1562	5034	12190	4584	2548	3718	2604
Bagdad	6380	8445	6180	2568	7695	8150	8155	5814	7212	6066
Berlin	7158	7384	4638	575	5849	9992	6119	3776	5182	4026
Bombay	4831	8172	6992	4526	8810	6140	9818	7582	8952	7875
Buenos Aires	10516	7653	7964	6919	6148	7336	4609	5619	4902	5295
Callao	9760	5993	5806	6376	4155	8196	2619	3954	2990	3633
Cairo	7175	8925	6352	2218	7675	8720	7807	5502	6862	5701
Cape Town	8918	11655	10382	5975	10165	6510	8620	7975	8390	7845
Chicago	7510	4315	2310	4015	1741	9837	1690	750	827	727
Istanbul	7015	8200	5665	1540	6895	9189	7160	4825	6220	5060
Guam	....	3896	5225	7605	6255	3497	7690	7840	7895	8115
Honolulu	3896	....	2825	7320	2620	5581	3846	4992	4305	5051
Juneau	5225	2825	....	4496	1835	8162	3210	2647	2860	2874
London	7605	7320	4496	....	5496	10590	5605	3370	4656	3500
Los Angeles	6255	2620	1835	5496	....	8098	1445	2468	1695	2466
Melbourne	3497	5581	8162	10590	8098	....	8599	10553	9455	10541
Mexico City	7690	3846	3210	5605	1445	8599	....	2247	940	2110
Montreal	7840	4992	2647	3370	2468	10553	2247	....	1390	340
New Orleans	7895	4305	2860	4656	1695	9455	940	1390	....	1161
New York	8115	5051	2874	3500	2466	10541	2110	340	1161	....
Panama	9220	5347	4456	5310	3025	9211	1532	2545	1600	2211
Paris	7675	7525	4700	210	5711	10500	5800	3490	4846	3600
Rio de Janeiro	11710	8400	7611	5747	6330	8340	4810	5110	4798	4810
San Francisco	5952	2407	1530	5440	345	7970	1870	2557	1960	2606
Santiago	9946	6935	7320	7275	5595	7130	4122	5461	4553	5134
Seattle	5785	2707	870	4850	961	8330	2339	2309	2137	2440
Shanghai	1945	5009	4968	5841	6598	4967	8120	7141	7830	7460
Singapore	2990	6874	7375	6818	8955	3768	10495	9280	10255	9617
Tokyo	1596	3940	4117	6050	5600	5172	7190	6546	6993	6846
Wellington	4206	4676	7501	11790	6806	1655	7003	9206	7950	9067

FROM/TO	Panama	Paris	Rio de Janeiro	San Francisco	Santiago	Seattle	Shanghai	Singapore	Tokyo	Wellington
Azores	3918	1617	4312	5114	5718	4720	7324	8338	7370	11475
Bagdad	7807	2385	7012	7521	8876	6848	4468	4443	5242	9782
Berlin	5902	540	6246	5744	7842	5121	5323	6226	5623	11384
Bombay	9832	4391	8438	8523	10127	7830	3219	2425	4247	7752
Buenos Aires	3319	6891	1230	6487	731	6956	12295	9940	11601	6341
Callao	1450	6455	2400	4500	1548	4964	10760	11700	9740	6696
Cairo	7230	2020	6242	7554	8100	6915	5290	5152	6005	10360
Cape Town	7090	5732	3850	10340	5080	10305	8179	6025	9234	7149
Chicago	2320	4219	5320	1875	5325	1753	7155	9475	6410	8465
Istanbul	6797	1390	6420	6770	8230	6124	5084	5440	5649	10790
Guam	9220	7675	11710	5952	9946	5785	1945	2990	1596	4206
Honolulu	5347	7525	8400	2407	6935	2707	5009	6874	3940	4676
Juneau	4456	4700	7611	1530	7320	870	4968	7375	4117	7501
London	5310	210	5747	5440	7275	4850	5841	6818	6050	11790
Los Angeles	3025	5711	6330	345	5595	961	6598	8955	5600	6806
Melbourne	9211	10500	8340	7970	7130	8330	4967	3768	5172	1655
Mexico City	1532	5800	4810	1870	4122	2339	8120	10495	7190	7003
Montreal	2545	3490	5110	2557	5461	2309	7141	9280	6546	9206
New Orleans	1600	4846	4798	1960	4553	2137	7830	10255	6993	7950
New York	2211	3600	4810	2606	5134	2440	7460	9617	6846	9067
Panama	....	5440	3311	3349	3000	3680	9430	11800	8560	7580
Paris	5440	....	5710	5680	7300	5080	5855	6730	6132	11865
Rio de Janeiro	3311	5710	....	6655	1852	6945	11510	9875	11600	7510
San Francisco	3349	5680	6655	....	5960	692	6245	8440	5250	6800
Santiago	3000	7300	1852	5960	....	6466	11850	10270	10850	5925
Seattle	3680	5080	6945	692	6466	....	5780	8200	4863	7310
Shanghai	9430	5855	11510	6245	11850	5780	....	2395	1095	6080
Singapore	11800	6730	9875	8440	10270	8200	2395	....	3350	5360
Tokyo	8560	6132	11600	5250	10850	4863	1095	3350	....	5730
Wellington	7580	11865	7510	6800	5925	7310	6080	5360	5730	......

WORLD STATISTICAL TABLES

Elements of the Solar System

	Mean Distance from Sun: in Miles	in Kilometers	Period of Revolution around Sun	Period of Rotation on Axis	Equatorial Diameter: in Miles	in Kilometers	Surface Gravity (Earth = 1)	Mass (Earth = 1)	Mean Density (Water = 1)	Number of Satellites
MERCURY	35,990,000	57,900,000	87.97 days	59 days	3,032	4,880	0.38	0.055	5.5	0
VENUS	67,240,000	108,200,000	224.70 days	243 days†	7,523	12,106	0.90	0.815	5.25	0
EARTH	93,000,000	149,700,000	365.26 days	23h 56m	7,926	12,755	1.00	1.00	5.5	1
MARS	141,730,000	228,100,000	687.00 days	24h 37m	4,220	6,790	0.38	0.107	4.0	2
JUPITER	483,880,000	778,700,000	11.86 years	9h 50m	88,750	142,800	2.87	317.9	1.3	16
SATURN	887,130,000	1,427,700,000	29.46 years	10h 14m	74,580	120,020	1.32	95.2	0.7	17
URANUS	1,783,700,000	2,870,500,000	84.01 years	10h 49m†	31,600	50,900	0.93	14.6·	1.3	5
NEPTUNE	2,795,500,000	4,498,800,000	164.79 years	15h 48m	30,200	48,600	1.23	17.2	1.8	3
PLUTO	3,667,900,000	5,902,800,000	247.70 years	6.39 days (?)	1,500	2,400	0.03 (?)	0.01(?)	0.7(?)	1

†Retrograde motion

Facts About the Sun

Equatorial diameter		865,000 miles	1,392,000 kilometers
Period of rotation on axis		25-35 days*	
Orbit of galaxy		every 225 million years	
Surface gravity	(Earth = 1)	27.8	
Mass	(Earth = 1)	333,000	
Density	(Water = 1)	1.4	
Mean distance from Earth		93,000,000 miles	149,700,000 kilometers

*Rotation of 25 days at Equator, decreasing to about 35 days at the poles.

Facts About the Moon

Equatorial diameter		2,160 miles	3,476 kilometers
Period of rotation on axis		27 days, 7 hours, 43 minutes	
Period of revolution around Earth (sidereal month)		27 days, 7 hours, 43 minutes	
Phase period between new moons (synodic month)		29 days, 12 hours, 44 minutes	
Surface gravity	(Earth = 1)	0.16	
Mass	(Earth = 1)	0.0123	
Density	(Water = 1)	3.34	
Maximum distance from Earth		252,710 miles	406,690 kilometers
Minimum distance from Earth		221,460 miles	356,400 kilometers
Mean distance from Earth		238,860 miles	384,400 kilometers

Dimensions of the Earth

	Area in Sq. Miles	Sq. Kilometers
Superficial area	197,751,000	512,175,090
Land surface	57,970,000	150,142,300
Water surface	139,781,000	362,032,790

	Miles	Kilometers
Equatorial circumference	24,902	40,075
Polar circumference	24,860	40,007
Equatorial diameter	7,926.68	12,756.4
Polar diameter	7,899.99	12,713.4
Equatorial radius	3,963.34	6,378.2
Polar radius	3,949.99	6,356.7

Volume of the Earth	2.6×10^{11} cubic miles	10.84×10^{11} cubic kilometers
Mass or weight	6.6×10^{21} short tons	6.0×10^{21} metric tons
Maximum distance from Sun	94,600,000 miles	152,000,000 kilometers
Minimum distance from Sun	91,300,000 miles	147,000,000 kilometers

The Continents

	Area in: Sq. Miles	Sq. Km.	Percent of World's Land
Asia	17,128,500	44,362,815	29.5
Africa	11,707,000	30,321,130	20.2
North America	9,363,000	24,250,170	16.2
South America	6,875,000	17,806,250	11.8
Antarctica	5,500,000	14,245,000	9.5
Europe	4,057,000	10,507,630	7.0
Australia	2,966,136	7,682,300	5.1

Oceans and Major Seas

	Area in: Sq. Miles	Sq. Km.	Greatest Depth in: Feet	Meters
Pacific Ocean	64,186,000	166,241,700	36,198	11,033
Atlantic Ocean	31,862,000	82,522,600	28,374	8,648
Indian Ocean	28,350,000	73,426,500	25,344	7,725
Arctic Ocean	5,427,000	14,056,000	17,880	5,450
Caribbean Sea	970,000	2,512,300	24,720	7,535
Mediterranean Sea	969,000	2,509,700	16,896	5,150
Bering Sea	875,000	2,266,250	15,800	4,800
Gulf of Mexico	600,000	1,554,000	12,300	3,750
Sea of Okhotsk	590,000	1,528,100	11,070	3,370
East China Sea	482,000	1,248,400	9,500	2,900
Sea of Japan	389,000	1,007,500	12,280	3,740
Hudson Bay	317,500	822,300	846	258
North Sea	222,000	575,000	2,200	670
Black Sea	185,000	479,150	7,365	2,245
Red Sea	169,000	437,700	7,200	2,195
Baltic Sea	163,000	422,170	1,506	459

Major Ship Canals

	Length in: Miles	Kms.	Minimum Feet	Depth in: Meters
Volga-Baltic, U.S.S.R.	225	362	—	—
Baltic-White Sea, U.S.S.R.	140	225	16	5
Suez, Egypt	100.76	162	42	13
Albert, Belgium	80	129	16.5	5
Moscow-Volga, U.S.S.R.	80	129	18	6
Volga-Don, U.S.S.R.	62	100	—	—
Göta, Sweden	54	87	10	3
Kiel (Nord-Ostsee), W. Ger.	53.2	86	38	12
Panama Canal, Panama	50.72	82	41.6	13
Houston Ship, U.S.A.	50	81	36	11

Largest Islands

	Area in: Sq. Mi.	Sq. Km.		Area in: Sq. Mi.	Sq. Km.		Area in: Sq. Mi.	Sq. Km.
Greenland	840,000	2,175,600	South I., New Zealand	58,393	151,238	Hokkaido, Japan	28,983	75,066
New Guinea	305,000	789,950	Java, Indonesia	48,842	126,501	Banks, Canada	27,038	70,028
Borneo	290,000	751,100	North I., New Zealand	44,187	114,444	Ceylon, Sri Lanka	25,332	65,610
Madagascar	226,400	586,376	Newfoundland, Canada	42,031	108,860	Tasmania, Australia	24,600	63,710
Baffin, Canada	195,928	507,454	Cuba	40,533	104,981	Svalbard, Norway	23,957	62,049
Sumatra, Indonesia	164,000	424,760	Luzon, Philippines	40,420	104,688	Devon, Canada	21,331	55,247
Honshu, Japan	88,000	227,920	Iceland	39,768	103,000	Novaya Zemlya (north isl.), U.S.S.R.	18,600	48,200
Great Britain	84,400	218,896	Mindanao, Philippines	36,537	94,631	Marajó, Brazil	17,991	46,597
Victoria, Canada	83,896	217,290	Ireland	31,743	82,214	Tierra del Fuego, Chile & Argentina	17,900	46,360
Ellesmere, Canada	75,767	196,236	Sakhalin, U.S.S.R.	29,500	76,405	Alexander, Antarctica	16,700	43,250
Celebes, Indonesia	72,986	189,034	Hispaniola, Haiti & Dom. Rep.	29,399	76,143			

Principal Mountains of the World

	Feet	Meters		Feet	Meters		Feet	Meters
Everest, Nepal-China	29,028	8,848	Pissis, Argentina	22,241	6,779	Kazbek, U.S.S.R.	16,512	5,033
Godwin Austen (K2),			Mercedario, Argentina	22,211	6,770	Puncak Jaya, Indonesia	16,503	5,030
Pakistan-China	28,250	8,611	Huascarán, Peru	22,205	6,768	Tyree, Antarctica	16,289	4,965
Kanchenjunga, Nepal-India	28,208	8,598	Llullaillaco, Chile-Argentina	22,057	6,723	Blanc, France	15,771	4,807
Lhotse, Nepal-China	27,923	8,511	Nevada Ancohuma, Bolivia	21,489	6,550	Klyuchevskaya Sopka, U.S.S.R.	15,584	4,750
Makalu, Nepal-China	27,824	8,481	Illampu, Bolivia	21,276	6,485	Fairweather (Br. Col., Canada)	15,300	4,663
Dhaulagiri, Nepal	26,810	8,172	Chimborazo, Ecuador	20,561	6,267	Dufourspitze (Mte. Rosa), Italy-		
Nanga Parbat, Pakistan	26,660	8,126	McKinley, Alaska	20,320	6,194	Switzerland	15,203	4,634
Annapurna, Nepal	26,504	8,078	Logan, Canada (Yukon)	19,524	5,951	Ras Dashan, Ethiopia	15,157	4,620
Gasherbrum, Pakistan-China	26,740	8,068	Cotopaxi, Ecuador	19,347	5,897	Matterhorn, Switzerland	14,691	4,478
Nanda Devi, India	25,645	7,817	Kilimanjaro, Tanzania	19,340	5,895	Whitney, California, U.S.A.	14,494	4,418
Rakaposhi, Pakistan	25,550	7,788	El Misti, Peru	19,101	5,822	Elbert, Colorado, U.S.A.	14,433	4,399
Kamet, India	25,447	7,756	Pico Cristóbal Colón, Colombia	19,029	5,800	Rainier, Washington, U.S.A.	14,410	4,392
Gurla Mandhada, China	25,355	7,728	Huila, Colombia	18,865	5,750	Shasta, California, U.S.A.	14,162	4,350
Kongur Shan, China	25,325	7,719	Citlaltépetl (Orizaba), Mexico	18,855	5,747	Pikes Peak, Colorado, U.S.A.	14,110	4,301
Tirich Mir, Pakistan	25,230	7,690	El'brus, U.S.S.R.	18,510	5,642	Finsteraarhorn, Switzerland	14,022	4,274
Gongga Shan, China	24,790	7,556	Damavand, Iran	18,376	5,601	Mauna Kea, Hawaii, U.S.A.	13,796	4,205
Muztagata, China	24,757	7,546	St. Elias, Alaska-Canada			Mauna Loa, Hawaii, U.S.A.	13,677	4,169
Communism Peak, U.S.S.R.	24,599	7,498	(Yukon)	18,008	5,489	Jungfrau, Switzerland	13,642	4,158
Pobeda Peak, U.S.S.R.	24,406	7,439	Vilcanota, Peru	17,999	5,486	Cameroon, Cameroon	13,350	4,069
Chomo Lhari, Bhutan-China	23,997	7,314	Popocatépetl, Mexico	17,887	5,452	Grossglockner, Austria	12,457	3,797
Muztag, China	23,891	7,282	Dykhtau, U.S.S.R.	17,070	5,203	Fuji, Japan	12,389	3,776
Cerro Aconcagua, Argentina	22,831	6,959	Kenya, Kenya	17,058	5,199	Cook, New Zealand	12,349	3,764
Ojos del Salado, Chile-Argentina	22,572	6,880	Ararat, Turkey	16,946	5,165	Etna, Italy	11,053	3,369
Bonete, Chile-Argentina	22,541	6,870	Vinson Massif, Antarctica	16,864	5,140	Kosciusko, Australia	7,310	2,228
Tupungato, Chile-Argentina	22,310	6,800	Margherita (Ruwenzori), Africa	16,795	5,119	Mitchell, North Carolina, U.S.A.	6,684	2,037

Longest Rivers of the World

	Length in:			Length in:			Length in:	
	Miles	Kms.		Miles	Kms.		Miles	Kms.
Nile, Africa	4,145	6,671	São Francisco, Brazil	1,811	2,914	Ohio-Allegheny, U.S.A.	1,306	2,102
Amazon, S. Amer.	3,915	6,300	Indus, Asia	1,800	2,897	Kama, U.S.S.R.	1,262	2,031
Chang Jiang (Yangtze), China	3,900	6,276	Danube, Europe	1,775	2,857	Red, U.S.A.	1,222	1,966
Mississippi-Missouri-Red Rock, U.S.A.	3,741	6,019	Salween, Asia	1,770	2,849	Don, U.S.S.R.	1,222	1,967
Ob'Irtysh-Black Irtysh, U.S.S.R.	3,362	5,411	Brahmaputra, Asia	1,700	2,736	Columbia, U.S.A.-Canada	1,214	1,953
Yenisey-Angara, U.S.S.R.	3,100	4,989	Euphrates, Asia	1,700	2,736	Saskatchewan, Canada	1,205	1,939
Huang He (Yellow), China	2,877	4,630	Tocantins, Brazil	1,677	2,699	Peace-Finlay, Canada	1,195	1,923
Amur-Shilka-Onon, Asia	2,744	4,416	Xi (Si), China	1,650	2,655	Tigris, Asia	1,181	1,901
Lena, U.S.S.R.	2,734	4,400	Amudar'ya, Asia	1,616	2,601	Darling, Australia	1,160	1,867
Congo (Zaire), Africa	2,718	4,374	Nelson-Saskatchewan, Canada	1,600	2,575	Angara, U.S.S.R.	1,135	1,827
Mackenzie-Peace-Finlay, Canada	2,635	4,241	Orinoco, S. Amer.	1,600	2,575	Sungari, Asia	1,130	1,819
Mekong, Asia	2,610	4,200	Zambezi, Africa	1,600	2,575	Pechora, U.S.S.R.	1,124	1,809
Missouri-Red Rock, U.S.A.	2,564	4,125	Paraguay, S. Amer.	1,584	2,549	Snake, U.S.A.	1,000	1,609
Niger, Africa	2,548	4,101	Kolyma, U.S.S.R.	1,562	2,514	Churchill, Canada	1,000	1,609
Paraná-La Plata, S. Amer.	2,450	3,943	Ganges, Asia	1,550	2,494	Pilcomayo, S. Amer.	1,000	1,609
Mississippi, U.S.A.	2,348	3,778	Ural, U.S.S.R.	1,509	2,428	Magdalena, Colombia	1,000	1,609
Murray-Darling, Australia	2,310	3,718	Japurá, S. Amer.	1,500	2,414	Uruguay, S. Amer.	994	1,600
Volga, U.S.S.R.	2,194	3,531	Arkansas, U.S.A.	1,450	2,334	Platte-N. Platte, U.S.A.	990	1,593
Madeira, S. Amer.	2,013	3,240	Colorado, U.S.A.-Mexico	1,450	2,334	Ohio, U.S.A.	981	1,578
Purus, S. Amer.	1,995	3,211	Negro, S. Amer.	1,400	2,253	Pecos, U.S.A.	926	1,490
Yukon, Alaska-Canada	1,979	3,185	Dnieper, U.S.S.R.	1,368	2,202	Oka, U.S.S.R.	918	1,477
St. Lawrence, Canada-U.S.A.	1,900	3,058	Orange, Africa	1,350	2,173	Canadian, U.S.A.	906	1,458
Rio Grande, Mexico-U.S.A.	1,885	3,034	Irrawaddy, Burma	1,325	2,132	Colorado, Texas, U.S.A.	894	1,439
Syrdar'ya-Naryn, U.S.S.R.	1,859	2,992	Brazos, U.S.A.	1,309	2,107	Dniester, U.S.S.R.	876	1,410

Principal Natural Lakes

	Area in:		Max. Depth in:			Area in:		Max. Depth in:	
	Sq. Miles	Sq. Km.	Feet	Meters		Sq. Miles	Sq. Km.	Feet	Meters
Caspian Sea, U.S.S.R.-Iran	143,243	370,999	3,264	995	Lake Eyre, Australia	3,500-0	9,000-0	—	—
Lake Superior, U.S.A.-Canada	31,820	82,414	1,329	405	Lake Titicaca, Peru-Bolivia	3,200	8,288	1,000	305
Lake Victoria, Africa	26,724	69,215	270	82	Lake Nicaragua, Nicaragua	3,100	8,029	230	70
Aral Sea, U.S.S.R.	25,676	66,501	256	78	Lake Athabasca, Canada	3,064	7,936	400	122
Lake Huron, U.S.A.-Canada	23,010	59,596	748	228	Reindeer Lake, Canada	2,568	6,651	—	—
Lake Michigan, U.S.A.	22,400	58,016	923	281	Lake Turkana (Rudolf), Africa	2,463	6,379	240	73
Lake Tanganyika, Africa	12,650	32,764	4,700	1,433	Issyk-Kul', U.S.S.R.	2,425	6,281	2,303	702
Lake Baykal, U.S.S.R.	12,162	31,500	5,316	1,620	Lake Torrens, Australia	2,230	5,776	—	—
Great Bear Lake, Canada	12,096	31,328	1,356	413	Vänern, Sweden	2,156	5,584	328	100
Lake Nyasa (Malawi), Africa	11,555	29,928	2,320	707	Nettilling Lake, Canada	2,140	5,543	—	—
Great Slave Lake, Canada	11,031	28,570	2,015	614	Lake Winnipegosis, Canada	2,075	5,374	38	12
Lake Erie, U.S.A.-Canada	9,940	25,745	210	64	Lake Mobutu Sese Seko (Albert),				
Lake Winnipeg, Canada	9,417	24,390	60	18	Africa	2,075	5,374	160	49
Lake Ontario, U.S.A.-Canada	7,540	19,529	775	244	Karida Lake, Zambia-Zimbabwe	2,050	5,310	295	90
Lake Ladoga, U.S.S.R.	7,104	18,399	738	225	Lake Nipigon, Canada	1,872	4,848	540	165
Lake Balkhash, U.S.S.R.	7,027	18,200	87	27	Lake Mweru, Zaire-Zambia	1,800	4,662	60	18
Lake Maracaibo, Venezuela	5,120	13,261	100	31	Lake Manitoba, Canada	1,799	4,659	12	4
Lake Chad, Africa	4,000-	10,360-			Lake Taymyr, U.S.S.R.	1,737	4,499	85	26
	10,000	25,900	25	8	Lake Khanka, China-U.S.S.R.	1,700	4,403	33	10
Lake Onega, U.S.S.R.	3,710	9,609	377	115	Lake Kioga, Uganda	1,700	4,403	25	8

MAP PROJECTIONS

by Erwin Raisz

Our earth is rotating around its *axis* once a day. The two end points of its axis are the *poles*; the line circling the earth midway between the poles is the *equator*. The arc from either of the poles to the equator is divided into 90 *degrees*. The distance, expressed in degrees, from the equator to any point is its *latitude* and circles of equal latitude are the *parallels*. On maps it is customary to show parallels of evenly-spaced degrees such as every fifth or every tenth.

The equator is divided into 360 degrees. Lines circling from pole to pole through the degree points on the equator are called *meridians*. They are all equal in length but by international agreement the meridian passing through the Greenwich Observatory in London has been chosen as *prime meridian*. The distance, expressed in degrees, from the prime meridian to any point is its *longitude*. While meridians are all equal in length, parallels become shorter and shorter as they approach the poles. Whereas one degree of latitude represents everywhere approximately 69 miles, one degree of longitude varies from 69 miles at the equator to nothing at the poles.

Each degree is divided into 60 minutes and each minute into 60 seconds. One minute of latitude equals a nautical mile.

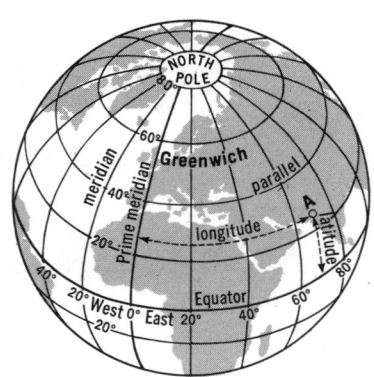

The map is flat but the earth is nearly spherical. Neither a rubber ball nor any part of a rubber ball may be flattened without stretching or tearing unless the part is very small. To present the curved surface of the earth on a flat map is not difficult as long as the areas under consideration are small, but the mapping of countries, continents, or the whole earth requires some kind of *projection*. Any regular set of parallels and meridians upon which a map can be drawn makes a map projection. Many systems are used.

In any projection only the parallels or the meridians or some other set of lines can be *true* (the same length as on the globe of corresponding scale); all other lines are too long or too short. Only on a globe is it possible to have both the parallels and the meridians true. The scale given on a flat map cannot be true everywhere. The construction of the various projections begins usually with laying out the parallels or meridians which have true lengths.

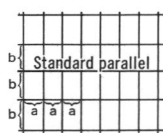

Rectangular Projection

RECTANGULAR PROJECTION — This is a set of evenly-placed meridians and horizontal parallels. The central or *standard parallel* and all meridians are true. All other parallels are either too long or too short. The projection is used for simple maps of small areas, as city plans, etc.

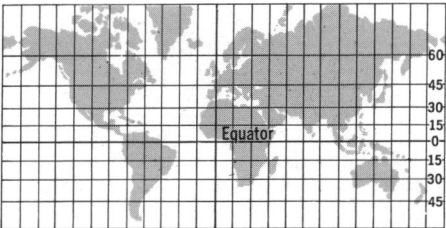

Mercator Projection

MERCATOR PROJECTION — In this projection the meridians are evenly-spaced vertical lines. The parallels are horizontal, spaced so that their length has the same relation to the meridians as on a globe. As the meridians converge at higher latitudes on the globe, while on the map they do not, the parallels have to be drawn also farther and farther apart to maintain the correct relationship. When every very small area has the same shape as on a globe we call the projection *conformal*. The most interesting quality of this projection is that all *compass directions* appear as straight lines. For this reason it is generally used for marine charts. It is also frequently used for world maps in spite of the fact that the high latitudes are very much exaggerated in size. Only the equator is true to scale; all other parallels and meridians are too long. The Mercator projection did *not* derive from projecting a globe upon a cylinder.

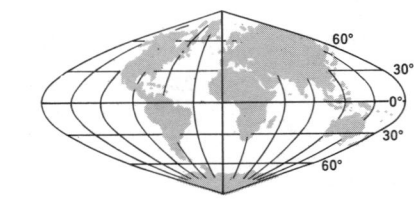

Sinusoidal Projection

SINUSOIDAL PROJECTION — The parallels are truly-spaced horizontal lines. They are divided truly and the connecting curves make the meridians. It does not make a good world map because the outer regions are distorted, but the central portion is good and this part is often used for maps of Africa and South America. Every part of the map has the same area as the corresponding area on the globe. It is an *equal-area* projection.

MOLLWEIDE PROJECTION — The meridians are equally-spaced ellipses; the parallels are horizontal lines spaced so that every belt of latitude should have the same area as on a globe. This projection is popular for world maps, especially in European atlases.

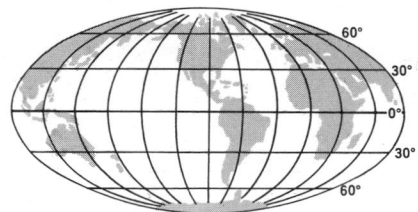

Mollweide Projection

GOODE'S INTERRUPTED PROJECTIONS—Only the good central part of the Mollweide or sinusoidal (or both) projection is used and the oceans are cut. This makes an equal-area map with little distortion of shape. It is commonly used for world maps.

Goode's Interrupted Projection

Eckert Projection

ECKERT PROJECTIONS — These are similar to the sinusoidal or the Mollweide projections, but the poles are shown as lines half the length of the equator. There are several variants; the meridians are either sine curves or ellipses; the parallels are horizontal and spaced either evenly or so as to make the projection equal area. Their use for world maps is increasing. The figure shows the elliptical equal-area variant.

CONIC PROJECTION — The original idea of the conic projection is that of capping the globe by a cone upon which both the parallels and meridians are projected from the center of the globe. The cone is then cut open and laid flat. A cone can be made tangent to any chosen *standard parallel*.

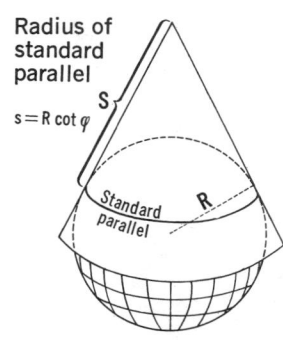

Radius of standard parallel

$s = R \cot \varphi$

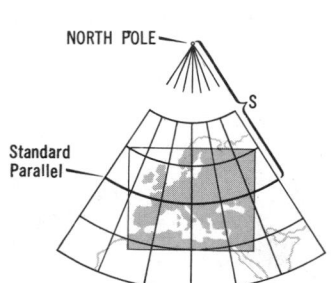

Conic Projection

The actually-used conic projection is a modification of this idea. The radius of the standard parallel is obtained as above. The meridians are straight radiating lines spaced truly on the standard parallel. The parallels are concentric circles spaced at true distances. All parallels except the standard are too long. The projection is used for maps of countries in middle latitudes, as it presents good shapes with small scale error.

There are several variants: The use of *two standard parallels,* one near the top, the other near the bottom of the map, reduces the scale error. In the *Albers projection* the parallels are spaced unevenly, to make the projection equal-area. This is a good projection for the United States. In the *Lambert conformal conic projection* the parallels are spaced so that any small quadrangle of the grid should have the same shape as on the globe. This is the best projection for air-navigation charts as it has relatively straight azimuths.

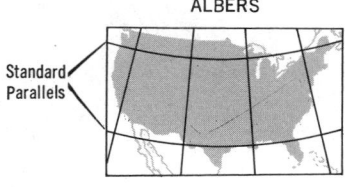

Albers Projection

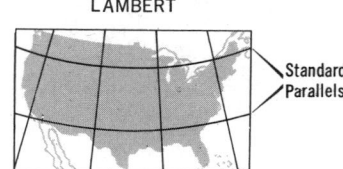

Lambert Conformal Conic Projection

An *azimuth* is a great-circle direction reckoned clockwise from north. A *great-circle direction* points to a place along the shortest line on the earth's surface. This is not the same as compass direction. The center of a great circle is the center of the globe.

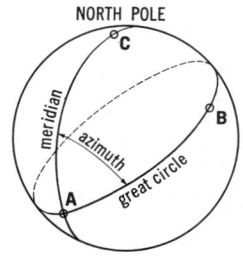

BONNE PROJECTION — The parallels are laid out exactly as in the conic projection. All parallels are divided truly and the connecting curves make the meridians. It is an equal-area projection. It is used for maps of the northern continents, as Asia, Europe, and North America.

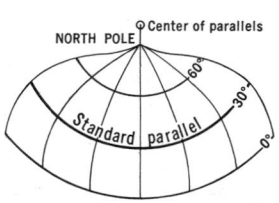

Bonne Projection

POLYCONIC PROJECTION — The central meridian is divided truly. The parallels are non-concentric circles, the radii of which are obtained by drawing tangents to the globe as though the globe were covered by several cones rather than by only one. Each parallel is divided truly and the connecting curves make the meridians. All meridians except the central one are too long. This projection is used for large-scale topographic sheets — less often for countries or continents.

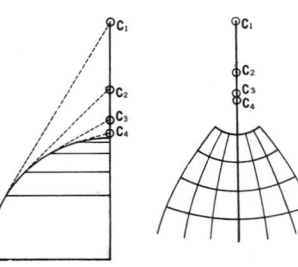

Polyconic Projection

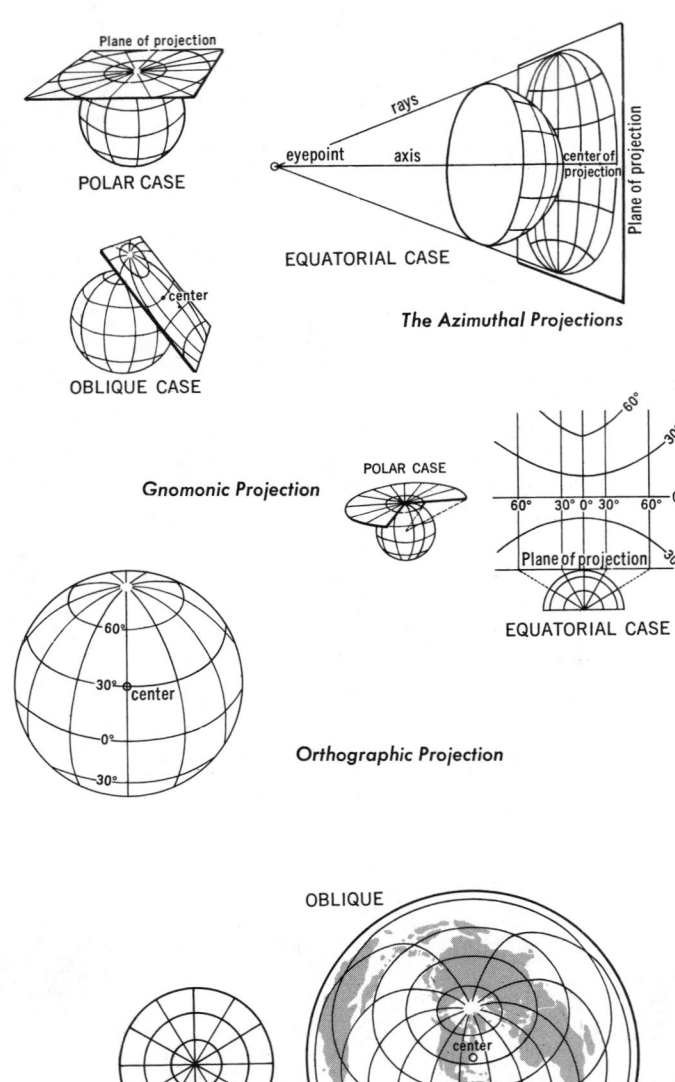

POLAR CASE

OBLIQUE CASE

The Azimuthal Projections

EQUATORIAL CASE

Plane of projection

rays

eyepoint   axis

center of projection

Gnomonic Projection

POLAR CASE

60°

30°

60° 30° 0° 30° 60° 0°

Plane of projection

EQUATORIAL CASE

Orthographic Projection

60°

30° center

0°

30°

OBLIQUE

center

POLAR CASE

Azimuthal Equidistant Projection

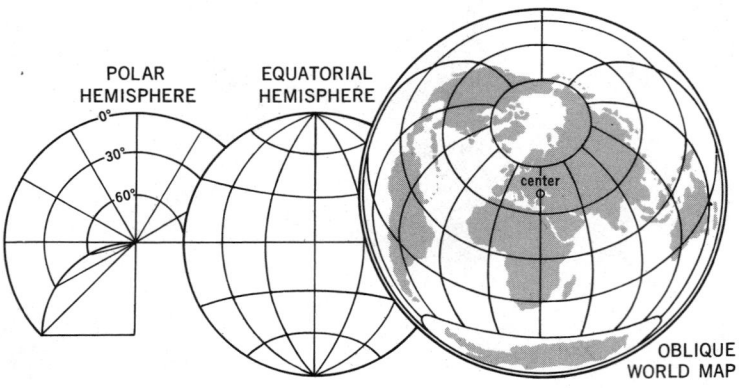

POLAR
HEMISPHERE

0°

30°

60°

EQUATORIAL
HEMISPHERE

center

OBLIQUE
WORLD MAP

Lambert Azimuthal Equal-Area Projection

THE AZIMUTHAL PROJECTIONS

In this group a part of the globe is projected from an eyepoint onto a plane. The eyepoint can be at different distances, making different projections. The plane of projection can be tangent at the equator, at a pole, or at any other point on which we want to focus attention. The most important quality of all azimuthal projections is that they show every point at its true direction (azimuth) from the center point, and all points equally distant from the center point will be equally distant on the map also.

GNOMONIC PROJECTION — This projection has the eyepoint at the center of the globe Only the central part is good; the outer regions are badly distorted. Yet the projection has one important quality, all great circles being shown as straight lines. For this reason it is used for laying out the routes for long range flying or trans-oceanic navigation.

ORTHOGRAPHIC PROJECTION — This projection has the eyepoint at infinite distance and the projecting rays are parallel. The polar or equatorial varieties are rare but the oblique case became very popular on account of its visual quality. It looks like a picture of a globe. Although the distortion on the peripheries is extreme, we see it correctly because the eye perceives it not as a map but as a picture of a three-dimensional globe. Obviously only a hemisphere (half globe) can be shown.

Some azimuthal projections do not derive from the actual process of projecting from an eyepoint, but are arrived at by other means:

AZIMUTHAL EQUIDISTANT PROJECTION — This is the only projection in which every point is shown both at true great-circle direction and at true distance from the center point, but all other directions and distances are distorted. The principle of the projection can best be understood from the polar case. Most polar maps are in this projection. The oblique case is used for radio direction finding, for earthquake research, and in long-distance flying. A separate map has to be constructed for each central point selected.

LAMBERT AZIMUTHAL EQUAL-AREA PROJECTION — The construction of this projection can best be understood from the polar case. All three cases are widely used. It makes a good polar map and it is often extended to include the southern continents. It is the most common projection used for maps of the Eastern and Western Hemispheres, and it is a good projection for continents as it shows correct areas with relatively little distortion of shape. Most of the continent maps in this atlas are in this projection.

IN THIS ATLAS, on almost all maps, parallels and meridians have been marked because they are useful for the following:

(a) They show the north-south and east-west directions which appear on many maps at oblique angles especially near the margins.

(b) With the help of parallels and meridians every place can be exactly located; for instance, New York City is at 41° N and 74° W on any map.

(c) They help to measure distances even in the distorted parts of the map. The scale given on each map is true only along certain lines which are specified in the foregoing discussion for each projection. One degree of latitude equals nearly 69 statute miles or 60 nautical miles. The length of one degree of longitude varies (1° long. = 1° lat. × cos lat.).